Reader's Guide to the

HISTORY OF

SCIENCE

Reader's Guide to the

HISTORY OF SCIENCE

edited by

ARNE HESSENBRUCH

FITZROY DEARBORN PUBLISHERS
LONDON • CHICAGO

British Library and Library of Congress Cataloguing in Publication Data are available

ISBN 1-884964-29-X

First published in the USA and UK 2000

Typeset by Florence Production Ltd, Stoodleigh, Devon
Printed and bound by The Bath Press

Cover design by Philip Lewis

CONTENTS

EDITOR'S NOTE

Aims, Scope, and Selection of Entries

The subject of the history of science has come of age. One can speak almost of a torrent of new books on the topic, especially if one includes the history of technology and medicine, as in this book. Among them are admirable examples of readable and authoritative treatments of large topics, addressed to a wide audience. However, a great deal of the recent work has reflected intense specialization within the subject; professional historians of science have increasingly been producing monographs addressed to a relatively restricted audience of fellow-specialists and their graduate students. However, it has become impossible to digest the literature in all subdisciplines, even for professional historians of science, while many of these debates have become confusing or even mystifying to a wider readership.

One positive feature, however, is the widening range of the historiography. What used to be called internal history remains important, but it is now complemented by a great diversity of other approaches. One can say generally that the 1980s saw a clash of traditional historiography with the sociology of science. In the 1990s debates on the role of gender in the history of science arrived on the scene, and now the cultural history of science has entered the mainstream. In future, this ought to enable mutual stimulation to a greater extent than is currently the case.

The aim of the *Reader's Guide to the History of Science* is to offer some help to those who wish to explore the riches of the writings on history of science in all its diversity. In the belief that a simple listing of books will not suffice for this purpose, the *Reader's Guide* takes the form of a series of essays that describe and assess books on some 500 different topics – some specialized and very specific, others much broader and more general. This approach is designed to help readers of various kinds and at various levels: students (both undergraduate and graduate) looking for assistance with their next assignment or research paper; teachers in schools, colleges and universities – and particularly those who are faced with the challenge of preparing courses or classes on topics in which they are not specialists; and those non-specialist readers who simply have an interest in a particular subject, and seek advice on what to read next.

Entries fall into three main categories, dealing respectively with individuals, disciplines and institutions, and broader themes. In cases where the literature on particular individuals is not substantial it has been subsumed under a broader theme. For instance, there are several entries entitled Women in Science (subdivided by discipline, for example, the physical sciences, medicine, life sciences) which collect the literature on individual women on whom too little has appeared to warrant an individual entry. The second category reflects another important genre. There are many histories of disciplines such as genetics, biology, physics, and chemistry, and of institutions such as the Royal Society of London. The third, more general, category covers literature on topics such as the Enlightenment or the Scientific Revolution. This category also contains entries on analytical concepts, such as Alienation, Discovery, and Experiments. The aim overall is that this kind of "multi-layered" approach will enable the user to navigate from the particular to the general, or vice versa, as his or her needs and inclinations dictate.

Even a volume with the generous proportions of this *Reader's Guide* cannot hope to be comprehensive in its coverage or in its treatment of each topic. Lines had to be drawn to make the project manageable within the scope of a single volume. Given that the approach had to be selective, the reader is entitled to know something of the principles underlying that selection. These are:

1. The emphasis is predominantly on books (and contributions to books), as opposed to articles in journals and magazines. Articles are normally included only when they are of seminal importance, or when there is no adequate treatment of a particular aspect of a subject in a book-length study.

2. The *Reader's Guide* is a guide to the secondary literature, and not to primary sources, or to collections of printed source material. There are two limited exceptions to this rule. An editorial introduction or editorial footnotes to a collection of source materials may justify the inclusion of the source materials. Second, translations of primary source material are included too.

3. For each entry, the contributor was free, within the editorial guidelines, to make his or her own choice of books to be discussed. In most cases, the emphasis is on more recently published work, but, where appropriate contributors were encouraged to include earlier books in order to sketch the historiographical development. New works appear constantly, and there has been no single cut-off point for inclusion of books in the *Reader's Guide*.

I would like to think of the *Reader's Guide* as a snapshot of the history of science at the beginning of the 21st century.

Arrangement of the Entries

Entries appear in alphabetical order; a complete list of them can be found in the **Alphabetical List of Entries** (p. xv). Where entries share the same general heading (e.g., China, Japan, Religion and Science), if there is a "general works" entry in such a group, it always precedes more specific subdivision.

While the overall arrangement of entries is alphabetical, there are other aids to facilitate access to the contents of the *Reader's Guide*. These are:

1. **Thematic List** (p. xxi). This should be consulted to see the full range of entries in the *Reader's Guide* on a particular subject area such as Institutions or Physical Sciences.

2. **Booklist Index** (p. 773). This lists in alphabetical order of author all books and articles discussed in any of the entries, and can be used to locate discussion of the work of particular historians.

3. **General Index** (p. 829). This lists individuals, themes and concepts mentioned in any of the entries. This index may be particularly useful for locating references to subject matters and individuals that do not have an entry of their own.

4. **Cross references**. At the end of the entries there are *See also* notes, which refer the reader to entries on related topics.

Format within Entries

Each entry begins with a list of the books/articles to be discussed. Publication details are provided, including dates of first publication and, where appropriate, the most recent revised edition. Reprints and paperback editions are normally omitted. In the text of each essay, the first significant mention of each author appears in capital letters. In cases where more than one item by the same author is discussed in the same entry, each item is introduced by the author's name in capital letters, followed by date of publication in parentheses. In a few cases, this would still be ambiguous, and here key words from the title are used instead of the year of publication. Although the list of books in each entry proceeds in alphabetical order of author, books are normally not discussed in the text in that order. It was left to the judgment of contributors to decide whether to discuss books in order of publication, or, more often, according to the subject matter and emphasis of each book.

Acknowledgements

Although, in his darker moments, the editor felt that this project sucked the life-blood out of him, he wishes to acknowledge the help that he received from a great number of people. First, I should like to thank all those who have written for this volume. I am deeply impressed with the generosity and professionalism of those who offered to contribute entries, in some cases many entries, and who encouraged others to do so also. In this respect a special thanks is due to Rhodri Lloyd Hayward. I am grateful to many of my friends and colleagues who have worked long and hard to help in different ways. The Advisers, some of whom I am also happy to count as my friends, were extremely helpful, both in the selection of entries to be included in the *Reader's Guide* and in aiding me in the search for contributors. I would also like to thank my mother who has helped me in more ways than I could possibly articulate.

The resources of many libraries but especially the Cambridge University Library and the Whipple Library of Cambridge University have been invaluable. I have also been able to make very good use of the Eureka database of the History of Science Society. It is interesting to ponder the role of the electronic media in the making of this book. When the project started, Fitzroy Dearborn did not have an email address, nor could they envisage a need for it. Contributions were received as typescript and sometimes on disk. Now, only a few years later, contributions are communicated as email attachments keeping the formatting intact. To begin with I checked all items against actual books, paper catalogues or computer catalogues in libraries, by the end of the project I received contributions and checked references without leaving my computer.

Particular thanks goes to Lesley Henderson at Fitzroy Dearborn whose unfailing good spirit and calm sense of what needs to be done saw me through moments of despair.

Thanks are also due to the editorial and production staff at Fitzroy Dearborn, and especially to Nina Bunton, Antonella Elisabetta Collaro, Jonathon Dore, Carolyn Dorée, Delia Gaze, Jill Halliday, Gillian Lindsey, Helena Lyons, and Michael Wardle.

The main midwives of the book are my children, Anna and Eric, who have always been able to dispel any sense of doom. At the age of seven Anna replied to the question of what she wanted to do as a grown-up: "I want to write a book this thick", indicating with her hands the approximate dimensions of the present *Reader's Guide*.

ARNE HESSENBRUCH

BOARD OF ADVISERS

CONTRIBUTORS

Joe Albree
Amir Alexander
Katharine Anderson
B.J. Andrews
Rima D. Apple
Jon Arrizabalaga
Richard Ashcroft
William J. Ashworth
Henry Atmore
Mike Ball
Josep Lluís Barona
Bruno Belhoste
Richard Bellon
Jim Bennett
Roberta E. Bivins
Christine Blondel
Ingemar Bohlin
Christian Bonah
Julia Borossa
Peter J. Bowler
Brian Bracegirdle
Patricia H. Bracegirdle
Robert Brain
Michael T. Bravo
Francesca Bray
Gunnar Broberg
Nathan Brooks
Randall C. Brooks
Reinhart Brüning
Robert Bud
Glenn E. Bugos
Hans Buiter
Vern L. Bullough
W.F. Bynum
Martin Campbell-Kelly
Beate Ceranski
Brigitte Chamak
Philippe Chavot
Xiang Chen
Peter E. Childs
Dan Ch. Christensen
John F.M. Clark
D.C.T. Cox-Maksimov
Catherine Crawford
Elisabeth Crawford

Maurice Crosland
Andrew Cunningham
Serafina Cuomo
Ann Dally
Ubiratan D'Ambrosio
Joseph W. Dauben
Frances Dawbarn
Dennis R. Dean
Soraya De Chadarevian
Silvia De Renzi
David H. DeVorkin
Arthur M. Diamond, Jr
Fokko Jan Dijksterhuis
Colin Divall
Igor S. Dmitriev
Mary J. Dobson
Brian Dolan
Michael Donnelly
Harold Dorn
Alice D. Dreger
Basileios Drolias
Richard Dunn
Frank N. Egerton
Ron Eglash
M.A. Elston
Moritz Epple
Christina Erneling
Henry Etzkowitz
Isobel Falconer
Fa-Ti Fan
Patricia Fara
Paul Lawrence Farber
Marianne P. Fedunkiw
Silvia F. de M. Figueirõa
Mark R. Finlay
Bernard S. Finn
Steve Fuller
Michael J. Galgano
Karl Galle
Ivana Gambaro
Kostas Gavroglu
Paulus Gerdes
Owen Gingerich
Jay E. Gladstein
Alexander Goldbloom

Catherine Goldstein
Graeme J.N. Gooday
Sarah Goodfellow
Matthew R. Goodrum
Michael D. Gordin
Michael John Gorman
Christoph Gradmann
Sally S. Graham
Helen P. Graves Smith
Jeremy Gray
Elizabeth Green Musselman
Joe Gross
Willem Hackmann
Elizabeth V. Haigh
Lesley A. Hall
Ernst P. Hamm
Kai Handel
Gary L. Hardcastle
Anne Hardy
Benjamin Harris
Keizo Hashimoto
Rhodri Lloyd Hayward
Michael Heidelberger
Cecil G. Helman
Colin A. Hempstead
John Heng
John Henry
Klaus Hentschel
Arne Hessenbruch
Matthias Heymann
Katherine Hill
Christine Hillam
Richard L. Hills
Andrew Hodgkiss
Susan Hoecker-Drysdale
Dieter Hoffmann
Graham Hollister-Short
S.W.F. Holloway
Gerald Holton
R.W. Home
John Honner
Brigitte Hoppe
Nick Hopwood
Peregrine Horden
Sally Horrocks
Steven Horwitz
Joel D. Howell
Robert G. Hudson
Toby E. Huff
Jeff Hughes
Brad D. Hume
Michael Hunter
Paul Israel
Myles W. Jackson
Frank A.J.L. James
Adrian Johns
Stephen B. Johnson
Stephen Johnston
Fredrik Jonsson
Thomas Junker

David Kaiser
Horst Kant
Carla Keirns
Jordan Kellman
William J. Kinsella
David Knight
Helge Kragh
Henry B. Kreuzman
Andreas Kühne
Kristine Larsen
Mark S. Lesney
Bruce V. Lewenstein
David C. Lindberg
M. Susan Lindee
Carlos López-Beltrán
Morris F. Low
James E. McClellan III
Gordon McOuat
Andreas-Holger Maehle
M. Eileen Magnello
Helmut Maier
Roderick Main
Marjorie Malley
Lara Marks
Ben Marsden
R.N.D. Martin
Anne Masseran
J. Rosser Matthews
Seymour H. Mauskopf
David Philip Miller
Eric L. Mills
Iwan Rhys Morus
A.M. Moulin
Peter Neushul
Phillip A. Nicholls
Henry Nielsen
Simon A. Nightingale
Richard Noakes
Derek Nuttall
Perry O'Donovan
David Oldroyd
Joan Garrett Packer
Gábor Palló
William Palmer
Alex Soojung-Kim Pang
Kim Pelis
Stephen Petrina
Naomi Pfeffer
Juan Pimentel
Trevor J. Pinch
Dorothy Porter
Roy Porter
Theodore M. Porter
Michael Power
Robert N. Proctor
Stephen Pumfrey
Kapil Raj
Sujantha Raman
Beatrice Rauschenbach
Hillary Ray

Günter Regneri
Horst Remane
Monika Renneberg
Brian R. Reynolds
Craig Rodine
Terrie M. Romano
Robert Rosenberg
Marc Rothenberg
Harry Rothman
Nicolaas A. Rupke
Torsten Rüting
Mike Saks
Christine F. Salazar
Andrew M.M. Samuel
José M. Sánchez-Ron
Margaret Schabas
Simon Schaffer
Londa Schiebinger
Arne Schirrmacher
Warren Schmaus
Claude Schnitter
Brigitte Schroeder-Gudehus
Michael Segre
Helaine Selin
Terry Shinn
Reinhard Siegmund-Schultze
Sergio Sismondo
Leo B. Slater
A.W. Sloan
David N. Smith
Geert Somsen
Sverker Sörlin
Richard Sorrenson
Lawrence Souder
Richard Staley

Larry Stewart
Steve Sturdy
Tracy L. Sullivan
Anne Summers
Charles Susskind
Zeno G. Swijtink
Jürgen Teichmann
Mary Terrall
Janet Tighe
Anthony S. Travis
Jennifer Tucker
Julianne Tuttle
Ton Van Helvoort
A. Bowdoin Van Riper
Keith Vernon
Antonio Augusto Passos Videira
Brant Vogel
Donald B. Wagner
Helen M. Ward
Kimberly Weathers
Paul Weindling
Sheila Faith Weiss
Simon Werrett
Richard S. Westfall
Paul White
Sven Widmalm
Gerhard Wiesenfeldt
Lise Wilkinson
Carolyn D. Williams
Philip K. Wilson
Alison Winter
Michael Wintroub
I. Richard Yeo
Elmer Yglesias
Robert M. Young

ALPHABETICAL
LIST OF ENTRIES

THEMATIC LIST

Entries by Category

Alternative Sciences

Analytical Concepts

Astronomy and Astrophysics

Almanacs
Astronomical Instruments
Astronomy: general works
Astronomy: non-European
Astrophysics
Big Bang Theory
Tycho Brahe

Nicolaus Copernicus
Cosmology
Galileo Galilei
Carl Friedrich Gauss
George Ellery Hale
Edmond Halley
William Herschel

Johannes Kepler
Particle Physics
Lambert Adolphe Jacques
    Quételet
David Rittenhouse
Space Science
Women in Science: astronomy

Chemical Sciences

Affinity
Alchemy
Atomism
Amedeo Avogadro
Adolf von Baeyer
Claude-Louis Comte de Berthollet
Jöns Jacob Berzelius
Biochemistry
Chemical Analysis
Chemical Revolution
Chemistry
Colloid Chemistry
Marie Curie

Humphry Davy
Drugs
Dyestuffs
Michael Faraday
Emil Fischer
Joseph Louis Gay-Lussac
Otto Hahn
Dorothy Hodgkin
Industrial Chemistry
Antoine Laurent Lavoisier
Justus von Liebig
Dmitrii Ivanovich Mendeleev
Walther Nernst

Organic Chemistry
Wilhelm Ostwald
Louis Pasteur
Pharmacology
Plastics and Polymers
Joseph Priestley
Carl Wilhelm Scheele
Spectroscopy
Valence
Women in Science: chemical
    sciences

Earth Sciences

Age of the Earth
Georgius Agricola
Agriculture
William Buckland
Cartography
Continental Drift

Georges Cuvier
Environmental Sciences
Geography of the Sciences
Geology
James Hutton
Charles Lyell

Meteorology
Oceanography
Paleontology
Physical and Human Geography
Niels Stensen

Education

Académie des Sciences
Accademia dei Lincei
Accademia del Cimento
CERN
École Polytechnique
Education
Engineering Schools

France: scientific and technical
    education
Gesellschaft Deutscher
    Naturforscher und Ärzte
Jesuits
Kaiser-Wilhelm-Gesellschaft zur
    Förderung der Wissenschaften

Muséum National D'Histoire
    Naturelle
Physikalisch-Technische
    Reichsanstalt
Scientification of Education
Universities

Engineering and Technology

Automobiles
Biotechnology
Calculating Devices
Electrical Engineering
Electrical Instruments
Engineering Schools
Engines: steam

Engines: turbo
Industrial Chemistry
Leonardo da Vinci
Metallurgy
Mills and Waterwheels
Photography
Printing

Werner von Siemens
Technology
Technology Transfer
Telegraphy
James Watt
Wind Turbines
Women in Science: technology

General Themes

Big Science
Capitalism and Science
Cartesianism
Colonialism and Science
Copernicanism
Degeneration
Dialectical Materialism
Education
Enlightenment
Ethnoscience
Exhibitions
Expeditions
Gender: general works
Gender and Identity
Gender and Sex
Graphical Method
Hermeticism
History of Science: general works

Humanism
Indigenous Knowledge Systems
Marxism and Science
Music and Science: antiquity to
    1700
Music and Science: since 1700
Newtonianism
Occult Sciences
Performance
Philosophy of Science
Polar Science
Popularization
Quantification
Religion and Science: general
    works
Religion and Science: Islam
Religion and Science: Medieval
Religion and Science: Renaissance

Research and Development
Romanticism
Scientific Illustration
Scientific Revolution
Scientification of Education
Sexuality
Themata
Third Reich and Science
Women in Science: general works
Women in Science: astronomy
Women in Science: chemical
    sciences
Women in Science: life sciences
Women in Science: medicine
Women in Science: physical
    sciences
Women in Science: technology

Individuals

Alfred Adler
Georgius Agricola
Archimedes
Aristotle
Amedeo Avogadro
Francis Bacon
Karl Ernst von Baer
Adolf von Baeyer
Joseph Banks
Gregory Bateson
Emil von Behring
Claude Bernard
Claude-Louis Comte de Berthollet
Jöns Jacob Berzelius
Marie François Xavier Bichat
Franz Boas
Herman Boerhaave
Niels Bohr
Ludwig Eduard Boltzmann
Robert Boyle
Tycho Brahe

William Buckland
George-Louis Leclerc, Comte de
    Buffon
Georg Cantor
Jean-Martin Charcot
Auguste Comte
Nicolaus Copernicus
Marie Curie
Georges Cuvier
Charles Darwin
Humphry Davy
John Dee
René Descartes
Pierre Maurice Marie Duhem
Émile Durkheim
Thomas Alva Edison
Paul Ehrlich
Albert Einstein
Euclid
Edward Evan Evans-Pritchard
Michael Faraday

Pierre Fermat
Enrico Fermi
Richard Feynman
Emil Fischer
Alexander Fleming
Howard Walter Florey
Michel Foucault
Benjamin Franklin
Joseph von Fraunhofer
Sigmund Freud
Galen
Galileo Galilei
Francis Galton
Luigi Galvani
Carl Friedrich Gauss
Joseph Louis Gay-Lussac
William Gilbert
Kurt Gödel
Johann Wolfgang von Goethe
Ernst Haeckel
Otto Hahn

George Ellery Hale
Edmond Halley
William Harvey
Friedrich August von Hayek
Werner Heisenberg
Hermann von Helmholtz
William Herschel
Heinrich Rudolf Hertz
David Hilbert
Hippocrates
Dorothy Hodgkin
Joseph Dalton Hooker
Alexander von Humboldt
John Hunter
James Hutton
Thomas Huxley
Christiaan Huygens
Carl Gustav Jung
Immanuel Kant
Johannes Kepler
John Maynard Keynes
Melanie Klein
Robert Koch
Max von Laue
Antoine Laurent Lavoisier
Ernest Orlando Lawrence
Gottfried Wilhelm Leibniz
Leonardo da Vinci
Claude Lévi-Strauss
Justus von Liebig
Carl Linnaeus
Joseph Lister

Konrad Lorenz
Charles Lyell
Trofim Denisovich Lysenko
Ernst Mach
Thomas Malthus
Etienne-Jules Marey
Alfred Marshall
Harriet Martineau
Karl Marx
Pierre-Louis Moreau de
    Maupertuis
James Clerk Maxwell
Lise Meitner
Gregor Mendel
Dmitrii Ivanovich Mendeleev
Marin Mersenne
Albert A. Michelson
John Stuart Mill
Robert Andrews Millikan
Gaspard Monge
John Napier
Walther Nernst
Salomon Neumann
Isaac Newton
J. Robert Oppenheimer
Hans Christian Ørsted
Wilhelm Ostwald
Paracelsus
Louis Pasteur
Ivan Petrovich Pavlov
Karl Pearson
Jean Piaget

Max Planck
Plato
Jules Henri Poincaré
Joseph Priestley
Pythagoras
Lambert Adolphe Jacques
    Quételet
Chandrasekhara Venkata Raman
Santiago Ramón y Cajal
David Rittenhouse
Wilhelm Conrad Röntgen
Henry Augustus Rowland
Ernest Rutherford
Carl Wilhelm Scheele
Friedrich Wilhelm Joseph von
    Schelling
Erwin Schrödinger
Seki Kowa
Werner von Siemens
Adam Smith
Herbert Spencer
Niels Stensen
Thomas Sydenham
J.J. Thomson
Alan Turing
Andreas Vesalius
Rudolf Virchow
Alessandro Volta
John Von Neumann
James Watt
William Whewell

Life Sciences

Aristotle
Bacteriology
Karl Ernst von Baer
Joseph Banks
Emil von Behring
Biochemistry
Biometrics, Statistical Biology,
    and Mathematical Statistics
Biotechnology
Botany: general works
Botany: Britain
George-Louis Leclerc, Comte de
    Buffon
Charles Darwin
Darwinism
Darwinism in Germany
DNA
Ecology
Embryology
Endocrinology
Ethology and Animal Behaviour

Eugenics
Evolution
Evolutionary Synthesis
Alexander Fleming
Francis Galton
Luigi Galvani
Genetic Engineering
Genetics: general works
Genetics: post-DNA
Ernst Haeckel
William Harvey
Heredity
Joseph Dalton Hooker
Horticulture
Human Genome Project
Alexander von Humboldt
John Hunter
Thomas Huxley
Robert Koch
Carl Linnaeus
Konrad Lorenz

Trofim Denisovich Lysenko
Etienne-Jules Marey
Gregor Mendel
Molecular Biology
Natural Selection
Ornithology
Paleontology
Louis Pasteur
Ivan Petrovich Pavlov
Physiology: France
Physiology: Germany
Santiago Ramón y Cajal
Niels Stensen
Respiration
Taxonomy
Veterinary Science
Andreas Vesalius
Virology
Vitalism
Women in Science: life sciences

Literature of Science

Almanacs
Encyclopedias

Journals
Literature and Science

Reading Culture and Science
Science Fiction

Mathematical Sciences

Accountancy
Algebra
Archimedes
Arithmetic
Artificial Intelligence
Axiomatics
Biometrics, Statistical Biology,
    and Mathematical Statistics
Calculating Devices
Georg Cantor
Chaos Theory
Computing
John Dee
René Descartes
Ethnomathematics
Euclid

Pierre Fermat
Function
Francis Galton
Carl Friedrich Gauss
Geometry
Kurt Gödel
Group Theory
David Hilbert
Christiaan Huygens
Gottfried Wilhelm Leibniz
Mathematical Instruments
Mathematical Modernity
Pierre-Louis Moreau de
    Maupertuis
Marin Mersenne
Gaspard Monge

John Napier
Number Theory
Karl Pearson
Jules Henri Poincaré
Probability
Pythagoras
Lambert Adolphe Jacques
    Quételet
Rational Mechanics
Seki Kowa
Set Theory
Statistics
Alan Turing
John Von Neumann

Medical and Health Sciences

Acupuncture
AIDS
Anatomy
Anti-Vivisection
Asylums
Claude Bernard
Marie François Xavier Bichat
Birth Control
The Body
Herman Boerhaave
Cancer
Cardiology
Jean-Martin Charcot
Clinical Science
Clinical Trials
Complementary Medicine
Dentistry
Doctor–Patient Relationship
Drugs
Paul Ehrlich
Embryology
Endocrinology
Epidemics
Epidemiology
Experimental Physiology
Fevers

Alexander Fleming
Howard Walter Florey
Forensic Sciences
Galen
Gynaecology
William Harvey
Health, Mortality, and Social
    Class
Herbalism
Hippocrates
Histology
Holistic Medicine
Homoeopathy
Human Genome Project
John Hunter
Hysteria
Immunology
Joseph Lister
Madness
Malaria
Medical Ethics
Medical Specialization
Medicine and Law
Medicine, Disease, and Health
Salomon Neumann
Neurosciences

Nursing
Nutrition
Obstetrics and Midwifery
Pain
Paracelsus
Pathology
Pharmacy
Plastic Surgery
Psychiatry
Psychoanalysis: conceptual
Psychoanalysis: gender
Psychoanalysis: institutional
Psychology
Public Health
Radiology
Reproductive Medicine
Sexuality
Surgery
Thomas Sydenham
Toxicology
Traditional Medicine
Andreas Vesalius
Rudolf Virchow
Virology

Medicine and Society

AIDS
Doctor–Patient Relationship
Epidemics
Health, Mortality, and Social
  Class

Medicine, Disease, and
  Health
Medicine and Law
Plague
Tuberculosis

Venereal Disease
Women in Science:
  medicine

National Histories

Africa: south of the Sahara
Africa: health and healing
Arabic Science
Australia and New Zealand
Brazil
Canada
China: general works
China: agriculture
China: astronomy and
  mathematics
China: medicine

China: natural history
Denmark
Egypt and Mesopotamia
France: scientific and technical
  education
Germanophone Areas
Greece: general works
Greece: medicine
Hungary
India: general works
India: medicine

International Science
Japan: general works
Japan: medicine
Japan: technology
Latin America
Netherlands: technology
Russia
Spain
Sweden
United States: general works
United States: women in science

Physical Sciences

Acoustics
Aether
Age of the Earth
Aristotle
Atomic Theory
Atomic Weapons
Atomism
Niels Bohr
Ludwig Eduard Boltzmann
Robert Boyle
CERN
Chaos Theory
Cryogenics
Marie Curie
René Descartes
Pierre Maurice Marie Duhem
Thomas Alva Edison
Albert Einstein
Electricity
Electromagnetism
Energy
Michael Faraday
Enrico Fermi
Richard Feynman
Benjamin Franklin

Joseph von Fraunhofer
Galileo Galilei
Galvanic Battery
Carl Friedrich Gauss
Joseph Louis Gay-Lussac
William Gilbert
Otto Hahn
Heat
Werner Heisenberg
Hermann von Helmholtz
Heinrich Rudolf Hertz
Christiaan Huygens
Max von Laue
Ernest Orlando Lawrence
Ernst Mach
Magnetism
Materials Science
James Clerk Maxwell
Lise Meitner
Albert A. Michelson
Robert Andrews Millikan
Walther Nernst
Isaac Newton
Nuclear Physics
J. Robert Oppenheimer

Optics
Hans Christian Ørsted
Wilhelm Ostwald
Particle Physics
Physical Chemistry
Physics: 20th century
Max Planck
Quantum Mechanics
Quantum Theory
Radioactivity
Chandrasekhara Venkata Raman
Relativity
Wilhelm Conrad Röntgen
Henry Augustus Rowland
Ernest Rutherford
Erwin Schrödinger
Solid State Physics
Spectroscopy
J.J. Thomson
Vacuum
Alessandro Volta
Women in Science: physical
  sciences

Science in "pre-modern" Cultures

Arabic Science
China: general works
China: agriculture
China: astronomy and
    mathematics

China: medicine
China: natural
    history
Egypt and Mesopotamia
Greece: general works

Greece: medicine
Medieval Science and Medicine

Scientific Instruments

Astrolabes
Astronomical Instruments
Blowpipe
Calculating Devices
Clocks
Computing

Electrical Instruments
Instrument Makers
Mathematical Instruments
Medical Instruments
Meteorological Instruments
Metrology

Microscopes
Navigational Instruments
Scientific Instruments: general
    works
Scientific Instruments: France
Telescopes

Social Sciences

Alfred Adler
Anthropology
Anthropometry
Archaeology
Atomic Weapons
Gregory Bateson
Franz Boas
Auguste Comte
Émile Durkheim
Eugenics
Edward Evan Evans-Pritchard
Michel Foucault
Sigmund Freud
Friedrich August von Hayek
Home Economics
Human Sciences
Hysteria

Carl Gustav Jung
Immanuel Kant
John Maynard Keynes
Melanie Klein
Claude Lévi-Strauss
Linguistics
Madness
Thomas Malthus
Malthusianism
Management Sciences
Alfred Marshall
Harriet Martineau
Karl Marx
John Stuart Mill
The Mind
Physical and Human Geography
Jean Piaget

Plato
Political Economy
Prehistory: archaeology and
    anthropology
Psychoanalysis: conceptual
Psychoanalysis: institutional
Psychoanalysis and Gender
Psychology
Psychophysics
Friedrich Wilhelm Joseph von
    Schelling
Adam Smith
Herbert Spencer
Social Sciences
Sociology
William Whewell

Societies and Institutions

Académie des Sciences
Accademia dei Lincei
Accademia del Cimento
Botanical and Zoological Gardens
British Association for the
    Advancement of Science
CERN
École Polytechnique
Engineering Schools
Galilean School
Gesellschaft Deutscher

Naturforscher und Ärzte
Global Organizations
Hospitals
Jesuits
Kaiser-Wilhelm-Gesellschaft zur
    Förderung der
    Wissenschaften
Muséum National D'Histoire
    Naturelle
Museums
Nobel Institution

Physikalisch-Technische
    Reichsanstalt
Rockefeller Foundation
Royal Institution
Royal Society of London
Russian Academy of Sciences
Smithsonian Institution
Societies
Universities

A

Académie des Sciences

Académie des Sciences, *Index biographique de l'Académie des Sciences du 22 decembre 1666 au 1er octobre 1978*, Paris: Gauthier-Villars, 1979

Briggs, Robin, "The Académie Royale des Sciences and the Pursuit of Utility", *Past and Present*, 131 (1991): 38–88

Crosland, Maurice P., *Science under Control: The French Academy of Sciences, 1795–1914*, Cambridge and New York: Cambridge University Press, 1992

Gillispie, Charles Coulston, *Science and Polity in France at the End of the Old Regime*, Princeton, New Jersey: Princeton University Press, 1980

Hahn, Roger, *The Anatomy of a Scientific Institution: The Paris Academy of Sciences, 1666–1803*, Berkeley: University of California Press, 1971

McClellan III, James E., "The Académie Royale des Sciences, 1699–1793: A Statistical Portrait", *Isis*, 72 (1981): 541–67

McClellan III, James E., *Science Reorganized: Scientific Societies in the Eighteenth Century*, New York: Columbia University Press, 1985

Outram, Dorinda, "The Ordeal of Vocation: The Paris Academy of Sciences and the Terror", *History of Science*, 21 (1983): 251–95

Paul, Charles B., *Science and Immortality: The Éloges of the Paris Academy of Sciences, 1699–1791*, Berkeley: University of California Press, 1980

Salomon-Bayet, Claire, *L'Institution de la science et l'expérience du vivant: Méthode et expérience à l'Académie royale des sciences 1666–1793*, Paris: Flammarion, 1978

Stroup, Alice, *Royal Funding of the Parisian Académie des Sciences during the 1690s*, (Transactions of the American Philosophical Society, 77/4) Philadelphia: American Philosophical Society, 1987

Stroup, Alice, *A Company of Scientists: Botany, Patronage, and Community at the Seventeenth-Century Parisian Royal Academy of Sciences*, Berkeley: University of California Press, 1990

Louis XIV and Jean-Baptiste Colbert founded the original Académie royale des sciences in 1666; since then it has occupied a distinguished place in the history of science and scientific institutions.

The Paris Academy was a new kind of scientific institution in the 17th century: an official organ of state devoted explicitly to the sciences. With academicians paid and research underwritten, the Paris institution was distinct from the traditional universities and from the Renaissance-style academies that preceded it. Reformed in 1699, the Academy ranked foremost among the great classical academies of the 18th century in terms of its membership, publications, expeditions, and research undertaken under its aegis. Closed by revolutionaries in 1793 and resurrected in 1795 as the First Class of the Institut de France, it continued after another constitution in 1803 as the Académie (or Académie royale) des sciences of the Institut, and so led French science in the 19th century. The Academy of Science is the premier scientific institution in France today and, along with the Royal Society of London (1662), the *grande dame* of learned scientific societies.

The Paris Academy has been thoroughly studied, and scholars have documented most stages in its long and distinguished history. In the 19th and early 20th centuries, the Academy itself and persons close to it produced a substantial body of work concerning the institution that serious students still need to consult. (That literature is accessible through more recent scholarly work discussed in this essay.) In this tradition the biographical index of members published by the ACADÉMIE DES SCIENCES remains an important resource for information about the institution and its members. In more recent years, however, a series of independent, professional historians of science has focused on the Academy, and it is through their studies that one should now broach the historiography.

HAHN remains the entry point for the history of the Academy from its foundation in 1666 to the early years of the 19th century. He underscores the distinct 17th-century phase of the Academy's history until its reform in 1699, and argues that the weaknesses of the Academy during this period stem from its "closed" nature (it met privately and published little), and from the failure of its early commitment to collective Baconian endeavors. Through her careful sifting of the financial records, STROUP (1987) clarifies the circumstances of the 17th-century Academy, documenting the erratic and often miserly support from the crown that also limited the Academy's initial effectiveness. STROUP (1990) covers much the same ground but with an important emphasis on botany and the life sciences in the early period of the institution's history. SALOMON-BAYET addresses the theme of experimentation in the life sciences in the shadow of the Academy with Foucauldian epistemological sophistication, illuminating the institution from the point of view of the life sciences across the 17th and 18th centuries. The pre-1699 phase of the Academy's history is now fairly well understood, although a full modern study of the Academy's early work in astronomy and geodesy remains to be written.

The formal reorganization of the Academy in 1699 created distinct categories of elected members and disciplinary fields, and otherwise transformed the institution into an active scientific center whose function was to judge and disseminate the approved scientific work of others. In its ensuing 18th-century phase the Academy reigned as Europe's leading scientific society, and this aspect of its history is the best studied. HAHN's focus is on the solidification of the Academy as an institution of the *ancien régime* in France and its travails to and through the revolutionary period. GILLISPIE provides additional context, and both emphasize the role of the Academy as a government institution providing technical and other useful services in exchange for the freedom to govern itself and science. Among the special studies of the Academy in the 18th century one needs to cite PAUL on the *éloges* of academicians published in the Academy's *Mémoires*; Paul underscores the rhetorical and ideological function of these *éloges* in helping to shape the modern image of science and scientists. McCLELLAN (1981) provides a statistical profile of the Academy's membership in the 18th century, albeit one that is somewhat too mathematically rigid. McCLELLAN (1985) sheds new light on the Academy's international relations and its place within the international organization of science at the time. BRIGGS offers an insightful study of the Academy's rather limited concern with technology and applied science in the *ancien régime*.

As part of their extirpation of *ancien régime* institutions, republicans in the National Convention suppressed the Academy of Science and other academies on 8 August 1793. Hahn is especially strong in tracing the demise of the old Academy and its revival in 1795 as the First Class of the Institut de France. OUTRAM examines the interregnum of the Terror and important continuities and discontinuities in the institutional history of the Academy from the point of view of the psychology of academicians in the turbulent months of 1793–95.

The 1992 volume by CROSLAND represents the first comprehensive study of the Academy in the 19th century, and it revises several cherished views. A former commonplace, for example, was that, with the growth and disciplinary specialization of science in the 19th century, the Academy became little more than a scientific hall of fame. Crosland, however, reveals the 19th-century Academy to have been of enormous influence and at the active center of contemporary French science and scientific research, and he documents how scientific life in and around a more democratic and discipline-oriented Academy orchestrated professional careers and a network of scientific institutions and appointments. The appearance in 1835 of the weekly *Comptes rendus* of the Academy and the elaboration of a system of prizes and grants thrust the institution to the forefront of French and world scientific production.

At the end of the 19th century the vitality of the Academy does seem to have declined in relation to other French scientific institutions and the rest of French science generally. Given the wealth of resources available to anyone approaching the history of the Academy of Sciences, the lack of a modern scholarly study of the Academy in the 20th century is all the more disappointing.

JAMES E. McCLELLAN III

Accademia dei Lincei

Accademia (L') dei Lincei e la cultura europea nel XVII secolo: Manoscritti – Libri – Incisioni – Strumenti scientifici, catalogue of the exhibition organized by A.M. Capecchi *et al.*, Rome: Accademia Nazionale dei Lincei, 1992

Biagioli, Mario, "Knowledge, Freedom and Brotherly Love: Homosociality and the Accademia dei Lincei", *Configurations*, 3 (1995): 139–66

Clericuzio, Antonio and Silvia De Renzi, "Medicine, Alchemy and Natural Philosophy in the Early Accademia dei Lincei", in *Italian Academies of the Sixteenth Century*, edited by D.S. Chamber and F. Quiviger, London: Warburg Institute, 1995

Convegno celebrativo del IV centenario della nascita di Federico Cesi, Acquasparta 7–9 ottobre 1985, Rome: Accademia Nazionale dei Lincei, 1986

Gabrieli, Giuseppe, *Contributi alla storia dell'Accademia dei Lincei*, 2 vols, Rome: Accademia Nazionale dei Lincei, 1989

Gardair, Jean-Michel, "I Lincei: i soggetti, i luoghi, le attività", *Quaderni storici*, 48 (1981): 763–87

Olmi, Giuseppe, "In essercitio universale di contemplatione e prattica: Federico Cesi e l'Accademia dei Lincei", in his *L'inventario del mondo: Catalogazione della natura e luoghi del sapere nella prima età moderna*, Bologna: Il Mulino, 1992

Raimondi, Ezio, "Scienziati e viaggiatori", in *Storia della Letteratura Italiana*, vol. 5, edited by Emilio Cecchi and Natalino Sapegno, Milan: Garzanti, 1967

The foundation of the Accademia dei Lincei by the Roman Prince Federico Cesi in 1603, and its subsequent enrolment of Galileo Galilei in 1611, have a secure place in the history of science. For a long time, however, discussions of the Accademia have had a somewhat ritual character, a nationalist historiography celebrating it as the pioneering first "scientific" academy and a model for later institutions. The recent general reassessment of such categories as scientific revolution and more specific studies of courtly culture have made it possible to reconsider the Accademia and its intellectual project. But so far the only extended analysis we have is OLMI's article, while the Accademia's immense archive has not yet been exploited.

ACCADEMIA, the catalogue of an exhibition organized in Paris in 1991, is a useful introduction to the history of the Accademia, as it offers a close view of documents, books and other objects which are not easily available. Exhaustive notes and remarkable illustrations document the wide range of the Accademia's interests very well.

GABRIELI's book gathers together the numerous papers he wrote for various journals between the 1920s and the 1940s. These were the result of his valuable archival research and were complemented by his publication in the 1940s of a large part of the correspondence of the Lincei. He concentrates primarily on the biographies and works of the members of the Accademia and these learned and meticulous profiles are still the starting point for research. His interpretation of the Accademia as a whole is, however, hagiographic: emphasising the role of the heroic scientist, Galileo Galilei, he builds for the Accademia the myth of a sudden turn from infatuation with late Renaissance natural philosophy and magic to the acquisition of the scientific method. In so doing, Gabrieli completely neglects crucial aspects of the activities of the Lincei, such as their medical and alchemical interests. These are the main subject of CLERICUZIO & DE RENZI's article. Focusing on the works of some of the Accademia's leading members, they show that an early interest in chemical and Paracelsian experimentation was by no means replaced by "more scientific" investigations. Rather, an updated knowledge of iatrochemistry, along with intense anatomical practice, remained an important feature of the medical activities and natural investigations of the numerous physicians among the Lincei.

In his still useful article, RAIMONDI analyses Cesi's intellectual project as part of the Prince's strong attack on the obsolete knowledge provided by the universities and endorsed in the courts. Cesi's violent antagonism to these sites of power led him to found a new and secluded institution, which with his utopian intentions should have been based on co-operation among scholars, direct observation of nature and the achievement of useful knowledge. Though this aim was only incompletely realised, Raimondi argues that the Lincei did achieve a major and far-reaching epistemological objective in developing a notion of accuracy and precision that was founded on their excellent use of scientific instruments like the microscope.

GARDAIR's paper is the first polemic challenge to the myth of national primacy. Basing his interpretation on statistical analysis, he points out that the Accademia actually organized rather few collective activities. By projecting backwards a stereotype of a "true" scientific institution, he argues that the Lincei were still trapped in courtly activities, and so developed only an amateurish approach to natural investigations. Although his statistics shed light on the social status and profiles of the Lincei, he fails to capture the distinctive features of the Accademia as an intellectual institution of court society.

One of the most balanced and well informed surveys of the Accademia is OLMI's article. He provides a thorough reading of the Accademia's still unpublished "Statute", and finds in the Lincei's commitment to a wide circulation of the results of its natural investigations one of the interesting novelties of its project. Furthermore, relying on the well-established political history of the Counter-Reformation, Olmi emphasises the complex relations between knowledge and political power in the first decades of the 17th century. Although Cesi declared that the price of the success of any innovative intellectual enterprise was complete neutrality on religious and political matters, almost all of the Lincei were in fact heavily involved in politics and diplomacy, especially on behalf of Galilei. But their considerable skills could not prevent the decline of the Accademia in the 1630s, when sudden political reversals unfavourably affected papal patronage.

More recently, BIAGIOLI has turned to gender history to make sense of the male bond and the rule of chastity that Cesi established for his Accademia. Undoubtedly, these were part of the military and aristocratic ethos he had inherited from his milieu, but, at the same time, brotherhood, freedom from sexual lust and seclusion ensured the Lincei the best conditions for the pursuit of their major epistemological aim, non-dogmatic knowledge and philosophical independence. Cesi's obsession with intellectual freedom can explain the main aporia of his project: the creation of an institution whose principal end was to put no constraint on its members. Moreover, this is the main feature of his Accademia, that, unlike later sites of natural research to which it has been compared inappropriately, it never became an articulated and regulated institution.

Although specific research has been done on other eminent members of the Accademia – such as Cassiano dal Pozzo, Giovanni Ciampoli and Johannes Faber – the life and intellectual background of its founder remains the principal topic for scholars. CONVEGNO, published for the centenary of Prince Cesi's birth, however, is a disappointing collection of papers of uneven quality. Among the best, Garin's article traces the late Renaissance philosophical sources of Cesi's plan, while Nicolò and Solina's contribution focuses on Cesi as a collector.

SILVIA DE RENZI

Accademia del Cimento

Altieri Biagi, Maria Luisa, "Lingua della scienza fra Sei e Settecento", in *Letteratura e scienza nella storia della cultura italiana*, edited by Vittore Branca, Palermo: Manfredi, 1978

Baldini, Ugo, "La scuola galileiana", in *Storia d'Italia*, edited by Gianni Micheli, Turin: Einaudi, 1980, 381–463

Biagioli, Mario, "Scientific Revolution, Social Bricolage, and Etiquette", in *The Scientific Revolution in National Context*, edited by Roy Porter and Mikulás Teich, Cambridge and New York: Cambridge University Press, 1992

Celebrazioni della Accademia del Cimento nel Tricentenario della Fondazione (Domus Galileiana, 19 June 1957), Pisa: Domus Galileiana, 1958

Galluzzi, Paolo, "L'Accademia del Cimento: 'gusti' del principe, filosofia e ideologia dell'esperimento", *Quaderni storici*, 16 (1981): 788–844

Middleton, W.E. Knowles, *The Experimenters: A Study of the Accademia del Cimento*, Baltimore: Johns Hopkins University Press, 1971

Poggi Salani, Teresa, Introduction to *Saggi di naturali esperienze*, by Lorenzo Magalotti, edited by Poggi Salani, Milan: Longanesi, 1976

Van Helden, Albert, "The Accademia del Cimento and Saturn's Ring", *Physis*, 15 (1973): 237–59

By the middle of the 17th century a group of natural philosophers, including Francesco Redi, Alfonso Borelli and Vincenzo Viviani, were in the habit of meeting in Florence at the court of the Grand Duke Ferdinando and his brother Leopoldo. Although they never subscribed to a formal charter and had different views on nature, for a period they worked together and conducted a range of physical experiments. A selection of their experimental trials was published after their erratic meetings had ended, in a book entitled *Saggi di naturali esperienze* (1667).

Since the 18th century, scholars have considered the Accademia del Cimento the first institution devoted entirely to experimental science. Positivist historiography has read its life, and especially its supposedly premature end, as an example of the interference of the Catholic Church in scientific activities in 17th-century Italy. Moreover, the Cimento's strong commitment to experimental trials has been explained as a strategic move to avoid philosophical issues that, after the Galilei affair, could become matters of dangerous conflict. In the last 20 years, however, all these assumptions, including the myth of the Cimento as a "scientific institution", have been questioned as scholars have fundamentally reassessed the status of natural investigations after Galilei's trial.

The principal aim of CELEBRAZIONI DELLA ACCADEMIA DEL CIMENTO is to celebrate the contributions made by members of the Accademia to various scientific fields. The most useful aspects of this work are the analytical description of archival material by Procissi, and the chapter by Righini Bonelli on the scientific apparatus owned and used by the Accademia.

The only book-length study on the Cimento is by MIDDLETON, who also presents a modern English translation of the *Saggi di naturali esperienze* and a valuable discussion of unpublished reports of the Accademia's experiments. His vast knowledge of archival sources makes this a detailed and still useful study. However, the account is largely descriptive, and Middleton does not really make the most of the rich material he has unearthed. This is clear, for instance, in the central chapter on the *Saggi*, in which he reconstructs their seemingly interminable editing and compares various extant drafts. Nevertheless, the only conclusion he offers is that the structure of the book clearly displays the Cimento's strong anti-Aristotelian bent, which, unfortunately, the Accademia could not openly state. Again, while Middleton acknowledges Prince Leopoldo's importance in establishing the Accademia, he does not tell us much about his intellectual background or his projects. On the whole, Middleton's evaluation is ambivalent: he admires the ingenuity of the experiments performed in the Accademia, but compares it unfavourably to other scientific institutions, especially the Royal Society. He seems to believe that the latter contributed much more to science.

Among the investigations not published in the *Saggi*, Middleton points to the usually neglected astronomical experiments carried out by the Cimento. Emphasising their importance to its history, VAN HELDEN's paper reconstructs the role of the astronomical models built by the Accademia in the long controversy between the astronomers Huygens and Divini about the rings of Saturn. To Prince Leopoldo's great embarrassment, both had dedicated their work to him and expected his authoritative approval. Taking the whole episode as an example of 17th-century intellectual negotiations, Van Helden focuses mainly on the Cimento's mastery of experimental technique in testing both hypotheses. He also underscores

the impartiality ostentatiously shown by Leopoldo until the Accademia obtained definitive evidence in favour of Huygens's work.

BALDINI's account of the Cimento is a section of his sweeping, but not very reader-friendly, article on the reworking of Galilei's heritage in the second half of the 17th century. To counteract the positivist dogma on the Church's negative role, he suggests that more "internal" reasons, such as an inadequate development of mathematics, were responsible for the decline of Italian science. But, since he is by no means an internalist historian, Baldini frames this intellectual crisis within the stagnating Italian economy and the lack of a dynamic bourgeoisie, with the consequent low demand for mathematical and technical skills. Therefore, while he fully acknowledges the importance of princely patronage in the laboratory activities of the Cimento, he believes that in the long run this typical courtly feature was a restraining factor in the history of Italian scientific investigations.

The most convincing and influential revision of the old historiography is GALLUZZI's paper. He stresses that princely patronage was not just an element in the history of this supposedly scientific enterprise, but rather the only reason for its existence. Far from being a scientific institution based on collaboration among researchers, the Cimento was one of the greatest successes in the cultural policy of the Medici. Prince Leopoldo's crucial role in setting the experimental agenda of the Accademia and in strongly promoting the publication of the *Saggi* are the strongest evidence for Galluzzi's thesis. Galluzzi further shows that the violent contrasts among members of the Cimento, both on relevant philosophical issues and on their careers, were cleverly hidden by the Prince. Through the Cimento he succeeded in building a long-lasting myth of his patronage and of neutral and consensual experimental knowledge. Galluzzi, however, is keen to emphasise that, like Borelli, not all members of the Accademia shared the Prince's conciliatory view and resented the interference of court patronage.

BIAGIOLI owes much to Galluzzi's thesis, but he develops a stronger sociological approach. His contribution is a section of a more general article in which, by comparing various national contexts in the late 17th century, he argues for the role of political power and court culture in structuring argumentative styles and scientific protocols. Thus, he understands the Cimento's celebrated empiricism as nothing but the outcome of a strict courtly rule that required princes to avoid harsh and status-tainting intellectual disputes. Only a science based on experimental trials and emptied of philosophical speculations allowed Leopoldo to take part in natural investigations and to be an authoritative patron. Biagioli invokes his status to make sense both of the institutional nature of the Accademia – a private rather than a public space – and of the content of its natural investigations. This is an interesting thesis, but since it is largely focused on Leopoldo, it is disappointing that the Prince remains a silhouette, and that almost nothing is said about his education, intellectual profile and political career between Florence and Rome.

In the 1970s scholars such as ALTIERI BIAGI drew attention to the making of a scientific prose in 17th-century Italy. The language used by Count Magalotti, analysed by POGGI SALANI, in writing the *Saggi*, and by other members of the

Cimento such as Redi, represented an important step in this direction. Now that courtly rhetoric and etiquette are at the centre of early modernists' concerns, such linguistic and literary researches may attract renewed interest.

SILVIA DE RENZI

Accountability

Ashworth, William J., "The Calculating Eye: Baily, Herschel, Babbage and the Business of Astronomy", *British Journal of the History of Science*, 27 (1994): 409–41

Kula, Witold, *Measures and Men*, translated by R. Szreter, Princeton, New Jersey: Princeton University Press, 1986

Lynch, Michael, *Scientific Practice and Ordinary Action: Ethnomethodology and Social Studies of Science*, Cambridge and New York: Cambridge University Press, 1993

Porter, Theodore M., *Trust in Numbers: The Pursuit of Objectivity in Science and Public Life*, Princeton, New Jersey: Princeton University Press, 1995

Power, Michael (ed.), *Accounting and Science: Natural Inquiry and Commercial Reason*, Cambridge and New York: Cambridge University Press, 1996

Shapin, Steven, *A Social History of Truth: Civility and Science in Seventeenth-Century England*, Chicago: University Press of Chicago, 1994

Accountability is a concept primarily associated with the idea of making the organisation and decision making apparatus of a government or public serving body answerable to the public, or a joint stock company responsible to its shareholders. At a time when there is such widespread mistrust of the institutions that combine to constitute what we loosely refer to as the State, the word accountability seems hardly to be out of the news. A form of accountability is seen as the means by which to preserve the integrity of (especially expert) institutions.

A useful starting point is a historical period when accountability in the above sense did not exist. During the 17th century, as SHAPIN has described, agreement about what constituted a piece of knowledge was reached through unspecified processes based on a set of social conventions. Veracity was a product of virtue defined by a gentlemanly code that gained its sense by a flourishing courtesy literature. The most important social characteristic was to be independent and therefore to seemingly have no reason to lie. Testimony lay at the core of economic truth-telling and was therefore implicit in relations of trust. An individual or an organisation was called to account not through a strict set of rules and set of ledger books, but via an unspecified code of economic behaviour played out in mainly face-to-face encounters.

Accountability was a term that emerged from the informational deluge of the late 18th century which accompanied the gradual forging of the notion of "the public". At the same time it witnessed the decline of genteel virtue and the *ancien régime*, with a movement towards specialisation and expert institutions. The notion of making people accountable for their actions or claims also finds an analogy in weights and measures. The work of KULA demonstrates that prior to the metric system, units of measurement referring to concrete objects such as the finger, foot and ell (elbow) were in everyday use. They had no abstract, standardized denomination. In short, accounting for the weight or measure of a commodity was a qualitative process that varied from region to region (and indeed within regions), and was suited to small communities. Kula argues that with the growth of the power of the state, increased commerce and expanding markets during the second half of the 18th century, weights and measures were increasingly made accountable to a standard meaning. The crucial impetus was the metrification of weights and measures in France, and its establishment in Europe during the 19th century. Metrological equality required measures to be independent of man and therefore seemingly morally neutral; this simultaneously required the equality of man before the law and the alienation of the commodity.

The late 18th-century legal philosopher Jeremy Bentham made accountability a cornerstone of his vast writings; the political radical Thomas Paine made it a key part of his pleas for social reform; and the stockbroker, member of parliament and political economist David Ricardo consistently pressured the government to make the Bank of England more accountable to parliament. Simultaneously, movements in science sought to make scientific claims more accountable. For example, ASHWORTH looks at the drive in 1820s London to police speculation in science and finance alike and to make both activities visibly accountable. Such a development required standardized tools (calculating tables and experimental apparatus) and indeed the idea of a generalized scientific method. Ideally, as Jeremy Bentham sought, the whole history of decision-making should be rendered visible and therefore accountable.

The contributors to POWER examine the function and character of economic calculation within science. They claim that to understand science we must examine the diverse array of expert scientific communities, the importance of lobbying for funds (and the bodies in charge of these funds), and the demands for public accountability. Power claims that science is now made accountable in economic terms through the use of accountancy, and there has been a shift from preoccupation with the scientificity of accounts to the financial accountability of science. In this sense science now has to be put into quantitative terms before it can be made accountable. Consequently, to obtain a better understanding of science we should look more closely at the practice of economic calculation. To do this we should make accountancy itself visible.

Numbers are the language we now generally associate with accountability. PORTER has traced the rise of trust in numbers in both science and politics to a desire to make decisions accountable – that is, literally to depersonalize the whole process and thus shift the onus to one not seemingly based on the interests of a particular social group. It was the insecure realm of social administration and policy, he argues, which introduced numerical objectivity (rather than the natural sciences). Moreover, it was propagated by those placed in a relative position of weakness within large bureaucracies – this can be seen particularly in the US during the 20th century. In short, accountability through standardized rules and impersonal numbers is a product of those primarily in a weak position. This formalization seemingly expels the need for personal trust. It is central, Porter argues, to a more open and therefore accountable society. In this sense trust in numbers is a fundamental axis in the functioning of a democratic society.

However, it could be argued that this process of depersonalization still shields the particular social interests hiding behind numbers. For SHAPIN, face-to-face contact and a more primordial form of trust remain necessities even to those practising science in modern democratic countries; and equally, this numerical depersonalized process continues to depend for its validity on an equally social and moral code of truth-telling. Therefore the important issues are: who deems what numbers are meaningful, and who is qualified to produce them? To understand the numbers you have to understand the people who produce them, and to understand what it is to be accountable you have to understand who legislates for this process.

Another way of looking at accountability within a scientific context is given to us by LYNCH. To appreciate the ethnomethodological approach we now have to shift our attention from the encompassing themes offered above, and travel to the more local and mundane. For Lynch and the ethnomethodologists there is no foundational, structuralist or materialist framework in which accountability should be situated. Rather, it is how the order and reason of scientific activities make themselves accountable within the setting in which it occurs. Accountability here does not retain some common features, but is simply concerned with observing how those involved in scientific practice make their activities accountable. Anyone who is a competent participant in the activity under scrutiny will recognize it as orderly, ordinary, and observable. Hence, through a number of ethnomethodological tools, those participants under examination can be held to account for their actions. Accountability, in this sense, is making the routine, taken-for-granted activities visible and recognizable (accountable). What it is to be accountable and give an account of the activity is reflexively embedded within the activity.

WILLIAM J. ASHWORTH

See also Accountancy; Quantification

Accountancy

Ashworth, William J., "The Calculating Eye: Baily, Herschel, Babbage and the Business of Astronomy", *British Journal of History of Science*, 27 (1994): 409–41

Babbage, Charles, *On the Economy of Machinery and Manufactures*, Philadelphia: Carey and Lea, 1832; London: 1832; 3rd edition, London: Knight, 1833

Hopwood, Anthony and Peter Miller (eds), *Accounting as Social and Institutional Practice*, Cambridge and New York: Cambridge University Press, 1994

Lowood, Henry, "The Calculating Forester: Quantification, Cameral Science and the Emergence of Scientific Forestry Management in Germany", in *The Quantifying Spirit in the 18th Century*, edited by Tore Frängsmyr, J.L. Heilbron and Robin E. Rider, Berkeley: University of California Press, 1990

Mumford, M.J. and K.V. Peasnell (eds), *Philosophical Perspectives on Accounting: Essays in Honour of Edward Stamp*, London and New York: Routledge, 1993

Noble, David, *America by Design: Science, Technology and the Rise of Corporate Capitalism*, New York: Knopf, 1977; Oxford: Oxford University Press, 1979

Porter, Theodore M., *Trust in Numbers: The Pursuit of Objectivity in Science and Public Life*, Princeton, New Jersey: Princeton University Press, 1995

Power, Michael (ed.), *Accounting and Science: Natural Inquiry and Commercial Reason*, Cambridge and New York: Cambridge University Press, 1996

Sterling, Robert, *Toward a Science of Accounting*, Houston, Texas: Scholars Book, 1979

Swetz, Frank, *Capitalism and Arithmetic: The New Math of the 15th Century*, La Salle, Illinois: Open Court, 1987

Taylor, Frederick, *The Principles of Scientific Management*, New York: Harper, 1911

At first glance the history of science and the history of accountancy have little to do with each other. "Heroic" conceptions of scientific activity have tended to exclude the influence of practices such as accounting, because they threaten to make either science too mundane or accounting "too interesting". However, increasing attention to the laboratory context of scientific activity, and the widespread recognition that science and society are a "seamless web", have created a new intellectual agenda that spans formerly distinct fields of inquiry.

The precise form of entanglement between scientific and accounting practice has only recently become an explicit object of interest, and the literature is far from extensive or well-developed. Broadly speaking, a convergence of research interests across the sociology of science, history of science, and accounting has occurred around three relatively discrete themes: the claims of accounting to be a science; accounting as a model of administrative objectivity; and the impact of accounting on science.

As far as the first theme is concerned, accountancy, like many other disciplines, has experienced "scientistic" longings, searching for legitimate foundations in a particular, and now largely discredited, model of natural science. This programme is not as implausible as it sounds, since systematic accounting techniques emerged in conjunction with developments in arithmetic. SWETZ analyses the cultural background of the *Treviso Arithmetic* and the commercial demands that drove arithmetical innovation, particularly in 14th- and 15th-century Italy where double-entry bookkeeping became well established and was famously codified by Luca Pacioli.

More recently, accounting scholars such as STERLING have pursued the dream of reconnecting accounting to its nobler "scientific" origins by transforming it into a science. MUMFORD & PEASNELL contains many essays that extend and criticise this dream although, apart from a few "realists" of economic measurement, it has not gained mass support, even though the rhetoric of science has proved convenient from time to time. Despite Sombart's bold claim that double-entry bookkeeping was born of the same spirit as the systems of Galileo and Newton, accounting researchers in the late 20th century aspire to be social scientists themselves and are less concerned about whether accounting is, or could be, regarded as scientific.

PORTER has argued that the scientistic aspirations of Sterling and others should not be dismissed out of hand. He claims that there is much to be learned about science from the "objectivity" debates of other disciplines. In particular, the claimed administrative objectivity and neutrality of accounting typify an important dimension of the social "trust in numbers". Practices of quantification in general, and of accounting in particular, crystallize social demands for forms of procedural fairness. Indeed, the imperatives of administrative consensus have almost become indifferent to the epistemological problem of whether accounting can give an accurate representation of the world. Accordingly, Porter's frame of reference is a history of objectivity in which science is one practice among many.

Despite Porter's rehabilitation of accounting as a (philosophically) interesting component of the history of objectivity, the economic and material basis of scientific activity is not a new theme. ASHWORTH explores the reciprocal relations between accountancy and astronomy in 19th-century Britain. This is not simply a question of business as a context for science, but of the co-production of key concepts in each field. LOWOOD makes these conceptual exchanges visible within the context of German forestry management, and in BABBAGE's *On the Economy of Machinery and Manufacturers* (1832) ideas of rational factory management correspond to those of a natural world system. Hence, notions of economy, calculation, balance, and precision have played decisive roles in the formation of both business and scientific practice, in which there are constant exchanges between intellectual and financial capital.

NOBLE shows how elements of Babbage's ideas were put into practice by TAYLOR some years later in North America. Taylor pioneered rational economic procedures in the form of cost accounting and statistical control, which constituted a re-engineering of the workplace. Critical analyses of Taylorism and other accounting-based reforms have revealed the way accounting is both constructed by social and economic demands and constitutive of its environment. The essays in HOPWOOD & MILLER are paradigmatic of this constructivist view of accounting: accounting techniques make organisations and individuals "visible" and "knowable" in economic terms. Financial statements, cash budgets and standard costing techniques are, like laboratory instruments, all ways of "representing and intervening".

These themes in the sociology of accounting meet the sociology of science in a number of the essays in POWER. This brings us full circle, from scientistic attempts to reform accounting to a consideration of the accounting-based reforms of public science that have taken place in many countries since the mid-1980s. Although there is no suggestion in these essays that public science has not always been shaped and made accountable in various ways to peers, patrons and the public, the financial accountability of science has intensified in recent years. And, despite earlier studies of the corporate laboratory within business history, it can be no accident that the "economics of science" is an emerging research programme in the 1990s, at a time when laboratory practice is itself being challenged and transformed by the need to give a financial account of itself. It is as if the distinction between factories and laboratories has become blurred, and the power of accounting techniques to represent scientific practice within policy contexts is transforming ways of thinking and speaking about scientific

practice. Hence, although the position of accountancy research within the history of science has been at best marginal, it is likely to assume greater importance in the future, as accountancy and scientific practices increasingly overlap.

MICHAEL POWER

See also Accountability; Quantification

Acoustics

Fletcher, Neville H. and Thomas D. Rossing, *The Physics of Musical Instruments*, New York: Springer, 1991
Hunt, Frederick Vinton, *Electroacoustics*, Cambridge, Massachusetts: Harvard University Press, 1954
Hunt, Frederick Vinton, *Origins in Acoustics: The Science of Sound from Antiquity to the Age of Newton*, New Haven, Connecticut: Yale University Press, 1978
Lindsay, R. Bruce (ed.), *Acoustics: Historical and Philosophical Development*, Stroudsburg, Pennsylvania: Dowden Hutchinson and Ross, 1971
Maley, V. Carlton, *The Theory of Beats and Combination Tones, 1700–1863*, New York: Garland, 1990
Palisca, C.V., "Scientific Empiricism in Musical Thought", in *Seventeenth Century Science and the Arts*, edited by Hedley Howell Rhys, Princeton, New Jersey: Princeton University Press, 1961
Rayleigh, Lord (John William Strutt), *The Theory of Sound*, 2 vols, London: Macmillan, 1877–78; reprinted, New York: Dover, 1945
Wood, Alexander, *The Physics of Music*, London: Methuen, 1945; 7th edition, revised by J.M. Bowsher, London: Chapman and Hall, and New York: Wiley, 1975

Historical literature about acoustics is, unfortunately, quite sparse. Acoustics is a "cross-roads" subject; its historical development can only be understood within the context of its relation to certain other sciences and arts, and this complexity perhaps explains the paucity of the literature. Nevertheless, the books and articles presented here are the most accurate and comprehensive currently available, and will provide a complete, if rather one-dimensional, history of the subject.

The best place to start is HUNT (1978). Unfortunately, the work is unfinished, and only the chapters that present the history of acoustics from ancient times to the 17th century are published in a complete form. The book's great strengths, however, are its comprehensive presentation of the scientific background of each era investigated and the stress it lays on the importance of the interrelations between acoustics and other sciences. In particular, it gives a good picture of developments in acoustics in association with developments in music.

Research in acoustics in the 16th and 17th centuries is the subject of PALISCA, who discusses the development of acoustics against the background of 17th-century empiricism and the scientific revolution. Palisca makes effective use of the fact that the evolution of acoustics is closely related to that of the theory of music and of the construction of musical instruments, in order to demonstrate the shift to empiricism that took place during this period.

MALEY looks at the development of ideas and beliefs concerning the combination tones, a subject that has been at the centre of acoustical research for at least three centuries, and which gives a useful picture of the progression of "acoustics" from merely a servant of music to a physical subject in its own right. Maley provides a clear picture of the ideas of the time (1700–1863), and lucidly describes the underlying physics of the problem.

HUNT (1954) contains a 91-page historical introduction to the problem of transducers and telephony, from the early 19th century through to the first decades of the 20th century. The inventions of the telegraph and telephone are covered in detail, and there is also an excellent discussion on the development of the field of electroacoustics (including a section on underwater acoustics and sonar). The references are extensive and together offer a complete guide to this particular subject.

WOOD covers in full the problem of the physics of music. The book assumes a minimal knowledge of physics, and so can be enjoyed by all those interested in the subject, whatever their background. Aside from this, Wood gives a great deal of historical information about almost everything related to the acoustics of music, including combination tones and temperament, musical instruments and the basic principles of musical theatre architecture. Unfortunately the book suffers from a lack of references to the original publications, but other books referenced by Wood would give this information.

FLETCHER & ROSSING's aim is similar to Wood's, but their book requires a greater knowledge of physics to be useful. Moreover, the historical elements are few, and mainly concern the physics of vibrations and the histories of individual instruments. The reference section lists other books giving the history of the development of different instruments.

LINDSAY has collected 39 original articles on subjects related to acoustics, ranging from those from antiquity (Aristotle and Vitruvius) to those from the end of the 19th century (Rayleigh). Matters discussed include acoustics in general, propagation of sound (in air or any other medium), the acoustics of theatres and the mathematics of acoustics. Some of the articles included were translated by Lindsay from their original language (Latin, German or French) for the first time. Lindsay's introduction also gives a short summary of the history of acoustics with useful references.

Finally, RAYLEIGH's *The Theory of Sound* should be included because the Dover edition has a useful introduction by R.B. Lindsay, which gives a short summary of the history of acoustics. Moreover, even though Rayleigh's book is not in fact a history of sound, the lack of a book in the literature that includes the original references for the mathematics of acoustics (vibration of strings, bars, plates, and membranes etc.) makes its inclusion something of a necessity.

BASILEIOS DROLIAS

See also Music and Science: Antiquity to 1700; Music and Science: since 1700

Acupuncture

Farquhar, Judith, *Knowing Practice: The Clinical Encounter of Chinese Medicine*, Boulder, Colorado: Westview Press, 1994

Geoffroy, Daniel, *L'Acupuncture en France au XIXe siècle*, Paris: Maisonneuve, 1986

Kuriyama, Shigehisa, "Interpreting the History of Bloodletting", *Journal of the History of Medicine and Allied Sciences*, 50 (1995): 11–46

Lu Gwei-Djen and Joseph Needham, *Celestial Lancets: A History and Rationale of Acupuncture and Moxa*, Cambridge and New York: Cambridge University Press, 1980

Saks, Mike, *Professions and the Public Interest: Medical Power, Altruism and Alternative Medicine*, London and New York: Routledge, 1995

Unschuld, Paul U., *Medicine in China: A History of Ideas*, Berkeley: University of California Press, 1985 (original edition, 1980)

As with many issues in Asian science and medicine, Joseph Needham's vast series *Science and Civilization in China* is the main point of departure for examinations of acupuncture, and the volume by LU & NEEDHAM is a separately published section of that series. As the title implies, this work is designed to supply the needs of two distinct groups of readers, the historians (whether of medicine, Chinese science, or the interchange between East and West) and those seeking a theoretical understanding of acupuncture medicine. Neither it, nor any of the other books in this entry, is intended as a practical guide to using the treatment. Lu & Needham begin by defining the body as it has been theorized in classical Chinese acupuncture texts, and then describe the growth of the therapy as a specialized medical practice. After an extensive discussion of "the possible physiological interpretations which look like giving it a rationale in terms of modern science", the authors examine acupuncture's reception and history in Asia and Europe. They conclude with an analysis of acupuncture's influence as a system of therapy. Ironically, considering their ample critique of Western medicine before the 20th century, *Celestial Lancets* is somewhat hampered by its authors' uncritical acceptance of the truth status and authority of Western scientific medicine. None the less, it remains a vital resource in studying acupuncture's historical development and diffusion, and an excellent starting point for those who wish to understand the traditions and theories underlying the therapeutic use of the needle in Chinese medicine.

UNSCHULD's work continues this tradition of Chinese medical scholarship, adding a strong interpretative and theoretical framework and a more critical stance on the value of scientific medicine. The book treats Chinese medicine as a whole, with acupuncture as one node within a wider network of treatments and ideologies of the body and disease. Unschuld argues that a complex culture inevitably produces a complex and often contradictory set of medical systems; these systems are characterized by both stable paradigmatic cores and "soft coatings", susceptible to the changing currents of their sociopolitical milieu. To make visible the ways in which change and diversity emerge within health care, Unschuld proposes a four-pronged approach, entailing chronological, linguistic, structural and socio-political analyses of medical systems. In the case of acupuncture, Unschuld illustrates the changing rationales offered for the treatment through the writings of individual practitioners at different periods in China's history. These individual voices are among the best features of the book, which draws its sources from the pre-history of China to its present.

Although these first works focus on acupuncture's Chinese roots and history, the therapy has been examined from several other perspectives. Its history in Europe and North America has been studied, though in less depth than its history in China. For example, GEOFFROY details the 17th- and 18th-century transmission of acupuncture to Europe, and its subsequent role in 19th-century French medical culture. The text is rich in contemporary French reports of needling, and describes both medical and popular responses to acupuncture. However, the author offers no explanation for the century-long delay between the initial transmission of information about the therapy and acupuncture's eventual adoption by the medical community, or for the fluctuating popularity of the technique in 19th-century France.

Acupuncture has also been used as a lens through which to examine alternative medicine, modalities of the clinical encounter, and the behaviors and motivations of professional groups. SAKS offers a survey of the British medical profession's historical and contemporary responses to acupuncture, documenting a persistent "climate of rejection", based not on the relative therapeutic merits of the needle but on the economic and political exigencies of the medical profession in Britain. Here, acupuncture acts as the stage on which Saks demonstrates his new method of assessing the motivations of professional groups; however, this approach fails to acknowledge the cultural attributes of acupuncture, and their effect on the response of the medical community and clientele. Moreover, in focusing so intently on the power of the medical profession to create this "climate of rejection", Saks falls into the trap of seeking a single explanation for a highly complex phenomenon. Nevertheless, the book begins to examine the long-term pattern of professional response to acupuncture in the West, and offers an example of the way in which acupuncture can act as a window through which to observe larger medical and cultural systems.

KURIYAMA's article also uses acupuncture as a means of investigating a broader set of issues. However, he shifts from studying acupuncture either alone or contrasted with modern Western medicine to a comparative analysis of the early histories of acupuncture and phlebotomy. The two therapies emerged synchronously and were initially quite similar, despite their geographical separation. Kuriyama uses comparisons between their diverging paths to illuminate underlying conceptual differences between Greek and Chinese ideas of health and disease. This article illustrates a new way of studying acupuncture and Chinese medicine; the rigid wall between analyses of Eastern and Western medicine is breaking down, and it is being replaced by historical work that looks, not at one side alone, but at each side as a guide to interpreting and understanding the other.

Finally, FARQUHAR, although not focusing solely on acupuncture, offers a vivid picture of the contemporary practice of Chinese medicine. Embedded within a broad ethnographic portrait are glimpses of acupuncture within its native context, practised as a living, and even as a mundane therapy. Farquhar examines Chinese medical praxis through its theory, institutions, practitioners and cases, but her emphasis is on the persistent particularity of diagnosis and on the skilled knowledge that is displayed and valued by practitioners of traditional Chinese medicine. Farquhar's text is certainly not designed to provide basic information about acupuncture or historical facts about needling; nevertheless, it canvasses and interrogates day-to-day clinical medicine in China and provides a useful foil to historical works on acupuncture.

ROBERTA E. BIVINS

See also China: medicine; Complementary Medicine

Adler, Alfred   1870–1937

Austrian psychologist

Adler, Kurt A. and Danica Deutsch (eds), *Essays in Individual Psychology: Contemporary Applications of Alfred Adler's Theories*, New York: Grove Press, and London: Evergreen Books, 1959

Bruder-Bezzel, Almuth, *Alfred Adler: Die Entstehungsgeschichte einer Theorie im historischen Milieu Wiens*, Göttingen: Vandenhoeck & Ruprecht, 1983

Hoffman, Edward, *The Drive for Self: Alfred Adler and the Founding of Individual Psychology*, Reading, Masachusetts: Addison-Wesley, 1994

Mosak, Harold H., "Adlerian Psychotherapy", in *Current Psychotherapies*, edited by Raymond J. Corsini and Danny Wedding, 4th edition, Ithaca, Illinois: Peacock, 1989

Sperber, Manès, *Masks of Loneliness: Alfred Adler in Perspective*, New York: Macmillan, 1974

Stepansky, Paul E., *In Freud's Shadow: Adler in Context*, Hillsdale, New Jersey: Analytic Press, 1983

Sweeney, Thomas J., *Adlerian Counseling*, Boston: Houghton Mifflin, 1975; 2nd edition, Muncie, Indiana: Accelerated Development, 1981

The literature on Alfred Adler tends to be determined by Adler's opposition to Sigmund Freud; even where it is biographical, much emphasis is put on the development of the Adlerian alternative in psychoanalysis, and the fact that both Adler and Freud were Viennese has prompted much of the literature to analyse Adler within the context of his home city.

Adler, according to SWEENEY in his overview account, began his career as an ophthalmologist in 1898, switched to general practice and then to neurology. He published his first psychological paper in 1904, and from 1907 to 1937 he became a catalyst in the field of psychotherapy. However, his name is not as well known as that of Freud, perhaps because he focused on teaching, rather than on publishing and promoting his theories.

Adler's idea of community was forged in his early years as a street urchin in the outskirts of Vienna. Even though he was Jewish, he grew up within a Christian community; Vienna at the time was anti-Semitic, and Freud, his contemporary who also lived in Vienna, had a very different childhood experience. SPERBER suggests that Adler's conversion from Judaism to Protestantism was not the result of a change in belief, but of a desire to escape the Viennese scorn of Jews, and he eventually became an atheist. Freud and Adler developed their theories at about the same time, but came to very different conclusions; in a very readable format, HOFFMAN outlines the effects of early developmental impressions on Adler, and traces his professional development, his relationship with Freud and the eventual breakdown of their relationship.

Sperber also examines the societal norms of Vienna and their influence on the development of the field of psychotherapy, and explains how Adler formulated his concepts of the unconscious, dream interpretation, repression, personality types, sexuality, social organization and authority, in contrast, and sometimes in opposition, to Freud's positions and attitudes. Sweeney provides an overview of Adler's theories, grouping his basic concepts under the following headings – socio, teleo, development, family constellation, life tasks, emotions, values, and validation.

ADLER & DEUTSCH have compiled papers that support and define the concepts and theories originally conceived by Alfred Adler. Theories of personality through to therapeutic interventions are presented, illustrated, and expounded on, showing how his basic theories of social interest, lifestyle, family constellation, and so on, can be applied to therapeutic situations.

Sweeney explains Adler's differing views on counselling and psychotherapy, with attitudes toward lifestyle and behavior indicated as determining factors. MOSAK provides an overview of the basic theory of Adlerian psychotherapy, comparing it to other systems and giving the historical background to its development. He includes a theory of personality and defines concepts such as lifestyle, social inferiority and the broader context of a therapeutic relationship. For the practitioner, helpful techniques are described, and case studies illustrate how social interactions can be addressed within a therapeutic relationship.

Sperber touches on Adler's theories of hysteria and psychosomatic illness, and promotes Adler's theory of learned behavior. Adler believed that individuality is shaped by one's environment and that traits are learned. He observed developmental behavior and formulated his theory of inferiority on a child's need for language, on physical and social development, and on the awareness of one's own consciousness. Adler expounds on the development of the subconscious in conjunction with his theory of repression.

Sweeney takes a more specific look at Adler's views on child guidance, counselling, consultation and group procedures. Adler saw child guidance as intertwined with life tasks; his theory is based on the influence of others on the child, and a child's need for social contact, and considers a child's behavior, whether disruptive or not, as goal-based with natural or logical consequences.

Hoffman traces how, later in life, Adler lectured throughout the US on the subject of society and the personality; through these lectures, he helped the general populace to define anxieties centered on social issues. Of interest is his discussion of personality and its draw. Hoffman suggests, however, that

Adler was often sought out as a lecturer because of his personality, rather than his tenets.

STEPANSKY examines Adler's later system of Individual Psychology against the backdrop of the Freudian years, and argues that the split between Freud and Adler should not dominate the critical assessment. Stepansky aims to evaluate Adler's status as educator and psychiatrist by placing him within a wider cultural and intellectual matrix.

BRUDER-BEZZEL goes even further in the attempt to contextualize Adler. She places Adler within the *zeitgeist* of his generation in Vienna, arguing that scientists and artists were moving away from causal–scientific thought towards holism, in which the driven psyche is replaced by the conception of the individual as an active subject. Within this, Bruder-Bezzel argues, Adler exposes masculinity as a posture, masking an inferiority complex born out of a fear of social degradation.

SALLY S. GRAHAM

See also Freud; Psychoanalysis: conceptual; Psychoanalysis: institutional

Aether

Cantor, Geoffrey and Michael J.S. Hodge (eds), *Conceptions of Ether: Studies in the History of Ether Theories, 1740–1900*, Cambridge and New York: Cambridge University Press, 1981

Doran, Barbara Giusti, "Origins and Consolidation of Field Theory in Nineteenth-Century Britain: From the Mechanical to the Electromagnetic View of Nature", *Historical Studies in the Physical Sciences*, 6 (1975): 133–260

Hunt, Bruce J., *The Maxwellians*, Ithaca, New York: Cornell University Press, 1991

Schaffner, Kenneth F., *Nineteenth-Century Aether Theories*, Oxford and New York: Pergamon Press, 1972

Schofield, Robert E., *Mechanism and Materialism: British Natural Philosophy in an Age of Reason*, Princeton, New Jersey: Princeton University Press, 1970

Swenson, Loyd S., *The Ethereal Aether: A History of the Michelson–Morley–Miller Aether-Drift Experiments, 1880–1930*, Austin: University of Texas Press, 1972

Whittaker, Edmund T., *A History of the Theories of Aether and Electricity from the Age of Descartes to the Close of the Nineteenth Century*, London and New York: Longmans Green, 1910

Wilson, David B., "The Thought of Late Victorian Physicists: Oliver Lodge's Ethereal Body", *Victorian Studies*, 15 (1971): 29–48

Wynne, Brian, "Physics and Psychics: Science, Symbolic Action, and Social Control in Late Victorian England", in *Natural Order: Historical Studies of Scientific Culture*, edited by Barry Barnes and Steven Shapin, Beverley Hills, California: Sage, 1979

Most early histories of the aether present a technical discussion of this unseen medium, rather than an examination of the broader intellectual contexts within which the concept of the aether was constructed. In recent years, historians have shown much more interest in how the aether performed specific functions within particular intellectual and cultural settings, and have developed historiographies appropriate to different phases of aether history.

The Cambridge mathematician Edmund WHITTAKER produced one of the first comprehensive surveys of the development of the concept of the aether from the earliest times, through the ideas of Newton and the problems of aberration, to the great 19th-century theories of Augustin Jean Fresnel, Augustin Cauchy, Louis MacCullagh, George Gabriel Stokes and William Thomson. He is concerned solely with the technical development of the aether, and makes free and anachronistic use of vector calculus notation throughout his discussion: the latter may benefit science students, but it effaces important historical connections between Victorian mathematical language and the mechanical models that informed them.

SCHAFFNER's short technical survey includes readings from primary sources and is aimed at science students interested in the history of science. The author concentrates exclusively on Fresnel's optical aether, the elastic solid aethers of George Green and MacCullagh, and the electromagnetic aethers of George Francis FitzGerald, Joseph Larmor and Hendrik Antoon Lorentz. Despite his cursory treatment of Michael Faraday and James Clerk Maxwell, the author succeeds in depicting a continuous 19th-century project to weld optical, mechanical, and electromagnetic aethers. This is the best place to begin grappling with the mathematical foundations of important 19th-century aether theories.

SCHOFIELD examines the effects of Newton's legacy on 18th-century aether concepts in physics, chemistry and physiology, and demonstrates the rich material available for 18th-century aether scholarship. He characterises the work of early Newtonians as "mechanists", who primarily used Newton's *Principia* to explain natural phenomena in terms of material particles acting under discoverable force laws. By 1740, a second generation of Newtonians, the "materialists", rejected this tradition and used Newton's *Opticks* to interpret phenomena such as heat and electricity in terms of a Newtonian imponderable material aether. The author's rigid distinctions between "mechanism" and "materialism", and between "force" and "imponderables", have been severely criticised: for instance, Newton and his readers did not recognise the distinction between aethers and forces, but regarded the aether itself as the agency of repulsive forces.

DORAN's lucid technical prose complements Schaffner's mathematical approach. She makes William Thomson a pivotal figure in the Victorian demechanisation of the aether, from atoms in a void acting at a distance to a non-material, continuous electromagnetic field whose dynamical structures produce discrete material atoms. Thomson's 1856 vortex-atom theory of matter "spawned an entire tradition of aether and matter based on the continuous nonmaterial plenum", and Faraday's crucial conversion to field theory, and Maxwell and Larmor's speculations on aether and matter, owed much to Thomson's thinking. In this account, aethers were constructed to solve internal problems in optics and electromagnetism rather than to express wider intellectual and metaphysical concerns.

Physicists and historians have typically cited the celebrated Michelson–Morley experiments of 1880 and 1887 as definitive evidence against the existence of a stagnant luminiferous aether. SWENSON insists, rather unconvincingly, that the experiments were not designed to search for an aether, but were originally intended to study the behaviour of light through moving media. This "social history" stresses the personalities and the vicissitudes of experiments, and charts the decline of the aether through statistical analysis. The experiment on the aether, he concludes, "derived its importance far more from what it suggested than from what it imposed".

WILSON uses Oliver Lodge – one of the great Victorian aether architects – to discuss the religious and metaphysical functions of the aether. He argues that Lodge's aether, as described in his *My Philosophy* (1933), continued and conflated four Victorian scientific traditions: a harmonious relationship between science and religion found in the writings of Maxwell, Stokes and William Thomson; psychical research, which had shown Lodge the reality of life after death; a premium on the unity of knowledge; and Victorian physicists' predilection for pictorial models of physical processes. The aether thereby answered Lodge's need to unify the organic and the inorganic, the spiritual and material, and the scientific and religious.

CANTOR & HODGE's book is a collection of essays from 10 leading historians of the aether. This remains one of the best books on the subject, not least for its consistent emphasis on the different theories as products of broader intellectual culture rather than a set of isolated concepts. Furthermore, each essay shows the kinds of historiographies demanded by aethers of a particular period. Four authors examine the Newtonian aethers in the 18th century: Heimann discusses imponderables; French examines physiology; Christie studies chemistry; and Cantor examines the theological significance of aethers. Despite the editors's claim for the fluidity of aether concepts within their chosen time period, a crucial historical discontinuity seems to have occurred during the 1820s, after which time "aether" became "ether" and subsequently performed specific functions within the emerging physical sciences. Hence, the following papers include Buchwald exploring the aether as a well-defined set of mathematical problems, and Siegel on how a universal dynamical aether functioned in Kelvin and Maxwell's project to unify heat, optics and electromagnetism. Wise's valuable essay powerfully traces the metaphysical roots of German field and aether concepts. The book includes a useful bibliography of secondary sources.

WYNNE explores the social functions of concepts of the aether by connecting Victorian Cambridge intellectuals' interests in physics, psychical research, and Tory politics. Their theorising on the aether and exploration of spiritual phenomena, he argues, were expressions of their political, moral, and social ideology: disclosure of a spiritual or transcendent order in the laboratory or the séance would undermine the materialistic viewpoint, while the declared unifying and spiritual properties of the aether would buttress their predominantly Tory political values against the socially disruptive and demoralising threats of industrialisation, mercantilism, and liberalism. Although crucial factual errors make his argument much stronger than it should be, Wynne's central contention remains tantalising.

HUNT shows that celebrated interpreters of Maxwell, such as George Francis FitzGerald and Oliver Lodge, devised mechanical models of the aether to explore, clarify, and illustrate key features of Maxwell's electromagnetic theories. The plausibility of these models derived from a strong Victorian tradition regarding aether and matter as fundamentally mechanical: for example, FitzGerald's vortex-sponge model conflated a Berkeleyan emphasis on matter in motion and a tradition of simple, complete and unified mechanical theories of the aether. Hunt also explores the crucial British and German hostility to the ontological significance of these models.

RICHARD NOAKES

See also Electromagnetism; Einstein; Maxwell; Michelson; Spiritualism

Affinity

Duncan, A.M., "The Functions of Affinity Tables and Lavoisier's List of Elements", *Ambix*, 17 (1970): 28–42

Hesse, Mary, *Forces and Fields: The Concept of Action at a Distance in the History of Physics*, London: Nelson, and New York: Philosophical Society, 1961

Jammer, Max, *Concepts of Force: A Study in the Foundations of Dynamics*, Cambridge, Massachusetts: Harvard University Press, 1957

Levere, Trevor H., *Affinity and Matter: Elements of Chemical Philosophy, 1800–1865*, Oxford: Clarendon Press, 1971

Metzger, Hélène, *Newton, Stahl, Boerhaave et la doctrine chimique*, Paris: Alcan, 1930

Nye, Mary Jo, *From Chemical Philosophy to Theoretical Chemistry: Dynamics of Matter and Dynamics of Disciplines, 1800–1950*, Berkeley: University of California Press, 1993

Roberts, Lissa, "Setting the Table: The Disciplinary Development of Eighteenth-Century Chemistry as Read Through the Changing Structure of Its Tables", in *The Literary Structure of Scientific Argument: Historical Studies*, edited by Peter Dear, Philadelphia: University of Pennsylvania Press, 1991, 99–132

Schofield, Robert E., *Mechanism and Materialism: British Natural Philosophy in an Age of Reason*, Princeton, New Jersey: Princeton University Press, 1970

Thackray, Arnold, *Atoms and Powers: An Essay on Newtonian Matter-Theory and the Development of Chemistry*, Cambridge, Massachusetts: Harvard University Press, and London: Oxford University Press, 1970

Tsukahara, Togo, *Affinity and Shinwa Ryoku: Introduction of Western Chemical Concepts in Early Nineteenth-Century Japan*, Amsterdam: Gieben, 1993

In this entry, affinity denotes a concept explaining the capabilities of chemical elements to combine. (Affinity sometimes refers to morphological similarities between natural history specimens, but this is not the usage explored here.) Since affinity is used in explanations relating to the behavior of physical bodies, it is relevant to the history and evolution of subjects such as physics, chemistry, and mineralogy, and it thus underscores the difficulties that exist in determining disciplinary distinctions within the physical sciences. This is a point raised by NYE, who uses the problem of categorizing people who define chemical affinity as a way of illustrating institutional and disciplinary dynamics in physics and chemistry.

Historically, chemical affinity is largely treated as a metaphysical issue but it is implicated in a central concern of the history of chemistry: do particles unite based on their physical properties, or are they held together by attractive forces or imponderable fluids? Thus, while relating to empirical accounts of chemical reactions, problems of affinity are frequently taken as metaphysical problems regarding the cause of combination.

Historiographic treatments of affinity commonly situate the debate within ancient, early-modern, and modern chemical philosophy. JAMMER is interested in the structure of philosophical debates, and his study analyses the logic in the construction of arguments about the concept of force. Rather than emphasising the philosophical challenges to the uses of this concept in physics (as those mentioned below), he looks for similarities in thought that associate force with what later becomes "work" in thermodynamics. Jammer adopts a broad chronological scope, tracing the development of these ideas from ancient Greece to modern Germany. Chemical affinity in particular is shown to be related to theories of mechanical phenomena or universal gravitation.

HESSE is also interested in the logical construction of theories of force that act on physical entities by considering, for example, realist arguments or hypothetico-deductive methods. She explores analogies and theoretical models in physics which work to illustrate the problem of bodies acting on one another at a distance. Like Jammer, Hesse works within a broad chronology, including atomism in antiquity, Cartesian mechanism, 18th-century elastic fluid theories, and the development of relativity theories. "Chemical affinity" is nowhere dealt with *per se*, but is discussed in relation to Newton's queries on the role of attraction and repulsion in the cohesion of particles. Hesse also discusses the problem of "action at a distance" in relation to philosophical considerations; for example, how metaphysical issues of spiritualism, voids in space, or ultimate particles were dealt with in religious and philosophical debate.

Within the framework of the development of modern chemistry, THACKRAY studies how Isaac Newton dealt with the forces that determine the structure of matter, and the subsequent spread of "Newtonianism", which here is a loosely defined methodological prescription that chemistry should be quantified through the measurement of forces. For Thackray, the effect of the "Cartesian legacy" on the philosophy of chemical combination was replaced by that of affinity theory, through the work of Newtonian experimental philosophy. Newton struggled with the problem of chemical combination and affinity, but his treatment of the problem was left incomplete. Newton raised the issue in "Query 31" of his *Opticks*, in which he stated: "Have not the small Particles of Bodies certain Powers, Virtues, or Forces, by which they act at a distance", but then left this as a proposition for the engagement of his successors. Thackray considers the ways in which 18th-century natural philosophers, such as Buffon, Macquer, and Bergman, worked with Newtonian equations for gravitational attraction in order to mathematicize laws of chemical affinity. An innovative research strategy for many of these scientists was assembling affinity tables, used to depict the degrees of force between chemicals. While Thackray places

Newton's work in connection with a subsequent research programme, METZGER concentrates on how the specific concept of chemical affinity is dealt with in the work of her three chosen individuals: Newton, Georg Ernst Stahl, and Herman Boerhaave. The affinity tables are discussed by DUNCAN and ROBERTS, who look at the relations between a particular aspect of chemical practice in the 18th century – the construction of affinity tables – and the way chemists defined their own scientific enterprise. Duncan lists how a number of 18th-century European chemists defined concepts of affinity, and then used different affinity tables to determine quantitatively the amounts of force in chemical attractions. Roberts considers how the growing uses of mathematics in chemistry in the 18th century, as represented in the increasing centrality of affinity tables, affected disciplinary views about the practice of chemistry.

Newtonian mathematical models are central to the study by SCHOFIELD. He focuses mainly on 18th-century debates on whether particles combined by their material shapes or by Newtonian forces acting at a distance, and examines how Newton's attempts to reconcile 17th-century corpuscularism with his ethereal philosophy were refined by his successors. Schofield adopts the tags "materialism" and "mechanism" to refer to the ways in which 18th-century materialists departed from the Aristotelian, scholastic tradition of associating primary particles with essential properties which determine chemical union, by invoking Newton's mechanism for active forces as a cause for the phenomenon.

LEVERE pursues and clarifies Schofield's account of this conceptual shift by extending the study to the 19th century. He examines the way a group of 19th-century chemists modified the concept of chemical affinity, and considers how experimental practices formed heuristic models with which chemists were able to conceptualise actions of affinity, and how metaphysical problems arising from the action of these invisible powers affect knowledge claims. Humphry Davy's experiments with the galvanic battery on the decomposition of matter are shown to provide a link between Davy's belief that all matter was electrically endowed and his association of chemical affinity with electricity. Levere then discusses at some length the impact of Michael Faraday's work on electrolytic decomposition, and Jacob Berzelius's and his contemporaries' researches in galvanism on the development of European chemical experimentation. Throughout, Levere emphasises individual biography, and the connections between chemical theory and contemporary philosophy and religion.

Finally, TSUKAHARA makes the concept of chemical affinity central to his account of the transfer of chemical theory from the West to Japan in the 19th century. He succinctly traces the history of the mechanical and dynamic conceptions of affinity in the West, then discusses conditions in Japan that made the transfer of this chemical theory difficult. In Japan, Buddhism, Shintoism, and Confucianism maintained different epistemological positions regarding atomic entities, their properties and interactions. Tsukahara reveals how Japanese natural philosophers, who attempted to engage with Western experimental practices, were forced to reconfigure their underlying metaphysical beliefs concerning invisible forces, and their propositions about the fundamental properties of matter.

BRIAN DOLAN

Africa: south of the Sahara

Doumbia, Salimata (ed.), *Mathématiques dans l'environnement socio-culturel Africain*, vol. 1, Abidjan: Institut de Recherches Mathématiques, 1984

Gerdes, Paulus, *Ethnogeometrie: Kulturanthropologische Beiträge zur Genese und Didaktik der Geometrie*, Bad Salzdethfurth/Hildesheim: Franzbecker, 1991

Gerdes, Paulus, *Geometria SONA: Reflexões sobre uma tradição de desenho em povos da África ao Sul do Equador*, 3 vols, Maputo: Instituto Superior Pedagógico, 1993–94; as *Une Tradition géométrique en Afrique: Les dessins sur le sable*, 3 vols, Paris: L'Harmattan, 1995

Gerdes, Paulus, "On Mathematics in the History of Sub-Saharan Africa", *Historia Mathematica*, 21 (1994): 345–76

Gerdes, Paulus and Gildo Bulafo, *Sipatsi: Technology, Art and Geometry in Inhambane*, Maputo: Instituto Superior Pedagógico, 1994

Liebenberg, Louis, *The Art of Tracking: The Origin of Science*, Claremont, South Africa: Philip, 1990

Niangoran-Bouah, G., *L'Univers Akan des poids à peser l'or* (English and French texts) 3 vols, Abidjan, Nigeria: Nouvelles Éditions Africaines, 1984–87

Obenga, Théophile, *La Philosophie africaine de la période pharaonique, 2780–330 avant notre ère*, Paris: L'Harmattan, 1990

Thomas-Emeagwali, Gloria (ed.), *The Historical Development of Science and Technology in Nigeria*, Lampeter, Wales, and Lewiston, New York: Edwin Mellen Press, 1992

Thomas-Emeagwali, Gloria (ed.), *Science and Technology in African History with Case Studies from Nigeria, Sierra Leone, Zimbabwe, and Zambia*, Lampeter, Wales, and Lewiston, New York: Edwin Mellen Press, 1992

Thomas-Emeagwali, Gloria (ed.), *African Systems of Science, Technology and Art: The Nigerian Experience*, London: Karnak House, 1993

Van Sertima, Ivan (ed.), *Blacks in Science: Ancient and Modern*, 2 vols, New Brunswick, New Jersey: Transaction Books, 1983

Zaslavsky, Claudia, *Africa Counts: Number and Pattern in African Culture*, Boston: Prindle Weber and Schmidt, 1973

Most histories of mathematics, science and technology devote a few pages to ancient Egypt and to northern Africa during the "Middle Ages". The history of science and technology in sub-Saharan Africa – like the history of Africa south of the Sahara in general – however, has only relatively recently enjoyed increased attention, as Eurocentric views have been losing their grip on historiography. The emerging literature can be divided into several genres: surveys based on a critical appraisal of existing written sources; studies that reflect on the methodology of reconstructing the history of science and technology within a context where few written sources are available; and analyses of specific themes using an interdisciplinary approach – from oral history and ethnography to archaeology.

In her classic study, ZASLAVSKY offers a preliminary survey of the available literature on the history of mathematics in sub-Saharan Africa. She discusses written, spoken and gesture counting, number mysticism, concepts of time, numbers and money, weights and measures, record-keeping (sticks and strings), mathematical games, magic squares, graphs, and geometric form; in addition Crowe contributes a chapter on geometric symmetries in African art. An overview of research findings since the publication of Zaslavsky's book can be found in GERDES (1994), along with sources on or related to mathematics in African history. Several references to physics, astronomy, cosmology, logic, philosophy, and technology are also included.

Several chapters of VAN SERTIMA deal with the history of science in Africa. Pappademos revises conventional assumptions about the role of Africans in the history of physics by outlining some of their contributions to measurement, mechanics, optics, astronomy, and metallurgy. Lynch and Robbins analyse evidence from Namoratunga, a megalithic site in north-western Kenya, that suggests that a prehistoric calendar based on detailed astronomic knowledge was in use in east Africa (c.300 BC). Lumpkin discusses the place of Africa in the mainstream of the history of mathematics.

THOMAS-EMEAGWALI (1993) includes a chapter on conceptual and methodological issues in science and technology in Nigerian history. The third and fourth chapters of GERDES (1991) are dedicated to the methodology of reconstructing elements of the early history of geometrical thinking through study of the relationships between the development of geometrical knowledge and socially/culturally important activities such as mat and basket weaving, pot making, and house building in Africa.

The emergence of scientific thinking in African hunter-gatherer societies is studied by LIEBENBERG. The principles of tracking, classification of signs, and spoor interpretation among the hunter-gatherers of the Kalahari in southern Africa are analysed. The book presents the hypothesis that the development of tracking probably played a significant role in the evolution of the scientific faculty. "The critical attitude of contemporary Kalahari Desert trackers, and the role of critical discussion in tracking suggest ... that the rationalist tradition of science may well have been practised by hunter-gatherers long before the Greek philosophic schools were founded."

The first volume of GERDES (1993–95) is dedicated to the analysis and reconstruction of mathematical elements in the sand drawing tradition of the Tchokwe and neighbouring peoples in Angola, Zaire and Zambia. Symmetries, classes, and algorithms for the execution of the drawings (called sona), and rules for the systematic construction of monolinear sona, are among the themes analysed. Volume 2 explores the educational and scientific potential of the (reconstructed) sona tradition, whereas volume 3 analyses traditions from ancient Egypt and Mesopotamia, from the Tamil of southern India, from the Celts of northern Britain and from North American Indians, which, from a technical point of view, bear similarities to the African sona tradition.

DOUMBIA analyses mathematical aspects of verbal calculation, gambling and board games of the Ivory Coast. GERDES & BULAFO study the development of the technological and geometrical knowledge of basket weavers in Mozambique's Inhambane province.

Each section of OBENGA contains the reproduction of an ancient Egyptian text, its translation and commentaries. A section on calendars includes a comparative description of ancient Egyptian, Fang, Mbochi (Congo), Borana (Ethiopia) and Dogon (Mali) astronomy. A section on metrology includes a comparison between the measures and numeration in ancient Egypt and the ones used by the Duala (Cameroon), Fang (Cameroon, Equatorial Guinea, Gabon), Yoruba (Nigeria), Ganda, BaNgongo (Congo) among others. NIANGORAN-BOUAH contributes to the reconstruction of the history and use of the gold weights of the Akan (Ghana, Ivory Coast).

Essays in THOMAS-EMEAGWALI (1992, *The Historical Development of Science and Technology in Nigeria*) analyse traditional methods of food processing, cassava-processing technology, textile technology, and pedagogy and science teaching in Nigeria. The text concentrates on the historical dimension, but approaches the subject within the context of multidisciplinary interpretation. THOMAS-EMEAGWALI (1993) includes essays on textile technologies of the 19th and early 20th centuries, traditional medicine, food processing, metal technology, and mechanics and engineering – the construction of fortifications – in pre-colonial Nigeria. THOMAS-EMEAGWALI (1992, *Science and Technology in African History*), presents case studies in the history of science and technology from Nigeria, Sierra Leone, Zimbabwe, and Zambia. In science, the areas of focus include arithmetic (pre-colonial central Sudan) and traditional medicine, as well as biologically-based warfare and control of water-based diseases (Nigeria). In technology, metallurgy (Nigeria), gold (Zimbabwe) and diamond mining (Sierra Leone), and glass-making (Nigeria) are studied. Two chapters discuss science and technology policies in Zambia and Nigeria, and the final chapter is dedicated to historical perspectives on technical co-operation in Africa. Kani concludes his contribution on arithmetic in pre-colonial central Sudan with the following criticism:

> Despite the availability of a great deal of literature on medicine, astrology, arithmetic and other related sciences, written in Arabic, Fulfulde, Hausa and other languages, little effort has been made to systematically study these sciences within the historical perspective. The intellectual output of the *cUlama* [scholars] in this area has been wrongly classified by our contemporary historians and social scientists under the rubric of "mysticism". A serious investigation into the literary output of the scholars of western and central Sudan, however, may reveal the fact that these scholars had explored agricultural, medicinal, astronomical and mathematical sciences long before the advent of colonial rule.

PAULUS GERDES

See also Astronomy: non-European; Ethnomathematics; Ethnoscience; Metrology

Africa: health and healing

Abdalla, Ismail H., *Islam, Medicine, and Practitioners in Northern Nigeria*, Lampeter, Wales, and Lewiston, New York: Edwin Mellen Press, 1997

Ackerknecht, Erwin Heinz, *Medicine and Ethnology: Selected Essays*, edited by H.H. Walser and H.M. Koelbing, Baltimore: Johns Hopkins Press, 1971

Conrad, Peter and Eugene B. Gallagher (eds), *Health and Health Care in Developing Countries: Sociological Perspectives*, Philadelphia: Temple University Press, 1993

Curtin, Philip D., *Disease and Empire: The Health of European Troops in the Conquest of Africa*, Cambridge and New York: Cambridge University Press, 1998

Evans-Pritchard, E.E., *Witchcraft, Oracles and Magic among the Azande*, with a foreword by C.G. Seligman, Oxford: Clarendon Press, 1937

Falola, Toyin and Dennis Ityavyar (eds), *The Political Economy of Health in Africa*, Athens: Ohio University Center for International Studies, 1991

Feierman, Steven, *Health and Society in Africa: A Working Bibliography*, Waltham, Massachusetts: Crossroads Press, 1979

Feierman, Steven, *Peasant Intellectuals: Anthropology and History in Tanzania*, Madison: University of Wisconsin Press, 1990

Feierman, Steven and John M. Janzen (eds), *The Social Basis of Health and Healing in Africa*, Berkeley: University of California Press, 1992

Harrison, Ira E. and Sheila Cosminsky, *Traditional Medicine: Current Research with Implications for Ethnomedicine, Ethnopharmacology, Maternal and Child Health, Mental Health and Public Health: An Annotated Bibliography of Africa, Latin America, and the Caribbean*, 2 vols, New York: Garland, 1976–84

Jacobson-Widding, Anita and David Westerlund (eds), *Culture, Experience and Pluralism: Essays on African Ideas of Illness and Healing*, Stockholm: Almqvist & Wiksell, 1989

Janzen, John M., *The Quest for Therapy in Lower Zaire*, Berkeley: University of California Press, 1978

Janzen, John M. and Steven Feierman (eds), "The Social History of Disease and Medicine in Africa", *Social Science and Medicine*, special issue 13 B/4 (1979): 239–356

Janzen, John M. and Gwyn Prins (eds), "Causality and Classification in African Health and Medicine", *Social Science and Medicine*, special issue 15 B/3 (1981): 169–437

Last, Murray, and G.L. Chavunduka (eds), *The Professionalisation of African Medicine*, Manchester: Manchester University Press/International African Institute, 1986

Loudon, J.B., *Social Anthropology and Medicine*, London and New York: Academic Press, 1976

Packard, Randall M., *White Plague, Black Labor: Tuberculosis and the Political Economy of Health and Disease in South Africa*, Berkeley: University of California Press, 1989

Sigerist, Henry E., *Primitive and Archaic Medicine*, Oxford and New York: Oxford University Press, 1951

Slikkerveer, Leendert Jan, *Plural Medical Systems in the Horn of Africa: The Legacy of "Sheikh" Hippocrates*, London and New York: Kegan Paul, 1990

Ulin, Priscilla R. and Marshall H. Segall (eds), *Traditional Health Care Delivery in Contemporary Africa*, Syracuse, New York: Maxwell School of Citizenship and Public Affairs, 1980

Vaughan, Megan, *Curing Their Ills: Colonial Power and African Illness*, Stanford, California: Stanford University Press, 1991

Yoder, P. Stanley (ed.), *African Health and Healing Systems: Proceedings of a Symposium*, Los Angeles: African Studies Center, 1982

It would be arrogant to attempt to summarize the history or the historiography of health and healing in Africa before defining what is meant by "health", "medicine", "healing", and "Africa". As a geographic entity, the continent of Africa has relatively clear boundaries, though the political and cultural boundaries within Africa and between Africa, Europe, and Asia have been more fluid. Culturally, politically, and economically, however, the North African countries on the Mediterranean, the West African countries that face the Atlantic, the East African societies with ties to the Middle East, and the southern African peoples are quite different from one another. The diversity of the African peoples and traditions, the varieties of social organization, and the differences in economies and ways of life, as well as many other factors, suggest that healing may be practiced differently, by different kinds of healers, and have varied social, political, technological, and material bases. What constitutes a healing activity is similarly difficult to articulate, since the boundaries between public and private, religion and medicine, and cure and care map differently compared to the Western doctor-patient relationship, in addition to varying from tradition to tradition and from place to place. These caveats make it crucial for the interested reader to consult materials on the specific peoples, places, and healing traditions of interest, and to be wary of making generalizations for other places, periods, peoples, or healing systems.

The study of health and healing in Africa has changed since Erwin Ackerknecht, Henry Sigerist, and E.E. Evans-Pritchard conducted studies of "primitive medicine" in Africa in the 1930s. SIGERIST and ACKERKNECHT displayed considerable sophistication in their analysis of medicine and culture, but their faith in modernism and in science as its tool to ease suffering and to bring greater equality of peoples now looks somewhat naive. African independence from colonial rule, the dialogue between European and African scholars of African cultures, and changes in the theoretical stances of anthropology have changed who studies whom, what, and for what purposes. Recent approaches have addressed the links between healing systems and cultures, and the coexistence of multiple healing traditions within particular societies. What has not changed but instead has expanded in histories of Western medicine in Western societies is the realization that, as Feierman notes in the introduction to his 1979 bibliography:

It is immediately clear to anyone attempting to define the scope of relations among medicine, disease, and social organization in Africa (or anywhere else) that no aspect of social life or human biology can legitimately be excluded. Changing settlement patterns, for example, lead to changes in disease patterns, which lead in turn to modified settlement patterns and sometimes to government intervention, producing in turn its own response. An individual who is ill might make use of local herbal knowledge or examine his or her place in neighborhood patterns of relationship, consult a diviner or attribute the illness to witchcraft, take part in a therapeutic spirit possession rite or visit a teacher learned in Islam, visit a hospital or simply go untreated.

The choice of terminology is important, since explicit or implicit comparisons to biomedicine have been encoded into many descriptions of ethnomedical practice. "Primitive" medicine has invidious evolutionary connotations in its comparison to "modern" medicine. "Traditional" medicine and "ethnomedicine" are used more flexibly, though they still reinforce the sense that ethnomedicine is unchanging or timeless, and by implication that traditional healers are uninterested in furthering their skills or learning new modalities.

Traditional African health and healing has been the province of anthropologists, sociologists, demographers, and historians. FEIERMAN (1979) and HARRISON & COSMINSKY provide entrées into the historical and anthropological literature on African health and healing. The essays in FEIERMAN & JANZEN give an introduction to the issues in African historical demography, African healing systems, and medicine in Africa before, during, and after the colonial period. This book is the best introduction to the central issues and aspects of the social study of African health. EVANS-PRITCHARD's discussion of Zande culture and the ways in which illness was explained and understood set a standard for ethnographic detail. Evans-Pritchard paid little attention to Zande disease classifications, and instead addressed their causal explanations based in witchcraft and spirit life. Though natural and supernatural explanations often existed for the same disease or accident, the power of supernatural explanations to answer the question "why me?" contributed to their importance. JANZEN & FEIERMAN and JANZEN & PRINS present important symposia discussing a variety of healing systems within different African cultures. Their emphases on health preservation and restoration as part of a larger social fabric of war, colonialism, and gender politics as well as the health valences of traditional settlement patterns, food production, and ways of cooking, place these works firmly within social anthropology as well as more narrowly medical anthropology. The essays in Janzen & Prins are particularly valuable for their discussions of disease causality, both personalistic (usually supernatural or intentional) and naturalistic (the sort of sickness that "just happens"). LOUDON presents a collection of essays on various diseases, treatment systems, and systems for explaining illness and misfortune, including an important essay by Gillies on "Causal Criteria in African Classifications of Disease". YODER's edited volume is also predominantly interested in explaining healing systems and the interaction among patients, families, and healers in eight case studies. Some of these take the approach of public health or that of health planning, providing a less individualistic perspective on health and healing, and the two commentaries included on the study of

African healing are valuable. FEIERMAN (1990) reminds the reader of the importance of change over time in Tanzania and the colonial history of the Shambaai peoples. Caring for people and the land and the interaction of colonial rulers and "peasant intellectuals", wisdom, and local knowledge are at the center of this work. Finally, VAUGHAN presents an evaluation of biomedicine as a colonial tool and contributes to the understanding of psychiatry and mental health as cultural phenomena. Her discussion of missionary medicine and government health education places health in a colonial discourse of politics, religious conversion, and economic exploitation. The portrait of the colonial administrator attempting to understand what counts as insanity in another culture, whose task is mystified rather than clarified by the use of a translator, since rendering another's words means giving them form and structure, is almost comic.

The presence of multiple healing systems in most African cultures, especially after colonization and biomedicine, has presented patients or their advocates with choices for the treatment of illness and misfortune. JANZEN (1978) gave the first forceful demonstration of therapeutic choice and the role of lay therapy managers in navigating the varied possibilities for explaining and treating illness. This work has been important in shifting the emphasis in the field from a view of biomedicine or traditional medicine as a simple and firm choice, and also in leading to the conclusion that therapeutic systems are not firmly or solely linked to a single cultural group, with each group having its own healing tradition. ABDALLA has pointed out the importance of Islamic prophetic healing as a third alternative in many places, including northern Nigeria, whose plurality of healing cultures he examines among the Hausa over the past four centuries. JACOBSON-WIDDING & WESTERLUND use pluralism as a guiding idea, and cultural anthropology and phenomenology as methods. A notable contribution by Susan Reynolds Whyte explores what it means to compare different African healers to biomedicine rather than to religious leaders. What, in the context of the East African cults of affliction, is the difference between religion and medicine? The contributors to ULIN & SEGALL present traditional medicine as part of a "worldwide drive to make health care accessible, affordable, and culturally relevant for all people". Similar concerns have been seen in the explicit endorsement of Chinese traditional medicine by the government of China since 1949 and the implicit license given to Curanderos in Mexico, where they provide primary health care to many in the population. SLIKKERVEER discusses the balance between biomedicine, Islamic medicine, and other healing systems in the northeast corner of Africa, largely in the present, as a contribution to health systems research and health policy. Slikkerveer argues that if biomedicine is unable to reach the rural populations, and the first therapeutic choice (help-seeking behavior) of individuals and groups is for other modalities, then this should be understood and used to advantage in health planning. The potentials of traditional healing as primary care viewed both by government officials and by healers themselves are most clearly addressed by the contributors to LAST & CHAVUNDUKA, who study the efforts of traditional healers to gain the protections of licensure and systematic control of training through professionalization and present in stark relief some of the questions of modernization, urbanization, population growth, commodification of health and healing and the legitimacy of traditional healing in post-colonial Africa.

Life and death as expendable or purchasable commodities rarely present an encouraging view of human nature. None the less, health conditions have been crucial to colonization, land use, labor, and trade. CURTIN explores the improvement of mortality rates in European military services in the mid-19th century. The improvement of mortality rates for troops occurred just before the waves of African colonization, and could not have been unrelated, he argues. PACKARD explores miners phthisis or tuberculosis among black diamond and gold miners in South Africa. The importance of nutrition and working conditions to life expectancy, and of political and economic power to the determination of those conditions, is a reminder of the class and race implications of employment policies and how and when money can buy or sell lives. FALOLA & ITYAVYAR include essays on African health services and health conditions with an emphasis on contemporary biomedical health service delivery, colonialism and its effects on African countries, and local versus international health planning. CONRAD & GALLAGHER also provide contemporary accounts from a health-services perspective, and place three pieces on Africa within a thematic organization that includes accounts of East Asian, Latin American, and other cultures.

The trade in ideas, medicinal substances, and practices that has led to the use of herbal medicines, charms, and divination in industrialized countries in European cultures is a separate movement. While the availability or visibility of ideas and practices from Africa in European cultures is the result of the usual rounds of trade, migration, and warfare that have been mixing peoples and their cultures for centuries, the critiques of science, technology, Western medicine, racism, and colonialism that are often encoded in the use of African healing modalities outside their cultures of origin highlight the importance of health and healing as part of larger social and cultural trends.

Interested readers are advised to search for monographs and articles on the specific traditions, peoples, or countries that interest them, since this summary is necessarily selective. Synthetic works on medical anthropology also often contain valuable material on particular traditions. A substantial volume of additional work exists in other fields relevant to African health conditions, including the contemporary demography of health and illness in Africa, particular diseases, population policy, and agriculture and food production.

CARLA KEIRNS

See also Traditional Medicine

Age of the Earth

Albritton Jr, Claude C., *The Abyss of Time: Changing Conceptions of the Earth's Antiquity after the Sixteenth Century*, San Francisco: Freeman Cooper, 1980

Burchfield, Joe D., *Lord Kelvin and the Age of the Earth*, New York: Science History Publications, 1975; with new afterword, Chicago: University of Chicago Press, 1990

Dalrymple, G. Brent, *The Age of the Earth*, Stanford, California: Stanford University Press, 1991

Dean, Dennis R., "The Age of the Earth Controversy: Beginnings to Hutton," *Annals of Science*, 38 (1991): 435–56

Gould, Stephen Jay, *Time's Arrow, Time's Cycle: Myth and Metaphor in the Discovery of Geological Time*, Cambridge, Massachusetts: Harvard University Press, 1987

Haber, Francis C., *The Age of the World: Moses to Darwin*, Baltimore: Johns Hopkins University Press, 1959

Rossi, Paolo, *The Dark Abyss of Time: The History of the Earth and the History of Nations from Hooke to Vico*, translated from the Italian by Lydia G. Cochrane, Chicago: University of Chicago Press, 1984 (original edition, 1979)

Rudwick, Martin J.S., "The Shape and Meaning of Earth History," in *God and Nature: Historical Essays on the Encounter Between Christianity and Science*, edited by David C. Lindberg and Ronald L. Numbers, Berkeley: University of California Press, 1986

The problem of determining the age of the Earth cuts across disciplinary boundaries: answers to the question, "How old is our world?" have been derived from biblical exegesis, physics, astronomy, chemistry, and various branches of geology. The implications of those answers, though felt most forcefully by geologists, have also reshaped ideas about biology, theology, and the aesthetics of nature. The literature on the age-of-the-Earth question is, accordingly, diverse and wide-ranging.

Western ideas about the age of the Earth were shaped, from ancient times to the end of the 18th century, principally by religious considerations. DEAN provides an overview of this era, briefly discussing Egyptian, Greek, Roman, and Jewish ideas before turning in detail to those of medieval Christendom. Criticism of these religiously oriented cosmologies began with the writings of medieval Aristotelians, Dean argues, and gained momentum in the Renaissance and Enlightenment as new methods of Biblical scholarship called old assumptions into question. Growing doubts about the literal reliability of Genesis led to the emergence, in the 18th century, of new chronologies which rested on geological rather than textual evidence.

Haber and Rossi both chronicle in detail the undermining and eventual collapse of Bible-based geochronologies. HABER's treatment spans the period between the recognition of fossils as once-living creatures in the 17th century and the publication of Darwin's theory of evolution in the mid-19th century, focusing on the way in which the new scientific ideas challenged and undermined orthodox Christian beliefs concerning Earth history. ROSSI's treatment covers a shorter period in greater depth and more intricate detail. It traces the evolution of early modern ideas about fossils, human history and language, while exploring their ties to each other and to the broader philosophical movements of late-17th and 18th-century Europe. Rossi argues that, in combination, these sets of new ideas created an entirely new view of the world's age and history that replaced the older view rooted in Christian orthodoxy. Haber, though somewhat dated and best read in conjunction with more recent works on science and religion, is the more accessible of the two treatments. Rossi's

wide-ranging, philosophically subtle analysis is more rewarding when read after Haber, or by those who already possess
a working knowledge of the ideas of René Descartes,
Giambattista Vico, and their contemporaries.

RUDWICK covers much of the same chronological ground
as Haber and focuses – as do both Haber and Rossi – on the
gradual decline of a Bible-centered view of Earth history. His
principal concern, however, is not with specific fossils or
Biblical texts, but with the cosmological systems derived from
them. Rudwick argues that specific, quantitative estimates of
the age of the Earth are less significant than the broad, qualitative patterns that link Earth histories constructed in particular times and places. He traces the impact of new ideas – first
in Biblical criticism and later in geology – on these patterns.

DALRYMPLE, a working geologist, is primarily concerned
with present-day scientific ideas about the age of the Earth and
the data on which they are based. His book begins, however,
with a historical survey. The chapter includes a few pages on
the Renaissance, but focuses on the 19th and early 20th
centuries – after the acceptance of the Earth's vast antiquity,
but before the widespread use of radioactive elements as
chronometers. Evidently writing with a geological audience in
mind, Dalrymple focuses on the "nuts and bolts" of these
calculations and makes free use of equations, graphs, and technical terminology. Readers without a scientific background may
find the level of detail off-putting, but Dalrymple's remains the
best survey of this often-neglected period in the history of
geochronology.

ALBRITTON, like Dalrymple, treats the age-of-the-Earth
problem as an episode in the history of geology. His book
is aimed at a general audience, however, and omits graphs
and equations in favor of period illustrations and a focus on
the scientific minds behind the key ideas. Albritton sees the
discovery of the Earth's antiquity as a central theme in the
development of geology. He traces the emergence of the idea
that the Earth has a long, complex history by showing its
impact on ideas about the history of life, the tempo of geologic
change, and the arrangement of the Earth's crust. The book
thus functions on two levels: as a history of ideas about the
age of the Earth, and as a history of ideas about the course
of Earth history. Its concluding chapters cover the same ground
as Dalrymple, but with less technical detail.

GOULD's analysis of three major British geologists –
Thomas Burnet, James Hutton, and Charles Lyell – is not,
strictly speaking, a study of ideas about the Earth's age. It is,
rather, an extended reflection on the nature of geologic time,
organized around two potent metaphors: time as a journey
with a finite beginning and end, and time as an endlessly
repeated cycle. Burnet saw the Earth as little older than 6000
years; Hutton and Lyell saw it as unimaginably old. Gould's
close analysis of their work traces the scientific, theological,
and philosophical implications of their very different views of
the past.

The British physicist William Thomson, later Lord Kelvin,
triggered an intense debate with a series of late 19th-century
papers that attacked Lyell's notion of an unimaginably old
Earth. Thomson argued that Lyell and his fellow geologists
had overestimated the Earth's age by orders of magnitude, and
so challenged the intellectual foundations of both British
geology and Darwinian evolution. BURCHFIELD analyzes

Thomson's critique, and the responses of British geologists and
biologists, in detail. He suggests that Thomson's arguments –
a potent force from 1862 until the early 20th century – brought
about the much-needed moderation of Lyell's more extreme
claims about the age of the Earth and the tempo of geological processes. Burchfield's work, like Albritton's, is written
with a broad audience in mind, linking ideas about the Earth's
age to contemporary geological practice.

A. Bowdoin Van Riper

See also Archaeology; Geology; Hutton; Prehistory:
archaeology and anthropology; Religion and Science: general
works; Time

Agricola, Georgius   1494–1555

German humanist and scientist

Adams, Frank Dawson, *The Birth and Development of the
Geological Sciences*, London: Baillière Tindall and Cox,
and Baltimore: Johns Hopkins Press, 1938

Bandy, Mark Chance and Jean A. Bandy (trans), *De Natura
Fossilium*, New York: Geological Society of America,
1955

Dibner, Bern, *Agricola on Metals*, Norwalk, Connecticut:
Burndy Library, 1958

Halleux, Robert, "La Nature et la formation des metaux
selon Agricola et ses contemporains", *Revue d'Histoire des
Sciences*, 27/3 (1974): 211–22

Halleux, Robert and Albert Yans, *Bermannus (Le Mineur):
Un dialogue sur les mines*, Paris: Les Belles Lettres,
1990

Hollister-Short, Graham, "The First Fifty Years of the
Rod-Engine (c.1540–c.1600)", in *Mining Before Powder*,
edited by Trevor D. Ford and Lynn Willies: *Peak District
Mines Historical Society: Bulletin*, 12/3 (Summer 1994):
83–90

Hoover, Herbert and Lou Henry Hoover (trans), *De Re
Metallica*, London: *Mining Magazine*, 1912; reprinted,
New York: Dover, 1950

Naumann, Friedrich (ed.), *Georgius Agricola: 500 Jahre:
Wissenschaftlicher Konferenz*, Basel: Birkhäuser, 1994

Suhling, Lothar, "Bergbau und Hüttenwesen in Mitteleuropa
zur Agricola-Zeit", in *Zwölf Bücher vom Berg- und
Hüttenwesen*, by Agricola, Munich: Deutscher
Taschenbuch, 1977, 570–88

Wilsdorf, Helmut, *Georg Agricola und seine Zeit*, vol. 1 of
Ausgewählte Werke, Berlin: VEB Deutscher Verlag der
Wissenschaften, 1956

It is likely that Georg Bauer latinized his name (Bauer = farmer
= Agricola) at the University of Leipzig. (The first recorded use
is in a receipted account of 1521.) He travelled to Italy to
further his medical education in 1523, and spent from 1524
to 1526 working in Venice, preparing the texts of the first
printed editions of Galen and Hippocrates. In 1527, after his
return to Germany, he took up the position of town physician
in St Joachimsthal (Jachymov), a post he held until 1530. These
years were spent gathering material for the series of books

on mineralogy, geology, and mining that he was to publish subsequently.

ADAMS, in his survey of the geological sciences from c.1500 to 1814 (the time of Berzelius's work on the chemical composition of minerals), devotes some 10 pages to Agricola, apostrophized as "the father of mineralogy", and as "one of the most outstanding figures in the history of geological science . . . of all time". The discussion is based on the two works in which Agricola developed his ideas about minerals and their classification, the *Bermannus* of 1530, and *De Natura Fossilium* (*Textbook of Mineralogy*) of 1546. In the latter work, Agricola reviews and rejects the ancient systems of classification of Aristotle, Avicenna, and Albertus Magnus, and in the process takes many sideswipes at magical and superstitious beliefs. He proposes instead a systematization based on the physical properties of "fossils"; i.e., of all the kinds of materials, such as earths, stones and minerals, dug from the earth's crust.

Although BANDY & BANDY supply only six pages of prefatory material to their translation, some of which is defective, their appreciation of Agricola's intellectual achievement is sharp and clear. Given the paucity of work in English on Agricola, DIBNER's contribution is to be welcomed, even though the treatment is somewhat elementary. Part of the book consists of a brief and not altogether accurate account of Agricola's life, which could have been corrected in the light of Wilsdorf's scrupulously researched biography of Agricola, a work actually cited in Dibner's bibliography. The bulk of Dibner's work consists of a chapter by chapter description of the 12 books of the posthumous *De Re Metallica* [On Mining] of 1556, with a generous selection of woodcuts from this work providing visual interest.

HALLEUX & YANS preface their translation of the *Bermannus* with a 20-page survey of Agricola's life and work up to the publication of this, his first work on mining, in 1530. Further sections examine the dialogue form that Agricola chose for this work, and its structure. The first part of the dialogue describes the scene of action, the topography of St Joachimsthal (now Jachymov); the second and larger part is an extended exercise in lexicography. The task Agricola set himself was to confront the mineralogical terms found in the classical medical vocabulary with the actual ores and metals extracted from the mountain range between Bohemia and Saxony.

HALLEUX undertakes a critical appraisal of Agricola's *De Ortu et Causis Subterraneorum* [On the Origin and Causes of Sub-Surface Phenomena] of 1546, in which Agricola, in his research into the nature of metals and the origin of their ores, reacted against earlier writers. He added quicksilver, antimony, and bismuth to the six metals of Aristotle, and modified the distinctive properties of metallic bodies. He criticized the Aristotelian theory of two-fold exhalation, and explained metals as frozen juices (*succi*), compounds of earth and water. He also rejected the alchemical ideas of Avicenna, Ibn Juljul, Albertus Magnus, and the Bergbüchlein. His criticism of Aristotle's ideas did not win much support from contemporaries such as Scaliger, Cardano, and Fallopius, but his demolition of the alchemists was successful.

A notion frequently encountered in the literature is that Agricola's *De Re Metallica* of 1556 remained for at least 150 years a standard work of reference for miners. HOLLISTER-

SHORT demonstrates that, as far as Book VI of the treatise is concerned, in which Agricola examines the machines used in mining, nothing could be further from the truth. Even before *De Re Metallica* came off Froben's presses in Basel, the speed of the development of a new type of water-pumping engine (the *Stangenkunst* or rod-engine) had already rendered obsolete virtually all of the older devices described by Agricola. The paper then goes on to trace the further development of the rod-engine up to c.1600.

The HOOVERS' preface to their translation of *De Re Metallica* (the only complete work of Agricola's, apart from *De Natura Fossilium*, to have been translated into English) is still the best critical appreciation (in English) of his life and work. Of *De Re Metallica* they remark that "while it is of the most general interest of all his works, yet from the point of view of pure science *De Natura Fossilium* and *De Ortu et Causis* . . . are works which deserve an equally important place". In Appendix A they present translations of key passages from *De Ortu et Causis* . . . in which Agricola refers to the role of erosion in the shaping of the earth's surface. Of greater interest, however, are his views on ore channels, on the origin of ground waters and gangue, and on the origin of metals and "juices" (*succi*). These reveal his belief that the deposition of ores, and the mineralization of rocks in general, took place subsequent to the formation of the containing rocks, and that channels were filled by circulating solutions to form mineralized veins.

The work edited by NAUMANN contains the best of the papers delivered at the symposium held in Chemnitz (Agricola's home from 1533 to 1555) in March 1994 to celebrate the 500th anniversary of Agricola's birth. Most of the 50 or so papers are arranged under six titles, following the pattern of the conference: 1. Agricola's place in the history of medicine, pharmacy, and science (eight papers); 2. the intellectual climate of his time (seven papers); 3. Agricola as a politician and diplomat (seven papers); 4. his work in the field of metallurgy (five papers); 5. his work in mining (11 papers); and 6. his life and times (seven papers). Unfortunately for English readers, only two papers are in English, and only one of these is directly concerned with Agricola himself. This is Nicoletta Morello's study (pp. 73–81) of Agricola's attempt to reconcile ancient and modern mineral nomenclature during the composition of the *Bermannus* of 1530 (the most widely read of all his works in his own time).

SUHLING, in an essay specially written for this reprint of the 1928 German translation of *De Re Metallica*, provides a five-part overview of central European mining and metallurgy in Agricola's time. He reviews: the importance of mining for the region extending from Alsace in the west to central Slovakia in the east; the significance of technological developments for production and as accelerators of social change; the place of *De Re Metallica* in European mining literature; the crisis in European mining in the mid-16th century brought on by imports of cheap silver from America and low-priced iron and copper from Sweden; and the importance of Agricola's work of 1556 for the history of technology. Suhling also supplies a chronological check-list of publications on Agricola from 1819 to 1974. A brief biographical sketch by Wilhelm Treue, also forming part of this appended material, has the great merit of citing a dedicatory letter written by Agricola in March 1546 to Georg von Komerstadt, as preface to his *De Veteribus et*

Novis Metallis [On Ancient and Modern Mining Sites]. This reveals how, even as Agricola rode home to Germany in the autumn of 1526, he was already fired by the ambition to make himself expert in all aspects of mining. The *Bermannus*, the first fruit of that decision, forms the link between Agricola's medical work in Venice and the new direction his research was to take from that time onward – i.e., from the medically valuable products of mining to the art of mining itself.

WILSDORF's study of Agricola's life and times remains the fundamental work of reference. The first quarter of the work consists of preliminary studies dealing with the nature of mining in Agricola's time in terms of zones of exploitation, the role of capital, the nature of mining law, the state of the art in respect of mining technology, the political situation in Saxony and Bohemia, and the situation in respect of previous Agricolan scholarship. Agricola's life and work then follows in a sequence of short chapters, with heavy emphasis on the period up to 1531, at which time he entered the service of Heinrich, Duke of Saxony. Even so, evidence for many important passages in Agricola's life depends on a decidedly sparse documentation. The closing chapters cover the corpus of Agricola's work, published and unpublished, including correspondence, translations, and lost works. Each episode in his life and work is supplied with a reference list of the pertinent literature. Wilsdorf later supplied the entry for Agricola in the *Dictionary of Scientific Biography*. Unfortunately, this is brief and misleading, and of very little value.

GRAHAM HOLLISTER-SHORT

Agriculture

Académie d'Agriculture de France, *Deux siècles de progrès pour l'agriculture et l'alimentation, 1789–1989*, Paris: Tec Doc, 1990

Berman, Morris, *Social Change and Scientific Organisation: The Royal Institution, 1799–1844*, London: Heinemann and Ithaca, New York: Cornell University Press, 1978

Boulaine, Jean, *Historie de l'agronomie en France*, Paris: Lavoisier Tec Doc, 1992

Brock, William H. and Susanne Stark, "Liebig, Gregory and the British Association for the Advancement of Science", *Ambix*, 37 (1990): 134–47

Chaplin, Joyce E., *An Anxious Pursuit: Agricultural Innovation and Modernity in the Lower South, 1730–1815*, Chapel Hill: University of Carolina Press, 1993

Dupree, A. Hunter, *Science in the Federal Government: A History of Policies and Activities to 1940*, Cambridge, Massachusetts: Belknap Press of Harvard University Press, 1957; reprinted Baltimore: Johns Hopkins University Press, 1986

Finlay, Mark R., "The Rehabilitation of an Agricultural Chemist: Justus von Liebig and the Seventh Edition", *Ambix*, 38 (1991): 155–67

Fox-Genovese, Elizabeth, *The Origins of Physiocracy: Economic Revolution and Social Order in Eighteenth-Century France*, Ithaca, New York: Cornell University Press, 1976

Fussell, G.E., *Crop Nutrition: Science and Practice before Liebig*, Lawrence, Kansas: Corando Press, 1971

Marcus, Alan I., *Agricultural Science and the Quest for Legitimacy: Farmers, Agricultural Colleges and Experiment Stations, 1870–1890*, Ames: Iowa State University Press, 1985

Moulton, Forest Ray (ed.), *Liebig and After Liebig: A Century of Progress in Agricultural Chemistry*, Washington, DC: American Association for the Advancement of Science, 1942

Munday, Patrick E., "Liebig's Metamorphosis: From Organic Chemistry to the Chemistry of Agriculture", *Ambix*, 38 (1991): 135–54

Osborne, Michael A., *Nature: The Exotic and the Science of French Colonialism*, Bloomington: Indiana State University Press, 1994

Palladino, Paolo, "Between Craft and Science: Plant Breeding, Mendelian Genetics and British Universities, 1900–1920", *Technology and Culture*, 34 (1993): 300–23

Palladino, Paolo, "Wizards and Devotees: On the Mendelian Theory of Inheritance and the Professionalisation of Agricultural Science in Great Britain and the United States, 1880–1930", *History of Science*, 32 (1994): 409–44

Palladino, Paolo, "Science, Technology, and the Economy: Plant Breeding in Great Britain, 1920–1970", *Economic History Review*, 49 (1996): 116–36

Rossiter, Margaret W., *The Emergence of Agricultural Science: Justus Liebig and the Americans, 1840–1880*, New Haven, Connecticut: Yale University Press, 1975

Russell, Sir E. John, *A History of Agricultural Science in Great Britain, 1620–1954*, London: Allen and Unwin, 1966

Schling-Brodersen, Uschi, "Liebig's Role in the Establishment of Agricultural Chemistry", *Ambix*, 39 (1992): 21–31

Tobey, Ronald C., *Saving the Prairies: The Life Cycle of the Founding School of American Plant Ecology, 1896–1955*, Berkeley: University of California Press, 1981

Wilmot, Sarah, *The Business of Improvement: Agriculture and Scientific Culture in Britain, c.1700–c.1870*, Bristol: Historical Geography Research Group, 1990

Agriculture remains a relatively neglected area in the history of science, despite the richness of the historical record and the breadth of the sciences that have historically been associated with agricultural improvement. Much of the current research remains confined to journals. None the less, there is a developing historiography of agricultural science, which can be divided either by chronology or, more interestingly, by national context.

The starting point for a study of British agriculture must be RUSSELL, who gives a narrative account of the rise and progress of agricultural science from the mid-17th to the mid-20th century. He places particular emphasis on theories of crop nutrition, a topic dealt with in more detail by FUSSELL, who looks at how humus theories of crop nutrition were related to practice, and by MOULTON, who looks at the impact of Justus von Liebig's mineral theory. Russell's commentary centres on the main figures involved but ignores the cultural, social, and political contexts within which they operated. While a useful source, then, one needs to be wary of Russell's rather dated account, which is best supplemented by WILMOT, who looks at how the taste for scientific and technical improvements in the 18th and 19th centuries shaped (and was shaped by) the rural communities in which these improvements were discussed and implemented. She examines the ways in which different social groups – landowners, tenant farmers, and labourers – were connected to the culture of improvement through local improving societies and strategies such as the awarding of medals and premiums to exemplary practitioners.

What these studies make clear is that 19th-century scientific agriculture was centred on chemistry. This is examined in detail by BERMAN, who, in his first three chapters, examines Humphry Davy's early career at the Royal Institution through a close study of manuscripts and printed material. In this period the Royal Institution functioned primarily as a laboratory for the landed improvers who managed the Board of Agriculture, a quasi-government institution founded in 1793. Taking a Marxist position, Berman shows how institutional factors led to important developments in agricultural chemistry, such as the development of a systematic programme of soil analyses. What Berman also makes clear is that in early 19th-century Britain agriculture was an important site for the development of science, in social and cognitive terms.

Taking a social constructivist view, PALLADINO (1996) has focused more specifically on the 20th century. He draws attention to the often ignored fact that agriculture was an important industry in early to mid-20th-century Britain and suggests that agriculture provides a particularly rich resource for the study of the complex relationship between science, technology, and the economy. Based on a survey of the four most important centres for plant breeding research, his central argument is that the nature of the relationship between theoretical science and technical improvement is a complicated one, grounded in social dynamics. Looking at the administrative and social structure of these centres, Palladino implicitly raises questions of how scientists and farmers interact. This issue is dealt with more fully by PALLADINO (1993), in which he identifies a multiplicity of practitioners and theorists, and examines the ways in which they are related. The negotiation of a social and intellectual space in which scientists could articulate their views about agriculture with authority proved to be of great importance.

PALLADINO (1994) concentrates on the way in which scientific theory – in this case Mendelian genetics – provided the rhetorical leverage for the positioning of science within agricultural discourse. Drawing out important differences between Britain and the US, Palladino argues that conflicts between more practically orientated figures, such as Edward Sloper Beavan, and more theoretically inclined geneticists, such as Sir William Dampier, had the effect of colonising an area of agriculture in much the same way that chemistry came to "scientize" agriculture in the 19th century. In Britain this came much later than it did in the US, where agricultural research was tied more closely to the universities. Palladino's primary interest is in the social organisation of science and technology, and especially the genesis of professional science. Accordingly, while he has written extensively on 20th-century British and American agriculture, his accounts in no way exhaust the topic. Indeed, such a focused attention on an area with which other scholars seem reluctant to engage is in danger of distorting the general picture of agriculture in the 20th century.

While his focus on the professionalization of agricultural science may be in danger of skewing the field, Palladino's study of British and American agriculture illustrates the richness of a comparative approach. His identification of a shift from practical to theoretical research has been more fully treated within the American context by MARCUS. He suggests that in the two decades between 1870 and 1890, the social organisation of agricultural research was such that it is profitable to speak of a shift from "scientific agriculture" to "agricultural science". Where technical and scientific improvement had once been the province of practising farmers, by the turn of the century such research agendas were being set and conducted by professional agricultural scientists based in universities. Similar themes are developed by DUPREE, who examines the political administration of agricultural research in America.

The historiography of American agriculture is much more extensive than that of Britain. Illustrating again the predominance of chemistry in the 19th century, ROSSITER examines the reception and dissemination of ideas concerning crop nutrition by charting Liebig's influence on the theory and practice of American agriculture in the period 1840–80. Focusing her study on three pioneering agricultural scientists and how they reacted to Liebig's ideas, she argues that Liebig's influence proved relatively short-lived. Concentrating on American agriculture in the 18th century, CHAPLIN shows how the modernisation of agriculture in the Lower South entailed the incorporation of Scottish political economy, which in turn generated interest in botany, technology, crop breeding, and technical innovation as strategies for economic development. Chaplin's monograph shows clearly how, at least in agriculture, economic thought and economic practice were intimately related to science and technology. Weaving the intellectual history of political economy and natural science together, she also places these in the local socio-economic context, highlighting at once the multifaceted nature of agriculture and the writing of its history. Taken together, these studies begin to offer a general picture of the development of agricultural science in modernity. A general shift from political economy to chemistry to genetics is evident, although this will undoubtedly need qualification and more detailed examination. Recognising such a trend, TOBEY suggests that the first half of the 20th century has, at least in the US, witnessed the blurring of such boundaries, through the emergence of agronomy and ecology within agricultural discourse.

OSBORNE argues that the growth of natural history societies in 19th-century France was intimately connected with imperialism, an important aspect of the history of agricultural research that is largely absent from the histories of American and British agriculture. In particular, he sees the development of an interest in Algerian agriculture as a product of the mobilisation of scientific organisations within an imperial agenda. More general studies of French agriculture are available. BOULAINE, for example, examines the history of agriculture from prehistory to the 20th century in much the same style as Russell, while the ACADÉMIE D'AGRICULTURE DE FRANCE has focused more narrowly on the two centuries since the French Revolution. One of the most interesting features of French agricultural research was that, unlike in Britain and the US, there was a lasting predominance of private research institutions. The most famous example is that of

Boussingault in Alsace, and it was not until after World War II that government institutes were established. Another important aspect of French agriculture was 18th-century physiocracy, an issue dealt with by FOX-GENOVESE. The physiocrats held that agriculture was the sole source of wealth and, as such, these works illustrate the importance of economic science in Enlightenment agriculture.

Studies of agricultural science, as we have seen, tend to concentrate on individuals or institutions. Rossiter focused on the reception of Liebig, and Liebig has provided an accessible and interesting point of entry in historical studies of agricultural science more generally. Several articles, considering the German, British, and American contexts, deal with his agricultural chemistry. Among these are the *Ambix* essays by MUNDAY, FINLAY, SCHLING-BRODERSEN and BROCK & STARK. Munday, arguing aggressively that Liebig scholarship has failed to take accurate note of the manuscript evidence, suggests that Liebig's turn to agricultural chemistry was part of a more general interest in the transformation of living bodies; a science of "metamorphoses", as he calls it. Finlay traces the reception of Liebig's ideas on agricultural chemistry from 1840 to 1862, when a seventh edition of his work in that area was published. Focusing especially on the German context, Finlay argues convincingly that the revised tone and content of the 1862 edition won back important support from the agricultural community. Brock & Starck look at the way in which Liebig utilised institutional support in Britain, in the form of the British Association for the Advancement of Science, in order to prepare an audience for his agricultural chemistry, while Schling-Brodersen considers the extent to which Liebig can be said to have inaugurated agricultural science in Germany. Also concentrating on Liebig's agricultural chemistry is the volume edited by Moulton, which contains essays examining Liebig's mastery of polemics, particularly in the disputes regarding his mineral theory of crop nutrition, and his general influence on the development of agricultural science. Also covered is Liebig's important contribution to the fertiliser industry. As with Russell, these studies are rather dated and Rossiter's work is, in part, a corrective to this collection.

Agriculture provides an interesting point of entry into wider historiographical debates, such as the professionalization of science, the relationship between science, technology, and economic development, the reception and establishment of ideas within specific communities, and the political aspects of government-funded research. Such fields, however, require further study, while other areas, such as the popularisation of agricultural science, the history of soil analysis, and the history of sewage irrigation, await investigation. It is to be hoped that these fields of research will attract interest in the future.

SIMON A. NIGHTINGALE

See also Liebig; Nutrition

AIDS

Altman, Dennis, *AIDS and the New Puritanism*, London and Sydney: Pluto Press, 1986

Berridge, Virginia, *AIDS in the UK: The Making of Policy, 1981–1994*, Oxford and New York: Oxford University Press, 1996

Berridge, Virginia and Philip Strong (eds), *AIDS and Contemporary History*, Cambridge: Cambridge University Press, 1993

Chirimuuta, Richard C. and Rosalind J. Chirimuuta, *Aids, Africa and Racism*, Stanhope, Derbyshire, 1987; revised edition, London: Free Association Books, 1987

Crimp, Douglas (ed.), *AIDS: Cultural Analysis/Cultural Activism*, Cambridge, Massachusetts: MIT Press, 1988

Fee, Elizabeth and Daniel M. Fox (eds), *AIDS: The Burdens of History*, Berkeley: University of California Press, 1988

Fee, Elizabeth and Daniel M. Fox (eds), *AIDS: The Making of a Chronic Disease*, Berkeley: University of California Press, 1992

Gallo, Robert, *Virus Hunting: AIDS, Cancer and the Human Retrovirus: A Story of Scientific Discovery*, New York: Basic Books, 1991

Garrett, Laurie, *The Coming Plague: Newly Emerging Diseases in a World out of Balance*, New York: Farrar Straus, 1994; London: Virago, 1995

Green, Edward C., *AIDS and STDs in Africa: Bridging the Gap Between Traditional Healing and Modern Medicine*, Boulder, Colorado: Westview Press, 1994

Grmek, Mirko D., *History of AIDS: Emergence and Origin of a Modern Pandemic*, translated by from the French by Russell C. Maulitz and Jacalyn Duffin, Princeton, New Jersey: Princeton University Press, 1990 (original edition, 1989)

Guibert, Hervé, *A l'ami qui ne m'a pas sauvé la vie*, Paris: Gallimard, 1990

Kirp, David L. and Ronald Bayer (eds), *AIDS in the Industrialized Democracies: Passions, Politics and Policies*, New Brunswick, New Jersey: Rutgers University Press, 1992

Mayes, Stephen and Lyndall Stein (eds), *Positive Lives – Responses to HIV: A Photodocumentary*, London and New York: Cassell, 1993

Montagnier, Luc, *Des Virus et des hommes*, Paris: Odile Jacob, 1994

Nelkin, Dorothy, David P. Willis and Scott V. Parris (eds), *A Disease of Society: Cultural and Institutional Responses to AIDS*, Cambridge: Cambridge University Press, 1991

Sabatier, Renée, *et al.*, *Blaming Others: Prejudice, Race and Worldwide AIDS*, London: Panos Institute, and Philadelphia, Pennsylvania: New Society, 1988

Seytre, Bernard, *Sida: les secrets d'une polémique: Recherche, intérêts financiers et médias*, Paris: Presses Universitaires de France, 1993

Shilts, Randy, *And the Band Played On: Politics, People and the AIDS Epidemic*, New York: St Martin's Press, 1987; Harmondsworth: Penguin, 1988

Thiaudière, Claude (ed.), *L'Homme contaminé: La tourmente du sida*, Paris: Autrement, 1992

Watney, Simon, *Practices of Freedom: Selected Writings on HIV/AIDS*, London: Rivers Oram Press, and Durham, North Carolina: Duke University Press, 1994

Since the US Federal Health authorities' first warnings in mid-1981 against what later came to be officially termed infection by HIV (Human Immuno Deficiency Virus) and AIDS (Acquired Immuno Deficiency Syndrome), this condition has been the topic of numerous historical studies. It has also prompted a renewed interest in the history of disease, particularly of those diseases that have been perceived in the West as similar to this unexpected pandemic, such as plagues, sexually transmitted diseases, tuberculosis, hepatitis B, and tropical diseases. To a great extent this editorial boom can be explained by the undisguised bewilderment that AIDS and other new, or newly emerging, infectious diseases – splendidly overviewed by Laurie GARRETT – have produced among the Western elites and common people, who look to the social responses to past diseases in order to find ways to confront more efficiently the new global health challenges.

Mirko Grmek, Randy Shilts, and Dennis Altman supply accounts, from different perspectives, of the outbreak and spread of AIDS in the 1980s. GRMEK reports the process of conceptualization of the new pandemic by North American and European clinical practitioners, epidemiologists and molecular biologists, and provides an interpretation of its origins and spread by incorporating results from the biological and epidemiological history of disease. SHILTS describes, by means of a vivid journalistic diary written in the US, the unstoppable progression of AIDS during the years of panic (1981–85). He denounces the valuable time wasted in the face of this epidemic as a result of the general institutional indifference (in medicine, public health, public and private scientific research agencies, and mass media). These only began to mobilize after the death of the Hollywood star Rock Hudson in October 1985. Finally, in a simultaneously personal and political fashion, ALTMAN accounts for the construction of AIDS as a new plague, and its impact on the American way of life in the age of the New Right and the Moral Majority (up to 1985). He lays particular emphasis on the early and active gay response to the situation, in contrast to the ambiguities in the response of the medical establishment and to the sensationalism of the media.

The two volumes edited by FEE & FOX (1988 and 1992) deal with a number of important issues concerning the social construction of AIDS and of AIDS policies from varied disciplinary perspectives (such as the history of medicine, social studies in medicine and science, political science, cultural studies and epidemiology). But in consonance with the changes in the dominant perceptions of AIDS between 1988 and 1992, the earlier volume emphasizes the analogies between the new pandemic and several historical instances of human diseases, while the later one approaches the history of AIDS as an issue fully inserted within contemporary history. In turn, the volume edited by NELKIN, WILLIS & PARRIS explores the impact of AIDS on social institutions, norms and values, interpersonal relationships and cultural representations.

While all these works, with the exception of Grmek, are excellent examples from a large literature concerned with AIDS in the US, much less attention has been paid to the history of AIDS and of AIDS policies in other parts of the world. Outstanding exceptions are Virginia BERRIDGE's thorough historical work analysing the first 14 years of AIDS policy in the UK, which represents a splendid model for future studies on other European countries; and the reader edited by Claude THIAUDIÈRE on the impact of AIDS on French civilization. Most of the rest consist of comparative studies of AIDS in different countries – far many more on developed countries

than on developing ones and the Third World – primarily focusing on issues of public policy, medical anthropology, public health and/or epidemiology, and rather obliquely on historical ones. KIRP & BAYER approach AIDS policy and politics in the developed world by comparing the responses of 11 industrialized democracies (Canada, Germany, Australia, Spain, Britain, France, The Netherlands, Denmark, Sweden, Japan and, again, the US). In contrast, the study by Edward GREEN deals with AIDS policies in sub-Saharan African countries (Swaziland, Liberia, Mozambique and South Africa) with particular emphasis on the relevant role of traditional healers, along with biomedical practitioners, in the containment of AIDS and other STDs.

Other works have focused on the relationship between AIDS and a number of "hot issues". The work of CHIRIMUUTA & CHIRIMUUTA and The Panos Institute Report by SABATIER et al. are written with a critical tone, denouncing racism and xenophobia. Richard and Rosalind Chirimuuta reveal the deeply racist ideology underlying the Western claims that "Africa is at the epicentre of the world AIDS pandemic", while Sabatier et al. deal with victimization of people affected by AIDS from the Third and the so-called Fourth Worlds (the destitutes in the First World). In other words, they focus on the use of some groups as scapegoats, as responsible for the origin and/or spread of AIDS. The interrelationship between AIDS and the mass media has been explored by Bernard SEYTRE, apropos of the long dispute between Luc Montagnier and Robert Gallo concerning priority in the HIV discovery and over the financial distribution of the patent rights for it. According to Seytre, beyond the big economic interests concerned, this controversy also represents a remarkably personalist media translation of the Franco–American polemics surrounding research on HIV and AIDS. The volume edited by BERRIDGE & STRONG explores, mainly in the case of the UK, US and France, the relationship between AIDS and Western contemporary history in two different ways: the larger agendas in medicine, public health, and social policy into which AIDS fitted, and AIDS itself as a part of the history of the 1980s.

Last, but not least, personal narratives of AIDS have been provided by individuals who have encountered the condition in a number of differing ways. The virologists Robert GALLO and Luc MONTAGNIER have done so from the perspective of their laboratory research on HIV. The French writer Hervé GUIBERT has described the experience of his own body's reaction to AIDS. Lyndall Stein from the British voluntary organization, the Terence Higgins Trust, with the collaboration of the photographer Stephen Mayes and others from the company Network Photographers, has collected pictures of and texts by people affected by AIDS (MAYES & STEIN). While cultural activists like Douglas CRIMP in the US and Simon WATNEY in the UK have used cultural analysis to explore the social and political meanings of AIDS.

JON ARRIZABALAGA

See also Epidemics; Epidemiology; Molecular Biology

Alchemy

Caron, M. and S. Hutin, *The Alchemists*, translated from the
    French by Helen R. Lane, New York: Grove Press and
    London: Evergreen Books, 1961 (original edition, 1959)

Debus, Allen G. and Robert P. Multhauf, *Alchemy and
    Chemistry in the Seventeenth Century*, Los Angeles:
    William Clark Memorial Library, University of California,
    1966

Dobbs, Betty Jo Teeter, *The Foundations of Newton's
    Alchemy or "The Hunting of the Greene Lyon"*,
    Cambridge and New York: Cambridge University Press,
    1975

Dreyfus, Hubert L., *Alchemy and Artificial Intelligence*, Santa
    Monica, California: Rand, 1965

Fauvel, John, Raymond Flood, Michael Shortland and Robin
    Wilson (eds), *Let Newton Be!*, Oxford and New York:
    Oxford University Press, 1988

Holmyard, Eric John, *Alchemy*, Harmondsworth: Penguin,
    1957; Baltimore: Penguin, 1968

Klossowski de Rola, Stanislas, *The Golden Game: Alchemical
    Engravings of the Seventeenth Century*, New York:
    Braziller and London: Thames and Hudson, 1988

Lindsay, Jack, *The Origins of Alchemy in Graeco–Roman
    Egypt*, London: Frederick Muller and New York: Barnes
    and Noble, 1970

Taylor, F. Sherwood, *The Alchemists: Founders of Modern
    Chemistry*, New York: H. Schuman, 1949; London:
    Heinemann, 1951

Vickers, Brian (ed.), *Occult and Scientific Mentalities in the
    Renaissance*, Cambridge and New York: Cambridge
    University Press, 1984

The alchemist's material goals were traditionally supposed to include the philosopher's stone, which would transmute base metals into gold; the elixir of life, which might be identical with the stone; and the homunculus, a miniature man, generated in a glass jar, who would possess and communicate superhuman knowledge. Alchemists themselves have defined their ultimate aims as intellectual enlightenment and spiritual redemption, to which Carl Gustav Jung and his followers would add psychological integration. Any manipulation of material substances is only a means to an end. Alchemy's scientific value has been hotly debated: did it foster the development of experimental method and sound theory, or only distract attention from the valuable chemical discoveries of practical investigators such as metallurgists, pharmacists, and Fellows of the Royal Society? The terms of this debate have themselves been condemned as inappropriate by scholars who have attempted to understand alchemy and alchemists on their own terms, within contemporary contexts. Controversy often focuses on the 17th century, which witnessed an unprecedented amount of alchemical publication, and the parting of the ways between alchemy and so-called modern science.

TAYLOR's brief but comprehensive survey takes a broad perspective, combining scientific rigour with sympathetic understanding of cultures and world views very different from that of the conventional 20th-century scientist, in which alchemy was, as he puts it, at once a craft and a creed. He traces alchemy's history from its ancient beginnings in far-off lands, through the rise of scientific method in 17th-century England, to its modern mystical and psychological applications. Plentiful illustrations are carefully integrated with the lucid, imaginative text.

HOLMYARD concentrates chiefly on the scientific implications of attempts to find the philosopher's stone, which he identifies with the elixir of life, from ancient China to 18th-century Europe. After the Royal Society's investigations into James Price's alchemical claims in 1783, no learned society since has been willing officially to notice alchemical claims. He sees Boyle's *Sceptical Chymist* (1661) as alchemy's death-warrant, though "it survived in apparent vigour for another century". Newton's interest in alchemy is mentioned, but not investigated. Within its conceptual and temporal limits, this is a thorough and authoritative survey. The glossary of technical terms is particularly useful.

CARON & HUTIN argue that alchemy has no history, in the sense that it claims to be a science that is complete and perfect. Unlike other sciences it does not evolve; rather, it is transmitted. Their lively general introduction covers alchemy's aims, theoretical structure, and methods – which are susceptible to change – from China in the 6th century BC to 20th-century Europe. It is lucidly written, with few technical terms, lavishly illustrated, and enhanced with vivid biographical and technical details, including descriptions of laboratory equipment and a recipe for the elixir of long life. Readers should remember the contingencies of translation: "Evranaeus Philaletha" is better known in England as "Eirenaeus Philalethes".

DREYFUS's trenchant rebuttal of exaggerated claims made for artificial intelligence in the 1950s and 1960s uses alchemists's attempts at transmutation as an analogy for the wishful thinking of pioneer computer programmers. He is unfair to alchemists, who, contrary to his assertion, had reasons to believe transmutation had actually been achieved. (Admittedly, they were not authentically "scientific" reasons.) Dreyfus misses an opportunity to draw an even closer parallel, by comparing the computer's potential with that of the homunculus: "wet engineering" with a vengeance!

Debus's paper in DEBUS & MULTHAUF argues that alchemy inspired "chemical philosophers" such as Paracelsus, Fludd and Van Helmont, who "helped formulate modern science by striving for the same goals as the mechanical philosophers, even though they were encouraged to do so by hypotheses and analogies which we today would reject outright". Multhauf's essay on scientific dialogues argues that the scientific revolution was not simply a sudden leap out of the darkness of antiquarianism and the occult into the "light" of rationalism.

LINDSAY's fascinating, scholarly study is the fourth book of a series on the life and culture of Roman Egypt. He accordingly conveys a strong sense of the links between alchemy and its social context, from Ionia in the 7th century BC to medieval Byzantium. Unfortunately, its sheer practicality was uncongenial to the aristocratic ethos of the mainstream philosophical tradition. Lindsay argues persuasively that its uniting of craft-processes with theoretical thought denied alchemy an accepted place in the ancient world.

DOBBS's important study presents Newton's alchemical investigations in a form that other historians of science have been unable to ignore. With impeccable scholarship, she combines broad historical perspective with detailed accounts of experiments, arguing that alchemy comprised one of the pillars that supported the structure of Newton's mature science.

VICKERS's compilation of essays is essential reading for students of Renaissance scientific historiography. He and his contributors examine the co-existence and interaction of occult and scientific modes of thinking, even in those scientists who themselves delivered sharp attacks on the occult mentality. Vickers recommends that historians of science should not ignore or deny the presence of this apparent contradiction; they should base their analyses on first-hand study of published texts and unpublished manuscripts, and should refine and deepen the intellectual models they use in attempting to understand the phenomenon. Alchemy is frequently discussed, appearing most prominently in Richard Westfall's contention that Newton derived his concept of force partly from the alchemical active principle.

FAUVEL *et al.* have combined with other contributors to produce a volume on Newton and Newtonianism whose clear style and attractive illustrations appeal to the general reader, while its academic rigour satisfies the demands of scholars. Newton's scientific theories are set within the context of his beliefs about Christian theology and classical culture. Studies of his occult interests, such as Jan Golinski's "The Secret Life of an Alchemist" and Piyo Rattansi's "Newton and the Wisdom of the Ancients", fall naturally into place. According to John Henry's "Newton, Matter, and Magic", Newton's alchemical studies laid the foundation for what eventually became particle physics.

KLOSSOWKI DE ROLA presents "a comprehensive selection of the finest engraved alchemical emblems of the 17th century, brought together for the first time". He transcribes and translates the inscriptions, as well as interprets the pictures, and, eschewing scientific terminology, tries to make alchemy intelligible in its own terms. Ultimately, however, he offers no instant enlightenment, claiming that the lesson of the Ancient Way can truly be learnt only by travelling on it. Reading must be supplemented by practice.

CAROLYN D. WILLIAMS

See also Occult Sciences

Algebra

Beaulieu, Liliane, *La Ribu: N. Bourbaki, 1934–1956*, Paris: Springer, 1995

Berggren, J.L., *Episodes in the Mathematics of Medieval Islam*, New York: Springer, 1986

Birkhoff, Garret, "The Rise of Modern Algebra to 1936", in *Men and Institutions in American Mathematics*, edited by J. Dalton Tarwater, John T. White and John D. Miller, Lubbock: Texas Tech Press, 1976

Bos, H.J.M., "On the Representation of Curves in Descartes' *Géométrie*", *Archive for History of Exact Sciences*, 24 (1981): 295–338

Busard, H.L.L., *Jordanus de Nemore, De Elementis Arithmetice Artis: A Medieval Treatise on Number Theory*, 2 vols, Stuttgart: Steiner, 1991

Corry, Leo, *Modern Algebra and the Rise of Mathematical Structures*, Basel: Birkhäuser, 1996

Crowe, Michael J., *A History of Vector Analysis: The Evolution of the Idea of a Vectoral System*, Notre Dame, Indiana: University of Notre Dame Press, 1967; reprinted, New York: Dover, 1985

Folkerts, M., *Zur Entwicklung der Algebra in Deutschland im 15. und 16. Jahrhundert*, Jahrbuch des Deutschen Akademie der Naturforscher Leopoldina, 1991

Grassmann, Hermann, *La Science de la grandeur extensive*, edited by D. Flamant, Paris: Blanchard, 1994

Klein, Jacob, *Greek Mathematical Thought and the Origin of Algebra*, translated from the German by Eva Brann, Cambridge, Massachusetts: MIT Press, 1968 (original edition, 1934)

Mahoney, M., "The Beginnings of Algebraic Thought in the Seventeenth Century", in *Descartes: Philosophy, Mathematics and Physics*, edited by Stephen Gaukroger, Brighton, Harvester Press, and Totowa, New Jersey: Barnes and Noble, 1980

Moore, G.H., "The Axiomatisation of Linear Algebra: 1875–1940", *Historia Mathematica*, 22/3 (1995): 262–303

Novy, Lubos, *Origins of Modern Algebra*, translated from the Czech by Jaroslav Taver, Prague: Academia, 1973

Rashed, Roshdi (ed.), *Diophante: Les Arithmétiques* (Books 4–7), Paris: Belles Lettres, 1984 (Arabic text with French translation)

Rashed, Roshdi, *Entre arithmétique et algèbre: Recherches sur l'histoire des mathématiques arabes*, Paris: Belles Lettres, 1984

Scholz, Erhard (ed.), *Geschichte der Algebra: Eine Einführung*, Mannheim: Wissenschaftsverlag, 1990

Sesiano, Jacques (ed.), *Books IV to VII of Diophantus's "Arithemetica" in the Arabic Translation Attributed to Qusta ibn Luqa*, New York and Heidelberg: Springer, 1982 (Arabic text with English translation)

Sinaceur, Hourya, *Corps et modèles: Essais sur l'histoire de l'algèbre relle*, Paris: Vrin, 1991

Unguru, S., "On the Need to Rewrite the History of Greek Mathematics", *Archive for History of Exact Sciences*, 15 (1975): 67–114

Waerden, Bartel Leendert van der, *Science Awakening*, translated from the Dutch by Arnold Dresden, 2 vols, Groningen: Noordhoff, 1954–74; New York: Oxford University Press, 1961

Waerden, Bartel Leendert van der, *A History of Algebra: From al-Khwarizmī to Emmy Noether*, New York: Springer, 1985

Whiteside, D.T. (ed.), *The Mathematical Papers of Isaac Newton*, vol. 5, Cambridge: Cambridge University Press, 1972

Wussing, Hans, *The Genesis of the Abstract Group Concept: A Contribution to the History of the Origin of Abstract Group Theory*, translated from the German by Abe Shenitzer, Cambridge, Massachusetts: MIT Press, 1984 (original edition, 1969)

Zaddach, Arno, *Grassmanns Algebra in der Geometrie*, Mannheim: Wissenschaftsverlag, 1994

Zeuthen, H.G., *Die Lehre von den Kegelschnitten im Altertum*, Copenhagen: Höst & Sohn, 1886; reprinted Hildesheim: Georg Olms, 1966

Scholars are divided on the issue of how to define algebra. The core concept is that of high school algebra, which teaches that the solutions of the equation $ax^2 + bx + c = 0$ are given by the formula $x = (-b \pm (b^2 - 4ac)^{1/2})/2a$ and that the equation $x^2 - a^2 = (x + a)(x - a)$ is an identity (true for all values of x and a). The use of letters for coefficients and unknowns, and of formal methods of deriving solutions, is characteristic of this form of algebra. For these reasons, MAHONEY argues that algebra did not exist before the 17th century. A less stringent view starts by observing that the word "algebra" derives from the Arabic *al-jabr* (meaning rearrangement), which appeared in the title of *al-Khwarizmi*'s book on the solution of quadratic equations (written in the 9th century), and that it therefore makes sense to include Arabic work of this sort. The broadest view is that any organised approach to the solution of questions about numbers that includes the systematic derivation of answers deserves to be called algebra. On this basis, early Babylonian solutions to questions about sums of unknown numbers and their squares, which closely resemble how one calculates the above formula step by step, count as algebra. This is the view of most of the authors collected in SCHOLZ (although others might argue that this is the study of numbers and not algebra). In the opinion of most scholars of Greek mathematics, the best approach to the material is via some books of Euclid's *Elements*, while Apollonius' *Conics* is as an account of algebraic identities proved geometrically, and for this reason they speak of Greek geometrical algebra, a term first coined by ZEUTHEN. A stern, if not always persuasive, study of this subject is UNGURU, who argues that this material is geometry and is travestied by translation into algebra.

A number of books and articles present the factual basis for engaging with the history of algebra. Greek geometrical algebra is described in WAERDEN (1961), while WAERDEN (1985) takes the story from *al-Khwarizmi* to his own time. BERGGREN describes Arabic work within the context of Islamic mathematics as a whole, while the articles in Scholz cover Greek, Arabic, and early modern algebra, and also describe the work of Doiphantus, algebra as applied to geometry, algebra and probability theory, algebraic number theory, and the rise of modern structural algebra. RASHED has written on other aspects of Islamic mathematics, especially the later algebraists.

More detailed studies include rival accounts of the work of Diophantus that draw on recently-discovered Arabic translations of lost Greek originals by RASHED and by SESIANO. The *Arithmetica* of Jordanus de Nemore, who was active in the early 13th century, was the standard source for theoretical arithmetic in the European Middle Ages; it is described in detail in the edition by BUSARD. The medieval algebraists or cossists (so-called because their name for the unknown was the "cosa" or thing) are described in specialist monographs, for which FOLKERTS may serve as an introduction. KLEIN remains a more provocative work, arguing that the decisive move in the creation of modern algebra was taken by Vieta, on the basis of an incorrect reconstruction of Greek ideas that found a common approach to the work of Apollonius and Diophantus.

Historical scholarship on Descartes was revitalised by BOS, who showed in detail just how important geometry was in *La Géométrie*, a work too often seen as simply the start of modern algebra. Literature in the philosophy of mathematics and the history of science has yet to grapple with the weight of Bos's account. For Newton's ideas on algebra and their impact, the starting point is WHITESIDE's monumental eight-volume edition of his work, especially volume 5.

Starting in the 19th century, algebra grew from its roots in the study of number-like objects. A useful overview is that by NOVY. An important breakthrough came with Hamilton's proposition of a system of "numbers" generalising the complex numbers, but at the price of abandoning the commutativity of multiplication. Whereas hitherto it had been assumed that *ab = ba*, this is not true of Hamilton's quaternions, and from their introduction (in 1843) two currents gradually diverged. One, described by CROWE, led to the modern use of vectors, especially in physics. (A recent account of the emergence of the concept of a vector space is MOORE in *Historia Mathematica*.) The other led to other systems of hypercomplex numbers (objects one can add, subtract, multiply together, and multiply by real numbers), later called algebra. At this point the subject of algebra, as a university topic, became the new structural analysis of these formal systems. A pioneer, neglected in his lifetime, was GRASSMANN, whose work is discussed by Crowe, and in more detail by ZADDACH. As such it now includes the theory of groups, the origins of which are thoroughly described by WUSSING. The history of the field concept (where the four arithmetical operations are permitted) includes generalisations of the real numbers, which led mathematicians into logic and model theory, as carefully described by SINACEUR.

The view of algebra in particular, and all pure mathematics more generally, as structural acquired widespread currency with its acceptance by Piaget (on which he based his analysis of the child's learning of mathematics), and with the "new mathematics" in the 1960s, which was allegedly also a response to the unexpected Russian lead in the space race. Key texts are the works of Emmy Noether and her school, widely disseminated as German mathematicians fled the Nazis, and that of Bourbaki, a French collective of mathematicians that began with the aim of helping French mathematicians to catch up with their German colleagues in the 1930s. The real difficulties in the mathematics has delayed the presentation of any kind of history of these 20th-century developments, but BEAULIEU considers the early days of Bourbaki and CORRY makes a broader investigation of the structural movement. The traditional view of the mathematician on the history is given in the cited article by BIRKHOFF.

JEREMY GRAY

See also Geometry

Alienation

Feuer, Lewis S., "What is Alienation? The Career of a Concept", in *Marx and The Intellectuals: A Set of Post-Ideological Essays*, New York: Anchor Books, 1969

Geyer, R. Felix and David Schweitzer (eds), *Alienation: Problems of Meaning, Theory and Method*, London: Routledge and Kegan Paul, 1981

Israel, Joachim, *Alienation from Marx to Modern Sociology: A Macrosociological Analysis*, Boston: Allyn and Bacon, 1971

Kaplan, Morton A., *Alienation and Identification*, New York: Free Press, 1976

Meszaros, Istvan, *Marx's Theory of Alienation*, London: Merlin Press, 1970; New York: Harper and Row, 1972

Mouledoux, Joseph C. and Elizabeth C. Mouledoux, *Alienation: A Critical Evaluation of Selected Empirical Studies*, Montreal: Canadian Sociology and Anthropology Association, 1975

Ollman, Bertell, *Alienation: Marx's Conception of Man in Capitalist Society*, Cambridge: Cambridge University Press, 1971; 2nd edition, 1976

Rotenstreich, Nathan, *Alienation: The Concept and Its Reception*, Leiden: E.J. Brill, 1989

Schacht, Richard, *Alienation*, with an introduction by Walter Kaufmann, New York: Doubleday, 1970; London: Allen and Unwin, 1971

Schmitt, Richard and Thomas E. Moody (eds), *Alienation and Social Criticism*, Atlantic Highlands, New Jersey: Humanities Press, 1994

Torrance, John, *Estrangement, Alienation and Exploitation: A Sociological Approach to Historical Materialism*, New York: Columbia University Press, and London: Macmillan, 1977

For four decades social scientists have debated the meaning of the concept of alienation and its potential for fruitful empirical analysis. The denotations of alienation as an historical, philosophical or theoretical phenomenon, or as a psychological variable to be operationalized, were heatedly disputed in the decades of Marxism's hegemony in Eastern Europe, and thus the problem of alienation is fundamental to discourses on the human experience of socialist and capitalist societies in the 20th century. In sociology and social philosophy, the fate of the concept of alienation has been inexorably linked to the question of philosophical continuity in the thought of Karl Marx, and much of the difficulty with the concept has related to deficiencies of conceptual clarity and specificity. Any theory of alienation involves assumptions about human nature and the relationship between the individual and society, and generally emphasizes society (socio–economic contexts) or the individual (psychological experience). Marx's definition of alienation refers to the exteriorization of work and/or human activity and its products or results – that is, a loss of personal control, and therefore a consequent absence of meaning, power, and self-fulfilment. Estrangement from others and from nature are further manifestations of alienation.

FEUER maintains that alienation has become the "key ethical concept" of the age. Its resurgence was based on a revival of the early writings of Marx, specifically the *Economic and Philosophic Manuscripts of 1844*, in which Marx had developed a theory of alienation. Feuer claims that the concept was associated particularly with sexual alienation, as reflected in the early romantic thinking of Marx, and that Marx and Engels later replaced the concept with "exploitation". Feuer

identifies six sociological modes of alienation, a phenomenon he claims as historically universal, and not in itself unique to modern class society. He considers the contemporary concept, "a concept of political theology", conveying a "mood of pervasive tragedy" and reflecting the self-alienation of the intellectual.

MESZAROS provides a clear examination of the Marxian meaning and usage of alienation. He explains the genesis and structure of Marx's theory of alienation including its economic, political, ontological–moral, and aesthetic aspects. With careful detail and precise use of Marx's German texts, Meszaros builds the evidence for the centrality and continuity of the theory of alienation within Marx's corpus. He deals with the controversy over Marx's concept, the problem of the individual in capitalist society, and finally the resolution of alienation in modernity through education. Within the Marxian context alienation is a concept of critique.

OLLMAN presents Marx's theory of alienation as contained in the *Economic and Philosophic Manuscripts of 1844* in relation to his conception of human nature, the four "relations" of alienation, and the labour theory of value in particular. In Ollman's perspective these relations of alienation are understood in combination with the theory of value in order to constitute "a useful aid for understanding capitalism . . . for those who share with Marx certain basic beliefs" – i.e. those, who see the ubiquity of alienated relations throughout capitalist society.

SCHACHT, in his 1970 exposition on alienation, attempts to clarify the origins of the concept and its philosophical, psychological and literary usage, and identifies basic contemporary issues of self and society deriving from the implications of alienation. Walter Kaufmann's introduction reminds us that "alienation is a central feature of human existence". Not wishing to discard the concept or ignore its realities, Schacht suggests a number of "issues" represented in the writings on alienation that lie somewhere between empirical propositions and philosophical assertions, but which are disappointingly obvious.

In an attempt to examine closely Marx's fundamental concepts of estrangement, alienation and exploitation, TORRANCE explores their potential as sociological concepts and their clarification in terms of property and class relations. The analysis is successful in demonstrating the heuristic possibilities of Marxian theory for identifying and understanding social and economic problems within contemporary society.

Particularly helpful in understanding the historical context of the concept and analysis of alienation within the discipline of sociology is ISRAEL's exploration of alienation in the theoretical writings of Marx, Weber, Simmel, and Durkheim. This work traces the analysis of alienation in theory and in applied research in macrosociology, social psychology and empirical sociology, and explores alienation's manifestations in the Soviet Union and Cuba. Israel maintains that a sociological understanding of alienation requires a shift, found even in Marx, from alienation to reification, "a process in which social relations gain the character of relations between things" and where social institutions gain independent powers over the members of society.

Attempts at operationalizing alienation in order to measure types and degrees among various groups and populations have been problematic, as a result of the use of mundane indicators and meagre, often inconsistent, theoretical frameworks. The leading empirical studies of alienation are critically reviewed in MOULEDOUX & MOULEDOUX, a rare work of this genre, which meticulously examines the quantitative and qualitative difficulties of the research, especially those generated by ahistorical, reductionist approaches. The authors conclude that, given the unsatisfactory quality of empirical studies of alienation, on the one hand, and the overly generalized views leading to "speculative conceptions of what man and society might become given the realization of a particular 'theory'", on the other, the concept of alienation offers little hope or help in understanding the human condition.

KAPLAN addresses some of the fundamental theoretical problems and inconsistencies in Marx's analyses of alienation, and maintains that alienation as a concept must be separated from ideology and understood as "a practical problem that requires different practical solutions at different times". To address and reduce alienation in these terms requires linking it, Kaplan claims, to identification – i.e. to a sense of membership in human groupings and to a constructive personal history.

In a more philosophical discussion, ROTENSTREICH traces the development and reception of the concept of alienation in its Hegelian and Marxian usage, particularly within the historical and economic domains. Moving to the personal realm, he maintains that alienation is an inevitable dimension of processes (even dialectics) of identity and creativity within the individual. The limited impact of the concept of alienation, related as it was to the Marxian critique of structures, may have spelled its own obsolescence.

Reflections on the theoretical and methodological complexities of the concept of alienation in sociology can be found in the collection edited by GEYER & SCHWEITZER. Here, analyses of conceptual and methodological problems stand alongside attempts to produce formal theories of alienation. The variety of cultural contexts and approaches of such work illuminate the controversial dimensions of the concept.

In a selection of previously published radical writings that consider human alienation in specific experiential contexts, SCHMITT & MOODY provide recent and sociologically-provocative considerations of alienation. The contexts of alienation considered here include work, gender, race, disability, old age, nature, and the relation of the individual to society. Alienation is used to refer to a range of human problems and their consequences, such as lack of autonomy, isolation, and discrimination. The volume is based on the contention that "alienation is indispensable for describing accurately the condition of oppressed groups in our society". Alienation may be observed and understood most meaningfully through such a spectrum of human experiences.

SUSAN HOECKER-DRYSDALE

See also Capitalism and Science; Marx; Marxism and Science; Sociology

Almanacs

Bosanquet, Eustace F., *English Printed Almanacs and Prognostications: A Bibliographical History to the Year 1600*, London: Chiswick Press, 1917

Capp, Bernard, *Astrology and the Popular Press: English Almanacs 1500–1800*, London: Faber and Faber, and Ithaca, New York: Cornell University Press, 1979

Drake, Milton (ed.), *Almanacs of the United States*, 2 vols, Metuchen, New Jersey: Scarecrow Press, 1962

Kelly, John T., *Practical Astronomy during the Seventeenth Century: A Study of Almanac-Makers in America and England*, New York: Garland, 1991

Perkins, Maureen, *Visions of the Future: Almanacs, Time and Cultural Change 1775–1870*, Oxford: Clarendon Press, and New York: Oxford University Press, 1996

Sommerfeldt, W.P. (ed.), *Den norske almanakk gjennom 300 år 1644–1944*, Oslo: Universitetets almanakkforlag, 1944

Stowell, Marion Barber, *Early American Almanacs: The Colonial Weekday Bible*, New York: Franklin, 1977

Originating in Europe in the 14th century, the almanac rapidly evolved from a relatively primitive form into a calendar or ephemeris in which were noted the positions of the heavenly bodies for regular intervals or specific dates. Additional information provided in almanacs has always been extremely diverse, and has included the times of the rising and setting of the sun, moon and certain stars, eclipses and conjunctions, weather forecasts, astrological predictions, days of historic and religious significance, medical advice, monetary tables, tide tables, tables of distances between towns and cities, literary contributions, and a wealth of other material. The relative emphasis of these different elements has also changed greatly over time. Following the introduction of printing, almanacs became extremely widespread, with print runs in the thousands by the 17th century. This can be explained in part by their practical domestic use; for instance, prior to the wide availability of clocks, almanacs could be used as a means of telling the time, while the weather forecasts that they usually contained were of vital importance in agriculturally-based communities, and the calendar could be used as a diary.

Much that has been written on the history of almanacs has tended to concentrate on those produced in particular countries. It is therefore quite easy to find studies for individual countries, but more difficult to find secondary sources that give a more general account. BOSANQUET provides, for instance, a survey of almanacs published in England up to 1600. The bulk of the work is a chronological listing of the almanacs published, with a short description of each, although the introduction includes a brief history of almanacs. DRAKE provides a similar resource for American almanacs for the period 1639–1850.

STOWELL, as the title indicates, underlines the huge cultural impact of the American almanac, given that, apart from the Bible, it was generally the only written material available in American homes. She chronicles the development of almanacs and their contents from the 17th century onwards, but with emphasis on the 18th century. Describing the main families publishing almanacs, such as the Ames and the Franklins, she also analyses the almanac as literature, paying particular attention to the expectations of the readership.

CAPP, again dealing largely with England, provides two main narratives. First, he uses an investigation of English almanacs to trace the development of astrology between 1500 and 1800.

Second, by analysing the range of subjects covered in almanacs, he attempts to explore the interests, attitudes, and needs of the English lower classes. Consequently, he includes sections on politics, society, religion, science and medicine, and history and literature, as well as tracing the general development of the almanac throughout the period. The author thus demonstrates how English almanac-makers advanced the practice of astrology at the popular level (which complemented the work of astrological consultants), while illustrating in addition the wide range of needs that almanacs fulfilled. This included, for example, giving advice on farming, news of highways and fairs, medical and sexual advice, tables of weights and measures and of interest and excise rates, popular science, and navigational aids. Furthermore, the book contains excellent appendices, listing not only all of the almanacs currently known to have been published in the period (with locations for extant editions), but also a list of their dedications and short biographical entries on each almanac author.

PERKINS extends chronologically the story developed by Capp and deals with almanacs in both England and Australia. Her central thesis is that the period 1775–1870 witnessed several important changes. First, astrology and prophecy gradually disappeared from the almanac, principally as a result of Whig reform of popular culture and the promotion of science. Second, new forms appeared, in particular the statistical almanac. Last, the traditional almanac declined in popularity, as a result of changing perceptions of the nature of time and the appropriation of many of its functions, such as weather forecasting, by other media, notably newspapers.

Despite the apparent limits implied by the title, KELLY provides an account that covers the development of the almanac from its origins in Europe in the 14th and 15th centuries, through England in the 16th and 17th centuries, to America during the colonial period. Concentrating on the technical aspects of production, the story begins with almanac-making, which required only a basic knowledge of arithmetic, geometry and astronomy, with the almanacs used for applications in astronomy, astrology and navigation. The account culminates in the production of national ephemerides, such as the Nautical Almanac, published in England from the 1760s, and the American ephemeris and nautical almanac, produced from 1852, by which time the emphasis was on the navigational applications of the astronomical information contained in these publications. This evolution, argues Kelly, reflected an increasingly sophisticated approach to computational astronomy, which was closely associated with the advancement of observational astronomy. Kelly's emphasis is on an analysis of the astronomical data used in the preparation of almanacs, and he adopts a comparative approach in order to demonstrate the dependence of American almanac-makers for their astronomical data on English ephemerides and planetary tables.

SOMMERFELDT contains essays on various aspects of Norwegian almanacs, with titles such as weather, medicine, astrology, prognostication and the role of time in social life. It also lists Norwegian almanacs and navigational calendars throughout history and includes a register of topics covered in almanacs of that country.

RICHARD DUNN

Anatomy

Choulant, Ludwig, *History and Bibliography of Anatomic Illustration*, edited and translated from the German by Mortimer Frank, New York: Schuman, 1945 (original edition, 1852)

Cole, F.J., *A History of Comparative Anatomy: From Aristotle to the Eighteenth Century*, London: Macmillan, 1944; reprinted, New York: Dover, 1975

French, Roger, "The Anatomical Tradition", in *Companion Encyclopedia of the History of Medicine*, vol. 1, London and New York: Routledge, 1994

Lind, L.R., *Studies in Pre-Vesalian Anatomy: Biography, Translations, Documents*, Philadelphia: American Philosophical Society, 1975

O'Malley, Charles D., *Andreas Vesalius of Brussels, 1514–1564*, Berkeley: University of California Press, 1964

Richardson, Ruth, *Death, Dissection, and the Destitute*, London and New York: Routledge and Kegan Paul, 1987

Roberts, K.B. and J.D.W. Tomlinson, *The Fabric of the Body: European Traditions of Anatomical Illustration*, Oxford: Clarendon Press, and New York: Oxford University Press, 1992

Singer, Charles, *The Evolution of Anatomy: A Short History of Anatomical and Physiological Discovery to Harvey*, New York: Knopf, and London: Kegan Paul Trench and Trubner, 1925; revised edition as *A Short History of Anatomy from the Greeks to Harvey*, New York: Dover, 1957

Both Charles Singer and F.J. Cole provide concise, readable surveys of the history of anatomy in Western society. SINGER is divided equally between the Greeks, the "Dark Ages", the Middle Ages and Renaissance, the era of William Harvey, and modern times. Profusely illustrated with the standard historical representations of anatomy, Singer's work explicitly makes no distinction between form and function. COLE provides a concise overview of "zootomy" from ancient Greece to the 16th century. Zootomy is defined as the pursuit of animal dissection to the point of indivisibility: i.e. animals were "resolved into their smallest parts". Animals have long been studied both for information about the specific animal's structure and to extrapolate those findings to the structure and working of humans. Cole explains that the homologies between "lower" animals and man have occupied the minds of many scientists and historians, particularly after the theory of evolution became more widely known. Cole discusses the "craft" of anatomy and the encyclopaedic compilations of comparative anatomy in the Renaissance. He proceeds to distinguish these contributions from the later "analysts" of anatomy, beginning with Marcello Malpighi. The Dutch contributions of Antoni van Leeuwenhoek, Jan Swammerdam, and Frederik Ruysch are discussed, as are the changing aspects of teaching anatomy to natural philosophers and artists since the Renaissance.

LIND examines the politico–cultural background of medieval scholasticism and Renaissance humanism before providing extensive "life and work" surveys of seven individuals who made significant contributions to anatomy between 1490 and 1543. Lind provides biographical sketches of Alessandro Achillini, Alessandro Benedetti, Gabriele Zerbi, Berengario de Carpi, Niccolo Massa, Andres de Laguna, Johannes Dryander, and Giovanni Battista Canano.

During the same year in which Copernicus' influential cosmological writing appeared and began to alter the macrocosmic way of seeing the universe, Vesalius published *De humani corporis fabrica* (1543), which began to shake Aristotelian microcosmic understandings of the human body. O'MALLEY provides the most complete investigation in English of the author and his work, arguably the most significant in the history of Western anatomy.

Procuring "specimens" for anatomical dissection has long vexed the educators of physicians. Surgeons also claimed that cadaveric human bodies were essential tools for improving their anatomical knowledge of the structures underlying the skin, as well as for practising their operative procedures. RICHARDSON provides an exhilarating account of the pinnacle of debate over the ownership of the body in her investigation of early 19th-century British medico–legal struggles. She discusses dissection as the ultimate fate of executed criminals, the frequent grave robbings, and the Anatomy Act of 1832, which legalized the procurement of the corpses of the poor, and in effect transferred the penalty of dissection from criminals to paupers.

Surgical treatises throughout history typically include an extensive section on anatomy. Anatomical knowledge was not only expected to be committed to memory, but put to practical use as well. Some historians have deemed that all improvements in the surgical art were solely due to advancements in anatomy. Gross anatomy – the structures visible at the dissection table – has recently been overshadowed by increasing interest in microscopic or cellular anatomy. The microscope distinctively changed the anatomical view of the body, but as FRENCH argues, the view of gross anatomical structures did not vanish into homogeneity. Rather, the diversity of structure was continued, even multiplied, at greater magnifications.

Anatomical writings are typically generously illustrated. CHOULANT analyzes the art and craftsmanship behind anatomical illustration as well as the graphic and plastic art forms. Brief attention is paid to pre-Vesalian art; instead, he concentrates his broad biographical and bibliographical coverage to post-Vesalian European anatomical illustration through the mid-19th century. This work focuses on human anatomy and the works which, through their lasting influence, are considered of key historical significance. ROBERTS & TOMLINSON review the same period as Choulant, though with less attention to detail, and then continue a discussion of European anatomical illustration through the 20th century.

PHILIP K. WILSON

Anthropology

Asad, Talal (ed.), *Anthropology and the Colonial Encounter*, New York: Humanities Press, 1993

De Waal Malefijt, Annemarie, *Images of Man: A History of Anthropological Thought*, New York: Knopf, 1974

Evans-Pritchard, E. E., *A History of Anthropological Thought*, edited by André Singer, London: Faber and Faber, and New York: Basic Books, 1981

Foucault, Michel, *The Order of Things: An Archaeology of the Human Sciences*, translated from the French by Alan Sheridan, London: Tavistock, and New York: Vintage, 1970 (original edition, 1966)

Goody, Jack, *The Expansive Moment: The Rise of Social Anthropology in Britain and Africa, 1918–1970*, Cambridge and New York: Cambridge University Press, 1995

Gould, Stephen Jay, *The Mismeasure of Man*, New York: Norton, 1981; revised and expanded edition, 1996

Haraway, Donna, *Primate Visions: Gender, Race, and Nature in the World of Modern Science*, New York: Routledge, 1989

Harris, Marvin, *The Rise of Anthropological Theory: A History of Theories of Culture*, New York: Crowell, and London: Routledge and Kegan Paul, 1968

Herbert, Christopher, *Culture and Anomie: Ethnographic Imagination in the Nineteenth Century*, Chicago: University of Chicago Press, 1991

Holmes, Lowell D., *Quest for the Real Samoa: The Mead/Freeman Controversy and Beyond*, South Hadley, Massachusetts: Bergin and Garvey, 1987

Honigmann, John J., *The Development of Anthropological Ideas*, Homewood, Illinois: Dorsey Press, 1976

Hyatt, Marshall, *Franz Boas, Social Activist: The Dynamics of Ethnicity*, Westport, Connecticut: Greenwood Press, 1990

Jarvie, I.C., *The Revolution in Anthropology*, London: Routledge and Kegan Paul, and New York: Humanities Press, 1964

Kuklick, Henrika, *The Savage Within: The Social History of British Anthropology, 1885–1945*, Cambridge and New York: Cambridge University Press, 1991

Kuper, Adam, *Anthropologists and Anthropology: The British School 1922–1972*, London: Allen Lane, and New York: Pica Press, 1973; 2nd edition, as *Anthropology and Anthropologists: The Modern British School*, London: Routledge and Kegan Paul, 1983

Leaf, Murray J., *Man, Mind and Science: A History of Anthropology*, New York: Columbia University Press, 1979

Lowie, Robert H., *The History of Ethnological Theory*, New York: Farrar and Rinehart, 1937

Payden, Anthony, *The Fall of Natural Man: The American Indian and the Origins of Comparative Ethnology*, Cambridge and New York: Cambridge University Press, 1986

Penniman, T.K., *A Hundred Years of Anthropology*, London: Duckworth, 1935; New York: Macmillan, 1936; 3rd edition, with contributions by Beatrice Blackwood and J.S. Weiner, London: Duckworth, 1965

Stanton, William, *The Leopard's Spots: Scientific Attitudes Toward Race in America, 1815–1859*, Chicago: University of Chicago Press, 1960

Stocking Jr, George W., *Race, Culture and Evolution: Essays in the History of Anthropology*, New York: Free Press, 1968

Stocking Jr, George W., *Victorian Anthropology*, New York: Free Press, and London: Collier–Macmillan, 1987

Stocking Jr, George W., *After Tylor: British Social Anthropology, 1888–1951*, Madison: University of Wisconsin Press, 1996

Urry, James, *Before Social Anthropology: Essays on the History of British Anthropology*, Chur, Switzerland, and Philadelphia: Harwood Academic, 1993

Anthropologists have a deep-rooted interest in the history of their discipline, perhaps in part because, faced with its fragmentation into various subdivisions and schools, history offers some coherence and stability. Departments of anthropology have their own required course in the history of the discipline with related textbooks and monographs, written mainly by anthropologists for anthropologists. These histories have two aims in common: to teach anthropology through a historical survey, and to provide polemical tools in the fight against rival programs. In the main, these functional histories have presented the history of anthropology as primarily a history of ideas in the "western" tradition. Historical bones to pick remain almost entirely internal, jointed by presentist pursuits.

A fine example of the textbook tradition, HONIGMANN presents the history of anthropology as a history of Western civilisation, from the creation of the science of "Man" by the Greeks and Romans, through the Middle Ages and the Renaissance, to the formative debates over "diffusionism" and "evolutionism" of the 19th and 20th centuries. DE WAAL MALEFIJT is another example along these lines. LEAF adopts a more philosophical viewpoint, presenting the history of anthropology as a history of underlying philosophical assumptions regarding the nature of man, mind and science, which reveal two major philosophical trends: "monism" and "dualism". Leaf's terms are rather idiosyncratic to say the least ("monism" here means a belief exclusively in the world of appearances), and he settles on the monistic view as the saviour of modern anthropology.

FOUCAULT radically challenges this "grand river" (or evolutionary) view of history and finds the science of man a rather recent discovery, enclosed in an episteme, bound on both sides, and doomed to pass away in the late modern period. Foucault moves away from the human subject as nodal in the history of anthropology, and finds wider morphological similarities between the sciences of man, linguistics, and the political economy of post-Enlightenment Europe.

Of prime concern to the textbook tradition is the supposed "revolution" (see JARVIE) in anthropology that took place in the early decades of the 20th century. From this point on, evolutionary accounts of human nature were replaced by functionalist and "diffusionist" accounts of culture, which were less concerned with tracing developments and classifications according to the degree of "primitive". The last detailed historical work from the early "evolutionist" school is PENNIMAN. Unluckily, just as the "functionalist school" was declaring evolutionism a dead letter in the 1930s, Penniman, curator of the Pitt–Rivers Museum in Oxford, linked the beginnings of modern anthropology with the biological revolution activated by Darwin's *Origin of Species*. Thus, Penniman's history was considered outdated at publication. Nevertheless, his work is still one of the best accounts of the emphasis on technology in late 19th-century anthropology – a subject often passed over by later historians. Subsequent editions of the work were increasingly concerned with the desperate attempt to reinstate Darwin's biological revolution at the centre of the history of anthropology in the face of the functionalist onslaught.

The founders of the "social anthropology" school at Oxford had their own view of the history of their subject. In a collection of lectures delivered by one of the patrons of the modern "diffusionist" school at the Institute of Social Anthropology, Oxford, EVANS-PRITCHARD related biographical stories of the "greats" of anthropology from Montesquieu to Robert Herz. These biographies were highly personal and intended to relay a sophisticated moral tale of the rise of the functionalist school. Following Evans-Pritchard, much of the history of anthropology has been told through biographies of the greats, one of the best examples being that on Franz Boas by HYATT.

In the main, histories since Penniman have stressed the progressive dissolution of the hegemony of evolutionism, its supposed racism, and its "acorn to oak" (to use Ernst Gellner's borrowing of a Hegelian term) view of necessary cultural development. LOWIE was first off the mark. As an early advocate of the "ethnographic turn", Lowie used his history to rage against evolution in favour of the diffusionist view of culture. As Darwin was jettisoned, the German/American anthropologist and founder of "cultural anthropology", Franz Boas, was made the hero of this story.

HARRIS marks a late and powerful reaction against this anti-evolutionism in the historiography of anthropology. In his massive, rollicking polemic against relativists, structuralists, and idealists of every kind, Harris spares no one the blame for the disintegration of the field: the French, structuralists, inductivists, and neo-Kantians are all responsible for turning anthropology from the "natural", while Boas is a "politically motivated" obscurantist. All this is done with consummate skill and remarkable historical rigour, making Harris's work the controversial standard for a number of years. His aim was to resurrect a form of "cultural materialism", later elaborated in his book by that title, which is a hybrid sort of materialism – an uneasy synthesis of Malthus and Marx, which constitutes a step beyond "cultural idealism" and owed much to the "hydraulic thesis" of Karl Wittfogel. Not surprisingly, Harris's detailed history culminates with Wittfogel and his hydraulic materialism as the modern defender of science against obscurantism. Harris thus sits happily within the history of ideas tradition, as he details the triumph of materialism and science over mysticism and idealism. Interestingly, however, his own theory of "cultural materialism" seems to point in a different direction, towards embedded practices and material grounds for belief, although there is little of this present in his history.

George Stocking is the exception to the rule regarding anthropologists writing their own history in reverse. Although trained as an anthropologist, Stocking is a one-man industry in the professional history of anthropology, from his editing of the exemplary University of Wisconsin series on the history of anthropology to his monographs on the history of modern, mainly British, anthropology.

STOCKING (1968), essentially a collection of essays, introduced a cautious yet powerful critique of the "presentism" of the field, taken from the then-fashionable "paradigmatic" approach of Thomas Kuhn. Stocking transcended the polemics of Harris and Lowie in order to regard the wider context of the history of modern anthropology, in which we find Boas reading Kant in German in the hope of finding a science of culture, we discover the persistence of the race problem in a growing liberal democracy, and we lay bare the institutional roots of a growing professionalism. Stocking uses his remarkable familiarity with archival and public texts to write a wholly interdisciplinary history of the field, although paradigms are soon lost and the early Stocking settles down to a history of ideas approach. In his account, the "race" concept looms over 19th-century debates concerning culture and peoples, and as he traces the rise of the competing "culture" concept in the gentle relativism of Boas and his school, it is very clear (for all his anti-presentism) where Stocking stands on the debate. None the less, he is extremely careful to illuminate the subtleties of the divisions over race, evolution and culture, and overdue distinctions are made between "evolutionist" and "racist", polygenist and monogenist, Darwinist and Lamarckian. Stocking also takes care to avoid a sort of conceptual whiggism: the culture concept means something quite different to Boas than to modern cultural anthropologists.

In STOCKING (1987) the focus is narrowed to Victorian anthropology, and here Stocking is more careful to attend to the narrative and institutional grounds in his historical account of the rise of anthropology. Race still looms large as Stocking concentrates on the effects of the "Darwinian Revolution"; while race is surely tied to evolutionism, he is careful to point out that evolutionism did not lead necessarily to racism. Indeed, Stocking sees liberal Darwinians as a bulwark against the rising racism of the structural anthropology school, and he follows the institutional wranglings of the competing anthropological societies. Stocking resurrects the Oxford anthropologist, Edward Tylor, as a pivotal figure, both as a follower of the Darwinian tradition and as the dominant player in the professionalization of the field. He explores the involvement of anthropologists in the imperial project and in the moderation of that project through groups such as the "protection of aborigines" movement. (Unfortunately, in this work "Victorian Anthropology" means Victorian England). In a lengthy and learned conclusion, he expands on the methodological problems involved in writing a history of anthropology, while steering a course between historicism and essentialism.

In his latest work, STOCKING (1996), he retraces the final steps in the professionalization and institutionalization of the field in England. Here Stocking draws on an increasingly "network" oriented historiography; the very success of institutionalization is intimately related to its ability to link up with other activities of much more acknowledged status – namely, the curation of collections of archaeological and ethnographic material, the study of the origin and development of religion, and the utilitarian needs of colonial administration. Stocking again de-emphasises the role of the idea of functionalism in the school of Malinowski, and offers instead an examination of the structures of professionalization and institutional grounding. But, in this, Stocking has narrowed his vision; wider questions of cultural context seem to evaporate, except insofar as they are immediately encompassed within the network of anthropological actors, and the history becomes progressively internalised.

KUPER also downplays the role of functionalism in the struggle of Malinowski's school against Victorian and Edwardian evolutionism. In Kuper's view, rising accumulation and field studies put paid to the kind of "armchair" anthropologising preferred by the 19th-century evolutionists. Kuper, like Harris, carves his history with a sharp polemical edge, and is especially brutal to the French structuralists and their Anglo-American followers. Taking a more social turn, URRY fills in some of the gaps between Stocking and Kuper.

As sociobiology thrust biologism back into anthropological debate in the 1970s, it is not surprising that historiographical controversy soon followed. GOULD's penetrating historical survey of the attempts by structural anthropologists and anthropometricists to measure racial, class and sexual difference was meant primarily as a first line of defence against this biological turn. The second edition appends a long attack on the recent attempt to "Bell curve" the concept of race. With this moral lesson foremost, much of the history gets compressed and even skewed, as the subtleties of the wider history of physical anthropology get lost in the telling. While this is certainly not pure contextualism, Gould still represents one of the best accounts of the French and American schools of measurement. For older pre-Darwinian ideas of race in anthropology, see the classic study by STANTON.

The "sociobiological turn" of the late 1970s inspired a furious debate over the historical worth of the main studies of the cultural school – mainly Margaret Mead's germinal work, *Coming of Age in Samoa* (1928). Freeman led a brutal historiographical cavalry charge against Mead in favour of sociobiology, and the cultural anthropologists fought back with their own histories and polemics. Some aspects of this debate can be found in HOLMES.

These historical debates still leave us at the level of the history of ideas, as they are remarkably unanthropological in their approach to the origins of ideas. GOODY is one dissenter, who writes as a participant observer in the process. Taking a cue from the functional trend in social anthropology, of which he was a main player, Goody's history traces the interactions between anthropological institutions and the intellectual life that exists within them, is constructed by them and, in turn, creates them. Goody recognises the internalism of the field and attributes the rise of Malinowski and his school to an institution-building that has internalised the scope of anthropology and declared as invalid questions asked by outsiders such as "Marxists, Weberians, sociologists and the public at large". Goody immerses himself in this internalisation and his history is very autobiographical. He is harshly critical of recent equations of anthropology with the imperialist project, and devotes a considerable part of his history to a polemic against KUKLICK, who sees the imperial anthropologists as necessarily "solipsists", imposing themselves and their "eurocentric" concerns on anthropological subjects. Goody feels that the story is much more complicated, indeed much more internal, than that.

Kuklick adapts many tools of recent Marxist criticism to her history in order to present anthropology as immersed in the ideological and utilitarian concerns of colonial Europe. In her final chapter, she shows a concern for the history of local knowledge, and for the involvement of the subject in the history of anthropology. That said, her subjects are given little voice, and end up as passive receptors in the colonial exercise.

HERBERT, in contrast, takes a postmodern approach. Opening a toolbox containing a jumble of Derrida, Foucault, Lacan, and so on, Herbert follows ethnographic imagery well beyond the confines of internal anthropological debates. He develops a "cultural studies" approach to the culture concept itself, following ethnographic imagery into missionary fieldwork in Polynesia, Mayhew's excursions in East London, and the novels of Trollope. He claims that the idea of culture, and indeed much of modern anthropology, was an ambiguous and sublimated response to the original-sin theology of John Wesley. Here we see a study of the place of anthropology that is reflexive, using anthropological and literary understandings of culture to study anthropology itself. However, Herbert still circles around one concept – culture – and his work would still settle comfortably into a history of ideas format.

Anthropology has recently discovered the problems of reflexivity, and the interaction of the anthropologist and his subject in the creation of beliefs and institutions. The role of the subject is beginning to be explored in the history of anthropology, as can be seen in Kuklick and others. PAYDEN has recovered the role of the American Indian in the move away from Enlightenment discourse on "human nature" towards the empirical study and historical relativism of 19th-century anthropology. The papers in ASAD begin an exploration into stories of the "anthropologised" in a colonial situation, while HARAWAY, writing as an ethnomethodologist, has exposed the history of primate anthropology to a feminist, and at times postmodern, gaze.

To date, however, the voice of those studied by anthropology has yet to be heard. Most histories of anthropology remain traditional in their approach, while anthropology itself has been recently facing a crisis in "reflexivity". A reflexive anthropological history of anthropology has yet to be written.

GORDON MCOUAT

See also Prehistory: archaeology and anthropology

Anthropometry

Barkan, Elazar, *The Retreat of Scientific Racism: Changing Concepts of Race in Britain and the United States Between the World Wars*, Cambridge and New York: Cambridge University Press, 1993

Bowler, Peter J., *Theories of Human Evolution: A Century of Debate, 1855–1944*, Baltimore: Johns Hopkins University Press, 1986

Gould, Stephen Jay, *The Mismeasure of Man*, New York: Norton, 1981; revised and expanded edition, 1996

Greenwood, Davydd J., *The Taming of Evolution: The Persistence of Nonevolutionary Views in the Study of Humans*, Ithaca, New York: Cornell University Press, 1984

Haraway, Donna, *Primate Visions: Gender, Race, and Nature in the World of Modern Science*, New York: Routledge, 1989

Hoyme, Lucile E., "Anthropology and Its Instruments: An Historical Study", *Southwestern Journal of Anthropology*, 9 (1953): 408–30

Hrdlicka, Ales, "Physical Anthropology: Its Scope and Aims; Its History and Present Status in America", *American Journal of Physical Anthropology*, 1/1 (1918): 3–23

Hughes, Miranda, "The Dynamometer and the Diemenese", in *Experimental Inquiries: Historical, Philosophical, and Social Studies of Experimentation in Science*, edited by Homer E. Le Grand, Dordrecht: Kluwer Academic, 1990, 81–98

Mann, Gunter and Franz Dumont (eds), *Die Natur des Menschen: Probleme der physischen Anthropologie und Rassenkunde, 1750–1850*, Stuttgart: Fischer, 1990

Schiebinger, Londa, *Nature's Body: Gender in the Making of Modern Science*, Boston: Beacon Press, 1993

Stanton, William, *The Leopard's Spots: Scientific Attitudes Toward Race in America, 1815–1859*, Chicago: University of Chicago Press, 1960

Stepan, Nancy, *The Idea of Race in Science: Great Britain, 1800–1960*, Hamden, Connecticut: Archon Books, and London: Macmillan, 1982

Very few studies exclusively devoted to anthropometry exist in the history of science. Broadly construed, the subject includes the use of various instruments to measure every facet of the human body, as well as experiment and statistical calculus. Practitioner accounts reveal the broad number of disciplines from which anthropometry can claim founders. HRDLICKA traces anthropometry back to the 17th century, pointing to Edward Tyson, Linnaeus, Buffon, George Cuvier, Johann Friedrich Blumenbach, Samuel Thomas Soemmering and others for the discipline's origin. The best historical account of anthropometric instruments is still the brief article by HOYME, who catalogues the principle instruments beginning in the 17th century. She describes their development, includes numerous illustrations, and uses this material culture to analyze how practitioners generated their hypotheses and theories.

Discussions of anthropometry appear in some of the classic studies in the science versus religion debate, especially in the history of evolutionary theory. STANTON's well-known study of race science in early 19th-century America remains the most relevant contribution. His work contextualizes American anthropometry in the development of European physical anthropology, and his analysis of the "misdirection" of research due to cultural factors resonates well with current historiographic trends. He analyzes the intersection of physical anthropology with evolutionary theory, religious debate, and the question of race. His argument that jousts with religious leaders kept American researchers from proceeding in an evolutionary direction remains unchallenged by more recent research.

Anthropometry has had a more prominent place in histories of race science. STEPAN's history of racial notions in physical anthropology and biology is mainly focused on Britain from 1800 to 1960, but she traces American and European influences. She examines the uncertainty many practitioners felt about the meaning of their measurements in debates over human evolution and their tendency to maintain views of racial fixity. A number of valuable essays on anthropometry in general and the problem of race in particular have been gathered into a volume edited by MANN & DUMONT. The authors have contributed important studies on key debates of the 18th and 19th-centuries in anthropometry including the interpretation of data, links with phrenology, and race. Kant, Herder, Buffon, Cuvier, Blumenbach, and Camper are all discussed, making this collection one of the most comprehensive examinations of the period in any language.

BARKAN compares late 19th- and 20th-century British and American research in biology and anthropology. He links theoretical debates with institutional and social developments and challenges the notion that the Holocaust was responsible for the decline of racial conceptions in science. Eugenics, genetics, and the rise of culture theory are all examined and Barkan develops an intriguing argument that "outsiders" (women, Jews, and "leftists") infused more egalitarian notions into science, which led to a fatal critique of race science.

Statistical analyses and bodily measures have been important in the development of the nature versus nurture controversy. GREENWOOD shows how anthropometric measures contributed to the persistence of non-evolutionary conceptions of human nature. He uses a generalized notion of humoral physiology as a foil to compare evolutionary and non-evolutionary views. His research reinforces points made in Stepan's book and provides an excellent, detailed discussion of anthropometry and the construction of racial and national characters. GOULD's *The Mismeasure of Man* is probably the most detailed study of anthropometric measures and biological determinism. Gould re-examined and replicated numerous anthropometric studies in areas ranging from craniometry to IQ testing, in an attempt to discredit arguments used by biological determinists and to show how *a priori* conceptions can influence the interpretation of data.

Anthropometry has also played an important role in the history of archaeology. BOWLER places archaeological and anthropometric work within the context of larger debates concerning human evolution. His summaries are the most technically proficient and comprehensive, though the book is difficult because it is organized by topic rather than chronologically, leaving the reader to form a comprehensive view.

Recent researchers have applied theories from the sociology of science, critical theory, and feminism to discuss anthropometry within a variety of new contexts. HUGHES uses a Latourian perspective to show how instruments could be used to enhance the credibility of expedition reports. One of the few current studies on 18th-century field experiments, it is a valuable history of the dynamometer and its role in strengthening the networks of knowledge and power. Historians examining sex and gender issues are also uncovering important evidence. SCHIEBINGER has a virtual monopoly on the 18th century with her exceptional analyses of anthropometric research on sex, race, and primatology. Her work includes discussions of important issues, including research on primate sexuality and the marginalization of women and non-white races. She successfully links these topics and shows how they fit with broader researches in comparative anatomy and natural history. HARAWAY's history of 20th-century primatology and physical anthropology combines the history of science with feminist and leftist critiques of both objectivity and the sociology of scientific knowledge. Most importantly, Haraway has gathered an impressive array of evidence, detailed analyses of texts, field research, and experimental research. Sometimes controversial, always engaging, Haraway and Schiebinger have both contributed important discussions on the permeable boundary between humans and apes, scientists and "others", without losing sight of specific researches or technical details.

BRAD D. HUME

See also Race

Anti-Vivisection

Cunningham, Andrew and Perry Williams (eds), *The Laboratory Revolution in Medicine*, Cambridge and New York: Cambridge University Press, 1992

French, Richard D., *Anti-Vivisection and Medical Science in Victorian Society*, Princeton, New Jersey: Princeton University Press, 1975

Jasper, James and Dorothy Nelkin, *The Animal Rights Crusade: The Growth of a Moral Protest*, New York: Free Press, 1992

Lederer, Susan E., *Subjected to Science: Human Experimentation in America Before the Second World War*, Baltimore: Johns Hopkins University Press, 1995

Ritvo, Harriet, *The Animal Estate: The English and Other Creatures in the Victorian Age*, Cambridge, Massachusetts: Harvard University Press, and Harmondsworth: Penguin, 1987

Rupke, Nicolaas A. (ed.), *Vivisection in Historical Perspective*, London and New York: Croom Helm, 1987

Ryder, Richard D., *Animal Revolution: Changing Attitudes Towards Speciesism*, Oxford and Cambridge, Massachusetts: Blackwell, 1989

Turner, James, *Reckoning with the Beast: Animals, Pain and Humanity in the Victorian Mind*, Baltimore: Johns Hopkins University Press, 1980

Opposition to scientific experiments on living non-human animals has as long a history as the practice itself; that is, it has existed at least since the classical Greek era. This opposition has been based on moral objections – to the allegedly deleterious impact of animal cruelty on humans; or to the apparent discounting of non-human animals' moral interests – and/or on critiques of the scientific utility of such experiments, said to arise from errors in extrapolating from one species to another, or from the mechanistic model of the human body that the experimental approach implies. The strength of such opposition has varied between countries and over time, as has historical interest. Not surprisingly, this historical interest has very often been the product of a prior commitment to the cause, just as serious consideration of the movement and its impact is generally absent from the historiography of biomedical and biological science.

An important exception is the volume of essays edited by RUPKE, the essential starting point for an overview of the history of the protest from antiquity to the 1970s, largely written from neutral perspectives. The essays cover the anti-vivisection movement in the United States, the United Kingdom and several European countries. Among the particular themes addressed are the role of women in the English protest and the response of British scientists to attack in the 1880s.

The most extensive body of historical research has focused on the late 19th and early 20th century in Britain. This was the place and time for very vigorous protest against what can now be seen as the laboratory revolution in medicine, and FRENCH's book on the British movement remains the central work. It considers the development and decline of the movement within the context of changes in science, in the medical profession and in attitudes to animals in the immediate post-Darwin period. His discussion of the significance of changes in public attitudes towards, and understanding of, science are relevant to debates in the 1990s. The collection edited by CUNNINGHAM & WILLIAMS provides the scientific context for the Victorian protest through detailed studies of laboratory practices and institutions. One essay (by Richards) specifically addresses the extent of suffering caused by late 19th-century animal experimentation and several other essays touch on the controversy. Turner and Ritvo both analyse changing attitudes and practices towards non-human animals in general in the Victorian period. TURNER focuses on conceptions of pain and suffering, and their implications for animal welfare campaigns in general, and for perceptions of alleged "scientific cruelty" in particular. RITVO describes the changing cultural significance of pets, wild animals and animal breeding in Britain. She analyses the function of animals as metaphors in Victorian society; for example, the ways in which they could symbolise class divisions. She argues that anti-vivisection offered a way in which troubled Victorians could reject modernist and materialist philosophies that valued progress (and hence science) above all else.

One of the long-standing claims of the anti-vivisection movement is that experimenting on animals places doctors at the top of a slippery slope towards experimenting on humans. The history of these claims and the relationship between human and animal experimentation and protests over it in the United States are discussed by LEDERER.

Not surprisingly, the upsurge of animal rights protests in many countries, particularly in the US and the UK, since the mid-1970s has stimulated fresh histories of the movement for animal protection in general, and also sociological interest in the present. Of the newer committed histories, that by RYDER, a leading English activist and originator of the term "speciesism", is one of the most comprehensive and accurate. Besides anti-vivisection, the course of protests against cruelty to farm animals and hunting are considered, mainly but not exclusively focused on Britain. JASPER & NELKIN present a similarly broad ranging analysis of the development of the American animal rights movement, including anti-vivisection protests, writing as academic sociologists but in a highly readable style. A brief historical overview is followed by detailed analysis of the different campaigns in the 1970s and 1980s.

M.A. ELSTON

See also Experimental Physiology

Arabic Science

Berggren, J.L., "History of Mathematics in the Islamic World: The Present State of the Art", *Bulletin of the Middle East Studies Association of North America*, 19 (1985): 9–33

Berggren, J.L., *Episodes in the Mathematics of Medieval Islam*, New York: Springer, 1986

D'Alverny, Marie-Thérèse, "Translations and Translators", in *Renaissance and Renewal in the Twelfth Century*, edited by Robert L. Benson and Giles Constable, Cambridge, Massachusetts: Harvard University Press, and Oxford: Clarendon Press, 1982

Huff, Toby E., *The Rise of Early Modern Science: Islam, China and the West*, Cambridge and New York: Cambridge University Press, 1993

Kennedy, Edward S. *et al.*, *Studies in the Islamic Exact Sciences*, Beirut: America University of Beirut Press, 1983

King, David A., *Islamic Mathematical Astronomy*, London: Variorum Reprints, 1986; 2nd revised edition, Great Yarmouth: Variorum, 1993

King, David A., *Astronomy in the Service of Islam*, Aldershot, Hampshire, and Brookfield, Vermont: Variorum, 1993

Lindberg, David C., *Theories of Vision from al-Kindi to Kepler*, Chicago: University of Chicago Press, 1976

Lindberg, David C., "The Transmission of Greek and Arabic Learning to the West", in his *Science in the Middle Ages*, Chicago: University of Chicago Press, 1978

Nasr, Seyyed Hossein, *Science and Civilization in Islam*, Cambridge, Massachusetts: Harvard University Press, 1968; 2nd edition, Cambridge: Islamic Texts Society, 1987

Rosenthal, Franz, *The Classical Heritage in Islam*, translated from the German by Emile and Jenny Marmorstein, Berkeley: University of California, 1975; London: Routledge, 1992 (original edition, 1965)

Sabra, A.I., "The Appropriation and Subsequent Naturalization of Greek Science in Medieval Islam: A Preliminary Statement", *History of Science*, 25 (1987): 223–43

Sabra, A.I., "Optics, Islamic", in *Dictionary of the Middle Ages*, edited by Joseph R. Strayer, vol. 9, New York: Scribner, 1987

Sabra, A. I., "Science, Islamic", *Dictionary of the Middles Ages*, edited by Joseph R. Strayer, vol. 11, New York: Scribner, 1988

Sabra, A.I., "Introduction" to *The Optics of Ibn al-Haytham*, edited and translated by Sabra, London: Warburg Institute, 1989

Saliba, George, *A History of Arabic Astronomy: Planetary Theories During the Golden Age of Islam*, New York: New York University Press, 1994

Saunders, J.J., "The Problem of Islamic Decadence", *Journal of World History*, 17 (1963)

Sayili, Aydin, *The Observatory in Islam, and Its Place in the General History of the Observatory*, Ankara: Türk Tarih Kurumu Busimevi (Turkish Historical Society Publication), 1960; New York: Arno Press, 1981

The term "Arabic science" is used here to denote the corpus of scientific knowledge that originated with the spread of Islam and the Arabic language throughout the Middle East towards the middle of the 8th century. The great bulk of that knowledge was recorded in Arabic, with later contributions in Persian. While many of the early translators and contributors to Arabic science were Christians and Jews who lived in an Islamic environment, at the peak of creativity – from the 12th to the 14th centuries – Muslims predominated. Nevertheless, all of these contributors were drawn from a variety of ethnic backgrounds representative of the peoples living within a vast region, stretching from present-day Morocco to Afghanistan, including Spain. This has led many to call this science either "Islamic" or "Arabic-Islamic" science.

Even today, however, there are no general histories of this tradition in astronomy, mathematics, optics, and medicine, which was the most advanced in the world from the 8th to the 14th centuries. Consequently, to attain an overall view of the nature, extent, and significance of the advances made by Arabic science, the reader must consult a variety of sources. This applies even more to such fields as alchemy, geography, and pharmacology.

The foundations of Arabic science laid by the classical Greek tradition have been sketched by ROSENTHAL, who provides vignettes, commentaries and selections from translations, adaptations, and further elaboration of Hellenic thought in such fields as philosophy, logic, medicine, geography, astronomy, musicology, the occult sciences, and literature. The work contains classifications of the sciences as understood by the Arabs, including the division between the Islamic or religious sciences, and those that the Arabs called the ancient or foreign Greek sciences. This account ought to be supplemented by SABRA (1988), which provides a more up-to-date survey of the early translators and commentators, along with a sketch of the evolving institutional structures. It offers concise assessments of significant achievements in Arabic astronomy, mathematics, optics, engineering, and timekeeping, which reflect current understandings in the history of those fields.

Although NASR is useful for its attempt to locate Arabic-Islamic science within a cultural and religious context, it is an idiosyncratic and somewhat dated view. The thrust of Arabic science is presented as one devoted to mystical unity, to gnosis, and Nasr argues that Arabic science deliberately took the path of the mystical unity of all knowledge, rather than the analytic one leading to modern science as we understand it. This is a position at odds with the view of leading contemporary historians of Arabic science, who have found that there were many innovations in its core disciplines that lead directly to modern science. Used with caution, Nasr's account contains helpful portraits of intellectual figures in the history of Arabic science along with important insights. It also offers translations from various Islamic authors. However, its accounts of major scientific figures need to be updated by reference to the *Dictionary of Scientific Biography*.

HUFF offers a broader, more current, and developmental view of the trajectory of Arabic science. It locates Arabic science within its religious, legal and institutional settings, and explores the relationship between law, the *madrasas* (Islamic colleges) and the pursuit of the natural sciences. Though focusing on developments in astronomy, it provides brief non-technical summaries of major scientific developments, as well as details of significant advances in medicine and medical education. As a sociological inquiry, it places more stress on the social and cultural context of Arabic science than on technical exposition. Its bibliography covers much of the technical literature in astronomy, mathematics, optics and medicine, as well as the specialized literature on Islamic law, philosophy and theology. Its comparative approach aids the understanding of contrasting patterns of development of science and society in Islam, China, and the European West during the golden era of Arabic-Islamic civilization.

Considerable progress in the understanding of the exact sciences in Arabic-Islamic civilization has been made since the early 1970s. BERGGREN's 1986 study is a good introduction to basic mathematical concepts and their development, including Islamic arithmetic, decimal fractions, square roots, algebra, geometry and trigonometry. BERGGREN's 1985 article gives a concise overview of these developments, but without historical and biographical sketches.

Of all the sciences pursued by the Arabs, astronomy has been the most extensively studied of late, though on the basis of only a small fraction of the scientific manuscripts known to exist. This has resulted in the discovery of Arabic treatises containing innovative reforms of the Ptolemaic models and the tantalizing suggestion that these reforms influenced Copernicus. The many Arab (and Persian) astronomers working in this astronomical tradition have been dubbed the Marāgha school because of their affiliation with the observatory built in Marāgha south-west of Tabriz in Iran c.1257–59, under the direction of Nasir al-Din al-Tusi (d.1274). SAYILI provides a pioneering general history of the development of the observatory in Islam, including Marāgha. It also contains an appendix devoted to the reasons for the decline of Arabic science.

The early results of the discovery (in the late 1950s) of the theoretical advances of the Marāgha astronomers are collected in KENNEDY *et al*. There the rolling device of two nested circles used to represent motion in a straight line, the "Tusi-couple", named after the astronomer al-Tusi, is identified, and suggestions are made that knowledge of this method was transmitted to Copernicus through channels yet to be verified. SALIBA represents the results of a second generation of historians of Arabic science studying these materials, and greatly amplifies the range of individuals associated with the Marāgha school and their accomplishments. Chapter 14 of this work is the most recent overview of these discoveries, their significance, and suggestions for future research.

The two books by KING (1986 and 1993) reveal the extreme sophistication of Islamic timekeeping and its relationship to mathematical astronomy from the early years of Islam to the 14th century. Although most of the papers are technical in nature, much can be learned from them by the general reader. These studies are the most extensive on the *zij* tables – that is, lists of planetary observations recorded systematically as ephemerides by location, along with advice for their use. Some of these tables contain over 250,000 entries and were meant to provide the basis for universal timekeeping.

King has pointed out the existence of both a folk (religiously guided) tradition of timekeeping and a more advanced tradition based on knowledge of mathematics and Ptolemaic astronomy throughout the history of Islam. It is the existence of these two separate traditions that accounts for the fact that many ancient buildings in the Middle East, including many mosques, are not perfectly aligned with Mecca – the direction called the *qibla* – even though the knowledge of such alignment was readily available. Chapter 3 of King's *Islamic Mathematical Astronomy* contains a valuable overview of the flourishing school of Mamluk astronomy of the 14th and early 15th centuries. In addition, King's work on the *muwaqqit*, the official timekeeper in the mosque, briefly reported in that chapter, represents an important yet still only vaguely understood aspect of Arabic science and its place in Islamic civilization.

Another field in which the Arabs excelled and contributed to universal science was optics. In many ways optics in the medieval period played a role similar to physics in the 20th century, bringing together observation, mathematics, theory and experiment. SABRA (1987) "Optics, Islamic", is a penetrating account of the development of optics from the Greeks (Euclid and Ptolemy), through the early Arab students of optics, the pioneering work of Ibn al-Haytham (d. c.1040), to Kamāl al-Din al Fāris (d. c.1320) and his European counterpart, Theodoric of Freiberg (d. c.1310). LINDBERG (1976) remains a useful study of the development of optics, but needs to be read in conjunction with more recent studies, such as the introduction to SABRA (1989), a translation of the first three books of Ibn al-Haytham's treatise on optics (*Kitāb al-Manāzir*). Sabra's discussion brings out the many innovative aspects of Ibn al-Haythams's work, noting especially the "modern" flavor of his procedures, and his commitment to the methods of observation and experiment. Sabra points to the direct link between Kamāl al-Din's successful explanation of the rainbow and his study of and commentary on al-Haytham's earlier treatise. Sabra highlights in addition the fact that Kamāl al-Din employed innovative experimental procedures.

There are other fields to which Arab scientists contributed, especially in medicine, but these are largely reported in specialized journals. Some are discussed in the 2nd edition of the *Encyclopedia of Islam*, though the reader must first determine the Arabic term for the subject. The best source for the lives and work of many significant Arab scientists is the *Dictionary of Scientific Biography*.

The problem that continues to fascinate all students of history, especially contemporary Muslims of the Middle East, is the question of exactly when and why Arabic science came to an untimely end, instead of giving birth to modern science? The more historians have studied and identified the scientific innovations of Arabic science – especially in astronomy, mathematics, and optics – the more pressing the question has become. For the profundity of those innovations suggests that Arabic science in various specialized areas was making considerable progress toward modern science, and, prior to the 14th century, was far more advanced than the West. Its subsequent decline is clearly a case of waning creativity. To grapple with this problem, SABRA (1987), "The Appropriation and Subsequent Naturalization of Greek Science in Medieval Islam", offers an overview of the development of Arabic science. It consists of a three-phase assimilation and maturation pattern followed by a fourth stage of decline. In this latter stage, according to Sabra, theoretical inquiry was placed in the service of religion, thereby deflecting the pursuit of theoretical innovation. King reiterates this theme in the first chapter of *Astronomy in the Service of Islam*.

Building on Sabra's insights, Huff maintains that the pursuit of the natural sciences in Islam was never fully institutionalized, since they were not incorporated into the curricula of the Islamic colleges (*madrasas*). In addition, he points to the great differences in legal conceptions between Islam and the West, and the fact that the West, through its legal revolution of the 12th and 13th centuries, created many spheres of legal autonomy for corporate bodies – cities and towns, guilds, and universities – which were absent in Islamic law. Consequently, the process of transmitting this Greek and Arabic scientific tradition to the West in the 12th and 13th centuries takes on considerable significance. D'ALVERNY and LINDBERG (1978) both provide overviews of this process. Once the Europeans had acquired this Greek and Arabic knowledge and placed it at the center of study in the universities, a platform of disinterested inquiry, largely free from political and religious censors, was created. This institutional structure, according to Huff, supported the continuous study of science, building freely on the advances of the Arabic-Islamic world that lacked such institutional arrangements. Huff also points out the underlying difference in conceptions of the rationality of man and nature that were built into the contrasting legal and theological structures of Islam and the West.

SAUNDERS is a thought-provoking essay on the general subject of decline in Islamic civilization. It covers a wide range of views of earlier writers, including matters of political stability and tolerance, racial mixing, competing linguistic communities, economic factors, foreign invasions, theological intolerance, and geographic dispersion.

TOBY E. HUFF

Archaeology

Bibby, Geoffrey, *The Testimony of the Spade*, New York: Knopf, 1956; London: Collins, 1957
Ceram, C.W. [Kurt Marek], *Gods, Graves, and Scholars: The Story of Archaeology*, translated from the German by E.B. Garside, New York: Knopf, 1951 (original edition, 1949)
Daniel, Glyn, *A Hundred and Fifty Years of Archaeology*, 2nd edition, London: Duckworth, 1975; Cambridge, Massachusetts: Harvard University Press, 1976
Daniel, Glyn (ed.), *Towards a History of Archaeology*, London and New York: Thames and Hudson, 1981
Stiebing Jr, William H., *Uncovering the Past: A History of Archaeology*, Buffalo, New York: Prometheus Books, 1993
Trigger, Bruce G., *A History of Archaeological Thought*, Cambridge and New York: Cambridge University Press, 1989
Willey, Gordon R. and Jeremy A. Sabloff, *A History of American Archaeology*, 2nd edition, San Francisco: W.H. Freeman, and London: Thames and Hudson, 1974; 2nd edition, San Francisco: W.H. Freeman, 1982
Winstone, H.V.F., *Uncovering the Ancient World*, London: Constable, 1985; New York: Facts on File, 1986

The popular image of archaeology owes more to romance than to realism. Images of gold-laden tombs and lost cities in the jungle abound, and the moment of discovery overshadows the long process of excavation, measurement, and laboratory analysis that inevitably follows. Popular histories of archaeology have traditionally reflected, and bolstered, the discovery-oriented image of the science. Since the mid-1970s, however, a series of new works has brought greater breadth and depth to the history of archaeology.

The classic work of the "great discoveries" school is *Gods, Graves, and Scholars*, published by the German archaeologist Kurt Marek under the pseudonym C.W. CERAM. Written with the stated intent of revealing the human drama behind dry excavation reports, it offers a parade of spectacular discoveries and colorful excavators. Beginning with the early civilizations of the Aegean – Crete, Mycenae, and Troy – it moves on to Egypt, Mesopotamia, and finally to Central America. The stories are exciting, and Ceram tells them well enough to send readers hunting for more detailed treatments. The whole, however, is somewhat less than the sum of its parts. The sheer diversity of Ceram's chosen subjects undercuts any sense that they form part of a single, larger story.

STIEBING's brisk survey tells many of the same stories that appear in Ceram. It places them, however, within a narrative substantially more integrated and wide-ranging. Sacrificing detail for geographic scope, Stiebing reviews pioneering excavations not only in the Mediterranean, Middle East, and Central America, but also in areas – such as East Asia, sub-Saharan Africa, and North America – that have traditionally received little attention from historians of archaeology. The survey extends, in principle, from the Renaissance to the present day, but the years before 1860 and after 1925 are covered only in a quickly-sketched overview. *Uncovering the Past* is, consequently, less a comprehensive history of archaeology than a study of what Stiebing describes as the discipline's coming of age.

Histories of archaeology, particularly general surveys, often focus on sites and artifacts while neglecting the ideas that guide their interpretation. TRIGGER redresses the balance in his densely packed, intensely analytical work – the outgrowth of a university course entitled "The History of Archaeological Theory". Ideas, and systems of ideas, take center stage throughout the book. Well-versed in the historiography of science, Trigger links the work of Soviet, European, and North American archaeologists not only to the work of their predecessors and contemporaries, but also to their cultural milieus. Trigger's discussion of the 20th century, which occupies more than half the text, achieves a level of analytical rigor and fine-textured detail unmatched elsewhere. Indeed, the book's sheer intellectual density is its principal drawback: the sections dealing with the later 20th century may be hard going for readers without some background in archaeology or its history. The book concludes with a comprehensive bibliography and an interpretative essay – invaluable tools for further research.

The surveys by Stiebing and by Trigger, read in conjunction, offer an excellent overview of the history of archaeology. They are not perfect complements, however, and can be usefully supplemented by the works below, which deal in greater depth with slightly narrower subjects.

DANIEL (1975), a modestly revised reprint of his earlier *One Hundred Years of Archaeology* (1950), focuses on the breakthroughs made – in Europe and the Middle East – by 19th-century Europeans. It treats the European pioneers in greater detail than Stiebing and with more assurance than Trigger. Although it has dated badly in some areas – particularly in its discussions of 19th-century geology and the impact of Darwinian evolution – its narrative core remains intact, and its treatments of archaeological field methods and the development of prehistoric chronologies remain unsurpassed. DANIEL's 1981 book consists of short papers that build on *150 Years of Archaeology* by treating specific aspects of the early (pre-1925) history of archaeology. The papers, though uneven in quality and approach, offer useful insights into archaeological thought in neglected areas such as Eastern Europe, Iberia, Belgium, and the British Commonwealth. As a group, they illuminate the connections between archaeological ideas and their cultural context.

Histories of the archaeological exploration and interpretation of particular regions abound. Trigger's bibliographic essay provides a useful guide, but three, in particular, are worthy of specific mention. WINSTONE offers a well-rounded treatment of archaeological work on the literate civilizations of the Aegean and Middle East that highlights the complementary roles played by artifacts and texts. Winstone treats the major civilizations in discrete chapters, but intersperses the chapters so that the work as a whole unfolds chronologically. The reader can thus choose to read the chapters about Mesopotamia, for example, as a group or within the context of the larger narrative. BIBBY, as the title of his work suggests, deals with pre-literate societies known only through their artifacts. Intended both as a history of archaeology and as an introduction to European prehistory, Bibby uses graceful prose and numerous illustrations to show how archaeologists have used artifacts to reconstruct the cultures that produced them. His focus on artifacts and their interpretation makes his work a useful supplement to Daniel (1975), which deals with many of the same sites, but places the interpretations within a broader theoretical context.

WILLEY & SABLOFF survey the history of archaeological research in the New World. They give some attention to key investigators and significant sites – providing extensive illustrations of both – but their principal concern, like Trigger's, is with ideas. The core of their work examines archaeologists's attempts, between 1840 and 1960, to classify the varied cultures of the Americas and to reconstruct their chronological relationships. They follow the American convention of treating archaeology as a branch of anthropology, rather than as an essentially autonomous discipline. Unfortunately, their survey offers only brief comments on the post-1960 era, when proponents of the "New Archaeology" reasserted the centrality of anthropological ideas within archaeology.

A. BOWDOIN VAN RIPER

See also Prehistory: archaeology and anthropology

Archimedes c.287–c.212 BC

Greek mathematician

Clagett, Marshall (ed.), *Archimedes in the Middle Ages*, 5 vols, Madison: University of Wisconsin Press, 1964–84

Dijksterhuis, Eduard Jan, *Archimedes*, translated from the Dutch by C. Dikshoorn, Copenhagen: Munksgaard, 1956; revised edition, with a new bibliographical essay by Wilbur Knorr, Princeton, New Jersey: Princeton University Press, 1987 (original edition, 1938)

Dollo, Corrado (ed.), *Archimede: Mito tradizione scienza*, Florence: Olschki, 1992

Favaro, Antonio, *Archimede*, Genoa: Formiggini, 1912

Heiberg, J.L., *Quaestiones Archimedeae*, Leipzig: Klein, 1879

Heiberg, J.L. (ed.), *Archimedes Opera Omnia, cum Commentariis Eutocii*, 3 vols, Leipzig: Tübner, 1880–81; reprinted, Stuttgart, Tübner, 1972–75

Knorr, Wilbur, "Archimedes and the *Elements*: Proposal for a Revised Chronological Ordering of the Archimedean Corpus", *Archive for History of Exact Sciences*, 19 (1978): 211–90

Laird, W.R., "Archimedes among the Humanists", *Isis*, 82 (1991): 629–38

Schneider, Ivo, *Archimedes: Ingenieur, Naturwissenschaftler und Mathematiker*, Darmstadt: Wissenschaftliche Buchgesellschaft, 1979

The importance of Archimedes lies both in his work (geometry, hydrostatics, statics, arithmetic) and in the scientific ideal he has embodied up to the present day. His name is linked to some geometrical discoveries, such as the formula for the volume of a sphere or that for the area of a circle, to his sophisticated demonstrative procedures, and to his combination of geometry and physics in order to study centres of gravity. Moreover, Archimedes is reported by several historians (Polybius, Livy, Plutarch) as having defended his city against the Romans by means of extraordinary war machines. The circumstances of his death (killed by soldiers when Syracuse was taken) and the fame of his inventions generated an anecdotal tradition, in which Archimedes gradually became the epitome of the man of genius, forced by the necessities of real life reluctantly to turn from his speculative pursuits to the practical applications of mathematics.

The scholarship on Archimedes has generally focused on his "scientific" production, comparing it to previous works, analyzing its demonstrative procedures or tracing links between the various texts of the corpus. Other issues include concern over the reliability of some of the reports on Archimedes' life, his lost works, and whether Plutarch's famous portrait, according to which Archimedes recoiled from the practical aspects of mathematics, is a "true" description. HEIBERG's (still standard) edition of Archimedes' *Opera Omnia*, (1880–81), was preceded by his doctoral dissertation (1879). The dissertation is a very good source of information on the extant manuscripts and their filiations, on language and terminology, and on testimonies regarding Archimedes and others he mentions in his work. Heiberg also put a number of new points on the agenda: the problem of the heuristic process behind Archimedes' finished and incredibly concise proofs, hypotheses on the nature of the lost works, and the problem of the chronology of the extant books. Although a definite answer to the question of dating is not given, the order in which Heiberg discusses the books was generally adopted as the standard chronological order, and remained unchallenged until Knorr's article.

One of four articles on Archimedes by Wilbur KNORR published in 1978, "Archimedes and the Elements" has given a new turn to studies on the subject. While reconsidering the chronology, he aims to reinsert Archimedes within the context of his times, when the circulation, production, and reproduction of texts were such that it is likely that most of them went through more than one edition or version (not necessarily at Archimedes' hands). Knorr postulates the existence of lost first editions of works such as "Spirals", whose traces survive in authors such as Hero and Pappus. Supported by linguistic usage and by Archimedes' own introductions to his works, Knorr establishes the dating of the texts on the basis of their lesser or greater similarity to Euclidean terminology and procedures – on the assumption that Archimedes would have been closer to Euclidean geometry in his early days, developing characteristic traits later on.

A more general survey is given in FAVARO's booklet, which focuses on the historical testimonies of Archimedes' life and achievements. Very comprehensively researched, it still is a standard work for a critical analysis of such sources as Silius Italicus or Diodorus. It is also the quickest method to discover which classical authors mention Archimedes.

DIJKSTERHUIS combines general background and mathematical results – it solves the problem of making the latter accessible to the modern reader by translating the propositions literally and paraphrasing the proofs. Dijksterhuis also brings up the problem of Archimedes' attitude to "practical" mathematics in relation to the interpretation of Archimedes' "Letter to Eratosthenes on the Method", in which geometrical results are attained via a combination of formulas on the centres of gravity and the division of areas into infinite lines. Archimedes himself says that his method is not to be considered rigorously demonstrative: yet, is it because of mechanics, or because of the use of infinitesimals? Dijksterhuis favours the latter hypothesis, within the wider framework of an interpretation that sees no stigma attached to mechanics in Archimedes' actual practice.

Another good survey is by SCHNEIDER – valuable for his vast knowledge of the literature on the subject, including histories of technology. Schneider aims to show how the different professional guises of Archimedes (engineer, mathematician, "scientist") hang together, and finds a sort of ideal unity between practice and theory in his astronomy and his building of astronomical instruments.

The remaining three works on the list deal with Archimedes' fortune in later times. The volume edited by DOLLO gathers various papers, both on Archimedes in his own time (e.g. Cambiano explores the relation between various heuristic stages in his work) and from late antiquity onwards (Rashed on Arabic reception, Baldini on Archimedes in the 16th century, Micheli on the 19th and 20th centuries). The book as a whole charts the significance of Archimedes not only as a source, but as a role-model for later generations of scientists.

CLAGETT's monumental publication is an incredibly rich collection of texts ranging from the 12th to the 16th centuries, which includes reworkings, commentaries, paraphrases of Archimedes' works, and some information on the anecdotal tradition linked to him. It is also an impressive testimony to the many different directions that could be followed starting from Archimedes' work, and to the vivacity of medieval "science".

Finally, LAIRD's all too short article fills an important gap – namely, the significance of Archimedes for Italian "humanist" mathematicians (Commandino, Tartaglia, Cardano, del Monte, Maurolico) and therefore for the 16th-century revival of Greek science. The author argues that Archimedes' pre-eminence (it was commonplace to mention him as the "prince of geometers") was increased by the interest in his historical persona, in its turn rekindled by the renewed success of authors such as Polybius and Plutarch. Laird adds another important chapter to the story of how Archimedes has been seen not only as a "scientist", but as the paragon of science, in its dialectic between the pure and the applied.

SERAFINA CUOMO

Aristotle 384–322 BC

Greek philosopher

Balme, D.M., L. Minio-Paluello, G.E.L. Owen and L.G. Wilson, entry in *Dictionary of Scientific Biography*, edited by Charles Coulston Gillispie, vol. 1, New York: Scribner, 1970

Boylan, Michael, *Method and Practice in Aristotle's Biology*, Washington, DC: University Press of America, 1983

Cole, F.J., *A History of Comparative Anatomy: From Aristotle to the Eighteenth Century*, London: Macmillan, 1944; reprinted, New York: Dover, 1975

Lang, Helen S., *Aristotle's Physics and Its Medieval Varieties*, Albany: State University of New York Press, 1992

Lloyd, G.E.R., *Early Greek Science: Thales to Aristotle*, London: Chatto and Windus, and New York: Norton, 1970

Lloyd, G.E.R., *Greek Science after Aristotle*, London: Chatto and Windus, and York: Norton, 1973

Randall, John H., *Aristotle*, New York: Columbia University Press, 1960

Solmsen, Friedrich, *Aristotle's System of the Physical World: A Comparison with His Predecessors*, Ithaca, New York: Cornell University Press, 1960

Aristotle's mark on Western thought has been comprehensive and enduring. In the sciences alone his influence continued to be felt in the fields of physics, cosmology, and biology well into the 17th century. As a result, the literature on Aristotle is rich in accounts of both his influences and his antecedents.

LLOYD (1970) traces early Greek speculations in astronomy, physics, biology, and mathematics in relation to the evolution of a scientific method. These histories of the ancient sciences culminate in Lloyd's penultimate chapter on Aristotle, in which his theories are compared with those of his predecessors. Lloyd sees Aristotle's qualitative approach to physics and biology as a step backwards from the atomists' earlier attempts at quantitative methods, and considers Aristotle's cosmology a clumsy response to earlier attempts to reduce irregular planetary motion to regular courses. However, Lloyd does see embodied within Aristotle's works three achievements in ancient science: first, the accumulation of much descriptive knowledge in the fields of biology and astronomy; second, the formulation of scientific problems such as the nature of change; and third, the development of methodological principles.

SOLMSEN's dense philosophical treatise attempts to link Aristotle with the pre-Socratics. In particular, he claims that Aristotle's debt is three-fold: that Aristotle inherited the subjects he addresses in his physical treatises from the pre-Socratics; that he takes up questions that are not arbitrary; and that his answers are not wholly original. Solmsen's route from Aristotle to the pre-Socratics is through Plato, specifically his later philosophy on genesis in the *Timaeus*, and on movement in the *Cratylus*, the *Sophist*, and the *Theaetetus*. Solmsen notes the Platonic components in Aristotle's system – his methodology, logical distinctions, and view of the nature of the cosmos – but he adds that the arguments in Aristotle's physics grew out of Plato's reactions to the pre-Socratics, in particular, to Parmenides and Zeno.

RANDALL claims that there is a clear disparity between Aristotle's scientific principles and his scientific practice. He acknowledges the explicit Platonism in Aristotle's notion of science: a formalism modeled on geometry, where structure is separated from experience. At the same time Randall notes Aristotle's indomitable empiricist proclivities, which became the basis of his functionalism. Randall's main theme is this tension between Aristotle the *logikos* and Aristotle the *physikos*, as it is lived out in his attempts to reintegrate Platonic structure into the experience of the world. Moreover, Randall follows this tension from Aristotle into later Greek and medieval Aristotelianism, and all the way up to modern times.

BOYLAN traces the development and practice of Aristotle's biology in order to rebut the claim that his actual biological investigations were inconsistent with his methodological principles. Boylan first lays out the context within which Aristotle's biology emerged, one that has its roots in Parmenides' distinction between *nous* and *aisthesia*. By Aristotle's time, these two concepts had become the basis of rationalism and empiricism, both of which Aristotle required in order to formulate valid explanations. Boylan examines in detail Aristotle's modes of biological explanation and then presents samples of his biological practice in order to show consistency between the two. Boylan concludes by describing the consequences of Aristotle's biology and its relevance to modern biology.

LLOYD (1973) shows how enduring were Aristotle's scientific doctrines, particularly in the fields of physics, mathematics, astronomy, and biology, from the times of his immediate successors at the Lyceum to the late Hellenistic and the Roman imperial eras. Lloyd draws a clear distinction between modern and ancient science, noting that the modern sense of science as a means to material progress never caught on in ancient times, despite the occasional interest and patronage shown by some monarchs in the possible technological by-products that could be used in warfare. Lloyd's conclusion is that no new rationale for scientific inquiry arises after Aristotle, and that the continuity of Aristotelian thought during these times is punctuated only by occasional variations in theory and practice.

LANG focuses on the medieval commentators of Aristotle's *Physics*. In maintaining a distinction between the *Physics* and Aristotelian physics, she shows how Aristotle's commentators radically reworked his arguments in order to redefine problems and offer their own solutions. She begins by establishing the unity among the rhetoric, logic, and context of the arguments in the *Physics* itself, and then systematically analyzes the way in which five commentators have reinterpreted his work. Lang first examines Philonus, who fashioned his own notion of nature as an intrinsic mover, a ploy that Lang sees as part of his program to reconcile Plato and Aristotle. Next she looks at Albertus Magnus: one of the first Latin commentators to rediscover Aristotle, he was a Neoplatonic thinker who interpreted the arguments in the *Physics* as a hierarchical treatment of forms of being. Lang moves on to describe how Aquinas altered the rhetorical and logical structures of the *Physics* when he divided the work up for classroom lectures; in so doing, Aquinas turns Aristotle's thesis of eternal motion into a proof of the existence of God. Lang then shows how Buridan supplemented and corrected Aquinas, although he agreed that the *Physics* is a proof of the existence of God. Finally, she examines the commentary of John Duns Scotus, who appropriated Aristotle's definition of place in the *Physics* to argue for the existence of angels.

COLE takes Aristotle's honorary title – "founder of biological science" – seriously, for, although he ostensibly traces the history of anatomy from Aristotle through Galen, Vesalius, Leonardo, and Harvey among others, Aristotle remains the norm by which his successors are gauged, as either progressive or retrograde. Cole points out many instances in which Aristotle's anatomies were often contradicted by later observers only to be vindicated by subsequent observers, as was the case, for example, with the description of cetacea as mammals and of sponges as animals. In addition, Cole seems to delight in pointing out the primacy of Aristotle's discovery whenever his successors claimed some new anatomical entity, calling them "the first after Aristotle to discover". Though his admiration for Aristotle is unabashed, Cole does not shrink from criticizing him for accepting without verification the reports of fishermen and hunters, and for denying on occasion the testimony of his own senses in favor of the logic of argument.

A concise but comprehensive account of Aristotle's science is the article by BALME *et al.* in the *Dictionary of Scientific Biography*. The author's rely heavily on the manuscript tradition to follow Aristotle's development in three areas: natural history and zoology; anatomy and physiology; and method, physics, and cosmology. In the subsection, "Natural History and Zoology", Balme notes how Aristotle's original plan for classifying animals evolved as he added more data from his ongoing observations. Sometimes, though, when empirical data were lacking, he changed his classification via *a priori* arguments and examples that were functionally, not morphologically, analogous. Wilson, in the subsection "Anatomy and Physiology", calls Aristotle the "founder of detailed anatomical study" for his careful observations of cardiovascular systems, offering in the process an explanation for Aristotle's miscounting of the number of cavities in the heart. Owen, in the subsection "Method, Physics, and Cosmology", traces

Aristotle's development of science in his early works, *Posterior Analytics*, *Topics*, *Physics*, *De caelo*, and *De generatione*, to find Plato's heavy imprint but no evidence yet of empiricism. In the last subsection, "Tradition and Influence", Minio-Paluello, by following Aristotle through Greek, Latin, and Islamic manuscripts, argues for two enduring aspects of his science: the methodological and the conceptual-linguistic.

LAWRENCE SOUDER

See also Greece: general works; Religion and Science: Medieval

Arithmetic

Ascher, Marcia and Robert Ascher, *Code of the Quipu: A Study in Media, Mathematics, and Culture*, Ann Arbor: University of Michigan Press, 1981

Cajori, Florian, *A History of the Logarithmic Slide Rule and Allied Instruments*, New York: Engineering News, and London: Constable, 1909

Cajori, Florian, *A History of Mathematical Notations*, vol. 1, Chicago: Open Court, 1928

De Morgan, Augustus, *Arithmetical Books from the Invention of Printing to the Present Time*, London: Taylor and Walton, 1847

Gillings, Richard J., *Mathematics in the Time of the Pharaohs*, Cambridge, Massachusetts: MIT Press, 1972

Hill, G.F., *The Development of Arabic Numerals in Europe, Exhibited in Sixty-Four Tables*, Oxford: Clarendon Press, 1915

Ifrah, Georges, *From One to Zero: A Universal History of Numbers*, translated from the French by Lowell Bair, New York: Viking, 1985 (original edition, 1981)

Knott, Cargill Gilston (ed.), *Napier Tercentenary Memorial Volume*, London and New York: Longmans Green, 1915

Menninger, Karl, *Number Words and Number Symbols: A Cultural History of Numbers*, translated by Paul Broneer, Cambridge, Massachusetts: MIT Press, 1969

Pullan, J.M., *The History of the Abacus*, London: Hutchinson, 1968; New York: Praeger, 1969

Schimmel, Annemarie, *The Mystery of Numbers*, New York: Oxford University Press, 1993

Seidenberg, A., "The Ritual Origin of Counting", *Archive for History of Exact Sciences*, 1 (1962): 1–40

Smith, David Eugene, *Rara Arithmetica: A Catalog of the Arithmetics Written Before the Year MDCI*, 2 vols, Boston and London: Ginn, 1908; 4th edition, New York: Chelsea, 1970

Yeldham, Florence A., *The Teaching of Arithmetic Through Four Hundred Years, 1535–1935*, London: Harrap, 1936

Zaslavsky, Claudia, *Africa Counts: Number and Pattern in African Culture*, Boston: Prindle Weber and Schmidt, 1973

History teaches us that the term arithmetic has carried much broader and multifaceted meanings than today's connotation. To the ancient Greeks who followed Pythagoras, *arithmetica* comprised the study of the theoretical properties of integers and rational numbers. (On the other hand, practical dealings with numbers in the classical Hellenic world was called *logistica*.)

In Europe, up to the Renaissance, mathematics was divided into what came to be known as the quadrivium: arithmetic, geometry, astronomy, and music. Only since the early decades of the 17th century has arithmetic slowly taken the shape we recognize today.

Some form of arithmetic is common to every civilization, and, as such, arithmetic precedes classical Greece by millennia. Menninger and Ifrah are two works that provide very broad coverage of the range of the history of arithmetic. The development of connections between counting numbers and the languages of many civilizations comprises almost half of MENNINGER, the Indo-European languages receiving the most extensive treatment. From number words, Menninger progresses to an account of pre-literate number systems, fingers, sticks, and knots. In Ifrah, this same material is covered with less general linguistic analysis. Both books contain several tables summarizing and comparing the terminologies that different peoples used for numbers, and both books are illustrated, Ifrah generously so.

The number sequence was not created or "made"; it grew and evolved slowly and randomly, along with man and his various languages. According to the conventional wisdom, the practical needs of the first societies of pre-literate humanity led to the development of counting, numerology, and arithmetic. On the other hand, SEIDENBERG argues forcefully that numbers did not exist prior to their ritual application, and that counting originated to mimic a portion of the Creation ritual. Connections between numbers and spiritual concerns have persisted throughout history. SCHIMMEL's book provides mystical and religious stories about each integer, from 1 to 40, as well as a few more, world-wide, and from cultures ancient to modern.

The arithmetic of the Incas of South America is presented with helpful photographs and many carefully labelled diagrams of quipus in ASCHER & ASCHER. The quipu was a system of knots tied in colored strings, which recorded numbers and on which have been found some arithmetic calculations, including multiplications and proportions. Arithmetic in sub-Saharan Africa is discussed in general terms in the first part of ZASLAVSKY. The last two chapters focus on the number systems of the Yoruba and Edo of Nigeria and several peoples of East Africa. Zaslavsky ranges from counting, games and number mysticism, the designation of numbers with fingers, sticks, bones, and strings, to practical matters of money, weights and measures.

The arithmetic of ancient Egypt, according to GILLINGS, was based on the two-times table and the ability to find two-thirds of any integer or rational number. Gillings discusses numerals in both hieroglyphics and hieratic script, analyzes many specific problems of pure and applied arithmetic taken from several papyri, and gives attention to the special role of fractions in ancient Egyptian arithmetic.

"An alphabet is . . . the highest stage in the development of writing", and the alphabets of many cultures have been employed to designate positive numbers. Beginning with a brief history of the alphabet, Menninger explains the Greek Attic and alphabetic numerals and Roman numerals, especially those of the Germanic states. The approach is more inclusive in Ifrah, in which many tables and diagrams support a generous account of the origins and development of Roman numerals.

Ifrah also discusses Phoenician, Hebrew, Greek, Syriac, and Arabic alphabetic number systems.

Alphabetic and other repetitive numeral systems, no matter how popular in their respective cultures, were not well designed for computations. For this purpose, the abacus was widely used in Greek and in Roman times. Menninger's account traces the use of various forms of the abacus from classical societies, through Russian and oriental cultures, to the Middle Ages and the beginning of the Renaissance in Europe. PULLAN repeats this story and adds a good deal of information on the jettons (the counters) used on European counting boards and gives some ideas on how contemporary teachers can use the abacus in their classes.

"The ultimate stage of numerical notation" is place-value notation, which arose sometime during the second millennium BC. The Babylonian sexigesimal (base 60) system originated with the organized study of astronomy (its influence through trigonometry and the measurement of time can be detected today) and has been preserved on numerous clay tablets. Accounts of these numerals can be found in many sources: Ifrah, Menninger, and general histories of mathematics. Ifrah and Menninger also contain chapters on the (base 10) place-value systems of China and Japan. The (base 20) and other numeral systems of the Maya of Central America and their interlocking calendars are well illustrated in Ifrah. Over the past few years, much progress has been made in the translation and interpretation of Mayan glyphs.

The Hindu-Arabic number system used by most of the world today originated in India, exactly when and where is apparently lost, and was perfected by the Muslims. The progression of the symbols for the digits on which this system is based is illustrated in diagrams in Ifrah. HILL's collection gives a very rich sense of this progress in Europe, as the Hindu-Arabic numerals gradually displaced the Roman numerals in the late Middle Ages and the Renaissance. The history of zero is examined in Menninger. The largest collection of arithmetic books published from incunabula to 1600 is described in SMITH; this is an annotated bibliography with almost every title page reproduced and additional features of some books also illustrated. DE MORGAN reviewed books in the British Museum, and with only a few exceptions made rather terse comments (there are no illustrations).

There currently exists a clear boundary between the algebra of solving equations and arithmetic computations – especially the Rule of Three, the Rule of False Position, and many numerical puzzles. This demarcation was not recognized until a separate notation for algebra had been created. In tracing this evolution in much detail, CAJORI (1928) also presents many examples of the variations on the basic arithmetic algorithms.

The deficiencies of these algorithms for many computations, especially in astronomy, were met with the invention of logarithms. KNOTT gives a careful explanation of John Napier's first formulation of logarithms, some personal accounts of Napier's life and times, and an account of the improvements by Napier and Henry Briggs that led to our common logs. The slide rule, based on logarithms of lengths, was invented by William Oughtred in 1632 and developed the following year. "Slide rules have been adapted to almost every branch of the arts in which calculation is required" (at least until the advent of electronic calculation in our own times), and their history is told in CAJORI (1909).

According to Robert Recorde (d. 1558), one of the earliest writers of mathematics textbooks in English, arithmetic "is marvellous, methinks, that such great matters may so easily be achieved by this Art". Using many examples and problems taken directly from English textbooks, YELDHAM traces the development of arithmetical pedagogy and teaching.

JOE ALBREE

Artificial Intelligence

Dreyfus, Hubert L., *What Computers Can't Do: The Limits of Artificial Intelligence*, New York: Harper and Row, 1972; revised edition, 1979

Fleck, James, "Development and Establishment in Artificial Intelligence", in *Scientific Establishments and Hierarchies*, edited by Norbert Elias, Herminio Martins and Richard Whitley, Dordrecht: Reidel, 1982

Ganascia, Jean-Gabriel, *L'Ame-machine: les enjeux de l'intelligence artificielle*, Paris: Seuil, 1990

Gardner, Howard, *The Mind's New Science: A History of the Cognitive Revolution*, New York: Basic Books, 1985

McCorduck, Pamela, *Machines Who Think: A Personal Inquiry into the History and Prospects of Artificial Intelligence*, San Francisco: W.H. Freeman, 1979

Searle, John, "Minds, Brains and Programs", *Behavioral and Brain Sciences*, 3 (1980): 417–57

Simon, Herbert A., *The Sciences of The Artificial*, Cambridge, Massachusetts: MIT Press, 1969; 3rd edition, 1996

Taube, Mortimer, *Computers and Common Sense: The Myth of Thinking Machines*, New York: Columbia University Press, 1961

Weizenbaum, Joseph, *Computer Power and Human Reason: From Judgment to Calculation*, San Francisco: W.H. Freeman, 1976

The expression "artificial intelligence" was coined by John McCarthy in 1956, officially declaring the birth of the field at a meeting held at Dartmouth College, New Hampshire. Pamela McCORDUCK, very much an enthusiast of the field, has written a detailed history in which she includes many interviews. She explains how this meeting gathered some 10 young mathematicians, psychologists, and electrical engineers who wanted to study the mind independently of its material manifestation in brains. Their project was based on the hypothesis that all the characteristics of intelligence could in principle be described precisely enough to permit their machine simulation. These young researchers all shared the belief that intelligence could be comprehended in a formal, scientific manner, and that the best instrument for the task was the digital computer. McCorduck describes this group of early researchers in artificial intelligence as a closed group, a "clan" whose nepotistic practices saw students pursuing the work of their pioneering mentors. McCarthy, Marvin Minsky, Herbert Simon, and Allen Newell made up the "hard core" of artificial intelligence. In 1957, McCarthy founded the first research center at the Massachusetts Institute of Technology (MIT), where work was oriented towards the construction of models and computer

programs devoted to problem solving and theorem proving, chess playing, and pattern recognition. At the Carnegie Institute of Technology (later Carnegie-Mellon University), Newell and Simon formed another group and conceived the General Problem Solver, which presumed that the methods used to resolve problems were independent of their contents. The mathematician Seymour Papert joined Minsky and McCarthy at MIT to work on the development of intelligence in children and to finish the Logo Project, with the aim of "teaching children to think". Following the first General Problem Solver programs, another approach, devoted to the production of expert systems, was developed. Contrary to General Problem Solver, expert systems like Dendral and Mycin were based on the idea that specialized knowledge was essential to the efficient resolution of a problem.

FLECK proposes a sociological view of science, and shows that a focus on intelligent behavior provides the disciplinary context (psychology) of artificial intelligence, while its goals are various, due to the great variety of social interpretations and linguistic applications of the very term "intelligence". This aspect of artificial intelligence is typical of any specialty based on a technique that can be put to diverse uses; thus Fleck sees the problem of conflict and competition in the field of artificial intelligence as being directly tied to the focus on intelligence, a term lacking a precise social and cognitive denotation. Fleck explains how the emergence of the field of artificial intelligence was consolidated by its success in obtaining the financial support of the United States government's Department of Defense, principally under the Advanced Research Projects Administration (DARPA) and the Air Force. DARPA's decision to finance only a small number of research groups helped to concentrate resources, and thus computers, in three centers, headed by Minsky at MIT, Newell and Simon at CMU, and McCarthy, working since 1962 at Stanford.

TAUBE criticized artificial intelligence as early as 1961, and since the 1970s increasingly virulent attacks have been levied at the field. DREYFUS's history of the domain is very critical, attacking its philosophical prejudices and what he sees as the naiveté of its fundamental hypotheses. He acknowledges the strengths of its technical achievements, but exposes the distance between pretensions and results, and refuses to grant artificial intelligence the privileged status it seems to claim for itself. Dreyfus sees artificial intelligence as a continuation of the occidental tradition begun by Plato, for whom all knowledge had to be expressible in the form of explicit definitions. WEIZENBAUM, who had been one of the members of the artificial intelligence "clan" at MIT, rose up in 1976 against "the imperialism of instrumental reason which would impose a machine regime on humanity". He raised the issue of morality, reckoning that computers should not be allowed to influence certain aspects of life. The machine metaphor as a description of the mind's functioning appears dangerous to him, and he believes that instead of revolutionizing the world, the use of computers has helped to protect and consolidate American social and political institutions. Weizenbaum also explains that most artificial intelligence work arises more from technology than from science.

In the face of criticism, proponents of artificial intelligence have published a number of books, attempting to disqualify their opponents and develop an epistemological conceptualization of the "sciences of the artificial". For SIMON, one of the pillars of the artificial intelligence community, constructivism – a philosophical movement that questions notions of reality and objectivity – provides support for these "new sciences". He invites us to view knowledge no longer as the unveiling of natural objects presumed to be independent of the observer, but as the invention or conception of artificial phenomena deliberately constructed by their observers. This conception of the "artificial" character of representations of knowledge and of their construction holds that our experiences of "natural" and "artificial" objects, whether material or logical, are equally "knowable".

A distinction between "weak" and "strong" artificial intelligence was proposed in 1980 by SEARLE, who strongly criticized the latter notion, which pretends that computers are capable of thought, comprehension, and learning. "Weak" artificial intelligence is more humbly directed to aiding our understanding of human behavior. According to Searle, the computer is a machine that performs formal operations, has no semantic knowledge, is devoid of intention, and is therefore a totally different kind of entity from the human being. GARDNER, author of a history of the cognitive sciences, believes that it no longer makes any sense to attack artificial intelligence since "after a period of exaggerated claims and sometimes superficial demonstrations, artificial intelligence has come to hold a humbler vision of itself". Like Gardner, GANASCIA describes the evolution of artificial intelligence towards a "cognitive pragmatics" in which, in the place of initial ambitions to produce or even reproduce intelligence, is now found a more measured ambition: to simulate cognitive activity within a narrow field of knowledge.

BRIGITTE CHAMAK

translated by Craig Rodine

See also Computing

Astrolabes

Bennett, J.A., *The Divided Circle: A History of Instruments for Astronomy, Navigation, and Surveying*, Oxford: Phaidon/Christie's, 1987

Gibbs, Sharon, Janice Henderson and Derek de Solla Price, *A Computerised Checklist of Astrolabes*, New Haven, Connecticut: 1973

Gunther, Robert Theodore, *The Astrolabes of the World*, 2 vols, Oxford: Oxford University Press, 1932; reprinted in 1 volume, London: Holland, 1976

Gunther, Robert Theodore, "The Astrolabe of Queen Elizabeth", *Archaeologia*, 86 (1937): 65–72

Hartner, Willy, "The Principle and Use of the Astrolabe", in *A Survey of Persian Art*, edited by Arthur Upham Pope, vol. 3, London and New York: Oxford University Press, 1939; reprinted in Hartner's *Oriens-Occidens*, edited by Gunther Kerstein, Hildesheim: Olms, 1968

King, David A., *Islamic Astronomical Instruments*, London: Variorum, 1987

Laird, Edgar and Robert Fischer (eds), *Pèlerin de Prusse on the Astrolabe: Text and Translation of His "Practique de astralabe"*, Binghamton, New York: Medieval and Renaissance Texts and Studies, 1995

Mayer, L.A., *Islamic Astrolabists and Their Work*, Geneva: Kundig, 1956

Michel, Henri, *Traité de l'astrolabe*, Paris: Gauthier-Villars, 1947; reprinted, Paris: Brieux, 1981

Morley, W.H., "Description of a Planispheric Astrolabe Constructed for Shah Sultan Husain Safawi . . .", London, 1856; reprinted in *The Astrolabes of the World*, edited by Robert Theodore Gunther, 2 vols, Oxford: Oxford University Press, 1932; reprinted in 1 volume, London: Holland, 1976

Neugebauer, Oscar, "The Early History of the Astrolabe", *Isis*, 40 (1949): 240–56

North, J.D. "The Astrolabe", *Scientific American*, 230 (1974): 96–106

Osborne, Marijane, "The Squire's 'Steed of Brass' as Astrolabe: Some Implications of the Canterbury Tales", in *Hermeneutics and Medieval Culture*, edited by Patrick J. Gallacher and Helen Damico, Albany: State University of New York Press, 1989

Poulle, Emmanuel, "La Fabrication des astrolabes au moyen âge", *Techniques et Civilizations*, 4 (1955): 117–28

Poulle, Emmanuel, "Le Quadrant nouveau medieval", *Journal des Savantes* (1964)

Poulle, Emmanuel, "Remarques sur deux astrolabes du moyen âge", *Physis*, 4 (1967): 161–64

Price, Derek de Solla, "An International Checklist of Astrolabes", *Archives Internationales d'Histoire des Sciences*, 34 (1955): 243–63, 363–81

Robinson, F.N. (ed.), *The Works of Geoffrey Chaucer*, 2nd edition, London: Oxford University Press, and Boston: Houghton Mifflin, 1957

Saunders, Harold N., *All the Astrolabes*, Oxford: Senecio, 1984

Stimson, Alan, *The Mariner's Astrolabe: A Survey of Known, Surviving Sea Astrolabes*, Utrecht: Hes, 1988

Turner, Anthony John, *The Time Museum: Catalogue of the Collection*, vol. 1, Rockford, Illinois, 1984

Turner, Anthony John, "Paper, Print, and Mathematics: Philippe Danfrie and the Making of Mathematical Instruments in Late 16th Century Paris", in *Of Time and Measurement: Studies in the History of Horology and Fine Technology*, edited by Turner, Aldershot, Hampshire, and Brookfield, Vermont: Variorum, 1993

Waters, David Watkin, *The Sea or Mariner's Astrolabe*, Coimbra: Junta de Investigações do Ultramar, 1966

The astrolabe, or star-finder, is a kind of analogue computer. A model of the heavens inscribed in brass, it was, at least in theory, capable of facilitating the making of a number of complex astronomical and geometrical calculations. In an era before accurate and portable clocks, the astrolabe could be used to tell the time, to measure altitude, and to determine geographical latitude and the direction of true north. Additionally, it played an important role in the casting of horoscopes, for it allowed astrologers to reference an "accurate" map of the heavens for any given time or locale.

The front of the astrolabe has a raised circumference called a *limb*; this is inscribed with a degree scale (usually a scale of hours), the interior of which (the *mater*) can be fitted with alternative plates (*tympanon*) which depict the night sky as stereographically projected on to the plane of the equator from different latitudes. An observer selects a plate and fits it into the *mater*, and by this means a system of celestial co-ordinates based on the reference point of the observer's horizon is established. Overlaid above this celestial template is a second projection: a moveable skeletal, or open plan, star map, known as the *rete* or spider, which points out prominent stars and the ecliptic of the sun. The *rete* can be rotated above the latitude plate so as to mimic the daily apparent motion of the celestial sphere; the changing positions of the stars in altitude and azimuth can thus be charted by reference to the plate lying below it. On the other side of the astrolabe is the *alidade*, a pivoted arm lying across the back face of the instrument, with small sighting holes that are raised above the astrolabe's plane. If the instrument is held vertically by the shackle and ring at the top or throne, the *alidade* can be used in conjunction with a fixed scale that runs along the outside rim of the instrument to measure the height of a given object. Thus, for example, to establish a model of the night's sky all that is required – at least in theory – is to measure the altitude of one of the stars on the *rete* by using the *alidade* and degree scale on the back of the astrolabe, and then to adjust the star represented on the *rete* to the appropriate altitude lines. By following this method, the time, as well as the positions of other celestial bodies, can be determined.

However, despite these putative practical uses in time-telling, surveying, and navigation, the cumbersome nature of handling the astrolabe in the field (in often less than perfect conditions), combined with limitations imposed by its necessarily small size (usually between 10 and 40 cm), the lack of textual corroboration of instances of use, and the precious nature of the materials used in its construction (typically gilt brass), make it extremely unlikely that the typical astrolabe was used for anything other than as a show-case item for purposes of display, or for didactic purposes in teaching the principles of astronomy and geometry. It is thus worth keeping in mind that, though many of the authors who write on the astrolabe acknowledge these practical difficulties in passing, most ignore them, and offer instead a detailed technical description of the construction, theory, and method of use of the instrument, without considering whether or not it was ever actually employed for practical purposes.

The astrolabe is of ancient Greek origin. While GUNTHER (1937) briefly discusses its early history, NEUGEBAUER is the most important source for the ancient history of the instrument, providing a survey of significant primary sources. The astrolabe more or less disappeared from Europe in late antiquity; however, it came to serve important ritual functions in Islam, being used for horoscopes, calendric reckoning of the month of fasting, and for the times of prayer. HARTNER provides a good general introduction to the Islamic astrolabe. KING is essential reading for those interested in the historical place of the astrolabe in Arabic science, religion, and culture. Another relevant work is that by MAYER, who provides biographical information (where available) on Islamic astrolabists, as well as referencing appropriate bibliography and extant instruments for each maker, including black and white plates of numerous instruments.

The best source for the history, description, use, and bibliography associated with the astrolabe is TURNER (1984), a superb volume of the Time Museum catalogue. If only one book is to be consulted, this should be it. MICHEL's volume is a classic modern account of the astrolabe, providing a detailed description of its various parts and functions, as well as the geometrical and astronomical theories on which they are based. NORTH provides a short, but elegant treatment of the theory and practices associated with the astrolabe's construction and use, while POULLE (1967) gives a historical account of the construction of the astrolabe in the Middle Ages. SAUNDERS's useful short account is particularly interesting insofar as he provides workable examples of laminated paper and plastic astrolabes.

BENNETT's gloss is especially important in that, unlike much of the literature on scientific instruments (which tends to be geared either towards the connoisseur or the specialist), he frames his discussion of "scientific" instruments within a larger historical and narrative context. Thus, he suggests that the main significance of the astrolabe is not to be found in its practical uses, but rather in its role in promoting mathematical and astronomical literacy, and in its commercial potential as a commodity that helped to establish centres of mathematical instrument-making. POULLE's articles (1964 and 1955) also touch on both of these themes, the former treating the didactic uses of the astrolabe, the latter the workshop of the 15th-century instrument maker, Jean Fusoris.

As would be expected, much of the literature on the astrolabe focuses on extant instruments in museum collections. TURNER (1984), in addition to its narrative history, description, and illustrations of the astrolabe, includes a catalogue – including colour plates – of the Rockford Illinois Time Museum collection. Though dated, GUNTHER's magisterial two-volume work (1932) is also a useful resource; it includes detailed descriptions, illustrations, and black and white pictures of a large number of instruments, information about their makers, transcriptions of relevant primary texts, and a still useful bibliography of sources (especially helpful with regards to the early modern period). PRICE provides a textual reference source for astrolabes in various collections around the world. However, GIBBS, HENDERSON & PRICE remains the most up-to-date work of this genre.

Despite the relatively large number of astrolabes held in museum collections around the world, those that had the widest popularity – and hence the greatest influence – no longer exist, for they were made of paper and wood. Unlike brass instruments, which were usually luxury items meant more for display than for use, paper instruments were both cheap and easy to manufacture. Consequently, it was probably in this form that astrolabes were most widely known and used. A brief discussion of these instruments and one of their makers, Philippe Danfrie, is given by TURNER (1993).

The most important early English work on the astrolabe is the *Treatise on the Astrolabe* written by Chaucer for his son, Lowys. This text consists largely of a translation of the Latin version of the Pseudo-Masha'allah treatise. Chaucer's is the earliest English-language text concerning the instrument, and is also significant in pointing to the place of astronomy in 14th century genteel culture, as well as to the importance attributed to the astrolabe as a didactic tool for the teaching of mathematics and astronomy. ROBINSON includes the text of Chaucer's *Treatise*, while OSBORNE discusses Chaucer's treatise and its significance with regards to its literary, scientific, and historical significance. Another medieval vernacular text concerning the astrolabe is Pèlerin de Prusse's *Practique de astralabe*. LAIRD & FISCHER published a modern critical edition of this text, which includes an English translation and a valuable introduction, and provides biographical information on de Prusse, as well as discussions of the practice of astrology at the court of Charles V and of the relationship between de Prusse's text and Chaucer's *Treatise*.

Although the astrolabe was essentially a showpiece with little practical use, a related instrument, the mariner's astrolabe, was just the opposite. Bearing more of a resemblance to a simple quadrant than a planispheric astrolabe, it was typically made of brass or iron, with the plates, inscriptions, and decorative paraphernalia removed as needless ornamentation interfering with functionality and adding cost. Little more than a heavily weighted circular ring, the mariner's astrolabe was an eminently practical instrument, of which very few survive. This was because, unlike most astrolabes held in museum collections, mariner's astrolabes were actually used. Indeed, many of the surviving examples of the mariner's astrolabe were found in salvaged shipwrecks or dredged up from the bottom of the sea. GUNTHER (1932) provides a brief discussion of the mariner's astrolabe. WATERS's treatment is more extensive, and deals in some detail with its use in solving practical problems of oceanic navigation. Extant instruments are documented by STIMSON, who also provides a valuable introduction to the history, use, and significance of the mariner's astrolabe as a navigational tool.

MICHAEL WINTROUB

See also Astronomical Instruments; Astronomy: general works; Navigational Instruments; Scientific Instruments: general works

Astrology

Barton, Tamsyn, *Ancient Astrology*, London and New York: Routledge, 1994

Curry, Patrick (ed.), *Astrology, Science and Society: Historical Essays*, Woodbridge, Suffolk: Boydell Press, 1987

Curry, Patrick, *Prophecy and Power: Astrology in Early Modern England*, Cambridge: Polity Press, and Princeton, New Jersey: Princeton University Press, 1989

Curry, Patrick, *A Confusion of Prophets: Victorian and Edwardian Astrology*, London: Collins and Brown, 1992

Garin, Eugenio, *Astrology in the Renaissance: The Zodiac of Life*, translated by Carolyn Jackson and June Allen, London and Boston: Routledge and Kegan Paul, 1983

Kitson, Anabella (ed.), *Astrology and History: Clio and Urania Confer*, London: Unwin Hyman, 1989

North, J.D., *Horoscopes and History*, London: Warburg Institute, 1986

Tester, S.J., *A History of Western Astrology*, Woodbridge, Suffolk: Boydell Press, 1987; New York: Ballantine Books, 1989

Thomas, Keith, *Religion and the Decline of Magic: Studies in Popular Beliefs in Sixteenth and Seventeenth Century England*, London: Weidenfeld and Nicolson, and New York: Scribner, 1971

Thorndike, Lynn, *A History of Magic and Experimental Science*, 8 vols, New York: Macmillan (vols 1–2) and Columbia University Press (vols 3–8), 1923–58

The literature covered in this entry is predominantly about astrology in the West, and does not cover in any detail Indian, Chinese, or Arabic astrology. Although numerous studies of the history of Western astrology exist, the majority suffer from two problems: first, many texts are written either by proponents or opponents of astrology, with the author's allegiances made explicit; second, although almost everyone imagines they know what astrology is, there is no single, simply defined entity that can be called astrology. Throughout history, there have been many different interpretations of the notion of celestial influence, and an equally wide variety of practices that can, at least in part, be called astrological. Adopting, for instance, the terms used by Patrick Curry, it is possible to delineate at least a tripartite division of astrology. The first part, high astrology, deals with natural philosophical questions about astrological influence and associated cosmological issues. The second, judicial astrology, encompasses the more practical predictive astrology found, for instance, in the calculation of birth charts (now referred to as horoscopes); these predictions rely on astronomical calculation and on complex rules of interpretation. The last, popular astrology, covers a wide variety of low-level practices, including simple predictions based only on the approximate positions of the sun or moon, the forecasts found in contemporary newspapers, and "natural astrology", which concerns only general predictions about such things as the weather. Different social and intellectual groups have used these forms of astrology in widely varying ways over history. Indeed, this tripartite division only partly reflects the true complexity of the situation, yet such complications are generally overlooked by texts attempting to narrate the history of astrology.

Early historians of science often treated astrology as one of the superstitions abandoned by the rational thinkers of the "scientific revolution". THORNDIKE challenged this view, tracing in eight volumes the history of the magical arts, including astrology, from the Roman Empire to the 17th century. The author's contention was that magic and experimental science were for a long time intimately linked, and that it was magicians who were the first to experiment, and who were thus the progenitors of modern science. The account is part chronological, part topical, with chapters on high astrology in particular appearing throughout. The work has been criticised, however, for inaccurately ascribing astrological and magical properties to the work of certain individuals and groups.

TESTER also provides an intellectual, rather than a practical, history. Tracing the origins of European astrology back to ancient Greece, the author concentrates on an analysis of primary sources, in particular those in Greek and Latin. The general argument is that there was little change in astrological theory from its origins until its supposed death in the 18th century. Although Tester promotes a more guarded approach than Thorndike regarding the description of particular authors as astrologers, (notably those from the Middle Ages), the work suffers from its attempt to cover so much ground.

Those works with a more limited scope have been more successful. The two collections of papers listed above, for example, provide interesting excursions into various topics within the history of astrology. KITSON includes entries that discuss the development of astrology in Mesopotamia, Greek and Roman astrology, Chaucer's and Spenser's astrology, astrological historiography in the Renaissance, Kepler's beliefs, some examples of electional astrology, and a discussion of astrology in 18th-century England. CURRY (1987) focuses on the period from the 13th to the 17th centuries, essays in this work including an excellent analysis of astrology's place in medieval thought, as well as discussions of medieval concepts of celestial influence, astrology at the late medieval English court, astrology in 17th-century England, and the beliefs of individuals such as Peter of Abano, Nicole Oresme, Kepler, Newton and Flamsteed.

A number of works also give more extensive treatments of specific periods in the history of astrology. BARTON admits that her treatment places its emphasis on the learned parts of astrology, due to the bias of the historical record. Nevertheless, she attempts to put ancient astrology – covering the period from its origins to the late Roman Empire – within its proper social, political, philosophical and religious contexts. The work also explores the practical workings of the subject, acknowledging the wide variety of astrological doctrines and interpretations, and emphasises that astrology should properly be viewed in terms of the Greek concept of "techne" (usually translated as "art").

NORTH also provides a technical exploration of the subject. The work is divided into two sections: the first concentrates on the development of the mathematical techniques for the division of the astrological figure into different houses, the central technical problem in judicial astrology; the second takes examples of astrological charts from Greek times to the 17th century and, by analysing their computation and application, demonstrates their use in historical interpretation.

GARIN, on the other hand, adopts a textual approach in his survey of Renaissance astrology. The four sections of the book deal with astrology and history, astrology and magic, neo-Platonic and Hermetic influences in astrology, and the criticism of the art. With an emphasis on continental philosophical works, this book centres on high astrology, and is more concerned with the impact of astrological ideas on Renaissance culture in general, than with the more limited context of the history of science.

A number of works on English astrology have, however, tried to encompass both high and low astrology. THOMAS's seminal work on the period 1500–1700 includes astrology as one of the magical arts in decline by the 18th century. The chapters on astrology illustrate the different types of practice in different social settings, thus combating the notion of astrology as a single entity, and provide information about the practices of working astrologers. The weakness of the work, however, lies in its attempt to compress too much information into a unified account, and in its placement of astrology primarily among the magical arts.

Patrick Curry, among others, has helped to reappraise this view, by placing astrology within its proper context, allied not only to magic, but also to mathematics, medicine, and other fields of knowledge. He has also helped to illustrate the

different types of astrology operating at different levels. In CURRY (1989), he discusses 17th-century England, adopting the tripartite division described above. In this way he explains how astrology died (high astrology disappeared from scientific and philosophical agendas), floundered (judicial astrology went into decline), and flourished (popular astrology thrived) into and beyond the 18th century. CURRY (1992) then traces some elements of this story into the early 20th century, beginning with the resurgence in astrology's popularity (including judicial astrology) in 19th-century England. Despite covering a period poorly documented by histories of astrology to date, this book is less useful to the historian of science, since by this time the division had opened up between astrology and "legitimate" science.

RICHARD DUNN

Astronomical Instruments

Bennett, J.A., *The Divided Circle: A History of Instruments for Astronomy, Navigation, and Surveying*, Oxford: Phaidon/Christie's, 1987

Brooks, Randall C., "The Development of Micrometers in the Seventeenth, Eighteenth and Nineteenth Centuries", *Journal for the History of Astronomy*, 12 (1991): 127–73

Chapman, Allan, *Dividing the Circle: The Development of Critical Angular Measurement in Astronomy, 1500–1850*, New York: Ellis Horwood, 1990; 2nd edition, Chichester, Sussex: John Wiley, 1995

Daumas, Maurice, *Scientific Instruments of the Seventeenth and Eighteenth Centuries and Their Makers*, translated from the French and edited by Mary Holbrook, London: Batsford, and New York: Praeger, 1972; reprinted, London: Portman Books, 1989 (original edition, 1953)

Gouk, Penelope, *The Ivory Sundials of Nuremberg 1500–1700*, Cambridge: Whipple Museum, 1988

Gunther, Robert Theodore, *The Astrolabes of the World*, 2 vols, Oxford: Oxford University Press, 1932; reprinted in 1 volume, London: Holland, 1976

Hearnshaw, J.B., *The Analysis of Starlight: One Hundred and Fifty Years of Astronomical Spectroscopy*, Cambridge and New York: Cambridge University Press, 1986; revised edition, 1990

King, Henry C., *The History of the Telescope*, Cambridge, Massachusetts: Sky, and London: Griffin, 1955

King, Henry C., *Geared to the Stars: The Evolution of Planetariums, Orreries, and Astronomical Clocks*, Toronto: University of Toronto Press, 1978

Ræder, Hans, Elis Strömgren and Bengt Strömgren (eds), *Tycho Brahe's Description of His Instruments and Scientific Work*, Copenhagen: Munksgaard, 1946

Thoren, Victor E., "New Light on Tycho's Instruments", *Journal for the History of Astronomy*, 4 (1973): 25–45

Van Helden, Albert, *The Invention of the Telescope*, Philadelphia: American Philosophical Society, 1977

Van Helden, Albert, *Measuring the Universe: Cosmic Dimensions from Aristardus to Halley*, Chicago: University of Chicago Press, 1985

The number of monographs dealing specifically with astronomical instruments is limited, and those that provide an analysis of their physical construction and limitations are even more rare. Until the 20th century, astronomy, navigation and surveying were closely linked, and several of the works discussed cross these lines. Astronomical instrument is used in a broad sense to include devices that were not normally used for scientific studies, for example, sundials.

The astrolabe has been used by astronomers, navigators, and surveyors for more than two millennia, and its construction reflects the state of understanding of astronomy as well as providing physical evidence of the abilities of its makers. GUNTHER produced the first exhaustive study of known astrolabes, and it is still the most scholarly work on the subject. It includes useful translations, especially of those originally in Arabic, while hundreds of photographs and illustrations show the inscriptions and details of the various components. There has been the occasional important astrolabe found since this monumental work was completed, but its primary shortcoming for modern scholars is the lack of discussion of fake instruments and how to identify them.

Sundials have been the topic of many books but one deserves special attention. GOUK's exemplary work considers a rather specific class of dial, but her approach should serve as a model for anyone investigating any type of scientific instrument. Her application of the material history approach covers the context within which they were made, marketed and used, as well as the factors that influenced their design and fabrication. She discusses the reasons why they were made in Nuremberg, and the technical and decorative details, including makers' marks, which allow working relationships to be followed. The catalogue provides details of specific instruments, which provides other researchers with materials for further investigation.

KING (1978) provides a point of entry into research on secondary astronomical instruments, such as planetariums, orreries, and astronomical clocks. Thoroughly researched, this study reveals that these instruments reflect not only the astronomical knowledge of the period but also the mechanical ingenuity of their makers. If one can overcome the overwhelming amount of detail, this work offers an absolute wealth of information on the makers, devices, and the evolution of the discipline.

The little-known work by RÆDER, STRÖMGREN & STRÖMGREN includes a translation of Tycho's *Astronomiae Instauratae Mechanica* (1598). Tycho's contribution in adapting instruments to enhance his ability to make observations is unquestionable. However, only a few of the instruments are described in detail elsewhere. This work also provides information on the astronomical and mathematical problems of interest to the great Danish astronomer, and here one finds the first discussion of buildings suited to astronomical observations. Another useful work on this subject is THOREN's paper on the accuracy of Tycho's instruments.

The primary tool of astronomers for 400 years has been the telescope, and two works outline its history. VAN HELDEN (1977) provides a careful and detailed analysis of the sources available in an attempt to resolve the question of who invented the telescope: to date, it is still the most creditable endeavour to resolve this question. Recent efforts to prove that the Englishman, Leonard Digges, discovered the optical principles necessarily remain conjectural; the fact that the concept did not spread suggests otherwise. KING (1955) remains the standard reference to the history of telescopes. It is unlikely to be replaced soon since it is comprehensive, well researched and provides a balanced assessment of the telescope's evolution up to and including the Hale 200 reflector on Mount Palomar, and of some of the research tools used with telescopes. King also provides biographical information on the individuals and firms involved.

A very different approach to the history of astronomical instruments is that used by VAN HELDEN (1985). Instead of discussing the instruments themselves, he has selected a problem faced by all astronomers – i.e., determining the size of the universe. By taking this approach, he analyses both the theories and the instruments at the disposal of Greek astronomers through to those of the 18th century. Here we discover more about the limitations of the instruments than their actual construction. (The limitations and errors of instruments are fundamental themes inadequately addressed by most historians of science.) One of the instruments important to van Helden's thesis is the astronomical micrometer: the invention, construction and evolution of this important device is discussed by BROOKS. HEARNSHAW, like van Helden, includes photographs and discusses the development and innovators of spectroscopic astronomy, but does not provide many details of the spectroscope's construction. None the less, Hearnshaw provides insight into its importance in revolutionizing astronomy from a science of position to one of astrophysics.

For an analysis of the European perspective on astronomical instruments and their development, one should read DAUMAS. His book covers other types of instruments as well, which helps place astronomical instrument developments in context with contemporary scientific technologies. He discusses the techniques of instrument making, the makers themselves and the inter-relationships between them. This is an area of research that requires much more work, because makers did not work in isolation. When researching the fabrication of instruments after the late 18th century, one soon concludes that components came from a range of specialized disciplines including founders, tube makers, engraving specialists and scale dividers, to name a few.

CHAPMAN's work on techniques of scale division emphasises the key role of scales of astronomical instruments to positional astronomy up to the mid-19th century. He concludes by presenting a graph of instrumental accuracy, and, like the practitioners of the times he analyses, he is somewhat optimistic of the positional accuracy they could routinely achieve, especially in the early 19th century. In a monograph with a similar title, BENNETT places astronomical instruments in relation to those of navigation and surveying to the end of the 19th century. Because of the wide range of instruments and the long time period covered, we do not find an exhaustive account of each, but it does provide the important conceptual and defining issues in instrument development that affected these three disciplines.

RANDALL C. BROOKS

See also Astrolabes; Mathematical Instruments; Navigational Instruments; Scientific Instruments: general works; Telescopes

Astronomy: general works

Hoskin, Michael (ed.), *The General History of Astronomy*, 4 vols, Cambridge and New York: Cambridge University Press, 1984–95

Hoskin, Michael (ed.), *The Cambridge Illustrated History of Astronomy*, Cambridge and New York: Cambridge University Press, 1997

Lankford, John (ed.), *History of Astronomy: An Encyclopedia*, New York: Garland, 1997

North, John, *The Fontana History of Astronomy and Cosmology*, London: Fontana, 1994; as *The Norton History of Astronomy and Cosmology*, New York: Norton, 1994

Pannekoek, Anton, *A History of Astronomy*, New York: Interscience, and London: Allen and Unwin, 1961

Selin, Helaine (ed.), *Encyclopaedia of the History of Science, Technology, and Medicine in Non-Western Cultures*, Dordrecht: Kluwer, 1997

Thiel, Rudolf, *And There Was Light: The Discovery of the Universe*, translated from the German by Richard and Clara Winston, New York: Knopf, 1957 (original edition, 1956)

Wilson, Robert, *Astronomy Through the Ages: The Story of the Human Attempt to Understand the Universe*, Princeton, New Jersey: Princeton University Press, and London: Taylor and Francis, 1997

There are a great many general histories of astronomy, testifying to the field's attraction to the general public. The night sky, space science, and cosmology all prove fascinating to an audience beyond academia. This entry covers the best-known older text (Pannekoek) and the most scholarly general history of astronomy (Hoskin). It also covers four popular histories that have been published recently, all of which contain references to further literature, and one text that aims to synthesize the academic contributions to the history of astronomy.

PANNEKOEK, a leading astronomer of his time, covers the history of astronomy from antiquity to the mid-20th century in more than 500 pages. The section on ancient science concerns Babylonian, Egyptian, Chinese, Greek, and Arabic astronomy; the section on astronomy in the scientific revolution covers Copernicus, Brahe, Kepler, and Newton; the section on "astronomy surveying the universe" covers celestial mechanics, photography, spectrography and gives an intellectual history of cosmology and stellar physics. Pannekoek follows an established tradition with this kind of coverage. THIEL is a similarly structured earlier example. Whereas Thiel emphasizes the maturing of astronomy and heroic discoveries, Pannekoek puts special emphasis on the role of quantification and the intellectual craving for beauty. In both books, the history of technology is confined to the provision of tools.

HOSKIN's encyclopedia (1997) is a beautifully illustrated history from prehistory to the 1980s (to the Hertzsprung-Russell diagrams and the Hubble constant) in nearly 400 pages. Both theory and instrumentation are discussed and depicted but mostly in separate sections, and so the connection between the two is not always addressed. The institutional history of astronomy is largely ignored. There is an appended chronology and a useful section on further reading.

LANKFORD is in encyclopedic format with entries arranged alphabetically. It includes articles on individuals, subfields of astronomy, institutions, instruments, and countries. There is a bibliography at the end of each entry. The entries are generally well-written and a good proportion of the authors are astronomers.

The coverage of non-Western cultures in general histories of astronomy is generally limited to ancient cultures, such as Babylonia, ancient Egypt, and ancient China, as we have seen for Pannekoek and Thiel above. SELIN fills that gap in that it covers comprehensively astrology, astronomical instruments and astronomy of Africa, native North America, the Australian Aboriginal peoples, China, Egypt, the Hebrew peoples, India, Indo-Malay Archipelago, the Islamic World, Mesoamerica and Tibet. Arranged alphabetically in some 1,100 pages, the entries are sometimes short (especially the biographical and descriptive entries) and sometimes long and fundamental (such as the entry on "Rationality, Objectivity, and Method").

NORTH aims to synthesize detailed research in a survey that is nearly 700 pages long. As with all books in the Fontana/Norton series in the history of science, it is targeted at general readers and students. Organized largely chronologically, each chapter has a bibliographical essay attached to it. Approximately one third of the book is allocated respectively to antiquity, Europe from the medieval period to William Herschel, and the rise of astrophysics to space observatories and Stephen Hawking. This is the least successful of the Fontana/Norton books: it is a story of progress and the bibliographies are highly selective. The author argues that science consists of reducing the observed to a series of rules. In LANKFORD, utility is presented as less important for the historical development of the subject than human feeling for system and order.

WILSON is a history written by an astronomer for a non-scientific audience – it explains the science very simply and avowedly without the use of mathematics. Arranged in three sections according to instrumentation (the naked eye, the telescope, and instruments capable of detecting radiation beyond the optical spectrum), the book includes, however, little discussion of the instrumentation. Wilson conceives of astronomical instruments as simply extending human perception.

The most useful general history for professional historians of science is HOSKIN (1984–95). Editors and authors include well-known names in the history of astronomy: Olaf Pedersen, René Taton, Curtis Wilson, Owen Gingerich, and Michael Hoskin himself. In progress since 1984, this collection was conceived as a seven-volume work in four parts (some volumes are in progress). The articles do not carry footnotes but there is an extensive section of further reading at the end of each. Each volume covers theory, experimentation, observational methods, and (for the relevant periods) observatories. There are also chapters under such headings as "Sociology of astronomy", which, however, is primarily an institutional history.

ARNE HESSENBRUCH

See also Astronomy: non-European; Astrophysics

Astronomy: non-European

Aveni, Anthony F. (ed.), *Archaeoastronomy in the New World*, Cambridge and New York: Cambridge University Press, 1982

Aveni, Anthony F. (ed.), *World Archaeoastronomy: Selected Papers from the 2nd Oxford International Conference on Archaeoastronomy*, Cambridge and New York: Cambridge University Press, 1989

Cornell, James, *The First Stargazers: An Introduction to the Origins of Astronomy*, New York: Scribner, and London: Athlone Press, 1981

Cullen, Christopher, *Astronomy and Mathematics in Ancient China: The Zhou Bi Suan Jing*, Cambridge and New York: Cambridge University Press, 1996

Haynes, Raymond et al., *Explorers of the Southern Sky: A History of Australian Astronomy*, Cambridge: Cambridge University Press, 1996

Ho, Peng Yoke, *Li, Qi, and Shu: An Introduction to Science and Civilization in China*, Hong Kong: Hong Kong University Press, 1985; Seattle: University of Washington Press, 1987

Hodson, F.R. (ed.), *The Place of Astronomy in the Ancient World: A Joint Symposium of the Royal Society and the British Academy*, London: Oxford University Press, 1974

Kaye, G.R., *Hindu Astronomy: Ancient Science of the Hindus*, Calcutta: Government of India Central Publications, 1924; reprinted, New Delhi: Cosmo, 1981

Kennedy, E.S., *Studies in the Islamic Exact Sciences*, Beirut: American University of Beirut, 1983

King, David A., *Islamic Mathematical Astronomy*, London: Variorum, 1986

Krupp, E.C., *Echoes of the Ancient Skies: The Astronomy of Lost Civilizations*, New York: Harper and Row, 1983

Nakayama, Shigeru, *A History of Japanese Astronomy*, Cambridge, Massachusetts: Harvard University Press, 1969

Ruggles, Clive L.N. and Nicholas J. Saunders (eds), *Astronomies and Cultures: Papers Derived from the Third Oxford International Symposium on Archaeoastronomy*, Niwot: University Press of Colorado, 1993

Selin, Helaine (ed.), *Encyclopaedia of the History of Science, Technology, and Medicine in Non-Western Cultures*, Dordrecht: Kluwer, 1997

Sen, S.N. and K.S. Shukla (eds), *History of Astronomy in India*, New Delhi: Indian National Science Academy, 1985

Swarup, G.A.K. Bag and K.S. Shukla (eds), *History of Oriental Astronomy: Proceedings of an International Astronomical Union Colloquium no. 91*, Cambridge: Cambridge University Press, 1987

Walker, Christopher (ed.), *Astronomy Before the Telescope*, London: British Museum Press, and New York: St Martin's Press, 1996

The study of the sky is arguably the first science. The peoples of the old and new worlds used the movement of celestial objects to keep time, to guide them in hunting, navigating and planting, and to predict and explain terrestrial events. Our knowledge of the astronomical activities of these peoples comes from a variety of sources, including written materials from literate civilizations and surviving instruments and observatories. There is a vast literature on European sites such as Stonehenge, but scholarly work on the rest of the world is much more limited. This imbalance is slowly being rectified.

Books on the history of astronomy tended to start with the Greeks, with a passing mention of the Arabs as translators of Greek science. This has changed in recent years. In 1972 a joint symposium of the Royal Society and the British Academy was held on astronomy in the ancient world. HODSON's edited collection of essays is one of the first to give scholarly credence to astronomy in non-European cultures. Astronomical theories and practices are examined in several ancient cultures: Babylonian, Egyptian, Polynesian and Micronesian, Chinese and Maya. An interesting section contains papers comparing astronomical alignments in several cultures. Three other volumes from symposia are included here, all resulting from the Oxford international conferences on archaeoastronomy. AVENI's collection on world archaeoastronomy (1989) contains articles from a variety of disciplines, including astronomy, history, and art. It includes overviews of Chinese, Maya, and Southwestern United States' astronomy, and other studies arising from ancient artifacts, such as books, pictographs, and string constructions.

Papers from the third Oxford conference edited by RUGGLES & SAUNDERS range from the editors' overview of the study of cultural astronomy, in which they explain how different cultures perceive and interpret the sky according to their own worldview, to those discussing Chinese, Mesoamerican, Indian, and Islamic astronomical practices and beliefs.

CORNELL gives equal weight to the astronomical discoveries and practices of the Egyptians, Europeans, Native Americans (North, Central, and South), Africans, and Asians. This is one of the first studies to look at the astronomy of sub-Saharan Africa with a careful scholarly eye (despite calling Africa the "Dark Continent"). The book is very readable and accessible, is a good introduction to the subject with a useful bibliography. KRUPP has written a variety of articles and books, and has edited volumes, both scholarly and popular, on astronomy in non-European cultures. His 1983 book discusses science, myth, religion, architecture, timekeeping, city planning, and cosmology. Rather than arranging the chapters by culture, Krupp takes a topic such as calendars and discusses the similarities and differences in Kenya, Egypt, China, and Peru. This approach gives an excellent synthesis of astronomical practices around the ancient world. Although most of the articles in WALKER focus on Europe, the collection includes the latest scholarship on Egypt, India, the Islamic world, China, Korea and Japan, the Americas, Africa, and, uniquely, Australian Aboriginal, Polynesian, and Maori astronomy. The bibliographies are extensive, and the book includes some wonderful illustrations. It is clear that these kinds of studies are becoming more comprehensive and are produced more frequently, which is a reflection of the recent changes in curricula in higher education away from an entirely Eurocentric perspective. SELIN's encyclopedia is the first compendium to bring together scholarly articles with bibliographies on all the sciences in many different cultures. The astronomy section includes essays on Africa, the Americas, Australia, China, India, the Islamic world, and Tibet, to name a few. This is a good starting point for scholars just beginning their research or embarking on a new field.

SWARUP & SHUKLA consists of 46 papers from a conference on the history of oriental astronomy. They range in depth and in breadth over the field, covering cultures from China and Japan to Java and Yemen, and ancient data relating to supernovae, eclipses and comets. There are essays on clocks, calendars, stars, medieval astronomical instruments and observatories.

SEN & SHUKLA's collection surveys the sources of Indian astronomy and the early development of astronomy in the Indus civilization. The essays deal with computations of mean and true longitudes, eclipses and equinoxes, phases of the moon and the setting of planets and stars, the Indian calendar and computations of time, and astronomical instruments and observatories. This is particularly noteworthy because the book was published in India, as much of the scholarly material on the East is published in the West. KAYE's book is an account of the astronomical material in early and medieval Hindu works, beginning with the early texts such as the Vedas and the Mahabharata. He describes eclipses, calculations of the length of the day, and the mean motions of planets as they were reported and interpreted in the Hindu literature.

KENNEDY is the father of modern Western scholarship on the Islamic exact sciences. This collection focuses largely on mathematical astronomy, including planetary theory, longitudes and latitudes, planetary and lunar visibility, eclipses, spherical astronomy and timekeeping, and mathematical astrology and methodology. Another section covers astronomical instruments, including the astrolabe and equatoria. KING's book on Islamic astronomy, which he calls the queen of sciences, is a collection of his own articles ranging from the history of Islamic astronomy and astronomical tables to Egyptian astronomical observations and Indian astronomy in 14th-century Fez. King writes about astronomical timekeeping in places such as Turkey and Syria, the determination of the direction of Mecca, and Islamic multiplication tables. His interests and scholarship are wide-ranging and insightful.

HO's work on China is part of an enormous scholarly effort begun by Joseph Needham. A third of this book is devoted to astronomy. The first section gives a clear overview of the concepts of Chinese philosophy, as it is necessary to understand these if one is to understand the science. Ho discusses Chinese astronomy from its beginning, some say from as far back as the 3rd millennium BC, to its heyday in the Song dynasty, AD 960–1279. He devotes chapters to stars and constellations, calendrical science, and astronomical record-keeping. CULLEN's book is a translation and interpretation of an ancient astronomical and mathematical text, and is so far the only English language book that deals exclusively with Chinese astronomy.

There is also a growing body of scholarship on astronomy in the Americas. One of the leading scholars of this movement is AVENI. His 1982 book is one of the first in a long list of books and edited volumes combining archaeoastronomy and cultural anthropology, producing some really excellent work on the meaning of astronomy within its cultural context.

Finally, there are two books on areas that have received much less scholarly attention. NAKAYAMA's work on Japanese astronomy describes the Japanese adaptation of traditional Chinese astronomy and of European techniques and cosmologic schemes after the scientific revolution. HAYNES's et al.'s work on Australian astronomy includes a significant chapter on the Aboriginal people, and brings to light some studies on the southern sky that have been quite neglected in the study of the history of astronomy.

The astronomy of the non-European peoples covers the globe (and the heavens) and ranges over five millennia. These books are just the beginning of what we hope will be a rich field of study for future scholars.

HELAINE SELIN

See also Arabic Science; Astronomy: general works; Astrophysics

Astrophysics

Berendzen, Richard (ed.), *Education in and History of Modern Astronomy*, New York: Academy of Sciences, 1972

DeVorkin, David H., *The History of Modern Astronomy and Astrophysics: A Selected, Annotated Bibliography*, New York: Garland, 1982

Edge, David O. and Michael Mulkay, *Astronomy Transformed: The Emergence of Radio Astronomy in Britain*, New York: Wiley, 1976

Gingerich, Owen (ed.), *Astrophysics and Twentieth-Century Astronomy to 1950* (vol. 4 of *General History of Astronomy*), Cambridge and New York: Cambridge University Press, 1984

Hearnshaw, J.B., *The Analysis of Starlight: One Hundred and Fifty Years of Astronomical Spectroscopy*, Cambridge and New York: Cambridge University Press, 1986; revised edition, 1990

Herrmann, Dieter B., *The History of Astronomy from Herschel to Hertzsprung*, translated from the German and revised by Kevin Krisciunas, Cambridge and New York: Cambridge University Press, 1984 (original edition, 1975)

Hirsh, Richard F., *Glimpsing an Invisible Universe: The Emergence of X-Ray Astronomy*, Cambridge and New York: Cambridge University Press, 1983

Hufbauer, Karl, *Exploring the Sun: Solar Science since Galileo*, Baltimore: Johns Hopkins University Press, 1991

Hynek, J.A. (ed.), *Astrophysics: A Topical Symposium Commemorating the Fiftieth Anniversary of the Yerkes Observatory and a Half Century of Progress in Astrophysics*, New York: McGraw-Hill, 1951

Jarrell, Richard A., *The Cold Light of Dawn: A History of Canadian Astronomy*, Toronto: University of Toronto Press, 1988

Lang, Ken R. and Owen Gingerich, *A Sourcebook in Astronomy and Astrophysics 1900–1975*, Cambridge, Massachusetts: Harvard University Press, 1979

Meadows, A.J., *Science and Controversy: A Biography of Sir Norman Lockyer*, Cambridge, Massachusetts: MIT Press, 1972

Paul, Erich Robert, *The Milky Way Galaxy and Statistical Cosmology, 1890–1924*, Cambridge and New York: Cambridge University Press, 1993

Plotkin, Howard, "E.C. Pickering and the Endowment of Scientific Research in America, 1877–1918", *Isis*, 69 (1978): 44–57

Smith, Robert W., *The Expanding Universe, Astronomy's "Great Debate" 1900–1931*, Cambridge and New York: Cambridge University Press, 1982

Smith, Robert W. *et al.*, *The Space Telescope: A Study of NASA, Science, Technology, and Politics*, Cambridge and New York: Cambridge University Press, 1989

Struve, Otto and Velta Zebergs, *Astronomy of the 20th Century*, New York: Macmillan, 1962

The history of modern astrophysics (as distinct from the history of astronomy or cosmology) has received only moderate attention from historians. The only journal dedicated to the specialty is the *Journal for the History of Astronomy* (Science History Publications) which until recently confined most of its attention to earlier periods. Likewise, earlier volumes of *Vistas in Astronomy* (Pergamon) sometimes contained useful review essays. Beyond the few monographic studies available (such as Edge & Mulkay and Hufbauer), the best places to find reliable contributions to the history of astronomy and astrophysics remain those journals central to the history and sociology of science and technology, which have full peer review and competent historiographical apparatus.

The origin and development of astrophysics can take various forms depending on the definition of the field. It was most common at first to associate astrophysics with spectrum analysis and the symbiotic growth of spectral series theory, but it was also associated with the allied field of solar physics. MEADOWS is a biography of Norman Lockyer, the eminent 19th-century editor of *Nature* and an advocate of spectroscopy for studying the sun, while HERRMANN provides a history of the spectroscopical analysis of the sun in the late 19th and early 20th centuries. HUFBAUER associates the origin of astrophysics with an even larger conceptual arena, which includes the constitution, lifetimes, and sources of energy of the sun and stars. Although large portions of the contemporary specialties of galactic and extra-galactic structure, as well as cosmology, fall outside the boundaries of astrophysics today, their origins and development in the 19th and 20th centuries helped to inform the growth of astrophysics also. For this reason, PAUL's history of statistical astronomy and SMITH (1982), which deals with the cosmological question of the expanding universe, both examine subject matter that at the time was not confined to strict disciplinary boundaries.

The term "astrophysics" appeared in the 1860s, when spectrum analysis was applied to the study of the sun and stars. The earliest use of the term has been attributed to Johann Carl Friedrich Zöllner of Leipzig in 1865, but the Greenwich astronomer Edwin Dunkin introduced the "astro-physicist" to the public in 1869, as an astronomer who examined the spectra of celestial objects and compared these to spectra revealed by gases in terrestrial laboratories. The earliest elucidation of astrophysics in its contemporary form came in the 1880s, as the theoretical and observational study of the physical condition of the sidereal universe. As the definition broadened, of course, the roots of astrophysics moved further back into history, at least to Newton.

The specialty of astrophysics has changed as it has acquired new theoretical and observational tools from physics: spectrum analysis, photography, photoelectric photometry, radiometry, and colorimetry were all applied to astronomical practice in the late 19th century, as were interpretative skills from mechanics, optics, the kinetic theory of gases and thermodynamics, electromagnetism, atomic physics, quantum mechanics, nuclear physics, and particle physics in the 20th century. HUFBAUER explicitly discusses some of these changes, and has interpreted them as stages in the formation of a specialty. He has provided the most complete contextual historical analysis of the nature of 19th- and 20th-century astrophysics, and the citations to which he refers provide an extensive introduction to both the primary and secondary literature needed to grasp the magnitude and flavor of the specialty. More extensive bibliographical information can be found in DeVORKIN, an annotated bibliography of the main literature.

Astronomical summaries and chronicles are also useful, and among the best are STRUVE & ZEBERGS, an accessible introduction to the field, and HEARNSHAW, which provides an exhaustive subject-based review of the growth of astronomical spectroscopy throughout the 20th century. Neither source transcends the tendency to evaluate historical events in terms of modern standards. Compendia written by a combination of historians and astronomers include LANG & GINGERICH, which offers excerpts from seminal papers with extensive commentaries on their scientific significance. BERENDZEN's and GINGERICH's volumes are collections of essays by astronomers and historians covering the history of the field to 1950. Articles by Strömgren, Whitford, Menzel, Oort, and Friedman in Berendzen's collection, reveal how astronomers themselves view the intellectual growth of their discipline. HYNEK is an insightful collection of essays reviewing the state of the specialty in the mid-20th century, from the standpoint of the growth of conceptual tools and techniques and observational methods. It provides extensive review articles by astronomers introducing the various areas of astrophysics, and planetary and stellar astronomy that form the core of the discipline of modern astronomy. It also provides detailed information on the growth of astronomical instrumentation.

As Hufbauer, Herrmann, Edge & Mulkay, and others interested in specialty formation have demonstrated, the best way to examine the origin and development of astrophysics is to understand how its various progenitors coalesced as a hybrid specialty, and how its practitioners defined themselves and their work in the production of journals, institutions, and modes of practice – especially, in the case of astrophysics, by the introduction of new and sometimes unproven analytical and observational tools. EDGE & MULKAY provide critical insight into the development of an instrumental specialty (radio wave detectors) that has had a great impact on astrophysical practice, as have HIRSH (X-ray detection) and SMITH *et al.* (the Space Telescope).

At the turn of the 20th century and for several decades afterwards, astronomy was one of the most expensive of the physical sciences, even though it remained the smallest in institutional terms. The scale of the enterprise centering on some of its major institutions can be deduced from various sources, especially the career of George Ellery Hale and institutional studies of major observatories. The juxtaposition of

PLOTKIN, on the late 19th-century American astronomer, Henry Pickering, and Smith *et al.*, on the Space Telescope, provides an excellent case study of how patronage patterns changed drastically in astronomy between 1900 and the 1970s and 1980s. Meadow's study of the life of Norman Lockyer further illuminates patronage, politics, and practice in early Victorian astrophysics, while JARRELL provides excellent insight into patterns of Canadian patronage.

DAVID H. DeVORKIN

See also Astronomy: general works; Astronomy: non-European

Asylums

Browne, W.A.F., *What Asylums Were, Are, and Ought to Be*, Edinburgh: Adam and Charles Black, 1837; reprinted, New York: Arno Press, 1976

Burdett, Henry, *Hospitals and Asylums of the World*, 4 vols, London: J. and A. Churchill, 1891–93

Castel, Robert, *The Regulation of Madness: The Origins of Incarceration in France*, translated by W.D. Halls, Berkeley: University of California Press, 1988

Digby, Anne, *Madness, Morality, and Medicine: A Study of the York Retreat, 1796–1914*, Cambridge and New York: Cambridge University Press, 1985

Donnelly, Michael, *Managing the Mind: A Study of Medical Psychology in Early Nineteenth-Century Britain*, London and New York: Tavistock, 1983

Dwyer, Ellen, *Homes for the Mad: Life inside Two Nineteenth-Century Asylums*, New Brunswick, New Jersey: Rutgers University Press, 1987

Esquirol, J.-E.-D., *Des Établissements des aliénés en France et des moyens d'améliorer le sort de ces infortunés*, Paris: Huzard, 1819

Foucault, Michel, *Madness and Civilization: A History of Insanity in the Age of Reason* (abridged edition), translated from the French by Richard Howard, New York: Pantheon Books, 1965; London: Tavistock, 1967 (original edition, 1961)

Goffman, Erving, *Asylums: Essays on the Social Situation of Mental Patients and Other Inmates*, New York: Anchor, 1961

Goldstein, Jan, *Console and Classify: The French Psychiatric Profession in the Nineteenth Century*, Cambridge and New York: Cambridge University Press, 1987

Grob, Gerald N., *The Mad among Us: A History of the Care of America's Mentally Ill*, New York: Free Press, 1994

Jones, Kathleen, *Asylums and After: A Revised History of the Mental Health Services, from the Early 18th Century to the 1990s*, London: Athlone Press, 1993

Rothman, David J., *The Discovery of the Asylum: Social Order and Disorder in the New Republic*, Boston: Little Brown, 1971; revised edition, 1990

Scull, Andrew T., *The Most Solitary of Afflictions: Madness and Society in Britain, 1700–1900*, New Haven, Connecticut: Yale University Press, 1993

Taylor, Jeremy, *Hospital and Asylum Architecture in England, 1840–1914*, London: Mansell, 1991

Asylums, or specifically lunatic asylums, were the precursor of the modern mental hospital; they provided the institutional context, and the field of observation, in which psychiatry emerged as a medical speciality. Although the term was occasionally used in the 18th century, it was applied more characteristically to the new purpose-built institutions for the insane that were planned and constructed in the first part of the 19th century. What were sometimes called "model asylums" marked the beginnings of comprehensive social and medical provision for the mentally disordered.

Initially the term asylum carried a quite positive connotation. The French psychiatrist ESQUIROL urged, for instance, that the new institutions designed for the insane "should be given a specific name which arouses no painful associations"; hence "asile" or asylum. This was the attitude typical of a generation or more of reform-minded psychiatrists and lay advocates for the insane. The first histories of asylums came out of these reform circles, although they were less histories than partisan manifestos parading the virtues of model asylums. BROWNE chronicled the abuse and neglect lunatics had suffered before, by way of vindicating the refuge which the new asylums offered. "What asylums ought to be" was at once an appropriate, humane setting for the treatment and care of the insane, and a carefully contrived instrument of that treatment. The watchword was "moral treatment", which implied a new attention to the psychological, emotional, and intellectual needs of the insane; rhetorically, the term "moral" was opposed both to "medical" and to "mechanical" treatments. DONNELLY describes these latter: the routine round of purges and bleedings, and close physical restraint.

The reformers' optimism about the therapeutic potential of asylums turned out to be fairly short-lived. By the second half of the 19th century many psychiatrists had been disabused of their more optimistic hopes for the therapeutic asylum; by then, asylums were more likely to be described realistically as simply custodial or grimly institutional. Perhaps for that reason the asylum has been more often considered for its social welfare functions than for its medical or scientific significance. Tellingly, histories of psychiatry have tended to treat the asylum, if at all, as a peripheral or background topic; it has figured more consistently in histories of social administration and as a specialist topic for architectural historians. JONES and GROB provide straightforward institutional histories of mental health policies in, respectively, Britain and the US. BURDETT highlighted in an encyclopedic survey the principal design issues in the building of hospitals and asylums in the latter part of the 19th century, a task recently repeated and deepened by TAYLOR. DWYER provides an interesting documentary account of "life inside" two 19th-century American asylums.

In the last several decades, historians of psychiatry have become interested again in the early, optimistic phase of the asylum, and in the connection between the early asylums and the emergence of scientific psychiatry. FOUCAULT stimulated, as well as provoked, much of this interest. His history of Western reason's encounter with "unreason" treats the asylum only summarily, but it concludes with a powerful re-evaluation of the accomplishments of early 19th-century lunacy reformers. By contrast to the mythic image of the psychiatric reformer, Philippe Pinel, liberating insane inmates from their chains, Foucault characterizes the model asylum as a new "moral imprisonment" of the insane, an interpretation challenged head-on by DIGBY in her study of the famous Quaker model asylum, the Retreat at York.

A second spur to this recent work was the American sociologist GOFFMAN. In adopting the title *Asylums* as emblematic for the "total institution", Goffman tried to highlight certain organizational similarities among mental hospitals, monasteries, concentration camps, and other closed institutions, notwithstanding their quite different purposes. The effect of his analysis was to induce skepticism about the avowed therapeutic aim of the mental hospital, and indirectly to question the legitimacy of psychiatry's power and authority; the book also provoked the curiosity of historians and historical sociologists about the origins of therapeutic confinement. ROTHMAN likewise employs the term asylum in a broad sense, referring to a whole array of institutional responses (lunatic asylums, penitentiaries, reformatories, orphanages) to the problems presented by deviant and dependent groups in early 19th-century America. While not denying the philanthropy of individual psychiatrists, he argues that the rationales for confining the mentally disordered had perhaps less to do with their specific condition than with a general programme of institution-building, spurred by a sense of anxiety amid the "disorders" of Jacksonian America. SCULL, among others, criticizes the narrowly American focus of Rothman's argument, pointing out that the American developments were in part modelled on, and otherwise paralleled by, developments in Europe. Scull's own interpretation stresses the broader, generic process of capitalist industrialization as the driving force behind institutional confinement; the asylum in turn came to serve ideally as a means to "remodel [the lunatic] into something approximating the bourgeois ideal of the rational individual". CASTEL, a sociologist and one-time collaborator of Foucault, provides a similar interpretation of developments in France, sharply stressing the social control functions of the asylum and its role in reinforcing disciplinary norms. GOLDSTEIN also documents the public security aspect of the asylum, but focuses more particularly on its role as the social and professional base on which psychiatrists in France secured their power and authority. Her analysis provides perhaps the clearest account of the centrality of the asylum to the formation of modern professional psychiatry.

MICHAEL DONNELLY

See also Hospitals; Madness; Psychiatry

Atomic Theory

Bohr, Niels, *Atomic Theory and the Description of Nature*, Cambridge: Cambridge University Press, 1934

Boorse, Henry A. and Lloyd Motz (eds), *The World of the Atom*, 2 vols, New York: Basic Books, 1966

Boorse, Henry A., *The Atomic Scientists: A Biographical History*, New York: John Wiley, 1989

Gamow, George, *Mr Tompkins Explores the Atom*, New York: Macmillan, 1944; Cambridge: Cambridge University Press, 1945

Keller, Alex, *The Infancy of Atomic Physics: Hercules in His Cradle*, Oxford: Clarendon Press, and New York: Oxford University Press, 1983

Makin, Stephen, *Indifference Arguments*, Oxford and Cambridge, Massachusetts: Blackwell, 1993

Mellor, David P., *The Evolution of the Atomic Theory*, Amsterdam, London, and New York: Elsevier, 1971

Melsen, Andras Gerardio Maria van, *From Atomos to Atom: The History of the Concept Atom*, translated from the Dutch by Henry J. Koren, Pittsburgh: Duquesne University Press, 1952

Nye, Mary Jo (ed.), *The Question of the Atom: From the Karlsruhe Congress to the First Solvay Conference, 1860–1911: A Compilation of Primary Sources*, Los Angeles: Tomash, 1984

Rocke, Alan J., *Chemical Atomism in the Nineteenth Century: From Dalton to Cannizzaro*, Columbus: Ohio State University Press, 1984

Atomic theory has evolved through five distinct periods: first, the ancient philosophical discussions on the nature of reality; second, the recovery of classical thought during the Middle Ages and Renaissance; third, the rise of mechanical theories in the 17th and 18th centuries; fourth, the 19th-century debates between chemists and physicists; and, finally, the transition from atomic to nuclear theory early in the 20th century.

The early Greek philosophers wanted to know what reality was made of: was reality a single whole substance or was it composed of many parts? If a single substance, how did change occur? And if reality was made of many parts, how could there be an infinite number of such parts? Leucippus and Democritus, in the 5th century BC, proposed that reality was composed of a finite number of small indivisible (*atomos*) particles that moved in an otherwise empty space, for if a void was not postulated then the particles would have nowhere to move. These teachings, to which Epicurus later subscribed, were taken up by Lucretius in Rome in the 1st century BC. The writings of these early atomists are found in most surveys of atomic theory, as in Boorse and MELLOR. The logic of these early arguments is scrutinised in great philosophical detail by MAKIN.

In MELSEN one finds references not only to the early atomists, but also to Aristotle's discussion, in his *Physics*, of the theory of minima, or smallest entities, and their composition into various substances. Melsen then offers a rare survey of the medieval philosophical discussions of Aristotelian minima. While less discussed than his metaphysics, Aristotle's minima influenced Renaissance natural philosophy and empirical mechanist scientific theories, beginning with Giordano Bruno, a bridge figure between the second and third periods of the development of atomic theory.

BOORSE provides lively biographies of all the major figures in the story of atomic theory. Its encyclopedic survey of the modern period begins with Descartes, Galileo, Boyle, Leibniz and Newton, the latter marrying mathematics to philosophy and observation in order to produce mechanical theories of atomic movement. Further, all the key texts written on atomic theory, from ancient to modern, are contained in the equally large companion volume edited by BOORSE & MOTZ.

In the 18th century, chemists such as Antoine Lavoisier had noted the conservation of weight in chemical reactions and the constancy of various combining ratios of weights for particular elements. Discoveries such as these led to John Dalton's *New System of Chemical Philosophy* (1808), in which he proposed that atoms had the properties of chemical elements and that atoms of different elements had different, but regular, weights. Chemists dealt with molecules rather than individual atoms, a molecule being the smallest amount of matter that could take part in a chemical reaction, but which often consisted of two or more atoms. For the first half of the 19th century, the chemists' atom held sway, as ROCKE explains in great detail.

With an increasing amount of experimental data available, and with conflicting positions being taken up by both advocates of the chemical atom and advocates of the more simple physicists's atom, as well as by the anti-atomists who refused to regard the atom as something real, the debate was keen and constantly changing. Furthermore, thermodynamic theory suggested that the underlying reality of the universe was not matter but energy: nevertheless, atomism offered the possibility of a unified science and the holy grail of a causal, rather than statistical, explanation of everything. This crucial fourth phase of atomic theory has been documented by NYE, who offers a comprehensive collection of all the key papers in the development of modern atomic theory from 1860 to 1911, as well as providing an authoritative introduction to the issues at stake. Stanislao Cannizzaro proves to be a central figure in these discussions.

KELLER describes the origins of modern atomic physics. The discoveries of the electron by J.J. Thomson and of radioactivity by Pierre and Marie Curie focused further attention on the physicists' atom. Atomic spectra implied regular electron energy levels, but how could all this be explained? In 1901, Jean Perrin proposed a solar model of the atom. Thomson then suggested a plum-pudding model, with negative electrons being embedded in a positive mass. Thomson's model, however, was in conflict with many observations. New discoveries and theories followed in rapid succession: in 1904 Lorentz proposed that mass may vary with motion, an idea taken up the following year in the relativity theory of Einstein; in 1905 Einstein also introduced Planck's constant to solve the problem of the photoelectric effect; by 1909 Poincaré was able to reduce chemistry to physics by the identification of the physical with the chemical atom; finally, in 1911, Ernest Rutherford proved experimentally that the atom consisted of a large, positively-charged nucleus surrounded by relatively small, negatively-charged orbiting electrons.

But the modern atom made no sense: the negatively-charged electrons should give off radiation and spiral into the positively-charged nucleus, so what kept Rutherford's atom stable? Niels BOHR suggested in 1913 that there was a lower limit to continuity in nature, and hence that the electrons were not allowed to collapse below energy levels determined by a ratio of Planck's constant, the quantum of action: in this way, stability was established for Rutherford's atom and quantum theory conceived. Bohr's popular essays on this topic enjoy classic status and introduce key ideas of quantum theory, including Heisenberg's contribution in 1925, while GAMOW offers an intimate, entertaining, and more accessible history of these developments.

After two and a half millennia, the philosophers' atom, moving in a void, has been replaced by the physicists' atom, in which space and matter are relativistically connected. Nuclear experiments would identify hundreds of sub-atomic particles, all possibly formed from various combinations of quarks, so that the elusive quark now became the new atom.

JOHN HONNER

See also Atomism

Atomic Weapons

Hershberg, James G., *James B. Conant: Harvard to Hiroshima and the Making of the Nuclear Age*, New York: Knopf, 1993

Hoddeson, Lillian *et al.*, *Critical Assembly: A Technical History of Los Alamos during the Oppenheimer Years, 1943–1945*, Cambridge and New York: Cambridge University Press, 1993

Holloway, David, *Stalin and the Bomb: The Soviet Union and Atomic Energy, 1939–1956*, New Haven, Connecticut, and London: Yale University Press, 1994

Hounshell, David A. and John Kenly Smith, Jr, *Science and Corporate Strategy: DuPont R & D, 1902–1980*, Cambridge and New York: Cambridge University Press, 1988

Lindee, M. Susan, *Suffering Made Real: American Science and the Survivors at Hiroshima*, Chicago: University of Chicago Press, 1994

Rhodes, Richard, *The Making of the Atomic Bomb*, New York: Simon and Schuster, 1986; Harmondsworth: Penguin, 1988

Sherwin, Martin J., *A World Destroyed: The Atomic Bomb and the Grand Alliance*, New York: Knopf, 1975; revised edition as *A World Destroyed: Hiroshima and the Origins of the Arms Race*, New York: Vintage, 1987

Walker, Mark, *German National Socialism and the Quest for Nuclear Power, 1939–1949*, Cambridge and New York: Cambridge University Press, 1989

More than any other scientific development in the 20th century, or perhaps in any century, the creation and use of atomic weapons in World War II have transformed the relationship of science to society. Not only has science been harnessed by the state in a manner infinitely more destructive than the extensive militarization of science before the advent of atomic weapons, but the debates and controversies within societies about the extent and prevalence of atomic weapons have generated new societal controls over scientific work. The history of the development of atomic weapons provides unique insights into the often fraught relations between 20th-century science and postwar society.

RHODES offers a broad survey in an accessible form, with his history of the American development of nuclear fission weapons at Los Alamos, New Mexico, and their use against Japanese civilians at Hiroshima and Nagasaki. He draws heavily on secondary literature to paint a picture of the project as a conflict between the internationalist ideals of scientists and the nationalist "death machine" that militarizes scientists' discoveries in a conscious attempt to subvert their ideals. As an introduction to the physics and politics of developing the bomb, this book is an excellent resource.

There is a series of more detailed studies on different aspects of the project. HODDESON *et al.* provide a highly technical history of the scientific work at Los Alamos. Based on archival documents, they trace the various scientific problems posed by the construction of a gun-type uranium bomb, and the more challenging implosion plutonium bomb. The emphasis throughout this book is on the bomb as "science", and not just the application of prewar physics. In this emphasis on the active and creative excitement of Los Alamos physicists, however, some of the destructive and moral implications of the weapons are lost.

HOUNSHELL & SMITH provide a different viewpoint of the work at Los Alamos. Instead of focusing on the scientists and their work on the Manhattan Project, they place the development of the bomb and the extensive uranium purification and plutonium production plants in the context of industrial history. Specifically, while tracing the history of DuPont as a giant of the American chemical industry, they devote considerable attention to the *engineering* of the bomb by industrial chemical engineers. As a complement to Hoddeson *et al.* this work is useful for showing how the Los Alamos project was directed from the start to be mass-produced as a tool of hostile statecraft.

As yet another aspect of the history of atomic weapons, SHERWIN discusses the complicated diplomatic political history surrounding the decision to use the bomb and the explicit denial of arms control arrangements with the Soviet Union. Sherwin concentrates on the decisions by president Truman and secretary of state Stimson about the choice of a target site, and the fear of the Soviet Union that motivated so many American decisions. The political picture presented is one of little doubt that the bomb would be used against Japan, and that the rejection of scientists' plans for arms control was a foregone conclusion. This political dimension nicely supplements the technical and engineering approaches of Hoddeson *et al* and Hounshell & Smith.

A biographical approach to similar material is offered by HERSHBERG in his biography of James B. Conant, a former president of Harvard and an atomic scientist and policymaker. Conant's career is traced through his early work mobilizing scientists for the bomb effort, through the early postwar attempts to control the bomb, and then to his outspoken opposition to an acceleration of the arms race. Hershberg's account reminds historians that the course of the history of atomic weapons was determined by individuals, and by using Conant as a tool to trace the contours of both science and diplomacy, Hershberg allows the personal side of atomic weapons to emerge.

For all the extensive study of the American development of atomic weapons, military nuclear projects in other nations have been relatively understudied, with some excellent exceptions. WALKER's concise and detailed history of the German uranium project traces the Nazi decision to begin a nuclear project, and then the fairly rapid rejection of nuclear bombs as unfeasible (a decision made by the German military), and a refocusing of war work on nuclear reactors to power military vehicles. Given that the prospect of a German bomb was a major incentive for the American Manhattan Project, Walker's study provides an illuminating insight into science-state relations under the Third Reich, and forcefully argues for the remoteness of a Nazi nuclear threat.

HOLLOWAY's magisterial study of the Soviet bomb is, on the other hand, a success story. He not only outlines the early attempts to initiate a nuclear project, begun in earnest only after Stalin saw the end of World War II approaching, but also documents the massive atomic "empire" built by prisoners and marshaled by Lavrenti Beria, head of the secret police. The book also extensively explores the importance of atomic espionage and the suitability of the Stalinist command economy in facilitating the Soviet atomic and hydrogen bombs. Diplomacy and the origins of civilian nuclear energy are also carefully presented.

A word should be said about the impact of atomic weapons on other sciences. It is widely acknowledged that the spectacular success of the Manhattan Project provided new political support and massive funds for the physical sciences. LINDEE's work on the American attempts to study the Japanese survivors of the bombings of Hiroshima and Nagasaki highlights how much of the new sciences of human genetics and population biology also rode in on atomic coattails. Her archival work on the American side of the project is regrettably not complemented by adequate study of Japanese perceptions of this work, but her integration of "big biology" into the atomic age of big physics was much overdue.

Even within the localized history of atomic weapons during and immediately after World War II, one can detect the complicated intertwining of science and society. As the history of atomic weapons is expanded in time and depth, the evidence of the relationship is broadened for all cultures and states. This feature makes this history an exceptionally good guide to social aspects of the history of science.

MICHAEL D. GORDIN

Atomism

Bailey, Cyril, *The Greek Atomists and Epicurus: A Study*, Oxford: Clarendon Press, 1928; New York: Russell and Russell, 1964

Brush, Stephen G., *Statistical Physics and the Atomic Theory of Matter: From Boyle and Newton to Landau and Onsager*, Princeton, New Jersey: Princeton University Press, 1983

Emerton, Norma E., *The Scientific Reinterpretation of Form*, Ithaca, New York: Cornell University Press, 1984

Freudenthal, Gideon, *Atom and Individual in the Age of Newton: On the Genesis of the Mechanistic World View*, Dordrecht and Boston: Reidel, 1986

Furley, David J., *Two Studies in the Greek Atomists: Study I, Indivisible Magnitudes; Study II, Aristotle and Epicurus on Voluntary Action*, Princeton, New Jersey: Princeton University Press, 1967

Furley, David J., *The Greek Cosmologists*, vol. 1: *The Formation of the Atomic Theory and Its Earliest Critics*, Cambridge and New York: Cambridge University Press, 1987

Kargon, Robert Hugh, *Atomism in England from Hariot to Newton*, Oxford: Clarendon Press, 1966

Knight, David M., *Atoms and Elements: A Study of Theories of Matter in England in the Nineteenth Century*, London: Hutchinson, 1967

Lasswitz, Kurd, *Geschichte der Atomistik, vom Mittelalter bis Newton*, 2 vols, Hamburg and Leipzig: Leopold Voss, 1890; reprinted, Hildesheim: Olms, 1963

Melsen, Andras Gerardus Maria van, *From Atomos to Atom: The History of the Concept Atom*, translated from the Dutch by Henry J. Koren, Pittsburgh: Duquesne University Press, 1952

O'Brien, D., *Theories of Weight in the Ancient World: Four Essays on Democritus, Plato and Aristotle: A Study in the Development of Ideas*, vol. 1: *Democritus, Weight and Size: An Exercise in the Reconstruction of Early Greek Philosophy*, Leiden: E.J. Brill, 1981

Pabst, Bernhard, *Atomtheorien des lateinischen Mittelalters*, Darmstadt: Wissenschaftliche Buchgesellschaft, 1994

Pyle, Andrew, *Atomism and Its Critics: Problem Areas Associated with the Development of the Atomic Theory of Matter from Democritus to Newton*, Bristol: Thoemmes Press, 1995

Rocke, Alan J., *Chemical Atomism in the Nineteenth Century: From Dalton to Cannizzaro*, Columbus: Ohio State University Press, 1984

Schofield, Robert E., *Mechanism and Materialism: British Natural Philosophy in an Age of Reason*, Princeton, New Jersey: Princeton University Press, 1970

Scott, Wilson L., *The Conflict Between Atomism and Conservation Theory, 1644–1860*, London: Macdonald, and New York: Elsevier, 1970

Thackray, Arnold, *Atoms and Powers: An Essay on Newtonian Matter-Theory and the Development of Chemistry*, Cambridge, Massachusetts: Harvard University Press, and London: Oxford University Press, 1970

Atomism was first propounded in the ancient world by a number of pre-Socratic Greek thinkers and can be said to have had a continuous history since then. Modern physical sciences are based on what is essentially an atomistic view of matter, although there are a number of crucial differences between ancient beliefs and contemporary theory. Most obviously, of course, atoms are no longer held to be indivisible. This is hardly a new modification of the ancient theory, however. Historically, there is a closely associated but separate tradition of what is usually called corpuscularianism, which explains physical phenomena in essentially atomistic terms, but which denies, or remains noncommittal about, the indivisibility of matter. Interparticulate void spaces were another distinguishing feature of ancient atomist theorising, but a number of thinkers have propounded systems that, while atomist, or corpuscularian, were also plenist. This survey does not confine itself to the history of atomism in the strict sense, but includes books that are concerned, either partly or entirely, with corpuscularian traditions. Accordingly, this survey, like the books it discusses, uses the term atomism in a loose sense, to refer to all particulate or corpuscularian theories of matter.

There are a number of great names in the history of science who played a major role in the history of atomism, but, because of limitations on space, the literature on these individual thinkers, some of it very important, has reluctantly been excluded in favour of more general surveys of the subject.

MELSEN provides the only survey that attempts to cover the history of atomism from its ancient origins to the 20th century. The author sees this history as falling into two distinct phases, a philosophical and a scientific phase, but this seems to be an idiosyncratic view prompted by the author's concern to defend pre-modern speculations about atoms as being concerned with problems that are beyond empirical science. Beginning, of course, with an outline of ancient Greek theories, Melsen then discusses the fortune of atomism during the Middle Ages and the Renaissance, before considering the new success of atomism in the 17th century. Although Melsen does well to recognise the importance of the Aristotelian tradition of *minima naturalia* (a belief that, although matter is infinitely divisible, in practical terms there are natural minima of substances that take place in chemical and physical operations) throughout the Middle Ages and Renaissance in keeping alive the notion of corpuscularianism, much of what he says is incomplete, or now out of date. In particular he emphasizes the role of the chemical *minima* tradition at the expense of the Renaissance revival of Epicureanism, and the more mathematical concerns of early mechanical philosophers such as Galileo, and Descartes. In keeping with his chemical orientation, Melsen's study of post-Newtonian developments concentrates on John Dalton and the development of the periodic system of the elements. Only when dealing with the 20th century does he pay sufficient attention to developments beyond chemistry.

Most other books on atomism focus on a smaller part of the picture (even though some of them are longer than Melsen's comprehensive study). We will consider these in a roughly chronological order of focus.

BAILEY's study of *The Greek Atomists and Epicurus* provides a still useful survey of the theories of Leucippus, Democritus and Epicurus, and the philosophical problems that they hoped to solve, although more recent commentators seem to agree that he is more reliable on Epicurus than on the pre-Socratic atomists. FURLEY (1987) also considers the background to the origins of atomism in the thought of Leucippus and Democritus, but finishes with a consideration of the earliest critiques of atomism, principally those of Plato and Aristotle. Furley sees atomism as the major representative of a particular world view, in which physical systems were seen as mechanistic and fundamentally inanimate, as opposed to the more animated, or organic, systems favoured by Plato, Aristotle, and the Stoics. The world view of the atomists was, according to Furley, fundamentally opposed to the teleological explanations that dominated the opposing world-view.

FURLEY (1967) and O'BRIEN are concerned with specific, but crucially important, aspects of ancient atomism. Furley's first study seeks to understand precisely what the ancient atomists meant by saying that a body was indivisible, and to discover the nature of what Epicurus referred to as the "minimal parts" of the indivisible atoms. His second study is concerned with the problem of the operation of the will in Epicurus, and the role of the swerve of the atoms, postulated by Epicurus, in solving this problem. O'Brien provides an extremely ambitious, but highly convincing account of the concept of "weight" in the atomic theory of Democritus and its role in explaining the motions of atoms. O'Brien believes that all previous attempts to understand the Democritean theory have been affected by the adverse criticisms of Aristotle.

LASSWITZ provides a classic study of the fortunes of atomism from the early Church Fathers, to Leibniz and Newton. A massive work of scholarship, *Geschichte der Atomistik* was the first account which, in spite of its title, took as its theme all corpuscularian traditions. Accordingly, it includes discussions of the Aristotelian *minima naturalia* tradition, the occasionalist-inspired discontinuous space, time and motion of the Islamic Mutakallimun thinkers, the medieval mathematical discussions of continuity, Renaissance discussions of the nature of elements, early modern theories of vibration, and of attraction, and the role of atomist conceptions of nature in the development of the mechanical philosophy and dynamic theory. In addition, it includes detailed surveys of the beliefs of individual thinkers.

PYLE covers much of the same ground as Lasswitz, though with a greatly reduced cast of characters, and with a somewhat narrower focus. Pyle is primarily concerned to re-consider the philosophical arguments raised by atomist notions such as indivisibility, the possibility of void space, and the nature of forms and qualities. Taking one of these major subject areas in turn, he studies the principal arguments that were raised about it during each of three chronological periods: classical antiquity, the Middle Ages and the Renaissance, and the 17th century. It is an indication of his primary concern with philosophical argument that he is content to provide the historical context for the issues he discusses from secondary sources.

The Middle Ages has usually been seen as a period when atomism all but disappeared, only to be revived in the Renaissance. PABST provides a corrective to this picture, showing that there was a continuity of corpuscular speculation throughout the Middle Ages, which differed markedly from ancient Greek theories, and which reached its greatest influence in the 12th century. With the triumph of the anti-atomistic Aristotelian philosophy by the end of this century, atomism declined in influence, winning only a handful of supporters throughout the 13th and 14th centuries.

EMERTON's study of the concept of form from the Middle Ages to the 18th century has much to say about the development of corpuscularian ideas. The standard Aristotelian view, known as hylomorphism, saw the body as an inseparable combination of matter and form. The substantial form of a table was the form that gave the requisite amount of matter its identity as a particular table. This is incompatible with the atomist view, in which tables, and all other bodies, are made up of countless invisible particles of matter that have their own individual forms. Emerton provides a careful and detailed account of the transformation of theories of form, which considers changes in chemical as well as physical traditions, and also includes a detailed consideration of early theories of crystallography.

The most useful survey of the development of atomism in 17th-century England is still to be found in KARGON. Decrying the "ahistorical" treatment provided by earlier writers on atomism (he only mentions Lasswitz by name), Kargon's professed aim is to take account of the "social, political, theological and personal, as well as scientific" concerns of his subjects. What this amounts to, however, is little more than a consideration of the religious implications of atomism, and the response of 17th-century thinkers to the perceived atheism of atomism.

For a real consideration of the socio-political background to atomism, consider FREUDENTHAL. He sets out by trying to understand the reasons for the fundamental rift in ideas on space as found in the thought of Newton (who insisted on the reality of an absolute space), and of Leibniz (who maintained that space was merely a relational concept). What follows, however, is a fascinating and well argued excursion into 17th-century political and social theory, and its effect on natural philosophy. Freudenthal's principal aim is to show that differing social relations can give rise to differing assumptions about correct procedures and ways of thinking, and so can lead to the establishment of different scientific theories. The fact that Newton lived in a society that had carried out the first bourgeois revolution caused him to have views about social relations that were significantly different from his Continental contemporary, Leibniz. According to Freudenthal, Newton's careful distinction between *essential* properties of bodies, like inertia, and so-called *universal* properties, like gravitation, echoed contemporary political theory. A single particle of matter in space could not have gravitational attraction, but it could have inertia, so inertia could be said to be essential, while gravitation has to be designated as universal. Freudenthal links this way of thinking, not found in Leibniz, to contemporary efforts in English civil philosophy to understand the nature of society in terms of the essential, pre-social, qualities of individual members of the society. In this way, contemporary political theory, stemming from political upheavals and the need to establish a basis for social stability, can be said to have affected the development of English science. Atoms were equated with political individuals, with their own essential qualities, and this suggested a specific view of a particle's qualities and of the nature of space. Freudenthal's claims have had very little impact on other studies of the 17th century in the history of science and have been subjected to rigorous criticism. Nevertheless, the book can be recommended as an ambitious, engaging and extremely thoughtful exercise in the historical sociology of scientific knowledge.

Thackray and Schofield provide the major studies on 18th-century atomism in Britain. THACKRAY shows how the Newtonian view of matter, which he characterizes in terms of belief in interparticulate forces and the "inertial homogeneity" of matter, played a major role in the development of chemistry throughout the century. Thackray is also aware of the importance of the institutional setting for the development of these ideas. SCHOFIELD covers much of the same territory, but he discerns differences in theorizing and practice that he takes to be the result of two separable traditions stemming from Newton's influence: one that relies on Newton's belief in particles endowed with various powers or forces capable of acting at a distance, and another that prefers to explain things in terms of refinements of Newton's aether theory. Here again, the author pays careful attention to the theological and institutional context of these ideas.

The crucial importance of corpuscular theories of matter, developed in the mechanical philosophy, to the development of modern theories of energy, work, heat, and other aspects of dynamics and thermodynamics is shown in SCOTT. Concentrating on developments in physical theory, Scott details the way in which attempts to understand what happens when atomic particles collide led to a host of new developments in physics.

Nineteenth-century developments are covered, particularly with regard to problems in chemistry, in KNIGHT and ROCKE. Both begin, after brief considerations of what went before, with the innovations of John Dalton and the problems arising from his theories. Knight succeeds in showing that 19th-century thinkers were deeply divided over the validity of atomic theory, many believing that the existence or otherwise of atoms was a metaphysical issue, scarcely relevant to the practice of science. Dalton's atomic theory could be seen merely as a theory about the combination of elements in definite proportions. Knight also considers the role of disciplinary divisions between chemists and physicists that helped to maintain a sceptical attitude toward the reality of atoms until about 1870, when physicists began to recognise that chemistry could be reduced to physics, and in particular to the second law of thermodynamics. Rocke concentrates on the work of chemists. Although recognising the contemporary scepticism towards atomism, Rocke considers the ways in which atomistic ways of thinking were adopted by research chemists during the period. Most chemists, in spite of professed scepticism, Rocke claims, tended to assume the existence of minimal parts in chemical operations. Rocke's story involves the history of stoichiometry – the development of the concepts of atomic weight and valency – and the kinetic theory of gases, but it also has much to say on the contemporary development of organic chemistry and its role in the establishment of a chemical atomic theory.

Although BRUSH invokes in his title the names of Boyle and Newton, his study is essentially concerned with the 20th-century development of quantum theory. Beginning with a survey chapter on the history of the kinetic theory of gases, Brush goes on to show the transition from these ideas into quantum theory; for example, by arguing for the role of concepts of the irreversibility and randomness of atomic motions in the formulation of Heisenberg's uncertainty principle. As well as providing a major study of the development of the Bohr model of the atom, and ideas about interatomic forces and chemical bonds, Brush also discusses the philosophical implications of a statistically-based mechanical theory, in which macroscopic behaviour is reduced to microscopic behaviour, which can only be understood in statistical terms.

The literature on the history of quantum theory is extensive, and developments in atomic and sub-atomic physics form a major part of that literature. But, given the enormous conceptual and contextual differences between modern particle physics and earlier corpuscularian speculations, it might be stretching notions of historical continuity too far to include them here, rather than under the heading of quantum theory.

JOHN HENRY

See also Atomic Theory; Quantum Theory

Australia and New Zealand

Fellows of the Australian Academy of Technological Sciences and Engineering, *Technology in Australia 1788–1988: A Condensed History of Australian Technological Innovation and Adaptation during the First Two Hundred Years*, Melbourne: Australian Academy of Technological Sciences and Engineering, 1988

Finney, C.M., *Paradise Revealed: Natural History in Nineteenth-Century Australia*, Melbourne: Museum of Victoria, 1993

Fleming, C.A., *Science, Settlers and Scholars: The Centennial History of the Royal Society of New Zealand*, Wellington: Royal Society of New Zealand, 1987

Home, R.W. (ed.), *Australian Science in the Making*, Melbourne, Cambridge and New York: Cambridge University Press/Australian Academy of Science, 1988

Home, R.W. and Sally Gregory Kohlstedt (eds), *International Science and National Scientific Identity: Australia Between Britain and America*, Dordrecht and Boston: Kluwer, 1991

MacLeod, Roy (ed.), *The Commonwealth of Science: ANZAAS and the Scientific Enterprise in Australasia, 1888–1988*, Melbourne and New York: Oxford University Press, 1988

Mellor, D.P., *The Role of Science and Industry*, in *Australia in the War of 1939–1945* series, Canberra: Australian War Memorial, 1958

Moyal, Ann, *"A Bright and Savage Land": Scientists in Colonial Australia*, Sydney: Collins, 1986

Schedvin, C.B., *Shaping Science and Industry: A History of Australia's Council for Scientific and Industrial Research, 1926–49*, Sydney and Boston: Allen and Unwin, 1987

Australia and New Zealand are predominantly (and in the case of Australia overwhelmingly) immigrant communities. From the arrival of the first British settlers in Australia in 1788, the indigenous peoples were devastated by European diseases and suppressed by force of European arms. Kept on the margins of the new societies established by the invaders, they, and the complex knowledge systems they had developed concerning the natural world, played effectively no role in the subsequent evolution of Western-style science in either country. These knowledge systems emerged within wholly non-literary cultures and so it is impossible to reconstruct their histories; the essay by Hiatt and Jones in HOME is a pioneering attempt, within the Australian context, to establish some generalizations about the knowledge systems themselves.

The recoverable history of science in Australasia is thus the history of Western science since European settlement. Long treated as peripheral to mainstream developments in the history of science, its systematic study has in recent years attracted wider interest, only partly as a result of a growing engagement by Australians and New Zealanders with all aspects of their respective national histories. In addition, historians of science, concerned with the changing nature of scientific practice, have begun looking to comparative studies in different locales, while a sharpened post-colonial sensibility has prompted renewed attention to the historical role played by science in the establishment of Western imperialist hegemonies. However, this wider consciousness remains largely confined to the journal literature; all the works discussed here address the history of science in Australia or New Zealand for its own sake, rather than for comparative or critical purposes.

Most of the works discussed relate to Australia, since there have been very few book-length studies of the history of science in New Zealand. FLEMING's work is nominally a history of a single institution, the Royal Society of New Zealand, but the Society and its predecessors have always occupied a central role in that nation's science and his book comes closest to a general survey. The approach adopted is descriptive rather than analytical.

Western science first came to the south-west Pacific with explorers such as James Cook, and afterwards with the early European settlers as part of their cultural baggage. Attempts to understand an unfamiliar environment were long perplexed by a Eurocentric world-view. Meanwhile, the peculiarities of Australasian natural forms had a profound impact on European thinking, and Australia and New Zealand long served as quarries for European science. Until relatively recently, both countries remained culturally bound to Britain and their science closely linked to, and in various ways dependent on, British scientific institutions. MOYAL's beautifully illustrated survey of the development of science in Australia in the 19th century, FINNEY's account of the growth of Australian scientific institutions during the same period, and the collection of essays edited by HOME, all have as a major theme the gradual erosion of this British dominance and the emergence of a self-sustaining Australian scientific community able to command authority comparable to that of the scientific heartland of western Europe.

A second collection of essays, edited by HOME & KOHLSTEDT, also addresses the issue of shifting authority in science, arguing paradoxically, on the basis of Australian case studies, that as scientists of an emerging nation become less dependent on those of a previously dominant metropolitan centre, far from becoming independent, they become increasingly embedded within international disciplinary networks. The converse of dependence in science proves to be not independence but interdependence; instead of authority being attributed automatically to the metropolitan centre, scientific participation and leadership become decentralized – not, however, all at once, but in different scientific fields at different rates.

The settlements in Australia and New Zealand were widely separated and for a long time the number of scientists active in any one settlement was very small. The resulting isolation, not only from European science but even from colleagues in the other settlements, has always been a significant factor in Australasian scientific life, and perhaps accounts for some of its most characteristic features. The regular congresses of the Australasian Association for the Advancement of Science (later ANZAAS), following its formation in 1888, quickly became the highlight of the region's scientific calendar, precisely because they provided opportunities for scientists in the different settlements to exchange ideas. In the volume of essays edited by MacLEOD for the Association's centenary, its history serves as a lens through which the work of the growing scientific communities of Australasia is surveyed.

Much of that growth resulted from the Australian and New Zealand governments' investment in science and the creation, in the 1920s, of the Council for Scientific and Industrial Research (CSIR) and the Department of Scientific and Industrial Research (DSIR) respectively. SCHEDVIN's history of CSIR, up to its reconstruction in 1949 and re-naming as CSIRO, is a persuasive account of the reasons for its creation, its pre-war preoccupation with agricultural research, and the impact of World War II and its aftermath on its activities.

The growth and diversification of the Australian scientific community during the 20th century is also a major theme of Home. Case studies covering biomedical research, optical and radio astronomy, and plant introduction, illustrate how and why this occurred in a number of widely differing contexts. As in Schedvin's study, World War II is seen as a major turning point.

Complementing this emphasis on the impact of World War II on the Australian scientific community, MELLOR details the vital contributions of that community to Australia's war effort during these years, when what had been a largely rural economy for the first time developed an extensive manufacturing capability. *Technology in Australia 1788–1988* offers a comprehensive account of Australian technological achievement over a much wider time span, with individual chapters written by experts in the respective technological fields.

R.W. HOME

Automobiles

Barker, Ronald and Anthony Harding (eds), *Automobile Design: Twelve Great Designers and Their Work*, Cambridge, Massachusetts: Bentley, 1971; 2nd edition, Warrendale, Pennsylvania: Society of Automotive Engineers, 1992

Bloomfield, Gerald, *The World Automotive Industry*, Newton Abbot, Devon: David and Charles, 1978

Day, John, *The Bosch Book of the Motor Car: Its Evolution and Engineering Development*, New York: St Martin's Press, 1976

Flink, James J., *The Automobile Age*, Cambridge, Massachusetts: MIT Press, 1988

Newcomb, T.P. and R.T. Spurr, *A Technical History of the Motor Car*, Bristol: Hilger, 1989

Sachs, Wolfgang, *For Love of the Automobile: Looking Back into the History of Our Desires*, translated from the German by Don Reneau, Berkeley: University of California Press, 1992

Scharff, Virginia, *Taking the Wheel: Women and the Coming of the Motor Age*, New York: Free Press, 1991

Ware, Michael E., *Making of the Motor Car, 1895–1930*, Buxton, Derbyshire: Moorland, 1976

Since the automobile as a technological and cultural phenomenon is still relatively new to mankind, most retrospective writing on the subject has appeared only in the past 20 years. The literature can be roughly divided into three types: popular, illustrated "coffee table" books; technical works appealing to engineers; and contextual approaches by social historians of technology.

Popular automotive history books first appeared in the 1950s and 1960s, and increased in number with the growth in collectors of antique cars. The genre matured in the 1970s, and numbers peaked in the second half of the decade, seemingly a reflection of widespread contemplation of the automobile's past and future after the oil crisis of 1974. Most of these books combine colour illustrations with photographs in an entertaining, popular format that also facilitates the learning process, but some have more educational value than others. The best open with descriptions of the steam road vehicles of the 18th and 19th centuries, and conclude with a survey of the latest prototypes and the impact of our car culture on the environment.

DAY made excellent use of the popular format, in his effort to impart the evolution and engineering development of the automobile in a way that both old and young readers can understand and enjoy. Unlike other popular books, the history of the car is conveyed through the technological evolution of its component parts, rather than by make and model. This approach provides much more detailed information on a wider selection of topics, and its encyclopedic arrangement makes for quick reference.

A more conventional approach to the history of automotive technology is provided by NEWCOMB & SPURR. The emphasis on text is supplemented by technical drawings of a uniform style. As is often the case with technical histories, the section dealing with various systems and components received more attention to detail and accuracy than the general synopsis. Readers, therefore, should be prepared to question the general narrative; for example, the authors perpetuate the myth that Eli Whitney successfully introduced interchangeable parts manufacture into the American small arms industry, even though it was proven more than 30 years ago that Whitney's muskets were never fully interchangeable.

A long-standing debate in the history of technology pits the idea of the hero-inventor, who revolutionizes a particular technology, against an evolutionary theory, that has each inventor "standing on the shoulders" of his predecessors. The collection of essays edited by BARKER & HARDING is interesting in this respect, because it shows how the individual nature of 12 successful automobile designers affected the vehicles they built. One can easily see, for example, how Henry Leland's perfectionism and Colin Chapman's self-confidence were reflected in the design of, respectively, Cadillac and Lotus cars.

WARE relies on period photographs, accompanied by short descriptions, to tell the story of automobile construction in the years before 1930. It is an uncommon approach, but his effort is highly rewarding and makes a valuable contribution to the understanding of vintage automobile design and construction. Ware's photographs depict processes that are not explained elsewhere; for example, how a wire-wheel assembler blows into a pitch pipe as he "tunes" the spokes to the correct tension. The reader can not only follow the complete construction process from start to finish visually, but compare how it was approached in different sized factories. Unfortunately, only British factories are depicted, but the introduction of mass production methods in the United States that began with the Ford Model T has been discussed in numerous other sources.

Although BLOOMFIELD did not write a historical work but a contemporary economic study, his book remains a valu-

able source for those studying automotive history, or the workings of the international automotive industry. The first half of the book explains production processes, marketing, economics, and management. The succeeding chapters describe the industry as it exists on different continents, and the final two discuss the international corporation, and trades and trends. Each chapter has a historical component and most of the graphs, charts and tables illustrate the changes in the automotive industry over several decades, providing historical information that is difficult or impossible to find in other secondary sources.

FLINK is representative of the new social historians who have written about the automobile in recent years. His approach is comparative, providing perspectives on the American automobile culture, and explaining developments elsewhere that have affected it. He believes that history is the product of human choice, made by the decisions of humans, rather than the inevitable result of impersonal forces, cultural or otherwise – thus his work deals with motives and personalities as well as behaviour and statistics. The following six general themes are discussed: the evolution of technology; mass-production techniques; business organization and marketing strategies; the diffusion of roads and the creation of a mass-market; the decline of mass transit; and the transformation of American life and institutions by mass automobility. He concludes that the automobile age ended in the early 1970s, and that the automobile has not been a historically progressive force for change in American civilization since at least the 1960s.

SACHS's look at the history of motoring from a German perspective is a refreshing and interesting complement to the more common view of car culture in the United States. Like Flink, Sachs feels that the age of the automobile has come and gone, but takes a more impassioned and pessimistic view, describing the history of the automobile as a morality play on the withering of a historical project. His book then, as he describes, is a eulogy to the bygone excitement caused by the automobile. He questions the notion of progress and argues that newer, less harmful desires are replacing our love for the automobile, and that those who still cannot tear themselves from the wheel will suffer from a bad conscience. Concluding that our car culture has developed to the point where those without automobiles are at a disadvantage, Sachs suggests we implement policies that aim to dismantle the political and economic assumptions of a society based on the automobile.

Believing in the importance of gender as a category of historical analysis, SCHARFF, herself a feminist scholar, joins other historians of technology who take the position that technology is "more than the product of pure rationality". Viewing the first three decades of motoring, she explains how women not only influenced the evolution of the automobile and the growth of car culture, but were also emancipated by it, as they moved from the passenger to the driver's seat.

BRIAN R. REYNOLDS

Avogadro, Amedeo 1776–1856

Italian physical chemist

Avogadro, Amadeo, *Opere scelte di Amedeo Avogadro publicata dalla R. Accademia della scienze di Torino*, Turin, 1911

Bonner, Joan Kirkwood, *Amedeo Avogadro: A Reassessment of His Research and Its Place in Early Nineteenth Century Science*, dissertation, Johns Hopkins University, Baltimore, 1974

Brooke, John H., "Avogadro's Hypothesis and Its Fate: A Case-study in the Failure of Case-studies", *History of Science*, 19 (1981): 235–73

Bykov, G.V., *Amedeo Avogadro: Ocherk zhizni i deiatel'nosti*, Moscow: Nauka, 1970

Fisher, Nicholas W., "Avogadro, the Chemists, and Historians of Chemistry", *History of Science*, 20 (1982): 77–102, 212–31

Morselli, Mario A., *Amedeo Avogadro: A Scientific Biography*, Dordrecht and Boston: Reidel, 1984

Rocke, Alan J,. *Chemical Atomism in the Nineteenth Century: From Dalton to Cannizzaro*, Columbus: Ohio State University Press, 1984

Amedeo Avogadro began his professional career as a lawyer in Turin. Expressing as much interest in natural philosophy as he did in law, he was appointed demonstrator at a college attached to the Academy of Turin in 1806, and on 7 October 1809 he became professor of natural philosophy at the College of Vercelli. Avogadro is known principally for "Avogadro's hypothesis" (1811), which states that gases of equal volumes contain the same number of molecules, given that temperature and pressure remain equal (also called the hypothesis of equal volumes, equal numbers). The reasons behind the 50-year neglect of Avogadro's hypothesis by the scientific community became, as BROOKE remarked, one of the great questions in the history of chemistry.

In his work on the life and scientific activities of Avogadro, MORSELLI investigates his accomplishments within a broad (political and scientific) historical context. In the first chapter, Morselli describes the life of the scientist, the greater part of which Avogadro spent in Turin, and discusses in detail the history of the Sardinian Kingdom, especially that of Piedmont, which remained for centuries strikingly remote from the cultural and historical centers of the peninsula. Morselli's account stresses the fact that Avogadro was an isolated figure working in an area shunned by practical chemists, and that his work belongs more to physics and physical chemistry than to chemistry. According to Morselli, Avogadro's hypothesis offered more than a method for determining atomic and molecular weights; without it, physical behavior and chemical combinations involving gaseous elements could not be explained. However, the cultural climate in the first decades of the 19th century had not reached the maturity necessary for the acceptance of ideas as hypothetical as those proposed by Avogadro. The author devotes the last chapters to Avogadro's investigations from the 1820s to the 1840s in the fields of physical chemistry and physics, and his final works. Morselli notes that these works show

the extent to which Avogadro lagged behind European science, as is evident from his magnum opus of almost 4000 pages, *Fisica dei corpi ponderabili* (1837–41), which was outdated even before it had been printed.

During the 1970s considerable progress was made in understanding the fate of Avogadro's molecular theory. BONNER has minutely examined the motivation of Avogadro's research within the context of the chemical tradition of Berthollet and Gay-Lussac (the study of molecules rather than atoms), and has demonstrated conclusively that in 1811 Avogadro was not trying to find an independent path to the solution of Dalton's problem. It is unfortunate that Bonner's study is available only in dissertation form, although her approach has been developed in BROOKE, FISHER, and ROCKE. All three works are similar in concept, and all three authors base their argument on the fact that it would be incorrect to accuse the chemists of the first half of the 19th century of prejudice, conservatism, or lack of foresight simply because they ignored Avogadro's theory for 50 years. In the early 19th century, two critical questions remained unresolved: how many atoms are there in an elementary molecule, and is this number the same for every element? According to Brooke, Fisher, and Rocke, such words as "atom" and "molecule" had no fixed or standardized meaning, certainly not the one we use today. Avogadro did not distinguish between the molecule and the atom of an element, as many had supposed, and while he did, on occasion, discuss the sub-units of the molecule, as Fisher remarks, "all these discussions have that lackadaisical quality which shows that the question is not one that the author considers of any importance". By 1860, both Avogadro's hypothesis and the assumption of sub-molecularity were derived from kinetic molecular theory. Moreover, the concept of a polyatomic elementary molecule was proved to be chemically useful in its own way.

Although the works of Brooke, Fisher, and Rocke are very similar in their ideas, it is important to point out some individual particularities. The goal of Brooke's paper is to raise a series of objections to the "case-study" approach which, according to his own view, "is not unanswerable but which seems to require consideration". Fisher's article stresses historiographical aspects of the question of the fate of Avogadro's hypothesis. Historians of chemistry refer frequently to the confusion in the first half of the 19th century that surrounded the definitions of atomic weights and molecular formulas, and the statement that it was the neglect of Avogadro's hypothesis that produced this confusion usually follows. According to Fisher, however, the confusion is likely to appear more important to 20th-century historians than it did to chemists at the time. They, at least, were familiar with the rules that allowed them to translate the weights of one system of atomic weights and chemical formulas into those of another. Rocke traces the development of chemical atomism, beginning with Dalton, through most of the 19th century, and covers a broad panorama of discussion. His book is clear in its structure and the breadth of the context is such that it is as useful for professional historians of chemistry as it is for those who are beginners in the field.

BYKOV includes an analysis of Avogadros's scientific and pedagogical activities as well as his biography. In the process of writing his book, Bykov relied on the work of an Italian chemist, Icilio Guareschi, "Amedeo Avogadro e la sua opera scientifica. Discorso storico-critico", which was published in 1911 in the collection of selected works of AVOGADRO. Bykov also had recourse to Avodagro's original works, and although his interpretation of the history of the formation of Avogadro's molecular theory and its fate must nowadays be considered outdated, his book remains interesting, if only for the fact that he presents a detailed analysis of Avogadro's works in the fields of chemistry and physics – especially his investigations in electricity, his studies of thermal properties of gases (his ideas on the connection between chemical affinity and specific heat), and his important works on atomic volumes, capillarity, chemical nomenclature, and so on. The works by Morselli and Bykov thus complement each other perfectly.

IGOR S. DMITRIEV

See also Affinity; Atomism

Axiomatics

Dummett, Michael, *Frege: Philosophy of Language*, London: Duckworth, and New York: Harper and Row, 1973

Gödel, Kurt, *Collected Works*, vol. 2: *Publications 1938–1974*, edited by Soloman Fefermann, *et al.*, Oxford: Clarendon Press, and New York: Oxford University Press, 1990

Hilbert, David, *Foundations of Geometry*, translated from the German by Leo Unger, Chicago: Open Court, 1971 (from the 10th German edition, 1899)

Hilbert, David, *Natur und mathematisches Erkennen: Vorlesungen, gehalten 1919–1920*, edited by David E. Rowe, Basel: Birkhäuser, 1992

Kennedy, Hubert C., *Peano: Life and Works of Giuseppe Peano*, Dordrecht: Reidel, 1980

Lowe, Victor, *Alfred North Whitehead: The Man and His Work, vol. 1 1861–1910*, Baltimore: Johns Hopkins University Press, 1985

Mehrtens, Herbert, *Moderne, Sprache, Mathematik: Eine Geschichte des Streits um die Grundlagen der Disziplin und des subjekts formaler Systeme*, Frankfurt: Suhrkamp, 1990

Monk, Ray, *Ludwig Wittgenstein: The Duty of Genius*, London: Jonathan Cape, and New York: Free Press, 1990

Moore, Gregory H., *Zermelo's Axiom of Choice: Its Origins, Development, and Influence*, New York: Springer, 1982

Mueller, Ian, *Philosophy of Mathematics and Deductive Structure in Euclid's Elements*, Cambridge, Massachusetts: MIT Press, 1981

Nagel, E., "The Formation of Modern Conceptions of Formal Logic in the Development of Geometry", *Osiris*, 7 (1939): 142–224

Panza, Marco and Jean-Claude Pont, *Espace et horizon de realité: philosophie mathématique de Ferdinand Gonseth*, Paris: Masson, 1992

Richards, Joan L., *Mathematical Visions: The Pursuit of Geometry in Victorian England*, Boston: Academic Press, 1988

Toepell, Michael-Markus, *Über die Entstehung von David Hilbert's "Grundlagen der Geometrie"*, Göttingen: Vendenhoeck & Ruprecht, 1986

The idea that mathematics should be formulated in terms of axioms specifying the rules of deduction of undefined objects – rules that are shown to be mutually consistent by means of a model that satisfied them – is essentially modern, and may be attributed to Peano and Hilbert in the 1890s. However, systems of axioms codifying the properties of intuitively understood terms that are too basic to be proved were defended by Aristotle, and were paradigmatically present in Euclid's *Elements*. Thereafter they presented a model of mathematics frequently extolled but seldom attained, and on occasion imitated in other fields (for example, by Spinoza). For a discussion of axiomatic mathematics in the ancient period that emphasises philosophical issues, see MUELLER.

Formal axiomatics drew its inspiration from several sources in 19th-century mathematics. The creation of geometries other than Euclidean, which seemed either equally plausible physically (i.e. non-Euclidean geometry) or logically more basic (i.e. projective geometry), cast doubt on the necessity of Euclid's system. The rigorisation of the calculus culminated in moves to base all of mathematics on arithmetic, which in turn was based on an emerging naive theory of sets. NAGEL's article argues for the influence of novel geometries on the creation of modern logic, while TOEPELL suggests that Hilbert's axiomatic formulation of geometry (his 1919–20 lectures on this topic are reprinted in HILBERT, 1992) was the result of the discovery that the new geometries produced new theorems expressing the dependence (or independence) of one classical theorem or concept on (or from) another. There is no comparable study of Peano and his school, although KENNEDY's book surveys Peano's life and work. This leaves important questions unanswered concerning the work of Russell and Whitehead, for whom Peano's logical interests were a turning point. Russell's philosophy of geometry is examined by RICHARDS, and Whitehead's intellectual life is described in detail by LOWE.

Hilbert's successes in geometry, extended by numerous authors, blossomed into a move to axiomatise many other branches of mathematics: the real and complex numbers, and algebraic structures (groups and fields). Hilbert himself pursued a deepening interest in the foundations of mathematics, and came to argue, contrary to the logicism of Russell, that logic was a branch of mathematics, specifically set theory. This had been axiomatised by Zermelo in 1908. While many scholars have argued that Zermelo did this with a view to excluding the growing list of paradoxes generated by the naive theory of sets, Zermelo's work is carefully analysed in MOORE, who disagrees with this judgement. Although Gödel's Theorem put an end to Hilbert's programme, the study of the foundations of mathematics has continued, and a large majority of philosophers of mathematics regard mathematics as reducible to, or even synonymous with, set theory. This was the influential view of Carnap, and, even though he opposed it, Gonseth gave greater clarity to it in his work than to his own ideas on evolving concepts. (See PANZA & PONT for a recent critical overview of Gonseth's work.) For the large and conflicting literature on Frege, see DUMMETT and the remarkable biography of Wittgenstein by MONK. There is no single comparable work on Hilbert; the philosopher's Hilbert is well presented in MEHRTENS, where it is central to his definition of the modern in mathematics, whereas the alternative opinion, that Hilbert always saw mathematics, however formal, as part of a problem formulating and solving activity with close links to physics, is well argued in Rowe (in his edition of Hilbert), who draws on the rich vein of Hilbert's unpublished lecture courses.

Two axiom systems are usually taken to underlie modern mathematics: that of Zermelo, as revised by Fraenkel in 1921 (the Zermelo–Fraenkel system), and the version proposed by von Neumann in 1925 and later adopted by Gödel. In either case, particular interest attaches to the independence (or other-wise) of each of two further axioms much used in mathematics: the axiom of choice, and the continuum hypothesis. Work by Gödel and Cohen established the independence of each of these from the Zermelo–Fraenkel system, the second volume of GÖDEL's *Collected Works* giving a good account of these developments.

JEREMY GRAY

See also Euclid; Gödel; Hilbert

B

Bacon, Francis 1561–1626

English philosopher and statesman

Anderson, Fulton H., *The Philosophy of Francis Bacon*, Chicago: University of Chicago Press, 1948

Jardine, Lisa, *Francis Bacon: Discovery and the Art of Discourse*, Cambridge and New York: Cambridge University Press, 1974

Leary Jr, John E., *Francis Bacon and the Politics of Science*, Ames: Iowa State University Press, 1994

Martin, Julian, *Francis Bacon, the State, and the Reform of Natural Philosophy*, Cambridge and New York: Cambridge University Press, 1992

Pérez-Ramos, Antonio, *Francis Bacon's Idea of Science and the Maker's Knowledge Tradition*, Oxford: Clarendon Press, and New York: Oxford University Press, 1988

Rossi, Paolo, *Francis Bacon: From Magic to Science*, translated from the Italian by Sacha Rabinovitch, London: Routledge and Kegan Paul, and Chicago: University of Chicago Press, 1968 (original edition, 1957)

Whitney, Charles, *Francis Bacon and Modernity*, New Haven, Connecticut: Yale University Press, 1986

"Around 1600 the English intellectual was more than half medieval, and around 1660 he was more than half modern", states ROSSI, who documents Francis Bacon's participation in this intellectual movement toward modernity, discussing his creative use, and reform of, medieval ideas. Rossi describes a number of instances in which Bacon's beliefs were taken from alchemical and magical sources; for example, his *Sylva Sylvarum* is a compilation of histories that culled many of its facts from the writings of Aristotle, Agricola, Della Porta, Cardano, and others. More importantly, Rossi argues that Bacon's approach to the aims and methods of science – his desire to discover the essence of things, in order that new effects could be produced by straightforward combination – was borrowed from the natural magic tradition of Agrippa and Campanella. Nevertheless, Bacon criticized that tradition for its individualism and vanity, believing that a collective and organized approach to science resulted in the more efficient production and more productive use of knowledge. In similar fashion, Rossi examines Bacon's interest in classical fables, and his innovative use of traditional and Ramist logic.

WHITNEY is also interested in Bacon as a thinker who stands on the brink of modernity, and in the contradictions that one finds in such a thinker. Whitney focuses on similar parts of Bacon's work to Rossi, and on similar combinations of the medieval and the modern, but approaches the text with the eye of a literary critic rather than an intellectual historian. Using the contrary themes of reform and revolution, which he finds implicit in Bacon's use of the term "instauration" (in Latin *instauratio* means both fulfilment and new beginning) to describe his proposal for the new learning, Whitney explores the conflict between Bacon's notion of traditional and new institutions. Bacon simultaneously hopes to restore an Adamic paradise, in which humans understand the nature of God's creations and have dominion over them, and to establish a completely new secular learning. This learning was to be religiously motivated, but rational and secular in its focus on nature, and, although Bacon's own writing is richly rhetorical and allegorical, his programme promised to lay nature transparent and bare. Whitney does not point to these and other contradictions merely to show Bacon's pre-modern status, but in order to reveal the tensions inherent within any claims to revolutions in understanding, which to be comprehensible must be seen in the context of the aims of social reform.

Bacon's *Novum Organum* pronounces itself a "logic", a way of systematically organising facts and ideas for the effective discovery and communication of knowledge. JARDINE takes this claim as her starting point, and discusses Bacon's writing as the embodiment of this new logic or dialectic. Jardine's Bacon is a well-educated, widely read, and extremely perceptive layman, but not a scholar: she argues that his contact with dialectic came through popular dialectic handbooks of the 16th century, and not with more scholarly treatises that were central to the Cambridge curriculum while he was a student there. His reforms are based on the realisation that traditional dialectic did not distinguish between contexts of discovery and communication, and therefore was not adequate for deriving new knowledge of nature, and his rules of discourse are organized around the discovery/communication divide. The bulk of Jardine's discussion lies in the analysis and elucidation of Bacon's rules of discourse, through readings that attempt to unify his work through its form.

Bacon famously connected natural philosophy and human welfare, through his belief in the potential usefulness of inventions. Thus he has been read as a spokesman for industrial science, claiming that scientific knowledge is essentially practical knowledge. PÉREZ-RAMOS emphasizes another connection between scientific knowledge and invention, by pointing to Bacon's interest in validating knowledge through the production of effects. Bacon can be situated within a scientific tradition, which includes Plato, Proclus, Vico, and Hobbes, embracing the idea that one can know the nature of a thing by making it. With the focus on "maker's knowledge", Bacon's emphasis on inventions becomes properly epistemological, because it occurs in part within the context of attempts to gain certainty. Thus Pérez-Ramos gives us a picture of Bacon as a philosopher of science, but not as the inductivist philosopher he has often been thought to be. (The book also includes a sketch of the remarkably variable history of readings of Bacon as philosopher of science.) Bacon's *inductio* is a set of methods – some verificationist, some deductive, and some analogical - designed to discover the *forms* of nature, and the rules of action under which nature operates and under which nature can be controlled. Although Pérez-Ramos does not try to fit all of Bacon's thinking into one picture, his vision of Bacon is that of a coherent and clever epistemologist, who has something to teach today's philosophy of science.

MARTIN asks a series of valuable questions about Bacon's motivations: why did Bacon, who was educated and trained as a statesman, and who was extremely ambitious in the pursuit of important positions, become interested in natural philosophy? How, in a more than busy life as an adviser to monarchs, gatherer of political intelligence and judge, could he have justified the time he spent on a plan to reform learning? To answer these questions, Martin looks at a conjunction of very particular facts about Tudor England and Bacon's resources and ambitions, attempting to unify his subject around his political life. Martin argues that Bacon inherited from Thomas Cromwell, through his father Nicholas Bacon, Lord Keeper, a vision of states as promoters of industry and welfare. From his political allegiances and his rebellion against his Cambridge education, he acquired a dislike of authoritarian Anglicanism and the Anglican-controlled learning of the universities. From his work as a lawyer and reformer of laws, he took a set of methods for establishing facts that could be transferred from legal to philosophical and historical realms. Martin thus makes Bacon's use of legal language and analogies central to his philosophical work. These contributions to Bacon's outlook allowed him to see an opportunity for the expansion of state authority and for a large new office for himself: Bacon said, ambitiously, "I have taken all knowledge to be my province".

LEARY in some ways expands on Martin's framework, examining Bacon's views of organization, and showing the congruities between Bacon's recommendations for the organization of science and states. In his analysis, Leary focuses more on texts than contexts, but he also includes a sketch of Bacon's life that helps to construct a picture of the politics behind Bacon's attempted reform of learning.

All of the above studies contain references to many other secondary sources. One not so recent study that deserves mention is ANDERSON, which serves as a good reference work on Bacon's philosophical thinking. Anderson discusses Bacon's ideas on the idols, materialism, classification, logic, and other philosophical topics in relation to Plato, Aristotle, and the atomists. The book is not particularly concerned with the more detailed historical context, but it remains useful because it treats many topics systematically.

SERGIO SISMONDO

Bacteriology

Baldry, P.E., *The Battle Against Bacteria: A Fresh Look*, Cambridge and New York: Cambridge University Press, 1976

Beeson, Paul B., "Infectious Diseases", in *Advances in American Medicine: Essays at the Bicentennial*, vol. 1, edited by John Z. Bowers and Elizabeth F. Purcell, New York: Josiah Macy Jr Foundation, 1976, 100–56

Brock, Thomas D., *Robert Koch: A Life in Medicine and Bacteriology*, Madison, Wisconsin: Science Tech, and Berlin: Springer, 1988

Bulloch, William, *The History of Bacteriology*, London and New York: Oxford University Press, 1938

Collard, Patrick, *The Development of Microbiology*, Cambridge and New York: Cambridge University Press, 1976

Cunningham, Andrew, "Transforming Plague: The Laboratory and the Identity of Infectious Disease", in *The Laboratory Revolution in Medicine*, edited by Cunningham and Perry Williams, Cambridge and New York: Cambridge University Press, 1992

De Kruif, Paul, *Microbe Hunters*, New York: Harcourt Brace, 1926

Delaunay, Albert, *L'Institut Pasteur: Des Origines à aujourd'hui*, Paris: France–Empire, 1962

Dubos, René J., *Louis Pasteur: Free Lance of Science*, Boston: Little Brown, 1950; London: Gollancz, 1951

Ford, William W., *Bacteriology*, New York: Hoeber, 1939

Foster, W.D., *A History of Medical Bacteriology and Immunology*, London: Heinemann, 1970

Geison, Gerald L., *The Private Science of Louis Pasteur*, Princeton, New Jersey: Princeton University Press, 1995

Koprowski, Hilary and Michael B.A. Oldstone (eds), *Microbe Hunters, Then and Now*, Bloomington, Indiana: Medi-Ed Press, 1996

Mochmann, Hanspeter and Werner Köhler, *Meilensteine der Bakteriologie: Von Entdeckungen und Entdeckern aus den Gründerjahren der Medizinischen Mikrobiologie*, Jena: VEB Fischer, 1984

Morange, Michel (ed.), *L'Institut Pasteur: contributions à son histoire*, Paris: La Découverte, 1991

Williams, R.E.O., *Microbiology for the Public Health: The Evolution of the Public Health Laboratory Service, 1939–1980*, London: Public Health Laboratory Service, 1985

Broadly speaking, the history of bacteriology can be subdivided into five or six periods. The first (5000 BC to 1675) was a period of speculation on the causes of phenomena such as diseases, fermentation, and putrefaction. The second (1675 to mid-19th century) was one of observation, magnification being achieved through microscopical techniques; this period starts with the work of Antoni van Leeuwenhoek, who was the first to visualize bacteria (from the Greek for Bakthrion, meaning "little stick"). In the third period (the mid-19th to 20th centuries), activity was focused on the isolation and cultivation of bacteria. With the discovery of cell-free fermentation at the end of the 19th century, physiological chemistry or biochemistry emerged as a separate discipline, resulting in the 1920s and 1930s in bacterial physiology. COLLARD's history of microbiology is organized along the lines of this periodization.

The discovery of the antibacterial drug sulphonamide in 1935 by Gerhard Domagk, and the subsequent discovery of antibiotics such as penicillin and streptomycin, could be interpreted as a transition to the next period, which was to be dominated by bacterial genetics, followed by its application in modern biotechnology and the techniques of genetic manipulation. It may be argued that another major transformation took place in the 1980s, as numerous problems in bacteriology/microbiology are now being redefined and investigated in terms of molecular evolution.

DE KRUIF's book is a compelling and popular account of the great names in bacteriology, centring on Van Leeuwenhoek, Lazzaro Spallanzani, Louis Pasteur, Robert Koch, Émile Roux and Emil Behring, Ilya Metchnikoff, Theobald Smith, Walter Reed, and Paul Ehrlich. Published in many languages, it has been reprinted time and again. Inspired by De Kruif's book, KOPROWSKI & OLDSTONE compiled a more specialized book, in which historical contributions on bacterial and viral diseases alternate with a discussion of the state of the art with regard to these particular disease agents.

FORD's book, which is more technical than De Kruif's, is a concise history of bacteriology up to the early 20th century. This book's guiding principle is the application of the microscope in solving fundamental problems, such as spontaneous generation, fermentation, and putrefaction. BULLOCH's work, also written in the 1930s, discusses the old doctrines regarding the nature of contamination, spontaneous generation and heterogenesis, the presence of specific elements in infectious diseases, and the classification of bacteria. Bulloch also addresses Louis Pasteur's work on virus vaccines, as well as doctrines regarding immunity, which is useful because the histories of vaccination and theories of immunity are closely intertwined with that of bacteriology. Chronologically, Bulloch ends his story at the turn of the century.

FOSTER's book differs from Bulloch's in that it is more medically oriented and continues its account up to 1938. Foster supplements Bulloch by paying more attention to the discovery of important pathogenic bacteria in man (streptococcus, staphylococcus, Escherichia coli and the agents of diphtheria, typhoid fever, pneumonia, etc.). It presents an analysis of how causal correlations between agent and disease were studied and how these discoveries were applied in the diagnosis, treatment and prevention of infectious disease. The book contains numerous figures on bacteriological techniques.

The development of antibacterial drugs since the mid-1930s is discussed in BALDRY, who uses common, military-inspired metaphors to describe the battle against microbial "invaders". The chapters are entitled: the unknown enemy; the enemy identified; the enemy named; defence measures; the enemy under attack; guided missiles; enemy resistance.

MOCHMANN & KÖHLER recount how Robert Koch's methods were used in the last quarter of the 19th century to isolate pathological organisms. In a collection of essays, they describe the discoverers and discoveries of these founding years of bacteriology. Their subjects include anthrax, diphtheria, the gonococcus, and the bacilli of lepra, tuberculosis, cholera, etc.

BROCK's biography of Robert Koch pays a great deal of attention to the techniques developed by this bacteriologist.

An engaging biography of Louis Pasteur is presented by DUBOS. René Dubos – born in France but employed for most of his academic career at the Rockefeller Institute in New York – emphasizes that Pasteur was an ecologist *avant la lettre*. In his view, Pasteur was greatly interested in the influence of environmental factors on bacteria: the environment exercises an enormous influence on the morphology and chemical activities of a specific microbial species. Dubos claims that Pasteur showed relatively little interest in classification and nomenclature, and concentrated on the general notion of physiology and function. (The closely related discipline of bacterial physiology was to become prominent in the 1920s and 1930s, through the work of Marjory Stephenson in England and Albert J. Kluyver in the Netherlands.)

GEISON's recent book on Pasteur is noteworthy because it is the first to make use of Pasteur's laboratory notebooks as a source of historical information. Geison concludes that in experimentation on humans, Pasteur did not comply with his own standards, which he defended publicly as crucial for the ethical behaviour of scientists and doctors. Furthermore, Pasteur's theories regarding immunity seem to be different from what can be found in his published work.

Based on his work on rabies, Louis Pasteur was given the opportunity to found a private research institute. DELAUNAY describes the history of the Pasteur Institute from its inception – the inauguration took place in 1888 – until just after World War II. He discusses the first "Pastorians", the services they rendered during World War I, and the work on BCG-vaccine, anatoxins, and sulphonamides. MORANGE edited a collection of essays on the Pasteur Institute and the Pastorians that places them within a wider context. The book also draws attention to the expansion of the Pasteur Institute through its branches all over the world.

A useful sketch of the contributions of American bacteriologists is presented by BEESON. The prominent late 19th-century bacteriologists he discusses include George M. Sternberg, William Henry Welch, Frederick George Novy, Simon Flexner, Daniel Elmer Salmon, and Theobald Smith, and he follows this with a discussion of some of the more recent American bacteriologists. Beeson pays special attention to the Rockefeller Foundation, the American counterpart of the illustrious research institutes of Pasteur and Koch in Paris and Berlin. In his account, Beeson uses various approaches. Sometimes he starts with a specific infectious disease, sometimes with a particular person and elsewhere with organizations or institutes.

In the literature discussed above there is hardly any mention of the application of bacteriology within public health laboratories or industry. Therefore, WILLIAMS's book on the Public Health Laboratory Service (PHLS) in Britain is an important addition to the literature on bacteriology. Before World War II, the activities of the Public Health Laboratories were limited to, for example, bacteriological tests on throat swabs, serological tests, and studies of the hygienic quality of milk and water. After the war, the PHLS expanded its activities, including several bacteriological laboratories for hospitals.

In an important essay, CUNNINGHAM arrives at a crucial conclusion for historians of science, which is hardly referred to in the other literature on bacteriology. He concludes that since the emergence of bacteriology in the second half of the 19th century, infectious diseases have been identified in the laboratory. Infectious diseases have thus been "redefined" relative to the pre-bacteriology era. Illustrating this by a case-study on the plague (bacillus), Cunningham shows that the final diagnosis of an infectious disease is no longer made through its symptoms and pathology, but through the identification of an alleged infectious agent. As the criteria for the identification of plague differ from those in use before bacteriological laboratories were available, Cunningham concludes that pre-laboratory plague and post-laboratory plague do not possess one consistent and continuous identity. This transformation of an illness by the diagnosis in a bacteriological laboratory is hardly ever recognized by historians of bacteriology. A general history of bacteriology based on this insight remains to be written.

TON VAN HELVOORT

See also Immunology; Koch; Pasteur

Baer, Karl Ernst von 1792–1876

Estonian-born German embryologist

Folia Baeriana series, Tallinn: Valgus, 1975–

Haacke, Wilhelm, *Karl Ernst von Baer*, Leipzig: Thomas, 1905

Meyer, Arthur William, *Human Generation: Conclusions of Burdach, Döllinger and von Baer*, Stanford, California: Stanford University Press, 1956

Ospovat, Dov, "The Influence of Karl Ernst von Baer's Embryology, 1828–1859: A Reappraisal in Light of Richard Owen and William Carpenter's 'Palaeontological Application of Von Baer's Law'", *Journal of the History of Biology*, 9 (1976): 1–28

Ottow, Benno, "K.E. von Baer als Kraniologe und die Anthropologen-Versammlung 1861 in Göttingen", *Sudhoffs Archiv für Geschichte der Medizin und Naturwissenschaften* 50, (1966): 43–68

Raikov, Boris Evgen'evic, *Karl Ernst von Baer, 1792–1876: Sein Leben und sein Werk*, translated into German by Heinrich von Knorre, Leipzig: Barth, 1968

Stieda, Ludwig, *Karl Ernst von Baer: Eine biographische Skizze*, Braunschweig: Vieweg & Sohn, 1878

STIEDA, who knew Karl Ernst von Baer personally, published an account of his life and work based on von Baer's autobiography, correspondence and literary bequest, and gives brief summaries and a bibliography of the writings. While HAACKE's biography is based on this book, his account of von Baer's work emphasises above all his teleological view of nature, of ontogenesis and evolution, and his reaction to Darwinism. The first comprehensive critical biography was produced by RAIKOV, with the use of material from the St Petersburg and Dorpat archives. Both von Baer's life and his varied scientific activities are presented in detail, and his views on the theory of heredity or evolution and on Darwinism are thoroughly discussed. This book also contains an extensive list of von Baer's published work, complete with annotations.

In recent years, von Baer's activities in the various sciences have been examined in a number of extensive specialist treatises. His fundamental contributions to animal evolution have been described in MEYER, a work that also contains an English translation of von Baer's commentary on his essay on mammalian eggs, which had just then been discovered. Insight into the complex history of von Baer's impact in the field of embryology is given by OSPOVAT, who claims that von Baer's theory of embryogenesis of four divergent types differs from the theory of recapitulation. He also holds that, since von Baer's theory linked embryology with palaeontology, it helped prepare the ground for Darwin's evolutionary thought among biologists prior to 1859. Von Baer's achievements of laying the foundations of craniology in Russia and of promoting the study of anthropology are appreciated by OTTOW, who has also published a collection of letters by von Baer to Richard Wagner in Göttingen.

The Estonian collection *Folia Baeriana* is an ongoing series, publishing a considerable number of smaller studies on von Baer's life and work. Contributions have appeared in Estonian, Russian, German, and English. The collection contains source material such as von Baer's graduation documents and genealogy (volume 1), and the autobiography of his ancestor Andreas von Baer (volume 2), which relates both family and political events between 1643 and 1707. There are discussions of von Baer's works in various scientific fields from zoology, evolution, and anthropology to geography (including his expeditions), and so on. Many of the contributions deal with his philosophical contemplations and his critical analysis of evolutionary thought. Von Baer's activities in the administration, promotion, and the popularisation of science also receive attention. The fourth volume contains a bibliography of the literature (until 1978) that has arisen from his professional interests, his life, and his work, since 1814.

BRIGITTE HOPPE

translated by Anna-Katherina Meyer

See also Embryology

Baeyer, Adolf von 1835–1917

German organic chemist

Baeyer, Adolf von, "Erinnerungen aus meinem Leben 1835–1905", in his *Gesammelte Werke*, 2 vols, edited by his "pupils and friends", Braunschweig: Friedrich Vieweg, 1905

Fruton, Joseph S., *Contrasts in Scientific Style: Research Groups in the Chemical and Biochemical Sciences*, Philadelphia: American Philosophical Society, 1990

Gienapp, Ruth Anne, entry in *Dictionary of Scientific Biography*, edited by Charles Coulston Gillispie, vol. 1, New York: Scribner, 1970

Huisgen, Rolf, "Adolf von Baeyers wissenschaftliches Werk: Ein Vermächtnis", *Angewandte Chemie*, 98 (1986): 293–311

Die Naturwissenschaften, special issue Adolf von Baeyer zur Feier seines 80 Geburtstages, 3 (1915)

Perkin, William Henry, "Baeyer Memorial Lecture", *Journal of the Chemical Society*, 123 (1923): 1520–46

Rupe, Hans, "Adolf von Baeyer als Lehrer und Forscher: Erinnerungen aus seinem Privatlaboratorium" in *Sammlung chemischer und chemisch-technischer Vorträge*, edited by H. Grossman, Stuttgart: Ferdinand Enke, 1932

Schmorl, Karl, *Adolf von Baeyer 1835–1917*, Stuttgart: Wissenschaftliche Verlagsgesellschaft, 1952

Wiedenmann, Evelin, *Die Konstruktion der richtigen Formel: Struktur und Synthese des dargestellt an Hand des Briefwechsels Baeyer–Caro*, PhD dissertation, Munich, Technische Hochschule, 1978

Willstätter, Richard, "Adolf von Baeyer" in *Das Buch der grossen Chemiker*, edited by Günther Bugge, vol. 2, Berlin: Chemie, 1930

Willstätter, Richard, *Aus meinem Leben: Von Arbeit, Musse und Freunden*, edited by Arthur Stoll, Weinhem: Chemie, 1949

Adolf von Baeyer received the Nobel prize in 1905 for his contribution to the development of organic chemistry and the chemical industry and for his work on organic dyestuffs and hydroaromatic compounds. He was a pupil of Kekulé and followed in the footsteps of Justig Liebig. He and his star student, Emil Fischer, dominated the development of organic chemistry for more than half a century.

Baeyer was primarily an empiricist. His goal was to uncover nature's secrets through the use of simple experiments and he used theories mainly as a guide for new experiments. FRUTON describes the large numbers of undergraduate and graduate students (about 450) who were educated in Bayer's brand of experimentalism in his teaching laboratories in Berlin (1860–70), Strasbourg (1872–75), and Munich (1875–1915).

In 1905 BAEYER's Complete Works were published, just in time to mark his 70th birthday. They contain an introductory autobiographical essay of some 50 pages in which he gives an account of his life and evaluates his scientific work in the period from 1865 to 1905. They also contain his essay on the history of the indigo synthesis. Fischer contributed his memories of Baeyer from his student days in Strasbourg in the years 1872–75.

The special issue of *Die Naturwissenschaften* in honour of his 80th birthday provides a celebratory account and an analysis of Baeyer's work by several authors, within the context of the general development of chemistry. The issue contains a biographical essay and a number of papers on the various topics of Baeyer's work: organic arsenic compounds in contemporary medicine, uric acids, indigos, the constitution of benzol, hydroaromatics, peroxides, phthaleines, and a paper on his attitude to the problem of the basic nature of carbon. HUISGEN discusses the breadth of Baeyer's work using the categorization of 16 themes that Baeyer had himself employed in the Complete Works.

The chemist WILLSTÄTTER's autobiography (1949) contains much information on Baeyer, such as his wish that none of his students would write a biography, with the justification that the autobiography already contained everything of importance. Willstätter provides biographical information

and discussions of Baeyer's scientific work, but the most interesting aspect of the book is the many anecdotes that shed light on Baeyer's personality and on his work as an academic teacher. Some of these stories were contained in WILLSTÄTTER's article on Baeyer for a volume on great chemists (1930). Baeyer is depicted as a leader and founder of organic chemistry in the age of analysis and synthesis. His main success was to explain the structure of organic compounds and to verify the concepts of structural chemistry devised by Kekulé, van't Hoff, and Le Bell.

One of Baeyer's assistants, RUPE, has collated several anecdotes and an account of Baeyer's working and private habits. He describes Baeyer's preference for doing experiments with very simple apparatus such as test tubes and glass rods in order to confirm his thoughts on the matter, and he describes Baeyer's extraordinary patience when performing an experiment. He characterizes his boss as strict but kind.

SCHMORL's 214-page biography published in 1952 describes Baeyer's life and work, and relates it to the *Zeitgeist* and to the institutional context. He notes Baeyer's contribution to the introduction of a new type of examination (*Verbandsexamen*) in 1897 as part of the professionalization of chemists. The book contains a bibliography of 20 further biographical essays and a list of Baeyer's major publications. One of these is William Henry PERKIN's Baeyer memorial lecture to the Chemical Society of London. Perkin was one of Baeyer's students and his lecture is a profound appreciation and analysis of his teacher's work. It is of course in English, as is GIENAPP's entry in the *Dictionary of Scientific Biography*, a concise essay that should probably be the first port of call for the neophyte.

WIEDENMANN's doctoral dissertation analyses the extensive correspondence (240 letters) between Baeyer and the spokesperson for the industrial dye industry, Heinrich Caro, with the aim of discussing the historical development of the structural analysis and synthesis of the dye indigo blue.

There are not many recent studies on Baeyer, despite the fact that his name is still prominent in chemical textbooks, for instance in the Baeyer-Villiger oxidation process and his tension theory. One reason for this may be that his organizational activities remained moderate in comparison with his student, Emil Fischer, and that he focused only on the generation of a research school. It may also be because most of his manuscripts were destroyed during World War II.

Horst Remane

translated by Arne Hessenbruch

Banks, Joseph 1743–1820

British explorer, naturalist, and scientific administrator

Beaglehole, J.C. (ed.), *The Endeavour Journal of Joseph Banks 1768–1771*, 2 vols, Sydney: Public Library of New South Wales/Angus and Robertson, 1962

Cameron, Hector Charles, *Sir Joseph Banks, KB, PRS: The Autocrat of the Philosophers*, Sydney: Angus and Robertson, 1952

Carter, Harold B., *Sir Joseph Banks (1743–1820): A Guide to Biographical and Bibliographical Sources*, Winchester, Hampshire: St Pauls Bibliographies/British Museum (Natural History), 1987

Carter, Harold B., *Sir Joseph Banks, 1743–1820*, London: British Museum, 1988

Dawson, Warren R., *The Banks Letters: A Calendar of the Manuscript Correspondence of Sir Joseph Banks Preserved in the British Museum, The British Museum (Natural History) and Other Collections in Great Britain*, London: British Museum, 1958

Gascoigne, John, *Joseph Banks and the English Enlightenment: Useful Knowledge and Polite Culture*, Cambridge and New York: Cambridge University Press, 1994

Mackay, David L., *In the Wake of Cook: Exploration, Science and Empire, 1780–1801*, London: Croom Helm, and New York: St Martin's Press, 1985

Maiden, J.H., *Sir Joseph Banks: The "Father of Australia"*, Sydney: New South Wales Government Printer and London: Paul, 1909

Miller, David, "Between Hostile Camps: Sir Humphry Davy's Presidency of the Royal Society of London, 1820–1827", *British Journal for the History of Science*, 16 (1983): 1–47

O'Brian, Patrick, *Joseph Banks: A Life*, London: Collins Harvill and Boston: Godine, 1987

Smith, Bernard, *European Vision and the South Pacific 1768–1850*, Oxford: Clarendon Press, 1960; 2nd edition, New Haven, Connecticut, and London: Yale University Press, 1985

Smith, Edward, *The Life of Sir Joseph Banks, President of the Royal Society with some Notices of His Friends and Contemporaries*, London: Bodley Head, and New York: John Lane, 1911; reprinted, New York: Arno Press, 1975

Although he was President of the Royal Society for more than 40 years, until recently Joseph Banks has received relatively scant attention from historians. The paucity of his original research, and the daunting bulk of his papers, have both contributed to his earlier neglect. Historians of science now portray him as an influential statesman of science, focusing rather on his administrative talents as an Enlightenment improver and scientific imperialist, than on the botanic practices and adventurous exploits emphasised by earlier biographers. Acclaimed since the early 20th century as the "father of Australia", much of the current interest in Banks is fuelled by Australian academics.

CARTER's biographical and bibliographical guide (1987) is an invaluable source of the primary and secondary material. The major section summarises the journals, correspondence and other documents scattered in more than 50 principal collections (those with 10 or more Banksian items) throughout the world. The book also includes detailed references to Banks's library and his specimen collections, as well as comprehensive lists of personalia, including portraits, caricatures, and a biographical bibliography of more than 100 articles and books. DAWSON is the other indispensable aid for negotiating Banks's huge legacy of archival manuscripts. Tabulated alphabetically, this book summarises the contents of some 7000 letters to and from Banks which are now in Britain, indicating for each one where the original is to be found. BEAGLEHOLE's edition of Banks's own account of his *Endeavour* voyage with James Cook, unpublished during Banks's lifetime, enables modern readers to enjoy this lively narrative portraying early European encounters with the Pacific. The substantial introduction includes valuable material about Banks as well as contemporary responses to the expedition.

Although there were numerous biographical memoirs published in the 19th century, the first substantial monograph was MAIDEN, a patriotic work intended to forge a heroic past for the Australian nation. Consequently, this book was primarily concerned with Banks's voyages and botanical activities. Less hagiographic than one might suspect, it relied primarily on stringing together lengthy, unedited transcripts from original documents, and was generously illustrated with portraits, manuscript facsimiles, and maps.

During the next 70 years, three far more systematic major biographies appeared, all intended to exploit the mass of surviving documents in order to resurrect the reputation of an uncommemorated scientific colossus. EDWARD SMITH's narrative celebrates Banks as a public benefactor of scientific progress. Written in a lively style enriched by plentiful background information, it still provides modern authors with a valuable cache of quotations, which are infuriatingly unreferenced. CAMERON oriented his text around establishing the importance of Banks's Australian connections and imperial influence, although it stolidly records many aspects of his Presidency and London life. Benefiting from these and other studies, O'BRIAN has drawn on the archives to construct a more intimate biography, describing Banks's experiences as an enthusiastic explorer and scientific innovator. Although less plodding, it is unfortunately relentlessly chronological and inadequately footnoted.

CARTER's biography (1988) is the Banksian bible, a meticulously researched account with over 50 pages of index entries to compensate for the absence of references. Drawing extensively on original sources, Carter devoted a quarter of a century to constructing a solid biographical framework, within which to unite two disparate images, the youthful dilettante explorer and the elderly aristocratic President. Intentionally eschewing thematic analyses, Carter compiled this immensely detailed chronology by dividing Banks's career into three successive stages: the traveller, the savant and "HM Minister of Philosophic Affairs". Although hardly bedtime reading, the wealth of contextual information made this a fascinating and essential resource for all subsequent studies of Banks.

MILLER's article introduced what has now become a standard phrase, the "Banksian Learned Empire", to describe a matrix of mutually supportive institutions associated with the Royal Society. Antithetical to other groups – notably geologists and mathematicians – these powerful constituencies revolved around antiquarian interests, investigations of natural history, and agricultural and horticultural concerns. GASCOIGNE's book – published after Carter's – sensibly allocates only an introductory chapter to sketching out Banks's life, aiming instead to relate him and his circle to major improvements of the period. This interpretative study explores Banks as an exemplar of the English Enlightenment, who encouraged the pursuit of natural knowledge for public benefit, and fostered its incorporation within polite culture. Implicitly endorsing this rhetoric of progress, Gascoigne structures Banks's life as one of development from virtuoso to botanist, and from anti-quarian to anthropologist. Nevertheless, by including agricul-tural and manufacturing topics, his utilitarian slant provides a valuable corrective to histories of science anachronistically based on modern disciplinary definitions.

Strangely, Gascoigne deliberately omits Banks's strategic manoeuvring to strengthen the Royal Society's influence on governmental policies, particularly Britain's mercantile impe-rial expansion. This vital aspect of his contribution to the Enlightenment establishment of science's cultural power has formed the subject of the most exciting recent studies. Through analysing exploratory missions financed by the state, MACKAY demonstrates Banks's crucial role in embedding scientific and commercial interests within colonial exploitation, and in forging the Royal Society's prestigious status as governmental adviser. In BERNARD SMITH's landmark text, which inves-tigates the relations between science and art by examining how Europeans represented their Pacific experiences, Banks emerges as an influential patron who moulded polite taste.

Variously satirised by his contemporaries as a foppish botanist and an imperious autocrat, the modern image of Banks is of a skilful political manipulator. As the rich archival material becomes increasingly accessible through publication, historians are profitably using Banks as a means to explore changing atti-tudes to knowledge around the end of the 18th century, a key period for the cultural legitimation of science as a powerful enterprise.

PATRICIA FARA

Bateson, Gregory 1904–1980

English-born American anthropologist

Bateson, Mary Catherine, *With a Daughter's Eye: A Memoir of Margaret Mead and Gregory Bateson*, New York: Morrow, 1984

Brockman, John (ed.), *About Bateson: Essays on Gregory Bateson*, New York: Dutton, 1977; London: Wildwood House, 1978

Donaldson, R., *Gregory Bateson Archive: A Guide/Catalog*, Ann Arbor: University Microfilm, International, 1987

Harries-Jones, Peter, *A Recursive Vision: Ecological Understanding and Gregory Bateson*, Toronto: University of Toronto Press, 1995

Howard, Jane, *Margaret Mead: A Life*, New York: Simon and Schuster, 1990

Lipset, David, *Gregory Bateson: The Legacy of a Scientist*, Englewood Cliffs, New Jersey: Prentice-Hall, 1980

Mead, Margaret, *Blackberry Winter: My Earlier Years*, New York: Morrow, 1972

Wilder-Mott, C. and John H. Weakland, *Rigor & Imagination: Essays from the Legacy of Gregory Bateson*, New York: Praeger, 1981

Gregory Bateson began his scientific career as an anthropo-logist, but scholars point out his transdisciplinary move-ment into psychiatry, linguistics, cybernetics, and ecology and evolution as his greatest scientific achievement – despite the resulting popular reputation he attained as a New Age guru.

DONALDSON serves as Bateson's chief archivist and provides a discussion of his work as a guide to the catalogued archives, including Bateson's most important publications.

LIPSET provides the closest to a definitive biography, taking advantage of Bateson's own critique given shortly before he died. The biography draws heavily on interviews, private documents, and letters, and it details the influence of Bateson's unique family background as the son of William Bateson, an atheist, and staunch Mendelian opponent of Darwinism. Bateson credited his interest in information theory and holistic systems to his father's abhorrence of the mechanistic aspects and "mindlessness" of Darwinian natural selection, which he claimed neglected the complexity and immaterial aspects of biological phenomena. His father concentrated especially on the evolution of pattern development, something that would presage Gregory Bateson's interests in holistic systems. Although Lipset discusses Bateson's association with Norbert Wiener and John von Neumann in cybernetics and communi-cations theory in the 1940s and 1950s, and his association with John C. Lilly and dolphin communication in the 1960s, he deliberately gives scant details of Bateson's failed marriage to Margaret Mead, except as it directly influenced his subse-quent work. That period of his early career and intellectual development as a young anthropologist resulted in *Naven: A Survey of Problems Suggested by a Composite Picture of the Culture of a New Guinea Tribe Drawn from Three Points of View* (1936) and is extensively treated in MEAD and BATESON and in HOWARD's biography.

WILDER-MOTT & WEAKLAND is based on an Asilomar conference held in Bateson's honor in 1978 and includes essays organized around four topics: context, theory, research, and provocations. Although the various authors include much that is an expansion and critique of Bateson's work, each details various facets of his epistemological enterprise. Most address the place of Bateson within the development of modern communications theory as presented in his central work, *Steps to an Ecology of Mind: Collected Essays in Anthropology, Psychiatry, Evolution and Epistemology* (1972). Bateson cham-pioned the idea of the recursive nature of mind and know-ledge, including scientific knowledge and envisioned a unity between knower and thing known, each influencing the other. He considered all "reality" to be a mental invention of the knower, constructed by the unique pattern of sensory ability and previous experience in systematic interaction with the known. This view suggests not only the theory-ladenness of data, but the very inability of data to exist without theory (whether sensory or intellectual) to recognize it: this is part of Bateson's view that all knowledge rests on the perception of difference, that must be invented or defined before it can be recognized. Language, especially in the use of metaphor, reifies this collaborative enterprise and fixes invented reality, limiting the ability to perceive alternatives. Errors in the use of language can thus create what Bateson, in his chief contribution to psychiatric theory, early defined as the double-bind, explicated in his book *Communication: The Social Matrix of Psychiatry* (in collaboration with Jurgen Reusch). Bateson originated the double-bind as a social theory of schizophrenia, which is postu-lated, not as an organic disease, but rather as a system of social pathology caused by self-contradictory linguistic traps that create mental states from which the victim cannot escape.

HARRIES-JONES further details how Bateson is considered a foundational thinker in the area of reflexive or recursive epistemology in science, bringing to the life sciences a holistic, systems-oriented approach as portrayed in his various writings, including both *Steps to an Ecology of Mind* and *Mind and Nature: A Necessary Unity* (1979). Bateson decried the various deterministic and materialist analyses proffered in the life sciences as a result of developments in molecular biology and molecular genetics, as well as in ecological modeling that relied on reductionist, quantitative analyses of energy. Harries-Jones discusses how Bateson produced difficult works with a variety of collaborators, facilitating (mis)interpretation by many as support of a New Age Gaia worship and "eastern" mysticism. Because of his charisma and obfuscatory style, Bateson was a popular figure throughout the 1960s and 1970s, embraced by a counter-culture with which he only partly agreed. He has been cited as a founder of postmodern skepticism concerning science and technology, a rebel philosopher of mind, and a New Age prophet of "deep" ecology. Bateson's claim of an intrinsic, systematic relationship between the knower and the known lent itself to mystical interpretation by many, as a perceived justification of personal knowledge, a de-legitimation of science, and a license for religious fabulism. Such beliefs ran counter to the atheistic Bateson's deeper meaning that declared that all knowledge, including religious dogmas and New Age ecologies, was constructed and thus subject to skeptical inquiry and the corruptions of language.

The essays in BROCKMAN, including Bateson's own afterword, detail how, according to Bateson, emotional knowledge and unconscious knowledge are valid, systematic approaches of the knower to the world, and have no more or less intrinsic credibility than conscious belief or linguistic constructs by scientists and philosophers. The essay by his daughter, Mary Catherine Bateson, shows how the highly subjective concepts of love and wisdom can be interpreted in a biologically-based, systematic or cybernetic fashion as relational states between an individual mind and its surroundings. Love is described as an internal, unconscious recognition of a beneficial systematic relationship between lover and loved, with wisdom the conscious recognition of these systematic interrelationships. Mind is seen as an immaterial (but not spiritual) state equated to a self-correcting system "immanent where there are a number of parts ... maintaining constants between the relations between the parts and relations to the environment". In such a definition, the human mind becomes one of a hierarchy of "minds" defined as all such systems from bacteria to Gaia, hence the easy absorption of such doctrines by popular adherents who saw Bateson's concept of "mind" as postulating human-style consciousness across the ecological sweep of micro-organisms to ecological super-organisms. Lipset discusses how, at the end of Bateson's life, religious questions absorbed him, including work with his daughter on his final (posthumously published) work, *Angels Fear: Towards an Epistemology of the Sacred*. Bateson's final years were spent at the Esalen Institute, "a community of alternative and supernatural psychotherapists in Big Sur, California", perhaps the ultimate affirmation of his interest and sympathy with the science of the avant-garde.

MARK S. LESNEY

See also Ecology

Bauer, Georg *see* Agricola, Georgius

Behring, Emil von 1854–1917
German bacteriologist and immunologist

Engelhardt, A. von, *Hundertjahrfeier der Geburtstage von Paul Ehrlich und Emil von Behring: Verleihung der Emil von Behring-Preise 1948, 1952 und 1954*, Marburg: N.G. Elwert, 1954

Fleck, Ludwik, *Genesis and Development of a Scientific Fact*, translated from the German by Fred Bradley and Thaddeus J. Trenn, Chicago: University of Chicago Press, 1979 (original edition, 1935)

Philipps-Universität, *Behring zum Gedächtnis* (conference) Berlin: Schultz, 1942

Unger, Hellmuth, *Unvergängliches Erbe: Der Lebensweg Emil von Behrings*, Berlin: Oldenburg, 1943

Weindling, Paul, "From Medical Research to Clinical Practice: Serum Therapy for Diphtheria in the 1890s", in *Medical Innovations in Historical Perspective*, edited by John V. Pickstone, London: Macmillan, and New York: St Martins Press, 1992

Zeiss, Heinrich and Richart Bieling, *Behring: Gestalt und Werk*, Berlin: Schultz, 1940; revised edition, 1941

A biography of Emil von Behring was originally planned by his widow, Else Spinola, who then encouraged Erich Wernicke to undertake the task. Wernicke had co-operated with Behring on the introduction of serum therapy, and he saw the project as a means of securing his place in the historical record. Else Behring then turned to a favoured former student, Alfred Goldscheider, who was an honorary professor in Berlin. That Else Behring was Jewish, and that Goldscheider was a baptised Jew, became a profound embarrassment to Nazi medical fanatics, for if Behring was to be a Germanic hero of science, his lack of interest in anti-Semitism was unfortunate. In 1937, the Berlin professor of hygiene, Heinrich Zeiss, joined forces on the biographical project with Richard Bieling, a virologist from the Behring-Werke, who was also active in typhus vaccine research.

ZEISS & BIELING's work is a classic of Nazi history of medicine. Zeiss (the main author) emphasized the interaction of cultural, physiological, philosophical, and local influences on Behring, thereby developing a geopolitical approach to scientific innovation. Keen to analyse irrational factors within creativity, Zeiss contacted the Secretary of the British Cremation Society in order to find out about Lytton Strachey's approach to an individual's political circumstances, and how context shaped personality. However, in place of Strachey's debunking of heroic figures, we find Zeiss's heroising of the mundane. Zeiss emphasised how Behring's discovery of serum therapy drew on his ability to think in terms of images and analogies, derived from the inspiration of Schopenhauer and Nietzsche – correctives to what Zeiss viewed as the superficialities of Kantian rationalism – and placed Behring within a tradition of "enthusiasm" (stretching from Paracelsus to Schopenhauer), so giving medical research the status of a spiritual mission. Thus, a new German ideology was formulated, in order to legitimate mass destruction as heroic and creative.

Although Behring was Koch's assistant for six years from 1886, Zeiss depicted Behring as quite independent from what was regarded as the excessively rigid, causal approach of Koch. Not only did Behring elaborate a humoral theory of immunity, he co-operated with Kitasato, Ehrlich, and Emil Roux in developing serum therapy. He therefore appears as a more internationalist figure than Koch, and (apart from Behring's debts to Ehrlich) this suited certain internationalists among the Nazi medical establishment. This geopolitical and Gestalt approach to scientific innovation countered Marxist and Soviet history of science based on dialectical materialism and economic determinants. There was also a striking conceptual parallel with the sociology of science as pioneered by the Polish immunologist, Ludwik FLECK, who emphasised thought-collectives. Fleck's study of the sociology of a scientific fact of 1935 had focused on Behring's Jewish contemporaries, Paul Ehrlich and August von Wassermann, and their relations to the Prussian state.

In December 1940, the National Socialists set out to celebrate 50 years of serum therapy with a major celebration of Axis and occupied nations at the University of Marburg, the extent of the celebrations indicating that Behring was a key figure in the pantheon of Nazi medical heroes. Hellmuth UNGER, the Nazi physician, euthanasia propagandist and planner, produced a noteworthy biography in this vein. The Behring cult became central to the Nazi attempt to mobilise medical research for the war in the east, as well as a symbol of German conquest. In order to create an appropriately inspiring scientific pedigree for bacteriology, legitimating its military and racial role under Nazism, it was important to construct a proto-Nazi image of the founding fathers of bacteriology as *Vorkämpfer* of Nazism. Such hero-worship reinforced the increasing prestige of the history of medicine, intended to give the German doctor a sense of mission in the promotion of genocide and aggression.

Nazi propaganda projected a heroised image of Behring; a postage stamp was issued, Behring was romanticised in Unger's popular biography, and articles on Behring proliferated in a wide variety of medical and technical journals – from an article by the SS hygienist, Mrugowsky, praising Behring for combining the skills of physician and medical researcher, to his crude heroisation in the journal for disinfectors. Research institutes were named after Behring as a founding father of bacteriology, and the celebrations served to launch a co-operative venture between IG Farben and the Behring Works, an IG subsidiary acquired in 1929. Their "Behring Institute for Experimental Therapy", was created for typhus vaccine production but was intended ultimately to become a central state serum institute. IG Farben's aim was to take over the leading role in serobacteriology from the Pasteur Institute and Rockefeller Foundation. Behring Institutes were to be established world-wide, in Rio de Janeiro and Buenos Aires, and in Nazi occupied Lemberg (Lwow).

During the 1950s there were further celebratory works on Behring's achievements (e.g. ENGELHARDT), largely promoted by the *Behringwerke*, which had survived a take-over by IG Farben. In order to rid Behring of the aura of Nazism,

he was celebrated jointly with Paul Ehrlich. Thereafter, historical interest in bacteriology and immunology languished until the 1980s, and little was done to mark the centenary of serum therapy.

WEINDLING's study examines the heroic claims for serum therapy. It has been pointed out that the use of the term "therapy" could easily be misunderstood, as the serum therapy neutralised the spread of diphtheria toxin, thus having more of a blocking than a curative effect. Although sometimes used prophylactically, systematic vaccination had to wait until the mid-1920s. This study indicates that it is necessary to place Behring within his cultural and institutional context in order to provide a critical historical assessment of the first generation of German immunologists.

PAUL WEINDLING

Bernard, Claude 1813–1878

French physiologist

Foster, Michael, *Claude Bernard*, New York: Longmans Green, and London: Unwin, 1899

Gendron, P., *Claude Bernard: rationalité d'une méthode*, Paris: Institut Interdisciplinaire d'Études Epistémologique, 1992

Grande, Francisco and Maurice B. Visscher (eds), *Claude Bernard and Experimental Medicine*, Cambridge, Massachusetts: Schenkman, 1967

Greene, Henry Copley, *Introduction to the Study of Experimental Medicine*, New York: Macmillan, 1927

Guillemin, Roger, Lucienne Guillemin and Hebbel H. Hoff (trans), *The Cahier rouge of Claude Bernard*, Cambridge, Massachusetts: Schenkman, 1967

Holmes, Frederick Lawrence, *Claude Bernard and Animal Chemistry: The Emergence of a Scientist*, Cambridge, Massachusetts: Harvard University Press, 1974

Olmsted, J.M.D, *Claude Bernard and the Experimental Method in Medicine*, New York: Schuman, 1952

Robin, Eugene Debs (ed.), *Claude Bernard and the Internal Environment: A Memorial Symposium*, New York: Dekker, 1979

Claude Bernard was one of the greatest medical scientists. He performed valuable work in many fields of physiology, but perhaps his greatest gift to posterity was his philosophical approach to science, and his clear enunciation of the scope and purpose of physiology. His experimental work, in which he was at first helped and encouraged by his teacher, François Magendie, extended from the comparative anatomy of the chorda tympani, to the functions of gastric and pancreatic juice and of the liver. Contrary to the belief at the time that an animal cannot form food materials, but can only break down those made by plants, Bernard proved conclusively that the liver can form glycogen. Later he showed that the body can convert cane sugar to glucose. He also studied the effects of drugs on his experimental animals. Perhaps his most important contribution to physiology was his concept of the *milieu intérieur*, the internal environment or tissue fluid in which all but the cells on the surface of the body live. It is the constancy of this internal environment that enables the whole body to move about in a great variety of external environments; all the vital mechanisms, varied as they are, have only one object, he explained, that of keeping constant the conditions of life in the internal environment.

FOSTER, Bernard's first English biographer, gives a clear and succinct account of his life, work, and philosophy. Bernard was gifted with both manual dexterity and imagination, but he would not allow the latter to influence experimental observations, writing: "Put off your imagination as you take off your overcoat when you enter the laboratory; but put it on again as you do your overcoat, when you leave the laboratory."

Bernard's ability was recognised not only by other scientists, who elected him to follow Magendie as professor at the Collège de France, but also later by the Emperor, Louis Napoleon, who financed two well-equipped laboratories for him. In addition to his chair at the Collège de France and later at the Sorbonne, he was elected to membership of the Académie des Sciences and created Chevalier of the Légion d'honneur.

In 1863, Bernard was unable, because of illness, to work in his laboratory for nearly a year; he spent this time writing his *Introduction à l'étude de la médecine experimentale*, generally regarded as his masterpiece, and the first of his works to be translated into English (see GREENE). His philosophy would be accepted by most modern philosophers of science: that the nature of our minds leads us to seek the essence or the *why* of things, and thus we aim beyond the goal that it is given us to reach, for experience teaches us that we cannot get beyond the *how*.

J.M.D. Olmsted published a biography of Bernard in 1939, but the later work, OLMSTED, written in collaboration with his wife, dated his earlier research. The work is more comprehensive than Foster's, and mentions the famous *Cahier rouge*, in which, from 1850 to about 1860, Bernard noted plans and ideas as they occurred to him. The Olmsteds describe and quote from Bernard's prolific publications and some contemporary criticism of them.

HOLMES examines not only Bernard's work, but also that of some of his contemporaries and the arguments between them. The book concentrates on experiments and writings between 1848 and 1865, Bernard's most productive period, and gives details of failures as well as successes.

GUILLEMIN, with the assistance of his wife and Hebbel H. Hoff, produced the first English translation of the *Cahier rouge*, which is more accurate and complete than the 1967 earlier French edition by M.D. Grmek. The *Cahier rouge* was lost for many years in the archives of the Collège de France, until Léon Delhoume discovered it and published an abbreviated version in 1942. The original is a small notebook bound in red cardboard, whereas most of Bernard's notebooks were black or green; it has 354 pages of manuscript with ideas for experiments, observations and comments on science in general, in random order as they occurred to him. Some of the experimental plans are illustrated by pen and ink sketches.

In his final years, Bernard was particularly interested in the phenomena of life common to plants and animals. His book, *La science expérimentale*, published in the year of his death, is as profound a work of philosophy as the much better-known *Experimental Medicine*, but has yet to be translated into other languages.

GRANDE & VISSCHER edited one of the numerous symposia published to commemorate the centenary of the publication of *Introduction à l'étude de la médecine experimentale* in 1867. Other symposia were held to commemorate Bernard's death in 1878; one of these, edited by ROBIN, describes advances in the fields he had studied, but others are merely general physiological symposia, published at this appropriate time. A more recent book, by GENDRON, comments on Bernard's philosophy and its application to experimental science. Bernard's outstanding ability was acknowledged during his life, and the passage of time has not dimmed his reputation.

A.W. SLOAN

Berthollet, Claude-Louis, Comte de   1749–1822

French chemist

Crosland, Maurice P., *The Society of Arcueil: A View of French Science at the Time of Napoleon I*, London: Heinemann, and Cambridge, Massachusetts: Harvard University Press, 1967

Cuvier, J.L.N.F., "Eloge historique de M. le Comte Berthollet", in his *Recueil des éloges historiques dans les séances publiques de l'Institut de France*, vol. 3, Paris, 1827, 179–227

Kapoor, Satish, "Berthollet, Proust and Proportions", *Chymia*, 10 (1965): 53–110

Kapoor, Satish, entry in *Dictionary of Scientific Biography*, edited by Charles Coulston Gillispie, vol. 2, New York: Scribner, 1970

Lemery, P. and R.E. Oesper, "Claude-Louis Berthollet (1748–1822)", *Journal of Chemical Education*, 23 (1946): 158–65 and 230–36

Sadoun-Goupil, Michelle, *Le Chimiste Claude-Louis Berthollet, 1748–1822: Sa vie, son oeuvre*, Paris: Vrin, 1977

Claude-Louis Berthollet (not to be confused with the other French chemist, Marcellin Berthelot) was an amiable and uncontroversial figure, whose biography has developed more by investigation of greater detail than by any radical new interpretation. Several studies reveal the interests of their respective authors as much as the life and work of their subject.

One of the first biographical studies of Berthollet was by CUVIER on behalf of the Académie des Sciences. Berthollet's origins in Savoy and his medical education are described before his arrival in Paris, where he turned to chemistry and was an early Lavoisier convert. He was employed at the Gobelins dyeworks, where he discovered the bleaching properties of chlorine. His friendship with Napoleon called for tactful biographical treatment under the Bourbon Restoration. Altogether he is presented in the heroic mould which characterised academic éloges.

CROSLAND's study of Berthollet concentrates on the chemist within the theme of patronage, and emphasises his relation with Napoleon Bonaparte. Berthollet bought a country house in the village of Arcueil, just outside the capital, where he set up a laboratory and gathered round him a group of talented young men, soon to be known as the Society of Arcueil. The total number of members of the group (including Laplace, who lived next door at Arcueil) never exceeded 15, yet Berthollet and Laplace succeeded in assembling the cream of the next generation of French scientists. It is argued that, just as Berthollet owed his social position and much of his fortune to Napoleon, many young scientists owed their subsequent careers to Berthollet. This provides a common theme of patronage. Younger members of the Society of Arcueil would present memoirs on Sundays, as a preparation for the final reading of the memoir on the following day at the First Class of the National Institute. Berthollet was able to champion the early election of his assistant, Gay-Lussac, and several other members of the Society.

SADOUN-GOUPIL's study of Berthollet is the only full-length biography of the chemist, and provides a useful complement to Crosland's approach since it concentrates on the science. More precisely it is divided (as are too many biographies of scientists) into two parts: the first 100 pages examine the life, the majority of the book then examining the work. Goupil found that Berthollet's early chemical research was very miscellaneous. His projects were always inspired by outside influences, either by the Académie des Sciences or by the Gobelins, where he was director of the dyeworks from 1784. Goupil asserts that Berthollet's work was completely lacking in any research programme until his return from the Egyptian expedition in 1799. What he had found in Egypt was large deposits of sodium carbonate (trona), which he concluded had been formed by the reaction between local limestone (calcium carbonate) and sodium chloride, from sea water. This was the reverse of the reaction that took place in the laboratory, and showed Berthollet that reactions depend not only on the substances present but also on their quantity. This was a major revision of the accepted laws of chemical affinity, and is seen as leading eventually to the law of mass action of Guldberg and Waage. Berthollet explained his ideas in two books: his *Recherches sur les lois d'affinité* (1801) was followed by the influential *Essai de statique chimique* (2 vols, 1803); Kapoor claimed that the latter was "the first work to undertake a systematic analysis of the methodology of chemistry". Sadoun-Goupil has seen the manuscript of the revised second edition of the *Essai de statique chimique*, which was never published, in which Berthollet developed his ideas on combining proportions.

It was this relativist interpretation of chemical reaction that led Berthollet to claim that the proportions of the constituents of a chemical compound are variable, an assertion disputed by Joseph Proust, who had an almost mystical view of Nature, "balance" in hand, forming compounds in fixed proportions. A detailed study of this famous controversy has been made in KAPOOR (1965). Berthollet believed that the composition of a compound would depend on the quantities of reagents present when it was formed, although he admitted some cases of fixed proportions. Both Proust and Berthollet were able to provide experimental results in support of their respective theories. In the end, Proust defined compounds as having fixed composition; substances with variable composition were solutions or mixtures. The controversy was carried on with great

politeness, and Berthollet was noted for his general friendliness even with those who disagreed with him.

KAPOOR (1970) provides a discussion of Berthollet in which he is represented as someone who (in contrast to Lavoisier) wanted to improve, rather than revolutionise, chemistry. His enthusiastic support of the ideas of the *Encyclopédie* reinforced his desire to put science to practical use. Nevertheless, Kapoor's treatment is almost entirely internalist. Although won over to Lavoisier's oxygen theory in 1785, Berthollet cast grave doubts on Lavoisier's view that oxygen was the universal principle of acidity. Kapoor shows a special interest in Berthollet's methodology and models, which were sometimes quasi-mechanical, as in the *Essai de statique chimique*.

MAURICE CROSLAND

Berzelius, Jöns Jacob 1779–1848

Swedish chemist

Brooke, John Hedley, "Chlorine Substitution and the Future of Organic Chemistry: Methodological Issues in the Laurent–Berzelius Correspondence (1843–1844)", *Studies in History and Philosophy of Science*, 4/1 (1973): 47–94

Dunsch, Lothar, *Jöns Jacob Berzelius*, Leipzig: Teubner, 1986

Jorpes, Johan Erik, *Jac. Berzelius: His Life and Work*, translated by Barbara Steele, Stockholm: Almqvist & Wiksell, 1966

Lundgren, Anders, *Berzelius och den kemiska atomteorin*, Uppsala: Almqvist & Wiksell, 1979

Melhado, Evan M., *Jacob Berzelius: The Emergence of His Chemical System*, Stockholm: Almqvist & Wiksell, and Madison: University of Wisconsin Press, 1981

Melhado, Evan M. and Tore Frängsmyr (eds), *Enlightenment Science in the Romantic Era: The Chemistry of Berzelius and Its Cultural Setting*, Cambridge and New York: Cambridge University Press, 1992

Söderbaum, Henrik Gustaf, *Jac. Berzelius: Levnadsteckning*, 3 vols, Uppsala: Almqvist & Wiksell, 1929–31

Solovev, Iurii Ivanovich and Victor Ivanovich Kurinnoi, *Jacob Berzelius: zhin i deiatelnost*, Moscow: Academy of Sciences, 1961

The scientific investigations of Jöns Jacob Berzelius cover almost all of the major chemical issues of the first half of the 19th century. His most popular works are those on stoichiometry, organic and inorganic compounds, and electrochemistry. Berzelius determined the atomic weights of 45 chemical elements, and developed the chemical symbols that are still in use today. He was also the author of a chemistry textbook and of the *Jahresberichte*, the annual reports on new achievements in chemistry and physics.

SÖDERBAUM's exhaustive three-volume biography in Swedish located Berzelius's importance in his early acceptance and experimental elaboration of John Dalton's atomic theory. However, this view does not do justice to the complex nature of Berzelius's debt to his predecessors' views on atomism, nor does it square with his initially very harsh judgment of Dalton's theory. None the less, this book contains a great deal of useful information.

JORPES's short work relies to some extent on Söderbaum, but includes excerpts from Berzelius's scientific correspondence. Jorpes describes the trajectory of the scientist's life, spicing it with interesting biographical detail, describing, for example, Berzelius's meeting with Goethe in Marienbad in 1822; the future Russian emperor Alexander II's visit to his Stockholm chemical laboratory in 1838; and the scientist's friendly relationship with the Swedish Royal Family.

Jorpes discusses the early 19th-century development of medicine, chemistry, physics, and other natural sciences in Sweden in great detail, pointing out that approximately 40% of the chemical elements known towards the end of the 19th century were discovered by Swedish chemists – including Berzelius, who co-discovered Cerium (Ce) (in collaboration with another Swedish chemist and manufacturer, Wilhelm Hisinger), Selenium (Se), amorphous Silicon, Zirconium, and Thorium. Jorpes's book will certainly be useful to a broad variety of readers, and especially to those who are new to the history of chemistry.

Like Jorpes, DUNSCH gives a short description of Berzelius's life and an overview of his scientific works, although emphasis is placed on his contribution to the development of the atomic theory.

The Russian language monograph by SOLOVEV & KURINNOI (in which chapters 2 and 3 are written by Igor S. Dmitriev) includes a short biography of the chemist as well as an analysis of the major areas of his scientific activities, with chapters on the following: the development of the theory of chemical proportions and the atomic theory; Berzelius's work on the system of symbols for the chemical elements and chemical nomenclature; the creation of electrochemical theory; and his investigations in mineralogy, organic and analytical chemistry, and catalysis. The authors also dedicate plenty of space to the textbook *Lehrbuch der Chemie*, on which Berzelius worked during most of his career, and to his famous *Jahresberichte*, which provided 27 annual overviews of Swedish contributions to the natural sciences (1821–47). The last chapter contains a detailed description of Berzelius's contact with Russian scientists, and notes how the ideas and discoveries made by Swedish scientists affected the development of chemistry in Russia. In addition, there are seven appendices, which include excerpts from Berzelius's correspondence with Dalton, Justus Liebig, Auguste Laurent, and fragments from his articles on isomerism and chemical proportions.

The first chapters of LUNDGREN are dedicated to Berzelius's early work, particularly his electrochemical researches of 1802–07 and 1808–10, and to his views on chemical affinity. Lundgren describes in detail the state of Swedish chemistry around 1800, in the wake of Lavoisier's anti-phlogistic theory, and emphasizes the special role played by Anders Ekeberg, one of Berzelius's teachers in Uppsala, who with Pehr Afzelius published the first (1795) Swedish chemical nomenclature compiled in accordance with Lavoisier's theory of oxygen. The author also notes the role of Christoph Girtanner, whose textbook Berzelius used in his studies, pointing out that Berzelius was educated in the spirit of Lavoisier's chemistry, and thus considered the problem of the ultimate structure of matter as metaphysical, and therefore as beyond the boundaries of scientific chemistry.

Most interestingly, Lundgren discusses Berzelius's views on Dalton's atomic theory; masterfully using a wide range of material, he analyses the causes and nature of the conflict between the two scientists. Prior to 1811, Berzelius was chiefly influenced by J.B. Richter's stoichiometric laws, the electrolytical decomposition of alkalis, and Dalton's law on multiple proportions, but not by his atomic theory of the structure of matter. Berzelius did not designate the smallest unit of proportions an atom, but "the absolute minimum". These minima can be difficult to find in the laboratory, and are sometimes only theoretically calculable. Furthermore, the minima bear no relation to Lavoisier's chemical elements, and so it is difficult to relate them to Dalton's atoms. Nevertheless, the most important difference between Dalton and Berzelius is that the former began with the atomic theory and used it to explain chemical proportions, while the latter first established the law of chemical proportions in his laboratory, and then looked for its explanation. Lundgren demonstrates how Berzelius gradually began to accept the atomistic terminology, while still rejecting Dalton's theory *per se*, and argues that this rejection was caused by the fact that some chemical combinations allowed by Dalton were not possible, according to Berzelius's laws of chemical proportions. This problem was solved in 1816, when the few combinations that failed to fit both theories came to be considered exceptions from the proportional laws.

The general conclusion to Lundgren's informative and interesting study is that Berzelius never claimed that atomic theory described reality, but that it was the most plausible and useful hypothesis available, allowing him to both systematize the ever-increasing amount of chemical information, and lay the foundation for the future development of chemistry. Lundgren's study is written in Swedish, but contains a useful summary in English entitled, "Berzelius and the chemical atomic theory".

MELHADO's book is a deep, multifaceted analysis of Berzelius's theoretical and experimental works, in which the author takes a generic approach to Berzelius's science. Almost one half of the book presents a broad overview of the development of chemistry in the 17th and 18th centuries. Describing how historical studies of 18th-century chemistry have traditionally focused on Lavoisier and the events of the chemical revolution, Melhado notes that, by selecting themes in the light of their relevance to later events, historians have ignored many other important themes – such as the achievements of Berzelius – which are of interest, not only in their own right, but also as precedents for 19th-century developments. He then goes on to examine a principal explanatory technique of chemistry in the 18th century, the two-component theories. These theories explained both the existence of generic groups of chemicals, like metals or acids, and the differences among members of these groups, with membership in genus depending on the presence of a generic ingredient. Being a property-bearing principle, the generic ingredient stamped its individuality on all members of the genus, the specificity of the different members of the genus being attributed to the presence of a different specific ingredient in each member. Melhado brings forward a number of examples showing the usage of this two-component approach, from the works of Georg Ernst Stahl, Torben Bergman, L. Guyton de Morveau, and Lavoisier among others.

The genesis and maturation of Berzelius's system is the subject of the second part of Melhado's study. Portrayed as a theory of salts, the system acquired its main outlines by 1813 through Berzelius's studies of inorganic chemistry, and received its final articulation in 1819 via its development in mineralogy and organic chemistry. Melhado argues that a major innovation of Berzelius's chemistry was to replace the hierarchical two-component theories, especially those of salts, with an approach that gave each component equal status. Melhado stresses also that Berzelius's concern for specificity is evident in his first experiments with the voltaic pile (1803), and persists through his stoichiometric studies. Electrochemistry determined qualitative specificity; stoichiometry determined quantitative specificity. Overall, Melhado's conclusions are well-argued and offer a new perspective on the development of chemistry at the time of the chemical revolution.

BROOKE's paper deals with the polemics that flared up in the 1830s and 1840s concerning Auguste Laurent and Jean-Baptiste Dumas's substitution theories. It was the notion that, in certain organic compounds, the highly electronegative element chlorine could replace, and essentially play the same role as, the electropositive element hydrogen, that evoked sharp objections from Berzelius. Historians have traditionally attributed Berzelius's persistent opposition to senile obstinacy and conservatism, assuming that the foundation for his obduracy lay in the electrochemical theory of chemical combination that he had introduced into the field of organic chemistry. However, the projection of this theory into the organic domain, by analogy with the electrochemical properties of inorganic salts, did have its own problems: in particular, that the majority of organic compounds are not ionic in character. The aim of Brooke's study is "to advocate at least a reprieve both for Berzelius and for the reputation of the electrochemical theory as it had been employed by the organic chemists of the 1830s". Brooke's main thesis is that Berzelius's primary motive for opposing Laurent and Dumas was neither a desire to defend his electrochemical theory, nor his commitment to the opinion that organic compounds really were no different from inorganic species. Rather, the decisive issue for Berzelius was the imminent inversion of a cherished regulative principle that he had long advertised as a *sine qua non* for the possibility of an organic chemistry. Berzelius had constantly maintained that the organic compounds theory could only progress if based on analogies borrowed from the inorganic domain. What was at stake in the substitution debates was, according to Brooke, not merely the truth or falsehood of a particular scientific theory, but a decision concerning nothing less than the entire future direction of theoretical organic chemistry.

MELHADO & FRÅNGSMYR's collection contains papers by Lundgren, Melhado, and Brooke that echo the concerns described above. In addition, the book includes two contrasting biographical portraits of Berzelius, as well as articles on such topics as isomorphism. All in all, this collection provides a very good introduction to Berzelius and the science of his time.

IGOR S. DMITRIEV

Bichat, Marie François Xavier 1771–1802

French anatomist and physiologist

Ackerknecht, Erwin H., *Medicine at the Paris Hospital, 1794–1848*, Baltimore: Johns Hopkins University Press, 1967

Coquerelle, Jules, *Xavier Bichat (1771–1802)*, Paris: Maloine, 1902

Dobo, Nicolas and André Role, *Bichat: La Vie fulgurante d'un génie*, Paris: Perrin, 1989

Duchesneau, François, *La Physiologie des lumières: Empirisme, modèles et théories*, The Hague: Nijhoff, 1982

Genty, Maurice, article on Bichat (1771–1802), in *Biographies médicales et scientifiques, XVIII siècle: Jean Astruc, Antoine Louis, Pierre Desault, Xavier Bichat*, edited by Pierre Huard, Paris: Dacosta, 1972

Haigh, Elizabeth, *Xavier Bichat and the Medical Theory of the Eighteenth Century*, London: Wellcome Institute, 1984

King, Lester Snow, *The Medical World of the Eighteenth Century*, Chicago: University of Chicago Press, 1958

Although acknowledged to be a hugely influential figure in the history of physiology and in the development of medicine and science in France from the time of his death, Bichat has long remained a somewhat elusive figure. His contributions were alluded to in various books and articles over the years, but it was difficult to pin down precisely his role, in either the history of medicine or the life sciences. The primary reason for the bewilderment appears to have been the fact that vitalist theory lost its authority, and even became a kind of embarrassment, in the 19th century; thus, while Bichat's tissue theory continued to be described and analyzed, its vitalist underpinning was ignored. In the 1960s, various works appeared that examined Bichat's work as a whole, analyzing it within the context of his predecessors and successors.

Some of the literature about Bichat, especially that written in France, confines itself largely to biographical study, and is designed to celebrate the short life of a national hero. It is, however, a useful place to start studying Bichat. Having done extensive archival work in a number of centres, COQUERELLE offers a profusion of details on the Bichat family, its genealogy, personal and professional letters, and a brief survey of Bichat's army and medical careers. A large part of the book is given over to reproducing eulogies and odes delivered in Bichat's honour. GENTY also deals with Bichat's family and his personal and professional life, with again just a cursory glance at his work. The most extensive work written in the hagiographic tradition is that of DOBO & ROLE, who examine in minute detail the years leading up to Bichat's arrival in Paris in 1794, and his apprenticeship to the surgeon Pierre Desault. While the latter third of the book summarizes his professional accomplishments, there is no attempt to evaluate his contributions to scientific scholarship, or to place it within its intellectual and academic context.

Both Ackerknecht and King evaluate Bichat's role in the development of physiological theory and medical practice, by including him in their treatments of more general themes. Most particularly, they evaluate his contributions to the development of theories of pathology, and both treat him as an intellectual giant. Concentrating on the new medicine that emerged as a result of the French Revolution, ACKERKNECHT shows how hospitals became the core of medical practice, teaching and investigation. He argues that Bichat was a leader in this transformation, on account of his contributions to anatomy and his location of pathological conditions in tissues, which he treated as the component parts of organs. In a work in which he illustrates ideas through the study of personalities, KING devotes a few pages to Bichat in a chapter on "The Rise of Modern Pathology". Dubbing him "one of the great geniuses of medicine", he argues that it was Bichat who placed the study of general pathology on a modern footing.

Duchesneau and Haigh both analyze Bichat's work more thoroughly, placing it firmly within the context of 18th-century developments in science in general, and the life sciences specifically. The authors cover many of the same topics: both analyze the vital properties that Bichat delineated, integrating his tissue theory into his vitalist ideology, and analyzing how his attitudes to vitalism led to the development of his *Anatomie générale*; and both contend that the debate, including Bichat's contribution to it, is central to the emergence of a distinct science of physiology at the end of the 18th century. The experience of reading the two works, however, is quite different.

DUCHESNEAU devotes the final chapter of his philosophical history to Bichat's work, treating it as the culmination of a century of vitalist theory and analysis, beginning with the anti-mechanism of Georg Ernst Stahl. There is an unrelenting quality to his massive, diligently researched and well-argued work, for Duchesneau confines himself strictly to his subject's scholarship. This valuable work is rigorous but tends to be turgid.

HAIGH's monograph opens with a sketch of Bichat's life and times. The book's central argument is that Bichat's work is the synthesis of two traditions of the analysis of organic functions. The first influence on his work was that of the physicians of the Montpellier medical school, and the second that of persons including Robert Whytt and Albrecht von Haller, who investigated the phenomena of bodily irritability and sensibility.

ELIZABETH V. HAIGH

See also Pathology

Big Bang Theory

Berger, André (ed.), *The Big Bang and Georges Lemaître*, Dordrecht: Reidel, 1984

Bertotti, Bruno, *et al.* (eds), *Modern Cosmology in Retrospect*, Cambridge and New York: Cambridge University Press, 1990

Godart, O. and M. Heller, *Cosmology of Lemaître*, Tucson, Arizona: Pachart, 1985

Kragh, Helge, *Cosmology and Controversy: The Historical Development of Two Theories of the Universe*, Princeton, New Jersey: Princeton University Press, 1996

Lightman, Alan and Roberta Brawer, *Origins: The Lives and Worlds of Modern Cosmologists*, Cambridge, Massachusetts: Harvard University Press, 1990

Tropp, Eduard A., Viktor Ya. Frenkel and Artur D. Chernin, *Alexander A. Friedmann: The Man Who Made the Universe Expand*, translated from the Russian by Alexander Dron and Michael Burov, Cambridge and New York: Cambridge University Press, 1993 (original edition, 1988)

Weinberg, Steven, *The First Three Minutes: A Modern View of the Origin of the Universe*, New York: Basic Books, 1977; revised edition, New York and Toronto: Bantam, 1984

Big Bang cosmology is generally understood as the theory that the world has had an origin in time in which the entire universe was in an ultradense state (perhaps of infinite density), which since then has expanded in agreement with the laws of general relativity. This kind of cosmological theory is thus a subclass of relativistic cosmology, as first pointed out by the Russian physicist, Alexander Friedmann, in 1922. However, it was only from about 1950 that Big Bang theory was developed into a physical cosmology, and it eventually (from about 1965) became the standard view of cosmologists. For this reason, the literature on the history of Big Bang theory is modern and limited. Very few books have taken up the topic, and much of the literature consists in articles published in technical journals.

Although Friedmann provided the mathematical foundation of Big Bang theory in 1922, his work was ignored, and it is questionable whether he thought of the Big Bang universe as anything other than a mathematical solution to Einstein's field equations. TROPP, FRENKEL & CHERNIN argue that Friedmann was the founder not only of the expanding universe, but also of the Big Bang universe. (The two concepts are different.) Based on new sources from Russian archives, they describe the short but eventful life of Friedmann, and focus on his seminal contributions of 1922 and 1924. The biography also includes a summary of later developments in Big Bang theory, which are not, however, quite reliable. It should be noted that this work, along with other Russian writings on Friedmann, are flavoured by a certain degree of Russian nationalism and hero-worship.

GODART & HELLER deal with the other candidate for the title of "the father of the Big Bang theory", the Belgian priest and physicist George Lemaître, giving a balanced evaluation of his contributions to cosmology. Godart was for a long period a junior collaborator of Lemaître, a fact that is reflected by the book's somewhat uncritical treatment of Lemaître's work and historical importance. This is a useful summary of Lemaître's career, but it is far from the full scientific biography that he deserves.

The same may be said of the volume edited by BERGER, which is the proceedings of a 1983 symposium in honour of Lemaître. Quite typical for the genre, it is an uneven mixture of scientific, biographical and historical articles. Among the historically interesting contributions are James Peeble's brief paper on Lemaître's influence on modern cosmology, William McCrea's survey of main trends in 20th-century cosmology, and, in particular, André Deprit's valuable biographical article. This is the most detailed description of Lemaître's life so far, but it unfortunately lacks references and documentation. Like Godart & Heller, the Berger volume belongs to the celebration literature, and concentrates more on depicting Lemaître as a precursor of modern cosmology than on analyzing his contributions within their historical context.

The volume edited by BERTOTTI *et al.* is also of conference proceedings, based on a meeting held in 1988, but is very different from Berger in content and scope. Bertotti is devoted entirely to the history of cosmology (c.1900–70), and is not "contaminated" by the many purely technical articles usually found in conference proceedings. It is a well organized work, covering most important aspects of modern cosmology. Two of the main contributors to the post-Lemaître Big Bang theory, Ralph Alpher and Robert Hermann, give a detailed account of their own (and George Gamow's) pioneering work, while other contributions related to Big Bang theory include articles by Robert Wagoner (on nuclear astrophysics), Woodruff Sullivan III (on Martin Ryle and radio astronomy), and Maarten Schmidt (on the discovery of quasars). The discovery of the cosmic microwave background radiation in 1965, the single most important factor in what has been called the "renaissance" of the Big Bang theory, is described by Robert Wilson, one of the discoverers (together with Arno Penzias) of the radiation. Taken together, Bertotti is possibly the best and most informative work on the history of modern cosmology at present. The fact that it does not deal specifically with Big Bang theory is not a disadvantage, for it is impossible to deal with the history of that theory independently of other developments in cosmology. For example, the rival Steady State theory is an integral part of the history of the Big Bang theory of the 1950s and early 1960s. The controversy between the Steady State theory and evolutionary cosmologies receives detailed and scholarly treatment in KRAGH, which also includes an account of the history of Big Bang theory. Unlike most other works, Kragh emphasizes the physical and observational, rather than the mathematical and conceptual, aspects of cosmology.

The theory that the universe had a violent beginning in time in a cataclysmic Big Bang became the standard view of cosmology in the mid-1960s, when cosmology experienced a major shift. It was only then, according to many astronomers and physicists, that cosmology became truly scientific, and based on a generally shared paradigm. It is this standard theory that is the subject of WEINBERG, a leading theoretical physicist and contributor to the interface between particle physics and cosmology. Although a popular work written by a scientist, Weinberg is historically sensitive, and one of the best works on the development of modern Big Bang theory. Weinberg is a pedagogical, yet historically reliable, work that is particularly strong in its analysis of the discovery of the cosmic microwave background, and its impact on the course of modern cosmology. In addition, the work goes beyond 1965, and provides a good account of the first attempts to understand the very early universe by means of the new theories of elementary particles to which Weinberg has himself been a major contributor.

More recent developments are covered in LIGHTMAN & BRAWER, a popular book that details how Big Bang cosmology has evolved during the 1970s and 1980s. It consists mainly of interviews with modern cosmologists, from pioneers such as Fred Hoyle and Allan Sandage, to the younger generation of Big Bang physicist-cosmologists such as Stephen Hawking, Alan Gut, and Andrei Linde. The inflationary universe – the theory that the very early universe experienced a drastic inflation – occupies a central theme in the book, which gives interesting information concerning the paradigmatic role played by Big Bang theory in modern cosmology. Lightman & Brawer is valuable because of the many interviews it includes, but neither it nor other works are comprehensive and coherent accounts of the history of Big Bang theory.

HELGE KRAGH

See also Cosmology

Big Science

Bacon, Francis, "New Atlantis", in *Selected Writings of Francis Bacon*, edited by Hugh G. Dick, New York: Modern Library, 1955

Galison, Peter and Bruce Hevly (eds), *Big Science: The Growth of Large-Scale Research*, Stanford, California: Stanford University Press, 1992

Jasanoff, Sheila, *et al.* (eds), *Handbook of Science and Technology Studies*, Thousand Oaks, California: Sage, 1995

Kevles, Daniel J., *The Physicists: The History of a Scientific Community in Modern America*, New York: Knopf, 1978; revised edition, Cambridge, Massachusetts: Harvard University Press, 1995

Price, Derek J. de Solla, *Science since Babylon*, New Haven, Connecticut: Yale University Press, 1961; revised edition, 1975

Price, Derek. J. de Solla, *Little Science, Big Science*, New York: Columbia University Press, 1963; revised edition as *Little Science, Big Science – and Beyond*, New York: Columbia University Press, 1986

Rhodes, Richard, *The Making of the Atomic Bomb*, New York: Simon and Schuster, 1986

Weinberg, Alvin M., *Reflections on Big Science*, Cambridge, Massachusetts: MIT Press, 1967

The term Big Science refers to large scale, highly organized research projects, employing large numbers of people over a long period of time, and usually supported through government funding. Two connections with technology are also usually implied: Big Science often employs "big technology", in the form of elaborate and expensive laboratory apparatus, and the advancement of new technologies is often offered as one of its purposes or justifications.

While the term is a 20th-century invention, the concept of Big Science is much older. In his fictional narrative, BACON portrays an island nation where peace and prosperity proceed from the process and products of organized scientific research. Here state-supported science, highly organized and fully institutionalized, is legitimized by its practical applications as well as by an appreciation of the value of knowledge for knowledge's sake. Two key attributes of Big Science are already present: substantial government support and a complex tension between "pure" and "applied" research.

Until recently, Big Science projects have been primarily within the physical sciences (although more lately biomedical, pharmaceutical, and genetic research have attained comparable levels of "bigness"). Thus KEVLES provides a useful history of how American physics evolved more and more toward the practices and institutions of Big Science. Relations among the professional physics community, academia, industry, government, and the military all figure in this story; but Kevles distinguishes the military connection as especially important. The contributions of physics to the technologies of the two world wars solidified the notion of science as essential to the national interest, and paved the way for the full-blown Big Science of the Cold War era. In a preface added to his 1995 edition, Kevles uses the demise of the Superconducting Supercollider, a premier project of American high-energy physics, as a case-study to illustrate the changing position of Big Science in a post-Cold War world.

The archetype of Big Science, and a key stimulus for its dramatic growth during the second half of the 20th century, is the legendary Manhattan Project. RHODES traces the roots of this project to small-scale, "pure" research beginning near the turn of the century, which contrasts sharply with the enormous, complex, goal-directed projects of World War II. A number of the central issues of Big Science emerge clearly: how does the practice of science change when it moves from the small laboratory to large institutions; what is the relationship between pure and applied research; how should scientists respond to the social consequences of their work?

WEINBERG, himself a director of a major laboratory with a primarily military mission, expounds on the problems and promises of Big Science from a viewpoint of scientific and technological optimism. Weinberg views science as essential to the solution of two inevitable, natural problems: a crisis in global energy supply and a crisis in information management. While recognizing that Big Science and the technologies it spawns create new problems of their own, he is confident that more Big Science can address some of these problems and that a separate community of humanists will somehow "supply those deeper values" that are needed to address the rest. As a Big Science administrator writing at a time of great enthusiasm for science and technology, and as a specialist in the physical sciences, Weinberg exemplifies the dominant paradigm of his times. Focusing on how Big Science should be managed, he assumes its inevitability as a social practice and – by today's standards – does not look deeply into how Big Science is conducted or at its broader social effects and implications.

Although the term "Big Science" never appears in PRICE (1961), he deals here with issues that are important to its explication. Noting that many ancient societies accomplished large-scale scientific projects, he asserts that these cultures were unlike our own "peculiarly" scientific one – modern Western science differs not simply quantitatively, but also qualitatively, from earlier modes of organized inquiry. Examining the relationship between science and technology, he concludes that the link between these domains is "weak but vital", rejecting a simple model of technology as driven directly by science. Toward the end of the book, Price explores the quantitative measurement of scientific activity, plotting over time such indicators as numbers of publications, journal titles, and scientific workers.

In PRICE (1963), he extends the same quantitative approach toward what he calls a "science of science". Writing within the same cultural context as Weinberg (to whom he attributes the invention of the term "Big Science"), he assumes that science is itself a social good, that its exponential growth is an inevitable natural process, and that one of the central problems posed by this growth is a vast proliferation of information. Price's chief concerns are with improving the efficiency and effectiveness of the scientific enterprise as given, rather than critiquing its consequences or its modes of organization. Nevertheless, his mathematical techniques are useful in identifying some of these organizational structures; his chapters on "invisible colleges" and "networks of scientific papers" are classic analyses that provided the framework for a generation of structural approaches to the sociology of science.

The volume edited by GALISON & HEVLY, produced some 30 years after those of Price and Weinberg, reflects a greatly changed approach to the analysis of Big Science. The concerns go beyond the optimization of science as a knowledge-producing machine to the consideration of how scientific communities are constructed within larger social, political, economic, and cultural contexts. Historical, anthropological, and sociological approaches provide insights useful for science policy analysis, for project and laboratory management, and for a broader view of Big Science as a complex phenomenon with a multitude of connections to the societies that host it symbiotically.

The essays collected by JASANOFF et al., continue in the same social constructionist tradition, but with a less historical and more sociological emphasis. Although the term "Big Science" appears only rarely in this thick volume, the concept is implicit throughout; this may reflect the extent to which the bigness of science and technology is now taken for granted. As Weinberg noted three decades earlier, science has become big in two ways: in the sizes of its individual projects as well as in its scope and scale as an overall enterprise. The latter aspect is apparent in the essays collected for the *Handbook*, which document the relationships between science and local and national government, the military, the mass media, and the public; as well as the relationships within and among scientific communities. Additionally, a section on theory and methodology in science studies reveals a new, self-conscious awareness among those who conduct such studies; perhaps the study of science, and of Big Science, is in the process of becoming Big Science itself.

WILLIAM J. KINSELLA

Biochemistry

Chittenden, Russell H., *The Development of Physiological Chemistry in the United States*, New York: Chemical Catalog Company, 1930

Chittenden, Russell H., *The First Twenty-Five Years of the American Society of Biological Chemists*, New Haven, Connecticut: American Society of Biological Chemists, 1945

Coley, Noel G., *From Animal Chemistry to Biochemistry*, Amersham, Buckinghamshire: Hulton, 1973

Florkin, Marcel, *A History of Biochemistry*, 5 vols, Amsterdam: Elsevier, 1972–86 (vols 30–33B of *Comprehensive Biochemistry*, edited by Florkin and Elmer H. Stotz)

Fruton, Joseph S., *Molecules and Life: Historical Essays on the Interplay of Chemistry and Biology*, New York: Wiley-Interscience, 1972

Fruton, Joseph S., *Contrasts in Scientific Style: Research Groups in the Chemical and Biochemical Sciences*, Philadelphia: American Philosophical Society, 1990

Goodwin, T.W., *History of the Biochemical Society, 1911–1986*, London: Biochemical Society, 1987

Holmes, Frederic L., *Hans Krebs*, 2 vols, Oxford and New York: Oxford University Press, 1991–93

Karlson, Peter, *Adolf Butenandt: Biochemiker, Hormonforscher, Wissenschaftspolitiker*, Stuttgart: Wissenschaftliche Verlagsgesellschaft, 1990

Kleinkauf, Horst, Hans von Döhren and Lothar Jaenicke (eds), *The Roots of Modern Biochemistry: Fritz Lipmann's Squiggle and Its Consequences*, Berlin: De Gruyter, 1988

Kohler, Robert E., *From Medical Chemistry to Biochemistry: The Making of a Biomedical Discipline*, Cambridge and New York: Cambridge University Press, 1982

Kornberg, Arthur *et al.* (eds), *Reflections on Biochemistry: In Honor of Severo Ochoa*, Oxford and New York: Pergamon Press, 1976

Kornberg, Arthur, *For the Love of Enzymes: The Odyssey of a Biochemist*, Cambridge, Massachusetts: Harvard University Press, 1989

Laszlo, Pierre, *Molecular Correlates of Biological Concepts*, Amsterdam: Elsevier, 1986

Leicester, Henry M., *Development of Biochemical Concepts from Ancient to Modern Times*, Cambridge, Massachusetts: Harvard University Press, 1974

Lipmann, Fritz, *Wanderings of a Biochemist*, New York: Wiley-Interscience, 1971

Needham, Joseph and Ernest Baldwin (eds), *Hopkins and Biochemistry, 1861–1947*, Cambridge: Heffer, 1949

Needham, Joseph (ed.), *The Chemistry of Life: Eight Lectures on the History of Biochemistry*, Cambridge: Cambridge University Press, 1970

Semenza, Giorgio and Rainer Jaenicke (eds), *Selected Topics in the History of Biochemistry: Personal Recollections*, 3 vols, Amsterdam: Elsevier, 1983–90

Slater, E.C., Rainer Jaenicke and Giorgio Semenza (eds), *Selected Topics in the History of Biochemistry: Personal Recollections IV*, Amsterdam: Elsevier, 1995

Srinivasan, P.R., Joseph S. Fruton and John T. Edsall (eds), "The Origins of Modern Biochemistry: A Retrospect on Proteins", *Annals of the New York Academy of Sciences*, 325 (1979): 1–375

Werner, Petra, *Otto Warburg: Von der Zellphysiologie zur Krebsforschung*, Berlin: Neues Leben, 1988

Biochemistry can be defined as the study of the composition of living organisms, and of the way in which the functions of these elements combine to result in the phenomenon called *life*. Interpreted in this broad way, the history of biochemistry begins in classical Greece. However, if we conceive of biochemistry as a specific scientific discipline, then its origins can be found in the first half of the 19th century, in vegetable and animal chemistry studied by chemists, as well as in physiological and clinical chemistry studied by physiologists, pathologists, and cytologists. The term biochemistry was first used by Felix Hoppe-Seyler in the opening issue of the *Zeitschrift für physiologische Chemie* in 1877.

Developments in bacteriology in particular offered chemistry a chance to contribute to the discovery of the solutions to problems related to infectious diseases and to agriculture. The discovery of cell-free fermentation by Eduard Buchner contributed to the formulation of a new paradigm explaining the processes of life, and biochemistry became the science of intracellular chemical conversions. Such new insights were stimulated by the development of new instruments from the 1920s onwards; for example, the ultracentrifuge, the x-ray diffraction apparatus, the electrophoresis apparatus, and the use of radioisotopes. Such techniques were used to isolate and characterize pure substances. In the 1950s, several (sub)disciplines branched off from biochemistry; e.g., molecular biology, molecular virology, and molecular genetics.

There are a number of books in which the leitmotif is formed by a specific theme from the history of biochemistry. LEICESTER describes the history of biochemical concepts from classical antiquity until the 1930s. He defines a biochemical concept as any hypothesis relating to a bodily function explained in terms of specific substances. He discusses, among other things, developments in the Hellenistic period, the early Middle Ages, the 17th century and later, as well as Chinese, Indian, and Arabic concepts. COLEY starts his history of biochemistry with the animal chemistry of the late 18th century. The study of diseases such as gout, diabetes, stomach disorders and urinary calculus using chemistry seemed promising for the treatment of such maladies. Coley pays much attention to Justus von Liebig's influential work *Animal Chemistry, or Organic Chemistry in Its Applications to Physiology and Pathology*, published in 1842; he also discusses extensively the work of the physiologist Claude Bernard. Besides chemists and physiologists, Coley also discusses physico-chemists such as Hermann von Helmholtz and Luigi Galvani. In physical chemistry, topics such as the conservation of energy, "electricity and life", electrolysis, osmosis, diffusion and colloids were intensively studied. Coley's treatise ends with a short discussion of several categories of substances that are crucial in biochemistry, such as purines, amino acids, polypeptides and proteins, enzymes, biological oxidation, vitamins, hormones, and the concept of macromolecules.

NEEDHAM's collection comprises eight essays on the history of biochemistry in the 19th and the first half of the 20th centuries. These essays discuss specific topics, such as the history of the study of photosynthesis, biological oxidation, hormones and vitamins. In his introductory essay, Needham discusses some early Chinese, Arabic and Indian influences.

In the United States, biochemistry arose in the medical schools, but most American biochemists were primarily educated as chemists. CHITTENDEN (1930) takes the reader from the 19th into the 20th century. The work begins with a comparison of physiological chemistry in the United States, France and Germany, and continues with the explosive growth of physiological chemistry in the US, providing a review of scientific findings by researchers from various universities and institutes. This culminates in a history of ideas, with only limited attention given to institutional history.

FRUTON (1972) is an extension of this form of internalistic history, in which the interplay between chemistry and biology is described historically through the discussion of five broad themes: the nature of enzymes; the chemistry of proteins; the chemical basis of heredity; the role of oxygen in biological systems; and the chemical pathways of metabolism.

SRINIVASAN, FRUTON & EDSALL is a collection in which scientists present a history of the biochemistry of proteins in the first half of the 20th century. Much attention is paid to the introduction of new instrumental techniques. The essays are grouped into five themes: protein structure; protein and amino acid metabolism; synthesis of essential amino acids; synthesis of proteins; and the emergence of the notion that nucleic acids are the carriers of genetic information to be translated into proteins.

In addition to the books mentioned above, there are many works concentrating on one individual, often a Nobel prize winner. For instance, on the occasion of the First International Biochemical Congress, a collection commemorating Frederick Gowland Hopkins was edited by NEEDHAM & BALDWIN. Hopkins played a crucial role in the establishment of biochemistry in England; his lecture "The Dynamic Side of Biochemistry", held in Birmingham in 1913, was a landmark in the history of biochemistry, and in 1929, Hopkins received the Nobel prize for physiology/medicine for his discovery of vitamins. The collection contains Hopkins's autobiography, a few of his lectures, and commentaries on Hopkins by colleagues and friends.

Otto Warburg was another highly influential biochemist from the early 20th century. He received the Nobel prize for physiology/medicine in 1931 for his discovery of respiratory ferments – which carry out the oxidative processes in cells – and their function. He furthermore introduced into biochemistry several new instruments, such as a special type of manometer. WERNER's biographical sketch of Warburg emphasizes the German societal context of Warburg's work in the interwar years, as well as after World War II.

KARLSON is a biographical portrait of Adolf Butenandt, who received the Nobel prize for physiology/medicine in 1939 for his work on sex hormones. In addition to his work on hormones, including the pheromones, Butenandt was also greatly interested in virus and cancer research, and was one of the driving forces behind virus research at the Kaiser Wilhelm Institutes in the 1930s and 1940s. Karlson's biography describes the institutional context of Butenandt's achievement in detail, and thus provides a general picture of biomedical research in Germany from 1920 to 1970. From 1960 to 1972, Butenandt was President of the Max Planck Gesellschaft, the successor of the Kaiser Wilhelm Institutes, which had been discontinued as an organization shortly after World War II.

Despite being half-Jewish, Warburg stayed in Germany after the National Socialist Party came to power. Many other scientists, however, fled the country, among them Hans Krebs, one of Warburg's co-workers. Krebs found a refuge in Sheffield, England, where he contributed to the elucidation of intermediary metabolism, especially through his discovery of the citric acid cycle in 1937. In 1953, Krebs was awarded the Nobel prize for physiology/medicine. HOLMES outlines Krebs's life from 1900 to 1937, based on laboratory notebooks, correspondence, published articles, Krebs's autobiography, secondary literature and interviews.

As the co-laureate of Krebs's Nobel prize, Fritz LIPMANN deserved his share of the prize for his discovery of co-enzyme A and its function in intermediary metabolism, and his autobiography was published in 1971. KLEINKAUF's collection contains biographical material on Lipmann, discussions of the history of research on bioenergetics, as well as contemporary implications of previous research efforts.

A final specific biochemical subject that deserves to be mentioned concerns the discovery of enzymes involved in the synthesis of ribonucleic acid and deoxyribonucleic acid. For his discovery of so-called RNA-polymerase, Severo Ochoa received the Nobel prize for physiology/medicine in 1959. This enzyme can synthesize RNA *in vitro* from individual nucleotide units. In KORNBERG *et al.*, about 40 scientists describe in more or less historical and autobiographical essays the developments with regard to energy metabolism, protein biosynthesis, regulation and the function of nucleic acids and the genetic code. Arthur Kornberg was Ochoa's co-laureate for his discovery of DNA-polymerase. KORNBERG (1989) is partly autobiographical and otherwise a quasi-scientific book in which the action of enzymes and the techniques that constitute the basis of contemporary recombinant DNA technology are explained.

The above books generally relate to the history of ideas and biographical accounts of scientists. Another type of history centres on institutes and organizations. More often than not, these aspects of the history of a discipline are treated separately, whereas ideally, the history of ideas, persons, and institutions ought to be integrated. A remarkable book in which the history of biochemistry is described as *independent* of theoretical notions is KOHLER, which aims to show that various styles or programmes within biochemistry arose as a consequence of specific institutional contexts, rather than from theories and concepts. Kohler distinguishes three different styles within pre-1940 biochemistry: clinical biochemistry; bioorganic and biophysical biochemistry; and biological biochemistry.

FRUTON (1990) describes the work of six research groups at German universities over the period 1830–1914. The author tries to establish correlations between the style of scientific leadership and its success, and finds that leadership in these various groups ranged from the quasi-military to the style of a senior adviser who left his pupils in complete freedom and acted only as a consultant.

In addition to institutes, professional organizations constitute a second type of establishment that is important for the development of a discipline. In 1906, the American Society of Biological Chemists split off from the American Physiological Society and became an independent body. CHITTENDEN (1945) contains short biographical essays on the founders of the society, as well as a brief description of the annual meetings of the society (the last one to be included took place in 1931). On the occasion of the 85th birthday of the British Biochemical Society, GOODWIN published a history of the foundation, established in 1911. His book relates the developments with regard to biochemistry, as well as the publications, international activities and educational activities of the society.

Finally, two serials have to be mentioned. FLORKIN and LASZLO together make up an intellectual history of biochemistry. The material is rather technical and as such is more of encyclopedic value than a readable history of biochemistry. This series was later supplemented by four collections of (auto)biographical essays by various biochemists; see SEMENZA & JAENICKE and SLATER, JAENICKE & SEMENZA.

TON VAN HELVOORT

See also Colloid Chemistry

Biometrics, Statistical Biology, and Mathematical Statistics

Blacker, C.P., *Eugenics: Galton and After*, Cambridge, Massachusetts: Harvard University Press, 1952

Box, Joan Fisher, *R.A. Fisher: The Life of A Scientist*, New York: John Wiley, 1978

Edwards, A.W.F., "Galton, Karl Pearson and Modern Statistical Theory", in *Sir Francis Galton, FRS: The Legacy of His Ideas*, edited by Milo Keynes, London: Macmillan, 1993

Eisenhart, Churchill, entry on Karl Pearson in *Dictionary of Scientific Biography*, vol. 10, edited by Charles Coulston Gillispie, New York: Scribner, 1974

Farrall, Lyndsay Andrew, *The Origins and Growth of the English Eugenics Movement, 1865–1925*, New York: Garland, 1985

Hilts, Victor L., *Statist and Statistician*, New York: Arno Press, 1981

Kendall, M.G. and R.L. Plackett (eds), *Studies in the History of Statistics and Probability: A Series of Papers*, vol. 2, London: Griffin, and Darien, Connecticut: Hafner, 1977

Kevles, Daniel J., *In the Name of Eugenics: Genetics and the Uses of Human Heredity*, New York: Knopf, 1985; Harmondsworth: Penguin, 1986; with a new preface, Cambridge, Massachusetts: Harvard University Press, 1995

MacKenzie, Donald A., *Statistics in Britain, 1865–1930: The Social Construction of Scientific Knowledge*, Edinburgh: Edinburgh University Press, 1981

Magnello, M. Eileen, "Karl Pearson: Evolutionary Biology and the Emergence of a Modern Theory of Statistics", DPhil dissertation, University of Oxford, 1993

Magnello, M. Eileen, "Karl Pearson's Gresham Lectures: W.F.R. Weldon, Speciation and the Origins of Pearsonian Statistics", *British Journal for the History of Science*, 29 (1996): 43–63

Magnello, M. Eileen, "Karl Pearson's Mathematization of Inheritance: From Ancestral Heredity to Mendelian Genetics (1895–1909)", *Annals of Science*, 55 (1998): 35–94

Matthews, J. Rosser, *Quantification and the Quest for Medical Certainty*, Princeton, New Jersey: Princeton University Press, 1995

Norton, Bernard, "Karl Pearson and Statistics: The Social Origin of Scientific Innovation", *Social Studies of Science*, 8 (1978): 3–34

Pearson, E.S. and M.G. Kendal (eds), *Studies in the History of Statistics and Probability: A Series of Papers*, vol. 1, London: Griffin, and Darien, Connecticut: Hafner, 1970

Pearson, E.S. *Student: A Statistical Biography of William Sealy Gosset*, edited by R.L. Plackett and G.A. Barnard, Oxford: Clarendon Press, and New York: Oxford University Press, 1990

Pearson, Karl, *The Life, Letters and Labours of Francis Galton*, 3 vols, Cambridge: Cambridge University Press, 1914–30

Porter, Theodore M., *The Rise of Statistical Thinking, 1820–1900*, Princeton, New Jersey: Princeton University Press, 1986

Provine, William B. (ed.), *The Origins of Theoretical Population Genetics*, Chicago: University of Chicago Press, 1971

Provine, William B., *Sewall Wright and Evolutionary Biology*, Chicago: University of Chicago Press, 1986

Stigler, Stephen M., *The History of Statistics: The Measurement of Uncertainty before 1900*, Cambridge, Massachusetts: Belknap Press of Harvard University Press, 1986

Walker, Helen, *Studies in the History of Statistical Method with Special Reference to Certain Educational Problems*, Baltimore: Williams and Wilkins, 1929; reprinted, New York: Arno Press, 1979

The term biometrics was coined by the biometrician and statistician, Karl Pearson, in 1893 to designate the measurement of life. From 1892 to 1936, he devised a series of biometrical methods (which he also referred to as mathematical statistics) that combined Cambridge Wrangler mathematics (such as matrix algebra) and the frequentist approach to probability. Pearson was instrumental in professionalizing the study of biometrics by establishing the Biometric School at University College London in 1893, the journal *Biometrika* in 1900 (with Francis Galton and W.F.R. Weldon and the Drapers' Biometric Laboratory in 1903.

Earlier applications of some type of statistics to problems of biology had been introduced by Galton, Weldon, and Adolphe Quetelet. Others who contributed to the development of biometrics include Francis Ysidro Edgeworth, George Udny Yule, William Sealy Gosset, and Ronald A. Fisher, who established collectively the modern theory of mathematical statistics. Though mathematical statistics can be applied to a number of disciplines, biometrics still refers to the application of mathematical statistical methods to problems of biology.

Karl Pearson, who lectured and wrote extensively on the history of statistics, provided his own account of the history of biometry. PEARSON placed Weldon at the centre of his own biometric innovations and emphasized Weldon's application of biometrical methods to problems of Darwinian evolution and natural selection. Some years later PEARSON (1914–30) examined Galton's contributions to statistics addressing, in particular, Galton's use of the normal curve, the median and quartile measures, as well as correlation and regression. Pearson also discussed developments leading up to his work on correlation and regression.

PEARSON & KENDALL contains several reprinted articles in which Karl's son, Egon (an accomplished statistician in his own right), examined how his father's statistical methods and theories arose from attempting to solve real problems in evolutionary biology. Egon, who placed Weldon's influence before that of Galton in the development of his father's work, was concerned with the priority given to Galton in the historiography of Pearsonian statistics. EISENHART, who provided a technical description of Pearson's principle contributions to biometrics and mathematical statistics, also regarded Weldon's role as central to the emergence of Pearsonian biometrics. EDWARDS considered Pearson's statistical work to have been influenced by Weldon and Edgeworth. MAGNELLO (1996) argued that Pearson's earliest statistical lectures (which he delivered at Gresham College) arose from problems associated with speciation arising from Weldon's impetus. Magnello also argued that the statistical resolution of Weldon's data led to Pearson's earliest statistical innovation for curve-fitting and to his finding a goodness of fit test for asymmetrical distributions. Additionally, Weldon's interests provided the wider basis of a program that underpinned Pearson's longer-term statistical work.

HILTS has argued that, for Pearson, biometry was a field primarily defined by its attempt to apply quantitative methods to demonstrate the existence of natural selection. He also argued that Pearson's work led to a divorce of mathematical-statistical theory from a direct connection with its earlier use in vital and social statistics.

One of Pearson's students, Helen WALKER, has provided an internalist account of the discipline and discussed the origins of certain technical terms used in mathematical statistics (nearly half of which were devised by Pearson). In assessing the changes that statistical theory was undergoing towards the end of the 19th century, STIGLER regarded Galton, Pearson, and Edgeworth as the three principal contributors who helped to create a statistical revolution.

Using a sociological framework, FARRALL attempts to analyse the development of Pearson's biometrics. Farrall claims that Pearson's biometrics bore no relation to Pearson's mathematical statistics and that biometry became a methodology of causation for eugenics. According to Farrall, Pearson and his students "defined statistics outside the context of the discipline of mathematics", and Farrall then concludes that neither eugenics nor biometry passed into the canons of 20th-century science as recognized specialities. Farrall's ideas were later endorsed by a number of historians of science. NORTON argues that Farrall provided "an excellent account of some of the stages involved in setting up Pearson's department of Applied Statistics". He also claims that Pearson's positivism was the crucial factor in the development of his statistical work and that biometry was formulated and constructed without theory. MACKENZIE has argued subsequently that "biometry as a speciality within professional biology must be judged a failure".

This historiographical tendency to link the methodological infrastructure of Pearsonian biometrics to his methodology of eugenics is deeply problematic, because it does not address the complexity and the totality of the different methodologies that Pearson devised in his laboratories. Pearson himself remarked that his "work in the eugenics laboratory was confined to a relatively narrow field, having nothing to do with statistical theory or its general application to biology". Nevertheless, BLACKER believes that Pearson's biometry was to have formed

the scientific basis of eugenics, while Farrall maintains that the bond between the Eugenics Laboratory and the Biometric Laboratory lay in techniques of research consisting of statistical analysis of large masses of observations. This view has continued to be espoused by a number of scholars. Norton states that "in Pearson's time statistics was always associated with eugenics" and Mackenzie claims that little demarcation could be made between the methods used in Pearson's Eugenics and Biometric Laboratories. KEVLES considers that Pearson's statistical techniques were developed in the Biometric Laboratory and the analysis was carried out in the Eugenics Laboratory, and that the symbiosis was so close as to make the distinction meaningless. PORTER, who espouses Mackenzie's social-constructivist analysis, asserts that Pearson's eugenic convictions provided the principal explanation for the enthusiasm with which he took up the study of statistics.

MAGNELLO has, however, argued that Pearson not only had separate goals for his Biometric and Eugenics Laboratories, but that he devised and deployed different quantitative procedures and statistical methods, and also used different types of instruments for the various problems that arose in the laboratories. Pearson's work in the Biometric School from 1892 to 1903, and in the Drapers' Biometric Laboratory from 1903 to 1936 was underpinned by his goodness of fit testing, his chi-square goodness of fit test, 18 methods of correlation, the use of a higher form of algebra (i.e. matrix algebra), statistical and experimental studies of natural selection, craniometry and physical anthropology. This biometrical work led subsequently to the emergence and development of the modern theory of statistics in the 20th century. While Pearson used four of his 18 methods of correlation in the Galton Eugenics Laboratory, the dominant methodology in this laboratory from its establishment in 1907 until Pearson's retirement in 1933 involved, rather, the use of a complex interconnecting set of family pedigrees and actuarial death rates.

MATTHEWS examined the debates over the use of quantitative and statistical methods for medical research during the 19th century. His interest in biometrics centred on the debates between the biometrician Major Greenwood and the bacteriologist Almroth Wright soon after Pearson devised most of his biometrical methods.

Various scholars have contributed articles in KENDALL & PLACKETT's volume, on topics including R.A. Fisher's concept of sufficiency, the discovery of the method of least squares, and the development of the notion of statistical dependence. The subsequent development of biometrical methods by Fisher has been examined by his daughter, Joan Fisher BOX, who assessed her father's contributions to statistics in relation to his work at Rothamsted Experimental Station, University College London and Cambridge. Fisher's role in the advancement of Mendelian genetics, which he achieved by determining the biometrical properties of Mendelian populations, has been discussed by PROVINE, who also examined the background to the discipline of population genetics (which synthesized biometrics, Mendelism and Darwinism) from the collaborative work of Fisher, Sewall Wright, and J.B.S. Haldane.

M. EILEEN MAGNELLO

See also Eugenics; Galton; Genetics: general works; Pearson; Statistics

Biotechnology

Bauer, Martin (ed.), *Resistance to New Technology: Nuclear Power, Information Technology, and Biotechnology*, Cambridge and New York: Cambridge University Press, 1995

Benninga, H., *A History of Lactic Acid Making: A Chapter in the History of Biotechnology*, Dordrecht and Boston: Kluwer, 1990

Brock, Malcolm V., *Biotechnology in Japan*, London and New York: Routledge, 1989

Bud, Robert, *The Uses of Life: A History of Biotechnology*, Cambridge and New York: Cambridge University Press, 1993

Bull, Alan T., Geoffrey Holt and Malcolm D. Lilly, *Biotechnology: International Trends and Perspectives*, Paris: Organisation for Economic Co-operation and Development, 1982

Cook-Deegan, Robert, *The Gene Wars: Science, Politics and the Human Genome*, New York: Norton, 1994

Galambos, Louis, *Networks of Innovation: Vaccine Development at Merck, Sharp & Dohme, and Mulford, 1895–1995*, Cambridge and New York: Cambridge University Press, 1995

Hall, Stephen S., *Invisible Frontiers: The Race to Synthesise a Human Gene*, New York: Atlantic Monthly Press and London: Sidgwick and Jackson, 1987

Kay, Lily E., *The Molecular Vision of Life: Caltech, the Rockefeller Foundation, and the Rise of the New Biology*, New York : Oxford University Press, 1993

Kenney, Martin, *Biotechnology: The University-Industrial Complex*, New Haven, Connecticut: Yale University Press, 1986

Kloppenburg, Jack Ralph, Jr, *First the Seed: The Political Economy of Plant Biotechnology 1492–2000*, Cambridge and New York: Cambridge University Press, 1988

Parascandola, John (ed.), *The History of Antibiotics: A Symposium*, Madison, Wisconsin: American Institute of the History of Pharmacy, 1980

Rimmington, Anthony, *Technology and Transition: A Survey of Biotechnology in Russia, Ukraine, and the Baltic States*, Westport, Connecticut: Quorum Books, 1992

Sharp, David H., *Bioprotein Manufacture: A Critical Assessment*, Chichester: Ellis Horwood and New York: Halsted Press, 1989

Sharp, Margaret, *The New Biotechnology: European Governments in Search of a Strategy*, Brighton: Science Policy Research Unit, University of Sussex, 1985

Teitelman, Robert, *Gene Dreams: Wall Street, Academia and the Rise of Biotechnology*, New York: Basic Books, 1989

For all its widely discussed industrial importance, the category of biotechnology is notoriously ambiguous; two quite different concepts emerged when formal definitions were sought in order to rescue policy makers at the beginning of the 1980s. In the reports of the OECD and the European Federation of Biotechnology, biotechnology was formally defined in terms of the application of biological understanding to the production of useful products. BULL, HOLT & LILLY provide an exhaustive listing. On the other hand, in the US in particular, there has been an alternative usage exclusively in terms of applied molecular biology, which draws on only recombinant DNA technology, with occasional use of contemporary discoveries of monoclonal antibodies.

Despite the apparent divergence between these interpretations, there remains a deep-seated connection that has been explored by BUD. The word "biotechnology" itself has been in use since the beginning of the 20th century, to express the goal of using living beings in order to create a new technology. As early as World War I, such products as acetone and lactic acid made by fermentation had seemed to herald a new industrial era. This use led to formulations of an ideal for biotechnology that has lasted to the present day, having been co-opted as the new possibilities for recombinant DNA technology came to be voiced in the late 1970s.

The great hopes for fermentation technology early in the 20th century have tended to be forgotten. The detailed account of the history of lactic acid manufacture by BENNINGA is exceptional. It offers a rare combination of technological detail and industrial insight into a chemical that, unlike most other products of the chemical industry, has been the product of growth in mild conditions, rather than of synthesis from coal products or oil in harsh conditions.

Much better known as a triumph of fermentation technologies is the development of penicillin during World War II, which seemed to prove to the pharmaceutical industry, and even to some chemists, that a new industrial era had begun. Other antibiotics followed quickly, as did artificial steroids such as cortisone, vitamins, single-cell proteins grown on petroleum, and starch (heralded as a potential cure for the world's food problems), and for a time alcohol was seen as a possible alternative to the finite supplies of oil. The development of penicillin itself has been served by a vast literature, covering its discovery by Fleming, its isolation by Florey and Chain, and its production in wartime America. PARASCANDOLA provides an introduction to the literature on an international level.

Outside the penicillin saga, however, the intense excitement over other post-war fermentation products has largely been forgotten. The development of gasohol still awaits its historian. The history of single-cell protein has been partially explored by David SHARP, who focuses on western European developments, and in particular the endeavours of BP and ICI, who during the 1960s and 1970s saw fermentation-based biotechnology as the key to their development. RIMMINGTON should be used to provide an alternative, Soviet perspective, for in the Soviet Union the dream of single-cell protein lasted longer and led to the commercial development of a major industry that ended only with the Union itself. While penicillin had been developed in Britain and America, it was in Japan during the 1950s and 1960s that fermentation technology was most extensively developed. The Japanese developed a world-leading enzyme industry and a philosophy of biomass-based industry. BROCK describes the interaction between such home-grown concepts and the inspiration provided by American developments.

The essentially utilitarian, and indeed device-orientated, approach to biotechnology inherent within even apparently abstract studies has been explored by KAY, who focuses on Caltech in the 20th century. The industrial use of classical genetics is another route to the development of biotechnology, and the links between the generalised exploration of living organisms and its sequel, in which recombinant DNA came to the fore, is well described by KLOPPENBURG. His study of the history of the American seed industry reveals the tension between an industrial model of agriculture, with a highly capitalised techno-science base, and an emphasis on self-sufficient communities meeting local needs. This may have been highlighted by recent issues in biotechnology, but it reaches back earlier through the 20th century. GALAMBOS also explores the boundary between traditional techniques and the new genetic technologies, showing the continuity within one company, Merck, between the era of traditional vaccine research and the era of recombinant DNA.

The great period of biotechnology was undoubtedly the decade from 1975 to 1985, when the implications of recombinant DNA seemed endless. An overall account has been provided from an American perspective by KENNEY. A more journalistic account, without footnotes but with vivid, well-researched and accurate detail, is provided by HALL in his description of the race during the 1970s to be the first with a genetically engineered source of the small, but clinically crucial, protein, insulin. The network of small companies and their search for finance from Wall Street is brilliantly rehearsed by TEITELMAN, in a work that is well-researched despite its lack of scholarly apparatus.

Two kinds of response to Wall Street's enthusiasm for biotechnology have been explored. On the one hand, European governments were terrified that they would be left behind, as they had in the development of information technology. Maragaret SHARP has documented their response. On the other hand, members of the public both in Europe and in America were anxious that their safety and culture were being compromised by over-enthusiastic scientists and business interests. Many of the essays brought together by BAUER are concerned with this phenomenon of resistance.

Any treatment of biotechnology today ought to include a reference to the so-called Human Genome project, which promises to present a host of commercial prospects as well as institutional and ethical challenges. The outstanding insider's view is provided by COOK-DEEGAN. He covers not just the details of American endeavours but also puts them within the context of world-wide developments. It is appropriate that his book is entitled *Gene Wars*; this captures not just the idea of a competition between teams to be the first to sequence certain genes, but also represents the contest over how to define the very meaning and significance of the multiple human genome projects currently in progress.

ROBERT BUD

See also DNA; Human Genome Project

Birth Control

Gordon, Linda, *Woman's Body, Woman's Right: A Social History of Birth Control in America*, New York: Grossman, 1976; revised edition as *Woman's Birth, Woman's Right: Birth Control in America*, New York: Penguin, 1990

Himes, Norman E., *Medical History of Contraception*, Baltimore: Williams and Wilkins, 1936

McLaren, Angus, *Birth Control in Nineteenth-Century England*, London: Croom Helm, and New York: Holmes and Meier, 1978

McLaren, Angus, *A History of Contraception: From Antiquity to the Present Day*, Oxford and Cambridge, Massachusetts: Blackwell, 1990

Reed, James, *The Birth Control Movement and American Society: From Private Vice to Public Virtue*, Princeton, New Jersey: Princeton University Press, 1978

Riddle, John M., *Contraception and Abortion from the Ancient World to the Renaissance*, Cambridge, Massachusetts: Harvard University Press, 1992

Soloway, Richard Allen, *Birth Control and the Population Question in England, 1877–1930*, Chapel Hill: University of North Carolina Press, 1982

The history of birth control has been written from a number of perspectives, ranging from concern with the role that contraception has played in the decline of fertility, interest in the development of contraceptive techniques, to social and political movements that have canvassed for better education in reproductive limitation and access to contraception. Many of the earlier texts on the history of birth control were in fact written by those who were active in the struggle. Much of the literature also focuses on the impact that birth control has had on sexual attitudes and relations between men and women, as well as on the overall social, political, and economic fabric of society. Historians have shown increasingly that the issue of birth control was not just a matter of finding an appropriate and effective technology, but was intricately tied to questions about population growth, the position of women in society, social and economic resources, and concerns of nationalism, race, and class. All these factors had an important influence not only on the degree to which birth control was accepted within a society, but also on the extent to which men and women were motivated to use contraception. As several historians have demonstrated, although the decline in fertility has been most marked in the last two centuries, the desire for and practice of fertility control is not a recent phenomenon and can be traced back to ancient societies. Many have also argued that the knowledge and practice of birth control were never just a matter of access to contraceptive technology, but were intricately linked with the conflicts between personal desire, collective interest and public policy.

Some of the earliest literature on the topic was written in the early 20th century by those who were heavily involved in the fight for the acceptance and promotion of birth control. One of the most influential accounts of the history of contraception from this period is that by the American sociologist, Norman HIMES. His work provides a detailed, albeit incomplete, account of different contraceptive techniques from the ancient Egyptians to the early 20th century. The book was written at a time when birth control was still considered a taboo issue, and its underlying message is to show not only the continuous desire of humans to limit their fertility through the ages, but also the ways in which the recent decline in fertility and the increasing resort to birth control might be seen as a sign of progress for civilization.

Many of the more recent historians, such as Linda Gordon, James Reed, Richard Soloway, and Angus McLaren, accept the premise of earlier historians such as Himes that the search for a means to limit fertility and its practice is an age-old phenomenon. They emphasize, however, that the control of reproduction was shaped and guided by family forms, gender roles, and social, political, and economic attitudes. GORDON tells the history of birth control from the perspective of women in America and their fight to control their own fertility. At the heart of Gordon's book are figures such as Margaret Sanger, whose aim in providing contraception was to enable women to control their fertility and thus to empower them in other spheres of their lives. REED similarly deals with Sanger's fight for contraception, but he also shows the ways in which birth control was not only a concern of female activists, but was also demanded by many medical men, who were involved in this area as a result of their concern over population growth. While these men did not always share the same vision as the women reformers, their efforts were vital in the campaign to win acceptance for contraception. SOLOWAY also illustrates the importance of politics and economics in the fight for access to contraceptives in Britain in the late 19th and early 20th centuries. He examines the ways in which different British generations viewed the issue of birth control and the population question in relation to their expectations regarding the future of their society and empire, and by their ideas on progress and civilization.

The importance of setting birth control within particular cultural, social, and political contexts is also the concern of McLAREN (1990). Like the three authors mentioned above, McLaren provides an analysis of contraception and birth control movements in the late 19th and early 20th centuries, but his work also goes back to ancient Greece. Challenging historians who have focused on the history of birth control from a demographic and economic perspective, he shows, like Gordon, Reed, and Soloway, that the history of contraception must be placed within particular social and cultural contexts that change over time.

Such a history of contraception in Victorian Britain is provided by McLAREN (1978). By returning to this period, McLaren challenges much of the recent historical literature on birth control, which tends to depict the late 18th and 19th centuries as a period of revolutionary change in the practice and knowledge of fertility control. RIDDLE similarly argues that ancient societies had an extensive knowledge of plants and other devices that could be used as contraceptives. Riddle not only provides an extensive catalogue of the different types of plants that were used, but indicates the surprising disappearance of contraceptive knowledge over time. As he argues, classical and medieval sources indicate a much greater knowledge of birth control than Renaissance writers. Indeed, premodern parents could probably predict the extent of their food supply and resources, and accommodate their fertility patterns accordingly, through a diet using specific herbs, or the taking of certain drugs to induce late menstruation. Riddle concurs with McLaren that the disappearance of contraceptive knowledge had much to do with the changing attitudes of the Church and legal systems towards fertility control, but additionally he hypothesises that it was also linked to the gradual professionalization of medicine, which created an increasing division between orthodox medicine and "quackery", and to the gradual transference of the compounding and dispensing of drugs from the medical man to the pharmacist.

LARA MARKS

Blowpipe

Anderson, R.G.W., "Instruments and Apparatus", in *Recent Developments in the History of Chemistry*, edited by C.A. Russell, London: Royal Society of Chemistry, 1985

Burchard, U., "Geschichte und Instrumentarium der Lötrohrkunde", *Wissenschaftliches Jahrbuch*, Deutsches Museum, 1993

Burchard, U., "The History and Apparatus of Blowpipe Analysis", *Mineralogical Record*, 25 (1994): 251–77

Campbell, W.A., "The Development of Qualitative Analysis 1750–1850: The Use of the Blowpipe", *University of Newcastle upon Tyne Philosophical Society*, 2 (1971–72): 17–24

Dumas, Maurice, *Scientific Instruments of the Seventeenth and Eighteenth Centuries and Their Makers*, translated from the French by Mary Holbrook, New York: Praeger and London: Batsford, 1972 (original edition, 1953)

Gonzalez, E.L., "Bochard de Saron and the Oxyhydrogen Blowpipe", *Bulletin for the History of Chemistry*, 4 (1989): 11–15

Greenaway, F., *Chemistry, 1: Chemical Laboratories and Apparatus to 1850*, London: HMSO, 1966

Jensen, W.B., "The Development of Blowpipe Analysis", in *The History and Preservation of Chemical Instrumentation*, edited by John T. Stock and Mary Virginia Orna, Dordrecht and Boston: Reidel, 1986, 123–49

Landauer, J., *Blowpipe Analysis*, London, Macmillan, 1879; reprinted, London and New York: Macmillan, 1984

Turner, Gerard L'E., *Nineteenth-Century Scientific Instruments*, London: Sotheby, and Berkeley: University of California Press, 1983

Although the blowpipe is an instrument widely used by practitioners from a range of scientific backgrounds – including chemists, mineralogists and geologists – and despite its being in common use for centuries, the literature on the history of the blowpipe is sparse and often sketchy. It has been mainly identified as a chemical instrument, and most references to blowpipes are found in accounts of forms of "dry analysis" and subsequent "discoveries" of elements such as nickel and titanium. Only a handful of articles suggest ways in which the history of this instrument could inform issues, such as the development of experimental skills, the consequences of alterations in the design of the instrument, and the effects the instrument had on local economies – particularly in mining districts, where blowpipes were used to identify the ore content of minerals. The most comprehensive literature is in the form of reprints or early editions of textbooks that instruct in blowpipe analysis.

BURCHARD's two lengthy articles (1993 and 1994) trace the use of blowpipes by an array of individuals throughout Europe in the 18th and 19th centuries, the latter article being an almost complete translation of the former. The articles are organized principally geographically, with sections containing brief chronologies of the literature and references to practitioners recognized as pioneers in blowpipe analysis. Burchard also includes a brief descriptive catalogue of different blowpipe designs, and accounts of chemicals and associated apparatus used in experimental trials. Both articles are generously illustrated with contemporary book engravings as well as with modern colour photographs of extant blowpipe kits in different museums. A well-researched bibliography makes these valuable reference works.

CAMPBELL contributes an account of the use of the blowpipe as part of a wider project about the history of chemical experimentation from the mid-18th to the mid-19th century. Here he focuses principally on the activities of Swedish chemists and mineralogists such as Cronstedt, Bergman, Gahn, and Berzelius, and offers comments about the kinds of apparatus they used. He provides a table indicating the variety of supplies included in blowpipe kits, and a table of flame coloration that was used as a reference to identify the presence of particular elements under examination. These suggest interesting avenues for research, in order to connect the apparatus with the experimental skills necessary to make reliable correlations between flame colours and traces of hidden elements.

The intriguing paradox between the simplicity in the design of the blowpipe and the complexity in its use is nowhere fully explored, but JENSEN does note the importance of examining in detail communities of chemists among whom skilled techniques in the use of the blowpipe were transmitted. Burchard also alludes to the importance of skilled training in his account of the steps of preparation for conducting blowpipe experiments. Burchard, Campbell, and Jensen are all similar in the respect that they identify applied research in 18th-century Sweden, sponsored by the Board of Mines, as central to the development of blowpipe analysis. It is from here that they all begin to trace the subsequent dissemination of literature on the subject to other European sites. GREENAWAY supports this model by showing some simple changes in the design of the blowpipe that begin in Sweden and finish in England. GONZALEZ departs from this model by briefly introducing the place of blowpipe analysis in French chemical practices.

ANDERSON mentions blowpipe analysis in a rapid discussion of the development and use of a range of chemical apparatus. Different kinds of blowpipes are discussed throughout the chapter on chemistry in TURNER, which provides information on such matters as prices, the types of kits available, and the blowpipe's relation to associated kinds of chemical instruments, although this information is particularly relevant to Britain. The information in DUMAS is very brief, but placed within a catalogue context of a number of contemporary chemical instruments.

LANDAUER's book offers a historical sketch of the use of blowpipes by various practitioners (similar to the accounts by Burchard, Campbell, and Jensen), and then describes in detail the necessary apparatus and techniques. Most of the book is a compendium of experimental results.

Taken together, these articles and books offer glimpses of ways in which the blowpipe can be related to geographical settings, training practices, and related experimental apparatus.

They provide a suggestive guide to initiating future research, in order to develop more theoretical views on the place of instrumentation within experimental cultures.

BRIAN DOLAN

Boas, Franz 1858–1942

German-born American cultural anthropologist

Andrews, J.J. et al., Bibliography of Franz Boas, American Anthropological Association, 1943, 67–109

Codere, Helen (ed.), Kwakiutl Ethnography, by Franz Boas, Chicago: University of Chicago Press, 1966

Harris, Marvin, The Rise of Anthropological Theory: A History of Theories of Culture, New York: Crowell, and London: Routledge and Kegan Paul, 1968

Hatch, Elvin, Theories of Man and Culture, New York: Columbia University Press, 1973

Helm, June (ed.), Pioneers of American Anthropology: The Uses of Biography, Seattle: University of Washington Press, 1966

Lowie, Robert H., The History of Ethnological Theory, New York: Farrar and Rinehart, 1937

Silverman, Sydel (ed.), Totems and Teachers: Perspectives on the History of Anthropology, New York: Columbia University Press, 1981

Stocking Jr, George W., Race, Culture and Evolution: Essays in the History of Anthropology, New York: Free Press, 1968

Stocking Jr, George W. (ed.), Objects and Others: Essays on Museums and Material Culture, Madison: University of Wisconsin Press, 1985

Stocking Jr, George W., The Ethnographer's Magic and Other Essays in the History of Anthropology, Madison: University of Wisconsin Press, 1992

Franz Boas's anthropological scholarship is broad and ethnological in both range and character, incorporating physical anthropology, linguistics, and archaeology. Boas's scholarship thus has relevance for the historically-informed disciplines of physical anthropology, linguistics, and archaeology. However, at the centre of Boas's conceptual apparatus is culture, and hence he is described as a cultural anthropologist.

The bibliography fashioned by ANDREWS et al. functions as a general guide to the breadth of Boas's scholarly concerns. Implicitly, the bibliography informs us that at the turn of the 19th century it was legitimate and acceptable for a scholar to pursue a wide range of interests. In Boas's case, the range included anthropometry and race, general ethnology, the classification of languages, ethnography, and the collection of items of material culture for anthropological museums. HATCH has argued that Boas was very much a product of his times, a broadly based scholar who fused scientific positivism with philosophical idealism.

STOCKING (1968) provides a detailed biographical and intellectual portrait of Boas's academic shift of orientation from physics, through geography, to ethnology and anthropology as part of his German education. Stocking notes the amount of overlap existent between ethnological and geographical scholarship in Germany during the 19th century. Between 1883 and 1884, Boas conducted research among the "Eskimo" of Cumberland Sound, ostensibly for cartographical purposes. On his return to Germany, he took up the position of assistant at the Royal Ethnological Museum in Berlin.

At the natural science end of Boas's range of scholarly concerns is his interest in aspects of physical anthropology and anthropometry – the person as species. Stocking (1968) argues that these interests can be studied within the intellectual context of evolutionary thought, and have implications concerning the late 19th-century development of eugenics and theories of race. Parmenter, in HELM, argues that, having moved to America, Boas was living in a society that was a "melting pot" for different peoples, a natural laboratory for Boas's revolutionary ideas on race. Stocking argues that Boas's critique of racial formalism, based on anthropometric and general physical anthropological research carried out on existent and incoming immigrants to the US, offered a scientific means of accounting for the differences between peoples. As STOCKING (1992) argues, in an account of science and politics in Boas's research into race, the dominant liberal individualism of American political thought was generally open to his cultural explanation of the differences between peoples.

In SILVERMAN, Lesser begins with the assumption that modern (American) anthropology began with Boas and his interest in cultural arrangements. Stocking (1968) takes the position that while the development and application of culture by Boas and his students contributed significantly to the establishment of American anthropology, their collected works did not amount to a systematic theory of culture. The position HARRIS adopts is in part supportive of Stocking: characterizing Boas's works as "historical particularism", Harris suggests that the broad eclecticism of Boas and his students perpetuated the lack of any systematic orientation in the study of culture. In contrast, Lesser, in Silverman, treats Boas in a more empirical sense as the "great theorist of modern anthropology".

LOWIE makes a convincing plea for Boas to be understood principally as a field worker. Rohner, in Helm, provides an account of Boas's major contributions to ethnography, in particular his collaborative researches with Hunt and others among the then rapidly declining peoples of the North West Coast. The range of publications, research directions, collections of items of material culture and museum exhibits and exhibitions that arose from this research is vast. CODERE argues that many students of Boasian scholarship find the vastness, complexity, and eclecticism inherent in the North West Coast materials impenetrable. Codere's collection of Boas's Kwakiutl ethnography is organized with the specific aim of presenting these materials in an accessible manner. Adhering to conventional anthropological, epistemologically-informed categories, Codere arranges the Kwakiutl ethnographic materials within areas that include, for example, mythology and language, material culture and art, and rituals and ceremonies.

Stocking (1992) discusses the highly ambitious project Boas had for the study of the American Indian languages, including those of the North West Coast peoples, which included their classification and the production of a handbook or guide for their study. Jacknis, in STOCKING (1985), comments on another aspect of Boas's North West Coast researches – their

significance for ethnological museums. Jacknis characterizes Boas as an anthropologist in a "museum age"; after his year at the Royal Ethnological Museum in Berlin, and after his arrival in America, Boas worked with Frederick Putnam, and in 1896 he was appointed assistant curator of ethnology and somatology at the American Museum of Natural History, a position he held until 1905. During this time, Boas pioneered styles of display for the various items of North West Coast material culture that he, his students and assistants collected.

Boas joined Columbia University as a lecturer in physical anthropology in 1896, and from 1899 until his retirement in 1936 he held the post of professor of anthropology, training many of the significant American anthropologists of the 20th century.

MIKE BALL

The Body

Bordo, Susan, *Unbearable Weight: Feminism, Western Culture, and the Body*, Berkeley: University of California Press, 1993
Bynum, Caroline, "Why All the Fuss about the Body? A Medievalist's Perspective", *Critical Inquiry*, 22 (1995): 1–33
Foucault, Michel, *Discipline and Punish: The Birth of the Prison*, translated from the French by Alan Sheridan, New York: Pantheon, and London: Allen Lane, 1977
Gould, Stephen Jay, *The Mismeasure of Man*, New York: Norton, 1981; revised and expanded edition, 1996
Hunt, Lynn (ed.), *Eroticism and the Body Politic*, Baltimore: Johns Hopkins University Press, 1991
Laqueur, Thomas, *Making Sex: Body and Gender from the Greeks to Freud*, Cambridge, Massachusetts: Harvard University Press, 1990
Schiebinger, Londa, *Nature's Body: Gender in the Making of Modern Science*, Boston: Beacon Press, 1993
Young, Katharine (ed.), *Bodylore*, Knoxville: University of Tennessee Press, 1993

Since the 1980s, the study of the body has emerged as the focus of vital and important scholarship. From Aristotle's proposition that women are merely imperfect men, to recent attempts to discover neurological markers for homosexuality, the body has often been seen as a microcosm reflecting transcendent truths about the individual and nature. Scholarship in anthropology, folklore, sociology, history, and the history of science has demonstrated, however, that the body cannot be taken as a given, or universal constant. It is rather a cultural artifact, inscribed, encoded, contested, and performed. Inspired by feminism, and by a reaction to Christian and Cartesian traditions that privilege the abstract and intellectual over the physical, the body is presently being explored as a product of biological theory, as the site of individual expression and resistance to institutional control, as a politicized entity, as a complex symbol of conscious and unconscious myths, beliefs, and desires, and as metaphor, text, and icon. Treating the body as a social as well as a biological construct makes possible, among other things, a new examination of beliefs concerning identity, the self, the political, and the cultural.

The body has also served historically to bolster scientific ideas of biological difference, justifying the identification and subsequent treatment of certain groups, such as the Hottentots and the Jews, as essentially different, even sub-human. GOULD was one of the first to document the politics of biological interpretations of the body, particularly with regard to race. He shows how the human body has been scientifically examined and found to "prove" various racist, classist, and sexist beliefs. From theories of polygyny, through craniology, phrenology, and the development of IQ tests, Gould offers a history of biological determinism as well as a critique of the faulty reasoning behind it. The scientific, political, and institutional power of the European male are evident in this account of who has historically (mis)measured whom.

SCHIEBINGER continues Gould's historical account, focusing on how gender became one potent principle organizing the 18th-century understanding of nature – a matter of consequence in an age that looked to nature as the guiding light for social reform. Through carefully argued case studies, Schiebinger shows how body politics has extended to scientific understandings of non-human nature, illustrating how contemporary beliefs about sexual difference and characteristics influenced botanical taxonomy, zoological nomenclature, and conceptions of race.

LAQUEUR focuses specifically on the ways in which sexual difference has been mapped on to the body. His compelling and controversial thesis argues that, until the 18th century, western civilization worked on a single-sex model within which all bodies were essentially the same in form and content: the female represented simply a less developed form than the male. During the 18th century, however, a two-sex model arose, which emphasized instead the profound differences between the sexes. As a result, the boundaries between the sexes became less flexible, and sex a more rigid and defining category.

FOUCAULT is often credited with initiating a critical approach to the body as the site of institutional control of the individual. In *Discipline and Punish*, he proposes that modernity is marked in part by a shift in the locus of society's power, from control over the physical body to control of the abstract individual. Transgression of societal laws is no longer punished with bodily pain, but with the restriction of personal liberty; a penalty once enacted on the body is now visited on the heart and soul of the individual. According to Foucault, the essential coercive violence of the state, once a highly physical, visible, and public spectacle, has become covert and abstract.

HUNT's edited volume explores the body as both political and erotic, demonstrating that these areas are far from mutually exclusive. In European history, the merging of the political and sexual is most evident in the person of the traditional monarch, but Hunt's collection shows that it is also evident in beliefs about the robustness of the aristocracy and/or the rising bourgeoisie. The strength of any particular social group or class, Hunt maintains, was represented especially by the bodies of its women, which could indicate either health or decay, nurturance or corruption. The book is divided into three chronological sections, each containing essays by a historian, an art historian, and a literary critic, which explore the multivalence and ambiguity of the female body in France during the 18th and 19th centuries.

In a more contemporary and philosophical vein, BORDO examines the meaning of the female body and feminism in contemporary American culture. She adds depth to her analysis by asking how it is that women experience their own bodies. In particular, she discusses anorexia nervosa, reproductive rights, and advertising as "crystallizations of culture".

A similar anthropological/folkloric approach, with a refreshing and all-too-rare sampling of cross-cultural perspectives, is provided by YOUNG. The essays in this volume work from the assumption that the body is socially invented, "a constellation of symbolic properties", and examine topics from Moroccan body painting to a Hakka Chinese ritual of mourning.

BYNUM's essay provides a concise, provocative, and readable discussion of why it is that the history of the body and the issues that surround it seem so pressing and intriguing at the close of the 20th century. She maintains that contemporary discussion of the body is haunted by a form of traditional western dualism, which wants both to glorify and escape the physical body. She also notes a schism between the issues addressed by scholarship about the body, and the anxieties surrounding it that are expressed in popular culture; for example, the ethics of organ transplantation. She proposes that academic treatments of the body have been too abstract and narrowly focused on issues of gender and sex, and calls for a scholarship that incorporates the real, physical body, which works, desires, and dies.

Bynum's critique of recent scholarship is well taken. As Gould has demonstrated, historically the archetypical body has been the white European male, and scholarship critical of this tradition has focused perhaps too exclusively on the white European female as his foil. Cross-cultural studies offer models of the body that challenge not only the centrality of sexual difference to identity, but also our understanding of the individual as a social, temporal, and physically bounded entity.

SARAH GOODFELLOW

Boerhaave, Herman 1668–1738

Dutch physician and professor of botany, chemistry, and medicine

Cunningham, Andrew, "Medicine to Calm the Mind: Boerhaave's Medical System and Why It Was Adopted in Edinburgh", in *The Medical Enlightenment of the Eighteenth Century*, edited by Cunningham and Roger French, Cambridge and New York: Cambridge University Press, 1990

Kegel-Brinkgeve, Elze and Antonie M. Luyendijk-Elshout (eds), *Boerhaave's Orations*, translated from the Latin by Kegel-Brinkgeve and Luyendijk-Elshout, Leiden: E.J. Brill and Leiden University Press, 1983

Lindeboom, G.A., *Herman Boerhaave: The Man and His Work*, London: Methuen, 1968

Lindeboom, G.A. (ed.), *Boerhaave and His Time*, Leiden: E.J. Brill, 1970

Lindeboom, G.A., *Boerhaave and Great Britain: Three Lectures on Boerhaave with Particular Reference to His Relations with Great Britain*, Leiden: E.J. Brill, 1974

Metzger, Hélène, *Newton, Stahl, Boerhaave et la doctrine chimique*, Paris: Alcan, 1930

Probst, Christian, *Der Weg des ärztlichen Erkennens am Krankenbett: Herman Boerhaave und die ältere Wiener medizinische Schule*, vol. 1, Wiesbaden: Steiner, 1973

Underwood, Edgar, *Boerhaave's Men at Leyden and After*, Edinburgh: Edinburgh University Press, 1977

Given Herman Boerhaave's central role in early 18th-century science and medicine, surprisingly few studies have focused on him or his writings. There is a particular scarcity of works attempting to relate his many and diverse fields of study (ranging from medicine, chemistry, and botany to philology and divinity) to his central position in the academic world and to his adoption of Newtonian philosophy, or indeed to the context of the Dutch Enlightenment and Leiden University. However, the most recent works by Kegel-Brinkgeve & Luyendijk-Elshout and by Cunningham are important contributions in this area.

The starting point for any research on Herman Boerhaave is still the biography by LINDEBOOM (1968), the only comprehensive account of Boerhaave's life. Drawing on a large amount of unpublished material, Lindeboom discusses in detail Boerhaave's life, his academic career, his personality, and his philosophical views. With regard to his scientific work, Lindeboom stresses Boerhaave's medical achievements, in both theoretical medicine and the development of clinical teaching. This approach leaves considerably less room for Boerhaave's activities in chemistry and botany, whereas his importance for the development of natural philosophy – as one of the first adherents of Newton on the Continent – is only dealt with in passing.

METZGER gives a clearer view of the way in which Boerhaave adopted experimental philosophy and iatrochemistry, and Newtonian ideas of matter, and transformed them in the development of his own chemical theories. Embedded within the framework of the history of ideas, she uses the *Elementa chemiae* – especially the notion of fire – to emphasize the eclecticism of Boerhaave, who used doctrines from different and non-cohesive contexts to explain chemical phenomena, without transforming them into one coherent synthesis.

The 13 articles in LINDEBOOM (1970) cover a broad range of subjects concerning the philosophical views of Boerhaave, his medical practice, and his relation to other scientists. The selection of the articles was obviously intended to show as many facets of his work as possible, thus giving an overall view of the diversity of Boerhaave's activities. However, as these facets remain somewhat detached from each other, and the methodological approaches vary significantly, there remains the difficulty of finding a coherent analytical concept with which to describe Boerhaave's science as a whole.

One such tool is offered by KEGEL-BRINKGEVE & LUYENDIJK-ELSHOUT, in their analysis of Boerhaave's academic orations and sermons within the university context. Though in principle a text edition, the introduction and commentary occupy nearly half of the book. In a detailed account, they show how Boerhaave used the possibilities of well-defined academic rhetoric at different stages of his career in order to obtain institutional approval for himself and his views on medicine, philosophy, and religion. The particular historiographical value of this study lies in the fact that the themes of his orations differ significantly from the subjects of his ordinary lectures or his textbooks. Thus, attention is drawn to topics that played a central role in Boerhaave's activities but have generally been ignored by more discipline-oriented historiographies.

The role of Boerhaave within the communications network of 18th-century academics is studied by LINDEBOOM (1974). He outlines the particularly close ties between Britain and The Netherlands, which is important for an understanding of the manner in which Boerhaave availed himself of English philosophical ideas for his teaching. Without going into much detail, Lindeboom describes Boerhaave's individual contacts with some British scholars of medicine, botany, chemistry, and the classics in an attempt to reveal his influence on British 18th-century intellectual life.

A different approach to this question is taken by UNDERWOOD, who follows the careers of 746 English-speaking students at Leiden University. The book gives an illustration of the lives of Boerhaave's students, their relations to the university, and their intellectual interests. In the second part of his book, Underwood gives their biographies after having left Leiden. Although emphasis is placed on those students who afterwards became medical teachers, especially at Edinburgh, their career patterns remain heterogeneous, making it difficult to understand what it meant to be "Boerhaave's man" after graduation.

The studies by Probst and Cunningham investigate Boerhaave's role in medical innovations made elsewhere, while highlighting aspects of Boerhaave's own medical ideas. PROBST concentrates his account of the pragmatic Vienna medical school on 18th-century medical practice and its relation to teaching and theorizing. Using medical history records by Boerhaave and his Viennese followers van Swieten, de Haen, and Stoll as sources, Probst tries to analyze the perceptions and actions of the physician at the sickbed, and their effects on the development of iatromechanical methodology in medicine.

CUNNINGHAM, on the other hand, examines the eminent success of Boerhaave's medical system, exemplified by the adoption of Boerhaavian methods in the new Edinburgh school. Cunningham characterizes this system by linking it to Boerhaave's theological and philological studies. Just as the message of the scriptures brought him peace, his medical system had to follow the same clear, simple, and anti-sectarian principles, avoiding conflict and metaphysical speculation. In Edinburgh, where an open conflict between the professions of physician and surgeon-apothecary had erupted, the acceptance of Boerhaave's system led to conciliation and the emergence of the "general practitioner" as a new medical professional.

GERHARD WIESENFELDT

Bohr, Niels   1885–1962

Danish physicist

Aaserud, Finn, *Redirecting Science: Niels Bohr, Philanthropy, and the Rise of Nuclear Physics*, Cambridge and New York: Cambridge University Press, 1990

Beller, Mara, "The Birth of Bohr's Complementarity: The Context and the Dialogues", *Studies in History and Philosophy of Science*, 23 (1992): 147–80

Blay, Michel, *et al.*, "Bohr et la complémentarité", *Revue d'Histoire des Sciences*, 38/3–4 (1985)

Darrigol, Olivier, *From c-Numbers to q-Numbers: The Classical Analogy in the History of Quantum Theory*, Berkeley: University of California Press, 1992

Favrholdt, David, *Niels Bohr's Philosophical Background*, Copenhagen: Munksgaard, 1992

Faye, Jan, *Niels Bohr: His Heritage and Legacy: An Anti-Realist View of Quantum Mechanics*, Dordrecht: Kluwer, 1991

Faye, Jan and Henry Folse (eds), *Niels Bohr and Contemporary Philosophy*, Dordrecht: Kluwer, 1994

Folse, Henry, *The Philosophy of Niels Bohr: The Framework of Complementarity*, Dordrecht: North-Holland, 1985

French, A.P. and P.J. Kennedy (eds), *Niels Bohr: A Centenary Volume*, Cambridge, Massachusetts: Harvard University Press, 1985

Heilbron, J.L. and Thomas S. Kuhn, "The Genesis of the Bohr Atom", *Historical Studies in the Physical Sciences*, 1 (1969): 210–90

Hirosige, Tetu and Sigeo Nisio, "Formation of Bohr's Theory of Atomic Constitution", *Japanese Studies in History of Science*, 3 (1964): 6–28; 9 (1970): 35–47

Meyer-Abich, Klaus Michael, *Korrespondenz, Individualität, Komplementarität: Eine Studie zur Geistesgeschichte der Quantentheorie in den Beiträgen Niels Bohrs*, Wiesbaden: Steiner, 1965

Moore, Ruth, *Niels Bohr: The Man, His Science, and the World They Changed*, New York: Knopf, 1966

Murdoch, Dugald, *Niels Bohr's Philosophy of Physics*, Cambridge and New York: Cambridge University Press, 1987

Pais, Abraham, *Niels Bohr's Times: In Physics, Philosophy, and Polity*, Oxford: Clarendon Press, and New York: Oxford University Press, 1991

Petruccioli, Sandro, *Atoms, Metaphors, and Paradoxes: Niels Bohr and the Construction of a New Physics*, Cambridge and New York: Cambridge University Press, 1993

Röseberg, Ulrich, *Niels Bohr: Leben und Werk eines Atomphysikers 1885–1962*, Stuttgart: Wissenschaftliche Verlagsgesellschaft, 1985; 3rd edition, Berlin: Spektrum, 1992

Rosenfeld, Léon, Introduction to *On the Constitution of Atoms and Molecules: Papers of 1913*, by Bohr, Copenhagen: Munksgaard, 1963

Rosenfeld, Léon, *et al.* (eds), *Niels Bohr: Collected Works*, 9 vols to date, Amsterdam: North-Holland, 1972–

Rozental, Stefan, *Niels Bohr: His Life and Work as Seen by His Friends and Colleagues*, Amsterdam: North-Holland and New York: Interscience, 1967

Niels Bohr, one of the central figures in the development of modern physics, is best known for his model of the atom with electrons orbiting a nucleus, and for his contributions to the development of quantum physics, especially the principles of correspondence and complementarity. His work has prompted a large secondary literature. After presenting texts for the beginner and Bohr's complete works, a main source for the serious scholar, this essay will survey biographies, the work on the atomic model (early and late), Bohr's influence on other scientists, on the principles of correspondence and complementarity, and on epistemology and ontology.

The well-selected anthology by FRENCH & KENNEDY can be highly recommended for the reader who is not yet familiar with Bohr's *oeuvre*. It collects brief, personal memoirs by some of Bohr's colleagues, and brief historical sketches of his contributions to the theory of the atom, of the periodic system, of his discussion with Einstein on paradoxes of quantum mechanics, and of his later work in nuclear physics. It also includes his institutional activities as head of the newly founded Universitetets Institut for Teoretisk Fysik in Copenhagen, and his engagement in world politics and issues raised by the atomic bomb after World War II. Interspersed are reprints of original papers and newspaper articles, as well as many illustrations.

ROSENFELD *et al.* (1972) includes all of Bohr's scientific papers, as well as hitherto unpublished manuscripts and (unfortunately, only selected) letters from his scientific correspondence. (Danish documents are also printed in English translation.) The volumes also contain brief introductory headnotes of varying length and quality.

Most biographical studies on Bohr have a rather distasteful, hagiographic tone when detailing the way in which the work of the "great, wise man" came into conflict with many world leaders, and with "sinister" Winston Churchill in particular. In MOORE's account of Bohr's meeting at Downing Street on 16 May 1944, in which he tried to convince Churchill of the need for concerted action with Russia in order to prevent the use of atomic weapons, Churchill is simply the impatient bad guy. The complex situation and the many political constraints of the time are much better described in chapter 11 of RÖSEBERG's biography, which is, moreover, richly illustrated and contains a good bibliography of primary and secondary literature concerning Bohr. Though full of pertinent details, PAIS's biography does not really achieve a well-rounded portrait of Bohr; in particular, the philosophical aspects of his *oeuvre*, squeezed by Pais into two brief chapters, are not successfully examined. A facet forgotten in most biographies is Bohr's talent as a fund raiser, meticulously described in AASERUD's institutional history of the emergence of a nuclear science program at the Copenhagen institute, as a result of Bohr's skilful science management which was sensitive to changes in the funding policy of the Rockefeller Foundation. In particular, Aaserud shows that when the latter decided to increase research funding of biology, Bohr immediately created a biological research program headed by George Hevesy.

Several studies address the genesis and reception of the atomic model. ROSENFELD (1963) gives the standard internalist account, with its usual emphasis on Rutherford's alpha-scattering measurements as the empirical clue. More interesting is the dispute between Hirosige & Nisio and Heilbron & Kuhn about which resources proved the most important for the development of the Bohr atomic model. HIROSIGE & NISIO (1964) point to the importance of the work of Hantaro Nagaoka, who had developed a Saturnian atomic model in the tradition of J.J. Thomson, in the hope of understanding the difference between line and band spectra. Furthermore, they conjecture that it was Planck's theory of radiation of 1910–12 that suggested to Bohr the quantum condition defining the stationary states of hydrogen. Despite explicit refutation by Hirosige & Nisio and others, HEILBRON & KUHN argue that John W. Nicholson's atomic model with quantized angular momenta was nevertheless instrumental in the formation of Bohr's model. They claim that it shifted the discussion from a mainly chemical context to spectroscopy, as Nicholson tried to explain certain wavelengths of prominent, but unaccounted, spectral lines in the solar corona. Backed by their study of Bohr's correspondence, they in turn attempt to refute Hirosige & Nisio's claim concerning the impact of Planck's second theory, which is rebutted in HIROSIGE & NISIO (1970).

There are also several studies of the history of the atomic model after Bohr's initial publication in 1913. A fairly technical, but illuminating, discussion of the development from the Bohr atom of 1913, up to the unsuccessful theory of Bohr, Kramers and Slater of 1924, is provided in DARRIGOL's study of the varying use of analogical arguments in the development of quantum theory. Further hints on the relation of Bohr's atomic theory to chemistry between 1913 and 1925 can be found in Helge Kragh's contribution to BLAY et al., in which he argues that the Bohr program was immunized against possible objections from the chemists by its narrow definition within physicalist terms.

After World War I, Bohr gathered large crowds of enthusiastic graduate students and researchers around him; many of these later wrote of the importance to their scientific development of this period of their lives, because of Bohr's extraordinary talent in creating an atmosphere for discussion. Evidence of this can be found in ROZENTAL and in the aforementioned biographies. Given the generally hagiographic tone of the biographies, J.L. Heilbron's sarcastic tone in his contribution to Blay et al. is very refreshing; he analyses why Bohr, in particular, attracted so many intelligent young scientists, all of whom were initiated into the "Copenhagen spirit" and became converts during more or less extended research visits. Alluding to Bohr's proverbial darkness, Heilbron concedes that, as a sage, Bohr spoke in riddles and parables, both hard to grasp and hard to compose. He analyses the psychological mechanisms by which the circle of "brilliant, aggressive disciples" around the "master guru" was formed, the mode of diffusion of the spirit, and the strategies created for suppressing dissent and combating unorthodox interpretations of the quantum riddles by figures at the fringe of the Bohr circle, such as Wolfgang Pauli and Pascual Jordan.

The full depth of Bohr's usage of the principles of correspondence and of complementarity is explored in parts 2 and 3, respectively, of MEYER-ABICH, unfortunately written in a style even heavier than Bohr's original. Meyer-Abich's approach is firmly rooted in the tradition of the history of ideas, with its tendency to retrace Bohr's thinking back to William James, Søren Kierkegaard, and, ultimately, to Socrates. Complementary to this, BELLER's paper on the genesis of Bohr's complementarity principle uncovers the underlying network of implicit scientific dialogues in his Como lecture of 1927. She argues that virtually every sentence of this famous talk is an implicit argument with leading physicists of the time, a quite plausible idea given Bohr's tendency toward "dialectic reasoning" in endless discussions with his colleagues. The root of complementarity is thus seen in Bohr's realization that a "happy marriage" between Schrödinger's wave mechanics and Heisenberg's quantum mechanics is feasible, on the basis of de Broglie's wave-packets.

PETRUCCIOLI offers a different version of Bohr's route to complementarity. He finds that Bohr's earlier struggles to achieve an epistemologically consistent view of atomic physics led directly to complementarity, but he also examines Bohr's later usage of the complementarity principle, and the 1924 virtual oscillator model of the atom by Bohr, Kramers, and Slater. The strength of Petruccioli's account lies in his close analysis of Bohr's use of metaphors, and the linguistic base of his interpretation of physics. Moreover, he is also careful to compare Bohr's claims with actual facts and results.

The clearest introduction to Bohr's philosophy of physics, and to the genesis, meaning, and later extension to psychology and biology of his complementary principle, is provided by FOLSE, who argues against a phenomenalist interpretation of Bohr. For Folse, complementarity is merely a conceptual framework for an epistemological analysis of the measurement of processes of observational interactions (which cannot be subdivided into separate interacting systems), which does not exclude ontological suppositions about an independent, but interacting physical reality.

FAYE & FOLSE is the best survey of the many different perspectives on Niels Bohr in contemporary philosophy. In it, competing camps claim Bohr as their own, but there are also interesting contributions on the Bohr-Einstein debate. Don Howard illuminates the importance, and systematic role, played by classical concepts in Bohr's philosophy of physics, and Paul Hoyningen-Huene analyses Bohr's argument for the irreducibility of biology to physics.

A scholarly war is currently raging concerning the extent of the influence that the Copenhagen philosophy professor, Harald Høffding had on Bohr. FAYE has collected evidence of such an influence, both indirectly through the friendship of Bohr's father, who taught physiology at Copenhagen university with Høffding, and directly, since Bohr took part in Høffding's course on propaedeutic philosophy in 1903. FAVRHOLDT, on the other hand, has vigorously attacked Faye's thesis, and has scrutinized all the evidence regarding philosophical influences on Bohr (Høffding or Kierkegaard, James or Kant), sometimes correcting Faye's over-enthusiasm, and sometimes bordering on the pedantic. Favrholdt argues that there was no intense mentor-pupil relationship between Bohr and Høffding, just a courteous relation between a young student and his father's friend; the alleged homologies and similarities between Høffding's philosophy of mind and psychology, and Bohr's philosophy of quantum mechanics, such as "a blurred distinction between subject and object", are partially refuted by Favrholdt, and partially rejected as methodologically insufficient grounds for claiming influence of any sort. Faye describes Bohr as an objective anti-realist, holding that "truth is a concept which relates to circumstances whose occurrence or non-occurrence is, in principle, empirically accessible to our cognitive capacities". Others, such as Folse, declare him an instrumentalistic realist, with a theory of meaning close to pragmatism, since, for Bohr, physical predicates have meaning only insofar as they can be used "to make an assertion which has effects that might conceivably have a bearing on practice". As might be clear from these quotes, this often-repeated, terminological reshuffling of Bohr's unsystematic remarks by professional philosophers is not very helpful from a historical point of view, since Bohr did not simply think as a systematic philosopher, or in terms of the philosophical schools of his day, about epistemological and ontological affairs, but rather in terms of problems that originated in physics, but which crossed disciplinary borders.

KLAUS HENTSCHEL

Boltzmann, Ludwig Eduard   1844–1906

Austrian physicist and philosopher of science

Broda, Engelbert, *Ludwig Boltzmann: Man, Physicist, Philosopher*, translated from the German by Larry Gay and Engelbert Broda, Woodbridge, Connecticut: Ox Bow Press, 1983

Brush, Stephen G., *The Kind of Motion We Call Heat (A History of the Kinetic Theory of Gases in the 19th Century)*, 2 vols, Amsterdam: North-Holland, 1986

Curd, Martin Vincent, *Ludwig Boltzmann's Philosophy of Science: Theories, Pictures and Analogies*, PhD dissertation, University of Pittsburgh, 1978

D'Agostino, Salvo, "Boltzmann and Hertz on the BILD-Conception of Physical Theory", *History of Science*, 28 (1990): 380–98

Dugas, René, *La Théorie physique au sens de Boltzmann et ses prolongements modernes*, Nêuchatel: Griffon, 1959

Hiebert, Erwin N., "Boltzmann's Conception of Theory Construction: The Promotion of Pluralism, Provisionalism, and Pragmatic Realism", in *Pisa Conference Proceedings*, vol. 2, edited by J. Hintikka, D. Gruender and E. Agazzi, Dordrecht: Reidel, 1980

Hörz, Herbert and Andreas Lass, *Ludwig Boltzmanns Wege nach Berlin: Ein Kapitel österreichisch-deutscher Wissenschaftsbeziehungen*, Berlin: Akademie, 1989

Jungnickel, Christa and Russell McCormmach, *Intellectual Mastery of Nature: Theoretical Physics from Ohm to Einstein*, 2 vols, Chicago: University of Chicago Press, 1986

Klein, Martin J., "The Development of Boltzmann's Statistical Ideas", *Acta Physica Austriaca*, supplement 10 (1973): 53–106

Stiller, Wolfgang, *Ludwig Boltzmann: Altmeister der klassischen Physik, Wegbereiter der Quantenphysik und Evolutionstheorie*, Thun/Frankfurt: Deutsch, 1989

Videira, Antonio Augusto Passos, *Atomisme épistémologique et pluralisme théorique dans la pensée de Boltzmann*, PhD dissertation, Equipe Rehseis-University of Paris VII, 1992

Wilson, Andrew D., "Mental Representation and Scientific Knowledge: Boltzmann's Bild Theory of Knowledge in Historical Context", *Physis*, 28 (1991): 769–95

Until quite recently, Ludwig Eduard Boltzmann's passionate defence of atomism, and his seminal contributions to statistical mechanics and the kinetic theory of gases, were the main reasons for the interest shown by historians and philosophers of science. However, Boltzmann's philosophical undertakings have received more attention since the end of the 1970s.

With his biography of Boltzmann, the only one existing to date, the Austrian physical chemist Engelbert BRODA has helped to bring Boltzmann to the attention of historians of science. It is the first work to attempt a general presentation of Boltzmann's achievements, with biographical information and an analysis of his scientific contributions, along with critical comments about his philosophical enterprise. However, as Broda himself concedes, Boltzmann's writings are not faultless, partly because of his sparing use of primary sources.

DUGAS also provides a general analysis of Boltzmann's scientific and philosophical thought. Beginning with the interest raised during the 1950s by the causal interpretation of quantum mechanics, Dugas endeavours to show, through Boltzmann's example, that dogmatism should not be accepted among scientists. Dugas's intention, then, is to present the Austrian physicist's notion of physical theory, and how this notion was consolidated by means of mechanical models and analogies. Dugas aims to establish the fruitfulness of Boltzmann's ideas and methods, when correctly employed.

KLEIN aims to show how Boltzmann's recourse to statistical concepts was in keeping with the principles underlying the world picture of classical mechanics; i.e., the way in which Boltzmann used statistics for reconciling the irreversibility of thermodynamics with the reversibility of mechanics. Klein describes how the criticism heaped on Boltzmann during the 1870s only spurred on his research program, which had as its goal the establishment of a mechanical foundation for his second principle of thermodynamics.

BRUSH, a collection of previously published papers, places Boltzmann's ideas within the scientific context of the 19th century. It analyses the unfolding of statistical mechanics and of the kinetic theory of gases throughout that century.

CURD's doctoral thesis is arguably the first work to attempt a circumstantial understanding of Boltzmann's arguments in favour of atomism and of a mechanistic view of the world. Curd shows why Boltzmann became involved in the explicit formulation of a philosophy of science that was significantly influenced by the writings of Hertz and Maxwell, and places Boltzmann's philosophical thought between realism and instrumentalism.

The interest of HIEBERT's work resides in his attempt to shed light on the motives that led Boltzmann to develop his own philosophy of science, despite having repeatedly expressed a profound loathing of philosophy. Faced with intense and severe criticism at the turn of the 19th century, Boltzmann devoted himself to philosophy in an attempt to justify his own scientific methods. Hiebert, like Curd, argues that Boltzmann's conceptual structure is a standard example of philosophical positivism.

In his article on the physical theory worked out by Hertz and Boltzmann, D'AGOSTINO shows how, despite his great admiration for Hertz, the development of Boltzmann's epistemological system made him reject some of the theses upheld by Hertz.

WILSON aims to settle some of the still undecided questions about the origins of Boltzmann's epistemological edifice. He points out that Boltzmann's philosophy of science does not spring from his readings of Hertz. Indeed, the inception of Boltzmann's philosophy is placed in his period as a student at the Gymnasium in Linz, where he encountered the thought of Robert Zimmermann, a partisan of Herbart, Fichte, and Kant. Discussing Zimmermann's influence, Wilson makes clear in what measure Boltzmann may be considered a neo-Kantian.

VIDEIRA's main purpose is to put into relief the systematic character of Boltzmann's thought. For this purpose, the significance of his theoretical pluralism is analysed; in Boltzmann's work, identical phenomena may be explained in different manners and within different contexts, such as his unwavering defence of atomism, and his steadfast refusal to convert scientific and philosophical theses into dogmas.

JUNGNICKEL & McCORMMACH analyse the emergence during the 19th century of theoretical physics, to a large extent a German phenomenon. They discuss the questions German physicists raised, the methods they used and the results they obtained within the context of the institutionalization of theoretical physics. On account of all his academic activities, Boltzmann is properly considered as one of the first theoretical physicists in the modern sense, and he features in four large chapters.

Marxist thinkers have always been interested in Boltzmann, whom they have consistently considered a materialist scientist and philosopher as a result of his continued support of atomism. As examples of this adoption of Boltzmann's work by Marxist intellectuals, I have chosen two recent publications. The first, by HÖRZ & LASS, discusses the motives that led Boltzmann to decline the invitation to replace Kirchhoff as the new professor of theoretical physics at the University of Berlin. Besides briefly commenting on Boltzmann's life, career, and work, they stress the personal and scientific relationship between Boltzmann and Helmholtz. Following the Marxist tradition, the authors propose that many of Boltzmann's scientific and philosophical conceptions may be correctly understood only when characterised as dialectic and Marxist.

The second Marxist work about Boltzmann is STILLER; the author is a physical chemist from the former East Germany. Addressed to the cultivated general public, it is not intended as a biography, but instead presents Boltzmann's life and work within a global context. Its greatest merit is the prominence it gives to contemporary opinion of Boltzmann's scientific and philosophical achievements.

ANTONIO AUGUSTO PASSOS VIDEIRA

Botanical and Zoological Gardens

Bendiner, Robert, *The Fall of the Wild, The Rise of the Zoo*, New York: Dutton, 1981
Berrall, Julia S., *The Garden: An Illustrated History*, New York: Viking Press, 1966; Harmondsworth: Penguin, 1978

Blunt, Wilfrid, *The Ark in the Park: The Zoo in the Nineteenth Century*, London: Hamish Hamilton, 1976
Bramwell, D. *et al.* (eds), *Botanic Gardens and the World Conservation Strategy*, London: Academic Press, 1987
Brockway, Lucile H., *Science and Colonial Expansion: The Role of the British Royal Botanic Gardens*, New York: Academic Press, 1979
Fletcher, Harold R. and William H. Brown, *The Royal Botanic Garden, Edinburgh. 1670–1970*, Edinburgh: HMSO, 1970
Gager, C. Stuart, *Botanic Gardens of the World: Materials for a History*, New York: Brooklyn Botanic Garden Record, 1937; 2nd edition, 1938
Hahn, Emily, *Animal Gardens*, New York: Doubleday, 1967
Howard, Richard A., Burdette L. Wagenknecht and Peter S. Green (eds), *International Directory of Botanical Gardens*, Utrecht: International Bureau for Plant Taxonomy and Nomenclature, 1963
Hyams, Edward, *Great Botanical Gardens of the World*, photographs by William MacQuitty, London: Nelson and New York: Macmillan, 1969
Hyams, Edward, *A History of Gardens and Gardening*, New York: Praeger, and London: Dent, 1971
Jarvis, Caroline (ed.), *International Zoo Yearbook*, London, published annually
Kirchshofer, Rosl (ed.), *The World of Zoos: A Survey and Gazetteer*, translated from the German by Hilda Morris, New York: Viking Press, 1968 (original edition, 1960)
Meyer, Alfred (ed.), *A Zoo for All Seasons: The Smithsonian Animal World*, Washington, DC: Smithsonian Exposition Books, 1979
Pei Sheng-Ji, *Botanical Gardens in China*, Honolulu: University of Hawaii Press, 1984
Prest, John, *The Garden of Eden: The Botanic Garden and the Re-Creation of Paradise*, New Haven, Connecticut: Yale University Press, 1981
Shetler, Stanwyn G., *The Komarov Botanical Institute: 250 Years of Russian Research*, Washington, DC: Smithsonian Institution Press, 1967
Solit, Karen D., *History of the United States Botanic Garden, 1816–1991*, Washington, DC: Government Printing Office, 1993
Wyman, Donald, "The Arboretum and Botanical Gardens of North America", *Chronica Botanica*, 10 (1947): 395–498
Zoological Parks and Aquariums in the Americas, 1906–1987, Wheeling, West Virginia: American Association of Zoological Parks and Aquariums, published annually

Although there is a vast literature on the subjects of botany and zoology, and considerable material on museums of natural history and on gardens in general, works devoted specifically to botanical and zoological gardens are more limited. Almost every major botanical and zoological garden offers publications covering its own history and the nature and extent of its individual collections. For comprehensive surveys of these (including information about ownership, average attendance figures, annual operating budgets, the number of species or specialty exhibits maintained in each facility), see HOWARD, WAGENKNECHT & GREEN, JARVIS, and *Zoological Parks and Aquariums in the Americas, 1906–1987*. The latter provides basic information, including a list of member institutions in the US and Canada, and pertinent local information, including hours, rates, facilities, numbers of employees and volunteers, educational programs, species on exhibit, as well as attendance figures and annual budgets.

For the most part, works surveyed here are representative of the most useful resources currently available to anyone interested in learning more about botanical and zoological gardens around the world. First botanical gardens are considered, and then publications related to zoological gardens.

Botanical Gardens

GAGER presents the results of a questionnaire sent to "all gardens of record", and covers both botanical gardens in their own right and those affiliated with university departments of botany or other institutions. Not included are nature preserves, public parks, flower gardens, or private collections of trees or shrubs. Thus, the book is limited to institutions and gardens whose primary aim is botanical research, teaching, or both. As a guide to the "history of botanical gardens", it includes both functioning gardens (as of 1938), as well as some notable examples of those no longer in existence, including the botanical gardens of Epicurus, Aristotle, and Theophrastus in antiquity. For gardens in operation, each entry includes as much information as supplied by each institution as possible, including the names of directors, garden revenues, the extent of holdings of both libraries and herbaria, special lectures, courses offered, and the extent of the botanical collections exhibited or maintained by each garden listed.

WYMAN provides a more detailed study limited to the arboretums and botanical gardens of North America. Wyman, then horticulturist at the Arnold Arboretum of Harvard University, also includes information on colonial gardens, with a bibliography and maps, one showing climate and temperature variations across the country over the years, and another locating the "active arboretums and botanical gardens of North America". Wyman notes that as a result of World War II, many gardens closed permanently (all of which are listed), while a number of new arboretums and botanical gardens subsequently came into existence. Like Gager, Wyman is based on responses received from questionnaires sent to more than 200 institutions throughout North America. Arranged alphabetically, he also provides local descriptions and notes special features, including the number of species and variations in each collection, library holdings, special events, publications of each garden, and a list of references about the garden in question. Among the illustrations (which are not limited to North America), Wyman includes the early garden at the University of Montpellier, France (1596), and the famous Hortus Botanicus, Linnaeus' Trädgård in Uppsala, Sweden.

BERRALL offers an illustrated history of gardens from the time of the Pharaohs in ancient Egypt, surveying ancient Mesopotamian, Persian, Greek and Roman gardens, Islamic gardens, and medieval monasteric and castle gardens. Italian Renaissance gardens, and the extraordinary example of the gardens at Versailles, are followed by examples of English garden traditions, and the gardens of Japan and China. Among the drawings, engravings, paintings, and photographs used to illustrate this book, some are reproduced in color. Although not strictly devoted to botanical gardens, many of the gardens covered here represent serious research facilities.

SHETLER represents another genre of writings on botanical gardens, devoted to institutional history. In celebrating the 250th anniversary of the Komarov Botanical Institute, Shetler focuses on the history of botanical research in Leningrad/St Petersburg conducted at three facilities: the Imperial Botanical Gardens of St Petersburg (1823–1931), the Botanical Museum of the Academy of Sciences (1835–1931), and the Botanical Garden of the Academy of Sciences (1713–1812). The Komarov Botanical Institute incorporated the legacy of all three institutions when it was founded in 1931, and celebrated the 250th anniversary of botanical research in Leningrad in 1966. Shetler includes a discussion of the Institute's herbarium, library, public museum, and the "Department of Living Plants", i.e., the botanical garden.

HYAMS (1969) covers the great botanical gardens of the world with full-color illustrations. Italian gardens include the important research centers at Padua, Pisa and Palermo, including the Villa Taranto, and all of the great northern European gardens are here: Leiden, Munich, and Berlin-Dahlem, Paris (Jardin des Plantes), Vienna (Schönbrunn), and London (Kew). Scandinavia is represented by Göteborg and the famous garden of Linnaeus at Uppsala. North America is represented by the Arnold Arboretum (Harvard University), the Longworth and Huntington gardens, and Montreal (Canada), among others. The section on the Soviet Union includes gardens in Moscow, Minsk, Kiev, Yalta, and Tashkent, the section on the tropics ranges over Brazil, Ceylon, India, Singapore, and Uganda, while the southern hemisphere is represented by Christchurch (New Zealand), Melbourne and Sydney (Australia), and Kirstenbosch and Stellenbosch (South Africa). Botanical gardens in Japan are also covered. In addition, ground plans of historic gardens, a map showing the locations of the world's botanical gardens, and illustrations in both black and white and color are provided, along with an index. Like Berrall, Hyams (1969) is not devoted specifically to botanical gardens, although, again, many of the gardens covered here may also be counted among the world's important research centers.

FLETCHER & BROWN offer another example of an institutional history, this one celebrating the tercentenary of the Edinburgh gardens. The frontispiece depicts Sir Robert Sibbald, founder (with Sir Andrew Balfour) of the garden; dissatisfied with the state of medicine at the time, these two physicians founded a physic garden for medicinal and other plants, and the original plot of 180 square yards eventually grew into the great Botanical Garden at Inverleith. This history of the gardens and the important research sponsored by the Royal Botanic Garden in Edinburgh, is nicely illustrated with ground plans and photographs of the gardens and of the individuals most responsible for their development.

HYAMS (1971) offers an extensively illustrated guide to gardens around the world, from Chinese garden art and pre-Columbian gardens, to New York roof garden terraces and the fountains at Longword gardens in Pennsylvania. Along the way, it covers African gardens in the Dar-al-Islam, medieval gardens, and Renaissance, French and English gardens. But again, like both Hyams (1969) and Berrall, Hyams (1971) is devoted to gardens in general, not botanical gardens in particular, although these do figure to a considerable extent.

BROCKWAY concentrates on the role of colonial expansion, especially the British experience in the Indies, China and the New World. The book discusses seed and plant transfers, new food staples and plantation crops, along with the roles of learned societies and botanical gardens in supporting botanical research – especially at Kew in London, where quinine, rubber, and sisal were all studied. Brockway, in addition to stressing the importance of British botanical science in studying and developing plant resources, is also interested in analyzing "the social and political implications of scientific research" within the context of colonial expansion.

PREST, while not a history of botanical gardens *per se*, is concerned with the "great age" of botanical gardens, following the discovery of the New World. It examines in particular six European gardens that achieved pre-eminence: Padua, Leiden, Montpellier, Oxford, Paris, and Uppsala. The Oxford garden, divided into four quadrants representing the four continents, Europe, Asia, Africa and the Americas, was typical. Such gardens were intended to serve as living encyclopedias, in which plants were laid out for ready reference. Prest also studies botanical gardens as "re-creations" of the Garden of Eden. This book, handsomely illustrated, also covers formal gardens like those at Chatsworth, and college gardens such as the one at Wadham College, Oxford.

PEI reflects a growing interest in gardens and their history throughout Asia. This study, published by the Harold L. Lyon Arboretum in Hawaii, evolved from a lecture given at the Arboretum, and gives a brief history of botanical gardens in China. As early as the Song Dynasty (AD 420–79), a garden of medicinal plants, the Du-Le Garden, was being studied in China, for which there is even a contemporary guide by Si-Ma Qian. Palace and private gardens are also discussed. Following the founding of the People's Republic of China in 1949, Pei reports on two major conferences on botanical gardens held in China, in 1963 and 1978, and in 1981 the Chinese Association of Botanic Gardens was established in Wuhan. Among the gardens covered in Pei, the earliest was founded in Nanjing in memory of Sun Yat-Sen in 1928, and later rebuilt in 1954 with a herbarium of 520,000 specimens. Other botanical gardens were founded in Lushan (1934), Kunming (1951), Beijing (1955, with a herbarium of more than one million specimens), Guangzhou (1956), Hangzhou (1956), Wuhan (1956), Guilin (1958), Xi'an (1959), Xishuangbanna (1959), and most recently, Shanghai (1973).

BRAMWELL *et al.* represents a growing interest in the role botanical gardens can play in ecological research and the conservation of wildlife in all its forms. This volume, based on a conference held in Las Palmas, Gran Canaria in 1985 (which brought together 175 botanists and botanical garden managers from 39 countries), discusses the role of botanical gardens in implementing world conservation strategies. In particular, this volume focuses on how gardens can be effective in both plant conservation efforts and in the maintenance of plant diversity. Reports from local communities range from Nancy (France) and Córdoba (Spain), to Xishuangbanna (China) and Mexico, among many others. Topics discussed range from the computerization of garden records to the role

of the International Association of Botanic Gardens (IABG) in conservation world-wide.

SOLIT studies yet another major institution, the US Botanic Garden. Although discussed by the founding fathers, it was not until the Presidency of James Monroe that an act was signed in 1829 to establish a National Botanic Garden. Charged with collecting plants from all over the world, this first national garden survived little more than 20 years, and was disbanded in 1837. Just five years later, however, the idea was revived, largely as a result of new interest roused by the plants collected by the Wilkes expedition to the South Seas. Solit describes the history of the institution, the significance of the Wilkes Expedition (1838–42), the achievements of the garden under the direction of William Smith, and its fortunes under the directorship of George Wesley Hess, and then gives details of its current functions, largely unchanged from its original Congressional mandate, to collect, cultivate, and grow various "vegetable productions" and to display them to the public for their enjoyment and education.

Zoological Gardens

JARVIS, although published annually, includes a brief history of zoos, from that of Queen Hatshepsut of Egypt to the "parks of intelligence" maintained by King Hui of Liang in ancient China. Marco Polo noted the splendid menageries of Kublai Khan at Xanadu, and, earlier, Alexander the Great kept strange animals as tribute from lands he conquered, which were available to Aristotle for academic study. In the modern era, Jarvis describes the great zoos of Britain, France, Germany, Russia, Japan, and the US.

HAHN concentrates on "zoos of the past, and the institution as it exists today". Practical discussion includes dealers and how they supply animals to zoos, both public and private. Unfortunately, there is nothing here on Latin America, and no zoos are covered in Spain or Portugal, or any of the reserves in Africa.

KIRCHSHOFER includes a number of articles written by directors of prominent zoos, and is devoted to various aspects of the practical operation of zoos and to various philosophies concerning their functions in modern society. A.C.V. van Bemmel (of the Blijdorp Zoo in Rotterdam) considers the "zoological garden as asylums for threatened species", while H. Hediger of Zurich examines the transformation "from cage to territory" – from the 19th-century concept of menageries, to the current fashion for exhibiting animals in habitats. Heinrich Dathe (of the Friedrichsfelde Zoo, Berlin) offers a day-to-day portrait of the life of a zoo director, while Walter Fiedler of the Schönbrunn Zoo (Vienna) describes the history of the "oldest zoo in the world" (dating from 1452). Kirchshofer provides a useful gazetteer of the zoological gardens of the world, a survey of zoos and public aquariums, as well as introductory essays by region.

BLUNT focuses on zoos in the 19th century, beginning with the zoological garden established in Regent's Park, London, in 1828. This was supported by the Zoological Society of London, which was granted its charter in 1829, and was first headed by Sir Humphry Davy, President of the Royal Society, and Sir Stamford Raffles. The history of the Zoological Society, and the roles of Sir Richard Owen, Thomas Henry Huxley, and Philip Lutley Selater, are also discussed.

MEYER is a beautifully illustrated history of the National Zoo in the US, including a history of the "evolution of the zoo", and covers such subjects as the art of acquisition, keepers and curators, feeding times, science and health, and the doctoring of exotic animals, along with the role of research and the study of animal behavior. It also provides a "who's who" of zoos, but only public institutions are listed, and no account is given of aquariums, private, or commercial zoos. Major exhibits and recent trends related to zoos in America are also covered.

BENDINER considers the changing role of zoos and their value in breeding endangered species. He is in favor of zoos because "in what remains of the wild", orang-utans, Siberian tigers, one-horned rhinoceroses, and green turtles – to name but a few – "are not destined to run free and multiply at all but rather to sink into the zoological burial ground that already contains the last remnants of the dodo, the woolly mammoth and the passenger pigeon". Emphasis here is given to the Bronx Zoo (New York), the San Diego Wild Animal Park (California), England's Whipsnade Zoo, and the Frankfurt Zoo in Germany. The importance of zoos for "informing the public, for furthering scientific study, and, above all, for providing a safety net for [endangered] species", is stressed. National parks and preserves in India and Africa are also covered. Menus for feeding animals at the National and London zoos are provided, while Bendiner also discusses outstanding examples of "habitat" zoo designs at Chester (England), Rotterdam, San Diego, and the Bronx.

JOSEPH W. DAUBEN

Botany: general works

Christensen, Carl Frederik Albert, *Den danske Botanik's Historie*, vols 1–2, Copenhagen: Haderups, 1924–26

Collander Runar, *The History of Botany in Finland 1828–1918*, translated from the Finnish by David Barrett, Helsinki: Societas Scientiarum Fennica, 1965

Davy de Virville, Adrien, *Histoire de la Botanique en France*, Paris: Comité Français du VIIIe Congrès International de Botanique Paris-Nice, 1954

Eriksson, Gunnar, *Botanikens historia i Sverige intill år 1800*, Uppsala: Almqvist & Wiksell, 1969

Ewan, Josef (ed.), *A Short History of Botany in the United States*, New York: Hafner, 1969

Green, Joseph Reynolds, *A History of Botany, 1860–1900: Being a Continuation of Sachs's "History of Botany, 1530–1860"*, Oxford: Clarendon Press, 1909; New York: Russell and Russell, 1967

Green, Joseph Reynolds, *A History of Botany in the United Kingdom from the Earliest Times to the End of the 19th Century*, London: Dent, and New York: Dutton, 1914

Humphrey, Harry Baker, *Makers of North American Botany*, New York: Ronald Press, 1961

Mägdefrau, Karl, *Geschichte der Botanik: Leben und Leistung großer Forscher*, Stuttgart: Fischer, 1973; 2nd edition, 1992

Meyer, Ernst Heinrich Friedrich, *Geschichte der Botanik*, vols 1–4, Königsberg: Bornträger, 1854–57; reprinted, Amsterdam: Asher, 1965

Möbius, Martin, *Geschichte der Botanik von den ersten Anfängen bis zur Gegenwart*, Jena: Fischer, 1937

Morton, A.G., *History of Botanical Science: An Account of the Development of Botany from Ancient Times to the Present Day*, London and New York: Academic Press, 1981

Sachs, Julius, *History of Botany, 1530–1860*, translated from the German by H.E.F. Garnsey, revised by I.B. Balfour, Oxford: Clarendon Press, 1890 (original edition, 1864)

Weevers, Theodorus, *Fifty Years of Plant Physiology*, translated from the Dutch by A.J.M.J. Rant, Amsterdam: Scheltema & Holkema, 1949

In the early 19th century a number of surveys of the history of botany were published, based on the work of well-known writers and organised as chronological histories of the botanical literature. Botanists of our own time have tried to grasp both the inner logic of scientific development and, above all, the differentiation of botany into its modern sub-disciplines. A substantial genre deals with the development of botany within the borders of national states.

The general overview by MÖBIUS dedicates only 20 pages to the scientific approaches of antiquity and the Middle Ages; the development since the 16th century takes up 350 pages, applications from agriculture to pharmacology 30 pages, and notes on research tools (such as botanical gardens and microscopy) 15 pages. The book amply refers to events, dates, and authors to map the development of taxonomy and of the botanical sub-disciplines, including morphology, cytology, anatomy, evolution, the various aspects of physiology, plant geography, and phytopalaeontology. However, Möbius offers merely a catalogue of dates, rather than an account of the inner logic of scientific development, and his work contains many errors with respect to first names, dates, and the biographical sketches in the footnotes. To the critical reader the book may serve as a reference work for a historical introduction into the various aspects of botany.

While retaining the main categories of Möbius's history, MÄGDEFRAU disregards systematic plant classification (taxonomy) and emphasizes particular individuals and their achievement. Original works are carefully documented, and many achievements described more fully than in earlier attempts. Some are even acknowledged for the first time, such as phytoecology, pathology, and palaeontology, which Mägdefrau presents a detailed analysis of the original works. Since all scholarly details are reliable and supported by references to the literature, the book can be recommended as a sound introduction to the fundamental problems of botany and to the development of its insights.

The British botanist MORTON has also produced a general survey of the history of botany from prehistoric times to the 20th century. In 11 chapters (supplemented by references to sources and the secondary literature) he discusses the chief lines of development, from early botany to the foundation of scientific botany in antiquity, and its continuation since the Renaissance to the modern specialisation of botanical sub-disciplines. In this account, only events that led to modern developments are deemed relevant. As in Möbius and Mägdefrau, the history of medieval botany is interpreted as a period of scientific stagnation and is paid scant attention. But, in contrast to earlier works, Morton includes developments in ancient China, the Americas, and other non-European countries. The history of botany in the 20th century is dealt with until about 1930, and, since the book skips a number of contentious areas, it can merely serve as an introduction.

The early history of botany from antiquity to the age of humanism is detailed in the four volumes by MEYER, who aimed at a complete listing of all authors and texts on botany known in his day. His extensive commentaries on the works are scholarly and fairly balanced. Even so, not all of his statements comply with modern standards of historical objectivity, for although a botanist of considerable philological skill, Meyer still tried to discover the biological knowledge of his own age in the earlier sources. However, the many carefully established details render his collection a reference work that is still useful.

SACHS has written a history of botany between around 1500 and the mid-19th century. His survey cites the most important authors of the period under consideration, but fails to evaluate adequately their writings, and contains neither footnotes nor references. The selection of events and the historical opinions of this positivist professional botanist are single-mindedly focused on a confirmation of the growth of knowledge of particular "facts". The work is thus useful merely for introductory information. GREEN (1909) is a study of the following period, from 1860 to 1900. It contains footnotes and references and deals with the main subject areas of botany, namely morphology with taxonomy and phytopalaeontology, plant anatomy and plant physiology, with the exception of taxonomy and plant geography. The emergent areas of research, such as evolution, bacteriology, microbiology, ecology as well as evolutionary biology, are only mentioned in passing. In the main, Green offers an introduction to the most important foundations of modern botany. The beginnings of modern plant physiology in the first half of the 20th century are discussed in detail by WEEVERS.

A number of special publications trace the history of botany in particular countries. CHRISTENSEN offers a detailed study of the history of botany in Denmark between c.1600 and 1912. He discusses the history of botany in the universities, the work of outstanding individuals, and special activities such as the compilation of a *Flora Danica* and scientific expeditions; also discussed are Danish contributions to the development of modern botany, morphology, taxonomy, anatomy, plant geography, plant physiology and plant pathology, mycology, microbiology, and so on. The book contains a useful biography of original literature.

GREEN (1914) presents a careful analysis of the history of botany in England, Scotland and Ireland from the early modern era up till about 1900. Consulting original literature and biographical material, he discusses the work of British botanists and their reaction to international developments, in particular to the work of Linneaus. He also gives an account of the history of botany in the universities and botanical institutions. A chronological table displays the most important events between 1516 and 1900, which are also discussed in the text.

A history of botany in Finland, focusing on the period 1828–1918, has been compiled by COLLANDER. The book describes the outstanding contributions by the Nylander brothers and by Frederik Elfving; it also offers an account of the rise of specialist institutions, and of the rise of botany in the educational system. In addition, Collander thoroughly discusses modern developments in physiology, phycology, mycology, ecology, and taxonomy.

In co-operation with a number of specialists, DAVY DE VIRVILLE has published a study of French botany between the 16th and 20th centuries. Referring to a wealth of biographical detail (supplemented by photographic portraits and illustrations) as well as original literature, this book gives a particularly detailed account of French contributions to modern aspects of botany in the 19th and early 20th centuries. Apart from morphology, anatomy and physiology, the book deals with the then important cryptogamy, phytogeography, pathology and palaeontology, as well as agronomical, pharmaceutical and silvicultural botany. There is a separate chapter on the notion of "species" and the beginnings of the theory of evolution.

ERIKSSON contains the early history of Swedish botany up to 1800. Based on original texts, this study gives a detailed account of university history, which began as early as the late Middle Ages (when the University of Uppsala was founded). Eriksson also discusses the important achievements of Swedish botanists, including the systematic work of Linneaus, whose impact on his successors is depicted along with later innovations in plant physiology and investigations of cryptogams.

HUMPHREY's alphabetical compilation of 122 short biographies of botanists active in North America was followed by EWAN's introductory survey on the history of botany in the United States, which concentrates on the period between 1850 and 1950.

BRIGITTE HOPPE

translated by Anna-Katherina Meyer

Botany: Britain

Allen, David Elliston, *The Botanists: A History of the Botanical Society of the British Isles through a Hundred and Fifty Years*, Winchester: St Paul's Bibliographies, 1986

Bower, Frederick Orpen, *Sixty Years of Botany in Britain (1875–1935): Impressions of an Eyewitness*, London: Macmillan, 1938

Clokie, Hermina Newman, *An Account of the Herbaria of the Department of Botany in the University of Oxford*, London: Oxford University Press, 1964

Desmond, Ray, *Kew: The History of the Royal Botanic Gardens*, London: Harvill Press with the Royal Botanic Gardens, Kew, 1995

Fletcher, Harold Roy and William H. Brown, *The Royal Botanic Garden Edinburgh, 1670–1970*, Edinburgh: HMSO, 1970

Gage, Andrew Thomas, *A History of the Linnean Society of London*, London: Linnean Society, 1938

Gage, Andrew Thomas and William Thomas Stearn, *A Bicentenary History of the Linnean Society of London*, London and San Diego: Academic Press, 1988

Green, Joseph Reynolds, *A History of Botany, 1860–1900: Being a Continuation of Sachs's "History of Botany,*

1530–1860", Oxford: Clarendon Press, 1909; New York: Russell and Russell, 1967

Green, Joseph Reynolds, *A History of Botany in the United Kingdom from the Earliest Times to the End of the 19th Century*, London: Dent, and New York: Dutton, 1914

Harvey-Gibson, Robert John, *Outlines of the History of Botany*, London: A. and C. Black, 1919

Walters, Stuart Max, *The Shaping of Cambridge Botany: A Short History of Whole-Plant Botany in Cambridge from the Time of Ray into the Present Century*, Cambridge and New York: Cambridge University Press, 1981

Until recently, writing general surveys of scientific disciplines has been out of fashion. In Britain, especially, this is in marked contrast to the beginning of the 20th century when, motivated by Julius Sachs's *History of Botany* (1875; English translation, 1890), and anxious to justify investment in laboratories and equipment, leading figures of the first generation of professional botanists produced accounts of the origin of their discipline. In *A History of Botany, 1860–1900*, Joseph Reynolds GREEN (professor of botany at the Pharmaceutical Society of Great Britain before becoming Hartley Lecturer in vegetable physiology at Liverpool University, 1907–14) has written one of the very best accounts of the period in which the foundations of the discipline were laid. Taking his cue from Sachs, the material is set out in three divisions: morphology (and classification), anatomy, and physiology. With a good index and a comprehensive bibliography, this remains a splendid account of the body of work to which British botanists aspired to contribute. Green's story really begins with the Reformation and the establishment of university and private herbal and physic gardens, and covers the period from the foundation of the Oxford Botanic Garden in 1621 to the surrender of the Chelsea Physic Garden by the Apothecaries's Company in 1899. As one might expect from someone involved with the Pharmaceutical Society for 20 years, the account is particularly strong on the relationship between botany and areas such as pharmacy, chemistry, and medicine.

In an attempt to temper Green's enthusiasm for all things German, Robert John HARVEY-GIBSON (a friend and colleague of Green) published his *Outlines of the History of Botany* in 1919. The text is based on a lecture course given to third-year students at Liverpool University (where the author was professor of botany from 1894 to 1921). Although the main body of the book concerns the story from Linnaeus to 20th-century laboratory-based botany, it is structured in a progressive, phylogenetic form, beginning with plant knowledge in antiquity and ending with the modern fields of reproduction, nutrition, ecology, sensitivity, morphology, taxonomy, evolution, palaeobotany, and anatomy. It is an attractively written account that, as the author intended, preserves the style of the lecture room.

To get the most out of these accounts one should bear in mind their historical context, and, to this end, excellent insight is provided by BOWER's autobiography. Bower was professor of botany at Glasgow University for 40 years (1885–1925), and his book provides a portrait of the moribund state of the discipline in Britain in the last quarter of the 19th century. In

the 1870s, a student in the natural sciences with an interest in botany who desired more than a course in descriptive botany and herborizing excursions, was reliant on German text-books. (This was at Cambridge University, where there had been a chair of botany for more than 150 years). There is an edge to this short account that makes it a good read: as Bower puts it, while Hugo von Mohl, Wilhelm Hofmeister, and Julius Sachs were setting the plant side of biology aglow with a new synthetic flame in Germany, "official botany at Cambridge had been splitting analytically the varieties of *Rubus*". He attributes the development of the discipline in Britain to the provisions of the 1870 Education Act, which introduced science to the national curriculum in schools, thereby creating the demand for teachers and for teachers of teachers. These demands were first met by Thomas Henry Huxley's Normal School of Science at South Kensington, London and, later, by the expanding university sector. This is a book as much about education and science as it is about botany and botanists. After Cambridge, Bower studied under Sachs at the University of Würzburg (1879) and with Anton de Bary at the University of Strasbourg (1879). In these continental research institutions he learned skills in preparing, treating, preserving, and observing material for biological inquiry. From 1880, he worked as an assistant to Daniel Oliver at University College, London, and as a demonstrator and lecturer at the Normal School of Science. At the same time he pursued his own research interests at the newly established Jodrell Laboratory at the Royal Botanic Gardens, Kew, until his appointment as Regius Professor of Botany at Glasgow in 1885. In his account of his experience of all these institutions, personae, pedagogy, and botany are given equal status. Despite the title, the focus of the book is primarily on the period 1870–90, and those interested in the nature of the new botany will find chapter 10, "The Morphological Kaleidoscope", of much value. Here, Bower describes the way in which the perspective shifted from the old paradigm, based on a fully organized land plant (constituted by root, stem, leaf, and hair), to the propagative organs of the more rudimentary forms. The result was that, far from any spore-producing form originating as a metamorphosed stem, leaf, pinna, or hair, the reverse is seen to be the outcome of the comparison, thereby producing a stable basis "for opinions that were to prove themselves more in accord with evolutionary theory".

While the general survey literature on botany is sparse, there is a good body of literature on British botanical institutions. Not surprisingly, the Royal Botanic Gardens, Kew, has received most attention, the most recent (and finest) study being DESMOND. This is an excellent institutional history, richly illustrated and with a great deal of supplementary material, including a bibliography, a biographical register of the statesmen, patrons, administrators, scientists, gardeners, and plant collectors associated with the gardens, notes on archival sources, a detailed index, and a chronology. Information on everything from annual attendance figures (1841–1994), opening times, and admission charges to the water supply is provided among the 15 appendixes.

FLETCHER & BROWN details 300 years of what is now the Royal Botanic Garden, Edinburgh, organised chiefly around biographical chapters on the keepers and curators. Although all of the major developments are mentioned, including the garden's various locations around the city during its early history and, once it had settled at Inverleith in 1823, its expansions, amalgamations, constructions, and reorganisations, little or nothing is done with this catalogue of detail. Apart from the front and back matter, the chapters are divided into four parts, which are separated by "Interludes" providing information on developments in botany elsewhere in Britain and beyond. However, these "Interludes" are as eclectic as the main parts are tedious. Some information is provided on the history of the Royal Caledonian Horticultural Society and on the Botanical Society of Edinburgh.

GAGE & STEARN's book is an in-house history based on the Linnean Society's extensive records. This is an updated version of GAGE, and there is very little mention of anything not immediately associated with the Society, and almost no discussion or analysis of the material provided. On the other hand, with a good index and with nearly a third of the book given over to the presentation of information concerning the Society's collections, publications, prize-winners, officers, and so forth, it is an indispensable factual resource for anyone researching the oldest active biological society in the world.

ALLEN is an account of the Botanical Society of the British Isles. Originally the Botanical Society of London, this was one of the plethora of scientific societies established in the capital during the 1820s and 1830s. Not only did this group seek to distinguish themselves from the Linnean Society of London, it was also in competition for membership with the Royal Botanical Society and the Medico–Botanical Society. Ostensibly a collecting co-operative established for the organized exchange of herbarium specimens, its quarrelsome membership represented disparate views concerning what the Society was about. This is a comprehensive account of a society that was dependent on slender resources, and was unclear about its purpose and, as a consequence, had an intermittent history. The text and the supporting notes are rich with suggestions and references, and there are helpful appendices on members.

An important resource for the history of botany at Oxford is CLOKIE, which has a wealth of biographical information, including a biographical register of collectors stretching to nearly 150 pages. Finally, WALTERS is an account of botany at Cambridge. The author is a former director of the Cambridge University Botanic Garden, and the book is a commemorative volume celebrating the sesquicentenary of John Stevens Henslow's new botanic garden. However, it does provide a history from John Ray (a fellow at Trinity College, who had a small botanic garden near his college rooms) onwards. Walters contrasts the histories of botany and zoology, the former traditionally having a strong presence due its inclusion within medical teaching, the latter being largely absent from the university curricula until a chair was founded in 1869, arguing that botany was shaped by this need to be useful in medicine, and that Henslow's garden was a significant step in the process which made botany a discipline in its own right. There are many pleasing illustrations and a bibliography, but no footnotes and no references to archival material.

PERRY O'DONOVAN

Boyle, Robert 1627–1691

Anglo-Irish natural philosopher and chemist

Birch, Thomas, "The Life of the Hon. Robert Boyle", in his *The Works of the Honourable Robert Boyle*, London: Miller, 1744; 2nd edition, 6 vols, London: Rivington, 1772

Clericuzio, Antonio, "A Redefinition of Boyle's Chemistry and Corpuscular Philosophy", *Annals of Science*, 47 (1990): 561–89

Frank Jr, Robert G., *Harvey and the Oxford Physiologists: A Study of Scientific Ideas and Social Interaction*, Berkeley: University of California Press, 1980

Hall, Marie Boas, *Robert Boyle and Seventeenth-Century Chemistry*, Cambridge: Cambridge University Press, 1958; New York: Kraus, 1968

Hall, Marie Boas, *Robert Boyle on Natural Philosophy: An Essay with Selections from His Writings*, Bloomington: Indiana University Press, 1965

Harwood, John T. (ed.), *The Early Essays and Ethics of Robert Boyle*, Carbondale: Southern Illinois University Press, 1991

Hooykaas, Reijer, *Robert Boyle: A Study of Science and Christian Belief*, with a foreword by J.H. Brooke and Michael Hunter, Lanham, New York: University Press of America, 1997 (original edition, 1943)

Hunter, Michael (ed.), *Robert Boyle: By Himself and His Friends*, London: Pickering, 1994

Hunter, Michael (ed.), *Robert Boyle Reconsidered*, Cambridge: Cambridge University Press, 1994

Hunter, Michael, "How Boyle Became a Scientist", *History of Science*, 33 (1995): 59–103

Jacob, J.R., *Robert Boyle and the English Revolution*, New York: Franklin, 1977

Kaplan, Barbara Beguin, *"Divulging of Useful Truths in Physick": The Medical Agenda of Robert Boyle*, Baltimore: Johns Hopkins University Press, 1993

Klaaren, Eugene M., *Religious Origins of Modern Science: Belief in Creation in Seventeenth-Century Thought*, Grand Rapids, Michigan: Eerdmans, 1977

Maddison, R.E.W., *The Life of the Honourable Robert Boyle, F.R.S.*, London: Taylor and Francis and New York: Barnes and Noble, 1969

Sargent, Rose-Mary, *The Diffident Naturalist: Robert Boyle and the Philosophy of Experiment*, Chicago: University of Chicago Press, 1995

Shapin, Steven, *A Social History of Truth: Civility and Science in Seventeenth-Century England*, Chicago: University of Chicago Press, 1994

Shapin, Steven and Simon Schaffer, *Leviathan and the Air-Pump: Hobbes, Boyle, and the Experimental Life*, Princeton, New Jersey: Princeton University Press, 1985

Webster, Charles, *The Great Instauration: Science, Medicine and Reform, 1626–60*, London: Duckworth, 1975; New York: Holmes and Meier, 1976

Westfall, Richard S., *Science and Religion in Seventeenth-Century England*, New Haven, Connecticut: Yale University Press, 1958

There is currently no work that satisfactorily binds together a narrative of Robert Boyle's life with an exposition of his ideas:

readers will therefore have to effect their own synthesis by separately consulting biographies and primarily thematic studies that sometimes make selective use of biographical detail. This is both the cause and symptom of a continuing tendency to consider Boyle's thought as a unitary system, as if his ideas hardly evolved in the 40 years of his active life as a natural philosopher, and as if he were little affected by the intellectual trends of his day. To a large extent, both the separation of his life from his ideas, and the reification of his thought as a system, can be traced back to the text of Boyle on which scholars still rely, Thomas BIRCH's edition of 1744 (reprinted in 1772), to which Birch's life of Boyle was prefixed. Birch printed Boyle's works more or less in order of publication but without dates, and the reader has therefore to turn to the accompanying "Life" in order to discover the actual year in which each work appeared. It is hoped that a new edition, currently in preparation, will use more intellectual rigour and sensitivity when detailing the dates of composition and publication of Boyle's writings, his intellectual evolution, and his relationship to his context.

For Boyle's life, the fullest narrative remains that of Birch, which reprints many key letters and other documents. It is usefully supplemented by MADDISON, which gives more accurate texts of certain important sources such as Boyle's will, but which is similarly limited to a purely narrative structure. Those who wish to consult the most telling biographical texts concerning Boyle — memoirs by Boyle himself and by those who knew him well — will find these provided in HUNTER (1994), *Robert Boyle: By Himself and His Friends*, accompanied by a lengthy introductory essay that uses this data to explore Boyle's intellectual personality. In addition, key evidence concerning Boyle's intellectual characteristics in the earliest phase of his career (1640s), before he turned to natural philosophy, and when, as is now generally acknowledged, he saw his role in life as that of a moralist, is to be found in HARWOOD.

A synopsis of current approaches to Boyle's ideas is to be found in HUNTER's *Robert Boyle Reconsidered*, which includes studies ranging from the sources of Boyle's experimental practice, to his rhetorical strategy and his philosophical outlook. The coverage is deliberately slanted towards facets of his ideas that might initially seem surprising in the work of a leading advocate of the mechanical philosophy, and which in the past have been neglected. The essays thus include up-to-date accounts of such topics (of which book-length treatments are not yet available) as Boyle's interest in alchemy, and his views on things beyond the rational. Hunter's introduction uses the findings of the essays to present a view of Boyle as a man whose great "scrupulousness" in his religious and private affairs was mirrored in his intellectual life by an obsession with detail and an insistence on getting to the bottom of any question to which he devoted himself. Arguably, this does much to explain his distinctiveness and profundity as a thinker.

This volume also offers a survey of the historiography of Boyle, pointing out how study of him in the post-war years was inhibited by the mismatch between his rather diffuse empiricism and the emphasis on heroic syntheses of mathematicised physics that characterised the classic post-war view of the scientific revolution. In part, this explains why Boyle received less attention than he might have done at that time,

considering his significance. It also had the effect of encouraging the principal author who did study Boyle at the time, Marie Boas Hall, to make as "rational" and mechanistic an interpretation as possible of Boyle's ideas, and to neglect aspects of them — such as alchemy — that failed to fit into this scheme. Her work is also flawed by an unfortunate obtuseness towards facets of Boyle's ideas that she deemed non-scientific. Nevertheless, there is still something of value to be found in Hall's studies, particularly HALL (1958), which combines a brief intellectual biography of Boyle with detailed attention to his eclectic theory of matter — which he christened "corpuscularianism" — and his views on chemical composition; it also includes "A Digression on Air". However, although she made a pioneering attempt to place Boyle within an intellectual context, the need for a reconsideration of Boyle's ideas on such subjects is made clear by the recent revaluation of his corpuscular philosophy by CLERICUZIO, which stresses the extent to which Boyle's explanations of chemical phenomena were not confined to purely mechanical principles. A further, more general, view of Boyle is to be found in the book-length interpretative essay prefixed to HALL (1965), a collection of extracts from Boyle's writings illustrating his outlook as a natural philosopher and his views on a wide range of scientific phenomena.

A classic study of Boyle's attempts to harmonise science and religion is HOOYKAAS, originally published in 1943 but only recently translated into English. This expounds Boyle's epistemological and theological ideas and seeks to illustrate their sophistication and deep compatibility; in the process, it offers great insight into many aspects of Boyle's thought, although more recent studies have to some extent duplicated (or superseded) its findings. A better-known study written from a similar viewpoint is provided by WESTFALL, though its extensive attention to Boyle's thought is placed within the context of an account of the ideas of contemporaries such as Newton, which illustrates the strong voluntarist tendencies that mitigated the drift towards Deism in the period. A further, comparable study is KLAAREN, which places Boyle within a more portentous context of issues involving the move towards modernisation and secularisation, and, partly for this reason, is less successful in doing justice to Boyle, though it is not without value.

In the 1970s and 1980s, the leading trend in Boyle studies was to attempt to place him more closely within his social and political context. One such attempt was made by WEBSTER, who deals with Boyle within the context of the circle of intellectuals surrounding Samuel Hartlib, with its emphasis on the amelioration of human life. A study focused more specifically on Boyle is that of JACOB, who argues that the impact of the English Revolution caused Boyle to question his aristocratic upbringing, and to adopt a more meritocratic ethos influenced by the Hartlib circle. It also claims that Boyle's natural philosophy was predicated on a dialogue with the radical sects that sprang up during and after the Civil War, and argues that, after the Restoration, Boyle not only continued to engage in similar debates but also sought to link science with the pursuit of empire and national prosperity. These views have been widely influential and form the cornerstone of the so-called "Jacob thesis" concerning the affiliations of the new science in the late 17th and early 18th centuries as a whole. On the other hand, their evidential basis is flimsier than most who have accepted them realise; an alternative reading of some of the key evidence is offered by HUNTER (1995), who also offers a reconsideration of Boyle's links with the Hartlib Circle.

A more recent and rather different contextualist study of Boyle is by SHAPIN & SCHAFFER. They also see Boyle's natural philosophy as predicated on the need for political stability, but they integrate this more fully with the actual content and method of Boyle's natural philosophy than Jacob, who tended to take Boyle's science for granted and to extrapolate from it in order to elucidate a broader strategy. Shapin & Schaffer argue that Boyle's use of experiment, his appeal to "matters of fact" that might be consensually agreed, and his tendency to favour and emphasise these rather than hypotheses that were liable to prove contentious, were all deeply ideological in intent, gauged to counter the divisive effects of rival natural philosophies, particularly that of Thomas Hobbes, on whose debate with Boyle their book is focused. This book has been very influential, raising new and quite profound questions about how different types of intellectual activity were validated in Boyle's time, and problematising historical constructs that had long been taken for granted. It has undoubtedly stimulated fresh thought on many related issues. On the other hand, it can be criticised for lavishing undue attention on Boyle's debate with Hobbes, neglecting the more sustained concern shown in Boyle's writings for the continuing vitality of scholastic modes of thought. In addition, it invests Boyle with a greater decisiveness than was in fact the case, eliding the complexities and tensions in his intellectual personality, and hence paradoxically underwriting the traditional view of Boyle as a consummate apologist for the new science, albeit from a novel point of view.

More recently, SHAPIN has sought to present Boyle as the paragon of a certain ideal of intellectual life, which was itself the basis for the way in which knowledge claims were formulated and adjudicated at the time. Thus the desiderata of a natural philosopher, and the appropriate codes of practice in the scientific community of the day, are seen as predicated on genteel ideals that Boyle above all exemplified, with claims to "truth" being filtered through socially-defined criteria of credibility and trustworthiness. As with Shapin & Schaffer, this book is at its strongest in setting out theoretical paradigms that informed intellectual life at the time; it is at its weakest in exploring how these worked in practice, and how they interacted with a range of other factors in explaining the complexity of Boyle's attempts to make sense of the natural world.

An alternative account of Boyle is that of SARGENT, who consciously confronts the social constructivism of the Shapin/Schaffer approach, offering instead a considered restatement of the value of a more intellectualist view of Boyle's ideas. Her book traces the various sources of Boyle's experimental method, creating a profile of his practice and emphasising his complexity as a thinker and the subtlety of his position on many issues. Indeed, she stresses the danger of oversimplifying Boyle by constricting him within modern philosophical categorisations, and she interestingly discusses various aspects of modern interpretations of his thought, not least in her voluminous endnotes. The book is perhaps at its weakest in dealing with the aspects of Boyle's thought that fit least well into her intellectualist framework, notably his voluntarism and his stress on things beyond reason – his receptiveness to

alchemy and to non-mechanical explanations in natural philosophy. On these – as on such topics as Boyle's interest in the ideas of van Helmont – fuller studies by other authors will have to be awaited. Sargent none the less provides an up-to-date and useful synthesis of many aspects of Boyle's thought.

Lastly, Boyle's medical writings have been the subject of two studies. KAPLAN's full-length book attempts a general survey of Boyle's medically-related research, dwelling particularly on the application of his corpuscularian ideas to the workings of the human body, and his interest in the impact on the body of environmental factors. On the other hand, her work ignores some key themes in Boyle's writings on such subjects, and it is particularly weak on his ambivalent position in relation to the virulent debates on health care that went on at the time. As far as Boyle's involvement in research on the medical sciences is concerned, a more searching and contextualised account is provided by FRANK in his study of the school of "Oxford physiologists", with whom Boyle was associated from the mid-1650s to the mid-1660s. As with most other aspects of Boyle, however, the final word on his ideas on such topics and the manner in which he presented them has by no means been said.

MICHAEL HUNTER

See also Experiments; Royal Society of London

Brahe, Tycho 1546–1601

Danish astronomer

Dreyer, J.L.E., *Tycho Brahe: A Picture of Scientific Life and Work in the Sixteenth Century*, Edinburgh: A. and C. Black, 1890; 2nd edition, New York: Dover, 1963

Dreyer, J.L.E. (ed.), *Tychonis Brahe Dani Opera Omnia*, 15 vols, Copenhagen: Gyldendal, 1913–29

Friis, F.R., *Tyge Brahe: En historisk Fremstilling efter trykte og utrykte Kilder*, Copenhagen: Gyldendal, 1871

Friis, F.R., *Tychonis Brahei et ad eum doctorum virorum Epistolae ab anno 1568 ad annum 1587 nunc primum collectae et editae a F.R. Friis cum effigie Tychonis Brahei et exemplo ipsius manus*, Copenhagen: G.E.C. Gad, 1876–86

Gade, John Allyne, *The Life and Times of Tycho Brahe*, Princeton, New Jersey: Princeton University Press, 1947

Gassendi, Pierre, *Tychonis Brahei, equitis Dani, astronomorum coryphaei, vita . . .*, Paris, 1654

Nielsen, Lauritz, *Tycho Brahes Bogtrykkeri: En bibliografisk-boghistorisk analyse*, Copenhagen: Valdemar Pedersen, 1946

Norlind, Wilhelm, *Tycho Brahe: Mannen och verket – Efter Gassendi översatt med kommentar*, Lund: Gleerup, 1951

Norlind, Wilhelm, *Tycho Brahe: En levnadsteckning med nya bidrag belysande hans liv och verk*, Lund: Gleerup, 1970

Petersen, Arthur, *Tyge Brahe*, Copenhagen: Udvalget for Folkeoplysningens Fremme i Kommission hos G.E.C. Gad, 1924

Ræder, Hans, Elis Strömgren and Bengt Strömgren (eds), *Tycho Brahe's Description of His Instruments and Scientific Work*, Copenhagen: Munksgaard, 1946

Shackelford, Jole, "Paracelsianism and Patronage in Early Modern Denmark", in *Patronage and Institutions: Science, Technology, and Medicine at the European Court, 1500–1750*, edited by Bruce T. Moran, Woodbridge, Suffolk, and Rochester, New York: Boydell and Brewer, 1991

Thoren, Victor E., *The Lord of Uraniborg: A Biography of Tycho Brahe*, Cambridge and New York: Cambridge University Press, 1990

Wittendorff, Alex, *Tyge Brahe*, Copenhagen: Gad, 1994

Zeeberg, Peter, *Tycho Brahes "Urania Titani": Et digt om Sophie Brahe*, Copenhagen: Museum Tusculanums, 1994

Tycho Brahe is best known for his system of the world, which effectively constitutes a compromise between the ancient geocentric and Copernicus's heliocentric systems. The Tychonic system has the Earth at the centre, with the Moon and the Sun revolving around it, but with the planets moving around the Sun. To a lesser extent, Tycho is also known for his meticulous observation of the positions of celestial bodies, which improved significantly on the precision of contemporary astronomical tables; much of Johannes Kepler's work was only possible on the basis of Tycho's superior observations. Tycho's achievement in precision was only superseded with the invention of the telescope, introduced a few years after his death. The most recent research attempts to address aspects of Tycho's life that do not fit neatly with his contribution to the progress of astronomy.

THOREN is an authoritative and detailed biography of more than 500 pages that draws together the research on Tycho. It provides a chronological account of his life with detailed footnotes, drawing both on the historical sources on Tycho and to some extent on Danish historical literature (although the latter is often misquoted). It does not eschew the technical aspects of Tycho's work, some of which is explained with very clear illustrations.

Thoren's biography continues a tradition in which Tycho's astronomical achievements are presented against the background of his life. The first in line was GASSENDI, a French Jesuit and supporter of the Tychonic world system who moved in the circles of Seigneur de Montfort, whose salons constitute something like a pre-history of the Académie des Sciences. Gassendi used Tycho's own publications and correspondence with the Landgrave of Kassel's astronomers, but he also wrote to Ole Worm in Copenhagen and obtained information that can no longer be found elsewhere. Gassendi established the basic facts of Tycho's life, which are followed by all subsequent biographers: the noble background; the observation of the new star; the travels abroad; the loss of his nose in a duel; the establishment of the great observatory of Uraniborg on the island of Hven in the Danish Sound; the great precision measurement of stellar and planetary positions performed there over decades with a large staff; Tycho's loss of royal patronage due to his haughtiness and insubordination; and his emigration to the court of Rudolph II in Prague, where he met Johannes Kepler, who subsequently inherited Tycho's observations. Gassendi knows his astronomy, but the account is by no means just technical, and the story includes some amusing asides, such as a moose getting drunk on strong beer. Gassendi's 1654 monograph is rare, but it has been translated into Swedish in NORLIND (1951), along with comments on historical sources and explanations of astronomical terminology.

In fact, Friis, Dreyer, and Norlind all collected and published historical sources on Tycho as well as writing scholarly biographies. FRIIS (1876–86) encompasses 63 Latin letters from Tycho's correspondence in the period 1568–87. DREYER (1913–29), a massive 15-volume collection of the complete works and correspondence, is almost comprehensive; however, none of the texts is translated, and for this reason, Tycho's *Astronomiae instauratae mechanica*, which on account of its description of his astronomical instrumentation provides material of general interest, has been translated into English in RÆDER, STRÖMGREN & STRÖMGREN.

FRIIS (1871) in Danish, DREYER (1890) in English, and NORLIND (1970) in Swedish, all provide biographical accounts following Gassendi's plot. All are well footnoted, especially Norlind (1970). All contain appendices: Friis (1871) has 22 manuscripts and letters in German and Danish; Dreyer (1890) includes a catalogue of Tycho's manuscript observations and a list of his pupils and assistants; Norlind (1970) attempts to reconstruct the contents of the Uraniborg library with a brief discussion of each book. All three authors are meticulous with their historical data, and all emphasise Tycho's scientific attitude as witnessed by the precision of his work and by his rejection of a strictly causal relationship between stars and humans. Tycho argued that humans were endowed with a free will and could counteract the influence of the stars.

In addition to these scholarly biographies, there are also a number of popular versions. GADE (in English) is more concerned with readability than with historical accuracy and as such succeeds admirably. PETERSEN (in Danish) cleverly mixes modern and earlier forms of Danish to recount the usual plot in readable form, and with a delightfully archaic tone.

Only very recently has Gassendi's plot, with its emphasis on Tycho as an astronomer, begun to be revised. ZEEBERG prints and translates into Danish a 605-line Ovidian epic poem written by Tycho, in the name of his sister Sophie to her beloved. Zeeberg places the poem within the noble discourse of the time and explains its many astrological, Paracelsian, and alchemical references. The book not only sheds much light on the relationship between Tycho and his sister, who was intimately engaged in Paracelsian medicaments and seems to have participated in much of the work at Uraniborg, but also reveals much regarding Tycho's intellectual activity, which has been ignored in the biographies of the Gassendi tradition, with its emphasis on Tycho as a moderniser of astronomy. SHACKELFORD has provided much of the background knowledge with which Tycho's non-astronomical work can be understood. Tycho's impact extended beyond astronomy. He set up an early printing shop where he produced his manuscripts. NIELSEN examines the influence of his printing press by tracking the books that were printed and bound there.

WITTENDORFF is the latest biography, that in quite a few points deviates from the usual story. For instance, it makes Tycho's Paracelsian leanings central to his life and work – a belief-system in which the universe is conceived as an organism within which everything is interrelated, and which therefore creates a multiplicity of significant links between micro- and macrocosm, such as Moon-silver-brain, and Jupiter-tin-liver. Tycho's chemistry and astronomy are thus not distinct activities but are intimately linked. Wittendorff also describes Tycho's haughtiness and harsh treatment of his subjects as normal behaviour for a 16th-century Danish nobleman. Wittendorff is a general historian who has published on witch-hunts in 17th-century Denmark, and he is most successful when discussing the politics surrounding Tycho's fall from grace. He describes Tycho's stated belief in a free will that can counteract astrological influences as consonant with the politics of religious consent pursued by Frederik II. This policy was also consonant with Melanchthon's conception of humanity as unprovable by reason, and Melanchthonian thought was influential at the University of Copenhagen. Wittendorff also shows how Melanchthonian thought (Philippism) was under attack throughout the Protestant lands; the anti-Philippist view gained power in Denmark with Frederik II's successor, Christian IV, who oversaw a systemic shift towards a strong and authoritative state, which engendered hostility to the notion of individual will and responsibility. This shift brought with it stricter controls, including witch-hunts, and Tycho's science had no place in this new conception of the state. Wittendorff argues that this is the main reason for Tycho's downfall, even if personal animosities and Tycho's less than diplomatic behaviour did not help. Unfortunately, Wittendorff's book does not contain footnotes.

The introduction of broader historical perspectives to Tycho scholarship has thus revised some of the received wisdom of previous biographies. It is to be expected that further attention to the culture and politics of court and state, and to the now alien aspects of Tycho's work, will further enhance our understanding of his life and career, without affecting his status as by far the best astronomical observer of the pre-telescopic age.

ARNE HESSENBRUCH

Brazil

Azevedo, Fernando de, *Brazilian Culture: An Introduction to the Study of Culture in* Brazil, translated from the Portuguese by William Rex Crawford, New York: Macmillan, 1950 (original edition, 1943)

Azevedo, Fernando de (ed.), *As ciencias no Brasil*, 2 vols, São Paulo: Melhoramentos, 1955

Benchimol, Jaime Larry and Luiz Antonio Teixeira, *Cobras, lagartos & outros bichos: uma historia comparada dos institutos Oswaldo Cruz e Butantan*, Rio de Janeiro: UFRJ, 1993

Britto, Nara, *Oswaldo Cruz: a construcão de um mito na ciencia brasileira*, Rio de Janeiro: Fiocruz, 1995

Dantes, M.A.M., "Institutos de pesquisa cientifica no Brasil", in *Historia das ciencias no Brasil*, edited by Mario Guimaraes Ferri and Shozo Motoyama, vol. 2, São Paulo: EDUSP, 1980

Domingues, M.H.B., "A ideia de progresso no processo de institucionalizacao nacional das ciencias no Brasil: a Sociedade Auxiliadora da Industria Nacional", *Asclepio*, 48/2 (1996): 149–62

Ferri, Mario Guimaraes and Shozo Motoyama (eds), *Historia das ciencias no Brasil*, 3 vols, São Paulo: EDUSP, 1979–81

Figueirõa, S.F. de M., "Charles Frederic Hartt and the 'Geological Commission of Brazil' (1875–1877)", *Earth Sciences History*, 13/2 (1994): 168–73

Figueirõa, S.F. de M., *As ciencias geologicas no Brasil: uma historia social e institucional (1875–1934)*, São Paulo: Hucitec, 1997

Fonseca, M.R.G.F. da, "Ciencia e identidade na America Espanhola (1780–1830)", in *Historia da ciencia: o mapa do conhecimento*, edited by Ana Maria Alfonso-Goldfarb and Carlos A. Maia, São Paulo: EDUSP, 1995, 819–36

Lopes, M.M., "Brazilian Museums of Natural History and International Exchanges in the Transition to the 20th Century", in *Science and Empires: Historical Studies about Scientific Development and European Expansion*, edited by Patrick Petitjean, Catherine Jami, and Anne Marie Moulin, Dordrecht and Boston: Kluwer, 1992, 193–200

Maio, Marcos Chor and Ricardo Ventura Santos (eds), *Raca, ciencia e sociedade*, Rio de Janeiro: Fiocruz/Centro Cultural Banco do Brasil, 1996

Schwartzman, Simon with Antonio Paim *et al.*, *Formacão da comunidade cientifica no Brasil*, São Paulo: Nacional, 1979

Stepan, Nancy, *Beginnings of Brazilian Science: Oswaldo Cruz, Medical Research and Policy, 1890–1920*, New York: Science History Publications, 1976

In the early 1980s, there were only a few works on the history of science in Brazil, and they all focused on the foundation of landmark institutions: the University of São Paulo (1934) and a number of microbiology research institutes, the Bacteriologico (1892), the Manguinhos (1899), the Butantan (1901), and the Pasteur (1903). These studies generally emphasized the bookish, non-experimental, and backward character of earlier scientific activity. These early works were mainly produced by non-historians with a positivist bias and a Eurocentric historiographical attitude: if science in Brazil did not resemble science in Europe, then it was inferior and unimportant. This framework led to a narrow view of the past that ignored the concrete scientific practices in Brazil, which after all did have a material existence in libraries, archives, and museums.

The most complete and theoretically consistent formulation of this framework – although inspired by a different philosophical basis – is found in the seminal work of Fernando de Azevedo (1894–1974), a sociologist and scholar of wide interests. His first book, AZEVEDO (1943), included one long chapter on Brazilian scientific culture. Azevedo's main contribution was his innovative attempt to explain the scientific development in Brazil in terms of the country's economy, political life, educational conditions, and religious beliefs. His central thesis was that the backwardness of science in Brazil was the result of the obscurantist policy, favourable to economic exploitation, imposed by the civil and religious (Catholic) authorities in Portugal. The sciences developed only with industrialization and urbanization. This idea was further developed in the 2-volume work edited by AZEVEDO (1955), which includes texts by several distinguished Brazilian scientists.

Up to the 1970s, studies on the history of science in Brazil retained the same general framework, but a number are still useful. STEPAN traces the roots of scientific development in Brazil. She focuses on the history of the Bacteriologico and Manguinhos institutes, and adopts the diffusion model proposed by George Basalla in 1967. This model is now considered outdated because it denied the existence of science in the so-called "pre-scientific" phase and stressed the contribution of foreign scientists during the "colonial" phase. Its Eurocentricity is anchored in "modernization theory".

SCHWARTZMAN's on the formation of the Brazilian scientific community focuses on the presence of foreign scientists (especially travellers) in the country during the 19th century. It also points out the weakness of the institutional base, stating that scientific activity in Brazil was performed only by Europeans attracted by the conditions offered by the Brazilian emperor. Schwartzman argues that prior to the first decades of the 20th century science in Brazil was strictly applied science, but he perceives a more substantial scientific tradition than his predecessors had acknowledged.

The 3-volume work edited by FERRI & MOTOYAMA can be regarded as updating Azevedo (1955). It has a similar theoretical framework, organized by discipline. The biggest difference is to be found in its inclusion of chapters on more recent disciplines such as space science, and on non-disciplinary themes such as the history of scientific institutions. The chapter on the history of scientific institutions (written by Maria Amelia DANTES) deserves mention, because it represents a turning point in the historiography of science in Brazil. Compared to most earlier works, which tended to be rather anecdotal and hagiographic, it is a professional treatment of history, using both primary and secondary sources, and places the research in its historical context. In the early 1980s, this paper stimulated a new and fertile line of research at the time when there was a renewed interest in the history of science and technology in Latin America generally.

Since then, it has been possible to write the history of actual scientific practices as they developed into local scientific institutions, within a local, national, and international context. Instead of looking for important contributions to international science, historians of Brazilian science now prefer to write of everyday scientific life, stressing its advancements, contradictions, continuities, ruptures, and historical limits, without pursuing a nationalistic agenda.

BENCHIMOL & TEIXEIRA is a comparative history of two research institutions that have been important in the field of microbiology since their foundation at the beginning of the 20th century: the Butantan and Manguinhos institutes. This pioneering comparative history demonstrates that both organizations followed similar institutional and paradigmatic trajectories; their dissimilarities lay in their different strategies, the political and scientific interests of their staffs, the personal disputes that arose in each organization, and, finally, in their different contacts in the market for vaccines.

BRITTO interprets several biographies of the important Brazilian scientist Oswaldo Cruz (founder of the Manguinhos Institute) and shows how his life has been re-told, reinvented, and manipulated by different groups fighting over his legacy. The construction of Cruz's image served a number of purposes, from the promotion of a national campaign for sanitation to much more theoretical agendas.

The article by DOMINGUES demonstrates how ideas of progress and civilization (conceived as essential and achievable national aims) defined and developed the scientific enterprise of the Sociedade Auxiliadora da Industria Nacional (Society for the Improvement of National Industry), founded in 1827, Brazil's first year of independence.

The works by Figueirõa investigate the institutionalization of the geological sciences in Brazil from the end of the 18th century to the first decades of the 20th. FIGUEIRÕA (1994) describes the impact of the Geological Commission of Brazil in the 1870s. FIGUEIRÕA (1997) shows that, contrary to expectations, agricultural interests were much more important than those related to mining in determining the growth and specialization of geological institutions.

FONSECA focuses on a comparison between the development of Brazil and Mexico in the late 18th and early 19th centuries. She shows that the research agenda of the time was strongly related to natural history and to using the natural products of the New World. Ultimately the agenda was embedded in questions of national identity and what constituted a "civilized", autonomous nation in Latin America.

LOPES examines the institutional development of natural history, especially in Brazilian museums, demonstrating how these institutions were deeply transformed in the 19th century as a result of changes both in the boundaries between scientific disciplines and in models for the popularization of science.

The book by MAIO & SANTOS is a stimulating collection of papers discussing the strong, complex interrelation between science and race in the shaping of modern notions of hygiene in Brazilian society around 1900.

SILVIA F. DE M. FIGUEIRÕA

British Association for the Advancement of Science

Armytage, W.H.G., *Sir Richard Gregory: His Life and Work*, London: Macmillan and New York: St Martin's Press, 1957

Basalla, George, William Coleman and Robert H. Kargon (eds), *Victorian Science: A Self-Portrait from the Presidential Addresses of the British Association for the Advancement of Science*, New York: Doubleday, 1970

Cannon, Susan Faye, *Science in Culture: The Early Victorian Period*, New York: Science History Publications, and Kent: Dawson, 1978

Collins, Peter, "The Origins of the British Association's Education Section", *British Journal of Educational Studies*, 27 (1979): 232–44

Howarth, O.J.R., *The British Association for the Advancement of Science: A Retrospect, 1831–1921*, London: The Association, 1922; 2nd edition, 1931

Lodge, Oliver, *Advancing Science; being Personal Reminiscences of the British Association in the Nineteenth Century*, London: Benn, 1931

McGucken, William, "The Social Relations of Science: The British Association for the Advancement of Science, 1931–1946", *Proceedings of the American Philosophical Society*, 123 (1979): 236–64

MacLeod, Roy and Peter Collins (eds), *The Parliament of Science: The British Association for the Advancement of Science, 1831–1981*, Northwood, Middlesex: Science Reviews, 1981

Morrell, Jack and Arnold Thackray (eds), *Gentlemen of Science: Early Years of the British Association for the Advancement of Science*, Oxford: Clarendon Press, and New York: Oxford University Press, 1981

Morrell, Jack and Arnold Thackray (eds), *Gentleman of Science: Early Correspondence of the British Association for the Advancement of Science*, London: Royal Historical Society, 1984

Historical information on the British Association for the Advancement of Science is patchy, though there is a considerable literature dealing with its foundation at York in 1831. The various explanations advanced for the founding of the British Association include: the desire to increase the professionalization of science; a reaction provoked by John Herschel's failure to be elected President of the Royal Society in 1830; a reaction against Charles Babbage's controversial text *Reflections on the Decline of Science in England and on Some of Its Causes* (1830); the need of the provinces to assert some kind of independent intellectual existence in response to London centralization; and, the need to promote the Humboldtian sciences. Most of the literature stemming from these positions is discussed and evaluated by CANNON and Roy MacLeod in MacLEOD & COLLINS.

The most detailed analysis of the founding of the British Association and its early years until 1844 is MORRELL & THACKRAY (1981), while MORRELL & THACKRAY (1984) includes many of the letters on which they had based their analysis. They examine the origins of the British Association, how it quickly evolved, how its structure was devised in terms of disciplinary sections, how it was decided which town would host the annual meetings, how the Presidents were chosen, what actually happened at annual meetings, and so on. They describe the formation of an institution which, in many ways, is recognisably the one that exists today.

After 1844, we know much less about the British Association. For instance, apart from what is in HOWARTH, we know very little about the superintendence by the British Association of the Kew Observatory between 1841 and 1871. But this was not the only place where the British Association supported research. Though we know comparatively little about it in the post-1844 period, the provision of funds to individual researchers was a key feature of the activities of the British Association almost from its inception until the 1940s, when its funding role diminished.

The British Association has met annually since 1831 apart from 1917, 1918 and the years 1940–46. It has generally met in some regional centre of Britain apart from the 1931 meeting in London, the 1957 meeting in Dublin and the years 1884, 1897, 1905, 1909, 1914, 1924, and 1929 when it met in either Canada, South Africa, or Australia. (The imperial role of the British Association is discussed by Michael Warboys in MacLeod & Collins.) At its annual meetings the President, always distinguished and usually a scientist, provides an address. Extracts from many of the addresses delivered in the 19th century are collected in BASALLA, COLEMAN & KARGON. Although addresses were normally safe pronouncements from the establishment, John Tyndall's address to the 1874 meeting in Belfast, in which he argued that theology had no role to play in science, provoked serious controversy.

The Belfast address highlights one of the weaknesses of much of the literature on the British Association. There is a tendency to concentrate on a particular, crucial event that occurred at a meeting, and there are several examples of these: Richard Owen coining the term dinosaur (Plymouth, 1842); Samuel Wilberforce asking after Thomas Huxley's grandparentage (Oxford, 1860); the Australian meeting being interrupted by the outbreak of war in 1914 when all the delegates were still at sea; the teach-in on secrecy and defence science at the 1970 meeting at Durham; and the debate on the sociology of science (Loughborough, 1994). Many of these events, but not all, have a literature devoted to them, but most tend to ignore (or are unaware of) the institutional contexts that gave rise to them; for instance, the Zoology and Botany section played a key role in arranging the meeting, the outcome of which was the confrontation between Huxley and Wilberforce. With the exception of the early period and COLLINS's study of the Education Section, very little is known about the sections and how they were organized and run. This is all the more unfortunate since the organization of the vast bulk of the programme of any annual meeting fell, and still falls, to the sections, with little central control or direction. However, since most active members of the British Association belonged to the General Committee, some degree of collegiality was ensured. Again, there is little published on the General Committee and here, as elsewhere, one has to read accounts by or about participants at annual meetings (such as LODGE) to gain some appreciation of how the British Association operated.

One area of its history where the British Association is well served is the period between 1918 and 1946, during which time the centenary of the British Association was commemorated with the re-publication of HOWARTH. This book, written by its Secretary, was in fact the first full-length history of the British Association, and as such is still a useful source on topics that have not been discussed subsequently. Howarth's vision of the development of the British Association was very much influenced by the concerns of the inter-war period: it was during this time that the assumption that science was always for the moral good came to be challenged, as the use of scientific products during World War I, and the supposed role of science-based technologies in bringing about mass unemployment, gave rise to unease about the relationship between science and society. In the 1930s, the British Association responded strongly to these concerns. Richard Gregory, editor of *Nature*, was a key figure in getting the British Association to adopt a realistic (instead of utopian) approach to the relationship between science and society. How this was achieved, particularly with the formation of the "Division for the Social and International Relations of Science" in 1938, is related in McGUCKEN, in Collins's paper in MacLeod & Collins, and in Gregory's biography by ARMYTAGE. With the coming of war in 1939, the British Association, with Gregory as its President, ceased annual meetings until 1947 (Dundee), and was kept going by Gregory and by the Division, who together organized a few war-time conferences discussed in McGucken. Nothing has yet been written on how the British Association has developed in the ensuing years.

FRANK A.J.L. JAMES

Buckland, William   1784–1856

British geologist and clergyman

Davies, Gordon L., *The Earth in Decay: A History of British Geomorphology, 1578–1878*, London: Macdonald and New York: American Elsevier, 1969

Edmonds, J.M., "*Vindiciae Geologicae*, published 1820: The Inaugural Lecture of William Buckland", *Archives of Natural History*, 18 (1991): 255–68

Gillispie, Charles Coulston, *Genesis and Geology: A Study in the Relations of Scientific Thought, Natural Theology, and Social Opinion in Great Britain, 1790–1850*, Cambridge, Massachusetts: Harvard University Press, 1951

Gordon, Elizabeth O., *The Life and Correspondence of William Buckland*, London: John Murray, 1894

Hooykaas, Reijer, *Natural Law and Divine Miracle: A Historical-Critical Study of the Principle of Uniformity in Geology, Biology, and Theology*, Leiden: E.J. Brill, 1959

Rudwick, Martin J.S., *Scenes from Deep Time: Early Pictorial Representations of the Prehistoric World*, Chicago: University of Chicago Press, 1992

Rupke, Nicolaas A., *The Great Chain of History: William Buckland and the English School of Geology, 1814–1849*, Oxford: Clarendon Press, and New York: Oxford University Press, 1985

William Buckland's eclectic research interests touched on many of the major geological issues of the early 19th century. He contributed to debates on the role of glaciers in shaping the landscape and the proper relationship between geology and religion. His palaeontological work helped to establish the viability of using rocks and fossils to reconstruct the ancient environments of which they were once a part. Most of the available literature on Buckland is narrowly focused, treating one aspect or another of his work in isolation.

GORDON remains, unfortunately, the only comprehensive biography. Written by Buckland's daughter, it is a characteristic Victorian life-and-letters volume: hagiographic in tone and filled with carefully-chosen anecdotes. Buckland emerges from its pages as a paragon of Victorian virtue – a stern but loving father, exemplary Christian, inspiring teacher, dedicated public servant. His delight in shocking middle-class audiences with mildly off-color remarks is quietly passed over. More significantly, Gordon's treatment of her father's scientific work is relatively shallow; she gives considerable attention to the nuts and bolts of his career – society memberships, professional meetings, and the like – but treats his ideas largely by quoting extensively from his own writings. The shallowness is, to some extent, a product of the fact that life-and-letters volumes were not meant to be scientific treatises. However, Gordon was further hampered by the passage of 40 years, in which virtually all of Buckland's colleagues had died. The work therefore lacks the sense of immediacy and first-hand knowledge that the best life-and-letters biographies can provide.

The first modern historical studies of Buckland focused on his ideas about geology and religion, particularly his belief in the reality and geological significance of Noah's flood. Each of Buckland's three major works had a strong religious dimension, and GILLISPIE discusses this aspect of his work in detail.

Gillispie's principal concern is to locate Buckland within the cultural context of early 19th-century Britain – a society desperately concerned about the corrosive effects of science on religion. He regards Buckland's work as a product of its time, rejecting claims that Buckland bent his geology to match his theology, and arguing that Buckland's science and religion were both shaped by a firm conviction that a clear understanding of nature would not conflict with the revealed word of God.

Buckland acted not only within the British geological community, but also within a larger, international community of scientists. HOOYKAAS, in a study of the philosophical tensions within that larger community, uses Buckland's work to exemplify a particular, "progressionist" view of Earth history. He focuses on the contrast between Buckland's essentially deistic view of Earth history, and his insistence that new species were periodically introduced by divine intervention. Hooykaas's analysis concludes with a useful discussion of the complex relationship between progressionists such as Buckland, transmutationists such as Jean Baptiste Lamarck, and uniformitarians such as Charles Lyell.

DAVIES discusses Buckland's substantial contributions to geomorphology – the study of the Earth's surface and the processes that shape it. He argues that Buckland's early works reflect a deep concern with reconciling Genesis with geology, while later writings show Buckland distancing himself from Biblical sources and down-playing the geological significance of Noah's flood. Davies emphasizes Buckland's role in using Louis Agassiz's ideas about glacial erosion to explain geological formations in Britain. Buckland's passionate advocacy of the glacial theory, Davies argues, ultimately transformed both his own work and that of his colleagues.

RUDWICK assesses Buckland's similarly pioneering role in the study and reconstruction of ancient environments. He cites Buckland's investigation of bone-filled Kirkdale Cavern in the early 1820s as a major influence on subsequent efforts to reconstruct, and visually depict, the pre-human past. Buckland's key innovation, Rudwick argues, was his belief that an accurate model of a long-vanished environment could be assembled from fragmentary evidence such as fossil bones, preserved animal tracks, and petrified feces. Buckland's work thus played a role in transforming geology from a classificatory into an interpretative, historical science.

Rudwick, Davies, Hooykaas, and Gillispie all treat specific aspects of Buckland's work within the context of closely related intellectual developments. RUPKE, on the other hand, treats Buckland's geological and palaeontological work as a coherent whole, and is concerned with placing Buckland's work within its social, as well as intellectual, context. Rupke presents Buckland as a leading member of the "English School of Geology" – a small but influential group of geologist-clerics who taught at Oxford and Cambridge in the first half of the 19th century. Rupke sees Buckland's interest in the reconstruction of past environments as characteristic of the English School, and indicative of its historically-oriented approach to geology. He contrasts Buckland's work with that of the rival Scottish School, centered in Edinburgh and concerned primarily with the causes of geologic change. Rupke's analysis of the English School's views on geology and religion provides an interesting counterpoint to the earlier work of Gillispie and Hooykaas. The strong religious overtones in Buckland's early work owes much, Rupke argues, to the English School's need first to justify and then to preserve a place for geology within the intensely clerical culture of Oxford and Cambridge. Based on extensive research in unpublished sources, Rupke is the most comprehensive treatment available of Buckland's scientific career.

Buckland's 1819 inaugural lecture as Reader of Geology at Oxford was his key attempt to establish a place for geology at the university. EDMONDS examines the sources and content of the lecture in detail, comparing the published version, *Vindiciae Geologicae* (1820), with its source material – particularly the work of Buckland's Cambridge-based colleague, William Daniel Conybeare. Conybeare was a leading member of Rupke's "English School", and Edmonds thus provides an interesting supplement to Rupke's larger study, illuminating one significant aspect of the personal and professional relationships within the group.

A. BOWDOIN VAN RIPER

See also Geology

Buffon, Georges-Louis Leclerc, Comte de 1707–1788

French naturalist

Bachelard, Gaston, *La Formation de l'esprit scientifique*, Paris: Vrin, 1938

Buffon 88: Actes du Colloque internationale pour le bicentenaire de la mort de Buffon, Paris: Vrin, 1992

Fellows, Otis E. and Stephen F. Milliken, *Buffon*, New York: Twayne, 1972

Gerbi, Antonello, *The Dispute of the New World: The History of a Polemic, 1750–1900*, translated from the Italian by Jeremy Moyle, Pittsburgh: University of Pittsburgh Press, 1973 (original edition, 1955)

Hanks, Lesley, *Buffon avant l'histoire naturelle*, Paris: Presses Universitaires de France, 1966

Heim, Roger (ed.), *Buffon*, Paris: Muséum Nationale D'Histoire Naturelle, 1952

Hémon, Félix, *Eloge de Buffon*, Paris, 1878

Lovejoy, A.O., "Buffon and the Problem of Species", *Popular Science Monthly*, 79 (July–December 1911): 464–73, 554–67

Roger, Jacques, Introduction, to *Les Epoques de la nature*, Mémoires du Muséum National D'Histoire Naturelle, Sciences de la terre, vol. 10, Paris: Editions du Muséum, 1962

Roger, Jacques, *The Life Sciences in Eighteenth-Century French Thought*, edited by Keith R. Benson, translated from the French by Robert Ellrich, Stanford: Stanford University Press, 1997 (original edition, 1963)

Roger, Jacques, *Buffon: A Life in Natural History*, edited by L. Pierce Williams, translated from the French by Sarah Lucille Bonnefoi, Ithaca, New York: Cornell University Press, 1997 (original edition, 1989)

Wilkie, J.S., "The Idea of Evolution in the Writings of Buffon", *Annals of Science*, 12/1 (March 1956): 48–63; 12/3 (September 1957): 212–27, 255–66

George-Louis Leclerc, Comte de Buffon was one of the most prolific scientists of the 18th century, making original and significant contributions to topics ranging from the tensile strength of wood to probability theory. His most substantial contribution, however, and the one that has generated by far the most historical scholarship, was in natural history. Beginning with his 22-volume, *Histoire naturelle générale et particulière*, Buffon was the central figure in the study of plants, animals and geographical features and their global distribution during most of his lifetime. His death in 1788 pre-dated the emergence of biology as a special science of the living by just over a decade, but when the prehistory of that crucial development is considered, Buffon's name is always central to the discussion.

Buffon's fortunes among commentators and historians have risen and fallen periodically since his death, partly in response to changing scientific and historical approaches. A dearth of historical treatments of Buffon during most of the 19th century can be attributed to the unpopularity of his flamboyant style of literary–philosophical reflection on nature. The most complete 19th-century treatment by HÉMON, himself a literary critic, emphasized this aspect of Buffon's work. BACHELARD represents the culmination of this trend, singling out Buffon as an example of the "pre-scientific mind", and using him to demonstrate the pitfalls that the careless contemplation of nature could encounter in the absence of rigorous scientific method. Much of what has been written since then has aimed to overturn that image.

Since the publication of Darwin's *Origin of Species* (1859), debate has raged as to the historical precedents and origins of his concept of species, and Buffon has been one of the most controversial figures in this history. Indeed, the species concept has often been taken to be one of the most central and defining elements of Buffon's thought. LOVEJOY outlines the 19th-century contributions to this debate, lays out Buffon's contribution to the idea of evolution, and defines the terms in which the problem has been argued ever since.

HEIM's collection of essays marks the dawn of the modern appreciation of Buffon. It seeks, for the first time, to put Buffon's scientific thought in the context of his life and times, focusing on his biography, the requirements of his post as director of the King's Gardens and of his business affairs, and his religious and philosophical predilections. Heim opened the floodgates for a thorough reconsideration of Buffon's life and his scientific legacy.

In 1956 to 1957, in the definitive treatment of Buffon's ideas on evolution, WILKIE revisited the issues raised earlier by Lovejoy. ROGER (1962), an introduction to one of Buffon's later and previously lesser-known works, offers a detailed analysis of Buffon's scientific thought, especially his cosmology and philosophy of nature, and their origins, with special attention to Buffon's unique conception of natural change over time. ROGER (1997) remains the definitive treatment of the scientific and philosophical debates in the life sciences, especially in France, of Buffon's time. In a long chapter devoted to Buffon, he analyses Buffon's concept of species and biological change, and his theory of generation.

Inspired by this new recognition of the significance of Buffon in the history of the life sciences, HANKS provides the first book-length reconsideration of a heretofore little-known part of Buffon's biography, his early life and publications, including his mathematical and statistical treatises. FELLOWS & MILLIKEN attempt to restore to Buffon some of the status as a thinker and writer he enjoyed during his lifetime by devoting a full-length English-language monograph to his life and works. Without analysing the genesis and meaning of Buffon's scientific ideas in depth, this accessible work provides an excellent overview, and remains the best introduction to Buffon in English.

Buffon 88 unites the work of nearly all the students of Buffon's life and thought who were trained after the post-World War II renewal of interest in Buffon. These scholars deepen our understanding of the many connections between his private life and his scientific work, his place in Enlightenment philosophy, his general philosophy of science, his approach to and philosophy of nature, his views on organic matter, and give the first deep consideration of his writings on humans and their relation to animals and the natural world, a topic pursued further in the first chapter of GERBI. The volume also contains a series of essays on the history of perceptions and evaluations of Buffon's work, and a thorough bibliography of works by and on Buffon published between 1954 and 1991.

ROGER's *Buffon: A Life in Natural History* is the first substantially researched, full-length biography of Buffon, and will remain the definitive source on Buffon's life for decades to come. Roger provides an integrated account of the origin, genesis, and context of the tremendous diversity of subjects that commanded Buffon's attention. Roger also provides an integrated framework for understanding these projects, showing how, taken together, they reveal a way of interpreting nature that was unique to Buffon, but had far-reaching consequences for the methods and direction of the life sciences. Roger has established that, while Buffon's developmental view of the living world may not have anticipated evolution, it was a crucial element in the growth of a unique science of the living.

JORDAN KELLMAN

See also Enlightenment; Evolution

C

Calculating Devices

Baxandall, David (ed.), *Calculating Machines and Instruments*, London: Science Museum, 1926; revised and expanded by Jane Pugh, 1975

Bryden, D.J., *Napier's Bones: A History and Instruction Manual*, London: Harriet Wynter, 1992

Cajori, Florian, *A History of the Logarithmic Slide Rule and Allied Instruments*, London and New York: Engineering News, 1909

D'Ocagne, Maurice, *Le Calcul simplifié: Graphical and Mechanical Methods for Simplifying Calculation*, translated from the French by J. Howlett and Michael R. Williams, Cambridge, Massachusetts: MIT Press, 1986 (original edition, 1928)

Horsburgh, E.M. (ed.), *Handbook of the Exhibition of Napier Relics and of Books, Instruments, and Devices for Facilitating Calculation*, Edinburgh: Royal Society of Edinburgh, 1914; as *Handbook of the Napier Tercentenary Celebration*, with a new introduction by Michael R. Williams, Los Angeles: Tomash, 1982

Kehrbaum, Annegret and Bernhard Korte, *Calculi: Bilder des Rechnens einst und heute (Images of Computing in Olden and Modern Times)*, Bonn: Nordrhein-Westfalischen Akademie der Wissenschaften, 1995

Marguin, Jean, *Histoire des machines et instruments à calculer: trois siècles de mécanique pensante, 1642–1942*, Paris: Hermann, 1994

Martin, Ernst, *The Calculating Machines (Die Rechenmaschinen): Their History and Development*, edited and translated from the German by Peggy Aldrich Kidwell and Michael R. Williams, Cambridge, Massachusetts: MIT Press, 1992

Turner, Anthony John, *Early Scientific Instruments: Europe, 1400–1800*, London: Sotheby, and New York: Philip Wilson, 1987

Williams, Michael R., *A History of Computing Technology*, Englewood Cliffs, New Jersey: Prentice-Hall, 1985; revised edition, Los Alamitos, California: IEEE Computer Society Press, 1997

The history of calculating devices reaches well beyond the boundaries of the history of science; business and accounting have made routine use of reckoning aids, and many special-purpose tools have been devised to reduce the burden of calculation within engineering disciplines. However, much of the modern impetus towards historical study in this area stems from efforts to construct a chronology for the history of computing. In the most schematic of lineages, the story begins in the 17th century with the adding and calculating machines of Blaise Pascal and Gottfried Wilhelm Leibniz, jumps to the Difference and Analytical Engines of Charles Babbage in the 19th century, and then passes on to the development of digital computers during and after World War II.

Thus the history of computing has given prominence to certain aspects of calculation, and rarely provides a balanced account; machines – especially digital machines – are highlighted, while the significance of alternative technologies is typically diminished. Yet the very term "calculation" suggests both the antiquity of the activity and the possible simplicity of its objects: "calculi" is the Latin for pebbles or stones, which were used for early arithmetical record-keeping and manipulation.

Among sources from the history of computing, WILLIAMS comes closest to providing a textbook account of calculation. Although directed towards 20th-century computing developments, leading to the mainframe digital computers of the 1960s, half of his presentation deals with the earlier history of calculation. He opens with ancient number systems and devices such as the abacus, and subsequently surveys mathematical instruments, calculating machines, and analogue devices. The material therefore includes 17th-century sectors, logarithmic slide rules, and Napier's bones, as well as contemporary adding and calculating machines, while the section on the 19th century offers planimeters, integrators, and tide predictors in addition to the more familiar machines of Babbage.

A richer visual sense of the development of calculating devices is offered by MARGUIN. Another general survey, this provides not only lavish illustrations but also many notes on both the structure and operation of calculating devices. By deliberately avoiding the era of the digital computer, Marguin not only gives more detail on, for example, the elaborate and often decorative machines of the 18th century, but also devotes attention to topics such as the mass-produced office calculating machines of the early 20th century. KEHRBAUM & KORTE's book is in part a gallery of microscopic images of modern computer chips, but it also offers a generally reliable history of calculating machines, in both German and English. Although brief, the narrative includes material not readily accessible elsewhere, and is supplemented by photographs of a wide range of examples.

Much of the surviving record of calculating devices is now preserved in museums, and most large science museums have sought to acquire comprehensive collections of calculating arte-facts. Rather than the developmental exposition of synthetic surveys, their catalogues document specific instruments and machines, and often find space for objects that would not fit neatly into a more connected narrative. BAXANDALL is a standard point of reference for the collection of the Science Museum, London.

There are few monographic treatments available on indi-vidual instruments and machines. CAJORI made a first attempt at unravelling the complex early history of the slide rule, but he later abandoned a number of his claims. Despite such problems, and the difficulty of fully recording the wealth of 18th- and 19th-century instruments, in the absence of more accurate and comprehensive accounts his text has been republished several times. BRYDEN offers a focused account of a popular calculating aid first introduced in the 17th century, "Napier's bones". Published in conjunction with the creation of a facsimile set of these calculating rods, Bryden not only traces the history of the various forms of the device, but also details how they were used.

A broader overview, covering the heyday of the mathemat-ical instrument maker, and a useful bibliography are provided by TURNER. The instruments discussed include medieval and Renaissance astrolabes and quadrants, which could be used to solve astronomical problems without recourse to spherical trigonometry, and also the various early modern sectors and slide rules – which spared draughtsmen, engineers, and other technical practitioners geometrical and logarithmic calculations with pen and paper.

In the absence of modern historical accounts of 19th- and 20th-century developments in calculating instruments and machines, contemporary reviews have taken on historical significance and often provide the only avenue for further research. Some of the most valuable original sources have recently been republished by the Charles Babbage Institute. HORSBURGH includes a historical section commemorat-ing John Napier, but also presents a range of calculating machines from the beginning of the 20th century, together with "mathematical laboratory instruments" such as the integrating devices used by naval architects. D'OCAGNE, one of the prime proponents of graphical problem-solving through nomography, provides a systematic survey of calcu-lation. MARTIN is a detailed collection of notes on calculat-ing machines; although offering a retrospective on their historical development, its value lies in the author's firsthand descriptions of machines from the first quarter of the 20th century.

Accessible accounts of the more recent history of calculating devices are not yet available. Historians of computing rarely dwell on the plethora of mechanical, electromechanical, and electronic calculating machines produced since the 1940s, preferring to focus on major trends in mainframes or the devel-opment of the personal computer. The rapid proliferation of hand-held electronic calculators in the early 1970s remains largely in the domain of popular memory, but early models have already become collectors' items, extending the existing market in antique office equipment. Indeed, there is now not only a specialist society for collectors of electronic calculators,

but also a group (the Oughtred Society) devoted to the collec-tion and study of slide rules.

STEPHEN JOHNSTON

Canada

Bogaard, Paul A. (ed.), *Profiles of Science and Society in the Maritimes prior to 1914*, Sackville, New Brunswick: Acadiensis Press/Mount Allison University, 1990

Chartrand, Luc, Raymond Duchesne and Yves Gingras, *Histoire des sciences au Québec*, Montreal: Boréal, 1987

Dufour, Paul and John de la Mothe (eds), *Science and Technology in Canada*, London: Longman, 1993

Eggleston, Wilfred, *National Research in Canada: The NRC 1916–1966*, Toronto: Clarke Irwin, 1978

Gingras, Yves, *Physics and the Rise of Scientific Research in Canada*, Montreal and Kingston: McGill-Queen's University Press, 1991; as *Les Origines de la recherche scientifique au Canada*, Montréal: Boréal, 1991

Hodgson, J.H., *The Heavens Above and the Earth Beneath: A History of the Dominion Observatories to 1946*, Toronto: Geological Survey of Canada, 1989

Jarrell, Richard A., *The Cold Light of Dawn: A History of Canadian Astronomy*, Toronto: University of Toronto Press, 1988

King, M. Christine, *E.W.R. Steacie and Science in Canada*, Toronto: University of Toronto Press, 1989

Richardson, R. Alan and Bertrum H. MacDonald, *Science and Technology in Canadian History: A Bibliography of Primary Sources to 1914*, Thornhill, Ontario: HSTC, 1987

Thomas, Morley, *The Beginnings of Canadian Meteorology*, Toronto: ECW Press, 1991

Thomson, Don W., *Men and Meridians: The History of Surveying and Mapping in Canada*, 3 vols, Ottawa: Queen's Printer for the Department of Mines and Technical Surveys, 1966

Wallace, W. Stewart (ed.), *The Royal Canadian Institute Centennial Volume, 1849–1949*, Toronto: Royal Canadian Institute, 1949

Zeller, Suzanne, *Inventing Canada: Early Victorian Science and the Idea of a Transcontinental Nation*, Toronto: University of Toronto Press, 1987

A study of scientific research in Canada might begin with a consideration of recent patterns. DUFOUR & DE LA MOTHE's collection of essays provides a summary of govern-ment and university activities since the 1960s. Of the indus-trialized countries, Canada has been among those spending the least on scientific research – a result of her economic ties with Britain and the United States, where companies frequently insist that research be carried out by their parent firms. Research is thus largely driven by government and carried out in its labo-ratories and, through government granting agencies, at univer-sities and "centres of excellence". Science is increasingly mission-oriented, and governments have defined research direc-tions that are deemed to be in the "national interest". Dufour touches on research related to energy, communications – including space-related applications – and resources.

The first stop for researchers of science in Canada before World War I is the invaluable work of RICHARDSON & MacDONALD. It provides bibliographic references for thousands of papers and works dealing with scientific topics to 1914; divided into author, title and subject catalogues, it has a monograph title index, and the subject catalogue is further divided into general, science, and technology categories.

ZELLER introduces the topics of geology, magnetism, meteorology, and botany in the 19th century in a well-rounded discussion, while providing an interesting analysis of how and why organized science emerged in a colonial environment. It is not surprising that the history of science in Canada is related to its huge geographic size and its hidden resources. The first scientific programme originating in Canada was initiated by the formation of the Geological Survey in 1842. Zeller examines the impetus and early history of the Geological Society of Canada (GSC) and of its founder, William Logan, and shows how, during the mid-19th century, immigrants became interested in botany as a cultural pastime.

The GSC became the model for other government agencies, including the Meteorological Service (MSC), the Survey and Mapping Branch, the Topographical Survey, and the Dominion Observatories. THOMSON provides a history of survey and mapping in Canada, and gives an account of "scientific" activities from the 16th and 17th centuries onwards. Significant contributions to the techniques of large scale photographic surveying, aerial surveying, topography, and airborne microwave surveying are chronicled. This series provides an extremely detailed history of a scientific discipline, but Thomson provides little analysis of the factors that shaped that history.

THOMAS chronicles the establishment of meteorological studies in Canada from the first formal research programme undertaken in 1839–40 (Sabine's international chain of magnetic and meteorological observatories) to the establishment of the MSC some 30 years later. He details the efforts made to establish a government meteorological service, and draws parallels, and discusses the working relationships, with American and European agencies. Additional problems were encountered in securing the participation of the various pre-confederation colonial governments. Thomas provides some history of meteorological theories, but this is largely a story of the perseverance of individuals, in particular George Kingston, founder of the MSC.

Both Hodgson and Jarrell provide a history of astronomy. HODGSON, an astronomer, provides a thoroughly researched work covering scientific activities, the construction of telescopes, and administrative issues of the Dominion Observatories in Ottawa and Victoria. He includes information on the time service, and the relationship of seismic groups to the astronomers. JARRELL covers a much broader time period, from the astronomical endeavours of 17th-century Jesuits to the university astronomy programmes of the 1980s. Unfortunately, he fails to provide a satisfactory analysis of the factors that shaped Canadian astronomical research, such as the controversy in the 1960s over the Mt Kobau Observatory, which divided professional astronomers – its aftermath has since defined all major astronomical projects. The research experience of university astronomy departments is typical, and is paralleled in other disciplines in their relationship to government and its funding agencies.

An important work is EGGLESTON's history, from 1916 to 1966, of the National Research Council of Canada, the foremost contributor to the progress of science in the country. Unfortunately, only sparse attention is paid to the details of scientific programmes. The periods of greatest productivity and highest reputation in the NRC's history have been under individuals such as H.M. Tory, A.G.L. McNaughton, and E.W.R. Steacie, who provided a rich environment for basic research. Tory was influential during a time of expansion in the 1920s and 1930s, which prepared the NRC for the important role it was to play during World War II – under the direction of General McNaughton, it was responsible for the construction of the first nuclear reactor outside the US. The NRC's growing stature continued under Steacie in the early 1960s, and Steacie's biographer, KING, also explains how he was able to establish an atmosphere that produced, directly or indirectly, three Nobel prize winners. Histories of the astrophysics, biological sciences, mechanical engineering, and physics branches of the NRC have been published.

Professional associations in Canada have had a limited impact on the direction of scientific research. WALLACE assesses the role of the Royal Canadian Institute during its first 100 years, but, with the increasing participation of government departments in research during and since World War II, the contributions of the Institute and the Royal Society of Canada have been largely restricted to influencing policy and to directing education in science, mathematics, and engineering. The role of the Royal Society in advancing physics is described in GINGRAS, who provides the most comprehensive and balanced discussion of the emergence of physics research, particularly in universities, from the 1870s to the 1960s. His work also covers the growth of Big Science and multi-national co-operation.

Regional issues in the history of science may be found in monographs edited by BOGAARD and by CHARTRAND, DUCHESNE & GINGRAS. The essays in the Bogaard are mainly presented from the perspective of sociological impact rather than of science *per se*. Chartrand, Duchesne & Gingras analyse the impact of scientific expeditions and institutions from the 17th to 20th centuries in Quebec, and describe the great impact on science made by the Jesuits and universities during this period. This work presents a more humanistic approach than many of the other works cited above.

RANDALL C. BROOKS

Cancer

Angier, Natalie, *Natural Obsessions: The Search for the Oncogene*, Boston: Houghton Mifflin, 1988

Austoker, Joan, *A History of the Imperial Cancer Research Fund, 1902–1986*, Oxford and New York: Oxford University Press, 1988

Ball, Howard, *Cancer Factories: America's Tragic Quest for Uranium Self-Sufficiency*, Westport, Connecticut: Greenwood Press, 1993

Clemmesen, Johannes, *Statistical Studies in the Aetiology of Malignant Neoplasms*, vol. 1, *Review and Results*, Copenhagen: Munksgaard, 1965

Cole, Leonard A., *Element of Risk: The Politics of Radon*, Washington, DC: American Association for the Advancement of Science Press, 1993

Efron, Edith, *The Apocalyptics: Cancer and the Big Lie: How Environmental Politics Control What We Know about Cancer*, New York: Simon and Schuster, 1984

Epstein, Samuel S., *The Politics of Cancer*, San Francisco: Sierra Club Books, 1978; revised edition, Garden City, New York: Anchor Press, 1979

Hien, Wolfgang, *Chemische Industrie und Krebs*, Bremerhaven, Germany: Wirtschaftsverlag, 1994

Hueper, Wilhelm C., *Occupational Tumors and Allied Diseases*, Springfield, Illinois: Charles C. Thomas, 1942

Moss, Ralph W., *The Cancer Industry: Unraveling the Politics*, New York: Paragon House, 1989

Patterson, James T., *The Dread Disease: Cancer and Modern American Culture*, Cambridge, Massachusetts: Harvard University Press, 1987

Proctor, Robert N., *Cancer Wars: How Politics Shapes What We Know and Don't Know about Cancer*, New York: Basic Books, 1995

Rettig, Richard A., *Cancer Crusade: The Story of the National Cancer Act of 1971*, Princeton, New Jersey: Princeton University Press, 1977

Richards, Evelleen, *Vitamin C and Cancer: Medicine or Politics?*, London: Macmillan, and New York: St Martin's Press, 1991

Ross, Walter S., *Crusade: The Official History of the American Cancer Society*, New York: Arbor House, 1987

Shimkin, Michael B., *Contrary to Nature*, Washington, DC: Government Printing Office, 1977

The bibliography of the history of cancer research is vast; this is a reflection both of the prevalence of the disease, which eventually strikes one in three persons in the wealthier nations of the world, and also of the vast sums of money that have been poured into the field. Cancer historiography is as politicized as cancer research, with opinions differing widely on how much attention should be given to genetics or viral research, radon or tobacco smoke, X-rays or nuclear fallout, "lifestyle" factors or environmental poisons, union activism or charitable interventions, and so forth and so on. Cancer's causes are so diverse, and the interests so complex, that one person's call for research in a particular direction may look to another like political grandstanding.

Many of the most useful introductions to the historical literature have been written either by cancer researchers or by activists involved in legal or political disputes. SHIMKIN is a good example of the former, while HUEPER combines both traditions. Hueper's work is the most comprehensive English-language history of occupational cancer. A German émigré who came to the United States in 1923 after working in a Ruhr Valley steel mill, Hueper documents both the social and technological circumstances leading to the discovery of the major industrial cancers of the 20th century (asbestos and X-ray cancer, the Schneeberger Krankheit, aniline bladder cancer, mule spinners' cancer, chimney sweeps' cancer, chromate, arsenic and nickel cancers, etc.). The book pays special attention to how particular technologies and work habits led to novel sorts of cancer – for example, the burning of soft coal in England resulted in chimney-sweeps' cancer, and the introduction of pneumatic equipment at the end of the 19th century led to lung-dust diseases.

AUSTOKER's history of the Imperial Cancer Research Fund is concerned less with the prevalence of cancer or its causes than with how Britain's foremost cancer research charity was organized to combat the disease. The emphasis is on the changing goals of the fund, though attention is also given to the growth of experimental cancer research, early 20th-century debates over viral agents, and the impact of World War I on the Fund. Austoker is a more comprehensive history than ROSS, which functions more or less as a palace history of the American Cancer Society.

PATTERSON provides a more cultural approach, looking at the changes in the popular understanding of cancer, and how politicians have responded to popular cancer fears. Attention is drawn to the struggles that led to the establishment of the American Society for the Control of Cancer in 1913 and of the National Cancer Institute in 1937; Patterson also explores why the American medical profession was so slow to admit that cigarettes could cause cancer, and how America's moon-shot technocratic optimism led Richard Nixon to declare "war on cancer" in 1971 – a topic also examined at length in RETTIG.

HIEN brings sociological methods to bear on the question of chemical industry cancers. The focus is on occupational medical ideology and practice in 20th-century Germany, especially the aniline cancers of dye workers and the arsenic cancers of vintners. His thesis is that, until the end of the Weimar period, aniline and other occupational cancers were widely discussed in both medical and labor literature, but that after World War II the entire subject was "dethematised" and largely forgotten. He also explores how employers used concepts of cancer predisposition and genetic susceptibility to screen out vulnerable workers from hazardous jobs, and how research traditions from the Nazi era persisted into more recent times.

The question of the role of occupational carcinogens and environmental pollutants in the overall cancer burden remains highly politicized; nowhere are the two opposing views more sharply contrasted than in Epstein and in Efron. EPSTEIN, an environmentalist, focuses on asbestos and petrochemical cancers to argue that governmental and corporate science have been negligent; EFRON, a libertarian, argues that environmentalists have exaggerated the cancer hazards of modernity, and that most cancers are not in fact preventable. Both produce historical narratives to support their theses, which are reviewed (along with the question of whether cancer rates are on the rise) in PROCTOR.

Many of the books on cancer are topical, responding either to new reports of a particular cancer hazard (such as radon in COLE), or to advances in a particular field of basic research (e.g. ANGIER's engaging popular history of the discovery of oncogenes), or to new legal or political environments, where issues of compensation come to the fore (e.g. BALL's history of the legal challenges posed by the lung cancer of the uranium miners' on the Colorado Plateau).

There has been surprisingly little attention to the history of cancer statistics, though CLEMMESEN contains an admirable discussion of early developments. Viral oncology is a relatively new field of historical interest, and we should be seeing more work in the history of cancer genetics. There are few book-length treatments of the history of cancer therapies, though there are several discussions of "alternative therapies" (e.g. RICHARDS and MOSS). Surprisingly little attention has been given to cancer theory and research outside the American and European contexts, and one can presumably expect to see this oversight redressed in the future. Future historians are also likely to focus increasing attention on particular types of cancer (breast cancer, lung cancer, leukaemia, etc.), recognizing that the material and social causes underlying different types of malignancy may be dramatically different, and that certain cancer sites have been slighted. We are likely to see the insights of body history brought to bear on cancer, illuminating both the cultural specificity of cancer attitudes and the diversity of tools used to understand and treat the disease. Historians will no doubt also continue to explore why cancer experts remain divided over the nature of the cancer problem, and what should be done about it.

ROBERT N. PROCTOR

Cantor, Georg 1845–1918

Russian-born German mathematician

Bell, E.T., *Men of Mathematics*, New York: Simon and Schuster, 1937; Harmondsworth: Penguin, 1953

Charraud, Nathalie, *Infini et Inconscient: essai sur Georg Cantor*, Paris: Anthropos, 1994

Dauben, Joseph W., *Georg Cantor: His Mathematics and Philosophy of the Infinite*, Cambridge, Massachusetts: Harvard University Press, 1979

Fraenkel, A., "Georg Cantor", *Jahresbericht der Deutschen Mathematiker-Vereinigung*, 39 (1930): 189–266; revised as the introduction to *Georg Cantor: Gesammelte Abhandlungen mathematischen und philosophischen Inhalts*, edited by Ernst Zermelo, Berlin: Springer, 1932

Grattan-Guinness, Ivor, "Towards a Biography of Georg Cantor", *Annals of Science*, 27 (1971): 345–91

Grattan-Guinness, Ivor (ed.), *From the Calculus to Set Theory, 1630–1910: An Introductory History*, London: Duckworth, 1980

Hallett, Michael, *Cantorian Set Theory and Limitation of Size*, Oxford: Clarendon Press and New York: Oxford University Press, 1984

Kimberling, Clark, "Emmy Noether", *American Mathematical Monthly*, 79 (1972): 136–49

Meschkowski, Herbert, *Probleme des Unendlichen: Werk und Leben Georg Cantors*, Braunschweig: Vieweg, 1967

Purkert, Walter and Hans Joachim Ilgauds, *Georg Cantor*, Leipzig: Teubner, 1985; 2nd edition, Stuttgart: Birkhäuser, 1987

Schoenflies, A., "Zur Erinnerung an Georg Cantor", *Jahresbericht der Deutschen Mathematiker-Vereinigung*, 31 (1922): 97–106

Schoenflies, A., "Die Krisis in Cantor's mathematischen Schaffen", *Acta Mathematica*, 50 (1927):1–23

The controversial mathematician Georg Cantor is universally recognized as the father of modern set theory. At the end of the 19th century, his remarkable approach to studying the mathematical infinite cast new light on a subject that has plagued mathematics since the time of the ancient Greeks.

As was common, Cantor initially thought that the infinite was inherently paradoxical, but, in the early 1870s, he was forced to consider the concept of mathematical infinity in greater detail. In 1873, Cantor made the major discovery that there are distinct differences between infinite sets – for example, the infinite set of all real numbers is strictly larger than the infinite set of all integers – and, eventually, he worked out the basic principles of both a theory of infinite point sets and of transfinite numbers, which together comprise the basis of what has come to be known as abstract set theory. However, despite the extraordinary effectiveness of Cantor's ideas, they, like the history of the infinite in mathematics itself, could not avoid controversy. As the infamous "paradoxes of set theory" were discovered at the end of the century by Cantor, Bertrand Russell and others chose to condemn transfinite set theory as mathematically inconsistent and therefore unjustifiable. The story of Cantor's great discoveries, and his equally remarkable life, is the subject of the works under review here.

Among contemporary mathematicians who knew Cantor, the first to write detailed accounts of his life and works were Arthur Schoenflies and Abraham Fraenkel. Of the few obituaries to appear shortly after Cantor's death, the most substantial is SCHOENFLIES (1922), and, within another decade, Abraham FRAENKEL completed a more detailed appraisal of Cantor's life and work. However, although full of useful details, both of these early appreciations have been superseded by the more extensive studies produced over the last 30 years.

More important, in fact, for understanding an important turning-point in Cantor's life and work is SCHOENFLIES (1927), which focuses on one especially sensational year – 1884, the year in which Cantor corresponded at length with the Swedish mathematician, Gösta Mittag-Leffler. As editor of the influential journal *Acta Mathematica*, Mittag-Leffler was in the process of publishing the heart of Cantor's new set-theoretic ideas in French translations, and thus of bringing the controversial theory to a truly international audience. It was also in 1884 that Cantor suffered the first of a series of nervous breakdowns that continued with increasing frequency and severity, especially after 1900, for the rest of his life. Their significance and nature – now understood to be manic depression – are among the most widely-debated, and often sensationalized, aspects of Cantor's career. Schoenflies presents texts (or excerpts) of 52 letters from 1884, mostly between Cantor and Mittag-Leffler. For the most part, Schoenflies allows the letters to speak for themselves, but he suggests that Cantor's nervous breakdown was due largely to stress over the failure to resolve his famous Continuum Hypothesis, which was further exacerbated by the mounting criticism of his work from his former teacher, Kronecker, with whom Cantor even attempted an unsuccessful reconciliation.

Cantor's first serious mental breakdown has always figured prominently in the more populist accounts of his life. Of these, none has treated his case with less reliability than BELL, who draws on the popular psychology of his day to produce a predictable, Freudian analysis. The book traces the roots of Cantor's mental instability back to childhood, and blames Cantor's father for having left his son with deeply-implanted neurotic anxieties which, Bell claimed, eventually led to his breakdown and hospitalization.

In addition to the medical questions surrounding Cantor's nervous breakdowns, another controversial question regarding Cantor is whether or not he was Jewish. Here, again, the most blatant example of an author mixing gossip with his own prejudice is E.T. Bell, who ascribes much of the hostility between Cantor and Kronecker to the fact that both were Jewish. But, as DAUBEN details, although Cantor's father had Jewish ancestors, Cantor's mother was a Roman Catholic, and Cantor himself was baptized and raised as a Protestant in the Evangelical Lutheran tradition. Moreover, later he professed that he followed no organized religion at all. Consequently, neither in a rabbinical sense, nor in the sense of a practised faith, can it be said that Cantor was Jewish, although it is clear that he was of Jewish ancestry.

Whether or not the question of Cantor's ancestry is of any direct relevance to his mathematics, it is unfortunate that the early, and subsequently most widely-read account of his life and work should be that provided by Bell. Fortunately, a number of more balanced and reliable accounts have recently appeared, assessing Cantor's career as a mathematician, and the true nature and significance of his personality. For example, on the subject of Cantor's infamous nervous breakdowns, GRATTAN-GUINNESS (1971) considers Cantor's mental illness from a clinical point of view, by reviewing his records preserved at the *Nervenklinik* in Halle. Reconstructing the outline of a case history, Grattan-Guinness explains that the attacks usually began suddenly in the autumn, when Cantor exhibited phases of excitement and exaltation; they ended just as suddenly, usually the following spring or summer, when the depressive phase began, and he would then be sent home to sit silent and motionless for hours on end.

A more recent and elaborate investigation of Cantor and his manic depression, paranoia, and other psychic problems, appears in the recent book by the psychoanalyst Nathalie CHARRAUD. She approaches Cantor's case from the point of view of the French theorist, Jacques Lacan, for whom the role of the father is especially important. Thus, the question of Cantor's relationship with his father plays an important part in Charraud's analysis, as does the famous "crisis" and nervous breakdowns Cantor experienced in 1884 and 1899, which ultimately involve what Charraud discusses as "the Death of the Other". Nevertheless, since most of Cantor's paranoid tendencies, along with his other delusions, plagued him (for the most part) after his professional career as a mathematician was over, it is doubtful that such psychohistory contributes much of value to our appreciation of Cantor's mathematics, or to the legacy of transfinite set theory.

GRATTAN-GUINNESS (1980) is not only concerned with Cantor's psychology, but with virtually every major aspect of Cantor's life, including his interest in music and the literary problem of the Bacon-Shakespeare controversy over the true authorship of Shakespeare's plays (Cantor championed Bacon). Grattan-Guinness includes the texts of 10 documents, mostly letters drawn from Cantor's previously unpublished correspondence of 1881–1905. It also spotlights the major "missing collections" among Cantor's papers, including many of his personal papers that were lost or destroyed during World War II, such as the Cantor-Dedekind correspondence. Remarkably,

only a year later, Clark Kimberling reported the discovery of the original Cantor-Dedekind correspondence, as described in KIMBERLING.

MESCHKOWSKI considerably revised his 1967 edition in 1983, as a result of the extensive amount of new research on Cantor. Both editions are sensitive to the "mathematics and metaphysics" in Cantor's work, but their focus is more on technical detail and less on the biographical or philosophical dimensions of Cantor's work, although these are by no means absent. Meschkowski also cites numerous personal documents in the hands of Cantor's relatives.

DAUBEN is more comprehensive in its treatment of the social background and psychological dimensions. This study takes advantage of earlier research and also draws on additional archival material in Germany and Sweden, tracing the progress of Cantor's work from his early study of point sets to the final emergence of an abstract theory of transfinite numbers, and his subsequent efforts to defend the theory from its mathematical, philosophical, and even theological critics. A closing epilogue assesses the significance of Cantor's personality, and an appendix includes previously unpublished correspondence.

PURKERT & ILGAUDS's biography contains a large number of new documents. Although essentially a chronological treatment, with brief, sometimes highly technical, descriptions of Cantor's mathematics, the book pays full attention to his philosophical, theological, and non-mathematical interests. Whereas the 1985 edition (135 pages) limited itself to material available only in the German Democratic Republic, the 1987 version (262 pages) draws heavily on the papers of Cantor, Klein, and David Hilbert at the *Niedersächsische Staats- und Universitätsbibliothek* in Göttingen. As a result, 49 (instead of five) documents make up the new appendix. Moreover, the authors have used the occasion of their new edition to rewrite portions of the old text for greater clarity. Comparisons between the two editions often reveal dramatic differences, some of them ideological; for example, in commenting on the dialectics of mathematical knowledge, the earlier edition states that only the materialistic point of view can provide successful explanations, while the later edition substitutes a new paragraph in which Cantor's Platonism is discussed instead. Similarly, where there are only passing references in the new edition to dialectics, the earlier edition discusses at some length the ideas of Marx, Engels, and Lenin. In both editions, however, the authors maintain that Cantor's theological efforts were scientifically fruitless.

None the less, if it is true that Cantor's theological beliefs were at all responsible for his faith in the correctness of his mathematics, and indeed supported him steadfastly despite what he considered strong opposition, then his theological concerns were, on the contrary, scientifically fruitful in the highest degree, as Dauben argues. Michael HALLETT has recently made exactly this point in detail, arguing that, insofar as Cantor's concept of the Absolute (theological) was later "transformed" or "translated" into his concept of the (now mathematical) absolute of collections too large to be sets, his theological concerns were of considerable importance.

The final chapter of both versions of Purkert & Ilgauds discusses some of the most important developments in mathematics since Cantor's day, especially those related to set theory.

Although Cantor's work is said to have led to an end of Platonism as a viable philosophy of mathematics (elsewhere Cantor is called the last of the Platonists), this is never really explained. (Surely one must count Kurt Gödel, for example, as a modern Platonist with very good credentials.)

Of all the works discussed here, those that contribute most to the historical understanding of Cantor's life and work are those by Meschkowski, Grattan-Guinness (1971), Dauben, and Purkert & Ilgauds. Above all, the many new documents brought to light in their research serve to substantiate recent conclusions drawn by mathematicians and historians about Cantor, his work, and the nature of the man who produced one of the truly great mathematical theories of the 19th century.

JOSEPH W. DAUBEN

See also Set Theory

Capitalism and Science

Aitken, Hugh G.J., *Scientific Management in Action: Taylorism at Watertown Arsenal, 1908–1915*, Princeton, New Jersey: Princeton University Press, 1985

Appelbaum, Herbert, *The Concept of Work: Ancient, Medieval and Modern*, Albany: State University of New York Press, 1992

Armstrong, Philip, Andrew Glyn and John Harrison, *Capitalism since 1945*, Oxford and Cambridge, Massachusetts: Blackwell, 1991

Banta, Martha, *Taylored Lives: Narrative Productions in the Age of Taylor, Veblen and Ford*, Chicago: University of Chicago Press, 1993

Braverman, Harry, *Labor and Monopoly Capital: The Degradation of Work in the Twentieth Century*, New York: Monthly Review Press, 1974

Hirsch, Joachim, "Fordism and Post-Fordism", in *Post-Fordism and Social Form: A Marxist Debate on the Post-Fordist State*, edited by Werner Bonefeld and John Holloway, London: Macmillan, 1991

Kolko, Joyce, *Restructuring the World Economy*, New York: Pantheon, 1988

Lipietz, Alain, *Mirages and Miracles: The Crisis in Global Fordism*, London: Verso, 1987

Merton, Robert, *Science, Technology and Society in Seventeenth Century England*, Bruges, Belgium: St Catherine Press, 1938; New York: Fertig, 1970

Noble, David F., *America by Design: Science, Technology and the Rise of Capitalism*, New York: Knopf, 1977; Oxford: Oxford University Press, 1979

Smith, David N., *Who Rules the Universities?: An Essay in Class Analysis*, New York: Monthly Review Press, 1974

Weber, Max, *General Economic History (1919–1920)*, translated from the German by Frank H. Knight, New York: Greenberg, and London: Allen and Unwin, 1927; with a new Introduction by Ira J. Cohen, New Brunswick, New Jersey: Transaction, 1987 (original edition, 1923)

Weber, Max, *The Protestant Ethic and the Spirit of Capitalism*, translated from the German by Talcott Parsons, London: Allen and Unwin, 1930; New York: Scribner, 1958 (original edition, 1920)

For Karl Marx and Max Weber, whose theories of capitalism still exert unrivalled influence, science and capitalism are indivisible. This is now manifested in two bodies of literature, the newly published works (and new editions of classics) by Marx and Weber themselves, and recent studies by contemporary scholars for whom the classics remain sources of inspiration.

Turning first to Marx, an understanding of his position on science and capitalism has been enriched by the recent appearance of his economic manuscripts of 1861–64. These were intended as early drafts of the first volume of *Capital*, in which Marx elaborates several key themes that he explains less fully elsewhere. Two of these themes merit special attention: noteworthy, first, is Marx's contrast between "the formal and real subsumption of labor to capital". Originally, Marx says, capitalism rests on a formal foundation, in which, though capitalists profit by hiring workers to produce for the market, they leave the traditional tools and methods of production unaltered – the actual labor of the new wage-earners (weaving, spinning, etc.) is still performed in the age-old manner. Hence, though this is formally "capitalism" – ever-expanding production for the market by producers hired by profit-seeking employers – it is not yet "really", fully capitalist. Indeed, labor is only "really subsumed" under capital, Marx says, when the tools and techniques of production arc so radically transformed that they grow too large and complex to be operated by individuals. Once this happens, artisans and farmers find that they have little choice in deciding whether to work for a capitalist; unable to buy or compete against power looms and cotton gins, they find themselves dependent on those who own the machines, and soon the workers become veritable "appendages of the machine", toiling in rhythms and at speeds dictated by the automatic operation of the machine.

Science enters this equation to the extent that capitalism now figures as a new and uniquely dynamic production system – a "mode of production", not simply a mode of profit-making. Capitalists, driven to accumulate capital on a global scale, find themselves forced continuously to revolutionize production, in the hope of cutting costs and thus underselling their competitors. Above all, this requires the application of science and engineering to production, and while this occurs haphazardly at first, applied science later becomes an integral feature of capitalist production.

For Marx, in other words, fully mature capitalism depends not only on the labor-power of the workers, but on the science and technology needed to unceasingly revolutionize the means of production. This, in turn, entails the transformation of science. Echoing the great Ricardian socialist, William Thompson, Marx claims that "science" was not originally distinct from labor, but was, rather, the intellectual dimension of labor, the mental aspect of a dual (mental and manual) production process. However, as science becomes ever more integrated into capitalist production, it becomes ever more foreign and external to the producer. Once a distillate of producers' "knowledge, observations and craft secrets", science now appears as a realm apart, personified by university-trained experts and resting "on the separation of the intellectual potentialities of the [labor] process from the knowledge, understanding and skill of . . . the masses of 'deskilled' workers".

Corporate science, in short, is an estranged form of the workers' intellectual life. And these workers, "deskilled" and divorced from institutional science, are often displaced bodily as well as intellectually. Science, in other words, far from being a neutral cumulation of knowledge, is in the corporate era an arm of capital itself. Integrated into production in countless ways, corporate science is "labor saving" – that is, it tends to displace workers, to permit proportionally fewer workers to produce at rising rates by operating ever more powerful machinery and equipment. Science thus lessens the employer's dependency on living labor, and thus also reduces labor's bargaining power.

Perspectives of this kind have been elaborated by many contemporary writers, including, most notably, BRAVERMAN, who interprets F.W. Taylor's system of "scientific management" as the culmination of precisely these trends. For Braverman, the main result of the Taylorist system, which swept American industry in the early 20th century, was the scientific "deskilling" of labor. This thesis has been amplified by many writers, while Taylorism in general has been analyzed by AITKEN. The cultural side of Taylorism, meanwhile, has been probed by BANTA, who offers a fascinating account of "Taylored lives" resulting from the scientific management of consumption and the adoption of the efficiency ethic.

There has also been a proliferation of related literature on two major post-Taylorist trends, which are commonly classed as "Fordist" and "post-Fordist". Fordism, briefly, is the Taylorism of the assembly line, in an age of mass production that is aimed at the new "mass market" of domestic consumers. Post-Fordism, in turn, is the diffraction of Fordist tendencies into the global arena, in a phase when production becomes "flexible" and Taylorist trends are modified by breakthroughs in robotics, microelectronics, and communications. Alternative versions of this theory have been offered, respectively, by partisans of the French "regulation school" (LIPIETZ), and by representatives of the German "reformulation school" (HIRSCH). Nevertheless, there is consensus that science is central to the ongoing transformations in post-war capitalist "regimes of accumulation", however these are defined.

Additional light on the contemporary fate of science and capitalism is provided by KOLKO, who gives a comprehensive, fact-laden survey of the restructuring of the world economy, sector by sector (from banking and the state, to the variety of new technologies in industry and agriculture); and by ARMSTRONG, GLYN & HARRISON, who offer a similarly detailed chronicle of post-war capitalism, period by period (from the uncertainties of post-war reconstruction though to the "great boom" which, ending in 1974, gave way to the new uncertainties and slowdown of the late 20th century). The reciprocal effects of capitalism on science in the realm of higher education have been charted by NOBLE, whose research focuses on the rise of the academic engineering discipline in the early 20th century, and by SMITH, who seeks to explain the larger dynamic at work in the interpenetration of corporate and academic science.

WEBER (1930), meanwhile, offers a triangulated version of the nexus of science and capitalism, in which culture is posited as a mediating variable. Like Marx, Weber defines "modern capitalism" as "a wholly capitalistic order of society", resting, essentially, on the formally free labor of workers employed by profit-seeking entrepreneurs. However, free labor can only systematically serve capitalist ends, Weber adds, when it is rationally organized on the foundation of "exact calculation", and the calculability of production depends, in turn, on modern science, "especially the natural sciences based on mathematics and exact and rational experiment". In other words, for Weber, as for Marx, science is woven into the very fiber of capitalism. Capital accumulation presupposes calculation, and calculation, in turn, presupposes science. Science, then, in this conception, is a cultural, and perhaps even a cognitive, prerequisite for capitalist enterprise.

This is not to say, however, that the causal arrow flies in only one direction. On the contrary, Weber is well aware that capitalism, by its "union with science", gives scientific research a new shape and impetus, and, perhaps even more importantly, argues that capitalism arose in conjunction with a new, ascetic, Protestant ethic, which gave a powerful stimulus to "demagicalized" world-views. Scientific world-views, while not expressly affirmed by ascetic Protestantism, were nevertheless reinforced by this anti-magical trend, and in many places science took on Protestant overtones. MERTON later wrote a famous and ingenious dissertation in which this thesis was elaborated in connection with 17th-century English science. Merton's book, which touched comparatively lightly on the theme of capitalism, inspired an entire literature of commentary and debate, most of which, however, leaves capitalism almost entirely in the shade.

More recent works of Weberian cast generally show a fuller appreciation of capitalism's relationship with science as well as with Protestantism. APPELBAUM, for example, inserts a Weberian discussion of ascetic Protestantism into a larger account of the occidental concept of work, paying close attention throughout to the technologies of work which, in the modern era, are so closely connected with scientific inquiry. WEBER (1927), his final lecture notes collected after his sudden death in 1920, reveal a similar emphasis. Here, in contradiction to the conventional belief that Weber advocates an "idealist" causal schema in which ideas drive social relations, he gives equal weight to the role of material and ideal factors. Further, science, in this account, is significant for capitalism on both sides of the equation; while science is plainly an "ideal" force resting on ideation, it is also a material force, embodied in the utterly material reality of the ascending productive forces, which reach their highest point, Weber says, in the form of coal and iron, transformed into means of machine production by the union of production with science.

DAVID N. SMITH

See also Marx; Marxism and Science; Merton Thesis

Cardiology

Acierno, Louis J., *The History of Cardiology*, London and New York: Parthenon, 1994

Burch, George E. and Nicholas P. DePasquale, *A History of Electrocardiography*, Chicago: Year Book, 1964; 2nd edition with a new introduction by Joel D. Howell, San Francisco: Norman, 1990

Comroe, Julius H. and Robert D. Dripps, *The Top Ten Clinical Advances in Cardiovascular-Pulmonary Medicine and Surgery, 1945–1975*, vol. 2, Washington, DC: Department of Health, Education and Welfare, 1978

Fishman, Alfred P. and Dickinson W. Richards (eds), *Circulation of the Blood: Men and Ideas*, New York: Oxford University Press, 1964

Fye, W. Bruce, *American Cardiology: The History of a Specialty and Its College*, Baltimore: Johns Hopkins University Press, 1996

Gorny, Philippe, *Histoire illustrée de la cardiologie: De la préhistoire à nos jours*, Paris: Dacosta, 1985

Howell, Joel D., "Soldier's Heart: The Redefinition of Heart Disease and Specialty Formation in Early Twentieth-Century Great Britain", in *The Emergence of Modern Cardiology*, edited by W.F. Bynum, C. Lawrence and V. Nutton, London: Wellcome Institute, 1985

Lawrence, Christopher, "Moderns and Ancients: The 'New Cardiology' in Britain 1880–1930", in *The Emergence of Modern Cardiology*, edited by W.F. Bynum, C. Lawrence and V. Nutton, London: Wellcome Institute, 1985

Leibowitz, J.O., *The History of Coronary Heart Disease*, London: Wellcome Institute, and Berkeley, University of California Press, 1970

Lüderitz, Berndt, *A History of the Disorders of Cardiac Rhythm*, Armonk, New York: Futura, 1995

Neill, Catherine A. and Edward B. Clark, *The Developing Heart: A "History" of Pediatric Cardiology*, Dordrecht and Boston: Kluwer, 1995

Paul, Oglesby, *Take Heart: The Life and Prescription for Living of Dr Paul Dudley White*, Cambridge, Massachusetts: Harvard University Press, 1986

Shumacker Jr, Harris B., *The Evolution of Cardiac Surgery*, Bloomington: Indiana University Press, 1992

Snellen, H.A., A.J. Dunning and A.C. Arntzenius (eds), *History and Perspectives of Cardiology: Catheterization, Angiography, Surgery, and Concepts of Circular Control*, The Hague: Leiden University Press, 1981

Cardiology is now held to be the study of the heart and its diseases, although the field is at times taken also to encompass the study of blood vessels and their diseases. As one of a number of organ- or system-based specialities within medical practice, the history of cardiology could be described as starting with the division of medical knowledge and clinical practice, a process generally thought to have taken place during the late 19th and early 20th centuries. None the less, some writers have taken the history of cardiology to include the history of ideas about the heart and its diseases, which leads to a much longer history.

ACIERNO provides a comprehensive review of ideas about the heart, from the beliefs and myths of early man to the medical technology and knowledge of the latter part of the 20th century. GORNY provides a similarly broad scope, in a book that, like Acierno's, has many well-reproduced illustrations. One of the most common forms of heart disease today is coronary heart disease, the blockage of the blood vessels supplying the heart itself, which is often perceived as chest pain that may be a manifestation of angina or myocardial infarction (heart attack). LEIBOWITZ traces ideas about coronary heart disease back to antiquity and gives a full account of changing ideas about this process, focusing on the 18th and

19th centuries. LÜDERITZ covers another common type of cardiac disease, abnormalities of the heart's rhythm. Heart disease in children is often of a different character than that seen in adults, and is more likely to be a result of congenital abnormalities of the heart's development; NEILL & CLARK describe the history of ideas about heart disease in children.

In the late 20th century, cardiology has come to be perceived as a high-technology, invasive, and aggressive enterprise. Some of the technology is discussed in FISHMAN & RICHARDS, who focus on changing ideas about cardiovascular physiology, including ideas about the electrical action of the heart. BURCH & DEPASQUALE cover the history of instruments that record the electrical action of the heartbeat: the electrocardiogram has been central not only for diagnosing cardiac disease but also for enabling its treatment – a treatment that has often become dependent on the ability to insert various devices into the chambers of the heart, both to make measurements and to intervene surgically. SNELLEN, DUNNING & ARNTZENIUS emphasize these sorts of invasive manoeuvers, including many personal reminiscences of key events. Obviously, the history of cardiac surgery is not as long as the history of ideas of the heart: SHUMACKER gives a useful account of the technical events related to the ability successfully to operate on the heart.

The preceding works are primarily addressed to a medical audience, and reflect in large part what has been termed an "internalist" approach to the history of medicine – that is, they tend to focus on events within the medical world, and have a generally laudatory and celebratory tone. Thus, the apparent triumphs of cardiology have encouraged histories that are effectively eulogies to the inventors and surgeons concerned. An overt attempt to produce such a history can be found in COMROE & DRIPPS: they identified the "top ten" clinical advances and prepared a detailed listing of names, dates, and references for the key contributions of knowledge, technique, and equipment for each of these advances. While making no attempt to situate this list within a historical context, the volume is extremely useful as starting point for further analysis.

Although medically-trained people – and almost all of the historical literature on cardiology has been written by people with medical training, mostly by practitioners of cardiology or cardiac surgery – have devoted considerable attention to changing ideas about the heart, there has been much less of an attempt to situate the history of those ideas and events within a larger social context. One way to do so is to pay attention to clinicians whose careers have reached beyond the medical world. PAUL gives a breezy, enjoyable biography of Paul Dudley White (1886–1973), a physician who played a crucial role in the history of American cardiology. Paul describes in detail White's role in treating the 1955 myocardial infarction suffered by the American president, Dwight Eisenhower; Eisenhower's return to the presidency marked a conspicuous development in the advice typically given to people who had suffered such a trauma, which had previously warned against a return to normal life.

The relationships between science and clinical practice may seem obvious today, but the historical transition for cardiology was complex. LAWRENCE gives an account of how changing concepts of heart disease led to a new approach to clinical issues and problems. He explains how experimental physiologists created a new concept of the heart, based on function rather than structure, that was soon applied to diseases of the heart as well as to normal functioning.

If the history of cardiology is conceptualized as the history of a group of individuals choosing to define themselves in terms of an area of knowledge or practice – i.e. a medical speciality – then it is clearly a study that must be to some extent specific to a given nation. Most works on this topic examine Britain and the United States. On Britain, HOWELL explains how World War I and post-war tensions, caused by high pensions and a faltering economy, led to the formation of the first group of British Cardiologists. FYE explores the creation of cardiology in the United States in some detail, particularly the two dominant professional organizations (the American Heart Association and the American College of Cardiology), and provides a comprehensive account of how cardiology has responded to the dramatic late 20th-century changes in medicine's political economy. What is generally lacking in the literature on the history of cardiology is attention to events outside the US and Europe, or attention to the social history of cardiology – that is, the history of heart disease as experienced by ordinary men and women.

JOEL D. HOWELL

Cartesianism

Ariew, Roger and Marjorie Grene (eds), *Descartes and His Contemporaries: Meditations, Objections and Replies*, Chicago: University of Chicago Press, 1995

Brockliss, L.W.B., *French Higher Education in the Seventeenth and Eighteenth Centuries: A Cultural History*, Oxford: Clarendon Press and New York: Oxford University Press, 1987

Clarke, Desmond M., *Occult Powers and Hypotheses: Cartesian Natural Philosophy under Louis XIV*, Oxford: Clarendon Press, and New York: Oxford University Press, 1989

Garber, Daniel, *Descartes' Metaphysical Physics*, Chicago: University of Chicago Press, 1992

Lennon, Thomas M., John M. Nicholas and John W. Davis, *Problems of Cartesianism*, Kingston and Montreal: McGill-Queen's University Press, 1982

Mouy, Paul, *Le Développement de la physique Cartésienne 1646–1712*, Paris: Vrin, 1934

Rosenfield, Leonora Cohen, *From Beast-Machine to Man-Machine: Animal Soul in French Letters from Descartes to La Mettrie*, New York: Oxford University Press, 1941; revised edition, New York: Octagon Books, 1968

Sutton, Geoffrey V., *Science for a Polite Society: Gender, Culture and the Demonstration of Enlightenment*, Boulder, Colorado: Westview Press, 1995

Verbeek, Theo, *Descartes and the Dutch: Early Reactions to Cartesian Philosophy, 1637–1650*, Carbondale: Southern Illinois University Press, 1992

The early modern French mechanist philosopher, René Descartes (1596–1650), had an enormous influence on the development of modern thought. Yet, the number of direct and orthodox followers of Descartes was never great. Without a doubt, the philosopher himself was partly responsible for this

restriction; according to his philosophical rhetoric, only Descartes himself, unaided by past or present authority, could begin and complete the enterprise of natural philosophy and metaphysics. In this way, Descartes proclaimed his thought to be the source, as well as the culmination, of all true knowledge. Hence, any orthodox follower of Descartes was left with a bare minimum of duties beyond the dissemination of the teachings of the master. Nevertheless, this mythology of absolute philosophical triumph concealed a series of intractable problems that proved more than sufficient to nurture a dynamic legacy. This is, in the end, the best definition of Cartesianism: a creative attempt to confront the many intrinsic ambiguities within Descartes's metaphysics and natural philosophy.

Physics was central to Descartes's conception of natural philosophy. The classic, general account of the history of Cartesian physics is to be found in MOUY's work from the 1930s. This should be supplemented, however, with more recent works, such as GARBER's detailed monograph. Garber emphasizes the crucial opposition to atomism in Descartes's physics – i.e. the denial of atoms and the void in favor of the notion of an indefinite divisibility of matter, and the idea of space as a plenum. By focusing on Descartes's account of motion, Garber shows that for Descartes physics and metaphysics formed an inextricable whole. The laws of motion governing the physical universe were at every instant ordained by divine omnipotent will, and, as a consequence, Garber is led to emphasize the centrality of the *Principles of Philosophy*, Descartes's textbook version of his thought, published in 1644.

For the influence of Descartes's thought in fields of natural philosophy other than physics, the literature is rich in general works, but very poor in specific monographs. ROSENFIELD provides a somewhat dated introduction to the theme of Cartesian physiology and psychology.

Ariew & Grene and Verbeek both give the history of the first reception of Descartes's metaphysical physics. Before Descartes published his foremost metaphysical work, *Meditations on First Philosophy*, he submitted the manuscript to a number of prominent members of the European intellectual community, in order to solicit their responses to his work. ARIEW & GRENE's collection of articles analyses the exchanges between Descartes and these chosen few, while providing some noteworthy articles on the Epicurean mechanism of Gassendi and the mathematical models of Mersenne. VERBEEK focuses on the Dutch reception of Descartes's legacy, emphasizing its academic nature; it was in the Dutch universities that Descartes's thought first underwent the transformation from independent philosophy into academic course work, facilitated by Descartes's own experiment in the genre, the *Principles of Philosophy*. While Descartes was still residing in the Low Countries, the philosopher also won his first disciples and fought his first intellectual battles. Among these Dutch followers were men such as Arnold Geulinex, Adriaan Heereboord, Joannes de Raey, Henri de Roy (Regius) and Burchardus de Volder. After them, Lodewijk Meyer and Baruch Spinoza appropriated and radicalized Descartes's ideas to an extreme that would have probably greatly upset their author.

There is not yet any full-length work on the reception of Descartes's thought in England. As a small remedy, the collection edited by LENNON, NICHOLAS & DAVIS includes, among several other useful pieces, an article by Allan Gabbey on the important role played by Henry More in introducing Cartesian thought to an English audience in the 1650s and 1660s.

In contrast, the French brand of Cartesianism has been better served in the secondary literature. The years 1660–1700 mark the reluctant, but widespread, reception of Descartes's metaphysical physics within French natural philosophy. CLARKE notes that this period of gradual dissemination coincided with the most active years of Louis XIV's reign, and proposes that the political and religious policies pursued by the monarch significantly influenced the growth of Cartesianism in France. The core of this movement consisted in a close-knit community of Cartesians, including Gerauld de Cordemoy, Claude Gadroys, Nicolas Malebranche, Nicholas-Joseph Poisson, Pierre-Sylvain Regis and Jacques Rohault. Their principal contribution to French natural philosophy was an insistence on a new, mechanical mode of scientific explanation.

Both Brockliss and Sutton describe the wider effects of Cartesian mechanism on French culture and education. BROCKLISS points to the years 1690–1740 as a period of Cartesian dominance in the teaching of university physics. SUTTON gives the fascinating history of Cartesian thought in salon culture; he argues that this brand of Cartesianism functioned more or less as a creative art, because the mechanical world view promoted was vague enough to allow for a wide range of improvisation. Besides some general outlines, the Cartesian thinker had almost no rules to confine his creativity, a freedom that appealed to specialist and amateur alike.

FREDRIK JONSSON

See also Descartes

Cartography

Bagrow, Leo, *History of Cartography*, edited by R.A. Skelton, translated from the German by D.L. Paisey, Cambridge, Massachusetts: Harvard University Press, and London: Watts, 1964 (original edition, 1951)

Crone, G.R., *Maps and Their Makers: An Introduction to the History of Cartography*, London: Hutchinson, 1953, 4th edition, 1968; 5th edition, Hamden, Connecticut: Archon, 1978

Harley, J.B. and David Woodward (eds), *The History of Cartography*, vol. 1: *Cartography in Prehistoric, Ancient, and Medieval Europe and the Mediterranean*; vol. 2, book 1: *Cartography in the Traditional Islamic and South Asian Societies*; vol. 2, book 2: *Cartography in the Traditional East and Southeast Asian Societies*, Chicago: Chicago University Press, 1987–94

Kain, Roger J.P. and Elizabeth Baigent, *The Cadastral Map in the Service of the State: A History of Property Mapping*, Chicago: University of Chicago Press, 1992

Miller, Konrad, *Mappaemundi: die ältesten Weltkarten*, 6 vols, Stuttgart: Roth, 1895–98

Nordenskiöld, A.E., *Periplus: An Essay on the Early History of Charts and Sailing-Directions*, translated from the Swedish by Francis A. Bather, Stockholm: Norstedt, 1897; reprinted New York: Burt Franklin, 1962(?)

Rudwick, Martin, "The Emergence of a Visual Language for Geological Science, 1760–1840", *History of Science*, 14 (1976): 149–95

Widmalm, Sven, *Mellan kartan och verkligheten: geodesi och kartläggning, 1695–1860*, Uppsala: Institutionen för idé- och lärdomshistoria, 1990

J.B. Harley's introduction to the first volume of HARLEY & WOODWARD provides a wonderful historical account of the emergence of the history of cartography. Here we learn about the early modern fascination with antique maps, the use of the discipline as a handmaiden for exploration and the science of geography, the role of map libraries and the antiquarian map trade, and their impact on the subject matter in cartographic history. We then learn about the professionalization of the history of cartography since the 1930s, symptomized by the appearance of the journal *Imago Mundi* from 1935 and prompted by the rise of cartography itself. Since the 1970s, the field has become much more transnational and open to interpretations of cartography not just as a precise science. Maps are now studied as artefacts that communicate on many levels, some of which transcend many cultures, and interpreting a map requires an understanding of the culture in which it was produced.

NORDENSKIÖLD and MILLER are two of the classic histories of cartography, and have survived as fundamental references, the former on portolan charts (the Mediterranean navigational charts of the late Middle Ages), the latter on the *mappaemundi* (medieval encyclopedic works reflecting, among many other things, the state of geographical knowledge). Both books were written in the late 19th century when the history of cartography was conceived as subservient to geography. Nordenskiöld, for example, was himself an explorer, the first successfully to navigate the Northwest Passage, and a collector of maps.

BAGROW and CRONE are two of the first and still influential syntheses of the field from the period when the history of cartography was gradually professionalizing. From a modern perspective, however, these syntheses are selective in significant ways. Bagrow (the founder of *Imago Mundi*) ends his history in the 18th century when craftsmanship in mapmaking was superseded by the machine. Accordingly, he excludes scientific methods of mapmaking, the selection of data, and the compilation of maps. Crone is still an excellent summary of the history of cartography. It treats maps simultaneously as scientific reports, historical documents, research tools, and objects of art. If any serious criticism can be levelled at it, it is that non-Western mapping is essentially ignored.

KAIN & BAIGENT provide a history of cadastral (property) mapping from the 16th century in the Netherlands, Scandinavia, Germany, the Habsburg lands, France, England, and Wales, and in the colonial settlements of North America, Australia, New Zealand, and India. They argue that cadastral maps are partisan in that they provide comprehensive information to be used to the advantage of some and to the detriment of others, and they document this by looking at the tax struggles in the 18th and 19th centuries. They also show that cadastral maps have a chequered past that reflects the turbulence of political history.

HARLEY & WOODWARD aims to be truly universal; two of the projected six volumes have so far appeared. The books are well produced (including high quality colour reproductions of maps) and the authors avoid a reductionist approach to cartography. For instance, it is emphasized that East Asian maps were employed for education, for aesthetic appreciation, to express emotional states, to represent power, to settle disputes, to symbolize submission or subordination, and to promise immortality. In order to carry out historical work on maps, one has to be eclectic: one needs grounding in the history of science and technology, art, literature, government, economics, religion, and philosophy – in short one needs the polymath range of the mapmakers themselves. The contributions to this large publication do indeed show how a history of cartography can pursue these many lines.

Rudwick and Widmalm illustrate many of the themes in the history of cartography and yet their subject matters lie squarely within the history of science, testifying to the common ground between the two fields. In the period between the late 18th century and 1840, geology could be said to have emerged as a selfconscious new discipline with clearly defined goals and well-established institutional forms. RUDWICK shows that in this period an integrated visual-and-verbal mode of communication emerged as well. Late 18th-century publications on geology and related matters contained few illustrations, and were often of poor quality. However, there was a need to describe the topography and to depict causal and temporal interpretations of observed structural configurations. In the decades around 1800 new technologies of representation emerged: aquatints, wood engravings, steel engravings, and lithographs, and they had an impact on the emergence of ever more abstract, formalized, and theory-laden modes of representation. At the end of the paper, Rudwick represents the narrative of the paper in a diagram. He thus departs from his analysis in prose and employs a mapping technique developed in the study of geology. Rudwick is well aware of this reflexive move in that he analyses geology but uses a geological tool with which to do so.

WIDMALM's history of geodesy and cartography explicitly takes its starting point in J.B. Harley's calls for an eclectic history of maps and then consciously shifts to concerns that are more clearly within the genre of the history of science: the book examines debates over the shape of the earth (Newton v. Cassini, or oblate v. oblong), the shift at the time of Bessel and Gauss away from an implicit faith in the mathematical modeling of the earth's shape toward the actual mapping of an acknowledgedly irregular earth, as well as the link between (military) discipline and precision. Widmalm does address issues in the Harleyan history of cartography, such as the symbolic meaning of maps in the context of a science in need of funding from the nation-state, but the emphasis is more on the organization and material effort required to produce maps and how this changed institutional, professionalizing, and theory-related aspects of science. Widmalm's focus is on the history of science in Sweden, but he is very attentive to the history of international links and institutions, and the book can thus be read also as a European history of geodesy and mapmaking, with special emphasis on one particular nation-state.

ARNE HESSENBRUCH

CERN

Galison, Peter, *How Experiments End*, Chicago: University of Chicago Press, 1987

Goldsmith, Maurice and Edwin Shaw, *Europe's Giant Accelerator: The Story of the CERN 400 GeV Proton Synchroton*, London: Taylor and Francis, 1977

Grinevald, Jacques *et al.*, *La Quadrature du CERN: Essai indisciplinaire*, Lausanne: Editions d'en bas, 1984

Hermann, Armin *et al.*, *History of CERN*, 3 vols, Amsterdam: North-Holland, 1987–96

Knorr-Cetina, Karin, *Epistemic Cultures: How the Sciences Make Knowledge*, Cambridge, Massachusetts: Harvard University Press, 1999

Pickering, Andrew, *Constructing Quarks: A Sociological History of Particle Physics*, Edinburgh: Edinburgh University Press, and Chicago: University of Chicago Press, 1984

Taubes, Gary, *Nobel Dreams: Power, Deceit and the Ultimate Experiment*, New York: Random House, 1986

CERN (the acronym is derived from the name of the provisional organization of 1952 to 1954, the Conseil Européen pour la Recherche Nucléaire) is a premier example of Big Science, a laboratory for relations between science and governments and for European co-operation, as much as for particle physics. The literature on CERN ranges from a multi-volume history of the organization, works written for a popular audience, to social science studies exploring the dynamics of large scientific collaborations and the nature of their achievements.

HERMANN *et al.* have produced a detailed history of the origins and establishment of the organization. The first volume is a chronological account, covering the post-war conception of the organization to the successful convention of 1954. It includes a useful description of the emergence of the field of particle physics and provides case studies of the roles played by France, Germany, the United Kingdom and Italy in the creation of the laboratory. The second volume, extending to around 1966, is organized thematically. It analyses, for example, the development of machines and the organization of research, and the functioning of CERN as an international body controlled by a mixture of scientists and government administrators. A forthcoming third volume, edited by Krige, takes the account further; this volume retains the mix, characteristic of the earlier volumes, of both technical accounts – e.g. the evolution of wire chambers – and studies of more general interest – such as Pèstre's account of the Gargamelle bubble chamber collaboration. Massively documented and including extensive bibliographies, these volumes will be the standard source for the history of CERN.

In the second category of literature, GOLDSMITH & SHAW provide a celebratory account of the design and construction of the Super Proton Synchroton at CERN in the 1970s, the second generation of CERN accelerators. Their summary of CERN's origins and workings, however, has been superseded by the accounts in Hermann *et al.* GRINEVALD *et al.* offer an example of the political (and, indeed, moral) critique that is part of the heritage of the social history of science. Here, the social and political dimensions of science, especially Big Science, assume a sinister aspect that can approach caricature.

The authors note the self-perpetuating nature of an institution permanently staffed with accelerator builders, and its resulting tendency, they claim, to "technological giantism". The costliness of high energy physics, too, is a familiar but real target. The authors also maintain that CERN and its users systematically underplay the applications of its research to atomic energy, or laser weaponry research. More contentiously, they claim that particle physics mounts a deception in presenting its subject as a fundamental study of nature, and they see the repeated discoveries of particles since the 1950s as an endless spiral. Their case is eroded, however, by the book's deliberate naivety: the argument for CERN's impurity depends on an artificial construct of the purity of science.

TAUBES is another highly coloured account aimed at a popular audience, without the dogmatism of Grinevald *et al*. This portrait of CERN could certainly be used to support an antagonistic view towards science, though Taubes himself finds high energy physics an obsessive but exhilarating activity. He concentrates on personalities, particularly the abrasive Carlo Rubbia, an Italian-born physicist who won a Nobel prize in 1984 for discovery of the W and Z particles. The book details the construction of Rubbia's experiment at CERN, the conflicts spawned within the huge collaboration responsible for it, and the competition between American and European physics communities.

High energy physics has often served as a focus for social studies of science, many of which devote attention to CERN. PICKERING's history is a key text in this field, concentrating on the practices of the high energy physics community in the 1960s and 1970s. The account of the emergence of the quark theory is of general relevance to a historical understanding of CERN, though Pickering's portrait of the high energy physics community and its resources is international in scale and does not closely delineate the middle ground between macro (high energy physics in general) and micro (individual) levels of scientific practice that could illuminate the particular context of CERN. More accessible than Pickering, GALISON uses a case study approach to analyze the relationship between observation and theory in modern physics; he contrasts neutral current experiments at Fermilab (the EA1 spark chamber) and CERN (the Gargamelle bubble chamber) in the early 1970s to explore the technologies and sociology of giant accelerator physics. Galison focuses on the increasingly involved process of data analysis – of sorting signals from the background "noise" of elaborate machinery and then elevating signals into conclusive evidence of natural phenomena. He sees this process as the major shift in the practice of 20th-century physics, significantly altering earlier conceptions of experiment.

Finally, there is a contemporary ethnography of CERN, from KNORR-CETINA, a sociologist who followed the later stages of the UA2 experiment (1987–1990), and one of the successive (and ongoing) experiments in the Large Hadron Collider, ATLAS. Knorr-Cetina adopts a method she calls "comparative optics", in which she uses her investigations of a physics laboratory and a molecular biology laboratory to illuminate the distinctive practices and, she argues, epistemologies of different branches of natural science. Her principal concern lies with epistemology, and the study seeks to move social construction beyond the practice of fact-making to the "structures of thought" that underlie it. In an argument that continues Galison's emphasis on data analysis, Knorr-Cetina presents the virtues of negative knowledge in high energy physics, where all evidence is defined by what it is not. Twisting the literature's preoccupation with the function of technology in constructing knowledge, she suggests that machines display fuller human identities in the laboratory than the physicists who build and operate them. Suitably and often divertingly reflexive, this analysis also provides a valuable discussion of the aims and politics of constructionism.

KATHARINE ANDERSON

See also Big Science

Chaos Theory

Abraham, Ralph H. and Christopher D. Shaw, *Dynamics: The Geometry of Behavior*, 4 vols, Santa Cruz, California: Aerial Press, 1982–88; 2nd edition, Redwood City, California: Addison-Wesley, 1992

Abraham, R., *Chaos, Gaia, Eros: A Chaos Pioneer Uncovers the Three Great Streams of History*, San Francisco: HarperCollins, 1994

Bass, Thomas A., *The Eudaemonic Pie*, Boston: Houghton Mifflin, 1985

Briggs, John and F. David Peat, *Turbulent Mirror: An Illustrated Guide to Chaos Theory and the Science of Wholeness*, New York: Harper and Row, 1990

Eglash, Ronald Bruce, *A Cybernetics of Chaos*, PhD dissertation, University of California, Santa Cruz, 1992

Franks, J., "Review of *Chaos: Making of a New Science* by James Gleick", *The Mathematical Intelligencer*, 11 (1987): 65–71

Gleick, James, *Chaos: Making of a New Science*, New York: Viking, 1987; London: Heinemann, 1988

Kellert, Stephen H., *In the Wake of Chaos: Unpredictable Order in Dynamical Systems*, Chicago: University of Chicago Press, 1993

Lyotard, Jean-François, *The Postmodern Condition: A Report on Knowledge*, translated from the French by Geoff Bennington and Brian Massumi, Minneapolis: University of Minnesota Press, and Manchester: Manchester University Press, 1984 (original edition, 1979)

Mandelbrot, Benoit B., *The Fractal Geometry of Nature*, San Francisco: W.H. Freeman, 1982

Pagels, Heinz R., *The Dreams of Reason: The Computer and the Rise of the Sciences of Complexity*, New York: Simon and Schuster, 1988

Porush, D., "Rewriting Chaos: A Study in the Popular Making of a New Science", *Society for Social Studies of Science*, November 1989

Prigogine, Ilya and Isabelle Stengers, *Order Out of Chaos: Man's New Dialogue with Nature*, New York: Bantam, and London: Heinemann, 1984

Waldrop, M. Mitchell, *Complexity: The Emerging Science at the Edge of Order and Chaos*, New York: Simon and Schuster, 1992

The family of mathematical systems referred to as "chaos theory" or "non-linear science" has received an extraordinary amount of attention in both popular and scholarly texts, although rigorous historical research has lagged behind this enthusiasm. Chaos theory can be divided into three areas of mathematics. In fractal geometry, the measure of symmetry between scales can be quantitatively measured for natural shapes, and artificially simulated in graphics. In dynamical systems theory, simple ("low-dimensional") difference (or differential) equations are shown to be capable of either short-term uncertainty in the relation of initial conditions to final conditions (fractal basin boundaries), or of infinitely long-term aperiodic fluctuations (chaotic attractors), with extreme sensitivity to initial conditions in both cases. In complexity theory, aggregate self-organizing systems – a large number of homogenous individual units – exhibit coherent collective behavior ("emergent phenomena").

GLEICK's popular history of dynamical systems theory and fractal geometry set off an explosion of interest, and has been the subject of much debate. In the pure mathematics community this is best represented by FRANKS, who opposed Gleick's implication that chaos theory was the dawning of a new holistic approach to science, and suggested that it was, rather, a direct outcome of digital computers. Although Gleick's rejoinder (published at the end of Frank's review) did not defend the "holism" thesis – he merely denied that he had missed the significance of digital computing – nevertheless, a large number of "new age" texts subsequently seized on, and made popular, the idea that chaos theory heralded a new holism in science.

More serious critique, however, was provided by PORUSH, who claimed that Gleick's lack of attention to the "order out of chaos" work by Prigogine (described in PRIGOGINE & STENGERS) was the result of an ideological bias. Porush saw the focus on deterministic aperiodicity as a reflection of Western traditions linking social control with science, and contrasted this with Prigogine's "open system" emphasis. However one sides in this debate, it is crucial to understand that the term "chaos" was used by Prigogine in its older sense of random white noise spectra, not in the new sense of deterministic aperiodicity (typified by "pink" or "1/F" noise spectra). This confusion was accelerated by Stewart Kauffman's neologism "antichaos" and Christopher Langton's phrase "the edge of chaos", both referring to self-organizing phenomena. Fortunately, an excellent account of this complexity theory terminology, along with brief historical portraits of the scientists and institutions involved, can be found in WALDROP.

More specialized histories are also available. MANDELBROT provides his own conceptual genealogy in an appendix to his seminal work on fractal geometry, and ABRAHAM & SHAW have put together a similar listing for the precursors to dynamical systems theory. BASS gives an entertaining account of the UC Santa Cruz "Chaos Cabal", as well as exploring some of the connections between gaming and mathematics in the history of statistics and information theory. Ueda's early work in Japan has been published by Aerial Press, and a brief history of numerical measures of complexity can be found in PAGELS.

Cultural analysis of these histories have run from the most optimistic of new age holism advocates (e.g., BRIGGS & PEAT), to the most cynical of postmodern deconstructionists (e.g., LYOTARD). A more balanced approach can be found in KELLERT, who gives some good historical details on deter-

minism in the philosophy of science, although his conclusion makes a rather unreflective use of essentialist feminist science theory. EGLASH constructs a critique of the claims for chaos theory as inherently ethical by documenting its use in military and labor management discourse, and by studying the ideological interpretations of its creators. ABRAHAM's holism manifesto, while celebrating a wild counter-cultural *jouissance*, does include many scholarly historical details, ranging from archaeological data on "chaos" concepts in the ancient world, to Kovalevsky's influence on Poincaré. Particularly important is his argument that the AAAS meeting of 1974 condemning Velikovsky should be seen not as the modern debunking of pseudo-science, but rather as a continuation of outdated quasi-religious dogma on the stability of the solar system.

RON EGLASH

Charcot, Jean-Martin 1825–1893
French pathologist and neurologist

Evans, Matha Noel, *Fits and Starts: A Genealogy of Hysteria in Modern France*, Ithaca, New York: Cornell University Press, 1991

Freud, Sigmund, "Charcot" in *The Standard Edition of the Complete Psychological Works of Sigmund Freud*, vol. 3: *Early Psychoanalytic Publications*, edited by James Strachey, London: Hogarth Press, 1962

Goldstein, Jan, *Console and Classify: The French Psychiatric Profession in the Nineteenth Century*, Cambridge and New York: Cambridge University Press, 1987

Guillain, Georges, *J.-M. Charcot, 1825–1893: His Life – His Work*, edited and translated from the French by Pearce Bailey, London: Pitman, and New York: Hoeber, 1959 (original edition, 1955)

Harris, Ruth, "Introduction", to Charcot's *Clinical Lectures on Diseases of the Nervous System*, London and New York: Tavistock/Routledge, 1991 (original edition 1872–87)

Micale, Mark, "Hysteria Male/Hysteria Female: Reflections on Comparative Gender Construction in Nineteenth-Century Medicine", in *Science and Sensibility: Essays on Gender and Scientific Enquiry, 1780–1945*, edited by Marina Benjamin, London and Cambridge, Massachusetts: Blackwell, 1992

Owen, A.R.G., *Hysteria, Hypnosis and Healing: The Work of J.-M. Charcot*, London: Dobson, and New York: Garrett, 1971

Showalter, Elaine, *The Female Malady: Women, Madness and English Culture, 1830–1980*, New York: Pantheon Books, 1985; London: Virago, 1987

In his obituary of Jean-Martin Charcot, FREUD enumerated the many achievements of his mentor and former teacher. In Freud's view, Charcot was responsible for rescuing the affliction of hysteria from the realms of superstition; his great abilities, together with his position as neurologist at the Salpêtrière, gave Charcot the opportunity to establish the framework of a detailed nosology for this flux of protean nervous conditions.

Alongside this clinical success, Freud also detailed Charcot's literary and political achievements, arguing that he deserved respect both for his historiographical work, which had brought the literature on demonology back to medical attention, and for his extensive political contacts, which had made him a key player within the Third Republic. The many different aspects of Charcot's life and career, outlined by Freud, have been more systematically explored in the writings of modern medical historians.

The hagiographical approach is continued in the biography of Charcot by GUILLAIN. In a narrative laced with respect and affection, Guillain traces the life of the physician, through his Parisian childhood and medical training to his eventual appointment as director of the Salpêtrière. The author details Charcot's high standing among both his family and the international community, portraying his subject as a determined genius who successfully mediated the public and private realms. The second half of Guillain's work contains an exposition of Charcot's medical and physiological research. As a summary this piece is extremely useful, since it charts the development of Charcot's most famous work on hysteria from his earlier investigations of chronic rheumatism, muscular dystrophy, muscular sclerosis, and cerebral localization.

Hysteria is at the centre of consideration in OWEN's work. Having previously published on psychical research, Owen concentrates on the more dramatic and sensational aspects of Charcot's career. He provides a detailed synopsis of Charcot's work on hysteria, recounting the development of his four-stage model of the affliction and locating his research on hypnotism within the wider context of 19th-century mesmerism. Particular attention is paid to Charcot's research on metallotherapy, faith healing, and the supernatural in history. This last topic is related to Charcot's republican sympathies, and he emerges from this history as one of the major agents of secularization in France.

The connection between medicine, secularisation, and republican politics provides the central theme of GOLDSTEIN, who examines the resurgence of hysteria in late 19th-century France. Eschewing the psycho-historical explanations offered by Freud and feminist historians, Goldstein argued that the category received its form and definition through the persistent and internecine warfare that existed between the Third Republic and the clerical establishment. Charcot's project of retrospective diagnosis, his attempt to uncover the role of hysteria in the trials and witchcraft persecutions of 17th-century France, is depicted as a double-edged strategy to establish medical, rather than clerical, authority over this aspect of human experience and behaviour. This strategy established both the material reality of hysteria across history, and the cruel incompetence of the clergy when confronted by this disease.

Charcot's extension of the hysteria diagnosis to men has been explored by MICALE. He contrasts the large number of case histories published by Charcot with its low recorded incidence, citing this as evidence of a general attempt to defeminize hysteria. Moreover, Micale demonstrates that these case histories comprised a notably virile selection of the labouring classes, rather than the nervous, effete figures more usually associated with hysteria in the popular imagination. This new masculine association, in Micale's view, advanced the neurological and genealogical model of hysteria over and above the traditional gynaecological explanation. The latter part of Micale's work is devoted to an analysis of the complex interaction between Charcot's need to establish the virile nature of his male patients and the gendered symptomatology of hysteria. He shows how the female characteristics of this disease, such as the hysteric's sensitivity to ovarian compression, were transposed on to male patients, while at the same time Charcot maintained a sex distinction when ascribing causes of the disease.

Most of Micale's material is ignored in the portrait of Charcot developed by EVANS. Evans is attentive to the question of domination in Charcot's work, arguing that his conceptualization of hysteria can be seen as an ideological attempt to disenfranchise unruly women. She details the physical violation involved in experimental techniques, such as ovarian compression, and the mental suppression and control engendered by the practice of hypnosis. Such medical theories and techniques, Evans argues, were not only an attack on hysterical woman, but a criticism of the female sex as a whole. They reduced the authentic capriciousness of womanhood to the realms of mental pathology. A more tempered feminist account is offered by SHOWALTER, who recognizes Charcot's attempts to destigmatize and desexualize hysteria, yet argues that his method still repressed the patient. In particular, she points to the way Charcot gave precedence to the visual rather than the verbal in his representation of hysteria, suggesting that this led to the exclusion of the hysteric's voice and experience.

A fine overall summary of these many approaches to the work of Charcot is provided by HARRIS in her introduction to his *Clinical Lectures*. Harris emphasizes the combination of science and art in Charcot's work, suggesting that this explains both his nosological success and his public influence. The greater part of her summary is devoted to Charcot's work on hysteria in the male, an account that remains very close to that formulated by Micale. However, Harris's piece also covers Charcot's research on hysterical children and parental authority; his visual representations of hysteria; his hypnotic and metallotherapeutic practice; and his dramatic attempts to establish an audience that would sustain his personality and ideas.

RHODRI LLOYD HAYWARD

Chemical Analysis

Brock, William H., *From Protyle to Proton: William Prout and the Nature of Matter, 1785–1985*, Bristol and Boston: Hilger, 1985

Brock, William H., *The Fontana History of Chemistry*, London: Fontana, 1992; as *The Norton History of Chemistry*, New York: Norton, 1993

Bud, Robert and Gerrylynn K. Roberts, *Science versus Practice: Chemistry in Victorian Britain*, Manchester: Manchester University Press, 1984

Golinski, Jan, *Science as Public Culture: Chemistry and Enlightenment in Britain, 1760–1820*, Cambridge and New York: Cambridge University Press, 1992

Hamlin, Christopher, *A Science of Impurity: Water Analysis in Nineteenth-Century Britain*, Bristol: Hilger, and Berkeley: University of California Press, 1990

Knight, David, *Humphry Davy: Science & Power*, Oxford and Cambridge, Massachusetts: Blackwell, 1992

Melhado, Evan M., *Jacob Berzelius: The Emergence of His Chemical System*, Stockholm: Almqvist & Wiksell, and Madison: University of Wisconsin Press, 1981

Oldroyd, David R., "Edward Daniel Cooke, 1769–1822, and His Role in the History of the Blow-Pipe", *Annals of Science*, 29 (1972): 213–35

Russell, Colin A., *Edward Frankland: Chemistry, Controversy and Conspiracy in Victorian England*, Cambridge and New York: Cambridge University Press, 1996

Russell, Colin A. (ed.), *Recent Developments in the History of Chemistry*, London: Royal Society of Chemistry, 1985

Russell, Colin A., Noel G. Coley and Gerrylynn K. Roberts, *Chemists by Profession: The Origins and Rise of the Royal Institute of Chemistry*, Milton Keynes: Open University Press, 1977

Szabadvary, Ferenc, *The History of Analytic Chemistry*, Oxford: Pergamon Press, 1966; revised and shortened version in *Comprehensive Analytical Chemistry*, vol. 10, edited by Cecil L. Wilson and David W. Wilson, Amsterdam: Elsevier, 1980

Chemical analysis represents something of a historiographical paradox: while biographies of individual chemists, and more thematic histories of chemistry, almost universally discuss the development of analytical techniques, there is relatively little literature on the history of chemical analysis itself. Thomas Thomson's inclusion of a long chapter on the history of chemical analysis in the second volume of his *History of Chemistry* (1831) was slow to develop into a common trend, and it was not until the translation of SZABADVARY's work in 1966 that a whole monograph devoted to the subject was available in English. In recent decades, however, chemical analysis has come to occupy the attention of an increasing number of scholars, even if it does remain a somewhat peripheral topic in the history of chemistry more generally. This essay will review the literature on late 18th- and 19th-century European developments, and will avoid mention of areas covered more thoroughly by separate entries in this book. This is particularly the case with Lavoisier and French chemical analysis during the chemical revolution of the late 18th century.

Although drawing on rather dated material, and now more than 10 years old itself, the survey of the literature on the history of chemistry by RUSSELL (1985) provides a good point of entry into the subject of chemical analysis. Chapter 8 looks at various types of analytical techniques – from combustion analysis to spectrometry and titrimetry – and offers short reviews and references to a selection of relevant literature. A second point of entry is provided by chapter 5 of BROCK (1992), in which he examines the development of various analytical techniques and the central problems associated with them, including the supply of adequate scientific instruments. Brock then goes on to discuss in more detail the problems encountered by Liebig in his development of techniques for analysing organic compounds.

As the above brief surveys suggest, historians generally locate the emergence of modern analytical techniques in the second half of the 18th century and chart its development through the 19th century. In Sweden, as MELHADO shows with reference to Bergman and Berzelius, the economic importance attached to mining and related industries had created the space in which chemists could develop proto-professional careers as mineralogical analysts. Dealing more particularly with the theoretical aspects of Berzelius's chemistry and its interaction with chemical practice, Melhado none the less shows that the rise of analytical chemistry was intimately bound up with the emergence of commercial and industrial interests. This particular theme is further examined by BUD & ROBERTS, in their study of the relationship between pure and applied chemistry in Victorian Britain. Again, although perhaps not their central argument, they do show that analytical expertise was crucial for the professional and institutional development of chemistry. Indeed, it is the question of professionalization that has most often concerned historians who write about chemical analysis. KNIGHT, in his biography of Humphry Davy, also draws attention to the way in which utilitarian concerns affected the type and nature of analyses undertaken by chemists. RUSSELL, COLEY & ROBERTS offer the most detailed and extensive study of this area, examining the role of the Royal Institute of Chemistry in the development of the chemical profession, and placing particular emphasis on the role of analytical skills and expertise. In short, during the first half of the 19th century in Britain, independent analysts benefited most, while by the turn of the century corporate chemists, working directly for industrial firms, rose to prominence. Similarly, HAMLIN, in his excellent study of the analysis of water, offers an account of the rise of the public analyst. Exploring the social and intellectual dynamics through which analysts approached the public health problems associated with municipal water supplies, Hamlin charts the development of expertise in analytical chemistry and places this within its social, political, and economic contexts. Hamlin also focuses on Edward Frankland, an important figure in the history of chemical analysis, whose contributions to chemical theory and practice are dealt with by RUSSELL (1996).

Questions concerning the relationship between analytical methods, modern economic culture and the professionalization of chemistry represent only one aspect of the history of chemical analysis. Other studies focus on the material culture of chemical analysis; for example, OLDROYD, in a now rather dated article, examines the work of Edward Daniel Clarke in order to explore the history of the development of technical instruments in the analysis of alkaline earth metals. BROCK (1985) also describes the instruments and apparatus used in chemical analysis in a short section, and places this within the context of the development of analytical chemistry and its more general theoretical implications. Focusing on the Glaswegian, John Joseph Griffin, BROCK (1992) has also discussed the trade in, and design of, analytical instruments.

Similar themes are explored by GOLINSKI, but his concern is more with the way in which such material cultures could be manipulated for rhetorical effect. In a fascinating study of the public nature of scientific display, Golinski suggests that public construction of scientific culture opens up possibilities for the manipulation by chemists of their own expertise and the public understanding of science in such a way as to enhance their own careers. Golinski thus provides a historiographical bridge between studies of the public nature of science and the professionalization of science. In his final chapter, he relates this directly to chemical analysis and analysts, showing how the utilitarian concerns of 19th-century Britain affected the development of analytical chemistry itself.

Chemical analysis is represented by a sparse and scattered selection of studies, the more important and accessible of which have been dealt with here. However, the topic itself remains understudied, and if the history of the practice of chemistry is to be understood more thoroughly this situation needs to be rectified.

SIMON A. NIGHTINGALE

Chemical Revolution

Bensaude-Vincent, Bernadette, *Lavoisier: Mémoires d'une revolution*, Paris: Flammarion, 1993

Bensaude-Vincent, Bernadette and Ferdinando Abbri (eds), *Lavoisier in European Context: Negotiating a New Language for Chemistry*, Canton, Massachusetts: Science History Publications, 1995

Clow, Archibald and Nan L. Clow, *The Chemical Revolution: A Contribution to Social Technology*, London: Batchworth Press, 1952

Conant, James Bryant, "Case 2: The Overthrow of the Phlogiston Theory: The Chemical Revolution of 1775–1789", in *Harvard Case Histories in Experimental Sciences*, vol. 1, Cambridge, Massachusetts: Harvard University Press, 1957

Donovan, Arthur L., *Philosophical Chemistry in the Scottish Enlightenment: The Doctrines and Discoveries of William Cullen and Joseph Black*, Edinburgh: Edinburgh University Press, 1975

Donovan, Arthur L., *Antoine Lavoisier: Science, Administration, and Revolution*, Oxford and Cambridge, Massachusetts: Blackwell, 1993

Golinski, Jan, *Science as Public Culture: Chemistry and Enlightenment in Britain, 1760–1820*, Cambridge and New York: Cambridge University Press, 1992

Gough, J.B., "Lavoisier and the Fulfillment of the Stahlian Revolution", *Osiris* (special issue), 2nd series, 4 (1988): 15–33

Guerlac, Henry, "Some French Antecedents of the Chemical Revolution", *Chymia*, 5 (1959), 73–112

Guerlac, Henry, *Lavoisier – the Crucial Year: The Background and Origins of His First Experiments on Combustion in 1772*, Ithaca, New York: Cornell University Press, 1961

Holmes, Frederic Lawrence, *Lavoisier and the Chemistry of Life: An Exploration of Scientific Creativity*, Madison: University of Wisconsin Press, 1985

Holmes, Frederic Lawrence, *Eighteenth-Century Chemistry as an Investigative Enterprise*, Berkeley: Office for History of Science and Technology, University of California, 1988

Hufbauer, Karl, *The Formation of the German Chemical Community, 1720–1795*, Berkeley: University of California Press, 1982

Kuhn, Thomas S., *The Structure of Scientific Revolutions*, Chicago: University of Chicago Press, 1962; revised edition, 1970

McEvoy, John G., "Joseph Priestley, 'Aerial Philosopher': Metaphysics and Methodology in Priestley's Chemical Thought, from 1762 to 1781", *Ambix*, 25 (1978): 1–55, 93–116, 153–75; 26 (1979): 16–38

Meinel, Christoph, "Artibus Academicis Inserenda: Chemistry's Place in Eighteenth and Early Nineteenth Century Universities", *History of Universities*, 7 (1988): 89–115

Perrin, Carleton E., "The Triumph of the Antiphlogistians", in *The Analytic Spirit: Essays in the History of Science in Honor of Henry Guerlac*, edited by Harry Woolf, Ithaca, New York: Cornell University Press, 1981, 40–63

Perrin, Carleton E., "The Chemical Revolution: Shifts in Guiding Assumptions", in *Scrutinizing Science: Empirical Studies of Scientific Change*, edited by Arthur Donovan, Larry Laudan and Rachel Laudan, Dordrecht and Boston: Kluwer, 1988, 105–24

Perrin, Carleton E., "Research Traditions, Lavoisier, and the Chemical Revolution", *Osiris* (special issue), 2nd series, 4 (1988): 53–81

Roberts, Lissa, "A Word and the World: The Significance of Naming the Calorimeter", *Isis*, 82 (1991): 199–222

Siegfried, Robert, "The Chemical Revolution in the History of Chemistry", *Osiris* (special issue), 2nd series, 4 (1988): 33–50

Siegfried, Robert and B.J. Dobbs, "Composition: A Neglected Aspect of the Chemical Revolution", *Annals of Science*, 24 (1968): 275–93

Thackray, Arnold, *Atoms and Powers: An Essay on Newtonian Matter-Theory and the Development of Chemistry*, Cambridge, Massachusetts: Harvard University Press, and London: Oxford University Press, 1971

The study of scientific revolutions has figured very prominently in the modern history and philosophy of science, and perhaps the most seminal book for both of these fields is KUHN. Kuhn saw the chemical revolution as a particularly clear-cut and illuminating example of a scientific revolution. Moreover, revolutionary language about the transformations in late 18th-century chemistry originated with the contemporary practitioners, particularly Priestley and Lavoisier.

According to Kuhn, each community of scientists is normally guided in its research by a paradigm, often embodied in a major textbook written by a founder-scientist. However, in the course of normal scientific research, scientists encounter observational or experimental "anomalies", the accumulation of which leads to a community "crisis". In response, a new paradigm is produced and triumphs over its predecessor, by persuasively accounting for the crisis-producing anomalies. The process of paradigm conflict and change is what Kuhn terms a scientific revolution.

The paradigms that Kuhn identified as in conflict in the chemical revolution were the phlogiston theory, and Lavoisier's anti-phlogistic chemistry as embodied in his *Traité élémentaire de chimie* (1789). The initiation of the chemical revolution was marked by a singular document: a sealed note deposited by Lavoisier with the Secrétaire perpétuale of the Académie des Sciences on 1 November 1772, which Kuhn characterized as the new paradigm "in embryo". In this document, Lavoisier recounted his experiments on the combustion of phosphorus and sulphur the previous August. He noted that great quantities of air united with the combustibles and caused weight gains in the products of these combustions. Lavoisier suggested that these findings might characterize combustion in general as well as calcination of metals.

According to the phlogiston theory, combustion and calcination were similar decomposition reactions in which combustibles and metals gave off a principle of inflammability called phlogiston. Substances rich in phlogiston were readily combustible and phlogiston also produced the peculiar features that characterize metals. Metals were produced from their calces (ores, oxides generally in modern terms) through the firing of the calces with charcoal. This process enabled the phlogiston-rich charcoal to supply phlogiston to the calces to produce the metal. Hence, metallic calces should be chemically simpler than metals; the metals were compounds of their calx and phlogiston. Kuhn asserted that the sealed note was a response to a crisis in chemistry that had developed by the early 1770s from anomalies to the phlogiston theory arising from two sources: the proliferation of new gases since Joseph Black had identified "fixed air" (CO_2) in 1756, and the increasing concern on the part of chemists with weight gain during the calcination of metals. What moved this crisis into revolution was the discovery of a new gas which supported combustion vigorously. Although made by a number of chemists, Kuhn concentrated on the discoveries by Priestley (1774) and Lavoisier (1775): Priestley, still adhering to the phlogiston theory, named the gas "dephlogisticated air"; however, under the name "oxygen", subsequently given to it by Lavoisier, this gas became the centerpiece of a new theory of combustion and calcination that was almost a mirror-image of the phlogiston theory. According to the oxygen theory, these reactions were in fact syntheses in which oxygen gas united with the combustibles and metals.

The rest of Kuhn's sketch of the chemical revolution could be termed "the overthrow of the phlogiston theory" and its supplanting by the oxygen theory of combustion and calcination. This reflected the prevalent view of the chemical revolution (e.g. CONANT). However, Kuhn offered only the most cursory sketch of the process of paradigm conflict and triumph.

When Kuhn's book was published, Lavoisier and the chemical revolution were among the most prominent subjects of research in the nascent discipline of the history of science. There had already been impressive French scholarship on this subject, which has been joined by British and American scholarship. Henry Guerlac and his students constitute the central research school on Lavoisier and the chemical revolution of the post-Kuhnian quarter century. In GUERLAC (1961), the personal background and origins of Lavoisier's chemical studies are rooted in the mid-1760s and Germanic chemical influences. In fleshing out the details of Lavoisier's life and complex scientific career, features of Lavoisier's scientific style and practice receive greater prominence as delineators of the chemical revolution: the "book-keeping" style of his gravimetric chemistry (resulting in the principle of the conservation of matter), the linguistic and epistemological influence of the Abbé de Condillac, the denomination of oxygen as the principle of acidity, and conception of "matter of heat" or "caloric" heat as an imponderable material substance (these last two simultaneously undergoing positive re-evaluation).

By the 1970s, scholars began to challenge the primacy given to the Lavoisian focus for comprehending 18th-century chemistry and the chemical revolution. SIEGFRIED & DOBBS suggest that the classification of earths and salts, and the movement for nomenclature reform based on the classification of these substances, was of comparable importance to the overthrow of the phlogiston theory. THACKRAY's study of the 18th-century "Newtonian dream", the quest for a dynamical chemistry of affinity forces, provided an image of late 18th-century chemical concerns startlingly different from the traditional Lavoisian-centered picture.

Meanwhile, others were studying the chemical activities and the formation of scientific communities outside France: DONOVAN (1975) in Scotland and HUFBAUER in Germany. There were also some detailed biographical studies of protagonists in the chemical revolution other than Lavoisier; McEVOY's series of essays on Priestley are perhaps the most elaborate, and situated Priestley's chemistry in a broad philosophical and theological context. Returning to Lavoisier, DONOVAN (1993) offered the novel suggestion that he should not even be viewed primarily as a chemist; rather, his orientation was that of an experimental physicist, which accounts for the peculiar features of his methodology – such as his insistence on complex instrumentation and quantitative precision. HOLMES (1985) gives the most intricately detailed study of Lavoisier's scientific practice yet to appear. However, he shifts the emphasis away from simply "the overthrow of the phlogiston theory" (although this is not neglected), to a consideration of Lavoisier's studies of vital chemical phenomena.

By the late 1980s, the first essays attempting a synthesis of these decades of scholarship on the chemical revolution appeared in time for the bicentenary of the publication of Lavoisier's Traité élémentaire de chimie (1789). Their focus has been on Lavoisier and Priestley as the chief protagonists of the chemical revolution. In the case of Lavoisier, in particular, the scholarship continues to be prodigious. But the details of Kuhn's analysis of the chemical revolution have been modified, amended, and even contradicted. Although the supplanting of the phlogistic explanation of combustion and calcination by the oxygen theory is still important, it has lost some of its centrality, as other aspects of Lavoisier's thought, research methodology, and actual investigations have come to be studied in detail. The paradigmatic status of the phlogiston theory itself has been seriously problematized by studies of 18th-century research; for example, it only became widely taught in France at the same time that Lavoisier himself was entering into chemical studies, and it is now clear that, for many areas of chemical investigation (the chemistry of organic substances and chemical affinity theory), the phlogiston theory was at most of marginal importance.

Perhaps of greatest importance, the crisis in the phlogiston theory in the early 1770s, so central to Kuhn's dynamics of the chemical revolution, has been shown to have been largely fictitious. Neither the English pneumatic chemists, nor even Lavoisier himself (at least initially) viewed their research as raising any serious difficulty for phlogistic chemistry; on the contrary, they saw this research as positively extending the domain of the phlogiston theory (PERRIN, 1988, "Research Traditions, Lavoisier, and the Chemical Revolution").

Moreover, detailed studies of Lavoisier's research in the 1770s, particularly by Holmes (1985) and Perrin (1988), "Research Traditions, Lavoisier, and the Chemical Revolution", have implicitly disputed Kuhn's denomination of the sealed note as a "paradigm in embryo", and have emphasized the complex, contingent and sometimes contradictory directions of Lavoisier's thought and work in subsequent years. The most appropriate metaphor for Lavoisier's theoretical position in these years might be "double vision", for he held what retrospectively appear to be incompatible beliefs concerning phlogistic chemistry and the "new" chemistry for several years. There is certainly no evidence for a sudden "gestalt shift" on his part from phlogiston to oxygen, and the process by which other chemists and scientists were converted to the antiphlogistic chemistry was neither simple nor sudden (PERRIN, 1988 "The Chemical Revolution: Shifts in Guiding Assumptions"). Indeed, what has been most striking is the analysis of the entrepreneurial role of Lavoisier himself in "selling" his new chemistry to his colleagues in France and abroad (PERRIN, 1981).

It should be obvious that "the characteristics of [scientific revolutions] which emerge with particular clarity" in the study of the chemical revolution are not so clear to present-day scholars as they were to Kuhn. Some scholars have even suggested decentering Lavoisier from the discourse on the chemical revolution: in the case of GOUGH, returning to Georg Ernst Stahl, the originator of phlogiston chemistry; and in the case of SIEGFRIED, going forward to John Dalton, the developer of the chemical atomic theory. Perhaps HOLMES (1988) provides the most provocative decentering of the chemical revolution, when he depicts a mosaic of century-long research traditions independent of phlogiston chemistry, notably the chemistry of salts and plant chemistry: "Lavoisier reconstructed not the whole of chemistry, but only a crucial domain within a larger science."

In the 1990s, a research orientation new to the history of chemistry focused on textual analyses: the structure of chemical texts, their choice of terms, their audiences, their relationship to contemporary social contexts and their political rhetoric. Kuhn may have provided a point of departure by his suggestion that paradigms were embodied in scientific textbooks and that the cumulative view of scientific progress was an artifact of "textbook" science, but these analyses go far beyond anything implied by Kuhn. Associated with this textual orientation has been the study of the reception of the new chemistry (and new chemical nomenclature) outside of France. BENSAUDE-VINCENT situates Lavoisier's career and the concept of the chemical revolution within social and cultural contexts, while BENSAUDE-VINCENT & ABBRI provide a comparative study of Lavoisier's chemistry in various parts of Europe. ROBERTS attends to the spread of instrumentation and terminology, while GOLINSKI relates the social role of British chemists to the structural and rhetorical style of their chemical writings.

Although Kuhn had highlighted the role of "scientific communities" in his dynamics of paradigm reception and articulation, there was little historical literature on this subject when *The Structure of Scientific Revolutions* was published. Since then, there have been important studies on the social and professional organization and status of chemistry in the 18th

century: in Scotland by DONOVAN (1975), in Britain by Golinski, in Germany by Hufbauer, and in the German universities by MEINEL. Yet we still lack a European-wide study of the formation of the chemical discipline in the 18th century. Nor, amazingly, do we have a study for France remotely comparable to Hufbauer's for Germany. Detailed studies of the profiles and roles of sub-groups within each chemical community, (for example, the apothecaries), are also needed.

Finally, a word on one aspect of 18th-century chemistry that was completely absent from Kuhn and has been largely ignored since then: the technological context. Chemistry was (and is) the quintessential "mixed" science, as much concerned with making and developing useful materials and products as generating scientific knowledge, and this was already recognized in the 18th century. The focus on technological utility was highlighted in some of the earlier literature; for instance CLOW & CLOW, the first modern book entitled *The Chemical Revolution*, was subtitled "A Contribution to Social Technology". The perceived (or hoped for) utility of chemistry for a range of professional, practical, and industrial activities played a major role in the professional formation of chemistry in the mid-18th century. The time has come for new scholarship on the technological context of 18th-century chemistry and the chemical revolution.

SEYMOUR H. MAUSKOPF

Chemistry

Bensaude-Vincent, Bernadette and Isabelle Stengers, *A History of Chemistry*, translated from the French by Deborah van Dam, Cambridge, Massachusetts: Harvard University Press, 1996

Beretta, Marco, *The Enlightenment of Matter: The Definition of Chemistry from Agricola to Lavoisier*, Canton, Massachusetts: Science History Publications, 1993

Brock, William H., *The Fontana History of Chemistry*, London: Fontana, 1992; as *The Norton History of Chemistry*, New York: Norton, 1993

Corsi, Pietro and Claudio Pogliano (eds), *Storia delle Scienze 4*, Torino: Einaudi, 1994

Crosland, Maurice P., *In the Shadow of Lavoisier: The Annales de Chimie and the Establishment of a New Science*, Chalfont St Giles, Buckinghamshire: British Society for the History of Science, 1994

Golinski, Jan, *Science as Public Culture: Chemistry and Enlightenment in Britain, 1760–1820*, Cambridge and New York: Cambridge University Press, 1992

Hammond, P.W. and Harold Egan, *Weighed in the Balance*, London: HMSO, 1992

Hoffmann, Roald, *Chemistry Imagined: Reflections on Science*, Washington, DC: Smithsonian Institution Press, 1993

Hudson, John, *The History of Chemistry*, London: Macmillan, and New York: Chapman and Hall, 1992

Knight, David, *Ideas in Chemistry: A History of the Science*, London: Athlone Press, and New Brunswick, New Jersey: Rutgers University Press, 1992; 2nd edition, 1995

Mason, Stephen F., *Chemical Evolution: Origins of the Elements, Molecules and Living Systems*, Oxford:

Clarendon Press, and New York: Oxford University Press, 1991

Nye, Mary Jo, *From Chemical Philosophy to Theoretical Chemistry: Dynamics of Matter and Dynamics of Disciplines, 1800–1950*, Berkeley: University of California Press, 1993

Russell, Colin A. (ed.), *Recent Developments in the History of Chemistry*, London: Royal Society of Chemistry, 1985

Russell, Colin A., Noel G. Coley and Gerrylynn K. Roberts, *Chemists by Profession: The Origins and Rise of the Royal Institute of Chemistry*, Milton Keynes: Open University Press, 1977

The history of chemistry has been a focus of interest in recent years, with important books being written both by practising chemists and by historians of chemistry. Part of the reason for this is the unease that chemists feel about the reputation of their science. Around 1800, large audiences flocked to hear chemical lectures, and chemistry was considered to be useful as well as exciting: Lavoisier had worked on gunpowder, Humphry Davy on fertilizers, and the life of the novice and chemical expert was understood to be spiced with interest and danger. Now, schoolchildren find chemistry dull, while explosives and fertilizers seem as much a threat as a boon. Perhaps the history of chemistry might enliven interest in a fascinating subject.

Lavoisier and his associates gave the science a new, technical vocabulary, designed to eliminate metaphor and render chemical writing factual, brief and precise, and thus unattractive to the outsider. Since then, nomenclature of compounds has become increasingly rebarbative, and the dependence on symbols and equations has made chemical publications forbidding. Thus, it is difficult to present the history of chemistry as momentous and interesting, which it undoubtedly is, without using language that inhibits those without considerable knowledge of the science, who may continue to consider it highly technical, and rather alarming. "Chemistry" used cheerfully to be called "stinks"; now, more sinisterly, the word "chemicals" usually means "poisons".

It is perhaps odd to study the history of chemistry apart from that of other sciences. Experimental physics and Linnean botany were in different ways important models for Lavoisier, while chemists such as Michael Faraday strayed across what are now well-policed boundaries. The very handsomely-illustrated CORSI & POGLIANO, which covers the 19th and 20th centuries, has three chapters on chemistry, by John Brooke, David Knight and Stephen Mason, and thus places the science in its intellectual context among other sciences. It is manifest after all that the frontiers between sciences are socially constructed.

HOFFMANN is an extremely distinguished chemist, and his book is the record of an exhibition mounted at various places in the US and in Germany, and contains collages illustrating historical themes. Hoffmann's text includes poems – like Davy, he is a published poet – and is attractively written. Refusing to reduce chemistry merely to physical laws, Hoffmann asserts that chemistry is a creative process and that its central quality is synthesis. An ambitious popular work by another distinguished chemist is MASON, which brings together the history of chemistry and the (chemical) history of the universe. There is no doubt that both these authors make chemistry momentous, and draw fruitfully upon its long history (although Mason's highly-compressed text is not always easy going), in order to show relevance to the chemistry of today.

The history of chemistry and chemical institutions is charted by RUSSELL, COLEY & ROBERTS, written to mark the centenary of the Institute of Chemistry. This, in a great disruption, had parted from the Chemical Society of London in 1877, and after a century apart, as a professional and a learned body respectively, they came together again as the Royal Society of Chemistry in 1977. The authors used this opportunity to write a social history of chemistry, raising all sorts of general questions as they handled sometimes parochial issues, avoiding both chemical and sociological jargon.

HAMMOND & EGAN have continued in this vein with their history of the Laboratory of the Government Chemist in Britain. This began with the testing of tobacco and alcoholic drinks for taxation purposes from 1842, but grew with the importance of the science, and acquired functions in what we would call consumer protection. The adulteration of foodstuffs, the limits of analysis (with the development of physical methods in chemical practice), and the emergence of careers in chemistry (with tensions between civil servants and outside consultant chemists), are all covered in a readable and stimulating work.

CROSLAND has approached the subject rather differently, studying in particular the journal that Lavoisier and his associates published to promote his chemical revolution. Not only do we discover why some issues were on blue paper, and learn a lot generally about scientific publication at a period when the journal began to be more important than the book, but we also find out a great deal about the chemical revolution and the dynamics of science in revolutionary and Napoleonic France, especially Paris. We learn much about how chemistry was perceived c.1800 as the basic science of the day, offering both utility and theoretical excitement, and about the French scientific community when it led the world in most fields. The study of the journal also opens up foreign connections, and there are interesting questions raised about intellectual communication: study abroad, and foreign contacts, were particularly important in chemistry. This journal was also a major factor in making the careers of many chemists.

Lavoisier effectively made chemistry a French science, and BERETTA charts its history and development up to and beyond Lavoisier's work. Beretta reveals that Lavoisier's associates did not like being seen as the full supporting cast for a chemical star, and that chemists abroad often referred to the new chemistry as "French", seeing it as the product of a committee rather than an individual. Exactly how much was Lavoisier's own is still being debated, but his role in making a science out of the unsystematized practices of pharmacy, metallurgy and gas-manipulation was clearly crucial. Beretta's study of the definition of chemistry in the preceding centuries does help us to focus clearly upon its transformation at the end of the 18th century, and the close study of language, naming, and theory makes the book valuable.

GOLINSKI concentrates on the period of the chemical revolution, and suggests that an enlightened attitude to new knowledge, such as Joseph Priestley's belief that science had the potential to empower the many, gave way to the idea that chemistry was necessarily a spectator-sport, practised by the talented and privileged few. The idea is a fascinating one, and directly relates to the idea of "two cultures" and to modern problems with chemistry; certainly, science in the 19th century became a method of social mobility for ambitious young men, rather than a force for democracy. Golinski is very learned, and so, unfortunately, is his language, which also draws heavily upon what literary critics are pleased to call theory.

We can confine this survey to recent works because of RUSSELL, whose essays and bibliographies make it an excellent place to start. A crop of general histories of chemistry appeared in the early 1990s: part of a useful series of histories, BROCK is a *tour de force*, achieving a good mixture of the survey and the close case-study. The bibliography is extensive and helpful, and the writing clear and unpretentious, managing to deal with a very wide variety of people, places, and times. It would be difficult to recommend this book too highly.

HUDSON's book is explicitly addressed to students and practitioners of chemistry, and aims to enrich their studies by introducing a historical dimension. It is a very useful introduction for those who might feel alarmed by more self-conscious historical writing, like that of NYE, who is concerned with the growth of research schools and disciplines, especially from the later 19th century – thus covering some of the same ground as Brock. The two books complement each other: Nye emphasizes how those who control the language in chemistry control the science, and she creates a Darwinian-style picture of competitive schools headed by powerful individuals, and also of different national traditions. Her language is not lively, but the structural formulae, like those in Hoffmann, have been specially drawn, and both books make much of their implications. Nye's introduction and conclusion raise general questions with which all historians of chemistry should be concerned.

BENSAUDE-VINCENT & STENGERS have organized their book with a strong thematic emphasis; Bensaude-Vincent has also written a biography of Lavoisier, and as we might expect their book is particularly strong on the chemical revolution. Nevertheless, its treatment of the subject is lucid and remarkably extensive, and its European perspective makes it a valuable counterpoise to Brock's.

Even more thematically organized is KNIGHT, which sets out to be a biography of the science, running from the occult science of alchemy, through the reduction of chemistry to physics, and to the emergence of chemistry as the service science of the 20th century. The book sets out to be accessible to readers with or without knowledge of modern chemistry, who may have believed that physics and biology were the only interesting physical sciences.

We have glanced at the history of an institution, a laboratory, and a journal, as well as at more general histories; for chemistry is a vast topic, and its history – apart perhaps from the chemical revolution and the overthrow of the phlogiston theory – has been little noted among philosophers of science and general historians. This is a pity, for the close relations of theory and experiment in the science, and its utility, make it distinct and instructive, and its history has the potential, as some of these authors show, to be absorbing and entertaining.

DAVID KNIGHT

China: general works

Bodde, Derk, *Chinese Thought, Society, and Science: The Intellectual Background of Science and Technology in Pre-Modern China*, Honolulu: University of Hawaii, 1991

Elvin, Mark *et al.*, "Symposium: The Work of Joseph Needham", *Past and Present*, 87 (1980): 17–53

Nakayama, Shigeru and Nathan Sivin (eds), *Chinese Science: Explorations of an Ancient Tradition*, Cambridge, Massachusetts: MIT Press, 1973

Needham, Joseph (ed.), *Science and Civilisation in China*, 7 vols, Cambridge: Cambridge University Press, 1954–

Needham, Joseph, *The Grand Titration: Science and Society in East and West*, Toronto: University of Toronto Press, and London: Allen and Unwin, 1969

Needham, Joseph, *Science in Traditional China: A Comparative Perspective*, Cambridge, Massachusetts: Harvard University Press, 1981

Orleans, Leo A. (ed.), *Science in Contemporary China*, Stanford, California: Stanford University Press, 1980

Ronan, Colin A. (ed.), *The Shorter "Science and Civilization in China": An Abridgement of Joseph Needham's Original Text*, 5 vols, Cambridge: Cambridge University Press, 1978–81

Sivin, Nathan (ed.), *Science and Technology in East Asia*, New York: Science History Publications, 1977

Sivin, Nathan, "Science and Medicine in Imperial China – The State of the Field", *Journal of Asian Studies*, 47 (1988): 41–90

SIVIN (1988), a long review article, is the best guide to current scholarship on the subject of science and medicine in China, offering perceptive comments and an extensive bibliography.

NEEDHAM's monumental project *Science and Civilization in China* (1954–), covers a wide range of topics in Chinese science and technology, and promises to conclude with an examination of the social background. The series is divided into seven volumes, each of which contains several parts, with each part devoted to a scientific subject. Needham's work has revolutionized our understanding of traditional Chinese science, and for decades it held authority on many of the subjects it examined. The scheme of the work is explained in volume 1; it is Needham's belief that ancient and medieval sciences of different civilizations met and merged into a stream of modern science, which appeared around the 17th century and had no cultural boundaries, and his aim is to bring to light pre-17th-century Chinese contributions to the development of modern science. By now, Needham's conceptual framework and style of scholarship seem old-fashioned, and he eventually conceded a little to criticisms of his social and economic generalizations, his traditional approach to the history of science, and his almost mystical view of the course of civilization. Nevertheless, Needham (1954) remains absolutely the most comprehensive and important work on this subject. RONAN provides an abridged version, now in its fifth volume.

Beginners and non-specialists may find Needham's grand *oeuvre*, or even the abridgement, overwhelming. Fortunately, two books of a manageable size provide a good sample of

Needham's work. NEEDHAM (1969) is a collection of eight of his important early essays, and is concerned primarily with the issues of science and social change, Chinese contributions to the development of "modern universal science", and Chinese and Western attitudes toward nature and time. In NEEDHAM (1981), a series of lectures delivered before a largely Chinese audience in the early 1980s, he ventures further into areas of alchemy, medicine, and the biological sciences. Both works aim to place the history of Chinese science within a global context.

The symposium in ELVIN et al. consists of three long critical essays of high quality, in which Needham's work on Chinese philosophy of nature, mathematics, and astronomy is examined. The introduction by Elvin effectively points out the limitations of Needham's whiggism.

Originally written for inclusion in *Science and Civilization in China*, but published separately because of the author's scholarly disagreement with Needham, BODDE's book has paradoxical features: on the one hand, Bodde takes pains to argue against Needham's generally more favorable view of the effects of traditional Chinese thought and society on the development of science; but on the other hand, he shares with Needham the same approach and conceptual framework. Bodde examines the Chinese language, concepts of time and space, religion, government and society, morals and values, and attitudes to nature, and in the end produces something like a balance-sheet assessing the positive and negative effects of Chinese thought and society on the development of science. The negative elements ultimately overpower the positive, and as a result he concludes that modern science did not (and could not) arise from China.

The volume edited by NAKAYAMA & SIVIN, though uneven and largely superseded, is still valuable for its topical variety and informative bibliography. About half of the 10 essays are devoted to discussing Needham's work, including that by A.C. Graham, an expert on Chinese philosophy. The other essays explore some of the then new research areas in the history of Chinese science, such as medicine and optics.

SIVIN (1977) has gathered 19 articles on the history of east Asian science originally published in *Isis*, the premier American journal of the history of science, in a single volume. With one or two exceptions, all the essays concern China. The introductory essay brings together the themes covered in this miscellaneous collection and provides a good overview of the state of the field in the late 1970s. Meanwhile, science in contemporary China has attracted increasing scholarly interest, and the thick volume edited by ORLEANS may provide a convenient starting point. It includes more than two dozen substantial papers, covering all major disciplines of the natural and social sciences.

FA-TI FAN

China: agriculture

Bray, Francesca, *Agriculture*, vol. 6, part 2 of *Science and Civilisation in China*, edited by Joseph Needham, Cambridge: Cambridge University Press, 1984

Chao, Kang, *Man and Land in Chinese History: An Economic Analysis*, Stanford, California: Stanford University Press, 1986

Elvin, Mark, *The Pattern of the Chinese Past*, London: Eyre Methuen and Stanford, California: Stanford University Press, 1973

Hsu, Cho-yun, *Han Agriculture: The Formation of Early Chinese Agrarian Economy, 206 BC–AD 220*, edited by Jack L. Dull, Seattle: University of Washington Press, 1980

Huang, Philip C.C., *The Peasant Economy and Social Change in North China*, Stanford, California: Stanford University Press, 1985

Huang, Philip C.C., *The Peasant Family and Rural Development in the Yangzi Delta, 1350–1988*, Stanford, California: Stanford University Press, 1990

Perdue, Peter C., *Exhausting the Earth: State and Peasant in Hunan, 1500–1850*, Cambridge, Massachusetts: Harvard University Press, 1987

Perkins, Dwight H., *Agricultural Development in China, 1368–1968*, Edinburgh: University of Edinburgh Press, and Chicago: Aldine, 1969

Rawski, Evelyn Sakakida, *Agricultural Change and the Peasant Economy of South China*, Cambridge, Massachusetts: Harvard University Press, 1972

Unlike some other branches of knowledge, it is impossible to write an internalist history of agriculture. Although such factors as climate, ecology, and the inherent dynamics of certain cropping systems exercise constraints on how an agricultural system can develop, the evolution of a country's farming practices and knowledge cannot be understood in isolation. Such social, economic, and political factors as who owned land, how it was distributed, how rents and taxes were levied, and the role of the state all play an important role in the history of agriculture.

From before the founding of the empire in 220 BC, and right through to the People's Republic, the Chinese state has always played an active role in "encouraging agriculture". This involved investment in infrastructure, such as dams and irrigation systems, the opening up of new land, dissemination by officials of new crops and techniques, and fiscal policies to encourage their adoption. But the state tended to disapprove of entrepreneurial activity and of the commercialisation of farming, and the beneficiaries of its policies were small peasant farmers rather than the gentry, the rich landlord class from whom the state's officials were drawn. As the population grew from a 100 million in the 10th century to more than 400 million by 1850, landlordism increased (although the land was almost all rented out to peasants on small farms, rather than managed in large estates), and the amount of land available to feed each individual fell. Most scholars agree, however, that it was only at the end of the 18th century that a vicious cycle of rural impoverishment set in. It is the social questions arising from this historical trajectory that have set the agenda for almost all the works discussed here.

Unlike other civilisations, in which either the educated elite had little interest in technical matters or periods of disruption leave blanks in the historical record, the Chinese elite and the Chinese state were obsessed with agriculture, and there are no gaps in the record after the founding of the empire – though of course some periods or aspects are better documented than others. BRAY is the only work that attempts a complete historical survey. Written as part of Needham's study of all the Chinese sciences from their origins up to the incursion of the West, it focuses on the evolution of agriculture as a technology, tracing the development of cultivation methods and field systems, of implements and machinery, and of crops and their varieties. Unlike any of the other works, it is lavishly illustrated.

An advantage of the thematic approach is that it provides a more thorough understanding of the practicalities of farming. A disadvantage is that it becomes more difficult to draw an overall picture of Chinese agriculture in any one period, or to discuss the interactions between farming and society that either encouraged or impeded its development over time. One prominent theme in the history of Chinese agriculture is that of "development" versus "stagnation": ELVIN is a study of China between c.900 and the modern era, and treats agriculture as one theme in an exploration of the reasons behind China's failure to sustain the economic transformations and the innovative brilliance that distinguished its culture between 900 and 1400. Why did China not develop industrial capitalism, or undergo a scientific revolution? Part of the answer, Elvin says, lies in the nature of Chinese rice farming technology; it could only produce quantitative growth, and absorbed the extra labour offered by increases in population only at the cost of diminishing returns – what Elvin calls "involution". True "development" would have required a qualitative transformation in labour productivity, such as that experienced in the industrialising West with agricultural mechanisation.

PERKINS prefigures Elvin's arguments in his analysis of the relations between population, agricultural methods, and output. He is more positive in his assessment of how well Chinese agriculture succeeded in sustaining a growing population, arguing that until about 1800 it was essentially a success story; however, he argues that all significant technical innovations had been disseminated throughout China by 1400. Only in the 1960s did a true process of modernisation begin, with a total restructuring of rural production. Although less technical than Perkins, CHAO takes a similar stance in his re-examination of demography and agriculture, but looks more closely at issues such as rural class structure.

Although Perkins and Chao, like Elvin, freely acknowledge that crop breeding, the use of new fertilisers, and improved irrigation practices were important in increasing yields subsequent to that date, all of them agree that this kind of improvement was far outstripped by the significance of mechanical inventions. To uphold their argument of technical stagnation, both Perkins and Chao compare the major treatises of the 17th and 18th centuries with a famous treatise of 1313, remarking that the former record no important implements or machinery not already documented in the precursor of 1313.

Chinese writers have produced a series of great agricultural treatises over the centuries. However, since they combine description with prescription they should not be treated as an infallible guide to local practice, as both RAWSKI and PERDUE demonstrate. The techniques they advocate were often adopted much later than Perkins suggests, when local conditions made this desirable or inevitable. Rawski looks at how differences in access to markets in the 17th and 18th centuries affected farming practices in neighbouring localities, and led to new geographical patterns of specialisation: populous regions that became rich through producing large rice surpluses started to specialise in other, more profitable, commodities, and new centres of rice production developed to fill the gap. Perdue examines the gradual and differentiated intensification of agriculture in a remote province, focusing on the negotiations and conflicts between officials, landlords, and peasants, and underlining the key role played by the late imperial state in promoting technical development and in attempting to control the degradation of resources.

HSU, like Perdue, believes that agricultural change and "peasant rationality" cannot be understood without reference to the framework of action imposed by the state. His study examines farming techniques in the context of the shifting balance of power between state and landowning elites in the early empire, and its effect on peasant farmers, whom he sees as responding rationally to markets whenever this was feasible. At the other end of the historical spectrum, HUANG (1985) examines the question of "rationality", once China entered the modern world economy. He asks why "managerial farming", apparently the economically rational solution to the conditions of North China, was so limited in its development, and concludes that early 20th-century peasants operated according to different forms of rationality – market-oriented or Chayanovian – depending on the size of their enterprise. HUANG (1990) also addresses the question of involution, this time looking at China's traditionally most advanced economic region, and bringing his study right up to the present day. He argues that only with the post-1980 abandonment of collective production did true qualitative development and an increase in rural prosperity become possible.

FRANCESCA BRAY

China: astronomy and mathematics

Chen Zungui, *Zhongguo tianwenxue shi* [History of Chinese Astronomy], 3 vols, Beijing: Kexue Chubanshi, 1980

Cullen, Christopher, *Astronomy and Mathematics in Ancient China: The Zhou bi suan jing*, Cambridge: Cambridge University Press, 1996

Ho Peng Yoke, *Li, Qi and Shu: An Introduction to Science and Civilization in China*, Hong Kong: Hong Kong University Press, 1985

Keizi Hashimoto, *Xu Guang-Qi and Astronomical Reform: The Process of the Chinese Acceptance of Western Astronomy*, Osaka: Kansai University Press, 1988

Lam, Lay Yong and Ang Tian Se, *Fleeting Footsteps: Tracing the Conception of Arithmetic and Algebra in Ancient China*, Singapore and River Edge, New Jersey: World Scientific, 1992

Li Yan and Du Shiran, *Chinese Mathematics: A Concise History*, translated from the Chinese by John N. Crossley and A.W.-C. Lun, Oxford: Clarendon Press, 1963

Libbrecht, Ulrich, *Chinese Mathematics in the Thirteenth Century: The Shu-Shu Chiu-Chang of Ch'in Chiu-shao*, Cambridge, Massachusetts: MIT Press, 1973

Major, John S., *Heaven and Earth in Early Han Thought: Chapters Three, Four and Five of the Huainanzi*, with an appendix by Christopher Cullen, Albany: State University of New York Press, 1993

Martzloff, Jean-Claude, *A History of Chinese Mathematics*, translated from the French by Stephen S. Wilson, Berlin and New York: Springer, 1997 (original edition, 1988)

Needham, Joseph, *Science and Civilization in China*, vol. 3: *Mathematics and the Sciences of the Heavens and the Earth*, Cambridge and New York: Cambridge University Press, 1959

Qian Baocong (ed.), *Zhongguo shuxue shi* [History of Chinese Mathematics], Beijing: Kexue Chubanshu, 1964 and 1981

Yabuuti Kiyosi, *Chugoku no tenmonrekiho* [History of Chinese Astronomy], Tokyo: Heibonsha, 1969 and 1994

Yabuuti Kiyosi, *Chugoku no Sugaku* [Chinese Mathematics], Tokyo: Iwanami shoten, 1974 and 1994

Zhongguo tianwenxue shi [History of Chinese Astronomy], Beijing: Kexue Chubanshu, 1987

NEEDHAM's monumental and pioneering work introduced Chinese traditional astronomy and mathematics to Western readers, and encouraged subsequent generations to explore this subject and to attempt to gain further knowledge of the field. It remains one of the best introductions to the topic, blazing a trail through the hitherto unknown Chinese texts on astronomy and mathematics.

HO provides a good introduction to the basic concepts of Chinese mathematics and astronomy, such as *li* (which Needham translates as pattern), *qi* (pneuma), and *shu* (number). The translations are of course awkward, as there are no English words that refer unambiguously to the Chinese concepts. Ho's discussion is not chronological but conceptual, and is helpful for a historical understanding of Chinese science in general. To some extent, the rest of the literature is divided up into the history of astronomy on the one hand, and the history of mathematics on the other, and the literature will be covered in that order.

CHEN's three-volume work documents the entire Chinese history of astronomy, and is intended for specialists. There are many quotes from the primary literature and as such the book is a very useful source, although the citations are not always entirely reliable. Chen was trained in Japan in the pre-Communist era, and he does not espouse the nationalism of some of the later works.

ZHONGGUO is a good basic text on the history of astronomy in China from ancient times to the present day, and provides a useful overview. The emphasis is very much on Chinese achievements, and it is symptomatic that the treatment of the introduction of Western astronomy into China in the 17th century is a little hostile.

YABUUTI (1969) is a collection of essays on mathematical astronomy, and examines the importation of the calculation methods of Islamic astronomy into China in the 13th century. These methods were developed in order to predict the orbits of the planets, sun, and moon – corresponding to what would now be called celestial mechanics, except that the calculational methods were not accompanied by our conception of celestial bodies moving in space.

CULLEN provides a translation and contextualisation of the *Zhou bi suan jing*, one of the oldest classics of Chinese cosmology and mathematics, that is traditionally dated to the western Zhou period, in the 11th century BC. Cullen describes in full the development of the cosmology of a round heaven and a square earth, and he explains the background to the *Zhou bi*, its origins, and later history.

Cosmological thought is also foregrounded in the chapters of the *Huainanzi*, a treatise of the 2nd century BC (early Han dynasty); three chapters of which are translated in MAJOR. The *Huainanzi* is a compilation of monographs on natural philosophy and statecraft, of which chapter 3 concerns astronomy and astrology, chapter 4 calendrical sciences, and chapter 5 geography.

KEIZI HASHIMOTO describes the introduction of European astronomy into 17th-century China, focusing especially on the role played by the Tychonic compromise between geocentric and heliocentric models of the universe. The Jesuits brought the *Astronomia Danica* to China, where they had it translated into Chinese. It had been written by one of Tycho's students, Longomontanus, and it contained a Tychonic theory of planetary motion. The Jesuits, Jacobus Rho and Adam Schall von Bell, were instrumental in effecting the translation, but the main translator was in fact Xu Guangqi (1562–1633), a high-ranking official who was to become prime minister of China.

In the history of mathematics, there are both general histories and translations of seminal texts. LI & DU provide a readable and popular general history. Li Yan was the founding father of the Chinese history of mathematics; it was he who initiated the discipline in China, unearthing much of the mathematics done in China in the past, and most historians of mathematics in China today are Li's students.

QIAN is very much to be recommended, as an excellent introduction to Chinese mathematics that covers the history comprehensively while providing the necessary detail. YABUUTI (1974) is a readable and popular text covering developments until 1900. A French translation of this text by Catherine Jami and Kaoru Baba will soon be available.

MARTZLOFF is the only general text in a Western language on the history of Chinese mathematics, an English edition of which is to appear shortly. Divided into two parts (on context and content), it is implicitly anti-Marxist and anti-Needham; for example, Martzloff ends his study at 1600, the point at which Needham postulates the beginning of the confluence of the great rivers of Eastern and Western science. One of the major problems with this work is that its translations into French are idiosyncratic. For example, Martzloff emphasises the absence of copulas in the Chinese language, using question marks and exclamation marks to denote the strangeness of the Chinese texts, and the result is at times nonsensical. Martzloff also ignores almost all contemporary French work in the field.

There are two translations of important Chinese texts into Western languages: Lam & Se, and Libbrecht. LAM & SE have translated the *Sunzi suanjing* (*The Mathematical Classic of Sun Zi*) of approximately AD 400 which describes and gives examples of rod numerals, and the processes of multiplication and division. Lam & Se chose this text, rather than the very first text on Chinese arithmetic, *Jiu zhang suanshu* (*Nine Chapters on Mathematical Art*), in order to analyse the evolution of arithmetic, and its subsequent extension into algebra, within the Chinese context.

LIBBRECHT is a pioneering book in a Western language, which translates and annotates Qin Jiushao's monumental

13th-century work. Qin's work was ground breaking, revealing the emergence of techniques for dealing with equations quite similar to algebra. The 13th century is considered the golden age of Chinese mathematics, and this translation makes a substantial text available, with extensive annotations and only a few mistranslations.

KEIZO HASHIMOTO

China: medicine

Andrews, Bridie J., *The Making of Modern Chinese Medicine, 1895–1937*, dissertation, University of Cambridge, 1996

Benedict, Carol, *Bubonic Plague in Nineteenth-Century China*, Stanford, California: Stanford University Press, 1996

Bray, Francesca, *Technology and Gender: Fabrics of Power in Late Imperial China*, Berkeley: California University Press, 1997

Croizier, Ralph C., *Traditional Medicine in Modern China: Science, Nationalism and the Tensions of Cultural Change*, Cambridge, Massachusetts: Harvard University Press, 1968

Farquhar, Judith, *Knowing Practice: The Clinical Encounter of Chinese Medicine*, Boulder, Colorado: Westview Press, 1994

Furth, Charlotte, *A Flourishing Yin: Gender in China's Medical History, 970–1670*, Berkeley: University of California Press, 1997

Harper, Donald J., *Early Chinese Medical Literature: The Mawangdui Medical Manuscripts*, London: Kegan Paul, 1997

Katz, Paul R., *Demon Hordes and Burning Boats: The Cult of Marshal Wen in Late Imperial Chekiang*, New York: State University of New York Press, 1995

Keegan, David, *The Huang-ti nei-ching: The Structure of the Compilation, the Significance of the Structure*, dissertation, University of California, Berkeley, 1988

Kleinman, Arthur K. *et al.* (eds), *Medicine in Chinese Cultures: Comparative Studies of Health Care in Chinese and Other Societies*, Bethesda, Maryland: National Institutes of Health, 1975

Kleinman, Arthur K., *Patients and Healers in the Context of Culture: An Exploration of the Borderland Between Anthropology, Medicine and Psychiatry*, Berkeley: University of California Press, 1980

Lu Gwei-Djen and Joseph Needham, *Celestial Lancets: A History and Rationale of Acupuncture and Moxa*, Cambridge and New York: Cambridge University Press, 1980

McKnight, Brian E., *The Washing Away of Wrongs: Forensic Medicine in Thirteenth-Century China*, Ann Arbor: Center for Chinese Studies, University of Michigan, 1981

Needham, Joseph and Lu Gwei-Djen, *Spagyrical Discovery and Invention: Physiological Alchemy*, in *Science and Civilisation in China*, vol. 5, Cambridge: Cambridge University Press, 1983

Sivin, Nathan, *Traditional Medicine in Contemporary China: A Partial Translation of Revised Outline of Chinese medicine (1972) with an Introductory Study on Change in Present-day and Early Medicine*, Ann Arbor: Center for Chinese Studies, University of Michigan, 1987

Unschuld, Paul U., *Medicine in China: A History of Ideas*, Berkeley: University of California Press, 1985 (original edition, 1980)

Unschuld, Paul U. (ed. and trans), *Nan-Ching: The Classic of Difficult Issues, with Commentaries by Chinese and Japanese Authors from the Third through the Twentieth Century*, Berkeley: University of California Press, 1986

Unschuld, Paul U., *Medicine in China: A History of Pharmaceutics*, Berkeley: University of California Press, 1986 (revised and enlarged translation of *Medicine in China: The Nan-Ching*, 1986)

Unschuld, Paul U., *Forgotten Traditions of Ancient Chinese Medicine: The I Hsüeh Yüan Liu Lun of 1757 by Hsü Ta-Ch'un*, Brookline, Massachusetts: Paradigm, 1990

Wong, K. Chimin and Wu Lien-teh, *History of Chinese Medicine*, 2nd edition, Shanghai: National Quarantine Service, 1936; reprinted, New York: AMS Press, 1973; also reprinted, Taipei: Southern Materials Center, 1985

Zhao Bichen, *Traité d'alchimie et de physiologie taoïste: Introduction, traduction et notes par Catherine Despeux*, Paris: Les Deux Océans, 1979

Works on Chinese medical history in Western languages may be divided into three main types: annotated translation, formal history, and historically-informed anthropology. The genres will be considered in that order.

HARPER provides critical annotated translations of the seven medical manuscripts recovered in 1973 from a tomb at Mawangdui sealed in 168 BC. These texts include discussions of physiological theories and pathology, recipe manuals for the treatment of ailments, sexual treatises, and illustrations of health-nurturing exercises. As such, they provide unique access to the range of medical concerns of China in the 3rd and early 2nd century BC. One of Harper's main findings is that incantations, exorcising rituals, and other magical techniques were interspersed without prejudice among recipes for the compounding of medicines and for therapeutic treatments. He argues that, "The blanket repudiation of magical practices by professional physicians implied in the extant historical documents and *belles-lettres* of the Han period reflects only the fortuitous preservation of the opinions of those hostile to magic." KEEGAN's dissertation uses texts from the same excavation to reconstruct a theory of how the earliest extant recensions of the *Huangdi nei jing* (Yellow Emperor's Inner Canon/Classic) may have been constructed from collations of such shorter texts.

McKNIGHT translated and annotated the *Xi yuan lu* (*Washing Away of Wrongs*), the manual of forensic medicine first written for imperial magistrates in the 13th century, and supplemented and annotated in different editions for the rest of China's imperial history. This work is unique in the Chinese tradition for its description of the human skeleton, although this knowledge was used for determining whether a person had received injuries before death rather than for strictly medical purposes.

Paul Unschuld aims to make the original Chinese medical literature available in Western languages; all his works contain substantial translated passages, and two are primarily translations with annotations. UNSCHULD (1986) provides a translation of both the received canonical text of the *Classic of Difficult Issues* and 20 different Chinese and Japanese commentaries on it, providing powerful evidence for the importance of the exegetical tradition in the development of Chinese medicine. In UNSCHULD (1990), he explores the theoretical writing of an 18th-century "Confucian" medical scholar, Xu Dachun, *Forgotten Traditions*. Unschuld's two volumes entitled *Medicine in China*, UNSCHULD (1985) and UNSCHULD (1986), also contain long translated passages, which he uses to good effect in order to demonstrate the range of therapies present in the medical literature of China, making the point that not all medicine was of the "rational" secular kind. His text-based, chronological approach sometimes means that the *History of Pharmaceutics* volume, in particular, sometimes reads like a well-annotated bibliography. None the less, Unschuld's publications are an essential introduction to the history of Chinese medicine.

Unschuld's concern to describe the history of less orthodox therapies is one he shares with Harper, but such topics were unfashionable in the 1970s and 1980s, and explicitly rejected by Needham and Sivin in their efforts to upgrade Western perceptions of Chinese medical accomplishments.

Catherine Despeux's translation and study of ZHAO BICHEN's Daoist (Taoist) manual of "inner (or physiological) alchemy" written in the 1890s shows that the author made use of Western physiological texts, then newly available in Chinese translation, to confirm the Daoist view of the importance of the brain and spinal cord in these practices. (There is little role for the brain or spinal cord in orthodox Chinese medicine.) Despeux's useful introduction places this late 19th-century text within the context of the history of Daoist meditative practices, which are clearly explained.

SIVIN's translation of a mainland Chinese introductory textbook (for physicians of Western medicine studying Chinese medicine) of 1972, documents the Communist medical orthodoxy of this period, while his introduction places it in its historical context. In his view, the ongoing reforms to orthodox Chinese medicine result in more rather than less incoherence, since aspects of Western medicine are being borrowed without any overall plan of development. The English terms he has coined to represent Chinese medical terminology are a useful reference guide, and have been generally adopted by later historians. Sivin translates only the first, theoretical part of the textbook, and does not discuss *materia medica* or Chinese-medical formulary.

The development of the history of Chinese medicine in Western languages continues to be intimately related to political and scholarly developments in China. Thus, WONG & WU, writing in the 1930s, criticized aspects of Chinese medicine that they perceived to be superstitious or non-rational. Their scope is large, and the book contains much useful historical data, especially on the history of Western medicine in China. However, even their version of the history of Chinese medicine, from which the most offensively irrational elements had been purged, was still too unscientific for many Chinese modernizers of the early 20th century, and CROIZIER describes the battles between the modernizers and the supporters of Chinese medicine as a vital component of China's

cultural heritage. If Croizier's dichotomy between so-called cultural conservatives and cultural modernizers is a little overdrawn, ignoring the ways in which conservatives modernized Chinese medicine in this period, his book remains the most useful and politically-informed study of medicine (and, to some extent, Chinese cultural history) in this period. ANDREWS's dissertation problematizes Croizier's assumption of conservatives versus progressives, and attempts to find reasons both for the early Chinese disinterest in Western medicine, and the influence of Western medicine on Chinese medicine in the 20th century. She argues that "traditional" Chinese medicine is in fact largely a new, sanitized product of the 20th century that accommodates much Western medical theory.

The great emphasis on tonics and the nurturing of vitality in Chinese medicine and healing is reflected in other activities and therapies aimed at the promotion of longevity, such as martial arts, *qigong*, *taijiquan*, and meditative and alchemical practices. There are as yet no satisfactory monographs in Western languages on the history of Chinese physical exercise techniques, but there is growing interest in what NEEDHAM & LU term physiological alchemy in volume 5 of *Science and Civilisation in China*. Here they examine the corpus of Daoist literature concerned with the achievement of immortality, and discuss methods of producing life-extending elixirs from bodily substances and meditative practices. As biochemists, they are concerned to establish the scientific bases of such practices.

The diversity of Chinese medical history is further developed by the work of Charlotte Furth and Francesca Bray on women's medicine as a specialty within Chinese medicine, and on gender issues within orthodox medicine. FURTH reconstructs the rich, but neglected, learned tradition of "medicine for women" (*fuke*) over the long span of the Song, Yuan, and Ming Dynasties (970–1644). Through use of case histories and literary sources, she locates medicine within the context of the social relations of family life. Challenging holistic interpretations, she shows how *fuke* was influenced by changing social and intellectual patterns, how it revealed conflicting patient voices, and was clinically pluralistic. Furth addresses theoretical issues concerning the history and anthropology of the body through the analysis of the relationship of language, text, and practice. Similar issues are taken up by BRAY in chapters 6 to 9, in which she discusses the technologies of reproduction and fertility control available to Chinese women in late imperial China. A theme of Bray's work is the way technology is used to negotiate power relations. More functionalist in her approach than Furth, Bray considers why the orthodox medicine of a society in which women without sons were considered to be social failures, accepted abortion, and portrayed the treatment of any menstrual irregularity (which might include early pregnancy) as essential to a woman's basic health. The apparent paradox is resolved once we realize that biological and social motherhood were distinct. China was monogamous, and wives were the legal mothers of children born to their husband's concubines. Thus, polygyny benefited elite women by allowing them to appropriate the fertility of women lower down the social scale, with medical theory justifying such exploitation.

BENEDICT examines an epidemic of bubonic plague that began in south-west China in the 18th century, spread throughout much of southern China in the 19th century, and eventually exploded on the world scene as a global pandemic. She offers an analysis of how economic growth and development along China's south-western frontier produced ecological changes in the 18th century that promoted the spread of plague; the geographical diffusion of the disease closely followed the growth of inter-regional trade networks, particularly the domestic trade in opium, in the 19th century. Discussion of late 19th-century foreign interventions during plague outbreaks along China's southern coast links the history of plague to the political impact of imperialism on China. Finally, the book documents the emergence of police-directed plague control measures during the New Policies reform era (1900–11), arguing that such initiatives were consistent with a more general trend toward state penetration of local society in the final decade of Qing rule.

KATZ's study of the cult of the epidemic-fighting deity, Marshal Wen, in the late imperial Zhejiang province is intended to demonstrate the existence of an important and often overlooked social space within Chinese society. Rather than engaging with the vexed question of whether there was a "civil society" or a public sphere within China, Katz argues that local temples and their festivals were:

> an important Chinese public space where opinions were formed and manipulated, where significant elite activism took place, where merchants attempted to increase their power and prestige, where conflicts could be resolved in a semi-institutional setting, and in where both state and society attempted to assert their interests while also compromising with each other.

For historians of medicine, the studies by both Katz and Benedict provide concrete examples of how communities attempted to deal with outbreaks of epidemic disease in Chinese history.

The Communist promotion of the new technique of "acupuncture analgesia" during the Cultural Revolution of 1966–76 prompted a great deal of Western interest in the late 1970s, and it was to meet this demand that LU & NEEDHAM published their study of the history of acupuncture. Their biological training and commitment to the scientific basis of acupuncture led them to devote much of the book to theories of its physiological action in Western terms. Nevertheless, the historical survey they provide is meticulously documented and engagingly written.

Finally, the following are anthropological studies of medicine in China. The extent to which the secular "Chinese medicine" of most 20th-century writing represents only a fraction of healing practices in Chinese history again became evident in the 1970s with the publication of anthropological studies of different Chinese healing practices. The volume edited by KLEINMAN et al. is a useful collection of such studies, although its anthropological reports are all restricted to Chinese communities outside the People's Republic of China. This was because fieldwork was not then possible in mainland China, and because many "popular" or "folk" healing practices had been discouraged by the Communist government.

KLEINMAN's monograph is an important study of the ways that culture shapes an individual's perception of bodily health and illness (medical phenomenology). His insights are a useful resource to historians wishing to understand the possible subjective meanings of Chinese medical writings.

During the early 1980s, it again became possible for anthropologists to conduct fieldwork in mainland China, and FARQUHAR's book is the result of 18 months of participant observation at the Guangzhou College of Traditional Chinese Medicine, 1982–84. Her main argument is that both the theories and the literature of Chinese medicine may be properly understood only in relation to clinical practice, as the social dimensions of the clinical encounter do not merely affect medical practice, they constitute it. Farquhar suggests that this insight may also be applied to Western biomedicine. Her work combines close readings of the Chinese medical literature with ethnographic observations, which are then analyzed within their social and historical contexts, providing another useful resource for historians of medicine.

B.J. ANDREWS

See also Acupuncture

China: natural history

Bretschneider, Emil, *On the Study and Value of Chinese Botanical Works, with Notes on the History of Plants and Geographical Botany from Chinese Sources*, Foochow, China: Rozario Marcal, 1870
Bretschneider, Emil, "Botanicon Sinicum: Notes on Chinese Botany from Native and Western Sources", *Journal of the North-China Branch of the Royal Asiatic Society* (new series), 16 (1882): 18–230; 25 (1893): i–ii, 1–468; 29 (1896): 1–623
Hu, Shiu Ying, "History of the Introduction of Exotic Elements into Traditional Chinese Medicine", *Journal of the Arnold Arboretum*, 71 (1990): 487–526
Laufer, Berthold, "Sino-Iranica: Chinese Contributions to the History of Civilization in Ancient Iran", *Publications of the Field Museum of Natural History* (anthropological series), 15 (1919): i–iv, 185–630
Li, Hui-Lin (ed.), *Nan-fang ts'ao-mu chuang: A Fourth Century Flora of Southeast Asia*, Hong Kong: Chinese University Press, 1979
Needham, Joseph, "Botany," in his *Science and Civilization in China*, vol. 6, part 1, Cambridge and New York: Cambridge University Press, 1986
Schafer, Edward H., *The Golden Peaches of Samarkand: A Study of T'ang Exotics*, Berkeley: University of California Press, 1963
Schafer, Edward H., *The Vermilion Bird: T'ang Images of the South*, Berkeley: University of California Press, 1967
Schafer, Edward H., *Shore of Pearls: A Study of Hainan Island and Its History*, Berkeley: University of California Press, 1970
Unschuld, Paul U., *Medicine in China: A History of Pharmaceutics*, Berkeley: University of California Press, 1986 (original edition, 1980)

Accounts of the development of Chinese natural history are few: there is no broad synthetic work available in English, and much of the existing literature is densely packed with specialized detail and esoteric terminology, which always tend to dampen the enthusiasm of a beginner.

Edward Schafer has written a number of excellent books on medieval Chinese perceptions of, and experiences in, other lands. They contain rich information about natural history writing in medieval China. The best known of them is probably SCHAFER (1967), an erudite account of the 7th- and 8th-century Chinese images of the conquered southern regions. The reader is invited to accompany this eminent sinologist through the riches of ethnographical and natural historical descriptions, culled from contemporary Chinese literature. The chapters are divided by subject – peoples, animals, plants, and so on. Schafer suggests that, trapped by their preconceptions and literary techniques, the Chinese first used expressions from the established literary tradition, relying on clichés and stereotypical images. Only after a long period were new images and metaphors discovered, which would eventually be assimilated into mainstream Chinese literature. SCHAFER (1963) and SCHAFER (1970) are written in the same vein, but cover respectively a larger (Samarkand in Central Asia) and a smaller (Hainan Island, close to the Vietnamese border) geographical region.

UNSCHULD's survey of Chinese herbal writing is also fairly accessible. Unlike Schafer, he does not try to capture the cultural imagination of a particular era, but attempts to trace and analyze the intellectual tradition of Chinese pharmaceutical writing. This work consists of an introductory essay and a succession of histories and close readings of dozens of medicinal herbals. It has many well-chosen excerpts from primary texts. The first part of HU's wide-ranging article has a brief account of the history of Chinese materia medica. By comparing the plants included in ancient Chinese pharmacopoeias, Hu demonstrates that many traditional Chinese medicinal plants were originally exotics introduced from Central Asia and other regions in different periods. Although its general conclusion is not new, this article is valuable for its original research and useful tables.

Volume 6 of NEEDHAM's *Science and Civilization in China* is devoted to biology, agriculture, and medicine, areas in which the Chinese lore of natural history lies. Part 1, on botany, has been published, and is the most comprehensive work on that subject. It begins with modern geo-botany, explaining the geographical setting of China's flora, and then proceeds to examine the Chinese systems of plant terminology and nomenclature. When turning to the botanical literature and its content, Needham organizes his investigation according to literary genres and chronology. In accordance with the whole Needham series, this work covers only the period before the 17th century. To historians, one limitation of Needham's encyclopedic approach is that it fails to give the cultural context of the age in which the botanical literature was produced.

Needham's book benefits a great deal from the efforts of two erudite precursors, Bretschneider and Laufer. Both were prolific authors, and much of their writing remains invaluable. BRETSCHNEIDER (1870) draws heavily on traditional Chinese botanical texts and aims to persuade Western botanists of the scientific value of these sources. It contains illustrations copied from a 19th-century Chinese botanical encyclopedia. BRETSCHNEIDER (1882–96) is an expanded version of the 1870 volume. Both works are basically organized by plant families and have become standard texts in the study of traditional Chinese botany. LAUFER's monograph examines the cultural contacts between ancient Iran and China, with emphasis on cultivated plants and products. It also uses many primary Chinese sources.

LI has translated one of the first Chinese botanical texts into English, with a long introduction and knowledgeable commentaries. The original text was traditionally alleged to have been written in the 4th century, but scholars generally now agree that it could only have been composed centuries later. In any case, it remains a representative and entertaining piece of Chinese botanical literature.

FA-TI FAN

Clinical Science

Booth, Christopher C., *Doctors in Science and Society: Essays of a Clinical Scientist*, London: British Medical Journal, 1987

Booth, Christopher C., "Clinical Research", in *Companion Encyclopedia of the History of Medicine*, edited by W.F. Bynum and Roy Porter, 2 vols, London and New York: Routledge, 1993

Bynum, W.F., *Science and the Practice of Medicine in the Nineteenth Century*, Cambridge and New York: Cambridge University Press, 1994

Clouser, K. Danner (ed.), special issue on "Clinical Medicine as Science", *Journal of Philosophy and Medicine*, 2/1 (1977)

Corner, George W., *A History of the Rockefeller Institute, 1901–1953*, New York: Rockefeller Institute Press, 1964

Harden, Victoria A., *Inventing the NIH: Federal Biomedical Research Policy, 1887–1937*, Baltimore: Johns Hopkins University Press, 1986

Harvey, A. McGehee, *Science at the Bedside: Clinical Research in American Medicine, 1905–1945*, Baltimore: Johns Hopkins University Press, 1981

Hollman, Arthur, *Sir Thomas Lewis: Pioneer Cardiologist and Clinical Scientist*, Berlin: Springer, 1997

King, Lester S., *Medical Thinking: A Historical Preface*, Princeton, New Jersey: Princeton University Press, 1982

Matthews, J. Rosser, *Quantification and the Quest for Medical Certainty*, Princeton, New Jersey: Princeton University Press, 1995

Meynell, G.G., *Materials for a Biography of Dr. Thomas Sydenham: A New Survey of Public and Private Archives*, Folkestone, Kent: Winterdown Books, 1988

Rothman, David J., *Strangers at the Bedside: A History of How Law and Bioethics Transformed Medical Decision Making*, New York: Basic Books, 1991

Warner, John Harley, "The History of Science and the History of Medicine", in *Constructing Knowledge in the History of Science*, edited by Arnold Thackray, *Osiris* (1995), 2nd series, vol. 10

Clinical science is to some degree a phenomenon of the 19th century, as the growth of academic medicine has created a new kind of research-orientated clinician. More generally, of course, a great deal of the medical knowledge of the past has been gleaned at the bedside, and thus can be called clinical. Accordingly, BOOTH's useful survey (1993) of what he calls clinical research begins in antiquity, but concentrates on modern times, when a more formal association between bedside investigation and academic medicine was established.

KING has analysed the issues that have historically confronted doctors seeking to make intellectual sense of a variety of signs, symptoms, and complaints from their patients. He is concerned with the systems of thought behind the creation of the "clinical entity" (disease or syndrome), and with the variety of methods employed to establish chains of causation in the clinical setting. MEYNELL explains that Thomas Sydenham (1624–89) was particularly important in demonstrating that careful bedside observation can reveal specific diseases which, despite individual variation from patient to patient, are sufficiently constant to be classified. One of the essays ("Clinical science in the Age of Reason") in BOOTH (1987; Booth is himself a clinical scientist) examines the ways in which 18th-century clinicians attempted to further the Sydenhamian programme. Their methods included the increasing use of multiple case reporting, and the attempt to evaluate various forms of therapy, most famously in James Lind's work on scurvy, and William Withering's introduction of digitalis in the treatment of dropsy (oedema).

BYNUM has used the relationship between basic science and clinical practice during the 19th century as a way of assessing how science influenced clinical practice. The development of more systematic diagnostic tools, symbolised above all by the stethoscope, (invented by René T.H. Laënnec in 1816), and the correlation of the signs and symptoms of disease with the changes observed at autopsy, were the hall-marks of the hospital, or clinical, approach. In a historiographically rich essay, WARNER has astutely analysed the variety of connotations that the word "science" had for 19th-century doctors, arguing that clinical science continued to have its own traditions and methods, and was not simply the adaptation of laboratory attitudes and findings at the bedside.

The phrases "clinical science" and "clinical research" have acquired somewhat different meanings since the late 19th century, a development associated above all with the rise to prominence of American medical education and research. HARVEY has described a range of issues instrumental in this phenomenon, but confirms that the rise of the full-time academic clinician was especially important. Important institutions included the medical schools at Johns Hopkins, Columbia, Harvard, Chicago, Yale, Michigan and other elite American universities. Money from private foundations, above all the Rockefeller Foundation, was crucial, and the Rockefeller Institute (now Rockefeller University) in New York City had an attached hospital devoted to clinical research. CORNER provides a history of the Rockefeller Institute.

Although philanthropy continues to be important in funding American clinical research, the dramatic expansion since World War II has largely resulted from government funds, both at the massive National Institutes of Health (the history of which can be found in HARDEN) in Bethesda, Maryland, and through the university medical schools.

Sir Thomas Lewis (1881–1945) was the central figure in British developments. He was an early pioneer in the emerging speciality of cardiology, but he became increasingly preoccupied with more general aspects of what he called clinical science. His small Department of Clinical Research at University College Hospital, London was funded principally by the Medical Research Council, the British government's mechanism for channelling public money into biomedical research. HOLLMAN has produced a full biography of Lewis, while BOOTH (1987) analyses the reasons why Lewis's general influence was not as catalytic as it might have been.

Clinical research, by definition, involves human subjects, and ethical issues now figure prominently in public perceptions of the field. Both ethical and conceptual aspects of clinical science were considered in a special issue of the *Journal of Philosophy and Medicine*, edited by CLOUSER. More specifically, ROTHMAN has surveyed the ways in which informed consent and patients' rights have interacted with the problems and power of high-tech medicine, in areas such as organ transplantation, brain death, and human experimentation. At a more routine level, new drugs and therapeutic procedures must be rigorously compared with existing alternatives. This requires experimental design to eliminate, or at least minimise, participant bias, and proper controls. MATTHEWS has analysed the quantitative impulse in clinical medicine from the time of Pierre Louis (1787–1872) to the development of the modern double-blind clinical trial by Sir Richard Doll (b. 1912) and Sir Austin Bradford Hill (1897–1991).

W.F. BYNUM

Clinical Trials

Armitage, Peter, "Trials and Errors: The Emergence of Clinical Statistics", *Journal of the Royal Statistical Society*, 149 (1983): 321–34

Armitage, Peter, "Bradford Hill and the Randomised Controlled Trial", *Pharmaceutical Medicine*, 6 (1992): 23–37

Bull, John P. "The Historical Development of Clinical Therapeutic Trials", *Journal of Chronic Diseases*, 10/3 (1959): 218–43

Cox-Maksimov, Desirée C., The Making of the Clinical Trial in Britain 1910–1945: Expertise, the State and the Public, dissertation, Cambridge University, 1997

Lilienfield, Abraham, "Ceteris Paribus: The Evolution of the Clinical Trial", *Bulletin for the History of Medicine*, 56 (1982): 19–29

Marks, Harry M., "Notes from the Underground: The Social Organisation of Therapeutic Research", in *Grand Rounds: One Hundred Years of Internal Medicine*, edited by Russell C. Maulitz and Diana E. Long, Philadelphia: University of Pennsylvania Press, 1988

Marks, Harry M., *The Progress of Experiment: Science and Therapeutic Reform in the United States, 1900–1990*, Cambridge and New York: Cambridge University Press, 1997

The randomised controlled clinical trial (RCT) has been hailed as a revolutionary innovation, and has been widely accepted as the standard for determining the therapeutic efficacy of medicines and medical techniques. Defended as unbiased and scientific, the method involves randomly sorting patients into a "control" group (treated in the usual way), and a "test" group (to which the medical therapy on trial is given). In the case of the double-blind RCT, neither the subject nor the investigator knows the identity of individual members of the groups.

RCT has recently become the subject of scholarly attention and there is little in the way of published work on it. Histories of this medical innovation are transmitted orally by those who remember the early clinical trials of Austin Bradford Hill, or who are involved in the shaping of the present-day RCT. Many of the short historical articles published on the RCT, written by physicians and statisticians, place heavy emphasis on the origin of randomisation and in particular on Austin Bradford Hill, who introduced randomisation into the trial of streptomycin in 1946–48. This clinical trial is generally defined as the first proper RCT, and the RCT itself as an essentially British invention. Accounts by the physician John P. Bull, the medical statistician Peter Armitage, and the epidemiologist Abraham Lilienfield have become significant examples of these early histories.

More recently, concerned with how particular therapies have acquired cultural meanings, scholars have produced historical and sociological studies of specific clinical trials. Clinical trials have also been used as evidence in thematic histories of human experimentation, most of which focus on experimentation in America. However, the making of the clinical trial in other cultures, particularly Britain, invites historiographic inquiry into how histories of the clinical trial should be periodized, and how they should expose moral issues of the method – issues that have yet to be addressed. COX-MAKSIMOV's dissertation deals with the development of the clinical trial in Britain during the first part of the 20th century, showing how the clinical trial was shaped by, and helped to shape, the state, and exploring the relationship between the trial, the state and the British public.

At present, the historical accounts of John P. Bull, Peter Armitage, Abraham Lilienfield, and the historian of medicine, Harry Marks, have emerged as standard texts on the subject. BULL, a physician who was involved in non-randomised clinical trials with plasma substitutes on burns patients at the MRC Burns Unit in Birmingham during the late 1940s and 1950s, wrote his history of the clinical trial in 1951. He argued that the conduct of "clinical trials" can be traced back to the ancient Egyptians. Bull's history is based on the premise that experiments designed to assess the value of therapeutic procedures on patients have always been an essential feature of medicine, and that therapeutic procedures have always been "clinical trials". Highlighting historic events – such as Avicenna's rules for testing drugs, Francis Bacon's suggestion of a committee of physicians to judge therapeutic efficacy, James Lind's comparative trial of scurvy "cures", and P.C.A. Louis's application of his numerical method in the clinic – Bull presents a linear account of the development of the clinical trial. The implication in this narrative is that, cumulatively, these historic experiments made the clinical trial progressively more scientific. The discovery of new drugs (such as salvarsan, digitalis, insulin, and penicillin) and the multitude of patients produced by World War I, provided the materials and the opportunity

for the conduct of increasingly sound clinical trials in the 20th century. Although Bull notes that Bradford Hill's introduction of randomisation modernised the clinical trial, he places it within a much larger, historical context of continuous human experimentation.

Peter Armitage is a medical statistician who experienced first-hand the establishment of medical statistics as a field in its own right. As a past president of the Royal Statistical Society, and now a retired professor of the department of biomathematics at Oxford University, ARMITAGE (1983) presents the RCT as a crucial part in the creation of medical statistics. In this article, in which he traces the historical influences of Philippe Pinel, P.C.A. Louis, and Claude Bernard on the evolution of medical statistics, Armitage argues that the "modern era" of medical statistics started with the streptomycin clinical trial associated with Austin Bradford Hill. ARMITAGE (1992) connects Bradford Hill's personal history with the evolution of the clinical trial in Britain. Armitage, who knew Bradford Hill personally, takes Bull's account as the pre-history of the RCT. He notes that Bradford Hill learned his statistics from Karl Pearson and Major Greenwood, and argues that, as a member of the Medical Research Council's (MRC) Statistical Committee, Bradford Hill was first involved in advising on the statistical analysis of the therapeutic trials organised by the MRC's Therapeutic Trials Committee during the 1930s. However, he does not provide archival evidence for this, nor does he show how the Statistical Committee, or the Therapeutic Trials Committee, made their judgements about the therapeutic efficacy of substances they accepted for clinical trial. Armitage argues that Bradford Hill clarified his ideas about the design and benefit of randomisation in therapeutic trials during the 1930s, publishing many of them in his series on statistics and medicine in *The Lancet* in 1937. Significantly, he claims that, although this innovation was originally discovered by R.A. Fisher in 1923, "Hill would have accepted randomisation on common-sense grounds and would have been unimpressed by Fisher's sophisticated advocacy". Armitage argues that in 1946, within the context of rationed supplies of streptomycin donated to the MRC from America, Bradford Hill, who sat on the MRC's *ad hoc* committee set up to organise the streptomycin trials, suggested the randomisation of patients and treatments. He offers Bradford Hill's promotion of the RCT during the 1950s and 1970s as an explanation for its institutionalization.

Abraham LILIENFIELD, an eminent American epidemiologist, divides the clinical trial into separate components – comparative therapeutic analysis, randomisation, and blind or masked therapeutic assessment – and likens these so-called historical variables to the factors of an epidemiological equation in order to show how the RCT came into being. Systematically charting evolutionary paths for each of these components, he argues that the main goal of each, and their fusion in the clinical trial, is to achieve *ceteris paribus*, "all other factors being equal", and that these different species of therapeutic trial were united in the clinical trial during the 20th century. In tracing the history of comparative studies, hinted at in the Old Testament but actively pursued in the comparative studies of Lind in the 18th century, through to the 20th century, Lilienfield argues that it is from this strand that controls, alternating controls and controlled series originate.

He demonstrates that the concept of controls can be found in the late 19th century. While Lilienfield stands with Armitage in crediting the discovery of randomisation to R.A. Fisher, he dates J. Burn's trial of sanocycin (gold therapy) for pulmonary tuberculosis in Michigan as the first recorded, randomised controlled trial. This was also the first blind trial.

Harry Marks, now professor of the history of medicine at the Johns Hopkins University, has written an intellectual history of the clinical trial. MARKS (1988), in his historiographical article on the clinical trial, argues that it was a part of an impetus for co-ordinated clinical research, and that the conviction that careful organisation and management would make clinical research more efficient and credible was central to the development of the RCT in America during the 20th century. MARKS (1997), based on his doctoral dissertation, examines the beliefs and activities of a disparate group, which he labels "therapeutic reformers", who operated through institutional structures (such as the Council of Pharmacy and Chemistry, the US Food and Drug Administration, and various universities) and used the science of controlled experiments to direct medical practice. In so doing, they framed the randomised controlled clinical trial during the first part of the 20th century, and furthered its institutionalization in America from the 1950s onwards. In this social and intellectual history of therapeutic experiments in the 20th century, Marks argues that, while laboratory sciences provided the standard of the "well-controlled" experiment for medicine, during the second half of the century the clinically-based, randomised controlled trial offered a new standard of scientific excellence.

D.C.T. Cox-Maksimov

Clocks

Andrewes, William J. H. (ed.), *The Quest for Longitude*, Cambridge, Massachusetts: Collection of Historical Scientific Instruments, Harvard University, 1996

Bedini, Silvio, *The Pulse of Time: Galileo Galilei, the Determination of Longitude, and the Pendulum Clock*, Florence: Olschki, 1991

Bedini, Silvio, *The Trail of Time: Time Measurement with Incense in East Asia*, Cambridge and New York: Cambridge University Press, 1994

Cipolla, Carlo, *Clocks and Culture, 1300–1700*, London: Collins, and New York: Walker, 1967

Dohrn-van Rossum, Gerhard, *History of the Hour: Clocks and Modern Temporal Orders*, translated from the German by Thomas Dunlap, Chicago: University of Chicago Press, 1996 (original edition, 1992)

Landes, David S., *Revolution in Time: Clocks and the Making of the Modern World*, Cambridge, Massachusetts: Harvard University Press, 1983

Needham, Joseph, Wang Ling and Derek J. de Solla Price, *Heavenly Clockwork: The Great Astronomical Clocks of Medieval China*, Cambridge: Cambridge University Press, 1960; 2nd edition with supplement by John H. Combridge, 1986

Sherman, Stuart, *Telling Time: Clocks, Diaries, and English Diurnal Form, 1660–1785*, Chicago: University of Chicago Press, 1996

Sobel, Dava, *Longitude: The True Story of a Lone Genius who Solved the Greatest Scientific Problem of His Time*, New York: Walker, 1995; London: Fourth Estate, 1996

The literature on clocks in this entry can be grouped into several types. One concerns itself with the experience of time in different historical periods, one can be described as economic history, one addresses time in different cultures (specifically Western or non-Western), and the last concerns itself with the problem of longitude.

DOHRN-VAN ROSSUM's book is primarily a history of medieval time with a brief summary of developments up to the creation of standardized "world time" in the late 19th century. But the book can also serve as a historiographical guide, since it rehearses much of the history of time and clocks, and indeed argues against most of it. One main line of argument seeks to debunk the theory that clocks provided primarily a means of control, particularly over work time. Against Jacques Le Goff in particular, who called the medieval communal clock a distant precursor of Taylorism, Dohrn-van Rossum arrays a great many historical sources to argue that time-keeping was not a story of special interests prevailing against opposition. He acknowledges that a wide range of innovations in temporal organization was made, but he denies any overarching explanation, such as the logic of capital. With regard to narrow history of science and technology themes, he also argues against Lynn Thorndike, Lewis Mumford, and Alistair Crombie that the division of the hour into 60 minutes had not become customary as the framework of thought and action by 1345, but only in the late 17th century.

Cipolla and Landes are economic historians who both locate a part of European economic and imperial success in the history of clocks. CIPOLLA uses the development of tower clocks from 1300 to 1700 to depict the gradual artisanal development of precision mechanics out of the practice of blacksmiths. He describes the increasing miniaturization resulting from accumulating skills.

LANDES is an eminent economic historian with a passion for antique clocks. He argues that the mechanical clock was a seminal invention that helped turn Europe from a peripheral outpost into a hegemonic aggressor. He describes the technical development of the clock over 500 years before turning to an economic history of clocks. There is much detail on individual clockmakers and guilds, especially in Switzerland and Britain. The emphasis is always on economic competition, and the book concludes with the decline of the mechanical clock when it had to face competition from quartz clocks made in Japan and the US.

As is often the case, most of the literature on clocks is based on Western material, and both Needham, Ling & Price, and Bedini (1994) are correctives that emphasize East Asian achievements.

Joseph Needham had originally argued that the mechanical clock was the last specifically European invention to be imported into China. NEEDHAM, LING & PRICE describe Su Song's clock of AD 1090 with many attractive illustrations from newly discovered historical sources, and argue, retracting the original claim, that a chain of technical development could be traced from ancient Chinese water clocks to medieval

European clocks. Su Song's clock was the last missing piece, in that it contained a device resembling an escapement.

BEDINI (1994) attempts to resurrect, Needham-style, an East Asian concern with time measurement. It contains many reproductions of Chinese and Japanese incense seals, containers that burn incense within a specific period of time, and it reveals many historical sources that discuss incense as a measurement of time. Attention is paid to incense timers in religious life and to their wider use as revealed, for example, in poetry.

Within the European history of clocks, most of the literature covers the 17th and especially the 18th century. The issue in this period was finding longitude, especially for navigation purposes. Whereas latitude can be found with comparative ease (in the northern hemisphere by observing the altitude of the polar star over the horizon), no straightforward way of determining longitude is available. Finding longitude at sea became urgent once seafarers began to cross oceans, and by the 18th century large prizes were offered for a solution to the problem. The last four items in this entry all address this issue in one way or another.

BEDINI (1991) describes Galileo Galilei's work on pendulum regulators and clockwork inventions that were intended as solutions to the longitude problem. Bedini also traces the successful application of Galileo's clocks in Florence and Tuscany, along with the circumstances that led to this aspect of Galileo's work being ignored. Bedini argues that Galileo, and not Christian Huygens, should be regarded as the inventor of the pendulum-regulated clock. The book contains several photographic replications of clocks and manuscripts.

SHERMAN juxtaposes the development of the diurnal narrative structure in English literature with that of clocks in the period 1660 to 1785. This narrative is based on daily and dated entries such as a diary or a travel journal. For Sherman, Samuel Pepys's diary, Joseph Addison and Richard Steele's *Spectator*, Samuel Johnson's *A Journey to the Western Islands of Scotland*, and James Boswell's *The Journal of a Tour to the Hebrides* map the main route by which the diurnal narrative assumed cultural dominion. Sherman notes that the widely publicized quest for longitude in the 18th century contributed to a new sense of time just when time became a main organizing principle in travel journals and magazines with daily installments.

ANDREWES is a collection of papers from a Harvard conference on the problem of longitude. It is lavishly illustrated and contains much information on the solutions proposed. If one were to know the exact time, then one could determine longitude from the position of any of the fixed stars rotating constantly from east to west. One proposed solution was to read the time by using the position of the moon against the fixed stars, another to make chronometers that would run sufficiently exactly even when carried on ocean-going ships. SOBEL focuses on the most famous solution to the problem, the clocks produced by John Harrison. As the full title of the book accurately reveals, the complicated story is collapsed into one of a hero against a villainous system – the British Board of Longitude – that delayed paying out the prize Harrison so richly deserved. The book consequently provides a good read, and it is indeed a bestseller.

ARNE HESSENBRUCH

Colloid Chemistry

Ede, Andrew G., *Colloid Chemistry in North America: The Neglected Dimension*, PhD dissertation, University of Toronto, Ann Arbor: UMI, 1993

Florkin, Marcel, *A History of Biochemistry*, New York: Elsevier, 1972 (vol. 30 of *Comprehensive Biochemistry*, edited by Florkin and Elmer H. Stotz)

Furukawa, Yasu, *Inventing Polymer Science: Staudinger, Carothers, and the Emergence of Macromolecular Science*, Philadelphia: University of Pennsylvania Press, 1998

Morgan, Neil, "The Strategy of Biological Research Programmes: Reassessing the 'Dark Age' of Biochemistry, 1910–1930", *Annals of Science*, 47 (1990): 139–50

Olby, Robert C., *The Path to the Double Helix*, London: Macmillan, and Seattle: University of Washington Press, 1974

Somsen, Geert J., *"Wetenschappelijk Onderzoek en Algemeen Belang": De Chemie van H.R. Kruyt (1882–1959)* (summary in English), Delft: Delft University Press, 1998

From about 1900 until World War II, colloid chemistry was a highly respected scientific field that attracted thousands of researchers. Its domain included the study of economically vital substances, such as rubber, cellulose, fibers, and plastics, as well as the chemistry of proteins and the living cell. Several Nobel prizes were awarded to colloid chemical investigations and the field's significance for industry and medicine was widely acknowledged. In the 1930s, however, it started to lose its dominance in those areas to the emerging disciplines of molecular biology and polymer chemistry, and was forced into a marginal position. The spectacular rise and fall of the field has frequently been noted in the histories of those supplanters (as well as biochemistry) but the perspective of hindsight has too often distorted its analysis. Too little has yet been written on the development of colloid chemistry in its own right.

In his multi-volume history of biochemistry FLORKIN provides two chapters on colloid chemistry, which are notorious for their pejorative tone. The author's phrase "the Dark Age of Biocolloidology" indicates his view that colloid chemistry retarded the development of what he terms a scientific biochemistry. This view underlines his whole treatment of the subject.

OLBY presents a solid and comprehensive intellectual prehistory of the double helix discovery of Watson and Crick, and does not share Florkin's harsh judgments of colloid chemistry. Olby discusses the field in chapters that deal with the first step toward the double helix: the establishment of the concept of the macromolecule. This led to the overthrow of the previous "aggregate theory", which Olby more or less identifies with colloid chemistry. The latter equation may be oversimplifying matters, however, since it does not do justice to the complex nature of the field. The adoption of the methods of physical chemistry, moreover, made most colloid chemists ignore chemical structure (whether aggregate or macromolecule) altogether.

MORGAN is one of the few scholars to have studied colloid chemistry as a separate subject. His article is an account of the program of the Cambridge colloid scientist William Bate Hardy, who offered an alternative to his colleague Frederick Hopkins's biochemistry in the chemical study of life. Whereas Hopkins studied the dynamics of metabolism, Hardy examined the structure of the cell at the colloidal level. Morgan argues that Hardy's program was a vigorous and intelligible part of the reductionist development of biochemistry, bridging 19th-century (microscopic) cell biology and 1930s (molecular) protein studies.

FURUKAWA offers a study of the establishment of polymer chemistry and focuses on the struggles for the recognition of the concept of macromolecules. His book gives extensive descriptions of the campaigns of Hermann Staudinger, who introduced this concept, and the epoch-making work of Wallace Carothers, which led to its general acceptance. Furukawa has collected an impressive amount of material, but tends to lump together all opposition to the macromolecule, inappropriately equating colloid chemistry with the aggregate theory.

EDE is a wide-ranging study of colloid chemistry in the US, where it became popular in the 1920s. He discusses the research and discipline building of such colloid chemists as Wilder Bancroft, Harry Holmes, and Jerome Alexander in the wake of Wolfgang Ostwald's lecture tour just before World War I. Ede provides useful statistics on publications and people active in the field, establishing that colloid chemistry was a thriving enterprise.

SOMSEN presents a thesis on the Dutch chemist Hugo Kruyt, who was the leader of a large research school in colloid chemistry in the interwar period. There is a chapter on the history of the field in general, which examines its rise after the convergence of medical, industrial, physical, and chemical interests around 1900. The chapter also analyses the concerns of leading colloid chemists such as Wolfgang Ostwald, Herbert Freundlich, Georg Bredig, and Wilder Bancroft, who focused on the physical-chemical properties of colloid particles rather than their molecular structure. Kruyt, whose work is thoroughly discussed in a separate chapter, investigated the stability of colloids from a similar point of view.

GEERT SOMSEN

See also Biochemistry

Colonialism and Science

Basalla, George, "The Spread of Western Science", *Science*, 156 (1967): 611–22

Brockway, Lucile H., *Science and Colonial Expansion: The Role of the British Royal Botanic Gardens*, New York: Academic Press, 1979

Home, R.W. (ed.), *Australian Science in the Making*, Melbourne, Cambridge and New York: Cambridge University Press/Australian Academy of Science, 1988

Kumar, Deepak (ed.), *Science and Empire: Essays in Indian Context, 1700–1947*, Delhi: Anamika Prakashan, 1991

Lafuente, Antonio and José Sala Catalá (eds), *Ciencia colonial en América*, Madrid: Alianza, 1992

Lafuente, Antonio, A. Elena and M.L. Ortega (eds), *Mundialización de la ciencia y cultura nacional: Actas del Congreso Internacional "Ciencia, descubrimiento y mundo colonial"*, Madrid: Doce Calles, 1993

McClellan III, James E., *Colonialism and Science: Saint Domingue in the Old Regime*, Baltimore: Johns Hopkins University Press, 1992

MacLeod, Roy and Philip F. Rehbock (eds), *Nature in Its Greatest Extent: Western Science in the Pacific*, Honolulu: University of Hawaii Press, 1988

Meade, Teresa and Mark Walker (eds), *Science, Medicine and Cultural Imperialism*, London: Macmillan, and New York: St Martin's Press, 1991

Osborne, Michael A., *Nature, the Exotic, and the Science of French Colonialism*, Bloomington: Indiana University Press, 1994

Petitjean, Patrick, Catherine Jami and Anne Marie Moulin (eds), *Science and Empires: Historical Studies about Scientific Development and European Expansion*, Dordrecht and Boston: Kluwer, 1992

Pyenson, Lewis, *Cultural Imperialism and Exact Sciences: German Expansion Overseas, 1900–1930*, New York: Peter Lang, 1985

Pyenson, Lewis, *Empire of Reason: Exact Sciences in Indonesia, 1840–1940*, Leiden: E.J. Brill, 1989

Pyenson, Lewis, "Pure Learning and Political Economy: Science and European Expansion in the Age of Imperialism", in *New Trends in the History of Science*, edited by R.P.W. Visser *et al.*, Amsterdam: Rodopi, 1989, 209–78

Pyenson, Lewis, *Civilizing Mission: Exact Sciences and French Overseas Expansion, 1830–1940*, Baltimore: Johns Hopkins University Press, 1993

Reingold, Nathan and Marc Rothenberg (eds), *Scientific Colonialism: A Cross-Cultural Comparison*, Washington, DC: Smithsonian Institution Press, 1987

Sangwan, Satpal, *Science, Technology, and Colonisation: An Indian Experience, 1757–1857*, Delhi: Anamika Prakashan, 1991

Science & Empire Newsletter, Joint publication of NISTADS (New Delhi) and REHSEIS (Paris)

Stearns, Raymond Phineas, *Science in the British Colonies of America*, Urbana: University of Illinois Press, 1970

Struik, Dirk J., "Early Colonial Science in North America and Mexico", *Quipu*, 1 (1984): 24–54

Historians of science have only recently begun to investigate connections between science and European colonialism and imperialism. The explosion of research in the last two decades has produced an entire scholarly industry, referred to as "Science and Empire Studies".

BASALLA is the founding father of historical inquiry into the subject. Based largely on the American experience, Basalla presented a three-stage model for colonial science, wherein a colony serves first as a site for initial explorations, then as an outpost of metropolitan scientific establishments, and finally as the seat of autonomous scientific traditions. Basalla's article continues to be cited and to structure presentations in the field. The collections by HOME, by MacLEOD & REHBOCK, and by LAFUENTE & CATALA, for example, are organized around the principles sketched by Basalla. However, other historians have found Basalla's model somewhat simplistic, and have proposed several more sophisticated alternatives. Roy MacLeod wrote an especially influential article exploring metropolitan perspectives on colonial science and center-periphery relations, published in the collection edited by REINGOLD & ROTHENBERG.

Although the study of colonial science has matured to the point where teams of scholars currently pursue a variety of research programs, a single individual, Lewis Pyenson, is its most accomplished practitioner. He has opened up new territory and sharpened questions for debate in his trilogy concerning German (PYENSON, 1985), Dutch (PYENSON, 1989), and French (PYENSON, 1993) colonial and scientific traditions. Pyenson focuses on the exact, mathematical sciences, and his works are among the most detailed and wide-ranging of any inquiry into the subject. A problem in Pyenson's approach is that one cannot automatically conflate the exact sciences with theoretical science, or the qualitative sciences with applied science, as he attempts to do. In Pyenson (1989), he proffered a new model for science within various colonial contexts according to either the functionary, commercial, or research orientation of the mother country. Pyenson's model is presently being explored further, notably by Japanese researchers.

An early bias towards the history of science in the Anglo-Saxon colonial world has been largely overcome, but the story of science in the former British colonies remains the best documented. STEARNS is a good introduction to the progress of science in the British colonies in America, while the early study by BROCKWAY broke new ground in examining the role of botanical gardens in the British empire of the 19th century. REINGOLD & ROTHENBERG's collection remains a landmark volume, particularly in its treatment of Australia and the United States; it contains papers from an international conference on science in colonial settings held in Australia in 1981. More recent collections edited by HOME and by MacLEOD & REHBOCK demonstrate the existence of a vibrant community of Australian researchers investigating the interplay of European science and colonialism in the Pacific.

The history of science in the colonial experience of the French was a major lacuna that has recently been partially filled. OSBORNE's study of 19th-century French acclimatization projects inaugurated the subject. Pyenson (1993) surveys French scientific functionaries stationed at various outposts around the French colonial empire in the 19th and 20th centuries. McCLELLAN's study of French science and Old Regime colonialism restores a major episode lost to the historiography, and offers a key point of chronological comparison. The volume edited by PETITJEAN, JAMI & MOULIN arose from a UNESCO conference in Paris in 1990; its papers are global and comparative in scope, but bespeak a robust community of French researchers.

The interplay of science and colonialism in the Americas represents a vast field that Iberian, Latin-American, and North American historians are currently attacking with vigor. The article by STRUIK is an early attempt to address the phenomena, and the journal in which it appeared, *Quipu*, marked the beginning of an effort to organize the study of colonial science in the Americas. The volume edited by LAFUENTE & CATALÁ presents 17 case studies by specialists concerning various stages of American colonial and scientific

development, and it represents the maturation of colonial science studies by another impressive community of scholars. An international congress sponsored by the American, Spanish, and Latin American societies for the history of science, held in Madrid in 1991, likewise exemplifies the energy with which scholars are presently pursuing the topic of colonial science in the Americas, as does the resulting volume edited by LAFUENTE, ELENA & ORTEGA, which contains more than 60 articles devoted to science in the colonial world of the Americas.

Yet another notable community of researchers has recently begun to examine the case of India. The collection of 14 papers edited by KUMAR in 1991 is an outgrowth of an international conference held in India in 1985 to discuss thematic links between science and empire. The volume by SANGWAN presents an overview of science and technology in the period of dominion by the East India Company. In 1990 a consortium of French and Indian researchers formalized an international collaborative network devoted to the study of colonialism and science, and their newsletter, *Science and Empire*, has become a major source of information about the field. Out of this group, and from other works in progress, will doubtless come even more sophisticated analyses of the Indian case.

As McClellan points out in MEADE & WALKER, yet another notable collection of case studies, too often in the literature the emphasis has been on science as some sort of transcendent entity, whose connection to colonialism is almost accidental. Initial historical studies, especially, dealt mostly with the effects of the colonial experience on science and the scientific enterprise. Only with more recent historiographical trends has attention shifted to an examination of the role and effect of science on the processes of colonization. This more recent work shows that the dynamic in the history of colonial science stems primarily from the role that science plays in colonialism, and not the other way around. In other words, the historical motive force in colonial science derives, in the first instance, from the various strategies of the colonial and imperialist powers involving science. A full synthetic treatment of the role of science in the colonial experience remains to be written.

JAMES E. McCLELLAN III

Complementary Medicine

British Medical Association, *Report of the Board of Science and Education on Alternative Therapy*, London: BMA, 1986

British Medical Association, *Complementary Medicine: New Approaches to Good Practice*, Oxford and New York: Oxford University Press, 1993

Bynum, W.F. and Roy Porter (eds), *Medical Fringe and Medical Orthodoxy, 1750–1850*, London: Croom Helm, 1987

Cooter, Roger (ed.), *Studies in the History of Alternative Medicine*, London: Macmillan, and New York: St Martin's Press, 1988

Fulder, Stephen, *The Handbook of Complementary Medicine*, Sevenoaks, Kent: Coronet, 1984; 3rd edition, Oxford and New York: Oxford University Press, 1996

Gevitz, Norman (ed.), *Other Healers: Unorthodox Medicine in America*, Baltimore: Johns Hopkins University Press, 1988

Porter, Roy (ed.), *Medicine: A History of Healing*, London: Ivy Press, 1997

Saks, Mike (ed.), *Alternative Medicine in Britain*, Oxford: Clarendon Press, and New York: Oxford University Press, 1992

Sharma, Ursula, *Complementary Medicine Today: Practitioners and Patients*, London and New York: Routledge/Tavistock, 1992; revised edition, 1995

Complementary medicine is a term often used to describe the range of unorthodox therapies – including, among many others, acupuncture, aromatherapy, chiropractic, herbalism, and osteopathy – that have recently become more popular with the general public, and which are seen to complement the practice of orthodox medicine. This usage is well illustrated by the work of SHARMA, who draws on her own small-scale empirical research to highlight the position of both practitioners and patients of complementary medicine in modern Britain. Such unorthodox therapies are also sometimes referred to by other terms in the literature, as, for instance, "traditional" or "holistic" medicine. However, as SAKS notes in his edited overview of this field, neither of these concepts is very helpful as a blanket description of such practices. The term "traditional" medicine may well apply to historically well-established techniques such as the laying on of hands, but is not appropriate for relatively new forms of unorthodox medicine, such as chiropractic or biofeedback. Similarly, the notion of all unorthodox therapy being "holistic" does not readily apply to the use of formula acupuncture for the treatment of medically defined symptoms, or the restricted employment of osteopathy for the treatment of back pain alone, since these applications cannot necessarily be seen to unite mind and body in diagnosis and treatment.

Many unorthodox therapies, of course, fit the "holistic" mould in this sense. It is precisely here, however, that the concept of "complementary medicine" is at its most vulnerable, in so far as orthodox medicine tends to be based on a divergent, mechanistic, biomedical approach in which the body is treated as a machine in which the malfunctions of its constituent parts need to be repaired on breakdown. In this frame of reference, "holistic" therapies such as spiritual healing cannot be seen as complementary, since they typically view health and illness in terms of the interrelationship of mind, body, and spirit. As is indicated in the useful collection by GEVITZ on unorthodox therapies in the United States in the 19th and 20th centuries, this disjuncture is most starkly illustrated by the founding principle of homeopathy – the stimulation of the healing force of the individual; this contradicts the basic tenets of allopathic orthodoxy, which is arguably further undermined by the associated homeopathic belief that the more dilute a substance the higher its potency.

Such an interpretation rests on the continuation of a significant difference between the underlying principles of orthodox and unorthodox medicine, with dissonant conceptual frameworks for diagnosis and treatment. However, as FULDER observes in his comprehensive handbook examining many practical facets of complementary therapies, even in such circumstances it is still possible to see unconventional medicine as acting in partnership with medical orthodoxy. He points to instances in China and in India, where therapies at present defined as orthodox and unorthodox medicine in the West have been successfully wedded together in practice, notwithstanding the apparent technical incompatibility of the systems of thought involved. This may chart a way forward for the employment of the term "complementary" medicine, especially as the recent text edited by PORTER highlights that Eastern health philosophies are increasingly being adopted alongside more biomedical frames of reference in Western societies; otherwise, it may be necessary to consign it only to such cases where the philosophical basis of the unorthodox therapies concerned has been stripped of its classical content, or fits in other ways with the prevailing patterns of biomedicine.

It is important, however, not to lose sight of the historical dimension to the debate. The scholarly volumes edited by BYNUM & PORTER and COOTER reveal that in Britain, in the period up to the mid-19th century before biomedicine rose to ascendancy, there was both a stronger appreciation of the way in which illness was fundamental to the whole person, and greater overlap between the practice of medical doctors and other competing practitioners. It was only with the increasing unification of the medical profession around biomedical orthodoxy from the latter half of the 19th century onwards, that the notion of "complementary" medicine seemed to be of diminishing relevance, except in instances where the unconventional therapies involved were more directly linked philosophically to orthodox medicine.

Readings in the collection by SAKS suggest that the hegemony of biomedicine was reinforced by a range of professional social control mechanisms, spanning formal and informal disciplinary measures to the regulation of entry to medical schools and promotion opportunities within the medical profession. As such, Saks argues that the term "alternative medicine" may well provide a better general description of the position of unconventional therapies in 20th-century Britain. Like the term "unorthodox medicine", it is wider ranging in its coverage, referring not so much to the specific nature of the therapies concerned – which can be very variable – as to their political marginality within the dominant health care system. Such marginality is based on the fact that they do not normally receive the support of the medical establishment in areas such as research funding and inclusion in the mainstream medical curriculum. Also implicit in the notion of alternative medicine is that it is a relative concept, the precise detail of which may change over time – hence the claim that the alternative medicine of today may become the orthodoxy of tomorrow.

In this vein, the applicability of the more limited notion of "complementary" medicine may also itself be a fluid concept. Certainly, with increasing consumer demand for the therapies that this term is intended to cover, and growing public awareness of the limits of modern medical orthodoxy, the BRITISH MEDICAL ASSOCIATION (1993) revised its stance on their acceptability. It now advocates, among other things, raising awareness of complementary medicine in medical education, and collaboration with non-medical practitioners of unconventional therapies. Admittedly, it is possible to have reservations about how far this symbolises a fundamental shift in the position of the medical establishment, and to suspect that this is perhaps more an attempt to retain its dominant position in a situation of flux. However, there does seem to have been a significant contemporary change in its ideology in comparison with the earlier report of the BRITISH MEDICAL ASSOCIATION (1986), which disparagingly stressed the alternative, rather than complementary, nature of unorthodox medicine, accentuating its unscientific nature in the wake of the march of progress of orthodox medical science.

MIKE SAKS

See also Acupuncture; Herbalism; Holistic Medicine; Homeopathy

Computing

Aspray, William F. (ed.), *Computing Before Computers*, Ames: Iowa State University Press, 1990

Aspray, William F., *John von Neumann and the Origins of Modern Computing*, Cambridge, Massachusetts: MIT Press, 1990

Campbell-Kelly, Martin (ed.), *Works of Babbage*, 11 vols, London: Pickering, and New York: New York University Press, 1989

Ceruzzi, Paul E., *Reckoners: The Prehistory of the Digital Computer: From Relays to the Stored Program Concept, 1935–1945*, Westport, Connecticut: Greenwood Press, 1983

Croarken, Mary, *Early Scientific Computing in Britain*, Oxford: Clarendon Press, and New York: Oxford University Press, 1989

D'Ocagne, Maurice, *Le Calcul simplifié: Graphical and Mechanical Methods for Simplifying Calculation*, translated from the French by J. Howlett and Michael R. Williams, Cambridge, Massachusetts: MIT Press, 1986 (original edition, 1928)

Goldstine, Herman H., *The Computer: From Pascal to von Neumann*, Princeton, New Jersey: Princeton University Press, 1973

Nash, Stephen G. (ed.), *A History of Scientific Computing*, Reading, Massachusetts: Addison-Wesley, 1990

Randell, Brian, *Origins of Digital Computers*, Berlin and New York: Springer, 1973; 3rd edition, 1982

Stern, Nancy, *From ENIAC to UNIVAC: An Appraisal of the Eckert-Mauchly Computers*, Bedford, Massachusetts: Digital Press, 1981

Williams, Michael R., *A History of Computing Technology*, Englewood Cliffs, New Jersey: Prentice-Hall, 1985; revised edition, Los Alamitos, California: IEEE Computer Society Press, 1997

Since the 1950s, the term "computing" has been appropriated for all forms of information processing, from mathematical and control applications, to business data processing. Within the context of the history of science, the term computing is normally restricted to numerical algorithms, and practical computing in science and engineering.

An excellent overview of the entire field of the history of computing is given in ASPRAY's edited collection of essays by five leading scholars in the history of computing. More demanding technical and mathematical overviews are given by WILLIAMS, GOLDSTINE, and RANDELL (in descending order of accessibility).

The prehistory of computing has a strong antiquarian as well as academic interest. Calculating aids included the abacus and the counting table, while computing methods included finger and pen reckoning, and the use of rudimentary mathematical tables. Algorithms developed in Babylonian, and other civilisations have also been the subject of research. These topics are all well covered, in a non-antiquarian manner, by Williams.

In the 16th century, John Napier was responsible for the most important calculating innovation, logarithms, as well as for a number of calculating aids of lesser importance, such as Napier's Bones. Logarithmic and other tables were the mainstay of computing until the 20th century. Much of this computing was performed by teams of human computers – the term "computer" invariably referring to the occupation of a human being who performed calculations. These topics are covered by both Williams and Goldstine.

Charles Babbage occupies an important place in 19th-century computing because of his lifelong attempts to build an automatic calculating engine, starting in 1820. Babbage designed two engines: the Difference Engine to produce mathematical tables, and the much more ambitious, general-purpose Analytical Engine, which embodied almost all the important characteristics of a modern electronic computer. Babbage has received almost too much attention in the history of computing, and there are more than 150 books and articles in the secondary literature. The best source is the collected works of Babbage, in CAMPBELL-KELLY.

After Babbage's failure to construct his calculating engines, practical computers turned into small scale, non-automatic, digital and analog calculating aids. The most important digital devices were adding and calculating machines, such as the Arithmometer and Brunsviga. While digital calculating machines worked on numbers directly, analog instruments represented numerical quantities by some physical property (such as the length, weight, or angular velocity of a solid, the volume of a liquid, or the electrical resistance of a conductor). In analog computing, instead of attempting the analytical solution of a mathematical system, the solution space was explored by constructing a physical model, or analog. Examples of important 19th-century analog devices include slide rules, nomograms, planimeters, and tide predictors. A contemporary survey of both digital and analog instruments is given by D'OCAGNE.

In the 1880s, Herman Hollerith invented punched-card machinery in response to the demand for the automation of statistical information processing for the US population census. This technology was subsequently exploited commercially by IBM. Between the two world wars, punched-card machinery was used for large scale digital calculations, such as the production of the Nautical Almanac in Britain. During the same period, analog computing reached its apogee through the differential analyser invented by Vannevar Bush. The only other method of doing large-scale calculations was by using teams of human computers, often augmented by logarithmic tables or calculating machines. Computing between the wars in

Britain is covered by CROARKEN, while Goldstine discusses the US scene.

In the late 1930s there were a number of attempts to construct an automatic calculating machine, of the kind originally envisaged by Babbage, using modern electro-mechanical technologies. The most important of these projects was the IBM Automatic Sequence Controlled Calculator built for Harvard University during the years 1937–43. Although the Harvard machine was slow (about three operations per second), the fact that it was fully automatic enabled it to be used for simple repetitive calculations, such as those in ballistics work and mathematical tables. CERUZZI gives an excellent overview of the Harvard machine and other contemporary projects.

During World War II, there were several attempts to construct electronic computing machines in the US, Britain, and Germany. By far the most important of these projects was the ENIAC, constructed at the Moore School of Electrical Engineering at the University of Pennsylvania, 1942–45. The most significant characteristics of the ENIAC were that it was fully automatic and operated at 5000 operations per second – a thousand times as fast as any previous calculating technology. The ENIAC project is well described in all the general histories of the computer; the best monographic study is STERN.

In the summer of 1944, the American mathematician John von Neumann became an adviser to the ENIAC project. At this time the ENIAC, though not yet complete, was seen to have a number of shortcomings: in spite of its 18,000 electronic tubes, it had a capacity of just 10 numbers; and programming the machine took many hours or even days. To overcome these deficiencies, von Neumann and the members of the ENIAC design group established a new computer design, known as the EDVAC. In June 1945, von Neumann produced the First Draft of a Report on the EDVAC on behalf of the Moore School group. This report defined the "stored-program computer" on which the academic discipline of computer science and the computer industry are founded. Unfortunately, because of von Neumann's sole authorship of the report, the role of his colleagues was slighted and the invention is often known as the "von Neumann architecture". The failure of von Neumann's collaborators to gain full credit resulted in much acrimony. ASPRAY's 1990 book contains the most objective account of this controversy.

The stored program computer created a new paradigm in computing. By the early 1950s, several prototype computers had been demonstrated in Britain and the US, and by the end of the decade an industry had been established. Over the next 20 years computing was transformed: analog instruments became largely obsolete, while non-electronic digital technologies, such as punched-card machines and desk calculators, were rendered uneconomic. In science and engineering, the feasibility of low-cost calculation transformed the economy of research and development: in place of analytical investigation and model building, the computer enabled the substitution of techniques of numerical approximation and simulation. There is no comprehensive history of post-World War II scientific computing, but NASH includes some useful material.

MARTIN CAMPBELL-KELLY

See also Artificial Intelligence

Comte, Auguste 1798–1857

French sociologist

Gouhier, Henri, *La Jeunesse d'Auguste Comte et la formation du positivisme*, 3 vols, Paris: Vrin, 1933–41

Gouhier, Henri, *La Philosophie d'Auguste Comte: Esquisses*, Paris: Vrin, 1987

Lacroix, Jean, *La Sociologie d'Auguste Comte*, Paris: Presses Universitaires de France, 1956, 4th edition, 1973

Lévy-Bruhl, Lucien, *The Philosophy of Auguste Comte*, translated from the French by Kathleen de Beaumont-Klein, New York: Putnam, and London: Sonnenschein, 1903 (original edition, 1900)

Mill, John Stuart, *Auguste Comte and Positivism*, London: Trubner, 1865

Ostwald, Wilhelm, *Auguste Comte: Der Mann und sein Werk*, Leipzig: Unesma, 1914

Pickering, Mary, *Auguste Comte: An Intellectual Biography*, Cambridge and New York: Cambridge University Press, 1993

Auguste Comte invented the term "sociology" and was a most influential social theorist. He argued for the need for a basic and unifying social science, which would both explain the existing social organization and guide social planning for a better future. He discerned three stages or states of intellectual development: the theological, the metaphysical, and the scientific. In the final state, a spiritual priesthood consisting of secular sociologists was to work out the details of a new social order. The actual administration of the state Comte would leave to businessmen and bankers, whereas private morality was the province and responsibility of womanhood. In later life, Comte advocated that this new social order was to be adapted to the organizational structure of the Catholic church, divorced from its supernaturalism.

In his very detailed study, GOUHIER (1933–41) examines the development of Comte's thinking up to the split with his teacher, Saint-Simon (1824), their relationship, and his attitude towards the aftermath of the French Revolution. He shows that Comte's turn towards the "Religion de l'Humanité" was established very early, and that it was a direct continuation of similar aims of the revolutionary years. He also provides a comprehensive bibliography of Comte's widespread correspondence.

GOUHIER (1987), which includes a biographical portrait and a bibliography, combines several essays concerning the "Opuscule fondamental", the philosophy of history, the philosophy of religion, medieval thought, *règne du coeur*, Comte's relationship to positivism in 1830, and his relation to Blainville. One of Gouhier's aims is to gather material for a critical edition of Comte's *Plan* of 1822, and for that purpose he examines successively the 1822, 1824, and 1854 editions, as well as P. Laffitte's edition of 1895. His fruitful observations on the original manuscript, and on the significant additions made in 1824, show convincingly the historical development of Comte's "first system".

Gouhier shows how Comte took from the biologist Blainville – with whom he became acquainted through Saint-Simon – the fundamental themes of his biological philosophy, revealed in

1838 in the third volume of his *Cours de philosophie positive*. The philosopher and the biologist supported each other in their systematic and historical conceptions of knowledge. The severity of Comte's judgement on the death of this former friend is due to the fact that Blainville could never go beyond the theological state of man's mind, in philosophy or in politics.

LACROIX explores Comte's philosophy, his (subjective and objective) sociology and politics, his predecessors (Aristotle, Bergson, de Bonald, Bossuet, Hobbes, de Maistre, and Saint-Simon), his critiques of political economy, and his thoughts on social classes, progress, ethics and religion. He describes Comte's positivism as the development of a scientific and religious philosophy into a kind of social humanism, describing a "priesthood of humanism" as the final purpose of positivism.

LÉVY-BRUHL presents a four-part survey of Comte's philosophy, with sections on: the philosophical problem, including the law of the three states; his classification of sciences, theory of science, and philosophy of science (especially mathematics, astronomy, physics and chemistry, biology and psychology); considerations on the social sciences (including social statics and dynamics); and his principles of morals and the idea of humanity. Lévy-Bruhl argues that the discovery of the law of the three states simultaneously founded sociology and realised the uniformity of human knowledge. Uniformity enabled the rational classification of the sciences; the philosophy of sciences is grounded on the hierarchy of sciences, the unity of method, the uniformity of knowledge, and the tendency of all sciences towards sociology.

MILL was concerned mainly with part 1 of Comte's *Cours de philosophie positive*, which had already exerted enormous influence on contemporary European thinkers, concentrating on Comte's doctrine of the development of the human mind, the law of the three states, the classification of the sciences, and the philosophy of science. Mill criticizes both the method of the positive science, (for the lack of a touchstone for an inductive proof), and the fact that psychology was not included in Comte's classification. Mill argues that Comte's conception of history is incomplete, and even incorrect, with regard to English affairs. He also bemoans the lack of a link between historical speculation and practical conclusions, and denies that Comte created social science. In part 2, the focus is on Comte's ethical and religious writings from 1851 to 1856.

OSTWALD's "psychographic" biography distinguishes three periods in Comte's life, each interrupted by depression: 1) youth and writings until the conception of the *Philosophie positive*; 2) the 12 years taken to complete the *Philosophie positive*; and 3) the period in which Comte tried to realise practical conclusions and returned to the Catholic church. The first period, with its distinctly romantic features, is acknowledged as Comte's most productive one. Ostwald especially deals with Comte's relationship with Henry de Saint-Simon and, later, with Clotilde de Vaux. In the third period, he examines Comte's "mystical" features and intellectual longsightedness.

PICKERING concentrates on Comte's career to 1842, the period when he made his principal contributions to modern culture – the establishment of positivism and sociology. In contrast to current assumptions, she points out that Comte was always aware of the human drive towards emotional and spiritual fulfilment, as well as the drive towards political activism and social reform. Chapter 1 places Comte's life (to 1817) within the historical context of post-revolutionary France; chapters 2 to 5 deal with Saint-Simon and his journalistic endeavors, and with his split with Comte in 1824; chapters 6 to 8 concentrate on Comte's personal and intellectual concerns in the years 1824–28 (such as the Scottish Enlightenment, and the doctrines of Herder, Kant, and Hegel); chapters 9 to 13 cover Comte's role within scientific circles; and chapters 14 and 15 analyse his ideas in his "Cours de philosophie positive". In the conclusion, Pickering states that there was no sudden break in 1842, and refutes the contention that Comte developed from an arid scientific thinker into a zealous religious reformer.

BEATRICE RAUSCHENBACH
translated by Anne Hessenbruch

Continental Drift

Carey, S. Warren, *Theories of the Earth and Universe: A History of Dogma in the Earth Sciences*, Stanford, California: Stanford University Press, 1988

Glen, William, *The Road to Jaramillo: Critical Years of the Revolution in Earth Science*, Stanford, California: Stanford University Press, 1982

Hallam, Anthony, *A Revolution in the Earth Sciences: From Continental Drift to Plate Tectonics*, Oxford: Clarendon Press, 1973

LeGrand, H.E., *Drifting Continents and Shifting Theories: The Modern Revolution in Geology and Scientific Change*, Cambridge and New York: Cambridge University Press, 1988

Marvin, Ursula B., *Continental Drift: The Evolution of a Concept*, Washington, DC: Smithsonian Institution Press, 1973

Menard, H.W., *The Ocean of Truth: A Personal History of Global Tectonics*, Princeton, New Jersey: Princeton University Press, 1986

Oreskes, Naomi, *The Rejection of Continental Drift: Theory and Method in American Earth Science*, New York: Oxford University Press, 1999

Schwarzbach, Martin, *Alfred Wegener: The Father of Continental Drift*, translated from the German, Madison, Wisconsin: Science Tech, 1986 (original edition, 1980)

Stewart, John A., *Drifting Continents and Colliding Paradigms: Perspectives on the Geoscience Revolution*, Bloomington: Indiana University Press, 1990

Wood, Robert Muir, *The Dark Side of the Earth*, London: Allen and Unwin, 1985

In stark contrast to 19th-century geology, 20th-century earth science has received little attention from historians except for the theory of continental drift, on which a sizeable body of historical literature has been accumulating. The concept of continental drift was first put forward in a modern scientific form by Alfred Wegener in his *Die Entstehung der Kontinente und Ozeane* (1915), and in the first chapter of its 4th edition (1928), Wegener briefly discussed the work of some of his predecessors. The South African drift proponent Alex. L. Du Toit, in the second chapter of his *Our Wandering Continents: An Hypothesis of Continental Drifting* (1937), considered the history of the drift idea, citing authors as far back as Francis Bacon to whom he (incorrectly) attributed "the germ" of the drift notion.

No book-sized historical study of the theory of continental drift appeared until the early 1970s, when, in the wake of the remarkable confirmation of Wegener's views in the form of plate tectonics with its drift mechanism of sea-floor spreading, both geologists and historians of science began looking at the historical development of continental "mobilism" versus "fixism".

Among the early works on the subject were MARVIN and HALLAM, who both wrote "internalist" accounts, describing the geological and geophysical facts, discoveries, hypotheses and arguments for and against continental drift. Milestones in their stories are the appearance of Wegener's book; the 1926 Symposium to debate Wegener's views organised by W.A.J.M. van Waterschoot van der Gracht, under the auspices of the American Association of Petroleum Geologists; the 1950s evidence from palaeomagnetism; the 1960s hypothesis of sea-floor spreading; the emergence of plate tectonics around 1970; and, in Hallam's book, the application of plate tectonics to continental geology.

Hallam's and Marvin's accounts are similar in the sense that each depicts the history of continental drift theory as a gradual, if at times dramatic, process of verification of an initially disregarded revolutionary concept. The same basic picture is painted by SCHWARZBACH in his readable and highly sympathetic account of Wegener's life and accomplishments; Schwarzbach casts the hero of his story in the role of the scientific prophet of truth, initially ignored but ultimately proved right.

GLEN selects from the various intellectual strands of the plate tectonics theory the study of palaeomagnetism, and especially of the magnetic polarity-reversal time-scale, which became an essential part of the Vine-Matthews-Morley hypothesis connecting magnetic reversal belts of the ocean floors with the spreading of these floors. Glen made use of the fact that the majority of the scientists concerned were still alive by interviewing them, and thereby produced a deft combination of oral and documentary history.

Hallam and Marvin aspired to something more than a straightforward geological account. In the early 1970s, there existed among historians of science a keen interest in Thomas S. Kuhn's paradigm theory of scientific change, and both Hallam and Marvin responded to this by concluding that earth science, in accepting plate tectonics, had undergone a revolution in the Kuhnian sense. Others, too, have seen in the triumph of the new global tectonics a characteristic instance of Kuhnian paradigm change. More comprehensively, LeGRAND and STEWART discuss not only Kuhn's views, but also those of other philosophers of science, such as Imre Lakatos and Larry Laudan, using the historical development of the revolution in earth science – recounted by Stewart in considerable geological-cum-geophysical detail – as a testing ground for models of scientific change.

Several of the histories of the continental drift theory are written by people who themselves were (or are) actively involved in plate tectonics research. In addition to Glen, Hallam and Marvin (all geologists), there have been Menard and Carey. MENARD focuses on the vast amount of new ocean floor data collected mainly during the period 1950–70, and is written from a "Pacific" point of view, counter-balancing the traditionally heavy "Atlantic" slant of the historiography of marine geology. As a prominent participant in the global tectonics revolution, Menard was able to draw on personal correspondence and other relevant records to tell an insider's tale, mixing his discussion of geological evidence with details of personalities, their interaction, co-operation and confrontations.

CAREY was one of the few champions of Wegener's theory during the years when it was still unfashionable. In 1956, he organised a classic symposium on continental drift at the University of Tasmania in Hobart. In Carey's substantial contribution to the symposium volume, he championed earth expansion as the mechanism of continental break-up, and became in later years a staunch opponent of the concept of sea-floor spreading. His book is the most complete presentation of the theory of earth expansion. The dignity of his intelligently argued account is somewhat impaired by the fact that Carey has cast himself in the role of a martyr-genius, ignored by the dogmatic earth science establishment.

A particular puzzle of the continental drift to plate tectonics story has always been the question of why the acceptance of Wegener's theory was delayed for approximately half a century. Most authors address this conundrum, attributing the delay to the geophysical inadequacy of Wegener's tentatively proposed drift mechanism of Polflucht combined with tidal friction. Sea-floor spreading, in this perception, has been the key to the ultimate acceptance of continental mobilism by the world's community of earth scientists.

Wood and Oreskes offer a very different solution, arguing that professional and national factors were crucial. WOOD, in his provocative account, maintains that the debate about Wegener's theory represented a clash of two professions, and that the ultimate victory of drift was one of whole-earth geophysicists over hammer-and-chisel field geologists. ORESKES challenges the notion that lack of an adequate mechanism led to the rejection of drift. She points to the fact that opposition to Wegener was considerably more widespread among American than European geologists, and that this opposition was expressed in a surprisingly vitriolic fashion. According to Oreskes, the American geological community saw in Wegener's theory a threat to its methodological principles and standards of practice of earth science.

With Oreskes's work, the historical study of continental drift theory is taking a turn away from a preoccupation with the content of scientific arguments, and towards an attempt to locate these arguments within the complexity and diversity of actual geological work, with the recognition of the constitutive importance of such factors as regionality, territoriality and convention.

NICOLAAS A. RUPKE

See also Oceanography

Copernicanism

Blumenberg, Hans, *Die kopernikanische Wende*, Frankfurt: Suhrkamp, 1965

Blumenberg, Hans, *The Genesis of the Copernican World*, translated from the German by Robert M. Wallace, Cambridge, Massachusetts: Harvard University Press, 1987 (original edition, 1975)

Born, Max, *Einstein's Theory of Relativity*, translated from the German by Henry L. Brose, New York: Dutton, n.d. ("after 1922"); London: Methuen, 1924, revised edition, edited by Günther Leibfried and Walter Biem, New York: Dover, 1962

Dreyer, John Louis Emil, *History of the Planetary Systems from Thales to Kepler*, Cambridge; Cambridge University Press, 1906; 2nd edition, as *A History of Astronomy from Thales to Kepler*, New York: Dover, 1953

Du Bois-Reymond, Emil, "Darwin und Kopernicus", in *Drei Reden*, Leipzig, 1884

Galilei, Galileo, *Dialogue Concerning the Two Chief World Systems: Ptolemaic and Copernican*, translated by Stillman Drake, foreword by Albert Einstein, Berkeley: University of California Press, 1962

Gingerich, Owen, "From Copernicus to Kepler: Heliocentrism as Model and as Reality", in *Proceedings of the American Philosophical Society*, 117/6 (1973): 513–22

Goethe, Johann Wolfgang von, *Schriften zur Farbenlehre, 1790–1807*, volume 23, part 2, of *Sämtliche Werke*, edited by Manfred Wenzel, Frankfurt: Deutsche Klassiker, 1991

Johnson, Francis R., *Astronomical Thought in Renaissance England: A Study of the English Scientific Writings from 1500 to 1645*, Baltimore: Johns Hopkins Press, 1937

Koyré, Alexandre, *The Astronomical Revolution: Copernicus, Kepler, Borelli*, translated from the French by R.E.W. Maddison, London: Methuen and Ithaca, New York: Cornell University Press, 1973 (original edition, 1961)

Kuhn, Thomas S., *The Copernican Revolution: Planetary Astronomy in the Development of Western Thought*, Cambridge, Massachusetts: Harvard University Press, 1957

Lambert, Johann Heinrich, *Cosmologische Briefe über die Einrichtung des Weltbaues*, Augsburg: Kletts Wittib, 1761

Rheticus, Georg Joachim, "The Narratio prima" in *Three Copernican Treatises*, edited and translated by Edward Rosen, New York: Columbia University Press, 1939; 3rd revised edition, New York: Octagon Books, 1971

Zinner, Ernst, *Entstehung und Ausbreitung der copernicanischen Lehre: Zum 200 jährigen Jubiläum der Friedrich-Alexander-Universität zu Erlangen*, Erlangen: 1943; revised edition, Munich: Beck, 1988

In his *De revolutionibus orbium coelestium libri VI*, Nicolaus Copernicus challenged Ptolemy's geocentric cosmology with his own heliocentric system, an act of paramount significance for the future development of both astronomico-scientific and philosophical thought. Accordingly, secondary literature on Copernicus tends to focus either on the more historical and astronomical, or on the more philosophical, aspects of Copernicus's work.

The beginnings of a comprehensive astronomical representation of Copernican cosmology can already be found in the work of Copernicus's only pupil RHETICUS. As a co-editor of *De revolutionibus*, Rheticus's qualifications were outstanding, and he initiated the representation of the new cosmology in a didactically structured, secondary work.

Of paradigmatic importance for a study of the spread of Copernican thought at the time is JOHNSON's work on astronomy and the English Renaissance. Since, in the relatively closed world of early modernity, conditions in the various European countries were not fundamentally different, Johnson is important for the overall reception of Copernican thought – the available specialist publications on the reception of Copernicus in Germany, Italy, and France are less broad in their approach. The German edition of Copernicus's *Collected Works* is planning an annotated edition with the title "receptio Copernicana" for volume 8. This volume, which is to offer a critical edition of Erasmus Reinhold's and Nicolaus Mulerius's commentaries on Copernicus for the first time, is expected to appear in a few years.

GALILEI, who became the most important populariser of Copernicanism, is responsible for the glorification of Copernicus's work, and for describing it as a "closed system". As a result of the Catholic Church's dogmatic insistence on Ptolemaic cosmology, on the basis of Aristotelian physics, the heliocentric system had to remain "hypothetical" until the 18th century, when it was liberated with Newtonian mechanics. The empirical proof of the correctness of the Copernican system did not occur until the mid 19th century, when in 1851 Jean-Bernard-Léon Foucault demonstrated the rotation of the earth, and the Königsberg astronomer, Friedrich Wilhelm Bessel, in 1838 measured the parallax of fixed stars.

However, during the Enlightenment the scientific community had already, in principle, ceased to doubt the truth of Copernican cosmology. Authors such as LAMBERT, who considered the Copernican reform merely a beginning of a fundamental cosmological reconstruction, already related Copernicanism to the wider context of a new physical world view. With GOETHE's claim that "among all discoveries and beliefs none had a greater impact on the human spirit than the teaching of Copernicus", the idea of the significance of the Copernican conception of the world entered also into general cultural discourse. Following him, several popular authors of the 19th century concerned themselves with Copernicanism, and eventually scholarship developed a new focus in the study of the life and work of Copernicus.

Under the impact of the pervasive scientific euphoria of his age, DU BOIS-REYMOND, president of the Prussian Academy of Sciences, dedicated a considerable portion of his work to studies in the history of science. Comparing Copernicus to Charles Darwin, he represented both as founders of a new conception of man's place within nature.

Unlike the philosophy of the Stoa, Copernicus did not charge geocentric or heliocentric cosmology with implications for the status of man in society and the world. In this sense Copernicus was no Copernican, as BLUMENBERG (1965) convincingly argues in an essay on the "Copernican turn". In the more recent philosophical literature, the notion of a "Copernican turn" is frequently used as a metaphor employing the new cosmology as a point of reference in the consideration of man's place within the wider world. Following Blumenberg, who has dedicated a series of valuable books and essays to reflection on the philosophical and ideological consequences of Copernicanism, the "re-construction of the universe designated a change of human identity". Blumenberg's writings do not provide easy reading since he employs occasionally complex philosophical terminology, yet, they are indispensable for those who seek an in-depth, argumentative discourse as a means to approach this multi-faceted topic. BLUMENBERG (1985) treats the prehistory of the new cosmology in detail: Copernicus's contemporaries, the complexities of the reception of Copernicanism until the end of the Enlightenment, and the influence of Kant's *Critique of Pure Reason* on its reception in the late 18th and early 19th centuries. By use of hermeneutic methods, Blumenberg provides intense textual criticism, and has only one flaw – the absence of references to, or study of, original sources.

A seminal treatment of the latter is provided in the work of the German historian of astronomy, ZINNER. His excellent presentation of the overall history of Copernican teaching, which has recently appeared in a revised edition, has the advantage over the majority of the literature cited here, in that it offers an exhaustive and reliable treatment of the complex problem of the sources. Zinner starts with Babylonian and Copernican astronomy, gives ample attention to Peurbach and Regiomontanus, and ends with the completion of the Copernican revolution by Johannes Kepler. In an appendix, Zinner reconstructs Copernicus's library, and supplies a register of his astronomical observations and instruments. This material offers verifiable clues to the decisive philosophical and scientific influences on the formation of the new cosmology.

There are also occasional attempts on the part of scientists to negotiate the philosophical aspects of Copernicanism. Above all, BORN can count as representative of other, less prominent authors. His essay on Einstein's relativity theory convincingly – and with reference to Copernicanism – developed the notion that in modernity, "the man of astronomy has ceased to be of any importance, perhaps except for himself".

Apart from these more philosophical attempts to trace the reception of Copernicanism over time, there are a number of studies favouring an internal, that is empirico-historical, approach. Large sections of DREYER's instructive and eminently readable account of the history of astronomy are devoted to Copernicus's discovery and the evolution of Copernicanism, and his exposition provides a qualified introduction to the problem. His book encompasses the entire prehistory of Copernicanism, proceeding from Greek antiquity via Cusanus to Copernicus and, fittingly, ending with Kepler, who completed the new cosmology. Even more profound is GINGERICH's excellent study, which contrasts the heliocentric model with physical reality, and thus subjects Copernicanism to a historical criticism from a modern point of view. Gingerich proved himself an authoritative Copernicus scholar, not least by his complete census of copies of *De revolutionibus* still in existence, as well as by his analysis of their hand-written comments in the margins.

Reconciliations of the empirico-historical and philosophical approaches to the topic are rare, but there are two authors who have succeeded admirably. With the work of the French historian of science, Alexandre Koyré, and Harvard's philoso-pher of science, Thomas S. Kuhn, the representation of Copernicanism in the 20th century yet again underwent a thorough revision. Already a classic, KOYRÉ's work on the cosmological revolution is required reading. Using Copernicus, Borelli, and Kepler as his main protagonists, Koyré describes the history of astronomical change, and the philosophical problems it produced.

KUHN developed his model of paradigmatic change from his detailed knowledge of the genesis of Copernican cosmology, and employed it to distinguish between cumulative and revolutionary phases in the history of science. His choice of the genesis and spread of Copernicanism for his case study was by no means accidental: the assimilation of Copernican thought up to Kepler constitutes a conclusive demonstration of the manner in which scientific paradigms can change.

ANDREAS KÜHNE

translated by Anna-Katherina Mayer

See also Cosmology; Galilei

Copernicus, Nicolaus 1473–1543

Polish astronomer, physician, and economist

Armitage, Angus, *The World of Copernicus (Sun, Stand Thou Still)*, New York: New American Library, 1951

Baranowski, Henryk, *Bibliografia Kopernikowska 1509–1971*, 2 vols, Warsaw: Panstwowe Wydawnictwo Naukowe, 1958–73

Baranowski, Henryk, "Copernican Bibliography: Selected Materials for the Years 1972–1975", in *Nicolas Copernicus: Quincentenary Celebrations*, Wrocław: Ossolineum, 1977

Birkenmajer, Ludwik Antoni, *Mikolaj Kopernik*, Krakow: Academia Litterarum Cracoviensis, 1900

Biskup, Marian, *Regesta Copernicana: Calendar of Copernicus' Papers*, translated by Stanisław Puppel, Wrocław: Polish Academy of Science Press/Ossolineum, 1973

Curtze, Maximilian, *Nicolaus Coppernicus: Eine biographische Skizze*, Berlin: Paetel, 1899

Gassendi, Pierre, *Tychonis Brahei equitis Dani, astronomorum coryphaei, vita . . .*, Paris, 1654

Hamel, Jürgen, *Nicolaus Copernicus*, Heidelberg: Spektrum, 1994

Hipler, Franz, "Die Biographen des Nikolaus Kopernikus: Ein Gedenkblatt zur vierten Säkularfeier seines Geburtstages", *Altpreussische Monatsschrift*, 10 (1873): 193–218

Kesten, Hermann, *Copernicus and His World*, translated from the German by E.B. Ashton and Norbert Guterman, New York: Roy, and London: Secker and Warburg, 1945

Prowe, Leopold, *Nicolaus Coppernicus*, 2 vols, Berlin: 1883–84; reprinted, Osnabrück: Otto Zeller, 1967

Rosen, Edward, *Three Copernican Treatises*, New York: Columbia University Press, 1939; 3rd revised edition, New York: Octagon Books, 1971

Rosen, Edward, entry in *Dictionary of Scientific Biography*, edited by Charles Coulston Gillespie, vol. 3, New York: Scribner, 1971

Rosen, Edward, "Copernicus' Translation of Theophylactus Simocatta", in *Minor Works*, by Copernicus, edited by Pawel Czartoryski, translated by Rosen with Erna Hilfstein, Warsaw: Polish Scientific Publishers and London: Macmillan, 1985; Baltimore: Johns Hopkins University Press, 1992

Rosenberg, Bernhard-Maria, "Das ärztliche Wirken des Frauenburger Domherrn Nicolaus Copernicus", in *Nicolaus Copernicus zum 500. Geburtstag*, edited by Friedrich Kaulbach, Udo Wilhelm Bargenda and Jürgen Blühdorn, Cologne: Böhlau, 1973

Sommerfeld, Erich, *Die Geldlehre des Nicolaus Copernicus: Texte, Übersetzungen, Kommentare*, Berlin: Akademie, 1978

Starowolski, Szymon, *Scriptorum Polonicorum Hekatontas seu centum illustrium Poloniae scriptorum elogia et vitae*, Frankfurt: 1625

Swerdlow, Noel M. and Otto Neugebauer, *Mathematical Astronomy in Copernicus' De revolutionibus*, New York: Springer, 1984

Wasiutynski, Jeremi, *Kopernik*, Warsaw: Przeworski, 1938

Nicolaus Copernicus must be classed with Erasmus of Rotterdam and Paracelsus as among the most outstanding personalities of early modernity. He is most famous for only one aspect of his work, his heliocentric model of the universe, which has often been taken as the starting point of the scientific revolution.

The scholarship on Copernicus is now so extensive that it barely allows for an overall view. Generally speaking, biographical research on Copernicus was always hampered by a great scarcity of sources. Copernicus's scientific correspondence is lost in its entirety, except for the 1524 letter on the theory of trepidations to Bernhard Wapolski, the head of the cathedral chapter of Frauenburg. Also preserved are 20 letters regarding medical and administrative matters written or dictated by Copernicus, and 120 files and documents that mention him as a witness or author. As a result of the chaos during numerous wars in Ermland, this body of work is now scattered over several archives in Poland, Germany, and Sweden. A portion of the documents from the time of Copernicus's studies in Bologna, Padua, and Ferrara is kept in Italy.

Georg Joachim Rheticus (1514–76) was Copernicus's sole disciple. From his stay in Ermland of nearly three years, from 1539 to 1541, and from Copernicus's communications, he knew more about his teacher's life in the circle of the confratres in the cathedral chapter of Frauenburg than any of his contemporaries. On the basis of this, Rheticus elaborated a biography to which he himself repeatedly referred, but the manuscript of which is now considered irretrievably lost.

The first authors to attempt the life and significance of Copernicus, in the form of brief and descriptive essays, were the Polish scholar Szymon STAROWOLSKI (1588–1656), and the French scientist, theologian, and philosopher Pierre GASSENDI (1592–1655). Both of them worked exclusively with printed sources, and did not make use of the manuscripts then available. Copernicus's unpublished work probably suffered the greatest damage at the hands of Johannes Broscius (1581–1652), professor of mathematics and astronomy at the university of Krakow. Around 1612, Broscius visited Ermland to collect documents for a biography on Copernicus. He took a number of letters and documents with him to Krakow, to utilize them merely for succinct notes and marginalia. Following his death, his entire Copernicus collection was lost. In these 17th-century biographies we already find the plethora of errors and orally-transmitted legends and anecdotes that remain part of the Copernicus literature up to the present.

Meticulous archival research has made letters, documents, and memoranda available, but some only in the 20th century. With their aid, the essential phases of Copernicus's life can be reconstructed. An annalistic register of all available evidence with immediate reference to Copernicus, comprising 520 contemporary documents, has been provided by BISKUP. His manuscript index, in the form of a calendar, forms the basis of all modern biography on Copernicus. Except for minor corrections during the past few years, this index represents the state of the art in Copernicus research.

The Copernicus quatercentenary in 1873 inspired a variety of scholarly activity in Poland and Germany. On the basis of the sources available in Prussia, the Ermlandic church historian and literary scholar HIPLER attempted to evaluate critically and honour all biographical work on Copernicus up to his day. His essay, which is worth reading even today, uncovered the difficulties with which biographical studies of Copernicus are generally confronted, and further developed a hermeneutic model for critical reflection on the fragmentary information on Copernicus's life.

For a brief and readable introduction to the life of Copernicus, the biographical sketch by the Ermlandic historian and scientist, CURTZE, can be recommended. Although the biographical details, and the majority of dates, in the book are in need of correction, in principle, and especially for didactic purposes, Curtze's little book is suitable as a reliable introduction, comprising the most important stages of Copernicus's life. In the English-speaking world, the same purpose is served by Rosen's essays, which have also eliminated a few of Curtze's errors on the basis of improved access to historical sources. Rosen is considered one of the most important Copernicus editors of the post-war period, and he is a major force behind the Polish edition of Copernicus's *Complete Works* which appeared simultaneously in the US.

As a result of its comprehensive treatment of the stages of Copernicus's life and its cultural, political, and scientific context, the biography by PROWE is regarded as unsurpassed to the present, despite some corrections recommended by more recent biographical research. Along with an analysis of the conditions of Copernicus's life, Prowe also developed an image of the Early Renaissance in Krakow, northern Italy, and Ermland. Although the author makes explicit his own standpoint, as a Protestant and a member of the German majority in Eastern Prussia, this does not compromise his differentiated historical judgment. None of the later biographies has succeeded in drawing a comparably multi-layered and historically-based picture of Copernicus. Prowe's work should be viewed within the context of the general rise of historical interest in the sciences in the second half of the 19th century, which also attempted novel historiographical approaches. Prowe, Hipler, and Curtze were all early modernists, and all three worked in eastern Prussia all their lives, displaying a distinct enthusiasm for regional history.

The most likely candidate for a comparison with Prowe's study is the biographical study by BIRKENMAJER, a well-known Polish Copernicus-scholar, which has a broad basis but with an emphasis on astronomy. Polish biographies of Copernicus of a later date can neither claim equal thoroughness with regard to astronomical and historical detail, nor are they free from nationalistic undertones, as displayed in WASIUTYNSKI's otherwise very readable work.

In the decades following Prowe, a number of Copernicus biographies have appeared that are sufficiently informative with regard to Copernicus's life, and which also convey the theoretical tools required for the study of his astronomical work. Candidates for successful compliance with such criteria are ARMITAGE's biography, and also ROSEN's biographical sketches of 1971 in the *Dictionary of Scientific Biography* and *Three Copernican Treatises*, which, though brief, are both reliable and full of detail. However, there is still need for a new scholarly biography that would process all the results and new historical sources on Copernicus over the past 100 years. Even the most recent German Copernicus biography, by HAMEL, cannot remedy this shortcoming, despite being well-written and reliable.

The eminent historians of science, SWERDLOW & NEUGE-BAUR, in their meticulous work, have almost exclusively focused on a discussion of mathematical and astronomical questions. For a reader whose interests are primarily in astronomy, their work is indispensable.

Apart from these general biographies, there are a number of studies on specific aspects of Copernicus's work, such as his activities as a physician, and his administrative and economic endeavours. In this context, SOMMERFELD's essay merits special attention. Containing critical editions and translations into German of all of Copernicus's economic treatises, it deals exhaustively with this aspect of Copernicus's work with detailed and knowledgeable commentaries. Among the wealth of minor studies concerning medicine and pharmacy, ROSENBERG's essay deserves special mention. Presenting Copernicus within the context of late medieval medicine, it edits extracts of his recipes, dietary prescriptions, and medical marginalia. In contrast to his work in astronomy, this area of Copernicus's activities requires a detailed knowledge of the attendant historical circumstances.

A thorough analysis of Copernicus as a humanistic author, and as a translator of the letter of the Byzantine poet and scholar Theophylakos Simokattes, has been provided by ROSEN (1985), within the "Kleine Schriften" of the Polish edition of the *Complete Works*.

The number of laudatory poems, plays, and biographical novels on Copernicus is legion. Frequently these have added to the legends and errors already incorporated in the tradition. While, as a rule, this corpus has no relevance for the tasks of scholarly biography, KESTEN's biography constitutes an exception worth mentioning. Although it exaggerates Copernicus's revolutionary impetus, in contrast to other fictional treatments of the subject it draws on original sources and strives for historical stringency and precision.

The comprehensive and factually reliable bibliography by BARANOWSKI (1958–73) is imperative for a scholarly study of Copernicus life and work. It also covers peripheral secondary literature. However, even with the supplement of 1977, it unfortunately excludes material after 1975. Also to be recommended is ROSEN's selective bibliography of secondary literature (in *Three Copernican Treatises*, 1939; revised, 1971), which restricts itself to essential studies of more recent date. While covering only the period from 1939 to 1970, it offers the advantage of a critical assessment of Copernicus scholarship with detailed annotations; even if not always in agreement with these evaluations, the reader is thus provided with suitable landmarks for the navigation of the biographical literature on Copernicus.

ANDREAS KÜHNE

translated by Anna-Katherina Mayer

Cosmology

Crowe, Michael J., *Modern Theories of the Universe*, New York: New American Library, 1963; reprinted as *Modern Theories of the Universe, from Herschel to Hubble*, New York: Dover, 1994

Kerszberg, Pierre, *The Invented Universe: The Einstein-De Sitter Controversy (1916–17) and the Rise of Relativistic Cosmology*, Oxford: Clarendon Press, and New York; Oxford University Press, 1989

Kragh, Helge, *Cosmology and Controversy: The Historical Development of Two Theories of the Universe*, Princeton, New Jersey: Princeton University Press, 1996

Merleau-Ponty, Jacques, *Cosmologie du XX siècle: Étude épistémologique et historique des théories de la cosmologie contemporaine*, Paris: Gallimard, 1965

North, John D., *The Measure of the Universe: A History of Modern Cosmology*, Oxford: Clarendon Press, 1965; New York: Dover, 1990

North, John D., *The Fontana History of Astronomy and Cosmology*, London: Fontana, 1994; as *The Norton History of Astronomy and Cosmology*, New York: Norton, 1994

Paul, Erich R., *The Milky Way Galaxy and Statistical Cosmology, 1890–1924*, Cambridge and New York: Cambridge University Press, 1993

Smith, Robert W., *The Expanding Universe: Astronomy's "Great Debate" 1900–1931*, Cambridge and New York: Cambridge University Press, 1982

Cosmology is both one of the oldest and one of the most recent areas of science. Man has always been interested in the world at large, and has always asked questions about its origin, size, and ultimate fate. For a very long period, scientific cosmology has been considered part of astronomy, the "universe" being limited to the solar system, the stars, and, since the 19th century, the nebulae. Because of astronomy's central position in the history of science, this kind of limited cosmology (or cosmogony) is very well described in a large number of books dealing with the history of astronomy. However, from about 1900, a new and much wider concept of cosmology arose, and the first models of the entire universe were proposed. The literature on the history of this new phase of scientific cosmology is relatively modest, and is mostly concerned with pre-1945 developments.

NORTH (1994) is one of many comprehensive histories of astronomy, but, contrary to most other works, it is oriented as much towards cosmology as towards classical astronomy. North takes seriously the fact that cosmology experienced a revolution with the theory of relativity, and provides a coherent history of that revolution within the larger historical context of astronomy and physics. In non-technical language, he also covers the importance of progress in observational technologies, without which the cosmological theories would have remained mathematical exercises of academic interest only. This work, which follows developments up to about 1990, includes a valuable bibliography.

Although Einstein's general theory of relativity heralded a revolution in cosmology, the field had already experienced a major reorientation in the late 19th century. Independent of Einstein, astronomers discovered and analyzed a new "realm of the nebulae". This development, being mainly observational and depending on telescope technology, is given a modern treatment in CROWE, starting with William Herschel's nebular universe, and ending with Edwin Hubble's celebrated establishment of a linear relationship between the distances and redshifts of the nebulae. Crowe includes many of the central sources, while its pedagogical style makes it useful for courses in the history of cosmology.

Partly overlapping with Crowe, PAUL is a more specialized and scholarly work on a major tradition in cosmology at the end of the 19th and beginning of the 20th centuries. This "statistical" cosmology tried to establish the size and composition of the universe in terms of star systems similar to the Milky Way. Paul describes statistical cosmology as a research program with phases of progress and decline. His detailed study is revealing also regarding the dynamics of scientific disciplines.

The so-called Great Debate took place about 1920, and was concerned with the size of the Milky Way relative to that of the entire material universe. This is a main subject of Crowe, and is treated in even more depth in SMITH, a standard work on cosmology during the first three decades of the 20th century. Smith gives a precise account of this phase, which led to Hubble's recognition in 1925 that the galaxies (nebulae) are far removed from the Milky Way, and then to Hubble's even more important correlation between red shifts and galactic distances. The linear correlation is usually referred to as the expansion of the universe, but, as discussed by Smith, at first neither Hubble nor others drew this conclusion from the 1929 data.

Smith only refers rather briefly to the relativistic cosmology, which, during the 1920s, had very little connection with observational astronomy. On the whole, the literature on modern cosmology has been preoccupied with either theory or observations, and physical approaches to cosmology have been largely ignored. KERSZBERG is an impressive example of the theoretically oriented literature. It gives a very detailed account of the first phase of relativistic cosmology, in particular the pioneering contribution by Einstein, and the alternative suggested by Willem de Sitter. Kerszberg is concerned with the theoretical and philosophical aspects of early relativistic cosmology – i.e., before the expanding universe became a reality in 1930. On this subject, Kerzberg is an excellent work, but it is also a difficult one that requires considerable knowledge to be useful.

The emphasis on theoretical and conceptual issues is also characteristic of the only two books that offer a comprehensive and penetrating analysis of the development of modern theoretical cosmology, namely NORTH (1965) and MERLEAU-PONTY. The two works have much in common. Not only did they appear the same year, but both are also ambitious attempts to draw philosophical consequences from the developments they analyze. Written just before the Big Bang renaissance of 1965, these works may now appear somewhat dated and unappreciative of physical cosmology, but they are unrivalled when it comes to pre-1960 theoretical cosmology. (Apart from an apologizing preface, the 1990 Dover edition of North is identical to the 1965 edition.) Merleau-Ponty, unfortunately never translated into English, pays much attention to foundational and philosophical questions of cosmology, and not least to the unorthodox theories of Arthur Eddington, Edward Milne, and others. The same is true of the better-known book by North (1994), the second half of which is philosophical rather than historical in nature. Dealing with highly complex subjects, neither of these works makes easy reading; the necessary mathematical background is presupposed in North, whereas Merleau-Ponty has chosen to collect the equations in an appendix.

A more modern account is offered in KRAGH, which deals comprehensively with developments between 1920 and 1970, and focuses on the two rival conceptions of the universe, the evolutionary and the Steady State models. By emphasizing observational and nuclear-physical developments, Kragh is a valuable supplement to the works of North and Merleau-Ponty. In particular, it analyzes in detail the situation in the 1960s, in which the new physical Big Bang cosmology became firmly established. On the other hand, neither Kragh nor any other work deals satisfactorily with the post-1970 development.

HELGE KRAGH

See also Big Bang Theory

Court Society

Apostolidès, Jean-Marie, *Le Roi-machine: spectacle et politique au temps de Louis XIV*, Paris: Editions de Minuit, 1981

Biagioli, Mario, "Scientific Revolution, Social Bricolage, and Etiquette", in *The Scientific Revolution in National Context*, edited by Roy Porter and Mikulás Teich, Cambridge and New York: Cambridge University Press, 1992

Biagioli, Mario, *Galileo, Courtier: The Practice of Science in the Culture of Absolutism*, Chicago: University of Chicago Press, 1993

Biagioli, Mario, "Etiquette, Interdependence, and Sociability in Seventeenth-Century Science", *Critical Inquiry*, 122 (1996): 93–238

Eamon, William, *Science and the Secrets of Nature: Books of Secrets in Medieval and Early Modern Culture*, Princeton, New Jersey: Princeton University Press, 1994

Elias, Norbert, *The Court Society*, translated from the German by Edmund Jephcott, New York: Pantheon

Books, and Oxford: Blackwell, 1983 (original edition, 1969)

Evans, R.J.W., *Rudolf II and His World: A Study in Intellectual History, 1576–1612*, Oxford: Clarendon Press, 1973; reprinted, London: Thames and Hudson, 1997

Findlen, Paula, *Possessing Nature: Museums, Collecting, and Scientific Culture in Early Modern Italy*, Berkeley: University of California Press, 1994

Greenblatt, Stephen, *Renaissance Self-Fashioning: From More to Shakespeare*, Chicago: University of Chicago Press, 1980

Marin, Louis, *Portrait of the King*, translated from the French by Martha Houle, Minneapolis: University of Minnesota Press, 1988 (original edition, 1981)

Moran, Bruce T., "German Prince-Practitioners: Aspects in the Development of Courtly Science, Technology, and Procedures in the Renaissance", *Technology and Culture*, 22 (1981): 253–74

Moran, Bruce T., "Patronage and Institutions: Courts, Universities, and Academies in Germany: An Overview 1500–1750", in *Patronage and Institutions: Science, Technology, and Medicine at the European Court, 1500–1750*, edited by Moran, Woodbridge, Suffolk, and Rochester, New York: Boydell and Brewer, 1991

Revel, Jacques, "The Uses of Civility", in *A History of Private Life* vol. 3: *Passions of the Renaissance*, edited by Roger Chartier, translated from the French by Arthur Goldhammer, Cambridge, Massachusetts: Belknap Press of Harvard University Press, 1989 (original edition, 5 vols, 1985–87)

Smith, Pamela H., *The Business of Alchemy: Science and Culture in the Holy Roman Empire*, Princeton, New Jersey: Princeton University Press, 1994

Tribby, Jay, "Cooking (with) Clio: Eloquence and Experiment in Seventeenth-Century Florence", *Journal of the History of Ideas*, 52 (1991): 417–39

Tribby, Jay, "Body/Building: Living the Museum Life in Early Modern Europe", *Rhetorica*, 10 (1992): 139–63

Westman, Robert, "The Astronomer's Role in the Sixteenth Century: A Preliminary Study", *History of Science*, 18 (1980): 105–47

Whigham, Frank, *Ambition and Privilege: The Social Tropes of Elizabethan Courtesy Theory*, Berkeley: University of California Press, 1984

ELIAS is the starting point for anyone interested in court culture. He argues that the court's ethic of consumption and display formed not only the basis for elaborate networks of patronage, but was also integral to the delineation of hierarchies of social status and honour, to the development of the modern bureaucratic state, and to the sociogenesis of individual identity. He describes the court as a site in which individuals and groups were both distinguished from one another and bound together by elaborate codes of honour, etiquette, and civility. Elites, he argues, attempted to define and preserve their privileged positions within the status hierarchy by creating exclusionary cultural distinctions based on etiquette, manners, speech, dress, and knowledge; conversely, these modes of distinction were adopted by those of lesser status in attempts to reposition themselves closer to the centres of power. It is

through the monarchy's strategy of elusive proximity – of playing one group off against another – that the engines of cultural production were driven; and it is through precisely these strategies of social and epistemic distinction that the king's power came to be articulated as being absolute.

There were essentially two separate traditions associated with the notion of civility, one represented by Erasmus, and the other by Castiglione. It was Erasmus's hope that civility would provide a common point of reference for social discourse in a world that was experiencing dramatic and tumultuous change. For Castiglione, on the other hand, the social practices associated with a courtier's honour were established to create, and maintain, social distinctions, not elide them. REVEL's elegant contribution to *A History of Private Life* explores the tensions inherent in these two traditions, through an analysis of the categories of civility, etiquette, and politeness in the 16th and 17th centuries.

Through a series of case studies (the writing of history, the design of money, portraiture, cartography, and pageantry), MARIN analyses the meaning of representation and its metonymic relationship to monarchical power. APOSTOLIDÈS examines a variety of courtly activities (painting, sculpture, ballet, poetry, and the casting of medallions), and illustrates how these were constitutive of a new ideology of spectacle, in which state, citizens, and power were all given meaning by reference to the symbolic body of the king. Both authors, like Elias, focus on 17th-century France, showing how status position was dependent on the ability to articulate a representation of the king, and of kingship that unambiguously glorified royal power and prestige. These authors thereby illustrate the dialectic nature within which intellectuals legitimated their cultural production and augmented their social standing, while at the same time showing how this cultural production came to legitimate the image and authority of absolutism.

GREENBLATT explores the context of elite literary culture in 16th-century England. He outlines the social and psychological anxieties concomitant with social and economic mobility, and how these anxieties intertwined with an awareness of the malleability of individual self-identity. In his account, such 16th-century manuals of court behaviour as Castiglione's *Book of the Courtier* are examined as practical guides for "self-fashioning" in a society whose "members were nearly always on stage". Yet, the significance of Greenblatt's book rests more in the detailed analysis of More, Tyndall, and Wyatt, among others, and the ways in which he describes the complex filiations between cultural production, individual psyche, and institutional power as creating the conditions for negotiated processes of "self-fashioning".

WHIGHAM also focuses on Elizabethan courtly behaviour, analysing the manner in which the literary genre of the courtesy book contributed to an understanding of the social hierarchy as a human construct. He argues that this resonated closely with the idea that the self could be similarly constructed. Accordingly, he argues that courtesy books (as "how-to" manuals for self-fashioning) provided critical resources for the strategic transformation of the self, as a means of navigating social space.

EVANS closely examines the intellectual and cultural milieu of the court of Rudolph II (patron of the likes of Tycho, Kepler, Dee, and Bruno), and, more generally, the mental universe of the court in late 16th-century Europe. He reveals significant connections between diverse elements of early modern culture, showing how the observation and practical investigation of nature were characteristics not only of "science", but of artistic, literary, philosophical, and occult practices as well. He explains that this "heightened awareness of a world of observation" was closely linked – through magic and the occult – to intuitions of an underlying cosmic order sanctioning existing hierarchies of power. His book is something of an obituary of this world view, for it characterises the development of pansophistic thought – in all is manifold forms – as a kind of intellectual consolation for the perceived decadence of life in the Rudolphine court, and for the political, social and economic decline brought on by the Thirty Years' War.

WESTMAN, in his seminal article, argues that the princely court provided an alternative space to the more rigid pedagogical structure of the university. It was thus by moving to the court that practitioners of mathematics and astronomy were able to transform the social status of their disciplines and legitimate their practices. This was possible insofar as "science" (its skills, its instrumentation, its presumed utility, and its glamour) epitomised courtly imperatives of consumption and display, and was thus construed as a means of enhancing the prestige and honour of both princes and practitioners.

A number of scholars have explored the close relationship between the princely court, the procedural values of "science", and the development of the bureaucratic state. MORAN (1991), for example, argues that aristocratic support for "science" was enlisted by adapting technical and scientific roles and procedures to the special projects of princes. He argues that exact and critical observation, collection of information, and the development of collaborative efforts through informal routes of communication, were closely linked to the development of administrative structures of the state, associated with political consolidation, territorial expansion and commercial growth. Pointing to the practical involvement of princes in mathematics, astronomy, instrument-making, mining, and cartography, MORAN (1981) expands the patronage model of court to include princes who were not only patrons but also practitioners. He argues for an understanding of early modern science that is far more sensitive to context than was previously the case, seeing princely concern for observational detail and mechanical extravagance as being closely related to artistic values associated with the courtly style of Renaissance mannerism.

BIAGIOLI (1993) takes up Westman's hypothesis, that the court contributed to the cognitive legitimation of the new science, by providing a locale outside the university for the social legitimation of its practitioners. He refines this idea through writing a detailed microhistorical account of Galileo's social trajectory in the Medician court. The book traces Galileo's court-based articulation of a new socioprofessional identity – that of court philosopher – and examines the relationship between this identity and Galileo's work. Arguing that "patronage was an institution without walls", Biagioli makes a forceful case for the ways in which patronage dynamics informed the social world within which Galileo produced and presented his science. Galileo, he argues, was able to build a constituency for his discoveries only insofar as he was able to present them in terms congenial to court culture. Thus Galileo

was not simply a mathematician/astronomer, but a courtly philosopher and retainer who strove to produce natural philosophical gifts – such as the "Medician stars" (the moons of Jupiter) – which would contribute both to his own, and his prince's, glory.

BIAGIOLI (1996) reflects on the significance of his study of Galileo, arguing that there was not one, but two "scientific revolutions" in the 17th century. The first is well-known, and concerns conceptual changes in fields such as physics, medicine, and astronomy. The second, however, though just as significant, has until recently remained obscure, being concerned less with science *per se* than with its socio-cultural context; mainly, the transformation of the socioprofessional identity of the "scientist", through a shift in the institutional locus from the universities to the court. BIAGIOLI (1992) takes this a step further, arguing that the move from the university to the court was followed by a move from the court to the academy. This entailed a corresponding shift in the attribution of credibility, away from a reliance on a personal bond with the prince and towards the collective sanction of a community of equals. Yet, despite the seeming distance between the court and the scientific academy, Biagioli maintains that the dispositions of *civilité* and *politesse* remained poignant and powerful factors, conditioning academic forms of sociability and cognitive legitimation. Thus, he concludes with the suggestion that the conditions of possibility of our own evidentiary standards, practices of authorship, and notions of collaboration – though first articulated within the context of 17th-century scientific academies – ultimately derive from the form of life first established at court.

EAMON focuses on the changes in both scientific practices and personnel that accompanied the move from universities to the court. He argues that this shift entailed a transformation in the "logic of scientific discovery", from an essentially scholastic mode of deductive reasoning, to one based on the primacy of inductive logic, experience, and exploration. Eamon suggests that this new mode of doing science mirrored the dominant value-system of the court, and can be compared with the archetypal noble pursuit of the hunt. The shift to the court also resulted in a dramatic change in the scientific work-force: thus, formerly marginal, and indeed, suspect disciplines (such as engineering, mathematics, alchemy, and magic) gained in status, as they came to be seen in terms of the technical and practical expertise they could provide in furthering princely power and prestige. In this regard, Eamon argues that the occult sciences were particularly well-suited to the court and its patronage networks, because they fit neatly into a value-system within which curiosity was considered definitive of elite identity. Who better to inspire this curiosity than the magus, whose hunt for nature's arcane secrets and marvellous rarities was combined with a theatrical view of science which aimed not simply to inform, but to delight and astonish?

The title of FINDLEN points to the close relationship of knowledge and power, for, in her view, acts of possession were visible signatures of social status. Findlen argues that the possession of such qualities as curiosity and civility were definitive of Italy's patrician elite. Displayed at court (through the diverse mediums of speech, etiquette, dress, and collections of art and nature), the possession of curiosity and civility was among the principle expressions of the cultivated man – and hence, a clear sign of his social mastery. Like Biagioli, Findlen borrows heavily from Elias in explaining the 17th-century discipline of natural history and its drive to master nature, with reference to the social logic of the court. In the 16th century, naturalists collected everything indiscriminately in their attempts to construct a microcosm of the universe. In the 17th century, on the other hand, collections came to be distinguished for their exoticism – that is, by the wonder that they could inspire. As Findlen puts it, the 17th century reinvented the museum as "a Baroque theatre of Marvels". Findlen understands the 17th century's emphasis on curiosity and civility as being crucial to the disciplinary formation of natural history. But she sees this "progress" as moving in a non-linear fashion, for, citing museum catalogues as evidence, she interprets the shift from the Renaissance to the Baroque as a shift from professionalism to dilettantism, from collecting as a professional activity to collecting as a noble pastime – that while 16th-century catalogues were directed at apothecaries and physicians, 17th-century catalogues were directed at a courtly audience. Indeed, she suggests, this changed emphasis reflects an overall transformation of collecting, from a practice that centred on utility to one that reflected instead an ethic of courtly virtuosity. This change of emphasis came from the top down, for it was inspired in its entirety by elite sensitivity to the necessity and importance of displaying civility and curiosity. Civility, Findlen explains, shaped the paradigm of collecting, as it embodied the self-conscious connection between possession and power, display and self-display. Collecting curiosities and possessing nature were, in this sense, a means of articulating social differences; they were not simply philosophical tropes, but social attributes central to Italy's patrician culture. In search of patronage, early modern naturalists thus fashioned their practices in imitation of court spectacles (as gifts). Knowledge, says Findlen, was simply another form of display, for by making their collections and experiments of interest for their courtly patrons, naturalists were legitimating their philosophical as well as their social positions. Indeed, it was through the courtly valorisation of curiosity that naturalists were able to escape the authority of ancient texts, and step into and engage directly with nature herself.

TRIBBY (1992) discusses how Francesco Redi, a 17th-century Italian natural philosopher, framed his experimental work on snakes as a theatrical display to delight and amuse potential patrons. He argues that Redi used his experiments to appeal to courtly conventions by drawing his audience into decorous conversation with both marvellous objects and ancient authorities; thus, Redi was able to legitimate both his own status and the cognitive worth of his experiments. TRIBBY (1991) suggests a connection between the display of objects in early modern collections and the courtly imperative of display of the civil body. He maintains that the courtier's use of collections as a strategy of social/status distinction was similar to other forms of status-conscious behaviour, such as those involving gesture, manners, speech, and dress, etc.

SMITH examines the relationship between alchemy, commerce, and political power in the German-speaking courts of the late 17th century. Focusing on the career of Johann Becher, she describes how he used his alchemical and mechanical knowledge in an attempt to secure patronage. Promising that his schemes would yield tremendous returns and immortal

renown, Becher (like Eamon's magus) was exemplary of a new type of expertise, one in which esoteric knowledge claimed a privileged place within the management of Church and state. What is of particular interest here is Smith's account of how Becher, in attempting to navigate the vagaries of court society, used his knowledge of the alchemical and mechanical arts to mediate between a ruling elite, hostile to merchant capital but in great need of money, and various practical commercial schemes, such as workshops and slave colonies in the New World. In this way, Smith demonstrates how the "business of alchemy" played a role in creating a tenuous alliance between the values of a rising commercial class and the values of a courtly elite.

MICHAEL WINTROUB

Cryogenics

Anderson, Jr, Oscar Edward, *Refrigeration in America: A History of a New Technology and Its Impact*, Princeton, New Jersey: Princeton University Press, 1953

Dahl, Per Fridtjof, *Superconductivity: Its Historical Roots and Development from Mercury to the Ceramic Oxides*, New York: American Institute of Physics, 1992

Gavroglu, Kostas and Yorgos Goudaroulis, *Methodological Aspects of the Development of Low Temperature Physics, 1881–1956: Concepts out of Context(s)*, Dordrecht: Kluwer Academic, 1989

Gavroglu, Kostas and Yorgos Goudaroulis (eds), *Through Measurement to Knowledge: The Selected Papers of Heike Kamerlingh Onnes, 1853–1926*, Dordrecht: Kluwer Academic, 1991

Gavroglu, Kostas, *Fritz London: A Scientific Biography*, Cambridge and New York: Cambridge University Press, 1995

Hård, Mikael, *Machines are Frozen Spirit: The Scientification of Refrigeration and Brewing in the 19th Century – A Weberian Interpretation*, Frankfurt: Campus, and Boulder, Colorado: Westview Press, 1994

Mendelssohn, Kurt, *The Quest for Absolute Zero: The Meaning of Low Temperature Physics*, London: Weidenfeld and Nicolson, and New York: McGraw Hill, 1966

Scurlock, Ralph G. (ed.), *History and Origins of Cryogenics*, Oxford: Clarendon Press, and New York: Oxford University Press, 1992

Thevenot, Roger, A *History of Refrigeration Throughout the World*, translated from the French by J. C. Fidler, Paris: International Institute of Refrigeration, 1979

Woolrich, Willis Raymond, *The Men Who Created Cold: A History of Refrigeration*, New York: Exposition Press, 1967

Cryogenics is the science of the production and effects of very low temperatures, and its history is closely tied to that of the refrigeration industry. The literature covered in this entry includes histories of the refrigeration industry and superconductivity, historical publications by scientists in the field, and monographs on prominent individuals: Carl von Linde, Heike Kamerlingh Onnes, and Fritz London.

WOOLRICH is intended for the non-specialist. It traces the development and use of refrigeration by the Gulf States of North America, Australia, and western Europe, and the emphasis is on economically feasible machine designs that enabled the large-scale commercial use of refrigeration. There are also short biographical notes on a large number of engineers.

ANDERSON is a historian who attempts to relate the development and utilisation of the refrigeration industry to "national development". The author deals systematically with the technical aspects as well as the uses of the refrigeration industry in the US between 1830 and 1950. One of the work's great strengths is its extensive references to technical reports and other publications of the US Department of Agriculture.

A collection of essays tracing the development of various aspects of low temperature physics in different countries is edited by SCURLOCK. In the introduction, Scurlock emphasises the interaction of training, research, and industrial innovation in the development of cryogenics. Despite the acknowledged omission of the USSR, which played such a major role in low temperature physics, the essays present a valuable overview of what happened in many countries and of certain commercial firms (e.g. British Oxygen). Of particular interest are the two long articles on the US (comprising a third of the book). The book ends with an article by the editor on the future trends in cryogenics.

The main focus of GAVROGLU & GOUDAROULIS (1989) is methodological. On the basis of extensive archive material, they discuss and classify what they term as new phenomena and unexpected results, and propose a taxonomy of a series of theoretical and experimental tests in the history of low temperature physics. The authors claim that, notwithstanding the immense technical difficulties involved, the fundamental difficulty in the search for a satisfactory explanation of superconductivity and superfluidity was conceptual. They use a critical Lakatosian approach to analyse systematically the new concepts and their continuous metamorphoses, and are led to the schema "concepts out of context(s)" which they propose as a heuristic device for understanding the way concepts acquire new and novel meanings. There is special emphasis on the so-called macroscopic character of these low temperature phenomena, which can only be comprehended in purely quantum mechanical terms.

MENDELSSOHN, one of the pioneers of low temperature physics research, presents the various phases in the history of cryogenics, from the mid-19th century to the period after World War II. His emphasis is on the experiments, but he also includes sufficient theoretical details. There are many references to research at the Royal Institution in London, where James Dewar liquefied hydrogen for the first time in 1898.

One of the past presidents of the International Union of Refrigeration, THEVENOT presents an impressive narrative of the history of cold. It is not the author's intention to write a historical work as such, but he successfully presents an exhaustive quasi-reference book, especially for the historian of technology. Although covering the scientific developments, much more interesting are the sections on how the refrigeration industry was used in various countries, and the way refrigeration was applied to agriculture and the food industry. There is extensive discussion of the household refrigerator and air conditioning. The comparison of the situation in different countries during three different periods (early 20th century, and before and after World War II) is also very informative. In the extensive chronological list included at the end of the book, a number of not so well-known instances in the development of cryogenics are noted.

Contributing to the history and sociology of technology, HÅRD recounts how thermodynamics influenced the development of refrigeration technology. More specifically, the book concentrates on Carl von Linde, whose innovations radically changed the researches in low temperature physics as well as the refrigeration industry. Despite the fact that Linde was heavily supported by the brewing industry, the processes and machines that bear his name were the major players in his successful bid, starting in the mid-1870s, to make liquid air available cheaply in large quantities. The author approaches the material through a Weberian method of analysis, using the notions of theoretical, formal, and practical rationalization processes articulated in Weber's numerous works.

DAHL traces the development of superconductivity from 1911, when Heike Kamerlingh Onnes first discovered the phenomenon, to its more recent use in the building of accelerators for elementary particles. The book's main emphasis is on experimental developments, and it analyses in detail almost all of the related papers published by Kamerlingh Onnes in the *Communications from the Physical Laboratory* of Leiden. Of particular interest is the section concerning the Meissner experiment of 1933, which, contrary to the expectations of the physicists, showed that superconductors were diamagnetic, thus transforming radically the focus of subsequent theoretical research.

GAVROGLU & GOUDAROULIS`s 1991 work is a selection of papers by Heike Kamerlingh Onnes, divided into five categories: 1) those referring to the plans for developing the cryogenic laboratory at Leiden ("the coldest spot on earth") and to the planned experiments for reaching progressively lower temperatures; 2) Kamerlingh Onnes's extensive theoretical researches on the equation of state, and his classic papers on the liquefaction of helium; 3) papers concerning the properties of liquid helium; and 4) and 5) papers on his electrical and magnetic researches at low temperatures. The book has a long historical introduction, editorial notes, and a comprehensive list of Kamerlingh Onnes's publications, and extensive use is made of the hitherto unpublished correspondence between James Dewar and Heike Kamerlingh Onnes.

GAVROGLU has written a scientific biography of Fritz London who, together with his brother Heinz, was in 1935 the first to propose a satisfactory phenomenological theory of superconductivity, introducing the concept of macroscopic quantum phenomena to account for both superconductivity and superfluidity. In this context, Fritz London proposed that superfluidity was a case of Bose–Einstein condensation. The book includes an examination of other proposed theoretical schemata concerning low temperature phenomena and traces, through the use of much archival material, disputes, and discussions involving London and several other protagonists of low temperature physics.

KOSTAS GAVROGLU

Curie, Marie 1867–1934

Polish-born French chemist and physicist

Cotton, Eugénie, *Les Curies*, Paris: Seghers, 1963

Curie, Eve, *Madame Curie*, translated from the French by Vincent Sheean, New York: Doubleday, 1937; London: Heinemann, 1938

Curie, Marie, *Pierre Curie*, translated from the French by Charlotte and Vernon Kellogg, New York: Macmillan, 1923

Davis, John L., "The Research School of Marie Curie in the Paris Faculty, 1907–14", *Annals of Science*, 52 (1995): 321–55

Fölsing, Ulla, *Marie Curie: Wegbereiter einer neuen Naturwissenschaft*, Munich: Piper, 1990

Giroud, Françoise, *Marie Curie: A Life*, translated from the French by Lydia Davis, New York: Holmes and Meier, 1986 (original edition, 1981)

Klickstein, Herbert S., *Marie Sklodowska Curie: Recherches sur les substances radioactives: A Bio-Bibliographical Study*, Philadelphia: Mallinckrodt Classics of Radiology, vol. 2, 1966

Ksoll, Peter and Fritz Vögtle, *Marie Curie*, Reinbeck bei Hamburg: Rowohlt, 1988

Pflaum, Rosalynd, *Grand Obsession: Madame Curie and Her World*, New York: Doubleday, 1989

Pycior, Helena M., "Marie Curie's 'Anti-Natural Path': Time only for Science and Family", in *Uneasy Careers and Intimate Lives: Women in Science, 1789–1979*, edited by Pnina G. Abir-Am and Dorinda Outram, New Brunswick, New Jersey: Rutgers University Press, 1987, 190–215

Pycior, Helena M., "Reaping the Benefits of Collaboration while Avoiding Its Pitfalls: Marie Curie's Rise to Scientific Prominence", *Social Studies of Science*, 23 (1993): 301–23

Pycior, Helena M., "Pierre Curie and 'His Eminent Collaborator Mme Curie': Complementary Partners", in *Creative Couples in the Sciences*, edited by Pycior, Nancy G. Slack and Pnina G. Abir-Am, New Brunswick, New Jersey: Rutgers University Press, 1996, 39–56

Quinn, Susan, *Marie Curie: A Life*, New York: Simon and Schuster, and London: Heinemann, 1995

Reid, Robert, *Marie Curie*, New York: Saturday Review Press, 1974

Wołczak, Olgierd, *Maria Skłodowska-Curie und ihre Familie*, Leipzig: Teubner, 1977

The life of Marie Curie has attracted numerous biographers and a multitude of admiring and curious readers. However, the romance inherent in her life has led Curie's biographers to focus more on its personal aspects, and much less on her scientific work and its broader context and significance.

Basic elements of her life, work, views, and personality can be gleaned from Marie CURIE's biography of Pierre Curie, which includes her perspective on her scientific collaboration with her husband. At the urging of the American journalist, Marie Mattingley Meloney, who wrote the book's acclamatory introduction, Curie appended autobiographical notes to this work.

Eve CURIE portrays her mother as an idealistic, disinterested woman, who was tough and persevering, while remaining inwardly tender and fragile. This biography, published just three years after Marie Curie's death, is the source for many subsequent biographical works. Eve Curie has adroitly woven together selections from private correspondence, quotations from friends and relatives, and excerpts from documents and published texts, with a warp provided by the experiences of her own childhood and youth. The result is a compelling account with the immediacy of first-hand knowledge, and is both aesthetically pleasing and emotionally uplifting, but it remains unsatisfactory for the historian. By consistently presenting Marie Curie in the most favorable light, less flattering interpretations remain unconsidered, and important aspects that clash with the ideal image are glossed over. As was common for the time, notes, bibliography, and index are not included.

Eugénie COTTON, a friend of the Curie family, based her biography on her own reminiscences of Marie Curie and Curie's sister, Helena, and on Eve Curie's biography. The second half of Cotton's book focuses on the life of Irène Curie, who is regarded as a disciple of her mother.

It was not until 1967 that a biographer presented cracks in this idealized image. REID shows us a woman who could be stubborn as well as persistent, annoying as well as analytical, cold as well as objective, haughty as well as self-assured, emotionally vulnerable as well as strong and loyal, and sometimes unwise or indiscreet in her personal life while remaining organized and logical in her scientific work. One has the feeling that Reid emerged from his research with a personal dislike for his subject, which has colored his interpretations of her motives and actions, as well as his estimation of her scientific worth. However, although Reid has not written a scientific biography, he devotes a portion of the text to the scientific background, content, and context of Marie Curie's work. He appears to have been the first biographer to elaborate on connections between the chronic illnesses of the Curies and the radioactive substances with which they worked, and he skillfully integrates this material into his story, providing a readable, popular biography.

As a journalist, GIROUD has added germane material from news events of the time to a matrix based on the biographies by Eve Curie and Reid. Her perceptiveness in discerning thematic elements in Marie Curie's life, and her success in integrating these throughout the text, make for smooth and insightful reading. Originally entitled *An Honorable Woman*, Giroud shows us the meaning of this attribute in pre-war France, and how Marie Curie lost and regained it in the eyes of the public, all the while taking us through the life of what, we are led to infer, always was an honorable woman. Curie's Polish roots, her emotional dependence on motherly women, her transformation from one scornful of social conventions and monetary matters to a skilled fund-raiser and figurehead for French science, are deftly traced. However, this is not a scientific or scholarly biography, and the reader should not rely on the small amount of scientific and historical information provided.

PFLAUM makes use of the earlier biographies, supplemented with material from her own interviews with 18 relatives, friends, and colleagues of Marie Curie. Having received access to previously closed correspondence between Marie Curie's daughter, Irène, and Irène's husband, Frédéric Joliot, she moves into a biography of this scientific couple midway through the book. Pflaum provides some new material and interesting detail, although the sometimes awkward phrasing and shifting foci of the text detract from the readability of her book.

The most comprehensive personal biography of Marie Curie is by QUINN, who makes adept use of the diary kept by Curie after her husband's death, not released to scholars until 1990. Quinn also uses family material previously available only in Polish, translations from Swedish documents concerning Marie Curie's Nobel prize (1911), and testimonials from friends at the time of the scandal concerning Curie's relationship with her colleague, Paul Langevin, in the development of a rich, multifaceted portrait of her subject. Quinn brings new perspectives and insights to this biography – for example, drawing attention to Curie's apparent emotional neglect of her children – and tackles modern issues and concerns, such as the role of feminism in Marie Curie's life, and the ethics of the Langevin affair, although here she does not succeed in avoiding anachronism. She uses vignettes of life in the Curie laboratory to illustrate Curie's relationship with her students, and appraises the extent of her knowledge of the hazards of radioactivity. In order to give a complete picture of Marie Curie, Quinn also supplies useful, readable background information on turn-of-the-century science, and on Curie's work within that context.

For the German reader, WOŁCZAK, KSOLL & VÖGTLE, and FÖLSING provide summaries of Marie Curie's life and work. Fölsing focuses on modern sociological concerns, such as women in science, marriage and careers, and feminism.

Intimations that Pierre Curie was largely responsible for his wife's success, and that Marie Curie's reputation exceeded the quality of her scientific work, first surfaced among Curie's contemporaries, and have continued to reappear as recently as Pflaum's biography. PYCIOR (1987) counters these allegations by analyzing Curie's contributions to radioactivity up to 1903, the year in which she shared the Nobel prize with Pierre Curie and Henri Becquerel. Pycior shows how Pierre and Marie Curie took pains to ensure that she would be recognized as an independent researcher, in spite of the obstacles posed by her gender and her marriage to a respected physicist. The key was their publication policy; Marie Curie published a number of papers under her own name, the contributions of Pierre and Marie Curie to their joint publications were carefully distinguished, and self-citation kept the contributions of each partner in view. On the other hand, PYCIOR (1993) shows how Curie's career development and professional style were profoundly influenced by her family situation, first as a daughter and sister in her family of origin, then as the wife of a well-known physicist, mother, and widow. Finally, PYCIOR (1996) takes the innovative approach of tracing and analyzing the dynamics of the Curies' scientific collaboration, and uncovers a multifaceted complementarity in personalities, styles, aspirations, and interests, which led to the remarkable success of their collaboration.

KLICKSTEIN considers Marie Curie's doctoral thesis to be the culmination of her creative science, and views her later research as primarily a consolidation of this earlier work. On the question of Curie's contribution to the collaboration with her husband, Klickstein concludes, from an analysis of the Curies' laboratory notebooks, that this work was truly a joint enterprise.

Several writers have commented on connections between Marie Curie and the scientific career of her daughter, Irène Curie, including Cotton and Pflaum. Meanwhile, DAVIS has investigated Curie's influence on her students during an earlier period, analyzing her role as director of a research school before the outbreak of World War I.

MARJORIE MALLEY

Cuvier, Georges 1769–1832

French anatomist and paleontologist

Appel, Toby A., *The Cuvier–Geoffroy Debate: French Biology in the Decades Before Darwin*, Oxford and New York: Oxford University Press, 1987

Bourdier, G.C., entry in *Dictionary of Scientific Biography*, edited by Charles Coulston Gillispie, vol. 3, New York: Scribner, 1971

Coleman, William, *Georges Cuvier, Zoologist: A Study in the History of Evolution Theory*, Cambridge, Massachusetts: Harvard University Press, 1964

Eiseley, Loren C., *Darwin's Century: Evolution and the Men Who Discovered It*, New York: Doubleday, 1958; London: Gollancz, 1959

Flourens, M.J.P., *Cuvier: Histoire de ses travaux*, 2nd edition, Paris: Paulin, 1845

Mayr, Ernst, *The Growth of Biological Thought: Diversity, Evolution, and Inheritance*, Cambridge, Massachusetts: Harvard University Press, 1982

Outram, Dorinda, *Georges Cuvier: Vocation, Science and Authority in Post-Revolutionary France*, Manchester: Manchester University Press, 1984

Outram, Dorinda, "Uncertain Legislator: Georges Cuvier's Laws of Nature in Their Intellectual Context", *Journal of the History of Biology*, 19 (1986): 323–68

Rudwick, Martin J.S., *The Meaning of Fossils: Episodes in the History of Palaeontology*, London: Macdonald, and New York: Elsevier, 1972

Theunissen, Bert, "The Relevance of Cuvier's Lois Zoologiques for His Palaeontological Work", *Annals of Science*, 43 (1986): 543–56

Georges Cuvier's early biographers were mainly concerned with his personality and character, partly as a result of Cuvier's careful construction of his own image during his lifetime – he was a master at putting forward his claims to scientific achievement. More recently, scholars have examined his scientific work and the effects of the socio-political environment on his career.

FLOURENS was a pupil of Cuvier and later inherited Cuvier's post of permanent secretary of the Académie des Sciences. His biography includes a short autobiography based on an abbreviated version of Cuvier's manuscript prepared by his widow. The original has been lost, and sections unacceptable to his wife and others close to him may have been excised.

BOURDIER describes the young Cuvier as a precocious child with an astonishing memory. According to Bourdier, Cuvier had great admiration for the work of Buffon from whom he learned much, but, unlike the latter, he failed to view phenomena within the time dimension. The brilliance of his career was partly a consequence of the importance of his work; he gathered some 13,000 items for the Museum d'Histoire Naturelle in Paris, delivered reports on the progress of scientific research for the Académie, and published three general works on zoology, including *Le Règne animale* (1829). Cuvier also had great ability as a teacher, and was influential in the field of higher education. Establishing a reputation as a devoted servant of the monarchy, he became councillor of state in 1814. Bourdier faults him for being authoritarian, somewhat "Germanic" in mentality, and surrounding himself with collaborators who did not challenge his ideas sufficiently.

COLEMAN's purpose is to outline the major features of Cuvier's zoological theory and practice. Never before had an experienced anatomist so thoroughly studied the remains of extinct animals. Cuvier believed the universe was orderly, and his main purpose was to discover the laws that govern the natural world. He was not an adventurous thinker, and the ideas gained from his early experience stayed with him. Aristotle's functional conception of the organism was of primary importance to his thinking, and he was opposed to the evolutionary ideas of Lamarck. Immutability was the essence of Cuvier's doctrine; variation affected only unimportant parts of an organism. Each taxonomic category was a sharply defined and morphologically stable unit, and his principle of the correlation of parts, although lacking in empirical justification, was at the heart of his work in comparative anatomy. His second anatomical rule was the principle of the subordination of characters, with the "type" concept a practical tool for the systematization of animal species. His *Leçons d'anatomie comparée* (1800) was the first truly complete work in the history of comparative anatomy. Coleman contends that Cuvier focused the attention of botanists and zoologists on the problem of biological adaptation because he emphasized the functional integrity of the individual organism.

OUTRAM (1984) examines issues relevant to the formation of Cuvier's career. Rather than providing a general account of his scientific work, she is concerned with how Cuvier arrived at a conscious knowledge of his own scientific vocation, and his subsequent interaction with the French scientific and social/political world. He was undoubtedly a gifted naturalist from childhood, who benefited from a rigorous and systematic German education, and from seven years of intensive reading and fieldwork in Normandy as a young man. His move to Paris was a gamble; he was admitted to the Institut de France at the age of 26 as a result of the upheaval in the scientific world caused by the Terror. Cuvier developed a "cosmopolitan ethos" through his move from a small dynastic state, the principality of Montebeliard, to a large nation-state, and his tenure at the Museum accelerated the progress of his work and offered him great visibility to the public. Cuvier was regarded by contemporaries as a great manipulator of patronage in the fields of science and education; he used his power to insist on norms and research programs to which he was committed, but Outram argues that his career was one of continuous controversy, because there was no universally accepted synthesis in natural science and thus conflict in ideas was an inescapable fact of public life.

APPEL examines the best-known instance of conflict in Cuvier's professional career: his acrimonious debate with his erstwhile colleague and collaborator, Geoffroy Saint-Hilaire.

The latter was as noted in his day as Cuvier in the fields of comparative anatomy and zoology. The two had worked together to augment the Museum's collections, but they soon developed a scientific rivalry. Geoffroy espoused the morphological approach to animal structure, which was known in France and Britain as "philosophical anatomy". This debate is now regarded most often as a confrontation between a teleological and a morphological approach to nature. Both Cuvier and Geoffrey defended extreme positions, and the debate exposed the untenability of both their views. Appel also looks at the controversy within the context of different scientific methodologies. Cuvier championed the naturalist's role as empiricist, one who gathers "positive facts"; he saw speculation and hypothesis as dangerous to orthodox religious and social beliefs, fearing above all a return to revolution and rule by the mob. In addition, Appel examines the personalities, institutions and micropolitics of science in Cuvier's day, recognizing that Cuvier exploited all the authority of his multiple positions to combat Geoffrey's approach to anatomy.

OUTRAM (1984) remarks that Michel Foucault (in *Les Mots et les choses*, 1966) sees Cuvier's work as marking the end of "history" as it had been understood by the 18th century. Cuvier contributed to a new arrangement of knowledge as a result of his focus on function over organic structure: classification no longer arises from order but from function, which is related to environment. Foucault refers to Cuvier's "fixism", which defines a stability of being for an organism, which can thus possess a history.

OUTRAM (1986) continues to examine Cuvier's work and life, this time within the context of the developing French life sciences of his time. When Cuvier arrived in Paris, zoology and anatomy were ripe for conceptual reorientation. He was receptive to the ideas of Bichat's newly-developed physiology, and the work of the botanist de Jussieu gave him the real basis for his classificatory work on the lower groups of animals. From German science, Cuvier used his interest in the physiological comparison of animals as the basis of his classification, but rejected *Naturphilosophie*. He also rejected embryological hypotheses as important in the history of life. Cuvier thus altered the relationships between different fields of knowledge, rather than expanding their content. His eclectic applications meant that little of his own work was completely coherent (his observational correlations were ambiguous as laws), and although his achievement in taxonomy was considerable, the rest of his work needed the support of his political and social power. His title as "legislator" of natural history was more a claim than a reality.

Cuvier's role in the history of palaeontology is described by RUDWICK. The development of stratigraphy linked Cuvier's anatomical work to the mainstream of contemporary geological research. Cuvier's work with Alexandre Brongniart, which produced *Essai sur la geographie mineralogique des environs de Paris* (1808) revealed that fossils could identify in great detail the individual strata within a formation – older beds had radically different bones from those of present-day animals. Cuvier and Brongniart also incorporated a biological approach, emphasizing the ecological implications of characteristic faunas. Cuvier's catastrophism explained the extinction of functionally well-adapted animal species; he believed that these events were regular episodes in the history of the Earth, and he explained the apparent appearance of new species as resulting from migration. Rudwick also links Cuvier's growing sense of progression in the natural world to the concerns of the natural theologians in England, who supported the argument from design, although Cuvier preferred to keep science and religion separate. Finally, Rudwick concludes that Cuvier's conception of sudden revolutions and his sense of an emerging progressive element to Earth's history ultimately made Darwin's theory convincing.

MAYR asserts that, prior to Darwin no one produced more new knowledge that ultimately supported the theory of evolution than Cuvier, despite being totally opposed to the idea itself – his arguments against it were so convincing that no French scientist was able to argue its case for the next 50 years. Most important was Cuvier's discovery of new characters and types of organization related to the internal anatomy of the vertebrates, and he also initiated the study of the comparative anatomy of the invertebrates. His emphasis was still Aristotelian, based on classification from the top down, and he was still in search of the essence or true nature of each group. Cuvier's division of the natural world into four groups, or *embranchements*, with no internal gradations is characteristic of his essentialist attitude. Mayr believes Cuvier ignored the fossil evidence because he was a conservative by nature, and, although perceptive and well-informed, always an adherent of the *status quo*.

EISELEY traces the discoveries of the scientists who paved the way for Darwin. He calls Cuvier the magician of the charnel house, because he developed a method of recognizing a given animal from fragments of its bones. His principle of correlation posited that all anatomical structures were intimately related to the life of the entire organism. Cuvier demonstrated anatomically that certain broad groups represented such divergent anatomical organization that they would not fit into a single unilineal ascending system such as the "scale of being", which dominated thinking in the 18th century. In his Parisian studies he noted a remarkable succession in the appearance of the different species, even hypothesized "secret reasons" for relationships in anatomical structure, but perhaps rejected evolution as a theory because it reminded him too much of the ascending scale he wished to avoid.

THEUNISSEN argues that Cuvier's *lois zoologique* played an important role in his palaeontological investigations. It is a misconception that his main concern in *Recherches sur les ossemens fossils* (1812) was the reconstruction of extinct animals; rather, most of his work deals with the identification, description, and classification of fossil remains. On this level he successfully applied his anatomical rules, but his ultimate claim that he could reconstruct extinct animals from their fossil fragments by means of his *lois* must be seen in the light of his great talent for publicity and propaganda. Even today, his fame is to a considerable extent connected to his renown as a person who could restore a complete fish from one fish bone.

JOAN GARRETT PACKER

D

Darwin, Charles 1809–1882

British naturalist

Barlow, Nina (ed.), *The Autobiography of Charles Darwin*, London: Collins, and New York: Harcourt Brace, 1958; reprinted, New York: Norton, 1993

Beer, Gillian, *Darwin's Plots: Evolutionary Narrative in Darwin, George Eliot, and Nineteenth-Century Fiction*, London and Boston: Routledge and Kegan Paul, 1983

Browne, Janet, *Charles Darwin*, vol. 1, *Voyaging*, London: Jonathan Cape, and New York: Knopf, 1995

Burkhardt, Frederick *et al.*, *The Correspondence of Charles Darwin*, Cambridge: Cambridge University Press, 1985–

Colp Jr, Ralph, *To Be an Invalid: The Illness of Charles Darwin*, Chicago: University of Chicago Press, 1977

De Beer, Gavin, *Charles Darwin: Evolution by Natural Selection*, London: Nelson, and New York: Doubleday, 1963

Depew, David J. and Bruce H. Weber, *Darwinism Evolving: Systems Dynamics and the Genealogy of Natural Selection*, Cambridge, Massachusetts: MIT Press, 1995

Desmond, Adrian and James Moore, *Darwin*, London: Michael Joseph, and New York: Viking Penguin, 1991

Ghiselin, Michael T., *The Triumph of the Darwinian Method*, Berkeley: University of California Press, 1969

Gruber, Howard E., *Darwin on Man: A Psychological Study of Scientific Creativity*, New York: Dutton, and London: Wildwood House, 1974

Himmelfarb, Gertrude, *Darwin and the Darwinian Revolution*, London: Chatto and Windus, and Garden City, New York: Doubleday, 1959

Kohn, David, "Theories to Work By", *Studies in History of Biology*, 4 (1980): 67–170

Kohn, David (ed.), *The Darwinian Heritage: Including Proceedings of the Charles Darwin Centenary Conference*, Princeton, New Jersey: Princeton University Press, 1985

Kohn, David, "Darwin's Ambiguity", *British Journal for the History of Science*, 22 (1989): 215–39

Limoges, Camille, *La Sélection naturelle: études sur la première constitution d'un concept (1877–1859)*, Paris: Presses Universitaires de France, 1970

Manier, Edward, *The Young Darwin and His Cultural Circle*, Dordrecht and Boston: Reidel, 1978

Mayr, Ernst, *One Long Argument: Charles Darwin and the Genesis of Modern Evolutionary Thought*, Cambridge, Massachusetts: Harvard University Press, 1991

Ospovat, Dov, *The Development of Darwin's Theory: Natural History, Natural Theology, and Natural Selection, 1838–1859*, Cambridge and New York: Cambridge University Press, 1981

Richards, Robert J., *Darwin and the Emergence of Evolutionary Theories of Mind and Behavior*, Chicago: University of Chicago Press, 1987

Vorzimmer, Peter J., *Charles Darwin: The Years of Controversy: The Origin of Species and Its Critics, 1859–1882*, Philadelphia: Temple University Press, 1970; London: London University Press, 1972

Young, Robert M., *Darwin's Metaphor: Nature's Place in Victorian Culture*, Cambridge and New York: Cambridge University Press, 1985

Darwin scholarship may be divided roughly into three categories: those examining the construction of Darwin's scientific views, their reception, and Darwin's biography. In the commentary to follow, little attention is paid to the literature on reception; instead, the focus is on biography and construction.

For the serious researcher, the publication of Darwin's thousands of letters in BURKHARDT *et al.* is a necessity; this project is proceeding chronologically, and had reached 1864 in 1999. All extant letters received and written by Darwin are published and footnotes are provided. The scholarly apparatus is meticulous, with footnotes and appendices enriching the letters for the modern scholar. To a large extent, modern scholarship on Darwin follows in the wake of the publication of this correspondence; for example, Darwin's increasing interest in botany in the 1860s is beginning to be reflected in current scholarship (the emphasis of earlier studies was largely on his zoological work.)

However, for the beginner, the Darwin Correspondence is forbidding in its sheer number of volumes and its abundance of detail. BARLOW is the obvious starting point, providing Darwin's autobiography in full. In an earlier transcript, published a few years after his death, passages deemed religiously imprudent by some members of his family had been left out. Even in its bowdlerised version, however, Darwin's own account stressed his indebtedness to the thinking of Malthus. The nature of that link remains one of the chief concerns of Darwin historians.

Though a number of biographies, and some other historical literature, did appear before the end of the 1950s, it was then that the first great surge of historical interest in Darwin occurred. This was directly related to the general acceptance of the theory of natural selection by scientists in the preceding decades. HIMMELFARB's book, one of the best to emerge in the 1950s, is interesting, particularly because it deviates from the currently developing trend. While most interpretations were informed by a reverential attitude towards Darwin's achievement, Himmelfarb took the liberty of finding fault both with his personality and his science, and for this she has suffered much condemnation.

DE BEER, one of the leading exponents of the above-mentioned trend, did for Darwin what Ernest Jones had previously done for Freud. Vigorously minimising the significance of Malthus, and aiming at a wide readership, this book has been held for decades to be the best scientifically-informed biography of Darwin. Thus a division opened up as the Darwin industry took off in the 1960s, between, on the one hand, specialised studies on various aspects of the emergence of evolutionary biology, and, on the other, the popularly accessible biography, new incarnations of which have been constantly forthcoming.

GHISELIN gives a biologist's assessment of Darwin's contribution to science, as well as a historical exposition. As in the case of De Beer's study, the object is to celebrate Darwin as the father of modern biology. VORZIMMER, by contrast, equally based on current scientific views on the nature of selection and variation, gives prominence to Darwin's lapses from true belief. He examines Darwin's reaction to objections prompted by the *Origin of Species*, and suggests that this was conditioned by ambiguities and weaknesses in the initial theory, which led to increasing confusion, and ultimately to Darwin's resignation to the critics.

YOUNG contains a series of essays that were written some 15 years before being collected in this volume. When they were first published, the essays constituted a radically new departure in Darwin studies, introducing a contextualist approach. While the contextualising of Darwin's science has moved ahead, in some respects proceeding along lines rather different from those suggested by Young, his texts remain provocative reading, and constitute one of the most vigorous attempts to situate Darwin's work within a strict ideological framework.

A second main tendency within Darwin historiography, the textual approach, has precipitated numerous close examinations of Darwin's manuscripts – in particular, a set of notebooks dating from the late 1830s and early 1840s. The first great landmark of the textual approach was by LIMOGES. In the tradition of French epistemology, Limoges emphasises ruptures along Darwin's path to natural selection; these have been disputed, as have many of its specific claims, but the attention Limoges paid to the detailed contents of archival material set a standard for subsequent workers in the field.

GRUBER treats the birth of Darwinism as a case-study for the psychology of scientific creativity, stressing the purposeful yet gradual nature of what might appositely be termed the embryology of complex ideas. The notion of a delay, from the conception of the theory of natural selection around 1838 to its publication 20 years later, is central to this interpretation, and is accounted for by the risk of persecution that the promulgation of evolutionary ideas presumably entailed. The same psychological explanation is advocated in COLP, a tediously

detailed report on Darwin's illness, which is, however, the best guide to the substantial literature on this subject.

MANIER inspects a diverse catalogue of texts, ranging from poetry to moral philosophy, which, in the course of Darwin's notebook period, may have left distinct and permanent traces on his thinking. The precise use Darwin made of the various ideas he encountered in his reading remains unclear, however, because the focus on the continuous shifts in Darwin's species theorising exhibited by Gruber is lacking. The value of Manier's interpretation lies, rather, in its broadening of the intellectual context in which the Darwinian conception of nature was generated. This is also true of BEER, which remains foremost among several contributions to Darwin scholarship made by students of literature. In this book, the analysis of the *Origin* is enriched by an examination of its narrative techniques, although no attempt is made at demonstrating for what purpose a particular means of expression was chosen.

Prior to the advent of the Darwin industry, Darwin's science was generally assumed to be in conflict with the Christian religion. While several authors have argued that this conflict was not present in the reception of his views, OSPOVAT has done most to demonstrate that neither did such a simple antagonism inform their construction. Though by no means labelling the *Origin* a religious tract, Ospovat claims that the theory of natural selection was devised within a framework of natural theology that Darwin did not abandon until the mid-1850s. Interestingly, from such a perspective the delay problem (why Darwin only published his theory decades after its conception) dissolves into a series of questions concerning the ways in which Darwin's species theory changed during the period between his Malthusian insight and publication.

When KOHN's article appeared in 1980, there was little doubt that this was the best study to date of the development of Darwin's thinking over the supposedly decisive years from 1837 to 1839. As with Ospovat, and practically every other revisionist interpretation in the history of science, its leading thesis is the historicist one: that the appearance of things alters dramatically when they are placed within their historical context. In Kohn's case, the basic claim is that, far from inevitably leading to the mature theory of natural selection, Darwin's pre-Malthusian work on species falls into distinct phases, each with its own rationale. For instance, Darwin's understanding of the practice of breeding, traditionally assumed to have led him ineluctably towards the notion of natural selection, is shown here to have long barred his step in that direction.

Though Kohn at an early stage welcomed broad contextualising, such as the work by Young, his first paper was itself a narrow textual study. KOHN (1985) is a collection in which the whole range of approaches employed in the Darwin industry is represented. KOHN's 1989 article is an interesting attempt to reconcile his early reconstruction of Darwin's road to natural selection with the interpretation offered by Ospovat, and, more generally, to resolve the differences between accounts highlighting the continuity from natural theology to Darwinian selection, and those that have continued to assume a break. In addition, this paper serves as an illustration of the level of sophistication that the best scholars in the area have now attained, combining intimate knowledge of Darwin's manuscripts with a keen appreciation of the broader context.

Of course, contextualising efforts of this kind oppose the histories of scientists, such as De Beer and Ghiselin. A later specimen of that genre is MAYR, which compiles arguments previously published by the same author and remains largely out of touch with recent developments in the field. However, there exists a group of historians who take an intermediate position, between the search for ever richer contexts on the one hand, and scientists' limited conception of history on the other. One of the strongest defences of the intermediate position is RICHARDS, an intellectual history that locates Darwin's work among theories of mind and behaviour in a manner that serves to legitimise modern sociobiology.

In the last few years, the rift between the biography genre and more specialised studies has been healed. Written in a style designed to appeal to the general reader, DESMOND & MOORE's work exploits the full range of specialist scholarship to provide a stirring portrait of Darwin, while at the same time exploring a number of disturbing tensions. Indeed, the popular idiom of the book has not prevented its authors from making an original contribution to the contextualisation of Darwin's work, expanding Young's politicising approach and offering an interesting new theory for the delay in publication of the *Origin*. BROWNE, the first of two volumes, also reveals a complete command of current research in this area, without making any populist concessions. The context within which this extensive biography sets Darwin's life and work is less permeated by class struggle, but it is exceedingly rich in a number of other respects, particularly the psychological.

Finally, mention should be made of a new comprehensive history of Darwinian biology. DEPEW & WEBER's book differs from the synthetic overviews that appeared a generation before, by devoting much more space to the development of evolutionary biology from Darwin onwards, rather than to events leading up to the publication of the *Origin*. While offering an interesting account of the birth of Darwinism, this volume chiefly addresses the changing standing of selectionism within the biological community, since the forging of the evolutionary synthesis in the 1930s and 1940s. As surely as the Darwin industry has arisen in the shadow of the neo-Darwinian establishment, the fortunes of those recent developments are crucial in determining the premises of future historical research on Darwin.

INGEMAR BOHLIN

See also Darwinism; Evolution; Natural Selection

Darwinism

Bowler, Peter J., *Evolution: The History of an Idea*, Berkeley: University of California Press, 1984; revised edition, 1989

Bowler, Peter J., *Darwinism*, New York: Twayne, 1993

Glick, Thomas F. (ed.), *The Comparative Reception of Darwinism*, Austin: University of Texas Press, 1974; with a new preface, Chicago: University of Chicago Press, 1988

Hull, David L., "Darwinism as a Historical Entity: A Historiographic Proposal", in *The Darwinian Heritage*, edited by David Kohn (see below), 773–812

Kohn, David (ed.), *The Darwinian Heritage: Including Proceedings of the Charles Darwin Centenary Conference*, Princeton, New Jersey: Princeton University Press, 1985

Mayr, Ernst and William B. Provine (eds), *The Evolutionary Synthesis: Perspectives on the Unification of Biology*, Cambridge, Massachusetts: Harvard University Press, 1980

Mayr, Ernst, *The Growth of Biological Thought: Diversity, Evolution, and Inheritance*, Cambridge, Massachusetts: Harvard University Press, 1982

Mayr, Ernst, "What is Darwinism?", in *One Long Argument: Charles Darwin and the Genesis of Modern Evolutionary Thought*, Cambridge, Massachusetts: Harvard University Press, 1991

Moore, James R., "Deconstructing Darwinism: The Politics of Evolution in the 1860s", *Journal of the History of Biology*, 24 (1991): 353–408

Oldroyd, David R., *Darwinian Impacts: An Introduction to the Darwinian Revolution*, Kensington: New South Wales University Press, Atlantic Highlands, New Jersey: Humanities Press, and Milton Keynes, Buckinghamshire: Open University Press, 1980; revised edition, Atlantic Highlands: Humanities Press, and Milton Keynes: Open University Press, 1983

Ruse, Michael, "Darwinism", in *Keywords in Evolutionary Biology*, edited by Evelyn Fox Keller and Elisabeth A. Lloyd, Cambridge, Massachusetts: Harvard University Press, 1992

Smocovitis, Vassiliki Betty, *Unifying Biology: The Evolutionary Synthesis and Evolutionary Biology*, Princeton, New Jersey: Princeton University Press, 1996

Ever since the term "Darwinism" was introduced in the early 1860s, there has been controversy over its meaning; even within the scientific context, Darwinism cannot be identified as a clear entity. One reason for this fluidity in meaning is that Darwin himself propounded several different theories in his *Origin of Species* (1859), as well as in other writings. Some authors, for example, refer to the theory of common descent as Darwinism, while others use the term to refer to Darwin's theory of natural selection. Another reason for the controversy is that Darwinian theories of evolution have changed quite fundamentally since the 1860s. The modern scientific Darwinism – as the synthetic theory of evolution is sometimes called – is in some respects quite different from Darwin's original theory. In addition, the term "Darwinism" has been used to refer to various kinds of philosophies, and political or social movements. The ideological and scientific forms of Darwinism have varied strongly over time and within different national contexts. The importance of Darwinism for evolutionary biology, and the expansion of Darwinian theories into the social and political context, have both contributed to the great influence that Darwin's ideas have had on Western culture. The following account will focus on the history of scientific Darwinism, while the specialized literature on various brands of social Darwinism, and related movements like eugenics, is ignored.

Recent discussions of the term "Darwinism" have led to a consensus that a variety of contradictory meanings do indeed exist, and have instigated the search for a method of discerning between correct and misleading meanings. HULL argues that the difficulties can be overcome by selecting an "exemplar", analogous to the practice of a taxonomist who selects a type specimen in order to connect a species to a name. RUSE finds essentially two meanings within Darwinism: a metaphysical and a scientific meaning. There is some overlap, but in major respects the two Darwinisms are seen as quite different, with only the scientific Darwinism unambiguously tied to the work of Darwin himself. MAYR (1991) approaches the problem of finding the appropriate meaning of Darwinism by excluding definitions that are misleading or unrepresentative of Darwin's thought. He comes to the conclusion that under these premises two meanings have had the widest acceptance: until the 1930s, Darwinism meant explaining the living world by natural processes; however, since the 1940s – i.e., after the evolutionary synthesis – the term "Darwinism" has meant the theory of evolution by natural selection. These and other attempts to find the authentic Darwinism are criticised by MOORE as unhistorical and uninteresting; instead, he traces the prolifer-ation of the term "Darwinism" and Darwin-related vocabu-lary, and interprets its function within public and professional discourse.

The history of Darwinism as an evolving scientific theory is described in the various general books on the history of the theory of evolution. The most comprehensive recent accounts can be found in BOWLER (1984) and in MAYR (1982). Mayr is primarily interested in the development of scientific ideas originating from Darwin's theories, while Bowler gives more room to the social implications and religious and moral problems of Darwinism. BOWLER (1993) is a concise introduction to Darwinism as a scientific and social topic. These and other aspects are also discussed in OLDROYD, which also gives a very helpful overview demonstrating the influence of Darwinism on other scientific disciplines, including theology, philosophy, psychology, anthropology, literature, and music.

Where Darwin's theories were imported into various local contexts, and translated and integrated into other scientific traditions, the resulting Darwinisms vary quite significantly. GLICK is a wide-ranging study, and includes discussions of some usually neglected areas, such as Mexico and the Islamic world. The reception of Darwinism in major scientific centres of the 19th century is also analysed in various chapters of KOHN.

The history of 20th-century scientific Darwinism is usually tied to the synthetic theory of evolution, as, from the 1940s onwards, this theory has dominated evolutionary biology. The most comprehensive account is still provided by MAYR & PROVINE, but, in her recent work, SMOCOVITIS considers some of the central questions from a more contextualized standpoint.

THOMAS JUNKER

See also Darwin; Evolution; Evolutionary Synthesis; Natural Selection

Darwinism in Germany

Cittadino, Eugene, *Nature as the Laboratory: Darwinian Plant Ecology in the German Empire, 1880–1900*, Cambridge and New York: Cambridge University Press, 1990

Harwood, Jonathan, *Styles of Scientific Thought: The German Genetics Community, 1900–1933*, Chicago: University of Chicago Press, 1993

Junker, Thomas, *Darwinismus und Botanik: Rezeption, Kritik und theoretische Alternativen im Deutschland des 19. Jahrhunderts*, Stuttgart: Deutscher Apotheker, 1989

Junker, Thomas and Marsha Richmond (eds), *Charles Darwin's Correspondence with German Naturalists: A Calendar with Summaries, Biographical Register and Bibliography*, Marburg: Basilisken-Presse, 1996

Kelly, Alfred, *The Descent of Darwin: The Popularization of Darwinism in Germany, 1860–1914*, Chapel Hill: University of North Carolina Press, 1981

Mayr, Ernst and William B. Provine (eds), *The Evolutionary Synthesis: Perspectives on the Unification of Biology*, Cambridge, Massachusetts: Harvard University Press, 1980

Montgomery, William Morey, "Germany", in *The Comparative Reception of Darwinism*, edited by Thomas F. Glick, Austin: University of Texas Press, 1974, with a new preface, Chicago: University of Chicago Press, 1988

Montgomery, William Morey, *Evolution and Darwinism in German Biology, 1800–1883*, dissertation, University of Texas, Austin, 1974

Mullen, Pierce C., *The Preconditions and Reception of Darwinian Biology in Germany, 1800–1870*, dissertation, University of California, Berkeley, 1964

Nyhart, Lynn K., *Biology Takes Form: Animal Morphology and the German Universities, 1800–1900*, Chicago: University of Chicago Press, 1995

Rádl, Emanuel, *Geschichte der biologischen Theorien in der Neuzeit*, vol. 2, Leipzig: Wilhelm Engelmann, 1909; reprinted, Hildesheim and New York: Georg Olms, 1970

Weindling, Paul J., "Darwinism in Germany", in *The Darwinian Heritage*, edited by David Kohn, Princeton, New Jersey: Princeton University Press, 1985

Charles Darwin's *Origin of Species* was very successful in Germany. Within a few years of publication in 1859, Darwin's theories gained widespread popularity; they were not only discussed in scientific circles, but became part of the common knowledge of a wide audience. This enthusiastic reception seems even more significant when compared to the rather diffi-dent reactions in France. German *Darwinismus*, as promoted by Ernst Haeckel and other semi-popular authors, was more outspoken, speculative, and had a stronger ideological flavour than Darwin's original theories, but remained always in touch with its scientific representatives, such as Carl Gegenbaur and August Weismann. Darwin's popularity in German scientific circles during the first half of the 20th century is shown by the fact that important architects of the latest version of Darwinism – the synthetic theory of evolution – such as Ernst Mayr and Bernhard Rensch, were educated in Germany. In recent decades, however, historians of science have devoted very little attention to the history of Darwinism in Germany, and there is nothing to compare to the excitement created by the so-called Darwin Industry. One of the reasons seems to be that, since 1945, evolutionary biology in Germany was identified with the atrocities of the Nazi regime. This is confirmed by the fact that most of the work that touches on the topic of Darwinism in Germany deals only with the political and ideological context of social Darwinism, or eugenics.

Under these circumstances it seems understandable that the most comprehensive treatment of German Darwinism in the 19th century was written by the Czech zoologist, Emanuel RÁDL, in 1909. Rádl gives a very detailed and careful account of the discussions in various scientific disciplines, as well as a good introduction to the social and political context. Rádl was a stern critic of Darwin's theory, and he obviously enjoyed the "decay" of Darwinism around the turn of the century, but his book is still the most extensive overview of 19th-century Darwinism in Germany.

In the 1960s and 1970s, two American doctoral dissertations were written – but never published – that cover much of the same ground. MULLEN is mostly concerned with the scientific preconditions that made Darwin's success in Germany possible. MONTGOMERY gives a much more detailed picture of the different versions of Darwinian, semi-Darwinian and anti-Darwinian theories within German biology. In his last chapter, he includes a brief account of the ideological questions involved. A condensed version of MONTGOMERY's dissertation, which gives some of his major findings, appeared as a chapter of *The Comparative Reception of Darwinism*, edited by Thomas F. Glick (1974). In 1985, Paul J. WEINDLING published a short overview of the history of Darwinism in Germany; Weindling confines his account to the scientific and ideological role of Ernst Haeckel, and the discussions around this controversial biologist. Haeckel was important, because in his person two strands of Darwinism blended: evolutionary morphology and popular *Darwinismus*.

The popularization of Darwinism in Germany has been analysed in an important work by KELLY, who gives an account of the influence of the liberal German popular science tradition on the reception of Darwinism, and traces the fortunes of Darwin's theories in right-wing social Darwinian, as well as Marxist, circles. Lynn NYHART treats the history of evolutionary morphology in Germany during the 19th century in great detail. During much of this century, animal morphology was the field in which Darwin's theory of common descent had its most rewarding applications. The reception of Darwin's theories in German botany is discussed in two recent books: JUNKER follows the controversies surrounding Darwinism in the different fields of botany during the first decades after the publication of the *Origin of Species*, and gives a picture of the great diversity of theoretical and empirical consequences that emerged; CITTADINO focuses on one particular Darwinian research school – plant ecology, in the tradition of Simon Schwendener and Gottlieb Haberlandt. From a different angle, 19th-century German Darwinism is approached via a calendar of Darwin's correspondence with German naturalists constructed by JUNKER & RICHMOND. This compilation of summaries of about 1200 letters gives an impressive picture of the far-reaching impact that Darwin had in Germany. The introduction examines the question of the extent to which the different reactions to Darwin can be accounted for by the social, religious, geographic and professional background of the various naturalists. Darwin's correspondence shows how much the so-called external factors influenced the reception of his theories in Germany, and that the distribution of approval or opposition follows certain patterns.

All the books treated so far deal with 19th-century biology. There has been little detailed analysis by science historians of 20th-century Darwinism in Germany. One of the few exceptions is HARWOOD on the German genetics community, who describes in one chapter the theoretical controversies in evolutionary biology that developed in the first decades of the 20th century. Other information can be found in MAYR & PROVINE's book on the evolutionary synthesis, which primarily gives biographical accounts of German Darwinians before 1945. In summary, there is a significant contrast between the importance and popularity of Darwinism in German culture and science through much of the 19th and 20th centuries, and the hesitation by historians of science to deal with these issues.

THOMAS JUNKER

Davy, Humphry 1778–1829
British chemist

Davy, John, *Memoirs of the Life of Sir Humphry Davy*, 2 vols, London: Longman Rees Orme Brown and Green, 1836

Davy, John (ed.), *The Collected Works of Sir Humphry Davy*, 9 vols, London: Smith Elder, 1839–40; reprinted, New York, 1972

Forgan, Sophie (ed.), *Science and the Sons of Genius: Studies on Humphry Davy*, London: Science Reviews, 1980

Fullmer, June Z., *Sir Humphry Davy's Published Works*, Cambridge, Massachusetts: Harvard University Press, 1969

Hartley, Harold, *Humphry Davy*, London: Nelson, 1966

James, Frank A.J.L., "Davy in the Dockyard: Humphry Davy, the Royal Society and the Electro-Chemical Protection of the Copper Sheeting of His Majesty's Ships in the mid 1820s", *Physis*, 29 (1992): 205–25

Knight, David, *Humphry Davy: Science & Power*, Oxford and Cambridge, Massachusetts: Blackwell, 1992

Miller, David Philip, "Between Hostile Camps: Sir Humphry Davy's Presidency of the Royal Society of London, 1820–1827", *British Journal for the History of Science*, 16 (1983): 1–47

Paris, John Ayrton, *The Life of Sir Humphry Davy*, London: Colburn and Bentley, 1831

Russell, Colin A., "The Electrochemical Theory of Sir Humphry Davy", *Annals of Science*, 15 (1959): 1–25; 19 (1963): 255–71

Thorpe, Thomas Edward, *Humphry Davy: Poet and Philosopher*, London: Cassell, and New York: Macmillan, 1896

Treneer, Anne, *The Mercurial Chemist: A Life of Sir Humphry Davy*, London: Methuen, 1963

There seem to be two chief problems in studying the life and work of Humphry Davy: first, his career had several unusually distinct phases; second, from the mid-19th century until fairly recently there has been a tendency to see Davy through the early biographies of his one-time protégé, Michael Faraday.

The first two biographies of Davy, published in the 1830s – Paris and DAVY (1836) – exacerbated the first of these problems, summed up by the comment of the Swedish chemist, Jöns Jacob Berzelius, that Davy's work constituted "only brilliant fragments". That is, while Davy could and did have brilliant scientific insights, he was unable to develop and sustain a system of chemistry in the way that Berzelius had done. A similar comment could have been applied to Davy's life as a whole, and such a view is implied by PARIS, who highlighted Davy the parvenu and social climber by charting his rise from his humble beginnings as the son of a Cornish woodcarver, to his presidency of the Royal Society. Suitably outraged by Paris's sneers, Davy's younger brother, John Davy, produced a biography that showed that Davy's rise was due to merit. He also published some of Davy's works posthumously, and edited DAVY (1839–40) which collected virtually all of the published works. These works are listed in FULLMER, together with Davy's other publications, translations, etc.

The standard version of Davy's biography which emerged during the 19th century (given its fullest expression in THORPE), viewed his career as fragmentary, blamed his wife, the wealthy bluestocking Jane Davy, for his failure to produce any original research after their marriage in 1812, and attributed the row with Faraday over priority in liquefying chlorine, and his election to the Royal Society, to Davy's jealousy. The relationship between Davy and Faraday was particularly stressed in the 19th-century biographies of Faraday. Though Faraday had sought to be fair to Davy (to whom after all he owed his scientific career), it was his adverse remarks concerning Davy that were repeated by later commentators. For example, Thorpe damningly commented, "The jealousy thus manifested by Davy is one of the most pitiful facts in his history."

Much 20th-century writing on Davy has struggled to overcome this critical heritage which, despite its simplistic view, gained wide currency. TRENEER gives a fairer account of Jane Davy than those of the 19th century, while HARTLEY avoids most of the problems inherent in any study of Davy's life by concentrating almost entirely on his science. The process of viewing Davy's biography on its own terms began with the set of essays edited by FORGAN. In this collection, various aspects of Davy's career are analysed and his links with contemporary medicine, science, fishing, and poetry examined. Thus Michael Neve looks at Davy's early career and his work with Thomas Beddoes at the Pneumatic Institution in Bristol, where he made his first major chemical experiments on the physiological effects of laughing gas (nitrous oxide). In Bristol (as Trevor Levere here and elsewhere relates), Davy became friends with the poets Samuel Taylor Coleridge, Robert Southey, and William Wordsworth, the second edition of whose *Lyrical Ballads* he edited. Indeed, Coleridge, whose philosophy profoundly influenced Davy's thought, somewhat generously commented that, "if Davy had not been the first Chemist, he would have been the first Poet of his age".

With the exception of Knight's essay on Davy's *Salmonia*, the rest of Forgan is concerned with Davy's chemical work, which he carried out while professor of chemistry at the Royal Institution between 1802 and 1812, and which is, with the possible exception of the miners' lamp (which has a literature of its own), the most widely discussed area of Davy's career. The many papers by Knight provide excellent studies of various aspects of Davy's chemistry, and indeed other aspects of his life. Davy's work on electrochemistry – for instance, the isolation of sodium and potassium and his development of a theory of electrochemical actions – is discussed by RUSSELL, and also receives considerable attention in Hartley. The practical and disastrous application of electrochemical methods to Royal Navy ships is narrated in JAMES. That Davy was able to supervise the attachment of electrochemical protectors to the whole fleet was partially due to his being President of the Royal Society at the time. The failure of the method contributed to his overall failure as President between 1820 and 1827, which is ably analysed by MILLER. These two papers deliberately seek to place Davy's life and work within the wider social and institutional context of 1820s England.

A cumulative effect of all these studies was the persistence, and in fact reinforcement, of the 19th-century image of the fragmentary nature of Davy's life and work. This problem was finally and brilliantly overcome by KNIGHT's biography, which exposes an internal consistency running through Davy's philosophy and poetry that gives coherence to his life, work, and thought. Furthermore, by taking Davy on his own terms and in his own time, Knight is able to deal with the vexed issues of the influence of Jane Davy and the Davy/Faraday relationship by going beyond the rather simplistic 19th-century interpretations. By demonstrating the consistency that existed in Davy's life and work (which had, for one reason or another, escaped most contemporary observers, especially in the latter part of Davy's life), and by fully contextualising Davy's relationships, Knight provides a biography that will serve as the interpretative framework for Davy studies for the foreseeable future.

FRANK A.J.L. JAMES

Dee, John   1527–1608

English alchemist, astrologer, and mathematician

Clulee, Nicholas H., *John Dee's Natural Philosophy: Between Science and Religion*, London and New York: Routledge, 1988

Deacon, Richard, *John Dee: Scientist, Geographer, Astrologer and Secret Agent to Elizabeth I*, London: Muller, 1968

French, Peter J., *John Dee: The World of an Elizabethan Magus*, London: Routledge and Kegan Paul, 1972

Sherman, William H., *John Dee: The Politics of Reading and Writing in the English Renaissance*, Amherst: University of Massachusetts Press, 1995

Shumaker, Wayne (ed.), *John Dee on Astronomy*, Berkeley: University of California Press, 1978

Taylor, E.G.R., *Tudor Geography, 1485–1583*, London: Methuen, 1930; New York: Octagon Books, 1968

Yates, Frances A., *Theatre of the World*, London: Routledge and Kegan Paul, and Chicago: Chicago University Press, 1969

Yates, Frances A., *The Occult Philosophy in the Elizabethan Age*, London and Boston: Routledge and Kegan Paul, 1979

As a result of the interest aroused by certain aspects of his life, notably his magical activities and his association with the court of Elizabeth I, John Dee has received attention from biographers and historians ever since his death. Yet the extraordinary complexity and range of his activities, reflected in the collection of works contained in his vast library, has also caused great difficulty among those trying to assess his life. Dee's activities included astrology, mathematics, cartography, cryptography, alchemy, angelology, antiquarianism, medicine, and law – testifying to his belief that by mastering all disciplines and all books he would apprehend the mystery of God's universe. However, this breadth of knowledge creates problems, particularly in its amalgamation of supposedly dubious activities (notably the occult) with more legitimate ones. This problem is further compounded by the fact that Dee produced only a handful of published works, the long-term significance of which has been unclear.

The tendency of many texts has been to concentrate on only a fraction of Dee's activity. TAYLOR is typical of this trend: in her account of Tudor geography and navigation, Dee's role as writer and adviser on all aspects of the practical mathematical arts is central, and the book excellently conveys Dee's importance in these areas. The confined subject matter of the work, however, means that Dee's other work at this time is excluded, and that his occult practices in particular are almost wholly ignored. Similarly, SHUMAKER, in the long introductory essay to a translation of Dee's *Propaedeumata Aphoristica*, concentrates on the mathematical aspects of his career. Indeed, the essay suggests that the practices of mathematics and of magic were antithetical, and that each stage of his intellectual development took Dee further from applied mathematics. DEACON, conversely, concentrates on Dee's magical activities, on his conversations with angels and on the romantic image of Dee as a secret agent. Again, only a partial picture of Dee emerges from this account, with the more mundane aspects of his work in the practical mathematical arts taking the sidelines.

It was Frances Yates who greatly changed this piecemeal method of viewing Dee's life work, initiating from the 1950s a series of studies that attempted to account simultaneously for Dee's occult as well as his more "legitimate" mathematical endeavours, which culminated in YATES (1969) and YATES (1979). However, most of these works have attempted to achieve this synthesis by placing Dee within a single intellectual tradition. For Yates, this was the "Occult Philosophy", a distinct intellectual tradition that blended Hermeticism and Neoplatonism with Christian Cabala, and which prefigured the scientific revolution of the 17th century – primarily through its identification of knowledge with power. Dee emerges from these studies as an iconic figure, precisely because of his blend of the occult with practical mathematics. In Yates (1969), it is suggested that Dee was the propagator of Vitruvian ideas in England, predominantly through his *Mathematicall Praeface*.

This, Yates argues, also sheds light on Elizabethan theatre. In Yates (1979), Dee emerges as the characteristic philosopher of Elizabethan England, as a key influence in English literature and as the leader of the Elizabethan Renaissance, with the *Mathematicall Praeface* now interpreted as its manifesto. According to Yates, Dee was responsible for developing Renaissance occult philosophy in scientific directions, and is credited as the father of the Rosicrucian phase of the Hermetic movement that was to emerge fully formed on the Continent in the following century.

Following in Yates's footsteps, FRENCH has provided the most recent attempt at a comprehensive biography of Dee. In this account, French explores all of the areas of Dee's activity – magical and non-magical – and illustrates Dee's importance in Elizabethan society; for example, through the "Sidney circle". Here, Dee is presented as a Hermetic magus – a philosopher-magician aspiring, through study of the arcane sciences as dictated by the Hermetic corpus, to understand the fabric of the cosmos and to achieve union with the divine. Thus, according to French, Dee's study of magic provides the continuity with which to characterise his whole life.

More recent works have criticised the attempts made by Yates, French and others to identify a single intellectual tradition within which Dee can be placed. Rather, they have sought to localise Dee within his immediate context, and to embrace the contradictions and changes of orientation evident across his career. CLULEE divides his analysis of Dee's natural philosophy into four main sections centring on his three major printed texts – the *Propaedeumata Aphoristica*, the *Monas Hieroglyphica*, and the *Mathematicall Praeface* – and on the group of manuscripts relating to the angelic conversations, referred to as the *Libri Mysteriorum*. Clulee traces through these sections the additional theme of the changing social dimension of Dee's intellectual career. Concentrating on the years 1542–89, the book concentrates on exposing the sources that contributed to the formation and expression of Dee's ideas – for example, the influence of the writings of Roger Bacon is emphasised – and provides an impressively detailed exploration of the development and meanings of Dee's major works.

SHERMAN, on the other hand, attempts to shift attention from Dee's intellectual allegiances to his professional and social roles, and places emphasis on Dee's political and imperialist ideas. Moving away from the idea of Dee as an isolated intellectual (as typified, for instance, by French), Sherman considers him instead as a player in the patronage game, describing Dee's connections to the academic, courtly, and commercial circles of his day. Like Clulee, Sherman shows that Dee's ideas did not fit simply within one intellectual tradition, but changed markedly with context and time. Sherman also makes an interesting analysis of Dee's manuscript material and, most importantly, of his reading methods. In this treatment, Dee's massive library assumes central importance, and is shown to be a valuable, practical resource used by many of Dee's contemporaries.

RICHARD DUNN

See also Court Society; Hermeticism

Degeneration

Chamberlain, J. Edward and Sander L. Gilman (eds),
Degeneration: The Dark Side of Progress, New York:
Columbia University Press, 1985

Jones, Gareth Stedman, *Outcast London: A Study in the
Relationship Between the Classes in Victorian Society*,
Oxford: Clarendon Press, 1971; New York: Pantheon
Books, 1984

Nordau, Max, *Degeneration*, translated from the German,
introduction by George L. Mosse, Lincoln: University of
Nebraska Press, 1968 (2nd edition, 1893)

Nye, Robert A., *Crime, Madness and Politics in Modern
France: The Medical Concept of National Decline*,
Princeton, New Jersey: Princeton University Press, 1984

Pick, Daniel, *Faces of Degeneration: A European Disorder,
c.1848–c.1918*, Cambridge and New York: Cambridge
University Press, 1989

Soloway, Richard A., "Counting the Degenerates: The
Statistics of Race Deterioration in Edwardian England",
Journal of Contemporary History, 17 (1982): 137–64

Soloway, Richard A., *Demography and Degeneration:
Eugenics and the Declining Birthrate in Twentieth-Century
Britain*, Chapel Hill: University of North Carolina Press,
1990

CHAMBERLAIN & GILMAN argue that, through the second
half of the 19th century, degeneration was as widespread
and encompassing a term as evolution, with which it was
commonly, and oppositionally, associated. The positivistic,
scientific, and optimistic impetus of the 19th century was seemingly threatened by the social and cultural pathologies symptomatic of degeneration, the dark side of progress. This
collection of essays provides a very wide-ranging survey of the
subject, and is therefore a good place to start. Chamberlain &
Gilman claim that, from being the opposite side of a basically
progressive current of Western thought, degeneration gradually came to acquire a more actively generative character – as
a producer of decay and deterioration – which became pervasive throughout European culture. In these essays, degeneration is discussed by a number of authors as it occurred within
a spectrum of disciplines. Although degeneration originated in
biology and medicine, it came to be associated with many new
social sciences – such as sociology, sexology, and psychiatry –
which were fashioned in large part in order to study the
processes and products of degeneration. Several of the authors
in this volume, and in the other works discussed here, indicate that its most pervasive influence was perhaps to be found
in the arts, which were undergoing the painful birth of
modernism.

PICK identifies degeneration as a European disorder, in his
comparative study of its various manifestations in France, Italy,
and Britain. Principally examining the medical concepts, Pick
also shows how the language and imagery of degeneration were
translated into other areas, such as novels. In France, where
the idea originated in the work of the psychiatrist B.A. Morel,
the notion resonated powerfully within a context of declining
economic and political power after the debacle of the Franco-
Prussian war, finding popular dissemination in the novels of
Émile Zola. Lombroso's anthropometrical study of hereditary

criminality took place in post-unification Italy, where degenerate types – those believed to be incapable of being transformed into Italians – needed to be identified. In Britain,
degeneration was most closely associated with the social problems of cities, recognised by investigators such as Henry
Mayhew, William Booth, and Rowntree. Although not as influential with social reformers as in other countries, the novels
of writers such as Arthur Conan Doyle and Bram Stoker reflect
contemporary fears of the degenerate. Pick suggests that an
important feature across the three countries was a general shift
in the perception of degeneration, which was first regarded as
a disease affecting individuals, but was gradually believed to
affect groups or crowds.

NYE looks most closely at the developing medical interpretation of criminality in France, which came to rest increasingly
on notions of degeneration. In the late 19th century, with
economic decline and increasing ritual migration and vagrancy,
moral panic focused on the recidivist and habitual criminal,
while other social problems, such as intemperance, also came
to be pathologised as symptoms of degeneration. Nye notes a
hardening of attitudes towards criminals which accompanied
this increasing desire for the hereditary taint to be removed
from society, and goes on to trace the beginnings of attempts
at national regeneration through the development of sports and
social hygiene. Although not a particular focus of the book,
he too suggests that probably the best way for someone today
to appreciate the strength of feeling that degeneration aroused
at the turn of the century is to look at the contemporary art
and literature.

The degeneracy of artistic life at the end of the 19th century
formed the principal focus of the damning criticisms of
Max NORDAU. Although a primary source, written in 1897,
the introductory essay by George L. Mosse offers a valuable
insight into the mentality and motivations of the author of one
of the most important documents of the *fin de siècle*. Mosse
argues that Nordau epitomised a form of high bourgeois
culture that lauded scientific progress, individualistic moral
worth, industry, and a positivistic belief in an optimistic
future. Nordau's diatribe against the depraved and degenerate
artistic, literary and theatrical pioneers of modernism, such as
the Impressionists, Ibsen, and Nietzsche, lambasted their acceptance of moral relativism, nihilistic pessimism, and indulgent
sensuality which, he argued, derived from degenerative mental
illness caused by excessive ego-mania, pessimism and mysticism.

Urban degeneration, particularly the problem of the
residuum of outcast London, was the principal cause for
concern in Britain, and forms the focus of JONES's detailed
analysis of the social and economic bases of the middle-class
fear of the East End. Mid-century concerns about the unremit-
tingly lower class population of that part of London reached
a climax during the 1880s, with a series of strikes and marches
by people from the East End into the fashionable West End.
Apart from the direct threat to civilised society, this was a
worrying case of social and moral canker infecting the very
heart of Empire. Jones charts the casualisation of the labour
force by the de-industrialisation of central London, and the
mounting housing problems occasioned by slum and railway
clearance through the mid-19th century, which placed intoler-
able strains on the local residents. Booth's survey, however,

showed that the problems were not as bad as feared, in particular that the residuum was in fact only very small, and, while it was still feared that the respectable working classes may yet be infected, the more restrained dock strike of 1889 went a long way towards alleviating middle-class fears and strengthening policies of environmental improvement.

SOLOWAY (1990) traces the background of ideas on degeneration that fed into the eugenics movements. He argues that the fundamental issue of differential birth rates and excessive fertility of the hereditarily unfit was the starting point for much eugenical thinking. More useful for our purposes is his article (SOLOWAY, 1982) which looks at the near panic resulting from revelations that up to three-fifths of volunteers to the forces during the Boer War were rejected as unfit to serve. Coming amid the several military debacles of the Boer War, these findings suggested a race suffering from serious decline.

Fears about degeneration subsided during the 20th century, particularly during World War I, when many urban social problems were resolved on the Western Front, and poverty was proved not to be hereditarily fixed in the populations of city centres. The new interpretations offered by genetics, and the racist atrocities perpetrated by those who persisted in believing in hereditary taint, undermined the currency of degeneration, particularly in scientific circles. Although relatively short-lived, however, all the authors emphasise that degeneration was one of the key organising concepts of the late 19th century.

KEITH VERNON

Denmark

Billeskov Jansen, F.J., *Liv og lærdom: kapitler af dansk videnskabs historie*, Copenhagen: Gyldendal, 1983

Christensen, Dan Ch., *Det Moderne Projekt: Teknik og Kultur i Danmark-Norge 1750–(1814)–1850*, Copenhagen: Gyldendal, 1996

Garboe, Axel, *Geologiens historie i Danmark*, vol. 1: *Fra myte til videnskab*; vol. 2: *Forsekere og resultater*, Copenhagen: Reitzels, 1959–61

Hessenbruch, Arne, "The Spread of Precision Measurement in Scandinavia, 1660–1800", in *The Sciences in the European Periphery during the Enlightenment*, edited by Kostas Gavroglu, Dordrecht: Kluwer, 1999

Holter, Heinz and K. Max Møller (editors), *The Carlsberg Laboratory, 1876–1976*, Copenhagen: Rhodos, 1976

Lomholt, Asger, *Det Kongelige Danske videnskabernes selskab, 1742–1942: samlinger til selskabets historie*, 5 vols., Copenhagen: Munksgaard, 1942–73

Nielsen, Henry and Birgitte Wistoft, *Industriens Mænd: Et Krøyer-maleris tilblivelse og industrihistoriske betydning*, Århus: Klim, 1996

Pedersen, Olaf, *Lovers of Learning: A History of the Royal Danish Academy of Sciences and Letters, 1742–1992*, Copenhagen: Munksgaard, 1992

Pedersen, Olaf, *Strejflys: træk af dansk videnskabs historie, 1917–92*, Copenhagen: Munksgaard, 1992

Söderqvist, Thomas, *Hvilken kamp for at undslippe: En biografi om immunologen og nobelpristageren Niels Kaj Jerne*, Copenhagen: Borgen, 1998

In terms of volume and institutionalization, Danish history of science has lagged behind that of the English-speaking world. Until recently, most monographs were in-house histories or disciplinary histories tending toward hagiography. Recently, a considerable amount of work has appeared by professional historians of science. This entry covers two overviews of the Danish Academy of Sciences, a sweeping history of Danish geology, and then seven works dealing with more focused time periods, roughly in chronological order.

PEDERSEN's *Lovers of Learning* gives an overview in just over 300 pages of the history of the Royal Danish Academy of Sciences. It was commissioned to celebrate the Academy's 250th anniversary and is intended for a foreign audience. Pedersen, himself an Academy member, surveys the general history of imperial Denmark and its possessions: Norway, Schleswig-Holstein, Iceland, and the Faeroe Islands, and places the history of the Academy in this context. The creation of the mighty Carlsberg Foundation (with capital from the brewery) in 1876 is described as the crucial event in the Academy's history. The Foundation was set up under the auspices of the Academy and subsequently the patronage of science and culture was securely in its hands. The 20th century is described primarily through the Academy's international joint ventures and collaborations. The book is a good read and contains many excellent illustrations.

LOMHOLT renders a history of the Academy, with a detailed description of the manuscripts in its archives. Volume 1 contains a history of the Academy's foundations, the development of its rules and regulations, and its insignia. There is a complete list of members, presidents, and secretaries. Volume 2 describes the Academy's publications and international cooperative ventures, along with the state of its finances over the centuries. The third volume describes the archival collections connected with special projects, such as an authoritative dictionary of the Danish language, and volume 4 describes the maps and the manuscripts related to mapping and surveying. Volume 5 is an index of manuscripts and drawings, including some reproductions.

GARBOE is a history of Danish geology from runic creation stories to the 20th century. The focus is on the big names of Danish geology: Nicolaus Steno, Johan Georg Forchhammer, Johannes Frederik Johnstrup, and Knud Johannes Vogelius Steenstrup. These are presented in biographical accounts with much emphasis on the personal and institutional connections. Volume 1 takes the story up to 1835, when the first comprehensive overview of Denmark's geology was published by Forchhammer. There is quite a substantial correspondence between Forchhammer and Lyell, and Garboe presents at least their personal relationship (Lyell visited Forchhammer in Denmark), if not the international context of geological professionalization. A good half of volume 2 describes the work of Forchhammer's many students, especially the surveys of Denmark's northern possessions – Greenland, Iceland, and the Faeroes – but also the work of Peter Wilhelm Lund in Brazil. The latter half is concerned with the founding of geological institutions such as Copenhagen University's Mineralogical Museum (1831), Denmark's Geological Survey (1888), and the Danish Geological Association (1893).

HESSENBRUCH argues that precision measurement developed in 18th-century Scandinavia because of the demand for it within the military-fiscal states of Denmark-Norway and Sweden-Finland, almost constantly interlocked in expensive wars. Precision measurement helped minimize resistance to indirect taxes. He describes the gradual development of an infrastructure of measurement comprising the circulation of instruments and people: the former being subject to increasingly disciplined regimes of calibration, the latter to increasing professionalization.

CHRISTENSEN gives a splendidly illustrated overview of technology in Denmark-Norway between 1750 and 1850. He describes both the techniques for the making of industrial products, such as the metal plough, and the development of institutional structures for their production and diffusion. Pivotal to the argument of the book is the use of technological development in that which general historians agree is central to the period: agricultural reform. Christensen develops a comprehensive view, interrelating communication (especially within masonic lodges with their international contacts), science, investment (products bought from outside the village), politics and political economy, and the lobbying for a host of new social structures (wage labour, enclosure, abandonment of villeinage). The book has prompted a vigorous debate.

HOLTER & MØLLER is an in-house celebration of the Carlsberg Laboratory which was established (with the help of the financial muscle of the Carlsberg brewery) with the purpose of pursuing "pure" research at a time when this was rare. The laboratory had two departments: chemistry and physiology. Biographies of the heads of the departments form the main part of the book. The editors argue that this narrative structure is appropriate given the patriarchal form of organization chosen by the founder, J.C. Jacobsen. He modelled the laboratory explicitly on Pasteur's, claiming this would result in the beneficial impact of science on human civilization as a whole.

NIELSEN & WISTOFT's analysis of Peder Severin Krøyer's painting *The Men of Industry* is a delightful look at the networks of industrial Copenhagen at the turn of the century. It combines excellent reproductions of the whole painting and of details along with an analysis of newly-found archival material illuminating both the genesis of the painting and the selection of men to be portrayed. The book reveals just why prosopography is such a powerful tool. The painting depicts 53 men of Danish industry in a Copenhagen electricity plant in 1903. It was commissioned by Gustav Hagemann, a particularly influential industrialist. He selected the 52 other individuals, and the archival material allows the authors to examine the relationship between Hagemann and every single one of them. They trace personal relations among the industrial elite which go beyond straightforward institutional affiliation, and thus they are able to illuminate connections that would be lost by histories focusing on any particular educational institution, industry, or administrative branch.

PEDERSEN's *Strejflys* is a collection of essays on 20th-century science in Denmark. It contains 17 essays, 15 of which cover a different scientific discipline or practitioner: biomedicine, archaeology, Niels Bohr, history, geology, Oriental philology, deep sea research, meteorology, particle physics, astronomy and astrophysics, dentistry, insulin, chemistry, medieval philology, and literary studies. The last two entries cover aspects of history of science policy. Each chapter is written by a participant in the historical development described.

BILLESKOV JANSEN's collation of newspaper articles and other conversational publications is an intriguing tour through Danish intellectual history. Some 20 essays range from the 17th to the 20th centuries and from Steno to the use of Victor Hugo in Danish schools. His insights into Ørsted's views on religion, art, and Kant, and on his integration of science into this general world-view, are informative and concise. There are further essays on topics such as Thomas Kingo's topographical-historical topography, Christian Gottlieb Kratzenstein, and Harald Høffding.

SÖDERQVIST's biography of Niels Kaj Jerne, the immunologist who received the 1984 Nobel prize for medicine and physiology, is organized around the moment of his inspirational discovery of the natural selection theory of antibodies. Söderqvist argues that Jerne's private life is more important for the development of his scientific theory than the theory's scientific and institutional context. This is in accord with Jerne's own emphasis on the striking moment of discovery when he was crossing a bridge in Copenhagen on an afternoon in 1954. Jerne lived a peripatetic life, and the reader gets an insight not only into scientific and cultural life of mid-20th-century Copenhagen, but also of Jerne's interactions at Caltech, Pittsburgh, Frankfurt am Main, Basel, and the United Nations.

ARNE HESSENBRUCH

Dentistry

Bennion, Elisabeth, *Antique Dental Instruments*, London and New York: Sotheby's, 1986

Cohen, R.A. (ed.), *The Advance of the Dental Profession: A Centenary History, 1880–1980*, London: British Dental Association, 1979

Donaldson, J.A., *The National Dental Hospital, 1859–1914*, London: British Dental Association, 1992

Hillam, Christine (ed.), *The Roots of Dentistry*, London: British Dental Association, 1990

Hillam, Christine, *Brass Plate and Brazen Impudence: Dental Practice in the Provinces, 1755–1855*, Liverpool: Liverpool University Press, 1991

Hoffmann-Axthelm, Walter, *History of Dentistry*, translated from the German by H.M. Koehler, Chicago: Quintessence, 1981 (original edition, 1973)

Ring, Malvin E., *Dentistry: An Illustrated History*, New York: Abrams, 1985

Weinberger, Bernhard Wolf, *An Introduction to the History of Dentistry*, 2 vols, St Louis, Missouri: Mosby, 1948

Dentistry has, by and large, developed alongside medicine, and its interaction with the state, other than within the school health service, is relatively recent. These facts go some way to explain, perhaps, why dentistry has attracted little attention from historians of medicine, who have seen it as peripheral to their concerns. The result is that very few references to dentistry are to be found in works of social or medical history; the bulk of writing in English on the subject is currently to be found in a few unpublished theses, two small journals – the *Bulletin of the History of Dentistry* (the publication of the American Academy of the History of Dentistry), and *Dental Historian* (produced by the Lindsay Society for the History of Dentistry)

– and in a relatively small number of more extended texts, usually available only in specialist dental libraries. Occasional articles are to be found in the dental press. This corpus reflects both the different aspects of the history of dentistry (clinical, scientific, social, and professional), and different approaches to the writing of history.

The reader seeking a quick overview of the scope of the subject might find HILLAM (1990) a useful starting point. This short (73-page) work is arranged thematically, containing sections on dental disease, treatment, practitioners, patients, and dental literature, together with a chronology and glossary. A high proportion of the illustrations are in colour. It is aimed at the general reader, and designed as an easily accessible text in order to arouse the interest of practitioners in their past.

Many lengthier works concern themselves principally with chronicling the history and lineage of clinical techniques and scientific ideas, though rarely placing them within a broader historical context. Both WEINBERGER (volume 1) and HOFF-MANN-AXTHELM are chronologically comprehensive in their approach, ranging from early historic times to the end of the 18th and the beginning of the 20th centuries respectively. Their source material consists mainly of printed texts, early manuscripts, archaeological evidence and artefacts; both are scholarly, well-referenced books, containing black and white illustrations. While Hoffmann-Axthelm is generally considered to be the modern reference book in this area, Weinberger draws perhaps on a wider range of sources and is more analytical. Of the two, he has more to say on the social history of dentistry and dentists (based mainly on observations made by 18th- and 19th-century practitioners), although some of his comments on the European context have been superseded by subsequent research. In the second volume, he deals at length (408 pages) with dental practice in the United States up to the early 19th century, and includes valuable biographical studies (including an exhaustive examination of George Washington's dental problems) and a wealth of primary sources.

RING's book is organised around a similarly chronological framework. The high proportion of excellent illustrations (many in colour) necessarily limits the scope and originality of the text, but the book fulfils its declared purpose as an illustrated history of dentistry. There is a useful bibliography, but no references.

BENNION provides "a history of dentistry through its instruments". Chapters are devoted to extracting and excavating instruments, artificial teeth, anaesthetic equipment, mirrors and scalers, and oral hygiene. The profusely illustrated text is unreferenced, but is followed by a short bibliography. A useful section of the book is a directory of 18th- and 19th-century instrument makers in the United Kingdom, parts of Europe and North America.

Writers of the early 20th century were often more concerned to provide an honourable lineage for the modern clinician, than to study the development of dental practice from the historian's perspective. Thus, extended texts treating dentistry as a social phenomenon, and examining the emergence of its practitioners as a group, are as yet few and far between. Since the 1980s, however, more interest has been taken in the medical and pharmaceutical history of dentistry. HILLAM (1991) is concerned with the development of practice outside London between 1755 and 1855, and her study is based on a wide variety of primary sources. She examines such aspects as trade origins and education, income and wealth, numerical expansion, geographical distribution, mobility, etc. The relatively short text (148 pages) is supplemented by a "register" of more than 1100 dentists, compiled from the surviving provincial trade directories published before 1856. The book is fully referenced and has a bibliography.

Where Hillam investigates the issues pertinent to the period 1755–1855 (growth in demand, pressure for reform, dental treatment as an expression of fashion, etc.), DONALDSON, while ostensibly concerned with the history of the National Dental Hospital (the first such establishment in London) from 1859 to 1914, deals also with dental education and the workings and problems of a 19th-century voluntary hospital. This book, although brief, is scholarly and well-referenced. A number of other short histories of dental schools or hospitals have been written in recent years. Their main concern has been to commemorate the contribution of individuals to their respective institutions.

In the process of examining the development and activities of the British Dental Association during the first 100 years of its existence from 1880, COHEN also deals with dental legislation, international dental meetings, and the position of dentists in the armed forces. Concise histories of the different branches of the Association are included, compiled from minutes books. Valuable appendices include a chronology, notes on all the presidents of the Association, life members, etc., and while not referenced, the book is well indexed.

Hillam (1991), Donaldson, and Cohen, taken together, form something of a trilogy, offering a picture of the development of the profession from the mid-18th to the late 20th centuries. Work currently (1996) in progress on a number of fronts promises to produce fuller and historically broader studies of dentistry and dental practice in the 17th and 18th centuries.

CHRISTINE HILLAM

Descartes, René 1596–1650

French natural philosopher

Baillet, Adrien, *The Life of Monsieur Descartes*, 2 vols, translated from the French by S.R., London: Simpson, 1693; reprinted New York: Garland, 1987 (original edition, 1691)

Chappell, Vere and Willis Doney, *Twenty-Five Years of Descartes Scholarship, 1960–1984: A Bibliography*, New York: Garland, 1987

Cottingham, John (ed.), *The Cambridge Companion to Descartes*, Cambridge and New York: Cambridge University Press, 1992

Garber, Daniel, *Descartes' Metaphysical Physics*, Chicago: University of Chicago Press, 1992

Gaukroger, Stephen (ed.), *Descartes: Philosophy, Mathematics and Physics*, Brighton: Harvester Press, and Totowa, New Jersey: Barnes and Noble, 1980

Gaukroger, Stephen, *Descartes: An Intellectual Biography*, Oxford: Clarendon Press, and New York: Oxford University Press, 1995

Lindeboom, G.A., *Descartes and Medicine*, Amsterdam: Rodopi, 1979

Sebba, Gregor, *Bibliographia Cartesiana: A Critical Guide to the Descartes Literature, 1800–1960*, The Hague: Nijhoff, 1964

Sepper, Dennis L., *Descartes' Imagination: Proportion, Images, and the Activity of Thinking*, Berkeley: University of California Press, 1996

Shea, William R., *The Magic of Numbers and Motion: The Scientific Career of René Descartes*, Canton, Massachusetts: Science History Publications, 1991

Voss, Stephen (ed.), *Essays on the Philosophy and Science of René Descartes*, New York: Oxford University Press, 1993

The natural philosophy of the early modern French mechanist René Descartes poses an unusually complex problem of interpretation for the historian of science. Few thinkers of the modern era have so deliberately created a mythology to accompany and flatter their work as Descartes; according to this mythology, only Descartes himself, without aid from past authority or contemporary peers, could initiate and complete the great human projects of metaphysics and natural philosophy. The construction of this myth of heroic self-origination necessarily involved a comprehensive denial and concealment of all intellectual influences on the philosopher. The first task of the historian of science in dealing with Descartes must therefore be to recover that historical context that he so deliberately sought to conceal.

Unfortunately, much of the traditional scholarship has accepted Descartes's own mythology at face value, painting him as the father of a new philosophical absolutism, promoting a rationalist method and a mind-matter dualism without nuances or compromises. SEBBA's comprehensive annotated bibliography, and the more recent but also more cursory work by CHAPPELL & DONEY, reveal that the emphasis within Descartes studies is on metaphysics and epistemology. Sebba contains an annotated list of all literature on Descartes between 1800 and 1960, an analytical survey, and is well indexed. Chappell & Doney is less ambitious, listing alphabetically the Descartes literature from 1960 to 1984. However, both mention new scholarship that points the way to a surprisingly subtle and complex body of thought on Descartes, far beyond the simple slogans of his mythology.

A critical, historically sensitive introduction to the life and thought of this "other" Descartes may be found in the collection of articles edited by COTTINGHAM. Among the many excellent pieces in the book, Amélie Oksenberg Rorty's article, "Descartes On Thinking with the Body", stands out as an especially articulate attack on simplistic interpretations of Cartesian dualism. As the title suggests, Rorty demonstrates the important role played by the body in Descartes's account of human consciousness. For a more specialized monograph on the subject, SEPPER offers a look at the theoretical prominence of the bodily imagination in Descartes. By attending to Descartes's borrowings from the medieval doctrine of the internal senses, Sepper is able to characterize Descartes's dualism as a more or less dialectical exchange between abstraction and image, mind and body, thereby seriously undermining the myth of Descartes as the archetypal rationalist and dualist.

The best guide to the historical context of Descartes's thought may be found in the biographical scholarship, which often manages to expose many of the roots of his intellectual development. A good starting point is BAILLET's classic 17th-century biography. Although it does not meet modern standards of historical scholarship and has to be read with great caution, it offers fascinating insights into the philosopher's culture and society. SHEA's book provides a good contemporary introduction to the genre, with an entertaining and lucid account, focusing mainly on Descartes's early writings in natural philosophy. This biography is particularly useful for its presentation of Descartes's mathematical style. However, as a whole, Shea's book has recently been superseded by the more ambitious and substantial biography by GAUKROGER (1995), which charts in great detail the entire span of Descartes's life. Unfortunately, Gaukroger promises more than he manages to deliver in terms of historical context; the author's attempt to ground Descartes's intellectual mind-frame within his social and cultural surroundings remains rather half-hearted. Gaukroger is at his best when he maps out the diverse character of Descartes's career. He points to at least three decisive stages of development, ranging from the early focus on natural philosophy and method, to the famous absorption with metaphysics of the middle period, and the final turn towards the psychology and physiology of the passions in the late works. This diversity of interests poses an intriguing problem of interpretation, since it clashes decisively with Descartes's own ideal about the unified nature of all human knowledge. How should the different directions of his thought be measured against each other? Gaukroger wants to suggest that the metaphysical writings of the middle period were written mainly to serve as window-dressing for the earlier ventures in natural philosophy. In his opinion, the metaphysical works must be understood as the product of political prudence, an attempt to legitimize the mechanist physics with the religious authorities. Yet he leaves the broader implications of this claim undefended. There is not yet any general work on the political implications of Descartes's natural philosophy; indeed, the philosopher never developed an explicit theory of politics in the traditional sense. Nevertheless Descartes's general vision of scientific and technological progress obviously offers a crucial foundation for modern political thought. To Descartes, the project of natural philosophy promised human society radical power over the natural world, a power potentially without limit.

Contrary to Gaukroger (1995), GARBER asserts that for Descartes physics and metaphysics formed a unified whole, and that the laws of motion governing the physical universe were at every instant ordained by divine omnipotent will. As a consequence, Garber is led to stress the central role of the *Principles of Philosophy*, Descartes's textbook version of his thought, written long after the natural philosophy of the early period. GAUKROGER (1980) and VOSS both focus on the foundations of Descartes's mathematics and physics, and give an incisive background to this quarrel between physics and metaphysical physics. Gaukroger (1980) is a little narrower, focusing on the philosophical foundation of Descartes's mathematical physics, while Voss is somewhat broader, and also contains a remarkable attack by John Schuster on the centrality of method in Descartes.

As noted, the literature on Descartes's physics and mathematics is plentiful and excellent. Unfortunately, this cannot be said of his other writings in natural philosophy. The few monographs on his medicine and physiology are of inferior quality. LINDEBOOM is a serviceable account that includes sections on Descartes's physiology as well as a brief examination of his hopes of extending human life. This poverty of interpretation is quite distressing, considering that Descartes himself, in the *Discourse on the Method*, described human health and longevity as the foremost goals of his natural philosophy. Perhaps medicine and physiology could therefore be said to form the central concern of Descartes's natural philosophy.

FREDRIK JONSSON

See also Scientific Revolution

Dialectical Materialism

Graham, Loren R., *Science, Philosophy, and Human Behavior in the Soviet Union*, New York: Columbia University Press, 1987 (revised version of *Science and Philosophy in the Soviet Union*, 1972)

Joravsky, David, *Soviet Marxism and Natural Science, 1917–1932*, New York: Columbia University Press, and London: Routledge and Kegan Paul, 1961

Joravsky, David, *The Lysenko Affair*, Cambridge, Massachusetts: Harvard University Press, 1970

Krementsov, Nikolai, *Stalinist Science*, Princeton, New Jersey: Princeton University Press, 1997

Weiner, Douglas R., *Models of Nature: Ecology, Conservation, and Cultural Revolution in Soviet Russia*, Bloomington: Indiana University Press, 1988

Wetter, Gustav A., *Dialectical Materialism: A Historical and Systematic Survey of Philosophy in the Soviet Union*, translated from the German by Peter Heath, London: Routledge and Kegan Paul, and New York: Praeger, 1958 (original edition, 1952)

Dialectical materialism was the official philosophy of science in the Soviet Union. It was promoted by state-sponsored philosopher-courtiers, and in many ways determined the discourse of science and technology in the USSR. The historiography of dialectical materialism has in the past been heavily colored by Cold War ideologies in both East and West. Several of the important non-Soviet works will be examined here.

In the most general sense, the tenets of dialectical materialism as it evolved in the Soviet context are an amalgam of statements made by V.I. Lenin on science and on Machian positivism before the Russian Revolution, and several late-19th-century texts by Friedrich Engels on the dialectics of nature. The basic elements of the philosophy are an ontology of matter-energy and an application of dialectical methods as the only correct way of reasoning in the sciences, which are themselves subdivided into several interacting but non-reductive levels, such as the social sciences, the life sciences, and the physical sciences.

Thus far, the ideas appear to be rather vague, and that was indeed the assessment of them in the early Soviet Union. JORAVSKY's 1961 monograph on the evolution of a Soviet philosophy of the natural sciences in the 1920s traces in great detail the different schools of interpretation of dialectical materialism and how both natural scientists and Marxist philosophers (and, to a much lesser degree at this stage, bureaucrats) negotiated the complicated meanings of the philosophy in a highly charged political context. As both an introduction to dialectical materialism and a survey of radically different interpretations, Joravsky's ground-breaking work is an excellent resource.

For a more detailed look at the actual philosophical claims of dialectical materialism, WETTER is a standard reference. He articulates the origins of the philosophy of nature and of dialectics back to Hegel and through various interpretations in the Russian context. The philosophical work is impressive but at times tedious, and there is little development of a historical context in this already lengthy tome. There is some discussion of the impact of dialectical materialism on Soviet science, which follows the philosophical analysis. The assumption by Wetter, a quite common assumption for German scholars working on this topic in the 1950s, is that dialectical materialism conceptually *mattered* for Soviet scientists.

For American authors, this claim has been much more controversial. The most famous example of dialectical materialism being invoked to justify a scientific viewpoint as valid, and not merely to explain it, is the notorious Lysenko affair, in which agronomist Trofim Lysenko managed to convince the Soviet state to ban genetics as a "bourgeois" science. JORAVSKY (1970) treats this incident at length, and makes a strong argument for the Lysenko affair being typical of Soviet state-science interactions. He claims that Lysenkoism was an instance of state-sponsored ideology being imposed by political bosses on scientists who wanted nothing to do with dialectical materialism – with disastrous consequences.

KREMENTSOV takes an entirely different view of the Lysenko affair's relation to dialectical materialism, but with a similar fundamental message. For him, dialectical materialism is the language in which Stalinist science was conducted. Both geneticists and Lysenkoists used this language to try to garner state patronage. It happens that in the heat of battle, the Lysenkoists won and managed to convince the state to oppress their opponents, but the opposite would have been the case had the geneticists won. Here, dialectical materialism is not a matter of conviction: it is a rhetorical tool used to accomplish an end. There is an affinity with Joravsky (1970) here: no scientists actually believe dialectical materialism in the Soviet Union, they have to use it or face destruction. Krementsov differs only in that he points out that the geneticists used the same ruses and techniques.

GRAHAM's magisterial text begs to differ. Looking closely at debates about dialectical materialism after Stalin's death in 1953, he traces how dialectical materialism was sincerely embraced by certain scientists to achieve major scientific advances in fields as disparate as relativity theory, quantum mechanics, cybernetics, origin of life, psychology, and linguistics. Graham does not see the pronouncements in favor of dialectical materialism as "window dressing" or the vestiges of totalitarianism, but as a positive world-view that scientists used to advance their various disciplines. He also points out several purely philosophical discussions of the metaphysics implied by dialectical materialism, further showing that the meaning of this supposedly "monolithic" philosophy was by no means settled. This stance in a Cold War context was received negatively by many who wanted to insist that the role of dialectical materialism exemplified by the Lysenko affair was typical. Graham's denial of this view is now widely accepted.

Largely inspired by Graham's work, there have appeared recently several excellent studies of specific disciplines to examine how dialectical materialism was actually introduced, negotiated, and used in several fields. WEINER's study of the rise of ecology in the Soviet Union points to ways in which dialectical materialism was both opportunistically and sincerely used by ecologists to set up a wide network of nature preserves. In the end, however, I.I. Prezent, Lysenko's future henchman, crushed ecology by using similar dialectical materialist arguments. The merit of Weiner's work lies in showing just how complicated such philosophical positions became when worked out in localized fields at definite times. The generalizing position so common on both sides of the Cold War has loosened its grip on studies of the history of dialectical materialism.

MICHAEL D. GORDIN

Discipline

Abbott, Andrew, *The System of Professions: An Essay on the Division of Expert Labor*, Chicago: University of Chicago Press, 1988

Bechtel, William (ed.), *Integrating Scientific Disciplines*, The Hague: Nijhoff, 1986

Ben-David, Joseph, *Scientific Growth: Essays on the Social Organization and Ethos of Science*, Berkeley: University of California Press, 1991

Dogan, Mattie and Robert Pahre, *Creative Marginality: Innovation at Intersections of the Social Sciences*, Boulder, Colorado: Westview Press, 1990

Fuchs, Stephan, *The Professional Quest for Truth: A Social Theory of Science and Knowledge*, Albany: State University of New York Press, 1992

Fuller, Steve, *Social Epistemology*, Bloomington: Indiana University Press, 1988

Geison, Gerald L. and Frederic L. Holmes (eds), *Research Schools: Historical Reappraisals*, special issue of *Osiris*, 8 (1993)

Graham, Loren, Wolf Lepenies and Peter Weingart, *The Functions and Uses of Disciplinary Histories*, Dordrecht: Reidel, 1983

Klein, Julie Thompson, *Interdisciplinarity: History, Theory and Practice*, Detroit: Wayne State University Press, 1990

Merz, John Theodore, *History of European Scientific Thought in the Nineteenth Century (1904–12)*, 4 vols, New York: Dover, 1965

Messer-Davidow, Ellen, David R. Shumway and David J. Sylvan (eds), *Knowledges: Historical and Critical Studies in Disciplinarity*, Charlottesville: University Press of Virginia, 1993

Olesko, Kathryn M., *Physics as a Calling: Discipline and Practice in the Königsberg Seminar for Physics*, Ithaca, New York: Cornell University Press, 1991

Toulmin, Stephen, *Human Understanding*, Oxford: Clarendon Press, and Princeton, New Jersey: Princeton University Press, 1972

Whitley, Richard, *The Intellectual and Social Organization of the Sciences*, Oxford: Clarendon Press, and New York: Oxford University Press, 1984

There have always been scientific disciplines, in the sense that one speaks of monastic and other forms of religious discipline: namely, a set of practices that are cultivated and transmitted by a group of specially trained people. However, as the authors in GEISON & HOLMES claim, the rise of the modern university system in the 19th century has caused historians to reconceptualize this older sense of discipline as a "school", especially stressing the localized and face-to-face character of its knowledge transmission. In contrast, "discipline" is now reserved for more far-flung epistemic regimes, that rely heavily on common textbooks and other formal means of knowledge transmission. OLESKO goes further, correcting the pervasive view (originating with Michael Polanyi and Thomas Kuhn) that scientific schools are grounded primarily in "tacit knowledge". She argues that this grossly underestimates the role of teaching by explicit precept, which is essential if the knowledge produced by schools is to achieve disciplinary status.

MERZ still provides the most comprehensive historical account of how the emergence of national university systems in Europe created the modern disciplinary mentality, and its attendant hierarchies and turf wars. According to Merz, scientific orientations that began as world views (e.g., atomism, vitalism, etc.) are eventually reduced to disciplinary proportions as they confront each other in the laboratory and the corridors of academic politics. Historians of science may have ignored disciplines (until the recent sociologization of their field), because disciplines are more easily tracked by their teaching and administrative functions than by their research functions. Yet, most general histories of science have been of the research frontier. The contributors to GRAHAM, LEPENIES & WEINGART look at this problem from the standpoint of the disciplines themselves (both the natural and the social sciences), the histories of which most often serve to motivate contemporary research agendas.

A good sociological complement to Merz is BEN-DAVID, who stresses the importance of the changing academic labour market to the incidence and resolution of cross-disciplinary turf wars. Ben-David is especially astute on the role of labour migration in the rise of new disciplines, as a shrinking job market forces academics trained in one field to find work in another. The emergence of experimental psychology as a result of medical scientists moving to philosophy departments is a case in point.

WHITLEY hit on the fruitful idea of explaining the differences between disciplines in terms of organizational sociology. He isolates two variables as being of particular significance: the degree to which practitioners can agree on an appropriate problem, and the degree to which they depend on each other for a solution. Whitley supposes that a discipline ranking high on both variables (e.g., physics) is ideal because it will allow piecemeal growth and rapid diffusion of innovations. FUCHS, whose own work is based on Whitley's model, draws the opposite conclusion, largely as a result of his own postmodernist scruples. In terms of promoting the creativity of its practitioners and preventing premature closure on debate, broadly "hermeneutical" disciplines, which rank low on both variables, are normatively most desirable.

ABBOTT, a major sociologist of the professions, argues that disciplinary credentials enabled the liberal professions to consolidate their power base in the early 20th century. The force of these credentials was to suggest that, say, psychiatrists were not beholden to special interests (unlike pastoral priests), but only to the truths that their field can uncover by its disciplined methods. In some cases, this meant that people studying for the professions had to take science courses.

In the philosophy of science, disciplines have only attracted the attention of the few who seek units of analysis in which social and epistemic factors cannot be neatly disentangled. The logical positivists and Karl Popper held that disciplines were at best expedient, at worst atavistic, ways of dividing up what they regarded as science's unified quest for truth. TOULMIN was the first philosopher to present a discipline-based account of scientific change, in which "discipline" clearly means an institution larger than a school. He identified disciplines in terms of their forums for evaluating knowledge claims; i.e. who reads you rather than who trains you. FULLER extends this viewpoint in a strongly sociological direction, using it as a basis for rethinking the philosophy of science more generally. In particular, he stresses the constructed character of disciplinary boundaries, as they simultaneously open and close possibilities for inquiry. Fuller suggests that these can be manipulated according to the epistemic needs of the society in question.

The past 10 years have witnessed an efflorescence of work on "interdisciplinarity". All of it aims to correct the idea that knowledge can be represented as a "map" with well-defined disciplinary boundaries. However, the alternative images of knowledge associated with interdisciplinarity are strikingly different. The contributors to BECHTEL, mostly biologically-orientated philosophers and scientists, imagine that increasingly specialized disciplines are like islands that require the building of interdisciplinary bridges. The contributors to MESSER-DAVIDOW, SHUMWAY & SYLVAN, strongly influenced by Michel Foucault's work on disciplinarity in carceral institutions, see academic disciplines as repressing people and phenomena that deviate from their norms. Interdisciplinarity for them turns out to be the revenge of the repressed. They relate historical and contemporary cases that threaten the legitimacy of current disciplinary boundaries, if not academic disciplines altogether.

There are also more moderate images of interdisciplinarity. KLEIN's comprehensive survey reveals that the problem-solving orientations of government and business – more than marginalized academics – have typically fostered interdisciplinary work. Her paradigm case is the transient interdisciplinary team whose members return to their home disciplines after their work is over. However, she notes that sometimes these teams leave lasting "transdisciplinary" traces – such as systems theory – that influence several disciplines without replacing them. DOGAN & PAHRE argue that the best interdisciplinary work is done, not by "interdisciplinarians", but by scholars trying to reconcile the competing normative demands of two or more disciplines in which they were trained.

STEVE FULLER

Discovery

Blachowicz, James, "Discovery as Correction", *Synthèse*, 71 (1987): 235–321

Boden, Margaret A. (ed.), *Dimensions of Creativity*, Cambridge, Massachusetts: MIT Press, 1994

Cushing, James T., *Theory Construction and Selection in Modern Physics: The S Matrix*, Cambridge and New York: Cambridge University Press, 1990

Fleck, Ludwik, *Entstehung und Entwicklung einer wissenschaftlichen Tatsache*, Frankfurt: Suhrkamp, 1980 (1935)

Gooding, David, *Experiment and the Making of Meaning: Human Agency in Scientific Observation and Experiment*, Dordrecht and Boston: Kluwer, 1990

Gruber, Howard E., *Darwin on Man: A Psychological Study of Scientific Creativity*, New York: Dutton, and London: Wildwood House, 1974

Hanson, Norwood R., *Patterns of Discovery: An Inquiry into the Conceptual Foundations of Science*, Cambridge: Cambridge University Press, 1958

Hull, David L., *Science as a Process: An Evolutionary Account of the Social and Conceptual Development of Science*, Chicago: University of Chicago Press, 1988

Kantorovich, Aharon, *Scientific Discovery: Logic and Tinkering*, Albany: State University of New York Press, 1993

Knorr-Cetina, Karin, *Die Fabrikation von Erkenntnis: Zur Anthropologie der Naturwissenschaft*, Frankfurt: Suhrkamp, 1984

Kuhn, Thomas S., *The Structure of Scientific Revolutions*, Chicago: University of Chicago Press, 1962; revised edition, 1970

Musgrave, Alan, "Is There a Logic of Scientific Discovery?", *LSE Quarterly*, 2–3 (1988): 205–27

Nersessian, Nancy J., "How Do Scientists Think? Capturing the Dynamics of Conceptual Change in Science", in *Cognitive Models of Science*, edited by R. Giere, Minneapolis: University of Minnesota Press, 1992, 3–4

Nickles, Thomas (ed.), *Scientific Discovery, Logic, and Rationality*, Dordrecht and Boston: Reidel, 1980

Nickles, Thomas (ed.), *Scientific Discovery: Case Studies*, Dordrecht and Boston: Reidel, 1980

Pickering, Andrew, *Constructing Quarks: A Sociological History of Particle Physics*, Edinburgh: Edinburgh University Press, and Chicago: University of Chicago Press, 1984

Shrager, Jeff and Pat Langley (eds), *Computational Models of Scientific Discovery and Theory Formation*, San Mateo, California: Morgan Kaufmann, 1990

Simonton, Dean Keith, *Scientific Genius: A Psychology of Science*, Cambridge and New York: Cambridge University Press, 1988

Thagard, Paul, *Conceptual Revolutions*, Princeton, New Jersey: Princeton University Press, 1992

Weisberg, Robert W., *Creativity: Genius and Other Myths*, New York: W.H. Freeman, 1986

Zahar, Elie, "Logic of Discovery or Psychology of Invention?", *British Journal for the Philosophy of Science*, 34 (1983): 243–61

By distinguishing between the "context of discovery" and the "context of justification", the analytical philosophy of science – comprising logical empiricism (Carnap, Hahn, Neurath, Schlick, and others) and critical rationalism (Popper) – staked out an independent subject area. This school, which dominated philosophy for half a century, excluded the "context of discovery" from philosophical studies, assigning it to such disciplines as the history of science, psychology, or sociology. However, in the 1970s, a group of "friends of discovery" began to challenge the isolation of the philosophy of science from the empirical disciplines, and especially from the history of science, and to turn their attention to the "context of discovery". From this very heterogeneous group, and partly through interdisciplinary work, a multiplicity of approaches began to evolve, each developing its own peculiar relationship with the history of science.

One approach deals with "discovery" as logical deduction, thus following the positivistic tradition. ZAHAR uses the second Newtonian Law to demonstrate the hypothesis that "scientific discovery" is not inductive, and does not require psychological explanations, but proceeds essentially by deduction. According to this historical reconstruction, Newton arrived at his law through the Cartesian principle of inertia and Kepler's laws. MUSGRAVE also favours a deductive logic of discovery, and proceeds by exposing the usually suppressed discipline/subject-specific conditions of scientific argumentation. This pattern of deductive reasoning can also be found in Musgrave's account of Rutherford's discovery of atomic structure.

BLACHOWICZ describes the mechanism of scientific discovery as the "logic of correction", in which the dynamic, constructive, "semi-inference pattern" of scientific research controls mistakes by reporting discrepancies between observation and prognosis. In this system, the deduction of the new theory is replaced by heuristic rules that fail to provide one-to-one correspondence.

Central to GOODING's understanding of scientific "discovery" is his emphasis on the importance of the use of instruments in observation. By systematically analyzing experimental procedures through laboratory books and drawings by André Marie Ampère, Jean Baptiste Biot, Humphry Davy, and Michael Faraday, he illustrates the important role of the experiments themselves, as a result of a process Gooding calls "black-boxing".

The "historicist" approach also analyzes case studies, but focuses on the local micro-structure of scientific research. The two collections edited by NICKLES display a preference for a historiography that is not reconstructed from the perspective of current scientific knowledge. Apart from Newton's discovery of gravitation, the first volume is chiefly concerned with methodological questions, while the second volume focuses on the Copernican era, the history of biology since Darwin, and the development of "plate tectonic theory" in geology. HANSON, who has made a substantial contribution to the revived interest in "discovery", is the inspiration for many of the contributions from the domain of physics.

Inspired by a detailed medical case study, FLECK responded to Popper's "Logic of Scientific Discovery" of 1934 by developing an alternative model, in which the dynamic aspects of scientific research are emphasized. Psychological, as well as sociological, factors enter into this theory, which describes discovery as a change in the style of thinking, both within the scientific "thought-collective" and in the scientist's everyday life.

On the basis of historic case studies, KUHN developed a model that distinguishes between successive phases of normal and revolutionary science. Accordingly, he identified two kinds of discoveries, on the one hand those that contribute to a further articulation of the paradigm currently adhered to, and, on the other hand, those that help remove anomalies that remained unsolvable within the normal scientific process. In the latter case, however, the old paradigm is left behind and a new one conceived in a revolutionary leap.

CUSHING's detailed case study deals with "S-matrix theory", whose further articulation later proved a dead end. Cushing provides an internal history of this episode of high energy physics, and avoids the charge of present-centredness by focusing on the temporary successes, as well as the ultimate failure, of "S-matrix theory".

The sociological approach to "discovery" was adopted by PICKERING in his massive case study, also on high energy physics. His model describes the dynamics of scientific practice as "opportunism in context". KNORR-CETINA applied her ethnographic method to everyday life in an American large-scale laboratory for microbiological research, which she observed over an extended period of time. On this site, she claimed, reality is not so much described as constructed, and this construction is determined by a number of decisions during scientific operations that are made on the basis of an opportunistic logic. This rationality of decision is transepistemic, and not confined to the scientific community.

Scientific discovery can also be considered from a psychological perspective; for example, BODEN claims that the psychological contributions to her collection are compatible with those by the two historians, who emphasize the sociological aspects of creativity. WEISBERG attempts to unmask the myth of the genius as a romantic exaggeration, using numerous examples from science and art. In his reading, scientific problem-solving does not significantly differ from everyday problem-solving, and he illustrates this using the cases of the discovery of the double-helix by Crick and Watson, and Darwin's theory of evolution through natural selection.

SIMONTON presents a multi-phase "chance configuration model", according to which, in the first purely statistical phase of a discovery, intellectual elements (such as facts, principles, relations, rules, laws, formulas, or images) permute. In the second (and likewise internal) phase, a selection is made, in that only the stable configurations of these elements become conscious. In order to become acceptable for the scientific community, these stable units must then be expressed in a linguistic or mathematical form that is suitable for communication.

Boden defines creativity as the representation, elaboration, and transformation of structured conceptual spaces. With the computer-simulation of these spaces she links up with yet another (fifth) approach to the description of "discovery": the development of mechanized intelligence. Conceptual analysis is of central importance for THAGARD's analysis of the chemical revolution through Lavoisier, of the Darwinian and geological revolutions, and of further examples from physics.

According to his model, in a revolution, concepts can be added (for example, oxygen) or removed (for example, phlogiston), and conceptual branches can be reassigned (for example, by viewing man as a kind of animal), or the entire conceptual tree can be reorganized (for example, "species", which previously denoted a mere similarity, with Darwin became a historical characteristic). The variety and interdisciplinarity of computational philosophy of science are reflected in a collection of conference papers edited by SHRAGER & LANGLEY.

Another approach to "discovery" is that of evolutionary epistemology. From this perspective, HULL presents his massive case study in biological systematology, in which he includes social components. KANTOROVICH also develops his theory of discovery on the evolutionary model, along with the social and psychological models of creativity. Supplementing Simonton's approach with a more detailed analysis of the "sociohistorical setting" of "epistemic co-operation", Kantorovich ascribes central importance to non-intentionality and "serendipitous discovery". According to Kantorovich, precisely the most interesting cases of creativity are unamenable to a logic of discovery, and are adequately characterized in a naturalistic theory only through his "tinkering" model.

The "cognitive history of science" constitutes an interdisciplinary approach, in which the social and cognitive dimensions of knowledge production are interlinked. This approach draws on the biography of the scientist, both as an individual and as a member of a research team. In his study of Darwin, GRUBER takes up Piaget's model of development and emphasizes the need to view creativity, not merely as an activity, but as a process within a network of enterprise.

NERSESSIAN, in her case study of Faraday and Maxwell, elucidates above all the role of thought experiments, analogies, and visual representations. For the historical reconstruction of the emergence of the concept of "field", she draws on scientists' sketches and lab books in order to convey the greater importance – for creativity – of visual, abstract, mental models, as opposed to propositional representation.

REINHART BRÜNING

translated by Anna-Katherina Mayer

DNA

Crick, Francis, *What Mad Pursuit: A Personal View of Scientific Discovery*, New York: Basic Books, 1988; London: Weidenfeld and Nicolson, 1989
Kevles, Daniel J. and Leroy Hood (eds), *The Code of Codes: Scientific and Social Issues in the Human Genome Project*, Cambridge, Massachusetts: Harvard University Press, 1992
Krimsky, Sheldon, *Genetical Alchemy: The Social History of the Recombinant DNA Controversy*, Cambridge, Massachusetts: MIT Press, 1982
Krimsky, Sheldon, *Biotechnics & Society: The Rise of Industrial Genetics*, New York: Praeger, 1991
Nelkin, Dorothy and M. Susan Lindee, *The DNA Mystique: The Gene as a Cultural Icon*, New York: Freeman, 1995
Portugal, Franklin H. and Jack S. Cohen, *A Century of DNA: A History of the Discovery of the Structure and Function of the Genetic Substance*, Cambridge, Massachusetts: MIT Press, 1977
Sayre, Anne, *Rosalind Franklin and DNA*, New York: Norton, 1975
Watson, James D., *The Double Helix: A Personal Account of the Discovery of the Double Helix*, New York: Atheneum, and London: Weidenfeld and Nicolson, 1968
Wright, Susan, *Molecular Politics: Developing American and British Regulatory Policy for Genetic Engineering, 1972–1982*, Chicago: University of Chicago Press, 1994

DNA, the chemical substance of which genes are made, is the only molecule to which an entry is dedicated in this Guide, and one of the few key words that appear as an abbreviation, which testifies to its currency in our culture. The book that made it a household name was *The Double Helix*, WATSON's first-hand account of the discovery of the structure of DNA, which reads like a detective story and introduced a new method of reporting scientific progress, with scientists portrayed as all too human. This ruthless and competitive style of research of the late 1960s has, however, since been taken as characteristic of the work of molecular biologists more generally.

CRICK persuaded Harvard University Press not to publish Watson's account, but later collaborated on the production of a BBC film on his and Watson's common venture. He has given his own version of the events leading to and following the suggestion of the double helix as the structure of DNA in his autobiography, which also covers Crick's involvement in later investigations regarding the coding mechanism of DNA. While also drawing on personal recollections, Crick's account is more settled than Watson's, and broader in scope.

SAYRE, a non-scientist and friend of the late Rosalind Franklin, took over the task of rehabilitating Franklin's name in the field of DNA, after Watson's caricature of her work in *The Double Helix*. Based on extensive interviews with Franklin's colleagues and friends, and on a careful study of reports, letters, and published material, Sayre reconstructs Franklin's important contribution to the establishment of the molecular structure of DNA, and portrays a lively picture of her as a person. Sayre suggests that *The Double Helix* could not have been written as it was if Franklin had still been alive. She further suggests that Watson's misrepresentation of Franklin was intended to justify and win sympathy for his and Crick's unfair appropriation of Franklin's data. While not a central theme, the book also draws attention to the general problems faced by woman scientists in the 1950s and after.

PORTUGAL & COHEN present a history of DNA, spanning the discovery of nucleic acids by Miescher in 1869 and the solution of the genetic code in the late 1960s. The aim of the authors is to place recent developments in perspective, and to present a comprehensive and accurate account of scientific developments. Thoroughly researched, but relying also on the authors' own experience in the field of nucleic acid research and on oral recollections by other participants, the book offers original and detailed information on scientific developments, as well as useful notes on the lives of the scientists involved, their careers, and collaborations. Richly illustrated and annotated, the book is a useful reference tool.

With the development of techniques that could combine and multiply DNA segments of disparate organisms, and the ensuing debate concerning the development and uses of these techniques, DNA became an object of public concern, industrial interest, and government policy. KRIMSKY (1982) analyses the reasons that induced scientists to draw attention to the hazards of recombinant DNA technologies, the public response to the questions raised by the scientists, and the changes the recombinant DNA debate produced in the relations between science and society. His main interest lies in examining how scientific decisions and social relations affect each other. WRIGHT's account focuses on the policy aspect of the debate; she offers a fine-grained comparative analysis of the making and subsequent dismantling of policies regulating recombinant DNA technologies in the US and the UK, and of the links between power, structural bias, and discursive practice in policy formation. The book also offers ample material on the rise of genetic engineering firms, and on the growing role of commercial interests in molecular politics. The growing industrial exploitation of recombinant DNA technologies also forms the focus of KRIMSKY (1991), which deals with genetic engineering. He analyses how the commercialisation of molecular biology has affected the social relationship of research, and the boundaries between academia and industrial science. Discussing the debates on the release of genetically engineered organisms in the environment, and on the regulation of human genetic engineering, he suggests new ways of assessing the new technologies.

The project of the 1990s of mapping and sequencing all the DNA of the human genome commands high investments, and has inspired many promises and fears. KEVLES & HOOD offers a good introduction to the history and politics, as well as the scientific, social, legal, and ethical issues of the Human Genome Project. This informative and thought-provoking collection comprises essays by scientists, historians, and sociologists, and by both advocates and critics of the ambitious technological project.

NELKIN & LINDEE explore the meaning of the gene in late 20th-century popular culture. DNA is what makes the gene a concrete entity, and the genetic essentialism diagnosed by Nelkin & Lindee thus relies crucially on DNA and its iconographic representation, the double helix.

SORAYA DE CHADAREVIAN

See also Genetic Engineering; Genetics: general works; Human Genome Project

Doctor–Patient Relationship

Fissell, Mary Elizabeth, *Patients, Power, and the Poor in Eighteenth-Century Bristol*, Cambridge and New York: Cambridge University Press, 1991
Foucault, Michel, *The Birth of the Clinic: An Archaeology of Medical Perception*, translated from the French by A.M. Sheridan Smith, London: Tavistock, and New York: Pantheon, 1973 (original edition, 1963)
Hunter, Kathryn Montgomery, *Doctors' Stories: The Narrative Structure of Medical Knowledge*, Princeton, New Jersey: Princeton University Press, 1991
Jewson, Nicholas D., "Medical Knowledge and the Patronage System in Eighteenth-Century England", *Sociology*, 8 (3 September 1974): 369–85
Jewson, Nicholas D., "The Disappearance of the Sick Man from Medical Cosmology", *Sociology*, 10 (2 May 1976): 225–44
Kawakita, Yosio, Shizu Sakai and Yasuo Otsuka (eds), *History of the Doctor-Patient Relationship: Proceedings of the 14th International Symposium on the Comparative History of Medicine – East and West, September 3–9 1989*, Tokyo: Ishiyaku, 1995
Porter, Dorothy and Roy Porter, *Patient's Progress: Doctors and Doctoring in Eighteenth-Century England*, London: Polity Press and Stanford: Stanford University Press, 1989
Porter, Roy (ed.), *Patients and Practitioners: Lay Perceptions of Medicine in Pre-Industrial Society*, Cambridge: Cambridge University Press, 1985
Porter, Roy, "Rise of the Physical Examination", in *Medicine and the Five Senses*, edited by W.F. Bynum and Roy Porter, Cambridge and New York: Cambridge University Press, 1993
Reiser, Stanley Joel, *Medicine and the Reign of Technology*, Cambridge and New York: Cambridge University Press, 1978
Shorter, Edward, *Bedside Manners: The Troubled History of Doctors and Patients*, New York: Simon and Schuster, 1985

In recent years, the patient has become increasingly important to the history of medicine. In traditional histories, the sick person was virtually invisible, the focus being on successive clinical innovations and great medical lives. Social historians began to include the patient in the 1960s and 1970s, and they now accept as a matter of course that their field of study goes well beyond the history of great discoveries and medical ideas. More generally, the experience of patients, and their active role in treatment, have become central features of histories, sociologies, and contemporary criticisms of modern medicine.

Nicholas Jewson's two papers put forward a suggestive, if sketchy, model of changing doctor-patient relations: JEWSON (1976) offers a programmatic argument, to which JEWSON (1974) contributes in a more chronologically focused manner. His work is more of an argumentative sketch than a robust history, but it develops a number of provocative and influential ways of understanding illness. Jewson argues that, before the late 18th century, the sick told their doctors what was wrong with them, explained how they had come to be ill, and the doctor gave advice as to the best treatment on the basis of this "patient's narrative". These exchanges were part of a deferential patronage relationship, as doctors relied on wealthy clients for their living. Jewson claims that this structure of "bedside medicine" changed dramatically with the development of the hospital as a site for medical training and practice. While the patient had once been regarded as a whole person, a "sick man" or woman, a new emphasis on anatomical dissection in medical education, the introduction of new physical techniques for examining the inside of the body, and other developments, changed the ways in which doctors learned about illness, and the "patient's narrative" declined, according to Jewson, with the rise of the new "hospital medicine". Later in the 19th century, the growing importance of the new laboratory sciences further removed the patient from the process of diagnosis. "Laboratory medicine" involved removing samples from the body for analysis in the austere preserve of the laboratory.

There is now a considerable literature on 18th-century doctors and patients. PORTER & PORTER's book is one of the most substantial and readable, reconstructing a world of health and illness from the patient's viewpoint. The authors describe the co-operative dialogues that took place between the sick and their doctors or attendants, and portray these exchanges as extensions of other social relations (such as family hierarchy and employment). This is also the framework for PORTER (1985), the essays in which explore the varieties of sickness experience, showing how these drew on and affected cultural and individual experience within a wide spectrum of socio-economic and religious contexts. This collection portrays patients as real people with an active voice in their own care. A number of historians have also focused more specifically on the issue of the patient's "narrative". Among them, FISSELL makes the strongest case for its existence and importance, building her argument on a social history of the relationship between doctors and patients in Bristol.

FOUCAULT was enormously influential in developing the "hospital medicine" model that is Jewson's middle-stage of medical history. During the 19th century, anatomy and the dissection of corpses became a substantial component of medical education, and students increasingly spent time in hospital training (as opposed to private apprenticeships). This was part of a transformation of medical practitioners into a disciplined body, and patients (in doctors' eyes) into living corpses, a collection of bodily parts that could be examined directly using the new knowledge and techniques of professional medicine. REISER stresses the power of technology, allowing doctors to gain access to the invisible inner spaces of the body. However, the extreme possibilities of medical technology were not realised, at least not when they were first introduced. Nineteenth-century hospital casebooks record narrative histories that were clearly dictated by even the poorest patients, and, as PORTER (1993) shows, even after the new techniques and technologies were generally available, their use was inhibited by many patients' distaste for the necessary breaches of propriety that physical examination involved.

In the late 19th and early 20th centuries, the laboratory became increasingly important to medical practice, and scientific medicine was underwritten by a number of government-sponsored health insurance programmes. This is one of the themes explored in KAWAKITA, SAKAI & OTSUKA, a volume unique for its comparative approach, juxtaposing essays on Japan, China, England, and America. While it is a rather slight proceedings of a conference on the same subject, it is nevertheless useful for opening up new avenues of study.

Contemporary historical accounts and sociological study have revealed the persistence of medical story-telling or "narratives" even to the present, despite staggeringly complex and accelerating technological innovation. It would be possible to complain, as does Edward SHORTER (among others), that the trajectory of medical development over the past two centuries has been inexorably to erase the patient from the process of diagnosis and to alienate doctor from patient. Nevertheless,

whatever force this complaint has (and, clearly, it has a great deal), modern medicine has not completely removed the patient's "voice" (however one would define this term) from the process of diagnosis. Although the patient's words are no longer vested with the kind of authority that Fissell and others believe was given to those of their early modern counterparts, sociological works, such as HUNTER, argue that storytelling and extended dialogues between doctor and patient continue to be a fundamental part of medicine, however inconspicuous they may have become within modern representations of medical knowledge.

ALISON WINTER

Drugs

Amberger-Lahrmann, Mechthild and Dietrich Schmähl (eds), *Gifte: Geschichte der Toxikologie*, Berlin: Springer, 1988

Chast, François, *Histoire contemporaine des médicaments*, Paris: La Découverte, 1995

Dousset, Jean-Claude, *Histoire des médicaments des origines à nos jours*, Paris: Payot, 1985

Haas, Hans, *Spiegel der Arznei: Ursprung, Geschichte und Idee der Heilmittelkunde*, Berlin: Springer, 1956; expanded edition as *Ursprung, Geschichte und Idee der Arzneimittelkunde*, Mannheim: Bibliographisches Institut, 1981

Issekutz, Bela, *Die Geschichte der Arzneimittelforschung*, translated into German by Adám Farag, Budapest: Akademiai Kiado, 1971 (original edition)

Kreig, Margaret Baltzell, *Green Medicine: The Search for Plants that Heal*, Chicago: Rand McNally, 1964; London: Harrap, 1965

Kuhlen, Franz-Josef, *Zur Geschichte der Schmerz-, Schlaf- und Betäubungsmittel in Mittelalter und früher Neuzeit*, Stuttgart: Deutscher Apotheker, 1983

Mosig, Alfred and Gottfried Schramm, *Der Arzneipflanzen- und Drogenschatz Chinas und die Bedeutung des Pên-ts'ao kang-mu*, Berlin: Volk und Gesundheit, 1955

Ropp, Robert S. de, *Drugs and the Mind*, New York: St Martin's Press, 1957; London: Victor Gollancz, 1958

Schneider, Wolfgang, *Lexikon zur Arzneimittelgeschichte: Sachworterbuch zur Geschichte der pharmazeutischen Botanik, Chemie, Mineralogie, Pharmakologie, Zoologie*, 7 vols, Frankfurt: Govi, Pharmazeutischer, 1968–75

Weatherall, M., *In Search of a Cure: A History of Pharmaceutical Discovery*, Oxford and New York: Oxford University Press, 1990

A broad survey of therapeutic concepts, and of the knowledge and use of drugs in both the past and the present, is provided by HAAS. The book discusses the scientific basis of drug use, and, in addition to modern science, covers empirical trials, the theory of foreign bodies, magic, the humoral doctrine and gross pathology, early chemistry, natural philosophy, and vitalism. This discussion is followed by a history of the drug trade, of chronopharmacology, of addictive drugs that have long been used in all civilizations, and of the isolation of highly effective pure substances. Finally, Haas discusses procedures for the discovery of new remedies, and the problems and risks that accompany the use of drugs and medicaments in the modern world. For the student, this lucidly arranged text is a good introduction to pharmacology, as it draws on a wide range of original texts as well as on secondary literature.

An excellent reference work on the history of particular drugs and medications is the extensive lexicon by SCHNEIDER, which is based on original texts. Its six volumes of monographs on particular drugs are supplemented by a general index in a seventh volume. Remedies and preparations are classified into the following sets, each of which is covered in an individual volume: animal drugs, pharmacological remedies, pharmaceutical chemicals and minerals (additions in volume 6), secret drugs and specialities (until 1900) and, the most extensive group, herbal remedies. The selection is based on the practice that was gradually introduced in the 16th century by the official pharmacopoeia that came into force in German lands, and which also had an impact on neighbouring countries. Each drug is listed by its historical name, and is identified by its synonyms and modern scientific term. This listing is followed by a historical account, which draws on important source material and names the various forms of drugs and preparations, as well as giving the chief indications for use. Schneider also notes the point at which older drugs were discarded, and he comments on their significance in the present.

ISSEKUTZ gives a detailed survey of the history of modern pharmaceutical research. A brief account of the history of therapeutic forms and pharmacological ideas is followed by a history of the description of natural agents, as well as of the synthesis of drugs. The great profusion of drugs and medications is classified into pharmacological, biochemical, and pharmaceutical-chemical groups. These include substances that act on various parts of the nervous system, cardiacs, hypotonics, chalogogs, diuretics, vitamins, hormones, chemotherapeutics such as dye stuffs, heavy metals, sulfonamides, antibiotics, cytostatics, and so on. Issekutz quotes extensively from both original publications and secondary literature, and the chemical structure of pure substances is often illustrated by the chemical formulae. A chronological table from pre-Christian times to 1964 lists the most important pharmaceutical discoveries. The book is a key reference work for the history of particular drugs and the main pharmaceutical groups.

The monograph by WEATHERALL is a survey of the development of modern pharmacological research and its medical foundations from 1650 to 1950. Each chapter begins with a chronological chart of its main themes, and the footnotes list the most important sources and secondary literature. The first chapter provides a historical account of the beginnings of medicine, drug therapy, and systematic pharmacological research and its curative effects. This account is followed by an appreciation of the advances in chemistry, pharmacology, and pharmaceutical chemistry since the 19th century, of the ensuing rise of immunotherapy and chemotherapy, and of the development of insights into the physiological and microbiological foundations of medicine. Weatherall also discusses the significance and mechanism of important new drugs, such as hormones, vitamins, sulfonamides, antibiotics, cytostatics (together with the risks attached to treatments for tumours), and psychopharmacological drugs. Lastly, he deals with the problems that arise

in the treatment of vascular and circulatory diseases, whose causes are still largely unknown. Above all, the book offers insight into the problems of modern pharmacology and drug therapy.

DOUSSET provides an introductory survey of the history of medication up to the present day. The book provides a summarized bibliography of more recent books and journals; its footnotes mostly refrain from critical discussion, and merely elaborate on material in the main text. Nevertheless, this study is based on original literature from which Dousset quotes extensively. Structured chronologically, it covers the chief cultural periods from antiquity to the Enlightenment (including non-European civilizations), as well as the 19th and 20th centuries. The main lines of development in the history of medicine, therapy, and pharmacy, as well as the most important remedies and drug groups, are described impressively and to the point. The basic features of the history of alchemy and chemistry are mentioned, and the discovery and development of new drug groups since the 19th century are described. An appendix defines fundamental terms, such as chronopharmacology, and lists medicinal plants that are important to this day, including those of exotic origin. Unfortunately, there is no index of subjects or persons.

Extensive indexes, references to literature, and quotations from original material in the footnotes can be found in CHAST's excellent work on the history of medications introduced since the 19th century, a period characterised by the discovery of chemotherapeutical drugs. Chast describes the conditions for their use, as determined by chemistry, physiology, pharmacology, genetics, and microbiology. Medications are classified according to their pharmacological effects into analgetica, psychotherapeutica, cardiaca, aseptica, sulfonamides, antibiotics, immunotherapeutica, etc. The latest biotechnological developments and successes, such as the production of insulin, are discussed, together with hopes for future gene therapy.

AMBERGER-LAHRMANN & SCHMÄHL's collection contains detailed contributions by a number of authors on the history and current state of knowledge of the toxic effects of drugs and chemicals available on the market. Eight detailed chapters (with quotations from original literature) consider, from a historical point of view, the toxicology of common drugs and narcotics, and other potent medications and stimulants from coffee to tobacco. The toxicology of biologically effective rays, carcinogenic substances, and industrial chemicals are discussed in a similar manner. Lastly, the volume describes the history of forensic toxicology, and the emergence of laws regulating the industrial use of chemicals, supplemented by a historical table of these regulations. The book is a fundamental introduction to the history and problems of toxins and their effects on the human organism.

Relying on travel reports and his own field studies, KREIG portrays the long history and sometimes world-wide use of powerful herbal drugs, especially those of non-European origin – such as strophantine, quinine, curare, chaulmoogra-oil, rauwolfia, and extracts of fungi and algi. She then proceeds to expound the future usefulness of continued world-wide research into herbal drugs. MOSIG & SCHRAMM reveal an important non-European tradition of chiefly herbal, but also animal and mineral, drugs. They describe the basic features of traditional Chinese medicine, the impact of which continues to this day, and analyze ancient China's extensive major pharmacological work. A compilation of the first medications introduced in the West (and still imported predominantly) from China is followed by a list identifying, for the first time, in modern scientific Latin nomenclature around 350 medicinal and toxic plants used in Chinese medicine. This work, which has been compiled on the basis of original Chinese texts, is of outstanding value, not least because these plant products and the active ingredients extracted from them are also used in the West.

KUHLEN is concerned with the history of a particular and frequently used drug group – pain-killers, soporifics, narcotics, and anaesthetics. Two chapters expound in great detail the diverse interpretations and theories of sleep and pain, from primitive cultures to the present. This is followed by an account of the most common analgesics, soporifics, and anaesthetics (occasionally supplemented by the recipe in use) from early history until the 19th century. The book concludes with a *Pharmacopoea Diabolica* (100 pages), which discusses the most important drugs and formulae employed in witchcraft on the basis of literary sources from antiquity to modernity. Kuhlen thus offers, for the first time, an account of the empirical and rational foundations of both therapeutic and ritual uses of analgetics and psychopharmacological drugs.

Psychopharmacological drugs used in both primitive and civilized cultures are studied by ROPP, who describes the methods of application and stimulating effects of certain drugs (such as mescaline and marihuana) and potions. The problems associated with addictive drugs and the condition of addiction itself, as well as the biochemistry of intoxication, are explored, along with the therapeutic use of psychopharmacological drugs. The book serves as an introduction to the problems and the cultural-historical background of psychoactive drugs.

BRIGITTE HOPPE

translated by Anna-Katherina Mayer

Duhem, Pierre Maurice Marie 1861–1916

French physicist and philosopher of science

Brenner, Anastasios, *Duhem, Science, réalité et apparence: La relation entre philosophie et histoire dans l'oeuvre de Pierre Duhem*, Paris: Vrin, 1990

Jaki, Stanley L., *Uneasy Genius: The Life and Work of Pierre Duhem*, The Hague: Nijhoff, 1984

Jaki, Stanley L., *Reluctant Heroine: The Life and Work of Hélène Duhem*, Edinburgh: Scottish Academic Press, 1992

Lowinger, Armand, *The Methodology of Pierre Duhem*, New York: Columbia University Press, 1941

Maiocchi, Roberto, *Chimica e filosofia: Scienza, epistemologia, storia e religione nell'opera di Pierre Duhem*, Florence: La Nuova Italia, 1985

Martin, R.N.D., *Pierre Duhem: Philosophy and History in the Work of a Believing Physicist*, La Salle, Illinois: Open Court, 1991

Miller, D.M., entry in *Dictionary of Scientific Biography*, vol. 4, edited by Charles Coulston Gillispie, New York: Scribner, 1971

Paul, Harry W., *The Edge of Contingency: French Catholic Reaction to Scientific Change from Darwin to Duhem*, Gainesville: University Presses of Florida, 1979

Probably of most historical interest for his pioneering studies in the history of medieval science, Pierre Duhem was primarily a first rank physicist with distinctive views on the nature of physical theory, who also wrote about the history of more recent physics. It is almost universally agreed that there must be a connection between his different concerns, so that no account of Duhem's physics, his philosophy, or even his politics or religion, is irrelevant to understanding his historical work.

Duhem's scientific interests are the main concern of MILLER's extended article, which contains a full bibliography. Duhem was a mathematical physicist who aimed to give an abstract coherent mathematical account of nature as experimentally determined. Opposed to atomic explanations and an admirer of Helmholtz and Gibbs, he contributed significantly to the final form of the theory of heat (thermodynamics), with particular attention to its applications to chemistry and electrical phenomena, hydrodynamics and the theory of electricity. At the same time, a series of brilliant monographs explored the historical antecedents of the debates in which he was engaged. He saw his version of thermodynamics as the key science in a future unification of theoretical physics, for which he proposed Rankine's name "Energetics". LOWINGER argues that Duhem's philosophical ideas, and therefore presumably his historical writing, are no more than an apology for the energetics. In this Lowinger can appeal to much in Duhem's own writings: he always said that he was a physicist and that physics was his prime motivation.

Many critics have objected to the alleged positivistic tendency in Duhem's work. What positivism amounted to in practice has been examined in detail by MAIOCCHI with a full bibliography, who finds that, in so far as it affected the teaching and practice of physics, it generated a culture deeply hostile to theory, suspicious of any generalization over and above experiment. It was also, in contrast to later 20th-century positivism, historically minded, and expected the development of physics to show continuity. Thus, Maiocchi finds, many of the most widely discussed features of Duhem's work do not in fact belong to him, but to the positivist tradition he inherited. According to Maiocchi, Duhem was most original when he was subverting positivism. Duhem the theoretical physicist needed space for theory and a rationale for his pursuit of theoretical coherence. In his analysis of experiment, he showed that the statement of experimental results ineluctably involved theory, so that the positivist suspicion of theory was baseless and incoherent. Moreover, experimental tests involved many other theories besides those at issue (holism), so that experimental refutation was never logically decisive. He also argued that those who denied that physical theory had to be grounded in reality left themselves no grounds to resist the (in Duhem's view) absurd result of the collapse of physical theory into a heap of incoherent models.

Since according to positivists – and most non-positivists – facts are supposed to be used as independent checks on theories, Duhem's critique of experiment has provoked energetic debate. BRENNER's detailed examination links it to the debates of the turn of the 19th and 20th centuries, particularly with Poincaré and Le Roy. He emphasizes Duhem's own claim that history was for him a testing ground for his methodological ideas, and explores the limitations of Duhem's holism. In contrast to other philosophers such as Popper, Duhem assigns a decisive role to common sense. For him, it protects physicists from absurd conclusions, guides their judgement in assessing the significance of experimental results, and within the historical context helps them to choose the new hypotheses their judgement deems necessary. Brenner seems to accept the traditional view that Duhem's historical research is driven by the doctrine of the continuous development of physics.

However, the continuity thesis did not lead Duhem's positivist predecessors to an interest in medieval science, the most interesting and original feature of Duhem's later work, nor does it explain his interest in such non-scientific subjects during his lifetime. It has been usual at this point to consider Duhem's openly avowed Catholicism, interpreted as his conformity to the neo-Scholasticism (Thomism) enforced by the hierarchy of the period. JAKI (1984), with the fullest bibliography in print to date of Duhem's writings, attempts to read Duhem in this way. He points to texts from his early and middle period in which Duhem seems to assert that in metaphysics he is a Thomist, and to Duhem's habit of publishing in neo-scholastic journals. Jaki reads Duhem's methodology as a kind of common sense realism and thus from his point of view approaches the position of Maiocchi. PAUL takes a similar line, but recognizes the difficulties: contemporary and later neo-scholastics, if not explicitly objecting to Duhem's views, showed plentiful signs of embarrassment. It is also puzzling that if neo-scholasticism was influential in his thinking, it led to an interest in medieval science only late in his career.

There may be something in all these theories of Duhem, but none of them suffices to encompass the totality of his work. Duhem's great concerns were to defend his physics, to construct an account of physics acceptable to positivists, and to defend his church and its dogma. But not all these considerations weighed equally all the time in every part of his work, and there is evidence of philosophical sources other than positivism and neo-scholasticism. If Duhemian history had conformed entirely to the guidelines of his *Théorie Physique*, it would have been like the work of Mach and Dühring, or of the older generation of scientist historians, containing nothing but material, logically analysed, germane and internal to the science in question. But Duhem's *Système du Monde* gives itself a far wider remit than the internal history of cosmology, since it brings philosophy, theology, and much else besides into its compass. It is externalist, even though it certainly qualifies as intellectual history. MARTIN widens the consideration of Duhem's philosophical motivations to include Pascal's *Pensées*, for which there was a vogue in French culture at the time, and points to a variety of friendships and associations opposed to the neo-scholastics, many of whom Duhem violently disliked. He presents the discovery of medieval science (datable to November 1904) as the "disastrous" encounter of theory with fact, and goes on to suggest that Duhem's anti-scholastic

instincts led him to base his new medieval history on those aspects of the Middle Ages least favourable to a neo-scholastic programme.

Finally, JAKI (1992) is chiefly notable for his detailed investigation of the long delays in the publication of the latter five volumes of the *Système du Monde*.

R.N.D. MARTIN

Durkheim, Émile 1858–1917

French sociologist

Alexander, Jeffrey C., *Theoretical Logic in Sociology*, 4 vols, Berkeley, California: University of California Press, 1982–83

Besnard, Philippe (ed.), *The Sociological Domain: The Durkheimians and the Founding of French Sociology*, Cambridge and New York: Cambridge University Press, 1983

Clark, Terry N., *Prophets and Patrons: The French University and the Emergence of the Social Sciences*, Cambridge, Massachusetts: Harvard University Press, 1973

Hall, Robert T., *Emile Durkheim: Ethics and the Sociology of Morals*, New York: Greenwood Press, 1987

Jones, Robert Alun, *Emile Durkheim: An Introduction to Four Major Works*, Beverly Hills, California: Sage, 1986

LaCapra, Dominick, *Emile Durkheim: Sociologist and Philosopher*, Ithaca, New York: Cornell University Press, 1972

Lukes, Steven, *Emile Durkheim: His Life and Work: A Historical and Critical Study*, New York: Harper and Row, 1972; London: Allen Lane, 1973

Mestrovic, Stjepan G., *Emile Durkheim and the Reformation of Sociology*, Totowa, New Jersey: Rowman and Littlefield, 1988

Parsons, Talcott, *The Structure of Social Action*, New York: McGraw-Hill, 1937; 2nd edition, Glencoe, Illinois: Free Press, 1949

Pickering, W.S.F., *Durkheim's Sociology of Religion: Themes and Theories*, London and Boston: Routledge and Kegan Paul, 1984

Schmaus, Warren, *Durkheim's Philosophy of Science and the Sociology of Knowledge: Creating an Intellectual Niche*, Chicago: University of Chicago Press, 1994

Turner, Stephen P., *The Search for a Methodology of Social Science: Durkheim, Weber, and the Nineteenth-Century Problem of Cause, Probability, and Action*, Dordrecht: Reidel, 1986

Wallwork, Ernest E., *Durkheim: Morality and Milieu*, Cambridge, Massachusetts: Harvard University Press, 1972

Serious historical scholarship concerning Émile Durkheim began in the early 1970s. Before then, writers often forced Durkheim into one or another of the Procrustean beds of contemporary "isms" in the social sciences, treating him either as a saint or a scapegoat in order to legitimize their own ideas. PARSONS provides a paradigm example: he interpreted Durkheim's intellectual development as a gradual movement, first away from "positivism", which Durkheim supposedly believed to reduce the behavior of social actors to merely a response to conditions in the physical environment, and towards the "voluntarism" to which Parsons himself subscribes, in which the behavior of social actors is explained in terms of the internalization of norms and values. Parsons then criticized Durkheim for failing to rest content with voluntarism, and turning instead to the sociological study of religion in a final, "idealist" stage, in which theory took precedence over empirical fact.

In the 1970s, the historicist movement in the history of sociology attempted to understand the classics within their social and intellectual context, rather than from the point of view of sociology's present concerns. The historicists challenged Parson's assumption that Durkheim's goal was to explain the behavior of individual social actors in the first place, and showed that Durkheim instead sought to understand collective phenomena. LUKES combined a historical biography with a critical analysis of Durkheim's work, provided a definitive bibliography of the known works of Durkheim at that time, and established a numbering system for referring to Durkheim's scattered publications. However, sometimes Lukes's criticisms reflect a failure to understand Durkheim's thought within the context of the philosophical tradition in which he was educated. LACAPRA tried to show how Durkheim's views on philosophy, sociology, and public policy form an integrated whole, although he did not relate Durkheim's moral philosophy to his metaphysics and epistemology. WALLWORK provided a more complete analysis of Durkheim's moral philosophy, and demonstrated how it depended on a realist philosophy of social relations, thus showing that Durkheim was never the positivist that Parsons claimed. JONES has published some important papers in defense of the historicist movement, and his 1986 text provides a brief introduction to Durkheim's major works from this perspective. The best part of Jones's work is his analysis of Durkheim's last major work, *The Elementary Forms of the Religious Life* (1912).

Other scholars in the 1970s and 1980s addressed the institutional context of Durkheim's thought. CLARK located the development of Durkheimian sociology within the history of the French educational system, and compares this tradition to other sociological movements at the time in France. Unfortunately, he tended to treat the Durkheimians as a united whole, and did not explore the subtle intellectual disagreements and social dynamics within the group. The collection of essays in BESNARD is much more successful in analyzing the intellectual and social relations among the group of scholars associated with Durkheim and the journal, *L'Année sociologique* (1898–1913). Besnard's lead essay on the founding of the journal is especially useful for undermining the notion that the Durkheimians formed a "school" of thought under the direction of Durkheim, while essays by Karady, Weisz, Vogt, and others advance our knowledge of the Durkheimians' academic setting. The volume also contains an illuminating autobiographical essay by Durkheim's nephew and collaborator, Marcel Mauss.

ALEXANDER found French academic politics important for explaining Durkheim's thought. He dismissed as so much intellectual fashion recent scholarship that tended to see a great deal of continuity in Durkheim's thought, and offered a re-interpretation in which Durkheim opportunistically made radical shifts in his published views in order to advance his career. Alexander also argued that Durkheim's methodology remained the same, and thus cannot account for these shifts in Durkheim's sociological positions. However, Alexander did not provide an adequate analysis of Durkheim's methodology. As a result, he did not fully understand the arguments in Durkheim's more substantive, empirical works and saw differences among these works that were not really there.

Since the early 1980s, scholars have tended to see Durkheim as motivated by intellectual concerns at least as much as by his desire for career advancement. HALL saw Durkheim's thought as directed towards the goal of establishing morality on a scientific basis, which Durkheim attempted through founding a sociology of morals, and regarded Durkheim's interest in the sociology of knowledge and collective representations merely as a means to that end. PICKERING interpreted Durkheim's intellectual development as culminating in his theory of religion as the fundamental social phenomenon, a theory presented in Durkheim's last and greatest work, *The Elementary Forms of the Religious Life*. MESTROVIC read Durkheim as concerned above all with the crisis of individualism in modern society; according to Mestrovic, Durkheim attempted to address this crisis through a sociological theory of the collective representations that unite people into a society, a theory that must be understood against the background of a philosophical tradition concerned with problems of mental representation.

A concern for Durkheim's intellectual goals leads naturally to a concern for his views on the methods appropriate for achieving those goals. Thus, scholars have come to appreciate the importance of Durkheim's philosophy of science, as expressed in *The Rules of Sociological Method* (1895) and elsewhere, for understanding his empirical and theoretical work in sociology. TURNER illuminated the relationship between Durkheim's philosophy of science and the methods he employed in his work, *Suicide* (1897). He showed that Durkheim maintained a realist commitment to social forces and employed a method of causal analysis appropriate to discovering these hidden entities. SCHMAUS expanded this project, showing the relationship of Durkheim's metaphysics and philosophy of scientific method to all of his major empirical works, including *The Division of Labor in Society* (1893) and *The Elementary Forms of the Religious Life*. Schmaus has thus been able to re-establish the intellectual continuity of Durkheim's thought.

WARREN SCHMAUS

See also Sociology

Dyestuffs

Beer, John J., *The Emergence of the German Dye Industry*, Urbana: University of Illinois Press, 1959; reprinted, New York: Arno Press, 1981

Clow, Archibald and Nan L. Clow, *The Chemical Revolution: A Contribution to Social Technology*, London: Batchworth Press, 1952 (chapters 9–12)

Edelstein, Sidney M., *Historical Notes on the Wet-Processing Industry*, New York: Dexter Chemical Corporation, 1972

Fox, Maurice R., *Dye-Makers of Great Britain, 1856–1976: A History of Chemists, Companies, Products and Changes*, Manchester: Imperial Chemical Industries, 1987

Fox, Robert and Agustí Nieto-Galan (eds), *Natural Dyestuffs and Industrial Culture in Europe, 1750–1880*, Canton, Massachusetts: Science History Publications, 1998

Haber, L.F., *The Chemical Industry During the Nineteenth Century: A Study of the Economic Aspect of Applied Chemistry in Europe and North America*, Oxford: Clarendon Press, 1958; corrected edition, 1969

Haber, L.F., *The Chemical Industry, 1900–1930: International Growth and Technological Change*, Oxford: Clarendon Press, 1971

Homburg, Ernst, Harm Schröter and Anthony S. Travis (eds), *The Chemical Industry in Europe, 1850–1914: Industrial Growth, Pollution and Professionalization*, Dordrecht: Kluwer, 1998

Hounshell, David A. and John Kenly Smith, Jr, *Science and Corporate Strategy: Du Pont R & D, 1902–1980*, Cambridge and New York: Cambridge University Press, 1988

Meyer-Thurow, Georg, "The Industrialization of Invention: A Case Study from the German Chemical Industry", *Isis*, 73 (1982): 363–81

Robinson, Stuart, *A History of Dyed Textiles: Dyes, Fibres, Painted Bark, Batik, Starch-Resist, Discharge, Tie-Dye, Further Sources for Research*, Cambridge, Massachusetts: MIT Press, 1969

Robinson, Stuart, *A History of Printed Textiles: Block, Roller, Screen, Design, Dyes, Fibres, Discharge, Resist, Further Sources for Research*, Cambridge, Massachusetts: MIT Press, and London: Studio Vista, 1969

Rosetti, Giovanventura, *The Plictho: Instructions in the Art of the Dyers, which Teaches the Dyeing of Woollen Cloths, Linens, Cottons, and Silk by the Great Art as well as by the Ccommon*, translated from the Italian by Sidney M. Edelstein and Hector C. Borghetty, Cambridge, Massachusetts: MIT Press, 1969 (original edition, 1548)

Steen, Kathryn, "Wartime Catalyst and Postwar Reaction: The Making of the United States Synthetic Organic Chemicals Industry, 1910–1930", PhD dissertation, University of Delaware, 1995

Travis, Anthony S., Willem J. Hornix and Robert Bud (eds), "Organic Chemistry and High Technology, 1850–1950", *British Journal for the History of Science*, special issue, 25 (March 1992), 1–167

Travis, Anthony S., *The Rainbow Makers: The Origins of the Synthetic Dyestuffs Industry in Western Europe*, Bethlehem, Pennsylvania: Lehigh University Press, and London: Associated University Presses, 1993

Travis, Anthony S., *From Turkey Red to Tyrian Purple: Textile Colours for the Industrial Revolution*, Jerusalem: Sideny M. Edelstein Library, Hebrew University of Jerusalem, 1993

Travis, Anthony S., Ernst Homburg and Harm Schröter (eds), *New Technologies, Political Frameworks, Markets and Companies Determinants in the Development of the European Chemical Industry, 1900–1939*, Dordrecht: Kluwer, 1998

Verg, Erik, Gottfried Plumpe and Heinz Schultheis, *Milestones: The Bayer Story, 1863–1988*, Leverkusen: Bayer, 1988

The history of dyestuffs, both natural and synthetic, invariably transcends the boundaries of science and technology, and encompasses economic, social, and cultural history. There are also close links with developments in chemistry, textile production, conservation, and, for natural dyes, botany. Several studies of lasting value appeared during the 1950s, 1960s, and 1970s, although the topics were rarely pursued in great depth. Natural dyes featured as part of more general histories of industries and trades in particular geographical areas, and of these CLOW & CLOW is particularly noteworthy, dealing with lichen and other dyes in Scotland during the first industrial revolution. The two volumes by Robinson are excellent introductions to the varied uses to which dyes were put. ROBINSON (1969, *A History of Dyed Textiles*) covers textile dying from antiquity to the 20th century. It is a brief global overview (112 pages) mainly organized by technique. ROBINSON (1969, *A History of Printed Textiles*) covers the history of textile printing in similar length. There is a brief global section on the technique in antiquity; the main section covers Britain to the mid-20th century; and the last section contains brief chapters on various European nations, the US, and India. Each of Robinson's books contains an appendix on further sources including further reading, museums and centres with textile collections, and libraries and booksellers with specialist holdings of textile literature.

EDELSTEIN's monograph brings together many of his published articles that deal with natural dyes in Europe and the Americas during the 16th to 19th centuries. Edelstein and Borghetty's translation of ROSETTI, the first book for the professional dyer published in Venice in 1548, is a valuable record of European dyes in use just before the time when new avenues of maritime trade would supplement some of them, and displace others. All the above mentioned studies pay careful attention to technical details, though apart from Clow & Clow they lack critical content. No less valuable are the many articles dealing mainly with natural dyes and their application published in *Ciba Review* (1937–1971).

The synthetic dye industry was mainly the outcome of William Henry Perkin's discovery in 1856 of the coal tar dye known later as mauve. The numerous accounts of the history of synthetic dyes that appeared from the end of the 19th century are the source for BEER's study, which emphasizes the origins of the German synthetic dye (and organic chemical) industry. Beer set new standards in the historiography of dyes and remains the most readable account of late 19th-century developments. In particular, he elucidates, for both the general reader and the specialist, the close relationship between science and technology. HABER's two volumes place the synthetic dye industry within the context of the modern chemical industry, including diversification into pharmaceuticals and explosives, products that employed the same intermediates as those from which coal tar dyes were produced, and electrochemistry and high pressure processes. The behemoth IG Farbenindustrie AG was the outcome of mergers among the principal German dye manufacturers that began, as both Beer and Haber describe, at the turn of the century.

More recent studies dealing with dyestuffs have been stimulated by growing interest in the emergence of science-based industry following Perkin's discovery. TRAVIS (1993, *The Rainbow Makers*) extends Beer's work, and pays close attention to developments in Britain and France, where the modern dye industry originated. The emphasis is on technical detail, patent litigation, the close connection between dye chemistry and classical organic chemistry and technology transfer to Germany. Several contributions to TRAVIS, HORNIX & BUD delineate the mainly German mastery of synthetic dye chemistry through organizational and manufacturing strategies, and control over patents. Highlights include scientific studies on aniline dyes (1860–66); synthetic alizarin, which replaced the natural dye from the root of the madder plant (1869, but also manufactured in England by Perkin); azo dyes (from 1875); synthetic indigo (BASF and Hoechst, 1897); direct azo dyes that attached to fibres without the aid of mordants (1884); and indanthrene dyes (1901). FOX provides an uncritical technical history of synthetic dyes in Britain, but is useful because it brings the story up to recent times with competent accounts of phthalocyanine dyes (1930s), fibre-reactive dyes (1956), and dyes for synthetic fabrics. VERG, PLUMPE & SCHULTHEIS's book is the most useful company-sponsored study based on archiveal material, in this case of the German Bayer firm. STEEN provides the most thorough analysis of the emergence of the United States dye industry, a relative latecomer among the industrial nations, in part because of German hegemony up to World War I. As in Europe, the synthetic dye industry was of tremendous strategic importance during the war. This, as Steen describes, had a tremendous impact on both wartime strategies and post-war planning. HOUNSHELL & SMITH's book on the DuPont company demonstrates the impact of that firm. In addition to dyestuffs research, they also describe the inauguration of research at DuPont into dye intermediates associated with bladder tumours. HOMBURG, SCHRÖTER & TRAVIS and TRAVIS, HOMBURG & SCHRÖTER both include English translations of Dutch, French, and German studies on the history of dyes, both natural and synthetic, their environmental impacts, and the role of the dye industry both during and after World War I. MEYER-THUROW's important study on the industrial research laboratory in the German dye industry focuses on its origins in Bayer, the organization of research within the chemical industry, and its links with tertiary education institutions. Meyer-Thurow also analyses the ambiguity of the status of intra-industry research and invention, paying particular attention to the perceived lack of autonomy of industrial chemists in comparison with those in academia.

The importance of natural dyes in the first industrial revolution are highlighted in TRAVIS (1993, *From Turkey Red*), and analysed in detail in the contributions to FOX & NIETO-GALAN. The latter also makes available in English studies on the history of dyes from various European authors. Historical studies on natural dyes (and often on synthetic dyes) appear as articles in journals, particularly the following: *Textile History, Journal of the Society of Dyers and Colourists, Textile Chemist and Colorist, American Dyestuff Reporter, Technology and Culture, History and Technology, Isis* and *British Journal for the History of Science*.

ANTHONY S. TRAVIS

See also Industrial Chemistry

E

École Polytechnique

Belhoste, Bruno, Amy Dahan Dalmedico and Antoine Picon
(eds), *La Formation polytechnicienne, 1794–1994*, Paris:
Dunod, 1994

Callot, Jean-Pierre, *Histoire et prospective de l'École
polytechnique*, revised edition, Paris: Limoges, 1993
(original edition, 1958)

Fourcy, Ambroise, *Histoire de l'École polytechnique*, Paris:
printed privately, 1828; edited by Jean Dhombres, Paris:
Belin, 1987

Langins, Janis, *La République avait besoin de savants: les
débuts de l'École polytechnique – l'École centrale des
travaux publics et les cours révolutionnaires de l'an III*,
Paris: Belin, 1987

Lesourne, Jacques (ed.), *Les Polytechniciens dans le siècle,
1894–1994*, Paris: Dunod, 1994

Livre de Centenaire, 1794–1894, 3 vols, Paris: Gauthier-
Villars, 1894–97

Pinet, Gaston, *Histoire de l'École polytechnique*, Paris:
Baudry, 1887

Shinn, Terry, *L'École polytechnique, 1794–1914*, Paris:
Presses Universitaires de la Fondation Nationale des
Sciences Politiques, 1980

Established during the French Revolution, the École
Polytechnique is both an institution of higher learning in engineering, and a research establishment. Its foundation constituted
the appearance of a new type of scientific institution, inspired by
Enlightenment figures whose influence in the 19th century was
considerable. Though its scientific importance has waned in the
20th century, it continues to play a notable role in French scientific life. There is an abundant historical literature on the École,
which dates from just after its foundation in 1794 and has continued ever since. During the past 20 years, the historiography
of the École has been profoundly renovated, first by English-language, and more recently by French, historians.

The first important work on the history of the École
Polytechnique is by FOURCY, published originally in 1828 and
in a new edition (1987), which includes an important introduction by Dhombres and a bibliography of several hundred
items. Fourcy, the École's librarian, systematically used the
sources available to him to write an erudite yet hagiographic
chronology, which for a long time remained the best reference
on the beginnings of the École. However, the book is written
in an outmoded style, only covers the initial period of the
École's history (1794–1814), and deals primarily with institutional aspects.

Since Fourcy's work, a number of other official (or semi-
official) publications have been devoted to the history of the
École Polytechnique. The most interesting were published
around the time of the school's centennial, from 1880 to 1890.
The book by PINET, who, like Fourcy, was the École's
librarian, covers the period from the school's origins to the
beginning of the Third Republic. It is an institutional history,
organized like Fourcy's according to the successive reorgani-
zations of the École. Its principle interest is its solidly documented study of the classes of students (*promotions*), their
collective rites, and their political engagements (especially
during the Revolution of 1830). The LIVRE DE CENTE-
NAIRE, a collective work published between 1894 and 1897,
completes Fourcy's book, containing, for the most part, notices
on graduates (many of whom also taught at the École) who
distinguished themselves in the fields of technology and the
sciences.

The historiography of the École remained little changed up
to the end of the 1970s. Historical studies since the centenary
were essentially hagiographic and commemorative, and written
largely by alumni, of which the best example is CALLOT. The
revision of this very mediocre historiography is due to English-
language historians, who have produced work that is both
erudite and critical.

The work by the historian and sociologist of science Terry
SHINN, focusing on the period 1794–1914, is a social history
based on research in the École's archives, primarily the register
of matriculated students. Using a statistical analysis of
these data, Shinn exposes the increasingly elite recruitment of
the school during the 19th century, which thus actively
contributed, despite its meritocratic ideology, to the reproduction of the managing classes. This critical and well-argued
study breaks with the self-satisfied conventional discourse of
traditional historiography, but its analysis of 19th-century
mechanisms of social reproduction suffers from a certain sociological schematism, and it lacks any historical information on
the École's functioning and teaching.

The works by LANGINS are also based on research in the
École's archives, but their inspiration is very different. Her
major work mentioned here (which must be supplemented by
a number of articles by the same author), has entirely revised
our knowledge of the École's beginnings. Describing the reality
of teaching at the École with finesse, Langins inaugurates a
kind of analysis unknown to traditional historiography, which

was limited almost exclusively to prescribed texts and programmes. This book revives the day-to-day beginnings of the École Polytechnique, painting a picture – far removed from the school's legend and barely suspected when reading the ancient authors – of the students' lack of industry and attention, of make-shift teaching, of delays in building works, and of political troubles, which marked the early period of activity at the school. Thus, one can measure, on the ground and in the midst of crisis and war, the distance between the founders' extraordinarily ambitious project and the improvised reality.

More recently, a number of historians, principally French, have pursued the lines of research laid out by Langins, again relying on the establishment's archives. The celebration of the École's bicentennial gave much impetus to these works, whose main concerns one can perceive by consulting the collective works published on the occasion. In particular, BELHOSTE, DAHAN DALMEDICO & PICON's book is the first documented study in two centuries of the instruction given at the École. Research on the history of the École remains active to this day; the interested reader will find a number of quality studies in the *Bulletin de la SABIX* (Société des amis de la bibliothèque de l'École polytechnique).

BRUNO BELHOSTE

translated by Craig Rodine

See also Education; France: scientific and technical education; Monge; Universities

Ecology

Acot, Pascal, *Histoire de l'écologie*, Paris: Presses Universitaires de France, 1988

Allen, T.F.H. and Thomas W. Hoekstra, *Toward a Unified Ecology*, New York: Columbia University Press, 1992

Beckel, Annamarie L., with Frank N. Egerton, *Breaking New Waters: A Century of Limnology at the University of Wisconsin*, Madison: Wisconsin Academy of Sciences, Arts and Letters, 1987

Bowers, Janice Emily, *A Sense of Place: The Life and Work of Forrest Shreve*, Tucson: University of Arizona Press, 1988

Bowler, Peter J., *The Fontana History of the Environmental Sciences*, London: Fontana, 1992; as *The Norton History of the Environmental Sciences*, New York: Norton, 1993

Bramwell, Anna, *Ecology in the 20th Century: A History*, New Haven, Connecticut: Yale University Press, 1989

Browne, Janet, *The Secular Ark: Studies in the History of Biogeography*, New Haven, Connecticut: Yale University Press, 1983

Cittadino, Eugene, *Nature as the Laboratory: Darwinian Plant Ecology in the German Empire, 1880–1900*, Cambridge and New York: Cambridge University Press, 1990

Cramer, Jacqueline, *Mission-Orientation in Ecology: The Case of Dutch Fresh-Water Ecology*, Amsterdam: Rodopi, 1987

Croker, Robert A., *Pioneer Ecologist: The Life and Work of Victor Ernest Shelford, 1877–1968*, Washington, DC: Smithsonian Institution Press, 1991

Crowcroft, Peter, *Elton's Ecologists: A History of the Bureau of Animal Population*, Chicago: University of Chicago Press, 1991

Deléage, Jean-Paul, *Histoire de l'écologie: une science de l'homme et de la nature*, 2nd edition, Paris: La Découverte/Seuil, 1993

Drouin, Jean-Marc, *Réinventer la nature: l'écologie et son histoire*, Paris: Desclée de Brower, 1991; 2nd edition, Paris: Flammarion, 1993

Dunlap, Thomas R., *Saving America's Wildlife*, Princeton, New Jersey: Princeton University Press, 1988

Egerton, Frank N., "A Bibliographic Guide to the History of General Ecology and Population Ecology", *History of Science*, 15 (1977): 189–215

Egerton, Frank N., "The History of Ecology: Achievements and Opportunities", *Journal of the History of Biology*, 16 (1983): 259–311; 18 (1985): 103–43

Fralish, James S., Robert P. McIntosh and Orie L. Loucks (eds), *John T. Curtis: Fifty Years of Wisconsin Plant Ecology*, Madison: Wisconsin Academy of Sciences, Arts and Letters, 1993

Golley, Frank Benjamin, *A History of the Ecosystem Concept in Ecology: More than the Sum of the Parts*, New Haven, Connecticut: Yale University Press, 1993

Hagen, Joel B., *An Entangled Bank: The Origins of Ecosystem Ecology*, New Brunswick, New Jersey: Rutgers University Press, 1992

Kingsland, Sharon E., *Modeling Nature: Episodes in the History of Population Ecology*, Chicago: University of Chicago Press, 1985

Kwa, Chunglin, "Radiation Ecology, Systems Ecology and the Management of the Environment", in *Science and Nature: Essays in the History of the Environmental Sciences*, edited by Michael Shortland, Oxford: British Society for the History of Science, 1995, 213–49

McIntosh, Robert P., *The Background of Ecology: Concept and Theory*, Cambridge and New York: Cambridge University Press, 1985

Maienschein, Jane, James P. Collins and John Beatty (eds), "Reflections on Ecology and Evolution", *Journal of the History of Biology*, 19 (1986): 167–312

Meine, Curt, *Aldo Leopold: His Life and Work*, Madison: University of Wisconsin Press, 1988

Mills, Eric L., *Biological Oceanography: An Early History, 1870–1960*, Ithaca, New York: Cornell University Press, 1989

Mitman, Gregg A., *The State of Nature: Ecology, Community and American Social Thought, 1900–1950*, Chicago: University of Chicago Press, 1992

Real, Leslie A. and James H. Brown (eds), *Foundations of Ecology: Classic Papers with Commentaries*, Chicago: University of Chicago Press, 1991

Sheail, John, *Seventy-Five Years in Ecology: The British Ecological Society*, Oxford and Boston: Blackwell, 1987

Shortland, Michael (ed.), *Science and Nature: Essays in the History of the Environmental Sciences*, Stanford in the Vale: British Society for the History of Science, 1993

Söderqvist, Thomas, *The Ecologists: From Merry Naturalists to Saviours of the Nation: A Sociologically Informed*

Narrative Survey of the Ecologization of Sweden, 1895–1975, Stockholm: Almqvist & Wiksell, 1986

Steinhaus, Edward A., *Disease in a Minor Chord: Being a Semihistorical and Semibiographical Account of a Period in Science When One Could Be Happily Yet Seriously Concerned with the Diseases of Lowly Animals Without Backbones*, Columbus: Ohio State University Press, 1975

Steleanu, Adrian, *Geschichte der Limnologie und ihrer Grundlagen*, Frankfurt: Haag & Herchen, 1989

Trepl, Ludwig, *Geschichte der Ökologie vom 17 Jahrhundert bis zur Gegenwart: Zehn Vorlesungen*, Frankfurt: Athenäum, 1987

Troyer, James R., *Nature's Champion: B.W. Wells, Tar Heel Ecologist*, Chapel Hill: University of North Carolina Press, 1993

Walter, Heinrich, *Bekenntnisse eines Ökologen: Erlebtes in acht Jahrzehnten und auf Forschungreisen in allen Erdteilen*, Stuttgart: Fischer, 1980

Weiner, Douglas R., *Models of Nature: Ecology, Conservation, and Cultural Revolution in Soviet Russia*, Bloomington: Indiana University Press, 1988

Wilson, Edward O., *Naturalist*, London: Allen Lane, 1985; Washington, DC: Island Press/Shearwater Books, 1994

Worster, Donald, *Nature's Economy: A History of Ecological Ideas*, San Francisco: Sierra Club Books, 1977; 2nd edition, Cambridge and New York: Cambridge University Press, 1994

Worthington, E. Barton, *The Ecological Century: A Personal Appraisal*, Oxford: Clarendon Press, and New York: Oxford University Press, 1983

Botanists and zoologists began attempting to organize the science of ecology in the 1890s, but studies on ecological questions had begun with the ancient Greeks, and the science was named and defined by a German follower of Charles Darwin in 1866. The boundaries of ecology are difficult to define, for this science easily merges with kindred disciplines such as biogeography, evolution, parasitology, and oceanography and also with applied sciences such as agriculture, forestry, fish and wildlife management, and pollution abatement. Ecology is the most diverse science, and, despite unifying concepts, most ecologists think of themselves as being either plant ecologists, animal ecologists, limnologists, or marine ecologists. However, some ecologists define themselves in terms of a research methodology, for example, population ecologists, community ecologists, ecosystem ecologists.

Historians of science responded more slowly to this bewildering diversity than they did to the much more cohesive science of genetics, organized at about the same time. Since the 1980s historians have been making up for a slow start. McINTOSH provides a bibliographical guide in his discussion of efforts to cope with various recalcitrant ecological questions, as seen in British and American ecological literature. ALLEN & HOEKSTRA attempt to resolve these paradoxes by establishing an explicit scale of magnitudes that encompass all ecological investigations. These three ecologists, drawing on earlier science and histories of ecology, provide a way for historians to ascertain whether ecologists who disagreed with each other were interpreting the same question differently or were studying different kinds of topics.

French scholars have demonstrated the most skill in writing general histories of ecology that convey sound judgments about what is most important and how topics are related historically. DROUIN's is a remarkably concise account, showing good mastery of both ecology and the history of ecology literature. DELÉAGE provides an equally sound survey at greater length, with more diagrams, and an annotated bibliography. ACOT is as concise as Drouin, but lacks knowledge of the careers of non-French ecologists; half of his history is on ecology and human affairs, focusing particularly on France.

The prominent American environmental historian, WORSTER is a superb stylist; the second edition of his history includes two new chapters. His heroes include Gilbert White, Henry Thoreau, and Rachel Carson, and he judges professional ecologists according to whether they seemed to defend the environment or were little more than capitalistic tools for its exploitation. The plant ecologist TREPL provides an overview that draws heavily on his own speciality and on Worster's volume, and he sometimes relies on a German-language sourcebook instead of the original literature. The gigantic English-language source book compiled by REAL & BROWN is too important to ignore here; it has extensive historical introductions to its six parts. Broadest of all in scope, BOWLER places ecology within the context of the history of the environmental sciences; he achieves an important synthesis that nevertheless dwells too long on his own speciality of evolution while neglecting limnology and the history of meteorological instruments. SHORTLAND edits 10 substantial articles (the first by Bowler), which explore the history of particular environmental science topics; the range of topics is weighted toward ecology. One example is KWA's evaluation on a contentious aspect of ecosystem ecology: the relationship between radiation ecology and managing the environment. BRAMWELL, a British intellectual historian, promises in her title far more than she delivers. Her concern is to defend conservative scholars and to discredit radical environmental authors. Readers interested in the history of science will find her discussion of Ernst Haeckel, the namer of ecology, especially interesting.

Plant ecologists have shown great interest in their collective past, as seen in the works by McIntosh, Allen & Hoekstra, and Trepl. CITTADINO provides an excellent survey of early plant ecology in Germany and its empire. He also sheds welcome light on the contentious question of what credit Darwin deserves for encouraging the development of ecology. The traditions that Cittadino describes were still important for the development of WALTER, whose own phytogeographical investigations carried him throughout the former German empire and beyond. FRALISH, McINTOSH & LOUCKS provide a history of a leading American school of plant ecology, John T. Curtis, since World War II. BOWERS is a botanist who writes about ecologists who studied Arizona's desert plants, culminating in her biography of Forrest Shreve. TROYER wrote a comparable biography of B.W. Wells, a plant ecologist who devoted most of his researches to the vegetation of North Carolina.

Many animal ecologists are attracted to population studies, and two excellent works illustrate different approaches to that history. KINGSLAND describes progress in the development of mathematical models to portray animal population changes that were developed in Europe, America and Australia, while

CROWCROFT has written the history of the Bureau of Animal Population, an ecological school where he trained, that emphasizes the correlation between the natural history of species and their population changes. The ecologist CROKER wrote the biography of a leading American ecologist, Victor Ernest Shelford, who was concerned with the interactions between animals and plant communities. WILSON is the founder of sociobiology, a subdiscipline that lies between animal ecology and evolution, and he is also a leading entomologist. His autobiography provides valuable insights into his achievements.

Limnology reached a somewhat separate status as a science by 1902 but has attracted fewer historians than other branches of ecology. STELEANU writes its history from 1640 to 1960, drawing on the writings of fellow limnologists, but not on those by historians of science. BECKEL & EGERTON use oral history to tell the story of the leading school of limnology at the University of Wisconsin during the tenure of its first two generations of leaders. CRAMER also describes the achievements of a limnology group – in The Netherlands.

Marine ecology is closely allied to both oceanography and fisheries management and is included in histories of these subjects. The oceanographer and biologist MILLS keeps the emphasis on marine ecology in his sophisticated history, and he places his survey within the contexts of these other disciplines. He also emphasizes the relationship between institutions and the advancement of science.

Although science is international, scientists live within nations, and their national contexts are meaningful for understanding scientific progress. Three monographs illustrate this approach: the ecologist SHEAIL provides an authoritative chronicle of the oldest ecological society (the British Ecological Society); the historian WEINER gives an outstanding survey of Russian and Soviet ecology and its applications; and SÖDERQVIST describes the struggles of scientists in a new field who attempted to find employment within a tradition-bound society.

Applied ecology is often tied to a national context. MEINE provides an excellent specific example in his biography of a leading American wildlife manager, Aldo Leopold. The treatment of wolves and coyotes is used by DUNLAP to show the slow impact of ecological understanding on American government policy. The careers of some applied ecologists have both national and international aspects, and two such scientists tell their own story: STEINHAUS is a California entomologist who was active in combatting threats to crops, nationally and internationally; WORTHINGTON is a British expert who spent most of his career assisting African countries to manage their fisheries, but at times also helped his native land to manage its resources.

There are some histories of ecological topics. An elegant example is the collection of articles from a symposium on ecology and evolution that MAIENSCHEIN, COLLINS & BEATTY organized and to which they contributed. MITMAN shows how the Chicago school of ecology was strongly influenced by one of its leaders to study cooperation and community in nature, because of his concern for peace in human society. BROWNE focuses on evolutionary rather than ecological aspects of biogeography, in the years 1675–1860, and in her haste to champion Darwin she overlooks some contributions made by lesser figures. However, her book provides

assistance for those interested in ecological aspects of biogeography.

A major approach to ecology since World War II – particularly in America – is the study of ecosystems, and there are two recent histories that describe both scientific developments and the importance of social context. HAGEN, a historian, inevitably brings a somewhat different perspective to the task than the ecologist GOLLEY, who contributed decisively to this speciality and provides an insider's viewpoint in the best history ever written by an ecologist. Nevertheless, many readers may be more struck by the similarities than by the differences in their works.

FRANK N. EGERTON

See also Environmental Sciences

Edison, Thomas Alva 1847–1931

American inventor

Baldwin, Neil, *Edison: Inventing the Century*, New York: Hyperion, 1995

Carlson, W. Bernard and Michael E. Gorman, "Understanding Invention as a Cognitive Process: The Case of Thomas Edison and Early Motion Pictures, 1888–91", *Social Studies of Science*, 20 (1990): 387–430

Conot, Robert, *A Streak of Luck: The Life & Legend of Thomas Alva Edison*, New York: Seaview, 1979

Dyer, Frank L. and Thomas C. Martin, *Edison: His Life and Inventions*, 2 vols, New York and London: Harper, 1910

Friedel, Robert and Paul Israel, *Edison's Electric Light: Biography of an Invention*, New Brunswick, New Jersey: Rutgers University Press, 1986

Hendricks, Gordon, *The Edison Motion Picture Myth*, Berkeley: University of California Press, 1961

Hughes, Thomas, *Networks of Power: Electrification in Western Society, 1880–1930*, Baltimore: Johns Hopkins University Press, 1983

Israel, Paul, *Edison: A Life of Invention*, New York: John Wiley, 1998

Jehl, Francis, *Menlo Park Reminiscences*, Dearborn, Michigan: Edison Institute, 3 vols, 1937–41

Josephson, Matthew, *Edison: A Biography*, New York: McGraw-Hill, 1959

Millard, Andre, *Edison and the Business of Innovation*, Baltimore: Johns Hopkins University Press, 1990

Musser, Charles, *The Emergence of Cinema: The American Screen to 1907*, New York: Scribner, 1990

Musser, Charles, *Before the Nickelodeon: Edwin S. Porter and the Edison Manufacturing Company*, Berkeley: University of California Press, 1991

Schallenberg, Richard H., *Bottled Energy: Electrical Engineering and the Evolution of Chemical Energy Storage*, Philadelphia: American Philosophical Society, 1982

Vanderbilt, Byron, *Thomas Edison: Chemist*, Washington, DC: American Chemical Society, 1971

Wachhorst, Wyn, *Thomas Alva Edison: An American Myth*, Cambridge, Massachusetts: MIT Press, 1981

Thomas Edison is internationally recognized as the signature inventor of the modern age, having contributed to a remarkable range of technologies that underlie electric light and power, communications, and popular entertainment. He was a central figure in the creation of the research and development laboratory, although he became the symbol of the quintessential lone inventor.

Although numerous biographies of Edison have appeared, most chroniclers begin with a large debt to the authorized biography written in 1910 (and enlarged in 1929) by DYER & MARTIN. It relies heavily on Edison's reminiscences and those of his associates. While filled with good stories and extensive quotations from Edison himself, its details are not always reliable and, like most subsequent biographies, it tells Edison's life largely through his most well-known inventions. However, Dyer & Martin provide a good technical discussion of these inventions and furnish insight into Edison's inventive and business methods.

JOSEPHSON's authorized biography was the first to put the inventor's life in any context, focusing on Edison's method of invention and the business climate in which he worked. Although relying primarily on Dyer & Martin and various reminiscences for information about Edison's method, Josephson made an important contribution by highlighting the transitional nature of Edison's laboratories at Menlo Park and West Orange during a period when inventive activity shifted increasingly from individual inventors to teams of scientists and engineers working in modern industrial research laboratories. However, Josephson's analysis was colored by his earlier work on the Gilded Age captains of American industry, which led him to a naive view of the inventor's convoluted business arrangements. He was also hindered by the lack of adequate archival organization and finding aids at the Edison National Historic Site. More importantly, the nascent state of the history of technology provided little technical context for Edison's work.

CONOT appeared during the centennial of Edison's inventive work on electric lighting and aimed to demythologize the inventor. He was the first biographer to make extensive use of original documents, but that use is amateurish and inaccurate. Furthermore, his citations to both primary and secondary material often prove inadequate and incorrect and the result is an error-filled book that cannot be trusted to provide a factual account of Edison's life. His portrayal of Edison's family relationships is his major contribution. BALDWIN's biography extends that portrayal, but otherwise suffers from a lack of technical understanding of Edison's work and businesses.

WACHHORST provides a detailed analysis of the way that biographies, newspapers, and magazines have portrayed Edison and how these various public images of him relate to larger issues in American cultural history, particularly to perceptions of science and technology. However, he does not examine Edison's own role in creating his public image.

ISRAEL, who has been working with the Edison archive for nearly two decades, provides the most recent and detailed examination of Edison's life and work. He produces the fullest account of Edison's approaches to his various inventions and places each in a larger business context. Paying particular attention to the inventor's formative early years in the telegraph industry, Israel shows how Edison was influenced by the dominant American pattern of cooperative shop invention and how he came to combine it with a laboratory model of research in his own successively larger "invention factories". Israel demonstrates the importance of the telegraph industry as well in giving Edison an appreciation for the growing influence – for better or worse – of corporate business structures as an environment for innovation. Israel pays considerable attention to Edison's public image and is the first to point out how Edison's work as a press-wire operator taught him the power of the news media, which he used to full advantage throughout his career. Edison emerges as a pivotal figure not only in the shift from invention to industrial research but also in the nation's definitions of science and technology.

Besides these biographical studies, there are several books that examine Edison's work on particular technologies. HUGHES, writing about Edison's work in electric lighting, was the first scholar sufficiently sophisticated to create a context for Edison's inventive work. Beginning with a series of articles in the mid-1970s, he introduced Edison the professional inventor-entrepreneur, who presided over all aspects of invention from conceptualization to commercialization. Edison's success at overseeing all aspects of invention and development, according to Hughes, stemmed from his consideration of economic and social factors and from his concern with systems rather than individual components in his conceptualization of problems and in his approach to their solution. Furthermore, Hughes sees an important key to Edison's success in the inventor's ability to use knowledge and insights gained from previous inventions.

JEHL provided the basis (before Hughes) for the interpretation of Edison's electric lighting activities. However, his work has two principal flaws: he wrote more than 50 years after the activities described, largely reconstructing his account from newspaper reports and miscellaneous documents that he had kept or that were collected by Ford; and he arrived at Menlo Park nearly six months after work had begun on the electric light experiments (six months later than he claimed).

Using archival materials, FRIEDEL & ISRAEL follow the inventor and his staff from the beginning of the electric light research to the opening of the Pearl Street central station four years later. They focus on the period of initial research and development at the Menlo Park laboratory, trying to corroborate various reminiscences, particularly those of Edison and of Jehl. Their analysis of the methods and roles of Edison and his associates raised new questions about Hughes's earlier interpretation of this subject, particularly the systems approach he saw as central to Edison's work. Friedel & Israel describe Edison's initial concept of an electric lighting system as unsophisticated and conclude that he only began to articulate a more sophisticated understanding of the relationship between components as his experiments forced him to take that approach.

MUSSER is the principal historian of Edison's influence on the cinema industry. In both his books he touches only briefly on Edison's work as an inventor, but offers a thorough business history and cultural analysis of the early film industry. HENDRICKS gives a detailed account of Edison's inventions for the cinema, arguing that his assistant William Dickson was the primary inventor. Although Hendricks claimed that he approached the problem with an open mind, he did not interpret even the most ambiguous pieces of evidence in Edison's favor and merely replaces one heroic inventor with another. CARLSON & GORMAN's more nuanced telling takes into account Edison's collaborative approach to invention, demonstrating the importance of both men's contributions.

SCHALLENBERG devotes a chapter to an examination of Edison's work on a commercial alkaline storage battery. He challenges the traditional story by going to the original documents, particularly the notebooks, to show that Edison was not blindly empirical, as had been traditionally claimed, but that he relied on previous work by others in the field.

VANDERBILT, a professional chemist, focuses on the role of chemistry in Edison's work, looking at the state of the art as revealed in the published literature of the time and comparing Edison's knowledge and achievements to those of other chemists and inventors. He also pays attention to Edison's manufacturing activities in organic chemistry, particularly during World War I. Vanderbilt bases his study on secondary works rather than on original documents; like Josephson, his analysis was further hindered by the limited available scholarship on the various technologies that were important to Edison's career.

MILLARD offered the first careful examination of the West Orange laboratory. He focuses on the relationship between Edison's extensive manufacturing concerns and the activities of his laboratories, and although he does not detail the laboratory's research efforts he provides the first significant investigation of the role of this important institution.

PAUL ISRAEL AND ROBERT ROSENBERG

Education

Argles, M., *South Kensington to Robbins: An Account of English Technical and Scientific Education since 1851*, London: Longman, 1964

Brock, W.H., *H.E. Armstrong and the Teaching of Science, 1880–1930*, Cambridge: Cambridge University Press, 1973

Debus, Allen G., *Science and Education in the Seventeenth Century: The Webster-Ward Debate*, London: Macdonald, and New York: American Elsevier, 1970

Dyhouse, Carol, *Girls Growing Up in Late Victorian and Edwardian England*, London and Boston: Routledge and Kegan Paul, 1981

Heward, C.M., "Industry, Cleanliness and Godliness: Sources For and Problems in the History of Scientific and Technical Education and the Working Class, 1850–1910", *Studies in Science Education*, 7 (1980): 87–128

Morrell, J.B., "The Chemist Breeders: The Research Schools of Liebig and Thomas Thomson", *Ambix*, 19 (1972): 1–46

Ringer, Fritz K., *Education and Society in Modern Europe*, Bloomington: Indiana University Press, 1979

Sanderson, M.J., *The Missing Stratum: Technical School Education in England, 1900–1990s*, London: Athlone Press, 1994

Education covers a vast range of ideas and practices, from the most advanced level research and training to elementary socialisation, all of which may incorporate, or be based on, aspects of science. The emphasis here is on science in schools, which is very much a recent phenomenon; mass schooling only became available during the 19th century, and mass schooling at secondary level, where most scientific education is done, only during the 20th century. It is important also to look at technical education, because scientific education has commonly been provided in that guise.

The emergence of modern science has had potentially profound implications for methods of education. DEBUS looks at the effects of the discoveries of the scientific revolution on traditional education provided by the universities in the 17th century. It is primarily a reprint of some contemporary texts that discussed this question but, in an introductory essay, he discusses the challenge posed to a scholarship that tended to look back to ancient authority, by the new modes of enquiry, which sought to make original discoveries. Modern science ultimately had an important effect on ways of learning, as well as doing, science in the universities. MORRELL's seminal paper, comparing the chemical laboratories of Liebig at the University of Giessen with that of his contemporary, Thomson, at Glasgow, although mainly concerned with the formation and characteristics of research schools, is also an account of new ways of "breeding" chemists. Liebig is often credited with establishing the basic model of a research laboratory, adopted by universities across the world; he also launched innumerable careers of people who went on to re-create the model.

The incorporation of science into school curricula also had potentially significant implications. In his introductory essay to a collection of writings by H.E. Armstrong, BROCK shows how Armstrong's heuristic methods of science teaching were very different from the prevailing ethos still infected by a tradition of "payment by results". Armstrong argued that science should be taught heuristically; i.e., that pupils, through experimental work, should discover things for themselves, with only discreet direction by the teacher. This was somewhat at odds with the usual methods of demonstration or rote learning, and although his methods gained considerable popularity from the late 19th century, they frequently proved to be slow, expensive, and not entirely amenable to a system driven by an exam syllabus. The principles, however, have had a lasting effect on science education, particularly in Britain.

Science education became more widespread with the wider emergence of state-run educational systems during the 19th century. ARGLES follows a common format in his factual account of the development of state scientific and technical education in England from the mid-19th century. Science education was seen to be important in providing a more systematic basis for technical occupations, and it was advocated as a means of creating better craftsmen and artisans. Impelled by the state of the economy and its performance relative to that of other countries, a whole series of government inquiries considered the place and purpose of science in schools and other educational institutions. SANDERSON's more critical study takes up the question that seems to preoccupy most historians of scientific and technical education in England – whether it was lacking in some way, or was otherwise connected with Britain's relative economic and industrial decline. His analysis focuses on the provision of specifically technical secondary schools through the 20th century. Although generally a defender of Britain's record of support for science, especially at higher levels, Sanderson does identify a deficiency; whereas most other industrially advanced nations had secondary level technical schools, which produced significant numbers of adolescents for industrial employment or higher education, Britain's secondary technical schools did not become an equal branch of secondary education, and were ultimately absorbed into general secondary schools. Sanderson also considers the issue of the relative status accorded to different aspects of the curriculum; in many European countries, scientific education has been deemed of lower status, both socially and academically, than the traditional liberal subjects of education. RINGER's statistically rich study of the development of educational systems in Germany, France, and England from the 19th century, although not primarily concerned with scientific education, provides an excellent comparative basis for the different countries.

Most accounts of scientific education, particularly in schools, tend to focus on what was provided, particularly by the state; there are much fewer discussions of the nature of the curriculum or the response of students. HEWARD's article provides something of a prolegomenon to these questions in a useful critique-cum-bibliographical essay, which also offers some interpretations and analyses. A significant point is that working class education in the early 19th century contained a strong tradition of scientific study; how this was assimilated into a state-run system that largely down-played science remains unexplored. Unfortunately, the title is a little misleading in that, while it reminds us that education for most people for most of the time has been a form of more or less overt socialisation in which science has played its part, the author does not really provide any particular evidence for the reasonable assessment that science education was primarily devoted to instilling habits of industry, cleanliness, and godliness.

DYHOUSE does consider one crucially important area in which the curriculum of science education has been discussed, that of women and girls. For large parts of the 19th and 20th century, scientific arguments have been advanced to debar women from higher education or from particular aspects of the curriculum. The most obvious division of science education by gender was probably at the turn of the century when fear of national decline, high infant mortality, and feminism prompted educationalists to replace science subjects for girls with domestic science – cookery, hygiene, and household economy – as more suitable preparation for their proper function in life as mothers and housewives. More or less overt influences on the choice of subjects by girls continues to the present, with significant gender imbalances in the study of sciences; chemistry and physics for boys, biology and domestic science for girls.

KEITH VERNON

See also École Polytechnique; Engineering Schools; France: scientific and technical education; Universities

Egypt and Mesopotamia

Bardinet, Thierry, *Les Papyrus médicaux de l'Egypte pharaonique: Traduction intégrale et commentaires*, Paris: Fayard, 1995

Benoit, Paul, Karine Chemla and Jim Ritter (eds), *Histoire de fractions, fractions d'histoire*, Basel: Birkhaüser, 1992

Caveing, Maurice, *La Constitution du type mathématique de l'idéalité dans la pensée grecque*, vol. 1: *Essai sur le savoir mathématique dans la Mésopotamie et l'Égypte anciennes*, Lille: Presses Universitaires de Lille, 1994

Friberg, Jöran, *A Survey of Publications on Sumero-Akkadian Mathematics, Metrology and Related Matters (1854–1982)*, Göteborg: Chalmers University of Technology and the University of Göteborg, 1982

Friberg, Jöran, "Mathematics", *Reallexikon der Assyriologie und Vorderasiatischen Archäologie*, 7 (1989): 531–85

Gillings, Richard J., *Mathematics in the Time of Pharaohs*, Cambridge, Massachusetts: MIT Press, 1972

Høyrup, Jens, "Algebra and Naive Geometry: An Investigation of Some Basic Aspects of Old Babylonian Mathematical Thought", *Altorientalische Forschungen*, 17 (1990): 27–69, 262–354

Høyrup, Jens, *In Measure, Number and Weight: Studies in Mathematics and Culture*, New York: State University of New York Press, 1994

Leitz, Christian, *Studien zur ägyptischen Astronomie*, Wiesbaden: Harrassowitz, 1989

Lucas, Alfred, *Ancient Egyptian Materials and Industries*, London and New York: Longmans Green, 1926; 4th edition, revised by J.R. Harris, London: Arnold, 1962

Neugebauer, Otto, *The Exact Sciences in Antiquity*, Copenhagen: Munksgaard, 1951; Princeton, New Jersey: Princeton University Press, 1952; 2nd edition, Providence, Rhode Island: Brown University Press, 1957

Neugebauer, Otto, *A History of Ancient Mathematical Astronomy*, 3 vols, Berlin: Springer, 1975

Nissen, Hans J., Peter Damerow and Robert K. Englund, *Archaic Bookkeeping: Writing and Techniques of Economic Administration in the Ancient Near East*, translated from the German by Paul Larsen, Chicago: University of Chicago Press, 1993 (original edition, 1990)

Nunn, John F., *Ancient Egyptian Medicine*, London: British Museum Press, and Norman: University of Oklahoma Press, 1996

Powell, Marvin, "Masse und Gewichte", *Reallexikon der Assyriologie und Vorder-asiatischen Archäologie*, vol. 7, Berlin: de Gruyter, 1989

Ritter, Jim, "Babylone–1800" and "Chacun sa vérité", in *Éléments d'histoire des sciences*, edited by Michel Serres, Paris: Bordas, 1989: 17–37, 39–61; English translation in *The History of Scientific Thought: Elements of a History of Science*, edited by Serres, Oxford and Cambridge, Massachusetts: Blackwell, 1995

Ritter, Jim, *Les Pratiques de la raison en Mésopotamie et en Egypte aux IIIe et IIe millénaires*, Thèse, Villetaneuse: Université de Paris 13, 1993

Rochberg, Francesca, "Babylonian Astronomy and Calendar", in *Civilizations of the Ancient Near East*, vol. 3, edited by Jack M. Sasson, New York: Scribner, 1995

Mesopotamia and Egypt used to be poor relations in the history of science, useful only as a foil for the so-called Greek miracle, the birth of real science and mathematics. However, new archeological discoveries, the study of newly-uncovered texts, and reappraisals of those already known from the point of view of an enlarged range of questions have changed this image in the last few decades. More than in other areas of the history of science, older syntheses and the popular expositions based on them may prove to be at best obsolete, or even misleading. Fortunately, there are recent and extensive bibliographies for both primary and secondary sources of Mesopotamian mathematics (e.g. see FRIBERG, 1982, which includes commentaries), for Mesopotamian medicine, and for Egyptian mathematics and medicine (see RITTER, 1993).

Although now challenged in various respects, NEUGEBAUER (1952) remains the classical non-technical synthesis of Egyptian and Babylonian mathematics and astronomy, unequalled in its scope and valuable for its methodological prudence. The focus is on transmission to the Greek world but, in opposition to the traditional view that pre-Greek texts are mere compilations of recipes for the purposes of everyday life, Neugebauer emphasizes the general ideas underlying the problems and their solutions, especially in the case of Mesopotamian science – which he interprets, for example, as searching for a theory of quadratic equations.

Part of BENOIT, CHEMLA & RITTER is devoted to the determination, use, and development of the notion of fractions and their computational use in Egypt and Mesopotamia. The importance of metrology for the evolution of the notion of fractions is stressed, and various types of texts (e.g. economic, juridical, and religious) are taken into account in a cultural, comparative perspective.

CAVEING is a critical and epistemological study of Babylonian and Egyptian mathematical texts that aims at an analysis of the procedures rather than the results. In particular, his examination of the original succession of the problems, irrespective of their apparent subject matter, reveals other coherent groupings. The book also examines various standard misunderstandings of the nature of pre-Greek mathematics.

The standard presentation of the mathematical achievements in Egypt, from the point of view of a mathematician, is GILLINGS, in which the classification of problems is thematic and modernized.

POWELL and FRIBERG (1989) contain exhaustive presentations of, respectively, the metrological and mathematical textual corpus of Mesopotamia. Powell summarizes recent, important findings concerning the various metrological systems used in Mesopotamia in various sorts of texts, and gives a clear and reasoned discussion of the evidence for each known or proposed Mesopotamian unit of length, area, volume, and weight. Where actual physical standards are known, as in the case of weights, he provides an overview of possible absolute values. Friberg organizes his material, which covers more than 3000 years, by periods and mathematical themes (in a modernized presentation), and includes descriptions of the available tablets and information on terminology and results. The final pages discuss the problem of the transmission of Babylonian mathematics, and the evidence for a possible common origin of the mathematics of various civilizations.

NISSEN, DAMEROW & ENGLUND synthesize fundamental recent discoveries concerning the beginnings of writing and number systems within a cultural context, emphasizing the earliest archaic texts from Uruk. Structures and lines of development, of economic texts in particular, are provided, as well as specific details on the evolution of written symbols and arithmetic.

HØYRUP (1990) contests, on etymological grounds, the interpretation of the content of some Old Babylonian texts as a rhetorical algebra, and suggests that they were in fact derived from considerations of line segments and thus are better described as a naïve geometry. This description is then used to reject categorizations of the Mesopotamian way of thinking as "cold-savage" or "mythical-poetic".

HØYRUP (1994) adopts a cultural anthropological approach. Several chapters are devoted to Mesopotamian mathematics (often in comparison to Greek or Islamic mathematics), underlining the importance of the educational context, the progressive professionalization of scribes, and the relationships between the social environment and the conceptual and theoretical aspects of the mathematics.

The relevant parts of NEUGEBAUER (1975) (Book 2, volume 1 for Babylonia; Book 3, volume 2 for Egypt; and relevant sections in volume 3 – e.g., on calendars) are comprehensive and detailed surveys of ancient mathematical astronomy. They show, in particular, how Babylonians worked out a theoretical arithmetical astronomy without an underlying geometrical model (unlike the Greeks), and stress the relationship between available mathematical tools and the development of scientific theory. The latest additions to our knowledge of Babylonian astronomy and calendrics are to be found in ROCHBERG (1995).

LEITZ argues that most historians of science (including Neugebauer) have dismissed Egyptian astronomy, while Egyptologists have been interested only in its role in the construction of calendars and the determination of an absolute chronology. He discusses in detail these latter questions (including the question of the orientation of temples), and concludes that the Egyptians knew about observation and measurement, but that their methods of representation differed from those of the Greeks.

A thematic survey of what was known of Egyptian technology in the 1960s is given in LUCAS, which examines the presentation, uses, and treatment of each material and technique thoroughly.

BARDINET examines the character of Egyptian medical thought; he describes in detail the magical protective sentences at the beginnings of most texts, analyzes the underlying physiological concepts, and shows the importance of the role played by what the Egyptians saw as four pathogenic factors circulating in the body. A full French translation of many of the Egyptian medical papyri is also given. For an overview of medical knowledge in Ancient Egypt, see NUNN, which describes the various papyri, the concepts used in anatomy, physiology, and pathology, and the evidence (human remains, representation of bodies, and texts) from which information can be obtained concerning illnesses and different types of healers. Other chapters are devoted to the relationship of Egyptian medicine to magic, its use of plants, and a detailed study of various diseases and their treatment.

RITTER (1993; part of which is summarized in RITTER, 1989, and in Benoit, Chemla & Ritter) delineates, from both sociological and textual criteria, certain areas that were privileged by the Mesopotamians and Egyptians – including divination, medicine, jurisprudence, and mathematics in Mesopotamia, and medicine and mathematics in Egypt – and analyses what the author calls the "rational practices" associated with the evolution of these areas. In medicine, he reveals that the usual discrimination between magical and scientific medicine does not correspond to the distinctions made between practitioners in these civilizations. In mathematics, a developed algorithmic interpretation allows specific features (and errors) in the texts to be taken into account.

CATHERINE GOLDSTEIN

Ehrlich, Paul 1854–1915

German medical scientist and immunologist

Apolant, H. *et al.*, *Paul Ehrlich. Eine Darstellung seines wissenschaftlichen Wirkens*, Jena: G. Fisher, 1914

Bäumler, Ernst, *Paul Ehrlich: Scientist for Life*, New York: Homes and Meier, 1984

Cambrosio, Alberto, Daniel Jacobi and Peter Keating, "Ehrlich's 'Beautiful Pictures' and the Controversial Beginning of Immunological Imagery", *Isis*, 84 (1993): 662–99

Dieterle, William, *Dr Ehrlich's Magic Bullet*, Hollywood: Warner, 1940 (film)

Engelhardt, A. von, *Hundertjahrfeier der Geburtstage von Paul Ehrlich und Emil von Behring. Verleihung der Emil von Behring-Preise 1948, 1952 und 1954*, Marburg: N.G. Elwert, 1954

Fleck, Ludwik, *Genesis and Development of a Scientific Fact*, translated from the German by Fred Bradley and Thaddeus J. Trenn, Chicago: University of Chicago Press, 1979 (original edition, 1935)

Himmelweit, Fred (ed.), *The Collected Papers of Paul Ehrlich*, 3 vols, London: Pergamon Press, 1956–60

Liebenau, Jonathan, "Paul Ehrlich as a Commercial Scientist and Research Administrator", *Medical History*, 34 (1990): 65–78

Marquardt, Martha, *Paul Ehrlich als Mensch und Arbeiter*, Stuttgart: Deutsche Verlags-Anstalt, 1924; enlarged edition as *Paul Ehrlich*, London: Heinemann, 1949; New York: Schuman, 1951

Mazumdar, Pauline, "The Antigen-Antibody Reaction and the Physics and Chemistry of Life", *Bulletin of the History of Medicine*, 48 (1974): 1–21

Parascandola, John, "The Theoretical Basis of Paul Ehrlich's Chemistry", *Journal of the History of Medicine*, 36 (1981): 19–43

Silverstein, Arthur M., *A History of Immunology*, San Diego, California: Academic Press, 1989

Although Paul Ehrlich is one of the best-known pioneers of German medical science, there is no full-scale biography that does him justice. He has been an elusive figure in the history of immunology for a number of reasons. Although held in high esteem by research-oriented physicians, his science was often far beyond the grasp of his contemporaries, and, while his 60th-birthday Festschrift of 1914 offered a prosaic account of his academic achievements, few historians have understood the complex and sophisticated theories he advanced.

During the Weimar Republic some minor biographies appeared, including that of MARQUARDT, who published an initial study of Ehrlich in 1924, but the salvarsan therapy for syphilis (first published in 1910) remained controversial and subject to criticisms from nature therapists. After 1933, Ehrlich's Jewish identity meant that he was mentioned only in a perfunctory manner; in Behring biographies and ceremonies, the lack of reference to Ehrlich, without whom the antitoxin serum could never have been clinically applied or manufactured, and the muted references to other Jewish researchers such as August Paul von Wassermann, confirmed how the history of medical science was to project a distorted ideology of the Germanic scientific genius.

Nevertheless, Ehrlich was less marginalised elsewhere. Ludwik FLECK, the Polish immunologist, focused on the Wassermann reaction, and mentioned Ehrlich in passing in his classic study of the social epistemology of science. Fleck depicted Ehrlich as a "great theoretician", and as adept in visual representation. In the US, a spectacular film by DIETERLE, portraying Ehrlich as a rebel, was released in 1940.

In 1951, Ehrlich's secretary, Martha Marquardt, republished her vivid portrait of Ehrlich. Her recollections concerning Ehrlich's behaviour and politics are of immense value. Meanwhile, Sir Henry Dale, who had studied in Ehrlich's institute and deeply admired his genius, encouraged critical appreciation of his science. Dale supported Fred HIMMELWEIT, a bacteriologist who had emigrated to Britain, in his endeavour to translate Ehrlich's scientific papers. In post-war West Germany, Ehrlich received renewed attention – often with Behring, whose birth-year he shared – providing a cover for Nazi sympathisers in order to legitimate their positions.

BÄUMLER has gathered together the sources from the Hoechst pharmaceutical company, although he did not have access to the important collection of Ehrlich's personal papers currently located at the Rockefeller Archive Center. Bäumler's biography is a useful account, but, written from the viewpoint of a research scientist, is much too narrow in focus.

There is no full-scale study of the history of the Institute for Serum Testing and Experimental Therapy (later the Paul-Ehrlich Institute) in Frankfurt, to which Ehrlich moved in 1899. However, Bäumler and LIEBENAU have examined relations with the pharmaceutical industry, notably with Hoechst, and reveal them to be vital to the development of the Frankfurt Institute.

A number of historians of medical science have grappled with Ehrlich's immunology. PARASCANDOLA has examined the theoretical basis of Ehrlich's chemistry, while MAZUMDAR has analysed the antigen-antibody reaction. Both are historically nuanced and carefully bring out the complexities of Ehrlich's ideas. SILVERSTEIN regards Ehrlich's side chain theory as a conceptual precursor of modern immunological theories of idiotypes. Latterly, CAMBROSIO, JACOBI & KEATING have embarked on a social interpretation of Ehrlich's immunology.

Notwithstanding the above studies, the links and relationships that so concerned Ehrlich have eluded historians when piecing together the diverse aspects of Ehrlich's mercurial thought and meteoric career. It is to be hoped that the broadening of concern with Ehrlich's science will at last lead to a balanced biographical evaluation.

PAUL WEINDLING

Einstein, Albert   1879–1955

German-born Swiss theoretical physicist

Beller, Mara, Jürgen Renn and Robert S. Cohen (eds), *Einstein in Context, Science in Context* (special issue), 6/1 (1993)

Cassidy, David, *Einstein and Our World*, New Jersey: Humanities Press, 1995

Clark, Ronald W., *Einstein: The Life and Times*, Cleveland: World, 1971; London: Hodder and Stoughton, 1979

Einstein, Albert, *The Collected Papers of Albert Einstein*, presently being published in a continuing series with various editors, the first 5 volumes dealing with the period 1879–1914, Princeton, New Jersey: Princeton University Press, 1987–

Fölsing, Albrecht, *Albert Einstein: A Biography* , translated from the German by Eward Osers, New York: Viking, 1993 (original edition, 1993)

Frank, Philipp, *Einstein: His Life and Times*, translated from the German by George Rosen, edited and revised by Shuichi Kusaka, New York: Knopf, 1947; London: Jonathan Cape, 1948

Friedman, Alan J. and Carol C. Donley, *Einstein as Myth and Muse*, Cambridge: Cambridge University Press, 1985

Glick, Thomas F., *Einstein in Spain: Relativity and the Recovery of Science*, Princeton, New Jersey: Princeton University Press, 1988

Hermann, Armin, *Einstein: Der Weltweise und sein Jahrhundert. Eine Biographie*, Munich: Piper, 1994

Highfield, Roger and Paul Carter, *The Private Lives of Albert Einstein*, London: Faber and Faber, 1993; New York: St Martin's Press, 1994

Holton, Gerald and Yehuda Elkana (eds), *Albert Einstein: Historical and Cultural Perspectives*, Princeton, New Jersey: Princeton University Press, 1982

Holton, Gerald, *Thematic Origins of Scientific Thought: Kepler to Einstein*, Cambridge, Massachusetts: Harvard University Press, 1973; revised edition, 1988

Klein, Martin J., "Einstein's First Paper on Quanta", *Natural Philosopher*, 2 (1963): 59–86; "Einstein and the Wave-Particle Duality", *Natural Philosopher*, 3 (1964): 3–49; "Einstein, Specific Heats, and the Early Quantum Theory", *Science*, 148 (1965): 173–80; "Thermodynamics in Einstein's Thought", *Science*, 157 (1967): 509–16

Kuhn, Thomas S., *Black-Body Theory and the Quantum Discontinuity, 1894–1912*, New York: Oxford University Press, 1978; revised edition, Chicago: University of Chicago Press, 1987

Kuznetsov, Boris G., *Einstein*, translated from the Russian by V. Talmy, Moscow: Progress, 1965 (original edition, 1962)

Moszowski, Alexander, *Einstein the Searcher: His Work Explained from Dialogues with Einstein*, translated from the German by Henry L. Brose, London: Methuen, 1921; New York: Dutton, 1922 (original edition, 1921)

Pais, Abraham, *"Subtle is the Lord . . .": The Science and the Life of Albert Einstein*, Oxford and New York: Oxford University Press, 1982

Pyenson, Lewis, *The Young Einstein: The Advent of Relativity*, Bristol and Boston: Adam Hilger, 1985

Reiser, Anton, *Albert Einstein: A Biographical Portrait*, New York: A. and C. Boni, 1930; London: Thornton Butterworth, 1931

Ryan, Dennis P. (ed.), *Einstein and the Humanities*, Westport, Connecticut: Greenwood Press, 1987

Sayen, Jamie, *Einstein in America: The Scientist's Conscience in the Age of Hitler and Hiroshima*, New York: Crown, 1985

Schilpp, Paul Arthur (ed.), *Albert Einstein: Philosopher–Scientist*, Evanston, Illinois: Library of Living Philosophers, 1949

Seelig, Carl, *Albert Einstein: A Documentary Biography*, translated from the German by Mervyn Savill, London: Staples Press, 1956 (original edition, 1950)

Great scholarly interest in Albert Einstein dates from 1919 when results confirmed his prediction, based on the general theory of relativity, that starlight is bent in the vicinity of the sun. Together with his contributions to physics (to special and general relativity, quantum theory, and debates on the interpretation of quantum mechanics in particular), and the significance this work has had for philosophies of science, Einstein's outspoken pacifism and Zionism, and his role in the instigation of the atom-bomb project in the United States, have contributed to unprecedented interest in him as a cultural figure. Biographies have often been intended for wide readership, with contributions from scientists and others connected with Einstein. He has been presented as the pinnacle of scientific achievement and as an important moral figure, from the time of World War II virtually embodying the conscience of science. The most detailed and significant studies of Einstein's contributions to physics have often been offered in the context of the different theories on which he worked, while studies of Einstein have significantly shaped our understanding of the history of theoretical physics. A further area of scholarship is on Einstein's rise as a public figure, and the impact of his work on culture and scholarship in the 20th century.

The extremely valuable ongoing publication of EINSTEIN presents his complete writings and correspondence, as well as related material important to an understanding of his work, life, and times. Annotations and editorial notes present these resources within the context of careful overviews of present scholarly understanding.

There has been considerable interest in Einstein's personality, and many of the more important biographies have used direct contact with Einstein to offer a privileged perspective. Both Einstein's own testimony, often reflected in aphoristic sayings, and characteristic parables of his behaviour have been important in shaping images of the man. Following his death, documentary biographies have supplemented reminiscences and references to published writing, drawing on an increasingly wide range of archival sources (which initially had been restricted by the Einstein Estate).

The earliest depiction of Einstein based on personal contact was MOSZOWSKI's 1921 book, which developed from the author's conversations with Einstein from 1916 to 1920. Discursive in style, it covers topics such as Einstein's views on contemporary education, scientific discovery and music, and aims to portray the universality of his intellectual concerns and his lively wit and breadth of personality. REISER describes Einstein as a dreamy youth with an independent and growing interest in mathematics and physics, and a desire to sift the essential from the inessential that was rarely satisfied in his secondary and tertiary education. Employment in the Patent Office in Bern provided a practical counterpoise against pure intellectual creativity. Reiser sketches Einstein's career, his work, and his role in public life after World War I, suggesting that his science, art, and religion originate from the same sources. Einstein certified this biography, written under a *nom de plume* by his son-in-law Rudolf Kayser, to be "duly accurate".

FRANK describes Einstein's personality and environment in broad philosophical terms. Einstein's physics is depicted as involving a revolution in philosophical conceptions of nature, and Frank (a physicist and logical positivist) describes how it was open to philosophical and religious interpretations far removed from the scientific realm. Written in the late 1940s, the book discusses Einstein's principled rejection of quantum mechanics because of its indeterminism, and his advocacy of the atom bomb. Whereas previous biographers had stressed an unusual unity, Frank saw many unresolved contradictions in Einstein's character, stemming from his intense social conscience and his equally intense aversion to intimate relationships.

Declaring that the essential in a man of his type was his thought rather than his action, Einstein's autobiographical notes (published in SCHILPP) outline the general orientation that led him to physics, and the main lines of development of his thought. After describing his epistemological views, Einstein delineates the principal features of 19th-century theory, mounting a critique of mechanics as a foundation for physics and describing the development of electromagnetic theory and Planck's work on heat radiation. He then describes the conceptual constraints and guiding insights that provided a framework for his own development of early quantum theory, special relativity and general relativity. He discusses also his critique of the epistemological stance of quantum mechanics, and his own expectations for the development of a unified field theory. In addition to giving Einstein's autobiographical notes, Schilpp indicates the main features of early scholarly commentary on Einstein. Papers reviewing different aspects of Einstein's scientific work are contributed by physicists such as Wolfgang Pauli, Max Born, and Niels Bohr, and a number of philosophers present different interpretations of relativity and quantum theory, within the context of discussions of the epistemological implications of these theories, and the volume concludes with Einstein's response.

SEELIG was the first to make extensive use of documentary evidence. He constructs a portrait of Einstein's career using his letters and material obtained through interviews, in addition to the sources available to previous authors. KUZNETSOV focuses more closely on Einstein's physics, drawing heavily on Einstein's autobiographical notes. Kuznetsov argues that Einstein's physical insights required a conscious epistemological and ontological credo, and that his work on Brownian motion and the relativity theories in turn gave clarity to his epistemological views.

CLARK uses correspondence extensively in order to discuss the myth and reminiscence that dominate earlier works on Einstein, in what can be termed scholarly journalism. Relating Einstein's public statements to their political and social contexts, Clark develops a complex – but not always consistent – picture of Einstein's views and their ramifications for his collaborators. He links Einstein's career and early work in physics with contemporary politics: the rise of modern Germany, the development of nuclear weapons, and the growth of Zionism. Central features are Einstein's ambivalence towards his German and Jewish heritage, and the fact that he often worked for individualist and internationalist political ideals at variance with those around him. Recent German publications, such as by HERMANN, have offered similarly detailed portraits of Einstein. By some distance, the most valuable, comprehensive, and historically sensitive biography is FÖLSING; drawing on the contributions of recent specialist scholarship, and the documentary resources of the Einstein Archive, the book puts Einstein's physics at the centre of his personality while developing an insightful and considered treatment of the many dimensions of his personal and public life.

SAYEN's detailed study of Einstein's non-scientific work in America and his reaction to contemporary events (from the rise of Nazism to the Cold War and McCarthyism) counters the perception of Einstein as impractical and naive in political affairs. Sayen argues that in matters concerning truth and justice, Einstein saw no distinction between large problems and small, and that he approached political events from a primary concern with truth and justice.

HIGHFIELD & CARTER provide a portrait via Einstein's relations with his family. The book draws on new material, especially the correspondence with his first wife, Mileva Marić, which reveals that Einstein's close relationships were marked by an ambivalence combined with a lack of self-awareness, manifested in cycles of emotional engagement and distance. The authors discuss previous biographers' interpretations of Einstein's personal life and the sources available to them, arguing that Einstein's Estate had actively sought to control his image by suppressing potentially unfavourable archival material.

Detailed studies of Einstein have been extremely important for our understanding of the history of theoretical physics and the philosophy of science in the 20th century, and it is possible to mention only some of the more important contributions by historians of science. HOLTON's interest in the nascent phases of science led him to investigate the importance of the Michelson–Morley experiment, Ernst Mach's philosophy of science, and various electrodynamical approaches to the formation of Einstein's special relativity. In common with the majority of commentators, Holton argues that Einstein developed a highly distinctive interpretation of unparalleled fruitfulness.

KLEIN's papers (1963, 1964, 1965 and 1967) provide a sensitive treatment of Einstein's early publications on thermodynamics and quantum theory. KUHN's revisionist study, focusing on the relation between the interpretation of theory and familiarity with highly specific mathematical techniques, emphasized that Einstein was the first to recognize individual quantization of energy in Planck's law of black-body radiation. Both Klein and Kuhn show that Einstein's independent development of statistical mechanics led him to acquire an unusual (for the time) facility with Boltzmann statistics. It enabled him to explain the photoelectric effect in his argument for the quantization of light, a new interpretation of Planck's law, a quantum theory of specific heats, and the argument that light showed properties of both waves and particles.

PAIS combines a deft overview with attention to technical detail, tracing Einstein's contributions to physics and outlining his life. Pais, a theoretical physicist of the following generation, attempts to understand both the evolution of work now thoroughly absorbed within the fabric of physics, and the source of Einstein's trenchant criticism of quantum mechanics. For Pais, Einstein's particular greatness lies in his invention of invariance principles and use of statistical fluctuations. There are two strands in this most complete treatment of Einstein's scientific work: the first proceeded from special to general relativity, the second from statistical physics to quantum theory. From the 1920s, Einstein sought a synthesis of both in a field theory that would unify gravitation and electromagnetism while being strictly causal (deterministic), with the particles of physics emerging as special solutions of the general field equations, and the quantum postulates derived as a consequence of those field equations.

PYENSON illuminates aspects of Einstein's career by examining the social circumstances of his youth, the culture of mathematics in Germany, and Einstein's early collaborators. From studies of Einstein's teachers and his examination performance, of the Einstein family electro–technological business, and of emancipated urban Jews in the late 19th century, Pyenson provides a rare attempt to relate Einstein's perspective on physics and mathematics, to the image of him as an outsider, and to his early environment.

The papers in HOLTON & ELKANA investigate the main lines of Einstein's "influence". They include historical perspectives on Einstein's scientific contributions, discussions on the reception of his scientific ideas, his impact on scholarship and 20th-century culture, his reaction to developments in the Jewish world, and his relation to the nuclear age. RYAN constitutes a collection of unusually eclectic (and often suggestive) papers by scholars from different fields celebrating Einstein as an intercultural and interdisciplinary phenomenon. It includes contributions on ethics and epistemology, religion, metaphysics, the history and philosophy of science, literature, politics and education and psychology.

GLICK's richly contextual study of Einstein's trip to Spain in 1923 provides the most detailed account of his dual activities in physics and Zionism, and of the reception he received on such journeys. The book illustrates the multi-level discussion of scientific ideas in different domains of discourse (scientific, intellectual, and popular) in a country undergoing scientific modernization, and explores Einstein's interaction with the Spanish intelligentsia.

FRIEDMAN & DONLEY examine the relationship between Einstein as cultural myth and inspirational muse. Observing common themes in a range of cultural revolutions in physics, art, and literature in the early 20th century, the authors trace the process whereby new ideas in physics – relativity and quantum theory – became public property and were used by artists, especially writers. They also analyse the image of Einstein in advertising, showing that Einstein's positive image assumed a tragic aspect after 1946, through the popular (but historically inaccurate) association of the equation $e = mc^2$ with the atom bomb.

BELLER, RENN & COHEN aim to establish links between the different branches of recent scholarship. They include papers on Einstein's early professional context, emphasizing the value of his employment in the Patent Office in Bern for his approach to theoretical physics; on the reception and development of his work on gravitation and quantum theory, and the nature of the anti-Einstein campaign in Germany; on experimental tests or applications of different consequences of relativity; and on Einstein's philosophical approach to quantum mechanics, field theory and causality. CASSIDY, intended for nonspecialists, provides a brief overview of Einstein's impact on physics and culture, both through his new views of nature, and through the rise of the status of the theoretical physicist (of which Einstein was a central exemplar). The author also relates the main concerns and debates of previous historical scholarship.

RICHARD STALEY

See also Quantum Mechanics; Quantum Theory; Relativity

Electrical Engineering

Appleyard, Rollo, *The History of the Institution of Electrical Engineers, 1871–1931*, London: Institution of Electrical Engineers, 1939

Bowers, Brian, *A History of Electric Light and Power*, New York: Peregrinus, and Stevenage, Hertfordshire: Peregrinus/Science Museum, 1982

Cowan, Ruth Schwartz, *More Work for Mother*, London: Free Association Books, and New York: Basic Books, 1989

Dunsheath, Percy, *A History of Electrical Engineering*, London: Faber and Faber, and New York: Pitman, 1962

Hollister-Short, Graham and Frank A.J.L. James (eds), *History of Technology*, vol. 13, London: Mansell, 1991

Hughes, Thomas P., *Networks of Power: Electrification in Western Society, 1880–1930*, Baltimore: Johns Hopkins University Press, 1983

Reader, William J., *A History of the Institution of Electrical Engineers, 1871–1971*, London: Peregrinus, 1987

Roberts, G.K., "Electrification", in *Science, Technology and Everyday Life, 1870–1950*, edited by Colin Chant, London and New York: Routledge/Open University, 1989

APPLEYARD's history of the Institution of Electrical Engineers is a celebratory work written with two purposes in mind; first, to mark the centenary of Faraday's discovery of electromagnetic induction, and second, to record the first 60 years of the

Institution of Electrical Engineers. The work presents a laudatory history of electrical engineering in the UK, and reports the growing importance of electricity in British life and the increasing sense of worth experienced by electrical engineers. Its approach is partisan, as might be expected from such a work, but it nevertheless remains a good introduction to the institutional history of the IEE, and gives a reasonably well-integrated account of the technological, educational, and social issues. Also, although hagiographic in form, Appleyard's biographies of the presidents of the Institution are useful cameos of those who formed and directed its trajectory in the first 60 years of its existence. Nearly 50 years after the appearance of Appleyard, READER's history was published to mark the centenary of the Institution. Reader's treatment is in marked contrast to Appleyard's, for although they deal with the same subject and have access to similar sources, their approaches reflect not only half a century of change, but also different historiographical attitudes. Reader examines the introduction and incorporation of electronics in his history, but also records and discusses the differences of opinion that arose from time to time, relating both to technicalities – for example, the disputes between William Henry Preece and a number of opponents – and to the form and future of the Institution.

ROBERTS, while limited in extent, covers a wide range of ideas. She shows how technological, scientific, and economic factors acted in concert in the development of electrical engineering, and how experiences in the US and Britain can throw some light on the processes of innovation and social change. Her treatment of the effects of electricity on industry and the home is particularly good, as is her discussion on the efforts made to interest women in the potential inherent in electrical power. The bibliography is full and comprehensive, making it very easy to extend the introductory studies in the chapter. COWAN is not restricted to the effects of electrification on the home and on the roles and responsibilities of women, but, by embedding electricity in the domestic situation, she has provided an insightful study of the interdependence of modern technologies. Her work demonstrates that the trajectories of technologies are neither predictable nor determined simply by technical or social factors, and is a fine example of the contextual approach to the history of technology.

HUGHES has produced perhaps the finest history of electrical engineering of recent years. His work attempts to discover order in the construction of electrical power systems as they developed in the years 1880–1930. With careful, detailed comparisons between the systems of Berlin, Chicago, London, and California, Hughes illuminates points of similarity, driven mainly by technological considerations, and points of difference, resulting mainly from cultural differences. In order to impose some structure on a complex history, Hughes introduces and defends some interesting ideas – including reverse salients, conflict and resolution, and technological momentum – some of which have been incorporated into modern approaches to the history of technology. This strongly analytical work underlines and clarifies the complex, social nature of electrical power systems, which involve the action and interaction of artefacts, engineers, entrepreneurs, users, and consumers.

BOWERS's work is a synoptic introduction to the history of electrical engineering, and forms a good entry into the subject. Organised into four sections – origins, practical possibilities, public supply, and the consumer – Bowers's account begins with Thales of Miletus and ends with "The Electrical World" of the late 20th century. He outlines the major stages in the development of modern electrical power systems, from the points of view of production, distribution, and supply. While he concentrates mainly on the UK, he does not imply that electrical engineering is a British phenomenon, and gives due regard and credit to the traditionally significant figures in the story of electric light and power. An earlier, and internal, history of electrical engineering is contained in DUNSHEATH; Dunsheath was an engineer and a president of the Institution of Electrical Engineers, and his interest lay in recounting the history of electrical engineering artefacts and methods. His careful, detailed study of machines and techniques is a useful adjunct to the more general works of Bowers and Roberts, the social history of Cowan, and the systems approach of Hughes.

In spite of the importance of electrical engineering to modern life, its history has not been the subject of many books. A recent collection of papers, partly redressing the balance, is HOLLISTER-SHORT & JAMES. Taken together these papers provide a mosaic of the history of electrical engineering, from its beginnings in telegraphy to the early development of television. The approaches range from the biographical to the largely internal, and, although readers would need to construct their own syntheses of the various elements provided, together these papers present a coherent, modern approach to the history of electrical engineering.

COLIN A. HEMPSTEAD

Electrical Instruments

Ben-Chaim, Michael, "Social Mobility and Scientific Change: Stephen Gray's Contribution to Electrical Research", *British Journal for the History of Science*, 23 (1990): 3–24

Brown, Neil, "Charging for Electricity in the Early Years of Electrical Supply", *IEE Proceedings – A*, 132 (1985): 513–24

Cattermole, M.J.G. and A.F. Wolfe, *Horace Darwin's Shop: A History of the Cambridge Scientific Instrument Company, 1878 to 1968*, Bristol: Hilger, 1987

Dunsheath, Percy, *A History of Electrical Engineering*, London: Faber and Faber, and New York: Pitman, 1962

Gee, Brian, "Electromagnetic Engines: Pre-Technology and Development Immediately Following Faraday's Discovery of Electromagnetic Rotations", *History of Technology*, 13 (1991): 41–72

Gooday, Graeme, "Precision Measurement and the Genesis of Physics Teaching Laboratories in Victorian Britain", *British Journal for the History of Science*, 23 (1990): 25–51

Gooday, Graeme, "Teaching Telegraphy and Electrotechnics in the Physics Laboratory: William Ayrton and the Creation of an Academic Space for Electrical Engineering, 1873–84", *History of Technology*, 13 (1991): 73–114

Gooday, Graeme, "The Morals of Energy Metering: Constructing and Deconstructing the Precision of the

Victorian Electrical Engineer's Ammeter", in *The Values of Precision*, edited by M. Norton Wise, Princeton, New Jersey: Princeton University Press, 1995

Gooding, David, "'In Nature's School': Faraday as an Experimentalist", in *Faraday Rediscovered: Essays on the Life and Work of Michael Faraday, 1791–1867*, edited by Gooding and Frank A.J.L. James, London: Macmillan, and New York: Stockton Press, 1985

Hackmann, W.D., *Electricity from Glass: The History of the Frictional Electrical Machine, 1600–1850*, Alphen aan den Rijn: Sijthoff & Noordhoff, 1978

Heilbron, J.L., *Elements of Early Modern Physics*, Berkeley: University of California Press, 1982

Hunt, Bruce, "Michael Faraday, Cable Telegraphy and the Rise of Field Theory", *History of Technology*, 13 (1991): 1–19

Hunt, Bruce, "The Ohm is Where the Art Is: British Telegraph Engineers and the Development of Electrical Standards", *Osiris*, 2nd series, 9 (1993): 48–64

Hunt, Bruce, "Scientists, Engineers and Wildman Whitehouse: Measurement and Credibility in Early Cable Telegraphy", *British Journal for the History of Science*, 29 (1996): 155–69

Lyall, Kenneth, *Electrical and Magnetic Instruments, Catalogue 8*, Cambridge: Whipple Museum, 1991

Morus, Iwan, "Telegraphy and the Technology of Display: The Electricians and Samuel Morse", *History of Technology*, 13 (1991): 20–40

O'Connell, Joseph, "Metrology: The Creation of Universality by the Circulation of Particulars", *Social Studies of Science*, 23 (1993): 129–73

Phillips, V.J., *Waveforms: An Early History of Oscillography*, Bristol: Hilger, 1987

Schaffer, Simon, "A Manufactory of Ohms: Late Victorian Metrology and Its Instrumentation", in *Invisible Connections: Instruments, Institutions, and Science*, edited by Robert Bud and Susan Cozzens, Bellingham, Washington: SPIE Optical Engineering Press, 1992, 23–56

Senior, John, "Rationalising Electrotherapy in Neurology", 1860–1920, unpublished D.Phil. thesis, University of Oxford, 1994

Smith, Crosbie and M. Norton Wise, *Energy and Empire: A Biographical Study of Lord Kelvin*, Cambridge and New York: Cambridge University Press, 1989

Stock, John T. and Denis Vaughan, *The Development of Instruments to Measure Electric Current*, London: Science Museum, 1983

Turner, Gerard L'E., *Nineteenth-Century Scientific Instruments*, London: Sotheby, and Berkeley: University of California Press, 1983

Williams, Mari E.W., *The Precision Makers: A History of the Instruments Industry in Britain and France, 1870–1939*, London and New York: Routledge, 1994

During the last two centuries, instruments have been a crucial resource in creating, exploring, and embodying knowledge of electrical science. A wide variety of electrical instruments has been invented in this period, and can be considered in a number of different ways. The scope of these instruments has broadened from the display of static discharges to the gauging of direct, and later alternating, currents, along with the closely associated parameters of resistance, voltage, and self-induction. Central to this evolution were the successive commercial stimuli of public lecture demonstrations, telegraphy, electric power and lighting, and electronic engineering. In very general terms, the overall trend up to the late 20th century has been to give an increasing status to metrological techniques; this reflects changes in the interests of instrument users, from the desire to create enlightening performances, to the desire to exploit fully the power of mathematical theory and its commercial applications. In this respect, a particularly useful historical distinction can be made of instruments that display electrical behaviour, between those that qualitatively indicate electrical magnitude, and those that measure it quantitatively in systematic units.

Although few historians cover all relevant issues with equal thoroughness, here are some important concerns raised in the literature discussed below: i) operational mechanism (electrostatic, electromagnetic or electrothermal); ii) mode of manufacture (specialist customized devices or mass-produced standard models); iii) the anticipated context of the user (standards laboratory, lecture theatre, power station); iv) the context-specific design characteristics (accuracy, portability, robustness); v) skill required in regular usage (specially trained expertise for fragile research apparatus, or rudimentary abilities for off-the-shelf devices); and vi) the audiences by which instruments and their usage are adjudicated (entertainment-seeking populace, institutional meetings, commercial customers, college students, or discerning antiquarians).

HEILBRON provides an extremely detailed history of electricity in the 18th century, describing both the institutional and scientific development, without, however, relating one to the other. The other literature on the period is more focused. Of great importance in the story of electricity was the development of the frictional machine, a topic central to HACKMANN. The frictional "electrical machine", first shown by Francis Hauksbee Snr in 1705, was developed in Britain and Germany in the 1740s for spectacular demonstrations of electrical effects, and by the end of the century such machines could accomplish the electrocution of small animals, magnetize needles and melt several yards of wire. BEN-CHAIM describes Stephen Gray's researches for the Royal Society in the 1720s and 1730s, which showed the possibility of "communicating" electrical effects along metallic wires, and the comparative difficulty of doing so with other (insulating) materials. In 1745–46, the Leyden jar – the ancestor of the capacitor (American: condenser) – was invented; this device was a particularly fertile, if controversial, resource for Benjamin Franklin in debates over the competing "fluid" theories of electricity in the 1750s and 1760s. Electrometers, based on the earlier pithball electroscope, were developed in the 1760s and 1770s as metal-leafed devices that qualitatively registered the presence of electricity. Around 1785, Charles Coulomb used an apparatus based on an electrometer stalk to develop his quantitative "Newtonian" inverse square law of electrostatic force – a law somewhat contested outside France. The development of the instrument-making trade is obviously an important backdrop to this story.

Heilbron's large monograph concludes with a new electrical phenomenon that emerged in the latter phases of Coulomb's researches. In 1791, Luigi Galvani claimed the discovery of "animal electricity" in the twitching legs of a newly killed frog, and five years later Volta developed the metallic "pile" to argue for the inorganic nature of this new phenomenon. The unresolved relationship between the three species of electricity – common, animal, and voltaic – and the "magnetic" fluid stimulated new debates and instrumental innovations in the early 19th century. STOCK & VAUGHAN relate how, in 1819–20, Hans Christian Ørsted of Denmark explored the remarkable deflections of a compass needle in the vicinity of a wire connected to a "voltaic" pile. In the flurry of international interest that followed, Johann Salomo Christoph Schweigger and Johann Christian Poggendorff harnessed Ørsted's finding in a device that used the deflection of a compass needle to indicate the size of voltaic effect ("current") in a wire. This "multiplier" or "galvanoscope" was developed by Claude Servais Matthias Pouillet in 1837 into the quantitative instrument familiar to modern readers as the tangent galvanometer. Such devices became prototypes for several generations of measuring and indicating instruments used in the new technologies of electrochemistry and telegraphy, as well as in associated "philosophical" researches.

GOODING shows that the emblematic form of the Ørsted phenomenon for English researchers was the "pocket" rotation apparatus that Michael Faraday produced in 1821. Most of Faraday's time, though, was spent preparing his apparatus for popular lectures on his recent electrical research at the Royal Institution. At these lectures, Faraday displayed his 1831 "discovery" of electromagnetic induction; this was soon employed, as GEE points out, by inventive contemporaries in prototype electrical motors. HUNT (1991) discusses Faraday's occasional involvement with Charles Wheatstone and Latimer Clark in the early development of cable telegraphy. MORUS emphasizes that telegraphy was one of several exciting new technologies, widely addressed by populist lecturers contemporary (and competing) with Faraday. Sturgeon and Barlow in Britain, and Morse and Henry in the US, developed electrical instruments for the theatrical display of telegraphy, electrical engines, and voltaic piles to inquisitive fee-paying audiences. Technical details of some of these instruments are elegantly, if idiosyncratically, catalogued by TURNER.

DUNSHEATH locates the history of telegraphy within a tradition of engineering instrumentation. He writes with particular regard for the various ingenious forms of sending, receiving, and line-testing equipment (such as bridges and potentiometers) devised by Wheatstone and others for use on overland lines from the late 1830s. With several undersea cables in place by the mid-1850s, commercial ambitions were directed towards a transatlantic cable, first laid in 1857–58 but which ceased operating soon after. The mirror-galvanometer devised by Sir William Thomson (later Lord Kelvin) for reading the faint messages that this cable transmitted in its last dying weeks was crucial. SMITH & WISE's study of Kelvin also emphasises such instrumental developments. HUNT (1993) discusses the mirror-galvanometer within the development of electrical standards. The conclusions of the official enquiry into the expensive breakdown of this cable recommended greater precision in the quality control measurements for telegraphic manufacture and maintenance, especially for the electrical resistance of cable materials. HUNT (1996)

examines the dispute between scientists and more practically-based telegraph engineers in the apportioning of blame for the failure of the cable, and how scientists managed to make their theoretical techniques indispensable in further cable-laying. SCHAFFER shows that this was followed by a competition between the British Association for the Advancement of Science and the Anglo-German Siemens company to establish international standards of electrical measurement, especially for resistance. GOODAY (1990) shows how the instrumentation and material standards of telegraphy were deployed in the first British teaching laboratories in physics in the 1860s, and GOODAY (1991) does the same for the first electrical engineering laboratories during the 1880s.

WILLIAMS provides a detailed, comparative study of the instrument-makers involved in the precision area of the electrical industry in France and Britain from 1870 up to the eve of World War II. Several of the instrument companies that grew to eminence in serving the international telegraph industry, such as Elliotts of London and James White in Glasgow, continued to thrive as the new industries of electrical power and light rose in the early 1880s. Dunsheath explains, and LYALL catalogues, the proliferation of ammeters, voltmeters, shunts, wattmeters dynamometers and so forth employed by electrical engineers in the construction, maintenance and running of their networks. These authors also deal with the new instruments created in the 1890s to deal with the challenges of the alternate current technology that was becoming a serious commercial rival to direct current schemes.

For more detailed studies, GOODAY (1995) relates the original work of William Edward A. Ayrton and John P. Perry in inventing and naming the ammeter and voltmeter in the years 1880–84. He deals especially with their efforts to develop direct-reading dials to replace the earlier time-consuming methods of multiplying galvanometer readings by proportional constants, or of constructing daily calibration charts for non-linear devices. BROWN surveys the multiplicity of early domestic power meters available up to 1892, and their dual role of satisfying the generating companies economic interests, and yet also of reassuring the consumer of the fairness of commercial charging. SENIOR's highly original thesis deals with the controversial attempts to adapt electrical instrumentation to medical diagnosis and treatment in Britain between 1860 and 1920. PHILLIPS's account of the invention of the oscillograph by William Duddell for analysing AC waveforms in the mid-1890s should be read in conjunction with CATTERMOLE & WOLFE's story of the Cambridge Scientific Instrument Company, which mass-produced these devices.

DUNSHEATH and STOCK & VAUGHAN give selective surveys of the genesis of electronic equipment. In the late 1890s, the cathode ray tube was an essential resource for many researchers, especially those working on X-rays and the electron. This tube was transformed by Fleming and De Forest into the "valve" (American: "tube") that enabled electronic amplification of electrical signals. This valve was especially invaluable for early "wireless" radio technology, being replaced after World War II by the semiconductor transistor. For the measurement devices described above, valves and later transistors were put to work in the Avometer – a multipurpose and conveniently portable device that could be used to measure current, voltage or resistance as appropriate. Another important application of electronics in the 1960s was the introduction of digital technology that enabled users to make precise numerical readings by merely glancing at an LED display.

Historical scholarship on electrical instruments has now begun to synthesize museological and antiquarian traditions with the more radical approaches of sociology and cultural studies. Drawing substantially on the work of Bruno Latour, O'CONNELL emphasizes that voltage standards have never been unproblematic, self-contained reference points in electrical measurement; rather, they need frequent human attention, the allocation of expensive resources, and a high degree of specialized skills in order to behave in anything like a "universally" standardized way. Gooday (1995) argues that late 19th-century practices in the representation of electrical measurement reveal significant differences; while electrical engineers cherished the utilitarian efficiency of the direct-reading ammeter and voltmeter, many physicists preferred the self-helpful rigour required in using tangent-galvanometers to gain "authentic", but painstaking, access to electrical "realities". HUNT (1996) shows that, in the battle over attributing blame for the failure of the first Atlantic cable, the instruments involved were not only the subject of politically-loaded scapegoating, but could also be imputed intriguing gender characteristics. Future studies must surely offer even more valuable insights on the human practice of using electrical instruments.

GRAEME J.N. GOODAY

See also Electrical Engineering; Electricity; Electromagnetism; Galvanic Battery; Instrument Makers; Telegraphy

Electricity

Appleyard, Rollo, *The History of the Institution of Electrical Engineers, 1871–1931*, London: Institution of Electrical Engineers, 1939

Bowers, Brian, *A History of Electric Light and Power*, New York: Peregrinus, and Stevenage, Hertfordshire: Peregrinus/Science Museum, 1982

Burns, R.W., *British Television: The Formative Years*, Stevenage, Hertfordshire: Peregrinus/Science Museum, 1986

Byatt, I.C.R., *The British Electrical Industry, 1875–1914: The Economic Returns of a New Technology*, Oxford: Clarendon Press, and New York: Oxford University Press, 1979

Coopersmith, Jonathan, *The Electrification of Russia, 1880–1926*, Ithaca, New York: Cornell University Press, 1992

Dunsheath, Percy, *A History of Electrical Engineering*, London: Faber and Faber, and New York: Pitman, 1962

Hackmann, W.D., *Electricity from Glass: The History of the Frictional Electrical Machine, 1600–1850*, Alphen aan den Rijn: Sijthoff & Noordhoff, 1978

Heilbron, J.L., *Electricity in the 17th and 18th Centuries: A Study of Early Modern Physics*, Berkeley: University of California Press, 1979

Hollister-Short, Graham and Frank A.J.L. James (eds), *History of Technology*, vol. 13, London: Mansell, 1991

Hughes, Thomas P., *Networks of Power: Electrification in Western Society, 1880–1930*, Baltimore: Johns Hopkins University Press, 1983

James, Frank A.J.L., "Davy in the Dockyard: Humphry Davy, the Royal Society and the Electro-Chemical Protection of the Copper Sheeting of His Majesty's Ships in the mid 1820s", *Physis*, 29 (1992): 205–25

Luckin, Bill, *Questions of Power: Electricity and Environment in Inter-War Britain*, Manchester: Manchester University Press, 1990

McMahon, A. Michal, *The Making of a Profession: A Century of Electrical Engineering in America*, New York: Institute of Electrical and Electronic Engineers, 1984

Mottelay, P.F., *Bibliographical History of Electricity & Magnetism*, London: Charles Griffin, 1922

Nye, David E., *Electrifying America: Social Meanings of a New Technology, 1880–1940*, Cambridge, Massachusetts: MIT Press, 1990

Papers Presented at the IEE Annual Weekend Meetings on the History of Electrical Engineering, 1973

Electricity is not only a fundamental force of nature, but the technological process of electrification has transformed society in ways unimaginable a century or so ago. It is therefore not surprising that there is a vast literature on electricity and electrical technology, of which the above is only a small sample. This sample has been selected to give a broad overview of major topics, and many of the texts contain extensive bibliographies for further reading on more specific subjects. MOTTELAY provides some indication of the large quantity of early literature on electricity. Furthermore, the biographies of many of those who studied electricity – such as Joseph Priestley, Benjamin Franklin, Charles Coulomb, Alessandro Volta, Humphry Davy, Hans Christian Ørsted, André-Marie Ampère, Michael Faraday, Charles Wheatstone, James Clerk Maxwell, William Thomson (Lord Kelvin), Thomas Alva Edison, Alexander Bell, Oliver Heaviside, William Henry Preece, R.E.B. Crompton, Joseph Swan, Heinrich Hertz, Guglielmo Marconi, and Alan Turing, as well as company histories such as those of GEC, Ferranti, Siemens, Westinghouse, and IBM – contain a great deal of information about the history of the understanding of electricity and of its use.

From the ancient Greeks until the end of the 18th century, the only form of electricity that could be studied under controlled conditions was static electricity, generated by rubbing glass with a fabric such as silk. By the 17th century, this process had been mechanised by the rotation of glass plates, spheres, or cylinders across a material such as catskin, either to create a discharge or to be stored in Leyden jars. This form of electricity is the subject of HACKMANN (whose focus is on the instrumentation) and HEILBRON (who gives a comprehensive account of work with electricity throughout Europe), and they show the sophistication that experimental and theoretical studies of electrostatics had reached by the end of the 18th century. Neither of them studies later developments of the production of static electricity involving Wimshurst machines or van der Graff generators. The only other form of electricity that could be studied before the 19th century was lightning; there was considerable effort during the 18th and 19th centuries to combat the effects of lightning by developing efficient lightning conductors, but, surprisingly, there has been no full scale study of this.

HOLLISTER-SHORT & JAMES show how Volta's invention of the electric battery at the end of the 18th century allowed, during the first third of the 19th century, a transformation in the understanding of electricity, and an extension of the uses of electricity both for scientific research and, for the first time, practical purposes. Davy's electrochemical experiments, Ørsted's discovery of electromagnetism, Ampère's theories of electro-dynamics, Faraday's discoveries of electromagnetic rotations and induction, were all predicated on Volta's invention. Furthermore, Faraday's enunciation of the field theory of electromagnetism permitted Thomson, Maxwell and Heaviside, in their different ways, to produce mathematical equations that described the behaviour of electricity, and thus paved the way for the work of Hertz and Marconi on what became known as radio.

Technological applications of electricity from batteries, and from the new understanding of electrical phenomena they engendered, evolved in the early 19th century. One of the earliest applications, invented by Davy in the 1820s for the protection of the copper sheets of ships and discussed in JAMES, was not a practical success, despite the large resources committed to the project. However, the electric telegraph developed by Cooke, Wheatstone and others in the 1830s did fundamentally and irrevocably transform communication technology; it is discussed in BOWERS (within a history of electric light and power) and DUNSHEATH (within a more general history of electrical engineering), as well as in some of the essays in Hollister-Short & James (a special issue devoted to the history of electrical engineering to mark the bicentenary of the birth of Faraday).

It was the enormous growth of electric telegraphy that prompted the formation of the Society of Telegraph Engineers in 1871. Later (1889) this society became the Institution of Electrical Engineers, discussed in APPLEYARD. The reason for this change in name was that by the 1880s the technological applications of electricity were going far beyond electric telegraphy, and there was a recognition of the necessity for a professional institution (like those for civil and mechanical engineers) to develop standards both for the use of electricity and for the practice of electrical engineers themselves. In very broad terms, a similar pattern of professionalization and institutionalization was followed in the United States, and this is discussed in McMAHON, although in Russia it was very different, as COOPERSMITH shows.

The use of electricity for lighting, power supply, and traction was, by the 1880s, becoming a practical possibility. Previous attempts to use electricity as the source of illumination for lighthouses (by Faraday using arc lamps in the 1850s and 1860s), or for traction (by Moritz Jacobi and by Robert Davidson using electric motors in the 1830s), had failed. What gave the impetus to the technological use of electricity was the independent invention by Swan and Edison of the filament lamp in the late 1870s, discussed in both Bowers and Dunsheath. However, the spread of the use of electricity for technological purposes was not particularly rapid, and the economic reasons for this in Britain are examined in BYATT, which also provides an account of the development of electricity supply and of the manufacture of electrical plant.

The enormous social impact of electrification is implicit in many studies, but is brought out explicitly in NYE in the case of the United States, and in the classic study by HUGHES in a comparison of Berlin, London and Chicago. Of course, there was a perceived downside to the process of electrification, for instance in the disfigurement of landscapes by electric pylons. This and other similar topics form the subject of LUCKIN.

Most of the studies of the development of heavy electrical engineering tend to stop in the 1930s, when the major problems of the use and distribution of electricity had been overcome. In the ensuing years, innovation in using electricity centred on "lighter" engineering projects, such as the development of radio, telephone, radar, television (discussed in BURNS), and computer technology. There is a rapidly developing literature on these subjects as the sources become available to undertake scholarly study, and much useful material is to be found in the volumes of *PAPERS PRESENTED AT THE IEE* dealing with the post-1940 period.

FRANK A.J.L. JAMES

See also Galvanic Battery

Electromagnetism

Aitken, Hugh G.J., *Syntony and Spark: The Origins of Radio*, New York: Wiley, 1976

Buchwald, Jed Z., *From Maxwell to Microphysics: Aspects of Electromagnetic Theory in the Last Quarter of the Nineteenth Century*, Chicago: University of Chicago Press, 1985

Cahan, David (ed.), *Hermann von Helmholtz and the Foundations of Nineteenth-Century Science*, Berkeley: University of California Press, 1993

Harman, Peter Michael, *Energy, Force, and Matter: The Conceptual Development of Nineteenth Century Physics*, Cambridge and New York: Cambridge University Press, 1982

Harman, Peter Michael (ed.), *Wranglers and Physicists: Studies on Cambridge Physics in the Nineteenth Century*, Manchester: Manchester University Press, 1985

Hendry, John, *James Clerk Maxwell and the Theory of the Electromagnetic Field*, Bristol and Boston: Adam Hilger, 1986

Hesse, Mary B., *Forces and Fields: The Concept of Action at a Distance in the History of Physics*, London and New York: Nelson, 1961

Hunt, Bruce J., *The Maxwellians*, Ithaca, New York: Cornell University Press, 1991

Jungnickel, Christa and Russell McCormmach, *Intellectual Mastery of Nature: Theoretical Physics from Ohm to Einstein*, vol. 2: *The Now Mighty Theoretical Physics 1870–1925*, Chicago: University of Chicago Press, 1986

Kargon, Robert and Peter Achinstein (eds), *Kelvin's Baltimore Lectures and Modern Theoretical Physics: Historical and Philosophical Perspectives*, Cambridge, Massachusetts: MIT Press, 1987

Schaffner, Kenneth F., *Nineteenth-Century Aether Theories*, Oxford and New York: Pergamon Press, 1972

Siegel, Daniel M., *Innovation in Maxwell's Electromagnetic Theory: Molecular Vortices, Displacement Current, and*

Light, Cambridge and New York: Cambridge University Press, 1991

Smith, Crosbie and M. Norton Wise, *Energy and Empire: A Biographical Study of Lord Kelvin*, Cambridge and New York: Cambridge University Press, 1989

In 1820 Hans Christian Ørsted showed that an electric current can prompt a kick in a magnetic needle. Faraday is one of the more famous researchers of these effects, but electromagnetism only really became a prominent part of physics in the latter half of the 19th century with the growth of telegraphy and the work of such individuals as William Thomson (Lord Kelvin), James Clerk Maxwell, and Hermann von Helmholtz. This entry covers the literature on the period between Faraday and relativity theory.

HARMAN (1982) provides an introduction to the theories of electromagnetism in the mid-19th century, while SCHAFFNER is a good collection of sources on the aether versions of electromagnetism (containing papers by Augustin Jean Fresnel, Jean Gabriel Stokes, Albert A. Michelson & Morley, Green, Louis MacCullagh, William Thomson, George Francis FitzGerald, Oliver Heaviside, Larmor, and Hendrick Anton Lorentz). HESSE gives a basic philosophical account of the way in which the development of electromagnetism involved major metaphysical debates on the contrasts between action at a distance and field theories.

A number of books analyse Maxwell's work on the development of the equations bearing his name. HENDRY has chosen what he describes as a narrow set of concerns: the technical details of physical theory and scientific methodology. He shows how Maxwell took up Faraday's "lines of force" and developed them into a full-blown electromagnetical theory, at a time when the energy principle was still being expounded, and how, in Maxwell's later work, the synthesis of Lagrangian dynamics and energy conservation played a significant role. SIEGEL focuses on Maxwell's development of the concept of the displacement current in 1861, while working on electromagnetic equations, and investigates Maxwell's electromagnetic theory of light within the context of the molecular vortex model.

The articles in HARMAN (1985) analyse a number of aspects of physics at Cambridge University, the institution where Maxwell became a professor, and where a great deal of electromagnetic research took place. The book begins with Sir Edmund Whittaker, whose *History of the Theories of Aether and Electricity* (1951–53) famously failed to mention Einstein. Whether it makes sense to talk of a Cambridge school does not become clear, however. Topics covered include education, relations with other disciplines (such as physical geology), William Thomson, and Maxwell. A paper by Jed Buchwald describes a method developed at Cambridge for explaining electromagnetic phenomena without recourse to microphysics by altering the field equations.

Maxwell's equations in modern-day physics textbooks look very different from the equations that Maxwell devised. HUNT describes the genesis of the equations that all physicists now know, by looking at the self-designated "Maxwellians": G. F. FitzGerald, Oliver Lodge, Oliver Heaviside, and Heinrich Hertz. It was, for instance, only with Heaviside that one gets the convenient notation with "curl", and so forth. Hunt shows,

through the example of Heaviside, who was an employee of a telegraph company, that the theory had great relevance for the practical concerns of electrotechnology. Whereas Hunt focuses on the people who were in correspondence and in effect came to define Maxwell's work, BUCHWALD's notion of the concept is much broader: everyone who took up the Maxwell equations and worked with them qualifies as a Maxwellian. Electromagnetism is thus equated with Maxwellian physics. Buchwald's main concern is to depict the development from electromagnetism, focusing on the field, to a physics containing electrons. While Buchwald ignores the concomitant history of technology, AITKEN provides a most useful complement, detailing the developments from electromagnetic experimentation to usable radio waves.

KARGON & ACHINSTEIN reprint 20 lectures that Lord Kelvin gave in Baltimore, first published in 1904. In addition, a number of rather disparate papers investigate various historical and philosophical topics. Norton Wise and Crosbie Smith, for instance, analyse the historical shift from a focus on dynamical models of the aether to Maxwellian mathematical structures.

SMITH & WISE's extensive biography of William Thomson (Lord Kelvin) is the first book that brings the connection with electrotechnology to the fore. The authors show in great detail Kelvin's simultaneous concern for physical theory, the instrumentation for use in both telegraphic practice and physics laboratories, and his involvement in practical and financial telegraphic affairs. Kelvin was prominent in all fields, and Smith & Wise highlight how closely related these fields actually are. Their book is a forceful argument for a history of electromagnetism that uses more historical sources than scientific journals.

CAHAN's edited volume consists of three sections on Helmholtz as physiologist, physicist, and philosopher. The second section contains a number of very good papers on the history of electromagnetism. Buchwald, for example, argues that Helmholtz conceived and developed the notion that physics is the science of objects that interact through system energies that are determined by the physical states of the objects at any given moment, and that this had a wealth of implications for both theory and experiment. Walter Kaiser shows Helmholtz's central role in introducing Maxwell's work to German physicists; in this, and in the guidance of a great number of students, Maxwell was instrumental in the formation of what was to be called "classical" electrodynamics. Kaiser finds it ironical that it was one of Helmholtz's students, Heinrich Hertz, who, with his detection of electromagnetic waves, vindicated Maxwell's theory, and put into question the predictive capacity of Helmholtz's rival version of electromagnetic theory.

JUNGNICKEL & McCORMMACH's grand institutional history of physics in Germany, culminating in the development of theoretical physics, also emphasises Helmholtz's tremendous influence on the development of the field, and shows how his electrodynamics was pursued by his students, who went on to occupy a great many university chairs in the newly-united Germany.

SIMON SCHAFFER

See also Aether; Electrical Engineering; Electrical Instruments; Electricity; Helmholtz; Hertz; Maxwell

Embryology

Cole, Francis Joseph, *Early Theories of Sexual Generation*, Oxford: Clarendon Press, 1930

Dinsmore, Charles E., *A History of Regeneration Research: Milestones in the Evolution of a Concept*, Cambridge and New York: Cambridge University Press, 1991

Dunstan, G.R., *The Human Embryo: Aristotle and the Arabic and European Tradition*, Exeter: University of Exeter Press, 1990

Farley, John, *Gametes and Spores: Ideas About Sexual Reproduction, 1750–1914*, Baltimore: Johns Hopkins University Press, 1982

Gasking, Elizabeth B., *Investigations into Generation, 1651–1828*, London: Hutchinson, and Baltimore: Johns Hopkins University Press, 1967

Gilbert, Scott F. (ed.), *A Conceptual History of Modern Embryology*, Baltimore: Johns Hopkins University Press, 1991

Horder, T.J., J.A. Witkowski and C.C. Wylie (eds), *A History of Embryology*, Cambridge and New York: Cambridge University Press, 1986

Needham, Joseph, *A History of Embryology*, Cambridge: Cambridge University Press, 1934; revised edition, with Arthur Hughes, New York: Abelard-Schuman, 1959

Oppenheimer, Jane, *Essays in the History of Embryology and Biology*, Cambridge, Massachusetts: MIT Press, 1967

Twentieth-century scientists have inherited complex problems about reproductive generation and regeneration from their intellectual forebears. However, questions such as the difference between inert and animate matter, the point at which the soul becomes integrated into the body, and the feasibility of spontaneous generation, have to some extent been replaced by concerns over tissue culture technique, cellular growth, and differentiation, and the influences that organize embryogenesis as an orderly, predictable process.

Questions about how we come to be recognizably human through embryonic development, why some children resemble one parent more than another, and how twins arise have always concerned natural philosophers. Until the 19th century, the preformation theory predominated in embryological thought. This theory proposed that the embryo existed in a fully preformed, yet miniature, state prior to conception, and embryonic development occurred by an increase in size of the pre-existent embryo. Arguments arose between preformationists over whether the preformed entity existed in the ovum or the sperm. However, experimental findings that chicks arose, after fertilization, from a homogenous living matter that gradually unfolded in a regularly observed order to form the fully-formed fetus, gained support for the theory of epigenesis. Many materialists opposed the epigenesis account of embryonic creation, as they deemed it implied that an essential or vital force was inherent in living matter.

DUNSTAN gathered 15 essays from the Constantinus Africanus Colloquy of 1988 that addressed ways in which some of the long-standing questions surrounding embryology were answered throughout history. This work begins with a discussion of how the unseen embryo became human according to Greek thought. Other contributors address Arabic science and religious thought, Maimonides and the fetus as a natural miracle, planetary influence over embryonic development, the soul and the embryo in the Renaissance, and in the 19th and 20th centuries the human embryo's legal rights.

Cole, Needham, and Gasking provide three rather traditional chronological histories of embryology. COLE focuses on the preformation doctrine, from the 17th-century development of the microscope through to the mid-19th century. The use of the microscope allowed a whole new world to appear to natural philosophers, but histories of embryology often neglect to mention that the diverse ways of describing the particulate appearance of nature, as well as the ineptitude of many of those using the early microscope, restricted any micro-world concepts from gaining immediate universal acceptance. Giving equal space to four chronological eras – antiquity, the Renaissance, the 17th century, and the 18th century – NEEDHAM's survey depicts embryology as a succession of progressive advancements. GASKING examines the interconnections between the factual discoveries of generation – the term used throughout history to indicate the coming into existence of a new organism – and the theoretical opinions advanced by scientists. Gasking concentrates on the study of development from William Harvey's publication of *Exercitationes de Generatione Animalium* in 1651, to Karl Ernst von Baer's announcement in 1828 of the identification of the mammalian egg. Harvey broke away from Aristotelian thinking, claiming that the egg was not produced by intermingling with other secretions, but was itself the initial primordium – *ex ova omnia*. Harvey viewed all types of generation, including human, as special cases exemplified by the study of the hen.

Picking up from the 18th century, FARLEY's work begins at the time when Linnaeus had developed a classificatory scheme on the ambiguity of the sexual organs. He examines work during the period on such questions as the universality of sexual reproduction, the nature of the substances liberated by plant and animal sexual organs, and the role these substances might play. Farley ends with a discussion of Frank Lillie's work on fertilization, and, in a provocative conclusion, argues that general biological instruction about sexual reproduction in the late 20th century (excluding discussion of sex hormones) is "basically identical to the views that were propagated in 1914".

Few, if any, embryologists around the world have devoted as much study to the history of embryology as Jane M. Oppenheimer. The cited work includes "intellectually teasing and historically remarkable" problems that embryological thinkers have faced. Unlike other histories, OPPENHEIMER presents her essays in reverse chronological order, claiming that "we understand our contemporaries more clearly than our earlier predecessors ... [thus] the design of the volume is ... intended to conduct us from what we know best towards what we see only more dimly". Topics discussed include the problems and concepts explored through experimental embryology (including an extensive bibliography), embryology and evolution, the non-specificity of the germ layers, and the experimental investigations of Ross Harrison, Baer, John and William Hunter, Sir Thomas Browne, William Harvey and William Gilbert.

Several books expand the focus of embryological histories by addressing the concept of the philosophy of embryology.

DINSMORE has collected papers first presented at the American Society of Zoologists' symposium of 1988 on the history of regeneration research. Regeneration, it is argued, is one biological field where theoretical models have dominated experimental findings for centuries. Even today, planaria regeneration is one of the most widely used "experiments" to introduce children to the wonders of nature. Theories on lizard tail regeneration, crayfish appendage replacement, and the regenerative capacity of the polyp are reconsidered in specific historical contexts in an attempt to dispel the myths and erroneous beliefs surrounding regeneration. The life and contributions of R.A.F. de Réaumur, Abraham Trembley, and Lazzaro Spallanzani are selectively discussed as having framed the questions that have become fundamental to present-day developmental biology. An interesting review of the 19th-century nerve-dependent regeneration studies, and observations on bioelectric phenomena, is presented in the context of varied expressions of the generative response.

HORDER, WITKOWSKI & WYLIE have collected papers devoted to the scientific and philosophical concepts of embryological preformation, induction, regeneration and reduction. Highlights of the careers of August Weismann, Thomas Hunt Morgan, Ross Harrison, Hans Spemann, and C.H. Waddington are discussed. Beyond the scope of other collections, this work also devotes considerable attention to the teaching traditions in embryology.

GILBERT's work turns readers' attention to the broader world of developmental biology – the science that includes the study of embryology as well as that of gene activity, regeneration, and intracellular functions. The availability of monoclonal antibodies, antisense mRNAs, and confocal microscopes allows new investigative ways of analyzing the development of frogs, chicks, and sea urchins. This interdisciplinary collection begins with an examination of the tradition of comparative embryology based on the chick embryo. The mosaic developmental patterns of embryos are discussed, as are the ways in which personal and national ideologies have shaped the interpretations of the mosaic experiments. Spemann's concept of "induction" is discussed in the context of experiments on lens and neural tube formation. More than other collections on embryology history, this work includes discussion of state-of-the-art investigations into the development of the critically – important cell surface, the formation of molecules responsible for adhesion between cells, and the conceptualization of the embryo in biochemical terms.

PHILIP K. WILSON

Encyclopedias

Arnar, Anna Sigridur (ed.), *Encyclopedism from Pliny to Borges*, Chicago: University of Chicago Press, 1990

Becq, Annie (ed.), *L'Encyclopédisme: Actes du Colloque de Caen*, Paris: Editions Amateurs de Livres, 1991

Collison, Robert, *Encyclopaedias: Their History Throughout the Ages: A Bibliographical Guide*, New York: Hafner, 1964

Darnton, Robert, *The Business of Enlightenment: A Publishing History of the Encyclopédie, 1775–1800*, Cambridge, Massachusetts: Belknap Press of Harvard University Press, 1979

Hahn, Roger, "Science and the Arts in France: The Limitations of an Encyclopedic Ideology", *Studies in Eighteenth-century Culture*, 10 (1981): 77–93

Hughes, Arthur, "Science in English Encyclopedia, 1704–1875", *Annals of Science*, 7 (1951): 340–70; 8 (1952): 323–67; 9 (1953): 233–64; 11 (1955): 74–92

Kafker, Frank A., "Notable Encyclopedias of the Seventeenth and Eighteenth Centuries: Nine Predecessors of the *Encyclopédie*", *Studies on Voltaire and the Eighteenth Century* (special issue), 194 (1981)

Kafker, Frank A. (ed.), "Notable Encyclopedias of the Late Eighteenth Century: Eleven Successors of the *Encyclopédie*", *Studies on Voltaire and the Eighteenth Century* (special issue), 315 (1994)

McArthur, Tom, *Worlds of Reference: Lexicography, Learning and Language from the Clay Tablet to the Computer*, Cambridge and New York: Cambridge University Press, 1986

Proust, Jacques, *L'Encyclopédie de Diderot et D'Alembert*, Paris: Hachette, 1985

Sarton, George, *A Guide to the History of Science: A First Guide for the Study of the History of Science, with Introductory Essays on Science and Tradition*, Waltham, Massachusetts: Chronica Botanica, 1952

Shorr, Philip, *Science and Superstition in the Eighteenth Century: A Study of the Treatment of Science in Two Encyclopedias of 1725–1750*, New York: Columbia University Press, and London: King, 1932; reprinted, New York: AMS Press, 1967

Thorndike, Lynn, "Encyclopedias of the Fourteenth Century", in *A History of Magic and Experimental Science*, vol. 3, New York: Macmillan and New York: Columbia University Press, 1924

Thorndike, Lynn, "L'Encyclopédie and the History of Science", *Isis*, 6 (1924): 361–86

Wells, James M., *The Circle of Knowledge: Encyclopedias Past and Present* (exhibition catalogue), Chicago: Newberry Library, 1969

Yeo, Richard, "Reading Encyclopedias: Science and the Organization of Knowledge in British Dictionaries of Arts and Sciences", *Isis*, 82 (1991): 24–29

Since the collections of Roman writers such as Varro and Pliny the Elder, scientific knowledge of various kinds has been included in works of encyclopedic aspiration. Although the term "encyclopedia" appears not to have been used in a title until 1559, the task of summarising the subjects deemed worthy of a place in the Greek "round of learning" was influential in the creation of the compendia of the Middle Ages. By the 18th century, dictionaries of arts and sciences (often titled "encyclopedias") made a special point of their treatment of scientific knowledge and, importantly, of arts and crafts, previously excluded from the status of *scientia*.

SARTON recognised this presence of science in encyclopedias, remarking that, "historians of science need not only the latest encyclopedias but also the old ones . . . [which] offer one of the simplest means of recapturing the educated opinion of earlier times". Since this declaration, historians of science have used encyclopedias as sources, but have not been leaders in the study of encyclopedias as cultural phenomena. Most work on the compiling, editing, organising, and selling of encyclopedias has been done by librarians, historians of publishing, and intellectual historians interested in the French *Encyclopédie* and its contributors.

The indispensable survey by COLLISON charts the major changes in size, content, and format of Western (and some other) encyclopedias since the pre-Christian era. The place of science within them is not his main concern, although he is alert to the importance of geometry and astronomy in the quadrivium of the university curriculum covered by the medieval encyclopedias. THORNDIKE (1924) gives a more detailed account of how some encyclopedic works of the 14th century incorporated natural knowledge. In a narrative that extends from papyrus to new information technology, McARTHUR views encyclopedias as one of the ways humans have stored knowledge. Although not focusing on science in any detail, he notes the appeal to "scientific" method and system in the organisation of some of these works. Other recent overviews, deriving from library exhibitions of encyclopedic texts and cabinets of curiosity, are offered by WELLS and ARNAR. Both include some description of the astonishing miscellanies published during the Renaissance, and document the considerable presence of scientific and technical information in the engraved plates carried by encyclopedias from the 18th century onwards.

Most work on encyclopedias of the Enlightenment focuses on the famous *Encyclopédie* begun by Diderot and D'Alembert in 1751, several writers regarding it as a powerful force for the interpretation and diffusion of science. THORNDIKE's 1924 article in *Isis* discusses the *Encyclopédie*'s attitude to science, observing that the affirmation of recent scientific theories is more often linked to a dismissal of medieval beliefs than to an attack on prevailing religious orthodoxy. HAHN also rejects the view that the work was a *machine de guerre* in the critique of Church and State, and says its attempt to align science with the mechanical arts and crafts was a more radical, though partly unsuccessful, aspect. PROUST offers a critical account of the ideological programme of the *Encyclopédie*; and DARNTON provides a definitive examination of the publishing history of the *Encyclopédie methodique*, begun in 1781 as the successor to the first version, noting the inclusion of major articles on the sciences, some written by leading experts, and arranged within 26 disciplinary volumes. The two collective volumes edited by KAFKER (1981 and 1994) are valuable discussions of the European forerunners and successors of the *Encyclopédie*; some of the chapters consider the scientific content of dictionaries, such as John Harris's *Lexicon Technicum* (1704). The volume of conference papers edited by BECQ includes approaches from literary history and philosophy, which compare encyclopedias from different countries and periods.

Apart from Thorndike, there are some other exceptions to the absence of work by historians of science on encyclopedias. SHORR provides an analysis of the treatment of science in Ephraim Chambers's *Cyclopedia* (1728) and Johann Zedler's *Grosses vollständiges Universal Lexicon* (1732–59), suggesting that these works are useful indexes to contemporary ideas about science. From this premise, he considers the extent to which they assimilated the "new science" of the 17th century, finding that although they did generally reject magical and occult explanations of natural phenomena, they had not broken completely with medieval views on a number of topics. HUGHES, in a series of articles written at the time of Sarton's comments, examines the ways in which particular scientific topics – such as animistic qualities, atomism, heat, theories of the earth, and final causes – were treated in different editions of British encyclopedias from 1704 to 1875. In particular, he notes the way in which some entries were carried over across several editions, making them out of step with scientific advances. He sees the ninth edition of the *Encyclopedia Britannica* as breaking with this uneven coverage of previous editions, and as providing a synthesis of major scientific theories, such as the conservation of energy. The article by YEO complements these two earlier studies; he stresses the importance of the organisation of scientific (and other) material, making the point that although most encyclopedias after 1700 were alphabetical, the intellectual appeal of systematic arrangement remained throughout the Enlightenment. The *Encyclopedia Britannica* (first edition 1771) prided itself on treating the major sciences as coherent wholes within large treatises, even though these were placed under the appropriate letter of the alphabet. The *Encyclopedia Metropolitana* (1817–45) went further, partially adopting a systematic classification devised by Samuel Taylor Coleridge (his treatise on this is reprinted in Collison) that placed subjects in the order in which they were to be read. It boasted original articles by John Herschel on sound and light, but the length and detail of these (and others) made them inappropriate for the general reader, although some were issued separately as texts for use in university courses. Yeo argues that, by the early 19th century, encyclopedias no longer displayed the relationships between the sciences on a map of knowledge, or as a circle of sciences, but, instead, generally marked the boundaries between specialist disciplines.

I. RICHARD YEO

Endocrinology

Bliss, Michael, *The Discovery of Insulin*, Chicago: University of Chicago Press, and Toronto: McLelland and Stewart, 1982; London: Macmillan, 1987

Borell, Merriley, "Organotherapy, British Physiology and the Discovery of Internal Secretion", *Journal of the History of Biology*, 9 (1976): 235–68

Brooks, Chandler McC. *et al.*, *Humors, Hormones and Neurosecretions: The Origins and Development of Man's Present Knowledge of the Humoral Control of Body Function*, Albany: State University of New York, 1962

Clarke, Adele, "Controversy and the Development of Reproductive Science", *Social Problems*, 37 (1989): 18–37

Gruhn, John G. and Ralph R. Kazer, *Hormonal Regulation of the Menstrual Cycle: The Evolution of Concepts*, New York: Plenum Medical Books, 1989

Hall, Diana, "Biology, Sex Hormones and Sexism in the 1920s", *Philosophical Forum*, 5 (1974): 81–96

McCann, S.M. (ed.), *Endocrinology: People and Ideas*, Bethesda, Maryland: American Physiological Society, 1988

Medvei, Victor Cornelius, *A History of Endocrinology*,
    Lancaster: MTP Press, 1982

Medvei, Victor Cornelius, *The History of Clinical
    Endocrinology: A Comprehensive Account of
    Endocrinology from Earliest Times to the Present Day*,
    Carnforth, Lancashire, and Pearl River, New York:
    Parthenon, 1993

Oudshoorn, Nelly, *Beyond the Natural Body: An
    Archaeology of Sex Hormones*, London and New York:
    Routledge, 1994

Welbourn, Richard B. (ed.), *The History of Endocrine
    Surgery*, New York: Praeger, 1990

By far the most useful single survey of the development of endocrinology is MEDVEI (1993), a compendious history that is effectively a second, revised edition of MEDVEI (1982). He traces the emergence of modern knowledge from the ancient Chinese and Hindu traditions, through early research into the functions of what subsequently came to be known as the endocrine organs, to the most recent researches in endocrinology proper. His narrative is strong on biographical and institutional details, as well as on the intellectual content of endocrinological knowledge, and is the obvious starting point for anyone beginning to read in this area. More detail on specific topics may be found in two volumes by practising endocrinologists, which take a similarly presentist perspective on the growth of the field, particularly as it developed from the end of the 19th century. The essays edited by McCANN each take as their topic the growth of knowledge of a particular hormone or hormone complex, and will be more useful for those investigating specific episodes in the history of endocrinology than for readers interested in the development of the field as a whole. BROOKS *et al.* offer a useful account of the development of ideas on endocrine control, and valuable detail on the role of the nervous system, including recent knowledge of neurosecretions and nervous regulation of endocrine processes – a topic barely covered by Medvei.

As will rapidly become apparent to anyone reading in the history of endocrinology, the rapid development of scientific knowledge of endocrine function and internal secretions from the end of the 19th century depended heavily on the integration of clinical experience with laboratory-based research. This is clear, for instance, from the essays on the development of endocrine surgery edited by WELBOURN. As in McCann's volume, the essays are organised around particular endocrine organs, without any further attempt at chronological or thematic integration, but they do much to illustrate the close relationship between the development of scientific knowledge and clinical practice in this field. The extent to which the growth of laboratory-based research was itself driven by hopes of therapeutic success is made clear by BORELL, who details the debt of early endocrinology to the scientifically dubious, but commercially successful, use of animal organ extracts to treat a wide range of conditions. These therapeutic hopes were realised most spectacularly some 30 years later, in 1921–22, when a team of researchers at the University of Toronto isolated insulin and successfully demonstrated its value in the treatment of diabetes. BLISS unpicks the events leading up to and immediately following this important event in the history of endocrinology, and challenges any simplistic supposition that the discovery of insulin was merely a matter of putting into practice the insights provided by experimental science. In particular, he highlights the fact that scientists were initially sceptical about the success of insulin therapy, that there was great difficulty in obtaining conclusive therapeutic proof, and that the press and the drug company, Eli Lilly, played an important role in ensuring that early tests were pursued to a successful conclusion.

Another important factor in the growth of endocrinology from the late 19th century was the expectation that it would provide insights into the biology of sex and gender, and thus yield new techniques for regulating both sexual behaviour and reproduction. The political and social dimensions of this history are largely missing from the work of GRUHN & KAZER, who offer a straightforward internalist and progressivist account of the development of reproductive endocrinology. Nevertheless, their book provides a useful, if somewhat sketchy, overview of scientific developments in this field. The wider, social expectations shaping research into sex hormones from the 1920s are described in the papers by CLARKE and HALL.

OUDSHOORN develops these insights further by charting the complex interactions between physicians' therapeutic aspirations, the growth of the pharmaceutical industry, and the conduct of research into sex hormones up to the development of the contraceptive pill. Her work, which looks especially at the Netherlands, stresses the way in which gendered assumptions and practices determined both the kind of research that was conducted, and the kind of medical innovations that proved commercially viable. In particular, she makes clear that the existence of a specialism of gynaecology, and the absence of an equivalent specialism of male medicine, was an important factor in the successful development and marketing of hormone preparations aimed primarily at women rather than men.

STEVE STURDY

See also Gynaecology; Pharmacology

Energy

Brush, Stephen G., *The Temperature of History: Phases of
    Science and Culture in the Nineteenth Century*, New York:
    Franklin, 1978

Caneva, Kenneth L., *Robert Mayer and the Conservation of
    Energy*, Princeton: Princeton University Press, 1993

Cardwell, Donald S.L., *From Watt to Clausius: The Rise of
    Thermodynamics in the Early Industrial Age*, London:
    Heinemann, and Ithaca, New York: Cornell University
    Press, 1971

Cardwell, Donald, *James Joule: A Biography*, Manchester:
    Manchester University Press, 1989

Dahl, Per F., "Ludvig A. Colding and the Conservation of
    Energy", *Centaurus*, 8 (1963): 174–88

Elkana, Yehuda, *The Discovery of the Conservation of
    Energy*, Cambridge, Massachusetts: Harvard University
    Press, and London: Hutchinson, 1974

Forrester, John, "Chemistry and the Conservation of Energy:

The Work of James Prescott Joule", *Studies in History and Philosophy of Science*, 6 (1975): 273–313

Fox, Robert (ed.), *Reflexions on the Motive Power of Fire: A Critical Edition with the Surviving Scientific Manuscripts*, by Sadi Carnot, translated, with an introduction by Fox, Manchester: Manchester University Press, and New York: Lilian Barber Press, 1986

Heimann, Peter M., "Conservation of Forces and the Conservation of Energy", *Centaurus*, 18 (1974): 147–61

Heimann, Peter M., "Helmholtz and Kant: The Metaphysical Foundations of *Über die Erhaltung der Kraft*", *Studies in the History and Philosophy of Science*, 5 (1974): 205–38

Heimann, Peter, "Mayer's Concept of 'Force': The 'Axis' of a New Science of Physics", *Historical Studies in the Physical Sciences*, 7 (1976): 277–96

Hiebert, Erwin N., *Historical Roots of the Principle of Conservation of Energy*, Madison: Madison State Historical Society of Wisconsin, 1962

Hutchison, Keith, "W.J.M. Rankine and the Rise of Thermodynamics", *British Journal for the History of Science*, 14 (1981):1–26

Kuhn, Thomas S., "Energy Conservation as an Example of Simultaneous Discovery", in *Critical Problems in the History of Science*, edited by Marshall Clagett, Madison: University of Wisconsin Press, 1959: 321–56

Lindsay, Robert Bruce, *Julius Robert Mayer: Prophet of Energy*, Oxford: Pergamon Press, 1973

Mach, Ernst, *History and Root of the Principle of the Conservation of Energy*, translated from the 2nd edition and annotated by P.E.B. Jourdain, Chicago: Open Court, 1911 (original edition, 1872)

Morus, Iwan Rhys, "Correlation and Control: William Robert Grove and the Construction of a New Philosophy of Scientific Reform", *Studies in the History and Philosophy of Science*, 22 (1991): 589–621

Sarton, George, "The Discovery of the Law of Conservation of Energy", *Isis*, 13 (1929): 18–44

Sibum, Otto, "Reworking the Mechanical Value of Heat: Instruments of Precision and Gestures of Accuracy in Early Victorian England", *Studies in the History and Philosophy of Science*, 26 (1995): 73–106

Smith, Crosbie, *The Science of Energy: The Construction of Energy Physics in the Nineteenth Century*, London: Athlone Press, 1998

Smith, Crosbie and M. Norton Wise, *Energy and Empire: A Biographical Study of Lord Kelvin*, Cambridge and New York: Cambridge University Press, 1989

Stewart, Balfour, *The Conservation of Energy: Being an Elementary Treatise on Energy and Its Laws*, London: King, and New York: Appleton, 1874

Tait, P.G., *Sketch of Thermodynamics*, Edinburgh: Edmunston and Douglas, 1868; revised edition, Edinburgh: Douglas, 1877

Wise, M. Norton, "German Concepts of Force, Energy, and the Electromagnetic Ether: 1845–1880", in *Conceptions of Ether: Studies in the History of Ether Theories, 1740–1900*, edited by G.N. Cantor and M.J.S. Hodge, Cambridge and New York: Cambridge University Press, 1981, 269–307

From the 1850s commentators have promoted distinct histories of energy that serve competing national, professional, or epistemological interests. Nineteenth-century positivist narratives and 20th-century chronicles of scientific ideas single out lone prophets, or discoverers, of the law of energy conservation or of its perceived pre-requisites. But there is an alternative to this obsession with determining priority and with celebrating real or imagined founders. The thesis that there were multiple, largely independent, discoveries of the conservation law has a long history, and there has been much debate over the possibility of a group phenomenon of simultaneous discovery, which they attribute to scientific, technological, and cultural trigger-factors that were specific to the period 1830–50. Such a neat retrospective reconstruction blurs distinctions in scientific thought, intention, and practice, however, and some degree of clarification comes only when scholars turn again to individuals and their astonishingly varied cultural resources (in the life sciences, chemistry, physics, technology, philosophy, and religion), rival conceptions of the natural world, local skills, and competing agendas for scientific reform.

Within this diversity, there remains a split between those commentators who – in history as in science – emphasize philosophical guidance and those who favour empirical grounding. While some scholars trace the philosophical roots of a particular energy concept from the ancients through to Enlightenment rational mechanics, others lay stress on a mid-19th century cultural symbiosis of engine practice, work measurement, and the science of heat. One historian deploys a social contextualist model to analyse the construction, during the third quarter of the 19th century, of an expansive programme of energy-based physics. More generally, analysts locate the spaces of energy physics; trace the language of energy as it replaced vocabularies of natural powers, Newtonian forces, *Kraft*, and work; find energy's place in popular culture and literature; and examine the parallels between energy physics and varieties of 19th-century political economy.

A handful of disparate individuals dominates the literature. The Heilbron physician Robert Mayer linked the indestructibility of *Kraft* to notions of causality and animal heat in Liebig's *Annalen der Chemie* in 1842; the Mancunian James Prescott Joule deployed a paddle-wheel apparatus in Oxford in 1847 to argue from the evolution of heat by fluid friction – and other experiments – to the universal existence of a mechanical equivalent of heat; in Berlin in the same year the mechanical speculations of the polymath Hermann Helmholtz failed to slough off Kantian influences and appeared as *Über die Erhaltung der Kraft*. Immediately, men of science constructed serviceable accounts of their own or others' roles in generating the energy conservation law. John Tyndall at the Royal Institution promoted the more speculative Germans and downplayed Joule's merely experimental work (SMITH). A Dane, Ludvig Colding, reinterpreted a series of frictional experiments, designed in 1843 to substantiate a principle of the perpetuity of force, and in 1856 staked a claim to priority for the energy conservation law (DAHL).

Responding primarily to Tyndall, Tait, and Stewart placed popular histories of energy within early expositions of the new science of thermodynamics. TAIT marginalizes Mayer, and instead favours the British natural philosophers, with James Prescott Joule seen as the experimental founder, and with

William Thomson, Macquorn Rankine and, perhaps, Rudolf Clausius, as the elaborators of the two fundamental laws of energy conservation and dissipation. STEWART's universe is a vast physical machine governed by the laws of energy alone. His brief history of energy and energy conservation is thus an account of the entire cosmos: it traces a serpentine path from the ancients' knowledge of the "essential unrest and energy of things"; to the contemporary industrialist's search for clear conceptions of work; the engineer-physicist's empirical certainty of the impossibility of perpetual motion; the speculations on force transformations of Mayer and William Robert Grove, to the (apparently) triumphant and incontrovertible – since experimental – labours of Joule.

MACH is a vehicle for a positivist scientific epistemology, stressing the historical contingency of physical hypotheses and arguing for the displacement of mechanics from the core of physics. Paradoxically, for Mach it is the mechanist Helmholtz who is responsible for making the energy conservation law universal. Mach nevertheless argues that the philosophical kernel of energy conservation, the principle of the exclusion of perpetual motion, is a historical and logical precursor to mechanical notions.

SARTON reproduces and comments on papers by Mayer (1842), Joule (1843), and Carnot (a manuscript, recovered in 1878, abandoning the conservation of caloric energy and propounding the equivalence of heat and work). Mayer's conservation discovery was an intuitive flash of genius comparable to a religious conversion, while the more mundane Joule was a laboratory "metrologist" with a mission for precision who, for the empiricist Sarton, provided the essential completion of Mayer's laudable insight.

The locus classicus for the simultaneity thesis is KUHN. The author groups a dozen Europeans who between 1830 and 1850 pondered the metaphysics of force, or practised the sciences of heat and electricity. All made statements that in retrospect could be interpreted as partial or complete formulations of energy conservation in nature: Mayer, Joule, Colding, and Helmholtz combined a general conservation law with concrete quantitative applications; Carnot, Marc Séguin, Holtzmann, and G.A. Hirn computed a conversion factor between heat and work; Mohr, Grove, Faraday, and Liebig described a world of phenomena (chemical affinity, electricity, heat, light, and magnetism) manifesting a single transformable indestructible force. Here was a flurry of near simultaneous and, in most cases, independent "discovery". But Kuhn has no interest in priority or prerequisites. He sees a confluence of three period-specific "trigger-factors": the availability of conversion processes; a concern with engines matched by rapid changes in heat theory; and the prominence in physics of frameworks of unity and harmony among natural phenomena, through German Naturphilosophie or through ideas of correlation.

HEIMANN (Centaurus, 1974) argues against Kuhn's interpretation. The "conversion process" trigger was hardly new: even by the end of the 18th century natural philosophers had discerned a balanced and unified nature wherein interconvertible powers acted as manifestations of a single force. Moreover, the concept of force was not so vague and malleable as Kuhn demanded: rather, it had multiple but distinct meanings from which a new concept of energy was eventually disentangled. Other authors take a fresh look at the supposed simultaneous

discoverers: DAHL sees Colding as a protégé of the Naturphilosophe Ørsted, for whom the immaterial forces of a unified nature were transformable but imperishable manifestations of God's intellectual power; LINDSAY scours Mayer's writings for vestiges of energy and gives him the indelible stamp of a tragically neglected but mentally unbalanced prophet.

More usefully, if paradoxically, some writers suggest that an energy-centred historiography has obscured the wider strategies or intellectual intentions of the participants. MORUS shows that Grove, in and beyond his notorious Correlation of Physical Forces, aimed simultaneously to reform the scientific polity and restructure the natural word. HEIMANN (1976) sees the substance of Mayer's work blurred both in the priority disputes of the 1860s and by those who, while correlating unknowing energy pioneers, portray "On the forces of inorganic nature" (1842) as the first publication of the law of conservation of energy, despite the author's explicit rejection of the idea that heat is motion. For Heimann, the kernel of Mayer's "thought" comprised a concept of force (invariable in quantity but transformable in quality), a theory of the relations between different forces (with the indestructibility of forces following from an equality of cause and effect), physiology as a central resource. Kant (on causality), Leibniz (on force), and Naturphilosophie were three red herrings.

CANEVA goes beyond Heimann's concentration on Mayer's texts, and examines the immediate context of his work and the literature he "likely knew" to make the fine structure of Mayer's thought historically intelligible. Mayer was no physicist but he did interact with chemists and spiritualists, and medicine, physiology, and theology formed the common basis for discussions of the soul, vital force, and the body. Unusually, Mayer followed Lavoisier on animal heat emphasizing analogies between organisms and work-performing machines, and seeking a tractable concept of force designed as an antidote to materialism. Caneva's Mayer is, like Heimann's, relatively immune to the constitutive action of "extra-scientific factors" such as social situation and religion: such factors, Caneva believes, play a subsidiary rather than an explanatory role.

HEIMANN (1974) suggests that the portrayal of Mayer's one-time champion Helmholtz as a Kuhnian simultaneous discoverer has resulted in the crude collapse of the Erhaltung der Kraft (1847) into an enunciation of the conservation principle. Heimann studies Helmholtz's individual intentions and immediate stimuli and discovers, inter alia, a desire to extend Liebig's correlation of heat, chemical activity and muscular work in studies of animal economy; a strong residue of Kant; and, pace Mach, an ontology of matter and central forces as the optimum (since mechanical) grounding of energy conservation.

Far removed from this heady metaphysics, FORRESTER separates Joule from fellow electro-chemists Faraday and Grove by asserting that Joule alone ascertained the mechanical equivalent of heat and worked to make this constant (appear) universal. Having examined Joule's quantitative programme and charted the emergence of the "first law" from what was essentially chemical research, he observes that placing the work within a physical context and refashioning Joule as an experimental physicist was a re-interpretative achievement. Forrester echoes Sarton's comment that in the 1840s Joule could not claim to be a member of a physical community; and Dahl agrees that, repeatedly, conservation laws were adumbrated by those outside professional natural philosophy.

Forrester says little about the social or technological context. CARDWELL (1989), however, introduces Joule as a business man *manqué* with a career trajectory that saw him transformed from an utopian Manchester electrician to the lofty social and scientific heights of the Royal Society of London. Alliances with powerful individuals and the broad-based British Association for the Advancement of Science conferred credibility on Joule and stability to his experimental construction of the mechanical value of heat. Cardwell contrasts Joule's physical dexterity with the mathematical gymnastics of his collaborator William Thomson. SIBUM goes further, locating Joule's uniquely skilled thermometric manipulations within the commercial environment of the Joule family brewery: a "gestural knowledge" gained there informed Joule's numerical fixing of the mechanical equivalent of heat. SMITH & WISE concentrated on Thomson as a Glasgow college professor of natural philosophy, co-establishing a science of thermodynamics with Clausius and Rankine.

HUTCHISON's analysis of Rankine – his idiosyncratic molecular vortex formulation of thermodynamics, his coinage of the terms "actual" and "potential" energy, and his aspiration towards a general science of energetics (1855) – takes place within an internalist framework. Smith & Wise choose a broader contextualist canvas. Thomson bypassed Hiebert's rational mechanics, looked to the macroscopic work-based engineering mechanics of the French, and by 1851 had formed a vigorous hybrid of Carnot and Joule. Industry – shipbuilding, steam-engines and railways – reflected and informed the energy physics of Thomson as he set about training energy physicists in the Glasgow laboratory, and warranting the submarine telegraphers whose expertise was to be embodied in precise resistance measurement standards built upon absolute energy-based units.

While studies of individuals have thus benefited from the illumination of the social and technological contexts, a traditional alternative has been to maintain *contra* Kuhn that any adequate history of energy must trace its historical roots and provide acute philosophical analysis of an energy concept. HIEBERT eschews 19th-century contextual history and instead extends part of Mach's programme, locating ancient, early modern, and Enlightenment authors who discussed the conservation of quantities related to motion (Descartes's momentum; Leibniz and the 18th-century rational mechanists' *vis viva*). Their writings, it transpires, were antecedents of the factors essential to the formation of the conservation of energy concept.

In ELKANA's philosophically sensitized history of energy in the 19th century, the creator of a good scientific concept must be philosophically informed, since concept creation originates in basic metaphysical principles. The principle of conservation of something in nature – the search for constancies or regularities in a world of change – leads from a state of essential confusion (*pace* Heimann) by a process of clarification to the development of a mature concept of energy conservation. Considerations of perpetual motion, rational mechanics, and thermodynamics had little to do with this emergence. Four factors were essential: a belief in conservation; the conceptual correlation of Newtonian and Lagrangian mechanics; the reduction of animal heat to inanimate law; and the mathe-matical expression of a conservation law. Conveniently, the philosophically astute Helmholtz managed uniquely to synthesize these factors in the watershed of the *Erhaltung*.

The most striking contrast to this school comes with those who *cash out* Kuhn by emphasizing the interplay of engineering traditions, political economy, and theoretical accounting in heat engine practice. The steam engine most clearly instantiated the correlation of natural powers by demonstrating an equivalence of chemical affinity, heat and mechanical work. Thus FOX elucidates Sadi Carnot's general analysis of the effects of heat engines, and his debt to the Parisian *écoles*, political economy, and international engineering contexts. CARDWELL (1971), powerfully states the historical symbiosis of the technological and the theoretical, as engine practice and the science of heat were jointly and painstakingly reconstructed during the first half of the 19th century. The partnership was unequal: attempts to theorize practice were, in Cardwell's terms, inadequate until about 1850. In the classic formulation, science – here, the science of energy – owed more to the steam engine than the steam engine owed to science.

SMITH uses the term "energy" as an actors' category, avoiding the linguistic and historical violations of rational reconstruction and simultaneous discovery theses. He studies the period in which a new discourse of "energy" accompanied the re-focusing and re-structuring of texts and practices in science and technology. For a self-conscious and aggressive alliance of north British scientific engineers and natural philosophers active between 1845 and 1880, the "science of energy" was more than a conceptual reorganization and unification of the natural physical world; it consolidated a credible, quasi-professional, and ultimately international community; it generated authoritative, exportable, and marketable natural knowledge; it mapped a morality decrying waste as man's failure to make optimal use of God's gifts; and it enshrined Whig values of progress and reform. Protagonists embarked on an expansive entrepreneurial programme, annexing staff and territory within the physical, geological and life sciences. In fierce and protracted boundary disputes, British natural philosophers struggled to enforce the rival histories and mythologies of the new science. Coming full circle, Smith explains why Tait caricatured Mayer as a dilettantish, speculative, and unschooled philosophical foil to the decisive, gentlemanly – and British – experimentalist, Joule. Locating in Newton the essentials of energy conservation, the north British natural philosophers invented not a continental but a British tradition for the universal and timeless natural fact of energy.

In more specialist studies, energy has been re-located within contexts of aether conceptions, psychophysics, energetics, economics, and literature. WISE studies the interconnections between German concepts of force, energy, and ether in the third quarter of the 19th century. He investigates the theorizing and the often idealist philosophical concerns of physicists who, while eschewing speculative *Naturphilosophie*, constructed ethers to show unity in nature. Wise focuses upon the electromagnetic ethers, considering the tensions between action-at-a-distance theories – such as Weber's where force was considered as a relation – and field theories, where fields were entities that carried the power to effect action locally in the form of force or, increasingly, as potential energy. Wise shows, *inter alia*, how Weber's collaborator, the Leipzig professor

Gustav Theodor Fechner, used energy to underpin a new empirical psychology or psychophysics. By about 1870, energy had become the symbol of unity in nature so that, in the following decades, Ostwald and other energeticists could insist that in physics an ontology of energy should be substituted for mechanical, kinetic, and atomic alternatives. BRUSH, finally, links the history of energy and thermodynamics with popular literary culture.

BEN MARSDEN

See also Engines: steam; Heat; Helmholtz

Engineering Schools

Buchanan, R.A., *The Engineers: A History of the Engineering Profession in Britain, 1750–1914*, London: Kingsley, 1989

Calvert, Monte Alan, *The Mechanical Engineer in America, 1830–1910: Professional Cultures in Conflict*, Baltimore: Johns Hopkins University Press, 1967

Day, Charles R., *Education for the Industrial World: The Écoles d'Arts et Métiers and the Rise of French Industrial Engineering*, Cambridge, Massachusetts: MIT Press, 1987

Fox, Robert and Anna Guagnini (eds), *Education, Technology and Industrial Performance in Europe, 1850–1939*, Cambridge and New York: Cambridge University Press, 1993

Gispen, Kees, *New Profession, Old Order: Engineers and German Society, 1815–1914*, Cambridge and New York: Cambridge University Press, 1989

Locke, Robert R., *The End of the Practical Man: Entrepreneurship and Higher Education in Germany, France, and Great Britain, 1880–1940*, Greenwich, Connecticut: Jai Press, 1984

Lundgreen, Peter, "Engineering Education in Europe and the USA, 1750–1930: The Rise to Dominance of School Culture and the Engineering Profession", *Annals of Science*, 47 (1990): 33–75

Noble, David F., *America by Design: Science, Technology and the Rise of Corporate Capitalism*, New York: Knopf, 1977; Oxford: Oxford University Press, 1979

Until quite recently, the historiography of engineering schools – at least that written in English – rarely rose above the level of commemorative or descriptive narratives of particular institutions. However, the recognition by historians of science and technology that the practices and disciplines of engineering cannot be understood merely as an adjunct to those of the natural sciences has contributed to a growth in comparative and analytical studies of engineering schools. The interest of economic historians in assessing the contribution of systems of industrial research and training to economic performance has also increased research in this field.

Rather surprisingly, given the industrial and technical achievements of Britain and the US, we lack good full-length studies of engineering schools in these countries. The strength of the Anglo-American tradition of apprenticeship meant that,

on both sides of the Atlantic, formal schemes of education arrived comparatively late in the 19th century. The success of practical cut-and-try approaches to technical innovation for a long time militated against the emergence of more systematic engineering research in the universities. CALVERT's pioneering study of the professionalization of American mechanical engineers is still worth reading as an introduction to the eventual establishment of engineering schools in the US. His concepts of school and shop culture, and his analysis of the evolution of the former as both a cause and consequence of the founding of a formally organised engineering profession, still inform much of the Anglo-American literature. While Calvert contrasts the engineering schools' theoretical approach to formal learning and research with the more empirically-based and informal modes of learning and innovation associated with engineering workshops, he stresses that in reality "shop" and "school" culture formed a continuum. This insight has encouraged a sensitivity in more recent studies to the differences that existed between engineering schools – both within and between national systems.

An acknowledgement of such diversity is not, however, one of the more obvious strengths of NOBLE's ambitious study of the evolution of corporate capitalism in the US. As part of this much wider analysis, Noble seeks to show how engineering schools became subordinated to the imperatives of industrial capital rather than those of particular professional groups. More recent and more detailed case-studies, particularly of chemical engineering, suggest that he overstates his point.

As far as Britain is concerned, BUCHANAN does not offer the level of theoretical sophistication or comprehensiveness of several of the other studies discussed here. Buchanan understands the emergence and development of engineering schools before World War I within the context of the fragmented organisational structure of the engineering professions, but he does not relate this to an explicit theory either of professionalization or of the wider development of British society. Nevertheless, for readers who do not have the time to search the specialist literature for more recent and detailed work that has yet to appear in book form, this volume offers a useful and accessible summary of the development of British engineering schools, as well as a guide to much of the older literature.

International comparisons are a welcome aspect of much recent writing. LOCKE is primarily interested in comparative economic performance; he presents a substantial study of British, French and German responses to the economic challenge posed from the later 19th century by the school culture of American engineers. His conclusion that the German system of technical education was superior to that of the other two European countries is, however, vitiated by a somewhat thin and tendentious interpretation of British developments.

LUNDGREEN challenges the over-generalised, technocratic assumptions that inform studies such as Locke's by developing a brief but suggestive comparison of engineering schools in Britain and the US with those in France and Germany. Informed by the kind of argument pioneered by Calvert, Lundgreen suggests that the evolution of national styles of academic forms of education and research is best understood in terms of the variety of interests and particular circumstances of the engineering professions in each of these countries. Debates about the economic pros and cons of engineering schools should be seen as reflecting a mobilisation of cultural resources by professional groups to further their position, rather than the progress of a historical cause in its own right. Thus, the academic training of engineers destined for service with the state established a model for private industry in continental Europe that was largely absent in Britain and the US. After about 1870, however, there was a degree of international convergence, as engineering graduates and professors in the engineering schools succeeded in using growing fears about the international competitiveness of their national economies to argue for a decisive shift towards school culture.

FOX & GUAGNINI's valuable collection extends the empirical base for further work of this kind, although, apart from the editors's introductory remarks, there is little attempt explicitly to draw international comparisons. The national studies of engineering schools encompass England, France, Germany, Belgium, Sweden, Spain, Italy and the US. Despite the volume's title, few of the essays try to assess the economic effectiveness of engineering schools; instead the emphasis is on understanding the growth and development of these schools in the context of the often conflicting demands of each country's employers and educational providers. The clear conclusion is that cultural prejudice against manufacturing was pervasive throughout much of Europe in the 19th and early 20th centuries. The bibliography, while far from comprehensive, is of very considerable value to anyone wishing to pursue matters further.

GISPEN provides a model study of how the search by engineers for social status throughout the 19th century shaped the development of engineering schools and of the disciplines taught therein. His analysis of the stratification of engineering schools, as both a product and a cause of tensions within the emerging German engineering profession, shows how necessary it is that any discussion of "national styles of engineering culture" must also comprehend the complexities to be found in any given country. Initially, many German educationalists stressed the general and theoretical nature of engineering knowledge, in an attempt to emulate the ideology of knowledge-for-its-own-sake favoured by a bureaucratic elite which – suitably reformed from its pre-industrial origins – continued to dominate Bismarckian society. From the 1870s, however, industrial capitalists supported teachers and schools that sympathised with shop culture, just as the state swung its support behind a massive expansion of technical education. The resultant oversupply of engineers severely compromised attempts before World War I to further the social standing of the engineering profession.

Social stratification and social mobility are also important aspects of DAY's analysis of the French Écoles d'Arts et Métiers. His focus on a secondary stratum of engineering schools is still fairly unusual in the literature of any country. Day suggests that within the French context these humbler schools made significant contributions to economic development, through the occupation by their graduates of key positions in the management of railways and the engineering industries. The schools also provided an important means of social mobility for those who were excluded by reason of social class from elite engineering schools such as the École Polytechnique.

While there are still considerable gaps in our understanding of the history of engineering schools, particularly for the period after World War II, the recent literature displays a maturity of analysis that bodes well for further research.

COLIN DIVALL

See also École Polytechnique; Education; France: scientific and technical education

Engines: steam

Barton, D.B., *The Cornish Beam Engine*, Truro, Cornwall: privately printed, 1969

Buchanan, R.A. and George Watkins, *The Industrial Archaeology of the Stationary Steam Engine*, London: Allen Lane, 1976

Cardwell, D.S.L., *From Watt to Clausius: The Rise of Thermodynamics in the Early Industrial Age*, London: Heinemann, and Ithaca, New York: Cornell University Press, 1971

Clark, Daniel Kinnear, *The Steam Engine: A Treatise on Steam Engines and Boilers*, 2 vols, London and New York: Blackie, 1890

Dickinson, Henry Winram and Rhys Jenkins, *James Watt and the Steam Engine*, Oxford: Clarendon Press, 1927

Dickinson, Henry Winram, *A Short History of the Steam Engine*, Cambridge: Cambridge University Press, 1939; 2nd edition, London: Frank Cass, 1963

Ewing, Sir J.A., *The Steam-Engine and Other Heat-Engines*, Cambridge: Cambridge University Press, 1894; 4th revised edition, 1926

Farey, John, *A Treatise on the Steam Engine, Historical, Practical and Descriptive*, London: Longmans, Rees, Orme, Brown and Green, 1827; reprinted, Newton Abbot, Devon: David and Charles, 1971

Galloway, Elijah, *History and Progress of the Steam Engine*, London: Thomas Kelly, 1829

Hills, Richard L., *Power from Steam: A History of the Stationary Steam Engine*, Cambridge and New York: Cambridge University Press, 1989

Hunter, Louis C., *A History of Industrial Power in the United States, 1780–1930*, vol. 2: *Steam Power*, Charlottesville: University Press of Virginia, 1985

Hunter, Louis C. and Lynwood Bryant, *A History of Industrial Power in the United States, 1780–1930*, vol. 3: *The Transmission of Power*, Charlottesville: University Press of Virginia, 1991

Lindqvist, Svante, *Technology on Trial: The Introduction of Steam Power Technology into Sweden, 1715–1736*, Stockholm: Almqvist & Wiksell, 1984

Neilson, Robert M., *The Steam Turbine*, London: Longmans Green, 1902

Richardson, Alex, *The Evolution of the Parsons Steam Turbine*, London: Engineering, 1911

Rolt, L.T.C. and J.S. Allen, *The Steam Engine of Thomas Newcomen*, Hartington, Derbyshire: Moorland, and New York: Science History Publications, 1977

While various people had tried to harness the power of steam from antiquity up to the end of the 17th century, the first person to have real success was Thomas Savery. Savery patented his steam pump in 1698, and his book *The Miner's Friend*

(1702) is a fine example of a sales brochure, explaining how the engine worked and its various uses, and it is a charming work. The engine that had much greater success and formed the basis for later developments was that of Thomas Newcomen, who ran an engine near Dudley Castle in 1712. ROLT & ALLEN give a good account of Newcomen's life, the origins of his engine, how Newcomen had to collaborate with Savery owing to Savery's prior patent, and the subsequent spread of the Newcomen engine across Britain. LINDQVIST tells of the problems facing Mårten Triewald when he introduced the Newcomen engine to Sweden. It is a fascinating tale of struggle against severe weather, a lack of skilled workmen, and the difficulties in adapting the pumping engine in order to work a mine hoist.

It was James Watt who, with his vital patent for the separate condenser in 1769 and his subsequent patents (ending in 1784) for rotative motion, first made the Newcomen engine more economical, and then adapted the engine to drive directly different kinds of mills. DICKINSON & JENKINS's book remains the most authoritative account of Watt's work, and shows the enormous range of inventiveness that enabled Watt to adapt the Newcomen engine to so many different uses. BARTON covers the further development of the Watt engine, by men such as Trevithick and Woolf, which gave increased power and economy to the Cornish copper mining industry. Here the steam engine reached its first zenith of efficiency.

Behind the application of the steam engine to industry lay the various theories of how it actually functioned. The science of thermodynamics arose out of the study of steam power. CARDWELL examines the early hypotheses of people like Watt, and shows how these were corrected by the work of James Prescott Joule, with his advocacy of the kinetic theory of heat around the mid-19th century. The new theories of Joule and Clausius were explained by W.J.M. Rankine, whose *A Manual of the Steam Engine and Other Prime Movers* (1859) led to the more economical compound engines used in the ocean-going ships of Elder, and other Scottish shipbuilders. This book became a standard text on the subject for many years.

Later text books are by Clark and Ewing, both of which contain historical elements. CLARK was written during the heyday of steam power in the 1890s, and his many illustrations of boilers, pumping engines, winding engines, mill engines, and railway locomotives show what was being made at that time. While Clark does cover the theory, EWING concentrates far more on this aspect, showing how thermodynamic principles were being applied to steam engines, which led to the Uniflow, and to turbines during World War I.

Since the early 19th century, there have been many histories written on the steam engine. FAREY is one of the earliest, and is still considered one of the most authoritative, even though only the first volume was published in the author's lifetime. Not only was Farey a skilled illustrator, but he also knew engineers, including James Watt, and as a result his book is full of many detailed descriptions of engines. The much shorter history by GALLOWAY is more general in its approach, has a useful list of steam engine patents, and covers some of the more obscure inventors.

For many years, the standard history of the steam engine was by DICKINSON, despite having been written in the 1930s, before the end of the steam era. For reciprocating engines, Dickinson concentrates mainly on the early period, (with the years 1850–1930 covered in a single chapter), and describes many different types of boilers, including a good account of the development of the steam turbine.

BUCHANAN & WATKINS's book gives an outline history, and then describes the mechanical principles and constructional details of the steam engine, but most useful are the notes on some of the builders of stationary engines and a gazetteer of preserved engines in Britain. While such a list soon becomes out of date, it does help to discover possible survivors. HILLS centred his history on the textile mill engine because that was developed into a most sophisticated and reliable type. However, this is set against other possible influences – such as the Cornish engines, the compound steamship engines, and electricity generating engines – so the work is also a general history of the stationary steam engine. A few textile mills employed turbines, but these were very rare.

For a consideration of all aspects of steam power in one country, one must turn to HUNTER's trilogy on industrial power in the United States. The second volume covers the steam engine up to c.1900, from the earliest atmospheric engine operating in the US in 1755. Lynwood Bryant took up the challenge of completing Hunter's work on his death, and the final volume (HUNTER & BRYANT) examines the transmission of power from steam to petroleum, with of course the important role of electricity, in the early 20th century.

Today, for commercial purposes, the steam turbine is the only user of steam power, for the generation of electricity. The most important early pioneer of the steam turbine was Charles A. Parsons, who took out his world-famous patent in 1884. RICHARDSON covers the theory and early evolution of both axial and radial flow types. The turbine proved to be particularly well suited for both electricity generation and ship propulsion, and quickly enabled much larger power outputs to be achieved in both these applications. While Richardson concentrates only on Parsons, NEILSON describes the work of other inventors, such as Carl Gustaf De Laval and Patrik Rateau as well as C.E. Auguste Parsons, giving the theoretical background to their different designs.

RICHARD L. HILLS

See also Heat; Thermodynamics

Engines: turbo

Constant, Edward W., *The Origins of the Turbojet Revolution*, Baltimore: Johns Hopkins University Press, 1980

Gunston, Bill, *The Development of Jet and Turbine Aero Engines*, Sparkford: Patrick Stephens, 1995

Heathcote, Roy, *The Rolls-Royce Dart: Pioneering Turboprop*, Historical Series, no. 18, Derby: Rolls-Royce Heritage Trust, 1992

Miller, Ronald and David Sawers, *The Technical Development of Modern Aviation*, London: Routledge and Kegan Paul, 1968

Neville, Leslie E. and Nathaniel F. Silsbee, *Jet Propulsion Progress: The Development of Aircraft Gas Turbines*, New York: McGraw-Hill, 1948

Norbye, Jan P., *The Gas Turbine Engine: Design Development Applications*, Radnor, Philadelphia: Chilton, 1975

Schlaifer, Robert, *Development of Aircraft Engines*, Boston: Division of Research, Graduate School of Business Administration, Harvard University Press, 1950

While the potential of the gas turbine engine for aircraft propulsion was known before World War II, primarily to engineers, and was restricted to secrecy during the war, it became common knowledge in the years immediately after. Considering the fact that the turbojet was expected to revolutionize flight, it is not surprising that numerous texts appeared in the late 1940s describing the progress of jet propulsion.

One text from this period, NEVILLE & SILSBEE, is a straight-forward narrative intended for students, businessmen, and professionals. The authors present the fundamentals of the gas turbine engine, in both turbojet and turboprop variations, with an outline of its development in Germany, Britain, and the United States. The chapters on the navy-industry team and on government research provide useful examples of how organizations affect the development of technology, and the chapters on tough problems and new horizons offer an interesting view on the state of gas-turbine development from the perspective of 1948. Many photographs and illustrations are provided, including a large fold-out cross-section drawing of each of the two German jet engines that saw service during the war. The chronology of events and glossary of technical terms are helpful, but those interested in the first years of turbojet development will find the comprehensive bibliography particularly useful, as it lists the earliest books on the subject and almost 200 articles.

Both Miller & Sawers's general text and Schlaifer's specialized history are considered by Constant to be essential historical accounts. MILLER & SAWERS discuss the improvement of the airplane in the 50 years following World War I. They offer only a brief description of the invention of the jet engine, but the value of their book comes from the examination of the impact of gas turbines on aircraft design, aviation in general, and the commercial air line industry. Also of interest is the extensive bibliography, and the statistical data contained in the numerous tables and appendices.

SCHLAIFER's detailed look at the development of aircraft engines in Britain, Germany, and the United States between the two world wars was initiated by the Harvard Business School, as a study of relations between government and industry. The United States was successful in the development of air-cooled engines, while Britain and Germany led in the development of liquid-cooled and gas turbine engines. Schlaifer sought to determine whether this might be explained in part by the differing relationships between the engine manufacturers and the governments in those countries, and his technical history was written with this goal in mind. He finds that, in its early stages, the development of the turbojet was supported by companies in Britain and Germany that had not previously manufactured aircraft engines. The gas turbine was backed neither by government nor by the engine industry, because both concentrated on solving the immediate problems of existing engine designs. The reason that the United States lagged behind in turbojet development, he concludes, was not due to an inferior government-industry relationship, but to a failure to realize the utility of the turbojet. Simply put, Frank Whittle, Hans Joachim Pabst von Ohain, and Herbert Wagner were not Americans.

While the turbojet engine was revolutionizing flight after World War II, numerous companies began to explore the practicality of applying the gas turbine engine to the automobile and other land vehicles. Experimentation began at Rover, which built the first gas-turbine car in 1950, and peaked at Chrysler, which field-tested 50 gas turbine cars among 203 participants between 1963 and 1966. NORBYE presents detailed case studies of the work done at Rover and Chrysler, as well as that done by General Motors, Ford, Volkswagen, Austin, Fiat, and other projects, including the Bluebird CN-7. These case studies are not limited to automobiles, but include trucks, buses, and trains. Also of interest are the sections on gas turbine design, and the "pre-history" and "modern history" of the gas turbine engine. However, the reader should take note that Norbye believed that the application of the gas turbine to land vehicles was only a matter of time and this bias is reflected in his writing. Although he wrote with optimism for the success of the gas turbine, he did not omit the inherent disadvantages or problems with its development.

HEATHCOTE's account of the development of the "pioneering" Dart turboprop engine is based on a lecture he first gave to the Rolls Royce Heritage Trust in 1985, as part of an effort to preserve the company's engineering history. Since work on the design began in 1945, more than 7,000 Dart engines have been produced for use in nine different types of military and commercial aircraft. Heathcote, therefore, provides a unique case study of the development and use of a single gas turbine design, complete with photographs, detailed drawings, and a fold-out colour cross-section illustration.

More recent, full-length technological histories of turbojet development have been provided by Constant and by Gunston. CONSTANT stresses historical theory, and is interested in the implications of the "turbojet revolution" for models of technological change within the new field of the history of technology. He argues that, although the turbojet was dependant on prior technology and required the successful co-evolution of piston aero-engines and streamlined airframes, it was not a simple, linear extrapolation of prior technology. The turbojet was "revolutionary" since it "very nearly extinguished the technological tradition founded upon piston engines and propellers". His thesis is that major advances in theoretical aerodynamics led a handful of men to radically new assumptions about possible aircraft speed and potential gas turbine efficiency. Of particular value is Constant's analysis of the "structural antecedents" and "prior technology", which includes water turbines, turbine pumps, steam turbines, turbo air compressors, and the first internal combustion gas turbines.

GUNSTON, on the other hand, provides a neutral narrative for engineering students, but avoids complicated mathematical formulae and specialized terminology that might frighten off the more casual reader. His book is in two parts, with the first describing the operation of gas turbines and the second their historical development. The second part starts with the pre-war pioneers and ends with the maturation of turbojet design by 1960. It also describes the development of rockets, ramjets, powered lifts, turboprops, propfans, and helicopter engines.

Almost every page has a detailed and precise cross-section illustration or diagram.

BRIAN R. REYNOLDS

See also Automobiles; Space Science

Enlightenment

Baker, Keith Michael, *Condorcet: From Natural Philosophy to Social Mathematics*, Chicago: University of Chicago Press, 1975

Cassirer, Ernst, *The Philosophy of the Enlightenment*, translated from the German by Fritz C.A. Koelln and James P. Pettegrove, Princeton, New Jersey: Princeton University Press, 1951 (original edition, 1932)

Darnton, Robert, *Mesmerism and the End of the Enlightenment in France*, Cambridge, Massachusetts: Harvard University Press, 1968

Engelhardt, Dietrich von, *Historisches Bewusstsein in der Naturwissenschaft: Von der Aufklärung bis zum Positivismus*, Freiburg: K. Alber, 1979

Foucault, Michel, *Madness and Civilization: A History of Insanity in the Age of Reason*, translated from the French by Richard Howard (abridged edition), New York: Pantheon Books, 1965; London: Tavistock, 1967 (original edition, 1961)

Foucault, Michel, *The Order of Things: An Archaeology of the Human Sciences*, translated from the French by Alan Sheridan, New York: Pantheon Books, and London: Tavistock, 1970 (original edition, 1966)

Gascoigne, John, *Cambridge in the Age of the Enlightenment: Science, Religion and Politics from the Restoration to the French Revolution*, Cambridge and New York: Cambridge University Press, 1989

Gay, Peter, *The Enlightenment: An Interpretation*, 2 vols, New York: Knopf, 1966–69

Golinski, Jan, *Science as Public Culture: Chemistry and Enlightenment in Britain, 1760–1820*, Cambridge and New York: Cambridge University Press, 1992

Hankins, Thomas L., *Science and the Enlightenment*, Cambridge and New York: Cambridge University Press, 1985

Hundert, E.J., *The Enlightenment's Fable: Bernard Mandeville and the Discovery of Society*, Cambridge and New York: Cambridge University Press, 1994

Kant, Immanuel, "What is Enlightenment?", translated from the German by Lewis White Beck, in his *Philosophical Writings*, edited by Ernst Behler, New York: Continuum, 1986

Kiernan, Colm, *The Enlightenment and Science in Eighteenth-Century France*, 2nd edition, Banbury, Oxfordshire: Voltaire Foundation, 1973

Koselleck, Reinhart, *Critique and Crisis: Enlightenment and the Pathogenesis of Modern Society*, translated from the German, Oxford: Berg, and Cambridge, Massachusetts: MIT Press, 1988 (original edition, 1959)

Lepenies, Wolf, *Das Ende der Naturgeschichte: Wandel kultureller Selbstverständlichkeiten in den Wissenschaften des 18. und 19. Jahrhunderts*, Munich: Hanser, 1976

Porter, Roy, "The Enlightenment in England", in *The Enlightenment in National Context*, edited by Roy Porter and Mikulás Teich, Cambridge: Cambridge University Press, 1981

Rousseau, G.S. and Roy Porter (eds), *The Ferment of Knowledge: Studies in the Historiography of Eighteenth-Century Science*, Cambridge and New York: Cambridge University Press, 1980

Rousseau, G.S., *Enlightenment Crossings: Pre- and Post-Modern Discourses: Anthropological*, Manchester: Manchester University Press, and New York: St Martin's Press, 1991

Rousseau, G.S., *Enlightenment Borders: Pre- and Post-Modern Discourses: Medical, Scientific*, Manchester: Manchester University Press, and New York: St Martin's Press, 1991

Rousseau, G.S., *Perilous Enlightenment: Pre- and Post-Modern Discourses: Sexual, Historical*, Manchester: Manchester University Press, and New York: St Martin's Press, 1991

Stafford, Barbara Maria, *Body Criticism: Imaging the Unseen in Enlightenment Art and Medicine*, Cambridge, Massachusetts: MIT Press, 1991

If there is a quintessential Enlightenment it would probably be French, although it is KANT who is credited with coining the concept. Enlightenment, he announced, was man's escape from self-incurred tutelage through the free use of reason. Kant's belief that reason, freely used, assured progress in the arts, sciences and especially religion, was less controversial than his conviction that the potential for Enlightenment was greatest under the reign of an absolutist monarch, such as Prussia's Frederick the Great. Kant's essay, and its famous dictum that his was not "an enlightened age" but an "age of enlightenment", is an example of the progressive, political and polemical character of much of the literature of the Enlightenment.

The distinguished neo-Kantian Ernst CASSIRER treats the sciences, religion, historical writing, legal and political theory, and the aesthetics of the 18th century within the context of a unified "philosophy of the Enlightenment". Not merely the combined ideas of its leading thinkers, this philosophy is characterized by a "method" of thinking that relied, above all, on Newton's rules of philosophizing, and stands in contrast to the all-encompassing "systems" of 17th-century philosophers, such as Descartes and Leibniz. Cassirer's is a profoundly learned and perceptive work, and it is entirely appropriate, in keeping with his own tradition, that he locates the beginning of the Enlightenment in Newton's method and its culmination, and eclipse, in the work of Kant.

Gay and Koselleck are important post-war interpreters of the Enlightenment. GAY portrays the *philosophes* as a "family" united by a single style of thinking, which was dependent on the paganism of classical antiquity, was directed against Christianity, and drew from the natural sciences. Above all, Gay sees the *philosophes* as united in their "pursuit of modernity" – of freedom grounded in reason. Although the Enlightenment was marked by a pervasive faith in the progress of the natural sciences – by a hope in the promise of Newton's science rather than Newton's God – Gay finds that its modernity was most evident in the "moral sciences": it was sociology, psychology, political economy, and modern education that gave the *philosophes* their hope of overcoming Christian pessimism and the fatalism of fortune. Although he calls his book a "social history" of the *philosophes*, his approach displays less sociology than liberal teleology: for Gay, the end of the Enlightenment, the program of the *philosophes* put into practice, is the founding of the United States.

KOSELLECK's post-war, central European perspective is decidedly less optimistic. Although science is not treated explicitly, he links an analysis of social conditions with the history of ideas – via a discussion of anonymous pamphlets and the great works of 18th-century thinkers – and presents an elegant and incisive argument that offers an effective framework for understanding the Enlightenment. Using Hobbes as his starting point, Koselleck argues that the modern state, especially in its absolutist form, was the product of early modern religious wars. A crucial feature of the Enlightenment state was the sharp distinction it drew between the realm of politics and the inner, moral world. Thus the Republic of Letters, the Masonic lodges and secret societies acted at once as critics of, and havens from, absolutism. Supported by a progressive philosophy of history that assured them of their goals, yet bereft of the concept of "crisis", Enlightenment critics failed to see the hypocrisy of their moral and non-political critique. For Koselleck, the culmination of the Enlightenment was neither a better philosophy nor a model Republic, but the French Revolution and the Terror.

FOUCAULT (1970) is much more than a narrow treatment of the human sciences. Avoiding intellectual biography, as well as the history of theories and concepts, Foucault aims to uncover the unspoken presuppositions that inform the discourse of a given time. Foucault's aim is to show how knowledge was arranged in the "Classical" era (c.1660–1800), and this task he calls "archaeology", because it uncovers a distinct layer of history that has no smooth connection with preceding or succeeding eras. He argues that the Classical period had neither biology nor life, only living things seen through the grid of natural history; no historical philology, just a general grammar that seeks to name everything; no political economy, just the analysis of wealth. It was an age concerned with ordering and naming, with taxonomies, as epitomized by the 17th- and 18th-century table. This discourse disappeared around 1800, supplanted by the new organizing principles of analogy, succession, and history of the modern era. Foucault's highly selective choice of sources has infuriated some historians, but his prose, interpretations, and insights have inspired many others.

Written after the appearance of T.S. Kuhn and Foucault, and during the first flush of contextual, "external" histories of science, the collection of historiographic essays in ROUSSEAU & PORTER are the product of scholars' keen awareness that the history of science was no longer the province of scientists, but a prestigious discipline with its own methods. Several themes emerge from these attempts to give direction to a new generation of scholars: an historicist emphasis on understanding 18th-century science according to its own terms and categories; skepticism about the explanatory power of broad categories such as Newtonianism, and about the possibility of a comprehensive and unified treatment of Enlightenment science; and a consideration of the ways in which science is used and given meaning by its wider social and political contexts.

HANKINS has similar doubts about Newtonianism in his concise overview of Enlightenment science, a work that is organized along the lines of 18th-century categories, such as experimental physics, natural history and physiology, and the moral sciences. Hankins manages to discuss a broad range of problems and controversies in Enlightenment science. The intellectual and philosophical contexts of the sciences, particularly various versions of the mechanical philosophy, are considered, but the social and political meanings of science are barely mentioned.

KIERNAN's essay on the history of ideas argues that the French Enlightenment was fractured by a pervasive debate between mechanists and organicists. Thus, the many philosophical and ideological differences between Voltaire and Rousseau, for example, come to the fore and, to a certain extent, have their source in the former's mechanistic physical science and the latter's organic life science. Kiernan is able to make some interesting and unusual connections, but his analysis is flawed by a failure to historicize his subjects' notions of science.

Darnton, Gascoigne and Golinski address aspects of Enlightenment science with an eye to shedding light on broader issues. DARNTON's original and valuable study on the mentality of the French on the eve of the Revolution restores Anton Mesmer to his place as one of that era's "most-talked about men". Mesmerism and animal magnetism are portrayed as radical scientific movements that were suited to the literate French public at a time when many new – and unusual – theories of the universe were being put forth. Mesmer's reliance on invisible forces had analogies in Newton's gravity, Franklin's electricity, and the "miraculous" gases of balloonists. Mesmer's struggles with the established science of the academies appealed to radicals, who were also drawn to those versions of mesmerism that offered unified explanations of the forces governing nature, society, and politics. Mesmerism survived the Enlightenment only as spiritualism, a romantic shadow of its former, more radical, self. Indeed, Darnton's portrayal of educated French society's fascination with Mesmer, "the first German romantic to cross the Rhine", suggests that the Enlightenment itself was waning on the eve of the Revolution.

The richly detailed studies of Gascoigne and Golinski are part of a larger body of scholarship on science in the English and Scottish Enlightenment, much of which builds on PORTER's essay. Porter makes the case for an English Enlightenment, arguing that England led other nations in free-thinking, empiricism, and utilitarianism. The pragmatism of its commercial culture meant that England was almost the only country in which the hopes of enlightenists were not thwarted by the political and social order. The dilemma of the English Enlightenment, Porter argues, was that of satisfying individual and group demands within a "familiar social frame". GASCOIGNE also makes the case for a "corrective to the largely Francocentric view of the Enlightenment, which views it largely as a clash between the apostles of reason and the clerical defenders of tradition". He describes a "holy alliance" between latitudinarian natural theology and Newtonian natural philosophy in Hanoverian England, and especially at Cambridge. This alliance between religion and science is shown to be an integral and,

Gascoigne argues, fruitful aspect of the English Enlightenment.

GOLINSKI examines the techniques, apparatus, and rhetoric of chemistry in order to show how science was constructed as a public culture in England and Scotland, and to undermine the "idealist" view that Lavoisier's accomplishments gave chemistry a scientific basis and led to the reorganization of the discipline. Thus, Joseph Priestley opposed Lavoisier's complex, expensive apparatus and emphasis on calculation skills, because they gave precedence to the private rights of élites over the autonomous judgement of the broader public. In an analysis not unlike Darnton's treatment of mesmerism, Thomas Beddoes's experiments with nitrous oxide are shown to be "emblematic" of the cultural and political meaning of scientific debates. Whereas Beddoes saw utility in the gas, the conservative Edmund Burke saw the effects of the gas as symptomatic of the delusion and hysteria of radical thought. Humphry Davy's ability to a mobilize a monied, middle- and upper-class audience to support the demands of his chemical practices in effect undermined the egalitarian ideals of Priestley's science, and propped up the authority of the scientific expert – another legacy of the Enlightenment.

The Enlightenment project of founding social science is taken up in Hundert's study of the Anglo-Dutch physician and satirist, Bernard Mandeville, and in Baker's work on M. de Condorcet. HUNDERT argues that Mandeville's paradoxical thesis, that society is an agglomeration of individuals united not by a common moral standard but by their passions, offered European intellectuals – including, Rousseau, Hume, and Smith – a means of subjecting not the economy, but society itself, to systematic analysis. The mechanistic, physiological underpinnings of Mandeville's reductionist anatomy of the passions are carefully explained, as are Mandeville's resonances throughout the 18th century. Indeed, Hundert argues that Mandeville's "vocabulary of the passions" shaped talk about society and the self, until it was supplanted by a more dynamic, romantic "language of the emotions". BAKER addresses Condorcet's goal of unifying the existing fragments of a moral and political science into a social science, which, in turn, would serve as the essential condition of a rational social and political order. In an analysis that treats many of the most prominent Enlightenment intellectuals, Baker explores Condorcet's efforts to develop an elaborate calculus, which balanced the greater responsibility of the enlightened minority against the political claims of the unenlightened majority. Condorcet's attempt to reconcile scientific elitism with democratic liberalism is said to make him a founder of a liberal concept of social science.

ENGELHARDT and LEPENIES both examine the relationship between historical thought and science in the 18th and 19th centuries. Engelhardt's thesis is that historical consciousness was an integral part of the self-understanding of Enlightenment natural philosophers; their view that the history of science was a discontinuous process marked by breaks from the past served, ultimately, to legitimate their science. Lepenies focuses on the years 1775–1825 with the aim of showing how the ahistorical natural history of the 18th century gave way to transformism and, eventually, a 19th-century history of nature. Lepenies argues that the great natural histories of the 18th century, especially that of Buffon, continued to thrive in the 19th century, but only as a part of literature, not as

science – a conclusion that has a parallel in Foucault's work on insanity.

Foucault (1965), Rousseau (1991), and Stafford cut across traditional disciplinary boundaries and undermine received views of the Enlightenment, epitomized by Cassirer and Gay. FOUCAULT (1965) argues that in the 18th century, the age of reason, madness was seen not against the background of medicine, but of "Unreason". The treatment of madness as pathology only became possible when reformers such as Philippe Pinel and William Tuke explained madness as the "psychological effect of a moral fault". This moral perception of madness was the nucleus for all the concepts that the 19th century called "scientific, positive, and experimental", and the so-called "liberation of the insane" was in fact nothing more than a "gigantic moral imprisonment". Foucault's heroes are not reformers, but those brilliant individuals such as Friedrich Hölderlin and Nietzsche, who, by "their own strength" kept the life of "Unreason" alive, if only in literature.

The three volumes by ROUSSEAU (1991), written over a 25-year span, represent his intellectual odyssey from a traditional historian of ideas to a "post-disciplinary" scholar. His essays cover science and literature, the history of medicine, studies of gender and sexuality, and literary studies. All are unified by a fascination with fields on the margins of traditional scholarship and by an underlying historicism. Although his approach is excessively autobiographical, these papers do serve as one example of how the changing meaning of historicism over the past three decades has left its mark on Enlightenment studies.

STAFFORD's magnificently illustrated volume juxtaposes an enormous, and sometimes overwhelming, array of evidence from the sciences, medicine, literature, and philosophy, with reproductions of engravings, paintings, caricatures, etc., to demonstrate how the Enlightenment visualized the invisible, especially in medicine. However, Stafford's work is more than a book on the relations between Enlightenment art and science; it is also an extended attack on "logocentrism", abstract schemata, and the philosophical prejudices against "seeing". She aims to show that visual and analogical reasoning were an important part of 18th-century culture. However, there are times when the thread of her argument is barely visible, and it seems fitting that it is, at those times, unified more by numerous reproductions than by a single, sustained line of reasoning. It is also unsurprising, and ironic, that Stafford's rejection of Kant's Enlightenment is entirely polemical.

ERNST P. HAMM

Environmental Sciences

Bocking, Stephen, *Ecologists and Environmental Politics: A History of Contemporary Ecology*, New Haven, Connecticut: Yale University Press, 1997

Bowler, Peter J., *The Fontana History of the Environmental Sciences*, London: Fontana, 1992; as *The Norton History of the Environmental Sciences*, New York: Norton, 1993

Bramwell, Anna, *Ecology in the 20th Century: A History*, New Haven, Connecticut: Yale University Press, 1989

Friedman, Robert Marc, *Appropriating the Weather: Vilhelm Bjerknes and the Construction of a Modern Meteorology*, Ithaca, New York: Cornell University Press, 1989

Glacken, Clarence J., *Traces on the Rhodian Shore: Nature and Culture in Western Thought from Ancient Times to the End of the Eighteenth Century*, Berkeley: University of California Press, 1967

Goudie, Andrew, *Environmental Change*, Oxford and New York: Clarendon Press, 1977

Goudie, Andrew, *The Human Impact: Man's Role in Environmental Change*, Oxford: Blackwell and Cambridge, Massachusetts: MIT Press, 1981; as *The Human Impact on the Natural Environment*, Oxford: Blackwell, and Cambridge, Massachusetts: MIT Press, 1986

Hayward, Tim, *Ecological Thought: An Introduction*, Cambridge: Polity Press, and Cambridge, Massachusetts: Blackwell, 1995

Jardine, Nicholas, James A. Secord and Emma C. Spary (eds), *Cultures of Natural History*, Cambridge and New York: Cambridge University Press, 1996

Livingstone, David N., *The Geographical Tradition: Episodes in the History of a Contested Enterprise*, Oxford and Cambridge, Massachusetts: Blackwell, 1993

Shortland, Michael (ed.), *Science and Nature: Essays in the History of the Environmental Sciences*, Stanford in the Vale: British Society for the History of Science, 1993

Smith, Michael L., *Pacific Visions: California Scientists and the Environment, 1850–1915*, New Haven, Connecticut: Yale University Press, 1987

Söderqvist, Thomas, *The Ecologists: From Merry Naturalists to Saviours of the Nation: A Sociologically Informed Narrative Survey of the Ecologization of Sweden, 1895–1975*, Stockholm: Almqvist & Wiksell, 1986

Worster, Donald, *Nature's Economy: The Roots of Ecology*, San Francisco: Sierra Club Books, 1977; as *Nature's Economy: A History of Ecological Ideas*, Cambridge and New York: Cambridge University Press, 1985

Environmental science was born in the late 1970s, reflecting a growing concern for the environment, and an increasing awareness of the involvement of the sciences in the development of the environment as a social issue. The role of science in this regard has been multifaceted; on the one hand, it is through advances in science that new products, processes, and technologies have emerged that have proved to be damaging to the environment; on the other hand, it is often science that establishes these environmental effects, and analytical science that reveals the deeper significance and consequences of these effects for the earth as a whole. It can even be argued that science has been a crucial player, along with the media, politics, and social movements, in the whole process of the cognitive and cultural construction of "the environment" in the post-World War II period. Today there exists a discipline, with some institutional autonomy, under the name of "environmental science".

The rising interest in the history of the environmental sciences also reflects changes in the agenda of historians of science. Whereas in the past attention was typically focused on theoretical watersheds, "revolutions", and clashes between individual scientists or different schools of thought that formed now-existing disciplines, interest has been growing in recent years in more integrated approaches. Life sciences and earth sciences are integral to the study of imperial expansion, global communication networks, and the growth of academies, botanical and zoological gardens, observatories, museums and other institutions or social spaces for collecting, displaying, disseminating, and utilizing science. One aspect of this new research agenda has been the role played by science in the development of cultural attitudes towards nature, and in the territorial domination and exploitation of natural resources, and the environmental consequences.

The environmental sciences should not be confused with "environmentalism". One meaning of the latter concept is that environmental factors, such as climate, influence humans and culture in a significant way, as was claimed in the Greek treatise *Airs, Waters, Places* of the 5th century bc, customarily attributed to Hippocrates. (Another meaning, that does not concern us here, is the "Green" ideology as conceived by, for example, the environmental movement.) Environmentalism, in the Hippocratic sense, plays an important role in the history of disciplines such as medicine, psychology, anthropology, and sociology. The history of environmentalism is relevant to the history of the environmental sciences in so far as these sciences (for example, geography) have included environmentalist ideas.

Given the fact that the "environmental sciences" have been established fairly recently, the body of literature treating it exclusively or in a targeted manner is not yet large, nor easily identifiable. The concept itself has been in use since the late 1970s, but was not investigated in any depth until the early 1990s. SHORTLAND is one of the few contributions to the field, with essays ranging from the history of climate history (T.S. Feldman) and American pest-control research (Palladino), to a study of the, mostly unsuccessful, attempts to establish human ecology in the US (Cittadino).

To date, there is one comprehensive work that both uses and, in essence, launches the concept as a general field: BOWLER. This is an overview, covering a wide range of geological and biological sciences, and excluding large parts of the chemical, physical, and medical sciences, with a few exceptions – such as geophysics, oceanography, and meteorology. Bowler's definition of the environmental sciences seems to suggest that they are concerned primarily with the natural environment, and not, for example, with city or work environments. In that sense, the concept can be seen as a late 20th-century version of the old concept of natural history, although with slightly different boundaries. The environmental sciences, Bowler suggests, are a projection retrospectively made on sciences such as geology, geography, zoology, evolution theory, paleontology, and oceanography, whose protagonists had no notion of an all-encompassing framework at the time they were working.

Bowler draws attention to the methods by which knowledge concerning the environment is produced, and to the growth of knowledge that has gradually constructed, from antiquity to the present, what can be termed "the environmental world view" (a term not used by Bowler). Although he deals briefly with the complex relationship between environmental science and environmental concern, and its sociological manifestations (groups, movements), this 600-page volume is primarily a work in the genre of the history of the science. The chapters are devoted to classical history of science themes such as "the great instauration", "theories of the earth", and "the age of evolution", with such figures as Aristotle, Buffon, Humboldt, Lyell, Darwin, and Wegener central to Bowler's sweeping coverage. None the less, the book's scope and themes produce a narrative that reveals the deep historical patterns that lie beneath contemporary issues and debates.

There are other overviews which, although they do not use the term "environmental sciences", have contributed to their history. Among those is GLACKEN's seminal history of geographical thought, which provides similar insights to Bowler's, but with greater emphasis on ideas and less emphasis on the science. Glacken is, for example, not particularly interested in how knowledge was won, i.e. the scientific method, nor does he care particularly for controversy or social context. Rather, he concentrates on the leading texts, and the way in which they have influenced changing conceptions of the environment.

Glacken's book is an intellectual history of ancient and early modern geography, which is perhaps the most significant science to the development of the environmental sciences. Geographers are concerned with the earth, with climate, and with the human impact on the environment world-wide. Another useful overview of the intellectual traditions of the discipline is LIVINGSTONE, which begins in the Renaissance and places its main emphasis on the 19th and 20th centuries, when geography was institutionalized as an academic discipline. Livingstone considers geography from the perspective of the history of science, and explores the role of geographical exploration in the growth of knowledge, citing the Swedish natural historian Anders Sparrman, who traveled with Thomas Cook on his second circumnavigation of 1772–75: "Every authentic and well-written book of voyages is, in fact, a treatise of experimental philosophy." In his quest to delineate the geographical project, Livingstone draws other environmental sciences into the picture, including geology, natural history, biology, and meteorology. He stresses the spatial dimension of these sciences, pointing especially to Humboldt and his role in the development of the concept of "the region", the environmental conditions of which serve as the constituting elements of the geographical patterns of different life forms.

General textbooks of physical geography sometimes function as inventories of progress in the environmental sciences. Good examples are GOUDIE (1981), and GOUDIE (1977), which cite the regular pre-20th century precursors – Buffon, Humboldt, Lyell, Marsh, etc. – but also the 19th-century Scottish scientist, Mary Somerville, who revealed close links between 19th-century environmental science and present-day concerns when she wrote: "Man's necessities and enjoyments have been the cause of great changes in the animal creation, and his destructive propensities of still greater."

Ideally, in order to reach an understanding of the environmental sciences, they must be considered both as separate disciplines and in the light of the environmental issues with which they have become associated over the past two decades. Many works on the history of the environmental sciences provide the former, but few the latter. Among those that meet both qualifications, most are on the history of ecology. The seminal work in this field is by WORSTER. It begins with the reflections of the parish priest, Gilbert White on rural English Selborne in the mid-18th century, and ends with the less harmonious ecology of the 1980s and 1990s. There is, argues Worster, a tension at the heart of the ecological tradition, as an "Arcadian", holistic approach has from the outset been challenged by an "imperial", more rationalistic and atomistic, approach, in line with Enlightenment science and quantification.

A number of more specialised studies have followed. SÖDERQVIST, focusing on Swedish developments, gives a sociologically and theoretically informed analysis of why, after World War II, four successive generations of ecologists came and went before the discipline became not only accepted but fashionable, and in the 1960s and 1970s received substantial funding and political wooing. BOCKING provides a study of ecologists at four institutions – the Nature Conservancy of Great Britain, the Oak Ridge National Laboratory and Hubbard Brook Ecosystem Study, both in the US, and the University of Toronto fisheries research in Ontario, Canada. Bocking's analysis demonstrates that, although there have been links between the science of ecology and the growth of environmental awareness, the post-World War II period is characterized by the need among ecologists to navigate between external demands and the more narrowly defined agenda of their science. HAYWARD presents the significance of ecological scientific results and theories for ethics and philosophy, thus pointing to one of the most important effects of the environmental sciences – their influence on environmental ideas and, indirectly, on the media, politics, economics, and the social debate at large. BRAMWELL, a British sociologist, is more critical, especially regarding what she interprets as the "brown", or fascist, tendencies of ecologism.

Of the environmental sciences, only ecology has been generously analyzed from the vantage point of late 20th-century environmentalism. However, there are also examples from other fields. For meteorology, there is FRIEDMAN, who explores the connections between early 20th-century meteorology, the Bjerknes school of Norway, and the increasing awareness of climate change. Increasingly, a modern environmental dimension becomes visible in works on the geosciences.

A sign of the close historical relationships between natural history, that nebulous and holistic 18th- and 19th-century field of enquiry, and the emerging environmental sciences is a collection of articles edited by JARDINE, SECORD & SPARY. The 25 or so articles may not elaborate on the links between their respective subjects – botanical gardens, zoos, gender, biogeography, travel, anthropology, field studies, etc. – and current environmental concerns. However, the contextual *raison d'être* of the volume, as spelled out by the editors ("Through historical studies we can hope to regain the natural and human worlds that we are in danger of losing") and by Secord in his concluding essay ("The Crisis of Nature" – "a bold enquiry into the past can uncover the basic structures . . . of change which lie behind our current dilemmas") – lies in the growing awareness of the historical roots of the environmental situation, and the still reverberating implications of natural history and what Secord terms "its successor disciplines" – i.e., largely, the environmental sciences.

SMITH is an interesting contribution to the role of environmental science, which shows how scientists in fact construct the image of the territory they are investigating, and how their descriptions of (and, more often than not, their affection for) such territories play an important role in the creation of individual, regional, and national environmental awareness. Smith's example is California in the period 1850–1915, but his work might serve as a useful model for other periods and regions.

SVERKER SÖRLIN

See also Ecology; Meteorology

Epidemics

Creighton, Charles, *A History of Epidemics in Britain*, 2 vols, Cambridge: Cambridge University Press, 1891–94; 2nd edition, with additional material by D.E.C. Eversley, E. Ashworth Underwood and Lynda Ovenall, London: Frank Cass, and New York: Barnes and Noble, 1965

Kraut, Alan M., *Silent Travelers: Germs, Genes, and the "Immigrant Menace"*, New York: Basic Books, 1994

Mack, Arien (ed.), *In Time of Plague: The History and Social Consequences of Lethal Epidemic Disease*, New York: New York University Press, 1991

McNeill, William H., *Plagues and Peoples*, New York: Anchor Press, 1976; Oxford: Blackwell, 1977

Nikkiforuk, Andrew, *The Fourth Horseman: A Short History of Epidemics, Plagues and Other Scourges*, Canada: Penguin, 1991; London: Fourth Estate, 1992

Ranger, Terence and Paul Slack (eds), *Epidemics and Ideas: Essays on the Historical Perception of Pestilence*, Cambridge: Cambridge University Press, 1992

Rosenberg, Charles E., *Explaining Epidemics and Other Studies in the History of Medicine*, Cambridge and New York: Cambridge University Press, 1992

Walter, John and Roger Schofield (eds), *Famine, Disease and the Social Order in Early Modern Society*, Cambridge and New York: Cambridge University Press, 1989

The history of epidemics as a general phenomenon, as opposed to that of specific outbreaks of disease, has been relatively neglected until recently. With the emergence of the global AIDS pandemic in the 1980s, however, historical interest in epidemics revived. Most of the available literature is in essay form, with a focus on specific diseases or on specific aspects of epidemic outbreaks. A rare attempt at a synthesis of "major changes in patterns of pestilential infection" is provided by McNEILL. Spanning human history from the early hunter-gatherers to the 20th century, McNeill demonstrates the impact of epidemic disease on human societies in the context of their ecological environment. The interplay of disease agent, human host, and natural environment is a central theme of this readable overview, which sets the biological experience within a social and cultural framework. In contrast, CREIGHTON's two-volume account of epidemics is essentially antiquarian in its approach, focusing on the date and nature of different disease outbreaks, ranging from the unspecific plagues of the classical period to the 19th-century scourges of measles, typhus, and smallpox. Still valuable as a factual resource, Creighton's interpretative observations must be treated with great care: he was an anti-vaccinationist, for example, and also rejected the

concept of cholera as a water-borne disease. NIKKIFORUK's popular account, written in a fashionable but tiresomely cynical style, is a modern variant of Creighton, although focused on a narrower range of diseases, and with a quite specific propagandist message. The warning that man's abuse of his environment leads to epidemic disaster is central to the accounts of bubonic plague, syphilis, smallpox, influenza, and AIDS.

Recent scholarly contributions amplify the historical concerns indicated by McNeill, and serve as a corrective to the older and popular literature. The essays collected by WALTER & SCHOFIELD spring essentially from the traditions of historical demography, and, in their concern with food-prices, famines, popular unrest, and mortality peaks, provide a social and economic dimension to discussions concerning disease patterns. The relationship between disease and nutrition has a significance beyond the phenomena of epidemics, and the studies in this book usefully detail the minute patterns of daily existence of the early modern past. Important points to emerge from these discussions are the absence of correlations between mortality peaks and years of high prices, and the contrasting experiences of England and France.

The essays collected by RANGER & SLACK focus on the way epidemics have influenced social, political, and theological ideas. Despite the wide range of their coverage – from classical times to 20th-century Britain – these essays demonstrate that epidemics have provoked very similar responses in very different times and places, but that man's perception of such events is determined by the contemporaneous social and political milieu. The immediate intellectual response to epidemic events may be similar as regards actions and blame, but individual societies will construct very different interpretations on these events for themselves.

The emphasis on epidemics as "socio-cultural events as much as biological and medical ones" is also central to the collection edited by MACK, which is specifically intended to provide a historical context for AIDS. Important issues include the definition and control of epidemics, the effects of new technologies and scientific research on perceptions of disease, and the moral and ethical responsibilities – both of society towards the victims of plague, and of the victims to society in return. Of special interest are contributions by Joshua Lederberg and Lewis Thomas, who take respectively a pessimistic and an optimistic view of the potential of modern medical science to limit the emergence of new epidemics. Five of the essays by ROSENBERG relate directly to epidemics, and these include some of the most influential recent contributions to the field. "Cholera in 19th-century Europe" is a classic, which sets out the ways in which disease can be used as a "sampling device" for the analysis of social, economic, and intellectual relationships, while "Framing Disease" explores the factors that determine how societies explain such disease. The other three essays address historical issues raised by AIDS, such as how societies construct their responses to disease, and how epidemics are defined, described, and explained. Although intended to provide a historical background for AIDS, these essays are important also for the historical understanding of epidemics in general.

The diversity of case histories and intellectual contributions contained in these essay collections can usefully be put in perspective by KRAUT's analysis of the American Association of Immigrants and the introduction of epidemic disease. Cholera and AIDS perhaps predictably figure in this account, but so do the untypical epidemics poliomyelitis (not an obviously contagious disease) and tuberculosis (long term and chronic, though known by 1900 to be infectious), so demonstrating that social reactions to "epidemics" can relate to untypical, as well as typical, disease outbreaks.

ANNE HARDY

See also AIDS; Epidemiology; Fevers; Plague; Tuberculosis, Venereal Disease

Epidemiology

Creighton, Charles, *A History of Epidemics in Britain from AD 644 to the Present Time*, 2 vols, Cambridge: Cambridge University Press, 1891–94, 2nd edition, with additional material by D.E.C. Eversley, E. Ashworth Underwood and Lynda Ovenall, London: Frank Cass, and New York, Barnes and Noble, 1965

Etheridge, Elizabeth W., *Sentinel for Health: A History of the Centers for Disease Control*, Berkeley: University of California Press, 1992

Evans, Richard J., *Death in Hamburg: Society and Politics in the Cholera Years, 1830–1910*, Oxford: Clarendon Press, and New York: Oxford University Press, 1987

Feinstein, Alvan R., *Clinical Judgment*, Baltimore: Williams and Wilkins, 1967

Greenwood, Major, *Epidemiology, Historical and Experimental*, Baltimore: Johns Hopkins University Press, 1932

Hardy, Anne, *The Epidemic Streets: Infectious Disease and the Rise of Preventive Medicine, 1856–1900*, Oxford: Clarendon Press, and New York: Oxford University Press, 1993

Hirsch, August, *Handbook of Geographical and Historical Pathology*, translated from the second German edition by Charles Creighton, 3 vols, London: New Sydenham Society, 1883–86

Hopkins, Donald R., *Princes and Peasants: Smallpox in History*, Chicago: University of Chicago Press, 1983

Lilienfeld, Abraham M. (ed.), *Times, Places, and Persons: Aspects of the History of Epidemiology* (conference proceedings), Baltimore: Johns Hopkins University Press, 1980

McNeill, William H., *Plagues and Peoples*, New York: Anchor Press, 1976; Oxford: Blackwell, 1977

Matthews, J. Rosser, *Quantification and the Quest for Medical Certainty*, Princeton, New Jersey: Princeton University Press, 1995

Shephard, David A.E., *John Snow: Anaesthetist to a Queen and Epidemiologist to a Nation*, Cornwall, Canada: York Point Publishing, 1995

Shrewsbury, J.F.D., *A History of Bubonic Plague in the British Isles*, Cambridge: Cambridge University Press, 1970

Slack, Paul, *The Impact of Plague in Tudor and Stuart England*, London and Boston: Routledge and Kegan Paul, 1985

Snow, John, *Snow on Cholera*, with an introduction by Wade Hampton Frost, New York: Commonwealth Fund, and London: Milford/Oxford University Press, 1936

Wilkinson, Lise, "Epidemiology", in *Companion Encyclopedia of the History of Medicine*, edited by W.F. Bynum and Roy Porter, 2 vols, London and New York: Routledge, 1993

Winslow, Charles-Edward Amory, *The Conquest of Epidemic Disease: A Chapter in the History of Ideas*, Madison: University of Wisconsin Press, 1943; reprinted, Madison: University of Wisconsin Press, 1980

Zinsser, Hans, *Rats, Lice and History*, Boston: Little Brown, 1935

Epidemics have always been a feature of settled human societies, and the importance of epidemic disease as a major determinant of human history is now widely appreciated. McNEILL has differentiated between the microparasitism of "germs" of all kinds, and the macroparasitism of wars, conquests and political repression – each can lead to profound social disruption. The study of epidemics has a long tradition, occupying a particularly important niche in the Hippocratic writings, and even predating them. Nevertheless, as WILKINSON has pointed out in her synoptic account of the subject, epidemiology as a word and a discipline is a product of the 19th century. She has argued for a tripartite periodisation: the first period stretched from antiquity to the early 19th century, during which epidemics were usually described qualitatively; the second period lasted about a century, and began when more systematic social and medical statistics and, eventually, the germ theory of disease allowed observers to account for the biological and demographic features of epidemic diseases; we are still in the third period, during which the discipline has become increasingly concerned with chronic diseases.

The classic accounts of HIRSCH and CREIGHTON were written during the second period and reflect the statistical orientation of that era. Hirsch's volumes first appeared in the 1860s, before the cognitive framework of the germ theory was in place; Creighton worked a generation later, and was anomalous in his passionate adherence to older, miasmatic notions of epidemic disease causation. At the same time, both works scoured a wide range of printed and archival sources in search of material, and record much of continuing historical value. WINSLOW's monograph provides a useful post-bacteriological account of what until recently was still complacently called "the conquest of epidemic disease".

Traditional epidemiological scourges included plague, smallpox, measles and what is now called "typhus", but was historically regarded as part of a much larger disease category known as "fever". Disease-specific monographs offer handy insights into earlier modes of medical thought. For plague, the monographs of SHREWSBURY and SLACK may be mentioned. Shrewsbury sought to exploit modern bacteriological knowledge within a historical framework, and despite the volume's modernist cast, it contains much of interest. Slack approached the early modern experience of bubonic plague from a social and political stance, though without neglecting contemporary medical conceptualisations or the ways in which medical ideas were translated into practical action. HOPKINS offered a useful overview of the history of smallpox (a disease that never conformed to the ordinary miasmatic paradigm). ZINSSER's well-known account of "typhus" is triumphalist in its orientation, but still a work of powerful historical synthesis. Zinsser had himself contributed to the modern scientific understanding of the etiology and epidemiology of the disease, but his monograph takes account of the social and cultural dimensions of typhus.

Among 19th-century epidemic diseases, cholera reigned supreme. It catalysed public health action, encouraged attempts at international sanitary cooperation, and generated much medical debate about the nature and mode of the spread of the disease. The investigations of John SNOW (1813–58) during the London epidemics of 1848 and 1854 are now viewed as brilliant epidemiological demonstrations of the disease's specificity, and its spread through faecal-contaminated water. FROST reproduced and introduced Snow's texts in the early 20th century, and SHEPHARD has recently produced a reasonable full-length biography of this remarkable anaesthetist and general practitioner. Although Snow's work did have some contemporary impact, it is more appreciated now than it was in the 19th century, as EVANS's study of cholera, public health and politics in Hamburg demonstrates. HARDY's fine monograph on epidemic diseases in late 19th-century London astutely analyses the interplay between investigation and practical action.

The collection of essays edited by LILIENFELD remains a helpful introduction to several major epidemiologists of the second period, including William Farr (1807–83), and Joseph Goldberger (1874–1929), as well as Pierre Louis (1787–1872), who may be described as a "clinical epidemiologist". In addition, the volume highlights the importance of statistics to epidemiology, following the mathematical work of Karl Pearson (1857–1936) and his student Major Greenwood (1880–1949), who became professor of epidemiology at the London School of Hygiene and Tropical Medicine (LSHTM). GREENWOOD's own historical writings are still of value, but, more significantly, his department at the LSHTM was instrumental in the transition of the discipline to its modern form.

As epidemiology has come to be concerned with all forms of disease in populations, and not simply with acute epidemics, its methods and institutional links have changed. No comprehensive historical study of its modern development exists. However, several important features have been examined. FEINSTEIN's monograph, though now somewhat dated, offers insights into the nature of modern clinical epidemiology, and also draws on a good deal of historical material. In particular, Feinstein deftly analyses the ways in which the mathematical tools of field epidemiologists can be applied to the clinical setting. The AIDS epidemic threw into prominence the principal monitoring agency in the United States, the Centers for Diseases Control (CDC), the history of which has been well chronicled by ETHERIDGE.

MATTHEWS has recently analysed quantitative thinking in medicine, and his volume contains a good discussion of the relationship between Pearson and Greenwood, as well as the fundamental work of Austin Bradford Hill (1897–1991) in medical statistics and the planning of "double-blind" clinical trials. No examination of 20th-century epidemiology omits the studies of Hill and Richard Doll (b. 1912) on the relationship between cigarette smoking and lung cancer. Beginning in the late 1940s, they designed a number of methodologically sophisticated investigations that did much to introduce the public to the notion of "risk factors" associated with a variety of diseases, life styles, and medical and surgical therapies. Matthews has argued that the decline of medical authority during the past few decades has contributed to the public's demand that medical pronouncements and new treatments be subjected to tests of statistical significance. Several historians are presently working on aspects of this important dimension of modern medicine, to which epidemiology is crucial.

W.F. BYNUM

See also Epidemics; Plague; Public Health

Error Theory

Bru, Bernard, "Laplace et la critique probabiliste des mesures géodesiques", in *La Figure de la terre, du XVIIIe siècle a l'ère spatiale*, edited by Henri Lacombe and Pierre Costabel, Paris: Gauthier-Villars, 1988, 223–44

Colclough, A.R., "Two Theories of Experimental Error", *Journal of Research of the National Bureau of Standards*, 92 (1987): 167–85

Czuber, Emanuel, *Theorie der Beobachtungsfehler*, Leipzig: Teubner, 1891

Daston, Lorraine, "The Moral Economy of Science", in *Constructing Knowledge in the History of Science*, Osiris (special issue), edited by Arnold Thackray, 10 (1995): 3–24

Hon, Giora, "Towards a Typology of Experimental Errors: An Epistemological View", *Studies in History and Philosophy of Science*, 20 (1989): 469–504

Knobloch, Eberhard, "Historical Aspects of the Foundations of Error Theory", in *The Space of Mathematics: Philosophical, Epistemological, and Historical Explorations*, edited by Javier Echeverria, Andoni Ibarra and Thomas Mormann, Berlin: De Gruyter, 1992, 253–79

Mendoza, Eric, "Physics, Chemistry and the Theory of Errors", *Archives Internationale d'Histoire des Sciences*, 41 (1991): 282–306

Olesko, Kathryn M., *Physics as a Calling: Discipline and Practice in the Königsberg Seminar for Physics*, Ithaca, New York: Cornell University Press, 1991

Rider, Paul R., *Criteria for Rejection of Observations*, St Louis, Missouri: Washington University Studies, 1933

Sheynin, O.B., "Theory of Errors", in *Companion Encyclopedia of the History and Philosophy of the Mathematical Sciences*, vol. 2, edited by Ivor Grattan-Guinness, London and New York: Routledge, 1994

Stigler, Stephen M., *The History of Statistics : The Measurement of Uncertainty before 1900*, Cambridge, Massachusetts: Belknap Press of Harvard University Press, 1986

Swijtink, Zeno G., "The Objectification of Observation: Measurement and Statistical Methods in the Nineteenth

Century", in *The Probabilistic Revolution*, vol. 1: *Ideas in History*, edited by Lorenz Krüger *et al.*, Cambridge, Massachusetts: MIT Press, 1987, 261–85

Wise, M. Norton (ed.), *The Values of Precision*, Princeton, New Jersey: Princeton University Press, 1995

To have a concept of error, and a systematic approach towards error, one needs a concept of truth, and a method of reasoning towards truth. The method of reasoning concerned in the Theory of Error is the instrumental method, as used in the experimental and observational sciences. This method not only includes observing nature by means of instruments – i.e., disciplining perception by registering nature's effects on instruments – but also making a record, whether on tablets, paper, tape, or discs, of what is observed – as in astronomical records, laboratory notebooks, or surveying logs. In self-recording instruments, these records are obtained without an intervening human observer. The Theory of Error provides a means of handling the observational record, and much effort has been put into simplifying and automating the often laborious calculations. Error theory also structures the observational process itself, by linking the precision desired to the "design" of the experiment: by determining how many and what data are collected; by instructing how the instruments are to be fine-tuned; and by determining what collateral observations should be made for the correction of raw data. Finally, as in Jean Charles de Borda's repeating circle and the German answer, Friedrich Wilhelm Bessel's reiterating circle, error theory has shaped the very design of scientific instruments.

The expression "Theory of Errors" was coined around 1760 by the Enlightenment natural philosopher Johann Heinrich Lambert, for the systematic treatment of that part of the variation in experimental and observational quantitative data that does not derive from variations in the material studied, but is caused by instrumental drift, observers lapses, and other sources of error. Truth and error thus signal the separation between the object of knowledge on the one hand, and the knower and method of knowing on the other. Thus, DASTON discusses error theory as part of the moral economy of mechanical objectivity, since its mechanical rules of calculation eliminate personal judgment in the treatment of the observational record.

In 1722, before Thomas Simpson, Lambert, and Joseph Louis Lagrange made error theory probabilistic in the latter half of the 18th century, Roger Cotes applied the mathematics of the differential calculus to obtain maximal bounds of error. In geodesic triangulation, for instance, the problem was raised of what shape of triangle would minimize the final error. SHEYNIN calls this the determinate branch of error theory, since it concerns the question of how error bounds are propagated through a series of calculations that combine measurements from a complicated network of points. BRU discusses how questions of determinate error theory shaped the practice and reporting of the survey expeditions sent out by the Paris *Académie des Sciences* to Lappland (April 1736–August 1737, led by Maupertuis) and Peru (1735–43, led by Pierre Bouguer and Charles-Marie de La Condamine) to determine the figure of the earth. These expeditions, together with the surveys for a new map of France, placed the problem of random error in geodesic measurements at the center of attention of mathematical astronomers, such as Jean Baptiste Delambre and Pierre Simon Laplace, in the second half of the 18th century.

Probabilistic error theory assumes that errors have a frequency distribution. This distribution is used to calculate the reliability of estimates made on the basis of the observational record. The theory of errors was an important playing field for the development of inferential statistics in the early 19th century. It was in this field that advanced probability mathematics was kept alive in the second half of the 19th century, after the disintegration of the classical conception of probability. During the 19th century, the theory of errors was dominated by the method of least squares of A.M. Legendre and Carl Gauss, and by the law of error, the normal distribution that came up in one of Gauss's justifications of the method of least squares. The theory had a coherency that one would expect of something so named, but the actual use of error theory based on least squares varied greatly, and many fields of science outside astronomy and geodesy dealt with errors in data in a less systematic manner than the strictures of least squares demanded. Today, the field of error theory shows a patchwork of approaches and techniques, from the Kalman filter to Goldberger-Theil estimators.

Hon and Colclough give a conceptual discussion of measurement error. HON argues that, since it is mathematically-based and thus does not consider the causes of errors or the context in which they arise, the traditional classification of errors into random and systematic is inappropriate for the historiography of experimental science. He considers an ideal chronology for experimentation, and proposes a four-fold typology of experimental errors, based on four stages of experimentation: i) laying down the theoretical framework; ii) constructing the apparatus and making it work; iii) taking observations or readings; iv) processing and interpreting the recorded data. This paper provides illustrations from the history of science, such as the Millikan-Ehrenhaft dispute on the nature of the electron, and William Herschel's discovery of Uranus.

COLCLOUGH clarifies traditional error theory, with its classification of errors into random and systematic, and contrasts it with the so-called "randomatic theory" that emerged in the recent history of the Bureau International des Poids et Mesure, in which systematic errors are treated within subjective Bayesian probability theory, and are incorporated into a total probabilistic estimate of uncertainty. The distinction between random and systematic error is fluid, since by changes in experimental design a source of systematic error can be transformed into a source of random error, as when the arms of a balance are randomly rotated in a weighing, or the start pulse in time-of-arrival correlators is randomly chosen.

SWIJTINK argues that exclusively numeric approaches to error (as in least squares) are only to be expected when calculators have no close acquaintance with the individual phenomena that have given rise to the data – as happens when there is division of labor between experimenters or observers and calculators, or when data are read off from instruments and the phenomenon is not otherwise accessible to the experimenter, or when data sets become unwieldy, large, and complicated. In such situations, all the information that calculators have on a phenomenon is of a numerical nature. Since there is no qualitative evidence present that could impede the inference, the method of least squares can be mechanically applied, within the constraints of the principle of total evidence. Sometimes, however, internal evidence suggested that least squares could not be mechanically applied before certain "outliers" – data with unexpectedly large residuals – were removed from the data set. To make this procedure objective, theoreticians of error theory proposed a large number of significance tests, "rules for the rejection of outliers", in order to identify outliers. RIDER is a secondary source listing, and discusses many of the rules for the rejection of outliers that were proposed during the 19th and early 20th centuries. Historiographically it is not sophisticated, but it is as yet the only discussion of this important part of error theory.

There exists no book-length treatment of the history of error theory, but a number of sections in STIGLER deal with the development leading up to the method of least squares. It is a story of statistical failure by a leading mathematician, Leonard Euler, and statistical success by a major astronomer, Tobias Mayer. Mayer worked on the perturbations in the movement of the moon, a problem of navigational significance, since a method of finding longitude depended on it. CZUBER has a historical section that remains useful. He surveys Gauss's two proofs to provide foundations for the method of least squares: the first based on the principle of maximum likelihood, and the assumption that the mean is the most likely value; the second on a minimization of loss, measured in terms of the square of the error. Czuber then contrasts these with Laplace's approach, which was independent of any special law of probability for the individual errors, but assumed a very large number of observations. Also described are the approaches of Gotthilf Hagen and Peter Guthrie Tait, which are based on assumptions about the elementary causes of error, and other justifications of the normal law by Robert Adrain, William Herschel, and William Fishburn Donkin. More than 40 papers by Oscar Sheynin provide a rich documentation for a history of error theory from Al-Burini to Dmitri Mendeleev (see Sheynin for further references). KNOBLOCH is particularly informative on the foundational debates of the 19th century; by exposing the complexity of the issues involved – concepts of proof, rigor, strictness, and experience – he shows why there was such long dispute over the foundations of the method of least squares.

Although no systematic overview exists, it is commonly agreed that the use of error theory in the different branches of science varied greatly in the 19th century. OLESKO is a fascinating study of the Königsberg Seminar for Physics founded by Franz Ernst Neumann in 1834. Neumann adopted the instrument analysis of the astronomer Friedrich Wilhelm Bessel, including his use of least squares, and transformed it into a new style of precision measurement and precision calculation in his study of heat, magnetism, and optics. MENDOZA argues that in the first half of the 19th century, formal error theory, in the sense of the method of least squares, was restricted to astronomy and geodesy. Early uses of error theory in chemistry occurred around the mid-19th century, first in Germany – not in the reduction of a single experiment by the observers themselves, but in the recalculations of data obtained by others, especially in discussions of William Prout's hypothesis that all atomic weights are multiples of that of hydrogen. Around the same time, experimenters in physics (Mendoza's material here is mainly from England and France) were mostly concerned with eliminating gross systematic error, but rough measures of uncertainty, based on the difference between extreme measurements, were in use, as was subjective choice of "best data". After 1870, textbooks for students taking practical physics laboratory – modeled on Friedrich Kohlrausch's *Leitfaden der praktischen Physik*, written for laboratory practice in Göttingen – made error theory a minor part of laboratory calculations; in Britain this was often embedded in a discourse about visual inspection and judgment. As in chemistry, error theory entered physics more seriously in the 1920s, in the books of tables of physical constants, with which calculators without first-hand knowledge of experimental runs had to find the most probable value between differing determinations.

A history of error (avoidance) is at the same time a history of the attempt to attain precision and accuracy, and the accompanying scientific sensibilities: see the papers in WISE, especially Kathryn Olesko's discussion of the exact sensibility in 19th-century Germany, where precision measurements and the numerical discipline of error analysis were used to discipline laboratory training, and instil students with the purportedly "masculine" virtues of honesty, integrity, and earnestness.

ZENO G. SWIJTINK

See also Measurement; Objectivity; Statistics

Ethnomathematics

Ascher, Marcia, *Ethnomathematics: A Multicultural View of Mathematical Ideas*, Pacific Grove, California: Brooks/Cole, 1991

Ascher, Marcia and Robert Ascher, *Code of the Quipu: A Study in Media, Mathematics, and Culture*, Ann Arbor: University of Michigan Press, 1981

Bishop, Alan J., *Mathematical Enculturation: A Cultural Perspective on Mathematics Education*, Dordrecht and Boston: Kluwer, 1988

Closs, Michael P. (ed.), *Native American Mathematics*, Austin: University of Texas Press, 1986

Crump, Thomas, *The Anthropology of Numbers*, Cambridge and New York: Cambridge University Press, 1990

D'Ambrosio, Ubiratan, "Ethnomathematics and Its Place in the History and Pedagogy of Mathematics", *For the Learning of Mathematics*, 5/1 (1985): 44–48

D'Ambrosio, Ubiratan, *Etnomatemática: arte ou técnica de explicare e conhecer*, São Paulo: Ática, 1990

Gerdes, Paulus, *Ethnogeometrie. Kulturanthropologische Beiträge zur Genese und Didaktik der Geometrie*, Bad Salzdethfurth: Franzbecker, 1991

Gerdes, Paulus, *Women and Geometry in Southern Africa: Suggestions for Further Research*, Maputo: Universidade Pedagógica, 1995

Høyrup, Jens, *In Measure, Number, and Weight: Studies in Mathematics and Culture*, Albany: State University of New York Press, 1994

Nissen, Hans J., Peter Damerow and Robert K. Englund, *Archaic Bookkeeping: Writing and Techniques of Economic Administration in the Ancient Near East*, translated from the German by Paul Larsen, Chicago:

University of Chicago Press, 1993 (original edition, 1990)

Wilder, Raymond L., *Mathematics as a Cultural System*, Oxford and New York: Pergamon Press, 1981

Zaslavsky, Claudia, *Africa Counts: Number and Pattern in African Culture*, Boston: Prindle Weber and Schmidt, 1973

Ethnomathematics may be defined as the study of the history and practice of mathematics within diverse cultural contexts. It is a relatively new field of interest that lies at the confluence of mathematics, cultural anthropology, and the history of science. The prevailing academic view during the first half of the 20th century was that mathematics was a universal, basically aprioristic form of knowledge. A reductionist tendency dominated by and large mathematics education, implying culture-free cognition models.

One of the first mathematicians to challenge this view was Raymond Wilder, in his address to the International Congress of Mathematicians in 1950, entitled "The Cultural Basis of Mathematics". His thesis, later elaborated in WILDER, may be summarized thus: each culture has its own mathematics, which evolves and dies with the culture. He considers professional mathematics a cultural system, and studies examples of cultural patterns observable in, and "laws" governing the evolution of, this mathematics. The reflections of Wilder did not find much support in the 1950s and 1960s.

In the late 1970s and early 1980s, awareness of the societal and cultural aspects of their discipline began to grow among mathematicians and mathematics educators. One of the important factors contributing to this gradual development was the failure of the hasty transplantation of the "New Mathematics" curriculum from North to South during the 1960s. It was within this context that the Brazilian D'Ambrosio – often called the intellectual "father of ethnomathematics" – launched his ethnomathematical programme, described in Portuguese in D'AMBROSIO (1990), and in a shorter statement in English in D'AMBROSIO (1985). His programme seeks to explain the processes of generation, transmission, and institutionalization of knowledge in diverse cultural systems, and the interactive forces working on and between these three processes. Each cultural group has its own form of mathematizing, and this should be the starting point in mathematics education. In particular, he calls attention to the mathematical practices of the colonized peoples and marginalized population groups, and recommends the incorporation of their knowledge into school education.

A cultural perspective on mathematical education is also presented by BISHOP, who sees certain mathematical activities as common to all human societies throughout history: counting, locating, measuring, designing, playing, and explaining. The process of enculturation through mathematical education into the internationally dominant mathematics of today is then analyzed.

Common conceptions of geometry in the historiography of mathematics are analyzed and criticized in GERDES (1991). He contributes to the elaboration of a methodology for reconstructing (elements of) the early history of geometrical practices embedded in culturally important activities, such as mat and basket weaving, pot making, and house building. On the basis of the first results obtained by applying this methodology, he criticizes the conjecture of a ritual origin of geometry, and reflects on the genesis of ancient geometry. The final chapter deals with possible implications for the teaching of geometry. Female geometrical practices in southern Africa are analyzed in GERDES (1995).

The American mathematician ASCHER became increasingly conscious of the omission, or misinterpretation, of "traditional" peoples in the mathematics literature. For her, ethnomathematics has the goal of broadening the history of mathematics to include a multicultural, global perspective, and thus of enlarging the history of mathematics from treating primarily the "Western" professional class called mathematicians, to involving all types of people. From this perspective, numbers, tracing graphs in the sand, logic of relations, chance and strategy in games and puzzles, the organization and modeling of space, symmetrical strip decorations among "traditional" peoples – including the Inuit, Navajo, and Iroquois of North America, the Incas of South America, the Malekula, Waripiri, Maori of Oceania, the Tchokwe, Bushoong, and Kpelle of Africa – are analyzed. In an earlier study (ASCHER & ASCHER) she made with her husband, an anthropologist reconstructs the cultural context of the "quipu" of the Inca – knotted colored cords, used to record and transmit information throughout their vast empire – and analyzes the mathematical ideas incorporated in them.

Not all authors of studies belonging to the field of ethnomathematics as defined above used the expression "ethnomathematics". For example, in the 1970s, ZASLAVSKY was concerned with the "sociomathematics" of Africa – the applications of mathematics in the lives of African people, and, conversely, the influence that African institutions have had upon the evolution of their mathematics. From this perspective, she discussed numbers and numeration systems, mathematical recreations, pattern and shape, and presented short regional studies of Southwest Nigeria and East Africa. Today, however, Zaslavsky uses the concept of ethnomathematics to characterize her work.

Further examples of the variety of studies that belong to the domain of ethnomathematics are those of Nissen, Damerow & Englund, Høyrup, Closs and Crump. NISSEN, DAMEROW & ENGLUND – archaeologist, mathematician and historian respectively – use philological research and computer analyzis to decipher much of the numerical information contained in the earliest clay tablets from Babylonia (proto-cuneiform script). In reconstructing both the social context and the function of the notation, they consider how the development of these written records affected patterns of thought, the concept of number, the evolution of arithmetic, and the administration of household economics.

HØYRUP's collection of papers provides a sociocultural study of the changing modes of mathematical thought throughout history – in Sumero-Babylonia, Mesopotamia, Ancient Greece, the European Middle Ages, the formation of Islamic mathematics, and the Renaissance. The final chapter, written together with B. Booß-Bavnbek, is an essay on the implications, past and present, of military involvement in the mathematical sciences for their development and potential.

CRUMP is an attempt, by an anthropologist, to find out how people from a wide range of diverse cultures, and from different historical contexts, use and understand numbers. The opening chapters lay the basis for examining the way numbers operate in different contexts, by considering ontological, cognitive, and linguistic aspects. Subsequent chapters deal with specific themes such as cosmology, politics, measurement, time, money, music, games, and architecture.

CLOSS includes contributions on number systems and their "cultural ecology" among various Indian peoples from North, Central, and South America. Earlier mathematical ideas among the Inca, Maya, and Aztec are also discussed.

PAULUS GERDES

See also Africa: south of the Sahara; Egypt and Mesopotamia; Ethnoscience

Ethnoscience

Ascher, Marcia, *Ethnomathematics: A Multiculural View of Mathematical Ideas*, Pacific Grove, California: Brooks/Cole, 1991

Bernal, Martin, *Black Athena: The Afroasiatic Roots of Classical Civilization*, 2 vols, New Brunswick, New Jersey: Rutgers University Press, 1987–91

Catalá, José Sala, *Ciencia y técnica en la metropolización de América*, Madrid: Doce Calles, 1994

Cavalli-Sforza, L. Luca, Paolo Menozzi and Alberto Piazza, *The History of the Geography of Human Genes*, Princeton, New Jersey: Princeton University Press, 1994

Clark, Grahame, *Space, Time and Man: A Prehistorian's View*, Cambridge and New York: Cambridge University Press, 1992

Closs, Michael P. (ed.), *Native American Mathematics*, Austin: University of Texas Press, 1986

Crombie, A.C., *Styles of Scientific Thinking in the European Tradition: The History of Argument and Explanation, Especially in the Mathematical and Biomedical Sciences and Arts*, 3 vols, London: Duckworth, 1994

D'Ambrosio, Ubiratan, *Etnomatemática: arte ou técnica de explicar e conhecer*, São Paulo: Ática, 1990

D'Ambrosio, Ubiratan, "The Cultural Dynamics of the Encounter of Two Worlds after 1492, as Seen in the Development of Scientific Thought", *Impact of Science on Society*, 167 (1992): 205–14

D'Ambrosio, Ubiratan, "The History of Mathematics and Ethnomathematics", *Impact of Science on Society*, 170 (1993): 369–77

Diop, Cheikh Anta, *Civilization or Barbarism: An Authentic Anthropology*, Brooklyn, New York: Lawrence Hills Books, 1991

Dorn, Harold, *The Geography of Science*, Baltimore: Johns Hopkins University Press, 1991

Gerdes, Paulus, *Ethnomathematics and Education in Africa*, Stockholm: Stockholms Universitet, 1995

Graham, A.C., *Disputers of the Tao: Philosophical Argument in Ancient China*, La Salle, Illinois: Open Court, 1989

Guidoni, Enrico, *Primitive Architecture*, translated by Robert Erich Wolf, New York: Abrams, 1975

Jollivet, Marcen, *Sciences de la nature: sciences de la société*, Paris: CNRS Editions, 1992

Jones, Prudence and Nigel Pennick, *A History of Pagan Europe*, London and New York: Routledge, 1995

Lefkowitz, Mary, *Not Out of Africa: How Afrocentrism Became an Excuse to Teach Myth as History*, New York: Basic Books, 1996

Montellano, Bernard R. Ortiz de, *Aztec Medicine, Health and Nutrition*, New Brunswick, New Jersey: Rutgers University Press, 1990

Needham, Joseph, *The Shorter Science and Civilization in China*, abridged by Colin A. Ronan, 5 vols, Cambridge and New York: Cambridge University Press, 1978–95

Pennick, Nigel, *Sacred Geometry: Symbolism and Purpose in Religious Structures*, Wellingborough, Northamptonshire, 1980; San Francisco: Harper and Row, 1982

Raskin, Marcus G. and Herbert J. Bernstein, *New Ways of Knowing: The Sciences, Society and Reconstructive Knowledge*, Totowa, New Jersey: Rowman and Littlefield, 1987

Rescher, Nicholas, *The Development of Arabic Logic*, Pittsburgh: University of Pittsburgh Press, 1991

Seal, Brajendranath, *The Positive Sciences of the Ancient Hindus*, London and New York: Longman, 1915

Steward, Julian H., *Handbook of South American Indians*, vol. 5, *The Comparative Ethnology of South American Indians*, Washington, DC: Bureau of American Ethnology, 1949; vol. 6, *Physical Anthropology, Linguistics and Cultural Geography of South American Indians*, 2nd edition, New York: Cooper Square, 1963

Sugimoto, Masayoshi and David L. Swain, *Science and Culture in Traditional Japan AD 600–1854*, Cambridge, Massachusetts: MIT Press, 1978

Vitruvius, Marcus, *The Ten Books on Architecture*, translated by Morris Hicky Morgan, Cambridge, Massachusetts: Harvard University Press, 1914

Ethnoscience is the study of the mode, style or, technique of the explanation and understanding of natural phenomena within a distinct cultural system. Ethnoscience thus offers to the history of science a broad historiography, because it allows for a better understanding of the (multi-)cultural dynamics that generated science. Ethnoscience can therefore be seen as a transdisciplinarian approach to the history of science, and a history of the ethnosciences cannot be distinguished from the broad history of human science and behaviour.

The literature is varied and includes books that one would not initially identify with ethnoscience. The species *homo sapiens* has inhabited the Earth for at least the last 50,000 years. CAVALLI-SFORZA, MENOZZI & PIAZZA study the cultural evolution of *homo sapiens* over this long period of time, while CLARK locates the earliest scientific thinking within the first perceptions of space and time.

The development of techniques for survival and the search for explanations of birth and death both originated in the drive to describe and understand the natural environment and observable phenomena. These quests and consequent human behaviours grew together symbiotically, in accordance with the varied answers offered by different local environments and habitats, as discussed by DORN. Health has always affected man's view of the world, and MONTELLANO discusses the pre-Columbian tradition of medicine, health, and nutrition.

Once a corpus of knowledge has been generated, it must be intellectually organized into what have become known as systems of knowledge, or logic. This development is discussed for Chinese philosophy by GRAHAM, for Hindu science by SEAL, and for Arabic logic by RESCHER.

The results of this cumulative process of the generation and organization of knowledge depend both on communication within a culture, and on a dynamic process of encounters between different cultures. This has given rise to conflicts of interpretation and to a manipulation of the historical record. The current controversy on Afrocentrism is a good illustration of how cultural dynamics can be used to serve political ends (see, in particular, the books by Bernal, Diop, and Lefkowitz). BERNAL argues that the Egyptian, and thus African, legacy has been eliminated from the canon of antiquity, and gives instances of such limitations in a number of human sciences in the 18th and 19th centuries. DIOP's book claims that Ancient Egypt was an African civilization and that all strata of the population had a large proportion of blacks. LEFKOWITZ, a classicist, argues that virtually all the claims made by Afrocentrists can be shown to be without substance, such as the African descent of Socrates and Cleopatra, and that Greek philosophy had been "stolen" from Egypt.

Just as in every other civilization, those around the Mediterranean developed techniques for survival and a set of structured explanations with which to describe and understand the natural environment and observable phenomena, and there exist registers of the techniques and explanations of the Greek and Roman civilizations of some 3,000 years before the Christian era. These structured systems, obviously all interrelated and with indistinguishable disciplinary boundaries, are now known as philosophy, mathematics, religion, art and science, and were the result both of classical attempts to understand and manipulate the environment and of dynamic encounters with other civilizations, mainly those of Egypt and Babylonia, but also with the pagan civilizations of northern Europe, southern Africa, and the East. Certainly, all these cultural encounters were determinant in the gradual construction of the corpus of knowledge that we today identify as European medieval science. This knowledge relied on characteristic styles of observation, identification and description, experimentation and theorization for the prediction and explanation of natural phenomena, and for the development of methods of survival and transcendence. This is clearly shown in the comprehensive work by CROMBIE, while the pagan contribution is discussed in JONES & PENNICK.

A discussion of the methodology of research in ethnoscience within the European context can be found in JOLLIVET, while STEWARD is a study of the South American Indians. During the 15th and 16th centuries, Europeans encountered many quite different natural and cultural environments and, with the ensuing conquests, colonizations and intracultural developments, European medieval science evolved into what became known as modern science. Particularly important to the new science was the recognition that space and time are culturally bound. The European encounters with Far Eastern cultures, mainly those of China and India, are well documented in for example, the abridgement of the monumental work by NEEDHAM on China, and the study by SUGIMOTO & SWAIN on Japan. Unfortunately, little work has yet been done on the European encounter with the American civilizations, but CLOSS offers a good synthesis.

The Europeans discovered that these alien cultures had developed different styles of observation, identification and description, experimentation and theorization for the prediction and explanation of natural phenomena, and had thus built up different corpora of knowledge, parts of which were absorbed by the conquerors and colonizers and incorporated into the European corpus of knowledge. GUIDONI is a study of architecture and urbanization within different cultural environments. For the colonization of the Americas, CATALÁ offers a valuable discussion of the role of science and technology in the process of urbanization.

These corpora of knowledge were organized coherently by the indigenous cultures over the centuries, in response to their specific natural and cultural environments. Many still persist within the cultural memory, some preserving their original structure and most naturally modified by a similar process of cultural dynamics. These are the ethnosciences, as discussed by ASCHER (mathematics), GERDES (mathematics and education) and D'AMBROSIO (mathematics and science). For urban classical antiquity, the best source is VITRUVIUS, which is the most comprehensive account of Roman science and technology.

Most of these ethnosciences were ignored and even suppressed by the Europeans, as they were (and in many cases still are) regarded as either superstition or folklore. However, as a practice, ethnoscience is working to uncover those elements from outside Europe that have played a part in the complex interplay of cultural dynamics that has shaped modern science. With the growing trend towards multiculturalism, ethnoscience is becoming recognized as a valid subject to be taught in schools; one which enhances creativity, offers a broad vision of mankind, and reinforces cultural self-respect. In everday life, the ethnosciences are increasingly recognized as systems of knowledge that offer the possibility of a more favourable and harmonious relation of human behaviour to nature, and in the professions, particularly in medicine, the ethnosciences are seen as facilitating the incorporation of natural rhythms of life in the cure process (for a broad discussion of this, see RASKIN & BERNSTEIN).

The historiographical approach to ethnoscience relies on monuments, tools, art, and a reinterpretation of texts not usually regarded as relevant to the history of science. Particularly important are the Bible, the Qu'ran and the Talmud, as shown by PENNICK in his work on religious structures and the origins of geometry. For day to day life, the *Farmer's Almanack* and similar books are also very important.

UBIRATAN D'AMBROSIO

See also Africa: south of the Sahara; Africa: health and healing; Ethnomathematics; Orientalism

Ethology and Animal Behaviour

Boakes, Robert, *From Darwin to Behaviourism: Psychology and the Minds of Animals*, Cambridge and New York: Cambridge University Press, 1984

Boas, George, *The Happy Beast in French Thought of the Seventeenth Century*, Baltimore: John Hopkins Press, 1933

Burkhardt, Richard W., "On the Emergence of Ethology as a Scientific Discipline", *Conspectus of History*, 7 (1981): 62–81

Burkhardt, Richard W., "The Development of an Evolutionary Ethology", in *Evolution from Molecules to Men*, edited by D.S. Bendall, Cambridge and New York: Cambridge University Press, 1983

Burkhardt, Richard W., "Darwin on Animal Behaviour and Evolution", in *The Darwinian Heritage*, edited by David Kohn, Princeton, New Jersey: Princeton University Press/ Nova Pacifica, 1985

Burkhardt, Richard W., "Theory and Practice in Naturalistic Studies of Behaviour Prior to Ethology's Establishment as a Scientific Discipline", in *Interpretation and Explanation in the Study of Animal Behaviour*, vol. 2, edited by Marc Bekoff and Dale Jamieson, Boulder, Colorado: Westview Press, 1990

Durant, John R., "Innate Character in Animals and Man: A Perspective on the Origins of Ethology", in *Biology, Medicine and Society 1840–1940*, edited by Charles Webster, Cambridge and New York: Cambridge University Press, 1981

Durant, John R., "The Making of Ethology: The Association for the Study of Animal Behaviour, 1936–1986", *Animal Behaviour* (1986): 1601–16

Klopfer, Peter H., *An Introduction to Animal Behaviour: Ethology's First Century*, Englewood Cliffs, New Jersey: Prentice-Hall, 1967; 2nd edition, 1974

Leary, David E., "The Fate and Influence of John Stuart Mill's Proposed Science of Ethology", *Journal of the History of Ideas*, 43 (1982): 153–62

Richards, Robert J., *Darwin and the Emergence of Evolutionary Theories of Mind and Behaviour*, Chicago: University of Chicago Press, 1987

Salisbury, Joyce E., *The Beast Within: Animals in the Middle Ages*, New York: Routledge, 1994

Singer, .B., "History of the Study of Animal Behaviour", in *The Oxford Companion to Animal Behaviour*, edited by David McFarland, Oxford and New York: Oxford University Press, 1981; revised edition, 1987

Sobol, Peter G., "The Shadow of Reason: Explanations of Intelligent Animal Behaviour in the Thirteenth Century", in *The Medieval World of Nature: A Book of Essays*, edited by Joyce E. Salisbury, New York: Garland, 1993

Sparks, John, *The Discovery of Animal Behaviour*, London: BBC/Collins, and Boston: Little Brown, 1982

Thorpe, W.H., *The Origins and Rise of Ethology: The Science of the Natural Behaviour of Animals*, London: Heinemann, and New York: Praeger, 1979

Tinbergen, Nikos, "Ethology", in *Scientific Thought, 1900–1960: A Selective Survey*, edited by Rom Harré, Oxford: Clarendon Press, 1969

As designations of fields of systematic study, "comparative psychology", "animal behaviour", and "ethology" are terms that orginated in the 19th century; yet knowledge of, and writing on the subject of animals stretches much further back in time. Any history, therefore, immediately confronts the difficulty of chronological parameters. Although relying on archaeological and anthropological evidence for an account of prehistoric animal behaviour studies, SINGER provides a concise but comprehensive intellectual history of the subject from Palaeolithic man to Tinbergen. Inextricably entangled in persistent debates about distinctions between humans and non-human animals, however, histories of animal behaviour often begin with Aristotle. SPARKS follows this model, and provides a broad, general overview of the subject. An unabashedly whiggish account of the history of animal "habits", this book was written as a companion to six one-hour television films. Lavishly illustrated, it recounts the history of animal behaviour, broadly construed, through a series of vignettes of Western naturalists and intellectuals from Aristotle to the present.

Apart from Singer and Sparks, histories of ethology and animal behaviour are predominantly disciplinary histories, which seek to understand the formation of an institutionalized science. An exploration of the historiography of instinct, intelligence, reason, habits, character, and morals provides greater scope. Through an intellectual history of early "comparative psychology", SOBOL analyses the various ancient and medieval strategies for dealing with distinctions between the mental powers of humans and animals. Because medieval commentators gravitated towards Aristotle's *De anima*, he argues, the emphasis of most discussions fell on internal powers of sense, or the *estimativa*, of animals. Aquinas and Descartes subsequently established instinct and animal behaviour as the centre of an enduring debate. SALISBURY explores more fully the *mentalité* that lay behind medieval relationships between humans and animals. She examines animals as property, food, sexual partners, and metaphoric exemplars, and argues that, by the 12th century, a blurring of former distinctions between animal and human had begun, through the medium of fables and bestiaries.

Writing in the tradition of the history of ideas, BOAS coins the word "theriophily" to identify a persistent mode of thought that acknowledged admiration for the character and behaviour of animals. As a minor variant on Primitivism, this elevation of animality had ancient origins, but it rose to prominence in the 16th century as one facet of the books of paradoxes. According to Boas, Descartes conceived his mechanization of animals as part of a sustained attack on theriophily.

Both BURKHARDT (1990) and THORPE begin their searches for ethology's antecedents in the 18th century. Whereas Thorpe asserts that ethology first appeared in late 18th-century France, Burkhardt studiously avoids a progressionist history. Although he seeks to demonstrate that distinctions between learned and innate animal behaviour pre-dated Lorenz, he emphasizes the different social and cultural motivations for such investigations. Similarly, RICHARDS rejects a progressionist disciplinary history, in favour of an "evolutionary" intellectual one. He explores instinct, reason, and morals in relation to developmental theories about mind and behaviour, by linking nascent sensationalist epistemology to the emergence of evolutionary theories at the turn of the 18th century. In addition, he demonstrates that sensationalism produced a wide spectrum of natural theological opinion on the continuity of human and animal capabilities, prior to Darwin.

As a comparative and evolutionary analysis of naturalistic observations of animal behaviour, ethology traces the greatest portion of its intellectual roots to Darwin. Both Richards and BURKHARDT (1985) demonstrate that considerations of animal instincts, intelligence, and habits were an integral part of the development and final formulation of Darwin's theory of evolution. Prior to reading Malthus, in fact, Darwin accorded instinct and habit central roles in his explanation of the transmutation of species. Historians of ethology universally agree, however, that Darwin was not the founder of the discipline of ethology. In addition, opinion is divided over the impact of evolutionism on both behaviourism and ethology.

BOAKES balances historical teleology and contextualism in his examination of the systematic investigation of animal minds between 1870 and 1930. Although sensitive to intellectual, personal, institutional, and disciplinary allegiances and affiliations, Boakes is principally interested in the manner in which the study of mammalian behaviour had an impact on human psychology. Ranging across a variety of national contexts, he demonstrates how evolutionary concerns merged with experimental psychology to produce a tradition of behaviourism in North American psychology. Richards, in contrast, views Watsonian behaviourism as an impediment to theorizing about the evolution of mind and behaviour. Behaviourism, Boasian environmentalism, and logical Positivism, he argues, obstructed research in Anglo-American evolutionary biopsychology between 1920 and 1960. BURKHARDT (1983) contends that Lorenz's attempts to build a distinct scientific discipline precluded the development of an evolutionary ethology. Determined to distinguish his programme for the naturalistic study of animal behaviour from contemporary animal psychology, Lorenz emphasized the invariability of instinctive behaviour, and thereby overlooked intraspecific variation. Ethologists did not fully appreciate the multifarious relationship between environmental pressures and animal behaviour until Tinbergen's work in the 1950s and 1960s.

After tracing the impact of John Stuart Mill's suggested science of ethology, LEARY concludes that the intellectual history of the projected study of the formation of human character is separate from that of the creation of a biological science of instinctual animal behaviour. Motivated by his search for the "roots of sociobiology", DURANT (1981) is less convinced about such a distinction. Employing a three-tiered chronological intellectual history, he explores the interests and attitudes that lay behind the development of ethology, and concludes that anthropomorphism played a significant methodological and intellectual role in this process. BURKHARDT (1981) also examines ethology in relation to sociobiology. He argues that the sociobiology debate was, at a professional level, a struggle over disciplinary boundaries. This provides him with a springboard to investigate the origins of ethology. He interprets Lorenz's efforts to promote theories of endogenous activities in the 1930s as self-conscious attempts to establish a scientific discipline. Moreover, Burkhardt raises a number of pertinent issues. Through his examination of Lorenz's history of ethology, he questions the role of legitimation in practitioners' accounts. In a similar vein, he scrutinizes Lorenz's apparent flirtation with Nazism, and judges the relevant ethological papers as either acts of expediency or of opportunism.

Tinbergen, Thorpe, and Klopfer provide practitioners' accounts of the history of ethology. Largely confined to the 20th century, each of their expositions contrasts early European ethology with the American predominance of behaviourism and comparative psychology. THORPE, a key participant in the post-war creation of an "English school of ethology", maintains a distinction between ethology and comparative psychology as a central theme of his history. KLOPFER, who wishes to provide an instructional text for students of ethology, presents a more consensual history, which subsumes American comparative psychology and neurophysiology within post-war ethology. Although evolutionary zoologists and ethologists clearly emerge the victors, TINBERGEN also recounts a story of conflict, followed by "convergence and fusion". As a complement to Thorpe and Tinbergen, DURANT (1986) sheds further light on the institutionalization of ethology in Britain, through his investigation of the origins of the Association for the Study of Animal Behaviour.

JOHN F.M. CLARK

See also Lorenz

Euclid   *fl. c.*300 BC

Greek mathematician

Fowler, David, *The Mathematics of Plato's Academy: A New Reconstruction*, Oxford: Clarendon Press, and New York: Oxford University Press, 1987; corrected edition, 1990

Heath, Thomas L. (ed. and trans.), *The Thirteen Books of Euclid's Elements*, 3 vols, 2nd edition, Cambridge: Cambridge University Press, 1926; New York: Dover, 1956

Knorr, Wilbur, *The Evolution of the Euclidean Elements: A Study of the Theory of Incommensurable Magnitudes and Its Significance for Early Greek Geometry*, Dordrecht: Reidel, 1975

Knorr, Wilbur, "Pseudo-Euclidean Reflections in Ancient Optics: A Re-examination of Textual Issues Pertaining to the Euclidean *Optrica* and *Catoptrica*", *Physis*, 31 (1994): 1–45

Lloyd, G.E.R., *Magic, Reason and Experience*, Cambridge and New York: Cambridge University Press, 1979

Mueller, Ian, *Philosophy of Mathematics and Deductive Structure in Euclid's Elements*, Cambridge, Massachusetts: MIT Press, 1981

Murdoch, John, entry in *Dictionary of Scientific Biography*, edited by Charles Coulston Gillispie, vol. 4, New York: Scribner, 1971

Szabó, Arpad, *The Beginnings of Greek Mathematics*, translated from the German by A.M. Ungar, Dordrecht: Reidel, 1978 (original edition, 1969)

Considering the immense importance of his major work, the *Elements* (c. 4th century BC), perhaps the most influential scientific work of all time, remarkably little is known about Euclid as a person. In 13 books, almost all of which are arranged in a rigorous, deductive structure, the whole of "elementary geometry" is covered, from the definitions of point and line, to the mutual ratios of three-dimensional regular bodies. The text's influence is the result not only of the fact that it examines most of plane and solid geometry in what has since been called Euclidean space, but also that it constitutes a logical model for mathematicians, philosophers, and scientists in general.

There are numerous concerns arising from the *Elements*, ranging from issues relating to the text itself (cross-references, logical dependence of one part on the other, terminology), to the sources used (it is generally acknowledged that Euclid drew much from previous mathematicians). Moreover, considerations on the structure of the *Elements*, its completeness and the reason why it "works" so well, have led to the conception of different notions of space, and to reflections on the relation between mathematics and reality. For an inkling of many such problems of interpretation, it is best to start with HEATH.

Although not flawless, this English version of the *Elements* is particularly valuable for its rich commentary, which reaches far beyond the original text. Heath makes connections with other mathematicians, both ancient and modern, informs on later developments of one theorem or the other, and traces the reception history where appropriate. Also, the book points to the problems linked to Euclid's meta-mathematical stances: for example, are the *Elements* organized following Aristotle's criteria for scientific demonstration as expressed in the *Posterior Analytics*? These questions are further complicated by cases such as the parallel postulate, which relies on conventional, but not absolutely self-evident, notions of geometrical space. Rejection of the parallel postulate triggered the elaboration of non-Euclidean geometries.

The problem of the relation, in Euclid's *Elements* – and, by extension, in classical Greek mathematics generally – between philosophy and mathematics is discussed in SZABÓ. He argues for the dependence of mathematical practice upon contemporary philosophical discussions, not just for Euclid but for earlier mathematicians like the Pythagoreans. Szabó's philology is certainly impressive, and his thesis has notable consequences for the issue of the historical origins of Greek mathematics, which would have been made possible only by the presence of philosophical debate.

LLOYD's examination of the development of forms of argumentation and demonstration as found in the *Elements* places the text firmly within the wider social and cultural context of the Greek world. He argues for a link between the dialectic method of argumentation, rhetoric and deductive demonstration, on the basis not so much of influence or primacy, as of their operation within a shared "public sphere" where all these forms of persuasion were employed.

A different reaction to Szabó has come from Knorr, who has argued, on the contrary, that mathematics developed following essentially its own agenda. His main contribution to Euclid studies, however, arguably remains his first book, KNORR (1975), which is concerned chiefly with the theory of incommensurables. Here the author examines early Greek mathematics in order to establish the background for the *Elements*, from which Euclid plucked results and procedures. The resulting picture is complex, in which, while the contributions of pre-Euclidean geometers are examined in their variety, Euclid himself is presented as someone with well-defined criteria of rigour and validity, reflected in his work.

A new perspective on the contents of the *Elements* is provided by FOWLER. The author argues that, for the ancient Greeks at least until the first centuries AD, the notion of "ratio" did not have any connotation of our operation of division. Rather, it was equivalent to a repeated reciprocal subtraction (anthyphairesis) between any two homogeneous magnitudes. The contention has important consequences for our notion of what Euclidean mathematics was all about (for example, Fowler argues that the maths of book 2 was completely non-arithmetized), and of the relation it upheld between numbers, magnitudes in general, and reality. The author checks his argument against Plato's mathematics curriculum in the *Republic*, which comprises astronomy, music and logistic, and applies it also to books 4, 10, and 13 of the *Elements*, and to some geometrical papyri. The result, complemented by his *faux*-Socratic dialogues, is supremely entertaining.

The most extensive survey available is probably by MUELLER, who focuses again on the deductive structure of the *Elements*: how different sections of the text interrelate, how certain propositions are used to support others, etc. The author avails himself of modern logic notation on some occasions, and extracts the mathematical significance of the various books that make up the *Elements* by comparing them with analogous issues in the modern philosophy of mathematics. There are also some useful appendices that summarize the *Elements* and lay down its contents in symbolic notation.

KNORR (1994) is a token article on the less-explored area of the other Euclidean works (the *Optics* and *Phenomena*), the study of which is vital if the usual image of Euclidean mathematics as perfectly disembodied and abstract is to be qualified. These texts deal with mathematics applied to physical phenomena, and were enormously influential during the Middle Ages and later. MURDOCH's article is an exhaustive yet self-contained survey of the Euclid tradition over the centuries, from Greek antiquity (including a history of the manuscripts) to the medieval versions in Arabic, Greek-Latin and Arabic-Latin. From the 15th century onwards, Western editions abounded, as did Western attempts at completing or updating Euclid. Murdoch provides a full bibliography, as well as a filiation tree of "the major versions of Euclid's *Elements* in the Middle Ages and the Renaissance". His account terminates with Girolamo Saccheri's *Euclidis ab omni naevo vindicatus* (1733) – "Euclid emended from every error" – which, rather ironically, is usually indicated as the beginning of non-Euclidean geometries.

SERAFINA CUOMO

Eugenics

Adams, Mark B., "Eugenics in Russia, 1900–1940", in *The Wellborn Science: Eugenics in Germany, France, Brazil, and Russia*, edited by Adams, New York and Oxford: Oxford University Press, 1990

Allen, Garland E., "The Eugenics Record Office at Cold Springs Harbor, 1910–1940: An Essay in Institutional History", *Osiris*, 2 (1986): 225–64

Bock, Gisela, *Zwangssterilisation im Nationalsozialismus: Studien zur Rassenpolitik und Frauenpolitik*, Opladen: Westdeutscher, 1986

Farrall, Lyndsay Andrew, "The Origins and Growth of the English Eugenics Movement", PhD dissertation, Bloomington: Indiana University, 1970; as *The Origins and Growth of the English Eugenics Movement, 1865–1925*, New York: Garland, 1985

Graham, Loren R., "Science and Values: The Eugenics Movement in Germany and Russia in the 1920s", *American Historical Review*, 82 (1977): 1135–64

Haller, Mark H., *Eugenics: Hereditarian Attitudes in American Thought*, New Brunswick, New Jersey: Rutgers University Press, 1963

Kevles, Daniel J., *In The Name of Eugenics: Genetics and the Uses of Human Heredity*, New York: Knopf, 1985; Harmondsworth: Penguin, 1986; with a new preface, Cambridge, Massachusetts: Harvard University Press, 1995

Kühl, Stephan, *The Nazi Connection: Eugenics, American Racism, and German National Socialism*, New York and Oxford: Oxford University Press, 1994

Ludmerer, Kenneth Marc, *Genetics and American Society: A Historical Appraisal*, Baltimore: Johns Hopkins University Press, 1972

McLaren, Angus, *Our Own Master Race: Eugenics in Canada, 1885–1945*, Toronto: McClelland and Stewart, 1990

Mazumdar, Pauline M.H., *Eugenics, Human Genetics and Human Failings: The Eugenics Society, Its Sources and Its Critics in Britain*, New York and London: Routledge, 1992

Mehler, Barry Alan, "A History of the American Eugenics Society, 1921–1940", PhD dissertation, University of Illinois, 1988

Pauly, Philip J., "Essay Review: The Eugenics Industry – Growth or Restructuring", *Journal of the History of Biology*, 26 (1993): 131–45

Proctor, Robert, *Racial Hygiene: Medicine under the Nazis*, Cambridge, Massachusetts: Harvard University Press, 1988

Roll-Hansen, Nils, "Geneticists and the Eugenics Movement in Scandinavia", *The British Journal for the History of Science*, 22 (1989): 335–46

Schneider, William H., *Quality and Quantity: The Quest for Biological Regeneration in Twentieth-Century France*, Cambridge and New York: Cambridge University Press, 1990

Stepan, Nancy Leys, *The Hour of Eugenics: Race, Gender, and Nation in Latin America*, Ithaca, New York: Cornell University Press, 1991

Weindling, Paul, *Health, Race and German Politics Between National Unification and Nazism, 1870–1945*, Cambridge and New York: Cambridge University Press, 1989

Weingart, Peter, Jürgen Kroll and Kurt Bayertz, *Rasse, Blut und Gene: Geschichte der Eugenik und Rassenhygiene in Deutschland*, Frankfurt: Suhrkamp, 1988

Weiss, Sheila Faith, *Race Hygiene and National Efficiency: The Eugenics of Wilhelm Schallmayer*, Berkeley: University of California Press, 1987

In 1883, the British biometrician Francis Galton, a cousin of Charles Darwin, coined the term "eugenics" to denote the social uses to which an understanding of heredity could be employed to "improve" the genetic substratum of a given population. During the first four decades of the 20th century, eugenic movements achieved a certain intellectual vogue in many Western, and in several non-Western, countries.

Since the 1970s, there has been a growing preoccupation with eugenics on the part of historians of science and social historians. Indeed, during the 1990s there was such a burst of scholarly production on the topic that PAULY was perhaps justified in speaking of a veritable "eugenics industry" in his review of the field. It is not difficult to understand both the initial and continuing appeal of the subject. As an international social movement, in which scientists and medically-trained professionals were frequently in the vanguard, eugenics is one of the best sites to examine the multifaceted interactions between science and society. In the light of recent scholarship, emphasis should be placed on the word multifaceted: historians now realize that eugenics not only meant very different things within different national contexts, but that even within nations differences in interpretation among practitioners were often substantial. In addition, it is not unusual to find individual eugenicists renegotiating their understanding of the term over time. Since the 1990s, several scholars have gone beyond an analysis of things said and done "in the name of eugenics" during the first four decades of the 20th century, to examine the link between this so-called old eugenics and developments in human genetics after World War II. Given the opportunities and dilemmas currently posed by reproductive technologies, gene therapy, and above all, the human genome project, interest in the history of eugenics is not likely to fade in the foreseeable future.

Viewed until recently as the "normal" pattern for eugenic movements world-wide, Anglo-American eugenics was practically the sole focus of investigation prior to the early 1980s. HALLER, followed by LUDMERER, are the appropriate starting points for a discussion of the history of American eugenics. While both authors agree on the origin, growth, and the reasons for the decline of eugenics in the United States, their emphasis is different. Haller, a social historian, is at pains to situate America eugenics within the broader history of hereditarianism in the US. He offers a topical approach to the subject, dedicating chapters to the issues of eugenics and the problem of the feeble-minded, eugenics and race, eugenics legislation, etc. Ludmerer, a historian of genetics, has a narrower focus: unlike Haller, who discusses the pre-history of American eugenics, Ludmerer concentrates on its so-called heyday, the years 1905–30, and stresses the use (and, for Ludmerer, more often misuse) by American eugenicists of genetic theories to gain support for eugenic legislation.

In more recent years, historians have begun to challenge some of the important theses of Haller and Ludmerer. In his institutional study of the United States Eugenics Record Office, ALLEN takes issue with Haller's and Ludmerer's position that scientific advances in genetics are the key factor in explaining the decline of the American movement; the rise of Nazi racial hygiene, as well as changing social and economic forces in the US, were, according to Allen, more responsible for the declining fortunes of American eugenics. MEHLER, the first prosopographical study of an American eugenics institution, the American Eugenics Society, is even more uncompromising in its rejection of the thesis that advances in genetics reformed eugenics in the US. Moreover, Mehler also takes issue with other basic tenets of the historiography of American eugenics; not only does he emphasize continuity rather than change in the period between 1920 and 1940, but he argues that, contrary to the position articulated by Ludmerer, the eugenics project was not discredited in the US because of developments in Nazi Germany – individual American geneticist's criticism of overtly "pseudoscientific" racist eugenics notwithstanding. Certainly McLAREN's work on eugenics in Canada, another Anglo-American movement, suggests that Canadian sterilization legislation, at least in British Columbia, did not appear until the Nazi take-over. KÜHL's monograph supports Mehler's position, by documenting the degree to which American eugenicists both actively supported the draconian Nazi sterilization law of 1933, and took pride in serving as a role model for Nazi race hygiene. He also points to the continuing legacy of eugenics and scientific racism, by examining the contemporary practices of the US-based Pioneer Fund.

Although written in 1970, FARRALL's dissertation still remains an important point of departure for anyone wishing to investigate eugenics in Britain. Farrall examines British eugenics from its beginnings until 1925, from the perspective of both social history and the history of science. He places particular emphasis on the intellectual and social origins of the movement, and contends that eugenics in Britain is in the social-political tradition of "middle-class radicalism". Farrall also documents the controversy between the British biometricians and the Mendelians, and he argues for the significance of this conflict in shaping British eugenics. The activities of the Galton Eugenics Laboratory serve as a major focus of his study. MAZUMDAR's monograph, an institutional history of the British Eugenics Society and one of the most important of the numerous books and articles written on the history of British eugenics in the last 25 years, addresses critical issues that have either been ignored in the historiography, or have failed to receive the in-depth treatment they deserve. Employing a wealth of archival material previously unavailable to historians, Mazumdar argues that British eugenics sought a solution to the problem of the residuum: the urban underclass. What separated the British Eugenics Society from numerous other organizations dedicated to solving the problem of pauperism was its emphasis on biology in the aetiology of poverty. Mazumdar provides the most solid treatment to date of the role of scientific methodology in the British eugenics movement. In so doing, she challenges the assumption that the Mendelian and biometrical genetical approaches informing the early movement were totally incompatible, and that this incompatibility led to significant rifts in the society. In her discussion of developments during the 1930s, Mazumdar pays particular attention to the "new alignment of method and ideology" advocated by left-wing British eugenicists such as Lancelot Hogben and J.B.S. Haldane, as they embraced the mathematical-statistical approach to heredity first advanced in Germany. Mazumdar's exploration of the British-German intellectual connection is one of her book's major strengths.

Although both Mazumdar and Kühl offer a much needed comparative dimension to their respective analyses, neither author attempted to provide a fully-fledged comparative history of eugenics in more than one country. For Anglo-American eugenics, this history is lucidly chronicled by KEVLES. Not only does Kevles's lengthy study demonstrate the social and political heterogeneity of the Anglo-American movement, and dispel any lingering assumptions that eugenics attracted only right-wing racist fanatics; it is also the first work to venture into the uncharted waters of the history of human genetics. His distinction between "mainline" and "reform" eugenics in the Anglo-American tradition has found general acceptance among historians, as the work of ROLL-HANSEN on eugenics in the Nordic countries makes clear.

Second only to the historiography of Anglo-American eugenics in terms of size and maturity is the secondary literature dealing with German race hygiene. Given the legacy of eugenics or *Rassenhygiene* – the latter was the term most frequently used by German eugenicists – for the racial policies of the Third Reich, it is perhaps not surprising that the earliest scholarly treatment of the subject tended to subordinate race hygiene to the broader themes of either the history of European racism, or the development of *völkisch* thought. Through an examination of the writings of Wilhelm Schallmayer, one of the two co-founders of German eugenics, WEISS contextualizes the origins of eugenics in Germany in order to lay bare its "logic". In so doing, she challenges the then widespread assumption that German eugenicists were primarily concerned with breeding a better "Aryan race". According to Weiss, early German race hygiene was a technocratic-managerial strategy for increasing Germany's national efficiency and cultural superiority, through the rational management of population.

Virtually all of the subsequent literature on the history of German eugenics is far broader in scope than Weiss's monograph, and deals primarily with the later period of the movement, especially with the development of race hygiene during the Weimar Republic and under the Nazis. In his highly readable book, PROCTOR focuses on German race hygiene under the swastika as part of a larger study of the fortunes of the German biomedical community during the Third Reich. He demonstrates that German physicians, always in the vanguard of the German race hygiene movement, not only supported most elements of the Nazi racial project, but indeed were instrumental in constructing them. In her thoroughly researched study of one of the key components in this racial project, the mandatory sterilization law of 1933, BOCK not only provides a comprehensive account of the origins and application of the infamous Law for the Prevention of Genetically Diseased Progeny, but also offers a masterful hermeneutical analysis of the sexual and racist politics that underlay it. Her major theoretical contribution – that all forms of genetic essentialism used to discriminate between so-called "more valuable" and "less valuable" lives deserve the pejorative label "racism" – continues to be debated among scholars working on German eugenics.

Of the two major accounts of the history of German race hygiene from its turn-of-the century beginnings to its post-1945 transformation into human genetics – that of WEINDLING and of WEINGART, KROLL & BAYERTZ – the former's work is unquestionably the superior. The great strength of Weindling's authoritative study is that it contextualizes the history of race hygiene, by situating it within the broader development of Germany's state-organized health care system. Using more than 30 different private, state, and federal archives to document his study, Weindling stresses how eugenics in Germany became intertwined with a myriad of often conflicting social and political debates among public health administrators, scientists, and physicians – all of whom were preoccupied with managing the nation's health. According to Weindling, the important differences between German race hygiene and eugenics movements elsewhere cannot be understood apart from the larger tradition of the German biomedical community. Both Weindling and Weingart, Kroll & Bayertz offer a solid analysis of the "Faustian bargain" between German eugenics and the Nazi state. Weingart, Kroll & Bayertz devote far more time to examining the post-World War II developments in human genetics in Germany than does Weindling.

If scholars have heretofore been unduly preoccupied with Anglo-American and German eugenics, there has been a trend in recent years to examine developments in other countries, for the light they can shed on the multifaceted nature of the movement, and the role of the biomedical sciences within particular national contexts.

One of the axioms of the early historiography of eugenics was that it was intricately linked with the rise of neo-Darwinism and Mendelian genetics. The important studies of SCHNEIDER on French eugenics and STEPAN on eugenics in Latin America criticize the assumption that a eugenics based on non-Mendelian views of heredity (in these cases, neo-Lamarckism) was somehow non-scientific. Moreover, they deftly explore the intellectual roots of French and Latin American eugenics in the medical movement known as "puericulture" – a movement that combined pronatalism with a concern for the pre-natal and post-natal care of children. The emphasis on "negative eugenics" in both France and Latin America was far milder than in Anglo-Saxon countries.

As editor of the first anthology dealing with the comparative history of eugenics, ADAMS has probably done more than anyone to help correct the myopic vision that underlay much of the older historiography of the movement. His own extensive work on the history of eugenics in Russia goes well beyond GRAHAM's pioneering treatment of the subject, as he demonstrates the remarkable durability of the movement as it was forced to adapt to the political changes in the former Soviet Union. His study is a reminder of that which has often fascinated scholars preoccupied with the history of "the science of human breeding": the great diversity of social and cultural projects undertaken under the banner of eugenics.

SHEILA FAITH WEISS

See also Galton

Evans-Pritchard, Edward Evan 1902–1973

British social anthropologist

Asad, Talal (ed.), *Anthropology and the Colonial Encounter*, New York: Humanities Press, and London: Ithaca Press, 1973
Beidelman, T.O. (ed.), *The Translation of Culture: Essays to E.E. Evans-Pritchard*, London: Tavistock, 1971
Beidelman, T.O., *A Bibliography of the Writings of E.E. Evans-Pritchard*, London: Tavistock, 1974
Burton, John W., *An Introduction to Evans-Pritchard*, Fribourg, Switzerland: University Press, 1992
Cunnison, Ian and Wendy James (eds), *Essays in Sudan Ethnography presented to Sir Edward Evans-Pritchard*, London: Hurst, and New York: Humanities Press, 1972
Douglas, Mary, *Evans-Pritchard*, Brighton, Sussex: Harvester Press, 1980
Geertz, Clifford, *Works & Lives: The Anthropologist as Author*, California: Stanford University Press, 1988
Hatch, Elvin, *Theories of Man and Culture*, New York: Columbia University Press, 1973
Kuper, Adam, *Anthropologists and Anthropology: The British School, 1922–1972*, London: Allen Lane, and New York: Pica Press, 1973

The scholarship of Edward Evan Evans-Pritchard is tidy and sharply focused in its substantive, theoretical, and methodological concerns. As a corpus, it has attracted attention from a range of disciplines, and its influence, therefore, extends way beyond the confines of anthropology.

BEIDELMAN (1974) serves as a good introduction to the literature, indicating something of Evans-Pritchard's prodigious academic output, while intellectually contextualizing his classic works on ethnographic fieldwork. The bibliography is preceded by a biographical sketch, which reveals that Evans-Pritchard and Raymond Firth were Bronislaw Malinowski's first students in London, and, significantly, that Evans-Pritchard was also trained by Charles Seligman. Much of Evans-Pritchard's academic reputation rests on his fieldwork-based ethnographic studies of the Azande and Nuer.

The foreword in CUNNISON & JAMES is notable for its contextualization of Evans-Pritchard's researches among the Azande, Nuer, and other peoples of the Sudan and its borders, and the influence these researches had on comparative anthropology. Reference is made to Evans-Pritchard's fieldwork "apprenticeship" with Charles and Brenda Seligman, assisting in their "survey" of the Sudan. Evans-Pritchard's fieldwork among the Azande was partly funded by the colonial government of the Sudan. Cunnison & James detail how, shortly after Evans-Pritchard's 20 or so months of fieldwork with the Azande, Sir Harold MacMichael a Sudan colonial administrator with more than some insight and understanding of the people of the Sudan, requested that Evans-Pritchard study the apparently warlike Nuer, with whom the colonial administration were experiencing problems.

In the book edited by ASAD, A.G.M Ahmed closely examines the generally tenuous, but none the less for some among the current generation of scholars consequential, links between anthropology and colonialism during the colonial era. Writing from the perspective of the colonized, Ahmed points to the informed administrators, including MacMichael, receiving some education in anthropology, but argues that they shared with the missionaries, traders, and the like a more or less common viewpoint about the colonies.

BIEDELMAN (1971) is a collection of essays dedicated to Evans-Pritchard. While the essay by Hallpike addresses the complexities involved in cross-cultural comparison, its theory and method, drawing extensively on the writing of Evans-Pritchard and Radcliffe-Brown, Gough's essay re-examines one of Evans-Pritchard's classics, *Nuer Kinship*.

Evans-Pritchard's empirical findings and researches were firmly established as classics of African ethnography during the first half of the 20th century. KUPER presents a concise and incisive characterization of British anthropology during the 1930s and 1940s – when most of the close-knit circle of Malinowski's and Radcliffe-Brown's students, the second generation of fieldworkers, published their ethnographic monographs – and indicates Evans-Pritchard's position within it. Kuper describes Malinowski's powerful influence over social anthropology at the time, and the growing importance of Radcliffe-Brown. In certain subtle ways, however, Evans-Pritchard's classic studies served to modify aspects of Malinowskian fieldwork orthodoxy, by consciously limiting it to a problem-centred ethnographic focus used to explore theoretical and philosophical concerns.

During the second half of the 20th century, Evans-Pritchard's African ethnographies came to stand for something beyond fieldwork, and they were scrutinized metaphorically for an assessment of their epistemological foundations. Scholars such as Burton, Douglas, Geertz, and Hatch have unpacked the epistemological dimensions of Evans-Pritchard's works. HATCH offers us a comparison of Radcliffe-Brown and Evans-Pritchard, suggesting that while each employs a similar conceptual apparatus organized around structure function system and the like, there are none the less significant differences in their respective employment of them.

In a book ostensibly designed for a general audience, DOUGLAS fashioned what is probably the current definitive work on Evans-Pritchard's epistemology. Consciously taking certain liberties with the historical location of epistemological concerns, Douglas indicates that many of Evans-Pritchard's ethnographical interests were somewhat in advance of their academic time and vogue – most notably, his concern with issues from within the sociology of knowledge, and his application of these issues within everyday contexts, such as Azande or Nuer social arrangements and practical reasoning. Douglas draws attention to what she believes comprises a cohesive research programme underlying Evans-Pritchard's apparently disparate empirical investigations. Employing an ethnomethodological sense of the concept of accountability, Douglas reviews Evans-Pritchard's study of witchcraft among the Azande and political arrangements among the Nuer. From this vantage point, witchcraft is concerned with the social accountability of persons in society, and the Nuer (a tribe without rulers) makes persons accountable through the institutions of kinship and bridewealth. Thus, what initially seem to be the exotic, bizarre behaviour and social arrangements of the Azande and the Nuer, in Evans-Pritchard's analysis are transformed into the rational and logical. Meanwhile, BURTON sets out to underline common themes within Evans-Pritchard's classic works on the Azande and Nuer religion, arguing that they are concerned with the symbolic mediation of social organization and values.

As employed within anthropology, ethnography has two distinct senses – as a fieldwork method, and also as a written ethnographic report – and it is the latter with which GEERTZ is principally concerned in his consideration of Evans-Pritchard. Geertz focuses on the study of Evans-Pritchard's ethnographies as textual products, examining his brilliant prose style, and surmising on Evans-Pritchard's likely awareness of this, and hence of his self-presentation to the audience in his texts. For Geertz, at the heart of Evans-Pritchard's success is his ability to construct believable and visualizable textual representations of exotic cultural arrangements.

MIKE BALL

See also Anthropology

Evolution

Bowler, Peter J., *Evolution: The History of an Idea*, Berkeley: University of California Press, 1984; revised edition, 1989

Bowler, Peter J., *The Non-Darwinian Revolution: Reinterpreting a Historical Myth*, Baltimore: Johns Hopkins University Press, 1988

Desmond, Adrian, *The Politics of Evolution: Morphology, Medicine, and Reform in Radical London*, Chicago: University of Chicago Press, 1989

Eiseley, Loren C., *Darwin's Century: Evolution and the Men Who Discovered It*, Garden City, New York: Doubleday, 1958; London: Gollancz, 1959

Glass, Bentley, Owsei Temkin and William L. Straus (eds), *Forerunners of Darwin, 1745–1859*, Baltimore: Johns Hopkins University Press, 1959

Glick, Thomas F. (ed.), *The Comparative Reception of Darwinism*, Austin: University of Texas Press, 1974; with a new preface, Chicago: University of Chicago Press, 1988

Greene, John C., *The Death of Adam: Evolution and Its Impact on Western Thought*, Ames: Iowa State University Press, 1959

Himmelfarb, Gertrude, *Darwin and the Darwinian Revolution*, London: Chatto and Windus, and New York: Doubleday, 1959

Hull, David L. (ed.), *Darwin and His Critics: The Reception of Darwin's Theory of Evolution by the Scientific Community*, Cambridge, Massachusetts: Harvard University Press, 1973

Mayr, Ernst, *The Growth of Biological Thought: Diversity, Evolution, and Inheritance*, Cambridge, Massachusetts: Harvard University Press, 1982

Moore, James R., *The Post-Darwinian Controversies: A Study of the Protestant Struggle to Come to Terms with Darwin in Great Britain and America, 1870–1900*, Cambridge and New York: Cambridge University Press, 1979

Richards, Robert J., *Darwin and the Emergence of Evolutionary Theories of Mind and Behavior*, Chicago: University of Chicago Press, 1987

Roger, Jacques, *Les Sciences de la vie dans la pensée française du dix-huitième siècle*, Paris: Armand Colin, 1963

Ruse, Michael, *The Darwinian Revolution: Science Red in Tooth and Claw*, Chicago: University of Chicago Press, 1979

Young, Robert M., *Darwin's Metaphor: Nature's Place in Victorian Culture*, Cambridge and New York: Cambridge University Press, 1985

A great boost was given to modern scholarship on the history of evolutionism by the centenary of the publication of Darwin's *Origin of Species* in 1959. The books by Greene and Eiseley, and the volume edited by Glass, Temkin & Straus, are products of this period. To a large extent, they helped to define the framework within which the subject would be studied over the next few decades, and much of the subsequent work has, in effect, been devoted to filling in the details of the picture they outlined. However, some more recent work has challenged aspects of the earlier scheme, on the grounds that it focused too strongly on the central role of Darwin's theory. BOWLER (1984) provides an overview of modern work, with a substantial bibliography.

Of the earlier studies, GREENE's is by far the most thorough and authoritative, although it takes the story only as far as the immediate impact of Darwin's ideas. Greene is concerned to explore the interaction of evolutionism with religious values, and he is personally suspicious of the extreme materialist interpretation of Darwinism. For him, the central theme in the development of evolutionism is the challenge offered by materialism to the old world view, in which nature was a divine contrivance. The account by HIMMELFARB shows how dislike of the Darwinian world view can lead to the production of a thoroughly unsympathetic account of Darwin's life, as well as of his influence. EISELEY offers a more idiosyncratic account; written in a highly-readable style, it has had much influence, not all to the good. To some extent, Eiseley helped to define the kind of Darwin-centered view of the history of evolutionism that some later historians have questioned: the advent of Darwinism became the central episode, with everything that happened both before and after related to this event. The far more authoritative survey by MAYR provides, to some extent, a more recent extension of this model, at least in the post-Darwinian period. As a leading modern Darwinist, Mayr naturally gives that theory a central role in the history of the subject.

The emergence of naturalistic alternatives to the concept of divine creation in the 18th and early 19th centuries has attracted the attention of several historians. Greene provides a detailed account of these early ideas, making it clear where they differed from the approach later taken by Darwin. Eiseley, however, tends to treat earlier writers such as Buffon as "precursors of Darwin", providing a selective account of their work that concentrates only on those areas where it could be argued that they had anticipated Darwin's views. The very title of the work edited by GLASS, TEMKIN & STRAUS seems to encapsulate this approach, although individual essays in the volume are more sophisticated. Since much of the 18th-century work was by French naturalists, ROGER's massive survey of the period is particularly impressive, and does a great deal to reveal the very non-Darwinian context within which these early ideas were articulated.

DESMOND's account of the early 19th-century British debates highlights a forgotten period in the development of evolutionism. His study makes it clear that the subject was being hotly debated, with all its radical implications made clear, in the decades before Darwin published. In effect, Darwin's *Origin of Species* appears as the last act in a drama whose protagonists were conservatives, trying to preserve as much as possible of the old, static world-view, and middle-class and radical thinkers, arguing for a dynamic view of nature more compatible with a progressionist model of social history.

The traditional historiography treats the development and publication of Darwin's theory of natural selection as the defining events in the development of modern evolutionism. These topics are dealt with separately in this volume. Much attention has been focused on the relationship between Darwin's scientific studies of biogeography, variation and heredity, and the social context within which he worked. YOUNG's book brings together a collection of his pioneering articles, which stress the extent to which Darwinism was integrated into the ideology of the Victorian middle class. With this interpretation, the concepts of the "struggle for existence" and the "survival of the fittest" become (as originally suggested by Marx and Engels) to some extent projections on to nature of the values of free-enterprise individualism. Desmond's analysis of the pre-Darwinian debates offers an extension of this technique, taking into account the many different factions within British society that were coming to grips with the new philosophy of scientific naturalism. Few historians now doubt that the social context was important, both in shaping Darwin's own thoughts, and in conditioning the acceptance of his theory by scientists and by the general public. Many, however, find it difficult to ignore the unique character of Darwin's scientific work. His development of a theory that transcended the ideology of his time was made possible by insights that were shaped by his scientific studies. His biogeography, and his emphasis on evolution as a process that adapted populations to changes in their environment, led him to visualize the history of life as a tree with many branches, not as a ladder leading up the stages of development toward humankind. RUSE provides an overview of the "Darwinian revolution" which seeks to balance the scientific and social influences.

Studies of the reception of Darwinism have focused on both the scientific debates and on the broader implications of the theory. HULL provides an overview of the scientific arguments, with selections from reviews of Darwin's *Origin of Species*, while the survey edited by GLICK reveals the extent to which the reception of Darwinism varied from one country to another. With the exception of France, most national scientific communities accepted the basic idea of evolution within a decade or so, but there was far less enthusiasm for the mechanism of natural selection. By the 1870s, most paleontologists were interpreting the fossil record as evidence of evolution, anatomical resemblances were being seen as evidence of common descent, and geographical distribution was being explained in terms of the origin and migration of species. To some extent, support for "Darwinism" stemmed from the growing enthusiasm for a naturalistic philosophy, especially among the new generation of professional scientists. Yet conservative thinkers were also able to take on board the general concept of evolution, although they preferred less materialistic mechanisms, such as "Lamarckism" (the inheritance of acquired characteristics). Neo-Lamarckism was particularly strong in America, where the scientific legacy of Louis Agassiz ensured that many biologists saw evolution as the unfolding of a developmental pattern, under the influence of goal-directed forces.

Scientists and non-scientists alike were affected by the debate over the wider implications of Darwinism. MOORE challenges the conventional image of a "war" between science and theology, with evolutionism as one of the battlefields. He argues that, despite the initial outcry, many religious thinkers were able to come to terms with Darwinism, provided they could interpret the theory in a way that preserved some aspects of the old teleological world view. Lamarckism gained support as an alternative to natural selection, because it retained a sense of purpose in nature's activities. Although Darwin himself insisted that most variation is random, he was not averse to the implication that natural selection would work toward progress in the long run. For many Darwinists, selection merely weeded out the less successful products of some more purposeful mechanism, for the production of new characters.

RICHARDS studies the application of evolutionism in another controversial area: the origins of the human mind. Here again, the initial hostility to the prospect of the animal ancestry of humankind was soon overcome. The idea of progress was used to argue that nature had been designed to move steadily up the scale of development toward human mental and moral faculties. Like Moore, Richards challenges the conventional view that Darwinism was perceived as an amoral philosophy at variance with all traditional values. Whatever the perception of modern Darwinists such as Mayr, the 19th-century evolutionists modified the logic of Darwin's theory to evade its more materialistic implications.

At the purely scientific level, Darwin's theory of divergent, adaptive evolution driven mainly by natural selection is seen as the foundation stone of modern evolutionism. Eiseley and Mayr both recognize that 19th-century biologists brought forward many objections against natural selection. They preserve a Darwin-centered historiography by concentrating on those areas where we know, with hindsight, that Darwin was in error: his views on heredity and variation. For Eiseley, natural selection simply could not work properly as a theory without the particulate conception of heredity provided by Gregor Mendel and his posthumous followers, the 20th-century geneticists. Genetics is thus presented as the missing piece in the Darwinian jigsaw puzzle: once put in place, the whole evolutionary picture is complete. Mayr recognizes that the eventual synthesis of Darwinism and genetics was a more complex affair. Darwin's own theory of heredity, pangenesis, arose from a pre-genetical viewpoint that did not distinguish between the transmission of characters from parent to offspring, and the development of those characters in the individual organism. The early geneticists concentrated on the transmission of hereditary units; they were saltationists, who thought that new characters were produced by sudden jumps, and as a result they rejected both natural selection and the belief that evolution is driven by adaptive pressures. Nevertheless, Mayr accepts a main line of events forming a sequence, leading from Darwin's original formulation of natural selection, to the theory's triumphant link with genetics in the 1930s and 1940s. Mayr insists that both field naturalists and mathematical population geneticists were involved in the synthesis.

Drawing on the new perceptions of late 19th-century Darwinism offered by writers such as Moore and Richards, BOWLER (1988) offers a protest against the historiography in which the introduction and perfection of the selection theory form the main sequence of events. He argues that if 19th-century Darwinists, and those evolutionists who styled themselves as Lamarckians, rejected the materialistic interpretation

of the theory of natural selection, then we should not try to understand the original Darwinian revolution through a conceptual framework determined by the values of modern Darwinism. Evolutionism was accepted despite the lack of enthusiasm for natural selection, and we should focus less on the initial debates over the selection theory, and more on the alternative forms of evolutionism that flourished in the late 19th century. The advent of genetics, and the synthesis with selectionism, represent a separate, and later, set of events, which should not be treated as merely the last stages of a process initiated by Darwin. Far from ushering in an age of materialism in 1859, the *Origin of Species* was incorporated into a modernized version of the old world view, in which the idea of progress and the concept of nature as a purposeful entity were preserved, until more comprehensively challenged by the new sciences and the new cultural forces of the 20th century. The hostility felt by many early geneticists towards the selection theory indicates that the new science of heredity was no mere spin-off from the original form of Darwinism, but arose from the collapse of a developmental view of nature into which Darwinism had at first been incorporated. Only in the aftermath of that collapse was it possible for the majority of scientists to understand the materialistic implications of the selection theory.

PETER J. BOWLER

See also Darwin; Darwinism; Evolutionary Synthesis; Natural Selection

Evolutionary Synthesis

Adams, Mark B., "The Founding of Population Genetics: Contributions of the Chetverikov School, 1924–1934", *Journal of the History of Biology*, 1/1 (1968): 23–39

Adams, Mark B., "La Génétique des populations était-elle une génétique évolutive?" in *Histoire de la génétique: Pratiques, techniques et théories*, edited by Jean-Louis Fischer and William H. Schneider, Paris: ARPEM, 1990, 153–71

Adams, Mark B. (ed.), *The Evolution of Theodosius Dobzhansky: Essays on His Life and Thought in Russia and America*, Princeton, New Jersey: Princeton University Press, 1994

Cain, Joseph Allen, "Common Problems and Cooperative Solutions: Organizational Activity in Evolutionary Studies, 1936–1947", *Isis*, 84/1 (1993): 1–25

Dietrich, Michael R., "Richard Goldschmidt's 'Heresies' and the Evolutionary Synthesis", *Journal of the History of Biology*, 28/3 (1995): 431–61

Grene, Marjorie (ed.), *Dimensions of Darwinism: Themes and Counterthemes in Twentieth Century Evolutionary Theory*, Cambridge and New York: Cambridge University Press, 1983

Mayr, Ernst and William B. Provine (eds), *The Evolutionary Synthesis: Perspectives on the Unification of Biology*, Cambridge, Massachusetts: Harvard University Press, 1980

Mayr, Ernst, *The Growth of Biological Thought: Diversity, Evolution and Inheritance*, Cambridge, Massachusetts: Harvard University Press, 1982

Mayr, Ernst, *One Long Argument: Charles Darwin and the Genesis of Modern Evolutionary Thought*, Cambridge, Massachusetts: Harvard University Press, 1991

Paul, Diane B. and Barbara A. Kimmelman, "Mendel in America: Theory and Practice, 1900–1919", in *The American Development of Biology*, edited by Ronald Rainger, Keith R. Benson and Jane Maienschein, Philadelphia: University of Pennsylvania Press, 1988, 281–310

Provine, William B. (ed.), *The Origins of Theoretical Population Genetics*, Chicago: University of Chicago Press, 1971

Provine, William B., *Sewall Wright and Evolutionary Biology*, Chicago: University of Chicago Press, 1986

Smocovitis, Vassiliki Betty, *Unifying Biology: The Evolutionary Synthesis and Evolutionary Biology*, Princeton, New Jersey: Princeton University Press, 1996

The history of the evolutionary synthesis is populated with scholars, such as Ernst Mayr, William Provine, and Stephen Jay Gould, who have commitments within both biology and history, and whose work in each discipline is to some extent synergistic. Ernst Mayr's centrality to both the evolutionary synthesis and the history of biology makes it unsurprising that he has become the main figure in the reconstruction of the history of the event. The dean of US historians of biology during his tenure at Harvard, Mayr trained most of the historians who have written on evolutionary synthesis. Provine, who did not study with Mayr, also combines history and biology in his work, and in turn trained Smocovitis at Cornell. Finally, Gould's commentary on the evolutionary synthesis complements his larger work on Darwinism and Neo-Darwinism.

Little of the existing work explicitly addresses the position of the evolutionary synthesis within the struggle for authority and resources. While there are brilliant intellectual histories of the evolutionary synthesis, the social and institutional story is only just beginning to be written. The rhetoric of the unification of biology by evolutionary theory also reveals tensions within the biological sciences, taking an aggressive stance toward both the reductionist experimental research programs that gained prominence in 20th-century biology, and toward the service role that biology has traditionally performed for medicine and agriculture. The disciplines for which the evolutionary synthesis is central – such as paleontology, systematics, and field biology – are precisely those that are unlikely to make practical contributions to either healing or food production. This provides an explanation for the lack of appeal of the synthesis for such disciplines as microbiology, physiology, and embryology, which were already securely placed as biomedical disciplines.

The remainder of this essay is divided into three parts. The first provides an account of the synthesis through the first generation of historiography, culminating in Mayr & Provine's edited volume. Next follows a discussion of the second generation of works that challenge these initial interpretations. The essay concludes with a discussion of the rhetoric of the unification of biology and the struggle for institutional resources,

issues that are relevant to the evolutionary synthesis but remain unresolved within its literature.

Taken together, the first generation of works by Adams, Mayr, Provine, and the contributors to Mayr & Provine, present an admirable portrait of the intellectual history of the evolutionary synthesis, exploring both the history of ideas and the disciplinary dynamics of 20th-century evolutionary biology. As described by PROVINE (1971) and MAYR & PROVINE, the evolutionary synthesis was a process that occurred in stages between 1900 and 1947. The first stage consisted of the merging of Mendelian and Darwinian views within theoretical population genetics, which had taken place by the early 1930s. The second stage brought population genetics to paleontology, geology, and a range of other disciplines. The contributors to Mayr & Provine also argue that the synthesis was the driving force for the unification of the biological sciences in the 20th century. This volume published in 1980 contains the writings of participants in the synthesis and of historians of biology who gathered at Ernst Mayr's invitation in 1974 to reflect on the event. Organized by country and discipline, Mayr & Provine's collection presents the classic tale of the evolutionary synthesis, and is the starting point for anyone interested in its intellectual history.

The fusion of Mendelian heredity and Darwinian evolution into the modern Neo-Darwinian evolutionary synthesis is a commonplace of both biology textbooks and histories of modern biology. The textbooks generally lament that Darwin did not read Mendel's landmark article of 1865 on heredity in *Pisum sativum* (pea plant) because it was published in the obscure *Proceedings of the Brünn Natural History Society*. This notion is countered in the historical literature by the wide circulation of the journal in European libraries, Mendel's correspondence with the prominent plant breeder Karl Wilhelm von Nägeli, and the probable lack of impact of Mendel's pea research on Darwin's broad and synthetic hereditary thinking.

According to Provine (1971), the followers of Mendel and Darwin in Britain around 1900 had moved from independent lines of work to active conflict. The British biometricians (who, under the leadership of Karl Pearson, called themselves the Darwinians) and the Mendelians (following William Bateson, and influenced by Hugo de Vries), all of whom believed in the evolution of species by descent with modification, were in vicious contention over its mechanism. Provine's classic work addresses this dispute, and describes its eventual solution by R.A. Fisher, J.B.S. Haldane, and Sewall Wright, whose creation of theoretical population genetics took account of both continuous and discontinuous variation in populations by mathematical modelling, successfully integrating the perspectives of both camps. Wright's career is profiled in the admirable intellectual biography by PROVINE (1986). The transition from mathematical models to natural populations was made in the 1920s and 1930s by a school of field biologists surrounding Sergei Sergeevich Chetverikov in Moscow, as shown by ADAMS (1968).

If, as Provine contends, the creation of population genetics as a solution to the tensions between the biometricians and the Mendelians was the first stage of the synthesis, the contributors to Mayr & Provine describe a second stage that began with Theodosius Dobzhansky. Dobzhansky's intermediate position between laboratory and field biology permitted him to bridge the concerns of naturalist-systematists and geneticists.

MAYR (1982) provides the most synthetic modern account of the history of biology from Aristotle to the present. Mayr places Darwin's theory of evolution by descent with modification at the turning point, from an era characterized by the description of diversity to one that concentrated on the explanation of evolutionary mechanisms. The evolutionary synthesis emerges within Mayr's narrative to clarify the relationship between evolution and inheritance, solving the second great problem in the biological sciences that leads to our modern understanding of the field. MAYR (1991) takes up where Mayr (1982) leaves off, exploring Darwinism and Neo-Darwinism in greater depth, and presenting in coherent narrative form a story that the essays in Mayr & Province leave the reader to reconstruct from the different contributions. Meanwhile, beginning a more skeptical historiography, Shapere (in Mayr & Province) questions what was synthesized, when, and by whom, and even calls into question the notion of a true synthesis.

Having inherited a timeline and story from the first generation, the second wave of historical works on the evolutionary synthesis challenged this historical picture by developing a social approach. Taking Provine as their starting point, PAUL & KIMMELMAN put the British biometrician-Mendelian debate into perspective with their social history of agricultural genetics in the United States, where applied projects and plentiful jobs permitted biometrical and Mendelian approaches to coexist in relative peace.

Some of the essays in GRENE, based on a conference of 1981, take an even more critical, and far more social, stance than Shapere, presenting new interpretations of the roles of several disciplines and discussing the social commitments of some synthesizers. Gould's discussion of the exclusion of Alfred C. Kinsey and Richard Goldschmidt, and the value of "heretics" in cementing the orthodox view of the synthesis and of Neo-Darwinian evolution, is a classic example of "negative solidarity" (in which participants can agree that a third party is wrong, without necessarily agreeing on the reasons for that judgment, thus uniting them in opposition). Gould suggests that the synthesis had as much to do with the limitation of perspectives as it did with the synthesis of theories and methods.

As ADAMS (1990) notes in his discussion of the relationship of population genetics and mechanisms of change within species (microevolution) with the problem of the evolution of new species (macroevolution), Dobzhansky and the synthesizers reduce macroevolution to population genetics. This redefinition allows Dobzhansky and others to contend that the problem of evolution is solved through their genetic studies of populations. Moving beyond the history of ideas and disciplines, the essays on Dobzhansky in ADAMS (1994) display a sensitivity to family, national context, and social issues.

DIETRICH's work on Goldschmidt provides a thoughtful and important analysis of the role of this controversial figure. Goldschmidt, one of the most prominent geneticists of the 1930s and 1940s, argued in *The Material Basis of Evolution* (1940) that there was an unbridgeable gap between the mechanisms of change within and between species (microevolution

and macroevolution). Dietrich's study explores in detail both the institutional and conceptual implications of Goldschmidt's objections, and his "heretical" status.

CAIN's history of the synthesis provides a further foray into the institutional dynamics of the episode, furnishing an analysis of social networks and professional problems, and explaining some of the problems that the synthesis solved for its participants. SMOCOVITIS, basing her work on more recent cultural history and theory, presents some of the social networks and institutional politics of the synthesis from an outsider's perspective. Her historiographical chapter is useful for laying out the literature and her narrative for synthesizing the state of the field. She asks, but does not entirely answer, questions about the meaning of the unification of biology.

Even the second generation of synthesis literature leaves many questions unanswered. What does it mean for biology to be "unified"? Is the notion of the unification of biology the product of a naïve comparison of biology with physics and chemistry, working under the assumption that those sciences are unified in some way that biology is not? If mimicry of chemistry and physics is the method, is the motive to increase the epistemological status of biology as a whole, or of just some of the biological sciences, and finally, did it succeed? If, indeed, there was a unification of biology through the evolutionary synthesis, did this unification change funding patterns or biological practice? Further studies of funding, institutional settings, and analyses of the wider claims concerning unification and epistemology present clear opportunities.

CARLA KEIRNS

See also Darwinism; Evolution; Natural Selection

Exhibitions

Allwood, John, *The Great Exhibitions*, London: Studio Vista, 1952

Bennett, J.A., *Science at the Great Exhibition*, Cambridge: Whipple Museum, 1983

Bennett, Tony, *The Birth of the Museum: History, Theory, Politics*, London and New York: Routledge, 1995

Brain, Robert, *Going to the Fair: Readings in the Culture of Nineteenth-Century Exhibitions*, Cambridge: Whipple Museum, 1993

Ferguson, Eugene, "Technical Museums and International Exhibitions", *Technology and Culture*, 1/1 (1965): 30–46

Geddes, Patrick, *Industrial Exhibitions and Modern Progress*, Edinburgh: Douglas, 1877

Giedion, Siegfried, *Space, Time, and Architecture: The Growth of a New Tradition*, Cambridge, Massachusetts: Harvard University Press, and London: Milford/Oxford University Press, 1941; 5th enlarged edition, 1967

Greenhalgh, Paul, *Ephemeral Vistas: The Expositions Universelles, Great Exhibitions, and World's Fairs, 1851–1939*, Manchester: Manchester University Press, 1988

Hafter, Daryl, "The Business of Invention in the Paris Industrial Exposition of 1806", *Business History Review*, 58 (1984): 317–35

Kusamitsu, Toshio, "Great Exhibitions Before 1851", *History Workshop*, 9 (1980): 70–89

Nye, David, "Electrifying Expositions, 1850–1939", in *Fair Representations: World's Fairs and the Modern World*, edited by Robert W. Rydell and Nancy E. Gwinn, Amsterdam: VU University Press, 1994, 140–56

Rydell, Robert W., *All the World's a Fair: A Vision of Empire at American International Expositions, 1876–1916*, Chicago: University of Chicago Press, 1984

Rydell, Robert W., "The Fan Dance of Science: American World's Fairs in the Great Depression", *Isis*, 76 (1985): 525–42

Rydell, Robert W., *The Books of the Fairs: Materials about World's Fairs, 1834–1916 in the Smithsonian Institution Libraries*, Chicago: American Library Association, 1992

Rydell, Robert W. and Nancy E. Gwinn (eds), *Fair Representations: World's Fairs and the Modern World*, Amsterdam: VU University Press, 1994

Schaffer, Simon, "Late Victorian Metrology and Its Instrumentation: A Manufactory of Ohms", in *Invisible Connections: Instruments, Institutions, and Science*, edited by Robert Bud and Susan E. Cozzens, Bellingham, Washington: SPIE Optical Engineering Press, 1991

Schroeder-Gudehus, Brigitte and Anne Rasmussen, *Les Fastes du progrès: Le guide des expositions universelles, 1851–1992*, Paris: Flammarion, 1992

International Exhibitions – also called Great Exhibitions, Universal Expositions, and World's Fairs – have been a source of important literature within the history of science and technology since they began with the Great Exhibition of 1851. The 19th-century Scottish scientist and urban sociologist GEDDES provided an exemplary account of exhibitions and their putative value for modernization and progress, while BRAIN presents excerpts from the vast exhibition literature of the 19th century on a variety of themes, ranging from their organization and promotion, architecture and display design, classification systems, science and technology, nationalism and internationalism, and the varied pronouncements on the exhibition experience, ranging from the euphoric to the dystopic.

ALLWOOD contains a wealth of general information about international exhibitions, along with an abundance of iconographic material. GREENHALGH provides the most thorough general critical interpretation of the exhibitions, delineating skilfully the interconnections between commodity culture, imperialism, and the invention of national and international traditions at exhibitions.

Several excellent reference volumes provide bibliographic guidance to the exhibitions. SCHROEDER-GUDEHUS & RASMUSSEN cover the entire exhibition movement, offering a remarkably thorough bibliography of both the primary and secondary literature on the international exhibitions. RYDELL (1992) offers a critical annotated bibliography of the historiography of exhibitions and should be regarded as the indispensable guide to the historical literature.

The international exhibition movement was preceded by a half-century of national and local industrial exhibitions, which had begun during the French Revolution. HAFTER examines how the pressures of international industrial competition prompted French officials to enlist scientists and engineers to serve on juries and to set criteria for originality for the appraisal of commercially viable inventions. The aim of the exhibitions, she argues, was to facilitate French efforts to catch up with the English standard in several branches of industry.

The legacy of such techniques of public display continued in museums, including many science and technology museums that were the direct offspring of the international exhibitions. FERGUSON surveys this relationship between specific international exhibitions and many of the world's most important science museums, including the London Science Museum, the Vienna Technical Museum for Industry and Trade, the Deutsches Museum in Munich, and the Museum of Science and Industry in Chicago. Tony BENNETT provides a critical Marxist and post-structuralist interpretation of the 19th-century museum and its genesis in the "exhibitionary complex". He argues that the public display of disciplines such as social statistics, hygiene, anthropology, and natural history made visible to a broader public the techniques through which the authorities came to know and govern modern populations, as a means of fostering self-governance and consensus in the new public sphere of the 19th century. RYDELL (1984) considers the role of anthropology in the Chicago Columbian Exposition of 1893, and reveals its importance as the unifying concept of the exhibition and its potency in promoting values of old racism and new imperialism in the turn-of-the-century United States.

GIEDION argues that the engineering-oriented architecture of international exhibitions exerted a decisive influence on modern design.

Another wellspring of recent interest in international exhibitions among historians of science derives from their role in promoting the culture of precision measurement, metrology, and standardisation. J.A. BENNETT provides a survey of the classes of scientific instruments shown at the Great Exhibition of 1851. SCHAFFER examines the negotiations between leading international physicists over the determination of standard measurements of electricity at the Paris International Electrical Exposition of 1881. He shows how the exhibition served as the general marketplace and public forum for the international science community, and how the wrangling over electrical standards extended the influence of international juries over technical standards and metrologies in many different spheres of industry. NYE delineates the imprint of exhibitions on the modern popular notion of electricity itself; while visitors to early exhibitions had no trouble understanding the drive-shafts, gears, valves, pulleys, and other mechanisms of steam-driven machinery, the largely invisible workings of electricity skewed presentation in favor of effects rather than internal workings, in entertainment rather than education. Finally, RYDELL (1985) examines the role of scientists and scientific displays at the American World's Fairs of the 1930s, arguing that exhibitions of that period buttressed popular respect for scientists as experts having answers to social as well as scientific problems.

ROBERT BRAIN

See also International Science

Expeditions

Beaglehole, J.C., *The Exploration of the Pacific*, London: A. and C. Black, 1934; 3rd edition, 1966

Brannigan, Augustine, *The Social Basis of Scientific Discoveries*, Cambridge and New York: Cambridge University Press, 1981

Broc, Numa, *La Géographie des philosophes: geographes et voyageurs français au XVIIIe siècle*, Paris: Ophrys, 1975

Cannon, Susan Faye, *Science in Culture: The Early Victorian Period*, Kent: Dawson, and New York: Science History Publications, 1978

Carter, Paul, *The Road to Botany Bay: An Essay in Spatial History*, London and Boston: Faber and Faber, 1987

Dening, Greg, *Mr Bligh's Bad Language: Passion, Power, and Theatre on the Bounty*, Cambridge and New York: Cambridge University Press, 1992

Lafuente, Antonio and Antonio Mazuecos, *Los caballeros del punto Fijo: ciencia, política y aventura en la expedición geodésica hispanofrancesa al virreinato del Perú en el siglo XVIII*, Barcelona: Serbal, and Madrid: CSIC, 1987

Latour, Bruno, *Science in Action: How to Follow Scientists and Engineers through Society*, Cambridge, Massachusetts: Harvard University Press, 1987

Laurens, Henry, *L'Expedition d'Egypte, 1789–1801*, Paris: Collin, 1990

Livingstone, David, *The Geographical Tradition: Episodes in the History of a Contested Enterprise*, Oxford and Cambridge, Massachusetts: Blackwell, 1993

Malinowski, Bronisław, *A Diary in the Strict Sense of the Term*, translated from the Polish by Norbert Guterman, New York: Harcourt Brace, and London: Routledge and Kegan Paul, 1967; 2nd edition with a new introduction, London: Athlone Press, and Stanford, California: Stanford University Press, 1989

Miller, David P. and Hans P. Reill (eds), *Visions of Empire: Voyages, Botany, and Representations of Nature*, Cambridge and New York: Cambridge University Press, 1996

Smith, Bernard, *European Vision and the South Pacific, 1768–1850*, Oxford: Clarendon Press, 1960; 2nd edition, New Haven, Connecticut, and London: Yale University Press, 1985

Stefánsson, Vilhjálmur, *The Friendly Arctic: The Story of Five Years in Polar Regions*, New York: Macmillan, and London: Harrap, 1921; revised edition, New York: Macmillan, 1943

Although numerous works connected with the term "scientific expeditions" are currently available, for the most part they make oblique references to what is a vast domain with partially concealed and ill-defined boundaries. Many concepts and facts clutter this evidently diffuse topic, as the relationship between science and travel has not only been protracted, but prolific and entangled. In this essay, expeditions are distinguished and separated from the subject of geographical exploration, a connected but different subject. If one were to examine the history of scientific travellers or voyaging scientists, one would have to go back to the time of Pliny or Ptolemy. If, on the other hand, one conceives of a scientific expedition as a self-conscious exercise in organisation and planning, wherein a group of experts is despatched, typically from an institutional centre to a periphery, with the purpose of researching and/or disseminating scientific descriptions, measurements or cadres, the topic is much more manageable. In the Western world, the phenomenon of scientific expeditions has been linked to the emergence and consolidation of nation states since the beginning of the early modern age, and, especially, to three distinctive aspects of European expansion: the progressive institutionalization of science; the professionalization of scientists; and the disciplined management and coordination of travelling labour. During the 15th, 16th and 17th centuries, border areas (America, in particular) were visited by European naturalists, cartographers and seafarers, who contributed to the growth of practical mathematics, natural philosophy and natural history, modifying the sciences and establishing new metaphysical assumptions. LIVINGSTONE's scholarly study is the only history of geography, spanning the early modern period to the end of the 19th century, which ties expeditions to wider social and religious contexts. Though by no means exhaustive, it is becoming a standard point of departure for further studies.

The Enlightenment was, however, the period of scientific expeditions *par excellence*, due to the concurrence of the "second phase of discoveries", the rise of the classification systems in the field of botany, advancements in nautical astronomy, and the consolidation of the great scientific institutions (the Académie des Sciences and the Royal Society of London, in particular). The scholarly contributions in this area are, nevertheless, dispersed; it is common, even for this period, to find the most insightful pages on scientific expeditions in books devoted to a different subject matter. For example, while studying the transition, in France, from humanistic geography to the emergence of embryonic sciences on the earth and the human being, BROC's study of 18th-century geography, written in the best scholarly tradition of the history of ideas, refers with regularity to French explorations and scientific voyages to America, the Islamic lands, the East and the Pacific as sources for the new knowledge.

Circumnavigations and the great Pacific expeditions are probably the topics most thoroughly analysed: BEAGLEHOLE's authoritative study of Cook's voyages and journals, and SMITH's path-breaking study of the aesthetic issues of visual descriptions, depict the vicissitudes weathered by Anson, Byron, Cook, Bougainville and La Pérouse, and are of seminal importance for the histories of science, anthropology and art. America, for her part, continued to be a privileged setting for debates about the New World. In the second half of the 18th-century, the Spanish monarchy despatched to the New World a substantial number of expeditions that preceded Alexander von Humboldt's expedition to New Spain. Many travelling naturalists of this period spread the Linnean nomenclature throughout the Americas, while others completed the cartography of its coastline.

CARTER's important and highly readable account of Cook's arrival in Australia borrows from anthropology and literary theory in order to discuss the significance of naming. He contrasts the explorer's and the botanist's attitudes towards naming, which he argues reflect fundamental disagreements about the nature of language, representation, and the roles of expedition members. This theme is extended and expanded in MILLER & REILL, an eclectic and informatively edited collection of essays addressing the visual languages of botany in this period.

LAFUENTE & MAZUECOS give an excellent account of the expeditions organised to solve metropolitan scientific controversies, such as the Hispanic-French geodesic expedition to the Kingdom of Quito, led by La Condamine, Juan and Ulloa, whose aim was to gauge the meridian degree, and to settle the issue of the shape of the earth that had divided Newtonians from Cartesians for decades. The authors analyse the complex interplay between science and politics on board an expedition that turned into an itinerant academy. The idea of expeditions as generators of scientific data, spaces for experimentation, indeed as travelling laboratories, is successfully developed and elaborated by Bruno LATOUR.

In the period straddling the transition between the 18th and 19th centuries, two major developments in the history of scientific expeditions accompanied the more general proliferation of forms of travel. First, the voyage to Spanish America by Alexander von Humboldt (who, significantly, regarded himself as a scientific traveller rather than an explorer) ushered in a cosmopolitan philosophy of scientific travel, fieldwork, and precision measurement under the label *physique du globe*. CANNON, in her classic essay, recognised that cultures of precision, calibration, institutionalization, and an international cosmopolitanism were particularly characteristic of the 19th-century "Humboldtian sciences", once more highlighting geography's indebtedness to expeditions as a source of knowledge. The second major development in the history of scientific expeditions was the incorporation of science into imperial occupation and acquisition, underlined by the scale and extent of Napoleon's expedition to Egypt. Indeed, LAURENS, in a thorough treatment of Napoleon's army of scientists in Egypt, argues that power and knowledge, the Armée d'Orient and the Commission des Sciences et Arts, converged and became indistinguishable within the sacred civilising project.

At the end of the 19th century a new form of expedition emerged, explicitly anthropological in character, and exemplified by Haddon's team of field-workers in the Torres Strait (1898). A self-conscious concern with delineating techniques that could be taught, practised and repeated characterises much early 20th-century literature on expeditions. MALINOWSKI's field notes combined a self-conscious individuality, bureaucratic-like record-keeping, and disciplined study as the conditions of extended fieldwork. In spite of his ambivalent attitudes towards the people he studied, his work remains a foundation for British social anthropology, a rite of passage for anthropology initiates.

Although some scientific travellers had throughout the centuries adopted the customs and manners of the places they visited, utilising indigenous techniques as an expeditionary strategy only acquired the status of "knowledge" in the 20th century. STEFÁNSSON's travel narrative, based on his Canadian Arctic Expedition (1913–17), nicely illustrates how some scientific travellers learned from, and openly embraced, indigenous strategies for hunting and living off the land.

Sociological critiques of the concept of expeditions are a relatively recent phenomenon. BRANNIGAN, though sometimes overlooked, is a milestone in science studies. He uses Columbus's most famous voyage to argue that scientific discoveries can be understood in terms of socially constructed (phenomenological) acts of knowing, the projections of social categories brought from home. DENING's unconventional, but humorous and wise, anthropological study of Captain Bligh takes the expedition, quite literally, to be a theatre of empire, a stage on which the actors make and remake history through their performances. In this and other works, Dening makes seminal contributions to anthropological history, in contrast to a standard work such as Latour, for whom expeditions are ultimately an institutional means of collecting, classifying, recording and describing a heterogeneous field, with those inscriptions that are most immutable, transferable and replicable having an agency of their own.

JUAN PIMENTEL AND MICHAEL T. BRAVO

See also Humboldt; Polar Science

Experimental Physiology

Coleman, William and Frederic L. Holmes (eds), *The Investigative Enterprise: Experimental Physiology in Nineteenth-Century Medicine*, Berkeley: University of California Press, 1988

Frank Jr, Robert G., *Harvey and the Oxford Physiologists: A Study of Scientific Ideas*, Berkeley: University of California Press, 1980

French, Richard D., *Anti-Vivisection and Medical Science in Victorian Society*, Princeton, New Jersey: Princeton University Press, 1975

Fye, W. Bruce, *The Development of American Physiology: Scientific Medicine in the Nineteenth Century*, Baltimore: Johns Hopkins University Press, 1987

Geison, Gerald L., *Michael Foster and the Cambridge School of Physiology: The Scientific Enterprise in Late Victorian Society*, Princeton, New Jersey: Princeton University Press, 1978

Geison, Gerald L. (ed.), *Physiology in the American Context, 1850–1940*, Bethesda, Maryland: American Physiological Society, 1987

Hodgkin, A.L. *et al.*, *The Pursuit of Nature: Informal Essays on the History of Physiology*, Cambridge: Cambridge University Press, 1977

Lesch, John E., *Science and Medicine in France: The Emergence of Experimental Physiology, 1790–1855*, Cambridge, Massachusetts: Harvard University Press, 1984

Rothschuh, Karl E., *History of Physiology*, translated from the German and edited by Guenter B. Risse, Huntingdon, New York: R.E. Krieger, 1973 (original edition, 1953)

Although physiology became a rigorously experimental discipline only during the 19th century, the study of animal functions has a long history. No recent attempt has been made to survey the whole subject, but ROTHSCHUH's monograph is still useful as a guide to the main themes, discoveries, and individuals, from antiquity to the early 20th century. Originally published in German, it contains good discussions of continental teacher-pupil relationships; the English edition provides additional material on British and American physiologists, though omitting some references to continental primary and secondary sources.

Among early experimentalists, William Harvey (1578–1656) is a pivotal figure, steeped in Aristotelianism, yet systematic in his hands-on approach to the functional problems that intrigued him – above all, the motions of the heart and the circulation of the blood. The study by FRANK demonstrates Harvey's immediate legacy among a group of Oxford disciples, such as Richard Lower (1631–92), John Mayow (1643–79) and Thomas Willis (1621–75), who extended his investigations on the blood, respiration and circulation. Harvey continued to be invoked as an inspiration by many 17th- and 18th-century experimentalists.

Nevertheless, it is common to regard François Magendie (1783–1855) as the first thoroughly modern physiologist, through his attempt to isolate questions of function from those of structure, his disregard for metaphysical issues, and his cool, not to say cruel, vivisection techniques. LESCH's study of "the emergence of experimental physiology" in France between 1790 and 1855 naturally places Magendie centre-stage, although he also analyses the institutional, organisational, and technical innovations effected by a generation of investigators that saw itself robbed by the early death of Xavier Bichat (1771–1802). Lesch is sensitive to the importance of medical experience in the training of this post-Bichat generation, in which students would acquire surgical skills and identify clinical problems demanding physiological explanations. Physiology was to remain closely tied to medicine for much of the century, despite the clarion call of Magendie's pupil, Claude Bernard (1813–78), in his *An Introduction to the Study of Experimental Medicine* (1865), for doctors to recognise the independent importance of laboratory sciences such as physiology.

In the German-speaking world, the establishment of institutes of physiology (among many other academic disciplines) provided more physical and intellectual space for the subject. The institutionalization of experimental physiology in Heidelberg, with the active research and training institute of Carl Ludwig (1816–95) in Leipzig, and the formation of a "school" of metabolism in Munich, are just three German themes explored in the outstanding collection of essays edited by COLEMAN & HOLMES. The volume's sub-title refers to "experimental physiology in 19th-century medicine", and the authors have taken their brief seriously; they examine the variety of pedagogical initiatives within medical education, as practical physiological experience became an increasingly routine part of a medical student's training, while at the same time scrutinising the research strategies instrumental in defining the profession of physiology in France, the German-speaking lands and, to a lesser extent, Britain. The equipment on which physiologists came to rely – the kymograph, sphygmograph, collecting apparatus, and, above all, the microscope – is also given appropriate attention.

One key British centre, the University of Cambridge, and its prime figure, Michael Foster (1836–1907), are the subject of GEISON (1978). Foster went as praelector in physiology to Trinity College, Cambridge, in 1870, and although he did not acquire a university chair for 13 years, he managed, through his astute political sense, the excellence of his teaching, and an ability to excite his students about research, to create what Geison accurately describes as a "school", with a series of related research problems – the origins and control of the heart beat, the nature of cardiac contractility, the functions of the autonomic nervous system – which his students tackled with remarkable success. Foster was also instrumental in founding a professional society and journal devoted exclusively to physiology.

Experimentation often required the use and sacrifice of laboratory animals, and although anaesthesia could control the pain, a tide of public sentiment, especially in Britain, rose against the employment of animals for experimental purposes. The best study of the anti-vivisection movement in the late 19th century is that of FRENCH. He demonstrates how fundamental the anti-vivisectionist threat was to the creation of group cohesion among physiologists, other medical scientists and the medical profession more generally, and although the scientific community was unable to prevent the passage through Parliament of the Cruelty to Animals Act (1876), this failed to disrupt the development of experimental medical science in late Victorian Britain. Indeed, by creating definite ethical boundaries, the Act helped to protect experimentalists from the anti-vivisectionists. French also provides a cogent analysis of the composition and strategies of the major anti-vivisection organisations.

The 19th-century American physiological scene has been explored by FYE. He examines the careers of four experimental physiologists, including H. Newall Martin (1848–96) at Johns Hopkins and Henry P. Bowditch (1840–1911) at Harvard, as they attempted to establish practical physiology teaching and research laboratories in their universities. Fye argues that the establishment of the American Physiological Society in 1887 represented a turning point for scientific medicine in the United States, although the fact that all of the 28 founding members were based in a few elite East Coast institutions highlights the marginality of experimental medicine in the country more generally. Nevertheless, Fye's account is one of several that remind us that the medical educational reforms associated with the Flexner Report of 1910 were well under way before the end of the 19th century.

In many ways, the 19th-century origins of experimental physiology have been examined more systematically than its 20th-century manifestations. However, GEISON (1987) contains a collection of essays that scrutinise many aspects of the emergence of American physiology on to the world stage. These essays deal with both institutional and conceptual matters, and although the volume was published to coincide with the centenary of the American Physiological Society, the authors, mostly professional historians, have avoided a narrow celebratory tone. HODGKIN *et al.* produced a more informal volume of autobiographical essays, at the time of the centenary of the Physiological Society in Britain.

W.F. BYNUM

See also Anti-Vivisection; Physiology: France; Physiology: Germany

Experiments

Cohen, H. Floris, *The Scientific Revolution: A Historiographical Inquiry*, Chicago: University of Chicago Press, 1994

Crombie, Alistair C., *Robert Grosseteste and the Origins of Experimental Science, 1100–1700*, Oxford: Clarendon Press, 1953

Galison, Peter, *How Experiments End*, Chicago: University of Chicago Press, 1987

Gooding, David, Trevor Pinch and Simon Schaffer (eds), *The Uses of Experiment: Studies in the Natural Sciences*, Cambridge and New York: Cambridge University Press, 1989

Gower, Barry, *Scientific Method: A Historical and Philosophical Introduction*, London and New York: Routledge, 1997

Hacking, Ian, *Representing and Intervening: Introductory Topics in the Philosophy of Natural Science*, Cambridge and New York: Cambridge University Press, 1983

Harré, Rom, *Great Scientific Experiments: Twenty Experiments That Changed Our View of the World*, Oxford: Phaidon Press, 1981; New York: Oxford University Press, 1983

Heidelberger, Michael and Friedrich Steinle, *Experimental Essays: Versuche zum Experiment*, Baden-Baden: Nomos, 1998

Holmes, Frederic L., "Do We Understand Historically How Experimental Knowledge Is Acquired?", *History of Science*, 30 (1992): 119–36

Koyré, Alexandre, "The Origins of Modern Science: A New Interpretation" [Review of Crombie 1953], *Diogenes*, 16 (1956): 1–22

Kuhn, Thomas S., "Mathematical vs. Experimental Traditions in the Development of Physical Science", *Journal of Interdisciplinary History*, 1/7 (1976): 1–31; reprinted in *The Essential Tension: Selected Studies in Scientific Tradition and Change*, by Kuhn, Chicago: University of Chicago Press, 1977

Licoppe, Christian, *La Formation de la pratique scientifique: le discours de l'expérience en France et en Angleterre, 1630–1820*, Paris: Découverte, 1996

Price, Derek J. de Solla, "Of Sealing Wax and String", *Natural History*, 93/1 (1984): 48–57

Schmitt, Charles B., "Experience and Experiment: Comparison of Zabarella's View with Galileo's in *De Motu*," *Studies in the Renaissance*, 16 (1969): 80–138

Shapin, Steven and Simon Schaffer, *Leviathan and the Air-Pump: Hobbes, Boyle, and the Experimental Life*, Princeton, New Jersey: Princeton University Press, 1985

Teichmann, Jürgen, Wolfgang Schreier and Michael Segre, *Experimente die Geschichte machen*, Munich: Bayerischer Schulbuch, 1995

Although experimentation is a very important element in modern scientific methodology there is no adequate systematic treatment of its history and its contribution to the Scientific Revolution. We also lack an account of the origin and development of its notion, of its rise to a central place in scientific method, of its diffusion into the different sciences, and of the variety of its different forms. There have been some treatments of the general history of experiment, but these have often been examples of a superficial and restricted Whig history, combined with a poor philosophy of science, repeating the same old well-worn stereotypes over and over again.

The most hackneyed idea of all concerns Galileo as the founder of experimentation. His particular contribution might be a good start for a treatment of experiment, because it is not only important in its own right, but also because it often serves as a battleground of different conceptions of science in general. From the title of SCHMITT's article one might be misled to think that he only deals with a minor aspect of Galileo's attitude towards experiment. Yet his treatment is scattered with many rich asides to the literature on experiment in general.

Perhaps the most daring and far reaching attempt to deny Galileo the title of the first experimenter is by CROMBIE. He sees experimental science of the modern world created by 13th-century philosophers of the West transforming Greek geometrical method and uniting it with the experimental habit of the practical arts. With this view, Crombie opposed the standpoint of Alexandre KOYRÉ and others that dominated the field from the 1920s up to the 1970s. For Koyré the undeniable verificationist spirit of medieval methodology does not suffice to mark the rise of experimental science. This step was achieved by Galileo, but in a way that owes very little to experimentation. Koyré saw Galileo's deed precisely in the overcoming of Aristotelian empiricism and 13th-century positivism and by replacing it with a mathematical Platonist ontology that put theory first. True experimental research is only possible, if questions to nature are posed in a suitable mathematical language.

It might sound paradoxical, but Thomas KUHN extended Koyré's approach in a certain sense and yet at the same time made room for Crombie's emphasis on experimental autonomy. He identified two separate traditions in the history of empirical science with their own characteristic way of experimentation, the classical (mathematical) and the Baconian (experimental). These traditions existed in relative isolation side by side until the early 19th century when they merged. Kuhn agrees with Koyré that the achievements of the Scientific Revolution have little to do with new experiments, instruments and observations, but everything to do with a revolution of ideas. He regards this revolution as happening mainly in the classical tradition where experimentation occured rarely and was exclusively used for theory testing *ex post*, thus being subordinate to theory. For the Baconian tradition, however, which was guided by the corpuscular philosophy, he concedes experimentation a leading and constitutive role in the creation and formation of many scientific disciplines, such as chemistry and the sciences of heat, magnetism, and electricity.

In PRICE's opinion, the Scientific Revolution was not so much the result of a grand theoretical paradigm shift but largely of the invention and use of a series of technological devices and "instruments of revelation," like the telescope and the microscope, which expanded the reach of science in many unforeseen directions. He sees the history of science as primarily an advancement of autonomous technology, which is in a second step "being puzzled out by theoreticians and resulting in the advancement of knowledge".

The potentialities of both Kuhn's and Price's approach to explore and to strengthen the peculiarities of experiment were neglected for a long time; both history and philosophy of science were largely theory dominated and took experiment as an unproblematic appendix of theoretical work. This situation changed radically with the appearance of the studies by Hacking and by Shapin & Schaffer. HACKING stresses on the one hand the autonomy and variety of experimentation and its different relationships to theory, calculation, model building and technology, giving a rich array of examples from the history of science to emphasize his points. On the other hand, he takes intervention in the laboratory as a crucial step in his argument for scientific realism, which makes up the central core of his philosophy of science: "It is not thinking about the world but changing it that in the end must make us scientific realists." This does not mean that *any* experimentation on a theoretical entity is supposed to prove its existence, but only its manipulation "in order to experiment on something else" need do that. So, as in Hacking's example, the successful spraying of artificially produced positrons on a niobium ball guarantees their existence.

SHAPIN & SCHAFFER's book is an extended study of the social forms of knowledge making. They take as their case the 1660s controversy between Boyle and Hobbes over the generation of knowledge by experimenting with the air-pump, and they try to show that this was in fact a debate about the social order of the time. They argue that the problem of generating knowledge is a political problem; the determination of a scientific fact derives from the outcome of a negotiation between scientists and is thus socially constructed. Combining the approach of Shapin & Schaffer with the perspective of "cultural history," LICOPPE gives a detailed account of how the attitude *vis-à-vis* experience and experiment has developed in the Baconian tradition of France and England and how the description of experiments in scientific accounts has changed in the period of 1630–1820.

In the wave of renewed interest in experiment, several edited volumes have appeared. The collection by GOODING, PINCH & SCHAFFER contains essays on the use of instruments in experimentation (especially in the 18th century), on Galileo's experimental discourse, on experimental work in the 19th and 20th centuries (Fresnel's and Poisson's optics, Faraday's "magnetic curves", cloud chambers, Morpurgo's search for free quarks) and experimental validation of elementary particle theory.

The claim raised by Shapin & Schaffer and sustained by volumes such as Gooding *et al.* that experiment was systematically neglected by earlier history of science was somewhat damped and relativized by HOLMES. He shows that the historians of science did not neglect experiment but that the questions posed have changed. After a detailed critique of Shapin & Schaffer's methodology he still sees the possibility to separate the cognitive side of experiment from its social one. In another criticism of Shapin & Shaffer, COHEN doubts whether their results can be taken as representative for the development of science on the continent (where the social order of the Restoration was not an issue) or for experimentation in

the mathematical tradition. (Chapters 2 and 3 include discussions of Crombie, Koyré, Kuhn and others on experiment and experimental science during the Scientific Revolution; see especially pages 184–89.)

What Shapin & Schaffer have done for the 17th century GALISON has in a way achieved for the 20th century. He shows how physicists separate real effects from the artefacts of instruments and the environment. His study analyses traditions of instrumentation, the role of computer simulation, and how experimental results are achieved in collective collaboration. His focus is not on theory but on the laboratory of the experimenter in microphysics.

HARRÉ is an appealing example of the literature on "great experiments", for the wide variety and concise analysis of the experiments treated as well as for the philosophical lessons drawn from them. He takes a fresh look at many famous and influential experiments, but also chose samples that are typical for a research programme or stand out because of their elegance. The reader will find a rich array of categories in which different experiments can be sorted according to their role. The temporal scope spans from Aristotle to Michelson, from Theoderic of Freiberg to the Stern-Gerlach experiment, from William Beaumont to J.J. Gibson's work on perception and to F. Jacob on transfer of genetic material. Another good example of this genre is TEICHMANN *et al.* who present the history of physics in a series of some 30 experiments, from antiquity to superconduction and laser technology.

GOWER gives an historical and philosophical selective overview of scientific method, from Galileo, Bacon and Newton, from the Bernoullis and Bayes, from 19th century methodologists, to Keynes and Ramsey, Reichenbach Popper and Carnap, with a concluding chapter on the present revival movement of experiment. Throughout, Gower stresses the role of ideas about experiment and about probability in scientific method.

HEIDELBERGER & STEINLE present new perspectives on experiment bringing philosophical, historical and disciplinary aspects together. Many historical case studies are given: from the first beginnings of experimentation in antiquity and from alchemy of the Middle-Ages to electrodynamics, energy-physics, spectroscopy and chemistry of the 19th century, and finally to psychology, physics and fluid dynamics of present-day science. In philosophical chapters, the concept of "experimental systems", the different roles of experiments, their changing significance and their empirical import are reflected on. There are also two chapters on the intricacies of replicating historical experiments.

[Written in 1995. Two important works have appeared subsequently: *The Mangle of Practice,* by Andrew Pickering, Chicago: University of Chicago Press, 1995 and *Image and Logic* by Peter Galison, Chicago: University of Chicago Press, 1997]

MICHAEL HEIDELBERGER

See also Measurement; Scientific Instruments; Scientific Revolution

F

Fact

Barnes, Barry, *Interest and the Growth of Knowledge*, London and Boston: Routledge, 1977

Bloor, David, *Knowledge and Social Imagery*, London and Boston: Routledge and Kegan Paul, 1976; 2nd edition, Chicago: University of Chicago Press, 1991

Collins, Harry M. and Trevor Pinch, *The Golem: What Everyone Should Know about Science*, Cambridge and New York: Cambridge University Press, 1993

Gibson, Roger F., *The Philosophy of W.V. Quine: An Expository Essay*, Tampa: University Presses of Florida, 1982

Goodman, Nelson, *Fact, Fiction and Forecast*, London: University of London, 1954; Cambridge, Massachusetts: Harvard University Press, 1955

Hanfling, Oswald (ed.), *Essential Readings in Logical Positivism*, Oxford: Blackwell, 1981

Hanson, Norwood R., *Patterns of Discovery: An Inquiry into the Conceptual Foundations of Science*, Cambridge: Cambridge University Press, 1958

Harré, Rom, *Great Scientific Experiments: Twenty Experiments that Changed Our View of the World*, Oxford: Phaidon Press, 1981

Kitcher, Philip, *The Advancement of Science: Science without Legend, Objectivity without Illusions*, New York: Oxford University Press, 1993

Kuhn, Thomas S., *The Structure of Scientific Revolutions*, Chicago: University of Chicago Press, 1962; revised edition, 1970

Latour, Bruno and Steve Woolgar, *Laboratory Life: The Social Construction of Scientific Facts*, Beverley Hills, California: Sage Publications, 1979; as *Laboratory Life: The Construction of Scientific Facts*, with a new postscript, Princeton, New Jersey: Princeton University Press, 1986

Laudan, Larry, *Science and Relativism: Some Key Controversies in the Philosophy of Science*, Chicago: University of Chicago Press, 1990

Longino, Helen E., *Science as Social Knowledge: Values and Objectivity in Scientific Inquiry*, Princeton, New Jersey: Princeton University Press, 1990

Quine, Willard van Orman, "Two Dogmas of Empiricism", *Philosophical Review*, 40 (1952): 20–43, reprinted in his *From a Logical Point of View: Nine Logico-philosophical Essays*, Cambridge, Massachusetts: Harvard University Press, 1953; revised edition, 1961

Shapin, Steven and Simon Schaffer, *Leviathan and the Air-Pump: Hobbes, Boyle, and the Experimental Life*, Princeton, New Jersey: Princeton University Press, 1985

The standard view of science is that it is based solely on value-free and theory-neutral facts. Scientists gather neutral empirical facts, either by observing the world directly or through instrumentation, and these facts then serve as the basis for the verification or falsification of scientific theories.

The standard view is most closely associated with the logical positivists, although they did not endorse a single, homogeneous view of science. HANFLING's anthology is a collection of writings from the logical positivists of the Vienna Circle, and the pieces by Carnap, Schlick, and Neurath illustrate the depth of disagreement on two issues – the nature of protocol statements (the neutral report of observed empirical facts), and the nature of verification (the relation between facts and theory). These essays reveal a sophistication not often attributed to the logical positivists, who recognized significant gaps between the empirical facts, the report of the facts, and the scientific theories that are supported by those facts.

The standard view of facts and their role in grounding scientific claims have been challenged on two fronts. First, it has been argued that scientific theories are underdetermined by the evidence (i.e., facts). QUINE brought attention to this argument, originally formulated by Pierre Duhem and frequently referred to as the Duhem-Quine thesis. It asserts that empirical facts are not enough to establish a single theory, as there are always alternative theories that are consistent with the facts. Thus, facts do not and cannot serve as the sole basis for accepting or rejecting scientific theories. This essay is notoriously difficult, but GIBSON provides a clear, concise, and carefully explained account of this and other major themes in Quine's philosophy.

Hanson and Goodman raise the second criticism, that of the theory-ladenness of observation. HANSON argues that what one observes is the result of one's background beliefs and the context of the observation. He asks rhetorically, "Would Sir Lawrence Bragg and an Eskimo baby see the same thing when looking at an X-ray tube?", and proceeds to argue that there are no neutral observations of facts. GOODMAN raises the same issue by examining the problem of induction, and by introducing the new riddle of induction. The point of Goodman's new riddle is that there is no neutral description of the facts. Two individuals can look at the same thing and yet describe it in two different ways. These different descriptions are not merely different ways of expressing the same phenomenon, because they have different intentional meanings. As a result, the descriptions support different predictions about future observations and thus different scientific theories.

KUHN is important for two reasons. First, he brought together the philosophical concerns about facts raised by Quine, Hanson, and Goodman, and the historical study of science, and introduced the concept of a paradigm to explain how psychological, sociological, economic, and historical factors shape how one observes the world and views the relationship between these "facts" and a theory. This aspect of his work led to charges of relativism, but he consistently and strongly denied such an interpretation of his position. Second, Kuhn's critique of the role of facts in science influenced others to pursue the social element in science. Prior to Kuhn, the examination of external influences on science was limited to cases in which science had gone wrong; it was believed that a sociological study could reveal nothing about good science because it is determined by the facts, while, in the case of "bad" science, it could uncover what pulled science away from the facts. However, Kuhn's historical study illustrated that facts are never theory-neutral and that, even if they were, they would not be robust enough to point to a single theory. This opened the door to the sociological study of all science, the good and the bad.

This was the impetus behind the strong programme, and the sociology of scientific knowledge (SSK). Both BARNES and BLOOR argue that all science is influenced by sociological factors, and, thus, sociology can investigate all scientific knowledge as social phenomena. The social dimension is essential for identifying facts and the links between facts and scientific theories.

In examining the SSK, it is important to recognize a crucial ambiguity in how the word "fact" is used. "Fact" can refer to the state-of-affairs in the world, or it can refer to the linguistic report of the state-of-affairs. If "fact" is used in the first sense, the social construction of scientific facts entails a radical relativism in which the world itself is a social construction, and thus scientific theories are also pure social constructions. If "fact" is used in the second sense, then the position is far less radical and asserts the existence of a world, a reality, independent of the social context. It claims that our descriptions (i.e. the "facts") and scientific theories are thus constrained by both the world and social factors.

LATOUR & WOOLGAR's book is the result of the two years spent by Latour in the laboratory at the Salk Institute in La Jolla, California, observing the scientists as an anthropologist would observe a tribe from another culture, and reveals the social and political process at work in the laboratory in creating scientific facts and grounding scientific claims. Latour & Woolgar argue that a statement made by an individual scientist becomes a fact as it becomes increasingly entrenched within the scientific community and the particularities of experimenter, laboratory, etc. are removed, and they appear to be endorsing the radical constructivist position.

SHAPIN & SCHAFFER, leading advocates of SSK, provide a careful examination of the role of experimental facts in 17th-century science. Their book centers on the controversy between Hobbes and Boyle regarding the significance of the air pump experiments. Using this case, the authors argue that the facts that resulted from the experiments are not the neutral recording of nature, but the result of the apparatus, the descriptions of the experiments that are disseminated, and the community that legitimated the results. The debate is thus presented as being between two competing views of science (i.e., Hobbes's deductivism and Boyle's experimentalism), with important implications for both science and the social order.

COLLINS & PINCH, also leading advocates of SSK, present a series of case studies in science. While the book is aimed at a general audience, it is based on careful scholarly studies by the authors and other sociologists and historians of science. Furthermore, the bibliographic references provide an excellent source for further study of the scientific cases and the SSK approach. The case studies aim to show that scientists "cannot settle their disagreements through better experimentation" because experiments do not provide theory-neutral facts. Facts are representations by scientists, and thus they rest in part on the scientists' credibility. Scientific facts are constructed when scientists reach an agreement.

In contrast, HARRÉ's case studies illustrate the role played by facts and experience in determining the acceptance of scientific theories. He divides the cases into those that illustrate facts deciding between rival hypotheses, facts providing inductive support for a law, and surprising facts leading to new scientific theories. Harré, like Collins & Pinch, addresses a general audience, but also gives excellent references for further scholarship.

Laudan, Kitcher, and Longino reject SSK, the social construction of scientific facts, and attempt to establish the objectivity of science. KITCHER refers to the standard view of facts and their role in grounding scientific theories as "Legend". He does not wish to re-establish Legend, but he believes that the theory-ladenness of facts and underdetermination of theory have been greatly exaggerated. He provides insightful critiques of Latour and Shapin & Schaffer, while recognizing that science is done by individuals within a social, historical, and economic context.

LAUDAN provides a critique of the constructivist view of scientific facts using a different approach, investigating the issues via a dialogue between a realist, a positivist, a pragmatist, and a relativist. There are few references or footnotes in the texts, as here the ideas take center stage.

An analysis that captures both the empirical and the social side of science is provided by LONGINO, which acknowledges both that there can be no neutral reports of empirical facts, and that the relation between facts and theories is dependent on the social context. The objectivity of science is preserved in Longino's contextual empiricism by the social context of science. Her analysis is especially insightful because it bridges philosophical, historical, sociological, and feminist approaches to science.

HENRY B. KREUZMAN

See also Measurement; Objectivity; Observation; Sociology of Science

Faraday, Michael 1791–1867

British chemist and physicist

Agassi, Joseph, *Faraday as a Natural Philosopher*, Chicago: University of Chicago Press, 1971

Bence Jones, Henry (ed.), *The Life and Letters of Faraday*, 2 vols, London: Green, 1870

Bowers, Brian and Lenore Symons, *Curiosity Perfectly Satisfyed: Faraday's Travels in Europe, 1813–1815*, London: Peregrinus/Science Museum, 1991

Bulletin for the History of Chemistry, no. 11 (1991)

Cantor, Geoffrey, *Michael Faraday: Sandemanian and Scientist: A Study of Science and Religion in the Nineteenth Century*, London: Macmillan, and New York: St Martin's Press, 1991

Cantor, Geoffrey, David Gooding and Frank A.J.L. James, *Faraday*, London: Macmillan, 1991; as *Michael Faraday*, Atlantic Highlands, New Jersey: Humanities Press, 1996

Faraday, Michael, *Experimental Researches in Electricity*, 3 vols, London: Quaritch, 1839–55

Faraday, Michael, *Experimental Researches in Chemistry and Physics*, London: Taylor and Francis, 1859

Gladstone, John Hall, *Michael Faraday*, London: Macmillan, and New York: Harper, 1872

Gooding, David, "Final Steps to the Field Theory: Faraday's Study of Magnetic Phenomena, 1845–1850", *Historical Studies in the Physical Sciences*, 11 (1981): 231–75

Gooding, David, *Experiment and the Making of Meaning: Human Agency in Scientific Observation and Experiment*, Dordrecht and Boston: Kluwer, 1990

Gooding, David and Frank A.J.L. James (eds), *Faraday Rediscovered: Essays on the Life and Work of Michael Faraday, 1791–1867*, London: Macmillan, and New York: Stockton Press, 1985

Hadfield, Sir Robert A., *Faraday and His Metallurgical Researches, with Special Reference to Their Bearing on the Development of Alloy Steels*, London: Chapman and Hall, 1931; Cleveland, Ohio: Penton, 1932

James, Frank A.J.L. (ed.), *The Correspondence of Michael Faraday*, 3 vols, London: Institution of Electrical Engineers, 1991–96

Jeffreys, Alan E., *Michael Faraday: A List of His Lectures and Published Writings*, London: Chapman and Hall, 1960

Kahlbaum, Georg W.A. and Francis V. Darbishire (eds), *The Letters of Faraday and Schoenbein, 1836–1862*, London: Williams and Norgate, 1899

Martin, Thomas (ed.), *Faraday's Diary*, 7 vols and index, London: Bell, 1932–36

Physis, 29 (1992): 121–225

Riley, James Frederic, *The Hammer and the Anvil: A Background to Michael Faraday*, Clapham, Yorkshire: Dalesman, 1954

Thompson, Silvanus P., *Michael Faraday: His Life and Work*, London: Cassell, and New York: Macmillan, 1898

Tweney, Ryan D. and David Gooding (eds), *Michael Faraday's "Chemical Notes, Hints, Suggestions and Objects of Pursuit" of 1822*, London: Peregrinus/Science Museum, 1991

Tyndall, John, "On Faraday as a Discoverer", *Proceedings of the Royal Institution*, 5 (1868): 199–272; as *Faraday as a Discoverer*, 5th edition, London: Longman, 1894

Williams, L. Pearce, *Michael Faraday: A Biography*, London: Chapman and Hall, and New York: Basic Books, 1965

Williams, L. Pearce, Rosemary FitzGerald and Oliver Stallybrass (eds), *The Selected Correspondence of Michael Faraday*, 2 vols, Cambridge: Cambridge University Press, 1971

From the time of his death in 1867, Michael Faraday has been the subject of almost continuous study, and today there is a veritable "industry" devoted to Faraday studies, from a wide range of disciplinary perspectives. In the 20th century most work on Faraday can be divided into that which analyses his life and work, and that which publishes his manuscripts.

This distinction does not, however, hold for most 19th-century studies of Faraday, which, in the convention of Victorian life and letters, published much manuscript material within their narratives. Some of this material is still useful today; for instance, what remains of Faraday's letters to his wife, Sarah, and his autobiographical jottings, can only be found in the biographies written by Tyndall, Bence Jones, Gladstone and Thompson. The first three knew Faraday personally in the latter part of his life, and all four were given access to his papers by the family, although the Faraday's relations clearly exercised careful control over his papers and guided what was written about him. Some of the alterations between the first and second editions of Bence Jones were made at the insistence of the family.

Faraday's widow, and later a niece and nephew, distributed some of his papers to other family members, and gave what they viewed as his scientific papers to appropriate institutions. The Royal Institution thus received his laboratory notebook (published in Martin), the Royal Society his diploma book, Trinity House his correspondence with them (now in the Guildhall Library, London), Trinity College, Cambridge, his letters from William Whewell, and the University of Basle his letters from Christian Friedrich Schoenbein (published in KAHLBAUM & DARBISHIRE). Finally, in 1915, a large collection of letters and other papers was deposited in the Institution of Electrical Engineers. Since then, comparatively little has come from the family, despite the current generation's eagerness to locate what still clearly existed in the late 1890s, when Thompson had access to it. The dispersal of the Faraday archive, and presumed loss of some of it, has meant that a comprehensive, properly contextual biography has yet to be written. Even so, there has been ample material available to enable many biographies to be written and specialist studies undertaken.

Faraday's 19th-century biographers had different aims from their 20th-century counterparts. TYNDALL, Faraday's successor at the Royal Institution, was the first; his book originated in two lectures delivered at the Royal Institution, and portrayed Faraday as a romantic philosopher and one of the great experimentalists. BENCE JONES, Secretary of the Royal Institution, 1860–73, and Faraday's physician, is the longest biography, and portrays Faraday's work as being driven by his genius. GLADSTONE, who held Faraday's Fullerian Professorship of Chemistry, 1874–77, was a deeply religious man; his is not so much a conventional biography as a portrait of Faraday, concentrating to a large extent on his character and Sandemanian religious beliefs. THOMPSON, an electrical engineer working at the end of the 19th century, was in a position to appreciate, as his predecessors had not, the long-term importance of Faraday's work on electromagnetism, particularly his enunciation of field theory. Tyndall, Gladstone and Thompson all share the tendency to concentrate on those areas in Faraday's life and science with which they were themselves connected. Thus Tyndall emphasised Faraday's work on diamagnetism rather than his electrical work in the 1830s (indeed Tyndall is notably weak on Faraday's early life), whereas Thompson did the reverse. It is worth noting that all these books went into two or more editions, thus indicating the existence of a large readership with a strong interest in Faraday.

While these books acknowledged that Faraday carried out applied scientific work, especially for the state and its agencies, they failed to emphasise its importance. Such work was crucial both to his career, by the contribution it made to his research, and to an understanding of how the role of scientific advice in society changed during the 19th century. The image that thus came across from these early studies was that of a lone man of science, working with only one assistant in his basement laboratory. Furthermore, because of the importance of Faraday's work, there was, until recently, a tendency to study Faraday in isolation from the various social contexts in which he operated, thus helping to sustain the early image of the lone genius.

This image was also reinforced by the fact that, until the very end of the 19th century, the only easily available texts were his research papers, virtually all of which he collected together in four volumes published between 1839 and 1859, in FARADAY (1839–55) and FARADAY (1859). The image persisted into the 20th century, and was given fresh impetus in 1931, when the centenary of Faraday's discovery of electromagnetic induction was celebrated. This event produced a whole clutch of hagiographical texts, most of which are derivative of the 19th-century biographies, and none of which is cited above. However, the celebrations also produced two texts of lasting worth. MARTIN published the whole of Faraday's laboratory notebook, which is an invaluable resource for Faraday scholars. Though this seven-volume work gave support to the prevailing image of Faraday, a partial corrective was supplied by the other useful text produced at this time – HADFIELD, which drew attention in a sustained way, for the first time, to the importance of Faraday's applied scientific work. This book, however, did not substantially affect Faraday's image of being primarily, if not solely, a researcher.

It was JEFFREYS's listing of the lectures delivered by Faraday that first showed just how wide a range of interests Faraday had beyond scientific research. Nevertheless, historians did not immediately take up the implied challenge of studying Faraday's interests as a whole. WILLIAMS's long biography sought to show that Faraday was heavily influenced by German metaphysics, and by a force atom theory of matter propounded by the 18th century Jesuit natural philosopher Roger Joseph Boscovich. Furthermore, Williams argued that Faraday had secretly held these views from a very early point in his career, and that they guided the entire course of his experimentation

and theorising. This idealist thesis was widely criticised, for example by AGASSI, and others such as Thomas Kuhn, who commented that if Boscovichian atoms were as important to Faraday as Williams made out, then there ought to be more literary evidence.

It was not until the realisation, in the 1970s and 1980s, of the intrinsic importance of experimentation to the construction of scientific knowledge that historians were able to come to grips with Faraday's experiments on their own terms. Thus GOODING (1981 and 1990), some of the essays in GOODING & JAMES, as well as many other papers by Gooding, emphasise the centrality of experiment, rather than presumed theory, in Faraday's research. Indeed, Gooding's work, particularly on Faraday's discovery of electromagnetic rotations in 1821, helped pioneer the way for the study of how experimental investigation is conducted, and how it relates to other aspects of science and society.

In the same period, other features of Faraday's life started receiving proper attention. Although it was known that Faraday's religion was important to him personally, apart from Gladstone and also RILEY (which provided much useful background on Sandemanianism in north west England), little attention had been paid to it. There was a tendency to assume that Faraday separated his science from his religious belief. CANTOR shows that this was far from the case, and that in studying the natural world in his laboratory, Faraday was studying the world that he knew that God had created.

The great interest shown in Faraday during the last 20 years, both in his own right and as a source of information on how science actually works, means that the problems caused by the dispersal of his archive need to be addressed before a fully rounded image of him can emerge. The publication of much of Faraday's manuscripts is well advanced. TWENEY & GOODING published Faraday's notebook of 1822, which was in fact kept during the mid-1820s, when Faraday was looking for the problems that he would spend much of the 1830s solving. An invaluable feature of this book is that the editors include a glossary of scientific words, defined in contemporary 1820s terms. BOWERS & SYMONS feature what has survived of the diary Faraday kept on his tour of the Continent with Humphry Davy between 1813 and 1815.

JAMES aims to publish every extant letter to and from Faraday. (WILLIAMS, FITZGERALD & STALLYBRASS selectively published around a sixth of Faraday's letters, with at least 20 of the letters misdated by anything up to 10 years.) These volumes not only deal with Faraday's research work, but demonstrate, in a way other sources do not, the importance of Faraday's work in applied science, and his place in 19th-century society. Whether one is considering his chemical analytical work for the Admiralty, or his improvement of optical glass for the Royal Society and Board of Longitude, or his enquiry for the Home Office into the Haswell Colliery explosion in 1844, or his teaching of chemistry to cadets at the Royal Military Academy, or his work on the ventilation and lighting of lighthouses for Trinity House (with which more than 10% of the letters are concerned), much new light has been cast by Faraday's correspondence on what used to be little known aspects of his career. By the time of the completion of the correspondence, and the publication of other of his manuscripts, Faraday will, with the obvious exception of

Charles Darwin, be one of the most completely documented men of science in the 19th century.

The process of assimilating all the new evidence that has become available to produce a fuller, more contextualised, understanding of Faraday's life and his place in 19th-century science and society has run in tandem with the publication of his manuscripts. The new wave of Faraday studies received its initial impetus from the essays published in Gooding & James. Besides the studies of Faraday's experimental work mentioned above, this volume contained, among others, essays by Sophie Forgan on Faraday's role in the Royal Institution, by Gertrude Prescott on Faraday's connection with the art world, and by Ryan Tweney on Faraday's work from the perspective of cognitive psychology. Since then, many papers on various aspects of Faraday's life and work have been published in a variety of journals. Special mention should be made of BULLETIN FOR THE HISTORY OF CHEMISTRY and PHYSIS, both of which devoted issues to new studies of Faraday. In the former, for example, June Fullmer and Mel Usselman deal with Faraday's election to the Royal Society, Cantor discusses Faraday's lecturing style, Harold Goldwhite examines his work on fluorine, while James looks at Faraday's connections with the Admiralty and the army. In the special issue of Physis, Howard Fisher discusses Faraday's rhetorical style, while Gooding looks at the role of mathematics in his science, and Tweney analyses Faraday's acoustical work.

Though CANTOR, GOODING & JAMES's book, which provides a short biography of Faraday, was aimed at a lay audience, it does gather together most of the strands of Faraday scholarship from the past 20 years or so. Because the book relies on recent research, it presents a rather different vision of Faraday from that of the 19th-century; Faraday is now firmly located within his scientific and social contexts, and he is seen to be an active member of society, spending only some (and not a very high proportion at that) of his time in the laboratory. With the continuing publication of still more material, together with the new, detailed studies of various aspects of his life and work appearing every year, it seems unlikely that this will be the definitive word on the life and work of Faraday.

FRANK A.J.L. JAMES

Fermat, Pierre 1601–1665

French mathematician

Andersen, Kirsti, "The Mathematical Technique in Fermat's Deduction of the Law of Refraction", *Historia Mathematica*, 10 (1983): 48–62

Breger, Herbert, "The Mysteries of Adaequare: A Vindication of Fermat", *Archive for History of Exact Sciences*, 46 (1994): 193–219

Cifoletti, Giovanna Cleonice, *La Méthode de Fermat: Son statut et sa diffusion: algèbre et comparaison de figures dans l'histoire de la méthode de Fermat*, Paris: Société française d'histoire des Sciences et des Techniques, 1990

Goldstein, Catherine, "Le Métier des nombres aux 17e et 19e siècles", in *Eléments d'Histoire des Sciences*, edited by Michel Serres, Paris: Bordas, 1989; as *A History of Scientific Thought: Elements of a History of Science*, edited by Michel Serres, translated from the French, Oxford: Blackwell, 1995

Goldstein, Catherine, *Un Théorème de Fermat et ses lecteurs*, Paris: Presses Universitaires de Vincennes, 1995

Hofmann, Joseph E., "Über zahlentheoretische Methoden Fermats und Eulers, ihre Zusammenhänge und ihre Bedeutung", *Archive for History of Exact Sciences*, 1 (1961): 122–59

Hofmann, Joseph E., "Pierre Fermat: Ein Pionier der neuen Mathematik", *Praxis der Mathematik*, 7 (1965): 1–23; reprinted in his *Ausgewählte Schriften*, Hildesheim: Olms, 1990, 402–24

Itard, Jean, *Essais d'histoire des mathématiques*, edited by Roshdi Rashed, Paris: Blanchard, 1984

Machabey, Armand, *La Philosophie de Pierre de Fermat: mathématicien, humaniste et conseiller au Parlement de Toulouse*, Liège: Dynamo-P. Aelberts, 1949

Mahoney, Michael S., *The Mathematical Career of Pierre de Fermat, 1601–1665*, Princeton, New Jersey: Princeton University Press, 1973; revised edition, 1994

Sabra, A.I., *Theories of Light: From Descartes to Newton*, London: Oldbourne, 1967; Cambridge and New York: Cambridge University Press, 1981

Strømholm, Per, "Fermat's Method of Maxima and Minima and of Tangents. A Reconstruction", *Archive for History of Exact Sciences*, 5 (1968): 47–69

Weil, André, *Number Theory: An Approach Through History from Hammurapi to Legendre*, Basel: Birkhäuser, 1984

Pierre Fermat occupies a somewhat paradoxical place in the history of mathematics. He is considered to be one of the 17th-century founders of modern mathematics, launching, for example, analytic geometry (at the same time as Descartes), probability theory (with Pascal), and above all modern number theory. But he left only rare, sketchy, often undated documents, which raise delicate questions of interpretation, and he produced no philosophical work as such, or even commentaries on his mathematical conceptions. For all these reasons, the range of historiographical attention lavished on him is much narrower than that on, say, Descartes or Galileo.

There are two classical, well-balanced surveys of Fermat's life and works; one in French, which is to be found in the collection of essays by ITARD, and one in German by HOFMANN (1965). In both cases, Fermat's results and methods are presented in modernized settings and notation, from a retrospective point of view (corresponding roughly to the level of undergraduate mathematics of the authors' times). Itard organizes his material thematically, and stresses areas in which Fermat's achievements were of lasting importance (e.g. number theory, and the calculus of variations stemming from his optical investigations). Hofmann adopts a more strictly chronological order, intercalating personal data with hints on Fermat's mathematical evolution and results, with precise references and quotations from the sources.

The little known MACHABEY attempts to characterize Fermat's mathematical practice. He suggests that Fermat derived his general theories from careful analyses of specific examples, and then sought analogies to extend his methods and proof schemes to other applications. Machabey relates this approach to Fermat's reading of Francis Bacon.

MAHONEY (a shorter version appears as the article on Fermat in the *Dictionary of Scientific Biography*) is the only book-length scientific biography of Fermat. Mahoney's aim is to provide a contextual approach to Fermat, by anchoring his work in the sequel to Vieta's programme. He argues that Fermat inherited from Vieta both an algebra (including a symbolic theory of equations) and an analytical research programme that could be applied to a wide range of problems taken from various Greek texts (Appollonius, Pappus, Archimedes, and Diophantus). After a biographical chapter, Mahoney proceeds, through a close reading of a selection of texts, to show how this specific analytical approach shaped an important part of Fermat's achievements: his analytic geometry, extrema and tangents, quadrature methods, and a part of his number theory (while his optical and combinatorial studies are relegated to an appendix). Emphasis throughout is placed on a comparison with Descartes's approach.

Besides these general presentations, historiographical works have focused on specific subfields. Some of these are discussed below, and further references can be found in the general presentations mentioned above.

The determination of the related problems of extrema and tangents is described by Fermat in various short (often undated) writings, and has raised several traditional groups of questions, concerning: whether there are one or several methods; the relationships between the various versions given by Fermat; how the chronological evolution of his thought on these themes should be reconstructed; how this work relates precisely to other achievements (centers of gravity, quadratures, etc.); and whether these results allow Fermat to be considered a precursor of differential calculus.

The classical paper on these questions is STRØMHOLM, who distinguishes two main "methods" (for Strømholm, justification of the proposed algorithms), details their chronology, and describes the polemic with Descartes concerning tangents. He concludes that Fermat failed to prove rigorously the general validity of his techniques, but succeeded in creating a powerful tool for the calculus.

CIFOLETTI re-examines these questions from a new perspective, and shows that the notion of method itself implicit in Fermat (passed on from Ramist circles to Vieta's heirs) makes it possible to make global sense of his various presentations. An important feature of the method is the finite incrementation of the variable in an equation, associated with the specific problem under study, and the use of comparison by a kind of equality (*adæquatio*), inspired by a Diophantine tradition. The transformation of the procedure to an infinitesimal one (and the consequent construction of Fermat as a precursor of calculus) is followed through the works of Fermat's diffusers and successors: Pierre Herigone, Frans van Schooten, Christiaan Huygens, and Joseph Louis Lagrange. The book also contains a critical overview of the literature on these issues. Some new philological details are given in BREGER, although he does not take Cifoletti's arguments into account.

The essential point of departure for Fermat's work in number theory is the second chapter of WEIL. Weil uses Fermat's writings (in particular the summing up of his results given in a letter of 1659 to Carcavi), to introduce theoretical concepts, methods, and ideas still important in number theory. Through accurate, often modernized, mathematical analysis, he indicates the relationships between various aspects of Fermat's work, and stresses their meaning for future developments in the field. (Appendices also transplant Fermat's results to the frameworks of modern algebraic number theory and algebraic geometry.) See also Itard and HOFMANN (1961) for interesting complements.

GOLDSTEIN (1989) explores social aspects of Fermat's number theory, in particular how the specificity of 17th-century work on numbers, and the rules of the network within which Fermat operated, concurred to hamper detailed publication and development of proofs. GOLDSTEIN (1995) focuses on the single number theoretical proof left by Fermat, and analyzes its various descriptions and commentaries, both by historians of mathematics of the 19th and 20th centuries, and by mathematicians of Fermat's time (in particular Frenicle de Bessy). The aim of the book is to understand how the various historical and cultural contexts of these descriptions have led to the highlighting and/or rewriting of certain aspects of the text. The book includes complete references to works on Fermat's number theory, and a critical introduction to the available biographical documents and narratives.

The optical results of Fermat are described in SABRA. The work begins with the controversy between Descartes (and later his followers) and Fermat on the refraction law. Fermat criticized Descartes's justification (thereby throwing the result itself into doubt), and proceeded to apply his method of extrema and the principle that nature takes the shortest path to discover the true law of refraction; because his result coincided with Descartes's, he then reinterpreted his approach as a correct *demonstration* of the sine law. Sabra also discusses the variants of the economy principle used by Fermat. A detailed mathematical reconstruction of Fermat's texts and arguments on this topic is offered in ANDERSEN.

Fermat's results concerning analytic geometry or theory of probability have been mainly studied in connection with Descartes and Pascal respectively – see the notices on these authors as well as the general references given above.

Catherine Goldstein

Fermi, Enrico 1901–1954

Italian-born American physicist

Amaldi, Edoardo, "Neutron Work in Rome in 1934–1936 and the Discovery of Uranium Fission", *Rivista di Storia della Scienza*, 1 (1984): 1–24

Belloni, Lanfranco, *Da Fermi a Rubbia: Storia e politica di un successo mondiale della scienza italiana*, Milan: Rizzoli, 1988

Fermi, Enrico, *Collected Papers*, 2 vols, Chicago: University of Chicago Press, 1962–65

Fermi, Laura, *Atoms in the Family: My Life with Enrico Fermi*, Chicago: University of Chicago Press, 1954

Holton, Gerald, "Fermi's Group and the Recapture of Italy's Place in Physics", in his *The Scientific Imagination: Case Studies*, Cambridge and New York: Cambridge University Press, 1978

Maiocchi, Roberto, *Non solo Fermi: I fondamenti della meccanica quantistica nella cultura italiana tra le due guerre*, Florence: Le Lettere, 1991

Pontecorvo, Bruno, *Enrico Fermi: Ricordi di allievi ed amici*, translated from the Russian, Pordenone: Edizioni Studio Tesi, 1993 (original edition, 1972)

Segré, Emilio, *Enrico Fermi: Physicist*, Chicago: University of Chicago Press, 1970

Enrico Fermi, who won the Nobel prize for physics in 1938, has played a particularly important role in the history of physics, both in Italy and in the United States, where he emigrated in 1938 in order to escape the racial laws that threatened his family. His life and work have been celebrated by physicists in both countries. In Italy he is remembered as the founder of the 20th-century Italian school of physics, and in America as one of the fathers of the atomic bomb.

His scientific papers and review articles have been brought together in FERMI (1962–65), a work divided into two volumes, the first covering the Italian period, 1921–38, and the second the American period, 1939–54. The work opens with a biographical introduction written by Emilio Segré, another Nobel prizewinner, and follows with Fermi's contributions to science, complete with copious introductory notes written by some of his closest colleagues and collaborators: Edoardo Amaldi, Enrico Persico, Franco Rasetti, and Segré in the first volume and H.L. Anderson, Albert Wattenberg, Alvin M. Weinberg, and Segré in the second.

Other essays by contemporary physicists (including S.K. Allison, H.A. Bethe, and Eugene Wigner), together with the most interesting of the introductory notes from the *Collected Papers* are published in a volume edited in Moscow in 1972 by PONTECORVO, another important scientist who trained in the Fermi school. An Italian translation of this work was published in 1993.

An account of the research carried out in Rome between 1934 and 1936 by Fermi and his group is given in AMALDI, which follows a traditional historiographical approach. Amaldi, one of the key figures alongside Fermi in this extraordinary period of Italian physics, relates, with the careful attention that distinguishes his historical articles, both the discovery of artificial radioactivity induced by neutrons, and the discovery of so-called "slow neutrons" that were to play such an important part in the realisation of the first controlled chain reaction. The extensive bibliography that follows this article gives a complete picture of the scientific activity of the group in Rome during those years. Other articles by Amaldi published elsewhere do not add substantially to the information supplied in this article.

In addition to the accounts and historical reconstructions provided by his closest collaborators, Fermi has also been studied by a number of historians. HOLTON, in his collection of "case studies" published in 1978, analyses Fermi as a "phenomenon", a precocious genius and autodidact who quickly raised the profile of Italian physics, rescuing it from its institutional weaknesses and gaining for it full international recognition. Holton's thematic analysis examines Fermi's scientific style and methods of research, and especially the structure and organisation of the Roman group. This group was set up by Fermi in the Institute of Physics at the University of Rome, and became of crucial importance to the subsequent development of physics in Italy.

BELLONI also pays particular attention to the Fermi group and its legacy in the first chapters of a book that recounts, in a lively style, the success story of Italian physics from the 1930s to the 1980s. (The Nobel prize for physics was awarded to Fermi in 1938 and to Carlo Rubbia in 1984.)

MAIOCCHI provides a different point of view. While acknowledging the central role played by the Roman group in raising the level of research in Italian physics to international standards, he argues that Fermi's school represented only one of the components of the Italian scientific environment – possibly the most important from a scientific point of view, but not the most important from a philosophical one. He provides an unusual picture of Italian intellectual life under fascism, with much discussion of the great methodological and philosophical problems raised by quantum mechanics, and underlines the implementation of, and the pragmatic approach to, the new theories that characterised the scientific practice of Fermi's school.

The life of Enrico Fermi has been related in two lengthy biographies and another more concise biography to be published shortly. The biography written by his wife, Laura FERMI (1954), traces the personal life of the physicist from infancy to the years spent in the laboratory of Los Alamos during World War II, from the research in Rome to his work in Chicago in the last months before his premature death.

SEGRÉ, on the other hand, has written a scientific biography without over-indulging in technical details. His concern is to convey a sense of Fermi's personality and of his legacy to contemporary physics. The role played by social, cultural, or philosophical factors in directing Fermi's research activity is not given particular attention, yet the text remains fundamental in providing a picture of one of the protagonists in the history of 20th-century physics.

IVANA GAMBARO

translated by Sarah Morgan

See also Nuclear Physics; Quantum Mechanics

Fevers

Ackerknecht, Erwin H., *Medicine at the Paris Hospital, 1794–1848*, Baltimore: Johns Hopkins Press, 1967

Bulloch, William, *The History of Bacteriology*, London and New York: Oxford University Press, 1938

Bynum, W.F. and V. Nutton (eds), *Theories of Fever from Antiquity to the Enlightenment*, London: Wellcome Institute, 1981

Estes, J. Worth, "Quantitative Observations of Fever and Its Treatment before the Advent of Short Clinical Thermometers", *Medical History*, 35 (1991): 189–216

King, Lester S., *The Medical World of the Eighteenth Century*, Chicago: University of Chicago Press, 1958

Kiple, Kenneth F. (ed.), *The Cambridge World History of Human Disease*, Cambridge and New York: Cambridge University Press, 1993

Kluger, Matthew J., *Fever: Its Biology, Evolution and Function*, Princeton, New Jersey: Princeton University Press, 1979

Nesse, Randolph M. and George C. Williams, *Evolution and Healing: The New Science of Darwinian Medicine*, London: Weidenfeld and Nicolson, 1995

Neuburger, Max, *The Healing Power of Nature*, translated from the German by L.J. Boyd, New York, 1932

Nicolson, Malcolm, "The Art of Diagnosis: Medicine and the Five Senses", in *Companion Encyclopedia of the History of Medicine*, edited by W.F. Bynum and Roy Porter, 2 vols, London and New York: Routledge, 1993

Reiser, Stanley Joel, *Medicine and the Reign of Technology*, Cambridge and New York: Cambridge University Press, 1978

Smith, Dale C. (ed.), *On the Causes of Fever (1839)* by William Budd, Baltimore: Johns Hopkins University Press, 1984

Spink, Wesley W., *Infectious Diseases: Prevention and Treatment in the Nineteenth and Twentieth Centuries*, Folkestone: Dawson, and Minneapolis: University of Minnesota Press, 1978

Winslow, Charles-Edward Amory, *The Conquest of Epidemic Diseases: A Chapter in the History of Ideas*, Princeton, New Jersey: Princeton University Press, 1943; reprinted; Madison: University of Wisconsin Press, 1980

In modern medicine, fever is a clinical sign, defined as body temperature elevated above the normal (98.6°F, 37°C). A fever can be caused by a variety of factors, the most common being infection. The biological significance of this body response to infection is complicated, as it may be adaptive rather than pathological. KLUGER has examined the biology of fever in the animal kingdom more generally, and has provided evidence that the modern practice of reducing fever with aspirin or other drugs may actually prolong the period of illness. NESSE & WILLIAMS have looked at fever within the context of what they call "Darwinian medicine", and have concluded that while fever may produce uncomfortable symptoms, it almost certainly does have a protective value. Although argued from a different historical context, fever as part of the body's response to illness falls within the Hippocratic notion of the "healing power of nature", which NEUBURGER analysed in the early 1930s. A new monograph on the topic is a desideratum.

Traditionally, fever has been considered as a disease *per se*, further described according to various clinical features; thus, a fever might be described as intermittent, ephemeral, continuous, or hectic. The collection of essays edited by BYNUM & NUTTON considers many theoretical debates on the nature of fever, from antiquity to the work of William Cullen (1710–90). The paper by Lonie on the fever tradition in 16th-century medical writings is especially suggestive. Several of the authors remark that excess heat was conceived as only part of the earlier definitions of fever: a rapid pulse, shivering and sweating were also part of the disease. As KING has shown, fever as a disease in itself was of great interest to 18th-century nosologists, or disease classifiers. As the most common human affliction, fevers generated a large literature, which extended not only to descriptions of how best to differentiate fevers clinically, but also to their presumed causes, and to their transmission – either from person to person (contagious), or via the medium of the atmosphere (miasmatic).

NICOLSON has shown that, within traditional medical thinking, "fever" was diagnosed at the bedside, on the basis of the patient's history and what the doctor could discover by his ordinary senses. ACKERKNECHT's account of the rise of the "Paris school" of the early 19th century argues that a greater emphasis was placed on the pathological signs of disease. Increasingly, doctors looked for the lesions of disease as the basis of the newer nosology. SMITH has shown that although leaders of the Paris school, such as Xavier Bichat (1771–1802), continued to keep a diagnostic category called "essential fevers" (those with no definable pathological lesions), many of the fevers began to be distinguished on pathological grounds. Thus, "hectic" fever was seen as a clinical manifestation of "phthisis" or consumption (roughly equivalent to modern tuberculosis), and typhus and typhoid fevers began to be separated on the basis of lesions discovered at post-mortem.

ESTES has examined attempts made by doctors during the 18th and early 19th centuries to study quantitative aspects of fever, including changes in heart-rate, respiration and blood-flow. This pathophysiological approach was facilitated by the introduction of short, easy-to-use clinical thermometers in the mid-19th century. Carl Wunderlich (1815–77) in Germany made thermometry central to his physiological conception of disease, and, by taking the patient's temperature at regular intervals, was able to distinguish various kinds of fever by the pattern of fluctuation over time. As REISER has shown, the fever chart became a familiar part of a patient's hospital record from this period, and fever became defined simply as an elevated body temperature rather than a disease in itself.

The work of Pasteur, Koch and others on the germ theory of disease offered a new paradigm for understanding fevers in terms of their causative agents, as analysed by BULLOCH. More than any other discipline, microbiology brought the laboratory closer to the bedside, and led to the optimism of the first half of the 20th century, which held that the infectious diseases could be controlled, if not completely eradicated. WINSLOW's work is a good example of the historical literature produced in that age of optimism. SPINK also provides accounts of the most important infectious diseases, and offers a useful, if predictable, summary of the interpretation of fever from antiquity to the 20th century. Modern short summaries of the history and geography of the major infectious fevers can be found in the massive volume edited by KIPLE, many of which were defined fairly precisely on clinical or pathological grounds before the etiological agent was discovered. In the case of some diseases – such as yellow fever, or typhoid fever – the modern name still bears the trace of the older formulation, when the fever was the disease, with an appropriate descriptive modifier placed in front.

W.F. BYNUM

See also Bacteriology; Epidemics; Medical Instruments

Feynman, Richard 1918–1988

American theoretical physicist

Feynman, Richard P., *Surely You're Joking, Mr. Feynman!
Adventures of a Curious Character*, as told to Ralph
Leighton, edited by Edward Hutchings, New York:
Norton, 1985

Feynman, Richard P., *What do You Care What Other People
Think? Further Adventures of a Curious Character*, as told
to Ralph Leighton, New York: Norton, 1988

Gleick, James, *Genius: The Life and Science of Richard
Feynman*, New York: Pantheon, 1992

Gribbin, John and Mary Gribbin, *Richard Feynman: A Life
in Science*, New York: Dutton, 1997

Mehra, Jagdish, *The Beat of a Different Drum: The Life and
Science of Richard Feynman*, Oxford: Clarendon Press,
and New York: Oxford University Press, 1994

Schweber, S.S., *QED and the Men Who Made It: Dyson,
Feynman, Schwinger, and Tomonaga*, Princeton: Princeton
University Press, 1994

Surpassed in his field only by Albert Einstein, the American theoretical physicist Richard Feynman remains a cultural icon, a symbol of the quintessential "curious character" and "eccentric genius". Feynman was the consummate calculator, who delighted in "getting the numbers out" of abstruse-looking mathematics. His famous approach to quantum electrodynamics (QED), built in the late 1940s around the so-called Feynman diagrams, immediately became a calculational necessity, eclipsing rival approaches that offered dizzying series of integrals instead of intuitive pictures. This work, completed before Feynman had turned 30 years old, earned him a Nobel prize, awarded in 1965. Feynman's name appears throughout many other branches of physics as well: he co-authored an important version of the weak-interaction theory in 1957, developed a theory of superfluidity in the same years, helped to reintroduce the study of gravitation in the early 1960s, and created the "parton" model in the late 1960s as an intuitive approach to the high-energy scattering of strongly-interacting particles. The work for his dissertation, on the path-integral approach to non-relativistic quantum mechanics, together with his Feynman diagrams, have come to redefine the very language with which theoretical physicists pose questions and seek solutions for describing the physical world.

Late in his life, while battling cancer, Feynman published two collections of anecdotes about his life. Based on tape-recorded interviews with his friend Ralph Leighton, the stories in Feynman's own two books have become legendary. In FEYNMAN (1985) we learn of his early fascination for tinkering with radios, and of his father's insistence that authority for its own sake deserved little respect. Once at college, the young Feynman learned to trade his skills in mathematics and physics for socializing tips from his upper-classman fraternity brothers. While on sabbatical years later in Brazil, Feynman nurtured his famous enchantment with bongo drumming. Always an inveterate code-cracker, Feynman tells of his safe-cracking antics in wartime Los Alamos, of his attempts to decipher the Dresden codex, and of his short career as an amateur biologist. FEYNMAN (1988) covers his participation

in the investigation of the 1986 *Challenger* space shuttle disaster. Ever the showman, he famously solved the puzzle behind this tragedy by dipping a small piece of rubber from the shuttle O-ring into a cup of ice water, to demonstrate before a press conference that the rubber lost elasticity at cold temperatures. These two collections contain virtually no discussion or description of Feynman's physics, and focus instead on his own self-fashioning as a quirky genius.

GLEICK's biography offers the best survey of Feynman's life and work. Written with a novelist's flair, it follows Feynman from his childhood in Far Rockaway, New York, to his undergraduate and graduate studies at MIT and Princeton. Later chapters tell dramatically of his wartime work at Los Alamos, his short stint at Cornell after the war, and his emergence at Caltech as the center of a cult of personality. Gleick has drawn on unpublished sources and a large number of interviews with Feynman's family and colleagues to paint this portrait, and provides readable, non-technical explanations of Feynman's most important scientific work. Though the biography carries the title "Genius," Gleick remains critical when treating Feynman's own carefully crafted self-image, and draws only in limited ways on his 1985 and 1988 books.

SCHWEBER offers the only truly historical account of Feynman's early work. Utilizing unpublished notebooks, correspondence, and diaries, in addition to a wealth of published sources, this rather technical account places Feynman's approach to quantum electrodynamics in a particular historical and intellectual context. The roots of Feynman's work from the late 1940s become clear by examining his graduate studies at Princeton under John Wheeler on advanced and retarded potentials in electrodynamics, on positrons as electrons moving backwards in time, and on a unique approach to quantum mechanics, based on summing up all the possible paths a quantum system could follow. Schweber contrasts this detailed study of Feynman's early work with similar studies of Julian Schwinger, Freeman Dyson, and Sin-itiro Tomonaga, and places this work in the broader context of American theoretical physics immediately after World War II. Though his treatment of Feynman's early work is largely biographical, it covers only the period to the late 1940s, and does not include work from later in Feynman's career.

At first, MEHRA's biography looks like a mixture of both Schweber's and Gleick's approaches: it combines technical discussion of Feynman's physics with biographical details of his upbringing and life outside, as well as inside, science. Unfortunately, this surface appearance proves thin upon reading. Mehra, trained as a physicist and not as a historian, bases his book almost entirely on a series of interviews conducted with Feynman a few weeks before Feynman's death. Details not taken from these interviews are simply lifted, uncritically, from Feynman's two books. The descriptions of Feynman's physics, moreover, though full of technical detail, are far less clear than the technical treatment in Schweber or the more narrative discussions in Gleick.

Finally, the biography by the science writers GRIBBIN & GRIBBIN is nothing short of hagiography. There are no equations in this book, and many of the descriptions of Feynman's physics are well done. However, no new research seems to have been conducted in order to write this study: practically all of the passages not attributed directly to Feynman's two books come from the interviews between Mehra and Feynman. The single benefit of this book is its brevity. Gleick's book, however, remains by far the most worthwhile study for the reader interested in a balanced, non-technical introduction to Feynman's life and work.

DAVID KAISER

Fischer, Emil 1852–1919

German chemist

Bergmann, Max (ed.), *Untersuchungen aus verschiedenen Gebieten/Vorträge und Abhandlungen allgemeinen Inhalts von Emil Fischer*, edited by Max Bergmann, 8 vols, Berlin: Springer, 1924

"Dem Andenken an Emil Fischer", in *Die Naturwissenschaften*, 7 (1919): 843–80

Fischer, Emil, *Aus meinem Leben*, Berlin: Springer, 1922; reprinted Berlin and New York: Springer, 1987

Fruton, Joseph Stewart, *Contrasts in Scientific Style: Research Groups in the Chemical and Biochemical Sciences*, Philadelphia: American Philosophical Society, 1990

Hoesch, Kurt, *Emil Fischer, Sein Leben und Werk: Im Auftrage der Deutschen Chemischen Gesellschaft dargestellt von Kurt Hoesch* (special issue of the *Berichte der Deutschen Chemischen Gesellschaft*), Berlin: Chemie, 1921

Johnson, Jeffrey Allan, *The Kaiser's Chemists: Science and Modernization in Imperial Germany*, Chapel Hill: University of North Carolina Press, 1990

Kauffman, George B. and Paul M. Priebe, "Emil Fischer's Role in the Founding of the Kaiser Wilhelm Society", *Journal of Chemical Education*, 66 (1989): 394–400

Remane, Horst, *Emil Fischer*, Leipzig: Teubner, 1984

In his time, Emil Fischer was known as the secret prince of chemists. In 1900, he opened what was then the largest and most modern institute of chemistry in the world, at the University of Berlin (now the Humboldt University), which he developed into a much-visited centre of research and education. In 1902 he received the Nobel prize for chemistry for his work on the synthesis of sugar and purines. Following this, he worked with similar energy and success on the chemistry of amino acids and polypeptides.

The emphasis in Fischer's work was very much on experimentation rather than theoretical speculation, and he used a combination of experiment and deft systematisation in order to map most of the chemistry of organic materials. In the course of his career, Fischer published more than 600 scientific articles, which have been collected in eight volumes, partly by himself and, after his death, by BERGMANN. The titles of the eight volumes give an indication of the main areas of his work, in rough chronology: triphenyl methane dyestuffs, hydrazine, and indoles (one volume); purines (one volume); carbohydrates and enzymes (two volumes); amino acids, polypeptides, and proteins (two volumes); and dyestuffs (one volume). Fischer attained a mastery of the synthesis and analysis of organic compounds that was not surpassed until the 1960s.

The first spate of works on Fischer was published just after his death in 1921. This first wave of publication then subsided,

and was only revived in the 1980s when some of Fischer's manuscripts became publicly available.

HOESCH's biography is an early overview of Fischer's life and works. The account is quite voluminous (480 pages) and Fischer's scientific contributions take up most of the space. The work has been criticised for its pathos and for being inexact, although the latter criticism is not justified.

As early as 1919, "DEM ANDENKEN AN EMIL FISCHER", a special issue of the journal *Die Naturwissenschaften*, celebrated Fischer's most important contributions with articles by his friends and students – in which Harries gave an overview of his scientific works, Abderhalden described Fischer's importance for physiology and medicine, von Weinberg detailed Fischer's activities during World War I, and Trendelenburg discussed his contribution to scientific work in Germany.

During recuperative journeys to Locarno and Karlsbad a year before his death, FISCHER (1922) had written the beginnings of his autobiography up to 1900, which was published posthumously in 1922. Fischer sketches a career that led him from Strasbourg, via Munich, Erlangen, and Würzburg, to Berlin. However, while there are detailed impressions of the institutions in which he worked, and of colleagues and friends, there is little mention of his private life and barely any references to his scientific work. The reprint of 1987 contains an introduction and epilogue by Bernhard Witkop, which includes a discussion of Fischer's scientific work and institutional contributions.

The revival of Fischer scholarship in the 1980s brought a change of emphasis towards issues of science organisation and science policy. REMANE provided a brief overview in 1984. Fischer was a member of the (Prussian) Academy of Sciences in Berlin where he regularly (once or twice a year) reported on the progress of his chemical works, thus propagating the most recent chemical knowledge. During the war, he was widely engaged as organiser and co-ordinator of various war committees on the requisitioning of substitutes for nutritional and feeding elements.

In 1989, KAUFFMAN & PRIEBE published a discussion of Fischer's role in the foundation and organisation of the Kaiser Wilhelm Gesellschaft (now renamed as the Max Planck Gesellschaft). They focus on Fischer's contribution to the establishment of a completely new type of research institution, that was independent of the university structures and funded jointly by the state and private industry. JOHNSON has shown that these new research centres were important for the leadership that German chemistry obtained before World War I, and he discusses developments during the war.

FRUTON's study of research groups in the chemical and biochemical sciences contains a substantial section (some 60 pages) on Fischer. He examines Fischer's scientific style, arguing that his success was due to his clear conception of science and to the international orientation of his school. According to Fruton, Fischer had 108 doctoral and post-doctoral students between 1892 and 1919. He also describes Fischer's work on the three main constituents of our nutrition – carbohydrates, proteins, and lipids – and its importance for the development of biochemistry at the turn of the century.

HORST REMANE

translated by Arne Hessenbruch

Fleming, Alexander   1881–1955

British bacteriologist

Clark, Ronald W., *The Life of Ernst Chain: Penicillin and Beyond*, London: Weidenfeld and Nicolson, and New York: St Martin's Press, 1985

Hare, Ronald, *The Birth of Penicillin, and the Disarming of Microbes*, London: Allen and Unwin, 1970

Hobby, Gladys L., *Penicillin: Meeting the Challenge*, New Haven, Connecticut: Yale University Press, 1985

Macfarlane, Gwyn, *Howard Florey: The Making of a Great Scientist*, Oxford and New York: Oxford University Press, 1979

Macfarlane, Gwyn, *Alexander Fleming: The Man and the Myth*, Cambridge, Massachusetts: Harvard University Press, and London: Chatto and Windus, 1984

Maurois, André, *The Life of Sir Alexander Fleming*, translated from the French by Gerard Hopkins, New York: Dutton, and London: Jonathan Cape, 1959 (original edition, 1959)

NOVA, "The Rise of A Wonder Drug", Deerfield, Illinois: Coronet Films and Video, 1986

Alexander Fleming is known for his discovery of the antibiotic penicillin in 1928. As a result, in 1945, the Scottish bacteriologist shared the Nobel prize in physiology or medicine with Howard Florey and Ernst Chain. In the post-war years he received countless awards throughout the world and joined the ranks of the most recognized scientists of the 20th century. Fleming is the subject of several biographical accounts and appears in numerous histories of antibiotics.

MACFARLANE (1984) stands out as by far the most comprehensive and accurate of the biographies, while HARE provides an excellent account of the sequence of events leading to Fleming's discovery. However, there remains a plethora of volumes that perpetuate the many myths and falsehoods that surround the penicillin story; MAUROIS's authorized biography, for example, typifies the tendency of Fleming biographers to focus chiefly on anecdotal material, with very little hard analysis of Fleming's scientific career.

HARE's account is the best first-hand description of Fleming's work. The author worked at St Mary's Hospital in London, at the time of Fleming's discovery, and was among those who witnessed his early penicillin research. Hare was the first to give a detailed description of the astonishing sequence of events leading to Fleming's discovery. The book is not a complete biography, focusing specifically on Fleming's research, but it directly inspired Macfarlane's revisionist biography.

Macfarlane (1984) is the only purely biographical account of Fleming's life that is properly documented; his background in medicine, and intimate knowledge of the Oxford Group's research, enabled him to answer many important questions left untouched by previous biographers. In particular, Macfarlane gives a detailed account of the of events leading to the contamination of Fleming's petri dish with penicillium notatum, and addresses Fleming's failure to develop penicillin during the 12 years following his discovery. Macfarlane also explains why the "Fleming myth" obscured the equally important work of Howard Florey, Ernst Chain, and Norman Heatley at Oxford,

through which the therapeutic powers of penicillin were discovered and proved. Macfarlane does not neglect Fleming's early life and career, and adds to the material contained in Maurois's more anecdotal work.

Much can be learned about Fleming from his collaboration with Florey and Chain. MACFARLANE (1979) is the most comprehensive source on Howard Florey, an Australian pathologist, and CLARK is a biography of Ernst Chain.

Hare chronicles Fleming's discovery of "lysozyme" in 1921, an antibiotic substance that he isolated from a sample of his own nasal mucus. Further investigation showed that lysozyme was also present in human blood serum, tears, saliva, pus, and milk. Fleming had discovered a universal biological protective mechanism, that killed and dissolved most of the airborne bacteria that exposed areas of the body. Surprisingly, the discovery of lysozyme, since recognized as fundamentally important, received little attention from the scientific community. Hare attributes the neglect of lysozyme to, "Fleming's inability to express himself clearly and lucidly in either words or print". Despite the lack of recognition, Fleming continued to investigate antibiotics.

In September 1928, Fleming noticed that a mold was growing in a petri dish containing strains of staphylococci, and that bacteria surrounding the mold were being destroyed. Macfarlane argues that it is likely that the source of the mold spores was the laboratory below Fleming's, where the mycologist C.J. La Touche was growing molds for research on allergies. Because of his interest in antibiotics, Fleming was conditioned to recognize immediately that an agent capable of dissolving staphylococci could be of great biological significance. He preserved the original culture plate and made a subculture of the mold in a tube of broth. Fleming's mold was later identified as penicillium notatum.

In his famous paper of 1929, "On the Antibacterial Action of Cultures of a *Penicillium*, with Special Reference to Their Use in the Isolation of B. *influenzae*", Fleming described his use of penicillin to isolate B. influenza, a bacteria that was not vulnerable to penicillin. The paper includes a description of the mold extract and lists the sensitive bacteria. Most importantly, Fleming suggests that penicillin might be used in the treatment of infection. In addition to describing his experiments, Fleming also states that the name "penicillin" should be used to describe the mold broth filtrate. His description of penicillin has since been regarded as one of the most important medical papers ever written.

During 1929, Fleming continued to investigate the antibiotic properties of penicillin, collecting data that clearly established the chemotherapeutic potential of penicillin. He was unable to purify and concentrate penicillin adequately, and hence did not conduct clinical tests in order to prove the effectiveness of the antibiotic *in vivo*. The significance of Fleming's discovery was not recognized until 1940, when Howard Florey and Ernst Chain discovered the enormous therapeutic power of penicillin. This is described in both Macfarlane (1979) and Clark.

HOBBY's book is the best overall description of the roles played by Fleming, Howard Florey, Ernst Chain and numerous other scientists in the discovery, development, and eventual mass production of penicillin. The author benefits from extensive personal participation in penicillin research, as a scientist employed by the Pfizer Corporation. The book includes extensive footnotes, and is the most complete overall history of penicillin available. Hobby's only setback is her focus on the role of Pfizer, above all other penicillin producers.

NOVA's outstanding film includes several important interviews with participants in the penicillin story. Macfarlane, Hare and Hobby provide a large portion of the narrative in this valuable primary source of historical data. All of the above authors place Alexander Fleming within the context of the overall history of penicillin. In doing so, they banish many of the historical inaccuracies, and provide well balanced accounts of one of the 20th century's greatest discoveries.

PETER NEUSHUL

See also Bacteriology; Drugs; Florey; Pathology; Pharmacology

Florey, Howard Walter   1898–1968

Australian pathologist

Baldry, P.E., *The Battle Against Bacteria: A History of the Development of Antibacterial Drugs, for the General Reader*, Cambridge: Cambridge University Press, 1965

Bickel, Lennard, *Rise Up to Life: A Biography of Howard Walter Florey Who Gave Penicillin to the World*, London: Angus and Robertson, 1972; New York: Scribner, 1973

Clark, Ronald W., *The Life of Ernst Chain: Penicillin and Beyond*, London: Weidenfeld and Nicolson, and New York: St Martin's Press, 1985

Hare, Ronald, *The Birth of Penicillin, and the Disarming of Microbes*, London: Allen and Unwin, 1970

Hobby, Gladys L., *Penicillin: Meeting the Challenge*, New Haven, Connecticut: Yale University Press, 1985

Macfarlane, Gwyn, *Howard Florey: The Making of a Great Scientist*, Oxford: Oxford University Press, 1979

Macfarlane, Gwyn, *Alexander Fleming: The Man and the Myth*, Cambridge, Massachusetts: Harvard University Press, and London: Chatto and Windus, 1984

NOVA, "The Rise of A Wonder Drug", Deerfield, Illinois: Coronet Films and Video, 1986

Ratcliff, J.D., *Yellow Magic: The Story of Penicillin*, New York: Random House, 1945

Williams, Trevor I., *Howard Florey: Penicillin and After*, Oxford and New York: Oxford University Press, 1984

During the early 20th century, scientists were aware of antibacterial substances but had not realized their full potential for the treatment of diseases in the human body. BALDRY provides a general introduction to antibiotics that is comprehensible to the general reader. Alexander Fleming discovered the antibiotic penicillin in 1928, but was unable to duplicate his laboratory results in clinical tests and, as a result, did not recognize the medical potential of penicillin as an antibiotic. MACFARLANE (1984) and HARE provide the most detailed accounts of Fleming's career, which also contain much about Howard Florey. Between 1935 and 1940, penicillin was purified, concentrated, and clinically tested by the pathologist Florey,

the biochemist Ernst B. Chain, and members of their Oxford Research Group. Their achievement has since been regarded as one of the greatest medical discoveries of the 20th century.

Florey is the subject of biographies by Bickel, Macfarlane and Williams. Of these, MACFARLANE (1979) is the most insightful. Macfarlane worked at Oxford and was an acquaintance of Florey's for 20 years. His book makes extensive use of the Florey archives at the Royal Society, and is an excellent blend of both personal and archival data. All three biographies describe how Florey decided to pursue a career in medicine at an early age, rather than entering into the family business. He finished his degree at the University of Adelaide in 1922 and, with the help of a Rhodes Scholarship, continued his education at Oxford, England, where he studied under the great neurophysiologist, Sir Charles Sherrington. Florey completed his doctorate at Cambridge, and in 1935 returned to Oxford as professor in charge of the Sir William Dunn School of Pathology.

Macfarlane is firm in his belief that a large amount of the credit given to Alexander Fleming should really have gone to Florey's Oxford Group, because they demonstrated the clinical effectiveness of penicillin. Macfarlane (1979) devotes considerable attention toward debunking what he refers to as the "Fleming Myth". BICKEL is a broader assessment of Florey and penicillin generally, and includes an interesting examination of the important role played by Florey's wife, Mary Ethel Florey. Bickel's only drawback is that the book is not completely documented. Although repeating much of what is covered in these two volumes, WILLIAMS does add to the story with information on Ernst Chain and his relationship with Florey. Williams worked for Chain during the 1940s, and provides excellent insight into the personality of his mentor. The union of Florey's medical knowledge and Chain's biochemical expertise proved to be an ideal combination for exploring the antibiotic potential of penicillin, a topic also covered in CLARK's biography of Chain, which includes four chapters on his work on penicillin.

Williams also focuses on the British biochemist Norman Heatley, a key member of the Oxford group, who has long been neglected by penicillin scholars. Heatley developed methods for measuring and producing penicillin, and his efforts ensured that enough penicillin was available to conduct chemical and clinical experiments, a fact that comes out clearly in NOVA. Clark describes how Florey and Chain began their investigation with a literature search in which Chain came across Fleming's work, and they then added penicillin to their list of potential antibiotics.

In May 1940, Florey's clinical tests of the crude penicillin proved its value as an antibiotic. Following extensive controlled experiments with mice, the Oxford Group concluded that they had discovered an antibiotic that was non-toxic and far more effective against pathogenic bacteria than any of the known sulpha drugs. Bacteria susceptible to the antibiotic included those responsible for gas gangrene, pneumonia, meningitis, diphtheria, and gonorrhoea. American researchers later proved that penicillin was also effective against syphilis. In January 1941, Florey injected the first of many volunteers with penicillin and found that there were no side effects to treatment with the antibiotic. The impact of Florey's discovery is best described in general works on penicillin.

The best of these is HOBBY's outstanding assessment of penicillin, from its discovery in 1928 to its mass production by the end of World War II. Hobby provides an overall description of the roles played by Fleming, Florey, Chain, and numerous other scientists in the discovery, development, and eventual mass production of penicillin. The author benefits from extensive personal work with penicillin, as a scientist employed by the Pfizer Corporation. Her book includes detailed footnotes and is by far the best documented text on penicillin, completely superseding earlier comprehensive efforts, such as RATCLIFF. Nova's film version of the penicillin story provides a well-balanced account of Florey's contribution, and is a valuable source of primary data. Macfarlane, Hare, Hobby, and Norman Heatley are among those appearing in the film.

Penicillin was the most important "wonder drug" of the 20th century. By refining and testing penicillin, Florey and his co-workers took a major step towards banishing scourges such as pneumonia, meningitis, and syphilis. Penicillin and other antibiotics also had a broad impact on medicine, as major operations such as heart surgery, organ transplants, and the management of severe burns became possible once the threat of bacterial infection was minimized. Florey's Oxford Group used a winning combination of outstanding medical and chemical expertise to make one of the greatest discoveries in the history of mankind.

PETER NEUSHUL

See also Bacteriology; Drugs; Fleming; Pathology; Pharmacology

Forensic Sciences

Browne, Douglas G. and Alan Brock, *Fingerprints: Fifty Years of Scientific Crime Detection*, London: Harrap, 1953; New York: Dutton, 1954

Chaillé, Stanford, "Address on Medical Jurisprudence", in *Transactions of the International Medical Congress of Philadelphia, 1876*, edited by John Ashhurst Jr, Philadelphia: printed for the Congress, 1877, 167–204

Clark, Michael and Catherine Crawford (eds), *Legal Medicine in History*, Cambridge and New York: Cambridge University Press, 1994

Crawford, Catherine, "A Scientific Profession: Medical Reform and Forensic Medicine in British Periodicals of the Early Nineteenth Century", in *British Medicine in an Age of Reform*, edited by Roger French and Andrew Wear, London and New York: Routledge, 1991

Crowther, M. Anne and Brenda White, *On Soul and Conscience: The Medical Expert and Crime: 150 Years of Forensic Medicine in Glasgow*, Aberdeen: Aberdeen University Press, 1988

Desmaze, Charles, *Histoire de la médecine légale en France: d'aprés les lois, registres et arrêts criminels*, Paris: Charpentier, 1880

Fischer-Homberger, Esther, *Medizin vor Gericht: Gerichtsmedizin von der Renaissance bis zur Aufklärung*, Berne: Huber, 1983

Forbes, Thomas Rogers, *Surgeons at the Bailey: English Forensic Medicine to 1878*, New Haven, Connecticut, and London: Yale University Press, 1985

Ginzburg, Carlo, "Morelli, Freud and Sherlock Holmes: Clues and Scientific Method", *History Workshop Journal*, 9 (1980): 5–36; reprinted as "Clues: Roots of an Evidential Paradigm" in his *Myths, Emblems, Clues*, London: Hutchinson, 1986; as *Clues, Myths and the Historical Method*, Baltimore, Maryland: Johns Hopkins University Press, 1989

Hammond, P.W. and Harold Egan, *Weighed in the Balance: A History of the Laboratory of the Government Chemist*, London: HMSO, 1992

Havard, John D.J., *The Detection of Secret Homicide: A Study of the Medico-Legal System of Investigation of Sudden and Unexplained Deaths*, London: Macmillan, and New York: St Martin's Press, 1960

Mohr, James C., *Doctors and the Law: Medical Jurisprudence in Nineteenth-Century America*, New York and Oxford: Oxford University Press, 1993

Nemec, Jaroslav, *Highlights in Medico-legal Relations*, Bethesda, Maryland: US Department of Health and Welfare, 1976

Thorwald, Jürgen, *The Century of the Detective*, translated from the German by Richard and Clara Winston, 3 vols, London: Thames and Hudson, and New York: Harcourt Brace, 1965–66 (original edition, 1965)

Trovillo, Paul V., "A History of Lie Detection", *Journal of the American Institute of Criminal Law and Criminology*, 29 (1938–39): 848–81; 30 (1939–40): 104–19

Wilson, Lindsay B., *Women and Medicine in the French Enlightenment: The Debate over "Maladies des femmes"*, Baltimore: Johns Hopkins University Press, 1993

If forensic science is defined as the application of scientific knowledge to the purposes of the law, its scope is extremely wide. It comprises a group of somewhat disparate applied sciences, whose histories have been shaped by the character of different legal systems and governments, as well as by the ambitions of practitioners in different periods and cultures. The existing historiography is weighted toward the use of medical expertise in the procedures of criminal justice. This is partly because of the enduring public fascination with crime, and partly because the use of non-medical sciences by legal systems was relatively rare until the later 19th century. The literature can be grouped into popular accounts, practitioners's histories, institutional and social histories, and cultural-historical approaches.

NEMEC is a useful and delightful chronicle, containing a paragraph on each of the 549 events in medico-legal history, from the 4th century BC to 1973. Originally published as a catalogue to accompany an exhibition at the US National Library of Medicine, it was greatly expanded for this edition, and has extensive references and indexes. Nemec's research was global, and the compendium is particularly valuable for its Central and Eastern European coverage.

Popular histories of scientific detection are legion. Among them, THORWALD and BROWNE & BROCK are notable for their comprehensiveness and their international scope. Thorwald recounts the stories of research and discovery in anthropometry, fingerprinting, forensic photography, serology, ballistics, toxicology, and forensic pathology, providing short bibliographies on 150 topics. His three-volume series provides the fullest account in English of forensic science in Germany and France in the 19th and 20th centuries. Browne & Brock trace the origins and development of fingerprint classification systems throughout the world. Their aim was to assess the competing claims of several figures in the history of fingerprints, and they elevate William Herschel, Edward Richard Henry, and Juan Vucetich while demoting Francis Galton and Henry Faulds.

Practitioners' histories of forensic science have often carried a reformist agenda. CHAILLÉ was one of 10 accounts commissioned for the American Centennial to portray advances made in the medical sciences during the century after Independence. While charting the progress of toxicology and forensic medicine, the author, a professor of pathology at New Orleans, described the institutional history of legal medicine in several countries; he showed that the United States had signally failed to promote the field, and argued for the adoption of the German model of "State Medicine". Similarly, HAVARD's study of the operation of the English coroner's inquest system over the centuries is a sustained critique of its deficiencies from a scientific point of view.

DESMAZE is a lawyer's history of medico-legal legislation, procedures, and cases in France from the 13th to 19th centuries. A jurisconsult to the Parisian court of appeal, Desmaze sought to inspire respect for French legal institutions, and to demonstrate the contributions of medical science to social defense. By documenting the growing importance of legal medicine in 1880, he hoped to persuade law students to seek training in the subject.

FORBES was interested in assessing the knowledge and techniques that English surgeons applied in medico-legal postmortems during the 18th and 19th centuries. A professor of anatomy, Forbes drew on his clinical experience to illuminate the efforts of his predecessors, and, by studying the proceedings of Old Bailey trials from the late 17th century to 1878, he brought routine medico-legal practice to light, mapping its development from a modern medical perspective.

TROVILLO is a detailed history of lie-detection, written by a forensic psychologist at the Chicago police science laboratory in the 1930s. Trovillo sought to apportion credit, and to influence the direction of future research, in what he showed was an extremely heterogeneous field. Above all, he wanted to facilitate acceptance of his branch of forensic science in the courtroom, by demonstrating the long academic lineage and experimental sophistication of deception tests.

There are some important monographs on individual institutions. HAMMOND & EGAN's history of the Laboratory of the Government Chemist documents a thriving realm of state-funded forensic science in Victorian Britain, in the detection of revenue fraud in the Customs and Excise laboratories. An insider's history (both authors had distinguished careers in the Laboratory), it describes the instruments and techniques by which salaried chemists in the 19th century detected adulteration in tobacco, tea, coffee, pepper, spirits, and wine, analyzing thousands of samples annually, and giving expert testimony in prosecutions. The book charts the steady expansion of government regulation, and the scientific, technical, and administrative developments that controlled it, up to 1991.

Social historians CROWTHER & WHITE focus on the department of forensic medicine at Glasgow University. Glasgow acquired a regius professorship in 1839, and became a centre of international importance in the early 20th century. Three phases are identified: an early period in which Scottish forensic medicine was combined with public health (drawing on the continental tradition of medical police); a "heroic" phase, characterized by the all-round medical expert; and the modern period, marked by teamwork and ever-increasing specialization.

CLARK & CRAWFORD explore the social, legal, and political history of legal medicine in Europe and America from the 17th to the 20th centuries. The 14 essays draw on recent doctoral theses and forthcoming monographs. Topics include early modern practice, infanticide, abortion, the growth of medico-legal science, medical police, the insanity defense, the politics of the coronership, and the creation of forensic-science laboratories.

CRAWFORD describes the professional culture that fuelled the rise of forensic medicine in early 19th-century England. MOHR traces in 19th-century America both the rise and fall of "medical jurisprudence" – the state-backed, public-spirited science that the early enthusiasts envisaged. He shows how social, political, and ideological factors led to the demise of this vision after mid-century, as free-market ideology, perceived abuses of the insanity defense, and the adversarial exertions of lawyers, made Jacksonian Americans unwilling to cede authority to medical men. The sudden growth of malpractice suits put American doctors on the defensive, increasing their distaste for the courtroom, and by 1900 medical jurisprudence had virtually disappeared from professional training in the United States.

Many historians have been interested in the power relations brought into play by medico-legal activity. In her reading of the early modern European literature, FISCHER-HOMBERGER discerns inter-professional jostlings for authority among surgeons, physicians, midwives, and apothecaries. She argues that the intellectual history of forensic medicine between the 16th and 18th centuries reflects the growing desire of physicians to establish pre-eminence over other practitioners, whose skills and experience were devalued as forensic medicine became a more learned science.

WILSON is concerned with the interplay of gender and knowledge, and finds in forensic medicine a rich field for reflection. Her study of women and medicine in 18th-century France uses medico-legal *causes célèbres* to illuminate the cultural politics of Enlightenment medical theory. The controversies generated by these cases raise questions about medical authority over empirics, women, the family and inheritance. Through discussing these questions, Wilson examines the ways in which Enlightenment science was gendered, and demonstrates how these debates penetrated literate culture.

GINZBURG explores the methodological parallels between psychoanalysis, criminal detection, and connoisseurship in their use of symptoms, clues, and pictorial marks. He argues that an evidential paradigm emerged in the humanities towards the end of the 19th century; expert analysis of obscure, trivial traces would permit comprehension of an important and otherwise unattainable reality. Ginzburg traces this particularizing epistemology back to ancient conjectural and divinatory methods, which were suppressed by the Platonic emphases of modern science, and then revived in the epistemology of the novel and the human sciences. The fascinations of forensic science appear to be deeply rooted in Western culture.

CATHERINE CRAWFORD

Foucault, Michel 1926–1984

French philosopher and historian

Armstrong, David, *The Political Anatomy of the Body: Medical Knowledge in Britain in the Twentieth Century*, Cambridge and New York: Cambridge University Press, 1983

Bernauer, James W., *Foucault's Force of Flight: Towards an Ethics of Thought*, Atlantic Highlands, New Jersey: Humanities Press International, 1991

Dean, Mitchell, *Critical and Effective Histories: Foucault's Methods and Historical Sociology*, London and New York: Routledge, 1994

Dews, Peter, *Logic of Disintegration: Post-Structuralist Thought and the Claims of Critical Theory*, London and New York: Verso, 1987

Diamond, Irene and Lee Quinby (eds), *Feminism & Foucault: Reflections on Resistance*, Boston: Northeastern University Press, 1988

Dreyfus, Hubert L. and Paul Rabinow (eds), *Michel Foucault: Beyond Structuralism and Hermeneutics*, Hemel Hempstead, Hertfordshire: Harvester Wheatsheaf, and Chicago: University of Chicago Press, 1982; 2nd edition, 1983

Eribon, Didier, *Michel Foucault, 1926–1984*, translated from the French by Betsy Wing, Cambridge, Massachusetts: Harvard University Press, 1991; London: Faber and Faber, 1992 (original edition, 1989)

Fraser, Nancy, *Unruly Practices: Power, Discourse, and Gender in Contemporary Social Theory*, Minneapolis: University of Minnesota Press, 1989

Gutting, Gary, *Michel Foucault's Archaeology of Scientific Reason*, Cambridge and New York: Cambridge University Press, 1989

Jones, Colin and Roy Porter, *Reassessing Foucault: Power, Medicine and the Body*, London and New York: Routledge, 1994

Kusch, Martin, *Foucault's Strata and Fields: An Investigation into Archaeological and Genealogical Science Studies*, Dordrecht and Boston: Kluwer, 1991

Martin, Luther H., Huck Gutman and Patrick H. Hutton (eds), *Technologies of the Self: A Seminar with Michael Foucault*, Amherst: University of Massachusetts Presss, 1988

Megill, Allan, *Prophets of Extremity: Neitzsche, Heidegger, Foucault, Derrida*, Berkeley: University of California Press, 1985

Miller, James, *The Passion of Michel Foucault*, New York: Simon and Schuster, 1993

Poster, Mark, *Foucault, Marxism and History: Mode of Production versus Mode of Information*, Cambridge: Polity Press, and New York: Blackwell, 1984

Rose, Nikolas, *Governing the Soul: The Shaping of the Private Self*, London and New York: Routledge, 1990

Sawicki, Jana, *Disciplining Foucault: Feminism, Power and the Body*, London and New York: Routledge, 1991

Sedgwick, Peter, *Psycho-Politics: Laing, Foucault, Goffman, Szasz and the Future of Mass Psychiatry*, New York: Harper and Row, 1982

Sheridan, Alan, *Michel Foucault: The Will to Truth*, London: Tavistock, 1980

Smart, Barry, *Foucault, Marxism and Critique*, London and Boston: Routledge and Kegan Paul, 1983

Still, Arthur and Irving Velody (eds), *Rewriting the History of Madness: Studies in Foucault's "Histoire de la Folie"*, London and New York: Routledge, 1992

The work of Michel Foucault has generated a massive secondary literature; his corpus, which addresses subjects as varied as medical diagnosis, penal policy, the rise of sexology and the ethics of self culture, has instigated a wide and many-layered debate. At its most straightforward, this debate has centred on issues of interpretation and clarification, as commentators have tried to render Foucault's often opaque work accessible to the general reader. On a more critical level, many authors have questioned the efficacy of Foucault's *oeuvre*, arguing that it is beset by failures of chronology and theoretical consistency. Finally, there has been a concerted attempt by historians to transcend this purely theoretical debate, by demonstrating the productiveness of Foucault's concepts and theories when applied to the history of science and medicine.

Since most of the commentaries on Foucault duplicate one another in approach and interpretation, it has been necessary to arrange this bibliography around the various themes of his work, rather than the individual secondary sources. For readers desiring a general introduction to Foucault's work, the best overviews are provided by Dreyfus & Rabinow and Gutting. DREYFUS & RABINOW supply a close and often critical reading of Foucault's work, dividing it into two major projects: an "archaeology", which consists of Foucault's reflections on the autonomy and historicity of language; and a "genealogy", describing the constitution and discipline of the modern subject. They situate these projects within the framework of continental theory and Anglo-American ordinary language philosophy, treating them as general contributions to modern anthropology. From this perspective, Foucault's work appears as a partial failure, since the gaps and contradictions that exist among his many case studies mitigate against the formulation of any universal theory of the human condition. GUTTING's work is far more sympathetic, approaching Foucault as a historian and philosopher of science working in the tradition of Bachelard and Canguilhem. He refuses to read Foucault's work as an attempted global theory, stressing instead how it has emerged out of pragmatic positions developed during his historical investigations. This standpoint allows Gutting to take an exegetical approach to Foucault's texts, reading them individually for each of their many and varied arguments, rather than reducing them to parts symbolic of a whole.

Foucault's first major works, which focused on the experience of madness, have been explored by Megill and Sedgwick. MEGILL locates these works within that romantic tradition of European philosophy and literature that stressed the value of extreme experience. This tradition provided Foucault with a perspective that undid the myth of psychiatry's progressive humanitarianism, revealing instead the repeated emergence of new forms of domination, from exclusion to inner control. This anti-psychiatric romanticism has been criticised by SEDGWICK, who argues that Foucault's prioritisation of madness over reason reduces it to a cultural stereotype, glossing over the very real misery engendered by the experience of mental illness. Moreover, Sedgwick argues that Foucault's idealistic advocacy of a dialogue between psychiatry and "unreason", which would lead to the reintegration of madness and civilisation, disguises the positive role of medicine and the need for a general social transformation in the liberation of the mentally ill. Such criticisms have been widely contested by the contributors to the volume by STILL & VELODY, in particular by Colin Gordon. Many of these authors claim that the criticisms directed against *Madness and Civilisation* have mistakenly relied on a heavily abridged version of his work. For these writers, the minor problems of chronology and historical accuracy associated with Foucault's exploration of medicine and madness should not distract from the philosophical or ethical urgency of his work.

The collection edited by JONES & PORTER provides the best introduction to Foucault's *The Birth of the Clinic*. Armstrong's and Osborne's essays in the volume contextualise Foucault's work on medical history, distinguishing it from the contemporary developments in anti-psychiatry. They show how Foucault moved away from his romantic preoccupation with human experience, towards a concern with the actual constitution of medicine's objects, the latter ranging from the space of the hospital to the individuality of the patient. Examples of this process are provided by the other contributors, whose studies range from the formation of the mouth in dentistry to the creation of the prison psychiatric service. Wider historical case studies can be found in the work of Rose and Armstrong; ROSE has described the constitution of modern subjectivity through the therapeutic interventions of counsellors and psychologists, while ARMSTRONG has traced the extension of medical power beyond the space of the clinic into the life of the family and the home.

Gutting and SHERIDAN give supportive readings of *The Order of Things*. They argue that this work can be seen as a rationalisation of Foucault's earlier writings, in which he consistently denigrated the narrative form of historiography in favour of a synchronic analysis of discrete and discontinuous historical episodes. These authors argue that the work successfully mediates between structuralism and historicism, revealing how the general form and organisation of knowledge is specific to a given historical period. Criticisms of this argument can be found in the works of Dreyfus & Rabinow and KUSCH, who suggest that this project foundered on internal contradictions, was beset by an all-encompassing relativism, and was bereft of any privileged standpoint that could explain the historical movement from one system of knowledge to another.

The books by SMART and by POSTER offer overarching assessments of Foucault's work, giving particular focus to his theory of power and its relationship to the tradition of Western Marxism. They concentrate on *Discipline and Punish*, in which Foucault developed a decentred and productive model of power, in opposition to the widely-held belief that power was a centralised negative force, repressing and constraining the population. DEWS has criticised the radical implications of this model of power; he argues that if truth and individuality are produced by power, then there can be no stable position from which one can critique the effects of domination. In response, several authors, including DEAN, have argued that such criticisms fail to recognise the dynamic nature of Foucault's conception of power, which stresses how the development of new practices and knowledge can constitute points of resistance.

In his attention to the local application of power and his problematisation of the body and sexuality, Foucault moved onto a terrain already explored by feminist scholars. For authors such as Sawicki and Fraser, Foucault's work has provided analytical tools for confronting the various disciplinary practices through which women are subjected. SAWICKI discusses Foucault's work in relation to the debate on new reproductive technologies, while FRASER's collection ranges between criticisms of Foucault's notion of the body, to applications of his theories to dietary and beauty concerns. Contributors to the volume by DIAMOND & QUINBY have considered the challenge that Foucault's work poses for the discourse on gender, given his refusal of any normative idea of womanhood and his suspicion of the rhetoric of liberation. Many of the contributors use this refusal to justify their own pragmatic critiques of Foucault, arguing that his refusal of value robs his philosophy of any radical or critical force.

BERNAUER's work has concentrated on Foucault's final writings, which explore the more reflexive strategies of self constitution embodied in the religious practices of the early Christians and the ancient Greeks. Bernauer follows Foucault's assessment of these practices, arguing that the marriage of theory and action reveals the moral effect of academic philosophy. Applications of this theory can be found in the volume edited by MARTIN, GUTMAN & HUTTON, which tackles confessional practices within various group and systems, ranging from New England Puritanism to psychoanalysis.

Given Foucault's intimate concern with the construction and contestation of identity, it was perhaps fitting that his death was followed by the publication of a clutch of contrasting biographies. With an irony that has been lost to few of Foucault's followers, his work and philosophy have been attributed to formative psychosexual experiences by MILLER. Other biographers have been more sympathetic to Foucault's project. ERIBON in particular has pursued the ecstatic intention of his work, refusing to relate the writer's life to any core identity, and describing instead the production of the philosopher by the social world.

RHODRI LLOYD HAYWARD

France: scientific and technical education

Boudon, Raymond, *L'Inégalité des chances: la Mobilité sociale dans les societés industrielles*, Paris: Colin, 1973

Bourdieu, Pierre and Jean-Claude Passeron, *Les Héritiers: les étudiants et la culture*, Paris: Éditions de Minuit, 1964

Day, Charles R., *Les Écoles d'Arts et Métiers: l'enseignement technique en France, XIXè–XXè siècle*, Paris: Belin, 1991

Nye, Mary Jo, *Science in the Provinces: Scientific Communities and Provincial Leadership in France, 1870–1930*, Berkeley: University of California Press, 1986

Paul, Harry W., *From Knowledge to Power: The Rise of the Science Empire in France, 1860–1939*, Cambridge and New York: Cambridge University Press, 1985

Pestre, Dominique, *Physique et Physiciens en France, 1918–1940*, Paris: Éditions des Archives Contemporaines, 1992

Picard, Jean-François, *La République des savants: la Recherche française et le CNRS*, Paris: Flammarion, 1990

Picon, Antoine, *L'Invention de l'ingénieur moderne: L'École des ponts et chaussées, 1747–1851*, Paris: Presses de l'École Nationale des Ponts et Chaussées, 1992

Shinn, Terry, "The French Science Faculty System, 1808–1914: Institutional Change and Research Potential in Mathematics and the Physical Sciences", in *Historical Studies in the Physical Sciences*, 10 (1979): 271–332

Shinn, Terry, *L'École Polytechnique, 1794–1914*, Paris: Presses de la Fondation Nationale des Sciences Politiques, 1980

Shinn, Terry, "Des sciences industrielles aux sciences fondamentales: La Mutation de l'École supérieure de physique et de chimie (1882–1970)", in *Revue Française de Sociologie*, 22/2 (1981): 167–82

Thépot, André, *Les Ingénieurs du Corps des Mines du XIXè siècle (1810–1914): Recherches sur la naissance et le développement d'une technologie industrielle*, dissertation, Paris: Université de Paris X-Nanterre, 1991

Weiss, John Hubbel, *The Making of Technological Man: The Social Origins of French Engineering Education*, Cambridge, Massachusetts: MIT Press, 1982

Weisz, George, *The Emergence of Modern Universities in France, 1863–1914*, Princeton, New Jersey: Princeton University Press, 1983

Zwerling, Craig S., *The Emergence of the École Normale Supérieure as a Center of Scientific Education in Nineteenth-Century France*, New York: Garland, 1990

There exists an abundant and conceptually rich literature dealing with French science, technology, and education. This stems in part from attempts by eminent French scholars to understand their society in terms of the structure of education and its links with the production of social class, cultural norms, and societal reproduction. Bourdieu & Passeron and Boudon figure prominently in this sociological and historical project. BOURDIEU & PASSERON regard scientific training (particularly high mathematics and science) as a mechanism of social selection that has operated historically to preserve a largely traditional élite, and to perpetuate its legitimacy within a framework of modern values and norms. In short, science education is societal reproduction. Such education is, by implication, very often intellectually, socially, and politically conservative. Conversely, BOUDON sees education in terms of meritocracy. In France, talented and dynamic individuals are drawn to schools of high science where potential is transformed into achievement. Education, notably in science and technology, is, in this view, connected with political, economic and cognitive competence, and, above all, it functions as a mechanism that nourishes and renews the national élite. The studies that focus even more specifically on French science and technical education also tend to raise broad questions of a relation between, various forms of cognition, on the one hand, and on the other, issues of authority, profession-building, and the socio-professional functions of graduates possessing different kinds of knowledge in the informal, yet predominant, French occupational and political hierarchy.

France boasts two main categories of scientific/technical educational institutions – the *grandes écoles* and the science faculties. The first *grandes écoles* were established in the 18th century, and were responsible for France gaining the well-deserved reputation of superlative scientific training, while providing a backdrop for a host of remarkable engineering feats and scientific achievements throughout the 18th and early 19th centuries. The science faculties only became a force in the late 19th century, and their position in French intellectual life has long been complex, and often precarious. Day, Picon, Shinn, Thépot, Weiss, and Zwerling have all explored episodes in the history of many of the principal *grandes écoles*. THÉPOT, PICON, and SHINN (1980) have focused on the most powerful and prestigious schools in the *grandes écoles* constellation – the École de mines, the École de ponts-et-chaussées and the École polytechnique. Each of these schools contributed significantly to France's technical and scientific accomplishments, particularly during the decades that immediately followed their creation. They also constituted the foundation of France's immensely powerful technocracy, and Shinn (1980) has suggested that the connection between the form of rigidly deductive knowledge ingrained by these institutions, and the authority-orientated careers of their graduates, often hampered the *grandes écoles* and their alumni in fulfilling the functions of technical innovation and scientific exploration. In their studies of the École centrale and the École supérieure de physique et de chimie, WEISS and SHINN (1981) document an inverse correlation between ascendency of institutions, in the *grandes écoles* hierarchy, and commitment to practical technical problem-solving and innovative research.

In his study of a different sub-set of schools, the École des arts et métiers, DAY shows that recruitment of students from the lower-middle classes, a curriculum of pragmatic engineering, and the pursuit by graduates of careers in technology are the rule for the less well-placed *grandes écoles*. This category of school enabled French industry to perform effectively in mechanics throughout the 19th century. However, the new demands resulting from the second industrial revolution in electricity and certain areas of chemistry raised severe problems of adaptation. The new situation found a solution only with the establishment of a supplementary cluster of *grandes écoles* in the 20th century, particularly (and often belatedly) after 1945. Such low-level institutions as the École des arts et métiers, despite their technological merits, never strove to participate in the growth of scientific knowledge. Indeed, this is the case for the majority of the *grandes écoles* constellation.

While cutting-edge science and research were generally sacrificed to political, social and technocratic authority at the allegedly most scientifically-orientated *grandes écoles*, such as the École polytechnique, ZWERLING reveals that another *grande école*, the École normale supérieure, was an exception of singular significance. This school was established during the Revolution, in order to train school teachers for the better secondary schools. Gradually, however, it attracted a growing number of gifted and scientifically ambitious students. This was the case of the chemist and biologist, Louis Pasteur, and when, in 1864, Pasteur became the school's director, he quickly imbued it with a research spirit and function, transforming the École normale supérieure into the nation's most advanced institution of scientific training. By the end of the 19th century, this institution was training more than two-thirds of France's science faculty staff and roughly one-third of the staff of certain *grandes écoles*. Although today occupying a somewhat diminished monopoly in research, the École normale supérieure nevertheless remains the country's foremost site of research training, in disciplines extending from high mathematics to macroscopic and microscopic physics, and to many areas of chemistry.

Science was slow to develop in French universities. The main function of the science faculties re-created in 1808 was to award the coveted secondary school *baccalaureat* and to offer low-level diplomas in higher education – to an extent that entailed minimal instruction. Nye, Paul, Shinn (1979) and Weisz all agree that the universities had relatively little to do with science before the last third of the 19th century, with the exception of the Sorbonne, and the sporadic activities of a few provincial faculties such as Strasbourg. University faculties only became a scientific force in the 1880s and 1890s. WEISZ argues that the new emphasis on university scientific research was principally a product of professional manoeuvring by teachers, as they sought to acquire material advantage and heightened occupational and social status in the fluid arena of republican politics. SHINN (1979) links the swift rise and abundance of science at the faculties to a complex combination of factors, which include, first, the use by republican politicians of the new experimental, inductive-based science at the faculties as a rhetorical and political device to attack and discredit conservative political forces allied to the traditional *grandes école* and committed to a form of relatively esoteric, mathematical and deduction-inspired cognition; second, the infusion of massive financial and material resources into the universities; third, the forging of an alliance between emergent technical science at the faculties and local industry; and last, the employment by the faculties of recently graduated research-minded *normaliens*.

In her exhaustive study of a sample of provincial science faculties, NYE unearths a few instances of success from the first half of the 19th century. She notes that it was not until later that these institutions came into their own, and draws attention to the considerable contribution to areas of technology and engineering made by the science faculties. Heightened faculty activity was in part, suggests Nye, a consequence of a general tendency (in France and elsewhere) to invest in education and research in engineering and science. PAUL deals obliquely with science faculty development, above all in the realm of applied science; his book examines the French science system in broad perspective, and emphasizes the fragile, patchwork character of the national science/technology enterprise. It thus comes as no surprise when Paul insists on France's constant need to improvise additional new educational and research arrangements in order to sustain adequate levels of performance.

Fully consistent with this perspective, the golden age of science at the faculties proved short-lived. PESTRE's history of French physics during the inter-war years indicates that the range of instruction shrunk after 1918, as did student enrolment and the number of teaching personnel. In the first half of the 20th century, the faculties, like most of the *grandes écoles*, lagged far behind in the teaching of up-to-date topics, such as theoretical and experimental microscopic physics, many domains of macroscopic physics, and many branches of chemistry. Although they were not intended to function as sites for science training, PICARD intimates that, in the 1920s and 1930s, France's gradually emerging private and public research funding agencies and newly created public research institutes allowed science to survive the frequently depressed and lacklustre inter-war decades, fostering some research, and also providing training grounds for a future generation of often brilliant scientists. While science was always alive at the École normale supérieure, France's full capacity in science education was achieved only in the 1960s and 1970s, in certain *grandes écoles*, like the École supérieure de physique et de chimie, and at certain science faculties, like Orsay, Grenoble, Lyon, and Strasbourg.

TERRY SHINN

See also École Polytechnique; Education; Universities

Franklin, Benjamin   1706–1790

American political leader, scientist, and inventor

Cohen, I. Bernard, *Benjamin Franklin: His Contribution to the American Tradition*, Indianapolis: Bobbs Merrill, 1953

Cohen, I. Bernard, *Franklin and Newton: An Inquiry into Speculative Newtonian Experimental Science and Franklin's Work in Electricity as an Example Thereof*, Philadelphia: American Philosophical Society, 1956

Cohen, I. Bernard, *Benjamin Franklin's Science*, Cambridge, Massachusetts: Harvard University Press, 1990

Darnton, Robert, *Mesmerism and the End of the Enlightenment in France*, Cambridge, Massachusetts: Harvard University Press, 1968

Heilbron, J.L., *Electricity in the 17th and 18th Centuries: A Study of Early Modern Physics*, Berkeley: University of California Press, 1979

Labaree, Leonard W. *et al.* (editors), *The Papers of Benjamin Franklin*, New Haven, Connecticut: Yale University Press, 1959– (34 vols through 1998)

Lemay, J. A. Leo (ed.), *Reappraising Benjamin Franklin: A Bicentennial Perspective*, Newark: University of Delaware Press, 1993

Van Doren, Carl, *Benjamin Franklin*, New York: Viking Press, and London: Putnam, 1939

Benjamin Franklin has been described as the most famous 18th century American after George Washington, so it is not surprising that the literature on him is very large. He is the author of the famous *Poor Richard* almanac, he was chief spokesman for the British colonies in talks in London about self-governance, he had a hand in the drafting of the Declaration of Independence and the Constitution, he secured military aid from France, founded what was to become the University of Pennsylvania, and served as postmaster of Philadelphia. This entry could not possibly do justice to the literature that has poured forth on this famous man, and it will thus focus on the literature dealing explicitly with Franklin's scientific work, primarily his work on electricity.

LABAREE *et al.* is a collection of Franklin's papers. It aims to be comprehensive, and so far 34 volumes have been published, taking us up to 1781. It is the backbone of scholarly work on Franklin.

VAN DOREN is the best-known general biography, against which most subsequent biographies are measured. Within the more than 800 pages, a mere 26 are devoted to Franklin's electrical science. It was this perceived deficit that COHEN (1953) addressed. The book is in the series entitled *Makers of the American Tradition*, and Cohen uses Franklin to argue that science is a crucial part of this tradition. Cohen focuses strictly on the question of Franklin's contribution to American sources of pride, and issues such as education or the role of economics in electricity are not discussed. COHEN (1956) is an extensive study (more than 600 pages) comparing Franklin to Newton. The main point is that Franklin contributed significantly to the generation of a theory of electricity resembling Newton's theory of gravity, in that both are characterized by inverse-square laws and central forces. Franklin thus contributed to the introduction of Newtonian science into new fields of natural philosophy. Cohen covers in great detail both the Newtonian tradition and Franklin's work on lightning conductors and electrical theory.

COHEN (1990) is a collection of eight essays from the period 1943–54. There are also three new chapters. It is partly thanks to Cohen's work in books and articles that biographies of Franklin in the 1970s paid more attention to his science that did Van Doren.

HEILBRON is a comprehensive history of electricity in the 17th and 18th centuries in which Franklin plays an important role. Heilbron describes the science of electricity at that time as frivolous and bogged down in metaphysics and magic. Into this world stepped a few extraordinary individuals, Franklin being the most important of them, who bring order and quantification on the basis of clear-headed and commonsensical experiments.

LEMAY contains two articles on Franklin's science. J.L. Heilbron compares Abbé Nollet (also a prominent 18th-century electrician) and Franklin: both were inventors, students of handicraft, literary figures, popularizers, analogizers, theorizers, travelers, tutors, experimenters, academicians, and professors. Otto Sibum's is the only paper that attempts to situate Franklin's science in the context of his other activities, especially his economic thinking. Sibum argues that there is a fundamental relationship between Franklin's creation of quantitative concepts created to handle electrical artifacts and his economic theories. His mundane concern with bookkeeping enabled the formulation of "plus" and "minus" electricity and "conservation of charge". Sibum argues further that by the 1780s, Franklin's bookkeeping principles were generally accepted, which led to balancing (in algebraic form) achieving the status of a natural law. This was most importantly expressed by Coulomb within the Laplacian programme of science.

DARNTON describes Mesmerism in 18th-century France in the context of general French culture. He depicts a society with odd and fascinatingly superstitious concerns. One chapter describes the work of a committee of experts examining and eventually debunking Mesmer's claims; one of the members of the committee, serving to shore up its authority, was Benjamin Franklin.

ARNE HESSENBRUCH

Fraunhofer, Joseph von   1787–1826

German physicist

Abbe, Ernst, "Gedächtnissrede auf Joseph Fraunhofer", in *Gesammelte Abhandlungen II, Wissenschaftliche Abhandlungen aus verschiedenen Gebieten Patentschriften Gedächtnisreden*, Hildelsheim, Zürich and New York: Georg Olms, 1989

Helmholtz, Hermann von, "Festbericht über die Gedenkfeier zur hundertjährigen Wiederkehr des Geburtstages Josef Fraunhofer's", *Zeitschrift für Instrumentenkunde*, 7 (1887): 114–28

Jackson, Myles W., "Artisanal Knowledge and Experimental Natural Philosophers: The British Response to Joseph Fraunhofer and the Bavarian Usurpation of Their Optical Empire", *Studies in History and Philosophy of Science*, 25 (1994): 549–75

Jackson, Myles W., "Illuminating the Opacity of Achromatic Lens Production", in *The Architecture of Science*, edited by Peter Galison and Emily Thompson, Cambridge, Massachusetts: MIT Press, 1999

Merz, Sigmund, *Das Leben und Wirken Fraunhofers*, Landshut: Thomann'schen Buchhandlung, 1865

Rohr, Louis Otto Moritz von, *Joseph Fraunhofers Leben, Leistungen und Wirksamkeit*, Leipzig: Adakemische Verlagsgesellschaft, 1929

Roth, Günther D., *Joseph von Fraunhofer: Handwerker-Forscher-Akademiemitglied, 1787–1826*, Stuttgart: Wissenschaftliche Verlagsgesellschaft, 1976

Sang, Hans-Peter, *Joseph von Fraunhofer. Forscher. Erfinder. Unternehmer*, Munich: Glas, 1987

Utzschneider, Joseph von, *Kurzer Umriß der Lebens-Geschichte des Herrn Dr Joseph von Fraunhofer*, Munich: Rösl'schen Schriften, 1826

There has been a fairly substantial amount of secondary literature dealing with Joseph von Fraunhofer, the optician and skilled artisan who used the dark lines of the solar spectrum, which now bear his name, in order to calibrate the manufacture of achromatic lenses. The earliest biography was written by his close friend and co-director of the Optical Institute, Joseph von Utzschneider. Published only months after Fraunhofer's death, UTZSCHNEIDER offers an informative account of the origin of the Optical Institute, where Fraunhofer was employed from 1806 until his death. Utzschneider's work also includes a discussion of Fraunhofer's childhood, how he came to the attention of the author, and how his workmanship placed Bavaria on the scientific and technological map. It also details the context within which Fraunhofer manufactured his world-renowned achromatic lenses.

Throughout the second half of the 19th century, Fraunhofer became a key figure in Germanic hagiographies; Merz, Abbe, and Helmholtz all consider Fraunhofer the father of German optics and precision mechanics. MERZ, whose father was Fraunhofer's apprentice and successor, emphasized Fraunhofer's success at manufacturing achromatic lenses and his instigation of optical precision in Germany. ABBE, who worked with Otto Schott at the Carl Zeiss Works on the improvement of achromatic lenses for microscopes and telescopes, underscored Fraunhofer's ability to fuse optical theory and practice with entrepreneurial values. Fraunhofer's Optical Institute, Abbe argued, was the forerunner of the Carl Zeiss Company, and he hoped that the Prussian government would continue subsidizing the Carl Zeiss Works, just as Maximilian I initially patronized Fraunhofer's work. HELMHOLTZ, being the spokesperson for both the German physics community and Germany's *Bildungsbürgertum*, stressed Fraunhofer's artisanal knowledge of optical glass production. He stressed that it had always been the ability of German leaders to recognize and co-ordinate the labour of skilled artisans in the fields of science and technology, and that such wisdom was destined to make the infant Reich a great nation. Artisanal labour, Helmholtz argued, formed the backbone of the *Bildungsbürgertum*, and Fraunhofer was the archetypal example of a working-class orphan who improved his socio-economic status to the level of the upper-middle-class as a result of his intellect, perseverance, and the sagacity of Bavarian reform-minded bureaucrats.

The most extensive and indeed informative biography of Fraunhofer is ROHR, which covers the technical aspects of Fraunhofer's research on optical lenses to a much greater extent than any other work. This work gives in-depth coverage of Fraunhofer's childhood and education as an apprentice, and draws upon Utzschneider's biography in order to describe the origins of the Optical Institute. However, the real value of the text is Rohr's detailed descriptions of Fraunhofer's lenses, comparing them to other lenses of the period, as this allows the reader to appreciate fully the superiority of Fraunhofer's workmanship.

More recent biographies by ROTH and SANG do not offer such an in-depth analysis, but they do both add more of a contextual approach. Both Sang and Roth discuss, for example, the importance of Napoleon's orders to produce a topographical map of his newly-acquired territory, Bavaria. The Optical Institute supplied lenses for astronomical instruments, such as telescopes and a heliometer, and ordnance surveying instruments, such as theodolites. Roth, like Helmholtz, emphasizes the importance of Fraunhofer's artisanal knowledge and abilities, and includes him in the history of German technology. Sang, like Abbe, discusses the entrepreneurial importance of the Optical Institute to Bavaria.

More recent work on Fraunhofer by Myles W. Jackson has continued along the lines of contextual analysis: JACKSON (1996) explores the significance of monastic culture to Fraunhofer's optical lens enterprise, as his laboratory was the secularized Benedictine cloister at Benediktbeuern. He has also analyzed the British response to Fraunhofer's artisanal knowledge: JACKSON (1994) argues that the British failure to "reverse engineer" Fraunhofer's lenses and prisms raises several interesting questions concerning the communicability of artisanal knowledge, the replacement of artisans by machinery, the British trade school curricula, and the politics of labour.

MYLES W. JACKSON

See also Astronomical Instruments; Optics

Freud, Sigmund   1856–1939
Austrian neurologist and psychoanalyst

Anzieu, Didier, *Freud's Self-Analysis*, translated from the French by Peter Graham, London: Hogarth Press/Institute of Psycho-Analysis, 1986

Appignanesi, Lisa and John Forrester, *Freud's Women*, London: Weidenfeld and Nicolson, and New York: Basic Books, 1992

Bakan, David, *Sigmund Freud and the Jewish Mystical Tradition*, Princeton, New Jersey: Van Nostrand, 1958; London: Free Association Books, 1990

Doolittle, Hilda, *Tribute to Freud*, New York: Pantheon, 1956; reprinted, Oxford: Carcanet, 1971

Ellenberger, Henri F., *The Discovery of the Unconscious: The History and Evolution of Dynamic Psychiatry*, London: Allen Lane, and New York: Basic Books, 1970

Gay, Peter, *Freud: A Life for Our Time*, London: Dent, and New York: Norton, 1988

Gellner, Ernest, *The Psychoanalytic Movement, or, The Cunning of Unreason*, London: Paladin, 1985; as *The Psychoanalytic Movement: The Cunning of Unreason*, Evanston, Illinois: Northwestern University Press, 1986

Ginzburg, Carlo, "Morelli, Freud and Sherlock Holmes: Clues and the Scientific Method", in *The Sign of Three: Dupin, Holmes, Peirce*, edited by Umberto Eco and Thomas Sebeok, Bloomington: Indiana University Press, 1983, 81–118

Jones, Ernest, *Sigmund Freud: Life and Work*, 3 vols, London: Hogarth Press, 1953–57; as *The Life and Work of Sigmund Freud*, New York: Basic Books, 1953–57

Krüll, Marianne, *Freud and His Father*, translated from the German by Arnold J. Pomerans, New York: Norton, 1986 (original edition, 1979)

Laplanche, Jean and Jean-Bertrand Pontalis, *The Language of Psycho-Analysis*, translated from the French by Donald Nicholson-Smith, London: Hogarth Press, 1973; New York: Norton, 1974 (original edition, 1967)

McGrath, William J., *Freud's Discovery of Psychoanalysis: The Politics of Hysteria*, Ithaca, New York: Cornell University Press, 1986

Mannoni, Octave, *Freud: Theory of the Unconscious*, translated from the French by Renaud Bruce, London: NLB, and New York: Pantheon, 1971; London: Verso, 1985 (original edition, 1968)

Marcus, Steven, *Freud and the Culture of Psychoanalysis: Studies in the Transition from Victorian Humanism to Modernity*, London and Boston: Allen and Unwin, 1984

Masson, Jeffrey Moussaieff, *The Assault on Truth: Freud's Suppression of the Seduction Theory*, London: Faber and Faber, and New York: Farrar Straus and Giroux, 1984

Rieff, Philip, *Freud: The Mind of the Moralist*, New York: Viking Press, 1959; 3rd edition, Chicago: University of Chicago Press, 1979

Roazen, Paul, *Freud and His Followers*, London: Allen Lane, and New York: Knopf, 1975

Robert, Marthe, *From Oedipus to Moses: Freud's Jewish Identity*, New York: Anchor Books, 1976; London: Routledge and Kegan Paul, 1977

Schorske, Carl E., *Fin-de-Siècle Vienna: Politics and Culture*, New York: Knopf, 1979; London: Weidenfeld and Nicolson, 1980

Sulloway, Frank, *Freud: Biologist of the Mind: Beyond the Psychoanalytic Legend*, London: Burnett Books, and New York: Basic Books, 1979

Swales, Peter, "Freud, His Teacher and the Birth of Psychoanalysis", in *Freud: Appraisals and Reappraisals: Contributions to Freud Studies*, vol. 1, edited by Paul Stepansky, Hillsdale, New Jersey: Analytic Press, 1986, 3–82

Wollheim, Richard, *Freud*, London: Fontana, 1971; 2nd edition, 1991

Yerushalmi, Josef Hayim, *Freud's Moses: Judaism Terminable and Interminable*, New Haven, Connecticut: Yale University Press, 1991

The scholarship devoted to Sigmund Freud is vast, and at times highly polemical. Indeed, texts proposing to address psychoanalysis as a discipline, frequently end up as texts on its founding father. In addition to identifying the main introductory conceptual and historical texts, the following selection will provide a guide to some of the contrasting approaches to Freud and his thought.

Although there are many biographies of Freud in circulation, JONES and GAY are the two to be recommended. The former, written by Freud's English disciple, has been condemned as hagiographic, but, despite a distinct tendency to mythologise the founder of psychoanalysis, the three-volume work nevertheless provides an incomparable mine of information about Freud, his career, his milieu, and the birth and development of the psychoanalytic movement. Gay is a more recent, and more manageable, book. Although offering an admiring account of the genius Freud, this narrative is somewhat more balanced than Jones's, acknowledging Freud's human failings, including his notorious intransigence towards dissenters. The book provides a useful first approach to the socio-historical context of the inception of psychoanalysis. It makes good use of Freud scholarship, and it includes an extensive bibliographical essay, which should be particularly noted.

MANNONI and WOLLHEIM stand as the best short, conceptual guides to Freud's system of thought. Mannoni, which also provides a cohesive account of Freud's life, focuses on the core psychoanalytic concept of the unconscious. Wollheim is a dense text requiring hard work from the beginner, who will, however, be rewarded for his or her perseverance with a very good general account of Freud's changing and multi-layered theories.

LAPLANCHE & PONTALIS's dictionary of Freud's terminology is an indispensable reference tool. A work of impeccable scholarship, it traces the development of every main psychoanalytic concept in Freud's writings, and (less thoroughly) in

those of his principle colleagues, such as Ferenczi and Abraham. The text also makes some reference to more recent, mainly Lacanian, developments of psychoanalytic thought. The work is historically sensitive and philosophically rigorous. However, its ideal use should be to refer the reader back to Freud's writings, rather than to act as a substitute summary of them.

The early phase of Freud's career has attracted particular attention. ANZIEU recounts Freud's self-analysis through a meticulous close reading of his first major psychoanalytic work, *The Interpretation of Dreams*, with the aim of explaining how the main psychoanalytic concepts came into being. Although this account is largely internal to the texts examined, it is very informative and useful, particularly if read in conjunction with other texts dealing with this material from a socio-historical perspective. Of these, SCHORSKE and McGRATH remain exemplary. Both regard a successful reading of the birth of psychoanalysis as dependent on an understanding of the social conditions and the politics of *fin-de-siècle* Vienna. Schorske writes more generally, Freud and psychoanalysis forming one strand of a wider story, while McGrath provides a more detailed analysis, specifically reading Freud's early work against the politics of the last decades of the Hapsburg empire.

Other scholars have emphasised particular, and sometimes differing, aspects of the socio-cultural context within which Freud worked. One approach is concerned with the question as to what extent psychoanalysis is "a Jewish Science". BAKAN, ROBERT, and YERUSHALMI all share a preoccupation with Freud's relation to Judaism, but their approaches vary widely. Bakan is mainly concerned with finding parallels between Freud's techniques and talmudic interpretations, and therefore remains very narrow and rather literal-minded in its focus. Robert stands out as one of the earliest texts to treat in depth the issue of psychoanalysis as emerging from a liberal bourgeois Viennese culture, sustained by an extensive but uneasily assimilated Jewish minority. Unlike the works above, which mainly address Freud's early career, Yerushalmi's allusive and evocative text tackles the issue of Judaism and psychoanalysis through a reading of Freud's late text, "Moses and Monotheism".

SWALES is exemplary of a certain type of research into Freud's background that can be termed deliberately iconoclastic. With the help of careful archival research, as well as a close reading of Freud's correspondence and published works, Swales's aim is to reconstruct a hidden historical truth about Freud, his early patients, and the birth of the psychoanalytic movement, seeking to use this truth to challenge the received histories of psychoanalysis, and ultimately the foundations of psychoanalysis itself. Although the material Swales uncovers is often of great interest, his work is overly bound up with his none-too-hidden agenda and his belief in a certain transparency of facts, and must be approached with some caution.

Freud's renunciation of the seduction theory (whereby neurosis was the result of some form of sexual abuse experienced in childhood) in favour of the Oedipus Complex (a network of loving and hating feelings that the child experiences towards its parents), has attracted much criticism and controversy. KRÜLL's work treats this question with depth and sensitivity, looking for explanations within Freud's own family background. Her research is particularly interesting when it touches on the issue of Jewish migration patterns in Eastern and Central Europe, and the question of the assimilation of Jews into an urban bourgeoisie. MASSON's text is much better known than Krüll's, despite being less nuanced and reliable. Masson himself has achieved a degree of notoriety, and has incurred the wrath of the psychoanalytic establishment, through his rather naive denunciation of Freud as a fundamentally dishonest man, who shifted positions out of an excessive desire for professional recognition.

SULLOWAY also seeks partly to discredit Freud's achievements, and does so by reading his theories as having developed in a direct line from the biological sciences of the later part of the 19th century. According to Sulloway, Freud sought to keep these links hidden, in order to postulate an original scientific theory of the mind, but his work remained a "cryptobiology".

Although providing much painstaking and valuable information on the scientific context from which psychoanalysis arose, Sulloway's account remains a partial one, and one that is perhaps ultimately less useful, because more narrow, than other contextualist ones, such as McGrath's, and particularly ELLENBERGER's, which stands as a monumental achievement. Presented as a history of dynamic psychiatry in general, it shows Freud's theory not so much as the culmination of a logical progression towards the truth about the human mind, but as one theory among many. He tells a broad, sweeping story, which unfolds over time and across national cultures, takes into account different kinds of discourses, and also provides detailed discussions of the systems of thought of a few outstanding figures, namely Janet, Freud and Adler.

GINZBURG's essay is included here as an example of a sharp and concise contextualist argument about the links between Freud's theory of interpretation and the art of diagnostics in late 19th-century scientific medicine. Ginzburg provides an illuminating connection, via a common professional training in medicine, between Freud and the art historian Morelli, inventor of a method for distinguishing real paintings from fakes, and Conan Doyle, also a former physician, as personified in his famous character Sherlock Holmes.

ROAZEN's text constitutes something of a departure, setting Freud's life and work within the context of the intricate network of friends and colleagues working alongside him in the years when psychoanalysis was becoming a discipline and a movement. As well as standing, to some extent, as the first institutional history of the beginnings of psychoanalysis, this text is notable for the way it unearthed and preserved a whole series of life-works and life-stories which had been overshadowed by an exclusive focus on Freud. Nevertheless, our knowledge of Freud is undoubtedly augmented by an awareness of the professional context within which he functioned.

Writing with a greater theoretical sophistication than Roazen, APPIGNANESI & FORRESTER also place Freud within a network of associates, albeit female ones. Starting from the fact that most of Freud's early patients were women, and that psychoanalysis had initially attracted a far higher number of female practitioners than other comparable professions, the authors address the ambivalent relationship between women and psychoanalysis. The text is composed of a series of intellectual biographies of the women who have helped shape psychoanalytic thought, as Freud's patients and/or

colleagues. It concludes with a cohesive and illuminating account of Freud's changing theories of femininity, and the history of their reception during the 20th century.

DOOLITTLE'S text constitutes an example of one woman's account of her analysis with Freud. It is included in this selection as one of the most evocative reports of Freud at work, a case history from the patient's perspective.

MARCUS, RIEFF and GELLNER all offer different slants on the question of the relationship between Freud's thought and theories of society and culture. Marcus writes primarily as a literary critic, and the main body of his text consists of a series of thoughtful analyses of Freud's case histories, considered mainly in terms of their literary textuality, and within the context of modernist writing in general. Rieff's and Gellner's texts are more sociologically slanted. Gellner examines the ways in which Freud's thought has functioned as a rallying point in the fundamentally secular 20th century, serving as a palliative to a whole set of anxieties no longer assuaged by religion. Rieff's text is more sympathetic to Freud than the fundamentally cynical Gellner; it offers a thoughtful and thought-provoking account of Freud as the creator of a moral and ethical system for what Rieff calls "psychological man". This is a creature inherently of the 20th century, which, according to these three authors, and indeed most of the authors under review, bears the indelible influence of Sigmund Freud.

JULIA BOROSSA

See also Psychoanalysis: conceptual; Psychoanalysis: institutional

Function

Bottazzini, Umberto, *The Higher Calculus: A History of Real and Complex Analysis from Euler to Weierstrass*, translated from the Italian by Warren van Egmond, New York: Springer, 1986 (original edition, 1981)

Brill, A. and M. Noether, "Die Entwicklung der Theorie der algebraischen Functionen in älterer und neuerer Zeit", *Jahresbericht der Deutschen Mathematiker-Vereinigung*, 3 (1892–93): 107–566

Cauchy, Augustin-Louis, *Cours d'analyse – analyse algébrique*, edited by Umberto Bottazzini, Bologna: CLUEB, 1990

Hawkins, Thomas W., *Lebesgue's Theory of Integration: Its Origin and Development*, Madison: University of Wisconsin Press, 1970; 2nd edition, New York: Chelsea House, 1975

Medvedev, Fyodor A., *Scenes from the History of Real Functions*, translated from the Russian by Roger Cook, Basel: Birkhäuser, 1991 (original edition, 1975)

Michel, A., *Constitution de la théorie moderne de l'intégration*, Paris: Vrin, 1992

Youschkevitch, A.P., "The Concept of Function up to the Middle of the 19th Century", *Archive for History of Exact Sciences*, 16 (1976): 37–85

Function is a central concept in mathematics, alongside number, shape, set, and transformation (a special case of function). It replaced earlier concepts, such as curves or equations, in the 18th century, largely thanks to the work of Hans Euler. This important development is described in a seminal paper by YOUSCHKEVITCH, who also discusses the later contributions of Peter Lejeune Dirichlet and the much less well-known Russian, N.I. Lobachevskii.

Modern mathematics distinguishes several types of function that have distinct, if overlapping, theories. Algebraic functions are those defined implicitly by polynomial equations, and their history was described in considerable mathematical detail by BRILL & NOETHER (two leading mathematicians of their day) in 1894. Although their account is selective, the most obvious change in emphasis has been the rise, already underway in the 1890s, of topological methods. This is discussed more fully in BOTTAZZINI, which is also the first book to describe the closely related history of analytic functions. A fuller treatment, but one focused on Cauchy's discovery of the first theory of analytic functions and richer in the institutional side of the story, is Bottazzini's edition of CAUCHY. Analytic functions have rigidity properties that make them inappropriate for many physical applications, although there is a vital special class of harmonic functions that satisfy the defining equations of potential theory.

The (usually) more relevant theory of differentiable functions was isolated much later, and has never been described in a single specialised treatise. A recent work covering differentiable continuous, and merely integrable, functions is that of MEDVEDEV, which is particularly useful for its information on Russian mathematicians. HAWKINS contains a good account of Lebesgue's discovery of the concept of measure that today bears his name, and how it rapidly became the standard theory of integration. Other concepts of integration, and the use of integration in the study of topological groups and spectral theory, are described by MICHEL.

JEREMY GRAY

Functionalism and Structuralism: biological sciences

Appel, Toby A., *The Cuvier-Geoffroy Debate: French Biology in the Decades Before Darwin*, New York: Oxford University Press, 1987

Coleman, William, *Biology in the Nineteenth Century: Problems of Form, Function, and Transformation*, New York: Wiley, 1971

Desmond, Adrian, *The Politics of Evolution: Morphology, Medicine, and Reform in Radical London*, Chicago: University of Chicago Press, 1989

Gould, Stephen J., *Ontogeny and Phylogeny*, Cambridge, Massachusetts: Belknap Press of Harvard University Press, 1977

Lenoir, Timothy, *The Strategy of Life: Teleology and Mechanics in Nineteenth Century German Biology*, Dordrecht: Reidel, 1982

Nyhart, Lynn K., *Biology Takes Form: Animal Morphology and the German Universities, 1800–1900*, Chicago: University of Chicago Press, 1995

Ospovat, Dov, *The Development of Darwin's Theory: Natural History, Natural Theology, and Natural Selection, 1838–1859*, Cambridge and New York: Cambridge University Press, 1981

Panchen, Alec L., "Richard Owen and the Concept of Homology", in *Homology: The Hierarchical Basis of Comparative Biology*, edited by Brian K. Hall, San Diego: Academic Press, 1994, 22–62

Rehbock, Philip F., *The Philosophical Naturalists: Themes in Early Nineteenth-Century British Biology*, Madison: University of Wisconsin Press, 1983

Richards, Robert J., *The Meaning of Evolution: The Morphological Construction and Ideological Reconstruction of Darwin's Theory*, Chicago: University of Chicago Press, 1992

Rupke, Nicolaas A., *Richard Owen: Victorian Naturalist*, New Haven, Connecticut: Yale University Press, 1994

Russell, E.S., *Form and Function: A Contribution to the History of Animal Morphology*, London: John Murray, 1916; with an introduction by George V. Lader, Chicago: University of Chicago Press, 1982

Sloan, Phillip Reid, "On the Edge of Evolution", in *The Hunterian Lectures in Comparative Anatomy May–June, 1837*, by Richard Owen, edited by Sloan, Chicago: University of Chicago Press, and London: Natural History Museum, 1992, 3–72

Most historical studies of biological functionalism and/or structuralism focus on 19th-century animal morphology. The functionalist epistemology was teleological, attributing purposiveness, whereas the structuralist approach (also referred to as "idealist", "transcendentalist", "morphological", "formalist" or "philosophical" – terms used loosely and synonymously in much of the English literature) discarded "final causes" and stood for organic "archetypes" or, more radically, "unity of type" in the organic world. Some authors, such as COLEMAN, take part of the epistemological meaning out of the terms "form" and "function", equating the latter, for example, with "physiology".

The classic account of the subject is RUSSELL, which describes the history of animal morphology as a debate on the primary explanatory feature of organic structure as either form or function. Russell identified George Cuvier as representative of the functionalist approach, and Étienne Geoffroy Saint Hilaire of the structuralist. Russell recognised three phases of the history of morphology: a pre-evolutionary phase, dominated by the idealist notions of Geoffroy and the German *Naturphilosophen*; an evolutionary phase, which followed the appearance of Darwin's *Origin of Species* (1859); and a third, early 20th-century phase, during which the historical approach to morphology was abandoned for a causal approach.

More recent studies discuss the extent to which Darwin was indebted to the functionalist and formalist approaches. OSPOVAT has shown that Darwin's theory of natural selection owed much to the functionalism of British natural theology, which co-opted Cuvier in support of its design argument. Moreover, he points out that the teleology of natural theology did not predominate in Britain untill 1859, as was commonly assumed, but was challenged during the decades 1830–60 by several biologists who imported German morphology and embryology. The importance of German "philosophical anatomy" for British biology of this period has also been stressed by REHBOCK, who focuses on the Edinburgh connection and the influence of Robert Knox, and his pupil Edward Forbes.

In a broadly ranging history of the notion of embryological recapitulation, GOULD discusses the transcendental origins of the theory that ontogeny recapitulates phylogeny, and its relation to German *Naturphilosophie*, in particular the work of Lorenz Oken and Johann Friedrich Meckel. Gould maintains that Darwin was not influenced by the recapitulation theory of the *Naturphilosophen*. RICHARDS takes issue with this, and argues that the German historicism present in the thesis – that the embryo recapitulates the forms of the species taxonomically below it – significantly guided Darwin in his theory of organic evolution. He accuses Gould of an ideological and unfounded attempt to separate Darwin from German teleological morphology – an attempt allegedly motivated by Gould's desire to keep his hero clean of the "political Prussianism", racism, and Nazism that are frequently associated with the development of German morphology in the 19th century.

A similar belief in the importance of German cognitive influences on British biology is expressed by SLOAN, who makes a detailed case for the thesis that Richard Owen, during his time as Hunterian Professor at the Royal College of Surgeons, produced a philosophically motivated, and intellectually coherent, reconciliation of traditional functionalism with German transcendentalism, the latter introduced into the College by the surgeon, Joseph Henry Green, a disciple of Coleridge.

One of Owen's claims to fame was his definition of the concept of homology, and PANCHEN demonstrates that to Owen the criterion of homology was less embryological development, and more Geoffroy's "principle of connections" derived from comparative anatomy.

In recent years, historical studies of the pre-Darwinian functionalists and structuralists have acquired a new focus of research, namely the socio-political purpose to which these different epistemologies were put. For the Paris Museum of Natural History, APPEL gives a fine sketch of the famous Cuvier-Geoffroy debate of 1830, held before the Académie, on the issue of "unity of composition" in the animal kingdom. For many years, Cuvier had avoided an open clash with Geoffroy, but, Appel maintains, in 1830, with political tensions building up to the revolution of that year, Cuvier may have decided that it was imperative to destroy the basis of theories that he believed were destabilising society. Cuvier's position represented the Catholic and royalist *status quo*, whereas Geoffroy's views went hand-in-hand with republicanism, and a drive towards liberalisation.

DESMOND views the adoption of German morphology by Owen and his circle in London as an establishmentarian ploy to subdue the evolutionary radicalism of Robert E. Grant at London University, and of lesser figures at the private medical schools, where Geoffroy's morphology-based transformism was cultivated by the underdogs of the British class hierarchy.

RUPKE makes a sharp distinction between Owen's functionalist and his formalist studies, taking issue with Sloan and arguing that no coherence between the two was achieved. Owen's choice of subject matter and epistemology were to a significant extent determined by the politics of his career objectives as curator, first of the Hunterian Museum and later of the natural history collections at the British Museum. Functionalism served to please and placate Owen's institutional patrons, who were Oxbridge Anglicans, committed to the design argument of natural theology. German formalism, by contrast – and here Rupke differs from Desmond – helped Owen (who did not belong to the Oxbridge élite) to establish a metropolitan, professional identity, separate from, and free of, the domination of the institutions of natural theology. A common denominator of Appel's, Desmond's and Rupke's studies is the assumption that the institutional setting, career objectives, and social conditions were formative of attitudes towards functionalist or structuralist approaches.

In a majority of the studies of 19th-century British morphology, it is assumed that German biology of the period was dominated by the *Naturphilosophie* of Oken and other "transcendentalists". LENOIR argues, however, that, distinct from the tradition of idealist morphology, a workable programme of research was developed by a well-connected group of biologists, Karl Ernst von Baer prominent among them, who unified teleological and mechanistic models of explanation. NYHART takes a different perspective, showing how the morphology of Oken's generation continued to flourish during Russell's second, evolutionary phase, especially at Jena, in the work of Carl Gegenbaur and Ernst Haeckel. Rejecting the "institutional context" as an adequate framework of explanation, Nyhart instead uses a "generational analysis", describing German morphology in terms of six "generational cohorts" of practitioners.

NICOLAAS A. RUPKE

G

Galen c.130–c.201

Greek physician

Ilberg, Johannes, "Über die Schriftstellerei des Klaudios Galenos", *Rheinisches Museum für Philologie* (new series) 44 (1889): 207–329; 47 (1892): 489–514; 51 (1896): 165–96; 52 (1897): 591–623

Kudlien, Fridolf and Richard E. Durling (eds), *Galen's Method of Healing: Proceedings of the 1982 Galen Symposium*, Leiden: E.J. Brill, 1991

Lloyd, G.E.R., *Greek Science after Aristotle*, New York: Norton, and London: Chatto and Windus, 1973

Lloyd, G.E.R., *Methods and Problems in Greek Science*, Cambridge and New York: Cambridge University Press, 1991

Nutton, Vivian (ed.), *Galen: Problems and Prospects*, London: Wellcome Institute, 1981

Smith, Wesley D., *The Hippocratic Tradition*, Ithaca, New York: Cornell University Press, 1979

A Greek-speaking Roman citizen from Pergamon in Asia Minor, Galen was for a long time second only to Hippocrates as one of the most famous names in ancient medicine. In Galen's case, however, a large corpus of writings – both medical and philosophical – has been transmitted under his name (and is with all probability actually Galen's work). These writings are also our main source for details about his life.

ILBERG's four articles discuss the chronology of Galen's life and works, and, together with LLOYD (1973), which provides a brief outline of Galen's life, medical theories, and practice, they form a helpful introduction for those who are unfamiliar with the topic.

KUDLIEN & DURLING, directed at students of classical medicine and philosophy, is a collection of papers focusing on one of Galen's best-known works, the *Method of Healing*. Style and context, the scientific base for Galen's surgery, his logic and therapy, as well as textual transmission in Arabic, Latin, and Middle English translations, are some of the aspects investigated.

LLOYD (1991) explores Galen's attitudes to his predecessors, namely Herophilus, Erasistratus, and, in particular, Hippocrates. The author examines the alternatives to Galen's choice of Hippocrates as his ideal – claiming that this was not an automatic preference, but the outcome of careful deliberation – and the factors influencing his choice.

The papers in NUTTON are scholarly writings (in English, French, German, and Italian), for a fairly specialised audience, on a variety of topics relating to Galen, such as the relation of his work to the Second Sophistic, his method of diagnosis, his epistemology, his religious belief, and also on translations of his works and textual transmission in later periods.

Despite the title, SMITH's book is not about Hippocratic medicine, but concerns the ways in which people of later eras have emulated or imagined in Hippocrates qualities that reflected their own ideals. Beginning with modern (post-1500) interpretations, Smith then moves backwards to Galen's Hippocratism, and then to the period between 400 BC and AD 200. In the section on Galen, which opens with a brief outline of Galen's life, the author examines where and to what extent Galen followed Hippocrates, the effects of Hippocratism on his medicine, and the degree of reliability provided by Galen's evidence for the reconstruction of previous traditions. The book is not overly technical, but it requires some preliminary understanding of Greek medicine.

CHRISTINE F. SALAZAR

Galilean School

Andersen, Kirsti, "Cavalieri's Method of Indivisibles", *Archive for History of Exact Sciences*, 31 (1985): 291–367

Arrighi, G. *et al.*, *La scuola galileiana: prospettive di ricerca*, Florence: La Nuova Italia, 1979

Baldini, Ugo, "La scuola galileiana", in *Storia d'Italia*, edited by Gianni Micheli, Turin: Einaudi, 1980, 381–463

Caverni, Raffaello, *Storia del metodo sperimentale in Italia*, 5 vols, Florence: Civelli, 1891–1900; reprinted in 6 vols, New York: Johnson Reprint, 1972

Favaro, Antonio, *Amici e corrispondenti di Galileo*, 4 vols, Venice: Ferrari, 1894–1919; edited by Paolo Galluzzi, 3 vols, Florence: Salimbeni, 1983

Galluzzi, Paolo, "L'Accademia del Cimento: 'gusti' del principe, filosofia e ideologia dell'esperimento", *Quaderni Storici*, 16 (1981): 788–844

Giusti, Enrico, *Euclides reformatus: La teoria delle proporzioni nella scuola galileiana*, Turin: Bollati Boringhieri, 1993

Koyré, Alexandre, *The Astronomical Revolution: Copernicus-Kepler-Borelli*, translated from the French by R.E.W. Maddison, London: Methuen and Ithaca, New York: Cornell University Press, 1973 (original edition, 1961)

Maffioli, Cesare S., *Out of Galileo: The Science of Waters, 1628–1718*, Rotterdam: Erasmus, 1994

Middleton, W.E. Knowles, *The Experimenters: A Study of the Accademia del Cimento*, Baltimore: Johns Hopkins University Press, 1971

Procissi, Angelo, *La collezione galileiana della Biblioteca Nazionale di Firenze*, 3 vols, Rome: Instituto Poligrafico dello Stato, 1959–94

Segre, Michael, *In the Wake of Galileo*, New Brunswick, New Jersey: Rutgers University Press, 1991

Targioni-Tozzetti, Giovanni, *Notizie degli aggrandimenti delle scienze fisiche accaduti in Toscana nel corso di anni LX del secolo XVII*, 3 vols, Florence: Bouchard, 1780; reprinted in 3 vols, Bologna: Forni, 1967

Torrini, Maurizio, *Dopo Galileo: Una polemica scientifica, 1684–1711*, Florence: Olschki, 1979

Although some of Galileo's followers already referred to themselves as a "school" in Galileo's lifetime, this concept – like that of a "follower" – is vague and rather difficult to define. This may in part explain why, despite Galileo's many admirers, the importance of some of their works, and the quantity of sources available, the spread of Galileo's ideas has been little studied. Even those intellectuals closely associated with Galileo are still relatively unknown, and only recently has the study of their work gained a certain impetus. The literature can be classified under the sub-groupings of general works and works on particular topics.

A general outline of Galileo's principal followers (Torricelli, Cavalieri, Viviani, and some of the members of the Accademia del Cimento) in the quarter of a century after Galileo is given by SEGRE. BALDINI offers a detailed presentation of the Galilean school in the broad sense of the term, attempting, in a traditional historiographical style, to account for contemporary intellectual streams and social context. ARRIGHI *et al.*, the proceedings of a congress held in 1978, is also a helpful introduction to the topic. PROCISSI is an outstanding catalogue of the Galilean Collection of manuscripts in the Biblioteca Nazionale Centrale in Florence; the second and third volumes of this catalogue present the manuscripts relating to Galileo's *Discepoli*, giving broad additional information that cannot be found elsewhere.

Since modern scholarship on the Galilean school is still in its infancy, pioneering works on the subject are still of interest, especially as indications of sources. TARGIONI-TOZZETTI is an impressive, 18th-century description of the development of science in Tuscany in the 17th century, focusing on Medici patronage, while FAVARO is a collection of biographies of people related to Galileo. An alternative approach can be found in CAVERNI's unusual, monumental study, which boldly claims that too much credit had been given to Galileo at the expense of others, including some of his followers.

Developments in astronomy soon after Copernicus are explored by KOYRÉ, which rightly emphasizes the importance of Borelli's contribution, in particular to the unification of terrestrial and celestial physics. Despite his excellence and scientific versatility, Borelli remains little studied; Koyré is a valuable contribution to the field, and highlights the *a priori* approach common to both Borelli and early modern science.

MIDDLETON is primarily a translation of *Saggi di naturali esperienze*, published by the Accademia del Cimento in 1667, but has useful introductory and final chapters, appendices and footnotes, which contain considerable, and at times more interesting, information and indications of sources. The relation between the Academy's empirical "ideology" with the patronage of Prince Leopold de' Medici is explored by GALLUZZI.

ANDERSEN gives a technical presentation of Cavalieri's Theory of the Indivisibles, while a technical study of the mathematics of Galileo's followers is also offered by GIUSTI, which concentrates on the investigation of Euclid's Theory of Proportions from Galilean predecessors to his followers. The book covers the work of Torricelli, Borelli, Viviani, Noferi and Marchetti, and shows both the dullness of mathematical investigation in the Galilean circles in the second half of the 17th century, and the fact that Galileo's followers were far from being as compact a school as has traditionally been held. TORRINI is an interesting, detailed, partly technical study of some specific cases of criticism of Galilean science (atomism in particular), and accounts for the response by Galileo's followers.

A recent, excellent, broad study of the development of fluid mechanics in Italy from Galileo's day to the first quarter of the 18th century is given by MAFFIOLI. Rightly claiming that too much attention has been given to Galileo and his followers at the expense of other scientists of the period, he nevertheless acknowledges, in Part II under the title "From Castelli to Borelli", the contribution of Galileo's followers, foremost among them Castelli.

MICHAEL SEGRE

Galilei, Galileo   1564–1642

Italian astronomer, mathematician, and natural philosopher

Agassi, Joseph, "On Explaining the Trial of Galileo", *Organon*, 8 (1971): 137–66; reprinted in his *Science and Society: Studies in the Sociology of Science*, Dordrecht: Reidel, 1988, 321–51

Biagioli, Mario, *Galileo, Courtier: The Practice of Science in the Culture of Absolutism*, Chicago: University of Chicago Press, 1993

Cooper, Lane, *Aristotle, Galileo, and the Tower of Pisa*, Ithaca, New York: Cornell University Press, 1935

Damerow, Peter *et al.*, *Exploring the Limits of Preclassical Mechanics*, New York: Springer, 1991

Drake, Stillman, *Galileo at Work: His Scientific Biography*, Chicago: University of Chicago Press, 1978

Finocchiaro, Maurice A., *Galileo and the Art of Reasoning: Rhetorical Foundations of Logic and Scientific Method*, Dordrecht: Reidel, 1980

Finocchiaro, Maurice A. (ed. and trans.), *The Galileo Affair: A Documentary History*, Berkeley: University of California Press, 1989

Frajese, Attilio, *Galileo matematico*, Rome: Studium, 1964

Galluzzi, Paolo (ed.), *Novità celesti e crisi del sapere: atti del convegno internazionale di studi galileiani*, Florence: Barbèra, 1984

Gebler, Karl von, *Galileo Galilei and the Roman Curia*, translated from the German by Mrs George Sturge, London: Kegan Paul, 1879; reprinted, Merrick, New Jersey: Richwood, 1977

Koyré, Alexandre, *Galileo Studies*, translated from the French by John Mepham, Hassocks, Sussex: Harvester Press, 1978 (original edition, 1939)

McMullin, Ernan (ed.), *Galileo: Man of Science*, New York: Basic Books, 1967

Morpurgo-Tagliabue, Guido, *I processi di Galileo e l'epistemologia*, Milan: Edizioni di Comunità, 1963; Rome: Armando, 1981

Olschki, Leonardo, *Galilei und seine Zeit*, Halle: Niemeyer, 1927

Paschini, Pio, *Vita e opere di Galileo Galilei*, 2nd edition, Rome: Herder, 1965

Pedersen, Olaf, *Galileo and the Council of Trent*, new edition, Studi Galileiani, vol. 1, no.1, Vatican City: Specola Vaticana, 1991

Redondi, Pietro, *Galileo: Heretic*, translated from the Italian by Raymond Rosenthal, Princeton, New Jersey: Princeton University Press, 1987; Harmondsworth: Penguin, 1989 (original edition, 1983)

Renn, Jürgen, "Proofs and Paradoxes: Free Fall and Projectile Motion in Galileo's Physics", in *Exploring the Limits of Preclassical Mechanics*, edited by Peter Damerow, Gideon Freudenthal, Peter McLaughlin and Jürgen Renn, New York: Springer, 1991

Santillana, Giorgio de, *The Crime of Galileo*, Chicago: University of Chicago Press, 1955; London: Mercury Books, 1961

Segre, Michael, *In the Wake of Galileo*, New Brunswick, New Jersey: Rutgers University Press, 1991

Shea, William, *Galileo's Intellectual Revolution: Middle Period, 1610–1632*, New York: Science History Publications, 1972

Shea, William, "Galileo in the Nineties", *Perspectives on Science*, 2 (1994): 476–87

Viviani, Vincenzio, *Racconto istorico della vita del Sigr. Galileo Galilei . . .*, 1717; reprinted in vol. 19 of *Le opere di Galileo Galilei* (National Edition), edited by Antonio Favaro, Florence: Barbera, 1890–1909

Wallace, William S., *Galileo and His Sources: The Heritage of the Collegio Romano in Galileo's Science*, Princeton, New Jersey: Princeton University Press, 1984

Wisan, Winifred L., "The New Science of Motion: A Study of Galileo's *De moto locali*", *Archive for History of Exact Sciences*, 13 (1974): 103–306

Wohlwill, Emil, *Galilei und sein Kampf für die copernicanische Lehre*, 2 vols, Leipzig: Voss, 1909–26; reprinted, Wiesbaden: Sändig, 1969

The Galilean bibliography contains thousands of books and articles. A list of items was published by Antonio Favaro and Alarico Carli in *Bibliografia galileiana (1568–1895)* (Rome, 1896); a first supplement was published by Guiseppe Boffito, in *Bibliografia galileiana (1896–1940)* (Rome: Libreria dell Stato, 1943), and a second was published as an Appendix to McMULLIN, bringing the Galilean bibliography to 3794 items. A third supplement is now being compiled. A helpful review essay of works on Galileo is SHEA (1994). The literature can be divided into biographies, more general works, items dealing with particular aspects of Galileo's work, his trial, and the social background, and, finally, edited collections of articles.

There are many biographies of Galileo. The earliest, written in Italian by his pupil VIVIANI (1622–1703), was the most influential text on Galileo until the beginning of the 20th century, if not to date. Drafted in 1654, it appeared posthumously in 1717, was republished many times and occasionally translated, although not into English. Viviani's sketch presents Galileo as a Renaissance genius and a practical man. It relates the famously doubtful stories of Galileo's discovery of the principle of the pendulum's isochrony by observing the oscillations of a lamp in the cathedral of Pisa, and his refutation of Aristotle by experiments performed from the top of the Leaning Tower. As such it became the cornerstone of the tradition in the historiography of science, presenting Galileo as the founder of modern experimental science. This view was seriously questioned in the 20th century, especially by Wohlwill, Cooper, Koyré, and Shea (1972). However, taken within its contemporary literary context, Viviani's essay is as balanced and accurate as possible, and is a typical example of a Renaissance biography.

A detailed (more than 700 pages), scholarly and well-written biography of Galileo was written between 1942 and 1944 by Monsignor PASCHINI. Based mainly on Galileo's correspondence, it focuses more on the events of Galileo's life than on the development of his science, and, though inevitably outdated in some respects, it remains a good reference for many details of Galileo's life. Another detailed, more recent, biography is by leading Galilean scholar, the late Stillman Drake. DRAKE concentrates on Galileo's work, presenting it chronologically, and summarizes some of Drake's other contributions to Galilean scholarship, such as his outstanding study of Galileo's working manuscripts. It contains as an appendix a helpful collection of brief biographies of Galileo's correspondents. Drake's general approach to the history of science is inductive, and he ascribes the same quality to Galileo's science. It avoids delving into the philosophical and social context, has no particular thread except for chronology, and jumps from one topic to another, sometimes confusing the reader.

Modern Galilean studies began at the end of the 19th century, when Antonio Favoro collected Galileo's work into the superb "National Edition", and a series of important and erudite Galilean studies were published soon after. One of them, by WOHLWILL, summarizes 40 years of Galilean research in two volumes, and gives particular attention to Galileo's campaign for Copernicanism and his clash with the Church. Although the book relies to a great extent on sources available before the publication of the National Edition, it contains much information and many remarks that have still not lost their validity. It was Wohlwill's rigour that brought him to question the truthfulness of Viviani's description and to break with the traditional characterization of Galileo.

Another major work written in the first half of the 20th century is OLSCHKI, which is the last of three volumes devoted to the emergence of early modern science as part of the general new culture, paying particular attention to its literary aspects. The result is an interesting study of Galileo's work within the context of Renaissance literature. One chapter of this book was translated into English, and published under the title "Galileo's literary formation" in McMullin.

KOYRÉ collected a series of studies of Galileo's science that appeared in the 1930s. One claim from this period was that Galileo's view of method had much in common with the Platonic and, more specifically, Archimedean methodology. Koyré's main and controversial conjecture is that neither experience nor experiment played an essential role in Galileo's work; he even suggested that some experiments Galileo described had never actually been performed. The work contains many inaccuracies (see Finocchiaro), and has been criticized for making blanket claims about Galileo. None the less, it marked a turning point in Galilean studies.

FINOCCHIARO (1980) focuses on the *Dialogue* and offers critical, balanced discussions of Galileo's work and of the secondary literature, based on careful textual examination of Galileo's writings from different points of view – such as rhetoric, science, methodology, religion, and logic. An appendix offers a page concordance of the editions of the *Dialogue*.

Many works focus on particular aspects of Galileo's work. One of the most challenging topics is Galileo's early manuscripts, which were not intended for publication but can offer a clue to his sources. Father WALLACE has written a series of studies of some of Galileo's early Latin manuscripts on physics and logic, stressing the influence of the Jesuits of the Roman College on the young Galileo.

COOPER, a professor of English at Cornell, translated and commented on the literature relevant to the Leaning Tower story in a small book, for the use of English-speaking readers. He repeated Wohlwill's doubts, and added further arguments pointing to the lack of evidence behind the story. His direct and humorous approach to breaking a taboo gave rise to strong, at times irrational, criticism, and it took some time for the book to be acknowledged as important to Galilean studies.

In the most recent and thorough study of Galileo's mechanics, RENN claims that modern mechanics developed from a pre-classical conceptual frame. He studies the dawn of Galileo's mechanics, concentrating particularly on the period 1600–04, and relates Galileo's work in this period to the later *Discorsi*. Renn uses Galileo's working manuscripts, and critically considers the various studies on the early stages of Galileo's mechanics.

In a lucid study of Galileo's science and methodology, SHEA (1972) concentrates on the "middle period" of his work, between Galileo's return to Florence and the appearance of the *Dialogue*. WISAN's technical study of Galileo's work on local motion – one of the two "new sciences" introduced in the *Two New Sciences* (1638) – attempts a reconstruction of the development of this science. It conjectures that Galileo started off from medieval concepts, to which he applied Greek mathematics and experiment to achieve the final "modern" formulation.

There are very few studies of Galileo's mathematics. FRAJESE is a clear, general presentation of the subject, unfortunately out of print and not easy to find.

There is a broad range of literature on Galileo's trial and, because of the delicacy of the topic, it is difficult to find an unbiased account. For this reason FINOCCHIARO (1989) is particularly helpful, and sufficient for a non-specialist. A documentary history of the developments of the case (1613–33),

and as such primarily a reliable English translation of the essential texts and documents, it nevertheless provides – through its introduction, chronology of events, biographical glossary, and notes – a first-rate framework for a critical interpretation of the affair.

Non-specialist readers will also find the following works suitable as an introduction. MORPURGO-TAGLIABUE is a thorough, erudite study of the epistemological aspects of Galileo's trial, while AGASSI gives a controversial, insightful analysis of the intricate intellectual tangle involving theology, philosophy, and science. REDONDI is an outstanding, controversial study written in a refreshing style; it takes its cue from an anonymous denunciation in the Vatican files of Galileo's theory of matter as presented in *The Assayer* (of 1623). Redondi claims that this was the main cause of Galileo's misfortune, since it questioned transubstantiation. Whether this conjecture is true or false, it is to Redondi's credit that he draws attention to the importance of atomism in Galileo's work, and presents a colourful description of the Roman scientific *milieu* of the day.

For those interested in the history of the literature on the Galileo Affair, there is GEBLER, an outstanding pioneering work that also presents the earliest collection of documents related to Galileo's trial. Gebler provided the material for SANTILLANA, which is a stimulating story of Galileo's trial and can serve as a general introduction to Galileo's life. It has been criticized for being popular, inexact, and biased in favor of Galileo, but it remains an accessible account in English. PEDERSEN is one of the recent studies promoted by Pope John Paul II to propagate a better understanding of the Galileo Affair. Outlining its development, the book reconstructs with great clarity the theological origins of the blunder, in a rather apologetic narrative.

BIAGIOLI's masterly work is one of the few devoted to the social matrix of Galileo's work, examining the mutual interaction between Galileo's science and his career objectives at the Tuscan court (i.e., after 1611). It is an erudite, complex, and exciting work, taking court etiquette as a departing point, and making broad use of recently developed methods from the sociology of science and the anthropology of knowledge.

SEGRE outlines the work of Galileo's leading followers (Torricelli, Cavalieri, Viviani, and some of the members of the Accademia del Cimento) in the quarter of a century after Galileo's death. It relates their work to Galileo's, and attempts to offer a better understanding of Galileo's work, showing in particular how some aspects of the Galileo myth originated from the work of these direct followers.

There are many collections of works on Galileo in several languages that contain excellent contributions, two of which will be helpful to the reader seeking a general presentation of Galileo's work. McMULLIN covers Galileo's work in general and, though it is by now somewhat old-fashioned, remains a basic work. It contains 23 articles in English, divided into five parts under the following titles: introduction to Galileo; background; Galileo's contributions to science; Galileo as a philosopher of science; and postscript. The 1967 edition of the book contains as an appendix a Galilean bibliography for the years 1943–64, but this important supplement was unfortunately not included in the 1988 edition. GALLUZZI is an impressive collection of papers presented to the international congress held in March 1983 in Pisa, Venice, Padua, and Florence, in order to commemorate the 350th anniversary of the publication of Galileo's *Dialogue*. It contains 39 articles in Italian, English, and French, divided into four groups examining Galileo's writings, his optics and the nature of light, Galileo's interlocutors, and the diffusion of the Galilean cosmology.

MICHAEL SEGRE

See also Accademia del Cimento; Court Society; Galilean School; Telescopes

Galton, Francis 1822–1911

British hereditarian, statistician, and eugenicist

Blacker, C.P., *Eugenics: Galton and After*, Cambridge, Massachusetts: Harvard University Press, 1952

Bowler, Peter J., *Evolution: The History of an Idea*, Berkeley: University of California Press, 1984; revised edition, 1989

Bowler, Peter J., *The Mendelian Revolution: The Emergence of Hereditarian Concepts in Modern Science and Society*, London: Athlone Press, and Baltimore: Johns Hopkins University Press, 1989

Bynum, W.F., "The Historical Galton", in *Sir Francis Galton, FRS: The Legacy of His Ideas*, edited by Milo Keynes, London: Macmillan, 1993

Cowan, Ruth, "Francis Galton's Contribution to Genetics", *Journal of the History of Biology*, 5 (1972): 389–412

Cowan, Ruth, "Francis Galton's Statistical Ideas: The Influence of Eugenics", *Isis*, 63 (1972): 509–28

Cowan, Ruth, "Nature and Nurture: The Interplay of Biology and Politics in the Work of Francis Galton", *Studies in the History of Biology*, 1 (1977): 133–208

Edwards, A.W.F., "Galton, Karl Pearson and Modern Statistical Theory", in *Sir Francis Galton, FRS: The Legacy of His Ideas*, edited by Milo Keynes, London: Macmillan, 1993

Fancher, Raymond E., "Biographical Origins of Francis Galton's Psychology", *Isis*, 74 (1983): 227–33

Forrest, D.W., *Francis Galton: The Life and Work of a Victorian Genius*, London: Elek, and New York: Taplinger, 1974

Froggatt, P.C. and N.C. Nevin, "Galton's 'Law of Ancestral Heredity': Its Influence on the Early Development of Human Genetics", *History of Science*, 10 (1971): 1–27

Galton, Sir Francis, *Memories of My Life*, London: Methuen, 1908

Hilts, Victor L., *Statist and Statistician*, New York: Arno Press, 1981

Kevles, Daniel J., *In the Name of Eugenics: Genetics and the Uses of Human Heredity*, New York: Knopf, 1985; Harmondsworth: Penguin, 1986; with a new preface, Cambridge, Massachusetts: Harvard University Press, 1995

MacKenzie, Donald A., *Statistics in Britain, 1865–1930: The Social Construction of Scientific Knowledge*, Edinburgh: Edinburgh University Press, 1981

Magnello, M. Eileen, "Karl Pearson's Gresham Lectures: W.F.R. Weldon, Speciation and the Origins of Pearsonian Statistics", *British Journal for the History of Science*, 29 (1996): 43–63

Magnello, M. Eileen, "Karl Pearson's Mathematization of Inheritance: From Ancestral Heredity to Mendelian Genetics (1895–1909)", *Annals of Science*, 55 (1998): 35–94

Olby, Robert, "The Dimensions of Scientific Controversy: The Biometrician–Mendelian Debate", *British Journal for the History of Science*, 74 (1989): 299–320

Pearson, Karl, *The Life, Letters and Labours of Francis Galton*, 3 vols in 4 parts, Cambridge: Cambridge University Press, 1914–30

Porter, Theodore M., *The Rise of Statistical Thinking, 1820–1900*, Princeton, New Jersey: Princeton University Press, 1986

Stigler, Stephen M., *The History of Statistics: The Measurement of Uncertainty before 1900*, Cambridge, Massachusetts: Belknap Press of Harvard University Press, 1986

Swinburne, R.G., "Galton's Law: Formulation and Development", *Annals of Science*, 24 (1965): 227–46

A Victorian polymath, Francis Galton was educated at Birmingham and Cambridge. He left Cambridge after inheriting his father's money, which enabled him to pursue his own interests. Much of the scholarship on Galton has focused on his work in anthropology, heredity, statistics, and eugenics, but he also made contributions to fingerprinting, photography, and meteorology. Apart from two biographies, most of Galton's historiography is centred on various aspects of his scientific ideas and theories.

GALTON provided the earliest account of his life in an autobiography written when he was 86 years old. Although he discusses his family life and education, the largest portion of the book is devoted to his travels. He also discusses his work in anthropometrics and heredity, and he mentions briefly his statistical innovations. The first biography of Galton came from his friend and protagonist Karl PEARSON, who was asked to undertake the writing of this biography by the Galton family after Galton's death in 1911. This was a project that Pearson had hoped initially to have completed in one year, but because of other commitments, the outbreak of World War I, financial restraints, and a desire to provide a complete portrayal of Galton, the project took him 20 years to complete, resulting in a four-part, three-volume work. In this monumental biography, Pearson endeavoured to give an account of Galton's scientific work and his social ideas, and he collected a substantial amount of Galton's published and unpublished papers, as well as his correspondence, in order to make Galton's work accessible to future generations. Although the length of this work has been criticised, such a detailed exposition has, none the less, made it an invaluable source of primary material for nearly all other accounts of Galton (as Pearson had intended).

Drawing on some of Galton's papers and much of Pearson's biography, BLACKER (secretary to the Eugenics Society for more than 20 years) provided the first compact account of Galton's life. Some 26 years after Blacker's book was published, FORREST wrote a biography of Galton in an attempt to give a more balanced account of Galton's life. Unlike Blacker, Forrest used archival material from University College London, the Eugenics Society, and the Royal Geographical Society, however, as BYNUM has noted, Forrest made little attempt to examine archival material from other societies with which Galton was connected.

HILTS is interested in the role of statistics within the context of 19th-century social sciences; he focuses on Galton's use of statistics in anthropology in connection with the problem of heredity. COWAN, who traces the development of Galton's hereditarian ideas, establishes the following three arguments: Galton provided an operational definition of the word heredity; his socio–political ideologies influenced his hereditarian and eugenic programme; and his statistical innovations were a consequence of his eugenic ideas. KEVLES discusses Galton's role as the founder of the eugenics movement, while MACKENZIE's interest in the rise of the professional middle class is central to his assessment of the extent to which Galton's work corresponded to the author's theory of the social construction of knowledge. MacKenzie argues that eugenics was intimately connected to the social groups to which Galton belonged, and the promotion of eugenics thus became a central goal of his statistical theory.

SWINBURNE is concerned with the underpinnings of Galton's theory of ancestral heredity. Although he acknowledged that the fundamental contribution of Galton's correlation helped scientists to look for statistical relationships rather than explaining phenomena with rigid laws of causation, he believes that Pearson introduced enormous mathematical complications into Galton's primitive theory. FROGGATT & NEVIN, who examine the genesis of Galton's law of ancestral heredity, also share Swinburne's interpretation of Galton's and Pearson's statistical work. MAGNELLO (1998) however, argues that Pearson's so-called "mathematical complexity" enabled him in 1896 to achieve a mathematical resolution of multiple correlation and of multiple regression, adumbrated in Galton's Law of Ancestral Heredity of 1885. Hence, while a number of historians of science have examined how Galton's development of simple correlation and simple regression led to further statistical developments by Pearson, Magnello has also argued that when Pearson applied his own agenda to Galton's law of ancestral heredity, Pearson not only devised the product–moment correlation coefficient and simple regression, but he also formulated the following statistical methods: multiple correlation, part and partial correlation coefficients, multiple regression, the standard error of estimate (for regression), and the coefficient of variation.

STIGLER, who views Galton as a romantic figure in the history of statistics, emphasizes the conceptual breakthroughs that Galton made in statistics in the last half of the 19th century. Stigler also recognizes that even though correlation is the statistical concept most often associated with Galton, it played only a minor role in his work (whereas the statistical concept of regression featured more prominently). PORTER argues that Charles Darwin's provisional hypothesis of pangenesis was Galton's starting point in biology, and that pangenesis provided the concept that led Galton to his statistical investigation of heredity. EDWARDS considers R.A. Fisher to have been the real inheritor of Galton's statistical innovations, rather than Pearson. Galton's influence on the statistical work of Pearson has also been of interest to a number of scholars. Although much of this scholarship has emphasised Galton's role in the development of Pearsonian statistics, MAGNELLO (1996) argues that Pearson and Galton not only maintained divergent hereditarian and evolutionary views, but that their statistical outlooks differed considerably. She has further argued that while Galton influenced Pearson's later statistical work on correlation, it was the zoologist, Walter F.R. Weldon, who provided the earliest and most significant link in the development of Pearsonian statistics.

BOWLER, who is particularly interested in Galton's evolutionary thinking, shows that Galton's statistical approach opened the way to a more detailed understanding of the mechanism of natural selection. Bowler also argues that Galton played a critical role in hereditarian thinking in the 19th century, when he moved away from the unproductive approach of using developmental and embryological ideas by focusing on the physiological level of inheritance instead. OLBY considers Galton to have laid the foundation of particulate heredity by reformulating Darwinian evolution in terms of discontinuous variation, thus leading to Galton's development of a "hard" theory of heredity. FANCHER discusses Galton's ideas of intelligence, and argues that his conflict-laden attitudes toward his own intellectual abilities shaped his hereditarian views of intelligence. BYNUM recently provided an overall assessment of the scholarship on Galton that demonstrates the multifaceted interests and outlooks that historians have sustained concerning Galton.

M. EILEEN MAGNELLO

See also Eugenics; Heredity; Pearson; Statistics

Galvani, Luigi 1737–1798
Italian physiologist

Bernardi, Walter, *I fluidi della vita: alle origini della controversia sull'elettricità animale*, Florence: Olschki, 1992

Clarke, Edwin and L.S. Jacyna, *Nineteenth-Century Origins of Neuroscientific Concepts*, Berkeley: University of California Press, 1987

Dibner, Bern, *Galvani–Volta: A Controversy that Led to the Discovery of Useful Electricity*, Norwalk, Connecticut: Burndy Library, 1952

Dibner, Bern, *Luigi Galvani*, Norwalk, Connecticut: Burndy Library, 1971

Heilbron, J.L., "The Contributions of Bologna to Galvanism", *Historical Studies in the Physical and Biological Sciences*, 22 (1991): 57–85

Kipnis, Naum, "Luigi Galvani and the Debate on Animal Electricity, 1791–1800", *Annals of Science*, 44 (1987): 107–42

Pera, Marcello, *The Ambiguous Frog: The Galvani–Volta Controversy on Animal Electricity*, translated from the Italian by Jonathan Mandelbaum, Princeton, New Jersey: Princeton University Press, 1992 (original edition, 1986)

Luigi Galvani is best remembered for his contributions to physiology, and in particular for his claim in 1791 that he had demonstrated the existence of an "animal electricity" responsible for producing muscular motion in living creatures. Apart from helping to inspire the electrical experiments on human cadavers that Mary Shelley would later credit with breathing life into Victor Frankenstein's hideous progeny, Galvani's announcement stimulated a vigorous controversy over the validity of his claims and, through the efforts of Alessandro Volta, to demonstrate that Galvani's twitching frog-legs derived their energy from metallic sources rather than from any innate force in the animal tissues themselves, which led indirectly to the development of the first electrochemical, or "voltaic", battery.

The two works by Dibner are slim volumes from the Burndy Library's series of occasional publications in the history of science. While their streamlined accounts lend a somewhat teleological air to the events they describe, they provide clear and concise narratives for anyone seeking a basic introduction to the making of Galvani's reputation. DIBNER (1952) is primarily concerned with events leading toward the development of the battery, and so focuses on details of the experimental results published by Galvani and Volta and on the competing explanations they gave for each other's results. DIBNER (1971) provides additional biographical material on Galvani, with brief descriptions of his family, education, and professional career. Both works, like most of the Burndy Library publications, are illustrated throughout with a fine array of images drawn from relevant contemporary sources.

KIPNIS provides a more detailed discussion of the physiological context within which Galvani's work appeared. Taking issue with earlier historical accounts, that viewed Galvani from the vantage point of modern physiology and thereby dismissed his idea of an electrical vital force as rather naive and misguided, Kipnis examines why Galvani's work attracted such intense interest among his contemporaries, and why the theory of animal electricity outlived even Volta's attempt to refute it. Toward this end, he surveys ideas on electricity and the nervous fluid that predated Galvani, and then discusses how these strands of thought fed into Galvani's own work and the diverse reactions of his contemporaries, many of whom refused to side entirely with either Galvani or Volta in the ensuing debate.

CLARKE & JACYNA discuss Galvani within the sweep of their broader survey of the development of modern concepts in the neurosciences, and their treatment of his work focuses on its relation to changing theories of nerve function in the 18th and 19th centuries. From this perspective, they chronicle the rise, decline, and subsequent triumph of the idea that the nervous impulse might be electrical, and describe some of the links that were made between theories of the nerves and debates on other topics such as general brain function and the phenomena of the electric fish. Like Kipnis, they are willing to explore the more grandiose of Galvani's ideas through constructive historicism, and, indeed, throughout their work argue for the strongly positive influence of a "romantic" philosophy of nature in stimulating concerns for unity, synthesis, and general laws in the life sciences that were instrumental in the nervous system's rise to prominence in medical and physiological thought.

PERA's book returns to a rather tight focus on the debate between Galvani and Volta, but at the same time provides the most detailed account of this exchange presently available.

While he begins by discussing the use of electricity as a means for displaying marvelous visual effects in 18th-century polite society, Pera's primary motivation is that of a philosopher examining the clash of scientific theories in cases where experimental results yield rival and incompatible interpretations. With this aim in mind, he probes the early training of both Galvani and Volta for signs of potentially formative influences on the contrasting theoretical frameworks from which they would later interpret identical phenomena, and he casts each salvo of their debate in the form of competing epistemological propositions, some of which are said to represent "crucial experiments". His discussions are thus indebted to the treatments of similar themes by philosophers of science such as Karl Popper, Paul Feyerabend, and especially Thomas Kuhn, whose work he also examines critically.

By contrast, BERNARDI's work is substantially framed as a response to the philosophically-oriented tradition of treating the Galvani–Volta debate as a textbook example of the clash of incommensurable gestalts. A historian who has written or edited several other volumes on the 18th-century life sciences, Bernardi instead focuses on the multiplicity of ways in which the controversy over animal electricity was inextricably bound up with ongoing debates in medicine, physiology, and other aspects of the life sciences. From this standpoint, he criticises Pera's presentation as employing an overly idealised framework that privileges clarity in logic over breadth in historical coverage, and he argues that the animal electricity debate is better viewed as a point of convergence for diverse theoretical interests, instead of as a collision between two largely monolithic worldviews. His survey of material covers a wide range of Italian primary texts and manuscript sources, and also provides a useful entry point into the substantial secondary literature in Italian on Galvani and his work.

Stepping back from the tradition of intellectual history, HEILBRON places Galvani's work in the social and institutional context of Bologna, where Galvani was raised, educated, and spent his entire professional life. In doing so, he describes the responsibilities and practices of Galvani's colleagues in Bologna, gives excerpts from the public lectures he was required to present, and provides other illuminating details concerning the influence of the university's evolving bureaucratic structure on the course of his career. Heilbron's account thus engages not simply what Galvani did or how he framed his theories, but where he learned his skills and how his research came to bear its particular methodological integration of exact anatomy combined with physical and chemical experimentation. While Heilbron leaves off at the point of Galvani's debate with Volta, where many other accounts largely begin, he offers a welcome complement to the other works described here, by providing an initial link between the animal electricity debate and its broader social history.

KARL GALLE

See also Electricity; Galvanic Battery; Volta

Galvanic Battery

Dibner, Bern, *Early Electrical Machines*, Norwalk,
    Connecticut: Burndy Library, 1957

Golinski, Jan, *Science as Public Culture: Chemistry and
    Enlightenment in Britain, 1760–1820*, Cambridge and
    New York: Cambridge University Press, 1992

Heilbron, J.L., *Electricity in the 17th and 18th Centuries:
    A Study of Early Modern Physics*, Berkeley: University of
    California Press, 1979

Mauro, Alexander, "The Role of the Voltaic Pile in the
    Galvani–Volta Controversy Concerning Animal vs.
    Metallic Electricity", *Journal of the History of Medicine*,
    24 (1969): 140–50

Ockenden, L., "The Great Batteries of the London
    Institution", *Annals of Science*, 2 (1937): 183–84

Pera, Marcello, *The Ambiguous Frog: The Galvani–Volta
    Controversy on Animal Electricity*, translated from the
    Italian by Jonathan Mandelbaum, Princeton, New Jersey:
    Princeton University Press, 1992 (original edition, 1986)

Schallenberg, Richard H., *Bottled Energy: Electrical
    Engineering and the Evolution of Chemical Energy
    Storage*, Philadelphia: American Philosophical Society,
    1982

Sudduth, William, "The Voltaic Pile and Electro-Chemical
    Theory in 1800", *Ambix*, 27 (1980): 26–35

Sutton, Geoffrey, "The Politics of Science in Early Napoleonic
    France: The Case of the Voltaic Pile", *Historical Studies in
    the Physical Sciences*, 11 (1981): 329–66

There is no substantial history on the galvanic battery; instead, information has to be gleaned from general histories of electricity, the debates over animal electricity, and accounts of early electrochemistry. Few studies pay much attention to the physical construction of the instrument, and terms such as "galvanic battery", "voltaic pile", and "galvanism" often seem to confuse different kinds of physical apparatus with theories of electricity or imponderable fluids. "Voltaic pile" and "galvanic apparatus", or "battery" sometimes appear to be used interchangeably, but it is worth noting that the "pile" generally refers to a single cell, while an apparatus that connects a number of these cells is referred to as a battery.

Mauro and Pera specifically examine the metaphysical and philosophical implications of the theories of electrical fluid, as drawn out in the conflict between Galvani and Volta concerning the visible contractions of a frog's leg, when nerves and muscles touch metal. Although incidental to the main theme of the rhetoric of the theoretical debate, PERA notes that one of the celebrated outcomes of this debate was the construction of the "Voltaic pile", which is the focus of one chapter. Throughout the book, the pile is considered as one among many types of electrical instruments, including Leyden jars, electrophores, conductors, and socks with static-cling. Nevertheless, despite the lack of concentration on the battery, Pera uses his account of the metaphysical issues implicit within the debate to illustrate the influence of theory on the uses of these instruments. MAURO, on the other hand, concentrates specifically on the theories that associated the phenomena of chemical electricity and animal electricity, while SUDDUTH briefly discusses the ways in which the chemical theory of

electricity (as caused through the contact between the metal plates of the Voltaic pile) affected pre-existing theories of the role of electricity in late 18th-century anti-phlogistic debates.

HEILBRON explores the changing relations between theories of electricity and physical science. In his ambitious history, he acknowledges that apparatus plays a role in the development of theories of electricity, although yet again batteries do not receive significant treatment. References to Galvani and galvanism are mentioned in relation to the debate with Volta, but are situated within the much larger context of physical and chemical theories of electricity. SCHALLENBERG examines technological developments in electrical generation in the 19th century, as well as the subsequent development of the storage battery and its affect on the 20th-century transportation industry. He discusses the technical aspects of electrochemical polarisation in the Voltaic pile, and the affects of placing electrodes in different solutions. By considering the structural variations of electrical instrumentation – through (galvanic) batteries, electromagnetic galvanometers, etc. – he traces some debates about the origins of chemical electromotive forces. DIBNER systematically examines the structural design of electrical apparatus over three centuries, and places a brief discussion of Volta's piles within a chronology of his other experiments, mainly his researches on electrostatics.

Schallenberg mentions in his study how, shortly after the introduction of the Voltaic pile into Britain about 1800, the electric current was itself a phenomenon for theoretical inquiry. Only after the concentrated efforts of a small group of experimentalists was the battery employed as a tool for analysis of other materials. Using historiographic models from the sociology of scientific knowledge, GOLINSKI considers the ways early 19th-century British natural philosophers attempted to make the galvanic battery an uncontroversial and unproblematic instrument for chemical researches, by close examination of the activities of Humphry Davy and his colleagues at the Royal Institution, where the battery became a famous centrepiece of the equipment in the new laboratory.

At about the time when Davy's public lectures, which demonstrated the powers of the battery, were becoming well-known to the British élite, researches on galvanism were increasingly being replicated elsewhere. OCKENDEN provides a brief physical description of the batteries constructed at the London Institution in the first half of the 19th century. Replication of galvanic experiments was in no way limited to Britain; as SUTTON points out, Napoleon heavily patronised researches in galvanism, providing ample funds with which Parisian natural philosophers attempted to construct the largest battery yet made during the 1810s. It quickly becomes apparent that further studies, which compare the pursuit of galvanic researches around Europe in the early 19th century, would be a welcome contribution to scholarship in the history of the physical sciences.

BRIAN DOLAN

See also Chemistry; Electrical Instruments; Electricity; Galvani; Volta

Gauss, Carl Friedrich 1777–1855

German mathematician, astronomer, and physicist

Bühler, W.K., *Gauss: A Biographical Study*, Berlin: Springer, 1981

Dunnington, Guy Waldo, *Carl Friedrich Gauss, Titan of Science: A Study of His Life and Work*, New York: Hafner, 1955

May, Kenneth O., entry in *Dictionary of Scientific Biography*, edited by Charles Coulston Gillispie, vol. 5, New York: Scribner, 1972

Merzbach, Uta C. (ed.), *Carl Friedrich Gauss: A Bibliography*, Wilmington, Delaware: Scholarly Resources, 1984

Peters, C.A.F. (ed.), *Briefwechsel zwischen C.F. Gauss und H.C. Schumacher*, 6 vols, Altona: Esch, 1860–65; reprinted in 3 vols, Hildesheim and New York: Olms, 1975

Reich, Karin, *Carl Friedrich Gauss, 1777–1977*, Munich: Moos, 1977

Sartorius von Waltershausen, W., *Gauss zum Gedächtniss*, Leipzig: Hirzel, 1856

Schering, Ernst, *Carl Friedrich Gauss Werke*, 12 vols in 14, Göttingen: Gesellschaft der Wissenschaften zu Göttingen, 1863–1933

Schilling, C., *Briefwechsel zwischen Olbers und Gauss – im Auftrage der Nachkommen*, 2 vols, Berlin: Springer, 1900–09 (part 2 of *Wilhelm Olbers: Sein Leben und Werke*)

von Auwers, G.F.J.A., *Briefwechsel zwischen Gauss und Bessel*, Leipzig: Engelmann, 1880 (compiled by the Prussian Akademie der Wissenschaften)

Carl Friedrich Gauss was a prolific polymath who served all his professional life at the University of Göttingen in the Kingdom of Hanover, now Germany. He has proved very influential in the fields of mathematics, astronomy, physics, geodesy, and surveying. Many of Gauss's manuscripts have been published and his collected works have been republished in an accessible form. However, despite the meticulous collation of primary sources, there have been only a few biographical studies. Given Gauss's continuing importance in the world of science and mathematics, this calls for an explanation: presumably it is because his work is highly technical and not accessible to anyone without at least university-level mathematics. However, Gauss's work also encompasses many activities with important social repercussions, such as his work in surveying and insurance mathematics. Some of the biographical studies present Gauss's work withsin a very narrow technical context, without attempting to set it in its social and institutional context. Writing a biography of Gauss clearly requires both technical skill and historical sophistication, and this might well explain the scarcity of biographies.

MAY's entry on Gauss in the *Dictionary of Scientific Biography* is the best place to start as, on some 16 pages, Gauss's various activities are presented. While these activities are dealt with sequentially, May makes up for this by providing an illustration showing the links between them. In this illustration, a field of activity is represented by a box, with arrows between the boxes, the size of which indicates the degree of linkage. There are six large boxes, representing the major fields of Gauss's work: empirical arithmetic, number theory, geodesy, analysis, geomagnetism, and astronomy. There are eight smaller boxes representing more marginal fields: insurance; probability and statistics; algebra, geometry, miscellaneous physics, electricity, capillarity, and dioptrics. In addition, the illustration includes some of the apparatus in the development of which Gauss had a hand: the photometer, telegraph, magnetometer, and heliotrope. It is this great diversity that has caused most of the research on Gauss to deal only with separate parts, rather than the whole, from a historical perspective.

There is a great deal of such literature. MERZBACH provides a 550-page bibliography including much information on such secondary sources, most of them focusing on only one aspect of Gauss's life or scientific work. However, Merzbach also provides information on primary sources and Gauss's correspondence, and she lists the locations where his manuscripts are held. More such short notices have appeared in the journal *Mitteilungen der Gauss-Gesellschaft*.

Most biographies rely to a great extent on SARTORIUS for details about Gauss's private life. Sartorius was an old friend, and his book is a paean to Gauss. He recounts many events and pronounces on a number of topics, such as Gauss's character, religious attitude, and his reasons for turning down jobs at other German universities.

DUNNINGTON is a compendium of personal information and received stories about Gauss. The personal information covers such topics as genealogy, friends, students, honours received, books borrowed, and courses given at the university. There is a large bibliography, but not as large as that of Merzbach.

For the celebration of the 200th anniversary of Gauss's birth, REICH wrote a short biography, which again dissects Gauss into mutually separate spheres. It is anecdotal and provides a smattering of the science. The book ends with a 23-page year-by-year timeline in the style of Werner Stein's *Kulturfahrplan*, juxtaposing in four columns events in Gauss's life with events in science and mathematics, in culture, and in politics. This timeline typifies the historiographical approach: juxtaposition replaces contextualisation. None the less, it is an accessible book with illustrations and a pleasing coffee-table format.

BÜHLER is the best scholarly biography. It describes the mathematics in quite some detail, but can still be read with profit by the non-mathematical reader. Bühler examines Gauss's work in the context of his jockeying for position in academia, and in the context of the absence of tables, slide rules, and other mathematical devices. Bühler is also concerned to locate the connections between the diverse fields. He gives many examples: he describes the close connection between pure mathematics and the calculations for the perturbations of Ceres, the largest known asteroid in the solar system; he notes Gauss's pleasure in finding the arithmetico–geometric mean (pure sophisticated mathematics) in the perturbations of Pallas, the second largest known asteroid; and he shows the direct relationship between the method of least squares (Gauss's principal tool for the reduction of his geodetic observations) and conformal mapping (the theoretical fruit of his efforts). Within the context of Gauss's work on weights and measures and on standards for the measurement of terrestrial magnetism, Bühler notes that Gauss seems to have preferred non-Euclidean geometry, because of the existence of an absolute length in non-Euclidean systems.

As mentioned, the bulk of the literature is concerned with the publishing and republishing of primary and secondary material. The 12-volume SCHERING contains the collected works. The original concept was to publish the works in volumes containing separate topics, in conformance with much of the historiography in evidence. However, it turned out not to be possible to pursue this design consistently, which led to several supplementary volumes.

The various volumes of the correspondence were edited without a general plan. Only the correspondence with Friedrich Wilhelm Bessel (VON AUWERS) contains a reliable and useful index. This, SCHILLING (correspondence with Wilhelm Olbers), and PETERS (correspondence with Heinrich Christian Schumacher) all project a vivid picture of the difficulties with which Gauss had to contend when surveying in the field, and all three books allow the reader to see in detail how the correspondents treat issues of, for instance, mathematics, astronomy, and practical surveying as of a piece. It should be mentioned that Gauss's correspondence with other individuals (Alexander von Humboldt, Wolfgang Bolyai, Christian Ludwig Gerling, Sophie Germain, B. Nicolai) has also been published, but it is not as voluminous and so is not discussed in this entry.

ARNE HESSENBRUCH

See also Geometry; Number Theory; Probability

Gay-Lussac, Joseph Louis 1778–1850

French chemist and physicist

Arago, Dominique François Jean, "Gay-Lussac", in *Oeuvres*, 17 vols, Paris, 1854–62; (*Notices biographiques*, vol. 3, 1–112)

Biot, Jean-Baptiste, "Notice sur Gay-Lussac", *Mélanges scientifiques et littéraires*, vol. 3, Paris, 1858, 125–42

Blanc, Edmond and Léon Delhoume, *La Vie émouvante et noble de Gay-Lussac*, Paris: Gauthier-Villars, 1950

Coyac, J., *et al.* (eds), *Gay Lussac: La Carrière et l'oeuvre d'un chimiste français durant la première moitié du XIXe siècle*, Palaiseau: École Polytechnique, 1980

Crosland, Maurice P., *The Society of Arcueil: A View of French Science at the Time of Napoleon I*, London: Heinemann, and Cambridge, Massachusetts: Harvard University Press, 1967

Crosland, Maurice P., *Gay-Lussac, Scientist and Bourgeois*, Cambridge and New York: Cambridge University Press, 1978

The first two substantial biographical treatments of the life and work of Gay-Lussac were written for major scientific institutions by former fellow-students at the École Polytechnique, who had also been fellow-members of the Society of Arcueil and of the Académie des Sciences. BIOT, as a physicist commissioned by the Royal Society of London, emphasised the contribution of his friend to that science – for example, describing Gay-Lussac's study of the thermal expansion of gases, which produced the misleadingly named "Charles law". Biot also discussed the rivalry between Gay-Lussac and Davy.

The second biographer, ARAGO, as both a close friend of Gay-Lussac and secretary of the Académie des Sciences, delivered the éloge. Admitting that the chemist was known for his cold reserve, Arago, by way of contrast, recounted several youthful exploits of his friend. A key event in Gay-Lussac's life was Berthollet's decision to take the young graduate under his wing, and Arago emphasised his courage in undertaking two major balloon ascents to acquire meteorological and magnetic data, while as a laboratory scientist he had been involved in several serious accidents when his apparatus had exploded. Arago was also concerned to emphasise Gay-Lussac's scrupulous honesty, claiming that "he honoured France by his moral qualities". Gay-Lussac had engaged in collaboration with several contemporaries, notably Humboldt and Thenard, and Arago summed up his relative contributions to the respective sciences of physics and chemistry by describing him as "physicien ingénieux, chimiste hors de ligne".

The 19th-century eulogies by Gay-Lussac's contemporaries were followed by a considerable period of neglect, which only ended with the centenary of the scientist's death in 1950. This provided an opportunity for BLANC & DELHOUME, two local historians from the Limousin, the birth place of Gay-Lussac, to produce a full-length biography. The title of the book betrays the authors's motivation, and the French historian of science, Maurice Daumas, wrote scathingly of the work, suggesting that pious intentions were not enough. Lacking confidence in their own abilities, Blanc & Delhoume reproduced extensive extracts from other works, notably Arago's éloge, and, while giving full attention to their subject's political life, quoted liberally from the parliamentary record. A bonus, however, is the inclusion of the text of a number of letters.

It was partly as a reaction to this local study that CROSLAND (1978) set out to provide an integrated interpretation of the life and work of Gay-Lussac, based on manuscript sources found in family papers and in the archives of the many institutions to which he had belonged. Crosland claims that Gay-Lussac belonged to the first generation of young men able to profit from the free scientific education made available as a by-product of the revolution. He passed an entrance exam to enter the École Polytechnique, where he studied chemistry, physics and mathematics, and, on graduation, worked as an assistant to Berthollet and was soon appointed as professor at his old school. Other academic appointments followed, as well as consultancy work. Thus Gay-Lussac is presented as an early professional scientist who, having been trained in science, was able to make science his career. This provides a contrast with the previous generation, one of whom, the great chemist Lavoisier, earned his living as a tax collector, and practised science only in his spare time.

The book makes much of the rivalry between Gay-Lussac and his contemporary, Davy. Both were interested in isolating new elements, and both were working on chlorine and iodine at around the same time. Gay-Lussac suspected that chlorine could not be decomposed, but submitted to the authority of Berthollet in not staking a claim, thus leaving Davy with the credit for having discovered it as an element. Also, Gay-Lussac was affected by the French spirit of positivism *avant la lettre*, which hesitated to draw bold conclusions from the accumulation of experimental evidence. The exception to this generalisation is his obsession with discovering regularities that he could claim as laws of nature: e.g., his law of combining volumes of gases.

The inclusion of the word "bourgeois" in the title of Crosland (1978) was intended to place Gay-Lussac within his social context. In his later life, he attained wealth and social position, much of his income relating to his work on applied rather than pure science, to the embarrassment of several biographers. Arago was particularly keen to defend his friend against the accusation that he had betrayed the true cause of science for financial gain, while BIOT excused him on the grounds that he had to provide for a large family. However, there was also a social context for Gay-Lussac's pure science, as a member of the Society of Arcueil and later of the Académie des Sciences. CROSLAND (1967) argues the importance of patronage in his career through his "adoption" by Berthollet, who had bought a house at Arcueil, just outside Paris. Gay-Lussac profited greatly from the patronage of the senior and well-connected Berthollet, and also, by association, with younger members of the Society of Arcueil, with whom he collaborated, both informally and formally.

Finally, on the occasion of the bicentenary of Gay-Lussac's birth, an international colloquium was held in Paris in 1978. Published in COYAC et al., the papers cover his physics (adiabatic expansion of gases), and his contributions to volumetric analysis.

MAURICE CROSLAND

See also Berthollet; Davy

Gender: general works

Bacus, Elisabeth A., Alex W. Barker and Jeffrey D. Bonevich (eds), *A Gendered Past: A Critical Biography of Gender in Archaeology*, Ann Arbor: University of Michigan Museum of Anthropology, 1993

Barad, Karen, "A Feminist Approach to Teaching Quantum Physics", in *Teaching the Majority: Breaking the Gender Barrier in Science, Mathematics, and Engineering*, edited by Sue V. Rosser, New York: Teacher's College Press, 1995

Biology and Gender Study Group, "The Importance of Feminist Critique for Contemporary Cell Biology", in *Feminism and Science*, edited by Nancy Tuana, Bloomington: Indiana University Press, 1989, 172–87

Dohm, Hedwig, *Die wissenschaftliche Emancipation der Frauen*, Berlin, 1874

Erikksson, I.V, B.A. Kitchenahm and K.G. Tijdens (eds), *Women, Work, and Computerization: Understanding and Overcoming Bias in Work and Education*, Amsterdam: North-Holland, and New York: Elsevier, 1991

Fedigan, Linda, "Is Primatology a Feminist Science?", in *Women in Human Evolution*, edited by Lori D. Hager, New York and London: Routledge, 1997

Gero, Joan M. and Margaret W. Conkey, *Engendering Archaeology: Women and Prehistory*, Oxford and Cambridge, Massachusetts: Blackwell, 1991

Haraway, Donna J., *Primate Visions: Gender, Race, and Nature in the World of Modern Science*, New York and London: Routledge, 1989

Haraway, Donna J., "Situated Knowledges: The Science Question in Feminism and the Privilege of Partial Perspective", in her *Simians, Cyborgs, and Women: The Reinvention of Nature*, London: Free Association, 1990; New York: Routledge, 1991

Harding, Sandra, *The Science Question in Feminism*, Ithaca, New York: Cornell University Press, 1986

Harding, Sandra, *Whose Science? Whose Knowledge? Thinking from Women's Lives*, Ithaca, New York: Cornell University Press, and Milton Keynes, Buckinghamshire: Open University Press, 1991

Hubbard, Ruth, *Profitable Promises: Essays on Women, Science and Health*, Monroe, Maine: Common Courage Press, 1994

Keller, Evelyn Fox, *Reflections on Gender and Science*, New Haven, Connecticut: Yale University Press, 1985

Keller, Evelyn Fox, *Secrets of Life, Secrets of Death: Essays on Language, Gender and Science*, New York: Routledge, 1992

Longino, Helen, "Can There Be a Feminist Science?", in *Feminism and Science*, edited by Nancy Tuana, Bloomington: Indiana University Press, 1989, 45–57

Martin, Emily, "The Egg and the Sperm: How Science has Constructed a Romance Based on Stereotypical Male-Female Roles", *Signs: Journal of Women in Culture and Society*, 16/3 (1991): 485–501

Mastroianni, Anna, Ruth Faden and Daniel Federman (eds), *Women and Health Research: Ethical and Legal Issues of Including Women in Clinical Studies*, vol. 2, Washington, DC: National Academy Press, 1994

Maurer, Margarete, *Frauenforschung in Naturwissenschaften, Technik und Medizin*, Vienna: Wiener Frauenverlag, 1993

Merchant, Carolyn, *The Death of Nature: Women, Ecology, and the Scientific Revolution*, New York: Harper and Row, 1980

Merchant, Carolyn, *Earthcare: Women and the Environment*, New York: Routledge, 1996

Schiebinger, Londa, *Nature's Body: Gender in the Making of Modern Science*, Boston: Beacon Press, 1993

Schiebinger, Londa, "Creating Sustainable Science", in *Women, Gender, and Science*, edited by Sally Gregory Kohlstedt and Helen Longino, Chicago: University of Chicago Press, 1997

Spanier, Bonnie B., *Im/partial Science: Gender Ideology in Molecular Biology*, Bloomington: Indiana University Press, 1995

Wylie, Alison et al., "Philosophical Feminism: A Bibliographic Guide to Critiques of Science", *Resources for Feminist Research/Documentation sur la Recherche Feministe*, 19/2 (1990): 2–36

The study of gender in science is very old, stretching back at least to Christine de Pizan's *The Book of the City of Ladies* (written in 1405), in which she surveyed women's original contributions to the arts and sciences. Through the centuries, feminists such as François Poullain de la Barre, Anna van Schurman, Dorothea Leporinin Erxleben, Antoinette Blackwell, and Charlotte Perkins Gilman often employed scientific arguments in their efforts to open universities to women. At the end of the 19th century, the German author DOHM presented a strikingly modern critique of the biological determinists Rudolf Virchow and Theodor von Bischoff, who argued that something in women's physical or intellectual nature prohibited them from producing great science. However, despite scattered interest in the question of gender and science over the centuries, it did not become part of the modern discipline of the history of science founded in the 1920s and 1930s. Since the 1970s, however, interest in gender in science has grown by leaps and bounds. Bibliographies include WYLIE *et al.*, which focuses on questions of methodology and epistemology within the English-speaking realm, and MAURER, which provides an analytical guide to both English and German sources.

Research on gender in science breaks down into several areas – the history of women in science, the analysis of sexual science, and the study and remediation of substantive epistemic gender bias. The last is treated in this entry.

Gender analysis of science in the 1980s centered on critiques of objectivity, the association of women with nature, and the question of producing a feminist science. KELLER (1985), using object-relations theory, argued that defining traits of modern Western science, such as objectivity and reason, are not gender neutral, but are directly associated with Western masculinity. She also revealed how conceptual dualities (subject/object, fact/value, masculine/feminine) have tended to exclude women and their interests from science. MERCHANT (1980) discussed the historical gendering of nature as female. Her analysis of the scientific revolution showed how Europeans abandoned the ancient personification of an organic, feminine Nature, and adopted instead an image of nature as inorganic and mechanized, an image that lifted many traditional ethical restraints on its exploitation. Despite the shift in representations of nature, conventional associations between nature and women have persisted, in both the work of many traditional scientists and essentialist strains of ecofeminism. Taking up the controversy surrounding the possibility of creating a feminist science, LONGINO refuted the notion that women carry with them the seeds of an alternative epistemology (often envisioned as built on traditionally feminine qualities, such as caring, cooperation, holism, and so forth), arguing instead for a "process-based" methodology that would allow for the evaluation of feminist values as constituents of scientific theories and practices.

Feminist science theory is as extensive as science theory and feminist theory combined. HARDING (1986) laid out the distinctions between essentialism, liberalism, stand-point theory, poststructuralism, and postmodernism in gender studies of science. Liberal feminism, still the dominant form of feminism within European and North American sciences, regards women as intellectually and physically the potential equals of men, and strives to help women realize that potential through education and special intervention programs. Difference feminism, including its more Marxist manifestation in stand-point theory, diverges from liberalism in emphasizing gender distinctions, not sameness, between men and women. (It differs from essentialism in seeing these differences as not inborn and hardwired, but instilled by culture and hence subject to change). Both liberalism and difference feminism have undergone exten-

sive critiques from postmodernists, who argue that sexual difference is not the only politically potent fault plane, and that race, class, ethnicities, sexual preference, etc. complicate prematurely reified categories. Postmodernists, while theoretically astute, have been criticized, in turn, for presenting little positive vision for political innovation. More recent developments in feminist science theory have emphasized gender as one analytic among many, required for creating socially and environmentally responsible science. These include agential realism (BARAD), resolute objectivity (HARDING, 1991), situated knowledge (HARAWAY, 1990), partnership ethics (MERCHANT, 1996), and sustainable science (SCHIEBINGER, 1997).

In the late 1980s and 1990s, historians began moving beyond what many saw as overly general theories and notions, to develop fine-grained analyses of gender dynamics in specific scientific discoveries, theories, nomenclatures, instruments, techniques, and objects of science, thus demonstrating in precise ways how gender relations inform science. The majority of this work has been in the life and behavioral sciences, where research objects are sexed, or easily imagined to have sex and gender. The Swarthmore College BIOLOGY AND GENDER STUDY GROUP and MARTIN, for example, have analyzed how biologists have rewritten the story of human conception. The classical "passive" egg is no longer seen as drifting aimlessly along the fallopian tube until captured by the heroic, active sperm, but portrayed as an active agent, directing the growth of microvilli (small finger-like projections on its surface) that tether the sperm, and releasing digestive enzymes that allow a sperm to enter it. Martin discusses the ensuing problems of the regendered egg and sperm which, now in tune with more current gender stereotypes, are often portrayed as "partners" – much like a dual-career couple – working together toward successful fertilization. SPANIER, in her work on microbiology, discusses how the gendering of the cell nucleus (as masculine) and the cytoplasm (as feminine or maternal) accounts at least in part for the late discovery of mitochondrial DNA. SCHIEBINGER (1993) discusses 18th-century natural history, developing case studies that focus on the sexing and gendering of plants, the origin of the intersecting categories of sex and race in anthropology, and the gender inequalities embedded in Linnaean botanical taxonomies and the coining of the taxon, Mammalia. KELLER (1992) reveals how in the 20th century the masculine-identified public sphere and the feminine-identified private sphere have structured important aspects of population genetics and mathematical ecology. She argues that geneticists' notions of individualism have led them to treat reproduction as if individuals simply reproduce themselves, effectively bypassing the complexities entailed in sexual difference, the contingencies of mating, and fertilization. Keller likens the biologists' atomic individual to the heuristic individual portrayed by mainstream Western political and economic theorists – both are "simultaneously divested of sex and invested with the attributes of the 'universal man' (as if equality can prevail only in the absence of sexual differentiation)". Feminists have also criticized molecular biology for its reductionistic treatment of living organisms, converging on James Watson's "master molecules" (his own term) and his notion that understanding the gene and its sequences are the ultimate goal of biology. HUBBARD argues that the "geneticization" of North America – currently driving the costly Human Genome Project – actually threatens health, by diverting attention and resources from the poverty and malnutrition afflicting much of the world's population.

It is not only in the life and behavioral sciences that fine-grained analyses of gender dynamics have been developed. In archaeology, GERO & CONKEY have shown how gender inequalities in intellectual authority have played a role in determining what counts as archaeological evidence. Stone tools and bone fossils figure among the most highly-prized data for archaeologists, in a way that has associated males and male activities with human evolution. BACUS, BARKER & BONEVICH annotated bibliography provides a thorough guide to the gender critique of archaeology. In computer science, North American literature has emphasized cognitive and social differences between, for example, boys' and girls' learning styles and interests, access to machines, and the gendered culture of computing, while Scandinavian literature (ERIKKSSON et al.) explores how computer applications can be designed to break down traditional divisions of labor. In the environmental sciences, MERCHANT (1996) has drawn fine distinctions between liberal, cultural, social, and socialist ecofeminism, and offers a comparative study of feminist environmental initiatives within three political contexts: Sweden, the United States, and Australia.

The negative program for gender scholars is the study of bias in the structure and substance of science, but gender critique can also open doors to new fields of inquiry, new questions, projects, and insights in history and also in science – and thus to a more positive program. Historians of gender in science not only cultivate an appreciation of the sciences, but often seek to change them.

The feminist ferment of the past decade has in many instances reshaped what is known and knowable: the simple process of taking feminists (men and women) seriously as makers of knowledge, and a far greater inclusion of females as subjects of research, has had a tremendous impact on the methods, manners, and priorities in many of the sciences. Two leading examples of how gender analysis has contributed to creating new knowledge are found in the bio-medical sciences and primatology. MASTROIANNI et al., provide a collection of essays that show how the combined efforts of academic analysts, lobbyists, doctors, and government leaders led to the Women's Health Initiative, and the founding of the US National Institutes of Health's Office of Women's Health Research. Fundamental insights from the feminist critique of medicine have informed new research and new policies. In primatology, FEDIGAN, extending HARAWAY's (1989) broad cultural history, argues that primatology, as it is currently practised, is a feminist science. While this may be overstated, primatologists, perhaps more than practitioners in other fields of science, have incorporated gender history and analysis into their discipline. As empirically-grounded and theoretically-informed gender analysis proceeds, historians will continue to give more attention to how inquiry into gender dynamics is changing science theory and practice.

LONDA SCHIEBINGER

Gender and Identity

Benjamin, Marina (ed.), *A Question of Identity: Women, Science and Literature*, New Brunswick, New Jersey: Rutgers University Press, 1993

Butler, Judith, *Gender Trouble: Feminism and the Subversion of Identity*, New York: Routledge, 1990

Carnes, Mark C. and Clyde Griffen (eds), *Meanings for Manhood: Constructions of Masculinity in Victorian America*, Chicago: University of Chicago Press, 1990

Foucault, Michel, *The Use of Pleasure*, vol. 2 of *The History of Sexuality*, translated from the French by Robert Hurley, New York: Pantheon Books, 1985 (original edition, 3 vols, 1976–84)

Greenblatt, Stephen, *Renaissance Self-Fashioning: From More to Shakespeare*, Chicago: University of Chicago Press, 1980

Haraway, Donna J., *Simians, Cyborgs, and Women: The Reinvention of Nature*, London: Free Association Press, 1990; New York: Routledge, 1991

Irigaray, Luce, *Speculum of the Other Woman*, translated from the French by Gillian C. Gill, Ithaca, New York: Cornell University Press, 1985 (original edition, 1974)

Jacobus, Mary, Evelyn Fox Keller and Sally Shuttleworth (eds), *Body/Politics: Women and the Discourses of Science*, New York: Routledge, 1990

Mangan, J.A., and James Walvin (eds), *Manliness and Morality: Middle-Class Masculinity in Britain and America, 1800–1940*, Manchester: Manchester University Press, and New York: St Martin's Press, 1987

Poovey, Mary, *Uneven Developments: The Ideological Work of Gender in Mid-Victorian England*, Chicago: University of Chicago Press, 1988; London: Virago, 1990

Roper, Michael and John Tosh (eds), *Manful Assertions: Masculinities in Britain since 1800*, London and New York: Routledge, 1991

Scott, Joan Wallach, *Gender and the Politics of History*, New York: Columbia University Press, 1988

Showalter, Elaine, *The Female Malady: Women, Madness and English Culture, 1830–1980*, New York: Pantheon, 1985; London: Virago, 1987

Resources for constructing accounts of gender and identity are wide-ranging and still under-utilized in science studies. These categories have been employed most powerfully, on the one hand, by feminist philosophers in order to critique masculine ways of knowing and coercing nature, and on the other hand, by historians seeking to recover the contributions of women to a male-dominated profession. Much feminist criticism of the sciences has drawn on psychoanalytic accounts of knowledge and power, of a kind that feature prominently in French feminist writings. In IRIGARAY, thought and language appear as bi-polar, hierarchical structures characteristic of Western patriarchy since Plato, in which women function as the primordial object of knowledge for the male subject. The author follows Lacan in viewing the development of the child as a process in which libidinal drives are suppressed, and a direct, emotive relation with the mother replaced by representational thought; the voice of the mother is effectively silenced through the production of language by the independent self. Thus women exist only as nurturing foundations for male subjectivity, and can never be knowing subjects themselves, unless the entire masculine system of representation that has fetishized them is overturned – a task taken up by Irigaray's own style of radical (un)writing.

Similarly, many of the articles in JACOBUS, KELLER & SHUTTLEWORTH present the sciences as projections of a masculine sexual identity, continually subverted by female desire. Thus while the sciences and technologies of diet, fitness, pharmaceuticals and cosmetic surgery seek to normalize women's bodies, male practitioners, driven by womb envy and castration anxiety, endeavour to define, contain, and ultimately usurp the maternal function – an enterprise resisted by the ineffable forces of female procreativity and motherhood. In SHOWALTER, modern psychiatry is likewise approached as an apparatus of bourgeois patriarchy, shaping the identity of women as the subordinate complements of men, while enabling scientific practitioners to play the role of hero, healer, and conqueror of the asocial passions and disorders of wild femininity. But if women were forced into categories of insanity, madness, and illness when they failed to conform to male-prescribed models, some varieties of female hysteria are also treated as genuine forms of protest in a society with few possibilities for resistance to gender norms.

While such studies seem to rely on, or to construct, stable identities for women and men, others view identity as the result of negotiations that are always ongoing. BUTLER rejects modern feminism's search for an authentic woman's voice, by posing identity as a transient, performative act. Casting off the model of the unitary subject, the author shows how categories like sex, the body and desire, which often serve as the fixed substratum of gender in feminist writings, are in fact normative ideals that create the illusion of a natural basis for identity. HARAWAY also expresses this postmodern version of the proliferating, contradictory self, via a thorough critique of naturalistic accounts of the human subject in contemporary science and literature. From women's primatology and science fiction, the author extracts figures such as the ape and cyborg, which trouble the boundaries between nature and culture, human and machine. Such entities are recruited to a new ontology, and politics envisioned as lying beyond racist, sexist and capitalist traditions that appropriate nature for the production of culture, or reproduce the self from reflections of the other.

In the introduction to BENJAMIN, the editor notes the tendency of feminist accounts, despite their proliferation, to remain isolated from other critical inquiries into the history of science. But if much recent sociology of science has failed to consider the intimate connection between gender and knowledge production highlighted by feminist critics, the essays that follow, exploring the great diversity and fluidity of masculinist scientific constructions of women in travel literature, medicine, discourses on luxury, population, and happiness, suggest ways of introducing gender analysis into the history of science mainstream. Here, the more systematic efforts of Poovey and Scott, in the fields of social and political history, are particularly relevant. Through a series of case studies, including childbirth under chloroform and divorce law, POOVEY argues that the same ideology that trivialized or demonized sexual desire in women also served to depoliticize class relations, limit competition, and provide emotional access to the elusive opportunities of an expanding capitalist empire. In SCOTT, too, gender operates not merely within the confines of private life, but at every level of social existence, underpinning the functioning of state, empire, class, and labour. This well-known account challenged the tradition of social history, in which gender identity was an objective category of historical existence, creating different needs and experiences, which in turn validated the exclusion of women from historical narratives, such as the rise of civilization.

Sophisticated historical accounts, which show the negotiated, temporal process of building gender identity and scientific knowledge, and the crucial role of this process in the fabrication of a more general culture, remain almost exclusively focused on women. In effect, the very force of feminist critiques of masculinity as an omnipresent oppressive structure have tended to obviate historical inquiries into the social construction of masculinity, while the rich field afforded by women in science has served to reinforce the view of gender identity as a problem faced primarily by women. This breach, still virtually unacknowledged in the history of science, has been noted by scholars in other fields, most of whose inquiries have been directed toward forms of masculine identity that lie on the margins of the heterosexist culture attacked by feminist writings. But public school rituals, youth organizations, adventure literature, and blood sports have provided the authors in MANGAN & WALVIN with rich materials for rewriting the history of British imperial expansion and home rule as manifestations of predominant masculine traditions. Similarly, the essays in CARNES & GRIFFEN explore Victorian fraternal institutions, where ritual enactments of ancient patriarchy provided relief from the psychic pressures of capitalism, and a release from the maternal nurture and sentimental ideals of the home. The collection edited by ROPER & TOSH differs from these accounts, in exhibiting the fragility of masculinity alongside its function as a foundation of men's dominion in the home, workplace, and politics. Thus men appear as both oppressors and oppressed, besieged by fantasies of a power that is never possessed, but must be continuously reasserted.

Though not explicitly styled as gender studies, several works on self-fashioning show the elaborate social work involved in adopting and reshaping a masculine identity, which is every bit as complex and contingent a cultural form as femininity. In FOUCAULT, the history of sexuality is approached not in the manner of the author's previous works – as a set of oppressive practices and interdictions – but rather as a mode by which individuals make themselves into works of art and vehicles for truth. The patriarchal power play enacted in the body, marriage, homosocial relations, and elaborate codes of vigilance, is staged as a process of sexual self-construction among the male elites of ancient Greece and Rome. GREENBLATT likewise shows the ways in which self-mastery and the power to shape others are integrated, effectively recasting accounts of the state, of the family, and of religious institutions as narratives of self-formation. Here, a history is also offered of the kind of bi-polar identity structure depicted and denounced in Irigaray and Butler; for Renaissance self-fashioning always unfolds in relation to a perceived other, who, as a bastion of evil, ignorance or deceit, must be repeatedly reinvented along with the self, and whose destruction entails a loss of self.

Frankly presentist and highly reflexive, many of the works assembled here raise questions regarding the function of history in shaping the present – a political drama unfolding within the authors themselves, who present their own identities as under construction. In Scott, a historian of women comes to terms with post-structuralism, and struggles to bind feminist politics with academic gender studies. In Haraway, the narrative describes how an unmarked, socialist, feminist biologist becomes a white, Euro-American, middle-class woman professional, defending multiculturalism from its enemies. Foucault writes a history of the self that is also an exercise of the self; for, as Greenblatt maintains, the questions we ask of our material are guided by the questions we ask ourselves.

PAUL WHITE

Gender and Sex

Bleier, Ruth, *Science and Gender: A Critique of Biology and Its Theories on Women*, New York: Pergamon Press, 1984

Cadden, Joan, *Meanings of Sex Difference in the Middle Ages: Medicine, Science, and Culture*, New York and Cambridge: Cambridge University Press, 1993

Dreger, Alice Domurat, *Hermaphrodites and the Medical Invention of Sex*, Cambridge, Massachusetts and London: Harvard University Press, 1998

Fausto-Sterling, Anne, *Myths of Gender: Biological Theories about Women and Men*, New York: Basic Books, 1985; 2nd edition, 1992

Fee, Elizabeth, "Nineteenth Century Craniology: The Study of the Female Skull", *Bulletin of the History of Medicine*, 53 (1979): 415–33

Gilman, Sander L., *Sexuality: An Illustrated History: Representing the Sexual in Medicine and Culture from the Middle Ages to the Age of AIDS*, New York: Wiley, 1989

Gould, Stephen Jay, *The Mismeasure of Man*, New York: Norton, 1981; revised edition, 1996

Laqueur, Thomas, *Making Sex: Body and Gender from the Greeks to Freud*, Cambridge, Massachusetts: Harvard University Press, 1990

Moscucci, Ornella, *The Science of Woman: Gynaecology and Gender in England, 1800–1929*, Cambridge and New York: Cambridge University Press, 1990

Nye, Robert A., *Masculinity and Male Codes of Honor in Modern France*, New York and Oxford: Oxford University Press, 1993

Oudshoorn, Nelly, *Beyond the Natural Body: An Archeology of Sex Hormones*, London and New York: Routledge, 1994

Russett, Cynthia Eagle, *Sexual Science: The Victorian Construction of Womanhood*, Cambridge, Massachusetts: Harvard University Press, 1989

Schiebinger, Londa, *The Mind Has No Sex? Women in the Origins of Modern Science*, Cambridge, Massachusetts: Harvard University Press, 1989

Schiebinger, Londa, *Nature's Body: Gender in the Making of Modern Science*, Boston: Beacon Press, 1993

Terry, Jennifer and Jacqueline Urla (eds), *Deviant Bodies: Critical Perspectives on Difference in Science and Popular Culture*, Bloomington: Indiana University Press, 1995

Since the 1970s, historians have focused attention on the role played by science and medicine in defining sex and gender differences. Scholars have begun to reveal the politics of gendered bodies; the ways in which cultural restrictions have been inscribed into, or effaced from, seemingly stable and ahistorical bodies. The process is often concurrent with, or even dependent on, the growth of ideals of objectivity that have tended to routinize and idealize body types. Until recently, there have been two poles in this debate: nurture, that perceived sexual differences as the product of history, and therefore of socialization; and nature, that something in the physical, psychological, and intellectual nature of women prohibits them from producing great arts and sciences. The distinction is significant: if gender roles or personality traits are rooted in the body, traceable ultimately to congenital or genetic factors, it is easier to argue that the predominant division in privilege between the sexes is natural, and that efforts to transform social relations between men and women are misconceived or foolhardy. If, by contrast, gender roles are rooted in culture, they are malleable and can be changed. More recently, scholars, of varying political stripes, have begun to emphasize the dialectic between biology and culture. In this area three categories of analysis are commonly distinguished: sex (distinctly male or female anatomy and physiology); gender (self or social identification); and sexuality (sexual desires or acts).

Historians of science have been particularly interested in how scientific characterizations of sex and gender have contributed to the historical exclusion of women from science, documenting how concepts of sex and gender change with shifting social circumstances. CADDEN and others have traced "sexual science" back as far as Aristotle, who argued, among other things, that woman is colder and weaker than man, and that woman – an incomplete and "monstrous" version of man – does not generate the heat necessary to "cook" the blood, and thus purify the soul. In her study of the meanings of sex difference in the Middle Ages, Cadden also analyzes the ways in which thinkers such as Hildegard of Bingen and Constantine the African discuss sex determination of the embryo, pleasure, sexuality, and so forth.

SCHIEBINGER (1989) shows how these types of argument were given empirical foundations in the 17th and 18th centuries, with "the scientific revolution in views of sexual difference". In a study of the first European anatomical illustrations of female skeletons, she reveals how anatomical illustrators self-consciously sought to capture the essence of femininity and masculinity, through models that were chosen to represent both contemporary ideals and classic representations of female and male forms. She argues further that these languid ladies of bone came to life only in the heat of Enlightenment debates over the "woman question" (i.e. whether or not women were physically and intellectually capable of becoming fully enfranchised citizens). FEE and in greater detail GOULD trace how, in the 18th and 19th centuries, craniometrists accounted for alleged sexual differences in intellectual achievement by measuring skulls. (Anatomists assumed that the larger male skulls were loaded with heavier and more highly-powered brains.)

Russett and Moscucci have explored the complex and powerful Victorian construction of womanhood. RUSSETT provides a close reading of Victorian ideals of women's brains and beauty, and delineates how women were cut to fit sexist theories of evolution, intelligence, and the conservation of energy. Mid-Victorian social Darwinists, for example, invoked evolutionary biology to argue that woman was a man whose evolution – both physical and mental – had been arrested in a primitive state. MOSCUCCI, in her study of the rise of gynaecology in England, shows how the politics of professionalization meshed with sexual politics to create a "science of woman", and a market for that science.

Fausto-Sterling and Bleier discuss recent controversies over sex differences. BLEIER explores scientific theories of sex-specific brain lateralization, and of the evolution of "man the hunter", and shows that the alleged evidence for these theories can be questioned or reinterpreted. FAUSTO-STERLING similarly analyses studies that purport to show evidence for genetic sex differences in IQ, and studies that portray women and men as slaves to their "hormonal hurricanes". Both Fausto-Sterling and Bleier highlight the general neglect of issues of learning and culture in sex-difference research. They demonstrate that contemporary studies of sexual differences are often not profoundly different from those by Aristotle and others, in that they again seek to provide scientific justification for enduring divisions in power and privilege between the sexes.

Many historians go beyond showing how "gendered" traits have been attributed to sex, to demonstrate that important aspects of sex (i.e. anatomy and physiology) are also constructed. LAQUEUR argues, in his study of the "making of sex", that if gender is constructed, at some level so too must be sex, for "almost everything one wants to say about sex – however sex is understood – already has in it a claim about gender. Sex . . . is explicable only within the context of battles over gender and power". In this survey of the history of sex, Laqueur identifies a foundational paradigm shift, one in which an older, Galenic "one sex" model, (in which female sexual organs were conceived as essentially the same, but merely a less perfect versions of men's), gave way in the 18th century to a "two sex" model of radical biological divergence between men and women. For the "one sex" model, Laqueur offers as evidence the fact that in the early modern period the word "testes" applied to the gonads of both sexes, and that Vesalius's drawing of a vagina closely resembles his drawing of a penis. Laqueur uses the works of Freud and others for illustrations of the two-sex model. Cadden and others, however, have argued that the historical record is more complex than Laqueur suggests, and that multiple models of sexuality occur in most historical periods.

In the same way that the 165-pound white male body has long served as the "gold standard" for mainstream biological sciences, the middle-class white female body has dominated gender studies of science. Historians have paid relatively little attention to scientific accounts of manhood. This imbalance is due in part to the interest among feminist scholars in women's history; "men's studies" is a relatively new field, and scholars are just now beginning to recover the history of masculinity. NYE has provided a detailed account of the construction of masculinity in modern France, and the role of science and medicine in that construction. Nye and others (e.g., Dreger, Schiebinger (1993), Oudshoorn, Bleier, Terry & Urla) have also demonstrated that scientific concepts of the "true nature" of the sexes have been largely dependent on the assumption that heterosexuality is the natural form of sexuality.

Race is also being newly theorized in relation to sex. GILMAN has discussed how black females (and by various degrees of skin hue, other non-European women) did not fit the much-touted ideals of European womanhood. Gould, Russett, SCHIEBINGER (1993), and others, have also shown how, in the United States and Europe, certain scientific ideas about masculine and feminine "natures" depended on and bolstered contemporary assumptions about "race" and "natural" hierarchies.

Several recent studies have focused on anatomically "deviant" bodies, and their treatment in science and medicine. These studies have sought to determine the origin and uses of concepts of "normal" sex. In an examination of the biomedical treatment of hermaphrodites, for instance, DREGER has shown how biomedical technologies (conceptual and surgical) have been deployed to bring apparently anomalous bodies into line with received views of sex; "deviant" bodies are thereby employed to strengthen paradigms they might otherwise threaten. Similarly, OUDSHOORN has shown, through her "archeology of sex hormones", how endocrinology has been used to construct (conceptually and chemically) "naturalized" female and male bodies. TERRY & URLA provide useful insight into how science and popular culture can function as co-workers in the construction of "normal" and "deviant" sex and sexuality.

Today, in the heat of the Women's Health Initiative, grave concerns have been raised about inadequate knowledge of the female body. There is, however, a certain irony in this regard. Scientists have tended to slight research concerning women's health, while all too often jumping to reductionistic, biologistic explanations of human inequality. Western science has wrought a double-edged sword of sexual science – the simultaneous exaggeration of sexual differences, often to the detriment of women, and the neglect of differences, the study of which might benefit women's health and well-being.

ALICE D. DREGER AND LONDA SCHIEBINGER

Genetic Engineering

Bennett, David, Peter Glasner and David Travis, *The Politics of Uncertainty: Regulating Recombinant DNA Research in Britain*, London and Boston: Routledge and Kegan Paul, 1986

Bud, Robert, *The Uses of Life: A History of Biotechnology*, Cambridge and New York: Cambridge University Press, 1993

Cantley, Mark F., "The Regulation of Modern Technology: A Historical and European Perspective" in *Biotechnology*, vol. 12, edited by H.-J. Rehm and G. Reed, Weinheim, Germany: VHC, 1995, 505–681

Goodfield, June, *Playing God: Genetic Manipulation and the Manipulation of Life*, New York: Random House, 1977; London: Abacus, 1978

Grobstein, Clifford, *A Double Image of the Double Helix: The Recombinant DNA Debate*, San Francisco: W.H. Freeman, 1979

Hall, Stephen S., *Invisible Frontiers: The Race to Synthesise a Human Gene*, New York: Atlantic Monthly Press, and London: Sidgwick and Jackson, 1987

Krimsky, Sheldon, *Genetic Alchemy: The Social History of the Recombinant DNA Controversy*, Cambridge, Massachusetts: MIT Press, 1982

Lear, John, *Recombinant DNA: The Untold Story*, New York: Crown, 1978

Old, R.W. and S.B. Primrose, *Principles of Gene Manipulation: An Introduction to Genetic Engineering*, Berkeley: University of California Press, 1980; 5th edition, Oxford: Blackwell, 1994

Tiley, Nancy, *Discovering DNA: Meditations on Genetics and a History of the Science*, New York: Van Nostrand Reinhold, 1983

Watson, James D. and John Tooze, *The DNA Story: A Documentary History of Gene Cloning*, San Francisco: W.H. Freeman, 1981

Wright, Susan, *Molecular Politics: Developing American and British Regulatory Policy for Genetic Engineering, 1972–1982*, Chicago: University of Chicago Press, 1994

Genetic engineering is the popular term for genetic manipulation, by which new combinations of genetic material can be created in the laboratory and transferred to, and propagated within, organisms in which they do not naturally occur. Much of the underlying knowledge and techniques were developed during the 1960s and early 1970s, and although widely regarded at the time as a revolutionary development in biology for which Nobel prizes were awarded, few suspected how rapidly it would provide the technical basis for a new biotechnology industry. Its arrival also stimulated a vigorous debate about the political, social, and ethical issues surrounding recombinant DNA research and its application.

There are few accessible historical accounts of the scientific developments leading to genetic engineering. WATSON & TOOZE, however, provide an exceptionally clear chapter on genetic engineering's roots in several fields of modern biology, including: DNA biochemistry; bacteriophage genetics; the genetics of bacterial antibiotic resistance; bacterial gene regulation; virology; various methodological advances in agarose gel electrophoresis; and nucleic acid blotting, cutting and joining DNA molecules. In their view, recombinant DNA and sequencing were extraordinary technical developments that saved molecular genetics from a future of gradual atrophy, and rebutted those who had suggested that the double helix and associated DNA research offered little of practical social value. OLD & PRIMROSE's textbook contains some useful historical sketches on the research fields feeding into genetic engineering, including "Restriction: From a Phenomenon in Bacteriological Genetics to a Biological Revolution", and "Bacteriophage Lambda: Its Important Place in Molecular Biology and DNA History".

Other writers, such as TILEY, have covered these historical origins, while avoiding the "hard" science. Tiley's treatment is more general and philosophical, beginning with the early history of genetics. In 1973, Herbert Boyer, Stanley Cohen and collaborators at the universities of Stanford and California developed the techniques for using plasmids – circular pieces of DNA found in many bacteria – as vectors for cloning foreign genes, and their techniques were patented in 1979. (A copy of the patent can be found in Watson & Tooze.) The availability of such techniques opened up the possibility of using recombinant research on all kinds of foreign DNA, including higher plants and animals. There followed over several years, to the late 1970s, intense dissension within the recombinant DNA research community on two counts: commercialisation of research, and fears about the safety and ethical implications of the research.

In his stimulating account of the race by three different teams of scientists to be the first to clone and express a human insulin gene, HALL shows how the injection of commerce and research regulation, into a field previously free from both had an overwhelming effect on the lives of many of the scientists involved. More than any other source, Hall's book, based on more than 90 interviews, brings vividly to life the scientific work in the laboratory, and the highly competitive and stressful atmosphere in which it was conducted. His detailed account provides information about the personal background of the scientists, including the usually unsung post-doctoral students – who did so much of the actual work – and the commercial interests developing around, and within, the first attempt to do something "useful" with genetic engineering. His account of how both Biogen and Genentech, pioneering genetic engineering firms, came into being, and their association with rival participants in the race, is illuminating.

Since the creation of Genentech and Biogen in the mid-1970s, hundreds of so-called New Biotechnology firms have been formed, many evolving directly out of academic research. Most commentators have tended to view contemporary biotechnology as the industrial offspring of genetic engineering. BUD's history of biotechnology is an excellent antidote to this erroneous and over-simplistic view. He shows how biotechnology can be seen as a wedding of genetics and industrial microbiology: historically, prior to 1980, biotechnology evolved primarily through aspects of engineering; however, after the development of genetic engineering, the popular perception of the industry shifted, to that of a field defined by its biological feasibility. Bud also notes a radical shift from the pre-World War II tradition of genetic engineering, which emphasised people, to one emphasising the production of proteins – although with the rise of the Human Genome Project, there may yet be a revival of the eugenics agenda.

As already mentioned, fears about the potential hazards of recombinant DNA research were quickly raised, and a protracted debate over the nature of its regulation ensued. The standard history is KRIMSKY, while LEAR provides a detailed, exposé-style account of the debates. Watson & Tooze bring together an outstanding collection of about 140 key documents grouped into 16 chapters and prefaced by short introductions, a reading of which reveals Watson's feeling, in retrospect, that the furore and consequent regulations were unnecessary – and even amounted to a self-inflicted wound by the scientists concerned. However, it is fair to say that the document collection is comprehensive enough to allow the reader to arrive at perhaps quite contrary conclusions. GOODFIELD, who interviewed many of the participants in the debate at the time of the Asilomar Conference in 1975, believes that the real historical significance of the debate was that it marked a mutation in the traditional social contract between the scientific community and society. Scientists would no longer be able to claim to be moral innocents, merely seeking the truth for the potential benefit of all; a new contract was developing, within which scientific freedom could be subject to extra-scientific constraints. GROBSTEIN, in his clear study of the background and course of the debate, reaches a similar conclusion. He uses a metaphor of the "double image" of the double helix to emphasise the contradiction between genetic engineering's potential for good – the resolution of ancient uncertainties regarding disease and famine – and evil – creating new social dangers and uncertainties. Genetic engineering is, he suggests, perhaps to be seen as a contemporary version of the Faustian bargain.

The moratorium on recombinant research in the mid-1970s had a world-wide effect. BENNETT, GLASNER & TRAVIS provide a thorough account of the development of the British response, and, in particular, of the Genetic Manipulation Advisory Group, which had the responsibility of vetting UK recombinant DNA research. The subsequent history of genetic engineering regulatory policy provides general insights into the nature of the struggle, between those who feel modern technology is being allowed to advance too rapidly and should be more strictly regulated, and those seeking a laissez-faire approach. In the US, and to some extent the UK, the record was one of a progressive and fairly rapid weakening of regulatory control. WRIGHT, in her outstanding history of this process, makes a convincing case that this largely resulted from a structural bias in the policy process, engendered by commercial interests. On the other hand, the European Union, dominated by transgovernmental regulatory policy, seems to have been more immune to such interests, and more open to "Green" pressure groups. Indeed, CANTLEY develops a well-documented counter-perspective to Wright, in which the history of regulation by Brussels is read as "a story of arrested development".

HARRY ROTHMAN

See also Biotechnology; Genetics: post-DNA; Molecular Biology

Genetics: general works

Bowler, Peter J., *The Mendelian Revolution: The Emergence of Hereditarian Concepts in Modern Science and Society*, Baltimore: Johns Hopkins University Press, and London: Athlone Press, 1989

Brock, Thomas D., *The Emergence of Bacterial Genetics*, Cold Spring Harbor, New York: Cold Spring Harbor Laboratory Press, 1990

Carlson, Elof Axel, *The Gene: A Critical History*, Philadelphia: Saunders, 1966

Cook-Deegan, Robert, *The Gene Wars: Science, Politics, and the Human Genome*, New York: Norton, 1994

Dunn, L.C., *A Short History of Genetics: The Development of Some of the Main Lines of Thought, 1864–1939*, New York: McGraw-Hill, 1965; reprinted, Ames, Iowa: Iowa State University Press, 1991

Judson, Horace Freeland, *The Eighth Day of Creation: Makers of the Revolution in Biology*, New York: Simon and Schuster, 1979; expanded edition, Plainview, New York: Cold Spring Harbor Laboratory Press, 1996

Mayr, Ernst, *The Growth of Biological Thought: Diversity, Evolution, and Inheritance*, Cambridge, Massachusetts: Belknap Press of Harvard University Press, 1982

Olby, Robert C., *Origins of Mendelism*, New York: Schocken Books, and London: Constable, 1966; 2nd edition, Chicago: University of Chicago Press, 1985

Portugal, Franklin H. and Jack S. Cohen, *A Century of DNA: A History of the Discovery of the Structure and Function of the Genetic Substance*, Cambridge, Massachusetts: MIT Press, 1977

Provine, William B., *The Origins of Theoretical Population Genetics*, Chicago: University of Chicago Press, 1971

Sap, Jan, *Beyond the Gene: Cytoplasmic Inheritance and the Struggle for Authority in Genetics*, Oxford and New York: Oxford University Press, 1987

Stubbe, Hans, *History of Genetics: From Prehistoric Times to the Rediscovery of Mendel's Laws*, translated from the German by Trevor R.W. Waters, Cambridge, Massachusetts: MIT Press, 1972 (original edition, 1963)

Sturtevant, A.H., *A History of Genetics*, New York: Harper and Row, 1965

Watson, James D. and John Tooze, *The DNA Story: A Documentary History of Gene Cloning*, San Francisco: W.H. Freeman, 1981

The general works on the history of genetics can be divided into two categories: those dealing with the history of classical or Mendelian genetics, often as it intersects with the history of evolution and the evolutionary synthesis, and those dealing with the more recent history of molecular genetics and modern gene technology. As a relatively new field of scientific inquiry, genetics was named only in the early 1900s, by William Bateson. As a result, much of the early historical treatment of genetics has been in-depth chronologies and elaboration of sources and subjects rather than interpretive studies.

Several early treatments of the history of genetics were written by research practitioners in the field. These include DUNN, Stubbe, Sturtevant, and CARLSON. These are primarily chronologies of people, ideas and events, highlighting developments before and after Mendel. STUBBE, for example, presents an in-depth discussion of reproduction and heredity in the classical world from the Greeks and Romans through to the Middle Ages. Much of the book highlights the pre-Mendelian situation and culminates in the "rediscovery" of Mendel and the beginnings of chromosome theory. STURTEVANT deals primarily with the 20th century, detailing topics such as biochemical genetics, mutation, and maternal effects, or history organized around organisms: drosophila, oenothera, and the genetics of man.

OLBY concentrates on 19th-century and earlier developments in plant hybridization and hereditarian theory in plants and animals, including studies of Darwin, the plant hybridist Charles Naudin, and the statistician Galton as necessary figures in the development of classical genetics, required to set Mendel and Mendelism in historical context. Olby espouses a constructionist view of genetics, where knowledge is underdetermined by facts and meanings depend on the pre-suppositions of the observer. He provides biographical bases for the variance in the response of these scientists to the new knowledge, and presents Mendel as more influenced by the ideas and traditions that defined Galton's, rather than Darwin's, view of heredity.

BOWLER provides an interpretive look at the development of classical genetics primarily after 1900, concentrating especially on the links established between chromosomal behavior, organismal phenotype, and Mendel's "laws". These set the stage for the concept of the gene as material embodied in DNA – the foundation of the subsequent development of molecular genetics. Bowler discusses the status of heredity before Darwin, the problem of heredity in evolution and development, and the work of Mendel and his "re-discovery" in 1900 by scientists who would promote Mendelism. Critical to the development of "classical genetics" was the work of Thomas Hunt Morgan and others on the fruit fly, *drosophila*, whose utility as an experimental organism would prove the ideal system from which to develop gene and mutation theory. Bowler's crucial interpretive point is that the development and acceptance of Mendelism was a Kuhnian-style scientific revolution, and that Mendelism was a socially constructed science, functionally serving human needs and linked to the politics of heredity, as well as intellectual and institutional constraints, rather than objective truth.

PROVINE outlines the history of theoretical population genetics as a critical component not only of genetics as a whole, but of the development of the evolutionary synthesis in the mid-20th century. Within the synthesis, Darwinian evolution became compatible and explicable within a classical genetics framework. According to Provine, the argument that occurred between the Darwinians and the Mendelians, and the Mendelians and the biometricians, informed and directed the development of classical genetics and paved the way for synthesis, but only after years of bitter feuding.

According to BROCK, although seemingly a subdiscipline, bacterial genetics proved instrumental in defining and developing genetics as a whole, providing the crucial link between the classical and molecular. Using a traditional history of ideas approach, Brock, like Provine, places the psychology of individual scientists and the sociology of institutions as background rather than foreground to the development of the science. The chapters are thematic rather than chronological, dealing with the roots of bacterial genetics in classical genetics and bacteriology, and with such subjects as mutation, transduction and transformation, and gene expression and regulation – each being treated in separate chapters.

SAP deals with one of the most significant controversies of the 20th century, on the nature of hereditary transmission – the existence of maternal or cytoplasmic inheritance separate from chromosomal inheritance. The author presents the controversy as based on disciplinary conflict, status and the struggle for authority, as much as one of conflicting scientific theories.

MAYR spends considerable time detailing the role and development of genetics. The final third of his book, entitled *Variation and Inheritance*, is a chronological history of the breeding experiments which led to the recognition of germ cells, and to various theories on the nature of inheritance from Darwin and Galton through to Mendel. Subsequent developments from Mendel's rediscovery through to the double helix are detailed, highlighting such figures as Hugo DeVries, Morgan, James Watson, and Francis Crick. The entire work is a history of modern biology as seen through the lense of the evolutionary synthesis, told by one of its scientific developers and promoters, near the end of his career.

PORTUGAL & COHEN provides one of the first chronicles of the discovery and structure of DNA, and the development of the genetic code. JUDSON is a definitive and lively biographical approach to the birth of modern molecular genetics, relying heavily on personal interviews with the scientists involved, from Pauling to Watson and Crick to François Jacob and Jaques Monod; afterwords are included on the roles of Rosalind Franklin and Erwin Chargaff. WATSON & TOOZE's annotated documentary history includes letters, cartoons, legislative documents, and newspaper and journal articles on the development of recombinant DNA in its early years of regulatory crisis. COOK-DEEGAN outlines the most modern developments in genetic science, including the creation of the human and other genome projects. It is a synthesis of scientific developments within the social and political contexts. This is an approach that all modern histories of genetics seem to require, especially given the ideologically charged nature of the concept of the gene, as discussed by so many of these writers, from Olby and Bowler to Cook-Deegan.

MARK S. LESNEY

See also DNA; Mendel; Molecular Biology

Genetics: post-DNA

Bud, Robert, *The Uses of Life: A History of Biotechnology*, Cambridge and New York: Cambridge University Press, 1993

Cook-Deegan, Robert, *The Gene Wars: Science, Politics and the Human Genome*, New York: Norton, 1994

Judson, Horace Freeland, *The Eighth Day of Creation: Makers of the Revolution in Biology*, New York: Simon and Schuster, 1979; expanded edition, Plainview, New York: Cold Spring Harbor Laboratory Press, 1996

Kevles, Daniel J., *In the Name of Eugenics: Genetics and the Uses of Human Heredity*, New York: Knopf, 1986; Harmondsworth: Penguin, 1986; with a new preface, Cambridge, Massachusetts: Harvard University Press, 1995

Krimsky, Sheldon, *Genetic Alchemy: The Social History of the Recombinant DNA Controversy*, Cambridge, Massachusetts: MIT Press, 1982

Nelkin, Dorothy and M. Susan Lindee, *The DNA Mystique: The Gene as a Cultural Icon*, New York: Freeman, 1995

Olby, Robert C., *The Path to the Double Helix*, Seattle: University of Washington Press, 1974

Wright, Susan, *Molecular Politics: Developing American and British Regulatory Policy for Genetic Engineering, 1972–1982*, Chicago: University of Chicago Press, 1994

The majority of post-war studies of genetics by geneticists, journalists, critics of science, and government agencies or consultants, focuses on the problems and questions raised by the great progress made in the field during this period. There are also several scholarly studies exploring human genetics, genomics, genetic engineering, and biotechnology. Relatively little work has been done on the technical history of post-DNA genetics, perhaps because so many different scientific fields are involved, and because the molecular tools growing out of DNA research are now applied to so many scientific problems. There is, in other words, no single discipline, research school, or intellectual problem that can claim to represent genetics in the molecular age. It should be noted that some of the more celebratory accounts of the changing scientific meaning of DNA can also provide a general insight into the broad reconfiguration of genetics after 1953 – from an emphasis on bodily traits, to a fascination with molecular structure and molecular codes. Like most post-war topics, this one offers many opportunities for further research.

A good starting place is JUDSON, who approaches the rise of molecular genetics as a grand adventure story. Technically his work is pre-DNA, since he explores how nucleic acids came to be the central problem of molecular biology, but much of what happened after 1953 reflects the political and intellectual forces he chronicles. His interest in the scientists involved, and his meticulous recording of their perceptions and interpretations, are the great strengths of the book. Judson wants to capture the scientific ideas and personalities, and while the result is not analytical, it is filled with detailed and clear explanations of the science, and gives some amusing anecdotes.

OLBY covers similar ground, but in a different style, focusing on the many strands of science, ideology, and technology that led to the elucidation of the structure of DNA. Olby explores the concept of long-chain molecules, including: W.T. Astbury's work in the 1930s on the structure of the proteins and nucleic acids; bacterial transformation and its importance to DNA; the intellectual migrations of physicists and others to biological problems between 1930 and 1950; and, finally, how all these led to James Watson and Francis Crick's new interpretation. Olby proposes that Rosalind Franklin was neither ignorant nor unreasonable in her reluctance to accept a double helix. He also explores why the implications of Erwin Chargaff's data on complementarity were not immediately grasped by Watson and Crick, and clarifies why it was so difficult to choose between proteins and nucleic acids as the hereditary material. He does expend some unnecessary energy establishing time lines and priorities – who knew what, and when – but this is an instructive text, with only a mild case of what Olby himself identifies as "precursor disease".

KEVLES provides a broader perspective, by placing genetics – particularly human genetics – within the context of eugenics. Much of this book explores the Anglo-American eugenics movements, but in the final chapters Kevles presents an overview of post-war human genetics. Most importantly, he directly links developments in contemporary genetics to eugenics, and shows that they are part of the same history. With an attention to social and political issues, he introduces the problems posed by genetic engineering and biotechnology.

The common perception that biotechnology began with recombinant DNA is refuted by BUD, who looks back to the 1920s in order to claim the Hungarian pig farmer Karl Ereky as a founding father. Bud somewhat obsessively follows the vocabulary of genetics (words such as biotechnology and zymotechnology) through 300 years of brewing, agriculture, microbiology, and genetics, arguing that when biotechnology became genetics in the 1970s, it incorporated many older ideas concerning the transformation of biological entities into factories, and the construction of new economies based on biological mass production. Bud also compares public concerns about genetic engineering to those about nuclear technologies and the chemical industry.

KRIMSKY's study provides a sustained exploration of these public concerns by examining the recombinant DNA debates in Cambridge and beyond in the 1970s. He assumes an internalist/externalist dichotomy, identifying some issues as internal to the science, and others as political or social issues that affected the form of the debate. For his purposes, the external political questions loom large. At the same time, he documents the important role of scientists themselves in the public debate, showing that in many ways they participated in the creation of the controversy.

With her comparative approach, WRIGHT brings questions of hazards posed by genetic engineering into a cultural context. She suggests that the crucial difference between British and American controls on genetic engineering – the fact that British limits applied to all sectors, including industry – was a consequence of the British emphasis on workplace rather than environmental hazards. She argues that controls were dismantled discursively in both Britain and America, as the burden of proof shifted from those supporting genetic engineering (who once had to prove it was safe), to those questioning it (who now had to prove that it was not). The economic potential of the biotechnology industry, she suggests, was the proximate cause of this transformation in both settings. She points out that technical resolutions were (and remain) impossible: the question of the risks posed by genetically engineered organisms is dauntingly complex, although scientists have commonly appealed to technical data in order to resolve disputes.

NELKIN & LINDEE examine how this technical appeal to genetics plays out in popular culture, examining the images and metaphors of heredity that appear in newspapers, television, advertising, fiction, film, comic books, and other media. They argue that the images of the gene as powerful, deterministic, and central to personal identity have been promoted by leading scientists involved with the Human Genome Project, and also explore how institutions – the courts, schools, employers – use genetic data to justify and legitimate policies and practices.

The political origins of the Human Genome Project are explored by COOK-DEEGAN, in his insider's account of the process of getting HGP through the funding maze in Washington. For some commentators, the genome project, now an international activity aimed at the creation of a map of all human DNA (with mouse and plant DNA thrown in as well), is a striking manifestation of the ideological and political power of DNA. Cook-Deegan explores how promoters framed DNA as profitable territory – linked to international competition in the biotechnology industry – and how the expectations of scientists intersected with Congressional interests.

M. Susan Lindee

See also Biotechnology; Molecular Biology

Genius

Abrams, M.H., *The Mirror and the Lamp: Romantic Theory and the Critical Tradition*, Oxford and New York: Oxford University Press, 1953

Aris, Rutherford, H. Ted Davis and Roger H. Stuewer (eds), *Springs of Scientific Creativity: Essays on Founders of Modern Science*, Minneapolis: University of Minnesota Press, 1983

Engell, James, *The Creative Imagination: Enlightenment to Romanticism*, Cambridge, Massachusetts: Harvard University Press, 1981

Friedel, Robert, "Defining Chemistry: Origins of the Heroic Chemist", in *Chemical Sciences in the Modern World*, edited by Seymour H. Mauskopf, Philadelphia: University of Pennsylvania Press, 1993

Golinski, Jan, *Science as Public Culture: Chemistry and Enlightenment in Britain, 1760–1820*, Cambridge and New York: Cambridge University Press, 1992

Levere, Trevor H., *Poetry Realized in Nature: Samuel Taylor Coleridge and Early Nineteenth-Century Science*, Cambridge and New York: Cambridge University Press, 1981

Manuel, Frank E., *A Portrait of Isaac Newton*, Cambridge, Massachusetts: Belknap Press of Harvard University Press, 1968

Merton, Robert K., "Singletons and Multiples in Science", in his *The Sociology of Science: Theoretical and Empirical Investigations*, edited by Norman W. Storer, Chicago: University of Chicago Press, 1973 (essay originally published, 1961)

Schaffer, Simon, "Scientific Discoveries and the End of Natural Philosophy", *Social Studies of Science*, 16 (1986): 387–420

Schaffer, Simon, "Genius in Romantic Natural Philosophy", in *Romanticism and the Sciences*, edited by Andrew Cunningham and Nicholas Jardine, Cambridge and New York: Cambridge University Press, 1990

Slade, Joseph W. and Judith Yaross Lee, *Beyond the Two Cultures: Essays on Science, Technology, and Literature*, Ames: Iowa State University Press, 1990

Yeo, Richard, "Genius, Method, and Morality: Images of Newton in Britain, 1760–1860", *Science in Context*, 2 (1988): 257–84

Historical studies of scientific genius fall into two broad categories; those that explore the intellectual history and/or social construction of scientific genius, and those that seek to discover the springs of scientific creativity.

Regarding the first category, scholars agree that modern notions of genius, including scientific genius, grew out of 18th-century debates over aesthetics, epistemology, and psychology. These debates arose partly in response to the radical accounts of mind put forth by Descartes and Locke. The literary historians ABRAMS and ENGELL both offer extensive intellectual histories of how reason and imagination were redefined, so that genius, originally defined as skill in copying, was recast as an inborn creative urge. Both authors base their analyses on mostly British and German sources, with Abrams focusing on the Romantic period, and Engell concentrating more on the 18th century. Neither author discusses the intellectual history of scientific genius itself, but they do both explore how the thinkers who devised modern notions of genius built upon, or explicitly rejected, conceptions of mind intrinsic to the new scientific philosophy. LEVERE describes how Coleridge rejected the Newtonian model of practising science, in which, he claimed, the mind was a mere passive spectator. Instead, Coleridge, building upon Schelling's philosophy, developed an elaborate theory of creativity as the organic, dynamic outgrowth of an active mind engaging with nature.

More recent studies analyze specific constructions of scientific genius, and the circumstances in which they were cast. Some of these constructions are to be found in popular biography. YEO examines numerous British biographies of Newton, for a long period the icon of scientific genius, and finds shifting formulations of method and imagination in portrayals of Newton's genius. Yeo states that 18th-century accounts incorporated ideals from natural theology and the Baconian credo in order to portray Newton as a moral, industrious, methodical discoverer of divine creation. By the mid-19th century, biographies by Brewster and Whewell portrayed Newton as an extraordinary personality, whose achievements could never be reduced to method. The collection by SLADE & LEE, hailing from the discipline of literature and science, contains a section entitled "Scientists and Inventors as Literary Heroes", which examines American and British popular biographies of the 19th century. FRIEDEL surveys depictions of the chemist in American encyclopedias, textbooks, and magazine articles from the early 19th century to c.1920. He finds that the image of the heroic chemist, wielding power to remake the world, emerged over the course of the century as tensions regarding the purpose of chemistry were confronted and resolved within the discipline.

Schaffer and Golinski, drawing upon recent sociological approaches to science, interpret attempts by individual natural philosophers to define scientific genius as bids for status and power. SCHAFFER (1990) surveys the German and British arenas, from c.1770 to 1840, and finds that the nature of scientific genius was hotly debated both outside and inside the scientific community. Schaffer relates these debates (including Edmund Burke's rabid attacks against genius-as-Illuminatus) to the political tumult of the times, as well as to complex and important changes taking place within the culture of the scientific community. SCHAFFER (1986) critiques attempts by philosophers of science to codify the logic of scientific discovery, arguing instead that the very identity of the discoverer, and the moment of discovery, is determined only after negotiations within the scientific community. Schaffer examines British and French cases from the end of the 18th century in order to demonstrate how the model of the heroic discoverer developed during the period served to legitimize emerging stratification within changing scientific institutions. In chapter 7 of GOLINSKI, studies from the laboratory, the lecture hall, and journals reveal how Humphry Davy publicly presented his own genius, using a strategy devised to impose knowledge claims and procure resources. Golinski dwells especially on how Davy deployed expensive instruments to master not only nature, but also his audiences and professional rivals, and is the only one of these authors who analyzes how the process of defining scientific genius affected the actual knowledge produced.

Within the second category of the history of scientific genius, several works seek to discover the springs of scientific creativity through biographical studies of exceptional scientists. MANUEL's biography includes a Freudian analysis of Newton's separation anxiety, mother fixation, Puritan shame, survivor guilt, and other afflictions, in a search for the roots of Newton's enormous creativity and drive. In his introduction, Manuel discusses the issue of scientific genius in general, and asserts that he does not presume to have unlocked the secret of Newton's genius with his analysis. The collection edited by ARIS, DAVIS & STUEWER contains 12 biographical sketches, mostly of physicists, including Galileo, Newton, Joule, Gibbs, Schrödinger, and Einstein. Each essay tries to account for, or at least describe, its subject's scientific creativity. Thomas Hughes's article is the most unusual, comparing Elmer Sperry's scientific creativity to artistic creativity as portrayed in Thomas Mann's *Doctor Faustus*, concluding that both types of creative endeavor entail an endless Romantic quest. C.W.F. Everitt's long article on Maxwell probes deeply into cultural circumstances, personal experiences, and quirks of personality, most notably Maxwell's masochism. William T. Scott's article describes Polanyi's attribution of creativity partly to community and tradition. Even those essays that offer no new interpretations of scientific genius could serve as provocative readings in undergraduate courses.

In an entirely different vein, MERTON seeks out the springs of scientific creativity through sociological, as opposed to biographical, study. Merton (representing an older genre of science sociology than that from which Schaffer and Golinski draw) defines the scientific genius simply as one who is a prolific publisher of discoveries and theories, and especially who is involved in multiple discoveries (such as Wallace and Darwin). Merton uses this quantifiable definition to investigate scientific discovery as arising from social process. Additional articles in parts four and five of Merton's collection explore these and related issues.

JULIANNE TUTTLE

Geography of the Sciences

Aveni, A.F. (ed.), *Archaeoastronomy in the New World: American Primitive Astronomy*, Cambridge and New York: Cambridge University Press, 1982

Clagett, Marshall, *Ancient Egyptian Science: A Souce Book*, 2 vols, Philadelphia: American Philosophical Society, 1989–95

Crosby, Alfred W., *Ecological Imperialism: The Biological Expansion of Europe, 1900–1900*, Cambridge and New York: Cambridge University Press, 1986

Dorn, Harold, *The Geography of Science*, Baltimore: Johns Hopkins University Press, 1991

Gillispie, Charles Coulston (ed.), *Dictionary of Scientific Biography*, vol. 15, New York: Scribner, 1978

Huff, Toby E., *The Rise of Early Modern Science: Islam, China, and the West*, Cambridge and New York: Cambridge University Press, 1993

Livingstone, David, *The Geographical Tradition: Episodes in the History of a Contested Enterprise*, Oxford: Blackwell, 1993

McClellan III, James E., *Colonialism and Science: Saint Domingue in the Old Regime*, Baltimore: Johns Hopkins University Press, 1992

Nasr, Seyyed Hossein, *Science and Civilization in Islam*, Cambridge, Massachusetts: Harvard University Press, 1968; 2nd edition, Cambridge: Islamic Texts Society, 1987

Needham, Joseph, *Science and Civilization in China*, 6 vols, Cambridge and New York: Cambridge University Press, 1954–86

Needham, Joseph and Lu Gwei-Djen, *Trans-Pacific Echoes and Resonances: Listening Once Again*, Singapore: World Scientific, 1985

Rotberg, Robert I. and Theodore K. Rabb (eds), *Climate and History: Studies in Interdisciplinary History*, Princeton, New Jersey: Princeton University Press, 1981

Sivin, Nathan, "Why the Scientific Revolution Did Not Take Place in China – or Didn't It?", in *Transformation and Tradition in the Sciences*, edited by Everett Mendelsohn, Cambridge and New York: Cambridge University Press, 1984, 531–54

Stahl, William H., *Roman Science: Origins, Development and Influence to the Later Middle Ages*, Madison: University of Wisconsin Press, 1962

Worster, Donald, *Nature's Economy: A History of Ecological Ideas*, Cambridge and New York: Cambridge University Press, 1977; revised edition, 1985

In the history of science, geography has appeared in three kinds of studies: regional examinations of non-Western science; comparative histories of science; and efforts to account for the development of scientific cultures in terms of environmental factors. The flagship of this tradition is now NEEDHAM's monumental study of science and civilization in China. Its geographical slant reflects Needham's Marxist convictions insofar as he calls attention to the material setting (environmental and ecological) in which Chinese science and technology developed. In the first volume, he announced that a major comparative theme of the work would address the question of why modern science arose in Europe and not elsewhere, and he indicated that a full analysis would involve "an examination of the concrete environmental factors of geography, hydrology, and the social and economic system that was conditioned by them". SIVIN has reviewed the issues, and has concluded that the comparative history of science across geographical frontiers is not yet well enough developed to resolve them fruitfully.

Unlike Needham, some historians have confined the comparative history of science to studies of different regional traditions, without bringing environmental conditions into play. In a recent book on Islam, China and the West, HUFF has explicitly taken up some of the comparative issues raised by Needham, but his main interest is intellectual and institutional history, and neither ecological nor environmental conditions are considered. DORN has explored the other end of the historiographical spectrum, by emphasizing the significance of geographical factors in comparing scientific cultures. Dorn applies Marx's Asiatic Mode of Production in a modified interpretation (that owes as much to the "hydraulic hypothesis" of American anthropologists as it does to historical materialism) to an analysis of the differences between the scientific cultures of the ancient Orient, ancient Greece, and modern Europe.

Most regional studies have neither confronted the issues of the comparative history of science, nor have they attempted (with the exception of Needham and Dorn) to correlate the development of the scientific enterprise with the constraints and opportunities of local geographical conditions. For Islam, much work has been published in research journals, although NASR remains a useful survey. STAHL covers "Roman science", treating Latin, Greek and Byzantine sources as a single tradition. A recent addition to the regional history of science is CLAGETT's major study of ancient Egyptian science, in which lengthy commentaries are combined with translations of original documents. A peculiar difficulty confronts the historian of the scientific cultures of Egypt and the other ancient civilizations; although all of those civilizations developed mathematics and astronomy, often at impressive levels of originality, their practitioners have remained shrouded in anonymity. Not a single scientific biography can be written for the scribes that practised their profession in many parts of the Old and New worlds over periods of thousands of years (with the few exceptions who, in late periods, made contact with Greek science). For GILLISPIE's *Dictionary of Scientific Biography,* the biographical approach proved impossible for these civilizations and, instead, a series of topical essays was included in volume 15.

Still another approach to the sciences of the ancient civilizations across the world has been taken, mainly by archaeologists, in what has been designated "archaeoastronomy". AVENI was a pioneer, and remains a leading figure in this field, which is especially well developed in the study of the ancient civilizations of North, Central and South America, since so little written evidence has survived and so much needs to be recovered from archaeological artifacts. Because some of the features of the civilizations of the New World and East Asia display strong similarities, questions have been raised about the possibilities of eastward diffusion across the Pacific. NEEDHAM & LU reviewed the great mass of evidence and concluded that while "there is a multitude of culture-traits which point to influences from, and contacts with, the Old World", there is "nothing [that] can in any way diminish the profound originality of the Amerindian civilizations, especially in Meso-America and South America".

One field of the history of non-Western science that has recently attracted interest is colonial science – the study of the European scientific tradition transplanted in diverse geographical settings by European settlers. McCLELLAN has presented a model of colonial science within the context of traditional Haiti, tracing the pattern of research contacts with the mother country (France) and emphasizing the patronage of the enterprise by state institutions.

Climatological and epidemiological factors represent fields of research that the historian of science with geographical interests may also wish to explore. Early in the century, climatological history was discredited by raciological biases. ROTBERG & RABB have edited a collection of articles that herald a new approach to the subject, without an ideological agenda, including studies of the effects of climate on history, as well as of the history of climate itself. On the historical consequences of disease patterns across the world, CROSBY is of interest to the general historian as well as to historians of science and medicine.

As environmental concerns have forced themselves on scholars in many disciplines, the history of those concerns has been taken up in several studies. WORSTER has reviewed the subject in terms of intellectual history, while LIVINGSTONE shows that the history of geography has recently begun to reflect the themes developed within the history of science over the past 35 years.

HAROLD DORN

See also Physical and Human Geography

Geology

Adams, Frank, *The Birth and Development of the Geological Sciences*, New York: Dover, 1938

Ellenberger, François, *Histoire de la géologie*, 2 vols, Paris: Technique et Documentation, 1988–94; vol. 1, *Des Anciens à la Première Moitié du XVIIe siècle*; vol. 2, *La Grand Éclosion et ses prémices 1660–1810*

Dean, Dennis, *James Hutton and the History of Geology*, Ithaca, New York: Cornell University Press, 1992

Flett, John Smith, *The First Hundred Years of the Geological Survey of Great Britain*, London: HMSO, 1937

Geikie, Archibald, *The Founders of Geology*, London and New York: Macmillan, 1897; 2nd edition, 1905; 2nd edition reprinted, New York: Dover, 1962

Gillispie, Charles Coulston, *Genesis and Geology: A Study in the Relations of Scientific Thought, Natural Theology, and Social Opinion in Great Britain, 1790–1850*, Cambridge, Massachusetts: Harvard University Press, 1951

Glen, William (ed.), *The Mass-Extinction Debates: How Science Works in a Crisis*, Stanford, California: Stanford University Press, 1994

Gould, Stephen Jay, *Wonderful Life: The Burgess Shale and the Nature of History*, New York: Norton, 1989; London: Hutchinson Radius, 1990

Greene, Mott T., *Geology in the Nineteenth Century: Changing Views of a Changing World*, Ithaca, New York: Cornell University Press, 1982

Herries Davies, Gordon L., *The Earth in Decay: A History of British Geomorphology, 1578–1878*, London: Macdonald, and New York: Elsevier, 1969

Herries Davies, Gordon L., *North from the Hook: 150 Years of the Geological Survey of Ireland*, Dublin: Geological Survey of Ireland, 1995

Laudan, Rachel, *From Mineralogy to Geology: The Foundations of a Science, 1650–1830*, Chicago: University of Chicago Press, 1987

Lyell, Charles, *Principles of Geology*, London: John Murray, 1830; reprinted, 3 vols, Chicago: University of Chicago Press, 1990–91

Metzger, Hélène, *La Genèse de la science des cristaux*, Paris: Alcan, 1918; new edition, Paris: Blanchard, 1969

Oldroyd, David R., *The Highlands Controversy: Constructing Geological Knowledge through Fieldwork in Nineteenth-Century Britain*, Chicago: University of Chicago Press, 1990

Oldroyd, David, *Thinking about the Earth: A History of Ideas in Geology*, London: Athlone Press, and Cambridge, Massachusetts: Harvard University Press, 1996

Porter, Roy, *The Making of Geology: Earth Science in Britain, 1660–1815*, Cambridge and New York: Cambridge University Press, 1977

Rudwick, Martin J.S., *The Great Devonian Controversy: The Shaping of Scientific Knowledge among Gentlemanly Specialists*, Chicago: University of Chicago Press, 1985

Rupke, Nicolaas A., *Richard Owen: Victorian Naturalist*, New Haven, Connecticut: Yale University Press, 1994

Sarjeant, William A.S., *Geologists and the History of Geology: An International Bibliography from the Origins to 1978*, New York: Arno Press, and London: Macmillan, 1980; supplements, *1979–1984* (2 vols) and *1985–1993 and Additions*, Malabar, Florida: Krieger, 1987–96

Secord, James A., *Controversy in Victorian Geology: The Cambrian–Silurian Dispute*, Princeton, New Jersey: Princeton University Press, 1986

Stafford, Robert A., *Scientist of Empire: Sir Roderick Murchison, Scientific Exploration and Victorian Imperialism*, Cambridge and New York: Cambridge University Press, 1989

Thompson, Susan J., *A Chronology of Geological Thinking from Antiquity to 1899*, Metuchen, New Jersey: Scarecrow Press, 1988

Whewell, William, *A History of the Inductive Sciences*, 3 vols, London: John Parker, 1837–57; reprinted, Hildesheim and New York: Olms, 1976

Wilson, Leonard, *Charles Lyell, the Years to 1841: The Revolution in Geology*, New Haven, Connecticut: Yale University Press, 1972

Zittel, Karl von, *History of Geology and Palaeontology to the End of the Nineteenth Century*, translated from the German by Maria Ogilvie-Gordon, London: Walter Scott, 1901; reprinted, New York: Hafner, 1962 (original edition, 1899)

There is one aspect of the history of geology, i.e. plate tectonics that has received close attention, but there are still many gaps in the literature, with room, for example, for detailed book-length studies of the histories of sedimentology, petrology, metamorphism, geochemistry, modern crystallography, studies of the different geological systems, geological travel, geological investigations in specific countries, branches of geophysics such as seismology and gravimetry, geology and literature, and the industrial and economic significance of geology. However, it is intended that such topics be addressed in a new series, *Studies in the History and Philosophy of the Earth Sciences* (Athlone Press).

Despite the paucity of books on some aspects of the history of geology, there is a large, though scattered, literature. Among the different genres there are bibliographies, philosophical works, internal histories, general surveys, examinations of the interplay between theology and geology, sociologically informed studies, institutional histories, and biographies of geologists.

For bibliographical information, readers are well served by SARJEANT and THOMPSON. The journal *Earth Sciences History* is devoted exclusively to the history of geology, and each issue includes a list of recent publications in the field.

Among the early studies, LYELL's historical introduction to his *Principles of Geology* (1830) influenced subsequent writers considerably, to the extent that 19th-century geologists regarded the work of many of their early, pre-Lyellian predecessors as belonging to a dark age. However, commentators such as Roy PORTER have described Lyell's history as a polemical document, tailored to the needs of Lyell's uniformitarian geology: that natural agents now at work on and within the Earth have operated with general uniformity through long periods of time. Thus Lyell's history made favourable mention of those among his predecessors who wrote in such a way that they might seem to support a uniformitarian geology, while non-uniformitarians and those who speculated about cosmology, were treated unfavourably or ignored. Lyell's work may have been methodologically partisan, but it was successful for many years in effecting a separation of geology from questions of cosmology, or cosmogony; the study of the Earth as a planet by geologists is largely a 20th-century activity.

Just as Lyell's history was tailored to his philosophy of geology, so WHEWELL's *History of the Inductive Sciences* (1837–57) was interwoven with his ideas about the philosophy of science. Thus he was interested in the way in which the history of science manifested the establishment of general laws and the gradual clarification of so-called "fundamental ideas". Whewell wanted geology to be a science, not a "promiscuous assemblage of desultory essays". For geology, Whewell considered the special feature of what he termed the "palaetiological sciences", and thought that the investigations of Alexander von Humboldt, for example, were beginning to lead to the recognition of such laws. In his history of geology, he addressed several of the grand problems – such as the question of "progressive development" (evolution) – that were exciting people at that time. Whewell, a mineralogist among many other things, also treated the history of mineralogy.

In keeping with the tradition established by authors such as Lyell, much history of geology has been written by geologists, rather than historians (or philosophers) of science, and some of the specific concerns of the scientist–historians have permeated their work. GEIKIE's beautifully written, Whiggish text is still the *entrée* to the study of the history of geology, despite the book's nationalistic tendencies. Geikie gave considerable attention to the debate between the supporters of the German geologist Abraham Gottleb Werner (Neptunists) and those of the Scotsman James Hutton (Vulcanists), favouring the latter to the extent that the English-language histories of geology began to recognise the full significance of Werner's work only in the second half of the 20th century. ZITTEL's more sober, but duller, account of the early history of geology remains an important 19th-century German counterweight to Geikie, and provides information about early geochemistry, petrology, and stratigraphy that is difficult to locate elsewhere.

Another geologist, ADAMS, provided much information about the early history of geology, particularly mineralogy. As was often the case among scientists in the 1930s, he thought that philosophical speculation was inimical to the proper development of science, and he argued that such speculations had not helped the emergence of the geological sciences. Earlier, by contrast, METZGER had emphasized the importance of philosophical ideas in the early development of crystallography, as she did likewise in her studies of the borderland of chemistry and earth science. More recently, ELLENBERGER has provided an extremely detailed account of almost all the primary and secondary literature relating to geology to around 1800, accepting the important role of philosophy in the development of scientific ideas. He has gone back to original sources wherever possible, and has found, thereby, some errors in earlier work.

For general surveys of the history of geology, see for example Laudan or Oldroyd (1996). LAUDAN's book is more detailed, but covers a limited period. She rightly emphasizes the importance of Werner, using the term "Wernian radiation" for the process by which Werner's ideas were spread and applied by his students in many parts of the world. Laudan examines the "logic" of Lyell's geology closely, seeing him as applying the Newtonian principle of *verae causae*. (The geologist had to think of, and investigate, "true causes", which might have operated so as to produce the effects observable in the field). Laudan also claims that William Smith, who proposed the principle that strata might be identified by their fossil contents, did not always practise what he preached, sometimes identifying strata by their lithologies. OLDROYD (1996) considers parts of geology such as geophysics, geochemistry, and sedimentary cycling, and some aspects of petrology – topics that are not much covered in other general texts.

GILLISPIE's entertaining, indeed exuberant book examines the relationship between geology and theology in Britain in the heyday of natural theology. It is critical of early efforts to reconcile the results of the emerging science of geology with religious/theological beliefs, and was perhaps unduly censorious of such attempted reconciliations, being extremely disparaging towards Wernerians such as Richard Kirwan. Nevertheless, Gillispie opened the way in the postwar period for historical studies of geology, and revealed the possibilities for exciting work in this area by students of intellectual history. Even so, only one area of the history of geology – the so-called "plate tectonics revolution" – has been accorded close historical scrutiny, and this by authors with significantly different historiographical perspectives.

For the study of particular periods, mention should be made of GREENE's *Geology in the Nineteenth Century*, though the title is somewhat belied by the book's content, since it is largely concerned with the history of theories of mountain-building. The text gives an authoritative broad treatment of much that was of prime importance in geological theory in the 19th century, and does not follow any particular philosophical "line", other than perhaps showing a general concern with empirical knowledge.

The study of geological controversies has received some detailed attention, being a field where issues in the sociology of scientific knowledge have been usefully explored. RUDWICK's minute scrutiny of the social processes involved in the establishment of the Devonian System draws on the work of theorists such as Harry Collins and Pierre Bourdieu, and has been regarded as a major landmark in the historiography of science. The significance of power and position in the geological community for the construction of knowledge is emphasised, the argument being illustrated by interesting diagrams showing shifts in theoretical position and changes in the "agnostic field" of the geological community. Rudwick is interested in the construction of scientific knowledge, but does not suggest that

scientific knowledge is "nothing but" a social construction. In this and other work, he has emphasised the importance of "visual imagery" in geology. Also concerned with the history of Palaeozoic geology, SECORD has unravelled the complexities of the debate between Roderick Murchison and Adam Sedgwick about the Cambrian–Silurian boundary, and helpfully elucidated stages in the debate by means of diagrams. OLDROYD (1990) has dissected "The Highlands Controversy" from a Latourian perspective, and has replicated some of the 19th-century fieldwork in the Scottish Highlands. He has thereby investigated the way in which such fieldwork was conducted and has illustrated its significance to geological debate. In a useful essay introducing a collection of papers on a current debate (on mass-extinction), GLEN examines an ongoing controversy. In such an "unclosed" case, we do not as yet know what the final consensus will be, hence, Whiggish anachronism is suitably restrained.

There are useful social and institutional histories of geology, especially that by PORTER, while early texts such as that by FLETT often offer helpful empirical information. Most institutional histories, however, have to date been published with the support of the institutions concerned and generally are not "critical" histories, although they typically display interesting "inside" knowledge of the workings and personalities of an organisation.

Among the several branches of geology, paleontology has relatively modern texts, as for example that by Rudwick, and GOULD's remarkable study of the history of the Burgess Shale fossils. Gould's book reveals much about the workings of geology as a social system and a cognitive activity, and shows how observations may be radically influenced by theoretical suppositions. The history of geomorphology has at least one notable text, by HERRIES DAVIES (1969), who has also published an exemplary history of geological mapping in Ireland (1995).

A limited number of geologists have received detailed biographical treatment. One may cite, for example WILSON on Lyell, DEAN on Hutton, RUPKE on Owen, and STAFFORD on Murchison. Wilson's book has been surprisingly controversial, being at the centre of a debate that took place in the 1970s about the virtues and vices of uniformitarianism, and the extent to which Lyell was or was not an empiricist. DEAN controversially accepts the designation of Hutton as "the father of modern geology", and examines in detail the response to his work in 19th-century journals. RUPKE offers a detailed examination of Owen, and destroys some of the old canards about this man, which grew up in part because of his rivalry with T.H. Huxley, the successful Darwinian. Rupke links Owen's paleontological work to his investigations in comparative anatomy, his philosophical ideas, as well as his social position in the British scientific establishment. His book sets new standards for detailed biographical studies in the history of geology. STAFFORD's biography is interesting for the way in which Murchison is represented as an ardent nationalist, who was adept in the power politics of the scientific community of his day. It can be seen as a historical case-study of "how to succeed in science".

While there has been some criticism of the work of geologist–historians by historians of geology, it seems likely that in the future, as in the past, the pioneer historical work will continue to be undertaken by geologists, who have a clear understanding of where the important and interesting topics are to be found. It should be mentioned that geology has already shown itself to be a field particularly well-suited to historical studies of scientific controversies and processes of theory change.

DAVID OLDROYD

Geometry

Atzema, E.J., *The Structure of Systems of Lines in 19th Century Geometrical Optics*, Utrecht: Rijksuniversiteit, 1993

Bonola, Roberto, *Non-Euclidean Geometry: A Critical and Historical Study of Its Development*, translated from the Italian by H.S. Carslaw, Chicago: Open Court, 1912; reprinted, New York: Dover, 1955 (original edition, 1906)

Bos, H.J.M., "On the Representation of Curves in Descartes' *Géométrie*", *Archive for History of Exact Sciences*, 24 (1981): 295–338

Bos, H.J.M. *et al.*, "Poncelet's Closure Theorem", *Expositiones Mathematicae*, 5 (1987): 289–364

Brigaglia, Aldo and C. Ciliberto, *Italian Algebraic Geometry Between the Two World Wars*, translated from the Italian by Jeanne Duflot, Kingston, Ontario: Queen's University, 1995 (original edition, 1993)

Chasles, M., *Aperçu historique sur l'origine et le développement des méthodes en géométrie*, Brussels: Academy Royale, 1837

Chemla, K. and S. Pahaut, "Préhistoire de la dualité: Explorations algébriques en trigonométrie sphérique", in *Sciences à l'époque de la Révolution Françaises: recherches historiques*, edited by Roshdi Rashed, Paris: Blanchard, 1988

Coolidge, Julian Lowell, *A History of Geometrical Methods*, Oxford: Clarendon Press, 1940; New York: Dover, 1963

Dieudonné, Jean Alexandre, *Cours de géométrie algébrique*, vol. 1, Paris: Presses Universitaires de France, 1974

Field, J.V. and Jeremy Gray (eds), *The Geometrical Work of Girard Desargues*, New York: Springer, 1987

Gray, Jeremy, *Ideas of Space: Euclidean, non-Euclidean, and Relativistic Geometry*, Oxford: Clarendon Press, and New York: Oxford University Press, 1979; 2nd edition, 1989

Gray, Jeremy, *Linear Differential Equations and Group Theory from Riemann to Poincaré*, Basel: Birkhäuser, 1986

Gray, Jeremy, "Algebra in der Geometrie von Newton bis Plücker", in *Geschichte der Algebra: Eine Einführung*, edited by Erhard Scholz, Mannheim: Wissenschaftsverlag, 1990, 265–90

Gray, Jeremy, "Möbius's Geometrical Mechanics", in *Möbius and His Band: Mathematics and Astronomy in Nineteenth-Century Germany*, edited by John Fauvel, Raymond Flood and Robin Wilson, Oxford and New York: Oxford University Press, 1993, 78–103

Gray, Jeremy and D.E. Rowe, *Klein's Evanston Colloquium Lectures and Other Works*, New York: Springer, 1996

Heath, Sir Thomas Little, *A History of Greek Mathematics*, 2 vols, Oxford: Clarendon Press, 1921; New York: Dover, 1981

Heath, Sir Thomas Little (ed.), *The Works of Archimedes*, Cambridge: Cambridge University Press, 1897; New York: Dover, 1953

Jones, Alexander (ed. and trans), *Book 7 of the Collection*, by Pappus of Alexandria, with commentary, New York: Springer, 1986

Knorr, Wilbur, *The Evolution of the Euclidean Elements: A Study of the Theory of Incommensurable Magnitudes and Its Significance for Early Greek Geometry*, Dordrecht: Reidel, 1975

Knorr, Wilbur, *The Ancient Tradition of Geometric Problems*, Basel: Birkhäuser, 1985; 2nd edition, New York: Dover, 1993

Lloyd, G.E.R., *Early Greek Science: Thales to Aristotle*, London: Chatto and Windus, and New York: Norton, 1970

Lloyd, G.E.R., *Greek Science after Aristotle*, London: Chatto and Windus, and New York: Norton, 1973

Parshall, Karen Hunger and David E. Rowe, *The Emergence of the American Mathematical Research Community, 1876–1900: J.J. Sylvester, Felix Klein, and E.H. Moore*, Providence, Rhode Island: American Mathematical Society, and London: London Mathematical Society, 1994

Paul, M., *Gaspard Monges, "Géométrie Descriptive" und die École Polytechnique*, Bielefeld: Universität Bielefeld, 1980

Pont, Jean-Claude, *L'Aventure des parallèles: histoire de la géométrie non euclidienne, précurseurs et attardés*, Berne and New York: Peter Lang, 1986

Reich, Karin, "Die Geschichte der Differentialgeometrie von Gauss bis Riemann (1828–1868)", *Archive for History of Exact Sciences*, 11 (1973): 273–382

Reich, Karin, *Die Entwicklung des Tensorkalküls: Von absoluten Differentialkalkül zur Relativitätstheorie*, Basel: Birkhäuser, 1994

Richards, Joan L., *Mathematical Visions: The Pursuit of Geometry in Victorian England*, Boston: Academic Press, 1988

Scholz, Erhard, "Hermann Weyl's 'Purely Infinitesimal Geometry'", *Proceedings of the International Congress of Mathematicians, Zürich, 1994*, edited by S.D. Chatterji, Basel: Birkhäuser, 1995

Sigurdsson, S., "Unification, Geometry and Ambivalence: Hilbert, Weyl, and the Göttingen Community", in *Trends in the Historiography of Science*, edited by Kostas Gavroglu, Jean Christianidis and Efthymios Nicolaidis, Dordrecht: Kluwer, 1994, 355–67

Struik, Dirk Jan, *A Concise History of Mathematics*, New York: Dover, 1948; London: Bell, 1954

Struik, Dirk Jan, *Lectures on Classical Differential Geometry*, Cambridge, Massachusetts: Addison-Wesley, 1950

Taton, René, *L'Oeuvre mathématique de G. Desargues*, Paris: Vrin, 1951; 2nd edition, 1988

Taton, René, *L'Oeuvre scientifique de Monge*, Paris: Presses Universitaires de France, 1951

Toomer, G.J. (ed.), "On Burning Mirrors", in *Diocles on Burning Mirrors: The Arabic Translation of the Lost Greek Original*, New York: Springer, 1976

Torretti, Roberto, *Philosophy of Geometry from Riemann to Poincaré*, Dordrecht: Reidel, 1978

Whiteside, D.T. (ed.), *The Mathematical Papers of Isaac Newton*, vol. 6, Cambridge: Cambridge University Press, 1974

Ziegler, Renatus, *Die Geschichte der geometrischen Mechanik im 19. Jahrhundert*, Stuttgart: Steiner, 1985

While all mathematical cultures have shown some degree of interest in geometry, the Greeks were the first to do so systematically. The standard English introduction to Greek geometry remains the work of HEATH (1921), although it is often naive. Later works have either attempted to situate Greek mathematics within a wider scientific or intellectual enterprise (see the works by LLOYD), or have focused on individual mathematicians: see, for example, HEATH (1953) for Archimedes, TOOMER's Diocles, and JONES's Pappus, although there is no English edition of Apollonius. KNORR (1975) attempts to shift attention to the problem-solving aspects of Greek mathematics and away from the emphasis on theory-building of earlier scholarship, while KNORR (1985) considers the commentating tradition and its implications for modern editions of classical works.

The first decisive shift away from Euclidean-style reasoning in geometry, and the first enlargement of the scope of the subject, came with Descartes's essay *La Geometrie*, for which the starting point in contemporary scholarship is now BOS. Bos shows for the first time how Descartes's essay proposed that geometrical problems could be translated into algebraic terms, solved there, and the solution turned back into geometry. The essay gives a series of good, but not convincing, arguments that this can always be done, and Bos shows the inconsistency of Descartes's ideas on how to define a curve. Descartes's work led to a general acceptance of the notion that the analysis of a problem virtually amounts to a proof, for this was how his use of algebra came to be regarded. It enlarged geometry, by establishing a rough and ready (and at times obscured) equivalence between curves and equations between two variables. His successor, Isaac Newton, brought an unrivalled ability in Euclidean geometry to bear on the analysis of nature in his *Principia* (1687); the richest account of this and all Newton's mathematics remains the eight-volume edition of his work by WHITESIDE (see especially volume 6).

Descartes's exact contemporary, Girard Desargues, had a grasp of classical Greek geometry (notably that of Apollonius), and a commitment to architecture – for example, teaching perspective to stonemasons. Sustained by the interest of friends in the circle around Mersenne, he circulated a 30-page essay outlining a thoroughly projective geometry. Although the 16-year-old Blaise Pascal responded enthusiastically, and his friend the painter and teacher found outlets for more of Desargues's ideas, the original essay fared poorly; only one copy survives today. An English edition, with commentaries on the learned and practical traditions of his day, can be found in FIELD & GRAY and a French one in TATON (1951).

Later generations of mathematicians preferred to use the calculus to do systematically what Newton had done by hand. Strictly geometrical works were few in the 18th century, the most successful being those by Euler and his Swiss contemporary, Cramer. Neither has received the full attention of historians.

The French Revolution saw a complete overhaul of French education and the creation of the École Polytechnique, with the mathematician Gaspar Monge at its head. His original discoveries included descriptive geometry, which was taught to all "polytechnicians" as part of their education as future military engineers. Monge's life and work are described from a traditional point of view by TATON (1951). A more recent work by PAUL gives a much fuller account of the École Polytechnique, the changes in personnel and subsequent changes in syllabus. The most important of Monge's students was Poncelet, who, when taken prisoner during the Napoleonic invasion of Russia, extended descriptive geometry and thereby re-discovered projective geometry. (Desargues's work being by then almost forgotten.) Poncelet greatly extended the theory, albeit in ways few have found truly acceptable or comprehensible (see BOS *et al.*), and for a time he had many followers, notably CHASLES, whose *Aperçu* remains a fine account of the history of geometry to date. However, the French mathematicians' disdain for algebraic methods meant that they were soon surpassed by German geometers, and the strictly synthetical approach to projective geometry may indeed be one type of mathematics that has died as a research subject. There is no satisfactory account of this part of the history of mathematics, although an old-fashioned account, strong on re-working the mathematics and short on context, will be found in COOLIDGE. An interesting light on duality in projective geometry, and on the origin of the key terms "pole" and "polar", is cast by CHEMLA & PAHAUT. GRAY (1993) examines the life and times of the important mathematician and astronomer, and first German projective geometer, A.F. Möbius; German geometrical work is described more briefly in GRAY (1990). The later history of projective geometry and its ramifications for what was called higher geometry (in which the primitive objects are not points, but lines, spheres, or other figures in another space) has never been adequately documented (there is only Coolidge's account). However, the origins of line geometry in work on optics is described by ATZEMA, and the use of line geometry to reformulate mechanics is described in ZIEGLER. Between them these works show how connections between mathematics and its applications were made in the 19th century.

During the late 1820s and early 1830s the first accounts of non-Euclidean geometry, the first physically plausible alternative to Euclidean geometry, were discovered and published. There has been a considerable amount of literature on this. BONOLA remains the classic account, strong on the mathematics but devoid of any other perspective. GRAY (1979), while also sticking closely to the mathematics, argues for a three-stage process, with the actual discovery by János Bolyai and Nikolai Lobachevskii coming second, and depending crucially on its ontological obscurity; clarity came with Riemann's ideas in the 1850s and their gradual acceptance. The numerous minor figures and their works, mostly aimed at defending Euclid, are described at length in PONT, which provides material for a community-based analysis. The only attempt to give non-Euclidean geometry a fully contextualised analysis is RICHARDS, whose account may owe much to the peculiar features of British intellectual life in the mid-19th century. Non-Euclidean geometry became a staple of philosophers of geometry when it was used by Poincaré to anchor what is called his conventionalism; this and the history of such ideas from Riemann to Poincaré, are described by TORRETTI.

Nevertheless, non-Euclidean geometry also had, and continues to have, a significant role in mathematics; the technical side until the 1880s is described in GRAY (1986).

The profusion of geometries led Felix Klein to formulate his so-called Erlangen Program in 1872, which achieved prominence in the 1890s; this defined geometry as a space and a group of transformations of that space, and Klein used it to organise the various geometries into a hierarchy. A recent reprint of Klein's original essay in English, with other essays by Klein and an account of his career and influence (especially in America), will be found in GRAY & ROWE, while PARSHALL & ROWE give a much fuller account of the American story.

Although the first applications of the calculus to the study of geometry are as old as the calculus itself, the subject of differential geometry began again with Gauss, who in the 1820s showed that the geometry on a surface can be described intrinsically (i.e. independent of any embedding of the surface in a three-dimensional space). A generation later, Riemann showed that indeed all geometry (except that of curves) may be formulated intrinsically. Aspects of this story are discussed in STRUIK (1948), with background comments of a Marxist persuasion, and in more mathematical detail in STRUIK (1950) on classical differential geometry, which contains many historical notes. The best systematic overview is that of REICH (1973), which also sticks closely to the mathematics. Developments after Riemann have not been well described, with the exception of the recent book by REICH (1994), which traces the emergence of the tensor concept, and thus investigates the mathematical pre-history of Einstein's theory of gravitation. However, the later story, covering the 20th century and the eclipse of Klein's ideas, has never been told. The work of E. Cartan and Weyl awaits the historian, although for Weyl one may consult SCHOLZ (1995) and SIGURDSSON.

Axiomatic geometry is described in the entry on axiomatics; like later differential geometry, it too represented a way beyond Klein's unification. However, once axiomatising became orthodox in mathematics, interest switched back to the traditional subjects of differential and algebraic geometry. In algebraic geometry, the leading role was assumed for a time by Italian mathematicians (Segre, Castelnuovo and Enriques, Severi) who relied to varying extents on a formidable intuition. By the 1920s, insurmountable obstacles with this work, especially when dealing with higher-dimensional problems, inclined mathematicians, especially outside Italy, to build up algebraic methods. Van der Waerden and Zariski took over ideas from Emmy Noether, and established the ambiguous subject of commutative algebra, one half of which looks to geometry. Again, neither the Italians nor the algebraists have had their due attention from historians. For an account of the 1920s and 1930s, which also explores issues arising from the Fascist rule (almost all Italian geometers were Jewish), see BRIGAGLIA & CILIBERTO.

Although close to these developments, the influential French mathematician André Weil (one of the seven founders of Bourbaki) put forward his own reformulation of algebraic geometry in the 1940s. However, this was overtaken a generation later by Grothendieck's ideas. Understandably, in view of the technical difficulties within all this work, historical accounts have only been written by mathematicians, notably Grothendieck's co-author, DIEUDONNÉ, who provides a masterly re-write of the material in the tradition of Coolidge.

JEREMY GRAY

See also Algebra; École Polytechnique; Euclid; Gauss; Mathematical Modernity; Newton; Rational Mechanics

Germanophone Areas   1780–1871

Brunschwig, Henri, *Enlightenment and Romanticism in Eighteenth-Century Prussia*, translated from the French by Frank Jellinck, Chicago: University of Chicago Press, 1974 (original edition, 1947)

Cahan, David (ed.), *Hermann von Helmholtz and the Foundations of Nineteenth-Century Science*, Berkeley: University of California Press, 1993

Cunningham, Andrew and Nicholas Jardine (eds), *Romanticism and the Sciences*, Cambridge and New York: Cambridge University Press, 1990

Gregory, Frederick, *Scientific Materialism in Nineteenth-Century Germany*, Dordrecht and Boston: Reidel, 1977

Olesko, Kathryn M. (ed.), "Science in Germany: The Intersection of Institutional and Intellectual Issues", *Osiris*, second series, 5 (1989)

Olesko, Kathryn M., *Physics as a Calling: Discipline and Practice in the Königsberg Seminar for Physics*, Ithaca, New York: Cornell University Press, 1991

Stichweh, Rudolf, *Zur Entstehung des modernen Systems wissenschaftlicher Diszipinen: Physik in Deutschland, 1764–1890*, Frankfurt: Suhrkamp, 1984

Turner, R. Steven, *In the Eye's Mind: Vision and the Helmholtz-Hering Controversy*, Princeton, New Jersey: Princeton University Press, 1994

The period 1780–1880 witnessed the emergence of German science, from an activity of a small group of *Naturphilosophen*, whose works were often ridiculed by French savants and British experimental natural philosophers, to a massive, well-orchestrated effort of natural and physical scientists, many of whom were considered to be among the best in the world. Beginning with the Romantic era of German science, CUNNINGHAM & JARDINE have edited a collection of well-informed essays for the student interested in the relationship between nature and culture in the German territories from c.1790 to 1830. Articles in this collection examine *Naturphilosophie*, German Romantic biology and physics, English Romanticism and political thought, Romantic genius, and the relationship between science and literature. Goethe, in particular, is well represented throughout a majority of essays. Many of the individual authors provide a very helpful further reading list after each of their articles.

BRUNSCHWIG is a very intriguing and highly controversial, sociological and psychological account of the early Romantics and the *Naturphilosophen*. It offers a general social history of the early Romantics, including their views on nature, their literary achievements, their genius cult, and their revolutionary tendencies.

For another outstanding collection of essays on German science, one should consult OLESKO (1989). This volume of

Osiris brings both an intellectual and an institutional approach to an analysis of the development of German science from the late 18th to the early 20th centuries. Topics covered include science and political reform during the late 18th century, the relationship between science and education during the mid-19th century, the rise of scientific institutions and the rise of the Reich, and the interplay between science and political institutions.

The third collected volume of essays that should be consulted is CAHAN, which, like Olesko, offers intellectual and institutional histories of Helmholtz, Germany's spokesperson for science during the second half of the 19th century. The essays are divided into three sections, each section corresponding to a different aspect of the polymath's life: physiology, physics, and philosophy.

The most ambitious analysis of German science in general, and physics in particular, is STICHWEH. Adopting a macro-sociological approach, Stichweh argues that northern Germany's rapid evolution during the second half of the 19th century into a modern, functionally differentiated society was the result of a vast social evolution that gave rise to, among many other things, scientific disciplines such as physics.

Two recent works examine the German scientific community during the 19th century. The first is OLESKO (1991), which offers an impressive account of the Königsberg physical seminar and the scientific practices of its students, who studied under Franz Ernst Neumann. Olesko offers a history of the discipline of physics, while also shedding light on the importance of error analysis and measurement, the role of pedagogy in the enterprise of physics, and the transmission of skills and practices from colleague to colleague, and from professor to student.

The second recent work dealing with the scientific community in Germany is TURNER, a clever analysis of the controversy in physiological optics between Helmholtz and Ewald Hering, which erupted in the German territories in the 1860s. Turner scrutinizes the views of the two differing camps by offering detailed accounts of the physiological optics involved, as well as the epistemological differences of the two men, their methods of training scientists, and how the controversy was played out through to the early 20th century.

Another important text dealing with the German biological community is GREGORY, which offers an impressive intellectual history of materialism – which dominated German philosophical circles, particularly surrounding Feuerbach, during the 1830s, 1840s, and 1850s – and its influence on the biological theories of Karl Voigt, Jacob Moleschott, Ludwig Büchner, and Heinrich Czolbe. This work is particularly effective in demonstrating the links between scientific theory and political ideology.

MYLES W. JACKSON

Gesellschaft Deutscher Naturforscher und Ärzte

Lampe, Hermann and Hans Querner (eds), *Die Vorträge der allgemeinen Sitzungen auf der 1.-85. Versammlung, 1822–1913*, Hildesheim: Gerstenberg, 1972

Lampe, Hermann, *Die Entwicklung und Differenzierung von Fachabteilungen auf den Versammlungen von 1828 bis 1913: Bibliographie zur Erfassung der Sektionsvorträge*, Hildesheim: Gerstenberg, 1975

Pfannenstiel, Max, *Kleines Quellenbuch zur Geschichte der Gesellschaft Deutscher Naturforscher und Ärzte: Gedächtnisschrift für die hundertste Tagung der Gesellschaft*, Berlin: Springer, 1958

Querner, Hans and Heinrich Schipperges (eds), *Wege der Naturforschung 1822–1972, im Spiegel der Versammlungen Deutscher Naturforscher und Ärzte*, Berlin: Springer, 1972

Schipperges, Heinrich (ed.), *Die Versammlung Deutscher Naturforscher und Ärzte im 19. Jahrhundert*, Stuttgart: Gentner, 1968

Schipperges, Heinrich, *Weltbild und Wissenschaft: Eröffnungsreden zu den Naturforscherversammlungen 1822 bis 1972* (Schriftenreihe zur Geschichte der Versammlungen deutscher Naturforscher und Ärzte: Dokumentation und Analyse. Herausgeber: Hans Querner. Band III) Hildesheim: Gerstenbera, 1976

Sudhoff, Karl, *Hundert Jahre Deutscher Naturforscher-Versammlungen. Gedächtnisschrift zur Jahrhundert-Tagung der Gesellschaft Deutscher Naturforscher und Ärzte Leipzig, im September 1922*, Leipzig: Vogel, 1922

Sudhoff, Karl, *Rudolf Virchow und die Deutschen Naturforscherversammlungen*, Leipzig: Akademische Verlagsgesellschaft, 1922

Zevenhuizen, Erika, *Politische und weltanschauliche Strömungen auf den Versammlungen Deutscher Naturforscher und Ärzte von 1848 bis 1871*, Berlin: Ebering, 1937

There is no complete study of the Gesellschaft Deutscher Naturforscher und Ärtze (Society of German Naturalists and Physicians), because the diversity of subjects has prevented a detailed examination. The present literature is introductory, but it does provide a general survey.

The society was founded in Leipzig on 18 September 1822, by the natural scientist and philosopher Lorenz Oken (1779–1859). The origin and history of the society are documented in the source book by PFANNENSTIEL. This contains original documents concerning the origin of the Society – such as Oken's invitation of 1821 to a meeting of naturalists and physicians in Leipzig, published in his journal *Isis* – and the reorganization of the Society in Göttingen in 1950, personal memories (such as confessions, the experiences of Jakob Nöggerath or Friderich Eser), chapters dealing with "characters and situations" showing the social background, and a list of 100 meetings, the cities in which they took place, the secretaries, the chairmen of the society, and their first and second deputies from 1891 to 1958.

SUDHOFF (1922, *Hundert Jahre*), an archivist of the society, examines the founding assembly of about 20 scholars against the politico-historical background, and in the light of Oken's aim of German intellectual unity by way of scientific collaboration and co-operation. Sudhoff also discusses the meetings in Munich (1827), Berlin (1828; chairman, Alexander von Humboldt (1769–1859)), and his new idea of differentiation between scientific disciplines), Heidelberg (1829; internationality on behalf of science), Vienna (1832), Stuttgart (1834; scientific national education), Jena (1836), Freiburg (1838), and Regensburg (1849). In his famous speech at the 40th meeting in Hanover in 1865, Rudolf Virchow (1821–1902) spoke of the importance of the natural sciences to national development, and urged that the meetings of the Society should represent German science as deeply connected with the life of the nation. In Sudhoff's opinion, the Society's first half-century was concentrated on the national effects of "German thought" and the creation of a successful German natural science, whereas the second half-century was engaged in presenting scientific results to the united German nation.

Sudhoff's list of titles of lectures held at the first 86 meetings is incomplete and at times incorrect. Improved lists were published in 1972 by LAMPE & QUERNER, with further bibliographical data; they present a list of publications corresponding to the subjects of the 1,000 or so lectures, with the names of the lecturers. It was Alexander von Humboldt who introduced the sessions of special scientific disciplines at the meeting in Berlin in 1828, despite Oken's original intention. The expansion of these sessions in the decades up to 1913 reflects the process of scientific specialization and variety during this period, which was closely connected to the growth of knowledge in medicine and the natural sciences.

The background to this development was an altering conception of "science": on the one hand, the development away from "Romanticism" towards a positivistic attitude, and, on the other hand, the introduction of new methods in science and medicine. In this sense, these specialized sessions threatened the very basis of the society's meetings of naturalists and physicians. This process of specialization is very well documented in LAMPE, which presents the lectures of the various disciplines until 1913 with a bibliography.

Three main periods in the history of the Society of Naturalists and Physicians have to be differentiated: the peripatetic period, 1822–54, with its sympathy for "nature"; the second period, 1854–90, the meetings of which took place against the ideological background of scientific unity; and the third period, 1890–70, of "realistic" science. SCHIPPERGES (1976) presents the inaugural lectures, which show the characteristic features and Weltanschauung of the different periods.

The remaining books deal with specific subjects in the history of the society: for example, SUDHOFF (1922, Rudolf Virchow) compiles the most important speeches of Rudolf Virchow, the most prominent German physician at the meetings of the society between 1858 and 1887, which show the general development of natural science and medicine. Sudhoff argues that, by reading the extracts or summaries of these speeches, the reader should be able to make his own decision on Virchow as either reactionary or progressionist. Nevertheless, Sudhoff describes Virchow's basic national conception of the 1860s and 1870s as progressionist.

The thesis of ZEVENHUIZEN concentrates on the period 1848–71, interpreting it from an ideological viewpoint and arguing that here one can discern the seeds of the Third Reich. She describes the importance of the meetings in the political (the concept of German union) and the social (such as the discussion on public health) spheres, and especially emphasizes the incipient discussion of Darwinism – arguing that in this period the scientific, rather than the ideological, content of the theory of evolution dominated.

SCHIPPERGES (1968) presents a collection of treatises resulting from a meeting of historians of science at Heidelberg University. These papers deal with the constitution of the Society, the idea of evolution, Virchow's position in the meetings, the importance of Helmholtz and Virchow for the history of science, and the character of a section for scientific pedagogics. Three hypotheses were developed: 1) that the notion of national unity as a fundamental motive for the meetings was combined with the idea of a scientific union, as well as with the social movement – and that it was for this reason that the society received political authorization, and the meetings of the naturalists became a sort of "National Institute"; 2) that the belief in progress, based on the new method of the exact sciences against the background of the concept of evolution, was combined with the national idea; and 3) that, as a result, science took on a missionary character, penetrating other fields of the cultural and public life, possibly as some kind of substitute for religion.

QUERNER & SCHIPPERGES, a collection of several treatises by different authors, examines several periods and subjects, including: physiology (especially the discussion about vitalism and mechanism); hygiene; the philosophy of nature and theory of science in the second half of the 19th century; biology c.1900 (cell research, the theory of evolution, and genetics); quantum theory and the theory of relativity at society meetings of the years 1906–20; the role of chemistry until the foundation of the German Chemical Society; and meetings in general from 1920 to 1960. Diversity is precisely the advantage of this volume, as it presents some aspects of the different sciences up to modern times, thus preparing a basis for further research in these fields.

BEATRICE RAUSCHENBACH

See also Germanophone Areas; Kaiser-Wilhelm-Gesellschaft; Romanticism; Virchow

Gilbert, William 1544–1603

English physician and natural philosopher

Boyer, Carl P., "William Gilbert on the Rainbow", *American Journal of Physics*, 20 (1952): 416–21

Daujat, Jean, *Origines et formation de la théorie des phénomènes électriques et magnétiques*, 3 vols, Paris: Hermann, 1945

Freudenthal, Gad, "Theory of Matter and Cosmology in William Gilbert's 'De Magnete'", *Isis*, 74 (1983): 22–37

Harré, Rom (ed.), *Early Seventeenth Century Scientists*, Oxford and New York: Pergamon Press, 1965 (chapter 1)

Hesse, Mary B., "Gilbert and the Historians", *British Journal for the History of Science*, 11 (1960): 1–10, 130–42

Jones, Richard Foster, *Ancients and Moderns: A Study of the Background of the Battle of the Books*, St Louis, Missouri: Washington University Press, 1936; 2nd edition as *Ancients and Moderns: A Study of the Rise of the Scientific Movement in Seventeenth-Century England*, 1961

Kelly, Sister Suzanne, *The De Mundo of William Gilbert*, Amsterdam: Hertzberger, 1965

Mottelay, P. Fleury (trans), *William Gilbert of Colchester, Physician of London: On the Loadstone and Magnetic Bodies*, London: Bernard Quaritch, and New York: Wiley, 1893; as *De Magnete*, New York: Dover, 1958

Pumfrey, Stephen, "Magnetical Philosophy and Astronomy, 1600–1650", vol. 2, part A of *The General History of Astronomy*, edited by R. Taton and C. Wilson, Cambridge and New York: Cambridge University Press, 1989, 45–53

Pumfrey, Stephen, "'O Tempora! O Magnes!' A Sociological Analysis of the Discovery of Secular Variation in 1634", *British Journal for the History of Science*, 22 (1989): 181–214

Robinson, John, *The System of Mechanical Philosophy*, Edinburgh: John Murray, 1822

Roller, Duane H.D., *The "De Magnete" of William Gilbert*, Amsterdam: Hertzberger, 1959

Thompson, Silvanus P. (trans), *On the Magnet*, London: Chiswick Press, 1900; New York: Basic Books, 1958

Thompson, Silvanus P., *Gilbert, Physician: A Note Prepared for the Three Hundredth Anniversary of the Death of William Gilbert of Colchester*, London: Chiswick Press, 1903

Zilsel, Edgar, "The Origins of William Gilbert's Scientific Method", *Journal of the History of Ideas*, 2 (1940): 1–32

Until the 1960s, scholars were interested in William Gilbert as an exemplar of modern scientific practice during an early stage of the scientific revolution, and hence as a provider of clues about how science emerged. There were two foci: Gilbert's creation of a new science of magnetism, and his experimental method. Subordinate themes included his scientific debts, particularly to craftsmen and navigators (Gilbert's theory of terrestrial magnetism promised great advances in compass use), and his relation to his court contemporary and equal in anti-Aristotelian empiricism, Francis Bacon. More recent attention has returned to that which many 17th-century scientists found impressive: his magnetic dynamics for a Copernican universe, and his systematic attempt to supersede Aristotelian natural philosophy, particularly of the earthly, sublunar region. Gilbert studies are bedevilled by an almost complete absence of primary sources, except for his two books, the famous *De Magnete* and the posthumous *De Mundo*. This has allowed historians to interpret Gilbert and his work in a wide variety of ways.

The sparse biographical details concerning Gilbert's rise from Cambridge student to London court physician became of interest in the late 19th century, and two scientists, MOTTELAY and the electrical engineer THOMPSON, prepared celebratory English translations of *De Magnete*. Mottelay's widely available biographical memoir, and Thompson's notes prepared for a tercentenary edition (1903), are still useful, but ROLLER's research exposed their common tendency to exaggerate the accomplishments of their scientific hero.

Famous scientists from Galileo, to Sir Christopher Wren and Joseph Priestley, praised the new, remarkably experimental approach of Gilbert's work on magnetism and electricity. ROBINSON consolidated what can be called the empiricist myth of Gilbert, praising his "unwearied diligence . . . and incessant occupation in experiments, [which] have left very few facts unknown to him". JONES is a more recent and influential example; arguing that the scientific spirit required 17th-century natural philosophers to break experimentally from the bookish authority of ancient sources, he deemed Gilbert to be more important than Bacon (who criticised him), and identified a 17th-century "Gilbert tradition" of magnetic and navigational research in England.

Gilbert's novel and beautiful series of experiments, proving the earth's magnetism using spherical magnets and small needles to replicate terrestrial phenomena in the laboratory, have attracted more sophisticated and philosophically-informed analyses of his method. One problem for naive empiricist readings is that Gilbert manifestly did not have experimental proof for his two most precious conclusions: that magnetism demonstrated the earth's possession of a kind of soul, and that this soul moved the earth in Copernican rotations. BOYER was typical in dividing Gilbert's mentality between a forward-looking tendency towards experimentation and a backward-looking tendency towards Neoplatonism, exemplified in his metaphysical cosmology. HESSE's neat review, written when Hempel's hypothetico-deductivism was the dominant model of scientific reasoning, collapsed this tension by insisting that such "hypotheses" gave necessary direction to Gilbert's researches. Likewise, HARRÉ's summary of Gilbert's work aimed to show the methodological importance of hypotheses, models, and clearly designed experiments to the scientific revolution. Although it remains the best single treatment, readers must be aware of Harré's modern bias, evident in his distaste for Gilbert's cosmology, and in the common fault of excessive attention to Gilbert's brief writings and experiments on electricity, which were designed to distinguish electric attraction from the greater marvel of magnetism. A much fuller, and generally very sensitive, commentary on *De Magnete* was provided by ROLLER, which remains the starting point for any serious study of Gilbert's magnetic philosophy. Roller also included a pre-history of work on magnetics, although this, and post-Gilbertian work, is much more fully summarised in the little-known, but painstaking volumes of DAUJAT.

In contrast to these internalist analyses, though no less convinced of Gilbert's modernity, is ZILSEL's Marxist account. Zilsel concluded that modern scientific method emerged from a synthesis, made possible by capitalism, of systematic philosophical intellectual knowledge and the practical hand knowledge of craftsmen. He was struck, not merely by Gilbert's experimentalism, but also by his open reliance on, and appreciation of, miners and farmers who knew the earth's composition, and of navigators and instrument-makers who knew how compasses actually behaved at sea. Zilsel pointed in particular, and over emphatically, to Robert Norman, the unschooled discoverer of magnetic inclination, as a source of Gilbert's method. Less dogmatically, but still sociologically, PUMFREY (1989, "O Tempora! O Magnes!") has also linked Gilbert's approach, conclusions, and posthumous success to the values and practices of London's maritime community.

Zilsel's Marxism led him to concur that Gilbert's cosmology was a residuum of woolly, medieval philosophising. That common, but suspect, assessment became untenable after KELLY, a critical exposition of Gilbert's untranslated *De Mundo*, and a companion volume both to the simultaneous reprinting of the first edition (1654) of *De Mundo* and to Roller's study of *De Magnete*. Kelly also analysed its origins, as a collection of more or less finished manuscripts, and the light it cast on Bacon's poor opinion of Gilbert's work, and she compared Gilbert's cosmology with contemporary systems. Kelly was clearly disappointed that *De Mundo* contained no new, "modern" insights, being a typically discursive, thoroughly unexperimental work of anti-Aristotelian natural philosophy. Nevertheless, this study confirmed for non-Latin readers that Gilbert's major interest was not magnetism *per se*, but a new magnetic philosophy of a noble, living, moving earth.

Now that Gilbert has been reinstated as a late Renaissance natural philosopher who happened to argue experimentally, his cosmological concerns have been reinstated. FREUDENTHAL was surely right to argue that, within the context of his meta-physics, Gilbert must have been a thorough Copernican, despite having used evasive language about the Earth's annual motion in both works. Historians such as Baldwin and PUMFREY (1989, "Magnetical Philosophy and Astronomy"), have detailed the considerable impact, on both sides of the 17th-century Copernicanism debate, of Gilbert's magnetic dynamics, despite their failure to conform to modern standards of exper-imental proof. Indeed, the question now seems to be not, "why was Gilbert ahead of his time", but, "why did *De Magnete* adopt an experimental proof structure"? The answer may lie in a reworking of Zilsel's thesis, allied to a consideration of Gilbert's position within the structure of Elizabethan court patronage of practical science.

STEPHEN PUMFREY

See also Court Culture; Magnetism; Scientific Revolution

Global Organizations

Ascher, Charles S., *Program-Making in UNESCO, 1946–1951: A Study in the Processes of International Administration*, Chicago: Public Administration Service, 1951

Caldwell, Lynton Keith, *International Environmental Policy: Emergence and Dimensions*, Durham, North Carolina: Duke University Press, 1984; 2nd edition, 1990; revised edition with Paul Stanley Weiland, 1996

Daniel, Howard, *One Hundred Years of International Cooperation in Meteorology, 1873–1973*, Geneva: World Meteorological Organization, 1973

Detter de Lupis, Ingrid, "The Human Environment: Stockholm and Its Follow Up", in *Global Issues in the United Nations' Framework*, edited by Paul Taylor and A.J.R. Groom, New York: St Martin's Press, and London: Macmillan, 1989

Fenner, F., *Smallpox and Its Eradication*, Geneva: World Health Organization, 1988

Finnemore, Martha, "International Organizations as Teachers of Norms: The United Nations Educational, Scientific, and Cultural Organization and Science Policy", *International Organization* (1994): 565–97

Holly, Daniel A., *L'UNESCO, le Tiers-Monde et l'économie mondiale*, Montreal: Presses de l'Université de Montréal, and Geneva: Institut Universitaire de Haute Études Internationales, 1981

Jacobson, Harold K., "WHO: Medicine, Regionalism, and Managed Politics", in *The Anatomy of Influence: Decision-Making in International Organizations*, edited by Robert W. Cox and Harold K. Jacobson, New Haven, Connecticut: Yale University Press, 1973

Preston, William, Edward S. Herman and Herbert I. Schiller, *Hope and Folly: The United States and UNESCO, 1945–1985*, Minneapolis: University of Minnesota Press, 1989

Sathyamurthy, T.V., *The Politics of International Cooperation: Contrasting Conceptions of UNESCO*, Geneva: Droz, 1964

Schroeder-Gudehus, Brigitte, "Collaboration scientifique et coopération intellectuelle: un chapitre dans les déboires de la Société des Nations", *Revue d'Allemagne* (1989): 357–77

Sewell, James, *UNESCO and World Politics: Engaging in International Relations*, Princeton, New Jersey: Princeton University Press, 1975

Stedman, Bruce J., "The International Whaling Commission and Negotiation for a Global Moratorium on Whaling", in *Nine Case Studies in International Environmental Negotiation*, edited by Lawrence E. Susskind, Esther Siskind and J. William Breslin, Cambridge, Massachusetts: Program on Negotiation at Harvard Law School, 1990

WHO: Four Decades of Achievement, Geneva: World Health Organization, 1988

The WMO Achievement: 40 Years in the Service of International Meteorology and Hydrology, Geneva: World Meteorological Organization, 1990

The majority of the studies on UNESCO, a member organ-ization of the United Nations, are programmatic or (more recently) apologetic, and few venture beyond rhetoric and generalities when it comes to an overall evaluation of its scien-tific activities. The publications by the WHO and the WMO are the former kind. Among the exceptions, SEWELL is partic-ularly valuable, as he pays consistent and thorough attention to UNESCO's involvement with science, describing critically the pressures and manoeuvres necessary to ensure, during the planning stage of the mid-1940s, the inclusion of science among the responsibilities of the new organization – which, instead of "UNECO", became the United Nations Educational, Scientific, and Cultural Organization. Sewell also examines the influence, during the 1940s and 1950s, of the "science lobby", the competition within the organization between education and science, and the politics of project planning and management involving high-level officials, member-states, and professional constituencies, such as the International Council of Scientific Unions (ICSU). His analysis includes information on the various scientific projects initiated (e.g. the Arid Zone Project) and sponsored by UNESCO, such as the creation of CERN.

ASCHER provides little-known details on the earlier years, especially on the budgeting process and the difficulties encoun-tered by both high-ranking personnel within the organization and members of national delegations (mostly newly recruited from academia) in adjusting to the constraints of collective action, such as priority setting, bargaining, and effective management. On a more conceptual level, SATHYAMURTHY examines briefly, and from a perspective that reflects the concerns of the early post-war period, the potentially conflicting views that shaped the understanding of UNESCO's role in world affairs at its inception – i.e. on the one hand, functionalism and, on the other, scientific evolutionism.

During the 1960s, when UNESCO became increasingly concerned with international development, the priorities of its scientific involvement shifted accordingly, the official discourse forcefully restating the importance of scientific research as a cornerstone of modernization, if not as a pre-investment for industrialization. As a consequence, the few authors who devote more than passing attention to the "science" part of UNESCO's mission generally concentrate on its contribution to Third World development. Writing from a Marxist viewpoint, HOLLY exposes the organization's efforts to encourage the development of scientific and technical capabilities in Third World countries as essentially a way to secure the reproduction of the capitalist system in these regions. UNESCO's strong belief in the deployment of appropriate research, organization, and science policies is also explored by FINNEMORE, who evaluates the impact of this type of assistance on the recipient countries.

UNESCO is not, indeed, the only organization within the United Nations system to be involved with science, nor is it the first attempt by a world organization to mobilize science in order to enhance international understanding and to provide mankind with a sense of common identity. SCHROEDER-GUDEHUS studies its predecessor, the League of Nations' Committee of International Intellectual Co-operation, and the reasons for its largely ineffectual efforts to overcome the reticence of national scientific communities. Today, practically all specialized agencies of the United Nations – such as WMO (World Meteorological Organization), WHO (World Health Organization), FAO (Food and Agriculture Organization) – and programmes – such as "Man and the Biosphere" in the 1960s, or, more recently, UNEP (United Nations Environment Programme) – bear some direct or indirect relation to science and technology, as do major mobilising events, such as the numerous United Nations Conferences – for example; on the Peaceful Uses of Atomic Energy (in Geneva 1955 and 1958), and on Science and Technology for Development (Geneva 1962 and Vienna 1979). Their work and the problems they face are frequently analysed as part of larger studies of the United Nations system (such as DETTER DE LUPIS's review of the origins and upshots of the 1972 UN Conference on the Human Environment in Stockholm), or of international scientific cooperation in general (such as JACOBSON's, CALDWELL's and STEDMAN's writings on, respectively, WHO, international environmental policies generally, and whaling).

All agencies and programmes produce official (administrative and technical) reports of their activities, and they also publish, albeit less regularly, case studies – such as FENNER's collective volume on the eradication of smallpox. Anniversaries usually set off the production of historical, although not always critical, overviews of the agencies' missions and accomplishments: some, such as DANIEL for WMO, reach back to 19th-century cooperation; others, such as WHO and WMO in the late 1980s, limit their histories to their existence within the United Nations "family".

Most of these studies tend to focus on political aspects of the functions and activities of international organizations: i.e.

the decision-making process, the structures and mechanisms of co-ordination, and the conflicts of interest. As these conflicts do not only arise among organization members, or between members and the organization's bureaucracy, but can also involve domestic constituencies – such as national scientific communities – it may be useful also to turn to studies of national policies: the withdrawal of the United States from UNESCO, for instance, has been analysed in detail by PRESTON, HERMAN & SCHILLER.

BRIGITTE SCHROEDER-GUDEHUS

See also International Science

Gödel, Kurt 1906–1978

Austrian-born American logician and mathematician

Dawson Jr, John W., "The Published Work of Kurt Gödel: An Annotated Bibliography", *Notre Dame Journal of Formal Logic*, 24 (1983): 255–84; 25 (1984): 283–87

Dawson Jr, John W., "Kurt Gödel in Sharper Focus", *Mathematical Intelligencer*, 6 (1984): 9–17

Feferman, Saul, "Gödel's Life and Work", introduction to vol. 1 of Gödel's *Collected Works*, Oxford: Clarendon Press, and New York: Oxford University Press, 1986, 1–34

Goldstern, Martin and Haim Judah, *The Incompleteness Phenomenon: A New Course in Mathematical Logic*, Wellesley, Massachusetts: Peters, 1995

Hofstadter, Douglas R., *Gödel, Escher, Bach: An Eternal Golden Braid*, New York: Basic Books, 1979

Kreisel, Georg, "Kurt Gödel", *Biographical Memoirs of Fellows of the Royal Society*, 26 (1980): 149–224; 27 (1981): 697; 28 (1982): 719

Kreisel, Georg, "Gödel's Excursions into Intuitionistic Logic", in *Gödel Remembered*, edited by Paul Weingartner and Leopold Schmetterer, Naples: Bibliopolis, 1987, 65–186

Nagel, Ernst and James R. Neuman, *Gödel's Proof*, New York: New York University Press, 1958

Shanker, S.G. (ed.), *Gödel's Theorem in Focus*, London and New York: Croom Helm, 1988

Van Heijenoort, Jean (ed.), *From Frege to Gödel: A Source Book in Mathematical Logic, 1879–1931*, Cambridge, Massachusetts: Harvard University Press, 1967

Wang, Hao, *Reflections on Kurt Gödel*, Cambridge, Massachusetts: MIT Press, 1987

Weingartner, Paul and Leopold Schmetterer (eds), *Gödel Remembered*, Naples: Bibliopolis, 1987

Kurt Friedrich Gödel was nicknamed "Mr Why" as he was growing up, and seems to have approached everything he did with great intensity. Crucial to his development as a mathematician were the lectures he heard as a student at the University of Vienna by Rudolph Carnap on mathematical logic, as well as his reading of David Hilbert's and Wilhelm Ackermann's *Grundzüge der theoretischen Logik* (1928) (translated as *Principles of Mathematical Logic* in 1950), in which the completeness of the axioms for first-order predicate calculus was raised as an open question. This was to become the subject of Gödel's dissertation, for which he received his PhD from the University of Vienna in 1929. Gödel's thesis, published in 1930, established that the axioms for first-order predicate calculus are indeed complete.

Gödel next set out to do the same for David Hilbert's program in general, which sought to establish the consistency of mathematics itself, viewed as a formal system. What Gödel eventually found was that any mathematical system containing arithmetic is incomplete – that it is possible to generate statements that cannot be proven to be either true or false. Gödel published his incompleteness results in 1931, and these became the subject of immediate mathematical interest. Subsequently, Gödel began to concentrate on one of the major open problems in mathematics, Georg Cantor's Continuum Hypothesis, which was intimately related to the Axiom of Choice. Finally, in 1937, Gödel succeeded in establishing the consistency not only of the Axiom of Choice, but also of the Continuum Hypothesis.

In March 1940, Gödel and his wife, Adele, moved permanently to the United States, where he had been offered a professorship at the Institute for Advanced Study at Princeton. Having established the consistency of both the Continuum Hypothesis and the Axiom of Choice, Gödel concentrated his first efforts at the Institute on trying to show that they were also independent, results that were successfully established by Paul Cohen of Stanford University in 1963. At about this same time, Gödel's interests began to change, and he increasingly turned away from mathematical problems towards esoteric philosophical issues and unusual cosmological models in which time was bi-directional, for, mathematically, time travel was assumed to be logically possible.

Gödel revolutionized logic and made some of the most fundamental contributions to the foundations of mathematics in the 20th century. As Saul Feferman has emphasized, Gödel's "were among the most outstanding contributions to logic in this century, decisively settling fundamental problems and introducing novel and powerful methods that were exploited extensively in much subsequent work".

Although there is an extensive literature by mathematicians on Gödel's contributions to logic and its bearing on mathematics, especially its foundations, the evaluation of his life and work only began in earnest after his death in 1978. Prior to that, the significance of Gödel's most salient achievement was made accessible to a wider audience thanks to NAGEL & NEUMAN, who give an easy-to-follow explanation of Gödel's famous incompleteness theorem of 1931. Above all, Nagel & Neuman present in an intelligible fashion the basic ideas behind Gödel's proof, including the important concept of Gödel numbering.

Less than a decade later, VAN HEIJENOORT included translations of four of Gödel's most important contributions with introductions and very useful commentaries. This source book covers the history of mathematical logic, from its beginnings with Frege to the remarkable results achieved by Kurt Gödel. Among the works that van Heijenoort translates, with extensive commentary and explanatory remarks, are Gödel's "The Completeness of the Axioms of the Functional Calculus of Logic" (1930), "Some Metamathematical Results on Completeness and Consistency" (1930), "On Formally Undecidable Propositions of *Principia Mathematica* and Related Systems I"

(1931), and "On Completeness and Consistency" (1931). The first of these was a rewritten version of Gödel's doctoral dissertation at the University of Vienna, which established that the first order predicate calculus is complete (i.e. that every valid formula is provable). While pointing out that Gödel also managed to establish, besides completeness, the Löwenheim-Skolem theorem that a satisfiable formula is khi-zero-satisfiable, Van Heijenoort also lists later proofs of Gödel's result, including proof-theoretic versions. The following year, Gödel introduced his method of arithmetization in order to prove a theorem that has since become one of the most influential results, and methods, of modern mathematical logic – namely, "On Formally Undecidable Propositions of *Principia Mathematica* and Related Systems I" (1931). Basically, this involved an analysis of the proposition "I am not provable", which Gödel approached in terms of Cantor's diagonal procedure. This led Gödel to construct a proposition that can be neither proven nor disproven (i.e., neither the proposition nor its negation can be established in the formal system Gödel used). Van Heijenoort offers a brief yet very useful overview of the major results that followed upon Gödel's publications of 1931, which serves to illustrate the deep influence that Gödel's results and methods have had on the foundations of mathematics. The value of the translation presented here is enhanced by Gödel's own explanatory annotations, including a new note (1963) in which he acknowledges Turing's general definition of a formal system, along with correspondingly general versions of several of Gödel's own theorems.

In popularizing Gödel's work, no one has brought his ideas to a wider public audience more than HOFSTADTER. The "Eternal Golden Braid", the subtitle of this Pulitzer prize-winning book, is a reference to Bach's *Musical Offering*, an improvisation that inspired Hofstadter to "improvise" a "meta-musical offering" of his own. Hofstadter includes ideas of recursion, self-reference, and parallels drawn between Bach's improvisations, the drawings of Escher and Gödel's incompleteness theorem (which in one version Hofstadter interprets as, "For each record player there is a record which it cannot play"). In addition to a brief history of logic and the paradoxes of set theory, Hofstadter also discusses mechanical reasoning, computers, and the debate over artificial intelligence. Along the way he considers such topics as "meaning and form" in mathematics, Zen Buddhism and its bearing on Gödel-numbering, a variety of computer languages including BlooP, FlooP and GlooP, the relevance of the Turing test for artificial intelligence, and the question of whether or not free will and human consciousness are at all related to Gödel's theorem. Hofstadter, a computer scientist by training, uses as recurring themes the works of Bach and Escher, primarily as metaphors to explore and explain ideas from logic, biology, psychology, physics, and linguistics, and to probe the question of how it is possible that we are unable to understand the nature of our own thinking. Here Gödel's theorems are presumably relevant, because they concern the ability of any human language, mathematical system, computer program, or thought process to talk about itself in an unending "mirroring" of reality.

KREISEL (1980–82) is much more technical, offering a detailed, scholarly analysis of Gödel's work by one of the most prominent logicians of the 20th-century. Kreisel knew Gödel as a colleague at the Institute for Advanced Study in Princeton, primarily in the late 1950s and 1960s. Kreisel was thus intimately familiar with Gödel's work, and explores its many facets in considerable detail. While Kreisel (1980–82) stresses the significance of Gödel's work relative to formal systems and sets, emphasizing various kinds of definability that have turned out to be more important than Gödel's work on intuitionistic logic, KREISEL (1987) explores the latter's connections with constructivity, the principal element of intuitionistic logic.

DAWSON (1983–84) offers an annotated bibliography of Gödel's published works. Unlike earlier bibliographies that Dawson cites, this annotated bibliography includes all known publications by Gödel, including articles, abstracts, and translations, 1930–81; reviews written by Gödel, 1931–36, after which he apparently declined to write any more; and correspondence and remarks by Gödel published by others. In three appendices, Dawson also includes an index of reviews of Gödel's publications, a list of published photographs of Gödel, and a cross-referenced index to translations of his works listed by language. There is also a very useful bibliography of references.

DAWSON (1984) is more expository in character, and describes Gödel as a "reclusive genius whose incompleteness theorems and set-theoretic consistency proofs are among the most celebrated results of 20th-century mathematics, yet whose life history has until recently remained almost unknown". Dawson seeks to redress inconsistencies between different accounts of Gödel's life, and to substantiate or refute various rumors that have circulated, using primary sources to place Gödel in sharper focus. Dawson, who spent two years cataloguing the Gödel papers at the Institute for Advanced Study in Princeton, also uses personal interviews and correspondence with many individuals who knew Gödel personally to produce this authoritative, if brief, account of Gödel's life and work.

FEFERMAN offers a more detailed, yet still relatively succinct, evaluation of Gödel's life and work, and is easily the most readable, informative study of Gödel written for non-mathematicians, but with sufficient technical detail to make clear the significance of his achievements. Beginning with a synopsis of Gödel's life and career, Feferman paints a detailed portrait of Gödel's experiences as a student in Vienna and his subsequent travels to America, where he eventually settled at the Institute for Advanced Study in 1940. Feferman also discusses Gödel's "Works, thought and influence", and includes a number of photographs.

WANG provides personal reminiscences of Gödel based largely on his contact with Gödel at the Institute for Advanced Study in the 1970s. After a "chronology" giving a year-by-year schematic account of Gödel's life, Wang provides further details of Gödel's life and career, followed by brief descriptions of his major mathematical and philosophical papers. These include observations on Gödel's proof of the completeness of elementary logic, the incompletability of mathematics, Cantor and set theory, and Russell's mathematical logic, among other related topics.

WEINGARTNER & SCHMETTERER comprises papers presented at a symposium convened to bring together scholars who had known Gödel personally, in order to discuss not only scientific and philosophical, but also personal issues. For example, Gödel's brother Rudolf gives a brief, personal account of him, which offers some interesting psychological insights –

that he was "a bad loser, who could cry intensely when he lost", and that he was a depressive, troubled by "feelings of inferiority". In addition to his severe medical problems, including bladder and kidney complaints, Rudolf Gödel notes that "my brother was of an unstable mental disposition . . . After the murder of Professor Schlick [of the Vienna Circle], he had a 'nervous breakdown' and was in a sanatorium for some time. Later too there were occasional mental crises". By contrast, Taussky-Todd recalls the years that she and Gödel spent as fellow students at the University of Vienna, from 1925 onwards, while Stephen Kleene describes Gödel's subsequent influence in the history of logic, mathematics, and foundations. Kleene attended Gödel's path-breaking lectures in Princeton in 1933 and 1934, and, as a student of Alonzo Church at Princeton in 1934, was again exposed to Gödel's work. Kleene's article stresses in particular his own collaboration with J. Barkley Rosser and its relation to Gödel's work, as well the results of Alan M. Turing, who took his PhD with Church at Princeton in 1936, and succeeded in reinterpreting Gödel's first undecidability theorem (1931). Kreisel, also in Weingartner & Schmetterer, focuses on recent research in intuitionism, but mentions his contacts with Gödel after World War II, including Gödel's teachers and friends at the University of Vienna, and describes Gödel's reception at Princeton, his views on Church, the work of Kleene and Rosser, and developments over the years related to Gödel's interest in intuitionistic logic, the foundations of logic and mathematics, and related philosophical questions. Kreisel stresses above all Gödel's intuitionistic logic, which was not covered in his biography of Gödel of 1980–82, and also includes his own reminiscences of him, beginning in the mid-1950s (which Kreisel provides, he says, as an "antidote" to most reminiscences of Gödel which stem mainly from the 1970s). However, the complex arguments and technical nature of Kreisel's article make it difficult to follow.

SHANKER was inspired, according to its editor, by the need to understand the relevance of Gödel's theorems for modern metaphysics and their relation to the "mechanist thesis". He was concerned that Gödel's methods were inaccessible to anyone but trained mathematical logicians, and this collection of articles seeks to provide "a lucid introduction to the mechanics and mathematical import of Gödel's proof". It begins with a short biographical sketch of Gödel by John Dawson, followed by an overview of the basic features of his mathematical logic by Kleene. Dawson, in a second article devoted to "The Reception of Gödel's Incompleteness Theorems", explores the remarkable fact that Gödel's revolutionary ideas and methods were almost immediately accepted by contemporary logicians. Solomon Feferman explores Gödel's reluctance to make better known his philosophical commitment to a realist, essentially Platonist account of mathematics, despite his insistence that a realist view of mathematics was essential to the remarkable discoveries he made in the late 1920s and early 1930s. Feferman further considers whether or not Gödel's Platonism kept him from investigating certain areas of mathematical logic, including aspects of truth and computability, which were major concerns of other logicians at the time. In one of three concluding papers, Michael Resnik ("On the Philosophical Significance of Consistency Proofs") considers their relevance to the apparent failure of Hilbert's Programme to establish the consistency of mathematics. This leads in turn to a paper by

Michael Detlefsen ("On Interpreting Gödel's Second Theorem"), which concludes that it does not imply the failure of Hilbert's Programme. In a similar vein, but drawing heavily on Wittgenstein's critique of Gödel's First Incompleteness Theorem, Shanker analyzes the consistency and decision problems, in order to resolve the foundational crisis that was precipitated by Cantor's paradoxes of set theory and was exacerbated by Gödel's theorems. Unfortunately, both Wittgenstein and Shanker inherited Russell's reluctance to distinguish between formal theories and their models, and the lack of such a distinction often leads, as in this case, to irrelevant or inaccurate interpretations of results in mathematical logic.

Among the most recent attempts to explain comprehensively yet intelligibly the importance of Gödel's many contributions to modern mathematics, logic, and philosophy is GOLDSTERN & JUDAH. The main goal of this book is to explain why all reasonable mathematical systems are necessarily incomplete; i.e., that there will always be mathematical problems that cannot be resolved. This is, of course, the major result of Gödel's incompleteness theorem, which assumes a fundamental role throughout Goldstern & Judah, a work designed as the basis of a two-semester course in mathematical logic. Goldstern & Judah demonstrate the persistent interest in (and importance of) Gödel's provocative and profound contributions to modern logic and philosophy, including the foundations of mathematics.

JOSEPH W. DAUBEN

See also Cantor; Mathematical Modernity; Set Theory

Goethe, Johann Wolfgang von   1749–1832

German poet, scientist, and court official

Amrine, Frederick, Francis J. Zucker and Harvey Wheeler, *Goethe and the Sciences: A Reappraisal*, Dordrecht: Reidel, 1987

Hansen, Adolph, *Goethe's Metamorphose der Pflanzen: Geschichte einer botanischen Hypothese*, Giessen: Tölpelmann, 1907

Hansen, Adolph, *Goethes Morphologie: Metamorphose der Pflanzen und Osteologie*, Giessen: Tölpelmann, 1919

Jackson, Myles W., "A Spectrum of Belief: Goethe's 'Republic' Versus Newtonian 'Despotism'", *Social Studies of Science*, 24 (1994): 673–701

Jackson, Myles W., "Natural and Artificial Budgets: Accounting for Goethe's Economy of Nature", *Science in Context*, 7 (1994): 409–31

Kuhn, Dorothea and Wolf von Engelhardt (eds), *Goethe: Die Schriften zur Naturwissenschaft: Vollständige mit Erläuterungen versehene Ausgabe im Auftrage der Deutschen Akademie der Naturforscher Leopoldina*, 11 + 11 vols, Weimar: Böhlaus Nachfolger, 1947–

Magnus, Rudolf, *Goethe as a Scientist*, translated from the German by Heinz Norden, New York: Schuman, 1949 (original edition, 1906)

Matthaei, Rupprecht, *Goethe zur Farbe und Farbenlehre*, Weimar: Die Gedenkstätten der deutschen Klassik, 1955

Nisbet, H.B., *Goethe and the Scientific Tradition*, London: Institute of Germanic Studies, 1972

Schöne, Albrecht, *Goethes Farbentheologie*, Munich: Beck, 1987

Semper, Max, *Die geologischen Studien Goethes*, Leipzig: Veit, 1914

Sepper, Dennis L., *Goethe Contra Newton: Polemics and the Project for a New Science of Color*, Cambridge and New York: Cambridge University Press, 1988

Steiner, Rudolf, *Goethes Weltanschauung*, Weimar: Emil Felber, 1897

Stephenson, R.H., *Goethe's Conception of Knowledge and Science*, Edinburgh: Edinburgh University Press, and New York: Columbia University Press, 1996

Wells, George A., *Goethe and the Development of Science, 1750–1900*, Alphen aan den Rijn: Sijthoff & Noordhoff, 1978

The secondary literature that deals with Johann Wolfgang von Goethe's views on nature could fill major libraries. Indeed, it has been (rather conservatively) estimated that there are well over 5,000 books and articles on this particular topic. Goethe has been elevated to the status of national hero in Germany, especially on account of his literary productions, and this has increased the attention paid to his writings on morphology and other scientific topics. Furthermore, Goethe's polemic against Newton and the reductionist view of nature has also struck a chord with many who are disaffected with modern science.

For the purposes of this essay, the literature has been divided into accounts of Goethe's scientific work, attempts to use Goethe as an authority for particular views of nature and society, and studies attempting to place Goethe within the history of science.

Goethe's writings on scientific topics have been conveniently gathered in the luxurious KUHN & VON ENGELHARDT, a collection reflecting the iconic position that Goethe holds in Germany. It contains 11 volumes, which reproduce Goethe's texts with extensive footnotes, and 11 accompanying volumes (not all of which have appeared to date) of commentaries, and provides a mine of information for the serious scholar, but is intimidating in its monumental concern with detail. Goethe's scientific works have been divided into scientific disciplines, and thus there are volumes on geology and mineralogy, optics, morphology (including botany), and other miscellaneous topics.

This categorisation stems from the "classic" studies of the first half of the 20th century, which concentrated on Goethe's work in specific disciplines, despite the fact that Goethe was not a professional or a specialized scientist. HANSEN (1907) and HANSEN (1919) are the seminal works on Goethe's botanical and morphological writings respectively, while MATTHAEI is the most comprehensive account of Goethe's theory of colors, and Goethe's geology is covered by SEMPER.

Goethe's iconic status has made it attractive to use his scientific work to bolster particular scientific arguments or interpretations. One of the earliest and most influential of such cases is STEINER, which stresses Goethe's organic, dynamic depiction of nature, and his diatribes against reductionist, Cartesian and mechanist accounts. Steiner started an educational movement in late 19th-century Europe that based its teachings on

Goethe's doctrines of holism, vitalism, and pantheism. Hence, Steiner's work is a hagiographic account of Goethe and his work and is often used by theosophists, and Germanists interested in either formulating "alternatives to modern science" or in salvaging Goethe's reputation as a scientist.

Much of the secondary literature on Goethe has attempted either to vindicate or debunk his views on nature, and often, by extension, to argue for or against modern science. Recently, SEPPER has offered a detailed summary of Goethe's infamous polemic against Sir Isaac Newton's doctrine of light and colors, but then proceeds to determine, rather ahistorically, which of the two scientists was correct. Similarly, AMRINE, ZUCKER & WHEELER contains 20 essays discussing Goethe's epistemology, color theory, morphology, and even psychoanalytic method. This work is more concerned with questioning whether Goethean science is a valuable alternative to modern science, rather than offering a historical or explanatory account of Goethe's scientific aims. There is, however, an impressive bibliography, of both primary and secondary sources, following the collection of essays, which is very useful to the scholar interested in Goethe's multifarious investigations of nature.

In the third category of literature on Goethe, there have been many influential works that offer a more sophisticated account of his view of nature – most of which could be described as intellectual histories. SCHÖNE argues that Goethe's stance against the Newtonians needs to be understood as a type of natural theology, and convincingly demonstrates that Goethe's rhetoric is saturated with Biblical passages and references to Martin Luther's Reformation. NISBET focuses on the forces that influenced Goethe's thinking, by discussing the importance of Plato, Kant, Spinoza, Francis Bacon and the empirical tradition to Goethe's physical and biological investigations. It is a very well written account and should be consulted for a general overview of Goethe's *Naturanschauung*.

STEPHENSON, a Professor of German, argues that Goethe deployed a novel mode of writing in order to reenact and describe the processes of nature. However, he fails to address the non-literary resources that Goethe employed, such as the colored card exercises, and, as (yet another) treatment of Goethe's scientific writings as representation, Stephenson offers the historian of science nothing new. He is also unaware of recent work on Goethe and Newton dealing with relevant issues, such as authority, the communicability of natural knowledge, and replication.

Other texts offer a more general account of Goethe's intense and highly varied investigations of nature. MAGNUS provides an intellectual history of Goethe's botany, zoology, geology, morphology, mineralogy and color theory, for many years representing the most thorough account of Goethe's contributions to the study of nature. Another thorough account, with a similar orientation, is WELLS, which emphasizes Goethe's views of nature, and compares and contrasts them with other views of the period.

More recent studies have offered a cultural history of Goethe's works, by analyzing them within the context of late 18th-century and early 19th-century Weimar, and by making use of sources that were not considered relevant for Goethe's "scientific" work in the "classic" studies of the early 20th century – i.e., his pronouncements on politics and administration. For example, JACKSON (1994, "A Spectrum of Belief") has argued that Goethe linked Newton's *Opticks* and its followers to tyranny, and contrasted this with his own theory of freedom. In the same fashion, Goethe attacked the private knowledge held by the illuminated circles of the late Enlightenment and the Roman Catholic Church, and countered such knowledge with a more accessible epistemology, as reflected in the ease of his color games and his assault on the privacy of Newtonian prisms. His views on nature contrasted enlightened despotism, which he considered a legitimate form of government, with unenlightened despotism, which he equated with tyranny. JACKSON (1994, "Natural and Artificial Budgets") has also argued that the organizing principles of nature were the same, for Goethe, as the methods for investigating it. Goethe's administrative rhetoric – which included words such as budget, balance, economy, law, and order – was also applicable to the relationships inside both the organization of the State and natural philosophy, as evidenced by the importance of the concept of the budget to both Goethe's administrative duties and morphological investigations.

MYLES W. JACKSON

See also Romanticism

Graphical Method

Brain, Robert M. and M. Norton Wise, "Muscles and Engines: Indicator Diagrams and Helmholtz's Graphical Method", in *Universalgenie Helmholtz: Rückblick nach 100 Jahren*, edited by Lorenz Krüger, Berlin: Akademie, 1994

Brain, Robert M., "Standards and Semiotics," in *Inscribing Science*, edited by Timothy Lenoir, Stanford: Stanford University Press, 1996

Braun, Marta, *Picturing Time: The Work of Etienne-Jules Marey (1830–1904)*, Chicago: University of Chicago Press, 1992

Daston, Lorraine and Peter Galison, "The Image of Objectivity", *Representations*, 40 (1992): 81–128

Frank Jr, Robert G., "The Telltale Heart: Physiological Instruments, Graphic Methods, and Clinical Hopes, 1854–1914", in *The Investigative Enterprise: Experimental Physiology in Nineteenth-Century Medicine*, edited by William Coleman and Frederic L. Holmes, Berkeley: University of California Press, 1988

Funkhouser, H.G. "Historical Development of the Graphical Representation of Statistical Data", *Osiris*, 3 (1937): 269–404

Hills, R.L. and A.J. Pacey, "The Measurement of Power in Early Steam-Driven Textile Mills", *Technology and Culture*, 13 (1972): 25–43

Hoff, Hebbel E. and L.A. Geddes, "Graphic Recording before Ludwig: An Historical Summary", *Archives Internationales d'Histoire des Sciences*, 12 (1959): 1–25

Holmes, Frederic L. and Kathryn M. Olesko, "Precision's Images: Helmholtz and Graphical Methods in Physiology", in *The Values of Precision*, edited by M. Norton Wise, Princeton, New Jersey: Princeton University Press, 1994

Krohn, Roger, "Why Are Graphs so Central in Science",
   Biology and Philosophy, 6 (1991): 181–206

Lawrence, Christopher, "Physiological Apparatus in the
   Wellcome Museum 1: The Marey Sphygmograph",
   Medical History, 22 (1978): 196–200

Lawrence, Christopher, "Physiological Apparatus in the
   Wellcome Museum 2: The Dudgeon Sphygmograph and
   Its Descendents", *Medical History*, 23 (1979): 96–101

Lawrence, Christopher, "Physiological Apparatus in the
   Wellcome Museum 3: Early Sphygmanometers", *Medical
   History*, 23 (1979): 474–79

Lenoir, Timothy, "Helmholtz and the Materialities of
   Communication", *Osiris*, 9 (1993): 183–207

Lynch, Michael and Steve Woolgar (eds), *Representation in
   Scientific Practice*, Cambridge, Massachusetts: MIT Press,
   1990

Owens, Larry, "Vannevar Bush and the Differential Analyzer:
   The Text and Context of an Early Computer", *Technology
   and Culture*, 27/1 (1986): 63–95

Schaffer, Simon, "Self-Evidence", *Critical Inquiry*, 18 (1992):
   327–67

Tufte, Edward R., *The Visual Display of Quantitative
   Information*, Cheshire, Connecticut: Graphics Press, 1983

As a central and time-honoured technique of imaging and measurement, the graphic method of representing scientific phenomena or data, by lines and points in a co-ordinate-system, has acquired a substantial literature examining its historical emergence and significance. With some exceptions, the publications surveyed here concern the production of graphic representation using self-registering or automatic recording instruments. Other publications consider statistical graphics, or scientific representation, in a more general sense.

Several works on scientific representation provide excellent frameworks for considering the use of graphic images in sociological, ethnomethodological, and philosophical terms. The essays in LYNCH & WOOLGAR present multiple approaches to graphs, diagrams, equations, models, photographs, instrumental inscriptions, written reports, computer programs, and hybrid forms of these. Among the essays in this volume, Latour furnishes a particularly influential model for examining these forms of representation, showing how specific optical and material features serve to bind social networks of scientific communication over spatial and temporal distance.

Although presented not as a work of history of science, but as a primer on graphical excellence for both the scientist and layperson, TUFTE nevertheless contains many insightful discussions of historical materials over two centuries of graphical practice, including the early economic charts of William Playfair, and the graphic methods of Minard and Marey. In the second half of the book, the author provides a theory of data graphics, suggesting why some graphics might be better than others, as well as changes and improvements in design. In every aspect of its production, this book exemplifies its proposition that graphic excellence derives from the same principles of design at work in successful art, architecture, and prose.

A central concern of all graphic representation has been its status as "objective" knowledge of the world. KROHN argues that statistical graphs enable the scientific researcher to imagine, or "see through them", to the physical processes and materials that they represent. But, he argues, the "objectivist" language of graphs is most effective when it allows a comparison between the incommensurable media of numbers, words and images, and thus permits the revision of scientific concepts. DASTON & GALISON consider the "objectivist" notion of the graphic method in historical terms, as a characteristic element of the more general emergence of what they term "mechanical objectivity". Along with photography and kindred techniques of atlas-making, the graphic method gained its objective status from the promise of machines to replace the weary, imperfect, and wilful human observer. Objectivity derived less from the graph's reference to nature, than from its adequacy as a representation of certain pre-selected and standardized objects of research. SCHAFFER argues that the adoption of self-registering instrumentation accompanied a decline in the rituals of public natural philosophical performance, and the evidential context that surrounded them. In place of the stable and carefully enclosed communities of 18th-century natural philosophy, the new science of the 19th century embodied skill in self-recording instruments, thereby establishing new conditions for the acceptance of evidence.

The earliest uses of the graphic method were found in mechanical engineering. HILLS & PACEY describe the mechanical and commercial considerations of the measurement of power in early steam-driven textile mills, which led to the development of the Indicator Diagram by John Southern, an associate of James Watt and Matthew Boulton. They demonstrate how the problem of supplying steam power demanded a reliable measure to potential customers, a problem solved by attaching a self-registering apparatus to a manometer, in order to record the relations of pressure and volume in the piston of the engine. HOFF & GEDDES survey a number of instruments which followed in the wake of the Indicator Diagram, including self-registering dynamometers, chronographs, and devices used by ballistics experts and telegraphers to measure extremely brief intervals of time.

The introduction of the graphic method into physiology was modelled on the techniques and methods of the engineers and physicists. BRAIN & WISE show how the German physiologists Carl Ludwig and Hermann Helmholtz looked to Indicator Diagrams and self-registering dynamometers as a means of measuring the internal processes of physiological function in terms of dynamical mechanical concepts, particularly those involving the critical variable of time. HOLMES & OLESKO argue that Helmholtz developed the graphic method less as a matter of precision measurement, for which he used other non-graphic techniques, than as a means of visualizing and communicating the phenomena of physiological function.

LENOIR considers Helmholtz's graphic representations of the velocity of nerve transmission in relation to the burgeoning telegraph industry, showing how these interests intersected and furnished an abundance of analogies central to the development of sensory physiology. BRAIN examines the application of the methods of the physiological laboratory to the new science of experimental phonetics, arguing that the graphic method played a critical role in the conceptual foundations of modern linguistics.

BRAUN examines the work of Étienne-Jules Marey, who was probably the most important and influential proponent of the graphic method during the 19th century. This beautifully produced book is distinguished by its use of hitherto unpublished archival photographs, which accompany valuable chapters on the extension of the graphic method to chronophotography, and the development of early cinematographic apparatus.

The application of the methods of physiological graphic recording became a cardinal feature of the new science-based medicine of the late 19th century. LAWRENCE (1978 and 1979) argues that the new self-registering instruments, such as the sphygmograph, stood at the center of British controversies between advocates of traditional clinical practice and proponents of the new scientific medicine. At issue was the status of the physician's extensive sensory and textual training, as well as the authority it conferred on the traditional gentleman doctor. Opponents of the graphic recording instruments argued that its widespread use would degrade this medical authority, while promoters asserted that it would bring medicine in line with modern science, and would thereby improve medical practice and prestige. FRANK considers the aims of some of the proponents of the new medical instruments, examining how, despite the relative failure of the sphygmograph to gain widespread clinical application, it cleared a path for the development and ultimate success of the electrocardiogram as a cornerstone of clinical apparatus.

In an excellent survey of statistical graphics, FUNKHOUSER attributes their early development to William Playfair's tenure as a draughtsman for James Watt. Funkhouser appraises the history of statistical graphics, with special attention to the various forms of representation, the spheres of application, and questions of standardisation.

OWENS describes the early 20th-century attempt to use graphic recording devices as the basis for an analogue computer. With the help of the differential analyzer, Vannevar Bush sought to mechanize the calculus as an aid to solving complex problems of physics and chemistry.

ROBERT BRAIN

Greece: general works

Clagett, Marshall, *Greek Science in Antiquity*, New York and London: Abelard-Schuman, 1957

De Santillana, Giorgio, *The Origins of Scientific Thought: From Anaximander to Proclus 600 BC to 300 AD*, Chicago: University of Chicago Press, and London: Weidenfeld and Nicolson, 1961

Dijksterhuis, E.J., *The Mechanization of the World Picture*, translated from the Dutch by C. Dikshoom, Oxford: Clarendon Press, and New York: Oxford University Press, 1961 (original edition, 1950)

Farrington, Benjamin, *Science and Politics in the Ancient World*, London: Allen and Unwin, 1939; New York: Oxford University Press, 1940; 2nd edition, London: Allen and Unwin, 1965; New York: Barnes and Noble, 1966

French, Roger, *Ancient Natural History: Histories of Nature*, London and New York: Routledge, 1994

James, Peter and Nick Thorpe, *Ancient Inventions*, New York: Ballantine Books, 1994; London: Michael O'Mara, 1995

Lindberg, David C., *The Beginnings of Western Science: The European Scientific Tradition in Philosophical, Religious, and Institutional Context, 600 BC to AD 1450*, Chicago: University of Chicago Press, 1992

Lloyd, G.E.R., *Early Greek Science: Thales to Aristotle*, New York: Norton, and London: Chatto and Windus, 1970

Lloyd, G.E.R., *Greek Science after Aristotle*, New York: Norton, and London: Chatto and Windus, 1973

Lloyd, G.E.R., *Magic, Reason and Experience: Studies in the Origin and Development of Greek Science*, Cambridge and New York: Cambridge University Press, 1979

Lloyd, G.E.R., *Science, Folklore and Ideology: Studies in the Life Sciences in Ancient Greece*, Cambridge and New York: Cambridge University Press, 1983

Lloyd, G.E.R., *The Revolutions of Wisdom: Studies in the Claim and Practice of Ancient Greek Science*, Berkeley: University of California Press, 1987

Lloyd, G.E.R., *Methods and Problems in Greek Science*, Cambridge and New York: Cambridge University Press, 1991

Neugebauer, Otto, *The Exact Sciences in Antiquity*, Copenhagen: Ejnar Munksgaard, 1951; 2nd edition, Providence, Rhode Island: Brown University Press, 1957

Rochberg, F. (ed.), "The Cultures of Ancient Science: Some Historical Reflections", *Isis* (special issue), 83/4 (1992)

Sarton, George, *Ancient Science and Modern Civilization*, Lincoln: University of Nebraska Press, and London: Edward Arnold, 1954

General works on ancient Greek science started to appear around the late 1920s and early 1930s, but it was not until World War II that the subject flourished dramatically. The postwar surveys by DIJKSTERHUIS, who focused on the clockwork metaphor in science, and by SARTON, the renowned founder of the journal *Isis*, both offered broader views that spanned from the Pythagoreans to the 17th century. Sarton's book contains lectures on Euclid, Ptolemy, and the end of Greek science and culture, and attempts to place this science within context by describing such institutions as the Alexandrian Museum and Library. Writing in the 1950s, Sarton argued that in antiquity, as in the present, non-conformists were persecuted and exiled, and that such refugees carried vital wisdom and knowledge with them overseas. In accordance with the high status of classical studies, the bulk of the material on science in antiquity during the 1950s and early 1960s is focused on Greek science. CLAGETT, for example, undertakes to define science, and to describe the continuity from Greek to modern thought; thus science is the orderly and systematic comprehension, description and/or explanation of natural phenomena, along with the tools necessary for that undertaking (especially mathematics and logic). Aiming to produce more than a mere catalogue of knowledge, Clagett analyses the relative importance of revelation, authority, reason, experience, and experimentation.

Throughout the 1960s, the influence of the Near East grew. NEUGEBAUER is a very good example, as he emphasizes Egyptian and Babylonian science and its transmission during Hellenistic times. Limiting himself to a study of mathematics and astronomy in antiquity, Neugebauer stays very close to the sources and his account is narrowly internalistic. DE

SANTILLANA set out to discover the science (apart from numerical science) that had gone unnoticed in classical texts, due to the fact that classicists by and large are not trained in the sciences. FARRINGTON discerns an emergence of a mode of thought in the 6th and 5th centuries BC in which science was a part of man's technique for controlling the natural environment. He is dismissive of Plato, since on the whole the philosopher was opposed to observation and experimentation.

Geoffrey Lloyd introduced socio-economical and political elements into the discussion in the late 1970s and 1980s. Already, in LLOYD (1970) he had focused on criticism and debate within Greek city states, beginning with Miletus, arguing that a new critical spirit was introduced into man's attitude to the world of nature, and that this should be seen as a counterpart to, and offshoot from, the contemporary development of the practice of free debate and open discussion within the context of politics and law. This theme has continued in all of Lloyd's subsequent works. LLOYD (1973) carries the overview of Greek science further in the chronology, these two early works together covering all of ancient Greece. LLOYD (1979) engages with studies in anthropology, philosophy, and the sociology of science (such as Popper, Kuhn, Lakatos, and Feyerabend), and the development of literacy. The problem is that the "irrational" can be found in all periods of Greek thought, even when science and philosophy were emerging as "recognisable inquiries", and Lloyd juxtaposes Greek thought with that of non-Greek non-modern cultures. The underlying theme of LLOYD (1987) is an exploration of the relationship between the various attempts at early science and the prevailing ideology of the time (where "ideology" in a broad sense covers "the ideas or beliefs that underpinned fundamental social structures or that corresponded to the views or ideals of the ruling elite"); it is worth mentioning in particular the chapter on "Dogmatism and Uncertainty", in which he tackles Kuhn's model of scientific paradigms. LLOYD (1991; his selected papers from the past 30 years) includes new commentaries that present the recent developments and problems that today's historian of science must confront in ancient Greek science, including a variety of methodological-historiographical issues.

In general, all these works reap the fruits of an increase of research into ancient science, thus providing extensive (and much needed) bibliographies. This systematization of the field matured during the 1990s in two ways. First, a realization has developed for the need to give a larger audience more facts and explanations, which has produced superior (general) ancient science books like LINDBERG, who points out that fully two-thirds of his bibliography on ancient science had not been available to Lloyd in the early 1970s. Lindberg is an account of both ancient and medieval science, the latter being his field of expertise. Indeed, one of the aims of the book is to point to the continuity between ancient and medieval science, which had been obscured by the disciplinary border between the two fields. However, while most of the book is concerned with later developments, there are still five chapters on Greece, covering the cosmos, Aristotle's philosophy of nature, Hellenistic natural philosophy, the mathematical sciences, and medicine. The aim is synthetic rather than encyclopedic, and the historical development is set within a largely

educational context. Meanwhile, FRENCH offers a more focused account of ancient natural history that is reminiscent of Lloyd's earlier agenda, always maintaining a strong awareness of the social context.

JAMES & THORPE is a collection of extraordinary facts and curiosities from before 1492, the year of Columbus's transatlantic crossing. This is a history of achievements in the mould of Needham (although much less scholarly), covering medicine, transport, sexual toys, military technology, personal effects, food, drink and drugs, urban life artifacts, agricultural and domestic technology, and, finally, communication techniques.

The second aspect of this increased systematization of the 1990s is illustrated by ROCHBERG, a special issue of *Isis*, which contains four papers on the current state of the field. In the introduction, Rochberg points to the hitherto unused Near Eastern and South Asian sources that have now become available, and encourages the use of these sources as an antidote to the Hellenophilia that has tended to skew the historiography. A widening of the historical perspective should enable us to understand the complexities of, and (to our eyes) contradictions in, the culture of ancient science.

ELMER YGLESIAS

Greece: medicine

Flashar, Hellmut (ed.), *Antike Medizin*, Darmstadt: Wissenschaftliche Buchgesellschaft, 1971

Kudlien, Fridolf, *Der Beginn des medizinischen Denkens bei den Griechen von Homer bis Hippokrates*, Zurich and Stuttgart: Artemis Verlag, 1967

Lloyd, G.E.R., *Science, Folklore and Ideology: Studies in the Life Sciences in Ancient Greece*, Cambridge and New York: Cambridge University Press, 1983

Longrigg, James, *Greek Rational Medicine: Philosophy and Medicine from Alcmaeon to the Alexandrians*, London and New York: Routledge, 1993

Phillips, E.D., *Greek Medicine*, London: Thames and Hudson, 1973; Philadelphia: Charles Press, 1987

Temkin, Owsei and C. Lilian Temkin (eds), *Ancient Medicine: Selected Papers of Ludwig Edelstein*, translated from the German by C. Lilian Temkin, Baltimore: Johns Hopkins University Press, 1967

Traditionally, most general works on the history of medicine begin with a summary of Greek medicine, which is usually treated as an important step in the development that finds its logical culmination in modern medicine. The other main approach to Greek medicine consists in detailed examinations of specialised topics, the majority written by and for classicists. It is therefore relatively difficult to find monographs that are both exhaustive and useful, but much interesting material can be found in certain collections of essays.

TEMKIN & TEMKIN's book is a posthumously edited selection of papers by Ludwig Edelstein on various aspects of Greek medicine. (Although intended for an academic audience, most of them can be understood without previous knowledge of Greek medicine.) Along with several papers on Hippocratic medicine, subjects discussed include the Methodists, Empiricism, the relation of medicine to religion and magic, anatomy, dietetics, and medical ethics.

FLASHAR has edited a collection of essays and articles written between 1905 and 1965, and added a useful bibliography up to 1970. The essays cover Hippocratic medicine, Diocles of Carystus, Herophilus, links with philosophy (pre-Socratic to post-Aristotelian), the Empiricists, Celsus (the only excursion into Roman medicine), Galen, late antiquity and Byzantium.

KUDLIEN offers a useful introduction to the concept of disease in Greek medicine. Starting with the Homeric epics, he argues for a development from supernatural explanations for non-traumatic afflictions, via the concept of disease as a type of wound, to a rational conception of disease. He is sceptical about borrowings from Egyptian medicine, but stresses the influence of pre-Socratic natural philosophy and of Ionian historiography. Although a rather scholarly work (containing some Greek), this is still accessible to non-classicists.

LLOYD uses the ulterior dimension of anthropology in his discussion of Greek popular beliefs and their interaction with scientific theorising, beginning with a study of Greek zoological taxonomy. Parts II and III are more specifically about Greek medicine, namely the repercussions of the assumed inferiority of the female sex on medical theory and practice, and the relation between folklore and "high" science in pharmacology, anatomy, and gynaecology.

The main claim of LONGRIGG is that the Greeks invented rational medicine, whereas in earlier times and in other cultures medicine had been largely an irrational combination of magic and religion. The attitude that led to the consideration of causes and symptoms of disease in natural (i.e., not supernatural) terms, claims Longrigg, is the same as the one first applied by Ionian natural philosophers in their search for the causes of natural phenomena. As clear evidence for this influence, he quotes the adoption of the Ionic dialect by the medical authors. The role of (Platonic, Aristotelian, and subsequent) philosophy in the further development of Greek medicine is also examined.

PHILLIPS gives a fairly straightforward introduction for those with little or no familiarity with the topic, in particular regarding the pre-Socratics, folk medicine, and the cult of Asclepius. His approach would now be considered old-fashioned, as he opposes "sensible treatment" and "bizarre theory" – criticising the Greeks for not being "fully scientific" – and lists the extracts under modern medical categories.

CHRISTINE F. SALAZAR

Group Theory

Hawkins, Thomas, "Wilhelm Killing and the Structure of Lie Algebras", *Archive for History of Exact Sciences*, 26 (1982): 127–92

Hawkins, Thomas, "Hesse's Principle of Transfer and the Representations of Lie Algebras", *Archive for History of Exact Sciences*, 39 (1988): 41–73

Hawkins, Thomas, *The Dedekind–Frobenius Correspondence in Context*, New York: Springer, 1996

Mackey, George W., *The Scope and History of Commutative and Noncommutative Harmonic Analysis*, Providence,

Rhode Island: American Mathematical Society/ London Mathematical Society, 1992

Montesinos, José María, *Classical Tessellations and Three-Manifolds*, New York: Springer, 1987

Nicholson, Julia, "The Development and Understanding of the Concept of Quotient Group", *Historia Mathematica*, 20/1 (1993): 68–88

Scholz, Erhard, *Symmetrie, Gruppe, Dualität*, Basel: Birkhäuser, 1989

Waerden, B.L. van der (ed.), *Sources of Quantum Mechanics*, Amsterdam: North-Holland, 1967; New York: Dover, 1968

Weyl, Hermann, *Symmetry*, Princeton, New Jersey: Princeton University Press, 1952

Wussing, Hans, *The Genesis of the Abstract Group Concept*, translated from the German by Abe Shenitzer with Hardy Grant, Cambridge, Massachusetts: MIT Press, 1984 (original edition, 1969)

Group theory has its origins in several branches of 19th-century mathematics: number theory, geometry, and the theory of equations (Galois theory). All this was described in detail in the pioneering work by WUSSING, which is written in the traditional mode of the history of ideas common in the history of mathematics. One source for these ideas ignored by Wussing was crystallography, which has been described by SCHOLZ, who also amplifies a picture of how pure and applied mathematics are constituted and then interact. Only a few later developments have been described, notably NICHOLSON's account of the emergence of the quotient group.

Once the subject of group theory had been delineated, with its own problems and techniques (many created by the French mathematician, Camille Jordan), it was discovered that it reached into many other branches of mathematics. The most important has proved to be the connection with ordinary and partial differential equations. This was opened up by Sophus Lie, who hoped to generalize Galois's theory of polynomial equations. Lie's ideas were often obscurely expressed, and were treated from a different point of view by Killing, and then brought together and made rigorous by Élie-Joseph Cartan in his theory of what are called Lie algebras. In the 1930s, for various reasons it was discovered that there was a richer theory of Lie groups (which are both groups and topological manifolds) – roughly speaking a Lie algebra is a tangent space to a Lie group – and that Lie groups and Lie algebras are central to quantum mechanics. Prominent in this work was Hermann Weyl, who extended Cartan's classification of the algebras to the groups. This convoluted story has for many years been the subject of a succession of papers by HAWKINS (1982, 1988), which are rich in mathematical detail – for example, they sketch the way in which Lie pursued his *idée fixe* about Galois theory over many years, which has never been explained before – and also describe the professional and institutional dimension of the story.

It turned out in the 1890s, that many difficult questions about groups could be answered only by formulating them in terms of what are called group representations. These present a group as a set of matrices acting on a vector space – oddly reversing the historical attempt to elucidate the underlying abstract structure of many concretely presented groups.

A leader in this work was Georg Frobenius, whose path to this discovery was described on the basis of recently found correspondence by HAWKINS (1996). The crucial contribution of Weyl was to generalize that work to the representation theory of compact Lie groups. Unfortunately, neither historians of mathematics nor historians of science have come forward to describe these developments, so important and rich in historical questions. Historians of science have tended to gloss over mathematical developments, while mathematicians tend to leave out the social and historical dimensions. Within its narrow self-imposed limits, however, the account by MACKEY is lucid concerning the mathematics, and the source book edited by van der WAERDEN gives another bird's-eye view from that perspective.

Since any symmetrical object may be described by means of the non-trivial group of its symmetries, discussions of symmetry and group theory tend to blur into one another. A discussion of the symmetries of cultural artefacts as well as natural objects was initiated by the innovative book by WEYL, a pioneering work in the cultural history of mathematics. Crystallographers and quantum chemists continue to make considerable use of group theory, and the symmetries of tessellations, wallpaper patterns and many Islamic designs can be described using a two-dimensional version of the chemists notation (see MONTESINOS). This has led to a greater appreciation of the geometrical accomplishments of Islamic art, although a full-scale mathematical monograph is still lacking.

JEREMY GRAY

See also Geometry

Gynaecology

Dally, Ann, *Women under the Knife: A History of Surgery*, London: Hutchinson Radius, 1991; New York: Routledge, 1992

Drife, James, "Gynaecology", in *The Oxford Medical Companion*, edited by John Walton, Jeremiah A. Barondess and Stephen Lock, Oxford and New York: Oxford University Press, 1994, 682–85

Ehrenreich, Barbara and Deirdre English, *Complaints and Disorders: The Sexual Politics of Sickness*, Old Westbury, New York: Feminist Press, 1973

Graham, Harvey, *Eternal Eve: The History of Gynaecology and Obstetrics*, London: Heinemann, 1950; New York: Doubleday, 1951; revised as *Eternal Eve: The Mysteries of Birth and the Customs That Surround It*, London: Heinemann, 1960

Kerr, J.M. Munro, R.W. Johnstone and Miles Philips (eds), *Historical Review of British Obstetrics and Gynaecology, 1800–1950*, Edinburgh: Livingstone, 1954

Moscucci, Ornella, *The Science of Woman: Gynaecology and Gender in England, 1800–1929*, Cambridge and New York: Cambridge University Press, 1990

Peterson, M. Jeanne, *The Medical Profession in Mid-Victorian London*, Berkeley: University of California Press, 1978

Ricci, James V., *One Hundred Years of Gynaecology 1800–1900*, Philadelphia: Blakiston, 1945

Shorter, Edward, *A History of Women's Bodies*, New York: Basic Books, 1982

Wangensteen, Owen H. and Sarah D. Wangensteen, *The Rise of Surgery: From Empiric Craft to Scientific Discipline*, London: Dawson, and Minneapolis: University of Minnesota Press, 1978, 209–45

Gynaecology is the study of disorders of women's reproductive organs, other than in pregnancy and childbirth. It has, along with obstetrics, been an area of medical practice that has evoked bitter controversy in recent times, mainly between feminists and medical practitioners. The history of female surgery by DALLY was written, in part, as an attempt to explain each side to the other.

Gynaecology has both medical and surgical aspects. It has existed throughout civilization, but developed during the 19th century as an important part of abdominal surgery; when, with anaesthesia and asepsis, surgery was made safer in the second half of the 19th century, it became possible to operate on the abdomen with no more than a 20–30 % mortality, a figure then regarded as acceptable. The easiest abdominal operation to perform was ovariotomy, the old name for removal of the ovaries, and many surgeons learned their craft through practising this operation. It was performed on a wide scale, and for reasons that today would be regarded as malpractice; for example, since it was believed that virtually anything wrong with a woman was due to derangement of her reproductive organs, the operation was performed for hysteria, for vague symptoms, and even for behaviour that did not conform to the Victorian view of femininity. Surgeons learned how to manage and manipulate the inside of the abdomen by practising ovariotomy, and the tendency of women to be compliant probably also played a part in the development of this surgical industry. Today, gynaecology is regarded as a surgical, rather than a medical, specialty, though some doctors call themselves "medical gynaecologists". The literature on this subject, both primary and secondary, is huge.

For a useful, quick guide, written from the "march of progress" point of view, see DRIFE in the *Oxford Medical Companion*. He succinctly describes how gynaecology developed, and is now developing, from the earliest practices to modern triumphs, such as cancer surgery, minimally invasive surgery (performed with a laparoscope), reproductive medicine (largely concerned with infertility), sexual gynaecology, uro-gynaecology, and so on. A wonderful source for the study of 19th-century gynaecology is RICCI's detailed guide, which reveals its triumphalist approach in its subtitle, "A Comprehensive Review of the Specialty During its Greatest Century". This book contains many details and important references, but does not refer to the extensive criticism of the subject or to its failures. Ricci, in fact, goes to some lengths to conceal the worst excesses and events in the history of gynaecology; for instance, the index makes no mention of ovariotomy (except in children), or of Battey's notorious operation of removing normal ovaries for theoretical disorders elsewhere in the body or mind.

KERR, JOHNSTONE & PHILIPS endorse Ricci with a specifically British account, written by eminent British gynaecologists of the time. GRAHAM gives a livelier, though less exhaustive account in his study of midwifery, in an entertaining chapter entitled "Gynaecology made Safe". WANGENSTEEN & WANGENSTEEN contains a chapter giving a fascinating history of surgery, which places gynaecology within its surgical context. All these books are of the "march of progress" kind, and all fail to question what happened or why, or attempt to give the subject a historical context.

A powerful and readable (if somewhat extreme) introduction to the modern criticism of gynaecology can be found in the pamphlets of EHRENREICH & ENGLISH. For a more scholarly, overall view see MOSCUCCI, which is a model of balanced analysis. Moscucci shows how gynaecology developed against the background of a growing medical profession, the increasing power of doctors, and significant changes in male/female relations. PETERSON's book is a scholarly and readable history of the medical profession in the 19th century, against which the history of gynaecology can be viewed.

During the late 19th century, surgeons also learned to remove the womb (hysterectomy), an operation that is often criticized today, not because it is inherently bad, but because it is sometimes done for "trivial" reasons. (As in the postmenopausal woman who doesn't "need" her womb and may be better off without it.) Surgeons also developed operations for replacing what they regarded as malpositioned wombs (e.g., retroflexed or pointing backwards, now regarded as a common, normal variation), and an increasing number of women submitted to major surgery, as well as to the procedure of "Dilatation and Curettage", which became nearly universal for gynaecological complaints until its recent discrediting. Discussions of these, from whatever point of view, are to be found in most of the books mentioned, as well as in SHORTER, who, as always, sheds new light on the subject.

ANN DALLY

See also Obstetrics and Midwifery

H

Haeckel, Ernst 1834–1919

German zoologist

Bölsche, Wilhelm, *Haeckel: His Life and Work*, translated from the German by Joseph McCabe, London: Fisher Unwin, and Philadelphia: Jacobs, 1906; revised edition, London: Watts, 1909 (original edition, 1900)

Engelhardt, Dietrich von, "Polemik und Kontroversen um Haeckel", *Medizinhistorisches Journal*, 15 (1980): 284–304

Gasman, Daniel, *The Scientific Origins of National Socialism: Social Darwinism in Ernst Haeckel and the German Monist League*, London: Macdonald, and New York: Elsevier, 1971

Gursch, Reinhard, *Die Illustrationen Ernst Haeckels zur Abstammungs- und Entwicklungsgeschichte: Diskussion im wissenschaftlichen und nichtwissenschaftlichen Schrifttum*, Frankfurt: Peter Lang, 1981

Krausse, Erika, *Ernst Haeckel*, Leipzig: Teubner, 1984; 2nd edition, 1987

Nyhart, Lynn K., *Biology Takes Form: Animal Morphology and the German Universities, 1800–1900*, Chicago: University of Chicago Press, 1995

Sandmann, Jürgen, *Der Bruch mit der humanitären Tradition: Die Biologisierung der Ethik bei Ernst Haeckel und anderen Darwinisten seiner Zeit*, Stuttgart and New York: Fischer, 1990

Uschmann, Georg, *Geschichte der Zoologie und der zoologischen Anstalten in Jena, 1779–1919*, Jena: Fischer, 1959

Weindling, Paul, "Ernst Haeckel, Darwinismus and the Secularization of Nature", in *History, Humanity and Evolution: Essays for John C. Greene*, edited by James R. Moore, Cambridge and New York: Cambridge University Press, 1989

Ernst Haeckel, the evangelist of German Darwinism, was one of the most controversial scientists of his age. His legacy remained contested in the first decades of the 20th century, as admirers and detractors, especially in the different German states, produced the scientist in their own, or in their opponent's, image. To some in the German Empire, including Haeckel himself, his Darwinism underwrote the biological regeneration of German imperial power, but to many skilled workers he was a freedom fighter who justified their faith in the progress towards socialism. His followers continued to struggle over his mantle until the collapse of the Weimar Republic, when some presented him as a forerunner of the Nazis. After the division of Germany, the centre of Haeckel research at the University of Jena became part of the German Democratic Republic (GDR), and historians there revived the socialist tradition of celebrating Haeckel as a fighter for a materialist world-view. Significant work has also been done in the Federal Republic of Germany, and anglophone historians have made important contributions. I shall first review some biographies, then consider works on Haeckel's relation to National Socialism, and finally turn to more detailed studies of Haeckel's place within academic zoology and public debate.

There is no full-scale scholarly biography of Haeckel. However, it was Haeckel's friend BÖLSCHE who, launching his own career as the most prolific science writer of his generation, wrote the first life. Bölsche immodestly, but truthfully, reckoned that he had laid the foundation for all future biographies, and his remains the only book-length life available in English. His hero is a pioneer of a scientific world-view, a scientist aware of his responsibility to root out superstition and dogma. This great storyteller entertainingly weaves the episodes of Haeckel's earlier career into a plea for the cultural value of natural science. The most recent and useful biography is KRAUSSE's short, reliable and fact-filled introduction; she places Haeckel within the history of the life sciences as a charismatic, but blemished, champion of materialism. WEINDLING's balanced and synthetic biographical article engages critically with the above literature, and the single most helpful evaluation of Haeckel's life and work.

Whereas Krausse presents Haeckel as essentially progressive, GASMAN's highly controversial polemic accused him and the Monist League – the organization founded to propagate his nature religion – of being "the scientific origins of National Socialism". Gasman claimed that Haeckel's Romantically-tinged materialism became the ideology of German fascism, and that his Social Darwinism produced the "Final Solution". Evolutionary biology is deeply implicated in the crimes of the Third Reich, but, as Weindling points out, Gasman's book is gravely flawed. The causal argument of this dated genre of intellectual history does not past muster alongside more recent studies of science and National Socialism. The elderly Haeckel did abandon his earlier liberalism and move to the far right, but only tendentious selection of evidence can implicate him in the rise of National Socialism. His work was in fact used in politically opposed ways, and its meaning remained disputed even under the Nazis, but Gasman's account took at face value the histories that sought to align Haeckel's authority with that of the "new state". Nevertheless, Gasman remains the only extended history of the Monist League since those of its founders.

SANDMANN's history of ideas is in a similar vein; he condemns Haeckel for founding a moral system within evolutionary biology, and for sanctioning inhumane actions in the supposed interest of future generations, thus paving the way to Auschwitz, but his work compares unfavourably to histories of racial hygiene that contextualize such ideas and developments.

Haeckel made his career out of crossing boundaries, and, as with his anti-clerical writings, he courted controversy by flouting distinctions between academic zoology and popular science. We lack fine-grained analyses of the relations between his activities in different arenas, but we do have substantial studies placing Haeckel within university life, and some useful investigations of Haeckelian controversy in and beyond academia. Georg USCHMANN was the most distinguished of the GDR directors of the Ernst Haeckel House, the prophet's shrine and archive. His learned, very detailed, and by no means Marxist-Leninist, history of Jena zoology is a meticulous and exceptionally rich book, based on thorough archival research. He describes how the bastion of German Darwinism was built, showing how Haeckel gained the first chair of zoology at Jena and constructed the institutions of the discipline, and detailing Haeckel's often stormy relations with students and associates.

While Uschmann focused on Haeckel as the key figure of zoology at Jena, NYHART's landmark work of institutional sociology includes an analysis of the fate of Haeckel's evolutionary morphology within the disciplinary system of the German universities. In spite of Uschmann's observation that Haeckel founded no school in the strict sense, it has generally been assumed that he none the less dominated late 19th-century morphology. Nyhart demonstrates not only why he ultimately failed to establish his approach within German zoology, but also how the view that he had swept all before him was generated. One important reason for Haeckel's increasing isolation from the zoological community was, she shows, that his dogmatic and speculative publicity-seeking clashed with the professionalizing ethos of the 1890s. But Bölsche provides a salutary reminder that many contemporaries defended the popularizers of Darwinism, of whom none had greater authority than Haeckel, against the censure of professors and bureaucrats.

GURSCH offers a thorough presentation of the recurrent controversies over the illustrations in Haeckel's works, which dogged much of his career with accusations of forgery. While chiefly concerned with the propriety, or misconduct, of Haeckel and his attackers, this dissertation shows the potential for further study of the contested standards of embryological images in different kinds of publication.

ENGELHARDT surveys the major themes and controversies surrounding Haeckel, and indicates how analysis of his work can shed light on the character and status of the natural sciences in the late 19th century. Insisting that Haeckel's project cannot be understood unless the zoological specialist and the monist are seen as one, he proposes that Haeckel's goal was to transcend increasingly specialized, positivist science, but that

this was problematical because it extended the principle of Darwinism to the whole of human culture.

NICK HOPWOOD

See also Darwinism in Germany

Hahn, Otto 1879-1968

German physical chemist

Baumer, Franz, *Otto Hahn*, Berlin: Colloquium, 1974

Berninger, Ernst, *Otto Hahn: Eine Bilddokumentation: Persönlichkeit, wissenschaftliche Leistung, öffentliche Wirkung*, Munich: Moos, 1969

Gerlach, Walther, *Otto Hahn (1879–1968): Ein Forscherleben unserer Zeit*, edited by Dietrich Hahn, Stuttgart: Wissenschaftliche Verlagsgesellschaft, 1984 (original edition, 1968)

Hahn, Otto, *A Scientific Autobiography*, translated from the German and edited by Willy Ley, New York: Scribner, 1966 (original edition, 1962)

Hahn, Otto, *My Life: The Autobiography of a Scientist*, translated from the German by Ernst Kaiser and Eithne Wilkins, New York: Herder and Herder, and London: MacDonald, 1970 (original edition, 1968)

Hermann, Armin, *The New Physics: The Route into the Atomic Age: In Memory of Albert Einstein, Max von Laue, Otto Hahn, Lise Meitner*, translated from the German by David Cassidy, Bonn-Bad Godesberg: Inter Nationes, 1979 (original edition, 1979)

Hoffmann, Klaus, *Schuld und Verantwortung: Otto Hahn, Konflikte eines Wissenschaftlers*, Berlin and Heidelberg: Springer, 1993

Krafft, Fritz, *Im Schatten der Sensation: Leben und Wirken von Fritz Strassman*, Weinheim: Chemie, 1981

Shea, William R. (ed.), *Otto Hahn and the Rise of Nuclear Physics*, Dordrecht: Reidel, 1983

Sime, Ruth Lewin, "The Discovery of Protactinium", *Journal of Chemical Education*, 63 (1986): 653–57

Sime, Ruth Lewin, "Lise Meitner and the Discovery of Fission", *Journal of Chemical Education*, 66 (1989): 373–76

Sime, Ruth Lewin, *Lise Meitner: A Life in Physics*, Berkeley: University of California Press, 1996

Stolz, Werner, *Otto Hahn, Lise Meitner: Mit 20 Abbildungen*, Leipzig: Teubner, 1983

The starting point for biographers of Otto Hahn has been Hahn's autobiographical works, the personal and anecdotal HAHN (1970), in which his reminiscences are interspersed with interviews designed to clarify his statements, and the more technical HAHN (1966). Both works are designed for the lay reader. In contrast to his biographers, who tend to focus narrowly on his role in the discovery of nuclear fission, Hahn presents the broad scope of his radiochemical researches. The attractive personal characteristics recounted in nearly all the biographies – his charm, amiability, modesty, humor, perseverance, and conscientiousness – can be inferred from both these books. Hahn's avowed aversion to the Nazis and his refusal to join the Nazi Party became well-known, as did his claim of ignorance regarding the applications of nuclear energy. From Hahn himself also came the oft-repeated but inadequate description of a diligent, hard-working scientist lacking in intellectual brilliance but with much common sense.

Several popular biographies of Hahn have been written by German physicists that reflect both their authors's scientific orientations and their national sympathies. BERNINGER, who has also written a text on radioactivity, summarizes Hahn's scientific work and post-World War II efforts for peace, including some illustrations not available elsewhere. GERLACH likewise provides authoritative scientific summaries of his colleague Hahn's researches, and stresses Hahn's opposition to nuclear warfare. To Gerlach's text, Hahn's grandson, Dietrich Hahn, has added excerpts (selected from a collection he published previously) from testimonials to Hahn. STOLZ's brief, combined biography of Hahn and Lise Meitner focuses on their joint work, particularly the discovery of fission, and notes the tension between his biographees over the issue of credit for the discovery. Like the other physicists, Stolz emphasizes Hahn's efforts to ban nuclear weapons and to encourage peaceful use of nuclear energy. All these biographies are full of praise for Hahn, with Stolz becoming openly defensive regarding the tragedies of World War II.

SHEA has compiled a volume of diverse essays connected with the history of nuclear physics. Several of these are reviewed separately below.

Although HERMANN's well-illustrated documentary work concentrates on Einstein, the author supplies information on Hahn's scientific career, supplemented by discussions of science under the Nazis and Hahn's internment in England. Hermann takes pains to distance Hahn from National Socialism, pointing out his lack of involvement with the German bomb project, and highlighting his role in rebuilding the German science establishment after the war. He suggests that Hahn's scientific successes were due more to his character – his scientific "integrity and honesty" – than to his intellectual abilities. The book is rather disjointed, since it contains several distinct themes and the documentary material is not integrated into a continuous narrative.

Most writers have accepted the popular assumption (legitimized by the award of the Nobel prize of 1944 to Hahn alone) that Hahn was the sole discoverer of nuclear fission, albeit assisted by Fritz Strassmann who was working under his direction. Drawing on documents and correspondence, Fritz Krafft shows that, on the contrary, the participation of Meitner and Strassmann was essential. In his article in Shea, Krafft abstracts a list of necessary internal (scientific) and external conditions, and identifies the unique combination of characteristics of the three members of the Berlin team as one of the essential external conditions. Krafft also believes that the isolation and interdependency of the team workers, created by the political circumstances in Nazi Germany, were crucial for the discovery.

KRAFFT is primarily a documentary, with the author's interpretations presented mainly in the first third of the book. Krafft includes much personal correspondence between Hahn, Meitner, and Strassmann, often letting their words speak for themselves, and reveals how both Strassmann and Meitner spent their post-war careers in Hahn's shadow, their own achievements of 1934–38 sinking into oblivion. Although Krafft locates the cause in a combination of personality differences between the three co-workers, and a snowballing effect of a media eager to create a sensation, he shows Hahn acquiescing in the popular rewriting of the discovery, thus leaving his image somewhat tarnished.

BAUMER relies heavily on Hahn's autobiographies. He provides some scientific background, but is most interested in the ethical and psychological issues that impinge upon Hahn's life, beginning with Germany's use of gas warfare during World War I. Writing with a flair for the dramatic, Baumer delves into the politics of Nazi Germany in order to try to uncover Hahn's psychological state and motives. Clearly sympathetic to his subject, Baumer emphasizes Hahn's work for disarmament after World War II, and his advocation of peaceful uses for nuclear energy. Baumer suggests that, although Hahn did not consciously believe a bomb was feasible, at some level he did sense the broader implications of the discovery of fission. He cites correspondence between Hahn and Meitner, but does not mention the friction that developed after Hahn alone was awarded the Nobel prize.

Responding to controversies concerning Hahn, HOFF-MANN sets out to distinguish truth from legend in Hahn's life, focusing on the ethical issues surrounding the discovery of nuclear fission. Was Hahn responsible for the bomb? Did he help the Nazis in war research? Should he alone have received the Nobel prize for the discovery of fission? No, no, and yes, respectively, according to Hoffmann. In this updated version of his 1978 biography, Hoffmann suggests that Hahn's struggle with ethical issues led him to new insights and knowledge, while also benefiting humanity through his post-war work for disarmament and the peaceful use of nuclear energy. Although not personally responsible, Hahn felt a burden of guilt for the bomb, which led him to work indefatigably for scientific responsibility. Although Hoffmann acknowledges Meitner's disappointment at having been absent from the momentous discovery, he dismisses the idea that she should have shared in the Nobel prize. He accepts Hahn's delineation of the discovery as limited to the final chemical separations, and repeats his claim that if Meitner had stayed in Berlin she might have kept him and Strassmann from accepting their chemical results (which defied the current physical theory). Hoffmann surmises that Hahn was considered suitable for the Nobel prize because of his research record, while the relatively unknown Strassmann was not. Hoffmann illustrates the political, ethical, and interpersonal aspects of Hahn's life with excerpts from Hahn's correspondence. However, he does not supply much scientific background, and by trying to trace the theme of atomic energy through Hahn's career, Hoffmann falls into anachronisms and a simplistic analysis of physics at the turn of the century.

Through careful and comprehensive research, SIME (1989) and SIME (1996) demonstrate Meitner's central role in the discovery of fission, and develop an unflattering analysis of Hahn's behavior towards his long-term collaborator. Sime contends that in order to save himself and his Institute, Hahn deliberately distanced himself from the non-Aryan Meitner and her field of physics by maintaining that the discovery of fission was a feat of chemistry alone. Although Hahn tried to ameliorate the eclipse of Strassmann, Sime maintains that he never tried to make restitution to Meitner. She believes that Hahn's nationalism blinded him to the extent of Germany's ethical failings, as well as to his responsibility to Meitner, and led him to distort the story of the discovery of fission.

Extrapolating from the kind of information on Hahn's postwar activities that impressed Hoffmann, Lawrence Badash (article in Shea) concludes that Hahn was a leader in the development of the notion of social responsibility among 20th-century scientists.

Hahn's extensive and fruitful work on radiochemistry before the mid-1930s has attracted less attention than the fission researches. Ernest Berninger (article in Shea) examines Hahn's relatively unknown, but highly significant, discovery of nuclear isomerism, while SIME (1986) finds that the discovery of protactinium by Hahn and Meitner was primarily due to Meitner's efforts, and Thaddeus J. Trenn (article in Shea) clarifies Rutherford's initial reaction to Hahn's discovery of radiothorium.

MARJORIE MALLEY

Hale, George Ellery 1868–1938

American astrophysicist

Goodstein, Judith R., *Millikan's School: A History of the California Institute of Technology*, New York: Norton, 1991

Kargon, Robert H., "Temple to Science: Cooperative Research and the Birth of the California Institute of Technology", *Historical Studies in the Physical Sciences*, 8 (1977): 3–31

Kevles, Daniel J. (ed.), *Guide to the Microfilm Edition of the George Ellery Hale Papers, 1882–1937*, Pasadena: Carnegie Institution and the California Institute of Technology, 1968

Kevles, Daniel J., "Into Hostile Political Camps: The Reorganization of International Science in World War I", *Isis*, 62 (1971): 47–60

Kevles, Daniel J., "Hale and the Role of a Central Scientific Institution in the United States", in *The Legacy of George Ellery Hale: Evolution of Astronomy and Scientific Institutions, in Pictures and Documents*, edited by Helen Wright, Joan N. Warnow and Charles Weiner, Cambridge, Massachusetts: MIT Press, 1972, 273–82

Kohler, Robert E., *Partners in Science: Foundations and Natural Scientists, 1900–1945*, Chicago: University of Chicago Press, 1991

Osterbrock, Donald E., *James E. Keeler: Pioneer American Astrophysicist and the Early Development of American Astrophysics*, Cambridge and New York: Cambridge University Press, 1984

Osterbrock, Donald E., *Pauper & Prince: Ritchey, Hale & Big American Telescopes*, Tucson: University of Arizona Press, 1993

Reingold, Nathan and Ida H. Reingold, "Astronomy: The Lure of the Sun", in *Science in America: A Documentary History, 1900–1939*, edited by Reingold and Reingold, Chicago: University of Chicago Press, 1981, 56–8

Tobey, Ronald C., *The American Ideology of National Science, 1919–1930*, Pittsburgh: University of Pittsburgh Press, 1971

Van Helden, Albert, "Building Large Telescopes, 1900–1950", in *Astrophysics and Twentieth-Century Astronomy to 1950*, Part A, edited by Owen Gingerich, Cambridge and New York: Cambridge University Press, 1984, 134–52

Wright, Helen, *Explorer of the Universe: A Biography of George Ellery Hale*, New York: Dutton, 1966; reprinted Woodbury, New York: American Institute of Physics, 1994

The career of George Ellery Hale included a great many activities in the fields of astrophysics and scientific organization, and consequently the scholarship concerning him is diverse, falling into three main (though overlapping) categories. The most voluminous works on Hale concern his activities as an astrophysicist; in particular, the observatories and large telescopes erected on his initiative. Hale's role as an organizer, of astronomy and general science in the United States and internationally, is treated in several works on the history of early 20th-century science, of which only a sample can be mentioned here. Finally, some historians have dealt with Hale's activities as an institution builder outside of astronomy and general scientific co-operation – most importantly, his role in creating Caltech. (Another significant example, not dealt with here, is the Huntington Library).

The general point of departure for both historians and laymen interested in Hale is WRIGHT's comprehensive and panegyric biography, which traces the subject from cradle to grave – a suitable approach in this case, as Hale was conspicuously a product of upbringing and milieu (his Chicago-industrialist father giving his scientific endeavour life-long support), and was active until his death in 1938, when the 200-inch reflector at Palomar, perhaps the greatest of his many schemes, was still under construction. In Osterbrock's distinguished body of work on early American astrophysics, Hale figures prominently. OSTERBROCK (1984), the biography of Keeler, contains a wealth of information concerning Hale's early career, while OSTERBROCK (1993) gives a broader and more nuanced picture of Hale's later scientific activities than Wright. Osterbrock's forthcoming book on the Yerkes Observatory will hopefully be of the same calibre. For the very serious Hale student, an important body of source material, described by KEVLES (1968), is available on microfilm from the archives of the California Institute of Technology.

Hale's importance lies less in his technical scientific work than in his visionary organizational approach, by which he, influenced for example, the policy of scientific support adopted by the Carnegie Institution, as detailed by KOHLER. At the scientific institutions that he planned and/or directed – most importantly the Yerkes, Mount Wilson, and Palomar observatories, and the California Institute of Technology – cross-disciplinary approaches were explored by the aid of ever-more expensive and sophisticated technology. In this sense he was one of the important founders of "Big Science". The Palomar 200-inch telescope, especially, is an early example of the industrial approach to research. These aspects of Hale's work are given due emphasis by VAN HELDEN and KEVLES (1972). The latter sees Hale as a visionary who, not least in his endeavour to re-organize the National Academy of Sciences around 1914, attempted to create a system of scientific collaboration that would come to fruition with the rise of accelerator physics.

Hale's not very successful attempt to reform the National Academy – described also by TOBEY, and commented on by REINGOLD & REINGOLD in connection with the publication of some relevant documents – was typical of a desire to promote scientific co-operation that persisted throughout Hale's career. During World War I, Hale urged, with some success, for a closer collaboration between scientists and the military, thus participating in moulding yet another important characteristic of 20th-century science. His co-operative activities were given an international scope early on, with the creation of the International Union for Cooperation in Solar Research in 1905. After the war, Hale, as has been described by KEVLES (1971), was a major force in the creation of the International Research Council, which was to re-establish international co-operation among the formerly allied and neutral countries.

KARGON has emphasized the co-operative agenda behind Hale's initiative to convert Throop Polytechnic Institute at Pasadena into a Californian institute of technology, the history of which is narrated in more detail by GOODSTEIN. Here the inter-disciplinary character of Hale's co-operative ideal came to the fore, with Caltech (together with Hale's observatory on Mount Wilson) furnishing a basis for co-operative work in physics, chemistry, and astronomy.

Despite the fact that he was not a very original researcher, Hale must be counted among the most influential scientists of the 20th century – if only because he was strongly associated with a number of important organizational trends. Hale championed the marriage of fundamental research and capital (and to some extent of science and the military state), the ever-closer dependence of science on both large-scale and very sophisticated technology, and the organizing of scientific work into hierarchical institutional systems. His career will always remain an important starting point for investigations into these developments.

SVEN WIDMALM

See also Big Science

Halley, Edmond 1656–1743

English astronomer and natural philosopher

Armitage, Angus, *Edmond Halley*, London: Nelson, 1966

MacPike, Eugene Fairfield (ed.), *Correspondence and Papers of Edmond Halley*, Oxford: Clarendon Press, 1932

Robinson, Arthur H., *Early Thematic Mapping in the History of Cartography*, Chicago: University of Chicago Press, 1982

Ronan, Colin A., *Edmond Halley: Genius in Eclipse*, New York: Doubleday, 1969; London: Macdonald, 1970

Schaffer, Simon, "Halley's Atheism and the End of the World", *Notes and Records of the Royal Society*, 32 (1977): 17–40

Thrower, Norman J.W., *The Three Voyages of Edmond Halley in the Paramore, 1698–1701*, 2 vols, London: Hakluyt Society, 1980–81

Thrower, Norman J.W. (ed.), *Standing on the Shoulders of Giants: A Longer View of Newton and Halley*, Berkeley: University of California Press, 1990

Edmond Halley's biographers mostly celebrate him as England's second greatest scientist, the "genius in eclipse" still commemorated for his comet, yet ironically doomed to historical obscurity by the very man whose heroic status he helped to secure, Isaac Newton. Since historians of science now play down individual achievement in order to concentrate on contextualised analyses, Halley has recently featured as an important actor rather than as the single focus of attention.

MacPIKE provides the readiest access to older studies. In addition to Halley's own correspondence and unpublished papers, this book reproduces and appraises 18th- and 19th-century biographies. The opening two accounts, though partial, include valuable details about Halley's life. Martin Folkes's eulogising memoir presents Halley not only as the intimate friend of Newton, but as an energetic and gifted astronomer whose dedicated talents won him royal patronage. Jean-Jacques d'Ortous de Mairan based his éloge on Folkes's account, but added further tributes to his talents, such as his poetic abilities. MacPike's brief essay on Halley's character and personality provides a well-footnoted survey of the biographical literature then available.

The subsequent Halleian secondary literature – or lack of it – reflects changing fashions within histories of science, and exemplifies the distortions generated by historians seeking to impose current categories on natural philosophers of earlier centuries. Faced with the diversity of Halley's concerns, and an apparent paucity of personal details, biographers from various disciplinary backgrounds have tunnelled back into Halley's life to produce articles narrating his pioneering initiatives in modern specialities, such as engineering, cartography, geophysics and magnetism. Halley himself slips between these fractured representations, a problem compounded by the tendency to ignore aspects of his life – such as his religious beliefs, and his historical investigations – which might distort the conventional vision of the scientific innovator, but which could provide a unifying thread.

Both written by scientists, the only two books devoted to Halley, Armitage and Ronan, are hagiographic accounts oriented around the concept of scientific progress. Part of the "British Men of Science" series, ARMITAGE is explicitly a historical evaluation of Halley's scientific research. After a chronological account of his early life, the book is arranged predominantly by topics, such as physics of the earth and atmosphere, astronomy and general science, sometimes rather oddly juxtaposed (e.g., "Diver and Mint-Master"). Written in a pedestrian style, this account interleaves Halley's work with brief summaries of contemporary knowledge of the natural world, relying on the *Philosophical Transactions* as a major source of information. RONAN is structured chronologically around Halley's life, and includes a much fuller account of his maritime expeditions. Far less dry, and virtually free of diagrams and equations, this is an equally old-fashioned narrative, but one that makes a brave attempt to integrate Halley's personal life with his experimental and theoretical investigations.

THROWER's account (1980–81) of Halley's three voyages in the *Paramore* between 1698 and 1701 is an illuminating, if restricted, study. The first volume prints the manuscript versions of Halley's log books, together with more than 100 other documents relating to these journeys, and the maps and articles he produced. This original material provides the basis for Thrower's long and amply referenced essay. By including items such as the comments of Halley's rebellious crew, confrontations with hostile foreign administrators, Admiralty instructions, and financial details, Thrower vividly reconstructs Halley's maritime experiences. This study offers the opportunity to revise conventional portraits of the objective scientific explorer and nautical expert.

THROWER's edited volume (1990) is an extraordinarily heterogeneous collection of essays occasioned by the near-coincidence, in 1985, of Halley's comet and the tercentenary of Newton's *Principia*. Unsurprisingly, the most exciting contribution is by Simon Schaffer, who discusses the disputes surrounding the return in 1759 of the comet, which only then acquired Halley's name. Although, according to David Hughes's paper, Halley only dedicated 3% of his life to comets, the composition of this book reflects how successfully the propagandists described by Schaffer established Halley's triumphant posthumous status as cometary predictor. Rather disappointingly, few of these articles provide dramatic reinterpretations; instead they reiterate fragmented versions of Halley as military engineer, skilled navigator, and theoretical barometrician. However, the generous footnotes facilitate access to primary references, and the diverse earlier studies of Halley.

Some of this previous work exemplifies the value of appraising Halley's concerns within their contemporary context. Instead of marginalising Halley's alleged atheism, SCHAFFER demonstrates how religious issues were central to his depictions of the universe. Backed by research in ancient records, Halley's arguments of natural philosophy were rooted in his desire to render his cosmology consistent with biblical texts. ROBINSON's discussion tends more towards retrospective evaluation, but it similarly highlights the value of releasing Halley from modern disciplinary categories. Thematic maps – displaying the geographic distribution of features such as weather or population – only became a common way of communicating information during the 19th century, but Halley set influential precedents. Thus, although Robinson's analysis is primarily concerned with the chronology of cartographic innovation, it indicates how Halley might be incorporated within themes favoured by interdisciplinary historians of science, such as scientific imperialism, iconographic representation, and the commercialisation of natural philosophy.

During his long life, Halley held several important administrative positions, generated a large body of experimental results and theories, and participated in an international network of scientists and academics. A new biography of Halley could yield a fascinating account of the cultural impact of natural philosophy, during a period crucial for the establishment of public science.

PATRICIA FARA

See also Astronomy: general works; Newton; Newtonianism

Harvey, William   1578–1657

English physician

Bylebyl, Jerome J. (ed.), *William Harvey and His Age: The Professional and Social Context of the Discovery of the Circulation*, Baltimore: Johns Hopkins University Press, 1979

Chauvois, Louis, *William Harvey: His Life and Times, His Discoveries, His Methods*, London: Hutchinson, and New York: Philosophical Library, 1957

Frank, Robert Gregg, *Harvey and the Oxford Physiologists: A Study of Scientific Ideas and Social Interaction*, Berkeley: University of California Press, 1978

Franklin, Kenneth J., *William Harvey, Englishman, 1578–1657*, London: MacGibbon and Kee, 1961

French, Roger, *William Harvey's Natural Philosophy*, Cambridge and New York: Cambridge University Press, 1994

Keele, Kenneth D., *William Harvey: The Man, the Physician, and the Scientist*, London: Nelson, 1965

Keynes, Geoffrey, *The Personality of William Harvey*, Cambridge: Cambridge University Press, 1949

Keynes, Geoffrey, *The Life of William Harvey*, Oxford: Clarendon Press, 1966

Malloch, Archibald, *William Harvey*, New York: Hoeber, 1929

Pagel, Walter, *New Light on William Harvey*, Basel and New York: Karger, 1976

Pagel, Walter, *William Harvey's Biological Ideas: Selected Aspects and Historical Background*, Basel and New York: Karger, 1967

Power, D'Arcy, *William Harvey*, London: Fisher Unwin, 1897; New York: Longmans Green, 1898

Whitteridge, Gweneth, *William Harvey and the Circulation of the Blood*, London: Macdonald, and New York: Elsevier, 1971

Wyatt, R.B. Hervey, *William Harvey (1578–1657)*, London: Leonard Parsons, and Boston: Small Maynard, 1924

William Harvey is viewed as a pivotal figure in the history of modern medicine. A physician, he is best known for his work on the circulation of the blood, *Exercitatio anatomica de motu cordis et sanguinis in animalibus* (1628) – also known by the shorter title, *De motu cordis* – and his writing on generation, *Exercitationes de generatione animalium* (1651).

POWER is one of the many 19th-century biographies of Harvey, and is a straightforward, glowing, and non-critical portrayal of one of the most revered English physicians. It is written in the "popular" style, and so is readable, chronological, and contains many interesting contextual details of English history and, more specifically, of European medicine in the late 16th and early to mid-17th centuries. There are also many excerpts of documents relating to Harvey, such as the "allegation" concerning his marriage license to Elizabeth Browne, and translations from Harvey's writings from the Latin, presumably by Power himself.

Although many of Harvey's biographers are fellow Englishmen, it is notable that he has also French disciples. CHAUVOIS, for example, which was published both in French and English, is an advocate of the experimental method as used by

Harvey, rather than the "ratiocination" of Harvey's contemporary, Descartes. His work is thus not solely a biography, but gives also the medical and philosophical context of Harvey's work.

KEYNES (1949) is an elaboration of a Linacre lecture, and, like Power, is more concerned with the man than with the written works. A surgeon himself, Keynes states that this "is an attempt to put before you the personality of a great man rather than a criticism or appreciation of his contribution to science". KEYNES (1966) is a longer, more intensive, biography; elaborating from his Linacre lecture, and using many of Power's sources, Keynes depicts Harvey as a dynamic figure working among his colleagues, patients, and the courts of James I and Charles I. There are many useful details: for example, in order to clarify the misconceptions garnered from the often-used account of Harvey's life by Aubrey, Keynes includes Aubrey's account in full (as well as Harvey's will, prescriptions, and the reception of Harvey's doctrine during his lifetime). There are also 32 black-and-white plates to augment the biography. Nevertheless, Keynes does not profess to analyze Harvey's work outside its relation to his life; for useful descriptions of Harvey's work, one has to turn to other sources.

KEELE is the obvious complement to Keynes, as he analyzes how Harvey made his discovery on the circulation of the blood, and concentrates on *De Motu Cordis* and *De Generatione Animalium*, and the reception they received. Keele is keen to bring out Harvey's close philosophical relationship with Aristotle, making full use of the annotated translations of Harvey's lectures and *De Motu Locali Animalium*. Keele ends his book on an interesting note: linking Harvey's discovery and methods with subsequent ideas and discoveries of the 20th century (like many who write on Harvey), Keele acknowledges that the meticulous experimental method he used is as significant as the discovery of the circulation of the blood itself.

PAGEL (1967) sets Harvey's work in the context of contemporary European thought, aligning him with Fabricius and a renewed Aristotelianism, while criticizing previous interpretations of the influence of Galileo and Bacon. Pagel also evaluates the originality of idea and method of many of Harvey's predecessors, including Servetus, Columbus, Vesalius, and Cesalpinus, and compares their relative positions. He tackles the issue of the dates of Harvey's manuscripts, arguing that Harvey delayed publication because he wanted to be sure of his discovery, given that it flew in the face of thousands of years of accepted doctrine, not because he was afraid of the charge of religious heresy. PAGEL (1976) builds on his earlier text and assumes knowledge of it. At the time of writing this second work, Pagel believed that many modern interpretations of Harvey had not clarified, but had rather obscured, major elements of his discovery, including its date. At the centre of Pagel's "new" reading is a study based on Aristotelianism, particularly the degree to which Harvey was influenced by final causes. Pagel also looks at the biological notion of tissue irritability, and the concept of instrumentality in the "plastic virtue" of genitures, and goes on to set Harvey's work within the context of his predecessors and successors, giving considerable space to the work of Johannes Walaeus, whom he credits with confirmation of Harvey's discovery.

Whitteridge is a prominent Harvey-scholar; as well as producing new editions of Harvey's *Prelectiones* and *De musculis*, she edited *De motu locali animalium* in 1959. The text noted here, however, WHITTERIDGE, is an overview of Harvey's work and its impact on later 17th-century science.

BYLEBYL's collection of three long articles is another of the more recent treatments. This is a work that sets Harvey in various contexts and builds on philosophical and sociological evaluations, containing essays by Jerome Bylebyl, Robert Frank and Charles Webster. Bylebyl examines the typical approach to disease taken by physicians trained in the classical tradition, arguing "that in this tradition no sharp distinction could be made between normal physiological processes . . . and the abnormal effects of disease and therapy", and, hence, a conception of circulation was not easy to realize. Frank's essay examines the effect Harvey's work had on his professional reputation, on the work of his professional colleagues, and, more generally, on the status of the medical profession within English society. Webster, in turn, reverses the looking glass in order to reflect how the characteristics of Jacobean London, and the status of the medical profession, may have influenced the scientific views and work of physicians like Harvey.

Instead of rewriting the interpretations of Harvey's work or of the man himself, FRANK's monograph examines physiology as a discipline, particularly within the scientific community at Oxford during the Commonwealth and Restoration periods. (An interesting table of major and minor scientists of the period, listing their Oxford affiliations, scientific friends and dates of major publications, is included.) This book not only examines the work by Harvey, but also the research on respiration, on the nature of blood, and on muscle contraction in animals. Frank begins his epistemological and sociological study in 1628, with Harvey's assertions on the circulation of the blood, and evaluates their effect over the following half century.

The most recent work listed is FRENCH's text on Harvey's natural philosophy. He, too, moves away from biography in order to analyze a major change in natural philosophy resulting from Harvey's work, particularly from Harvey's experimental methodology. French argues that Harvey's anatomy was theocentric and contributed to a revolution in science. In order to evaluate Harvey as a catalyst for new ideas, the author posits a framework for "modes of exposition and evaluation of knowledge" in the 17th century, and within this studies the reactions of Harvey's contemporaries to his research. Unlike Frank, French examines the continental reactions also, revealing the importance of personal communication in spreading the new discoveries in natural philosophy. Fundamental to the revolution, and the criticism, was the role of religion, the soul having now been displaced as the impulse behind the motion of the heart by the new mechanistic model, proven by vivisection and experimentation.

Finally, among the vast number of biographies are brief works by Wyatt, Malloch, and Franklin. The earliest of the three, WYATT, is part of a series on prominent British men and women of science; Wyatt states that he relied on the work of others, including Power, of details of Harvey's life and the history of physiology, and most interesting is his final chapter, in which he notes how Harvey's work influenced other notable scientists – such as Lavoisier, Hooke, Malpighi and Boyle –

and, hence, the dynamism of physiological science of the period.

MALLOCH offers brief synopses of the major points of Harvey's life, and frankly states that others have done more comprehensive research on any single topic, from Harvey's predecessors in circulatory research to analyses of his writings.

FRANKLIN, another physician himself, had investigated the history of circulatory research in the 1920s, and offers his *A Short History of Physiology* as "background" to his biography of Harvey. This biography benefits from Franklin's long-standing study of the subject, and includes concise summaries of the work of his predecessors – going as far back as Aristotle, Alcmaeon, and Chalcedon – and a lengthy bibliography of further reading. Franklin's translations on the circulation treatises were published in 1963 as *The Circulation of the Blood and Other Writings*.

MARIANNE P. FEDUNKIW

Hayek, Friedrich August von

1899–1992

Austrian-born British economist and social theorist

Boettke, Peter J., "Hayek's *The Road to Serfdom* Revisited: Government Failure in the Argument Against Socialism", *Eastern Economic Journal*, 21/1 (1995): 7–26

Burczak, Theodore A., "The Postmodern Moments of F.A. Hayek's Economics", *Economics and Philosophy*, 10/1 (1994): 31–58

Butos, William N., "The Hayek-Keynes Macro Debate", in *The Elgar Companion to Austrian Economics*, edited by Peter J. Boettke, Aldershot, Hampshire: Edward Elgar, 1994

Butos, William N. and Roger Koppl, "Hayekian Expectations: Theory and Empirical Applications", *Constitutional Political Economy*, 4/3 (1993): 303–29

Caldwell, Bruce, "Hayek's Transformation", *History of Political Economy*, 20/4 (1988): 513–41

Colonna, M., H. Hagemann and O.F. Hamouda (eds), *The Economics of F.A. Hayek*, 2 vols, Aldershot, Hampshire: Edward Elgar, 1994

Garrison, Roger, "Time and Money: The Universals of Macroeconomic Theorizing", *Journal of Macroeconomics*, 6/2 (1984): 197–213

Gray, John, *Hayek on Liberty*, Oxford and New York: Blackwell, 1984; 3rd edition, London and New York: Routledge, 1998

Kirzner, Israel M., *Competition and Entrepreneurship*, Chicago: University of Chicago Press, 1973

Kukathas, Chandran, *Hayek and Modern Liberalism*, Oxford: Clarendon Press, and New York: Oxford University Press, 1989

Lavoie, Donald C., *National Economic Planning: What is Left?*, Cambridge, Massachusetts: Ballinger, 1985

Lavoie, Don, *Rivalry and Central Planning: The Socialist Calculation Debate Reconsidered*, Cambridge and New York: Cambridge University Press, 1985

Madison, Gary B., "Hayek and the Interpretive Turn", *Critical Review*, 3/2 (1989): 169–85

O'Driscoll, Gerald P., *Economics as a Coordination Problem: The Contributions of Friedrich A. Hayek*, Kansas City: Sheed Andrews and McMeel, 1977

O'Driscoll, Gerald P. and Mario J. Rizzo, *The Economics of Time and Ignorance*, Oxford and New York: Blackwell, 1985

Selgin, George A. and Lawrence H. White, "How Would the Invisible Hand Handle Money?", *Journal of Economic Literature*, 32 (1994): 1718–49

Thomsen, Esteban F., *Prices and Knowledge: A Market-Process Perspective*, New York: Routledge, 1992

Weimer, Walter B., "Hayek's Approach to the Problems of Complex Phenomena: An Introduction to the Psychology of the Sensory Order", in *Cognition and the Symbolic Processes*, vol. 2, edited by Weimer and D. Palermo, Hillsdale: Lawrence Erblaum, 1982

Although known primarily as an economist, Friedrich August von Hayek made contributions to a variety of fields, mostly in the social sciences. Much of the recent scholarship on Hayek has attempted to establish links between his work on economics, theoretical psychology, social science methodology, and political philosophy.

Specifically, this literature has focused on what CALDWELL has termed "Hayek's Transformation". In the 1920s and 1930s, Hayek was very much a technical economist, but by the 1950s he had virtually abandoned technical economics for broader issues in social theory. Caldwell argues that Hayek's participation in the debate over the feasibility of economic calculation under socialism (as well as his ongoing criticism of the emerging Keynesian revolution) led him to realize that his differences with his contemporaries were deeply rooted in his understanding of the task of the social sciences in general, and economics in particular.

An overview of Hayek's contributions to economics can be found in O'DRISCOLL, while COLONNA, HAGEMANN & HAMOUDA provide a representative sampling of commentary on his economics. The unifying thread of Hayek's work is the explanatory problem posed by the fact that economic coordination in market economies occurs spontaneously; i.e., as the result of human action, but not human design. Hayek saw the fundamental task of economics as explaining how the fragmentary and frequently tacit bits of knowledge held by individuals are communicated and used by others, and unintentionally produce order. These Hayekian themes have been explored most effectively by KIRZNER, who argues that it is entrepreneurial activity that increasingly co-ordinates knowledge that has been unintentionally generated by the competitive behavior of individuals involved in the market.

To most economists, Hayek is best known for his argument that prices are information signals to market participants. THOMSEN tries to separate Hayek's emphasis on dis-equilibrium from the equilibrium reading of this argument favored by most economists. Thomsen argues that the informational role of prices has to be understood as part of the competitive discovery process, in which they provide information to participants attempting to co-ordinate their behavior.

Hayek's monetary theory, which won him the Nobel prize in 1974, has been addressed by Butos and Garrison. BUTOS gives a clear overview of Hayek's differences with Keynes, many of which centered on the role of microeconomic issues and Keynes's understanding of what he saw as "macro-economic" phenomena. Of particular importance is Hayek's theory of capital, which counters the Keynesian proclivity to portray capital and investment as abstract, homogenous aggregates. Keynes overlooked the various microeconomic processes by which concrete, heterogeneous capital goods were used in the real world.

GARRISON attempts to place Hayek's contribution within the contemporary macroeconomic spectrum. Hayek believed that money was neither a veil that overlaid an otherwise perfectly equilibrating economy, nor was it unable to contribute to the coordination of economic activity. Rather, money, when it is supplied properly, does indeed create a climate where market coordination processes can operate to the best of their ability, but, when mishandled, money can be a major source of disruption to that process. As Garrison elucidates, Hayek argued that inflation would lead to inappropriately low rates of interest, which would provide mistaken information to entrepreneurs. Those entrepreneurs would then erroneously invest in more time- consuming processes of production, causing the boom of the business cycle. Only when the inflation ceased, and the real inter-temporal preferences of consumers became clear, would the mistakes be revealed and the downturn ensue.

As a result of his research on money Hayek believed that central banks had to be instructed in order to avoid inflation. He vacilated on how precisely this should take place, and by the 1970s he began to advocate opening up the production of money to the competitive forces of the market. SELGIN & WHITE provide an overview of the recent literature focusing on the various alternative interpretations of the significance of competition in money. This area has become one of the most important and exciting extensions of Hayek's work.

Along with his work on monetary theory, Hayek's contribution to the field of comparative economic systems is perhaps his most noteworthy achievement. Following on Mises's claim that a socialist economy would have no way of allocating resources rationally in the absence of market prices, Hayek argued that this was because planners would lack the knowledge disseminated by money prices in a competitive market. At the time of the debate in the 1930s and 1940s, Hayek was generally believed to have been wrong, and neoclassical economists largely accepted the view that attaining economic equilibrium was independent of the form of capital ownership. In two different works, Lavoie has both clarified and extended this Hayekian argument, by linking it to more contemporary views of the nature of knowledge and the informational properties of mass communication systems. Lavoie shows how Hayek's argument was misunderstood by the economics profession as a result of its dependence on Walrasian models, which treated important economic data as objectively given. LAVOIE (1985, *Rivalry and Central Planning*) is generally credited with having effectively reinterpreted Hayek's argument and undermined the confidence in the conclusion the profession had reached between the wars.

Hayek's argument about prices, socialism, and knowledge was ably extended by LAVOIE (1985, *National Economic Planning: What is Left?*). Here Lavoie ties Hayek's work to both the Kuhnian revolution in the philosophy of science, and

to Michael Polanyi's work on tacit knowledge. Lavoie argues that the problem facing planners is how to obtain the specific knowledge embedded in the minds and practices of market participants. In the same way that freedom of scientific inquiry allows scientists to explore the unknown, and just as the institutions of science create self-correcting processes that generate scientific knowledge, so the institutions and freedom of activity associated with capitalism generate similar self-correcting and self-organizing processes; in Hayek's famous phrase, the market is a spontaneous order. As a result of this reinterpretation of Hayek's work, and its empirical confirmation in the problems faced by the economies of Eastern Europe and the former Soviet Union, economists have generally reverted to Hayek's opinions of 60 years ago.

Hayek's lesser-known work in theoretical psychology and social science methodology grew out of his frustration at how the project of economics was understood by a growing number of his contemporaries. What links both investigations is a further refinement of the subjectivist approach to economics and the social sciences, as the study of the workings of the mind has obvious implications for the study of human beings in the social world. BUTOS & KOPPL provide an excellent start in this direction by linking Hayek's theory of the mind to a theory of expectations, and using that to explore aspects of Hayek's economic and political thought more broadly. WEIMER has shown the relevance of Hayek's work to contemporary trends in psychology. Although not referring to Hayek's work on the mind explicitly, O'DRISCOLL & RIZZO develop a radical and thorough-going subjectivist economics that owes much to Hayek's conception of the social sciences. There are also important points in common between Hayek's methodological work and the ongoing interpretative/postmodern turn in philosophy, and these issues are explored by MADISON.

Toward the end of his life, Hayek was best known for his work on political philosophy, and as a defender of classical liberalism. The two most notable sympathetic, but critical, overviews are by Gray and Kukathas. GRAY's work attempts to locate Hayek's contribution within the history of liberal thought; though largely positive, Gray does highlight some of the tensions between Hayek's apparently conservative belief in the power of evolved institutions, and his more prescriptive attempts to limit the power of the state. That theme is also central to the work by KUKATHAS, which compares and contrasts Hayek's political philosophy with that of contemporary liberals, such as Rawls. Kukathas's major contribution is to show how these tensions in Hayek trace back to the dual influence of Kant and Hume: Hayek's emphasis on spontaneous order and the priority of received traditions reflects his Humean heritage, while his concern with human freedom is undeniably Kantian. Kukathas argues that Hayek's work was ultimately unable to bridge this conflict.

Perhaps Hayek's best-known book is *The Road to Serfdom* (1944), in which he argued that any attempts to move toward a socialist economic system were bound to result in a society increasingly dominated by a totalitarian state, despite the best intentions of those involved. BOETTKE argues convincingly that Hayek's "serfdom" thesis must be understood within the context of his more technical work on the impossibility of socialist calculation. Hayek took it for granted that studies of economics had established that socialism was impossible, and was interested in explaining what would happen when attempts to implement it encountered this fact. Hayek's claim that total-itarianism would emerge was conditioned on the belief that, faced with the inability to plan an economy rationally, socialist leaders would have to rely on political rationales for their decisions, and thus those who were most effective at wielding political power would rise to the top. In Boettke's interpretation, *The Road to Serfdom* was prophetic in explaining how the perhaps noble intentions of the Russian Revolution might result in the horrors of Stalinism.

Whatever tensions have been identified in Hayek's thought, he has left a body of work that spans a number of disciplines, and has made a major contribution to the rebirth of classical liberalism, both in the academy and in politics.

STEVEN HORWITZ

See also Keynes; Political Economy

Health, Mortality, and Social Class

Abraham, Laurie Kaye, *Mama Might Be Better Off Dead: The Failure of Health Care in Urban America*, Chicago: University of Chicago Press, 1993

Buhler-Wilkerson, Karen, *False Dawn: The Rise and Decline of Public Health Nursing, 1900–1930*, New York: Garland, 1989

Coleman, William, *Death is a Social Disease: Public Health and Political Economy in Early Industrial France*, Madison: University of Wisconsin Press, 1982

Duffy, John, *The Sanitarians: A History of American Public Health*, Urbana: University of Illinois Press, 1990

Eyler, John M., *Victorian Social Medicine: The Ideas and Methods of William Farr*, Baltimore: Johns Hopkins University Press, 1979

"Health Inequalities in Modern Societies and Beyond", *Social Science and Medicine* (special issue), edited by Eero Lahelma and Ossi Rahkonen, 44/6 (March 1997)

Katz, Michael Barry, *In the Shadow of the Poorhouse: A Social History of Welfare in America*, New York: Basic Books, 1986; revised edition, New York: Basic Books, 1996

McKeown, Thomas, *The Role of Medicine: Dream, Mirage, or Nemesis?*, London: Nuffield Provincial Hospitals Trust, 1976; Princeton, New Jersey: Princeton University Press, 1979

Meckel, Richard A., *"Save the Babies": American Public Health Reform and the Prevention of Infant Mortality, 1850–1929*, Baltimore: Johns Hopkins University Press, 1990

Rosen, George, *A History of Public Health*, New York: MD Publications, 1958; revised edition, Baltimore: Johns Hopkins University Press, 1993

Rosner, David (ed.), *Hives of Sickness: Public Health and Epidemics in New York City*, New Brunswick, New Jersey: Rutgers University Press (for the Museum of the City of New York), 1995

Rosner, David and Gerald Markowitz, *Deadly Dust: Silicosis and the Politics of Occupational Disease in Twentieth-Century America*, Princeton, New Jersey: Princeton University Press, 1991

Sellers, Christopher C., *Hazards of the Job: From Industrial Disease to Environmental Health Science*, Chapel Hill: University of North Carolina Press, 1997

Starfield, Barbara, "Child Health and Public Policy", in *Children and Health Care: Moral and Social Issues*, edited by Loretta M. Kopelman and John C. Moskop, Dordrecht and Boston: Kluwer, 1989, 7–21

Tomes, Nancy, "The Private Side of Public Health: Sanitary Science, Domestic Hygiene, and the Germ Theory, 1870–1900", *Bulletin of the History of Medicine*, 64/4 (1990): 509–39

In mid-19th-century Liverpool, middle-class life expectancy was 35 years of age, tradesmen and their families had a life expectancy of 22 years, and laborers, servants, and others in the working class could expect, on average, to live to the age of 15. Although the slums of Liverpool at the height of the Industrial Revolution were a particularly noxious place to live, class differentials in morbidity (sickness) and mortality (death) have been a constant finding since the reliable collection of vital statistics.

Fundamentally, health inequalities and differential mortality are part of the larger demographic project and of the histories of urbanization, poverty, labor, health, and medicine within and across cultures, and the best studies take on several of these aspects. Instead of attempting to cover such a sweeping landscape in such a short space, this review concentrates on class-based differences in sickness and death, and some of the historic responses to those inequalities, with emphasis on literature on the United States to illustrate the kinds of material bearing on this issue. The McKEOWN debate, arising from Thomas McKeown's argument that rising living standards, and not specific medical interventions, explain the steady decline in mortality from tuberculosis since about 1800 – the most famous explication of historical demography – is not centrally about class differences, and therefore will not be addressed directly. Both McKeown's argument and the varying responses of critics are now so well covered that they need no further explication here.

The literature can be divided into the following categories: the sanitarians; occupational health and "child-saving"; and modern analyses of socioeconomic factors in health, and will be discussed in that order. The common theme of these three threads is the finding that it is not the individual failings of poor people, but broader social conditions that precipitate class-based mortality. Nearly all argue therefore that the solutions must be social.

The statistical strand in the history of public health, exemplified by William Farr in Britain and Louis-René Villermé in France, was never entirely separate from the complementary work by the sanitarians Edwin Chadwick, Alexandre Parent-Duchâtelet, Rudolf Virchow, Lemuel Shattuck, John H. Griscom, and others. Both sides played a part in illustrating the living conditions of the working classes, writing the various reports on the *Sanitary Condition of the Laboring Classes* that were published in the 1840s and 1850s, and proposing solutions. EYLER's intellectual biography of Farr places the statistician within the context of British medical thought, and explicates the relationship between his statistical work and the reforms in public health in 19th-century Britain. COLEMAN's incisive treatment of Villermé describes his landmark work in the statistical demonstration of social and health inequalities, but also places him within a conservative school of French economists who laid the blame for these inequalities on workers' lack of hygiene and personal responsibility, rather than on industrial or urban conditions.

A large body of work on the history of health reform and public health gives additional background to the discovery of the correlation of poverty with illness in the work of these statisticians. Studies of individual cities, states, provinces, and countries supplement full-length biographies of Virchow, Chadwick, John Simon, Villermé, and other founders of public health. ROSEN's classic study of the history of public health as public works and policy, originally published in 1958, was reprinted in 1993. Following, in part, a style of grand narrative and history as progress that is currently unfashionable, Rosen none the less provides a wealth of detail on public health in Western history, concentrating on its full flowering in 19th-century urban sanitation. Subsequent scholarship on public health takes Rosen as the starting point. The movement in the United States is well-characterized by DUFFY'S encyclopedic (if somewhat cluttered) study of professionalization and the spread of local initiatives across the decentralized landscape of US federalism. ROSNER's edited collection presents some of the best recent work on the sanitary school of public health in the US, using New York City as an exemplar and lens for discussing the kinds of conditions and activities that can be found in cities large and small.

The fundamental political, scientific, and moral issue – of whether poor people are sick because they are poor or poor because they are sick, with all of the attendant hypothesizing about destitution, laziness, and responsibility – remains contentious. In addition, the status of modern scientific medicine relies in large part on its ability to find technical – not social – answers to medical problems. Systematic explanations and broader social responses have been suggested along a number of lines by reformers within and outside the health professions. The "sanitary" approach emphasized urban infrastructure, but, as TOMES demonstrates, it contained analogues in home construction and sanitary devices that allowed the middle and upper classes to protect themselves against water-borne disease and sewer gas.

Occupational health and the study of the effect of working conditions on class-based mortality presents some of the most interesting recent work on class and health. ROSNER & MARKOWITZ concentrate on a single disease and category of worker, spinning out the rise and fall of silicosis during the interwar and immediate postwar period in the United States. SELLERS looks at the workplace and the discipline of occupational health, documenting the rise of professionalism, disciplinary change, and the changing medical and toxicological understandings of the industrial environment in the US.

Starfield and Meckel are examples of the final approach, placing responsibility at the social or institutional level through their studies on the health of children. STARFIELD makes the common moral argument that children have a special claim on community resources, because of their lack of behavioral culpability for sickness or poverty, and because child health

has life-long implications for economic and social opportunities. MECKEL explores how that argument was put into practice by middle-class social reformers fighting infant mortality in the United States and Canada, and shows the problems raised by the intervention of middle-class reformers into working-class families. BUHLER-WILKERSON examines the interactions between the professionalization of nursing and a social medicine perspective, and shows how both are thwarted by class differentials between visiting nurses and poor mothers. KATZ, in his history of social welfare in the United States and several other related works, uses both quantitative social history and policy studies to place health visiting and public health interventions directed towards family and home environments within the broader context of social welfare in the US.

Continuing the work of Farr, Villermé, and their contemporaries, the study of class-based health inequalities is a staple of modern epidemiology and medical sociology, and is a sufficiently active area of research for *Social Science and Medicine* to dedicate its second symposium issue (March 1997) to HEALTH INEQUALITIES. Medline, the major medical database compiled under the authority of the United States National Library of Medicine, contains 32,288 citations to socioeconomic factors in health from 1966 to September 1997. Current demographic and public health research on class-based health inequalities attempts to isolate income, education, plumbing and public works, family structure, and dozens of other variables in the hopes of finding a point of intervention that is both technically and politically acceptable. This demographic work has received a thoughtful phenomenological counterweight from ABRAHAM, who shows the labyrinthine and manifestly unjust workings of the US health system, through the experiences of a poor family in a Chicago ghetto.

CARLA KEIRNS

See also Nursing; Public Health; Toxicology

Heat

Badcock, A.W., "Physics at the Royal Society, 1660–1800, I. Change of State", *Annals of Science*, 16/2 (1960): 95–115

Brush, Stephen G., *The Kind of Motion We Call Heat: A History of the Kinetic Theory of Gases in the 19th Century*, Amsterdam: North-Holland, 1976

Cardwell, D.S.L., *From Watt to Clausius: The Rise of Thermodynamics in the Early Industrial Age*, Ithaca, New York: Cornell University Press, and London: Heinemann, 1971

Fox, Robert, *The Caloric Theory of Gases from Lavoisier to Regnault*, Oxford: Clarendon Press, 1971

Guerlac, Henry, "Chemistry as a Branch of Physics: Laplace's Collaboration with Lavoisier", *Historical Studies in the Physical Sciences*, 7 (1976): 193–275

Heilbron, J.L., "Weighing Imponderables and Other Quantitative Science around 1800", *Historical Studies in the Physical and Biological Sciences*, Supplement to vol. 24, part 1 (1993)

Layton Jr, Edwin T., and John H. Lienhard (eds), *History of Heat Transfer: Essays in Honor of the 50th Anniversary of the ASME Heat Transfer Division*, New York: American Society of Mechanical Engineers, 1988

McCormmach, Russell, "Henry Cavendish on the Theory of Heat", *Isis*, 79 (1988): 37–67

McKie, Douglas and Niels H. Heathcote, *The Discovery of Specific and Latent Heats*, London: Edward Arnold, 1935

Middleton, W.E.K., *A History of the Thermometer and Its Use in Meteorology*, Baltimore: Johns Hopkins University Press, 1966

Roberts, Lissa, "A Word and the World: The Significance of Naming the Calorimeter", *Isis*, 82 (1991): 198–222

Roller, Duane, "The Early Development of the Concepts of Temperature and Heat: The Rise and Decline of the Caloric Theory", *Harvard Case Histories in Experimental Science*, Cambridge: Massachusetts: Harvard University Press, 1957, 119–214

Heat is a rather nebulous subject within the history of science. In general terms, heat from c.1840 to the present is usually referred to via the disciplines of thermodynamics, heat transfer, or low-temperature physics. From the late 18th century up to c.1840, discussions of heat focus on the caloric theory, and are usually to be found under that name. Prior to 1600, heat is typically discussed as fire, one of Aristotle's four elements or, alternatively, the alchemical or Paracelsian concept of fire. When the term "heat" is used in the history of science, it generally refers to the middle period, from 1600 to 1800 – succeeding Aristotelian and alchemical ideas of fire, but preceding the ascendancy of the caloric theory. This period marks the invention of the thermoscope and thermometer, and the beginning of quantitative research into heat phenomena.

It can be difficult for readers or researchers investigating heat to unify the topic; this is because of the great diversity of both heat phenomena and the historical representations of heat by scientists and historians through the ages. In addition to the topics mentioned above, information and investigations on heat can be found under many other names, including "cold", "state changes", "radiation", "convection", and "thermometry", and there is no single work or group of works that covers all periods or topics. This article will discuss only those works relevant to the period 1600 to 1800.

Most of the significant work on heat was performed from the late 1950s to the early 1970s, at which point its popularity faded. There is now, in the mid-1990s, a mild resurgence of interest.

ROLLER was among the first to overview the subject. His case study remains a satisfactory introduction to the subject, with one very serious drawback: its lack of footnotes and references. In his account, the thermometer is the most important early development, the first significant discoveries with the thermometer being made by Joseph Black on specific and latent heat. Benjamin Thomson (Count Rumford) plays a major role in Roller's account, in accordance with the prevailing interpretation of the time, whereby the origins of the kinetic theory were given primacy.

FOX overturned the conventional story regarding the role of Rumford and the kinetic theory in his definitive work on the caloric theory of gases, showing the caloric theory to be much more important in the early history of heat. He provides a comprehensive review of the research traditions concerning heat in the late 18th century; according to Fox, these were the French caloric theories developed by Lavoisier and Laplace; the Scottish school, from Black to Irvine and Crawford, and the work of the German and Swiss scientists Lambert, Saussure, and Pictet. He regards the work of Rumford as "a red herring" for the historian, along with kinetic theory in general at this time.

The still-authoritative account of the development of the thermometer is to be found in MIDDLETON. Although the focus of this work is an internalist account of the development of thermometric instruments, Middleton is attentive to the research performed using the instruments. He pays a great deal of attention to meteorology, but also discusses the theories and observations of medical doctors and natural philosophers. Middleton's work remains very useful, due to his careful documentation and the breadth of his evidence.

A much more recent study of 18th-century instrumentation and its usage is to be found in HEILBRON. His work focuses on the use of quantitative techniques in science, with the increasing demands for precision in 18th-century science, and their relation to the theories of imponderable fluids. Although this work focuses on the last decades of the 18th century, and spills over into the 19th century in its study of heat, Heilbron's description of the use of thermometric instruments, and their relation to theory, is thoroughly up-to-date. He convincingly uses historiographical conceptions of the interrelationships between theory and experimentation, and between external social values, culture and internal development.

McKIE & HEATHCOTE's work remains remarkably resilient. After nearly 60 years, it is still the definitive work on the "discovery" of specific and latent heat by Joseph Black and others in the mid-18th century. This internalist work retains its value because of the very high quality of its research, and the soundness of its interpretation – that the work of Black is the foundation of the science of heat. While recognizing the primacy of Black, McKie & Heathcote give ample attention to the more obscure work of Black's contemporaries on the same subject, thus fending off potential rival interpretations.

CARDWELL's book contains detailed descriptions of the work of James Watt on the steam engine, and of Watt's relationship to Black. Like Middleton, Cardwell places emphasis on meteorology. Although he deals primarily with the development of thermodynamics in the 19th century, Cardwell's emphasis on technological change results in his first few chapters providing significantly different interpretations of important events in the history of heat than that of other scholars.

The remaining works are less significant than those described above. BADCOCK's monograph is a good example of a paper that would normally be overlooked, since it focuses on Royal Society reports on changes of state, typically water to ice or steam. BRUSH's work is significant, primarily for its description of the kinetic theory of heat in the 19th century, but he briefly discusses 18th-century precursors. McCORMMACH focuses on the debate between the kinetic and caloric theories in the late 18th century in the research of Henry Cavendish. The caloric theory was placed on solid ground by Lavoisier and Laplace, an event described in GUERLAC's classic monograph. The collection by LAYTON & LIENHARD is mentioned here because of its useful bibliography, and shows once again how significant information can be found in unexpected places, this time in the history of technology, in a volume on heat transfer. Finally, the monograph by ROBERTS shows the influence of recent trends in the social construction of science and rhetoric, using the example of the controversy between Lavoisier and Irvine on the nature of the caloric theory.

STEPHEN B. JOHNSON

See also Engines: steam

Heisenberg, Werner   1901–1976

German theoretical physicist

Blum, Walter, Hans-Petr Dürr and Helmut Rechenberg (eds), *Gesammelte Werke /Collected Works*, Berlin: Springer, 1985–

Cassidy, David C., *Uncertainty: The Life and Science of Werner Heisenberg*, New York: W.H. Freeman, 1992

Eckert, Michael, "Primacy Doomed to Failure: Heisenberg's Role as Scientific Advisor for Nuclear Policy in the FRG", *Historical Studies in the Physical and Biological Sciences*, 21/1 (1990): 29–58

Frank, Charles (ed.), *Operation Epsilon: The Farm Hall Transcripts*, London: Institute of Physics, and Berkeley: University of California Press, 1993

Geyer, Bodo, Helge Herwig and Helmut Rechenberg (eds), *Werner Heisenberg. Physiker und Philosoph*, Berlin and Oxford: Spektrum, 1993

Heisenberg, Elisabeth, *Inner Exile: Recollections of a Life with Werner Heisenberg*, translated from the German by S. Cappellari and C. Morris, Boston: Birkhäuser, 1984 (original edition, 1983)

Hermann, Armin, *Werner Heisenberg in Selbstzeugnissen und Bilddokumenten*, Reinbek: Rowohlt, 1976

Jammer, Max, *The Conceptual Development of Quantum Mechanics*, New York: MacGraw-Hill, 1966; 2nd edition, Woodbury, New York: American Institute of Physics, 1989

Jungk, Robert, *Brighter than a Thousand Suns: A Personal History of the Atomic Scientists*, translated from the Swedish by James Cleugh, New York: Harcourt Brace, and London: Gollancz/Rupert Hart-Davis, 1958 (original edition, 1956)

Kleint, Christian and Gerald Wiemers (eds), *Werner Heisenberg in Leipzig, 1927–1942*, Berlin: Akademie, 1993

Mehra, Jagdish and Helmut Rechenberg, *The Historical Development of Quantum Theory*, vol. 2 *The Discovery of Quantum Mechanics, 1925* and vol. 3 *The Formulation of Matrix Mechanics and its Modifications 1925–1926*, Berlin and New York: Springer, 1982

Powers, Thomas, *Heisenberg's War: The Secret History of the German Bomb*, New York: Knopf, 1993

Walker, Mark, *German National Socialism and the Quest for Nuclear Power, 1939–1949*, Cambridge and New York: Cambridge University Press, 1989

Walker, Mark, "Physics and Propaganda: Werner Heisenberg's Foreign Lectures under National Socialism", *Historical Studies in the Physical and Biological Sciences*, 22/2 (1992): 339–89

The most comprehensive biography of Werner Heisenberg is CASSIDY's 550-page account, which avoids the trap of uncritical hagiographic admiration. It is well-researched and full of quotations, in many cases from unpublished documents. Heisenberg's problematic traits of character (e.g., his extreme competitiveness), his much-debated stance as an "apolitical" scientist, and even his nationalistic sympathies, are discussed frankly and embedded within the norms and values of his day. In particular, Heisenberg's role during the Nazi era is described in illuminating detail and with great sensitivity. However, Cassidy's biography is weak in its discussion of Heisenberg's physics, perhaps as a result of constraints imposed on a popular biography at a trade press. With only a handful of exceptions, formulas are avoided altogether. Thus, Heisenberg's attempts around 1924 to save the old quantum theory, and his later endeavors to achieve a unified theory of matter, are discussed only sparingly. Furthermore, the endnotes are cumbersome, and the 27 chapter headings (such as "fresh fruits", or "an unending loneliness") are unhelpful orientation aids.

For a quick chronological overview of Heisenberg's life, it is advisable to start with a glance at HERMANN's booklet, which provides a fair portrait of Heisenberg in a dense sequence of well-chosen quotes and photographs, but which touches only briefly on the many technical aspects of his life in science. HEISENBERG, his widow's recollections, are openly apologetic and in places actually erroneous. However, regarded as an account by one of his closest companions, this work has its own psychohistorical qualities. Covering Heisenberg's years as professor of physics at the University of Leipzig, KLEINT & WIEMERS's excellent anthology not only contains several biographical essays, but also some very useful prosopographical information on his students and colleagues during that time. The Leipzig period is also the main focus of GEYER, HERWIG & RECHENBERG, a collection of papers given at the 1991 conference on Heisenberg in Leipzig. However, several other papers deal with Heisenberg's physical and philosophical work on quantum mechanics, elementary particle physics, and philosophy, and his personal relations with several other physicists.

Readers looking for a thorough description of Heisenberg's formulation of matrix mechanics in July 1925, and the subsequent history, should turn to volumes 2 and 3 of MEHRA & RECHENBERG's *magnum opus* on the history of quantum theory and quantum mechanics, which makes use of all the scholarly literature published prior to 1981, and of Heisenberg's still unpublished correspondence, located at the Max-Planck Institute for Physics in Munich. (A selected edition of Heisenberg's scientific correspondence in the style of the Pauli edition is in preparation.)

A more condensed account of this episode is given in two 50-page chapters of JAMMER's concise book on the conceptual development of quantum mechanics, which relied more heavily on published sources. Heisenberg's *Collected Works*, edited by BLUM, DÜRR & RECHENBERG, contains brief editorial introductions to each section, but these are often too sketchy and rarely written from a historical point of view: intended as concise systematic overviews of the respective fields, they cannot replace the scholarly secondary literature.

Heisenberg's research in nuclear physics under the aegis of the so-called *Uranverein* deserves special mention here. When JUNGK published his famous book on the development of the atomic bomb, he relied heavily on undocumented information obtained from interviews with Heisenberg, von Weizsäcker, and a dozen other important German figures. The impression resulting from this oral history was that this group, and Heisenberg in particular, had consciously prevented any decisive breakthrough in German nuclear research. However, WALKER's well-documented monograph (1989) on the German development of "Uranium Machines" shows conclusively that this version is one of the many myths surrounding the German project. Walker argues that the decision on whether or not to develop the bomb lay in the hands of high-ranking Nazi officials, such as Rust, Speer, and Göring. Furthermore, according to Walker, it is simply not true to state that German physicists sought only peaceful applications of nuclear energy; at least until 1942, Heisenberg and others, in particular Kurt Diebner and Paul Harteck, did what they could to push the military applications forward. This does not eliminate the possibility of Heisenberg's relief when the *Heereswaffenamt* decided that it was unfeasible to pursue that avenue, under the restraints of the war economy and increasing air-attacks that repeatedly destroyed key sites for the production of heavy water and other crucial supplies. Walker's lucid account of the achievements and failures of the German atomic scientists during the Nazi period picks up the many documentary traces, and is both authoritative and well-written.

For technical details of the research conducted at Leipzig, which Heisenberg directed until 1942, the pertinent sections in Kleint & Wiemers's anthology can also be consulted, with Blum, Dürr & Rechenberg covering the later research at the Kaiser Wilhelm Institute for Physics, Berlin, although both texts deal only with the research that was to lead to the nuclear reactor.

The most recent occurrence of the myth that German scientists actively prevented the development of the atomic bomb can be found in POWERS. This book is interesting because of the documentation of Allied preparations to kidnap and assassinate Heisenberg in order to slow down the German uranium project. However, for his plot to work, Powers systematically over-emphasises Heisenberg's importance, and even falls into the trap of providing an apologia, by assuming that Heisenberg actually "falsified the mathematics" in order to obstruct or delay progress in the military applications of nuclear energy.

Regarding Heisenberg's personal stance during the Nazi period, WALKER (1992) examines Heisenberg's lectures in the countries occupied between 1939 and 1945, and offers some revealing insights. Although Heisenberg's obligatory reports to the Foreign Office after such trips were certainly less opportunistic and obsequious than, say, Pascual Jordan's, his foreign colleagues got the impression that he was deeply convinced of German victory and of Germany's cultural superiority. After all, this spirit of cultural imperialism was the motive behind the Nazi government's sending prominent intellectuals into occupied countries, and whether he realized it or not, Heisenberg thus functioned as a propagandist for the Third Reich.

FRANK has recently published the English transcripts of recordings made by the British secret service during the post-war internment of Heisenberg and nine other important German physicists at Farm Hall, Godmanchester, England. Among many other things, these transcripts reveal the personal relations between these men, and help us to understand the emergence of some of those myths exposed by Walker. For example, after the initial shock of the news of the American atomic bombs dropped on Japan, Carl Friedrich von Weizsäcker, Heisenberg, and others gradually worked their way to a (counter-factual) consensus opinion on their own motives – namely, that they had consciously chosen not to develop such a bomb – which they later spread on numerous other occasions.

Despite interesting sections both in Cassidy's and Hermann's biographies, Heisenberg's role as science politician in post-war Germany has been less intensively studied than his earlier activities. One notable exception is ECKERT's essay, which gives an uncritical account of Heisenberg's efforts to become Germany's foremost scientific personality and adviser, as well as the reasons for his ultimate failure in this endeavor.

KLAUS HENTSCHEL

See also Bohr; Quantum Mechanics; Quantum Theory; Schrödinger; Third Reich and Science

Helmholtz, Hermann von 1821–1894
German physicist and physiologist

Cahan, David (ed.), *Letters of Hermann von Helmholtz to His Parents, 1837–1846*, Stuttgart: Steiner, 1993

Cahan, David (ed.), *Hermann von Helmholtz and the Foundations of Nineteenth-Century Science*, Berkeley: University of California Press, 1993

Cahan, David (ed.), *Science and Culture: Popular and Philosophical Essays*, Chicago: University of Chicago Press, 1995

Cohen, Robert S. and Yehuda Elkana (eds), *Epistemological Writings*, translated from the German by Malcolm F. Lowe, Dordrecht: Reidel, 1977 (original edition, 1921)

Eckart, Wolfgang U. and K. Volkert (eds), *Vorträge eines Heidelberger Symposiums anläßlich des einhundertsten Todestages*, Pffaffenweiler: Centurus-Verlaagsgesellschaft, 1996

Hoffmann, Dieter and Heinz Lübbig (eds), *Hermann von Helmholtz (1821–1894). Berliner Kolloquium aus Anlaß des 100. Todestages*, Braunschweig: PTB, 1996

Hoffmann, Dieter and Horst Kant, *Hermann von Helmholtz – Bibliographie der Schriften von und über ihn*, Weinheim: VCH, 1997

Hörz, Herbert, *Physiologie und Kultur in der zweiten Hälfte des 19. Jahrhunderts. Briefe an Hermann von Helmholtz*, Marburg: Basilisken-Presse, 1994

Kirsten, Christa *et al.* (eds), *Dokumente einer Freundschaft: Briefwechsel zwischen Hermann von Helmholtz und Emil du Bois-Reymond*, Berlin: Akademie, 1986

Königsberger, Leo, *Hermann von Helmholtz*, translated from the German by Frances A. Welby, Oxford: Clarendon

Press, 1906; New York: Dover, 1965 (original edition, 1902–03)

Kremer, Richard L. (ed.), *Letters of Hermann von Helmholtz to His Wife, 1847–1859*, Stuttgart: Steiner, 1990

Krüger, Lorenz (ed.), *Universalgenie Helmholtz: Rückblick nach 100 Jahren*, Berlin: Akademie, 1994

Lipschitz, Rudolf, *Briefwechsel mit Cantor, Dedekind, Helmholtz, Kronecker, Weierstrass und anderen: Bearbeitet von W. Scharlau*, Braunschweig: Vieweg, 1986

Rechenberg, H., *Hermann von Helmholtz: Bilder seines Lebens und Wirkens*, Weinheim: VCH, 1994

Siemens-Helmholtz, Ellen von (ed.), *Anna von Helmholtz: Ein Lebensbild in Briefen*, 1929 Berlin: Verlag für Kulturpolitik

Turner, Steven, *In the Eye's Mind: Vision and the Helmholtz-Hering Controversy*, Princeton, New Jersey: Princeton University Press, 1994

Werner, P. (ed.), *Kunst und Liebe müssen sein: Briefe von Anna von Helmholtz an Cosima Wagner, 1889 bis 1899*, Bayreuth: Druckhaus, 1993

Research on Hermann von Helmholtz has increased significantly in recent times, for two reasons: the publication of numerous editions of his correspondence since 1986 has stimulated much research on the scholar's life and works; and, the 100th anniversary of Helmholtz's death was celebrated with a number of conferences, seminars and symposia, many of which have resulted in a publication.

Faced with the abundance of literature, the reader is well advised to start with the volumes edited by CAHAN (*Hermann von Helmholtz and the Foundation of Nineteenth-Century Science*, 1993) and by KRÜGER. Both give an excellent synopsis of the current state of Helmholtz research and an introduction to his polymathic activities. The various aspects of Helmholtz's research are treated competently in an array of essays, in which his (co-)discovery of the law of energy conservation (his most famous achievement) and his invention of the ophthalmoscope are appreciated in as much detail as his other fundamental contributions to the development of science in the 19th century – in classical physics, especially thermodynamics and electrodynamics, medicine, physiology, psychology and mathematics. Also covered is Helmholtz's keen interest in the implications of philosophical, cognitive and scientific theory issues for the actual practice of science. Taken together, Cahan and Krüger offer a broad range of studies on the (in Krüger's words) "interdisciplinary mental power of a polymathic genius", the analysis expanding beyond the narrower confines of exact science and cognitive theory into Helmholtz's public role as a "Chancellor of the sciences", scientific "mandarin", and *Kulturträger* in the German Empire.

Nevertheless, these edited volumes do not amount to a modern scientific biography, which is unfortunately still awaited. Meanwhile, the three volumes by KÖNIGSBERGER, from the early 20th century, remains the standard for anyone who wants to follow Helmholtz's life and works chronologically, although the hagiographical elements, and the frequently uncritical and selective use of the historical sources, make the biography useful only when approached with caution. However, the virtues of Königsberger's biography include its rich detail, and the privileged access its author had to the

Helmholtz papers, including the family correspondence, which makes the biography a gold mine of sources; there are letters and documents (sometimes reproduced only in fragments) which appear nowhere else and are now lost.

The biography by RECHENBERG was published in the centennial year of 1994; it leans respectfully but critically on Königsberger, elaborating a "mosaic" of the great scholar in 43 short sections. Its strengths are to be found in the presentation of the scientific *oeuvre* and its links with modern physics. The contextualisation of Helmholtz's work is comparatively brief, however; only rarely does the author attempt to explain how Helmholtz became who he was or what determined his activities, and no new sources or archival material are used to any significant extent.

TURNER does not pretend to be a biography, although it contains much detail concerning Helmholtz's life and works, and on the social and intellectual background. This is a brilliant and fertile study of the development of the theory of perception and colour in the late 19th century, the strength of the study lying in the fact that Turner does not restrict himself to a narrow internalism, but instead sets the theory of colours in a wider context. For instance, the case of the discussions between Helmholtz and Hering on the theory of colour is analysed within the context of the general role that scientific controversies played in the establishment of scientific theory. The book also contains an abundance of illuminating insights into the 19th-century German university system, the process of institutionalization, and science's place within them.

Further information regarding specific aspects of Helmholtz's life and works can be found in the edited volumes by ECKART & VOLKERT, and by HOFFMANN & LÜBBIG, both of which contain the proceedings from symposia organised on the centenary of Helmholtz's death. Naturally, there is great variability, both in terms of content and quality, and there are also some overlaps. However, there is much to be found on Helmholtz as organic physicist, on the physiology of sight, and on Helmholtz's role as cultural icon and political representative of science, and the footnotes are extensive.

Until the mid-1980s, the image of Helmholtz was largely determined by Königsberger's biography, by Helmholtz's impact upon science, and by a few manuscript publications, especially Anna Von Helmholtz. In the last 10 years this has changed, and it has become apparent that Helmholtz's daughter, Ellen von SIEMENS-HELMHOLTZ, carefully selected the manuscripts to be published with the aim of aggrandizing her father. Today there are several editions of Helmholtz's correspondence which allow a firsthand examination of his life and work, and not least of his personality.

KIRSTEN *et al.*, Helmholtz's correspondence with perhaps his closest friend and colleague, Emil DuBois-Reymond, gives important insights into the former's intellectual development, his relation to the field of physiology, and also the changes in the role of science and in scientists' perception of their role within the *Kaiserreich*.

HÖRZ examines Helmholtz's relationship with physiology and physiologists of his time. This correspondence makes it evident just how much the "organic physicists" in the mid-19th century saw themselves as a secret society, as they struggled to establish their (scientific) view of physiology. However, the very long and sometimes doctrinaire introductions are a blemish.

LIPSCHITZ, the correspondence between Helmholtz and Rudolf Lipschitz, is much more modest, documenting Helmholtz's attitude to contemporary mathematics, and especially his position at the University of Bonn, the circumstances of both his call and departure.

In all the above editions of Helmholtz's correspondence, the mature, established and successful Helmholtz is in focus. The two volumes by CAHAN allow interesting glimpses of the process of maturation in a genius. The reader learns details of the circumstances of the young student, his likes and dislikes, his (political) attitudes, but also the everyday problems and conflicts that he encountered early in his very successful career. These editions are very useful for the reader who wants to unearth the origins and patterns of Helmholtz's thought and personality.

WERNER's selection of letters between Helmholtz's first wife and the wife of the composer Richard Wagner shows Helmholtz's and his family's close links with musicians, and simultaneously how intimately Helmholtz was rooted in, and identified himself with, Wilhelminian society. Indeed, this throws light on Helmholtz's famous textbook on the perception of sound, which had a great cultural impact.

Faced with the wealth of secondary literature and editions of correspondence, one ought not to forget Helmholtz's scientific publications. HOFFMANN & KANT contains a bibliography that brings together primary material published in the *Gesammelte Schriften* and in Cahan (1993), and it also lists relevant secondary literature. Helmholtz's main works have all been translated into English. COHEN & ELKANA (1977) is a recent edition of his epistemological writings, and CAHAN (1995) contains his popular and philosophical essays, providing another important source for the discovery of Helmholtz's life, work, and personality.

DIETER HOFFMANN

translated by Arne Hessenbruch

Herbalism

Anderson, Frank J., *An Illustrated History of the Herbals*, New York: Columbia University Press, 1977

Arber, Agnes, *Herbals, Their Origin and Evolution: A Chapter in the History of Botany, 1470–1670*, Cambridge: Cambridge University Press, 1912; Darien, Connecticut: Hafner, 1970

Blunt, Wilfrid and Sandra Raphael, *The Illustrated Herbal*, London: Lincoln, 1979; revised edition, 1994

Fischer, Hermann, *Mittelalterliche Pflanzenkunde*, Munich: Oldenbourg, 1929

Nissen, Claus, *Die botanische Buchillustration: Ihre Geschichte und Bibliographie*, 2 vols, Stuttgart: Hiersemann, 1951, supplement, 1966

Rohde, Eleanour Sinclair, *The Old English Herbals*, London: Longmans Green, 1922

Schreiber, Wilhelm Ludwig, *Die Kräuterbücher des XV. und XVI. Jahrhunderts* [supplement to the facsimile edition of Peter Schöffer's *Hortus Sanitatis Deutsch (Gart der Gesundheit)*], edited by Reimar Walter Fuchs, Munich: Münchener Drucke, 1924

Singer, Charles, "The Herbal in Antiquity and Its Transmission to Later Ages", *Journal of Hellenic Studies*, 47 (1927): 1–52

Early herbals and herbaria, characterized by their descriptions (and usually illustrations) of mostly medicinal and useful plants, are mentioned in the general surveys of the history of botany. In addition, a number of specialist monographs are dedicated to herbals. The most comprehensive account to date of the history and bibliography of illustrated botanical works is NISSEN, which deals with herbals and their history from the early advanced civilizations, antiquity and the Middle Ages (that is, before such works appeared in print), to modernity. Works since the 17th century are classified according to their country of origin, into European and non-European, for they frequently already contain the basic inventories of regional floras. Nissen also analyses the history of botanical book illustration and its artists, and supplements his account by detailed references to the literature and to the biographies of both the botanists and artists. This descriptive section is followed by a thorough and excellent bibliography that aspires to the highest degree of comprehensiveness. A supplement updates the bibliography with literature up to the 1960s.

ANDERSON presents a selection of 30 outstanding herbals from antiquity to the early 17th century. Dedicating a chapter to each, he examines the historical significance of these books by reproducing illustrations and title pages, and by summarizing their contents. A bibliography of the most important editions and literary references supplements the text.

Equally careful bibliographical references characterize the survey by BLUNT & RAPHAEL, which above all documents the history of illustrations, from the miniatures and woodcuts in early prints to the copper engravings of the 18th century, in magnificent and frequently coloured reproductions. A carefully prepared text comments on the contents and the historical significance of the herbals under consideration. The book is of special value for its reproductions of illustrations from medieval manuscripts and rare early modern prints, which are not easily accessible.

All of the above three works mention in passing the involved history of textual traditions. Dedicated exclusively to this history of the traditions of classical texts is the thorough study by SINGER, which analyses the filiation of copies and editions of the most important texts known at the time. All later statements and graphical schemes rely on this study.

A history of herbals of the Middle Ages (comprising both Latin European and Muslim regions), including early prints from c.1500, has been compiled by FISCHER. The book is based on manuscript studies, and provides detailed information on the contents and plant inventories (with synonyms) of the most outstanding books. SCHREIBER provides a survey of the best-known early printed herbals of the 15th and 16th centuries. The supplemented reprints are useful bibliographical references.

ARBER is the first attempt to integrate into the history of botany the tradition and botanical contents of printed herbals, from between 1470 and 1670. She takes account of the tradition of medieval (Dioscorides Pseudo-Apuleius) texts and describes innovations that originated in various European countries during the Renaissance. She also discusses the various methods of plant description and classification, and analyses the craftsmanship of botanical illustrations. Further, Arber studies the peculiar interpretations offered by herbals concerning the properties of plants; i.e., the doctrine of signatures and the inclusion of astrological readings. Her work remains a fundamental introduction to the history of herbals during this important period.

ROHDE has supplied an extensive treatise (with a detailed bibliography) on Anglo-Saxon herbals between the 8th and the 17th centuries, locating the originals of medieval and early modern manuscripts, as well as of early prints, which are scattered over a number of college and private libraries. These (often anonymous) original texts, their contents and significance within the tradition, are thoroughly analysed. Outstanding 16th- and 17th-century herbaries, by English authors such as William Turner, John Gerarde and John Parkinson, receive extensive appreciation. A separate chapter is exclusively dedicated to herbals containing plants that were newly discovered in the Americas. Rohde also comments in detail on the herbals of the late 16th and 17th centuries, which give magical, astrological, and superstitious interpretations of certain plants. This thorough and ambitious book is an indispensable reference work for those studying the history and bibliography of herbals, and their relationship with corresponding continental botanical writings of the Middle Ages and early modern period.

BRIGITTE HOPPE

translated by Anna-Katherina Mayer

See also Botany; Drugs; Natural History

Heredity

Borie, Jean, *Les Mythologies de l'hérédité au XIXe siecle*, Paris: Galilee, 1981

Churchill, Frederick B., "From Heredity Theory to Vererbung: The Transmission Problem, 1850–1915", *Isis*, 78 (1987): 337–64

Delage, Yves, *L'Hérédité et les grandes problèmes de la biologie générale*, 2nd edition, Paris: Reinwald, 1903

Dowbiggin, Ian R., *Inheriting Madness: Professionalization and Psychiatric Knowledge in 19th-Century France*, Berkeley: University of California Press, 1991

Hilts, Victor, *Statist and Statistician: Three Studies in the History of 19th-Century English Statistical Thought*, New York: Arno Press, 1981

López-Beltrán, Carlos, "Forging Heredity: From Metaphor to Cause, a Reification Story", *Studies in the History and Philosophy of Science*, 25/2 (1994): 211–35

Lucas, Prosper, *Traité philosophique et physiologique de l'hérédité naturelle dans les états de santé et de maladie du système nerveux*, 2 vols, Paris: Mason, 1847–50

Olby, Robert C., *Origins of Mendelism*, New York: Schocken Books, and London: Constable, 1966; 2nd edition, Chicago: University of Chicago Press, 1985

Pick, Daniel, *Faces of Degeneration: A European Disorder, c.1848–c.1918*, Cambridge and New York: Cambridge University Press, 1989

Robinson, Gloria, *A Prelude to Genetics: Theories of Material Substance of Heredity, Darwin to Weissman*, Lawrence, Kansas: Coronado Press, 1979

Roger, Jacques, *Les Sciences de la vie dans la penseé francaise du dix-huitième siècle*, Paris: Armand Colin, 1963

Russell, Nicholas, *Like Engend'ring Like: Heredity and Animal Breeding in Early Modern England*, Cambridge and New York: Cambridge University Press, 1986

Williams, Elizabeth A., *The Physical and the Moral: Anthropology, Physiology, and Philosophical Medicine in France, 1750–1850*, Cambridge and New York: Cambridge University Press, 1994

The field of heredity was essentially a 19th-century phenomenon, which collapsed into genetics during the 20th century. The adoption of Mendelism after 1900 as the research strategy for exposing the basic regularities of character transmission from parents to offspring restricted, reorganized, and radically altered the nature of the questions surrounding heredity. Such a collapse was reinforced by the fact that heredity was a key explanatory concept of Darwin's work, and that Mendelian genetics was eventually articulated along with Darwinism under the same triumphant theoretical banner.

As a result a degree of historiographical distortion dominated for a long period. Historians of biology focused on a few conceptual lineages related to the explanatory problems of Darwinism, from soft to hard inheritance, or from the inheritance or non-inheritance of acquired characteristics. Lamarck, Darwin, Mendel, Galton, and Weissman would typically be mentioned as the main contributors to the pre-genetics era, and earlier writers, such as Maupertuis or William Lawrence, were mentioned only in so far as they "anticipated" ideas that were to become crucial for Darwinism and genetics.

Recent work by several historians has helped change the general understanding of the development of the concept of heredity (or biological inheritance) from early modern times to the 1850s, when the need for a full blown theory of heredity was first manifested in Prosper LUCAS. Following the publication of this work, the concept of heredity was transformed during the second half of the 19th century, when an increase in experimental and theoretical activity was aimed at constructing an account of the dynamics of character transmission. It is now possible to trace the contribution of several quite independent research traditions to such developments, and three main strands can be mentioned.

The first strand is the tradition of plant hybridization that began with Linnaeus and gave rise to the work of Gregor Mendel, and which has been carefully followed and described by OLBY. The main task of these researches was to explore, through the controlled crossing of varieties, the boundaries of plant species.

The second strand was linked to animal breeding, its main purpose being to control the characteristics of domesticated animals. RUSSELL provides a good exposition of the practical concepts of heredity in relation to cattle-breeding practices in early modern England. There remains a need for a book-length monograph examining the whole tradition of animal breeding (which had a great influence on Darwin) and the development of ideas on inheritance; as yet, only some unpublished theses and a few scholarly papers have been written on the subject.

Within both of these strands there was no theoretically oriented work on the concept of heredity, although some patterns and regularities of resemblances and variation were systematized for practical purposes. It was within the third strand that the concept of heredity acquired its explanatory independence within the medical tradition, prompted by Enlightenment materialism, and centered on the causal influence of bodily and moral features of parents in those of their offspring.

ROGER's masterly work makes a clear distinction between traditional disputes around the issue of generation from the 16th to the 18th centuries, and the more specific, and posterior disputes around heredity. HILTS's early work on the ethnological origin of Francis Galton's views on heredity pointed towards a whole area of undisturbed historical evidence on the construction of some key features of the concept of biological inheritance. LÓPEZ-BELTRÁN has argued that 18th- and early 19th-century discussions among medics and anthropologists (linked with the concepts of constitution, hereditary disease, and diathesis) provided the arena for an autonomous, physical, causal view of heredity among humans. It seems clear that the "reified" concept of *hérédité* was first employed, with a causal explanatory purpose, by French medical men early in the 19th century. An insightful description of how the French search for a physical science of man within its 18th- and 19th-century medical communities made possible the emergence of heredity as a theoretical resource is found in WILLIAMS.

Within the context of the professionalization of psychiatry after 1848, DOWBIGGIN has found that the appeal to heredity as an efficient and independent cause for mental disease provided a useful tool for discipline demarcation and legitimation against rivals in the control of the insane. PICK gives a rich description of the cultural and social context of 19th-century France, in which hereditarianism was linked to important social issues (e.g. mental health and hygiene). He also describes how Morel's concept of *Degenerescence* revealed national and cultural anxieties common in 19th-century Europe.

Heredity was such a pervasive 19th-century French myth that it had a profound effect on many fields, including literature. BORIE offers a compelling analysis of how scientific, hereditarian views of human nature were introduced as narrative-guiding devices in the works of, among others, Balzac and Zola.

LUCAS's mid-century treatise constitutes an amazing marshalling of previously published sources from all ages, concerning hereditary transmission of all sorts of characteristics, although his theoretical scheme was not as influential as his skilful deployment of bookish evidence. Darwin, Galton, Ribot, De Candolle, and many other authors read this work carefully, and J.A. Thomson was not far off the mark when he stated that Lucas had convinced his generation of "the facts of heredity".

Heredity was an established scientific subject by 1850. CHURCHILL has described the transition from the genealogical, physiological view, promoted by physicians and zoologists, to a new kind of biological theory of heredity (*Vererbung*) that incorporated the late 19th-century findings in cytology and development, and documents the proposals that aimed to solve the transmission and developmental problems within a single scheme. DELAGE is an exhaustive and detailed exposition of the multiplicity of hypotheses that existed at the turn of the century concerning the basis of heredity. ROBINSON gives an evaluation of many of these, within what she calls the search for a material substance of heredity.

CARLOS LÓPEZ-BELTRÁN

See also Darwinism; Genetics: general works

Hermeticism

Clulee, Nicholas H., *John Dee's Natural Philosophy: Between Science and Religion*, London and New York: Routledge, 1988
Copenhaver, Brian (ed.), *Hermetica: The Greek Corpus Hermeticum and the Latin Asclepius in a New English Translation with Notes and Introduction*, Cambridge and New York: Cambridge University Press, 1992
Festugière, A.-J., *La Révélation d'Hermès Trismégiste*, 4 vols, Paris: Librarie Lecoffre, 1944–54 (especially vol. 1: *L'Astrologie et les sciences occultes*)
Fowden, Garth, *The Egyptian Hermes: A Historical Approach to the Late Pagan Mind*, Cambridge and New York: Cambridge University Press, 1986
French, Peter J., *John Dee: The World of An Elizabethan Magus*, London: Routledge and Kegan Paul, 1972
Merkel, Ingrid and Allen G. Debus (eds), *Hermeticism and the Renaissance: Intellectual History and the Occult in Early Modern Europe*, Washington, DC: Folger Shakespeare Library, and London: Associated University Presses, 1988
Righini Bonelli, M.L. and William R. Shea (eds), *Reason, Experiment and Mysticism in the Scientific Revolution*, London: Macmillan, and New York: Science History Publications, 1975
Schmitt, Charles B., "Reappraisals in Renaissance Science", *History of Science*, 16 (1978): 200–14
Vickers, Brian (ed.), *Occult and Scientific Mentalities in the Renaissance*, Cambridge and New York: Cambridge University Press, 1984
Westman, Robert S. and J.E. McGuire, *Hermeticism and the Scientific Revolution*, Los Angeles: University of California Press, 1977
Yates, Frances A., *Giordano Bruno and the Hermetic Tradition*, Chicago: University of Chicago Press, and London: Routledge and Kegan Paul, 1964
Yates, Frances A., "The Hermetic Tradition in Renaissance Science", *Art, Science and History in the Renaissance*, edited by Charles S. Singleton, Baltimore: Johns Hopkins Press, 1967; reprinted in her *Ideas and Ideals in the North European Renaissance: Collected Essays*, vol. 3, London and Boston: Routledge and Kegan Paul, 1984
Yates, Frances A., *The Rosicrucian Enlightenment*, London and Boston: Routledge and Kegan Paul, 1972

Hermeticism is a label that is used in at least two different ways. First, it can refer to the beliefs and practices of late ancient syncretic writers who presented themselves as, or saw themselves as, followers of Hermes Trismegistus, Thrice-Great Hermes. Second, and more commonly among historians of science, it is used to refer, in a very loose way, to a set of beliefs supposedly inspired by the 15th-century rediscovery in the Latin West of the Hermetic writings, which arguably influenced certain late Renaissance and early modern natural philosophers, and thereby played a significant part in the scientific revolution. This second meaning of the term derives essentially from a number of highly controversial works by Frances A. Yates, and the claim that Hermeticism played a major role in the scientific revolution is often referred to as the Yates thesis. Yates herself used to differentiate these two senses of Hermeticism, by referring to the teachings of the Hermetic writings and the beliefs of their authors and immediate followers as *Hermetism*, while reserving *Hermeticism* to refer to the broader tradition that she saw as stemming ultimately from Hermetism – but few have accepted this special terminology.

The Hermetic writings, which emanate from the Greco-Egyptian culture of Hellenistic, Roman, and early Christian times, have been effectively divided into two parts. The *Corpus Hermeticum* consists of 17 separate treatises, written in Greek, and a dialogue, known as the *Asclepius*, which only survives in a Latin version. These are usually referred to by scholars as the "philosophical" Hermetica, in order to distinguish them from the more technical writings, concerned principally with the occult sciences of astrology, alchemy, and natural magic. The separation of these two kinds of Hermetic writing seems to have taken place in late antiquity or the early Middle Ages by Christians who were evidently offended by the emphasis on the occult in the technical writings, but more tolerant of the "philosophical" works with their emphasis on salvation through knowledge of God. A detailed analysis of the technical writings can be found in FESTUGIÈRE. He concludes that there is nothing original in any of the Hermetic writings, but that they are all derivative of beliefs that can be found in earlier Greek magical writings. This judgement undoubtedly remains valid, even though Festugière was mistaken in believing that the Hermetic writings originated exclusively from Greek sources. The more eclectic origins of the Hermetic writings and their significance are discussed in FOWDEN, and in the introduction of COPENHAVER's new English translation of the *Corpus Hermeticum*.

The Hermetica gained authority from the mistaken belief that they were written by an Egyptian sage who lived around the time of Moses, or even earlier. When the Greek *Corpus Hermeticum* was rediscovered by the Latin West and translated into Latin by Marsilio Ficino in 1463 and published in 1471, Hermes came to be regarded as the founder of theology. His authority was enhanced for Christians by the fact that he seemed to prefigure by many centuries some of the mysteries of Christianity. In fact this was hardly surprising, given the date that these writings were composed, but Renaissance thinkers had no suspicions that the Hermetic works were written in the Christian Era.

There can be no doubt, therefore, that the Hermetic writings were immensely influential on Renaissance intellectuals. What is much more controversial, however, is the claim, hinted at by Frances Yates in 1964, and stated more directly in 1967, that Hermetic ideas or Hermetic ways of thinking played a major role in the scientific revolution.

YATES (1964) provides an excellent and accessible general survey of the influence of Hermeticism in the Renaissance, as well as a major study of Giordano Bruno. Of more relevance here, however, is the fact that in the closing pages she draws some parallels between Renaissance Hermeticism and the new approaches to natural philosophy. Francis Bacon's *New Atlantis*, she states, is Hermetic, while Bruno is representative of those for whom the "Hermetic impulse" provided the motive force behind the formulation of a new cosmology: Bruno's animistic universe "would turn into something like the mechanical universe of Isaac Newton, marvellously moving forever under its own laws". Such throw-away speculations were made more trenchant in YATES (1967), when the Renaissance magus is declared to be the immediate ancestor of the 17th-century scientist, and the Hermetic revival is hailed as the major force "which turned men's minds in the direction out of which the scientific revolution was to come". YATES (1972) takes the story further, by linking Rosicrucianism, which needless to say she regarded as a Hermetic movement, to Francis Bacon, the Hartlib Circle and other groups that were the initial inspiration for the Royal Society of London, and to Isaac Newton.

Yates's claims were highly speculative, based on no real historical evidence, and intended merely to be suggestive, but, for a while, her suggestions were taken far more seriously than, with hindsight, they seem to deserve. Numerous works by other scholars talked glibly of Hermetic influences, or located various Renaissance and early modern thinkers within what was presented as a flourishing and undeniable Hermetic Tradition. FRENCH, for example, is a study of the Elizabethan sage John Dee as "England's first Hermetic magus", as well as "a respected practical scientist". Although there is much of value in this book, it must now be treated with caution, and should only be read in conjunction with the much more reliable study by CLULEE, written after the Yates thesis had had its day.

The Yates thesis, perhaps because of its unexpected authoritativeness, soon began to draw severe criticism of two kinds. First, there were those who had been opposed to earlier historiographical suggestions that the origins of modern science in the late 16th and 17th centuries owed something to magical traditions. Most of this literature appeared as articles in academic journals, or in general collections of essays. One famous example of this kind of attack on the Yates thesis is to be found in RIGHINI BONELLI & SHEA; Paolo Rossi, an author who had previously pointed to magical influences upon Francis Bacon (*Francesco Bacone: Dalla Magia alla Scienza*, Bari, Editori Laterza, 1957), in a discussion entitled "Hermeticism, Rationality and the Scientific Revolution", rejected the role of Hermeticism in the scientific revolution, claiming that "the refutation of the priestly idea of knowledge inherent in hermeticism" was among the essential and decisive factors in "modern thought". He also decried the latest historiographical image of Bacon as a "transformer of hermetic dreams", and affirmed, in his conclusion, that the true role of the history of science is to show how logical rigour, experimental control, and the publication of results and methods can lead to the advance of civilisation. Rossi's views are then taken even further by A. Rupert Hall in an attack on "Magic, Metaphysics and Mysticism in the Scientific Revolution" in the same volume, which he declares to be irrelevant to an understanding of the supremely rational pursuit of modern science.

WESTMAN & McGUIRE's book contains two separate papers attacking the Yates thesis. Westman's "Magical Reform and Astronomical Reform: The Yates Thesis Reconsidered" takes issue with Yates's suggestion that the analogy between God and the visible splendour of the sun, which can be found in the Hermetic corpus, was an inspiration behind the Copernican revolution in astronomy. Westman convincingly refutes this. McGuire's article is entitled "Neoplatonism and Active Principles: Newton and the *Corpus Hermeticum*", and argues that the seemingly Hermetic elements in Newton's thought could have originated with the Cambridge Platonists, and especially Henry More. McGuire concludes that the Hermetic world-picture did not play a significant role in shaping Newton's thought.

The editor's introduction to VICKERS surveys the historiography of the role of magic in the scientific revolution. After a brief discussion, Vickers rejects the Yates thesis as "almost wholly unfounded", but he recognises that her claims are separate from the broader historiographical issue of the possible influence of magical traditions on science. This is to repeat the point that was first urged in SCHMITT; pointing out that Hermeticism in the Renaissance was merely one strand in a rich fabric of magical or occult traditions, and one which depended on a much broader Neoplatonic philosophy, Schmitt concluded that Hermeticism should not, and cannot, be seen as the driving force behind any significant historical developments. What Yates had done, in other words, was to cause scholars to think erroneously that they were focusing on Hermeticism, when they were in fact looking at broader Neoplatonic or magical traditions; or she had encouraged them to use the label "Hermetic" to refer to a wide variety of different magical and mystical traditions, when that label should have been reserved for historical developments that did genuinely stem from the Renaissance revival of the *Corpus Hermeticum*.

Although this kind of use of the label "Hermetic" is now largely passé, it has not entirely disappeared. Of the 20 essays in MERKEL & DEBUS, for example, only eight deal with Hermeticism in the proper, restricted sense, the others being concerned with various other aspects of the magical tradition (even though two of these misleadingly use the word Hermetic in their titles). In their introduction, the editors admit that their aim of gathering together a collection of papers that would explicate the diverse and "largely contradictory elements" of the supposedly Hermetic tradition fell short of their expectations, and failed to draw a sharper profile of Hermeticism. They explicitly reject the conclusion that Hermeticism is a fallacious historiographical category, however, but give no good reason for this resolution.

JOHN HENRY

See also Dee; Occult Sciences

Herschel, William   1738–1822

German-born British astronomer

Bennett, J.A., "'On the Power of Penetrating into Space': The Telescopes of William Herschel", *Journal for the History of Astronomy*, 7 (1976): 75–108

Crowe, Michael J., *The Extraterrestrial Life Debate, 1750–1900: The Idea of Plurality of Worlds from Kant to Lowell*, Cambridge and New York: Cambridge University Press, 1986

Crowe, Michael J., *Modern Theories of the Universe: From Herschel to Hubble*, New York: Dover, 1994

Dreyer, J.L.E. (ed.), *The Scientific Papers of Sir William Herschel*, 2 vols, London: Royal Society, 1912

Hoskin, Michael A., *William Herschel and the Construction of the Heavens*, London: Oldbourne, 1963

Lubbock, Constance A., *The Herschel Chronicle: The Life Story of William Herschel and His Sister Caroline Herschel*, Cambridge: Cambridge University Press, and New York: Macmillan, 1933

Schaffer, Simon, "'The Great Laboratories of the Universe': William Herschel on Matter Theory and Planetary Life", *Journal for the History of Astronomy*, 11 (1980): 81–111

Schaffer, Simon, "Herschel in Bedlam: Natural History and Stellar Astronomy", *British Journal for the History of Science*, 13 (1980): 211–39

Sidgwick, J.B., *William Herschel: Explorer of the Heavens*, London: Faber and Faber, 1953

William Herschel, one of the most eminent astronomers of all time, was born at Hanover on 15 November 1738, the son of a military bandsman, Isaac Herschel. William joined the band of his father's regiment in 1753, and as a military musician visited England briefly in 1756. After the defeat of the Duke of Cumberland by the French at Hastenbeck, the young oboe player in the Hanoverian Foot Guards decided to pursue a musical career in England, where he arrived in November 1757. Settling initially in London, from 1760 Herschel had a number of musical appointments in the north of England. Then, in 1766, he was appointed organist at the Octagon Chapel in Bath. While at Bath, Herschel began to develop his philosophical and scientific interests. In 1773, he began constructing telescopes and making astronomical observations, and fame came with his discovery, in March 1781, of what became known as Uranus. Herschel was the first person in recorded history to discover a new planet, and the subsequent patronage of George III and his earnings from the construction and sale of telescopes enabled him to abandon professional musicianship. Leaving Bath with his sister Caroline (who had joined him in 1773), Herschel moved first to Datchet (1782), then to Old Windsor (1785), and finally to Slough (1786), where he spent the rest of his life. It was during the course of the second of three "reviews" of the sky prior to 1783 that Herschel had discovered Uranus. In 1783, he began a systematic examination of the heavens that was completed in 1802. Herschel employed telescopes of his own design and construction that were of unprecedented power. He discovered more than 800 multiple stars (only a few dozen had been known before), and some 2,500 nebulae and star clusters (just over 100 had been identified before him). On the basis of these discoveries, Herschel developed his account of the "construction of the heavens".

The literature on William Herschel is notable for the stress placed on his observational cosmological work, which derives from the contrast between his work and that of other 18th-century cosmologists. The theories concerning the large-scale structure of the universe, propounded by Immanuel Kant, Thomas Wright and J.H. Lambert, were speculative cosmologies unaccompanied by any significant additions to empirical knowledge. Herschel, on the other hand, did make major empirical contributions, and his cosmological speculations are often treated as grounded in his vast observational program. However, in recent years, historians of science have re-evaluated the "empirical" Herschel, presenting an astronomer who engaged in very broad physical speculation, and whose whole astronomical career might be understood in terms of a larger natural historical project, the guiding philosophical tenets of which included adherence to the doctrine of the plurality of worlds.

DREYER remains an indispensable source, since it collects Herschel's scientific papers, mainly from the *Philosophical Transactions* of the Royal Society of London between 1780 and 1818, and also includes unpublished scientific and biographical materials. LUBBOCK is also very valuable for its presentation of correspondence between Herschel and his sister Caroline, who lived with him from 1773, and became a very able astronomer in her own right, assisting Herschel during his arduous telescopic observations.

SIDGWICK is in many ways the most accessible of the numerous biographies of Herschel. It does much to bring Herschel's character alive, stressing the continuities between his musical, mathematical, philosophical, and astronomical interests. It gives readable accounts of his observational work, and yet appreciates some of the deeper philosophical roots of Herschel's imaginative interpretation of his observations.

HOSKIN is the most influential interpretation of Herschel's scientific work and philosophical temper. It provides clear and authoritative accounts of the discovery of Uranus, the work on double stars and the solar motion, the observations of nebulae, and Herschel's two major renderings of the "construction of the heavens". The volume includes extensive extracts from Herschel's key papers dealing with these topics. Hoskin argues that, despite his achievements, Herschel was isolated from his contemporaries, partly by the unique power of his instruments, but more importantly by his bold and dogmatic theoretical stances and arguments.

CROWE (1994) is useful in placing Herschel in relation to his predecessors and successors in stellar astronomy and cosmological theorising, and in providing a clear statement of the major historiographical questions concerning Herschel's approach and achievements. Crowe also provides extensive extracts from key papers. CROWE (1986) argues that speculative philosophy, notably a belief in the plurality of worlds, played a crucial role in Herschel's creative work.

A number of more specialised papers have made important contributions to an understanding of Herschel's activities. BENNETT examines as working instruments the telescopes that Herschel built for his own use, showing how the changing designs can be understood, at least in part, as responses to the theoretical problems that Herschel progressively faced. Bennett explains in detail how the push for ever bigger telescopes, in order to gather more light and achieve greater "penetrating power" into space, was tempered by issues of optical quality and ease of use. Herschel's famous 40-foot telescope, a magnificent technical achievement in construction, was, however, a failure as a working instrument.

SCHAFFER (1980, "Herschel in Bedlam") provides an important reinterpretation of Herschel's project, as part of the discourse of natural history as described by Michel Foucault. Conceiving Herschel's work as concerned with identifying natural types of astronomical objects in series and relating them through physical law, Schaffer provides a coherent understanding of Herschel's work and explains why his contemporaries and successors could never entirely embrace his ideas and approach. Schaffer pinpoints precisely the reasons why his contemporaries felt they detected heterodoxy verging on madness in some of Herschel's contributions.

SCHAFFER (1980, "The Great Laboratories") attempts further integration by spelling out the relations between Herschel's cosmology, his theory of matter, and the idea of the plurality of worlds. Schaffer depicts Herschel's cosmology as the product of a complex, carefully articulated philosophical system of great scope, and assimilates it with such systems as James Hutton's geology and Laplace's astronomy, both of which attracted much scientific and theological opprobrium. As Schaffer claims, the reaction to Herschel's cosmology can only be fully understood if one appreciates the company which his work was thought to keep. This Herschel is a far cry indeed from the patient, sober, and empirical observational astronomer.

DAVID PHILIP MILLER

See also Astronomy: general works; Telescopes

Hertz, Heinrich Rudolf   1857–1894

German physicist

Buchwald, Jed Z., *The Creation of Scientific Effects: Heinrich Hertz and Electric Waves*, Chicago: University of Chicago Press, 1994

Fölsing, Albrecht, *Heinrich Hertz: Eine Biographie*, Hamburg: Hoffmann & Camp, 1997

Hertz, Johanna (ed.), *Erinnerungen, Briefe, Tagebücher: Heinrich Hertz*, Leipzig: Akademische Verlagsgesellschaft, 1927; revised, bilingual edition as *Erinnerungen, Briefe, Tagebücher/Memoirs, Letters, Diaries: Heinrich Hertz*, edited by Mathilde Hertz and Charles Susskind, Weinheim: Physik, and San Francisco: San Francisco Press, 1977

O'Hara, J.G. and W. Pricha, *Hertz and the Maxwellians: A Study and Documentation of the Discovery of Electromagnetic Wave Radiation 1873–1884*, London: Peter Peregrinus/Science Museum, 1987

Susskind, Charles, *Henrich Hertz: A Short Life*, San Francisco: San Francisco Press, 1995

Wiesbeck, Werner (ed.), *100 Jahre elektromagnetische Wellen/100 Years Electromagnetic Waves*, Berlin: VDE, 1988 (conference proceedings)

Heinrich Hertz's work is well documented by two volumes of his collected papers – on electric waves (1892) and on other miscellaneous physics topics (1895) – and by his monograph *Principles of Mechanics, Presented in a New Form* (1894). All three were promptly translated into English and published in 1893, 1896, and 1899 respectively. The last was reprinted (New York: Dover, 1956) with an added introduction by R.S. Cohen and an extensive updated bibliography, having proved to be of abiding interest to an entirely different scholarly community, the philosophers of science.

BUCHWALD's work (the first of a projected two volumes examines Hertz's highly original approach to science in great detail. Buchwald's extensive treatment (329 pages of text, 80 pages of appendices, 48 pages of notes, and a 13-page bibliography) is intended in the main for historians (and philosophers) of science; scientists, and engineers. Buckwald places Hertz's work in a Helmholtzian tradition. He shows that Helmholtz developed an electromagnetic theory in which everything had to be formulated in terms of system energies and he argues that this defines the coherence and unity of the work of both Helmhotz and Hertz. He contrasts this with Weberean electrodynamics. In a Weberean laboratory one builds, and having built, one analyzes. In the Helmholtzian laboratory one builds, probes, and mutates until the device behaves as a system in a satisfactory manner. Hertz imbibed this approach to physics and Buchwald is at pains to point out that Helmholtzian ways drove the experimenter to constantly look for new effects, including the discovery of what we know call radio waves. In describing the numerous experimental set-ups and conceptualizations, Buchwald uses contemporary language and refrains from explanations in modern terms.

FÖLSING's volume is the only full biography of Hertz and he makes full use of the extensive private papers left by Hertz. Its is a readable account, filled with delightful anecdotes and numerous examples of Hertz's wonderfully understated humour. Fölsing is very good at explaining Hertz's physics in a simple manner, while always keeping the end point – Hertz's discovery of radio waves – in mind.

Johanna HERTZ edited the first collection (now out of print) of her father's memoirs, letters and diaries, which also contains a charming account of Hertz's youth by his mother. On Johanna Hertz's death in 1966, the underlying materials were revised by her sister Mathilde to produce a bilingual version (German and English), which also includes an appreciation of Hertz's achievements by Max von Laue, taken from his entry on Hertz in the bibliographical dictionary *Die grossen Deutsche*.

O'HARA & PRICHA's book is an excellent 150-page account of the discovery of electromagnetic-wave radiation, that draws mainly on some four dozen letters exchanged between Hertz and his British colleagues (now in the collections of the Deutsches Museum in Munich), as well as additional correspondence and other materials held by the Royal Society, Trinity College, Dublin, University College, the Institution of Electrical Engineers, and the Science Museum in London. These items attest to the warm esteem in which Hertz was held by his contemporaries in Britain, as reflected by the award of the Royal Society Rumford Medal to him in 1890, so different from the disdain that was to be his posthumous portion in the priority controversies over radiotelegraphy.

SUSSKIND fills gaps in previous accounts of Hertz's life, which pay scant attention to his ancestry, his relationships with colleagues in Germany and elsewhere, his interest in the study of hardness, and his persona in general. The subtitle "A Short Life", refers both to his early demise (aged 36), and to the size of this 185-page biography.

WIESBECK presided over an international meeting at Karlsruhe celebrating the centenary of Hertz's discovery of the equivalence between electric and light waves. The circumstances, and many ramifications, of this achievement were set forth by an international group of contributors, who discussed the manifold aspects of his accomplishment, and of its theoretical and practical consequences on such diverse fields as higher education, communication, astrophysics, and the environment.

CHARLES SUSSKIND

See also Electromagnetism; Maxwell

Hilbert, David 1862–1943

German mathematician

Berliner, Arnold (ed.), "David Hilbert zur Feier seines sechzigsten Geburtstages", *Die Naturwissenschaften*, 10/4 (1922): 65–103

Blumenthal, Otto, "Lebensgeschichte", in *Gesammelte Abhandlungen* by Hilbert, 3 vols, Berlin: Springer, 1932–35; reprinted, 3 vols, New York: Chelsea, 1965, 388–429

Bottazzini, Umberto, *Il flauto di Hilbert: Storia della matematica moderna e contemporanea*, Turin: UTET, 1990

Corry, Leo, "David Hilbert and the Axiomatization of Physics (1894–1905)", in *Archive for History of Exact Sciences*, 51 (1997): 83–198

Fang, Joong, *Hilbert*, vol. 2 of *Towards a Philosophy of Modern Mathematics*, Hauppauge, New York: Paidaia Press, 1970

Gochet, Paul (ed.), "Hilbert", *Revue Internationale de Philosophie*, 47/4 (1993): 249–353

Mehrtens, Herbert, *Moderne–Sprache–Mathematik: Eine Geschichte des Streits um die Grundlagen der Disziplin und des Subjekts formaler Systeme*, Frankfurt: Suhrkamp, 1990

Peckhaus, Volker, *Hilbertprogramm und kritische Philosophie: Das Göttinger Modell interdisziplinärer Zusammenarbeit zwischen Mathematik und Philosophie*, Göttingen: Vandenhoeck & Ruprecht, 1990

Reid, Constance, *Hilbert*, Berlin and New York: Springer, 1970; reprinted with a new foreword but without the formerly appended abridged version of Weyl's paper (see below), New York: Copernicus, 1996

Rowe, David, *Felix Klein, David Hilbert, and the Göttingen Mathematical Tradition*, dissertation, City University of New York, 1992; abridged version, as "Klein, Hilbert and the Göttingen Mathematical Tradition", *Osiris*, 5 (1989): 186–213

Toepell, Michael-Markus, *Über die Entstehung von David Hilberts "Grundlagen der Geometrie"*, Göttingen: Vandenhoeck & Ruprecht, 1986

Weyl, Hermann, "David Hilbert and His Mathematical Work", *Bulletin of the American Mathematical Society*, 50 (1944): 612–54; reprinted in his *Gesammelte Abhandlungen*, edited by K. Chandrasekharan, vol. 4, Berlin and New York: Springer, 1968, 130–72

David Hilbert is often considered the most important mathematician of the 20th century; he founded influential and fruitful research programs that still continue to enthrall mathematicians. He gained great prominence with his axiomatization of Euclidean geometry in 1899, and particularly when he gave a list of problems in his Paris speech of 1900 that set an agenda for generations of mathematicians. His axiomatic method (or "thinking") spread and redefined many disciplines. While some of his ideas on finitism and formalism, which became prominent under the term *Hilbertprogramm* in the 1920s as an answer to the foundational crisis, did not turn out tenable in the long run, they were indispensable steps in the development of modern mathematics.

Unlike his fellow scientists in other fields, there is as yet no critical biography that conforms to basic historiographical standards, and this is perhaps a problem of sources. Meanwhile, the larger philosophical literature has partly redefined a rather archetypical Hilbert, that seems at odds with his private papers and historical studies, taking into account his unpublished work.

Hilbert's contemporary and first doctoral student, BLUMEN-THAL, gives a straightforward description of Hilbert's scientific life in the last volume of the Collected Works. He provides a general perspective on Hilbert's *oeuvre* and tries to illuminate his more general intentions behind his single works. More specific historical accounts of Hilbert's share in the development of algebra, geometry, analysis, physics, and philosophy in the period before the *Hilbertprogramm* can be consulted in a special number of *Die Naturwissenschaften*, published on the occasion of Hilbert's 60th birthday and edited by BERLINER, with contributions from well-known students of Hilbert.

WEYL's obituary became very influential in its division of Hilbert's mathematical life into five clear periods and in the personal way in which he paid tribute to his teacher – although it seems, at times, that he is revealing more of his own struggles than those of his master. Taking up Weyl's metaphor of Hilbert as the Pied Piper of 20th-century mathematics, BOTTAZZINI offers a recent and readable overview of the history of modern mathematics, with special emphasis on Hilbert's work and role.

The only fully-fledged biography of Hilbert is by REID and is aimed at a wide readership. It is a sympathetic account by a layman, based mainly on the reminiscences of Hilbert's students and colleagues. Because of the nature of the relationship between author and subject, it is a "romantic" book that suffers from a certain "mathematical innocence" at the time of writing. However, it has benefited much from the assistance of Richard Courant and Paul Ewald, and is quite a reliable source of information about Hilbert's life despite its romanticization of his personality. Unfortunately, no references are given, and thus it is a difficult record for historians of science, who have to check on unpublished material to verify the information. The first edition includes an abridged version of Weyl in which, however, the passages mentioned above have been omitted.

FANG's book is more of a biography than a contribution to the philosophy of mathematics as is intended, and is essentially a compilation of mainly published information ranging from scientific works to anecdotes about Hilbert and German academics of his time. Because there is no critical distance between the author and his subject, the book is in parts simplistic, speculative, and hagiographic; it is designed to inform and to kindle the interest of those new to the history of mathematics.

ROWE, on the other hand, provides in his dissertation a thorough grounding in Hilbert's – and Felix Klein's – work and role within the institutional history of mathematics and within Wilhelmian society. While the first two parts are mainly a study of Klein's career and mission, Hilbert features prominently in the third. These mathematician's break with neohumanist ideals of science, as separate from public and economic concerns, made them contrasting "activists for the mission of mathematics". Hilbert is portrayed more as an ahistorical thinker and *Fachmathematiker* (a mathematician concerned only with his field). Noteworthy is Rowe's attempt to shed light on Hilbert's personality by dismissing the traditional and unverified picture of a naive eccentric or ivory tower dreamer. Unconventionality, for example, is identified not as naivety but as an expression of independence and power.

For MEHRTENS, who aims at a social history of mathematics enriched with French poststructuralist thought, Hilbert serves prominently as the "director–general" of a "company of modern mathematics". As a proponent of modernism in mathematics, closely related to the modernization of discipline, profession, and society, Hilbert is seen as opposed to countermodernists such as intuitionists (Luitzen Egbertus Jan Brouwer) and enemies of progress who try to ban new techniques (Leopold Kronecker). This unusual interpretation is based on an intimate knowledge of the sources.

As in the historical research on Hilbert, the question of his influence on other fields has attracted steadily increasing interest, and a number of more specialized publications that also contain biographic material should be noted. PECKHAUS's book discusses Hilbert's influence on the development of critical philosophy in Göttingen; his efforts to promote Leonard Nelson give interesting insights into Hilbert's social and political ideas. Similarly, although less extensive, the book by TOEPELL and the collection of articles edited by GOCHET are worth consulting for information on further details of Hilbert's thought and its development regarding geometry, finitism, formalism, logic, and infinity. A comprehensive account of Hilbert's early aims and activities in physics is given in CORRY, which is typical of a number of recent articles that try to reconstrue Hilbert's views as different from that of the formalists.

ARNE SCHIRRMACHER

See also Algebra; Geometry

Hippocrates   c.460–377 or 359 BC

Greek physician

Di Benedetto, Vincenzo, *Il medico e la malattia: la scienza di Ippocrate*, Turin: Einaudi, 1986

Langholf, Volker, *Medical Theories in Hippocrates: Early Texts and the "Epidemics"*, Berlin and New York: De Gruyter, 1990

Lasserre, François and Philippe Mudry (eds), *Formes de pensée dans la collection hippocratique: Actes du IVe Colloque International Hippocratique*, Geneva: Droz, 1983

Lloyd, G.E.R., *Methods and Problems in Greek Science*, Cambridge and New York: Cambridge University Press, 1991

Potter, Paul, *Short Handbook of Hippocratic Medicine*, Quebec: Sphinx, 1988

Smith, Wesley D., *The Hippocratic Tradition*, Ithaca, New York: Cornell University Press, 1979

Temkin, Owsei and C.L. Temkin (eds), *Ancient Medicine: Selected Papers of Ludwig Edelstein*, Baltimore: Johns Hopkins University Press, 1967

Temkin, Owsei, *Hippocrates in a World of Pagans and Christians*, Baltimore: Johns Hopkins University Press, 1991

Although arguably the most famous name in the history of medicine, his name and place of origin, Cos, are the only facts known about Hippocrates. With the exception of two mentions in Plato (whose lifetime overlapped with his), all testimonials come from sources written after Hippocrates' death, when he had already become a legendary figure. Thus, we have a variety of possible dates of birth and death, as well as a gamut of legends about Hippocrates' achievements. Since none of the works in the Hippocratic Corpus mentions their authors' names, it is impossible to determine, based on available evidence, whether any of them were written by Hippocrates himself. (Nevertheless, speculation on "authentic" works has been a popular endeavour since antiquity.) Given the paucity and unreliability of extant sources, it is not surprising that there are no scholarly works on Hippocrates as a person, but much work has been done on what is termed Hippocratic medicine.

DI BENEDETTO concentrates on the concept of disease in Hippocratic medicine, especially on the notions of crisis and signs, as well as "tendency and probability", which considers the applicability of general concepts to the individual. He includes a section on mental disorders, and a discussion of the treatises on "bone surgery" as a foundation for the development of anatomy as a science. This is a densely-argued, scholarly book by a well-known philologist.

The first part of TEMKIN & TEMKIN's edited collection of Ludwig Edelstein's papers, deals with Hippocratic medicine in a way that at the time was considered revolutionary. In particular, the chapter (originally a monograph) on the Hippocratic oath must be counted as among the most incisive works on the topic to date. While it had been generally accepted that the oath was sworn by all (or most) Greek physicians at the beginning or end of their training, Edelstein was the first to point out that it corresponded closely to Pythagorean ideas, but not to Hippocratic practice. His hypothesis, therefore, is that it was presumably used only by a Pythagorean minority among Greek doctors.

Examining early works within the Hippocratic tradition, LANGHOLF presents a detailed and intricate discussion of such topics as the notion of *krisis* and critical days, research methods, criticism, scepticism, and prognosis. He studies the application and evolution of medical theories in the Hippocratic Corpus, and the extent to which various theories are compatible with each other.

For readers with some background knowledge in Greek medicine, literature, or philosophy, the 43 contributions to LASSERRE & MUDRY provide further insights into a varied selection of aspects, including the influence of literacy on the development of medicine, old age in the Hippocratic Corpus, and the influence of Ionian natural philosophy.

Two chapters in LLOYD treat specific problems concerning the Hippocratic writings. The first seeks to establish who is attacked in the treatise *On Ancient Medicine*, and suggests the medical writers Philolaus, Polybus, and Petron. The second paper re-examines the "Hippocratic question", i.e., the external and internal evidence for the authenticity of some works in the Corpus. Lloyd argues for a cautious and sceptical approach, as definitive proof cannot be produced.

POTTER's slim booklet gives an excellent, brief introduction for readers who need a succinct evaluation of Hippocratic medicine. He touches on the question of authorship, gives an outline of medical theory and practice, as well as a résumé of all surviving treatises (with references to printed editions). Potter is thus the best starting point for those completely unfamiliar with the topic.

Smith and Temkin have both chosen the "afterlife" of Hippocratic medicine as their topic of research. In part 3 ("From Hippocrates to Galen") of his book, SMITH examines in particular the questions of how the Hippocratic Corpus was assembled, how it was read, and by what stages Hippocrates acquired his status as the "father of medicine". He then goes on to explore how writers described their own notion of medical practice, and how they related to the earlier tradition, particularly to Hippocrates.

TEMKIN investigates the position of Hippocratic medicine in the first six centuries of the Christian era, during the transformation of the pagan Graeco-Roman culture into a Christian one. He examines the relationship between secular medicine and religion in pagan, Jewish, and Christian thought, and concludes that the Hippocratic works remained authoritative and that there was no far-reaching accommodation, science and practice remaining essentially the same.

CHRISTINE F. SALAZAR

See also Greece: medicine

Histology

Bracegirdle, Brian, "The History of Histology: A Brief Survey of Sources", *History of Science*, 15 (1977): 77–101

Bracegirdle, Brian, *A History of Microtechnique: The Evolution of the Microtome and the Development of Tissue Preparation*, London: Heinemann, 1978; 2nd edition, Lincolnwood, Illinois: Science Heritage, 1986

Clarke, George and Frederick H. Kasten, *History of Staining*, 3rd edition, Baltimore: Williams and Wilkins, 1983

Hughes, Arthur, *A History of Cytology*, London and New York: Abelard-Schuman, 1959

Mandl, Louis, *Anatomie Microscopique*, 2 vols, Paris: Baillière, 1838–57

Mann, Gustav, *Physiological Histology: Methods and Theory*, Oxford: Clarendon Press, 1902

Paget, James, *Report on the Chief Results Obtained by the Use of the Microscope in the Study of Human Anatomy and Physiology*, London: Churchill, 1842

Histology, the study of the microscopic structure of tissues, is rich in primary source material, both original papers and texts designed for student use. Secondary sources, however, are relatively rare, and a full history of histology has yet to be compiled.

Nevertheless, HUGHES provides a good starting point. In a useful and succinct text, this work offers a brief outline of the development of microscopical observation from the 17th century, including the history of the instrument, the introduction of techniques such as fixing, staining, and sectioning, and the roles of the various workers in the field. He places the microscopical observation of cells within this context, and explores the development of cell-theory and its place in biology. For a short, broad sweep of the history of histology, BRACE-GIRDLE (1977) gives a chronological account based on both primary and secondary sources, and sets the history within the milieu of the scientific enquiry of the period. BRACEGIRDLE (1986), a history of microtechnique, traces the origin and development of the manipulations needed to prepare biological specimens for examination under the light microscope. In particular, he discusses the evolution of the microtome, a vital but neglected instrument. The book is based on a comprehensive study of the literature and of thousands of actual preparations, and full documentation is included. The chapter "Microscopy, Microtomy and Histology in the Nineteenth Century" will be of particular interest, offering a brief history of histology, based on the literature and set within the context of the developing understanding of the structure of the retina. A brief history of the teaching of histology as an element of medical education is also included.

In 1842, PAGET asserted that, in the preceding decade, in no department of medical science had there been so great an addition of facts than in minute anatomy, and in none had the access to knowledge been more difficult. He remedied the situation with his first *Report*, which brought together the conclusions of workers in Britain and Europe, which had until then been scattered in monographs and journals. Paget's compilation, together with his comments and footnotes, gives an accurate picture of the understanding of the structure of the tissues, and the techniques used in microscopical observation at that period.

Paget's report, one of a series that reviewed new work in histology, is complemented by the remarkable and important volumes of MANDL, the first of which gives a detailed account of the history of the development of understanding of the structure of tissues. The author describes the conclusions of the key workers on the microscopic structures, and gives details of the techniques used to elucidate them. He then describes his own research, and contrasts his results with those of other researchers in the field. The volume is accompanied by an atlas of plates of the microstructures, as described and interpreted in the text, enabling the reader to follow the discussion of the development of understanding of the structure of each tissue. The volumes are fully documented, and include details of original papers written over the previous two centuries. This was a remarkable work, but is now not well known.

Half a century later, understanding had advanced to the stage where MANN felt it necessary to broaden the concept of histology, from being simply concerned with microstructure, in order to make the subject more valuable to the physiologist by emphasising function. In his detailed account of what he called physiological histology, he introduces each section – on fixation and cell structure, on coagulation, on injection, on sectioning, on staining, and on the making of microscopical preparations – with a useful historical account of the development of each technique, placing his description of contemporary practice within that context. Mann compares and contrasts the effect of the various processes on the tissue concerned, and discusses the relative advantages of their use in determining structure and function. This was a landmark text in its day, and remains a valuable milestone.

A useful collection of chapters on staining had been compiled by Conn in 1948, and was revised and supplemented by CLARKE & KASTEN in 1983. Each chapter deals either with an important individual in the history of staining, such as Paul Ehrlich, or with the history of the development of special techniques in histology, such as the development of aniline dyes. This is a general book for the interested student of the history of histology, rather than one for those seeking specific instruction, although the very full bibliography will go far towards supplying that need.

Textbooks on histology have been published freely since the early 1800s, some of them in a large number of editions. These can provide valuable evidence of the progress of the science over perhaps 50 or more years, in a way that cannot be emulated by any publication lacking good and plentiful illustrations. Far too many have been written for any to be singled out for specific mention, but recourse to a selection will flesh out the bones provided by the specific texts mentioned above.

PATRICIA H. BRACEGIRDLE

See also Microscopes; Physiology

History of Science: general works

Asimov, Isaac, *Asimov's Chronology of Science and Discovery*, New York: Harper and Row, 1989, London: Grafton, 1990; revised and illustrated edition, New York: HarperCollins, 1994

Brush, Stephen G., *The History of Modern Science: A Guide to the Second Scientific Revolution, 1800–1950*, Ames: Iowa State University Press, 1988

Bynum, W.F., E.J. Browne and Roy Porter (eds), *Dictionary of the History of Science*, London: Macmillan, and Princeton, New Jersey: Princeton University Press, 1981

Darmstaedter, Ludwig (ed.), *Ludwig Darmstaedters Handbuch zur Geschichte der Naturwissenschaften und der Technik: In chronolgischer Darstellung*, 2nd edition, Berlin: Springer, 1908; reprinted New York: Kraus, 1960

Gillispie, Charles Coulston, *The Edge of Objectivity: An Essay in the History of Scientific Ideas*, Princeton, New Jersey: Princeton University Press, 1960; 2nd edition with a new foreword, 1990

Gillispie, Charles Coulston, *Dictionary of Scientific Biography*, 16 vols, New York: Scribner, 1970–80; vols 17–18 edited by Frederic L. Holmes, 1990

Isis Current Bibliography of the History of Science and Its Cultural Influences, Chicago: University of Chicago Press / History of Science Society, 1989–

Marcorini, Edgardo (ed.), *The History of Science and Technology: A Narrative Chronology*, translated from the Italian, 2 vols, New York: Facts on File, 1988 (original edition, 1977)

Neu, John (ed.), *Isis Cumulative Bibliography, 1966–1975: A Bibliography of the History of Science Formed from Isis Critical Bibliographies 91–100, Indexing Literature Published from 1965 through 1974*, 2 vols, London: Mansell / History of Science Society, 1980–85

Neu, John (ed.), *Isis Cumulative Bibliography, 1976–1985: A Bibliography of the History of Science Formed from Isis Critical Bibliographies 101–110, Indexing Literature Published from 1975 through 1984*, 2 vols, Boston: G. K. Hall / History of Science Society, 1989

Neu, John (ed.), *Isis Cumulative Bibliography, 1986–1995: A Bibliography of the History of Science Formed from the Isis Current Bibliographies*, Canton, Massachusetts: Science History Publications, 1997

Olby, R.C. *et al.* (eds), *Companion to the History of Modern Science*, London and New York: Routledge, 1990

Whitrow, Magda (ed.), *Isis Cumulative Bibliography: A Bibliography of the History of Science Formed from Isis Critical Bibliographies 1–90, 1913–1965*, 6 vols, London: Mansell / History of Science Society, 1971–84

This entry examines the literature that in some way or other aspires to cover all of the history of science. One book that covers the canon of the history of science is GILLISPIE's *Edge of Objectivity*. It is a highly readable and often witty history from Newton through Darwin to Einstein. Many historians of science, perhaps even the majority, now reject this canon because of its celebration of scientific greats and its promotion of the genre of history of ideas. In the foreword to the second edition, Gillispie defends himself against what he calls sociopolitical reductionism, reaffirming his opinion that science is unique in that it transcends culture. From another perspective, one could see this not as an argument against "sociopolitical reductionists" but rather as a topic that they address. Still, it may well be that modern-day history of science is so diverse that its practitioners can relate only through a concerted rejection of the canon.

The three following items attempt to cover not only the canon in the history of science, but science universally in time and space. All tacitly emphasize science in the Western world, where virtually all the "discoveries" that are described were made.

DARMSTAEDTER *et al.* is a chronological listing of scientific and technological firsts. It is intended as a celebration of progress. Covering all periods and all of the natural sciences and technology, it categorizes strictly by time, which, except for the early period, means by year. The events are simply mentioned and not commented upon.

ASIMOV is also a chronological listing, but it juxtaposes scientific events with a rubric titled "In Addition", very much in the tradition of the German *Steins Kulturführer*. This category provides a context for science by looking at political history, with occasional comments on the social history of technology, catastrophes, and demographic data.

MARCORINI is also a chronological account covering all of time and the entire Western world. It is the collected work of some 40 Italian authors and it describes in simple prose events and important developments in the history of science. One could describe it as a halfway house between a chronological listing and straightforward history; hence the title "narrative chronology".

Other comprehensive works on the history of science are organized by categories other than time.

GILLISPIE's *Dictionary of Scientific Biology* (DSB) remains the largest and most used reference work in the history of science. It categorizes by individual scientist and not by time, unlike the above mentioned books. Its scope is all of time and it attempts to be global, especially by including lenghty articles on relatively unknown Chinese scientists. Each entry contains a short biographical paragraph followed by a detailed bibliography of primary and secondary sources. One can criticize it for its emphasis on ideas and established names (and its de-emphasis on support staff), but no historian of science could do without it, and it is an appropriate entry point for the neophyte.

BYNUM *et al.* was explicitly thought of as a small corrective to the lack of emphasis in the *DSB* on concepts such as the atom, the unconscious, and Mendelism, as opposed to Dalton, Freud, and Mendel. As a dictionary it contains an alphabetical listing of the concepts with brief explanations; there is also an analytical index.

OLBY *et al.* is a collection of essays that is intended to cover much of the ground in the history of science without any claim to universality. In 1,000 pages it contains 67 essays of roughly 20 pages, each of which introduces a particular topic. These essays are divided into six sections: history of science in relation to neighbouring disciplines; analytical perspectives (such as Marxism or gender); philosophical problems (e.g. rationality, realism); turning points (e.g. scientific revolution, energy, Darwin, genetics, Keynesian economics); topics and interpretations (e.g. Newtonianism, probability, physiology, and experimental medicine); and themes (e.g. religion, nationalism and internationalism, war, professionalization, science and the public).

The format of BRUSH resembles that of the present book. It is intended as a guide to undergraduate education in the history of science from the period 1800 to 1950. The chapters look at biology, anthropology, psychology, physics, mathematics, astronomy, and philosophical and sociological approaches. Each topic is outlined with readings followed by a brief expository essay ("synopsis") which is again followed by a bibliography on, typically, four or five selected aspects of the synopsis.

The *ISIS CURRENT BIBLIOGRAPHY* is a continuation of the bibliography that George Sarton started in the first volume of *Isis* in 1913. For many years the bibliography was published once a year as a normal issue of *Isis*, but in 1989 the journal and the bibliography were separated with the aim of letting libraries catalogue and shelve the bibliography in the reference section. WHITROW, NEU (1980–85), and NEU (1989) provide cumulative bibliographies taken from *Isis* over consecutive periods. Taken together, these bibliographies are the single most important reference work for secondary literature in the history of science (broadly construed so as to include technology and medicine). The original *Isis* bibliography was critical in the sense that each item was commented upon. In the

Current Bibliography this is no longer the case, although sometimes a summary by the author is included. The *Current Bibliography* is divided up into four parts: general references and tools; special points of view (e.g. philosophy of science, scientific instruments); histories of each of the sciences; and a chronological classification. The latter is by far the largest, reflecting the growth in studies of particular places and times. Book reviews are in a separate section. There is an extremely useful name index.

ARNE HESSENBRUCH

Hodgkin, Dorothy   1910–1994

British chemist

Ewald, P.P., *Fifty Years of X-Ray Diffraction*, Utrecht: Oosthoesk's Uitgeversmaatschappij, 1962

Farago, Peter, "Interview with Dorothy Crowfoot Hodgkin", *Journal of Chemical Education*, 54/4 (1977): 214–15

Goldwhite, Harold, "Dorothy Mary Crowfoot Hodgkin", in *Women in Chemistry and Physics: A Biobibliographic Sourcebook*, edited by Louise S. Grinstein, Rose K. Rose and Miriam Rafailovich, Westport, Connecticut: Greenwood Press, 1993

Hudson, Gill, "Unfathering the Thinkable: Gender, Science, and Pacificism in the 1930s", in *Science and Sensibility: Gender and Scientific Inquiry, 1780–1945*, edited by Marina Benjamin, Oxford and Cambridge, Massachusetts: Blackwell, 1991

Kass-Simon, G. and Patricia Farnes, *Women of Science: Righting the Record*, Bloomington: Indiana University Press, 1990

McGrayne, Sharon Bertsch, *Nobel Prize Women in Science: Their Lives, Struggles, and Momentous Discoveries*, Seacaucus, New Jersey: Carol, 1993

Opfell, Olga S., *The Lady Laureates: Women Who Have Won the Nobel Prize*, Metuchen, New Jersey: Scarecrow Press, 1978; 2nd edition, 1986

Wolpert, Lewis and Alison Richards, *A Passion for Science*, Oxford and New York: Oxford University Press, 1988

Most accounts of Dorothy Hodgkin's life point out that she was the only recipient of the Nobel prize for chemistry in 1964, yet, beyond her distinction as the solo recipient, little is made of this award. A notable exception is the very personal account by OPFELL, who writes at length concerning the circumstances surrounding Hodgkin's acceptance of the prize, although Hodgkin herself valued her membership of the Royal Society above the Nobel prize. Most accounts of her life seem to focus on three areas: feminist issues of science, scientific accomplishments, and politics.

Hodgkin's own words are available from a number of published interviews. One frequently quoted interview is by FARAGO, in which Hodgkin narrates the now well-known story of her childhood among intellectual achievers and social activists, her early struggles to enter the male-dominated colleges at Cambridge and Oxford, and her work in X-ray crystallography. Farago attempts to break out of these encyclopedic concerns by asking questions about gender issues,

although Hodgkin's responses here seem to indicate a soft stance toward sexism in the sciences.

Another opportunity to hear Hodgkin speak on her own behalf is in WOLPERT & RICHARDS. They present a concise summary of Hodgkin's life and works, and then proceed to elicit some interesting comments from Hodgkin regarding her modest regard for her own academic development and scientific accomplishments, her aesthetic appreciation of the scientific, and her respect for the boundaries between science and politics.

As a woman scientist in a male-dominated field, and a Nobel prizewinner besides, many commentators have tried to make ideological use of Hodgkin's life. KASS-SIMON & FARNES, for example, claim that Hodgkin, in spite of her accomplishments, was initially passed over for the Nobel prize in 1962 in favor of Perutz and Kendrew, and was slighted in the literature about Nobel laureates when she finally received it. Kass-Simon & Farnes try to make reparations to Hodgkin by inferring that there has been a concerted mobilization among certain women crystallographers, in order to confer on them their deserved recognition and to push for the recruitment of more women into their ranks.

In a similar ideological vein, McGRAYNE offers an explanation for Hodgkin's choice of specialty. McGrayne notes that it was fashionable for late 19th-century British women of leisure to take up an interest in crystals as a hobby. Moreover, women of Hodgkin's social position were encouraged to pursue practical subjects such as chemistry. As McGrayne follows Hodgkin's education and early research, she cites many instances in which Hodgkin had to suffer the effects of sexism at Oxford and Cambridge.

The most radical ideological interpretation of Hodgkin's life comes from HUDSON. In the course of defending her feminist perspective of science, she conscripts Hodgkin as an exemplar of the new scientist, combining science, politics, and motherhood. Hudson advocates a "science for the people", which includes elements of pacifism, co-operation, and humanitarianism, and suggests that Hodgkin's practice of science illustrates all of these. Hodgkin herself, however, publicly maintained a disjunction between science and politics.

GOLDWHITE offers an especially full account of Hodgkin's political life. Though she claimed to keep her scientific and political personas separate, Hodgkin could not always avoid the political consequences of practising science. Her political life becomes most noticeable with her foundation of the International Union of Crystallography, as her effort to include all crystallographers brought her into conflict with Cold War politics – particularly from the United States. Goldwhite shows that Hodgkin's insistence on internationalism was absolute, and cites her ongoing relationships with scientists in the Soviet Union, North Vietnam, and China during the Cold War years.

Most accounts of Hodgkin's scientific work highlight her X-ray photographs of penicillin, vitamin B-12, and insulin crystals. Most accounts also describe her methods: she preferred small-scale projects, and she readily embraced other disciplines. Hodgkin was one of the first crystallographers to enlist the aid of computers, and EWALD describes in detail Hodgkin's efforts to use computers in the analysis of vitamin B-12. Ewald also cites many occasions when Hodgkin was universally praised for her contributions to crystallography and to science in general, the most notable perhaps being W.L. Bragg's comment that Hodgkin's work on penicillin "broke the sound barrier".

LAWRENCE SOUDER

Holistic Medicine

Alster, Kristine Beyerman, *The Holistic Health Movement*, Tuscaloosa: University of Alabama Press, 1989

Cant, Sarah and Ursula Sharma, *A New Medical Pluralism? Alternative Medicine, Doctors, Patients and the State*, London: UCL Press, and New York: Garland, 1999

Gordon, James S., *Holistic Medicine*, New York: Chelsea House, 1988

Jewson, Nick, "The Disappearance of the Sick-Man from Medical Cosmology, 1770–1870", *Sociology*, 10/2 (1976): 225–44

Leathard, Audrey (ed.), *Going Inter-Professional: Working Together for Health and Welfare*, London and New York: Routledge, 1994

Lyng, Stephen, *Holistic Health and Biomedical Medicine: A Countersystem Analysis*, Albany: State University of New York Press, 1990

McKee, Janet, "Holistic Health and the Critique of Western Medicine", *Social Science and Medicine*, 26/8 (1988): 775–84

Pietroni, Patrick, *The Greening of Medicine*, London: Gollancz, 1991

Saks, Mike, *Professions and the Public Interest: Medical Power, Altruism and Alternative Medicine*, London and New York: Routledge, 1995

Stalker, Douglas and Clark Glymour (eds), *Examining Holistic Medicine*, Buffalo, New York: Prometheus Books, 1985

Holistic medicine is, essentially, the engagement of the whole person in the promotion of health and the prevention of illness – a medicine in which the person is seen as a unique being, consisting of mind, body, and spirit, and existing within a context of the wider social and cultural environment. In this sense, as the frequently cited article by McKEE illustrates, holistic medicine is often contrasted with orthodox biomedicine, derived from the philosophical mind-body dualism of Descartes, which tends to view the body as a symptom-bearing organism, separate from the mind and akin to a machine, whose parts need to be repaired on malfunction.

GORDON traces the notion of holistic medicine back to the concept of "holism", developed by the South African philosopher, Jan Christian Smuts, in the 1920s in order to counter natural scientific reductionism, and to enable recognition of the fact that, as is so often the case in science and nature, the whole is greater than the sum of its parts. More recently, the features of holistic medicine have been highlighted by increased criticism of the biomedical approach. As PIETRONI clearly documents, for all its highly successful interventions based on drugs and surgery, the biomedical approach has come increasingly under attack for, among other things, its limited efficacy, the iatrogenic dangers that it presents, and its depersonalisation of the patient. This leads Pietroni to elaborate the concept of holistic medicine and to advocate a more person-centred, inter-professional approach to medical practice, with greater emphasis on self-care, and a more reciprocal relationship between patient and practitioner.

Nevertheless, the concept of holistic medicine cannot be fully understood without reference to the historical development of orthodox biomedicine, as demonstrated by the case of Britain. Here, as JEWSON observes in his seminal paper, two or three centuries ago there was a far more eclectic approach to health care than today, with a far greater understanding of the need to ensure that individual health systems were in a state of balance within a context of greater self-responsibility for health. However, the rise of an organised, unified and exclusionary medical profession by the mid-19th century was associated with the ascendance of biomedical orthodoxy. Within this new frame of reference, there was a shift away from "bedside medicine", in which affluent clients directly influenced their own diagnoses and treatments, towards first "hospital medicine", in which the disease rather than the whole person was the key focus, and then "laboratory medicine", in which the body was perceived as a complex of cells, through which the patient was further objectified by, and subordinated to, the medical investigator.

This development helps to explain why a number of the more holistic alternative approaches are largely employed outside medical orthodoxy, as therapies such as classical acupuncture and homeopathy, which are person-centred and based on the notion of stimulating the life force, can be seen to run against the mainstream principles of the current medical establishment. However, as critics in the volume edited by STALKER & GLYMOUR controversially argue, the credentials of exponents of such apparently holistic therapies cannot always be taken at face value. Stalker & Glymour suggest that often the claims of holistic practitioners unjustifiably stereotype the nature of biomedicine, and that their client-centred practices are seldom linked coherently to holistic beliefs. McKEE has also commented that, notwithstanding the recent growth of holistic health centres, even therapists with a whole-person approach do not necessarily take broader social determinants of illness into account in their work, and still less play a leading role in promoting inter-professional care, as might be expected within a wider holistic framework.

Conversely, as ALSTER notes in her sophisticated overview of the holistic health movement, orthodox medicine itself stems historically from holistic roots, as epitomised by the work of the Greek physician, Hippocrates, in the 5th century BC, who was well aware of the relation of both environment and the emotions to illness. Alster claims that modern medical orthodoxy has also recently striven to become more holistically oriented, partly in response to the increasing critique of biomedicine and to growing public demand. This reform was initially focused most heavily on allied health professionals, and has subsequently taken many forms. As Gordon underlines, it has now stretched to include the use of unorthodox therapies by some medical practitioners, the enhancement of the communication skills of doctors in dealing with patients, and heightened understanding of the medical implications of family and social networks. Contributors to the pioneering book by LEATHARD, on collaborative working in health and welfare, also emphasize that practitioners based in the social and behavioural sciences, such as counsellors and social workers, are increasingly working in multi-professional teams. LYNG, meanwhile, in a more philosophically-based volume, documents the holistic shift in medicine in recent times from hospital-based services to primary health care, and the greater medical emphasis on public health issues and self-responsibility for health.

However, this shift towards a more holistic approach by orthodox medicine has occurred within distinct limits, exemplified by the restricted involvement of doctors in unorthodox practice. As SAKS stresses in his historical account of the British medical response to acupuncture, its main contemporary medical employment has been as an analgesic, justified by orthodox neurophysiological theorising, rather than as a wider therapy linked to the traditional concept of balancing the forces of Yin and Yang. He also indicates that, while there has been improved collaboration between doctors and alternative practitioners such as acupuncturists, this has tended still to be shaped by relationships of orthodox medical dominance – thus highlighting the problems of achieving holistic inter-professional collaboration within the health care division of labour. It is interesting to note, too, that, as Lyng critically observes, even where recent efforts have been made to develop a less reductionist, biopsychosocial model within medicine based on more equal relationships with clients and a wider view of environmental influences on health, these have been bounded by positivistic biomedical beliefs. CANT & SHARMA, in their useful review of the new medical pluralism, stress that the integration that has occurred is insignificant. However, the balance of the literature to date suggests that, despite recent changes, holistic medicine as a concept may not yet have been translated fully into practice, in either medical or non-medical circles.

MIKE SAKS

See also Acupuncture; Complementary Medicine; Doctor–Patient Relationship; Homeopathy; Quackery

Home Economics

Apple, Rima D., "Science Gendered: Nutrition in the United States, 1840–1940", in *The Science and Culture of Nutrition, 1840–1940*, edited by Harmke Kamminga and Andrew Cunningham, Amsterdam: Rodopi, 1995, 129–54
Apple, Rima D., "Constructing Mothers: Scientific Motherhood in the Nineteenth and Twentieth Centuries", *Social History of Medicine*, 8 (1995): 161–78
Cravens, Hamilton "Establishing the Science of Nutrition at the USDA: Ellen Swallow Richards and Her Allies", *Agricultural History*, 64 (1990): 122–33
Nerad, Maresi, "Gender Stratification in Higher Education: The Department of Home Economics at the University of Berkeley, 1916–1962", *Women's Studies International Forum*, 10 (1987): 157–64
Okey, Ruth, "A Woman in Science: 1893–1973: Autobiographical Article", *Journal of Nutrition*, 118 (1988): 1425–31
Rossiter, Margaret W., *Women Scientists in America: Struggles and Strategies to 1940*, Baltimore: Johns Hopkins University Press, 1982
Rossiter, Margaret W., "Mendel the Mentor: Yale Women Doctorates in Biochemistry, 1898–1937", *Journal of Chemical Education*, 71 (1994): 215–19
Rossiter, Margaret W., *Women Scientists in America: Before Affirmative Action, 1940–1972*, Baltimore: Johns Hopkins University Press, 1995
Saidak, Patricia, "Home Economics as an Academic Science", *Resources for Feminist Research/Documentation sur la recherche féministe*, 15 (1986): 49–51
Stage, Sarah and Virginia B. Vincenti (eds), *Rethinking Home Economics: Women and the History of a Profession*, Ithaca, New York: Cornell University Press, 1997

Home economics is also known as domestic science, domestic economy, and even household science, the proliferation of names indicating the discipline's lack of clear definition. The field is often denigrated as "women's work" and accused of lacking scientific basis, and these charges have obscured the scientific roots and content of home economics. Despite these negative connotations, or perhaps because of them, the discipline has provided a space for women to pursue research careers. Historians have only recently begun the critical study of home economics, recognizing its importance in the history of science and in women's history.

Home economics was crystallized in the work of Catherine Beecher, an educational reformer convinced that women needed scientific knowledge in order to successfully fulfil their socially-sanctioned domestic roles of wife, mother, and home-maker. Her *Treatise on Domestic Economy* (1841) presented scientific principles for women's domestic tasks. As APPLE (1995, "Constructing Mothers") has shown, Beecher and her followers did not intend that women should become scientific researchers and creators of new knowledge; rather, they were expected to learn appropriate science in order to maintain healthy households. Formal science education was available to few women in the 19th century, but home economics instruction reached many through advice books, home medical manuals, and women's magazines.

At the turn of the century, one person dominated the field of home economics, Ellen Richards, who trained in chemistry at Vassar College and the Massachusetts Institute of Technology. CRAVENS has analyzed her importance in establishing a scientific basis for the study of human nutrition in the United States, focusing on her work in the 1890s with the New England Kitchen in Boston, and the Rumford Kitchen at the Chicago World's Fair of 1893. These kitchens did more than supply food for the poor; Richards viewed them as experiment stations, using current scientific principles to devise nutritious, inexpensive meals and to educate the public in food preparation and nutrition. For Richards, home economics was a path to social reform (science would benefit individuals, households, and the larger public), as well as a venue in which women could pursue science.

Stage in STAGE & VINCENTI has analyzed Richards's role in establishing home economics firmly within the American educational system. In 1899, Richards presided over the first Lake Placid Conference, which sought to establish the parameters of the field and to coin a generally accepted name for it. Though Richards promoted "domestic science", tying the kitchen to the laboratory with an emphasis on chemistry and sanitation, the group agreed on "home economics", connecting the field with the emerging social science disciplines. The name was firmly established in 1909 with the founding of the American Home Economics Association. Richards worked to separate home economics from mere household arts; in particular, she hoped to establish home economics at the elite women's colleges of the east. In this she was largely unsuccessful, and, instead, collegiate-level home economics became integral to the public land-grant universities of the mid-west and west.

The pivotal work of ROSSITER (1982) allows a fuller appreciation of the role of home economics as a scientific career for women in the first half of the 20th century, as promulgated by these institutions. Just as land-grant universities sought to train rural men in scientific agriculture, they also sought to train women in "scientific home-making". These courses needed scientifically-trained women as instructors, and thus home economics encompassed both practical and scientific education. By the 1910s, academic-based departments of home economics flourished in schools such as Cornell University, Teachers College Columbia University, and the University of Illinois.

Women interested in scientific careers were frequently directed into nutrition, which dominated most academic home economics departments. This is described in APPLE (1995, "Science Gendered"), and the autobiography of OKEY provides further illustration. ROSSITER (1994) has traced the careers of women who trained in the 1920s and 1930s under Lafayette B. Mendel, a physiological chemist at Yale University. Many of them achieved notice in the field of nutrition, however, frequently within home economics departments, a situation that served to marginalize, minimize, and undervalue their notable achievements. In a careful analysis of gender and bureaucracy, NERAD discloses the process by which home economics at a leading research institution, the University of Berkeley, was denied resources, prestige, and eventually its existence, despite the presence and leadership of Agnes Faye Morgan. When Morgan began there in 1916, she was determined to create and maintain a research-based department, which she did by hiring women with doctorates in chemistry, and by establishing demanding science courses for home economics students. This research focus conflicted with goals imposed on the department from the outside; the university administration expected students to be trained in practical courses, as the State needed graduates prepared to teach home economics courses in primary and secondary schools. Following Morgan's retirement in 1954, nutrition was reorganized on the Berkeley campus, and the home economics department was disbanded.

This history of Berkeley is more detailed than most, but it is not unique. ROSSITER (1995) analyzes the post-World War II transformation of the discipline, as women were admitted to other areas of the university, a lack of home economics fellowships discouraged graduate students, and, most significantly, the gender composition of the field changed. When men moved in, departments and schools of home economics were disbanded, their names were changed, and the concept of home economics was dismissed.

Home economics represented an important arena for women researchers; however, not all home economists were research scientists. The articles in STAGE & VINCENTI address the diversity of the field. For example, Julia Grant examines the importance of child psychology in home economics, focusing on the child development work of Margaret Wyle at Cornell University College of Home Economics. Her study highlights the role of home economics in disseminating scientific knowledge. Lisa Mae Robinson describes how other home economists were employed in government agencies, or by commercial concerns.

Throughout the 20th century, home economists found employment in a variety of venues within academia, teaching, government, and industry. These positions increased women's career opportunities and helped expand the field, but at the cost of creating subfields with competing visions and missions, thereby making it more difficult for home economics to present a clear identity. Though the more recent history of home economics has focused on the United States, SAIDAK's work suggests that the discipline faced similar contradictions in Canada. Other researchers are examining comparable strains in other industrialized countries, such as Norway, Sweden, New Zealand, and Australia. Since the early 20th century, home economists have struggled to define their field, which culminated with the conference in Scottsdale, Arizona in October 1993, "Positioning the Profession for the 21st Century", where, following heated debate, the profession united behind the new name of "family and consumer sciences".

RIMA D. APPLE

See also Education; Gender and Identity; Gender and Sex; Nutrition

Homoeopathy

Cook, Trevor M., *Samuel Hahnemann: The Founder of Homoeopathic Medicine*, Wellingborough, Northamptonshire: Thorsons, 1981

Coulter, Harris L., *Divided Legacy: A History of the Schism in Medical Thought*, 3 vols, Washington DC: Wehawken, 1973–77; 2nd edition, as *Divided Legacy: The Conflict Between Homeopathy and the American Medical Association*, Richmond, California: North Atlantic Books, 1982

Danciger, Elizabeth, *The Emergence of Homoeopathy: Alchemy into Medicine*, London: Century, 1987

Kaufman, Martin, *Homoeopathy in America: The Rise and Fall of a Medical Heresy*, Baltimore: Johns Hopkins Press, 1971

Nicholls, Phillip A., *Homoeopathy and the Medical Profession*, London and New York: Croom Helm, 1988

Rothstein, William G., *American Physicians in the Nineteenth Century: From Sects to Science*, Baltimore: Johns Hopkins University Press, 1972

Homoeopathy is a system of medicine developed by the German physician Christian Friedrich Samuel Hahnemann (1755–1843); it involves the treatment of illness by drugs that, in a healthy person, are known to produce the particular symptom complex experienced by the patient. This is the doctrine, to use Hahnemann's own phraseology, of *similia similibus curentur* – let likes be treated by likes. Homoeopathy thus stands in marked contrast to "allopathic" (orthodox or "scientific") medicine, which tries to remove or oppose disease causes, and to suppress or alleviate symptoms.

Hahnemann's ideas eventually emerged as the *Organon of the Rational Art of Healing* in 1810, but his work on the development of homoeopathy in fact dates from the 1790s. Following experiments on himself, Hahnemann noticed that quinine (Peruvian bark or "cinchona", as it was known at the time) seemed to produce the kinds of symptoms that, in cases of fever, it was known to be effective against. To this idea of treatment based on symptom similarity, Hahnemann subsequently added a second, and more controversial, principle: the concept of the infinitesimal dose. By the successive dilution and shaking of the medicinal substance, Hahnemann argued that the vital, healing energy of the drug was released: this was known as "potentisation". As far as orthodox medical practitioners at the time were concerned, however, this process meant that homoeopathic remedies could contain no active medicine at all, and so any healing effect had to be merely placebo reaction.

Homoeopaths are still contesting this argument as vigorously today as when the charge was first levelled. Whether or not the claim was true seemed to matter little to its clients, however. In Britain and India, continental Europe and America, homoeopathy rapidly acquired a substantial following among patients and practitioners in the 19th century, and fierce personal and political struggles soon ensued between homoeopathic and orthodox doctors.

Hahnemann himself was inevitably a primary focus for much of this opprobrium. An accessible biography for the general reader, which details much of the opposition – as well as the eventual respect and support that Hahnemann won from influential patients and patrons – is drawn by COOK. The reader should note, however, that Cook, having acted as the managing director of one of the leading homoeopathic pharmaceutical companies in Britain (Nelson and Co. Ltd.) is not an unsympathetic reporter, and Hahnemann emerges from his writing as both hero and saint. However, if the tendency to eulogise is ignored, the book is a useful summary of what is known of Hahnemann's life.

As far as a discussion of homoeopathy as a system of medicine is concerned, COULTER is essential and provocative reading. Coulter's argument is that Hahnemann's work represents the fullest articulation of a particular therapeutic tradition that can be traced back to the Hippocratic writings, and which focuses on the encouragement of the body's own healing processes, as indicated by the observation of signs and symptoms. Coulter calls this the "empirical" tradition, and he contrasts this with the "rationalist" approach, represented by the hypothesis of "hidden" disease causes, internal to the human organism, and the attempt to expel, dilute, or oppose them. Western scientific (or "allopathic") medicine is the contemporary expression of this tradition, although Coulter suggests that it too can be traced back to the earliest Greek physicians.

According to Coulter, it is possible to see the entire history of medical thought in terms of a "schism" between the rationalist and empirical approaches. Rationalism, in Coulter's view, has traditionally been the dominant mode of practice, because,

as an occupational ideology, it is more attractive, and potentially more lucrative, to any group of people dependent on the practice of medicine for their livelihood. For the social scientist, Coulter's argument is attractive, in that he explains the adoption of particular therapeutic regimes in terms of the occupational interests of groups of practitioners, rather than in terms of objective efficacy. His thesis, however, is not without its problems. The epistemological stance that Coulter adopts is an unreconstructed and unconvincing version of empiricism, and his interpretation of particular medical thinkers is open to question. It should also be remembered that Coulter writes as a partisan: he is an unashamed advocate of homoeopathy as the only "true" medicine.

While Cook is interested in the man, and Coulter in the system of medicine that he created, the books by Kaufman, Nicholls and Rothstein represent academic interest in the political history and sociology of homoeopathy as an occupational community.

KAUFMAN's focus is on the struggle for professional supremacy between homoeopaths and regular practitioners in America between 1820 and 1960. The concern here is much less with the theory and practice of homoeopathy, but rather with issues such as arguments over the control of medical education and licensing, professional honour and integrity, and the control of institutions such as hospitals and medical schools. Indeed, the decline of homoeopathy is largely explained by its increasing therapeutic convergence with regular practice, as competition in the medical marketplace forced first orthodox doctors to abandon heroic medicine (violent purging and bleeding of the patient), and then homoeopaths to adopt allopathic initiatives in hygiene, pain relief, and diagnostic technologies.

NICHOLLS, covering a similar period, produces a comparative picture for Britain. Many of Kaufman's findings and conclusions are endorsed by this study. Based to a large extent on research conducted at the library of the Faculty of Homoeopathy in London, this book also contains a useful evaluation of Coulter.

ROTHSTEIN's focus, although also on America, is wider than Kaufman's, in the sense that he incorporates a fuller treatment of other medical movements, such as the Thomsonians, Botanics, and Eclectics, as well as the homoeopaths. His analysis, however, is distinguished (and to some extent dated) by the argument that the reason for the eventual decline of these rival groups of practitioners was, in the end, their lack of scientific basis.

The last text discussed here represents a change of focus. Written by a homoeopath and lay practitioner – and intended more for a general rather than an academic audience – DANCIGER's book is included because it highlights an aspect of homoeopathy that has often appealed to certain kinds of (often, but by no means exclusively, lay) practitioner; i.e., its connection with magical, metaphysical and astrological interpretations of the universe. Danciger suggests that the origins of some of Hahnemann's thinking are to be found in the work of the alchemist Paracelsus (1493–1591), and the Hermetic influences on medical thinking to which his work gave rise. Hahnemann himself always denied a Paracelsian influence, but it is difficult to ignore Danciger's case, especially given the metaphysical power that Hahnemann attributed to potentised remedies. This Paracelsian background has encouraged some homoeopaths (see chapter 15 of Nicholls, for example) to emphasise that homoeopathic remedies act spiritually, and to describe and prescribe remedies in terms of their form and function in nature (the doctrine of correspondence or "signatures"), rather than in terms of the symptoms that they are able to produce. In these respects, it is noteworthy that metaphysical philosophers and thinkers, such as Swedenborg and Rudolf Steiner, have exerted considerable influence on the development of homoeopathic thought after Hahnemann. Needless to say, homoeopathic physicians, anxious to provide serious experimental evidence that homoeopathic remedies are medicinally active, have been anxious to distance themselves from this interpretation of Hahnemann's work.

PHILLIP A. NICHOLLS

See also Holistic Medicine

Hooker, Joseph Dalton   1817–1911
British botanist and traveller

Allan, Mea, *The Hookers of Kew, 1785–1911*, London: Michael Joseph, 1967

Barton, Ruth, "'An Influential Set of Chaps': The X-Club and Royal Society Politics, 1864–85", *British Journal for the History of Science*, 23 (1990): 53–81

Browne, Janet, *The Secular Ark: Studies in the History of Biogeography*, New Haven, Connecticut: Yale University Press, 1983

Browne, Janet, *Charles Darwin*, vol. 1: *Voyaging*, London: Jonathan Cape, and New York: Knopf, 1995

Desmond, Ray, *Kew: The History of the Royal Botanic Gardens*, London: Harvill Press/Royal Botanic Gardens, 1995

Huxley, Leonard (ed.), *Life and Letters of Sir Joseph Dalton Hooker*, 2 vols, London: John Murray, and New York: Appleton, 1918; reprinted New York: Arno Press, 1978

MacLeod, Roy M., "The Ayrton Incident: A Commentary on the Relations of Science and Government in England, 1870–1873", in *Science and Values: Patterns of Tradition and Change*, edited by Arnold Thackray and Everett Mendelsohn, New York: Humanities Press, 1974, 45–78

Stevens, Peter F., *The Development of Biological Systematics: Antoine-Laurent De Jussieu, Nature, and the Natural System*, New York: Columbia University Press, 1994

Turrill, W.B., *Pioneer Plant Geography: The Phytogeographical Researches of Sir Joseph Dalton Hooker*, The Hague: Nijhoff, 1952

Turrill, W.B., *Joseph Dalton Hooker: Botanist, Explorer, and Administrator*, London: Nelson, 1963

During a long and productive life, beginning two years after the battle of Waterloo and ending three years before the assassination of Franz Ferdinand in Sarajevo, Joseph Dalton Hooker not only witnessed fundamental transformations in the understanding, practice, and organization of British science, but also acted as one of the principal architects of these changes. His accomplishments ran deep and wide: he produced vigorous and influential taxonomic and biogeographical research (exploring on every continent); he served as director of Kew, the Royal Botanic Gardens, and president of both the British Association for the Advancement of Science and the Royal Society; he gave seminal botanical advice and personal support to his close friend Charles Darwin; and enjoyed intimate personal and professional relationships with numerous other pre-eminent scientific authorities throughout the world.

Up to the 1980s, historians of science tended to place conceptual questions of scientific theory at the center of their investigations, and, since Hooker was not responsible for any major theoretical innovation, he has not received attention commensurate with his standing during the 19th century. (His important contributions to Darwin's development of natural selection do mean that he appears frequently, but virtually always as an ancillary, within the pages of the Darwin industry's vast production.) Hooker remains without a living biographer, so the comprehensive treatments of his life tend to be dated, although still useful. New historical research on institutions, professionalization, discipline formation, sites of research, and the role of epistemic traditions, has not yet fully included him. Information on his work in systematics remains frustratingly scant (reflecting the neglect of the history of systematics generally), although more is known about him as a biogeographer. The development of Kew is also beginning to attract attention, both for its domestic influence and as an important center for the Empire.

TURRILL (1963), a Kew botanist who wrote his biography in retirement, makes a helpful and concise, factual assessment of Hooker's long scientific and administrative career. ALLAN's infectious enthusiasm and deep affection for Hooker and his father Sir William, the subjects of her chatty, charming joint biography, make her work as pleasant as it is informative, especially on the Hookers' family life, although this tenderness too often teeters on the brink of hagiography. Similarly, once the now-routine warning against the hagiographic inclinations of the Victorian "Life and Letters" has been made – the cannily-edited letters published within and the accompanying elucidation, in particular, must not be taken at face value – HUXLEY's two-volume memorial serves as the most comprehensive and serviceable source of information on the abundant accomplishments of Hooker's life and science, and includes a complete bibliography of his numerous printed works.

STEVENS identifies the work of Antoine-Laurent de Jussieu as the backbone of modern systematics, since it firmly established the "natural system" in both the theory and the practice, with Hooker standing prominent among the subsequent generation of French and British botanists who expanded and modified Jussieu's proposals. Unfortunately for students of Hooker, although he wanders on to Steven's stage repeatedly in small cameo appearances, he never gets to hold the spotlight for long at any one time. Stevens also ends his study in 1859, placing much of Hooker's most mature work outside its boundaries. None the less, this book does contain important, if restricted and scattered, observations concerning Hooker's work, providing an essential examination of the context from which it emerged, and offering fruitful suggestions for future historical research. (Among the most interesting is Stevens's observation that "it is not clear how the field observations of botanical explorers like J.D. Hooker affected their classificatory work".)

TURRILL (1952) provides the most copious source of information about Hooker's biogeography. Turrill devotes separate chapters to the numerous and diverse regions studied by Hooker, and extensive primary-source quotation presents the flavor of his writing, in addition to its content. BROWNE (1983) places this biogeographical work within the broader context of European science, and ties it more fully into Hooker's interest in taxonomy, and his ongoing discussions with Darwin on evolution theory.

Kew served with exemplary utility as a base for all Hooker's impressively extensive and fruitful explorations, both physical and intellectual. Its comprehensive herbarium (originally belonging to his father) allowed him access to thousands of specimens, which were absolutely essential to his classificatory work. Moreover, it provided him, for much of his life, with an indispensable source of personal income, and his science with funding, legitimization, and an institutional base. Kew operated as a Hooker-family fiefdom for nearly 65 years, during which time it expanded significantly in both size and scientific importance. Sir William became director in 1841, while his son was still on his maiden scientific voyage aboard the H.M.S. *Challenger*, and would remain so until his death in 1865. Joseph succeeded him and maintained the post, until turning it over in 1885 to William Thistelton-Dyer, his son-in-law, who would hold the reins for the next 20 years. DESMOND, a former Kew librarian who has published regularly on the history of the Gardens for nearly 30 years, certainly could claim to be the foremost expert on its development; his work is the first place to turn when tracing the long, defining and mutually-beneficial relationship between Hooker and the Gardens.

BARTON finds a number of "warring interest groups", fractured by disciplinary rivalries, class interests, and research priorities, operating within the Royal Society of the mid-19th century, and identifies the "X-Club", of which Hooker was a conspicuous member, as the dominant interest group of the mid-Victorian period. This dining club, which also claimed Thomas Huxley, John Lubbock, and John Tyndall as members, stood for professional research and a naturalistic world view, and against aristocratic and ecclesiastic patronage. Barton makes the compelling case that Hooker's Royal Society presidency can only be evaluated within the context of the confrontations between the various interest groups. The X-Club, of course, did not operate merely within the politics of the Royal Society, and received one of its most consequential and gruelling public tests in the dramatic and acrimonious "Ayrton Controversy" of the 1870s. As Gladstone's First Commissioner of Works, Acton Smee Ayrton had jurisdiction over Kew, and began attempts to limit its budget and Hooker's independence as director. Backed by X-Club colleagues, Hooker resisted both, arguing that the Commissioner's directives would destroy Kew as a viable scientific institution. Ayrton and his allies insisted that Hooker's insubordination represented a serious breach of public accountability, and the conflict ended up on the floor of Parliament before it, somewhat inconclusively, subsided. MacLEOD argues that the incident "marked one stage in the transformation of the amateur natural scientist into the professional scientific civil servant".

Desmond contains another judicious account, while Allan provides a rabidly partisan one.

Darwin initiated correspondence with Hooker in 1843, and quickly determined that his sharp-minded younger colleague would make an unparalleled sounding-board for his theories. Within a short time, professional exchange enlarged into an enduring friendship, which would play a central role in the scientific and personal lives of both men. In the first volume of her biography of Darwin, BROWNE (1995) provides a detailed and gracious portrait of the beginnings of this important relationship. Since only this volume has reached print, we must wait patiently for her to take the story beyond 1856.

RICHARD BELLON

See also Botany: Britain

Horticulture

Amherst, Alicia, *A History of Gardening in England*, London: Bernard Quaritch, 1895; New York: Dutton, 1910

Desmond, Ray, *A Dictionary of British and Irish Botanists and Horticulturists, Including Plant Collectors and Botanical Artists*, London: Taylor and Francis, 1977; revised edition, London: Taylor and Francis/Natural History Museum, 1994

Desmond, Ray, *Bibliography of British Gardens*, Winchester: St Paul's Bibliographies, 1984

Elliott, Brent, *Victorian Gardens*, London: Batsford, and Portland, Oregon: Timber Press, 1986

Goode, Patrick and Michael Lancaster (eds), *The Oxford Companion to Gardens*, Oxford: Oxford University Press, 1986

Harvey, John, *Mediaeval Gardens*, London: Batsford, and Beaverton, Oregon: Timber Press, 1981

Huxley, Anthony Julian, *An Illustrated History of Gardening*, London: Royal Horticultural Society, and New York: Paddington Press, 1978

Jacques, David, *Georgian Gardens: The Reign of Nature*, London: Batsford, 1983; Portland, Oregon: Timber Press, 1984

Thacker, Christopher, *The History of Gardens*, London: Croom Helm, 1979

Horticultural history, as distinct from natural histories or histories of botanical science, is a relatively young discipline, and one whose rapidly increasing popularity is evidenced by the plethora of publications and courses generated in recent years. The subject spans the diverse fields of biography, design theory, institutional history, sociology, spatial science, and international relations, and examines the creation and cultivation of the "civilizing" of nature for human ends.

The systematic study of garden history may be said to have begun in Britain at the end of the 19th century, with the publication of Alicia AMHERST's classic text, *A History of Gardening in England* (1895). This popularly acclaimed volume, following a strictly chronological infrastructure, traced the history of garden design from the knot gardens of monastic origin to the municipal bedding schemes of the High Victorians. Her innovative integration of chapters on contemporary garden literature at each formative stage of horticultural history, and the cumulative list of printed books on gardening that she included in the appendix, were to provide a useful starting point for her late 20th-century disciples. After the 3rd edition of the book appeared in 1920 there was a surprising lull until the foundation of the Garden History Society in 1965 by Christopher Thacker, which heralded the appropriation of horticultural history as a peculiarly 20th-century phenomenon. The inaugural members of the society reshaped the subject in the 1960s within rigidly academic parameters and – through their journal *Garden History* and the later publication of John Dixon Hunt's *Journal of Garden History* – a new style of historical writing emerged.

Late 20th-century histories of horticulture have tended toward four structural emphases: thematic, biographical, chronological, and regional. Thematic studies adopt a conceptual approach, by addressing such issues as the picturesque, landscape gardening, women in gardening, and revivalism. Biographical studies have tended to focus on either the exponents and practitioners of these concepts or the plant hunters, plantsmen and women, and nurserymen responsible for the fabric of the garden. The chronological approach is widely adopted, almost invariably opening with a discussion of "the first garden" – Eden – and subsequent attempts to recreate paradise by the sublimation of the natural world.

Regional studies frequently overlap with chronological or thematic ones, considering the Renaissance garden in Italy, the French formal garden of the 18th century, and the philosophical importance of elements of design in the Japanese garden, for example. Studies of the relationship between national identity and garden design concepts have yielded interesting regional variations, and have informed readings of international co-operation and antagonism throughout history. The most noteworthy exception to this fourfold structural conformity is the *The Oxford Companion to Gardens*, edited by GOODE & LANCASTER, which favours a non-linear approach, including 1,500 entries written by various contributors on the history and design of gardens worldwide. It is an invaluable introductory text to a range of issues in horticultural history, but its claims to comprehensiveness necessarily limit the depth of its analysis, making it an ideal introductory guide to the subject, and particularly to the way in which horticultural history writing has evolved into a modern interdisciplinary discourse.

If Goode & Lancaster provide a model for style, then the first textbook for the historian of British horticulture must undoubtedly be the one by Desmond, whose companion volumes on gardens and gardeners are indispensable works of reference. Desmond's annotated guides constitute a tertiary resource providing tools for research without authorial comment. DESMOND (1977) lists a wide, but not fully comprehensive range of secondary sources, including alphabetically arranged biographical entries, the location of manuscripts and portraits where known, and publications by and about the named individuals, and is cross-referenced by occupation. DESMOND (1984) lists secondary literature, including journal articles and books that discuss the gardens, and contains cross-references to counties.

Most general gardening histories tend to be polarised – aiming either for mass appeal or analytic specialism. In his *Illustrated History of Gardening*, Anthony HUXLEY adopts an idiosyncratically thematic approach, in an anecdotal introduction aimed at the amateur enthusiast. Huxley's work is directed toward a specific market, catered for by lavish illustration and a narrative unhindered by academic footnotes. The "coffee-table book" approach to grand narrative history characterizes the early reception of garden history as a not entirely serious scholarly pursuit, and has now been largely superseded by a more rigorous academic agenda.

Inhabiting the grey area between the readership of amateur gardeners and professional garden historians, the works of Harvey, Jacques and Elliott, which concentrate on specific periods, have a broad appeal, for both the serious student of horticulture and the enthusiastic amateur. Each writer focuses on the relationship of individuals to the defining movements of the age, and the progressive tendency of landscape aesthetics to be redefined in response to wider historical phenomena. Thus, Jacques connects picturesque improvement with social control and Elliott considers the Victorian garden, not as a wholly artificial construct, but as a stage on which the political and intellectual concerns of the age were played out. ELLIOTT reads the creation of the Victorian garden as an act of rebellion against the 18th-century landscape park. His meticulously researched text focuses on the three forces that marked this transition from gardens as works of nature to gardens as works of art: technological advances, the rise of the head gardener, and the artistic ferment spread by the contemporary proliferation of gardening magazines. In the Victorian garden he shows how technical innovation and social change were brought into conflict with tradition.

John HARVEY's reading of the medieval garden is informed by his conviction that the garden reflects societal values of spirituality and transcendalism. His study is also concerned to expand the concept of the garden to include a wider environmental aesthetic that, during the Middle Ages, came to embrace landscaped parkland and woodland. He takes a European-wide perspective for his examples, stressing their common cultural background, to prove that "national distinctions in gardening were comparatively slight".

David JACQUES's work charts the development in English garden design from William Kent's Natural Style, first seen in 1733, to the beginnings of the gardenesque, which he arbitrarily assigns to the year 1825. Unlike Harvey, he restricts himself to a discussion of English and Welsh gardens, with glancing references to the rest of Europe. He disassociates his work from formal horticultural history, attempting instead a history of taste and design as made manifest in the Georgian garden.

Arguably the most highly regarded general history of horticulture is Christopher THACKER's book of 1979. Until the 1960s, biographical studies of influential figures like Lancelot "Capability" Brown, William Kent, Humphrey Repton, and Gertrude Jeykll had been the staples of horticultural publishing, but Thacker extended the scope of the debate to contextualize these figures within a discipline increasing in academic legitimacy. Thacker's intellectual focus is on the transience of gardens and their role in the artistic life of the nation. He introduces his study with the qualification that "though gardens are old, the writing on their history is still new and adventurous", and it is this spirit of novelty and adventure that informs his revisionist reading of garden history.

HELEN M. WARD

See also Botanical and Zoological Gardens; Botany; Nature

Hospitals

Ackerknecht, Erwin H., *Medicine at the Paris Hospital, 1794–1848*, Baltimore: Johns Hopkins University Press, 1967

Fissell, Mary E., *Patients, Power and the Poor in Eighteenth-Century Bristol*, Cambridge and New York: Cambridge University Press, 1991

Foucault, Michel, *The Birth of the Clinic: An Archaeology of Medical Perception*, translated from the French by A.M. Sheridan Smith, New York: Pantheon, and London: Tavistock, 1973

Gelfand, Toby, *Professionalizing Modern Medicine: Paris Surgeons and Medical Science and Institutions in the 18th Century*, Westport, Connecticut: Greenwood Press, 1980

Howell, Joel D., *Technology in the Hospital: Transforming Patient Care in the Early Twentieth Century*, Baltimore: Johns Hopkins University Press, 1995

Pickstone, John V., *Medicine and Industrial Society: A History of Hospital Development in Manchester and Its Region, 1752–1946*, Manchester: Manchester University Press, 1985

Risse, Guenter B., *Hospital Life in Enlightenment Scotland: Care and Teaching at the Royal Infirmary of Edinburgh*, Cambridge and New York: Cambridge University Press, 1986

Rosenberg, Charles, *The Care of Strangers: The Rise of America's Hospital System*, New York: Basic Books, 1987

Stevens, Rosemary, *In Sickness and in Wealth: American Hospitals in the Twentieth Century*, New York: Basic Books, 1989

Taylor, Jeremy, *Hospital and Asylum Architecture in England, 1840–1914: Building for Health Care*, London and New York: Mansell, 1991

Thompson, John D. and Grace Goldin, *The Hospital: A Social and Architectural History*, New Haven, Connecticut: Yale University Press, 1975

Warner, John Harley, *The Therapeutic Perspective: Medical Practice, Knowledge, and Identity in America, 1820–1885*, Cambridge, Massachusetts: Harvard University Press, 1986

Hospitals have existed, in one form or another, since antiquity, but it is only since the 18th century that they have been devoted primarily to the provision of medical care, as distinct from generalised charitable relief and religious succour. This change in the purpose of hospitals was intimately related to other changes, both in the aim and orientation of charitable and state welfare, and in the organisation of medical practice. The medicalisation of hospitals and the professionalization of medicine proceeded hand-in-hand, and both were mediated by changes in the technical constitution of medical knowledge

and practice. By the early 19th century, hospitals had become one of the key sites for the development of new forms of medical knowledge and technique. Historians of medical science, and of medical practice more generally, have consequently been at pains to elucidate the relationship between the development of hospitals as institutions, and the intellectual and technical innovations that took place within them.

Some historians have gone so far as to locate the beginnings of modern medical science at a specific moment in hospital history – namely, the reform and reorganisation of the Paris hospitals during the French Revolution. ACKERKNECHT offers the most accessible version of this thesis. He argues that the overthrow of the *ancien régime* and the ensuing democratisation of the Paris hospitals provided an opportunity for a new generation of doctors to reassess the teachings of their predecessors, and to seek new forms of medical knowledge through the systematic conduct of scientific methods: autopsies, vivisection, and clinical experimentation. FOUCAULT's notoriously difficult but historiographically ground-breaking study, *The Birth of the Clinic*, covers much the same period and developments, but from a rather different perspective. Where Ackerknecht sees progress in medical knowledge, Foucault sees a leap into a quite other universe of discourse. The reform of the hospitals did not simply encourage the adoption of better, more objective methods of scientific investigation, says Foucault; rather, the adoption of such methods itself resulted from the articulation of completely new structures of thought and language, which made possible new objects of knowledge and new encounters between doctors and the sick. Foucault's aim is to dig beneath the new scientific knowledge and methods, and to reveal the novel discursive structures around which, he argues, such science took shape. Readers should be warned, however, that Foucault is not particularly interested in explaining how or why this transformation came about. His chief concern is with what he calls "genealogy": for Foucault, the universe of scientific discourse first articulated in the Paris clinics continues to frame much of our present-day thought and knowledge. *The Birth of the Clinic* should thus be read not simply as an attempt to recover the past, but as an attempt to excavate the bare bones of the present; it is as much a work of philosophy as of history proper.

More recently, other historians have questioned and qualified the notion that the French Revolution marked a uniquely important moment of transformation within the medical sciences. The events played out during the Revolution now need to be seen within the context of longer-term changes in hospital medicine, both in France and elsewhere. GELFAND, for example, looks at the rise of surgery in 18th-century Paris, analysing the dynamic relationship between social status, the pursuit of technical skill, and the articulation of systematic scientific knowledge. As he makes clear, the emergence of hospital-based medical schools at this time was crucial in providing a setting in which such knowledge and techniques could be both developed and disseminated. FISSELL's study of 18th-century Bristol relates the growth and medicalisation of British hospitals during this period to shifts in the system of domestic care and private and state philanthropy. Within this context, she shows how the rise of dissection and the emergence of anatomical ideas about disease were facilitated by a wider tendency for polite culture to objectify the poor and repudiate the vernacular. By contrast, RISSE is concerned almost exclusively with the internal routines of hospital life in late 18th-century Scotland. He looks in detail at the practices of diagnosis and therapy in order to show that, despite a relative lack of interest in dissection, hospital medicine in Scotland (as in France and England) was approaching a more physical conception of disease, and a more skeptical attitude towards received medical theory.

The period from the mid-19th century onwards saw the arrival of a second, and more sustained, wave of technical development in hospital medicine. New laboratory-based technologies – including bacteriology, antisepsis, X-rays, and a host of new therapeutic substances and regimes – now began to be integrated into hospital practice, and especially into the clinical training of a new generation of doctors. A number of historians have sought to explain these innovations in relation to the social and institutional development of hospitals within particular national or regional contexts, including ROSENBERG (who covers the period 1800–1920) and STEVENS (20th century) for the United States, and PICKSTONE for the north-west of England. These authors all take a similar view of the relationship between medical laboratories and the growth and development of hospital medicine. They argue that new laboratory technologies were not, on the whole, adopted because they led unproblematically to improvements in medical efficacy. On the contrary, the supposed superiority of new, over older, techniques of diagnosis and treatment was commonly a matter of intense medical debate; and even when such technologies were put to use on the wards, it was frequently as a means of reinforcing, rather than challenging, more established forms of practice. Rather, these historians seek to explain the spread of the new medical sciences and technologies by showing how they were implicated in more general changes within the culture of hospital medicine: from care to cure; from moral education to technical control; from philanthropic patronage to professional autonomy; and from individualism to a corporate division of labour. Within this emerging culture, they argue, laboratories came to be valued because they held a promise of technical innovation, they offered a source of esoteric professional knowledge, and they could be used to define universally applicable standards of practice.

A number of historians have pursued similar insights through more narrowly focused studies of hospital practice. WARNER examines the practice of therapeutics in American hospitals in the decades of the mid-19th century, charting the growing tendency for doctors to appeal to laboratory-based physiology and pharmacology rather than synoptic theories of illness and its treatment, in order to legitimise their therapeutic practices. He relates this to the search for a single and uncontroversial body of knowledge on which doctors could build a unified and coherent professional identity. HOWELL looks at the adoption and development of new technologies, especially diagnostic technologies – such as urinalysis, X-rays, and blood analysis – in American hospitals. He argues that such technologies were adopted, not because they were seen to offer more precise or reliable methods of diagnosis, but chiefly because a display of technological virtuosity served to enhance the cultural authority of hospital doctors. Howell also suggests that the spread of these technologies might have been implicated in the promotion of "scientific management", in particular the development of standardised systems of clinical records, as a means of ensuring the efficient management of an increasingly specialised division of medical labour.

Finally, it is worth bearing in mind that hospital buildings themselves may be regarded as medical technologies, designed to assist in the management of patients and their diseases. In this respect, the books by THOMPSON & GOLDIN and TAYLOR throw an interesting side-light on the history of medical science and technology by looking at the development of hospital architecture in, respectively, the United States and Britain. Both make clear how changing notions of disease aetiology and prevention, and shifts in the social relations of medical practice, combined to produce striking changes in the physical structure and spatial organisation of hospitals.

STEVE STURDY

See also Medical Instruments; Medical Specialization; Professionalization

Human Genome Project

Bishop, Jerry E. and Michael Waldholz, *Genome: The Story of the Most Astonishing Scientific Adventure of Our Time: The Attempt to Map All the Genes in the Human Body*, New York: Simon and Schuster, 1990

Cohen, Daniel, *Les Gènes de l'espoir: A la découverte du génome humain*, Paris: Laffont, 1993

Cook-Deegan, Robert, *The Gene Wars: Science, Politics and the Human Genome*, New York: Norton, 1994

Cooper, Necia Grant (ed.), *The Human Genome Project: Deciphering the Blueprint of Heredity*, Mill Valley, California: University Science Books, 1994

Davis, Joel, *Mapping the Code: The Human Genome Project and the Choices of Modern Science*, New York: John Wiley, 1990

Jordan, Bertrand, *Travelling Around the Human Genome: An In-situ Investigation*, Paris: Editions INSERM, 1993

Kevles, Daniel J. and Leroy Hood (eds), *The Code of Codes: Scientific and Social Issues in the Human Genome Project*, Cambridge, Massachusetts: Harvard University Press, 1992

Lee, Thomas F., *The Human Genome Project: Cracking the Genetic Code of Life*, New York: Plenum Press, 1991

Lewontin, R.C., *The Doctrine of DNA*, London: Penguin, 1993

Shapiro, R., *The Human Blueprint: The Race to Unlock the Secrets of Our Genetic Code*, New York: St Martin's Press, 1991

Wills, Christopher, *Exons, Introns and Talking Genes*, New York: Basic Books, 1991

The Human Genome Project is an ambitious international research programme designed to produce complete genetic and physical maps of the human genome. The project was first mooted in the early 1980s, and officially launched in October 1990 in the US as one of the most ambitious and exciting scientific ventures of the 20th century, which would produce a "book of man" containing the key to understanding the code of human life. It was from its onset, however, an extremely controversial project, and was widely opposed due to its cost – an estimated \$3 billion over 15 years, its questionable scientific value, and its ethical implications.

There are a number of popular accounts of the origins and nature of the programme; for example, Bishop & Waldholz, Cooper, Davis, Lee, Shapiro, and Wills. Of these BISHOP & WALDHOLZ, and WILLS lay particular emphasis on the potential medical outcomes of the human genome project. DAVIS, LEE, and SHAPIRO also provide popular histories of the science behind the project, covering much of the same ground, usually along the lines of, "From Mendel to the human genome project, via the double helix and recombinant DNA". COOPER is a multi-author work, lavishly illustrated, with clear explanations of the human genome project technology and discussions with important genome scientists.

The problem with many of these accounts is that they tend to over-emphasize the scientific (especially human genetics) origins of the human genome project, whereas, in fact, it could also be regarded as a technological vision, established after much political lobbying by research bureaucracies. COOK-DEEGAN's detailed accounts of the politics of the origin of the human genome project lend support to that view. He argues that, while it would have been logical for the human genome project to have emerged from human or medical genetics, that is not in fact how it happened. None of the original protagonists, he claims, was a specialist in human genetics; rather, the human genome project was initially based on a technological vision of systematically applying the tools of molecular genetics to sequence the entire human genome, and only later did human geneticists recapture part of the project by redefining its goals. Furthermore, the nature of the human genome project was such that it called for the building of new bureaucratic structures for carrying out and overseeing the research; Cook-Deegan's account of the politics of their establishment in the US is fundamental to understanding the history of the human genome project. He shows, for example, that the reasons US Department of Energy (DOE) supported the human genome project were rooted in decades of research that they had financed into the genetics of Japanese survivors of the atomic bombing of Hiroshima and Nagasaki. He perceives a further link between the human genome project and nuclear weapons programmes, tracing some of the roots of the computational tools of the human genome project to Stanislaw Ulam's fusion group at Los Alamos in the 1950s. The strength of Cook-Deegan's work lies in his willingness to explore the politics and intrigues surrounding the human genome project; for example, the struggle for control of the US human genome project between the DOE and the National Institutes of Health (NIH), the rise and fall of James Watson as Head of the NIH Office of Human Genome Research, and the controversy over NIH patent applications for DNA sequences.

The human genome project is not actually a unitary project funded by a single source and managed as a single programme. It consists of several national and international programmes conducted in numerous institutes, funded from a variety of sources, and it also studies non-human genomes. The individual research goals, strategies and resources of the various programmes may vary, but *in toto* they all contribute to the basic goal of the human genome project, to map the human genome. Perhaps the most accessible account of this variety is to be found in JORDAN, whose book is based on visits to more than 100 genome laboratories. An interesting account by an individual, of his research within the context of international competitiveness and the struggle to raise funds and develop quick moving opportunistic strategies, is provided by COHEN, a French genome researcher.

The role of "instrumentalities", i.e., research technology, instruments, and methods, is paramount in the human genome project, yet the history of these instrumentalities and their coming together within the context of the project remains to be comprehensively covered. None of the reading materials provides, on its own, an adequate history of the instrumentalities of the human genome project; several, however, deal with particular aspects of that history. A general introduction to the history of gene mapping and sequencing is provided by Judson in KEVLES & HOOD.

Both Wills and Shapiro provide useful material on the invention of DNA sequencing methods by Frederick Sanger, and by Allan Marshall Maxam and Walter Gilbert. Wills describes the first attempts to automate DNA sequencing by Hood's team at CalTech and Applied Biosystems, a start-up company who developed the first commercial gene sequencer machine, and whose successors are now regarded as indispensable for the large-scale rapid sequencing necessary for the human genome project. Shapiro provides information on David Schwartz who developed pulsed field gel electrophoresis, and on Kary Mullis, awarded a Nobel prize in 1993 for his invention of the polymerised chain reaction (PCR), said to be the most significant technical innovation in molecular biology of the 1980s. Bishop & Waldholz give a history of mapping techniques, such as the restriction-fragment-length polymorphisms tool. Computation and the human genome project is well dealt with in Cooper, though in an ahistoric fashion.

Not everyone has seen the human genome project as an unmitigated blessing. LEWONTIN provides one of the strongest cases against it, arguing that it is poor science because of its ideological bias towards biological determinism, and, further, that it is in danger of becoming dominated by commercial interests. Kevles & Hood contain several chapters by critics of the human genome project along similar lines, as well as dealing with the project within the context of the history of eugenics. The attempt to institutionalize ethical considerations within the human genome project is presented by Cook-Deegan, who describes how James Watson established (within the NIH genome programme) ELSI (Ethical, Legal and Social Implications of Human Genome Research), in order to anticipate such concerns.

HARRY ROTHMAN

See also Biotechnology; Genetic Engineering

Human Sciences

Bryson, Gladys, *Man and Society: The Scottish Inquiry of the Eighteenth Century*, Princeton, New Jersey: Princeton University Press, 1945

Curti, Merle, *Human Nature in American Thought: A History*, Madison: University of Wisconsin Press, 1980

Foucault, Michel, *The Order of Things: An Archaeology of the Human Sciences*, translated from the French by Alan Sheridan, New York: Pantheon Books, and London: Tavistock, 1970 (original edition, 1966)

Fox, Christopher, Roy Porter and Robert Wokler (eds), *Inventing Human Science: Eighteenth-Century Domains*, Berkeley: University of California, 1995

Gusdorf, Georges, *Les Sciences humaines et la pensée occidentale*, 15 vols, Paris: Payot, 1960–88

Jones, Peter (ed.), *The "Science of Man" in the Scottish Enlightenment: Hume, Reid and Their Contemporaries*, Edinburgh: Edinburgh University Press, 1989

Kristeller, Paul Oskar, *Renaissance Concepts of Man and Other Essays*, New York: Harper and Row, 1972

Smith, Roger, *The Fontana History of the Human Sciences*, London: Fontana Press, 1997; as *The Norton History of the Human Sciences*, New York: Norton, 1997

At their broadest, the human sciences encompass disciplines as diverse as political science, economics, sociology, natural history, psychology, anthropology, theology, astrology, rhetoric, history, and the history of science itself. They are a heterogeneous assembly of subjects, loosely linked by an unstable concept of man, and as such are continually seeking some form of definition. The history of the human sciences can be seen as an ongoing contribution to this attempted project of self-demarcation, the literature of which is both reflexive and polemical, forced into a series of very open value-judgements in the attempt to discriminate between scientific and literary approaches and the natural and cultural domains.

The most sustained attempt to portray the history of the human sciences appears in the untranslated work of Georges GUSDORF. In 15 volumes, and over 3 million words, Gusdorf provides a global narrative of man's attempt to make sense of his being and position in the world. The work stretches from the cosmobiological ideas of classical Greek philosophy through to the evolutionary schemes of 19th-century neurobiology. His approach is influenced by Husserlian phenomenology, with Gusdorf paying close attention to the ways in which linguistic innovation has brought about a reorientation of man's social and intellectual horizons. Within these volumes, the history of the human sciences appears as an epic tragedy, in which the outer world and man's inner being are surrendered to mathematization and representation.

FOUCAULT's *The Order of Things* is probably the most influential and controversial work in the history of the human sciences. In reaction against Gusdorf's idea that these disciplines have a long history stretching back to ancient times, Foucault argued that the human sciences represented a discrete and distinctly modern phenomenon originating at the end of the 18th century. This period saw the articulation of "man" as a "difficult object", who is both subject and source of representation; the human sciences are novel insofar as they attempt to comprehend the individual in both his empirical and transcendental aspects. In Foucault's view, disciplines such as biology, economics, and philology, which treat man as a part of nature and society, are engaged in a continual traffic with those disciplines such as psychology, sociology, and literary criticism which analyse the meaning of society for man. The human sciences emerge at the crossing point of these disci-plines. Moreover, Foucault believed that this point itself was transitory, as "countersciences" such as ethnology, linguistics, and psychoanalysis reveal sources for man's nature and representations that lay beyond the human in the unconscious structures of language.

The essays of KRISTELLER provide a counterbalance to Foucault's exclusive concentration on the concept of man in the modern period. Kristeller eschews any unifying idea of the Renaissance, arguing that the concept of man must be situated within a whole complex of theological, ethical, and scientific problems, such as dignity, free will, and predestination. He concentrates on the Italian humanists Marsilio Ficino, Francesco Petrarch, and Pietro Pomponazzi, who believed that the philosophical examination of man's status in the natural and spiritual worlds would encourage his moral transformation. Kristeller downplays the novelty of the Italian humanists, arguing instead that their work should be seen as a response to the discoveries of science and exploration, from within an Aristotelian and Neo-Platonic framework.

The Scottish Enlightenment, which many have identified as the true origin of the human sciences, is well covered in the secondary literature. BRYSON's volume provides a clear (if dated) introduction to this era. Influenced by the sociology of postwar America, Bryson treats the contributions of individuals such as David Hume, Thomas Reid, and Adam Ferguson as signs of a larger shift in culture, brought about through changes in economic and social organization. She believes that Scottish philosophy was characterized by a scientific optimism that imported the Newtonian faith in natural laws into the new arenas of human nature and society. For Bryson, it is this enduring faith in the scientificity of the human sciences that joins 18th-century moral philosophy to the modern disciplines of sociology and psychology.

Bryson's work should be supplemented by the essays contained in JONES. Against Bryson's attempt to establish the continuity of Scottish moral philosophy and modern disciplines, the contributors to this volume attempt to uncover the radical difference that exists between Enlightenment culture and the contemporary world. Hume's conceptions of aesthetics, religion, woman, and the crowd are analyzed, demonstrating their relationship to the conservative concerns of 18th-century Edinburgh. This stress upon the social context of Scottish philosophy is extended into essays on Hume's followers, such as Reid, Adam Smith, and John Boswell.

A more substantial consideration of the relationship between human science and Enlightenment culture is presented in the collection of essays edited by FOX, PORTER & WOKLER, which address a range of writings and subjects from across 18th-century Europe. Most of the essays are divided along modern disciplinary lines – Gary Hatfield writes on psychology, David Carrithers on sociology, Wokler on anthropology, and Porter on medicine, etc. – yet with the purpose of destabilizing these respective fields. This deconstructive theme is pursued through an admixture of close analysis with theoretical insights from writers such as Habermas and Foucault. Concentrating on the specific contexts and local disputes within which the disciplines were founded, these essays demonstrate the historical contingency of the modern human sciences.

This theme of the interaction between human science and political aspiration is explored in the work of CURTI, who examines how the notion of man has been deployed in North American culture, demonstrating its implications in ideological controversies over race, class, and gender. His work takes a broad historical sweep, moving from the European neo-Platonic philosophy imported by the Pilgrim Fathers through New England theology, Jamesian psychology, and other intellectual traditions specific to the United States, to the modern emergence of socio-biology. Curti's close attention to the political uses of the human sciences results in a narrative that integrates both élite and popular conceptions of mankind.

The many conflicts surrounding the origins and nature of the human sciences are subsumed into a global narrative within the work of Roger Smith. SMITH provides the first truly comprehensive account of these disciplines, beginning with the meditations of the Renaissance humanists and ending with the "death of man" pronounced by contemporary post-structuralists. His work demonstrates a lively awareness of the ideological function of previous textbook histories in this area, drawing attention to ways in which these traditional narratives have been used to establish the professional identity of the human sciences. As a counterpoint, Smith's book provides a generous perspective on the sciences of man. His work embraces the hard sciences, from natural philosophy through to neuroscience, alongside disciplines excluded from the traditional pantheon, such as theology, physiognomy, and spiritualism. This is a lucid and decentred account, in which the sciences of man emerge out of series of overlapping intellectual movements and genres. Supplemented by a long and detailed bibliographic essay, Smith's book is the essential starting point for anyone embarking on the history of the human sciences.

RHODRI LLOYD HAYWARD

See also Enlightenment; Humanism; Political Economy; Psychology; Sociology

Humanism

Bylebyl, Jerome, "The School of Padua: Humanistic Medicine in the Sixteenth Century", in *Health, Medicine and Mortality in the Sixteenth Century*, edited by Charles Webster, Cambridge and New York: Cambridge University Press, 1979

Cochrane, Eric, "Science and Humanism in the Italian Renaissance", *American Historical Review*, 81 (1976): 1039–57

Duhem, Pierre, *Le système du monde: Histoire des doctrines cosmologiques de Platon à Copernic*, 10 vols, Paris: Hermann, 1913–59

Kristeller, Paul Oskar, *Renaissance Thought and Its Sources*, edited by Michael Mooney, New York: Columbia University Press, 1979

Nutton, V., "Humanistic Surgery", in *The Medical Renaissance of the Sixteenth Century*, edited by A. Wear, R.K. French and I.M. Lonie, Cambridge and New York: Cambridge University Press, 1985

Reeds, Karen Meier, *Botany in Medieval and Renaissance Universities*, New York: Garland, 1991

Rose, Paul Lawrence, *The Italian Renaissance of Mathematics: Studies on Humanists and Mathematicians from Petrarch to Galileo*, Geneva: Droz, 1975

Rummel, Erika, *The Humanist-Scholastic Debate in the Renaissance and Reformation*, Cambridge, Massachusetts: Harvard University Press, 1995

Sarton, George, *The Appreciation of Ancient and Medieval Science during the Renaissance, 1450–1600*, Philadelphia: University of Pennsylvania Press, 1955

Shapiro, Barbara, "Early Modern Intellectual Life: Humanism, Religion and Science in Seventeenth Century England", *History of Science*, 29 (1991): 45–71

Siegel, Jerrold E., *Rhetoric and Philosophy in Renaissance Humanism: The Union of Eloquence and Wisdom, Petrarch to Vella*, Princeton, New Jersey: Princeton University Press, 1968

Toulmin, Stephen, *Cosmopolis: The Hidden Agenda of Modernity*, New York: Free Press, 1990

Trinkaus, Charles, *In Our Image and Likeness: Humanity and Divinity in Italian Humanist Thought*, 2 vols, London: Constable, and Chicago: University of Chicago Press, 1970

According to KRISTELLER's widely accepted interpretation, Renaissance humanism was primarily a literary and cultural movement promoting the "studies of humanity" (*studia humanitatis*) – grammar, rhetoric, poetics, history, and ethics – through the recovery of classical Greek and Latin sources. It flourished in the city states of 15th-century Italy, particularly Florence, but did not firmly take root in other parts of Europe until the middle of the 16th century. Kristeller's circumscribed understanding of humanism contrasts with that of earlier authors, who tended to conflate the humanist movement with the whole of Renaissance culture and thought. By contrast, Kristeller argued that, in areas of study and practical achievement outside the humanities, the humanists were concerned mainly with the literary and rhetorical merits of classical texts. Although they supplied the scholarly methods, ideals, and activities that stimulated a classical revival in other disciplines, they did not directly influence what was appropriated from ancient sources. Hence Renaissance writers who shared a common formation in the humanities often held diverse and even opposing philosophical, political, natural scientific, and religious views.

Despite the merits of Kristeller's interpretation of humanism, historians have found it difficult to distil the purely literary and rhetorical interests of humanists from their specific commitments in other fields of human endeavour. Often the methodological goals and assumptions of the humanists shaped their theological and philosophical views in quite subtle ways. For instance, in theology, TRINKAUS has shown how the humanists' regard for rhetoric led to a heightened awareness of the human being as "a living, feeling subject". This was the phenomenological starting point for what Trinkaus has called "rhetorical theology" (*theologia rhetorica*), a characteristically humanist approach to moral and religious questions that emphasised the freedom and value of human actions. Similarly, in philosophy, SIEGEL concluded that humanists such as Leonardo Bruni and Lorenzo Valla glossed over, reinterpreted and even rejected parts of the works of Plato and Aristotle, because they considered these writings to be inimical to the practice and teaching of rhetoric.

The humanist movement, moreover, was not a static entity over time; various factors shaped its development, particularly during the 16th century. RUMMEL suggested that shifting professional boundaries, and the fragmentation of Western Christianity, helped to polemicise the debate between scholastics and humanists. As a result, humanism, which began as "an élitist literary movement", came to rival scholasticism as a generalised approach to truth-seeking.

Rummel surmised that neither scholasticism nor humanism had the last word in this raging debate, because both were swept aside in the 17th century by a new intellectual current, scientific empiricism. The relationship between humanism and science, however, remains a topic that is vigorously discussed. Although SARTON acknowledged the stimulating influence of the humanists' recovery of classical works on mathematical and scientific topics, he contrasted their "imitative" approach to scientific inquiry, which was mired in the past, with the "creative" experimental style of a handful of contemporaries, such as Petrus Severinus and Andreas Vesalius.

Other authors have assessed the relationship between humanism and science more positively, as a result of two trends in scholarship – detailed studies of the involvement of humanists in scientific investigations, and a reconsideration of scientific empiricism. COCHRANE's paper set the stage in both respects. He argued that the accepted caricature of humanists as scholars concerned only with bookish learning needed to be revised. The humanists, he claimed, emphasised the significance of observation, and were favourably disposed to technological innovation. Moreover, their approach to investigations in nature bore resemblance to certain features of scientific methodology, which had been overlooked by earlier historians writing from a strictly positivistic perspective. The humanists, Cochrane suggested, understood the historical character of scientific learning and the importance of communication, persuasion, and other rhetorical skills in advancing scientific opinions.

Among those studying the interaction of humanism and science, ROSE has argued against DUHEM's well-known view that, relative to the influence of the medieval, scholastic tradition in mathematics and mechanics, the classical Greek heritage that was recovered by humanists contributed little to the development of a mathematical physics by Galileo and others. Rose concluded that the debt of Galilean science to humanism was both technical and "psychological". Its content was shaped by the mathematical tools of the Greeks, particularly Diophantus, Pappus and Archimedes, whose works were either unknown or ignored in the Middle Ages, and its impetus for change came, at least initially, from the humanists' enthusiasm for a fresh approach to learning. In a different area of science, BYLEBYL and, more recently, NUTTON have documented the influence of the humanists' revival of Galen on anatomy, clinical medicine, and surgery, showing that this influence extended far beyond the recovery and analysis of texts. The Galenic ideal of linking theory with praxis, causal knowledge with useful skills in surgery, provided the framework within which a significant reorientation in medicine took place during the Renaissance. REEDS provided evidence for an analogous conceptual shift in Renaissance botany. SHAPIRO has recently shown important congruences in methodological goals and assumptions between the Renaissance humanists and early 17th-century English scientists. Humanist views on the importance of practical knowledge, the powers and limitations of human reasoning, the probable nature of knowledge, and the need for experience, created an intellectual and cultural milieu in which the scientific endeavours of the Royal Society gained ready acceptance. On the continent, TOULMIN suggested that the eventual triumph of Cartesian rationalism amounted to a rejection of the humanist roots of science. According to Toulmin, this was a turning point in history, which had significant but dire consequences for modern culture.

In summary, historians and philosophers today tend to regard humanism as a movement that had an impact far beyond literary studies and education. In science, it was one factor that helped to prepare the way for the conceptual and methodological transformations of the 16th and 17th centuries.

JOHN HENG

See also Scientific Revolution

Humboldt, Alexander von   1769–1859

German naturalist and traveller

Banse, Ewald, *Alexander von Humboldt: Erschliesser einer neuen Welt*, Stuttgart: Wissenschaftliche Verlagsgesellschaft, 1953

Beck, Hanno, *Alexander von Humboldt*, 2 vols, Wiesbaden: Steiner, 1959–61

Biermann, Kurt R., *Alexander von Humboldt*, Leipzig: Teubner, 1979

Botting, Douglas, *Humboldt and the Cosmos*, London: Joseph, and New York: Harper and Row, 1973

Bowen, Margarita, *Empiricism and Geographical Thought: From Francis Bacon to Alexander von Humboldt*, Cambridge and New York: Cambridge University Press, 1981

Bruhns, Karl (ed.), *Life of Alexander Humboldt*, translated from the German by Jane and Caroline Lassell, 2 vols, London: Longman, 1873; reprinted, Boston: Lee and Shepard, 1973 (original edition, 3 vols, 1872)

Cannon, Susan Faye, *Science in Culture: The Early Victorian Period*, New York: Science History Publications, and Folkestone, Kent: Dawson, 1978

Dangel, Anneliese, *Alexander von Humboldt: Sein Leben in Bildern, 1769–1859*, Leipzig: Enzyklopädie, 1959

De Terra, Helmut, *Humboldt: The Life and Times of Alexander von Humboldt, 1769–1859*, New York: Knopf, 1955

Deutsche Akademie der Wissenschaften zu Berlin, *Alexander von Humboldt: Wirkendes Vorbild für Fortschritt und Befreiung der Menschheit*, Berlin: Akademie-Verlag, 1969

Ertel, Hans (ed), *Alexander von Humboldt, 14.9.1769–6.5.1859: Gedenkschrift zur 100. Wiederkehr seines Todestages: Herausgegeben von der Alexander von Humboldt–Kommission der Deutschen Akademie der Wissenschaften zu Berlin*, Berlin: Akademie-Verlag, 1959

Hein, Wolfgang-Hagen (ed.), *Alexander von Humboldt: Leben und Werk*, Frankfurt: Weisbecker, 1985

Kellner, Charlotte, *Alexander von Humboldt*, London and New York: Oxford University Press, 1963

Klencke, Hermann, *Alexander von Humbold: Ein biographisches Denkmal*, Leipzig: Spamer, 1851

Krammer, Mario, *Alexander von Humboldt: Mensch, Zeit, Werk*, Berlin: Gebrüder Weirs, 1954

Linden, Walther, *Alexander von Humboldt: Weltbild der Naturwissenschaft*, Hamburg: Hoffmann & Campe, 1940

MacGillivray, William (ed.), *The Travels and Researches of Alexander von Humboldt: Being a Condensed Narrative of His Journeys in the Equinoctial Regions of America, and in Asiatic Russia; Together with Analyses of His More Important Investigations*, Edinburgh: Oliver and Boyd, and London: Simpkin and Marshall, 1832; 3rd revised edition, 1836; New York: Harper, 1853

Meyer-Abich, Adolf, *Alexander von Humboldt, mit Selbstzeugnissen und Bilddokumenten*, Reinbek bei Hamburg: Rowohlt Taschenbuch, 1967

Pfeiffer, Heinrich (ed.), *Alexander von Humboldt: Werk und Weltgeltung*, Munich: Piper, 1969

Pratt, Mary Louise, *Imperial Eyes: Studies in Travel Writing and Transculturation*, London and New York: Routledge, 1992

Schultze, Joachim H., *Alexander von Humboldt: Studien zu seiner universalen Geisteshaltung*, Berlin: De Gruyter, 1959

Like Charles Darwin, Alexander von Humboldt has himself become a field of historical scholarship; the literature on Humboldt is vast, and its bibliography fills several volumes. Entire catalogues have been published, listing Humboldt studies in German, Polish, Russian, and Spanish, dozens of biographies of Humboldt have been written, and many volumes of collected essays on Humboldt and his impact have been edited.

The "Humboldt industry" curve, tracing the output of books and papers over time, has not followed an even course, but shows distinct peaks. Book-length studies of Humboldt started to appear during the last third of his life. In the course of the two decades following his death in 1859, a first modest publication peak took place, centred on the centenary of his birth in 1869. This was followed by a long flat stretch, and then new peaks emerged, first around 1959, the centenary of Humboldt's death and, a decade later, around 1969, the bicentenary of his birth.

The first book on Humboldt appeared in 1832, following in the wake of Humboldt's second major journey of exploration, his expedition to Russia and Siberia in 1829, and was heavily indebted to Humboldt's own account of his earlier American journey, the *Personal Narrative of Travels to the Equinoctial Regions of the New-Continent*, (1799–1804, first English translation, 1814–29). The book was written by the Edinburgh botanist MacGILLIVRAY, who presented his hero in the role of "Humboldt-the-explorer". MacGillivray's account of Humboldt was a success; it appeared in several new editions, and was translated into several languages. "Humboldt the celebrated traveller" has remained a *leitmotif* of part of the subsequent biographical literature. A recent example is the engagingly written and well-illustrated biography by the explorer, BOTTING, who followed in Humboldt's footsteps in South America and Asia.

Also during Humboldt's lifetime, a more Germanic interpretation of his significance was given by KLENCKE, who intended to bring Humboldt's "high spiritual standpoint" to bear on the "German national conscience". In Klencke's account, *Kosmos* was the high point and the epitome of Humboldt's works. Like MacGillivray's biography, Klencke's was a success, published in several editions and languages.

The centennial anniversary of Humboldt's birth formed the occasion for the publication of the first major and authoritative biography, the multi-author, three-volume work edited by BRUHNS, which has remained a valuable source of information, especially on bibliographical details, ever since. The Bruhns biography is comparable to the "Life and Letters" of eminent Victorians, in that it was the "authorised" biography, based on unpublished letters and other private papers made available by relatives and officialdom. Significant in the type-casting of Humboldt was the fact that the book was not written by a single author, but by a team of scientists, drawn from Humboldt's circle of friends and colleagues. The first volume, written by Julius Löwenberg, covers the early part of Humboldt's life up to 1799, and also the first two episodes of travel and exploration to America and Asia. The second volume covers Humboldt's years in Paris (1808–26), written by Robert Avé-Lallemant, and Alfred Dove's account of his Berlin period (1827–59). In the third volume, Humboldt's contributions to the world of learning are discussed: his mathematics, astronomy and mathematical geography by Bruhns himself; his terrestrial magnetism and parts of physics and chemistry by Gustav Wiedemann; his meteorology by H.W. Dove; his geology by Julius Ewald; his social geography, ethnography, economics, and historiography by Oskar Peschel; his plant geography and botany by J.V. Carus; and finally his physiology by Wilhelm Wundt. Thus a vision of Humboldt was created that included the "Romantic explorer" of MacGillivray and the "noble mind" of Klencke, but which added the image of a giant of scientific learning, the scope of whose accomplishments matched that of the philosophical universalism of *Kosmos*.

During the approximately 80 years that followed, the flow of Humboldt studies was reduced to a trickle of mainly small-scale publications, discussing Humboldt in relation to Darwin, Leopold von Buch, Johannes Müller or Alexander's brother, Wilhelm von Humboldt. Interestingly, during the jingoistic exchanges between German academics and the Anglo-French during World War I concerning which of the warring parties had produced the superior culture, little if no use was made of Humboldt's name and reputation by the German side. Significant, too, is that during the Third Reich, Humboldt was no Nazi favourite, and appears to have been a difficult subject for fascism to use, one reason perhaps being that his philo-semitism was a matter of public record. Nevertheless, LINDEN did make an attempt to incorporate Humboldt in the conception of a Greater Europe of German National Socialism.

In stark contrast to its insignificant role in the ideological battles that accompanied the two world wars, Humboldt scholarship became a major instrument of German cultural politics in the post-1945 period. The name of Humboldt came to stand for what was, and had all along been, positive about Germany and its culture: neither militarism nor totalitarianism, but rather humanism, democracy, and cosmopolitan liberalism. Humboldt was put forward as "the good European", representing a Germany with which one could co-exist and co-operate.

Such use of Humboldt was made by DE TERRA, who was born and educated in Germany, but who later emigrated to the United States. The date of the preface to his book coincided with the 150th anniversary of Humboldt's arrival in Philadelphia, on his return home from his tour of the Americas in the years 1799–1804. De Terra's is a substantial, although traditional, biographical account, following the course of Humboldt's life via his early years in Germany, his exploration of the Americas, his Parisian years, his return to Berlin and the Asian journey, his time in Prussian state service, and the writing of *Kosmos*. Original detail was added where de Terra, in pursuing his own archaeological researches, had followed in Humboldt's footsteps in Central and South America, and in Asia. Novel, too, is his emphasis on the North American connection, with an entire chapter on Humboldt's visit to Jefferson, a concluding chapter on his popularity in Canada and the US, and de Terra's assertion that Humboldt's personal acquaintance with the young American Republic had made him a staunch believer in the future of democracy.

In Germany, new Humboldt biographies began to appear in the early 1950s, such as those by KRAMMER and BANSE, although most were traditional hagiographies, adding little new material. It is noteworthy, however, that these books showed the beginning of an intra-German polarisation in the post-war orientation of Humboldt scholarship. During the division of Germany between 1945 and 1990, both East and West claimed Humboldt for itself, portraying him in colours that matched those of their respective post-Nazi political banners. Krammer, for example, writing for the East, claimed Humboldt for Berlin, and described his significance using socialist rhetoric.

The East-West rift in Humboldt scholarship became clearly visible in 1959, when meetings were organized on both sides to commemorate the centenary of Humboldt's death. Two separate Humboldt committees were formed, each publishing its own commemorative volume, and both containing a range of specialised contributions, mainly on aspects of Humboldt's scientific activities. The East German volume, edited by ERTEL, was wrapped in various socialist watchwords, and attempted to identify Humboldt with the cause of international communism. SCHULTZE's West German volume, however, turned the Humboldt celebrations into an occasion for post-war reconciliation, with an emphasis on Humboldt's universality and cosmopolitanism; moreover, four North Americans and two South Americans were included in the group of 13 contributors.

In the single-author Humboldt biographies that appeared on the occasion of the 1959 centenary, a similar ideological East-West contrast could be observed. In East Germany, DANGEL's charming, but insubstantial, iconographic treatment of Humboldt's life portrayed her hero as a democrat, who had stood up for repressed peoples and for the common man. BECK, by contrast, who by now had become West Germany's leading Humboldt scholar, presented Humboldt as the good and, in some ways superior, German scientist, whose memory could help re-establish international contacts, especially with the enemies and victims of the Nazi period. Beck's elaborate, two-volume study finally replaced Bruhns's three-volume 19th-century biography as the most detailed, comprehensive and authoritative account of Humboldt's life and work.

During the 1959 commemoration, the East German volume attracted several West German contributions. By 1969, however, the East-West polarity had intensified, and cross-border co-operation was no longer possible. The volume edited by the DEUTSCHE AKADEMIE DER WISSENSCHAFTEN ZU BERLIN – an East German institution – claimed that the only legitimate heir to Humboldt's humanistic ideas was the "socialist humanism" of the DDR, and that West Germany, because of its persistence with a modernised form of Hitler's fascism, had no right to use Humboldt's name. The larger part of the volume was written by Kurt-R. Biermann, East Germany's answer to West Germany's Hanno Beck, and the entire volume was published in both German and Spanish. Humboldt was made an instrument of DDR foreign policy towards Latin America, and in the preface East Germany was portrayed as the state that interacted with Central and South America in a Humboldtian manner, unlike West Germany's pursuit of a neo-colonialist policy.

The Western commemoration of 1969 was less argumentative and defensive than its Eastern equivalent. PFEIFFER, general secretary of the Alexander von Humboldt-Stiftung, edited a collection of papers that examined in detail Humboldt's significance for the humanities and the sciences, and added a first chapter by Werner Heisenberg drawing on Humboldt's universality. The Humboldt interpretation of this volume differed little from the stance the West had adopted in 1959, Humboldt's reputation being used as a tool of international post-war reconciliation or, in the case of Beck – one of the contributors – of renewed German self-aggrandisement.

The political function served by Humboldt's name in the post-war period elicited the surmise that he was a homosexual, and as such, inappropriate and undesirable. MEYER-ABICH, for one, objected to the use of Humboldt's passionate letters to lieutenant Reinhard von Haeften as evidence of his sexual orientation.

German Humboldt studies of the post-war period have uncovered and made use of new source materials, and an ever-increasing variety of aspects of Humboldt's life and work has been examined. However, none of the leading Humboldt biographers has managed to rise beyond traditional Humboldt hagiography, with a political twist. BIERMANN, in a well-written and authoritative biography, reiterated East German claims that Humboldt belongs to the socialist cause. On the West German side, the collection of essays edited by HEIN elaborated on Humboldt's universality, with a range of splendidly illustrated essays on detailed aspects of Humboldt scientific work, including the physiological experiments of his early years.

It has been left to English-language publications to turn Humboldt scholarship away from conventional hagiography. Writing in the early 1960s, KELLNER still repeated much of the traditional accounts, which were her main source of information, but her book was published in connection with the International Geophysical Year, and laid emphasis on Humboldt's work in geomagnetism. CANNON, publishing in the late 1970s, formulated the fruitful concept of "Humboldtian science", by means of which Humboldt's contemporary influence could be defined, measured, and assessed. Less hagiographical yet, BOWEN knocks cracks in Humboldt's libertarian pedestal, arguing that *Kosmos* was not as universal in scope as traditionally asserted, and reflects a much diminished agenda, omitting his earlier interest in human geography. This impoverishment she attributes to Humboldt having succumbed to the pressures of reactionary politics in his Berlin environment. PRATT, focusing on Humboldt's American travel writing, is less interested in the objectivity of his scientific documentation, and more in the subjectivity and Eurocentricity of the image of Latin America that was created in Humboldt's travel accounts. These authors no longer see it as their primary task to tell the story of Humboldt's greatness, but offer instead a nuanced interpretation of his influence, his successes, and his failures.

NICOLAAS A. RUPKE

See also Expeditions

Hungary

Fischer, Holger and Ferenc Szabadváry (eds), *Technologietransfer und Wissenschaftsaustausch zwischen Ungarn und Deutschland: Aspekte der historischen Beziehungen in Naturwissenschaft und Technik*, Munich: Oldenburg, 1995

Héberger, Károly (ed.), *A Müegyetem története 1782–1967*, 8 vols, Budapest: Mimeo, 1979

Kovács, László (ed.), *Fejezetek a magyar fizika elmúlt 100 esztendejéböl*, Budapest: Eötvös Loránd Fizikai Társulat, 1992

Pach, Zsigmond Pál (ed.), *A Magyar Tudományos Akadémia másfél évszázada, 1825–1975*, Budapest: Akadémiai Kiadó, 1975

Palló, Gábor, *Radioaktívitás és a kémiai atomelmélet* [Radioactivity and the Atomic Theory], Budapest: Akadémiai Kiadó, 1992

Priszter, Szaniszló (ed.), *Az Eötvös Loránd Tudományegyetem Természettudományi Karának Története*, Budapest: Eötvös Loránd Tudományegyetem, 1991

Radnai, Gyula and Rezsö Kunfalvi, *Physics in Budapest: A Survey*, Amsterdam: North Holland, 1988

Sinkovics, István (ed.), *Az Eötvös Loránd Tudományegyetem története, 1635–1985*, Budapest: Eötvös Loránd Egyetem Tanacsa, 1985

Szabadváry, Ferenc and Zoltán Szökefalvi-Nagy, *A kémia története Magyarországon* [History of Chemistry in Hungary], Budapest: Akadémiai Kiadó, 1972

Szénássy, Barna, *History of Mathematics in Hungary until the 20th Century*, translated from the Hungarian by Judith Pokoly, text revised by János Bognár, Budapest: Akadémiai Kiadó, 1992 (original edition, 1970)

Zemplén, M. Jolán, *A magyarországi fizika története 1711-ig* [Physics in Hungary up to 1711], Budapest: Akadémiai Kiadó, 1961

Zemplén, M. Jolán, *A magyarországi fizika története a VIII.században: a fizika szaktudománnyá válik* [Physics in Hungary in the 18th Century: Physics becomes a Speciality in Science], Budapest: Akadémiai Kiadó, 1964

The history of Hungarian science began to develop in the 1960s. The main goal then as now was to collect information about the past of science in the country, which has resulted in a series of books of more descriptive than analytic character. Since the authors have come from various fields of the natural sciences, their books mostly focus on the scientific achievements of Hungarian scientists, and less on their social and cultural context. From the 1970s, collective volumes have been published on the most important scientific institutions, mainly universities and the Hungarian Academy of Sciences. Whatever the subject of these books, they aim to give information about the past instead of interpreting the history in any specific framework.

There is virtually no literature on the history of science in Hungary in Western European languages. RADNAI & KUNFALVI is one of the exceptions, providing a brief overview of Hungarian physics in English. With its 84 pages it resembles a Baedeker of the history of physics in Hungary from the 15th century up to the 1970s. Mention is made of the most important researchers, professors, science organizers and organizations, including their most significant results. The book is richly illustrated with interesting photographs. Apart from this book and Fischer & Szabadváry (which is in German, see below), the literature is in Hungarian.

ZEMPLÉN's book (1961) provides a brief overview of the Middle Ages, and paints a picture of 16th- and 17th-century physics in Hungary. The influences of Copernicus and Descartes are the main concern, but medicine, alchemy, technology, and astronomy are also included, as is the teaching in schools of various confessions. Even some early atomists and *philosophiae naturalis* are studied.

In her second volume ZEMPLÉN (1964) traced the influence of Copernicus up to that of Newton. Since physics was an activity performed primarily in schools, her most important sources are the textbooks that contain chapters on fields such as mechanics, optics, and thermodynamics. Higher technological education began in the 18th century, and its curriculum also included physics. Astronomy developed vigorously with the new observatories built in this period. Electricity emerged in physics textbooks through the description of phenomena such as lightning, static electricity, and Galvanism. Zemplén ends her book with an examination of the popular scientific literature in Hungarian that emerged at the end of the period, as opposed to the earlier Latin literature.

KOVÁCS, a 294-page volume on the last 100 years of physics in Hungary, concerns a number of topics: periods, emigration, and local history. There are chapters on the period at the turn of the century, focusing on Lorand Eötvös (by Gy. Radnai) on the interwar period, characterized by the reception of modern physics (L. Fustoss); and on the state socialist period (G. Palló). The emigration of physicists is discussed by two contributors (Gy. Marx and Zs. Makra). Finally, Kovács provides an account of physics in a number of cities such as Szeged, Debrecen, and Kolozsvar and on some high schools that educated outstanding physicists.

SZABADVÁRY & SZÖKEFALVI-NAGY, a 365-page history of Chemistry, begins with the Hungarian alchemists of the 15th and 16th centuries followed by the first mineral water analysts and the discussion on the phlogiston theory in Hungary. In the 18th century, chemical analysis gained ground and reached its peak with the discovery of tellurium. Lavoisier's influence in Hungary can be detected as early as around 1790. During the period between 1848 and 1918, chemistry departments were founded in universities, and associations and journals were established. Discussion of the scientific results of the period is organized by disciplinary branches: analysis, inorganic and organic chemistry, physical chemistry, agricultural chemistry, and chemical technology. The book ends with a short overview of research in the interwar period.

PALLÓ analyses turn-of-the-century Hungarian chemistry through the reception of the changing structural terms: atoms, molecules, chemical bond. The process is considered a Kuhnian revolution, which was received very quickly by Hungarian chemists but primarily in popular scientific works or university textbooks. Research followed a more traditional pattern, prevalently in chemical analysis. This state of affairs is explained by the social position of the chemist community at the time.

According to SZÉNÁSSY's book, the earliest signs of mathematical knowledge in Hungary can been found in 15th-century documents. But since some students attended the universities in Paris, Bologna, and Padua even in the 12th century, and since monastic schools were also established at that time, mathematical knowledge should have been present in Hungary and it is assumed that the relevant documents must have vanished. In the 17th and early 18th centuries, books on elementary arithmetic and geometry were published, while research in mathematics began in the 18th century. The science of mathematics reached a very high level in the early 19th-century works of Farkas and János Bolyai (father and son), when János Bolyai formed the first non-Euclidian geometry. The later success of mathematics began around the turn of the 20th century. Szenássy enumerates the results in 381 pages and gives biographical sketches in an appendix.

The history of the Hungarian Academy of Sciences runs in parallel with the history of the various branches of science. PACH, an edited volume of more than 500 pages, gives an institutional history from 1825 to 1975, including a study of the context of national science policy, which exerted an unusually strong influence on the Academy. All chapters contain sections on the history of ideas in the social sciences, the natural sciences, technology, and the agrarian sciences in Hungary. The sequence of chapters begins with 1825–31 and 1831–49, and then it follows the 11 political periods of the country, proving the central role of the Academy in Hungarian science, particularly after World War II, when the Soviet model prevailed and the Academy became the hub of a network of research institutes.

Sinkovics and Priszter both provide histories of Eötvös University. The former is a general history; the latter is a history only of the faculty of sciences. SINKOVICS describes how the most important Hungarian university was established in 1635 and eventually relocated to Budapest in 1784. Though the faculty of science was organized only in 1949, various disciplines of science were taught as early as the 17th and 18th centuries. Moreover, in 1782 the Institutum Geometrico-Hydrotechnicum was set up to train engineers. Sinkovics gives an institutional history in chronological order, including statistics and the most important professors, and the context of political history is also given. PRISZTER is organized by disci-

plines. It discusses the most important scientific results achieved not only within the faculty but also those of earlier times.

Since its establishment in 1782, the technical university has been an important site of the mathematical, physical, and chemical sciences. HÉBERGER, an 8-volume, 2,000-page history adheres to the conventional political periodization and enumerates the most important events from an institutional point of view. Within this structure, the chairs of the natural sciences are also described, including some famous professors and their scientific results. In the field of the natural sciences, the Technical University has always been a rival of Eötvös University and has sometimes been more open to modern ideas (for instance, in theoretical physics at the beginning of the 20th century, or in organic chemistry in the interwar period). The eighth volume contains important statistics and biographical sketches of the professors.

The volume edited by FISCHER & SZABADVÁRY provides a 357-page survey of a most decisive element in the history of science in Hungary: the relationship with the German scientific and technical community in the period from the 15th century until World War II. Von Stromer examines the dissemination of special metallurgical processes in the 15th century; Heckenast discusses the transfer of iron technology; Endrei describes the textile industry; and Paulinyi gives an overview of technology transfer in the late 19th century. Kaiser examines a special case of the relationship between the universities; and Vamos pursues the same topic but in more general terms. Included also are two overviews of scientific contacts: one for the 16th–18th centuries (Volker), in the 20th century (Palló), and analyzed in the field of geography in the interwar period (Fischer). In the editors' introduction the general features of this wide-ranging system of relations are studied in the political and historical context.

GÁBOR PALLÓ

Hunter, John 1728–1793

British surgeon and natural historian

Dobson, Jessie, *John Hunter*, Edinburgh: E. and S. Livingstone, 1969

Gloyne, Stephen Roodhouse, *John Hunter*, Edinburgh: E. and S. Livingstone, and Baltimore: Williams and Wilkins, 1950

Gross, S.D., *John Hunter and His Pupils*, Philadelphia: Blakiston, 1881

Holmes, T., *Introductory Address Delivered at St. George's Hospital, October 2, 1893, on the Centenary of John Hunter's Death*, London: Adlard, 1893

Kobler, John, *The Reluctant Surgeon: A Biography of John Hunter*, New York: Doubleday, and London: Heinemann, 1960

Noble, Iris, *Master Surgeon: John Hunter*, New York: Messner, 1971

Nuland, Sherwin B., "'Why the Leaves Changed Color in the Autumn': Surgery, Science, and John Hunter", in his *Doctors: The Biography of Medicine*, New York: Knopf, 1989

Oppenheimer, Jane M., *New Aspects of John and William Hunter*, New York: Shuman, 1946

Qvist, George, *John Hunter, 1728–1793*, London: Heinemann, 1981

Most biographies of John Hunter can be placed somewhere between the two extremes of the laudatory chronicle and the critical historical work. The laudatory chronicles, written by physicians for physicians, tend to date from an earlier period, although there are important exceptions.

Beginning in the 1830s, and occurring at more or less regular intervals since then, a Hunterian Oration, many on Hunter himself, is given at St George's Hospital, London. An example of this, leaning toward the laudatory, is the short work by HOLMES, a transcript of his speech to the surgeons of St George's toward the end of the 19th century. The intention of this work is to present Hunter as an inspiration to others, and, with this goal in mind, Holmes is very clear in describing Hunter's contribution to science and medicine. This work also has a very personal quality; Holmes was himself a surgeon at St George's Hospital, and he writes of Hunter with an almost familial affection. This is a short and fairly superficial account of Hunter's life, but the footnotes are extensive and add a great deal of depth.

Written slightly early than Holmes, GROSS also produced a very laudatory (and sometimes repetitive) work, in an attempt to promote Hunter's life and works as an example to American surgeons. Short on details, the brief work is as useful in informing the reader about surgery in Gross's time as it is in describing Hunter. For example, Gross discounts Hunter's vitalism, claiming that anyone of education "knows that life is a function of organic structure", not "something super-added". The last quarter of the book provides a nice description of some of Hunter's more illustrious pupils.

At the other extreme of Hunter scholarship is the critical biography. While the laudatory works are meant to inspire, the critical works aim to increase historical accuracy. A wonderful example of critical scholarship is QVIST. This is an outstanding short volume, making extensive and clear use of illuminating examples. One of the strengths of the book, and an example of carefully argued critical history, is the chapter on "Health". Qvist makes a compelling argument that Hunter's alleged self-inoculation with gonorrhea and syphilis originated in an "irresponsible misinterpretation" by D'Arcy Power in his Hunterian Oration in 1925; using examples of other medical experiments in Hunter's time, examining Hunter's writing style, and placing Hunter's use of human subjects within the context of late 18th-century experimental ethics, Qvist claims that Hunter inoculated another man and not himself. Qvist also challenges traditional scholarship on Hunter's development of his surgical procedure for popliteal aneurism. He did not, according to Qvist, deduce the procedure from his observation of collateral circulation in a stag, as the stag experiment never actually occurred. Among other interpretations challenged by Qvist is the traditional one that Hunter did not express himself well in writing.

The most comprehensive of the critical histories is DOBSON. This biography makes very extensive use of letters, often reprinting them in full. Dobson aims to dispel several myths about Hunter's life, including the one that his childhood was underprivileged; this myth was created, Dobson writes, in order to make his life into a glamorous tale from "gutter to palace". Dobson manages to bring historical accuracy to Hunter's life while remaining an admirer. This work is accessible to scholars; references are clearly laid out and a separate bibliography follows each chapter, with an additional, comprehensive bibliography at the end. For extensive detail and scholarly accessibility, this work is the most complete. KOBLER's biography is also very extensive; however, while his critical history is not "flawed by either idolatry or hatred", the lack of noted references makes it frustrating for the more serious scholar.

OPPENHEIMER's work is not a biography but is an important critical work. Its value lies in the attention it brings to the relationship between Hunter and his brother-in-law, Sir Everard Home, who burned many of Hunter's surviving manuscripts 30 years after Hunter's death. Home has been much maligned by historians; according to Oppenheimer, his name has become "a byword for apostasy, for ingratitude, for infidelity to himself, to his family and to science". Oppenheimer brings to light many overlooked details in Home's life, and partially raises him from ignominy. The second half of the book is devoted to John's older brother, William, and ascribes to him a great deal of the credit for John's surgical success. This, too, is contrary to more popular portrayals.

There are also recent works that are laudatory rather than critical. NULAND, in his very popular compilation of biographical sketches, devotes one chapter to Hunter. This is a very short work, but he aims to make Hunter's life memorable, and in so doing he tends toward sensationalism. Nuland does not incorporate any of the challenges to traditional Hunterian scholarship, and his lack of reference to Qvist's scholarship is disappointing, while references are not footnoted. As a brief, popular overview, however, this chapter is effective.

Two book-length works also written for general readers fall roughly in-between the laudatory and critical extremes. NOBLE's book is written in narrative style for a young-adult audience. The events of Hunter's life are highly embellished, but there are worthwhile insights among the padding. Noble is very successful in demonstrating that Hunter's quarrel with his brother, William, for example, was based on a complex set of reasons and not solely on their dispute over priority to discoveries in placental anatomy, as many other biographers suggest. This work is colorful, easy reading, and engaging. GLOYNE's work, written for an adult audience, is similar to Noble's, in that he recognizes Hunter's accomplishments without deifying him. Again, this work is not scholarly, references are not cited, and Gloyne does not attempt to challenge traditional scholarship. The book is full of details of Hunter's life, though sometimes presented in such a dense and dry manner that it is easy to lose sight of the larger picture. One of the most helpful aspects of this book is the great care taken concerning Hunter's publications, with even differences between editions being described.

JAY E. GLADSTEIN

See also Surgery

Hutton, James   1726–1797

British geologist and philosopher

Albritton Jr, Claude C., *The Abyss of Time: Changing Conceptions of the Earth's Antiquity after the Sixteenth Century*, San Francisco: Freeman Cooper, 1980

Chorley, Richard J., Anthony J. Dunn and Robert P. Beckinsale, *The History of the Study of Landforms, or the Development of Geomorphology*, vol. 1: *Geomorphology before Davis*, London: Methuen, and New York: Wiley, 1964

Craig, Gordon Y., D.B. McIntyre and C.D. Waterston, *James Hutton's Theory of the Earth: The Lost Drawings*, Edinburgh: Scottish Academic Press/Royal Society of Edinburgh, 1978

Dean, Dennis R., "The Age of the Earth Controversy: Beginnings to Hutton", *Annals of Science*, 38 (1981): 435–56

Dean, Dennis, R., "James Hutton's Place in the History of Geomorphology", in *History of Geomorphology: From Hutton to Hack*, edited by Keith J. Tinkler, Boston: Unwin Hyman, 1989, 73–84

Dean, Dennis R., *James Hutton and the History of Geology*, Ithaca, New York: Cornell University Press, 1992

Geikie, Archibald, *The Founders of Geology*, London and New York: Macmillan, 1897; 2nd edition, 1905; reprinted New York: Dover, 1962

Haber, Francis C., *The Age of the World: Moses to Darwin*, Baltimore: Johns Hopkins Press, 1959

Herries Davies, Gordon L., *The Earth in Decay: A History of British Geomorphology, 1578–1878*, London: Macdonald, and New York: Elsevier, 1969

James Hutton presented his famous geological theory in two forms: first as a long scientific paper (1785, 1788) and then as a lengthy book. Though highly controversial at the time, Hutton's *Theory of the Earth* (2 vols, Edinburgh, 1795; vol. 3, London, 1899) is now regarded by many historians as the modern beginning of two sciences, geology and geomorphology. Despite a number of striking passages, Hutton's book was in general poorly written and in consequence became known primarily at second hand, as summarized by his critics and supporters. Hutton's controversial ideas included a uniformitarian concept of geological forces; unlike those theorists who attributed the origin of landforms to causes no longer in operation, Hutton assumed that the forces working today are those that have always been in operation. Given the almost imperceptible slowness with which these forces work, Hutton's assumption perforce required an immense extension in the presumed age of the earth.

GEIKIE was the first major writer on the history of geology to emphasize Hutton's role as one of the founders of modern science. Another practising geologist, Geikie had an expert's understanding of the geological sites with which Hutton had been familiar. He was also a fine writer, and his book remains readable today. However, much of his evidence was derived from secondary sources, and has now been superseded.

Geikie was also responsible for the belated publication (from an incomplete manuscript) of the third volume of Hutton's *Theory*. Although an important source of information regarding Hutton's fieldwork in support of his theory, it remained little utilized until a remarkable series of illustrations, dating from Hutton's time and intended to accompany the theory, came to light (see CRAIG, McINTYRE & WATERSTON). In addition to the drawings, which were presented both as a bound volume and as an accompanying portfolio, Craig, McIntyre & Waterston were able to include other new and relevant facts. Stimulated by this attractive publication, historians produced a number of further Huttonian studies.

Among these is DEAN (1992), the first comprehensive treatment of Hutton as a geologist, which synthesizes all available biographical information, provides the most comprehensive bibliography of Hutton's own publications in all areas, summarizes each of his geological ones, and recounts each of the major responses to Hutton's theory by his friends and foes, ending with Geikie. The book also contains an extensive bibliography of Hutton scholarship, from the 18th century to the 1990s.

In parts one to three of CHORLEY, DUNN & BECKINSALE, Robert P. Beckinsale presented what is now a somewhat old-fashioned, but still influential, view of Hutton, his predecessors, and his successors from the standpoint of geomorphology, the study of landforms. Like his opinions, Beckinsale's methods (which are those of the work as whole) also strike one as rather out-of-date; relying heavily on apt but lengthy excerpts from generally well-known sources, the volume is as much an anthology as a study. Nevertheless, this characteristic remains useful to those who have only limited library resources at their disposal. Three volumes of this lengthy history have been published, with at least two more planned.

In another older book, HERRIES DAVIES, then writing as G.L. Davies, ably and often eloquently reviewed the history of geomorphology in Britain from 200 years before Hutton's time to 100 years after. As many of his examples are taken from lesser-known and often neglected sources, Davies is a very useful supplement to Chorley, Dunn & Beckinsale. The chief liability of his work is its exclusively British emphasis, for, in the second half of the 19th century, many of the most significant geomorphological theories were being proposed by Americans, such as Powell and Dana, who had been exposed to unprecedented sights like the Grand Canyon and Hawaii. Chorley, Dunn & Beckinsale's book includes these American developments. After thoughtful consideration of both these volumes, as well as other sources, Dennis R. Dean, in DEAN (1989) and DEAN (1992), came to regard the second volume of Hutton's *Theory of the Earth* (1795) as the effective founding of geomorphology.

Three authors have written about Hutton and the age of the earth. Though superseded in many respects by more recent and more specialized studies, HABER still provides a useful overview of the entire topic. ALBRITTON restricts his account to the period of modern science (as opposed to Biblical scholarship, included in the account by Archbishop Ussher), but although attractively written and illustrated, his chapter on Hutton contains errors. DEAN (1981) elaborates Haber's basic perspective with much new information, and is superior to both Albritton and Haber in its more detailed attention to Hutton, who believed that the Earth was vastly old but (publicly, at least) had no quarrel with the Biblically-derived assumption that mankind itself was no more than 6,000 years old. The antiquity of man was firmly established during the later 19th century by Charles Lyell's *The Geological Evidences of the Antiquity of Man* (1863), and by a series of further contributions by fellow geologists.

DENNIS R. DEAN

See also Age of the Earth; Geology

Huxley, Thomas 1825–1895

British biologist

Barton, Ruth, "'An Influential Set of Chaps': The X-Club and Royal Society Politics, 1864–85", *British Journal of the History of Science*, 23 (1990): 53–81

Bibby, Cyril, *T.H. Huxley: Scientist, Humanist and Educator*, London: Watts, 1959; New York: Horizon Press, 1960

Desmond, Adrian, *Thomas Huxley: The Devil's Disciple*, London: Michael Joseph, 1994

Di Gregorio, Mario A., *T.H. Huxley's Place in Natural Science*, New Haven, Connecticut: Yale University Press, 1984

Irvine, William, *Apes, Angels, and Victorians: The Story of Darwin, Huxley, and Evolution*, New York: McGraw-Hill, 1955; as *Apes, Angels, and Victorians: A Joint Biography of Darwin and Huxley*, London: Weidenfeld and Nicolson, 1956; as *Apes, Angels, and Victorians: Darwin, Huxley, and Evolution*, New York: Meridian Books, 1962

Lightman, Bernard, *The Origins of Agnosticism: Victorian Unbelief and the Limits of Knowledge*, Baltimore: Johns Hopkins University Press, 1987

Paradis, James G., *T.H. Huxley: Man's Place in Nature*, Lincoln: University of Nebraska Press, 1978

Richards, Evelleen, "Huxley and Women's Place in Science: The 'Woman Question' and the Control of Victorian Anthropology", in *History, Humanity and Evolution: Essays for John C. Greene*, edited by James R. Moore, Cambridge and New York: Cambridge University Press, 1989

Turner, Frank, *Contesting Cultural Authority: Essays in Victorian Intellectual Life*, Cambridge: Cambridge University Press, 1993

Winsor, Mary P., *Starfish, Jellyfish, and the Order of Life: Issues in Nineteenth-Century Science*, New Haven, Connecticut: Yale University Press, 1976

Best known for his public support of Darwin in the evolutionary debates of the 1860s and 1870s, and for his role as spokesmen for a new group of professional practitioners that came to dominate scientific institutions in the second half of the 19th century in Britain, Thomas Huxley is among the figures most widely referred to in the secondary literature on Victorian science. Assessments of his work have been quite various: he has been hailed as a leading promoter of meritocracy, a tireless opponent of clerical and aristocratic forms of authority, and a progressive representative of workers and women. He has also been portrayed as the architect of a new élitism of experts, the high-priest of a religion of science, and

an ideologue of middle-class patriarchy. Huxley scholarship is thus a fair indicator of the range of concerns that have occupied historians of Victorian science for several generations, and of historiographic debates that are still ongoing.

Among the earlier works, BIBBY is the most extensive account of Huxley's career as a popular lecturer and science teacher at South Kensington, and includes discussions of Huxley's activities on the London School Board, and on the governing bodies of Eton, Aberdeen, and the University of London. Very useful in matters of detail, Bibby reproduces the hagiographic style of Victorian biography, and reveres the liberal values that Huxley tried to mobilize against theologians, spiritualists, and anti-vivisectionists. A more playful, if still honorific, portrait is IRVINE, which dramatizes Huxley's personality and accomplishments through a running contrast with Darwin – the former portrayed as a "butterfly", whose poetic flights illuminate and overawe the Victorian public; the latter as a "crustacean", sedentary and fixed on a single idea.

A favorite reference point for historians of the natural sciences in the Victorian period, Darwin has been ubiquitous within studies of Huxley's zoology and paleontology. As part of a larger examination of the search for a natural order of marine invertebrates in the decades before the *Origin of Species*, WINSOR places Huxley's early work on polyps and acalephs firmly within an idealist tradition of science (here Quinarianism), and concludes that it was precisely this romantic devotion to a symmetrical, hierarchical system of affinities and analogies that prepared him to receive favorably the theory of natural selection. In a broad survey of Huxley's scientific memoirs, DI GREGORIO also places Huxley "in the footsteps of Darwin", although it was Haeckel who, according to the author, finally converted Huxley to natural selection in the late 1860s.

Since the 1970s, Huxley's wide-ranging career has been approached most often through the category of "professionalization". The essays collected in TURNER portray Huxley as a member of a rising scientific community, struggling against an older clerical caste for cultural hegemony. According to Turner, the naturalism that Huxley and others in his reforming circle espoused was part of an ideology designed to advance the authority of one professional group over another. This recasting of the history of ideas as social history has characterized the writing on Victorian science and religion of the past 20 years, much of which continues to place Huxley in a leading role. LIGHTMAN, for example, adopts Turner's thesis as background for a study featuring Huxley as the preacher of an agnostic catechism – a holy trinity of scientific (un)belief. Likewise, BARTON presents the intellectual labour of Huxley's "X-Club" – a small group of practitioners that began to meet regularly in London in the 1850s – as a strategic campaign to wrest control of the scientific world from clerical and theological dominion. In a more literary study, PARADIS makes Huxley the author of a secular scientific personae that came to the fore in the classroom, the public lecture hall, and the popular press of late Victorian Britain. But while Paradis also reserves a role for Huxley as a cultural critic of the scientific authority that he helped to construct, such reflexivity is not granted to Huxley in RICHARDS, which claims that his democratizing rhetoric and educational reforms were in fact totally in the service of the rigidly exclusive, male-dominated professions.

Renewed interest in Huxley may be excited by DESMOND, the first large-scale biography since the respectful *Life and Letters* composed by his son, Leonard, in 1900. As in his novelistic *Darwin* (co-written with James Moore), the subject of Desmond's work is heroic, the social context chiefly one of class-conflict, and the movement between individual agency and class determinism extremely rapid. Rich in family history and the crises of the young man in search of a career, the narrative dwells most on the fate of evolutionary theory. Framed by the drama of Chartists in the streets and a rising bourgeoisie, the plot casts Darwin and his work as instruments of Huxley's own ambitions (which were in turn those of the middle-class), and thus offers an alternative to the conventional view of Huxley as "Darwin's Bulldog".

PAUL WHITE

See also Darwin; Evolution; Hooker

Huygens, Christiaan   1629–1695

Dutch mathematician and physicist

Andriesse, C.D., *Titan kan niet slapen: Een biografie van Christiaan Huygens*, Amsterdam: Contact, 1993

Bell, Arthur E., *Christiaan Huygens and the Development of Science in the Seventeenth Century*, London: Arnold, 1947

Bos, Henk, *et al.* (eds), *Studies on Christiaan Huygens: Invited Papers from the Symposium on the Life and Work of Christiaan Huygens*, Lisse: Swets & Zeitlinger, 1980

Fournier, M., "Huygens' Designs for a Simple Microscope", *Annals of Science*, 46 (1989): 575–96

Hooykaas, Reijer, *Experientia ac ratione: Huygens tussen Descartes en Newton*, Leiden: Museum Boerhaave, 1979

Huygens, Christiaan, *Oeuvres complètes*, 22 vols, The Hague: Nijhoff, 1888–1950

Palm, Lodewijk (ed.), "Huygens" *Zeventiende eeuw* (special issue), 12/ (1996)

Shapiro, Alan, "Kinematic Optics: A Study of the Wave Theory of Light in the Seventeenth Century", *Archive for the History of Exact Sciences*, 11 (1973): 134–266

Taton, René, *et al.*, *Huygens et la France: Table ronde du Centre National de la Recherche Scientifique, Paris, 27–29 mars 1979*, Paris: Vrin, 1982

Van Helden, Albert, "Eustachio Divini Versus Christiaan Huygens: A Reapprraissal", *Physis*, 12 (1970): 36–50

Van Helden, Anne and R. Van Gent, *Een vernuftig geleerde: De technische vondsten van Christiaan Huygens*, Leiden: Museum Boerhaave, 1995

Westfall, Richard S., *Force in Newton's Physics: The Science of Dynamics in the Seventeenth Century*, London: Macdonald, and New York: Elsevier, 1971

Yoder, Joella G., *Unrolling Time: Christiaan Huygens and the Mathematization of Nature*, Cambridge and New York: Cambridge University Press, 1988

Yoder, Joella G., "Christiaan Huygens' Great Treasure", *Tractrix*, 3 (1991): 1–13

Unlike some other protagonists of the scientific revolution, Christiaan Huygens has not given rise to a strikingly large number of scholarly studies. One reason for this may be found in the transitional character of his science, standing as it did between Galileo and Descartes on the one hand and Newton and Leibniz on the other. Another reason might be the absence of cohesion between the various parts of Huygens's science. This is one of the main themes in the chapter on Huygens in WESTFALL, an excellent and unsurpassed study of Huygens's contributions to mechanics. Westfall carefully analyses Galilean and Cartesian influences, the tension between both approaches, and Huygens's kinematic treatment of mechanics. Westfall argues that Huygens did not pursue dynamics to the same extent as Newton because of his adherence to the mechanical philosophy of nature.

Another reason for the relative neglect of Huygens may, surprisingly, be his own writings. In a thorough and erudite manner, the 22 volumes of HUYGENS make all parts of his versatile science accessible, but the nature of the editorial comments may have discouraged prospective students of Huygens. Reservations have been made (for example, by Yoder) regarding the editors' handling and interpretation of Huygens's papers, although the *Oeuvres complètes* still enjoy a reputation for their accuracy and completeness.

In 1979, two conferences were held to commemorate the 350th anniversary of Huygens's birth, and both resulted in a collection of papers on Huygens's life and work. BOS *et al.*, the first of these collections, is the principal starting point for scholarship, as the versatility of Huygens's science is demonstrated in valuable papers on the various disciplines and areas to which he contributed. For instance, Bos discusses the development and character of Huygens's mathematics, Alan Gabbey his mechanics, and Henricus Adrianus Marie Snelders his theory of matter. Bos also contains a biographical sketch, which gives an excellent impression of Huygens's life.

Bos supersedes much previous historical work on Huygens, in particular BELL. Although still much read, this biography does not meet modern standards of historical scholarship, for, like the editors in their comments and annotations on the *Oeuvres complètes*, Bell treats Huygens's science out of historical context, and along modern scientific lines.

SHAPIRO is a searching study of Huygens's theory of light. Shapiro traces the development of 17th-century explanations of light in terms of waves and the difficulties this raised. *Traité de la lumière* is seen as the culmination of previous attempts by Hobbes, Hooke, and Pardies to understand the kinematics of wave propagation and to explain rectilinear propagation of light. Shapiro argues that the key to Huygens's success was his "ability to rise above mechanism and to treat the wave theory of light purely kinematically".

Bos also contains Albert Van Helden's overview of the content and nature of Huygens's astronomical work. Van Helden argues that Huygens was a brilliant thinker in astronomy, rather than a dedicated observer, and that this is illustrated by the genesis of the ring system, Huygens's explanation of the strange appearances of Saturn. Van Helden has also treated Huygens's astronomy in various other works. In VAN HELDEN, he analyses the dispute following the publication of *Systema Saturnium* (1659); this unequal match between an eminent scientist and a simple artisan, which was only superficially on observation and the quality of telescopes, was disastrous for Divini.

Huygens's versatility poses a problem for historians of science, as it is difficult to form a coherent picture of his scientific personality, and of his place within the scientific revolution. Part of the problem is that Huygens was not a philosopher, unlike many protagonists of the scientific revolution, and that he never provided an account of his scientific objectives. He appears rather as an eclectic, who pragmatically solved problems as they appeared using a variety of methods and practices.

TATON *et al.*, the second volume commemorating Huygens's 350th anniversary, partly overlaps with the content of Bos and partly extends the discussion. Huygens's relations with French scientists are extensively explored, for example in the papers of Taton, Belaval, and Picolet. In general Taton is a more fragmented collection than Bos, as most of the papers focus on particular topics from Huygens's *oeuvre*, rather than striving after synthetic questions and answers. For example, in Bos, Leopold treats Huygens's relationship with instrument makers in general, while in Taton he focuses on his invention of the spiral spring for watches.

HOOYKAAS also resulted from the commemorations of 1979, and is unique for its treatment of Huygens's religious attitude. As with metaphysical statements, religious statements are almost absent from Huygens's work, and Hooykaas attempts to interpret and explain the developments in Huygens's religious views, and the influences of his Calvinist upbringing and the Parisian circles.

YODER (1988) is without doubt the most important contribution to Huygens scholarship since the 1979 conferences, examining in detail the relationship between mathematics and physics in the *Horologium Oscillatorium* of 1673. Yoder elaborates the image of Huygens as an eclectic: he was usually spurred to action by a problem posed by another, pursued it systematically and thoroughly to its solution, and substantiated it by carefully prepared experiments. His consistent appeal to mathematics while investigating nature was crucial, and can be characterized as applying Archimedes's approach to Galileo's science of motion.

Yoder is currently preparing a catalogue of the manuscripts of Huygens, which will make the *Oeuvres complètes* more applicable to contemporary historical problems. In YODER (1991), she sketches some of the problems with the *Oeuvres complètes*, and the editors' influence on the current configuration of the manuscripts. Unfortunately, the editors have separated the manuscripts into categories determined by their historical and scientific outlook, without recording the original order.

FOURNIER treats an aspect of Huygens's science not covered in Bos and Taton: his contributions to microscopes and microscopical observing. This paper principally treats Huygens's designs for single microscopes during 1678, and describes Huygens's approach to the subject and its influence on the development of the microscope. It contains references to the work of Fournier on Huygens's microscopical observations.

The need for a state-of-the-art biography of Huygens is not wholly met by ANDRIESSE, but it is still a commendable attempt to clarify the genius of Huygens and explain his personality. Utilizing Freudian theory, Andriesse claims that Huygens escaped from life into science, and collapsed when his work was severely attacked. Irrespective of the value of this claim, Andriesse paints a vivid picture of Huygens's youth and maturity, and the development of his science.

VAN HELDEN & VAN GENT focus on Huygens's dealings with instruments; ranging from clocks and telescopes to carriages and wind gauges, they reveal the diversity of his contributions to the development of 17th-century instruments, and include an overview of the instrument makers with whom Huygens worked and the nature of their collaboration.

The 300th anniversary of Huygens's death in 1995 was commemorated with a conference on his life and work in Leiden. Most of the papers in English, French and Dutch have been published in PALM, which increase understanding of several aspects of Huygens's science, most notably his thoughts on dynamics, in papers by Mormino and Nauenberg, and his efforts to solve the problem of finding longitude at sea, in papers by Jonkers and by Schliesser and Smith. Van Helden, Yoder and Andriesse raise interesting views on several aspects of Huygens's science, and thus offering a greater understanding of his personality, and of his science in general.

FOKKO JAN DIJKSTERHUIS

See also Académie des Sciences; Astronomy: general works

Hysteria

King, Helen, "Once Upon a Text: Hysteria from Hippocrates", in *Hysteria Beyond Freud*, edited by Sander L. Gilman *et al.*, Berkeley: University of California Press, 1993

MacDonald, Michael, *Witchcraft and Hysteria in Elizabethan London: Edward Jorden and the Mary Glover Case*, London: Tavistock, and New York: Routledge, 1991

Micale, Mark S., *Approaching Hysteria: Disease and Its Representations*, Princeton, New Jersey: Princeton University Press, 1995

Showalter, Elaine, *The Female Malady: Women, Madness, and English Culture, 1830–1980*, New York: Pantheon Books, 1985; London: Virago, 1987

Veith, Ilza, *Hysteria: The History of a Disease*, Chicago: University of Chicago Press, 1965

Clinically, hysteria was always a mysterious disease, and thus it is unsurprising that it has been interpreted historically in radically different ways. In a widely-read work that has achieved the status of a minor classic, the American medical historian, Ilza Veith, approached hysteria as a real disease, whose nature was long misunderstood, but was finally discovered and explored by a succession of heroic, pioneering figures.

Although named by the Greeks, the existence of hysteria, VEITH contended, has been known to doctors, East and West, at least from 1800 BC. Medieval Christendom's gestalt-switch, treating psychosomatic symptoms as the stigmata of Satan, had entailed a gigantic regression. Fortunately, far-sighted Renaissance physicians, such as Johannes Weyer, recaptured hysteria from the theologians, regarding it as a disease not a sin.

Nevertheless, true understanding (and treatment) continued to be hamstrung by a fallacious medical materialism, which misconstrued hysteria as organic – standardly, an abnormality of the womb, or, in later centuries, of the nervous system and brain-stem. Veith particularly deplored the "increasingly sterile and repetitive neurological basis that had emanated from Great Britain for nearly two hundred years", sparked, above all, by George Cheyne's "nervous" theory, whose "affectation and absurdities are such that it scarcely merits elaborate discussion". Even the Scottish iatromechanist's "references to his own distress", Veith uncharitably grumbled, "seem inconsequential". Not least, she argued, somatic theories had been marred by misogyny; overall, such ideas were the obstacles that "so long stood in the way of [hysteria] being recognized as a psychical disorder".

Fortunately, according to Veith, a counter-interpretation had emerged, albeit by fits and starts. Brave spirits such as Paracelsus, Edward Jorden, Thomas Sydenham, Franz Anton Mesmer, Philippe Pinel, Ernst von Feuchtersleben, and Robert Carter began to develop "an amazing amount of anticipation" of the insight that hysteria was psychogenic, the monster child of emotional trauma aggravated by bourgeois sexual repression, especially in females. Veith concluded with the triumph of that insight in Freud, and the ensuing freedom from this libidinal straitjacket that led, she claimed, to the disorder's demise in the 20th century.

It says something for the vitality of medical history that, 25 years later, Veith's recension appears hopelessly outdated. For one thing, this is heroes-and-villains history, and Veith was particularly generous to those who "anticipated" Freud's psychosexual theory. Among these, the mid-Victorian London practitioner, Robert Carter, received her most fulsome praise, for having effected "a greater stride forward [than] all the advances made since the beginning of its history". This rosy interpretation of Carter grates, however, upon a modern generation primed upon anti-psychiatry and feminism. After all, it was precisely his judgment that hysteria was psychogenic that enabled Carter to indict hysterical women as not sick but swindlers, sunk in "moral obliquity", cynically exploiting the sick role in order to manipulate their families, and getting perverse sexual kicks out of the repeated vaginal examinations they were given. Carter, however, saw through their tricks and advocated their subjection to ordeal by psychiatric exposure. With Dora's case in mind, we might wryly agree with Veith that Carter did indeed "anticipate" Freud, but such a compliment would, of course, be backhanded, underlining that Freud could also be a misogynistic blamer of victims, and a therapeutic bully. Faced with the deviousness of hysterics, Freud confided to Fliess his sympathy for the "harsh therapy of the witches' judges".

Within the last decade, there has been an enormous surge of new and more sophisticated scholarship on hysteria. This is the result of many developments, including the revaluation of Freud, contemporary feminism, the current epidemic of anorexia nervosa and multiple personality disorder, and controversies within psychiatric classification. A full listing and evaluation of the new historiography is to be found in Micale, but a few key contributions may be discussed here.

The classical historian, KING, has radically undermined Veith's account, by denying, on the basis of impeccable textual scholarship, that the Greeks identified a disease essentially identical to the hysteria of later ages and known by that name. Greek physicians recognized disorders involving peculiarities of behaviour and bodily disturbances; they also appreciated that women frequently suffered from gynaecological complaints, stemming from the womb. But they did not build all these features into a disease called hysteria. That was the work of later medical men and scholars, who then transposed their new disease concept ("hysteria") on to the Greeks, so as to confer upon it a proper pedigree and gravity. King's contribution thus undermines the idea that hysteria is an objective disorder known throughout history, suggesting that it is rather a relatively recent diagnostic category.

MacDONALD has argued that it was in the early modern era that medical practitioners found this new disease concept helpful, primarily within the context of their need to come up with a medical alternative to attributions of witchcraft and possession, in the case of women exhibiting disturbing behaviour. Edward Jorden's *A Briefe Discourse of a Disease Called the Suffocation of the Mother* (1603), praised by Veith as pioneering, is identified by MacDonald as a key text in this disease-creating process. The Renaissance invention of hysteria was, in MacDonald's view, an expression of interprofessional rivalry between clergy and physicians, and an attempt to medicalize the control of unruly women.

This gender dimension is also central to Elaine SHOWALTER's reading of 19th- and early 20th-century hysteria. Her interpretation emphasizes how the Victorian epidemic of hysteria was the product of the growing cultural hegemony of medicine, which, within a broadly patriarchal society, was beginning to be threatened by movements for the emancipation of women. But she also casts doubt on the more extreme modern feminist analyses: on the one hand, those who view hysteria as the archetypal state of utterly repressed Victorian doll's-house wives and ladies, and on the other, those who, rejecting this kind of victimology, treat hysteria as an expression of political protest.

Developing Showalter's subtler readings, MICALE, in the most recent and comprehensive reassessment of hysteria, has emphasized the great fluidity and flexibility of the disease label as a resource in the negotiation of a variety of "sick roles". Like Showalter, Micale demonstrates that the hysteria diagnosis was not restricted to women. (It was, for instance, applied to shell-shock victims in World War I.) Not least, his careful reconstruction of the work of Charcot ("the Napoleon of the neuroses") remonstrates against crude demonizations of the doctors by historians who, with hindsight, "know better". Hysteria may have disappeared, but its historiography is advancing.

ROY PORTER

See also Charcot; Freud; Gynaecology; Madness

I

Ideology

Barnes, Barry, *Interests and the Growth of Knowledge*, London and Boston: Routledge and Kegan Paul, 1977

Berman, Morris, "'Hegemony' and the Amateur Tradition in British Science", *Journal of Social History*, 8 (1975): 30–50

Canguilhem, Georges, *Ideology and Rationality in the History of the Life Sciences*, translated from the French by Arthur Goldhammer, Cambridge, Massachusetts: MIT Press, 1988 (original edition, 1977)

Feyerabend, Paul, *Against Method: Outline of an Anarchistic Theory of Knowledge*, London: NLB, and Atlantic Highlands, New Jersey: Humanities Press, 1975; reprinted New York and London: Verso, 1993

Geertz, Clifford, "Ideology as a Cultural System", in his *The Interpretation of Cultures: Selected Essays*, New York: Basic Books, 1973; London: Fontana Press, 1993

Habermas, Jürgen, "Technology and Science as 'Ideology'", in his *Toward a Rational Society: Student Protest, Science, and Politics*, translated from the German by Jeremy J. Shapiro, Boston: Beacon Press, and London: Heinemann, 1970; reprinted Boston: Beacon Press, 1989

Hessen, B., "The Social and Economic Roots of Newton's 'Principia'", in *Science at the Cross Roads: Papers Presented to the International Congress of the History of Science and Technology*, London: Kniga, 1931; reprinted London: Frank Cass, 1971

Kennedy, Emmet, *A Philosophe in the Age of Revolution: Destutt De Tracy and the Origins of "Ideology"*, Philadelphia: American Philosophical Society, 1978

McLellan, David, *Ideology*, Milton Keynes, Buckinghamshire: Open University Press, and Minneapolis: University of Minnesota Press, 1986; 2nd edition, New York: Harcourt Brace, 1995

Mannheim, Karl, *Ideology and Utopia: An Introduction to the Sociology of Knowledge*, translated from the German by Louis Wirth and Edward Shils, London: Routledge and Kegan Paul, 1946; several reprints including San Diego: Harcourt Brace Jovanovich, 1985 (original edition, 1929)

Outram, Dorinda, "Science and Political Ideology, 1790–1848", in *Companion to the History of Modern Science*, edited by R.C. Olby *et al.*, London: Routledge, 1990

Rosen, George, "The Philosophy of Ideology and the Emergence of Modern Medicine in France", *Bulletin of the History of Medicine*, 20 (1946): 328–39

Vovelle, Michel, *Ideologies and Mentalities*, translated from the French by Eamon O'Flaherty, Cambridge: Polity Press, and Chicago: University of Chicago Press, 1990 (original edition, 1982)

Young, R.M., "Science *is* Social Relations", *Radical Science Journal*, 5 (1977): 65–129

Young, R.M. "Science, Ideology and Donna Haraway", *Science as Culture*, 3 (1992): 165–207

Although akin to nailing jelly to a wall, attempted explications of the protean term "ideology" have come both thick and fast throughout its relatively brief history. Any attempt to grapple with the multifarious meanings of ideology must, therefore, begin with McLELLAN's concise introduction to the subject. From its late 18th-century origins to the more recent declaration of its demise, McLellan charts the vagaries – Marxist, historist, structuralist, postmodernist – of ideology. He demonstrates how debates about ideology have been subsumed within struggles to define the nature of knowledge, truth and human society.

The early history of the term, as told by KENNEDY, explains much about the trajectory of its later meanings, and its intimate association with science. Antoine Destutt de Tracy coined the word *idéologie* in 1796 as a label for his "science of ideas". The culmination of Enlightenment faith in reason and progress, it was founded upon the sensationalist epistemology of the French *philosophes*, who associated with Abbé Etienne de Condillac. As ROSEN demonstrates, the *Idéologues'* influence contributed to a revolutionary paradigm shift in Western medicine – the rise of "Paris medicine", or the "clinical gaze". Between 1799 and 1804, however, Napoleon Bonaparte rendered ideology a pejorative term after his strident authoritarianism clashed with the republicanism of the *Idéologues*.

Focusing on the same period, OUTRAM places ideology within the historiography of science. Combating notions of science and ideology as single autonomous entities, she demonstrates the complexity of the relevant historiographical issues by focusing on the period 1790–1848. During this time, she argues, the Industrial and French revolutions effected new social and political groupings; for the first time, ideology became a fundamental part of a nascent non-consensual politics. And science became incorporated into resultant discussions about the nature of authority.

Inspired by the German historicist tradition, MANNHEIM presents the sociology of knowledge as the descendant of ideology. Referred to as "perspective", his is a total conception of ideology. Sensitive to the contextual nature of thought and to the role of the unconscious, Mannheim calls for the systematic analysis of knowledge within its historical and social settings. Believing that the natural sciences do not constitute such "situationally-bound thinking", he aspires to a sociology of knowledge modelled on their methods. Consequently, he proclaims a belief in "relational", rather than relative knowledge.

As a member of the Soviet delegation at the Second International Congress of the History of Science and Technology in London in 1931, HESSEN struck at the heart of the historiography of science with a Marxist analysis of Newton and the Scientific Revolution. In spite of explicit Marxist statements, he presented an at times nuanced, contextualist account of the religious and economic considerations that lay behind Newton's science. Most recently, sensitive readings of Hessen have become part of a revisionist rebuttal of the post-war Anglo-American idealists, who dismissed him as a Marxist zealot.

VOVELLE charts the manner in which adherents of the *Annales* school made the journey "from the cellar to the loft" – from a concern for social structures to a concern for collective attitudes and representations. As the *Annales* attempted to distance themselves from the crude socio-economic reductionism of vulgar Marxist historiography, they rejected studies of ideology, or "systematic thought", in favour of quantitatively-based studies of collective consciousness or sensibility over long periods of time. Promoting *mentalité* as a belief system or worldview, Vovelle, in effect, provides a new name and methodology for Mannheim's "total ideology", in reaction to the "perceived ideology" dominant in intellectualist historiography.

Alternatively, BERMAN espouses an organicist variant of ideology in reaction to the Marxist historiography of science of the 1930s, and seeks a theoretical framework for the social relations of science during the Industrial Revolution, which does not attempt a reductionist explanation of scientific theories in terms of the socio-economic needs of a nascent industrial society. In Antonio Gramsci's elaboration of the psychological or cultural dimension of class, he claims to discover a useful way forward. Using a simplistic definition of "hegemony" as "cultural supremacy", Berman then attempts to explain the persistence of the gentleman-amateur tradition in British science.

For the social and cultural anthropologist GEERTZ, an analysis of ideology necessarily entails grappling with Mannheim's Paradox – where does ideology end and science begin? The answer, he contends, lies in linguistics. "Interest" and "strain" theories have been inadequate because they have lacked an appreciation of the processes of symbolic formulation. The sociology of knowledge, he asserts, should be called the "sociology of meaning". Within Geertz's "intricate symbolic webs", science and ideology are distinct cultural systems. And, as the "critical dimension" of culture, science provides the necessary buffer and critique for ideology.

Clearly cognisant of common intellectual influences, the Edinburgh School espoused a similar conception of ideology as part of their new sociology of knowledge, or the "strong programme". Unlike Mannheim and R.K. Merton, they did not exclude mathematics and natural science from their examination. As BARNES proclaims, all knowledge is open to the same questioning. Nevertheless, his self-proclaimed goal of achieving a "naturalistic" understanding of knowledge signals his non-allegiance to relativism. Within his instrumental view of knowledge, ideology is the "covert interest" embodied in rationalization and persuasion, and science encompasses the "overt interest" of prediction, manipulation, and control. Admittedly, these interests are difficult to disentangle, and yesterday's ideology may become today's science. Consequently, knowledge must be located within its social and cultural contexts.

A representative of the post-1960 French history and philosophy of science, CANGUILHEM supports many of the same suppositions. A historian of the biological and medical sciences, he acknowledges a role for "scientific ideology" within his analysis of the history of changing concepts and models. Canguilhem asserts that ideology entails a mistaken belief that is close to the truth. As such, it plays an active role in the formation of scientific knowledge. Although different in its meanings and assumptions, ideology often precedes science. Thus, "the past of a present-day science is not the same thing as that science in the past."

The chief architect of an influential variant of "critical theory", HABERMAS provides a German philosophical and sociological critique of positivism and its pitfalls. Specifically, he identifies the search for a "science of society" as a dehumanizing endeavour, because it denies human free will and introspection in the name of deterministic laws. Although he rejects a correspondence theory of truth, he does not make the leap into a sea of relativism. Instead, he maintains a hold on a transcendent standard of knowledge or behaviour, by positing universal procedures of argumentation that are grounded in language. However, his critical gaze identifies a potentially invidious mixture of ideology and science. In the late 19th century, he argues, science and technology were united and yoked to state interventionism. The result has been the "scientization of politics", or a veiled ideology that has manifested itself in the rise of a technocratic consciousness.

Within Anglo-American scholarship, R.M. Young has been one of the most vocal proponents of a Marxist historiography of science that has highlighted the miscible nature of science and ideology. In his early contributions, YOUNG (1977) promoted "socialist science". This, he argues, comes with the realization that "science *is* social relations". Science, he proposes, should not be considered a value-neutral study of a reified nature. Rather, it is one manifestation of the social relations and conceptual framework shaped by ideology. More recently, YOUNG (1992) has declared that the ideology/science dichotomy is *passé* because positivistic notions of science are "utterly discredited". He asserts that the union of the history of ideas with cultural history has undermined the privileged epistemological status of science. Echoing Richard Rorty's postmodernism, Young contends that all that remains for historians of science is to tell "the best stories that we can".

A self-described proponent of intellectual anarchy, FEYERABEND argues that when a science purports to be the only correct method and to contain the only true theories, it has itself become ideology or second-rate myth. For Feyerabend, there is no fixed method or theory of rationality; the only certainty is that "anything goes". Truly to strive for objective knowledge, a plurality of opinions must be explored. The privileged status given to modern western science places a slavish acceptance on one method, when all should be considered.

JOHN F.M. CLARK

Immunology

Bibel, Debra Jan (ed.), *Milestones in Immunology: A Historical Exploration*, Madison, Wisconsin: Science Tech, 1989

Cambrosio, Alberto and Peter Keating, *Exquisite Specificity: The Monoclonal Antibody Revolution*, Oxford and New York: Oxford University Press, 1995

Charlesworth, Max, et al., *Life Among the Scientists: An Anthropological Study of an Australian Scientific Community*, Melbourne and New York: Oxford University Press, 1989

Corbellini, Gilberto, *L'evoluzione del pensiero immunologico*, Turin: Boringhieri, 1990

Daëron, Marc, et al., *L'Immunité, cent ans après Pasteur*, Paris: Nathan, 1996

Gallagher, Richard B., et al. (eds), *Immunology: The Making of a Modern Science*, San Diego, California: Academic Press, 1995

Goodfield, June, *An Imagined World: A Story of Scientific Discovery*, New York: Harper and Row, 1981

"Immunology as a Historical Object" (special issue), *Journal of the History of Biology*, 27 (1994): 375–594

Martin, Emily, *Flexible Bodies: Tracking Immunity in American Culture from the Days of Polio to the Age of AIDS*, Boston: Beacon Press, 1994

Mazumdar, Pauline M.H. (ed.), *Immunology, 1930–1980: Essays on the History of Immunology*, Toronto: Wall and Thompson, 1989

Mazumdar, Pauline M.H., *Species and Specificity: An Interpretation of the History of Immunology*, Cambridge and New York: Cambridge University Press, 1995

Moulin, Anne Marie, *Le Dernier Langage de la médecine: Histoire de l'immunologie de Pasteur au Sida*, Paris: Presses Universitaires de France, 1991

Silverstein, Arthur M., *A History of Immunology*, San Diego, California: Academic Press, 1989

Tauber, Alfred I., *Metchnikoff and the Origins of Immunology: From Metaphor to Theory*, New York: Oxford University Press, 1991

Tauber, Alfred I., *The Immune Self: Theory or Metaphor?*, Cambridge and New York: Cambridge University Press, 1994

The history of immunization is at least as ancient as the practice of inoculation against smallpox which, relayed by Jennerian vaccine, led to the eradication of the disease in 1980. However, the science of immunology is hardly more than a century old; the term "immunology" was generally adopted at the beginning of the 20th century, and first referred to the science of bodily resistance to diseases ascribed to the newly – discovered germs, a resistance originating in a network of cells and molecules the study of which still continues.

Novels and early literature concentrated on grand narratives of the main episodes of the medical fight against disease, the most famous being Paul de Kruif's *Microbe Hunters* (1926). Nevertheless, there was no comprehensive account published on what seemed an esoteric science before the 1980s, and the first books were mainly intellectual accounts. SILVERSTEIN and MOULIN provide general overviews. Mapping the main discoveries, they aim to identify the controversies and to position immunology within the context of the other biological sciences. But where Silverstein traces the history in terms of the most important conceptual threads, and composes each chapter as a self-contained account of one immunological problem, Moulin's history is more discursive, pivoting around the emergence of a new conception of physiological function, the "immune system" – a unique system of interacting cells and molecules reaching far beyond anti-infectious resistance. Silverstein, a professional immunologist turned historian, reviews the many experimental facets of immunity. By contrast, Moulin's work reflects her holistic philosophical concern; she opts for a rounded presentation of a general scientific discourse, which reappraises the traditional issues of the normal and the pathological, and the newer issues of the uniqueness of the individual.

Other authors present anthologies of the major texts, accompanied by a detailed introduction and commentaries on both the science and the scientists. BIBEL groups the "milestone papers" loosely into sections inspired by heterogeneous criteria (such as immunotherapy, immunochemistry, cells, and interactions). CORBELLINI's choice reflects his commitment to a more theoretical approach, studying the work of biological thinkers such as McFarlane Burnet. In the 1960s, Burnet introduced the "self" metaphor within immunology – the concept that the immune system learns to distinguish the body's own antigens from foreign antigens at an early stage of life – and fathered the theory of clonal selection. The description of immunology by Burnet as the "science of self and nonself" has certainly helped to popularize the field, even if its meaning has remained controversial.

MAZUMDAR (1995) is primarily a biography of the Austrian immunologist Karl Landsteiner, whose half a century of work on immunity touched on almost all the issues discussed by Silverstein and Moulin. Updating her pioneering thesis (1976) on Landsteiner, Mazumdar focuses on specificity, describing an ongoing debate between a discontinuist and a continuist view of immune phenomena. She analysed this debate as a dialogue between "unitarians" and "pluralists" pursued through different episodes over three generations, and concluding, after World War II, with the controversy over the number of genes (one or many?) involved in the Rhesus blood groups.

Other recent work tends to cover later developments and to clarify recent controversies. Both MAZUMDAR (1989) and GALLAGHER et al. offer reminiscences and reflections by immunologists who are still active in the discipline, and who have contributed innovative concepts or techniques. While forcibly impressionist, the two books offer first-hand material on two scientific generations. DAËRON et al. presents the latest trends of research in molecular immunology, questioning their link with the issues raised at the turn of the 20th century.

Accompanying developments, both conceptual and technological, in immunology and the explosion of research linked to the AIDS epidemic, some books address the subject from a very different viewpoint. Anthropologists have investigated the new scientific tribe and its vision of the world. In 1970, when immunological knowledge was still esoteric, GOODFIELD gave an ethnographical account of scientific activity, viewed through the daily life of an ordinary immunologist whose work had been briefly hailed as a landmark in therapeutics. CHARLESWORTH *et al.* investigate a famous Australian institution dedicated to immunology, revealing how immunological research shaped national politics and public health. MARTIN, an American anthropologist, relies on extensive interviews and popular literature in order to examine the spread of scientific knowledge on the immune system among the public. She reveals the way in which powerful metaphors of the fighting organism shaped the understanding of immunity, both for medical people and patients, and characterizes immunological thinking as a pattern of postmodern thought. In particular, Martin shows how people actively used the notion of the immune body to organize and comprehend their lives.

Again using ethnological methods, such as participant observation and interviews, in exploring the practices of "laboratory life", CAMBROSIO & KEATING have focused on an immensely successful innovation in terms of science and business: hybridoma, or the making of homogenous antibodies of a predetermined specificity, on a previously impossible scale. Their study of what they conceive as a practical cosmology was for them a way of exploring general questions raised by social studies of science: for example, the two-way interaction between science and technique, and the formation of new entities inspired by experimental systems and/or theories. Following Thomas Kuhn, they have challenged the currently-received ideas on the logical necessity of discovery and universal standardization, and have presented the dynamics of scientific innovation as a contingent process.

Burnet's definition of immunology in the 1960s as the science of "self and nonself", even though it does not reflect the present state of the discipline, has raised the question of metaphors and their inescapable role in science. TAUBER (1991 and 1994) first traced the genesis of the metaphor of self through Metchnikoff's zoological work, and details the genealogy of ideas on immune tolerance (versus rejection) in the organism. It can be predicted that forthcoming books will focus more on detailed analyses of theories and practices of experimental science, and of the immunological language, such as are found in a special issue of the *JOURNAL OF THE HISTORY OF BIOLOGY*. They will very likely also consider how immunology faces the challenge of disease and death, and the justifications for its disciplinary boundaries.

A.M. MOULIN

See also AIDS

India: general works

Baber, Zaheer, *The Science of Empire: Scientific Knowledge, Civilization, and Colonial Rule in India*, Albany: State University of New York Press, 1996

Bose, Devendra Mohan, Samarendra Nath Sen and B.V. Subbarayappa (eds), *A Concise History of Science in India*, New Delhi: Indian National Science Academy, 1971

Habib, S. Irfan and Dhruv Raina, "The Introduction of Scientific Rationality into India: A Study of Master Ramchandra – Urdu Journalist, Mathematician and Educationalist", *Annals of Science*, 46/6 (1989): 597–610

Kumar, Deepak, *Science and the Raj*, New Delhi, Oxford, and New York: Oxford University Press, 1995

Malamoud, Charles, "Hierarchie et technique", in *Histoire et linguistique: Actes de la table ronde*, edited by Pierre Achard, Max-Peter Gruenais, and Dolores Jaulin, Paris: Editions de la Maison des Sciences de l'Homme, 1983

Raj, Kapil, "La Construction de l'empire de la géographie: l'odysée des arpenteurs de Sa Très Gracieuse Majesté, la reine Victoria, en Asie centrale", *Les Annales*, 6 (1997)

Although India figures among the five largest scientific communities in the world – among the first 10 in terms of its publications – and that science and its history have played a crucial role in the emergence of a national identity in the country over the past century, there is surprisingly little serious work on the history of science in India. There are no departments of the history of science in any Indian university, but bookshops carry numerous far-fetched books and tracts proving that the Vedas expounded the principles of thermodynamics and relativity 3,000 years ago, and polemics about the "scientific temper" figure regularly in the leading national newspapers.

BOSE, SEN & SUBBARAYAPPA, despite its age – it was published almost 30 years ago – and its superficial treatment of the subject (615 pages plus a bibliography and an index covering 2500 years) remains the only general introduction to the subject. After a brief survey of written source materials, the book covers astronomy, mathematics, medicine, chemical practices, alchemy, agriculture, botany, zoology, and cosmology, and ends with the introduction of Western science to the Indian subcontinent in the 19th century. However, the authors say little about the relationship of this knowledge to that of contemporary Greece, China, and the Arab world, the whole question being relegated to a summary, four-page section entitled, "Interrelationship between Indian and Greek, Arabic and Chinese mathematics and the part played by Indian mathematics in European renaissance", which claims priority for India. Moreover, only 37 of its pages are given to the 1000 years of close Indo–Arab contact. Apart from ignoring the question of where and when exactly, in the vast subcontinent, the scientific practices described occurred and who, in a highly differentiated society, practised them, the book does not mention the peculiar nature of knowledge practices within largely oral traditions and the problem of suitable source materials with which to take this characteristic into account.

The nature of orality within the classical Indian context and its relationship to the written tradition (writing has co-existed with orality in India since at least the beginning of the 1st millennium BC) is clearly rendered by MALAMOUD. By articulating orality, socio–intellectual hierarchies, and scientific and technical knowledge within the context of Vedic Hinduism, he brings out the needs and specific nature of Hindu mathematics and linguistics.

Most of contemporary writing on the history of science is devoted to the introduction and practice of modern science from the 18th century onwards. The subjects treated range from the reception of Western science within the context of colonialism to its appropriation, institutionalisation and the indigenous response, both in the form of its practice by Indians and the part it played in the emergence of a nationalist ideology. KUMAR's book, based on a close examination of archival records, deals with the first generation of Indian scientists working in the Western tradition and their frustrations – including lack of both funding and international recognition. His almost total reliance on bureaucratic reports, and his treatment of these questions within the narrow framework of primary anti-colonialism, severely restrict the range of questions he raises.

In a 300-page book that straddles three millennia of Indian science, BABER level-headedly, if inevitably cursorily, examines the interplay between religious and cultural factors and the emergence of a characteristic scientific and technical practice prior to European colonisation, before going on to analyse the role of Western science and technology in the consolidation of the British empire in India. He shows how both the Indians and Britons were active in the introduction and establishment of scientific and technological institutions in the subcontinent, thereby calling into question the rather simplistic notion of a forcibly imposed intellectual tradition in a colonial context. However, Baber says little about the meaning of science in the constitution of a national identity, and even less about the widespread attempts to popularise it among the mass of the South Asian populace.

These questions are at the core of HABIB & RAINA's work. In this study of one of the major popularisers of modern science in mid-19th-century India, the authors attempt to understand the meaning of science for such intellectuals, and to locate the positivist bias of their politics within the context of British colonialism. They thus bring to the fore the appropriation and redefinition of modern science in a non-Western situation.

Finally, a quite different set of problems – the making of new and important knowledge through the interaction of indigenous and British cognitive and material practices in colonial India – has recently been examined. Posed within the context of colonial scientific and technological institutions, which of necessity employed both Europeans and Indians, these studies bring to light the hybrid nature of many knowledge practices of the colonial period, and throw into question simplistic ideas of knowledge diffusion and appropriation. Through an analysis of terrestrial surveying, especially the Indo–British mapping of central Asia and Tibet in the 19th century, RAJ, for example, seeks to show how Victorian geography and the British empire were co-produced within the same act.

KAPIL RAJ

India: medicine

Bala, Poonam, *Imperialism and Medicine in Bengal: A Socio-Historical Perspective*, London and Newbury Park, California: Sage, 1991

Jeffery, Roger, *The Politics of Health in India*, Berkeley: University of California Press, 1988

Leslie, Charles (ed.), *Asian Medical Systems: A Comparative Study*, Berkeley: University of California Press, 1976

Leslie, Charles and Allan Young (eds), *Paths to Asian Medical Knowledge*, Berkeley: University of California Press, 1992

Mazars, Guy, *La Médecine indienne*, Paris: Presses Universitaires de France, 1995

Van Alphen, Jan and Anthony Aris (eds), *Oriental Medicine: An Illustrated Guide to the Asian Arts of Healing*, London: Serindia, 1995; Boston: Shambala, 1996

Wujastyk, Dominik, *The Roots of Ayurveda: Selections from Sanskrit Medical Writings*, New Delhi: Penguin, 1998

Zimmermann, Francis, *The Jungle and the Aroma of Meats: An Ecological Theme in Hindu Medicine*, Berkeley: University of California Press, 1987

To subsume the healing practices of the Indian subcontinent under any one name is inevitably to oversimplify the complex and inter-related medical systems of that region. The major traditions of South Asian medicine – Ayurveda, Unani Tibb, and Siddha (or Cittar) medicine – have co-existed and interacted for centuries. Moreover, all have affected and been modified by that imperial immigrant, Western medicine. It is also important to note that descriptions of Indian medicine are too often tainted by one of three characteristic ideological stances: orientalist pseudo-mysticism, nationalist mythologizing, and Western bowdlerization. Finally, the Western reader will soon become aware that all European-language treatments of South Asian medicine are susceptible to errors and biases introduced in translation. This caveat aside, WUJASTYK has produced elegantly clear translations from a range of Sanskrit medical texts. The selections are well chosen and represent important periods and themes in the history of Ayurveda, while the introduction usefully contextualizes the original texts.

For general information about the nature and theoretical underpinnings of the three regional medical systems of the Indian sub-continent, a modern and lucid source is MAZARS. Possibly the most valuable and unique feature of this slender text is its rich bibliographical annotation; each feature of Indian medicine discussed in the text is accompanied by footnotes listing alternative analyses and sources of further information. After a brief, rich, and theoretically neutral discussion of the history of medicine in India from the Vedas to the present, Mazars then turns to the task of explaining the theory and practice, in particular of Ayurveda. He concludes with short chapters on the historical emergence of the medical profession in India, and the relationship between modern science and Ayurvedic medicine.

Taken as a group, the four essays on India contained in VAN ALPHEN & ARIS indicate the medical diversity of the subcontinent in uncontentious and fairly clear language. The first sketches out a historical overview of these systems and their interactions with each other, with Siddha, and with Western medicine. This is followed by three articles describing the historical and contemporary practices of Ayurveda and Unani Tibb, India's two major therapeutic modes. Although these articles are necessarily brief, they benefit from their place within a collection of similar essays on other Asian medical systems, and from the volume's vivid and lush illustrations.

The two collections edited by Charles Leslie also consider the medical practices of India within a comparative context. LESLIE is now somewhat dated: the initial essay, describing the history of Indian medicine, for example, leans heavily and uncritically on Western anatomy in critiquing its Ayurvedic counterpart, and case studies in later essays are similarly flawed. However, the nine essays devoted to South Asian medicine demonstrate the use of historical, anthropological, and sociological techniques to address the regional (as opposed to "cosmopolitan" or Western) medical systems. Most authors focus either on uncovering contemporary interactions between Western and indigenous systems, or on the relationship between the broader culture and its medical practices. However, LESLIE & YOUNG remedy the tendency to judge Indian medicine by Western standards, and includes substantially more material relating to issues of gender. These volumes are useful in terms both of the information they present, and of the range and variety of approaches to the practice of medicine in India that they employ.

JEFFERY follows a slightly different exploratory path. His study is intended to bridge the divide between uncritically descriptive accounts of health provision in India, and aggressively dismissive (and often economically deterministic) critiques of the health services as imperialist institutions. He examines the making and changing of health policy over time, seeking to assess the sources and significance of changes in the Indian health care system, from the age of empire to the present. The work is divided into two major parts: first, a discussion of the impact of British rule on health and the style of health care in India up to Independence; and second, a detailed analysis of post-Independence health policy. The latter part is the more innovative, but both are full of new material and offer a useful perspective on the questions raised by Leslie *et al*.

Jeffery's student, BALA, continues his politically-aware approach in her history of imperialism and medicine in Bengal. This is not a "balanced" survey; rather, Bala presents a committed critique of historical and contemporary (Anglo-European) responses to indigenous Bengali medical practices. Thus, Bala considers "the impact of British rule" in terms of its role as "the last of a series of major challenges facing Indian medicine". None the less, she presents a valuable analysis of the roles played by the imperial state, caste, professionalization, and the explanatory power of science, in the spread of Western medical practices in Bengal, and of nationalism (and caste, again) as a force behind the re-evaluation and reintroduction of indigenous medicine.

ZIMMERMANN moves away from this concern with the politics of interactions between western and indigenous medicine. Instead, he investigates a far more ancient, and still continuing set of interactions: the communication between human society and its environment. He uses Ayurvedic medicine – and in particular the central role of diet and food in Ayurvedic theory – as a lens through which to examine this relationship. Simultaneously, he studies the physical environment from which Aurvedic practitioners drew their evidence and in which they formed their theories for clues about the origins and significance of Ayurveda's different categories – the way in which "biogeography was absorbed into theraputics". This is an intriguing, if often frustrating and sometimes self-referential text; it illustrates a new way to use studies of medicine and studies of the environment.

ROBERTA E. BIVINS

See also India: general works; Indigenous Knowledge Systems

Indigenous Knowledge Systems

Appiah, Kwome Anthony, *In My Father's House: Africa in the Philosophy of Culture*, London: Methuen, and New York: Oxford University Press, 1992

Berlin, Brent, *Ethnobiological Classification: Principles of Categorization of Plants and Animals in Traditional Societies*, Princeton, New Jersey: Princeton University Press, 1992

For the Learning of Mathematics, (special issue) 14/2 (1994)

Freeman, Milton M.R. and Ludwig N. Carbyn (eds), *Traditional Knowledge and Renewable Resource Management in Northern Regions*, Edmonton, Alberta: Boreal Institute for North American Studies, 1988

Hamill, James F., *Ethno-Logic: The Anthropology of Human Reasoning*, Urbana: University of Illinois Press, 1990

Hountondji, Paulin J., *African Philosophy: Myth and Reality*, translated from the French by Henri Evans and Jonathan Rée, Bloomington: Indiana University Press, and London: Hutchinson, 1983 (original edition, 1977)

Hyndman, D., "Conservation Through Self-Determination: Promoting the Interdependence of Cultural and Biological Diversity", *Human Organization*, 53/3 (1994): 296–302

IWGIA, *Indigenous Self-Development in the Americas: (Conference proceedings)*, Copenhagen: International work Group for Indigenous Affairs, 1989

Juma, Calestous, *The Gene Hunters: Biotechnology and the Scramble for Seeds*, Princeton, New Jersey: Princeton University Press, 1989

Mudimbe, V.Y., *The Invention of Africa: Gnosis, Philosophy, and the Order of Knowledge*, Bloomington: Indiana University Press, and London: Currey, 1988

Peek, Philip M. (ed.), *African Divination Systems: Ways of Knowing*, Bloomington: Indiana University Press, 1991

Rodwin, Lloyd (ed.), *Shelter, Settlement and Development*, Boston: Allen and Unwin, 1987

Sanford, G.A., *A Capacity for Agricultural Change: Indigenous Technical Knowledge and the New York State Agricultural Society in the Transformation of US Agriculture, 1830–1862*, Ames: Iowa State University Research Foundation, 1988

Slikkerveer, L. Jan, P. Nkwi, V. Kimani and D.M. Warren (eds), *Ethnomedical Systems in Sub-Saharan Africa*, Leiden: African Studies Centre, 1991

Wiredu, J.E., "How Not to Compare African Thought with Western Thought", in *African Philosophy: An Introduction*, edited by Richard A. Wright, Lanham, Maryland: University Press of America, 1979

Zaslavsky, Claudia, *Africa Counts: Number and Pattern in African Culture*, Boston: Prindle Weber and Schmidt, 1973

Indigenous knowledge systems are currently of interest for their straightforward epistemological opposition to primitivism, as well as for their potential application to education and development. However, as JUMA argues, the historical origins of this discipline are to be found in colonial exploitation. The term "indigenous" is itself highly contentious; while the survival of traditional non-state societies is threatened by modernization, it is nevertheless through the discursive constructions of "the authentic native" that colonial and neo-colonial political economies have created this threat. Defining the terms is defining the field. Thus we might wish to exclude SANFORD's "indigenous technical knowledge", since it refers almost exclusively to white farmers in New York State, while arguing that a vernacular knowledge, such as Latin American peasant architecture – the topic of RODWIN – should be included, even though it is an utterly "inauthentic" mixture of indigenous, colonial, and modern traditions.

An excellent history of the theoretical debates within the African context can be found in APPIAH, who begins with ethnophilosophy. His analysis weaves between the positions of WIREDU, who critiques the focus on a comparison with Western science rather than religion (noting that it leaves the superstitions and folk philosophies of the West unexamined), and HOUNTONDJI, who argues against any mimetic comparison, suggesting that ethnophilosophy and its allies are dressing European motivations in autochthonous garb. As in MUDIMBE's Foucauldian discourse analysis, Appiah's dialectical contour maps African epistemology as a historical process, rather than as an object of strictly pre- or post-Western presence. His strongest statement is focused on Evans-Pritchard's classic Azande study, showing that the supposed self-limiting system of explanation for failures in Azande magic are quite similar to the theory-laden observations and resistance to new paradigms described in the sociology of Western science.

A similar rejection of the "closed world" portrait underlies the review of studies on African divination in PEEK, who notes that Evans-Pritchard himself was interested in the possibilities for a more reflexive comparison of knowledge systems. Theoretical analysis within the Native American context can be found in IWGIA. A more abstract, Chomskian approach is reviewed in HAMILL's outline towards an anthropology of logic, which also focuses on Native American societies.

The most successful outcomes in research and application of indigenous knowledge systems have been in ethnobotany, traditional medicine, ethnomathematics, and natural resource management. A good history of ethnobotany can be found in the introduction to BERLIN, although in his critique of cultural relativism he tends to downplay the role of intentionality. Stronger support for conscious invention – and hence syncretic applications – is provided in the traditional medicine literature; see SLIKKERVEER *et al.* for a review of this work in Sub-Saharan Africa. The history of ethnomathematics in several different areas of the world can be found in the special issue of *FOR THE LEARNING OF MATHEMATICS*. The most important monograph on African ethnomathematics is ZASLAVSKY, the introduction of which also gives a good history. Applications in natural resource management for North America are reviewed in FREEMAN & CARBYN. HYNDMAN, focusing more on tropical resource management, offers an incisive analysis of the various strategies linking traditional knowledge systems with the political economy of indigenous self-determination.

RON EGLASH

See also Africa: south of the Sahara; Africa: health and healing; China: general works; China: medicine; India: general works; India: medicine

Industrial Chemistry

Aftalion, Fred, *A History of the International Chemical Industry*, translated by Otto Theodor Benfey, Philadelphia: University of Pennsylvania Press, 1991

Campbell, W.A., *The Chemical Industry*, London: Longman, 1971

Campbell, W.A., "Industrial Chemistry", in *Recent Developments in the History of Chemistry*, edited by C.A. Russell, London: Royal Society of Chemistry, 1985

Clow, Archibald and Nan L. Clow, *The Chemical Revolution*, London: Batchworth Press, 1952

Forbes, R.J., "Chemical, Culinary and Cosmetic Arts", in *A History of Technology*, vol. 7, *From Early Times to the Fall of Ancient Empires*, edited by Charles Singer, E.J. Holmyard and A.R. Hall, Oxford: Oxford University Press, 1954 (chapter 11 and chapters in subsequent volumes)

Haber, L.F., *The Chemical Industry During the Nineteenth Century: A Study of the Economic Aspects of Applied Chemistry in Europe and North America*, Oxford: Clarendon Press, 1958; corrected edition, 1969

Haber, L.F., *The Chemical Industry, 1900–1930: International Growth and Technological Change*, Oxford: Clarendon Press, 1971

Hardie, D.W.F. and J. Davidson Pratt, *A History of the Modern British Chemical Industry*, Oxford: Pergamon Press, 1966

Ihde, Aaron J., *The Development of Modern Chemistry*, New York: Harper and Row, 1964

Morris, P.J.T. and Colin A. Russell, *Archives of the British Chemical Industry 1750–1914: A Handlist*, London: British Society for the History of Science, 1988

Morris, Peter J.T., W.A. Campbell and H.L. Roberts, *Milestones in 150 Years of the Chemical Industry*, London: Royal Society of Chemistry, 1991

Reader, W.J., *Imperial Chemical Industries: A History*, 2 vols, London: Oxford University Press, 1970–75

Smith, John Graham, *The Origins and Early Development of the Heavy Chemical Industry in France*, Oxford: Clarendon Press, and New York: Oxford University Press, 1979

Spitz, Peter H., *Petrochemicals: The Rise of an Industry*, New York: John Wiley, 1988

Travis, Anthony S., *The Rainbow Makers: The Origins of the Synthetic Dyestuffs Industry in Western Europe*, Bethlehem, Pennsylvania: Lehigh University Press, and London: Associated University Presses, 1993

Trescott, Martha Moore, *The Rise of the American Electrochemicals Industry, 1880–1910: Studies in the American Technological Environment*, Westport, Connecticut: Greenwood Press, 1981

Warren, Kenneth, *Chemical Foundations: The Alkali Industry in Britain to 1926*, Oxford: Clarendon Press, and New York: Oxford University Press, 1980

Both early and recent histories of industrial chemistry are shrouded in mystery: its beginnings are unrecorded and obscure, because the earliest chemical industries (soap, glass, brewing, and distilling) left no records, and their discoverers and pioneers are unknown; and today's history of the modern chemical industry is protected by patent and corporate secrecy, so that the details emerge only years later. The early years are covered by FORBES in, chapter 11 of the first volume *A History of Technology*, while subsequent volumes in this series cover aspects of the chemical industry in different periods and provide a useful starting point. The chemical industry is a very broad topic covering several centuries, many countries, and a wide variety of important products, pioneering industrialists, and major companies. It is convenient, therefore, to consider the topic in this review under two broad headings: general surveys; and specific topics, periods, or products, including company histories and biographies of industrial chemists. There is a wealth of material available, and this entry does not claim to be exhaustive, particularly when it comes to dealing with individual companies or entrepreneurs.

Industrial chemistry is not well served by general histories of chemistry, in which it is usually an incidental rather than a major theme. IHDE gives industrial developments substantial coverage in several chapters, but the strongest feature is its detailed bibliography. Early single-volume histories of industrial chemistry are now outdated but still provide useful introductions. HARDIE & PRATT is particularly useful for its snapshot of the British chemical industry, while CLOW & CLOW is one of the most readable and detailed thematic surveys of the early chemical industry in the British Isles, with particular reference to Scotland and the period 1750–1830. The international chemical industry is covered by AFTALION, the most recent and broad coverage of the growth of the chemical industry worldwide. CAMPBELL (1985) gives a useful overview of the chemical industry, expanded in MORRIS, CAMPBELL & ROBERTS, which looks at the development of specific industries over the past 150 years, including a number not usually covered in such histories.

The growth of industrial archaeology as a discipline has left the chemical industry largely untouched. CAMPBELL (1971) surveys the industry as part of a series on industrial archaeology, but his work is an illustrated survey of the history of industrial chemistry, considered product by product, without any real reference to industrial archaeology as such. Within the relatively new discipline of industrial archaeology, the archaeology of the chemical industry is a neglected area.

Scotland, the north of England, and France were pioneer areas in the large-scale production of chemicals. Clow & Clow look particularly at the early importance of Scotland, while SMITH examines the development of the heavy chemical industry in France. HABER (1958) and HABER (1971) give a detailed picture of the growth of the chemical industry, with particular attention to economic factors, during the 19th century and from 1900 to 1930 respectively. Haber also pays attention to the international dimensions of the industry, since the focus shifted from England to Germany and then to the US as leaders in the production of industrial chemicals.

The story of the chemical industry is a complex one, given the range of products and the many different processes which have evolved for individual products. The industry underpinned the industrial revolution in many areas, particularly the textile industry, and yet its role is usually underplayed in books on the Industrial Revolution. The change in the industry from small-scale production to large-scale industrial enterprise is one of the major success stories of the 19th century. Moreover, the response of the industry to the demands for larger quantities of established and new products enabled many other industries to develop and grow during the 19th and 20th centuries. Just as Liebig once said that the production of sulphuric acid was the best measure of a country's economic prosperity, so the health of the chemical industry in general, or the availability of its products, was often the essential, though usually hidden, backbone of industry in the newly-industrialized countries. This is still true today, although the specific products have changed in importance. Nevertheless, sulphuric acid is still the chemical produced in the largest quantity in modern economies, so Liebig's dictum still holds.

Specific industries and products have been covered in various studies – for example, the alkali industry (WARREN), petrochemicals (SPITZ), and dyestuffs (TRAVIS). Petrochemicals, in particular, are at the heart of the modern chemical industry, and Spitz traces the growth of industrial organic chemicals, from dependence on coal as a raw material, a resource dominated by the German chemical industry in the late 19th century, and the shift of power to the US with the rise of the oil industry. It is encouraging to see the increasing number of detailed studies focusing on specific industries or products. Each of the products mentioned above is sufficiently important to warrant its own story, and cannot be adequately treated in single-volume histories.

The list above is not exhaustive and pays no attention to important sectors of the chemical industry, such as the gas industry, fertiliser industry, and metallurgical industries. TRESCOTT recounts the rise of industrial electrochemistry, dominated in the early years by the US with its wealth of hydroelectricity, and charts the growth in importance of aluminium.

Supplementing the coverage of particular periods and products are the company histories, which give a detailed look at the growth and development of important players in the world chemical industry. Several detailed company histories are now available, but just one will be cited here as an example, the study of ICI by READER. MORRIS & RUSSELL gives an invaluable guide to the manuscript sources on important chemical firms in Britain.

Another important source of information on the history of industrial chemistry are biographies or autobiographies of important chemical industrialists, e.g. Nobel, Du Pont, Tennant, Muspratt, and Albright. The early history of industrial chemistry was dominated by such entrepreneurs, while the 20th century has been dominated by large companies produced by mergers within one country (such as ICI) or multinationals (such as Unilever). There is no space in this review to list the many biographies available, but this is not to diminish their importance, because they are a valuable supplement to the more general works.

PETER E. CHILDS

See also Chemistry; Dyestuffs

Information

Bar-Hillel, Yehoshua, *Language and Information: Selected Essays on Their Theory and Application*, Reading, Massachusetts: Addison-Wesley, 1964

Beniger, James R., *The Control Revolution: Technological and Economic Origins of the Information Society*, Cambridge, Massachusetts: Harvard University Press, 1986

Buckley, Walter (ed.), *Modern Systems Research for the Behavioral Scientist: A Sourcebook*, Chicago: Aldine, 1968

Castells, Manuel, *The Informational City: Information, Technology, Economic Restructuring and the Urban-Regional Process*, Oxford and Cambridge, Massachusetts: Blackwell, 1989

Dretske, Fred, *Knowledge and the Flow of Information*, Cambridge, Massachusetts: MIT Press, 1981

Krippendorff, Klaus (ed.), *Communication and Control in Society*, London: Gordon and Breach, 1979

Lamberton, D.M. (ed.), *Economics of Information and Knowledge: Selected Readings*, Harmondsworth: Penguin, 1971

Machlup, Fritz, *Knowledge: Its Creation, Distribution and Economic Significance*, vol. 1, Princeton, New Jersey: Princeton University Press, 1980

Mosco, Vincent and Janet Wasko (eds), *The Political Economy of Information*, Madison: University of Wisconsin Press, 1988

Poster, Mark, *The Mode of Information: Poststructuralism and Social Context*, Cambridge: Polity Press/Blackwell, and Chicago: University of Chicago Press, 1990

Rogers, Everett M., *A History of Communication Study: A Biographical Approach*, New York: Free Press, 1994

Shannon, Claude E. and Warren Weaver, *The Mathematical Theory of Communication*, Urbana: University of Illinois Press, 1949

Webster, Frank, *Theories of the Information Society*, London and New York: Routledge, 1995

Wiener, Norbert, *Cybernetics: Or Control and Communication in the Animal and the Machine*, Cambridge, Massachusetts: Technology Press, 1948; 2nd edition, Cambridge, Massachusetts: MIT Press, 1961

Along with Norbert Wiener's *Cybernetics*, Shannon & Weaver's *Mathematical Theory of Communication* is generally regarded as the pioneering text of the late 1940s, as this work was highly influential in the development of an important new sub-discipline that overlapped both the natural sciences and engineering: information science. A separate line of inquiry into the economic role of information has since led to claims that the advanced industrial countries have become "information societies", "knowledge economies", and so forth, while for some theorists this transformation is due to a widespread scientification of society. This line of research, which began in the 1960s, includes different approaches from economics and social theory; economic studies tend to classify and measure the information sector in the economy today, while social theory research is rooted in the history of industrialization and social change.

SHANNON & WEAVER exemplify the "bits" view of information – namely, that all units of information are equivalent and that their content or meaning is irrelevant to their analysis. In contrast with common sense usage, measures of the amount of information at a specific point are measures of uncertainty. This is because Shannon (like his predecessor, R.V.L. Hartley) was addressing a specific problem of electrical engineering – the transmission of a message from one point and its faithful reproduction at another, as in radio broadcasts, for example.

Both Buckley and Krippendorff provide summaries of the idea of cybernetics developed by WIENER, and its subsequent applications. Cybernetics is the science of communication and control, originally developed for automated systems, in which information transmission is central. KRIPPENDORFF notes that cybernetics has found a wider audience in engineering than social science, but believes that the more difficult social problems also require a cybernetic approach which, according to him, eschews the technological fix and promises a systemic analysis. Social problems are linked to circular flows of information between spheres normally considered autonomous – economy, society, culture, etc. – and he suggests that cybernetics can help understand the feedback between these processes. BUCKLEY is an exhaustive source on the applications of information theory in the systems research tradition in behavioural science. One of the authors in this edited volume, Brillouin, compares information to entropy. He makes a distinction between "absolute information" (which exists as soon as one person has it) and "distributed information" (product of the amount of absolute information and the number of people who have it), and proposes that the former progressively loses its value, just like the degradation of available energy in the second law of thermodynamics. Another contributor, Rapoport, is critical of grand speculations about the implications of information theory for explaining everything from specific natural and social processes to life itself. Against Brillouin, he warns that measures of "amount of information" cannot be extended to answer questions about how much a person knows.

Similarly, the logician BAR-HILLEL states that most information theorists misinterpret engineering measures of information as measures of meaning or semantic content. Working with Carnap, he sketches a theory of semantic information that has no intrinsic connection to the mathematical theory of communication (or what he calls the statistical theory of signal transmission). He notes that in Britain "information theory" has remained rooted in the philosophy of science, while it quickly became a subset of communications theory in the United States.

The philosopher DRETSKE's semantic theory of information is rooted in the new communications theory, as he believes that meaning is not the only semantically relevant concept. Dretske argues that information itself should not be confused with meaning: information has an objective existence prior to interpretation, and it is only by taking this "pure" view of information – from cognitive psychologists and computer scientists – that epistemologists can understand knowledge, which Dretske defines as information-caused belief.

ROGERS takes a biographical approach to the history of communication theory, casting his net beyond Shannon, Weaver and Wiener. The Frankfurt School's work on the new informational media, as well as Lazarsfeld's study of propaganda, are also chronicled. Despite their differences, these represent the more traditional social science concerns, especially in comparison with the eclecticism of much cybernetics-influenced research.

A good introduction to the early attempts by economists to theorize information is LAMBERTON, which contains most of the classic pieces by economists such as Arrow, Boulding, and Stigler. The basic assumption is that economic systems are activated by decisions that link information flows to the objectives of individuals and firms. Traditional economics bypassed this, assuming that the firms have perfect information about factor supply and product demand, and that consumers have perfect information about prices or the characteristics of goods. Unlike later work in political economy, the early efforts mostly studied information as an intermediary in production (as in science and research & development) and market exchange, rather than as a commodity in itself.

MACHLUP's opus represents the most exhaustive effort to date in mapping the production, distribution, and use of knowledge in the post-war US economy. Unlike some of his counterparts in economics, he is scornful of attempts to provide simple measures of what is ultimately an intersubjective phenomenon. Machlup notes that information could potentially be distinguished as the "raw data" making up the flow or process by which knowledge (the stock of interpreted data) is transmitted. However, he prefers to stick to everyday usage, in which "knowledge" and "information" tend to occur interchangeably. Like Brillouin, Machlup distinguishes between socially new knowledge (that no one has had before) and subjectively new knowledge (the production of old knowledge in new minds). This helps clarify the argument that knowledge plays an increasingly important role in the economy; usually this claim refers to the former sense, but within Machlup's terminology it refers to the latter.

CASTELLS claims that capitalism has progressed to an informational mode of development, in which information – once, along with capital and labour, only a factor of production in the manufacture of goods – is now the primary raw material, processing tool, and final product in a majority of economic processes. Castells believes this is the result of the widespread application of science in every aspect of industry, which has led to both new "science-based" industries (such as biotechnology) and the transformation of older sectors (such as steel).

POSTER, like Castells, reconfigures Marx in order to propose a shift from the mode of production to the mode of information in late capitalism. While humans have been exchanging information since the beginning of language, electronically mediated exchange, he claims, has changed the way we perceive reality, as it subverts both traditional meanings of self and the social relations assumed in classical social theory. Poster tries to demonstrate this by a highly selective examination of new modes of information exchange, such as electronic databases and electronic writing.

WEBSTER reviews the classic works in social theory on the information society. He takes issue with influential theorists such as Bell and Baudrillard, who claim that information technologies have fundamentally altered some aspects of social relations. Such claims typically underpin either a liberal optimism that these changes are for the better, or a postmodern belief in the collapse of meaning itself as people are constantly bombarded with information. Webster sides with theorists such as Herbert Schiller, who analyze the changes in terms of traditional political economy.

MOSCO & WASKO is a good introduction to this latter mode of analysis. The authors's central concern is to examine how power (held by corporations and states) shapes the production and distribution of information, as the "information society" is mainly about the commodification of information – as Mosco puts it, it is a "pay-per" society.

Finally, BENIGER is the ultimate synoptic work on the origins of the information society, bringing together both the systems research on information processing in living systems and the historical study of industrialization. Beniger concludes that the emergence of the information society is the result not of recent changes, but of revolutionary advances in the speed of material processing that began in the late 19th century. This "Control Revolution" is a complex of technological and economic changes which has made information processing more important than the processing of energy. Replacing the bureaucracy developed in the 19th century, computer technology is simply the latest mechanism of societal control.

SUJANTHA RAMAN

See also Computing; Instrument as Embodied Theory; Journals; Social Sciences

Instrument as Embodied Theory

Bachelard, Gaston, *Les intuitions atomistiques: essai de classification*, Paris: Boivin, 1933

Bachelard, Gaston, *The New Scientific Spirit*, translated from the French by Arthur Goldhammer, Boston: Beacon Press, 1984 (original edition, 1934)

Dewey, John, "Nature, Means and Knowledge", in *Experience and Nature*, Chicago and London: Open Court Publishing, 1925

Duhem, Pierre, *The Aim and Structure of Physical Theory*, translated from the French by Philip P. Wiener, Princeton, New Jersey: Princeton University Press, and London: Oxford University Press, 1954 (2nd French edition, 1914)

Gaukroger, Stephen, "Bachelard and the Problem of Epistemological Analysis", *Studies in the History and Philosophy of Science*, 7 (1976): 189–244

Gooding, David, Trevor J. Pinch and Simon Schaffer (eds), *The Uses of Experiment: Studies in the Natural Sciences*, Cambridge: Cambridge University Press, 1989

Gutting, Gary, *Michel Foucault's Archaeology of Scientific Reason*, Cambridge: Cambridge University Press, 1989

Harding, Sandra G. (ed.), *Can Theories Be Refuted? Essays on the Duhem-Quine Thesis*, Dordrecht: Reidel, 1976

Kvell, D.F. (ed.), "The Question Concerning Technology", in *Basic Writings: From "Being and Time" (1927) to "The Task of Thinking" (1964)*, edited by David Farrell Krell, London: Routledge and Kegan Paul, 1978; revised and expanded edition, San Francisco: Harper SanFranciso, 1993

Ihde, Don, *Instrumental Realism: The Interface Between the Philosophy of Science and the Philosophy of Technology*, Bloomington: Indiana University Press, 1991

Latour, Bruno and Steve Woolgar, *Laboratory Life: The Social Construction of Scientific Facts*, Beverley Hills, California: Sage, 1979; as *Laboratory Life: The Construction of Scientific Facts*, with a new postscript, Princeton, New Jersey: Princeton University Press, 1986

McAllester Jones, Mary, *Gaston Bachelard, Subversive Humanist: Texts and Readings*, Madison: University of Wisconsin Press, 1991

Quine, Willard van Orman, "Two Dogmas of Empiricism", *From a Logical Point of View: 9 Logico-Philosophical Essays*, Cambridge, Massachusetts: Harvard University Press, 1953; revised edition, 1961

The description of a scientific instrument as a "reified theory" was formulated by the French physicist-turned-philosopher, Gaston Bachelard (1884–1962). Bachelard wrote in a French philosophical tradition that gave primacy to theory rather than experiment, in contrast to the British, German, and American logical positivists and empiricists, for whom scientific instruments held little interest, regarding them as little more than passive, theory-independent objects that simply mediated the all-important experimental "data" to an observer. In the past two decades, however, Bachelard's thesis has been a valuable launch-point for the work of a growing number of post-positivist historians and philosophers of experiment.

An important predecessor of Bachelard was another physicist-turned-philosopher, Pierre DUHEM, who, in *The Aim and Structure of Physical Theory*, strongly emphasized the importance of theory in interpreting the operation and results of instrumental activity. In a somewhat Platonic vein, Duhem argued that the significance of an instrument's readings rested only on the theoretical ideas that underlay its operation, not on its material characteristics. "It would be impossible to use the instruments we have in physics laboratories", he wrote, "if we did not substitute for the concrete objects composing these instruments an abstract and schematic representation which mathematical reasoning takes over ... [and] if we did not submit this combination of abstractions to deductions and calculations involving the assimilation of theories". While Duhem thus gave philosophical visibility to the use of scientific instruments, his reductionist argument portrayed them merely as passive embodiments of theoretical ideas, not as epistemologically important in their own right.

Bachelard's examination of the instrument-theory relationship has a somewhat different emphasis. In his account of "phenomenotechnique" (usually translated as phenomenotechnics), there is less of a hierarchical division between theory and experiment than in Duhem's writings, and a much greater stress on the constructive role of theory in experimentation. As he wrote in BACHELARD (1934), "phenomena must ... be carefully selected, filtered and purified; they must be cast in the mould of scientific instruments and produced at the level of these instruments. Now instruments are just materialized theories. The phenomena that come out of them bear on all sides the mark of theory." Bachelard argued that the phenomena of modern physics – for example, the traces of subatomic particles – were not "naturally" given, but were constituted through human engagement with nature, specifically through instrumental and theoretical interpretation. For Bachelard, the role of instruments was to help "concretize the abstract", as only instruments could "realize" the possibilities produced by a scientific theory.

The specific description of an instrument as "un théorème réifié" appears in BACHELARD (1933), in which he describes the apparatus of Millikan and of Stern & Gerlach as being "thought directly" in terms of the electron and the atom respectively. Hence, whereas Duhem raised the epistemological profile of instruments only to subordinate them to the dominance of theory, Bachelard dissolved the theory-instrument distinction without eliminating reductively the autonomous material status of instruments. The subtleties of these issues within "phenomenotechnics" are examined by GAUKROGER, who helpfully locates them within the wider context of Bachelard's epistemological analysis of the differentiation of scientific discourse from non-scientific discourse. GUTTING usefully points to the ways in which this aspect of Bachelard's work served as an important source for his intellectual successors, George Canguilhem and Michel Foucault. Since little of Bachelard's epistemological critique of instruments is available in the English language, some readers may find it useful to refer to McALLESTER JONES's survey of translated extracts from major Bachelard texts.

Bachelard's analysis of "phenomenotechnique" has been taken up by LATOUR & WOOLGAR in their celebrated anthropological analysis of how scientific phenomena are constructed in the laboratory. Specifically, they look at the way in which biochemical entities – which have otherwise only a theoretical existence – are effectively constituted by the outcome of instrumental activity in bioassays. However, Latour & Woolgar diverge from Bachelard in arguing that these phenomena are constructed only from the material resources of the laboratory, and by down-playing the importance of theory. None the less, Latour & Woolgar's work is also historically significant as (probably) the first book in the English language to give a sustained application of Bachelardian analysis to scientific practice.

The collection of essays in GOODING, PINCH & SCHAFFER reveals how a Bachelardian perspective can illuminate historical writing on instruments. For example, Hackmann's essay raises many valuable points about the importance of both "passive" and "active" devices in European natural philosophy of the 17th and 18th centuries. Explicitly invoking Bachelard's characterization of "un théorème réifié", Hackmann suggests that much can be learned, not by treating a historical instrument as merely synonymous with its pictorial representation, but rather by attempting to recreate its past usage as a theoretically-embedded material resource. In his article "Glass Works", Schaffer draws upon the same Bachelard quote in order to analyse Isaac Newton's difficulties with the critics of his optical experiments with prisms. Schaffer's account nevertheless powerfully subverts the thrust of Bachelard's original arguments, by showing how the status of an instrument can become highly problematic when observers disagree about the integrity of the theory embodied within it. Much subsequent historical scholarship has highlighted the way in which scientific instruments cease to be "transparent" mediators of "Nature" when the theoretical status of their operations is contested.

This important development in the historiography of instruments relates to another of Duhem's ideas, that it is never possible for a single "crucial experiment" to decide which of two rival theories is correct. Duhem's theory-centred argument for this is that "an experiment in physics can never condemn an isolated hypothesis but only a whole theoretical group". From this, the American philosopher Willard QUINE formulated the so-called Duhem-Quine thesis, that no observation can ever decisively refute a theoretical claim. Observational tests rely on many fallible auxiliary hypotheses, especially approximations and assumptions concerning the operation of instruments, so if an observation does not match a theoretical claim it may simply be that an auxiliary hypothesis has failed. The possibility of radical scepticism therefore arises: how can one ever be sure that an apparent empirical falsification of a theoretical claim might not later be overturned by the identification of a hitherto unseen failed hypothesis? (See HARDING for a full discussion of this.) If instruments are as theoretically charged as Duhem and Bachelard maintained, there is plenty of scope for illuminating study of the problematic role of instruments in both creating and resolving theoretical controversy.

A number of philosophers of science, however, have taken an opposing view and granted more importance to instruments than to theory. The American instrumentalist, John DEWEY, argued (historically) that the sciences were "borne of the arts", and that the tool-bearing operations of commerce and industry are the definitive characteristic of modern scientific practice. Theory, as a second order production created in order to assist in the control and manipulation of "Nature", was for Dewey just the subordinate tool of instrumental practice. As an existential phenomenologist, Martin HEIDEGGER argued that the theories and practices of modern science (but not those of ancient Greece) were all subordinate to the operations of "Technology". He claimed that even the theoretical imperative to examine and investigate nature as a calculable and orderable system of information was typical of an exploitative, "technological" attitude towards the earth's resources. Dewey and Heidegger's positions might both be summed up as "theory is a disembodied technology".

A somewhat different approach has been adopted by the phenomenologist Don Ihde. IHDE contends that instruments have long been employed as direct extensions of human perceptual apparatus, indeed as sensory tools that are effectively "embodied" in the observational practices of the subject. In this respect, he emphasizes that instruments have often been used for investigating phenomena regardless of their theoretical standing, preferring (in implicit contrast to Bachelard and

Duhem) to speak of science – including theoretical science – as being "technologically embodied". Drawing upon the work of other phenomenologically-inclined philosophers of instruments, such as Patrick Heelan, Robert Ackermann, and Ian Hacking, Ihde presents a stimulating, if by no means conclusive, inversion of the Bachelardian thesis.

There is clearly much scope for further debate concerning the theory-instrument relationship among historians, philosophers, and sociologists of science and technology.

GRAEME J.N. GOODAY

See also Information; Scientific Instruments: general works; Sociology of Science

Instrument Makers

Bedini, Silvio A., *Thinkers and Tinkers: Early American Men of Science*, New York: Scribner, 1975

Bennett, J.A., *The Divided Circle: A History of Instruments for Astronomy, Navigation, and Surveying*, Oxford: Phaidon/Christie's, 1987

Clarke, Tristram N., Alison D. Morrison-Low and Allen D.C. Simpson, *Brass and Glass: Scientific Instrument Making Workshops in Scotland as Illustrated by Instruments from the Arthur Frank Collection at the Royal Museum of Scotland*, Edinburgh: National Museum of Scotland, 1989

Clercq, P.R. de (ed.), *Nineteenth-Century Scientific Instruments and Their Makers*, Leiden and Amsterdam: Museum Boerhaave/Rodopi, 1985

Daumas, Maurice, *Scientific Instruments of the Seventeenth and Eighteenth Centuries and Their Makers*, translated from the French and edited by Mary Holbrook, London: Batsford, and New York: Praeger, 1972; reprinted, London: Portman Books, 1989 (original edition, 1953)

Millburn, John R., *Benjamin Martin: Author, Instrument-Maker, and "Country Showman"*, Leiden: Noordhoff, 1976; *Supplement*, London: Vade-Mecum Press, 1986

Taylor, E.G.R., *The Mathematical Practitioners of Tudor and Stuart England, 1485–1714*, London: Cambridge University Press/Institute of Navigation, 1954

Taylor, E.G.R., *The Mathematical Practitioners of Hanoverian England, 1714–1840*, London: Cambridge University Press/Institute of Navigation, 1966

Turner, Anthony John, *Early Scientific Instruments: Europe, 1400–1800*, London: Sotheby, and New York: Philip Wilson, 1987

Turner, Anthony John, *From Pleasure and Profit to Science and Security: Etienne Lenoir and the Transformation of Precision Instrument-Making in France, 1760–1830*, Cambridge: Whipple Museum, 1989

Zinner, Ernst, *Deutsche und niederländische astronomische Instrumente des 11–18 Jahrhunderts*, Munich: Beck, 1956; 2nd edition, 1967

Anyone writing on the history of scientific instrument makers is faced with a number of problems: the definition of scientific instruments as opposed to instruments serving other purposes; the relation between instrument makers and scientists; the connections between the development of scientific culture and the instrument-making trade in general; and the relation of instrument-making to other crafts. However, while these topics are extensively treated in the discussed studies, the possibility that the (generally) lower social rank of instrument makers might involve different kinds of knowledge, such as skill, has yet to be incorporated.

The classic of the field is still DAUMAS, which gives an almost comprehensive account of the development of instrument-making in early modern Europe (with an emphasis on France). Daumas covers social and economic factors, the impact of scientific activities and problems on instrument-making, as well as minute descriptions of technical processes. According to Daumas, the central characteristic of the period is the close collaboration and occasional competition between scholars and craftsmen. Part of the French historiographical tradition, this work is essentially a narrative of progress – a long and evolutionary process that led to the maturity of precision instruments in the early 19th century.

In certain respects the study by TURNER (1987) can be regarded as a successor to Daumas. While both are concerned with the relation between scientists and instrument makers, Turner focuses more strongly on institutional aspects, questions of patronage, and the social uses of instruments. His approach is broader, both chronologically and thematically, as he includes late medieval and Renaissance developments, as well as instruments used in everyday life or for teaching purposes. While Turner himself calls his book a work of "haute vulgarisation", as reflected in the narrative and the rich edition, it comes with a large number of annotations and an extensive bibliography.

A good survey of instrument-making in the 19th century is offered by the collection edited by CLERCQ. Most of these essays concentrate on the social and economic processes that led to a greater separation between instrument makers and scientists, and transformed the instrument-making trade into an industrialized enterprise. The arrangement of the articles emphasizes the different national contexts, with some of the papers including extensive lists of instrument makers, thus providing a reference guide for the respective national trades.

The history of mathematical (as opposed to optical or philosophical) instrument makers has been studied by BENNETT. Dealing mainly with England, he focuses on the relation between the manufacturing of instruments and the developments in navigation, surveying, and astronomic observation, which led to a growing demand for precision instruments and increasing specialization in the trade. The book is clearly intended for a more general audience, as it is richly illustrated and does without footnotes, but it does contain a long bibliography.

The works by Bedini, Clarke, Morrison-Low & Simpson, Taylor, and Zinner are all geographically limited and encyclopedic in character. The two books by TAYLOR (1954 and 1966) form an extensive study of the history of mathematical practitioners – i.e. those making mathematical instruments, or using them for practical purposes – in England, France, Italy, and America. Both volumes consist of two parts, the first being a chronological narrative of the general history, and the second consisting of nearly 3,000 short biographies. Taken together, these works are an indispensable reference guide to the field.

BEDINI places his study within the context of American settlement, analysing how mathematics in America was transformed by the immigrant instrument makers and their use of the different material resources available. Intending to highlight the "little men of science", Bedini gives detailed accounts of many individual biographies, accompanied by descriptions and illustrations of the instruments used.

ZINNER limits his book to makers of astronomic instruments, giving short biographies with lists of manufactured instruments, introduced by a short history of instrumentation in astronomy. The fact that he restricts himself to the German region is particularly awkward, as his study is the only reference guide to medieval instrument makers.

While the three above-mentioned works aim to be comprehensive in their field, CLARKE, MORRISON-LOW & SIMPSON consciously restrict their study of Scottish instrument makers to workshops represented in one collection, ranging from the 18th to the early 20th century. As a result, they are able to provide detailed accounts of every instrument manufacturer covered, followed by extensive references and a description of the instruments produced. This presentation gives the reader a chance to look for typical strains of Scottish instrument workshops, and makes the volume more a tool for historians than a book intended for the general reader.

Millburn and Turner (1989) are biographies of individual instrument makers, which highlight certain aspects representative of the history of instrument-making in general. MILLBURN's account of the life of Benjamin Martin aims to show the social, economic, and scientific factors that promoted instrument-making and public lecturing in 18th-century England. In a chronological narrative, Martin is described as a popularizer of science who turned to the business of manufacturing and retailing instruments. This biography gives a good insight into the context of 18th-century instrument-making, and long appendices facilitate access to the source material used by Millburn.

TURNER (1989) portrays Etienne Lenoir as a key figure in a crucial period of French instrument-making. By the mid-18th century, French workshops were regarded as inferior to their English counterparts, as a result of the lower social standing of French craftsmen. Turner analyses how this situation was changed dramatically by the political reforms of the French Revolution, the introduction of the metric system, and the need for precision instruments in science, all of which placed the artisan Lenoir at the center of academic life. As Turner has marked this book as a work in progress for a larger study not yet published, it is by no means exhaustive, although it is a very useful introduction to the relationship between instrument-making and science around 1800.

GERHARD WIESENFELDT

See also Astronomical Instruments; Electrical Instruments; Mathematical Instruments; Meteorological Instruments; Scientific Instruments: general works

Internalism versus Externalism

Brown, James Robert (ed.), *Scientific Rationality: The Sociological Turn*, Dordrecht: Kluwer, 1984

Bukharin, Nikolai (ed.), *Science at the Crossroads: Papers Presented to the International Congress of the History of Science and Technology Held in London from June 29th to July 3rd, 1931 by the Delegates of the Soviet Union*, reprinted with new Foreword by Joseph Needham and new Introduction by Gary Werskey, London: Cass, 1971

Cohen, H. Floris, *The Scientific Revolution: A Historiographical Inquiry*, Chicago: University of Chicago Press, 1994

Fuller, Steve, *Philosophy of Science and Its Discontents*, Boulder, Colorado: Westview Press, 1989; 2nd edition, New York: Guilford Press, 1993

Kuhn, Thomas S., *The Essential Tension: Selected Studies in Scientific Tradition and Change*, Chicago: University of Chicago Press, 1977

Lakatos, Imre, "History of Science and Its Rational Reconstructions", in *Scientific Revolutions*, edited by Ian Hacking, Oxford and New York: Oxford University Press, 1981

Merton, Robert, *Science, Technology and Society in Seventeenth Century England*, Bruges, Belgium: St Catherine Press, 1932; New York: Fertig, 1970; with new introduction, Atlantic Highlands, New Jersey: Humanities Press, 1978

Proctor, Robert N., *Value-Free Science? Purity and Power in Modern Knowledge*, Cambridge, Massachusetts: Harvard University Press, 1991

Schäfer, Wolf (ed.), *Finalization in Science: The Social Orientation of Scientific Progress*, translated from the German by Pete Burgess, Dordrecht and Boston: Reidel, 1984

Shapin, Steven, "Discipline and Bounding: The History and Sociology of Science as Seen Through the Externalism-Internalism Debate", *History of Science*, 30 (1992): 333–69

Young, Robert, "The Historiographic and Ideological Contexts of the Nineteenth Century Debate on Man's Place in Nature", in *Changing Perspectives in the History of Science: Essays in Honour of Joseph Needham*, edited by Young and Mikuláš Teich, London: Heinemann, 1973

In terms of sheer erudition and insight, the articles by Young and Shapin provide ideal introductions to the internalist-externalist debate within the historiography of science. Nevertheless, the two decades separating the articles seem to colour significantly the concerns of the two self-styled externalists: Young sees the debate as simultaneously concerned with defining the past and the future of science, and hence his principals range far beyond the guild of professional historians; Shapin, however, treats the debate as a largely rhetorical diversion from the more technical concerns of historians coming to grips with the past.

YOUNG portrays externalism as the attempt to penetrate the ideological character of the history of a science regarded as the logical unfolding of timeless ideas, or "internalism". According to Young, the Soviet contributors to the BUKHARIN volume (notably Boris Hessen) radicalized British scientists such as J.D. Bernal and Joseph Needham, who were interested in reorienting their research to the public good. As these contributors saw it, the internal history of science was under-motivated, without a clear grounding in the material conditions of life. This opened the door to accounts that portrayed science as directed towards political and economic ends, the goodness of which depended on the class interests that stood to benefit. In the 1970s, West German scholars, influenced by Kuhn and Habermas, staked out a middle position between internalism and externalism in this sense. SCHÄFER gathers the historical papers associated with this short-lived movement, which portrays science as internally driven (as a paradigm) until diminishing returns on puzzle-solving makes it ripe for external direction, or "finalization".

SHAPIN begins with Merton, who is credited with having conceived of "internal" and "external" as complementary "factors" that influence the course that science takes, to varying degrees at different times. MERTON's sense of internalism accepts at face value the idea that science has a natural trajectory, which external factors can either hasten or delay. During the Cold War, external factors became increasingly associated with sources of ideological distortion, which were thought capable of inhibiting science at any moment. At that point, philosophy of science's "demarcationist" project started to influence the historiography of science, notoriously in the form of LAKATOS's programme of rational reconstruction, which would purge history of all its arational elements. The ensuing debate among historically-minded philosophers and sociologists is captured in BROWN, which includes some extended discussion of Paul Forman's thesis that some very "arational" factors occasioned the "rational" adoption of the indeterminacy interpretation of quantum mechanics in Weimar Germany.

Despite their somewhat different starting points, Young and Shapin foreground the externalist tradition, whereas KUHN is largely responsible for conveying the opposite impression to the recent generation of historians: namely, that externalism was proposed in response to internalism. For Kuhn, "externalism" stands for a culturally embedded understanding of science that is designed to enrich the internalist's picture, typically by drawing on a wider range of scientists (not just geniuses) and sources (not just published works). Kuhn turns internalism into a very broad church, whose members – including Comte, Sarton, Duhem, and Koyré – would otherwise seem to have little in common but an interest in the history of science. According to Kuhn, the tendency to read the past in terms of the present is the only flaw in (some versions of) internalism, for which externalism can be seen as a corrective. Otherwise, he presents externalist historiography as a refinement of internalism.

Finally, the internalist-externalist distinction may be conceptualized as a boundary that scientists themselves regularly construct in order to retain their autonomy. In his panoramic survey of the history of this activity, PROCTOR observes that autonomy has usually been part of a Faustian bargain. Whether it was Plato's Academy, the Charter of the Royal Society, or the modern German university, scholars managed to safeguard the integrity of their practices by agreeing to perform administrative functions for the state. But because these functions were in practice not clearly separable from their research, over time factors previously regarded as "external" to science have become "internalized". For example, IQ tests were originally designed to sort students into academic classes, but eventually became the principal instrument for testing theories about human cognitive differences. FULLER explores how this sense of internalization has caused much confusion among philosophers of science, as to the exact causes for the internal trajectory they seem to discern in the history of science.

The scientific revolution of the 17th century is probably the historical episode that has been most contested by internalist and externalist accounts. The second part of COHEN takes stock of virtually all the accounts that have been advanced, and reaches some interesting conclusions. His criterion for whether an account is "internalist" or "externalist" depends upon whether early modern science is said to have arisen from the previous history of scientific thought, or from roughly contemporary non-scientific events. According to Cohen, most internalist accounts show how the early moderns drew on their precursors but not how they managed to go beyond them, while externalist accounts are much better at explaining the institutional persistence of the scientific revolution than its actual origins. Cohen recommends that the strengths of internalist and externalist approaches can be used to greatest effect by posing the question of origins in terms of cross-cultural comparison: why Western Europe rather than ancient Greece, Islam, India or China? Cohen then provides an illuminating but inconclusive survey of this literature.

STEVE FULLER

International Science

Bulkeley, Rip, *The Sputniks Crisis and Early United States Space Policy: A Critique of the Historiography of Space*, Bloomington: Indiana University Press, and London: Macmillan, 1991

Crawford, Elisabeth, *Nationalism and Internationalism in Science, 1880–1939: Four Studies of the Nobel Population*, New York and Cambridge: Cambridge University Press, 1992

Crawford, Elisabeth, Terry Shinn and Sverker Soerlin (eds), *Denationalizing Science: The Contexts of International Scientific Practice*, Dordrecht: Kluwer, 1993

Forman, Paul, "Scientific Internationalism and the Weimar Physicists: The Ideology and Its Manipulation in Germany after World War I", *Isis*, 64 (1973): 151–80

Fruton, Joseph S., *Contrasts in Scientific Style: Research Groups in the Chemical and Biochemical Sciences*, Philadelphia: American Philosophical Society, 1990

Haas, Ernst B., Mary Pat Williams and Don Babai, *Scientists and World Order: The Uses of Technical Knowledge in International Organizations*, Berkeley: University of California Press, 1977

Haas, Peter M., "Banning Chlorofluorocarbons: Epistemic Community Efforts to Protect Stratospheric Ozone", in *Knowledge, Power, and International Policy Coordination*, *International Organization* (special issue), 46/1 (1992): 187–224

Home, R.W. and Sally Gregory Kohlstedt (eds), *International Science and National Scientific Identity: Australia between Britain and America*, Dordrecht: Kluwer, 1991

Kevles, Daniel J., "Into Hostile Political Camps: The Reorganisation of International Science in World War I", *Isis*, 62 (1971): 47–60

"Les Congrès scientifiques internationaux", *Relations internationales*, no. 62 (Summer 1990): 111–222

Meinel, Christoph, "Nationalismus und Internationalismus in der Chemie des 19. Jahrhunderts", in *Perspektiven der Pharmaziegeschichte*, edited by P. Dilg, Graz: Akademische Druck-u. Verlagsanstalt, 1983

Nowotny, Helga and Ulrike Felt, *After the Breakthrough: The Emergence of High-Temperature Superconductivity as a Research Field*, Cambridge and New York: Cambridge University Press, 1996

Pancaldi, Giuliano, "Scientific Internationalism and the British Association", in *The Parliament of Science: The British Association for the Advancement of Science*, edited by Roy MacLeod and Peter Collins, Northwood, Middlesex: Science Reviews, 1981

Polanco, Xavier, *Naissance et développement de la science-monde: production et reproduction des communautés scientifiques en Europe et en Amérique latine*, Paris: Éditions de la découverte/Conseil de l'Europe/Unesco, 1990

Sarton, George, "L'Histoire des sciences et l'organisation internationale", *Isis*, 29 (1938): 311–25

Schroeder-Gudehus, Brigitte, *Les Scientifiques et la paix: la communauté scientifique internationale pendant les années vingt*, Montreal, Presses de l'Université de Montréal, 1978

Skolnikoff, Eugene B., *The Elusive Transformation: Science, Technology, and the Evolution of International Politics*, Princeton: Princeton University Press, 1993

Teich, Albert H., "Politics and International Laboratories: A Study of Scientists' Attitudes", in *Scientists and Public Affairs*, edited by Albert H. Teich, Cambridge, Massachusetts: MIT Press, 1974

Woolf, Leonard S., *International Government: Two Reports Prepared for the Fabian Society Research Department*, London: Allen and Unwin, and New York: Brentano, 1916

The term "international science" is an ambiguous one, sometimes because it has ideological overtones analogous to "scientific internationalism", while at other times it is used merely to express the independence of scientific knowledge from national boundaries, or the internationalisation of scientific activities. In any case, international science – as an ideology, a political commitment, or a practice – has only recently become an object of critical historical analysis. Although the rapid expansion of international scientific cooperation and organisation that took place prior to World War I and up to World War II, and its possible political significance, had certainly not gone unnoticed, most of the writings during that period were speculative rather than analytical, although some remain an invaluable source material, such as Leonard WOOLF's work on science as a model for world government and George SARTON's enthusiastic call for international organisation (1913–39).

During the years immediately following World War II, the public image of international science was dominated by the traditional notion that "true" science is neutral and above politics, and of "true" scientists being impervious to nationalist passion (i.e. more resourceful than politicians in showing the way towards mutual understanding and peace), thanks to their commitment to rationality, their common values and language, and the authority that came from a long tradition of international cooperation. This frequently blurred perception of scientific internationalism, both as the pursuit of universally valid knowledge and as a political attitude, was further fostered by experiences such as the Pugwash movement of the 1950s and 1960s and, on a more theoretical level, by the commitment to a rational, functional world order radiating from the United Nations.

In the 1960s and 1970s, historical research turned to a more critical examination of politics within the international scientific community, and particularly of that community's credentials in matters of mutual understanding, international conciliation, and peace. Relying heavily on public and private archives, the first studies focused, not surprisingly, on the inter-war period when, notwithstanding the end of military conflict, the international scientific community continued to be deeply split. FORMAN, reaching beyond the case of the Weimar physicists, provides critical insight into the nationalistic foundations of the scientists' commitment both to the norms of their profession and their internationalist ideology. Studying the same period, SCHROEDER-GUDEHUS places particular emphasis on the scientific community's divisiveness as a problem of foreign policy when, in the mid-1920s, leaders of science in all former belligerent countries moved far more slowly than their governments towards the resumption of normal international relations. KEVLES considers the domestic dynamics of American participation in the reorganisation of international science during and after World War I.

The late 1970s and early 1980s produced a considerable contingent of secondary works corroborating the sobering evidence of the earlier studies, and demolishing the legend of science and scientists as intrinsically unifying factors among divided nations. Research on the topic was infused with new excitement in the early 1980s, when access to the Nobel archives made it possible to look beyond the discourse of the institution, and to evaluate and quantify the resistance of both jurors and nominators to the pressures of national loyalties. CRAWFORD explores this material, showing both the political even-handedness of the Swedish Academy, and the extent to which the nominating records reflected national "myopia" or bias.

The interest in this particular aspect of international science – i.e. its relation to both nationalism and (political) internationalism – has since then declined, especially with the new research directions in the sociology of science that are beginning to erode the very foundation of the claim that science, being universal, is a prime mover of worldwide consensus and peace. Indeed, doubts are cast on the universality of science itself, as the generation of scientific knowledge emerges from these researches as an essentially social process, and as this knowledge, instead of being determined exclusively by "nature", is revealed as a social construct. Research on international science has therefore shifted from interest in the dynamics of transnational integration to the impact of local tradition, culture, and politics on scientific practice and content. More emphasis is given to the study of national styles of research, to science at centres and peripheries, or to the effects, in practice and content, of the international migration of scientists. Studies on the origins and development of various forms of exchange and cooperation bring to light motivations for international activities that reach beyond the imperatives of rationalisation, productivity and efficiency, and which range from institutional and professional strategies to political expediency. In this vein, both MEINEL (regarding 19th-century chemistry) and PANCALDI (regarding the British Association for the Advancement of Science) explore the passage from 18th-century cosmopolitanism to 19th-century internationalism, and the latter's close links with nationalist concerns already examined by Forman (within the context of Weimar Republic physics).

As the focus of mainstream research is shifting away from the essence of scientific internationalism *per se*, secondary literature relevant to the study of international science may be hidden within works whose main focus lies in the structures and mechanisms of the production and diffusion of knowledge. FRUTON's work on 19th-century research groups in chemistry and biochemistry is a good example, offering valuable data and analysis in its sections on "influence abroad". Other examples include the contributions to HOME & KOHLSTEDT's study of the emergence of Australian science, which explore the structure of international science within a colonial context. The basically inegalitarian structure of the so-called "international scientific community" is also the subject of POLANCO's collective volume on "world science", which examines, using a sociological approach combined with bibliometrical methods, the comparative development of science in Europe and Latin America.

The ever-expanding globalisation of research, and especially the geographic dispersal of scientific activities within multinational companies, has led CRAWFORD, SHINN & SOERLIN to contend that "international science" has become a misnomer, as it suggests a continuing tension between international and national motivations that has essentially disappeared within a steady process of denationalisation. NOWOTNY & FELT, taking issue with this conclusion, demonstrate that, even within the geographically highly dispersed research effort on superconductivity, national identification had far from disappeared; rather, phases of nationally- and internationally-oriented discourse and practice alternated or developed in parallel.

The mobilisation of science in order to solve transnational problems and, more generally, to further the common well-being of mankind, was generally considered one of the more powerful factors of international functional integration. As a whole, the extensive literature on this subject, and on the political and scientific aspects of international organisations in general, consists of work undertaken within the framework of contemporary political analysis, rather than from the vantage point of the history of science. There are, however, studies focusing on science or scientists in particular, such as TEICH's analysis of the attitudes of scientists working in international laboratories, or the research by HAAS, WILLIAMS & BABAI on the possible impact of the increasing infiltration of science and scientists within international organisations, both volumes making extensive use of semi-directed interviews. In a more recent article, HAAS demonstrates the positive influence of transnational "epistemic communities" (i.e. knowledge-based networks of specialists) on intergovernmental efforts of policy coordination. A broader view of the interaction of science and international affairs is taken by SKOLNIKOFF, whose book reflects not only the state of research in this field but also considerable practical experience on the borderlines of international technology and international politics.

One has to turn to case studies to learn about the interplay, within the scientific community, of the need for transnational collaboration and the promotion of strictly national, institutional, or disciplinary concerns; international congresses, organisations, or projects provide avenues of professional influence and power at the same time as they facilitate intellectual exchange and synergy. In "*LES CONGRÈS SCIENTIFIQUES INTERNATIONAUX*", several authors explore the social dynamics of these gatherings, which, from the late 19th century onwards, became a dominant feature of scientific communication. Since World War II, the growing dependence of military power on advances in certain disciplines has brought more players on to the scene. BULKELEY describes the powers and interests at work in the creation and management of one of the major international research projects of the post-war period, the International Geophysical Year.

BRIGITTE SCHROEDER-GUDEHUS

See also CERN; Global Organizations

J

Japan: general works

Bartholomew, James R., *The Formation of Science in Japan: Building a Research Tradition*, New Haven, Connecticut: Yale University Press, 1989

Nakayama Shigeru, David L. Swain and Yagi Eri (eds), *Science and Society in Modern Japan: Selected Historical Sources*, Tokyo: University of Tokyo Press, 1973; Cambridge, Massachusetts: MIT Press, 1974

Nakayama Shigeru, *Academic and Scientific Traditions in China, Japan, and the West*, translated from the Japanese by Jerry Dusenbury, Tokyo: University of Tokyo Press, 1984

Nakayama Shigeru, *Science, Technology and Society in Postwar Japan*, New York: Kegan Paul, and London: Routledge, 1991

Sugimoto, Masayoshi and David L. Swain, *Science and Culture in Traditional Japan, AD 600–1854*, Cambridge, Massachusetts: MIT Press, 1978

Traweek, Sharon J., *Beamtimes and Lifetimes: The World of High Energy Physicists*, Cambridge, Massachusetts: Harvard University Press, 1988

Watanabe, Masao, *The Japanese and Western Science*, translated from the Japanese by Otto Theodor Benfey (original edition, 1976), Philadelphia: University of Pennsylvania Press, 1990

For many years there were few books on the history of Japanese science available in English. When Japan hosted the 14th International Congress of the History of Science in 1974, a great effort was made to collect and translate a cross-section of historical studies that emphasized the "externalist" approach to the history of science, and the people involved in this project have since dominated the field. NAKAYAMA, SWAIN & YAGI's book was, for a long time, the only major English-language source on 20th-century Japanese science. The volume reflects the importance of Marxist thought in the post-war Japanese academic world, and is especially useful for those interested in the history of Japanese physics, as historians working in that area have been particularly prominent in the profession in Japan.

It was not until 1978 that a general history of pre-modern Japan was published. Like Nakayama, Swain & Yagi, it was part of the East Asian science series, under the overall editorship of Nathan Sivin, published by the Massachusetts Institute of Technology. SUGIMOTO & SWAIN is a useful reference

book for the period up to the Meiji Restoration in 1868. An interesting historiographical feature of the book is the way in which it categorizes Japanese history in terms of domestic development and foreign influence, the latter being depicted as waves of influence from China and the West. The planned companion volume, on science since the end of the Tokugawa period, has failed to materialize, but Bartholomew and Nakayama have fortunately helped to fill the gap.

It took 10 years for Nakayama's book to appear in English. NAKAYAMA (1984) portrays Sugimoto & Swain's waves of foreign influence as paradigms that shaped the Japanese consciousness and interpretations of natural phenomena. He argues that the paradigms of Western scientific thought could not be subsumed under traditional Japanese paradigms of knowledge. Instead, the imported paradigm of Western science was introduced as an established canon to be readily translated and systematically introduced by the state via the establishment of a government educational system. Meiji Japan was more concerned with the construction of an institutional system by which to transplant Western paradigms, rather than with the actual content.

WATANABE has also been an important figure in the history of Japanese science. While some of his papers have been published in English, it took 14 years for his work of 1976 to reach an English-speaking audience. He agrees with Nakayama that the Japanese approach to science has been largely instrumental. In the rush to learn and adopt the latest developments, traditional Japanese concepts and attitudes to nature have been neglected. Watanabe attributes the environmental problems faced by Japan during the 1970s to a lack of affinity with nature, and believes that this has resulted in a certain poverty within Japanese science, combined with an absence of values normally associated with modern science in the West.

Important monographs on the history of Japanese science appear to take a great deal of time to be translated from Japanese to English, or from doctoral dissertation to published book. BARTHOLOMEW falls into the latter category, but it was well worth the wait. The most authoritative English-language source on the establishment of modern science in Japan, this book details how the roots of Japanese science can be found in the Tokugawa period (17th to mid-19th century), how a scientific community was formed in the Meiji period (mid-19th to early 20th century), and how the infrastructure to support scientific research was created. Bartholomew focuses on the years 1868–1921, looking especially at the case of medical research and the career of Kitasato Shibasaburō.

In recent years, much scholarship has attempted to explain Japan's economic success. NAKAYAMA (1991) critically examines the mechanisms by which Japan has promoted science and technology for such ends, highlighting its historical development and social context since the end of World War II. He portrays Japanese history in terms of the interests of four sectors – academic, public, private, and citizen – and the key issues creating conflict: democracy versus technocracy in science, changing models of Japanese science, the expansion and limits of academic science, high economic growth and private science, the relative weakness of public science, the possibility of a science that serves the needs of the people, the microelectronics revolution, and competition and co-operation between Japan and the United States.

TRAWEEK provides a much-needed comparative study of Japanese and American high energy physicists. Effectively an ethnography of the physics communities in two countries, Traweek asks how physicists construct their world, and how they represent it as free of their own agency, emotions, and considerations of gender and national culture. To do this, she examines laboratory spaces, detectors that are used in experiments, how physicists are trained to become members of their respective communities, features of life in these communities, strategies for staying at the cutting edge of knowledge-creation, and the meaning of "time" in the lives and minds of physicists. A sophisticated anthropological study in the vein of "laboratory" studies made elsewhere, Traweek raises many issues regarding cultural difference and the social construction of knowledge.

MORRIS F. LOW

Japan: medicine

Beukers, Harm *et al.* (eds), *Red-Hair Medicine: Dutch–Japanese Medical Relations*, Amsterdam: Rodopi, 1991

Bowers, John Z., *Western Medical Pioneers in Feudal Japan*, Baltimore: Johns Hopkins Press, 1970

Bowers, John Z., *When the Twain Meet: The Rise of Western Medicine in Japan*, Baltimore: Johns Hopkins University Press, 1980

Huard, Pierre, Zensetsou Ohya and Ming Wong, *La Médecine Japonaise: des origines à nos jours*, Paris: Dacosta, 1974

Jannetta, Ann Bowman, *Epidemics and Mortality in Early Modern Japan*, Princeton, New Jersey: Princeton University Press, 1987

Lock, Margaret M., *East Asian Medicine in Urban Japan: Varieties of Medical Experience*, Berkeley: University of California Press, 1980

Nakayama Shigeru, *Academic and Scientific Traditions in China, Japan, and the West*, translated from the Japanese by Jerry Dusenbury, Tokyo: Tokyo University Press, 1984

Ohnuki-Tierney, Emiko, *Illness and Culture in Contemporary Japan: An Anthropological View*, Cambridge and New York: Cambridge University Press, 1984

Rosner, Erhard, *Medizingeschichte Japans*, Leiden: E.J. Brill, 1989

Siary, Gerard and Herve Benhamou (eds), *Médecine et société au Japon*, Paris: L'Harmattan, 1994

NAKAYAMA has suggested that Chinese and Western paradigms of medical knowledge were able to co-exist peacefully, as there was little overlap in their areas of strength and so not much need for competition. The introduction of Western medicine through Dutch studies during the Tokugawa period has been the object of study by a number of European scholars. HUARD, OHYA & WONG is essentially a reference book that provides attractive medical illustrations, a historical chronology, a bibliography, and many facts and historical materials relating to the origins of Japanese medicine from ancient times until 1970.

ROSNER presents a general history of Japanese medicine from the Heian period (794–1185), through to the Kamakura (c.1185–1333), Muromachi (c.1333–1573), and the Tokugawa (c.1600–1868) periods. BEUKERS *et al.* provide more substantial histories of the influence of the Dutch on the direction of medicine in Japan during the Tokugawa period, while an introductory chapter surveys the preceding period. The volume is particularly strong in its use of Dutch sources, with a useful bibliography of studies on Japanese–Dutch medical relations by Dutch authors, and specialist chapters on anatomy, Dutch surgery, smallpox, ophthalmology, and the career of J.L.C. Pompe van Meerdervoort. However, the influence was not all in one direction, and a study of the role of Japanese and Dutch physicians in the introduction of acupuncture into Western medicine is also included.

As its title suggests, BOWERS (1970) is interested in the contributions of important foreigners in the shaping of Tokugawa medicine. Written in a highly readable, narrative form, Bowers considers the activities of physicians including Willem Ten Rhijne, Engelbert Kaempfer, Carl Pieter Thunberg, Philipp Franz Balthasar von Siebold, and J.L.C. Pompe van Meerdervoort. The work remains a classic, along with BOWERS (1980), which explores the activities of the key players of the 19th century, most notably Otto Mohnike, J.K. van den Broek, William Willis, and Erwin Baelz.

Many accounts have been written by physician-historians, and tend to be either chronological surveys, compilations of facts, or biographies. JANNETTA, however, reviews the history of major epidemics during the Tokugawa period with certain key questions in mind. Using Japanese sources and death records to examine the prevalence of smallpox, measles, dysentery, and cholera, she finds that smallpox was a major killer that lowered fertility, depressing the rate of population growth. She also points out the lack of plague epidemics, which she links to the absence of certain species of rats and rat-fleas, as Japan's relative isolation made it difficult for some diseases to reach the islands.

SIARY & BENHAMOU show the diversity of approaches to the history of Japanese medicine that are now appearing, with chapters surveying studies of the history of medicine, public health, representations of illness, and the way in which the Japanese have dealt with mental health.

As anthropological studies of the urban Japanese, Ohnuki-Tierney and Lock enable us to ask complex questions relating to medicine, which previously the historical records had prevented scholars from posing. OHNUKI-TIERNEY suggests that most societies including Japan, have a pluralistic system of medicine, where by medical pluralism has become embedded in its culture and society. She argues that differences in attitudes to health and illness are related to how the self is perceived in a given culture, and that certain values and ideologies affect the way in which the sick, the handicapped, and the aged are viewed.

LOCK has examined the revival of interest in traditional East Asian medicine in Japan, attributing some of its popularity to the impact of the mass media, the interest of foreigners, disenchantment with synthetic medicines, and a heightened interest in holistic approaches to medicine. She traces the philosophical foundations and historical development of East Asian medicine in Japan, and explores contemporary attitudes to health and illness, the interrelationship of socialization practices and medical beliefs, and aspects of the East Asian medical system, including herbal therapy, acupuncture, moxibustion, and massage. Lock suggests that the pluralistic approach to medicine in Japan might be usefully incorporated into medical practice in the West.

MORRIS F. LOW

Japan: technology

Coaldrake, William H., *The Way of the Carpenter: Tools and Japanese Architecture*, New York: Weatherhill, 1990

Kenney, Martin and Richard Florida, *Beyond Mass Production: The Japanese System and Its Transfer to the US*, New York: Oxford University Press, 1993

Morris-Suzuki, Tessa, *The Technological Transformation of Japan: From the Seventeenth to the Twenty-First Century*, Cambridge and New York: Cambridge University Press, 1994

Okimoto, Daniel I., *Between MITI and the Market: Japanese Industrial Policy for High Technology*, Stanford, California: Stanford University Press, 1989

Samuels, Richard J., *The Business of the Japanese State: Energy Markets in Comparative and Historical Perspective*, Ithaca, New York: Cornell University Press, 1987

Samuels, Richard J., *"Rich Nation, Strong Army": National Security and the Technological Transformation of Japan*, Ithaca, New York: Cornell University Press, 1994

Wray, William D. (ed.), *Managing Industrial Enterprise: Cases from Japan's Prewar Experience*, Cambridge, Massachusetts: Council on East Asian Studies, Harvard University, 1989

Japan's phenomenal economic growth has provided the incentive for many recent studies of Japanese technology. This literature is multi-disciplinary in nature, although many studies adopt a historical perspective. SAMUELS (1987) pioneered the use of historical case studies in the study of the Japanese political economy. Effectively a series of mini-histories of energy sources such as coal, electric power, oil, and nuclear power, Samuels traces the role of government-industrial relations in the energy industry, to argue that the prevalence of "reciprocal consent" serves to enhance state power and private power, and is able to accommodate considerable diversity and conflict. It is agreed that the state has jurisdiction in energy markets while private industry retains control.

SAMUELS (1994) argues that insecurity provides the key to understanding the Japanese political economy and the development of technology. The Japanese hoped to achieve technological autonomy, and thereby enhance national security, through the indigenization of technology, the diffusion of know-how throughout the economy, and widespread efforts to encourage the companies that received such technology. Samuels focuses on the controversy surrounding the US-Japan FSX fighter co-development agreement. He provides histories of arms production and the aircraft industry in Japan in order to contextualize the debate, and explores the strategic relationship between the military and civilian economies, and technonationalism within these histories.

OKIMOTO has examined the role of the industrial policy of the Ministry of International Trade and Industry (MITI) in Japan's economic success. The long reign in government of the Liberal Democratic Party (LDP) is seen to have allowed MITI to control the formulation of industrial policy. A low level of defence expenditure also enhanced MITI's flexibility in policymaking, helped along by a large population, Japanese industrial organization, certain Japanese values, and a dynamic private sector. The book includes a chapter on industrial policy directives for high technology, such as industrial targeting, national research projects, government financing, research subsidies, tax policies, administrative guidance, and home market protection.

KENNEY & FLORIDA look at the situation when the Japanese system is transferred to the US. By examining automobile assembly and parts, and the steel and electronics industries, they provide evidence of the transformation of the organization of work and production into a new form, which melds intellectual and physical labor and changes the factory into a laboratory for product and process innovation.

It would be wrong, however, to view Japan's technological transformation as a post-war economic miracle. As COALDRAKE shows, Japanese artisans and master carpenters have long developed ingenious tools and techniques that enabled the construction of elaborate, traditional timber-frame buildings. He traces the invention and evolution of tools from before the Jōmon period (c.10,000–300 BC) to almost the present day, and explores in great depth the actual materials and methods used in the design and construction of buildings. In the process, he provides details of religious rituals associated with the Way of the Carpenter, the transmission of knowledge from master to disciple, the organization of guilds, the apprenticeship system, and the divisions of labor.

MORRIS-SUZUKI is able to reconcile the broader picture, given by books that emphasize the role of government and management in Japan's rapid technological transformation with Coaldrake's view of a technology in which artisans work in small, traditional workshops. She uses the concept of social networks of information to argue that new ideas were quickly transmitted from large enterprises to small workshops and factories that were often found in regional areas. This process was facilitated by social institutions such as local trade associations, research laboratories, and technical high schools found in the periphery, and educational bodies and research institutes in the centre. All these bodies contributed to the importation, modification, and development of technology that has been an integral part of Japan's industrialization.

WRAY fills in some of the details, with case studies that include the Meiji government's model silk-reeling factory that began operations at Tomioka in 1873; the financing and management of Japanese railway companies c.1890; the relation between the Mitsubishi *zaibatsu* and the Japanese Mail Steamship Company (NYK); the chemical industry; and the important role of the Institute of Physical and Chemical Research established in Tokyo in 1917.

MORRIS F. LOW

Jesuits

Baldini, Ugo, *Legem impone subactis: studi su filosofia e scienza dei gesuiti in Italia, 1540–1632*, Rome: Bulzoni, 1992

Baldini, Ugo (ed.), *Christoph Clavius e l'attività scientifica dei Gesuiti nell'età di Galileo*, Rome: Bulzoni, 1995

Bangert, William J., *A History of the Society of Jesus*, St Louis: Institute of Jesuit Sources, 1972; revised edition, 1986

Costantini, Claudio, *Baliani e i Gesuiti*. Milan: Giunti, 1969

Dainville, François de, *L'Education des Jesuites: XVIe–XVIIIe siècles*, edited by Marie-Madeleine Compère, Paris: Editions de Minuit, 1978

Dear, Peter, *Discipline & Experience: The Mathematical Way in the Scientific Revolution*, Chicago: University of Chicago Press, 1995

D'Elia, Pasquale M., *Galileo in China: Relations Through the Roman College Between Galileo and the Jesuit Scientist-Missionaries (1610–1640)*, translated from the Italian by Rufus Suter and Matthew Sciascia, Cambridge, Massachusetts: Harvard University Press, 1960 (original edition, 1947)

Evans, R.J.W., *The Making of the Habsburg Monarchy, 1550–1700: An Interpretation*, Oxford: Clarendon Press, and New York: Oxford University Press, 1979

Feldhay, Rivka, *Galileo and the Church: Political Inquisition or Critical Dialogue?* Cambridge and New York: Cambridge University Press, 1995

Feldhay, Rivka and Yehuda Elkana (eds), "'After Merton': Protestant and Catholic Science in Seventeenth-Century Europe", *Science in Context*, 3/1 (Spring 1989)

Giard, Luce (ed.), *Les Jesuites à la Renaissance: système educatif et production du savoir*, Paris: Presses Universitaires de France, 1995

Giard, Luce and Louis de Vaucelles (eds), *Les Jesuites a l'âge baroque, 1540–1640*, Grenoble: Millon, 1996

Jami, Catherine and Hubert Delahaye (eds), *L'Europe en Chine: Interactions scientifiques, religieuses et culturelles au XVIIe et XVIIIe siècles*, Paris: College de France, 1993

O'Malley, John W., *The First Jesuits*, Cambridge, Massachusetts: Harvard University Press, 1993

Spence, Jonathan D., *The Memory Palace of Matteo Ricci*, New York: Viking Penguin, 1984; London: Faber and Faber, 1985

Many of the recent approaches in the history of science towards patronage, ethnomethodology, institutionalization, and the relationship between scientific production and ideology, find a remarkably rich field of application in the Society of Jesus. The order, officially founded in 1540, rapidly established a reputation for universal learning by means of a network of colleges (really secondary schools) that expanded rapidly throughout the world. Although previous studies of Jesuit intellectual life have tended either to focus on the Jesuits as educators (DAINVILLE), or to emphasise the achievements of individual astronomers and mathematicians of the order (including Christoph Clavius, Athanasius Kircher, and Christoph Scheiner), more recently the enormous archival resources of the order have begun to be used in order to explore the institutional locus of Jesuit scientific activity.

Despite the renewed interest in Jesuit science, now that the traditional wrangles between Galileo's hagiographers and Jesuit apologists have widely lost their appeal, there is so far only one important monograph dedicated to the scientific activity of the order, BALDINI (1992). The central thesis of the book, is that the scientific activity of the Jesuits was decisively conditioned by a troubled relationship between the mathematicians and the philosophers of the order. Although the main concern of Baldini (who has recently published the correspondence of Christoph Clavius, in conjunction with Pier Daniele Napolitani) is the emergence of the "physico-mathematical" sciences in the Italian context, the source material that he cites and reproduces is likely to be of great value to scholars interested in all aspects of Jesuit cultural production. Of special importance, in this respect, are his rich treatments of the disciplinary hierarchy inherited by Jesuit colleges from the University of Paris where the early Jesuits had studied, and of the censorship of books and opinions within the order. BALDINI (1995), by contrast, is of mixed quality, but contains well-documented, helpful essays by Antonella Romano (on Jesuit mathematics in France) and Romano Gatto (on science in the Jesuit college of Naples, the subject of a new monograph by the same author).

An aspect of Jesuit science that Baldini somewhat neglects is experimentation, but this is discussed in depth in DEAR's book. In tracing the "mathematical way" in the scientific revolution, Dear associates two crucial, connected moves – the recognition of mathematics as a science, and the incorporation of particular experience-statements produced as a result of "special empirics" into natural philosophy – with the Jesuit followers of Christoph Clavius. Although Jesuit writers (notably Giuseppe Biancani, Giambattista Riccioli, and Christoph Scheiner) feature prominently in his book, Dear prefers to avoid invoking large-scale institutional features of the order as part of his explanatory framework for the phenomenon of Jesuit mathematical science.

The issue of censorship, and its effect on the participation of Jesuits involved in debates on scientific matters that transcended the bounds of the order, is also explored in COSTANTINI's case study of the correspondence between Giovan Battista Baliani and the Jesuit mathematician and architect, Orazio Grassi. Costantini's treatment has the added advantage of supplementing Baldini's work for the period of doctrinal reinforcement within the order throughout the 1640s and 1650s, which falls outside Baldini's temporal limits.

Despite the impressive documentary resources deployed by the works mentioned above, they arguably share a tendency to consider the Jesuit identity of a particular scientific practitioner only insofar as it is explicitly invoked by an individual involved in a specific debate – such as the debates on the fluidity of the heavens or on the Copernican theory that brought theology, natural philosophy, and astronomy into close contact in the mid-17th century. The essays by Harris and by Feldhay and Heyd, in FELDHAY & ELKANA, ostensibly motivated by a desire to broaden the domain of application of the Merton thesis linking scientific and technological innovation to the "Puritan ethos" in 17th-century England, mark an important development in the attempt to read the scientific production of individuals or groups of individuals within the order in terms of the institutional goals of the order as a whole.

One clear danger of such efforts, however, is that, by constructing a "blueprint" of Jesuit ideology on the basis of the prescriptive documents composed in the 16th century (especially the *Constitutions* and the *Ratio Studiorum*), scientific production will be viewed wholly in terms of this blueprint, even where local and temporary conditions might dictate a reversal of traditional priorities. FELDHAY's more recent monograph, which analyses the structure of the Jesuit order as a prelude to a reinterpretation of the Galileo trial, demonstrates the existence of a high degree of competition between the Jesuits and the older Dominican order for intellectual prominence during the early years of the 17th century. Feldhay argues that this competition, and the debate about divine foreknowledge on which it was centred, conditioned Jesuit "science policy" in important ways and helped to determine the positions adopted in Galileo's trial of 1632–33.

O'MALLEY, though wholly unconcerned with science, demonstrates the disagreements and radical changes of policy that occurred even during the early years of the society, as well as the emphasis placed on the subjection of all decisions to repeated review. Additionally, his book constitutes an invaluable, and highly readable guide to the organization of the order at its outset. GIARD & VAUCELLES contains a number of studies that supplement O'Malley and provide useful background to the social history of the order in the first century of its existence. Taken together, these works go some way towards supplanting the simplistic and often triumphalist narrative provided by BANGERT, though the latter remains useful as a chronological overview of the history of the order. The essays collected in GIARD, preceded by an extremely rich synthesis by the editor, use the tools of the social historian to situate scientific and pedagogical practice within this complex and changing institutional structure. Many of the essays in this volume (such as those by Lohr, Harris, Brockliss, and Lerner) explore the interesting grey area between the teaching of natural philosophy in Jesuit colleges and the prosecution of "scientific research".

Rather less attention has been given to the period after 1650, although EVANS provides a stimulating discussion of Jesuit cultural politics in the Habsburg lands in the second half of the 17th century. His discussions of Jesuit alchemical writings, universal language schemes, perpetual motion machines, and Egyptology are highly sensitive to the political concerns and changing intellectual tastes of the Habsburg dynasty. Moreover, by placing these works within the context of the intellectual production of competitors for Habsburg patronage, he casts new light on the voluminous works of Athanasius Kircher, Gaspar Schott, Christoph Scheiner, and many other Habsburg-friendly Jesuits. Jesuit scientific enterprises in the 18th century have so far been almost entirely neglected in the literature, except for a few studies of better-known figures, such as Roger Boscovich.

Geometry, astronomy, and artificial magic also played a crucial role in the Jesuit mission to China, and this has been the subject of numerous studies, including SPENCE's valuable but structurally contrived analysis of the world of Matteo Ricci, and D'ELIA's apologetic but well-documented discussion of Ricci's immediate followers. The conference proceedings edited by JAMI & DELAHAYE provide a starting point for the exploration of Jesuit scientific activity during the period of the Chinese rites controversy, which was to play a decisive role in the lead-up to the general suppression of the order in 1773.

MICHAEL JOHN GORMAN

See also Galilei; Religion and Science: Christianity: Renaissance

Journals

Bazerman, Charles, *Shaping Written Knowledge: The Genre and Activity of the Experimental Article in Science*, Madison: University of Wisconsin Press, 1988

Crosland, Maurice P., *In the Shadow of Lavoisier: The Annales de Chimie and the Establishment of a New Science*, Chalfont St Giles, Buckinghamshire: British Society for the History of Science, 1994

Hall, A. Rupert and Marie Boas Hall (eds), *Correspondence, of Henry Oldenburg*, 13 vols, Madison: University of Wisconsin Press, and London: Mansell/Taylor and Francis, 1965–86

Houghton, Bernard, *Scientific Periodicals: Their Historical Development, Characteristics and Control*, Hamden, Connecticut: Linnet Books, and London: Bingley, 1975

Hufbauer, Karl, *The Formation of the German Chemical Community, 1720–1795*, Berkeley: University of California Press, 1982

Hull, David L., *Science as a Process: An Evolutionary Account of the Social and Conceptual Development of Science*, Chicago: University of Chicago Press, 1988

Kronick, David A., *A History of Scientific and Technical Periodicals: The Origins and Development of the Scientific and Technical Press, 1665–1790*, Metuchen, New Jersey: Scarecrow Press, 1961; 2nd edition, 1976

Kronick, David A., *Scientific and Technical Periodicals of the Seventeenth and Eighteenth Centuries: A Guide*, Metuchen, New Jersey: Scarecrow Press, 1991

Meadows, A.J., *Science and Controversy: A Biography of Sir Norman Lockyer*, Cambridge, Massachusetts: MIT Press, and London: Macmillan, 1972

Meadows, A.J. (ed.), *The Development of Science Publishing in Europe*, Amsterdam and New York: Elsevier, 1980

Piternick, Anne, "Attempts to Find Alternatives to the Scientific Journal: A Brief Review", *Journal of Academic Librarianship*, 15 (1989): 260–66

Publication of scientific research findings in periodicals has historically been the main kind of formal communication in science. Although one can find precursors, the first major scientific journals were produced in the 17th century, namely the *Philosophical Transactions of the Royal Society of London* and the *Journal des Scavans*, both beginning in 1665. Many early journals were associated with scientific societies, and the production of a journal became an important aspiration of any serious scientific organization. Journal literature grew at an exponential rate, becoming more specialised in its coverage. The journal evolved not only as a form of communication, but also as the centre of a system of quality control based on what is now called peer review. Editorial and refereeing practices were developed to try to ensure the flow of appropriate and accurate material to the readership. This also slowed down publication, and created a niche for more "newsy" journals, especially in the 19th century, and for journals published on a weekly basis. *Nature* is among the most celebrated of these weekly publications, and is also a prime example of commercial journal publishing, which began seriously in the 19th century. As the pace of scientific work further increased in the 20th century, scientists have relied more heavily on more immediate, informal communication. However, journals have remained important as publishers of record, and as systems of quality control. The complex culture of journal practices will not be as readily superseded by the "electronic journal" as the abstract advantages of that technology might lead one to think.

Compared with the literature on the analogous topic of scientific societies, the literature on scientific journals is not extensive. Standard scholarship has preoccupied itself with documentation of the numbers, variety, and growth of periodical publications at various epochs in various countries, and with locating the scientific journal in the wider world of private and commercial publishing. Very few major studies of particular scientific journals have been produced; until recently, the study of editorial and quality control practices has been the preserve of the sociologist of contemporary science than that of the historian. But recent work on the rhetoric of scientific communication has renewed interest in journals as media, and as an important site for the study of the evolution of practices of scientific communication. The view increasingly is that constituting knowledge and communicating it are not separate activities pursued serially, but rather one process.

HALL & HALL's edition allows the interested and diligent reader to trace in detail the evolution of Henry Oldenburg's wide circle of correspondence into the fledgling *Philosophical Transactions*. This process reveals that the scientific journal was not born fully formed, but instead evolved from private and informal literary communications, and only gradually acquired modern forms of editorial and quality control.

KRONICK (1961) provides a general overview of the history of scientific journals up to 1790, but concentrates on an examination of the forms of scientific serial publication – namely, the substantive journal, the abstract journal, and the review journal. He also provides useful quantitative information on the numbers and types of publications, produced by subject area and country. KRONICK (1991) is a guide to 17th- and 18th-century scientific and technical periodicals, which includes alphabetical, name and title indexes. HOUGHTON gives a brief, less detailed survey than Kronick, but brings the major

outlines of journal development up to recent times. He also provides a lucid introduction to the recent history of secondary bibliographic tools, such as the *Science Citation Index*, and the important retrieval and analytical work that can be done with them.

MEADOWS (1980) includes useful historical studies. Particularly notable is the essay by W.H. Brock on commercial science journals in Victorian Britain, which demonstrates that commercial journals significantly outnumbered those sponsored by scientific societies, showing that the proliferation of journals did not simply mirror the growth in the number of scientific societies. Brock also provides an incisive study of commercial journals, by concentrating on five editors and the various journals with which they were associated. A second notable essay, by May Katzen, deals with the changing appearance of research journals, and points to the interaction of conventions of presentation, the needs of scientific communities, and the available technologies of printing, composing, paper making, and so on. The early years of *Nature* are detailed in MEADOWS's biography (1972) of its founding editor, Sir Norman Lockyer.

Journals can be useful foci for the study of wider developments, as exemplified in CROSLAND's study of the *Annales de Chimie*. Making a virtue of the patchy documentary base for a study of the journal, Crosland focuses on the *Annales* to examine the career of the new chemistry, and French and European chemical and scientific journals more generally. HUFBAUER manages to characterize the otherwise obscure German chemical community by building outwards from Crell's *Chemische Annalen*. HULL's evolutionary account of how science develops provides fascinating insights into the recent history of the journal *Systematic Zoology*, arguing that it has become a meeting-point for the exercise of power and the transformation of knowledge in modern biology.

As accounts of scientific writing have increasingly emphasized its persuasive character, and its role in constituting knowledge rather than just reporting or communicating it, so journals and other scientific texts have been studied for their rhetorical characteristics. BAZERMAN gives a pioneering analysis of the development of the genre of the experimental article in science. His episodic approach deals first with 17th-century cases, notably the *Philosophical Transactions*, and how experimental reports in that journal changed from 1665 to 1800, and how the roles of editors, authors, and readers were constituted. Bazerman's second major area of study is 20th-century physics, in which he examines not only the experimental report but also the reading habits of physicists. Finally, he discusses aspects of the rhetorical features of the social sciences, as revealed through journal literature.

Current fascination with electronic journals often assumes that the traditional journal can be replaced, and the problems of information "explosion" solved, more readily than is the case. A fine study of the failure of numerous attempts in recent history to replace the scientific journal is provided by PITERNICK. This book highlights the more than functional nature of the journal, and its deep cultural and, indeed, ergonomic significance and satisfactions.

DAVID PHILIP MILLER

See also Information; Societies

Jung, Carl Gustav 1875–1961

Swiss psychiatrist and psychologist

Brome, Vincent, *Jung: Man and Myth*, London: Macmillan, and New York: Atheneum, 1978

Brooke, Roger, *Jung and Phenomenology*, London and New York: Routledge, 1991

Charet, F.X., *Spiritualism and the Foundations of C.G. Jung's Psychology*, Albany: State University of New York Press, 1993

Franz, Marie-Louise von and James Hillman, *Lectures on Jung's Typology*, New York: Spring, 1971

Franz, Marie-Louise von, *Psyche and Matter*, Boston: Shambhala, 1992

Homans, Peter, *Jung in Context: Modernity and the Making of a Psychology*, Chicago: University of Chicago Press, 1979

Jung, Carl Gustav, *Memories, Dreams, Reflections*, edited by Aniela Jaffe, translated from the German by Richard and Clara Winston, New York: Pantheon Books, and London: Routledge and Kegan Paul, 1963 (original edition, 1962)

Jung, Carl Gustav et al., *Man and His Symbols*, London: Aldus Books, and New York: Doubleday, 1964

Samuels, Andrew, *Jung and the Post-Jungians*, London and Boston: Routledge and Kegan Paul, 1985

Stevens, Anthony, *Archetype: A Natural History of the Self*, London: Routledge and Kegan Paul, 1982

Carl Gustav Jung's work ranges widely over many different fields, from the natural sciences to comparative mythology and religion, and has stimulated a corresponding diversity of secondary studies. The transmission of his ideas has also been influenced by the impact of Jung's multi-faceted and highly charismatic personality.

An accessible introduction to the central concepts of Jung's psychology is provided by JUNG et al. Conceived and edited by Jung, and co-written by him with "four associates whom he considered best equipped to explain his work", this book (richly illustrated in most editions) represents the classical Jungian view of consciousness and the unconscious; dreams, symbols and archetypes; the modern relevance of myths; the process of individuation; and the significance of these concepts within science, therapy, and the arts.

Until recently, JUNG's biographers have tended to be either former colleagues or committed enthusiasts, basing their accounts on Jung's somewhat self-mythologizing *Memories, Dreams, Reflections*. "Recorded and edited" (in fact, largely composed) by Aniela Jaffé, this is itself as much biography as autobiography. Anecdotal in style, the book covers Jung's life from beginning to end, but is concerned almost exclusively with inner events, including numerous candid accounts of paranormal and mystical experiences, and, in a section written by Jung himself, a refreshingly uninhibited expression of his late thoughts on a number of key issues.

Of the available biographies, BROME's is probably the most balanced. Sympathetic but non-partisan, he gives many details concerning Jung's outer life and major relationships, affirming his extraordinary personality while avoiding idealization by reporting some of his more questionable traits. However, while giving a broad and informative picture, this work, like many others, perhaps accepts too readily the basic structure of Jung's life given in *Memories, Dreams, Reflections* and does little independent digging below the surface.

A pioneering attempt at fuller contextualization was made by HOMANS, in his cogent analysis of the psychobiographical, religious, and sociological factors that influenced the origin and development of Jung's thought, and the threefold nature of his mature identity as psychologist, social critic, and prophet. Homans elucidates the way in which individuation, the "core process" of Jung's psychology, is an attempt to integrate traditional (especially religious) and modern (especially psychoanalytic) approaches to life. By framing his insights in terms of theoretical perspectives other than either Jungian or strictly Freudian, Homans distances himself from the too familiar polarization between these schools.

An even closer historical investigation of the origins and background of Jung's thought can be found in CHARET who, using what he calls a "psychologically informed historical method", presents a well-researched, persuasive, but perhaps slightly over-played thesis arguing for the pervasive influence of spiritualism on the development of Jung's principal concepts and concerns. Particularly valuable is Charet's revelation of the possible ancestral origins of the split within Jung's personality between the religious and the scientific, and the careful tracing of the implications of this split throughout Jung's life.

For an understanding of the post-Jungian scene, one can turn to SAMUELS's comprehensive and authoritative survey. He identifies three main schools, differentiated according to the emphasis and weight given to various theoretical and clinical aspects of Jung's psychology: the Classical school, which follows Jung's own priorities and emphasizes the concept of the self and its symbolic expressions; the Developmental school, which gives more importance to personal development and the analysis of transference and countertransference; and the Archetypal school, which pays greatest attention to particularized archetypal imagery. Orienting within this broad classification, Samuels explores how the major Jungian themes have been variously extended or modified. He also draws numerous comparisons and contrasts with Freudian and post-Freudian psychoanalysis, and indeed reveals the pervasive influence of Jung's ideas on contemporary analysis and psychotherapy in general.

Jung frequently characterized his approach to knowledge as phenomenological. BROOKE picks up on this and skilfully recasts Jung's psychology in terms consistent with existential phenomenology as developed from Martin Heidegger and Maurice Merleau-Ponty, arguing that such an enterprise recovers insights discernible in Jung's writings but obscured because of his inadequate grasp and inconsistent application of the phenomenological method – insights, for instance, into the need to overcome the separation of self from world, so that the body can be appreciated as psychological and the psyche as corporeal. In return, Jung's psychology is shown to be able to give depth to the insights of existential phenomenology.

One aspect of Jung's work that has been particularly influential is his theory of psychological types, with its concepts of the two attitudes of extroversion and introversion, and of the four functions of thinking, feeling, sensation, and intuition.

The Myers-Briggs Type Indicator (MBTI), at present one of the most widely used diagnostic personality tests, is based on Jung's theory. FRANZ & HILLMAN explore some of the important aspects of this typology. Franz, after a lucid general exposition, focuses on the concept of the "inferior" function (i.e. whichever of the four in any particular case is least developed), characterizing the ways in which this function is manifested for each of the different personality types, as well as the role it plays in psychic development. Hillman, in turn, concentrates on the (culturally neglected) feeling function, emphasizing both Jung's achievement in having differentiated it as a function, and the importance of its contribution to our sensitivity when reading Jung's work itself. Historically informed and subtly insightful, Hillman explores the difference between inferior feeling and negative feelings, and the relationship of the feeling function to the mother complex, the anima, and education.

A courageous attempt to bring the specifically scientific status of Jung's ideas more sharply into focus was made by STEVENS. Drawing knowledgeably on the findings of ethology and socio-biology, while also remaining true to Jung's own formulations, he explores the nature of a number of central archetypes – the mother, the father, the animus and anima, the shadow, etc. – conceived as phylogenetically-acquired biological entities. He also invokes modern neurology in order to suggest that the Jungian attitude, and functional types, may be explicable in terms of the bi-camerality of the brain.

Jung was deeply preoccupied with the enigma of the relationship between psyche and matter, and in particular with the possible parallels between his own depth psychology and recent developments in subatomic physics. (He maintained a close collaborative friendship with Wolfgang Pauli between 1932 and Pauli's death in 1958.) FRANZ's collection of papers deals ably with these issues, expounding and extending Jung's late thinking on the relationship of medieval alchemy to modern science, on the hypothesis that psyche and matter might share a common substrate, on the nature of number and time, and, above all, the phenomenon of synchronicity – the meaningful acausal paralleling of inner psychic experiences with outer physical events.

RODERICK MAIN

See also Psychoanalysis: conceptual; Psychoanalysis: institutional

K

Kaiser-Wilhelm-Gesellschaft zur Förderung der Wissenschaften

Brocke, Bernard vom and Hubert Laitko (eds), *Die Kaiser-Wilhelm-/Max-Planck-Gesellschaft und ihre Institute: Studien zu ihrer Geschichte: Das Harnack-Prinzip*, Berlin and New York: Walter de Gruyter, 1996

Burchardt, Lothar, *Wissenschaftspolitik im Wilhelminischen Deutschland: Vorgeschichte, Gründung und Aufbau der Kaiser-Wilhelm-Gesellschaft zur Förderung der Wissenschaften*, Göttingen: Vandenhoeck & Ruprecht, 1975

Engel, Michael, *Geschichte Dahlems*, Berlin: Spitz, 1984

Generalverwaltung der Max-Planck-Gesellschaft zur Förderung der Wissenschaften e.V., *50 Jahre Kaiser-Wilhelm-Gesellschaft und Max-Planck-Gesellschaft zur Förderung der Wissenschaften, 1911 [-] 1961: Beiträge und Dokumente*, Göttingen: Die Gesellschaft, 1961

Hauke, Petra, *Bibliographie zur Geschichte der Kaiser-Wilhelm-/Max-Planck-Gesellschaft zur Förderung der Wissenschaften (1911–1994)*, 3 vols, Berlin, 1994

Henning, Eckart and Marion Kazemi, *Chronik der Kaiser-Wilhelm-Gesellschaft zur Förderung der Wissenschaften*, Berlin: Max-Planck-Gesellschaft, 1989

Henning, Eckart, Marion Kazemi and Dirk Ullmann (eds), *50 Jahre Max-Planck-Gesellschaft zur Förderung der Wissenschaften*, 2 vols, Berlin: Dunckler & Humblot, 1998

Johnson, Jeffrey Allan, *The Kaiser's Chemists: Science and Modernization in Imperial Germany*, Chapel Hill: University of North Carolina Press, 1990

Kohl, Ulrike, *Die Kaiser-Wilhelm-Gesellschaft zur Förderung der Wissenschaften im Nationalsozialismus - Quelleninventar*, Berlin: Archiv zur Geschichte der Max-Planck-Gesellschaft, 1997

Macrakis, Kristie, *Surviving the Swastika: Scientific Research in Nazi Germany*, Oxford and New York: Oxford University Press, 1993

Planck, Max (ed.), *25 Jahre Kaiser Wilhelm-Gesellschaft zur Förderung der Wissenschaften*, 3 vols, Berlin: Springer, 1936–37

Rasch, Manfred, *Geschichte des Kaiser-Wilhelm-Instituts für Kohlenforschung, 1913–1943*, Weinheim: VCH, 1989

Vierhaus, Rudolf and Bernhard vom Brocke, *Forschung im Spannungsfeld von Politik und Gesellschaft: Geschichte und Struktur der Kaiser-Wilhelm-/Max-Planck-Gesellschaft*, Stuttgart: Anstalt, 1990

Wendel, Günter, *Die Kaiser-Wilhelm-Gesellschaft, 1911–1914: Zur Anatomie einer imperialistischen Forschungsgesellschaft*, Berlin: Akademie, 1975

The Kaiser-Wilhelm-Society for the Promotion of the Sciences (KWG) was founded, after many years of debate, on 11 January 1911, and its first two research institutes (the KWI for Physical Chemistry and Electrical Chemistry, and the KWI for Chemistry) opened in October 1912. Though formally attached to the university, the KWIs were exclusively dedicated to research, and thus constituted a specific mode of interaction between science, the state, and the economy. The new model for the organization of research that the KWG represented reflects the structural changes that science underwent around 1900, and overall this model proved formidably effective in subsequent years. After World War II, the KWG continued under a new name as the Max-Planck-Society for the Promotion of the Sciences (MPG). For political reasons this change of name formally designated a refoundation, which took place in Göttingen on 26 February 1948. Since 1960 the general administration of the MPG has had its seat in Munich, and its more than 75 institutes, independent research stations, and groups are spread thoughout Germany.

The series "Veröffentlichungen aus dem Archiv zur Geschichte der Max-Planck-Gesellschaft" contains several useful historical surveys. Three of them are included here. HENNING & KAZEMI provide an extremely useful compilation of the most important dates in the history of the KWG and its institutes. (A very short version of this can also be found in Vierhaus & vom Brocke.) Especially helpful are the references provided in each entry to the corresponding files in the MPG archive. The extensive bibliography by HAUKE is also a crucial document for those working on the KWG/MPG. Finally, KOHL is a highly useful guide to the historical sources for the period of national socialism.

Jubilees commonly offer an opportunity for more extensive publication, and this has also been the case for the anniversaries of these institutions. It must be noted, however, that PLANCK and GENERALVERWALTUNG DER MAX-PLANCK-GESELLSCHAFT, the publications celebrating the 25th and the 50th anniversary of the KWG/MPG, respectively, do not really provide historical accounts in the proper sense, but instead offer surveys of the development of the society. The three volumes of Planck include the so-called *Handbuch der KWG*, which gives a brief introduction to the origin, aims, and administrative structure of the institutes (and reproduces some of the documents relating to their foundation). Another volume reports on the scientific work of the institutes, and includes a number of general accounts of the respective scientific disciplines. The third volume contains essays on various humanistic themes, representing the work of the relevant institutes. The Generalverwaltung der Max-Planck-Gesellschaft does not offer a well-knit historical account either, but essentially amounts to a reprint of certain documents relating to the history of the society, supplemented by brief portraits of its former presidents. In 1998, the 50th anniversary of its foundation, the Max-Planck-Gesellschaft published an extensive history (more than 1300 pages): HENNING, KAZEMI & ULLMANN. There are useful references to the archival sources. The second volume contains biographies of all members.

In the 1960s, historiography of the sciences gradually began to move towards a critical evaluation of the history of the KWG/MPG. Two thorough monographs, by BURCHARDT and by WENDEL, on the origins of the KWG and the foundation of the first institutes before World War I appeared almost simultaneously, in 1975. For an understanding of their respective approaches one should bear in mind that Burchardt appeared in the former Federal Republic, while Wendel's book was produced in the former East Germany. Like most subsequent works, both of these monographs focus on the creation of the working conditions required for research, and not on the scientific results that were ultimately achieved. Apart from the motives of the respective founders, Burchardt concentrates on the financial structure of the institutes, pointing out their differences in organization, while Wendel, whose book is based on his unpublished doctoral thesis of 1965, conceives the process of foundation as an interplay of the interests of science, economy, and the state. Wendel also makes more of a point than Burchardt in analyzing the social and economic contexts of specific operations on the part of economic and political groups. In this, he is guided by a Marxist interpretation, according to which science develops into a force of production.

Unlike the above-named works (which focus on the beginnings of the KWG), the monograph by MACRAKIS constitutes the first attempt at a critical evaluation of the society under National Socialism, analyzing the complex mechanisms that left the KWG in an ambiguous position of resisting, and yet becoming entangled in, political machinations. In the introduction, Macrakis discusses the development of the KWG after its foundation and during the Weimar Republic. The main section analyzes how the society's structures and traditions changed (or, rather, adapted) under National Socialism, demonstrating that adherence to tradition helped to guarantee the continued existence of the KWG. While most of the chapters deal with the society as a whole, two chapters concentrate on events within particular institutes. Macrakis uses the wide spectrum of biological and medical research, from successful pure science to Nazi eugenics and racial doctrine, to demonstrate the complexity of state interference in research. He also discusses the interactions between science, the military, and the National Socialist state, using the example of the "Uranium project".

The book by ENGEL is not really a history of the KWG, but rather an urban history of the town of Dahlem, which is now part of Berlin. None the less, the KWG has decidedly left its mark on Dahlem, for the first Kaiser-Wilhelm-Institutes of 1912 were located there; and, moreover, of the 36 institutes administrated by the KWG in 1933, 16 were located in Berlin,

and 12 of those in Dahlem. Thus, Engel's documented presentation combines local history with the history of science. From Dahlem's origins as a hamlet until after World War II, he depicts the architectural and social development of what was to become an exclusive residential area, knitting into his account how the evolving town was moulded into a "Science-Landscape", above all by the KWG, but also by other scientific institutions (such as the Preussische Geheime Staatsarchiv, the Botanical Gardens, and, after World War II, the Free University of Berlin).

The volume edited by VIERHAUS & VOM BROCKE, on the occasion of the 75th anniversary of the society, attempts a critical historical account of the entire history of the KWG/MPG. However, even this work does not reach beyond the 1950s, and, rather than a narrative history, it is a collection of essays by more than 20 authors. The book is divided into three parts: the first, "On the History of the Kaiser-Wilhelm-/Max-Planck-Gesellschaft" (460 pages), charts the historical development of the society until the refoundation of the MPG, in five chapters. The seven chapters that comprise the second part of the book, "Personalities and Structures" (218 pages), give a survey of the motives and goals of leading individuals associated with the KWG, such as Adolf von Harnack, Albert Einstein, Fritz Haber, and Emil Fischer, and also elucidates some structural aspects of the KWG – for example, its financial structure, its relations to the industry during the Weimar Republic, and Dahlem's great importance as the KWG's settlement area – and also offers a study of publicly funded research institutions for comparison. The third part, which consists of eight chapters, considers the various aspects of the "International Relations of Science" (214 pages), from Germany's bilateral relations – with France, the United Kingdom, the US, the USSR, and Japan – to an account of cultural politics abroad, emphasising the importance of the Nobel prize.

Work on the history of the KWG as a whole initially eclipsed the study of individual KWG institutes. A number of smaller investigations and treatises (including doctoral dissertations) have been undertaken, as cited in Hauke's bibliography. However, to date there is still no major comprehensive historical monograph on the individual institutes and research stations. Among the few existing works on the topic is RASCH's study of the Institute for Research on Coal, which to some extent may also serve as a reference work. Located in Mühlheim an der Ruhr, this KWI was the first institute outside Berlin, and from the very beginning, and to a larger extent than the other institutes, it was geared towards applied research – i.e., towards the interests of the powerful major industries in the Rhineland. The various research topics of the institute are analyszd within the context both of its organization and its general scientific policy between 1913 and 1943, when Franz Fischer was in charge of the institute as its first director.

One of the starting points for the foundation of the KWG was a debate, at the beginning of the 20th century, over the setting up of an Imperial Chemical Institution (Chemische Reichsanstalt). As a result of this debate, the first two institutes of the KWG were dedicated to research in chemistry; JOHNSON gives a detailed analysis of the history of these two institutes within the context of contemporary social and scientific developments. Starting with their origin, he depicts the background of the project of an Imperial Chemical Institution and its development into the relevant Kaiser-Wilhelm-institutes, as well as their role in World War I. Precisely because the early history of the KWG is so closely linked to the rise of these chemical institutes, a comparison of this study with publications by Burchardt and Wendel shows the importance of this alternative approach, which has brought to light new source material from the institutes' archives.

The fundamental work by Vierhaus & vom Brocke also made visible this deficit in the research on the KWG/MPG to date, for a reasonably objective general picture of the Gesellschaft can emerge only after its history has been supplemented by a differentiated history of the individual institutes and their interaction with the KWG. The collection by BROCKE & LAITKO, which treats the history of the KWG/MPG mainly as a history of its institutes, represents a step in this direction. The editors avoided a mere enumeration of the histories of individual institutes by adopting as their guiding model the so-called Harnack principle – that is, the traditional KWG practice of organizing institutes around famous scientific personalities. In the first five chapters, they discuss the available source material and the methods for the study of the KWG and its institutes. A second part (likewise of five chapters) puts the Harnack principle under scrutiny, clarifying to what extent it remained fictional and was actually realized, and considers whether it can still be implemented today. Part 3 contains brief historical introductions to 12 institutes, and, in accordance with the motto of the work, it concentrates on their respective founders. Finally, the fourth part discusses topics such as inventive activity in the institutes, the deployment of major equipment within the KWG, and the use of quantitative methods for the historiography of the KWG/MPG. Drawing on the material supplied by the various contributions to the volume, and attempting an evaluation of their more general implications, a concluding essay analyzes in detail both the potential and the limits of a research organization research that centres on particular individuals.

HORST KANT

translated by Anna-Katherina Mayer

See also Education; Universities

Kant, Immanuel 1724–1804

German philosopher

Adickes, Erich, *Kant als Naturforscher*, 2 vols, Berlin: De Gruyter, 1924–25

Butts, Robert E. (ed.), *Kant's Philosophy of Physical Science: Metaphysische Anfangsgründe der Naturwissenschaft, 1786–1986*, Dordrecht: Reidel, 1986

Eisler, Rudolf, *Kant-Lexikon: Nachschlagewerk zu Kants sämtlichen Schriften, Briefen und handschriftlichem Nachlass*, Berlin: Mittler, 1930

Fischer, Kuno, *Immanuel Kant und seine Lehre*, 2 vols, 3rd edition, Munich: Basserman, 1882; 5th edition, Heidelberg: Winter, 1909–10

Friedman, Michael, *Kant and the Exact Sciences*, Cambridge, Massachusetts: Harvard University Press, 1992

Hoppe, Hansgeorg, *Kants Theorie der Physik: Eine Untersuchung über das Opus postumum von Kant*, Frankfurt: Klostermann, 1969

McLaughlin, Peter, *Kant's Critique of Teleology in Biological Explanation: Antinomy and Teleology*, Lewiston, New York, and Lampeter, Dyfed: Edwin Mellen Press, 1990

Plaass, Peter, *Kant's Theory of Natural Science*, translated from the German, with an introduction by Alfred E. Miller and Maria G. Miller, Dordrecht and Boston: Kluwer, 1994 (original edition, 1966)

Apart from two standard works on Kantian philosophy, this entry focuses above all on literature dealing with Immanuel Kant's influence on the natural sciences, especially physics and biology, and vice versa, presenting such controversial points of view as those propounded by Adickes and by Plaass.

FISCHER's work remains the most comprehensive biography of Kant and also the most extensive presentation of his writings and doctrines. Its merit lies in the contextualization of Kant's life and doctrines in their historical and philosophical setting. The origins of his critical philosophy are discussed against the background of empiricism (Francis Bacon, John Locke, George Berkeley, David Hume) and rationalism (René Descartes, Benedict de Spinoza, Gottfried Wilhelm Leibniz, Christian von Wolff). Kant's writings are surveyed and divided, according to special subjects, into: pre-critical writings from 1740 to 1770; writings from 1770 to 1780; and the critical writings from 1780 to 1800. Fischer's main aim is to point out Kant's philosophical development. The first volume covers the natural philosophical inquiries into force and matter, motion, and silence; natural historical inquiries into cosmogony, geology, and geography; metaphysical inquiries into the origins and principles of knowledge; the transformation of metaphysics under the influence of empirism; the influence of Jean-Jacques Rousseau and Emanuel Swedenborg on Kant; and the foundation of the critical philosophy (for example, the method of critique of reason), transcendental aesthetics, transcendental analytics, and doctrine of schematism and the thing-in-itself. The second volume deals with the metaphysics of nature (such as the concept of motion, matter and its forces, and phoronomy, dynamics, and mechanics) and morals (for instance, human liberty, and practical reason), Kant's doctrine of religion, the Critique of Judgment and – finally – his own critique of Kant's philosophy. Fischer's very detailed work is useful for beginners as well as for advanced students of Kant's philosophy.

EISLER provides a comprehensive reference work to all known written material on Kant until 1930, compiling the most important quotations on specific Kantian nomenclature (such as category, experience, faculty of judgment, object, purpose/purposiveness, reason, space, time, and the understanding). Each entry contains a short, explanatory introduction, followed by quotations from Kant himself.

ADICKES discusses Kant from a neo-Kantian perspective. He examines Kant as a naturalist, especially in *Thoughts on the True Estimation of Living Forces* (1746), *Universal Natural History and Theory of the Heavens* (1755), *Meditationes de igne* (1755), *Physical Monadology* (1756), and *Metaphysical*

Foundations of Natural Science (1786). Adickes argues that Kant was not a scientist in the true sense of the word, because of his lack of clarity and exact (mathematical) calculations and also as a result of the vagueness of his terminology. But in *Thoughts*, Adickes discovers a brilliant anticipation of modern metageometry and in *Physical Monadology*, the dynamical theory of matter that he regards as Kant's everlasting contribution. The doctrine of motion and the concept of matter provided in the *Metaphysical Foundations* reveal the disadvantageous consequences of Kant's transcendental method – for instance, it could not prove the three mechanical principles. Moreover, Kant's hypothesis of the aether (especially in *Meditationes*) could not explain the states of aggregation, cohesion, elasticity, liquidity, and solidity. In 1755, Kant developed a theory of the heavens resembling that of modern astronomy, and in his natural history of the heavens he created the Nebular Hypothesis, which he developed in great detail.

PLAASS offers a very different approach to Kant's theory of natural science. In particular, he gives an exegesis of the Preface to Kant's *Metaphysical Foundations* and investigates the relationship between this and the *Critique of Pure Reason*, structurally and methodologically. He argues that the "Copernican turn" (the assumption that the subjectively necessary conditions of experience determine the necessary conditions of objects of possible experience) of the *Critique* had to be repeated in the *Foundations* as the means of applying the general metaphysics to matter, thereby creating the special metaphysics of nature. So the *Foundations* reveal the consequent development of the transcendental principles as metaphysical determinations of matter. Further, the metaphysics of nature is structured to include the *a priori* synthetic principles of mathematics, in terms of which the objects and laws of physics have to be described.

BUTTS presents a collection of essays on the *Metaphysical Foundations* outlining approaches to Kant's philosophy of physics. Part 1 is an introduction to Kant's Newtonianism: Friedman's paper gives the most detailed and comprehensive treatment of both the physics and the method of argument employed in Kant's justification of Newton, emphasizing the phenomenology. Brittan completes this picture, providing more details on the science and Kant's Newtonian intentions, emphasising the Dynamics. Shea provides an exposition of Kant's *Universal Natural History and Theory of the Heavens*. The papers by Buchdahl, Butts, and Kitcher in part 2 deal with more general aspects of Kant's scientific methodology, while the papers by Harper, Okruhlik and Duncan in part 3 investigate special problems of Kant's philosophy of physics. Böhme's paper in part 4 is a controversial and unorthodox reading of Kant's epistemology: in his opinion Kant's epistemology is a theory of scientific knowledge, not a general theory. All contributors are agreed that Kant regarded the physical synthesis worked out by Newton as the best example we have, both of reliable theoretical knowledge and of justified method in science and in metaphysics, and in this sense Kant was the philosopher of Newtonian physics.

FRIEDMAN considers such Kantian thoughts as a model of fruitful philosophical engagement with the sciences, and an understanding of these thoughts within their 18th-century context as most relevant for 20th-century problems also. He investigates Kant's engagement in the pre-critical (including the *Inaugural Dissertation*, Kant's new conception of the relationship between space and ultimate substances), the critical (*Prolegomena*, *Metaphysical Foundations*, *Critique of Pure Reason*: the division of the faculties of understanding and sensibility; the spatio-temporal "schematism" of categories), and the post-critical period (*Opus postumum*), where Kant deals with chemistry, and especially the theory of heat. Friedmann tries to show that central aspects of the Kantian philosophy respond to the theoretical evolution and conceptual problems of contemporary mathematical science.

HOPPE's main subject is Kant's question in *Opus postumum* (1796–1803; first published 1938) on the possibility of physics as an empirical science. This question is understandable only against the background of the *Critique of Pure Reason* (1781, 1787), *Metaphysical Foundations*, and the introduction to *Critique of Judgement* (1790), where Kant deals with the metaphysics of nature as a transition from pure to empirical knowledge. In order to be science, physics has to be 1) objective, 2) be law-like knowledge, 3) a system of empirical knowledge. Hoppe argues that Kant tries to achieve this in *Opus postumum* through the schematism of *a priori* terms of motive powers, and that Kant completes the transition with the term "experiment", which is grounded in the action of the subject (self-objectivation).

McLAUGHLIN wants to read Kant's critique of teleology – the second part of the *Critique of Judgment* – as a philosophy of biology. There Kant systematically pursues the question of the extent to which the mechanistic mode of explanation itself constantly forces the introduction of teleological principles into science. The reconstruction of Kant's "critique" follows three steps: after presenting basic problems of biological explanation in the 18th century (the theory of organism; the focus on "objective purposiveness" and "natural purpose"), he analyses Kant's most important conceptual instrument for solving such problems – the argumentational figure of the antinomy – and, finally, he analyses the application of the antinomy of judgement in the Dialectic of Teleological Judgement. Here Kant holds on to mechanistic reductionism as the only legitimate kind of explanation in science, but he establishes standards to be met by any possible future mechanistic explanation of the organism.

BEATRICE RAUSCHENBACH

See also Enlightenment; Newtonianism

Kepler, Johannes   1571–1630

German astronomer

Aiton, E.J., A.M. Duncan and J.V. Field (trans), *The Harmony of the World*, Philadelphia: American Philosophical Society, 1997

Beer, Arthur and Peter Beer (eds), *Kepler: Four Hundred Years: Proceedings of the Conference Held in Honour of Johannes Kepler*, Oxford and New York: Pergamon Press, 1975

Caspar, Max and Walther von Dyck (eds), *Johannes Kepler in seinen Briefen*, 2 vols, Munich and Berlin: Oldenbourg, 1930

Caspar, Max (ed.), *Bibliographia Kepleriana: Ein Führer durch das gedruckte Schrifttum von Johannes Kepler*, Munich: Beck, 1936; 2nd edition, edited by Martha List, 1968

Caspar, Max, *Kepler*, translated from the German and edited by C. Doris Hellman, London and New York: Abelard-Schuman, 1959; with a new introduction by Owen Gingerich, New York: Dover, 1993 (original edition, 1948)

Donahue, William H. (trans), *The New Astronomy*, Cambridge and New York: Cambridge University Press, 1992

Duncan, A.M. (trans), *The Secret of the Universe*, with an introduction and commentary by E.J. Aiton, New York: Abaris, 1981 (original edition, 1621)

Dyck, Walther von and Max Caspar (eds), *Gesammelte Werke*, 20 vols, Munich: Beck, 1937–97

Field, J.V., *Kepler's Geometrical Cosmology*, Chicago: University of Chicago Press, and London: Athlone Press, 1988

Gingerich, Owen, *The Eye of Heaven: Ptolemy, Copernicus, Kepler*, New York: American Institute of Physics, 1993

Hübner, Jürgen, *Die Theologie Johannes Keplers zwischen Orthodoxie und Naturwissenschaft*, Tübingen: Mohr, 1975

Jardine, Nicholas, *The Birth of History and Philosophy of Science: Kepler's "A Defense of Tycho Against Ursus" with Essays on Its Provenance and Significance*, Cambridge and New York: Cambridge University Press, 1984

Koestler, Arthur, *The Watershed: A Biography of Johannes Kepler*, New York: Anchor Books, 1960

Koyré, Alexandre, *The Astronomical Revolution: Copernicus, Kepler, Borelli*, translated from the French by R.E.W. Maddison, London: Methuen, and Ithaca, New York: Cornell University Press, 1973 (original edition, 1961)

Kozhamthadam, Job, *The Discovery of Kepler's Laws: The Interaction of Science, Philosophy, and Religion*, Notre Dame, Indiana: University of Notre Dame Press, 1994

Pantin, Isabelle (ed. and trans), *Discussion avec le Messager Céleste: Rapport sur l'Observation des satellites de Jupiter*, Paris: Belles Lettres, 1993

Rosen, Edward (trans), *Kepler's Somnium: The Dream, or Posthumous Work on Lunar Astronomy*, Madison: University of Wisconsin Press, 1967

Rosen, Edward, *Three Imperial Mathematicians: Kepler Trapped Between Tycho Brahe and Ursus*, New York: Abaris Books, 1986

Segonds, Alain (trans), *Le Secret du monde*, Paris: Belles Lettres, 1984

Simon, Gérard, *Kepler: astronome, astrologue*, Paris: Gallimard, 1979

Stephenson, Bruce, *Kepler's Physical Astronomy*, New York and Berlin: Springer, 1987

Stephenson, Bruce, *The Music of the Heavens: Kepler's Harmonic Astronomy*, Princeton, New Jersey: Princeton University Press, 1995

Voelkel, James R., "The Development and Reception of Kepler's Physical Astronomy 1593–1609", PhD dissertation, Bloomington, Indiana University Press, 1995

Wallis, Charles Glenn (trans), *Epitome of Copernican Astronomy: Books IV and V, The Harmonies of the World*, Chicago: Encyclopedia Britannica, 1952

Wilson, Curtis, *Astronomy from Kepler to Newton: Historical Studies*, London: Variorum, 1989

Scholarship on Johannes Kepler (including translations of his work) has been slow off the mark compared with that on his more accessible contemporary, Galileo. In the latter case there have been half a dozen biographies in recent years, from many different viewpoints. The only major biography of Kepler (not counting that by the novelist Arthur Koestler) was published in the 1940s and most serious study on Kepler is carried primarily by articles and translations.

In the surge of interest accompanying the quadricentennial of Kepler's birth in 1971, several symposia volumes or compendia were published, the most comprehensive of which was edited by BEER & BEER. In this, I. Bernard Cohen suggests that the 20th-century renaissance in Keplerian studies could in part be attributed to the style and reputation of Albert Einstein, whose search for aesthetic unities more closely resembled those of Kepler than the empirical approach long associated with Galileo. In 1971, all of Galileo's major works were available in English, but the only English-language translations of Kepler's works were portions of his *Epitome of Copernican Astronomy* and his *Harmony of the Worlds*. A quarter of a century later translations had finally become available in English, joining the earlier German translations of several key works.

Keplerian studies today rest fundamentally on the 20-volume edition of his works (DYCK & CASPAR), published by the Kepler Commission of the Bavarian Academy of Sciences. It was envisioned in the late 1920s by DYCK & CASPAR, who, as a preliminary, published a two-volume German edition of letters (CASPAR & DYCK 1930), which remains unrivalled as a translated source of Kepler's correspondence. After Dyck's death, Caspar continued to amass an archive of 15,000 Keplerian manuscripts, and in 1937 brought out volume 3, the *Astronomia nova*, the first of the planned series to appear. In 1956, Franz Hammer and, later, Volker Bialas continued as editors, and the series contains all of Kepler's printed corpus and correspondence, although several volumes of manuscript material, plus the comprehensive index, are still under preparation. This reference set essentially replaces the 19th-century Frisch edition, which is however, still useful for its index and extensive documentation of Kepler's mother's trial for witchcraft.

The standard biography is CASPAR (1959). Caspar relied heavily on the introductory material he had prepared for the main volumes in the collected edition, and on the German edition of letters. Curiously, Caspar included virtually no references in his biography, although it is full of quotations from the letters and books. This lacuna has been filled by Gingerich and Alain Segonds in the recent Dover edition, which contains nearly 1200 citations; this edition also contains a bibliography of recent articles relating to Kepler.

CASPAR (1968) is a second edition of his excellent bibliography (1936), edited by his long-time assistant Martha List, and provides a wealth of publication information on all known printed works by Kepler, as well as an extensive bibliography of articles. An extension of the bibliography to 1974, prepared by List, is included in the Beer & Beer symposium volume. A new and extensively revised edition of the *Bibliographia Kepleriana* is expected within the next few years; it will extend the bibliography to more recent articles, list a few recently discovered original items, and incorporate world-wide locations of the printed copies of all the Keplerian texts.

The original publication in German of Caspar (1959) in 1948 provided grist for the distinguished novelist Arthur KOESTLER to prepare *The Watershed*, a biographical section of *The Sleepwalkers: A History of Man's Changing Vision of the Universe*, in which he analyzed Kepler from the viewpoint of the psychology of discovery. Although controversial in its interpretation, Koestler's vivid moulding of Caspar's material helped to spark a renewed interest in Keplerian studies, and led to a major revision of the traditional picture of Kepler as a curve-fitting mystic, who finally made empirical sense of Tycho Brahe's treasure trove of observations. The anthology by Curtis WILSON, and the major book by Alexandre Koyré, showed Kepler guided by a highly unusual physical sense (uncommon among astronomers, who were supposed at the time to work geometrically, without physical considerations). Addressing the technical issues, these and other researchers have reminded readers that Tycho Brahe's observations were not sufficiently precise to define an ellipse without guidance from physical considerations, which Kepler sought in theoretical magnetical speculations. Furthermore, GINGERICH's study of the surviving manuscript legacy (primarily in St Petersburg, Russia) has revealed that Kepler's most important work, his *Astronomia nova*, was far from a linear autobiographical presentation of his researches, but rather a complex and carefully crafted account; this and other of his articles are collected in his anthology. VOELKEL carries this theme further, showing the rhetorical construction of the *Astronomia nova*, as well as describing the intense interaction with the correspondent David Fabricius that helped shape Kepler's argument. STEPHENSON (1987) is the most comprehensive study of Kepler's physical astronomy, not only concerning the *Astronomia nova*, but also the relevant parts of the *Epitome*, including the complex lunar theory.

In looking back over his early years, Kepler stated that all his ideas found their inception in his *Mysterium cosmographicum* of 1596, wherein he demonstrated his unabashed Copernicanism, his quest for answers to fundamental questions such as why there is so much empty space in the Copernican system, and his attempt to derive planetary speeds from physical principles. This work is now available in an English translation by DUNCAN, with extensive notes by Eric Aiton. A particularly well-annotated edition has been produced in French by SEGONDS, indispensable to any student of Kepler's earliest studies; the appendices and notes occupy fully half of the volume. An extended analysis of this work, as well as its relation to Kepler's *Harmonice mundi*, has been given by FIELD, who focuses on one of Kepler's major preoccupations, his search for the geometrical plan according to which God created the universe.

Kepler's greatest work, *Astronomia nova*, stands with Ptolemy's *Almagest*, Copernicus's *De revolutionibus* and Newton's *Principia* as one of the great foundation stones of mathematical astronomy. His *opus magnum* describes his attack on Mars, his discovery of the non-uniform orbital velocity of the earth, and what are now known as Kepler's first two laws of planetary motion. It was, nevertheless, deemed too technical for the Great Books of the Western World series (published by Encyclopedia Britannica), which included the other three works but opted to represent Kepler by his more cohesive account given in the central part of his longest work, *Epitome of Copernican Astronomy*. For this purpose they commissioned a useful, though unannotated, translation by WALLIS.

In 1961, KOYRÉ published an extended analysis of the *Astronomia nova*, in which he partially took into account the newly published Keplerian correspondence. An English translation of the *Astronomia nova*, long awaited, finally materialized through the sustained effort of William H. DONAHUE, who repeated all of Kepler's computations, not always with complete success, and in the process unearthed several archaeological layers in the construction of the book.

Remarking on Kepler's *Harmonice mundi*, Caspar stated that, "this book was his mind's favorite child . . . With the accuracy of a researcher, who arranges and calculates observations, is united the power of shaping of an artist, who knows about the image, and the ardor of the seeker for God, who struggles with the angel. So his Harmonice appears as a great cosmic vision, woven out of science, poetry, philosophy, theology, mysticism . . . " In this work Kepler sought a unified picture of cosmic harmony as revealed in geometry, astrology, music, and astronomy. In the course of his investigations, he stumbled across the so-called harmonic law (Kepler's third law of planetary motion), a theoretical derivation of which he attempted to provide in his *Epitome*. Partially translated into English in the Great Books series (with some excellent footnotes on the musical annotation), a fully annotated translation of the *Harmony* has been done by AITON, DUNCAN & FIELD. STEPHENSON (1995) clears up several misconceptions that exist in earlier secondary literature, and places Kepler's harmonic approach into a wider context, including its inspiration from Ptolemy's *Harmonics* and 17th-century ideas on musical harmony and cosmic consonances.

The complexity of Kepler's thought is revealed in several studies that examine both these and other minor works. Kepler was trained in the Lutheran seminary at Tübingen, and he originally anticipated a career as a clergyman. Unwilling to accept all the details of the Lutheran Formula of Concord, he eventually found himself excommunicated, although he was always a devout Christian, and believed that God was being celebrated through his discoveries. The most extensive treatment of Kepler's theology is given by HÜBNER. Because theological ideas played such a fundamental role in Kepler's thought, these were intimately bound up with his astronomical researches, a theme explored by KOZHAMTHADAM, although the causal connections between his theology and the shaping of his astronomical discoveries are necessarily only speculative. In his search for cosmic harmony and unity, Kepler always assumed a connection between human souls at birth and the position of the planets, even though he rejected most of traditional astrology. SIMON has examined this intertwining of the physical astronomy and Kepler's attempts to produce a physical astrology.

A Keplerian work of considerable importance for establishing his philosophy of science remained unpublished in his lifetime. Written at the behest of his sometime patron, Tycho Brahe, the *Tract against Ursus* defended Tycho against a charge of plagiarism, but Kepler used the occasion to address broader issues. In preparing a translation and commentary, Nicholas JARDINE argues that this is a key not only for understanding Kepler's mature works, but important for the light it sheds on the emergence of modern assumptions about the nature of science and scientific progress; hence he has called it "the birth of the history and philosophy of science". Concentrating more squarely on the plagiarism issue, ROSEN (1986) considered the three successive Imperial Mathematicians in Prague (Ursus, Tycho, and Kepler) and produced a useful compendium of translated sources.

The rich fabric of Kepler's contribution becomes even clearer by examining additional minor works, several of which now have translations and informative analyses. For example, Kepler was the first astronomer of note to comment on Galileo's new telescopic discoveries, and his "conversation" with the *Sidereus nuncius* has been translated into English by Edward Rosen (1967) and into French, with a very scholarly and extensive set of notes, by PANTIN; a whimsical and brief New Year's offering, a theoretical explanation of why snowflakes have six corners, is considered a pioneering work in crystallography; Kepler's *Dioptrice* gave the first optical theory of the telescope and proposed a new arrangement of lenses that was soon widely adopted; and his *Stereometria* is a foundation work in the prehistory of the calculus. A science fiction work of Kepler's later years (propagandizing for the Copernican arrangement), the *Somnium*, has had more than one translation, of which the best is ROSEN (1967).

Perhaps it is as a result of his multifaceted personality and contributions, which might prove daunting to scholars, that no major biography of Kepler has appeared in nearly half a century. A modest but steady stream of doctoral dissertations and articles attests to a lively interest in Kepler's role in early modern science, and with the completion of the collected works, which has so far taken nearly seven decades, the time is ripe for a fresh consideration of this remarkable genius.

OWEN GINGERICH

See also Astronomy: general works; Copernicanism; Scientific Revolution

Keynes, John Maynard 1883–1946

British economist

Friedman, Milton, *A Theory of the Consumption Function*, Princeton, New Jersey: Princeton University Press, 1957

Hansen, Alvin, *A Guide to Keynes*, New York: McGraw-Hill, 1953

Harrod, R.F., *The Life of John Maynard Keynes*, London: Macmillan, 1951; New York: St Martin's Press, 1963

Howson, Susan and Donald Winch, *The Economic Advisory Council, 1930–1939: A Study in Economic Advice during Depression and Recovery*, Cambridge and New York: Cambridge University Press, 1977

Kahn, Richard F., *The Making of Keynes' General Theory*, Cambridge and New York: Cambridge University Press, 1984

Keynes, Milo (ed.), *Essays on John Maynard Keynes*, Cambridge and New York: Cambridge University Press, 1975

Leijonhufvud, Axel, *On Keynesian Economics and the Economics of Keynes: A Study in Monetary Theory*, New York and London: Oxford University Press, 1968

Lucas Jr, Robert E., *Studies in Business-Cycle Theory*, Cambridge, Massachusetts: MIT Press, and Oxford: Blackwell, 1981

Moggridge, D.E., *Maynard Keynes: An Economist's Biography*, London and New York: Routledge, 1992

Patinkin, Don, "*Anticipations of the General Theory?*" *and Other Essays on Keynes*, Chicago: University of Chicago Press, and Oxford: Blackwell, 1982

Shackle, G.L.S., *The Years of High Theory: Invention and Tradition in Economic Thought, 1926–1939*, Cambridge: Cambridge University Press, 1967

Skidelsky, Robert, *John Maynard Keynes*, 2 vols, London: Macmillan, 1983–92; New York: Viking, 1986–94

Stein, Herbert, *The Fiscal Revolution in America*, Chicago: University of Chicago Press, 1969; revised editions, Washington, DC: AEI Press, 1990 and 1996

John Maynard Keynes is historically important mainly as one of the two or three most highly respected economists of the 20th century. Nevertheless, he also deserves some attention for his influence on government policies and, to a lesser degree, as a member of the culturally significant Bloomsbury Group.

The distinguished mainstream Keynesian economist HARROD wrote the first major biography of Keynes. Harrod's biography has been supplanted by more recent work, and is now mainly of interest for its early contribution to the promotion of Keynesian doctrines. Some critics of the work note that it omits personal information that might be viewed as unfavorable to Keynes. Keynes's nephew, Milo KEYNES, has edited a useful collection of essays by distinguished scholars that supplements the Harrod biography in a variety of directions. As might be expected, the essays, except for Harry Johnson's, present a favorable picture of Keynes. Another account written by a friend, is by Sir Richard KAHN, who was one of Keynes's students and later, during the period of the writing of the General Theory, a collaborator. Kahn emphasizes the importance of Keynes's growing role as a practical policy adviser for the development of his views. He also suggests that Keynes's disputes with his Cambridge colleagues were less acrimonious than many have believed.

SKIDELSKY has written the most readable, complete and useful biography; it emphasizes Keynes's personal life and his involvement in the world of policy and culture. Skidelsky's work is unsurpassed for sheer detail on Keynes's personal life, but this has led some critics to argue that such detail obscures Keynes's main claim to fame – his contributions to economics. MOGGRIDGE's book covers much the same territory as Skidelsky, but with a drier style, somewhat less emphasis on personal matters and somewhat more emphasis on economics. Moggridge incorporates insights he has learned in his years of co-editing the collected works of Keynes. Moggridge's volume covers all of Keynes's life, while Skidelsky's second volume (of a projected three) concludes with 1937, the year following the publication of the General Theory.

Within the economics profession there have been lively and continuing debates on the nature of Keynes's central message in his General Theory. The mainstream view uses mathematical apparatus, such as the IS-LM equilibrium graphs, of the Nobel prize winner Hicks to clarify what Keynes really meant. Hicks's simple diagrams, analogous to supply and demand diagrams in neo-classical price theory, have the advantage of simplicity, policy relevance, and fruitfulness in leading to additional research. In addition, they provided an interpretation of Keynes that was most compatible with the existing body of neo-classical theory. An early summary of the mainstream view (and one that was partially responsible for its popularization) is HANSEN. Two main non-mainstream lines of interpretation have garnered considerable attention: the first, explored by LEIJONHUFVUD and Clower, emphasizes the inter-temporal disequilibrium aspects of Keynes's message, while the other non-mainstream interpretation emphasized the impact that expectations (both rational and irrational) have on the economy. This interpretation was advocated by Joan Robinson, the later Hicks, and perhaps in its most extreme form by SHACKLE.

PATINKIN also entered the interpretative fray in order to discover the accuracy of the usual view that the Keynesian revolution was a case of multiple co-discovery, with Keynes's theory having been independently discovered by one or more of Michal Kalecki, Erik Lindahl, Gunnar Myrdal, Bertil Ohlin or Knut Wicksell. Patinkin marshals evidence to conclude that Keynes's "central message" was his Theory of Effective Demand, and goes on to conclude that the alleged co-discoverers did not have the Theory of Effective Demand as their "central message" and hence cannot be considered to have been co-discoverers. Patinkin's interpretation of Keynes's central message has been adopted by many Keynes scholars, including Moggridge and Skidelsky.

The most famous opponent of Keynes, the Nobel prize-winner Milton FRIEDMAN, in one of his most celebrated works, criticized Keynes's view that the poor consume a greater percentage of their income than the rich. This claim was used by some Keynesians to justify redistribution to the poor in order to stimulate the economy. Contrary to Keynes's view, Friedman found evidence that when income is properly interpreted as "permanent income" nearly all income groups consume roughly the same percentage of their income (about 90%). Encouraged by the Keynes-refuting stagflation of the 1970s, the Nobel prizewinner LUCAS and other "new classical economists" elaborated a rational expectations theory that criticized the role Keynes gives to irrational expectations in influencing macroeconomic magnitudes, such as the rate of unemployment.

Keynes's influence on policy has been much discussed and documented. From an emphasis on original sources and reports, HOWSON & WINCH analyze Keynes's dominant role in the 1930s on Britain's Economic Advisory Council, and its successor organization, the Committee on Economic Information. The authors suggest that the policy problems that Keynes faced in his dealings with the Council help to explain his movement from his orthodox neo-classical views in his *Treatise on Money* to his revolutionary views in the General Theory.

In a stimulating and well-documented book, STEIN contradicts the commonplace view that Keynes's General Theory influenced the depression-era economic policy of the Roosevelt administration in the United States. Stein does not deny, however, that Keynes, and especially the mainstream Keynesians, were an important influence on United States policy after World War II.

ARTHUR M. DIAMOND, JR

Klein, Melanie 1882–1960
Austrian-born English psychoanalyst

Doane, Janice and Devon Hodges, *From Klein to Kristeva: Psychoanalytic Feminism and the Search for the "Good Enough" Mother*, Ann Arbor: University of Michigan Press, 1992

Grosskurth, Phyllis, *Melanie Klein: Her World and Her Work*, London: Hodder and Stoughton, and New York: Knopf, 1986

Hinshelwood, R.D., *A Dictionary of Kleinian Thought*, London: Free Association, 1989; revised edition, London: Free Association, and Northvale, New Jersey: Aronson, 1991

Hughes, Judith M., *Reshaping the Psychoanalytic Domain: The Work of Melanie Klein, W.R.D. Fairbairn and D.W. Winnicott*, Berkeley: University of California Press, 1989

King, Pearl and Riccardo Steiner (eds), *The Freud–Klein Controversies, 1941–45*, London and New York: Routledge/Tavistock, 1991

Mitchell, Juliet (ed.), *The Selected Melanie Klein*, Harmondsworth: Penguin, 1986; New York: Free Press, 1987

Riviere, Joan (ed.), *Developments in Psycho-Analysis*, London: Hogarth Press, 1952; New York: Da Capo, 1983

Rose, Jacqueline, *Why War? Psychoanalysis, Politics and the Return to Melanie Klein*, Oxford and Cambridge, Massachusetts: Blackwell, 1993

Sayers, Janet, *Mothering Psychoanalysis: Helene Deutsch, Karen Horney, Anna Freud and Melanie Klein*, London: Hamish Hamilton, 1991

Segal, Hanna, *Klein*, Brighton, Sussex: Harvester Press, 1979; as *Melanie Klein*, New York: Viking, 1980

Spillius, Elizabeth Bott (ed.), *Melanie Klein Today: Developments in Theory and Practice*, 2 vols, London and New York: Routledge, 1988

Melanie Klein's position as a highly influential and, at times, controversial figure in the development of psychoanalytic theory and therapy has been unassailable since the 1920s. She is considered one of the most innovative thinkers after Freud, a pioneer in the field of child-analysis, whose theories place emphasis on the first few months of psychic life. However, it is only relatively recently that her work has begun to be seriously discussed outside the boundaries of her discipline.

Segal and Mitchell both supply useful overviews of Klein's work and are a good place to start. SEGAL is a self-professed follower of Klein and, as such, provides an "authorised" version of her theories. While clear and concise, the book is nevertheless somewhat misleading, precisely because it provides a reading of Klein's work that is overly neat, and almost schematic. In contrast, MITCHELL's account, organized as an introductory chapter with explanatory notes framing a representative selection of Klein's own writings, draws out more successfully the complexities and inconsistencies of her system of thought, and contextualises it through a thoughtful and informative comparison with those theories of Freud from which it derives and deviates.

GROSSKURTH's biography of Klein is the most complete account of her life and the professional context in which she worked. This was a controversial book when it first appeared, as it proposed to unveil a figure who had been consistently mythologized (and demonized) by the psychoanalytic establishment. It forms a richly detailed psychological portrait of Klein, and follows her complex relationships with family members, colleagues, and rivals. However, Grosskurth's description of Klein's concepts is less than reliable. Moreover, although the book does give an account of the controversies surrounding the figure of Klein, it does not theorise them adequately.

KING & STEINER's massive, but carefully edited and well introduced, tome provides the reader with the archival documentation concerning the main institutional event surrounding Klein: the so-called Controversial Discussions, which opposed her followers to those of Anna Freud. The critical apparatus provided by the editors, as well as the actual documents reprinted here (such as letters, reports, and minutes of meetings), form an invaluable guide to understanding Klein's historical place within British psychoanalysis, as well as her institutional importance.

HUGHES is also of much use in positioning Klein. The approach is different from that taken in King & Steiner, as it emphasises clinical practice and writing, rather than institutional politics. Hughes reads Klein's work, with special emphasis on her book-length case history *Narrative of a Child Analysis*, alongside the contributions of Winnicott and Fairbairn. She argues that all three form parallel strands of a theoretical restructuring of psychoanalysis, particularly in Britain.

RIVIERE's anthology, containing important essays by Klein's colleagues, appeared as an aftermath to the events recorded in King & Steiner and, as such, stands as a kind of manifesto for a consolidated Kleinian movement within British psychoanalysis. SPILLIUS's two-volume anthology brings the reader up to date on the way Klein's theories have been adopted and used by psychoanalysts since that time. It forms, in the main, a good and representative selection of Kleinian psychoanalytic writing. However, the effect is undermined by a spurious division of the essays into a volume devoted to "mainly theory" and another one devoted to "mainly practice". The nature of the complex interrelationship of theory and practice in psychoanalysis is, needless to say, inadequately addressed.

HINSHELWOOD provides a generally sound account of the development and uses of Kleinian terminology, and this book is a useful reference tool. However, some of its shortcomings must be noted, the main one being its explicit assumption of the primacy of clinical experience of a quasi-mystical sort pertaining to "archaic" and "unknowable" regions of the mind. This assumption is not scrutinised or put in a historical perspective. The volume itself is divided into two parts: the first part consists of several articles tracing the development of those concepts that Hinshelwood regards as fundamental to

Kleinian theory; the second part consists of more succinct entries arranged in alphabetical order, but which at times seem arbitrary in their selection. The result is factually accurate, but lacks sufficient conceptual sophistication and historical acumen.

SAYERS presents Klein's life and work as part of a general narrative of the shift in the psychoanalytical movement from a father-centred and patriarchal theory, to a mother-centred one that appeals to a feminist political agenda. Sayers provides a concise reading of Klein's life and work, as well as that of three other pioneering female psychoanalysts, Helene Deutsch, Karen Horney, and Anna Freud. The focus is on the idea of "mothering", understood on two levels that Sayers sees as interrelated: biographical, concerning these women's relationships with their mothers and (if applicable) their children; and theoretical, referring to the search for an understanding of the feminine.

DOANE & HODGES also concentrate on the mothering bond in psychoanalysis, and seek to illustrate the ways in which it has been taken up by feminist theory. In so doing, they place Klein's work in a foundational position. Although this book is very helpful in situating Klein within a feminist discourse that has traditionally not recognized her influence, the treatment given to her theories is too sketchy to stand on its own.

ROSE's collection of wide-ranging essays integrates psychoanalytic history, psychoanalytic theory, and feminist thought. On the one hand, Klein's work is read within the context of the debates outlined in King & Steiner; for example, the author explores the implications of the "Controversial Discussions" for a theorization of the limits of knowledge and self-knowledge in psychoanalysis. On the other hand, Rose also tackles literary texts and contemporary political issues, and proposes using Klein's theories, namely negativity and unconscious phantasy, as effective analytical tools in the effort to understand our status as political subjects.

JULIA BOROSSA

See also Psychoanalyis: conceptual

Knowledge and Power

Abercrombie, Nicholas, Stephen Hill and Bryan S. Turner, *The Dominant Ideology Thesis*, London and Boston: Allen and Unwin, 1980

Bacon, Francis, *The Works of Francis Bacon*, edited by James Spedding, Robert Leslie Ellis and Douglas Denon Heale, 14 vols, London: Longman, 1857–74; Boston: Brown and Tuggart, 1860–64

Barnes, Barry, *The Nature of Power*, Cambridge: Polity Press, and Urbana: University of Illinois Press, 1988

Box, Ian, *The Social Thought of Francis Bacon*, Lewiston, New York and Lampeter, Dyfed: Edwin Mellen Press, 1989

Clegg, Stewart R., *Frameworks of Power*, London: Sage, 1989

Foucault, Michel, *Discipline and Punish: The Birth of the Prison*, translated from the French by Alan Sheridan, London: Allen Lane, and New York: Pantheon Books, 1977 (original edition, 1977)

Foucault, Michel, *Power/Knowledge: Selected Interviews and Other Writings, 1972–77*, edited and translated from the French by Colin Gordon, Brighton, Sussex: Harvester Press, and New York: Pantheon Books, 1980

Latour, Bruno, *We Have Never Been Modern*, translated from the French by Catherine Porter, Hemel Hempstead, Hertfordshire: Harvester Wheatsheaf, 1992; Cambridge, Massachusetts: Harvard University Press, 1993 (original edition, 1991)

Law, John (ed.), *Power, Action and Belief: A New Sociology of Knowledge?*, London and Boston: Routledge and Kegan Paul, 1986

Mannheim, Karl, *Ideology and Utopia: An Introduction to the Sociology of Knowledge*, translated from the German by Louis Wirth and Edward Shils, London: Routledge and Kegan Paul, and New York: Harcourt Brace, 1936 (original edition, 1929)

Marx, Karl and Friedrich Engels, *The German Ideology*, London: Lawrence and Wishart, 1938; edited by S. Ryazonskaya, Moscow: Progress, 1968

Rouse, Joseph, *Knowledge and Power: Toward a Political Philosophy of Science*, Ithaca, New York: Cornell University Press, 1987

The equation of knowledge and power, first made famous by Francis BACON, has become central to our understanding of both science and society. Yet our interpretation of this equation has not remained constant; over the centuries, both knowledge and power have been reinterpreted in the light of new insights and political programmes. For Bacon, knowledge was powerful because it allowed man to increase his practical strength and so transform the natural world. This power granted by understanding was, however, limited to the government of nature. As Ian BOX has shown, Bacon's understanding of the relationship between knowledge and power never extended into the social realm. His repeated conceptualisation of the true society as a kind of desire-free utopia excluded the need for a form of knowledge aimed at government or social control.

The simple equation of knowledge and power formulated by Bacon was contested by MARX & ENGELS, who argued that knowledge not only produced power but was itself produced by power, since the means of cultural production were controlled by the dominant classes. Thus culture had an ideological function, providing a rationalisation for the social inequalities maintained by class division. Against Bacon, who had believed that knowledge was powerful because it offered a true representation of the world, Marx argued that the power it granted the dominant classes stemmed from its distortion of external reality: culture and knowledge prevented the masses from reaching a true and revolutionary consciousness of their social conditions.

Throughout the 20th century, Marx's ideas on the social bases and ideological function of knowledge have been consistently refined. In 1929, Karl MANNHEIM contested the polemical understanding of ideology contained in Marx's work. He argued that although power could distort knowledge in particular cases, it also produced the general structures of thinking. Whereas power and knowledge had remained extrinsic to each other in the models proposed by Bacon and

Marx (knowledge could grant a certain power; power could prevent the uptake of knowledge), in Mannheim's account it was power, or the social structure, which actually produced the shape of knowledge.

The Marxist theory that society was governed by a single dominant ideology was severely criticised by ABERCROMBIE, HILL & TURNER. These authors tested the dominant ideology thesis at four levels: 1) the demonstration of a dominant ideology's existence; 2) the identification of transmitting institutions; 3) the ideology's actual influence on the subordinate classes; 4) the impact on the ruling classes. Taking as their case studies Catholic feudalism and early capitalism, the authors argued that their overarching rationales had failed to penetrate through to the level of popular culture. They thus concluded that the dominant ideology should be seen as those shared values that bound the ruling classes, rather than as the agent of social control.

This movement away from a centralised notion of knowledge and power is reflected in the work of Barnes and Foucault. Drawing on the theories of American ethnomethodologists and his own previous work in the sociology of science, BARNES constructed a model of social power that was distinctive on two counts. First, he criticised the dominant model of post-war sociology, which had suggested that social cohesion was achieved through a process of internal socialisation – i.e., the creation within the individual of a series of intellectual norms. Instead, Barnes argues that our own knowledge of society developed in public discourse was sufficient in itself to create this cohesion. Second, he reversed the familiar priority of power over knowledge, arguing that it was knowledge that revealed to us the horizons of our discretion and so governed our future action.

The most famous contemporary model of the relationship between power and knowledge has been articulated by Michel Foucault, both in his history of the prison, FOUCAULT (1977), and in the collection of essays and interviews that was specifically named to direct attention to the link between knowledge and power, to the point where the two cannot be distinguished, FOUCAULT (1980). Foucault employed a rigidly historicist approach to power, arguing that it had no stable core, but was simply the matrix of relations operating at a given time. Previous authors had been mistaken, he suggested, since they still worked from a 17th-century model that depicted power as something concentrated in the hands of the few. In contrast, Foucault believed that power was global, being distributed throughout society. Instead of being possessed by individuals, it existed as a collection of discrete strategies disconnected from any authorial agency. It was intimately related to knowledge, however, since language and investigation define the scope of power's domain.

The relationship between this theory and the material world is explored in John LAW's collection. Bringing together a range of writers from the Marxist through to the Foucauldian traditions, Law traces the gradual dissolution of the boundary between knowledge and social structure. In place of the grand schemes that had attributed the shape of culture to the interests of individuals and society as a whole, Law advances the idea that each of these phenomena are produced through a series of local interactions. Law's own study of Portuguese navigation in the 16th century, and the contributions to his volume by Callon and Latour, explicitly develop this theme. Their studies recognise the possibility that power could be contested, and describe many and various techniques that emerge for reducing an individual's discretion. However, this concern with the production of docility could be seen as going beyond Foucault, for it encompassed both human and non-human agents; the studies by Law and Callon, for example, describe how subjects as diverse as scientists and sailors, scallops and astrolabes, have been incorporated into networks of power.

Bruno LATOUR has argued that this dissolution of the boundaries between the social and the material, or the human and the non-human, can be seen as the final undoing of the modernist project. Contemporary society has been forced to deal with a series of crises, such as the AIDS virus and the ozone hole, which breach the boundaries between the social and the scientific. These mediating items, which Latour terms quasi objects, establish a connection between the political and the natural worlds that has sustained so-called primitive societies. Within Latour's polemical presentation, the history of theorising on knowledge emerges as a series of detours in which we return to one starting point, only to recognise that place for the first time.

Two works that take a synoptic view of the power–knowledge debates are to be recommended. Joseph ROUSE integrates the latest ideas in this debate with small scale studies of laboratory work, giving some idea of how these theories can be used in practice. Stewart CLEGG locates the ideas of Barnes, Foucault and Latour within the context of more traditional sociological approaches to power, demonstrating how their cognitive approach developed through local case studies can be fruitfully extended into theories of government and the state.

RHODRI LLOYD HAYWARD

See also Bacon; Marx Foucault

Koch, Robert 1843–1910

German physician and bacteriologist

Brock, Thomas D., *Robert Koch: A Life in Medicine and Bacteriology*, Madison, Wisconsin: Science Tech, and Berlin: Springer, 1988

Bulloch, William, *The History of Bacteriology*, London and New York: Oxford University Press, 1938

Carter, K. Codell, "Koch's Postulates in Relation to the Work of Jacob Henle and Edwin Klebs", *Medical History*, 29 (1985): 353–75

Eckart, Wolfgang U., "Friedrich Althoff und die Medizin", in *Wissenschaftsgeschichte und Wissenschaftspolitik im Industriezeitalter: Das System Althoff in historischer Perspektive*, edited by Bernhard vom Brocke, Hildesheim: Lax, 1991, 375–404

Elkeles, Barbara, "Der 'Tuberkulinrausch' von 1890", *Deutsche Medizinische Wochenschrift*, 115 (1990): 1729–32

Eschenhagen, Gerhard, *Das Hygiene-Institut der Berliner Universität unter der Leitung Robert Kochs 1883–1891*, Dissertation, Berlin: 1983

Evans, Richard J., *Death in Hamburg: Society and Politics in the Cholera Years, 1830–1910*, Oxford: Clarendon Press, and New York: Oxford University Press, 1987

Gradmann, Christoph, "Auf Collegen zum fröhlichen Krieg", *Popularisierte Bakteriologie im Wilhelminischen Zeitalter, Medizin, Gesellschaft und Geschichte*, 13 (1994): 35–54

Heymann, Bruno, *Robert Koch. I. Teil 1843–1882*, Leipzig: Akademische Verlagsanstalt, 1932

Mendelsohn, John Andrew, *Cultures of Bacteriology: Formation and Transformation of a Science in France and Germany, 1870–1914*, Dissertation, Princeton, New Jersey: Princeton University Press, 1966

Möllers, Bernhard, *Robert Koch: Persönlichkeit und Lebenswerk, 1843–1910*, Hanover: Schmorl & von Seefeld, 1950

Schlich, Thomas, "'Wichtiger als der Gegenstand selbst' – Die Bedeutung des fotografischen Bildes in der Begründung der bakteriologischen Krankheitsauffassung durch Robert Koch", in *Neue Wege in der Seuchengeschichte*, edited by Martin Dinges and Thomas Schlich, Stuttgart: Steiner, 1995

Weindling, Paul, "Scientific Elites and Laboratory Organisation in Fin-de-Siècle Paris and Berlin: The Pasteur Institute and Robert Koch's Institute for Infectious Diseases Compared", in *The Laboratory Revolution in Medicine*, edited by Andrew Cunningham and Perry Williams, Cambridge and New York: Cambridge University Press, 1992

The historiography on Robert Koch is to some extent still marked by the hagiographies produced by Koch's contemporaries: the many scientific, biographical, and anecdotal texts, films and even novels, do not always convey reliable or even valuable information. Considering his importance as a pioneer in microbiology, there has been little professional historical research on Koch, compared with that on Louis Pasteur. Only since the 1980s has research on Koch moved from biography to a broader history of science.

There are more than a dozen biographies of Koch, the earliest from 1890, yet only three deserve mention. HEYMANN provides the best account of Koch's early years up to 1882. Based on Koch's scientific writings, private letters, and even laboratory notes, the book combines a psychological understanding of its subject with a thorough description of Koch's scientific work, down to specific laboratory procedures. Unfortunately, the second volume of his biography has never been published. MÖLLERS, who was one of Koch's last collaborators, has produced the most popular German-language biography, which gives a rounded picture of the man and the scientist. It is exhaustive on Koch's scientific work, public and private life, but somewhat less analytic on scientific matters, and it does have a slight hagiographic slant. BROCK is the present-day state-of-the-art biography, offering an excellent assessment of Koch's scientific work. It is devoid of any hagiography, but the author adds little that is new to our knowledge of Koch's personal life, having relied on Heymann and Möllers.

BULLOCH's 1938 history of bacteriology (1938) is by no means outdated, and depicts Koch in rich detail in the context of the emerging bacteriology of his age. Since the 1980s, research has placed Koch within a broader history of science, with some authors investigating the cognitive structure of Koch's bacteriology. First, CARTER has investigated the philosophical foundations of Koch's etiological understanding of disease. Using the example of Koch's postulates, Carter emphasised the role of specific micro-organisms as a (in a strict sense of the word) necessary cause of a specific disease, and stressed that the procedures laid down by Koch in his famous postulates for identifying a causal agent of a disease did not demand sufficiency of explanation. More recently, SCHLICH has explored the epistemological foundations of Koch's bacteriology from another perspective, in order to show the importance of the techniques of visualisation – dyeing and microphotography, in particular – for the development and propagation of bacteriology. GRADMANN has placed Koch's bacteriological concept of infectious diseases within the intellectual context of his age, by showing the mutual influence of scientific concepts of infectious agents and contemporary political concepts.

Another group of texts considers the political and institutional framework of Koch's bacteriology in the 1880s and 1890s. ESCHENHAGEN's notable account of Koch as director of the Department of Hygiene at Berlin University is based on primary sources from Prussian governmental archives.

ELKELES examines Koch's ill-fated attempt to cure tuberculosis with the invention "Tuberkulin", while WEINDLING has undertaken a comparative analysis of Koch's Institut für Infektionskrankheiten in Berlin and the Institut Pasteur in Paris. A point that is obvious in all these texts has been explicitly tackled by ECKART – the dependence of Koch's career on the steady support of the Prussian administration, and of the Ministerialdirektor, Friedrich Althoff, in particular. EVANS, in his study on the Hamburg cholera epidemic of 1892, offers an example of the influence that Koch and his school exerted on the public hygiene of *fin de siècle* Germany.

MENDELSOHN has provided an intellectual history of bacteriology as a juxtaposition of two distinct and separated research schools: the French and the German. While Koch's school was characterized by its decidedly medical background – the emphasis was on the etiology of disease and germs as pathogens – Pasteurian microbiology is shown, by contrast, to have had its roots in the agricultural technology of fermentation processes and to have focused its research on the physiology of micro-organisms. Both schools only gradually merged into an international science of bacteriology during the 1890s, a development accompanied by the shift towards immunological and epidemiological questions.

CHRISTOPH GRADMANN

L

Latin America

Ascher, Marcia and Robert Ascher, *Code of the Quipu: A Study in Media, Mathematics, and Culture*, Ann Arbor: University of Michigan Press, 1981

Azevedo, Fernando de (ed.), *As ciências no Brasil*, 2 vols, São Paulo: Melhoramentos, 1955

Babini, José, *La evolución del pensamiento científico en la Argentina*, Buenos Aires: La Fragua, 1954

Basalla, George, "The Spread of Western Science", *Science*, 156 (May 1967): 611–22

Cueto, Marcos (ed.), *Saberes andinos: ciencia y tecnología en Bolivia, Ecuador y Perú*, Lima: Instituto de Estudios Peruanos, 1995

Gortari, Eli de, *La ciencia en la historia de México*, Mexico City: Fondo de Cultura Económica, 1963

Lafuente, Antonio, Alberto Elena and María Luisa Ortega (eds), *Mundialización de la ciencia y cultura nacional*, Madrid: Doce Calles, 1993

López Austin, Alfredo, *Cuerpo humano e ideología: las concepciones de los antiguos nahuas*, Mexico City: Universidad Nacional Autónoma de México, 1984

Peset Reig, Jose Luis (ed.), *Ciencia, vida y espacio en Iberoamírica*, 3 vols, Madrid: CSIC, 1989

Pyenson, Lewis, "Macondo científico: instuciones científicas en América Latina a principios del siglo XX", in *1907–1987: la junta para ampliación de estudios e investigaciones científicas 80 años después*, vol. 2, edited by José M. Sanchez Ron, Madrid: Consejo Superior Investigaciones Cièntificas, 1989

Quevedo, Emilio (ed.), *Historia social de la ciencia en Colombia*, 10 vols, Santa Fe de Bogotá: Colciencias, 1993

Safford, Frank, *The Ideal of the Practical: Colombia's Struggle to Form a Technical Elite*, Austin: University of Texas Press, 1976

Saldaña, Juan José (ed.), *Historia social de las ciencias en América Latina*, Mexico City: Porrúa/UNAM, 1996

Stepan, Nancy, *Beginnings of Brazilian Science: Oswaldo Cruz, Medical Research and Policy, 1890–1920*, New York: Science History Publications, 1981

Trabulse, Elías, *Historia de la ciencia en México: éstudios y textos*, 4 vols, Mexico City: Conacyt/Fondo de Cultura Económica, 1983–85

Trabulse, Elías, *Ciencia y tecnología en el Nuevo Mundo*, Mexico City: El Colegio de México/Fondo de Cultura Económica, 1994

Yepes, Ernesto (ed.), *Estudios de historia de la ciencia en el Perú*, 2 vols, Lima: Consejo Nacional de Ciencia y Tecnologia, 1986

The history of Latin American science is still a young discipline; only barely institutionalized, it is, however, dynamic and with good prospects for the immediate future. For example, the Latin American Society for the History of Science and Technology (SLHCT) was set up in 1982, and held its first conference in Havana in 1985. The first issue of its journal, *Quipu*, appeared in 1984, and this is the main reference work available to any reader interested in the subject, and a good indication of the work by leading experts in the field.

Before comprehensive studies of Latin American science as a whole became available, there existed only a few, though insightful, local and national monographs, such as the pioneering work by BABINI on Argentina, and the more recent one by YEPES on Peru. Some were written from a Weberian perspective (e.g. AZEVEDO on Brazil), and others followed a materialist analysis (e.g. GORTARI on Mexico). There are compilations that include both studies and texts, whose aim is to highlight the scientific contribution of Latin America, such as the classic work by TRABULSE (1983–85), also on Mexico. There are also modern works focusing on social aspects of science, such as QUEVEDO's on Colombia, a work of synthesis that stands comparison with European books regarding its methodological thoroughness and thematic scope.

In general, two factors have encouraged studies of Latin American science in the last 25 years: first, the development of this discipline itself, the goals and scope of which are now wider, transcending the narrow domain formerly reserved for the exponents of "mainstream" theories; and second, Latin American historians' efforts to find a common language from which to approach the development and specific features of science in the "periphery". With Reingold's thesis on the American scientific method in mind, it is only fair to acknowledge the doubly exceptional character of Latin American scientific procedures: because Spanish and Portuguese penetration took place in the more densely populated areas (especially Mesoamerica and the Andean region), indigenous cultures managed to survive for a longer period and, as a result, syncretism between autochthonous, and European knowledge was (and still remains) greater. The Latin American case reflects the endeavour to rescue the "secret history" from oblivion (in Trabulse's words), the "unchronicled" past (CUETO) of a region on which European scientific revolutions had a marginal effect, and whose contribution to the advancement of the history of that science was also marginal.

With the exception of a few works devoted to the study of science in pre-Colombian cultures (mostly Aztec and Inca cultures – e.g. LOPEZ AUSTIN and ASCHER & ASCHER), most books have dealt with the colonial and modern periods. As a result, it is understandable that the study of Latin American science has been influenced by analyses of the spread and rejection of European paradigms, science in the periphery, and the phenomenon of dependence. Such studies have been conducted against the backdrop of colonialism, in both its formal and informal variants; the origins and causes of scientific and technical backwardness remain the issues to elucidate, and the debate has often been articulated in a nationalist (or imperialist from the old metropolis) language.

Also within this dialectic between European and local science, the books that shed light on the former indebtedness to the latter, the expansion or even construction of modern science from an American basis, are abundant as well. The most remarkable example is that of knowledge associated with geography and natural history; TRABULSE (1994) focuses on the double role played by America in the reception and transformation of geographic, cartographic, astronomic, and metallurgical knowledge during the 16th, 17th, and 18th centuries.

Among the comprehensive studies available on the topic, three can be singled out. The first, in three volumes and edited by PESET REIG, comprises numerous contributions on disparate topics: life sciences, technology, urbanism and the city, geography, navigation, and scientific expeditions. This book has the virtue of being encyclopedic; its 80 or so articles are the result of extensive research carried out on specific aspects by experts from different countries (mostly Spanish and Latin American). Most readers will find something in these works relevant to their own research or of interest to them.

The second study, edited by LAFUENTE, ELENA & ORTEGA four years later, shows the prevalence of some of the tendencies outlined in the previous volume, such as the importance of studies devoted to Latin American Enlightenment. Though less detailed, it has the advantage of including numerous North American historians, so that what had been hitherto a dialogue becomes a wider discussion. Readers will find here less empirical research and more attempts at comparative analysis, such as that of scientific associationism and the spread of science. For example, BASALLA discusses his famous and controversial argument, which has been described as the starting shot for the discourse on colonialism and science.

The third comprehensive work is that published under the supervision of SALDAÑA. It is fair to say that this is the first real synthesis of the history of Latin American science – it is not a collection of articles, but a systematic and well-arranged book. The work offers a veritable social history of science that treats the Latin American space as a unified geographical and cultural region. Its 15 chapters were written by leading specialists (Vessuri, Cueto, Arboleda, Quevedo, Estrella, and Saldaña himself), who describe the landmarks in this discipline, ranging from pre-Colombian medicine and astronomy, to academic science and 19th-century scientific policy, the natural history

of the Renaissance, the spread and adaptation of modern science during the Enlightenment, public health, and 19th-century positivism.

Although works devoted to the modern period out-number those available for other periods, there are good monographs on different aspects of Latin American science, during the age of new independent nations. SAFFORD's book describes the endeavour of the Colombian ruling classes to train elite engineers in the 19th century, and testifies to the difficulties arising from the adaptation of foreign models and the transformation of local cultural values. STEPAN, in her study of the Brazilian institution "Oswaldo Cruz", tackles the issue of excellence in the periphery, and the institutionalization of microbiology at the beginning of the 20th century. PYENSON, finally, in a small but insightful work, tries to combat the narrow-mindedness inherent in nationalism, which is a persistent trait of Latin American historiography. Resorting to García Márquez's image, he describes the light and shadow of Latin American scientific institutions at the turn of the century, places in which rationality is still haunted by a dim, but magical and erudite past.

JUAN PIMENTEL

Laue, Max von 1879–1960
German theoretical physicist

Ewald, P.P., "Max von Laue", *Biographical Memoirs of the Royal Society*, 6 (1960): 135–56

"Feierstunde zu Ehren von Max von Laue an seinem 80. Geburtstag", *Mitteilungen der Max-Planck-Gesellschaft*, 6 (1959): 323–66

Hermann, Armin, entry on Laue in *Dictionary of Scientific Biography*, edited by Charles Coulson Gillispie, vol. 8, New York: Scribner, 1980

Herneck, Friedrich, *Max von Laue*, Leipzig, 1979

Hildebrandt, G., "Max von Laue, der 'Ritter ohne Furcht und Tadel'", in *Berlinische Lebensbilder 1: Naturwissenschaftler*, edited by Hildebrandt and W. Treue, Berlin: Colloquium, 1987

Laue, Max von, *Gesammelte Schriften und Vorträge*, 3 vols, Braunschweig: Vieweg, 1961

Meissner, W., *Max von Laue als Wissenschaftler und Mensch: Sitzungsberichte der Bayerischen Akademie der Wissenschaften, Mathematisch-Naturwissenschaftliche Klasse*, Munich: Verlag der Bayerischen Akademie der Wissenschaften, 1960, 101–21

Päsler, M., "Leben und Wissenschaftliches Werk Laues", *Physikalische Blätter*, 16 (1960): 552–67

Über das Persönliche und Wissenschaftliche Wirken von Albert Einstein und Max von Laue, 21, East Berlin, 1980

Max von Laue was a scientist of world renown, who was awarded the Nobel prize for his contribution to the discovery of X-ray diffraction. Despite being an outstanding physicist of the 20th century, and despite the fact that his scientific papers and lectures have been published in a three-volume edition, historians of science have paid scant attention to his work. While there are plenty of obituaries and memorial essays by his colleagues, students, and historians of physics, there is no biography of academic quality. Anyone desiring to work on Laue should therefore start with LAUE, which also contains the 1952 autobiographical notes, "Mein physikalischer Werdegang"; these detail the most important stages in his life, his relations with his colleagues, the motivation for his work, and, especially, his philosophical attitude. Laue did not develop his own philosophical system and it is difficult to place him within a particular philosophical category, but he did grant philosophy a central role. He maintained "that all science needs to group around philosophy as a common centre and it is the purpose of science to serve philosophy. Only in this way can the unity of scientific culture be preserved in the face of the fragmentation accompanying specialisation."

Because there are a few comprehensive historical studies of Laue, HERMANN's entry in the *Dictionary of Scientific Biography* is to be recommended as an introductory text. Without providing much detailed information, Hermann gives an instructive overview of Laue's life, and especially of his scientific accomplishments. The focus is on the discovery of the diffraction of X-rays by crystals and his contributions to the theory of relativity; unfortunately, Laue's works on thermodynamics and superconductivity are omitted. The reader also learns little about Laue's activities in the organisation of science and in politics, which were especially important in the post-World War II period. Information on this aspect of Laue's life has to be gleaned from the anniversary publications and obituaries – "FEIERSTUNDE", Päsler, Meissner, and Ewald – although these can be hagiographic and unreliable, perpetuating uncritically well-known myths and legends.

EWALD contains the most authentic description of the discovery of X-ray interference, and its roots in the Munich scientific environment of the late Wilhelmine era. It also contains a bibliography of Laue's writings. Laue's contribution to the theory of superconductivity is mentioned in detail in MEISSNER's obituary, although the relation between Laue's work and that of one of the London brothers is not told quite truthfully – modern work on superconductivity gives a much more differentiated picture. In addition, Meissner describes Laue's brave behaviour during the Nazi era, which brought him international acclaim. It is in reference to this that HILDEBRANDT's essay is subtitled "Knight Without Fear and Blame"; he adds little to our knowledge of Laue during the Nazi period, but gives an instructive and knowledgeable overview of Laue's collected works, and of his participation in the reconstruction of science in Germany after World War II. The same can be said of PÄSLER's commemorative address.

The papers by HERNECK, a Marxist historian of science from the German Democratic Republic, present in a popular way Laue's most important scientific contribution, the discovery of X-ray interference. This is integrated with his work on the theory of relativity and superconductivity within the wider history of physics, and in so doing Herneck manages to keep Laue's personality in the foreground. Laue's role in the Berlin scientific community of the 1920s and 1930s is described, including his admiration for his supervisor Max Planck, his relation to Einstein, and his conflicts with the Nazis.

The appreciation of Laue's role in post-war Germany (especially in West Berlin) focused mainly on his initiatives in the 1957 declaration of the "Göttingen Eighteen" (a group of West German physicists who protested publicly against the atomic armament of the West German army, and who vigorously rejected participation in any research related to military technology), and his initiatives for collaboration and dialogue with the East Berlin academy of science. On the occasion of the centenary of Laue's birth, a history of science colloquium took place in East Berlin, which resulted in the *ÜBER DAS PERSÖNLICHE . . .* This contains a contribution on Laue as a physicist, and an article on his relation to scientific institutions in Berlin. His contribution to the Physikalische Kolloquium of the university and his philosophical position are also covered in detail – although the account is not always free of the ideological, Marxist-Leninist blinkers so typical of the time.

DIETER HOFFMANN

translated by Klaus Staubermann

Lavoisier, Antoine Laurent   1743–1794

French chemist, financier, and administrator

Bensaude-Vincent, Bernadette, *Lavoisier: mémoires d'une révolution*, Paris: Flammarion, 1993

Beretta, Marco, *The Enlightenment of Matter: The Definition of Matter from Agricola to Lavoisier*, Canton, Massachusetts: Science History Publications, 1993

Berthelot, Marcellin, *La Révolution chimique: Lavoisier*, Paris: Alcan, 1890

Berthelot, Marcellin, "Notice historique sur Lavoisier", *Mémoires de l'Académie des Sciences de l'Institut de France*, 45 (1889): xix–lxxii

Crosland, Maurice P., *Historical Studies in the Language of Chemistry*, London: Heinemann, and Cambridge, Massachusetts: Harvard University Press, 1962; 2nd edition, New York: Dover, 1978

Crosland, Maurice P., "Lavoisier's Theory of Acidity", *Isis*, 64 (1973): 306–25

Daumas, Maurice, *Lavoisier, Théoricien et expérimentateur*, Paris: Presses Universitaires de France, 1955

Demeulenaere-Douyère, Christianne (ed.), *Il y a 200 ans Lavoisier*, Paris: Technique et Documentation-Lavoisier, 1995

Donovan, Arthur (ed.), "The Chemical Revolution: Essays in Reinterpretation", *Osiris*, 2nd series, 4 (1988): 5–231

Donovan, Arthur, *Antoine Lavoisier: Science, Administration and Revolution*, Oxford and Cambridge, Massachusetts: Blackwell, 1993

Dumas, Jean-Baptiste, *Leçons sur la philosophie chimique*, Paris: Bechet Jeune, 1836; reprinted, Brussels: Editions "Culture et Civilisation", 1972

Duveen, Denis I. and H.S. Klickstein, *A Bibliography of the Works of Antoine Laurent Lavoisier, 1743–1794*, London: Dawson, 1954; *Supplement*, London: Dawson, 1965

Goupil, Michelle (ed.), *Lavoisier et la Révolution chimique*, Paris: SABIX-École Polytechnique, 1992

Grimaux, Edouard, *Lavoisier, 1743–1794, D'Après Sa Correspondance, ses manuscrits, ses papiers de famille et d'autres documents inédits*, Paris: Alcan, 1888

Guerlac, Henry, *Lavoisier – The Crucial Year: The Background and Origin of His First Experiments on Combustion in 1772*, Ithaca, New York: Cornell University Press, 1961

Holmes, Frederic L., *Lavoisier and the Chemistry of Life: An Exploration of Scientific Creativity*, Madison: University of Wisconsin Press, 1985

McKie, Douglas, *Antoine Lavoisier: The Father of Modern Chemistry*, London: Gollancz, 1935; Philadelphia: Lippincott, 1936

McKie, Douglas, *Antoine Lavoisier: Scientist, Economist, Social Reformer*, London: Constable, and New York: Schuman, 1952

Poirier, Jean-Pierre, *Lavoisier: Chemist, Biologist, Economist*, translated from the French by Rebecca Balinski; Philadelphia: University of Pennsylvania Press, 1996 (original edition 1993)

Siegfried, Robert and B.J. Dobbs, "Composition: A Neglected Aspect of the Chemical Revolution", *Annals of Science*, 24 (1968): 275–93

Despite the importance of the "chemical revolution" associated with Antoine Laurent Lavoisier, there were few early biographical studies of the chemist, while much of his work soon came to be taken for granted, as chemistry moved into such new 19th-century dimensions as atomic theory and electrochemistry. There may have been some jealousy of Lavoisier among his former colleagues because of his superior wealth, and his execution at the height of the Terror was certainly an embarrassment in the more stable period which followed. When DUMAS gave his famous lectures in 1836, he could claim that Lavoisier had been forgotten. For Dumas, Lavoisier alone was the founder of modern chemistry, and he had died the death of a martyr. It was customary for the Académie des Sciences to deliver an *éloge* of its more important members yet this duty was ignored until 1889, the centenary of the political revolution, when BERTHELOT took on the task. Like Dumas, he presented Lavoisier in a heroic mould: he alone was responsible for the new chemistry, an interpretation to be disputed later (e.g. see GOUPIL, chapter 1). The latest analyses have raised the question whether Lavoisier was not rather the leader of a team working in the Paris Arsenal. Berthelot, however, could not have provided an authoritative *éloge* without the work of GRIMAUX, published in the previous year. Although Grimaux covers all aspects of Lavoisier's life, he gives special emphasis to the final months after his arrest as one of the tax "farmers", and some key documents are reproduced in an appendix. Grimaux had taken great trouble to trace Lavoisier's family papers, his library, apparatus, notes and correspondence in order to reconstruct his career, and all subsequent authors are indebted to him, perhaps none more than McKIE (1952). However, Grimaux was so grateful to the heirs of Lavoisier for making these papers available to him that he scrupulously avoided offending the family by mentioning any evidence that might have been unfavourable to Lavoisier. The later dispersion of some of those primary sources has seriously hindered Lavoisier studies, which still lag behind the study of many other major figures in the history of science.

Of vital importance to any study of Lavoisier is the central problem of the nature of his progress towards the theory of oxygen. This issue occupied GUERLAC, who in a carefully documented study suggests that it was in 1772 that the amateur scientist was to begin the study of gases that led to his later understanding of oxygen. Unfortunately, subsequent evidence has shown that, several years before, Lavoisier had embarked on a study of the four Aristotelian elements, one of which (air) was to provide the key to combustion. Most older studies of Lavoisier have focused on combustion and the phlogiston theory as the central question, notably McKIE (1935). CROSLAND (1973) and others, however, have argued that the oxygen theory was equally a theory of acidity (oxus = acid). SIEGFRIED & DOBBS have also pointed out that the theory involved a completely new idea of chemical composition, since metals were now seen as simple substances, while calces ("oxides") were compounds. Earlier studies were often preoccupied with questions of priority, discussing, for example, the meaningless question of whether Lavoisier was really the "discoverer" of oxygen, a title often claimed for Priestley. Lavoisier himself was notorious for his failure to acknowledge his debt to others, especially the British pneumatic chemists.

This brings us to the question of the "chemical revolution" of the 18th century. It used sometimes to be claimed that Robert Boyle was "the father of chemistry", but although Boyle challenged several traditional ideas, he did not lay the foundations of a new chemistry – this is usually claimed as the achievement of Lavoisier 100 years later. The "chemical revolution" is usually regarded as a paradigmatic example of a revolution in science, although occasionally this view has been attacked, for example by German scholars wishing to claim greater importance for their fellow-countryman Stahl, and also by BENSAUDE-VINCENT, who resurrects the claims of Stahl and raises the question whether too much importance has not been attached to the name of Lavoisier, especially in French schools. Bensaude-Vincent has also contributed a useful book to the Lavoisier bicentenary commemoration, documenting the gradual emergence of Lavoisier's new ideas. She devotes a whole chapter to the balance, an instrument that Lavoisier used to maximum effect by means of a methodology that sharply distinguishes him from some of his contemporaries, such as Priestley. DONOVAN (1988) is one of those who, while accepting the epoch-making nature of Lavoisier's work, suggests that it might have involved the creation of a new science, rather than the modification of a pre-existing one.

Lavoisier's chemical revolution was based partly on the list of simple substances or elements, which he published in his *Traité* (1789), and was consolidated by the establishment of a new journal, the *Annales de chimie*. Yet the most fundamental step in establishing the new science was neither the publication of a textbook nor a journal; rather, it was the introduction of a new language for chemistry. The collaboration of Lavoisier with Guyton de Morveau, Berthollet and Fourcroy in 1787 in the publication of their *Méthode de nomenclature chimique* has been described by many authors including CROSLAND (1962). A more up-to-date survey of the history of chemical language, culminating in the Lavoisier reform, and emphasising the influence of Condillac on him, is that given by BERETTA (1993). This collaboration on chemical nomenclature provides further evidence that Lavoisier did not work alone. The language played a fundamental part in establishing the new theory, since, once people spoke of "oxide of mercury" and "sulphuric acid", it was difficult to think in terms of the old phlogiston theory.

Some of the details of Lavoisier's career in the Académie des Sciences are difficult to follow because of the system of dating used, and here DAUMAS's book is useful, in providing a chronology of Lavoisier's major contributions to the Academy. Unfortunately it is not entirely accurate, since even Daumas does not seem to have been fully aware of Lavoisier's habit of re-writing early memoirs in the light of subsequent knowledge. His book would have also been improved if he had been aware of various books and articles on Lavoisier published in English. DUVEEN & KLICKSTEIN provide a comprehensive bibliography of Lavoisier, listing first contributions to period-ical works, then separate works and finally collected works. Lavoisier's laboratory note-books were studied by BERTHELOT (1890), who provided invaluable documentation for those wishing to study the development of Lavoisier's ideas. The best microstudy of this area is, however, that provided by HOLMES, whose study of scientific creativity focuses on Lavoisier's biochemistry. Whereas most historians have been content to study Lavoisier's ideas on combustion, Holmes is concerned to show how these ideas were applied to the study of respiration. He also deals with the question of the analysis of vegetable and animal matter, in which Lavoisier was a pioneer.

Whereas most biographies of Lavoisier concentrate on his contributions to chemistry, two recent studies have attached special attention to his other work as an economist and administrator. Indeed, POIRIER at first sight is more concerned with his work as a financier than as a chemist, which is hardly mentioned at all in the second half of the book. Poirier, who has made use of unpublished manuscript material, also calls attention to Lavoisier's interest in agriculture and education, and his political position in the French Revolution. Poirier raises the question of continuity between the various activities of one man; for example, it may be no coincidence that the first man to write full chemical equations was also involved in book-keeping. The author of the *Traité élémentaire de chimie* (1789) was simultaneously the author of a treatise on economics, *De la richesse territoriale du royaume de France* (1791). When commissioned to write about Lavoisier, DONOVAN (1993) independently decided to emphasise his subject's contribution to administration, based on Lavoisier's training as a lawyer. Like Poirier, Donovan describes his employment in the collection of taxes, which provided him with a large income. Both deal with Lavoisier's involvement in commissions of the Académie des Sciences, notably those dealing with saltpetre, mesmerism, and the reform of weights and measures. Most authors seem to agree that the Academy was doubly important in Lavoisier's life, in providing him first with an audience for his scientific work, and second with lucrative employment. Later he was to repay his debt by guiding both the Academy and the government in, for example, the commission on the Paris Hôtel-Dieu.

One of the latest publications on Lavoisier is DEMEULE-NAERE-DOUYÈRE, the proceedings of a conference organised by the Académie des Sciences to mark the bicentenary of Lavoisier's death. Although this contains some uncritical general tributes from modern scientists, it also includes papers by historians of science, for example on Lavoisier's apparatus, on the journal founded by Lavoisier, the *Annales de chimie*, and on relevant historiography.

Finally, we may consider the reception of Lavoisier's new chemistry. Bensaude-Vincent is particularly good at examining the "conversion" of chemists from theories of phlogiston to the oxygen theory. She points out that many chemists accepted only parts of the new theory, and that of those who accepted the theory in its entirety, many were critical of some aspects of the nomenclature – there was also always the question of how this should be translated into other languages. DONOVAN (1988) contains papers describing the acceptance of Lavoisier's ideas in other countries.

MAURICE CROSLAND

See also Chemical Revolution; Priestley

Lawrence, Ernest Orlando   1901–1958
American physicist

Childs, Herbert, *An American Genius: The Life of Ernest Orlando Lawrence*, New York: Dutton, 1968

Davis, Nuel Pharr, *Lawrence and Oppenheimer*, New York: Simon and Schuster, 1968

Heilbron, J.L., Robert W. Seidel and Bruce R. Wheaton, *Lawrence and His Laboratory: Nuclear Science at Berkeley, 1931–1961*, Berkeley: Office for History of Science and Technology, University of California, 1981

Heilbron, J.L. and Robert W. Seidel, *Lawrence and His Laboratory: A History of the Lawrence Berkeley Laboratory*, vol. 1, Berkeley: University of California Press, 1989

Hughes, Thomas P., *American Genesis: A Century of Invention and Technological Enthusiasm*, New York: Viking, and Harmondsworth: Penguin, 1990

Livingston, M. Stanley, "Early History of Particle Accelerators", in *Advances in Electronics and Electron Physics*, vol. 50, New York and London: Academic Press, 1980

Ernest Lawrence was the first American to be awarded the Nobel prize in 1939 for work done at a state university, based on his invention of a new, circular form of particle accelerator (the "cyclotron") capable of making particles move at great velocities, and thereby inaugurating the age of nuclear physics. His pioneering work led to the establishment of the Radiation Laboratory – now the Lawrence Berkeley National Library – and increasing activity by a number of young colleagues, several of them future Nobel prizewinners: L.W. Alvarez, Owen Chamberlain, E.M. McMillan, Glenn Seaborg, and E.G. Segrè. Lawrence's life has been minutely documented, not always sympathetically.

CHILDS is the most detailed biography (513 text pages, with more than 300 index entries pertaining to Lawrence), commissioned by the Regents of the University of California, and intended for the general public; nevertheless, the scientific contents are skilfully rendered and amply illustrated. The materials assembled for the book are in the Berkeley university archives.

DAVIS is a somewhat sensationalized dual biography of Lawrence and J.R. Oppenheimer, former colleagues and collaborators whose friendship ended when Oppenheimer lost his government clearance, because of his alleged Communist sympathies and his stated opposition to the development of the hydrogen bomb. The book is also of interest as a revealing commentary on the fate of American science under the short-lived sway of the ultra-conservative US Senator, Joseph McCarthy, whose avid pursuit of Communists and other "subversives" tended to dominate the American political scene during the 1950s. Davis's sympathies in these controversies usually rest with Lawrence.

HEILBRON, SEIDEL & WHEATON is a 100-page, profusely illustrated booklet, produced at Berkeley on the 30th anniversary of the "Rad Lab". Of particular interest are the illustrations, which depict some of the original instruments (many of them since discarded) and their sites.

HEILBRON & SEIDEL is the first volume of what remains the best source of information on Lawrence *qua* scientist, written by professional historians of science with a strong background in physics, and equipped with a 50-page bibliography devoted almost entirely to science publications. It is, hands down, the most professional and thorough work about Lawrence to have appeared to date.

HUGHES provides a concise account of the circumstances that led the US, between the two World Wars, to "invent and produce the future by design", in large part by making state and federal governments major partners in the planning, management, and financing of increasingly elaborate projects – from bridges and dams to science laboratories, including those developing new weapons. The success of such weapons in ending World War II played a crucial part in how such projects would continue to be managed after the war, a development in which Lawrence participated vigorously, as leader and innovator.

LIVINGSTON, Lawrence's graduate student from 1928 to 1931 and his collaborator until 1934, played a substantial part in the design of early cyclotrons, including a method of beam focusing by electromagnetic means, and other important contributions. Livingston had been disappointed not to be named co-inventor of the cyclotron when Lawrence applied for a patent in 1932 (although he never exploited it financially), a perceived slight that may have decided him to quit Berkeley in 1934, for what proved to be an extraordinarily successful career, with successive appointments at Harvard, the Brookhaven National Laboratory, and the National Accelerator Laboratory in Batavia, Illinois.

CHARLES SUSSKIND

See also Big Science; Nuclear Physics

Leibniz, Gottfried Wilhelm 1646–1716

German philosopher and mathematician

Aiton, E.J., *Leibniz: A Biography*, Bristol and Boston: Hilger, 1985

Bertoloni-Meli, Domenico, *Equivalence and Priority: Newton versus Leibniz*, Oxford: Clarendon Press, and New York: Oxford University Press, 1994

Garber, D., "Leibniz and the Foundations of Physics: The Middle Years", in *The Natural Philosophy of Leibniz*, edited by Kathleen Okruhlik and James Robert Brown, Dordrecht and Boston: Reidel, 1985

Hall, A. Rupert, *Philosophers at War: The Quarrel Between Newton and Leibniz*, Cambridge: Cambridge University Press, 1980

Hoffman, Joseph E., *Leibniz in Paris, 1672–1676: His Growth to Mathematical Maturity*, Cambridge and New York: Cambridge University Press, 1974

Kabitz, Willy, *Die Philosophie des jungen Leibniz*, Heidelberg: Winter, and New York: Olms, 1909

Meyer, Rudolf Walter, *Leibniz and the Seventeenth Century Revolution*, translated from the German by J.P. Stein, Cambridge: Bowes and Bowes, and Chicago: Regnery, 1952; reprinted, New York: Garland, 1985 (original edition, 1948)

Supplementa 17, *Leibniz à Paris (1672–1676)*, vol. 1, Les Sciences, 1978

Gottfried Wilhelm Leibniz died in 1716, hailed as the "premier metaphysician in Europe" (*Mercure de France*, 1716). A significant part of his contribution to metaphysics was his work in natural science and mathematics that occupied him throughout his life, but especially during the 30-year period, 1665–95. Co-inventor of the infinitesimal calculus, he coined the term "dynamics" for the area of physical science that lay at the centre of his interests, and was much engaged in the discussion of technical innovations, especially in mechanics. He was interested in new developments in chemistry, natural history, and observational astronomy, but did not do significant work in these areas himself. Leibniz founded the Berlin Academy of Sciences in 1719, and engaged in much historical work, publishing some of his findings. His best known work was a popular book on political theology.

Though Leibniz was a major participant in the scientific revolution, there has been little historical analysis of his role in this major series of events and developments. Most of the literature relates not to Leibniz's science but to his philosophy, or rather to those parts of his philosophy that are active resources in schools of philosophy. The selection of books discussed below has been guided by the search for exceptions to this rule.

KABITZ was an editor of the main edition of Leibniz's collected works. The interest of this work from 1909 is that it can help historians explain how and why Leibniz became interested in science in the first place. Based on original documents from the 1660s, Kabitz tries to trace the intellectual and political path that led Leibniz to his interest in the new science, and seeks to outline his early scientific interests. Though necessarily dated in its approach and rather limited in scope, it remains the only work that does this clearly. The scientific interests remain close to the centre of the narrative and are not displaced by the philosophy.

SUPPLEMENTA 17 picks up the story where Kabitz leaves off, with Leibniz's stay in Paris from 1672 to 1676. The chapters by H.J.M. Bos and M.B. Hall gather some of the basic material on the two most important relationships developed by Leibniz during the Paris period, those with Christiaan Huygens in Paris and Henry Oldenburg in London. These are useful for guiding the reader to the relevant primary source material. More controversial is HOFFMAN, an apologia that deals largely with the conditions in which Leibniz developed his ideas on the calculus, and is intended to answer the charges of misconduct and plagiarism levelled at him by English mathematicians.

One of the key activities with which Leibniz was much involved during the Paris years was the development of a calculating machine of his own invention. There is no comprehensive historical account of this important episode, but AITON provides a good introduction as part of an intellectual biography intended to cover the whole of Leibniz's career. Written by an accomplished historian of mathematics, Leibniz's mathematical interests are never far from the centre of Aiton's narrative, although reasonable, if rather dry, coverage is also given to the key personal and political events in Leibniz's life. For more information on these the reader should go to MEYER, originally entitled *Leibniz und die europäische Ordnungskrise*, which focuses on placing Leibniz within the political context of his time. Although containing little on Leibniz's science, this book is an essential complement to any research strategy that seeks to place Leibniz's scientific work in context.

Leibniz's move to Hanover in 1676 inaugurated a productive career in philosophical and scientific journalism, with which he made his mark on the science of his day. A good introduction to the central concerns of this period is GARBER's extensive essay in Okruhlik & Brown. A useful corrective to whiggish approaches to Leibniz, which judge all his scientific work as steps toward the metaphysical theory of monads that he developed many years later, Garber seeks to show how the natural philosophy developed by Leibniz in the decade 1685–95, was founded on both a realist approach to bodies, similar to dominant trends in the work of the Royal Society and the Paris Academy of Sciences, and a concern with the theological dangers associated with the new sciences that again was common to many other leading figures in the scientific revolution. Somewhat marred by a rigidly intellectualist approach, Garber's analysis is nevertheless an essential propaedeutic for contextual historians who wish to understand how Leibniz's gradual divergence from the scientific consensus of the day emerged from a common agenda.

The dramatic consequences of Leibniz's divergence from the scientific consensus are nicely covered by HALL, who does not make the mistake of overly concentrating on the formal *causus belli* – the charges and countercharges of plagiarism with regard to the invention of the calculus – but instead introduces the reader to the wide range of issues that divided Leibniz and his small band of followers from the triumphant Newtonians after 1700. Informed by his acquaintance with the crucial documents (gained while editing Newton's correspondence), this gripping tale is essential reading for all those interested in scientific controversy. It is nevertheless (in secular terms) an Anglican approach to the debates; Hall's sense of cool reason is perhaps not the best tool for understanding the baroque tapestry of philosophy, politics, and intrigue that motivated Leibniz's war effort.

BERTOLONI-MELI describes in detail an earlier part of the tale told by Hall – namely, Leibniz's attempt to develop a cosmological model that could compete with the one that had already made Newton's reputation. Inspired by the conviction that even the nastiest brawls can be intellectually productive, Bertoloni-Meli's detailed and sophisticated account seeks to show how a discreditable attempt by Leibniz to hide the extent of his reading in Newton's *Principia* was turned to good account by the development of mathematical techniques that could completely transform Newton's work. As a study in mathematical creativity and grand larceny, this is a peerless, imaginative, and salutary account.

Bertoloni-Meli's tale overlaps in period with Garber and thematically with Hall, and together these works show how

closely the science, philosophy, and politics of this period and milieu were intertwined, and how the "premier metaphysician in Europe" was one of the productions of the newly institutionalized science of his day.

JOE GROSS

See also Newton; Rational Mechanics

Leonardo da Vinci 1452–1518

Italian painter, sculptor, architect, and engineer

Clark, Kenneth, *Leonardo da Vinci*, Cambridge: Cambridge University Press, and New York: Macmillan, 1939; 2nd edition, Cambridge: Cambridge University Press, 1952; Baltimore: Penguin, 1958

Dionisotti, Carlo, "Leonardo uomo di lettere", *Italia medioevale e umanistica*, 5 (1962): 183–216

Duhem, Pierre, *Études sur Léonard da Vinci*, 3 vols, Paris: Hermann, 1906–13

Freud, Sigmund, *Leonardo da Vinci and a Memory of His Childhood*, translated from the German by Alan Tyson, London: Hogarth Press, 1957; New York: Norton, 1964 (original edition, 1910)

Fumagalli, Giuseppina (ed.), *Leonardo, omo sanza lettere*, Florence: Sansoni, 1938

Galluzzi, Paolo and J. Guillaume (eds), *Leonardo da Vinci: Engineer and Architect*, Montreal: Montreal Museum of Fine Arts, 1987

Gille, Bertrand, *The Renaissance Engineers*, translated from the French, London: Humphries, 1966 (original edition, 1964)

Kemp, Martin, *Leonardo da Vinci: The Marvellous Works of Nature and Man*, London: Dent, and Cambridge, Massachusetts: Harvard University Press, 1981

Maccagni, Carlo (ed.), *Leonardo nella scienza e nella tecnica*, Florence: Giunti Barbera, 1975

O'Malley, C.D. (ed.), *Leonardo's Legacy: An International Symposium*, Berkeley: University of California Press, 1969

Pedretti, Carlo, *Leonardo Architect*, translated from the Italian by Sue Brill, New York: Rizzoli, 1985; London: Thames and Hudson, 1986 (original edition, 1981)

Rosci, Marco, *The Hidden Leonardo*, translated from the Italian by John Gilbert, Chicago: Rand McNally, 1977; Oxford: Phaidon, 1978 (original edition, 1977)

Leonardo from Vinci, in Tuscany, was an engineer, mathematician and artist. He worked at the court of several princes in Italy and France, the most famous being Ludovico Sforza and Francis I. His lasting fame is thanks to his paintings, which include the *Mona Lisa* and the *Last Supper*, and to his prophetic "inventions" of the parachute, the bicycle, the diving suit and the tank, which, in most cases, are nothing but sketches and projects in his notebooks, and were never actually built. As well as painter, sculptor (his most famous statue, a massive bronze equestrian monument of Sforza's father, was never completed) and feast organizer, Leonardo was employed chiefly as a (military) engineer, in charge of fortifications and water channels. He also tackled mathematical problems, such as squaring the lunules or doubling the cube, illustrated Luca Pacioli's book *De divina proportione*, drew anatomical sketches of great precision, and was interested in mechanics (the trajectory of projectiles and stability of architectural arches). He never published a book, and his production is amassed, often chaotically, in several *Codices*.

Not long after his death, and possibly even during his lifetime, he was considered to be a multifaceted genius as a result of his prodigious skills and personal qualities – the true Renaissance man. Anecdotes in the early literature depict Leonardo as brilliant and gifted, but also a restless dreamer. He was aware of the exceptional nature of his career (an illegitimate son, he was an apprentice in a Florentine artist's workshop before moving to Milan), and often proudly contrasted his own upbringing with that of the courtiers who would have been his superiors in learning. Leonardo is thus sometimes seen as the representative of the up-and-coming urban middle class, which, even when employed in traditionally humble, manual professions, brought to these a whole new "empirical" view of the world.

Leonardo's opinions on subjects such as knowledge and how to attain it have to be gathered from several scattered remarks, but seem to fit the picture, in that they stress the importance of experience, of visual knowledge, and of direct evidence over and above abstract speculation. Leonardo also pointed out the special character of mathematical knowledge, whose degree of certainty makes it more reliable than other types of approach to reality – he had great enthusiasm for Archimedes, Euclid, and Hippocrates of Chios, even though he had to teach himself Latin and apparently never knew Greek. Thus, although never a humanist in the literary sense of the word, he did prize the past as the place to look for epistemological models, while at the same time appreciating the positive differences of the present day.

Most of the extant literature focuses on Leonardo as a genius or as an artist: it extols Leonardo's mechanical feats and presents him as an exceptional, fertile mind, sprung more or less out of nowhere, an all-rounded scientist *ante litteram*. Alternatively, it analyzes his use of drawing, his knowledge of anatomy, and the problems of authenticity of some works that seem to exist in multiple copies (the *Virgin of the Rocks* is an example).

What seems to fascinate FREUD, among others, is Leonardo's unsteadiness of character, the fact that he left nearly all the works of his post-Milan period unfinished, his asystematicity. Freud underlines the artist's ambivalent relationship to his works and his cool rejection of or indifference to anything sexual – which formed the image of the genius. The father of psychoanalysis claims that Leonardo's exceptional personality was the result of his emotions being subjected to the investigation impulse – investigation was substituted for sexual activity, the reasons for this dating back to his infancy. Moreover, unfinished works would most successfully embody the impossibility of expressing his total vision of reality.

DUHEM's work, for all its obvious limitations (a full corpus of Leonardo's works was not available to him), was instrumental in putting the "genius" back into the image of Leonardo. Duhem placed Leonardo in context, pointed out his debt to his predecessors (mainly Albert of Saxony, Nicholas of Cusa, and John Buridan), and traced some lines of transmission for the medieval tradition of mechanics, which Leonardo probably knew second-hand. Duhem's study also served to give a more balanced view of the Middle Ages, a period when mathematics, mechanics, and philosophy were actively pursued and appreciated.

GILLE's book, focuses on the (mainly) German and Italian traditions of practical engineering and construction of machines, starting from the 13th and 14th centuries. The author provides useful information on people such as Filippo Brunelleschi, Mariano Taccola, and Francesco di Giorgio Martini – the last having worked with the young Leonardo. With the aid of numerous reproductions from the manuscript illustrations, Gille's Leonardo comes to life as the particularly brilliant exponent of a whole current of mechanical practitioners who participated in the public life of their time, while working as artists or architects. Great attention is devoted to Leonardo's machines with an economic potential (a spinning jenny, a felt-cutter) and to his theoretical remarks on "method".

FUMAGALLI's title is meant to shed light, rather provocatively, on another aspect of the Leonardo myth: his proud self-declaration of ignorance and illiteracy. An annotated anthology with long introductions, the book is an important collection of Leonardo's most literary and literate passages, from his travel notes to the descriptions of his "visions". Fumagalli's criteria may be outdated in that she wants to "reach to the spirit of the great genius", but her results nevertheless form a very nuanced picture, in which Leonardo again comes across as very much a man of his time. DIONISOTTI's article takes as its starting point a passage in the *Codex Atlanticus*, a catalogue of Leonardo's library that ranges from Poggio Bracciolini and Petrarch to Valturius's *On Military Matters*. Dionisotti links Leonardo's bibliographical choices on the one hand to the Italian culture of the time, with emphasis on Florentine authors, and on the other hand to Leonardo's own written works, none of which was ever published.

Three collective volumes have been included here, because scholarship on Leonardo is so varied and vast that a general survey will always tell only part of the story. These texts have the double advantage of covering many topics, and of grouping contributions from many countries. O'MALLEY's collection includes Clark on ancient inspirations for Leonardo's drawings; Keele on the physiology of the senses, which Leonardo studied in conjunction with their geometry and mechanics, concluding that sensorial perception is the result of movement and percussion; Reti on Leonardo the technologist, with his interest in the efficiency of machines and in the sources of power for mechanical movement; Heydenreich on architecture; and Dibner on automation.

The volume edited by MACCAGNI includes articles by Rose on Leonardo's view on the certainty of mathematical knowledge; by Bruins on his theory of centres of gravity and possible relations with ancient sources; and by many others on a myriad of topics that concerned Leonardo, such as astronomy, hydrology, anatomy, and spontaneous generation. The last two articles, by Arrighi and Vasoli, are also valuable, as they draw a wider picture of art, technology and science in the Renaissance.

While uneven in quality, this collection is a useful starting-point (including good bibliographies) for the study of some of the many facets of the Leonardo phenomenon.

Published on the occasion of an exhibition of Leonardo's drawings and models, GALLUZZI & GUILLAUME's book contains articles by all the contemporary leading Leonardo scholars (Pedretti, Galluzzi, Marinoni, Kemp, Scaglia, Firpo), with a focus on his technology and architecture, and a particular eye to the relation between technology and theory. Of special interest is Firpo's article on Leonardo's plans for an ideal city (Sforzeide), which has usually been read as embodying class divisions into its urbanistic structure. Firpo, via a different interpretation of the drawings, claims that Sforzeide was indeed planned as an aristocratic society, but one in which the interests of everybody had been considered, thanks to Leonardo's multi-layered functional structure.

Another "must" in Leonardo studies are the large, illustrated coffee-table books. Two of the best representatives of this type are Pedretti and Rosci. PEDRETTI's volume is a corpus of Leonardo's architectural studies, organized chronologically with places and dates, and with a focus on special problems (fictive architecture, industrial design, ornaments and emblems, etc.) and several excursus with complementary material. The author considers Leonardo's later years in Florence (1503–06), usually seen as a decline, but fundamental, because Leonardo "began to express the heroic ideals and sense of civic pride which the city of Florence" was renewing. His role as architect ran hand in hand with this renewed civic sense, and helped generate Leonardo's concept of "total design".

ROSCI's book quotes and discusses previous opinions on Leonardo's life and career, which provides a useful bibliographical tool. The book, however, is especially valuable for its stunning iconographical apparatus, which is both extensive and accurate (often reproducing several different versions of one work), and provides a number of revealing close-ups.

Kemp and Clark are organized as biographies, with a strong emphasis on Leonardo the artist. KEMP's book is intended to be "about Leonardo as a whole". The narrative is chronological, following Leonardo in his travels around Italy, and aims to describe, at each stage, everything in which Leonardo was engaged. The resulting picture is an awesome portrait of someone who carried on several lines of research at the same time and excelled in most of them, but we also get more than a glimpse of the lively cultural environment that gave Leonardo much inspiration, and of his meetings with people (Ludovico Sforza, Martini, Pacioli), who steered his career in new directions.

CLARK's biography of Leonardo the artist has become a classic. Clark's picture may depend to some extent on psychological explanations, but the result is eminently readable and rests on solid knowledge of the subtleties of Leonardo's production. (The author has also catalogued one of the largest collections of Leonardo's drawings, at Windsor). Clark sees artistic production as based mainly on the development of the artist's spirit – as a progressive widening of the soul that, drawing fruitfully on scientific theories and on meetings with other painters, engineers, and mathematicians, combined all these ideas into greater and greater artistic works. As no contemporary survey of a more critical kind is available, for

example on Leonardo's professional roles assessed on contemporary criteria, Clark's text remains one of the best examples of its genre: the (historically sophisticated) re-affirmation, after centuries of historical enquiry, of the figure of the true Renaissance man.

SERAFINA CUOMO

Lévi-Strauss, Claude 1908–

French anthropologist and structuralist

Badcock, C.R., *Lévi-Strauss: Structuralism & Sociological Theory*, London: Hutchinson, 1975; New York: Holmes and Meier, 1976

Boon, James A., *From Symbolism to Structuralism: Lévi-Strauss in a Literary Tradition*, Oxford: Blackwell, and New York: Harper and Row, 1972

Gardner, Howard, *The Quest for Mind: Piaget, Lévi-Strauss and the Structuralist Movement*, New York: Knopf, 1973; 2nd edition, Chicago: University of Chicago Press, 1981

Geertz, Clifford, *Works and Lives: The Anthropologist as Author*, Stanford, California: Stanford University Press, 1988

Harris, Marvin, *The Rise of Anthropological Theory: A History of Theories of Culture*, London: Routledge and Kegan Paul, and New York: Crowell, 1968

Hayes, E. Nelson and Tanya Hayes (eds), *Claude Lévi-Strauss: The Anthropologist as Hero*, Cambridge, Massachusetts: MIT Press, 1970

Jenkins, Alan, *The Social Theory of Claude Lévi-Strauss*, London: Macmillan, and New York: St Martin's Press, 1979

Lapointe, François H. and Claire C. Lapointe, *Claude Lévi-Strauss and His Critics: An International Bibliography of Criticism 1950–1976*, New York: Garland, 1977

Leach, Edmund, *Claude Lévi-Strauss*, London: Fontana, and New York: Viking Press, 1970; revised edition, 1974

Pace, David, *Claude Lévi-Strauss: The Bearer of Ashes*, London and Boston: Routledge and Kegan Paul, 1983

Sperber, Dan, *On Anthropological Knowledge: Three Essays*, Cambridge and New York: Cambridge University Press, 1985

Sturrock, John (ed.), *Structuralism and Since: From Lévi-Strauss to Derrida*, Oxford and New York: Oxford University Press, 1979

For an anthropologist to achieve the level of eminence attained by Claude Lévi-Strauss in the second half of the 20th century, with no notable fieldwork-based research to his credit, is exceptional. The bulk of his scholarship involves a highly imaginative and ebullient form of "armchair anthropology", which is employed in order to provide different ways of exploring existent anthropological themes. At the centre of his concerns is the heuristic question of what it is to be human, and the relation of nature to culture. Lévi-Strauss's structuralism has had a distinguished multi-disciplinary significance.

The bibliography by LAPOINTE & LAPOINTE serves as a general guide to both the span of Lévi-Strauss's major works and the criticism they received, alongside a basic biographical sketch. The provisional nature of this work must be emphasised. While the bibliography was up to date when published, Lévi-Strauss has himself published since, and there are as yet no signs of an end to his productive scholarship. It should be noted that, unsurprisingly, a proportion of the references cited in the bibliography are publications in the French language.

The range of analysis of Lévi-Strauss's works is broad, although there is a tendency for many commentators to contextualise his work within the broader scholarship of social theory and the history of knowledge. BADCOCK is notable in this respect, tracing Lévi-Strauss's intellectual ancestry through the work of, among others, Freud, Sartre, Marx, Durkheim, Mauss, Comte, and Rousseau, while arguing that cultural arrangements and behaviours comprise a form of communication, the language of culture. In contrast, HARRIS is content to focus his treatment of Lévi-Strauss around an examination of "Mauss's gift to Lévi-Strauss" and Durkheim's "present" of the "Conscience Collective". Harris characterizes Lévi-Strauss's structuralism as rooted firmly in the European cultural idealist tradition (which for Harris is historical and non-empiricist in the positivist sense), while exhibiting a firm interest in the mental structures that govern thinking. For Harris, Lévi-Strauss's employment of the Hegelian concept of dialectics is totally idealist, something he considers to be a feature of structuralism's development beyond ontological to epistemological concerns.

The aspects of Lévi-Strauss's works that reveal psychological concerns are placed in sharper relief by GARDNER. In a comparison of Lévi-Strauss with Piaget, Gardner indicates something of the centrality of binary opposition to Lévi-Strauss's works, as an implicit model of how the mind works. For Gardner, the structuralist quest is for a method of reducing complex, apparently disparate, bodies of empirical data to their internal structural principals, which are frequently displayed as the transformation of binary opposites, such as nature and culture.

JENKINS attempts to explore Lévi-Strauss's scholarship as a working example of social theory by examining it as a form of semiotics, the study of signs and symbolism. The structural linguistics of Roman Jakobson and the Prague school, and the semiotics of Ferdinand de Saussure, are introduced as foundational to Lévi-Strauss's structuralism. Jenkins takes the position that, as a form of analytical machinery, the epistemological justification of the structural method – as a comparative analytical scheme for reducing complex bodies of data to elementary forms – is essentially flawed. Subjecting Lévi-Strauss to an empirical, rather than metaphorical, reading, Jenkins is generally critical of the structuralist project. While structure serves as a broadly employed root metaphor for science and the post-Enlightenment world, Jenkins – like Radcliffe-Brown, who had previously criticized the work of Lévi-Strauss's along the same lines – suggests that Lévi-Strauss's methodological prescriptions for a "science of the concrete" is found wanting because it has no adequate substantive foundations.

LEACH is, however, far more enthusiastic about Lévi-Strauss's project. Employing a range of illustrative materials, Leach argues that the work of Lévi-Strauss should not be taken literally, but explored as offering imaginative metaphorical devices that offer new vantage points on a range of conven-

tional problems, and are "good to think with". Leach examines Lévi-Strauss through his contributions to the major substantive areas of anthropological study, including kinship, totemism, the savage mind, and mythology. SPERBER argues persuasively that the works of Lévi-Strauss, while exhibiting on the surface a certain opacity and abstruseness (reliant as they are, in part, on analytical intuition), none the less as a corpus demonstrate an essential intellectual integrity. While Sperber amplifies certain of these matters in STURROCK, PACE'S consideration of Lévi-Strauss is directed towards an examination of his significance within Boasian-influenced theories of cultural relativism.

HAYES & HAYES is a series of studies of anthropological texts as texts, a method that has recently enjoyed something of a vogue; the collection is, however, concerned with the literary character of the works, rather than with any empirical contents. BOON offers a reading of Lévi-Strauss's works that combines anthropology with literary studies and criticism. For Boon, a powerful analogy can be fashioned from a comparison of Lévi-Strauss's written works with those of a range of French literary figures who can be collectively described as "symbolists". Boon sees Lévi-Strauss as working from the assumption – for example, in the study of mythology – that different cultures have their own texts which, in certain crucial respects, exhibit similarities and can be seen as analogous. In this respect, people from one culture have the ability to read the texts of other cultures and to discover themselves within them, suggestive of a common humanity. GEERTZ also explores Lévi-Strauss's work as text and, focusing largely around a consideration of *Tristes tropiques*, goes beyond Boon's analysis. Geertz alerts us to some of the literary strategies employed by Lévi-Strauss in his works, while noting that they are notoriously difficult to read because they are multi-layered and metaphorically rich. For Geertz, these works are self-consciously fashioned products, designed to display the author's structural concerns.

MIKE BALL

See also Anthropology

Liebig, Justus von 1803–1873

German chemist

Brock, William H., *Justus von Liebig: The Chemical Gatekeeper*, Cambridge and New York: Cambridge University Press, 1997

Caneva, Kenneth L., *Robert Mayer and the Conservation of Energy*, Princeton, New Jersey: Princeton University Press, 1993

Finlay, Mark R., "Quackery and Cookery: Justus von Liebig's Extract of Meat and the Theory of Nutrition in the Victorian Age", *Bulletin of the History of Medicine*, 66 (1992): 404–18

Fruton, Joseph S., *Contrasts in Scientific Style: Research Groups in the Chemical and Biological Sciences*, Philadelphia: American Philosophical Society, 1990

Holmes, Frederic L., "Introduction", in *Animal Chemistry, or Organic Chemistry in Its Applications to Physiology and*

Pathology, by Liebig, edited by William Gregory, New York: Appleton, and London: Taylor and Walton, 1842; reprinted, New York: Johnson, 1964

Holmes, Frederic L., "The Complementarity of Teaching and Research in Liebig's Laboratory", *Osiris*, 5 (1989): 121–66

Kohut, Adolf, *Justus von Liebig: Sein Leben und Wirken*, Giessen: Roth, 1904

Morrell, J.B., "The Chemist Breeders: The Research Schools of Liebig and Thomas Thomson", *Ambix*, 19 (1972): 1–49

Moulton, Forest Ray (ed.), *Liebig and after Liebig: A Century of Progress in Agricultural Chemistry*, Washington, DC: American Association for the Advancement of Science, 1942

Munday, E. Patrick, *Sturm and Dung: Justus von Liebig and the Chemistry of Agriculture*, dissertation, Cornell University, Ithaca, New York, 1990

Rossiter, Margaret W., *The Emergence of Agricultural Science: Justus Liebig and the Americans, 1840–1880*, New Haven, Connecticut: Yale University Press, 1975

Schling-Brodersen, Ursula, *Entwicklung und Institutionalisierung der Agrikulturchemie im 19. Jahrhundert: Liebig und die Landwirtschaftlichen Versuchsstationen*, Braunschweig: Braunschweiger Veröffentlichungen zur Geschichte der Pharmazie und der Naturwissenschaften, 1989

Teuteberg, Hans-Jürgen, *Die Rolle des Fleischextracts für die Ernährungswissenschaften und den Aufstieg der Suppenindustrie*, Stuttgart: Steiner, 1990

Volhard, Jakob, *Justus von Liebig*, 2 vols, Leipzig: Barth, 1909

In the past few decades, there has been a significant revival in Liebig scholarship. Just as Liebig's career touched on the history of several sciences – including chemistry, physiology, agriculture, nutrition, public health, and medicine – interpretations of his career have touched on virtually all of the issues in the historiography of 19th-century science. Liebig's polemical and tendentious style, combined with the vast collections of correspondence and other primary source materials, make him an especially engaging and fascinating personality. The continual publication of newly-released letters and other primary source materials has further contributed to the emerging scholarship.

At present, though, the most complete biographies of Liebig remain those written by KOHUT and by VOLHARD in the first decade of the 20th century. Both authors had ties to Liebig and his family, and relied extensively on sources that had been edited and distorted by those – including Liebig himself – who promoted the chemist's legendary biography. The resulting works can be classified as hagiography. Kohut compares Liebig to German heroes such as Bismarck, Luther, and Alexander von Humboldt, while Volhard stresses Liebig's role as a founder of Wilhelmine Germany's industrial and chemical might. These works have become sources for many of the assumptions and legends about Liebig's role as an innovative teacher, tireless researcher, and selfless servant to humanity.

MUNDAY's work stands at the opposite end of the spectrum. In a significant corrective to the Liebig mythology, Munday has unearthed, reread, and reinterpreted scores of letters and primary source materials that expose Liebig's career from his youthful adventures to his call to Munich in 1852. Munday skilfully locates Liebig's career within the social and political climate of Hesse-Darmstadt, and traces Liebig's intellectual development in the context of the evolving fields of organic chemistry, agricultural science, and plant physiology. Though Munday is often scathing in his critique of the historiography, blunt in his tone, and bold in his conclusions, there can be little doubt that his dissertation and published articles have challenged and largely overturned the traditional biographies.

The biography by BROCK may prove to be the new standard work. One of Brock's themes is that Liebig was able to expand and institutionalize the teaching of chemistry, and, through his imposing and lengthy influence over the discipline, was able to shape and popularize its development for decades. Brock's work also emphasizes Liebig's impact on Britain, where the German chemist achieved a legendary status in scientific, medical, agricultural, and political circles. Though more moderate than Munday in his tone and argument, Brock's study corroborates the emerging portrayal of a Liebig who was quite conscious of his position and influence within several scientific communities.

Among the significant monographs in Liebig scholarship, ROSSITER's has been especially influential. In a significant revision of the sketchy and celebratory essays edited by MOULTON, Rossiter provides a clear exegesis of the strengths and weaknesses of Liebig's agricultural chemistry. Rossiter focuses on Liebig's reception among three pioneering American scientists of the mid-19th century, and provides an examination of the factors that defined differences between American and continental science during an important phase in the early history of chemistry. She asserts that Liebig was an important influence in the United States, where worn-out soils and an absence of real challengers meant his ideas found a ready market. In the long run, however, the US commitment to the research agenda was weaker than that of the Europeans, with the consequence that Liebig's influence was short-lived.

SCHLING-BRODERSEN's history of German agricultural chemistry is an important parallel to Rossiter's. Her emphasis on the history of the discipline of agricultural chemistry means that Liebig's role is relativized. She stresses that Liebig's impact on the discipline was more as a propagandist than as an innovative researcher or theorist. She also explores the connections between agricultural chemistry and the emergence of German agricultural experiment stations, noting that Liebig's influence in agricultural circles was diminishing through the 1840s and 1850s.

Frederic L. Holmes has turned to Liebig repeatedly in his distinguished career as a historian of science. His lengthy "Introduction" to Liebig's *Animal Chemistry* (in HOLMES, 1964) is generally considered the starting point for any study of Liebig's physiology. Though highly speculative, Liebig's writings established the foundations for the quantitative thinking and experimental methodologies that shaped energy metabolism studies for decades. CANEVA's recent biography of the scientist Robert Mayer places Liebig's physiology in the context of contemporary German theological and philosophical disputes over the very meaning of science and nature.

Holmes has also joined the debate over the Liebig "research school". MORRELL contributed a significant article outlining the success of Liebig's research program, which he attributed largely to Liebig's charisma and mastery of financial considerations. HOLMES (1989) stresses the combination of externalist issues, including personal relationships and institutional considerations, and internalist, intellectual questions that shaped the Liebig laboratory and its research agenda. Moreover, Holmes's studies have pinpointed changes in Liebig's research agenda and his decision to allocate important research questions to his students. Holmes's colleague, FRUTON, goes further in his assertions that research schools like Liebig's are a key explanation for the rapid rise of science in the 19th century. Fruton's most important contribution is his in-depth prosopographical study, which traces the careers of hundreds of Liebig's Giessen students.

In a work that is framed as a history of the Knorr food products company, TEUTEBERG provides the most complete of several recent studies of the Liebig Extract of Meat Company. Though Liebig was not directly involved in this enterprise, the firm borrowed Liebig's ideas and his name to become an innovative producer of foods on an international and industrial scale. Teuteberg, FINLAY, and others have connected Liebig's Extract of Meat with the history of cookery, the social history of consumerism, the emergence of women as dispensers of nutritional knowledge, and with marketing strategies that seized upon the entrepreneurial scientist as an ideal.

Liebig historiography has been reshaped in recent years. Thanks to newly released documents, and the synthetic works by Munday, Brock, and others, Liebig scholarship is moving beyond the legends.

MARK R. FINLAY

Linguistics

Aarsleff, Hans, *From Locke to Saussure: Essays on the Study of Language and Intellectual History*, Minneapolis: University of Minnesota Press, 1982

Amsterdamska, Olga, *Schools of Thought: The Development of Linguistics from Bopp to Saussure*, Dordrecht: Reidel, 1987

Bassnett-McGuire, Susan, *Translation Studies*, London and New York: Methuen, 1980; revised edition, London and New York: Routledge, 1991

Botha, Rudolf P., *Challenging Chomsky: The Generative Garden Game*, Oxford and New York: Blackwell, 1989

Chomsky, Noam, *Cartesian Linguistics: A Chapter in the History of Rationalist Thought*, New York: Harper and Row, 1966

Dinneen, Francis P., *An Introduction to General Linguistics*, New York: Holt Rinehart and Winston, 1967

Foucault, Michel, *The Order of Things: An Archaeology of the Human Sciences*, translated from the French by Alan Sheridan, New York: Pantheon Books, and London: Tavistock, 1970 (original edition, 1966)

Harris, Roy, *Reading Saussure: A Critical Commentary on the "Cours de linguistique generale"*, London: Duckworth, 1986; La Salle, Illinois: Open Court, 1987

Hudson, Nicholas, *Writing and European Thought, 1600–1830*, Cambridge and New York: Cambridge University Press, 1994

Newmeyer, Frederick J., *Linguistic Theory in America: The First Quarter Century of Transformational Generative Grammar*, New York: Academic Press, 1980; 2nd edition, 1986

Padley, G.A. *Grammatical Theory in Western Europe, 1500–1700: The Latin Tradition*, Cambridge and New York: Cambridge University Press, 1976

Sebeok, Thomas A. (ed.), *Portraits of Linguists: A Biographical Source Book for the History of Western Linguistics, 1746–1963*, 2 vols, Bloomington: Indiana University Press, 1966

A historiographical survey of all the fields devoted to the study of language would be much broader than this one, which treats only the areas normally covered in today's linguistics departments. Such an unabashedly presentist strategy means that we shall not consider histories of rhetoric, hermeneutics or, for that matter, logic. However, virtually every book in our inventory touches on the history of these other fields to varying degrees. As might be expected, the professional linguists tend to marginalize these neighbouring fields more successfully than the professional historians.

FOUCAULT provides a convenient way of thinking about alternative frameworks for writing the history of linguistics. Throughout Western history, language as a coherent system of signs has been associated with fundamental ontology. However, the grounds of being have successively shifted since the Renaissance from God (or Creation), to Reason, to Man. Foucault maintains notoriously that the 20th-century pre-occupation with ruptures, not only between language and reality (ideology critique), but also within language itself (ranging from psychoanalysis to deconstruction), presages the dissolution of Man as a proper object of scientific enquiry.

At a finer grained level of analysis, historians have observed philosophical reorientations that run counter to general tendencies in the history of science. While the shift from the Middle Ages to the Renaissance is often read as a Neo-Platonic triumph over Aristotelianism, PADLEY notes that the scholastics typically had a more "Platonic" understanding of language than the humanists. Thus, the scholastics stressed distinctions between words, concepts, and things that the humanists then collapsed. Nevertheless, both groups envisaged a pristine pre-Babel tongue that was the ultimate object of their inquiries. Like many recent scholars, Padley assigns considerable importance to the work of Joseph Scaliger (1540–1609), a humanist who historicized the scholastic distinction between necessary and accidental features of language through cross-cultural comparisons of linguistic forms. He thereby not only rehabilitated the search for a "universal grammar", but also provided a "scientific" model of philological investigation – the two principal strands in subsequent linguistic inquiry.

Ideological differences between historians can be discerned by noticing when they begin and end their histories. AARSLEFF, perhaps the most distinguished American historian of linguistics, and SEBEOK, a semiotician noted for his work in animal communication, share a largely intellectual biographical approach. However, Aarsleff's collected essays reach back to Locke, whereas Sebeok's sourcebook of scientific memoirs begins with Sir William Jones, the man who hypothesized Sanskrit as the Ursprache in the late 18th century. Whereas Aarsleff ends with Saussure, Sebeok concludes with Benjamin Lee Whorf, the famous proponent of linguistic relativism. For Aarsleff, the history of linguistics revolves around debates concerning language's role as either constraining or enabling thought. Sebeok's concern, on the other hand, is whether the essence of humanity can be identified with a common underlying linguistic structure. A negative answer (as Whorf's work seems to imply) can then license the semiotician's urge to blur the boundary between human and non-human communication.

Dinneen and Newmeyer are practising linguists who write sophisticated textbook histories based broadly on the Chomskian paradigm of generative grammar, though they differ markedly over whether Chomsky marks a genuine break, or merely a watershed of sustaining themes, in the history of linguistics. DINNEEN stresses continuities, which he takes back to the debate between Plato and the Sophists over whether language is "natural" or "conventional". His history is organized around the exegesis of classic texts, which enables the effective display of recurrent lines of thought. NEWMEYER's history is occasioned by the need to export the Chomskian research programme outside the United States. The result is a rational reconstruction of theoretical elaborations and experimental tests in psycholinguistics, starting with Chomsky's ground-breaking monograph of 1957, *Syntactic Structures*. Professional historians will puzzle over Newmeyer's explicit disavowal of any "external" influences in the development of Chomsky's thought. Newmeyer's book is usefully read alongside CHOMSKY's own attempt to construct a research tradition, focused on the creative character of language use that goes back to Descartes, and includes Leibniz and (curiously) Karl Wilhelm von Humboldt. Finally, no rationally reconstructed historiography of Chomsky's research programme would be complete without an inventory of debates over its metaphysical hardcore, protective belt, and negative heuristic. BOTHA offers an ironic account of 96 such debates.

The only figure in the history of modern linguistics to receive nearly as much scholarly attention as Chomsky is Ferdinand de Saussure (1857–1913), the Franco-Swiss philologist normally credited with introducing a "structuralist" perspective that regards language as a closed system of signs. AMSTERDAMSKA draws on Mertonian and organizational sociology of science to characterize the 19th-century linguistics research communities from which de Saussure emerged, while HARRIS considers de Saussure's legacy for 20th-century linguistics from a largely hermeneutical standpoint. Amsterdamska casts de Saussure as someone who used his cultural marginality (the key sites for philology were in Germany) to achieve the level of both acceptance and detachment he needed from the research community in order to be innovative. However, according to Harris, because de Saussure's seminal *Course in General Linguistics* was not published until three years after his death, his legacy has turned out to be quite other than he might have expected. Whereas de Saussure understood the scientific study of language to be centred on the Durkheimian tension between collective coercion (*langue*) and individual freedom (*parole*), that tension is now normally read as being

about innate capacity versus manifest behaviour – a distinction that appears to anticipate the distinction drawn by Chomsky between linguistic competence and speech performance.

Two other aspects of language that receive increasing attention from historians are the role of translation in the transmission and expression of knowledge, and the significance of the transition from oral to print cultures. In her brief but focused history, BASSNETT-McGUIRE argues that translation has largely been a client-driven activity, except for the attempts to subsume translation under a "scientific" account of language. At those points, the idea of "semantic content" as a *sine qua non* of a good translation becomes prominent, though its influence in day-to-day translation practices remains elusive. HUDSON's equally brief and provocative history shows that not only was Marshall McLuhan correct in his assessment of the role that the printing press played in making Western culture more visually oriented, but also that Gutenburg's own contemporaries already held such a view. While Renaissance scholars esteemed print as a mark of the human, the beginnings of mass literacy witnessed in the 18th century created a nostalgia for orality among Enlightenment intellectuals, which evolved into the vexed views on the relationship between speech and writing that have predominated in the West since 19th-century Romanticism.

STEVE FULLER

See also Human Sciences; Social Sciences

Linné, Carl von *see* Linnaeus

Linnaeus, Carl 1707–1778
Swedish naturalist and physician

Allen, David Elliston, *The Naturalist in Britain: A Social History*, London: Allen Lane, 1977; 2nd edition, Princeton, New Jersey: Princeton University Press, 1994

Broberg, Gunnar, *Homo sapiens L.: Studier i Linnés naturuppfattning och människolära*, Uppsala: Lychnosbibliotek 1975

Broberg, Gunnar (ed.), *Linnaeus: Progress and Prospects in Linnean Research*, Uppsala: Almqvist & Wiksell, 1980

Carl von Linnés betydelse såsom naturforskare och läkare, Uppsala: Almqvist & Wiksell, 1907

Duris, Pascal, *Linné et la France, 1780-1850*, Geneva: Droz 1993

Frängsmyr, Tore (ed.), *Linnaeus: The Man and His Work*, Berkeley: University of California Press 1983; revised edition, Canton, Massachussetts: Science History Publications, 1994

Fries, Theodore Magnus, *Linné: Lefnadsteckning* 2 vols, Stockholm: Fahlcrantz, 1903; abridged edition, as *Linneaus: The Story of His Life*, translated into English by Benjamin Daydon Jackson, London: Witherby, 1923

Heller, John L., *Studies in Linnean Method and Nomenclature*, Frankfurt and New York: Peter Lang, 1983

Hofsten, Nils von, "Linnaeus's Concept of Nature", in *Kungl. Vetenskaps-Societeten i Uppsala Årsbok*, 1954

Larson, James L, *Reason and Experience. The representation of natural order in the work of Carl von Linné*. Berkeley: University of California Press 1971

Lindroth, Sten, "The Two Faces of Linnaeus", translated from the Swedish by Michael Srigley, in *Linnaeus: The Man and His Work*, edited by Tore Frängsmyr, Berkeley: University of California Press, 1983

Malmeström, Elis, *Carl von Linné*, Stockholm: Bonniers, 1964

Stafleu, Frans, *Linnaeus and the Linnaeans: The Spreading of Their Ideas in Systematic Botany, 1735–1789*. Utrecht: Oosthoek, 1971

Stearn, W.T., "An Introduction to the Species Plantarum and Cognate Botanical Works of Carl Linnaeus", in *Species plantarum* a facsimile of the 1st edition of 1753, 2 vols, London: Ray Society, 1957–59

Weinstock, John (ed.), *Contemporary Perspectives on Linnaeus*, Lanham, Maryland: University Press of America, 1985

Carl Linnaeus is primarily known for being the first to introduce a "scientific" taxonomic system of plants. His impact has been enormous, in Sweden and throughout the world. For this reason, the literature is substantial. The early literature is often hagiographic, but more recently much research has contextualized Linnaeus and analysed his impact on science and society.

Because of his central position in Swedish culture, much has been written on Linnaeus in Swedish. The Yearbook of the Swedish Linnaeus Society (*Svenska Linnésällskapets Årsskrift* 1917–) contains a large number of articles on Linnaeus as a person and a scientist, as well as his influence on different aspects of Swedish culture. Such articles often reveal hagiographic and nationalistic attitudes. It was during the nationalistic revival of the early 1900s that FRIES, the botanist and former rector of Uppsala university, who had unrestricted access to the archives, published the first full-length biography of Linnaeus. He eliminated some of the myths associated with Linnaeus's childhood and student years, but he did not really change the general image of the divinely-inspired scientist. Despite its simplistic psychology, it remains very useful on account of its wealth of information and mastery of sources, including those of the Linnean Society in London. The same is true of the volume celebrating the bicentenary of Linnaeus's birth, published by the Royal Swedish Academy of Science, which was written by a group of scientists paying homage to their great fellow-countryman. There are contributions by Otto Hjelt on medicine, Einar Lönnberg and Christian Aurivillius on zoology, C. Lindman on botany, A. Nathorst on geology, and Hj. Sjögren on mineralogy. So far, it has not been supplemented by any general evaluation of Linnaeus the scientist.

MALMESTRÖM, once bishop in Linnaeus's home town of Växjö, wrote his thesis on Linnaeus's theological ideas (*Carl von Linnés religiösa åskådning*, 1926), the divine justice or *Nemesis divina*. Because of their private nature, these notes were not published in full until 1968. Malmeström considers Linnaeus as a Protestant, discussing such topics as free will, retaliation and the theodicy, and sometimes making Linnaeus more of a philosopher than he actually was. HOFSTEN's essay on Linnaeus's concept of nature is of more direct relevance to the history of science, and marks a fairly early attempt by an accomplished zoologist and geneticist to contextualize Linnaeus within broader patterns of thought.

And yet, in LINDROTH's reevaluation of Linnaeus, he became almost a contemporary modern scientist. Lindroth's interpretation, which was criticized as an attack on national values, marked a turning point in the literature on Linnaeus. Here, Linnaeus became a more complex person – naive in many respects, vain and easily offended, a genius because of his sharp "intuitive eye", and a wonderful writer. Linnaeus's impressive command of language is apparent in his travelogues on the Swedish provinces and in his lectures and letters. Furthermore, Lindroth underlines Linnaeus's success as an entrepreneur in organising science and exploiting his social contacts. In particular, Lindroth reevaluates Linnaeus as a scientist, making him old-fashioned, unaware of what was going on in other fields of science, and also lagging behind in the experimental side of natural history. In contrast to earlier opinions, Linnaeus's genius was now presented as extremely one-dimensional: thus, he did not "make one single discovery", but was a scholastic and a system builder, belonging to an older episteme rather than to a modern. Today, Lindroth's interpretation might seem ahistoric, as it neglects the enormous impact and influence of Linnean science, which effectively led to the professionalization of natural history. From this perspective, such a statement as Linnaeus "did not discover anything" reveals an outdated view of the scientist's role. Nevertheless, it is important to stress the scholastic heritage, which can be traced to Linnaeus's years at high school in Växjö. Lindroth also drew on several Swedish authors, who in turn were inspired by Julius Sachs's *Geschichte der Botanik* (1875), which can be seen as an argument for physiological, rather than taxonomic, natural history.

STAFLEU gives a balanced view of Linnaeus, and assesses his influence in different countries – his strong appeal in Britain, his reluctant acceptance in France, and his academic successes in The Netherlands, Germany, and Russia. Stafleu's expert knowledge of taxonomic literature makes his book a first useful survey of the diffusion of the Linnean method, without, however, going very deeply into the sociological history of natural history. There are now two volumes, which discuss the diffusion of the Linnean method in greater detail within a national context. Stafleu should thus be supplemented for France by DURIS, and for Britain by ALLEN.

William T. STEARN, the doyen of Linnean scholars, reads Linnaeus from the perspective of a botanist, but includes many perceptive historical interpretations. From his rich production, the supplements to the facsimile of *Species plantarum* are especially useful for the understanding of Linnean technicalities.

LARSON offers a meticulous close-reading of the methodological texts without entering into the broader social contexts. FRÄNGSMYR contains Gunnar Eriksson's expert summary of the botanist Linnaeus, including new information of the genesis of the sexual system in his history of Swedish botany. Frängsmyr himself analyses Linnaeus's ideas about geology. In another chapter Broberg summarizes his dissertation, BROBERG (1975), which discusses Linnaeus's general attitude to natural philosophy, and his classification of man within the animal kingdom and into different varieties ("races"). The dissertation contains a chapter on double organisms, such as "zoophytes", which is also published in WEIN-STOCK; there is also a chapter on Linnaeus's ideas on the "electrical" nature of life. The collection of essays by HELLER originates from different periods, but have a philological or bibliographical theme in common. Certainly, Latin was important for the impact of Linneanism, which has made Latin a living scientific language up to the present day. Heller covers classical mythology, abbreviations, the origin of the binomial nomenclature, and trivial names. Essays of this kind show an interest in detail that is characteristic of much Linnean research. Potentially, the number of studies identifying persons or natural objects or allusions connected with the great Linnean catalogue of nature is unlimited.

At the bicentenary of Linnaeus's death, it might seem that the important aspects of Linnaeus and his influence have already been covered. As the editor of BROBERG (1980), I have to admit that it did not contain many new prospects. However, the articles by Smit, Shillito and Wheeler on Linnean zoology are substantial and too often neglected. Language problems (Swedish and Latin) seem to have raised barriers to international research. Looking to the future, genus studies on Linnean science are on their way, by Londa Schiebinger (on the word "mammal"), Janet Browne (popular botany), Ann B. Shteir (Flora's daughters in England), Lisbet Koerner (Goethe's botany), and others. And, indeed, we are still in need of a modern biography on Linnaeus.

GUNNAR BROBERG

See also Sweden

Lister, Joseph 1827–1912

British surgeon

Cameron, Hector Charles, *Joseph Lister: The Friend of Man*, London: Heinemann, 1948
Fisher, Richard B., *Joseph Lister, 1827–1912*, London: MacDonald and Jane's, and New York: Stein and Day, 1977
Godlee, Rickman John, *Lord Lister*, London: Macmillan, 1917; 3rd edition, revised, Oxford: Clarendon Press, 1924
Guthrie, Douglas, *Lord Lister: His Life and Doctrine*, Edinburgh: Livingstone, and Baltimore: Williams and Wilkins, 1949
Howie, W.B. and S.A.B. Black, "Sidelights on Lister: A Patient's Account of Lister's Care", *Journal of the History of Medicine*, 32 (1977): 239–51
LeFanu, William Richard, *A List of the Original Writings of Joseph, Lord Lister, O.M.*, London: Livingstone, 1965
Johnson & Johnson (Research Readers of the Scientific Department), *Lister and the Ligature: A Landmark in the History of Modern Surgery*, New Brunswick, New Jersey: Johnson and Johnson, 1925
Nuland, Sherwin B., "To Tend the Fleshly Tabernacle of the Immortal Spirit", in *Doctors: The Biography of Medicine*, New York: Knopf, 1988
Truax, Rhoda, *Joseph Lister: Father of Modern Surgery*, Indianapolis: Bobbs-Merrill, 1944; London: Harrap, 1947
Wellcome Historical Medical Museum, *Lister Centenary Celebration, American College of Surgeons*, London: Wellcome Historical Medical Museum, 1927

Joseph Lister's pioneering work in germ theory and asepsis merged science and medicine and brought on the modern practice of medicine. He is notable as both a surgeon and a researcher, possessing a passion for both fields.

GODLEE was Lister's nephew, and his is the most important of the biographies of Lister. Not only were personal memories readily available, but also all of Lister's papers, for the doctor knew that his biography was imminent. Unfortunately, according to Lister's wishes, Godlee omitted details of the doctor's private life. The result is an authoritative chronological volume of Lister's work, written in a style by, and for, the medical community. Although some parts may require careful reading, it is, however, basically accessible to the lay public.

CAMERON also drew on personal recollections, being the son of Lister's assistant (his father's reminiscences appear in the centenary publication). He relied heavily on Godlee's volume, but worked Lister's personal life into the professional accounts, and had the added benefit of his father's correspondence with Lister. He lamented the seemingly short shrift that Lister received in the historical record, and endeavored to revive his memory. The book is relatively short, at only 176 pages.

GUTHRIE's work was published almost simultaneously with Cameron's, but without any personal connection with Lister. This is one of the first works on Lister by an American. However, Guthrie was also a surgeon, and so the work again lacks real historical perspective. While it is somewhat more objective than Cameron's version, it still points to the same end. It provides mostly a solid chronology of events, and is the least readable of the volumes.

TRUAX is probably the only woman to have written a biography of Lister, and probably also the first from outside the medical world. She attributed Lister's apparent absence from the annals of medical history to his own modesty, which made him almost anonymous even in his own writings. This volume was written expressly for popular consumption, although the author admires her subject as much as those who worked directly with him. Her account emphasises his personal relationships, such as those with Queen Victoria and Edward VII, and with Louis Pasteur. In this way, Truax established how small the scientific community was at that time, despite the rebuke that Lister faced.

JOHNSON & JOHNSON focuses almost solely on Lister's use of catgut for suturing. They are quick to point out that he was not the first to employ this method, or even the first to use the aseptic technique, although he did much to popularize it. Their study is very short, only 89 pages, and the introduction is little more than a jumble of quotes and observations. However, the remainder of the volume is a compilation of excerpts from Lister's work on suturing, and is a good source for this often neglected, but important part of his career.

The WELLCOME HISTORICAL MEDICAL MUSEUM collection from the centenary of Lister's birth is an excellent source not only for the exhibited material, but also for a first-hand account of Lister's work, and for a concise biography of Lister by Cameron's father.

NULAND's work is the most recent on Lister. Although it contains only one chapter on the surgeon in a general "biography of medicine", it is all the better placed here, for Nuland does a superb job of chronicling the rise of modern medicine. Lister was undoubtedly a major influence on the development of medicine, and the magnitude of his contribution becomes especially apparent in the following chapter, on the eminent surgeon William Steward Halstead.

FISHER has contributed the most modern, full-length biography of Lister to the collection, relying on historical methods and working outside the realm of medicine. He places Lister's life within context and tracked down all possible sources beyond the family papers on which Godlee had relied, and includes everything in an excellent and comprehensive bibliography, which also has comments on Lister's most important works.

LeFANU compiled a bibliography of Lister's writings, an important source for primary research into his techniques. There are a few articles that he omitted, but Fisher made note of them in his own bibliography.

HOWIE & BLACK stumbled across a patient's diary, written during her eight-month stay in the Edinburgh Royal Infirmary under Lister's care in 1877. It is a rare and valuable account of Lister from a patient's perspective. In addition, it provides useful information on the Royal Infirmary at that period.

KIMBERLY WEATHERS

See also Surgery

Literature and Science

Anderson, Wilda C., *Between the Library and the Laboratory: The Language of Chemistry in Eighteenth-Century France*, Baltimore: Johns Hopkins University Press, 1984

Beer, Gillian, *Darwin's Plots: Evolutionary Narrative in Darwin, George Eliot, and Nineteenth-Century Fiction*, London and Boston: Routledge and Kegan Paul, 1983

Benjamin, Andrew E., Geoffrey N. Cantor and John R.R. Christie (eds), *The Figural and the Literal: Problems of Language in the History of Science and Philosophy, 1630–1800*, Manchester: Manchester University Press, 1987

Chartier, Roger, *The Cultural Uses of Print in Early Modern France*, translated by Lydia Cochrane, Princeton, New Jersey: Princeton University Press, 1987

Christie, John and Sally Shuttleworth (eds), *Nature Transfigured: Science and Literature, 1700–1900*, Manchester: Manchester University Press, 1989

Dear, Peter (ed.), *The Literary Structure of Scientific Argument: Historic Studies*, Philadelphia: University of Pennsylvania Press, 1991

Fish, Stanley, *Is There a Text in This Class?: The Authority of Interpretive Communities*, Cambridge, Massachusetts: Harvard University Press, 1980

Jordanova, Ludmilla, *Languages of Nature: Critical Essays in Science and Literature*, New Brunswick, New Jersey: Rutgers University Press, and London: Free Association Books, 1986

LaCapra, Dominick and Steven Kaplan (eds), *Modern European Intellectual History: Reappraisals and New Perspectives*, Ithaca, New York: Cornell University Press, 1982

Latour, Bruno, "Drawing Things Together", in *Representation in Scientific Practice*, edited by Michael Lynch and Steven Woolgar, Cambridge, Massachusetts: MIT Press, 1990

Lepenies, Wolf, *Between Literature and Science: The Rise of Sociology*, translated from the German by R.J. Hollingdale, Cambridge and New York: Cambridge University Press, 1988 (original edition, 1985)

Levine, George (ed.), *One Culture: Essays in Science and Literature*, Madison: University of Wisconsin Press, 1987

Pratt, Mary Louise, *Imperial Eyes: Travel Writing and Transculturation*, London and New York: Routledge, 1992

Serres, Michel, *Hermes: Literature, Science, Philosophy*, edited by Josue V. Harari and David F. Bell, Baltimore: Johns Hopkins University Press, 1982

Snow, C.P., *The Two Cultures and the Scientific Revolution*, Cambridge and New York: Cambridge University Press, 1959

The emergence of "literature and science" as a coherent subject is comparatively recent, and owes much to the progress of structuralism and post-structuralism with their emphasis on language as the substance of thought, the siege laid to realism by social constructivist accounts of knowledge, and the rise of cultural studies with their focus on representations. In America, the subject has begun to acquire the characteristics of a disciplinary field, with its own learned society, annual conference, quarterly journal (*Configurations*), and book series (published by the University of Wisconsin Press).

Some of the methodological approaches that have facilitated the conversion of scientific texts into literature, and of literature into history, are on display in LaCAPRA & KAPLAN, an essay collection in which intellectual historians, drawing on Derrida, Foucault, German hermeneuticists, and Anglo-American philosophers of language, try to negotiate a literary turn. According to this programme, the materials of intellectual history are no longer mined for ideas but for discourses and for the social worlds that these discourses express. Past and present, author and interpreter are conjoined in a process that the volume's commentator, Hayden White, finds deeply literary, because of its power to represent and refigure human nature and human history through linguistic form. Thus, the distinction between text and context is not ready-made, but produced both by the "great works" that intellectual historians study, and by the interpretative acts that intellectual historians perform.

In a sharper-edged, and altogether less solemn, attack on the boundaries separating literature from history, and text from interpretation, FISH confronts the ahistoric formalism predominant in literary studies before the 1970s, with the social construction of meaning by "interpretative communities" precisely situated in space and time. If the essays in LaCapra & Kaplan show how historians might enrol literary criticism in the analysis of discourse, the arguments of Fish suggest how literary critics might use social history to connect discourses with the groups and institutions that produce them. Applied to the history of science and its texts, such approaches have introduced into a field traditionally dominated by the history of ideas, and dependent on a strict demarcation of intellectual content from discursive form, a wide range of interpretations of science as culture.

In a number of works, these new resources have been used to restage a debate, epitomized in SNOW, about the relationship between the "two cultures" of the sciences and the arts. But whereas Snow looked mainly to the sciences to reform the arts, these authors write as humanist critics of a science grown mechanical and indifferent to social needs, and draw their moral examples from earlier times, when imagination and reason were still happily coupled. While the contributors to LEVINE, for example, exhibit the science and literature of ages past in "creative intercourse", the editor outlines a textual approach that "historicizes and humanizes" science, by discovering poetic leaps in biological reduction and literary devices in numerical abstraction. LEPENIES plots the rise of sociology in France, Germany, and Britain in the 19th century as a series of misguided methodological wars with the arts, and suggests that the virtue of sociology lies in the fact that it occupies a space between science and literature. More pointedly, the essays in JORDANOVA exploit the methods of literary criticism in an examination of the construction of "nature" and the uses of "nature", in order to construct models of human community, sexual relations, and femininity in the 18th and 19th centuries. In an introductory essay, Raymond Williams challenges historians to mediate between literary studies, with their particular ahistoricism, and the sciences, thus opening possibilities for cross-disciplinary collaboration, a more general education, and a more direct criticism of current uses of nature and the natural.

What these works accomplish using new conventions of literary and intellectual history, others achieve through style. In an extended treatment of the literary exchange between Darwinian theory and English fiction, BEER shows how each worked to refashion contemporary myths of inheritance, sensibility, female beauty, and male dominance. The use of metaphors, such as natural selection in the writings of Darwin, Eliot and Hardy, enabled a multivalent range of readings, rather than coercing a single logical meaning. Likewise, Beer's own strategy of persuasion rests on its use of metaphor, and its appeal is to a psychology of imagination that favors ambiguity over didacticism. Similarly, the collection of essays in SERRES actively constructs the common culture of science and literature by narrating a poetic journey to wisdom through fluctuating space and time. En route, the post-structuralist philosopher finds, for example, that Zola's novels and Turner's canvases display the operation of thermodynamic laws, and endow the elemental forces of fire and heat with new power and significance. However, it is chiefly Serres's own writing that demonstrates how scientific theories may acquire mythological form through literature.

Other approaches to the topic of science and literature seek to examine the psychological structures and discursive polarities on which these contemporary humanist critiques depend. For the early modern period, BENJAMIN, CANTOR & CHRISTIE examine how the construction of traditions of

philosophical rationalism and scientific empiricism required the generation and valorization of a series of opposites: poetry, rhetoric, and persuasion. Thus the truths of logic, for example, are effectually substantiated by the fictive self of the novel. Western philosophy and science emerge as strategies to escape deception through the continual fabrication of domains of error. In CHRISTIE & SHUTTLEWORTH, science and literature are neither necessary opposites nor creative partners in the generation of culture, but cultural artifacts themselves. Ranging from 17th-century experimental culture to late 19th-century popular science writing, these studies focus on the invention of scientific discourse as an impersonal, collective mode of pronouncing on the world. Integral to that invention was the active construction of literature as an opposite – as a storehouse of everything personal, fanciful, and erroneous. The studies also explore the value of this Manicheanism for novelists, poets, and other writers of "fiction", in their own efforts to claim the creative and moral high-ground. Attention to local historical contexts enables the contributors to examine precise relationships between modes of writing, institutions of learning, and the problems of authority that were being negotiated through particular forms of authorship. ANDERSON explores similar developments in the field of 18th-century chemistry, tracing the transformations in experimental practice, epistemology and nomenclature that brought forth the anonymous, neutral practitioner from the sociable world of the savant who was simultaneously "auteur", earning philosophic credit through literary facility and exchange.

Though not concerned explicitly with the categories of science and literature, several of the many works on the literary technologies of science are also highly relevant. The essays in DEAR examine the role of writing and publishing strategies in the shaping of knowledge and scientific community, and, through accounts of the scientific essay, journal article, textbook and table, show how theory construction, communication and acceptance form part of a single process. Resources for this form of analysis abound in LATOUR, which makes the production and manipulation of inscriptions – printed words, pictures, maps, charts – into the foundation of truth-claims, the basis of their persuasive power. In a radical inversion of the "world as text" of literary critics, and of the "past as discourse" of new intellectual historians, metaphor and theory appear not as psychological marvels, but as the technical recombination and superimposition of emblematic materials.

Despite fundamental differences of interpretation over the meaning of "science" and "literature", however, all of these projects tend to focus on great works, disciplines, and actors at institutional or intellectual centers. For many scholars in the field, genuine criticism or creativity require intellectual gravity. Thus the familiar authors surveyed in LaCapra & Kaplan appear as decisive critics of their age, even when the materials with which they worked were appropriated from popular culture. Likewise, the cultural history proposed by CHARTIER is explicitly directed against the encroachments of social historians from below (here the Annales school), whose work seems to deny the importance of productions of authentic learning. However, while the history of "science and literature", of discourses, print culture, and authorship, has been written largely from the standpoint of canonical figures, some studies are now underway that show that the traffic between science and literature was negotiated in many different social and cultural arenas, and not just among elites. One example is PRATT, which suggests that a close attention to readership and audience can show the "text" of Euro-imperialism to have been written by a whole range of figures at both the center and periphery, and to involve improvization at the frontier, and widespread appropriations of natural historical discourse and its rhetoric of neutral observation.

PAUL WHITE

See also Reading Culture and Science

Lorenz, Konrad 1903–1989

Austrian naturalist and philosopher

Burkhardt, Richard W., "On the Emergence of Ethology as a Scientific Discipline", *Conspectus of History*, 7 (1981): 62–81

Deichman, Ute, *Biologen unter Hitler: Vertreibung, Karrieren, Forschung*, Frankfurt and New York: Campus, 1992

Dewsbury, Donald A. (ed.), *Leaders in the Study of Animal Behavior: Autobiographical Perspectives*, Lewisburg, Pennsylvania: Bucknell University Press, and London: Associated University Presses, 1985

Evans, Richard I. (ed.), *Konrad Lorenz: The Man and His Ideas*, New York: Harcourt Brace Jovanovich, 1975

Heinroth, Katharina, *Oskar Heinroth: Vater der Verhaltensforschung, 1871–1945*, Stuttgart: Wissenschaftliche Verlagsgesellschaft, 1971

Kalikow, Theodora, "Konrad Lorenz's Ethological Theory: Explanation and Ideology, 1938–1943", *Journal of the History of Biology*, 16 (1983): 39–73

Lerner, Richard M., *Final Solutions: Biology, Prejudice, and Genocide*, University Park: Pennsylvania State University Press, 1992

Nisbett, Alec, *Konrad Lorenz: A Biography*, London: Dent, 1976; New York: Harcourt Brace Jovanovich, 1977

Richards, Robert J., *Darwin and the Emergence of Evolutionary Theories of Mind and Behavior*, Chicago: University of Chicago Press, 1987

Thorpe, W.H., *The Origins and Rise of Ethology: The Science of the Natural Behaviour of Animals*, London: Heinemann, and New York: Praeger, 1979

In 1973, the award of the Nobel prize in physiology or medicine to Karl von Frisch, Nikolaas Tinbergen, and Konrad Lorenz confirmed the international standing of ethology, the biological study of behaviour. Soon afterwards, an increasing number of studies appeared investigating the origins and growth of the discipline. They were based on scientists' reminiscences and scientific literature, and shared the problematic need to investigate the roots of the new discipline of ethology. It is in this context that studies on Lorenz's life and career first appeared.

NISBETT's biography offers an idyllic portrait of Lorenz, retracing his childhood, describing the origin of his love for animals, and the various conflicts he faced during the evolution of ethology. Nisbett notably comments on the way Lorenz opposed the American school of comparative psychologists; the

biological reductionism that Lorenz advocated contradicted the environmentalism supported by the American school, for Lorenz definitively opposed all kinds of scientific theories tied up with liberal or "pseudo-democratic" ideologies. A large part of EVANS's book is also devoted to this aspect of Lorenz's endeavours. However, both Nisbett and Evans may not have been sufficiently cautious, as they accepted at face value most of Lorenz's claims and reminiscences.

The work by THORPE reflects a different approach. Partly based on the author's own recollections, the book describes the development of animal behaviour studies from the late 19th century up to the 1970s. Lorenz appears as a crucial player in this development, as the theories he promoted constituted a synthesis of the different (and often contradictory) conceptual schemes current in the 1930s. Despite the fact that Lorenz's contribution had been largely acknowledged in the 1940s, it soon led to criticisms from American, Dutch, and British animal psychologists. None the less, Thorpe particularly insists on the way Lorenz's instinct theory had been adapted by British ethologists, and claims that the new scientific observations made in both Cambridge and Oxford were the basis for the transformation of Lorenz's first ethological theories.

Thorpe's historical account may well be complemented by the testimonies or articles written by leading ethologists, such as that edited by Dewsbury. In DEWSBURY, autobiographical essays by Eibl-Eibelsfeldt and Leyhausen underline the crucial part Lorenz played in the institutionalization of ethology in Germany and Austria after World War II. Those by Tinbergen, Hinde and Baerends bring new data on the early development of ethology in Britain and the Netherlands, and make a precise analysis of Lorenz's influence. Taken together, these essays permit an appreciation of the internationalization of ethology in the late 1940s, and also an understanding of why Lorenz's formulation led to so much criticism.

This historical literature produced by scientists is an important starting point for the historians of ethology. However, more detailed articles have been published that focus on precise points of Lorenz's life and career.

The roots of Lorenz's theory of instinctive behaviour had been investigated by BURKHARDT. Lorenz's first theoretical constructions reflect his desire to understand animal and human behaviour, and his attempt may be characterized as a study in "phylogenetic psychology", the end result of which is to describe human natural behaviour. Many of Burkhardt's conclusions are drawn from a meticulous reading of Lorenz's letters to Oskar Heinroth, edited by Katharina HEINROTH. RICHARDS's analysis demonstrates how Lorenz's constructs were the outgrowth of certain German scientific traditions. Lorenz benefited from several influences: that of Weisman, an ultra-Darwinian who considered natural selection as a blind mechanism; but also that of Haeckel and Ziegler, who described instinct as an inherited mechanism. In the end, Lorenz opposed the kind of vitalism advocated by Hans Driesch and Friedrich Alverdes.

Lorenz's theoretical choices had strong political implications in the 1930s, and Richards points out the relation of Lorenz's theories to National Socialist ideology. This point has been explored with more scrutiny by KALIKOW and DEICHMAN. Kalikow focuses her analysis on the articles Lorenz published between 1938 and 1942. Soon after the Anschluss, Lorenz started to explore human natural behaviour. His achievement was quite analogous to his previous studies of animal instinctive behaviour, as in both cases he considered instinct and emotions as if they were morphological characters that evolve thanks to the selection process. Lorenz's conception of evolution contradicted the Nazi conception of Aryan race. However, one idea that he stressed in several articles – that both behaviour and morality may regress as a result of progress – put him close to Nazi ideology. According to Lorenz's point of view, modern cities tended to transform human natural behaviour through a domestication mechanism.

DEICHMAN offers a similar analysis of Lorenz's writings. However, the use she makes of recently released archives helps to understand how Lorenz contended with Nazi principles. During the early 1940s, Nazi science appeared to be of major concern to Lorenz. After he published his first Nazified article, he was appointed professor of psychology at the University of Königsberg. Soon afterwards, he was requested to participate in the war effort and moved to Poznan. There he chose to study what he believed to be his own speciality, neurology and psychiatry, and worked with the psychiatrist Hippius to establish the psychological criteria used to recognize pure Germans from Polish or metis within a mixed population.

LERNER's book focuses also on aspects of Lorenz's writing previously analysed by Kalikow: the principle of degenerescence induced by a mechanism such as domestication. Lerner does not restrict his analysis to articles that Lorenz had published during the Nazi era. Hence a new aspect of Lorenz's philosophy is put under scrutiny: the actual significance of biological determinism as advocated by Lorenz, and the way it could affect real policy. Criticising Lorenz but also human sociobiology, Lerner wishes to warn readers about the use racists and reactionary movements may make of biological determinism.

PHILIPPE CHAVOT

See also Ethology and Animal Behaviour

Lyell, Charles 1797–1875

British geologist

Bailey, E. B., *Charles Lyell*, London: Thomas Nelson, 1962; New York: Doubleday, 1963

Bartholomew, Michael, "Lyell and Evolution: An Account of Lyell's Response to the Prospect of an Evolutionary Ancestry for Man", *British Journal for the History of Science* (1973): 262–303

Bonney, T.G., *Charles Lyell and Modern Geology*, London: Cassell, and New York: Macmillan, 1895

Cannon, Walter, "The Uniformitarian–Catastrophist Debate", *Isis* (1960): 38–55

Fox, Robert (ed.), "Lyell Centenary Issue: Papers Delivered at the Charles Lyell Centenary Symposium London 1975", *British Journal for the History of Science*, 9/2 (1976)

Gillispie, Charles Coulston, *Genesis and Geology: A Study in the Relations of Scientific Thought, Natural Theology, and Social Opinion in Great Britain, 1790–1850*, Cambridge, Massachusetts: Harvard University Press, 1951; with a foreword by Nicolaas A. Rupke, 1996

Gould, Stephen Jay, *Time's Arrow, Time's Cycle: Myth and Metaphor in the Discovery of Geological Time*, Cambridge, Massachusetts, and London: Harvard University Press, 1987

Hodge, Jonathan, "Darwin Studies at Work: A Re-examination of Three Decisive years (1835–37)" in *Nature, Experiment, and the Sciences: Essays on Galileo and the History of Science*, edited by Trevor H. Levere and William R. Shea, Dordrecht: Kluwer, 1990

Hooykaas, Reijer, *Natural Law and Divine Miracle: A Historical and Critical Study of the Principle of Uniformity in Geology, Biology, and Theology*, Leiden: E.J. Brill, 1959; 2nd edition, 1963

Hooykaas, Reijer, *Catastrophism in Geology: Its Scientific Character in Relation to Actualism and Uniformitarianism*, Amsterdam: North-Holland, 1970

Laudan, Rachel, *From Mineralogy to Geology: The Foundation of a Science, 1650–1850*, Chicago: University of Chicago Press, 1987

Lyell, Charles, *Sir Charles Lyell's Scientific Journals on the Species Question*, edited by Leonard G. Wilson, New Haven, Connecticut: Yale University Press, 1970

Lyell, Mrs [Katherine] (ed.), *Life Letters and Journals of Sir Charles Lyell*, Bart., 2 vols, London: John Murray, 1881; New York: AMS Press, 1983

Ospovat, Dov, "Lyell's Theory of Climate", *Journal of History of Biology*, 10 (1977): 317–39

Rudwick, Martin, "Lyell on Etna and the Antiquity of the Earth", in *Toward a History of Geology*, edited by Cecil J. Schneer, Cambridge, Massachusetts: MIT Press, 1969

Rudwick, Martin, "Charles Lyell's Dream of a Statistical Palaeontology", in *Palaeontology* (1978): 225–44

Rudwick, Martin, "Transposes Concepts from the Human Sciences in the Early Work of Charles Lyell", in *Images of the Earth: Essays in the History of the Environmental Sciences*, edited by Ludmilla Jordanova and Roy Porter, Chalfont St Giles: British Society for the History of Science, 1979

Rudwick, Martin, "introduction", to *Principles of Geology*, (reprint of the 1st edition), Chicago: University of Chicago Press, 1990

Wilson, Leonard, "The Origin of Charles Lyell's Uniformitarianism", in *Uniformity and Simplicity: A Symposium on the Principle of the Uniformity of Nature*, edited by Claude Albritton Jr, Boulder, Colorado: Geological Society of America, 1967

Wilson, Leonard, *Charles Lyell: The Years to 1841: The Revolution in Geology*, New Haven, Connecticut, and London: Yale University Press, 1972

Wilson, Leonard, "Geology on the Eve of Charles Lyell's First Visit to America, 1841", *Proceedings of the American Philosophical Society*, 124 (1980): 168–202

With a well-established position in the history of geology, Charles Lyell is renowned for his *Principles of Geology* (1830–33), his *Elements of Geology* (1838), and his *Antiquity of Man* (1863). He was controversial in his own day for the doctrine of "uniformitarianism" (as compared with "catastrophism" – the opposites being so named by William Whewell), and for his efforts to establish a general methodology for geology. Lyell is also well known for his influence on Darwin, his method for the subdivision of the Tertiary, his arguments for the great age of the Earth, his early deployment of the concept of metamorphism, his attempts to confirm geology as a naturalistic science distinct from cosmogony, his views on mankind's place in nature, and his work as an historian of geology. Not until the mid-20th century did the notion that the Lyellian method was the correct one for geology come under serious attack. It is still taught to students today.

Lyell was the subject of a Victorian "Life and Letters" edited by his sister-in-law Katherine LYELL, which contains an autobiographical fragment. There is also considerable extant manuscript material, most of it in private hands, which was used in WILSON (1972).

BONNEY produced the first full-scale biography of Lyell, drawing on manuscript sources. He expressed approval of Lyell's uniformitarianism, representing Lyell as an empiricist, with "experience . . . redolent, not of the dust of libraries, but of the sweetness of the open air". This field knowledge, Bonney averred, "did much to disarm opposition, and to open the way to victory [against "catastrophism"]. Another early "scientist-historian's" account of Lyell was the lively biography of BAILEY, which discussed the political context of Lyell's career.

Most historians today consider that Whewell's dichotomy does not do justice to all possible theoretical positions regarding the uniformity of nature that was obtained in 19th-century geology, or subsequently. However, Lyell's methodology for the geological research – perhaps not analysed closely enough at the time – proved highly successful in the 19th century. And conjoined with Darwinian theory, Lyell's geology succeeded, by the end of his century, in achieving "victory" against catastrophism in a hard-fought and complex controversy. Twentieth-century Lyellian historiography has likewise been contentious and significantly it has to an extent revised the earlier debates.

Situating his discussion in the context of the history of the relationships between science and theology, GILLISPIE suggested in an ebullient text – the first major work on the history of geology written by a professional historian of science – that Flood, or "diluvialist", geology was Lyell's chief target as he sought to establish a sound methodology for his science. Lyell, then, "prepared the way for Darwin", but did not at first see how to reconcile evolutionism and uniformitarianism. Gillispie further saw "[u]niformitarian presuppositions" as "those of optimistic materialism". He recognized that Lyell's doctrine did not rest on empirical results alone and maintained that Lyell "universalised the principle of uniformity and then arranged the facts in accordance with it".

CANNON objected that, in Gillispie's eyes, Lyell's difficulty in linking uniformitarianism and evolutionism was a kind of "logical peccadillo" whereas catastrophism and the problem of the Flood were really the big issues. But for Cannon this misrepresented the historical situation. In Cannon's view, it was "progressive development" rather than the question of the Biblical Flood that came to be "the great dividing point between Uniformitarianism and Catastrophism".

Close historical and philosophical analysis of uniformitarianism was undertaken by HOOYKAAS (1959), who maintained that uniformitarianism (or "actualism") was "not a law, not a rule established after comparison of facts, but a methodological principle". For Lyell, it was a multi-faceted set of assumptions made by scientists as they approach nature. The several "facets" of the principle were: that the laws of nature were constant: that geological processes were the same in the past as at present; that the energy of geological processes was uniform over time; that conditions on Earth were approximately constant; and that there was not geological "progress". But for Hooykaas uniformitarianism should be no more than a "methodological rule", or a set of assumptions serving as a guide for the conduct of geological research.

Developing the suggestions of Hooykaas, GOULD distinguished between what he called "methodological uniformitarianism" and "substantive uniformitarianism". The later, he claimed, was empirically incorrect, while the former merely asserted that the laws of nature are uniform. So he vaunted Lyellian principle for geology was little more than that which was common to all the physical sciences. Indeed, it was an unhelpful dogma, which might impede creative thinking in geology.

While Lyell was an empiricist, according to the earlier writers such as Bonney, HOOYKAAS (1970), submitted that empiricism was not the prerogative of uniformitarians, as Bonney had implied. For "catastrophists" such as Cuvier and Buckland could also claim to be empiricists, given that some geological evidence strongly suggests the occurrence of great floods, if not actually the Biblical deluge.

However, the view that Lyell's uniformitarianism was empirically grounded was restated by WILSON (1967), and in his first volume of his projected biographical trilogy on Lyell WILSON (1972) gave much attention to Lyell's travels and fieldwork, especially in the Auvergne and Italy. In contrast to Wilson, other historians, taking the lead from Hooykaas, have emphasized the rational aprioristic aspects of Lyell's geology. In particular, RUDWICK (1969) gave a valuable account of how Lyell reasoned actualisticaly about Etna, suggesting that his ideas and his approach were established at least in part before he viewed the rocks of the Auvergne and Sicily. In several later publications, the various arguments of which were brought together in 1990, RUDWICK has closely analysed Lyell's thinking, examining his "strategy" in composing his major work, and particularly his use of history for rhetorical purposes. He has shown for example, how Lyell deployed analogies from such fields as history, economics, and linguistics in his thinking and writing. Rudwick has also clarified the terms "gradualism" and uniformitarianism" using the term "directionalism" the latter distinguishing Darwin's uniformitarianism (say) from that of Lyell.

Lyell's historiography attracted considerable attention at the Centenary Symposium held in the geologist's honour in 1975 (FOX). Among the several interesting papers, Porter presented Lyell's history as a "complex polemic" intended to "chronicle all the obstacles to the emergence of the true [Lyellian] science of geology". It was, Porter opined, a "mythic history of geology". Also objecting to Lyell's historiography, Alexander Ospovat criticized Lyell's historical account of Werner; and McCartney showed that Lyell's historiography was indebted without proper acknowledgement to the work of the Italian, Giovanni Battista Brocchi.

Ruse (also in FOX) contended that Lyell's "system" was influenced by the philosophies of science of Herschel and Whewell, and was dependent on the Newtonian notion of *verae causae*. By arguing from the present to the past one could suggest "true causes" that might *actually* have operated so as to lead to the formation of the Earth as seen today. But Lyell's Earth showed no progression. Also at the Lyell Centenary Symposium, Bartholomew (in FOX) argued that although Lyell's *Principles* was well received as supposedly providing the correct method for geological enquiry the notion of non-progression was largely rejected by his contemporaries. It did no seem to agree with what could be observed in the stratigraphic record.

RUDWICK (1978) has analysed Lyell's method for subdividing the Tertiary according to the proportion of extant fossils contained in the different strata, and Dov OSPOVAT showed how Lyell's theory, according to which climate depended on whether high land was concentrated at equatorial or polar regions, might be used even to account for the occurrence of ice ages. Lyell's theory of climate and his methodology of science have been further analysed by LAUDAN.

In 1970, Wilson published the notebooks of Lyell that dealt with the questions of species (LYELL, 1970), and discussed his fluctuating thoughts about "progressive development" as well as his response to Darwin's theories. Lyell did not accept that the idea of progressive development/special creations, as favoured by the likes of Sedgwick, Roderick Murchison and Hugh Miller, since it seemed either to sustain a miraculous element in geology or to be the thin end of the wedge for the acceptance of transmutation/evolution. BARTHOLOMEW has examined Lyell's ideas on humans and the inclusion of mankind in Darwin's theory, emphasising that Lyell's initial rejection of transformism was not because evolution conflicted with his principles of scientific reasoning but because it ran counter to his version of deism. Lyell could not tolerate the idea of humans having evolved from some other biological species. Even when he reluctantly accepted Darwin's theory and published *The Antiquity of Men*, there was supposedly a "bound" from the most intelligent animals to mankind.

Lyell's role in the formulation of Darwin's theory has been analysed at the conceptual level by HODGE. According to his interpretation, Darwin largely derived his knowledge of Lamarck from Lyell's exposition and analysis of the Frenchman's transmutationist philosophy. And Darwin's thinking about biogeography during and after the *Beagle* voyage, which was central to his establishment of the notion of the occurrence of transmutation, was shaped by his intellectual response to Lyell's ideas about the coming-into-being and passing-away of species, matching ever-changing environmental circumstances.

Though WILSON presented a paper at the 1975 Symposium entitled "Charles Lyell's Concept of Uniformity: A Revolution in Geology", it was not published in Fox. Later, WILSON (1980) published a strongly-worded paper that attacked the work of Hooykaas, Rudwick, and Porter, and hinted that Hooykaas's writing on Lyell was influenced by religious considerations. Wilson also criticised Alexander Ospovat's discussion of Lyell's historical account of Werner.

The issues dividing Wilson from the other historians appear to have been partly personal, partly "philosophical", and partly to do with providing a just historical evaluation of Lyell. Broadly speaking, Wilson emphasises Lyell's empiricism and his leading position in the establishment of modern geology. His opponents have taken a more critical view and are more influenced by developments in the sociology of knowledge. But Wilson's book remains the only modern biography of Lyell. Though Wilson withdrew from Lyell's scholarship for some years, he is currently working on the volumes needed to complete his biographical project.

DAVID OLDROYD

Lysenko, Trofim Denisovich 1898–1976

Ukrainian geneticist and agronomist

Graham, Loren R., *Science and Philosophy in the Soviet Union*, New York: Knopf, 1972; London: Allen Lane, 1973

Huxley, Julian, *Heredity East and West: Lysenko and World Science*, New York: Schuman, 1949; as *Soviet Genetics and World Science: Lysenko and the Meaning of Heredity*, London: Chatto and Windus, 1949

Joravsky, David, *Soviet Marxism and Natural Science, 1917–1932*, New York: Columbia University Press, and London: Routledge and Kegan Paul, 1961

Joravsky, David, *The Lysenko Affair*, Cambridge, Massachusetts: Harvard University Press, 1970

Lecourt, Dominique, *Proletarian Science? The Case of Lysenko*, translated from the French by Ben Brewster, London: New Left Books, and Atlantic Highlands, New Jersey: Humanities Press, 1977 (original edition, 1970)

Medvedev, Zhores A., *The Rise and Fall of T.D. Lysenko*, translated from the Russian by I. Michael Lerner, New York: Columbia University Press, 1969

Popovsky, Mark, *The Vavilov Affair*, Hamden, Connecticut: Archon Books, 1984

Soyfer, Valery N., *Lysenko and the Tragedy of Soviet Science*, translated from the Russian by Leo Gruliow and Rebecca Gruliow, New Brunswick, New Jersey: Rutgers University Press, 1994

A considerable amount of scholarship on Trofim Lysenko has been conducted by biologists who studied and worked in the USSR in the years when genetics was a controversial, and even a banned, subject. Their recollections and analyses give a colour to the literature that comes of their personal acquaintance with some of the principal players in the drama, and their participation in outrageous events. Western trained scholars have tended to examine the debate at a distance, concentrating on the relationship between a dialectical materialist philosophy and the vagaries of total power, and analysing their combined effect on the pursuit of natural science.

Both Huxley and Joravsky were analysing the Lysenko phenomenon while he was still the favoured biologist of the Soviet regime. HUXLEY, a British biologist, described the Cold War in science that took hold shortly after Lysenko's triumphant take-over of Soviet genetics and agronomy – a time when the regime's scientists challenged the new orthodoxy only at the risk of their lives. In a brief but well-documented work, Huxley covers the ideological and scientific issues, and includes a chapter on "Genetics as a Science" for those who are not biologists. His aim is to disprove Lysenkoism and thus destroy the edifice, showing it to be non-scientific, while alluding also to the effects of regimented thought on other spheres of Soviet science and culture.

In a chapter on "The Crisis in Biology" in JORAVSKY (1961), the clash between "Morganism" and "Lamarckism" is explored. Joravsky argues that there was little in the Marxist heritage that portended serious conflict over biology, such that problems only began to emerge c.1931, by which time Lysenko had emerged as leader of a mass movement for the improvement of wheat culture.

At the time that MEDVEDEV wrote his book, he was head of a Soviet Department of Molecular Biology, and Lysenko was completely discredited, although still in possession of a small power base in the USSR. Medvedev describes the circumstances of the Lysenko take-over in biology, and the bizarre events that transpired between 1929 and 1964. He divides the book into three parts, approaching 1929–41 as a historian, and 1946–62 as a witness to the events. In the section covering the years 1962–64, he shows that Soviet attitudes to genetics and biology began to reverse within hours of Khrushchev's downfall in October 1964. Many of Lysenko's hare-brained schemes for planting and transforming species are detailed, and the system for political and ideological control of science indicted.

Popovsky and Soyfer, both citizens of the USSR, gained access to archival documents that supplemented earlier accounts of the Lysenko phenomenon. POPOVSKY employed cunning when the guards of police archives had begun to be unsure of themselves. With a journalist's eye, he examines the destructive effects of state control on the professional and private lives of individuals. The noted agronomist and botanist, Vavilov, who died in a prison hospital in 1943 of exhaustion and hunger, was the most eminent of the victims of the "Lysenko dictatorship", and Popovsky shows that the case against him had been prepared since 1931. The book suffers, however, from the lack of an index.

SOYFER's is the most complete and authoritative analysis so far of Lysenko's life and times, and a pleasure to read. Soyfer saw Lysenko's power at first hand while a student in the 1950s. In the 1970s, having been stripped of his scientific positions, he set out to find out all he could about Lysenko, drawing on extensive interviews, archives long inaccessible to scholars, and his own memories. The original Russian manuscript of this biography was circulated as a *samizdat* book, and smuggled to the West for publication. Soyfer shows how numerous careers were ruined and exposes many of Lysenko's breath-taking agronomic deceptions and confidence tricks. He relates the sustained challenges to Lysenkoism until Khrushchev was deposed, and continues the narrative to Lysenko's death.

Graham and Joravsky (1970) address the philosophical underpinnings of Lysenkoism. They both argue that nothing in the philosophical system of dialectical materialism lends obvious support to any of Lysenko's views.

JORAVSKY (1970) gives a detailed documentation of the arguments, squabbles, debates, and factions. There is a considerable amount of science in the book, and extensive discussion of the theories behind the debates in plant physiology and genetics. The pre-revolutionary background to the agronomic disputes is described, and Joravsky shows a good understanding of the theoretical basis for each argument, including the role played by Marxist philosophy. He also considers the main players besides Lysenko, consistently maintaining that scientists were subordinated to cranks.

GRAHAM's book, which contains a chapter on the genetics controversy, is concerned with the relationship between dialectical materialism and natural science. He argues that in the 1940s and 1950s, the worst threats to Soviet science came from third-rate people who tried to win Stalin's favour, among them Lysenko. His rise, therefore, was the result of a long series of social, political, and economic events, rather than of connections with Marxist philosophy. There are two useful appendices: the first, "Lysenko and Zhdanov", discusses the puzzle of Stalin's own son-in-law, who wrote, then recanted, an article in 1948, censuring people who tried to make fiefdoms of certain areas of science; the second, "H.J. Muller on Lenin and Genetics", reproduces an article of 1934 opposing Lysenkoism by the noted American Marxist biologist who became a senior geneticist of the Academy of Sciences in Moscow.

LECOURT provides a Marxist perspective of the Lysenko affair, and cautions that Marxists must not gloss over the crushing agricultural failure that followed the implementation of Lysenkoism after 1948. Lecourt focuses on what he considers to be Lysenko's bizarre exhumation of Bogdanov, Lenin's Bolshevik rival in philosophy, who was allegedly scorned by Soviet philosophers for more than 50 years, and blames the entire fiasco on this error.

ELIZABETH V. HAIGH

See also Genetics: general works; Marxism and Science; Russia

M

Mach, Ernst 1838–1916

Austrian physicist

Blackmore, John T., *Ernst Mach: His Work, Life, and Influence*, Berkeley: University of California Press, 1972

Blackmore, John T. and Klaus Hentschel (eds), *Ernst Mach als Aussenseiter: Machs Briefwechsel über Philosophie und Relativitätstheorie, mit Persönlichkeiten seiner Zeit*, Vienna: Braumüller, 1985

Blackmore, John T. (ed.), *Ernst Mach: A Deeper Look: Documents and New Perspectives*, Dordrecht: Kluwer, 1992

Cohen, Robert S. and Raymond J. Seeger (eds), *Ernst Mach: Physicist and Philosopher*, Dordrecht: Reidel, 1970

Diersch, Manfred, *Empiriokritizismus und Impressionismus: Über Beziehungen zwischen Philosophie, Ästhetik und Literatur um 1900 in Wien*, Berlin: Rütten & Loening, 1977

Feyerabend, Paul K., "Mach's Theory of Research and Its Relation to Einstein", *Studies in History and Philosophy of Science*, 15 (1984): 1–22; reprinted in Haller & Stadler, 1988 (see below)

Haller, Rudolf and Friedrich Stadler (eds), *Ernst Mach: Werk und Wirkung*, Vienna: Hölder-Pichler-Tempsky, 1988

Hentschel, Klaus, "On Feyerabend's Version of 'Mach's Theory of Research and Its Relation to Einstein'", *Studies in History and Philosophy of Science*, 16 (1985): 387–94

Hentschel, Klaus, "Die Korrespondenz Duhem–Mach: Zur Modellbeladenheit der Wissenschaftsgeschichte", *Annals of Science*, 45 (1988): 73–91

Hiebert, Erwin, "Mach's Philosophical Use of the History of Science", in *Historical and Philosophical Perspectives of Science*, edited by Roger H. Stuewer, Minneapolis, University of Minnesota Press, 1970

Hoffmann, Dieter and Hubert Laitko (eds), *Ernst Mach: Studien und Dokumente zu Leben und Werk*, Berlin: Deutscher Verlag der Wissenschaften, 1991

Mach, Ernst, *Knowledge and Error: Sketches on the Psychology of Enquiry*, translated from the German by Thomas J. McCormack and Paul Foulkes, Dordrecht: Reidel, 1976 (original edition, 1906)

Schorske, Carl E., *Fin-de-Siècle Vienna: Politics and Culture*, New York: Knopf, 1979

Stadler, Friedrich, *Vom Positivismus zur "wissenschaftlichen Weltauffassung": Am Beispiel der Wirkungsgeschichte von Ernst Mach in Österreich von 1895 bis 1934*, Vienna: Löcker, 1982

Thiele, Joachim (ed.), *Wissenschaftliche Kommunikation: Die Korrespondenz Ernst Machs*, Kastellaun: Henn, 1978

Wolters, Gereon, *Mach I, Mach II, Einstein und die Relativitätstheorie*, Berlin: De Gruyter 1987

The literature discussed below is divided into the following categories: Mach's own writings, and correspondence, biographies, discussions of Mach's attitude to perception, discussions of Mach's relation to Einstein and relativity theory, Mach as a historian of science, and finally literature on Mach's cultural context.

A study of the life and work of Austrian physicist, physiologist of perception, and philosopher, Ernst Mach, should begin with the reading of several of his works. Especially recommended is MACH, containing Robert Cohen's outstanding introduction. Excellent translations of Mach's *Mechanics* and his popular science lectures, by the American monists Paul Carus and J. McCormmack, are also available. It was through these works that Ernst Mach became well known in the US.

A good introduction to the study of Mach's scientific correspondence with physicists such as Gustav Robert Kirchhoff, Hermann Helmholtz, Ludwig Boltzmann, and Heinrich Hertz, and with philosophers such as Richard Avenarius, Franz Brentano, and Edmund Husserl, as well as with representatives of many other scientific disciplines, can be found in THIELE's detailed annotated edition. One disadvantage of this selected correspondence is that Thiele primarily published letters written to Mach that are available in the Ernst Mach Archive in Freiburg and, only in a few cases (as, for example, to the biologist Ernst Haeckel or the philosopher Wilhelm Schuppe) was he able to discover letters from Mach.

A far greater selection of letters from Mach from many different archives (including letters to Friedrich Adler, Joseph Petzoldt, Josef Popper-Lynkeus, and Wilhelm Jerusalem) can be found in BLACKMORE & HENTSCHEL's anthology, which was conceived as a supplement to Thiele's. The appendix to this anthology also includes facsimiles from Mach's last notebook, for the years 1909–16. The weakness of this edition is the paucity of annotations. Additional supplements to Thiele's edition can be found in HALLER & STADLER, and in the appendix to HOFFMANN & LAITKO. Mach's correspondence with Ostwald can also be found in BLACKMORE

(1992). Haller & Stadler and Hoffmann & Laitko include a complete Mach bibliography, while Stadler contains a list of Ernst Mach's correspondents in the Ernst Mach Institute of the Fraunhofer-Gesellschaft in Freiburg im Breisgau.

The only scholarly biography on Mach in English is BLACK-MORE (1972), in which the full range of Mach's life and work is covered. Especially noteworthy are the sections on Mach's early intellectual development, from which the motives for his phenomenalistic philosophy become clear, and on Mach and Buddhism, a topic also covered by Ursula Baatz in Blackmore (1992). Blackmore (1972) also touches on the thorny question of Mach's attitude towards atomism, and concludes that, unlike Ostwald, Mach did not accept the reality of atoms to his death, despite apocryphal anecdotes hinting to the contrary. The difficult period of Mach's two terms as rector at the University of Prague, then in the process of splitting into two separate (German and Czech) universities, are further illuminated by Dieter Hoffmann's contributions to Hoffmann & Laitko and Blackmore (1992).

Although Blackmore also covers Mach's studies on the perception of different shades of grey in fast-rotating patterns from 1875 onwards – which led to the discovery of the so-called Mach bands and his famous work on the photography of shock waves – the reader is nevertheless advised also to consult the more detailed essays on these aspects by Floyd Ratcliff, Wolfgang Merzkirch and Raymond Seeger in COHEN & SEEGER. Broader reflections on the impact of Mach's "analysis of sensations" for the development of his philosophical opinions can be found in Cohen's paper (also in Cohen & Seeger), in Leinfellner's and Swoboda's contributions to Haller & Stadler, and in Tembrock's contribution to Hoffmann & Laitko.

The question as to whether Mach finally accepted Einstein's theory of relativity is particularly controversial. Though the early Mach had pioneered the thorough application of the principle of relativity, and had criticized Newton for his concepts of absolute space and time, Blackmore concludes that the late Mach did in fact oppose the theory of relativity because of its formalistic approach, the conceptual problems with the postulate of constancy of the velocity of light in vacuum, and on methodological grounds. For WOLTERS, on the other hand, the anti-relativistic foreword in Mach's textbook on optics, published posthumously in 1921, is not an authentic piece, but rather a falsified text written by Mach's oldest son, Ludwig, who lived with his father in Vaterstetten near Munich from 1913 onwards, and performed optical experiments for Ernst Mach after the latter was partially paralyzed by a stroke. The high point of Wolters's book, which, unfortunately, occasionally reads like a polemic attack on all other Mach literature, is actually the detailed analysis of this very intense father-son relationship, which culminates in Wolters's thesis that Ludwig felt entitled to write under his father's name because he had always only executed his father's wishes. However, Ludwig was in fact far more under the influence of ardent anti-relativists, such as Hugo Dingler, than was his father. Further material and controversies on this issue can be found in Haller & Stadler, and in Blackmore (1992).

Aside from this unresolved controversy, it is undisputed that the early Einstein interpreted the theory of relativity as the direct outgrowth of Mach's philosophy of science, as shown by his letters to Mach and his obituary of Mach in 1916. Furthermore, both Goenner's contribution to Cohen & Seeger and Schmutzer's paper in Hoffmann & Laitko show that Mach's principle explaining inertia in terms of the mutual interaction of matter was an important heuristic principle in the development of the general theory of relativity.

The more philosophical impact of Mach's methodology on Einstein has been the subject of a study by Gerald Holton (in Cohen & Seeger). He claims that while the young Einstein was strongly influenced by Mach, he turned to a much more rationalistic world-view after 1920. However, FEYERABEND's effort to connect Mach's and Einstein's research practice is much shakier; his unconvincing, artificial separation of Mach's physical arguments (which Feyerabend accepts) from his philosophical outlook (which he dislikes) has been criticized in HENTSCHEL (1985), who in turn called for an integrated view of Mach, explaining Mach's astonishing variety of scientific interests as stemming from a common methodological root – the systematic correlation of different types of sense-perceptions.

Mach as a historian of science is the subject of HIEBERT and HENTSCHEL (1988). Both authors show how Mach's pioneering studies in the history of science were rooted in philosophical notions, and intertwined with empiricist and somewhat naive expectations of steady progress. Hentschel's study also quotes from Pierre Duhem's fairly critical review of Mach's history of mechanics. Further material on the reception of Mach's "historical-critical" analyses can be found in Haller & Stadler and Blackmore (1992).

A broad description of the cultural context of Mach's works can be found in SCHORSKE's book on fin-de-siècle Vienna. By his examination of the political environment, the literature of Schnitzler and Hoffmannsthal, Freud's psychoanalysis, the paintings of Klimt and Kokoschka, and the music of Schoenberg, Schorske makes the many different strands of Mach's works – e.g. his criticism of the integral subjects – comprehensible to the reader. If, on the contrary, one is interested in the impact of Mach's publications, especially on literature, ample material on this topic is available in DIERSCH's study on the significance of Mach's theory of perception for impressionism, and for the literature of the fin-de-siècle. The literary conversion of Mach's "Philosophy of the irrecoverable ego" is illustrated in the works of Hermann Bahr, whereas Diersch's interpretation of the characters of Arthur Schnitzler (such as Fräulein Else) considers also the implications of Freud's psychoanalysis.

STADLER discusses Ernst Mach's persistent effort to popularize science, and its effect on the Vienna "People's Education Movement" and the "Ernst Mach Society". Moreover, he examines the effect of Mach's epistemological "positivism" on the first and second Vienna Circle, from which proceeded, in turn, logical empiricism and the "Unity of Science" movement.

KLAUS HENTSCHEL

See also Atomic Theory; Einstein; Rational Mechanics

Madness

Foucault, Michel, *Madness and Civilization: A History of Insanity in the Age of Reason* (abridged edition), translated from the French by Richard Howard, New York: Pantheon Books, 1965; London: Tavistock, 1967 (original edition, 1961)

Gilman, Sander L., *Disease and Representation: Images of Illness from Madness to AIDS*, Ithaca, New York: Cornell University Press, 1988

Micale, Mark S. and Roy Porter (eds), *Discovering the History of Psychiatry*, New York: Oxford University Press, 1994

Roth, Martin and Jerome Kroll, *The Reality of Mental Illness*, Cambridge and New York: Cambridge University Press, 1986

Still, Arthur and Irving Velody (eds), *Rewriting the History of Madness: Studies in Foucault's "Histoire de la Folie"*, London and New York: Routledge, 1992

Szasz, Thomas S., *The Myth of Mental Illness: Foundations of a Theory of Personal Conduct*, New York: Hoeber-Harper, 1961; revised edition, New York: Harper and Row, 1974

Szasz, Thomas S., *The Manufacture of Madness*, New York: Harper and Row, 1970; London: Paladin, 1972

As is discussed in the entry on Psychiatry, ours is a cognitive world in which "madness" (or, more formally, "mental illness") is viewed as an objective disease condition, whose manifestations and treatment may be historically traced. In recent years, however, many sociologists of knowledge and social historians have maintained that the category of madness should rather be regarded as essentially a social or a discursive construct.

Two thinkers have been especially prominent in this development. The American (anti)-psychiatrist, Thomas Szasz, has argued in SZASZ (1961) that insanity is not a real disease; mental illness is rather a myth, forged by psychiatrists for their own greater glory, and, in SZASZ (1970), he details how, over the centuries, the medical profession and their supporters have been involved in this self-serving "manufacture of madness". Szasz indicts both organic psychiatry and the psychodynamic followers of Freud, whose notion of the unconscious in effect breathed new life into the obsolete metaphysical Cartesian dualism.

For Szasz, any expectation of finding the aetiology of mental illness in body or mind – above all, in some mental underworld – must be a lost cause, a dead-end, a linguistic error, and even an exercise in bad faith. "Mental illness" or the "unconscious" are not realities, and at most only metaphors. In promoting such ideas, psychiatrists have either been involved in improper cognitive imperialism, or have rather naively pictorialized the psyche – reifying the fictive substance behind the substantive.

Properly speaking, contends Szasz, insanity is not a disease with origins to be excavated, but a behaviour with meanings to be decoded. Social existence is a rule-governed game-playing ritual, in which the mad person bends the rules and exploits the loopholes. Since the mad person is engaged in social performances that obey certain expectations so as to defy others, the pertinent questions are not about the origins, but the conventions, of insanity. In this light, Szasz dismisses traditional approaches to the history of madness as questions *mal posées*, and aims to reformulate them.

To an extent reinforcing Szasz's critique of the epistemological status of insanity, FOUCAULT argues that mental illness must be understood not within the domain of positivist science, but as inscribed within discursive formations. To be precise, from classical through medieval times, "madness" was a voice that spoke its truth and was listened to, within a Platonic philosophy of poetic furore, an Aristotelian assumption of the mad genius, or the Christian doctrine of inspiration through divine or demonic possession. At a later stage, as part of the developments dubbed by Foucault as the "great confinement", madness was "shut up" (in both senses of the word), reduced to "unreason" (a purely negative attribute), and rendered the object of supposed scientific investigation.

Foucault's provocative formulations – which stand traditional history of psychiatry on its head, turning heroes of the standard story into villains – have been robustly rebutted by various professional psychiatrists. ROTH & KROLL, for instance, assert that such has been the stability of psychiatric symptoms presented in recorded history, that we may confidently affirm that madness is more than a label, a device for scapegoating deviants in the interests of social control, but is in fact a real disease, probably with a biological basis.

Historians have also taken issue with many of the empirical particulars of Foucault's reading of the transformations of madness and its treatment from medieval times to the 19th century. MICALE & PORTER and STILL & VELODY contain many essays offering detailed critiques, favourable and unfavourable, of Foucault's views. Micale & Porter offers a thorough historiographical survey of the history of psychiatry; the 15 essays in Still & Velody focus specifically and exclusively upon the implications of Foucault's work. The contribution by Colin Gordon ("Histoire de la Folie: An Unknown Book by Michel Foucault") to the latter volume points out that the currently available English translation of *La Folie et la déraison: Histoire de la folie à l'âge classique* is in fact an abridgement, which in important ways presents a misleading view of Foucault's complete work. Overall, it would seem that Foucault, who saw reason and society as involved in a joint mission (or even conspiracy) to control and silence madness, did not offer a more sophisticated historical view than traditional progressive or meliorist interpretations. Nevertheless, his emphasis upon the dialectic between reason and madness is surely valuable to historians.

That insight has been built on by GILMAN and others, who have examined madness as a particular mode of disease representation. Gilman argues that the image of the insane forms part of wider constructions of "self" and "other", whereby societies identify themselves by the projection of stigmatizing stereotypes. The mad form part of a world of the "other", also populated by (for example) blacks, homosexuals, criminals, and other "deviants". Such an approach to the history of perceptions appears to offer a fruitful entry into the analysis of language, myth, and metaphor respecting madness.

ROY PORTER

See also Asylums; Foucault; Psychiatry

Magnetism

Cawood, John, "The Magnetic Crusade: Science and Politics in Early Victorian Britain", *Isis*, 70 (1979): 493–518

Chapman, Sydney and Julius Bartels, *Geomagnetism*, 2 vols, Oxford: Clarendon Press, 1940; revised edition, 1962

Fanning, A.E., *Steady As She Goes: A History of the Compass Department of the Admiralty*, London: HMSO, 1986

Fara, Patricia, *Sympathetic Attractions: Magnetic Practices, Beliefs, and Symbolism in Eighteenth-Century England*, Princeton, New Jersey: Princeton University Press, 1996

Harris, William Snow, *Rudimentary Magnetism: Being a Concise Exposition of the General Principles of Magnetical Science*, London: John Weale, 1850; 2nd edition revised and expanded by Henry M. Noad, London: Lockwood, 1872

Home, Roderick W., "Introduction", in *Aepinus's Essay on the Theory of Electricity and Magnetism*, by F.U.T. Aepinus, edited by Home and P.J. Connor, translated by Connor, Princeton, New Jersey: Princeton University Press, 1979

Livingston, James D., *Driving Force: The Natural Magic of Magnets*, Cambridge, Massachusetts: Harvard University Press, 1996

McConnell, Anita, "Nineteenth-Century Geomagnetic Instruments and Their Makers", in *Nineteenth Century Scientific Instruments and Their Makers*, edited by Peter R. de Clercq, Leiden and Amsterdam: Museum Boerhaave/Rodopi, 1985

May, W.E., with a chapter by Leonard Holder, *A History of Marine Navigation*, Henley-on-Thames, Oxfordshire: Foulis, and New York: Norton, 1973

Mottelay, Paul F., *Bibliographical History of Electricity and Magnetism, Chronologically Arranged*, London: Charles Griffith, 1922; reprinted, New York: Arno Press, 1975

Pumfrey, Stephen, "William Gilbert's Magnetical Philosophy, 1580–1684: The Creation and Dissolution of a Discipline", Dissertation, Warburg Institute, University of London, 1987

Smith, Julian A., "Precursors to Peregrinus: The Early History of Magnetism and the Mariner's Compass in Europe", *Journal of Medieval History*, 18 (1992): 21–74

Verschuur, Gerrit L., *Hidden Attraction: The History and Mystery of Magnetism*, Oxford and New York: Oxford University Press, 1993

Warner, Deborah Jean, "Terrestrial Magnetism: For the Glory of God and the Benefit of Mankind", *Osiris*, 9 (1994): 67–84

Reflecting the consolidation of modern disciplinary boundaries, the history of magnetism has become increasingly fragmented into three major strands: the physics of magnets, geomagnetism (a 20th-century term), and navigational instruments. However, this separation distorts the historical picture, since these fields of investigation were formerly closely interlinked, only gradually drawing apart in the 19th century.

The scientific study of magnetism has a short formal history. In Europe, compasses became important navigational aids only in the 15th century, and the first systematic and comprehensive account was William Gilbert's Latin treatise *De Magnete* of 1600, not translated into English for nearly 300 years. Following the demise of Gilbert's animistic magnetic cosmology, the only major theoretical innovations were by René Descartes (in his *Principles of Philosophy* of 1644) and Franz Æpinus (in his *Essay on the Theory of Electricity and Magnetism* of 1759). However, magnetic phenomena and materials remained high on experimental agendas because of their enormous importance for navigation. Paralleling the establishment of geology, meteorology and pharmacology, construction of the new public science of magnetism entailed complex processes of social and epistemological legitimation, which included appropriating the expertise of traditional practitioners. After Hans Christian Ørsted's experimental demonstration in 1819 of the relationship between electrical and magnetic powers of nature, magnetism largely lost its distinct identity. Most modern accounts are framed by current theories of electromagnetism, thus concealing the important differences between the historical trajectories of electricity and magnetism before their unification.

MOTTELAY is a marvellous treasure trove of information, with anecdotes that make it far more fun to browse through than most chronological bibliographies. Mottelay – one of Gilbert's translators – interpreted his brief surprisingly widely, including items, such as sympathetic powders and mesmerism, which many compilers of his era would have rejected. While his analyses have been revised, and his details not always accurate, this remains a valuable starting point for research.

Unlike electricity, academic historians have written comparatively little about magnetism, although magnetic scientists have enriched their accounts of current research with discussions of their discipline's history. Among the more recent of these, LIVINGSTON entertainingly blends historical episodes with discussions of the properties of magnets and contemporary theories of their action; while apparently more scholarly, VERSCHUUR is ridden with factual errors, and disturbingly misinterprets sociological approaches to studying science's past. Fortunately for historians of science, Victorian scientific popularizers bequeathed more substantial studies. HARRIS is the most useful, starting – like most books on this subject – with a historical sketch. It then describes magnetic knowledge in the mid-19th century, including detailed discussions of navigational compasses and techniques for making artificial magnets. From the 20th century, the 40-page historical section in CHAPMAN & BARTELS's scientific textbook on geomagnetism remains unsurpassed for its factual information, although necessarily excluding the important role of magnetic evidence in validating continental drift. Comprehensive and reliable, it presents a chronological international survey of theoretical and experimental developments, including details of instruments.

Until recently, many academic articles revolved around priority debates on the origins of compasses. SMITH provides a detailed discussion of early European magnetic instruments and theories, with full references to the historical literature. PUMFREY's study is the best account of 17th-century magnetism. Historians often cite *De Magnete* as a Baconian exemplar of the new experimental approach to controlling nature, but Pumfrey revises this over-simplistic picture by showing how Gilbert intended his work to provide a complete magnetic cosmology. Gilbert portrayed the earth as a living organism in a vitalist universe, dynamically bonded by magnetic powers. During the 17th century, work on this new magnetic philosophy was sustained by three major interests: natural magicians claimed that it endorsed their practices; Jesuit philosophers explored its cosmological significance; and navigational improvers examined its value for explaining magnetic variation and measuring longitude at sea.

Gilbertian philosophy declined in Restoration England as new mechanical theories were developed, and there are now two good secondary texts describing 18th-century magnetism. HOME provides a useful discussion of theoretical and experimental work in Europe, but anachronistically excludes compasses and terrestrial magnetism, dealing only with topics that now belong to the domain of physics. In contrast, FARA provides a far more comprehensive study, analysing magnetism within the broader cultural context of 18th-century England. Fara retrieves the diverse implications of magnets and compasses, showing how, for people of this period, magnetic phenomena reverberated with a concealed symbolism of occult mystery, sexual attraction and universal sympathies, while, at the same time, navigational compasses heralded imperial expansion, commercial gain, and progress through inventive natural philosophy. Structured thematically, this interdisciplinary book uses magnetic practices, beliefs, and symbolism to explore historiographical issues such as commercialization, imperialism, technological innovation, and the roles of language. It reveals the contested rise to public power of natural philosophers, as they constructed the new science of magnetism by appropriating the skills and knowledge of experienced navigators.

For the 19th century, CAWOOD demonstrates the rewards of an analytical perspective by examining the political entrenchment of scientific research into terrestrial magnetism.

Studies of magnetic instruments are very patchy: this is a rich area for future research. Chapman & Bartels provide an overview, WARNER uses 17th- and 18th-century investigations of terrestrial magnetism to examine more general questions about the role of instruments, and McCONNELL relates the development of different instrument designs to the social separation of distinct groups of magnetic experts. For navigational compasses, there are two useful books by naval specialists: MAY includes extensive original research from the 14th century onwards, while FANNING provides detailed analyses of compass designs in the 19th and 20th centuries. However, although these books are rich in technical information, their historical approach is old-fashioned and limited. Although focusing on the 18th century, Fara presents a more substantial and contextualized analysis, not only describing changes in the construction, uses, and marketing of different types of magnetic instruments, but also investigating their symbolic significance. In addition, one chapter is devoted to a sociological case-study of the introduction of a new navigational compass design.

PATRICIA FARA

See also Electromagnetism; Gilbert; Mesmerism

Malaria

Ackerknecht, E.H., "Malaria in the Upper Mississippi Valley, 1760–1900", *Supplement to the Bulletin of the History of Medicine*, 4, Baltimore: Johns Hopkins Press, 1945

Bruce-Chwatt, Leonard J. and Julian de Zulueta, *The Rise and Fall of Malaria in Europe: A Historico-Epidemiological Study*, Oxford and New York: Oxford University Press, 1980

Carlson, Dennis G., *African Fever: A Study of British Science, Technology, and Politics in West Africa, 1787–1864*, New York: Science History Publications, 1984

Hackett, L.W., *Malaria in Europe: An Ecological Study*, London: Oxford University Press/Milford, 1937

Harrison, Gordon A., *Mosquitoes, Malaria and Man: A History of the Hostilities Since 1880*, New York: Dutton, and London: John Murray, 1978

Jarcho, Saul, *Quinine's Predecessor: Francesco Torti and the Early History of Cinchona*, Baltimore: Johns Hopkins University Press, 1993

Jones, W.H.S., *Malaria and Greek History*, Manchester: Victoria University Publications, 1909; reprinted, New York: AMS Press, 1977

Kiple, Kenneth F. (ed.), *The Cambridge World History of Human Disease*, Cambridge and New York: Cambridge University Press, 1993

Macdonald, George, *The Epidemiology and Control of Malaria*, London and New York: Oxford University Press, 1957

Ross, Ronald, *The Great Malaria Problem and Its Solution: From the Memoirs of Ronald Ross*, London: Keynes Press/BMA, 1988

Russell, Paul F., *Man's Mastery of Malaria*, London and New York: Oxford University Press, 1955

Targett, G.A.T. (ed.), *Malaria: Waiting for the Vaccine*, Chichester, West Sussex, and New York: John Wiley, 1991

The secondary literature on the history of malaria covers a wide range of different aspects of this disease. A number of texts discuss the paleogeography of malaria, as well as the origins of mosquitoes, parasites and human transmission. Several books describe the historical and geographical impact of malaria on ancient civilisations. Some are concerned with the global spread of malaria from the Old World to the New World, others with the historical epidemiology of malaria in different parts of the world during the recent past. A number of books deal with the discovery of the malaria parasite in the late 19th century and the subsequent unravelling of the role of mosquitoes in the transmission of malaria. Some of the literature focuses on 20th-century eradication and control programmes, other works adopt a historical perspective on the search for a cure or a malaria vaccine. There is also a growing literature on blood genetic polymorphisms in modern populations and their ancient association with malaria.

KIPLE provides the best short overview of the history and geography of malaria. In a section on the subject by Frederick Dunn (pp. 855–62), there is a well-presented outline of the aetiology of malaria (and a reminder that the disease was once believed to be caused by the "bad air" of the marshes, hence the term malaria from the Italian, *mala* and *aria*), its clinical manifestations and pathology, the epidemiology and control of malaria in the recent past, and a brief history of the global impact of the disease from the mid-Pleistocene to the 1980s. In most of the general and geographical sections of Kiple, malaria also receives attention as one of the major global diseases of the past and present.

Another excellent and broad ranging text on the history of malaria is BRUCE-CHWATT & De ZULUETA. As its title indicates, this book covers the rise and fall of malaria in Europe from its ancient origins to its final eradication from Europe in the mid-1970s. Historical material on the disease is presented on a country by country basis. For each region, there is information on the incidence of malaria, its demographic impact, major breakthroughs in understanding the factors of its transmission, types of eradication and control programmes conducted in the 20th century, and an insight into the leading figures in its history. This book also contains a number of superb illustrations on the history of malaria.

JONES's book on the influence of malaria on the course of Greek history is one of a number of classics to suggest that malaria has been a powerful force in human history. The historical role of malaria in other parts of the world is widely discussed in monographs and journal articles: ACKERKNECHT's paper on malaria in the Upper Mississippi Valley from 1760 to 1900 is one excellent case study, and CARLSON's work on Africa provides a stimulating account of the contemporary images and effects of malaria on the White Man's Grave, within the context of European medical and scientific thought.

The efforts and campaigns to cure, prevent, control or eradicate malaria from ancient times to the present are the subject of many writings. JARCHO presents a history of the early discovery of cinchona; this offers new material on a familiar theme – the importation of the Peruvian bark from South America to Europe in the 17th century, and its value as a drug at a time when malaria was a major problem in many parts of the world. HARRISON's book takes us forward in time to the campaigns to control and eradicate malaria, following the discoveries by Patrick Manson, Ronald Ross, Charles Laveran, Giovanni Grassi and others in the late 19th century concerning the role of the mosquito and parasite in the transmission of malaria. His narrative is less a medical than a military and social history, interweaving within his story both a history of the battles against mosquitoes and malaria, and a perceptive account of the hostilities within the scientific community in its endeavours to understand and fight the disease.

Some of the original and influential malaria studies, discussed by Harrison, are well worth reading. The memoirs of ROSS (part of which is reproduced with a short introduction by Bruce-Chwatt), and the 1937 text by HACKETT, are two examples that will enable the reader to gain a fuller picture of the dynamics of malaria discoveries and control strategies in the late 19th and early to mid-20th centuries. The studies of the 1950s, such as the mathematical and pioneering epidemiological work of MACDONALD, and the optimistic account of "man's mastery of malaria" by RUSSELL, also provide an important historical perspective on the subject of malaria.

TARGETT's work is a critical reminder that, notwithstanding the early knowledge and use of cinchona bark (containing quinine) as a malaria drug, and, in spite of the scientific discoveries and international efforts of the last few decades to eradicate or control malaria, scientists are still some way from finding a solution to the escalating global problem of malaria.

MARY J. DOBSON

See also Epidemics

Malthus, Thomas 1766–1834
British economist and clergyman

Ambirajan, S., *Malthus and Classical Economics*, Bombay: Jupiter Press, 1959

Bonar, James, *Malthus and His Work*, London: Macmillan, 1885; 2nd edition, London: Allen and Unwin, and New York: Macmillan, 1924

Dupâquier, J., A. Fauve-Chamoux and E. Grebenik (eds), *Malthus Past and Present*, London and New York: Academic Press, 1983

James, Patricia, *"Population" Malthus: His Life and Times*, London and Boston: Routledge and Kegan Paul, 1979

Meek, Ronald L. (ed.), *Marx and Engels on Malthus: Selections from the Writings of Marx and Engels Dealing with the Theories of Thomas Robert Malthus*, translated by Dorothea L. Meek and Ronald L. Meek, London: Lawrence and Wishart, 1953; New York: International Publishers, 1954

Petersen, William, *Malthus*, London: Heinemann, and Cambridge, Massachusetts: Harvard University Press, 1979

Smith, Kenneth, *The Malthusian Controversy*, London: Routledge and Kegan Paul, 1951; New York: Octagon Books, 1978

Turner, Michael (ed.), *Malthus and His Time*, New York: St Martin's Press, and London: Macmillan, 1986

Waterman, A.M.C., *Revolution, Economics and Religion: Christian Political Economy, 1798–1833*, Cambridge and New York: Cambridge University Press, 1991

The first edition of Thomas Malthus's *Essay on the Principle of Population* (1798) was intended to refute the revolutionary optimism of William Godwin and Condorcet, the author asserting that, "Population, when unchecked, increases in a geometrical ratio. Subsistence increases only in an arithmetical ratio." Malthus argued, in this and later works, that the poor would not ultimately benefit from increased benefits or lower food prices; rather, they would only multiply up to the limit of the available subsistence, at which point "positive" or "preventive" checks to further increase would take their inevitable toll. He offered only one way to break this vicious circle – "moral restraint", comprising premarital chastity and late marriage.

Malthus became a prominent figure in the history of sociology, politics, demography, economics, and birth control – the last is often associated with Malthus's name, despite his disapproval of artificial interference with human fertility. Furthermore, awareness of the "struggle" involved in staying alive led Charles Darwin and Alfred Wallace to formulate the theory of natural selection. From the first, Malthus's work has engendered controversy, often embittered by the fact that his theories – or, more commonly, ideas more or less directly derived from his theories – have led to so many practical applications in the modern world. How could he claim to have the interests of the poor at heart? How could he, as a clergyman, believe that God had made such niggardly provision for mankind? The most useful studies set Malthus's work within its contemporary context, as only then can its complexities, paradoxes, changes, and underlying consistency be appreciated.

BONAR guides the reader through the historical background and theoretical content of Malthus's works, paying most attention to the *Essay*, but using the full range of his writings to elucidate his views on politics, economics, and moral and political philosophy. He then turns to Malthus's contemporary and subsequent opponents, and concludes with a brief biography. Bonar is broadly, but not uncritically, sympathetic to Malthus, finding the *Essay* of 1798 too controversial in emphasis to be fully scientific, and attributing the notorious ratios to "the natural liking of a Cambridge man for a mathematical simile". He stands closest to Malthus on the issue of birth control, eloquently appealing to the sensibilities of those readers who have faith "in man's power to conquer nature by obeying her".

SMITH's purpose is to "rescue Malthus's contemporary critics from unjust neglect". He finds the *Essay* derivative and scientifically unsound; the 1798 version owed its popularity to its "graceful style" and good timing, as its doctrine was "convenient" for upper-class readers alarmed by growing social unrest; the second edition of 1803 was marred by "occasional exhortations, more appropriate to a pulpit than to a treatise on political economy". Insisting that, "The problem of human population is an ecological study", Smith maintains that the disasters prophesied by Malthus can be averted by fertilizers, factory farming, pesticides, atomic energy, and other exertions of human ingenuity. Smith's conclusions may be suspect by today's standards, but his collection of critical opinion on Malthus is very useful, and his analysis of the birth control controversy particularly cogent.

MEEK has assembled, in one conveniently compact volume, an interesting selection of references to Malthus by Karl Marx and Friedrich Engels, in writings on political theory, economics, and Darwinism. Meek largely supports their accusation that Malthus sinned against science by his "shameless and mechanical plagiarism" and the "*apologetic* character of his conclusions". The economist David Ricardo, arguably Malthus's greatest opponent, emerges as the book's hero, tirelessly defending the working classes from Malthus's fabrications. Meek believes that modern economists, following John Maynard Keynes, are using Malthus's doctrines to justify oppression and imperialism in capitalist countries facing "economic stagnation", while "the Soviet Union and the People's Democracies are growing from strength to strength".

AMBIRAJAN's lucid exposition of Malthus's economic theories offers a more favourable view, acknowledging the "apparent ruthlessness and real humanity" of Malthus's population theory, and taking it as a "timely warning". He admits that "the moralist in Malthus qualified (and to a certain extent confused) the social scientist", but nevertheless ranks Malthus with Adam Smith and Ricardo as one of the greatest classical economists. Malthus improved on Smith by his recognition that "Economics cannot be an exact science", while his disagreements with Ricardo were often questions of viewpoint or temperament rather than fundamental conviction.

JAMES has written the standard biography of Malthus. Combining rigorous intellectual analysis with sensitivity to personal matters, James convincingly relates published utterances to private circumstance. The occasional bitterness of the 1803 *Essay* is easier to understand when we reflect that Malthus was working "with no settled home, no secure income if he married, approaching middle age and deeply in love". Her book is packed with fascinating details about Malthus's friends, relations, and environment, including informative illustrations and a family tree.

PETERSEN, concentrating more on ideas than the man, gives the best general account of Malthus's work and its subsequent influence. He corrects many previous errors in Malthus scholarship, and vindicates his originality and importance, claiming that, by "examining in detail the relation of population growth to economic, social, and political development, Malthus did more than any of his predecessors or all of them together". Furthermore, his *Essay* was no "mere clue", but "the scaffolding on which Darwin and Wallace hung their data".

TURNER's critically objective collection of essays by an international panel of contributors covers a wide range of periods, places, and approaches. There are sections on "Demography and Malthusianism", "Land", "Labour", and "Capital". E.A. Wrigley places the enterprise neatly in perspective by observing that "it was Malthus's fate to frame an analysis of the relationship between population, economy and society during the last generation to which it was applicable".

DUPÂQUIER, FAUVE-CHAMOUX & GREBENIK's book is more concerned with rehabilitating Malthus by demolishing "those prejudices which prevented a scientific approach to Malthus's theories". This compilation has a similarly international flavour, discussing Malthus in relation to his historical context, religion, Malthusianism, Socialism and Darwinism. Linda Gordon offers a solitary, but most welcome, feminist contribution. A full-scale feminist analysis of Malthus is long overdue.

WATERMAN applies the theoretical insight of an economist to a vast array of theology, philosophy, and literature. He is the first to appreciate the depth and permanence of Malthus's commitment to Christianity, and to trace its full implications regarding Malthus's attempt to reconcile 18th-century optimistic theodicy with classical economics. This intellectually distinguished examination of Christian political economy marks a new departure in Malthus studies.

CAROLYN D. WILLIAMS

See also Darwinism; Malthusianism; Political Economy

Malthusianism

Benn, J. Miriam, *Predicaments of Love*, London and Concord, Massachusetts: Pluto Press, 1992

Boner, Harold A., *Hungry Generations: The Nineteenth-Century Case Against Malthusianism*, New York: King's Crown Press, 1955

Dupâquier, J., A. Fauve-Chamoux and E. Grebenik (eds), *Malthus Past and Present*, London and New York: Academic Press, 1983

Glass, D.V. (ed.), *Introduction to Malthus*, London: Watts, and New York: John Wiley, 1953

James, Patricia, *"Population" Malthus: His Life and Times*, London and Boston: Routledge and Kegan Paul, 1979

Ledbetter, Rosina, *A History of the Malthusian League, 1877–1927*, Columbus: Ohio State University Press, 1976

Malthus, Thomas Robert, *An Essay on the Principle of Population, and A Summary View of the Principle of Population*, edited by Antony Flew, Harmondsworth: Penguin, 1970

Petersen, William, *Malthus*, London: Heinemann, and Cambridge, Massachusetts: Harvard University Press, 1979

The use of the term "Malthusianism" has a certain ambiguity, for it can mean not only the "iron law of population" (i.e. that population increases geometrically while the means of subsistence increases only arithmetically) and its consequences for theories of political economy and practices of social welfare during the 19th century, but also what is more correctly described as "neo-Malthusianism", which aimed at the amelioration of the potential dangers of unrestricted breeding prophesied by Malthus, by advocating the use of some form of artificial contraception. This essay discusses works mainly concerning the first of these meanings, but includes a couple of works on the latter, as a specific theme within the wider history of birth control.

Malthusianism is a philosophy so intimately connected with one specific work of its first proponent, Thomas MALTHUS, that it seems logical to include a readily available edition of the text. The first edition of the *Essay on the Principle of Population* (1798) has been republished as a "Penguin Classic", along with the first edition of the *Summary View* (1830), and continues to be regularly reprinted. There is a substantial and useful introduction, and helpful editor's notes on the text. The suggestions for further reading include details of the more substantial annotated edition, and recommendations of editions of other works by Malthus.

BONER's study is the definitive work on the reception of Malthus's theory, and its rise and fall in 19th-century England. It is written from a particularly engaged stance, as indicated by Boner's statement in the Preface that it is a "history of the long and dramatic struggle by which his theory *as a whole* was exposed as an invidious and fallacious instrument for concealing exploitation and social injustice". Malthus's project, Boner suggested, was not "quite so academically innocuous" as it might appear. With the recrudescence of anxiety concerning the growth of population around the time of writing, this time on a global rather than a national scale, he felt that an account of the tenacity of Malthus's doctrine, and the long-drawn-out struggle to overthrow it, would operate prophylactically against the danger of the deployment of similar "possible instruments of class advantage" in the present or near future. Bearing in mind this ideological position, this is nevertheless a detailed and useful account of the debates about Malthusianism during the 19th century.

An almost contemporary volume, suggesting that the revival of anxieties about over-population in the era immediately following World War II (replacing the fears of population decline of the 1930s) had resuscitated interest in Malthus, is the GLASS collection, based on three talks broadcast on the BBC Third Programme. The volume includes a reprint not only of Malthus's *Summary View*, but also of his *Letter to Samuel Whitbread on the Poor Laws* (1807), and a bibliography of British publications on the Population Question (1793–1880), compiled by Glass and the eminent historian of birth control, J.A. Banks. In his Preface, Glass argues for the need to read what Malthus actually wrote, but also of the necessity for his prescriptions to be seen within their historical context. The essays include just such a study, by H.L. Beales on the historical context of the *Essay on Population*, plus an analysis by Glass (himself a demographer) of Malthus's theories on the limitation of population growth in the light of modern demography, and Alan T. Peacock's consideration of "Malthus in the Twentieth Century" as economic analyst.

Malthus's influence on 19th-century political economy, in particular its practical effect on the Poor Laws, has largely been seen as deleterious. Among the many essays dealing with aspects of Malthus and Malthusian thought – demography, economics, politics, and philosophy – DUPÂQUIER, FAUVE-CHAMOUX & GREBENIK includes a section examining the impact of Malthus on biological science, via his influence on Charles Darwin, with its implications for the development of evolutionary theory. The volume is a useful overview of modern scholarship from many countries, based on the proceedings of an International Conference on Historical Demography held under the auspices of UNESCO in 1980.

If there was a resurgence of interest in Malthus in the early 1950s, this volume, and the two biographically-orientated studies of Malthus that appeared almost simultaneously, suggest that the late 1970s was a period when attention was again drawn to him and his doctrines. JAMES remarks on the previous absence of any full-length biography, and the perpetuation of various incorrect statements about Malthus in works of reference. Based on a variety of sources, including papers still surviving in the hands of his descendants, her biography is a substantial and well-researched study of Malthus as an individual within his specific historical context, and includes consideration of his thought and its impact.

PETERSEN pays tribute to James's grasp of the details of Malthus's life and of his place in English history. Petersen, however, explicitly concentrates on Malthus's professional career, his thought and its reception, both during the 19th century and in the light of more recent scholarship on the Industrial Revolution, economic theory, and demography. Petersen sees Malthus as having been the victim of "terrible simplifiers", intent on imposing "discrete dualities" upon a complex system of thought.

While Dupaquier, in his editor's introduction to *Malthus Past and Present*, expressed an explicit desire to dissociate Malthus from "his embarrassing admirers – Drysdale and his disciples", those who accepted Malthus's law, but felt that human ingenuity was able to come up with the means to evade the worst-case scenario it implied, perhaps deserve some attention. BENN's volume is a meticulously researched recovery of the Drysdale family, and places the Malthusian League within the context of other late Victorian fringe bodies. LEDBETTER's account of the Malthusian League is rather more of an internalist history, but none the less a useful study. For the place of "Malthusianism" or "neo-Malthusianism" within the wider history of birth control, the reader is referred to the entry under that heading.

LESLEY A. HALL

See also Darwinism; Malthus; Political Economy

Management Sciences

Chandler Jr, Alfred D., *The Visible Hand: The Managerial Revolution in American Business*, Cambridge, Massachusetts: Belknap Press of Harvard University Press, 1976
Child, John, *British Management Thought: A Critical Analysis*, London: Allen and Unwin, 1969
Copley, Frank Barkley, *Frederick W. Taylor: Father of Scientific Management*, New York: Harper, 1923; reprinted, New York: Kelley, 1969
Gillespie, Richard, *Manufacturing Knowledge: A History of the Hawthorne Experiments*, Cambridge and New York: Cambridge University Press, 1991
Merkle, Judith A., *Management and Ideology: The Legacy of the International Scientific Management Movement*, Berkeley: University of California Press, 1980
Montgomery, David, *Workers' Control in America: Studies in the History of Work, Technology and Labour Struggles*, Cambridge: Cambridge University Press, 1979
Nelson, Daniel, *Frederick W. Taylor and the Rise of Scientific Management*, Madison: University of Wisconsin Press, 1980
Pollard, Sidney, *The Genesis of Modern Management: A Study of the Industrial Revolution in Great Britain*, Cambridge, Massachusetts: Harvard University Press, 1965
Sass, Steven A., *The Pragmatic Imagination: A History of the Wharton School, 1881–1981*, Philadelphia: University of Pennsylvania Press, 1982
Scott, William G., *Chester I. Barnard and the Guardians of the Managerial State*, Lawrence: University Press of Kansas, 1992
Waring, Stephen P., *Taylorism Transformed: Scientific Management Theory since 1945*, Chapel Hill: University of North Carolina Press, 1991
Wren, Daniel, *The Evolution of Management Thought*, 4th edition, New York: Wiley, 1994

Management science is about control, structure, information, and motivation – i.e. how to get individuals to function efficiently and coherently toward organizational goals. European militaries, the Roman Catholic Church, and colonial empires all had effective bureaucracies and people who thought deeply about management. The application of scientific norms and practices to management theory, however, came with the professionalization of educated, white-collar managers in the large integrated corporations that emerged between 1880 and 1920.

CHANDLER describes the evolution of management practice in these modern corporations by showing how managers adapted strategy and structure to the technical dimensions of various industries. Chandler's vision of the rise of managerial capitalism frames the work of historians focusing on specific areas of management practice – accounting, marketing, communication, and industrial research – and how emergent schools of management keep up with the broad trends in practice. Chandler also introduces Henry Varnum Poor, Frederick W. Taylor, financiers, board chairmen, independent management consultants, and others who explicated general theories of management. POLLARD, likewise, describes the broad accumulation of organizational skills antecedent to the British Industrial Revolution, and portrays the few attempts to systematize management thought.

Frederick Taylor, as the leading advocate of scientific management, figures prominently in all studies of management science. NELSON (1980) corrects COPLEY's exhaustive hagiography, and considers Taylor's key ideas on how to make work flow more efficiently through factories – time-and-motion studies, differential piece rate systems, and functional foremanship – as incremental improvements on ideas introduced by the systematic management movement. Other historians take up Harry Braverman's radical critique of scientific management as a means of shifting power on the shop floor from workers to management. MONTGOMERY provides the most balanced interpretation of scientific management on the shop floor in his wide-ranging history of American industrial relations. Other historians have explored how the quest for efficiency through scientific management extended into non-factory industries, the home, and government agencies.

Scientific management, in conjunction with Fordism, blossomed from practice into ideology. The historian Charles Maier first explored the centrality of managerial ideology in European political economy during the 1920s and 1930s. By boosting productivity and erasing radical unionism, technical experts then claimed, scientific management would lead society into a new era of harmony based on mass consumption. Several excellent monographs have explored the social and political conflicts engendered in different countries by the state's adoption of the role of agent of efficiency and general uplift, while others have looked at the professionalization of the social sciences in the service of the state. MERKLE, while making some sweeping political statements, reliably summarizes the reception of scientific management among rationalized, bureaucratic states predisposed to the gospel of efficiency, including socialist Russia, France, Germany, and Britain.

An exemplary study of management science is GILLESPIE's account of the social construction and acceptance of the Hawthorne Experiments. The experiments began in 1924 as a classical study of the impact of lighting on productivity at a Western Electric factory. Some "confusing" results led the experiment leader, Elton Mayo of the Harvard Business School, to question the basic Taylorist premises of the experiment. After filtering his ideas through a vast network of industrial managers and social scientists, which Gillespie richly describes, Mayo authoritatively attributed improved productivity to informal human relations, improved motivation, and general contentment among the test workers. The fields of industrial sociology, the social psychology of work, and personnel management all emerged from these experiments, and the foundations of management sciences shifted away from physiology and towards the social sciences.

The experiences of social scientists during World War II prompted further shifts in the conceptual foundations of management science. By the 1960s, the proliferation of - management theories fractured the field into administrative behavior, economic theories of the firm, program management, the decision sciences, artificial intelligence, human resources, and a variety of other interdisciplinary approaches to solving the problems of big business and big government. The most mathematical, statistical, and computer-prone of the new approaches – operational research and systems analysis – captured the title and spirit of "management science". As historians began to explore the content and origins of these management sciences in military programs and the computer sciences, some already addressed their political implications.

SCOTT's mix of social commentary and intellectual biography explains how Chester Barnard legitimated, codified, and institutionalized the managerial revolution in American business and politics during the 1940s and 1950s, proclaiming that the moral function of an executive was to maintain the organization as a system of cultural interrelationships. WARING glosses the work of many modern management theorists – particularly that of Herbert Simon and Peter Drunker – and describes such theorists as "mandarins" seeking to legitimate the role of the elite in American society. Likewise, CHILD describes the social construction of management thought in Britain that culminated in the Glacier Project – which brought task management to British factory floors – paying special attention to its legitimating functions.

There are no good synthetic surveys that integrate the three dominant perspectives on management thought – as science, as practice, and as ideology. Of the institutional histories of business schools, only SASS deals systematically with disciplinary genealogies in his comments on the proximity of economics to management education at the Wharton School. WREN's textbook treatment is the best available, though uncritical and America-centered. However, he does suggest several episodes in the history of management sciences – such as the work of Henri Fayol and Mary Parker Follet on administration and functional co-ordination – that deserve further study.

GLENN E. BUGOS

See also Capitalism and Science; Information; Social Sciences

Marey, Etienne-Jules 1830–1904

French physiologist

Brain, Robert, "The Graphic Method: Inscription, Visualization, and Measurement in 19th-Century Science and Culture", dissertation, University of California, Los Angeles, 1996

Braun, Marta, *Picturing Time: The Work of Etienne-Jules Marey (1830-1904)*, Chicago: University of Chicago Press, 1992

Dagognet, François, *Etienne-Jules Marey: A Passion for the Trace*, translated from the French by Robert Galeta, New York: Zone Books, 1992 (original edition, 1987)

Frank, Robert G., Jr, "The Telltale Heart: Physiological Instruments, Graphic Methods, and Clinical Hopes, 1854–1914", in *The Investigative Enterprise: Experimental Physiology in Nineteenth-Century Medicine*, edited by William Coleman and Frederic L. Holmes, Berkeley: University of California Press, 1988

Frizot, Michel, *La Chronophotographie*, Beaune: Association des amis Marey and Ministère de la Culture, 1984

Rabinbach, Anson, *The Human Motor: Energy, Fatigue, and the Origins of Modernity*, New York: Basic Books, 1990

Snellen, H.A. (ed.), *E.-J. Marey and Cardiology: Physiologist and Pioneer of Technology, 1830–1904: Selected Writings*, Rotterdam: Kooyker, 1980

Sauvage, Leo, *L'Affaire Lumière: du mythe à l'histoire: enquête sur les origines du cinéma*, Paris: L'herminier, 1985

Etienne-Jules Marey was a physiologist renowned for introducing graphic methods and automatic recording devices into the study of function in the animal body. Besides a vast legacy of instruments built for use in the experimental laboratory and the medical clinic, Marey also designed important apparatus of high-speed photography that served as the basis for the cinematograph and motion-pictures. For this reason he has earned an important place in histories of cinema and of photography more generally. His purely scientific work has been somewhat less thoroughly examined, although it has enjoyed a wave of interest over the last decade.

Most of the available literature examines either the cinematographic or the scientific work largely to the exclusion of the other.

Among the exceptions to this specialized approach are some of the better recent works. DAGOGNET, a historian and philosopher of science, presents an insightful survey of the whole of Marey's scientific work, drawing out central themes and showing how Marey's methods of "chronophotography" – his term for the method of decomposing motion into sequences of still photographic images taken at high speeds – grew out of his earlier approaches to physiological experiment. BRAUN, a historian of photography, similarly presents Marey's work in an integrated context, but the focus remains on the photographic work. Unlike Dagognet, Braun draws on extensive archival research, with detailed factual material about Marey's life and work. This is a beautifully produced book, with hundreds of photographs and other visual materials culled from archives and not published elsewhere. RABINBACH, a cultural historian, examines the growth of thermodynamic metaphors and conceptions of the human body in 19th and early 20th-century culture. He devotes a lengthy, central chapter of his book to the work of Marey, whom he views as pivotal figure in establishing both theoretical concepts and popular images of the body as a "human motor".

SNELLEN, a cardiologist and historian of medicine, examines Marey's early cardiological work and assesses its place in the longer history of the field. Snellen includes several of Marey's important writings on the heart and the circulation of the blood. Snellen also contains a complete bibliography of Marey's published work, which also reappears in Braun. FRANK, a historian of science, is interested in the transfer of scientific instruments and technologies from the physiological laboratory to the practice of clinical examinations. In this article he focusses especially on the cardiology of Marey and his successors such as the English physiologist John Burdon Sanderson and the Dutch cardiologist Willem Einthoven. Frank examines the invention of the sphygmograph, a device for recording arterial pulse in graphic form and its promotion as a tool for clinical diagnosis. BRAIN considers the development of the graphic method in the 19th century in a range of disciplines. In his account, Marey appears as a central figure in the promotion of the graphic method as a universal means of scientific communication.

Among the books which deal exclusively with Marey's chronophotography, FRIZOT's is the most comprehensive and insightful, and places Marey in a broader context of related photographic studies. Marey's role in the early history of cinematography has been entangled in debates about who was the "true" inventor of the cinematographic method. This complicated and perhaps badly posed question of priority has been further muddled by polemics and partisanship, often tinged with nationalistic passions. Accordingly, Marey's role has figured more prominently in French accounts and has been downplayed by English language author in favor of Thomas Alva Edison and others. SAUVAGE is a recent and the most judicious French account.

ROBERT BRAIN

See also Graphical Method; Photography

Marshall, Alfred   1842–1924

British economist

Bigg, Robert J., *Cambridge and the Monetary Theory of Production: The Collapse of Marshallian Macroeconomics*, London: Macmillan, and New York: St Martin's Press, 1990

Blaug, Mark, *Economic Theory in Retrospect*, Homewood, Illinois: Irwin, 1962; 4th edition, Cambridge and New York: Cambridge University Press, 1985

Coase, R.H., *Essays on Economics and Economists*, Chicago: University of Chicago Press, 1994

Eshag, Eprime, *From Marshall to Keynes: An Essay on the Monetary Theory of the Cambridge School*, Oxford: Blackwell, 1963

Groenewegen, P.D., *A Soaring Eagle: Alfred Marshall, 1842–1924*, Brookfield, Vermont, and Aldershot, Hampshire: Edward Elgar, 1995

Maloney, John, *Marshall, Orthodoxy and the Professionalisation of Economics*, Cambridge: Cambridge University Press, 1985; as *The Professionalization of Economics: Alfred Marshall and the Dominance of Orthodoxy*, New Brunswick, New Jersey: Transaction, 1991

Marshall, Mary P., *What I Remember*, Cambridge: Cambridge University Press, 1947

Pigou, A.C. (ed.), *Memorials of Alfred Marshall*, London: Macmillan, 1925

Reisman, David, *The Economics of Alfred Marshall*, New York: St Martin's Press, and London: Macmillan, 1986

Reisman, David, *Alfred Marshall's Mission*, New York: St Martin's Press, and London: Macmillan, 1990

Stigler, George J., *Production and Distribution Theories: The Formative Period*, New York: Macmillan, 1941

Whitaker, John K. (ed.), *Centenary Essays on Alfred Marshall*, Cambridge and New York: Cambridge University Press, 1990

Alfred Marshall is historically important because he was one of the three or four leading economic theorists of all time. His *Principles* is the last great comprehensive treatise on economics, constituting the core document of neo-classical economics and incorporating many of the tools of analysis that are currently central to the foundation of economics (which is called either "price theory" or "microeconomics").

Keynes's long biographical essay in PIGOU is a still useful, elegant and stimulating introduction to the life of Marshall. Keynes's sometime rival Schumpeter once described this essay as "the most brilliant life of a man of science I have ever read". Keynes was an admiring student of Marshall's (and Keynes's father had been an ally), so it may not be surprising that Keynes's essay has been criticized for being too protective of Marshall. The Nobel prize winner COASE, for example, has carefully collected evidence on Marshall's family background, and found it less distinguished than Keynes claimed. A brief source that enriches the biographical detail of Marshall's life is the memoir written by his wife, Mary MARSHALL, near the end of her long life.

GROENEWEGEN's careful and massive work will probably be the definitive biography of Marshall for a very long time to come. The author appears to have read and exploited nearly all known sources of archival information on Marshall's life, and to have subjected early drafts of his biography to useful criticism from several of the leading Marshall scholars. Although generally favorable to Marshall, Groenewegen does not shy away from issues that may show him in an unfavorable light, such as his attitude toward women.

Several useful summaries of various aspects of Marshall's views are available. Written in a non-technical style, REISMAN (1986) summarizes Marshall's positions on issues such as the evolutionary character of economics and how to lead a moral and good life. The Nobel prize winner STIGLER, in his published doctoral dissertation, devoted a chapter to explaining clearly Marshall's position on the key theoretical tools of marginal productivity. Late in his career, Stigler (in the WHITAKER volume) also summarized Marshall's main contributions. With characteristic Stiglerian mischief, he suggests that one of Marshall's contributions is to have delayed by a generation the dominance of the "abstract formalism" of the Walrasian general equilibrium economists. A "reader's guide" to Marshall's main work, the *Principles*, can be found in a chapter in BLAUG.

MALONEY incites controversy by arguing that Marshall's main contribution was not his addition to the toolbox of economics, but rather his successful efforts to complete the professionalization of economics. This professionalization is seen as accompanied by an increased emphasis on theory, by the goal of scientific objectivity, and by a sympathy toward the marketplace in policy analysis. A quite different view is presented in REISMAN (1990), which argues that Marshall's main objective was to benefit humanity through social reform.

Although Marshall's main contribution to economics is usually seen as his development of price theory, his writings on macroeconomics have received attention, both because they were considered important when they were written, and because there is interest in how they may have influenced Marshall's student and colleague, Keynes. In ESHAG's brief monograph tracing the development of macroeconomics from Marshall to Keynes, the author finds little in this area that is original to Marshall. BIGG's analysis is more favorable to Marshall, arguing that his macroeconomic theory was a progressive research program that contained the seeds that eventually grew into the Keynesian revolution.

ARTHUR M. DIAMOND, JR

See also Keynes; Political Economy

Martineau, Harriet 1802–1876

British writer and reformer

Basham, Diana, "The Demon Redeemed: Witchcraft, Mesmerism and Harriet Martineau's Ear-Trumpet", in *The Trial of Woman: Feminism and the Occult Sciences in Victorian Literature and Society* edited by Diana Basham, New York: New York University Press, 1992

Cooter, Roger, "Dichotomy and Denial: Mesmerism, Medicine and Harriet Martineau", in *Science and Sensibility: Gender and Scientific Enquiry, 1780–1945*, edited by Marina Benjamin, Oxford and Cambridge, Massachusetts: Blackwell, 1991

David, Deirdre, "Harriet Martineau: A Career of Auxiliary Usefulness", in *Intellectual Women and Victorian Patriarchy: Harriet Martineau, Elizabeth Barrett Browning, George Elliot*, Ithaca, New York: Cornell University Press, 1987

Hill, Michael R., introduction to *How To Observe Morals and Manners*, by Martineau, New Brunswick, New Jersey: Transaction, 1988

Hoecker-Drysdale, Susan, *Harriet Martineau: First Woman Sociologist*, Oxford: Berg, 1992

McDonald, Lynn, *Women Founders of the Social Sciences*, Ottawa: Carleton University Press, 1994

Martineau, Harriet, *Autobiography, with Memorials by Maria Weston Chapman*, 3 vols, London: Elder, 1877; Boston: Houghton, Mifflin, 1877

Pichanick, Valerie Kossew, *Harriet Martineau: The Woman and Her Work, 1802–76*, Ann Arbor: University of Michigan Press, 1980

Postlethwaite, Diana, *Making It Whole: A Victorian Circle and the Shape of Their World*, Columbus: Ohio State University Press, 1984

Rossi, Alice, "The First Woman Sociologist: Harriet Martineau", *The Feminist Papers: From Adams to de Beauvoir*, edited by Alice Rossi, New York: Columbia University Press, 1973

Webb, Robert K., *Harriet Martineau: A Radical Victorian*, London: Heinemann, and New York: Columbia University Press, 1960

Wright, T.R., *The Religion of Humanity: The Impact of Comtean Positivism on Victorian Britain*, Cambridge and New York: Cambridge University Press, 1986

Harriet Martineau has been studied as a public educator, journalist, historian and author of didactic literature. She wrote religious tracts, tales on political economy, historical novels, histories and moralistic tales for children, and nearly 2,000 newspaper leaders on a multitude of current issues in the 1850s and 1860s. However, Martineau also explored religion, philosophy, natural science and social science; examined the potential of associationist psychology, Comtean positivism, phrenology, and mesmerism; and determined how to apply a variety of theories and methodologies in conducting her own social research. Her research projects included macrosociological studies of America, Ireland, India, and the Middle East, explorations of socialization and human nature, qualitative and quantitative investigations of work, occupations and industries, and critical analyses of current history. Within the new perspective, she has been identified as the first woman sociologist, a popularizer of science, and an imposing figure in feminist causes and issues.

MARTINEAU wrote her *Autobiography* in 1855, in anticipation of her death, which in fact occurred 21 years later. In the account, she shapes her life as progressively rationalist, secular and autonomous, characterizing it as having reproduced Comte's Law of Three Stages, as her faith and intellect evolved from religion (Unitarianism), to philosophy, and finally to science. Within the limits inherent in such a construction of self, the book provides invaluable insights into Martineau's intellectual and emotional journey and into her persistent interests and scientific work, and also provides examples of her compliance and resistance as a Victorian woman of science.

Numerous biographies of Martineau appeared in the 19th and 20th centuries, and, more recently, a number of insightful literary studies. In general, these do not deal in significant measure with Martineau's concerns and accomplishments in science. One exception is DAVID, whose work on three Victorian intellectuals analyses aspects of Martineau's social thought, particularly on political economy, slavery, feminist politics and the novel *Deerbrook*, in which the protagonist, Edward Hope, is the doctor-scientist figure. Martineau's increasingly scientific perspective on societal change and social problems is emphasized in chapters 2 and 3.

No study of Harriet Martineau would be comprehensive without inclusion of WEBB's distinguished biography of 1960, unsurpassed in its breadth, historical detail and critical stance. Webb emphasizes the significance of the influence of Unitarianism, utilitarianism and necessarianism for Martineau's intellectual development, her penchant for principle, and her lifelong search for truth. Webb maintains that it is precisely Martineau's radicalism that drew her to concerns with human nature and social progress, and to science as perhaps the panacea for the problems of modernity. Webb points out that Martineau was "preaching sociology without the name" from the early 1830s, an observation that is more thoroughly developed in later works on Martineau.

Sympathetic, readable, and situated on solid historical ground is PICHANICK's life of Martineau, which examines particularly her role as historian and journalist, but also offers an appreciation of the influence of necessarianism and of Martineau's critical stance on Comte. Martineau's industriousness as a radical reformer was punctuated by impulsiveness and stubbornness, but "she was seldom seriously out of step with the more advanced opinions and trends of her day".

Other interpretations of Martineau accentuate her sociological research and writings, as well as her interests in parascientific phenomena including phrenology, mesmerism (animal-magnetism), and clairvoyance. In her collection of feminist writings, ROSSI emphasises the pioneering contributions of Harriet Martineau to feminist thought and social research, in a brief but salient introduction to an excerpt from Martineau's *Society in America*.

In the 1988 edition of Martineau's *How To Observe Manners and Morals* (1838), HILL introduces Martineau's important methodological treatise with a discussion of the theoretical and methodological resonances of her empirical work with the more commonly recognized figures in the history of sociological investigation. Martineau's approach to social research, as explicated in this methodological treatise, is outlined by Hill, who also considers Martineau's intellectual journey from metaphysics to empiricism and positivism. Hill rightly emphasizes that Martineau was not an uncritical social scientist, that she was highly innovative, and that her sociological work was most certainly within the accepted cannon.

An examination of the life and work of Harriet Martineau as a noteworthy founder of the sociological enterprise is presented in a biography by HOECKER-DRYSDALE. The underlying sociological orientation of Martineau's research and writings – from her earliest religious and philosophical period (her writings in *Unitarian Monthly Repository*), to her own literary illustrations of political economy, her empirical studies of America and the Middle East, and later to her expositions on science – provides the theme of this succinct biography. Martineau, like many Victorian intellectuals, believed in the emancipatory power of science and rational knowledge. Her translation and condensation of Comte's *Positive Philosophy* (1853), her original field research and analyses, and her proficiency in linking social research to public issues, properly place her among early sociologists and social scientists. Of particular importance are her systematic research practices: her macrosociological and comparative studies, her field methods (interviews, observation including participant observation, scientific note-taking, cross-checking of data) and analysis of census data, and her use of documents and of historical data in qualitative and quantitative analyses.

The methodological achievements in Martineau's research on American society, and many other subjects, would alone be grounds to establish her importance in the development of sociology. McDONALD underscores them in precisely that framework – Martineau as a woman methodologist within a male-dominated scientific tradition – showing the connections and influences among several generations of women in the social sciences.

Martineau's attraction to science can be attributed to a number of factors, including her early study of religion and philosophy and of literature, her precocious scepticism of patri-archal norms, her critical view of the Martineau family dynamics, and her own physical and psychological disabilities (a sickly constitution, deafness, impaired senses, childhood phobias, and anxieties). Added to these, prolonged illness in her third and fourth decades led her to mesmerism, which she subsequently claimed "cured" her abdominal maladies, and to phrenology, to which "science" she willed her head. Both contributed to her increasing support for the science of medicine, as COOTER demonstrates, and to her conviction that mesmerism was a path to the empowerment of women, as well as to her own independence, as explored by BASHAM.

POSTLETHWAITE examines the elements of materialism and spiritualism in Martineau's search for answers to the questions of human nature and scientific epistemology. She correctly claims that Martineau's *Letters on the Laws of Man's Nature and Development*, written with Henry G. Atkinson, is "a prototypical expression of (the) Victorian world view". Mesmerism, as experiential verification of scientific mysteries, held for them the promise of the unification of the irrational (religious or mystical) and the rational (scientific) realms.

While a thorough analysis of Martineau's position within 19th-century social science remains to be written, WRIGHT places her translation of Comte, her book on science with Atkinson, and her influence among positivist contemporaries within the sweep of Comtean positivism and his Religion of Humanity.

Martineau's own empirical research, sociological interpretations in theoretical and literary writings, methodological practices, analyses of social issues, problems, and social change, and commitment to a science of society constitute a broad and fascinating agenda for analysis.

SUSAN HOECKER-DRYSDALE

See also Comte; Mesmerism; Social Sciences; Sociology

Marx, Karl 1818–1883

German political theorist

Anderson, Kevin, *Lenin, Hegel, and Western Marxism*, Urbana: University of Illinois Press, 1995

Aronowitz, Stanley, *Science as Power*, London: Macmillan, and Minneapolis: University of Minnesota Press, 1988

Bhaskar, Roy, *Dialectic: The Pulse of Freedom*, London and New York: Verso, 1993

Braverman, Harry, *Labor and Monopoly Capital*, New York: Monthly Review Press, 1975

Colletti, Lucio, "Bernstein and the Marxism of the Second International", in his *From Rousseau to Lenin: Studies in Ideology and Society*, translated from the Italian by John Merrington and Judith White, London: New Left Books, and New York: Monthly Review Press, 1972 (original edition, 1969)

Engels, Friedrich, *Anti-Dühring: Herr Eugen Dühring's Revolution in Science*, Moscow: Progress, 1947; Cambridge: Polity Press, 1984

Hanson, Norwood Russell, *Patterns of Discovery: An Inquiry into the Conceptual Foundations of Science*, Cambridge: Cambridge University Press, 1958

Jay, Martin, *Marxism and Totality: The Adventures of a Concept from Lucács to Habermas*, Berkeley: University of California Press, 1984

Kautsky, Karl, *The Materialist Conception of History*, London: Macmillan, 1939; abridged by John H. Kautsky, translated from the German by Raymond Meer and John H. Kautsky, New Haven, Connecticut: Yale University Press, 1988 (original edition, 1927)

Kitching, Gavin, *Marxism and Science*, University Park: Pennsylvania State University Press, 1994

Marcuse, Herbert, *Soviet Marxism: A Critical Analysis*, New York: Columbia University Press, and London: Routledge and Kegan Paul, 1958

Marx, Karl, *Capital: A Critique of Political Economy*, translated from the German by Ben Fowkes, Harmondsworth: Penguin, and New York: New Left Review, 1976 (original edition, 1867)

Sayer, Derek, *Marx's Method: Ideology, Science and Critique in "Capital"*, Hassocks, Sussex: Harvester Press, and Atlantic Highlands, New Jersey: Humanities Press, 1979; 2nd edition, Brighton, Sussex: Harvester Press, 1983

Sohn-Rethel, Alfred, *Intellectual and Manual Labour: A Critique of Epistemology*, translated from the German by Martin Sohn-Rethel, London: Macmillan, and Atlantic Highlands, New Jersey: Humanities Press, 1978 (original edition, 1970)

Wetter, Gustav A., *Dialectical Materialism: A Historical and Systematic Survey of Philosophy in the Soviet Union*, translated from the German by Peter Heath, New York: Praeger, and London: Routledge and Kegan Paul, 1958; revised edition, Westport Connecticut: Greenwood Press, 1973

The debate over Karl Marx's critique of science began during his lifetime, and has never ceased. The starting point for this debate is MARX's magnum opus, *Capital*, to which he devoted most of his life. Volume 1 of this great unfinished work (1867) is the *locus classicus* of each of the most widely disputed themes in the literature on Marx and science: (a) the "scientificity" of Marx's method in general; (b) the scientificity of Marx's critique of capital in particular; and (c) the substance of Marx's critique of science as an institution.

The first of these questions, in particular, captured the imagination of a generation of early Marxists, thanks largely to the influence of a polemic by Marx's friend, ENGELS. Preoccupied with the generalizability of Marx's ideas, Engels drew from *Capital* a series of "dialectical" precepts which, he said, formed the conceptual basis of a "scientific socialist" theory which could be applied, with equal validity, to nature and society alike. Showing keen insight into the science of his day – focusing, for example, on matter and motion, Darwinian theory, and cell physiology – Engels argued for a unified Marxian science of society and nature that would be simultaneously historical, materialist, and dialectical.

The influence of this vision was immense. In the period from 1890 until World War I, Marxism as defined by Engels figured as the reigning orthodoxy in the swiftly growing international movement that marched under the flag of the "Second International". The one serious challenge to Engelsian doctrine in this period – Bernstein's claim that Marx's "scientificity"

had been eclipsed by his dogmatism – was anathematized by the leading socialist parties at the turn of the century. "Marxism" and "science" became virtual synonyms for socialists in this tradition.

KAUTSKY, the "pope" of the Second International, gave a further, Darwinian twist to Engelsian "historical materialism", coloring it with determinism. Stating that societies and species are both passive products of a uniform process of evolution, Kautsky added that humanity can only "adapt" to external change. Even revolution, in this vision, is construed as a form of evolutionary adaptation. Society is driven forward by "objective forces", not, Kautsky believed, by the subjective will or imagination of classes or nations.

Parallel views were elaborated by most of the other leading figures in European socialism in this period, including the founder of Russian Marxism, Plekhanov, who coined the term "dialectical materialism". Though there were minor differences in the opinions of the leading theorists of the Second International, they generally embraced an openly reductionist materialism, economic or even technological determinism, and a pre-critical epistemology anchored in the belief that objective reality is immediately "copied" by the human mind.

In his influential article of 1969, COLLETTI argued that this doctrine is not only simplistic, but remote from Marx's critique of political economy. The argument of *Capital* did not rest on the comparatively static, scholastic "laws" that Engels distilled from a mélange of Marx's footnotes and epigrams, but, rather, on subtle deductive reasoning about essence and appearance, abstract and concrete labor, the form and content of value, and a host of other issues to which Engelsian orthodoxy paid little attention. More recently, ANDERSON has argued that, though Russian Marxism in the era of the Second International was unique in its emphasis on materialist "dialectics", it was very nearly as reductionist in its materialism as Kautskyan orthodoxy.

After the Bolshevik Revolution of 1917, dialectical materialism was elaborated into a comprehensive new world-view, as WETTER has shown. Initially quite sophisticated, so-called "diamat" was soon transformed, under Stalin, into an all-embracing, anti-empirical, legitimating ideology serving the interests of the ruling bureaucracy, as MARCUSE explains. The well-known aberrations of this ideology (e.g. Lysenko's Lamarckian pseudo-genetics) are only the most extreme examples of the Stalinist disdain for truth.

Stalinism entered a period of acute crisis in 1956, with the suppression of the Hungarian uprising and Krushchev's disclosure of Stalin-era crimes. In the ferment of the following decades, a New Left began to reconsider not only Marx and Marxism, but positivism, psychoanalysis, and other orthodoxies. Critics of the Old Left found inspiration in the earlier heresies of György Lukács, Antonio Gramsci, Wilhelm Reich, and the Frankfurt School, whose criticisms of reification and authoritarianism seemed to lay a foundation for a new, more open and emancipatory Marxism.

Opposed by Louis Althusser, Galvano Della Volpe, and others who aspired to revitalize "scientific" orthodoxy by placing it on a new foundation, the neo-Marxists of the New Left were concerned, above all, with the palpable uncertainties of an era in which alienation was acute, and yet emancipation seemed deeply problematic. As JAY has shown, this prompted a rethinking of many of the main aspects of the relationship between Marxism and science.

SOHN-RETHEL, for example, united a critique of positivist epistemology with a return to Marx's critique of institutional science, claiming that knowledge has been systematically severed from the labor of the direct producers – a thesis further refined by ARONOWITZ, and especially by BRAVERMAN, whose own factory experience is used to describe the de-skilling process in the 20th century. New attention has also been devoted to the logical status of Marx's theory of value and alienated labor. This has yielded studies showing not only the richness, but also the counter-intuitive complexity of Marx's theory.

Colletti, who tried valiantly, but in vain, to reconcile Marx's notion of value with the tenets of normal science, ultimately turned away from Marx and dialectics altogether. SAYER, agreeing that Marx's theory departs from conventional norms of induction and deduction, nevertheless argues that Marx's logic is intelligible as an example of what the philosopher Peirce called "Retroductive inference" (as expounded by HANSON). Another noteworthy contribution to this debate comes from KITCHING, for whom Marx's theory of society is an example of conceptual critique rather than "science" in the strict sense.

Issues that remain to be adequately addressed in this connection include, among others, the logical status of several key categories Marx adapted from Hegel, including "reflection-determinations" and "existence-forms". Meanwhile, many writers now urge the "reconstruction" of historical materialism on a non-dialectical basis, although the opposite position is taken by BHASKAR, for whom Marx's greatest weakness was not an excess of dialectical imagination, but just the reverse – a failure to grasp that class, culture, and consciousness are no less contradictory than capitalism itself.

DAVID N. SMITH

See also Capitalism and Science; Evolution; Ideology; Marxism and Science; Political Economy

Marxism and Science

Bernal, J.D., *Science in History*, London: Watts, and New York: Cameron Associates, 1954

Childe, V. Gordon, *Man Makes Himself*, London: Watts, 1937; New York: Oxford University Press, 1939

Dorn, Harold, *The Geography of Science*, Baltimore: Johns Hopkins University Press, 1991

Farrington, Benjamin, *Greek Science: Its Meaning for Us*, 2 vols, Harmondsworth: Penguin, 1944–49; Baltimore: Penguin, 1953

Gould, Stephen Jay, "Sociobiology and the Theory of Natural Selection", in *American Association for the Advancement of Science Symposia*, (1980): 257–69

Graham, Loren R., "The Socio-Political Roots of Boris Hessen: Soviet Marxism and the History of Science", *Social Studies of Science*, 15 (1985): 705–22

Hessen, Boris, "The Social and Economic Roots of Newton's 'Principia'", in *Science at the Crossroads*, London: Kniga [1931]

Joravsky, David, *The Lysenko Affair*, Cambridge, Massachusetts: Harvard University Press, 1970

Lewontin, R.C., Steven Rose and Leon J. Kamin, *Not in Our Genes: Biology, Ideology and Human Nature*, New York: Pantheon Books, and London: Pelican, 1984

Lumsden, Charles J. and Edward O. Wilson, *Promethean Fire: Reflections on the Origin of Mind*, Cambridge, Massachusetts: Harvard University Press, 1983 (chapter 2 "The Sociobiology Controversy")

Needham, Joseph, *Science and Civilization in China*, Cambridge and New York: Cambridge University Press, 1954–86

Smith, Merritt Roe and Leo Marx (eds), *Does Technology Drive History? The Dilemma of Technological Determinism*, Cambridge, Massachusetts: MIT Press, 1994

Werskey, Gary, *The Visible College: The Collective Biography of the British Scientific Socialists of the 1930s*, New York: Holt Rinehart and Winston, and London: Allen Lane, 1978

Over the past 75 years, Marxists have exerted a strong influence on the history of science and technology while, conversely, theoretical Marxism has received little clarification in return. Marx's materialist interpretation of history – with its theory of historical stages, structural analysis of society in terms of economic base and cultural superstructure, dialectical principles with which to account for change, and suggestion that technology determines history – have all left their mark on the history of science and technology. Because Marxism has been, from its inception, both a system of thought and a program of political action, it has also embraced the principle of the unity of theory and practice. A corollary of that principle is the unity of science and technology that Marxist writers have consistently proclaimed – i.e. that science has flourished and benefited society when it has been stimulated by contact with the practical arts, technology, and medical practice. The general emphasis of these Marxist principles on material and institutional, rather than intellectual, factors has played a major role in the development of the sociological (externalist) branch of the history of science.

In 1931, the Soviet philosopher of science, Boris HESSEN, read a paper at the Second International Congress of the History of Science and Technology held in London, which was a canonical and provocative presentation of the Marxist historiography of science. He postulated that, in terms of base and superstructure, the themes of Newton's *Principia* had a strong dependence on the technical problems of an emergent capitalism in 17th-century England. The "Hessen thesis" was sharply debated, and for many years it enlivened discussions on the connections between science and society. GRAHAM has shown that the thesis did not spring from any Marxist interest in the history of science; rather, it was a tactical maneuver within the debate in the Soviet Union between doctrinal zealots, who repudiated Einstein and his physics, and modernizers, who held that the latest innovations in physical theory were potentially as socially relevant as Newton's physics once were.

A Marxist historiography of science was developed in Britain after the Russian Revolution. CHILDE and FARRINGTON, working on the prehistoric and classical eras respectively, consistently emphasized the unity of knowledge and technique – sometimes, indeed, obscuring all distinction between them.

BERNAL, who was a remarkable polymath as well as an eminent crystallographer and a member of the British Communist Party, produced a long survey of the history of science that is still in print. In 1954, NEEDHAM, an even more remarkable polymath who, as he put it, "fell in love with the Chinese people", launched a monumental study of the history of Chinese science and technology. It is based on an astonishing number of sources in Chinese, Japanese, and European languages, and covers a vast range of ideas and techniques, emphasizing their interdependence. The project is now in its fifth decade and will be completed by the Needham Research Institute, Cambridge, England. Although Needham conceded that "modern science" originated "only in Europe", his sympathetic acknowledgement of the diffusion of many scientific and technological innovations from China to the West, and his insistence that scientific development is to be accounted for by "concrete social reasons" rather than by the inspiration of geniuses, are at least vaguely consistent with his Marxist principles. While none of these British writers on the history of science is as explicitly doctrinal as Hessen, they have collectively influenced the subject by directing it towards an institutional and sociological approach, with an emphasis (sometimes exaggerated) on the interconnections between science and technology as joint components of the socio-economic basis of society. WERSKEY presents an informative and thoughtful account of the careers of these British Marxists.

Marx's theory of history includes a stage of historical development that he called the "Asiatic Mode of Production". This corresponds to what are generally known as the first civilizations in the Near and Far East and in the Americas, and postulates that much of the social organization of these civilizations, which are quite unlike the European model, was determined by their physical and environmental settings, requiring the intensification of agriculture through bureaucratic control of large-scale public works, generally in the form of irrigation projects. Although Needham resolutely avoided Marx's irritating "Asiatic Mode of Production" (which, ironically, was repudiated by Marxists and, in 1931, condemned in the Soviet Union), preferring instead to designate traditional China as "feudal bureaucratism", he endorsed the thesis that major cultural patterns of Chinese history can be explained by the material environment of an agrarian society dependent on artificial irrigation in semi-arid flood plains. Also, he specifically contrasted Chinese and Greek astronomy in terms of the divergent social effects determined by ecological differences. DORN has recently applied an apolitical interpretation of the Asiatic Mode of Production, along the lines of the "hydraulic hypothesis" adopted by some American anthropologists, to an analysis of the differences between the scientific cultures of the ancient Orient and ancient Greece, extending the argument in order to establish a generalized geographical approach to the social history of science.

Marx's famous aphorism, "the hand-mill gives you society with the feudal lord; the steam-mill, society with the industrial capitalist", with its forbidding implication of technological determinism, has been only slightly developed by historians of technology as a historical generalization. SMITH & MARX have now edited a collection of articles that may refocus the discussion. Another of Marx's aphorisms, "the ideas of the ruling class are the ruling ideas", seems to be finding expression (albeit without the distinctive class analysis) in the "social constructivism" that some historians of science have advocated in recent years.

As a result of its dual nature (as political program and theory of history), Marxism has often become embroiled in ideological conflict, which, in the Soviet Union, even led to the suppression of scientific research. In an effort to bolster agricultural production, Soviet authorities, in the notorious "Lysenko affair", favored a group of plant breeders, ideologues, and scientists who repudiated the science of genetics – immutable genes seemed to contradict dialectical materialism, which postulates incessant change – and for a few years in the 1940s, the political authorities went so far as to prohibit research in the field of genetics. JORAVSKY presents a thorough account of that doleful episode in the history of science.

In the US, a sharp controversy has erupted along another front of Darwin studies. In 1975, Edward O. Wilson published a massive survey of sociobiology, in which he included, as a tangential issue, the biological basis of human social behavior. Wilson's survey evoked an immediate condemnation, on both scientific and ideological grounds, by left-wing critics, including the scientists GOULD and LEWONTIN, ROSE & KAMIN. In terms that are more akin to political liberalism than theoretical Marxism, Wilson was accused of favoring a theory that provides a justification for "policies which led to the establishment of gas chambers in Nazi Germany". LUMSDEN & WILSON have summarized the controversy, which shows little sign of abating. Gould has also been a leading advocate, on scientific grounds, of the theory of "punctuated evolution", which may appeal to him ideologically because of its consistency with dialectical materialism, which postulates that all change is punctuated by relatively abrupt transformations.

HAROLD DORN

See also Capitalism and Science; Ideology; Marx; Social Sciences

Materials Science

Bever, Michael B. (ed.), *Encyclopedia of Materials Science and Engineering*, vol. 1, Oxford: Pergamon Press, and Cambridge, Massachusetts: MIT Press, 1986

Bijker, Wiebe E., *Of Bicycles, Bakelites, and Bulbs.: Toward a Theory of Sociotechnical Change*, Cambridge, Massachusetts: MIT Press, 1995

Brocke, Bernhard vom (ed.), *Forschung im Spannungsfeld von Politik und Gesellschaft. Geschichte und Struktur der Kaiser-Wilhelm-/Max-Planck-Gesellschaft*, Stuttgart: Deutsche Verlags-Anstalt, 1990

Hoddeson, Lillian *et al.* (eds), *Out of the Crystal Maze: Chapters from the History of Solid-State Physics*, Oxford and New York: Oxford University Press, 1992

Johnson, Jeffrey Allan, *The Kaiser's Chemists: Science and Modernization in Imperial Germany*, Chapel Hill: University of North Carolina Press, 1990

Köster, Werner, *25 Jahre Kaiser-Wilhelm-Institut für Metallforschung 1921–1946*, Stuttgart: Riederer, 1949

Kranzberg, Melvin and Cyril Stanley Smith, "Materials in History and Society", *Materials Science and Engineering*, 37 (1979)

Pusch, Richard, "Die Geschichte der Metallographie unter besonderer Berücksichtigung der mikroskopischen Prüfverfahren", *Practical Metallography*, 16 (1979)

Pyatt, Edward, *The National Physical Laboratory: A History*, Bristol: Adam Hilger, 1983

Serafini, Anthony, *Legends in Their Own Time: A Century of American Physical Scientists*, New York: Plenum Press, 1993

Servos, John W., *Physical Chemistry from Ostwald to Pauling: The Making of a Science in America*, Princeton, New Jersey: Princeton University Press, 1990

Seymour, Raymond B. (ed.), *History of Polymer Science and Technology*, New York: Marcel Dekker, 1980

Smith, Cyril Stanley, *A History of Metallography: The Development of Ideas on the Structure of Metals before 1890*, Chicago: University of Chicago Press, 1960; 2nd edition, Cambridge, Massachusetts: MIT Press, 1988

BEVER states that materials science emerged as a scientific discipline during the 1940s when military technology in particular required new engineering materials such as high-temperature metals for jet engines or nuclear reactors. The young academic discipline integrated the materials related research of older sciences that were its mother disciplines. Thus, the historiography of materials science must be divided into two main periods covering the materials related research of its mother-disciplines such as physics, chemistry, physical chemistry, and metallography up to the 1940s, and the period from the 1950s when the results of materials science became crucial for industrial (steel) and consumer (transistor) applications.

As the only study to give an overview of the subject, KRANZBERG & SMITH perfectly reflect the heterogenous character of materials science before and after 1950. They emphasize the significance of materials for mankind from the early times on and the contributions of chemistry, physics, and engineering to the field. A key question is the dichotomy between science and practice, and engineering respectively, reflecting the different cultures and the gulf between the communities, which was overcome only after the requirements of national security brought together scientists and engineers in research and development projects. The need for sophisticated materials for communication, space flight and atomic energy purposes mainly contributed to the evolution of the discipline under the appellation "materials science and engineering" in the 1950s and 1960s.

Tracing back the evolution of materials science in its mother disciplines, for the case of solid-state physics HODDESON *et al.* delineate the international discussion on the microstructure of metals from the 19th century on, before the emergence of quantum mechanics. Obviously, these investigations must be seen as a reaction to socio-economic needs, when the extreme increase in the production of steel for railroad and steam-engine purposes in the second half of the 19th century demanded a better knowledge of metal microstructure. The "externalistic" approach shows that the state effort in industrialized nations was responsible for the foundation of research institutions which was crucial for further investigation on materials and which integrated fundamental and applied research. On the other hand, industrial research establishments such as Edison's Menlo Park, the Bell Telephone Company, General Electric, Siemens, Krupp and I.G. Farben, established metallurgical and strength-of-materials laboratories. World War I then fostered the material supply for and the exchange of results and personnel among these institutions.

Moving over the watershed of 1950, the history of the National Physics Laboratory (NPL) is an example for the institutional attitude in the history of science. PYATT shows the state impact on the foundation and during the war years as well as the interdisciplinary character of the research program, when Walter Rosenhain became superintendent of the new Metallurgy and Metallurgical Chemistry Department in 1906. His department made a tremendous contribution to materials science with its "annual reports" on non-ferrous alloys which already covered a broad range of elements of modern materials science such as phase diagrams, chemical and microstructural constitution and the effects of processing on mechanical properties. In the history of the NPL, the period from 1945 to 1980 is labelled with "Materials Science" standing for the application of new techniques and methods with X-ray, ceramic and radioactive tracer sections but further indicating the emergence of the new discipline inside a national institution.

The history of the German "Kaiser-Wilhelm-Institut für Metallforschung" founded in 1921 which pursued a similar research program as the NPL is portrayed in its political and socio-economic aspects by the work of BROCKE. This is an institutional history at its best, but neglects the "internal" developments of the materials scientific questions and developments that directed the institutes research. JOHNSON follows this position on a smaller scale indicating the dominance of chemistry in Imperial Germany, which is expressed by the fact that the first director of the institute, Emil Heyn, was an analytic chemist. The whole body of research has thus to be taken from a classical jubilee work of its director KÖSTER who described his institutions history as if it mainly would follow an internal logic and one discovery leading to another. Only the combination of Brocke, Johnson and Köster can reveal the whole range of driving forces for the development of materials science in this institution.

The significance of chemistry and physical chemistry for the emergence of materials science is not limited on the analysis of the constituents of alloys. It expands on the theoretical basis such as the phase rule developed by J. Willard Gibbs. SERAFINI has chosen the biographical approach to the subject in order to examine the importance of an individuals life and character on his impact in physical chemistry and thus materials science. Not accidentally, the history of the phase rule and its relevance for metallurgical research is to be found in SERVOS's work on the history of physical chemistry.

Although metallography is still a main element in todays materials science studies only one profound history was written yet. Unfortunately, SMITH's work mainly covers its development from the early days up to the late 19th century and represents the old approach in history of science, excluding other than scientific driving forces. However, it is essential for any further study and the history of materials science as well as PUSCH's work which covers the years up to the 1940s from the German perspective.

Materials science also includes non-metal materials. The work of SEYMOUR carries a misleading title because it contains 18 internalistic articles on different polymers which were developed in the 20th century. Only two articles deal with general aspects of polymer science history and the history of polymer education. BIJKER adopts a different position in his monograph, which became a role model for history of science and technology during the 1990s. He develops the "social construction of technology" (and science) viewpoint in which he takes Leo Hendrik Baekeland and his works on polymers as a key example. He claims, that the scientist is a member of a relevant social group and who is reacting to demands from outside his community. In the case of Baekeland this was the demand for a cheap and inflammable plastic material to overcome the disadvantages of celluloid. A modern history of materials science still has to be written.

HELMUT MAIER

Mathematical Instruments

Bennett, J.A., *The Divided Circle: A History of Instruments for Astronomy, Navigation and Surveying*, Oxford: Phaidon/Christie's, 1987

Bennett, Jim and Stephen Johnston, *The Geometry of War, 1500–1750*, Oxford: Museum of the History of Science, 1996

Brown, Joyce, *Mathematical Instrument-Makers in the Grocers' Company, 1688–1800, With Notes on Some Earlier Makers*, London: Science Museum, 1979

Chapman, Allan, *Dividing the Circle: The Development of Critical Angular Measurement in Astronomy, 1500–1850*, New York: Ellis Horwood, 1990; 2nd edition, Chichester, Sussex: Wiley, 1995

Clifton, Gloria C., *Directory of British Scientific Instrument Makers, 1550–1851*, London: Zwemmer/National Museum, 1995

Gouk, Penelope, *The Ivory Sundials of Nuremberg, 1500–1700*, Cambridge: Whipple Museum, 1988

Hambly, Maya, *Drawing Instruments, 1580–1980*, London: Sotheby's, 1988

Taylor, E.G.R., *The Mathematical Practitioners of Tudor and Stuart England, 1485–1714*, Cambridge: Cambridge University Press/Institute of Navigation, 1954

Taylor, E.G.R., *The Mathematical Practitioners of Hanoverian England, 1714–1840*, Cambridge: Cambridge University Press/Institute of Navigation, 1966

Turner, Anthony John, *Early Scientific Instruments: Europe, 1400–1800*, London: Sotheby, and New York: Philip Wilson, 1987

Turner, Anthony John, *Mathematical Instruments in Antiquity and the Middle Ages: An Introduction*, London: Vade-Mecum Press, 1994

Turner, Gerard L'E., *Nineteenth-Century Scientific Instruments*, London: Sotheby, and Berkeley: University of California Press, 1983

Mathematical instruments are historically the earliest devices now subsumed under the general heading of scientific instru-

ments. They were used for calculation, observation and drawing in a range of mathematical arts, including astronomy, surveying, navigation, fortification, and gunnery. As a category, "mathematical instruments" gradually disappeared in the 19th century, buried under increasing specialisation and changing technology. Much of the history of mathematical instruments therefore appears under the guise of more broadly conceived histories of scientific instruments, or within the narrower bounds of accounts of particular disciplines or topics.

Taylor was one of the first to reveal the historical coherence of the mathematical arts and sciences as a tradition that actively continued through to the 19th century. Her two volumes on consecutive periods, TAYLOR (1954) and TAYLOR (1966), though largely bibliographical, nevertheless echo the interests of the mathematical practitioners themselves, by giving extended consideration to the manufacture and use of instruments. While frequently criticised on points of detail, Taylor has been the starting point for much subsequent research.

Historiography has focused on the Renaissance and early modern periods, which reflects the bulk of surviving instruments in museum and private collections. However, TURNER (1994) provides a first survey of ancient and early medieval instruments. This serves as a useful preface to TURNER (1987), which reviews the subsequent period. Although the latter work also considers the natural philosophical and optical instruments of the 17th and 18th centuries, it is nevertheless heavily concerned with mathematical instruments. Taken together, these two texts offer the best current synthesis for the period up to 1800, as well as detailed references to more specialised literature.

The 19th-century fragmentation of the tradition of mathematical instruments is reflected in the structure of TURNER (1983), in which such instruments are distributed through several separate chapters. Turner's account focuses on the instruments themselves, and, in a work aimed partly at collectors, he does not attempt a comprehensive review; in particular, such larger-scale devices as astronomical observatory instruments are omitted.

Apart from period-based studies, mathematical instruments feature prominently in many accounts of particular topics or disciplines. Against the background of such studies of individual mathematical arts or sciences, BENNETT is unusual in presenting the three areas of astronomy, navigation, and surveying as a coherent historical terrain. The juxtaposition is justified less on the level of theory than through their reliance on shared principles of instrumentation, and especially on the geometry of the graduated circle. Bennett serves not only as an introduction to these three principal areas of practical mathematics and their instruments, but also as a demonstration of how attention to instruments can structure historical inquiry itself.

CHAPMAN offers a more tightly focused account of astronomical instruments, and supplements Bennett's account in his attention to issues of construction, use, and accuracy. More than most authors, Chapman strives to reconstruct the working methods of makers and to assess and evaluate the technical frontier of precision.

Not all mathematical instruments represented the cutting edge of technology; sundials, for example, were often as much aesthetic objects as time-telling devices. Although concerned with only a small part of this large field, GOUK provides a model interdisciplinary study that addresses the principles, materials, manufacture, decoration and use of a particular type of sundial, as well as its market.

Drawing instruments, predominantly used professionally by architects and engineers, were also part of the repertoire of the mathematical instrument maker. Although partly a picture book for collectors, particularly in its presentation of cases of drawing instruments, HAMBLY is by far the most extensive survey of this class of instrument. The text is centred on the instruments themselves, and there is no systematic analysis of the relations between instrumentation and drawing practice. However, the development of all major drawing instrument types is covered.

In an area where much of the historiography has been written by museum curators, catalogues as well as monographs are a major medium of publication. BENNETT & JOHN-STON is an exhibition catalogue with an introductory essay that addresses the little-discussed area of the military uses of mathematical instruments.

Apart from period surveys and subject-based accounts, much recent work in instrument history has concerned itself with the identification of instrument makers and the development of their trade. Studies such as those of BROWN have reconstituted sequences of master-apprentice relations among mathematical instrument makers, establishing a continuous lineage of craft succession over literally hundreds of years. CLIFTON provides the results of a more systematic project to document English makers of all types of scientific instrument.

STEPHEN JOHNSTON

See also Astronomical Instruments; Calculating Devices; Instrument Makers; Navigational Instruments; Scientific Instruments: general works

Mathematical Modernity

Corry, Leo, *Modern Algebra and the Rise of Mathematical Structures*, Basel: Birkhäuser, 1996

Gray, Jeremy, "The 19th-Century Revolution in Mathematical Ontology", in *Revolutions in Mathematics*, edited by Donald Gillies, Oxford: Clarendon Press, and New York: Oxford University Press, 1992

Heims, Steve J., *John von Neumann and Norbert Wiener: From Mathematics to the Technologies of Life and Death*, Cambridge, Massachusetts: MIT Press, 1980

Heintz, Bettina, *Die Herrschaft der Regel: Zur Grundlagengeschichte des Computers*, Frankfurt: Campus, 1993

Mehrtens, Herbert, *Moderne, Sprache, Mathematik: Eine Geschichte des Streits um die Grundlagen der Disziplin und des Subjekts formaler Systeme*, Frankfurt: Suhrkamp, 1990

Mehrtens, Herbert, "Mathematics and War: Germany, 1900–1945", in *National Military Establishments and the Advancement of Science and Technology*, edited by Paul Forman and José M. Sánchez-Ron, Dordrecht and Boston: Kluwer, 1996

Parshall, Karen Hunger and David E. Rowe, *The Emergence of the American Mathematical Research Community, 1876–1900*, Providence, Rhode Island: American Mathematical Society, and London: London Mathematical Society, 1994

Peckhaus, Volker, *Hilbert-Programm und kritische Philosophie*, Göttingen: Vandenhoeck & Ruprecht, 1990

Pyenson, Lewis, *Neohumanism and the Persistence of Pure Mathematics in Wilhelmian Germany*, Philadelphia: American Philosophical Society, 1983

Reid, Constance, *Hilbert*, Berlin and New York: Springer, and London: Allen and Unwin, 1970

Reid, Constance, *Courant in Göttingen and New York: The Story of an Improbable Mathematician*, New York: Springer, 1976

Richards, Joan L., *Mathematical Visions: The Pursuit of Geometry in Victorian England*, Boston: Academic Press, 1988

Rotman, Brian: *Ad infinitum – The Ghost in Turing's Machine: Taking God Out of Mathematics and Putting the Body Back In: An Essay in Corporeal Semiotics*, Stanford, California: Stanford University Press, 1993

Rowe, David E. and John McCleary (eds), *The History of Modern Mathematics: Proceedings of the Symposium of the History of Mathematics, Vassar College, Poughkeepsie*, 2 vols, Boston: Academic Press, 1989

Rowe, David E. and Eberhard Knobloch (eds), *The History of Modern Mathematics* (sequel to the Symposium of the History of Mathematics), Boston: Academic Press, 1995

Scholz, Erhard, *Symmetrie, Gruppe, Dualität: Zur Beziehung zwischen theoretischer Mathematik und Anwendungen in Kristallographie und Baustatik des 19. Jahrhunderts*, Basel: Birkhäuser, 1989

The history of mathematics has only recently begun to focus on 20th-century developments. A key issue in approaching that last century is adequate periodization; it has long been apparent that during the final decades of the 19th century there was a slow but significant change within mathematical culture, from research and teaching to applications in various contexts. A promising proposal, made most forcefully by Herbert Mehrtens, is to regard the emergent mathematical culture as reflecting a period of "mathematical modernity", related to cultural modernity as a whole. Historical studies that substantiate this proposal are only just beginning to emerge, and, in the following discussion, some of these recent studies will be mentioned.

In research, a process of differentiation and diversification of mathematical fields accompanied the onset of mathematical modernity. For a sample of historical studies, mostly dealing with new fields constituted in that process but also with a variety of institutional aspects, see the volumes ROWE & McCLEARY and ROWE & KNOBLOCH. Linked to the internal differentiation of mathematical research fields was a revolution in the relations between mathematics and the natural sciences, and mathematics and technology. SCHOLZ draws on two interesting case studies; against the background of the dichotomy between "autonomous" and "heteronomous" processes of concept formation in mathematics, he discusses the abstract group concept in 19th-century crystallography, and the emergence of the geometric notion of duality, in connection with architecture and technical drawing.

The autonomous development of mathematics clearly rested on the new role and status of the mathematical profession. A good starting point for studies of this level of modernization is PYENSON's concise treatment of the reformation of mathematical education in Wilhelmian Germany, against the background of the neo-humanist ideal of pure mathematics. In particular, Pyenson highlights Felix Klein's institutional activities on behalf of the mathematics profession. Together with the British algebraist, Joseph J. Sylvester, Klein was also one of the key figures in the establishment of a mathematical research community in the US in the decades before 1900. The story of this influential development is told in great detail by PARSHALL & ROWE, who not only describe almost every individual involved in the project, but also emphasize how the mathematical ideas of the leading figures helped to shape the research traditions of the growing community. However, a complementary study of the tremendous growth of mathematics in the US in the early 20th century is still lacking, as are comparative studies of the development of mathematical research communities in the various imperialist countries.

Internal differentiation, the achievement of disciplinary autonomy, professionalization, and the spreading of mathematics over the industrialized parts of the globe, are just some of the changes that mark the onset of mathematical modernity. At a deeper level, traditional conceptions of what mathematics is actually about were threatened and finally abandoned. The best-known line of mathematical thinking which involved such a redrawing of the image of mathematics is the emergence of non-Euclidean geometries. RICHARDS discusses the reception of these geometries in Britain within the broader context of British geometrical traditions, from the Cambridge Tripos to debates on Euclid as a school book. The central issue in her narrative is the need for the rejection of the notion of geometry as describing some sort of spatial reality, which was finally accepted by British mathematicians after a variety of arguments and controversies. Most probably, the full (international) story of these developments will transcend Richards's national perspective in significant and interesting ways.

A similar developmental process in algebra during the 19th century led also to the explosion of the traditional concept of number. In a tightly-argued article, GRAY has described these and further developments as a "revolution in mathematical ontology", in the Kuhnian sense. In fact, it seems that much may still be gained from disentangling the various threads from what could be called the end of the conception of mathematics as a science of quantity, to the philosophical battles concerning the foundations of mathematics fought to this day.

The turn of the 20th century saw a radicalization of mathematical culture and a movement of committed modernists. Using an interpretative framework, based on both semiotics and David Hilbert's metamathematics, and focusing mainly on German developments, MEHRTENS (1990) depicts the rise of the axiomatic style in mathematics, and the continuing struggle between "moderns" like Hilbert and Felix Hausdorff and "counter-moderns" like Felix Klein or Luitzen Brouwer. For Mehrtens, the modernist approach to mathematics implied working on a language without fixed meaning, while his "counter-moderns" insisted that mathematical practice had to be rooted in the real world, via either intuition or application. Around this narrative core, Mehrtens groups a broad spectrum of issues, ranging from professionalization to a psychoanalytic sketch of the modern mathematical subject.

Mehrtens shares the general view that the central figure in the struggles concerning the shape of mathematical modernity was Hilbert. While little of Hilbert's mathematical research has as yet received adequate historical treatment, his metamathematical activities have occupied philosophers ever since. From a historical perspective, these are also discussed in PECKHAUS, who details Hilbert's efforts to establish a research tradition at Göttingen on the foundations of modern mathematics.

Following the lead of Hilbert's early work and Julius Dedekind's conceptual innovations in algebraic number theory, in Göttingen Emmy Noether and her followers created a mathematical discipline that carried "modernity" even in its name: modern algebra, understood as a science of algebraic structures. CORRY treats the rise of this discipline within a broad context; his main concern is the development of the image of mathematics with the growing faith in mathematical structures as the basis of all mathematical research – which sometimes bordered on myth-making, as reflected in the Bourbakist modern encyclopedia of mathematics.

In the formalist idea of mathematics as a language without fixed meaning, and the Bourbakist idea of mathematics as a science of pure structures, the 19th-century ideal of pure mathematics survived in a specifically modern form. It would, however, be misleading to locate the essence of mathematical modernity here. At least two issues have been brought into the discussion that counterbalance this view. The first is computing; while Mehrtens links the emergence of a mathematical theory of computing with his general interpretation (by pointing out the roots of Turing's ideas in both formalist metamathematics and the intuitionists' insistence on effective computability), HEINTZ parallels theories of automatic computing with theories of social rationalization – in both cases, she argues, a system of strict rules is seen as the organizing principle. The second issue relativizing the myth of purity in mathematical modernity is the role of mathematics in war. In an illuminating parallel biography, HEIMS has contrasted the contributions of Norbert Wiener and John von Neumann to US warfare in World War II, which resulted in their antagonist views on military technology in the post-war period. MEHRTENS (1996) discusses the German case in detail, based on his earlier interpretative framework.

Collecting references to the historical literature under the title of "mathematical modernity" leaves one with the impression that much has still to be done. This is due not only to the general scarcity of studies on 20th-century mathematical practices, but also to the fact that important issues for the construction of a coherent picture of modernity in mathematics still remain unresearched. One issue is the development of the relations between mathematics and the natural sciences – in particular physics, but also chemistry or biology. Another is the use of mathematical methods in the social sciences, first and foremost economics. On a different level lies the lack of critical, scientific biographies of the central actors. Apart from Heims's parallel lives, the best we have are REID's semi-popular, insufficiently documented presentations of Hilbert and Courant.

If most of 20th-century mathematics can be described as forming part of the epoch of mathematical modernity, the question is raised as to when this period came to an end. Mehrtens is quite strict on this point: "The history of mathematical modernity ended about twenty years ago." (Mehrtens, 1990) The semiotician, ROTMAN, goes one step further: jumping on the train of academic postmodernism, he sketches a radically revisionist critique of modern mathematics, based on his conviction that mathematics should be understood as no more or less than a real (as opposed to idealized) practice of dealing with material signs.

MORITZ EPPLE

See also Algebra; Geometry; Number Theory

Maupertuis, Pierre-Louis Moreau de   1698–1759

French mathematician and geodeist

Beeson, David, *Maupertuis: An Intellectual Biography*, Oxford: Voltaire Foundation at the Taylor Institution, 1992

Brunet, Pierre, *Maupertuis*, 2 vols, Paris: Albert Blanchard, 1929

Greenberg, John L., *The Problem of the Earth's Shape from Newton to Clairaut: The Rise of Mathematical Science in Eighteenth-Century Paris and the Fall of "Normal" Science*, Cambridge and New York: Cambridge University Press, 1995

Hoffheimer, Michael, "Maupertuis and the Eighteenth-Century Critique of Preexistence", *Journal of the History of Biology*, 15 (1982): 119–44

Pulte, Helmut, *Das Prinzip der kleinsten Wirkung und die Kraftkonzeptionen der rationalen Mechanik: Eine Untersuchung zur Grundlegungsproblematik bei Leonhard Euler, Pierre Louis Moreau de Maupertuis und Joseph Louis Lagrange*, Stuttgart: Steiner, 1989

Terrall, Mary, "The Culture of Science in Frederick the Great's Berlin", *History of Science*, 23 (1990): 333–64

Terrall, Mary, "Representing the Earth's Shape: The Polemics Surrounding Maupertuis's Expedition to Lapland", *Isis*, 83 (1992): 218–37

Terrall, Mary, "Salon, Academy and Boudoir: Generation and Desire in Maupertuis's Science of Life", *Isis*, 87 (1996): 217–29

Pierre-Louis Moreau de Maupertuis operated in and around the institutional centers of science in the Enlightenment. From the mathematics class of the Paris Academy of Sciences, he worked his way up the hierarchy to a pensioned position, before being recruited by Frederick II for the presidency of the Prussian Academy of Sciences in Berlin. He was well-known in England, and contributed to the *Philosophical Transactions* of the Royal Society. His reputation rests primarily on his contributions in three areas: the shape of the earth (geodesy), the principle of least action (mechanics), and the theory of generation and heredity (life science). His works on these subjects, written in a variety of genres for a range of audiences, have usually been treated in the historical literature as separate from each other, without a great deal of attention to the cultural and institutional contexts in which they were written and read.

The classic biography is that of BRUNET, which separates Maupertuis's life (vol. 1) from his works (vol. 2). The biographical narrative relies exclusively on sources located in Paris libraries in the 1920s, ignoring major collections of correspondence and manuscripts held elsewhere. Brunet is interested in Maupertuis as the first "French Newtonian", and his account of Maupertuis's science is a straightforward summary of the *oeuvre*, with little emphasis on historical context. The more recent work by BEESON is based on careful archival work, including substantial sources unknown to Brunet. Beeson focuses on Maupertuis's intellectual development, representing him as an empiricist who opposed the "rationalist methodology of Cartesianism". These categories are not particularly helpful in understanding the complexity of ideas and practices that defined science in this period. Beeson takes no notice of the historiography of science of recent decades.

GREENBERG's masterful treatment of geodesy gives a detailed account of the technical content of Maupertuis's papers on the subject, and chronicles the dispute that engaged the attention of many members of the Paris Academy for more than a decade. This is a valuable source on the mathematical aspects of the debate, showing how an emerging mathematical tradition in Paris drew on Newton, without imitating him. The dispute also prompted the Academy to mount measuring expeditions to the Arctic circle and the equator, Maupertuis leading the northern expedition. TERRALL (1992) analyzes the polemics prompted by Maupertuis's expedition, and examines the rhetorical strategies used by the opposing factions to defend results obtained with competing calculational, observational, instrumental, and literary techniques. Particular instruments and particular texts crystallized these disputed practices.

Maupertuis's articulation of the principle of least action as the foundation of mechanics, and the key to a proof of God's existence, embroiled him in further controversy. The principle was formulated explicitly as both physical and metaphysical, an economy principle for the universe and for physics. PULTE puts this principle into its mathematical and philosophical context; he attacks positivist accounts of the development of physics as the gradual and necessary abandonment of metaphysics, arguing that metaphysics and physics worked together to reinforce particular theories of science in the 18th century. The careful attention to metaphysics is unusual and salutary, though Pulte's account stresses the philosophical context to the exclusion of political and institutional settings for the practice of mechanics.

The institutional context is explored in TERRALL (1990), which discusses Maupertuis's development of the principle of least action, at an academy that included a class of speculative philosophy. Maupertuis's move from Paris to Berlin allowed him to pursue his project regarding the value of metaphysical foundations for physics, to which he enlisted the co-operation of Leonhard Euler. The natural efficiency and economy ingrained in the principle of least action resonated with the ideology that defined Frederick's Prussia. This article also analyses the version of enlightened absolutism that informed Maupertuis's autocratic rule as president of the Berlin Academy of Sciences.

HOFFHEIMER's article is a helpful introduction to Maupertuis's work on generation and heredity. He shows how Maupertuis used experimental and observational evidence to develop an epigenetic system that challenged the prevailing wisdom about the pre-existence of organic germs. TERRALL (1996) looks at the participation of these texts in a discourse of eroticism outside the academy. Speculative claims about organic matter and the forces guiding organization drew on the language of pleasure current in fashionable social circles, where women were key interlocutors, as well as on microscopy and animal breeding experiments. Incorporating gallantry and wit into reflections about the possibilities of a new science of life was a way of playing to different, but overlapping, audiences for scientific knowledge.

Maupertuis's work and career provide clear evidence for the kind of disciplinary, geographical, and stylistic boundary-crossing characteristic of the practice of science in the early modern period generally. Though many of his scientific claims and rhetorical strategies were innovative, he is perhaps most interesting for the variety of ways he played the field, at a time when there was no single route to fame and fortune in science. His name crops up in historical accounts of many different fields, from biology to linguistics, to mechanics and geography, but there is no satisfactory account of how the various pieces of his life and work fit together within the historical context.

MARY TERRALL

See also Enlightenment; Newtonianism; Rational Mechanics

Maxwell, James Clerk   1831–1879

British physicist

Bromberg, Joan, "Maxwell's Displacement Current and His Theory of Light", *Archive for the History of Exact Sciences*, 4 (1967): 218–34

Buchwald, Jed Z., *From Maxwell to Microphysics: Aspects of Electromagnetic Theory in the Last Quarter of the Nineteenth Century*, Chicago: University of Chicago Press, 1985

Hendry, John, *James Clerk Maxwell and the Theory of the Electromagnetic Field*, Bristol and Boston: Hilger, 1986

Hunt, Bruce J., *The Maxwellians*, Ithaca, New York: Cornell University Press, 1991

Larmor, Joseph (ed.), *Origins of Clerk Maxwell's Electric Ideas, as Described in Familiar Letters to William Thomson*, Cambridge: Cambridge University Press, 1937

Siegel, Daniel M., *Innovation in Maxwell's Electromagnetic Theory: Molecular Vortices, Displacement Current, and Light*, Cambridge and New York: Cambridge University Press, 1991

Smith, Crosbie and M. Norton Wise, *Energy and Empire: A Biographical Study of Lord Kelvin*, Cambridge: Cambridge University Press, 1989

Although short, James Clerk Maxwell's life was extremely interesting; not only from a scientific point of view (his work on the electromagnetic field and electromagnetic theory of light and his contributions to the statistical molecular theory put him alongside Newton and Einstein in a unique chapter of the history of science), but also because of the milieu in which he grew up and carried out his scientific career. It is not easy to capture such variety, which includes some of the most difficult and important scientific problems of the 19th century, in just one book of biographical character. This explains why there are so few biographies of merit on Maxwell.

Of all the single contributions that Maxwell made to physics, one stands out: the introduction of the displacement current. A question frequently asked of the Maxwell scholar is why it took him so long to introduce the displacement current when it was surely obvious to him that Ampère's law, which connects a current to the magnetic field, is mathematically inconsistent with the equation of continuity, which connects current to charge. Although many historians have confronted this question, especially BROMBERG in her seminal article of 1967, none is as complete and satisfactory as SIEGEL's book, in which it is shown that Maxwell did not introduce the displacement current for reasons of mathematical consistency to close currents that otherwise would be open, as is usually stated, but for reasons of mechanical consistency, to open currents that would otherwise be closed. Such "mechanical consistency" was related to the dynamical interdependence of electricity and magnetism; to illustrate this, Maxwell had to invent a complex mechanical contrivance that would faithfully imitate the dynamics of the ether. In *Innovation in Maxwell's Electromagnetic Theory*, Siegel also discusses the realism of Maxwell's resulting vortex system. Besides these questions, and closely related to them, Siegel also tackles the question of the assimilation of optics into the electromagnetic theory that resulted from the introduction of the new current.

Less detailed and authoritative than Siegel, and based essentially on published works and accounts instead of on manuscript sources, but nevertheless offering a valuable introduction to the whole problem of the development of Maxwell's electrodynamics is HENDRY's book. Basic questions, such as what Maxwell achieved in his electrodynamical theory, what his theory meant, and how it related to other works are clearly addressed here.

This last question, how Maxwell's work related to that of others, notably André Marie Ampère, Michael Faraday and William Thomson (Lord Kelvin), is, of course, central to any attempt to reconstruct the development of his electrodynamical theory. The relationship with the work of Ampère and Faraday has been considered much more often than the one with respect to Thomson, although Maxwell's dynamical theories mark a significant break with the ideals expressed by Thomson. A detailed and satisfactory analysis of Maxwell and Thomson's relationship, including the differences that set them apart (Thomson considered Maxwell's system of equations as metaphysical, a product of brains alone), is found in SMITH & WISE's biographical study of Kelvin.

No picture of the work of a central scientific figure is complete without taking into account also how his or her work was taken up by the scientific community. This question is particularly relevant in Maxwell's case. In 1873, he published his monumental and difficult *Treatise on Electricity and Magnetism*, which summarizes his previous electrodynamical studies. However, Maxwell's *Treatise*, which not only provided the mathematical tools for the investigation and the representation of the whole of the electromagnetic theory, but which altered also the very framework of both theoretical and experimental physics, did not immediately convince the scientific community. The concepts in it were strange as was the mathematics involved. When Maxwell died of cancer in 1879, midway through preparing a second edition of his *Treatise*, he had convinced only a very few of his fellow countrymen and none of his continental colleagues. That task fell to the "Maxwellians", men such as George Francis FitzGerald, Oliver Heaviside, Oliver Lodge, Joseph Larmor, and the German physicist Heinrich Hertz. The evolution of "Maxwell's Theory" in the years after Maxwell's death is the subject of two important books: HUNT's study of 1991 and BUCHWALD's account of 1985. Their subject-matter is, however, very different. While Buchwald pays special attention to phenomena such as the Hall effect and the problem of conductivity, Hunt bases his narrative on the extant correspondence between FitzGerald, Heaviside, and Lodge, combined with expositions of their published papers, with LARMOR (who is a prominent figure in Buchwald's book) and Hertz playing a secondary role. There is still, nevertheless, much to be said about the reception among other scientists of Maxwell's ideas and theories, including, for instance, the role played by Hermann von Helmholtz.

JOSÉ M. SÁNCHEZ-RON

See also Electromagnetism

Measurement

Adas, Michael, *Machines as the Measure of Men: Science, Technology, and Ideologies of Western Dominance*, Ithaca, New York: Cornell University Press, 1989

Diez, José, "A Hundred Years of Numbers: An Historical Introduction of Measurement Theory 1887–1990", *Studies in the History and Philosophy of Science*, 28 (1997): 167–85

Funtowicz, Silvio O. and Jerome R. Ravetz, *Uncertainty and Quality in Science for Policy*, Dordrecht: Kluwer, 1990

Gooday, Graeme, "Precision Measurement and the Genesis of Physics Teaching Laboratories in Victorian Britain", *British Journal for the History of Science*, 23 (1990): 25–51

Gooday, Graeme, "Instrumentation and Interpretation: Managing and Representing the Working Environments of Victorian Experimental Science", in *Victorian Science in Context*, edited by Bernard Lightman, Chicago: University of Chicago Press, 1997

Hunt, Bruce J., "Scientists, Engineers and Wildman Whitehouse: Measurement and Credibility in Early Cable Telegraphy", *British Journal for the History of Science*, 29/2 (1996): 153–70

Iliffe, Robert, "'Applatisseur du monde de Cassini': Maupertuis, Precision Measurement, and the Shape of the Earth in the 1730s'", *History of Science*, 31 (1993): 335–75

Johnston, Sean, "The Construction Of Colorimetry By Committee", *Science in Context*, 9 (1996): 387–420

Koyré, Alexandre, *Metaphysics and Measurement: Essays in Scientific Revolution*, London: Chapman and Hall, and Cambridge: Massachusetts: Harvard University Press, 1968

Kuhn, Thomas, "The Function of Measurement in Modern Physical Science", *Isis*, 52 (1961): 161–90; reprinted in *The Essential Tension: Selected Studies in Scientific Tradition and Change*, Chicago: Chicago University Press, 1977

Mackenzie, Donald, *Inventing Accuracy: A Historical Sociology of Nuclear Missile Guidance*, Cambridge, Massachusetts: MIT Press, 1990

Olesko, Kathryn M., "Precision, Tolerance, and Consensus: Local Cultures in German and British Resistance Standards", in *Archimedes: New Studies in the History and Philosophy of Science and Technology*, edited by Jed Z. Buchwald, Dordrecht: Kluwer Academic, 1996

Porter, Theodore M., *Trust in Numbers: The Pursuit of Objectivity in Science and Public Life*, Princeton, New Jersey: Princeton University Press, 1995

Schaffer, Simon, "Astronomers Mark Time: Discipline and the Personal Equation", *Science in Context*, 2 (1988): 115–45

Sibum, Otto, "Reworking the Mechanical Value of Heat: Instruments of Precision and Gestures of Accuracy in Early Victorian England", *Studies of the History and Philosophy of Science*, 26 (1995): 73–106

Smith, Crosbie and M. Norton Wise, *Energy and Empire: A Biographical Study of Lord Kelvin*, Cambridge and New York: Cambridge University Press, 1989

Sydenham, P.H., *Measuring Instruments: Tools of Knowledge and Control*, Stevenage: Peter Peregrinus, 1979

Wise, M. Norton (ed.), *The Values of Precision*, Princeton, New Jersey: Princeton University Press, 1995

The historiographical interest of this subject lies in the fact that measurement is never a simple process of quantifying empirical work. The reasons why scientists and technologist strive to measure things, and the means by which they do so, are by no means self-evident. Moreover, the important question of what constitutes "accuracy" or "precision" in a given measurement is tied up with issues of disciplinary power, commercial interest, experimental skill, and spatial management. The issue of standards for calibrating measurements is dealt with in this volume under the heading "metrology" – a term often misleadingly used as a synonym for "measurement".

SYDENHAM argues that while scientists and technologists like himself have produced ever more sophisticated measuring tools, they have not been able to explain very much about the process of measurement itself. The central problem is that no rigorous connection can be drawn between the results extracted from measuring instruments and the knowledge putatively built on them. He criticizes several major attempts to establish such a connection, and concludes that the meaning ascribed to any particular measurement depends on the conventions adopted by the user. He further suggests that to understand historically why certain measurement instruments and not others come to be given a special status among the scientific community, we should examine the contexts of commerce and engineering that generated them, looking particularly at the craft skills deployed in their creation and use.

Writing in the 1950s, KOYRÉ contended that measurement was a characteristic feature of modern science, judging that quantitative knowledge is fundamentally more valuable than the qualitative Aristotelian natural philosophy that preceded it. Yet he argues that previous historians had rarely studied past measurement experiments with sufficient historical sensitivity, criticizing them for writing about such experiments as though they had happened in a modern laboratory. Ironically, by looking more carefully at the conditions of Galileo's measurement experiments, Koyré concluded that Galileo could not possibly have undertaken them in the manner that he had claimed, since there were too many sources of error and inexactitude to arrive at results that were so congenial; as a platonist, Koyré inferred that Galileo must have intuited his results. His general contention is that measurement was such a problematic enterprise in the scientific revolution that it cannot have been as important as metaphysics in bringing about the development of modern science.

KUHN also presents a critical account of the epistemological functions of measurement in the paradigms and revolutions of modern physical science. Noting that no experiment ever gives *quite* the expected numerical result – an inevitable discrepancy known facetiously as the fifth law of thermodynamics – he raised important questions about what counted as "reasonable" agreement between a theoretical prediction and an experimental measurement that tested it. For example, while a mere order of magnitude similarity was considered reasonable in cosmology, within spectroscopy a concurrence of as many as six or eight significant figures was required to accomplish such "agreement". Kuhn observed that such elastic notions of "agreement" were more than just discipline-relative, they were also historically mutable. He concluded that decisions about when a measurement and a prediction were in "reasonable" agreement were of necessity conventional in character, and judgements could only be made by drawing on pedagogically-inculcated exemplars of previous good practice.

ADAS argues that a particular obsession with impersonal measurement through material technologies has historically been a feature unique to Western industrial/imperial concerns. He cites many examples of African and Asian cultures in the 18th and 19th centuries that relied on "natural" methods of quantification namely, bodily extension and seasonal, lunar and meteorological rhythms, to gauge distances and times. For such peoples the use of instrumental means could be "sinful", liable to bring bad luck to their user, or simply ill-suited to traditional everyday practices. These indigenous communities promoted values that were antithetical to the thrift, punctuality, and routinization that European colonial administrators believed to be essential to the successful functioning of advanced capitalist societies. Adas thus highlights the existence of some profound cultural presuppositions in Western notions of how measurement should be accomplished.

SMITH & WISE present a rich and detailed biography of a major 19th-century expert on measurement, William Thomson (later Lord Kelvin) in the contexts of his education in Cambridge and Paris, his Glasgow University chair, and the wider panoramas of Victorian imperialism and industry. This work shows how intimately linked were the industrial and intellectual rationales for developing schemes of thermal and electrical measurement. Most notable of all is that measurements of energy and efficiency were central to the interactions between thermodynamics and steam engineering, and between electrical theory and submarine telegraphy. The recurrent focus on the commercial environment of Glasgow illustrate how effective and important it is to locate a history of measurement in the immediate geographical setting of its practitioners.

SCHAFFER's article is a similarly localized study of George Biddell Airy's work as Astronomer Royal at the Greenwich Observatory in the mid-19th century. Airy's difficulties in achieving consistency in the astronomical measurements undertaken by his assistant observers led him to seek ways of independently calibrating their work. Schaffer shows that Airy accomplished this by determining the idiosyncrasies of each observer's reaction times in their individualized "personal" equation, and used this to recalculate their reports of stellar positions. A major feature of Schaffer's argument is that, to maximize the replicability of results and thus the reputation of work at Greenwich, Airy regulated his observers' work with a factory-like managerial supervision. Schaffer suggests that the practical effectiveness of Airy's measurement practices required a totalitarian degree of control over institutional workers.

PORTER draws out the alternative "democratic" associations of measurement in his broad study of the creation of objectivity through quantification in Europe and America in the 19th century. He argues that the development of rigorous schemes of quantification in areas such as accountancy, insurance, and civil engineering did not, as has often been tacitly maintained, derive from progressive imperatives inherent in these disciplines. Rather to gain authority within their respective cultural contexts, practitioners in these fields used abstract measurements to present an image of their work in the guise of objective impersonality. Porter's political argument is that such processes of quantification were adopted where no elites were strong enough to administrate through more traditional modes of authority, thereby forcing populations lacking trust in social institutions to acquiesce instead in the apparently implacable governance of numbers.

GOODAY's (1990) analysis of the genesis of physics laboratories in Britain in the 1860s and 1870s also gives a central explanatory role to the perceived cultural qualities of measurement. Seeking ways to promote the disciplinary and institutional expansion of experimental physics through novel kinds of laboratory teaching, physicists alluded to contemporary debates on the industrial and pedagogical efficacy of "accuracy" and "exactitude" in arguing that laboratories devoted to physical measurement would be an effective way of serving Britain's cultural and economic needs. Gooday shows that, having won the institutional space and resources needed for the task, and attracting students in significant numbers from various sections of the population, these physicists implemented a nationwide programme of laboratory measurement that was driven not by commitments to physical theory, nor (simply) to metrological standards, but rather to the cross-contextual imperative to measure for the virtues to be gained by measurement in itself.

Taking a less irenic view of the social consequences of quantification, HUNT examines the micro-politics of measurement in the diagnosis of the failure of the 1858 transatlantic telegraph cable. He looks at the way in which two principal groups of telegraph experts namely the "scientists" and the "practical men", singled out as a convenient scapegoat one individual allied with neither group who shared none of their measurement practices. The cable's electrician, E.O.W. Whitehouse was cast as the villain because of his idiosyncratic and persistent use of his own "magneto-electrometer" to measure the relevant electrical parameters of cable operation, giving readings that other practitioners deemed to have little physical significance. Hunt's conclusion is that highlighting Whitehouse's lack of credibility in telegraphic measurement enabled the leading participants in the cable enterprise to evade responsibility for their own part in the cable's failure.

OLESKO shows that throughout the last four decades of the 19th century there were stark differences between German and British techniques of accomplishing "accurate" measurements of electrical resistance. These differences concerned not only the material basis of resistance standards, Germans preferring liquid mercury to the British use of metal alloys, but also the protocols of processing measurement data. Olesko shows that the emphasis placed by Werner Siemens and Friedrich Kohlrausch on the importance of rigorous statistical analysis of errors led them to question results published by the British, the accuracy of which was premissed rather less transparently on the trustworthiness of the experimenters. She also tells how Ernst Dorn, recomputed the absolute value of the ohm in 1898 by a statistical analysis of both German and other researchers' results, each being "weighted", however, on the basis of its *prima facie* trustworthiness – rather than on the British model of "character" based determinations of accuracy.

MACKENZIE argues that the perceived necessity of ballistic "accuracy" in the deployment of intercontinental guided nuclear missiles from the 1950s to the 1980s was quite contingent on fluctuations in the agenda of US military policy. Increased "accuracy", being the enhanced capacity to land a nuclear warhead within a specified distance of its target, was not the inevitable direction of ongoing technical developments in ballistic engineering. The importance of Charles Stark Draper's (expensive) gyroscopic accomplishment range-accuracy was negated when the targeting of individual sites was displaced on the military agenda by that of blanket bombing. However, if the political context so demanded, there was every chance that accuracy could become strategically relevant once more. Even so it is clear there were different ways of construing the meaning and implementation of accuracy in the US and USSR that depended on subtle differences of cultural organization.

The papers collected together in the volume edited by WISE, map the striking historical contingencies in the epistemological, practical and moral value attributed to "precision". In Golinski's piece "The Nicety of Experiment", we see how Lavoisier's defence of his oxygen-based theory of chemical combustion by reference to precise measurements on reaction products was challenged by Priestley and others as no more than a rhetorical device. Gooday's chapter "The Morals of Energy Metering" shows that physicists challenged the precision of electrical determinations of Joule's constant made with ammeters and voltmeters, arguing that these engineering instruments were so decadently easy to use that the moral quality of the precision achieved was thereby vitiated. Warwick's chapter on "The Laboratory of Theory" draws attention to the way in which the calculation of mathematical tables evokes problems of exactitude in a manner directly analogous to the problems of physical measurement.

In his account of controversial French efforts to determine the curvature of the earth in the 1730s, ILIFFE has shown that many difficulties attended the practice of geodetic measurement out in the field. Maupertuis experienced great difficulties in overcoming the scepticism of critics regarding the deleterious effect on the calibration of his surveying instruments during the arduous journey to Lapland and of the inclement conditions encountered at the destination. As a defence against their challenges to the accuracy of his measurements, Maupertuis had only his reputation, the vouched good conduct of his teamsmen, and his rhetorical skill in reporting and debating, to support his conclusion that the earth's poles were indeed slightly flattened – not elongated as his adversaries so wished to prove. As Iliffe shows, these and other negotiating resources were barely sufficient to convince the Académie des Sciences of the credibility of his work – and it was thoroughly discredited a few decades later anyway.

Another recent historical theme is the difficulty of establishing unequivocally what it is that is being measured. SIBUM reconstructs James Joule's earliest attempts to establish the existence of a universal "mechanical equivalent of heat" in the 1840s, and showing thereby the problems of using highly localized measuring resources to persuade fellow British experimenters of an unexpected new result. In making detailed measurements on temperature rises induced in stirred water, he used thermometers and subtle techniques that were unique to Joule as a Manchester brewer's son with access to the temperature-controlled environments of the brewery industry. According to Sibum, the difficulties contemporaries had in replicating Joule's result arose because they did not have the "gestural knowledge" that Joule deployed to measure the amount of heat produced by frictional work. Such knowledge was in any case scarcely visible to them since reference to important aspects of it was absent from Joule's papers; much of Sibum's article is accordingly devoted to recovering this form of tacit knowledge, and recounts his attempts to infer how Joule conducted his experiments by reconstructing the environment and skills that Joule had originally employed.

GOODAY (1997) shows how academic physics laboratories in British cities of the 1860s to 1880s were afflicted with a range of chaotic disturbances that compromised – or even comprised – the identity of what physicists were attempting to measure. Rather than suppressing perturbations caused by vibration from passing vehicles and humans, as well as more inexplicable variations in readings, physicists explicitly highlighted this issue in published accounts of their experimental work. Gooday argues that this strategy of honesty was necessary since many readers would have doubted the credibility of experimental reports had reference to such well-known difficulties been omitted – despite the fact that such admissions presented critics with ammunition to challenge the integrity of the experimental environment employed. Only by the use of effective narrative methods could readers give credence to the author's claims about the nature of what was being registered in measurement experiments.

JOHNSTON discusses the complex process by which the measurement of colour emerged in the century or so up to World War II. The major difficulty in this project lay in the persistent disagreements among physicists, psychologist and photometrists about what actually constituted the nature of colour. Johnston relates how several attempts were made to negotiate a compromise between the commercial need for quantitative descriptions with the perceived subjectivity of colour judgement. He shows how contingently the international CIE colour system, numerically defining the three primary components of blue, green and red in a "psychophysical" scheme of colorimetry was formulated by international committees in 1939. The import of this paper is that this now well-entrenched scheme of colour quantification is strongly conventional in character, and the measurement of colour would subsequently have been conducted in a quite different fashion had the political manoeuvrings of transient committees been otherwise.

Measurement theories have won relatively little attention from historians, probably because such theories have often historically followed the successful practice of measurement, and thus have required little attention from historians seeking to account for the development of such practices. FUNCTOWICZ & RAVETZ discuss the ways in which the theorization of measurement emerged in the early 20th century as Norman Campbell and Percy Bridgman attempted to resolve uncertainties and ambiguities that arose in extant schemes of measurement. DIEZ argues that the now predominant measurement theory formulated by Suppes in 1951 was moulded from two distinct traditions: the work of Hermann von Helmholtz (1887), O. Hölder (1901) and Campbell (1920) on axiomatics and "real morphisms", and S.S. Stevens's classic article of 1946 on the theory of "scales" and transformations in measurement. Many historical questions still remain to be resolved concerning the relation between the theory and practice of measurement, and how – or indeed how far – measurements have come to be resiliently authoritative in scientific practices of the past.

GRAEME J.N. GOODAY

See also Metrology

Mechanization

Adas, Michael, *Machines as the Measure of Men: Science, Technology and Ideologies of Western Dominance*, Ithaca, New York: Cornell University Press, 1989

Barnett, George Ernest, *Chapters on Machinery and Labor*, Cambridge, Massachusetts: Harvard University Press, 1926; reprinted, Carbondale: Southern Illinois University Press, 1969

Giedion, Siegfried, *Technology and Western Civilization*, Oxford and New York: Oxford University Press, 1948

Habakkuk, H.J., *American and British Technology in the Nineteenth Century: The Search for Labour-Saving Inventions*, Cambridge: Cambridge University Press, 1962

Hounshell, David A., *From the American System to Mass Production, 1800–1932: The Development of Manufacturing Technology in the United States*, Baltimore: Johns Hopkins University Press, 1984

Hughes, Thomas P., "Machines, Megamachines, and Systems", in *In Context: History and the History of Technology – Essays in Honor of Melvin Kranzberg*, edited by S.H. Cutcliffe and Robert C. Post, Bethlehem, Pennsylvania: Lehigh University Press, and London: Associated University Presses, 1989

Jerome, Harry C., *Mechanization in Industry*, New York: National Bureau of Economic Research, 1934

Kranzberg, Melvin and Carroll W. Pursell Jr (eds), *Technology in Western Civilization*, 2 vols, Oxford and New York: Oxford University Press, 1967

Landes, David S., *The Unbound Prometheus: Technological Change and Industrial Development in Western Europe from 1750 to the Present*, Cambridge: Cambridge University Press, 1969

McPherson, Natalie, *Machines and Economic Growth: The Implications for Growth Theory of the History of the Industrial Revolution*, Westport, Connecticut: Greenwood Press, 1994

Mumford, Lewis, *Technics and Civilization*, London: Routledge and Kegan Paul, and New York: Harcourt Brace, 1934

Pollard, Sidney, *Peaceful Conquest: The Industrialization of Europe 1760–1970*, Oxford and New York: Oxford University Press, 1981; revised edition, 1982

Rosenberg, Nathan (ed.), *The American System of Manufactures: The Report of the Committee on the Machinery of the United States, 1855, and the Special Reports of George Wallis and Joseph Whitworth, 1854*, Edinburgh: Edinburgh University Press, 1969

Salter, Arthur James, *Modern Mechanization and Its Effects on the Structure of Society*, London: Oxford University Press, 1933

Sawyer, John E., "The Social Basis of the American System of Manufacturing", *Journal of Economic History*, 14 (1954): 361–79

Susskind, Charles, *Understanding Technology*, Baltimore: Johns Hopkins University Press, 1973

Over two millennia ago, Aristotle called politics "the most sovereign of all the arts and sciences". Arguably, technology has come to occupy much the same central position within contemporary society, although the fact is scarcely recognized. Nevertheless, this fact has been perceived by certain political scientists, economists, sociologists, and demographers, not to mention historians, over the last two centuries, who have turned to technology in order to gain a more complete understanding of their own disciplines. This phenomenon began with Adam Smith and Jean Baptiste Say, and continued with Charles Babbage and Karl Marx – all students of that great transition, the industrial revolution – and provides some evidence for supposing that technology (however defined) is the new "sovereign". Indeed, the Western world is what it is by reason of the technology that it has created. These writers fixed their gaze on the "engines" of change – the machines (the prime movers), and the machines driven by those prime movers – and on the social and economic consequences of what has proved to be a constantly accelerating process of mechanization.

Mechanization did not, of course, begin with the Industrial Revolution. The first decisive development, or perhaps the first visible evidence of such development, in the West belongs to the 12th century. A result of this long-standing fascination with technology, and especially with machines, is that the literature on the subject is very large, and is far from being the work of historians of technology. At the same time, because mechanization is so vast a subject, and so intimately linked with society, culture, and industrialization as a whole, it touches virtually everything, so that few writers have attempted to address it as an entity in its own right. Perhaps the nearest approaches to a comprehensive treatment of the subject are to be found in the works of Giedion and Jerome. Habakkuk's study, although concerned only with Britain and the United States in the 19th century, should also be mentioned as especially important in this respect.

BARNETT sought to study the human cost of mechanization as machines displaced skilled labour. By examining concrete cases, he hoped to quantify the scale and pace of the displacement of craftsmen by machines in printing, stone-cutting, and bottle manufacture. Predictably, perhaps, he found it impossible to generalize, as each case was really *sui generis*. It appeared for the most part, however, that skill nearly always retained its market value, even if adjustment was inevitable. (This is some way, however, from Schumpeter's conception of "creative destruction".)

Writing in the 1930s, SALTER saw in the evolving technology a possibility of the blight that 19th-century mechanization had visited on the Ruhr, the Pittsburgh region, and the Black Country in England, being lifted. Salter argued that a more sophisticated technology might permit the rehumanizing of the work-place, and bring with it a renewed emphasis on skills. He further argued that this was only possible however, with the political will to create adequate social structures capable of containing the destructive potential latent in Western technology.

MUMFORD's stated objective is clear and simple: to explain how the development of the machine has completely modified the material basis and cultural form of Western civilization during the last 1000 years. This involved examining the preliminary process of ideological and social preparation that has permitted the West to adapt its way of life to the pace and capacities of the machine.

JEROME's work is a wide-ranging review of the course of mechanization in the US from c.1890 onwards, in which he attempted to consider the economy as a whole. Perhaps the most valuable part of the book is his review, in chapter 6, of the variety of possible approaches to the problem of measuring the rate of change in mechanization. Despite the visible effects of mechanization, Jerome concluded that there was "no one adequate single measure", and that one must create "a composite picture afforded by a number of approximate assays". The evidence seemed to suggest (and this was in line with the teaching of the classical economists) that the rate of change in mechanization was relatively stable over time, although sectoral studies revealed vast differences; i.e. window glass was 98% machine-made, but bricklaying was 100% manual. Frederick Mills's introduction to Jerome's work is a valuable essay in its own right.

GIEDION called his work a contribution to anonymous history, because he was dealing with objects and processes normally ignored by historians. Giedion was not greatly concerned with the antecedents of the Industrial Revolution, since his target was to investigate what he called "high mechanization". This had begun in the United States after 1800, and involved the replacement of complicated craft skills by machine production using unskilled labour, the prerequisite of which was a highly developed division of labour. This had been recognized long before by Adam Smith in his classic description of pin manufacture: 18 workers, each of whom was responsible for one operation only, acting like a machine in the reduction of a strip of wire to final pin form. Full mechanization (c.1913–39) was represented by the assembly line, ". . . wherein the entire factory is consolidated into a synchronous organism". A series of case studies of how craft skills were taken over by machines includes, as an exemplary case, Linus Yale's work on locks, while further studies concentrate on bread-making, butchery, and the mechanization of the home. There is no triumphalism here; future generations, Giedion thought, would look back on these developments as "mechanized barbarism, the most repulsive barbarism of all". This is, indeed, a very long way from the optimism with which Karl Marx viewed the first flush of mechanization a century earlier.

There are a number of reasons why SAWYER's article makes extraordinarily interesting reading, the most important relating to its basic structure. Describing the period of the Marshall plan, when the US poured money and machines into Europe to rebuild its economy after 1945, Sawyer shows that the returns were regularly less than those yielded by similar investments in the US. British visitors to the US found no obvious technological explanation for superior American performance, and everything pointed to the crucial importance of socio-cultural factors. Sawyer then contrasts Europe with the US in the 1850s, revealing that, even at the time, the attention of British visitors was drawn as much to the "immense drive" of the people of New England as to their technological virtuosity.

HABAKKUK, in his classic work, questioned why some countries of European stock invented and adopted mechanical methods more rapidly than others. His objective was to explain the astonishingly rapid development of mechanization in the US in the 19th century; its progress was such that, as early as the 1850s, the US was already ahead of England – the home of the Industrial Revolution – in the development of automatic machinery. Was the key determinant the high price of American labour? Although Habakkuk felt justified in tackling the problem from this angle, it was no simple matter of cause and effect: "American inventive ingenuity was the result rather than the cause of mechanization". There was, for example, the question of factor endowment to consider, and ultimately perhaps something as indeterminate as "the restlessness of American life". It was possible furthermore to compile a formidable list of British inventions (cf. p.121) which, failing to flourish in Britain, were taken up in the US and which, when re-exported to Britain, were hailed as wonders of modernity and progress.

KRANZBERG & PURSELL's outline history, consisting of some 90 essays, has 10 that should be noted in particular. In volume 1, these are chapters 1, 23, 33, 38 and 45, the first of which, "The importance of technology in human affairs", makes the point that *homo sapiens* is also *homo faber*: that man makes tools but equally tools have made man, an idea at the heart of Marxian and post-Marxian thinking on the subject. In volume 2, chapters 2, 4, 23, 35 and 41 should be noted. The last of these is a salutary warning against attempting to extrapolate from current trends.

A comparative study of the course of European industrialization from 1750 to c.1950 is offered by LANDES, although he excludes any treatment of agriculture, transport systems, and demography. This study has the great merit of making clear and wide-ranging points on the important issues: for example, coal is termed "the bread of industry", and the effect of the Industrial Revolution world-wide is seen as akin to "Eve's tasting of the fruit of the tree of knowledge".

ROSENBERG's introduction to the *Reports* of 1855 is devoted to placing these documents in their historical context, and to presenting a valuable digest of the literature generated over the last 100 years by the debate over "the American system of manufactures" – the onset of full-blown mechanization. Of specific interest here was the development of special purpose machinery for working both wood and metal in the US, the New England states having taken up several ideas (often brought over to the US by the inventors themselves) that had failed to flourish in the UK.

SUSSKIND's contribution to the debate is valuable, not least for his examination of an astonishing paradox at the heart of Western culture: the prevalent denial of the central role played by technology in the formation of that culture. This is an extremely well-written work, that may inspire readers to seek out the literature referenced by the author.

POLLARD confines his study to the essential core of industrialization – power mechanization – and to an examination of the industrial development of Europe on a regional basis, the process "transforming and being transformed by [each] changing geographical setting and historical sequence".

HOUNSHELL provides a comprehensive analysis of the development of the best-known mass-production techniques in the US, from those used in the manufacture of sewing machines, wood-working machinery, agricultural machinery, the bicycle, and the automobile, to flexible mass-production pioneered by Alfred Sloan at General Motors in the 1930s. The sequence begins at the armouries at Springfield and Harper's Ferry, which in the 1850s were already specifying the interchangeability of parts when assigning contracts to outside suppliers.

HUGHES suggests that "the second discovery of America" is a more accurate phrase with which to describe the last two centuries of American history, than the more usual concept of "the frontier experience". This idea of a second discovery is based on the perceptions of European visitors in the early 1900s, who, seeing the vast mechanical development of the country, concluded that the US was "the nation of machines, megamachines, and systems", and that such figures as F.W. Taylor and Henry Ford best epitomized this phenomenon.

ADAS shows how, even at the beginning of their reconnaissance of the extra-European world in the 15th century, Europeans were accustomed to measuring the cultural level of the peoples they encountered by comparing their technical capacity with the European level of accomplishment – ". . . few disputed that machines were the most reliable measure of humankind". Such an outlook was long-lived, but around 1900 it began to give way to anxiety concerning the price that Europeans, and *a fortiori* the Americans, had paid, and would continue to pay, for their machine-dominated condition.

The basic question McPHERSON sets herself concerns one of the salient features of our period: why do such enormous disparities in wealth exist between states? These disparities are largely the product of industrial development, but this raises the question as to why so few countries have managed to make the transition to industrialization. She concludes that the "virtuous circle growth", characteristic of the West, is short-circuited when populations breed to subsistence.

GRAHAM HOLLISTER-SHORT

See also Alienation; Marx; Technology

Medical Ethics

Annas, George J. and Michael A. Grodin (eds), *The Nazi Doctors and the Nuremberg Code: Human Rights in Human Experimentation*, Oxford and New York: Oxford University Press, 1992

Beauchamp, Tom L. and James F. Childress, *Principles of Biomedical Ethics*, New York and Oxford: Oxford University Press, 1979; 4th edition, 1994

Campbell, Alastair, Grant Gillet and Gareth Jones (eds), *Practical Medical Ethics*, Auckland and New York: Oxford University Press, 1992

Engelhardt Jr., H. Tristram, *Foundations of Bioethics*, Oxford and New York: Oxford University Press, 1986; 2nd edition, 1996

Faden, Ruth R. and Tom L. Beauchamp, with Nancy M.P. King, *A History and Theory of Informed Consent*, Oxford and New York: Oxford University Press, 1986

Levine, Robert J., *Ethics and Regulation of Clinical Research*, Baltimore: Urban and Schwarzenberg, 1981; 2nd edition, 1986

Ramsey, Paul, *The Patient as Person: Explorations in Medical Ethics*, New Haven, Connecticut: Yale University Press, 1970

Sherwin, Susan, *No Longer Patient: Feminist Ethics and Health Care*, Philadelphia: Temple University Press, 1992

Veatch, Robert M., *A Theory of Medical Ethics*, New York: Basic Books, 1981

Medical ethics has now become a fully-fledged academic discipline in its own right, with the full panoply of journals, institutes and centres, international associations, graduate programmes, and so forth. This is a relatively recent state of affairs; until a generation ago, medical ethics was almost exclusively a question for doctors, as a matter of professional definition and self-regulation, and theologians, as a matter of pastoral guidance and what can loosely be called canon law. RAMSEY's important book reflects some of these earlier concerns, as expressed by an eminent Protestant theologian, and also looks forward to many of the concerns that characterize medical ethics in its contemporary form.

Three key events might define the situation in which this discipline began to take its modern shape: first, the Nuremberg Trial of doctors and bio-scientists involved in medical atrocities in the Nazi concentration camps; second, the rise of the welfare state and (partial) nationalization of medical care in Britain and elsewhere; and third, the liberalization of abortion law in Britain and the United States in the late 1960s and early 1970s. The first event had two effects: it undermined the medical (and scientific) profession's claims to self-policed integrity, and it placed patient consent at the centre of ethics, as opposed to "paternal" care. The patient's right, as a subset of human rights, to be free from coercion and to be treated as a self-determining individual, even – especially – *in extremis*, became recognized as of paramount importance. This issue, its history, significance, and ethical details are very well surveyed in the book edited by ANNAS & GRODIN, which helpfully supplies many of the key codes of ethics relevant to the medical profession and to patients. Its particular focus is on the rights of patients who are research subjects, but it is also relevant to other patients, and to "healthy volunteer" subjects in medical research. One important issue addressed is whether patient rights and physician obligations are culturally determined or are historical universals (and if the former, what should be done internationally). LEVINE's work is by far the best on the many aspects of research ethics, providing a sound treatment of the famous, central issue of "informed consent", while FADEN & BEAUCHAMP give a valuable, albeit US-centred, account of the legal and philosophical history of the concept.

The second event, the incorporation of much of the medical profession's sphere within the state, had a long history, but the significance of the creation of the British National Health Service is enormous. Ethically, it signalled a new set of obligations to what was once the "medical dyad" of doctor and patient. In fact, the Hippocratic Oath reminds us that the doctor also owed obligations to his professional peers, so this mythical dyad was in fact always a triad. But the state management of medicine has had wide-ranging cultural and political effects on the relations between doctor and patient, notably in formalizing and making visible the economic fact that medicine – like anything else – operates with scarce resources, and so choices must be made between patients, and between present and future opportunities. On the other hand, while some of these realities were already reflected in the ability to pay the doctor's fee, state provision was now intended to overcome the unjust distribution of access to health care by ability to pay, and replace it with distribution of access by need. Justice thus becomes a second central element in medical ethics. Important chapters on this are to be found in VEATCH (who favours a social contract model), Engelhardt (who uses a constructivist theory of rights), and Beauchamp & Childress.

The third event, the liberalization of abortion law, inaugurates three important themes. The first is the creation of "bioethics"; the second is the expansion of patients' rights within medical law to include freedom-to as well as freedom-from; and the third is the recognition of the ineluctability of moral pluralism. Bioethics is the study of ethical issues that shape and arise from innovations in the biosciences, including medicine. This inquiry has become detached from medical ethics as such, largely because the issues of religious ethics, social acceptability, and social and political power are broader and more complex than simply the resolution of the rights and duties involved in the medical encounter between a doctor and a patient. Often, the technical aspect of medical innovation is relatively straightforward, while the moral consequences are large. A good example is *in utero* screening of foetuses for some genetic disorders: while technically this is a straightfor-

ward procedure, it raises the possible ethical problem of the "routinizing" of abortion for "non-viable" foetuses. Bioethical issues are well surveyed in CAMPBELL, GILLET & JONES. Linked to this is the second issue of the increase in patients' rights: while it is increasingly accepted that a patient has the right actively to choose some course of treatment that the doctor cannot deny out of hand, it is not the state's business to legislate for those choices, although it is the state's business to protect the patients' liberty.

The history of medical ethics is often shaped by the history of medical law, as FADEN & BEAUCHAMP demonstrate, yet the law–ethics connection remains extremely unclear. And this raises the third issue concerning moral pluralism: states and philosophers recognize that on many moral questions related to the practice of medicine, traditions and arguments are in conflict, and that conflict is very likely incommensurable. This has the apparent consequence that no clear and incontestable foundation for medical ethics can be found.

Two responses to this deduction dominate medical ethics, and both are species of liberalism. The first response is to deny that there is an incommensurable dispute; instead, focusing on core values, and some analytically obvious features of the concept of medicine, should remind us of some central facts that any ethic must respect. Hence disagreements are merely disagreements about glosses on these facts and principles, and disputes are piecemeal and resolvable. This is the essence of the "principlist" approach of BEAUCHAMP & CHILDRESS. From these principles (beneficence, non-maleficence, autonomy, and justice), the various rights and duties can be derived; and while many issues are left open by this method, this is the normal human condition. This is essentially an ethical liberalism, taking freedom and respect as core ethical values.

The second response is a political liberalism, which takes the variability of ethical belief as irremovable, but the common need to live together as motivating some consensus concerning the rules of fair discussion and decision-making. This approach concentrates on a quasi-legal approach to "procedural justice". By far the most sophisticated approach to this is ENGEL-HARDT, a Roman Catholic who takes the postmodern social condition as his premise for an investigation into the need for a secular ethics in a pluralistic world. In Veatch there is valuable material on the different approaches of non-Christian religions to medical ethics, and in Campbell, Gillet & Jones attention is paid to multi-cultural issues beyond the religious. Veatch's social contract model stands as an alternative to Engelhardt and to Beauchamp & Childress, and may be aligned with either.

A valuable service performed by Beauchamp & Childress is the analysis of the application of various different moral theories to medical ethical problems. (Notably Utilitarianism, which has widespread support among philosophers, but has less popular appeal). New developments in medical ethics involve the application of feminist, narrative, and virtue ethics, focusing on the concept of care, and shifting the focus from medicine to health care more generally. Feminist approaches are discussed and exemplified in SHERWIN, and a useful survey of virtue and narrative ethics can be found in Campbell, Gillet & Jones. The crucial insight here is that the patient's experience now takes centre stage, rather than the "doctor's dilemma", and the period of a rather formalist approach to rights is now being replaced by a richer account of the social practices of health care and rights.

RICHARD ASHCROFT

See also Doctor–Patient Relationship

Medical Instruments

Blume, Stuart S., *Insight and Industry: On the Dynamics of Technological Change in Medicine*, Cambridge, Massachusetts: MIT Press, 1992

Bud, Robert and Deborah Jean Warner (eds), *Instruments of Science: An Historical Encyclopedia*, New York: Garland, 1997

Davis, Audrey B., *Medicine and Its Technology: An Introduction to the History of Medical Instrumentation*, Westport, Connecticut: Greenwood Press, 1981

Edmonson, J.M., "Asepsis and the Transformation of Surgical Instruments", *Transactions and Studies of the College of Physicians*, 13 (1991): 75–91

Hacking, Ian, *Representing and Intervening: Introductory Topics in the Philosophy of Natural Science*, Cambridge and New York: Cambridge University Press, 1983

Lawrence, Ghislaine, "The Ambiguous Artifact, Surgical Instruments and the Surgical Past", in *Medical Theory, Surgical Practice: Studies in the History of Surgery*, edited by Christopher Lawrence, London and New York: Routledge, 1992

Postel-Vinay, Nicolas, *A Century of Arterial Hypertension 1896–1996*, Chichester: Wiley, 1996

Reiser, Stanley J., *Medicine and the Reign of Technology*, Cambridge and New York: Cambridge University Press, 1978

Spink, M.S. and G.I. Lewis (eds and trans), *Albucassis on Surgery and Instruments: A Definitive Edition of the Arabic Text*, London: Wellcome Institute, 1973

Vetter, André and Marie-José Lamothe, *Les Outils du corps*, Paris: Hier et demain, 1978

Those familiar with the history of Western medicine will immediately recognize the contrasting images of medieval physician and barber-surgeon: the physician, attending to the art of diagnosis from theories and external observations, holds a urine glass to the light; the barber-surgeon, symbol of internal intervention and technical manipulation, holds a lancet over a patient whose blood flows into a bowl. As our historically informed observer would also know, these two medical practitioners were of strikingly different social status. The physician was a member of the urban, university educated elite; the barber-surgeon was apprentice-trained, usually poor, and living among the poor in towns and villages. Indeed, these representations underscore a fundamental dichotomy between theory and practice, art and technique, that to some extent continues to inform today's understanding of medical instruments.

Historians, perhaps influenced by this dichotomy, have long ignored the role of instruments in their studies of medical history. Often, when instruments have been acknowledged, they have served merely to illustrate texts, with the underlying assumption that their medical use was transparent. On display in texts, collectors' galleries, or public museums, these instruments have often been perceived as a kind of "cabinet of curious tools". An example of this approach is VETTER & LAMOTHE, which provides just such a richly-illustrated pageant of instruments from prehistory to modern times. Its visual and historical presentations suggest, somewhat anachronistically, that these instruments are the forerunners of modern medical technology.

Evidence of the value of examining instruments beyond their illustrative capacity has recently been tentatively provided in SPINK & LEWIS, a study of the Arab Andalusian manuscript of Zahrawi (10th century), better known as Albucassis, by the curators of an exhibition in Marburg, Germany. The text itself provides the first detailed representation of medical instruments; its illustrations schematically present surgical instruments (mainly cauters of various shapes), accompanied by brief indications of their use. The exhibition's curators fabricated realistic models from these illustrations, in an attempt to go beyond elliptic comment.

A combination of more recent concerns, however, has brought the study of medical instruments into the centre of numerous historical studies. These concerns range from the growing technological orientation of medical practice itself, to a heightened awareness of the importance of material culture evident in a variety of academic disciplines, from archeology and anthropology, to sociology. Between is a spectrum of social and cultural concerns about the changing nature of medical practice, the understanding of the body, and the treatment of the patient – central to all of which are medical instruments.

For an introduction to the kinds of questions raised by the historical study of instruments, one would do well to start with two texts: LAWRENCE and REISER. Lawrence's article is a kind of manifesto of medical instrument analysis, setting out a critique of traditional approaches and challenges for future directions. Although she does not believe that their study will reveal "new" knowledge about the past, Lawrence does think that investigation of instruments in action – as the outcome of the process of invention, as products or commodities, as designed and distributed by distinct individuals, or as employed (broadly speaking) by others – will raise new historical questions and provide unique historical insight. Reiser's text, on the other hand, is one of the earliest to place medical instruments in their socio-cultural context. His sweeping analysis examines instruments (including the microscope, stethoscope and sphygmomanometer), medical machines, and complex socio-technical environments (such as the diagnostic laboratory) as they were developed by inventors and adopted by medical practitioners. In so doing, Reiser argues that medical technologies not only produce information that must be interpreted, but that they also affect the practice of medicine – particularly the relationship of doctor and patient, and the latter's perception of his/her own body.

DAVIS is an early work in that direction. Relying on the analysis of many objects, this book focuses on the end of the 19th century as a critical time for the development of medical instrumentation. This argument is set in the context of medicine's quantitative turn, which Davis connects to forces such as the growing demand for the standardization of diagnosis procedures, the expansion of the medical profession, and the extension of experimental methods to medicine. Further, Davis connects her understanding of medical instrumentation to an important economic concern: the search for criteria for tabulating medical data, which was done primarily for the sake of insurance companies, eager to establish their business on a better knowledge of life expectancy. POSTEL-VINAY's recent book illustrates this trend with studies (and pictures of instruments) drawn from the field of hypertension, an area of particular interest for insurers.

Debates within the sociology of knowledge have provided some of the impetus for the growing historical interest in instruments. Advocates of the actor-network theory, such as Bruno Latour, have argued that serious analytic attention must be paid to objects, from laboratories to microbes, as actors in the construction of science. HACKING's classic text demonstrates the promise held by attending to science as it is practised, not simply as it is theorized – that is, as it intervenes, not just as it represents. In this way, he sheds light on the complex pattern that results from the interweaving of experiment, theory, invention, and technology, that is science in action. Those interested particularly in medical instruments will want to read his chapter on learning to see through the microscope.

In this spirit, museum curators have also begun to pay closer attention to the potential significance of their collections. The Science Museum in London and the Smithsonian Institution joined forces to compile the encyclopedic text–*Instruments of Science* (BUD & WARNER). Contributions by an interdisciplinary collection of authors treat not just the "instruments", but also the "machines" and the "tests", not just of science, but of medicine. Entries include more traditional objects, such as microscopes, and stethoscopes, but also extend to the intelligence test and the polygraph. Moreover, some challenge our understanding of "instruments" (beyond standard questions concerning their distinction from simple tools and more complex technological machines): for example, there are entries on E. coli, drosophila, and "the mouse". From a different museological perspective, scholars have started to look to museum displays in history as a focal point of scientific values and national identity. Within such public displays, instruments become powerful icons for the transmission of culture.

Alongside such broad-ranging treatments of medical instruments are more detailed monographs. Two exemplary studies are provided by Edmondson and Blume. EDMONSON looks to the laboratory, with its arsenal of glassware and engines, in telling the history of the so-called Pasteurian revolution and the impact of germ theory on medical practice. Specifically, he follows the transformation of surgical instruments, in their material construction (from precious wood to metal) and in their shape and design, as they moved toward increasing disposability and sterilizability. In this way, Edmonson investigates the historical marriage of biology and medicine, by studying the coming-together of medical and scientific instruments.

BLUME illuminates the complex set of concerns surrounding another instrumentally-guided medical conception, medical echography. A product of the collaboration of physicians and engineers, the echogram applies the methods of physicists to the exploration of the body. As the knowledge of physics arose from the weapons programs and defense funding of the post-war era, this medical technology came to represent not only the applications of "Big Science" and technology to medicine, but also the desire of some physicists to find "purer", biomedical applications for their knowledge. Moreover, such technologies of medical imagery, which allow physicians to explore the body without opening it, have done much to blur the distinctions between surgeons and physicians. Clinical consequences of this move still remain to be assessed.

From lancet and urine glass to echogram, medical instruments provide historians with a unique vantage point from which to view the development of medicine. They illuminate changes in a practitioner's education, in his/her relationship to patients, and even to those patients' understandings of themselves. The study of instruments production and evolution, and the techniques attached to their applications, can reveal the daily constraints that guide changes in medical practice. Moreover, instruments may further suggest ways in which medical practice helps to create cultures and change societies.

A.M. MOULIN AND KIM PELIS

Medical Specialization

Berlant, Jeffrey Lionel, *Profession and Monopoly: A Study of Medicine in the United States and Great Britain*, Berkeley: University of California Press, 1975

Bynum, W.F., C. Lawrence and V. Nutton (eds), *The Emergence of Modern Cardiology*, London: Wellcome Institute for the History of Medicine, 1985

Cone Jr, Thomas E., *History of American Pediatrics*, Boston: Little Brown, 1979

Cooter, Roger, *Surgery and Society in Peace and War: Orthopaedics and the Organization of Modern Medicine, 1880–1948*, London: Macmillan and University of Manchester, 1993

Crissey, John Thorne and Lawrence Charles Parish, *The Dermatology and Syphilology of the Nineteenth Century*, New York: Praeger, 1981

Dally, Ann, *Women under the Knife: A History of Surgery*, London: Radius, 1991; New York: Routledge, 1992

Donnison, Jean, *Midwives and Medical Men: A History of Inter-Professional Rivalries and Women's Rights*, London: Heinemann and New York: Schocken Books, 1977; 2nd edition, as *Midwives and Medical Men: A History of the Struggle for the Control of Childbirth*, New Barnet, Hertfordshire: Historical Publications, 1988

Eulner, Hans-Heinz, *Die Entwicklung der medizinischen Spezialfächer an den Universitäten des deutschen Sprachgebiets*, Stuttgart: Enke, 1970

Fye, W. Bruce, *American Cardiology: The History of a Speciality and Its College*, Baltimore: Johns Hopkins University Press, 1996

Goldstein, Jan, *Console and Classify: The French Psychiatric Profession in the Nineteenth Century*, Cambridge and New York: Cambridge University Press, 1987

Granshaw, Lindsay, *St. Mark's Hospital, London: A Social History of a Specialist Hospital*, London: King Edward's Hospital Fund, 1985

Leavitt, Judith Walzer, *Brought to Bed: Childbearing in*

America, 1750–1950, New York: Oxford University Press, 1986

Lomax, Elizabeth M.R., *Small and Special: The Development of Hospitals for Children in Victorian Britain*, London: Wellcome Institute, 1996

McGovern, Constance M., *Masters of Madness: Social Origins of the American Psychiatric Profession*, Hanover, New Hampshire: University Press of New England, 1985

Marland, Hilary (ed.), *The Art of Midwifery: Early Modern Midwives in Europe*, London and New York: Routledge, 1993

Maulitz, Russell C. and Diana E. Long, *Grand Rounds: One Hundred Years of Internal Medicine*, Philadelphia: University of Pennsylvania Press, 1988

Moscucci, Ornella, *The Science of Woman: Gynaecology and Gender in England, 1800–1929*, Cambridge and New York: Cambridge University Press, 1990

Peterson, M. Jeanne, *The Medical Profession in Mid-Victorian London*, Berkeley: University of California Press, 1978

Rosen, George, *The Specialization of Medicine with Particular Reference to Ophthalmology*, New York: Froben Press, 1944

Scull, Andrew, *The Most Solitary of Afflictions: Madness and Society in Britain, 1700–1900*, New Haven, Connecticut: Yale University Press, 1993

Shumacker Jr., Harris B., *The Evolution of Cardiac Surgery*, Bloomington: Indiana University Press, 1992

Stevens, Rosemary, *Medical Practice in Modern England: The Impact of Specialization and State Medicine*, New Haven, Connecticut: Yale University Press, 1966

Weisz, George, "The Development of Medical Specialization in Nineteenth-Century Paris", in *French Medical Culture in the Nineteenth Century*, edited by Ann La Berge and Mordechai Feingold, Amsterdam: Rodopi, 1994

Wilson, Adrian, *The Making of Man-Midwifery: Childbirth in England, 1660–1770*, Cambridge, Massachusetts: Harvard University Press, 1995

The specialization of knowledge and of occupational function are prominent features of modernity. The reasons for this are both obvious and contentious: the increase in knowledge makes it impossible for a single individual to master a single discipline, such as medicine or chemistry, much less several disciplines, or the whole encyclopedia. We rely increasingly on technology that we do not understand, and which someone else has to develop and mend when it goes wrong. The age of the Renaissance Man has gone forever.

At the same time, the extent to which specialization is inevitable and "natural", rather than the result of deliberate action by groups of "specialists", is not always clear. This is particularly true within medicine, as a broad occupational discipline and as a body of knowledge. Despite traditional medical occupational diversity in the distinction between physicians, surgeons, and apothecaries (the basic equivalents obtained throughout Europe with only minor variations), there was, until the 19th century, resistance among medical elites to the notion of specialization. Those who "specialized" were deemed to be quacks, and, indeed, three specialist

functions – cutting for bladder stone, setting bones, and operating for cataract – were often performed by itinerants with no formal training or qualifications. The classic account of the development of specialization by ROSEN took ophthalmology (and its relationship to cataract couchers) as its prime example. Rosen worked within the parameters of functionalist sociology, wherein specialization more or less naturally grows out of new knowledge, techniques, or diagnostic or therapeutic equipment. Thus, in this study, the ophthalmoscope, invented in the 1850s by Hermann von Helmholtz (1821–94), played a crucial role in stimulating the speciality of ophthalmology, with its formation of special societies and journals, and autonomous training programmes and standards.

COOTER has analysed the development of another modern speciality from the older occupational pattern – the emergence of orthopaedic surgery from the bone setters. The traditional account placed emphasis on the frequency of trauma during World War I as a stimulus to speciality formation, and while Cooter acknowledges the importance of the war, he emphasizes the calculated actions of individuals and groups, rather than the natural outcome of war and industrial accidents, as the major driving force. Within this scenario, power, prestige, and income become the central issues, while the techniques, training programmes, journals, and societies were part of the consequence, rather than the natural accompaniment of the new speciality.

Special hospitals also provided opportunities for doctors to observe and treat particular diseases or age groups. PETERSON has examined the foundation of special hospitals in mid-Victorian London within the context of the medical profession more generally. She notes that many of the special hospitals were established by ambitious men who had failed to obtain posts in the more prestigious general voluntary hospitals, and who thus sought to establish different niches for themselves. GRANSHAW'S history of St Mark's Hospital, London, for diseases of the colon and rectum provides a good example of the way in which a small hospital could become a leading centre in the gradual development of a surgical speciality, in this case devoted to surgery of the large bowel, and of the interaction between the surgeons and medical specialists in the field of gastroenterology.

LOMAX has examined children's hospitals in 19th-century Britain, and their role in the formation of paediatrics. American paediatrics is the subject of a monograph by CONE; like most historical literature produced by practitioners from within the speciality itself, Cone's narrative assumes that the development of paediatrics is essentially unproblematic.

Rosen had already noted that specialization was relatively easily accepted by the American medical establishment. The same was true in Germany, and EULNER's massive monograph documents the systematic growth of special chairs and institutes in many medical disciplines within the German university framework. Eulner was concerned with sciences such as anatomy, physiology, pharmacology, and pathology, as well as medical and surgical specialities. WEISZ provides a suggestive reading of the French scene, confined to the clinical specialities, but he is also working on a major comparative project that will examine the phenomenon of specialization in four countries: France, Britain, the United States, and Canada.

Curiously, psychiatry was not particularly successful in obtaining compulsory time in 19th-century medical curricula, despite being one of the earliest clinical specialities firmly to establish itself. By the mid-19th century, there were special societies and journals in Germany, France, Britain, and the United States devoted to the subject. SCULL has been particularly analytical in dissecting the aspirations – not always realized – of British alienists, as they were often called. These trappings of professional structure were matched by the provision of publicly-funded asylums, compulsory in England after 1845, although the optimistic belief that insanity treated early could be cured was not borne out in practice, and as the asylums filled up with patients with chronic disorders, the speciality became more administrative than curative. McGOVERN has examined the formation of the Association of Medical Superintendents of American Institutions for the Insane, and the moves by its founding fathers, from the mid-1840s, to secure a niche within the wider medical profession. GOLDSTEIN scrutinized parallel French developments, especially as seen through the intellectual and professional influence of J.E.D. Esquirol (1772–1840) and his pupils. In France, as elsewhere in Europe and North America, psychiatrists obtained a fair amount of public visibility, although it remained a relatively low-prestige speciality, isolated from mainstream medicine and surgery and their increasing association with laboratory science.

Dermatology represents another modern medical speciality with complicated historical roots. Skin diseases were traditionally considered to be the rightful province of the surgeon (they were often treated manually, by the application of an ointment or salve), and because a rash is one of the manifestations of syphilis, the treatment of venereal disease was often included within the surgeon's ken. There was never a complete surgical monopoly within skin and venereal diseases, however, and the fundamental modern monographs on dermatology were written in the early 19th century by Robert Willan (1757–1812) and Thomas Bateman (1778–1821) in Britain, and by Jean Louis Marc Alibert (1768–1837) in France. CRISSEY & PARISH have examined the intellectual and social development of dermatology and syphilology in 19th-century Europe and America.

Gynaecology was another contentious 19th-century speciality. Although, from the 1860's, it clearly benefited from the development of antiseptic surgical techniques, it had earlier roots in the American ovariotomists, and the increasing use of the vaginal speculum. MOSCUCCI has analysed the gender issues that the speciality raised, and the more general subject of women and surgery has been discussed by DALLY. Gynaecology has an intimate association with obstetrics, although the latter developed as a subject of male activity a century or so earlier, and often with acrimonious occupational boundary disputes with female midwives. WILSON has examined the subject for 17th- and early 18th-century England, highlighting in particular the specific social, as well as medical, conditions surrounding childbirth that led to the engagement of the male medical man. The longer-term relationships between midwives and medical men have been recounted by DONNISON and LEAVITT for England and the United States respectively, and the variety of different occupational structures surrounding childbirth in various national contexts is the subject of the collection of essays edited by MARLAND. By focusing on other "advanced" countries, such as The Netherlands, where home delivery by a female midwife is still the norm, the importance of human choice and social structures is highlighted.

All these and several other clinical specialities had achieved some visibility by the end of the 19th century, but the phenomenon has gathered momentum since then. What is called "internal medicine" in the US, and was the purview of the old consultant physician in Britain, has been divided into a variety of specialities, based on organ, system, or mode of causation. A fine collection of essays edited by MAULITZ & LONG examines a number of instances within the American context; these include the development of specialities in infectious diseases, diseases of the kidney (nephrology), gastrointestinal tract (gastroenterology), heart (cardiology), and joints (rheumatology). Other essays examine the growth of a specialist periodical literature and the politics of academic medicine.

STEVENS has provided a systematic analysis of specialization in modern Britain, where the role of the state in medical care and education has been more clearly defined. The central place of the general practitioner within British medicine has meant that speciality formation has developed within the context of a referral system, and that specialities are generally hospital-based.

In addition to ancillary specialities, such as radiology and anaesthesiology, medical and surgical specialities have continued to grow apace. Thus, paediatrics and surgery now have their own cadre of "subspecialities", such as paediatric neurology and endocrine surgery, most of these specialities and subspecialities having an internalist literature. Among the most sophisticated is the literature for cardiology; the essays edited by BYNUM, LAWRENCE & NUTTON examine several aspects of speciality formation, such as its relationship to the development of the electrocardiograph in the early 20th century, and its "naturalness" as a response to the increased incidence of cardiovascular disease. FYE has written a full account of cardiology in modern America, and the development of cardiac surgery as a highly visible surgical subspeciality has been described by SHUMACKER.

All this literature points to the fact that specialism raises, in miniature and in an intraprofessional setting, the same cluster of issues regarding power, prestige, and monopoly that are central to the politics of professionalism more generally. BERLANT offers a comparative account of the search for a medical monopoly in Britain and the United States.

W.F. BYNUM

See also Medical Instruments; Professionalization

Medicine and Law

Clark, Claudia, *Radium Girls: Women and Industrial Health Reform, 1910–1935*, Chapel Hill: University of North Carolina Press, 1997

De Ville, Kenneth Allen, *Medical Malpractice in Nineteenth-Century America: Origins and Legacy*, New York: New York University Press, 1990

Jasanoff, Sheila, *Science at the Bar: Law, Science, and Technology in America*, Cambridge, Massachusetts: Harvard University Press, 1995

Leavitt, Judith, *Typhoid Mary: Captive to the Public's Health*, Boston: Beacon Press, 1996

Mohr, James C., *Doctors and the Law: Medical Jurisprudence in Nineteenth-Century America*, Oxford and New York: Oxford University Press, 1993

Novak, William, *The People's Welfare: Law and Regulation in Nineteenth-Century America*, Chapel Hill: University of North Carolina Press, 1996

Rosenberg, Charles E., *The Trial of the Assassin Guiteau: Psychiatry and Law in the Gilded Age*, Chicago: University of Chicago Press, 1968; reprinted 1989

Rothman, David J., *Strangers at the Bedside: A History of How Law and Bioethics Transformed Medical Decision Making*, New York: Basic Books, 1991

Since at least the time of Alexis de Tocqueville's visit to North America in the middle of the 19th century, observers have remarked on the litigious nature of its citizens. A few others, mostly observers of the modern United States, have been equally impressed with American's dedication to a therapeutic culture. The juxtaposition of these two factors provides insight into an important nexus of power in American history – the volatile relationship between the medical and legal professions. Falling into the interstices between historical fields the long, intimate and often combustible partnership between the law and medicine in the US has received minimal sustained scholarly attention. Practitioners of the two professions have written, sometimes penetratingly, about the intersection of the two fields, but until recently few social scientists have addressed this topic. In these more recent works the 19th century has fared better than the colonial or 20th-century periods, but even in the 19th century we are just begining to understand what this relationship has meant for Americans and their development as a nation.

The best place to begin to get a sense of America's medico-legal culture is MOHR's study. Although dealing only with the 19th century, Mohr's book attempts to analyze physicians' contributions to both litigation and legislation. Mohr's recognition that understanding the relationship between medicine and the law requires familiarity with the doctor's role as expert witness and as policy maker is one of the book's strengths. It is also the source of one of its weaknesses : Mohr's failure to sustain such a broad analysis for the entire period. The physicians' role as policy maker, particularly in public health matters, disappears quickly from the book that devotes most of its attention to a detailed analysis of the various types of courtroom and profession building activities engaged in by 19th-century medico-legal practitioners.

NOVAK helps to fill in the gaps left by Mohr's analysis. Although health regulation is only one of Novak's case studies, he provides valuable insight into the nature of public health decision making. Drawing on analyses of local community records, Novak distances himself from the standard interpretation of 19th century as an era of minimal regulation and *laissez faire* ideals and paints a portrait of an America with a substantial culture of locally based regulation. For Novak, health regulation is an important manifestation of this often overlooked culture of local regulation. Although he overstates his distance from previous scholars, Novak none the less serves a useful purpose by bringing together both the medical and the legal historical literature.

There are a number of other more narrowly focused histories of 19th-century medico-legal topics that make evident the complexity and power of medical and legal collaboration in this era. Two of these works – Rosenberg's account of the trial of President Garfield's assassin Charles Guiteau and De Ville's analysis of the mid-19th century medical malpractice crisis – are particularly noteworthy. ROSENBERG has produced a nuanced reading of America's response to one of the most highly publicized trials of the 19th century. His account of Guiteau's insanity plea and the subsequent furor shows the consequences of the often esoteric intellectual debates between professionals for the broader community of American citizens. De VILLE's analysis of 19th-century medical malpractice cases attempts a similar contextualization of courtroom activity. Focusing his attention on the origins of modern medical malpractice, De Ville offers revealing insights into the nature of both medical and legal practice. He uses this analysis of the actual workings of the two professions to explain the rapid growth of this kind of litigation in the mid-19th century. De Ville also shows, as does Rosenberg, how powerful larger socioeconomic and political forces can dominate medico-legal cases.

Judith LEAVITT's book gives a similarly rich account of another case of interest to both the medical and legal professions. One of the earliest identified healthy carriers of disease, Mary Mallon alias "Typhoid Mary", became the focus of intense medical and legal attention in the early 20th century. Highlighting the transformation of Mallon from a test case for a new public health theory to a cultural icon, Leavitt gives an informative glimpse of the changing power dynamic between law and medicine in the early 20th century. As Leavitt's analysis makes clear, tensions within professions are often as important as tensions between professions. Claudia CLARK similarly addresses this question of intraprofessional conflict in her book about the women employed as watch dial painters in New Jersey and Connecticut. The radium present in the paint used by these women created health risks that neither the law nor medical science was ready to confront, as Clark's explanation of the sometimes arcane debates within medicine, radiation science, and the legal profession makes clear. She also explains that the professions of the law and medicine were not the only ones with a role in deciding the fate of the "radium girls" and of the new disease entity called radium necrosis. Insurance companies, voluntary women's organizations, newspapers, various local, state, and federal government agencies, not to mention an array of courts, institutions dedicated to scientific research, and corporations had an interest in this encounter between medicine and the law. As Clark's study demonstrates, occupational health is a particularly rich field in which to explore the working relationship between medicine and the law in the 20th century. It is out of this field of occupational health and a related one of health insurance that one of the most important aspects of 20th-century medical – legal debate was born – the debate over health rights. The relationship between medicine and law in post-World War II United States can not be understood without addressing the notion of health rights. The right to health has been interpreted variously to include such principles as a right to access to care, a right to make decisions about treatment and termination of care, and/or a right to die. Having had a tremendous impact on the nature of care, as well as the legal status of patients and health care providers, this debate over health rights has even helped create a new intellectual discipline, bioethics. The best book-length history of bioethics and of the mid-20th century debate about Americans' health rights is by David Rothman. ROTHMAN's book is a chronological reconstruction of the cases that led to the expansion of the role played by law and bioethics in medical decision making. The first attempt at a comprehensive analysis of the origins of the new field of bioethics, Rothman's book contains a sometimes too brief, but always thoughtful commentary on significant aspects of late 20th-century medical–legal culture. An equally thoughtful examination of some other aspects of contemporary medical–legal relations is by Sheila JASANOFF. Focusing her attention on several of the scientific issues of most pressing legal concern today such as euthanasia and genetic engineering, Jasonoff analyzes both the current the regulatory process and that of expert testimony. She argues persuasively that (medical) science and the law configure each other. Although promising a historical context, Jasonoff's account remains firmly in the late 20th century, with only cursory forays into the more distant past. These forays present scholars with an exciting agenda for future historical research. Such future research should build upon the foundations laid by such scholars as Mohr, Jasonoff, Clark and the others mentioned here. It would be particularly useful if these future scholars could explain how the arenas of policy making and the courtroom became so closely tied with the laboratory and the clinic in the therapeutic, yet litigious United States.

JANET TIGHE

Medicine, Disease, and Health

Beier, Lucinda McCray, *Sufferers & Healers: The Experience of Illness in Seventeenth-Century England*, London and New York: Routledge, 1987

Clark, George, *A History of the Royal College of Physicians*, 2 vols, Oxford: Clarendon Press, 1964–66

Cook, Harold J., *The Decline of the Old Medical Regime in Stuart London*, Ithaca, New York: Cornell University Press, 1986

Kealey, Edward J., *Medieval Medicus: A Social History of Anglo-Norman Medicine*, Baltimore: Johns Hopkins University Press, 1981

Loudon, Irvine, *Medical Care and the General Practitioner, 1750–1850*, Oxford, Clarendon Press, and New York: Oxford University Press, 1986

Orme, Nicholas and Margaret Webster, *The English Hospital, 1070–1570*, New Haven, Connecticut, and London: Yale University Press, 1995

Pelling, Margaret, *The Common Lot: Sickness, Medical Occupations and the Urban Poor in Early Modern England*, London and New York: Longman, 1998

Porter, Roy and Dorothy Porter, *In Sickness and in Health: The British Experience, 1650–1850*, London: Fourth Estate, and New York: Blackwell, 1988

Rubin, Stanley, *Medieval English Medicine: AD 500–1300*, New York: Barnes and Noble, and Newton Abbot, Devon: David and Charles, 1974

Webster, Charles, *The National Health Service: A Political History*, Oxford and New York: Oxford University Press, 1998

RUBIN provides a useful introduction to medieval medicine in England. Constructing a sound argument for its rational foundation, he places special emphasis, the title notwithstanding, on the Anglo-Saxon period. The study makes effective use of archaeological and paleopathological resources and contains fine discussions of leprosy and the development of medicine as a profession. Rubin describes most practitioners as individuals of good sense with a solid grounding in classical and contemporary knowledge. The survey includes valuable descriptions of the varieties of extant historical evidence in its appendices and is a good starting point for understanding medieval physicians and disease.

A richer and more thoroughly documented analysis of medieval medicine is offered by KEALEY. His approach, though also centered on practitioners, is more focused and thematic than that of Rubin. Examining the expansion of health care between 1100 and 1154, the work takes into account the contributions of faith healers and others as medical practitioners. The study presents important insights into charitable institutions and emphasizes the prominent role of secular, rather than ecclesiastical benefactors. Perhaps Kealey's most lasting contribution is his two useful appendices: the first identifies 90 physicians, while the second records 113 hospitals. The study relies extensively on charters and contemporary chronicles. As a consequence, it is less valuable treating medical studies or techniques than Rubin.

ORME & WEBSTER draw particular attention to the hospitals of south-west England stressing their charitable and religious functions. Though the authors identify many types and properly observe the diversity of these institutions, most hospitals cared for the sick poor and gave sustenance to travelers. The authors caution against accepting earlier arguments regarding the use of hospitals to segregate lepers from the rest of society. The study includes a rich bibliography and is a useful survey of hospitals from Anglo-Norman times through the Reformation.

Early efforts to professionalize medical practice are detailed in CLARK's survey of the Royal College of London from its chartering in 1518 through passage of the Medical Act of 1858. Drawing extensively on the College's own archives, Clark portrays the group initially as a professional entity serving London; however, it later evolved into a national self-serving elite. The College struggled against the barber-surgeons and apothecaries, and also worked to keep unlicensed practitioners from offering their services to the public. Success was limited because they lacked popular support. They did improve the standards and status of physicians by encouraging dissections, promoting lectures, and insisting on qualifying examinations for all practitioners. Although Galen's teachings dominated their examinations through the 16th century and the College was slow to recognize the contributions of William Harvey, Clark nevertheless sees the organization as a positive force through the next century. Volume 2 covers the period from the late 17th century through 1858. For Clark the College lost its direction early in the 18th century; yet regained its vigor by the reign of George III, when it labored conscientiously to improve treatment and conditions for the insane. It also helped establish national standards in the struggles to address disease and the causes and consequences of poverty. Overall, Clark sees the College providing pivotal leadership in the evolution of English medicine.

COOK focuses his study more narrowly, examining the Royal College of Physicians from its period of dominance in the 1630s through its decline in 1704. His revisionist analysis modifies Clark's interpretation of the 17th century. Cook presents a less attractive portrait of the College, though he does not echo those modern scholars who condemn it as simply seeking to retain its privileged status. Drawing from an impressive array of sources, such as malpractice proceedings, minutes of medical societies and licensing boards, printed treatises, and advertisements, he explains how the College ultimately failed to restrict practice by its rivals. Unlike Clark, he shows how the medical marketplace and developments in the education of physicians led to revisions in philosophy and practice. Competition fuelled publication of medical texts as practitioners sought to trumpet their successes and gain more patients. Finally, Cook interprets the College's political struggles through the late century and illustrates how these problems combined with market realities and changes in medical education to transform the group into a learned society after apothecaries gained the right to prescribe medicines. More balanced than Clark, he provides rich insights into the College's regulatory activities.

BEIER both complements and challenges Cook's conclusions. She rejects the idea of an organized medical profession in the 17th century; instead, she explains in far greater depth how all types of practitioners competed in a consumer-driven open market. Each tried to promote their own skills while discrediting rivals through extensive use of propaganda. Licensed practitioners might attack their antagonists' lack of formal training; however, they seldom criticized their diagnostic skills or success. In the second part of her study, she analyzes illness from the perspectives of healers and sufferers. Basing much of her discussion of healers on the casebook of Joseph Binns, a London barber-surgeon, she depicts a cautious healer who treated more than 600 people during his career. Binns followed traditional practices ranging from purges to blood-letting and each of his patients was treated over long periods with care taken to prevent infection. Beier concludes that barber-surgeons possessed greater manual skills and were more modern in their techniques than the members of the Royal College. The concluding sections of this important social history of medicine describes popular diseases and their victims. Many contemporaries believed God visited illness on humans either because of their sinfulness, or to educate. Others recognized the power of magic and trusted healing to amulets or charms. Beier provides a fascinating window into the world of popular medicine.

Studying the urban environment, age groups and gender, and occupations, PELLING offers a rich blend of essays to interpret the social history of medicine in early modern times. She emphasizes popular preoccupation with disease and disability and underscores Beier's findings about the variety of practi-

tioners who attended the poor and middling sorts. Local authorities retained several kind of medical practitioners to minister to the health needs of the poor. She also studies nutrition and moderation in medical diagnosis. Among her more significant analyses is a discussion of the 1570 household census for Norwich, UK. From this she gleans a wealth of information to illuminate public concern for the health needs of the poor and efforts to offer assistance. Her study supplies valuable insights into the omnipresence of disease, as well as treatment for children, the elderly, the disabled, and women.

A survey that continues Pelling's time frame through the long 18th century with a similar focus on the social history of medicine from the perspective of the sick is contributed by PORTER & PORTER. They use traditional literary evidence: diaries, autobiographies, correspondence, fiction and poetry creatively to explore health, sickness, and the relationship between suffering and the self. Sickness and death were constant and fears about them consumed most citizens. By the later 17th century, individuals became more concerned with prevention and health, though their lives remained dominated by life-threatening illness. The work is filled with detailed first-person descriptions of sickness and reveals the centrality of health concerns among everyday people.

Viewing a portion of the same period, although through a different lens, LOUDON describes the evolution of the general practitioner. In response to rising costs of medical education, new men, trained through practical apprenticeships with hospital experience, presented the types of care sick people wanted. They were accessible, reasonably priced, and their ability to deliver effective care for common ailments and minor injuries made them extremely popular. Loudon successfully uses account books from provincial practitioners to reveal dedicated, hard-working, able professionals. His analysis also adds to an understanding of an important dimension of the professional middle class in the 18th and 19th centuries.

No survey of medical history would be complete without mention of the National Health Service and its pre-eminent historian offers an important interpretation from its origins to the Blair administration. While WEBSTER's primary attention is drawn to the politics and bureaucracy of the NHS, he provides solid analyses of clinical advances and finances. The author credits the special circumstances of the war and the special vision of Aneurin Bevan for creating the system. If Bevan draws high praise for his commitment and stewardship, few of his successors are similarly singled out. Between 1964 and 1974 the Service peaked; yet even then it suffered from poor leadership, a complicated bureaucracy, and social and geographical inequalities. Webster explains how the Thatcherites worked to discredit the NHS by lengthening waiting lists for services, insisting on more central control of the system, and increasing the number and power of managers. He sees little hope for a return to Bevan's vision for the NHS under the Blair government.

MICHAEL J. GALGANO

See also China: medicine; Doctor–Patient Relationship; Greece: medicine; India: medicine; Health, Mortality and Social Class; Medieval Science and Medicine

Medieval Science and Medicine

Crombie, A.C., *Augustine to Galileo: The History of Science, AD 400–1650*, London: Falcon Press, 1952; 2nd edition, London: Mercury Books, and Cambridge, Massachusetts: Harvard University Press, 1961

García Ballester, L. *et al.* (eds), *Practical Medicine from Salerno to the Black Death*, Cambridge and New York: Cambridge University Press, 1994

Grant, Edward (ed.), *A Source Book in Medieval Science*, Cambridge, Massachusetts: Harvard University Press, 1974

Jacquart, Danielle and Claude Thomasset, *Sexualité et savoir médical au Moyen Age*, Paris: Presses Universitaires de France, 1985

Klein-Franke, F., *Vorlesungen über die Medizin im Islam*, Wiesbaden: Steiner, 1982

MacKinney, Loren, *Medical Illustrations in Medieval Manuscripts*, London: Wellcome Historical Medical Library, and Berkeley: University of California Press, 1965

Rahman, Fazlur, *Health and Medicine in the Islamic Tradition: Change and Identity*, New York: Crossroad, 1987

Schipperges, Heinrich, "La medicina en la edad media latina", in *Historia Universal de la Medicina*, vol. 3, edited by P. Laín Entralgo, Barcelona: Salvat, 1972

Siraisi, Nancy G., *Medieval and Early Renaissance Medicine: An Introduction to Knowledge and Practice*, Chicago: University of Chicago Press, 1990

Talbot, C.H. and E.A. Hammond, *The Medical Practitioners in Medieval England: A Biographical Register*, London: Wellcome Historical Medical Library, 1965

Ullmann, Manfred, *Islamic Medicine*, translated from the German by Jean Watt, Edinburgh: Edinburgh University Press, 1978 (original edition, 1970)

The breadth of the above title highlights the relevance of reference books intended to provide bibliographical guidance. Such is the case of GRANT's book, which, among the sources of medieval science, devotes a substantial part to medicine (more than 100 pages). Its contents are organized according to a selection of sources comprising medical theory, physiology, scientific methodology in medieval medicine, anatomy, clinical procedure, prognosis methods, specific treatment of some diseases, and the whole gamut of remedies used in therapeutics and surgery. This book, although not exhaustive, affords a good general view of the contents, ideas, and methods of medieval medicine, with references also to the Arabic tradition.

General works on medieval science, such as CROMBIE's, provide an excellent background and include specific articles on medieval medicine, covering both general biological conceptions and theories of disease, therapeutics, and the origins of the hospital.

GARCIA BALLESTER *et al.* comprises 10 contributions by different experts, and constitutes a magnificent revision of current research on medicine in medieval Western Europe. It tackles such disparate issues as the influence of astrology on medical practice, medical wisdom and practice in the 13th century through the figure of the surgeon Gulielmo da Saliceto, medieval theories and practices of phlebotomy, the medical and surgical professions in 14th-century Paris, the teaching of medicine and the royal surgeons in the Kingdom of Aragon in the 14th century, perceptions of and reactions to the Black Death, John Aderne and scholastic surgery, curative practices of medieval women, and the medical world of Jews, Muslims, and Christians in late medieval Spain.

The institutionalization of medical knowledge and the rise of the medical profession are treated in SIRAISI, which includes two chapters on anatomical and physiological knowledge, the problems posed by disease and its manifestation in the medieval world, medieval therapeutics, and surgeons and surgical professions. The last part of the book contains a good bibliographical guide to works available in English.

The chapter by SCHIPPERGES, although lacking bibliographical references, is a good summary of the foundations of medicine in the High Middle Ages, describing the organization of knowledge and its academic structure in connection with medieval arts. It provides interesting biographies of the main figures of monastic medicine, and sketches out the major routes along which the Graeco-Arabic tradition was assimilated.

MacKINNEY is a useful bibliographical guide to illustrated medieval manuscripts and medical miniatures available in collections in the United States, Canada, Britain, the Netherlands, France, Spain, Italy, Germany, Hungary, Yugoslavia, Poland, Russia, and Scandinavia.

Specific aspects of medical knowledge concerning anatomy, physiology, and the making of a medical discourse on sexuality and gender are meticulously analyzed, with abundant bibliographical material and records, in JACQUART & THOMASSET.

TALBOT & HAMMOND's work, is a biographical dictionary of medieval English physicians. It is wide-ranging, and includes references to positions held by the subjects and their places of practice. The available biographical data is drawn from archival registers and, often, with explanatory notes indicating the sources used.

The influence of the Arabic medical tradition on medieval Western Europe is highly important. Among the numerous books dealing with this topic, ULLMANN's summary of Islamic medical knowledge deserves special praise, while her analysis of the process of Islamization of the Greek medical tradition is also noteworthy. The same approach can be found in KLEIN-FRANKE's essays, which assume a diachronic perspective, spanning the period from the origins of Arabic medical thought to its encounter with the Greek tradition, in particular the Hippocratic texts and the writings of Galen. The second part of the book deals with dogmatic and empirical medicine, and the influence of religion on Islamic medicine.

Finally, RAHMAN affords a general view of health and medicine in the Islamic tradition, from its cosmological views and religious tenets, to sanitary institutions and medical ethics.

JOSEP LLUÍS BARONA

Meitner, Lise   1878–1968

Austrian physicist

Berninger, E.H., "Otto Hahn, Lise Meitner and Fritz Strassmann in Berlin wird die Kernspaltung entdeckt", in *Berlinische Lebensbilder: Naturwissenschaftler*, edited by W. Treue and G. Hildebrandt, Berlin: Colloquium, 1987

Ernst, Sabine (ed.), *Lise Meitner an Otto Hahn: Briefe aus den Jahren 1912 bis 1924*, Stuttgart: Wissenschaftliche Verlagsgesellschaft, 1992

Feyl, Renate, "Lise Meitner", in her *Der lautlose Aufbruch: Frauen in der Wissenschaft*, Berlin: Neues Leben, 1981

Frisch, O.R., "Lise Meitner", *Biographical Memoirs of Fellows of the Royal Society*, 16 (1970): 405–20

Herneck, Friedrich, "Otto Hahn and Lise Meitner" in his *Bahnbrecher des Atomzeitalters. Grosse Naturforscher von Maxwell bis Heisenberg*, Berlin: Morgen, 1965

Kerner, Charlotte, *Lise: Atomphysikerin: Die Lebensgeschichte der Lise Meitner*, Weinheim and Basel: Beltz, 1986

Krafft, Fritz, *Im Schatten der Sensation: Leben und Wirken von Fritz Strassman*, Weinheim: Chemie, 1981, 165ff

Rife, Patricia, *Lise Meitner*, Düsseldorf: Claassen, 1990

Sime, Ruth Lewin, *Lise Meitner: A Life in Physics*, Berkeley: University of California Press, 1996

Stolz, Werner, *Otto Hahn/Lise Meitner*, Leipzig: Teubner, 1983

The biographical literature on the outstanding 20th-century physicist, Lise Meitner, can be divided roughly into two parts. The first part consists of mainly older studies that treat her life and work, in a more or less hagiographic manner, in relation to that of her colleague, Otto Hahn. The second part consists of the more recent representations that, strongly influenced by the rise of the feminist movement, try to present Lise Meitner's biography within the context of women in science. Neither approach does full justice to Meitner, since she was neither a mere "co-worker" of Otto Hahn, nor was she an ambitious suffragette, or even a feminist.

The most reliable information on the life and works of Meitner can be found in the voluminous biography by SIME, which details her scientific achievements, and also the social and political problems, which shaped her life. Inevitably, the focus is on Meitner's emigration from Nazi Germany a few months before the momentous discovery that the uranium nucleus could be split; Sime describes the circumstances of Meitner's emigration, and also how she lost out on the deserved honours following the great scientific success. This fact, and her modest way of life in Swedish exile, have cast a shadow on an otherwise very successful career. However, Sime also makes it clear that Meitner's life cannot be interpreted as simply a question of martyrdom; she was not just a victim of social and personal discrimination, because there was also much happiness and success in her life, not least during the Berlin years and in her collaboration with Otto Hahn.

Sime's biography is complemented by the obituary by her nephew, Frisch, and by Krafft's book on Fritz Strassmann and the history of the discovery of uranium fission. Not surprisingly, FRISCH is not free from hagiographic elements, but he gives a very instructive and highly competent overview of Meitner's research: her early radio-chemical work and her important nuclear-physical investigations of the 1920s and 1930s, which led to the important discovery of uranium fission by Hahn and Strassmann in November 1938, just a few months after Meitner had escaped from Berlin. Frisch gives plenty of first-hand information about Meitner's contribution to the first interpretation of nuclear fission in 1938 and 1939, and the appendix gives a useful bibliography of her scientific publications. What Frisch reports from personal memory and experience, KRAFFT supports by documentary evidence integrated into a wider history of science, such as the historical background in physics prior to the discovery of uranium fission. In general, some of the strength of Krafft's study lies in its documentary style, since he systematically evaluates the existing and accessible documents for the first time: from laboratory records, letters and memories, to relevant original works.

As a spin-off from this project, ERNST has edited the correspondence between Otto Hahn and Lise Meitner – the result of a thesis supervised by Krafft. Unfortunately, this edition covers only the years 1912–24, and hence barely touches upon the later period, which is so exciting for nuclear physics. However, it is an excellent source for the study of the scientific work and personality of Meitner, particularly her early radio-chemical collaboration with Otto Hahn.

HERNECK's important work on "pioneers of the atomic age" provided the first overview of Meitner; it remains highly readable, and can therefore be recommended as an introduction to her life and work. Herneck's strength lies in its instructive presentation of the Berlin scientific community, and the role that Lise Meitner played in it. Furthermore, he gives a sensitive presentation of the congenial relationship between Lise Meitner and Otto Hahn. The latter is also the focus of BERNINGER's essay, but here the focus is shifted slightly more towards the social environment during the discovery of nuclear fission. In comparison to Krafft's study, the essay does not offer much that is new. Another good introduction is the brief biography by STOLZ, which offers an overview of Meitner's scientific achievements, and her sometimes dogmatic social and political engagement, especially in her efforts to achieve a peaceful use of nuclear energy.

Feyl, Kerner, and Rife are all concerned with a different kind of social and political engagement, tracing the destiny of Lise Meitner as a woman. FEYL does this in an easily readable, and quite stimulating, essay. KERNER's biography is an attempt to meet the demands of a popular science biography, distilled from the literature of the history of science. The biography gives new and interesting insights into the difficult years in Sweden, which are hardly mentioned in other publications, Sime's excepted. Finally, although RIFE claims to have produced the first comprehensive biography of Meitner, throughout the book her life, scientific successes, and failures are embedded in the social reality of the male-dominant scientific research community, sometimes very superficially. This is both an advantage and a disadvantage: on the one hand, Meitner's biography is understood as part and parcel of the history of science; on the other hand, the detailed categorization according to a general feminist theory leads to several exaggerations and factual misinterpretations. Moreover, the last two decades of Meitner's life are virtually excluded, being merely summarized in a short epilogue.

DIETER HOFFMANN
translated by Klaus Staubermann

See also Nuclear Physics; Women in Science: physical sciences

Mendel, Gregor 1822–1884

Austrian biologist and botanist

George, Wilma, *Gregor Mendel and Heredity*, London: Priory Press, 1975

Iltis, Hugo, *Life of Mendel*, translated from the German by Eden and Cedar Paul, London: Allen and Unwin, and New York: Norton, 1932 (original edition, 1924)

Jakubíček, Milan and Jaromir Kubíček, *Bibliographia Mendeliana*, Brno: Universitni knihovna v Brne, 1965

Krizenecky, Jaroslav (ed.), *Gregor Johann Mendel (1822–1884): Texte und Quellen zu seinem Wirken und Leben*, Leipzig: Barth, 1965

Olby, Robert C., *Origins of Mendelism*, London: Constable, and New York: Schocken Books; 1966; 2nd edition Chicago: University of Chicago Press, 1985

Orel, Vitezslav and Anna Matalová (eds), *Gregor Mendel and the Foundation of Genetics*, Brno: Mendelianum of the Moravian Museum in Brno and the Czechoslovak Society for the History of Science and Technology, 1983

Orel, Vitezslav, *Mendel*, translated by Stephen Finn, Oxford and New York: Oxford University Press, 1984; revised and expanded edition as *Gregor Mendel: The First Geneticist*, Oxford and New York: Oxford University Press, 1996

Sherwood, Eva R. and Curt Stern (eds), *The Origin of Genetics: A Mendel Source Book*, San Francisco: W.H. Freeman, 1966

Weiling, Franz (ed.), *Versuche über Pflanzenhybriden*, by Mendel, Braunschweig: Friedrich Vieweg, 1970

The foundations, development, and impact of Mendelism are described by OLBY, who consults original texts *in extenso* and supplements every chapter with notes for further reading. The book initially deals with Mendel's predecessors among plant breeders, from the first hybridization experiments of the 18th and early 19th centuries, to Linnaeus, Klreuter, C.F. Gaertner, Charles Naudin, Charles Darwin and Francis Galton. Olby then follows this with an account of the 19th-century debate on sexual and non-sexual reproduction, and of the possibilities, opened up by breeding, of producing hereditary varieties. He supplies a description of Mendel's career, and of the most important characteristics of his hybridization experiments. The 34 years of poor and hesitant reception that followed Mendel's publications of 1865–66 are described merely as a "pause"; Olby does not discuss this period in detail, and only the so-called re-discoveries of Mendel's law by Hugo De Vries, Carl Correns, Erich Tschermak, and William Bateson are conceded

some attention. A detailed appendix reproduces relevant passages from original texts in English translation, and illustrations and tables help make the book a very suitable introduction for students.

Mendel's life, work, and family history have been assembled by KRIZENECKY, a book full of archival material. It also contains an edition of Mendel's original publication of 1865 (for the first time revised on the basis of the manuscript), as well as a short autobiography and a commentary. A commemorative speech of 1902 and reminiscences (1928) by Mendel's nephew, A. Schindler, and the recollections of Mendel's death by A. Doupovec (1884) and by G. Niessl v. Mayendorf (1902), are followed by private correspondence on family matters. Mendel's genealogy, and the history of his ancestors and of his home region in the eastern part of North Moravia are described in great detail, and a chronological table concludes a very informative book.

WEILING's critical and annotated edition of Mendel's *Versuche über Pflanzenhybriden* can be recommended to students. It includes an account of Mendel's life and an appreciation of his work. Krizenecky also contains the classical text of 1865 (revised on the basis of the original manuscript), and other original papers (in the original language) on the reception of and debate over Mendelism between 1895 and 1904. An introduction by Nemec analyzes the achievements in botany after 1580, which made Mendel's research possible. A detailed commentary (about 40 pages) by the editor discusses the significance, for the development of early genetics, of particular texts that are reprinted in this volume.

SHERWOOD & STERN contains reprints of the classical writings in early genetics, which are published in their entirety, or in extracts in English translation. The foreword pays homage to Mendel's work and explains the editors' choice of material, while there are a number of footnotes and references for further reading which facilitate an understanding of the texts. The volume opens with Mendel's two major works on plant hybrids, along with his letters to C.W. Nägeli (1866–73). Extracts on *Pisum* etc., from the collection on hybrids by Focke (1881), are followed first by an introduction to works acknowledging Mendel's laws by De Vries and Correns (1900), then by their letters to the early Mendelian H.F. Roberts, conveying the circumstances of their respective studies of hybrids (1924–25), and lastly by R.A. Fisher's critical discussion (1936) of the interpretation of De Vries's, Correns's and Tschernak's work (which in the volume appears under the heading of "rediscovery"). Wright's short treatise of 1966, which follows, criticizes Fisher's claim that Mendel's number ratios were merely the result of calculations, and had not been reached through experimentation. The volume serves as an important introduction to Mendel's work and his research methods.

ILTIS presents an extensive account of Mendel's life and work, both in his profession and as a scientific researcher, and a history of Mendelism, including the development from around 1900 of the discovery that heredity is governed by law-like processes, which was intimately linked to the gradual acknowledgement of Mendel's laws. The book describes the history of empirical results and theoretical conclusions, and discusses the developments of Mendel's claims after 1900 – i.e. the influence of the chromosome theory of heredity, the theory of sex determination, developmental theories, and the Morgan Principles (of the behaviour of Mendelian factors). The book also touches on the discovery of the limits of Mendel's laws, and it traces the impact of plant and animal breeding on ideas of human genetics. This history describes only a few basic features of the impact of Mendelism in the first two decades of the 20th century.

A brief introduction to the life and work of Mendel is provided by GEORGE, whose amply illustrated book contains a chronology of Mendel's life and career. The book also serves as an introduction, both to the state of research into heredity around 1860, and to the relevant botanical and cytological knowledge. Mendel's hybridization experiments and his later research are described and commented on in great detail. There are discussions of later contributions to breeding (by Darwin, Galton, Focke, De Vries, Correns, Tschermak, Bateson), and of cytological genetics until around 1910. The book also provides a glossary and references to secondary literature, which, however, already needs updating.

The biography by OREL (1985) provides an introduction to the life and work of Mendel. It is based on extensive knowledge of original source material, as well as of the history of the scientific, cultural, and social contexts of Mendel's work. The book offers both an appreciation of Mendel's wide-ranging scientific research, complete with graphical representations, and an introduction to the reception of his ideas, which began already before the turn of the century. There are references for further reading, and the book was updated for a new edition in 1996.

OREL & MATALOVÁ is a collection of essays on the various aspects of Mendelism. This international volume provides information on contemporary developments in Bohemia and Brno, as well as in scientific research, and also sheds light on the pattern of scientific discovery and on aspects of Mendel's personal life. The book concludes with a discussion of the delayed acknowledgement of Mendel's laws, and an appreciation of the fundamental importance of Mendel's discovery for modern genetics.

JAKUBÍČEK & KUBÍČEK is a bibliography of all literature on Mendel until 1965. A bibliography of Mendel's own works is followed by a list of original publications on the discovery of Mendel's laws since. Finally, the bibliography lists literature on Mendel's life and work, classified in general accounts, documentation and correspondence and (earlier) bibliographies.

BRIGITTE HOPPE
translated by Anna-Katherina Mayer

See also Botany: general works; Botany: Britain; Genetics: general works; Heredity

Mendeleev, Dmitrii Ivanovich 1834–1907

Russian chemist

Figurovskii, N.A., *Dmitrii Ivanovich Mendeleev*, 2nd edition, Moscow: Nauka, 1961; 2nd edition, 1983

Kedrov, Bonifatii Mikhailovich, *Filosofskii analiz pervykh trudov D.I. Mendeleeva o periodicheskom zakone (1869–1871)*, Moscow: Akademii nauk SSSR, 1959

Kedrov, Bonifatii Mikhailovich and D.N. Trifonov, *Zakon periodichnosti i khimicheskie elementy: Otkrytiia i khronologiia*, Moscow: Nauka, 1969

Makarenia, A.A., I.N. Filimonova and N.G. Karpilo (eds), *D.I. Mendeleev v vospomonaniiakyh sovremennikov*, 2nd edition, Moscow: Atomizdat, 1973

Mladentsev, M.N. and V.E. Tishchenko, *Dmitrii Ivanovich Mendeleev, ego zhizn' i deiatel'nost'*, vol. 1, parts 1 and 2, Moscow and Leningrad: Akademiia nauk SSSR, 1938

Parkhomenko, V.E., *D.I. Mendeleev i russkoe neftianoe delo*, Moscow: Akademiia nauk SSSR, 1957

Pisarzhevskii, O., *Dmitry Ivanovich Mendeleyev: His Life and Work*, Moscow: Foreign Languages Publishing House, 1954

Pisarzhevskii, O., *Dmitrii Ivanovich Mendeleev*, Moscow: Guardiia, 1959

Van Spronsen, J.W., *The Periodic System of Chemical Elements: A History of the First Hundred Years*, Amsterdam: Elsevier, 1969

There is a vast literature on the life and work of Dmitrii Ivanovich Mendeleev, much of which relates to Mendeleev's discovery (1869) and subsequent elaboration of the periodic law of the elements. Other aspects of his exceptionally wide-ranging interests have been relatively neglected, however.

There is no fully satisfactory biographical study of Mendeleev in any language, including Russian. The most adequate biography is by FIGUROVSKII, which presents a standard chronological treatment of Mendeleev's life and work, and at least alludes to the many sides to Mendeleev's activities. Figurovskii includes separate chapters on Mendeleev's work on solution theory, economic studies, and metrological studies, as well as on various aspects of his work on the periodic law. However, the biography is far too short (258 pages of text) to allow for an in-depth coverage of any topic, including the work on the periodic law. Moreover, the author relied mainly on published materials, leaving virtually untapped the voluminous archival materials concerning Mendeleev.

MLADENTSEV & TISHCHENKO's two-volume work is more a compilation of excerpts from primary sources by and about Mendeleev, linked by the authors' commentaries, than a true biography. Still, the treatment does provide a strikingly vivid portrait of Mendeleev. The first volume (1938) covers only the early years of Mendeleev's life up to 1861; the second volume, which carries the treatment up to 1890 when Mendeleev resigned in protest from St Petersburg University, was completed prior to the authors' deaths in 1941, but not published until 1983. The first volume is arranged chronologically, while the second is organized in three main sections: family chronicle, scientific and pedagogical activities, and social and industrial activities.

The volume by MAKARENIA, FILIMONOVA & KARPILO is a useful collection of excerpts from memoirs, reminiscences, and other recollections of Mendeleev by students, friends, and colleagues. Many of these excerpts are taken from unpublished archival documents or from relatively obscure published sources.

PISARZHEVSKII (1959) is a quite short and, often unreliable biography, which sometimes verges on the hagiographic. However, an earlier version of this work, PISARZHEVSKII

(1954) has the value of having been translated into English. Other biographies of Mendeleev in English are highly inaccurate, have no scholarly value, and should be avoided.

By far the best work on Mendeleev deals with his discovery and research on the periodic law of the elements. Non-Russian scholars often describe this as work on the periodic table, while Russian and Soviet scholars emphasize that the merit of Mendeleev's work far exceeded simply devising a new table of the elements.

The most fundamental studies of Mendeleev's work on the periodic law have been written by KEDROV, who used archival documents to reconstruct the process by which Mendeleev came to his discovery. He shows that Mendeleev developed the essence of the periodic law on one specific day in 1869; Mendeleev then spent many years furiously elaborating the periodic law, confirming its features, and defending it from the numerous critics, both in Russia and the West. Kedrov emphasizes that Mendeleev came to the idea of the periodic law through writing a textbook on inorganic chemistry, a work that later became the famous *Principles of Chemistry*. Kedrov rejects the usual assertions of most Western historians of science, that Mendeleev's starting point was the external progression of elements by atomic weight. Instead, Kedrov demonstrates that Mendeleev began by focusing on groups of elements with similar properties, such as the halogens and alkali metals, and only later did he connect these distinct groups to the idea of ascending atomic weight. This process induced Mendeleev to include certain features in his periodic table that gave his overall scheme great flexibility and power. For example, Mendeleev left gaps in his system when necessary, assuming that these were undiscovered elements. The volume by KEDROV & TRIFONOV presents a useful summary of Kedrov's, and other Soviet scholars's, research on Mendeleev's periodic law.

One of the most contentious aspects of the periodic law is the question of priority. Some historians of science outside Russia do not give Mendeleev full, or sometimes even partial, credit for the periodic table. For example, VAN SPRONSEN concludes that no less than six scientists should share the credit for the discovery of the periodic table: Alexandre Chancourtois, John Newlands, William Odling, Hinrichs, Julius Meyer, and Mendeleev. In general, these works make little use of the extensive Russian-language secondary source literature and archival materials on Mendeleev. Russian and Soviet scholars such as Kedrov have shown the serious flaws in many of these accounts, and argue convincingly that the periodic table developed by Mendeleev was far better than those of the other contenders.

Throughout his life, Mendeleev devoted considerable time to interests other than chemistry, especially in the years after 1880. He was greatly interested in economic questions relating to Russia, and wrote many books and was consulted on various topics, including the coal industry, the tariff structure, petroleum production, and heavy industry. In addition, he conducted large-scale laboratory research on smokeless gunpowder, as a result of a commission from the Russian Naval Ministry. He was also actively involved in the regulation of the system of weights and measures in Russia, and served as the director of the Central Bureau of Weights and Measures from 1893 to 1907. These activities have attracted little attention from historians, and are only sketchily described in the biographies and other works mentioned above. One exception is the specialized study by PARKHOMENKO, which examines Mendeleev's involvement with questions of the production and uses of petroleum. This work is a solid technical treatment of Mendeleev's activities in this area, placed in the broader context of the early development of the Russian petroleum industry.

NATHAN BROOKS

See also Chemistry; Metrology; Russia

Mersenne, Marin   1588–1648

French mathematician and theologian

Beaulieu, Armand, "Bibliographie", in *Correspondance du P. Marin Mersenne, religieux Minime*, edited by Mme Paul Tannery and Cornélis De Waard, vol. 17, Paris: CNRS, 1988, 11–108

Crombie, A.C., *Styles of Scientific Thinking in the European Tradition: The History of Argument and Explanation especially in the Mathematical and Biological Sciences and Arts*, 3 vols, London: Duckworth, 1994

Dear, Peter, *Mersenne and the Learning of the Schools*, Ithaca, New York: Cornell University Press, 1988

Hine, William L., "Mersenne and Copernicanism", *Isis*, 64 (1973): 18–32

Hine, William L., "Mersenne Variants", *Isis*, 67 (1976): 98–103

Hine, William L., "Mersenne and Vanini", *Renaissance Quarterly*, 29 (1976): 52–65

Hine, William L., "Marin Mersenne: Renaissance Naturalism and Renaissance Magic", in *Occult and Scientific Mentalities in the Renaissance*, edited by Brian Vickers, Cambridge: Cambridge University Press, 1984

Lenoble, Robert, *Mersenne; ou, la naissance du mécanisme*, Paris: Vrin, 1943; 2nd edition, 1971

Tannery, Paul and Cornélis De Waard, "Note sur la vie de Mersenne", in *Correspondance du P. Marin Mersenne, religieux Minime*, edited by Mme Paul Tannery and de Waard vol. 1, Paris: Beauchesne, 1932

Tannery, Mme Paul [Marie] and Cornélis De Waard, *Correspondance du P. Marin Mersenne, religieux Minime*, vols 1–2, Paris: Beauchesne, 1932–33; vols 3–4, Paris: Presses Univérsitaires de France, 1945–55; vols 5–17: Paris: CNRS, 1959–88

The figure of Marin Mersenne had practically vanished from the history of science when a project to publish his vast correspondence was advanced by Paul Tannery around 1900. Though they acknowledged his acumen in music, the *philosophes* and their followers found Mersenne's books plodding, derivative, mediocre mere trifling antiquities; worse, he was often caricatured as a meddlesome and intolerant churchman (Mersenne was a Minim friar) unworthy of association with Descartes, Fermat, Galileo, Pascal, Huygens and Hobbes, his brilliant secular collaborators. Tannery was a devout Catholic and a talented scholar who took offense at this historiographical canard and endeavoured to restore Mersenne's legacy; when he died his wife Marie continued his plan to publish a richly annotated edition of Mersenne's massive correspondence. It opens with a biographical note by TANNERY & De WAARD featuring an evocative passage from the *éloge* penned shortly after Mersenne's death by Hilarion de Coste, his student and Minim brother. Their construction on this first-hand account is a concise and elegant testimonial that grounds all modern Mersenne studies.

Robert LENOBLE complemented the *Correspondance* project with an unabashedly sympathetic biography. Lenoble celebrates Mersenne's clever synthesis of natural philosophy and Christian doctrine into a workable institution. He champions Mersenne's curiosity, energy and enthusiasm, and grants him many of his proper discoveries and accredits him with crucial contributions; and valorizes the Minim's piety, sociability, and rectitude. This global review of Mersenne's mediation in philosophical affairs hints at the significance of trust, replication, and discipline in regimes of knowledge. However Lenoble, a priest keenly interested in the psychodynamics of development, decided that Mersenne's qualities had essentially inward, psycho-theological sources, and never pursued his fleeting sociological insights.

Instead, Lenoble represents Mersenne's personal growth from zealous polemicist to tolerant mechanist as emblematic of the very constitution of modern science. Thus Mersenne, unable quite to dominate the subjects of philosophy or theology, "merely" embodied their harmonious union in his mixed mathematics and his habits of association. By working to establish the moral economy of European science he did much to ensure its future; according to Lenoble, Mersenne heralds the advent of great things.

Peter Dear was dissatisfied with such an apology for Mersenne, whose subtle but powerful ideas, he argued, provided crucial philosophical underpinnings for the scientific revolution. Dear finds a deep structure within Mersenne's fragmentary *oeuvre*, the result of a dialectical confrontation among humanist-Ciceronian probabilism, Jesuit-Thomist eternalism, neo-Augustinian innatism and illuminationism, classical (pseudo-) Aristotelian mechanics, acoustical coincidence theory and Pythagorean harmonic theory, and anti-essentialist universal language schemes. It shows how Mersenne carefully selected and strategically deployed these orthodox resources in order to justify a strange, new mathematical natural philosophy in a hostile intellectual climate. Dear's meticulous reconstruction of esoteric doctrines and foregone habits of thought is sometimes dazzling. However, it yields a brilliant picture of Mersenne's philosophical craftwork, and is well worth the required effort.

Having described Mersenne's deeply conservative intellection, Dear argues for its political agency, claiming that Mersenne's subterfuge especially facilitated consensus on matters of natural knowledge in reactionary Catholic France. Mersenne's open association with powerful figures is never considered as a more likely source of social power than his subtle deployment of school doctrines; this overweening intellectualism mars an otherwise sensible account.

Of all the authors considered, William HINE attends most carefully to the work Mersenne assumed as a Catholic apolo-

gist. In a series of concise, trenchant studies Hine uses close textual analysis to discover Mersenne's subtle, sometimes arcane bibliographic practices. Thus we learn how thoroughly Mersenne obscured his engagement with Vanini, the Italian naturalist condemned for heresy, in biblical exegesis, and how strategically he bound and distributed his treatments of suspect topics. Hine deftly situates these author functions within the charged field of counter-Reform intellectual politics to reveal the force of Mersenne's operations.

Hine is largely concerned with Mersenne's commentary on Genesis, though later works figure in his studies of "Variants" and "Copernicanism". In his preoccupation with this huge Latin book and its reflection of Mersenne's fundamental motivations, Hine has left unexplored important aspects of Mersenne's life and work (travel, association, experiment); even so his articles vivify an engaged, pragmatic "party" intellectual who seems more historically authentic than the heroic character proffered in other accounts.

For Alistair Crombie Mersenne's interest in sensation, signs, and language expressed his "intellectual commitment" to an experimental physiological psychology that would ground all empirical knowledge, while his "moral commitment" to the study of nature, so conceived, was manifest in his faith and humility, and his patience, honesty, and openness with kindred spirits. CROMBIE supposes these commitments were shared by other philosophers, but argues that Mersenne pursued them in a distinct and superior "style", illustratively contrasted here with Galileo's. Thus Mersenne never insisted on his priority in matters Galileo, perhaps knowingly, appropriated; rather he challenged the Florentine's questionable experimental claims with respect and resolve. Considering Mersenne's prudent support of Galileo throughout his struggle with the Roman authorities, Crombie finds the Minim friar all the more virtuous.

Mersenne's gentle style produced "genuinely original contributions to scientific knowledge", which were subsequently obscured by the harmful effects of reputation and influence. This is framed in Crombie as "an exemplary historiographical problem" and resolved without an inkling that Mersenne, too, laboured to establish his reputation and influence and saw them contested along with his scientific claims. In this and other essential ways Crombie's asymmetrical treatment utterly fails as anthropology, despite its pretensions. Nevertheless, with copious extracts in translation and judicious commentary, Crombie provides the best available account of Mersenne's experimental form of life.

Armand Beaulieu's extended essay brings the "Mersenne business" up to date as of 1986–87. BEAULIEU summarizes not only the secondary literature but also the historical experience of the *Correspondance* team, and affirms Tannery's conviction that this project, diligently pursued, would provide a wealth of material for the socio-cultural history of early 17th-century European science.

CRAIG RODINE

Merton Thesis

Basalla, George, *The Rise of Modern Science: External or Internal Factors?*, Lexington, Massachusetts: Heath, 1968

Clark, Jon, Celia Modgil and Sohan Modgil (eds), *Robert K. Merton: Consensus and Controversy*, New York: Falmer Press, 1990

Cohen, I. Bernard (ed.), *Puritanism and the Rise of Modern Science: The Merton Thesis*, New Brunswick, New Jersey: Rutgers University Press, 1990

Conant, James B., *On Understanding Science: An Historical Approach*, New Haven, Connecticut: Yale University Press, and London: Oxford University Press, 1947

Dillenberger, John, *Protestant Thought and Natural Science: A Historical Interpretation*, New York: Abingdon Press, 1960; London: Collins, 1961

Feuer, Lewis, *The Scientific Intellectual: The Psychological and Sociological Origins of Modern Science*, New York: Basic Books, 1963

Fleming, Donald, "review of *The Scientific Intellectual*" Isis, 56 (1965): 369–70

Hill, Christopher, *Intellectual Origins of the English Revolution*, Oxford: Clarendon Press, 1965

Hooykaas, Reijer, *Religion and the Rise of Modern Science*, Edinburgh: Scottish Academic Press, and Grand Rapids, Michigan: Eerdmans, 1972

Hunter, Michael, *Science and Society in Restoration England*, Cambridge and New York: Cambridge University Press, 1981

Jacob, Margaret C., *The Newtonians and the English Revolution, 1689–1720*, Ithaca, New York: Cornell University Press, 1976; 2nd edition, New York: Gordon and Breach, 1990

Merton, Robert K., *Science, Technology and Society in Seventeenth Century England*, Bruges, Belgium: St Catherine Press, 1938; New York: Fertig, 1970

Purver, Margery, *The Royal Society: Concept and Creation*, Cambridge, Massachusetts: MIT Press, and London: Routledge and Kegan Paul, 1967

Weber, Max, *The Protestant Ethic and the Spirit of Capitalism*, translated from the German by Talcott Parsons, London: Allen and Unwin, 1930; New York: Scribner, 1958 (original edition, 1904)

Webster, Charles (ed.), *The Intellectual Revolution of the Seventeenth Century*, London and Boston: Routledge and Kegan Paul, 1974

Webster, Charles, *The Great Instauration: Science, Medicine, and Reform, 1626–1670*, London: Duckworth, and New York: Holmes and Meier, 1976

Westfall, Richard S., *Science and Religion in Seventeenth-Century England*, New Haven, Connecticut: Yale University Press, 1958

Zuckerman, Harriet, "The Other Merton Thesis", *Science in Context*, 3 (1989): 239–67

One of the most widely-discussed and controversial issues relating to the origins of the scientific revolution, and of modern science generally, is the role played by Puritanism in the rise of science in Britain (and in Europe wherever Protestantism was influential) and the United States. This discussion may also be approached in terms of the connections between science and religion, and, even more broadly, between science and philosophy.

Among the first to study seriously the connection between science and religion from a historical perspective was Alphonse de Candolle, whose *Histoire des sciences et des savants depuis deux siècles* (1873) included a section devoted to "The Influence of Religion on the Development of the Sciences" (translated in Cohen). De Candolle found what he took to be a strong correlation between scientists and sons of Protestant clergymen, and suggested it was celibacy that prevented priests from producing a similar legacy for science in Catholic countries! De Candolle found a peculiarly "Darwinian" influence here, and emphasized that his work investigated aspects of the correlation between "heredity and selection in the human species".

This theme was also pursued by the German sociologist, Max WEBER, not explicitly with reference to science, but in terms of the "Protestant ethic" and its presumed role in the rise of Western capitalism (1904). In this same spirit, the American sociologist, Robert K. Merton, published an article in 1936 devoted to "Puritanism, Pietism, and Science", which was followed two years later by MERTON, a monograph based on a dissertation he had completed at Harvard University. (The edition of 1970 also contains a select bibliography devoted to the Merton thesis). It was this work that eventually inspired the expression, the "Merton Thesis".

Merton's monograph (or STS, as it is often called in the vast literature stimulated by this important work) has had a seminal influence on studies related to the social dimensions of science in the half-century since it was written. As Cohen points out, the idea of the singular role of Puritanism (or of radical or ascetic Protestantism) in 17th-century science has come to be known as the "Merton thesis", a name that has gained official sanction in the foremost journal (and a dictionary) of the history of science.

Merton himself later described the "Merton Thesis" as the "Puritan Spur to Science" in a lengthy new preface for the reprint of his book in 1970. There he notes that his original study included among the "Motive Forces of the New Science" such Puritan concerns as affirming the "Glory of the Great Author of Nature", promoting a utilitarian respect for the "Comfort of Mankind", and supporting the concomitant "Shift to Science" and the "Process of Secularization", all of which were taking place in 17th-century England as both the scientific and political revolutions were underway. For readers desiring a succinct outline of the major subjects covered in STS, K.E. Dufin and Stuart W. Strickland have provided a useful overview in Cohen.

After reading Merton himself, COHEN's edited volume should be the natural starting place for anyone interested in learning more about the "Merton Thesis", as it includes critical reviews and a number of major studies. The book opens with a monograph-length study by Cohen himself devoted to "The Impact of the Merton Thesis", which totals more than 100 pages, includes a carefully annotated list of articles and books related to the "Merton Thesis", and serves as a very useful guide to the vast literature Merton's work has inspired. Another informative study is to be found in CLARK, MODGIL & MODGIL, in which Cohen in particular provides a detailed analysis of a number of works by authors who have examined the possible links between Protestantism (as well as Puritanism) and the rise of science in England, including R.K. Merton, James B. Conant, A. Rupert Hall, Richard Foster Jones, Marjorie Hope Nicolson, Walter Pagel, and Dorothy Stimson.

As a variation on the basic "Merton Thesis" and Merton's claim that the overwhelming majority of the early members of the Royal Society were Puritans, CONANT examines the important experimental work that was undertaken in Catholic Florence, another major center of activity crucial for the scientific revolution, "lest one become too engrossed with one county and the cultural effects of the Reformation". DILLEN-BERGER examines the "Merton Thesis" from yet another angle, in terms of the Puritans who did not embrace the new science, but rather condemned it as a distraction from the only thing that should matter in life, salvation. While questioning Merton's definition of "Puritan", Dillenberger also notes the strong representation of Puritans in the universities where science was practised, as well as among the early members of the Royal Society.

On the other hand, Christopher Hill, in Webster (1974), maintains that even after the Counter-Reformation, Protestant countries were more supportive of science than those countries dominated by Roman Catholics. By reducing the power of the priesthood and the authoritarianism of the Church, Hill maintains that Protestantism was naturally a "liberating force" for modern science. HOOYKAAS also agrees with Merton that Protestantism encouraged a positive environment for the study of science by emphasizing good works and utilitarianism, but he downplays the role of salvation. Alternatively, a major attempt to show that Catholics were positively receptive to the new science is an article by François Russo, originally in French but translated as "Catholicism, Protestantism and Science" in BASALLA. Russo, who is a Catholic Jesuit, argues that the Jesuits were actually more supportive of science than Protestants.

A controversial, negative critique of the "Merton Thesis" came from Lewis FEUER, who claims that it was not "ascetic Protestantism", but a "hedonist-libertarian" ethic that encouraged the new approach to nature reflected in experimental science. Like Dillenberger, Feuer questions Merton's terminology and the exact meaning of "Puritanism". In the revised edition (1970), Merton responds to Feuer in a lengthy preface, giving line-by-line quotations in order to show that Feuer's emphatic critique of the Merton Thesis involved straightforward misquotation. Additionally, anyone reading Feuer's book should also consult the largely negative review by FLEMING, who objects in particular to the vagueness of the term "hedonism" in Feuer's analysis, just as Feuer objects to the vagueness of the term "Puritan" in Merton's. Similarly, HUNTER argues that Merton's use of "Puritanism" is so vague and comprehensive as to be meaningless.

Another challenge to Merton has come from specific studies of the Royal Society. For example, PURVER claims that in terms of both the "testimony and actions" of its early members, the Royal Society was not a reflection of the Puritan ethic.

Theodore K. Rabb, writing on "Religion and the Rise of Modern Science" in Webster (1974), also fails to find that "radical Protestants" were over-represented in 17th-century English science. In Cohen, Rabb focuses instead on Baconianism in England, and its emphasis on the utilitarian value of the "new science", as having been more important than strictly Puritan religious motivations. Rabb argues that it was not because they were Protestants, or more specifically Puritans, that the founders of the new science in England were revolutionaries, but because they were Baconians.

Christopher HILL represents another important direction in research. Not only does Hill support Merton's connection between radical Protestantism and modern science, but he links the ideas of the new science to those championed by Puritans and Parliamentarians alike. Nevertheless, Hill only maintains that there is a "connection" – not necessarily a causal link – - and he broadens considerably the definition of radical Protestants to include all who were interested in reformation rather than separation from the Church prior to 1640. This serves to connect the basic Merton Thesis with larger moral and political issues. What Hill stresses are close connections between Protestantism, utilitarianism, and belief in progress.

JACOB also emphasizes political elements in her approach to 17th-century England and the scientific revolution, claiming that Anglicanism itself requires closer scrutiny as a link between the interests of early Puritan scientists and the new science associated with Newton and the founders of the Royal Society. Reformers within Puritanism had different interests – and a correspondingly different agenda – than the radical Puritans, and it was the conservatives among reform-minded Puritans, claims Jacob, who turned out to have been, predominantly, the scientific forerunners of Newton.

Merton's lengthy preface to the 1970 edition lamented above all the fact that the question of Protestantism's role in supporting modern science had unfortunately overshadowed other aspects of his work. He had actually devoted more space in the original book to the important roles economic and military interests played in stimulating scientific advance. This same point is emphasized explicitly in an article by ZUCKERMAN, in which she considers at length those parts of Merton's original work that were *not* concerned with the science–Protestantism connection.

An entire section of Cohen is devoted to "Charles Webster's Analysis of Puritanism and Science", beginning with an appreciation of "Charles Webster on Puritanism and Science" by Harold J. Cook. Cook notes that Webster stresses the social consequences of broadly Puritan reform, rather than the personal responses of various individuals to religious doctrine. Furthermore, he highlights Webster's contention that, while the Puritan revolution certainly influenced English society at large, it was through that revolution (rather than through doctrinal concerns about salvation) that Puritans so significantly influenced the course of English science.

WEBSTER (1974) reprints a number of articles that had initially appeared in *Past and Present*, all devoted to a variety of aspects of the "Merton Thesis", with an overview by Webster. WEBSTER (1976) also focuses on the problem of Puritanism and English science; although he admits that there were both Catholics in England (such as Richard Towneley and Kenelm Digby), as well as radical Protestants (such as

John Digby, Ralph Cudworth, and John Webster), who contributed to the scientific revolution, his conclusion emphasizes that there is ample evidence to suggest that the entire Puritan movement was conspicuous in its cultivation of the sciences.

WESTFALL, while accepting some vague, ill-defined connection between Puritanism and modern science, prefers to see this entire matter in terms of an "atmosphere more conducive to scientific investigation" than one fostered by Protestantism in any of its various forms. Westfall suggests it may simply have been the idea that nature is mechanical, material, or corpuscular that found a more sympathetic hearing among Protestants than Catholics, and that fortunately this approach turned out to be crucial to the success of the scientific revolution.

For anyone interested in reading more about Merton and the "Merton Thesis", Merton himself provides a useful guide to the literature on this subject to 1957 in Cohen. Here Merton also wrote a concluding piece, in which he re-emphasized an observation by Cohen that the triad of science, technology and society has become a prime semantic marker of the rapidly growing "social science of science". It is this recognition of the significance of the sociology of science that ultimately makes the Merton Thesis such an influential concept in the history of science, and so important for the on-going study of the origins and nature of the scientific revolution.

JOSEPH W. DAUBEN

See also Religion and Science: Renaissance; Scientific Revolution; Sociology of Science

Mesmerism

Crabtree, Adam, *From Mesmer to Freud: Magnetic Sleep and the Roots of Psychological Healing*, New Haven, Connecticut: Yale University Press, 1993

Darnton, Robert, *Mesmerism and the End of the Enlightenment in France*, Cambridge, Massachusetts: Harvard University Press, 1968

Ellenberger, H.F., *Discovery of the Unconscious: The History and Evolution of Dynamic Psychiatry*, London: Allen Lane, and New York: Basic Books, 1970

Ernst, Waltraud, "'Under the Influence' in British India: James Esdaile's Mesmeric Hospital in Calcutta, and Its Critics", *Psychological Medicine*, 25 (1995): 1113–23

Fara, Patricia, "An Attractive Therapy: Animal Magnetism in Eighteenth-Century England", *History of Science*, 33 (1995): 127–77

Gauld, Alan, *A History of Hypnotism*, Cambridge and New York: Cambridge University Press, 1992

Miller, Jonathan, "Mesmerism", in *Hidden Histories of Science*, edited by Robert Silvers, New York: New York Review of Books, 1995; London: Granta, 1997

Palfreman, Jon, "Mesmerism and the English Medical Profession: A Study of a Conflict", *Ethics in Science and Medicine*, 4 (1977): 51–66

Parssinen, Terry M., "Mesmeric Performers", *Victorian Studies*, 21 (1977): 87–104

Parssinen, Terry M., "Professional Deviants and the History of Medicine: Medical Mesmerism in Victorian Britain", in *On the Margins of Science: The Social Construction of Rejected Knowledge*, edited by Roy Wallis, Keele: University of Keele, 1979, 103–20

Winter, Alison, "Ethereal Epidemic: Mesmerism and the Introduction of Inhalation Anaesthesia to Early Victorian London", *Social History of Medicine*, 4 (1991): 1–27

Winter, Alison, "Mesmerism and Popular Culture in Early Victorian England", *History of Science*, 32 (1994): 317–43

Animal magnetism, or mesmerism, the creation of Franz Anton Mesmer (1734–1815), a Viennese physician, was a practice in which an individual was thought to influence another by a variety of personal gestures, sustained eye contact, and the direct influence of the will. Mesmer speculated that imponderable fluids, then thought to control the celestial and inorganic world, also determined the state of living things. He applied magnets to the bodies of patients with the intention of changing the rhythm and quantity of their magnetic fluid, and their "crises" signalled the restoration of health. Mesmer and his work were as controversial as they were popular during his lifetime, and his practice spread rapidly, despite the lack of any consensus on the nature, or even the reality, of the phenomena. By the mid-19th century, animal magnetism, or "mesmerism" as it was named by sceptics in order to deny the existence of the fluid, was practised and debated in much of Europe, America, and various colonial communities, notably British India.

A variety of other practices involving altered states of mind were inspired by, or related to, mesmerism; for example, the surgeon James Braid developed the practice of "hypnotism" in 1842 as an alternative to mesmerism, while the spiritualist movement, and the related practice of "table-turning" – in which vital powers (not muscular effort) were thought to make tables spin under certain conditions – were direct descendants of mesmerism. Furthermore, mesmerism and hypnotism played a critical role in the development of psychoanalysis at the end of the 19th century.

The importance of mesmerism to so many different scientific and medical enterprises was both a cause and a result of the difficulties involved in its classification. Was it therapeutic or pathological, natural or supernatural, a branch of physics, psychology, parapsychology, psychiatry, chemistry, or physiology? Diverse histories have given mesmerism a role in each practice and discipline, playing various features up or down according to the sympathies of the author. Questions of validity have also loomed as large within historical accounts as they did for the practitioners themselves: were the practitioners trustworthy natural philosophers and doctors, or charlatans and quacks; were the phenomena real or fraudulent; and if they were real, what was their cause?

There are, broadly speaking, two approaches to the history of mesmerism; the first treats it as an earlier form of a body of doctrine recognizable today (such as psychical research, psychoanalysis, or cognitive psychiatry), while the second treats the practice and its phenomena as an expression of, or a stimulus to, the culture of the period.

Disciplinary histories of mesmerism follow its travails through different periods and countries, isolating it (to varying degrees) from each local situation, rather than looking intently at a particular context and its cultural significance at any particular place and time. Mesmerism often gets at least a walk-on part in the history of psychiatry and psychoanalysis, not least because of the eerie similarities between the two pivotal men – two controversial "wizards" purveying radical accounts of the human mind, who rose to prominence in Vienna at the end of their respective centuries. In short, Mesmer can appear to be a prior incarnation of Freud, or, at the very least, the 18th-century healer can be shown to have begun investigations into the unconscious that were consummated by his 19th-century counterpart. These associations are exploited in ELLENBERGER's classic history of psychiatry and the unconscious, and in CRABTREE's scholarly portrayal of mesmerism as an embryonic form of modern psychological healing. In addition to psychiatry, other modern sciences of the mind can look to mesmerism as their ancestor; GAULD's massive study, the most empirically detailed source on the subject to date, is framed, in part, as a disciplinary history of hypnotism, while Jonathan MILLER argues that mesmeric phenomena display hitherto unrecognized components of modern cognitive psychology.

The second category of literature explores the cultural significance of mesmerism. DARNTON opened up the history of mesmerism as appropriate to cultural and social history by examining Mesmer's practice within the context of late-Enlightenment and revolutionary intellectual movements in France. After the Revolution, mesmerism's career continued, and FARA reconstructs the activity of mesmerists on both sides of the Channel. This is one of the most detailed and informative accounts yet available of mesmerism in the late 18th century, particularly for England. Studies of mesmerism in the Victorian period have often used the phenomenon as a means of testing the boundaries of legitimacy in the culture, or conversely, as a window on to other aspects of Victorian society. Studies of the relationship between orthodox and marginal intellectual communities, such as PALFREMAN's social history and PARSSINEN (1979), the latter adapting the sociology of knowledge to his own social history, use mesmerism as a case in point in distinguishing between "fringe" and "orthodox" medicine in early Victorian England, while WINTER (1991) argues that the distinction between what was proper and improper to medicine was not so easy to make during this period. ERNST's study of mesmerism in India argues that mesmerism failed as a medical technique administered to white patients by Indian practitioners because of discomfort at the necessary interracial contact. Other studies have used mesmerism to explore aspects of Victorian culture; WINTER (1994) examines how people used altered states in order to make polemical characterizations of "popular culture" and "the common people", and PARSSINEN (1977) uses mesmerism to understand Victorian itinerant lecturing activity.

ALISON WINTER

See also Magnetism; Quackery; Spiritualism

Metallurgy

Aitchison, Leslie, *A History of Metals*, 2 vols, London: MacDonald and Evans, and New York: Interscience, 1960

Allan, James W., *Persian Metal Technology, 700–1300 AD*, Oxford: Ithaca Press, 1979

Ashton, Thomas Southcliffe, *Iron and Steel in the Industrial Revolution*, Manchester: Manchester University Press, 1924; New York: Kelley, 1968

Beck, Ludwig, *Die Geschichte des Eisens in technischer und kulturgeschichtlicher Beziehung*, 5 vols, Braunschweig: Vieweg, 1884–1903

Chakrabarti, Dilip K., *The Early Use of Iron in India*, Delhi: Oxford University Press, 1992

Craig, Alan K. and Robert C. West (eds), *In Quest of Mineral Wealth: Aboriginal and Colonial Mining in Spanish America*, Baton Rouge: Louisiana State University Geoscience Publications, 1994

Forbes, R.J., *Metallurgy in Antiquity: A Notebook for Archaeologists and Technologists*, Leiden: E.J. Brill, 1950

Gille, Bertrand, *Les Origines de la grande industrie métallurgique en France*, Paris: Domat Montchrestien, 1947

Johannsen, Otto, *Geschichte des Eisens*, Düsseldorf: Stahleisen, 1924

Oddy, W.A. and W. Zwalf, *Aspects of Tibetan Metallurgy*, London: British Museum, 1981

Percy, John, *Metallurgy: The Art of Extracting Metal from Their Ores, and Adapting them to Various Purposes of Manufacture*, 3 vols, London: John Murray, 1861–70

Rostoker, William and Bennet Bronson, *Pre-Industrial Iron: Its Technology and Ethnology*, Philadelphia: privately published, 1990

Smith, Cyril Stanley, *A History of Metallography: The Development of Ideas on the Structure of Metals before 1890*, Chicago: University of Chicago Press, 1960

Smith, Cyril Stanley (ed.), *Sources for the History of the Science of Steel, 1532–1786*, Cambridge, Massachusetts: MIT Press, 1968

Tylecote, R.F., *A History of Metallurgy*, London: Metals Society, 1976; 2nd edition, London: Institute of Materials, 1992

Wagner, Donald B., *Iron and Steel in Ancient China*, Leiden: E.J. Brill, 1993

Wertime, Theodore A., *The Coming of the Age of Steel*, Chicago: Chicago University Press, 1962

There is not a great deal of literature that deals specifically with the history of metallurgy as a science, but there is a fair amount on metallurgy as technology, and, because of the dominant role of iron and steel, much has been written on the sub-field of ferrous metallurgy. Most of the general historical literature focuses on Europe. A number of monographs on metallurgy in China, Persia, Tibet, India, and Spanish America are included here to make up for the inevitable Eurocentrism.

SMITH is the most important author on metallurgy as a science. His 1960 general history outlines some important developments in metallurgical technology and the attempts at their explanation by 17th-century natural philosophers, then demonstrates the subsequent change especially with the introduction of crystallographic ideas and techniques in the 19th century. WERTIME is primarily an internalist history of technology touching also on developments in the science of ferrous metallurgy.

SMITH has also commissioned and edited translations of major primary sources for the history of the science of metallurgy. The most important one is his 1968 collection of scientific texts (as opposed to furnace design or the invention of new heavy machinery) between 1532 and 1786. The authors translated are: an anonymous German 16th-century author, Vannoccio Biringuccio, Giovanni Battista della Porta, Methurin Jousse, René Antoine Ferchault de Réaumur, Johann Andreas Cramer, Pierre Clément Grignon, Torbern Bergman, Louis Bernard Guyton de Morveau, and the joint authors Charles Auguste Vandermonde, Claude Louis Berthollet, and Gaspard Monge.

The above texts by no means do justice to the huge field of the science of ferrous metallurgy. For example, 18th-century Swedes, such as Sven Rinman and Torbern Bergman, discovered the important role of carbon in iron alloys and this has not yet been studied by an historian with knowledge of the Swedish language. And the 20th-century elucidation of the physics of the quench-hardening of steel has hardly been studied at all. These two examples are covered only very briefly in Smith (1960) and Wertime.

By contrast, the (European) history of metallurgical technology is so abundant that only a few works can be mentioned here. The best have been written by working engineers such as Percy, Aitchison, Tylecote, Beck, and Johannsen, no doubt because the subject makes heavy demands on the technical understanding of its historians.

PERCY, a physician turned metallurgist, was an admirable Victorian polymath, who knew as much chemistry as one could know in his time, was friendly with the leading English metallurgists, corresponded with scientists, engineers, and businessmen around the world, and drew on a wide variety of publications in English, Latin, French, and German. He made great efforts to cover the history of every aspect of the subject, and his book, though intended as a technical treatise, can still be read with profit as a general history of metallurgy.

AITCHISON is a well-written and superbly illustrated history from pre-historic to modern times, and is perhaps the best of a large number of "Whig" histories of metallurgy. As he writes, his book "is a typical success story, following the common sequence of humble beginnings, of growth to wealth, power and influence, and culminating in the acquisition of an almost unquestioned supremacy among the materials used by man". (This was written in 1960, before the plastic age.)

TYLECOTE is an encyclopedic history from the Neolithic period to 1950, which contains a lot of technical detail. It is the textbook on the subject for archaeologists, and is useful for anyone who needs a serious technical history.

FORBES is probably the best writer on metallurgy of ancient Greece and Rome. He deals with a great deal of archaeological material, but advances in archaeological methodology as well as new excavations make this part of his book rather dated. Readers should also be aware that its very full bibliography contains numerous typographical errors that make it difficult or impossible to find some of its references.

There is no history of metallurgy that works within the more sociologically oriented conceptual framework now commonly practised in academic departments of the history of technology, but scattered articles on various metallurgical topics can be found in such journals as *Technology and Culture* and *Technikgeschichte*.

The literature on ferrous metallurgical technology is especially rich. Beck and Johannsen are the classics of this specialization, giving great detail on all technical aspects. For earlier periods they are now out of date, but they remain valuable for medieval and later developments. BECK is the more ambitious of the two. In five large volumes it covers antiquity and Middle Ages, the 16th and 17th centuries, the 18th century, 1801–60, and 1860–1900. Each volume contains much on the development of technologies while also referring to the acquisition of raw materials and trade. The 1801–60 volume in particular emphasizes scientific developments. Each volume has a separate section describing the developments peculiar to particular regions, especially of the main European nation states. JOHANNSEN is much shorter, only 240 pages, and it deals with the technology of ferrous metallurgy only. But it covers the same time span as Beck.

ROSTOKER & BRONSON places the technological aspects of ferrous metallurgy in a broader historical context. It is a kind of textbook of ferrous metallurgy, written by an engineer and an anthropologist, and it also applies the technical insights gained to questions of ethnology and economic history. Unfortunately it is marred by numerous minor errors of fact, both technical and historical.

There are two classic economic histories of metallurgical industry that take the technology seriously: Ashton on Britain and Gille on France. ASHTON covers events and personalities in 18th-century Britain, detailing business structures, mechanical, and chemical processes, and the discovery of new sources of raw material and the expansion of markets. GILLE describes the generation of large-scale industry in the period from 1661 to 1789. He first discusses Jean-Baptiste Colbert, Louis XIV's controller general of finance, and his role in the development of the French economy. He then analyses the geographical-physical, technical, commercial, financial, and social conditions of French metallurgical development. Finally he details the concentration of industry culminating in large-scale factories.

Eurocentricity is a characteristic of most of the works discussed above. A list of some useful histories relating specifically to other parts of the world may remedy this to some extent: WAGNER on China, which also contains references to the fairly voluminous literature on the history of Chinese metallurgy; ALLAN on Persia; ODDY & ZWALF on Tibet; CHAKRABARTI on India; and finally CRAIG & WEST on pre-Columbian and colonial Spanish America.

DONALD B. WAGNER

See also Materials Science

Metaphor

Bloor, David, *Knowledge and Social Imagery*, London and Boston: Routledge and Kegan Paul, 1976; 2nd edition, Chicago: University of Chicago Press, 1991

Hannaway, Owen, *Chemists and the Word: The Didactic Origins of Chemistry*, Baltimore: Johns Hopkins University Press, 1975

Haraway, Donna, *Crystals, Fabrics, and Fields: Metaphors of Organicism in Twentieth-Century Developmental Biology*, New Haven, Connecticut: Yale University Press, 1976

Johnson, Mark (ed.), *Philosophical Perspectives on Metaphor*, Minneapolis: University of Minnesota Press, 1981

Keller, Evelyn Fox, *Secrets of Life, Secrets of Death: Essays on Language, Gender, and Science*, New York: Routledge, 1992

Leatherdale, W.H., *The Role of Analogy, Model and Metaphor in Science*, Amsterdam: North-Holland, and New York: Elsevier, 1974

Mirowski, Philip, *More Heat Than Light: Economics as Social Physics; Physics as Nature's Economics*, Cambridge and New York: Cambridge University Press, 1989

According to the positivist image, ideal scientific theories are axiomatic, mathematical structures that summarize and unify phenomena. Within this picture, there is usually no real place for metaphors; they are viewed as rhetorical flourishes or, sometimes, as aids to discovery, but they are never essential to the cognitive content of theories.

LEATHERDALE is a summary and elaboration of philosophical criticisms of the positivist view of metaphor in science. It includes a careful survey of arguments for and against the importance of metaphor put forward in the 1950s and 1960s, by, among others, Mary Hesse, Max Black, Stephen Toulmin, Peter Achinstein, Rom Harré, Mario Bunge, and E.H Hutton. For example, one chapter explores the debate over the importance of theoretical models, closely related to metaphors. Leatherdale sees philosophers as fundamentally divided on this issue: Hesse, Black, and others argue that models provide essential cognitive content to scientific theories, making those theories usable, fruitful, and representational, while philosophers such as Bunge and Pierre Duhem regard mathematical formalisms as completing the scientific project. Although the book is constrained by its conservative picture of science, it is useful for its systematic treatment of these issues, providing extensive lists of positions on, and possibilities for, the importance of metaphor in science.

JOHNSON is not primarily about science, but it is an excellent collection of philosophical perspectives on metaphor. Although the book is no longer fully up to date, it includes chapters representing the main positions on how and why metaphors are meaningful, and how they work cognitively or linguistically, including chapters by Max Black, Donald Davidson, John Searle, and George Lakoff and Mark Johnson.

One strong position on the relation of metaphor to science is that of BLOOR, which argues that scientific knowledge always reflects, in a number of senses, the social organization in which it is embedded. Most thoroughly explored is the claim, following Emile Durkheim and Mary Douglas, that images of the structure and status of knowledge are metaphors for society. However, this is taken only as a first step in the sociology of science, as can be seen most clearly in the "strong programme" in the sociology of science that has drawn on Bloor, and in the work of those who take scientific knowledge itself to be a metaphor for the society that creates it. Unlike Leatherdale, which argues that scientists use metaphors productively, the strong programme argues that science is essentially metaphorical.

A huge number of works in the history of science discuss particular metaphors. The following are a few examples, dealing with very different sciences that explicitly and prominently address metaphor, and thus add something to our understanding of the use of metaphor in science. MIROWSKI puts the study of metaphor to use in a critique of the theory of value in economics. Neo-classical economics appropriated, quite directly, the formalisms of the contemporary physics of energy (which had in its turn reflected some popular economic mores), resulting in a metaphorical connection between energy and value. Nineteenth-century physics, therefore, shaped much 20th-century economic research, in ways and directions of which the researchers have been largely unaware. That lack of awareness, Mirowski argues, has contributed to confusions, both because economists have not accepted the consequences of their metaphors, and because they have been unable to see the alternatives. Mirowski suggests, then, that economists examine new metaphors or models of value, some of which might lead to new solutions to long-standing problems.

HARAWAY also uses the study of metaphors in a constructive critique, attempting to revive a form of non-reductionism in biology. Following the work of Mary Hesse in arguing that metaphors are necessary to science because of their fertility, the book explores whether such a position can fit with a Kuhnian model of science, in which fertile metaphors are one component of paradigms. Haraway then studies the effects of a set of metaphors connected with organicism, an anti-reductionist position, on developmental biology. By looking at the work of three important and interesting 20th-century figures, she argues that the metaphors of organicism – crystals, fabrics, and fields – provide some consistent directions of thought and work, and thus might be thought of as contributing to a loosely structured paradigm. The paradigm may, though, be too loosely structured to be successful or analytically useful. Haraway's more recent work continues to focus on metaphors in biology, particularly on metaphorical relations between biological images and popular understandings of race, class, and gender.

The uses and effects of figurative scientific language are the focus of almost all of the essays in KELLER, which range widely over such topics as population genetics, the "competition" metaphor in ecology, and the Manhattan Project. The title essay juxtaposes Watson and Crick's assault on the "secret of life" and commonly-used metaphors of paternity, in descriptions of physicists who worked on the atomic bomb. The metaphors – some of them embedded in actions, rather than being wholly linguistic – surrounding these different secrets can be regarded through the lens of gender, which greatly affects the symbolic politics of life and reproduction.

HANNAWAY elucidates the beginnings of chemistry in a contrast between two readings of the metaphor of the "Book of Nature"; one by a Paracelsian physician, Oswald Croll, and the other by a humanist schoolteacher, Andreas Libavius. Libavius's *Alchemia* (1597) was a key source of chemical knowledge in the 17th century, and a model on which later chemistry text books were patterned. Reading the "Book of Nature" was not the only issue concerning metaphors over which Libavius and Croll disagreed, because the root of that conflict was the nature of language itself. The Paracelsian Croll saw power in the search for the Word of Creation, the true language whose metaphors would – with study – reveal nature's secrets. For Libavius, the Word was lost forever, and knowledge could stem only from the organization and use of literal languages. Thus Hannaway describes an important period in the de-figuralization of scientific language.

SERGIO SISMONDO

See also Rhetoric

Meteorological Instruments

Abbe, Cleveland, *Treatise on Meteorological Apparatus and Methods*, Washington, DC: Government Printing Office, 1888

Bolton, Henry Carrington, *Evolution of the Thermometer, 1592–1743*, Easton, Philadelphia: Chemical Publishing, 1900

Brush, Stephen G. and Helmut E. Landsberg, with Martin Collins, *The History of Geophysics and Meteorology: An Annotated Bibliography*, New York: Garland, 1985

Burkhardt, F., "Die Erfindung des Thermometers und seine Gestaltung im XVII. Jahrhundert", *Bericht des Pädagogiums*, Basel, 1867

Burkhardt, F., "Die wichtigsten Thermometer des achtzehnten Jahrhunderts", *Bericht der Gewerbeschule zu Basel*, 1871,

De Waard, Cornelis, *L'Expérience barométrique: Ses antecedents et ses explications*, Thouars: Imprimerie Nouvelle, 1936

Fleming, James Rodger, *Meteorology in America, 1800–1870*, Baltimore: Johns Hopkins University Press, 1990

Friedman, Robert Marc, *Appropriating the Weather: Vilhelm Bjerknes and the Construction of a Modern Meteorology*, Ithaca, New York: Cornell University Press, 1989

Goodison, Nicholas, *English Barometers, 1680–1860: A History of Domestic Barometers and Their Makers*, New York: Potter, 1968; revised edition, Woodbridge, Suffolk: Antique Collectors' Club, 1977

Meteorological Office of Great Britain, *Handbook of Meteorological Instruments: Part II*, London: HMSO, 1961

Middleton, W.E. Knowles, "The Early History of Hygrometry, and the Controversy Between de Saussure and de Luc", *Quarterly Journal of the Royal Meteorological Society*, 68 (1942): 247–61

Middleton, W.E. Knowles and Athelstan F. Spilhaus, *Meteorological Instruments*, 3rd edition, Toronto: University of Toronto Press, 1953

Middleton, W.E. Knowles, *The History of the Barometer*, Baltimore: Johns Hopkins Press, 1964

Middleton, W.E. Knowles, *A History of the Thermometer and Its Use in Meteorology*, Baltimore: Johns Hopkins Press, 1966

Middleton, W.E. Knowles, *Invention of the Meteorological Instruments*, Baltimore: Johns Hopkins Press, 1969

Middleton, W.E. Knowles, *The Experimenters: A Study of the Accademia del Cimento*, Baltimore: Johns Hopkins University Press, 1971

Multhauf, Robert P. "The Introduction of Self-Registering Meteorological Instruments", US National Museum (Smithsonian Institution) Bulletin 228, *Contributions from the Museum of History and Technology*, Paper 23 (1961): 95–106

Patterson, Louise Diehl, "Thermometers of the Royal Society, 1663–1768", *American Journal of Physics*, 19 (1951): 523–35

Patterson, Louise Diehl, "The Royal Society's Standard Thermometer 1663–1709", *Isis*, 44 (1953): 51–64

Shapin, Steven and Simon Schaffer, *Leviathan and the Air-Pump: Hobbes, Boyle, and the Experimental Life*, Princeton, New Jersey: Princeton University Press, 1985; revised edition 1989

Taylor, F. Sherwood, "The Origin of the Thermometer", *Annals of Science*, 5 (1942): 129–56

The history of meteorology has been divided into three periods: a speculative period from antiquity through the Renaissance; an empirical period, dating from the introduction of classical meteorological instruments, and ending some time between 1800 and 1920; and the final period, when meteorology, although tainted (as it were) by its prognostic end, attained some pretence to being an exact science. The history of meteorological instruments is intimately linked to this evolution. The first period is characterized as virtually instrument-free, in the sense that the instruments that were to become important in the later history of meteorology, such as the barometer and the thermometer, were employed for entirely different purposes. The second period is defined entirely by the instruments, which is clearly reflected in the histories. Modern meteorology, in contrast, is theory driven, and, consequently, discussion of instrumentation in the third period is sparse.

A fairly comprehensive bibliography of meteorology and meteorological instruments can be found in BRUSH & LANDSBERG, which reveals also the nationalistic bent of many of the histories. Serious historical accounts began toward the end of the 19th century in a number of European sources, but these rarely rose above the merely descriptive. BURKHARDT (1867 and 1871), for instance, briefly described the discovery of the thermometer and its development in the 17th century. ABBE, although not an explicit history, contains descriptions of a great variety of instrumentation, and thus remains a valuable source. BOLTON's history of the thermometer also focuses on descriptions of the development of the instrument itself. This antiquarian and positivistic genre has continued into the 20th century; GOODISON, for instance, provides vivid descriptions of many barometers, but in the complex descriptions surrounding the derivation of each apparatus, the history is lost.

Within the English-language literature of the 20th century, Middleton defines the field. A prolific writer, this meteorologist/

historian has an extensive body of work, from practical hand-books and historical articles in the 1940s and 1950s, followed by a comprehensive series of synoptic histories of instruments and early theoretical thought in the 1960s, to the study of early scientific academies in the 1970s. Following the positivistic genre at the onset, he developed a sympathy for earlier scientific belief systems, and matured into a scholar with an interest in the patronage and social interaction of early modern practitioners. His research is comprehensive, in terms of both secondary and primary sources. What little had been written in the field of meteorological instruments is synthesized in his corpus.

MIDDLETON & SPILHAUS begins its explication of the instruments with historical notes, and provides some information on 20th-century instruments in addition to information on earlier items. MIDDLETON (1964) is an invaluable and comprehensive history of the development of the barometer. It includes an historiographical analysis of the several debates surrounding the early history of the instrument, provides a summary of primary sources, and clarifies the arguments found elsewhere in the literature. MIDDLETON (1966) is narrow in scope, but it does consider the impact of the thermometer on a multitude of fields, and there is a good discussion of the conceptual shift from subjective to objective temperature. Middleton draws on much of the earlier, rather positivistic, secondary literature and his account is a great improvement on them. MIDDLETON (1969) is the major survey of the field; recapping the works on the barometer and thermometer, it proceeds to discuss most of the major instruments, and also a few minor ones, from antiquity to World War II. MIDDLETON (1971) is a study of Italy's first scientific academy, the birthplace of the thermoscope and the baroscope, and contains translations of some of the academicians' publications, placing them within their institutional, political, and intellectual contexts.

Aside from Middleton's work, the bibliography on meteorological instruments is sparse, and serious analysis even more so. The primary sources on early instruments are found in correspondence and reports, such as those from the *Transactions of the Royal Society*. They can also be found littered among the encyclopedic publications of several of the great lights of the 17th century (e.g. Hooke, Boyle, Pascal), but here the footnotes of secondary works provide the best guidance. One is almost better served with a synopsis from Middleton.

The most extensive work in the field concerns instruments the significance of which stretches far beyond the field – namely, the barometer and the thermometer. The history of the barometer is an important chapter in the history of the scientific revolution: the instrument itself was developed not to measure air pressure, but rather as a demonstration brought to the fore in the controversy over the existence of the vacuum, and nearly every general work on the period makes some mention of the Toricellian experiment. Middleton (1969, *Invention of the Meteorological Instruments*) is a good source here, while De WAARD, one of Middleton's key sources on the early history, places the barometric experiment within its philosophical context. SHAPIN & SCHAFFER's discussion of the role of experiment in the 17th century centers on the vacuum pump; while their account is clearly important on the one hand for an understanding of the barometer, on the other

hand, it is this kind of sociological analysis that promises to unravel the period of instrument invention later to become central to meteorology. With this kind of remit in mind, PATTERSON's work on the Royal Society is highly relevant, as it contains an interesting analysis of the collective process by which quantitative scales and physical standards came to be generally adopted.

The shift away from qualitative concepts of heat and cold, as represented by the thermometer, encapsulates the crucial shift of science toward number. However, much of the literature on the thermometer is impoverished, as it is obsessed with priority in the case of two central inventions. The first area of controversy, covered in TAYLOR and Middleton (1969), is over the invention of the modern thermoscope (non-quantitative thermometer), often attributed to Galileo. The second controversy concerns the final development of the Celsius scale. Many accounts of early thermometry betray the nationalistic bent of the historians.

Recent instruments remain for the most part unanalyzed, and technical works are often the only sources of information. For example, along with practical instruction, the METEORO-LOGICAL OFFICE OF GREAT BRITAIN offers a brief chronology of instruments up to the 1950s.

There remains much to be done in the field, particularly as the progress of certain instruments may prove to be telling indexes of social and cultural change. So far, the best accounts of how instrumentation and instrumental practice form a part of a larger social, political, and economic context can be found in histories of national meteorological programs: FLEMING is a good example, analyzing instrumental practice in 19th-century America, and examining the use of the telegraph; MULTHAUF relates the history of self-registering instruments, from their invention in the early-modern period to their adoption in organized institutional settings in the late 19th century; while the process by which economic and military necessity can interact with a theoretical program, through the mutually dependent rise of aviation, international observation, and thermodynamic upper-air modelling during and after World War I, is described in FRIEDMAN. There is still much room for the discussion of meteorological instruments in their social and cultural contexts.

BRANT VOGEL

See also Meteorology; Scientific Instruments: general works; Telegraphy

Meteorology

Fleming, James Rodger, *Meteorology in America, 1800–1870*, Baltimore: Johns Hopkins University Press, 1990

Friedman, Robert Marc, *Appropriating the Weather: Vilhelm Bjerknes and the Construction of a Modern Meteorology*, Ithaca, New York: Cornell University Press, 1989

Frisinger, H. Howard, *The History of Meteorology to 1800*, New York: Science History Publications, 1977

Heninger, S.K., *A Handbook of Renaissance Meteorology*, Durham, North Carolina: Duke University Press, 1960

Khrgian, A. Kh., *Meteorology: A Historical Survey*, vol. 1, revised edition, translated from the Russian by Ron

Harden, Jerusalem: Israel Program for Scientific Translation, 1970

Kutzbach, Gisela, *The Thermal Theory of Cyclones: A History of Meteorological Thought in the Nineteenth Century*, Boston: American Meteorological Society, 1979

Middleton, William E. Knowles, *A History of the Theories of Rain and Other Forms of Precipitation*, London: Oldbourne, 1965; New York: Watts, 1966

Shaw, William Napier, *Manual of Meteorology*, vol 1: *Meteorology in History*, Cambridge: Cambridge University Press, 1926

Spence, Clark C., *The Rainmakers: American "Pluviculture" to World War II*, Lincoln: University of Nebraska Press, 1980

Thomas, Morley, *The Beginnings of Canadian Meteorology*, Toronto: ECW Press, 1991

Meteorology lacks a rich historiography, a misfortune for which there are two possible reasons. First, until perhaps the advent of computers, chaos theory and fears of global warming, meteorology demonstrated little of the charisma and conspicuous progress that attracted an earlier generation of historians, and historical accounts written by meteorologists remained buried in specialist journals. Second, the term's contemporary meaning fails dismally to encompass its historical one; until the 19th century, meteorology referred broadly to phenomena of the air, including much that now falls under the guise of astronomy or geology, such as meteors and aurorae. More than most subjects, then, meteorology has historical boundaries that remain ill-defined and problematic in relation to the present discipline.

There are several surveys, most of which require some caution from a reader. FRISINGER's history, part of the historical monograph series of the American Meteorological Society, is widely accessible but of a length that allows for little more than chronology. Frisinger divides the subjects into three periods, and deals with the first two: the period of "speculation" dominated by Aristotle; the "dawn of scientific meteorology" in the 17th and 18th centuries; and, from the 19th century on, the coming of "meteorology as a physical science". Frisinger's emphasis is on the development of measurement, on which the advances of meteorology depend.

KHRGIAN can be difficult to locate, but contains information on eastern Europe and Scandinavia that cannot be found elsewhere in the literature: for example, accounts of weather information networks in Siberia in the 18th century. The narrative also suffers in parts from a breathless chronology, but at its best is far more comprehensive and suggestive than Frisinger. The chapters on climatology are a case in point, as is the brief discussion of medical ideas about climate. Carrying his account through to the 20th century, Khrgian covers institutional developments in Europe from the 18th century onwards, as well as providing a standard treatment of meteorological concepts and instruments.

A third and idiosyncratic survey, written at the end of World War I, comes from the early 20th-century head of the British meteorological office. William Napier SHAW was keenly interested in raising the profile of meteorology as a physical science, and distanced himself from both the practical applications and the pre-modern conceptions of the subject. Like Frisinger, his is ultimately an account of the triumph of exact measurement.

HENINGER was designed in part to serve students of Elizabethan literature, and remains an invaluable resource for those interested in this period, not least because of its bibliography and appendix of authors. Heninger integrates folkloric, literary and scriptural treatments with the natural philosophy of the period, still dominated by Aristotle's *Meteorologica*. The rich picture of meteorological knowledge that emerges is an interesting contrast to the surveys mentioned above.

MIDDLETON has produced another type of survey, following the development of a concept. His definition of "precipitation" is wide, however, (including winds and water vapours), so that the history is more comprehensive than its title might indicate. Middleton provides a context for meteorological thought, and links speculation to other philosophical debates, such as the influence of chemical and electrical theories on ideas about rain in the 18th century. This more concentrated approach also allows Middleton to discuss some practitioners, in contrast to the other somewhat disembodied surveys.

The best of the more detailed surveys is undoubtedly FRIEDMAN, which is both more and less than a biography. Concentrating on the career of Vilhelm Bjerknes (1862–1951), and the development of physical dynamic models of the atmosphere in the first quarter of the 20th century, Friedman details Bjerknes's struggle to further both the peripheral position of meteorology and his own position as a scientist in Scandinavia. The influence of World War I is brilliantly explored.

For those interested in further discussion of the development of storm theory, prior to the work of Bjerknes's Bergen school, KUTZBACH offers the 19th-century history in a scholarly account in the internalist tradition. There are three studies of meteorology in North America. FLEMING also covers the 19th-century storm theory debates, yet his account of the extensive and varied meteorological networks in the United States demonstrates how awkwardly theoretical concerns were placed in the work of organizations whose appeal and justification was practical forecasting. THOMAS supplies a pioneering account of meteorological services in Canada, covering the half-century following the foundation of the Toronto Magnetic and Meteorological Observatory in 1839. This study, based principally on the archives of the Toronto Observatory, sketches the personalities, observation programs, and institutional development of Canada's central observatory. SPENCE integrates discussions of advertising, public swindles, and ecological change into his history of experiments with rainmaking in the drought-ridden American West of the late 19th and early 20th centuries.

KATHARINE ANDERSON

See also Environmental Sciences; Meteorological Instruments

Metrology

Boudia, Soraya and Xavier Roqué (guest eds), "Science, Medicine, and Industry: The Curie and Joliot-Curie Laboratories" (special issue), *History and Technology*, 13 (1997): 241–343

Cahan, David, *An Institute for an Empire: The Physikalisch-Technische Reichsanstalt, 1871–1918*, Cambridge: Cambridge University Press, 1989

Cochrane, Rexmond, *Measures for Progress: A History of the National Bureau of Standards*, Washington, DC: National Bureau of Standards, 1966

Cronon, William, *Nature's Metropolis: Chicago and the Great West*, New York: Norton, 1991

Gordin, Michael, "Making Newtons: Mendeleev, Metrology, and the Chemical Ether", *Ambix*, 45 (1998): 96–115

Hessenbruch, Arne, "Geschlechterverhältnis und rationalisierte Röntgenologie", in *Geschlechterverhältnisse in Medizin, Naturwissenschaft und Technik*, edited by Christoph Meinel and Monika Renneberg, Bassum: GNT, 1996

Hessenbruch, Arne, "The Spread of Precision Measurement in Scandinavia 1660–1800", in *The Sciences in the European Periphery During the Enlightenment*, edited by Kostas Gavroglu, Dordrecht: Kluwer, 1999

Kula, Witold, *Measures and Men*, translated from the Polish by R. Szreter, Princeton, New Jersey: Princeton University Press, 1986 (original edition, 1970)

Latour, Bruno, *Science in Action: How to Follow Scientists and Engineers Through Society*, Milton Keynes: Open University Press, 1987

O'Connell, Joseph, "Metrology: The Creation of Universality by the Circulation of Particulars", *Social Studies of Science*, 23 (1993): 129–73

Olesko, Kathryn M., "Precision, Tolerance, and Consensus: Local Cultures in German and British Resistance Standards", in *Scientific Credibility and Technical Standards in 19th and Early 20th Century Germany and Britain*, edited by Jed Z. Buchwald, Dordrecht: Kluwer, 1996

Schaffer, Simon, "Late Victorian Metrology and Its Instrumentation: A Manufactory of Ohms", in *Invisible Connections: Instruments, Institutions, and Science*, edited by Robert Bud and Susan E. Cozzens, Bellingham, Washington: SPIE Optical Engineering Press, 1992

Schaffer, Simon, "Metrology, Metrication and Victorian Values", in *Victorian Science in Context*, edited by Bernard Lightman, Chicago: University of Chicago Press, 1997

Wise, M. Norton (ed.), *The Values of Precision*, Princeton, New Jersey: Princeton University Press, 1995

In the last two decades of the 20th centry, the history of metrology has developed from a disregarded part of the history of science, an unappealing process far from the heroic work of scientific genius, to one of the most theorized topics.

LATOUR describes a world in which the person who can rally the most (or most important) allies accrues the power. Scientific reporting makes it possible to collate scientific research, thus in a sense gathering together expert allies. For example, the experience of many bridge builders can be combined in order to generate an authoritative statement about the kind of bridge that will not fail in the future. An argument based on such collective experience will carry more authority than one based on a single observation. Inscriptions, especially numbers and graphs, facilitate such collation of evidence. The final chapter depicts metrology as sustaining science by setting up the infrastructure within which the results of measurements (inscriptions) can be communicated and understood.

WISE is a collection of papers on various aspects of precision measurement: censuses and the metric system in 18th-century France, Lavoisier, the cultural meaning of precision and accuracy in 19th-century Germany and Britain, Victorian insurance, the graphical method in physiology, electricity metering, the work ethic in light research, and the practice of mathematical calculation. Wise manages to tie these themes together by a stylistic innovation. In addition to an introduction, he has interjected three chapters that comment on the previous three or four papers. This generally works well in giving the book structure. Wise finds that all papers speak to the mediation of travelling objects, such as instruments within a metrological regime, unifying the concerns of centralized bureaucratic states, international commerce, and science.

SCHAFFER (1992) describes the reliance of the international telegraphic network on standards of measurement. He relates this to the very detailed organization of work practices in laboratories and in the world of telegraphy. He also examines the resistance in genteel late Victorian Cambridge to the introduction of rigorous laboratory practices into the otherwise "liberal education" of the university curriculum. Schaffer argues that metrology resembles a vanishing trick and that this constitutes its power. The tremendous work required in order to set up a metrological regime is completely ignored once it is established: calibrated instruments will then appear to reveal the laws of nature unproblematically. Historical work renders the vanishing trick visible again.

SCHAFFER (1997) examines metrology in the work of three prominent 19th-century British scientists. John Herschel argued against the claim that the measurement of the Earth quadrant by which the metre was defined was more exact than the imperial yard. The latter embodied superior British workmanship and discipline. Also, international trade at that time was primarily British, so it was felt that the world should adopt British units. Charles Piazzi Smyth argued that the imperial yard must be divine since it was embodied in the dimensions of the Great Pyramid. Schaffer shows how this claim could have made sense. Finally, Schaffer shows how James Clerk Maxwell endeavoured to soften the resistance to the foundation of the Cavendish Laboratory within Cambridge University by proffering a theological argument of the metrological work done there for the telegraphy industry. Metrology discovered equalities and these were signs of divine creation as witnessed in the absolute equalities of molecular dimensions. Schaffer shows how all three scientists skilfully fused tradition and innovation to make their cases.

O'CONNELL gives a readable overview of electrical standards from their 19th-century origins to the 1990s. He describes the circulation of instrumentation between a highly trusted physical embodiment of a standard and scientific laboratories in general. The error of local instruments is routinely corrected when calibrated with the circulating instruments coming from, for instance, a national standards bureau. This he compares to the periodic sacramental redemption from error within Catholicism. O'Connell sees a "Calvinist Revolution" in the shift towards so-called intrinsic standards in the second half of the 20th century. An example of this is the Josephson junction, which, is based on a quantum effect and is now the standard voltage measurement. Hence, it is not in need of periodic calibration, and in a sense authority has been devolved to the local level. O'Connell also describes the practice of the US Department of Defense, which used to dispatch surprise calibrators to its suppliers but it now relies on documentation from local calibrators.

HESSENBRUCH (1999) sets the development of 18th-century precision science in the context of the military-fiscal state. The "high science" of the Academies concerned itself with problems of measurement for taxation purposes, such as the evaluation of grain or alcohol. A metrological regime was developed in which calibration worked in the manner O'Connell termed Catholic. However, in contrast with the suddenness of O'Connell's revolution, Hessenbruch describes the ongoing work to decentralize the metrological regime. This has involved developing robust apparatus that can travel and is not sensitive to its surroundings, and also certifying the personnel using the instruments (mostly surveyors). The devolution of authority to local representatives was a part of the institutionalization of a civil service and of a community of instrument makers. Finally, Hessenbruch relates the fixing of metrological values to the contemporary fixing of monetary value.

KULA, a Polish economic historian who wrote during the Cold War, focuses on weights and measures in 18th-century Poland and France. He discusses the local cultures of measurement in loving detail, thus rendering the immense work required to standardize weights and measures comprehensible. He contrasts the anthropomorphic measures (such as the king's foot) of local customs with the "natural" measures of the metric system. Kula argues that the extensive local resistance to national standards can only be overcome in societies where two conditions are satisfied: a *de facto* equality of men before the law, and the alienation of the commodity – which is reminiscent of the transition from feudalism to bourgeois society in Marx's writings.

OLESKO examines the creation of the international standard of electrical resistance in the 19th century. By focusing on the German states and unified Germany, she aims to balance the accounts that hitherto have dealt primarily with the British side of the story. She finds that the German work was formed to a much larger extent by the culture of weights and measurements than in Britain where demands of the booming telegraphy industry were paramount. She also finds that the adaptation of foreign practices, such as standardized measurement, occurs in a manner that preserves the salient features of the local culture.

CRONON is a history of Chicago in the 19th century, and describes the developing role of Chicago as the most important trading place for the American Midwest. Three central chapters cover the history of trade in grain, meat, and lumber. Cronon shows how the measurement and pricing of the commodities radiated outwards throughout the entire trade network. The evaluation of grain for instance was related to issues of packing, shipping, and to the new practice of lumping together grain of "similar quality" from entirely different provenances. Cronon, brilliantly, also maps the movement of capital in the opposite direction of the movement of commodities. He is also attentive to the ecological changes wrought.

BOUDIA & ROQUÉ's work contains three papers on the active role of the Curies, and Marie Curie in particular, in the establishment of a radium economy centered on the use of radium in the therapy of skin diseases. They reveal the metrological commitment of the Curies in the service of that industry and show how intimate their connections were with both the industrial production of radium and the establishment of a market for it. In the introduction, Dominique Pèstre discusses the tensions in French scientific culture prompted by Marie Curie's metrological services to commercial enterprises run from within a state university putatively concerned with pure science.

HESSENBRUCH (1996) shows that the development of a factory-style cancer radiotherapy in the 1920s created sufficient demand to set up an elaborate and expensive metrological infrastructure for X-ray intensity. He shows that in this process women were systematically reified. Exact dosage made the delegation of some radiological work, such as turning the radiation source on and off, easier. Female X-ray assistants were increasingly classed as a part of the instrumentation both when patient fees were determined and also when responsibility was to be defined for litigation purposes. The radiologists who were keenest on precision measurement also classed the bodies of female patients (the large majority in radiotherapy) as machines without individuality.

The last three items in this entry are historical accounts of some of the main national standards laboratories: Germany, the US, and Russia. CAHAN covers the first half century of the Reichsanstalt, the world's first national standards laboratory. He describes in some detail the methods used in this institution, such as the development of standards, testing and certifying, which demonstrated some of the intellectual and social benefits that science and technology could contribute to modern society and to the modern nation-state. Cahan has used the Reichsanstalt's archives extensively and provides a very thorough account.

COCHRANE shows the development of US metrology from Independence through to the 1960s, focusing mainly on the National Bureau of Standards (NBS), the predecessor of the present-day National Institute of Science and Technology. Cochrane was invited to write the book by the NBS and had free access to the archives. He is attentive to the political difficulties that characterize its history in contrast to European standards bodies, where the central government's authority to issue standards has not been contested to the same extent. The book is comprehensive in its coverage of the many different activities at the NBS, and as a result provides an overview of the history of American industrial life in the 20th century.

GORDIN examines the work of Dmitrii Ivanovich Mendeleev, famed for the Periodic Table, in his capacity as Director of Russia's Chief Bureau of Weights and Measures, and as a pioneer of reforms in economics, military policy, popular education, and trade. He argues that all these activities "cohered incongruously" with Mendeleev's work on a chemical (meaning ponderable) ether and periodic order. Just as good education requires the circulation of inspectors coordinating teaching, so also a metrological regime requires circulation between a central standards bureau and local stations. Within a smoothly running functional regime, scientific measurements become orderly and the Periodic Table is easily shown. Mendeleev introduced the concept of the chemical ether to defuse the threat to the stability of the Periodic Table posed by the disintegration theory of radioactivity.

ARNE HESSENBRUCH

See also Measurement; Standardization

Michelson, Albert A.   1852–1931

German-born American physicist

Astronomische Nachrichten (special issue) 1982

Goldberg, Stanley and Roger H. Stuewer (eds), *The Michelson Era in American Science, 1870–1930*, New York: American Institute of Physics, 1988

Holton, Gerald, "Einstein, Michelson, and the "Crucial Experiment"", *Isis*, 60 (1969): 133–97; reprinted in his *Thematic Origins of Scientific Thought: Kepler to Einstein*, Cambridge, Massachusetts: Harvard University Press, 1973

Jaffe, Bernhard, *Michelson and the Speed of Light*, London: Heinemann, and New York: Anchor, 1960

Kevles, Daniel J., *The Physicists: The History of a Scientific Community in Modern America*, New York: Knopf, 1978; revised edition, Cambridge, Massachusetts: Harvard University Press, 1995

Michelson-Livingston, Dorothy, *The Master of Light: A Biography of Albert A. Michelson*, New York: Scribner, 1973

Reingold, Nathan, *Science in Nineteenth-Century America: A Documentary History*, New York: Hill and Wang, 1964

Serafini, Anthony, *Legends in Their Own Time: A Century of American Physical Scientists*, New York: Plenum Press, 1993

Swenson Jr, Loyd S., *The Ethereal Aether: A History of the Michelson–Morley–Miller Aether-Drift Experiments, 1880–1930*, Austin: University of Texas Press, 1972

The unique skills in optics of the American experimental physicist, Albert Abraham Michelson, has inevitably led to the appearance of hagiographic works on the scientist. MICHELSON-LIVINGSTON's biography certainly falls into that category, but her research on the topic was most thorough, and she does a fine job in presenting an accessible, layman's account of Michelson's work, covering topics as varied as the measurement of the velocity of light and of stellar diameters, the definition of the meter in terms of multiples of a spectral line wavelength, the search for an aether-wind, and materials testing. Her quotes from published and unpublished sources are well-chosen, and include many interesting newspaper clippings, as well as selections from Michelson's correspondence, and excerpts from interviews with his former co-workers and students.

Apart from this full biography, Michelson has also been the subject of several other less intensely researched popular accounts, such as those by SERAFINI and by JAFFE. As implied by Serafini's book title, Michelson was indeed a "legend in his own time": as the second president of the American Physical Society, the first American Nobel prize winner in the sciences,

and, first and foremost, the undisputed leading expert in the many applications of interference methods. Nevertheless, the hagiographic perspective has its severe limitations.

Contextual questions on such topics as, for example, the influence of training and of other scientists on Michelson's work, are considered in REINGOLD's anthology of science in 19th-century America. This anthology includes excerpts from the correspondence between Michelson and the classical mathematical astronomer, Simon Newcomb, the editor of the US navy's *Nautical Almanac*. Newcomb's early interest in the velocity of light inspired Michelson, who is now famous for his high-precision redeterminations of the light's velocity that originated from this contact.

Additional information on Michelson's scientific education in the Naval Academy is found in Kathryn Olesko's essay for GOLDBERG & STUEWER's anthology on the Michelson era in American science. According to Olesko, physics teaching in America in the 1870s was undergoing a reform that brought it closer to the European model of teaching-research laboratories and seminars. In the same volume, W.A. Koelsch looks at the network of scientists at Clark University, where Michelson taught between 1889 and 1893, and J.L. Michel at the "Chicago connection" between Michelson and Millikan from 1894 to 1921. The strength of Goldberg & Stuewer's anthology lies in its studies of a broader contextual nature, such as those by D.H. Stapleton and E.T. Layton, who argue for the thesis that new relations emerged between theoreticians, experimentalists, and instrument-producers. Stapleton, in particular, argues convincingly that Michelson's many successful experiments must be seen against the background of an exceptionally well-developed community of industry and higher education in the area around Cleveland and Pittsburgh.

Another important terrain covered in Goldberg & Stuewer is the national context of American science in the age of Michelson and beyond. KEVLES gives a brief summary of his book-length study of the social history of the physics community in America between 1870 and 1930, and E. Crawford and R.M. Friedman analyse the profile of American candidates for the Nobel prizes in physics and chemistry – Friedman, in particular, comparing the nominations of Michelson and G.E. Hale (one accepted in 1907, the other undeservedly unsuccessful).

Part II of Goldberg & Stuewer's anthology deals with Michelson's high-precision work in optics, especially with his most famous experiment, the interferometric search for an aether wind. In a special issue of *ASTRONOMISCHE NACHRICHTEN*, that appeared in 1982 as a centenary contribution to the first Michelson interferometer experiment performed in the winter of 1880–81 in Potsdam, we learn more about Michelson's stay in Berlin as the research guest of Helmholtz. However, the most detailed account is offered in SWENSON's monograph, a prototype of the "biography" of a certain type of experiment. Swenson not only covers the details of the 1881 experiment, but also its repetition, together with Morley, in 1886–87 at Western Reserve College. (For Michelson's correspondence with Morley see also Reingold). The experiment confirmed the unexpected null result, but Swenson also gives an account of the later repetitions, including that of D.C. Miller who, in the 1920s, claimed to have obtained positive results. Swenson's history shows that anomalous results – such as Michelson's and Morley's (placed against the background of classical electrodynamics), as well as Miller's (considered in relation to the special theory of relativity) – were not at all as fatal as would be supposed; on the contrary, the case shows just how much anomalies are ignored by the scientific community.

Another debated issue is whether the Michelson–Morley experiment was in fact instrumental in Einstein's formulation of the special theory of relativity. In contradiction to a strong textbook tradition, HOLTON, in a now-famous essay of 1969, argued that the usual assertion of a genetic link between the Michelson–Morley experiment and Einstein's special relativity theory is ill-founded, and that it was other experiments – such as aberration, Fizeau's ether-drag experiment, and the asymmetries of the classical account of induction – which were much more significant in the development of the work of the young Einstein.

KLAUS HENTSCHEL

See also Aether; Electromagnetism; Optics; Relativity

Microscopes

Bracegirdle, Brian, *A History of Microtechnique: The Evolution of the Microtome and the Development of Tissue Preparation*, London: Heinemann, 1978; 2nd edition, Lincolnwood, Illinois: Science Heritage, 1986

Bracegirdle, Brian (ed.), *Beads of Glass: Leeuwenhoek and the Early Microscope*, London: Science Museum, 1983

Bradbury, Savile, *The Evolution of the Microscope*, Oxford and New York: Pergamon Press, 1967

Clay, Reginald S. and Thomas H. Court, *The History of the Microscope*, London: Charles Griffin, 1932

Disney, Alfred N., *Origin and Development of the Microscope*, London: Royal Microscopical Society, 1928

Frison, Edouard, *L'Évolution de la partie optique du microscope au cours du dix-neuvième siècle*, Leiden: Rijksmuseum voor de Geschiedenis der Natuurwetenschappen, 1954

Hartley, W.G., *The Light Microscope: Its Use and Development*, Oxford: Senecio, 1993

Hawkes, Peter W. (ed.), *The Beginnings of Electron Microscopy*, Orlando, Florida: Academic Press, 1985

Petri, R.J., *Das Mikroskop: Von seinen Anfangen bis zur jetzigen Vervolkommnung für alle Freunde dieses Instruments*, Berlin: Schoetz, 1896

Ruska, Ernst, *The Early Development of Electron Lenses and Electron Microscopy*, translated from the German by Thomas Mulvey, Stuttgart: Hirzel, 1980 (original edition, 1979)

Schmitz, E.-H., *Handbuch zur Geschichte der Optik: Ergänzungsband II Das Mikroskop*, vol.1, Bonn: Wayenborgh, 1989; vol. 2, Edinburgh: Wayenborgh, 1990

Turner, Gerard L'E., *Essays on the History of the Microscope*, Oxford: Senecio, 1980

Turner, Gerard L'E., *The Great Age of the Microscope: The Collection of the Royal Microscopical Society Through 150 Years*, Bristol and New York: Hilger, 1989

The now ubiquitous microscope has a large literature, but, unfortunately, much of what has been written contains abundant half-truths and errors, and care is necessary in selecting sources. Virtually all the early books on the practice of microscopy contained historical sections, at least on the mechanical part of the instrument, the stand itself, while much less was written concerning the optics – despite the fact that the optics are the entire reason for the existence of the stand – and less still about the nature of what was seen with the instrument. Nowadays, in studying the history of the microscope, it is not desirable to use any work published before the very end of the 19th century. At that time, the well-known bacteriologist, PETRI, produced a book still useful for its full coverage, many references, and good illustrations. He provides a 250-page account of the simple microscope (where one lens forms the image), and of the compound (where an eyepiece further magnifies the image formed first by the objective). His details of what were then quite recently-developed instruments and optics are especially useful.

BRACEGIRDLE (1983), a small edited volume (only 76 pages), accompanied an exhibition that included all the known examples of Leeuwenhoek's simple microscopes. It contains chapters by Dutch and English specialists on Leeuwenhoek and his work, and illustrated descriptions of all the instruments. Leeuwenhoek undoubtedly discovered bacteria (without understanding what they were), and did much other useful work (albeit in a most secretive manner) for more than 50 years, but other treatments of him are merely laudatory.

FRISON is one of the very few writers to concentrate on the development of the optical system. His small book contains not only helpful, succinct accounts of the improvements in optical systems (including test objects) during the 19th century, but also a chronological table, some useful short biographies, and an excellent bibliography.

The early years of the history of the microscope have tended to interest authors disproportionately, and DISNEY is no exception. He based his long account of antiquity and the period up to the late 17th century on a series of texts, and provided a good bibliography and catalogue of the considerable collection of the Royal Microscopical Society. Such details of individual instruments are vital if the nuances of microscopical evolution are to be understood, but it should be noted that much of Disney has to be interpreted in the light of more modern work.

CLAY & COURT are equally concerned with the earlier period, although they do proceed to the 1830s. Their text is solidly based on an examination of many instruments and is valuable on that account alone, but (in spite of a recent reprint) this book must be read with even more caution than Disney, as many of their statements have been shown to be in error.

BRADBURY produced a bird's eye view of the history, and his work is interesting for having been written by a trained microscopist. This book is easy to read, and remains a good starting point, especially as he brings the story up to date and includes a little on the electron microscope.

TURNER (1980) provides further basic reading. This is a volume of reprinted essays, and the first two (on the study of the history of the microscope, and on a survey of sources for the history of optical instruments) are required reading for all those new to the subject. The other 10 essays by this doyen of the history of scientific instruments are all valuable in their different ways, but those on the microscope as a technical frontier in science and on microscopical communication require special notice.

TURNER (1989), a new catalogue of the collection of the Royal Microscopical Society, is also required reading. It includes details of individual makers and revealing insights of construction, and is a model of how a reasoned catalogue should be written. It provides accurate details of enough individual instruments to give a real feel for the microscope.

HARTLEY concentrates on the period post-1830, and displays unique insights into the practical use of the instrument. This is an especially valuable work, as it brings out the sheer intricacy of obtaining and interpreting high-power microscopical images.

Far and away the most comprehensive treatment of the history of the microscope is provided in the two large volumes by SCHMITZ. The books are fully illustrated with pictures of excellent quality, and, as a contrast to most writers on the subject, most of what he says is devoted to more modern instruments, especially those from Germany. He includes sections on the electron microscope and on other recent exotic instruments, and provides no fewer than 1158 main references, some of which contain many entries. This is a monumental and invaluable reference work.

BRACEGIRDLE (1978) is the only authoritative history of the microtome and of preparatory techniques ever written. The work is fully illustrated and referenced, in order to explain how the (largely biological) specimens were viewed by the optics on the stand. Fixing, sectioning, staining, and mounting are all key processes required to look at all but the simplest specimens, and all are brought together to show how particular structures were gradually elucidated.

It would not be sensible to describe only the history of the light microscope, for much detail that remained questionable with its use at the full extent of its resolution was solved only post-1945, by the electron microscope. Apart from the two general works mentioned above, which contain something on electron microscopy, RUSKA should certainly be read. Ruska was the founder of practical electron microscopy, and his book was translated by a prominent early British worker. In addition, the volume of reminiscences edited by HAWKES provides a first-hand account of the birth and early days of the subject. How valuable it would have been to have had available a similar book, published three centuries earlier, by the founders of light microscopy.

BRIAN BRACEGIRDLE

See also Bacteriology; Medical Instruments; Optics; Scientific Instruments: general works

Midwifery *see* Obstetrics and Midwifery

Mill, John Stuart 1806–1873

British philosopher and economist

Collini, Stefan, Donald Winch and John Burrow, *That Noble Science of Politics: A Study in Nineteenth Century Intellectual History*, Cambridge and New York: Cambridge University Press, 1983

Hollander, Samuel, *The Economics of John Stuart Mill*, 2 vols, Oxford: Blackwell, and Toronto: Toronto University Press, 1985

McRae, Robert F., *Introduction to A System of Logic: Ratiocinative and Inductive*, vols 7–8 of *Collected Works of John Stuart Mill*, edited by F.E.L. Priestley and J.M. Robson, Toronto: University of Toronto Press, 1973

Mill, J.S., *Autobiography*, Oxford: Clarendon Press, 1971

Nagel, Ernest (ed.), *John Stuart Mill's Philosophy of Scientific Method*, New York: Hafner, 1950

Robson, John M., *The Improvement of Mankind: The Social and Political Thought of John Stuart Mill*, Toronto: University of Toronto Press, and London: Routledge and Kegan Paul, 1968

Ryan, Alan, *J.S. Mill*, London and Boston: Routledge and Kegan Paul, 1974

Skorupski, John, *John Stuart Mill*, London and New York: Routledge, 1989

Wilson, Fred, *Psychological Analysis and the Philosophy of John Stuart Mill*, Toronto: University of Toronto Press, 1990

John Stuart Mill remains one of the towering figures of 19th-century philosophy. In the history of science, his contributions are in the fields of logic and scientific methodology, political economy and psychology.

MILL's *Autobiography* is the best place to begin. It is quintessentially Victorian in its restrained display of emotion and overriding self-command. A good general introduction to Mill's life and work is RYAN, which offers specific chapters on his logic and political economy. Another good overview, by ROBSON, focuses more on Mill as a social reformer than as a scientist. As general editor of the *Collected Works of John Stuart Mill*, and editor of *The Mill News Letter*, Robson can be counted on for an authoritative reading of the sources.

There is, unfortunately, no book specifically on Mill's logic and philosophy of science. The introductions by Nagel and by McRae are both somewhat dated but are, none the less, excellent for their genre. NAGEL emphasizes the extent to which Mill's logic served his more specific aim of elevating the status of the moral sciences. McRAE is more concerned with making sense of Mill's strict empiricism, and argues that Mill devised, at least to his own satisfaction, a non-circular solution to the problem of induction. SKORUPSKI, who offers the most detailed study to date on Mill's epistemology, is less sympathetic. He offers a particularly good critique of Mill's philosophical analysis of language and mathematics, and shows how Mill's deep commitment to empiricism got him into trouble. There is also a good chapter on Mill's methodological agenda for the moral sciences.

Samuel HOLLANDER gives a classic treatment of Mill's economics. Over 1,000 pages long, this is an exhaustive coverage of Mill's writings on the scope and method of economics, his theory of production and distribution, his monetary theory, and his policy recommendations and broader vision of economic welfare. Hollander's book is one of a series by him on the classical economists, which demonstrates that they were more neo-classical than has hitherto been recognized, more committed to a market mechanism that made distribution simultaneous with pricing, and more cognizant therefore of the demand-side of the economy. As a result, Mill served as the precise middleman between the theoretical advancements of David Ricardo (1817) and Alfred Marshall (1890). According to Hollander, Mill was not infected by the socialism of some of the lesser-known economists of the period, and thus did not pave the way for Marx. Mill is portrayed as a deeply reflective economist, with virtually no traces of dogmatism or sectarian alliances. The primary motivation for his *Principles of Political Economy* was to reaffirm and improve upon the core of Ricardian theory, and to put to rest the political controversies that surrounded that doctrine during the 1820s and 1830s.

One of the finest books to grace the field of intellectual history in the 1980s is the collaborative effort of COLLINI, WINCH & BURROW. Mill is but one of a large cast of characters in their narrative (others include Thomas Malthus, Walter Bagehot, and Henry Sidgwick), but he nevertheless played a prominent role in the conception of political science that emerged in Victorian England. In the specific chapter on Mill, Collini portrays him as highly ambivalent about the scientific status of political inquiry. On the one hand, Mill sought to develop and expand the programme of his father and the Philosophical Radicals, but, on the other, due in part to his appreciation for Romantic poetry, he wished to temper their naive positivism and highlight the art, as opposed to the science, of government.

WILSON's book offers a detailed study of Mill's associationist psychology and his assimilation of the work of Alexander Bain, and links these with his broader conception of Utilitarianism and economic well-being. On other facets of Mill's work – for example, his criticisms of William Hamilton and Auguste Comte, and of natural theology – one is best off foraging the journal literature. Brief overviews may also be found in Ryan and Skorupski.

MARGARET SCHABAS

See also Political Economy; Positivism

Millikan, Robert Andrews 1868–1953

American physicist

DuBridge, Lee A. and Paul S. Epstein, "Robert Andrews Millikan", *Biographical Memoire, National Academy of Sciences*, 33 (1959): 241–82

Epstein, Paul S., "Robert A. Millikan as Physicist and Teacher", *Reviews of Modern Physics*, (20 January 1948): 10–25

Hughes, Thomas P., *American Genesis: A Century of Invention and Technological Enthusiasm*, New York and London: Penguin, 1990

Kargon, Robert, *The Rise of Robert Millikan: Portrait of a Life in American Science*, Ithaca, New York: Cornell University Press, 1982

Kevles, Daniel J., entry on Millikan in *Dictionary of Scientific Bibliography*, edited by Charles Coulson Gillespie, vol. 9, New York: Scribner, 1974

Millikan, Robert A., *The Autobiography of Robert A. Millikan*, New York: Prentice-Hall, 1950; London: Macdonald, 1951

Robert Andrews Millikan is known primarily as the first physicist to measure the charge on the electron (1913), and as the first American-born scientist to receive the Nobel prize (1923). He is also remembered for his success, in 1920, in helping to transform Throop College of Technology in Pasadena (originally Throop Polytechnic Institute, a trade school founded in 1891) into the California Institute of Technology, long since one of the top US science and engineering universities, and an important factor in the emergence of Southern California as a major centre of modern industry. (It is generally known as Caltech, but Millikan preferred to call it CIT, presumably to establish its equivalence with the older, and equally prestigious Massachusetts Institute of Technology (MIT) in Boston). The literature consists of a bibliography and résumé assembled by Lee A. DuBridge (his successor as Caltech's chief executive) and Paul Epstein, a Caltech colleague, who also supplied an account of Millikan's scientific work and of his excellence as a teacher; several mentions in a survey of American inventors by T.P. Hughes; an exegesis of Millikan's contributions by Caltech historian of science and technology D.J. Kevles; and Millikan's autobiography. None of the books cited above mentions Millikan's considerable contributions as an author or co-author of textbooks, notably his *Mechanics, Molecular Physics, Heat and Sound* (Boston: Ginn, 1937, with Duane Roller and Earnest C. Watson), which introduced entire generations of college freshmen to physics and to the arts, through reproductions of classical science-related illustrations and portraits provided by Watson, a world-class collector in that genre.

DuBRIDGE & EPSTEIN's bibliography is a posthumous tribute to a greatly admired colleague, published six years after his death, and listing his nearly 300 scientific publications, while EPSTEIN is a listing of Millikan's scientific work (assembled on the occasion of his 80th birthday) that appears in somewhat condensed form in DuBridge & Epstein, and is classified by Kevles as "on the whole a useful contribution to Millikan's life".

HUGHES notes that Millikan could claim to have played a role in the introduction of the transcontinental telephone service in North America. Frank Jewett, an 1898 graduate from Caltech (when it was still the Troop Polytechnic Institute), had obtained a PhD in physics from the University of Chicago when he befriended Millikan, then a young instructor. Jewett went on to a brilliant career at AT&T, the long-distance arm of the Bell Telephone company, and was instrumental in forming the Bell Telephone Laboratories (later rising to become president). Jewett's first major success was to lead AT&T in establishing a telephone link with San Francisco in time for the 1915 Panama-Pacific International Exposition there, work in which a succession of Millikan's young doctoral students played major parts.

KARGON is the only full-length biography. The first half is devoted to Millikan's ancestry, youth, training, surroundings, and early career, and provides a great deal of relevant information not readily available elsewhere. The account of Millikan's spectacular success as a scientist is paralleled by the equally astonishing story of Caltech's rise in international prominence and fame, as one of the world's top institutions of advanced learning in science and engineering – an achievement that is scarcely thinkable without Millikan's organizational skills. His single-mindedness in bringing these skills to bear on Caltech's development is described in an even-handed, "warts and all" manner, which helps make his achievements appear particularly laudable.

KEVLES is a superb 20,000-word entry in the *Dictionary of Scientific Biography* devoted entirely to Millikan's scientific work. Despite its relative brevity, the entry is an outstanding summary of Millikan's scientific achievements.

MILLIKAN is an autobiography, not necessarily self-serving, but certainly no *apologia pro vita sua*, which would have been altogether out of the author's character. However, both Kargon and Kevles warn that, for example, the account of the author's role in Caltech's development is to be read with care, reflecting the controversies concerning the administration of Caltech that followed Millikan's retirement and the appointment of Lee A. DuBridge as Caltech's first president.

CHARLES SUSSKIND

See also United States: general works

Mills and Waterwheels

Apling, Harry, *Norfolk Corn and Other Industrial Windmills*, Norwich: Norfolk Windmills Trust, 1984

Gribbon, H.D., *The History of Waterpower in Ulster*, Newton Abbot, Devon: David and Charles, 1969

Hills, Richard L., *Power from Wind: A History of Windmill Technology*, Cambridge and New York: Cambridge University Press, 1994

Holt, Richard, *The Mills of Medieval England*, Oxford and New York: Blackwell, 1988

Hunter, Louis C., *A History of Industrial Power in the United States, 1780–1930*, vol. 1: *Waterpower in the Century of the Steam Engine*, Charlottesville: University Press of Virginia, 1979

Jespersen, Anders, *The Lady Isabella Waterwheel of the Great Laxey Mining Company, Isle of Man, 1854–1954: A Chapter in the History of Early British Engineering*, Virum, Denmark: Jespersen, 1954

Nasmith, J., *Recent Cotton Mill Construction and Engineering*, London: Heywood, 1894; 2nd edition, Manchester: Heywood, 1900

Reynolds, John, *Windmills and Watermills*, London: Evelyn, 1970

Shaw, John, *Water Power in Scotland, 1550–1870*, Edinburgh: Donald, 1984

Syson, Leslie, *The Watermills of Britain*, Newton Abbot, Devon: David and Charles, 1980

Wailes, Rex, *The English Windmill*, London: Routledge and Kegan Paul, 1954

Williams, Mike and D.A. Farnie, *Cotton Mills in Greater Manchester*, Preston, Lancashire: Carnegie, 1992

Wilson, Paul, *Water Turbines*, London: HMSO, 1970

The first important British study of the theory of wind and water power was by John Smeaton, whose paper published in the *Philosophical Transactions*, of 1759, described the tests he had carried out on model wind and water mills. For water mills, he showed that the overshot type was more efficient and, while his conclusions about the best type of sails for windmills were not so definitive, his work was not superseded until the closing years of the 19th century.

What Smeaton did for British mills, Evans's *The Young Mill-Wright's and Miller's Guide* did for those in America. His work, describing how to build corn and saw mills, was published in over 40 editions, and remained the standard reference work until the 1830s. He explained the theory, using Smeaton's work, and illustrated the workings of his cornmill, which was fully automated, from the conveyors lifting the grain from carts or boats to the flour falling into the sacks. Evans used wood technology, while Buchanan's *Practical Essays in Mill Work and Other Machinery* (1841), coming that much later in Britain, describes iron machinery. Evans concentrates on the prime movers, the waterwheels, but Buchanan looks at the means of transmission, such as gearing and shafting, which, along with machine tools, are featured in his volume of plates. Fairbairn pioneered the use of better cast iron beams for textile mills, and had improved the design of iron "suspension" waterwheels, as well as introducing lighter, quicker rotating wrought iron shafting. This, plus his work on steam engines, appears in Fairbairn's *Treatise on Mills and Millwork* of 1861–63, which has remained a much-consulted work, mainly because it is easier to read than, for example, Buchanan, in which the formulae for determining the correct proportions of parts are included in the text.

Fairbairn improved the design of iron-framed mill buildings, through testing beams with different sections, and examining mills where there had been a structural failure. Fairbairn's *On the Application of Cast and Wrought Iron to Building Purposes* (1854) is one of the first comprehensive studies of mill structures, examining particularly the use of cast iron for beams. It concludes with his work on tubular wrought iron bridges, illustrated by his final design for the bridge over the Rhine at Cologne. NASMITH describes the structural development of mills up to the end of the 19th century, by which time the stronger steel and concrete had been introduced and textile mills had reached their final evolution.

WILLIAMS & FARNIE is one of a trilogy of books published in 1992 with the assistance of the Royal Commission on the Historical Monuments of England, which survey the surviving textile mills in the Manchester, Macclesfield, and Yorkshire regions. This work gives a good historical survey of mill development, from the beginning of the expansion of the cotton industry around 1770 to the last traditional mill constructed in 1926, together with an inventory of selected mills.

Turning to water power, the best account of the history of the development, both of the theory and of actual mills, may be found in John REYNOLDS. Reynolds starts with antiquity, examines the spread of water power during the medieval period, and discusses the theoretical concepts propounded on the Continent during the 18th century. The introduction of the iron waterwheel during the Industrial Revolution, and the way in which the traditional vertical wheel was replaced by the turbine, are also covered. The first volume of HUNTER covers water power: for the early US colonists this was the major source of energy, and in the early 19th century water power was successfully developed for the major textile mills in, for example, Lowell, where the water turbine was adopted in order to gain as much power as possible from existing water resources. In comparison, SYSON is a slim volume; however, after a general introduction covering the historical development and workings of the mills, it contains excellent illustrations and descriptions, mostly of corn mills throughout the British Isles, although textile mills are rarely included. For the best study of any region of the UK, one must turn to SHAW, which covers virtually every water powered mill in Scotland during three periods, 1550–1730, 1730–1830, and 1830–1870. In each section, he subdivides the different industries – such as paper mills, coal mines, bleach fields, and so on – and thus outlines the development of both waterpower and the different Scottish industries. GRIBBON has done the same for Ulster, but here the number of mills is far less. Gribbon examines each industry individually, including the linen, iron, and cotton industries, as well as electricity. There is also a list of all the water turbines, generally with their horsepower.

As a comprehensive study of one waterwheel, JESPERSEN will remain outstanding. The famous Laxey wheel was built in 1854, just at the point when turbines were being introduced, and Jespersen covers the reasons for building the wheel, how it was built, its water supply, and its effectiveness. WILSON's small booklet shows most of the major types of water turbines, which have replaced the earlier waterwheels.

The other source of natural power for mills was the wind, and Reynolds has excellent illustrations of both types. Once again, corn mills predominate, but pumping mills and fulling mills are shown too, while the isometric drawings of the machinery inside the buildings are excellent. HILLS is the first general account of the development of wind power to have been published in Britain. Tracing the origin of the windmill from Persian horizontal mills around 900 AD, Hills shows that the main development lay in the West with the vertical windmill, which soon appeared in the traditional forms of both post and tower mills. The application of such mills to industry is explored, as well as how the sails were improved. In the middle of the 19th century, the American windpump spread across the world, and then early in the 20th century electricity began to be generated by wind, the major use today. HOLT looks at the origins of the windmill in Britain in the 12th century. He points out many possible early references, but his enthusiasm has led him to see a windmill in every ancient text, where probably none existed. The classic book is that by WAILES, who must have visited practically every windmill in Britain, as well as many on the Continent, selecting those he considered the most typical, and using them as examples of the different types of post, smock, tower and drainage mills. Their machinery and the men who worked them are also described. APLING gives the histories of the many corn mills in Norfolk, where the traditional windmill reached its final form – with a fantail to turn it into the wind, shutters on the sails to control the speed, and tall brick towers, often with six sails.

RICHARD L. HILLS

See also Wind Turbines

The Mind

Brazier, Mary A.B., *A History of Neurophysiology in the 17th and 18th Centuries from Concept to Experiment*, New York: Raven Press, 1984

Churchland, Paul M., *Matter and Consciousness: A Contemporary Introduction to the Philosophy of Mind*, Cambridge, Massachusetts: MIT Press, 1984

Gardner, Howard, *The Mind's New Science: A History of the Cognitive Revolution*, New York: Basic Books, 1985

Gregory, Richard L. and O.L. Zangwill (eds), *The Oxford Companion to the Mind*, Oxford and New York: Oxford University Press, 1987

Neuburger, Max, *The Historical Development of Experimental Brain and Spinal Cord Physiology Before Flourens*, edited and translated from the German by Edwin Clarke, Baltimore: Johns Hopkins University Press, 1981 (original edition, 1897)

Roccatagliata, Giuseppe, *A History of Ancient Psychiatry*, Westport, Connecticut: Greenwood Press, 1986

Smith, J.-C. (ed.), *Historical Foundations of Cognitive Science*, Dordrecht: Kluwer, 1990

Stagner, Ross, *A History of Psychological Theories*, New York: Macmillan, and London: Collier Macmillan, 1988

Studies of the mind span many disciplines and coalesce into many schools. The mind has been the subject of analysis by, among others, psychology, psychiatry, philosophy, and physiology, and these analyses have come to be labelled, for example, dualism, behaviorism, functionalism, and materialism. A helpful guide for negotiating this diverse intellectual landscape is GREGORY & ZANGWILL; its dictionary format and generous bibliographies make it a convenient starting point for exploring any one of the various aspects of the mind. Gregory & Zangwill can also serve as a welcoming rest stop, as all entries are accessible to the informed lay reader in need of basic definitions and tutorials.

CHURCHLAND presents an especially complete analysis of the different types of philosophical questions in the history of the studies of the mind. He devotes separate chapters to ontological questions (e.g. what is the nature of the mind?), semantic questions (e.g. how do terms and concepts for the mind get their meanings?), epistemological questions (e.g. how do we know whether other beings have minds?), and methodological questions (e.g. what is the proper discipline for studying the mind?). Though it touches on many specialties, Churchland's account is intended for a lay audience.

Soon after Descartes initiated the discussion of the mind-body problem, early experimental scientists were inventing and using new tools for understanding nature. BRAZIER illustrates the nexus between the conceptual philosophers and the experimental scientists, by following the lives of 17th- and 18th-century anatomists, equipped with Leeuwenhoek's microscope, as they attempted to construct a mechanistic model of the human nervous system. Since few could resist speculating on the location of the soul, Brazier's history becomes an interesting account of their attempts to place the seat of consciousness in, for example, the pineal gland, the cerebellum, the corpus callosum, and the spinal column. Brazier complements her history of the events in the laboratory and lecture hall with an account of the political influences, explaining how the anatomists' personal beliefs, and the contemporary ideologies of the Church and certain scientific societies, discouraged, if not stifled, materialist interpretations of anatomical discoveries.

NEUBURGER is another history of the mechanistic views of the human nervous system. Though tedious at times for his interminable advocacy of Baconian science, Neuburger supplements Brazier's account with details concerning actual experimental practices. Like Brazier, he notes how strong was the urge to locate the mind somewhere in the body, while pointing out the inconsistency of the use of the term "soul" among the experimenters of the time, some of whom claimed for it powers of reason and consciousness, and others merely sensation. As a strict empiricist, Neuburger focuses on the experiments themselves, an approach that makes his history interesting, if not macabre. In their zeal to locate the life force, experimenters made frequent use of vivisection and decapitation of both cold- and warm-blooded animals, as well as the by-products of the local gallows. Neuburger never flinches from these horrors, and in fact applauds the progress toward understanding functional differentiation in the nervous system, as experimenters learned to recognize ever more subtle differences in the behavior of their subjects.

ROCCATAGLIATA traces the healer's view of the mind in the ancient world, as he describes various approaches to psychiatry from pre-Homeric times to the end of the Roman Empire. Along the way, views of the mind or soul reflect various cultural, social, political, and economic influences. In Homeric times, a sacerdotal psychiatry regarded the soul as at the mercy of supernatural forces, and that healing could be achieved through song, dance, herbs, and dream interpretation. The Hellenic Greeks abandoned this demonology when they attempted to reduce the mind to atoms, in the Ionian naturalist manner. Roccatagliata notes that later thinkers either embraced or scorned the Ionian view of the mind according to their ideology: there were anti-democratic thinkers, like Plato, who preferred a hierarchical division of mind into three strata; while others, like the political strategists of the Roman Republic, found that Ionian materialism comported with their program to drive out superstitious practices. As the Roman Republic evolved into the Roman Empire, Roccatagliata finds influences, such that the individual soul became a part of a cosmic soul, just as the individual political states became part of the Empire. Roccatagliata ties the ultimate fortunes of ancient psychiatry to those of the Roman Empire. The ancient views of the soul then disappeared until the 16th-century rediscovery of the classical physicians, a point he makes in order to establish a continuity between ancient and modern psychiatry.

SMITH's collected essays attempt to establish an intellectual pedigree for cognitive science. Each essay variously interprets history in order to ground cognitivism in some earlier tradition of rationalism. In the process, the ontological and epistemological issues in the philosophy of mind and psychology emerge as the guiding forces for modern cognitive science, artificial intelligence, and connectionist research programs. Some essays find philosophical antecedents in the ancient Greeks: Plato's theory of recollection, for example is thought to suggest a cognitivist view. Other essays find shared philosophical commitments between Aristotle and contemporary functionalists. Still others claim some congruence between medieval scholastics and modern computationalists. While some of Smith's essays flirt at times with anachronism, they show some worthwhile conceptual parallels between cognitivists and earlier thinkers.

STAGNER looks for the antecedents of modern psychology, and, like Smith, trots out the classical Greek progenitors: Aristotle, he says, begat behaviorism, while Pythagoras instilled the modern preoccupation with numbers. However, Stagner tries to look beyond the classical Western canon and includes Judaic, Hindu, and early Christian antecedents of modern psychology. While the Western canon privileges the individual, takes reality to be objective and reducible, and sees the observer as independent of that reality, the Hindu tradition rejects egocentrism, and Judaism emphasizes faith rather than reason. Stagner attempts to show how these other traditions have softened an otherwise tough-minded Western perspective towards the study of the psyche.

GARDNER is a history of the cognitive sciences which breaks down the field into philosophy, psychology, artificial intelligence, linguistics, anthropology, and neuroscience, and then devotes a hefty chapter to the historical development of each. Each history revolves around some view of the mind, and taken as a group, they constitute the centerpiece of Gardner's work. His belief is that philosophy provided cognitive science with a list of questions about the mind, which he meticulously extracts from the debates between rationalists and empiricists from Descartes to Rorty. Under psychology, he rounds up various approaches to the mind from early introspectionist to empiricist, while his account of artificial intelligence is mostly concerned with how literally one can take the metaphor of a thinking computer. In linguistics, Gardner limits his scope to the roots and development of Chomsky's work and its effects on psychology. The efforts by anthropologists to arrive at basic modes of human perception through the empirical findings of case studies are also described, while Gardner's history of neuroscience follows the debate since Descartes over whether brain functions are localized or holographic.

LAWRENCE SOUDER

See also Artificial Intelligence; Psychiatry; Psychology

Molecular Biology

Abir-Am, Pnina, "The Discourse of Physical Power and Biological Knowledge in the 1930s: A Reappraisal of the Rockefeller Foundation's 'Policy' in Molecular Biology", *Social Studies of Science*, 12 (1982): 341–82
Gaudillière, Jean-Paul, "Biologie moleculaire et biologistes dans les années soixante: La Naissance d'une discipline: Le Cas français", PhD thesis, Paris VII, 1991

Judson, Horace Freeland, *The Eighth Day of Creation. Makers of the Revolution in Biology*, New York: Simon and Schuster, and London: Jonathan Cape, 1979; expanded edition, Plainview, New York: Cold Spring Harbor Laboratory Press, 1996

Kay, Lily E., *The Molecular Vision of Life: Caltech, The Rockefeller Foundation, and the Rise of the New Biology*, New York: Oxford University Press, 1993

Keller, Evelyn Fox, *A Feeling for the Organism: The Life and Work of Barbara McClintock*, San Francisco: W.H. Freeman, 1983

Kohler, Robert E., *Partners in Science: Foundation Managers and Natural Scientists, 1900–1945*, Chicago: University of Chicago Press, 1991

Olby, Robert C., *The Path to the Double Helix*, Seattle: University of Washington Press, and London: Macmillan, 1974

Yoxen, Edward, "Life as a Productive Force: Capitalising the Science and Technology of Molecular Biology", in *Science, Technology and the Labour Process*, edited by Les Levidow and Robert Young, London: CSE Books, and Atlantic Highlands, New Jersey: Humanities Press, 1981

More than other fields, the definition of molecular biology has been problematic and at the centre of much historical writing on the subject, both by participant scientists and historians. Especially in the American context, molecular biology is often equated with molecular genetics; some have taken Watson and Crick's suggestion of the double helix as the structure of DNA in 1953 as the origin of the new science, while others, notably biochemists, have stressed their participation and long-standing rights to the field now known as molecular biology. Furthermore, some see molecular biology as essentially a post-World War II development, while others have emphasized various attempts to promote it in the inter-war years. It is thus not easy to separate the history of molecular biology from that of DNA, genetics, or biochemistry.

The first, still most quoted, and recently reprinted book-length accounts of the history of the new field of molecular biology by non-participants were by Robert Olby and Horace F. Judson. Based on both primary sources and interviews, OLBY offers a wide-ranging account of studies in the structure and function of proteins and nucleic acids from around 1900 to 1953 – i.e. leading up to and including the discovery of the double helix. He provides an institutional reading of the (pre)history of molecular biology based on the notion of research schools, and supports the view, first presented by the British protein crystallographer, John Kendrew (but rejected by other contenders), that molecular biology originated from the merging of two research schools – the informational school centred on Max Delbrück and his phage work, and the structural school, an essentially British tradition based on the pioneering work in protein X-ray crystallography by William Astbury and Desmond Bernal. (According to this view, the first link between the two schools was established when James Watson from the phage school and Francis Crick from the British school met in Cambridge.) Olby also surveys more recent developments in the history of molecular biology, and his book remains a very useful resource for historians in the field.

In a more journalistic style, JUDSON tries to convey the excitement of the main discoveries in molecular biology, and to give a portrait of their makers. Descriptions of Judson's personal encounters with the scientists blend with long quotations from their conversations; based extensively on interviews, Judson reiterates the views of his main interlocutors, among them Max Perutz, Crick, Brenner, François Jacob, Jacques Monod, and Matthew Meselson.

KELLER's biography of corn geneticist, Barbara McClintock, offers a view on the new science from the perspective of someone who, through her work and her institutional affiliation with Cold Spring Harbor, a centre of genetic research and the site of Delbrück's celebrated phage courses, was both near to and marginalized by the new developments. Stretching from the early decades of the 20th century to the 1980s, when McClintock's work on the organization and control of genetic information gained wider recognition, Keller's account offers a penetrating analysis of the practice and language of molecular biology, and of the ways consensus was achieved among early molecular biologists. In more recent essays, Keller has offered a stronger gender reading of these issues.

The role of the Rockefeller Foundation in fostering the new field of molecular biology through its funding programme in the 1930s has attracted much attention by historians. In a widely debated article, ABIR-AM challenged the positive role attributed to the Rockefeller Foundation, by claiming that its policy in the 1930s supported the colonization of biology by physical scientists and their instruments, but that it failed to support really innovative projects aimed at recasting the biological sciences along non-reductionistic molecular lines. KOHLER takes a broader historical view on foundations and scientific patronage in early to mid 20th-century America. The Rockefeller Foundation programme of molecular biology in the 1930s is discussed as the product of a new system of patronage, based on a close relationship between programme director and prospective and actual grantees. From internal memoranda, diaries, and correspondence kept in the Foundation's archives, Kohler reconstructs the formation of the new interdisciplinary programme and its implementation, and concludes that the Foundation's patronage did not create new institutions in the life sciences, although it did change the behaviour and practices within existing institutions. KAY argues that the Rockefeller Foundation programme in molecular biology was based on the intervention and control of vital processes. According to Kay, this project reflected the Foundation's political agenda of "social control" that was grounded in the natural, medical, and social sciences. This thesis, which has not passed unchallenged, is developed in a rich account of the institutional and scientific development of the life sciences at Caltech, a prime site of the implementation of the Foundation's programme, from the 1920s to 1950s. According to the author, this does not represent "The Story", but with Morgan, Delbrück, Beadle, and Pauling situated at Caltech, it is an important aspect of the rise of the new biology.

Reviewing more recent developments, YOXEN's radical study considers the history of molecular biology as a research programme and technological project formed, organized, and regulated by economic and political forces. According to Yoxen, a successive alignment of interests of an emerging disciplinary elite in the life sciences with corporate capital has led to the increasing exploitation of biological knowledge as a productive force. This process, Yoxen suggests, has been aided by a reductionistic notion of life-as-programmed-nature that has been developed in the post-war years.

GAUDILLIÈRE's account of the French history of molecular biology draws attention to the importance of national research policies in the establishment of new scientific practices. However, the impact of government support for the promotion of molecular biology in France, Gaudillière suggests, can only be studied at the level of local choices and in the redefinition of local research practices. The establishment of a new common research culture of molecular biology is then examined, as the redefinition of local research cultures mediated through the circulation of tools, models, and new governmental research policies privileging these kinds of exchanges.

SORAYA DE CHADAREVIAN

See also DNA; Genetics: post-DNA; Rockefeller Foundation

Monge, Gaspard   1746–1818

French mathematician

Arago, François, "Eloge de Monge", *Oeuvres complètes*, vol. 2, Paris: Baudry, 1854

Aubry, Paul, *Monge: le Savant ami de Napoléon Bonaparte, 1746–1818*, Paris: Gauthier-Villars, 1954

Belhoste, Bruno and René Taton, "L'Invention d'une langue des figures", in *L'Ecole normale de l'an III: Leçons de mathématiques*, edited by Jean Dhombres, Paris: Dunod, 1992

Brisson, Barnabé, "Notice historique sur Gaspard Monge", Paris, 1818

Chasles, Michel, *Aperçu historique sur l'origine et le développement des méthodes en géométrie, particulièrement de celles qui se rapportent à la géométrie moderne*, Brussels: 1837; 2nd edition, Paris: Gauthiers-Villars, 1875

Dupin, Charles, *Essai historique sur les services et les travaux scientifiques de Gaspard Monge*, Paris: Bachelier, 1819

Launay, Louis de, *Un Grand Français: Monge, fondateur de l'École Polytechnique*, Paris: P. Roger, 1933

Taton, René, *L'Oeuvre scientifique de Monge*, Paris: Presses Universitaires de France, 1951

One can distinguish two basic foci of interest in studies devoted to Gaspard Monge: first, his contribution to the development of mathematics, and second his political role during the French Revolution and the Empire. The most recent works have placed an emphasis on his scientific activities under the *ancien régime*, as professor and academician.

The earliest studies are the work of Monge's disciples, all matriculates of the École Polytechnique. The engineer Barnabé BRISSON, Monge's nephew by marriage, published an interesting obituary in 1818, evoking the figure of the great professor. The following year, the mathematician Charles DUPIN published a remarkable, solidly-documented biographical essay, in which he sketched an extremely complimentary portrait of the scholar, and provided an early analysis of his

scientific work. Here Monge's definitive role in the creation of the École Polytechnique is clearly described, although, for political reasons, his engagement in the French Revolution is only very cautiously broached. The academic éloge delivered by François ARAGO on 11 May 1846 should be read with caution; even though the author knew Monge and had access to family reports, this text, written just before the revolution of 1848, is a politically charged hagiography of a democratic and republican *savant*.

Beyond these initial biographical works, there is the remarkable study by Michel CHASLES on the origins of modern geometry, published in 1837 in response to a question posed by the Académie de Bruxelles. Although it replaces Monge's own work on the history of geometry since antiquity, Monge is hailed by Chasles as the reformer of geometrical methods, the founder of modern geometry, and the leader of a new school of mathematicians.

After attracting much interest during the first half of the 19th century, the life and work of Monge were not the subjects of original research in succeeding decades, and it was only towards the mid-20th century that notable studies were published. Two new biographies then appeared, the first by Louis de LAUNAY (1933), and the second by Paul AUBRY (1954), which have not been superseded to this day. Although written in quite different styles (Aubry is much more sober that Launay), these two works are actually quite close in motivation and spirit; both authors benefited from the support and encouragement of Monge's descendants and drew essentially on the unpublished manuscript biography written at the end of the 19th century by the mathematician's great-grandson, Frédéric Eschasseriaux. Monge's scientific work is barely mentioned in Eschasseriaux's writings, but his political activity is described in detail. Launay and Aubry, neither of whom had much sympathy for the Jacobins, analyze the role Monge played during the Convention, searching in particular for attenuating circumstances. What emerges is a picture of a scholar lost in politics, naïve, and sometimes imprudent, but always acting in good faith. Much space is given to relations between Monge and Napoleon Bonaparte, in Italy, in Egypt and finally under the Council and the Empire, as Monge's correspondence with his wife, used by both authors, sheds light on various episodes in this authentic and reciprocal friendship between the general and the scientist. However, these two conventional biographies by amateur historians are hardly trustworthy, and leave numerous aspects of Monge's personal, political, academic, and scientific life in shadow. Thus, there is still no modern scholarly biographical study of the mathematician; awaiting this, one should not neglect the 19th-century notices discussed above.

There is, however, an exhaustive and carefully-argued study of Monge's work by René TATON. This book, capped by a brief but solid biographical notice, is based on an exhaustive inventory and analysis of Monge's manuscript papers and printed memoirs. Each theme – descriptive geometry, analytic geometry, infinitesimal calculus, the theory of partial differential equations, physics, technology, etc. – is covered in a separate article. This results in the image of a *savant generalist*, interested as much by questions of applied science as by pure mathematical theories. Even though Taton's thematic divisions prevent the chronological coherence of Monge's life work from emerging, this book, which will not soon be superseded, is by far the best work on Monge yet written.

BRUNO BELHOSTE
translated by Craig Rodine

See also École Polytechnique

Muséum National d'Histoire Naturelle

Appel, Toby A., *The Cuvier–Geoffroy Debate: French Biology in the Decades Before Darwin*, Oxford and New York: Oxford University Press, 1987

Burkhardt Jr, Richard W., *The Spirit of System: Lamarck and Evolutionary Biology*, Cambridge, Massachusetts: Harvard University Press, 1977; 2nd edition, 1995

Hamy, E.T., "Les Derniers Jours du Jardin du Roi et la fondation du Muséum d'Histoire Naturelle", in *Centenaire de la fondation du Muséum d'Histoire Naturelle, 10 Juin 1793–10 Juin 1893*, Paris: 1893

Laissus, Yves, "Le Jardin du Roi", in *Enseignement et diffusion des sciences en France au dix-huitième siècle*, edited by René Taton, Paris: Hermann, 1964; 2nd edition, 1986

Laissus, Yves, "Les Animaux du Jardin des Plantes, 1793–1934", in *Les Animaux du Muséum, 1793–1993*, edited by Yves Laissus and Jean-Jacques Petter, Paris: Imprimerie Nationale, 1993

Laissus, Yves, *Le Muséum d'Histoire Naturelle*, Paris: Découvertes Gallimard, 1995

Lemoine, Paul, *Le Muséum National d'Histoire Naturelle: son histoire, son état actuel*, Paris: Masson, 1935

Lepenies, Wolf, *Das Ende der Naturgeschichte: Wandel kultureller Selbstverständlichkeiten in den Wissenschaften des 18. und 19. Jahrhunderts*, Munich: Hanser, 1976

Limoges, Camille, "The Development of the Muséum d'Histoire Naturelle of Paris, c.1800–1914", in *The Organization of Science and Technology in France, 1808–1914*, edited by Robert Fox and George Weisz, Cambridge and New York: Cambridge University Press, 1980

Paul, Harry W., *From Knowledge to Power: The Rise of the Science Empire in France, 1860–1939*, Cambridge and New York: Cambridge University Press, 1985

Roger, Jacques, *Buffon: Un Philosophe au Jardin du Roi*, Paris: Fayard, 1989

Schnitter, Claude, "Le Développement du Muséum National d'Histoire Naturelle de Paris au cours de la seconde moitié du XIXème siècle: 'se transformer ou périr'", *Revue d'Histoire des Sciences*, 49/1 (1996)

Works devoted specifically to the history of the Muséum National D'Histoire Naturelle are few. However, listed below are certain works which, although not solely concerned with the museum, are worth investigating.

The centenary volume of the museum contains a study by HAMY that describes the transformation of the Jardin du Roi into the Muséum National d'Histoire Naturelle in 1793. The author recounts in great detail how this institutional creation of the *ancien régime* became a symbol of national unity under the Revolution, and describes the active role played by employees of the Jardin, particularly Daubenton and Fourcroy.

LEMOINE, the museum's director before World War II, wrote an institutional history that remains a valuable reference source. After recalling the history of the Jardin du Roi and its reorganization as the museum, Lemoine gives a history of its professorial chairs and their occupants.

The works of Laissus merit special consideration. As conservator of the museum's library, he enjoyed privileged access to the institution's archives. His short work, LAISSUS (1995), surveys the museum's history in words and images. Often informative and accurate, this chronological account extends from its beginnings to the present day, and covers, the time of the founding fathers, the second generation of administrators, competition with the university, and the colonial period.

LAISSUS (1986), in his history of instruction at the Jardin du Roi, includes a complete and detailed inventory of its scientific and academic personnel. Guy de la Brosse, founding father of the Jardin and the commanding figure of Buffon dominate this history, the latter emerging as the promoter of the naturalist-teacher vocation within the institution.

LAISSUS (1993) is a study of the museum's menagerie, and gives a precise account of the important moments in its creation and evolution. While giving the impression that, from its inception, the museum's professors never really paid much heed to the menagerie, Lassius does, however, fail to relate the life of the menagerie to that of the museum. The impressive notes included in these two works by Laissus include references to important primary resources.

The aforementioned works contain very little on the role and place of the museum within French science. Since no synthetic study of this question exists, the reader will have to consult related texts.

ROGER's biography of Buffon, one of the museum's spiritual fathers, provides a view of the institution's earliest years. Buffon trained Daubenton, the first director of the museum, who was, significantly, an important influence on Lamarck, and materially affected the beginnings of the museum through his administration of the Jardin du Roi, which became the theater of teaching and research for the most eminent naturalists. In his study of Buffon's life and work, Roger clarifies how far his philosophical and scientific intentions shaped the development of natural history, in spite – or perhaps because of – the contradictions they engendered.

LEPENIES, considering European science in the period 1775–1825, gives a refined analysis of the movement of natural history towards evolutionism. Reviewing the theories of *savants* influential in the museum's history, he shows how the marvellous and extraordinary – which animated the 18th-century science of Buffon, Daubenton and, to a certain degree, Lamarck – gave way little by little, under the influence of Saint-Hilaire and Cuvier, to a science that classified and normalized "the entities of everyday life". This book places the museum within the context of the history of ideas.

BURKHARDT's study of Lamarck usefully supplements Lepenies's analysis. The author rejects clichés surrounding Lamarck's work, and situates it within the contemporary intellectual context. The protégé of Buffon, and then of Daubenton, Lamarck had to develop his work in a transitional period, when collaboration and co-operation were becoming more typical in scientific work. His theory of evolution had close ties with his interests in chemistry, meteorology, geology, and zoology, yet his synthesis was criticized by Daubenton and even dissimulated in Cuvier's work. Burkhardt's study provides an idea of the intellectual discussions that took place in the museum at the turn of the 19th century.

APPEL's intellectual history of French biology at the beginning of the 19th century offers a detailed picture of the contemporary Parisian institutional context, in which the museum's two most celebrated professors, Cuvier and Geoffroy Saint-Hilaire, clashed in a debate before the Académie in 1830. In Appel's account, the museum, both witness and actor in this famous controversy, plays a major, perhaps too glorious, role. Long passages describe the research facilities the museum provided for its chairholders. Appel highlights a particularly interesting fact: during the revolutionary period, the museum's public and teaching vocation clashed with its role in the professionalization of zoology.

PAUL describes the strengths and weaknesses of French science between 1860 and 1939. The comparative roles of scholarly institutions and the state in French scientific policy-making are compellingly analyzed, and the difficulty of establishing a governmental science policy discussed. From this perspective, Paul briefly touches on the increasing marginalization of the museum in relation to the university. By the beginning of the 20th century, university professors effectively controlled French scientific life, while a century earlier this role had been largely the privilege of the museum's chairholders.

The alleged decline of French science during the 19th century, and the questions this raises, comprise the underlying theme of the collection edited by Fox and Weisz, in which LIMOGES's contribution concerns the development of the museum from 1800 to 1914. Using various statistical indicators, the author proposes a new interpretation, challenging the classical chronology. The most interesting and polemical aspect of this argument is the insistence on the rivalry between "experimentalists" and "naturalists", and on their attempts to gain power via the museum's institutional politics. The colonial orientation of the museum at the end of the 19th century thus appears as a justification for the renovation of naturalism.

SCHNITTER's study follows on the work of Limoges. It refines the chronology of the museum's evolution in the 19th century, concentrating on political events, the competition between the museum and the universities, and the roles of various players. Schnitter shows that the institution actively adapted itself to the changing political and academic contexts, and emphasizes the role of one of the museum's directors, the chemist Edmond Frémy. Under pressure from the museum's overseeing ministry, Frémy developed its educational function by introducing practical courses. Following on from this, the author interprets the museum's colonial orientation, demonstrated by Limoges, as a consequence of the competition that thus arose between the museum and the university of Paris.

CLAUDE SCHNITTER, ANNE MASSERAN
AND PHILIPPE CHAVOT
translated by Craig Rodine

See also Education; France: scientific and technical education

Museums

American Association of Museums, *The Official Museum Directory*, 26th edition, New Providence, New Jersey: Bowker, 1995

Findlen, Paula, *Possessing Nature: Museums, Collecting, and Scientific Culture in Early Modern Italy*, Berkeley: University of California Press, 1974

Finn, Bernard, "The Museum of Science and Technology", in *The Museum: A Reference Guide*, edited by Michael Steven Shapiro, Westport, Connecticut: Greenwood Press, 1990

Follett, David, *The Rise of the Science Museum under Henry Lyons*, London: Science Museum, 1978

Gordon, Robert B., "Material Evidence of the Manufacturing Methods Used in 'Armory Practice'", *Journal for the Society of Industrial Archaeology*, 14 (1988): 22–35

Hindle, Brooke, *Technology in Early America: Needs and Opportunities for Study*, Chapel Hill: University of North Carolina Press, 1966

Hudson, Kenneth and Ann Nicholls, *The Directory of World Museums*, New York: Columbia University Press, 1975; 2nd edition, New York: Facts on File, and London: Macmillan, 1981

Kohlstedt, Sally Gregory (ed.), *The Origins of Natural Science in America: The Essays of George Brown Goode*, Washington, DC: Smithsonian Institution Press, 1991

Morton, Alan Q. and Jane A. Wess, *Public and Private Science: The King George III Collection*, Oxford and New York: Oxford University Press, 1993

Sellers, Charles Coleman, *Mr. Peale's Museum: Charles Willson Peale and the First Popular Museum of Natural Science*, New York: Norton, 1980

Sinclair, Bruce, *Philadelphia's Philosopher Mechanics: A History of the Franklin Institute, 1824–1865*, Baltimore: Johns Hopkins University Press, 1974

Technology and Culture, 6/1 (1965): 1–82

Turner, Gerard L'E., *Essays on the History of the Microscope*, Oxford: Senecio, 1960

The World of Learning, 45th edition, London: Europa, 1994

Museums of science and technology are of special interest to historians for two reasons: first, as repositories of artefacts and documents they make available evidence that can be used in historical studies; and second, as cultural institutions they are, through their own histories, reflections of society's attitudes towards science and technology. FINN provides a comprehensive bibliography, together with a survey of the development of these museums.

Although museums of science and technology have existed since the Renaissance, serious use of them by historians is relatively recent. This has been hindered by the fact that there are no separate listings of such institutions. The best source remains HUDSON & NICHOLLS, an annotated directory of all types of museums, with detailed subject indexes (not to be found in the third edition). As HINDLE points out, in considering potentials for study, an additional problem has been the lack of adequate catalogues and research aids that would make the collections more readily accessible. An exception is Gerard Turner, who has been an effective advocate of accuracy and uniformity in collection catalogues. His influence can be seen on Morton & Wess, in their elegant description of instruments in the King George III Collection at the Science Museum in London (with items from the early 18th century up to the mid-19th century). Popular guide books are generally unsatisfactory for direct scholarly use, but they can supply a good idea of the collections, and therefore of what might be available on further investigation.

Some museums have archives and libraries. Catalogues of the latter are to be found by computer, on-line, and some of the former are in standard manuscript reference works – e.g. *AMERICAN ASSOCIATION OF MUSEUM*'s *The Official Museum Directory* (for the US), and *THE WORLD OF LEARNING* both contain some information on manuscript and book holdings.

There are very few monograph-length interpretative studies that have used museum artefacts as evidence. The principal medium for expression by museums is, of course, the exhibition. However, even though exhibitions in recent years have become increasingly scholarly, they suffer two major defects: they are not readily available, and almost inevitably they do not include references. The first problem can be overcome in part by converting the exhibition to published form, but such publications usually omit detailed references. The second problem remains unsolved.

Shorter interpretative studies occasionally appear in exhibition catalogues, as with the essays in MORTON & WESS, which use the *George III* instrument collection as a starting point for a discussion of the popularization of science. TURNER is more explicit in his examination of individual objects; the measurements on microscope lenses provide information about what early investigators could see, and tooling marks on the body of the instruments helped him to identify the instrument makers. GORDON turns his attention to gun parts that were supposedly manufactured as interchangeable, only to discover file marks that clearly indicate they were individually shaped. These studies are examples of a growing, but still modest, literature that shows how powerfully objects can speak to us if we know where and how to look.

The treatment of science museums as cultural institutions has been more extensive. FINDLEN supplies a detailed account of their development in Italy in the 16th and 17th centuries, with special emphasis on their role as public laboratories of natural history. Silvio Bedini, in a special issue of *TECHNOLOGY AND CULTURE*, covers all of Europe over a longer time-period, and in the process gives brief descriptions of a broad range of early museums. Eugene Ferguson, in the same issue, argues persuasively that most of the great technical museums of the 19th and early 20th centuries were inspired by the numerous large international industrial exhibitions, and thus were born with a guiding philosophy that combined exuberant public education, nationalism, and a positive and progressive view.

Both SELLERS and SINCLAIR convey important insights into two significant 19th-century American museums: the Peale Museum, as an expression of one man's enthusiasm for the marvels of America, and the Franklin Institute, as a scientific/technical establishment that gradually developed a public education role. KOHLSTEDT reprints some of G. Brown Goode's essays examining the Smithsonian's approach to exhibitions in the late 19th century. FOLLETT treats the critical years in the 1920s and 1930s, when the Science Museum in London emerged as a significant public institution.

Virtually all of these museums, in their exhibitions, continued to interpret the development of science and technology from an internalist and progressive point of view until well after World War II. Only in recent years, basically in accord with trends in academic historical practice, have they begun to frame their exhibitions within a broader social context. Little has been written about this development, although a feeling for it can be gained through published exhibition reviews, especially those that have appeared in *Technology and Culture* since the early 1970s.

BERNARD S. FINN

See also Public and the Private; Scientific Instruments: general works; Smithsonian Institution

Music and Science: antiquity to 1700

Amman, Peter J., "The Musical Theory and Philosophy of Robert Fludd", *Journal of the Warburg and Courtauld Institutes*, 30 (1967): 198–227

Barbour, J.M., *Tuning and Temperament: A Historical Survey*, East Lansing: Michigan State College Press, 1951

Coelho, Victor (ed.), *Music and Science in the Age of Galileo*, Dordrecht and Boston: Kluwer, 1992

Cohen, H.F., *Quantifying Music: The Science of Music at the First Stage of the Scientific Revolution, 1580–1650*, Dordrecht and Boston: Reidel, 1984

Crombie, A.C., *Science, Optics and Music in Medieval and Early Modern Thought*, London: Hambledon Press, 1990

Dear, Peter, *Mersenne and the Learning of the Schools*, Ithaca, New York: Cornell University Press, 1988

Drake, S., "The Role of Music in Galileo's Experiments", *Scientific American*, 232/6 (1975): 98–104

Gouk, P.M., "Newton and Music: From the Microcosm to the Macrocosm", *International Studies in the Philosophy of Science*, 1 (1986): 36–59

Kassler, Jamie C., *Inner Music: Hobbes, Hooke and North on Internal Character*, Madison-Teaneck, New Jersey: Fairleigh Dickinson University Press, 1995

Lippman, Edward A., *Musical Thought in Ancient Greece*, New York: Columbia University Press, 1964

McGuire, J.E. and P.M. Rattansi, "Newton and the Pipes of Pan", *Notes and Records of the Royal Society*, 21 (1966): 108–43

Palisca, C., "Scientific Empiricism and Musical Thought", in *Seventeenth Century Science and the Arts*, edited by H.H. Rhys, Princeton, New Jersey: Princeton University Press, 1961

Stephenson, Bruce, *The Music of the Heavens: Kepler's Harmonic Astronomy*, Princeton, New Jersey: Princeton University Press, 1994

Walker, D.P., *Studies in Musical Science in the Late Renaissance*, London: Warburg Institute, 1978

Studies in music and science explore the interrelations of practices now perceived as separate. This present-day separation thesis has allowed most scholars to assume a crude opposition between rigidly divided fields of "music" and "science", and to neglect the musical dimensions of scientific practice. Empirical historical studies, on the other hand, show music and science in a fertile, varied, and fluid relationship. The few who have investigated the musical aspects of scientific culture argue, unsurprisingly, that histories of science are thereby significantly enhanced.

Most of the accessible literature deals with the Western world, with the period from antiquity to the scientific revolution coherently worked out and subjected to critical re-evaluation. Scholars have frequently investigated music and science through the careers, contexts or milieus of characters prominent within standard histories of science – notably Robert Fludd (Amman), Johannes Kepler (Walker and Stephenson), Galileo (Crombie, Drake and Coelho), Marin Mersenne (Crombie and Dear), Isaac Newton (McGuire & Rattansi and Gouk), and the musicians and music theorists, Zarlino (Walker) and Galileo (Drake).

More rarely, scholars have analysed the interrelations between science and music thematically, according to categories, including: music and the cosmic harmony or harmonic science of the Greeks (Lippman); music as (a mathematical) science (Crombie); music as theory or speculative music (Kassler); music as practice, skill, or experiment (Palsica, Drake, and Gouk); music and its instrumentation or technology (Gouk and Kassler); music and theory/practice debates, focusing upon issues of tuning and temperament (Walker and Barbour), or the elaboration of a mechanical philosophy of nature (Cohen); the musical instrument as analogue for the human being (Kassler); music as therapy or medicine (Lippman, Crombie, Kassler and Dear); music institutionalized within scientific society (Gouk); and music as aural perception subject to psycho-physiological analysis, perhaps linked with aesthetics (Crombie and Kassler).

LIPPMAN clarifies the complex interplay of conceptions of harmony, musical aesthetics and musical philosophy in ancient Greek thought from Pythagoras, through Plato's *Timaeus*, to the Peripatetics. Natural order was central to conceptions of man, society, and art, and ideas of order, proportion, and reason were generalised as harmony – to which music lent elaboration and structure. In a philosophy that made numbers the essence of reality, the ratios of the integers 1 through 4 corresponded to consonant musical intervals. Universal harmony was thus instantiated by perfect musical proportions. Sonorous music, rather than ideal intellectual harmonies, had an ethical force, compelling human response or manifesting curative and soothing powers. Criticisms of such older, rational, and moral harmonic schemes came especially from the Peripatetics (notably Aristotle's pupil, Aristoxenus), who doubted the Platonic harmony of soul and cosmos, questioned the nature of the harmony of the celestial spheres, and transferred emphasis from speculative harmonic ontology to the practical empiricism and sensuality of musical sound.

CROMBIE's essays touch on science and music in the medieval and early modern periods, when, following Boethius, music was one division of mathematics in the university quadrivium. Boethius codified speculative music as *musica mundana* (encompassing the motion of the heavenly bodies and the cycle of the seasons), *musica instrumentalis* (practical music) and *musica humana* (dealing with the human body and soul). Crombie discusses each of these, locating Renaissance music as one of many pursuits within the arts that formulated, and sometimes responded to, pressing technical problems. Practitioners of "measured music" demonstrated a progressive rational control of materials, and a quantitative analysis of pitch and interval, which complemented the logical control of argument ostensibly achieved by the philosophers. Such technical problem-solving and theory-led material construction were, in Crombie's view, essential factors in the genesis of a recognisably modern science. Discussing Boethius and the Arabic commentator Avicenna, Crombie introduces the medicinal and therapeutic functions of early modern music, which involved attuning the soul to the harmony of the spheres, preparing it to see wisdom, responding to mental illness, and inducing calm.

WALKER mixes musicology, aesthetics, and the history of ideas in a classic collection of essays. This volume serves as a detailed agenda for scholars of music and science. Walker surveys the ancient and modern harmony of the spheres, not as literary trope but as natural knowledge fused with musical practice. He considers the disputes of the 1580s over singers' intonation between the practical musician Vincenzo Galilei and his theoretician teacher, Gioseffo Zarlino. Zarlino designed his neo-Pythagorean "just temperament", built upon the integers from 1 to 6 (the *scenario*), in order to cope effectively with the new polyphonic music, but, as Galileo insisted, the results were inappropriate to musical practice. Walker re-introduces Vincenzo's son, Galileo, in the role of musician, and describes how Kepler's elaborate and polyphonic celestial music drew inspiration from neo-Platonic number mysticism. He also re-examines the role of Mersenne, ponders the expressive value of intervals, and considers the views of 17th-century natural philosophers on intonation. On this last point, BARBOUR is the essential complement to Walker, providing an exhaustive historical and theoretical treatment of tuning systems, from the Greeks, through just intonation, to meantone and equal temperament. Barbour uses compositional and performance practice to gauge which scales were employed within different instrumental groupings.

AMMAN discusses Robert Fludd, whose "divine monochord", spanning the earthly and the Empyrean domains, was lodged within a rich musical cosmology and a grand history of the macrocosm. Fludd's philosophy was simultaneously neo-Platonic, panpsychic, alchemical, and cabbalistic, but there was still room for an elaborate harmonics. Amman explains how Fludd's idiosyncratic syncretism, his musical theorising, and his search for hidden essences rather than shadowy material imitations were decried as animistic poetic imagery by opponents who offered more restrained alternatives. Kepler's exclusively planetary harmonics and Mersenne's mechanistic harmonies of strings were, reciprocally, disparaged by Fludd, who deemed them preoccupied with superficial appearances or unduly limited in cosmic scope.

STEPHENSON uses one of these figures, Kepler, to show how neo-Platonic notions of harmony continued to underpin programmes of natural knowledge-making. He provides an extended exegesis of the *Harmonice Mundi* (1619), that sometimes obscure culmination of Kepler's speculations on planetary geometry and celestial music. Stephenson rehearses the long tradition of harmonic theorising that preceded Kepler;

noting that earlier studies have been too selective, he sketches the intellectual contexts of astrology, meteorology, and contemporary music theory. Kepler's eternal planetary music thus emerges as a timely revision of Ptolemy's mathematical harmonics, coherent with Kepler's programme of authorship, non-mystical, and modern in that it enshrines polyphonic theory and the new just intonation.

The musicologist PALISCA asserts that the reformed experimental and empirical science of the 17th century created a climate that favoured a parallel musical reform: experimental acoustics superseded the Pythagorean number mysticism on which the older musical theory had been founded, while practical music gained the status of an independent art, linked to rhetoric and poetry. Specifically, Palisca (in Coelho) insists that Vincenzo Galileo was an "experimental scientist", engaged in "a quest for scientific truth", using his lute as "laboratory equipment".

DRAKE inverts Palisca, and audaciously locates the origins of the new experimental manner of science in musical technique. In mechanics, Drake insists, experiments that constructed rather than confirmed laws were initially rare, but there were two such novelties: Vincenzo Galilei carried out musical experiments with weighted strings to argue against Zarlino's cosmic harmonies; his son, Galileo, exploited skills peculiar to the musician (accurate time measurement) in order to generate a mathematical law from experiments in mechanics with bodies on inclined planes. Experimentalism in music, typified by Vincenzo, generated an equivalent in mechanics, exemplified by Galileo. Musical practices essential in experiments are counted as crucial within Drake's historiographical framework. Cohen suggests that Drake overemphasises the experimental turn in Galileo's science, but saves something of his radical claim by returning to Crombie's point regarding the role played by the practical arts in the scientific revolution. Alternatively, COELHO and his contributors – among them music historians and historians of science – offer a more complex portrait of music-making in the age of the Galilei, including composition, the skilled construction and metaphysical import of Galileo's lute, and the practices of music-making in cultures of courtly patronage.

Studies of Galileo's contemporary and Fludd's critic, the Minim monk and diligent correspondent, Marin Mersenne, again respond to Walker's agenda. Traditional accounts note Mersenne's extensive experiments in acoustics (especially those concerning the relationship between the pitch of a string and its physical characteristics). Amman claims that in the compendious *Harmonie universelle* (1636–37), Mersenne responded to Fludd's poetic cosmology, digging the grave for ancient theories of *musica mundana* and of the harmony of the spheres. Crombie characterises Mersenne as a historian of ancient music, possessed of great knowledge of contemporary musical instruments, as befitted an individual whose scientific programme was largely experimental. Mersenne was, for Crombie, a religiously motivated psycho-physiological engineer who, by manipulating the emotions and dispositions of the soul induced by music, would surpass in rational controlling power the use of music in medicine or education available to antiquity. The medical science of hearing was invaded by those like Mersenne: quantifiers, mathematizers and mechanists of sounding bodies and of emotional states alike.

DEAR reminds us that Mersenne had a distinctive agenda for his mechanical natural philosophy – that co-operative research led to a cumulative acquisition of ratified facts made into science through mathematics. Within this programme, Mersenne centralised the sciences of music, mechanics, and optics. If Crombie and Amman portray Mersenne as revolutionary, Dear emphasises caution, continuity and the careful management of existing cultural resources in a search for religious harmony. Paralleling Stephenson, Dear responds to those who have isolated Mersenne's acoustics, by reconstituting the unity of Mersenne's work in music and in mechanics. As for the ancients, music provided the paradigm of harmony by which other mathematical endeavours could be developed and judged. Mersenne accomplished the harmonisation of mechanics through the mechanisation of music. Sounds were movements and, reciprocally, all movements were sounds, perceptible to the intellect if not to the ear. Harmony equated with divine wisdom ordering Creation, and thus the teachings of St Augustine (on universal harmony) sanctioned Mersenne's attempts to find manifestations of wisdom, number, and regularity in the mechanics of the physical world.

COHEN's masterly synthesis demonstrates the significance of music in the practice of 16th- and 17th-century natural philosophers (notably Kepler, the Galilei, Mersenne, Descartes and the Dutchmen, Beeckmann, Stevin and Huygens). From a Popperian perspective, Cohen focuses on the classic problems of musical consonance and the division of the octave. He examines competing mathematical, experimental and mechanistic approaches to the science of music. Purely numerical theories of consonance, dependent upon neo-Pythagorean conceptions of harmony and unity, were by 1650 replaced by explanations in terms of the physical properties of sound. Aesthetic considerations, Cohen claims, gave way to an acoustical view of the science of music as the science of sound. Cohen shows, furthermore, that one early corpuscularian who made music central to his theorising (Beeckman) was an important resource for the mechanical philosophising of Mersenne and Descartes. Cohen relates problems in musical science to the practical music of the day, identifying similarities between transitions in musical science and changes in composition, reflecting the transition from Renaissance to Baroque styles. Rudolf Rasch (in Coelho) provides a useful complement in a discussion of the practical musical knowledge, compositions, and musical acquaintances of Cohen's Dutchmen of science (including, here, Descartes).

Drake takes Galilean experiment, and Cohen writes of a richer fusion of experimental, mathematical and mechanical philosophies, in order to link musical science with the "origins" of modern science. Others echo Dear in their unwillingness to assimilate historical actors to either progressive big pictures, or standard syntheses in the history of science. McGUIRE & RATTANSI's now classic revamping of the great amphibian, Isaac Newton, places Hermetic, alchemical and theological practices centre stage. Their Newton was as much magician as mechanist; a speculative music theorist of the old school, he heeded the pipes of Pan, sought to re-establish the *prisca theologia*, and identified anticipations of the gravitational inverse square law of the *Principia* in reports of Pythagorean harmonies.

GOUK traces the theoretical roots of Newton's science against a backdrop of day-to-day experimental (and occasionally musical) practice in the Royal Society. The Society's versatile curator, Robert Hooke, promoted a musical ontology of particles vibrating at different frequencies coupled by sympathetic resonance. Hooke and Newton expounded different theories of light, but when they considered colour both developed analogies between light and sound. To explain this, Gouk places Newton within the context of Cambridge, viewed as a centre of speculative music study, and links his far from practical speculative music theory (allied to Zarlino's system of tuning) with his optical investigations. Newton's mechanics and musical speculations, Gouk claims, evolved simultaneously as integral parts of a much broader programme in chronology, alchemy and theology. Newton sought a unified harmonic theory of light and colour, and it was thus no accident that Newton's harmonic colour theory enshrined analogies between seven tones of an appropriately tempered musical scale and an equal number of colours in the visible spectrum.

Historians have thus provided studies showing a symbiosis of science and music within the context of the work of individual natural philosophers prominent, as cosmologists, mechanists or proponents of a new experimental life, in traditional accounts of the scientific revolution. KASSLER's period is the same, but her historiographical location is quite different. In perhaps the most ambitious and original work to consider music and the scientific revolution, the author examines questions of philosophy, physiology, aural perception and self-perception. Focusing upon the English philosophers Thomas Hobbes, Roger North, and (following Gouk) the ubiquitous Robert Hooke, Kassler shows how musical technologies (a bundle of lute strings, a consort of instruments, a bell) modelled "internal character" (a term embracing both aspects of physiology and ethics) and bodily action. The metaphors of Kassler's protagonists were thus grounded in instrumental experience and infused with social meaning.

BEN MARSDEN

See also Hermeticism; Scientific Revolution

Music and Science: since 1700

Anderson, John D., "Varèse and the Lyricism of the New Physics", *Musical Quarterly*, 75 (1991): 31–49

Christensen, Thomas, *Rameau and Musical Thought in the Enlightenment*, Cambridge and New York: Cambridge University Press, 1993

Cohen, Albert, *Music in the French Royal Academy of Sciences: A Study in the Evolution of Musical Thought*, Princeton, New Jersey: Princeton University Press, 1981

Cohen, H.F., *Quantifying Music: The Science of Music at the First Stage of the Scientific Revolution, 1580–1650*, Dordrecht and Boston: Reidel, 1984

Hankins, Thomas L. and Robert J. Silverman, *Instruments and the Imagination*, Princeton, New Jersey: Princeton University Press, 1995

Hatfield, Gary, "Helmholtz and Classicism: The Science of Aesthetics and the Aesthetics of Science", in *Hermann von Helmholtz and the Foundations of Nineteenth-Century Science*, edited by David Cahan, Berkeley: University of California Press, 1993

James, Jamie, *The Music of the Spheres: Music, Science and the Natural Order of the Universe*, New York: Grove Press, 1993

Jeans, James Hopwood, *Science and Music*, Cambridge: Cambridge University Press, 1938

Kassler, Jamie C., *The Science of Music in Britain, 1714–1830: A Catalogue of Writings, Lectures, and Inventions*, 2 vols, New York: Garland, 1979

Levenson, Thomas, *Measure for Measure: A Musical History of Science*, New York: Simon and Schuster, 1994

Needham, Joseph and Kenneth Robinson, "Sound (Acoustics)" in *Science and Civilization in China* by Joseph Needham, Cambridge and New York: Cambridge University Press, 1954

Tatlow, Ruth, *Bach and the Riddle of the Number Alphabet*, Cambridge and New York: Cambridge University Press, 1991

Turner, Anthony John, *Science and Music in Eighteenth-Century Bath* (exhibition catalogue) Bath: University of Bath, 1977

Wachsmann, Klaus P. and Russell Kay, "The Interrelations of Musical Instruments, Musical Forms and Cultural Systems in Africa", *Technology and Culture*, 12 (1971): 399–413

The boundaries of science and music continued to be re-drawn after 1700, ultimately establishing two quite distinct disciplines and sets of practices. Certainly, there are valuable studies on science-music interactions for the Enlightenment (Turner, Albert Cohen, Christensen), for Georgian Britain (Kassler), and for more recent times (Hankins & Silverman). The historical literature attempts, then, to capture the sporadic disentanglement of musical and natural philosophy, and simultaneously assembles a case for new science-music interactions at many levels, fragmenting in the process.

Thus, for the modern period scholars have explored: music and its instrumentation or technology (Kassler, Hankins & Silverman, Wachsmann & Kay); music as sound reduced to physics (Hatfield, Jeans); music as a component of polite culture or society (encompassing science) (Turner, Hankins & Silverman); music as propaganda for a favoured scientific methodology (Christensen); music institutionalized within scientific society (Albert Cohen); and music as aural perception subject to psycho-physiological analysis, perhaps linked with aesthetics (Hatfield). An exceptional polymath from the physical community has become the focus for one such study (Hatfield, on Helmholtz); musicians and music theorists are also prominent (Tatlow on J.S. Bach, Christensen on Rameau, and Anderson on Varèse). Recent attempts to deploy music in recapturing the elusive "big picture" history of science have been refreshing if not always entirely successful (James, Levenson). While scholars remain preoccupied with the Western world, suggestive readings can be found on African musical cultures (Wachsmann & Kay) and on Chinese music (Needham).

CHRISTENSEN argues that, during the Enlightenment, music theory became less prominent in the work of natural philosophers. Euler's magnum opus of musical harmonics, *Tentamen Novae Theorie Musicae* (1739), was perhaps the last gasp in a tradition in which significant explanatory force could be derived from unifying frameworks of cosmic harmony.

Philosophical attention shifted to studies of music theory, which were acoustical and analytic rather than organic and universal, and to investigations of music practice from an empirical, inductive or mechanical perspective. The absorption of music theory by practice continued, as did the shift from natural philosophy towards the practical musician who had little interest in cosmic theorising. Acoustical topics, on the other hand, were taken out of their musical context, to be treated as autonomous within natural science.

Historians have been correspondingly hard-pressed to develop alternative large-scale analyses of the relationship between Enlightenment music (as distinct from acoustics) and science. H.F. COHEN sketches the development of theories of consonance into the 18th and 19th centuries, but notes the loss of definition of music as a science in the Romantic era. JAMES, who supports his grand science-and-music synthesis of secondary sources with the familiar backbone of cosmic harmony, has conspicuously little to say about the Enlightenment, or any later age. In James's view, after Newton, the "grand theme" of cosmic harmony practically vanished from what he sees as legitimate modern science: if it still found artistic expression in Masonic works like Mozart's *Magic Flute*, it was surely, if temporarily, obliterated by Romantic ideals of individualistic artistic genius.

Authors with more limited aims have written convincingly on musical numerology, the pursuit of science and music in a cosmopolitan city, the institutionalization of music, the use of music as propaganda, and the scientification of music theory. TATLOW re-appraises the notorious claims of the musicologist Smend and his followers that J.S. Bach regularly used the natural-order number alphabet (A = 1 to Z = 24), and that Bach's music was otherwise suffused with cryptographic and perhaps cabbalistic signs, inherited from Renaissance neo-Platonism and other sources. Tatlow concludes that Smend's hypothesis is flawed, and cautions future musicologists against it; Bach was unlikely to have endangered his reputation by resorting to magical number alphabets, and there is no evidence that he used a number alphabet as part of a cabbalistic technique with theological intent in his compositions.

Cultural studies of Enlightenment music and science are ripe for further development. TURNER offers a tantalising account of science and music in Bath, a magnet for Georgian pleasure seekers. He focuses on the circle of William Herschel, the professional musician, amateur astronomer and maker of instruments both philosophical and musical. Few morals are explicitly drawn in the text of this exhibition catalogue, but the following points are implicit: music and natural philosophy shared cultures, practices, patronage networks, patterns of performance, audiences, and instrumental skills and technologies; the science of music was one route into theoretical and experimental natural philosophy (especially for readers, like Herschel, of Smith's *Harmonics* of 1749); a lucrative musical career could finance leisure for science, or for new forms of amateur astronomy; entrepreneurship in musical and scientific (more properly, philosophical) spheres could be cross-fertilising; similarly, there were parallel skills in the production and manipulation of musical and scientific instruments. Nevertheless, we are still waiting for a close study of music practice and performance in an age of popular scientific spectacle.

Albert COHEN offers instead an exhaustive, if sometimes antiquarian, account of the disciplinary, pedagogic, acoustical, craft/practice, and theoretical facets of music, in and around the foremost Parisian scientific society, the French Royal Academy of Sciences. The Academy's centralised authority made it a likely focus for committee-style reporting on acoustical matters and systems of tuning, a site of accreditation for innovative instrument makers, and the source of sanction for those venturing systematic theories of harmony. The Academy also pursued a role of policing disciplinary boundaries, pronouncing on whether or not the submissions it received did indeed qualify as musical science rather than as musical practice, which was insistently subordinated to it.

Within the same institutional context, CHRISTENSEN shows that music theory could draw on scientific context, and at the same time serve as unlikely propaganda for a favoured scientific methodology. Rameau claimed that he had, in two easy stages, achieved a novel and distinctively scientific theory of music, capable of changing the conceptualisation and pedagogy of tonal music: sceptical Cartesian introspection established the minimal empirical base of the *corps sonore*, and thereafter chains of deductive reasoning generated a revolutionary, elaborate and complete music theory rooted in the "fundamental base". During the 1750s, Rameau, variously dubbed the (inductive empiricist) Newton of harmony and the (rationalist) Descartes of music, thus delivered to the encyclopedist d'Alembert a paradigm of systematic rationalist method and synthetic deductive structure, neatly confirming – or at least conformable to – his scientific ideals. For Christensen, then, Rameau was not merely a composer; he was a harmonic theorist, working within the turbulence of the Enlightenment, interacting with the *philosophes*, attuned to and perhaps inspired by contemporary contexts of scientific method and experiment, and generating ideas that drew on materialist mechanism, the neo-Platonism of Mersenne, Locke's sensationalism, and also pantheistic and occasionalist doctrines, and that responded to the tension between Newtonian empiricism and Cartesian system building.

KASSLER's remit is far broader. In a critical bibliography of the science of music in Georgian Britain, Kassler seeks to show the historical integrity of science and music by assembling the writings, lectures and inventions (from the humble metronome to Schulze's musical balloon) of musicians, scientists, teachers, and amateurs. An important introductory essay draws together pedagogic and philosophical strands. For Kassler, the science of music reduces to doctrine in four areas of musical knowledge: the technical (performance and composition); the mathematical (tuning, temperament); the critical (examining musical excellence and sources of musical pleasure); and the physical (acoustics). Although Kassler's chosen genre is the history of musical ideas, the author does, nevertheless, provide copious information concerning institutions and personnel (pamphlet makers or instrument designers), digressing (as she has it) into social history when necessary, and thereby recovering the varied musical exploits of the Hanoverian mathematical practitioners. There can be no single grand narrative for science and music here: Kassler locates a complex but integrated Georgian science of music, wherein by 1830 nearly all the modern conceptual categories of theory and teaching were established, only to see it subsequently dismembered into separate disciplines, and finally fragmented into the specialisms of the 20th century.

Moving into the late 19th century, the literature becomes increasingly fragmented. Scientists and early historians (like Jeans) have chosen in this period to write about acoustics as a branch of rational mechanics, about the practical engineering science of auditorium design, or about the psychology, anatomy and physiology of aural (and, from that, musical) perception. HATFIELD, however, demonstrates that the polymath Hermann von Helmholtz could synthesise a new science of music, couched within a broader context of aesthetics. Helmholtz aspired to a reduction of musical perception to physiology and psychology combined. In his rejection of Euler's non-physical theory of consonance (based on the commensurability of ratios of pitch numbers of tones), and his replacement of it by a physical, physiological and psychological theory of consonance (based partly on the recognition of beats), Helmholtz exemplifies the shift from the natural harmonic order of the 16th and 17th centuries, through the rational mechanics and performing skills of music in the 18th century, towards 19th-century physical reductionism. Furthermore, for Hatfield, Helmholtz serves as an atypical example showing the relation of disciplines at a time of increasing separation and specialisation. Hatfield examines Helmholtz's application of sensory physiology and psychology to music (especially in the famous *Tonempfindungen*) and painting, and then analyses Helmholtz's account of the methodology of aesthetics, and of the thought processes of the artist and the scientist. Helmholtz increasingly saw a close relationship between the two, a relationship that came to exemplify his classical "aesthetics of science".

JEANS is a venture into the history of science and music, an accessible presentation of the state of the art of musical acoustics, and a popularisation of Helmholtz's *Tonempfindungen*. Jeans reviews tuning systems, pitch standardization, instrumentation, and even the evolution of the organs of hearing. He chooses examples from everyday technologies (church bells, domestic pianos, gramophones and Hammond organs) and builds up a theory of hearing from the timely analogy of the ear as telephone. Jeans insists that music is, in all its essentials, assembled from, and intelligible as, a superposition of basic sound-curves, simple tones, and harmonic oscillators. For him, "science and music" equates to an amalgam of sciences in their application to hearing, consonance, harmony, timbre, and hall design.

ANDERSON provides an effective response to a physicist's reductionism, and shows how Edgar Varèse modelled his compositional technique on (popularisations of) the new physics. Varèse combined novel electronic technologies with conventional instruments to capture a complex aesthetics of "intelligent" sounds, re-deploying the new scientific language in the titles and structures of his works ("plane", "sound mass", "collision", "repulsion", *Ionization*, and *Intégrales*). He imitated chemical interactions, Brownian motion, radioactivity, and, in his "projections" of sound in space, he mimicked the photon of quantum theory. Varèse claimed to be influenced by scientific figures as diverse as Wronsky, Helmholtz, and Paracelsus.

In complete contrast to the narrow and specialised foci of Anderson or Drake, James and Levenson offer broad-scale, popular, and synthetic introductions to the field of music and science. JAMES writes from outside the mainstream of the history of science. He is not embarrassed to pursue a grand theme of cosmic harmony from the Greeks, via such figures as the Jesuit and neo-Pythagorean practitioner of speculative music Athanasius Kircher, through to Stockhausen, locating only one major anomaly (the Romantic era). As an arts critic, James extends the familiar thesis of natural order to the musical world: he discusses Hindemith's opera *Die Harmonie der Welt* (based on Kepler's life), pigeonholes Schoenberg as the most mystical musician since Pythagoras, and takes us into a 20th-century age of cultural disunity, figuring the mathematically-trained Milton Babbitt and the stochastic music of Iannis Xenakis.

LEVENSON offers an eclectic history of science, grounded in music theory and practice. He locates successive eras of harmony, cataloguing, and fragmentation in science, and characterises these eras by the questions that indicated the dominant approach to knowledge of the natural world: "why", "what" (corresponding to the scientific revolution), and "how" (or "which") (corresponding to a post-Newtonian fission of the sciences). Levenson presents a series of instruments, both scientific (the microscope) and musical (the violin), and suggests that they contain archaeologies of ideas – as embodiments of the ways of finding out about the world, or as demonstrations of how we choose to use the knowledge we have, they represent the era in microcosm. In such an instrumental history, Levenson claims, the scientific and the musical shed light on each other. This loose metaphorical framework allows the author to integrate much of the standard music and science literature with a staggeringly diverse range of topics, including chaos theory, the HIV virus, and the interactions between composers of the 20th century and instruments reliant on digital, electronic, or computer technologies.

In their innovative and provocative work, HANKINS & SILVERMAN begin with the basic claim that instruments do scientific work, structuring scientific theory and moulding practice. The authors take instruments, many of them from the tradition of natural magic, and many of them concerned with the replication of sight and sound, and show them penetrating cultures of experimental natural philosophy, art and popular entertainment. These artifactual foci are frequently obscure (in present day terms) and are often musical. Looking at this apparently marginal material paraphernalia, they claim, discloses otherwise invisible connections in science historiography, while it simultaneously sharpens our historical appreciation of the true nature of scientific instruments. Kircher's celestial organ of the Creation could serve to represent the instruments as *emblem* in natural magic. The cat piano (described by Kircher in 1650) was regarded with mirth in previous ages but as inhumane in ours: as Darnton showed, it is this strangeness that provides access to otherwise unrecognised aspects of historical cultures. Instrumentalists, as natural philosophers or natural magicians, sought to imitate, to duplicate, to distort, or to record human perceptions of sight and sound. At a time when many instrumentalists were working out analogies between the senses, Louis-Bertrand Castel's ocular harpsichord served as a synesthetic thought experiment, as rhetoric, and as a way of getting back to the colour-tone analogy of Newton (studied by Gouk). If, from the 19th century, instruments imitating sight, hearing (the phonograph) and speech (like Wheatstone's speaking machines or Helmholtz's tuning-fork apparatus) lost their magic, in cinema and audio reproduction they retained their ability to entertain.

All the works above have shown a pronounced emphasis on things Western. Two works begin to redress the balance. WACHSMANN & KAY combine the disciplines of technology studies and ethnomusicology in order to delineate the interrelations of musical instruments, musical forms and cultural systems in Africa. They show that instruments and musical forms are intrinsically bound up with culture at the levels of social function (social order and instrumental usage reinforcing each other), belief about the nature of the universe (instruments might be images of the world or embody creation stories), and physiology or healing. For Wachsmann & Kay, studies of African musical technology entail and imply studies of the human body, and suggest the extension of their perspectives to Western music.

NEEDHAM & ROBINSON are concerned primarily with the physics of sound (acoustics). Nevertheless, their essay does give special access to a more general culture of mathematical harmonics, in which musical conceptions were intimately related to the structure of the universe, and, for example, musical resonance could be a basis for a correlation of natural and human events. These include correlations of sound with flavour and colour, the concept of *chhi*, classifications of sound by timbre and pitch, instruments like the pitch-pipe (itself the basis of a cosmic numerology), musical scales, tuning, musical metrology, and the evolution of musical temperament in China (where, Needham claims, equal temperament originated).

BEN MARSDEN

See also Acoustics

N

Napier, John 1550–1617

Scottish mathematician

Brown, P. Hume, "John Napier of Merchiston", in *Napier Tercentenary Memorial Volume*, edited by Cargill Gilston Knott, London: Longmans Green, 1915

Cajori, Florian, "Algebra in Napier's Day and Alleged Prior Inventions of Logarithms", in *Napier Tercentenary Memorial Volume*, edited by Cargill Gilston Knott, London: Longmans Green, 1915

Gibson, G.A., "Napier's Logarithms and the Change to Briggs's Logarithms", in *Napier Tercentenary Memorial Volume*, edited by Cargill Gilston Knott, London and New York: Longmans Green, 1915

Goldstine, Herman H., *A History of Numerical Analysis from the 16th Through the 19th Century*, New York: Springer 1977

Napier, Mark, *Memoirs of John Napier of Merchiston: His Lineage, Life and Times*, Edinburgh, 1934

Naux, Charles, *Histoire des logarithmes de Neper à Euler*, Paris: Blanchard, 1966

Shennan, Francis, *Flesh and Bones: The Life, Passions and Legacies of John Napier*, Edinburgh: Napier Polytechnic, 1989

Steggall, J.E.A., "A Short Account of the Treatise *De Arte Logistica*", in *Napier Tercentenary Memorial Volume*, edited by Cargill Gilston Knott, London: Longmans Green, 1915, 145–61

Whiteside, D.T., "Mathematical Thought in the Later 17th Century" in *Archive for the History of the Exact Sciences*, 1 (1960): 179–388

Most of the scholarship on John Napier has focused on his development of logarithms. Unfortunately, Napier's method of calculating by rods, his technological inventions, and his theological work, *A Plaine Discovery of the Whole Revelation of St John*, are less frequently discussed in the secondary literature.

NAPIER provides what information is available concerning Napier's life and work; it is based on meticulous research of the private papers of the Napier family, and is the source of most modern accounts. SHENNAN is the only modern, book-length, biography. Based upon Napier, Shennan presents an adequate overview of Napier's life and historical context, and makes it clear that in his lifetime he was famous, not for his work in mathematics and science, but rather for his work in theology and the occult. Shennan is not a historian of mathematics, and his book does not furnish a satisfactory account of Napier's mathematical contributions, but it at least points out Napier's interest in alchemy and the occult. Moreover, he describes some of the weapons Napier proposed to develop for the English government in 1596, his agricultural improvements, and his development of a hydraulic screw and revolving axle for keeping the level of water down in coal mines. This book is intended for a popular audience; it makes few references to primary source material and it is highly anecdotal. On the other hand, BROWN supplies not only a concise sketch of Napier's life, but also an explanation of the significance to Napier's development of the contemporary religious disputes. He convincingly argues that Napier's *A Plaine Discovery of the Whole Revelation of St John* forms an essential part of his biography, as both Napier and his contemporaries considered it of greater importance to the world than his invention of logarithms.

Napier's formulation of logarithms has been thoroughly explored by Gibson, Goldstine, Naux, and Whiteside. Sadly, most historical discussions of his logarithms are marred by translation into modern symbolism. Napier's original treatment used almost no notation, and his explanations are almost entirely verbal. The descriptions offered often fail to convey accurately Napier's geometric model of a correspondence between the terms of an arithmetic and a geometric progression, which was based on the idea of continuously moving points and utilized the concepts of time, motion, and instantaneous speed.

The chapter of GOLDSTINE'S book that covers the 16th and early 17th centuries examines work with exponents prior to Napier's discovery of logarithms, analyzes Napier's particular methods, and shows how Henry Briggs further developed Napier's ideas. Although Goldstine often describes Napier's methods using modern mathematical notation, he at least conveys the kinematic nature of his approach. Like Whiteside, he is mainly interested in explicating the discovery of specific mathematical ideas, and does not discuss in any detail the historical context or motivation for the logarithms. WHITESIDE claims that by the 17th century mathematics was too remote from any possible physical origins to be influenced by ideas "from without". His concern with Napier's logarithms stems from his idea that logarithms are a good example of how 17th-century mathematicians treated the notion of "function". Whiteside acknowledges Napier's use of kinematic methods, but his interest in logarithms as functions causes him to stress the structure on which the logarithmic computations are made, rather than the computations themselves. GIBSON presents Napier's construction of the logarithms concisely but clearly; he does not introduce modern notation unnecessarily, and thus succeeds in conveying Napier's actual mathematical practice. However, his main concern is with the defects in Napier's original conception and how these problems were overcome by Briggs's modifications. NAUX's book provides an account of Napier's work that is most faithful to the presentation given in the primary sources. He explores how the concepts of time, motion, and instantaneous speed allowed Napier to model a correspondence between an arithmetic and a geometric progression in order to create the logarithms. Naux supplies the most comprehensive, yet historical account of the development of logarithms.

STEGGALL offers the only discussion of Napier's work in algebra. Napier's original algebraic manuscript, copied by his son, Robert, for Henry Briggs, was lost in a fire, but a copy of the work was published in 1839 under the title *De Arte Logistica*. Steggall provides a complete description of the contents of the chapters, and he also explores Napier's view of numbers, especially "surd" or irrational numbers. The article is extremely useful for understanding Napier's later work with logarithms, and it supplies one of the few possible glimpses of Napier's earliest mathematical practice. CAJORI, on the other hand, does not so much discuss Napier's algebraic contributions as place them within their historical context. He also considers the disputes by historians concerning the priority of the actual invention, if not publication, of the logarithms. Joost Bürgi, a Swiss maker of watches and astronomical instruments, developed a system of logarithms independently of Napier, at about the same time. Cajori concludes that Napier and Bürgi were entirely independent of one another in their invention of the logarithms, and that Napier probably had a slight priority in terms of invention, and certain priority in terms of publication.

KATHERINE HILL

See also Algebra

National Styles of Reasoning

Beyerchen, Alan D., *Scientists under Hitler: Politics and the Physics Community in the Third Reich*, New Haven, Connecticut: Yale University Press, 1977

Crombie, A.C., *Styles of Scientific Thinking in the European Tradition: The History of Argument and Explanation*, 3 vols, London: Duckworth, 1994

Crosland, Maurice P., "History of Science in a National Context", *British Journal for the History of Science*, 10/5 (1977): 95–113

Daston, Lorraine and Michael Otte, "Style in Science", *Science in Context*, 4/2 (1991)

Duhem, Pierre, *German Science: Some Reflections on German Science*, translated from the French by John Lyon, La Salle, Illinois: Open Court, 1991 (original edition, 1915)

Fleck, Ludwik, *Genesis and Development of a Scientific Fact*, edited by Thaddeus J. Trenn and Robert K. Merton, translated from the German by Fred Bradley and Trenn, Chicago: University of Chicago Press, 1979 (original edition, 1935)

Paul, Harry W., *The Sorcerer's Apprentice: The French Scientist's Image of German Science, 1840–1919*, Gainesville: University of Florida Press, 1972

Reingold, Nathan, "The Peculiarities of the Americans; or, Are There National Styles in the Sciences?", *Science in Context*, 4/2 (1991): 347–66

Russell, Bertrand, *An Outline of Philosophy*, London: Allen and Unwin, 1927; as *Philosophy*, New York: Norton, 1927; revised edition, with an introduction by John G. Slater, London and New York: Routledge, 1995

Historians have long placed the study of science within national contexts, conventionally based on the simple appreciation, as CROSLAND puts it, "that science is a part of the intellectual life of a country and cannot be divorced from social, political, and religious history". Explicit focus on distinct "styles of reasoning" as a source and expression of such national differences is, however, fairly recent, although in some ways it may mark a return towards the old and persistent cliché that the French are rational, the Germans methodical and speculative, the British empirical, etc.

The notion of style is a borrowing from the humanities, in particular from critical vocabularies of the history of art, music, and literature. Historians of science use the term with varying emphases, but typically referring to some set of impersonal, tacit rules that govern or condition research programs; in the formulation of FLECK, a "thought style" is "the entirety of intellectual preparedness or readiness for one particular way of seeing and acting and no other".

CROMBIE has made the most ambitious attempt to apply an idea of style to the history of science. Although he stresses the role of language "mediating man's experience of nature and of himself both through common speech and through the technical discourse of the arts and sciences", in practice he gives no systematic treatment of national styles. Instead, he treats an international "culture-area", Europe, as the unit of analysis, and thus indirectly emphasizes the international, rather than the specifically national, contents of science.

DASTON & OTTE collect a series of critical reflections on the provenance of style, and its utility and limits in the historiography of science. While the phenomenon of national styles in science "eludes precise description", they claim that it "lends itself to detailed causal analysis", as several brief case studies presented are meant to illustrate. Various social units (or even individuals) may be the carriers of style, but "once the nation state takes charge of this aspect of culture, its prevailing values often color scientific style", a pattern evident since the emergence of cultural nationalism in the late 18th and 19th centuries. As a cautionary note, however, Daston & Otte add that "'national' may sometimes mask another, more decisive variable, such as degree of urbanization and/or economic development", as REINGOLD argues, for instance, in the case of contemporary American science, whose characteristics are sometimes attributed to a supposed cognitive and organizational style rather than (more realistically) to the distinctive pattern of US scientific institutions.

Style would seem to be a neutral, descriptive term, yet the very idea of national styles in science immediately raises a fundamental normative question: in Daston & Otte's words, "how pronounced must a national style be to threaten internationalism in science?" This was likewise a prominent theme in earlier writings that flirted with or embraced some notion of national mentalities. RUSSELL memorably lamented how the cultural background of scientists can intrude on even experimental work:

> Animals studied by Americans rush about frantically, with an incredible display of hustle and pep, and at last achieve the desired result by chance. Animals observed by Germans sit still and think, and at last evolve the solution out of their inner consciousness.

The French physicist DUHEM evaluated the national characteristics of science in a rather different spirit, openly praising the particular character of French science, in order to keep it free from the vices of German or British science. As PAUL argues, Duhem was one of many scientists in the late 19th and early part of the 20th centuries to be caught up in patriotic fervor, defending their own national traditions against the dangers of foreign influence.

At the extreme, national characteristics become national peculiarities or deviations. The distortions of science under totalitarian regimes represent perhaps the grossest aberrations from the ideal of the Republic of Science. BEYERCHEN, for example, describes the Nazi campaign to stigmatize "Jewish science", and the failed efforts to produce a distinctly "Aryan physics", "predicated on the view of reality that permeated National Socialist thought". However, if the notion of "national style" is stretched to cover such a disparate array of phenomena, it is difficult to see, in the end, what coherent significance the term might retain.

MICHAEL DONNELLY

See also International Science

Natural Law

Buckle, Stephen, *Natural Law and the Theory of Property: Grotius to Hume*, Oxford: Clarendon Press, and New York: Oxford University Press, 1991

Finnis, John (ed.), *Natural Law*, New York: New York University Press, 1991

Gierke, Otto, *Natural Law and the Theory of Society 1500–1800*, translated from the German by Ernest Barker, 2 vols, Cambridge: Cambridge University Press, 1934; 2nd edition, 1950 (original edition, 4 vols, 1868–1913)

Nettheim, Garth, "Human Rights: People's Rights", in *The Rights of Peoples*, edited by James Crawford, Oxford: Clarendon Press, and New York: Oxford University Press, 1988

Ruby, Jane E., "The Origins of Scientific 'Law'", *Journal of the History of Ideas*, 47 (1986): 341–59

Sargent, Rose-Mary, "Scientific Experiment and Legal Expertise: The Way of Experience in Seventeenth-Century England", *Studies in History and Philosophy of Science*, 20/1 (1989): 19–45

Shapiro, Barbara J., *Probability and Certainty in Seventeenth-Century England: A Study of the Relationships Between Natural Science, Religion, History, Law and Literature*, Princeton, New Jersey: Princeton University Press, 1983

Tuck, Richard, *Natural Rights Theories: Their Origin and Development*, Cambridge and New York: Cambridge University Press, 1979

Natural law arises from theories concerning the duties owed by citizens to God, the state or society, which originate in the mind or reason of God. Natural law thus expresses itself as a contract between man and God, and as such forms the beginnings of contract theory. Gierke, Tuck and Finnis all discuss the origins of natural law; using a historical approach, they describe the political appropriation of the theories of classical authors such as Aristotle, Plato, and Cicero, and, later, of Thomas Aquinas, and the subsequent development of the theories of natural rights and the creation of the monarch's divine right to rule. Natural law was not solely theoretical but was also applied by political rule, and later by policy – for example, it was used to legitimate the French absolutist regime. GIERKE sees the law as one-sided, and as a delimitation between the state and all other areas of society. Confining legal science to political theory, his work goes into considerable detail concerning how early natural law and its later developments structured the state. He also analyses the theory of the sovereignty of the ruler and of the mixed constitution.

TUCK examines the history of natural law in order to explain some of the problems in 20th-century rights theory. Although admitting that it is not obvious how a liberal theory emerged from 17th-century essays on the subject, he argues for an authoritarian, Grotian origin, that held that there was no private property in a state of nature, and that liberty itself was a kind of property, thus making contracts possible. He also maintains that Grotius's theory of the state was far more individualistic than those of his Protestant contemporaries, and that it had a contradictory duality, speaking the languages of both absolutism and liberty. Tuck also addresses current historiographical interpretations of natural law theory, by arguing that Immanuel Kant wrote out the contribution of ecclesiastics such as the Jesuits in order to make himself the conclusion of his version of history.

In his edited volumes, FINNIS analyses Thomist natural law theory and argues for an objective truth that exists independently of the order of nature. Explanations of things cannot, he claims, be discovered by direct speculation but by theology, and in this respect he is Thomist in his approach. By using "practical reasonableness" as a means of evaluating natural law, Finnis is also an idealist, opposed to positivism's empiricist philosophy. The other essays in the volumes take a philosophical approach, and dissect various aspects of natural law.

BUCKLE takes an intellectual historical approach, and contends that natural law was used to defend property. In proof of this, he follows the theme in the works of Grotius and Pufendorf's theory of the state and of the natural necessity of property, to the works of Locke and Hutcheson in the 18th century. His analysis of Hume's moral and political theory aims to resolve the philosopher's views on natural jurisprudence, and he does so by recourse to Newton. Contrary to some, Buckle argues that Hume did contribute to natural law theory, by showing that Hume borrowed Newton's experimentalism for his method of reasoning on moral subjects. Buckle disagrees with Tuck's interpretation of the Grotian (and later Hobbesian) tradition as having no place for a theory of property. Instead, he maintains that Tuck's contrast between absolutism and liberty is artificial, and that the right of property was very much part of the Hobbesian school of anti-absolutist political theory.

Ruby, Sargent, and Shapiro all discuss the role of natural law in science, focusing on Bacon, the experiential procedure of the common law, and the Royal Society. RUBY takes an epistemological approach, and argues that the term scientific law was first used in the 17th century, not a century or so later as some have maintained, and originated in the legal realm. Illustrating how scientific law was then used in the various texts she surveys, Ruby thus stakes a claim for the participation of clerics in the investigation of scientific laws.

Similarly, SARGENT also proposes that legal concepts were imported into the 17th-century scientific enterprise in her broader examination of the role of natural law in the practice of natural philosophy in England. She argues that scholars have neglected or misunderstood the legal concepts used by English experimentalists such as Boyle. In addition, she claims that Boyle combined empiricist and rationalist approaches to the study of nature in an eclectic fashion. Although asking the same sorts of questions concerning the nature of knowledge and its relation to the culture in which it is created, her conclusion is contrasted with that of Shapin & Schaffer's *Leviathan*, in which, she says, it is argued that Boyle was an empiricist, and that facts produced by experiment are arbitrary and influenced by their social and political environments. Sargent also argues that the boundary separating matters of fact from other considerations was not a creation of the experimentalists, but was already in use in the legal profession.

SHAPIRO takes another approach, and argues that the epistemological barriers between logic and rhetoric, and knowledge and opinion, were breached in 17th-century England, resulting in a distinct intellectual style that characterised inquiries into nature, religion, history, law, and literature. Rather than telling a story of legal procedure imported from the courts into the workings of the Royal Society, Shapiro maintains that concepts such as probability and degrees of certainty were simultaneously being worked out in the legal domain. She agrees that the dominant approach in English science was empirical, but adds that it was also probabilistic, because of a tension between the Baconian quest for certainty and the realisation that the results of empirical investigation could never be completely certain. Her characterisation of the "new science" as hostile to dogmatism, and her placing of authority with those scientists who were motivated by investigation (with Newton held up as the crowning glory of English science) and not by the desire to construct a "true" theory, should be read critically. Nevertheless, the chapter on law takes a sound historical and textual approach that begins appropriately with Roman law, and then gives a useful account of the

differences between Italian and French legal scholars. However, Shapiro does not mention that the central reason for the interest in quasi-Roman and Thomist concepts of natural law in the 17th century was a result of the need for expanded legal concepts, in order to justify and protect the use of land as capital and the commercial interests resulting from the increase in overseas trade – for example, Grotius worked as a lawyer for the Dutch East India Company. As such, the development of natural law reflected a shift in political power; it was no longer the monarchist political system that predominated and thus demanded protection and privilege, but rather individual and commercial rights (see the discussion of Buckle above).

From this change emerged the social contract theories of Locke, Hume, and Rousseau, in which, for instance, Rousseau's concept of natural rights contained natural freedoms that were to be protected from the power of the state. Later, the American and French revolutions used theories of natural law to argue for the institutionalization of natural and human rights – as in the United States's *Declaration of Independence* and France's *Declaration of the Rights of Man*.

Gierke also shows how, in the 19th century, positive rights, positivism, and utilitarianism developed out of natural law theories. On the one hand, Bentham's utilitarianism attacked the idea of natural rights in favour of using law as an active tool in his attempt to institutionalize his own ideas on social reform. On the other hand, John Stuart Mill fought to curb utilitarianism and to protect freedom of thought and expression. He favoured using rights theories to reduce the power of the state and to institutionalize a paternalistic form of liberalism.

The 20th century has seen an exciting revival in natural law theories and implications for natural law in the development of human rights law. The second volume of Finnis contains the work of current scholars, such as Dworkin and Hart, who have widened the scope of natural law. NETTHEIM shows how rights also include certain cultural rights; indigenous peoples, for example, have developed natural law theories that include a right to land as a way of maintaining their cultural heritage. In addition, the critical legal studies movement has taken root, and offers a continuing reassessment of the state of current natural law and rights theories.

HILLARY RAY

Natural Selection

Bowler, Peter J., *The Eclipse of Darwinism: Anti-Darwinian Evolution Theories in the Decades Around 1900*, Baltimore: Johns Hopkins University Press, 1983

Darwin, Charles, *On the Origin of Species by Means of Natural Selection; or, The Preservation of Favoured Races in the Struggle for Life*, facsimile of the original (1859) with an introduction by Ernst Mayr, Cambridge, Massachusetts: Harvard University Press, 1964

Darwin, Charles and Alfred Russel Wallace, *Evolution by Natural Selection*, edited by Gavin De Beer, Cambridge: Cambridge University Press, 1958

Darwin, Charles, *Charles Darwin's Natural Selection: Being the Second Part of His Big Species Book Written from*

1856 to 1858, edited by R.C. Stauffer, Cambridge and New York: Cambridge University Press, 1975

Darwin, Charles, *Charles Darwin's Theoretical Notebooks, 1836–1844*, edited by Paul H. Barrett *et al.*, Cambridge: Cambridge University Press, and Ithaca, New York: Cornell University Press, 1982

De Beer, Gavin, *Charles Darwin: Evolution by Natural Selection*, London: Nelson, and New York: Doubleday, 1963

Desmond, Adrian and James Moore, *Darwin*, London: Michael Joseph, and New York: Viking Penguin, 1991

Eiseley, Loren C., *Darwin's Century: Evolution and the Men Who Discovered It*, New York: Doubleday, 1958; London: Gollancz, 1959

Kohn, David (ed.), *The Darwinian Heritage: Including Proceedings of the Charles Darwin Centenary Conference*, Princeton, New Jersey: Princeton University Press, 1985

McKinney, H. Lewis, *Wallace and Natural Selection*, New Haven, Connecticut: Yale University Press, 1972

Mayr, Ernst and William B. Provine (eds), *The Evolutionary Synthesis: Perspectives on the Unification of Biology*, Cambridge, Massachusetts: Harvard University Press, 1980

Ospovat, Dov, *The Development of Darwin's Theory: Natural History, Natural Theology, and Natural Selection, 1838–1859*, Cambridge and New York: Cambridge University Press, 1981

Provine, William B. (ed.), *The Origins of Theoretical Population Genetics*, Chicago: University of Chicago Press, 1971

Vorzimmer, Peter J., *Charles Darwin: The Years of Controversy: The Origin of Species and Its Critics, 1859–82*, Philadelphia: Temple University Press, 1970; London: London University Press, 1972

Young, Robert M., *Darwin's Metaphor: Nature's Place in Victorian Culture*, Cambridge and New York: Cambridge University Press, 1985

Natural selection is the mechanism of evolution proposed by Charles DARWIN (1859) in his *Origin of Species*. The theory formed an integral part of the argument used by Darwin in order to convert the majority of scientists to an acceptance of the general idea of evolution. Following its synthesis with Mendelian genetics in the early 20th century, it has become the dominant explanatory tool of modern evolutionism. Many historical studies of evolutionism present the emergence of Darwin's theory as a central theme. More recently, however, historians have noted the lack of enthusiasm for natural selection among 19th-century evolutionists, and have drawn attention to the alternative mechanisms of evolution under consideration before the triumph of modern synthetic Darwinism.

As noted by Mayr in his introduction to the *Origin of Species*, natural selection presents evolution as a process that occurs in populations. There is no fixed "type" for the species, and the population exhibits a range of variation (now explained in terms of genetic differences) that organisms can transmit to their offspring. Selection occurs through the differential reproductive success of variant individuals: those best adapted to the local environment will leave more offspring, which will inherit their adaptive characters; less well-adapted individuals will not reproduce and may actually die. This is the process that Herbert Spencer called the "survival of the fittest". Darwin noted that differential reproduction would be intensified, because overpopulation tends to create a "struggle for existence" as organisms compete for scarce resources.

Darwin believed that the process that generates variant characters is essentially undirected (it is now attributed to genetic mutation). Selection alone changes the population in a direction determined by the requirements of adaptation. If part of the population migrates to a new environment, it will adapt and diverge from the original population, eventually forming a new species. The history of life must thus be represented as a divergent tree or bush, each branch continually subdividing as populations adapt to new environments. There can be no ladder of development leading toward a single goal. Natural selection is the most radically materialistic of all the mechanisms of evolution conceived by biologists.

Historians have devoted a great deal of effort to studying the process by which Darwin was led to the theory of natural selection. His *Theoretical Notebooks* from the late 1830s have been published (DARWIN, 1982), with commentaries indicating the latest thinking on their significance. His earliest accounts of the theory, from 1842 and 1844, are reprinted along with Alfred Russel Wallace's 1858 paper proposing a similar mechanism, in DARWIN & WALLACE. The "big book" on which Darwin was working, before being interrupted by Wallace's paper, has been edited and published as DARWIN (1975). Analysis of this wealth of original material has concentrated on certain key issues: (i) technical factors, including Darwin's views on heredity and variation, and the analogy with artificial selection; (ii) the religious and moral significance of his idea; and (iii) the role of free-enterprise individualism as an inspiration for Darwin's view of nature.

DE BEER's biography follows Darwin in emphasising the scientific discoveries leading to the theory. His work on biogeography during the voyage on HMS *Beagle* is stressed, especially his experience of local adaptation on the Galapagos islands. This is followed by his study of animal breeding, which led to a recognition that artificial selection can change the character of a population. Finally there is his recognition that population pressure generates a struggle for existence capable of serving as an equivalent selective power in nature.

The volume edited by KOHN brings together the best modern interpretations, and reassessments, of these factors. Frank Sulloway (pp. 121–54) surveys the impact of the *Beagle* voyage, warning that Darwin only recognized the significance of local geographical variation when he was on the point of leaving the Galapagos islands. David Kohn and Jonathan Hodge (pp. 185–206) study Darwin's early thoughts, noting that historians now question whether artificial selection actually played the role attributed to it in Darwin's later reconstruction of his discovery. His work on breeding certainly fuelled Darwin's understanding of variation, but it is possible that he put together the analogy with artificial selection only after conceiving how the natural version of the process might work. Hodge also stresses (pp. 207–44) the significance of Darwin's views on sexual reproduction, which lay at the heart of his vision of individual variation as a creative force. These ideas were very different from the modern geneticists' model of variation and heredity. Darwin did not see hereditary characters as units; he assumed that differences between the parents would blend together in the offspring, and thought that new characters were produced when changes in the environment interfered with the normal copying of parental characters through heredity.

Historians have also focused on Darwin's interest in the wider implications of his new theory. Traditionally, it has been assumed that the theory of natural selection undermines the logic of the argument from design used by natural theology. Where Paley saw the adaptation of an organ's structure to its function as evidence of design by a wise and benevolent Creator, natural selection sees only the product of a process of trial-and-error based on suffering and death. The possibility that Darwin found it much more difficult than the modern Darwinist to throw off the legacy of natural theology was stressed by OSPOVAT. Like Young, Ospovat noted that the theory of natural selection seems to portray nature as a purposeful entity very similar to the Creator. At first, Darwin thought that selection would operate only when the conditions changed, rapidly bringing the species back to a state of perfect adaptation; only when he realized that the pressure toward specialization would produce a constant elimination of the unfit, even in a stable environment, did he begin to abandon the belief that nature might be a divine contrivance. Where modern Darwinists argue that natural selection produces only adaptation, not progress, YOUNG, like many later writers, argues that the theory was meant to justify the belief that the struggle for existence had the long-term effect of driving living things to ascend the scale of organic complexity.

Young's argument is part of his wider campaign to insist that Darwin's theory must be understood as a reflection of the value system of the English middle classes. Ever since Marx and Engels noticed the congruence between the theory of the "survival of the fittest" and the competitive ethos of free-enterprise capitalism, socialist scholars have sought to portray Darwin's discovery as a projection of his class's value system onto nature. Young highlights the role of Thomas Malthus's principle of population-expansion as a key factor in the common context of social and scientific debate from which Darwin's theory emerged. DESMOND & MOORE also provide a relentlessly sociological account of Darwin's theory, although they regard his reluctance to publish as an indication that he (correctly, by the standards of modern Darwinists) saw how his vision of a world driven by struggle undermined the possibility of progress. Whether Darwin himself accepted or denied progress, these sociological accounts take it for granted that Darwinism only became popular because the theory became linked to the image of struggle as the motor of progress. This image was best expressed in Herbert Spencer's philosophy of evolution, although – as Bowler points out – Spencer was a Lamarckian, who believed that struggle was the spur to individual self-improvement. Natural selection was thus only one, and not necessarily the most obvious, application of the struggle metaphor to explain evolution.

In addition to controversies over Darwin's discovery of the selection principle, historians have also commented on the fact that the idea was independently conceived by A.R. Wallace in 1858. There have been some attempts to claim that Wallace has been given less credit than he deserves, although he came

on the scene nearly 20 years after Darwin had begun to develop the theory. McKINNEY gives a detailed account of Wallace's path towards natural selection. Malcolm Kottler in the Kohn volume (pp. 367–432) examines the differences perceived by some historians between the conceptions of selection developed by the two pioneers.

Whatever the popularity of a generalized form of Darwinism in the late 19th century, the theory of natural selection was subjected to a harsh critique. VORZIMMER provides an overview of the arguments, and of Darwin's responses. Many naturalists thought that species possess non-adaptive characters that cannot have been produced by natural selection. Another argument that has received much attention from historians was based on Darwin's pre-genetical view of variation and heredity. In 1868, Fleeming Jenkin claimed that if heredity involved the blending of parental differences, then the advantage enjoyed by a favoured individual would be halved in its offspring and eventually diluted beyond recognition. EISELEY argued that this argument undermined the case for natural selection, until the advent of Mendelian genetics in the early 20th century showed that inheritance is based on unit characters that cannot be diluted. He suggested that Darwin himself retreated from the selection theory and turned increasingly to the Lamarckian theory of the inheritance of acquired characters. This latter point exaggerates Darwin's despair, but, as BOWLER shows, non-Darwinian mechanisms of evolution flourished in the late 19th century. Many biologists thought that there must be some more purposeful or directed process for the generation of new characters, with natural selection merely weeding out the least successful.

PROVINE's account of the debates around 1900 shows that pro-Darwinists such as Karl Pearson were able to formulate theories of selection based on non-particulate models of heredity. At the same time, August Weismann began to discredit Lamarckism through his concept of the germ plasm – hereditary material that could transmit characters without being influenced by changes in the adult body. This viewpoint was built into the new genetics, although the early geneticists were saltationists, believing that new characters were produced instantaneously as units, without the need for selection of ordinary variation. Provine charts the process by which population geneticists such as R.A. Fisher brought the Mendelian and Darwinian perceptions together, by showing that mutations produced a pool of genetic variation in the population corresponding to Darwin's "random" variation. Selection boosted the frequency of genes which conferred adaptive benefit, and eliminated those less fitted to the environment. Natural selection thus emerged as the most plausible mechanism of evolution. The genetical theory of natural selection was now taken up by field naturalists and paleontologists, generating what has become known as the evolutionary synthesis. This process is described in MAYR & PROVINE's volume, with Mayr insisting that the naturalists were independently developing a more Darwinian concept of evolution based on local adaptation, which paralleled the geneticists' revival of the selection theory.

PETER J. BOWLER

See also Darwin; Darwinism; Evolution; Evolutionary Synthesis; Genetics: general works

Nature

Arnold, David, *The Problem of Nature: Environment, Culture and European Expansion*, Oxford and Cambridge, Massachusetts: Blackwell, 1996

Baldwin Jr., A. Dwight, Judith De Luce and Carl Pletsch (eds), *Beyond Preservation: Restoring and Inventing Landscapes*, Minneapolis: University of Minnesota Press, 1993

Collingwood, R.G., *The Idea of Nature*, Oxford: Clarendon Press, 1945; New York: Oxford University Press, 1960

Cronon, William (ed.), *Uncommon Ground: Toward Reinventing Nature*, New York: Norton, 1995

Crosby, Alfred W., *Ecological Imperialism: The Biological Expansion of Europe, 900–1900*, Cambridge and New York: Cambridge University Press, 1986

Evernden, Neil, *The Social Creation of Nature*, Baltimore: Johns Hopkins University Press, 1992

Glacken, Clarence J., *Traces on the Rhodian Shore: Nature and Culture in Western Thought from Ancient Times to the End of the Eighteenth Century*, Berkeley: University of California Press, 1967

Lovejoy, Arthur O. and George Boas, *Primitivism and Related Ideas in Antiquity*, Baltimore: Johns Hopkins Press, 1935

Merchant, Carolyn, *The Death of Nature: Women, Ecology, and the Scientific Revolution*, San Francisco: Harper and Row, 1980

Nash, Roderick, *Wilderness and the American Mind*, New Haven, Connecticut: Yale University Press, 1967; 3rd edition, 1982

Passmore, John, *Man's Responsibility for Nature: Ecological Problems and Western Traditions*, New York: Scribner, and London: Duckworth, 1974; 2nd edition, London: Duckworth, 1980

Soulé, Michael E. and Gary Lease (eds), *Reinventing Nature?: Responses to Postmodern Deconstruction*, Washington, DC: Island Press, 1995

Thomas, Keith, *Man and the Natural World: A History of the Modern Sensibility*, New York: Pantheon, 1983; Harmondsworth: Penguin, 1984

Torrance, John (ed.), *The Concept of Nature*, by Herbert Spencer, Oxford: Clarendon Press, and New York: Oxford University Press, 1992

Worster, Donald, *Nature's Economy: A History of Ecological Ideas*, Cambridge and New York: Cambridge University Press, 1977; 2nd edition, 1994

Worster, Donald (ed.), *The Ends of the Earth: Perspectives on Modern Environmental History*, Cambridge and New York: Cambridge University Press, 1988

The literature on nature in such fields as the history of ideas, philosophy, anthropology, and the history of religion is truly copious. Present knowledge suggests that views of nature differ substantially between cultures, regions, and periods of history. NASH shows that pre-agrarian societies generally tend to manifest a magical and respectful attitude towards nature that can be explained by their strong dependence upon it for their survival. Agrarian societies show a tendency to value cultivated land and, more generally, whatever is man-made, whereas nature in its pure form is considered threatening, even ugly; "wilderness" as a word for uncultivated nature is a product of agrarian societies. Modern industrial civilisation, originating in Europe, developed within scientific thought a view of nature as built by atoms, ruled by natural laws, and with an ultimate purpose to serve as a resource for humans. This point of view has been challenged by Romanticism, critics of civilization and other traditions, and in recent decades by arguments stemming from such diverse sources as ecological research, catastrophe and chaos theories, and from philosophic, economic, and feminist debates.

Older works on the history and usage of the concept that still merit attention are Lovejoy & Boas and Collingwood. COLLINGWOOD explains how Ionian philosophers in the 6th century BC already distinguished between things that were brought forth by human agency and those that occurred by themselves. From this grew a more precise and general division between *nomos* and *physis*, words that (roughly speaking) could be replaced by the later "culture" and "nature", although *nomos* also had a connotation of "norm" or "convention".

The reader of LOVEJOY & BOAS is carefully instructed in how the fundamental man-nature dualism developed within the Western world. Particularly in the Platonic and Christian traditions, a clear distinction was made between the natural and the supernatural, or metaphysical. The supernatural was eternal, unchangeable, spiritual, and divine; therefore it was superior to the natural, which was material, corporeal, and in constant flux. This view formed the basis of a hierarchical world view that has dominated in the West: man lived on Earth, in nature, and shared its sinfulness; on the other hand, man also had a soul, through which he had (potential) contact with the divine. When, in later scientific thought, nature was cast in the role of a grim and amoral arena for struggle and competition, the idea had roots in the older distinction between a male heaven and female earth. On the same intellectual foundation, it has been possible to value civilisation and culture in contrast to nature; through their virtue, morals, and social organisation, human societies stand above the proposed brutality, injustice, and capriciousness of nature.

The classical historical study of ideas on the relationship between man and nature in Western culture is GLACKEN. The backbone of this enormously rich work consists of three ideas that have been present in the history of Western thought from antiquity to the 18th century: first, that the Earth is fit for man to live on and that it is ultimately designed for man alone, as the highest being of creation, or for the hierarchy of life with man at the apex; second, that man's health and well-being is dependent on his natural environment (this idea is similar to what was later called environmentalism); and third (an idea that gradually gained ground but was not fully articulated until the late 18th century with Buffon), that man functions as a geographic agent who shapes, moulds, cultivates, but also destroys the earth once created for him. The relative importance of these ideas has varied greatly, but none was ever wholly out of focus. What is also evident to the reader of Glacken is that almost no single aspect of nature is lacking in the vast body of literature he examines, from the influence of climate on man, and nature as a source of norms and morals, to the idea that nature has seriously declined.

PASSMORE is a more selective overview, focusing particularly on the ethics of nature. A section of his book deals with both classical and Judeao-Christian ideas; the author finds, like exegetes and other scholars of the scriptures, that although there is a fundamentally anthropocentric perspective in the Bible and the Talmud, there are nuances to the picture. If man's domination of nature is one part of this picture, another is the idea of stewardship, in which man receives a divine mandate to care for nature while making use of it.

WORSTER (1977) is in the same vein as Glacken, but it covers the last three centuries, starting in a small English village in the latter half of the 18th century, and ending with the "chaos ecology" of the 1990s. Worster is interested in one particular aspect of nature – namely, the interrelatedness of different parts of the living whole, and how this has been observed, described, and valued. He therefore concentrates on philosophical ideas and scientific disciplines that deal particularly with this issue. In the latter half of the book, he increasingly focuses on the rise and development of ecology as a science. Ecology, Worster argues, carries twin traditions at the heart of its enterprise: one is an Arcadian, idyllic vision of nature, in which man fosters empathy with the creation and all life forms, even inorganic life; the other is the imperial vision – the distant, scientific gaze that seeks to dissect, analyse, decipher, control, and ultimately exploit nature and her resources and wealth.

WORSTER (1988) starts with Buffon, who is the end point of Glacken. According to Worster, in the late 18th century a new era begins, as Buffon is one of the first fully to accept and articulate the idea that the Earth undergoes change and that man is the principal agent. This marks a great divide in the history of man's view of nature: it is a revolution of thought, one may say, of the same magnitude as that of Adam Smith in the field of economics. Smith realised the potential of modern industrial economy, and proposed that it would necessarily continue until it had dominated the world. His contemporary, Buffon, said essentially the same about man as a geographical agent: that his progress will continue until there will be no nature left. Therefore, in Worster's interpretation, Buffon is also the invocator of environmental history: he is the first fully to realise that the history of nature is in essence a history of man's deeds and daily practices.

In the 1980s and, particularly, in the early 1990s there appeared a number of studies that to varying degrees have included a constructivist perspective. EVERNDEN is a full-scale, yet subtle and critical constructivist analysis; in discussing a very limited number of thinkers, Evernden nevertheless tries to give a chronological narrative of the construction of nature, from the Renaissance through to the 20th century. Starting with Pico della Mirandola's *Oration on the Dignity of Man* (1496), he describes how humanity has become increasingly separated from nature. With the appearance of such words as "humanism" and "humanitarian" (signifying that there is something human that exists in contrast to nature) came the idea of human will, compassion, and freedom to choose, with nature increasingly downgraded as lacking these elevated qualities. Nature does not feel and think, it lacks intentions, it cannot show care and compassion, and its actions do not occur by freedom but by necessity – precisely because of the inner imperative reason called "nature".

Evernden terms this ontological process of separation the social "creation" of nature, for, he suggests, in a certain sense "nature" did not exist before this process of construction occurred. Before the Renaissance, the human and the natural were mixed, while in the 20th century there were even more far-reaching attempts to minimise the human: from Freud, there is a line through to sociobiology and genetics that purports to posit driven nature within all human thought and action.

The constructivist approach has had a strong influence on historical work dealing with nature in the 1990s. A seminal example is a volume edited by the environmental historian, CRONON. This is a collection of papers by authors representing a wide array of disciplines and a variety of positions, but who, with a few exceptions, gather around a basic idea – namely, that the nature we cherish and hold on to in conservationist and environmentalist debates is in almost every aspect a socially and culturally constructed concept. The argument works on two levels. The first is a level of ideas: what is today conceived of as "nature" is in fact something that is historically recent; as Cronon points out in his introduction, "In Search of Nature", the appreciation of wilderness, a phenomenon perhaps peculiar to the North American experience, was by and large constructed by the urban upper and middle classes in the 19th and 20th centuries. The other level of the argument concerns "real" nature; i.e. the landscape as it is "out there". One of the valuable contributions of this volume is that it demonstrates the ambiguity of the places that constitute, or are part of, "nature". The chapters of the book point to a number of environments that do not commonly pass for "nature", but could indeed be subsumed under its name: in some cases we are dealing with culture – i.e. man-made landscapes – that are called nature, sometimes with places commonly understood as nature that have been turned into culture, such as national parks or nature monuments. In either case, it is increasingly unclear which is which. Cronon's comment on the contemporary notion of nature is that, whatever "it" may be, it is primarily, maybe solely, something that humans have agreed on to call by that name, and that, quite obviously, we will then have to accept that not all humans will agree.

When the line between nature and culture has become as blurred as it is today, it is unsurprising to find a growing opinion that completely denies the value of preservation. In BALDWIN, DE LUCE & PLETSCH, the editors state the overall theme of this interdisciplinary collection of papers:

> we can see how current development has transformed so much of nature in our lifetime; we are learning how nature had already been reshaped by our species in the past; and we are realizing that there is not much left to preserve in pristine state anyway. Furthermore, we are less and less clear about what it would mean to preserve nature.

However, SOULÉ & LEASE react specifically against such arguments; in their view nature does indeed exist "out there" and it requires human protection, at the very least for the sake of humanity. The volume documents the anxiety felt among environmentalists of the late 1990s.

As a background to the ongoing relativisation of the nature-concept is a new knowledge concerning the global transformation of nature. Not long ago, conventional wisdom held that in Africa, Asia, Australia, and the Americas, aboriginal populations, old as they are, had not in any deep or lasting sense affected their environment. Recent scholarship, however, has demonstrated that in virtually every corner of the world where humans have been present to any substantial degree there is evidence of an environmental impact. Much of the land was then taken over by European colonisers who moulded it further, bringing, even to those areas they did not actually cultivate, weeds, livestock, and disease, so that the encounter was also an ecological one, substantially changing biota and diminishing populations in overseas colonies. The single most influential book in this field is CROSBY, whose historical argument is informed by a mass of epidemiological, ecological, and other scientific data. Other historians have emphasized alternative aspects of the encounter, not least the scientific. A short but valuable introduction to this new knowledge of nature is ARNOLD.

Throughout Western history, and in particular during the half century or more after Darwin's *Origin*, nature served as a powerful metaphor for those considered less refined in (Western) culture and civilisation, particularly women, children and the lower social classes. However, this has not been the only use of the metaphor; far from being a denigration, the supposed presence of the "natural" in women has also been a cherished notion in feminism, and a vast literature has examined different aspects of the role of women in relation to nature. The identification of nature with the female is very old, and probably goes all the way back to the early fertility cults. In particular, MERCHANT epitomises this eco-feminist gospel. Her work is a survey of how important female images, gods, and metaphors have been in Western views of nature, but she also discusses female knowledge traditions and insights in fields such as botany and medicine. The Earth itself was female, often compared to the womb, and she suggests that this metaphor in fact functioned as a restraint on the exploitation of nature and her resources. THOMAS, whose empirical study covers England from 1500 to 1800, corroborates that these traditions were indeed common, even after the Renaissance.

The subtitle of Merchant, *Women, Ecology, and the Scientific Revolution*, should be interpreted to mean that the death of nature came with the suppression of female knowledge of nature and the "spontaneous" ecological truth that lay hidden within it. The book also allows for a critique of those (male) powers of Western science that have classified women according to an organic schema and thereby "naturalised" them. This approach is also adopted by some of Merchant's followers, who have written gendered environmental histories of science and society. This combination of perspectives creates, however, a complication: on the one hand, the view of the female principle as part of nature, and therefore possessing deeper insights, is interpreted as a male strategy for domination; on the other hand, the female principle is praised in a certain strand of feminist nature writing precisely as a part of nature.

TORRANCE gives an overview of these manifold concepts of nature. Focusing on scientific ideas on nature from several periods, this is a traditional interpretation of the history and usage of this complex word, providing concise and yet probing analysis. There are chapters on Greek antiquity, the Middle Ages, the scientific revolution, Darwin's conception of nature,

and, finally, two chapters on contemporary scientific views of nature, one by a biologist and one by a physicist.

SVERKER SÖRLIN

See also Ecology; Environmental Sciences

Navigational Instruments

Andrewes, William J.H. (ed.), *The Quest for Longitude: The Proceedings of the Longitude Symposium, November 4–6, 1993*, Cambridge, Massachusetts: Collection of Historical Scientific Instruments, Harvard University, 1996

Bennett, J.A., *The Divided Circle: A History of Instruments for Astronomy, Navigation, and Surveying*, Oxford: Phaidon/Christie's, 1987

Cotter, Charles Henry, *A History of the Navigator's Sextant*, Glasgow: Brown and Ferguson, 1983

Gould, Rupert Thomas, *The Marine Chronometer: Its History and Development*, London: J.D. Potter, 1923

Hitchens, Henry Luxmoore and W.E. May, *From Lodestone to Gyro-Compass*, London and New York: Hutchinson Scientific and Technical, 1952; revised edition, 1955

Mörzer Bruyns, W.F.J., *The Cross-Staff: History and Development of a Navigational Instrument*, Amsterdam: Vereeniging Nederlandsch Historisch Scheepvaart Museum; Rijksmuseum Nederlands Scheepvaartmuseum and Zutphen: Walburg Instituut, 1994

Randier, Jean, *Marine Navigation Instruments*, translated from the French by John E. Powell, London: John Murray, 1980 (original edition, 1978)

Sellés, Manuel A., *Instrumentos de navegación: del Mediterráneo al Pacífico*, Barcelona: Lunwerg, 1994

Stimson, Alan, *The Mariner's Astrolabe: A Survey of Known, Surviving Sea Astrolabes*, Utrecht: Hes, 1988

Waters, David Watkin, *The Art of Navigation in England in Elizabethan and Early Stuart Times*, New Haven: Yale University Press, 1958; Greenwich: Trustees of the National Maritime Museum, 1978

There are several museum catalogues devoted exclusively to navigational instruments, but for the most part the literature is scattered throughout books either with a larger remit or which focus on one type of instrument. There are also works on the history of navigation, but they rarely focus on the instrumentation.

RANDIER does focus on navigational instruments and is a fairly reliable account, although (as a work written for collectors) emphasis is placed on describing each individual instrument in turn. SELLÉS offers a Spanish perspective on the subject from the Renaissance to the 18th century. BENNETT's study extends to the late 19th century, and treats navigational instruments alongside those used for astronomy and surveying.

Of the books on individual types of instruments, STIMSON and MÖRZER BRUYNS, treating the mariner's astrolabe and the cross-staff respectively, both base their accounts on an international survey of all surviving examples. Thus, both books are catalogues as well as histories. Even though both types of instrument were common during the periods they were in use, the number of surviving instruments is sufficiently small to permit such treatment, and the results have the benefit of being firmly based on the material record.

No such approach is possible for the sextant, and COTTER has written a history with a stronger narrative line. At the same time, he concentrates more on the workings of the sextant and the developments in its optical geometry over time, than with the history of individual objects and their manufacture. The same general remarks apply to HITCHENS & MAY's history of the compass.

GOULD is still the standard history of the marine chronometer, and the author's careful and dedicated work has stood the test of time. ANDREWES contains valuable accounts of the histories of different methods of finding longitude, on land as well as at sea, but some of the contributions on the work of John Harrison are marred by an uncritical enthusiasm for their subject.

Among general histories of navigation, WATERS is notable for providing the background to many instruments, and for dealing successfully with the technicalities of the instruments themselves, although his study is limited in scope to England in the 16th and 17th centuries.

JIM BENNETT

See also Astrolabes; Astronomy: general works; Clocks; Scientific Instruments: general works

Nernst, Walther 1864–1941

German physical chemist

Anonymous, "Dem Andenken an Walther Nernst", *Naturwissenschaften*, 31 (1943): 257–75, 305–22, 397–415

Anonymous, "Über Walther Nernst aus Anlass seines 50. Todestages", *Wissenschaftliche Zeitschrift der Humboldt-Universität zu Berlin, Reihe Mathematik/Naturwissenschaften*, 4 (1992)

Barkan, Diana K., *Walther Nernst: Physicist as Chemist*, Cambridge: Cambridge University Press, 1997

Bartel, Hans-Georg, *Walther Nernst*, Leipzig: Teubner, 1989

Cherwell, Lord and Franz Simon, "Walther Nernst, 1864–1941", *Obituary Notices of the Fellows of the Royal Society*, 4 (1942): 101–12

Mendelssohn, Kurt, *The World of Walther Nernst: The Rise and Fall of German Science*, London: Macmillan, and Pittsburgh: University of Pittsburgh Press, 1973

There is so far only one substantial scholarly biography of Walther Nernst, despite the fact that he is regarded as a co-founder of physical chemistry, a trailblazer for quantum theory, and as one of the most important scientific personalities of the late 19th and early 20th centuries. The reader interested in Nernst's life and work can turn first to the small biography in German by BARTEL, one in a very useful series of biographies issued by the Teubner publishing house in Leipzig. This booklet gives an excellent and very readable overview of Nernst's scientific work and fascinating personality. It documents his role in the establishment of physical chemistry, and explains his fundamental scientific contributions in a style which is both popular and knowledgeable. Nernst's scientific high point came in 1905, with the discovery of the third theorem of thermodynamics – the so-called Nernst heat theorem. It was through this theorem that technical chemistry became a "calculating science", and it also opened up the entirely new fields of low temperature research and quantum theory. From 1910 onwards, Nernst, his collaborators and graduate students systematically examined the physical properties (especially the specific heats) of different materials at low temperatures. This research confirmed the heat theorem, but in addition revealed that it and the loss of heat of specific heats at low temperatures were both a consequence of the quantum concept of oscillating molecules and the exchange of energy between them. With this research, Nernst provided the still young and fragile quantum theory with one more pillar of experimental support, while becoming one of the theory's most ardent pioneers. He not only supported the theory in his research but also in his organisational work; for instance, he was one of the initiators of the Solvay Congress held in Brussels in 1911, which brought together all the leading physicists of the time to discuss the quantum theory, and the theory's peripheral status.

These sets of problems and questions – the transformation of classical physical chemistry and molecular physics into quantum physics – within Nernst's work is analysed in great detail and very convincingly in Diana Barkan's doctoral thesis. BARKAN shows that the interdisciplinary character of physical chemistry, with its diverse and to some extent competing research programs and traditions, had an impact upon this transformation, as did the pooling of experim-ental and theoretical methods. However, in addition to this methodological and internalist perspective, Barkan provides an abundance of interesting information concerning Nernst's personality, for instance his organization of the first Solvay conference in 1911 on the emerging quantum theory.

MENDELSSOHN, who himself belonged to the circle of students around Nernst in Berlin, focuses on Nernst's personality, but this work also fails to meet the standards of a modern scientific biography. The strength of the book is to be found in its vivid description of the atmosphere of Berlin during its scientific (and cultural) heyday, and of the interrelation of the scientific development with the personalities involved. In this way, the example of Nernst makes clear what made Berlin an international centre for technology and the natural sciences at the turn of the century. If one reads the book critically, there is no reason to be deterred by the lack of scholarly apparatus and the rendering of anecdotes, legends, myths and data which cannot always be substantiated.

CHERWELL & SIMON's obituary (Lord Cherwell is the physical chemist, Frederick Lindemann), and especially ANONYMOUS (1943), provide first-hand information on Nernst's work and personality. The latter in particular is an excellent introduction to specific technical aspects of Nernst's research. Schottky and Wietzel describe the foundations and application of the heat theorem, Bonhoeffer writes on Nernst's examination of the irritation of nerves, Hartech describes his work in photochemistry, and Eggert examines his role as a text book author.

Last, but not least, ANONYMOUS (1992), published by the Humboldt University on the 50th anniversary of Nernst's death, is to be recommended. Originating in a series of lectures held at a commemorative seminar, the volume includes specialised contributions judging Nernst's role from the perspective of the historian of science, documentation on the archives relating to Nernst's time in Berlin, and (most usefully) an extensive bibliography of primary and secondary sources.

DIETER HOFFMANN
translated by Arne Hessenbruch

See also Cryogenics; Physical Chemistry; Quantum Theory

Netherlands: technology

Bijker, Wiebe E., Thomas P. Hughes and Trevor J. Pinch (eds), <i>The Social Construction of Technological Systems: New Directions in the Sociology and History of Technology</i>, Cambridge, Massachusetts: MIT Press, 1987

Davids, C.A., "De technische ontwikkeling van Nederland in de Vroeg-moderne tijd. Literatuur, problemen en hypothesen", <i>Jaarboek voor de Geschiedenis van Bedrijf en Techniek</i>, 8 (1989): 9–29

Fischer, Emil J. (ed.), <i>Geschiedenis van de techniek: Inleiding, overzicht en thema's</i>, The Hague, 1980

Forbes, R.J., <i>Man the Maker: A History of Technology and Engineering</i>, New York: Schuman, 1950

Lintsen, Harry W. (ed.), <i>Geschiedenis van de techniek in Nederland: De wording van een moderne samenleving 1800–1890</i>, 6 vols, Zutphen: Walburg Pers, 1992–95

Pieterson, Maarten (ed.), <i>Het technisch labyrint: Een maatschappijgeschiedenis van drie industriele revoluties</i>, Meppel: Boom, 1981

The history of technology has been studied in the Netherlands by scientists and scholars of different backgrounds for at least 60 years, but only in the last 25 years has it been done within a stable institutional context. The study of the history of technology has a shorter tradition than it has in Britain and Germany, just as industrialization also came later to the Netherlands. A first wave of history of technology came in the 1920s and the 1930s. This first generation consisted of Dutch historians who focussed on the economic history of the Netherlands in the 16th, 17th, and 18th centuries. Their motivation was to understand the success of the Dutch economy in this period. DAVIDS gives an overview of the literature and historiographical problems concerning the early modern period. For a long time, the technological development in the Netherlands in the 19th and 20th centuries was not taken very seriously because the machines, skills, and knowledge were mainly imported. For several generations of historians technology was a black box: only invention was worthy of study whereas technology transfer was not.

Some engineers also contributed to the history of technology as a hobby. The most important Dutch historian of technology before the 1970s was R.J. FORBES, a chemical engineer working for the company Bataafse Petroleum Maatschappij, later renamed Koninklijke Shell. Forbes did much research, focussing at first on the history of mining, road building and materials technology, especially bitumen and petroleum.

A large part of his research dealt with antiquity, but later he broadened his field to other themes and periods. Forbes dealt with technological progress from the Stone Age to the 1930s, placing much importance on the role of inventors and technicians. Forbes was a professor at the Municipal University of Amsterdam, a position he held until his death in 1973. Although he had an outstanding reputation both in the Netherlands and abroad, this did not result in permanent institutions for the history of technology in the Netherlands.

In the 1970s the history of technology became for the first time a more widely studied subject within engineering circles and among scholars and university scientists. This new attention to the field was thanks to the widespread contemporary criticism of the role and side effects of modern technology. Only later did the discipline disengage itself from this political context. A working committee on the history of technology was founded at the Technical University of Twente as a result of which two text books were published: Fischer and Pieterson. FISCHER is an initial exploration of the field. The team of sociologists, historians, psychologists and other scholars and scientists led by PIETERSON of the University of Leiden was more ambitious. Their aim was to analyse the technical development within the broad framework of economic, political, social and cultural context. The book describes technical developments in three and a half centuries on three levels: the level of production (tools, machines, working procedures, innovations), its impact on daily life (the concept and consequences of industry and technology) and of legitimization (the ideological side). The book did not pay attention to specific Dutch developments, but concentrated on the most important international trends. Much attention was given to developments in Britain, Germany, and the United States. This emphasis on developments abroad was typical of the study of the history of technology in the Netherlands at the time. The book was definitely new in its emphasis on the connections between the different levels of analysis and on the different ways the technological development was connected to developments in the society. Even though the book contains minor errors, it is an original publication and still useful for educational purposes in some universities and schools.

BIJKER, HUGHES & PINCH describes the relation between technology and society as a "seamless web". Bijker and his co-authors attempt to define technology and technological processes and to identify the factors involved. They generally orient themselves towards sociological concepts and models. The book was the result of an international meeting at the Twente Technical University in 1984, which was attended by many internationally well-known historians and sociologists of technology. The approach of the scholars of the Twente University, the Social Construction of Technology (SCOT), resonated with other approaches such as technology assessment. For Bijker and his co-authors the technical development is the result of the interaction of technical, economical, social, political, cultural, psychological and geographical factors. They did not give priority to any one of these factors. Their approach is suitable for the examination of relations and dynamics of technological development.

The six volumes of LINTSEN were published between 1992 and 1995. The title translates as "The History of Technology in the Netherlands: The Emergence of a Modern Society

1800–1890". This work was the result of years of research on the history of engineering and industrialization in the Netherlands. Harry W. Lintsen who has worked on the occupational history of Dutch engineers was the fulcrum of the project. The first four volumes cover a wide spectrum: agriculture and nutrition; health, public hygiene and communications; textiles, cotton, lighting and construction; mining, machinery, steam technology, and chemistry; technology in the working environment; and technology and society. The volumes are divided into chapters on particular technologies or economic sectors. Volume 1, for example, contains chapters on foodstuffs, such as margarine, beer, and sugar. Each chapter gives an overview of developments with many excellent illustrations and some statistical tables. Volume 5 describes the development of technical education, while volume 6 attempts to integrate the diverse empirical descriptions into a methodological framework and to appease the intrinsic tension between micro- and macro-perspectives. These six volumes make clear that technology can not be regarded as a black box and that the diffusion of technology is a topic worthy of analysis: the application of technical knowledge, machines and skills developed in patterns that depended on the particular socio-cultural environment. Currently a follow-up project is under way on the history of Dutch technology from 1890 to 1970.

HANS BUITER

See also Education

Neumann, Salomon 1819–1908

German physician

Baader, Gerhard, "Salomon Neumann", *Mediziner*, in *Berliner Lebensbilder*, edited by Wilhelm Treue and Rolf Winau, Berlin: Colloquium, 1987, 151–74

Cohen, Hermann, "Salomon Neumann: Rede bei der Gedächtnisfeier der Lehranstalt für die Wissenschaft des Judentums", in *Jüdische Schriften*, vol. 2, Berlin: Schwentschke, 1924, 425–38

Hacking, Ian, *The Taming of Chance*, Cambridge and New York: Cambridge University Press, 1990

Karbe, Karl-Heinz, *Salomon Neumann (1819–1908): Wegbereiter sozialmedizinischen Denkens und Handelns*, Ausgewählte Texte, Leipzig: Johann Ambrosius Barth, 1983

Meyer-Neumann, Elsbeth, "S. Neumanns Wirksamkeit auf dem Gebiete der Sozialhygiene", *Sozialhygienische Mitteilungen*, 17 (1933): 14–19

Regneri, Günter, "Salomon Neumann's Statistical Challenge to Treitschke", *Leo Baeck Institute Yearbook*, vol. 43, 1998

Rosen, George, "What is Social Medicine? A Genetic Analysis of the Concept", *Bulletin of the History of Medicine*, 21 (1947): 674–733

Much commemorative literature can be found on Salomon Neumann, who was a prominent figure of the medical reform movement of 1848 in Berlin. Neumann pioneered occupational health statistics and tenaciously lobbied for sanitary reform, playing a crucial part in the hygienic clean-up of Berlin in the late 19th century. Yet there is unfortunately still no scholarly biography of Neumann. In the historical work done so far, he usually remains in the shadow of his friend and collaborator, Rudolf Virchow, who was both the founder of cellular pathology and a prominent politician. Also, the literature is frequently coloured by the period in which it was published, and Neumann's left-leaning politics or Jewishness accordingly emphasised or downplayed.

The only major work on Neumann is a study by the East German medical historian KARBE, whose focus is on public health issues and especially on Neumann's dominant role in the *Berliner Gesundheitspflegeverein* (Berlin Health Care Club), which offered the first health insurance of the German labour movement. Yet Karbe's claim that the former German Democratic Republic saw the realisation of Neumann's ideals of social medicine is, at the very least, misleading; one pertinent fact that he ignores, for example, is that Neumann, a radical democrat, regarded self-determination of both the patient and the physician as an important principle of public health. Nevertheless, this is a monograph-length study of Neumann in which he is not eclipsed by Virchow.

ROSEN argues that the intellectual climate in Germany in the mid-19th century was crucial for major theoretical formulations of social medicine. Despite highlighting the plea of the radicals in the medical reform movement that "medicine is a social science", an idea first formulated by Neumann, and quoting him quite frequently, Rosen clearly considers Virchow the leading light in the reform movement.

One of the chapters in HACKING is entitled "Chapter from Prussian Statistics", a straight, although unacknowledged, lift from the title of a book by Neumann. Hacking discusses the use and abuse of statistics in the process of constructing the "normal" state. During the wave of anti-semitism in Germany from 1879 to 1881, Neumann disproved the politically-charged claim that Germany had been the subject of massive Jewish immigration. According to Hacking, "Neumann was well placed to comment" on this demographic question and his study contained only official figures. However, the Prussian statistical bureau, which was loyal to the Bismarck administration (which for political expediency was happy with the argument for a large Jewish immigration), printed a "disdainful dismissal" of his study. Hacking comments that statistical practice had reached a phase in which "one needed a fund of amateur information to prevent abuse of numbers by the establishment". While this is surely a backhanded compliment to Neumann, the epithet "amateur" is surely not the most appropriate.

The discursive structures outside the scientific community of statisticians are examined by REGNERI, who describes the conditions that made Neumann an influential voice in the public debate on anti-semitism.

A general biographical account of Neumann is given by BAADER, in which Neumann's decision to get involved in municipal politics is described as a decisive move to put some of the ideas of the 1848 medical reform movement into practice.

COHEN argues that, in order to arrive at a holistic picture of Neumann, it is important to see the interrelation between his religious and scientific activities, as Neumann was active in Jewish circles in Berlin. Rather than viewing Judaism as a constraint on scientific research, Neumann emphasised how objectivity and scientific rigour were important for understanding the historic role and mission of Judaism.

Elsbeth MEYER-NEUMANN, Salomon Neumann's daughter, herself a medical doctor, gives a detailed account of her father's writings on social medicine and statistics. Her article was published at the beginning of the Nazi era, and Neumann's distinctive Jewish forename was reduced to an initial in the heading of the article, thus avoiding Nazi censorship. Meyer-Neumann does not bring much new information, but it is an interesting document for understanding the realities of publishing under the Nazi regime when compared with similar documents from other periods.

GÜNTER REGNERI

See also Public Health; Statistics; Virchow

Neurosciences

Finger, Stanley, *Origins of Neuroscience: A History of Explorations into Brain Function*, Oxford and New York: Oxford University Press, 1994

Harrington, Anne, *Medicine, Mind and the Double Brain: A Study in Nineteenth-Century Thought*, Princeton, New Jersey: Princeton University Press, 1987

Jacobson, Marcus, *Foundations of Neuroscience*, New York: Plenum Press, 1993

Jeannerod, Marc, *The Brain Machine: The Development of Neurophysical Thought*, translated from the French by David Urion, Cambridge, Massachusetts: Harvard University Press, 1985 (original edition, 1983)

Smith, Roger, *Inhibition: History and Meaning in the Sciences of Mind and Brain*, London: Free Association, and Berkeley: University of California Press, 1992

Stevens, Leonard A., *Explorers of the Brain*, New York: Knopf, 1971; London: Angus and Robertson, 1973

The history of the neurosciences has long been beset by a central tension. The term neuroscience has a relatively recent origin: it was coined after World War II, the result of an optimistic attempt to unite such varied approaches as the anatomical, the physiological, the psychological, and the psychiatric through the common organ of the brain. The holism and the modernity of the neurosciences, however, is not reflected in the discipline's historical literature. Whereas there are a large number of *festschrifts* and edited collections in this area, most of them concentrate on the infancy or the prehistory of the discipline. Moreover, such collections offer only the most fragmentary account of the subject, confounding the reader's attempt to achieve a general understanding of the social and intellectual context behind the current fascination with the human brain. This discussion is limited to works that make some sustained reference to 20th-century developments in the neurosciences.

The most obvious introduction to the general history of the neurosciences appears in the work of Stanley FINGER. In a lavishly illustrated large-format book, Finger attempts to cover the general development of ideas about the brain and nervous system from classical to modern times. The material is organized into seven sections, with each section covering a discrete structure–function relationship in the brain, such as the sensory system, the motor system, sleep and emotion. The format does not suit the material, projecting modern classification on to ancient belief systems. Likewise, the coverage is of necessity fairly superficial – moving from Babylonian sources through 19th-century psycho-physics to modern electrophysiological investigations in the space of a few pages. Without the space to provide any social context or sustained analysis, the narrative develops a fairly whiggish trajectory, occasionally descending into a rollcall of neurological pioneers and innovations. Despite these reservations, Finger's work remains a lucid, if occasionally inaccurate, introduction, providing ample references to support further research.

JEANNEROD's work follows Finger in its isolation of specific structure–function relationships as a key to understanding the development of the neurosciences. In *The Brain Machine*, he focuses on just one relationship, between the brain and physical action, arguing that animal movement has always been considered "a special index" of brain activity. Beginning with the work of René Descartes and Thomas Willis in the 17th century, he concentrates on the shifting boundary between reflex and voluntary action, arguing that these opposed models of activity support antagonistic conceptions of the human personality. Jeannerod himself is committed to a "physiology of spontaneity", which stresses the role of internal representations in the direction of action. Consequently, he provides a close survey of 20th-century developments in neurobiology, arguing that its dynamic has moved away from mechanistic models to a new emphasis on self-organization.

A more historicising and deconstructive approach to contemporary neuroscientific belief is provided by the work of Anne HARRINGTON. Her book traces the moral and medical issues that grew up around the concept of hemispheric difference in the second half of the 19th century. After providing a working map of theories of the dual brain in early 19th-century phrenology and physiological psychology, Harrington embarks on a detailed exploration of cerebral asymmetry in Victorian culture. Although she resists the idea that scientific investigation in this area was driven by social interests, she is attentive to the mundane implication of these ideas. Hypnotism, metallotherapy, and early investigations into psychotherapy and psychoanalysis are each shown to be profoundly influenced by the doctrine of hemispheric difference. In her closing chapter, Harrington considers the resurgence of interest in the concept of cerebral asymmetry which occurred in the 1950s.

Roger SMITH is probably the only author to attempt a history that integrates the modern development of neuroscience with its social and political context. Smith goes beyond the accounts offered by Harrington and Jeannerod, which simply rehearse the technical evolution of specific neuroscientific concepts and their subsequent impact on the public sphere. Instead, he outlines the persistent linguistic slippage that has occurred between neuroscience and popular languages, arguing that the elision has imparted new values and expectations to both discourses. Beginning with the moral psychology of mid-19th-century Britain, and ending with the 20th-century schools of Ivan Pavlov, Charles Scott Sherrington, and Sigmund Freud, Smith demonstrates how the scope and ambition of the neurosciences were predicated on the elasticity of its organizing concepts.

Leonard STEVENS is one of the few authors to attempt a synoptic account of the neurosciences in the 20th century. Although written for a popular audience, his work was produced in consultation with practising neuroscientists across Britain and America. He focuses on electro–physiological investigations, especially the more glamorous projects such as electroencephalography and the electrical stimulation of the brain. The presentation, however, is cool and lucid, possessing the single advantage of subsuming fairly dry material, such as experimental reports of synaptic transmission, into an overarching and engaging narrative. Although Stevens ignores the social dimension in the direction and evolution of the neurosciences, he is keen to emphasize the public impact of the discipline's discoveries, portraying it as the starting point for a reformation in concepts of learning, responsibility, and selfhood.

A more complex and considered account of the neurosciences in the 20th century has been developed in the work of Marcus JACOBSON. Jacobson is suspicious of attempts to subsume the complexity of the emergence of the discipline within a single narrative, and instead deploys a massive range of historical sources to produce a series of reflections on the practice and ethics of the science. Across five chapters, he considers the issues of theory formation, neuroreductionism, hero worship, and problems of disciplinary synthesis, and ethical issues. This examination focuses on key issues in the modern neurosciences, such as the role of the metaphor in brain models, the intellectual status of C.S. Sherrington and Ramón y Cajal Santiago, and the synthesis of discrete research programmes in neuron theory. His work provides a naturalistic justification of the history of the neurosciences, portraying this project as the conscience and collective memory of the profession.

RHODRI LLOYD HAYWARD

See also Anatomy; Physiology: France; Physiology: Germany; Psychophysics

Newton, Isaac 1642–1727

English physicist and mathematician

Bertoloni Meli, Domenico, *Equivalence and Priority: Newton versus Leibniz*, Oxford: Clarendon Press, and New York: Oxford University Press, 1993

Blay, Michel, *La conceptualisation newtonienne des phenomenes de la couleur*, Paris: Vrin, 1983

Brackenridge, J. Bruce, *The Key to Newton's Dynamics: The Keeper and the Principia*, Berkeley: University of California Press, 1996

Brewster, David, *Memoirs of the Life: Writings and Discoveries of Sir Isaac Newton*, 2 vols, Edinburgh: Constable, 1855; reprinted with an introduction by Richard S. Westfall, 2 vols, New York: Johnson, 1965

Castillejo, David, *The Expanding Force in Newton's Cosmos*, Madrid: Ediciones de Arte y Bibliofilia, 1981

Cohen, I. Bernard, *Introduction to Newton's "Principia"*, Cambridge: Cambridge University Press, and Cambridge, Massachusetts: Harvard University Press, 1971

Cohen, I. Bernard, *The Newtonian Revolution: With Illustrations of the Transformation of Scientific Ideas*, Cambridge and New York: Cambridge University Press, 1980

Dobbs, Betty Jo Teeter, *The Foundations of Newton's Alchemy: or "The Hunting of the Greene Lyon"*, Cambridge and New York: Cambridge University Press, 1975

Dobbs, Betty Jo Teeter, *The Janus Faces of Genius: The Role of Alchemy in Newton's Thought*, Cambridge and New York: Cambridge University Press, 1991

Dobbs, Betty Jo Teeter and Margaret C. Jacob, *Newton and the Culture of Newtonianism*, Atlantic Highlands, New Jersey: Humanities Press, 1995

Force, James E. and Richard H. Popkin (eds), *The Books of Nature and Scripture*, Dordrecht and Boston: Kluwer, 1994

Gandt, François de, *Force and Geometry in Newton's Principia*, translated from the French by Curtis Wilson, Princeton, New Jersey: Princeton University Press, 1995

Gjertsen, Derek, *The Newton Handbook*, London and New York: Routledge and Kegan Paul, 1986

Hall, A. Rupert and Marie Boas Hall (eds), *Unpublished Scientific Papers of Isaac Newton: A Selection from the Portsmouth Collection*, Cambridge: Cambridge University Press, 1962

Hall, A. Rupert, *Philosophers at War: The Quarrel between Newton and Leibniz*, Cambridge and New York: Cambridge University Press, 1980

Hall, A. Rupert, *Isaac Newton: Adventurer in Thought*, Oxford and Cambridge, Massachusetts: Blackwell, 1992

Hall, A. Rupert, *All Was Light: An Introduction to Newton's Opticks*, Oxford: Clarendon Press, and New York: Oxford University Press, 1995

Herivel, John, *The Background of Newton's "Principia": A Study of Newton's Dynamical Researches in the Years 1664–84*, Oxford: Clarendon Press, 1965

Jones, Peter (ed.), *Sir Isaac Newton: Manuscripts and Papers* (microfilm) Cambridge: Chadwyck-Healey, 1991

Koyré, Alexandre and I. Bernard Cohen (eds), *Isaac Newton's Philosophiae Naturalis Principia Mathematica*, 3rd edition with variant readings, 2 vols, Cambridge: Cambridge University Press, 1972

McGuire, J.E. and Martin Tamny, *Certain Philosophical Questions: Newton's Trinity Notebook*, Cambridge and New York; Cambridge University Press, 1983

Mamiani, Maurizio, *Isaac Newton filosofo della natura*, Florence: La Nuova Italia, 1976

Mamiani, Maurizio, *Il prisma di Newton: i meccanismi dell'invenzione scientifica*, Rome: Laterza, 1986

Manuel, Frank E., *Isaac Newton: Historian*, Cambridge, Massachusetts: Belknap Press, 1963

Manuel, Frank E., *A Portrait of Isaac Newton*, Cambridge: Massachusetts: Harvard University Press, 1968

Manuel, Frank E., *The Religion of Isaac Newton*, Oxford: Clarendon Press, 1974

Shapiro, Alan E., *The Optical Papers of Isaac Newton*, Cambridge and New York: Cambridge University Press, 1984–

Turnbull, H.W. *et al.*, *Correspondence*, 7 vols, Cambridge: Cambridge University Press, 1959–77

Wallis, Peter and Ruth Wallis, *Newton and Newtoniana, 1672–1975: A Bibliography*, Folkestone, Kent: Dawson, 1977

Westfall, Richard S., *Never at Rest: A Biography of Isaac Newton*, Cambridge and New York: Cambridge University Press, 1980

Whiteside, D.T. and M.A. Hoskins (eds), *The Mathematical Papers of Isaac Newton*, 8 vols, Cambridge: Cambridge University Press, 1976–81

The amount of scholarly literature on Isaac Newton is immense. WALLIS & WALLIS offers reliable and exhaustive guidance through the vast maze of literature on Newton to 1975. GJERTSEN is a bio-bibliographical dictionary of Newton's career, with useful entries on many of his colleagues, rivals, and disciples and chronological lists of his publications and manuscripts. The literature covered here includes publications of primary sources, biographies of Newton, and works focusing on particular aspects of Newton's concerns.

There is no general edition of the collected works and papers of Newton. Rather, there is a series of editions of his correspondence and of his particular fields of study. The editorial apparatus to these editions constitutes much of the best scholarship on Newton, but the compartmentalization of Newton's work is problematic. JONES, which is designed to accompany the microfilm of Newton's manuscripts, simply reproduces the *Catalogue of the Portsmouth Collection* acquired by Cambridge University Library in 1888 and the *Catalogue of the Newton Papers* sold at Sotheby's in 1936, together with a useful indication of all these papers' current location. It contains descriptions and summaries of each item: many quite full, some cursory or inaccurate. The *Correspondence* (TURNBULL *et al.*) is the necessary point of departure for anyone concerned with Newton's life as a whole, or with some segment of it. The editors have enhanced this aspect of the work by including a number of manuscripts that had not been published previously. They have also supplied translations of letters and manuscripts not in English, as well as elaborate annotations. The wealth of information in these notes (with a few exceptions) continues to be authoritative.

Newton's career in science began with a lengthy passage in an undergraduate notebook that he entitled, "Quaestiones quaedam philosophicae". Made known by A. Rupert Hall more than 40 years ago, this passage offers insight into the questions in natural philosophy that initially stimulated Newton's interest and continued to hold his attention throughout his career. The "Quaestiones" have remained prominent in Newton scholarship. The McGUIRE & TAMNY edition of the passage prints the original together with a "translation" into 20th-century English with all the abbreviations spelled out, and accompanies the two texts with thorough commentaries that establish the setting and explicate the problems to which Newton first addressed himself.

HALL & HALL is an edition of hitherto unpublished papers that made available to scholars a number of important, but previously unknown, manuscripts, for the most part on general issues of natural philosophy. These manuscripts have figured prominently in Newtonian scholarship ever since, and anyone interested in the development of Newton's conception of nature will need to become familiar with them. Interpretative

commentaries are included with the manuscripts, but inevitably, with the intense scrutiny these papers have received over more than 30 years, alternative interpretations have elsewhere been posited.

Mathematics was an early intellectual passion of Newton's, and his interest continued, with diminished intensity, throughout his life. Surprisingly, in view of the importance of his contribution to mathematics, very few of his papers had been published before the WHITESIDE & HOSKINS edition. This is the pre-eminent edition of Newton's scientific papers, with introductory essays and exhaustive footnote commentaries. Volume 1, which is of special interest, traces Newton's progress from self-taught student to inventor of the calculus.

SHAPIRO is an edition of Newton's optical papers. So far, only one of three projected volumes has appeared, containing the early Cambridge lectures in which Newton worked out the details of his theories of the heterogeneity of light and the phenomena of colours, and established the core of his contribution to the science of optics. The volume also contains Shapiro's explication of Newton's work.

HERIVEL contains the manuscripts on mechanics that preceded the *Principia*, introducing them with an interpretative narrative of Newton's developing grasp of the subject. The manuscripts go back to the same undergraduate years that witnessed the "Quaestiones quaedam philosophicae", when Newton made contact with the new conception of motion and attacked the problems of impact and circular motion. Herivel concludes with Newton's essay *De Motu* in its three versions, the first composed in 1684, and the manuscripts that accompanied them – in effect, the first drafts of what became the *Principia*. In his *Introduction to the Principia*, COHEN (1971) takes up the story where Herivel leaves off, focusing, as the title promises, on the composition of the book itself. Volume 6 of Whiteside & Hoskin's edition of the *Mathematical Papers* and the KOYRÉ & COHEN edition of the *Principia*, with variant readings from the first two editions and also from the extensive manuscript remains, complete the set of works necessary to the study of this central aspect of Newton's science.

As Cohen proceeded, his attention shifted away from the *Opticks* and toward the *Principia*, of which he was an editor, and a new English translation of that work is imminent. Unlike his earlier work, COHEN (1980) relates Newton (primarily the Newton of the *Principia*) to the ideas and the men who preceded him. Part I defends the concept of a Newtonian revolution, as distinct from the scientific revolution of which it formed the concluding chapter. Central to the Newtonian revolution is what Cohen calls the "Newtonian style", a reciprocal interchange between idealized mathematical theory and empirical measurements, by which the mathematical theory is continually refined in order to embody as fully as possible the complex reality of nature. The second part of the book, entitled "Transformations of Scientific Ideas", treats Newtonian physics as a development and enhancement of the earlier work of Kepler, Galileo, and Descartes.

There is no edition of Newton's extensive papers on alchemy, but some of the most important among them are published as appendices to both DOBBS (1975) and DOBBS (1991).

The first major biography of Newton, by BREWSTER, had access to the great trove of manuscripts then in possession of the Portsmouth family. However, Brewster was a busy scientist who was not prepared to devote a major portion of his career to plumbing the contents of an uncatalogued mountain of papers, and he was a century too early to benefit from the editions of papers mentioned above. He was also afflicted with a serious case of hero-worship, which tinted his perception of his subject. For all that, the *Memoirs* is a remarkable exercise in scientific biography, which held the field as the best source on Newton for more than a century. It can still be read with profit.

WESTFALL accepts that moral excellence does not necessarily accompany intellectual genius. This biography presents a portrait of a neurotic, tortured man, but also gives a detailed account of Newton's scientific achievements. Considering the alchemical papers as part of his scientific career, Westfall draws his account of Newton's religious opinions from manuscripts that were deposited in the Jewish National Library in Jerusalem only after the biography was well in progress. Newton's career as Master of the Mint is also described.

Frank Manuel came to Newton from Renaissance studies, where the split between mysticism and positivism did not exist; he thus had no compunction about studying Newton's various activities from a single perspective. MANUEL (1963) describes the profound methodological and metaphysical relationship between Newton's scientific and other work, including that on the prophetic books of the scriptures (e.g. his derivation of a chronology of ancient kingdoms). The essays in FORCE & POPKIN show that Newton sought to correct the errors he believed had been introduced into the Bible falsely to justify faith in the Trinity.

MANUEL (1974) made use of the Newton manuscripts that had recently been brought to light. The theological manuscripts sold at the Sotheby auction in 1936 had vanished for several decades; Abraham Yahuda, an Alexandrian Jew and friend of Einstein's, had bought them, and bequeathed them to the Jewish National Library in Jerusalem, where they are now known as the Yahuda manuscripts. This event, and Manuel's book, inaugurated serious scholarly study of the content of these papers.

Alchemy is a subject fraught with religious overtones, and Dobbs's work is as much concerned with an examination of the role of religion in Newton's career as a study of alchemy. Until recently, Newton's theological manuscripts were not available for scholarly study, and despite the fact that the manuscripts, which form an immense bulk, are now deposited in libraries, only a tiny fraction of them has been published. DOBBS (1991) is the most recent of the small number of works that rest on these manuscripts. The development in Dobbs's two books reflects the development within the history of science in general: DOBBS (1975) presents Newton's alchemy as a rational, controlled enterprise into fundamental properties of matter, which left major traces in his published work on gravity and light; in Dobbs (1991), emphasis is placed upon the profound relationship between Newton's alchemical work and his religious beliefs, especially his denial of the doctrine of the Trinity.

There are several monographs on special aspects of Newton's career. For his early work on optics, good studies are BLAY on the optical notebooks of the 1660s, MAMIANI (1976) on the Cambridge optical lectures, and MAMIANI (1986) on the development of the prism experiments from the mid-1660s. As part of his editorial work on Newton's correspondence, HALL (1980) produced a book on his notorious dispute with Leibniz on the invention of fluxions and on metaphysics. This chronological survey can now be complemented by a thorough analysis of mathematical and astronomical issues, raised during the dispute studied in BERTOLONI MELI. CASTILLEJO, an early student of the Yahuda manuscripts, eventually summarized some of his own sometimes idiosyncratic work on the relation between Newton's alchemy, theology, and prophetic interpretation. Recent important studies of the dynamics of the *Principia* are BRACKENRIDGE, on the opening sections of the book, and De GANDT, on the relation between geometry and dynamics. Hall has continued his work on the Newtonian legacy with an accessible biography, HALL (1992), and a well-written introduction to the *Opticks*, HALL (1995).

DOBBS & JACOB is the best introduction to Newton; it is very well written and is popular as a textbook. Building on the work by Thomas, Manuel, and Dobbs, the authors do justice to Newton's theology and alchemy, and, in the latter part of the book, they consider the significance of Newton to the Industrial Revolution.

RICHARD S. WESTFALL
reviewed by Simon Schaffer

See also Newtonianism; Scientific Revolution

Newtonianism

Burke, John G. (ed.), *The Uses of Science in the Age of Newton*, Los Angeles: University of California Press, 1983

Cohen, I. Bernard, *Franklin and Newton: An Inquiry into Speculative Newtonian Experimental Science and Franklin's Work in Electricity as an Example Thereof*, Philadelphia: American Philosophical Society, 1956

Ferrone, Vincenzo, *The Intellectual Roots of the Italian Enlightenment: Newtonian Science, Religion, and Politics in the Early Eighteenth Century*, translated from the Italian by Sue Brotherton, Atlantic Highlands, New Jersey: Humanities Press, 1995 (original edition, 1982)

Gascoigne, John, *Cambridge in the Age of the Enlightenment: Science, Religion and Politics from the Restoration to the French Revolution*, Cambridge and New York: Cambridge University Press, 1989

Guerlac, Henry, *Newton on the Continent*, Ithaca, New York: Cornell University Press, 1981

Guicciardini, Niccolò, *The Development of Newtonian Calculus in Britain, 1700–1800*, Cambridge and New York: Cambridge University Press, 1989

Heilbron, J.L., *Physics at the Royal Society during Newton's Presidency*, Los Angeles: William Andrews Clark Memorial Library, 1983

Jacob, Margaret C., *The Newtonians and the English Revolution, 1689–1720*, Ithaca, New York: Cornell University Press, 1976

Koyré, Alexandre, *Newtonian Studies*, Cambridge, Massachusetts: Harvard University Press, and London: Chapman and Hall, 1965

McMullin, Ernan, *Newton on Matter and Activity*, Notre Dame, Indiana: University of Notre Dame Press, 1978

Markley, Robert, *Fallen Languages: Crises of Representation in Newtonian England*, Ithaca, New York: Cornell University Press. 1993

Nicolson, Marjorie Hope, *Newton Demands the Muse: Newton's Opticks and Eighteenth Century Poets*, Princeton, New Jersey: Princeton University Press, 1946

Schechner Genuth, Sara, *Comets, Popular Culture and the Birth of Modern Cosmology*, Princeton, New Jersey: Princeton University Press, 1997

Shapiro, Alan E., *Fits, Passions and Paroxysms: Physics, Method, and Chemistry and Newton's Theories of Colored Bodies and Fits of Easy Reflection*, Cambridge and New York: Cambridge University Press, 1993

Stewart, Larry, *The Rise of Public Science: Rhetoric, Technology, and Natural Philosophy in Newtonian Britain, 1660–1750*, Cambridge and New York: Cambridge University Press, 1992

Thackray, Arnold, *Atoms and Powers: An Essay on Newtonian Matter-Theory and the Development of Chemistry*, Cambridge, Massachusetts: Harvard University Press, 1970

Thrower, Norman J.W. (ed.), *Standing on the Shoulders of Giants: A Longer View of Newton and Halley*, Berkeley: University of California Press, 1990

Just as Newton himself has been a frequent object of study, so his influence has been an important subject for the history of science. From Koyré onwards, Newtonianism has been on the agenda and, as a result, the literature is voluminous. The early investigators pioneered very close readings of the primary sources, and subsequent historians have tried to inform these readings with institutional history. Much recent scholarship has emphasised the theological import of Newtonianism, and has attempted to analyse which groups claimed to be Newtonians and for what reasons.

Toward the end of his illustrious career, Alexandre Koyré turned toward Newton. With I. Bernard Cohen, he prepared an edition of the *Principia* with variant readings, and although he produced no book devoted to Newton alone, he did write a number of major articles. Several of these are collected in KOYRÉ, published shortly after his death, its title consciously paralleling his epochal book on Galileo. Among the articles, "The Significance of the Newtonian Synthesis" has been especially influential.

COHEN has led Newton studies for four decades. As the title indicates, this work does not regard Newton in terms primarily of the scientific revolution that led up to him, but rather of the 18th-century investigations that he inspired. Cohen advances the thesis, which has been widely adopted, that two traditions flowed from Newton's work, one of mathematical physics based on the *Principia*, and another of experimental science that drew on the "Queries" attached to the *Opticks*. The book is primarily about electrical science in the 18th century, which Cohen treats as a Newtonian experimental science, the structure of which was shaped by Newton's speculations about the aether.

Proceeding further along the paths opened by Koyré, the philosopher and historian Ernan McMULLIN explores the meanings behind several of Newton's concepts introduced in the *Principia*, that together constitute the heart of the Newtonian image of physical reality. Thus, he carefully analyses what Newton understood the universal qualities of matter to be, what he meant by forces between particles, in what sense he thought activity could be ascribed to passive matter, whether he considered gravity essential to matter, what he regarded as the nature of the agencies that move matter, and similar questions central to the understanding of Newtonian science.

SHAPIRO explicates Newton's theory of the colours of solid bodies and follows its history until its demise in the mid-19th century. He covers most of the issues present in Newton's work on optics.

Newton's presidency of the Royal Society (1703–27) saw a systematic and coordinated defence of the principles of mechanics and optics he had established. HEILBRON describes these initiatives in detail, as well as the developments in natural philosophy and rational mechanics of the period, using the correspondence and journal books of the Royal Society.

In a provocative work, JACOB examines the political interests that drove the first generation of British Newtonians, including a discussion of the ideology of the early Boyle Lectures, the response to Newton's natural theology from Whigs and Deists, and the establishment of the Newtonian hegemony in British political thinking by 1721.

Cambridge University in the 18th century was soon dominated by the Newtonian curriculum of mathematics and natural philosophy. GASCOIGNE describes the "holy alliance" forged by Cambridge dons between Anglican orthodoxy and Newtonianism, then traces the various crises within the University community that saw Newton's reputation and the principles of his science become, by the century's end, matters of debate between orthodox and dissenting clerics.

It has often been argued that Newtonian mathematics was pursued more effectively in continental, rather than British, academies and institutions. However, as GUICCIARDINI argues, there continued a rich vein of work on fluxions by British mathematical practitioners in London, Cambridge, and Scotland throughout the 18th century. Much of this legacy has no doubt been ignored because of the highly successful campaign of mathematical reform launched by early 19th-century analysts, in Cambridge and elsewhere.

THACKRAY explores the legacy of Newton's speculations on the nature of chemical phenomena, published primarily in Query 31. He begins with Newton, and follows the tradition he established through the 18th and into the early 19th century, with emphasis on forces between particles and the attendant conception of the overwhelming preponderance of void space over solid matter.

STEWART shows that the spread of Newtonianism in England was concomitant with the development of a commercial and technological society in the first three decades of the 18th century. Projectors, as they were called, working at the Royal Exchange and in the network of coffee houses in London's financial district, developed a public culture of Newtonianism in which lectures on the new philosophy were accompanied by schemes for profitable engines such as pumps, water wheels, and coinage projects – all apparently credible because of their close link with the new truths of Newtonian mechanics. The preeminent expositor of these programmes was

John Desaguliers, Newton's lieutenant and the Royal Society's curator of experiments.

In a collection of essays, GUERLAC analyses the first responses to Newton's optical work in France, showing how the prismatic experiments were reproduced by the circles around Malebranche, and the labor of the Newtonian circle to win adherence among Paris academicians between 1710 and 1740.

FERRONE's excellent work provides a similar analysis for Italy. He shows how networks of liberal Catholic intellectuals in Rome and Bologna cultivated strong links with the Royal Society under Newton, successfully combating Cartesian and scholastic critics of Newtonian optics and planetary theory, and reinterpreting Newton for the Italian Enlightenment. Chief among these figures was Francesco Algarotti, whose "Newton for Ladies" was a best-selling handbook of popular Newtonianism. Ferrone also identifies the sources of criticism of Newtonian mechanics in Venice and Padua, which helped inaugurate the *vis viva* controversy from the 1720s onwards.

Cometography was a principal avenue for the development of Newtonianism in 18th-century Europe. The reappearance of comet Halley in 1986 prompted a conference on aspects of the comet work of Newton, the Newtonians, and Edmund Halley from which THROWER emerged. The book contains some useful studies of Newtonian sciences in Europe in the mid-18th century, such as Waff on the coordination and interpretation of observations of comet Halley in 1758–59, and a group of studies on the presence of Newton in the Greenwich and Paris observatories. A good discussion of the link between cometary theory and cosmology in Newtonianism is provided in SCHECHNER GENUTH.

There has been much discussion of the literary and cultural significance of Newtonianism. An early and masterly account was provided by NICOLSON, while more recent discussions of Newtonian culture are summarised in the essays in BURKE, and developed with special reference to the literary styles of Newtonian theology and natural philosophy in MARKLEY.

RICHARD S. WESTFALL
reviewed by Simon Schaffer

See also Enlightenment; Halley; Rational Mechanics

Nobel Institution

Bliss, Michael, *The Discovery of Insulin*, Chicago: University of Chicago Press, 1982

Crawford, Elisabeth and Robert Marc Friedman, "The Prizes in Physics and Chemistry in the Context of Swedish Science: A Working Paper", in *Science, Technology and Society in the Time of Alfred Nobel* (Nobel Symposium 52), edited by Carl Gustaf Bernhard, Elisabeth Crawford and Per Sörbom, Oxford and New York: Pergamon Press, 1982

Crawford, Elisabeth, *The Beginnings of the Nobel Institution: The Science Prizes, 1901–1915*, Cambridge and New York: Cambridge University Press, 1984

Crawford, Elisabeth, J.L. Heilbron and Rebecca Ullrich, *The Nobel Population 1901–1937: A Census of the Nominators and Nominees for the Prizes in Physics and Chemistry*, Berkeley: Office for History of Science and Technology, University of California, 1987

Friedman, Robert Marc, "Nobel Physics Prize in Perspective", *Nature*, 292 (1981): 793–98

Friedman, Robert Marc, "The Nobel Prizes and the Invigoration of Swedish Science: Some Considerations", in *Solomon's House Revisited: The Organization and Institutionalization of Science* (Nobel Symposium 75), edited by Tore Frängsmyr, Canton, Massachusetts: Science History Publications, 1990

Luttenberger, Franz, "Arrhenius vs. Ehrlich on Immunochemistry: Decisions about Scientific Progress in the Context of the Nobel Prize", *Theoretical Medicine*, 13 (1992): 137–73

Nagel, Bengt, "The Discussion Concerning the Nobel Prize for Max Planck", in *Science, Technology and Society in the Time of Alfred Nobel* (Nobel Symposium 52), edited by Carl Gustaf Bernhard, Elisabeth Crawford and Per Sörbom, Oxford and New York: Pergamon Press, 1982

Pais, Abraham, *Subtle is the Lord . . .: The Science and Life of Albert Einstein*, Oxford: Clarendon Press, and New York: Oxford University Press, 1982

Schück, Henrik *et al.*, *Nobel: The Man and His Prizes*, Stockholm: Sohlman, and Norman: University of Oklahoma Press, 1950; 2nd edition, Amsterdam: Elsevier, 1962

Zuckerman, Harriet, *Scientific Elite: Nobel Laureates in the United States*, New York: Free Press, 1977

The Nobel institution is important to the progress of science, both because the prizes in physics, chemistry and physiology represent three out of the original five Nobel prizes (the two others being the literature and peace prizes), and because of the weight they carry in the scientific reward system. The scientific part of the Nobel institution encompasses those who award the prizes (the Royal Swedish Academy of Sciences for the prizes in physics and chemistry, and the Karolinska Institute for the prize in physiology or medicine), the decision-making machinery for awarding the prizes, chiefly the Nobel committees, and the symbolic uses to which the prizes are put by and through the laureates.

The literature about the Nobel institution can be roughly separated into two broad categories: before and after the changes to the statutes of the Nobel Foundation in 1974. Access to documents at least 50 years old in the archives of the Royal Swedish Academy of Sciences and the Karolinska Institute is now permitted for the purpose of historical research. The most important documents in the archives are: the letters of nomination of candidates for the prizes; the reports on the candidates drawn up by the Nobel committees; the minutes of the Nobel committees; and the minutes of meetings of the Academy of Sciences and the Karolinska Institute concerning the Nobel prizes.

SCHÜCK *et al* is the major institutional history produced before the opening of the archives. Its authors were all associated with the Nobel institution, and prominent members of the Nobel committees describe the progress made in physics, chemistry, and medicine during the 20th century, limiting their perspective to work that was crowned by Nobel prizes. For each decision, only the prize winners are mentioned, never the unsuccessful candidates. ZUCKERMAN also belongs to the period before the opening of the archives. The careers of American laureates of 1901–72 are used to show how the process of accumulating advantages, chiefly those of education and research training, has produced the ultra-elite of Nobel laureates in the sciences. A historical perspective is offered through the study of the master-apprentice relationships, often encompassing several generations, that Zuckerman suggests are important for entering the ultra-elite.

The opening of the Nobel archives meant primarily that the study of the institution could encompass not just the laureates but the candidates as well. The names of all the candidates in physics and chemistry of 1901–37, as well as those of the people who nominated them, are listed in CRAWFORD, HEIL-BRON & ULLRICH. A new edition, including the years 1938–45, is in preparation.

The access to the archival material has made it possible to study the whole process of selecting prize winners, from nominations to the final decision. CRAWFORD describes this process with regard to the prizes in physics and chemistry, from 1901 to 1915. She uses as her starting-point the establishment of the institution, in the crucial years between Nobel's death in 1896 and the promulgation of the statutes of the Nobel Foundation in 1900, and then examines how the statutory rules were transformed into workable decision-making practices. She also describes how the Nobel prizes became the most important award in the sciences, in the eyes of both the public and the international scientific community.

Access to the archives has also meant that the research specialties of Swedish scientists who were the decision-makers for the Nobel prizes, and the local context of the decisions, can be used to throw light on the selection of prize winners. FRIEDMAN (1981), and then in more detail in CRAWFORD & FRIEDMAN, was the first to draw attention to the importance of this variable, which was illustrated through case studies of several decisions up to the 1920s. As a major influence on the early prize decisions, the authors stressed the experimentalist bias, which made members of the physics committee prefer work representing their own specialities of "measuring physics" (especially spectroscopy and metrology). FRIEDMAN (1990) goes one step further, and argues that the Nobel institution was used more directly by committee members, particularly in the 1930s, to further their disciplinary strategies and to garner additional resources – by, among other things, appropriating funds representing interest on the capital that had accumulated as a result of the prizes being reserved.

The main value of the materials in the Nobel archives lies in their ability to contribute to "puzzle-solving" in the history of science. This applies most directly to controversial prize decisions. PAIS, a biography of Einstein, Friedman (1981) and Crawford & Friedman, all examine the decision of the Nobel Committee for Physics in 1922 to award Einstein the 1921 prize for "his discovery of the law of the photoelectric effect", rather than for the theory of relativity cited by a majority of the nominators. NAGEL describes the lengthy deliberations that preceded the awarding of the 1918 physics prize in 1919 to Max Planck, for the discovery of energy quanta.

The studies cited above are all based on materials in the Nobel archives, found at the Center for History of Science of the Royal Swedish Academy of Sciences, and concern the prizes in physics and chemistry. By contrast, the prizes in physiology or medicine have not been extensively studied, perhaps because of the more restrictive policies with respect to archival access practised by the Karolinska Institute. The discussion by BLISS of the controversial decision to award J.J.R. MacLeod half of the 1922 Nobel prize in physiology or medicine for the discovery of insulin (the other half going to Fredrick Banting) represents the major study in the puzzle-solving genre. Finally, LUTTENBERGER shows how the conflict between Svante Arrhenius and Paul Ehrlich, concerning the chemical reactions of immune response early in the century, was brought into the debate concerning the Nobel prize awarded to Ehrlich (together with Ilya Mechnikov) in 1908. The article sheds important light on the procedures and policies that guided the decision-makers of the Karolinska Institute at this time.

ELISABETH CRAWFORD

See also Sweden

Nuclear Physics

Aaserud, Finn, *Redirecting Science: Niels Bohr, Philanthropy, and the Rise of Nuclear Physics*, Cambridge and New York: Cambridge University Press, 1990

Amaldi, Edoardo, "From the Discovery of the Neutron to the Discovery of Nuclear Fission", *Physics Report*, 3 (1984): 1–332

Crowther, J.G., *The Cavendish Laboratory 1874–1974*, London: Macmillan, and New York: Science History Publications, 1974

Fischer, Klaus, *Changing Landscapes of Nuclear Physics: A Scientometric Study on the Social and Cognitive Position of German-Speaking Emigrants Within the Nuclear Physics Community, 1921–1947*, Berlin: Springer, 1993

Heilbron, J.L. and Robert W. Seidel, *Lawrence and His Laboratory: A History of the Lawrence Berkeley Laboratory*, vol. 1, Berkeley: University of California Press, 1989

Hendry, John (ed.), *Cambridge Physics in the Thirties*, Bristol: Hilger, 1984

Hermann, Armin *et al.*, *History of CERN*, 3 vols, Amsterdam: North-Holland, 1987–96

Hiebert, Erwin, "The Role of Experiment and Theory in the Development of Nuclear Physics in the Early 1930s", in *Theory and Experiment: Recent Insights and New Perspectives on Their Relation*, edited by Diderik Batens and Jean Paul van Bendegem, Dordrecht: Reidel, 1988

Holton, Gerald, "Fermi's Group and the Recapture of Italy's Place in Physics", in *The Scientific Imagination: Case Studies*, edited by Holton, Cambridge and New York: Cambridge University Press, 1978

Mladjenović, Milorad, *The History of Early Nuclear Physics (1896–1931)*, Singapore, and River Edge, New Jersey: World Scientific, 1992

Pais, Abraham, *Niels Bohr's Times: In Physics, Philosophy and Polity*, Oxford: Clarendon Press, and New York: Oxford University Press, 1991

Rhodes, Richard, *The Making of the Atomic Bomb*, New York: Simon and Schuster, 1986

Shea, William R. (ed.), *Otto Hahn and the Rise of Nuclear Physics*, Dordrecht: Reidel, 1983

Six, Jules, *La Découverte du Neutron (1920–36)*, Paris: Editions du Centre National de la Recherche Scientifique, 1987

Stuewer, Roger H. (ed.), *Nuclear Physics in Retrospect: Proceedings of a Symposium on the 1930s*, Minneapolis: University of Minnesota Press, 1979

Stuewer, Roger H., "Mass-Energy and the Neutron in the Early Thirties", *Science in Context*, 6 (1993): 195–238

Weart, Spencer R., *Scientists in Power*, Cambridge, Massachusetts: Harvard University Press, 1979

Weiner, Charles (ed.), *Exploring the History of Nuclear Physics*, New York: American Institute of Physics, 1972

Weiner, Charles, "Institutional Settings for Scientific Change: Episodes from the History of Nuclear Physics", in *Science and Values: Patterns of Tradition and Change*, edited by Arnold Thackray and Everett Mendelsohn, New York: Humanities Press, 1974

Wilson, David, *Rutherford: Simple Genius*, London: Hodder and Stoughton, and Cambridge, Massachusetts: MIT Press, 1983

Mirroring their status in science and wider culture, nuclear physics and its practitioners have occupied a privileged place in the Anglo-American history of physics in the second half of the 20th century. It is paradoxical, then, that there exists no single comprehensive and authoritative critical history of the subject. Rather, the literature consists of a number of partial accounts covering various elements of the cognitive, biographical, disciplinary, and institutional aspects of the field. The literature can be conveniently divided into several genres: autobiographies and reminiscences of those who themselves took part in the development of nuclear physics; biographies of key individuals in the field; histories of the important institutions in the subject's development; and intellectual histories of the discipline.

These various accounts are best approached with caution, for they tend to overlap and co-define each other to a large extent, with the same unanalysed catalogue of events, individuals and institutions featuring as significant in each. This underlying, unifying master narrative in fact represents an implicit "canonical account" of the history of the subject, deriving largely from a reification of the post-war writings of nuclear scientists on the history of their subject. In this pervasive interpretation, key events in the pre-World War II period – the discovery of radioactivity (1896), the identification of the nucleus (1911), the elaboration of isotopes (1913, 1919), the splitting of the nucleus (1917, 1932), the discovery of the neutron (1932), artificial radioactivity (1934), and the liquid drop model of the nucleus (1936) – are identified and retrospectively given significance in terms of their contribution to the development of nuclear theory, its role in the later discovery of nuclear fission (1938), and the wartime development of atomic energy for military purposes.

This "internalist" narrative of theory is complemented by an "externalist" narrative (that these terms are appropriate indicates the relative historiographical underdevelopment of the field), which addresses the nuclear physics community and its institutions. Again, important individuals, developments and key institutions are essentially defined retrospectively. This literature largely emphasises the translation of pre-war European nuclear physics to the United States (particularly through the émigré Jewish nuclear physicists, who fleeing Nazi persecution, catalysed the Allied atomic weapons projects), the role of nuclear physicists (as opposed to the far more numerous engineers, chemists, metallurgists, etc.) in the development of atomic weapons during the war, and the creation of nuclear institutions and facilities (e.g. particle accelerators) in both the pre- and post-war periods.

Matters are complicated by the fact that much of the written history of pre-war nuclear physics is to be found in the numerous histories of the atomic bomb (of which RHODES is the most comprehensive and successful). However, insofar as it can be separated from the military story (a question upon which few historians have chosen to reflect), the history of nuclear physics *per se* has tended to be shaped around the same basic elements and plot.

The fission-directed teleological emphasis on nuclear theory – overt in Amaldi, for example, but widely, if implicitly, employed elsewhere – has had important consequences for the kinds of historical questions which have (and, more importantly, which have not) been asked in the history of nuclear physics. The role of experiment often remains in the background, for example, and the development of instrumentation is shown as essentially progressive and unproblematic. Instruments such as the Geiger counter or the Wilson cloud chamber are often seen as relatively straightforward windows on to nature, and tend to feature in terms of their contribution to the development of theory, when there is actually much evidence to suggest that experimental and theoretical nuclear physics have been relatively autonomous scientific disciplines.

More problematically, "nuclear physics" itself is typically regarded as a transcendent disciplinary category whose identity, integrity and significance, even in the pre-war years, are assumed to be self-evident. MLADJENOVIĆ, for example, attempts an overview of the early development of nuclear physics, without any reference to the historical specificity of the disciplinary category. He assumes that nuclear physics came into being with the identification of the nucleus in 1911, when in fact the term only came into use in the early 1930s, to signify a new disciplinary formation distinct from radioactivity and its mathematical-theoretical correlates.

In short, the historical literature on pre-war nuclear physics is largely driven by a retrospectively-defined, fission-directed canon of events, individuals and institutions, while that of war-time and post-war nuclear physics is dominated by histories of the development of the large institutions associated with Big Science. With these historiographical remarks in mind, let us now consider representative texts from each of the genres identified at the outset.

Few readers will need to be cautioned that the reminiscences of practitioners – unsurprisingly numerous in this field, given its prestige – should not be taken directly at face value, since they are highly selective accounts carefully filtered through individual institutional and disciplinary memory. Based on conferences held in 1968 and 1969, which brought long-eminent nuclear scientists and historians together to explore the history of nuclear physics, WEINER (1972) consists largely of transcripts of the exasperatingly free-wheeling discussions which ensued between the scientists, with occasional prompts from the historians. Although organised in two sections around the themes of "the emergency and growth of nuclear physics as a research field" and "the role of theory in the development of nuclear physics", both sections of the volume in fact focus largely on the development of nuclear theory in both the pre- and post-war periods, and thus present a rather limited version of the field's history.

STUEWER (1979) is a more rounded collection (the product of another conference), and consists of eight chapter-length historical memoirs by nuclear scientists, each of which is followed by a discussion involving both scientists and historians. The papers cover both theoretical and experimental aspects of nuclear physics at a number of institutions in the interwar period, and offer a nicely complementary set of perspectives on the historical development of the subject, while providing occasional illuminating insights into the sociological characteristics of the early nuclear physics community which can profitably be turned to historical account. Better structured and more rigorously documented than Weiner (1972), the volume nevertheless shares its assumption that scientists' history is relatively objective and value-free – a conceit which historians have only recently begun to question.

Despite its fairly narrow focus on the Cavendish Laboratory in the interwar period and its misleading title (it almost entirely neglects non-nuclear physics in interwar Cambridge), HENDRY's collection of reminiscences (some reprinted from elsewhere, and some specially commissioned) is likewise valuable, in that several of the essays give insights – often incidental to the author's main concerns – into day-to-day practices and social life at the Cavendish Laboratory and library. Particularly rich in detail are the chapters on the development of instrumentation (cloud chambers, electrical counting methods, and particle accelerators), while the reflections of a number of research students provide ample material for a social and cultural history of nuclear physics. The book also includes a useful chapter on the relations between nuclear physics and the electrical industry – a theme also pursued in Heilbon & Seidel. Hendry provides four brief contextual introductions and a bibliography, which form a useful starting point for further reading.

Though they vary enormously in scope, emphasis and depth of critical analysis, the many biographies of nuclear scientists now available collectively provide further useful insights into the interplay between individuals, institutions, ideas, and experiments in the history of nuclear physics. PAIS's recent biography of Niels Bohr is an archetypal scientific biography, in that the emphasis is on charting a linear sequence through the development of ideas in nuclear physics – the "canonical account" – and on identifying the contributions of the subject (Bohr) to the gradual revelation of that sequence. WILSON's is a less theory-dominated account – unsurprisingly, given that Rutherford was primarily an experimentalist – and provides a more rounded picture of the various contexts within which Rutherford worked, and of the research school that he created.

Sharing many of the characteristics of biographies are the various institutional histories. Again, it is important to remember the historiographical admonition that the "key" institutions, and hence those whose histories have been written, have been defined in retrospect largely by the scientists them-

selves. Given this caveat, WEINER (1974) is a good overview of the dynamics of the discipline in the 1930s. Although it never strays far from the canonical account of heroic individuals, and is over-reliant on reminiscence and anecdote, CROWTHER's celebratory centenary history of the Cavendish Laboratory remains the best source to date on the development of nuclear physics in Cambridge.

WEART's study nicely situates the development of nuclear physics in France within its social and political context, while HOLTON's work on the entry of Fermi and his group into nuclear physics research is one of the few accounts to cover Italian nuclear physics in some detail. AASERUD's account of nuclear physics at the Niels Bohr Institute in Copenhagen, like Heilbron & Seidel's of Berkeley, emphasises the importance of philanthropic organisations (particularly the Rockefeller Foundation) to the development of machine-based physics, on the promise of medical applications in the 1930s. SHEA's mixed bag of essays, though centred on the work of Otto Hahn and, inevitably, the discovery of nuclear fission, also offers interesting insights into the wider politics and practice of interwar nuclear physics.

HEILBRON & SEIDEL's comprehensive account of Ernest Lawrence's Berkeley Laboratory, the birthplace of the cyclotron, is in many ways an exemplary study of the interrelationships between the institutional, technical, and cognitive aspects of interwar nuclear physics. It also includes significant detail on the other individuals and institutions with which the Berkeley Laboratory engaged, and on the social and intellectual aspects of the international development of accelerator-based nuclear physics, and is among the best (and, at 600 pages, the weightiest) of recent scholarship on the subject.

Comparable in scale and scope is HERMANN et al., which provides invaluable coverage of the post-war development of nuclear physics. Focusing on the creation and operation of CERN, the European organisation for nuclear research, the volume nevertheless provides an indispensable overview both of the wider context in which nuclear physics developed in the post-war period, and of the scientific products of that development.

Other than biographies, autobiographical memoirs, and institutional histories, there are a number of histories of ideas in nuclear physics. The linear history of nuclear theory is best examined by AMALDI, which synthesises over 900 primary and secondary sources to produce a comprehensive account of the development of nuclear theory from 1932 to 1939. Though recognising the presence of instrumentation and experiment, both Amaldi and Mladjenovic see the development of theory as driving the history of the subject.

An important series of articles by Stuewer (see STUEWER 1993 and its bibliography) provides the basis for a deeper and more critical understanding of the development of interwar nuclear physics. Based on thorough archival research, as well as published materials, Stuewer's writings represent the most detailed analyses of the subject to date, and are indispensable for serious researchers. Though his works flesh out much of the detail on the historical development of the subject, Stuewer does, however, tend to follow the canonical account, in casting experiment in a relatively unproblematic, and subsidiary role to theory. This assumption is persuasively challenged by HIEBERT, who, while still offering primarily a fission-directed account, argues for the relative autonomy of pre-war experimental nuclear physics from theory. Recognising, moreover, the essentially retrospective nature of the history of the subject, Hiebert offers a useful, if brief, corrective to the canonical account implicitly accepted by so many writing on this subject.

A few accounts offer perspectives on the history of nuclear physics which do not wholly rely on (and in some cases even challenge) the canonical account. SIX's analysis of the discovery of the neutron modifies the standard interpretation (in which theoretical prediction of the particle in 1920 was eventually followed by unambiguous experimental demonstration in 1932), by emphasising the importance of instrumental traditions in different laboratories and their role in the constitution of phenomena. In a very different vein, FISCHER's scientometric study attempts to assess the importance of German émigré nuclear scientists to the development of nuclear physics, by mapping changing patterns of citation from the early 1920s through to the post-war period. Though the merits of such an approach may be open to question, it provides useful resources for a reassessment of the history of this field.

As recent anti-essentialist approaches begin to make a mark in the historiography of nuclear physics, we may expect a new, critical, non-linear and non-teleological history to emerge, which is sensitive to such issues as the reasons for the emergence of nuclear physics, the changing boundaries of the field and its relationship to particle and high-energy physics, the development of the relationship between experiment and theory, and the rich complexities of practice.

JEFF HUGHES

See also Atomic Theory; Big Science; Radioactivity

Number Theory

Chikara, Sasaki, Sugiura Mitsuo and Joseph W. Dauben (eds), *The Intersection of History and Mathematics*, Basel: Birkhäuser, 1994

Dauben, Joseph W. (ed.), *Mathematical Perspectives: Essays on Mathematics and Its Historical Development*, New York: Academic Press, 1981

Dickson, Leonard Eugene, *History of the Theory of Numbers*, 3 vols, Washington, DC: Carnegie Institute of Washington, 1919–23

Echeverria, Javier, "Observations, Problems and Conjectures in Number Theory: The History of the Prime Number Theorem", in *The Space of Mathematics, Philosophical, Epistemological and Historical Explorations*, edited by Echeverria, Andoni Iberra and Thomas Mormann, Berlin and New York: De Gruyter, 1992

Edwards, Harold M., *Fermat's Last Theorem: A Genetic Introduction to Algebraic Number Theory*, New York and Berlin: Springer, 1977

Edwards, Harold M. "Mathematical Ideas, Ideals, and Ideology", *Mathematical Intelligencer*, 14/2 (1992): 6–18

Ellison, W.J. and F. Ellison, "Théorie des nombres", in *Abrégé d'histoire des mathématiques: 1700–1900*, vol. 1, edited by J. Dieudonné, Paris: Hermann, 1978, 165–334

Goldstein, Catherine, "Le Métier des nombres aux 17e et 19e siècles", in *Éléments d'Histoire des Sciences*, edited by Michel Serres, Paris: Bordas, 1989; as *A History of Scientific Thought: Elements of a History of Science*, translated from the French, Oxford and Cambridge, Massachusetts: Blackwell, 1995

Goldstein, Catherine, *Un Théorème de Fermat et ses lecteurs*, Paris: Presses Universitaires de Vincennes, 1995

Gray, Jeremy, "The Nineteenth Century Revolution in Mathematical Ontology", in *Revolutions in Mathematics*, edited by Donald Gillies, Oxford: Clarendon Press, and New York: Oxford University Press, 1992

Kolmogorov, A.N. and A.P. Yushkevich (eds), *Mathematics of the Nineteenth Century: Mathematical Logic, Algebra, Number Theory, Probability Theory*, Basel: Birkhäuser, 1992

Pier, Jean-Paul (ed.), *Development of Mathematics 1900–1950*, Basel: Birkhäuser, 1994

Weil, André, *Number Theory: An Approach Through History from Hammurapi to Legendre*, Basel: Birkhäuser, 1984

Number theory is usually described as the field of mathematics that concerns the properties of integers, and the search for integral and rational solutions to certain problems. Although appearing at the end of the 18th century, the origins of the problems and methods have often been traced back either to Greek theoretical arithmetic or to Babylonian tablets. However, number theory has commingled with almost all branches of mathematics, in particular combinatorics, algebra, and, in more recent times, algebraic geometry, analytic functions, and group representation theory. Therefore, problems of demarcation (between number theory and the other available branches at any given period) and classification of methods or questions are particularly acute, although generally these have not been explicitly addressed in most historical narratives. This entry will concentrate on the Western modern period.

DICKSON's three volumes are a crucial bibliographical tool. They contain descriptions of every result published (or then known) from antiquity to World War I, arranged topically – the identification of these topics roughly reflecting the state of the field in the mid-19th century. Exact references are given, and the mathematical content of each paper is briefly explained (in modernized notation). The introductions to the volumes give some lines of internal development for each subject treated.

The main introduction to the history of number theory before 1800 is WEIL. After a brief chapter describing some ancient achievements in the field, the book details the lives and works of Fermat, Euler, Lagrange, and Legendre, before proceeding from detailed citation of the sources to complete mathematical analyses, in order to show the various threads leading towards current number theory. Weil covers Fermat's work on prime numbers and Diophantine equations, the introduction of analytic tools and proofs of Fermat's results by Euler, and Lagrange's classification of binary quadratic forms, among others. Appendices relate these results to more modern points of view.

A general survey of number theory after 1800, concentrating on results, is given in ELLISON & ELLISON. After a number of brief sections on the field before 1830, and a section on binary quadratic forms (one of the first topics to give rise to a unified presentation, according to modern standards), the classification follows the main trends of the subject: algebraic number theory, prime numbers, transcendental numbers, Diophantine approximations and equations, quadratic forms with several variables, additive number theory, and algebraic function fields. The central ideas, results, and works are introduced and explained, with cross references to related subjects.

Chapters 2 and 3 in KOLMOGOROV & YUSHKEVICH deal with number theory in connection with developments in algebra, and follow the evolution of results concerning some particular problems (e.g. arithmetic form theory, and the geometry of numbers). The authors also take into account work on these topics by Russian mathematicians such as Markov, Voronoi, and Bugaev.

Recent complements concerning special topics (reciprocity law, class field theory, Weil conjectures, Prime Number Theorem, etc.), or dealing with subsequent periods can be found in various chapters of CHIKARA, MITSUO & DAUBEN and PIER. There are also mathematical surveys for the works of the main number theorists (from Fermat onwards). The approach in most cases is essentially internalist, with emphasis on description and explanation of the main results. A few recent works have, however, used number theory to illustrate some general historical issues, or to raise other types of questions.

EDWARDS (1977) builds on a seminal series of articles in the *Archives for the History of the Exact Sciences*. The author mixes careful historical analysis, including hints from unpublished writings, with detailed mathematical hindsight, in order to arrive at an understanding of the (social, intellectual, and mathematical) circumstances surrounding Kummer's work on Fermat's Last Theorem, and the emergence of the notion of the mathematical ideal. Edwards, and also the essays by Merzbach and Neumann in DAUBEN, show how new archival work can provide insights into classical questions (e.g. the influence – or lack of it – of famous problems on the development of mathematics, or the role of computations in the emergence of new concepts). EDWARDS (1992) examines, for the case of ideal theory, the question of the acceptability of a definition or mathematical concept within a general intellectual framework.

GOLDSTEIN (1989) sketches the variation of social and intellectual conditions for the practice of number theory from the 17th up to the 19th century, and how these relate to the concrete work produced by mathematicians around the time of Fermat's Last Theorem. Particular emphasis is placed on the cultural nature of the form and necessity of mathematical proof.

ECHEVERRIA attempts to study the epistemological impact of experimental thinking – in particular, through the construction and examination of tables – in mathematics. He concentrates on the Prime Number Theorem (giving an asymptotic estimate of the distribution of prime numbers), proved at the end of the 19th century by analytical means, and shows how estimation formulas were proposed and derived from empirical investigations.

GRAY takes examples from the history of algebraic number theory (among others) to analyze what he calls the "ontological revolution" in 19th-century mathematics. Freedom in mathematical constructions (here the construction of ideal numbers)

is related to general Romantic conceptions of intellectual creation, and to philosophical debates on the relationship between human understanding and nature.

The focus of GOLDSTEIN (1995) is the social history of mathematics. Goldstein examines all the descriptions and analyses of a single theorem of number theory (proved in the 17th century) by contemporary mathematicians, and by historians (including mathematicians writing history) in the 19th and 20th centuries. The social and intellectual positions of these various readers are shown to have provided implicit hypotheses on the aim, nature, exercise, and history of number theory, and have shaped even the most technical of analytical details.

CATHERINE GOLDSTEIN

See also Fermat

Nursing

Abel-Smith, Brian, *A History of the Nursing Profession*, London: Heinemann, 1960
Baly, Monica E., *Florence Nightingale and the Nursing Legacy*, London: Croom Helm, 1986
Hudson Jones, Anne (ed.), *Images of Nurses: Perspectives from History, Art and Literature*, Philadelphia: University of Pennsylvania Press, 1988
Jones, Colin, *The Charitable Imperative: Hospitals and Nursing in Ancien Régime and Revolutionary France*, London and New York: Routledge, 1989
Nutting, M. Adelaide and Lavinia L. Dock, *A History of Nursing*, 4 vols, New York: Putnam, 1907–12
Petitat, André, *Les Infirmières: de la vocation à la profession*, Montreal: Boréal, 1989
Reverby, Susan M., *Ordered to Care: The Dilemma of American Nursing, 1850–1945*, Cambridge and New York: Cambridge University Press, 1987
Summers, Anne, *Angels and Citizens: British Women as Military Nurses, 1854–1914*, London and New York: Routledge, 1988

The historiography of nursing, perhaps more than that of any other branch of medicine, has until recent years been inextricably wedded to a narrative of progress, from ignorance, superstition and religious dogma to scientific and secular knowledge and practice. Both general histories of nursing, and biographies of Florence Nightingale (whose sanitary and educational reforms made a substantial impact in the three decades following the Crimean War of 1854–56), tended to distance 19th-century developments in hospital nursing from their origins in, on the one hand, domestic nursing by women of the working classes, and, on the other, nursing as an unremunerated vocation exercised by religious orders. Much of the literature reflects – and has only latterly begun to explore – the tensions inherent in perceptions of nursing as, by turns, an other-worldly vocation, an expression of the female instinct for caring, an unskilled occupation, and an educated profession. In many cases this has led to caricature and vilification of the working woman (Dickens's fictional character, Sarah Gamp, being seized on for propaganda purposes in the campaign to achieve national registration for nurses), and to a facile equation between religious organisations and a superstitious and fatalistic approach to death and disease.

Of all the progressive interpretations of history published by the nursing campaigners, the account given by NUTTING & DOCK is the most open-minded on the religious antecedents of the profession, and hence the most valuable. This two-volume work gives credit to the ideals that animated the medieval and later nursing orders, showing the clinical standards, high for their time, that their regulations imposed on them, and including a wealth of detail on developments in different countries – much of it fragmentary, which merits, and still awaits, further scholarly exploration.

JONES has produced a major contribution to the history of the nursing orders in France, and of the Filles de la Charité of St Vincent de Paul in particular, from the early 17th century to the 1860s. He is thus able to show that nursing as a religious vocation flourished in France, even in the teeth of the most aggressive trends towards modernisation and secularisation, and that nursing orders continued to take responsibility for the administration of hospitals, the management of pharmacies, the care of the insane, and for minor surgical procedures.

PETITAT derives similar insights from research on 20th-century Canada. In a study of changing concepts of vocation and profession in training schools and professional associations, he shows a "new tradition" of secular nursing emerging alongside, rather than evolving out of, the organisation of nursing by Catholic religious orders.

For the most part, the literature is still dominated by writers on and from the English-speaking world, which pioneered the modern secular profession of nursing. A ground-breaking study by ABEL-SMITH challenged the simplistic views of the reformers by treating nursing history as an aspect of British social and labour history, placing it within the context of class relations in 19th- and 20th-century British society and the development of its welfare services. His example was not immediately followed, but in the 1970s the explosion of interest in "history from below", oral and local history and women's history, produced a spate of independent and academic research on nursing which transformed the field. Among many notable publications, BALY must be singled out as the only monograph on Nightingale to focus on her work rather than on her personality. Based on an extensive reading in primary sources, hers is an impartial (and unflattering) account of the Nightingale Training School, which shows that nearly 15 years elapsed after the end of the Crimean War before it began to produce a reliable cohort of trained women. Baly also identifies the School's dubious legacies, in the form of the exploitation of trainee labour and excessive emphasis on the domestic service aspects of ward work. A complementary account in SUMMERS stresses the continuing importance of male nursing in the British Army between 1856 and 1914, and discusses the limited "feminization" of military nursing, within the context of women's intervention in other areas of public life during this period.

Of the many North American contributions to this "revisionist" historiography, the monograph by REVERBY covers the greatest amount of ground, exploring nursing as a branch of labour exposed to all the industrial and managerial fads and fashions of the wider world, while staying rather too closely to the professionalising narratives of the reformers, and

dismissing the skills of the "pre-reform" nurses a little summarily. The interesting topic of nursing iconography and its cultural resonances in the West is dealt with in a collection edited by HUDSON JONES, in which the modern architecture of hospitals, and representations of nursing from antiquity to the present day in literature, painting and sculpture, film and photograph, are analysed in chapters that are intellectually sophisticated without being disfigured by jargon.

It should be borne in mind that aspects of nursing history are inextricable from other social and medical developments, and must be studied through the histories of hospitals and kindred institutions, of midwifery and other specialisms, of plagues and epidemics, and of religious and charitable organisations. Among the last of these, the Red Cross, which has trained so many male and female nurses and paramedics for civilian and military emergencies, and in some societies sponsored the only non-denominational forms of medical provision, is of outstanding importance. Nursing history is a multi-faceted subject area in which many more noteworthy monographs may be anticipated. Important articles frequently appear in general historical journals as well as periodicals devoted to medical history, and professional nurses in many countries have formed historical societies that now publish research journals and bulletins of their own.

ANNE SUMMERS

See also Hospitals

Nutrition

Apple, Rima D., *Mothers and Medicine: A Social History of Infant Feeding, 1890–1950*, Madison: University of Wisconsin Press, 1987

Apple, Rima D., *Vitamania: Vitamins in American Culture*, New Brunswick, New Jersey: Rutgers University Press, 1996

Aronson, Naomi, "Fuel for the Human Machine: The Industrialization of Eating in America", PhD dissertation, Brandeis University, 1979

Carpenter, Kenneth J., *Protein and Energy: A Study in Changing Ideas in Nutrition*, Cambridge and New York: Cambridge University Press, 1994

Drummond, J.C. and Anne Wilbraham, *The Englishman's Food: A History of Five Centuries of English Diet*, London: Jonathan Cape, 1939; revised by Dorothy Hollingsworth, 1957

Goodman, David and Michael Redclift, *Refashioning Nature: Food, Ecology, and Nature*, London and New York: Routledge, 1991

Guggenheim, K.Y., *Basic Issues of the History of Nutrition*, Jerusalem: Akademia University Press, 1990; revised edition, Jerusalem: Magnes Press/The Hebrew University, 1995

Heischkel-Artelt, Edith (ed.), *Ernährung und Ernährungslehre im 19. Jahrhundert*, Göttingen: Vandenhoeck und Ruprecht, 1976

Kamminga, Harmke and Andrew Cunningham (eds), *The Science and Culture of Nutrition, 1840–1940*, Amsterdam: Rodopi, 1995

Komlos, John, *Nutrition and Economic Development in the Eighteenth-Century Habsburg Monarchy: An Anthropometric History*, Princeton, New Jersey: Princeton University Press, 1988

Levenstein, Harvey A., *Revolution at the Table: The Transformation of the American Diet*, New York: Oxford University Press, 1988

Liebig, Justus, *Animal Chemistry, or, Organic Chemistry in Its Applications to Physiology and Pathology*, London: Taylor and Walton, and New York: Appleton, 1842; reissued with an introduction by Frederic L. Holmes, New York: Johnson Reprint, 1964

Lusk, Graham, *Nutrition*, New York: Hoeber, 1933

McCay, Clive, *Notes on the History of Nutrition Research*, Bern: Hüber, 1973

McCollum, Elmer Verner, *A History of Nutrition: The Sequence of Ideas in Nutrition Investigations*, Boston: Houghton Mifflin, 1957

Mendel, Lafayette B., *Nutrition: The Chemistry of Life*, Hew Haven, Connecticut: Yale University Press, 1923

Smith, Edward, *Foods*, New York: Appleton, and London: H.S. King, 1873

Despite the significance of nutrition in both past and contemporary cultures, the topic has received relatively little attention from historians of science. While several practitioners' histories have described the progress of nutrition as a laboratory science, nutritional issues can often be encountered in social and cultural histories that are tangential to the history of science.

LIEBIG, with Holmes's thorough introduction to the 1964 edition, provides a starting point for the study of the history of nutrition. Liebig's text was bold in explaining the perceived shortcomings of his predecessors in the field, and in staking out his influential chemistry (and laboratory) based approach to nutrition and physiology. Holmes traces the history of these disputes, including Liebig's rivalries with the contemporary scientists G.J. Mulder, J.B. Boussingault, and J.B.A. Dumas. SMITH, a 19th-century text written for a popular audience, summarizes some of the early history of nutritional ideas and their implications for social reform.

McCOLLUM is probably the best-known and most complete practitioner's history of the science of nutrition. Tracing nutrition science from the early 19th century, McCollum emphasizes developments in laboratory science, beginning with the "older" understanding of nutrition – a body of assumptions that defined nutrition in terms of proteins, carbohydrates, fats, and minerals. McCollum places special emphasis on the paradigm shift to "newer knowledge" of nutrition that emerged in the early 20th century, when researchers – including McCollum himself – isolated and identified the amino acids and vitamins that also play crucial roles in human nutrition. DRUMMOND & WILBRAHAM (particularly in the edition revised by Hollingsworth) place a similar emphasis on the emergence of the nutrition sciences in the late 19th and early 20th centuries. Their work is broader than McCollum's, however, and also surveys the history of British daily food habits, gastronomy, and food production since the medieval period. Other authoritative practitioners' histories include MENDEL, which emphasizes the amino acid research of the early 20th century, and

LUSK, which emphasizes energy metabolism and dietetics studies. McCAY, who was a colleague of Mendel and Lusk, is a collection of posthumously published lecture notes on the history of nutrition and proteins. GUGGENHEIM, another practitioner/historian, has produced a collection of nine brief essays that are especially useful in their treatment of Galen, van Helmont, Boerhaave, and other names in the early history of ideas on nutrition.

CARPENTER's history of protein deficiency diseases is an example of recent studies on the medical and scientific aspects of nutrition history. Like McCollum, Carpenter's internalist approach reveals expertise as a nutrition scientist, but, unlike McCollum, Carpenter demonstrates how nutrition scientists' past models were often inadequate rather than heroic. Carpenter's works are also significant since they devote attention to developments in the past 50 years – an area of shaky ground for many historians of science. Carpenter also calls attention to a fundamental distinction between pre-World War II science, which was tied largely to individualistic research agendas, and post-war science, which has been more group- and grant-oriented. As a result, scientific truth and facts are now harder to locate and trace to individual scientists.

LEVENSTEIN demonstrates how the emergence of nutrition scientists, the industrialization of food production, and changes in consumer culture shaped American food habits between the years 1880 and 1930. This was a period when nutritionists held important positions in public and contributed to scientific discussions on urban poverty and social change, with much debate between "old" and "new" nutritionists. Levenstein reveals that scientists' motivations often went beyond the search for scientific truth. Wilbur Olin Atwater, for instance, hoped to find a more efficient diet for the working classes, while others linked food with national and racial health. Nutritionists' answers were not always heard, however, for business and industrial interests simultaneously pushed Americans to consume mass-produced, but less nutritious, foods.

ARONSON's dissertation, and the published articles that it produced, are important for their market-oriented analyses of nutrition science. Aronson forcefully describes the social context of nutrition science, connecting it with the rise of industrial capitalism. In contrast to the practitioners' histories, Aronson suggests that the scientists' real objective was not "newer knowledge"; instead, she locates early nutrition experts within a context of Taylorism, industrialization, and pressure to obtain the greatest labor efficiency of the working classes. Her work also addresses the important issue of "resistance to discovery", showing how cultural and institutional considerations delayed the discovery of vitamins.

The work by GOODMAN & REDCLIFT brings a parallel analysis into food and nutrition policies of recent times by focusing on the modern "agri-food system" that operates today. Western demand for export commodities from the developing world, and pressure from farmer-constituents at home, have affected the flow of nutrients around the world. The developing world – once self-sufficient in food – now relies on imported animal and vegetable proteins to keep workers employed and fed.

APPLE (1987) examines the history of artificial milk, showing how infant nutrition is at the intersection of a dialogue between the medical community, the business community, and mothers. Scientists and industrialists recognized that women comprised the primary market for their pronouncements about scientific feeding, and placed pressure on women to accept their teachings. In response, many women joined the debate, encouraged by the fact that the study of nutrition has been among the most open fields for female scientists. Apple concludes that women have played important roles, both as the subjects and as the objects of nutrition science.

APPLE (1996) describes the emergence of the vitamin supplement industry in the United States. As in her earlier work, Apple demonstrates that historically nutrition has been a battle between conflicting testimonies from the scientific community. Though middle-class American consumers face little risk of suffering a vitamin deficiency disease, the "ambiguous authority of science" has proven so persuasive that millions purchase and ingest vitamins and nutritional supplements none the less.

The recent emergence of anthropometric studies of history represents another trend in the history of nutrition, and works by KOMLOS are among the most respected in this genre. Komlos and other anthropometricians begin with an assumption that records of human height and weight are valid indices of the food habits and nutritive status of past societies. Anthropometricians have been able to show connections among demographic changes, fluctuations in the history of human height, the history of industrial development, commercialization of the economy, standards of living, and the development of government programs that responded to perceived crises in public nutrition.

The essays edited by KAMMINGA & CUNNINGHAM are representative of new directions in the history of nutrition. In their introductory essay, Kamminga & Cunningham assert that, "western society has become a nutrition culture", nutrition science affects medical practice, government policy, and popular culture in countless ways that are often overlooked. The contributed essays demonstrate that reciprocal interactions among western governments, public health officials, entrepreneurs, and citizens have shaped the nutritional discourse. HEISCHKEL-ARTELT's collection of essays offers a similar approach to issues in the history of nutrition in Germany, where cookbook authors, military planners, agricultural scientists, and practitioners of alternative medical therapies shaped the discourse of nutrition science decades before Britain and America.

As these recent works suggest, it seems likely that the history of nutrition will continue to attract attention from those interested in social history, women's history, cultural history, demography, and other branches of historical inquiry. While several histories focusing on nutrition scientists, their laboratories, and the relevant medical sub-disciplines have been written, vast opportunities remain for studies that locate nutrition at the intersections of social, cultural, economic, and scientific history.

MARK R. FINLAY

See also Agriculture; Liebig; Public Health

O

Objectivity

Daston, Lorraine and Peter Galison, "The Image of Objectivity", *Representations*, 40 (1992): 81–128

Gillispie, Charles Coulston, *The Edge of Objectivity: An Essay in the History of Scientific Ideas*, Princeton, New Jersey: Princeton University Press, 1960

Megill, Allen (ed.), *Rethinking Objectivity*, Durham, North Carolina: Duke University Press, 1994

Porter, Theodore M., *Trust in Numbers: The Pursuit of Objectivity in Science and Public Life*, Princeton, New Jersey: Princeton University Press, 1995

Proctor, Robert N., *Value-Free Science? Purity and Power in Modern Knowledge*, Cambridge, Massachusetts: Harvard University Press, 1991

Toulmin, Stephen, *Cosmopolis: The Hidden Agenda of Modernity*, New York: Free Press, 1990

Wise, M. Norton (ed.), *The Values of Precision*, Princeton, New Jersey: Princeton University Press, 1995

Although "objectivity" is a slippery term, most of the senses relevant to the history of science can be grouped into two related clusters: "absolute" and "mechanical" objectivity. In the scientific context, absolute objectivity is the ideal of perfect knowledge – knowledge that is true, regardless of perspective; therefore, absolute objectivity requires Thomas Nagel's "view from nowhere", or distanced, passionless researchers. Mechanical objectivity, on the other hand, is the ideal of perfect procedures for the performance of tasks; in this sense, the ideally objective scientific researcher would be machine-like in his or her adherence to the rules.

While GILLISPIE is a broad history of science, covering ideas and achievements from Galileo to Maxwell, it takes as its theme the gradual conquest, by austerity and distance, of ever-more topics in natural science. Gillispie defines the progress of science as the invention and utilization of tools, metrics and frameworks that eliminate subjectivity. There is a sense in which all histories of the progress of scientific knowledge are histories of objectivity, but this book is explicit in its recognition of this, and unusual in its dramatic, yet subtle, ambivalence about absolute objectivity – defining objectivity as a positive virtue that derives in part from the elimination of passion and intimacy with nature.

TOULMIN's main aim is to revive the humanist modernity he finds in the 16th century, but he simultaneously relates a speculative narrative on the rise of absolute objectivity as an ideal. Central to Toulmin's thesis is his contrast between Montaigne and Descartes: whereas Montaigne was comfortable with elements of subjectivism in knowledge, Descartes demanded austerity and distance on the part of the knower, or the creation of a stance that did not depend on the individual subject. Toulmin takes as a significant symbolic event the assassination of Henry of Navarre – possibly important for the young Descartes – after which there remained little possibility in Europe for political moderation. The drive for certainty or objectivity exemplified in Descartes's writings can then be seen as an attempt to disconnect philosophy and science from the political and economic uncertainties of the Thirty Years, War.

The ideal of absolute objectivity in science has a number of components, one of which is the ideal of value-freedom. PROCTOR shows that this concept has itself not been stable across contexts, having stood for a separation of theory and practice, the exclusion of ethical concerns from science, and the disenchantment of nature. The largest section of Proctor examines the 19th- and 20th-century, primarily German, contexts for the rise of value-freedom as an ideal in the social sciences. Proctor argues that, for German academics, the discourse of value-neutrality served to insulate and protect science from external controversies – parallel to the well-known insulation of the Royal Society from religious and political controversies – but it was articulated in opposition to, and used to combat, particular social movements. Thus, Proctor argues that value-neutrality needs to be understood in terms of political context.

MEGILL includes articles on both absolute and mechanical objectivity (and on other senses that do not fit neatly into this dichotomy). For example, a chapter by Mary Hawkesworth explores feminist arguments that link stances of absolute objectivity with the objectification of women. Although Hawkesworth regards the links between attempts at a distanced knowledge and objectification as weak, she finds much value in feminist criticisms of putatively objective knowledge, since those criticisms point out the failures of various strategies for obtaining objectivity. Thus, for example, intersubjective agreement cannot be a guarantor of objectivity, because it tends to reproduce social values. To move toward objectivity, we have to increase awareness of cognition as a human project with multiple influences.

Also in Megill are chapters by two of the prominent historians of science studying mechanical objectivity: Lorraine Daston on the "prehistory" of objectivity, and Theodore Porter on standardization. Daston argues that some European intellectual circles of the 17th century attempted to curtail divisive argument over theoretical speculations by creating a new emphasis on, and interest in, "Baconian" facts, particularly experimental facts. Although the concept of (mechanical) scientific objectivity as such is a later invention, community agreements around Baconian facts provided a surrogate for objectivity, since these facts were not open to question in the same way as theories. The term "objectivity" did not take on its current meanings and status until the 19th century, when expanding communities of researchers desired to eliminate idiosyncrasy. DASTON & GALISON picks up one part of this story in a study of representational techniques in scientific atlases, particularly of the human body. Daston & Galison argue that the search for objective representation was a moral, and not just a technical, issue, and was connected to a new image of the scientist as a paradigm of self-restraint. Thus, the choice of specimens for these atlases became a point of crisis, because it was necessarily a human choice. There were discussions over the merits of different types of specimens, and the range of specimens that should be presented. Interest in eliminating choice also led to increasing use of tools for mechanical representation, such as photography, which could be trusted for their impartiality, if not their accuracy.

PORTER is a wide-ranging and fascinating study of conflicts between informal expertise and mechanical objectivity: objectivity as a form of regulation that limits the discretion of knowledgeable experts. Whereas much of the recent study of science and technology has pointed to the indispensability of expertise and informal communities, Porter is interested in the development of rules and formal procedures that can be widely applied. For the most part, Porter focuses on public science, mathematics, and engineering; his chapter-length studies are of 19th-century British actuaries, the French Corps des Ponts et Chaussées, and the American Corps of Engineers in the 20th century. Particularly in the public arena, objectivity, in the form of ever more precise rules and procedures, is a response to weakness and distrust. Together the American Corps of Engineers and US bureaucracy developed uniform cost-benefit analysis procedures in order to limit pork-barrelling and possible disagreement, even though uniformity necessarily introduces its own forms of arbitrariness. In contrast, the French Corps des Ponts enjoyed more freedom, and could calculate costs and benefits in an atmosphere of relative trust, by claiming that they were acting in the interests of the general public.

The reduction and containment of subjectivity through mechanical objectivity is the result of many different processes. As a result, parts of the history of objectivity can be found in the mass production of instruments, the use of textbooks, and the standardization of measurement techniques and units. For example, WISE is a collection of papers by the participants of a Princeton University workshop on the interest in, and development of, precision measurements. The papers range from a collection of social statistics in 18th-century France, to late 19th-century measurements of energy in Britain. As Wise's commentary points out, almost all of the papers discuss both the social production of precision – the negotiation of what is to count as precise measurement, and the mobilization of resources in order to create precise measurements – and the unity that standardized precision measurements produce, in being used to end theoretical conflicts and shape new areas of research. Precision, like objectivity more generally, is a value that has particular social meanings and serves particular purposes.

SERGIO SISMONDO

See also Fact; Standardization

Observation

Brown, Harold I., *Observation and Objectivity*, New York and Oxford: Oxford University Press, 1987

Carnap, Rudolf, *Philosophical Foundations of Physics: An Introduction to the Philosophy of Science*, edited by Martin Gardner, New York: Basic Books, 1966

Churchland, Paul M., *Scientific Realism and the Plasticity of Mind*, Cambridge and New York: Cambridge University Press, 1979

Dretske, Fred, *Seeing and Knowing*, Chicago: University of Chicago Press, and London: Routledge and Kegan Paul, 1969

Fodor, Jerry, "Observation Reconsidered", *Philosophy of Science* (1983): 23–43

Hacking, Ian, *Representing and Intervening: Introductory Topics in the Philosophy of Natural Science*, Cambridge and New York: Cambridge University Press, 1983

Hanson, Norwood Russell, *Patterns of Discovery: An Enquiry into the Conceptual Foundations of Science*, Cambridge: Cambridge University Press, 1958

Kosso, Peter, *Reading the Book of Nature: An Introduction to the Philosophy of Science*, Cambridge and New York: Cambridge University Press, 1992

Maxwell, Grover, "The Ontological Status of Theoretical Entities", in *Scientific Explanation, Space, and Time, Minneapolis*, edited by Herbert Feigl and Maxwell, Minneapolis: University of Minnesota Press, 1962

Shapere, Dudley, "The Concept of Observation in Science and Philosophy", *Philosophy of Science* (1982): 28–59

Van Fraassen, Bas C., *The Scientific Image*, Oxford: Clarendon Press, and New York: Oxford University Press, 1980

Observation is of central importance to scientific work, because it is through observation that scientific theories are confirmed and refuted. As a result, in many discussions of the subject, an attempt is made to explain the reason why observation has the authority to adjudicate between competing scientific claims. Typically, these discussions concentrate on the case of visual observation.

CARNAP discusses the prevalent theory/observation dichotomy. According to this dichotomy, observation terms refer to the directly observable properties of objects, whereas theoretical terms refer to properties that are not directly observable. Here, the expression "directly observable" means "observable without recourse to intermediaries, such as an experimental apparatus or an inferential presupposition". So construed, the ability of observation terms to refer to directly observable properties seems to offer a straightforward explanation of why observation reports are valuable in testing scientific theories; in short, it is fairly easy to ascertain their truthfulness, since one need not perform any inferential steps or manipulate any physical intermediaries.

MAXWELL rebutted the tenability of Carnap's theory/observation dichotomy, by noting that many theoretical properties are, in fact, directly observable. For instance, the property "is a molecule" is presumably a theoretical property; however, there are circumstances in which this property can be directly observed, such as when we are dealing with an observable crystal that is known to be a single (very large) molecule. Similarly, some traditionally observable properties are, in some cases, unobservable – for instance, the distance between two atoms.

Subsequently, VAN FRAASSEN has attempted to resuscitate the observation/theory dichotomy by responding to Maxwell's criticism in the following way: by observable, we do not mean observable *tout court*, but observable for us, given our human limitations. After reinstating along these lines the observation/theory distinction, van Fraassen reaffirms the epistemic value of observations in providing us with information about the world, and relegates the non-observational, or theoretical, to what has only a pragmatic or instrumental value.

Generally in the literature, the presence of a strict theory/observation dichotomy has been discounted on the grounds that all observations are theory-laden. The most forceful defense of this argument can be found in HANSON, who borrows liberally from work in Gestalt psychology to prove his case. The theory-laden nature of observation, however, poses a problem, if one believes that experimental research is capable of guiding us toward more truthful theories about the world. The problem, simply, is that the informative value of an observation depends on the theoretical assumptions of the observer; change these assumptions, and what an observation tells us changes as well. In addition, the question arises, what gives observation the authority to decide between competing scientific theories, if its informative value is itself a product of an observer's theoretical perspective?

Various answers have been tendered to resolve this difficulty. SHAPERE argues that theory-ladenness would pose a problem for the objectivity of observations only if the theories behind the observations were themselves dubious – which is, of course, not necessarily the case. CHURCHLAND proposes that, because of the theory-laden nature of observation, it is possible to retool observations with new and better theories, thus allowing observers to see things more accurately than before (assuming, of course, that these theories are themselves more accurate). Indeed, he provocatively suggests that observers, if properly trained, could learn to observe directly the theoretical properties of physical objects. For instance, people could learn to see electromagnetic radiation of a certain wavelength, instead of seeing what we now call "colour". However, FODOR argues, on the basis of a "modularity" theory of mind, that the psychological processes underlying observation are not as plastic as Churchland believes. For Fodor, the "modules" underlying observation are constrained in such a way that the

theory informing observation is always the same – such a theory, he says, is "cognitively impenetrable" – and, moreover, he believes that this impenetrability (this "fixedness" in the nature of the theory-ladenness of observation) is the source of the objectivity of observations.

KOSSO maintains that observational objectivity can be assured by simply ensuring that, in a situation in which a theory is being subjected to experimental test, the theory behind our observations is not the same as the theory which is under test. However, BROWN has denied the need for such a requirement, claiming that observations can still be highly informative, even when the theory under test and the observation-theory are the same. This is because observations, in spite of their theory-ladenness, are the product of an physical interaction between an observer and the world; and this interaction can have unexpected results, no matter what an observer believes.

Another strategy, suggested by HACKING, which might be used to circumvent the relativistic implications wrought by theory-ladenness, is to test a theory using a variety of experimental strategies, each strategy involving different theoretical assumptions. If the same result should be found in each case, Hacking claims that this coincidence would be too remarkable to be the result of pure chance – the observations must be tracking some real feature in the world, despite their theoretical governance.

There is another tradition in recent work on observation that maintains that it is still possible to discuss observation as not theory-laden. For instance, DRETSKE argues for the presence of "non-epistemic seeing" – i.e. seeing that is devoid of conceptual content. According to Dretske, one can non-epistemically see a physical object if, independently of one's beliefs, one is able visually to differentiate this object from its immediate surroundings. Hacking proposes a similar theory (though without making any allusion to the work of Dretske) which he calls "entity realism", according to which it is possible for scientific researchers to observe physical processes without having any knowledge at all of what they are examining. Proof of entity realism can be found in any scientific laboratory; one can find technicians with practically no theoretical knowledge of what they are doing, but who can, nevertheless, make extremely accurate and informative observations. The reality of what is being observed in such a case is demonstrated by the ability of experimenters to interfere with the observed objects in predictable ways.

ROBERT G. HUDSON

See also Experiments; Objectivity; Paradigm

Obstetrics and Midwifery

Donnison, Jean, *Midwives and Medical Men: A History of Inter-Professional Rivalries and Women's Rights*, London: Heinemann, and New York: Schocken Books, 1977; 2nd edition, as *Midwives and Medical Men: A History of the Struggle for the Control of Childbirth*, New Barnet, Hertfordshire: Historical Publications, 1988

Drife, James, entry on "Obstetrics and Gynaecology", in *The Oxford Medical Companion*, edited by John Walton, Jeremiah A. Barondess and Stephen Lock, Oxford: Oxford University Press, 1994

Ehrenreich, Barbara and Deirdre English, *Witches, Midwives and Nurses: A History of Women Healers*, Old Westbury, New York: Feminist Press, 1973; London: Writers and Readers Publishing Cooperative, 1976

Gélis, Jacques, *History of Childbirth: Fertility, Pregnancy and Birth in Early Modern Europe*, translated from the French by Rosemary Morris, Cambridge: Polity Press, and Boston: Northeastern University Press, 1991 (original edition, 1984)

Graham, Harvey, *Eternal Eve*, London: Heinemann, 1950; 2nd edition, 1960

Leavitt, Judith Walzer, *Brought to Bed: Childbearing in America, 1750–1950*, New York: Oxford University Press, 1986

Loudon, I., *Death in Childbirth: An International Study of Maternal Care and Maternal Mortality, 1800–1950*, Oxford: Clarendon Press, and New York: Oxford University Press, 1992

Moscucci, Ornella, *The Science of Woman: Gynaecology and Gender in England, 1800–1929*, Cambridge and New York: Cambridge University Press, 1990

Munro Kerr, J.M., R.W. Johnstone and Miles H. Philips (eds), *Historical Review of British Obstetrics and Gynaecology, 1800–1950*, Edinburgh: Livingstone, 1954

Oakley, Ann, *The Captured Womb: A History of the Medical Care of Pregnant Women*, Oxford and New York: Blackwell, 1984

Shorter, Edward, *A History of Women's Bodies*, New York: Basic Books, 1982

The words "midwifery" and "obstetrics" are to some extent interchangeable, although where "midwifery" suggests to many people normal birth and the gentler art practised by midwives, the word "obstetrics" frequently suggests "progress", "interference", "male dominance", and surgery. Obstetrics is the branch of medicine concerned with pregnancy and childbirth. While men were excluded from taking part in it until the 16th century, from this period their influence increased, until by the 19th century it was completely in their control. Alongside this development, the treatment of childbirth became increasingly "scientific" and interventionist, although only in the last 60 years has it become safer for the mother. The Royal College of Obstetricians and Gynaecologists was founded in 1929 with maternal mortality in view. Maternal mortality has always been an important indicator of the state of obstetrical practice and of the maternity services. Only since the advent of the National Health Service in Britain (1948), has it gradually become the custom for most births to take place in hospital under the guidance, at least theoretically, of a consultant obstetrician.

For some years obstetrics has been the subject of acrimonious controversy. One side regards obstetrics as a progressive science, in which learned and increasingly "scientific" (male) obstetricians took over from ignorant (female) midwives, and have made childbirth increasingly safe, with the advent of new knowledge and "discoveries". This view is hospital-based and its advocates frequently include highly-trained doctors, who are likely to regard midwives as the handmaidens of obstetricians, and to believe that no pregnancy or birth can be regarded as normal until it is over.

For a quick and uncritical summary of this point of view, see DRIFE (a professor of obstetrics) in *The Oxford Medical Companion*. Drife does not mention either the controversy surrounding obstetrics, or the fact that pregnancy and childbirth are usually normal events, but instead summarizes the dangers to women (childbirth was one of the commonest causes of female death), and the enormous decrease in maternal mortality that has occurred during the 20th century. He covers antenatal care and the conquest of the dangerous complications of eclampsia and puerperal fever, and describes the development of obstetric techniques such as forceps, caesarean section, ultrasound, and foetal monitoring. However, Drife fails to mention any "non establishment" views; for example, that too many caesarean operations are done, or that many people, including some obstetricians, regard foetal monitoring as an unnecessary encumbrance that ties the mother to her bed and so increases the doctor's power. Drife then describes the development of pain relief and the way in which, once childbirth had become safer for the mother, interest in the baby increased, with the study of perinatal mortality (stillbirths and neonatal deaths) and development of new methods for ensuring that the baby is well grown, and for maintaining its oxygen supply during labour. He points out that perinatal mortality (deaths per 1,000 live births) was down from 70 in 1935 to 8 in 1990.

For a more detailed, older and equally uncritical account see GRAHAM Written under a pseudonym by Harvey Flack, a distinguished medical journalist who edited *Family Doctor*, the British Medical Association's lively journal for the lay public, this book is a delight to read, full of fascinating nuggets, although not very well referenced. The second edition (1960) is even less well-annotated because references and index were, regrettably, omitted. MUNRO KERR, JOHNSTONE & PHILIPS is a more solemn work from this side of the controversy, containing contributions from most of the establishment figures of mid 20th-century obstetrics, including one woman, Dame Anne Louise McIlroy, who was the first female professor of obstetrics and gynaecology in Britain.

The other side of the controversy presents obstetricians as power-seeking doctors, who usurp the normal functions of pregnancy and childbirth and treat them as diseases, thereby making them abnormal. People of this persuasion are largely feminists who believe that pregnancy and birth are normal processes that should be supervized by midwives, and require obstetric help only when something goes seriously wrong. For a quick, passionate introduction to this view see the pamphlet by EHRENREICH & ENGLISH, and for more detailed, closely argued, accounts, see OAKLEY and works by Edward Shorter. LEAVITT gives a useful feminist account of the history of obstetrics in America, beginning with early Europe.

For a more detailed, all-round assessment of the various problems, see DONNISON's scholarly book, which is essential reading for anyone wishing to understand the various side of the controversy, and also MOSCUCCI. LOUDON's lengthy work on maternal mortality is a great achievement, closely argued and packed with interesting facts about the history of many aspects of childbirth in general. Those who wish to wander further afield (at least to France), and gather unusual stories and information, will enjoy GÉLIS, while SHORTER also contains much information concerning other European countries.

ANN DALLY

See also Gynaecology

Occult Sciences

Clulee, Nicholas H., *John Dee's Natural Philosophy: Between Science and Religion*, London and New York: Routledge, 1988

Debus, Allen G., *Man and Nature in the Renaissance*, Cambridge and New York: Cambridge University Press, 1978

Eamon, William, *Science and the Secrets of Nature: Books of Secrets in Medieval and Early Modern Culture*, Princeton, New Jersey: Princeton University Press, 1994

Evans, R.J.W., *Rudolf II and His World: A Study in Intellectual History, 1576–1612*, Oxford: Clarendon Press, 1973

Luck, Georg (ed.), *Arcana Mundi: Magic and the Occult in the Greek and Roman Worlds: A Collection of Ancient Texts*, Baltimore: Johns Hopkins University Press, 1985

Merchant, Carolyn, *The Death of Nature: Women, Ecology and the Scientific Revolution*, New York: Harper and Row, 1980

Rossi, Paolo, *Francis Bacon: From Magic to Science*, translated from the Italian by Sacha Rabinovitch, London: Routledge and Kegan Paul, and Chicago: University of Chicago Press, 1968 (original edition, 1957)

Shumaker, Wayne, *The Occult Sciences in the Renaissance: A Study in Intellectual Patterns*, Berkeley: University of California Press, 1972

Thomas, Keith, *Religion and the Decline of Magic: Studies in Popular Belief in Sixteenth- and Seventeenth-Century England*, London: Weidenfeld and Nicolson, 1971

Thorndike, Lynn, *A History of Magic and Experimental Science*, 8 vols, New York: Macmillan (vols 1–2) and Columbia University Press (vols 3–8), 1923–58

Vickers, Brian (ed.), *Occult and Scientific Mentalities in the Renaissance*, Cambridge and New York: Cambridge University Press, 1984

Webster, Charles, *From Paracelsus to Newton: Magic and the Making of Modern Science*, Cambridge and New York: Cambridge University Press, 1982

Historically, the occult sciences were those that provided, or claimed to provide, knowledge of secret or hidden things. This designation should be considered in comparison with a science such as theology, the so-called queen of the sciences in the pre-modern period, which was supposedly based on revealed, rather than hidden, information. Similarly, a science such as astronomy provided knowledge of the motions of the stars, objects visible to everyone. The occult sciences, however, sought to reveal and understand natural operations and natural phenomena that could not be directly observed, but only known through their effects. Astrology, one of the most prominent and public of the occult sciences, for example, differed from astronomy because its subject matter was not the directly observable motions of the stars, but the unobservable influences that the stars had over events on earth.

It should be noted that it is anachronistic to equate the occult sciences with the pseudo-sciences, for the former were not regarded as bogus. Certainly, it was widely recognised that the occult sciences were much more capable of being exploited by charlatans and frauds than those sciences that dealt with a more open and more easily confirmed subject matter. But this was seen as an inevitable result of their (and human) nature, and was not regarded as an indication that the future could not be foretold, or that magnets could not attract iron, or that demons were not available to be summoned. The anachronistic assumption that the occult sciences were pseudo-sciences is perhaps responsible for the failure of a number of modern historians to acknowledge their positive and rational role in the development of early modern science. But in the pre-modern period there was nothing irrational about the science of alchemy, given that it was based on the matter theory of Aristotelianism. Similarly, there was nothing irrational about the belief in demons, at a time when the greatest minds of the age wholeheartedly accepted and promoted the teachings of the Christian Church.

The literature on the occult sciences is much more extensive than indicated here, as the selection has been restricted to books that deal with the tradition in a general way. Astrology and alchemy, two of the most historically important of the occult sciences, receive separate consideration. This selection has been further restricted by considering only those books which, at least arguably, show the historical relevance of the occult sciences to an understanding of the development of modern science.

LUCK is useful for showing the richness and extent of magical traditions in the ancient world. Given the influence of ancient Greek and Roman thought on medieval Europe, Luck's survey of ancient beliefs in magic, miracles, demonology, divination, astrology, and alchemy should be considered as providing additional perspectives on the nature of that influence. The bulk of the book is given over to translations of primary magical texts, but each section is prefaced by a detailed and judicious account of the magical tradition in question.

To pursue the next stage in the development of the magical tradition and its influence upon the development of Western science, it is hardly necessary to go beyond THORNDIKE. This monument to scholarship is devoted to the proposition that "magic and experimental science have been connected in their development; that magicians were perhaps the first to experiment; and that the history of both magic and experimental science can be better understood by studying them together". The gradual development of what we today call "science", Thorndike claims, on the basis of more than three decades of research, owes much to "that view of the world and mode of dealing with it, that theory and practice, which may be summed up by the word magic". Covering the period from the Roman Empire to the 17th century, the scope is as comprehensive as possible.

For a more succinct account of the links between magic and science, the reader might wish to take up WEBSTER, which suggests three main ways in which magic could be said to have influenced modern science: through concern with prophecy; through the belief in what Webster calls spiritual magic, but is more properly called natural magic; and through a continued belief in demonic magic. Pre-modern concerns with prophecy stimulated a keen interest in astrology, and therefore in astronomy, cosmology, and other related matters. Natural magic was based on the belief that many substances had hidden powers, or virtues, by which they could operate on, or bring about changes in, other substances or bodies. This belief stimulated an empirical search for the hidden powers of bodies – a concern for the usefulness of natural knowledge not found in the natural philosophy tradition – and a continued belief in the active nature of matter, which was to prove influential in certain versions of the mechanical philosophy. Webster's survey of continued belief in witches and demons among leading natural philosophers shows how traditional occult notions could be turned to provide support for the dualism between matter and spirit, which was a characteristic feature of most versions of the mechanical philosophy.

For all its brevity, Webster's book is erudite, scholarly and challenging. DEBUS, by contrast, is an introductory level textbook on science in the Renaissance and the early modern period. Although its focus is not primarily the occult sciences, it pays far greater attention to the role of magical traditions in the origins of modern science than other such introductory textbooks on the scientific revolution.

MERCHANT is also concerned with the nature of the scientific revolution, and her thesis has a number of important implications for the histories of magic and science. Characterizing the scientific revolution as the triumph of a mechanistic worldview closely associated with capitalistic and exploitative ambitions, over a supposedly more holistic, organic, and ecologically aware world-view, the rise of modern science is seen as a disenchantment of the world. During this process, Merchant argues, the previous order of the Great Chain of Being, with its correspondences linking different orders of being within the hierarchies of nature, had to be shown to be a bogus image of order, masking what was really a disordered and dangerous conception of the natural world. The European witch craze, among other things, is presented as part of this process of reconfiguring the earlier intellectual conception of nature, as a chaotic and potentially subversive force that needed to be brought under the control of the new science. Although certainly based upon an over-simplified view of the past, Merchant's book marshals its historical evidence well, is persuasively argued, and has proven immensely influential, particularly among feminist and "green" historians.

VICKERS provides a superb collection of essays by distinguished scholarly authors on a wide variety of topics, but all concerned with the relationship between magic and science. There are articles on Johannes Kepler, John Dee, Marin Mersenne, Francis Bacon and Isaac Newton, on archemastrie, analogy, astrology and numerology, alchemy, and demonology. There is even a highly useful article on the extent to which the occult sciences were studied and discussed in Oxford and Cambridge in the early modern period. The already considerable interest of the collection is enhanced by the fact that,

whereas all the contributors accept the undeniable influence of "occult mentalities" on "scientific mentalities", the editor, in his own paper and in his long introduction to the volume, takes the opposite line. While admitting that what he calls "Renaissance scientists" were able to operate simultaneously within two separate traditions (magic and science), Vickers insists that science and the occult went in different directions, and indeed always had done. It is an error, he therefore insists, to argue that, "the occult sciences in the Renaissance were productive of ideas, theories, and techniques in the new sciences". Within the anthology that he himself compiled, the editor stands out as a lone voice.

SHUMAKER provides a useful survey of the major beliefs held by some of the leading figures in Renaissance astrology, demonology, alchemy, Hermeticism, and what he calls "White Magic" – a term that, for him, embraces natural magic, astrological magic (in which the magus seeks to alter, not just read, the influence of the stars), and "spiritual or ceremonial" magic. Shumaker's overview of these occult sciences is accessible and generally reliable, and his brief discussions of the theory underlying each of the sciences are particularly helpful. This book also has a somewhat different interest for students of the history of the occult sciences; in the preface, Shumaker tells us that one of his reasons for writing the book was his awareness that the occult sciences were once again becoming highly attractive to university students and others involved in the "revolt against reason". Shumaker apologises therefore for "intrusive" passages in which he tries to bring "the shaky foundations of traditional occultism into the light".

While providing a rich and detailed account of the nature of Books of Secrets, their authors and their readership, EAMON also discusses the role of magic in both popular and elite culture. This work reveals the links between the magical tradition and technology (complex machines were regarded as occult because the way they worked was hidden), and the importance of magic within the culture of the court, and in the establishment of the earliest societies or academies devoted to the study of the natural world. It also discusses magic in relation to the epistemology of the new science.

Although CLULEE focuses upon a single individual, John Dee, his book is a superb guide to the occult sciences in the Renaissance, their place within the intellectual culture of the time, and their role in the development of modern science. By a close study of Dee's work, Clulee is able to show the richness, variety, and complexity of the occult sciences. Furthermore, a consideration of Dee's career and his efforts to gain patronage enables the reader to comprehend some of the ways in which the occult sciences, often opposed by the church, gained a new legitimacy, both intellectual and religious, in the Renaissance.

Similar lessons can be learned from the study of the Emperor Rudolf II and his intellectual milieu by EVANS. After a chapter in which he gives a detailed outline of the occult interests of Rudolf and his entourage, Evans goes on to argue that what Vickers would call the "occult mentality" was in fact a characteristic feature of late Renaissance European culture, and that Rudolf II was not alone in believing that it endorsed his own political position.

ROSSI's account of Francis Bacon is justifiably highly regarded, but magic plays only a small part in his story.

Although Rossi points to the "heritage of magic" in Bacon's attempted reform of natural philosophy, he quickly passes on to look at Bacon's criticisms of the magical tradition. Rossi concludes that the real model for Bacon's reform of natural philosophy was the supposedly collaborative and progressive work of elite craftsmen working in the mechanical arts. Rossi's work pre-dates that of Eamon, Clulee and Evans, and it is hard to accept the limited role he gives magic after reading their works. It seems likely, for example, that his emphasis on what he sees as the role of the mechanical arts might have to be reassessed, given that, as Thorndike and Eamon point out, machines were routinely regarded as magical contrivances by Bacon's contemporaries.

THOMAS is not directly concerned with the origins of modern science, but provides a wealth of information on magical beliefs in its period, detailing the nature and scope of magical ideas, and showing the universality of its persuasiveness across all orders of society. Strong on extensive and fascinating detail about occult beliefs, Thomas's book is less able to account for the decline of magic, which is supposedly its main theme. It is possible, he concludes, to link magic's decline with the growth of urban living, the rise of science, the ideology of self-help, and the rise of Protestantism with its opposition to the more magical–miraculous elements of Roman Catholicism. But Thomas seems to be well aware of the question-begging nature of all these explanations.

JOHN HENRY

See also Dee; Religion and Science: Renaissance; Scientific Revolution

Oceanography

Burstyn, Harold L., "Theories of Winds and Ocean Currents from the Discoveries to the End of the Seventeenth Century", *Terrae Incognitae*, 3 (1971): 7–31

Carpine, Christian, *Catalogue des appareils d'océanographie en collection au Musée Océanographique de Monaco*, 6 vols, Monaco: Le Musée, 1987–93

Deacon, Margaret B., *Scientists and the Sea, 1650–1900: A Study of Marine Science*, New York: Academic Press, 1971

LeGrand, H.E., *Drifting Continents and Shifting Theories: The Modern Revolution in Geology and Scientific Change*, Cambridge and New York: Cambridge University Press, 1988

McConnell, Anita, *No Sea Too Deep: The History of Oceanographic Instruments*, Bristol: Hilger, 1982

McConnell, Anita, *Directory of Source Materials for the History of Oceanography*, Paris: UNESCO, 1990

McIntosh, Robert P., *The Background of Ecology: Concept and Theory*, Cambridge and New York: Cambridge University Press, 1985

Mills, Eric L., *Biological Oceanography: An Early History, 1870–1960*, Ithaca, New York: Cornell University Press, 1989

Mills, Eric L., "The Historian of Science and Oceanography after Twenty Years", *Earth Sciences History*, 12/1 (1993): 5–18

Nelson, Stewart B., *Oceanographic Ships, Fore and Aft*, Washington, DC: Government Printing Office, 1971

Paffen, Karlheinz and Gerhard Kortum, *Die Geographie des Meeres: Disziplingeschichtliche Entwicklung seit 1650 und heutiger methodischer Stand*, Kiel: Geographisches Institüt der Universität Kiel, 1984

Reinke-Kunze, Christine, *Den Meeren auf der Spur: Geschichte und Aufgaben der deutschen Forschungsschiffe*, Herford: Koehlers Verlagsgesellschaft, 1986

Rice, A.L., *British Oceanographic Vessels, 1800–1950*, London: Ray Society, 1986

Schlee, Susan, *The Edge of an Unfamiliar World: A History of Oceanography*, New York: Dutton, 1973

Thomasson, E.M. (ed.), *Study of the Sea: The Development of Marine Research under the Auspices of the International Council for the Exploration of the Sea*, Farnham, Surrey: Fishing News Books, 1981

Wallace, William J., *The Development of the Chlorinity/Salinity Concept in Oceanography*, Amsterdam: Elsevier, 1974

Went, A.E.J., *Seventy Years Agrowing: A History of the International Council for the Exploration of the Sea, 1902–1972*, Copenhagen: International Council for the Exploration of the Sea, 1972

Wood, Robert Muir, *The Dark Side of the Earth*, London: Allen and Unwin, 1985

Oceanography – the description, analysis, and understanding of the physical, chemical, geological, and biological phenomena of the oceans – became differentiated from the geographical and biological sciences between about 1895 and the 1930s, and became fully professionalized only after World War II. The first period has received rudimentary historical attention; the second has received virtually no attention at all.

DEACON's account of the marine sciences from antiquity, through the scientific revolution, to 1900 is still unmatched in breadth and depth of scholarship. Centering on Britain, it concentrates mainly upon physical and geological studies of the oceans, except in the case of the Challenger Expedition, 1872–76, which in part owed its origin to biological problems.

Deacon's work is complemented by SCHLEE, which examines 19th-century marine science in the US, the origin of international co-operation around 1900, and the relationship between fisheries and studies of ocean circulation. The books by Deacon and Schlee encompass most of the historical work on oceanography carried out during the past 20 years. A synoptic review of the historical literature to 1990 is available in MILLS (1993), including references to publications resulting from the International Congresses on the History of Oceanography held in 1966, 1972, 1980 and 1987. Collectively, the Congress publications deal in a broad and unfocused way with all the subdisciplines of oceanography, and with related topics including navigation and hydrography.

McCONNELL (1990) provides a preliminary list of the resources available worldwide for the historical study of oceanography, including scientific collections, data, documents, instruments, and photographs.

In late 19th-century Europe, the oceans were studied by geographers, as outlined by PAFFEN & KORTUM, who discuss the German-language tradition of physical geography.

The transition from geography to a fully-differentiated science of oceanography has not yet been studied, but another influence, that of fisheries biology, is described by WENT, whose monograph is a chronological, administrative account, without historical analysis, of the International Council for the Exploration of the Sea (ICES), founded in 1902. A comprehensive study is still needed of how the Council influenced the development of professional marine science.

Subdisciplinary works are rare in the history of oceanography. BURSTYN's account of the "prehistory" of ocean circulation, dealing with concepts and descriptions of ocean currents from the ancients until the time of Newton, is a rich source of information and insights.

Biological oceanography originated during the second half of the 19th century, in studies of deep-water animals and in concerns about the depletion of northern European sea fisheries. Only the latter has been dealt with in major works, especially the monograph by Went on ICES, supplemented by THOMASSON, which includes biographical information and a useful collection of early photographs. A major theme in biological oceanography from the 1890s to the present has been the study of how marine production is controlled. MILLS (1989) offers a detailed account of how this work developed, discussing scientific, institutional, economic, and social issues. Some other aspects of biological oceanography are dealt with indirectly in the densely-packed compilation by McINTOSH, which mainly catalogues the literature of ecology, rather than oceanography.

Marine geology and geophysics have developed hand-in-hand with oceanography, in part because ships are needed for each, and the theory of plate tectonics, in particular, has provided a focus for marine geology and geophysics, as recounted in many recent publications. Among the most useful recent examples are WOOD's account of the scientific development of plate tectonics, with much biographical information, and LeGRAND's philosophically and sociologically oriented account of the plate tectonic revolution. The chemistry of the oceans is more sparsely served; WALLACE is the main source, which examines the determination of sea water composition.

Ships and scientific instruments have played a large part in determining the kinds of problems studied in oceanography, and the kinds of solutions deemed satisfactory. NELSON, RICE and REINKE-KUNZE consider oceanographic vessels from the national viewpoints of the United States, Britain and Germany. Each is a valuable and important historical account, but their national viewpoints preclude a broader view of how and why ships and their equipment were used.

The construction and use of many kinds of oceanographic instruments are described in McCONNELL (1982), based on – but not restricted to – the collections in the Science Museum in London. Another very valuable source is the series by CARPINE, including excellent photographs and a good descriptive text, based on the remarkable collection in the Musée océanographique de Monaco. Though valuable and indispensable, McConnell and Carpine are, however, only first steps toward a historical understanding of how technology entered and shaped oceanography.

Much of the early popular or hagiographic literature on the history of oceanography (not considered here) was preoccupied with personalities, or with the Challenger Expedition. Recent scholarship, as outlined above, has gone well beyond this, although large gaps still exist as written histories of oceanography have yet to come into their own.

ERIC L. MILLS

See also Environmental Sciences; Geology

Oppenheimer, J. Robert 1904–1967
American physicist

Boskin, Joseph and Fred Krinsky, *The Oppenheimer Affair: A Political Play in Three Acts*, Beverly Hills: Glencoe Press, 1968

Curtis, Charles P., *The Oppenheimer Case: The Trial of a Security System*, New York: Simon and Schuster, 1955

Davis, Nuell Pharr, *Lawrence and Oppenheimer*, New York: Simon and Schuster, 1969

Goodchild, Peter, *J. Robert Oppenheimer: Shatterer of Worlds*, London: BBC Books, 1980; Boston: Houghton Mifflin, 1981

Holloway, Rachel L., *In the Matter of J. Robert Oppenheimer: Politics, Rhetoric and Self-Defense*, Westport, Connecticut, and London: Praeger, 1993

Kevles, Daniel J., *The Physicists: The History of a Scientific Community in Modern America*, New York: Knopf, 1978; revised edition, Cambridge, Massachusetts: Harvard University Press, 1995

Major, John, *The Oppenheimer Hearing*, New York: Stein and Day, and London: Batsford, 1971

Nichols, K.D., *The Road To Trinity: A Personal Account of How America's Nuclear Policies Were Made*, New York: Morrow, 1987

Smith, Alice Kimball and Charles Weiner (eds), *Robert Oppenheimer: Letters and Recollections*, Cambridge, Massachusetts: Harvard University Press, 1980

Stern, Philip M., *The Oppenheimer Case: Security on Trial*, New York: Harper and Row, 1969; London: Hart-Davis, 1971

United States Atomic Energy Commission, *In the Matter of J. Robert Oppenheimer: Transcript of Hearing before Personnel Security Board and Texts of Principal Documents and Letters*, Cambridge, Massachusetts: MIT Press, 1971

J. Robert Oppenheimer played a significant role in the development of the atomic bomb during World War II. Ten years later, during the Korean War, he lost his security clearance. The academic literature on Oppenheimer is to be found in accounts of either of those two stories. The revocation of Oppenheimer's security clearance in particular has attracted much attention, especially because the case has offered a means of discussing the United States security services during the McCarthy era. There are some popular biographies on Oppenheimer, but so far scholarly attention has not been paid to his life as a whole.

The biography by GOODCHILD, the result of a television program for the BBC, is a useful introduction to Oppenheimer's career. The book contains many interesting images, and while Oppenheimer's life and work provides the backbone of the narrative, much attention is paid to the clear and simple explication of related matters, such as the workings of the atomic bomb. Goodchild describes sympathetically Oppenheimer's formative years, including his precocious youth in New York City and at Harvard, his venture to Europe for post-graduate study in physics, his treatment for depression, and his reputation as a bright and eccentric American student. Goodchild suggests that the depression derived from Oppenheimer's feeling that he was not making major contributions to the physics community. However, as early as the 1930s, he did exert an impact on the teaching of physics in American universities. Goodchild describes Oppenheimer's marriage to Kitty Harrison, a Communist party member, and how he was not the only American intellectual to find Communism alluring. Nevertheless, by the time of the revocation of his security clearance in the 1950s, his wife had left the party, and Oppenheimer himself never joined. Instead, the rise of Hitler and the accompanying intolerance for cultural and intellectual freedom increasingly occupied his concerns. In 1942, he became the scientific director of the Manhattan Project, the American effort to build an atomic bomb designed for use against Germany. In the summer of 1945, two types of atomic bombs were dropped on Hiroshima and Nagasaki, Japan. Oppenheimer emerged from the headlines of V-J Day as the "Father of the A-Bomb".

Until the explosion of the first Soviet nuclear device in 1949, and the success of the communist offensive in China in the same year, Oppenheimer's influence prevailed. That year, however, as chair of the General Advisory Council of the newly-created Atomic Energy Commission, he delivered the Council's majority opinion that the nation should not embark on a crash program to develop the more powerful, and potentially genocidal, hydrogen bomb. In the general intensification of the Cold War, Oppenheimer's position became more difficult.

Goodchild argues that Oppenheimer had hoped that more efficient fission weapons, and international control of such weapons, might truncate the nuclear arms race. Late in 1952, the H-bomb was given form when the first full-scale thermonuclear blast took place at Los Alamos.

NICHOLS argues that Oppenheimer's political beliefs and administrative actions delayed the development of the H-bomb, and that he was a security risk. Nichols claims that the US military and government policy-makers wanted thermonuclear weapons, and that as a result opposition to the development and deployment of such weapons systems had to be stifled at all levels: this meant silencing Oppenheimer. In 1953, the US military and the Atomic Energy Commission forced Oppenheimer into security hearings that often prohibited the presence of his own attorney. It is this case that has attracted most of the scholarship on Oppenheimer.

Soon after the end of the case, CURTIS published an account of the trial which, he argued, provided the first opportunity to understand the US security system. Written in a journalistic style, it quoted extensively from the trial transcripts. Curtis argues that Oppenheimer was innocent of any espionage for the Soviets, and that the security system was blatantly curbing the rights of individual citizens.

Around 1970, the issues of individual and civil rights came to the fore, and the professors of history and political science, BOSKIN & KRINSKY, treated the Oppenheimer trial as a test-case. They argued that the popular anxieties and prejudices of the McCarthy era influenced, if not determined, the outcome of the trial. Among these anxieties and prejudices they list the advent of the Soviet bomb in 1949, the general fear of Communism and of foreign (especially German) intellectuals, and, more specifically, Oppenheimer's marriage to a member of the Communist party, and his relations with a Communist paramour.

STERN is the most prodigiously researched study of the case (almost 600 pages long), on which subsequent literature draws; the scholarly apparatus is impeccable, with detailed notes and a section on the sources. Stern, a journalist, argues that while the trial has ended, the insidious system behind it remains.

The UNITED STATES ATOMIC ENERGY COMMISSION was originally published by the Government printing office in 1954, but this 1970 issue rendered it more widely available. It contains a foreword by Philip M. Stern.

MAJOR, a Professor of History at the University of Hull, sets the case squarely within the context of the McCarthy era and the heavy American losses in the Korean war. Major argues that Oppenheimer was destroyed by American anti-communism and by the cult of weapons of mass destruction, which were regarded as an embodiment of American national strength. He also argues that the case did much damage to America's reputation and to the principles associated therewith.

More recent publications have been less concerned with the conflict between individual rights and the US security system. HOLLOWAY analyses the rhetoric in the Oppenheimer case within the framework of communication studies, ignoring the political context. She develops a terminological algebra, arguing that Oppenheimer's rhetoric was flawed: for example, Oppenheimer's contextualisation of the allure of communism was bad rhetoric.

SMITH & WEINER was funded by the Oral History Program and Science and Technology Studies at the Massachusetts Institute of Technology, and is by far the best book for a reader primarily interested in the history of physics. While pointing out that Oppenheimer came to symbolise the bomb and analysing the problems related to this, the main emphasis is on Oppenheimer's role in physics and the development of the atomic bomb.

DAVIS is a journalistic tale of two "strong personalities" complementing each other: Ernest Orlando Lawrence, the experimental physicist, and Oppenheimer, the theoretical physicist. Covering the period from the 1920s to the 1950s, some dialogue and details are invented in order to enhance the narrative flow, but much of the physics is explained, and there is a useful glossary at the back.

In KEVLES's institutional history of 20th-century US physics, Oppenheimer crops up repeatedly: his background and early career, his work at Los Alamos, and the trial are all covered within the context of the general development of the discipline of physics.

ARNE HESSENBRUCH

See also Atomic Weapons; Lawrence; United States: general works

Optics

Buchwald, Jed Z., *The Rise of the Wave Theory of Light: Optical Theory and Experiment in the Early Nineteenth Century*, Chicago: University of Chicago Press, 1989

Cantor, G.N., *Optics after Newton: Theories of Light in Britain and Ireland, 1704–1840*, Manchester: Manchester University Press, 1983

Hakfoort, Casper, *Optics in the Age of Euler: Conceptions of the Nature of Light, 1700–1795*, Cambridge and New York: Cambridge University Press, 1995

Hall, A. Rupert, *All Was Light: An Introduction to Newton's Opticks*, Oxford: Clarendon Press, and New York: Oxford University Press, 1993

Kipnis, Naum, *History of the Principle of Interference of Light*, Basel: Birkhäuser, 1991

Lindberg, David C., *Theories of Vision from al-Kindi to Kepler*, Chicago: University of Chicago Press, 1976

Sabra, A.I., *Theories of Light: From Descartes to Newton*, London: Oldbourne, 1967; Cambridge and New York: Cambridge University Press, 1981

Schaffner, Kenneth F., *Nineteenth-Century Aether Theories*, Oxford and New York: Pergamon Press, 1972

Shapiro, Alan E., *Fits, Passions, and Paroxysms: Physics, Method, and Chemistry and Newton's Theories of Colored Bodies and Fits of Easy Reflection*, Cambridge and New York: Cambridge University Press, 1993

Steffens, Henry John, *The Development of Newtonian Optics in England*, New York: Science History Publications, 1977

Wheaton, Bruce R., *The Tiger and the Shark: Empirical Roots of Wave-Particle Dualism*, Cambridge and New York: Cambridge University Press, 1984

By focusing on the problem of vision, which necessitates discussion of the nature of light and its propagation, LINDBERG traces the development of optics for more than 2,000 years, from ancient Greece to the time of Kepler. Special attention is given to the contributions made by natural philosophers of the Islamic and European worlds, who established a vigorous optical tradition throughout the Middle Ages.

One of the most important contributors to optics in the 17th century was Newton. The first part of SHAPIRO's book studies Newton's theory of colored bodies and his theory of fits (the periodicity of light). In addition to historical analysis, Shapiro offers a philosophical discussion of the subject, because, in order to explain the formation and subsequent reception of Newton's theories, it is necessary to take into account Newton's methodology, in particular his view of hypothesis. The second part of the book traces the influences of Newton's theories of colored bodies and fits in the late 18th and early 19th centuries.

HALL gives a general account of one of the most important books in the history of optics: Newton's *Opticks*. Adopting a non-mathematical approach, Hall examines the book's context, preparation, evolution, and influence in Britain and Europe. According to Hall, Newton's approach to optical topics was physical, a result of his having been preoccupied by the physical nature of light and its interactions with matter.

SABRA provides a detailed examination of the Cartesian tradition in 17th-century optics, including the works of Descartes, Fermat, Hooke, and Huygens. By focusing on the problems and controversies regarding the nature of light and its properties, Sabra outlines the development of the wave theory in the 17th century – from Descartes's notion that the transmission of light was something like the transfer of energy, to Huygens's concept that light was a pulse phenomenon.

A popular conception is that optics in Britain entered an "age of Newton" in the 18th century, when Newton's orthodoxy inhibited the development of different points of view. STEFFENS, however, examines the progress of optics in 18th-century England, and details the concepts of the materiality of light, the forces of attraction and repulsion between light and matter. He then identifies the application of the principles of mechanics to the description and explanation of all optical phenomena as the major characteristics of Newtonian optics in 18th-century England, which was significantly different from Newton's optics of the 17th century.

CANTOR also challenges the popular conception regarding optics in 18th-century Britain, by concentrating on the evolution of the notion of light in natural philosophy. Cantor identifies four classes of theories concerning the nature of light, which include not only the well-known particle and wave theories, but also fluid theories – which conceived of light as a flow of a fluid, and vibration theories – which viewed light as something similar to sound. Cantor also covers the particle-wave controversy in the British Isles during the early 19th century – an example of a fundamental alteration in scientific style, which raised questions concerning the discipline's domain, methods, problems, training patterns, audience, and its connections with other disciplines.

HAKFOORT provides a supplement to "the age of Newton", by outlining a picture of "an age of Euler" in Germany from the 1750s to the 1790s. He begins with a careful examination of the non-confrontational relations between Newtonian "emission" theory and Cartesian "medium" theory in German-speaking areas of the Continent during the first half of the 18th century. He then shows how Euler established a wave theory of light on the grounds of the analogy between light and sound, and how the formulation of Euler's wave theory began a new age in optics, in which the struggle between the particle and wave traditions became an important theme.

Optics experienced a radical change in the early 19th century, when the wave theory of light replaced the particle theory to became the dominant tradition. KIPNIS discusses the contributions of Thomas Young in the rise of the wave theory. The central concept of Young's work was the interference of light, which, however, was almost unanimously rejected when it was first introduced. Kipnis reasons that Young's theory failed because it did not have the audience it needed; until the middle of the second decade of the century, optics was basically qualitative, and, under the circumstances, it was difficult for Young's theory, which provided no understanding of the physical aspect ·of interference, to receive a favorable hearing.

BUCHWALD stresses the contributions of another wave theorist, Augustin Fresnel, and in particular his work on the diffraction and polarization of light. The principal goal of Buchwald's work is to reveal that, in addition to the replacement of particles of light by waves as the tools of explanation, a deeper process also took place within the revolution, in which the ray was replaced by the wave front as a tool of analysis. This change was so profound that it was not clearly recognized, even by some of the wave theory's most vigorous advocates, such as Arago and Herschel. Buchwald also provides a unique discussion of the role of optical experiments, showing that the development of theory and experiment were tightly interwoven.

Optics in the second half of the 19th century was occupied by the discussion of aether. SCHAFFNER places the concept of aether in its historical context, discussing how the acceptance of the wave theory drew attention to the nature of the optical medium, and how later the development of Maxwell's electromagnetic theory of light led to the formulation of mechanical aether theories in order to explain physical optics. Schaffner also explains why the concept of aether failed, and how it was eventually eliminated from physics. The book also contains selected papers from the original literature.

WHEATON tells the story of the next revolution in the concept of light: from 1896, when most physicists were convinced that light consisted of wave disturbances in a medium, to the mid-1920s, when the concept of the wave-particle duality for both radiation and matter was widely accepted. By focusing on the development of the localized electromagnetic pulse theory of X-rays and gamma rays, Wheaton reviews the important role of experiment in this radical change of theory.

XIANG CHEN

See also Aether; Electromagnetism; Newton

Organic Chemistry

Benfey, O. Theodor, *From Vital Force to Structural Formulas*, Boston: Houghton Mifflin, 1964; reprinted Philadelphia: Beckman Center for the History of Chemistry, 1992

Leffek, Kenneth T., *Sir Christopher Ingold: A Major Prophet of Organic Chemistry*, Victoria, British Columbia: Nova Lion Press, 1996

Rocke, Alan J., *The Quiet Revolution: Hermann Kolbe and the Science of Organic Chemistry*, Berkeley: University of California Press, 1993

Slater, Leo, *Organic Synthesis and R. B. Woodward: An Historical Study in the Chemical Sciences*, PhD dissertation, Princeton University, 1997

Tarbell, Dean Stanley and Ann Tracy Tarbell, *Essays on the History of Organic Chemistry in the United States, 1875-1955*, Nashville, Tennesse: Folio, 1986

Todd, Alexander, *A Time to Remember: The Autobiography of a Chemist*, Cambridge and New York: Cambridge University Press, 1983

Travis, Anthony S., *The Rainbow Makers: The Origins of the Synthetic Dyestuffs Industry in Western Europe*, Bethlehem, Pennsylvania: Lehigh University Press, and London: Associated University Presses, 1993

Traynham, James G. (ed.), *Essays on the History of Organic Chemistry*, Baton Rouge: Louisiana State University Press, 1987

Verkade, Pieter Eduard, *A History of the Nomenclature of Organic Chemistry*, Dordrecht: Reidel, and Delft: Delft University Press, 1985

Williams, Trevor I., *Robert Robinson: Chemist Extraordinary*, Oxford: Clarendon Press, 1990

While the field of organic chemistry has deep roots in earlier iatrochemistry and pharmacy, it is largely a 19th- and 20th-century discipline. The books described below have been chosen to illustrate the range of the field itself as well as various historiographic approaches. Organic chemistry spans two centuries full of innumerable achievements and the work of countless scientists, but there are major historical roadmarks of organic chemistry that deserve special mention: the investigations of coal-tar derivatives, the rise of the synthetic-dye industry, the advent of structure theory and stereochemistry, the elaboration of theories of chemotherapy and the manufacture of pharmaceuticals, and finally the growth and use of petrochemicals as feedstocks. Emphasis on the 19th century in this article is an artifact of the available secondary literature in which the chemistry of the 20th century is underrepresented. Additional information pertinent to organic chemistry can also be found in the history of adjacent fields such as physical chemistry, polymers and plastics, and biochemistry.

Using the life of German chemist Hermann Kolbe as the vehicle, ROCKE examines the scientific reform movement of the late 19th century. In the short term, this "quiet revolution" led to the standardization of molecular formulas and atomic weights; in the longer term, it led to what is now referred to as modern chemistry. Rocke's volume is an important one for the history of science, but it also deserves some attention from non-history of science scholars: along with his treatment of Kolbe's efforts in the synthesis of acetic acid and the introduction of carboxylation, Rocke succeeds also in placing this reform movement, and German organic chemistry generally, in its political framework.

Detouring from the common road of history of science scholars, TRAVIS's *The Rainbow Makers* takes a fresh perspective on the rise of the synthetics dyestuff industry in the late 19th century. Beginning with Sir William Perkin and his discovery of mauve, Travis consistently emphasizes the importance of the technology gleaned from the natural dye industry, as opposed to solely academic chemical research, in the advancement of the aniline dye industry throughout Western Europe. His methodology is likewise unique: rather than rehashing the oft-used French and German sources, Travis chose to focus on a re-interpretation of the English sources.

BENFEY provides a solid background of the development of structural theory. Designed as a supplement for first-year chemistry students, it traces the history of chemical structure and organic chemistry through the 19th century, ending with the contributions of Kekulé and Couper. Benfey's close reading and extensive quotation of the primary sources provides an excellent window into the contemporary debates on structure theory.

Though originally intended to provide a comprehensive history of organic chemistry for the benefit of both the chemist and the historian, TARBELL & TARBELL has instead been recognized as an excellent technical reference for the field of organic chemistry. While highlighting the major American achievements in organic chemistry in both academic and industrial environments throughout the period 1875 to 1955, the Tarbells also succeed in tracing the development of modern chemical ideas and the interrelation between organic chemistry and other scientific disciplines. This book provides an excellent biographical introduction to a substantial segment of the academic organic chemists in the US.

TRAYNHAM addresses a diverse range of subjects relating to 19th- and 20th-century organic chemistry, from chemical nomenclature to late 19th-century Louisiana sugar chemists. Compiled on the occasion of the 16th annual Louisiana State University Mardi Gras Symposium in Organic Chemistry, these eight essays, thematically disparate, challenge many of the long-held ideas about the discipline of organic chemistry, making it an important work for chemists and historians alike.

VERKADE, a member of the IUPAC Commission on Nomenclature of Organic Chemistry for more than 40 years and chairman for the majority of that period, presents a clear and comprehensive history of chemical nomenclature in this English translation. His chapters are arranged almost chronologically, beginning with the Geneva Conference of 1892, allowing the reader to view the adoption of nomenclature as a process rather than a decree; it effectively demonstrates the difficulties surrounding chemical nomenclature, the eventual development of a nomenclature for organic chemistry, and the actors who made the entire process possible.

Little work is available on late 20th-century history of chemistry; what post-war organic chemistry literature exists, primarily consists of biographies and autobiographies. Notable among these are Jeffrey Seeman's fine series "Profiles, Pathways, and Dreams: Autobiographies of Eminent Chemists", printed beginning in 1990 by the American Chemical Society. This series now totals some 20 volumes, each of which is on a 20th-century chemist. Not all the biographies can be covered here. Four biographies will be presented below and the suggestion is that these 20th-century chemists as "a group" contributed to a larger edifice of knowledge and industry that can be seen collectively through their lives: organic chemistry has transformed the conceptions of bodies and materials by realizing a goal of molecular control conceived in the the second half of the 19th century. Four prominent organic chemists are described in the following works: There is an autobiography by TODD, a British biochemist (1907–97) whose research on the structure and synthesis of nucleotides, nucleosides, and nucleotide coenzymes gained him the 1957 Nobel prize for chemistry. The topic of WILLIAMS is Sir Robert Robinson (1886–1975), another British chemist and recipient of the Nobel prize for chemistry in 1947 for his research in plant biology, including alkaloids. LEFFEK is a biography of Christopher Ingold who contributed to the development of a general system of amino acids in the 1960s. SLATER has written on Robert Burns Woodward (1917–79), an American chemist best known for his syntheses of complex organic substances, including quinine (1944), cholesterol and cortisone (1951), and vitamin B12 (1971). He was awarded the Nobel prize for chemistry in 1965. In the main, these works focus narrowly on the lives of major figures. However, they do provide the reader with some insight into the practices and personalities of late 20th-century organic chemistry, a productive and historically interesting enterprise in both science and industry.

TRACY L. SULLIVAN AND LEO B. SLATER

See also Dyestuffs; Industrial Chemistry

Orientalism

Carrier, James G. (ed.), *Occidentalism: Images of the West*, New York: Oxford University Press, and Oxford: Clarendon Press, 1995

Clifford, James, "On Orientalism", in his *The Predicament of Culture: Twentieth-Century Ethnography, Literature, and Art*, Cambridge, Massachusetts: Harvard University Press, 1988, 255–76

MacKenzie, John M., *Orientalism: History, Theory and the Arts*, Manchester: Manchester University Press, 1995

Said, Edward W., *Orientalism*, New York: Pantheon, 1978; London: Routledge and Kegan Paul, 1979

Said, Edward W., *Culture and Imperialism*, New York: Knopf, and London: Chatto and Windus, 1993

Schwab, Raymond, *The Oriental Renaissance: Europe's Rediscovery of India and the East, 1680–1880*, translated by Gene Patterson-Black and Victor Reinking, New York: Columbia University Press, 1984 (original edition, 1950)

Sprinker, Michael (ed.), *Edward Said: A Critical Reader*, Oxford and Cambridge, Massachusetts: Blackwell, 1992

Orientalism, as a critical concept introduced by Edward Said, has generated a significant amount of literature and controversy in several disciplines, notably literary criticism, anthropology, and history. Since works dealing with, and influenced by, this concept are legion and diverse, one may best begin with Said's own writings.

SAID (1978) argues that orientalism is neither a mere scholarly tradition devoted to the study of non-Western (Middle Eastern) societies, nor just an imperialist institution, but a certain way of pursuing knowledge and, thus, of extending power. Said's orientalism manifests itself as the will to essentialize other societies, persistent attempts to project simplified images of the unfamiliar, and the struggle to create and maintain the other; the concept of orientalism, therefore, involves issues of representation, domination, and, implicitly, resistance. Said's analytic apparatus evolved out of Foucault's idea of discourse and Gramsci's idea of hegemony, and he applies this interpretative framework to the writing of British, French, and American orientalists from the 18th to the 20th centuries – many of them drawn from SCHWAB's old-fashioned, but erudite, account of European oriental studies. Said's project is simultaneously a theoretical proposal, a historical study, and a political polemic. By investigating their conceptual foundation, he calls into question the intellectual tradition of orientalist disciplines, and concludes his study with a passionate attack on contemporary oriental studies, urging for the development of new kinds of scholarship.

SAID (1993) continues and expands his original project by broadening his subject, from a particular scholarly tradition to the general relationships between culture and imperialism, addressing emphatically the issue of resistance. Western imperialism of the 19th and 20th centuries, he argues, was not merely economic and geopolitical, but is reflected in, and indeed justified by, the cultural vision held by many Europeans. By reading canonic novels, such as those by Austen, Dickens, and Kipling, in this light, he aims to show the ways in which narrative fiction has been permeated with the imperialist experience and imagination. In this post-colonial age, Said claims, imperialist culture still persists, but faces a growing resistance. Native writers are writing back, challenging the Western imperialist assumptions and struggling for liberation and cultural independence. In his conclusion, Said calls for a kind of cultural cosmopolitanism, which will go beyond the destructive conflicts between nationalist and imperialist cultures.

Said's work has been criticized on several fronts: his tendentious reading of sources, his theoretical inconsistency, and his neglect of issues of gender, postmodernism, and popular culture. CLIFFORD's celebrated essay review is a critical assessment of Said's theoretical framework. It argues that Said's humanist appropriation of Foucault is problematic, that his criticism of orientalism essentializes the West, and that his discourse analysis does not hold together. The nine essays collected in SPRINKER's volume are varied, uneven, and generally sympathetic to Said's theoretical and political position. More important among them are a friendly critique of Said's post-colonial cosmopolitanism, and an essay on anti-colonial nationalism. This volume also includes a long interview with Said, which contains illuminating biographical information and Said's comments on some current cultural and academic issues.

The most recent and comprehensive re-evaluation of this subject is MacKENZIE's learned and provocative book. As a fine imperial historian specializing in the late 19th and early 20th centuries, MacKenzie is not afraid to challenge Said's knowledge and interpretations of imperial history. He also takes issue with Said's historical method, and argues that Said has limited his study to elite culture, leaving out the whole problem of orientalism in popular culture. To illustrate his alternative approach, MacKenzie offers several suggestive essays on orientalism in art, architecture, design, music, and the theatre. He emphasizes the complexity and heterogeneity of Western images of other societies, and believes that orientalist elements in the Western arts play a more interactive and creative role than Said suggests. This book has an acute review of all major works on this subject and an excellent bibliography.

The volume edited by CARRIER provides an unusual perspective and suggests new directions for further discussion, as the introduction and several of the articles are substantial and perceptive. Inspired by Said's work, nine anthropologists employ their knowledge of colonial and other non-Western societies to investigate the perceptions and images of the West, emphasizing the multiplicity of occidentalism. These essays reveal that not only do members of non-Western societies have stereotyped images of the West, but Western people also have essentialist, selective conceptions of themselves. Therefore, any society's constructions of other societies can only be dialectically defined.

FA-TI FAN

See also Colonialism and Science

Ornithology

Anker, Jean, *Bird Books and Bird Art: An Outline of the Literary History and Iconography of Descriptive Ornithology*, Copenhagen: Levin & Munksgaard, 1938

Boubier, Maurice, *L'Évolution de l'ornithologie*, Paris: Alcan, 1925

Farber, Paul Lawrence, *The Emergence of Ornithology as a Scientific Discipline: 1760–1850*, Dordrecht and Boston: Reidel, 1982

Farber, Paul Lawrence (ed.), "The Historical Impact of Ornithology on the Biological Sciences", *Acta XIX Congressus Internationalis Ornithologici*, 2 (1986): 2717–759

Jackson, Christine E., *Bird Illustrators: Some Artists in Early Lithography*, London: Witherby, 1975

Jackson, Christine E., *Bird Etchings: The Illustrators and Their Books, 1655–1855*, Ithaca, New York: Cornell University Press, 1985

Lysaght, A.M., *The Book of Birds: Five Centuries of Bird Illustration*, London: Phaidon, 1975

Mullens, W.H. and H. Kirke Swann, *A Bibliography of British Ornithology from the Earliest Times to the End of 1912*, London: Macmillan, 1917

Newton, Alfred, *A Dictionary of Birds*, 4 vols, London: A. and C. Black, 1893–96

Nissen, Claus, *Die illustrierten Vogelbücher: Ihre Geschichte und Bibliographie*, Stuttgart: Hiersemann, 1953

Ronsil, René, *L'Art français dans le livre d'oiseaux: Elements d'une iconographie ornithologique française*, Paris: Société Ornithologique de France et de l'union Française, 1957

Sterling, Keir (ed.), *Contributions to the History of American Ornithology*, New York: Arno Press, 1974

Stresemann, Erwin, *Ornithology from Aristotle to the Present*, translated from the German by Hans J. Epstein and Cathleen Epstein, edited by G. William Cottrell, with bibliographic essay by Ernst Mayr on the history of American ornithology, Cambridge, Massachusetts: Harvard University Press, 1975 (original edition, 1951)

Whittell, Hubert Massey, *The Literature of Australian Birds: A History and Bibliography of Australian Ornithology*, Perth, Western Australia: Paterson Brokenstra, 1954

Works of literature on the history of ornithology vary considerably, depending on the author's purpose. A considerable body of work is devoted to helping the practising scientist locate early descriptions of a particular species, for the purposes of accurate naming and classification. Mullens & Swann, Whittell, and Newton are examples of such basic reference works for ornithologists which, nevertheless, contain vast amounts of information for the historian of science attempting to survey the literature. MULLENS & SWANN supply biographies and bibliographies of the major ornithologists of the past, and although WHITTELL focuses on Australia, because Australian birds were of such great interest, his historical introduction discusses European naturalists. NEWTON has a historical introduction that traces the development of the study of birds up to the 20th century.

Because birds are so striking in appearance, they have inspired much artistic reproduction, and illustrated bird books comprise many of the most beautifully produced volumes in printing history. These books are also of considerable scientific value, for ornithologists were able to capture the appearance of birds in the field, or of specimens that were later destroyed by insect pests. Scientists, art book collectors, and historians of illustration appreciate the craftsmanship and creativity of illustrated bird books, and historians of science have also made extensive use of them. Anker, Nissen, and Ronsil are three major reference guides to the illustrated bird book. They contain iconographic information, along with discussions of the artists, authors, and printers. ANKER is based on the collection in the University Library of Copenhagen, and is rich in iconographic information on 18th- and 19th-century bird books. NISSEN covers much of the same material, but has useful indices of artists, birds, geographical locations, and authors. RONSIL focuses on French publications, and contains technical information concerning the illustration process.

There is also an extensive literature on individual ornithologists who produced famous bird books (e.g. Gould, Audubon, and Lear). JACKSON (1985) provides a wealth of background information for appreciating the artistic work of the 19th century, the period of the most impressive illustrated bird books. JACKSON (1975) is especially important, because the invention of lithography in the 19th century allowed inexpensive and more accurate reproduction of bird drawings than anything previously available. Dozens of coffee-table books have also been published over the years, and LYSAGHT is an excellent example of their quality and value.

Histories of the study of birds from ancient times onwards generally construct a narrative starting with Aristotle and running to the present. This to some extent creates a false picture, as "ornithology" as a distinct science did not exist before the 19th century, and historians of science must of necessity extract sections of writing on birds from very disparate works. As a result, an impression is often given that a few ancient Greeks and Romans knew a little about birds, but that for many centuries the "subject" lay fallow, until its rediscovery in the Renaissance (i.e. 100 years later). Even then, little was done until, as a result of the hard work and intelligence of some 18th-century naturalists, the subject took off (partly due to the exploration of the period) and finally grew into a serious subject of scientific investigation in the 19th century. The histories of BOUBIER and STRESEMANN are not quite as crude as this suggests, but they each attempt to span periods from the Greeks to the present. Both books, however, are of great historical value, for they present thoughtful and carefully researched discussions of many of the principal figures in ornithology. In addition, they each analyze the central issues that have occupied ornithologists during the past century and a half. Stresemann is valuable particularly for his discussion of the broader biological context in which birds were studied, while Boubier stresses the development of systematics and the discovery of avian diversity.

The growth of the history of biology since the 1970s has produced many more specialized studies. Reprints of classical works are available, and anthologies of classical articles have been collected, for example in STERLING. FARBER (1986) contains an overview of the historical impact of ornithology by Ernst Mayr, as well as representative articles by historians of the life sciences on detailed topics. FARBER (1982) gives an account of the emergence of ornithology as a scientific discipline, and covers technical issues (such as the development of taxidermy), intellectual factors (the growth of classification systems), and the cultural context from which ornithology emerged.

PAUL LAWRENCE FARBER

Ørsted, Hans Christian   1777–1851
Danish natural philosopher

Billeskov Jansen, F.J., Egill Snorrason and Chr. Lauritz-Jensen (eds), *Hans Christian Ørsted*, 1987

Christensen, Dan Ch., "The Ørsted-Ritter Partnership and the Birth of Romantic Science", *Annals of Science*, 52 (1995): 153–85

Christensen, Dan Ch., "Romantic Natural Philosophy", in *The Golden Age Revisited: Art and Culture in Denmark 1800–1850*, edited by Bente Scavenius, translated from the Danish by Barbara Haveland and Jean Lundskar Nielsen, Copenhagen: Gyldendal, 1996

Dibner, Bern, *Oersted and the Discovery of Electromagnetism*, Norwalk, Connecticut: Burndy Library, 1961

Franksen, Ole Immanuel, *H.C. Ørsted: A Man of Two Cultures*, Birkerød: Strandbergs, 1981

Harding, M.C. (ed.), *Correspondance de H.C. Ørsted avec divers savants*, 2 vols, Copenhagen: Ascheoug, 1920

Knudsen, Ole, *Elektromagnetismens historie 1820–1831 og Faradays opdagelse af induktionen*, Copenhagen, 1980

Meyer, Kirstine, "The Scientific Life and Works of H.C. Oersted", in H.C. Ørsted, *Naturvidenskabelige Skrifter*, vols 1–3, Copenhagen: A.F. Host, 1920

Ørsted, Hans Christian, *Samlede og Efterladte Skrifter*, 9 vols, Copenhagen, 1851–52

Ørsted, Hans Christian, *The Spirit in Nature*, translated from the German by Leonora and Joanna B. Horner, in Bohn's Scientific Library, London, 1852

Ørsted, Matilde (ed.), *Breve fra og til Hans Christian Ørsted*, 2 vols, Copenhagen, 1870

Snelders, H.A.M., "Oersted's Discovery of Electromagnetism", in *Romanticism and the Sciences*, edited by Andrew Cunningham and Nicholas Jardine, Cambridge and New York: Cambridge University Press, 1990

Stauffer, Robert C., "Speculation and Experiment in the Background of Oersted's Discovery of Electromagnetism", *Isis*, 48 (1953): 33–50

Williams, L. Pearce, entry on *Ørsted* in *Dictionary of Scientific Biography*, edited by Charles Coulston Gillispie, vol. 10, New York: Scribner, 1974

No comprehensive biographical monograph on Hans Christian Ørsted has yet been written. Meanwhile, Kirstine MEYER's introduction to Ørsted's scientific writings, published on the occasion of the centenary of his famous discovery of electromagnetism in 1820, remains the best place to start. The contents of his scientific writings appear in the following order: electricity, electromagnetism, geology, chemistry, s ound, light, heat, compressibility, magnetism, mechanics, technology, natural philosophy, and teaching. Meyer attempts to normalize Ørsted's work, in the light of the positivist science prevalent in 1920, by downplaying the influence of speculative natural philosophy on his experimental endeavours. As a consequence, she separates the underlying Kantian and Romantic inspiration behind his hypothesis-making from his experimental activities as a natural philosopher, and denies that the latter was an outgrowth of the former. Meyer was writing at a time when philosophical considerations had been almost completely eradicated from scientific activity, and, instead of recognizing the stimulating effect of Kant's critical philosophy upon Romantic science, she quotes approvingly that "metaphysics ravaged science like a plague in the first years of the 19th century". This attempt at processing Ørsted in accordance with early 20th-century positivist views is supported further by the fact that Meyer edited only his scientific papers, and ignored his poetry and philosophical essays, and thus the persona was separated from his scientific enterprise. (See ØRSTED (1851–52), the first two volumes of which were translated into English and published separately as ØRSTED, 1852). Meyer's life of Ørsted – although valuable in its own right – therefore does not do justice to her subject.

ØRSTED (1870), edited by his daughter, contains letters in Danish to family and friends, including Adam Oehlenschläger, the Danish Romantic poet and playwright and Ørsted's brother-in-law. The HARDING supplement is a good companion to this volume, as it contains an almost complete collection of Ørsted's correspondence with scholars abroad, including Ritter, Berzelius, Davy, and Faraday.

Ørsted is known primarily by historians of science for his discovery of electromagnetism. DIBNER's monograph places Ørsted's discovery within a comprehensive narrative of the history of electrical science – preceded by Volta's pile and followed by Faraday's magnetoelectricity. Furthermore, Dibner relates these important discoveries to the wider technological developments associated with the telegraph and the electric motor.

Although STAUFFER generously acknowledges Meyer's sound and thorough analysis of the varied facets of Ørsted's scientific career, he finds that any speculation, no matter how fantastic, that leads to important experimental discovery deserves some notice, and ends up emphasizing "the significance of intellectual factors outside the realm of science as

potential influences upon the development of science". WILLIAMS goes even further, claiming that Ørsted's experiments were the direct result of his absorption in Kantian metaphysics. From this standpoint, metaphysics is even considered a prerequisite for the production of scientific knowledge.

KNUDSEN gives a detailed description of Ørsted's crucial experiment, and places his discovery of electromagnetism within the subsequent developments by Faraday and Maxwell. FRANKSEN demonstrates how Ørsted bridges the gap between the two intellectual realms of the sciences and the arts, and reprints a facsimile of his famous circular letter of July 1820, entitled: "Experimenta circa effecum conflictus electrici in acum magneticam". BILLESKOV JANSEN, SNORRASON & LAURITZ-JENSEN is a collection of essays examining Ørsted's life and accomplishments as physicist, chemist, and secretary of the Copenhagen Royal Academy of Sciences and Letters (1815–51), as well as his lack of competence as a mathematician. All essays are summarized in English.

SNELDERS endorses the view that Ørsted dissociated himself from Schelling's *Naturphilosophie*, and emphasizes the close friendship and collaboration with Ritter, including the latter's astrological prophesy that an outstanding discovery in the field of electricity was going to occur towards the end of 1819, or in the following year. Ritter died in 1810, but, "lo and behold Ørsted discovered in 1820 the effect of the electric 'conflict' upon the magnetic needle".

Arguing that the term *Naturphilosophie* defies attempts at definition and lacks analytical power, CHRISTENSEN shows that Ørsted joined Ritter in his contempt for Schelling's wild speculations, which were frequently based on the experiments of others. The partnership between Ritter and Ørsted was deeply rooted in original experimentation based upon Kantian epistemology, and the circumstances behind Ørsted's famous discovery appear to be adequately explained by the framework set up in Williams.

DAN CH. CHRISTENSEN

See also Denmark; Electromagnetism; Romanticism

Ostwald, Wilhelm   1853–1932

German physical chemist

Dunsch, Lothar, *Ein Fundament zum Gebäude der Wissenschaften: Einhundert Jahre Ostwalds Klassiker der exakten Wissenschaften (1889–1989)*, Leipzig: Geest & Portig, 1989

Hakfoort, Caspar, "Science Deified: Wilhelm Ostwald's Energeticist World-View and the History of Scientism", *Annals of Science*, 49 (1992): 525–44

Internationales Symposium anlässlich des 125: Geburtstages von Wilhelm Ostwald, Berlin: Akademie, 1979

Lotz, Günther et al., *Forschen und Nutzen: Wilhelm Ostwald zue wissenschaftlichen Arbeit. Aus seinen Schriften ausgewählt, bearbeitet und zusammengestellt anlässlich seines 125*, Berlin: Akademie, 1979; 2nd edition, 1982

Mittasch, Alwin, *Wilhelm Ostwalds Auflösungslehre*, Heidelberg: Springer, 1951

Niedersen, Uwe, " Energie, Glück und Autopoiese", *Selbstorganisation: Jahrbuch für Komplexität in den Natur-, Sozial, und Geisteswissenschaften*, 2 (1991): 245–69; "Leben, Wissenschaft Klassifikation – Aus dem Nachlass Wilhelm Ostwalds", 3 (1992): 279–308; "Ästhetik und Zeit. Wilhelm Ostwald über Kunst", 4 (1993): 251–95

Ostwald, Wilhelm, *Lebenslinien: Eine Selbstbiographie von Wilhelm Ostwald*, 3 vols, Berlin: Klasing, 1926–27

Rodnyj, N.I. and Ju.I. Solowjew, *Wilhelm Ostwald*, Leipzig: B.G. Teubner, 1977 (originally published in Russian 1969)

Servos, John W., *Physical Chemistry from Ostwald to Pauling: The Making of a Science in America*, Princeton, New Jersey: Princeton University Press, 1990

Walden, Paul, *Wilhelm Ostwald*, Leipzig: Engelmann, 1904

Wall, Florence E., "Wilhelm Ostwald: A Study in Mental Metamorphosis", in *Selected Readings in the History of Chemistry*, edited by Aaron J. Ihde and William F. Kieffer, Easton, Pennsylvania: American Chemical Society, 1965

Zott, Regine (ed.) *Wilhelm Ostwald und Paul Walden in ihren Briefen: Mit einem Begleittext: Paul Walden Wissenschaftler zwischen den Kulturen?* Berlin: ERS, 1994

Zott, Regine (ed.), *Wilhelm Ostwald und Walther Nernst in ihren Briefen sowie in denen einiger Zeitgenossen*, Berlin: Engel, 1996

Wilhelm Ostwald was a versatile scholar. He worked successfully in different areas such as physical chemistry (for which he received the Nobel prize in 1909), natural philosophy, history of science, science organization, and the theory of colours. He was also a very efficient teacher who helped place his students in academic positions throughout Europe. The literature on Ostwald consists of biographical studies, publications of his papers and manuscripts, and a few studies on specific aspects of his work.

OSTWALD's autobiography is a three-volume work. The first covers the period 1853 to 1887 when Ostwald lived in Riga and in Dorpat. The second covers his time in Leipzig from 1887 to 1905. The last volume deals with his post-academic life which he spent in his villa "Energie" and his travels until 1927. The autobiography is well written, accessible, and entertaining. Ostwald discusses his work, the people he encountered and the places in which he lived or visited. The structure is largely chronological but each chapter is devoted to a theme, such as the Electrochemical Society, energeticism, or universal languages.

RODNYJ & SOLOWJEW is one of the most comprehensive biographies, although it is not free from a certain dogmatic tendency. Written in the Soviet Union, the authors find Ostwald interesting because he was born and raised near Riga, and because he proclaimed himself an atheist and a pacifist. However, Rodnyj & Solowjew present a critical interpretation of Ostwald's life which they divide into three periods: the first is the "scientific" period, when he worked on electrochemistry and catalysis; the second is his "philosophical" period, when he developed a theory of energetics, anti-atomism, and natural philosophy; and the last is his "non-scientific" period, when he concerned himself with works of art, the establishment of a universal language, and the theory of colours.

Paul WALDEN, one of Ostwald's most successful students and a historian of chemistry, has written a biography, which covers the first period, from 1853 to 1887 when Ostwald moved from Riga to Leipzig. The author emphasizes Ostwald's role as an educator, displaying his loyalty to his former teacher.

In a brief but comprehensive biographical article WALL argues that Ostwald was able to see scientific problems in the larger context but not as distinct and simple tasks. As a result, he was a great inspiration ("catalyst") for the work of his students and colleagues. This, as opposed to a narrow specialism is the source of his success.

The INTERNATIONALES SYMPOSIUM is an East German collection of 20-odd, short essays on Ostwald's diverse activities. Several of them take their cue from Lenin's critique of Ostwald in *Materialism and Empirio-Criticism*. But not all: Dieter Hoffmann, for instance, analyzes K.W.F. Kohlrausch's attack on Ostwald's colour theory. He finds that most physicists and important institutions such as the Physikalisch-Technische Reichsanstalt (PTR) rejected it too.

MITTASCH was also one of Ostwald's students. In his monograph on Ostwald's concept of the initiation of chemical reactions, Mittasch discusses the implications of some central terms within the framework of Ostwald's natural philosophy – such as initiation (Auslösung) of a chemical reaction, energetics, and catalysis. Referring to an unpublished manuscript entitled "Julius Robert Mayer über Auslösung", written in 1914, he criticizes Ostwald for believing that catalysis only accelerates reactions and does not initiate them, because each thermodynamically possible reaction is always occurring albeit sometimes very slowly.

SERVOS has written a general history of physical chemistry, focusing mainly on American developments, within which Ostwald is presented as a pioneer. Servos points out that there are similarities between Ostwald and Pauling, in that they both aimed to unify within one theory all the chemical sub-disciplines.

HAKFOORT illustrates and discusses Ostwald's metaphysics in which everything can be explained in terms of energy and energy transformations, and further discusses how Ostwald considered science to be the modern and legitimate substitute for God: omniscient and perfectly good. Hakfoort is the only author who convincingly makes all of Ostwald's diverse activities appear as part of his larger conception of the world.

NIEDERSEN, in a journal devoted to a critique of the mechanistic world-view, is a selection of hitherto unpublished articles by Ostwald on the calculus of happiness, the cultural history of chemistry and aesthetics. Each publication is accompanied by a short essay, and many aspects of Ostwald's thought are expertly explained by Hakfoort.

DUNSCH is a celebration of *Ostwalds Klassiker*, the series of reprints of "classics" in the history of science that Ostwald initiated. It contains a biography of Ostwald, a publishing history based, because of scarce historical sources, primarily on correspondence, and a bibliography of the series. By 1989 the series contained 275 items, mostly papers from the 18th and 19th centuries.

LOTZ *et al* contains a large selection of Ostwald's papers in 11 categories such as "how to make discoveries", "how to do experiments", instrumentation, organization of scientific work, education, talent, and the history and future of science. The papers are sparsely footnoted and there is a short introduction.

ZOTT (1994) contains the correspondence between Ostwald and Walden in 205 pages. ZOTT (1996) contains that between Ostwald and Nernst in 230 pages. Both volumes are carefully edited with useful and brief footnotes.

ARNE HESSENBRUCH

P

Pain

Hodgkiss, Andrew, "Chronic Pain in Nineteenth-Century British Medical Writings", *History of Psychiatry*, 2 (1991): 27–40

Keele, Kenneth D., *Anatomies of Pain*, Oxford: Blackwell, and Springfield, Illinois: Thomas, 1957

Merskey, Harold and F.G. Spear, *Pain: Psychological and Psychiatric Aspects*, London: Baillière Tindall and Cassell, 1967

Morris, David B., "The Marquis de Sade and the Discourses of Pain: Literature and Medicine at the Revolution", in *The Languages of Psyche: Mind and Body in Enlightenment Thought*, edited by George Rousseau, Berkeley: University of California Press, 1990

Morris, David B., *The Culture of Pain*, Berkeley: University of California Press, 1991

Pernick, Martin S., *A Calculus of Suffering: Pain, Professionalism and Anaesthesia in Nineteenth-Century America*, New York: Columbia University Press, 1985

Rey, Roselyne, *History of Pain*, translated from the French by Louise Elliott Wallace, J.A. Cadden and S.W. Cadden, Cambridge, Massachusetts: Harvard University Press, 1995 (original edition, 1993)

Shorter, Edward, *From Paralysis to Fatigue: A History of Psychosomatic Illness in the Modern Era*, New York: Free Press, 1992

Until recently, pain has been a rather neglected topic in the history of science and medicine. Fortunately there is now growing interest, provoked by the appearance of specialised clinics devoted to pain in most first world countries, the foundation of the International Association for the Study of Pain in 1973, and a trend toward placing human corporeal experience more centrally within academic writing in the humanities.

Perhaps the most straightforward genre in the secondary literature is the history of medical ideas concerning the neuroanatomy and neurophysiology of pain. Two outstanding accounts are available in English, by Keele and Rey. KEELE's monograph is essentially organised around famous names in the history of pain, from antiquity to the mid-20th century. What this book misses in methodological sophistication is outweighed by the lucid summaries of the thought of these various authorities. One 40-page chapter, entitled "The Discovery of the Spinothalamic Tract", offers an exposition of the work by Charles Bell, François Magendie, Johannes Müller, Ernst Heinrich Weber, Gustav Fechner, Edouard Brown-Séquard, Schiff and William Gowers that remains an ideal starting point for any reader with an interest in 19th-century scientific writings on pain. However, virtually no context is provided within which to place these canonical experiments and authors.

REY's more recent and rather longer work, translated from the French, covers similar territory but with much more of an historian's eye, and is the most valuable work on the history of pain to date. In the introduction, a useful distinction is drawn between pain as an observable object of scientific enquiry and human suffering in a more general sense, often described through what she calls the "idioms of pain". Her book confines itself strictly to the former. Although more than 2,000 years are surveyed, the longest and strongest chapters are on the period from 1750 to 1950. Rey employs a range of historical methods, from analysis of the frequency with which different words for pain appear in Homer, Sophocles, and the Hippocratic Corpus, to a detailed conceptual history of "sensibility" in the 18th century. An effort is made to place the discoveries within their institutional and intellectual contexts, and there are inserts on religious attitudes to pain.

Rey advances several important arguments, each of which merits further research. She insists that the secularisation of pain was a prerequisite for its development into an object of scientific investigation; Protestantism, and a growing emphasis on individualism in the Renaissance, are credited with loosening the links between pain and original sin and the passion of Christ. It is suggested that the semiology of pain remained essentially Galenic until pathological anatomy placed special emphasis on spatial localisation, rather than on, say, the quality of the pain. Rey blames the separation of experimental physiology from clinical practice in 19th-century France for a loss of interest in psychological determinants of pain, such as mood and memory, in favour of the reductionist notion of a "pain pathway".

PERNICK examines medical practice, rather than elite theory, using quantitative methods in the service of social history, and discovers that only some patients were offered anaesthetics for surgery in North America in the period 1846–80, despite the fact that the techniques were widely available. The judgements made by physicians regarding the sensitivity to pain of women and men, young and old, black and white, are outlined. Pernick argues that tailoring the dose of anaesthetic according to the individual characteristics of the patient set the doctor apart from the quack with his "specifics". Thus what looks to us like rank prejudice once defined medical professionalism.

MORRIS (1991) cuts across the disciplinary boundaries between literary criticism, medical history, and contemporary medical practice to produce chapters on pain words, hysterical pain, visionary pain, pain and comedy, and tragedy and beauty. The chapter on de Sade is the most impressive, an expanded version of which can be found in MORRIS (1990). De Sade's literary treatment of pain is depicted as more than an appropriation of Enlightenment medical vocabulary, because a "transvaluation" of late 18th-century medical knowledge was at stake. There is something striking in the observation that de Sade wrote as the Parisian clinical method was born – a method in which, as Michel Foucault has argued, pain was reduced to a marker of tissue lesion for the medical gaze.

Lesion-less pain has been regarded as problematic since 1800. Three texts are useful on the history of such pain, often dubbed "hysterical", "psychogenic", or "somatised". MERSKEY & SPEAR, in an argument similar to Rey's, claim that pain psychology became neglected with the rise of neurophysiological knowledge in the 19th century. SHORTER, in a more recent book full of original source materials, surveys somatised symptomatology in the period 1800–1920, and concludes that motor symptoms were common in the mid-19th century, while sensory symptoms, such as lesion-less pain, came to the fore later. Shorter suggests that such somatised symptoms are socially constructed via the unconscious: thus, hysterical women stopped presenting a difficulty after 1900, because the sociocultural position of women changed and bedside neurological examination could distinguish hysterical motor symptoms from organic symptoms. HODGKISS takes issue with much of Shorter's methodology and many of his conclusions. He suggests that pain has been the most prevalent, and simultaneously the most theoretically problematic, lesion-less complaint since 1800, and that it is this historical invariance that demands explanation. The terminology and theorisation of lesionless pain in the 19th century is surveyed in detail, without post-Freudian assumptions, and the history of this type of pain is shown to be central to the development of the concept of neurosis.

ANDREW HODGKISS

See also Anatomy; Experimental Physiology; Neurosciences

Paleontology

Bowler, Peter J., *Fossils and Progress: Paleontology and the Idea of Progressive Evolution in the Nineteenth Century*, New York: Science History Publications, 1976

Bowler, Peter J., *Life's Splendid Drama: Evolutionary Biology and the Reconstruction of Life's Ancestry, 1860–1940*, Chicago: University of Chicago Press, 1996

Buffetaut, Eric, *A Short History of Vertebrate Paleontology*, London: Croom Helm, 1986

Desmond, Adrian, *The Hot-Blooded Dinosaurs: A Revolution in Paleontology*, London: Blond and Briggs, and New York: Dial Press, 1976

Desmond, Adrian, *Archetypes and Ancestors: Palaeontology in Victorian London, 1850–1875*, London: Blond and Briggs, 1982; Chicago: University of Chicago Press, 1984

Rainger, Ronald, *An Agenda for Antiquity: Henry Fairfield Osborn and Vertebrate Paleontology at the American Museum of Natural History, 1890–1935*, Tuscaloosa: University of Alabama Press, 1991

Rudwick, Martin J.S., *The Meaning of Fossils: Episodes in the History of Paleontology*, London: Macdonald, and New York: American Elsevier, 1972; revised edition, New York: Science History Publications, 1976

Rudwick, Martin J.S., *The Great Devonian Controversy: The Shaping of Scientific Knowledge among Gentlemanly Specialists*, Chicago: University of Chicago Press, 1985

There are many popular surveys of great fossil discoveries, but the works cited here take a more sophisticated approach, exploring how our understanding of the significance of fossils has changed through time. Recognizing that fossils are the remains of long-extinct organisms that can be used to reconstruct the history of life on earth required a number of conceptual innovations that spanned the 17th and 18th centuries. Moreover, once the prospect of a historical account of life's development was acknowledged, paleontologists continued to disagree over the nature of the process displayed by the fossil record.

RUDWICK (1972) charts these conceptual revolutions up to the early stages of evolutionary paleontology. He stresses that many 17th-century naturalists refused to accept that fossils were a clue to past forms of life, because they saw them as mere structures in the rock that might have been produced by other, non-organic, causes. Robert Hooke and Nicholas Steno pioneered the modern view, that fossils are the remains of animals and plants that have become mineralized in sedimentary rocks. They were immediately confronted by the prospect that – since many fossils do not correspond to known forms of life – species alive in the distant past must have become extinct. Many naturalists at first rejected extinction as incompatible with the Creator's wisdom and benevolence, and the fact of extinction was only established conclusively when Georges Cuvier reconstructed the remains of many vertebrate fossils around 1800. Comparative anatomy could now be used as a tool, both to identify the kind of animal from which a particular fossil bone had come, and to produce spectacular restorations of extinct animals that would become centerpieces in many natural history museums. Rudwick explores Cuvier's bold decision to erect a new science dealing with the history of life on earth.

A vital step in this process was a recognition of the fact that there was not a single extinct population, but a series of them defining a historical sequence of geological formations. Fossils, especially invertebrate fossils, thus became a prime tool for stratigraphy – the identification of strata and their correct positioning in the sequence. Establishing the modern stratigraphical column was a complex process, and RUDWICK (1985) uses a single example to illustrate how geologists negotiated a broadly acceptable interpretation of a particularly difficult collection of strata. Consensus over the stratigraphical role of fossils in general, and over the significance of particular episodes in the earth's history, was a product of much social activity among early 19th-century specialists.

Rudwick's broader survey also charts changing ideas through the 19th century concerning the pattern of development in the history of life, as revealed by the record. He links Charles Lyell's uniformitarian geology to his belief in a steady-state earth, which denied any cumulative change in the history of life. BOWLER (1976) focuses on the emergence of the more popular theory that living things have become more complex in the course of geological time, stressing that there were rival interpretations of the significance of progress and the exact structure of the divine plan of creation, even before the emergence of evolutionism.

DESMOND (1982) takes a detailed look at a series of debates centered on the advent of Darwinism, and argues that the interpretation of particular fossils was shaped by a naturalist's position within the wider debates. Thus Richard Owen's early reconstructions of dinosaurs were tailored to fit his anti-evolutionary position, allowing him to emphasize the discontinuity of the ascent of life. Desmond's work remains controversial, however, because other historians feel that he has exaggerated the role of social pressures in his interpretations of the factual evidence.

The later history of paleontology is only gradually being surveyed by professional historians. BUFFETAUT's general history is useful in this area, as it provides at least an overview of some evolutionary debates centered on fossils, and notes the role of Western imperialism in generating a wider geographical basis for paleontological knowledge. DESMOND (1976), which supports the modern claim that the dinosaurs were hot-blooded, is worth mentioning because of the wealth of historical background it offers to the different interpretations of dinosaur fossils.

RAINGER offers a detailed account of a particular episode in early 20th-century American paleontology. Henry Fairfield Osborn created an influential research-group studying vertebrate fossils at the American Museum of Natural History, exploiting his social connections with wealthy capitalists to obtain funds. Rainger analyzes Osborn's own anti-Darwinian version of evolutionism, based on his analysis of fossil sequences, and notes the increasingly pro-Darwinian stance adopted by Osborn's subordinates, William King Gregory and William Diller Matthew. BOWLER (1996) offers an overview of evolutionary debates, showing how paleontology took over from morphology as the chief source of evidence for reconstructing ancestries. He generalizes Rainger's analysis of Gregory's and Matthew's work, and argues that the greater availability of geographically-diverse evidence, coupled with geologists' increased ability to reconstruct past environments, transformed early 20th-century paleontology in a way that anticipated some of the insights of modern Darwinism.

PETER J. BOWLER

See also Darwinism; Evolution; Geology; Prehistory: archaeology and anthropology

Paracelsus   1493–1541

German alchemist and physician

Debus, Allen G., *The English Paracelsians*, London: Oldbourne, 1965; New York: Franklin Watts, 1966

Debus, Allen G., *The French Paracelsians: The Chemical Challenge to Medical and Scientific Tradition in Early Modern France*, Cambridge and New York: Cambridge University Press, 1991

Goodrick-Clarke, Nicholas, *Paracelsus*, Wellingborough, Northamptonshire: Crucible, 1990

Jacobi, Yolande (ed.), *Selected Writings*, translated from the German by Nornert Guterman, London: Routledge and Kegan Paul, and New York: Pantheon, 1951; revised edition, Princeton, New Jersey: Princeton University Press, 1969 (original edition, 1948)

Jung, Carl Gustav, "Paracelsus as a Spiritual Phenomenon", in his *Collected Works*, vol. 13, *Alchemical Studies*, translated from the German by R.F.C. Hull, Princeton, New Jersey: Princeton University Press, 2nd edition, 1969; London: Routledge and Kegan Paul, 1973

Pagel, Walter, *Paracelsus: An Introduction to Philosophical Medicine in the Era of the Renaissance*, New York: Karger, 1958; revised edition, 1982

Trevor-Roper, Hugh, "The Court Physician and Paracelsianisn", in *Medicine at the Courts of Europe, 1500–1837*, edited by Vivian Nutton, London and New York: Routledge, 1990

Webster, Charles, *From Paracelsus to Newton: Magic and the Making of Modern Science*, Cambridge and New York: Cambridge University Press, 1982

Webster, Charles, "Paracelsus, and 500 Years of Encouraging Scientific Enquiry", *British Medical Journal*, 306 (6 March 1993): 597 ff.

Most studies of Paracelsus open with an overview of his life, which serves as an introduction to a broader discussion of his work, generally emphasising those aspects of his heterodox philosophy that were informed by his dissenting and difficult personality.

An old but indispensable study is PAGEL, in which the multi-faceted nature of Paracelsus' medical doctrines and personality are examined within the Renaissance context. What Pagel terms the "interdependence and fusion of the scientific and non-scientific elements" provides the focus for an identification of the sources of influence in Paracelsus's work, as contemporary commentaries emphasise the problematical nature of Paracelsian medical doctrine, and demonstrate its mixed reception. The final section, entitled "Was Paracelsus a Scientist?", remains apposite for all students of the history of science and medicine, addressing the problem of reconciling the integral occult and mystical elements within the Paracelsian world-view with what are seen as his otherwise (proto) scientific medical doctrines.

An author who sees Paracelsus, not as a harbinger of the scientific revolution, but as the progenitor of modern-day alternative medical therapy – and therefore of topical interest – is GOODRICK-CLARKE. Selecting material that emphasises his view of Paracelsus as a holistic healer with occultist leanings,

Goodrick-Clarke's anthology offers a well-defined and contextualised introduction to the often difficult Paracelsian medicophilosophical terminology. Although the familiar themes of Paracelsus's heterodoxy are presented in a clear and accessible manner, it is necessary to bear in mind that organising the diffuse, confusing, and often contradictory Paracelsian corpus with a view to promoting a particular interpretation may invest the texts, perhaps unavoidably, with a sequential coherence that they do not in fact possess.

This is also true of JACOBI's older anthology (1951), which shares with Goodrick-Clarke the problem of otherwise useful chapter headings or subsections, which, because of the obvious need for organisation, may nevertheless mislead the reader into believing such topics as "alchemy", "magic", "religion", and "medicine" to be discrete categories in the Paracelsian worldview. In fact, as Pagel shows, they are subject to significant integration. It is necessary to Jacobi's view of Paracelsus as a divinely-inspired genius, working in "a free cosmos obedient only to his law, and ultimately subject only to the commandments of God", that she tidies up his infamously chaotic personality, attributing his less attractive qualities merely to "rumour" and "legend". Both this and the Goodrick-Clarke anthology include useful bibliographies, and are valuable as starting points or for reference.

Placing Paracelsus firmly within the scientific revolution, the collection of essays in WEBSTER (1982) represents a determination to remove the "wedge driven between the cultures of Paracelsus and Newton", and they are important for an appreciation of the wider framework within which Paracelsus worked, and within which his philosophy was received and developed. The essays provide a sense of continuity, rather than the more usual discontinuity, between the "magic" of Paracelsus and the "science" of Newton, and each draws upon issues of vital and continuing significance to both ages: prophecy, and spiritual and demonic magic. The theme of continuity is pursued, for the benefit of a readership of 20th-century physicians, in WEBSTER (1993), a short article written to mark the 500th anniversary of Paracelsus's birth. Webster suggests that his place in the encouragement of "scientific enquiry" may be understood as integral to "a new spirit of investigation", which inspired such figures as Francis Bacon, Thomas Boyle, Thomas Sydenham, and Thomas Willis, and the founders of the Royal Society. Moreover, he suggests that modern medicine may be the poorer for having "failed to capture Paracelsus's sensitivity" to the "environmental, social, spiritual, and moral dimensions of health".

Those who wish to explore more fully the reception and repercussions of the challenge posed by Paracelsus to traditional medical authority will be interested in Debus's large output on the subject. In particular, two studies place his teachings within contrasting contexts, the English and the French. DEBUS (1966) illustrates both the kinds of transmutation that Paracelsus's work and philosophy underwent, and the compromises needed to cleanse his medicine of its many mystical aspects before iatrochemistry (the use of chemical remedies) could be introduced into medical practice. DEBUS (1991) covers a period when medical practitioners were obliged to redefine explanations of disease and cure in chemical or mechanical terms. The debate centres on the response of the Medical Faculty of Paris, "one of the great European bastions of Galenism", and on the careers of the French iatrochemists.

The opinion, supported by many historians of science, that Paracelsus was responsible for no less than the "insertion of chemistry into medicine" is held by TREVOR-ROPER, who explains the success of this development in terms of the role of European princely patronage – a source of vital support in an age pre-dating research institutions, and fractured by religious tensions. Trevor-Roper describes how such obstacles might be circumvented or overcome in the courts, where princely support presented a powerful challenge to rival sources of authority.

Laying claims for Paracelsus as a "pioneer not only of chemical medicine but of empirical psychology", JUNG sees alchemy as representing a pathway, leading from the transformation and purification of the materials used by the alchemist to the transformation and purification of the alchemist himself: the search for a higher truth, both physical and spiritual, through a process of separation and rejection of the pure from the impure. Although probably difficult reading for those with little or no prior knowledge of Jungian psychology, it may nevertheless strike a chord with those for whom holism possesses both a Paracelsian and a modern resonance.

In addition, it should be noted that there exists a wealth of German scholarship on Paracelsus, such as that by Kurt Goldammer, which this author is not competent to review.

FRANCES DAWBARN

See also Alchemy; Occult Sciences; Scientific Revolution

Paradigm

Barnes, Barry, *T.S. Kuhn and Social Science*, London: Macmillan, and New York: Columbia University Press, 1982

De Mey, Marc, *The Cognitive Paradigm: An Integrated Understanding of Scientific Development*, Dordrecht and Boston: Reidel, 1982; 2nd edition Chicago: University of Chicago Press, 1992

Fleck, Ludwik, *Genesis and Development of a Scientific Fact*, edited by Thaddeus J. Trenn and Robert K. Merton, translated from the German by Fred Bradley and Thaddeus J. Trenn, Chicago: University of Chicago Press, 1979 (original edition, 1935)

Gutting, Gary (ed.), *Paradigms and Revolutions: Appraisals and Applications of Thomas Kuhn's Philosophy of Science*, Notre Dame, Indiana: University of Notre Dame Press, 1980

Hoyningen-Huene, Paul, *Reconstructing Scientific Revolutions: Thomas S. Kuhn's Philosophy of Science*, translated by Alexander T. Levine, Chicago: University of Chicago Press, 1993

Kitcher, Philip, *The Advancement of Science: Science Without Legend, Objectivity Without Illusions*, Oxford and New York: Oxford University Press, 1993

Kuhn, Thomas S., *The Copernican Revolution: Planetary Astronomy in the Development of Western Thought*, Cambridge, Massachusetts: Harvard University Press, 1957

Kuhn, Thomas S., *The Structure of Scientific Revolutions*, Chicago: University of Chicago Press, 1962; revised edition, 1970

Kuhn, Thomas S., *The Essential Tension: Selected Studies in Scientific Tradition and Change*, Chicago: University of Chicago Press, 1977

Lakatos, Imre, "Falsification and the Methodology of Scientific Research Programs", in *Criticism and the Growth of Knowledge*, edited by Lakatos and Alan Musgrave, Cambridge: Cambridge University Press, 1970

Laudan, Larry, *Science and Values: The Aims of Science and Their Role in Scientific Debate*, Berkeley: University of California Press, 1984

Margolis, Howard, *Paradigms & Barriers: How Habits of Mind Govern Scientific Beliefs*, Chicago: University of Chicago Press, 1993

Masterman, Margaret, "The Nature of a Paradigm", in *Criticism and the Growth of Knowledge*, edited by Imre Lakatos and Alan Musgrave, Cambridge: Cambridge University Press, 1970

Polanyi, Michael, *Personal Knowledge: Towards a Post-Critical Philosophy*, Chicago: University of Chicago Press, and London: Routledge and Kegan Paul, 1958

Shapere, Dudley, "The Structure of Scientific Revolutions", *Philosophical Review*, 63 (1964); reprinted in Gutting (1980)

For the purposes of this essay the literature directly relevant to the concept of paradigm will be sorted into four groups, concerning: (i) an analysis of the concept; (ii) its applications in historiography and the sociology of science; (iii) its use or applications in cognitive science; and (iv) its use in thought regarding science prior to its starring role in Kuhn (1962). The abundance of literature on paradigm means that only the most prominent works can be mentioned, and that some aspects (e.g. discussions dedicated to incommensurability, and identifications of current paradigms in the sciences) must be omitted.

KUHN (1962) is the locus of the paradigm literature, and a comprehensive bibliography of the topic would create a virtual subset of work on Kuhn's thought. In this work, paradigms are defined as "universally recognized scientific achievements that for a time provide model problems and solutions to a community of practitioners". As conceptually prior to (and extending beyond) the explicit rules, formulae, or methods that might be used to express them, paradigms take on the central role in Kuhn's theory of the structure of science. Acceptance of a paradigm in part delineates a scientific community, and the community's "normal science" is informed and directed by this paradigm – a process Kuhn likened to puzzle-solving. The priority of paradigms, their broad character (Kuhn described them as world-views), and the claim that a scientific revolution was the change of paradigms, led Kuhn to identify "revolutionary" science, which he compared to a Gestalt change or "conversion experience", and contrasted with the received view of scientific change as an accumulation. Kuhn's alleged relativism has since loomed in most discussion of paradigms.

Reactions to Kuhn (1962) were spirited, and concerned mainly with analysis of the concept and its consequences. MASTERMAN, a sympathetic critic writing from a scientific perspective, argued that Kuhn had used "paradigm" in 21 different senses, although these could be reduced to three classes: metaphysical, sociological, and artifact/construct paradigms. SHAPERE found "paradigm" in Kuhn's hands to be at once vague, general, mysterious, and misleading, and argued that on these grounds there perhaps was no such thing. LAKATOS rejected Kuhn's conclusion as "mob psychology", but retained aspects of Kuhnian paradigms in the "negative" and "positive" heuristics of his own account of science.

Responding to such criticisms in a postscript to the second edition of his work in 1970, Kuhn distinguished two senses of paradigm, renamed each, and has subsequently avoided the term altogether (see KUHN 1977). One sense – the "disciplinary matrix" – captures the range of ontological commitments and values shared by a scientific group, and amounts to a metaphysical view. "Exemplar" captures the second sense of paradigm, and refers to the solution schemata learned in the course of disciplinary scientific training. This clarification of the paradigm idea has found acceptance among many (including Kuhn's leading expositor, HOYNINGEN-HUENE), perhaps in part because the reformulations were accompanied by a tempering of the perceived relativism. LAUDAN, for example, has adopted this revision within an anti-relativist account of scientific change, arguing that an appreciation of scientific change requires taking Kuhnian paradigms (Laudan retains Kuhn's earlier term) as mixtures of theories, methods, and goals, but not as the "inextricable mix" Kuhn had described. So conceived, paradigm change can be piecemeal and, argues Laudan, rational. Similarly, KITCHER adopts elements of Kuhnian paradigms in his study of the advancement of science, although he emphasizes the continuity across changes in consensus practice. Both argue that a finer delineation of the features of science identified by Kuhn provides for an account of science as the rational growth of knowledge.

The concepts of a "disciplinary matrix" and an "exemplar" have also informed discussions of scientific paradigms within the social and cognitive sciences respectively. To the extent that the disciplinary matrix was taken to show that scientific change was beyond the reach of rational choice (because different matrices embodied different standards), the concept of a disciplinary matrix helped bring forth post-Mertonian sociologies of science like the Strong Programme, which regarded the content of science to be amenable to sociological study. For BARNES, for example, the disciplinary matrix idea supports a principle of symmetry in the explanation of scientific change: beliefs held to be true by our culture are to receive the same kind of explanation as beliefs that are held to be false. Hence, the sociology of science must address scientific content, not just its institutional trappings.

The significance of paradigms (or disciplinary matrices) within the social sciences does not depend on their relativism. For many, such as GUTTING, the interest of the concept lies in its placing of the locus of scientific authority within the scientific community, rather than with the individual or transcendent rules of method. The epistemological significance of the scientific community is a topic of much current research.

As Kuhn's disciplinary matrices have informed discussion in the social sciences, exemplars have had a role in cognitive science-based studies of science. The writings of Margolis and

De Mey are two notable attempts to incorporate this sense of paradigm into cognitive science. De MEY finds in Kuhn's notion of paradigm the starting point for a genuinely scientific science of science, while MARGOLIS takes "habits of mind" to be constitutive of paradigms. Like examinations of scientific communities, the formulation of paradigms as objects of study in cognitive science is also the topic of much current research.

Study of the paradigm concept easily leaves the mistaken impression that its origins lie with Kuhn. As one would suspect, and as Kuhn emphasized, his articulation of the concept had roots – for example, in the thought of the German physician FLECK, and the philosopher/psychologist POLANYI. In 1935, Fleck published an account of the development of the Wassermann reaction, which depended on the notion of a *Denkkollektiv* (usually rendered "thought collective"). A further source is KUHN (1957), which features what Kuhn called "conceptual schemes", which share many features with Kuhn's paradigms of 1962. Thus, although the discussion of paradigms since 1962 has been enormously rich and fruitful, the history of the concept before 1962 should not be neglected.

GARY L. HARDCASTLE

See also Sociology of Science

Particle Physics

Brown, Laurie M. and Lillian Hoddeson (eds), *The Birth of Particle Physics*, Cambridge and New York: Cambridge University Press, 1983

Brown, Laurie M., Max Dresden and Lillian Hoddeson (eds), *Pions to Quarks: Particle Physics in the 1950s*, Cambridge and New York: Cambridge University Press, 1989

De Maria, Michelangelo, Mario Grilli and Fabio Sebastiani (eds), *The Restructuring of Physical Sciences in Europe and the United States, 1945–1960*, Singapore and Teaneck, New Jersey: World Scientific, 1989

De Maria, M., M.G. Ianniello and A. Russo, "The Discovery of Cosmic Rays: Rivalries and Controversies between Europe and the United States", *Historical Studies in the Physical and Biological Sciences*, 22 (1991): 165–92

Galison, Peter L., *How Experiments End*, Chicago: University of Chicago Press, 1987

Galison, Peter L., *Image and Logic: A Material Culture of Microphysics*, Chicago: University of Chicago Press, 1997

Habfast, Claus, *Grossforschung mit kleinen Teilchen: DESY, 1956–1970*, Berlin: Springer, 1989

Heilbron, J.L. and Robert W. Seidel, *Lawrence and His Laboratory: A History of the Lawrence Berkeley Laboratory*, vol. 1, Berkeley: University of California Press, 1989

Hermann, Armin *et al.*, *History of CERN*, 3 vols, Amsterdam: North-Holland, 1987–96

Pickering, Andrew, *Constructing Quarks: A Sociological History of Particle Physics*, Edinburgh: Edinburgh University Press, and Chicago: University of Chicago Press, 1984

Pinch, Trevor, *Confronting Nature: The Sociology of Solar-Neutrino Detection*, Dordrecht and Boston: Reidel, 1986

Polkinghorne, John, *Rochester Roundabout: The Story of High Energy Physics*, New York: W.H. Freeman and Harlow, Essex: Longman, 1989

Schweber, Samuel S., "Some Reflections on Big Science and High Energy Physics in the United States", *Rivista di Storia della Scienza*, new series 2, (1994): 127–89

Traweek, Sharon, *Beamtimes and Lifetimes: The World of High Energy Physicists*, Cambridge, Massachusetts: Harvard University Press, 1988

Particle physics – or high energy physics, as the field is also known due to particle acceleration at high energies – has been the flagship of physics, and perhaps even of science, since World War II, and has also been an important issue of national prestige in the countries involved. It is therefore not surprising that its history has been of interest to both physicists and historians of science. The variety of approaches mirrors the many facets of this field, as well as different currents in science studies.

The review begins with a discussion of the historiographical literature in which the involvement of physicists plays a dominant role. The substantial volumes edited by BROWN & HODDESON and BROWN, DRESDEN & HODDESON both arose from symposia that brought together physicists and historians. Brown & Hoddeson deals mainly with cosmic ray physics and quantum electrodynamics, which are perceived as the roots of particle physics, while Brown, Dresden & Hoddeson examines the further development up to 1960. In the earlier collection, the articles (or talks) are almost exclusively by physicists, as the historians participated only in several round-table discussions, which are meticulously reported. This volume might therefore be considered a source rather than a study of the history of particle physics. There is presently no comprehensive study on cosmic ray physics. The article by DE MARIA, IANNIELLO & RUSSO, which deals with priority claims for the discovery of cosmic rays, is cited mainly as one of several smaller studies, several of which have been undertaken by the same authors.

In comparison to the first volume, Brown, Dresden & Hoddeson is more balanced, containing contributions by both historians and physicists on the development of the discipline in the 1950s. This period marks the transition from cosmic ray-dominated physics to particle physics, dominated by ever-growing accelerators and their laboratories. The importance of this new site is acknowledged by the 10 out of 47 articles dealing with "the new laboratory". The combination of accounts by both physicists and historians yields many exciting insights, both in this collection and that of DE MARIA, GRILLI & SEBASTIANI. Although the essays in the latter's collection deal with physics in general, particle physics is the subject of 25 of the 40 contributions – a result of the strong Italian commitment (both in physics and its historiography) to particle physics. The Italian collection covers roughly the same period as Brown, Dresden & Hoddeson, but it pays more attention to the impact of World War II on the development of particle physics. Many prominent physicists and historians contributed to both these works, and they can be usefully read as complementary volumes. As for the discovery of the antiproton, the books contain conflicting personal accounts – by Chamberlain and Piccioni in Brown, Dresden & Hoddeson, and a historical analysis of the subject by Heilbron in De Maria, Grilli & Sebastiani.

The theoretical high-energy physicist POLKINGHORNE recounts the history of his discipline by reviewing the series of Rochester Conferences between 1950 and 1980, which were (and still are) the most important conferences on the field. His factual account is interwoven with personal recollections and anecdotes, yet it still requires some basic understanding of the subject. The last 20 pages are devoted to a philosophical evaluation, in which Polkinghorne explains his adherence to "scientific realism".

Considering the importance of large laboratories for particle physics, it is no surprise that the history of several of them has been documented. HERMANN *et al* is the most comprehensive so far and deals with the complex history of the European laboratory CERN, whose status as an international laboratory has made it subject to extensive national and international political negotiations. Volume 1 mainly deals with these aspects, while volume 2 concentrates on the actual process of research. In contrast, HEILBRON & SEIDEL and HABFAST narrate the stories of two national laboratories. The former centers on the person of Ernest Orlando Lawrence, the founder and director of the Lawrence Berkeley Laboratory, and draws a vivid picture of both the internal and external aspects of nuclear and particle research up to World War II. Habfast, on the other hand, is mainly concerned with the political and administrative factors affecting the beginnings of the West German facility DESY, and deals only briefly with the cognitive issues. Both studies cover only the beginnings of their respective institutions, and sequels are to be expected.

The history of particle physics has also been the object of thrilling case studies, from the sociological point of view. Both Pinch and Pickering argue for a constructivistic position, which claims that scientific results are the process of social negotiations rather than nature's voice. PINCH examines a long-standing (and still open) controversy concerning the flux of neutrinos from the sun to the earth (i.e. an issue of non-accelerator particle physics as well as astrophysics). PICKERING, on the other hand, is concerned with the central developments of the discipline, especially the emergence of the quark concept and the unification theories. Both authors pay much attention to social dynamics within the scientific community, and provide fine-grained analyses of the genesis of theories and experiments, and of the competing interpretations of the latter. Thus, even for those who do not agree with the philosophical agenda of constructivism, both Pickering and Pinch are valuable reading.

TRAWEEK is a study from an anthropological viewpoint, and thus the most exotic among those reviewed here. The author describes the sites, artefacts, everyday life, dreams, etc. of high-energy physicists whom she has accompanied in a field study. Her study is perceptive in many details, and is also the sole work to pay attention to such issues as gender and culture.

In history, as well as in the sociology of science, in recent years the concept of "practice" – i.e. what scientists actually do (and not what they claim to do) in their day-to-day work – has become an important issue. GALISON (1987) takes this perspective in his analysis of how experiments end – i.e. how agreement is reached on the validity and meaning of a certain experiment. Although particle physics is not the central theme of his book, two of his three comprehensive case studies

(up to 100 pages long) are taken from this field: the discoveries of the muon and the weak neutral currents, and the controversies surrounding them. His book is also a thorough study of the relationship between theory and experiment. GALISON (1997) is an insightful history of material culture in 20th-century physics, ranging from Monte Carlo simulation to the architecture of institutes of physics.

Apart from Galison (1997), all the studies mentioned were written during the heyday of particle physics. The situation, however, has changed dramatically since the mid-1980s, and has given way to a general feeling of crisis among particle physicists. SCHWEBER gives not only a concise sketch of the connections between the political situation and the state of particle physics research (for example, military funding was forthcoming for a long while in the hope of some strategic spin-off), but also tries to assess new roles for the once mighty and now struggling discipline.

BEATE CERANSKI

See also Big Science; CERN; Physics: 20th Century; Solid State Physics

Pasteur, Louis 1822–1895

French chemist and bacteriologist

Balibar, Françoise and Marie-Laure Prévost (eds), *Pasteur: cahiers d'un savant*, Paris: CNRS, 1995

Cadeddu, Antonio, *Dal mito alla storia: biologia e medicina in Pasteur*, Milan: Francoangeli, 1991

Dagognet, François, *Méthodes et doctrines dans l'oeuvre de Pasteur*, Presses Universitaires de France, 1967

Debré, Patrice, *Louis Pasteur*, translated from the French by Elborg Forster, Baltimore, Johns Hopkins University Press, 1998 (original edition, 1995)

Dubos, René J., *Louis Pasteur: Free Lance of Science*, Boston: Little Brown, 1950; London: Gollancz, 1951

Geison, Gerald L., entry on Pasteur in *Dictionary of Scientific Biography*, edited by Charles Coulston Gillispie, vol. 10, New York: Scribner, 1974

Geison, Gerald L., *The Private Science of Louis Pasteur*, Princeton, New Jersey: Princeton University Press, 1995

Latour, Bruno, *The Pasteurization of France*, translated from the French by Alan Sheridan and John Law, Cambridge, Massachusetts: Harvard University Press, 1988 (original edition, 1984)

Latour, Bruno, *Pasteur: Une Science, un style, un siècle*, Paris: Perrin, 1994

Loir, Adrien, *A l'Ombre de Pasteur: le mouvement sanitaire*, Paris, 1938

Salomon-Bayet, Claire (ed.), *Pasteur et la révolution pastorienne*, Paris: Payot, 1986

Vallery-Radot, René, *The Life of Pasteur*, translated from the French by Mrs R.L. Devonshire, London: Constable, 1902; New York: McClure Phillips, 1906 (original edition, 1900)

Louis Pasteur's career has inspired numerous scholarly and popular accounts of his life and work. The diversity of perspectives to be found in these works reveals the methodological evolution, and the existence of national styles, within the history of science itself. Each study mentioned speaks to different audiences and considers a different subject, and, therefore, the reader interested in studying Pasteur is advised to select one book from each of two or three of the categories discussed below.

Within the category of general biography fall the studies by René Vallery-Radot, Adrien Loir, and Patrice Debré. VALLERY-RADOT (Pasteur's son-in-law) whose biography was in fact supervised by Pasteur himself, provides us with the standard starting reference on Pasteur. Accordingly, the author conveys not only information about Pasteur's life, but also something of the "mystique" of the early Pastorian school. LOIR's biography, too, was written by a witness, Pasteur's own nephew and assistant in the laboratory. This work, completed some 30 years after Pasteur's death, is, however, a slightly ironic collection of reminiscences that serves, when one can find it, to temper the exclusively laudatory tone of Vallery-Radot's account.

A second generation of biographical accounts includes school textbooks that served to consolidate Pasteur's status as a cultural icon. DUBOS's comprehensive biography stands somewhat as an exception. Written by a French-born bacteriologist who migrated to the Rockefeller Institute in the US between the two world wars, the book, a best-seller in his time, revealed the importance of the scientific context within which Pasteur's work evolved, and provided some clues to the genesis of his work on contagion and infection, virulence and vaccination.

DEBRÉ's recent biography draws on the two familial biographies and a re-reading of Pasteur's scientific work and bibliography, in order to present a synthetic view of the great man's life and work. The book embodies the argument for the marriage of medicine and scientific research, arguing that we remain in the Pastorian conceptual framework, which will continue to provide solutions for medical problems into the 21st century. In all, it is a modern introduction to Pasteur that also acts as a traditional monument to the Pastorian revolution.

Two books in particular shed light on Pasteur's scientific and intellectual career, Dagognet taking an epistemological approach, Latour a sociological one. Though strikingly different in their methodologies, both works are masterpieces of French scholarship, their portraits ultimately converging to provide a coherent image of Pasteur.

DAGOGNET has analysed Pasteur's thought as a philosophical system, identifying his postulates and type of logic. His thesis is that Pasteur devised an approach to biological functions that linked chemistry and medicine, and that this approach has formed the basis of current thinking on the scientific study of life. It is Dagognet's contention that Pasteur articulated his epistemological framework within the realm of chemistry and biology (fermentations) and subsequently applied it to medicine. Yet, in arguing for Pasteur's pre-medical articulation of his thought-system, Dagognet ends his own analysis by suggesting how this application worked in the study of diseases, without coming to grips with the germ theory. Within Pasteur's systematic philosophy, however, Dagognet noted an important element: flexibility. The man who applied the same conceptual framework to each of his general research

topics was able to adapt each application to the specificities of the subject, and to the vagaries of experimentation. In this way, he successfully mitigated absolute principles by consideration of real experimental conditions. Ultimately, Dagognet argues that Pasteur's program is defined both by absolute dogmas (i.e. germ specificity) and a flexible approach to applying these dogmas in research (i.e. germ attenuation and vaccine production).

The sociologically-oriented Latour, on the other hand, set out to question the traditional French assumption that Pasteur had transformed society, by attending to the real actors in this transformation. Relying on only three journals for evidence, LATOUR (1984) illustrates how doctors became scientists – or, more derisively, how they became the ventriloquists of microbes. The laboratory was at the centre of this shift in identity and, as such, became the focal point of medical diagnosis and power. Latour further argues that doctors accepted this role, not because it represented better science, but because it bettered their beleaguered image. Men in industry, agriculture, and food processing similarly embraced Pasteur's methods. In this way, the "Pastorian revolution" was not effected by a solitary genius, but by a handful of men who adopted and applied his methods to diverse aspects of society. More radically still, Latour attributes the success of the Pastorian program not to men, but to microbes, which provided a common focus, a "lever, with which to move" society. Here, for Latour, was the true revolution. This study marks the introduction of American methods of historical analysis to the Pastorian story, which analyse the ways in which professionals use science to further their own interests, as it shifts the portrait of Pasteur from "benefactor and truth-giver" to that of effective recruiter, the very definition of social success. Pioneering and beautifully written, Latour (1984) may perhaps be forgiven for overstating bacteriology's conquest of medicine, persuading the reader not so much by the force of its reasoning, as by the shock of its images and language. It may be more difficult for the new reader to perceive this shock; Latour's methods have, since their application to Pastorian history in 1984, themselves permeated historical ways of approaching scientific and medical subjects, and so now appear more familiar.

On the surface, Dagognet and Latour (1984) have presented strikingly different portrayals of Pasteur. Dagognet acts as philosopher, sensitive to Pasteur's system of thought; Latour is the sociologist, who deconstructs that thought. Beneath this conflicting surface, however, the two studies merge, as both focus on the coherence of Pasteur's life and work. Faithful to the French intellectual school of Georges Canguilhem, Dagognet characterises Pasteur's experimental work as a pattern of continuity ruptured by subject changes. The tension between absolute dogma and flexible adaptation is revealed when Pasteur, supporter of the dogmatic germ theory, worked on vaccines for diseases for which germs were not known (e.g. rabies); or when he set out to find preventative vaccines, only to discover that his first vaccine was, in fact, curative. Dagognet's Pasteur adapts to social demand, whereas Latour's Pasteur seems less of a genius, but rather more shrewd, methodically recruiting new followers while managing to retain the old. Dagognet shows how Pasteur moved to new subjects and capitalised on them by retaining, and modifying, older ideas; Latour, how Pasteur enrolled different categories of society until he ultimately enrolled society as a whole. Though these authors' methods seem opposed, they in fact unite when demonstrating the reasons for the continuity and success of Pasteur's work.

It is evident that the laboratory was central to Pasteur's work and public image. The recent publication of his laboratory notebooks and private correspondence has helped shift the tone of these studies from hagiographical to critical, revealing a Pasteur who consciously marketed himself and sometimes borrowed his science. For a concise introduction to Pasteur's experimental investigations, one might consult BALIBAR & PRÉVOST, who present some experiments completed by Pasteur, from optical isomerism to germ theory. Not all reviews in this multi-authored text, however, consulted Pasteur's laboratory notebooks, although they generally provide a multi-faceted and readable introduction to Pasteur's experimental investigations.

Recent works by Cadeddu and Geison provide detailed insight into Pastorian laboratory life. CADEDDU's account (in Italian) provides a precise, scientific re-reading of Pasteur's major medical discoveries by examining Pasteur's laboratory notebooks. The study of laboratory notebooks was pioneered by Frederic L. Holmes, who has successfully convinced historians of science that the traditional narrative of scientific discovery is overly simple and needs to be fundamentally re-examined, case by case. Accordingly, Cadeddu is interested in making comprehensible the mechanism of discovery that chanced to guide Pasteur, by returning methodically to the detailed accounts of his work that Pasteur himself provided. What arises is a less heroic description of Pasteur who, facing adversity, even resorted to manipulating data.

Geison established his reputation as the primary expert on Pasteur with his classic presentation of the scientist's work in GEISON (1974), in which he provided a well-balanced account of Pasteur's life and achievements. Geison's originality lay in voicing, and listening to, the arguments of Pasteur's critics. This article's long-anticipated sequel, GEISON (1995), again attends to the strategies of Pasteur's critics, and reveals the clinical, ethical, statistical, and scientific inconsistencies in Pasteur's work. Geison has attempted to present a complete portrait of Pasteur, with his desires for recognition and grandeur, but unfortunately neglects large sections of his work – for example, Pasteur's studies of silk worms, beer, and wine are omitted, when an understanding of these areas is essential for appreciating Pasteur's social success and his approach to biological beings.

Insight into the social context within which Pasteur conducted and extended his work is provided in SALOMON-BAYET. Indeed, it is difficult to talk about Pasteur without talking about his school, which is here depicted along with its impact on various segments of society. Popularising the phrase "Pastorian revolution", the contributors to this volume focus on the influence of what they term "the first medical revolution", identifying it with modern medicine. Their analysis starts with the institute established by Pasteur himself and bearing his name (founded in 1888), and effectively examines the Pastorian methods, their meaning, and their extension by subsequent generations of students. Analysing the "Pasteurisation of society", this volume studies the Pastorian revolution's impact on physicians, pharmacists, and the law,

underscoring its social as well as scientific contexts. Bodies, until then absent from the French Code, made their appearance in French law in the form of germs, and modification of this legislation eventually led to special legislation for the control of drugs.

Latour, who also contributed to the Salomon-Bayet volume (articulating his famous methodological "theatre of proof"), presents in LATOUR (1994) a lavishly-illustrated and sumptuously-narrated introduction to the society in which Pasteur worked. Written for the centenary of Pasteur's death, Latour's study highlights the technical transformations effected by the microbe's introduction to industry, colonial expansion, and emerging pathologies. Latour also attends, for the first time, to the material culture of Pasteur's work – his instruments and laboratory apparatus – to illuminate the relationships between society, medical technology and scientific ideas. In a book ostensibly celebrating Pasteur, Latour weds his sociology of science to the history of technology, providing exciting arguments for the study of the material culture of science.

A.M. MOULIN AND KIM PELIS

See also Bacteriology; Nutrition; Public Health

Pathology

Ackerknecht, Erwin H., *Rudolf Virchow: Doctor, Statesman, Anthropologist*, Madison: University of Wisconsin Press, 1953

Ackerknecht, Erwin H., *Medicine at the Paris Hospital, 1794–1848*, Baltimore: Johns Hopkins University Press, 1967

Foster, William Derek, *A Short History of Clinical Pathology*, Edinburgh: Livingstone, 1961

Foucault, Michel, *The Birth of the Clinic: An Archaeology of Medical Perception*, translated from the French by A.M. Sheridan Smith, London: Tavistock and New York: Pantheon Books, 1973 (original edition, 1963)

Howell, Joel D., *Technology in the Hospital: Transforming Patient Care in the Early Twentieth Century*, Baltimore: Johns Hopkins University Press, 1995

Jarcho, Saul (ed. and trans.), *The Clinical Consultations of Giambattista Morgagni: The Edition of Enrico Benassi (1935)*, Boston: Francis A. Countway Library of Medicine, 1984

Long, Esmond R., *A History of Pathology*, Baltimore: Williams and Wilkins, 1928; revised edition, New York: Dover, 1965

Long, Esmond R., *A History of American Pathology*, Springfield, Illinois: Thomas, 1962

Maulitz, Russell C., *Morbid Appearances: The Anatomy of Pathology in the Nineteenth Century*, Cambridge and New York: Cambridge University Press, 1987

Maulitz, Russell C., "The Pathological Tradition", in *Companion Encyclopedia of the History of Medicine*, 2 vols, edited by W.F. Bynum and Roy Porter, London and New York: Routledge, 1993

Nicolson, Malcolm, "Giovanni Battista Morgagni and Eighteenth-Century Physical Examination", in *Medical Theory, Surgical Practice: Studies in the History of*

Surgery, edited by Christopher Lawrence, London and New York: Routledge, 1992

Rather, L.J., *Addison and the White Corpuscles: An Aspect of Nineteenth-Century Biology*, London: Wellcome Institute of the History of Medicine, 1972

Rather, L.J., *The Genesis of Cancer: A Study in the History of Ideas*, Baltimore: Johns Hopkins University Press, 1978

Risse, Guenter B., *Hospital Life in Enlightenment Scotland: Care and Teaching at the Royal Infirmary of Edinburgh*, Cambridge and New York: Cambridge University Press, 1986

Rosenfeld, Louis, *Origins of Clinical Chemistry: The Evolution of Protein Analysis*, New York: Academic Press, 1982

Ideas of health and disease have always been linked, with the consequence that pathology – the study of disease (or, more literally, of suffering) – has long been part of organised medical thinking. Nevertheless, the term pathology was not introduced until the Renaissance, when Jean Fernel (1497–1558) divided medicine into three parts: physiology, pathology, and therapeutics. By then, post-mortem dissections were beginning to become more frequent, often within a medico-legal context, as doctors sought to determine the cause of sudden or unexpected death. LONG (1928) is the classic survey of pathology from antiquity to the early 20th century, and contains useful summaries of this older literature. As Maulitz has recently pointed out, however, the more systematic attempt to locate "the seats and causes of disease" is primarily of 18th-century origin.

Foremost among 18th-century exponents of the genre was G.B. Morgagni (1682–1771), who taught anatomy at Padua as well as carrying on an extensive consultative practice. Saul JARCHO's edition of his consultations offers important insight into Morgagni's approach to disease and its manifestations, and NICOLSON has examined aspects of his major pathological treatise of 1761. Morgagni's work was soon translated into English, although a good deal of the teaching at the institutes of pathology continued to rely on humoralism and what could be called "bedside physiology", as demonstrated by RISSE's study of the Royal Edinburgh Infirmary during the time of William Cullen (1710–90).

With the reorganisation of the French medical schools in 1794, however, the localist approach of surgery was grafted on to the more traditional holism of physic, and the pathological lesion came into its own as the defining characteristic of disease. FOUCAULT emphasises the extent to which this new orientation was central to "the clinic", and insists that the ideas developing within the French medical schools reflected more general shifts within the "epistemic" relations between knowledge and power in the period (c.1790–1830) which he identifies as spawning the modern. From a more empirical point of view, ACKERKNECHT (1967) supports the same conclusion, by showing how French doctors based their clinical diagnoses on the careful analysis of signs and symptoms during the lives of their patients, and correlated them with the lesions to be found in their corpses after death. In his monograph (1987) and overview article (1993) MAULITZ has analysed in much more detail this pathological tradition, noting that in the early decades of "Paris medicine" clinicians were

their own pathologists, and that the development of pathology in France as an independent discipline took several decades. He also scrutinises the intellectual ramifications of this new orientation in Britain, which encouraged what he calls "channel crossing", as British (and American) medical students began to study in Paris after the close of the Napoleonic wars.

This French medicine tended to be organ-based, even though one of its early leaders, Xavier Bichat (1771–1802), developed the idea of tissues as more fundamental units of function and disease. Bichat based his work on naked-eye anatomy supplemented with a simple hand-lens, but improvements in the reliability of the compound microscope from the late 1820s brought the microscope to the centre-stage in medicine and pathology. From the mid 19th century, the dominant figure in pathology was Rudolf Virchow (1821–1902), still best approached through the sympathetic biography, ACKERKNECHT (1953). For Virchow, the cell was basic to all biological functions, both normal and abnormal, and Virchow's work recast pathology within a cellular mould. Virchow naturally features in RATHER (1978), a fine study of the idea of cancers and their origins from antiquity to the end of the 19th century. The blood was an easy "tissue" to study microscopically, and inflammation and diseases of the blood also received much minute attention from the 1830s, as shown by RATHER (1972), a monograph on the white blood corpuscles.

By the late 19th century, pathology was beginning to emerge as a career specialism within medicine, as documented by LONG (1962) in his history of American pathology. Meanwhile, the development of bacteriology helped diversify the pathologist's diagnostic tasks, increasing the discipline's involvement with the diagnostic process. In many hospitals, the pathological laboratory was added to the morgue, as FOSTER's short history of clinical pathology makes clear. The microscopic analysis of biopsies and blood smears, and the chemical analysis of a variety of body fluids, including urine and blood serum, were gradually added to the pathologist's repertoire, and in turn led to the subsidiary occupations of laboratory technicians. HOWELL has examined aspects of this phenomenon in two American hospitals between 1900 and 1925, and one specialised dimension, protein analysis, has been described in ROSENFELD's comprehensive, though rather technical, monograph.

With the exception of bacteriology, however, modern pathology has been less well served historiographically than other medical sciences, such as physiology and biochemistry. This is particularly to be regretted, since pathology has played such an important role, conceptually as well as economically, in the transformation of hospital care in the 20th century.

W.F. BYNUM

See also Anatomy; Bacteriology; Hospitals

Pavlov, Ivan Petrovich 1849–1936

Russian physiologist

Asratian, Ezras A., *Ivan Petrovich Pavlov, 1849–1936*, Moscow: Nauka, 1974; German edition, Leipzig: Hirzel, 1978

Babkin, Boris P., *Pavlov: A Biography*, Chicago: Chicago University Press, 1949; London: Gollancz, 1951

Joravsky, David, *Russian Psychology: A Critical History*, Oxford and Cambridge, Massachusetts: Blackwell, 1989

Kreps, Evgeny M. (ed.), *I.P. Pavlov v vospominaniakh sovremenikov* [Pavlov in Reminiscences of Contemporaries], Leningrad: Nauka, 1967

McLeish, John, *Soviet Psychology: History, Theory, Content*, London: Methuen, 1975

Maiorov, F.P., *Istoriia ucheniia ob uslovnykh refleksakh* [History of the Teachings of Conditional Reflexes], Moscow and Leningrad: Nauka, 1948; revised edition, 1954

Mozzhukhin, A.S. and V.O. Samoilov, *I.P. Pavlov v Peterburgye, Petrogradye, Leningradye* [Pavlov in Petersburg, Petrograd, Leningrad], Leningrad: Lenizdat, 1977; revised and supplemented edition, 1989

Todes, Daniel P., "Pavlov and the Bolsheviks", *History and Philosophy of the Life Sciences*, 18 (1995)

Ivan Pavlov left only a brief autobiography, written around 1900, and a few pages of recollections of his childhood, both included in the fourth volume of the second edition of his *Complete Works*. W.H. Gantt's translation of Pavlov's "Lectures on Conditioned Reflexes" contains a biographical sketch, based on the translator's experience as a professional associate in Pavlov's laboratories between 1923 and 1929.

Studying the narratives of Pavlov's life and work, one must be conscious of bias as a result of ideology, and the fact that most authors were either students or disciples. Since Pavlov was made a hero and the leading figure of a monolithic "new Soviet" biology, medicine, and psychology during the Stalinist period, Soviet (and some uncritical Western) scholars and editors have described Pavlov "through red colored glasses" (as Gantt put it), adhering to the official narrative by suppressing or misrepresenting elements critical of Pavlov's life and work.

Aiming at the deconstruction of myths and the sharpening of critical judgment, JORAVSKY, who was denied access to Soviet archives even in the late 1980s, is helpful in giving a profound critique of sources and secondary literature. His extensive and trustworthy analysis, which contains several chapters on Pavlov and Pavlovianism, concentrates on historical causes and contexts accountable for the creation of the legend, and scrutinizes crucial tendencies in the history of Russian/Soviet science and society, as well as in Pavlov's life and work. Joravsky's critique does not, however, create a comprehensive picture of the man and his work; rather, he dismisses the latter as an "impossible project", which aimed to replace the "subjective" science of psychology with "objective" physiology.

BABKIN, one of Pavlov's oldest pupils who emigrated to Canada in 1920, gives an uncensored account, and the most complete up to World War I, based on personal and professional recollections and reveals the less flattering aspects of Pavlov's character and the origins of his scientistic creeds. Breaking with the clerical tradition of his parents, Pavlov had abandoned his theological studies at the seminary where he had first learned of the new ideas of the Russian intelligentsia in the 1860s. Under the influence of the Darwinian theory of natural selection, as popularized by Pisarev, Pavlov chose instead to study natural sciences at St Petersburg University in 1870, and Herbert Spencer became his "beloved author" (according to Pavlov's widow in her memoirs, as quoted in Kreps). In place of the religion of his ancestors, Pavlov substituted a monistic philosophy and secularized belief in natural science as the only true means of saving mankind. He became a skilled experimenter and imperturbable empiricist. When examining the period after the Russian Revolution, Babkin relies mainly on Pavlov's correspondence, a monograph by another colleague, and the memoirs of Pavlov's widow, to rationalize Pavlov's late endorsement of the Soviet regime as a patriotic response to the rise of fascism.

ASRATIAN's extensive biography, also published in German, provides first-hand recollections of the last 10 years of Pavlov's life (1926–36), when the author was one of the first few communists in Pavlov's laboratory. Asratian focuses on episodes that are supposed to show his teacher's views on the new Soviet order and on the Marxist world-view, which gradually changed from skepticism to sympathetic conviction. More than half the book deals with Pavlov's scientific work and concentrates on the studies of higher nervous activity: the investigation of the nervous control of behavior, through the analysis of the formation and phenomena of conditional reflexes. Pavlov embarked on this far-reaching research program when already in his fifties, after he was rewarded the Nobel prize for his studies on the regulation of digestive glands in 1904.

For readers of Russian, MAIOROV presents a detailed chronology of the history of this research program and its participants in the laboratory up to 1936, supplemented by a detailed bibliography and index. In the conclusion of the second edition, Maiorov was coerced into adopting the approved Stalinist and "Cold War" version, with Pavlov as the progressive dialectical materialist fighting, in the direct tradition of the Russian revolutionary democrats, against the reactionary tendencies of Western philosophies. Maiorov's conversion is a vivid illustration of the process of the establishment of the official mythology.

The merit of McLEISH's purely theoretical, and historically superficial, chapters on Pavlov's "New Science", and on "Pavlov and Lenin" is his attempt to explain to the Western reader the syntheses of Pavlovianism, Leninism, and dialectical materialism in the new Soviet psychology, by tracing philosophical and methodological confluences within these traditions.

An abundance of material, often anecdotal, is presented in KREPS's collection of reminiscences by Pavlov's contemporaries. Besides the accounts by 39 Soviet pupils and colleagues, there are short contributions by 12 Western physiologists who met Pavlov between 1906 and 1935 (such as W.B. Cannon, R.M. Yerkes, A.V. Hill, and H.W. Cushing). Pavlov's youngest son, Vsevolod, included his reconstruction of an interesting conversation between Pavlov and the writer Maxim Gorky in 1931; Gorky, who had convinced Lenin to support Pavlov in 1921, showed his continued interest in the development of Pavlov's science, and tried to convince Pavlov that its application would be compatible with Soviet attempts to create a "new man".

MOZZHUKHIN & SAMOILOV give a detailed account of Pavlov's scientific, social, and political life, and of his relationship with the Russian intelligentsia. The section describing Pavlov's work under the Soviet regime was completed in the 1989 edition, with the inclusion of material that had been suppressed until *glasnost*. The one great failing of this interesting and detailed work is that it lacks an index.

TODES, who has been working on Pavlov in about 20 Russian archives for several years, began to publish his results in the mid-1990s. His 40-page article on "Pavlov and the Bolsheviks" is the first description – thoroughly verified by sources – of Pavlov's "combative collaboration" with Soviet leaders, in building a scientific empire and defending Russian science as a whole. Besides substantiating the picture of the scientist's engaged and informed political stand as a "prosperous dissident", Todes provides deeper insights into Pavlov's life, scientistic philosophy, and *Menschenbild*, when confronted by Soviet experimentation and Stalin's purges. Todes describes Pavlov's maturing relationship with individual communists (notably Bukharin), and explains Pavlov's endorsement of Soviet achievements in his last years, which promoted the monopolization of his person and work by Soviet legend. Todes is currently preparing a book on Pavlov's laboratory and his early work on digestive glands, as well as a modern major biography based on the rich archive material he has been studying.

TORSTEN RÜTING

See also Physiology: France; Physiology: Germany; Russia

Pearson, Karl 1857–1936

British mathematician, statistician, and biometrician

Bowler, Peter J., *Evolution: The History of an Idea*, Berkeley: University of California Press, 1984; revised edition, 1989

Edwards, A.W.F., "Galton, Karl Pearson and Modern Statistical Theory", in *Sir Francis Galton, FRS: The Legacy of His Ideas*, edited by Milo Keynes, London: Macmillan, 1993

Eisenhart, Churchill, entry on Pearson in *Dictionary of Scientific Biography*, edited by Charles Coulston Gillispie, vol. 10, New York: Scribner, 1974

Farrall, Lyndsay Andrew, *The Origins and Growth of the English Eugenics Movement, 1865–1925*, New York: Garland, 1985

Froggatt, P.C. and N.C. Nevin, "Galton's 'Law of Ancestral Heredity': Its Influence on the Early Development of Human Genetics", *History of Science*, 10 (1971): 1–27

Hilts, Victor L., *Statist and Statistician*, New York: Arno Press, 1981

MacKenzie, Donald A., *Statistics in Britain 1865–1930: The Social Construction of Scientific Knowledge*, Edinburgh: Edinburgh University Press, 1981

Magnello, M. Eileen, "Karl Pearson's Gresham Lectures: W.F.R. Weldon, Speciation and the Origins of Pearsonian Statistics", *British Journal for the History of Science*, 29(1996): 43–63

Magnello, M. Eileen, "Karl Pearson's Mathematization of Inheritance: From Ancestral Heredity to Mendelian Genetics (1895–1909); *Annals of Science*, 55 (1998): 35–94

Norton, Bernard, "Karl Pearson and Statistics: The Social Origin of Scientific Innovation", *Social Studies of Science*, 8 (1978): 3–34

Olby, Robert, "The Dimensions of Scientific Controversy: The Biometrician–Mendelian Debate", *British Journal for the History of Science Commemorative Issue for Bernard Norton*, 74 (1989): 299–320

Pearson, Egon, "Karl Pearson: An Appreciation of Some Aspects of His Life and Work", Part 1, 1857–1905, *Biometrika* (1936): 193–257; Part 2, 1906–36, (1938): 161–248; reprinted Cambridge University Press, 1938

Porter, Theodore M., *The Rise of Statistical Thinking, 1820–1900*, Princeton, New Jersey: Princeton University Press, 1986

Provine, William B. (ed.), *Origins of Theoretical Population Genetics*, Chicago: University of Chicago Press, 1971

Riddle, Chauncey, *Karl Pearson's Philosophy of Science*, PhD dissertation, Columbia University, New York, 1958

Semmel, Barnard, "Karl Pearson: Socialist and Darwinist", *British Journal of Sociology*, 9 (1958): 111–25

Stigler, Stephen M., *The History of Statistics: The Measurement of Uncertainty before 1900*, Cambridge, Massachusetts: Belknap Press of Harvard University Press, 1986

Karl Pearson's voluminous published papers and mass of archival material have provided scholars with considerable scope for studying Pearson's work, which ranged from astronomy, mathematics, mechanics, meteorology, and physics to the biological sciences in particular (including anthropology, biometrics, evolutionary biology, epidemiology, eugenics, heredity, and medicine). Despite this abundant material, much of the scholarship on Pearson in the last 50 years has been dominated by discussions about the relationship of Francis Galton and the eugenics movement, and of Pearson and biometrics. This emphasis has resulted in the following conclusions: first, that Pearson was merely a "disciple" of Galton; second, that Pearson's principal contribution to statistical theory was the development of the mathematical theory for Galton's method of correlation and regression; and hence third, that that correlation was not only the dominant methodology in the Pearsonian corpus of statistics, but was therefore the dominant tool in the Galton Eugenics Laboratory. Considerably less attention has been given to Pearson's working relationship with his colleague and closest friend W.F.R. Weldon, and to the theoretical infrastructure supporting Pearson's statistical innovations.

Moreover, nearly all of the scholarship on Pearson's work in the Drapers' Biometric Laboratory and the Galton Eugenics Laboratory has been supported by the belief that the methods used by Pearson and his co-workers for biometrics and eugenics were inextricably bound to each other to the extent that no distinctions can be made between the methods, procedures, and tools of the two laboratories. This historiographical tendency to link *in toto* Pearson's work in the Galton Eugenics Laboratory to his work in the Drapers' Biometric Laboratory is probably the most problematic aspect in the historiography of Pearsonian statistics.

Some of the earliest work on Pearson arose from consideration of his positivistic epistemology, which formed the basis of his *Grammar of Science*. RIDDLE identified three main components of Pearson's epistemological writings, which included empiricism, a Kantian emphasis on the role of the mind in organizing and interpreting sensation, and a Cartesian faith in mathematics as the key to organized thought. Thus Riddle thought that Pearson's *Grammar of Science* was largely an attempt to impress the ideas of Mach upon the English-speaking world. SEMMELL, who was interested in Pearson's socio-political thought, examined Pearson's socialism and his Marxist lectures. He argued that Pearson's socialism was the keystone to his non-Spencerian social Darwinism. Unlike Spencer, Pearson did not stress the individualist struggle of economic competition, but emphasized the evolutionary struggle between tribes and nations. Consequently he adopted Spencer's competitive and highly individualist view of the economic struggle of the free market for the needs and methods of his social state.

FARRALL made one of the first attempts to analyse Pearson's statistical work within a sociological framework. The author used Hagstrom's account of disciplinary differences as a theoretical framework for the study of Pearson's attempts to establish eugenics and biometry as new disciplines, and pointed out that neither biometry nor eugenics became recognized scientific specialities, and suggests that Pearson's biometrics bore no relation to Pearson's statistics; biometry was viewed as a methodology of causation for eugenics.

NORTON argues that Pearson's statistics embodied the central tenets of his philosophy of science, and that his positivism is viewed as the crucial factor in the development of his statistical work. Norton also attests that Pearson had grown into a social Darwinist anxious to provide his particular form of Darwinism with a proper scientific basis. Biometry was thought to have been formulated and constructed "without theory" and thus was to be applied to eugenics.

MACKENZIE holds similar views to those of Farrall and Norton, although he places greater emphasis on eugenics and influences connected with the growth of a professional middle class. He adopts a social constructivist approach, and links Pearson's statistical work to eugenics by placing it in a wider context of social and political ideologies. This interpretation involved frequent recourse to Pearson's social and political views *vis-à-vis* his popular writings on eugenics. This approach, while indicating the political and social dimensions of science, has produced a rather mono-causal or uni-dimensional view of history. Building on much of this conventional scholarship, PORTER places the development of Pearson's statistics within the tradition of 19th-century pure mathematics.

Egon PEARSON and EISENHART have both provided comprehensive accounts of Karl Pearson's life. Both have emphasized Pearson's development of the modern theory of mathematical statistics and stressed the importance of Weldon's role in his work. Egon Pearson offers a fuller exposition of his father's life and work whereas Eisenhart gives a drier and more technical description of Pearson's seminal published papers.

Weldon's role in the production of Pearson's early published work has also been acknowledged by HILTS, STIGLER and EDWARDS and both BOWLER and OLBY have given Weldon greater priority than Galton in Pearson's development of statistics as it relates to problems of evolutionary biology. MAGNELLO (1996) examines Pearson's earliest statistical work in 30 of his (much neglected) Gresham lectures from November 1891 to May 1893, and argues that the Darwinian biological concepts at the centre of much of Weldon's statistical and experimental work provided the impetus for Pearson's earliest statistical innovation on goodness of fit testing in 1892. (This work led on to his single most important contribution to modern statistical theory when he devised the chi-square goodness of fit test in 1900.) It is argued that Weldon's interests also provided the wider basis of a programme that was the foundation for Pearson's longer term work, which may be distinguished in his corpus from the specifically Galtonian influences implied by Farrall, Mackenzie, and Norton.

MAGNELLO has also shown that Pearson not only had separate goals for his Biometric and Eugenics Laboratories, but that he devised and deployed different quantitative procedures and statistical methods, and also used different types of instruments for the various problems that arose in the laboratories. Pearson's work in the Biometric School from 1892 to 1903 and in the Drapers' Biometric Laboratory from 1903 to 1936 was underpinned by his goodness of fit testing, his chi-square goodness of fit test, 18 methods of correlation, the use of a higher form of algebra (i.e. determinental matrix algebra), statistical and experimental studies of natural selection, craniometry, and physical anthropology. This biometrical work led subsequently to the emergence and development of the modern theory of statistics in the 20th century. While Pearson used four of his 18 methods of correlation in the Galton Eugenics Laboratory, the dominant methodology in this laboratory from its establishment in 1907 until Pearson's retirement in 1933 involved, instead, the use of a complex interconnecting set of family pedigrees and actuarial death rates.

Pearson's role in the Biometrician-Mendelian dispute of 1900 aroused a series of debates that continued through most of the 20th century. Historians of science (including FROGGATT & NEVIN, Mackenzie, Norton, and PROVINE) who have claimed that Pearson rejected Mendelism and that continuous variation was the principal (if not only) form of biological and statistical variation he and the biometricians used, have typically relied on the views of Pearson's contemporaries, including biologists such as William Bateson, William Ernest Castle, and Reginald Punnett (all of whom believed that Pearson rejected Mendelism). MAGNELLO (1998) has shown instead that Pearson began to consider the role of discontinuous variation for problems of inheritance by the end of the 19th century (for which he devised a set of statistical methods as early as 1900). His work in the 20th century indicates that he accepted Mendelism as an alternative theory of inheritance for discontinuous variation while Galton's law of ancestral heredity could be used for continuous variation.

M. EILEEN MAGNELLO

See also Biometrics, Statistical Biology, and Mathematical Statistics

Performance

Biagioli, Mario, *Galileo, Courtier: The Practice of Science in the Culture of Absolutism*, Chicago: University of Chicago Press, 1993

Brain, Robert, *Going to the Fair: Readings in the Culture of Nineteenth-Century Exhibitions*, Cambridge: Whipple Museum, 1993

Golinski, Jan, *Science as Public Culture: Chemistry and Enlightenment in Britain, 1760–1820*, Cambridge and New York: Cambridge University Press, 1992

Hankins, Thomas L. and Robert J. Silverman, *Instruments and the Imagination*, Princeton, New Jersey: Princeton University Press, 1995

Morus, Iwan Rhys, "Different Experimental Lives: Michael Faraday and William Sturgeon", *History of Science*, 30 (1992): 1–28

Morus, Iwan Rhys, "Manufacturing Nature: Science, Technology and Victorian Consumer Culture", *British Journal for the History of Science*, 29 (1996): 403–34

Schaffer, Simon, "Natural Philosophy and Public Spectacle in the 18th Century", *History of Science*, 21 (1983): 1–43

Schaffer, Simon, "Self Evidence", *Critical Inquiry*, 18 (1992): 327–62

Shapin, Steven and Simon Schaffer, *Leviathan and the Air-Pump: Hobbes, Boyle and the Experimental Life*, Princeton, New Jersey: Princeton University Press, 1985

Sibum, Otto, "Reworking the Mechanical Value of Heat: Instruments of Precision and Gestures of Accuracy in Early Victorian England", *Studies in History and Philosophy of Science*, 26 (1995): 73–106

Winter, Alison, "Mesmerism and Popular Culture in Early Victorian England", *History of Science*, 32 (1994): 317–43

Most historians and sociologists would now agree with the observation that science is an inherently public activity, and not just an activity that goes on inside an individual scientist's head, or in the privacy of a laboratory. To count as knowledge, science has to command assent from others, and scientists must convince others that the world conforms to their views. Persuasion is therefore central to the consolidation of new scientific facts; in order to persuade, scientists have, in various ways, to perform for their audiences, and performance has therefore always been central to the fashioning of natural philosophy or science.

The texts examined here consider various aspects of scientists' performances, from the Renaissance to the late 19th century. This is not to imply that performance only became central to scientific practice in the 16th century, or that it is no longer central to contemporary practice. The limitation is simply a feature of the available literature.

BIAGIOLI analyses Galileo's career as a philosopher in terms of courtly performance, and shows how Galileo achieved success by adopting and adapting the complex protocols and rituals of Italian Renaissance court culture. Episodes such as Galileo's "invention" of the telescope, and his presentation of the Medicean stars to his patron, are portrayed as public performances within the context of court culture, as are Galileo's carefully staged disputes with other scholars. It was by placing himself in the public domain through such perfor-

mances that Galileo gained and maintained both his own reputation and that of his discoveries.

SHAPIN & SCHAFFER use an analysis of the dispute between Robert Boyle and Thomas Hobbes to argue that the carefully managed performance of an experiment for a selected audience of gentlemen philosophers was crucial for the creation of a fact. By convincing the Fellows of the Royal Society that the productions of Boyle's air pump were features of the natural world, rather than artefacts, Boyle could then use the gentlemanly status of his witnesses as a guarantor of his own and his experiment's veracity. The authors emphasise the central role played by such public performances before witnesses, and analyse the various technologies (literary, material and social) that could be exploited to translate experimental performances from the laboratory into natural facts.

SCHAFFER (1983) points to the proliferation of performances of natural philosophical experiment during the 18th century. Such performances, and the spectacles associated with them, were central to the establishment of new cosmologies throughout the century. SCHAFFER (1992) extends this argument; he focuses on the status of the natural philosopher and his performances, pointing in particular to the strategies adopted by different natural philosophers in order to establish their authoritative status. By examining the status of experiments performed on the experimenter's own body, Schaffer establishes the narrowing boundaries of scientific authority and credibility during the 18th century, which culminated in the cult of Romantic genius. He points also to the increasingly central role of self-registering instrumentation, which could be portrayed as allowing Nature to speak for herself, unmediated by human performance.

GOLINSKI follows the theme of genius, showing how Humphry Davy succeeded by fashioning himself as a flamboyant performer who appealed to the Romantic sensibilities of his audience by demonstrating his power over the spectacular displays of electricity produced by his batteries. The power of his performances was intended to convince his audience of his privileged access to the secrets of Nature.

MORUS (1992) focuses on the role of public performance in the self-fashioning of two early 19th-century experimental philosophers: Michael Faraday and William Sturgeon. He shows how such fashioning was designed to cultivate different audiences. Faraday, at the Royal Institution, tailored his performances to suit the expectations of his polite, gentlemanly audience, while Sturgeon adopted a more populist and egalitarian style. Their performances and the ways in which they represented their relationship with their experiments had clear consequences for their respective cosmologies. MORUS (1996) focuses on the popular exhibition halls, such as the Adelaide Gallery, where experimenters such as Sturgeon plied their trade. He argues that performances at such venues, where the public paid their shilling at the door to view natural, scientific, and technological wonders, placed nature within the context of consumer culture. Nature could thus be regarded as a commodity to be consumed like the other artefacts on show.

WINTER illustrates some of the problematics of performance. Focusing on mesmerism in early Victorian London, she draws attention to the difficulties encountered by experimenters, in distinguishing between their own performances and those of their subjects. For instance, John Elliotson at

University College London Hospital had great difficulty in persuading his audience that it was he, rather than his patient Elizabeth O'Key, who controlled the mesmeric performance.

SIBUM introduces the notion of "gestural knowledge" to encapsulate the complex relationship between the experimenter and his apparatus. Concentrating on James Prescott Joule's experimental work on determining the mechanical equivalent of heat, he draws attention to the tacit skills embodied in successful experimental performances. Sibum's work is unusual in that it is based on actual replications of historical experiments. He shows that Joule's background in the brewing industry provided crucial resources for his experimental work on the mechanical equivalent of heat, and draws attention to the difficulties of translating experimental performances convincingly from the private to the public domain.

BRAIN is a selection of contemporary sources designed to accompany a museum exhibition on the culture of 19th-century industrial and scientific exhibitions. His selections show how the placing of scientific instruments and apparatus in such a context played a crucial role in constructing the Victorians' perceptions of nature and science.

In a series of essays, HANKINS & SILVERMAN examine the cultural context of a range of scientific instruments. They draw attention to the ways in which such instruments were designed to exhibit the fabulous and the spectacular, and suggest that such displays were constitutive of the knowledge embodied in such instrumentation. Instruments were designed for public performance as much as for private experimentation, and were understood as such both by their makers and their audiences.

As this selection of texts makes clear, the concept of performance encapsulates a whole range of important issues central to the production, reproduction, and reception of scientific facts. This viewpoint draws attention to the fact that science is a practical activity embedded in material culture, and provides one avenue at least for trying to understand the ways in which science proliferates: how the locally contextualized products of a particular individual or laboratory can become recognized as routine parts of the world around us.

IWAN RHYS MORUS

See also Fact; Genius

Pharmacology

Ackerknecht, Erwin H., *Therapeutics: From the Primitives to the Twentieth Century*, New York: Hafner Press, 1973

Bynum, W.F., "Chemical Structure and Pharmacological Action: A Chapter in the History of Nineteenth-Century Molecular Pharmacology", *Bulletin of the History of Medicine*, 44 (1970): 518–38

Debus, Allen G., *The English Paracelsians*, London: Oldbourne, 1965; New York: Franklin Watts, 1966

Estes, J. Worth, *The Medical Skills of Ancient Egypt*, Canton, Massachusetts: Science History Publications, 1989; revised edition, 1993

Leake, Chauncey D., *An Historical Account of Pharmacology to the 20th Century*, Springfield, Illinois: Thomas, 1975

Lesch, John E., *Science and Medicine in France: The Emergence of Experimental Physiology, 1790–1855*, Cambridge, Massachusetts: Harvard University Press, 1984

Levey, Martin, *Early Arabic Pharmacology: An Introduction Based on Ancient and Medieval Sources*, Leiden: E.J. Brill, 1973

Liebenau, Jonathon, *Medical Science and Medical Industry: The Formation of the American Pharmaceutical Industry*, London: Macmillan/Business History Unit, University of London, and Baltimore: Johns Hopkins University Press, 1987

Nicholls, David, *Nineteenth-Century Britain, 1815–1914*, Folkestone, Kent: Dawson, and Hamden, Connecticut: Archon Books, 1978

Parascandola, John, "The Development of Receptor Theory", in *Discoveries in Pharmacology*, edited by M.J. Parnham and J. Bruinvels, Amsterdam and New York: Elsevier, 1985

Parascandola, John, *The Development of American Pharmacology: John J. Abel and the Shaping of a Discipline*, Baltimore: Johns Hopkins University Press, 1992

Riddle, John M., "Theory and Practice in Medieval Medicine", *Viator*, 5 (1974), 157–84; reprinted in his *Quid Pro Quo: Studies in the History of Drugs*, Aldershot, Hampshire: Variorum, and Brookfield, Vermont: Ashgate, 1992

Riddle, John M., *Dioscorides on Pharmacy and Medicine*, Austin: University of Texas Press, 1985

Sneader, Walter, *Drug Discovery: The Evolution of Modern Medicines*, Chichester, Sussex, and New York: Wiley, 1985

Swann, John P., *Academic Scientists and the Pharmaceutical Industry: Cooperative Research in Twentieth-Century America*, Baltimore: Johns Hopkins University Press, 1988

Voigts, Linda E., "Anglo-Saxon Plant Remedies and the Anglo-Saxons", *Isis*, 70 (1979): 250–68

Weatherall, M., *In Search of a Cure: A History of Pharmaceutical Discovery*, Oxford and New York: Oxford University Press, 1990

Knowledge of the action of drugs has been central to medicine for as long as healers have been a distinct body of practitioners. From the ancient world onwards, this knowledge has been consolidated and systematised in a number of distinct learned traditions, of which modern pharmacology – characterised by systematic experimental and clinical investigation of drug action – is only the latest. Two volumes taken together provide a very useful overview of the rise and fall of these different traditions. ACKERKNECHT concentrates on the changing theoretical frameworks within which therapeutics in general, and drugging in particular, were conceptualised, and describes how drug action was understood within each. LEAKE, by contrast, offers a more detailed account of the actual practices of drugging, with less discussion of the therapeutic theories by which such practices were rationalised.

More recent works have looked at some of these early pharmacological traditions in greater detail. ESTES includes a useful account of early Egyptian physiological theory and the drugs associated with it. RIDDLE (1985) describes in some detail the work of the Greco-Roman author Dioscorides, who systematised knowledge of *materia medica* on the basis of, among other things, empirical studies of the effects of drugs in health and illness. As Riddle makes clear, however, later writers largely ignored Dioscorides' system of drug classification, while assimilating many of the botanical and other remedies he described into the humoral theory of health and illness propagated, most influentially, by Galen. LEVEY shows how this humoral framework was expanded by Arabic physicians to accommodate not just Dioscoridean and Galenic, but also Indian remedies, within an eclectic and pragmatic system of drugging.

A similarly eclectic approach to therapeutics characterised medieval medical knowledge. Historians up to and including Ackerknecht tended to depict medieval pharmacy as little more than a degenerate form of classical learning, but more recent writers have challenged this view. The essays by RIDDLE (1974), and VOIGTS on Anglo-Saxon herbal medicine make a strong case for regarding it as an autonomously developing body of knowledge and practice, informed by a highly practical understanding of drug action, and sustained by trade with the Mediterranean and the Orient. The recovery of classical learning in the Renaissance helped to consolidate the Galenic tradition in the European medical schools, but this was challenged, during the 16th century, by renewed interest in vernacular knowledge and by the development of laboratory-based methods of investigation. The alchemical research of Paracelsus, in particular, was implicated in the growing popularity of a number of new chemical therapies, including mercury. No detailed account exists of Paracelsian therapeutic theory, but DEBUS stresses its importance in opening up humoral theory to reinterpretation, and in fostering a more reductively chemical understanding of illness and its treatment.

The period from the late 18th century onwards saw an enormous expansion and reorganisation of knowledge of drugs and their actions. There are considerable obstacles for anyone who would write a general history of these developments, however. While the growth of laboratory-based methods of scientific investigation was undoubtedly one of the key factors in the therapeutic revolution, pharmacological knowledge was not pursued within a single disciplinary framework, or through the adoption of a single central methodology. More even than other biomedical sciences, modern pharmacology is a hybrid discipline, which has progressed by cobbling together insights and information from a variety of settings, using a variety of experimental approaches: at the bedside, in academic laboratories, and in industry. Organising the history of modern pharmacology into a coherent narrative is consequently a problematic enterprise.

The best attempt in this direction is the book by WEATHERALL, which traces the rise of a number of different, and parallel, investigative strategies. Beginning with early studies of the chemistry of drugs, it moves on to the emergence of immunotherapy and chemotherapy later in the 19th century, and to attempts by physiologists to explain and predict the action of drugs in terms of their effects on the normal chemical processes of life. Weatherall also pays attention to the institutional developments that made such coherent strategies possible. However, while this historiographical approach works well for the 19th century, it breaks down thereafter,

because the commercially-driven search for new drugs became increasingly inter-disciplinary and opportunistic. Consequently, Weatherall is forced to abandon his account of particular investigative strategies, and to organise his 20th-century material in terms of a simple accumulation of knowledge of particular kinds of chemicals: hormones, antibacterials, cancer drugs, psychoactive chemicals, and so on. SNEADER adopts this kind of taxonomic framework from the very beginning, and, as a result, his book can hardly be considered a historical narrative in the normal sense. Rather, it offers a series of chapters on the development of different categories of drugs, characterised by their pharmacological action as it is now understood. What the book lacks in historical perspective, however, it makes up for in the wealth of pharmacological detail it amasses. It is consequently a useful resource for anyone interested in tracing the discovery of particular drugs and their medical uses.

Despite the many different routes to drug discovery, a distinct discipline of pharmacology began to establish itself in medical schools in the course of the 19th century. LESCH looks at developments in France, and especially in Paris, during the first half of the century. His research documents the growth of interest in isolating pure chemicals from herbal remedies, and in conducting experimental investigations into the physiological activity of those chemicals. Lesch locates this emerging research programme within the context of post-Revolutionary reforms in French medical practice and medical education. Spurred on by the therapeutic scepticism that had dominated clinical medicine during the Revolution, physicians joined with the emerging profession of pharmacy in search of a new body of empirically-based therapeutic knowledge. Experimental physiology in general, and pharmacological research in particular, was adopted as a promising way to generate such knowledge. As Lesch makes clear, the new pharmacology not only served to bolster the social standing of physicians and pharmacists, but also provided a new breed of career physiologists with useful experimental tools – "chemical scalpels" – with which to pursue their own programme of research into the fundamental processes of life.

By the end of the 19th century, such methods were also being adopted in Britain and America, where professional medical scientists now sought to extend their own forms of laboratory-based expertise more directly into the clinical setting. The promotion of pharmacology as a distinct discipline within the hierarchy of laboratory sciences provided one way of doing so. PARASCANDOLA (1992) illuminates the institutional dimension of the emergence of the new discipline, first in the German universities, and subsequently – in greater detail – in the United States. Parascandola's book does not deal, however, except in passing, with the methodological and intellectual content of pharmacology at this time. Readers interested in tracing some of the key theoretical and experimental programmes around which the new discipline took shape should consequently look at BYNUM's paper on the search for a relationship between molecular structure and pharmacological action, and at PARASCANDOLA (1985) on the development of the drug receptor theory. Even while pursuing such programmes, however, pharmacologists remained open-minded about possible sources of new drugs. NICHOLLS, for instance, shows that late 19th-century British doctors, including some of those now enshrined as founders of the science of pharmacology, were prepared to adopt homeopathic remedies while ultimately rejecting the theoretical system in which they were rooted.

One of the most powerful stimuli to the generation of new knowledge of drugs and their action came from the growth of the pharmaceutical industry. LIEBENAU charts the rise of science-based pharmaceutical production in the US from the late 19th century, and investigates the role that laboratories played in this highly competitive field of commercial endeavour. He shows that those companies that were able to claim that their products were manufactured to high standards of purity, validated by laboratory-based methods of production and quality control, secured an important competitive advantage within the pharmaceutical marketplace. This was particularly the case when drugs were sold, not to the general public, but directly to doctors, who themselves saw the deployment of laboratory-based knowledge as a way of reinforcing their own claims of objectivity and expertise.

Pharmaceutical companies were consequently quick to acquire laboratory research facilities, capitalising on the possibility of patenting manufacturing techniques and new synthetic preparations. In America, as in Britain and Germany, this enterprise rapidly snowballed into the enormous programme of research and development that now characterises the pharmaceutical industry. As SWANN makes clear, this process also depended heavily on research conducted within universities and other academic institutions, and did much to sustain the development of academic pharmacology during the 20th century.

STEVE STURDY

See also Drugs

Pharmacy

Cowen, David L. and William H. Helfand, *Pharmacy: An Illustrated History*, New York: Abrams, 1990

Foust, Clifford M., *Rhubarb: The Wondrous Drug*, Princeton, New Jersey: Princeton University Press, 1992

Holloway, S.W.F, *Royal Pharmaceutical Society of Great Britain, 1841–1991: A Political and Social History*, London: Pharmaceutical Press, 1991

Kremers Edward and George Urdang, *The History of Pharmacy: A Guide and a Survey*, Philadelphia: Lippincott, 1940; 4th edition, revised by Glenn Sonnedecker, 1976

Mann, Ronald D., *Modern Drug Use: An Enquiry on Historical Principles*, Lancaster, Lancashire: MTP Press, 1984

Riddle, John M., *Dioscorides on Pharmacy and Medicine*, Austin: University of Texas Press, 1985

Silverman, Milton and Philip R. Lee, *Pills, Profits and Politics*, Berkeley: University of California Press, 1974

Weatherall, M., *In Search of a Cure: A History of Pharmaceutical Discovery*, Oxford and New York: Oxford University Press, 1990

Although in need of major revision, Sonnedecker's 1976 edition of KREMERS & URDANG remains the best survey of the whole field. It traces pharmacy's evolution from the ancient empires of Babylonia – Assyria, Egypt, Greece and Rome – through the Middle Ages in Europe and the Arabic world, to the rise of specialized pharmacy in representative countries of Europe (Italy, France, Germany and Britain). Pharmacy in the United States is examined in some detail, and many examples are provided of contributions to science and society by pharmacists of various nationalities. An attractive visual companion to Kremers & Urdang is provided by COWEN & HELFAND with its large format, slick layout and heavy glossy paper. The 308 illustrations (half in colour, many full page) include examples of archaeological artefacts, portraits, paintings, prints, postcards, caricatures, and advertisements, as well as photographs of pharmacies and their equipment. The text is not as illuminating as the illustrations.

MANN has produced an encyclopedic reference work on the history of drugs. Considering its scope, it is a remarkably reliable chronicle of drugs, medicine, science, and world history from antiquity to the 1980s. There are nine carefully researched chapters and a concluding essay. The first three cover the ancient world, the civilizations of Greece and Rome, and the Middle Ages and Renaissance. Each of the next four chapters examine developments in a single century, from the 17th to the 20th. The last two chapters are mainly concerned with modern British drug regulation. There is no comparable single reference book on the primary literature of pharmaceutical history, as Mann diligently provides the reader with details of the editions, translations, and collections relating to whatever subject he handles. The text is scrupulously documented with 2,550 footnotes.

WEATHERALL focuses on the history of pharmaceutical research from 1880 to 1980, with particular reference to British contributions. The sequence of chapters deftly combines the virtues of both a chronological and a thematic treatment: insulin and steroid hormones (chapter 5) follow the first advances in chemotherapy (chapter 3) and precede vitamins (chapter 7) and antibiotics (chapter 9). Chapters 10–13 are mostly concerned with developments after 1945. The great strength of the book is its elucidation of complex scientific problems in clear non-specialist prose.

Throughout history, and in all cultures, medicine has been practised primarily by drug therapy. The history of pharmacy is, therefore, inseparable from the history of therapeutics. For 1,600 years the major source of European knowledge about medicinal substances was Dioscorides' *Materia Medica*, written in the 1st century AD, in which he assembled data on more than 1,000 natural drugs and prescribed some 4,700 therapeutic uses. RIDDLE argues that Dioscorides invented a "drug affinity" system that provides the organizing principle of his work. This attention to the therapeutic properties of drugs, and the theoretical structures such classification implies, raised pharmacy from an empirical art to a clinical science.

FOUST recounts the fascinating history of medicinal rhubarb. Marco Polo observed Chinese rhubarb in 1295, but it was not until the late 19th century that it was authoritatively established that the plant that produced the finest cathartic/laxative/restorative rhubarb roots was native to the highlands of western China, northern Tibet, and southern Mongolia. Foust describes the frustration Europeans experienced in trying to acquire the plant and master its special botanical and chemical properties. By the 18th century, the trade in rhubarb had become a major state monopoly for Russia and an important source of revenue for the East Indies companies. Foust's biography of a plant is a model of pharmaceutical history, being a synthesis of political, commercial, scientific, medical and cultural history.

The impact of the modern state on the development of the pharmaceutical profession is the central theme of HOLLOWAY's history of the Royal Pharmaceutical Society. He shows how the Victorian "laissez-faire" state handed over the regulation of the retail sale of poisons to a voluntary organisation of proprietor pharmacists. This led to the establishment of a statutory register which, in due course, became the criterion of qualification for dispensing drugs within the state health care system.

In spite of its age, SILVERMAN & LEE remains the best introduction to the issues involved in the modern revolution in drug therapy. Although concerned mainly with developments in the US since 1962, it discusses the major controversies in contemporary pharmacy in an even-handed manner. Among the subjects examined are the role of the pharmaceutical industry in research, production, promotion and pricing of drugs; the debate on generic prescribing and the related questions of safety, efficacy and quality; over-the-counter drugs; the rise of clinical pharmacy in the delivery of health services; and the role of the government (mainly the Food and Drug Administration) in drug development, control, and supervision. There are further sections on adverse drug reactions, on the prescribing practices of doctors, and on the future of prescription-only drugs.

S.W.F. HOLLOWAY

See also Drugs; Pharmacology

Philosophy of Science

Bloor, David, *Knowledge and Social Imagery*, London and Boston: Routledge and Kegan Paul, 1976; 2nd edition, Chicago: University of Chicago Press, 1991

Boyd, Richard, Philip Gasper and J.D. Trout (eds), *The Philosophy of Science*, Cambridge, Massachusetts: MIT Press, 1991

Earman, John, *Bayes or Bust?: A Critical Examination of Bayesian Confirmation Theory*, Cambridge, Massachusetts: MIT Press, 1992

Feyerabend, Paul K., *Against Method: Outline of an Anarchistic Theory of Knowledge*, Atlantic Highlands, New Jersey: Humanities Press, 1975; revised edition, New York and London: Verso, 1988

Gower, Barry, *Scientific Method: A Historical and Philosophical Introduction*, New York and London: Routledge, 1997

Hacking, Ian, *Representing and Intervening: Introductory Topics in the Philosophy of Natural Science*, Cambridge and New York: Cambridge University Press, 1983

Harding, Sandra G., *Whose Science? Whose Knowledge?: Thinking from Women's Lives*, Ithaca, New York: Cornell University Press, and Milton Keynes: Open University Press, 1991

Hempel, Carl Gustav, *Aspects of Scientific Explanation, and Other Essays in the Philosophy of Science*, New York: Free Press, 1970

Kitcher, Philip, *The Advancement of Science: Science without Legend, Objectivity without Illusions*, Oxford and New York: Oxford University Press, 1993

Kuhn, Thomas S., *The Structure of Scientific Revolutions*, 2nd edition, enlarged, Chicago: University of Chicago Press, 1970

Laudan, Larry, *Progress and Its Problems: Toward a Theory of Scientific Growth*, Berkeley: University of California Press, 1977

Popper, Karl, *The Logic of Scientific Discovery*, New York: Basic Books, and London: Hutchinson, 1959

Reichenbach, Hans, *Experience and Prediction: An Analysis of the Foundations and the Structure of Knowledge*, Chicago: University of Chicago Press, 1938; 3rd edition, 1961

Suppe, Frederick (ed.), *The Structure of Scientific Theories*, Urbana: University of Illinois Press, 1974

Tuana, Nancy, *Feminism & Science*, Bloomington: Indiana University Press, 1989

The philosophy of science is currently characterized by a wide variety of approaches, ranging from the logical analysis of central scientific concepts (e.g. explanation and confirmation), and historical and sociological investigations of the nature and method of science, to the examination of philosophical problems within individual sciences.

GOWER provides an introduction to the philosophy of science through a historical examination of scientific method. The scope of this work is broad. Discussing the ideas of Galileo, Bacon, and Newton on the role of experiments and the nature of scientific method, the 19th-century debate on the legitimacy of the hypothetical – deductive method, the origin and development of probability theory and the Bayesian approach to science, he then ties these historical discussions to 20th-century philosophers of science, such as Rudolf Carnap, Karl Popper, Thomas S. Kuhn, and Paul Feyerabend. This is a valuable study because it provides a clear and solid interpretation of major figures in the history and philosophy of science, and illustrates their influence on contemporary debates.

While logical positivism is no longer the dominant view in the philosophy of science, it has shaped most 20th-century debates. REICHENBACH provides an excellent account of the logical positivists' approach to science; he critically discusses the nature of verification, proposes a solution to the problem of induction, and introduces the distinction between the context of discovery and the context of justification. Like most logical positivists, he also believes that the philosophy of science should be concerned with logical analysis, that the history of science is irrelevant to the philosophy of science, and that physics is the ideal model for empirical knowledge.

HEMPEL's book is a collection of his most important essays on the philosophy of science. In the title essay, he defends an empiricist covering-law model of explanation, and in the section on the logic of confirmation he presents a purely syntactical analysis of confirmation. Hempel's essays are somewhat technical, but they are the touchstones for most subsequent work in these areas.

POPPER, although not a positivist (he considers himself an opponent of positivism), is very much in the empiricist tradition. Instead of arguing that verification by observation is what demarcates science from non-science, he argues that falsification provides the demarcation criterion: a theory is scientific, if it is open to falsification. His rejection of verification is a reaction to the problem of induction, which he believes the logical positivists never adequately resolved.

KUHN challenges the traditional view of science as a rational, progressive accumulation of empirical truths, arguing that observations are theory-laden and that they underdetermine scientific theories. He concludes that science develops, not by the steady accumulation of empirical knowledge, but by non-cumulative revolutions. Scientific revolutions do not just involve changes in scientific theory, but also changes in the criteria that an adequate theory must meet. In addition, Kuhn argues that, instead of focusing on logical and conceptual analysis, the philosophy of science should be grounded in the history of science. Kuhn was not alone in his critique of the logical positivists, and he synthesized various points from philosophy, history, and sociology. The result was that *The Structure of Scientific Revolutions* served as a point of reference from which a variety of new approaches to the philosophy of science emerged. This work, more than any other, is responsible for the current lack of unanimity within the philosophy of science.

FEYERABEND, noted for his polemical and witty style, argues that there is no single scientific method: that an examination of science reveals that psychological, sociological, economic, political, and historical factors, rather than an adherence to "the scientific method", determine the acceptance of scientific theories. BLOOR, a founder of the Strong Programme and the sociology of scientific knowledge, argues that scientific knowledge is a social phenomenon, and as such can be investigated and explained by sociology. Such a view is a development of Kuhn's and Feyerabend's view that science is shaped by external (such as psychological, sociological, economic, or historical) factors, and directly challenges the philosophy of science by calling for its replacement by the sociology of science.

SUPPE provides a collection of papers from a symposium held in 1969 to discuss the "acute state of disarray" of the philosophy of science. The papers in this volume reveal the depth of disagreement, but what is most valuable is Suppe's lengthy introduction and his afterword. These two essays constitute a classic analysis of the shift from a positivist to a post-positivist philosophy of science.

Laudan, Earman, and Kitcher attempt to re-establish the objectivity and rationality of science in the light of relativist criticisms raised by Kuhn, Feyerabend, and the defenders of the sociology of scientific knowledge. LAUDAN grounds the rationality of science in the progress of science, which he defines as a "research tradition's" ability to solve problems. A research tradition is shaped by sociological factors, but is nevertheless constrained by empirical observation. Thus, this approach recognizes both the social and the empirical elements in scientific knowledge. Moreover, he illustrates how bringing together the history and philosophy of science does not undermine the normative character of the philosophy of science.

Bayesianism is a different and, in many respects, more traditional approach to the philosophy of science. Its objective is to provide an analysis of confirmation using the probability calculus and Bayes's Theorem. Such a formal approach contrasts with the sociological, historical, and contextual analyses that emerged after Kuhn. EARMAN does not unequivocally endorse the Bayesian approach to science, but instead gives a balanced assessment of its successes and weaknesses. He also provides a careful interpretation of Thomas Bayes's original essay of 1763.

KITCHER gives a detailed analysis of three cases in the history of science – Galileo's argument for the heliocentric solar system, Lavoisier's rejection of the phlogiston theory, and Darwin's arguments for evolution – in order to defend the claim that science is progressive and rational. The scope of his analysis, in terms of both the history of science and the philosophy of science, is impressive. He does not endorse a logical positivist approach to science (what he calls "Legend"), but rather defends a view of rationality that recognizes social influences while giving priority to the empirical element in science. He also presents a critique of other current approaches to philosophy of science, including Bayesianism.

HARDING is one of the philosophers who have initiated and developed the feminist critiques of science. Like Kuhn, Feyerabend, and Bloor, she sees scientific knowledge as the result of its social context, and thus argues that the sexist and racist ideologies of Western society are embedded within Western science. Harding provides a critical examination of the various feminist approaches to science, and refines her epistemological standpoint. TUANA's collection of essays, which originally appeared in two special issues of *Hypatia: A Journal of Feminist Philosophy*, examines the relationship between feminism and science. These essays focus upon two themes: feminist theories of science, and case studies of gender biases in science. In addition, Tuana provides an excellent bibliography of feminism and science.

HACKING approaches the philosophy of science via the issue of scientific realism. He provides a sophisticated introduction to the issue of scientific realism (representing) and the nature of experimentation (intervening). He first examines and critiques a plethora of "realisms", and then, through a re-examination of the nature and role of experiments in science, argues for a realist's view of scientific entities.

BOYD, GASPER & TROUT is an excellent anthology of some of the most significant essays in the philosophy of science, covering the period from the logical positivists to the present. The volume is divided into two parts: essays that focus upon general themes in the philosophy of science, and essays that focus on individual sciences. The first section is thematically oriented around the major issues: confirmation, explanation, causation, realism, and reductionism. Each general topic starts with a synoptic introductory essay written by one of the editors, and then proceeds chronologically from some of the early classic essays to recent work: for example, the section on "Confirmation, Semantics, and Scientific Theories" starts with essays by Moritz Schlick, Carnap, and Carl Gustav Hempel and proceeds to essays by Bas van Fraassen, Larry Laudan, and Ian Hacking. The second part of the anthology reflects a recent trend in the philosophy of science; instead of examining science as a general phenomenon, it focuses on philosophical issues that arise within individual sciences, and contains an excellent collection of recent articles on the philosophy of physics, the philosophy of biology, the philosophy of psychology, and the philosophy of the social sciences.

HENRY B. KREUZMAN

See also Experiments; Instrument as Embodied Theory; Measurement; Objectivity; Themata

Photography

Benjamin, Walter, "The Work of Art in the Age of Mechanical Reproduction", in *Illuminations*, edited with an introduction by Hannah Arendt, translated from the German by Harry Zohn, New York: Harcourt Brace, 1968; London: Jonathan Cape, 1970 (original edition, 1955)

Braun, Marta, *Picturing Time: The Work of Etienne-Jules Marey (1830–1904)*, Chicago: University of Chicago Press, 1992

Darius, Jon, *Beyond Vision*, Oxford and New York: Oxford University Press, 1984

Daston, Lorraine and Peter Galison, "The Image of Objectivity", *Representations*, 40 (1992): 81–128

Edwards, Elizabeth (ed.), *Anthropology and Photography, 1860–1920*, New Haven, Connecticut: Yale University Press, 1992

Fox, Daniel M. and Christopher Lawrence, *Photographing Medicine: Images and Power in Britain and America since 1840*, New York: Greenwood Press, 1989

Gernsheim, Helmut, *A Concise History of Photography*, New York: Grosset and Dunlap, and London: Thames and Hudson, 1965; revised edition, New York: Dover, 1986

Gilman, Sander L. (ed.), *The Face of Madness: Hugh Diamond and the Origin of Psychiatric Photography*, Secaucus, New Jersey: Citadel Press, 1976

Ivins, William Jr., *Prints and Visual Communication*, New York: Da Capo Press, 1969

Lalvani, Suren, *Photography, Vision, and the Production of Modern Bodies*, Albany: State of New York Press, 1996

Lankford, John, "Photography and the Nineteenth-Century Transits of Venus", *Technology and Culture*, 28 (1987): 648–57

Pang, Alex Soojung-Kim, "Victorian Observing Practices, Printing Technology and Representations of the Solar Corona", *Journal of the History of Astronomy*, 25 (1994): 249–74

Rosenblum, Naomi, *A History of Women Photographers*, New York: Abbeville Press, 1994

Rothermel, Holly, "Images of the Sun: De La Rue, Airy and Celestial Photography", *British Journal for the History of Science*, 26 (1993): 137–69

Ryan, James R., *Picturing Empire: Photography and the Visualization of the British Empire*, Chicago: University of Chicago Press, 1997

Schaaf, Larry J., *Out of the Shadows: Herschel, Talbot and the Invention of Photography*, New Haven, Connecticut: Yale University Press, 1992

Sekula, Allan, "The Body and the Archive", *October*, 39 (1986): 3–64

Tagg, John, "Power and Photography – A Means of Surveillance: The Photograph as Evidence in Law", *Screen Education*, 36 (1980): 17–55

Thomas, Ann (ed.), *Beauty of Another Order: Photography in Science*, New Haven, Connecticut: Yale University Press, 1997

Trachtenberg, Alan (ed.), *Classic Essays on Photography*, New Haven, Connecticut: Leete's Island Books, 1980

Warner, Deborah Jean, "Lewis M. Rutherfurd: Pioneer Astronomical Photographer and Spectroscopist", *Technology and Culture*, 12 (1971): 190–216

The place of photography and photographic production in the history of science is a relatively new field of scholarship that reflects the growing interest in the relation between art and science, technology and culture, and scientific instruments and observing practices. There is a body of scholarship concerning the history of the medium, and currently the cultural and intellectual history of photography is gaining wider recognition. However, there is often little correspondence between writers in different fields of photographic writing, and although much has been written about artistic and documentary photography, the history of scientific photographs has generally been neglected. One cause of such neglect is the assumption that photography has a fixed identity, determined by its technical evolution. Another is that photographs and prints are incidental to the elaboration of scientific theory. Any new developments in photographic criticism within the history of science will require that historians address the medium itself, including its social and cultural properties; the differences of language and communicative mode that have developed across various photographic practices; its variety of roles within and outside professional scientific culture; and its complex relations with print culture and other visual media, including drawings.

A critical tradition of writing on photography began in the early 19th century, when many hailed it as a new medium of communication. It is worth noting that many of the writers contributing to the serious discussion of the medium have been photographers themselves. TRACHTENBERG contains classic essays on photography by individuals whose writings represent different moments in the development of thought about photography in the United States and Western Europe, including Louis Daguerre, William Henry Fox Talbot, Charles Baudelaire, Paul Strand, and more recent critics such as Walter Benjamin and Roland Barthes.

In his classic essay, "The Work of Art in the Age of Mechanical Reproduction", Walter BENJAMIN argued that photography democratized art by making reproductions available for dissemination to the middle and lower classes. In 1951 William IVINS, Jr wrote that photography freed artists from documentary reproductions and freed scientists from dependence on artists' imprecision. His book became a classic, documenting how the visual image achieved the communicative flexibility of the printed word. John TAGG, like Benjamin and Ivins, also explored how the medium exercised a kind of persuasion. Drawing on insights from what Michel Foucault called the "microphysics of power", Tagg explained that the power of photography rested not in the inherent properties of the medium, but in the institutional spaces that enabled photography to function, within certain contexts, as a kind of proof. Tagg's insights on the relationship between the state and new technologies of knowledge have provided a model for historians of science, especially those interested in the politics of visual evidence.

Among these are DASTON & GALISON, who locate photography in the evolution of western conceptions of objectivity. They argue that illustrated scientific atlases from the 18th and 19th centuries reflect a shift towards a new ideal of objectivity in the 19th century, one that valorized restraint and self-discipline and sought to eliminate the mediating presence of the observer.

There is a significant literature on the pioneering years of photography. GERNSHEIM's history is a comprehensive work on the social history of photography in the 19th century. SCHAAF has produced a well-documented source for the development of photography in England by the scientists, John Herschel and William Fox Talbot. ROSENBLUM's book on early women photographers is one of the few serious studies of women's involvement with the new medium.

Recent work on medical, astronomical, and anthropological photography provides important exceptions to the general neglect of scientific photographs. The two major comprehensive works on the historical applications of photography in science are Thomas and Darius. THOMAS presents a pioneering collection of photographs of scientific subjects. The contributors to the volume, which was published to accompany an exhibition at the National Gallery of Canada, consider the history of scientific photographs and the issues of representation that they inspired. Topics they consider include 19th-century astronomical and medical photography, 20th-century photographs of motion and matter, and non-optical photography. DARIUS presents 100 scientific photographs selected for their historical significance to science. The collection spans the history of photography from calotypes and daguerreotypes to digitally encoded photographs relayed from deep space. Photographic details accompany each image, along with specific references.

Monographs and case studies have explored special moments in the development of scientific photography. BRAUN's study of Etienne-Jules Marey documents the work of the French scientist whose methods of recording movement transformed conventional ways of visualizing time and space. GILMAN investigates the early history of psychiatric photography through the work of the English physician and photographer, Hugh W. Diamond. FOX & LAWRENCE present early photographs of hospital work and healthcare delivery, explicating the links between healthcare, photography, and consumerism in the late 19th and early 20th centuries. The application of photography to the 19th-century science of criminology is taken up by LALVANI. SEKULA's account of criminal photography demonstrates that photography was both a new way of seeing and a new way of being observed by the state.

The problems associated with employing photography as a tool of scientific observation are addressed by recent historians of astronomical photography. LANKFORD focuses on the debates in the international astronomical community surrounding the choice of photographic instrumentation for use in the transit of the Venus expeditions. WARNER has pioneered scholarship on the early history of astronomical photography in the United States. Her paper focuses on Lewis Rutherfurd's development of instruments for both astronomical photography and spectroscopy, such as telescopes, micrometers for measuring celestial photographs, multiprism spectroscopes, and diffraction gratings. She argues that the case of Rutherfurd reveals the interaction of mind and machine in the development of science and for that reason alone it is important to preserve and study material artefacts. ROTHERMEL's exploration of early celestial photography and the solar photography of Warren de la Rue suggests that the disputes over the legitimacy of the photograph as a scientific document in the 1850s and 1860s laid the groundwork for the later successes of the dry-plate period. PANG, who focuses on the photographic activities of scientists who organized solar eclipse expeditions in the Victorian and Edwardian eras, persuasively demonstrates that observing practices and instrument designs were shaped by the practices and culture of British tourism and imperialism.

Recent studies on the early history of anthropological photography reveal the collaboration of anthropology and popular culture in western constructions of race, gender, nation, and empire. EDWARDS's edited collection, the first serious study of the place of photography within anthropology, examines the content and social contexts of over 150 still photographs made in British anthropology between 1860 and 1920. RYAN discusses the place of photography within the imaginative geography of the British empire, its role in 19th-century explorations of Africa, the topographical and landscape work of commercial photographers, and the relationship between photography and science in the practice and representation of imperial warfare.

JENNIFER TUCKER

See also Anthropology; Astronomy: general works; Scientific Instruments: general works

Phrenology

Carnicer, Ramon, *Entre la ciencia y la magia: Mariano Cubí*, Barcelona: Seix Barral, 1969

Cooter, Roger, *The Cultural Meaning of Popular Science: Phrenology and the Organization of Consent in Nineteenth-Century Britain*, Cambridge and New York: Cambridge University Press, 1984

D'Orazio, H., *Gall e la prima diffusione della frenologia in Italia*, Sanità: Scienze e Storia, 1991

Haymaker, Webb and Francis Schiller (eds), *The Founders of Neurology*, Springfield, Illinois: Thomas, 1953, 2nd edition, 1970

Lanteri-Laura, George, *Histoire de la phrénologie: L'homme et son cerveau selon F.J. Gall*, Paris: Presses Universitaires de France, 1970

Lesky, Erna (ed.), *Franz Joseph Gall, 1758–1828: Naturforscher und Anthropologie: Ausgewählte Texte*, Bern: Huber, 1979

McHenry, Lawrence C. (ed.), *Garrison's History of Neurology*, Springfield, Illinois: Thomas, 1969

Martelli, F., L. Baratta and S. Arieti, "Considerazioni preliminari sull'origine della frenologia: l'opera di Vincenzo Malacarne", *Medicina nei Secoli* (1993): 405–18

Shapin, Steven, "Phrenological Knowledge and the Social Structure of Early Nineteenth-Century Edinburgh", *Annals of Science*, 32 (1973): 219–43

Temkin, Owsei, "Gall and the Phrenological Movement", *Bulletin of the History of Medicine*, 21 (1947): 275–321

Thearle, M.J., "The Rise and Fall of Phrenology in Australia", *Australian and New Zealand Journal of Psychiatry*, 27/3 (1993): 518–25

Young, Robert, entry on Franz Joseph Gall in *Dictionary of Scientific Biography*, edited by Charles Coulston Gillispie, vol. 5, New York: Scribner, 1976

The phrenological system represents the most extreme manifestation of the localistic perspective applied to the functions of the central nervous system. Its dissemination was widespread and controversial, not only in the European scientific circles of the late 18th century, but also in the salons of the aristocracy and considerable sectors of Enlightenment society. The scientific personality of its founder, the Austrian physician Franz Joseph Gall (1758–1828), its historical and intellectual background, and its expansion and controversy, have been soundly analyzed in the monograph by LESKY. Further, the famous French neurologist LANTERI-LAURA devoted a descriptive study to the contents and spread of phrenology through a detailed study of Gall's biography.

YOUNG provides a good summary of Gall's phrenological conceptions, his education, his original works, and some references to the impact of the phrenological movement and its dissemination throughout Europe. The same perspective is embraced with excellence by TEMKIN's article, in which the author magisterially establishes a link between Gall's scientific mentality and the success of his system, and the development of contemporary ideas about the nervous system and scientific mentalities.

Like other scientific systems that proliferated in Europe after the Enlightenment (e.g. mesmerism, Brownism, and Broussais's physiological medicine), Gall's phrenological doctrine had a great impact during its author's lifetime, but soon after his death lost currency, was discredited and abandoned in all scientific circles, and was even condemned by such mighty institutions as the Catholic Church.

After these early general assessments of phrenology, other works set out to analyse the reasons behind the swift expansion of phrenological ideas, and to examine their widespread reception within certain scientific circles and social gatherings. MARTELLI, BARATTA & ARIETI examine the connection between Gall's phrenological system and Vincenzo Malacarne's studies on cerebral anatomy, conducted mainly between 1760 and 1794. Malacarne claimed that mental illness had an organic nature that manifested itself in the alteration of the organs of the endocranium, and could be detected through an analysis of the skull's formation. The dissemination of the phrenological system and the early debate it sparked in Italy constitute the main purpose of D'ORAZIO's work.

COOTER examines the social uses of phrenology in early 19th-century Britain. Despite severe criticism of the evidence, phrenology was taken seriously in some quarters, and Cooter argues that this was because it met the needs of some radical social reformers. He stresses the authority of some scientists supporting phrenology, and demonstrates the need for a broader context of social history. Steven SHAPIN analyzes the scientific controversy sparked by phrenology in Edinburgh society, and highlights the implicit and explicit interests of both its advocates and detractors. The craving for social ascendancy, and the desire to depose and replace those who held the academic and scientific power, is part of the motivation that Shapin attributes to the followers of phrenology.

Other works tackle different contexts. Thus, CARNICER analyzes the spread of phrenology in Spain through the figure of Mariano Rubi, its main advocate and author of a book publicizing the phrenological system in Castilian. A similar approach can be found in the writings of Michael John THEARLE, concerning the reception of phrenology in Australia.

Some general books on the history of neurology, such as McHENRY, allude to the origins of phrenology and its links with the widespread tendency to locate cerebral functions, inaugurated in the 18th century.

Other works with a bio-bibliographical content devoted to the history of neurology include information on Franz Joseph Gall. For example, HAYMAKER & SCHILLER includes references to Gall's biography and also gives a detailed exposition of the phrenological doctrine.

JOSEP LLUÍS BARONA

See also Anatomy; Neurosciences

Physical Chemistry

Barkan, Diana K., *Walther Nernst: Physicist as Chemist*, Cambridge: Cambridge University Press, 1997

Cohen, Ernst, *Jacobus Henrikus van't Hoff: Sein Leben und Wirken*, Leipzig: Akademische Verlagsgesellschaft, 1912

Laidler, Keith J., *The World of Physical Chemistry*, Oxford and New York: Oxford University Press, 1993

Nye, Mary Jo, *From Chemical Philosophy to Theoretical Chemistry: Dynamics of Matter and Dynamics of Disciplines, 1800–1950*, Berkeley: University of California Press, 1993

Partington, J.R., *A History of Chemistry*, vol. 4, London: Macmillan, and New York: St Martin's Press, 1970

Root-Bernstein, Robert Scott, "The Ionists: Founding Physical Chemistry 1872–1890", PhD dissertation, Princeton University, New Jersey, 1980

Servos, John W., *Physical Chemistry from Ostwald to Pauling: The Making of a Science in America*, Princeton, New Jersey: Princeton University Press, 1990

The literature on the history of physical chemistry comprises studies of its precarious position between chemistry and physics, general histories, histories focusing on the main institutions, and biographical studies of the main contributors.

NYE's book is an attempt to present the history of the identity of chemistry during the 19th and 20th centuries, and to articulate the methodological complexity of the ambivalences concerning this identity. In many instances her book addresses the question of whether or not chemistry is reducible to physics directly, but it also examines this issue by studying the formation of the boundaries of physical chemistry, chemical physics, theoretical chemistry, and/or quantum chemistry. Nye argues that the legitimacy of theoretical chemistry and the drawing of disciplinary boundaries was the result of a whole network of factors resulting in the construction of the identity of the discipline. She examines such an identity through the systematic discussion of six elements in various cases. These elements are: the genealogy and historical mythology of heroic origins and episodes in the initial period of each discipline; a core literature defining archetypal language and imagery; practices and rituals that are codified and performed; a physical homeland, including institutions based on citizenship rights and responsibilities; external recognition; and shared values together with unsolved problems. Nye traces these elements in the Paris School of theoretical organic chemistry and in the London–Manchester School of theoretical organic chemistry, both for the period 1880–1930, in Christopher Ingold's attempt to integrate physical and organic chemistry, and in the development of quantum chemistry in the United States and Britain up to the end of the 1940s.

Both Laidler and Partington provide general histories of the field without asking the kinds of questions addressed by Nye. LAIDLER has presented the various developments in physical chemistry following a similar format to a typical textbook of physical chemistry. The book starts with a theoretical discussion of some issues in the philosophy of science, and there follows a comprehensive list of all the journals for physical chemistry. The sections on thermodynamics, kinetic theory, and statistical mechanics include some mathematics and many experimental results and there is an analytic discussion of chemical kinetics. Brief biographies of most of the well-known and some more minor figures mentioned in the book are found in an appendix.

Apart from his very influential textbooks, PARTINGTON also wrote extensively on the history of chemistry. The fourth volume contains a section on physical chemistry that provides a detailed narrative of the various developments. It stops in the early 1920s and the references to the original papers are still an invaluable asset in what is otherwise a "scientist's history".

SERVOS presents the emergence of physical chemistry in the United States by concentrating on a number of institutions and individuals who played a pivotal role in the development: MIT and William Albert Noyes's initiatives; the College of Chemistry at Berkeley and Gilbert Newton Lewis's unquestionable dominance in the forming of the academic culture in the US; Cornell and Wilder Bancroft's insistence on the possibilities provided by the phase rule and his influence through his editorship of the *Journal of Physical Chemistry*; the California Institute of Technology where Linus Pauling started his professional career and where he stayed to the end of his life. Of particular interest are the discussions of the process of "migration" of physical chemistry from Europe to the US, in particular of Wilhelm Ostwald's relationship with the many American students who spent time at his laboratory.

ROOT-BERNSTEIN's dissertation is a most thorough account of the rise of physical chemistry. It examines the work of the three "founders", Wilhelm Ostwald, Jacobus van't Hoff,

and Svante Arrhenius, and especially their thermodynamic theory of solutions based on ionic dissociation in electrolytes. These three, of course, were known as the Ionists. Max Planck's largely ignored theory of dissociation, first published in 1887, is also discussed. The analysis revolves around four themes: the different (national) research traditions of the ionists and Planck; the particularity of each investigator in the context of these traditions; how the reception of the innovations introduced by these researchers depended on the compatibility or incompatibility of their styles with the styles of other scientists; and, in contrast to Planck, whose work was at the forefront of a specialized field, how the Ionists's research resulted from the mixing of diverse old traditions and problems with new styles and techniques.

A biography of van't Hoff was written by one of his students, himself a significant figure in physical chemistry, Ernst COHEN. The author presents a detailed analysis of van't Hoff's work, including a wealth of personal data, a complete bibliography of van't Hoff's writings, a list of the honours he received, and a list of the obituaries written about him.

BARKAN has written a scientific biography of Walther Nernst (1864–1941) who won the Nobel prize in 1920 and was one of the main contributors to the study of electrolytic solutions, chemical thermodynamics, the theory of chemical equilibria, quantum chemistry, low temperature phenomena, and photochemistry. He formulated the third law of thermodynamics and exemplified the increasing connection between German technical industry and German academic science. The book discusses in detail the role played by Nernst and his colleagues in Berlin for the reception of Einstein's quantum theory of solids, and the events surrounding Nernst's organization of the first Solvay Conference in 1911, which consolidated the consensus around the newly emerging quantum theory.

KOSTAS GAVROGLU

See also Nernst; Ostwald; Quantum Theory

Physical and Human Geography

Agnew, John, David N. Livingstone and Alisdair Rogers (eds), *Human Geography: An Essential Anthology*, Oxford and Cambridge, Massachusetts: Blackwell, 1996

Beazley, C. Raymond, *The Dawn of Modern Geography* 3 vols, London: John Murray, 1897–1906; New York: Smith, 1949

Bunbury, E.H., *A History of Ancient Geography among the Greeks and Romans from the Earliest Times till the Fall of the Roman Empire*, 2 vols, London: John Murray, 1879; 2nd edition, 1883; New York: Dover, 1959

Hartshorne, Richard, *The Nature of Geography: A Critical Survey of Current Thought in the Light of the Past*, Lancaster, Pennyslvania: The Association, 1939

Johnston, R.J. and P. Claval, *Geography Since the Second World War: An International Survey*, London: Croom Helm, and Totowa, New Jersey: Barnes and Noble, 1984

Livingstone, David N., *The Geographical Tradition: Episodes in the History of a Contested Enterprise*, Oxford and Cambridge, Massachusetts: Blackwell, 1993

Stoddart, D.R., *On Geography and Its History*, Oxford and Cambridge, Massachusetts: Blackwell, 1986

Many geographers consider that their discipline is situated between the natural sciences and the social sciences and that it also acts as a bridge between the two fields. Because of the split that occurred in the 20th century between physical and human geography, there is also much debate about the place of geography. Perhaps as a result of such discussions, there is an established genre of the history of geography written by geographers, not all of which is whiggish – the epithet that is so routinely attached to natural scientists writing history. Human geographers, in particular, are keen to pick up on historiographical debates in the history of science. None the less, the history of geography is not well integrated into the history of science in the sense that very little history is written by non-geographers.

There is something like an established canon of (whiggish) the history of geography, the representatives of which have functioned as boosters. BUNBURY is a history of geography in antiquity in which he discusses the early precursors to the field such as Strabo and Eratosthenes. BEAZLEY argues that mankind made progress during the Dark Ages when the tide of life seemed to ebb, which led through a dawn with futile ventures and partial triumphs to the grandiose discoveries of Bartholomew Diaz (Cape of Good Hope, 1486), Christopher Columbus (America, 1492) and to Magellan's circumnavigation of the globe in 1520–22. In nearly 2,000 pages, Beazley chronicles the voyages of the travellers, the maps that were produced, and geographical theory of the time. HARTSHORNE argues that geography should be the study of material landscape features, both natural and cultural, according to their regional (or "chorographic") interrelations. His book attempts to show that this is what geography has always been about, intrinsically. Written in 1939, it provided a self-justification for the discipline of geography in the decades of its professionalization.

JOHNSTON & CLAVAL grapple with the theories of Kuhn, Popper and Lakatos, in their search for an appropriate contextual history. Its usefulness lies in its scope, which covers much more than the Anglo-Saxon world. In separate chapters, the history of geography of the following geographical areas is covered: France, Italy, Southeastern Europe, the Soviet Union, the United Kingdom, Poland, German-speaking countries, North America, the Netherlands (only human geography), Japan, the Spanish- and Portuguese-speaking world.

STODDART is a collection of essays inspired by the Gramscian notion of hegemony and written in opposition to the canon. Many of the essays are concerned with the institutionalization and professionalization of geography in the context of the British Empire, especially with the role of the Royal Geographical Society. Another important strand in the book is the influence of Darwin (and more generally biology) on geography, and the importation of notions such as organism and ecosystem.

AGNEW, LIVINGSTONE & ROGERS is a 696-page anthology of "classical" writings in human geography ranging from 19th-century practitioners, such as Peter Kropotkin (otherwise mainly known as a theoretician of anarchism) and Paul Vidal de la Blache to modern practitioners such as David Harvey and Allan Pred. The volume deals with power in the history of geography, and many articles are informed by Marx, Foucault or gender theoreticians (an article by Donna Haraway is included). Given the high level of concern for methodology, there is a curious lack of reflexivity with regard to the articles included. They are treated as great texts and their contextualization is minimal. A useful chapter by Horacio Capel describes the struggle for a disciplinary identity in the 19th century between geology, geophysics, cartography and meteorology. He argues that for France, Germany, Britain, the US, and Russia, geography owed its growth to the mushrooming of school geography with nationalist overtones.

LIVINGSTONE is a collection of eight essays on the history of geography in periods ranging from the Renaissance to the mid-20th century. He draws on the sociology of science in order to situate the history of geography in the contingent "messiness" within each period. Livingstone's historiography is clearly recognizable from the perspective of modern-day history of science: he is concerned, for example, with the negotiation of disciplinary boundaries, authority, religion, race, and quantification.

ARNE HESSENBRUCH

Physics: 20th century

Forman, Paul, "Behind Quantum Electronics: National Security as Basis for Physical Research in the United States, 1940–1960", *Historical Studies in the Physical and Biological Sciences*, 18 (1987): 149–229

Galison, Peter, *How Experiments End*, Chicago: University of Chicago Press, 1987

Galison, Peter, *Image and Logic: A Material Culture of Microphysics*, Chicago: University of Chicago Press, 1997

Hoddeson, Lillian *et al.* (eds), *Out of the Crystal Maze: Chapters from the History of Solid-State Physics*, Oxford and New York: Oxford University Press, 1992

Kevles, Daniel J., *The Physicists: The History of a Scientific Community in Modern America*, New York: Knopf, 1977; revised edition, Cambridge, Massachusetts: Harvard University Press, 1995

Kragh, Helge, *Cosmology and Controversy: The Historical Development of Two Theories of the Universe*, Princeton, New Jersey: Princeton University Press, 1996

Pickering, Andrew, *Constructing Quarks: A Sociological History of Particle Physics*, Edinburgh: Edinburgh University Press, and Chicago: University of Chicago Press, 1984

During the 20th century physics has gone from being a minor, backwater discipline to one commanding unparalleled prestige and government support, at least in the US. The century opened with conceptual upheaval, as special and general relativity, along with quantum mechanics, upset long-held worldviews. Physicists followed these theoretical developments, completed during the first quarter of the century, with excursions into studies of the atomic nucleus, relativistic quantum mechanics, and anti-matter. Even before World War II, physics and physicists had begun to move outside of purely academic settings, to work with and within industry. The push during the 1940s to enlist physics and physicists into wartime service, however, changed the very nature of the discipline: work on radar, proximity fuses, and the atomic bomb was completed in special interdisciplinary laboratories, and the US government provided nearly limitless funding. This shift to "big science" continued after 1945, as tremendous federal, and usually military, capital outlays paid for ever-larger, accelerators for investigating the sub-atomic realm. The war and its aftermath also marked a transition from the European domination of physics to increased American leadership. The scale of and support for physics during and after World War II brought with it tensions over what should actually be considered physics, how this work should be funded, and what roles physicists should play in the larger debates of national and international policy.

Most of the historical literature on 20th-century physics, especially that which treats work from the 1930s onward, has focused almost entirely on elementary nuclear and particle physics. This emphasis derives both from the unprecedented nature of the work completed at Los Alamos during World War II, and from the lasting influence held by this "Los Alamos generation" of high-energy physicists in the inner circles of political power throughout the Cold War. Topics that are not directly linked to high-energy particle physics, such as solid state physics (now usually called condensed matter physics), or gravitational physics, have remained little studied by historians. Although several historians have turned to these topics recently, much work remains to be done, if historians are to understand these areas with the same breadth and detail as particle physics.

KEVLES remains the best general introduction to the social and institutional changes within American physics during the 20th century. A constant theme throughout the study concerns the tensions between "best-science elitism" on the one hand, and the rhetoric of democratic pluralism on the other. The final third of the book focuses on the shifting political fortunes of the "Los Alamos generation" following the war, as they lobbied to form a civilian Atomic Energy Commission, a federally-funded National Science Foundation, and a standing Presidential Science Advisory Committee. Widespread disapproval of military-supported research on university campuses during the Vietnam War later helped to challenge the physicists' unquestioned authority. Certain intellectual developments, such as the birth of quantum mechanics and its role in helping to change the balance between experimental and theoretical physics in the US, are discussed in the book. Overall, however, there is no systematic attempt to relate the social, political, and institutional elements of the discipline to the content of science. Such shortcomings aside, Kevles's book offers a broad, well-written overview of the dramatic changes in physics throughout the 20th century.

FORMAN's article focuses more specifically on the question of military patronage for American academic physics during and after World War II. With unrelenting statistical detail, Forman demonstrates the qualitative change in the source and scale of funding for physics from the prewar trends. Debatably, Forman concludes that academic physicists capitulated their intellectual and moral independence in response to the influx of military dollars. Though many physicists claimed at the time to be fooling the military into supporting "basic" research, Forman argues that in the final analysis, it was the military who held the upper hand and ultimately determined the direction of physics research.

Against this backdrop of increased funding for postwar nuclear and particle research, PICKERING offers an important and detailed look into changes within elementary particle physics from the 1950s to the 1980s. Drawing explicitly on sociological categories, Pickering argues that the acceptance of the quark model by particle physicists by the early 1970s had more to do with "opportunism" among experimentalists and theorists than with any fundamental constituents of nature. The new gauge theories offered theorists a chance to extend several of their hard-won skills, while pointing to a host of potential new effects for experimentalists to search for and discover. Much of Pickering's detailed analysis of these subtle changes within theoretical physics and within experimental practice, however, may be read independently of his own constructivist conclusions.

Galison's two studies present a different view of the relationship between experiment and theory in elementary particle physics. Rather than a simple symbiosis, the author charts distinct traditions within experiment and instrument-design, which show no easy correlation with changes in theoretical physics. The case studies in GALISON (1987) chart the change in scale within elementary particle physics, from the 1910s through the 1970s; along with these changes in scale have come changes in how physicists work together in groups and evaluate each others' work. GALISON (1997) continues this line of argument by tracing two distinct traditions within particle physics instrumentation: an "image" tradition (Wilson cloud chambers, nuclear emulsions, and bubble chambers) focused on capturing single events photographically, and a "logic" tradition (Geiger counters, spark chambers) centered on the accumulation of large statistics rather than individual events. Galison's work thereby challenges accounts of 20th-century physics that are based solely on theoretical developments and changes.

The elementary particle physicists who were studied in such detail do not represent more than one-tenth of all the professional physicists in America, and yet historians know far less about the remaining majority. It is this majority that developed most of the practical advances offered by physicists during the 20th century, from materials science to communications technology. An important first step in charting the history of solid-state physics comes in HODDESON et al's collection. Essays included here, written both by historians and physicists, trace conceptual and experimental changes within solid state physics from the 1910s through the 1960s. An important area has been the study of superconductivity, and attempts to explain the phenomenon quantum-mechanically. Especially helpful for historians is Spencer Weart's contribution on the development of a self-identified community of solid state physicists. Weart focuses on how the group came to demarcate its subject with new journals, teach students with new textbooks, and share ideas in new conferences.

Finally, another area of 20th-century physics that has attracted limited historical attention is gravitation and cosmology. General relativity fell from most physicists' curricula during the 1930s and 1940s; physicists who reintroduced it during the 1950s often reformulated its key concepts. Yet many physicists only recognized the importance of studying gravitation only in the late 1960s, following the consolidation of the big bang model of cosmology. KRAGH's book is the first study by an historian of the complicated debates from the late 1940s through the mid-1960s between a steady-state model, in which the universe has existed for all times, and a big bang model, in which the universe began a finite time ago. When they began, these debates sparked the interest of very few physicists overall, and cosmology was often mocked as more speculation than science. The sophisticated interweaving of astronomy, gravitation, and nuclear physics, however, convinced some physicists to take the ideas seriously. During the past two decades, cosmology has been a "boom industry" within physics, and Kragh's book lays important groundwork for understanding this transition.

DAVID KAISER

See also Astrophysics; Cosmology; Nuclear Physics; Particle Physics; Solid State Physics

Physikalisch-Technische Reichsanstalt

Bortfeld, Jochen, Wilfried Hauser and Helmut Rechenberg (eds), *Forschen-Messen-Prüfen, 100 Jahre Physikalisch-Technische Reichsanstalt/Bundesanstalt*, Weinheim: Chemie, 1987

Bruch, Rüdiger vom and Rainer A. Müller (eds), *Formen ausserstaatlicher Wissenschaftsförderung im 19. und 20. Jahrhundert: Deutschland im europäischen Vergleich*, Stuttgart: Steiner, 1990

Buchheim, Gisela, "Die Gründungsgeschichte der Physikalisch-Technischen Reichsanstalt von 1872 bis 1887", in *Dresdener Beiträge zur Geschichte der Technikwissenschaften*, Dresden, 1981–82

Cahan, David, *An Institute for an Empire: The Physikalisch-Technische Reichsanstalt, 1871–1918*, Cambridge and New York: Cambridge University Press, 1989

James, Frank A.J.L., *The Development of the Laboratory: Essays on the Place of Experiment in Industrial Civilization*, London: Macmillan, and New York: American Institute of Physics, 1989

Kern, Ulrich, *Forschung und Präzisionsmessung*, Weinheim: Verlag Chemie, 1994

Lundgreen, Peter *et al.* (eds), *Staatliche Forschung in Deutschland, 1870–1980*, Frankfurt: Campus, 1986

Moser, Helmut (ed.), *Forschung und Prüfung: 75 Jahre PTR/PTB*, Braunschweig: Vieweg, 1962

Stark, Johannes (ed.), *Forschung und Prüfung: 50 Jahre PTR*, Leipzig: Hirzel, 1937

The Physikalisch-Technische Reichsanstalt (PTR) is one of the German research institutions that have received the most attention in the history of science. This is due to the fact that, for a decade around the turn of the 20th century, the PTR was a model institution for the development of physics and technology, especially in the field of modern precision physics and metrology; for example, its research in light technology and

the theory of radiation led directly to the formulation of the quantum hypothesis. The PTR was also a model for the structure of modern institutions, realizing an "institutional innovation principle" which had considerable effect, providing a precedent for today's Big Science centres.

BUCHHEIM is based on a thesis from 1978, and gives a very detailed overview of the negotiations for the creation of the PTR during the 15-year period prior to its actual inauguration. She points out the successful efforts of the electric industry, and especially of Werner von Siemens, to induce the state to establish an "institute for the experimental promotion of the exact sciences and precision technology". The state's involvement in research was intended to improve the general conditions of production. Within the context of her Marxist approach, Buchheim interprets the foundational history of the PTR as an early state monopolist use of science as a factor of production. The internal scientific and technological processes behind the foundation are not attended to in any great detail.

These processes are, however, emphasised by CAHAN, who sets the history of the PTR within the context of the "institutional revolution" in German physical research in the late 19th century. Cahan's book gives an overview of institutional physics in Germany and the history of the PTR up to World War I, the three decades that saw the scientific heyday of the institution, and in which it achieved national and international attention as a result of several acknowledged scientific and technological feats. KERN is a chronological follow-up to Cahan, examining the history of the PTR from the end of World War I until its reconstruction in 1948 as the Physikalisch-Technische Bundesanstalt (PTB), the metrological institution of the new Federal Republic of Germany. In contrast to Cahan, Kern limits himself to the presentation of scientific connections; the relation of the institution to the government, to other scientific institutions in Germany, and to the wider German society, is only mentioned briefly.

The reader wanting to learn more concerning the internal scientific problems in the development of modern metrology, and the activities of the PTR/PTB in this field, can find plenty of information in the commemorative publications on the occasion of the 50th (STARK), 75th (MOSER) and 100th (BORTFELDT, HAUSER & RECHENBERG) anniversaries of the institution. All these works offer uncritical and historically doubtful treatises of the PTR's history, along with brief histories of two further state metrological institutions: the Kaiserliche Normal-Eichungs-Kommission, and the Reichsanstalt for weights and measures, which were merged in 1923. In addition, Bortfeldt, Hauser & Rechenberg gives a brief overview of the development of institutionalized metrology in the East German state, the German Democratic Republic.

In Bruch & Müller, and in Lundgreen *et al*, the history of the PTR is presented as a prominent example of the relation between government and science. The German government is shown to have given applied science a dual function in the modernization of society: research and service. Lundgreen *et al* adopts the approach of science studies, and contains plenty of statistical material and synoptic overviews comparing the history of institutional metrology in Germany with other activities of governmental research, from deposit science (*Lagerstättenkunde*) and agriculture, to aviation and space research. BRUCH & MÜLLER's omnibus volume compares public with private support for science, and examines the historical development of such support on a national and international level. The topics covered stretch from the Kaiser-Wilhelm-Gesellschaft, to the Notgemeinschaft/Deutsche Forschungsgemeinschaft, and industrial patronage in Britain. Both books follow developments up to modern times.

JAMES's edited volume contains an abbreviated history of the PTR by David Cahan. The juxtaposition of this with the other articles in the volume enables an integration and comparison of the PTR's history with the histories of other important international laboratories of the 19th and 20th centuries – not only in scientific terms, but also in terms of architecture, personnel, and equipment.

DIETER HOFFMANN
translated by Klaus Staubermann

See also Metrology

Physiology: France

Albury, W.R., "Experiment and Explanation in the Physiology of Bichat and Magendie", *Studies in the History of Biology*, 1 (1975): 47–131

Bonah, Christian, *Les Sciences physiologiques en Europe: Analyses comparées du XIXe siècle*, Paris: Vrin, 1995

Canguilhem, Georges and Maurice Caullery, "Physiologie animale, chapitre VI", in *Histoire générale des sciences*, vol. 1, "Le Dix-neuvième siècle", edited by René Taton, Paris: Presses Universitaires de France, 1961

Canguilhem, Georges, "La Constitution de la physiologie comme science", in *Physiologie*, edited by Charles Kayser, vol. 1, Paris : Flammarion, 1963

Coleman, William, "The Cognitive Basis of the Discipline: Claude Bernard on Physiology", *Isis*, 76 (1985): 49–70

Dagognet, François, *Etienne-Jules Marey: A Passion for the Trace*, translated from the French by Robert Galeta, New York: Zone Books, 1992 (original edition 1987)

Debru, Claude, Jean Gayon and Jean-François Picard (eds), *Les Sciences biologiques et médicales en France, 1920–1950*, Paris: CNRS, 1994

Debru, Claude (ed.), *Essays in the History of the Physiological Sciences: Proceedings of a Symposium of the European Association for the History of Medicine and Health*, Amsterdam: Rodopi, 1995

Florkin, Marcel, *Léon Fredericq et les débuts de la physiologie en Belgique*, Brussells: Lebegue, 1943

Grmek, Mirko Drazen, *Catalogue des manuscrits de Claude Bernard, avec la bibliographie de ses travaux imprimes et des études sur son oeuvre*, Paris: Masson, 1967

Grmek, Mirko Drazen, *Raisonnement expérimental et recherches toxicologiques chez Claude Bernard*, Geneva: Droz, 1973; abridged edition as *Claude Bernard et la méthode expérimentale*, Paris: Payot, 1991

Holmes, Frederic L., *Claude Bernard and Animal Chemistry: The Emergence of a Scientist*, Cambridge, Massachusetts: Harvard University Press, 1974

Jacyna, L.S., "Medical Science and Moral Science: The Cultural Relations of Physiology in Restoration France", *History of Science*, 25/2 (1987): 111–46

Klein, Marc, *Regards d'un biologiste: Evolution de l'approche scientifique–l'enseignement medical strasbourgeois*, Paris: Hermann, 1980

Legée, Georgette, *Pierre Flourens 1794–1867: Physiologiste et historien des sciences*, Abbeville: Paillart, 1992

Lesch, John E., *Science and Medicine in France: The Emergence of Experimental Physiology, 1790–1855*, Cambridge, Massachusetts: Harvard University Press, 1984

Michel, Jacques (ed.), *La Necessité de Claude Bernard*, Paris: Meridiens Klincksieck, 1991

Olmsted, J.M.D., *François Magendie: Pioneer in Experimental Physiology and Scientific Médicine in XIXth Century France*, New York: Schumann, 1944

Olmsted, J.M.D., *Charles-Edouard Brown-Séquard: A Nineteenth Century Neurologist and Endocrinologist*, Baltimore: Johns Hopkins Press, 1946

Olmsted, J.M.D., *Claude Bernard and the Experimental Method in Medicine*, New York: Schumann, 1952

Paul, Harry W., *From Knowledge to Power: The Rise of the Science Empire in France, 1860–1939*, Cambridge and New York: Cambridge University Press, 1985

Rothschuh, Karl E., *History of Physiology*, translated from the German and edited by Guenter B. Risse, Huntington, New York: Krieger, 1973 (original edition, 1953)

Schiller, Joseph, *Claude Bernard et les problèmes scientifiques de son temps*, Paris: Les Editions du Cèdre, 1967

Physiology as a specialized discipline was founded during the 19th century, when it was characterized as an experimental science. The literature listed here deals with this process within the frontiers of the French national state. Physiology, in the narrow sense, is a pure science, concerned with the study of the functions and functioning of animal and human bodies. Nevertheless, a survey of the secondary literature on its development must not lose sight of the fact that these disciplinary changes occurred within a field of tensions, produced, on the one hand, by the nascent biological sciences (especially after the publication of Darwin's theory of evolution), and, on the other hand, by the expectations and ideas of medical practice. Physiology as an independent discipline was thus influenced from two sides and, in the wider meaning of the term, cannot therefore be unambiguously and entirely separated from these two neighbouring areas.

There are essentially two phases in the development of physiology in France, the first characterized by the rise of experimental physiology in the first half of the 19th century, and the second by the flowering and subsequent differentiation of the subject between 1850 and 1950.

The history of science has, according to its changing identity, approached physiology from various perspectives, under various main themes, and through several periods. The first phase of the history of physiology in France has attracted much attention from historians, who have concerned themselves with the original crystallization of modern physiology. At a time when Germany was steeped in Romantic thought, the first outlines of a scientific experimental physiology came into being in France. The interest in this development has been amplified by the fact that France is generally regarded as retaining the lead in the life sciences to this day. The second phase is largely dominated by studies on Claude Bernard, the outstanding personality of French physiology in the second half of the 19th century. There are two main reasons for this: first, Bernard's organistic-vivisectional perspective offers an influential alternative to the reductionist-physicalist orientation in physiology that became dominant in Germany from about 1850; second, Bernard is seen to buck the trend of French decline in the sciences from 1850 to 1900.

Initially, in the 1940s, OLMSTED wrote biographies of the three outstanding personalities of French physiology: François Magendie (1944); Charles-Edouard Brown-Séquard (1946); and Bernard (1952). FLORKIN's study of Léon Fredericq represents a comparable work for French-speaking Belgium in the 1880s. In many respects, these earlier works do not comply with the standards of modern biographical scholarship; their descriptive, and to some extent hagiographical, accounts lack virtually any contextualization in terms of the political and social context, as neither the connections and prerequisites for scientists' career strategies, nor the disciplinary and institutional organization, are described and analysed. However, in some cases – e.g. Olmsted (1946) – they remain the only work available on their particular subject.

ROTHSCHUH's account combined these eclectic accounts into a synthetic narrative of "all" individuals and discoveries of any importance in the history of physiology, and provides a succession of "great" discoverers and discoveries in the field. It contains an introduction to, and survey of, the events in the development of physiology within the European context and thus also in France. Guenter Risse has translated, reorganized, and expanded the book specifically for an English-speaking audience. This standard work is based on a first comprehensive presentation in Heinrich Borruttau's *Geschichte der Physiologie in ihrer Anwendung auf die Medizin bis zum Ende des Neunzehnten Jahrhunderts*, which originally appeared in 1903 in the *Handbuch der Geschichte der Medizin* by Neuburger and Pagel.

A stimulating, alternative presentation has been undertaken in CANGUILHEM & CAULLERY, and more thoroughly in CANGUILHEM. Canguilhem shifts the emphasis away from individual physiologists and master-apprentice relationships towards an internal history of ideas; the history of physiology thus becomes a history of its configuration of problems, its technologies, and its methodology. This account corresponds to the development of an epistemologically-orientated history of science that was so characteristic of France in the 1960s, and which was the outcome of the old institutional links between philosophy and the history of science in that country. Canguilhem's epistemological history of ideas is epitomized by his *bon mot* "the history of physiology has made itself relatively independent of the history of physiologists".

During the 1970s, historians of medicine and science renewed their interest in French physiology, and, in this process, Claude Bernard almost exclusively absorbed their attention as the central figure and emblem of this new, foundational medical science. The study of the manuscripts and laboratory diaries of the author of the "grande charte de la physiologie" – his *Introduction à l'étude de la médecine expérimentale* of 1865 – especially by GRMEK (1967), led to the excellent and detailed representations of Bernard's scientific practice and thinking in GRMEK (1973) and HOLMES, two

leading historians of science in France and the US respectively. Holmes deals chiefly with Bernard's early work, combining intellectual and cultural history; Grmek, on the other hand, stays closer to the French tradition of an event-centred history of ideas. These two studies largely take the place of earlier works by Olmsted and SCHILLER, and have been supplemented in the mid-1980s by COLEMAN's general essay on the significance of Bernard's work as a cognitive basis for the formation of physiology as a discipline in France. Yet the fascination with the personality and the influence of the "true" founder of French physiology has not abated: for example, in 1991, MICHEL's collection appeared, the result of a French conference on the continuing *"nécessité de Claude Bernard"*, at which various aspects of his work and thought, and his continuing impact were discussed.

With the exception of the personality of Bernard and the Parisian milieu, there have been few studies of French physiology during the second half of the 19th century. Compared with the treatment by historians of German physiology of the same period, the institutional development of French physiology as an orthodox medical discipline and the practical work in laboratories and classrooms have been largely ignored. On the one hand, this reflects a reorientation among Anglo-American historians over the past 20 years, who have transferred their interest to German physiology. On the other hand, this development indicates flaws in the perception of French representatives of the practice-focused historiography of science of the 1980s and 1990s. Even the sole exception to this, DAGOGNET's work on Jules Etienne Marey, does not substantially modify this observation.

During the 1980s there were renewed disputes over the early phase of French physiology. Unfortunately, LEGÉE's factual biography of Pierre Flourens ignores all modern historiographical approaches, and has similar flaws to the earlier work of Olmsted, discussed above. Meanwhile, English-speaking authors remain especially fascinated with this earlier phase in the history of French physiology. ALBURY thus came up with a comparative analysis of the use and function of experiments by Bichat and Magendie, and his study transformed the historical presentation from the biographical mode into a systematic and analytical intellectual history. LESCH, in the most detailed and comprehensive study of early French physiology to date, then completed this historiographical re-orientation in two important respects: first he expanded his analysis to include the underlying connections between physiology as a science and medicine as an art of healing, charting the impact of the latter on the development of the former and the significance of the former for innovations in the latter; and second, he integrated physiology as a science within its cultural and political contexts. Furthermore, JACYNA successfully produced a unique study that brings out the complexity of these interconnections between medical and moral science in Restoration France. A comparatively profound analysis of the relationship between positivism and French biology in the second half of the 19th century can be found in PAUL's even broader study of the significance of the rise of science within French society between 1860 and 1939. A number of very neglected, yet important essays on the history of French physiology can be found in KLEIN's collection, which has unfortunately appeared under an extremely misleading title; in fact, it contains accounts of the development of cell theory in France, the relationship between biology and philosophy (especially within the context of Bernard), and the emergence of endocrinology from physiology.

There are three further studies that are significantly removed from this general picture, and give an idea of historiographical developments in the 1990s. BONAH's comparative study of the history of physiology in Europe in the second half of the 19th century fits the various national formations of physiology into the larger framework of the biological sciences. This revision is carried out above all through a methodologically novel, scientometric handling of previously neglected source material, such as physiological journals from Germany, France, and Britain. It turns out that, in the second half of the 19th-century, physiology developed from a nationally-defined mongrel, born of medicine and natural science, into an international speciality of bodily functions, very much influenced by morphology. DEBRU, GAYON & PICARD, a collection of essays on the development of the biological and medical sciences in France between 1920 and 1950, examines for the first time some aspects of the development of French physiology after the turn of the century. Finally, DEBRU's collection of essays on the history of physiology addresses certain aspects of some neglected topics within French physiology, such as the concerns of endocrinology and physiology's links with medicine.

CHRISTIAN BONAH
translated by Anna-Katherina Meyer

See also Experimental Physiology; Physiology: Germany

Physiology: Germany

Bäumer, Beatrix, *Von der physiologischen Chemie zur frühen biochemischen Arzneimittelforschung: der Apotheker und Chemiker Eugen Baumann (1846–1896) an den Universitäten Strassburg, Berlin, Freiburg und in der pharmazeutischen Industrie*, Braunschweig: Apotheker, 1996

Ben-David, Joseph, *The Scientist's Role in Society: A Comparative Study*, Englewood Cliffs, New Jersey: Prentice-Hall, 1971

Bonah, Christian, *Les Sciences physiologiques en Europe: Analyses comparées du XIXe siècle*, Paris: Vrin, 1995

Cahan, David, *Hermann von Helmholtz and the Foundations of Nineteenth-Century Science*, Berkeley: University of California Press, 1993

Coleman, William and Frederic L. Holmes (eds), *The Investigative Enterprise: Experimental Physiology in Nineteenth-Century Medicine*, Berkeley: University of California Press, 1988

Cranefield, Paul F., "The Organic Physics of 1847 and the Biophysics of Today", *Journal of the History of Medicine and Allied Sciences*, 12 (1957): 407–23

Cunningham, Andrew and Perry Williams (eds), *The Laboratory Revolution in Medicine*, Cambridge and New York: Cambridge University Press, 1992

Hagner, Michael and Bettina Wahrig-Schmidt (eds), *Johannes Müller und die Philosophie*, Berlin: Akademie, 1992

Hagner, Michael and Hans-Jörg Rheinberger, *Die Experimentalisierung des Lebens: Experimentalsysteme in den biologischen Wissenschaften 1850–1950*, Berlin: Akademie, 1993

Krüger, Lorenz (ed.), *Universalgenie Helmholtz: Rückblick nach 100 Jahren*, Berlin: Akademie, 1994

Lenoir, Timothy, *The Strategy of Life: Teleology and Mechanics in Nineteenth Century German Biology*, Dordrecht and Boston: Reidel, 1982

Lenoir, Timothy, *Politik im Tempel der Wissenschaft: Forschung und Machtausübung im deutschen Kaiserreich*, Frankfurt: Campus, 1992

Lohff, Brigitte, *Die Suche nach der Wissenschaftlichkeit der Physiologie in der Zeit der Romantik: Ein Beitrag zur Erkenntnisphilosophie*, Stuttgart: Fischer, 1990

Rothschuh, Karl E., *Entwicklungsgeschichte physiologischer Probleme in Tabellenform*, Munich and Berlin: Urban Schwarzenberg, 1952

Rothschuh, Karl E., *Physiologie: Der Wandel ihrer Konzepte, Probleme und Methoden vom 16. bis 19. Jahrhundert*, Freiburg: Alber, 1968

Rothschuh, Karl E., *History of Physiology*, translated from the German and edited by Guenter B. Risse, Huntington, New York: Krieger, 1973 (original edition, 1953)

Schroer, Heinz, *Carl Ludwig: Begründer der messenden Experimental-physiologie, 1816–1895*, Stuttgart: Wissenschaftliche Verlagsgesellschaft, 1967

Tuchman, Arleen Marcia, *Science, Medicine and the State in Germany: The Case of Baden, 1815–1871*, New York: Oxford University Press, 1993

Turner, R. Steven, *In the Eye's Mind: Vision and the Helmholtz-Hering Controversy*, Princeton, New Jersey: Princeton University Press, 1994

Zloczower, Awraham, *Career Opportunities and the Growth of Scientific Discovery in Nineteenth Century Germany*, Jerusalem: Hebrew University, 1966; New York: Arno Press, 1981

Physiology in the German-speaking lands will be considered largely as a specialist experimental discipline of the 19th and 20th centuries. In view of the relatively late development of the German nation state, "Germany" will be equated with the "German-speaking lands", a position that largely corresponds to the scientific organization of the German states during the 19th century.

The historiography of physiology in Germany has followed a different line of development than that of France. ROTHSCHUH (1952) is the first serious, and at once outstanding, treatment of the history of German physiology; this collection "of all physiological discoveries" is still useful today, despite its rather one-sided national bias and its very positivistic orientation. This was followed a year later by ROTHSCHUH (1973), reorganized, expanded, and translated by Risse from the original edition of 1953. In this form it must still be regarded as the standard work on the subject. It is chiefly a history of "great" physiologists, rather than a representation of the cognitive developments and ideas of the subject, and Rothschuh directs his attention to teacher–pupil relations, and describes the scientists and their institutions. Towards the end of the 1960s, ROTHSCHUH (1968) followed Canguilhem's work on the history of ideas in physiology, and expanded his studies to comprise a detailed account of the changes in physiological concepts, problems, and methods between the 16th and the 19th centuries. Almost simultaneously, CRANEFIELD published an important essay on the physicalist and materialist orientation of German physiology since the mid-19th century, a development that is associated above all with the "Four of 1847": DuBois-Reymond, Helmholtz, Brücke, and Ludwig. Cranefield draws attention to the fact that the triumph of experimental physiology in the mid-19th century cannot be satisfactorily explained by the intellectual success of this leading group of physiologists. SCHROER supplements this first phase in the historical treatment of German physiology with a biographical study of its most important personality, Carl Ludwig, and his school. Yet, neither in its perspective nor in its analytical depth, does this presentation compare with the literature on its French equivalent, Claude Bernard.

Subsequent to these initial endeavours in the history of German physiology, academic interest in this early paradigm of German laboratory medicine all but disappeared for two decades, only to reappear with renewed vigour in the mid-1980s, when it constituted a veritable renaissance of the historiography of German physiology. In the meantime, a revolution had occurred within the history of science. The internalism–externalism debate of the 1970s and the "social studies of science" movement had fundamentally reorganized the perspectives, principal topics, and questions within the historical study of science. Also, in the meantime, the general political, economic, and scientific "take-off" of Germany after 1840 had begun to claim the attention of historians of science. The path-breaking studies by ZLOCZOWER and BEN-DAVID on the significance of the social role of scientists and the organization of scientific work had a fundamental impact on the manner in which German physiology has since been treated. Above all, the following themes were identified in the scientific development towards a modern Germany: the German university system as a market place characterized by competitive behaviour; state intervention with a view towards modernization; and systems theory. Within this argument, the discipline of physiology serves at least as an example of, or case for, ongoing general discussions of scientific development as it constitutes an independent topic in its own right.

From this background arose three crucial developments in the historiography of German physiology, in the wider sense. First, the search for the origins of the rapid development of physiology, which thus became the epitome of the development of German laboratory medicine. The evolution in Germany of the biological sciences from the Romantic movement of the early 19th century onwards has been studied above all by LENOIR (1982), who largely avoids an opposition of "external" (political, instrumental, economic, cultural, etc.) and "internal" (cognitive) factors, but attempts to weave them together within a single explanatory structure. A similar approach has been pursued by LOHFF, in her quest for the origins of scientificity in the physiology of the Romantic era. While Lenoir discusses the biology of the whole of the 19th century, Lohff confines herself exclusively to the Romantic period (i.e. 1800–30), and to physiology as a subdiscipline of medicine. In

this argument, Johannes Müller and his school assume cardinal importance, representing the transition from Romanticism to physicalist physiology. A collection edited by HAGNER & WAHRIG-SCHMIDT attempts, from various historical, philosophical, analytical, and social-constructivist perspectives, to determine the specific relationship between philosophy and physiology in, and following, the work of Müller.

Second, the question of the status of the laboratory and of experimental systems within scientific work became a focal point in the historiography of physiology, indicating a shift in the disciplinary perception of how the production of scientific knowledge actually functions. Also, this means a shift of interest, from a theoretical-cognitivistic logic of development, towards a complex, holistic analysis of discursive and non-discursive practices and conditions. The most detailed and convincing studies on the history of physiology have mostly remained within this domain, among them a collection by COLEMAN & HOLMES, whose editors are especially concerned to represent "scientific investigation" as a "nexus of overlapping, interlocking thought, actions and conditions", and thus to avoid imposing artificial demarcations. The volume contains excellent contributions by Holmes, Tuchman, Coleman, Lenoir, Frank, and Lesch, which chiefly, but not exclusively, deal with physiology in Germany. A second collection, edited by CUNNINGHAM & WILLIAMS, addresses the same issue in more general terms; using the history of physiology to discuss the development of ideas and procedures within laboratory medicine, the collection contextualizes this process within a network of channels and authorities, and within the framework of a pragmatic theory of science. A third, important contribution to this historiographical approach is yet another collection, edited by HAGNER & RHEINBERGER, which aims to alert the attention of historians to the importance of the scientific apparatus and the entire experimental side of the research process. For the editors, experimental systems (within this context) constitute precisely one of those moments in the process of scientific labour that can be claimed to represent the whole amalgam, consisting of research subject, theory, experimental arrangement, instruments, as well as disciplinary and social dispositions. Finally, and somewhat on the margins of the development charted here, TUCHMAN studies the impact of the politics of modernization of the state of Baden on Henle's idea of a scientific medicine, and the ways in which experimental physiology was fostered at the university of Heidelberg, especially after the appointment of Helmholtz in 1850. A collection by LENOIR (1992) in German, on the topic of research and power in the German empire, consists of new articles as well as ones previously published in English, and uses physiology in particular to state its case.

The third approach in the historiography of German physiology led to the rediscovery of a central personality of the discipline, Hermann von Helmholtz. While it is true that the biographical approach reappears in this third historiographical strand, this new work has nothing in common with the hagiographical biographies of the 1950s. In his brilliant book, TURNER studies the scientific controversy in which the two most important practitioners of 19th-century German physiology, E. Hering and Helmholtz, clashed on the topic of visual capacity and skills. Turner focuses on the influence of scientific research on this controversy, and the reciprocal influence of the controversy on scientific research. Overall, his study is based on an integrative concept of the production of scientific knowledge. CAHAN, in his detailed study of Helmholtz as co-creator of a new understanding of the sciences in the 19th century, returns, like Lenoir, to the relations between the general history of the German empire and the natural sciences of the same period. A third study on Helmholtz is the collection edited by KRÜGER, and despite being published under the somewhat dated title "Helmholtz: universal genius", the book contains a number of sound contributions by international experts on Helmholtz and German science during the empire. Nevertheless, this work lacks the internal coherence of the two studies mentioned above.

Two further works, which do not quite fit into the historiography of physiology depicted here, deserve to be mentioned. One is BONAH's comparative international study of the thematic development of physiology, which evolved as a specialist discipline above all in Germany in the second half of the 19th century. Bonah describes and analyzes the process in which physiology divided into three sub-disciplines, two of which – biochemistry and biophysics – went their own way. At the end of the 19th century, physiology thus became an international subject dealing largely with morphological and biological topics, and a great deal less concerned with experimental physiology than it had been 50 years earlier. BÄUMER's study of the early history of biochemical pharmacological research underlines this development in two respects: on the one hand, she depicts how the chemical aspect of physiology evolved into the independent discipline of biochemistry, and, on the other hand, she emphasizes the special relationship between physiological chemistry and the rising pharmaceutical industry during the German empire. In conclusion, it can be maintained that, particularly since the mid-1980s, German physiology has become a popular research topic in the history of science and medicine internationally, and, as a result, quite a number of publications of unusually high quality have become available over the past 20 years.

CHRISTIAN BONAH
translated by Anna-Katherina Meyer

See also Experimental Physiology; Physiology: France

Piaget, Jean   1896–1980

Swiss psychologist, philosopher, and biologist

Atkinson, Christine, *Making Sense of Piaget: The Philosophical Roots*, London and Boston: Routledge and Kegan Paul, 1983

Boden, Margaret A., *Jean Piaget*, New York: Viking Press, 1979; London: Fontana, 1994

Chapman, Michael, *Constructive Evolution: Origins and Development of Piaget's Thought*, Cambridge and New York: Cambridge University Press, 1988

Flavell, John H., *The Developmental Psychology of Jean Piaget*, New York: Van Nostrand, 1963

Gardner, Howard, *The Quest for Mind: Piaget, Lévi-Strauss and the Structuralist Movement*, New York: Knopf, 1973; 2nd edition, Chicago: University of Chicago Press, 1981

Hamlyn, D.W., *Experience and the Growth of Knowledge*, London and Boston: Routledge and Kegan Paul, 1978

Morss, John R., *The Biologising of Childhood: Developmental Psychology and the Darwinian Myth*, Hove, East Sussex: Earlbaum, 1990

Piaget, Jean, *Insights and Illusions of Philosophy*, translated from the French by Wolfe Mays, London: Routledge and Kegan Paul, 1965; New York: World, 1971 (original edition, 1965)

Piaget, Jean, "Autobiography", in *A History of Psychology in Autobiography*, edited by E.G. Boring, *et al.*, New York: Russell and Russell, 1968

Piattelli-Palmarini, Massimo (ed.), *Language and Learning: The Debate Between Jean Piaget and Noam Chomsky*, Cambridge, Massachusetts: Harvard University Press, and London: Routledge and Kegan Paul, 1980

Sugerman, Susan, *Piaget's Construction of the Child's Reality*, Cambridge and New York: Cambridge University Press, 1987

Sutherland, Peter, *Cognitive Development Today: Piaget and His Critics*, London: Chapman, 1992

Vidal, Fernando, *Piaget Before Piaget*, Cambridge, Massachusetts: Harvard University Press, 1994

In interpreting Jean Piaget's development and theories, most scholars rely on his own intellectual autobiographies, PIAGET (1968), and the more detailed PIAGET (1965). In these texts, Piaget claims that his ambition to trace and explain the origin of intelligence in biological terms was conceived early and consistently followed through, from his early studies of children's thought to his later structural analysis of thought processes. The new scientific field he founded – genetic epistemology – was to probe not only the origin and development of thought and intelligence in children, and the genesis of knowledge in different scientific fields, but also to solve entrenched philosophical issues connected with problems in empiricism and rationalism.

The most detailed study of Piaget's early influences and intellectual development is found in VIDAL. In his reconstruction of Piaget's early pre-psychological period, he questions some of Piaget's own descriptions of his development and influences. He also shows how Piaget's interests and training in natural history and metaphysics, his attempts to reconcile questions of fact and value, science and religion, were firmly rooted in the French-Swiss intellectual climate of the early 20th century. Piaget's fascination with life processes and biology, his adherence to Lamarckism instead of Darwinism, the influence of Bergson, and his interest in moral and social reform, are all explained by the influence of this intellectual and social milieu.

MORSS shows how Piaget's theory of the origin and development of intelligence in the child, like the corresponding accounts of, for example, Freud and Vygotsky, is to a large extent pre-Darwinian in its basic assumptions, and also relies on traditional associationist-sensationalist epistemology for its analyses of early mental functioning. The idea of recapitulation in the weak sense – i.e. the assumption that the same laws of development apply to the increase of knowledge in the human species and in the individual child, as well as in science and culture – was crucial to Piaget's whole scientific–philosophical enterprise.

SUGERMAN focuses on Piaget's early studies, which showed how children's thinking differs qualitatively from adult thinking by being animistic, magical, and illogical. She argues that Piaget's analysis of these modes of thinking, as well as the egocentrism underlying them, fails both on a descriptive and an explanatory level, and is based on contradictory or arbitrary analyses of children's behaviour and utterances. This applies not only to his studies of children's conceptions of physical and mental phenomena, but also to his account of children's moral development.

Flavell and Sutherland both concentrate on the psychological aspect of Piaget's theory. FLAVELL, one of the more sympathetic of Piaget's interpreters, presents, in addition to a description of the theoretical framework, a comprehensive account of Piaget's experimental work. SUTHERLAND telescopes the criticisms that have been raised among psychologists, beginning with Vygotsky's criticism of Piaget's account of children's egocentrism, continuing with the objections of behaviourists, interactionists, and cultural psychologists, and ending with the information-processing critique. He also discusses Piaget's implications for, and impact on, educational practices.

Piaget the polymath is one of the themes explored by BODEN, which also contains an important discussion of Piaget's role in the emergence of the so-called cognitive science paradigm in psychology. Piaget himself did not actively explore the assumption that mental processes are computational, and that the mind can be seen as a computer program, but he actively endorsed the idea. Boden also outlines Piaget's indebtedness to the Kantian philosophy. His attempt to give a developmental and biological interpretation to Kant's "static" and non-psychological categories of thought are critically discussed.

CHAPMAN argues that Piaget's guiding theme, or fundamental problem, was that of universals, or the relationships of the parts to the wholes. In biology, he was concerned with the relationship between the individual and the biological species, and in psychology with the problem of how the mind is able to conceptualise general terms. Chapman claims that Piaget attempts to synthesise realism and constructivism, by describing the mind as active in constructing the categories it uses without these being arbitrary or conventional. In discussing this, he relates Piaget's solution to both the philosophies of Kant and Hegel. Unlike most other scholars, Chapman also discusses Piaget's sociological writings. However, he regards Piaget's controversial stage theory – i.e. the claim that cognitive development proceeds by a succession of universal stages, where the subsequent stages are the necessary result of the preceding ones – as more descriptive than explanatory.

ATKINSON also explores the philosophical roots, especially the Kantian influence, of Piaget's ideas, and shows how different are Piaget's questions from the ones posed by traditional psychologists. Reconstructing Piaget's unique blend of the logical and the causal in his analyses, Atkinson argues that he actually mixes the two, as, for example, in his analysis of the nature and development of objective knowledge. She claims that his strong commitment to a biological or organism model of the mind – in which the idea of equilibration, or the "search" for a stable state, is seen as the motor of development – fails to take account of the inherent social aspects of cognitive development, and argues that assimilation and accommodation, the basic processes of moving toward increasingly stable cognitive equilibriums, are not sufficient to explain objective knowledge.

PIATTELLI-PALMARINI, in his introduction to the debate between Piaget and Chomsky in 1975, contrasts Piaget's constructivism with Chomsky's innatism. In contrast to Chomsky, Piaget assumes that the structure of the mind can form and develop without a programmme dictating all possible structures at the outset. Piaget sees the mind metaphorically as a flame, which keeps its structure in spite of constant exchange with the environment, whereas Chomsky's innatist conception of the mind has more in common with a crystal. Piatelli-Palmarini's introduction and editorial remarks attempt to locate the theories of both thinkers in relation to contemporary research programmes of both physics and biology.

HAMLYN is sympathetic to Piaget's attempts to find a way between empiricism and rationalism, and he considers Piaget's theory an improvement on both B.F. Skinner's behaviourism and Noam Chomsky's innatism. Nevertheless, he, like Atkinson, argues from a Wittgensteinian perspective that Piaget's approach to cognitive development is too individualistic, in that it neglects the fact that meaning, objectivity and knowledge are all irreducibly social concepts.

GARDNER, unlike Hamlyn and Piatelli-Palmarini, explores the similarities between Piaget and other structuralist thinkers, and places Piaget's theories firmly within the Cartesian tradition of looking for hidden universal structures behind diverse behavioural manifestations.

Piaget's structuralism, along with his biological approach to the mind and its development, place him in the mainstream of intellectual trends of the century. Yet he is set apart by his original and sometimes controversial use of these ideas, which have posed many challenging questions for philosophers and have led to fruitful empirical studies by psychologists.

CHRISTINA ERNELING

See also Linguistics; The Mind; Psychology

Plague

Arrizabalaga, Jon, "Facing the Black Death: Perceptions and Reactions of University Medical Practitioners", in *Practical Medicine from Salerno to the Black Death*, edited by Luis García-Ballester, Roger French, Jon Arrizabalaga and Andrew Cunningham, Cambridge and New York: Cambridge University Press, 1994

Biraben, Jean-Noël, *Les Hommes et la peste en France et dans les pays européens et méditerranéens*, 2 vols, Paris and The Hague: Mouton, 1975–76

Carmichael, Ann G., "Bubonic Plague", in *The Cambridge World History of Human Disease*, edited by Kenneth F. Kiple, Cambridge and New York: Cambridge University Press, 1993

Cipolla, Carlo M., *Public Health and the Medical Profession in the Renaissance*, Cambridge and New York: Cambridge University Press, 1976

Conrad, Lawrence I., "The Plague in the Early Medieval Near East", PhD dissertation, Princeton University, 1981

Dols, Michael W., *The Black Death in the Middle East*, Princeton, New Jersey: Princeton University Press, 1977

Hirst, L. Fabian, *The Conquest of Plague: A Study of the Evolution of Epidemiology*, Oxford: Clarendon Press, 1953

McNeill, William H., *Plagues and Peoples*, New York: Anchor Press, 1976; Oxford: Blackwell, 1977

The Plague Reconsidered: A New Look at Its Origins and Effects in 16th and 17th Century England, Matlock, Derbyshire: Social Science Research Council Cambridge Group for the History of Population and Social Structure, 1977

Slack, Paul, *The Impact of Plague in Tudor and Stuart England*, London and Boston: Routledge and Kegan Paul, 1985

Twigg, Graham, *The Black Death: A Biological Reappraisal*, London: Batsford, 1984; New York: Schocken Books, 1985

Ziegler, Philip, *The Black Death*, London: Collins, and New York: Davy, 1969

Bubonic plague, or the Black Death, has probably been the most lethal and disruptive disease in European history. The profound impact of its three pandemics (beginning respectively in the 6th, 14th, and 19th centuries: see CARMICHAEL's brief outline, and McNEILL, chapters 3 and 4) has provoked an enormous medical and historical literature. That literature has, however, tended to concentrate on a relatively limited number of controversies, concerning the manner of the disease's spread, and its economic and demographic consequences. Much of the best work has appeared in articles, not monographs, and the recurrent plagues of the later medieval and early modern periods have received far more attention from commendable historians than have the other two pandemics. This entry, therefore, follows the grain of modern scholarship in being mainly devoted to monographs concerned with the second pandemic. It is further confined to titles that should be found helpful in understanding the place of bubonic plague within the history of medicine and healing, rather than, for example, its relation to demography and religion.

Indispensable to any reading of the historiography is some awareness of the difficulties revealed by 20th-century plague cases, such as the complex biology and ecology of the plague bacillus and its rodent and insect hosts, and the various means by which the disease is transmitted to (and within) human populations. The current orthodoxy is briefly outlined in most of the monographs listed: for example, by ZIEGLER, still unsurpassed as an accessible yet responsible account of 14th-century plague; the contributions by L. Bradley and J.N. Biraben to THE PLAGUE RECONSIDERED; or by Slack, who offers a judicious analysis of national historiographical traditions concerning such matters as the role of the human flea. The orthodox account derives essentially from the reported experience of those combating the third pandemic in the early decades of the 20th century, of which HIRST is an admirably full history. Excellent use is also made of such information by, for instance, McNEILL, in his hypothetical reconstruction of the geographical origins of the Black Death within the ecological disturbance wrought on the Eurasian steppes by the burgeoning Mongol empire. A more systematic history of the evolution and impact of the first two pandemics can be found in volume 1 of BIRABEN, which is also notable

for its tentative ascription of the periodicity of epidemics to the effect of cycles of solar activity on the growth of rodent populations.

Despite such successes, it should not, however, be supposed that reports of the third pandemic constitute a secure and unproblematic body of knowledge on which historians can draw when attempting to grasp the character of earlier epidemics. This is partly because, as the minor epidemic in India of the mid-1990s attests, full ecological understanding, or even confident diagnosis, remains elusive. It is also because these discussions of the third pandemic make use of historical evidence to round out their picture of modern plague, so that when historians in turn resort to them for medical information they are completing a potentially vicious interpretative circle. Finally, it is also because the historical applicability of the orthodox view has been powerfully and comprehensively challenged.

TWIGG, a zoologist specializing in rodent biology and diseases, and writing therefore as an amateur historian, is none the less able to make effective use of the historical evidence to draw attention to the troubling discrepancies between the often limited mortality and slow spread of 20th-century plagues in India or North Africa, and the vastly more serious effects of the Black Death. He argues, indeed, that the Black Death was not bubonic plague at all, and instead proposes anthrax as the disease responsible for the pandemic of the 14th century. Although there are flaws in Twigg's comparisons, his argument has not to date been satisfactorily refuted in print, and his work is far from deserving its omission from most short bibliographies of the subject.

The plague bacillus was identified in 1894, during the early days of the struggle to contain the third pandemic, and only during subsequent years was its origin in a disease of rodents discovered. Before the 20th century, then, plague was a disease with a number of recognizable symptoms but no known aetiology. Defeating specific medical-scientific understanding, its analysis and treatment could only be subsumed under that of pestilence in general. Volume 2 of Biraben contains the most detailed conspectus of pre-modern conceptions of, reactions to, and remedies for the plague in Western Europe and the Mediterranean, but above all in France, from late antiquity to the end of the 17th century. The material is organized thematically rather than chronologically, and ranges from the presumed supernatural, ecological, and human causes of epidemics, to the various public health measures that were elaborated, first by Italian Renaissance states and then in European cities generally. The thematic approach successfully highlights the ultimate dependence of most of the ideas under review on the Hippocratic-Galenic medicine of antiquity, but some corrective to the static picture that results is also needed.

ARRIZABALAGA's study of the 14th-century treatises concerning the Black Death composed by medical practitioners working in the universities of Western-Mediterranean Europe is of especial interest here, for it reveals the immediate medical responses to the new disease, set down at a time when doctors could still imagine a cure to be possible. As for measures concerned with public, rather than individual, health – isolation hospitals, border controls, quarantine, and so on – of the numerous studies now available, two classics can be mentioned: CIPOLLA for Italy (one of his numerous short and readable monographs on this theme), and SLACK for Britain, which caught up only slowly with Italian thinking on this subject.

The above writings all deal with Western Europe, but there are also excellent and comprehensible works now available to the non-specialist wanting to range more widely. CONRAD and DOLS, for example, provide a full account of the impact of the plague on medical, religious, and administrative ideas in the Islamic Near East from the 6th to the 16th centuries.

PEREGRINE HORDEN

See also Epidemics; Epidemiology

Planck, Max   1858–1947

German theoretical physicist

Albrecht, Helmuth, "Max Planck: Mein Besuch bei Adolf Hitler – Anmerkungen zum Wert einer historischen Quelle", in *Naturwissenschaft und Technik in der Geschichte*, edited by Albrecht, Stuttgart: Verlag für Geschichte der Naturwissenschaft und der Technik, 1993

Darrigol, Olivier, *From c-Numbers to q-Numbers: The Classical Analogy in the History of Quantum Theory*, Berkeley: University of California Press, 1992

Hartmann, Hans, *Max Planck als Mensch und Denker*, Berlin: Siegismund, 1943; 4th edition, Basel: Ott, 1953

Heilbron, J.L., *The Dilemmas of an Upright Man: Max Planck as Spokesman for German Science*, Berkeley: University of California Press, 1986

Hermann, Armin (ed.), *Dokumente der Naturwissenschaft*, issues 11 and 12, Munich: Battenberg, 1969

Hermann, Armin, *Max Planck in Selbstzeugnissen und Bilddokumenten*, Reinbek: Rowohlt, 1973

Kangro, Hans (ed.), *Planck's Original Papers in Quantum Theory*, London: Taylor and Francis, 1972

Kangro, Hans, *Early History of Planck's Radiation Law*, translated from the German by R.E.W. Maddison, London: Taylor and Francis, 1976 (original edition, 1970)

Klein, Martin J., "Max Planck and the Beginnings of the Quantum Theory", *Archive for the History of Exact Science*, 1 (1962): 459–79

Klein, Martin J., "Planck, Entropy, and Quanta, 1901–1906", *The Natural Philosopher*, 1 (1963): 83–108

Kuhn, Thomas S., *Black-Body Theory and the Quantum Discontinuity, 1894–1912*, Oxford: Clarendon Press, and New York: Oxford University Press, 1978

Lowood, Henry, *Max Planck: A Bibliography of His Non-Technical Writings*, Berkeley: Office for History of Science and Technology, University of California, 1977

Vogel, Heinrich, *Zum philosophischen Wirken Max Plancks: Seine Kritik am Positivismus*, Berlin: Akademie, 1961

The theoretical physicist Max Planck has been the subject of several biographical studies, and he also figures prominently in the literature on early quantum theory and on studies of physics under National Socialism.

For his biographer John L. HEILBRON, Max Planck was not only the "dean and definition of theoretical physics in Germany" c.1900, but also an important science politician in the times thereafter, a "man of exceptional probity in positions of exceptional sensitivity". Heilbron describes as a "heroic tragedy" the fact that Planck's 19th-century Prussian idealism regarding science and the state were quite unfit to cope with political crises such as World War I and the seizure of power by the National Socialists in 1933. More than half of Heilbron's study, in which many quotes from Planck's letters are included (Planck's own papers were destroyed during an air raid), thus deals with Planck's science policy in Berlin.

As ALBRECHT has recently shown, the text of Planck's report on his meeting with Hitler in spring 1933, published in 1947, was significantly altered, with derogatory remarks about the "valueless Eastern Jews" changed into a "neutral" distinction between "valueless and valuable, the latter referring to old families with a good German cultural tradition". This shows the extent to which scientists were involved in "collaboration" with the Nazis, through their loyalties to both the state and their professions. A closer look at HARTMANN's study (1943) on "Max Planck, the German", reveals the extent to which historio-biographical literature was also tainted with Nazi ideology during the Nationalist Socialist period. The section on Planck's family, for instance, exemplifies "today's natural conception of the heredity of man and the hereditary nature of mental and intellectual abilities". It also contains excerpts from interviews that were broadcast on radio but not published elsewhere. HERMANN's handsome biography (1973) with interesting quotes from Planck's correspondence with W. Wien, von Laue, Sommerfeld and Einstein, aptly characterizes Planck, and is richly illustrated with contemporary photographs. Further studies of Planck's biography ought to make more use of the many non-technical writings that Planck published in newspapers and elsewhere. There is a handsome bibliography by LOWOOD, providing orientation through this "extraordinary maze of Planckiana".

Planck's defence of the realist world picture from the threat of, for example, Mach's phenomenalism, only touched upon by his other biographers, is the central issue of VOGEL's study of Planck's philosophy. This East German writer's aim is to claim Planck for the materialist camp: thus, in a blatantly politically motivated account, Planck's anti-positivism is drastically over-emphasized. This appropriation only works by suppressing Planck's early leanings towards Machianism and the religious (in fact pantheistic) strand in his writings, especially after 1930, and by the crude and altogether implausible identification of Planck's plea for a causal and realist philosophy of life with a specifically East German dialectic materialism.

KANGRO (1972) contains an (English and German) annotated edition of Planck's original papers from c.1900. HERMANN (1969) is a German-language anthology with brief introductory comments. Both provide an excellent introduction to Planck's contribution to quantum theory. For further background information, KANGRO (1976) on the history of Planck's radiation law is to be recommended. Kangro focuses on the experimental determinations of the law of black-body radiation, which were performed both at the Physikalisch-Technische Reichsanstalt and at the Charlottenburg Polytechnic c.1900. However, Wilhelm Wien's and Planck's efforts to find a formula covering the empirically-determined dependency of energy density on frequency, as well as several contemporary alternatives to Planck's formula rarely mentioned in other accounts, are also discussed. KLEIN (1962) gives a standard, but concise and lucid version of Planck's contribution to the beginnings of quantum theory at the turn of the 20th century. Rejecting the popular, but retrospective notion of a crisis c.1900, Klein shows how Planck came to the introduction of quanta by reasoning from the entropy of radiation, using techniques adapted (but modified) from Ludwig Boltzmann's memoir of 1877. The further development of Planck's thinking on entropy and quanta in the period 1901–06 is analyzed in KLEIN (1963).

Against this "standard" version of Klein and others, KUHN juxtaposes his "non-standard" account, arguing that the concept of energy quanta is not yet present in Planck's papers of 1900, but only comes with Einstein's rederivation of Planck's distribution law in 1906, which explicitly demands the restriction of energy to be integral multiples of h. Only at this stage of Kuhn's narrative do we meet such "converts to discontinuity" as Ehrenfest, Lorentz, and finally, albeit reluctantly, Planck himself, the most conservative of all the revolutionaries. Strangely enough, the quantum revolution is not only shifted from 1900 to 1906, but also tamed in Kuhn's narrative to such a degree that many have wondered whether this really is the work of the author of *The Structure of Scientific Revolutions*. In reply to these critics, Kuhn addresses this issue in his essay on "Revisiting Planck", also appended as an "afterword" to the second edition of his monograph. That Planck's slight shift of vocabulary (from "resonator" to "oscillator", and from "element" to "quantum") is seen by Kuhn to be "the central symptom of incommensurability" indicates the book's weak sense of Gestalt switch, and highlights the generally disappointing pallidness of Kuhn's account. The strength of Kuhn's book lies instead in its analysis of the further development of quantum theory up to Planck's second theory of 1911–12, and in its thorough study of the early reception of the theory within the physics community.

Readers not put off by integral signs will also profit from DARRIGOL's fairly technical exposition of the path that led Planck from concerns about irreversibility and resonators to black-body radiation and its statistics. His focus is on Planck's use of analogy to describe Boltzmann's gas theory, which Darrigol calls "horizontal analogy", in contrast to Ehrenfest's and Bohr's use of the correspondence principle as a "vertical analogy" for certain limiting cases.

KLAUS HENTSCHEL

See also Kaiser-Wilhelm-Gesellschaft; Quantum Theory; Third Reich and Science

Plastic Surgery

Gnudi, Martha Teach and Jerome Pierce Webster, *The Life and Times of Gaspare Tagliacozzi: Surgeon of Bologna, 1545–1599*, New York: Reichner, 1950

Gonzalez-Ulloa, Mario, *The Creation of Aesthetic Plastic Surgery*, New York: Springer, 1976

Haiken, Beth, "Body and Soul: Plastic Surgery in the United States, 1914–1990", PhD dissertation: University of California at Berkeley, 1994

McDowell, Frank (ed.), *The Source Book of Plastic Surgery*, Baltimore: Williams and Wilkins, 1977

Maltz, Maxwell, *Evolution of Plastic Surgery*, New York: Froben Press, 1946

Patterson, Thomas J.S. (ed. and trans.), *The Zeiss Index and History of Plastic Surgery, 900 BC–1863 AD*, by Edward Zeiss, Baltimore: Williams and Wilkins, 1977

Wallace, Antony F., *The Progress of Plastic Surgery: An Introductory History*, Oxford: Meeuws, 1982

Sushruta Samhita's claim that, "The love of life is next to our love of our own face, and thus the mutilated cry for help" transcends the course of history from the time of its original evocation in c.600 BC. Mutilation has, from the earliest of times up to the present, often been associated with war, and thousands of surgeons gained their experience treating the victims of naval and military conflicts. More than other medical practitioners, surgeons have historically been trained to acquire specific manual skills, and they frequently gained their initial experience treating the casualties of war. Surgical writings suggest that surgery was an art, or craft, whose practitioners joined unnaturally separated parts, separated preternaturally joined parts, removed superfluous parts, and supplied those parts that were wanting. Although among the more recent of modern surgical specialties, plastic surgery enables its practitioners to gain an aesthetic appreciation of their handiwork, as well as pecuniary reward. As stated by Alfred-Armand-Louis-Marie Velpeau, one of the founders of modern plastic surgery, "The operations whose object is to repair mutilations constitute one of the most brilliant triumphs of surgery."

No review of plastic surgery would be complete without mention of Gaspare Tagliacozzi, the Renaissance Bolognese surgeon who revived the rhinoplasty operation. In early modern history, many individuals had their noses severed in sword fights, bitten off by assailants, or structurally distorted due to complications of syphilis. GNUDI & WEBSTER recount Tagliacozzi's life and his modification of the traditional Indian method of reconstructing the human nose, by attaching a skin flap from the inner side of the arm to the mutilated site of the nose, and also critically review Tagliacozzi's classical writing, *De curtorum chirurgia per insitionem* (1597).

McDOWELL reprints a series of classical writings, in either their original language or translated into English, which were written before the appearance of a journal devoted to this surgical speciality. Although the articles are explicitly arranged to emphasize comparisons between "old" and "new" thinking, they also serve to demonstrate the continuity of using established techniques. The work is divided into sections discussing the origins of free skin grafting, rhinoplasty, cleft palate repair, lip flaps, otoplasty, and facial fractures, together with supplying useful biographies.

Maltz and Wallace trace the developments in plastic surgery in terms of "evolution" or "progress". MALTZ's chronology traces the evolution of the "science" of plastic surgery from the Chinese use of tannic acid in burn treatment c.5000 BC, to Max Thorek's operative nipple transplantation without the functional loss of lactation, as reported in 1945. WALLACE's very readable work is divided into sections covering burns and dressings, and gives a head-to-toe topography of the potential applications of plastic surgery.

GONZALEZ-ULLOA has collected a series of articles previously published in *Aesthetic Plastic Surgery*, the organ of the

International Society of Aesthetic Plastic Surgery. This work, and its nearly 100 graphic illustrations, trace the overall history of the specialty, followed by histories of the six most common aesthetic plastic surgery operations: blepharoplasty, rhytidectomy, rhinoplasty, otoplasty, mammaplasty, and abdominal dermolipectomy. The editor claims this "story of discovery" to be an "integrated [physical] geographical guide to the possible".

Zeiss reviewed the entire medical literature of plastic surgery in *Die Literatur und Geschichte der Plastischen Chirurgie* (1863). PATTERSON has reprinted a later English translation of this work, together with an extensive biography of Zeiss, a general history of plastic surgery that includes a discussion of Zeiss's coining of the term "plastic surgery", and a copious list of references. Four additional volumes have been published in this McDowell Series of Plastic Surgical Indexes: volume 2, the Patterson Index of Plastic Surgery, 1864–1920 (1978); volume 3, the Leuz Index, 1921–46 (1977); volume 4, the 25-year index of Plastic and Reconstructive Surgery, covering 1947–1971 (1971); and volume 5, the Honolulu Index of Plastic Surgery, 1971–76 (1976).

In one of the first major works to explore plastic surgery in more than a medico-surgical context, HAIKEN examines the developments of plastic surgery within the beauty-conscious culture of 20th-century America. She argues that in the early 20th century, "most Americans (particularly American women) had come to understand physical beauty as an external, independent – and thus alterable – quality, the pursuit of which demanded a significant amount of time, attention, and money". After this cultural change in the perception of beauty, elective or cosmetic desires began to rival reconstructive needs for practitioners of plastic surgery.

PHILIP K. WILSON

See also Surgery

Plastics and Polymers

Fenichell, Stephen, *Plastic: The Making of a Synthetic Century*, New York: Harper, 1996
Friedel, Robert, *Pioneer Plastic: The Making and Selling of Celluloid*, Madison: University of Wisconsin Press, 1983
Hounshell, David A. and John Kenly Smith, Jr, *Science and Corporate Strategy: Du Pont R & D, 1902–1980*, Cambridge and New York: Cambridge University Press, 1988
Manzini, Ezio, *The Material of Invention*, Milan: Arcadia, 1986; Cambridge, Massachusetts: MIT Press, 1989
Meikle, Jeffrey L., *American Plastic: A Cultural History*, New Brunswick, New Jersey: Rutgers University Press, 1995
Morawetz, Herbert, *Polymers: The Origins and Growth of a Science*, New York: Wiley, 1985
Morris, Peter J.T., *Polymer Pioneers: A Popular History of the Science and Technology of Large Molecules*, Philadelphia: Center for History of Chemistry, 1986
Morris, Peter J.T., *The American Synthetic Rubber Research Program*, Philadelphia: University of Pennsylvania Press, 1989
Mossman, S.T.I. and Peter J.T. Morris (eds.), *The Development of Plastics*, Cambridge: Royal Society of Chemistry, 1994
Seymour, Raymond B. (ed.), *Pioneers in Polymer Science*, Dordrecht and Boston: Kluwer, 1989

Since the creation of the first synthetic plastic, bakelite, in the early 20th century, plastics have transformed society. Loved for their utility but despised for their often negative environmental impact, plastics today can be found virtually everywhere. They constitute a major – and perhaps the most well-known – group of the polymer family, making them a sister to such materials as nylon, polyester, and synthetic rubber. Plastics undoubtedly simplify our lives; they also reflect the changing values of 20th-century society, emphasizing in many cases not only economy and convenience, but efficiency and versatility. Despite the environmental and social significance of plastics, historical writing on the material is rather scarce. Some excellent recent books redress this absence to a certain extent. However, there is still room for more scholarship in this area.

FENICHELL takes a candid look at the role of plastics in the modern age. From CDs to Tupperware, plastic's utilitarian nature has made it an inseparable part of life, and its omnipresence makes plastic part of popular culture. In accessible terms, Fenichell puts plastic in its proper context as both technological innovation and cultural icon, tracing its historical development from celluloid film through to its modern medical uses. The book does not ignore the plastic-related environmental and safety concerns, however; Fenichell devotes a chapter to the anti-plastics crusaders, notably Norman Mailer and Barry Commoner, and in his concluding chapter addresses current efforts to recycle plastics.

Much like Fenichell, MEIKLE seeks to examine plastic in its modern societal and cultural roles. Though he is moderately successful, his book is perhaps more useful as a history of the chemical and industrial development of plastic than an analysis of plastic culture per se. Meikle, a historian of science, demonstrates an excellent grasp of the technicalities of plastic, taking care to discuss it as the varied group of polymers it is, not solely as the generic term it has become. These technical details are particularly evident in his discussions of the development of celluloid, bakelite, and nylon.

MORRIS (1989) uses the case of the natural rubber shortage during World War II to investigate the drawbacks and merits of industry-wide cooperation and government sponsorship. After a thorough, critical examination of both the synthetic rubber project and the process by which scientific research becomes technological innovation, Morris ultimately supports the motivating factor of industrial competition, noting that the project's interrelation of academia, industry, and government did little to facilitate the final development of synthetic rubber.

Unlike most of the books on plastics reviewed here, MANZINI takes a more theoretical approach to the world of polymers and plastics, exploring the concept of matter and its relationship to material. In his study, Manzini seeks to emphasize the importance of human intervention, specifically in the form of design, to the creation of material (i.e., phenolic resin, polypropylene, and polystyrene) from matter. In his view, there are innumerable possibilities hidden within the "new materials", but there are also strict limitations of matter with which this potential must be reconciled.

Considered to be one of the foundational works on the history of industrial research and development, HOUNSHELL & SMITH seeks to illustrate the growth of research and development in Du Pont, one of the largest chemical companies. It is a thorough and scholarly investigation of science-based industry. Based largely on the internal archives of Du Pont, this book tends to focus less on the actual chemistry of discoveries such as nylon and Kevlar, choosing instead to view R & D from a management perspective. Though the authors are careful to note that the case of Du Pont should not be seen as representative of industrial R & D up to 1980, they succeed admirably in their efforts to chronicle the history of Du Pont including the company's great developments, difficulties, and eventual shift in the 1980s away from chemistry and toward the life sciences.

MORRIS (1986), a product of the Polymer Project of the Center for History of Chemistry (now the Chemical Heritage Foundation), presents a cogent and concise look at the history of polymer chemistry. Though Morris begins with a valuable introductory overview, which places polymers in a scientific and historical context, he spends the majority of the 88-page volume discussing the individual contributions of important polymer chemists such as John Wesley Hyatt, the Nobel laureate Giulio Natta, and Speed Marvel. Interspersed throughout these biographical accounts are timelines of innovations in polymer chemistry. Another notable book, SEYMOUR, takes a similar approach, focusing on the individuals behind the advent of polymers in 24 chapters, some of which were written by polymer chemists themselves.

There are several other notable books on plastics and polymers that may be of interest. FRIEDEL is an excellent book, examining the development, uses, and marketing of celluloid. MORAWETZ offers readers a comprehensive look at the history of polymers and plastics. In addition, the 20 papers that comprise MOSSMAN & MORRIS provide historians of science with analyses of the development of synthetic materials from a wide variety of perspectives.

TRACY L. SULLIVAN AND LEO B. SLATER

Plato 429–347 BC

Greek philosopher

Fowler, David, *The Mathematics of Plato's Academy: A New Reconstruction*, Oxford: Clarendon Press, and New York: Oxford University Press, 1987; revised edition, 1990

Friedländer, Paul, *Plato*, translated from the German by Hans Meyerhoff, 3 vols, New York: Harper and Row, and London: Routledge and Kegan Paul, 1958–69 (original 2 vol. edition, 1928)

Krämer, Hans Joachim, *Plato and the Foundations of Metaphysics: A Work on the Theory of the Principles und Unwritten Doctrines of Plato with a Collection of the Fundamental Documents*, edited and translated by John R. Catan, Albany: State University of New York Press, 1990

Kraut, Richard (ed.), *The Cambridge Companion to Plato*, Cambridge and New York: Cambridge University Press, 1992

Mohr, Richard D., *The Platonic Cosmology*, Leiden: E.J. Brill, 1985

Natorp, Paul, *Platos Ideenlehre: eine Einführung in den Idealismus*, Leipzig: Durr, 1903; 2nd edition, Leipzig: Meiner, 1921; Hamburg: Meiner, 1994

Scheffel, Wolfgang, *Aspekte der Platonischen Kosmologie: Untersuchungen zum Dialog "Timaios"*, Leiden: E.J. Brill, 1976

Wedberg, Anders, *Plato's Philosophy of Mathematics*, Stockholm: Almqvist & Wiksell, 1955

FOWLER examines early Greek mathematics within its historical context, and culminates with Euclid and Archimedes. In the first section, Fowler presents mathematical topics in the works of Plato (*Meno*, *Parmenides*: anthyphairetic ratio theory; *The Republic*, including astronomy and music theory), Aristotle, Euclid, and Archimedes, while the second section deals with Plato's Academy and the transmission of Greek texts up to the present day. The author studies arithmetised mathematics and calculations with fractions in order to highlight his argument that early Greek mathematics is non-arithmetised. In the third section, he examines the development of mathematics since the 17th century, and the influence of anthyphairetic ratio theory on Fermat, Lagrange, Legendre, Gauss, Galois, and others. This is an extremely useful work, especially for historians of mathematics.

FRIEDLÄNDER combines a biography of Plato with a presentation of his doctrines in the various dialogues, divided into early, middle, and late periods. There are chapters on Plato as an atomic physicist (*Timaeus*: the structure and splitting of atoms), as well as a geophysicist and geographer (*Phaedo*, *Timaeus*). After discussing modern opinions, he examines the fundamentals of Platonic physics, and pursues Plato's influence on modern natural science (suggesting that might be regarded as a forerunner of Dalton). In chapter 15, Friedländer describes how Plato combined Anaximander's and Parmenides' view of the earth (*Phaedo*: there are no caves any more, the earth's surface is a unity for human beings), and then follows the development of this conception in the works of Aristotle, through late antiquity, and into the Renaissance.

KRÄMER presents his theory of Plato's unwritten doctrine in four parts ("Schleiermacherism", the philosophical structure of the Platonic theory, its interpretations, and appendices), and locates the gap between Plato's written dialogues and the indirect (or intramural, esoteric) tradition arising from the unwritten doctrines as that between "writing" and "orality". Krämer argues that the indirect tradition contains very important concepts, such as the ultimate foundation – the subsequent fulfilment and completion of the ascending dialectic up to the final heights not mentioned in the dialogues. Part 2, in particular, presents the results and the achievements of the Tübingen School, and contains pages of anthology. In chapter 3, Krämer compares Platonism with transcendental philosophy, Hegelianism, phenomenology, and Heidegger.

KRAUT combines several essays by an international team of scholars on Plato's dialogues *Meno*, *The Republic*, *Sophist* and *Philebus*, and on Plato's views on ethics, knowledge, love, mathematics, poetry, politics, reality, and religion. It thus provides a good introduction to Platonic thinking, while the very detailed bibliography, arranged according to subject, provides a useful guide to further studies on Plato's philosophy.

MOHR deals with Plato's cosmology, especially in the *Timaeus* and the other cosmological writings (*Statesman*, *Phaedrus*, *Laws*, *Philebus* and *Sophist*). He covers the following subjects: "Metaphysics and the Characteristics of Platonic Forms" (as standards, measures, exemplars or paradigms); "Theology and the Platonic Demiurge" (a unique and rational god, described as a craftsman); "Bodies and Souls" (World-Soul); and finally "Space and the Status of the Material World" (space as a principle of existence for the phenomena).

NATORP's book founded a new era in research on Plato, the (Kantian) "idealistic" exegesis of the Platonic dialogues. Natorp equates the philosophy of Plato with the development of the doctrine of ideas, his central terms being "idea" and the "discovery of the logical". After discussing each of the Platonic dialogues, he then considers Aristotle's relationship with Plato and his critique of the doctrine of ideas. Even today, this book is considered as an important introduction to Plato's work and to "philosophical idealism".

After presenting two antique interpretations on cosmogony by Aristotle and Plutarch, SCHEFFEL discusses Plato's terms of space and soul, the doctrine of motion, and the difference between first and second causes as presented in *Timaeus*. Scheffel shows that the *Timaeus* discourse is a description of physical, cosmical reality. The problem concerning the connection of cosmic and chaotic movements, and the gap between ideal and physical reality, is analysed in Plato's use of the term "soul" in *Phaedrus* and *Timaeus*. The demiurge thus produces a cosmos combined with soul, and Scheffel argues that the doctrine of motion is a dynamic one, based on this cosmic soul.

After reviewing Greek mathematical knowledge in Plato's time, WEDBERG presents a general consideration of how Plato approached the philosophical problems presented to him by mathematics. In particular, he deals with Plato's philosophy of geometry and arithmetic, and the Aristotelian interpretation.

BEATRICE RAUSCHENBACH

See also Greece: general works

Poincaré, Jules Henri 1854–1912

French mathematician, physicist, and philosopher of science

Browder, Felix E. (ed.), *The Mathematical Heritage of Henri Poincaré*, Providence, Rhode Island: American Mathematical Society, 1983

Chabert, Jean-Luc and Amy Dahan Dalmedico, "Les Idées nouvelles de Poincaré", in *Chaos et Determinisme*, edited by Dalmedico, Chabert and K. Chemla, Paris: Seuil, 1992

Dantzig, Tobias, *Henri Poincaré, Critic of Crisis: Reflections on His Universe of Discourse*, New York: Scribner, 1954

Darboux, J.G., *Eloge historique de Henri Poincaré*, Paris: Gauthier-Villars, 1913

Dieudonné, Jean, entry on Poincaré in *Dictionary of Scientific Biography*, edited by Charles Coulston Gillispie, vol. 11, New York: Scribner, 1975

Giedymin, Jerzy, *Science and Convention: Essays on Henri Poincaré's Philosophy of Science and the Conventionalist Tradition*, Oxford and New York: Pergamon Press, 1982

Miller, Arthur I., "A Study of Henri Poincaré's 'Sur la Dynamique de l'électron'", *Archives for History of Exact Sciences*, 10 (1973): 207–328

Rougier, L., *La Philosophie géometrique de Henri Poincaré*, Paris: Alcan, 1920

Stump, D., "Henri Poincaré's Philosophy of Science", *Studies in History and Philosophy of Science*, 20 (1991): 639–57

Torretti, R., *Philosophy of Geometry from Riemann to Poincaré*, Dordrecht and Boston: Reidel, 1978

Volterra, Vito, Jacques Hadamard and Paul Langevin, *Henri Poincaré: L'Oeuvre scientifique, l'oeuvre philosophique*, Paris: Alcan, 1914

Jules Henri Poincaré was an extremely productive and creative scientist who made very important contributions to almost all mathematical fields. He was the founder of many major fields of contemporary mathematics, including algebraic and differential topology, dynamical systems, and ergodic theory, and also produced influential works in physics and the philosophy of science. Unfortunately, there is no satisfactory scientific biography of Poincaré, nor a deep critical analysis encompassing the breadth of his thought. This can perhaps be ascribed to the diversity of domains and problems considered by Poincaré, requiring a very broad knowledge in mathematics, physics, and the philosophy of science, and to the fact that only in recent years has the importance of his works become generally accepted.

An old eulogy by DARBOUX is still a valuable source, providing an account of Poincaré's life and the chronological development of his professional and scientific activities. Soon after Poincaré's death, VOLTERRA, HADAMARD, & LANGEVIN gave an overview of his main scientific works. The book is divided among the fields to which Poincaré contributed – mathematics (by Volterra), three body problems (by Hadamard), physics (by Langevin), and the philosophy of science (by Boutroux) – and is particularly interesting as it shows how he was perceived by important contemporary scientists. Langevin, for example, argues that one of the central features of Poincaré's work was his profound involvement in the physical research of his time, both theoretical and experimental. Boutroux states that Poincaré's philosophy of science is much influenced by his way of doing mathematics, and that the study of non-Euclidian geometry led him to his first philosophical musings. Poincaré always asserted that scientists' conventions (definitions, axioms, hypotheses) are freely conceived by the mind but suggested by external phenomena, and are chosen for the reasons of simplicity and adaptability to experience. His several disputations with the nominalists (e.g. LeRoy), and with the "logical" philosophers, such as Bertrand Russell, led him to render his thoughts on the foundations of science more precise. Boutroux suggests also that Poincaré's pragmatic view of mathematics led him to pioneer investigations on the psychological genesis of concepts such as space.

Up to now, the most complete and detailed description of Poincaré's mathematical works was given by Hadamard, in a paper published in 1921 and reproduced in the book edited by BROWDER. This collection also includes a great number of interesting mathematical papers on modern aspects of many fields in which Poincaré made important initial investigations. However, it is not comprehensive, as some disciplines – e.g. bifurcation theory – are not considered. A special essay on historical materials, including Hadamard's article, reproduces an analysis by P.S. Aleksandrov on the historical and mathematical roots of topology; from the beginning, Poincaré saw topology above all as a powerful instrument arising out of the classical branches of mathematics, and, as a great representative of classical mathematics, he "exploded" its tradition from within, opening it up to new methods of investigation.

DIEUDONNÉ, a leading bourbakist mathematician, wrote the entry on Poincaré for the *Dictionary of Scientific Biography*. Next to a synthetic introduction to Poincaré's most important mathematical works, Dieudonné pondered several of Poincaré's contributions to the foundations of mathematics. He argued that Poincaré never stated his ideas on these questions very clearly, mostly confining himself to criticizing the schools of Russell, Peano, and Hilbert. According to Dieudonné, Poincaré had a "blind spot" with regard to the formalization of mathematics, but his criticisms were probably the starting point for many fruitful mathematical developments. Poincaré seems to have been convinced that the Hilbert school's attempt to prove the non-contradiction of a system of axioms was hopeless, and eventually Kurt Gödel's theorem was to prove him right.

The most interesting aspect of DANTZIG's book is his point of view; not wishing to compose a traditional (or academic) commentary on Poincaré's scientific and philosophical ideas, the author chose instead to display the fecundity and beauty of Poincaré's thinking. Dantzig's book was written in the mid-1950s, when some of Poincaré's ideas were rarely discussed, and its main aim was to remind scientists that Poincaré's science and philosophy were still alive and useful.

In his classical work on Poincaré's geometrical philosophy, ROUGIER explains how the French mathematician arrived at a new solution for the old philosophical dichotomy between apodictical and assertoric truths, by means of an analysis of the true epistemological meaning of non-Euclidean geometries. As is well known, Poincaré's solution asserts that the mathematical (e.g. geometrical) principles are conventions. Along with other authors, Rougier believes that Poincaré's conventionalism is not well understood, and that this misunderstanding occurs because many interpreters of Poincaré's philosophy of geometry do not take seriously the mathematical method used by Poincaré for developing and basing his conventionalism. Rougier also discusses the mathematical concepts he considers necessary for a correct understanding of Poincaré's conventionalism.

TORRETTI also believes that Poincaré's conventionalism can only be judged if its mathematical origins are seriously considered. Unlike Rougier, however, Torretti analyses the genesis of Poincaré's geometrical conventionalism within the 19th-century context of the development of non-Euclidean geometries.

Within the last few years, many commentators on Poincaré's philosophical ideas have begun to criticize the standard, classical interpretation formulated by the Logical Positivists, with their emphasis on the rejection of theoretical entities. For example, both Stump and Giedymin claim that Poincaré's philosophy of science has previously been misinterpreted, and then attempt to provide the necessary historical and philosophical context required to explain its true meaning. STUMP argues that Poincaré's epistemological thinking contains more ideas than the frequently mentioned thesis of the conventionality of the metric, and that it is therefore important to take into consideration every scientific and philosophical topic analysed by Poincaré himself. Stump concludes that Poincaré explicitly argued in favor of a philosophy of science which contains a "hypothetical method" – i.e. a "middle ground" between the dogmatism of the old generation of French scientists and the fresh nominalistic opinions expressed by a new generation of French philosophers, such as E. LeRoy.

GIEDYMIN argues that in order to understand Poincaré's philosophy of science it has to be examined in its entirety. Poincaré developed what Giedymin calls his method of "structuralism realism" when searching for possible bases for the existence of objective knowledge and scientific progress, in the face of the replaceability of scientific theories.

The question of Poincaré's contribution to the genesis of relativity theory, (and why he himself failed to create it), has been discussed by many authors during the last two decades. For example, MILLER has made a detailed study of Poincaré's fundamental work on relativity, *Sur la dynamique de l'électron* (1906). Arguing that his physics is a reflection of his philosophy, Miller shows how Poincaré's strict adherence to a research program based on the electromagnetic world-view prevented him from understanding the universal applicability of the principle of relativity and, therefore, the importance of the constancy of the velocity of light in all inertial frames.

Interest in Poincaré's significance and influence, after a long eclipse during the period 1920–60 (with the exception of Birkhoff and the Russian school of mathematics), has been renewed in the last three decades. CHABERT & DALMEDICO have clearly described concepts and methods introduced by Poincaré that play a crucial role in the new area of chaotic non-linear dynamical systems. It is to be expected that future readings and studies of Poincaré's works will exhibit further unexpected aspects of his many deep and original insights within all fields of pure and applied mathematics and in the philosophy of science.

ANTONIO AUGUSTO PASSOS VIDEIRA

See also Chaos Theory; Electromagnetism; Positivism; Relativity

Polar Science

Armstrong, Terence, George Rogers and Graham Rowley, *The Circumpolar North: A Political and Economic Geography of the Arctic and Sub-Arctic*, London: Methuen, and New York: Wiley, 1978
Bloom, Lisa, *Gender on Ice: American Ideologies of Polar Expeditions*, Minneapolis: University of Minnesota Press, 1993

Bravo, Michael T., *Science and Discovery in the Admiralty Voyages to the Arctic Regions in Search of a North-West Passage (1815–1825)*, PhD dissertation, Cambridge University, 1992

Cawood, J., "The Magnetic Crusade: Science and Politics in Early Victorian Britain", *Isis*, 70 (1979): 493–518

Chaturvedi, Sanjay, *The Polar Regions: A Political Geography*, Chichester: Wiley, 1996

Damas, David (ed.), *Arctic*, Washington, DC: Smithsonian Institution, 1984

Elzinga, Aant, "Antarctica: The Construction of a Continent by and for Science", in *Denationalizing Science: The Contexts of International Scientific Practice*, edited by Elisabeth Crawford, Terry Shinn and Sverker Sörlin, Dordrecht and Boston: Kluwer, 1993

Fogg, G.E., *A History of Antarctic Science*, Cambridge and New York: Cambridge University Press, 1992

Frängsmyr, Tore, *Science in Sweden: The Royal Swedish Academy of Sciences, 1739–1989*, Canton, Massachusetts: Science History Publications, 1984

Freeman, M.M.R., "Ethnoscience, Prevailing Science and Arctic Co-operation", in *Arctic Alternatives: Civility or Militarism in the Circumpolar North*, edited by Franklyn Griffiths, Toronto: Science for Peace/Samuel Stevens, vol. 3, 1992

Friedman, Robert Marc, *Background to the Establishment of Norsk Polarinstitutt: Postwar Scientific and Political Agendas*, Umeå: Umeå Universitet, 1995

Iliffe, Robert, "'Aplatisseur du Monde et de Cassini': Maupertuis, Precision Measurement, and the Shape of the Earth in the 1730s", *History of Science*, 31 (1993): 335–75

Johnson, Samuel, *Journey to the Western Isles of Scotland* with *The Journal of a Tour to the Hebrides*, by James Boswell, edited with an introduction by Peter Levi, Harmondsworth: Penguin, 1984

Levere, Trevor H., *Science and the Canadian Arctic: A Century of Exploration, 1818–1918*, Cambridge: Cambridge University Press, 1993

Mauss, Marcel and Henri Beuchat, *Seasonal Variations of the Eskimo: A Study in Social Morphology*, translated from the French by James J. Fox, London: Routledge, 1979 (original edition, 1950)

Minority Rights Group (eds), *Polar Peoples: Self-Determination and Development*, London: Minority Rights Group, 1994

Petersen, M.J., *Managing the Frozen South: The Creation and Evolution of the Antarctic Treaty System*, Berkeley: University of California Press, 1988

Savours, A., "'A Very Interesting Point in Geography': The 1773 Phipps Expedition Towards the North Pole", *Arctic*, 37 (1984): 402–29

Scoresby Jr, William, *An Account of the Arctic Regions, with a History and Description of the Northern Whale Fishery*, Edinburgh: Constable, 1820; reprinted with an introduction by Sir Alister Hardy, Newton Abbot, Devon: David and Charles, and New York: A.M. Kelley, 1969

Sörlin, Sverker, "Hans W. Ahlmann, Arctic Research and Polar Warming: From a National to an International Scientific Agenda, 1919–1952", *Mundus Librorum*, (1996): 383–98

Stefansson, Vilhjalmur, *Hunters of the Great North*, New York: Harcourt Brace, 1922; London: Harrap, 1923

Tønnessen, J.N. and A.O. Johnsen, *The History of Modern Whaling*, translated by R.I. Christophersen, London: Hurst, and Berkeley: University of California Press, 1982

Williams, Glyndwr, *The British Search for the Northwest Passage in the Eighteenth Century*, London: Longmans for the Royal Commonwealth Society, 1962

Winter, Alison, "'Compasses All Awry': The Iron Ship and the Ambiguities of Cultural Authority in Victorian Britain", *Victorian Studies*, 38 (1994): 69–98

The history of the polar regions has been dominated until recently by two groups: historians of empire on the one hand, and scientific practitioners on the other. The former have tended to concentrate on exploration and geography, while the latter have addressed the other field sciences, producing passionate, well-informed, but internalist accounts. To gain an adequate appreciation of the regional character of polar science, the sources suggested here are those that make diverse links between fieldwork, experimentation, instruments, politics, law, and culture.

Alexander von Humboldt supposedly coined the term "circumpolar" in the early 19th century, when describing the climate, vegetation, and animal life in the northern zone of latitudes, in the context of a global perspective. The polar regions considered as a coherent concept was an abstraction of the period, emerging from the surveys carried out by naval officers and scientific supernumeraries, who charted not only the coastlines, but also the atmosphere, gravitational fields, magnetic fields, tides, ocean currents, and many other geophysical phenomena. These scientific travellers brought the northern regions into the emerging global consciousness, and challenged common misperceptions of distance by emphasizing their geographical proximity to northern Europe.

The role of the Arctic regions as a site for settling scientific disputes has a longer history. ILIFFE's clear exposé of the conflict between the followers of Newton and those of Jacques Cassini, as to the shape of the earth – was it oblong or flattened at the Poles? – examines the strategies employed to assume authority in judgements of precision, as rival approaches were reflected in different measurement practices. In his voyage to Lapland in 1728, Maupertuis used English instruments and particular triangulation methods to measure an arc of the meridian. With the help of a Swede, Anders Celsius, Maupertuis was thus able to bypass Cassini and move the dispute beyond the boundaries of the astronomical establishment in the French Academy. In challenging the apparent self-evidence of precision, this study offers a lesson equally applicable to studies of the "Humboldtian" surveys, which dominated polar science in the 19th and 20th centuries.

The natural history tour of the Arctic regions emerged during the second half of the 18th century, when new forms of travel, offering alternatives to the well-beaten path of the Grand Tour, emerged. WILLIAMS's classic study reminds us that James Cook's remit to discover a Terra Australis and a North-West Passage was linked to collecting, surveying, and solving the longitude problem within a wider European framework of imperial expansion. SAVOURS's audit of the aims, relevant theories, scientific instruments and experiments of John Constantine Phipps's expedition to the North Pole in 1773 is the only detailed study of the subject, which deserves further contextualization. Joseph Banks, after aborting a second journey with Cook, travelled to Staffa, and then Iceland, inaugurating a natural history tour that became something of an initiation for a new breed of aspiring educated travellers, such as Simon Pallas, William Jackson Hooker, Thomas Malthus, Edward Daniel Clarke and George Mackenzie. More popular tours, such as Thomas Pennant's, observing local inhabitants, commenting on the degenerate quality of the flora, and making notes about the process of land enclosure, soon followed. JOHNSON's and Boswell's famous diaries of their tour encouraged and perpetuated ill-founded stereotypes of the Highlands, and, more generally, the Arctic regions, as degenerate. This tradition of northern scientific travel has received remarkably little attention, but is crucial for making sense of long-standing European perceptions of the polar regions.

In contrast, SCORESBY, a whaler and student of Robert Jameson, wrote a two-volume study of the Arctic regions, a primary source that remains fascinating and instructive. His unprecedented studies of snow and ice, descriptions of flora and fauna, and investigations of climate, made him Humboldt's chief informant and authority on the Arctic regions. Ironically, the experience of whalers accounted for much of the best information about the natural history of the Arctic, as well as the eradication of marine mammals through over-fishing. TØNNESSEN's history of whaling since the era of steam provides a Norwegian perspective, highly relevant to an understanding of the past and present debates about conservation and quotas.

After the Napoleonic Wars had brought the capture of Matthew Flinders's expedition to Terra Australis, and expeditions to Africa had been ravaged by disease, the focus of British exploration shifted towards the cold, but more salutary, Arctic regions. Thereafter, the poles became the principal theatre for exercising Britain's national character through state-sponsored scientific expeditions. The ensuing century is the period of polar research most thoroughly covered by historians of science.

BRAVO's doctoral dissertation analyses the North-West Passage expeditions in the first 10 years (1815–25) as the product of a renewed alliance between the Royal Society and the Royal Navy, and investigates the social basis of the scientific field practices, as well as the ethno-cartographic encounters with Inuit. In this period, the Arctic regions acquired the status of Britain's privileged field laboratory. As Britain committed itself to the development of a national tradition of polar expeditions, men of science, such as Humboldt, were promoting the need for international co-operation in order to calibrate instruments and link observations made in different regions of the globe. Geomagnetic research problems in the 1830s and 1840s extended Britain's empire of ice to the Southern Ocean and Antarctica. CAWOOD's excellent account of the magnetic crusade picks up Cannon's idea of Humboldtian science, and gives a description of the emerging international "cosmopolitanism", in contrast to the strong nationalism associated with geographical exploration, and of the co-ordinated mapping programmes based on precision measurement by gentlemen savants and military elites.

LEVERE takes a longer view of this process, and gives the first thoroughly researched, comprehensive picture of a century of British scientific research in the Arctic, shedding light on previously obscure subjects, such the first International Polar Year – a landmark for international co-operation.

Nineteenth-century attitudes to Arctic science in this period were modulated by the prevailing tide of evangelicalism, both in terms of individual attitudes towards science and its public reception. WINTER's study of William Scoresby highlights the importance of evangelicalism to his science, and sheds light on the world of his contemporaries. Her analysis also suggests the relevance of a range of Victorian social issues to the polar expeditions and their public reception: mesmerism, cannibalism, and patriotic duty, for example, were all themes closely tied to the construction of the image of the heroic explorer.

Because of the international character of the Arctic regions, much pertinent material is in languages other than English. The literature on Nordic science within the Scandinavian context is particularly well developed, and although many dissertations are written in Nordic languages, summaries are often translated into English. FRÄNGSMYR's collection of essays, entirely in English, is an important resource because it shows how the Swedes mapped and appropriated their northern periphery.

Polar field research also played a crucial role in driving institutional developments. The foundation of a national polar institute in Britain in 1920 created a basis for co-ordinating and supporting scientific research in the polar regions. FRIEDMAN's exploratory essay on the post-World War II origins of Norsk Polarinstitutt in Oslo shows how national strategic interests were combined with support for geophysics.

New generations of scientific instruments created new research problems, as well as providing new approaches to old problems in the natural and social sciences. Co-ordinated studies of atmospheric properties during the first International Polar Year (1882–83), and experiments in radio propagation during the second (1932–33), made use of new kinds of electrical instruments, which could be both used and tested in extreme polar conditions. A much more explicit concern with techniques of polar travel and survival emerged at the beginning of the 20th century. MAUSS & BEUCHAT chose the Eskimoan way of life as their primary anthropological case study of techniques. On the Canadian Arctic expedition led by Stefansson, shipwreck proved fatal for the young Beuchat; STEFANSSON survived, and enjoyed lasting fame for openly embracing indigenous techniques of living as a practical strategy for Arctic survival.

Scientific research in the two polar regions has often been intertwined, although it has to some extent diverged in the course of the 20th century. Arctic states were already looking to their northern backyards as territories or colonies for the exploration of natural history in the 18th century, although more familiar and less exotic than the glowing reports of an unsighted Terra Australis. The importance of global physics in the 19th and 20th centuries situated common kinds of climatic problems and research methods in both regions. However, since the end of World War II, attention to more regional and local ecological and cultural features has sharpened the distinctions between the characteristics of the polar regions. Although both polar regions have been research sites for common institutions and scientists, there are two fundamental differences. The Arctic regions were first inhabited by indigenous peoples (later missionaries, fur traders, police, etc.), whereas Antarctica is still restricted to scientific parties. The sovereignty of the Arctic is predominantly managed by the nations that possess the Arctic territory, whereas the Antarctic continent is recognized internationally as a common heritage for humanity, according to the Antarctic Treaty that was renegotiated in 1991, with many more nations joining the original nine signatories.

ARMSTRONG, ROGERS & ROWLEY offer the best general overview of the scientific and industrial development of the Arctic regions up to the mid-1970s, written with the benefit of enormous personal experience. As an expression of a regional indigenous political identity, the term circumpolar is a comparatively recent phenomenon, part of a nascent post-colonialism, and a late 20th-century innovation. The histories of polar peoples, edited by the MINORITY RIGHTS GROUP, gives a useful (though teleological), historical treatment of the indigenous northerners according to nation state, and charts the recent emergence of circumpolar political movements. There is an enormous anthropological literature about Arctic peoples, much too large to summarize here. DAMAS's collection of essays on the anthropology and archaeology of Greenlandic and Canadian Inuit, Inuvialuit and Inupiat, provides a good cross-section and a mine of information replete with references to studies of the demographics, archaeology, and anthropology of Arctic North America.

FOGG brings his experience as a biologist to the only full-length study of the natural sciences in Antarctica. Although the work is obviously internalist, it does provide a useful point of departure for further research, especially concerning more recent institutional agreements pertaining to the International Geophysical Year, the Scientific Committee on Antarctica, and the Antarctic Treaty. CHATURVEDI, a political geographer, argues that the polar regions can be best understood as geopolitical arenas, laboratories for both the natural and social sciences. This book reflects the strength of interest in the politics of Antarctic science.

Within the changing political arenas of the poles, cultural critiques are a relatively recent phenomenon. The polar sciences have for so long been the preserve of men that it hardly needs pointing out. Nevertheless, the consequences of this for self-determination movements, together with the nuances of gender in landscape and visual representations, deserve further investigation. BLOOM's deconstructionist study of the gendered practices of American polar exploration is unsurprising, but fills a lacuna. Her deconstructionist approach shows the "Orientalist" construction of the Inuit (polar Eskimos) as feminized, submissive sources of labour and domesticity for Peary in his journey to the North Pole. However, her lack of awareness of either anthropological or Inuit sources is a serious shortcoming, and invites many of the criticisms and responses that followed the original publication of Edward Said's *Orientalism* thesis.

The International Geophysical Year (1957–58) was shaped by the politics of the Cold War. A strategic international agreement by a group of nine nations to keep Antarctica demilitarized, yet colonized exclusively for the purposes of the sciences, constituted a special laboratory with limited privileges of access. PETERSEN's history of the Antarctic Treaty System gives a good introduction and overview. ELZINGA is the only study of Antarctic science that takes its terms of reference from issues raised in the philosophy of science. The renegotiation of the treaty in 1991, to include other member states, raised important questions about the politics of polar scientific research: Chaturvedi's analysis has the advantage of including the perspectives of recent member nations.

The polar regions have occupied a special place as sites of experimental fieldwork for climatic change. Problems of atmospheric composition (such as the concentration of isotopes and ozone depletion), the melting of the ice sheets, and ocean circulation have received widespread attention. SÖRLIN, in a thought-provoking study of the Swedish glaciologist Hans W. Ahlmann, suggests that the rise of environmentalism in the 1960s mobilized national and international scientific research interests into more overtly socially-constructed, politicized phenomena.

The Arctic regions have recently been a focus for discussing and negotiating the obligations and debts of scientific research to local peoples and institutions. FREEMAN, an anthropologist and expert on debates about the future of indigenous whaling, has argued for the utility of a distinction between traditional ecological knowledge (TEK – a kind of indigenous knowledge) and prevailing science. Although these northern debates have not yet crystallized in terms satisfying for most historians or philosophers, they are none the less crucial sites for parallel environmental impact assessments, reworking codes of ethics, and rethinking issues of intellectual property. Summary studies of Arctic science are now beginning to address the complex cross-cultural context, and the questions of ownership of knowledge and licensing of research. It is safe to say that no single perspective dominates the historiography of the region, and debates about the future of the Antarctic Treaty are focusing on a range of interpretations of the notion of a common heritage.

MICHAEL T. BRAVO

See also Anthropology; Expeditions; International Science

Political Economy

Appleby, Joyce Oldham, *Economic Thought and Ideology in Seventeenth-Century England*, Princeton, New Jersey: Princeton University Press, 1978

Berg, Maxine, *The Machinery Question and the Making of Political Economy, 1815–1848*, Cambridge and New York: Cambridge University Press, 1980

Dobb, Maurice, *Theories of Value and Distribution since Adam Smith: Ideology and Economic Theory*, Cambridge: Cambridge University Press, 1973

Hirschman, Albert O., *The Passions and the Interests: Political Arguments for Capitalism Before Its Triumph*, Princeton, New Jersey: Princeton University Press, 1977

Hollander, Samuel, *Classical Economics*, Oxford and New York: Blackwell, 1987

Ingrao, Bruna and Georgio Israel, *The Invisible Hand: Economic Equilibrium in the History of Science*, translated by Ian McGilvray, Cambridge, Massachusetts: MIT Press, 1990

Maloney, John, *Marshall, Orthodoxy and the Professionalisation of Economics*, Cambridge and New York: Cambridge University Press, 1985

Mirowski, Philip, *More Heat Than Light: Economics as Social Physics, Physics as Nature's Economics*, Cambridge and New York: Cambridge University Press, 1989

Morgan, Mary S., *The History of Econometric Ideas*, Cambridge and New York: Cambridge University Press, 1990

Schabas, Margaret, *A World Ruled by Number: William Stanley Jevons and the Rise of Mathematical Economics*, Princeton, New Jersey: Princeton University Press, 1990

Schumpeter, Joseph Alois, *History of Economic Analysis*, New York: Oxford University Press, 1954; London: Allen and Unwin, 1955

If one includes works in languages other than English, there are well over 1,000 books that survey the history of political economy. Most, however, are traditional textbooks that offer little in the way of historical analysis. The most distinguished of this group, both in terms of comprehensiveness and transcendence of mere chronology, is SCHUMPETER. His erudition is evident on virtually every page, and no author has since given so much attention to the broader intellectual context, or imposed such strong judgements on past economists. Some, such as Léon Walras, are portrayed as heroic warriors, armed with analytical weaponry in order to combat ignorance and to advance the frontiers of knowledge. Others, such as Adam Smith and David Ricardo, are denigrated, either because they had nothing new to offer, or because they took economic theory on a long detour.

Much subsequent scholarship in the field, such as the contents of the journal *History of Political Economy*, begins by taking issue with the great, but idiosyncratic, Schumpeter. However, a strong residue of whiggism still remains in much of these studies, attempts to correct Schumpeter's distortions notwithstanding. This bibliography is limited to those synthetic treatments that wisely limit their temporal reach to either a decade or a century, and which manifest some awareness of the fact that current economists may not have captured the world more accurately than their predecessors.

APPLEBY offers a detailed study of the debates surrounding usury, trade, and money in Stuart England, and highlights the sophistication of the mercantilist literature and the entrenchment of capitalist ideology by William Petty and John Locke. Appleby helps to bring out the complex manner in which such ideas both reflect and shape the economic world. Unfortunately, there is no comparable study of Enlightenment political economy, although there are many good articles and studies of specific economists of the period, notably Adam Smith and François Quesnay. HIRSCHMAN provides a brief overview of the leading economic ideas of the 18th century, with an eye to the evolution of the concept of individual self-interest. But his primary aim is to use this historical account to cast aspersions on the present, and to intimate that the Montesquieu-Steuart vision, whereby commercial gain promotes civility and political liberty, was myopic.

The classical school, which Smith founded and which lasted until the 1870s, has been most thoroughly examined by scholars. BERG is noteworthy for her appraisal of the extent to which the advent of industry transformed 19th-century economic theory; mechanization and the displacement of labourers became a topic for heated debate among economists. HOLLANDER provides a balanced exegetical account of the main texts by the most prominent classical economists (Smith, Ricardo, Malthus, and Mill) organized by theme: value and distribution, capital, employment and growth, money and banking, and methodology. He also downplays the classical components in Marx, and uses this to develop his central thesis that the classical economists were more aligned with their neo-classical successors. The crux of his argument rests on the demonstration that, for classical economists, distribution and pricing were simultaneous rather than sequential.

DOBB, by contrast, underscores the theoretical and methodological discontinuities between the classical and neo-classical theories. He presents Ricardo as unquestionably the most brilliant theoretician, with Marx a close second. The Jevonian Revolution of the 1870s effectively retreated to a more superficial account, by whitewashing the questions of distribution and growth under the banner of individual choice as the proximate cause of all economic phenomena. MALONEY furthers this line of interpretation with a detailed study of the professionalization of economics in late Victorian England and the ideological components of neo-classical economics. The most prominent economist of the age, Alfred Marshall, is portrayed as a master of disguise, who cloaked the political dimensions of the subject, and thus made economic theory much more attractive to the status quo. Welfare economics, with its imputation of justice to market mechanisms, is depicted as the final deathblow to the classical economists' recognition of economic strife.

Three recent books have addressed the role of mathematics in the development of neo-classical economics. INGRAO & ISRAEL offer the most general account, insofar as they cover the period from Walras to Arrow-Debreu. They also acknowledge the advent of game theory with von Neumann and Morgenstern. SCHABAS describes how the mathematization of economic theory drew directly upon new ideas in logic and the philosophy of science. MORGAN takes up the more specific question of the empirical verification of economic theory via the emerging set of techniques known as econometrics, which consisted primarily of refined statistical manipulations until the probabilistic turn undertaken by Trygve Haavelmo in the 1940s. Her account appreciates the technical and broader philosophical problems that were confronted but never resolved.

The most controversial history of modern economics to appear of late is MIROWSKI, who argues that neo-classical economists dressed their subject in the mathematical and metaphorical garb of thermodynamics without laying the proper conceptual foundations. As a result, he claims, modern economics is thoroughly suspect in both its content and methods. While this account sounds too conspiratorial, he is to be commended for having drawn attention to the bilateral analogical trade between economists and physicists. Mainstream historians of science might well find this work the best place to start.

MARGARET SCHABAS

See also Capitalism and Science; Quantification; Social Sciences

Popularization

Bazerman, Charles, *Shaping Written Knowledge: The Genre and Activity of the Experimental Article in Science*, Madison: University of Wisconsin Press, 1988

Burnham, John C., *How Superstition Won and Science Lost: Popularizing Science and Health in the United States*, New Brunswick, New Jersey: Rutgers University Press, 1987

Caudill, Edward, *Darwinism in the Press: The Evolution of an Idea*, Hillsdale, New Jersey: Lawrence Erlbaum, 1989

Cooter, Roger, *The Cultural Meaning of Popular Science: Phrenology and the Organization of Consent in Nineteenth-Century Britain*, Cambridge and New York: Cambridge University Press, 1984

Cooter, Roger and Stephen Pumfrey, "Separate Spheres and Public Places: Reflections on the History of Science Popularization and Science in Popular Culture", *History of Science*, 32 (1994): 237–67

Fayard, Pierre, *La Communication scientifique publique: De La Vulgarisation à la mediatisation*, Lyon: Chronique Sociale, 1988

Gross, Alan G., *The Rhetoric of Science*, Cambridge, Massachusetts: Harvard University Press, 1990

Hilgartner, Stephen, "The Dominant View of Popularization: Conceptual Problems, Political Uses", *Social Studies of Science*, 20 (1990): 519–39

Kevles, Daniel J., *The Physicists: The History of a Scientific Community in Modern America*, New York: Knopf, 1977; revised edition, Cambridge, Massachusetts: Harvard University Press, 1995

Kevles, Daniel J., *In the Name of Eugenics: Genetics and the Uses of Human Heredity*, New York: Knopf, 1985; Harmondsworth: Penguin, 1986; with a new preface, Cambridge, Massachusetts: Harvard University Press, 1995

Kinsella, James, *Covering the Plague: AIDS and the American Media*, New Brunswick, New Jersey: Rutgers University Press, 1989

Klaidman, Stephen, *Health in the Headlines: The Stories Behind the Stories*, New York: Oxford University Press, 1991

LaFollette, Marcel C., *Making Science Our Own: Public Images of Science, 1910–1955*, Chicago: University of Chicago Press, 1990

Myers, Greg, *Writing Biology: Texts in the Social Construction of Scientific Knowledge*, Madison: University of Wisconsin Press, 1990

Nelkin, Dorothy, *Selling Science: How the Press Covers Science and Technology*, New York: W.H. Freeman, 1987; 2nd edition, 1995

Rydell, Robert W., *All the World's a Fair: Visions of Empire at American International Expositions, 1876–1916*, Chicago: University of Chicago Press, 1984

Rydell, Robert W., *World of Fairs: The Century-of-Progress Expositions*, Chicago: University of Chicago Press, 1993

Secord, Anne, "Science in the Pub: Artisan Botanists in Early 19th-Century Lancashire", *History of Science*, 32 (1994): 269–315

Sheets-Pyenson, Susan, *Cathedrals of Science: The Development of Colonial Natural History Museums During the Late Nineteenth Century*, Kingston, Ontario: McGill-Queen's University Press, 1988

Shinn, Terry and Richard Whitley (eds), *Expository Science: Forms and Functions of Popularisation*, Dordrecht: Reidel, 1985

Winter, Alison, "Mesmerism and Popular Culture in Early Victorian England", *History of Science*, 32 (1994): 317–43

Ziporyn, Terra, *Disease in the Popular American Press: The Case of Diptheria, Typhoid Fever, and Syphilis, 1870–1920*, New York: Greenwood Press, 1988

Popularization, as a historiographic concept, is a recent invention, deeply influenced by developments in the sociology of scientific knowledge. Although reference to popularization is common in some histories of science (such as those by KEVLES), the nature of popularization, and its relationship with other aspects of science, have only recently been addressed.

In the major works that consider popularization, two strands dominate. The first, emerging mainly from attempts by single authors to survey broad periods of time, takes the notion of "popularization" to be unproblematic – as the means by which the knowledge produced by scientists is distributed to audiences beyond the limits of professional research – and considers the images of science portrayed to the public, and their effects.

BURNHAM, for example, looks at popularization in the United States from 1800 to the 1970s. Concentrating on health, psychology, and the natural sciences, he traces the 19th-century growth of missionary zeal for science, when senior scientists used their pulpits and bully tactics to proselytize for a scientific approach to life. The enemy, they believed, were the dark forces of superstition and (later) the occult. Though their individual lectures and articles were concerned with specific scientific findings, the proselytizers' consistent message was of the value of science. However, Burnham argues that the 20th century brought specialization to popularization as well as to science, so, with the rise of "science educators" and "science journalists" who were not themselves scientists, came a fragmentation of the message. Instead of exalting "Science", popularization became the simplification of individual scientific findings, and, without a continued commitment to the scientific way of thinking, popularization became mere snippets of information, taken out of context. The general public were forced to accept science without understanding its deepest meanings, Burnham argues, and so, in the end, popularization led to blind faith in science – a kind of superstition, no better than the anti-science that the great popularizers of the 19th century had fought to banish.

LAFOLLETTE is also concerned with the influence of popularization on the public. Based on a quantitative analysis of nearly 700 articles taken from 11 American magazines published between 1910 and 1955, LaFollette describes a "myth of scientific differentness", in which scientists were routinely portrayed as possessing "an unusual combination of both insightful genius and physical stamina". A series of stereotypes portrayed scientists as wizards, experts, creators/destroyers, or heroes. Many of these articles were written by, or with clear co-operation from, the scientific community. Overall,

LaFollette argues, the image of scientists produced by these articles was very positive – of caring individuals using reliable methods to research important topics – but, at the same time, unfulfilled promises of a cure for cancer and anxiety about issues such as atomic weapons and chemical pollution, led the public to question this shiny image. Perhaps much of the current distrust of science, LaFollette argues, comes from the disjunction between an over-positive image and a more complex reality in which the public has come to recognize the limits of science.

Though less well-known and less comprehensive, other works in the survey tradition include RYDELL's two works on world fairs (which often celebrated the contributions of science and technology to national and international development), ZIPORYN's review of media coverage of diseases such as diphtheria, typhus, and syphilis in the years around 1900 (showing the way in which social issues of class and morality shaped the reports), and CAUDILL's review of media stories on Darwinism from the 1850s to the 1920s (demonstrating the impact of non-scientific social issues on the shape of scientifically-based media stories). A more recent subject for historical work on popularization is the natural history museum; the most comprehensive example is SHEETS-PYENSON's survey of colonial museums in Canada, Argentina, Australia, and New Zealand, in which she describes the local contingencies that shaped individual institutions, which were essentially based on imperial models. Although Sheets-Pyenson does not explicitly question the distinction between science and non-science, she does make clear that institutions of popularization such as museums drew much of their strength from the interaction of the forces of education, research, and local pride.

In the mid-1980s, at about the time that Burnham, LaFollette, and others were publishing their comprehensive surveys, a different group of historians (many of them European) came under the influence of the newly-developed sociology of scientific knowledge. Considering smaller pieces of history – i.e. case studies of particular incidents or contexts – these historians produced a second strand of research on popularization that questioned the sharp line between doing science and popularizing it, in general looking at popularization not as a product, but as a process.

A volume of 1985 edited by SHINN & WHITLEY contained a manifesto for "expository science", arguing that no fundamental difference distinguished science presented to scientists from science presented to non-scientists; the only differences were those of local rhetorical contingency – the choice of language, examples, and structures that were needed for different audiences. The ultimate claim, supported by cases ranging from early 19th-century geology lectures to Hollywood movies in the 1940s and Dutch sociology of the 1960s, was that "science" existed only insofar as it was represented in texts. Thus, the same scientific research presented in different texts became different "science".

The rhetorical ideas in the Shinn & Whitley volume have been developed in the literature of the sociology of science, often with extended reference to historical cases. BAZERMAN, for example, demonstrates the presence of rhetorical tropes in materials ranging from the first 150 years of the Royal Society's *Philosophical Transactions*, to spectroscopy and psychology articles in the 20th century. MYERS, focusing primarily on biology writing in the 20th century, compares rhetorical techniques in articles on the same topic that have appeared in technical, semi-technical, and popular literature, in order to develop a distinction between "narratives of science" (depersonalized, objectified) and "narratives of nature" (in which plants and animals play active, time-bound roles independent of the activities of the scientists). GROSS, pursuing a more theoretical goal, moves from Copernicus to Watson and Crick in order to demonstrate that science is fundamentally about persuasion, not about descriptions of nature.

COOTER examines the intertwined technical and social uses of phrenology in early 19th-century Britain. Despite withering criticisms of its empirical base, phrenology acquired significant social authority, he argued, because it met the needs of radical reformers attempting to reshape the social order. Phrenology was used by those appealing to the working classes to take unto themselves the power that was rightfully theirs. By examining the use of scientific ideas within popular contexts – and emphasizing the authority those ideas maintained through their espousal by people with scientific credentials – Cooter demonstrates the importance of treating popularization within the broad context of social history, not merely as a side-show to the development of science.

More recently, in 1994, COOTER & PUMFREY arranged for the publication of a series of articles in the journal *History of Science* that continue to seek an appropriate historiographic model for exploring popularization. Pointing to general historical research on the relationship between popular culture and "high" culture, and to attempts to mesh "the sociology of collective behaviour and the history of scientific ideas" for inspiration, they claim, however, that few models exist. Ultimately, the authors question whether the multiple topics of "popular science", "popularization", "pop science", and "populist science" (among other labels) can be fruitfully combined. Their programmatic statement is followed by two examples: the first by SECORD, who explores the relationship of recreational botany by the working classes to the pub culture in which it developed, and the second by WINTER, who looks at how elite and popular audiences construed mesmerism in different ways. In both cases, the authors seek to redefine the term "science", by exploring how multiple contexts produce a development of knowledge in many different directions.

We cannot yet know whether this second strand of historiography on popularization – based on constructivist notions of the relationship between audiences, texts, and science – will thrive. It competes not only with the traditional treatment of popularization as something separate from science (an approach that HILGARTNER argues to be a tool used by the scientific community for essentially political purposes), but with "recent histories" of popularization that focus almost exclusively on science journalism and its production. KINSELLA, for example, in his examination of the media coverage of AIDS, suggests that the failure of the media to cover the emerging epidemic sufficiently aggressively was partly responsible for its spread. KLAIDMAN's case studies of "health in the headlines" document the contingency that shapes particular incidents in media coverage, but without providing historical or historiographic contexts. NELKIN does a good job of pulling together disparate work on the nature of contemporary science journalism, but again fails to address historiographic questions concerning the place of popularization in the history of either science or journalism. These presentist works provide useful entrées to recent events, but are neither sensitive to the historical literature nor theoretically sophisticated in their definition of the contexts of popular science. Thus they provide, at best, raw material for historians to use in their own studies. (Another recent history, FAYARD's analysis of French popularization, does develop a theoretical model, but one not especially sensitive to historiographic traditions.) A resolution of the two major strands, yet to appear, would be a synthesis of the broad scope represented by Burnham and LaFollette with the nuanced understanding of the role of science in popular culture offered by works more explicitly influenced by sociological concerns.

BRUCE V. LEWENSTEIN

See also Journals; Performance; Public and the Private; Rhetoric; Sociology of Science

Positivism

Kolakowski, Leszek, *Die Philosophie des Positivismus*, translated into German from the Polish by Peter Lachmann, Munich: Piper, 1971

Kraft, Viktor, *Der Wiener Kreis: Der Ursprung des Neopositivismus: Ein Kapitel der jüngsten Philosophiegeschichte*, Vienna: Springer, 1950; 2nd edition, 1968

Mises, Richard von, *Positivism: A Study in Human Understanding*, Cambridge, Massachusetts: Harvard University Press, 1951

Plé, Bernhard, *Die "Welt" aus den Wissenschaften: Der Positivismus in Frankreich, England und Italien von 1848 bis ins zweite Jahrzehnt des 20. Jahrhunderts: Eine wissenssoziologische Studie*, Stuttgart: Klett-Cotta, 1996

Stadler, Friedrich, *Vom Positivismus zur "wissenschaftlichen Weltauffassung": Am Beispiel der Wirkungsgeschichte von Ernst Mach in Österreich von 1895 bis 1934*, Vienna: Löcker, 1982

Weiss, Burghard, *Zwischen Physikotheologie und Positivismus: Pierre Prevost (1751–1839) und die korpuskularkinetische Physik der Genfer Schule*, Frankfurt and Bern, New York: Peter Lang, 1988

Wright, T.R., *The Religion of Humanity: The Impact of Comtean Positivism on Victorian Britain*, Cambridge and New York: Cambridge University Press, 1986

Positivism is not a unique phenomenon in the modern history of philosophy and science, in terms of either its terminology or its reality. It unites very different movements (such as positivism during the French and English Enlightenment, empirio-criticism, and neo-positivism), and for that reason this entry presents different, but especially interesting, approaches to the history of science.

KOLAKOWSKI gives a survey of the most important epochs of positivistic thinking, including the Middle Ages, the 17th century, and the Enlightenment, with an emphasis on David Hume. He stresses the positivism of Auguste Comte, Claude Bernard, John Stuart Mill, and Herbert Spencer, but also examines "empirio-criticism" (Ernst Mach) and "conventionalism" (Henri Poincaré, Pierre Duhem, Edouard Le Roy), the "pragmatistic method" (Charles Sanders Pierce) and "Logical Empirism" (Ludwig Wittgenstein), arguing that all these are "cultural formations". He makes a distinction between "radical" and "milder" forms of positivism, and demonstrates how the radical form reduces all knowledge to biological reactions.

KRAFT examines the work of the "Vienna Circle" in the 1930s, which included Moritz Schlick, Friedrich Waismann, Otto Neurath, Rudolf Carnap, Kaufmann, Hahn, and Kurt Gödel. He sketches the circle's development into an international philosophical movement known as "Neo-Positivism", or "analytical philosophy", which was particularly pursued in the UK and the US (by Waismann and Neurath, and later by Ayer and Popper). He points out the common basis and scientific character of this philosophy – clarity, logical stringency, and sufficient foundation – and shows how the connection with the earlier positivism persists in its opposition to the old dogmatic-speculative metaphysics. He describes empiricism, new logics (Whitehead and Russell), and philosophy of language (Carnap and Wittgenstein) as the fundamental concepts of this philosophical circle, which was dealing with the analysis of knowledge, the theoretical foundations of mathematics, the natural sciences, psychology, and sociology, and regards the circle's championing of the scientific method as its lasting achievement.

MISES, known for his contributions to the theories of probability, statics, aerodynamics, and mechanical engineering (including water-power machines and kinematics), discusses an instrumentalistic theory of language – "connectivity" – as a pragmatic and regulative criterion for scientific method, axiomatics, mathematical logic and the relationship between mathematics and logic, the analysis of causality and probability, "Unified Science" (including its critics on two different fields of knowledge and method), and the possibility of a scientific ethics. Mises argues that scientific progress is only possible by following a number of rules: language has to be criticised; empirical statements must be the basis of all knowledge; empirical verification must be the scientific goal; coherence can only be established by attending to causality and probability; there must be only one method in the natural and the human sciences; metaphysical statements cannot claim objectivity; and there can be no objective scale of moral values.

PLÉ shows that the term "positivism" has been employed within differing intellectual and political endeavours. This very detailed investigation, based on new sources, demonstrates: 1) that positivism was a movement of disparate ideas, influenced by opposing traditions; 2) that it was embodied in particular social groups; and 3) that doctrines tagged "positivism" posited different solutions to the same question – the relationship between man and the scientifically perceptible world. The book's perspective is primarily sociological (Karl Mannheim's "sociology of knowledge"), and contains three parts: the first introduces new sources and develops an analytical framework for the theory and history of science; the second deals with the establishment of organisations and the founding of a "religion" in Britain and France; and the third part investigates Italian positivism juxtaposed with the French. Plé gives very detailed references to his sources, including positivistic writings, organised members, and their occupations in Britain and France.

WEISS concentrates on works of the corpuscular-kinetic oriented "Geneva School". After a reconstruction of Pierre Prevost's biography, he points out the specific "Geneva" style in science, which created a "Newtonianism", and its influence on Prevost's physics (especially magnetism and optics). Weiss reconstructs Prevost's most prominent contribution, the theory of "calorique rayonnant", its decline at the time of Fourier, and its subsequent renaissance in Scotland as a result of a "congruence of researching styles".

In order to show the impact of Comtean positivism on Victorian Britain, WRIGHT first describes the genesis of Comte's and Clotilde de Vaux's Religion of Humanity within its historical context, before analysing Comte's ideas. Chapter 2 deals with Comte's British followers, such as John Stuart Mill, George Henry Lewes, Harriet Martineau, George Holyoake, and Richard Congreve, while chapter 3 discusses "organised" positivism (the Centre for the Religion of Humanity). Chapter 4 examines positivism in the press and the universities (John Morley, Leslie Stephen, Henry Sidgwick), especially Cambridge (from a "institutional-sociological" point of view), and chapter 5 studies positivism in 19th-century fiction (e.g. by George Eliot, Mrs Humphrey Ward, George Meredith, and H.G. Wells). The last chapter shows the decline of positivism in Britain. Wright's hypothesis of a linear impact is, however, doubtful; in fact, there was a correlation between Comte's influence and the resistance to it.

STADLER provides a "bio-bibliographical" sketch of Ernst Mach's contribution as a physicist to psychology, the methodology of science and philosophy, and to the history of science and technology. He demonstrates the tendency and unity of Mach's monistic, natural scientific conception of science within the context of his biography and his (socio-political, democratic) influence on Vienna and Austria c.1900, showing the "Verein Ernst Mach" as a prototype of the Anglo-American "Unity of science" movement associated with Otto Neurath.

BEATRICE RAUSCHENBACH

See also Objectivity; Paradigm; Practice

Practice

Bourdieu, Pierre, *The Logic of Practice*, translated from the French by Richard Nice, Oxford: Polity Press/Blackwell, and Stanford, California: Stanford University Press, 1990 (original edition, 1980)

Buchwald, Jed Z. (ed.), *Scientific Practice: Theories and Stories of Doing Physics*, Chicago: University of Chicago Press, 1995

Bud, Robert and Gerrylyn K. Roberts, *Science Versus Practice: Chemistry in Victorian Britain*, Manchester: Manchester University Press, 1984

Collins, H.M., *Changing Order: Replication and Induction in Scientific Practice*, Beverly Hills, California, and London: Sage, 1995

Golinski, Jan, "The Theory of Practice and the Practice of Theory", *Isis*, 81 (1990): 492–505

Gooday, Graeme, "The Morals of Energy Metering: Constructing and Deconstructing the Precision of the Victorian Electrical Engineer's Ammeter and Voltmeter", in *The Values of Precision*, edited by M. Norton Wise, Princeton, New Jersey: Princeton University Press, 1995

Hessen, Boris, "The Social and Economic Roots of Newton's 'Principia'", in *Science at the Crossroads*, edited by N.I. Bukharin, *et al.*; 2nd edition, London: Frank Cass, 1971 (original edition, 1931)

Jordanova, Ludmilla, *Sexual Visions: Images of Gender in Science and Medicine Between the Eighteenth and Twentieth Centuries*, Hemel Hempstead, Hertfordshire: Harvester Wheatsheaf, and Madison: University of Wisconsin Press, 1989

Knorr-Cetina, Karin, *The Manufacture of Knowledge: An Essay on the Constructivist and Contextual Nature of Science*, Oxford and New York: Pergamon Press, 1981

Koyré, Alexandre, *Metaphysics and Measurement: Essays in Scientific Revolution*, London: Chapman and Hall, and Cambridge, Massachusetts: Harvard University Press, 1968

Kuhn, Thomas S., *The Structure of Scientific Revolutions*, Chicago: University of Chicago Press, 1962; revised edition, 1970

Latour, Bruno and Steve Woolgar, *Laboratory Life: The Social Construction of Scientific Facts*, Beverley Hills, California: Sage, 1979; as *Laboratory Life: The Construction of Scientific Facts*, with a new postscript, Princeton, New Jersey: Princeton University Press, 1986

Lynch, Michael and Steve Woolgar (eds), *Representation in Scientific Practice*, Cambridge, Massachusetts: MIT Press, 1990

Macintyre, Alasdair C., *After Virtue: A Study in Moral Theory*, London: Duckworth, and Notre Dame, Indiana: University of Notre Dame Press, 1981

Marsden, Ben, "Engineering Science in Glasgow: Economy, Efficiency and Measurement as Prime Movers in the Differentiation of an Academic Discipline", *British Journal for the History of Science*, 25 (1992): 319–46

Pickering, Andrew, *Science as Practice and Culture*, Chicago: University of Chicago Press, 1992

Pickering, Andrew, *The Mangle of Practice: Time, Agency and Science*, Chicago: University of Chicago Press, 1995

Ravetz, Jerome R., *Scientific Knowledge and Its Social Problems*, Oxford: Clarendon Press, and New York: Oxford University Press, 1971

Rouse, Joseph, *Knowledge and Power: Toward a Political Philosophy of Science*, Ithaca, New York: Cornell University Press, 1987

Secord, Ann, "Science in the Pub: Artisan Botanists in Early Nineteenth-Century Lancashire", *History of Science*, 32 (1994): 269–315

Shapin, Steven and Simon Schaffer, *Leviathan and the Air-Pump: Hobbes, Boyle, and the Experimental Life*, Princeton, New Jersey: Princeton University Press, 1985

Shapin, Steven, *A Social History of Truth: Civility and Science in Seventeenth-Century England*, Chicago: University of Chicago Press, 1994

Sibum, Otto, "Reworking the Mechanical Value of Heat: Instruments of Precision and Gestures of Accuracy in Early Victorian England", *Studies in History and Philosophy of Science*, 26 (1995): 76–106

Traweek, Sharon, *Beamtimes and Lifetimes: The World of High Energy Physicists*, Cambridge, Massachusetts: Harvard University Press, 1988

Warwick, Andrew, "Cambridge Mathematics and Cavendish Physics: Cunningham, Campbell and Einstein's Relativity", *Studies in History and Philosophy of Science*, (part 1) 23 (1992): 625–56; (part 2) 24 (1993): 1–25

Although much in vogue among historians of science, the term "practice" is none the less used by them in a variety of distinct ways. "Philosophical" traditions have long construed science as a body of abstract theory, in contrast with the application of science within industrial "practice". More recently, however, sociologists have portrayed science as a macroscopic cultural "practice" in its own right, while ethnographic studies since the late 1970s have analysed scientific disciplines microscopically as a complex of individual "practices" – i.e. utilizing distinct social, material, and literary techniques. The useful differentiation between the "macro" practice of science as a socio-cultural enterprise, and the individual "micro" practices of scientists' everyday work, is not acknowledged by all writers, with some confusing consequences. (Although all writers employ the noun "practice", British writers refer to the *practising scientist* or the "scientist who *practises*", while American authors use *practicing* and *practices* respectively.)

KOYRÉ's pre-war studies of Galileo's measurement experiments epitomize the common mid-20th-century interpretation of science as essentially a corpus of pure theory. His Platonist conviction that "nature" is fundamentally mathematical not material in character is manifest in his view that the "means" by which experiments are performed are "nothing more than theory incarnate". For Koyré, "good experiments" are good because they are "based on theory", not because they are executed by skilled practice (p. 113). The popularity of such a position among many post-war "intellectual" historians of science (if not historians of technology) can be related to their Cold War hostility to Marxist materialist doctrines on science. Most notorious in this respect was the view expounded by Soviet historian, Boris HESSEN, in 1931, that science is created and governed by economic demands, and is thus only a secondary by-product of technological "practice".

A more subtle form of the theory-practice nexus has been employed in historical studies of the (educational) relation between science and industry. BUD & ROBERTS's account of chemistry in 19th-century Britain presupposes a duality between academic "science" and commercial "practice", although it does address with some sensitivity the problems of creating and managing links between Victorian educational institutions and industry. MARSDEN's study of mid-19th-century engineering argues that this nexus was often contested, rhetorical, and distinctly local in character. He shows how W.J.M. Rankine attempted to synthesize fashionable themes of economy, efficiency, and measurement into a representation of "engineering science" that might persuade important Glaswegian audiences of the "harmony" of theory and practice. Such scholarship indicates that historians should not take at face value dichotomies constructed in the past between science and industrial practice.

Many historians now see that the sciences can be regarded as (macro) practices analogous to technologies. The origins of this view are usually traced to KUHN's famous treatise, which shows the value of seeing science as constituted by the day-to-day collective work of scientists. For Kuhn, the "practice" of science could not be reduced to the following of a well-defined set of explicit rational "rules", but rather involved learning to solve shared problems by reference to heuristic exemplars. Just as in the practice of medicine or law, argued Kuhn, practising scientists exercise "tacit" (non-articulable) knowledge and culturally-learned discretion in extending the scope of their shared paradigm. Although focusing on "macro" issues, Kuhn's analysis of individual (micro) practices within a paradigm was also informed by the hitherto-neglected work of Ludwik Fleck in the 1930s, on the chaotic genesis of the Wasserman reaction in diagnosing syphilis (Kuhn, pp. v–vii).

In the preface to PICKERING (1992), the author points out that few scholars immediately adopted Kuhn's concern with practice, the only exception being RAVETZ's imaginative study of the "craft" aspects of science. Certainly, in the 1970s, Edinburgh-based sociologists of knowledge were concerned with mapping congruencies between the social interests of scientists and the end product of scientific knowledge, rather than with the production processes. The Edinburgh-trained Pickering embraced the study of practice in recognition of the constructivist (and also Marxist) insight that the doing of science is in fact "real work", and thus worth studying in its own right. Drawing directly on Kuhn's arguments, Pickering defines (macro) practice as being the "creative extension" of an existing network of concepts to "fit new circumstances" (p. 4). Pickering also emphasizes the qualities of creativity and open-endedness in his definition of (micro) practices as the distinct acts of "making or unmaking" performed by scientists drawing upon the cultural resources of their field.

What makes the themes of open-endedness and creativity so central to "cultural" (macro) interpretations of practice is most clearly expressed in MACINTYRE's ethical writings. For Macintyre, a practice is a morally-laden enterprise: it is any coherent form of co-operative human activity through which goods internal to that form of activity are realised in pursuit of pertinent standards of excellence. The expected result of a practice, he maintains, is the systematic extension of humans' ability to achieve their ends in a virtuous manner. By Macintyre's criteria of creativity and virtue, science is thus a genuine practice, as is history, whereas planting turnips or bricklaying are not. This moral dimension of the cultural "practice" of science is epitomized in SHAPIN, a study of how codes of gentlemanly virtue governed the conduct of natural philosophy in late 17th-century England. In contrast, GOODAY demonstrates an absence of any similarly common moral basis to late 19th-century electrical practice, as conflicts arose between physicists and electrical engineers over the proper conduct of measurement work.

The collection edited by BUCHWALD shows that traditional epistemological debates about relativism can still be of interest for historians. In his paper, Peter Galison concedes that scientific practice is far from monolithic, typically consisting of dispersed sub-cultures bound together by transactions in local-ized "trading zones"; nevertheless, he also claims that each of these subcultures recognizes material constraints within its context that limit acceptable interpretations of the world. From a broader temporal perspective, Andrew Pickering's essay argues that such apparent constraints do not present insuper-able limits to practice, but are merely finite resistances that are often overcome by open-ended modelling. He cites Gell-Mann's and Zweig's proposal of fractional charges for "quarks" as a radical break with the long-held constraint that allowed only integral charges in particle physics.

Anthropological and ethnographic studies have been of great value in indicating how "micro" practices generate con-tingency in "macro" practice. LATOUR & WOOLGAR's classic study of the Salk Institute in California shows how individual biochemical facts of the world could be made and unmade in the messy complexity of everyday laboratory life. In her constructivist account, KNORR-CETINA offers a useful list of elements of individual techniques that constitute scientific practice (p. 136), emphasizing particularly the haphazard "deci-sion-ladenness" of any given scientific practice. TRAWEEK's study of high-energy physics laboratories reveals how gender issues are ubiquitous in the personnel imbalances, discursive practices, and modes of judgement exercized in their daily scientific practice. In a valuable, if selective, overview of this literature, GOLINSKI argues that such studies have done much to help historians develop a historiography that pays much closer attention to the (micro) practices of the past.

The French anthropologist, Pierre BOURDIEU, has proposed a theory of "habitus" that provides a broader framework within which to understand how culturally-grounded but diverse day-to-day micro practices of scientific work can somehow hang together in a coherent macro practice. Bourdieu defines habitus as the durable, but mutable, shared "disposi-tions" by which humans collectively generate and organize their daily practices. The routinization of these (micro) prac-tices make everyday life "regulated and regular without in any way being the product of obedience to rules", arising un-intentionally from the enmeshing of practices within a given social space. Applied to the practice of localized forms of science, the notion of habitus can be of considerable historical cogency: e.g. SECORD imaginatively deploys the notion of "habitus" to articulate the crucial role played by pub-life in early 19th-century Lancashire in sustaining a strong artisanal culture of botany.

Such anthropological studies of individual locations do not, however, help us to understand how a "macro" practice can extend with some homogeneity across a range of geographically dispersed sites. In the traditional philosophy of science (e.g. by Koyré), this difficulty did not arise: it was simply assumed that the rule-based methodology of science was universal in its applicability. COLLINS has shown, however, that the issue of replication is no simple matter: individual scientific practices do not generally readily spread uniformly from one site to many others just by scientists' adherence to published experimental rules or protocols. His sociological studies on the development of lasers show that experimenters have generally to travel to the location of the original experimental set-up and learn the necessary tacit knowledge in order to enable them to emulate the originator's "successful" practices.

The classic historical application of Collins's arguments is SHAPIN & SCHAFFER's study of the recurrent difficulties of Robert Boyle's contemporaries in attempting to replicate his experiments with airpumps. WARWICK has applied similar themes to the practice of theory, using the differential reception accorded to Einstein's 1905 work on special relativity as a case study with which to articulate the localized "practice-ladenness" of theoretical physics and mathematics in early 20th-century Cambridge. Equally stimulating is SIBUM's account of his painstaking efforts to reconstruct Joule's experiments on the "Mechanical Equivalent of Heat" in the 1840s. Sibum's work led to the recovery of some of the daily practices that were unique to Joule's Manchester brewery context: idiosyncratic, local practices that made it very difficult for Joule's contempo-raries, and also later scholars, to replicate his results.

Equally fruitfully, LYNCH & WOOLGAR look at the complexity and subtlety of the practices involved in con-structing and interpreting visual evidence. Papers in their joint volume show how the integrity of research tends to hinge on practices of transforming and "fixing" inscriptions into stable images, in order to persuade diverse audiences of the credi-bility of evidential claims made from them. It is clear, espe-cially from Bastide, Myers and Knorr-Cetina, that historians of science still have much to learn from historians of art about the social practices of encoding and decoding non-textual representations in the work of the past. Although not specifi-cally addressing the issue of practice, JORDANOVA usefully complements this literature with an analysis of the gendered character of visual representation in medical and scientific texts of the last two centuries.

Future historians of scientific practice may glean something of value from PICKERING (1995), if only perhaps the insight that the processes of science leave no element unchanged – be it fact, theory, instrument, or social relation – after their open-ended interaction with "practice". It will be more difficult for such historians, however, to make sense of the technological metaphor of the "mangle of practice", especially if they follow British readers in identifying the "mangle" as a wash-room device that simply restores wet clothes to a former state of dryness. Instead, historians may find more value in critical elab-orations of Heidegger's phenomenology of material "practices" by ROUSE. Certainly, it is easy to concur with Rouse that Heidegger's vocabulary of tools as "ready-to-hand" and serving human purposes, or as being merely "present-at-hand" and occupying a background role in investigation, may prove effec-tive in analyses of the geographical location of material prac-tices in scientists' immediate working environments.

Few can now doubt the centrality of "practice", in its many and varied forms, to the contemporary history of science. Many questions are left unanswered, however. Historians have not hitherto been deeply reflective about why (or indeed whether) they should be satisfied with historical explanations based on an ontology of "practice"; they perhaps have something to learn on this topic from ethnographers. Historians must also wrestle with the difficulties of recovering past forms of prac-tice from often meagre textual, visual, or material resources, and of devising persuasive means of representing past practices in their own historical writing.

GRAEME J.N. GOODAY

See also Measurement; Sociology of Science

Prehistory: archaeology and anthropology

Casson, Stanley, *The Discovery of Man: The Story of the Inquiry into Human Origins*, New York: Harper, and London: Hamish Hamilton, 1939

Cole, Thomas, *Democritus and the Sources of Greek Anthropology*, Cleveland, Ohio: Press of Western Reserve University, 1967

Daniel, Glyn, *The Idea of Prehistory*, Cleveland: World, 1963; 2nd edition, with Colin Renfrew, Edinburgh: Edinburgh University Press, 1988

Grayson, Donald K., *The Establishment of Human Antiquity*, New York: Academic Press, 1983

Guthrie, W.K.C., *In the Beginning: Some Greek Views on the Origins of Life and the Early State of Man*, London: Methuen, and Ithaca, New York: Cornell University Press, 1957

Jia, Lanpo and Huang Weiwen, *The Story of Peking Man: From Archaeology to Mystery*, translated from the Chinese by Yin Zhiqi, Beijing: Foreign Languages Press, and New York: Oxford University Press, 1990

Laming-Emperaire, Annette, *Origines de l'archéologie Préhistorique en France: des superstitions médiévales à la découverte de l'homme fossile*, Paris: Picard, 1964

Livingstone, David N., *The Preadamite Theory and the Marriage of Science and Religion*, Philadelphia: American Philosophical Society, 1992

Piggott, Stuart, *Ancient Britons and the Antiquarian Imagination: Ideas from the Renaissance to the Regency*, New York: Thames and Hudson, 1989

Popkin, Richard H., *Isaac La Peyrere (1596–1676): His Life, Work, and Influence*, Leiden and New York: E.J. Brill, 1987

Reader, John, *Missing Links: The Hunt for Earliest Man*, London: Collins, and Boston: Little Brown, 1981

Rossi, Paolo, *The Dark Abyss of Time: The History of the Earth and the History of Nations from Hooke to Vico*, translated from the Italian by Lydia G. Cochrane, Chicago: University of Chicago Press, 1984 (original edition, 1979)

Slotkin, J.S., *Readings in Early Anthropology*, Chicago: Aldine, 1965

Spencer, Frank, *Ecce Homo: An Annotated Bibliographic History of Physical Anthropology*, New York: Greenwood Press, 1986

Spencer, Frank, *Piltdown: A Scientific Forgery*, London and New York: Oxford University Press, 1990

Trinkaus, Erik and Pat Shipman, *The Neanderthals: Changing the Image of Mankind*, New York: Knopf, and London: Jonathan Cape, 1993

Van Riper, A. Bowdoin, *Men among the Mammoths: Victorian Science and the Discovery of Human Prehistory*, Chicago: University of Chicago Press, 1993

Wendt, Herbert, *In Search of Adam: The Story of Man's Quest for the Truth about His Earliest Ancestors*, translated from the German by James Cleugh, Boston: Houghton Mifflin, 1955

The term "prehistory" only came into common usage in the 19th century, yet the philosophical and scientific inquiry into the origins of human beings, and the early conditions and development of these first people, have had a continuous and unbroken history leading back to ancient Greece. Like many other modern scientific disciplines, prehistoric anthropology and archaeology emerged gradually out of more general philosophical questions. Early speculation about human prehistory by philosophers, historians, and scientists focused on such problems as the origins of the first people, their conditions of existence, and whether they were created with, or without, all the accoutrements of civilization – such as language, a knowledge of fire, metallurgy, agriculture, and the other arts and sciences. Recent histories of prehistoric anthropology and archaeology have demonstrated that many disciplines contributed to the development of these sciences; geology, biology, classical archaeology, history, and Christianity have all had a powerful role in shaping the development of the study of human prehistory. Yet, despite the diversity of opinions and theories that have been proposed to explain the origins and early conditions of mankind, and the differences in methods that have been employed in those inquiries, the history of prehistoric anthropology and archaeology show that many themes and assumptions have remained constant, from the earliest speculations of the Greeks to the most modern theories of paleoanthropology.

A good general introduction to the subject is provided by CASSON. Although the book is somewhat dated, it is comprehensive in its coverage, beginning with Greek biological and anthropological ideas, then tracing the impact of the voyages of discovery during the Renaissance, and the biological and geological discoveries of the 18th and 19th centuries. The unearthing of the remains of early civilizations by 19th- and 20th-century archaeologists, discussed in the final chapters of the book, reflect the important connections between prehistory and history proper.

Most general accounts of the study of prehistory locate the beginning of such investigations in the 17th century or later, yet many of the basic assumptions about, and models of, human prehistory have their origins in Greek and Roman theories. As GUTHRIE has shown, with the transition from the creation myths of the early Greeks to the philosophical speculations of the pre-Socratic natural philosophers, a new set of ideas and methods were introduced to explain the origin and earliest conditions of the first people. The book only covers the period up to Aristotle, yet it successfully shows that the roots of the rational inquiry into the obscure beginnings of human culture lie here.

COLE gives a much more detailed and extensive discussion of ancient Greek and Roman theories about human prehistory. The primary argument of the book is that some prominent accounts of prehistory, composed by both Greek and Roman authors, were based on ideas derived from Democritus. The enormous wealth of information culled from a host of ancient philosophers and writers, also serves as a thorough survey of Greco–Roman thought on the subject.

Despite the powerful impact of Christianity and scholasticism on medieval ideas about the origins of mankind and the earliest stages of human history, no adequate work on the subject exists. One valuable source of information about medieval and Renaissance views, however, is SLOTKIN. This is a source book composed of selections from major writers rather than a narrative history, yet it can be used to trace the course of medieval anthropological ideas.

Most histories of prehistoric anthropology and archaeology begin with the 17th or 18th centuries. DANIEL discusses the development of the idea of prehistory from the early works of 17th-century antiquaries to the present. The rise of modern geological theories, the study of human fossils and artifacts, and the excavations of ancient civilizations, are all considered central to this development. A great deal of attention is given to the improvement of archaeological research methods, while at the same time the influences of racial anthropology, historical linguistics, and the idea of diffusionism in shaping early conceptions of prehistory are explored.

LAMING-EMPERAIRE also emphasizes the importance of antiquarianism, geological theory, and the discovery and interpretation of human fossils and artifacts, in the rise of French prehistoric archaeology from the 17th to the 19th centuries.

WENDT devotes much more attention to the way the biological theories of the 18th and 19th centuries changed the scientific conception of man. Darwin's theory of evolution, and the subsequent debates over prehistoric artifacts, human remains and cave paintings in the last decades of the 19th century, lead Wendt to discuss the discovery of the Neanderthal, Cromagnon, Pithecanthropus, and Sinanthropus fossils of the early 20th century.

Besides these general histories, there are a number of very important studies that have a more limited scope. ROSSI's meticulous study of the intricate interaction, in the 17th and 18th centuries, between the debates over the meaning of fossils, the geological question of the history of the earth, scholarly arguments over the early history of ancient civilizations, and the rising interest in the question of the origins and early conditions of mankind, raises entirely new questions for the historian of prehistoric anthropology and archaeology. It demonstrates that inquiries into human prehistory were well developed at that time, and that ideas from many disparate disciplines helped shape the newly-emerging theories.

PIGGOTT examines the same period (17th–18th centuries) but his focus is entirely on antiquarianism and the archaeological investigation of British prehistory by British scholars.

POPKIN investigates the origin and development of yet another important theme of early modern anthropological thought, the pre-Adamite thesis. Much of the book is devoted to the ideas of Isaac La Peyrere, the main propounder of the thesis, and the subsequent reaction to his radical views that Adam was only the father of the Jews, and that God had created people before Adam.

While the debates over pre-Adamism were most prominent in the late 17th century, the theory continued to affect prehistoric anthropology into the 20th century. LIVINGSTONE explores the outlines of this history, revealing connections between monogenism/polygenism and pre-Adamism. He also argues that the pre-Adamite thesis can tell us a great deal about the relationship between science and religion.

GRAYSON is primarily concerned with the geological debates in the 19th century regarding the antiquity of man.

The discoveries by British and continental European geologists of human fossils and artifacts, sometimes in association with the bones of extinct animals, were interpreted in different ways. Grayson follows the development of these debates through the critical discoveries made at Brixham Cave, in England, which convinced many scientists of the great antiquity of fossil man.

VAN RIPER examines even more closely the work conducted at Brixham Cave. Starting with a discussion of early 19th-century archaeology and geology in Britain, the book proceeds to describe the significance of the way the excavations were organized and of the discoveries that were made there. The scientific and popular reception of this powerful evidence of human antiquity are treated in the final chapters.

A number of works have been written about the remarkable fossil discoveries of the 20th century. A general survey of the most important of these, from Neanderthal to the early discoveries of Louis Leakey, can be found in READER.

The impact of the discovery of Neanderthal fossils on the modern debate about human evolution, and the various schools of thought that have emerged about how Neanderthal should be interpreted, form the central themes of TRINKAUS & SHIPMAN. Their account of the history of Neanderthal research recognizes the important contributions made by physical anthropologists, anatomists, and those who searched for the fossil remains of human ancestors.

SPENCER (1990) analyses the historical and scientific context surrounding the discovery, study, and eventual rejection of the Piltdown fossils. By providing a wealth of detail about the state of anthropological and archaeological research into human origins in Britain during the first decades of the 20th century, Spencer helps to explain why the fossils were accepted. The subsequent debates about the fossils and the scientific theories constructed from them are treated at length, as are the events surrounding the final demonstration that the fossils were a hoax.

The excavations at Chou Kou Tien, which uncovered Peking Man, are related in JIA & WEIWEN. This work is significant not only as a history of the discovery of the Sinanthropus fossils by Davidson Black, but as one of the few histories that deal with the important role played by Chinese archaeologists in the excavation and study of these valuable fossils.

Lastly, SPENCER (1986) is a tremendously useful research tool for anyone interested in identifying the prominent writers on physical anthropology from the Renaissance to the present. The list of authors and books is lengthy, and the annotations give the reader a sense of the significance of each work. Since many of those books deal with issues related to the problem of human prehistory, this bibliography will prove invaluable to any researcher in this area.

MATTHEW R. GOODRUM

See also Age of the Earth; Anthropology; Archaeology

Priestley, Joseph 1733–1804

British chemist and clergyman

Anderson, R.G.W. and Christopher Lawrence (eds), *Science, Medicine and Dissent: Joseph Priestley (1733–1804)*, London: Wellcome Trust and the Science Museum, 1987

Bolton, Henry Carrington (ed.), *Scientific Correspondence of Joseph Priestley*, New York: privately printed, 1892; reprinted New York: Kraus, 1969

Crook, Ronald E., *A Bibliography of Joseph Priestley, 1733–1804*, London: Library Association, 1966

Gibbs, F.W., *Joseph Priestley: Adventurer in Science and Champion of Truth*, London: Nelson, 1965

Golinski, Jan, *Science as Public Culture: Chemistry and Enlightenment in Britain, 1760–1820*, Cambridge: Cambridge University Press, 1992

Lindsay, Jack (ed.), *Autobiography of Joseph Priestley*, Bath: Adams and Dart, 1970

McEvoy, John G. and J.E. McGuire, "God and Nature: Priestley's Way of Rational Dissent", *Historical Studies in the Physical Sciences*, 6 (1975): 325–404

McEvoy, John G., "Joseph Priestley, 'Aerial Philosopher': Metaphysics and Methodology in Priestley's Thought 1772–1781", *Ambix*, 25 (1978): 1–55, 93–116; 26 (1979): 16–38

Priestley, Joseph, *Memoirs of Dr. Joseph Priestley to the Year 1795. Written by Himself*, London: J. Johnson, 1806

Rutt, John Towill (ed.), *The Theological and Miscellaneous Works of Joseph Priestley, LL.D., F.R.S.*, 25 vols in 26, London: George Smallfield, 1817–31

Schaffer, Simon, "Priestley's Questions: An Historiographical Survey", *History of Science*, 22 (1984): 151–83

Schofield, Robert E., *The Lunar Society of Birmingham: A Social History of Provincial Science and Industry in Eighteenth-Century England*, Oxford: Clarendon Press, 1963

Schofield, Robert E. (ed.), *A Scientific Autobiography of Joseph Priestley (1733–1804)*, Cambridge, Massachusetts: MIT Press, 1966

Schofield, Robert E., *The Enlightenment of Joseph Priestley: A Study of His Life and Work from 1733 to 1773*, University Park: Pennsylvania State University Press, 1997

Joseph Priestley was a clergyman, political theorist, and physical scientist whose work contributed to advances in liberal, political, and religious thought as well as in experimental science. In the history of science, he has most commonly been depicted as a foil for Antoine Lavoisier in the chemical revolution of late 18th-century chemistry. Thus, Priestley's discovery of what Lavoisier was subsequently to call oxygen, while continuing to adhere to the old phlogiston theory has been employed to emphasize the revolutionary nature of Lavoisier's thinking. More recently, Priestley's emphasis on democratic values in science has been used to highlight Lavoisier's elitist form of science. Priestley's open support for the French Revolution resulted in a mob burning down his house, library, and laboratory, and he was driven from his home. Eventually, Priestley emigrated to the US. Priestley has been of interest not only to historians of science; there is also a tradition of scholarship on Priestley by dissenters. Priestley wrote on theological matters too, such as his six-volume history of the Christian Church.

BOLTON provides access to the part of Priestley's correspondence that was recognizable as science at the time of editing in 1892. RUTT, a co-dissenter and personal friend, republished a great deal of Priestley's work. The focus of these massive 25 volumes, as the title implies, is on theology, but much of Priestley's work, which ostensibly is more of a chemical nature, is included too.

PRIESTLEY's autobiography has been republished by LINDSAY, who provides a short introduction covering Priestley's career, his relations with David Hartley and Boscovich, and his doctrines of materialism and phlogiston.

There are two useful biographies of Priestley. GIBBS is reliable and fairly comprehensive: Priestley's science and its application to the arts is covered and there is a good account of his post-Revolutionary life, including a detailed description of the mobbing which led to his house being burnt down. Unfortunately the book is incompletely documented: there are few footnotes and only a short bibliographical essay.

SCHOFIELD's long-awaited volume (1997) covers only the first half of Priestley's life, although a second volume is planned. SCHOFIELD (1966) does not actually contain Priestley's autobiography. Rather, it depicts his life through a selection of slightly edited correspondence. It contains a very useful (but not comprehensive) index of Priestley's correspondents.

Much literature which is not of a biographical nature bears on Priestley: institutional history, works on specific aspects of Priestley's activites, and contextualisations of Priestley's written work within the society of his day.

CROOK is the standard bibliography, containing a listing of Priestley's own publications, including his many pamphlets. The physical details of each are described meticulously, and locations are listed of where each item can be found. Most of these locations are in the British Isles, but many are also in Canada, Germany, Switzerland, and the US. Priestley's nonperiodical publications are listed by category: theological and religious, political and social, educational and psychological, philosophical and metaphysical, historical, and scientific. The book also contains a section on secondary literature which, more than three decades later, is now out of date.

SCHOFIELD (1963) is an indispensable account of Priestley's principal philosophical network. The Lunar Society was a group of natural philosophers and industrialists in Birmingham with whom Priestley was involved for the central part of his career. The book describes the industrial context of the application of chemistry to the useful arts.

McEVOY & McGUIRE is a useful introduction for historians of science to Priestley's philosophical and theological thought. The authors argue that Priestley's constructive empiricism represents a major philosophical reform in 18th-century attitudes to science, and that Priestley sets out a way to link rationalism and empiricism: things are as they are because a wise God has made them so. McEVOY interprets Priestley's pneumatic chemistry in the light of his philosophical and theological convictions. For example, Priestley saw the qualities of different kinds of of air as a part of divine design. McEvoy argues, not always convincingly, that all parts of Priestley's chemistry can be linked to such convictions.

SCHAFFER surveys the strange contradiction in Priestley's scientific reputation – that he was too empirical, and guided too much by the mere appearances of chemical phenomena; and that he was too theoretically prejudiced, and thus too driven by an overarching commitment to the phlogiston theory. In order to resolve this apparent contradiction, it is argued that we need a developmental account of Priestley's natural philosophical work instead of assuming that he held one single set of methodological or chemical beliefs. Scahffer also points out that Priestley's scientific and political careers have been used to teach morals about the fate of the scientist, and this may help explain why he has been seen as both conservative and radical, empiricist and theoretician.

GOLINSKI is a history of chemistry in Britain in relation to the forms of civic life characteristic of the Enlightenment, a period when scientific practice and discourse became an established part of the public domain. The book contains two chapters on Priestley, who is interpreted as a communicator whose aspiration was to spread the knowledge of science.

ANDERSON & LAWRENCE is the first collection to bring together in one volume papers covering the various aspects of Priestley's work, such as science, applied science, philosophy and theology. There is a paper on the relation between Priestley and Whewell, and there are several good papers on Priestley's politics and millenarianism (Priestley was a millenarian in the sense that he believed that prophecies of the Scripture would be fulfilled and had a relevance to his day).

ARNE HESSENBRUCH

See also Chemical Revolution; Lavoisier

Printing

Atkins, William (ed.), *The Art and Practice of Printing*, 6 vols, London: Pitman, 1932–33
Bankes, Henry, *Henry Bankes's Treatise on Lithography*, (reprint of 1813 and 1816 editions), edited by Michael Twyman, London: Printing Historical Society, 1976
Berry, W. Turner and H. Edmund Poole, *Annals of Printing: A Chronological Encyclopedia from the Earliest Times to 1950*, London: Blandford Press, 1966
Bloy, C.H., *A History of Printing Ink, Balls and Rollers, 1440–1850*, Barnet, Hertfordshire: Wynkyn de Worde Society, 1967; New York: Sandstone Press, 1980
Carter, Harry, *A View of Early Typography up to about 1600*, Oxford: Clarendon Press, 1969
Clair, Colin, *A Chronology of Printing*, London: Cassell, and New York: Praeger, 1969
Legros, Lucien Alphonse and John Cameron Grant, *Typographical Printing Surfaces: The Technology and Mechanism of Their Production*, London: Longmans Green, 1916; New York: Garland, 1980
Moran, James, *The Composition of Reading Matter: A History from Case to Computer*, London: Wace, 1965
Moran, James, *Printing Presses: History and Development from the Fifteenth Century to Modern Times*, London:

Faber and Faber, and Berkeley: University of California Press, 1973
Moxon, Joseph, *Mechanick Exercises in the Whole Art of Printing, 1683–4*, edited by Herbert Davies and Harry Carter, London: Oxford University Press, 1958; New York: Dover, 1978
Reed, Talbot Baines, *A History of the Old English Letter Foundries*, London: E. Stock, 1887; edited and revised by A.F. Johnson, London: Faber and Faber, 1952
Steinberg, S.H., *Five Hundred Years of Printing*, Harmondsworth: Penguin, 1955; Baltimore: Penguin, 1961; 3rd edition, revised by James Moran, 1974; revised by John Trevill, London: British Library and New Castle, Delaware: Oak Knoll Press, 1996
Updike, Daniel Berkeley, *Printing Types: Their History, Forms and Use: A Study in Survivals*, 2 vols, Cambridge, Massachusetts: Harvard University Press, 1922; 2nd edition, London: Milford / Oxford University Press, 1937
Wallis, L.W., *A Concise Chronology of Typesetting Developments, 1886–1986*, London: Wynkyn de Worde Society/Lund Humphries, 1988

Printing embraces a number of inter-related trades, especially type designing and founding, the composition of text or display matter, producing an inked impression by means of letterpress, and lithographic, intaglio, or screen processes. Integral to these are various methods of printing surface production or duplication, and the manufacture of inks and rollers. The essentials of letterpress printing were applied to commercial uses from the middle of the 15th century, while lithographic and photogravure printing have been in use for 200 and 100 years respectively. Recent years saw the demise of letterpress with the introduction, first of photographic, and latterly of computerized typesetting linked to photo-offset lithography.

STEINBERG presents a wide over-view of the historical development of printing and its close links with the graphic images of typefaces and illustrations, as well as covering plenty of peripheral matter concerning both printing and publishing.

Two indispensable reference works are the annals or chronologies of BERRY & POOLE and CLAIR. These cover the international history of printing, placing particular emphasis on Britain and Europe, from the earliest Chinese attempts at printing up to the second half of the 20th century. Because of the date of their publication, neither work has chronicled the rapid developments in graphic technology since 1970.

MOXON was the first author to cover in great detail all the various processes involved in letterpress printing in the 17th century. The techniques he describes were virtually identical to those of the time of Gutenberg, and were still used in the early years of the 19th century. Comparison of Moxon's description of type-founding should be made with Reed who, while concerned mainly with the history of British type foundries, covers the technicalities of punch-cutting, matrix manufacture, and type casting over a period of 400 years. For a scholarly investigation of the methods of type-founding during the early years of printing, CARTER is an outstanding work, based on his Lyell Lecture of 1968. As well as explaining the technicalities and problems of type-founding, Carter gives a thorough account of the transition from gothic, or black-letter, to the roman and italic faces that came into general use during the 16th century.

The further development of type-founding, particularly as it occurred in England, is covered by REED, whose work was published at a time (1887) when type-founding had reached a peak of technical precision, and when the prodigious output of numerous foundries struggled to satisfy the huge demands of printers, whose only means of type-setting was by hand composition. Following the introduction of mechanical type-setting at the end of the 19th century, new techniques for the mass production of punches and matrices were introduced, and these are thoroughly described in the monumental treatise by LEGROS & GRANT.

MORAN (1965) provides the only comprehensive survey of the wide range of machines devised for the speeding up of type-setting from the 1820s to the 20th century. These included ingenious mechanisms for assembling and justifying pre-cast types, which gave way to the more successful devices that cast new type, either as solid "slugs" or as justified lines of separate characters. The subsequent development of photocomposition and computer typesetting is adequately covered by WALLIS.

General printing techniques, as practised for more than 100 years in the pre-computer era, are covered in the six-volume work edited by ATKINS. This describes the techniques used in the many ancillary processes, such as stereotyping, embossing, and book-binding, which had become integral to many of the larger printing establishments by the first quarter of the 20th century.

MORAN (1973) has brought together a wealth of information on the very wide range of machinery designed for letter-press printing, whether by hand or power, on separate sheets or from reels of paper. While some of his treatment of individual presses tends to be rather sketchy, his early death prevented a second, enlarged edition and, apart from the virtually unobtainable French book, *Les Machines à imprimer depuis Gutenberg*, there is no other work which covers this subject. Supplementary, in a sense, is the survey of printers' rollers and printing inks by BLOY; again, the only comprehensive work on these vital ingredients for any kind of printing process.

While letterpress was the only widely used printing process for 400 years, apart from intaglio as used particularly in the 17th and 18th centuries for copper-plate illustrations, maps, and musical scores, this has now given way to lithographic printing. Invented by Senefelder at the very end of the 18th century, the process soon spread across Europe as a new means of artistic expression. Its early development into a commercial process is well documented by BANKES, one of the first to exploit lithography. During the 19th century, first direct, then later offset, lithography developed into viable commercial printing methods, particularly when linked with photographic plate-making, a stage dealt with by Atkins.

No history of printing can divorce the printed image on paper from the technical means of obtaining the transfer of ink. The historical development of typefaces in Europe and the United States is covered in detail by UPDIKE in his two-volume work, although he virtually ignores the incredible range of large "display types" that evolved from c.1820 to become particularly prolific during the Victorian era.

DEREK NUTTALL

See also Reading Culture and Science

Probability

Dale, Andrew I., *A History of Inverse Probability: From Thomas Bayes to Karl Pearson*, New York: Springer, 1991

Daston, Lorraine, *Classical Probability in the Enlightenment*, Princeton, New Jersey: Princeton University Press, 1988

Grattan-Guinness, Ivor (ed.), *Companion Encyclopedia of the History and Philosophy of the Mathematical Sciences*, 2 vols, London and New York: Routledge, 1994

Hacking, Ian, *The Emergence of Probability: A Philosophical Study of Early Ideas about Probability, Induction and Statistical Inference*, Cambridge and New York: Cambridge University Press, 1975

Hacking, Ian, *The Taming of Chance*, Cambridge and New York: Cambridge University Press, 1990

Hald, Anders, *A History of Probability and Statistics and their Applications Before 1750*, New York: Wiley, 1990

Krüger, Lorenz, Lorraine Daston and Michael Heidelberger (eds), *The Probabilistic Revolution*, 2 vols, Cambridge, Massachusetts: MIT Press, 1987

Porter, Theodore M., *The Rise of Statistical Thinking, 1820–1900*, Princeton, New Jersey: Princeton University Press, 1986

Shapiro, Barbara J., *Probability and Certainty in Seventeenth-Century England: A Study of the Relationships Between Natural Science, Religion, History, Law, and Literature*, Princeton, New Jersey: Princeton University Press, 1983

Stigler, Stephen M., *The History of Statistics: The Measurement of Uncertainty Before 1900*, Cambridge, Massachusetts: Belknap Press of Harvard University Press, 1986

Von Plato, Jan, *Creating Modern Probability: Its Mathematics, Physics, and Philosophy in Historical Perspective*, Cambridge and New York: Cambridge University Press, 1994

The modern concept of probability has, like its companion the proverbial coin, two faces: probability is used to model random processes in the world, and to provide a structure for our uncertain inferences about that world – thus, probability is both ontological/objective and epistemic/subjective. When these inferences are based on many quantitative data, one speaks of statistical inference. But not all statistical inferences use a probabilistic model, and not all epistemic uses of probability start with many quantitative data points.

GRATTAN-GUINNESS contains short essays on practically all aspects of the history of probability and statistics. A collection of essays that places the history of probability within the history of science and culture in general is the two volume work by KRÜGER, DASTON & HEIDELBERGER.

HACKING (1975) analyzes how probability obtained a dual aspect in the 17th and 18th centuries, examining the reasons behind the conceptual merger of probable beliefs and chances, and the period when the entire mode of probabilistic conceptualizing began. Hacking sees the transformation of the medical or alchemical sign into a testimony of nature as the key to the emergence of the two-faced concept of probability – the frequency of a sign assigning a quantified probability to an opinion regarding its possible repetition. According to Hacking, there was a sudden appearance of this style of reasoning after *La Logique, ou L'Art de Penser* of Arnauld and Nicole (1662), which spans morals, politics, economics, and social affairs. Probability provided a new way of conjecturing, and at the same time a new mode of representing reality, opening the way for David Hume to formulate his sceptical problem of induction, since the difference between knowledge and belief had become a matter of degree.

HACKING (1990) covers the 19th century, the era of the slow erosion of determinism and the creation of a world subject to probabilistic laws. The avalanche of printed numbers poured out by European statistical offices provided seemingly stable regularities of social deviancy that were hard to brush aside as surface phenomena of underlying deterministic processes, and, in some circles at least, these were seen as expressions of statistical laws. Hacking is concerned with the conditions that made possible our present organization of concepts into two probability domains: those in the area of physical indeterminism, and those regarding statistical information collected for purposes of social control. This is a work of historical analysis of concepts; for Hacking, to invoke the history of a concept is to investigate the principles that caused it to be usable – when the sentences formed with the concept acquire for the first time a "positivity", becoming "up for grabs" as possibly true or false.

SHAPIRO discusses pervasive attitudes to the various degrees of conviction and proof in a number of discourses of 17th-century Britain: natural science, religion, history, law, and literature.

The history of the mathematics of probability and statistics is covered by Hald, Stigler, Dale, and Von Plato. HALD deals with probability theory and inference up to the late 18th century in the contexts of games of chance, astronomy, demography, and life insurance mathematics. There is a tripartite focus, on persons, problems, and methods. Persons include Cardano, Pascal, Huygens, Graunt, Montmort and de Moivre, whose *Doctrine of Chances* (2nd edition of 1738) established probability theory as a mathematical discipline with a defining set of problems and methods. Problems discussed include the duration of play problem, and Waldegrave's problem on a circular tournament. Methods of solution covered are infinite series, method of inclusion and exclusion, and generating functions.

STIGLER discusses the development of 19th-century statistics from the point of view of measurement. To be a basis for generalization, measurement data have to be comparable, and this requires an assessment of their accuracy, their variability, and their uncertainty. This assessment is the task of modern statistics. Stigler's topic is how a logic common to all empirical sciences emerged from the needs within diverse disciplines, focusing on probability-based statistical methods in the pre-

disciplinary period before 1900. Examining the combination of observations (especially the method of least squares) and the use of probability for inferential purposes in astronomy and geography, Stigler describes the struggle to extend these techniques to the human sciences by Quetelet, Lexis, and Fechner, and of the breakthrough in Francis Galton's studies of heredity, which established regression equations as a new type of law for the social sciences.

DALE discusses the work carried out on inverse probability (arguing from observed events to the probability of causes), from its inception in Thomas Bayes's *An Essay Towards Solving a Problem in the Doctrine of Chances* (1764), through the contributions of Pierre Laplace and Karl Gauss, Condorcet and George-Louis Leclerc Buffon, Siméon Poisson and Venn, and Karl Pearson, to the rise of sample theoretic and decision theoretic solutions concerning direct inference in the 1930s.

VON PLATO traces the development of modern probability into a field of pure mathematics in the period 1900–50, with an emphasis on foundational questions: the frequentism of Richard von Mises, the formal-mathematical framework of Andrei Kolmogorov's measure theoretic probabilities, and the subjectivism of Bruno de Finetti. The mid-section of his book deals with probability in statistical physics from Krönig to Gibbs and Khintchine, in quantum theory (with special attention to Heisenberg's uncertainty relation), and in dynamical systems – especially the work of Eberhard Hopf in the 1930s, who aimed for explanations of stable but irregular frequencies in a classical deterministic setting.

Daston and Porter are each masterly accounts of the development of probability and statistics written by historians of science. DASTON's work is a comprehensive discussion of classical probability theory from 1650 until its decline around 1840, in relation to games of chance, insurance, jurisprudence, political economy, associationist psychology (an area of overlap between objective and subjective senses of probability), religion, induction and the moral sciences. Daston shows how classical probability was conceived as a model of universal rationality – supposed to be the same for lawyer and merchant – and how it evaporated, because of both internal problems (as the St Petersburg problem) and changed social and political circumstances. Her work is a detailed study of preconditions of quantification, and of the changing notion of rationality.

PORTER is a study of the rise of probabilistic thinking in the period 1820–1900 in the social sciences, psychology, and physics. In the period to 1840, a growing chorus raised its voice against certain areas of classical probability, as judicial applications and the probability of causes, and in the *annus mirabilis* of 1842–43, a frequency interpretation of some sort was defended by four different writers. Parallel to this development, the probability of error theory found new applications, and further development, as the mathematics of mass phenomena in the work of Quetelet, Lexis, Maxwell and Galton, who thus identified a new category of knowledge. Order was found in large numbers, and the explanation of this order ranged from the typological interpretation of the early Quetelet, to efforts of population thinking in Galton and Karl Pearson.

ZENO G. SWIJTINK

See also Error Theory; Quantification; Statistics

Professionalization

Ben-David, Joseph, *The Scientist's Role in Society: A Comparative Study*, Englewood Cliffs, New Jersey: Prentice-Hall, 1971

Carr-Saunders, A.M. and P.A. Wilson, *The Professionals*, Oxford: Oxford University Press, 1933

Durkheim, Emile, *Professional Ethics and Civic Morals*, translated from the French by Cornelia Brookfield, London: Routledge and Kegan Paul, 1957; Glencoe, Illinois: Free Press, 1958 (original edition, 1950)

Farber, Paul Lawrence, *The Emergence of Ornithology as a Scientific Discipline, 1760–1850*, Dordrecht and Boston: Reidel, 1982

Freidson, Eliot, *Doctoring Together: A Study of Professional Social Control*, New York: Elsevier, 1975

Hughes, E., "The Making of the Physician", *Human Organisation*, 14 (1956): 22–25

Johnson, Terence J., *Professions and Power*, London: Macmillan, 1972

Kohlstedt, Sally Gregory, *The Formation of the American Scientific Community: The American Association for the Advancement of Science, 1848–1860*, Urbana: University of Illinois Press, 1976

MacLeod, Roy and Peter Collins (eds), *The Parliament of Science: The British Association for the Advancement of Science, 1831–1981*, Northwood, Middlesex: Science Reviews, 1981

Morrell, Jack and Arnold Thackray, *Gentlemen of Science: Early Years of the British Association for the Advancement of Science*, Oxford: Clarendon Press, and New York: Oxford University Press, 1981

Parsons, Talcott, *The Social System*, Glencoe, Illinois: Free Press, 1951; with new preface by Bryan S. Turner, London and New York: Routledge, 1991

Perkin, Harold, *The Rise of Professional Society: England since 1880*, London and New York: Routledge, 1989

Porter, Roy, *The Making of Geology: Earth Science in Britain, 1660–1815*, Cambridge and New York: Cambridge University Press, 1977

Reingold, N., "Definitions and Speculations: The Professionalisation of Science in America in the Nineteenth Century", in *The Pursuit of Knowledge in the Early American Republic: American Scientific and Learned Societies from Colonial Times to the Civil War*, edited by Alexandra Oleson and Sanborn C. Brown, Baltimore: Johns Hopkins University Press, 1976

Rudwick, Martin J.S., *The Great Devonian Controversy: The Shaping of Scientific Knowledge among Gentlemanly Specialists*, Chicago: University of Chicago Press, 1985

Rueschemeyer, Dietrich, "Doctors and Lawyers: A Comment on the Theory of the Professions", *Canadian Review of of Sociology and Anthropology*, 1 (1964): 17–30

Weber, Max, *The Protestant Ethic and the Spirit of Capitalism*, translated from the German by Talcott Parsons, London: Allen and Unwin, 1930; New York: Scribner, 1958; 2nd edition, 1976

Much scholarship over the past 60 years, mainly sociological, has analysed the mechanisms for, and the activities involved in, the development of the "professional" in modern society. "Professionalization" is a process, the end product being either a discipline, or a person with qualifications, in order to provide specialized social services. Many sociological studies have offered models for conceptualising the "steps" frequently associated with efforts to define and legitimate professional identity. Increasingly, however, historians have eschewed such models, due to their tendency to impose teleological narratives, and have opted to focus in detail on historically situated events – such as the establishment of academies, training programmes, or specialized journals – in order to point out the many contingencies and negotiations that affect the ultimate status of a body of knowledge and its practitioners in a certain social setting. The conclusion drawn is that what was eventually identified as a professional discipline did not necessarily have to take the form it did, and that historians should not use hindsight to assume that our admired professional disciplines were inevitable consequences of progress in society and the specialization of knowledge. Historians of science have usefully exploited the vast sociological literature, in order to examine the ways in which scientific disciplines have become accepted as bodies of expert knowledge with professional ethics that affect social and political policy. The present historiographic survey begins with a brief sketch of some sociological debates over relevant ways to conceptualize the function of professionals in modern society, then moves on to more detailed studies in the history of science, which provide some useful examples of how social categories can be historicised.

In his work of 1957 DURKHEIM pioneered the study of professional organizations when he investigated the secularization of the moral order of modern society. Durkheim suggested that professional ethics would replace religious values as the basis of social cohesion in modernity. During the 1930s, CARR-SAUNDERS & WILSON extended the Durkheimian model in establishing the "traits" that characterised the professions as "a collective orientation", combining "altruism" and "a commitment to service". PARSONS reinforced the idea that the professions realised common social goals and aims. Parsons claimed that professional occupations embodied the "primacy of cognitive rationality", thus making them the standard bearers of the institutionalization of science. Looking at the medical profession, Parsons traced the expression of cognitive rationality through mechanisms such as affective neutrality and the functional specificity of the professional role. In this way, he argued, doctors were able to emphasize the technical basis of their capacity to manage relationships of potential tension with patients. Both the trait model of Carr-Saunders & Wilson, and the functional analysis of Parson, have been severely criticised by more recent sociological analysis. JOHNSON, for example, has pointed out that both these models were ahistorical, and argued that the social status and function of occupational groups changed in relation to much broader social conditions prevailing at any particular time.

Taking up a number of themes from Johnson, FREIDSON shows that while the term professionalism has assumed a generic meaning, it actually represents the development of specific groups, such as the law and medicine, largely within the Anglo-American context. He argues that this static model of professionalism should be replaced by a historical typology of occupations, and that occupational groups should be examined with broader reference to changing patterns of social stratification. Moreover, RUESCHEMEYER has reinforced this view by suggesting that occupational groups need to be analysed historically in order to identify when market autonomy is achieved, by means of the social control of expert knowledge.

In this context, Freidson has highlighted the importance of various concepts developed by HUGHES in his analysis of "The Making of the Physician". Specifically, Freidson argues that "licence and mandate", as a means of achieving market monopoly over the supply of labour informed by expert knowledge, are especially useful for understanding professional development. Professional status is thus identified as an outcome of the reinforcement by the state of occupational power and control over a section of the labour economy. WEBER traces distinctions between professions, vocations, and the rise of bureaucratic society. In his analysis, professionals have occupations that achieve a market monopoly of the supply of labour trained in specialized knowledge. Linking qualifications with economics, the professions thus underlie the organization of modern society, which is marked by the operation of substantive rationality in the production of bureaucratic power. PERKIN also writes about the association between professions and the rise of corporate society, in which professionals produce new patterns of social organization. In this analysis, "bureaucratic corporatism" is taken to be the definitive characteristic of modernity.

BEN-DAVID provides a model for combining sociology with history, in tracing when the conception of a professionally qualified person in science replaced the idea that science could only be pursued by a minority with a vocation. Inspired by Weber on Puritanism, and by Durkheim's theories of the division of labour, Ben-David raises comprehensive sociological questions about how scientific knowledge might grasp and manage the affairs of modern society. His study considers the ways in which social and political support were used to legitimate scientific programmes, particularly those developed in universities. A predominate interest for Ben-David, who casts his comparative analysis in a broad historical light, is comparing the development of institutional science in Germany, Britain, and America. Comparisons throughout the book raise consistent questions about how different societies dealt with the tensions surrounding the drive for intellectual autonomy in science, while the moral values in scientific knowledge were increasingly scrutinised.

University settings are important sites for an analysis of the process of professionalization, because it is here that research interests are consolidated, and specific programmes reproduced, through training regimes that reinforce and stabilize areas of scientific knowledge. However, emerging professional communities are also often marked by attempts to forge a coherent identity by founding societies or institutions. A few studies of major scientific associations in Britain and America explore this point. KOHLSTEDT's study looks closely at the foundation of the American Association for the Advancement of Science in 1848 and its early years. The outbreak of the American Civil War in 1861 affected the operations of the Association and the subsequent profile of American science, which became more fragmented. These themes, in a similar chronological perspective, are highlighted succinctly by REINGOLD, in his essay on the 19th-century professionalization of American science. In both Reingold's and Kohlstedt's analyses, many of the associated activities of a major national institution follow various historical models for professionalizing disciplines – for example, publications were begun to promote scientific communication, and reward systems were designed to acknowledge innovative research.

Both Kohlstedt's book and the study by MORRELL & THACKRAY are sensitive to internal debates in their respective associations, regarding conflicting ambitions to define a public role for science. In these associations, conceptions of professionalism by their leadership mediate the relative status of the sciences, between, for example, the physical and natural sciences. Morrell & Thackray look in detail at the logistics of organising a travelling association from its foundation in 1831, and in the second half of their study they analyse the ideological frameworks that projected images of science as progressive, useful, and desirable. Science was nevertheless made professional under social and political pressures: government funding for research, religious dissension among factions of the largely Anglican members, and debates about university reform and science curricula, were all matters that affected the administration of the Association. The essays in the volume edited by MacLEOD & COLLINS explore various aspects of the relationship between the specialized sub-sections of the British Association for the Advancement of Science and its administration, which exercised intellectual control over what was endorsed as public and professional knowledge, and what ultimately shaped the character of Victorian science. A number of essays treat specific mechanisms of administration in the "Parliament of Science", including patronage networks, rewards for research, publishing policies, expert consultations, and the promotion of scientific education. For institutional histories, which provide models for examining conditions affecting the formation and status of professional identities in Western science in the 19th century, these provide useful places to begin. But studies of individual scientific disciplines can also be useful in thinking about the ways a body of knowledge and specialized practices become standardised and recognised as a professional activity.

The road to obtaining a professional status was never straightforward, as many studies in the history of science demonstrate. One example is PORTER's study of British geology in the 17th and 18th centuries. Porter set out to trace the long process by which diverse and largely isolated strands of research, into the mineralogy and stratigraphy of the earth, eventually came together to make an identifiable discipline of geology by the 19th century. The work of those who could be broadly identified as geologists in the 18th century was diverse: geology involved travel, forming natural history collections, mapping, and deciphering fossils, and these activities were informed by various political, cultural, and religious concerns, and found expression in local specialist societies and eventually in the foundation of the Geological Society of London in 1807. While Porter limits his study to Britain, he demonstrates the diversity of activities that historians must recognise, without assuming the inevitability of the ultimate boundaries of a scientific practice, and points out the specific, national character of the making of a professional scientific discipline.

RUDWICK continues the theme of the professional status of geology in 19th-century Britain, and provides a useful discussion of the 19th-century distinction between the "professional" and the "amateur". The members of the Geological Society were gentlemen, with wealth enough to enjoy expensive dinners while discussing the mineral wealth of the British Isles. The members of the Society engaged in open debates and published in the in-house journal, but were by no means the only practitioners with specialized knowledge, and indeed largely relied on the efforts of mineral collectors and land surveyors for their information. Rudwick examines how a debate between a number of individuals connected with the Geological Society worked to define the status of theories of the earth and practical fieldwork, and how this debate among the few potentially affected wider professional practices, along with definitions of specialized knowledge in geology.

A different model for the professionalization of science is offered by FARBER in his study of ornithology. Here the fragmentation of part of the life sciences into a body of specialized knowledge is explored, with Farber examining contributions defining ornithology from practitioners across Europe. While his study, which in part examines French science during the revolutionary decades, considers the effect of political upheavals on philosophical inquiry, his main concern is with the development of standardised methods of scientific practices that define the discipline.

Consolidating group interests and establishing criteria for expert knowledge in a new field typically involve institutional affiliation and the awarding of qualifications, but, as many of the above works show, every step towards professional identity is laden with contingencies. In sociological models, professionals provide specialized services and are in control of expert knowledge, but the nature and definition of that knowledge was shaped through internal and external conditions, which the historian must locate and relate to the changing values of scientific knowledge.

BRIAN DOLAN

See also Discipline; Societies; Universities

Progress

Basalla, George, *The Evolution of Technology*, Cambridge and New York: Cambridge University Press, 1988
Blumenberg, Hans, *The Legitimacy of the Modern Age*, translated from the German by Robert M. Wallace, Cambridge, Massachusetts: MIT Press, 1983 (original edition, 1966)
Bury, J.B., *The Idea of Progress: An Inquiry into Its Origins and Growth*, London: Macmillan, 1920; New York: Macmillan, 1932
Fukuyama, Francis, *The End of History and the Last Man*, New York: Free Press, 1992
Kuhn, Thomas S., *The Structure of Scientific Revolutions*, Chicago: University of Chicago Press, 1962; revised edition, 1970
Kumar, Krishan, *Prophecy and Progress: The Sociology of Industrial and Post-Industrial Society*, London: Allen Lane, and New York: Penguin, 1978
Lasch, Christopher, *The True and Only Heaven: Progress and Its Critics*, New York: Norton, 1991
Laudan, Larry, *Progress and Its Problems: Toward a Theory of Scientific Growth*, Berkeley: University of California Press, 1977
Laudan, Larry, *Science and Hypothesis: Historical Essays on Scientific Methodology*, Dordrecht and Boston: Reidel, 1981
Mandelbaum, Maurice, *History, Man and Reason: A Study in Nineteenth-Century Thought*, Baltimore: Johns Hopkins University Press, 1971
Nisbet, Robert, *History of the Idea of Progress*, New York: Basic Books, 1980; with a new introduction, New Brunswick, New Jersey: Transaction, 1994
Paepke, C. Owen, *The Evolution of Progress: The End of Economic Growth and the Beginning of Human Transformation*, New York: Random House, 1993
Pollard, Sidney, *The Idea of Progress: History and Society*, London: Watts, 1968; New York: Basic Books, 1969
Rescher, Nicholas, *Scientific Progress: A Philosophical Essay on the Economics of Research in Natural Science*, Pittsburgh: University of Pittsburgh Press, and Oxford: Blackwell, 1978

Progress is an unwieldy concept for the historian because science and/or technology has usually been taken as the source of all social progress. Moreover, in the 19th century, the concept was often treated as synonymous with evolution. Interestingly, internalist accounts of scientific progress that fail to refer to the social costs and benefits of science are of relatively recent origin and, as we shall see below, have obscured the original motivation for proposing theories of scientific progress.

NISBET is typical of popular histories that draw a straight line from the Greco-Roman quest for intellectual perfection and material comfort, through Judeo-Christian eschatology, to modern conceptions of progress. The compendious scholarship of BLUMENBERG provides an antidote to this narrative, which he calls the secularization thesis of progress. Instead, Blumenberg locates the origin of the idea of progress in the ascendancy of modernism, in a variety of 17th-century debates over the relative merits of ancient and modern learning. Part of the charge of the scientific revolution was to imagine a fresh start to knowledge, from which progress could be made through the accumulation of knowledge without divine intervention or guidance. This decidedly historical, yet atheological, view of progress was muddied in the 19th century as Hegel, Comte, and Spencer presumed that science had to replace religion on the latter's terms rather than its own; hence, progress became "salvation secularized". This has led to a backlash against progress, comparable to earlier backlashes against Christian salvation histories.

The equally compendious MANDELBAUM picks up the story where Blumenberg leaves off, in the 19th century. He focuses on the philosophical overreaction (especially by the proto-existentialists Kierkegaard, Schopenhauer and Nietzsche) to evidence that contradicted the historical trajectory charted by progressivist thinkers. Typically, this evidence revealed the contingent character of events previously deemed necessary, which was often sufficient to instil a general scepticism about historical knowledge, without explaining how humanity has managed to achieve as much as it has – especially granting trenchant error and irrationality. Indeed, the only progressivist belief that seems to have survived this revolt against reason is human malleability, although that now carries sinister connotations. Writing partly in response to the student revolts of the late 1960s, Mandelbaum suggests that the revolt against reason is itself symptomatic of the progressivist tendency to discount the old in favour of the new, regardless of its self-defeating consequences.

Most modern historiographical discussions of the concept of progress start with the work of J.B. Bury, a distinguished classicist and Regius Professor of History at Cambridge. Writing in the wake of World War I, BURY argued that belief in progress requires certain preconditions not met until the 16th-century European Renaissance. Before then, a comparative historical basis for evaluating cultures was generally lacking, while known episodes of material progress were typically short-lived, and accompanied by political corruption and moral decline. Beginning with the Enlightenment, progress became increasingly tied to underlying biological processes, first to individual maturation, and then to species evolution. During this period, technological control over nature was the surest measure of progress, but the destruction wrought by science-driven military operations led Bury to question the future applicability of the concept.

One important scientific response to Bury's scepticism was to couch the concept of progress in exclusively bio-evolutionary terms, and to expand the time-frame of its alleged occurrence to many thousands of years. BASALLA examines this move as it was executed by its most distinguished proponent, the Anglo-Marxist anthropologist V. Gordon Childe, who wrote in the 1930s and 1940s. Drawing on the latest findings of prehistoric archaeology, and the emerging neo-Darwinian synthesis, Childe argued that biological proof of progress could be found in increasing numbers of humans, able to meet their needs more efficiently while allowing an increasing number of other species to flourish. Basalla notes that the idea of human population growth as an unmitigated good now seems anachronistic, and that Childe's specific assertions about the correlation between population spurts and technical innovation (e.g. during the Industrial Revolution) do not stand under scrutiny.

A more optimistic view is given by POLLARD, an economic historian writing during the capitalist boom of the 1960s. He traces the original model for the dynamics of progress to the profitable returns on investment associated with the spirit of enterprise in the 16th century, although it would be another two centuries before Turgot and Condorcet brought intellectual achievements to the fore by explicating progress in terms of the logical unfolding of human nature. Pollard notes that unlike development theorists in his own day, who follow Marx in holding that political progress requires economic progress, these 18th-century thinkers proposed the opposite thesis, that material progress presupposes growth in the scope of human sympathy. In any case, Pollard finds the belief in progress, once institutionalized, to be ineradicable, as even the concept's critics grant at least humanity's increased collective control of nature.

FUKUYAMA, rejuvenating the Hegelian view of history, combined these strands of thought by arguing that mastery of the scientific method (roughly, applied Baconianism) potentially enables all cultures to orient their economies toward the production of innovations that will earn them wealth and respect in the world market. The fall of the Soviet Union in 1989 supposedly removed the final barrier to the realization of this global liberal utopia. In a more science-fictional vein, PAEPKE distinguishes between technoscientific and material progress, concluding that there is little reason to think that a world of human beings enhanced by gene therapy and wetware would want to increase the production and consumption of material goods. Such economic indicators of progress are themselves the products of the living conditions of 19th-and 20th-century humans.

The wave of post-industrial prognostications of the 1970s led KUMAR to stress the utopian and futurological character of progress, noting two distinct strands of recent progressivist thought: i) the consolidation and diffusion of the achievements of industrial societies – a view associated with Joseph Schumpeter and Daniel Bell, which conceptualizes future progress in terms of better management, largely through information technologies; ii) the decoupling of human welfare from industrial growth – traceable to the guild socialism of William Morris and John Ruskin in the late 19th century; this view has received renewed support from advocates of environmentalism, communitarianism, and appropriate technologies.

Among those who believe that the dissolution of the industrial economic base heralds the end of any credible conception of progress, LASCH is the most synoptic. He sifts through 200 years of mostly American critics of progress to identify a strand of populist communitarianism that was frequently dismissed as "provincial". Lasch is especially keen to show how progressivist intellectuals, under the rubric of "improvement", lined up behind the state to endorse coercive policies of social engineering that did more harm than good, by ignoring the character of local communities. While Lasch fully realizes that critics of progress were often aligned with racism, atavism, and anti-intellectualism, he nevertheless argues that their avowedly petty bourgeois perspective is more appropriate to social policy than that of a scientifically sanctioned philosopher-king.

Turning to "internalist" conceptions of scientific progress, Larry Laudan has been among the few historians and philosophers of science who have tried to distinguish and interrelate progress in science and progress in scientific methodology. LAUDAN (1981) argues that methodological progress has occurred only by reflection on the significance of scientific achievements, and not by philosophical dialectics. For example, Einstein's experimental demonstration of Brownian motion did more to vindicate the reality of atoms than the traditional metaphysical arguments for realism. Until the logical positivists' professionalized philosophy of science, the leading methodologists were not epistemologists, but practising scientists. Laudan suggests that the marked lack of progress in methodology since that time is at least partly due to the autonomy of philosophy of science from the conduct of science; nevertheless, he sees the roots of the malaise in the "self-corrective" theory of science proposed by C.S. Peirce at the end of the 19th century, as Peirce was more concerned with analysing the concept of probability implied by the theory, than with identifying instances of the purported self-corrections in the history of science.

Whereas 19th-century accounts of scientific progress typically focused on the nature and direction of science (e.g., toward a unified picture of reality), 20th-century accounts have been increasingly confined to establishing formal criteria of progress, without specifying an overarching telos. KUHN famously speaks of the history of science, on the model of biological speciation, as having progressed "from" but not "to", and imagines a seemingly endless functional differentiation of paradigms. LAUDAN (1977), building on the initiatives of Popper and Lakatos, offers a purely procedural definition of progressiveness: which of a set of competing research traditions solves the most empirical problems, while generating the fewest conceptual problems in the process. He judges each tradition against its own track record but not against each other's, thereby forgoing any substantive judgments of progress. RESCHER is closer to 19th-century accounts in supposing a single, continuous trajectory for basic research, but one that experiences diminishing returns on investment. Thus, he believes that for pragmatic reasons science will only asymptotically approach the truth in its inquiries.

STEVE FULLER

See also Evolution; Scientific Revolution

Psychiatry

Lewis, Sir Aubrey, *The State of Psychiatry: Essays and Addresses*, London: Routledge and Kegan Paul, and New York: Science House, 1967

Micale, Mark S. and Roy Porter (eds), *Discovering the History of Psychiatry*, New York: Oxford University Press, 1994

Scull, Andrew, *Museums of Madness: The Social Organization of Insanity in Nineteenth-Century England*, London: Allen Lane, and New York: St Martin's Press, 1979

Scull, Andrew, *Social Order/Mental Disorder: Anglo-American Psychiatry in Historical Perspective*, London: Routledge, and Berkeley: University of California Press, 1989

Scull, Andrew, *The Most Solitary of Afflictions: Madness and Society in Britain, 1700–1900*, New Haven, Connecticut: Yale University Press, 1993

Zilboorg, Gregory and George Henry, *A History of Medical Psychology*, New York: Norton, 1941

The recent publication of *DSM-IV*, the diagnostic manual of the American Psychiatric Association, has brought a fresh crop of disorder labels, and has confirmed the trend of mainstream psychiatry away from the psychogenic theories popular a generation ago, and towards a more organic basis. Meanwhile controversy rages, within and beyond the psychiatric profession, about the success (or rather failure) of policies of de-institutionalization and "community care". In such circumstances, psychiatry itself may seem somewhat disoriented, and it is perhaps no surprise that there continue to be many diverse approaches to the history of psychiatry, as the organized attempt to understand and treat mental illness.

During the first half of the 20th century, psychiatrists were sufficiently self-confident about their speciality to produce the first full-scale in-house histories of the field. The most widely read work in this frame was *A History of Medical Psychology* (1941), written by the Russian-born American psychoanalyst, Gregory ZILBOORG. Such so-called whiggish narratives typically presented a "progressive" historical movement, from barbarism to institutional humanitarianism, and from ignorance, religion, and superstition to modern medical science, and dramatically juxtaposed dark ages, enlightenments, and revolutions, which heralded the way to the present.

One influential statement of this kind of historical vision sums up the genre. "The story in its broad outlines is familiar and dramatic", wrote Sir Aubrey LEWIS, the distinguished senior psychiatrist at the Maudsley Hospital, in 1967:

> After the tortures and judicial murders of the Middle Ages and the Renaissance, which confounded demoniacal possession with delusion and frenzy, and smelt out witchcraft in the maunderings of demented old women, there were the cruelties and degradation of the madhouses of the 17th and 18th centuries, in which authority used chains and whips as its instruments. Humanitarian effort put an end to the abuses. Pinel in France, Chiarugi in Italy, Tuke in England inaugurated an era of kindness and medical care, which prepared the way for a rational, humane approach to the mastery of mental illness. In the 19th century the pathology of insanity was investigated, its clinical forms described and classified, its kinship with physical disease and the psychoneuroses recognized. Treatment was undertaken in university hospitals, out-patient clinics multiplied, social aspects were given increasing attention. By the end of the century the way had been opened for the ideas of such men as Kraepelin, Freud, Charcot and Janet, following in the paths of Kahlbaum and Griesinger, Conolly and Maudsley. In the 20th century psychopathology has been elucidated, and psychological treatment given ever widening scope and sanction. Revolutionary changes have occurred in physical methods of treatment, the regime in mental hospitals has been further liberalized, and the varieties of care articulated into one another, individualized, and made elements in a continuous therapeutic process that extends well into the general community, beginning with the phase of onset, *Stadium incrementi*, and proceeding to the ultimate phase of rehabilitation and social resettlement.

"This", concluded Lewis, "is the conventional picture, one of progress and enlightenment . . . [and] it is not far out".

Since the elaboration of that conventional view 30 years ago, numerous alternative historical views have been advanced, stimulated by medical sociology and not least the writings of Michel Foucault. The most complete collection of re-assessments of the nature, growth, and functions of psychiatry may be found in MICALE & PORTER. The 21 historiographical contributions to that volume move from antiquity to the present, and from the Old World to the New, examining both medical and dynamic psychiatry, and scrutinizing the profession, its claims to scientific knowledge, and its social role and impact. Between them these essays challenge, and in many cases destroy, the entire historical interpretation advanced above by Sir Aubrey Lewis. No single revisionist orthodoxy has, however, supplanted the whiggish reading of psychiatric progress adduced by Lewis, Zilboorg, and others.

The major revisionist author not personally represented in that collection is Andrew Scull, historian and sociologist at the University of California (San Diego), but in a series of essays collected in SCULL (1989), he offers the most comprehensive revisionist reading available. Scull tends to view Anglo-American psychiatry as essentially the construct of the emergent and then increasingly powerful body of medical men involved with the asylum business, in both its private and public sectors. The essays cover various aspects of the history of psychiatry in Britain and the United States, such as Anglo-American historiography of psychiatry, the rhetoric of morality, and the role of architecture and gender in psychiatry.

SCULL (1979) provides a history of psychiatry in England in a somewhat black-and-white form that was radically altered and augmented in SCULL (1993), which expands the argument to the 18th and 19th centuries. However, his main argument remains the same in both books – that in a capitalist society, with its increasing division of labour, madness ceased to be a matter for the family and steadily became commodified. Broad tendencies towards specialization led to mad-doctoring seeking to establish itself as a distinct department of medicine. Meanwhile, the insecure relations between commercial practice and professional ideals prompted aspirant mad-doctors (or alienists) to stake claims to privileged medico-scientific knowledge and therapeutic skills, over and against other healers, magistrates, and the public at large. Scull has contended that his "sociology of scientific knowledge" approach explains the key features of psychiatric theory and practice during the last couple of centuries, including its unresolved internal divisions (due to a lack of proper scientific basis), and the gross disparity between its claims to unique expertise and its continued therapeutic shortcomings. Many historians would dispute particular features of Scull's overarching view of the rise of the psychiatric profession, and its claims to scientific achievement, but his general vision of the relations between profession, knowledge, and power is persuasive.

ROY PORTER

See also Asylums; Foucault; Madness

Psychoanalysis: conceptual

Benjamin, Jessica, The Bonds of Love: Psychoanalysis, Feminism and the Problem of Domination, New York: Pantheon, 1988

Chodorow, Nancy, Femininities, Masculinities, Sexualities: Freud and Beyond, Lexington: University Press of Kentucky, and London: Free Association Books, 1994

Ellenberger, Henri F., The Discovery of the Unconscious: The History and Evolution of Dynamic Psychiatry, New York: Basic Books, and London: Allen Lane, 1970

Gay, Peter, Freud: A Life for Our Time, London: Dent, and New York: Norton, 1988

Greenberg, Jay R. and Stephen A. Mitchell, Object Relations in Psychoanalytic Theory, Cambridge, Massachusetts: Harvard University Press, 1983

Grosskurth, Phyllis, Melanie Klein: Her World and Her Work, London: Hodder and Stoughton, and New York: Knopf, 1986

Hinshelwood, R.D., A Dictionary of Kleinian Thought, London: Free Association Books, 1989; revised edition, London: Free Association Books, and Northvale, New Jersey: Aronson, 1991

Hughes, Judith M., Reshaping the Psychoanalytic Domain: The Work of Melanie Klein, W.R.D. Fairbairn and D.W. Winnicott, Berkeley: University of California Press, 1989

Jones, Ernest, Sigmund Freud: Life and Work, 3 vols, London: Hogarth Press, 1953–57; as The Life and Work of Sigmund Freud, New York: Basic Books, 1953–57

Laplanche, Jean and Jean-Bertrand Pontalis, The Language of Psycho-Analysis, translated from the French by Donald Nicholson-Smith, London: Hogarth Press, 1973; New York: Norton, 1974 (original edition, 1967)

Marcuse, Herbert, Eros and Civilization: A Philosophical Inquiry into Freud, Boston: Beacon Press, 1955; London: Routledge and Kegan Paul, 1956; 2nd edition, with a new preface by the author, New York: Vintage Books, 1962; London: Allen Lane, 1969

Mitchell, Juliet, Psychoanalysis and Feminism, London: Allen Lane, and New York: Pantheon, 1974

Mitchell, Stephen A. and Margaret J. Black, Freud and Beyond: A History of Modern Psychoanalytic Thought, New York: Basic Books, 1995

Newman, Alexander, Non-Compliance in Winnicott's Words: A Companion to the Work of D.W. Winnicott, New York: New York University Press, and London: Free Association Books, 1995

Roudinesco, Elisabeth, Jaques Lacan & Co.: A History of Psychoanalysis in France 1925–1985, translated from the French by Jeffrey Mehlman, Chicago: University of Chicago Press, and London: Free Association Books, 1990 (original edition, 1986)

Sutherland, J.D., Fairbairn's Journey into the Interior, London: Free Association Books, 1989

Wolfenstein, Eugene Victor, Psychoanalytic-Marxism: Groundwork, London: Free Association Books, and New York: Guildford Books, 1993

Young, Robert M., Mental Space, London: Process Press, 1994

No firm line can be drawn between the conceptual history of psychoanalysis and its historians, since many of the main theoretical innovators – for example, Freud – also wrote historical and conceptual overviews. A short list of key concepts would include the following: the unconscious, defence mechanisms of the ego (especially repression, sublimation, conversion, and denial), infantile sexuality, free association, the interpretation of dreams, the pleasure principle, the reality principle, the primary process, the secondary process, the libido theory, the psychopathology of everyday life, transference, countertransference, the Oedipus complex and constellation, topographic hypothesis (conscious, preconscious, unconscious), structural hypothesis (id, ego, superego), Eros, Thanatos, object relations, projective identification, psychotic anxieties, paranoid-schizoid and depressive positions, transitional objects and phenomena, container/contained, pathological organization, and narcissism. Differing psychoanalytic orientations have different lists. There are three main dictionary-style authoritative sources for the central concepts in psychoanalysis: LAPLANCHE & PONTALIS provide the most comprehensive examination of psychoanalytic concepts; HINSHELWOOD has 13 main entries in the Kleinian tradition, and more than 100 subsidiary ones; NEWMAN is less systematic, in line with Winnicott's more discursive style.

Freud introduced new ideas without discarding many of the old, while innovators among his followers claimed to be developing his ideas when they were, with hindsight, going beyond them, and sometimes even effectively opposing them. It is therefore very easy to lose one's bearings in the overlapping conceptual frameworks. For example, as we are told with great clarity by GREENBERG & MITCHELL, there are three pioneers of object relations theory. One, Melanie Klein, wrote using the biological rhetoric of instincts, but was probably the most radical in her departure from the Freudian biologistic libido theory. Donald Winnicott created an intermediate zone between the inner and outer worlds, treating his transitional objects and phenomena as neither subjective nor objective but partaking of both, while Klein drew a sharp boundary between the inner and outer, and focused on the inner world. Ronald Fairbairn claimed that a completely healthy person would have no internal objects, while Klein argued that internal objects were the basic resources of all thought. These major differences between the co-founders of object relations theory are highlighted to illustrate that the boundaries between psychoanalytic theories and theoriticians are often blurred.

For a narrative account of the history of psychoanalysis, the best-known and a reliable source is ELLENBERGER. Freud's most informed biographers, JONES and GAY, cover the evolution of the movement, its social relations, and its ideas. Jones, a central figure in the psychoanalytic movement, is more orthodox and glosses over some areas that might expose Freud to criticism, while Gay, a professional historian of ideas and social movements, is more up-to-date, scrupulous and wide-ranging. GROSSKURTH, a scholarly biographer, brings the story up to 1960, the year of Klein's death, with a searching account that spares no reputations. This study gives an excellent history of the British movement, with particular emphasis on the important "controversial discussions" of the 1940s, which centred upon the clash between Anna Freud's adaptive approach and Melanie Klein's focus on primitive anxieties.

Another central psychoanalytical concern is "ego psychology", which, along with Winnicott and Kohut, is discussed with some care in MITCHELL & BLACK's overview of the whole history of psychoanalytic thought. Another is the object relations tradition, pioneered by Klein, Fairbairn, and Winnicott. GREENBERG & MITCHELL provide the best overview of this tradition in relation to orthodox Freudianism, but their approach is, in my opinion, distorted by a strange obeisance to Sullivan. HUGHES analyses the development of object relations theory in the work of Klein, Fairbairn, and Winnicott with clarity and balance, from the point of view of a cultural historian. SUTHERLAND focuses on the development of Fairbairn's ideas with an excellent grasp of his analytic

roots, and in comparison with Kohut and Kernberg. A third major departure from orthodoxy is the work of the French psychoanalyst, Jacques Lacan, who claimed to be making a return to Freud, but those who have managed to tease out the meaning entangled within Lacan's labyrinthine linguistic style have found themselves in a strange place, where language is substituted for emotions. ROUDINESCO provides a vast panorama of the history of French psychoanalysis and its international relations, and describes Lacan's charismatic and disruptive influence in great detail.

YOUNG provides a setting for psychoanalysis within the history of scientific ideas, and focuses on the problematic place of mind in nature. He then turns to psychoanalytic theories of culture – in particular, those of Freud, Winnicott, and Meltzer. Young makes a detailed critique of the scientism of neo-Freudianism, and provides an exposition of the histories and current uses of the concepts of psychotic anxiety, counter-transference, projective identification, and transitional objects and phenomena. These are viewed from the perspectives of both individual psychoanalysis and the tradition of group relations founded by Bion.

A number of figures who proposed theoretical innovations that have their own adherents are under-represented in the above sources: Carl Jung, Wilhelm Reich, Alfred Adler, Sandor Ferenczi, Harry Stack Sullivan (for whom, see Greenberg & Mitchell and Mitchell & Black), Heinz Kohut, John Bowlby, Margaret Mahler, Wilfred Bion, Donald Meltzer, and Harold Searles (for the last three, see Young). Group relations and group analysis also have their own literatures and adherents. The same is true of radical and Marxist approaches to psychoanalysis; e.g., the work of Herbert MARCUSE (who historicises some of Freud's basic concepts by adding the performance principle, surplus repression, and repressive desublimation), Wilhelm Reich (an instinctual radical), Erich Fromm (a culturalist humanist), Otto Fenichel (who wrote a key textbook and provided a forum for radicals until his untimely death at the age of 49), Joel Kovel (an American drawing on critical theory), Eugene Victor WOLFENSTEIN (a psychoanalyst and political theorist who offers the best Marxist overview; Young provides leads to some of the above), and feminist psychoanalysts – such as Juliet MITCHELL (who turned feminists back to Freud in the 1970s), Nancy CHODOROW (who drew American feminists to psychoanalysis in the 1980s, and has recently taken stock of developments in feminist approaches to the subject), and Jessica BENJAMIN (who offers the best recent feminist analyses of gender and sexuality in psychoanalysis).

ROBERT M. YOUNG

See also Psychoanalysis: gender; Psychoanalysis: institutional

Psychoanalysis: gender

Appignanesi, Lisa and John Forrester, *Freud's Women*, London: Weidenfeld and Nicolson, and New York: Basic Books, 1992

Baruch, Elaine Hoffman and Lucienne Serrano (eds), *Women Analyze Women: In France, England and the United States*, New York: New York University Press, and London: Harvester–Wheatsheaf, 1988

Butler, Judith, *Gender Trouble: Feminism and the Subversion of Identity*, London and New York: Routledge, 1990

Chodorow, Nancy, *Feminism and Psychoanalytic Theory*, New Haven, Connecticut: Yale University Press, and Cambridge: Polity Press, 1989

Freud, Sigmund, "On the Psychical Consequences of the Anatomical Sex-Distinction", (1925)

Irigaray, Luce, *Speculum of the Other Woman*, translated from the French by Gillian C. Gill, Ithaca, New York: Cornell University Press, 1985 (original edition, 1974)

Kofman, Sarah, *The Enigma of Woman: Woman in Freud's Writings*, translated from the French by Catherine Porter, Ithaca, New York: Cornell University Press, 1985 (original edition, 1980)

Mitchell, Juliet, *Psychoanalysis and Feminism*, London: Allen Lane, and New York: Pantheon, 1974

Mitchell, Juliet and Jacqueline Rose (eds), *Feminine Sexuality: Jacques Lacan and the École Freudienne*, translated from the French by Jacqueline Rose, London: Macmillan, and New York: Pantheon, 1982

Person, Ethel, "Women in Therapy: Therapist Gender as Variable", (1983): 193–204

Stoller, Robert, *Sex and Gender*, 2 vols, London: Hogarth, 1968–75; New York: Science House, 1968

Wright, Elizabeth (ed.), *Feminism and Psychoanalysis: A Critical Dictionary*, Oxford and Cambridge, Massachusetts: Blackwell, 1992

The literature on psychoanalysis and gender is best approached by examining the problematic concept of "gender" itself. The use of gender as a descriptive category has been co-opted and popularised by feminist discourse. The term is generally made to stand for the social and cultural manifestation of "sex", a concept that, conversely, then becomes associated with a kind of biological given.

In FREUD's writings on sexuality and sexual difference, including the essay listed here, the gender/sex divide is not present. Nevertheless, Freud can be interpreted as arguing that, notwithstanding our biological sex, we become men and women in society, and it is precisely around this idea that the association between psychoanalysis and a feminist understanding of gender, as well as between psychoanalysis and a feminist politics, will come to be articulated.

Within the discipline of psychoanalysis itself, the concept of gender, as it is used in contemporary critical discourse, has received relatively little attention. However, the works of Stoller and Person form notable exceptions. STOLLER constitutes an important study of the question from a practitioner's point of view. Starting from clinical work with patients whose sense of their gender-identity is troubled and at odds with their biological sex, he argues for the introduction of the term "gender" into psychoanalytic discourse, particularly the concept of a core gender-identity. Crucially for Stoller, this identity is not one we are born with; rather, it is socially derived from the parents' certainty of their child's gender. PERSON addresses the role and effects of gender on the power differential within the analytic interaction. BARUCH & SERRANO seek to explore this very issue through a series of in-depth interviews with women analysts, working within different contexts and with different theoretical outlooks. The collection raises interesting questions about whether women, as patients and/or practitioners, might have a particular approach to analytic work, and what that approach might be. Ultimately, however, the material collected remains too diverse and unintegrated.

In the final essay of a very useful collection of writings on psychoanalysis and feminist theory, CHODOROW explicitly questions the absence of gender as an interpretative category in traditional psychoanalytic theory, even when it is authored by women. Having conducted extensive interviews with women who were pioneering professionals in the psychoanalytic movement, Chodorow observes that gender was not a salient category for them. This ties in with the view that, notwithstanding work such as Stoller's, gender is a term that truly came into its own with feminist theory and that theory's particular use of psychoanalysis. It is fruitful to read Chodorow alongside APPIGNANESI & FORRESTER. This latter book takes as its starting point the fact that a high percentage of Freud's most important patients, and (given the times) a startling ratio of his colleagues, were female. The text is organised around a series of intellectual biographies of the women who have helped shape psychoanalytic thought, as Freud's patients and/or colleagues. Its concluding chapters offer a cohesive and illuminating account of Freud's changing theories of femininity, and the history of their reception during the 20th century.

Although not explicitly about gender, MITCHELL constitutes a key text in an on-going debate about Freud's writings on femininity. Intervening at a time when Anglo-American feminists were overwhelmingly hostile to Freud and read his work as demeaning to women, Mitchell argued that psychoanalysis acts as a description of patriarchy, rather than a prescription for it. The text reviews Freud's basic theories of development, and defends Freud against his chief feminist critics, whom Mitchell reads as ultimately basing their arguments on biological givens. MITCHELL & ROSE is a collection of essential writings on femininity by the French psychoanalyst Jacques Lacan and members of his school. The essays, as well as the highly informative introductions by the editors, spell out a view of psychoanalysis in which subjectivity, as well as sexual difference, is socially constructed.

Kofman and Irigaray are both representative of a French feminist critical engagement with Freud's writings on femininity. KOFMAN offers a close philosophical critique of Freud, undermining psychoanalytical assumptions pertaining to the constitution of the female subject – for example, penis envy. IRIGARAY, a philosopher as well as a practising psychoanalyst who was initially a follower of Lacan, seeks to uncover the unconscious institutional fantasies at play in the construction of psychoanalytic theories. She shows how these theories deny women their specificity, always giving them a relational position *vis-à-vis* men. By arguing for women's difference, based, at least metaphorically, on her specific bodily experience, Irigaray's work might be read as laying itself open to charges of essentialism.

While engaging strategically, rather than directly, with Freud and Lacan, BUTLER nevertheless constitutes an important and controversial intervention into the debates on psychoanalysis and gender. The author seeks to undermine the dichotomy between sex and gender by maintaining that both are socially constructed. She argues the case for gender as something that is performed, and as such, ultimately unstable.

Finally, WRIGHT's critical dictionary of psychoanalysis and feminism is recommended as a map to what now forms a vast field of inquiry. It explicitly states as its aims the politicisation of psychoanalysis by feminism, refocusing the received understanding of psychoanalytic terms, as well as introducing new ones, including that of gender. The reader should find it a useful reference tool, and a guide to a whole series of discussions in which the question of gender figures explicitly and/or implicitly.

JULIA BOROSSA

See also Freud; Gender: general works; Psychoanalysis: conceptual

Psychoanalysis: institutional

Bernfeld, Sigfried, "On the Psychoanalytic Training System", *Psychoanalytic Quarterly*, 31 (1962): 453–82

Borossa, Julia, "Freud's Case Histories and the Institutionalisation of Psychoanalysis", in *Case Material and Clinical Discourse*, edited by Ivan Ward, London: Freud Museum, 1997

Colonomos, Fanny (ed.), *On Forme des Psychanalystes: Rapport original sure les dix ans de l'Institut Psychanalytique de Berlin; 1920–1930*, translated by Helen Stierlin and Marianne Henich, Paris: Denoel, 1985

Derrida, Jacques, *The Post Card: From Socrates to Freud and Beyond*, translated from the French by Alan Bass, Chicago: University of Chicago Press, 1987 (original edition, 1980)

Ellenberger, Henri F., *The Discovery of the Unconscious: The History and Evolution of Dynamic Psychiatry*, London: Allen Lane, and New York: Basic Books, 1970

Forrester, John, *The Seductions of Psychoanalysis: Freud, Lacan, and Derrida*, Cambridge and New York: Cambridge University Press, 1990

Freud, Sigmund, "On the History of the Psychoanalytic Movement" (1914)

Roazen, Paul, *Freud and His Followers*, London: Allen Lane, and New York: Knopf, 1975

Roudinesco, Elisabeth, *Jacques Lacan & Co: A History of Psychoanalysis in France 1925–1985*, translated from the French by Jeffrey Mehlman, London: Free Association Books, and Chicago: University of Chicago Press, 1990 (original edition, 1982–86)

Roustang, François, *Dire Mastery: Discipleship from Freud to Lacan*, translated from the French by Ned Lukacher, Baltimore: Johns Hopkins University Press, 1982 (original edition, 1976)

Turkle, Sherry, *Psychoanalytic Politics: Jacques Lacan and Freud's French Revolution*, New York: Basic Books, 1978; 2nd edition, London: Free Association Books, and New York: Guilford Press, 1992

The question of the institutional formation of psychoanalysis has traditionally been of great interest to both practitioners and historians of psychoanalysis, as it touches upon the very nature of psychoanalytic knowledge. It can be approached in two distinct, but related, ways. Some of the texts surveyed offer mainly a description and/or critique of the formal insti-

tutional accoutrements of the profession; for example, its training system. Others primarily address the ties that bind psychoanalysts to each other and to Freud, the founding father of their discipline. However, ultimately all authors are obliged to confront both aspects of the problem.

The reader might wish to start with ELLENBERGER. This sweeping text, a history of dynamic psychiatry across time and cultures, provides a contextual account of the development of psychoanalysis, setting it alongside comparable systems of thought. It shows how psychoanalysis as a practice is dependent on a particular patient–practitioner relationship, and shows the deployment of that relationship in parallel disciplines and discourses.

In a polemical text that stands as the first history of the psychoanalytic movement, FREUD stakes his claim as the originator of psychoanalysis, and recounts the break with his followers, Jung and Adler. Albeit obviously a partisan account, this text clearly shows that the profession is built upon a network of intricate interpersonal relationships.

COLONOMOS is a useful and helpfully-introduced collection pertaining to the archives of the first psychoanalytic training institute, founded in Berlin in 1920. Among the documents reprinted are reports by the faculty, in which searching questions already appear concerning what type of institution might best regulate the transmission of psychoanalytic knowledge. BERNFELD serves as the best-known example of an outright condemnation of psychoanalytic training institutes by a well-respected practitioner; describing them as "teacher-centred", and based on authoritarian, pre-psychoanalytic attitudes to knowledge, Bernfeld proposes a return to an informal model of training that was the norm in the early days of the psychoanalytic movement. BOROSSA recounts the historical debates surrounding the formation of psychoanalytic training institutes, and describes the ways in which Freud's clinical writing served a special institutional function.

ROAZEN and ROUSTANG both examine the history, and Roustang the theoretical nature, of the relationship between analyst and analysand, arguing that psychoanalysis as a profession depends on a structure of discipleship. Roazen is a more descriptive text, which recounts the life and work of the principal players in the early psychoanalytic movement – men and women whose lives have usually been eclipsed by Freud's. Roustang's text is reliant on psychoanalytic theory, particularly on the concept of transference (the feelings of love or hate experienced in the analytic situation, which are replays of similar feelings directed towards parental figures in early life). The text explores, with much acuity and depth, Freud's complex relationship with some of his principal followers, and probes the implications of one particular aspect of the psychoanalytical profession: the necessity of undergoing analysis of oneself in order to practice.

DERRIDA's profound and suggestive text is one of many books and articles in which the philosopher comments on the nature of the institution of psychoanalysis, and particularly on its indelible tie to its originator, Freud. In this particular text, he comments on Freud's late text, "Beyond the Pleasure Principle". He also investigates some of the implications of the writings of the French psychoanalyst, Jacques Lacan, who had himself questioned the theoretical and institutional foundations of the profession of psychoanalysis. The reader would find it helpful to read Derrida in conjunction with FORRESTER, as many of the thought-provoking essays in that book, while exploring the nature of the institution of psychoanalysis in an illuminating way, also act as a commentary on Derrida's writings, as well as Lacan's.

TURKLE and ROUDINESCO both examine the particular case of the institution of psychoanalysis in France, and the ways in which the figure of Jacques Lacan has been instrumental in shaping it. Turkle's account is primarily of a sociological bent and concentrates on 1968, a significant moment in French intellectual and political life and also the year of Lacan's rise to great fame. The question of the institution of psychoanalysis is central to Roudinesco's detailed and stimulating history of the French psychoanalytic movement. His text offers an illuminating historical and theoretical exploration of the many bureaucratic, institutional and personal controversies and struggles involved in the creation and consolidation of French psychoanalysis, while also exploring the vicissitudes involved in the formation of a specifically Lacanian psychoanalysis in France.

JULIA BOROSSA

See also Freud; Psychoanalysis: conceptual

Psychology

Ash, Mitchell G., "The Self-Presentation of a Discipline: History of Psychology in the United States Between Pedagogy and Scholarship", in *Functions and Uses of Disciplinary Histories*, edited by Loren Graham, Wolf Lepenies and Peter Weingart, Dordrecht: Reidel, 1983

Ash, Mitchell G. and William R. Woodward (eds), *Psychology in Twentieth-Century Thought and Society*, Cambridge and New York: Cambridge University Press, 1987

Baritz, Loren, *The Servants of Power: A History of the Use of Social Science in American Industry*, Middletown, Connecticut: Wesleyan University Press, 1960

Boring, Edwin G., *A History of Experimental Psychology*, New York: Century, 1929; 2nd edition, New York: Appleton Century Crofts, 1950

Burnham, John C., *Paths into American Culture: Psychology, Medicine, and Morals*, Philadelphia: Temple University Press, 1988

Danziger, Kurt, *Constructing the Subject: Historical Origins of Psychological Research*, Cambridge and New York: Cambridge University Press, 1990

Gould, Stephen Jay, *The Mismeasure of Man*, New York: Norton, 1981; revised and expanded edition, 1996

Herman, Ellen, *The Romance of American Psychology: Political Culture in the Age of Experts*, Berkeley: University of California Press, 1995

Kamin, Leon J., *The Science and Politics of I.Q.*, Potomac, Maryland: Erlbaum, 1974; Harmondsworth: Penguin, 1977

O'Donnell, John M., *The Origins of Behaviorism: American Psychology, 1870–1920*, New York: New York University Press, 1985

Samelson, Franz, "History, Origin Myth, and Ideology: Comte's 'Discovery' of Social Psychology", *Journal for the Theory of Social Behavior*, 4 (1974): 217–31

Samelson, Franz, "Rescuing the Reputation of Sir Cyril [Burt]", *Journal of the History of the Behavioral Sciences*, 28/3 (1992): 221–33

Sokal, Michael M., "Introduction", in *Psychological Testing and American Society, 1890–1930*, edited by Sokal, New Brunswick, New Jersey: Rutgers University Press, 1987

Young, Robert M., "Scholarship and the History of the Behavioural Sciences", *History of Science*, 2 (1966): 1–51

As explained by YOUNG, the history of psychology has until recently been a practitioner's discipline, uncontaminated by knowledge of the historiography of science. The model for practitioners' history has been BORING's justificatory textbook, based on his lectures at Harvard University from the 1920s to the 1940s. Attempting to further his disciplinary advancement, Boring asserted the superordinate status of laboratory-based research over its competitors, applied clinical and educational psychology, and over the philosophical psychology that was dominant at Harvard in the 1920s. Ignoring the warring epistemologies that divided the field, Boring suggested that they all contributed data to the progressive development of scientific facts. In contrast, as has been pointed out by ASH, subsequent textbook histories have admitted the existence of warring "systems" of psychology, while also promising that knowledge of their history will innoculate practitioners against philosophical sectarianism.

A genre suited to the division of psychology into subfields has been the history of research specialties (e.g. human development). In the 1970s, reform-minded practitioners challenged the whiggishness of most of these histories. In social psychology, SAMELSON (1974) disputed the standard history, and its presentist search for precursors to the experimentalism of the 1950s. Invoking Kuhnian sociology of science, Samelson charged traditional historians with creating origin myths for the operationalist bias that he deplored in post-World War II social research.

The subfield most studied, and marked by the most contentious historiography, is the psychology of intelligence and individual difference. Alarmed by the growing hereditarianism of the late 1960s, KAMIN wrote an exposé of the racism and nativism of the early 20th-century developers of intelligence testing in the US. GOULD then wrote a popular history linking hereditarianism in psychology with racist currents in 19th-century social science in Europe and America, asserting a continuity between Lombrosianism and conservative psychometricians in the era of the Vietnam War. These influential revisionist histories were debunked by SOKAL, who showed that psychology of the 1920s had much less social influence and was more politically diverse than was suggested by historians in the 1970s.

The career of the British hereditarian, Cyril Burt, has also become a historical controversy, initiated by KAMIN's accusation that Burt falsified his research data. After investigations by journalists and practitioner historians, Burt's dishonesty became generally acknowledged. Recently, hereditarians have attempted to restore Burt's reputation, writing monographs that SAMELSON (1992) has convincingly debunked.

More general histories of psychology have focused on specific eras, examining intellectual and institutional changes in the field. The most successful have been the analyses by historians of American social thought of the cultural significance of psychology in the 1920s, a period of rapidly changing social values. In a series of influential essays, BURNHAM suggested that behaviorism supplanted more instinctual psychologies, as popular concerns shifted from expressing the hidden self to regulating personal conduct. Accordingly, the influence of the behaviorist John Watson came more from his promotion of the ideology of social control, than providing a technology for its realization.

Twenty years after Burnham, O'DONNELL portrayed the rise of behaviorism as a struggle for institutional resources and inter-professional hegemony. As psychology was brought from Germany to the US, its content was adjusted in order to differentiate it from competing disciplines, better suit the resources of the university, and promise applicability to educational and business problems. The result was the "transformation of academic psychology from the science of consciousness to the science of behavior".

Investigations of psychology's usefulness to political elites and government bureaucrats have attempted to add a social context to the traditional history of ideas. ASH & WOODWARD present case studies of the adaptive forms taken by psychology, under conditions of political patronage or attack. Countries covered by these essays – some of which have now been expanded into monographs – include Austria (under the Social Democrats), Germany (under the Nazis), China, India, and the Soviet Union.

Because the US contains a majority of the world's psychologists and is a thoroughly psychologized society, much of the political history of psychology is focused on America; written as social history, it reflects the changing historiography of the progressive era and the modern welfare state. Reacting against the consensus history written during the Cold War, BARITZ portrayed industrial psychologists as the "self-castrating" minions of big business, "endangering ... the millions of workers who have been forced or seduced into submission to [their] ministrations." Recently, young historians influenced by social constructionism have written less conspiratorial accounts, showing how social issues have become psychologized by the mutual consent of experts, the state, and the populace. Notable is HERMAN's history of the political uses of psychology from World War II to the 1960s. The great change during this era, she demonstrates, was the addition of a subjective dimension to political discourse and social planning. While this sometimes served repressive ends (e.g. the CIA's programs in Vietnam), it also gave campaigns for racial justice and women's liberation an effective ideology for social change, such as consciousness raising.

From the perspective of the sociology of science, histories of psychological research are distinguished by their failure to question the language and social relationships of the laboratory. This has been remedied by DANZIGER's analysis of the development of the norms of psychological research. These norms include the study of the "abstract individual", which Danziger shows to be "the product neither of nature nor of society but of statistical construction". Like the distinction between "experimenter" and "subject", such constructions are "knowledge products", supplied by psychologists to administrators with social and financial power. The resulting patronage, Danziger suggests, has been crucial to the growth of psychology as both a profession and science.

BENJAMIN HARRIS

See also Heredity; Human Sciences; Psychophysics

Psychophysics

Boring, Edwin G., *History, Psychology, and Science: Selected Papers*, edited by Robert I. Watson and Donald T. Campbell, New York: Wiley, 1963 ("The Stimulus-Error", 255–73, "The Beginning and Growth of Measurement in Psychology", 140–58, and "Fechner: Inadvertent Founder of Psychophysics", 126–31)

Brozek, Josef and Horst Gundlach (eds), *G.T. Fechner and Psychology*, Passau, Germany: Passavia, 1988

Foucault, Marcel, *La Psychophysique*, Paris: Alcan, 1901

Gundlach, Horst, *Entstehung und Gegenstand der Psychophysik*, Berlin and New York: Springer, 1993

Heidelberger, Michael, *Die innere Seite der Natur: Gustav Theodor Fechners wissenschaftlich-philosophische Weltauffassung*, Frankfurt: Klostermann, 1993

Hornstein, Gail A., "Quantifying Psychological Phenomena: Debates, Dilemmas, and Implications", in *The Rise of Experimentation in American Psychology*, edited by Jill G. Morawski, New Haven, Connecticut: Yale University Press, 1988

Lennig, Petra, *Von der Metaphysik zur Psychophysik: Gustav Theodor Fechner (1801–1887)*, Frankfurt: Peter Lang, 1994

Link, Stephen W., *The Wave Theory of Difference and Similarity*, Hillsdale, New Jersey: Erlbaum, 1992

Murray, David J., *A History of Western Psychology*, Englewood Cliffs, New Jersey: Prentice-Hall, 1983; 2nd edition, 1988

Murray, David J., "A Perspective for Viewing the History of Psychophysics", *Behavioral and Brain Sciences*, 16/1 (1993): 115–86

Stevens, Stanley S., *Psychophysics: Introduction to Its Perceptual, Neural, and Social Prospects*, edited by Geraldine Stevens, New York: John Wiley, 1975; with a new introduction by Lawrence E. Marks, New Brunswick, New Jersey: Transaction, 1986

Titchener, Edward Bradford, "The Rise and Progress of Quantitative Psychology", in *Experimental Psychology: A Manual of Laboratory Practice*, vol. 2: *Qualitative Experiments*, Part 2: *Instructor's Manual*, edited by Titchener, London and New York: Macmillan, 1905

From its beginning, the historiography of psychophysics has suffered from severe limitations and distortions, as both historians of philosophy and historians of the more technical development of experimental psychology have tended to neglect or downgrade the philosophical context of the ideas of Gustav Theodor Fechner, the founder of psychophysics, and his critics. However, this context, essential for an understanding of the history of the subject, has recently been made the subject of several studies.

At the turn of the century, the first historian of psychophysics, Marcel FOUCAULT, distinguished three different phases in its history, corresponding to three different areas of the subject: 1) Fechner's original task of measuring sensations (and his elaboration of the logarithmic law relating sensation, strength, and physical stimulus); 2) the measurement of sensibility, relating more to the original work of Ernst Heinrich Weber than to the work of Fechner himself (by Delboeuf, Vierordt, Galton, and many Americans); and 3) the measurement of the duration of perceptual acts, giving way to a general quantitative analysis of perception (by Helmholtz, Wundt, and many others). Foucault's book is a meticulous and erudite treatment, mainly of the first phase, discussing many controversies and pulling together the most remote sources. He concludes that Fechner did not achieve his goal, as the measurement of the intensity of sensations is "chimerical", but he gives Fechner credit for being the "true founder of experimental psychology".

TITCHENER's much shorter treatment is heavily indebted to Foucault, and has served as the principal source for many later assessments. Whereas Foucault still discussed, at least to some extent, the neo-Kantian and mechanist background of Fechner's critics, this disappears from Titchener's account, so that the history of psychophysics appears as a merely technical development. Fechner is depicted as erring to an unfortunate extent, but as nevertheless capable of stimulating a whole new field of research. This interpretation has allowed BORING (who relied on Titchener) to include Fechner as the "inadvertent founder of psychophysics" in his gallery of founding fathers of experimental psychology (which includes, among others, Hermann von Helmholtz and Wilhelm Wundt). In the 1950s, the school of Stevens challenged the data and theories on which Fechnerian psychophysics had been based. In the final synopsis of his work, STEVENS continued the historiographic tradition of his teacher, Edwin Boring, and made his "New Psychophysics" with its power law appear as the final culmination of the scientific tradition of psychophysics.

Although HORNSTEIN is in the tradition of Titchener, Boring, and Stevens, the author did much preparatory work that enabled later historians to escape from the tradition's limitations. This tradition erroneously takes Boring's so-called "quantity objection" to the measurement of sensation – supposedly based on the "stimulus error" (of reading the character of the stimulus into the sensation) – as a revolt by metaphysical philosophers and introspectionists against the naturalization of psychical phenomena. As a consequence, the history of psychophysics appears to show psychologists choosing to ignore this and other objections, with this perspective nicely fitting Boring's version of the history of scientific psychology as a history of emancipation from metaphysics. Against this, HEIDELBERGER insists that the neo-Kantians and the scientists from the biophysics movement of 1847 formed an "unholy alliance" in their criticism of Fechner's original psychophysics, and that their "quantity objection" is a product of their reductionist materialist world-view and has nothing whatsoever to do with an anti-scientific metaphysics. From this perspective, Wundt's conception of psychology can be seen as an attempt to find a third way between Kantian *Erkenntnistheorie* and physiological reductionism.

In his account of the technical history of psychophysics, MURRAY (1993) concentrates on the search for a psychophysical law, and the measurement of the magnitude of sensation by a signal-to-noise relationship, in relation to the notion of work. MURRAY (1983) gives the most extensive and detailed overview of all three phases of the history of psychophysics to date. LINK examines Fechner's application of Gaussian error theory to human discrimination, and tells the story of the theorists and experimentalists who continued this direction beyond Fechner's pioneering work. In the debate about the quantity objection, and about the controversy between the log law and the power law, scaling has received far more attention than the development of threshold methods.

BROZEK & GUNDLACH is a collection of essays that gives a lot of background information and considers many topics around psychophysics, such as its genesis and interaction with other fields, its extension into experimental aesthetics, and its many controversies. GUNDLACH concentrates on the early history of psychophysics, providing, in particular, an extensive discussion of the relation of Fechner's psychophysics to Ernst Heinrich Weber's experimental work, and to the work of Daniel Bernoulli, Pierre-Simon de Laplace, and Siméon Poisson. He argues that Fechner has bewitched the tradition with a dubious ontology for psychophysics to this very day, and, consequently, he suggests a new and reformed conceptual foundation for psychophysics in order to resolve its "conceptual chaos" (or, in Boring's words, its "interminable Teutonic polemical talk").

HEIDELBERGER gives an exhaustive treatment of Fechner's life and work, and of the philosophical unity in his diverse thinking. He shows that Fechner's philosophy is much more coherent and rational than has been assumed, and that many problems with the interpretation of his work in psychophysics and elsewhere can be resolved if one takes this philosophy seriously into account. Heidelberger also shows how Fechner's statistical approach to science is an outgrowth of his probabilistic world view, and argues that Fechner's conception of science, influenced mainly by Ernst Mach, was an important step on the way to the philosophy of logical empiricism. LENNIG concentrates on the intimate interrelation of Fechner's metaphysics and his psychophysics and claims, in accord with Heidelberger, that it is not possible to separate Fechner as the irrational mystic from Fechner the exact scientist.

MICHAEL HEIDELBERGER

See also Error Theory; Helmholtz; Mach; Psychology

Public and the Private

Cooter, Roger, *The Cultural Meaning of Popular Science: Phrenology and the Organization of Consent in Nineteenth-Century Britain*, Cambridge and New York: Cambridge University Press, 1984

Cooter, Roger and Stephen Pumfrey, "Separate Spheres and Public Places: Reflections on the History of Science Popularization and Science in Popular Culture", *History of Science*, 32 (1994): 237–67

Desmond, Adrian, *The Politics of Evolution: Morphology, Medicine, and Reform in Radical London*, Chicago: University of Chicago Press, 1989

Eamon, William, *Science and the Secrets of Nature: Books of Secrets in Medieval and Early Modern Culture*, Princeton, New Jersey: Princeton University Press, 1994

Geison, Gerald L., *The Private Science of Louis Pasteur*, Princeton, New Jersey: Princeton University Press, 1995

Golinski, Jan, *Science as Public Culture: Chemistry and Enlightenment in Britain, 1760–1820*, Cambridge and New York: Cambridge University Press, 1992

Morton, Alan Q. and Jane A. Wess, *Public & Private Science: The King George III Collection*, Oxford and New York: Oxford University Press/ Science Museum, 1993

Shapin, Steven and Simon Schaffer, *Leviathan and the Air-Pump: Hobbes, Boyle, and the Experimental Life*, Princeton, New Jersey: Princeton University Press, 1985

Shapin, Steven, *A Social History of Truth: Civility and Science in Seventeenth-Century England*, Chicago: University of Chicago Press, 1994

Webster, Charles, *The Great Instauration: Science, Medicine and Reform, 1626–1660*, London: Duckworth, and New York: Holmes and Meier, 1975

In the early modern world, natural philosophy moved beyond the private preserve of the court to advocacy of the public benefits of natural knowledge. Moreover, scientific promise was transformed by an epistemological revolution that to some reformers implied a wide public dissemination of experimental knowledge. The 17th-century collapse of radical democratic visions of scientific and technical discourse was, as WEBSTER suggests, crucial to the promotion of national scientific institutions – ultimately leading to the Royal Society in England. A broad public agenda nevertheless failed but, as SHAPIN points out, it did produce the concept of experimental demonstration of endlessly repeatable truths. Thus, the replication of experimental results effectively imposed an audience on the natural philosopher. To follow SHAPIN & SCHAFFER, trust and truth merged in the respectable epistemology of display. This was one of the most crucial philosophical achievements of the early Enlightenment. There emerged in the 17th and 18th centuries an increasingly vast technology of display, and a market for apparatus whose purpose it was to make possible the public theatre of scientific discovery and the achievement of popular consent.

The most important reason for the success of experimental demonstrations was the existence of a public itself. EAMON argues that Robert Boyle clearly understood the duty of the natural philosopher to reduce the sense of wonder in the public to a demonstration of sensible effects. Entertainment was not the essential issue, a clarity of understanding was. This might well have been a naive hope, but the objective was far better served than one might expect by the public philosophers who followed him. As the early Newtonians soon realized, much could be achieved through the apparatus of display.

Perhaps the best analysis of the public/private divide is the important article by COOTER & PUMFREY on "Separate Spheres and Public Places". While popularization has been regarded as a kind of "umbrella term", it only addresses one aspect of the issues within science and society studies.

Dissemination thus appears as science moving from the inside out. Cooter & Pumfrey take pains to point out that the diffusionist, trickle-down, model of scientific culture is altogether inadequate. Indeed, recent studies such as the one by Desmond have clearly shown that an artisanal, evolutionary science emerged from theoretical considerations that did not sit very well in elite circles of early 19th-century London. The process of making science popular also "reconfigures the cultural context of scientific activity and hence – conceivably – reconfigures the nature of the science itself". There are a number of ways in which this appears to have occurred, partly by refining science in the image of princely patrons, partly by transforming the agenda of the questions that natural philosophers or scientists might seek to ask – this might well be considered in the explorations of electricity, magnetism, and pneumatic chemistry in the 18th century. Even the transformation of concepts of work, power and energy may owe more to the pressure of public understanding than has been appreciated. As MORTON & WESS suggest, demonstrations of mechanical powers were fundamental here.

Experiment in the 18th century became an instrument of the conquest of the public world. As GOLINSKI has demonstrated, the chemical discoveries at the end of the 18th century were transformed by the proposition of "public knowledge". Experimental demonstrations were "methods for converting private opinions into public facts". Golinski shows that Joseph Priestley's criticism of the ideas of Lavoisier were closely tied to his belief that Lavoisier's instruments were far too complex to achieve a public scientific culture. For Priestley, as for many of his followers, it was a fundamental Enlightenment ideal to comprehend "the great difference between seeing and reading". Simplicity of demonstration was essential. It is instructive, therefore, that within the context of the French Revolution these scientific democrats were assailed by Burke over scientific methods undermining established social and moral principles.

As COOTER has argued, the early 19th century witnessed widespread challenges to considered social and political orthodoxy. Mesmerists and phrenologists adopted a pseudo-Newtonian image by promoting a "simple, empirical, practical science [which] bespoke equal opportunity and social justice". Consequently, as science could be represented as liberating, then phrenologists opened avenues of access to a public world for their view of natural laws. They were "firmly convinced that they were democratizing the revolutionary truths of Nature and were teaching workers to 'think and judge for themselves'". The reasons for this were culturally complex, but the appearance of measure and classification in human behaviour promised an objective – and ultimately numerical – test for "social, economic, and intellectual success, on the one hand, and problems of crime, delinquency, and addiction, on the other".

For some historians and philosophers social influences appear antithetical to the scientific researcher, yet recent accounts of intense philosophical debates argue otherwise. In the early 19th century, social distinctions could be explained phrenologically, and notions of progressive development were promoted by English Lamarckians, thus sending Tories into a rage. DESMOND has shown that atomism and materialism were the alarms sounded in Britain for those fearing the biological imperatives of Lamarck and Geoffroy Saint-Hilaire. Few paleontological debates escaped the democratic consequences inherent in notions of progressive development. Fought out among the physicians and surgeons of London, the battle against the reformist Lamarckians represented "the failure of the ultraradical movement". The rapidly expanding scientific public clearly felt that philosophical debates had profound intellectual and social consequences.

A similar question arises in the marvellously ironic title of GEISON's *Private Science of Louis Pasteur*. Pasteur was the master manipulator in the political world and in the laboratory, with rhetoric as much a tool as his vials of desiccated spinal cords. Pasteur instinctively understood the "continuum between private thought or practices and public knowledge, whatever the field". Pasteur's rigidly controlled laboratories, none the less, generated as much image as they did bench work. Whether of anthrax or of rabies, Pasteur's public presentations were carefully contrived to represent the greatest achievement in the best possible public light. The reward was public funding as much as recognition. The creation of a Pastorian myth was successfully engineered by keeping the actual research result within the confines of the laboratory and by promoting real, if dangerous and unproven, successes in the treatment of disease. As in the case of Pasteur, acknowledgement of the public world lurks behind many a scientific legend.

LARRY STEWART

See also Experiments; Performance; Popularization

Public Health

Armstrong, David, *Political Anatomy of the Body: Medical Knowledge in Britain in the Twentieth Century*, Cambridge and New York: Cambridge University Press, 1985

Evans, Richard J., *Death in Hamburg: Society and Politics in the Cholera Years, 1830–1910*, Oxford: Clarendon Press, and New York: Oxford University Press, 1987

Fox, Daniel M., *Power and Illness: The Failure and Future of American Health Policy*, Berkeley: University of California Press, 1993

Hamlin, Christopher, "Predisposing Causes and Public Health in Early Nineteenth-Century Medical Thought", *Social History of Medicine*, 5 (1992): 43–70

Hardy, Anne, *The Epidemic Streets: Infectious Disease and the Rise of Preventive Medicine, 1856–1900*, Oxford: Clarendon Press, and New York: Oxford University Press, 1993

Kearns, Gerry, "Introduction: Urbanisation and the Epidemiological Transition", in *Urbanisation and Epidemiologic Transition*, edited by Marie C. Nelson and John Rogers, Uppsala: Reprocentralen HSC, 1989

McKeown, Thomas, *The Modern Rise of Population*, London: Arnold, and New York: Academic Press, 1976

Porter, Dorothy (ed.), *The History of Public Health and the Modern State*, Amsterdam: Rodopi, 1994

Riley, James C., *The Eighteenth-Century Campaign to Avoid Disease*, London: Macmillan, and New York: St Martin's Press, 1987

Rosen, George, *A History of Public Health*, New York: MD Publications, 1958; revised edition, Baltimore: Johns Hopkins University Press, 1993

Slack, Paul, *The Impact of Plague in Tudor and Stuart England*, London and Boston: Routledge and Kegan Paul, 1985

Webster, Charles, *Problems of Health Care: The National Health Service Before 1957*, London: HMSO, 1988

Weindling, Paul, *Health, Race and German Politics Between National Unification and Nazism, 1870–1945*, Cambridge and New York: Cambridge University Press, 1989

Public health has often been portrayed as a heroic progress from ignorance to knowledge, darkness to light, squalor to cleanliness, barbarism to civilization. More recent historiography, however, has explored the complex web of forces underlying changing demographic distributions of disease; contradictory theories of causation and prevention and their relationship to conflicting interests in the enforcement of health; the relationship of epidemics to social disruption and the politics of health and the state.

In his textbook, ROSEN argued that public health reform emancipated modern society from the primitive bondage of disease, but PORTER, in her introduction to *The History of Public Health and the Rise of the Modern State*, points out that sometimes this led to an expansion of authoritarian power. This has been illustrated by historians examining the influence of epidemic disease on social order in European societies from the early modern period. SLACK shows that plague control in Tudor and Stuart England generated draconian laws that forced people to die imprisoned in their own homes, which were overrun with infected rats, while EVANS elucidates how, 300 years later, cholera facilitated the Prussianization of Hamburg in 1892. Similarly, the late-medieval institution of quarantine by Italian city states stimulated the growth of secular bureaucratic government. Porter reveals that public health bureaucracy was, however, critically shaped by national, imperial, and international political cultures.

While HARDY demonstrates that the epidemics of the late 19th century were responsible for making disease prevention the prime focus of early public health reform, WEBSTER and FOX both portray how the role of preventive medicine radically diminished in the construction of health care provision in both Britain and the United States in the 20th century. Nevertheless, intellectual conflicts over disease theory provided one, among many, powerful ideological forces behind population health regulation. RILEY suggests that the 18th-century campaign to avoid disease revived Hippocratic preventive ideals regarding airs, waters and places, and HAMLIN has stressed how the long legacy of humoralism continued to frame the 19th-century debate between contagionism and anti-contagionism. While the "bacteriological revolution" has largely been dismissed by contemporary historians as instituting a historical "watershed" in public health practice, its significance in facilitating the invention of preventive medicine as a social science has been provocatively proposed by ARMSTRONG. Equally, WEINDLING has the examined the way in which post-Darwinian evolutionism imbued public health discourse with a new biological determinism which promoted racial theories of inevitable biological decline.

Since McKEOWN first tried to account for modern population growth, historical demographers have been measuring the contribution of public health reform. While debates have raged about the comparative role played by rising standards of living, little as yet has been resolved. KEARNS, however, has recently suggested how the matrix of economic, technological and social change, together with direct political intervention in public health, have combined to bring about networks of disease prevention that may be responsible for the epidemiological transition from infectious to chronic diseases in modern societies.

DOROTHY PORTER

See also Bacteriology; Epidemics; Epidemiology; Health, Morality and Social Class; Hospitals

Pythagoras 6th century BC

Greek philosopher and mathematician

Burkert, Walter, *Lore and Science in Ancient Pythagoreanism*, translated from the German by Edwin L. Minor Jr., Cambridge, Massachusetts: Harvard University Press, 1972 (original edition, 1962)

Fritz, Kurt von, *Pythagorean Politics in Southern Italy: An Analysis of the Sources*, New York: Columbia University Press, 1940

Heninger, S.K. Jr, *Touches of Sweet Harmony: Pythagorean Cosmology and Renaissance Poetics*, San Marino, California: Huntington Library, 1974

Huffman, Carl A., *Philolaus of Croton: Pythagorean and Presocratic*, Cambridge and New York: Cambridge University Press, 1993

O'Meara, Dominic J., *Pythagoras Revived: Mathematics and Philosophy in Late Antiquity*, Oxford: Clarendon Press, and New York: Oxford University Press, 1990

Timpanaro Cardini, Maria, *I Pitagorici: Testimonianze e frammenti*, 3 vols, Florence: La Nuova Italia, 1958–62

Van der Waerden, B.L., *Die Pythagoreer*, Zurich: Artemis, 1979

Vogel, C.J. de, *Pythagoras and Early Pythagoreanism*, Assen: Van Gorcum, 1966

Rather than Pythagoras, the title of this entry should perhaps read "Pythagoreans" or "Pythagorism", since what is known about the legendary founder of the school, who apparently lived in Southern Italy around the 6th century BC, is, indeed, mostly legendary. Literature on Pythagoras already flourished around the 2nd century BC, and anecdotes about him circulated widely: that he had a golden hip, and that he could perform miracles or remember all his previous lives, while those of the Pythagorean school were said not to eat broad beans or slaughtered animals, or divulge their mathematical discoveries. What we do know for certain about the Pythagorean movement, which persisted throughout the classical period (we find self-styled Pythagoreans at least up to the 4th century AD), is that in its early stages it was concerned with cosmology, mathematics and music, admitted women, and took an active part in political life, with Pythagoreans ruling cities such as Tarentum and Crotone.

TIMPANARO CARDINI's collection, which is a translation, with the original text, of the relative parts of the Diels-Krantz standard edition of the pre-Socratics, offers probably the most extensive commentary on extant testimonies and fragments on Pythagoreans. She cross-references most of them, quotes at length where necessary, and provides very useful introductions to each author. The third volume is a good selection of pseudo-Pythagorean works. This collection is a good starting-point from which to examine some of the most debated issues regarding the Pythagoreans, relating to the identification of "late" forgeries from early genuine theories; the division in the early theories between cosmology, numerology, and political theories; and the relation of the Pythagoreans to other Greek philosophers. For instance, debates continue regarding how far some Platonic theories, as expressed especially in the *Timaeus*, can be said to derive from the Pythagoreans, and the import of Pythagorean mathematics that went into Euclid's *Elements*. The ever-present fascination with the movement is the result of its pervasiveness, being (or presenting itself as) a comprehensive vision of the cosmos, within which macro- and micro-phenomena are made to correspond via number theory.

The interpretation given of Pythagorism will often depend on one's opinion on the reliability of the evidence. For example, BURKERT's enormously influential book arose partly from the author's wish to counteract interpretations that saw Pythagorean theories everywhere in Greek philosophy, under guises as different as "rational analysis" and "mysticism". With a philological precision that at times borders on the fastidious, Burkert sifts the surviving evidence, labelling most of it as later forgeries, reworkings or interpolations, and emphasizes the "anthropological" side of Pythagorism, rooted in popular lore, in contrast to what he considers later distortions of perspective, leading to the enquiries into mathematics and natural science. In fact, he denies that the early Pythagoreans engaged in anything like philosophy or science, and defines Pythagoras himself as a shaman. While offering a fascinating interpretation, Burkert's book underlines the fact that the divide between genuine and fake is value-laden, and parallels opinions on "good" and "bad" theories.

Similar underlying assumptions can be found in VAN der WAERDEN, an extremely comprehensive survey of the issues concerning the identity of the Pythagoreans and the nature of their activities. Van der Waerden endorses the idea that most of those activities were "scientific", and he places great weight on the alleged distinction, within the school, between mathematicians and mere auditors. While the latter were fed most of the foibles about reincarnation, cosmic returns, and diet prescriptions, the former were engaged in serious mathematics, and it is to them that most of the Pythagorean theories mentioned by Aristotle should be attributed. Moreover, Van der Waerden concludes that Book 2 of Euclid's *Elements*, the contents of which are traditionally described as geometric algebra, is "essentially due to the Pythagoreans", the dignity of the school depending on it having produced some "real science".

With greater focus on the historical aspects of our topic, FRITZ's slim volume analyzes in depth the sources for the Pythagoreans' political involvement in Southern Italy. His conclusions, aided by archaeological and numismatic evidence, fix a date for Pythagorean activities in Italy between

Pythagoras's acme and the emigration to the Greek mother-land, spanning more than two centuries. He also reaffirms the reliability of the evidence for the movement's political activities, which presents its members as having a very definite public profile, and an agenda that was much less esoteric and mystical than some later views would concede. VOGEL purports to analyze hitherto neglected evidence, in order to cast more light on the early phase of Pythagorism, and on Pythagoras himself. She is, again, particularly interested in the historical setting for the political and social activities of the Pythagoreans in Southern Italy, but her argument differs from that of Fritz, in that Vogel thinks philosophy and politics were not separated, and that the people who ruled did so *qua* Pythagoreans. The integration of philosophy and politics also meant that they "exerted a real influence over people's lives".

O'MEARA examines later Pythagorism (3rd–4th centuries AD) and examines its foremost authors, their relations to each other, and their attitude to philosophy and to the role mathematics should have in the acquisition of knowledge. The result is a very varied picture, in which some individuality of viewpoint is preserved, so vindicating the complexity of the Pythagorean field – in marked contrast to interpretations that tend to render certain related authors, like Iamblichus and Plotinus, under unifying labels. Another focus of interest in the book is the later attitude of Pythagorism to preceding philosophers, particularly Plato; O'Meara traces the ways in which Platonism and Pythagorism overlapped, mixed or contrasted, often on the crucial point of the nature of mathematical knowledge.

The most up-to-date study is HUFFMAN. Although concerned mainly with Philolaus, his survey is so exhaustive and thoroughly researched that new light is thrown on many other aspects and figures. The author, by means of a careful analysis of all the extant evidence (here collected and translated), manages to draw a balanced picture that projects Philolaus against his own philosophical background. In the special case of Aristotle's testimonies, Huffman sifts Aristotle's readings from Philolaus's own theories, which he interprets as a development of earlier pre-Socratic ideas.

Finally, HENINGER's book provides some insight into the later fortunes of Pythagorean theories. During the Renaissance there was a huge revival of beliefs about the divine order of the cosmos, the relation between microcosm and macrocosm, the harmony of the spheres, and the hidden properties of numbers. Heninger examines the way Renaissance culture disseminated these beliefs, with the help of a rich iconographical apparatus in which a mythically-represented Pythagoras appears quite frequently – although, needless to say, the Renaissance "movement" had little relation to the ancient one. Nevertheless, the book makes quite clear the enormous importance Pythagorism has had for Western culture.

SERAFINA CUOMO

See also Greece: general works; Plato

Q

Quackery

Bynum, W.F. and Roy Porter (eds), *Medical Fringe and Medical Orthodoxy, 1750–1850*, London: Croom Helm, 1987

Cook, Harold J., *The Decline of the Old Medical Regime in Stuart London*, Ithaca, New York: Cornell University Press, 1986

Cooter, Roger (ed.), *Studies in the History of Alternative Medicine*, London: Macmillan, and New York: St Martin's Press, 1988

Gentilcore, David, "Charlatans, Mountebanks and other Similar People: The Regulation and Role of Itinerant Practitioners in Early Modern Italy", *Social History*, 20/3 (1995): 297–314

Nutton, Vivian, "Idle Old Trots, Cobblers and Costardmongers: Pieter van Foreest on Quackery", in *Petrus Forestus Medicus*, edited by Henriette A. Bosman-Jelgersma, Amsterdam, 1997

Porter, Roy, *Health for Sale: Quackery in England, 1660–1850*, Manchester: Manchester University Press, 1989

Ramsey, Matthew, *Professional and Popular Medicine in France, 1770–1830: The Social World of Medical Practice*, Cambridge and New York: Cambridge University Press, 1988

Thompson, C.J.S., *The Quacks of Old London*, New York: Brentano, 1928

Weatherall, Mark W., "Making Medicine Scientific: Empiricism, Rationality, and Quackery in Mid-Victorian Britain", *Social History of Medicine*, 92 (1996): 175–94

From the works of early modern physicians, such as Laurent Joubert and James Primrose, to the broadsides of the 18th century and the medical journals of the Victorian era, the literature of medicine is littered with references to "quacks" and "popular errors". Early histories of medicine, from John Friend in 1715 to THOMPSON in 1925, stress a bi-polar divide between book learned, university-trained physicians and other forms of practitioner. Friend stressed the hierarchical divide that was found in Galen; physicians whose method was ratio based on both a reasoned understanding of disease and the body and practical experience, were considered superior to those practitioners whose knowledge was at best based on experience, and at worst on ignorance and superstition. By portraying itinerant practitioners as quacks and skilful dupes, who used theatre and verbose rhetoric to seduce their gullible audience, studies such as Thompson's have served to enforce this hierarchical model. Physicians appear as heroic and truthful custodians of medical knowledge treating helpless patients, while terms such as "charlatan" and "quack" are used in a manner that belies their historic complexity.

Recent texts have sought both to break down the dichotomy between learned and lay medicine, and to move the history of quackery away from the physician and towards the viewpoint of patients and the lay practitioners themselves. Focusing on the late 16th-century Dutch physician, Pieter van Foreest, NUTTON has illustrated how practices such as uroscopy, though frequently labelled as "quackery", had their roots in learned medicine. Patients, or perhaps more accurately, customers, are given far greater credit than in earlier accounts; they recognised the similarities between learned and lay uroscopy, and pilloried the individual bad practitioner, regardless of learning, rather than the treatment itself. "Quack" or "charlatan" could be used as a general term of abuse, both by laymen to describe physicians, or, in some cases, by physicians to describe other physicians. Therapeutic value for money, rather than book-learning, was a prime concern for most patients.

Patient expectations of charlatans and mountebanks have received colourful treatment in GENTILCORE's work on early modern Italy. Using the court records of *protomedici* in towns such as Siena and Florence, he has emphasised how, by providing a display that combined elements of theatre and preaching, itinerant practitioners provided a therapy that went far beyond the mechanics of pulling teeth or the sale of treacles and nostrums. This broad role was both recognised and tolerated, at least in part, by the civic authorities. Disputes usually occurred when itinerants infringed on the jurisdiction of the Church by practising religious healing.

The relationship between itinerant healers and authority, whether in the form of the state, civic government, or medical bodies, was generally weak in early modern Europe. As COOK has shown for England, attempts by physicians to regulate the practice of medicine in and around London through the formation of the Royal College of Physicians in 1518 had an extremely limited effect. Throughout this period, patients continued to have a broad choice of practitioners, whether licensed or not. In England, this situation was enforced, first by the granting of the so-called "Quack's Charter" in 1581, and secondly by the Rose Case (1702–04). The former supported the right of lay healers, in this case a woman,

Margaret Kennix, to administer cures, while the latter allowed apothecaries to practice medicine.

PORTER has emphasised the position of quacks within the growth of 18th-century commercial society. In a vivid and readable monograph, he illustrates how figures such as Sir William Read and James Graham were able to achieve considerable wealth and fame in an urban society that favoured dynamic entrepreneurship. As Porter noted in an 1986 essay, the oral and written language of quacks was that of the market and contemporary advertising. Quack healers took their cue from learned physicians, utilising the penny broadsheets and leaflets to advertise their services and products. In addition to what was often a common medical training, both groups shared a love for medical jargon and a populist patois. As with earlier periods, this was an era in which the combination of appropriate self-presentation and networks of contacts were vital for the successful practitioner. Porter's focus is essentially urban, and it is questionable whether such wealth and fame were available to itinerant healers operating elsewhere.

The relationship between medicine and professionalization is a key issue in RAMSEY's fine monograph. In a detailed study that draws on a broad range of source material, he contrasts the patchwork of local healers operating in late 18th-century France, with the picture that emerged after the French Revolution and the medical reforms initiated by the new Napoleonic bureaucracy. In part owing some of its theory to Foucault and Illich, this is a subtle assessment of the "medicalisation" of society by elite physicians and *officiers de santé*. As Ramsey points out, this was a slow process, in which healers, whether sanctioned by the state or otherwise, continued to provide similar therapies albeit under different guises.

The issue of professionalization has been central to studies dealing with 19th-century Britain. As Porter noted, legislative changes through the Apothecaries Act of 1815 and the Medical Act of 1858 did not produce a commercial advantage for "orthodox" physicians over lay practitioners. If anything, the role of individuals such as Thomas Holloway or companies such as the Boots Company only served to enforce the existing scenario. However, as WEATHERALL's study of the homeopath William Bayes suggests, by establishing or editing journals, such as the *Lancet* and the *British Medical Journal*, and sitting on hospital and university committees, physicians were able to influence appointments and the content of university syllabuses. This growing perception of lay medicine as a "fringe" or "alternative" source of healing receives excellent treatment in two volumes of essays, edited by Bynum & Porter and by COOTER. BYNUM & PORTER contains interesting papers by Michael Neve and Jonathan Barry, in which the association between quackery and popular culture is analysed, and a paper by Roger Cooter, in which the idea of either a single medical "orthodoxy", or a single "medical" fringe, is rejected.

ALEXANDER GOLDBLOOM

See also Complementary Medicine; Professionalization

Quantification

Brian, Eric, *La Mesure de l'État: administrateurs et géomètres au XVIIIe siècle*, Paris: Michel, 1994

Cartwright, Nancy, *Nature's Capacities and Their Measurement*, Oxford: Clarendon Press, and New York: Oxford University Press, 1989

Daston, Lorraine, *Classical Probability in the Enlightenment*, Princeton, New Jersey: Princeton University Press, 1988

Frängsmyr, Tore, J.L. Heilbron and Robin E. Rider (eds), *The Quantifying Spirit in the 18th Century*, Berkeley: University of California Press, 1990

Hacking, Ian, *The Taming of Chance*, Cambridge and New York: Cambridge University Press, 1990

Heilbron, J.L., *Electricity in the 17th and 18th Centuries: A Study of Early Modern Physics*, Berkeley: University of California Press, 1979

Porter, Theodore M., *Trust in Numbers: The Pursuit of Objectivity in Science and Public Life*, Princeton, New Jersey: Princeton University Press, 1995

Wise, M. Norton (ed.), *The Values of Precision*, Princeton, New Jersey: Princeton University Press, 1995

Woolf, Harry (ed.), *Quantification: A History of the Meaning of Measurement in the Natural and Social Sciences*, Indianapolis: Bobbs-Merrill, 1961

Quantification has long been regarded as central to science, and sometimes even as its defining feature. It is a very general rubric, generally covering measurement, enumeration, calculation, mathematization, and statistics. It is of great importance both in the social sciences, including social administration and public regulation, and in the natural and physical sciences. Much of the scholarship on quantification, historical as well as philosophical, reflects a particular concern for the social sciences. However, there is much research on the quantification of particular disciplines that is overlooked here.

The collection edited by WOOLF, which appeared first as an issue of *Isis*, was for two decades the standard work on the quantification of the natural and social sciences. It includes a well-known essay by Thomas Kuhn, in which he argues that the mathematization of experimental physics owed little to indiscriminate measurement; instead, it derived from the expansion of traditional mathematical sciences, such as mechanics and astronomy. Paul Lazarsfeld's presentation and defense in this volume of the quantitative tradition in sociology have also been influential.

Quantification has recently emerged as a central theme in studies of Enlightenment science. HEILBRON has written extensively on the quantification of experimental physics, beginning with this book on early modern electricity. In contrast to Kuhn, he sees the promiscuous measuring activities of experimental natural philosophers as defining a new, and historically important, variety of physical science. He also sees this quantitative impulse as reaching far beyond physics into chemistry, surveying, meteorology, and population statistics. The collection of FRÄNGSMYR, HEILBRON & RIDER, the product of a close collaboration, under a firm editorial hand, by scholars associated with the universities at Berkeley and Uppsala, gives a wide view of quantifying activity in the late 18th century.

DASTON writes about probability theory in the 17th and 18th centuries, which was related particularly to the quantification of the "moral sciences". Her book does not stress measurement or counting, but rather examines the ways in which the mathematics of chance served as a standard of rationality or good sense. BRIAN is also concerned with probability theory, but his attention is focused on its use by enlightened French administrators, in order to address population questions.

HACKING is one of several recent books on statistics in the 19th century. His argument connects the statistical social sciences and the natural sciences in several respects; most notably, he regards the "avalanche of printed numbers" produced in the early part of the century as evidence of a rift or discontinuity occurring around 1820 – an interpretation that is hard to reconcile with recent scholarship on the late Enlightenment. He also stresses the Baconian aspects of quantification.

The collection edited by WISE deals mainly with the late 18th and 19th centuries. Here, too, the administrative dimension of quantification is emphasized, in essays ranging over such diverse topics as teaching laboratories and seminars, experimental physics and chemistry, population estimation, physiological measurement, and insurance. Similarly, PORTER argues that the growth of quantification should be seen in relation to an accounting ideal, and not merely, or even mainly, as part of an effort to emulate physics. He suggests that, instead of the pursuit of quantitative rigor being the triumph of the scientific ideal, it in fact follows from a weakening of elites, and a decline of public faith in expert judgment. Nevertheless, obtaining consistent measurements is not easy, as it depends on the effective exercise of administrative power, and much of Porter's book is devoted to quantification in relation to accounting, insurance, regulation, and decision sciences such as cost-benefit analysis.

CARTWRIGHT is concerned mainly with relations between measurement and theory. She argues that statistical inference can accomplish little, unless theoretical expectations are fed into the analysis. Like several of the authors discussed here, she reverses the traditional hierarchy of sciences, and uses a social discipline, econometrics, in order to illuminate the uses of measurement and statistics in physics.

THEODORE M. PORTER

See also Accountancy; Measurement; Statistics

Quantum Mechanics

Cassidy, David C., *Uncertainty: The Life and Science of Werner Heisenberg*, New York: W.H. Freeman, 1992

Cushing, James T., *Quantum Mechanics: Historical Contingency and the Copenhagen Hegemony*, Chicago: University of Chicago Press, 1994

Darrigol, Olivier, *From c-Numbers to q-Numbers: The Classical Analogy in the History of Quantum Theory*, Berkeley: University of California Press, 1992

Dresden, Max, *H.A. Kramers: Between Tradition and Revolution*, Berlin and New York: Springer, 1987

Eckert, Michael, *Die Atomphysiker: Eine Geschichte der theoretischen Physik am Beispiel der Sommerfeldschule*, Braunschweig: Vieweg, 1993

Forman, Paul, "Weimar Culture, Causality, and Quantum Theory, 1918–1927: Adaptation by German Physicists and Mathematicians to a Hostile Intellectual Environment", *Historical Studies in the Physical Sciences*, 3 (1971): 1–115

Heilbron, J.L., *Historical Studies in the Theory of Atomic Structure*, New York: Arno Press, 1981

Heilbron, J.L., "The Earliest Missionaries of the Copenhagen Spirit," *Revue d'histoire des sciences*, 38 (1985): 195–230

Hendry, John, *The Creation of Quantum Mechanics and the Bohr-Pauli Dialogue*, Dordrecht: Reidel, 1984

Jammer, Max, *The Conceptual Development of Quantum Mechanics*, New York: McGraw-Hill, 1966

Kragh, Helge S., *Dirac: A Scientific Biography*, Cambridge and New York: Cambridge University Press, 1990

Mehra, Jagdish and Helmut Rechenberg, *The Historical Development of Quantum Theory*, 5 vols, Berlin and New York: Springer, 1982–87

Pais, Abraham, *Inward Bound: Of Matter and Forces in the Physical World*, Oxford: Clarendon Press, and New York: Oxford University Press, 1986

Robertson, Peter, *The Early Years: The Niels Bohr Institute, 1921–1930*, Copenhagen: Akademisk Forlog, 1979

Schweber, Silvan S., *QED and the Men Who Made It: Dyson, Feynman, Schwinger, and Tomonaga*, Princeton, New Jersey: Princeton University Press, 1994

Sopka, Katherine Russell, *Quantum Physics in America, 1920–1935*, New York: Arno Press, 1980

Stuewer, Roger H., *The Compton Effect: Turning Point in Physics*, New York: Science History Publications, 1975

Wheaton, Bruce, *The Tiger and the Shark: Empirical Roots of Wave-Particle Dualism*, Cambridge and New York: Cambridge University Press, 1983

By the time an elite group of physicists gathered for the first Solvay conference in 1911, the development of quantum theory in studies of black-body radiation, and Einstein's successful application of quantum concepts to the specific heats of solids, had prompted an increasingly general awareness of the new concept of a quantum of energy as a fundamental break from "classical" physics, and the search to understand where the quantum element should be located and the extent of its applicability. Following this initial establishment of "quantum theory" as a distinctive field of research, the most significant developments in quantum physics occurred in atomic theory, and the analysis of free radiation. The successes and failures of Bohr's quantum theory of the atom of 1913 (which, together with its elaboration in Sommerfeld's work, was later often described as "old quantum theory"), led first to the perception that a new form of mechanics was necessary to deal with atomic events, and then to the development of two consistent mathematical representations of "quantum mechanics" in 1925 and 1926. Following Schödinger's proof of the mathematical equivalence of matrix and wave mechanics, and the development of the still more general transformation theory by Paul Dirac and Jordan, a still controversial but widely accepted philosophical interpretation of the new theory was formulated. This combined Heisenberg's uncertainty principle and Bohr's principle of complementarity in the "Copenhagen interpretation". Von Neumann subsequently developed a mathematically rigorous formulation of abstract quantum mechanics in the arena of "Hilbert space" (1927–29).

The profusion of names in even this briefest of overviews is indicative of an important feature of the changing nature of the physics discipline during this period. Its expansion, begun in the 1880s, had led by the 1920s to a situation where, more than in any previous period, the intellectual development of the subject was the result of collaborative work rather than individual insight. The intellectual prestige of quantum mechanics has been reflected in a relative profusion of historical studies, many of which have had formations as their centre of gravity, and have emphasised developments up to 1930. Major issues have been the complex conceptual relations between mathematical formalism, interpretation, and experimental measurement, and the disciplinary interplay between theoretical and experimental physics and mathematics – most often described from the perspective of the theorist, rather than in terms of the dynamic of experimental (or mathematical) work.

Among works treating the development of quantum mechanics in its broadest scope, two particular studies may be singled out. The classic overview of the conceptual development of the subject (from the initial formulation of quantum theory to the development of the Copenhagen interpretation) is JAMMER. Originally designed to serve as a companion to courses in quantum mechanics, by providing a study of the origin and development of the concepts concerned, the book presents a very clear discussion confined to the treatment of published primary material and non-relativistic quantum mechanics of a finite number of degrees of freedom. MEHRA & RECHENBERG's five-volume treatment is, by contrast, an extremely detailed treatment of the subjects indicated by title. The authors utilise the interviews with physicists and the extensive correspondence collected for the Archive for History of Quantum Physics (available at the American Institute of Physics and other locations internationally), and previous writings by historians of physics, although they sometimes rely uncritically on the recollections of important quantum physicists.

Many important contributions have been concerned more specifically with particular lines of research in the development of quantum mechanics, or with methodological and historiographical themes. The lectures and articles collected together in HEILBRON (1981) provide a valuable overview of the role of developments of the theory of atomic structure (from 1900) in the invention of quantum mechanics, and several detailed studies. These include an important essay (with T.S. Kuhn) on the genesis of Bohr's quantum theory of the atom in 1913, and papers on Moseley's discovery of the formulas governing high frequency (X-ray) spectra of the elements and on the importance of the Kossel-Sommerfeld theory of X-ray spectra in refining quantum models of the atom. The essays trace the gradual process by which the concepts of Victorian physics were compromised by quantum principles, leading to the development of a model of the atom as a three-dimensional tracery of electron orbits tied together by ordinary forces limited by unpicturable quantum constraints.

It has been traditional to focus on Einstein's initially controversial theoretical contributions (from his introduction of the concept of light quanta in 1905, and of the first arguments for a union of wave and particle treatments in 1909), in discussing the development of a quantum theory of light. Two highly detailed studies of experiment have shown the quite different path taken by most physicists in order to take seriously the application of quantum theory to light and free radiation. WHEATON's account of research on free radiation (of X-rays, gamma rays, and light) between 1896 and the 1920s illuminates the empirical route by which many physicists became convinced that a consistent electromechanical explanation of radiation was not possible in principle. Discussing, in particular, impulse theories of X and gamma rays, the development of X-ray spectroscopy, and the absorption of radiation, Wheaton describes the work of Barkla, W.H. Bragg, Stark, Sommerfeld, Compton, and the de Broglie brothers, among others. He relates different responses to the paradoxical nature of X and gamma rays to different national traditions in physical argument and research, especially in Britain and Germany, and shows that a resolution of the paradoxes was forged through an appeal to indeterministic quantum theories, which saw both light and matter as sharing wave and particle characteristics, and brought together long-separated theoretical and experimental approaches. Wheaton argues that the development of two independently formulated versions of the new quantum mechanics was due to the virtual separation of the parent fields of research – spectroscopic analysis of atoms (matrix mechanics) and the statistical analysis of radiation (wave mechanics) – for the decade before their fusion through discussion of the light quanta.

STUEWER is devoted to understanding the empirical and theoretical developments that led to the discovery of the Compton effect: that a quantum of radiation undergoes a discrete change of wavelength (as a result of change in momentum) when it collides with an electron at rest in an atom. Stuewer's closely argued account describes the developments of radiation theory, especially concerning X-rays, in the first decades of the 20th century. Utilising A.H. Compton's research notebooks, it investigates in close detail the evolution of his experimental work, and his changing conception of X-ray scattering from 1913 to 1924. The book also investigates responses to Compton's work, supporting the view that, through the support they provided for the concept of light quanta (photons), the experiments were responsible for an important turning-point in radiation physics, and the development of quantum physics more generally.

The circumstances of the development and propagation of quantum mechanics in the fraught political climate of central Europe in the aftermath of World War I have often raised questions concerning the multi-directional relations between physical research, philosophical concerns, and wider (intellectual) culture. FORMAN's landmark article gives an account of the intellectual milieu in Germany between the wars, describing a widespread anti-scientific (Spenglerian and vitalist) sentiment. He argues that many physicists and mathematicians responded to this hostile cultural environment by embracing acausal (indeterministic) quantum physics – hence jettisoning the rigorous causality that was an oft-criticised feature of the scientific world picture – before this was fully justified, on technical grounds alone. Although the argument relies on a simple model of the relations between science and culture, it has been extremely important in stimulating scholarship on early 20th-century science.

HENDRY, intended to promote a serious interest in the history of science among physicists, and criticising Forman's article by focusing on internal reasons, seeks to relate the technical development of quantum mechanics, and the philosophical debate it occasioned, to more fundamental issues in the concepts used to describe the physical world (especially to a tension between demands for the consistent visualisability of physical knowledge, and physical operationalism). Drawing on the correspondence, Hendry focuses on the creative role played by Pauli in stimulating and shaping the research of both Bohr and Heisenberg, with his call for operational consistency and an operationally-defined system of concepts. The book then traces connections between epistemological and methodological problems encountered in general relativity and unified field theory, and in quantum theory (the duality of wave and particle pictures is a central issue). Hendry's study also investigates Pauli's role in the development of the old quantum theory, the virtual oscillator theory, and the genesis and evolution of the matrix formulation of quantum mechanics until the establishment of a definitive formulation and interpretation in 1927.

With the conviction that theoretical physics proceeds by building formal analogies between work in different areas, through the extension, combination, and transposition of available pieces of theory (with mathematics playing an important structuring role), DARRIGOL examines in detail the lines of conceptual argument that shaped the development of three important phases of quantum theory: Planck's law of black-body radiation; Bohr's correspondence principle; and Dirac's formulation of quantum mechanics. His study identifies the use of several different types of analogies with "classical" theories, and provides valuable insight into the changing relations between mathematical schemes and interpretation. Darrigol suggests that analogies usually work with "a touch of blindness", but argues that Bohr's correspondence principle provides a counter-example of an analogical principle that never concealed the contrasts between the old and new theories.

HEILBRON (1985) discusses the reception of Niels Bohr's principle of complementarity from 1927 (in Germany, Britain, and the United States), and describes the attempts made by Bohr and some of his followers (especially Pauli and Jordan) to derive a universal epistemology applicable also to the basic problems of psychology and biology. In the psychological portraits of Heilbron's account, Bohr plays the role of a sometimes reluctant guru, and the complementarity principle presents an opening towards vitalism, mysticism, and free will – and Nazism – to which the younger physicists around Bohr were variously susceptible.

CUSHING's concerns with the role played by historical contingency in the construction and selection of a successful theory are scientific, philosophical, and historical. Arguing that neither empirical nor logical (in)adequacy can explain present (or past) adherence to the Copenhagen interpretation over a causal, hidden-variable interpretation of quantum mechanics such as David Bohm's, Cushing analyses the different philosophical or metaphysical commitments that inform different schools in the development and interpretation of quantum mechanics. His study pays far greater attention to alternative formulations than is customary.

In addition to the studies outlined above, work oriented on the particular contributions of Einstein and Bohr has provided an initial focus for many discussions of quantum physics and the interpretation of quantum mechanics. In Einstein's case, historians have been particularly concerned to establish the conceptual origins of his contributions, while in Bohr's case the emphasis has been on exploring the principle of complementarity. The debate on the interpretation of quantum mechanics that these two sustained from 1927, and especially around the "Einstein–Podolsky–Rosen Paradox" of 1935, has also been a focus of on-going philosophical research, as an expression of contrasting attitudes towards the epistemological implications of quantum mechanics.

Three institutionally-based research centres were important in the formation and later propagation of matrix mechanics and the Copenhagen interpretation – Copenhagen (around Bohr), Göttingen (Born), and Munich (Sommerfeld) – while wave mechanics emerged through a line of research associated with Einstein, de Broglie, and Schrödinger. Many of the central figures in these developments, and especially the younger physicists (such as Pauli, Heisenberg, and Jordan), studied and worked in several of these centres. As the specialist studies above indicate, their research on quantum mechanics, and subsequent attempts to extend the theory beyond its initial application, reflect tensions between concerns and theoretical tools characteristic of the different schools. A number of works have discussed these schools primarily from the perspective of the social history of the physics discipline. ROBERTSON's survey of the lives and careers of the physicists at Bohr's institute, from its foundation in 1921 to 1930, offers an account of the conceptual development of quantum physics within the context of the institution's foundation and expansion, its position in Danish society, and its major role as a meeting-ground for physicists from Germany, Britain, and the United States. ECKERT's non-technical study is a "socio-biography" of Sommerfeld and his school from the late 19th century to the end of World War II, and examines the changing social context of theoretical physics. Eckert characterises theoretical physics, and atomic theory in particular, as rising from the ashes of World War I and economic inflation, comparing the adventure of quantum mechanics (as theory and in social terms) to an expedition – the first collective undertaking of theoretical physicists. Eckert argues that Sommerfeld's book *Atombau und Spektrallinien* played a principal role in motivating the post-war influx of physics students in the search for new foundations. He describes features of the group dynamics between the three principal schools in the formation of quantum mechanics, and briefly outlines the subsequent search for applications in the electron theory of metals by Sommerfeld's school and the rapid development of the hybrid sciences of quantum chemistry, molecular biology, and astrophysics.

Drawing on a wide range of sources in order to relate the internal history of physics, the sociological place of Americans within the international physics community, and the rise of scientific activity in the United States between 1920 and 1935, SOPKA's study places great importance on quantum physics in the passage of US physics to maturity. In particular, the book characterises the period immediately following the (European) formulation of quantum mechanics as one in which US theoreticians made important contributions to the further development of the subject (especially in quantum chemistry and the theory of magnetism), and the discipline of theoretical physics found a new status in regard to the more traditional US strength in experimental work. Sopka's account includes much useful and quantitative information on changing dynamics in the relations between European and US physicists.

More recently, biographical studies have outlined the distinctive perspectives exhibited in the research and philosophical outlook of physicists other than Einstein and Bohr, such as Heisenberg, Schrödinger, Dirac, Oppenheimer, and DRESDEN's study of Kramers. These studies have also shown the different roles that their contributions to quantum theory played in the careers of the physicists concerned, and often depict the physicists' orientation to the political events of the 1930s and to World War II. The books by Kragh and Cassidy are particularly important for their treatment of the attempts by different physicists to integrate quantum mechanics with special relativity, and to extend a quantum theoretical approach to nuclear theory.

CASSIDY's biography of Heisenberg, dealing in detail with the period up to 1945, discusses Heisenberg's work within the context of his education and his extraordinary career. Cassidy's treatment of Heisenberg's contributions to quantum mechanics (especially matrix mechanics and the uncertainty principle) and the subsequent development of quantum field theory, is at a level appropriate to an educated lay person, and provides a guide to more specific studies. In addition to his discussion of the evolution of Heisenberg's work, Cassidy also offers a sensitive treatment of the major issues that have been raised in the historiography of 20th-century physics more generally, and particularly in the discussion of physics in Nazi Germany and the issue of a German bomb.

KRAGH's scientific biography of Dirac provides a detailed study of the work of one of the foremost contributors to the formation of quantum mechanics and the instigator of many of the most important approaches to quantum field theory, and examines the central preoccupations and the philosophical approach implicit in Dirac's work. Kragh analyses the lines of thought that led to Dirac's important contributions (such as his development of the relativistic theory of the electron, and postulation of the positron), and describes his long attempts, from the mid-1930s, to find better equations for quantum electrodynamics, motivated by a dissatisfaction with the theory's divergence difficulties, and the search for a formulation exhibiting what Dirac described as "mathematical beauty".

The two major comprehensive studies of the attempt to extend quantum mechanical rules for mechanical systems to the electromagnetic field in a way that satisfies relativity – an approach that became known as quantum electrodynamics – and to extend quantum mechanics to the laws governing the nucleus, have been contributed by working physicists. Within the context of a history of particle physics from 1895, which stresses the evolution of ideas, the confusion attendant on and leading to progress, and the great changes of scale (both in the physics discipline and in the scope of its experimental possibilities), PAIS provides an important treatment of the evolution of relativistic quantum mechanics and quantum field theory for the period from the late 1920s to 1945. He describes

the often counter-intuitive development of theoretical and experimental insight that was involved in the development of new concepts of forces, and the postulation, detection, and production of a host of new particles through cosmic ray and accelerator physics. An episodic writing style conveys well the impression of a physics being built through the contributions of many figures. SCHWEBER discusses the experimental and theoretical development of quantum electrodynamics in detail, treating the period from 1927 to about 1950, and arguing that at this time the success of renormalisation theory in quantum electrodynamics (and its application to other field theories) made quantum field theory the most natural framework for the synthesis of quantum theory and special relativity. Schweber describes the development of renormalised field theory (echoing earlier stances in quantum mechanics) as an oscillation between a metaphysics based on particles, represented by the hole-theoretic point of view of Dirac and the work of Feynman, and one based on field theory, represented by Schwinger, Tomonaga, and Dyson. The argument proceeds through a discussion of a series of important conferences from the 1940s, and details the work of the latter four physicists, which are approached as different styles of reasoning. Schweber sets his work within the broader institutional and political context of the period, discussing in particular the importance of research conditions in the war-time laboratories of the US (and especially experimental work on microwaves) in shaping the character of post-war research in theoretical physics.

RICHARD STALEY

See also Bohr; Heisenberg, Quantum Theory; Schrödinger

Quantum Theory

Agassi, Joseph, *Radiation Theory and the Quantum Revolution*, Basel: Birkhäuser, 1993

Cahan, David, *An Institute for an Empire: The Physikalisch-Technische Reichsanstalt, 1871–1918*, Cambridge and New York: Cambridge University Press, 1989

Darrigol, Olivier, *From c-Numbers to q-Numbers: The Classical Analogy in the History of Quantum Theory*, Berkeley: University of California Press, 1992

Heilbron, J.L., *H.G.J. Moseley: The Life and Letters of an English Physicist, 1887–1915*, Berkeley: University of California Press, 1974

Heilbron, J.L., *Historical Studies in the Theory of Atomic Structure*, New York: Arno Press, 1981

Heilbron, J.L., *The Dilemmas of an Upright Man: Max Planck as Spokesman for German Science*, Berkeley: University of California Press, 1986

Hermann, Armin, *The Genesis of Quantum Theory (1899–1913)*, translated from the German by Claude W. Nash, Cambridge, Massachusetts: MIT Press, 1971 (original edition, 1969)

Jungnickel, Christa and Russell McCormmach, *Intellectual Mastery of Nature: Theoretical Physics from Ohm to Einstein*, vol. 2: *The Now Mighty Theoretical Physics, 1870–1920*, Chicago: University of Chicago Press, 1986

Kangro, Hans, *Early History of Planck's Radiation Law*, translated from the German by R.E.W. Maddison, London: Taylor and Francis, 1976 (original edition, 1970)

Klein, Martin J., "Max Planck and the Beginnings of Quantum Theory", *Archives for the History of the Exact Sciences*, 1 (1962): 459–79; "Einstein's First Paper on Quanta", *Natural Philosopher*, 2 (1963): 59–86; "Einstein and the Wave-Particle Duality", *Natural Philosopher*, 3 (1964): 3–49; "Einstein, Specific Heats, and the Early Quantum Theory", *Science*, 148 (1965): 173–80; "Thermodynamics in Einstein's Thought", *Science*, 157 (1967): 509–16; and "Mechanical Explanation at the End of the Nineteenth Century", *Centaurus*, 17 (1972): 58–82

Klein, Martin J., *Paul Ehrenfest: The Making of a Theoretical Physicist*, Amsterdam: North-Holland, and New York: Elsevier, 1970

Kuhn, Thomas S., *Black-Body Theory and the Quantum Discontinuity, 1894–1912*, Oxford: Clarendon Press, and New York: Oxford University Press, 1978

Wheaton, Bruce R., *The Tiger and the Shark: Empirical Roots of Wave-Particle Dualism*, Cambridge and New York: Cambridge University Press, 1983

The introduction of a physics of elementary discontinuity, which challenged the assumptions of the "classical" physics of the 19th century, and its subsequent incorporation within the (philosophically) novel and (empirically) highly successful quantum mechanical theory of the atom, has resulted in the initial formation of quantum theory having assumed a particular importance in the work of professional historians of science. An early manifestation of this interest was the collection in the 1960s of extensive correspondence and interview material, from the generation of physicists responsible for these developments, in the Archive for History of Quantum Physics (held in the American Institute of Physics and other locations internationally). Quantum physics is now one of the most thoroughly researched fields in the history of science, and the very prestige of the subject has exposed its historiography to particular challenges.

A first potential difficulty lies in the possibility that a teleological interpretation of the physicists' contributions, largely in terms of a particular understanding of quantum physics (actually formed retrospectively), could significantly obscure the complexities of the subject's development. In an exemplification of his well-known argument concerning the incommensurability of different scientific paradigms, Thomas S. KUHN's important work argued that such a retrospective reinterpretation had in fact occurred in the readings by earlier scientists and historians of Max Planck's derivation of his law of black-body radiation in 1900. Kuhn's research highlights the need for a critical approach to the relations between mathematical formalism and interpretation, one of the most fruitful methodological contributions yet made in the literature on quantum theory.

A second historiographical challenge stems from the very real possibility of configuring images of early 20th-century physics, largely in the light of our unusually extensive knowledge of quantum physics, which was in fact only a limited and perhaps highly idiosyncratic component of work in the physics discipline at the time. The virtues and limitations of one of the most insightful general overviews of the subject and discipline illustrate this point. JUNGNICKEL & McCORMMACH's major study offers an extremely valuable contextualisation of the conceptual history of quantum theory on a number of fronts: intellectually, by showing the context of a prior search for new foundations in which quantum physics was developed; and educationally and institutionally, by discussing the relations between physics research, pedagogy, journal policy, and academic appointments within the German university system. Drawing on institutional archives, the authors integrate their account of quantum theory into a demonstration of the increasingly strong disciplinary distinctions between theoretical and experimental physics in Germany. However, their decision to relate the rather unusual methodological aspects of their study to the conceptual history of the traditionally prestigious subjects of relativity and quantum theory, without discussing other research areas in comparable detail, means that it is difficult to evaluate critically the significance of these fields in the formation of the discipline (and vice versa). Despite the great strengths of historical research on quantum theory, the possible benefits of a more critical contextualisation of the various intellectual and institutional relationships have not yet been realised.

Quantum physics grew out of an earlier body of experimental and theoretical research devoted to the physics of radiation. CAHAN's study of the foundation and operation of the Physikalisch-Technische Reichsanstalt (PTR) in Berlin between 1871 and 1918 argues that a concern with establishing standards of luminous intensity and temperature measurement for the heating and lighting industries motivated the development of this field of research. In the late 1890s, the Optical Laboratory of the PTR devoted all its resources to the study of radiation physics, with significant improvements in instrumentation allowing a greater determination of the spectral distribution of radiation from a "black body" or cavity, and hence providing increasingly demanding tests for the theoretical work of physicists such as Wilhelm Wien and Max Planck. Cahan argues convincingly that the commitment of the PTR to respond to the practical needs of German industry indicates that more complex motivations were responsible for the timing and setting of the origins of quantum physics than accounts focused on experiment and theory alone have allowed.

The most thorough study of experimental work at the foundation of radiation physics is KANGRO. Kangro examines the period from the 1880s to 1901, and is particularly concerned to show the close interrelationships between theoretical and experimental work, and between physicists working in different centres with different instrumentation (especially between those in and around the PTR in Berlin and Friedrich Paschen in Hannover). He combats the view that quantum theory was Planck's alone, by paying attention to the less well-known contributions integral to the subject's development, but he also discusses the development of Planck's work in some detail, arguing that Planck was primarily concerned with the two constants of nature his law incorporated, k (Boltzmann's constant) and h (Planck's constant).

AGASSI presents a broad-ranging and critical, if somewhat impressionistic, study of the background to quantum theory, in radiation theory from 1800 (especially Kirchhoff's law) and spectroscopy. The book is aimed at science students and intends to present science as an activity that is in principle open (i.e. accessible to the public) and critical. Agassi believes that a reform of the etiquette of scientific research and of methods of writing history, in order to emphasise these features and to prevent intimidation of the student, to be important and interwoven tasks. His account critically discusses previous work (in particular that of Kuhn) and continually raises questions about scientific methodology and the historiography of science.

The most detailed studies of the initial conceptual development of quantum physics have raised the issue of authorship of the theory. KLEIN (1962–72) provides sensitive readings of the published papers of Planck and Einstein, and supports the traditional attribution of quantum theory to Planck – in the derivation of his law of 1900 for the spectral distribution of radiation, which drew on Boltzmann's combinatorial statistics. Einstein was then responsible for the most fruitful extensions of the theory to the behaviour of light (1905) and the specific heat of solids (1907), in the period when Planck's work first began to attract wider attention. Paul Ehrenfest is another physicist who was early to recognise quanta as an important feature of Planck's law, and KLEIN (1970) gives an account of his formation as a theoretical physicist. Using a combination of Ehrenfest's revealing correspondence and published resources, Klein discusses the physicist's studies in Vienna c.1900, his travels through Europe, and his calling to succeed H.A. Lorentz in Leiden in 1913. Arguing that Ehrenfest's contributions were most important for their critical analysis of foundational issues in the new physics, Klein shows that Ehrenfest's work on statistical mechanics developed out of his close study of the work of his first teacher, Ludwig Boltzmann. He then describes Ehrenfest's published analysis of the assumptions underlying Planck's derivation of the law, and discusses Ehrenfest's formulation of the adiabatic principle, which guided extensions of the statistical foundations of quantum theory in the later work of Bohr.

HERMANN's account was one of the earliest to make use of the correspondence and interviews gathered by the Archives for the History of Quantum Physics, and is presented in a series of chapters devoted to physicists who made important contributions in the period to 1913: Planck, Lorentz, Einstein, Stark, Haas, Sommerfeld, Nernst, and Bohr. Hermann argues that, while Planck's work introduced the physical constant h, it was only from 1908 that discussion of the principle of continuity began, which was then only a minor feature of the attempt to find a solution to the quantum problem.

KUHN's major and revisionist study built on earlier work that had established the gradual nature of the development of quantum theory, while problematising Planck's own understanding of black-body radiation and quantisation of energy in the period 1894–1912. Focusing on the relation between mathematical resources and conceptual understandings in theoretical physics (and the means by which these are assimilated), Kuhn argues that in 1900 Planck did not interpret the energy elements he took from Boltzmann's approach as involving the quantisation of energy, commonly seen as integral to his work (and its most revolutionary feature). Kuhn attributed this to Planck's incomplete understanding of Boltzmann's statistics, which he employed only late in his work for the 1900 derivation. Showing that facility with this form of statistics was

unusual in the period, Kuhn's study investigates in some detail the process by which the quantum physics of discontinuity became a major concern of the physics community. He argues that three principal features were important in this: the critical analysis of Planck's work by Einstein and Ehrenfest, on the basis of their independent work in statistical mechanics; successive demonstrations (by Lorentz in particular) that "classical" theory led to the Rayleigh-Jeans law of spectral distribution, rather than Planck's; and the empirical confirmation of Einstein's quantum theory of the specific heat of solids in Walter Nernst's Institute of Physical Chemistry in 1911. Following Kuhn's study, one might say that, while Planck was responsible for his law, "quantum theory" was only created after 1905, largely due to Einstein's contributions.

DARRIGOL's study includes a close technical analysis of Planck's work up to 1900, within the context of a discussion of the use by physicists of formal analogies with earlier work in a number of important phases of quantum physics. Darrigol combines Kuhn's thesis with the insight that Planck retained a non-statistical understanding of thermodynamic irreversibility, in order to explain more fully the particular character of Planck's use of Boltzmann's work. HEILBRON (1986) is an insightful account of Planck's role as a spokesman for the German physics community from the late 1890s to 1944, and discusses the relations between Planck's physics and his personal life, science policy, and philosophy of nature. Heilbron explores the biographical foundations for Planck's general theoretical goals, and his particular attitude to the issues of causality raised by interpretations of quantum mechanics. He also describes the challenges that World War I and the Third Reich posed for Planck's allegiance to a unitary world picture.

Following the initial establishment of quantum theory as a distinctive field of research, many of the most important developments in quantum physics occurred in atomic theory, and the analysis of free radiation. Work in these fields in the first two decades of the 20th century was central to the subsequent formation of quantum mechanics.

The lectures and articles collected together in HEILBRON (1981) provide an overview of the development of the theory of atomic structure in the period from 1900 to the invention of quantum mechanics in the 1920s, and several detailed studies. An essay (with Kuhn) on the genesis of Bohr's quantum theory of the atom is particularly important. Bohr's theory of 1913 was built on Rutherford's nuclear model of the atom, introducing the concept of stable "stationary states" for the orbital electrons, together with the assumption that electrons passing from one stationary state to another emitted electromagnetic radiation (where the relation between the frequency and amount of radiation was given by Planck's theory of black-body radiation). Heilbron and Kuhn show that the motivation for these innovations was the difficulty of adapting the mechanical stability of earlier models of the atom to electrons in the new planetary model. In addition to this study, Heilbron's papers on alpha and beta scattering and the Rutherford atom, on Moseley's discovery of the formulas governing high frequency (X-ray) spectra of the elements, and on the importance of the Kossel-Sommerfeld theory of X-ray spectra in refining quantum models of the atom, all draw extensively on manuscript and correspondence sources. The essays show strong continuities between the work of Bohr, Moseley, and Rutherford and the framework of atomic theory established earlier by J.J. Thomson, and trace the gradual process by which the concepts of Victorian physics were compromised by quantum principles, leading to the development of a model of the atom as a three-dimensional tracery of electron orbits tied together by ordinary forces limited by unpicturable quantum constraints. HEILBRON (1974), a biography of Moseley, describes the physicist's important work within the context of his upper-class upbringing, the transition through stages of apprenticeship and journeyman work, and his mastery of the emerging new field of quantum theory of the atom through the application of spectroscopic studies to atomic physics.

A second area that saw the gradual introduction of quantum theory was that of free radiation. Here, Einstein's early arguments for light quanta (1905), and for a fusion of wave and particle models in the treatment of light (1909), were not initially taken seriously by most physicists. WHEATON's account examines the emergence of what later came to be called the wave-particle duality in empirical work, discussing impulse theories of X and gamma rays, the development of X-ray spectroscopy, and the absorption of radiation, from 1896 to the 1920s. He describes how physicists such as Barkla, W.H. Bragg, Stark, and Sommerfeld sought to interpret various radiations in terms of either particles or waves, and relates the various strategies they developed to national traditions in physical research and argument. His study thus shows the manner in which the introduction of indeterministic quantum theories – fusing wave and particle characteristics for both matter and light – allowed an eventual resolution of the paradoxes.

RICHARD STALEY

See also Atomic Theory; Planck; Quantum Mechanics

Quételet, Lambert Adolphe Jacques

1796–1874

French astronomer and social statistician

Brian, Eric, "Statistique administrative et internationalisme statistique pendant la seconde moitié du XIXe siècle", *Histoire et Mesure*, (1989): 201–24

Hankins, Frank H., *Adolphe Quételet as Statistician*, New York: Columbia University Press, 1908; New York: AMS Press, 1968

Lazarsfeld, Paul, "Notes on the History of Quantification in Sociology – Trends, Sources, and Problems", *Isis*, 52 (1961): 277–333

Lottin, Joseph, *Quételet: Statisticien et sociologue*, Louvain: Institut Superieur de Philosophies, 1912; reprinted, New York: Franklin, 1969

Porter, Theodore M., *The Rise of Statistical Thinking, 1820–1900*, Princeton, New Jersey: Princeton University Press, 1986

Stigler, Stephen M., *The History of Statistics: The Measurement of Uncertainty before 1900*, Cambridge, Massachusetts: Belknap Press of Harvard University Press, 1986

Turner, Stephen P., *The Search for a Methodology of Social Science: Durkheim, Weber, and the Nineteenth-Century Problem of Cause, Probability, and Action*, Dordrecht and Boston: Reidel, 1986

There is almost no scholarship that addresses the wide range of Quételet's scientific activities. His career was commemorated by the Belgian Academy of Science on the centenary of his death, in four volumes that are not listed here because they were only distributed privately, and another commemoration took place in 1996, the bicentenary of his birth. Quételet's career was among the most distinguished in the history of Belgian science, and he was the driving force in the Belgian Academy for several decades after its refounding in the 1820s. He was also highly influential in the development of Belgian official statistics and of international statistical organizations. Most studies of his career, however, have focused on his work in social science, and, especially, on his efforts to make it statistical. The exception is BRIAN, who argues that Quételet's scientific program for administrative and international statistics was rather less successful than were the bureaucratic efforts of his contemporary, Xavier Heuschling.

In the 19th century, when "statistics" was a social rather than a mathematical science, Quételet was seen as a major social thinker, and his work inspired a large critical and reflective literature. The early 20th-century books by Hankins and Lottin, as well as the study in 1912 by Durkheim's student, Maurice Halbwachs, are all late products of this tradition. HANKINS, a young sociologist at Columbia University, considered Quételet in relation to the quantification of sociology. So, much later, did LAZARSFELD, an Austrian émigré to the United States and himself a noted social quantifier, who endeavored to separate Quételet's apparently laudable efforts to measure social phenomena from his discredited doctrine of *l'homme moyen*, the average man.

LOTTIN was a philosopher at the University of Louvain, interested as much in the moral as the sociological dimension of Quételet's work. His book addresses at length, and with much sympathy, the debates of the 1860s to the 1880s on the relation between Quételet's belief in the universality of statistical social laws and his commitment to human free will. Lottin's book remains by far the most complete account of Quételet's life and career, and relies extensively on quotations from Quételet's work, and that of his commentators and critics.

Three recent books devote chapters or long sections to Quételet's work in sociology and statistics. TURNER is particularly interested in attempts to establish social causality using statistical methods. PORTER considers Quételet's career from the standpoint of statistical thinking, and interprets his work on statistical regularities as helping to make credible a faith in mass regularity; he sees Quételet as inadvertently creating new resources that proved important for the population genetics of Francis Galton, and the statistical physics of James Clerk Maxwell. STIGLER provides a close examination of Quételet's methods of statistical analysis, presenting him as part of a worthy but, in its time, failed effort to extend the statistical successes of error theory in astronomy to the social sciences.

THEODORE M. PORTER

See also Astronomy; Social Sciences; Statistics

R

Race

Bernal, Martin, *Black Athena: The Afroasiatic Roots of Greek Thought*, 2 vols, New Brunswick, New Jersey: Rutgers University Press, and London: Free Association Press, 1987–91

Bullard, Robert D., *Dumping in Dixie: Race, Class and Environmental Quality*, Boulder, Colorado: Westview Press, 1990

Degler, Carl N., *In Search of Human Nature: The Decline and Revival of Darwinism in American Social Thought*, Oxford and New York: Oxford University Press, 1991

Diop, Cheikh Anta, *Civilization or Barbarism?: An Authentic Anthropology*, translated from the French by Yaa-Lengi Meema Ngemi, Brooklyn, New York: Lawrence Hill Books, 1991

Gould, Stephen Jay, *The Mismeasure of Man*, New York: Norton, 1981; revised and expanded edition, 1996

Harris, Marvin, *The Rise of Anthropological Theory: A History of Theories of Culture*, New York: Crowell, and London: Routledge and Kegan Paul, 1968

Herrnstein, Richard J. and Charles Murray, *The Bell Curve: Intelligence and Class Structure in American Life*, New York: Free Press, 1974

Lewontin, Richard C., Steven Rose and Leon J. Kamin, *Not in Our Genes: Biology, Ideology, and Human Nature*, New York: Pantheon Books, 1984

Myrdal, Gunnar, *An American Dilemma: The Negro Problem and Modern Democracy*, 2 vols, New York: Harper, 1944

Rushton, John Philippe, *Race, Evolution and Behavior: A Life History Perspective*, New Brunswick, New Jersey: Transaction, 1995

Stepan, Nancy, *The Idea of Race in Science: Great Britain, 1800–1960*, Hamden, Connecticut: Archon Books, and London: Macmillan in association with St Antony's College, 1982

Stocking Jr, George W., *Race, Culture and Evolution: Essays in the History of Anthropology*, New York: Free Press, 1968

Race became a politically controversial explanation for differences in the human condition as a result of two 19th-century scientific innovations: the techniques for measuring humans against a variety of dimensions, and the theories that defined the biological substratum as resistant to most environmental changes. This is spiritedly recounted and critiqued in GOULD.

Because 20th-century scientific racism tends to presuppose a sharp Darwinian distinction between "nature" and "nurture" as causes of human behaviour, it is often not appreciated that traditionally racism was associated with the hereditary transmission of acquired traits. Thus, pre-19th-century students of race accepted the unity of the human species, and explained persistent racial differences in terms of geographical segregation. This carried over into two features of modern racism: 1) presumed linkages between race and culture, or "blood and soil", which has been increasingly used to discipline national populations and restrict immigration; 2) the admission that general attitudes and abilities may be racially determined, yet subject to considerable expressive variation. Together these features have rendered scientific racism virtually unfalsifiable, and hence perennially ripe for revival. HARRIS (in particular, chapter 4), is a good source for the protean character of racism.

Racism became a tough-minded scientific attitude as hopes for universal Enlightenment appeared unrealizable. Whereas Lamarck continued to believe that the "perfectibility" of the species would come from the exposure of all races to a "civilized" upbringing, Voltaire and Hume had already concluded that the failure of certain races (especially Blacks) to become "civilized" of their own accord, implied that they were incapable of improving their condition, and were better left to their own devices, or, if already in captivity, be kept in nonage. These theorists saw history as having revealed the full potential of humanity. Combined with new quantitative techniques in comparative anatomy, including cranial measures that seemed to correlate with perceived racial differences, this view spawned various accounts of the multiple origins of humanity or "polygenesis" – which led some to argue for emergent species's differences. STOCKING (especially chapters 3 and 6) is the canonical source for these developments.

While most scientific racism is traceable to polygenesis, modern "humanistic" forms of racism are derived from the single-origin biblical account of the Fall and the dispersion of humanity. As BERNAL controversially argues, the Tower of Babel story legitimated the search of classical philology for the root of all "Indo–Aryan" languages. Each language was said to capture the soul of a race, whose degree of degeneration could be measured by its grammatical differences from the root-language. From this tradition came the idea of the Greeks as the unique racial source of Europe, which is probably still the most pervasive racist belief built into the general curriculum (and target of multiculturalism). Although Bernal is sometimes used today to support an "Afrocentrist" reorientation to the history of science, a much more appropriate source is the Senegalese ethnologist, DIOP, who explicitly tries to show, mainly through archaeological evidence and speculation, that the Greek achievement was largely a "stolen legacy" from Africa, especially Egypt.

Darwinian natural selection seemed to deny the inheritance of acquired traits, presumably including any long-term effects of social co-operation. Thus, racial conflict was portrayed as a biological eventuality, as periodic environmental changes forced different populations to compete for survival in the same space. As DEGLER points out, there were two main expressions of opposition to this Social Darwinist perspective, both usually associated with leftist causes. One was eugenics, which aimed to use biology as an instrument of public policy by "selecting" for desirable traits and against undesirable ones. The other, which managed to escape any links with Hitler or Stalin, was a methodological denial of biology's relevance to social explanation, usually by arguing that evolution's time scale is too long to operate at the level of specific cultures. Degler credits the anthropologist Franz Boas with this response, which seeped into American public policy through MYRDAL, whose work was used to justify massive housing, educational, and employment initiatives for Blacks in the 1960s.

However, by the late 1960s, doubts were already being raised concerning these initiatives, and whether their failures implied that scientific racism is, in some sense, true. The evidence was typically presented in the form of Blacks continuing to trail Whites in their performance on intelligence tests. The most thorough defence of this line of thinking, HERRNSTEIN & MURRAY, a psychologist and a political economist, is couched more in terms of cost-benefit considerations, (i.e. "Does welfare spending deliver proportional benefits?"), than any racist ideology. Interestingly, they argue that because other social indicators suggest an increasing democratization of American life, persistent class differences between groups must be due to something "deeper", outside the reach of public policy: i.e., inherent racial differences.

LEWONTIN, ROSE & KAMIN, three biologists, provide the best antidote to this renascent racism. They observe that intelligence levels within races vary more widely than between races, and that claims concerning the high heritability of intelligence can be explained by either genetic insensitivity to environmental change, or simply the limited range of environments to which the genes have been exposed. The last is especially damning to scientific racial policy, as it implies that history does not furnish a "natural laboratory" for assessing racial capacities. Moreover, the ranking of races seems to shift relative to perceived social achievement, with East Asians scoring higher than Whites in the tests RUSHTON administers. Lewontin, Rise & Kamin finally make the neat historical point that, just as Darwinism initially gave hope to racists, it later dashed those hopes once genetics showed that no essential definition could be given to species.

Nevertheless, racists commonly respond that critics demand a much higher level of statistical reliability for race-based social policies than for other such policies – such as smoking prohibitions or nuclear plant sitings – because critics can imagine the immediate personal risk associated with the targets of these policies, but not the collective risk entailed by continued pref-erential treatment for disadvantaged races. This objection has come full circle in the past 20 years, with the introduction of "environmental racism", a phrase coined by the American sociologist BULLARD to characterize the high correlation between the location of toxic waste dumps and minority communities, which sinisterly suggests that genocide may be a precondition to a clean environment.

And how do the slighted races themselves respond to scientific racism? STEPAN has pointed out that, unlike some recent "postmodernist" and "postcolonial" tendencies, educated members of the races regarded as inferior during the late 19th and early 20th centuries (especially Blacks and Jews) tended not to attack the scientific method, but to use it to combat racism's scientific pretensions. Three strategies emerged: 1) accept the racial stereotypes, but attribute them to environment rather than heredity; 2) reinterpret the stereotypes as positive; 3) deny the empirical basis of the stereotypes and/or their explanations.

STEVE FULLER

See also Anthropometry; Darwinism; Eugenics

Radioactivity

Badash, Lawrence, *Radioactivity in America: Growth and Decay of a Science*, Baltimore: Johns Hopkins University Press, 1979

Chalmers, Thomas W., *A Short History of Radioactivity*, London, 1951

Jenkins, E.N., *Radioactivity: A Science in Its Historical and Social Context*, London: Taylor and Francis, 1979; 2nd edition, London: Wykeham, 1979

Kauffman, George B. (ed.), *Frederick Soddy (1877–1956): Early Pioneer in Radiochemistry*, Dordrecht: Reidel, 1986

Keller, Cornelius, *Die Geschichte der Radioaktivität, unter besonderer Berücksichtigung der Transurane*, Stuttgart: Wissenschaftliche Verlagsgesellschaft, 1982

Malley, Marjorie, "The Discovery of Atomic Transmutation: Scientific Styles and Philosophies in France and Britain", in *History of Physics: Selected Reprints*, edited by Stephen G. Brush, College Park, Maryland: American Association of Physics Teachers, 1988, 184–95

Minder, Walter, *Geschichte der Radioaktivität*, Berlin: Springer, 1981

Mladjenović, Milorad, *The History of Early Nuclear Physics (1896–1931)*, Singapore, and River Edge, New Jersey: World Scientific, 1992

Pais, Abraham, *Inward Bound: Of Matter and Forces in the Physical World*, Oxford: Clarendon Press, and New York: Oxford University Press, 1986

Phillips, Melba Newell (ed.), *Physics History from AAPT Journals*, New York, American Association of Physics Teachers, 1985

Romer, Alfred, *Radiochemistry and the Discovery of Isotopes*, New York: Dover, 1970

Starosel'skaya-Nikitina, O.A., *Istoriya radioaktivnosti i voxniknoveniya yadernoy fiziki* [History of Radioactivity and the Beginnings of Nuclear Physics], Moscow: Izdatelstvo Akedemi Nauk SSSR, 1963

Trenn, Thaddeus J., *The Self-Splitting Atom: The History of the Rutherford–Soddy Collaboration*, London: Taylor and Francis, 1977

The brief works by Chalmers, Jenkins, Keller, Minder, and Mladjenovic on radioactivity were all written to elucidate ideas and practices in modern science. While Chalmers addresses engineers, Mladjenovic writes for physicists. Keller focuses on nuclear chemistry, Minder on physics, and Jenkins on the entire field, at a level accessible to the educated lay person. Since the model for these works is the science textbook, relevant secondary literature is rarely cited.

Of these five books, MLADJENOVIC's is the broadest in scope and the most historical in its orientation. Mladjenovic considers the development of key ideas, experiments, and techniques in radioactivity, although, unfortunately, his text suffers from an awkward and sometimes ungrammatical translation. CHALMERS's book, on radioactivity to c.1907, is a reprint of a series of expository journal articles in the style of Rutherford's textbooks. Neither notes nor a bibliography are included. Perhaps unique are his two interesting chapters on the histories of uranium and thorium. JENKINS intends his book to be socially and morally relevant, and to this end includes historical material of varying reliability. KELLER's focus is the discovery of transuranic elements, for which he supplies detailed information. His well-illustrated book also includes a brief summary of some of the early work on radioactivity. MINDER includes discussions of the prehistory of elementary concepts in physics, radiation shielding, and the uses of radioactivity. However, this is a textbook that makes little allowance for the historical development of research into radioactivity. Minder minimizes Rutherford's contributions while highlighting Becquerel's work, an unusual approach for a modern writer.

The physicist PAIS writes about radioactivity against the backdrop of 20th-century physics, starting from the discovery of X-rays and concluding with the discovery of W- and Z-bosons, taking the reader on an odyssey of progress to modern times. Nevertheless, this presentist approach does not lead Pais to sketch a simplistic linear history; his interest in the byways and particulars of the journey, his ability to delineate and connect important themes, his erudition, and his literary skill have produced an engaging, informative and intellectual history that is enjoyable to read. For the most part, the book's chapters can stand alone, which is an advantage for the reader who wishes to sample only the chapters relating to radioactivity. Pais has based his book on scientific publications, with some use of secondary sources.

STAROSEL'SKAYA-NIKITINA is a comprehensive study of the genesis and development of the main scientific ideas associated with radioactivity, based on both primary and selected secondary sources. The author's attempts to denote Russian precursors for certain ideas do not detract from the main narrative.

ROMER has prefaced a collection of reprints and translations of key papers concerning radiochemistry with an extended, detailed, and insightful essay on the history of radioactivity, from its discovery in 1896 to the recognition and recovery of isotopes in 1913. Based on the scientific literature, this accessible synthesis of the relevant scientific developments serves as a good introduction as well as a starting point for further investigations. The explanatory notes to the papers are also helpful.

Of the authors of histories of radioactivity, BADASH is the most attentive to modern historical questions and methodological canons. Using a wide range of both scientific and popular documents, he outlines the growth of radioactivity in America and its eventual decline. Badash demonstrates that radioactivity as a science disappeared in the 1930s, after radiochemistry had completed its work and radiophysics had transformed itself into nuclear physics. Since America was something of a scientific backwater during the first part of the 20th century, Badash includes extensive, illuminating discussions and analyses of European developments in his well written, engaging account. The disjunction between this book's stated focus and the European locale of the main action in radioactivity creates a weakness in organization, which is not eliminated by inevitably artificial attempts to provide coherence. However, Badash's attentiveness to the popular press and to applications of radioactivity is unique among the full-length works reviewed here, and the quantity of information assembled within its covers makes this book a useful resource.

TRENN has written a definitive work on the internal history of the disintegration theory of radioactivity. Intended as a case study of a scientific collaboration, this book shows that the strengths of both Soddy and Rutherford were essential to their joint work. Trenn uses published papers, laboratory notebooks, and secondary sources to take the reader through the thought-processes of Rutherford and Soddy as they worked through the various stages of their research. He sees as pivotal to the successful theory a change in view that made ray emission simultaneous with, rather than subsequent to, atomic change. However, Trenn may have underestimated the influence of current speculations about transmutation upon Rutherford and Soddy.

By comparing Rutherford's and Soddy's collaborative work to the parallel researches of Pierre Curie and André Debierne in France, MALLEY shows that the differing philosophies and styles of science practised by these two teams affected the outcome of their researches.

Other topics in the history of radioactivity are treated in the collections of individual papers edited by Kauffman and Phillips. KAUFFMAN has compiled a selection of essays on the life and work of the radiochemist, Frederick Soddy. These include articles on isotopes and isomers (N. Feather), the classification of the radioelements (J.W. van Spronsen), the atomic weight of lead of radioactive origin (G.B. Kauffman), radiochemistry (L. Badash), teaching (A.D. Cruickshank), the reception of Soddy's work in Russia and Japan (A. Krivomazov; M. Tanaka and K. Yamasaki), and Soddy's later work in economics (T.J. Trenn, H.E. Daley). S.B. Sinclair ("Radioactivity and Its Nineteenth-Century Background", p. 43–53) identifies three themes from 19th-century science (chemical, physical, and a combined area) that converge in radioactivity and connect to subsequent themes. Michael I. Freeman ("The Practical Significance of Radioactive Matter", pp. 171–76) points to Soddy's interest in the commercial availability and uses of radioactive substances, a subject generally slighted in the literature.

PHILLIPS's collection includes a paper in which Lawrence Badash documents the initial reactions to radioactivity and shows the changes produced by Marie Curie's entry into the field. In another article, Marjorie Malley analyzes the simultaneous discovery of the beta particle and the discovery's significance for the development of physics.

MARJORIE MALLEY

See also Curie; Nuclear Physics; Rutherford

Radiology

Brecher, Ruth and Edward Brecher, *The Rays: A History of Radiology in the United States and Canada*, Baltimore: Williams and Wilkins, 1969

Brown, Percy, *American Martyrs to Science Through the Roentgen Rays*, Springfield, Illinois: Thomas, 1936

Burrows, Edmund H., *Pioneers and Early Years: A History of British Radiology*, Alderney, Channel Islands: Colophon, 1986

Dibner, Bern, *The New Rays of Professor Roentgen*, Norwalk, Connecticut: Burndy Library, 1963

Eisenberg, Ronald L., *Radiology: An Illustrated History*, St Louis, Missouri: Mosby Year Book, 1992

Grigg, E.R.N., *The Trail of the Invisible Light: From X-Strahlen to Radio(bio)logy*, Springfield, Illinois: Thomas, 1965

Kaye, G.W.C., *X-Rays, An Introduction to the Study of Röntgen Rays*, London and New York: Longmans Green, 1914; 4th edition, 1923

Kevles, Bettyann Holtzmann, *Naked to the Bone: Medical Imaging in the Twentieth Century*, New Brunswick, New Jersey: Rutgers University Press, 1997

Mould, Richard F., *A History of X-Rays and Radium*, Sutton: IPC Buildings and Contract Journals, 1980

Mould, Richard F., *A Century of X-Rays and Radioactivity in Medicine: With Emphasis on Photographic Records of the Early Years*, Bristol, Philadelphia: Institute of Physics, 1993

Webb, Steve, *From the Watching of Shadows: The Origins of Radiological Tomography*, Bristol and New York: Adam Hilger, 1990

The material on radiology can be divided along chronological or thematic lines, and for the case of this review, the listed books have been divided into four types: national histories, general histories, clinical books, and selected biographies.

There are several histories of radiology in specific countries, and both Burrows and Mould (1993) focus on the history of British radiology. MOULD (1993) covers more than a century of developments, to the era of computerized tomography and diagnostic radiology of the 1990s. A photographic record with supporting text (rather than text with some pictures), it shows many different applications and elements of X-rays, from animal and dental radiographs, to photographs of early equipment, paintings, and museum artefacts. BURROWS covers the period from 1895 to c.1930, and gives much information on individual British radiologists, on the history of the most important radiological institutes, and on the radiological societies and their journals. There is also much information on instrument makers. The book's strength lies in its material on early X-ray departments in London and beyond, and on the pioneers, such as Britain's first woman radiologist, Florence Constance Stoney of the Royal Free Hospital. Brief biographies are also included.

The focus of the works by Brecher & Brecher and Brown is the history of radiology in North America. BRECHER & BRECHER concentrate on radiological ideas rather than specific individuals or institutions, and the emphasis is more technical than clinical. Hence, they look at the "Gas-Tube Gang", the dissemination of information via radiological organizations and publications, the rise of supervoltage and radioisotopes, and safety measures.

BROWN chronicles the work of 28 Americans who died as a consequence of their work in radiology. Brown, a historian, physician, and former president of the American Röntgen Ray Society, himself died from work with radiation. The text gives a personal side to the issue of safety and the relative lack of precautions that were taken in an era when the excitement of discovery overrode pain, amputations, and even death. For example, Brown notes in his biography of Stephen Clifton Glidden, a young surgeon who first lost an arm and then died, aged 47, from pulmonary metastasis, that Professor Novy of the University of Michigan met a friend of Glidden's on the day the surgeon died: "I hear that Steve Glidden is dead", remarked the professor, "and that you are preparing to do X-ray work. Why not go into something safe and sane, like aviation or the submarine service?"

The most prolific type of book on radiology, excluding clinical texts, is the general history, and most have been written since 1960. DIBNER's brief book is a basic history of the Röntgen ray, which ties together historical material, including pictures and excerpts from the popular press (this includes the English translation of Röntgen's announcement of his discovery in *The Electrician* of London). Although Dibner's history is not rigidly country-specific, there is a considerable amount of space devoted to the development of X-rays in the United States. MOULD (1980) is also relatively brief and easy-to-read, and highlights X-rays in the period press, including advertisements for radiological apparatus and supplies.

Grigg and Eisenberg have written much lengthier tomes; both are physicians and both use a thematic structure rather than a chronological, episodic framework. GRIGG has undertaken to describe, in almost 1,000 pages, the world history of the X-ray; this is a fine starting point for any research, particularly given its extensive annotated bibliography, and its wealth of material on American radiology. EISENBERG has also written a profusely illustrated history. After a general overview of "the early days", he surveys the technology of radiology, the development of clinical radiology, the emergence of imaging modalities (such as tomography and nuclear medicine), therapeutic applications, and the non-medical aspects of radiology. Eisenberg's book is, therefore, more modern in much of its content than Grigg's, which was published 27 years earlier.

WEBB is a medical physicist and, accordingly, his history of radiological tomography focuses on the development of imaging techniques. The work begins in the 1890s and describes the early techniques of stereoscopy and imaging that tried to go beyond straightforward X-ray photography. There is much emphasis on patents and the history of ideas. It is well illustrated, includes many informative tables, a helpful glossary, and an extensive bibliography.

KEVLES is part of the Sloan Technology Series and its richly illustrated text is divided into two periods: the first examines the discovery of the X-ray and its impact on the world to the mid-20th century; the second deals with the "sister technologies" that flourished after World War II – computerized tomography, magnetic resonance imaging, positron emission tomography, ultrasound and mammography – in tandem with, and dependent upon, the rise of television and computer technologies. This book goes well beyond the effect of successive imaging innovations upon science, as Kevles sets her chronicle within the context of the effect of each individual technology on 20th-century art, legal practice, and notions of privacy. The final chapter is reserved for a discussion of the concept of the "transparent body", as shown in film, art, and popular culture. Kevles includes a timeline (1873–1995) of major events in the history of radiology set against landmarks in history, science, law, and the arts, and her bibliography is divided into works on "History, Culture, and Society", "Law and Policy", "Fiction", "Medicine, Science, and Technology", and a list of almost 50 individuals whom she interviewed.

MARIANNE P. FEDUNKIW

See also Medical Instruments; Röntgen

Raman, Chandrasekhara Venkata

1888–1970

Indian physicist

Keswani, G.H., *Raman and His Effect*, New Delhi: National Book Trust, 1980

Krishnan, K.S., *Raman Effect: Discovery and After*, New Delhi: National Physical Laboratory, 1978

Mehra, Jagdish, entry on Raman in *Dictionary of Scientific Biography*, edited by Charles Couston Gillispie, vol. 11, New York: Scribner, 1975

Ramaseshan, S., *Scientific Papers of C.V. Raman*, 6 vols, Bangalore: Indian Academy of Sciences, 1988

Souder, Lawrence, "C.V. Raman", in *Notable Twentieth-Century Scientists*, edited by Emily J. McMurray, 4 vols, Detroit: Gale Research, 1995

Venkataraman, G., *Journey into Light: Life and Science of C.V. Raman*, Bangalore: Indian Academy of Sciences, 1988

Most extended accounts of Raman's life come from Indian presses. More widely available are two précis by Mehra and Souder. MEHRA writes a thoroughly detailed essay on Raman, tracing the technical history behind the Raman Effect and his studies in optics and acoustics, and pointing to some of the influences on his scientific thinking. SOUDER's précis is wholly non-technical, but it is rich in anecdotes illustrative of Raman's personality and scientific method.

Perhaps the most complete account of Raman's life is by VENKATARAMAN. Truly a scientific biography, this offers a technical account of Raman's work, at the level of *Scientific American*. However, a certain chauvinism is apparent in his account, as he uses the story of Raman's life to champion India's emergence within modern science. He appears particularly defensive when he retells the dispute over the primacy of the discovery of the Raman Effect, and the controversy between Max Born and Raman, when a scientific quarrel soured a collegial friendship. Nevertheless, this book is a comprehensive source of information about Raman's life and works, generously supplemented with both biographical and scientific illustrations, and fully indexed by name and subject.

RAMASESHAN introduces his edited volumes with interesting and varied commentaries on Raman's research papers and monographs: in volume 1, Ramaseshan suggests that Raman's work on the scattering of light was an attempt to correct Rayleigh's explanation of the blue appearance of the sea; in volume 2, on acoustics, he traces the influences of Helmholtz and Rayleigh on Raman's experiments with whispering galleries and Indian drums; the introduction to volume 3, on optics, acknowledges Raman's debt to Huyghens and Fresnel; volume 4 collects papers from a variety of topics, including a discussion of Raman's fascination for the phenomenological – in particular, the colors of minerals, the plumage of birds, and the brilliance of diamonds; in volume 5, on crystal dynamics, Ramaseshan offers some candid observations concerning Raman's personality – his stubbornness in the face of criticism, his dispute with the crystallographer Lonsdale, and his untoward criticism of Born. In the final volume, considering Raman's last decade, Ramaseshan summarizes his work on vision, and describes his struggle against depression.

Raman's compatriots have written most of his biographies, so their loyalty and admiration is understandable. KESWANI is no exception. He, like Venkataraman, uses Raman's story to promote India as an equal among modern, scientifically competent nations. Keswani, however, does not flinch from some of the unflattering details concerning the many controversies involving Raman, including the Born–Raman spat, the tension between Raman and Nehru over state funding of science, and the charge that Raman and K.S. Krishnan should have been named co-discoverers of the Raman Effect.

In his history of the Raman Effect, KRISHNAN also presents evidence suggesting that the author should have shared more of the credit for the discovery. According to this account, Krishnan was involved in all aspects of the work that led to the discovery: the brute laboratory work, the observations, the interpretations, the theorizing, and the publishing of the results. Krishnan also takes particular pains to document the primacy of the Indian discovery of the Raman Effect over the Russian and German efforts at that time. His account becomes more technical when he turns to the studies and applications that followed the discovery of the Raman Effect. Nevertheless, a lay reader will find of interest the frequent quotations from eminent scientists of the time, and the numerous extracts from the diaries of K.S. Krishnan.

LAWRENCE SOUDER

See also India: general works; Optics; Spectroscopy

Ramón y Cajal, Santiago 1852–1934

Spanish physician and histologist

ARBOR, *Número monográfico dedicado a la figura y la obra de Cajal*, 1983

Archivos de Neurobiología, *Número dedicado a la memoria de Cajal: Biografías y juicios de personalidades científicas españolas y extranjeras*, 1934

Cannon, Dorothy F., *Explorer of the Human Brain: The Life of Santiago Ramón y Cajal (1852–1934)*, New York: Schuman, 1949

Castro, Fernando de, *Cajal y la escuela neurológica española*, Madrid: Universidad Complutense, 1981

Durán Muñoz, García and Francisco Alonso Buron, *Cajal: Vida y obra*, Barcelona: Editorial Científico-Médica, 1983

Homenaje a Cajal: *Recordación de Cajal en el primer centenario de su nacimiento*, Mexico City, 1952

Rodríguez, Enriqueta Lewy, *Santiago Ramón y Cajal: el hombre, el sabio y el pensador*, Madrid: Consejo Superior de Investigaciones Científicas, 1987

The work of the famous Spanish neurohistologist has resulted in numerous studies and references to his life and writings, many of which Santiago Ramón y Cajal himself reflected in several memoirs published before his death, such as *El mundo visto a los ochenta años* (1934), *Charlas de café* (1932), and *Recuerdos de mi vida* (1923). Since his death in 1934, scientists, neurologists, disciples, and historians of medicine or science have praised his achievements and personality in numerous publications.

Shortly after his death, the journal *ARCHIVOS DE NEUROBIOLOGIA* devoted an issue to highlight the scientific importance of Cajal. This issue comprises first-hand information and personal testimonies and panegyrics by acquaintances or former disciples.

In Spain, the public image of Cajal epitomises the wise researcher – a figure regarded as a kind of archetype to be emulated by all those wishing to undertake scientific research. This exemplary image also had a particular impact among Spanish scientists exiled after the downfall of the Republican government at the end of the Spanish Civil War. Cajal's name was invoked in all cultural societies, journals, and scientific associations in exile and, in 1952, Spanish refugees in Mexico organized a homage, *HOMENAJE A CAJAL*, on the occasion of the centenary of his birth, in which some of his disciples and associates in Mexico participated. Then, in March 1983, the journal *ARBOR* devoted an issue to him, which included not only testimonies of those who, as Cajal's disciples, belong to the so-called "Spanish neurological school", but also contributions on his scientific activity by medical historians.

From a biographical perspective, several historical studies have tackled Cajal's science. The earliest is CANNON, which compiles abundant material on his private and family life and his scientific career. The two volumes by DURÁN MUÑOZ & ALONSO BURON include an interesting preface by P. Lain Entralgo and an epilogue by Severo Ochoa; the first volume reconstructs Cajal's biography, from childhood to the years of scientific prominence, while the second analyzes his intellectual career, especially his religious attitudes and beliefs and his

pedagogical concerns. Finally, this work includes a selection of unpublished writings and social commentaries, letters, poems, and documents which afford a broad view of Cajal's human and scientific personality.

RODRÍGUEZ, in a more succinct and up-to-date approach, analyzes Cajal's life, his academic and institutional activity, and his social and philosophical thought, and includes a useful up-to-date bibliography. CASTRO examines Cajal's scientific production against the background of the so-called "Spanish Neurological School". Although the book ignores some of his direct disciples (for example, those who conducted their scientific activity abroad, a corollary of the Republican scientific exile), it none the less provides an accurate review of the work carried out by Nicolas Achucarro, Pio del Rio-Hortega, J. Francisco Tello, and Fernando de Castro.

JOSEP LLUÍS BARONA

See also Neurosciences; Spain

Rationality

Barry, Brian and Russell Hardin (eds), *Rational Man and Irrational Society? An Introduction and Source Book*, Beverley Hills, California: Sage, 1982

Bellman, Beryl Larry, *Village of Curers and Assassins: On the Production of Fala Kpelle Cosmological Categories*, The Hague: Mouton, 1975

Benn, S.I. and G.W. Mortimore (eds), *Rationality and the Social Sciences: Contributions to the Philosophy and Methodology of the Social Sciences*, London: Routledge and Kegan Paul, 1976

Button, Graham (ed.), *Ethnomethodology and the Human Sciences*, Cambridge and New York: Cambridge University Press, 1991

Cazeneuve, Jean, *Lucien Lévy-Bruhl*, translated from the French by Peter Riviere, Oxford: Blackwell, and New York: Harper and Row, 1972 (original edition, 1963)

Coleman, James S., *The Mathematics of Collective Action*, London: Heinemann, and Chicago: Aldine, 1973

Coleman, James S., *Individual Interests and Collective Action*, Cambridge and New York: Cambridge University Press, 1986

Coleman, James S. and Thomas J. Fararo (eds), *Rational Choice Theory: Advocacy and Critique*, Beverly Hills, California: Sage, 1992

Elster, Jon, *The Cement of Society: A Study of Social Order*, Cambridge and New York: Cambridge University Press, 1989

Elster, Jon, *Nuts and Bolts for the Social Sciences*, Cambridge and New York: Cambridge University Press, 1989

Elster, Jon, *Solomonic Judgements: Studies in the Limitations of Rationality*, Cambridge and New York: Cambridge University Press, 1989

Evans-Pritchard, E.E., *Witchcraft, Oracles and Magic among the Azande*, Oxford: Clarendon Press, 1937

Evans-Pritchard, E.E., *The Nuer: A Description of the Modes of Livelihood and Political Institutions of a Nilotic People*, Oxford: Clarendon Press, 1940

Garfinkel, Harold, *Studies in Ethnomethodology*, Englewood Cliffs, New Jersey: Prentice-Hall, 1967; Cambridge: Polity Press, 1984

Garfinkel, Harold (ed.), *Ethnomethodological Studies of Work*, London and New York: Routledge and Kegan Paul, 1986

Hollis, Martin, *The Cunning of Reason*, Cambridge and New York: Cambridge University Press, 1987

Hollis, Martin and Steven Lukes (eds), *Rationality and Relativism*, Oxford: Blackwell, and Cambridge, Massachusetts: MIT Press, 1982

Lévi-Strauss, Claude, *The Savage Mind*, translated from the French, Chicago: University of Chicago Press, and London: Weidenfeld and Nicolson, 1966 (original edition, 1962)

Lévy-Bruhl, Lucien, *How Natives Think*, translated from the French by Lilian A. Clare, New York: Knopf, 1925; London: Allen and Unwin, 1926; with a new introduction, Princeton, New Jersey: Princeton University Press, 1985 (original edition, 1910)

Livingston, Eric, *An Ethnomethodological Investigation of the Foundations of Mathematics*, London: Routledge and Kegan Paul, 1986

Lukes, Steven, *Essays in Social Theory*, London: Macmillan, and New York: Columbia University Press, 1977

Lynch, Michael, *Art and Artifact in Laboratory Science: A Study of Shop Work and Shop Talk in a Research Laboratory*, London and Boston: Routledge and Kegan Paul, 1985

Sudnow, David, *Ways of the Hand: The Organization of Improvised Contact*, London: Routledge and Kegan Paul, and Cambridge, Massachusetts: Harvard University Press, 1978

Turner, Roy (ed.), *Ethnomethodology: Selected Readings*, Harmondsworth: Penguin, 1974

Wilson, Bryan R. (ed.), *Rationality*, Oxford: Blackwell, and Evanston, Illinois: Harper and Row, 1970

Within philosophy and the social sciences, there are a range of approaches to the study of the bases of rational behaviour and action. Broadly, the spectrum encompasses forms of calculative practical and custom-based reasoning. The literature can be divided into the study of these overlapping spheres of reasoning and rationality, which range from formalistic models to variants of the interpretation of culture.

What has become known as theories of rational choice – calculative reasoning – are frequently a formal orientation within social theory, which has its epistemological roots in the 17th and 18th-century rationalist philosophers, including Descartes, Spinoza, and Leibniz, and the classical utilitarian economics of Adam Smith and others. The conception of "economic rational man" is that of human beings in the systematic pursuit of their own interest.

COLEMAN (1973) provides an example of the abstract mathematical modelling of rational action, reducing it to formal choices. The formal mathematical modelling of social action is also evident in COLEMAN (1986), which explores rational action in terms of its relation to individual interest and collective political behaviours. Similar themes are pursued in BARRY & HARDIN, which is notable for also reprinting examples of classical works from within this tradition.

Elster sets out a view of rational action that focuses on the extent to which human actions privilege a normative dimension. ELSTER (1989, *Nuts and Bolts for the Social Sciences*) is designed to introduce a general audience to rational choice theory. ELSTER (1989, *The Cement of Society*) serves as a study of the relationship between norms and irrational action. ELSTER (1989, *Solomonic Judgements*) explores aspects of rational choice within the context of chance and probability.

Despite its impressive formal architecture, there is plainly less than equanimity among the proponents of rational choice theory. COLEMAN & FARARO provide an account of the strengths and weaknesses of rational choice theory, while HOLLIS offers a critique, indicating the limitations of the applicability of its models, and its links to a conception of norms as comprising types of prescriptive rules for behaviour.

At the level of practical reasoning, GARFINKEL (1967) established the phenomenologically-informed ethnomethodology around the study of members' methods for producing social organisation, which led to investigations of the internal rationality exhibited by the behaviours of cultural members. In philosophy, following Aristotle's distinction, practical reasoning concerns reasoning that has direct consequences for social activities, and is contrasted with theoretical reasoning. Garfinkel's classical ethnomethodological studies include the examination of practical reasoning in a range of everyday situations, and also formal organisational contexts – such as jurors deciding guilt or innocence, or the construction of psychiatric clinical records.

Examples of other ethnomethodological researches involve the study of the practical reasoning involved in other empirical areas, including science (LYNCH), jazz piano playing (SUDNOW), mathematics (LIVINGSTON), alchemy (Eglin, in GARFINKEL, 1986), Kpelle medicine (BELLMAN), and Lue ethnicity (Moreman, in TURNER). Sharrock and Anderson, in BUTTON, furnish an account of the epistemological foundations of ethnomethodology, and explore the notion of the social actor and social actions.

The attempt to understand and interpret the culturally-informed custom-based reasoning of members of other cultures has become known as the rationality debate. The origins of this debate can be traced to the works of Lévy-Bruhl; informed by the scholarship of the turn of the 20th century – including evolutionary thought, and aspects of Rousseau, Durkheim, and Mauss – LÉVY-BRUHL fashioned an interest in the primitive mentality while addressing such fundamental issues as "how natives think". CAZENEUVE provides an outline of Lévy-Bruhl's scholarship in these areas. The central issues were whether such a thing exists as a primitive mentality; whether the thought processes of peoples in the exotic, "simple" societies around the world; were, in any real respect, different from those of the peoples from the "developed" world, and whether these "primitive" peoples engaged in any form, of what has been termed, pre-logical thought. These types of problems came to inform the research of field-working anthropologists, notable among whom was Evans-Pritchard. He consciously employed these Lévy-Bruhlian problematics as a starting point for his now classic study, EVANS-PRITCHARD (1937); this ethnographic account of the Azande, and his later account of

Nuer culture (EVANS-PRITCHARD, 1940), presents these peoples as plainly logical, orderly, and prudential. While on the surface the behaviour of the Azande and Nuer people exhibit certain exotic (but superficial) institutional and custom-based differences, their essential humanity, and mental and rational capabilities, are treated as beyond reasonable doubt; they are merely the behavioural practices of other cultures. In short, Evans-Pritchard provided the peoples he studied with a believable rationality, which is every bit as human and sophisticated as those routinely attributed to the culture he represented. He thus fashioned a shared humanity in order to account for the often exotic behaviours found in other cultures. In this respect, Evans-Pritchard established squarely the issue of the relativism of cultural behaviour and arrangements as a central tenet of modern social anthropology, much as Boas had established it for cultural anthropology. Later LÉVI-STRAUSS, from a non-fieldwork base, constructed the argument that all humanity shares structural mental processes.

Evans-Pritchard's approach to the study of other cultures thus became the conventional anthropological wisdom, and became influential in other disciplines, such as philosophy and theology. A number of papers in WILSON elaborate on this issue: Horton offers a comparison of African traditional thought and Western science, focusing on a range of epistemological issues; Winch poses the question of how one can understand a primitive society; and Macintyre parodies an earlier work of Winch by exploring "the idea of a social science", while dissenting from Winch's views on the matter. Meanwhile, LUKES argues that sociologists and anthropologists employing the principles of relativism frequently treat empirically-discovered exotic practices which are *prima facie* irrational in a charitable manner, ascribing to them a rationality.

In HOLLIS & LUKES, Sperber, Gellner, and Lukes explore the panorama of relativism, while Hacking, Taylor, and Elster consider the potential of rationality as an epistemology. In BENN & MORTIMORE, the issue of rationality within a belief system is considered from a perspective that serves as an interface with rational choice theory.

MIKE BALL

See also Anthropology

Rational Mechanics

Alder, Ken, *Engineering the Revolution: Arms and Enlightenment in France, 1763–1815*, Princeton, New Jersey: Princeton University Press, 1997

Boss, Valentin, *Newton and Russia: The Early Influence, 1698–1796*, Cambridge, Massachusetts: Harvard University Press, 1972

Brian, Eric, *La Mesure de l'Etat: administrateurs et géomètres au XVIIIe siècle*, Paris: Michel, 1994

Gillispie, Charles, Robert Fox and Ivor Grattan-Guinness, entry on Pierre Laplace in *Dictionary of Scientific Biography*, edited by Charles Coulston Gillispie, vol. 15, supplement 1, New York: Scribner, 1976

Greenberg, John, *The Problem of the Earth's Shape from Newton to Clairaut: The Rise of Mathematical Science in Eighteenth-Century Paris and the Fall of "Normal"*

Science, Cambridge and New York: Cambridge University Press, 1995

Hankins, Thomas L., *Jean D'Alembert: Science and the Enlightenment*, Oxford: Clarendon Press, 1970

Jenni, Marcel (editor), *Leonhard Euler, 1707–1783: Beiträge zu Leben und Werk: Gedenkband des Kantons Basel-Stadt*, Basel: Birkhäuser, 1983

Lagrange, J.L., *Œuvres*, edited by J.-A. Serret, 14 vols, Paris: Gauthier-Villars, 1867–92

Laplace, Pierre Simon, marquis de, *Œuvres complètes*, 14 vols, Paris: Gauthier-Villars, 1878–1912

McClellan, James E. III, *Science Reorganized: Scientific Societies in the Eighteenth Century*, New York: Columbia University Press, 1985

Mach, Ernst, *The Science of Mechanics: A Critical and Historical Exposition of Its* Principles, translated from the German by Thomas J. McCormack, Chicago: Open Court, 1891, London: Watts, 1893; 6th edition (based on 9th German edition), La Salle, Illinois: Open Court, 1960 (original edition, 1883)

Truesdell, C., *Essays in the History of Mechanics*, New York: Springer, 1968

Woolf, Harry, *The Transits of Venus: A Study of Eighteenth-Century Science*, Princeton, New Jersey: Princeton University Press, 1959

The rational mechanics of the 18th century is not a topic that has been covered in great detail in the history of science. John Greenberg argues that Thomas Kuhn's influence may have something to do with this. In Kuhn's account, all sciences tread the path of quantification and mathematization. In the first scientific revolution astronomy and mechanics matured, and around 1800 a number of sciences followed suit, such as natural history, electricity, magnetism, and pneumatics. For this reason, there was no emphasis on the history of the already mathematized sciences. This entry includes the biographical material on the most prominent individuals who worked on rational mechanics: D'Alembert, Euler, Lagrange, and Laplace.

The monographs dealing with the topic of rational mechanics will be discussed first. The historiographical approach varies from institutional history and detailed descriptions of the technical problems of the period in the genre of the history of ideas to the study of the role of mathematical analysis in political institutions and engineering practice. The literature on the individuals will be presented afterwards.

McCLELLAN provides the main social context for rational mechanics. He gives an overview of academies of science throughout Europe in the 18th century. McClellan sees the age of academies as straddling two organizational revolutions in the history of science: the rejection of the university-based science of the 17th century and the professionalization and specialization of science in the 19th century. McClellan shows that the academies of the 18th century gave definition to the social role of the man of science and that the hierarchical and professional structure of the academies (in comparison with earlier times) allowed for efficient and informed judgment of work in mathematics, rational mechanics, and astronomy: for instance through prize contests.

TRUESDELL is a collection of articles, some of which deal with rational mechanics. Chapter 2, in particular, outlines the whole program of rational mechanics pursued between Newton and Lagrange to lay a formal basis for the science of motion in general so that that science can be shown to be deductive in form. Truesdell describes the culmination of rational mechanics in Lagrange's search for general formulae, the simple development of which gives the equations necessary for the solution of any problem: it is only with Lagrange that we get Newton's Laws.

GREENBERG argues that the evolution of Parisian mechanics was not a replacement of a Cartesian paradigm by a Newtonian one, as might be expected from Kuhn (hence the reference to "normal science" in the title). Rather, a complex process involving a great many areas of research took place. For instance, Greenberg describes in detail the development of the calculus. This sophisticated tool of mathematical analysis was mainly refined by fellows of German and French academies in order to deal with such problems as the shape of the earth. The main individuals discussed are Pierre Bouguer, Alexis-Claude Clairault, Alexis Fontaine des Bertins, and Maupertuis, as well as Euler.

WOOLF covers one of the most important collaborative efforts to test and apply Newtonian theory: that of the transits of Venus. The observations of these transits correspond to today's big science: Woolf lists 150 observations of the 1769 transit, and details the extensive collaboration and exchange of data. By measuring from distant points on the earth's surface the time that Venus appeared to spend crossing the surface of the sun, observers sought to establish the solar parallax and the sun's mean distance from the earth. Woolf focuses on the high science and ignores the fact that much of the interest in these events resulted from the opportunity to establish exact coordinates of the points of observation on earth, which was useful for such mundane matters as cadastral (property) mapping.

MACH's history of mechanics was the first of a trilogy of textbooks on mechanics, heat, and optics. It is not a history in a conventional sense, but an attempt to teach mechanics in a comprehensible way. Mach aimed to eliminate metaphysics from physics: in one succinct phrase he stated that we call those concepts metaphysical of which we have forgotten the origin. The book begins with Archimedes and ends with a discussion of the physics of his time (when statistical thermodynamics seemed hard to square with received mechanics), but the emphasis of the book is on the 18th century, and there is much discussion of Euler, D'Alembert, and Lagrange.

BOSS describes the introduction and development of rational mechanics at the St Petersburg Academy. He argues that Newton's impact was much greater than had hitherto been presumed. The book traces reactions to several aspects of Newton's work (mathematics, gravitation, optics), but much of it deals with rational mechanics and with Euler's contribution to it as a professor of the Academy.

ALDER examines French artillery between 1763 and 1815. This is a sophisticated argument about the relationship between theory and practice, economics and culture. Alder argues that there was an engineering science designed by the artillery which linked mixed analytical mathematics with technical drawing, that this allowed the controlled management of, and experimentation on, variable systems, and that this was why and how optimization became central to their way of working.

Alder thus shows exactly how the rational mechanics of the later 18th century fitted so well into the textbook training systems of a range of military-engineering sites.

BRIAN discusses the relationship between mathematical analysis and science and political institutions at end of the Ancien Régime, as personified by Condorcet, secretary of the Academy of Sciences, mathematician-philosopher, and friend and collaborator of Turgot, the reforming minister. Brian discusses statistics, but also astronomy, especially the theory of cometry and the emergence of philosophical probability.

There are very few biographical works on D'Alembert, Euler, Lagrange, and Laplace. However, the works of each of them have been republished in massive collections, some of them complete, such as LAPLACE. Because most of their work spans what now belongs to different disciplines, much of it highly technical, there is also much more literature on specific aspects of each these individuals' activities. The following studies have been chosen because they attempt a general picture, but also because they have excellent bibliographies.

HANKINS is a good intellectual biography of D'Alembert, with a detailed discussion of his mechanics. It also contains a good bibliography. D'Alembert is presented as important because he defined the methods by which mechanics was to be turned into a science.

JENNI's volume is a collection of essays on the various aspects of Euler's work, from his number theoretical writings to his optics and his relations with Lagrange. Several entries relate to his work on mechanics: much of his mathematical work explicitly so, and there are essays on theoretical hydraulics, shipbuilding and navigation, angular momentum, and celestial mechanics. About half of the essays are in German, the other half is in English and French. There is a very useful 40-page bibliography of secondary literature, including much in Russian.

The 14 volumes of Serret's edition of LAGRANGE include a biographical notice of Lagrange, written by Delambre, along with Lagrange's papers and monographs, and much of his correspondence with D'Alembert, Condorcet, Laplace, Euler, and others. There is no full-length biography of Lagrange.

GILLISPIE et al. is a monograph-length entry in a supplement to the Dictionary of Scientific Biography. Laplace's diverse activities are reflected in the structure of the piece, ranging from several fields of mathematics, celestial mechanics, and heat to the French Revolution and Laplace's role in the development of the metric system. There is a bibliography of both primary and secondary sources, which appears to be nearly comprehensive.

SIMON SCHAFFER AND ARNE HESSENBRUCH

Reading Culture and Science

Chartier, Roger, The Order of Books: Readers, Authors, and Libraries in Europe Between the Fourteenth and Eighteenth Centuries, translated from the French by Lydia G. Cochrane, Cambridge: Polity Press, and Stanford, California: Stanford University Press, 1994 (original edition, 1992)

Chartier, Roger and Henri-Jean Martin (eds), *Histoire de l'édition française*, 2nd edition, 4 vols, Paris: Promodis, 1982–86

Darnton, Robert, *The Business of Enlightenment: A Publishing History of the Encyclopédie, 1775–1800*, Cambridge, Massachusetts: Belknap Press of Harvard University Press, 1979

Darnton, Robert, *The Great Cat Massacre, and Other Episodes in French Cultural History*, Harmondsworth: Penguin, and New York: Basic Books, 1984

Eamon, William, *Science and the Secrets of Nature: Books of Secrets in Medieval and Early Modern Culture*, Princeton, New Jersey: Princeton University Press, 1994

Eisenstein, Elizabeth L., *The Printing Press as an Agent of Change: Communications and Cultural Transformations in Early Modern Europe*, 2 vols, Cambridge and New York: Cambridge University Press, 1979; abridged version, as *The Printing Revolution in Early Modern Europe*, 1983

Febvre, Lucien and Henri-Jean Martin, *The Coming of the Book: The Impact of Printing 1450–1800*, translated from the French by David Gerard, London: NLB, 1976; New York: Verso, 1990 (original edition, 1958)

Gingerich, Owen, "Copernicus's *De Revolutionibus*: An Example of Renaissance Scientific Printing", in *Print and Culture in the Renaissance: Essays on the Advent of Printing in Europe*, edited by Gerald P. Tyson and Sylvia S. Wagonheim, Newark: University of Delaware Press, and London: Associated University Presses, 1986, 55–73

Ivins, William M., *Prints and Visual Communication*, Cambridge, Massachusetts: Harvard University Press, 1953

Jardine, Lisa and Anthony Grafton, "'Studied for Action': How Gabriel Harvey Read His Livy", *Past and Present*, 129: 30–78

Latour, Bruno, "Drawing Things Together", in *Representation in Scientific Practice*, edited by Michael Lynch and Steve Woolgar, Cambridge, Massachusetts: MIT Press, 1990

McKenzie, D.F., *Bibliography and the Sociology of Texts*, London: British Library, 1986; 2nd edition, Cambridge and New York: Cambridge University Press, 1999

McLuhan, Marshall, *The Gutenberg Galaxy: The Making of Typographic Man*, London: Routledge and Kegan Paul, and Toronto: University of Toronto Press, 1962

Raven, James, Helen Small and Naomi Tadmor (eds), *The Practice and Representation of Reading in England*, Cambridge and New York: Cambridge University Press, 1996

Rudwick, Martin J.S., *Scenes from the Deep: Early Pictorial Representations of the Prehistoric World*, Chicago: University of Chicago Press, 1992

Secord, James A., "Introduction", to *Vestiges of the Natural History of Creation and Other Evolutionary Writings*, by Robert Chambers, edited by Secord, Chicago: University of Chicago Press, 1994

Sherman, William H., *John Dee: The Politics of Reading and Writing in the English Renaissance*, Amherst: University of Massachusetts Press, 1995

Stafford, Barbara Maria, *Artful Science: Enlightenment Entertainment and the Eclipse of Visual Education*, Cambridge, Massachusetts: MIT Press, 1994

Winkler, M.G. and Albert Van Helden, "Johannes Hevelius and the Visual Language of Astronomy", in *Renaissance and Revolution: Humanists, Scholars, Craftsmen, and Natural Philosophers in Early Modern Europe*, edited by J.V. Field and Frank A.J.L. James, Cambridge and New York: Cambridge University Press, 1993, 97–116

The material objects within which knowledge is contained and by which it is communicated are also everyday resources for historians of science. Their importance is signalled by the fact that the accepted turning-points in the history of science since the Renaissance are virtually all moments of publication. It is perhaps surprising, then, that those same historians have been relatively slow to appreciate that these objects have their own history. Practices governing the manufacture, distribution, and use of scientific texts have changed vastly over the centuries, and it is becoming increasingly clear that the course of these changes needs to be understood by historians of science. The current article thus serves to introduce a field vital to the history of science.

Interest in the cultural history of the book has until recently been greatest in France, where it was originally stimulated by FEBVRE & MARTIN. Febvre's interest in the subject derived from his pioneering work in the historiography of *mentalités*; his original project aimed at explaining the importance of the development of printing for the cultural transformations of the Renaissance, but the resulting book became the foundation of a tradition of *histoire du livre* which continues to thrive to this day. Its greatest testament is CHARTIER & MARTIN's book, which surveys the development and consequences of communication in manuscript and print. Similar grand projects are now under way in several other countries, including both Britain and the United States. They typically aim to explain the changing character of written and printed books through history, and their effects in a variety of cultural fields – including, but not especially, science.

It is possible to identify two major approaches within this historiography. The first is concerned primarily with the appraisal, and often the quantitative measurement, of production and distribution. It may justly be regarded as a descendent of the *Annaliste* predilection for "objectivity". This approach has been particularly effective in characterising the early decades of printing, when a huge quantitative transformation in the availability of books indeed occurred. The second approach, sometimes posited in opposition to this rather dry numerical enterprise, instead emphasises problems of reception. It tries to characterise the different practices of appropriation through which books have been put to use in different times and different settings, thereby tracing how they came to have what we might call "influences". Its attention therefore tends to be directed more at individual works and their differing fortunes. It is perfectly possible to combine both approaches, as in the case of Chartier & Martin.

For the historian of science, the major area of interest discussed by historians of the book has been the period between the invention of printing and that of the steam press – the period, that is, embracing the scientific revolution and the

Enlightenment. A number of conclusions have been posited as to the effects of changing communications on natural knowledge in this period, and a few warrant particular mention.

A major figure in the 1960s was Marshall McLUHAN, who explored the psychological consequences of typography and other media with a gleeful zeal, and attained something of the status of a guru. Others also pursued this interest in psychology, notably Walter J. Ong. McLuhan himself later suffered the fate of the fashionable, however, being widely castigated for premature and inadequately-based theorising. None the less, his work was always suggestive, and it seems that now, with the cultural dominance of electronic media poised to succeed that of print, it is being rediscovered and re-evaluated for its insights into "typographic man".

Elizabeth EISENSTEIN cited McLuhan as influencing her own decision to study the impact of printing in detail in the 1970s. It was Eisenstein who really forced Anglophone historians to recognise the subject, and her *Printing Press as an Agent of Change* remains a central document in the field. Readers have found it both infuriating and inspirational; Bruno LATOUR has rested his notion of "immutable mobiles" substantially on Eisenstein's suggestions.

EISENSTEIN is not a history of printing. Rather, it is a very long polemic, arguing for attention to be paid to the subject by historians of all fields, but especially of religion and science. Eisenstein posits three central effects of printing: multiplication, fixity, and juxtaposition. The press, she observes, permitted the manufacture of thousands of identical copies of texts, and their distribution across Europe and beyond to new and diverse audiences. It also allowed particular readers (the astronomer, Tycho Brahe, is her favourite example) to juxtapose copies of these books on one desk, and thereby to compare them directly. Tycho's successor, Kepler, could thus display the competing systems supported by Tycho, Copernicus, and Ptolemy side by side, and be confident that all three were accurate and credible representations. (This is the aspect singled out by Latour.) Without these factors, Eisenstein argues, the scientific revolution could not have happened: the "fixity" made possible by print enabled scientists to escape from the need always to doubt the reliability of their records, and to begin to build knowledge cumulatively for the future.

Bibliographers and historians of printing have questioned particular aspects of Eisenstein's account, such as its problematic assertion that the products of early presses can be characterised as identical "editions". Medievalists, too, have objected to her caricatured and anachronistic portrait of the book before printing. Historians of science will have their own quibbles, principally that her notion of the scientific revolution is crude and one-dimensional. Nevertheless, there is no denying the extensive influence of Eisenstein's work, and her effective creation of a new subject area. Successors to her interpretation include Latour, as already mentioned, and a number of historians working in the early modern period, notably William EAMON. Owen GINGERICH is also an important figure here; he has attempted a thorough quantitative and qualitative census of such important volumes as Copernicus's *De Revolutionibus*, and has thereby drawn important conclusions concerning distribution, readership, and censorship.

For the Enlightenment, Robert Darnton has been a major influence. DARNTON (1979), his detailed account of the making and distribution of certain editions of the *Encyclopédie*, draws extensively upon printers' archives. It says relatively little about the work's cultural content and reception, but does demonstrate exhaustively the economic and commercial labours upon which the Enlightenment depended. DARNTON (1984) concentrates on the "low-life" of French literary culture in the 18th century. Having excavated the complex culture of printing houses and their occupants (especially in the anthropological account of the "Great Cat Massacre" in Darnton, 1984), and shown that culture mattered for the kinds of public knowledge produced, Darnton's researches have restored to view the collective character of knowledge-making in the Enlightenment.

In the future, it seems likely that studies of the scientific book will advance in the three directions already charted. The first will see scholars use these approaches to investigate not just typography but reproducible images. The pioneering work of IVINS first raised general questions about the cultural consequences of such materials, but it is now being superseded by detailed discussions of the making, circulation, and use of printed images in specific cultural contexts. WINKLER & VAN HELDEN, for example, describe the astronomer Hevelius's strategies for buttressing the credit of his representations of the heavens. These included providing a minutely detailed account of their manufacture, which he claimed to have supervised personally, thus using his own stature to bolster the status of his images. STAFFORD recaptures an extraordinary world of visual virtuosity in 18th-century France, relating it (though in a rather piecemeal fashion) to Enlightenment initiatives in science and public reason, while RUDWICK's fine work analyses the visual creativity displayed in 19th-century pictorial representations of prehistory. At present, studies of typography and images remain rather artificially separate, although scholars like these are showing how they may be re-unified.

Second, the historiography of the book will surely continue the current trajectory of linking the making of inscriptions to their uses. A number of historians are now paying close attention to the practices of reading itself, one of which is CHARTIER, who has developed the "object study" as a means of tracking the different appropriations of a book by its various users. McKENZIE relates technical issues of typography to reception in similar vein. A rather different approach is adopted by JARDINE & GRAFTON, and SHERMAN, who analyse in close detail the annotations made on books by their readers (respectively Gabriel Harvey and John Dee), and use this material to reconstruct the processes through which printed texts have been made into instruments of action. Their work has so far centred on the Renaissance, but its implications deserve to be recognised farther afield. A beginning has been made by RAVEN, SMALL & TADMOR, which combines both approaches in order to suggest a composite history of reading over a longer term. Finally, SECORD has usefully applied this kind of work to the understanding of a major 19th-century scientific publication, Chambers's *Vestiges of the Natural History of Creation*. These initiatives will increasingly come to be seen as central to the emerging historiography of natural knowledge that identifies plausibility, not as an unchanging and intrinsic feature of texts themselves, but as an achievement constituted through the practical application of skills in particular locales. Within this context, scientific authorship, along with all the conventions of credit deployed in written and printed communication, will again become subject to intense historical study.

ADRIAN JOHNS

See also Journals; Popularization; Printing; Representation; Scientific Illustration

Relativity

Darrigol, Olivier, "The Electrodynamic Origins of Relativity Theory", *Historical Studies in the Physical and Biological Sciences*, 26 (1996): 241–312

Earman, John and Glymour Clark, "Relativity and Eclipses: The British Eclipse Expeditions of 1919 and Their Predecessors", *Historical Studies in the Physical Sciences*, 11 (1980): 49–85

Earman, John, Michel Janssen and John D. Norton (eds), *The Attraction of Gravitation: New Studies in the History of General Relativity*, Boston and Basel: Birkhäuser, 1993

Glick, Thomas F. (ed.), *The Comparative Reception of Relativity*, Dordrecht and Boston: Reidel, 1987

Glick, Thomas F., *Einstein in Spain: Relativity and the Recovery of Science*, Princeton, New Jersey: Princeton University Press, 1988

Goldberg, Stanley, *Understanding Relativity: Origin and Impact of a Scientific Revolution*, Boston: Birkhäuser, 1984

Hentschel, Klaus, *Interpretionen und Fehlinterpretationen der speziellen und der allgemeinen Relativitätstheorie durch Zeitgenossen Albert Einsteins*, Basel: Birkhäuser, 1990

Hentschel, Klaus, *Der Einstein-Turm: Erwin F. Freundlich und die Relativitätstheorie; Ansätze zu einer "dichten Beschreibung" von institutionellen, biographischen und theoriengeschichtlichen Aspekten*, Heidelberg: Spektrum, 1992

Holton, Gerald, *Thematic Origins of Scientific Thought: Kepler to Einstein*, Cambridge, Massachusetts: Harvard University Press, 1973; revised edition, 1988

Howard, Don and John Stachel (eds), *Einstein and the History of General Relativity*, Basel: Birkhäuser, 1989

Jungnickel, Christa and Russell McCormmach, *Intellectual Mastery of Nature: Theoretical Physics from Ohm to Einstein*, vol. 2, *The Now Mighty Theoretical Physics, 1870–1920*, Chicago: University of Chicago Press, 1986

McCormmach, Russell, "Einstein, Lorentz, and the Electron Theory", *Historical Studies in the Physical Sciences*, 2 (1970): 41–87

McCormmach, Russell, "H.A. Lorentz and the Electromagnetic View of Nature", *Isis*, 61 (1970): 459–97

Mehra, Jagdish, *Einstein, Hilbert, and the Theory of Gravitation: Historical Origins of General Relativity Theory*, Dordrecht and Boston: Reidel, 1974

Miller, Arthur I., *Albert Einstein's Special Theory of Relativity: Emergence (1905) and Early Interpretation (1905–1911)*, Reading, Massachusetts: Addison-Wesley, 1981

North, J.D., *The Measure of the Universe: A History of Modern Cosmology*, Oxford: Clarendon Press, 1965

Pais, Abraham, *"Subtle is the Lord . . .": The Science and the Life of Albert Einstein*, Oxford and New York: Oxford University Press, 1982

Pyenson, Lewis, *The Young Einstein: The Advent of Relativity*, Bristol and Boston: Adam Hilger, 1985

Stachel, John, "History of Relativity", in *Twentieth Century Physics*, edited by Laurie M. Brown, Abraham Pais and Brian Pippard, Philadelphia, Pennsylvania: Institute of Physics, 1995

Swenson Jr, Loyd S., *The Ethereal Aether: A History of the Michelson–Morley–Miller Aether-Drift Experiments, 1880–1930*, Austin: University of Texas Press, 1972

Vizgin, Vladimir P., *Unified Field Theories in the First Third of the Twentieth Century*, translated from the Russian by Julian B. Barbour, Basel and Boston: Birkhäuser, 1994 (original edition, 1985)

Warwick, A.C., "Cambridge Mathematics and Cavendish Physics: Cunningham, Campbell and Einstein's Relativity 1905–1911: Part 1: The Uses of Theory: Part 2: Comparing Traditions in Cambridge Physics", *Studies in History and Philosophy of Science*, 23 (1992): 625–56; 24 (1993): 1–25

Whittaker, Edmund, *A History of the Theories of Aether and Electricity*, 2 vols, London: Thomas Nelson, 1951–53; New York: Harper, 1960

Will, Clifford M., *Was Einstein Right? Putting General Relativity to the Test*, New York: Basic Books, 1986; Oxford: Oxford University Press, 1990; 2nd edition, New York: Basic Books, 1993

The theories of special and general relativity, foundational for modern physics and extremely significant in the popular notion of science, have attracted much attention from historians and philosophers of science. Studies of the subject have dominated our picture of the history of (theoretical) physics in the early 20th century, and have shaped our understanding of the nature of theoretical work in the sciences. Both theories are strongly associated with the contributions by Albert Einstein of 1905 (formulating the principle of relativity for rectilinear motion of constant velocity) and 1913–15 (generalising relativity to encompass accelerated motions and gravitation). In addition to numerous accounts of the inception of these theories (most often devoted to studies of Einstein's work), many treatments of the context within which relativity was developed and propagated can usefully be characterised as reception studies. One concern has been with understanding the nature of the response (or lack thereof) to relativity among physicists and mathematicians, outside the German-speaking community in which these theories were first developed. Here, Einstein's work has often been taken as unproblematically normative. A second focus has been on understanding the popular response to relativity and to Einstein, following the celebrated experimental confirmation of the general theory in 1919. Recently, historians have begun to question the effects of a primary orientation on Einstein for our appreciation of the work of other physicists, and have also argued that a concern with interpretative issues alone has obscured the role of more routine aspects, such as practical calculational techniques, in the development of theory.

Analysis of the Michelson-Morley ether-drift experiment of 1887 led to the development of the Lorentz-Fitzgerald transformation equations and the hypothesis that matter contracted with motion, the experiment providing one of the most important empirical justifications for special relativity. SWENSON's study provides the most complete account of the experiment, and is intended to redress the simplifications of many accounts that have focused primarily on Einstein and the advent of relativity. Detailing the many versions carried out from 1881 to the 1920s, and the wide variety of responses it engendered from physicists, Swenson argues that the experiment was important for what it suggested, rather than for imposing the abandonment of the ether or a particular interpretation of the Lorentz-Fitzgerald transformation equations.

Within the context of a technical intellectual history of the classical theories or ether and electricity, and also relativity and quantum theory to 1926, an early account by the British mathematical physicist and historian, WHITTAKER, assigned Einstein only a marginal role in the development of special relativity. Instead, Whittaker presented relativity as the result of the incremental development of insight in the work of Lorentz and Poincaré, with its origins in the theory of the ether and electrons. To some extent, the first studies of special relativity by professional historians of science were developed as a reaction against this perspective. Two main endeavours have been prominent: to establish the path taken by Albert Einstein to his 1905 paper, "On the electrodynamics of moving bodies", and to distinguish the character of Einstein's work in this field from those he drew on, or those who also made important contributions to it – such as Föppl, Mach, Lorentz, Poincaré, and Minkowski. HOLTON's essays often challenge physics textbook representations of history, and issues discussed by philosophers of science, such as the senses in which the contraction hypothesis could be described as "ad hoc". Examining the differences between the personal realm of science in the making ("the nascent phase") and the public, institutional aspects of science, several of Holton's studies explore tensions between the two realms. In his work on Einstein and the Michelson-Morley experiment, for example, he argues that the popular view that the experiment was crucial, often advanced for pedagogic reasons, is not supported by a study of the evidence concerning Einstein's own path to relativity, or the different statements Einstein subsequently made on the subject. Holton's study of Einstein's approach to electrodynamics argues persuasively that Einstein drew on Föppl's presentations of Maxwell's equations, as well as the work of Lorentz, Mach, and Poincaré. Holton's studies are framed as inquiries into historiographical issues, rather than as historical narratives.

In a group of papers analysing Lorentz's successive formulations of the electron theory, and the relation of Einstein's research to this program, McCORMMACH argues that physics in the first years of the 20th century was dominated by a turn to electrodynamics in general, and electron theory in particular. Electron theory, in his view, was first responsible for revealing the ways in which mechanical laws and concepts could be superseded, and for the elaboration of a constructive alternative ("electromagnetic") world view. This account sees relativity and quantum theory then emerging as transformations of an already existing concern with the foundations of physics and with building unitary world-views. The objectives of the original electromagnetic view were subsequently transmuted into a broader field-theoretic ideal for all of physics, exemplified in general relativity. In his discussion of Einstein's unpublished work towards a theory of electrons, McCormmach stresses continuities between Einstein's theoretical work and the approaches of his contemporaries.

McCormmach has also been concerned with charting the rise of theoretical physics as a sub-discipline in Germany. JUNGNICKEL & McCORMMACH's book is valuable for its presentation of a discussion of the major intellectual developments of physics, including surveys of special and general relativity, within a number of contexts central to the working life of physicists. One is the context of institutional developments within the university system, which saw the expansion of resources and positions devoted to physics in general, and theoretical physics in particular. Attention is also paid to pedagogy, in discussions on textbooks and lecturing in a number of fields, and to charting the impact of relativity on the research concerns reflected in the publication patterns of the principal German physics journals.

MILLER is the most highly technical and complete account of the emergence of special relativity between 1890 and 1911 (the date at which Max Laue's textbook on relativity appeared, marking the development of a stable interpretation of the theory amongst an élite group of physicists in Germany). The book takes its structure from Einstein's 1905 paper, offering analyses of the state of physical research at the time, the development of Einstein's thinking, and subsequent interpretations and elaborations of the area, for each section of the original publication. It is noteworthy for its discussion of experimental arrangements in the testing of electron theory, which played an important role in early attitudes to relativity. Despite its abundance of detail, like much literature on theoretical physics in this period, Miller's study suffers somewhat from a concentration on interpretational issues at the expense of explication of the routine calculational practices involved in theoretical work – and the importance of these more mundane dimensions of physics for the elaboration and use of a theory such as relativity.

PYENSON presents a range of valuable studies on figures around Einstein, investigating different areas of discourse in order to illuminate the tacit understandings and shared beliefs of the German intellectual milieu. In addition to studies of Einstein's early collaborators and Planck's role as editor of the primary physics journal in Germany, Pyenson has discussed the work of Minkowski and other Göttingen mathematicians. Here, Pyenson integrates technical studies of mathematical and physical theory into an account of disciplinary politics in the German mathematics and physics communities. His study of a Göttingen seminar on electron theory in 1905 examines different approaches to the field at the time that Einstein's work was being developed. However, in common with many other accounts, the study of a context important for relativity is to a large extent shaped by the assumption that Einstein's work is normative. Both the choice of topic and the ways in which it is discussed are subtly determined by a focus on Einstein's work. The unacknowledged implications of such approaches constitute some of the most important limitations of scholarship on relativity. Nevertheless, Pyenson has done more than most to explore a range of perspectives, and begins the task of building adequate social historical approaches to Einstein and relativity.

GOLDBERG's book is directed at a lay audience. Arguing that science is no more certain than any other body of knowledge, but that the processes of peer review and replication through the institutions of science ensure a kind of objectivity, his account of the special theory of relativity is presented as a case study of science in culture. Goldberg suggests that the responses of individual physicists reflect traditional national systems, and relates the nature of the assimilation of relativity in Germany, France, Britain, and America to the structure of their educational systems. Thus, he argues that the German university system, with many centres and a migration of students and professors, saw a rich variety of responses to relativity, ensuring its acceptance or rejection on the merits of the elaboration of its central ideas. In contrast, more hierarchical educational structures in France and Britain promoted a narrow range of responses, dominated by the preconceptions of a few influential approaches. Goldberg's most extended study is on relativity in the scientific community and popular culture in America to 1980, where he sees a form of pragmatism to have dominated research contributions and their presentation in physics textbooks.

WARWICK's study of work on electrodynamics in Britain argues that the nature of British responses to Einstein's special relativity cannot be understood by focusing narrowly on attitudes to the ether. Exploring the research of different mathematicians and physicists in Cambridge, Warwick shows that the most important unit of analysis in reception studies is not the nation, but (sub)disciplinary groups sharing an educational and research background, and argues persuasively that familiarity with specific "theoretical technologies" (mathematical techniques and resources utilised in routine work) shape a physicist's interpretative practices. The paper is exemplary, and is unusual in providing a close analysis of theoretical work in physics that takes seriously the important historiographical and methodological questions facing reception studies.

Detailed studies of the development of general relativity have most commonly been based on a close reading of a series of papers by Einstein from 1907 to 1916, with a discussion of the contemporary work of Abraham, Nordström, Mie, and Hilbert. In PAIS, an account of this kind is presented within the context of a discussion of Einstein's career and other work in physics. Pais's engaging accounts of both relativity theories incorporate reflections on his own working life as a physicist, and recollections of his contact with Einstein. MEHRA approaches the genesis of general relativity with the aim of illuminating the decisive role played by Hilbert in determining the form of the equations and the strict conditions to which they are subject. VIZGIN charts the development of unified geometrized field theories, from their pre-history in the electrodynamic field program and general relativity to the early 1930s. He argues that the distinctive feature of general relativity was its geometrization of a physical interaction, and shows that general relativity formed the basis for Hilbert's and Weyl's development, in 1915 and 1918 respectively, of theories unifying the electromagnetic and gravitational fields. NORTH's work is broader in focus, discussing relativity within a study of astronomical cosmology up to 1950, and considering early relativistic cosmology, the expanding

universe, kinematic relativity, and the steady-state theories of Bondi, Gold, and Hoyle. The scope of the book is extremely broad, with brief descriptive accounts of the contributions of a large number of mathematicians and physicists.

The most closely textured historical analyses of the general theory have also often charted the evolution of specific principles for their philosophical interest concerning concepts of space, time, and physical explanation. Important examples are the papers by Norton and Stachel on Einstein's route to the field equations, the equivalence principle, and the requirement of covariance in HOWARD & STACHEL, a volume that collects many important specialist studies of general relativity, and initiated a series of conferences (and associated volumes) on topics in the history of relativity. EARMAN, JANSSEN & NORTON, includes papers on disputes with Einstein, the empirical basis of general relativity, variational principles in the theory, its reception, and development, and cosmology.

Focusing on the career of Erwin Freundlich, the first German astronomer to support Einstein's treatment of gravitation with experimental studies, HENTSCHEL (1992) explores a chapter in early empirical work on general relativity from a number of perspectives. The book traces interdependent layers of meaning (biographical, institutional, disciplinary, and intellectual) revealed in Freundlich's efforts from 1911 to verify relativity through analysis of the bending of light rays and gravitational red-shift; in his institutional career and often antagonistic professional relationships; and in the construction of and debate on the architecturally-distinctive observatory, informally named the "Einstein Tower", which was built in Potsdam in 1920 to further Freundlich's research.

The dramatic announcement of British observations of the bending of starlight in the sun's gravitational field in November 1919 did much to stimulate widespread interest in Einstein and relativity, both in the public sphere and in mathematical and physical circles. EARMAN & GLYMOUR's important study situates the work of the British eclipse expeditions within the context of previous, unsuccessful attempts to measure deflection, and the attitude of the leading scientists involved (especially Eddington) to war-related chauvinism. Analysing the complexity of both theoretical and experimental argumentation, the paper argues that a false trichotomy between null, Newtonian, and Einsteinian predictions was presented, and that a result favourable to Einstein's prediction was only achieved by disregarding significant data. WILL's book, written for a popular audience and based on personal participation, is a study of experimental tests of general gravitation (of the bending of starlight, the perihelion of Mercury, and the gravitational red shift of light) that have taken place since the 1950s, with the renewal of interest in relativity based on theoretical and experimental astrophysics.

The articles in GLICK (1987) discuss numerous aspects of the reception of relativity in the US, Britain, Germany, France, Italy, Spain, Russia and the USSR, Poland, and Japan. The focus chosen ranges from studies of contributions to both special and general relativity by the physics and mathematics communities, to impressionistic surveys of responses to the theories (or Einstein's visit to a nation) in popular culture. However, the variety of subject matter and historiographical approaches somewhat diminishes the book's ability to fulfil its stated aim, to found a comparative study of the reception of relativity. GLICK (1988) is one of the most broad-ranging and complete studies of the discussion and impact of relativity within a single nation. In Spain, renewals of the mathematics and physics disciplines in the 20th century encouraged an early awareness of Einstein's work amongst limited circles. Exploring different contexts of reception, Glick argues that the main target for high level syntheses of relativity was the engineering discipline – the "scientific middle class" – and he also investigates the variety of responses from the Spanish intelligentsia, the media, and popular culture.

Engagement with relativity has been extremely important for numerous philosophical schools, and especially for neo-Kantians and logical positivists, who focused on the theory when developing their influential philosophies of science, and of space and time. HENTSCHEL (1990) is a study of the history of philosophical interpretations of relativity. He details the philosophical presuppositions of philosophers and scientists representing a wide range of viewpoints, and discusses their interpretations of relativity theory, revealing the close relationship between background and consequent interpretation.

Two recent articles provide valuable surveys of the history of relativity and, together with Warwick's papers, constitute a good starting point for further research. DARRIGOL's study is on the prehistory of special relativity, the range of approaches to electrodynamics around 1905, and Einstein's path to relativity. Describing late 19th-century European electrodynamical theory as a result of the encounter between German and Maxwellian approaches, Darrigol argues that it is this context of electrodynamic theory that provides the most appropriate environment for understanding the sources of Einstein's approach, rather than other possible contexts within physics, thermodynamics, electrotechnology, philosophy, or broader culture. The account stresses both the considerable links between Einstein's work and that of his contemporaries (particularly Poincaré), and the relative strengths of alternative theories. Darrigol argues persuasively that the work of previous historians has exhibited a teleological focus on Einstein, and that the unquestioned superiority of Einstein's approach (in 1905) is only a retrospective construction. STACHEL provides the single most comprehensive overview of the history of both theories, and a guide to previous literature that is especially valuable in the case of general relativity. Written in the concise but inclusive style of a review article in the physical sciences, the paper provides an extremely clear account, oriented around conceptual issues, of the origins and development of the theories, their application to various branches of physics, and experimental and observational testing.

RICHARD STALEY

See also Aether; Cosmology; Einstein; Electromagnetism

Religion and Science: general works

Barbour, Ian G., *Issues in Science and Religion*, Englewood Cliffs, New Jersey: Prentice-Hall, 1966
Brooke, John Hedley, *Science and Religion: Some Historical Perspectives*, Cambridge and New York: Cambridge University Press, 1991
Chant, Colin and John Fauvel (eds), *Darwin to Einstein: Historical Studies on Science and Belief*, London and New York: Longman, 1980
Dillenberger, John, *Protestant Thought and Natural Science: A Historical Perspective*, New York: Abingdon Press, 1960; London: Collins, 1961
Draper, John William, *History of the Conflict between Religion and Science*, London: H.S. King, and New York: Appleton, 1874; reprinted, Farnborough, Hampshire: Gregg International, 1970; abridged and edited by Charles T. Sprading, New York: Vanguard Press, 1926
Jaki, Stanley L., *Science and Creation: From Eternal Cycles to an Oscillating Universe*, Edinburgh: Scottish Academic Press, and New York: Science History Publications, 1974
Jaki, Stanley L., *The Road of Science and the Ways to God*, Edinburgh: Scottish Academic Press, and Chicago: University of Chicago Press, 1978
Kaiser, Christopher, *Creation and the History of Science*, London: Marshall Pickering, and Grand Rapids, Michigan: Eerdmans, 1991
Lindberg, David C. and Ronald L. Numbers (eds), *God and Nature: Historical Essays on the Encounter Between Christianity and Science*, Berkeley: University of California Press, 1986
Lovejoy, Arthur O., *The Great Chain of Being: A Study of the History of an Idea*, Cambridge, Massachusetts: Harvard University Press, 1936
Russell, Colin (ed.), *Science and Religious Belief: A Collection of Recent Historical Studies*, London: University of London Press/Open University Press, 1973
Russell, Colin, *Cross-Currents: Interactions Between Science and Faith*, Leicester: Inter-Varsity Press, and Grand Rapids, Michigan: Eerdmans, 1985
White, Andrew Dickson, *A History of the Warfare of Science with Theology in Christendom*, 2 vols, New York: Appleton, and London: Macmillan, 1896

It is commonly held in contemporary society that the scientific and religious world-views are incompatible. The fact that there are a number of prominent scientists who vigorously proclaim their Christianity and insist that their science is inspired and supported by their religion has little impact on the popular belief in the fundamental dichotomy of intellectual approach between science and religion. To a significant extent, it is the historiography of science that is responsible for this popular image. Beginning with Draper and White (both of which, incidentally, must be counted among the very earliest exercises in the history of science), historians of science have presented a picture of the relations between science and religion calculated to separate the one from the other, and to insist upon their categorical differences. Evidently, this early message from the incipient discipline of the history of science was widely accepted, and continues to shape the popular consciousness, while more recent work in the history of science and religion which has sought to correct this one-sided and biased picture, has not had the same impact upon the wider community. None the less, it is broadly true that a second wave of books on the history of science has tended to play down the antagonism between science and religion and has focused on the stimulus

Christianity frequently provided for science. The very latest developments in the history of science, represented here by Brooke and Lindberg & Numbers, have tried to give what is currently regarded as a more balanced picture, taking greater account of the undoubted hostility between science and religion visible from the historical record, while also acknowledging the more positive role of Christianity in providing both a metaphysical foundation for science, and the inspiration for a great number of individual scientists, from the Middle Ages to the present. The progress towards a more balanced approach has been given further momentum by the increased attention that Church historians have been paying to the historical relations between science and religion, seeking to counteract the earlier historiography for apologetic purposes.

Too polemical to count as a work of sound historical scholarship, DRAPER's survey is an attack upon what he saw as the intellectual pretensions of the Roman Catholic Church, which had recently declared so-called "Papal infallibility" and had insisted upon the superiority of "revealed doctrine" over the human sciences. Draper consistently presents his historical case-studies as the inevitable outcome of the expansive force of the untrammelled human intellect, best represented by scientific rationalism, and the repressive force of institutionalized human interests, represented by the Catholic Church. The essentially anti-Catholic nature of Draper's study is perfectly explicit, and he emphasizes the point by exonerating the Protestant and Greek Orthodox Churches from his strictures. The leading Protestant churches, he insists, have been averse to constraint and, except in rare instances, their opposition has never gone beyond exciting theological odium. Draper even went so far as to suggest that when Jean Calvin had Michael Servetus burned at the stake, the great Swiss Reformer was merely revealing the fact that he had not completely emancipated himself from Catholic ways.

WHITE followed Draper in seeing the relationship between science and religion as one of conflict, but rooted this antagonism in what he saw as two categorically distinct mentalities, invariably and unavoidably at odds with one another. These mentalities, according to the Comtean White, were the products of "two epochs in the evolution of human thought – the theological and the scientific". As with Draper, it is clear that White had a personal axe to grind, having met vigorous religious opposition to his proposed secularist Charter for Cornell University, with its emphasis on the importance of science in education. Like Draper, however, White was also willing to make concessions to religion. White's thesis included a sincere belief that science left free from interference, no matter how apparently religiously subversive, would always ultimately benefit religion. Although the main value of these two works is now as primary source materials for an understanding of the relations between science and religion in the second half of the 19th century, White's two-volume survey may still be cautiously used as a mine of fascinating information.

Although not written as a specific contribution to the debate on the relations between science and religion, LOVEJOY is one of the earliest books to present the other side of the coin. Lovejoy's famous essay is a study of "one of the half-dozen most potent and persistent presuppositions in Western thought", the notion of a "Great Chain of Being" and associated philosophical principles, such as the "principle of plenitude", from Plato and Aristotle to the 19th century. The Great Chain of Being refers to the hierarchical structure of the universe and everything in it, which from ancient times onwards was commonly supposed to exist, but which in the Christian era came to be seen as a consequence of God's goodness, wisdom, and omnipotence. The Christian theology underlying the concept of the Great Chain of Being, Lovejoy shows, linked God's attributes to the nature of Creation, so making natural theology possible, and having a direct influence upon cosmology, natural history and, later, the new science of biology. Lovejoy's study is, therefore, a fundamental source for understanding the role of Christian theology in scientific thinking. However, written very much from a philosophical perspective, it delves into the recondite niceties of the theology in a way that many readers will find demanding.

DILLENBERGER writes not on the history of the conflicts between theology and science, or of the harmony between the two, but of the changing relations between them. Accordingly, Dillenberger sees a divergence of science and theology at the end of the 16th and the beginning of the 17th centuries, particularly on the Continent, but discerns a convergence in later 17th-century England. Viewing these movements to and fro largely in terms of changes in the interpretation of nature and Scripture, and the relative authority accorded to each, Dillenberger manages to give a well-balanced account of the interactions between science and religion, from the Copernican revolution to the 20th century. The author's concern with balance, however, stems from his views on contemporary Protestant factionalism; the problems dealt with in the book, he insists, make sense only from a theological perspective that is not one of Protestant orthodoxy, Protestant liberalism, or Protestant fundamentalism – each of which erred either by capitulating to the new science or by defying it, when they should, presumably, have maintained the older traditional relationship of interconnectedness. The value of the book for historians of science, therefore, lies not so much in the history of science it contains, but in its parallel account of the history of theology.

Although written by a practising physicist, BARBOUR's book also has a theological agenda. Beginning with a brief account of how the prevailing view, that science and religion are two separate spheres that should attend to their own affairs, came to be established, the author goes on to argue that the absolute separation of science from religion is not possible. Divided into three substantial parts, only the first part of the book deals with historical material, covering developments in science, religion and the relationship between them from the 17th to the 20th centuries. The rest of the book deals with contemporary matters concerning the implications of the scientific method for theology, and its approach to an understanding of the world, and with the theological implications of new scientific ideas, such as the indeterminacy principle and theories of the origin of life. Like Dillenberger, the main interest of this book for the historian of science is in its historical and contemporary account of developments in theology and religious thought.

JAKI (1974) tries to account for the historical singularity of the rise of Western science, attributing it to the Christian notion of the deity as a transcendent creator and lawgiver. "To this belief", Jaki writes, "science owes its very birth and life".

It was Christian faith, according to Jaki, that enabled Western intellectuals to have confidence in the rationality of the universe, and a belief in the possibility of progress. The historical account deals at length with ancient, pre-Christian or non-Christian cultures, only reaching the Renaissance by chapter 11, and concluding with the 20th century at chapter 14.

JAKI (1978) also argues for the crucial role played by the religious world-view in the origin and development of science. Beginning with the claim that science found its road to unlimited advance when the Christian belief in the linearity of time replaced the cyclical notions of other ancient cultures, Jaki proceeds, through a densely-written, idiosyncratic survey of the history of science, philosophy, and religion, to conclude that theism remains "the most needed inspiration in this age of science". It is by no means clear at the end of this somewhat rambling book, however, whether we are to see theism as an inspiration to science, or merely to ourselves as moral beings.

Like Jaki, KAISER argues that the major contributors to science throughout 21 centuries were frequently inspired by the belief that God had created all things in accordance with laws that made the world comprehensible to humans. This "creationist tradition", as he calls it, began to unravel in the 12th century, with the separation of natural from revealed theology, but this did not give rise to a conflict between science and religion since both sides were rooted in the same tradition. However, the creationist tradition itself began to lose power in the 19th century as a result of fragmentation and secularization. Kaiser still manages to extend his survey into the 20th century, but only by pointing to supposed similarities between the thought of Niels Bohr and Albert Einstein to earlier theological traditions. This is by now so divorced from any consideration of historical context as to be merely suggestive; Bohr's and Einstein's concerns with "harmony", for example, are not analyzed in terms of contemporary attitudes among their fellow scientists, but merely likened to earlier religious beliefs.

RUSSELL (1985) provides what he calls a book for laymen in the history of science, and can be regarded, therefore, as a useful, concise introduction to the history of interactions between science and religion. Written by a historian of science, it is clear and reliable, without entirely avoiding the complexities of the issues. Russell writes with a strong and manifest Christian outlook, and does not simply use historical evidence to debate if science and religion are separate autonomous concerns, but insists ahistorically that they can accomplish more together than separately.

RUSSELL (1973) and CHANT & FAUVEL are collections of essays by various historians of science dealing with a variety of themes and topics within the interface of the histories of science and religion. Russell's collection covers the period from the 16th to the late 19th centuries, while Chant & Fauvel's covers the period from the 19th to the early 20th century. Both collections include a number of classic papers, and are well worth consulting for these, even though the collections as a whole cannot be relied upon to provide a full picture of the relations between science and religion during their respective periods.

For a collection of essays that does fulfil the role of a more or less comprehensive survey of this major theme, the reader should look no further than LINDBERG & NUMBERS.

Beginning with a survey of "Science and the Early Church", and ending with three articles on 20th-century issues, the articles cover all the major topics in the historiography of the subject. Written to a uniformly high standard, and displaying a greater concern with history than with Christian apologetics, the essays in this collection constitute an excellent guide.

This anthology is matched, if not excelled, in its usefulness by BROOKE, a continuous survey of the interactions of science and religion that is entirely reliable, and often more comprehensive, more detailed, and more nuanced in its judgements on a specific topic than the corresponding article in Lindberg & Numbers. Beginning with the scientific revolution, and ending with the 19th century, Brooke's survey needs supplementing for a full understanding of pre-16th-century, and for 20th-century developments. The strongest aspect of Brooke's survey is its subtlety and historiographical sophistication. For a full and judicious assessment of the implications of the historical evidence for the relations between science and religion in any given period, or with regard to any particular scientific or religious topic, it can hardly be bettered. Unique among surveys, it manages to cover all the ground, without resorting to sweeping generalizations or simplistic models. However, these strengths, as far as some are concerned, may be regarded as weaknesses, and because of its acceptance of complexity, this may not be the best book to use as a first introduction to this important historiographical theme.

JOHN HENRY

See also Merton Thesis; Religion and Science: Islam; Religion and Science: Medieval; Religion and Science: Renaissance

Religion and Science: Islam

al-Afghani, Jamal ad-Din, "Answer of Jamal ad-Din to Renan", in *An Islamic Response to Imperialism: Political and Religious Writings of Sayyid Jamal ad-Din "al-Afghani"*, edited by Nikki R. Keddie, Berkeley: University of California Press, 1968

Goldziher, Ignaz, "The Attitude of Orthodox Islam Toward the Ancient Sciences", in *Studies on Islam*, edited and translated by Merlin L. Swartz, New York and Oxford: Oxford University Press, 1981

Hoodbhoy, Pervez, *Islam and Science: Religious Orthodoxy and the Battle for Rationality*, London and Atlantic Highlands, New Jersey: Zed Books, 1991

Huff, Toby E., *The Rise of Early Modern Science: Islam, China and the West*, Cambridge and New York: Cambridge University Press, 1993

Huff, Toby E., "Islam, Science and Fundamentalism", *Journal for Arabic, Islamic and Middle Eastern Studies*, 2/2 (1995)

King, David A., "Science in the Service of Religion: The Case of Islam", *Impact of Science on Society*, 159 (1990)

Nasr, Seyyed Hossein, *Science and Civilization in Islam*, Cambridge, Massachusetts: Harvard University Press, 1968; 2nd edition, Cambridge: Islamic Texts Society, 1987

Renan, Ernest, "L'Islamisme et la science", in *Discours et conférences*, 6th edition, Paris: Calmann-Levy, 1919

Sabra, A.I., "The Appropriation and Subsequent Naturalization of Greek Science in Medieval Islam: A Preliminary Statement", *History of Science*, 25 (1987)

Tibi, Bassam, "The Worldview of Sunni Arab Fundamentalists: Attitudes Toward Modern Science and Technology", in *Fundamentalisms and Society: Reclaiming the Sciences, the Family, and Education*, edited by Martin E. Marty and R. Scott Appleby, Chicago: University of Chicago Press, 1993

Nineteenth-century Western scholars, examining the intellectual vitality of Arabic–Islamic civilization, concluded that Islam itself was inimical to the pursuit of science, despite the fact that certain European medieval scholars had referred to Arabic scientists as "our Arab masters". RENAN is the classic statement of the view that Islamic law, theology, and priest-craft interfered with the pursuit of science, and that, as long as Islam captivated the minds and hearts of the peoples of the Middle East, they would be unable to contribute to the advance of modern science.

AL-AFGHANI wrote a response to Renan's essay of 1883, in which, while granting the basic point of Renan's argument, he adopted Auguste Comte's positivist view, according to which mankind progresses through various intellectual stages – a theological, a metaphysical, and finally a rationalist stage, supportive of science. In their inception, he argued, all religions were intolerant of scientific and metaphysical thought, just as Christianity had been, but with progress Islam too would become supportive of scientific inquiry. On the other hand, the Arabs in the classical period had very quickly assimilated the Greek sciences and carried them to new heights of development and perfection, thereby showing their aptitude for scientific inquiry. However, Al-Afghani agreed that Islam was responsible for extinguishing scientific innovation in Arabic–Islamic civilization.

In this context, GOLDZIHER remains the best and most thorough exposition of the attitudes of the orthodox religious scholars toward the "foreign" or ancient sciences, as they were known to the Arabs. In general, these pious scholars regarded the study of the natural sciences as the first step toward impiety, and railed especially against the study of logic and philosophy as the ultimate destroyers of religious belief.

SABRA argues that parts of Islamic science performed an intermediary role between the ancient Greek and medieval Latin traditions. As a result the focus has been on a purportedly passive reception of Greek science and this received science was marginal. Sabra repudiates both. Greek science was actively appropriated, and it was thoroughly naturalized so that jobs became available for individuals with knowledge of astronomy and engineering.

KING's article in a United Nation's sponsored journal is aimed at the non-specialist. He surveys the way in which science, particularly astronomy, has been used for purposes relating to the Muslim religious life. Examples are the lunar calendar (which determines the beginning of Ramadan), astronomically define times of prayer, and the determination of the sacred direction of the Kaaba in Mecca. King distinguishes between mathematical and folk astronomy and argues that whereas the former has captured the attention of historians of science, the latter has actually had a much greater influence in Muslim life.

HUFF (1993) is the most recent attempt to explore the relationship between Islam and science, within the context of current understandings of the many innovations introduced by Arab science. This account locates both European and Arabic science within their philosophical, legal, and theological traditions. Huff shows that, while Europe experienced a legal revolution in the 12th and 13th centuries that created new spheres of legal autonomy (especially universities dedicated to the study of the natural sciences), the Islamic world continued to exclude the natural sciences from their institutions of higher learning (*madrasas*), and failed to separate, through legal reform, the sphere of religion from other activities. Huff also points out that, while Christian theology supported the view of a rational/causal universe, and the idea that humankind is endowed with creative rational capacities modeled after the divine, Islamic law and theology rejected the idea of divine rationality.

The debate concerning the compatibility of Islam with modern science has erupted in contemporary discussions focusing on the concept of an "Islamic science", namely a science derived from the Quran. While the belief that the Quran is the perfect model of all knowledge, including the sciences of medicine and astronomy, has existed since the early days of Islam, resurgent Islam of the last two decades has produced a more aggressive and explicit movement dedicated to the idea of "Islamic science". Prior to this development, the most significant work by a Muslim writer in a Western language, championing an alternative view of science, was NASR. This proclaimed the view that Arabic–Islamic scientists had always been committed to a spiritually unified conception of science, that of *gnosis*, and that Muslim scientists of the golden era deliberately chose the path of unified scientific and religious knowledge over that of modern science as we understand it.

HOODBHOY is an account by a Pakistani Muslim and Western-trained scientist who challenges both the foundations of the idea of an Islamic science, and the extravagant claims made by its proponents, including Nasr. In a chapter devoted to the study and public support of science in contemporary Muslim countries, the author concludes that support is extremely weak and the future dismal. He champions the rationalist tradition of Islam founded in the 8th century by the Islamic rationalists, the Mu'tazilites. An appendix called "They Call It Islamic Science" is a bold and trenchant scientific critique of the putative "scientific miracles" of the Quran, reported at a conference in Islamabad, Pakistan in 1987, and supported by President Zia ul-Haq.

TIBI is a recent survey of Sunni attitudes toward science and technology, based on both written sources – Arabic and English – and interviews with leading religious and secular figures in contemporary Egypt. It shows the various positions taken by Islamic fundamentalists, ranging from the view that the Quran is the blueprint for science and the view that the limited pursuit of science is permissible, to those who insist on the "Islamization" of science in the mold of those criticized by Hoodbhoy.

HUFF (1995) compares and contrasts theological and legal

conceptions in Islam and Christianity regarding the rationality of man and nature, and traces contemporary Islamic fundamentalist objections to the pursuit of science back to those early Islamic doctrines.

TOBY E. HUFF

See also Spain

Religion and Science: Medieval

Amundsen, Darrel W., "The Medieval Catholic Tradition", in *Caring and Curing: Health and Medicine in the Western Religious Traditions*, edited by Ronald L. Numbers and Darrel W. Amundsen, New York: Macmillan, 1986

Amundsen, Darrel W., and Gary B. Ferngren, "The Early Christian Tradition", in *Caring and Curing: Health and Medicine in the Western Religious Traditions*, edited by Ronald L. Numbers and Darrel W. Amundsen, New York: Macmillan, 1986

Armstrong, A.H. and R.A. Markus, *Christian Faith and Greek Philosophy*, London: Darton, Longman and Todd, 1960; New York: Sheed and Ward, 1964

Chenu, M.D., *Nature, Man, and Society in the Twelfth Century: Essays on New Theological Perspectives in the Latin West*, edited and translated by Jerome Taylor and Lester K. Little, Chicago: University of Chicago Press, 1968

Cochrane, Charles Norris, *Christianity and Classical Culture: A Study of Thought and Action from Augustus to Augustine*, Oxford: Clarendon Press, 1940; New York: Oxford University Press, 1944

Dales, Richard C., *Medieval Discussions of the Eternity of the World*, Leiden: E.J. Brill, 1990

Draper, John William, *History of the Conflict between Religion and Science*, London: H.S. King, and New York: Appleton, 1874; reprinted, Farnborough, Hampshire: Gregg International, 1970; abridged and edited by Charles T. Sprading, New York: Vanguard Press, 1926

Duhem, Pierre, *Medieval Cosmology: Theories of Infinity, Place, Time, Void, and the Plurality of Worlds*, edited and translated from the French by Roger Ariew, Chicago: University of Chicago Press, 1985 (original edition, 1913–17)

Funkenstein, Amos, *Theology and the Scientific Imagination from the Middle Ages to the Seventeenth Century*, Princeton, New Jersey: Princeton University Press, 1986

Grant, Edward, "Science and Theology in the Middle Ages", in *God and Nature: Historical Essays on the Encounter between Christianity and Science*, edited by David C. Lindberg and Ronald L. Numbers, Berkeley: University of California Press, 1986, 49–75

Grant, Edward, *Planets, Stars, and Orbs: The Medieval Cosmos, 1200–1687*, Cambridge and New York: Cambridge University Press, 1994

Jaki, Stanley L., *The Road of Science and the Ways to God*, Chicago: University of Chicago Press, and Edinburgh: Scottish Academic Press, 1978

Lindberg, David C., "Science and the Early Church", in *God and Nature: Historical Essays on the Encounter Between Christianity and Science*, edited by Lindberg and Ronald L. Numbers, Berkeley: University of California Press, 1986, 19–48

Lindberg, David C., "Science as Handmaiden: Roger Bacon and the Patristic Tradition", *Isis*, 78 (1987): 518–36

Lindberg, David C., *The Beginnings of Western Science: The European Scientific Tradition in Philosophical, Religious, and Institutional Context, 600 BC to AD 1450*, Chicago: University of Chicago Press, 1992

Lindberg, David C., "Medieval Science and Its Religious Context", *Osiris*, n.s., 10 (1995): 61–79

McEvoy, James, *The Philosophy of Robert Grosseteste*, Oxford: Clarendon Press, and New York: Oxford University Press, 1982

Steenberghen, Fernand Van, *Thomas Aquinas and Radical Aristotelianism*, Washington, DC: Catholic University of America Press, 1980

Steneck, Nicholas H., *Science and Creation in the Middle Ages: Henry of Langenstein (d. 1397) on Genesis*, Notre Dame, Indiana: University of Notre Dame Press, 1976

White, Andrew Dickson, *A History of the Warfare of Science with Theology in Christendom*, 2 vols, London: Macmillan, and New York: Appleton, 1896

Modern scholarship on science and medieval Christianity has been shaped by a long and bitter debate over the question: did Christianity obstruct or encourage scientific progress? 19th-century opinion portrayed the medieval church as broadly anti-intellectual and firmly opposed to genuine science, as a threat both to its authority and to the literal interpretation of the Bible; this view is frequently referred to as the "warfare model" or the "warfare thesis". Its great 19th-century formulators and defenders were DRAPER and WHITE, both of whom remain influential to this day.

The warfare model retains a strong following in the 20th century, but it has also been bitterly attacked by certain writers (many with a religious agenda), who have attempted to demonstrate that, far from restricting scientific advance, medieval Christianity offered a vital stimulus to the development of genuine science, in the form of fundamental assumptions about nature. The pioneer of this line of argumentation was DUHEM, whose writings on cosmology display the main features of this argument. JAKI, who argues that modern science would not exist without the assumptions of Christian theology concerning the orderliness and rationality of nature, is a vocal and belligerent contemporary representative of this point of view.

Although much scholarly energy continues to be dissipated in defense of one or the other of these polar opposites, scholarship of a more dispassionate and balanced sort has begun to appear. The key to a proper understanding of the interaction between medieval science and medieval Christianity is to recognize its complexity and variability. No particular form of relationship between these two powerful cultural entities characterizes the entire Middle Ages, or all of western Christendom at any particular medieval moment. The relationship varied with time, place, and the specific science–religion issue under consideration, while, with regard to a given time, place, and issue, we usually find that there were alternative opinions among the European elites who shaped religious practice and scientific belief. Much of the best literature, therefore, focuses on a narrow time period, or particular set of historical events, and on a specific area of interaction between science and religion.

Two further introductory points are in order. First, if, by "science", we mean something more or less identical with modern science, then there was no such thing during the Middle Ages. What we do find in the Middle Ages, however, are the ancestors of many of the pieces that make up modern science – ancestors that bear a family resemblance to their offspring without being identical to them. In short, medieval scholars had ideas about nature, techniques for exploring it, and languages for describing it. In the analysis below, these ancestors are referred to collectively as "natural philosophy" or "science" (the latter term employed in its very broadest sense); and, individually, by narrower terms such as "medicine" and "cosmology", representing identifiable medieval disciplines or subjects.

Second, we will make no headway in understanding the relationship of religion and natural philosophy during the Middle Ages until we discard the notion of religion (or theology) and natural philosophy as independent, rival entities, glaring at each other across clear and uncrossable disciplinary boundaries. We need to remind ourselves that religion and natural philosophy are abstractions rather than actual existent things. What did exist during the Middle Ages were highly educated scholars (some of them also active in the church bureaucracy) who held beliefs of both a theological and a natural philosophical sort. What must be appreciated is that the theologian and the natural philosopher were frequently the same person; the best medieval scholars tended to be universal scholars, with a scope that spanned the world of the intellect, including both theology and natural philosophy. With these introductory points behind us, let us analyze the available literature, beginning with the early Middle Ages and working forward chronologically from there.

COCHRANE's classic study offers a brilliant analysis of the impact of Christianity on the Greco-Roman world in the first four centuries of the Christian era, and a general perspective on Christian attitudes toward classical culture (including its natural philosophy). Cochrane argues, among other things, that the goal of many Christian thinkers (represented by St Augustine and others) was not the repudiation of natural philosophy and other intellectual activity, but its Christianization. Cochrane also serves as a model of sound historical methodology (sorely needed in this particular area of research) in his unwillingness to take sides in the struggles about which he writes.

ARMSTRONG & MARKUS examine the "dialogue" that took place in the minds of the early medieval Christians who sought ways of accommodating Biblical teaching with the content and methods of Greek philosophy, including its teachings about the material universe. In his broad survey of Christianity and natural philosophy in the early medieval period, LINDBERG (1986) occupies the middle ground between the warfare model and its polar opposite, denying that the Church "retarded or crushed science", while denying also that "Christianity offered major stimulus to scientific activity".

With CHENU we move to the 12th century, frequently regarded as a crucial transition period between the earlier and later Middle Ages. Several chapters of this book are devoted to an enthusiastic account of the assimilation of Platonic natural philosophy in 12th-century schools and its "transubstantiation" under Christian auspices. The results of this critically important development, according to Chenu, included the perception of the universe as a unified cosmos, a growing demand for the investigation of natural causes (secondary causes rather than the supernatural first cause), a belief in the power of human reason to discover the laws governing the behavior of things, and a technological revolution.

During the 12th century Greek and Arabic sources unknown during the early Middle Ages were recovered – most importantly the works of Aristotle and his Islamic commentators – and these new sources greatly complicated the relationship between science and religion in the 13th and 14th centuries. One of the towering intellects of the Middle Ages, whose career stretched from the 12th well into the 13th centuries, was the theologian and natural philosopher, Robert Grosseteste (1168–1253). The recent book by McEVOY brilliantly analyzes the integration of Christian theology and natural philosophy in the mind of this leading thinker. LINDBERG (1987) investigates the campaign of one of Grosseteste's great admirers and intellectual followers, Roger Bacon (mid-13th century), to save the new learning from its critics, by demonstrating its utility for Christendom and its ability to serve as the faithful and obedient handmaiden of theology and the Church.

STEENBERGHEN considers the debates that swirled through the University of Paris over the appearance of radical Aristotelianism in the 13th century. His main focus is on Thomas Aquinas (d.1274) and his response to the rationalistic tendencies of the Aristotelian tradition, and such Aristotelian claims as the eternity of the world.

STENECK examines the lectures on Genesis by a representative 14th-century thinker, Henry of Langenstein (d.1397), revealing how Langenstein integrated contemporary natural philosophy and the Genesis account of creation, producing in the process "a barely disguised scientific encyclopedia".

DALES is a thorough, scholarly, book-length analysis of debates over the possible eternity of the world, firmly defended by Aristotle but clearly at odds with the fundamentals of Christian theology. He reveals the complexity of the issues, the variety of positions adopted, and the range of strategies available for those who hoped for an accommodation between the claims of Christian theology and Aristotelian natural philosophy.

One of the areas of medieval scientific endeavor most likely to impinge on Christian belief was medicine, for here the naturalism of the Greek scientific tradition (a commitment to the investigation of the natural causes of things) collided directly with the supernaturalism of the Christian tradition. In their close examination of these developments, AMUNDSEN and AMUNDSEN & FERNGREN (the former for the medieval period, the latter for the patristic period) debunk the widely-held myth that Christians repudiated secular medical treatment, revealing just how complicated the genuine situation was, and showing how naturalistic medicine and supernatural beliefs managed to co-exist.

Another important area of encounter between Christian belief and the classical tradition was cosmology, owing to the presence in the Bible of what medieval scholars took to be cosmological claims. Medieval cosmological speculations, including their interaction with Christian theology, are dealt with exhaustively by GRANT (1994). The relationship between cosmology and theology also figures prominently in Duhem.

There have been several recent attempts to paint a picture of developments in the relationship between science and theology in the later Middle Ages with a broad brush. GRANT (1986) has examined the impact of Christian theology and the classical tradition in natural philosophy on one another, arguing that theology did not (on the whole) inhibit the development of a significant medieval natural philosophy, and that the later medieval period was one of relative tranquillity in the history of science–religion relations. FUNKENSTEIN, in a sweeping theoretical study, attempts to find in late medieval theology and metaphysics the origins for such ideals of 17th-century science as the mathematization and mechanization of nature. LINDBERG (1992) offers a survey of ancient and medieval science, in which religion and theology are integrated into the narrative. Finally, LINDBERG (1995) assesses recent developments in the history of science–religion interaction in the Middle Ages, and ventures a set of broad generalizations concerning its nature.

DAVID C. LINDBERG

See also Religion and Science: general works; Religion and Science: Islam

Religion and Science: Renaissance

Brooke, John Hedley, Science and Religion: Some Historical Perspectives, Cambridge and New York: Cambridge University Press, 1991

Cohen, I. Bernard (ed.), Puritanism and the Rise of Modern Science: The Merton Thesis, New Brunswick, New Jersey: Rutgers University Press, 1990

Funkenstein, Amos, Theology and the Scientific Imagination from the Middle Ages to the Seventeenth Century, Princeton, New Jersey: Princeton University Press, 1986

Grell, Ole Peter and Andrew Cunningham (eds), Medicine and the Reformation, London and New York: Routledge, 1993

Hooykaas, Reijer, Religion and the Rise of Modern Science, Edinburgh: Scottish Academic Press, and Grand Rapids, Michigan: Eerdmans, 1972

Klaaren, Eugene M., Religious Origins of Modern Science: Belief in Creation in Seventeenth-Century Thought, Grand Rapids, Michigan: Eerdmans, 1977

Kocher, Paul H., Science and Religion in Elizabethan England, San Marino, California: Huntington Library, 1953

Koyré, Alexandre, From the Closed World to the Infinite Universe, Baltimore: Johns Hopkins Press, 1957

Lindberg, David C. and Ronald L. Numbers (eds), God and Nature: Historical Essays on the Encounter Between Christianity and Science, Berkeley: University of California Press, 1986

Merton, Robert K., Science, Technology and Society in Seventeenth-Century England, Bruges, Belgium: St Catherine Press, 1938; New York: Fertig, 1970

Webster, Charles (ed.), The Intellectual Revolution of the Seventeenth Century, London and Boston: Routledge and Kegan Paul, 1974

Webster, Charles, The Great Instauration: Science, Medicine and Reform, 1626–1670, London: Duckworth, 1975; New York: Holmes and Meier, 1976

Westfall, Richard S., Science and Religion in Seventeenth-Century England, New Haven, Connecticut: Yale University Press, 1958

Wybrow, Cameron (ed.), Creation, Nature and Political Order in the Philosophy of Michael Foster (1903–1959): The Classic Mind Articles and Others, with Modern Critical Essays, Lewiston, New York, and Lampeter, Wales: Edwin Mellen Press, 1992

The Renaissance (treated here as the period embracing the Reformation and the Scientific Revolution, up to about the mid-17th century) has always been regarded by historians as a major period of significant interaction between science, or natural philosophy, and religion. The books covered here deal with general developments during this period. The list could easily be massively extended, however, by considering the literature on individual natural philosophers, many of whom feature prominently in the history of relations between science and the churches. Indeed, it seems true to say that all the leading contributors to the development of science during this period, as well as many of the lesser ones, manifest an explicit interest in the usefulness of their natural philosophies to theology and religion. The list of such concerned individuals would include not just Galileo, Kepler and Descartes, but also Marin Mersenne, Pierre Gassendi, Thomas Hobbes, Robert Boyle, and many more.

Although they are general works that cover more than just the Renaissance period, BROOKE and LINDBERG & NUMBERS cannot be bettered as convenient places to begin reading on this topic. Both offer up-to-date analyses of the major historiographical issues, as well as clear and accessible accounts of the most significant historical developments. Brooke provides a continuous narrative, while the anthology edited by Lindberg & Numbers includes six articles concerned with Renaissance developments (out of a total of 18). Both works are also invaluable for providing the medieval background, and for illustrating post-Renaissance developments.

Although the interactions between science and religion have been, and continue to be, a major theme in the history of science, the relations between religion and medicine have drawn surprisingly little attention by comparison. Grell & Cunningham and Kocher, however, go some way to redressing the balance. GRELL & CUNNINGHAM provide an anthology of eight papers by leading scholars covering topics from anatomy to spiritual healing, and regions from Denmark and Lutheran Germany to Italy and Spain. Although not comprehensive in its coverage, the standard of the papers is generally high, and the book therefore provides useful indications of the ways in which religion impinged upon the theory and practice of medicine during the 16th and early 17th centuries.

KOCHER is only concerned with developments in Elizabethan England, but provides an excellent survey of the relations between science and religion during this period. He also includes a couple of chapters on the history of medicine that aim to provide a general survey of interactions with contemporary religion, and are in many respects indicative of the wider European picture.

WESTFALL also restricts himself to England, but during the turbulent 17th century. In a thorough and detailed survey of the attempts made to persuade English natural philosophers to deny that their science was inimical to religion, and to present themselves as devout readers and interpreters of God's other book – the Book of Nature – Westfall persuasively argues that their work did in fact subvert revealed religion. By insisting upon the usefulness of the mechanical philosophy for proving the existence of God, the natural philosophers developed a natural religion that, according to Westfall, was indistinguishable from deism, and which promoted a morality based on rational demonstration and the concerns of the individual in society.

The so-called Puritanism-and-science thesis is a major subtheme in the historiography of relations between science and religion. Although suggestions of a link between the rise of science in 17th-century England and the flourishing of Puritan religious values had been stated earlier, the argument received its fullest treatment in the highly influential doctoral thesis of the sociologist Robert K. Merton. While careful to acknowledge the likely role of economic and political factors in the rise of science, and of what he viewed as science's own capacity for self-fertilization, MERTON wrote that, "Puritanism and ascetic Protestantism generally, emerges as an emotionally consistent system of beliefs, sentiments and action that played no small part in arousing a sustained interest in science". In fact, the thesis for which Merton's book is most renowned is confined essentially to three chapters (4 to 6), which begin with an exposition of the so-called "Protestant Ethic", then offer a pivotal account of Puritanism and the "motive forces of the New Science", and conclude with a would-be "experimentum crucis", a head-count of supposed Puritans among the membership of the Royal Society of London in its early years. In spite of vigorous opposition from a number of historians – who pointed out, for example, that the motive forces for science that Merton finds in Puritanism were found among many other religious groups, including in some cases even Catholics, and that his attribution of Puritanism to various thinkers was highly tendentious – Merton's thesis has never been entirely dismissed by historians of science.

WEBSTER (1974) includes an important set of papers by various historians disputing the Puritanism-and-science thesis, although here the case for the defense is put by the historian Christopher Hill, rather than by Merton himself. COHEN provides an extremely useful collection of items for those interested in the Merton thesis as a historiographical phenomenon; it includes a long survey of the impact of the Merton thesis since its publication, a bibliography of books and articles on the thesis, Merton's own chapter on the "Motive Forces of the New Science", an essay on Merton's other work in the sociology of science, a series of articles by other writers arguing the links between Puritanism, or at least Protestantism, and science, extracts from some notable discussions of Merton's thesis, a section devoted to the contributions of the historian Charles Webster to this historiographical debate, and three of Merton's own musings on his original thesis and its impact, written at different stages of his subsequent career. Although

concerned primarily with the Merton thesis itself, rather than with the relations between science and religion in 17th-century England, it none the less provides a valuable resource for revealing how historians have dealt with this particular aspect of the interface between science and religion.

WEBSTER (1975) is the major historical study written in support of the Puritanism-and-science thesis. A monumental and magisterial contribution to scholarship, it surveys in untiring detail early 17th-century attempts to reform education, natural philosophy, medicine, and other forms of knowledge of nature such as alchemy, husbandry, and agriculture. It also details the social and political context of the period of the Puritan Revolution. Although Puritanism figures largely in the book as a category, there is relatively little discussion of theology and religion. Webster does make one important addition to the list of supposed connections between the advancement of science and religious concerns, however: he shows the significance of millenarian expectations and their relevance to the attempts made to use natural philosophy for the "relief of man's estate".

For a deeper consideration of the role of theology in the rise of modern science, and one that emphasizes Protestant, if not necessarily Puritan, theology, we can consider HOOYKAAS. While cautiously acknowledging other factors, Hooykaas believes that a new approach to natural philosophy in the late Renaissance period was inspired by the Protestant encouragement to read the Bible for oneself. A new awareness of the transcendence of God, together with new efforts to read God's other book (Nature), Hooykaas suggests, led to an emphasis on voluntarism in theology (in which the world is seen as the creation of God's arbitrary will), and to empiricism in natural philosophy (since a world created by the arbitrary will of its creator cannot be rationally reconstructed).

Hooykaas presents his case as a major historical shift to empiricism from a rationalism that was primarily inspired by ancient Greek philosophy, but this is to overlook an alternative theology to voluntarism, usually called intellectualism, which held that God created the world to a rational pattern, and that it was possible in principle to "think God's thoughts after Him". An early, and rather philosophical analysis of these two theologies of Providence is provided by Michael Foster in WYBROW. Although not very well-known, Foster's three papers on these matters, originally published in the philosophical journal *Mind* in the 1930s and gathered together in this recent volume, have proved very influential among scholars working in this area, some of whom provide critical assessments in this useful tribute volume. Although he analyses both voluntarism and intellectualism, like Hooykaas, Foster believes that voluntarism has had the greatest impact on the historical development of science.

So, too, does KLAAREN, who focuses upon Robert Boyle's theologically-inspired natural philosophy as representative of the importance of voluntarism in the historical development of modern science. Boyle's thinking can be seen, according to Klaaren, as typical of a "major current of thought" in the 17th century, also manifested in the work of Francis Bacon, Isaac Newton and the early Royal Society. Nevertheless, Klaaren also provides an important, but brief, study of Johan Baptist van Helmont, in which his unique system of chemical philosophy is linked to the unorthodox tradition of Spiritualist theology.

This part of Klaaren's study is useful for demonstrating how even recondite and unorthodox theological positions may influence the theory and practice of natural science.

If Merton, Webster, Hooykaas, Foster and Klaaren are principally concerned to show the influence of theology and religion on the origins of modern science, FUNKENSTEIN seeks to illustrate the influence of natural philosophy on theology. In a major and fundamentally important study of the transformations of four specific areas of traditional theology, as a result of the arguments of natural philosophers, Funkenstein argues that theology was effectively secularized in the 17th century. The revival of so-called natural theology was only part of this story, Funkenstein insists, which also saw the natural philosopher taking over intellectual domains that had previously been the province of theologians. Funkenstein's story is one of dissolving or shifting disciplinary boundaries, in which natural philosophy begins to usurp the position of the former "queen of the sciences", theology, and to pronounce not only upon the existence and nature of God, but also upon the nature of right religion. This process should also be seen, according to Funkenstein, as another factor in the subsequent decline of religion and the secularization of our culture.

Although KOYRÉ's study of the development of the concept of infinite space pre-dates Funkenstein by over three decades, it can be regarded as a fifth case-study of the secularization of theology by natural philosophers. This classic study of Renaissance cosmology has much to say on the theories of the relationship of God to the world. While describing what he sees as the destruction of the cosmos and the geometrization of space, Koyré is led to consider theories of the divinization of space, in which the immensity of an infinite space is seen as an attribute of God. Koyré concludes, however, that space soon lost its attributive and substantial character, and became the void of the atomists, an uncreated nothingness that, instead of being the frame of God's presence and action, became the frame of the absence of all being, including God's.

JOHN HENRY

See also Merton Thesis; Religion and Science: general works

Representation

Blum, Ann Shelby, *Picturing Nature: American Nineteenth-Century Zoological Illustration*, Princeton, New Jersey: Princeton University Press, 1993

Coelho, Victor (ed.), *Music and Science in the Age of Galileo*, Dordrecht and Boston: Kluwer, 1992

Cohen, I. Bernard, *From Leonardo to Lavoisier, 1450–1800*, New York: Scribner, 1980

Daston, Lorraine and Peter Galison, "The Image of Objectivity", *Representations*, 40 (1992): 81–128

Ford, Brian J., *Images of Science: A History of Scientific Illustration*, London: British Library, 1992; New York: Oxford University Press, 1993

Levenson, Thomas, *Measure for Measure: A Musical History of Science*, New York: Simon and Schuster, 1994

Lynch, Michael and Steve Woolgar (eds), *Representation in Scientific Practice*, Cambridge, Massachusetts: MIT Press, 1990

Mazzolini, Renato G. (ed.), *Non-Verbal Communication in Science Prior to 1900*, Florence: Olschki, 1993

Pera, Marcello and William R. Shea (eds), *Persuading Science: The Art of Scientific Rhetoric*, Canton, Massachusetts: Science History Publications, 1991

Rudwick, Martin, "The Emergence of a Visual Language for Geological Science, 1760–1840", *History of Science*, 14 (1976): 148–95

Schiebinger, Londa, *Nature's Body: Gender in the Making of Modern Science*, Boston: Beacon Press, 1993

Shirley, John W. and David F. Hoeniger (eds), *Science and the Arts in the Renaissance*, Washington, DC: Folger Shakespeare Library, and London: Associated University Presses, 1985

Stafford, Barbara Maria, *Voyage into Substance: Art, Science, Nature and the Illustrated Travel Account, 1760–1840*, Cambridge, Massachusetts: MIT Press, 1984

Stafford, Barbara Maria, *Body Criticism: Imaging the Unseen in Enlightenment Art and Medicine*, Cambridge, Massachusetts: MIT Press, 1991

Stafford, Barbara Maria, *Artful Science: Enlightenment, Entertainment, and the Eclipse of Visual Education*, Cambridge, Massachusetts: MIT Press, 1994

Tufte, Edward R., *The Visual Display of Quantitative Information*, Cheshire, Connecticut: Graphics Press, 1983

Tufte, Edward R., *Envisioning Information*, Cheshire, Connecticut: Graphics Press, 1990

Wechsler, Judith (ed.), *On Aesthetics in Science*, Cambridge, Massachusetts: MIT Press, 1978

From an already rich tradition in philosophy and art criticism, aesthetics has recently gained a following in the history of science, especially over the last two decades. Aesthetics is concerned with representation as well as perception, meaning (within the context of the history of science) the historical representation of scientific ideas and practices. Most histories of scientific representation focus on the visual arts, both because traditionally the philosophical discipline of aesthetics has done so, and because the sciences have relied heavily upon visual representations (graphs, paintings, sketches, photographs) to communicate ideas. However, music and technology have frequently been vehicles for scientific communication – for example, Johannes Kepler expressed his planetary system using not only a concentric-sphere model, but also a harmonic series of notes on a musical scale. Additionally, historians have studied the rhetoric or discourse of science as an important aesthetic. Histories of representation and science, then, concentrate on the expression of scientific ideas – whether verbal, visual, musical, material, etc. Many of the scholars discussed here agree that scientists not only represent a world based on culturally-accepted aesthetic norms, but also see the world through glasses that are tinted by their culture's aesthetics. One can then argue that the distinction between perception and representation is essentially a false one.

A good way of approaching this complex area is to begin with the work of Edward R. Tufte, an inspirational author for many historians of technology and science. Unless borrowed from a library, his books can be difficult and costly to obtain: Tufte published both his books through a self-owned, independent press, and charges a little under $50 for each volume.

What they lack in availability, however, they easily make up for in quality. Tufte was among the first (and still among the most persuasive) to call attention to the historical importance of visual thinking for scientists and engineers, and his illustrations of this point are deservedly famous. TUFTE (1990) spans a wide range of images, while TUFTE (1983) concentrates on charts and graphs.

One predictable and necessary outcome of Tufte's work was the development of the history of scientific illustration, which was in turn influenced by the discipline of art history generally. A seminal article by RUDWICK argues that, during the period when geology was developing into a profession (1760–1840), it simultaneously adopted a predominantly visual mode of communicating its ideas. Rudwick's subsequent work in the history of stratigraphy and paleontology has elaborated on the notion that images are a vital and distinct form of argumentation for the sciences. Although focusing on 19th-century zoological illustration in America, BLUM elaborates extensively on Rudwick's thesis, as she weaves visual representations of zoology in the 19th century together with the social mores, instruments, and institutions that supported their production. Her emphasis is on the production and the producers of these images, rather than on the static images themselves. In another important article, DASTON & GALISON survey illustrations from the scientific revolution to 1900, in order to argue that late 19th-century scientists, in the interests of claiming objectivity, attempted to remove any indication that their images were the productions of human agents. Before then, the accuracy of an image derived from the authority of the image-maker, but in the Victorian era objective images had to be inscribed, not by the skilled eye and hand, but by the incorruptible, inhuman lenses of scientific instruments. In his general history of scientific illustration, FORD includes the entire chronology and most fields of science, but lacks the analytic punch of the aforementioned authors.

Outside of scientific illustration specifically, there are few book-length surveys on the history of scientific representation, but several earlier works still prove useful. COHEN's series of illustrated histories of science are intended to show how science was perceived by people in the past, in order to convey a sense of immediacy that is not always available through text alone. The authors in this series rarely analyze how images have changed science, but there is great value in the wealth of illustrations reproduced, the breadth of topics covered (these are no mere chronicles of "great discoveries" or portrait galleries of "great men"), and the often provocative juxtaposition of textual history and images.

Furthermore, several excellent edited volumes have been published recently. Rather than attempting a unified argument, these volumes usually gather together diverse approaches to representation in the history of science. For example, the 20 essays in MAZZOLINI feature virtually every time period and scientific field – themes include Victorian depictions of prehistoric life, representations of machinery in 15th-century Siena, and textbook illustrations in the 17th and 18th centuries – and are written by many of the most prominent historians of scientific representation. SHIRLEY & HOENIGER's contributors are primarily art historians who concentrate on three main aspects of the relationship between art and science during the Renaissance: the philosophical similarities and conflicts between them, science's connection with the practical arts, and the intertwining of science and art within the humanistic context. While this volume defines the arts almost exclusively as visual, COELHO's contributors look at the interaction between music and science during the same period. Also examining music's historical interface with science, the popular science writer LEVENSON makes a wider, but more episodic, chronological sweep, paying particular attention to cross-fertile histories of scientific and musical instruments.

While the above collections look at aspects of science that are more obviously open to aesthetic analysis (e.g. scientific illustrations and instrument design), the authors in WECHSLER take a broader view, claiming that formulas, models, theories, and the like are also influenced by aesthetic criteria. Here, scientists' output is studied as if it were an artistic production, since both artists and scientists are understood to be visual thinkers.

Historians of gender, race, sexuality, and science have used scientists' representations as a critical tool. Specifically, many have argued that Western scientists have used the white heterosexual male as the aesthetic standard to which all other races, sexualities, and genders were unfavorably compared. Most of the major studies in these areas deal with representation in some form, but SCHIEBINGER's collection of essays is the most comprehensive introduction to this vast literature, since she discusses both gender and race.

STAFFORD (1991), an art historian, examines the image of the body in the Enlightenment, when the human form was weighted heavily with cultural meanings. Since then, she argues, bodies have lost much of this meaning, largely because in the 20th century we no longer know how to read images. Stafford has written on another popular area within scientific representation, namely 18th- and 19th-century voyages to the "New World"; STAFFORD (1984) links the sublime with paintings produced by artists on the European ships. Her latest work, STAFFORD (1994), ties the author's earlier work into a unified history of how literary culture triumphed over "audio–visual" culture after the Enlightenment. Her fluid treatment of science, technology, and the arts is founded on her thesis that the boundaries between these activities are virtually indistinguishable.

Of late, sociologists of scientific knowledge and kindred anti-realists have been as vocal as analytical philosophers in defining the terms of the history of scientific representation. LYNCH & WOOLGAR's edited volume gathers together work on both historical and contemporary episodes. The contributors agree that scientists (or anyone else, for that matter) can only know the world through representations, and argue that these representations are all we have: we cannot appeal to any "objective" world from which is subtracted the social, economic, political, and cultural contexts. PERA & SHEA's collections of essays by historians and philosophers of science, while not taking the anti-realist approach of Lynch & Woolgar, continue an important aspect of that approach: namely, rhetoric as a tool for the representation of scientific ideas.

ANDREW M.M. SAMUEL

See also Reading Culture and Science; Rhetoric; Scientific Illustration

Reproductive Medicine

Clarke, Adele, "Controversy and the Development of Reproductive Sciences", *Social Problems*, 37 (1989): 18–37

Clarke, Adele, "Research Materials and Reproductive Science in the United States, 1910–1940", in *Ecologies of Knowledge: Work and Politics in Science and Technology*, edited by Susan Leigh Star, Albany: State University of New York Press, 1995

Martin, Emily, *The Woman in the Body: A Cultural Analysis of Reproduction*, Boston: Beacon Press, 1987; Milton Keynes: Open University Press, 1989

Moscucci, Ornella, *The Science of Woman: Gynaecology and Gender in England, 1800–1929*, Cambridge and New York: Cambridge University Press, 1990

Oudshoorn, Nelly, *Beyond the Natural Body: An Archaeology of Sex Hormones*, London and New York: Routledge, 1995

Pfeffer, Naomi "From Private Patients to Privatisation", in *Changing Human Reproduction: Social Science Perspectives*, edited by Meg Stacey, Newbury Park, California: Sage, 1992

Pfeffer, Naomi, *The Stork and the Syringe: A Political History of Reproductive Medicine*, Cambridge: Polity Press, and Cambridge, Massachusetts: Blackwell, 1993

Sandelowski, Margarete, "Failure of Volition: Female Agency and Infertility in Historical Perspective", *Signs*, 15 (1989): 465–99

Yoxen, Edward, "Historical Perspectives on Human Embryo Research", in *Experiments on Embryos*, edited by Anthony Dyson and John Harris, London and New York: Routledge, 1990

During the 20th century, doctors have acquired new ways of conferring biological parenthood on women and men who appear to be irremediably sterile. Although each new technique is heralded as a more effective treatment of sterility than its predecessors, PFEFFER (1993) shows that it is almost impossible to sustain such claims because the evidence is unreliable. Nevertheless, it is undoubtedly the case that virtually every new technique has provoked controversy, as shown by CLARKE (1989). Among the reasons she cites is their association with visionaries, in particular the eugenicists, who sought a scientific means of gaining control over reproduction in order to determine the direction of human evolution, both social and physical. The most vociferous and persistent opponents of reproductive technology are vitalists, who believe that materialist intervention in human procreation, especially by manipulating human gametes and embryos, is tantamount to murder and morally repugnant. Furthermore, where a sperm or egg is derived from another person, as is the case in artificial insemination using donated semen, the techniques are renounced because of the threat they are said to pose to the kinship relations that underpin the nuclear family. Although these arguments are more intensely expressed nowadays, YOXEN points out that, strictly speaking, the techniques are not new. He traces the origins of the scientific urge to manipulate human embryos to 19th-century anatomists, although conceding that before the 1960s they were collected for scientific investigation and not for clinical purposes. Furthermore, embryos were obtained fortuitously, after a reproductive "accident" such as miscarriage or abortion, whereas nowadays they are produced deliberately by in vitro fertilisation, which has raised new ethical concerns and, in some countries, has brought reproductive technology under the control of official regulations.

In addition to embryos, sperm, and eggs, live, fresh, and dead human and non-human animal tissues and body fluids were used, sometimes in vast quantities, in the development of techniques used by doctors in the treatment of sterility. Indeed, as CLARKE (1995) points out, securing reliable supplies of fresh and live materials, from the exotic to the mundane, became a large and time-consuming part of the daily work of reproductive scientists and their clinical colleagues who maintained the laboratories. OUDSHOORN describes how the isolation of male and female sex hormones – testosterone, oestrogen, and progestogen – in the 1920s and 1930s, now used extensively in reproductive medicine, was possible only where supplies of human and non-human ovaries and testes, blood and urine, were secured from abattoirs, hospitals, and farms. Because enormous quantities were sometimes needed, science-based pharmaceutical enterprises frequently monopolised scarce supplies, leaving short government-sponsored or academic scientists, and thereby stimulating unprecedented collaborations between individuals, disciplines, and institutions.

The birth in 1968 of Louise Brown, the first child conceived through in vitro fertilisation, was the product of one such collaboration: by exploiting the professional connections of the gynaecologist Patrick Steptoe, the scientist Robert Edwards gained access to human eggs with which he was able to carry out experiments on the technique of in vitro fertilisation. At first, their project caused consternation within the scientific and medical community; however, as PFEFFER (1992) points out, it quickly gave rise to a profitable infertility industry. It also changed the mix of professionals working within reproductive medicine: the investigation and treatment of involuntary childlessness had required the skills of gynaecologists, urologists, and endocrinologists; now it could be accomplished by a gynaecologist backed up by a technician with expertise in tissue culture and embryology.

The processes that give rise to the emergence of a medical specialty are complex and do not necessarily reflect the conditions that people complain of, and which doctors treat. MOSCUCCI argues that the medical specialty of gynaecology emerged in the 19th century as the "science of woman", a corollary to anthropology, the "science of man". The purpose of gynaecology was then to classify and regulate woman, and not to investigate and treat the conditions that troubled women. Moscucci's thesis also explains why andrology, a separate medical specialty for problems of the male reproductive system, has barely emerged. Hence, while "reproductive medicine" is an appropriate generic term that describes the investigation and treatment of involuntary childlessness, it has also the virtue of reminding us of the crucial, but changing, relationship between the clinic and the reproductive scientific community.

Increasingly in the 20th century, involuntary childlessness has been defined as a medical problem, yet, until fairly recently, its existence was rarely acknowledged. This is because of the hegemony of the "contraceptive hypothesis", which proposes that childlessness and small families are always the result of deliberate action. The hypothesis has conveyed the impression that fertility is rarely compromised, and has convinced us that the problem facing women and men is how to keep it in check. Pfeffer traces the origins of the contraceptive hypothesis to the end of World War II, when fear of a global "population explosion" emerged. Its influence can be seen everywhere. Social scientists investigating women's reproductive histories, for example, rarely ask about difficulties women may have had with respect to conception or maintaining a pregnancy. MARTIN's work provides a good example of this tendency; her schedule of questions leaps from the experience of menstruation to pregnancy and childbirth. The powerful institutional response to fear of population growth highlights the significance of the political context of reproductive medicine. It also explains why fertility and birth control are seen as public issues, whereas involuntary childlessness has been privatised and individualised. SANDELOWSKI calls infertility a "failure of volition"; none the less, it is a gendered condition, afflicting far more women than men.

NAOMI PFEFFER

See also Gynaecology; Medicine and the Law

Research and Development

Bowker, Geoffrey C., *Science on the Run: Information Management and Industrial Geophysics at Schlumberger, 1920–1940*, Cambridge, Massachusetts: MIT Press, 1994

Dennis, Michael Aaron, "Accounting for Research: New Histories of Corporate Laboratories and the Social History of American Science", *Social Studies of Science*, 17 (1987): 479–518

Edgerton, David and Sally Horrocks, "British Industrial Research and Development before 1945", *Economic History Review*, 47 (1994): 213–38

Edgerton, David, *Science, Technology and the British Industrial "Decline", 1870–1970*, Cambridge and New York: Cambridge University Press, 1996

Fitzgerald, Deborah, *The Business of Breeding: Hybrid Corn in Illinois, 1890–1940*, Ithaca, New York: Cornell University Press, 1990

Fukasaku, Yukiko, *Technology and Industrial Development in Pre-War Japan: Mitsubishi Nagasaki Shipyard, 1884–1934*, London and New York: Routledge, 1992

Goodchild, Peter, *J. Robert Oppenheimer: Shatterer of Worlds*, London: BBC, 1980; Boston: Houghton Mifflin, 1981

Gowing, Margaret, *Britain and Atomic Energy, 1939–1945*, London: Macmillan, and New York: St Martin's Press, 1964

Haber, L.F., *The Poisonous Cloud: Chemical Warfare in the First World War*, Oxford: Clarendon Press, and New York: Oxford University Press, 1986

Hoddeson, Lillian, *Critical Assembly: A Technical History of Los Alamos During the Oppenheimer Years, 1943–1945*, Cambridge and New York: Cambridge University Press, 1993

Jungk, Robert, *Brighter than a Thousand Suns: A Personal History of the Atomic Scientists*, translated from the German by James Cleugh, New York: Harcourt Brace, and London: Gollancz/Hart-Davis, 1958 (original edition, 1956)

Liebenau, Jonathan, *The Challenge of New Technology: Innovation in British Business since 1850*, Aldershot, Hampshire: Gower, 1988

MacKenzie, Donald A., *Inventing Accuracy: A Historical Sociology of Nuclear Missile Guidance*, Cambridge, Massachusetts: MIT Press, 1990

Mendelsohn, Everett, Merritt Roe Smith and Peter Weingart, *Science, Technology and the Military*, Dordrecht and Boston: Kluwer, 1988

Meyer-Thurow, Georg, "The Industrialisation of Invention: A Case Study from the German Chemical Industry", *Isis*, 73 (1982): 363–81

Mowery, David C. and Nathan Rosenberg, *Technology and the Pursuit of Economic Growth*, Cambridge and New York: Cambridge University Press, 1989

Noble, David F., *America by Design: Science, Technology and the Rise of Corporate Capitalism*, New York: Knopf, 1977; Oxford: Oxford University Press, 1979

Reader, W.J., *Imperial Chemical Industries: A History*, vol. 2: *The First Quarter Century, 1925–1952*, London: Oxford University Press, 1975

Reich, Leonard S., *The Making of American Industrial Research: Science and Business at GE and Bell, 1876–1926*, Cambridge and New York: Cambridge University Press, 1985

Smith Jr, John Kenly, "The Scientific Tradition in American Industrial Research", *Technology and Culture*, 31 (1990): 121–31

Research and Development (R&D) is best defined as organised, team-based scientific and technical research, combined with the refinement and improvement of existing products or processes. It is a potential source of both inventions and innovations, but its contribution to these processes has varied significantly over time and place. The history of R&D has been approached from several different perspectives, using a range of units of analysis from the nation state to the individual firm or laboratory. Treatments of R&D are often embedded in broader studies of science, technology and innovation. R&D has attracted scholars from a number of disciplines, reflecting the variety of institutional contexts in which it has taken place, the organisational structures that have provided funding, its varied goals, and the range of social groups that have been involved in and affected by it. Much of the literature has a strong North American and European bias, and falls into one of three interconnected areas: national systems of R&D; R&D in individual firms or industries; and military R&D. R&D also appears as a component of many more wide-ranging studies of science, technology, and society. NOBLE's important book is an essential starting point, which goes beyond the popular case-study approach to place the development of R&D within a wide-ranging analysis of the relationship between science, technology, and the rise of corporate capitalism.

Economists and economic historians have been interested in the history of R&D as an extension of their studies on the contribution of technology to economic growth and national competitiveness. Economists frequently draw on historical material to provide a background to their analyses of current events, and in so doing have made some important contributions. The work of MOWERY & ROSENBERG provides a good introduction to the literature. Here, and elsewhere, Rosenberg has argued for the importance of incremental change to economic growth, encouraging the historian to look not only for new discoveries, but also at more routine R&D work.

National systems of innovation have come to be regarded by many as playing an important role in economic performance, and this has led to several analyses of R&D capabilities at the level of the nation state, including state-funded R&D. Britain has been frequently identified as having a historically weak national R&D system, particularly within the industrial sector. However, this has recently been disputed by EDGERTON & HORROCKS, who draw on existing work as well as on new evidence regarding the R&D activities of British firms. EDGERTON has also argued that it is wrong to equate levels of spending on industrial R&D directly with economic growth, since countries that spent less on R&D grew more rapidly than Britain during the 1950s and 1960s.

Studies of R&D in individual firms and industries have enriched research at the level of the nation state, although as yet only a limited range of firms, industries and countries have been explored in detail. The electrical engineering and chemical industries in the US and Germany have received the most attention, in part because they have been identified as among the earliest sites for the development of industrial R&D in the late 19th century. In a pioneering and influential study, MEYER-THUROW wrote of the "industrialisation of invention" in the German dyestuffs industry in the 19th century, while REICH discusses the early years of research in the US electrical engineering industry. He notes the many different functions that R&D was called upon to fulfil, acting not only as a source of new products and processes, but also bringing prestige and access to knowledge generated elsewhere, enabling the control of rival technologies that could be used in defence of market positions. Drawing on Alfred Chandler's organisational approach, Reich and other scholars have produced detailed studies of the development of R&D within the large-scale industrial enterprise. SMITH's essay draws together these studies to explore what he identifies as the "scientific tradition in American industrial research". DENNIS, using much of the same literature, locates the corporate R&D laboratory within the social history of American science.

The quality and detail of this literature offers a benchmark against which to compare studies of other companies and nations, but the universal applicability of this model of industrial R&D has been questioned. As FUKASAKU's study of the Mitsubishi-Nagasaki shipyard in Japan reveals, the generation of new knowledge was not the only route to economic success. BOWKER's analysis of the French firm Schlumberger paints a very different picture of an R&D that takes place not in a laboratory, but out in the terrain of the oil field itself. This volume draws on a range of analytical approaches, including actor–network theory. The studies collected by LIEBENAU indicate something of the range of R&D activities conducted by British firms. By examining R&D in the US agricultural sector, FITZGERALD highlights the importance of including industries beyond those generally regarded as the most important users of R&D.

Perhaps the single most extensively documented R&D project in history is the United States Atomic Bomb project – the Manhattan Project. A large number of books examine this from a range of perspectives, from HODDESON's highly technical account, to GOODCHILD's popular biography of the project's director, J. Robert Oppenheimer. JUNGK's overview is a very readable introduction to events, although it should be supplemented by more recent works.

The British bomb project has been much less extensively explored, but the work of GOWING on this and the subsequent development of atomic energy in Britain provides an example of how large-scale military R&D projects were administered. HABER's examination of the poison gas programmes of Britain and Germany during World War I extends coverage of this issue, but it is only relatively recently, with the growth of interest in the emergence of a military–industrial–academic complex in the post-war United States, that these questions have been widely explored. Many of the essays collected by MENDELSOHN, SMITH & WEINGART cover this theme, while also considering contemporary developments in other nations. MacKENZIE has provided probably the most detailed study of the R&D process behind any post-war military technology, despite the secrecy of the research he examines. His aims are to understand the development of nuclear missile guidance systems as the product of specific social and political circumstances, and, by demonstrating the extent to which nuclear weapons were neither natural nor inevitable, to render a deadly technology passive.

While much of this recent work, particularly on the US, has focused on the interaction of the military, industry and the universities in the performance of war-like R&D, it is important to remember that this type of R&D has not always taken place with the same constellation of institutional actors. After World War II, university-based military science was never as important in Britain as in the US, and prior to the conflict, business enterprises were often responsible for the development of new weapons. Information on military R&D is often to be found in the histories of the individual firms that carried it out, although here, as elsewhere, their coverage is patchy and their R&D activities not always recorded in detail. READER, for example, includes a discussion of the oil from a coal programme carried out by ICI, with government support, in the late 1920s and 1930s.

SALLY HORROCKS

See also Capitalism and Science; Management Sciences; Technology

Respiration

Astrup, Poul and John W. Severinghaus, *The History of Blood Gases, Acids and Bases*, translated by Patrick Graham Jørgensen, Copenhagen: Munksgaard, 1986

Frank Jr, Robert G., *Harvey and the Oxford Physiologists*, Berkeley: University of California Press, 1980

Fruton, Joseph S., *Molecules and Life: Historical Essays on the Interplay of Chemistry and Biology*, New York: Wiley-Interscience, 1972

Goodfield, June, *The Growth of Scientific Physiology: Physiological Method and the Mechanist–Vitalist Controversy, Illustrated by the Problems of Respiration and Animal Heat*, London: Hutchinson, 1960; New York: Arno Press, 1975

Gottlieb, Leon S., *A History of Respiration*, Springfield, Illinois: Thomas, 1964

Holmes, Frederic L., *Claude Bernard and Animal Chemistry: The Emergence of a Scientist*, Cambridge, Massachusetts: Harvard University Press, 1974

Holmes, Frederic L., *Lavoisier and the Chemistry of Life: An Exploration of Scientific Creativity*, Madison: University of Wisconsin Press, 1985

Holmes, Frederic L., *Hans Krebs*, vol. 1: *The Formation of a Scientific Life, 1900–33*; vol. 2: *Architect of Intermediary Metabolism, 1933–37*, Oxford and New York: Oxford University Press, 1991–93

Holmes, Frederic L., *Between Biology and Medicine: The Formation of Intermediary Metabolism*, Berkeley: Office for History of Science and Technology, University of California, 1992

Keilin, David, *The History of Cell Respiration and Cytochrome*, prepared for publication by Joan Keilin, Cambridge: Cambridge University Press, 1966

Mendelsohn, Everett, *Heat and Life: The Development of the Theory of Animal Heat*, Cambridge, Massachusetts: Harvard University Press, 1964

In modern usage, the word respiration denotes two related, but distinct, sets of processes: first, the physical act of breathing, the transfer of gases from the lungs into the blood, and the distribution of these gases around the body; and second, the processes of aerobic metabolism taking place within the living body. This separation of meanings is relatively recent, however, and 19th-century scientists commonly included both aspects of respiration within the scope of their investigations. At the same time, many of those who worked on the chemical aspects of respiration were also interested in other chemical processes taking place within the body. Research into respiration and metabolism has therefore been closely intertwined in the past. This is reflected in the historical literature, and it is therefore convenient to consider the history of respiration and that of metabolism together.

GOTTLIEB is still probably the most useful introduction to the field as a whole; in just 100 pages, he provides a brief but valuable account of many of the main landmarks and controversies in the development of knowledge of respiration. He focuses mainly on research at the level of the organism, including the processes of breathing and respiratory exchange. MENDELSOHN examines the theories of animal heat and metabolism from the ancients onwards, concentrating especially on the 17th and 18th centuries. His concern is to show how vitalist concepts were gradually displaced by more materialist notions of life, which were informed by physical analogies and elaborated using physical and chemical techniques of experimentation. GOODFIELD offers a more detailed account of developments in respiration research during the first half of the 19th century, concentrating on experimental debates over the site and nature of the respiratory exchange, and on the generation of animal heat from Antoine Lavoisier to Claude Bernard. Her work is intended as a case study in the emergence of the new discipline of experimental physiology, characterised by a distinct body of knowledge and investigative techniques. In contrast to Mendelsohn's view of progressive materialism, she also stresses the fruitful interaction between reductionist or mechanistic programmes of investigation and the articulation of more holistic or vitalist approaches to the phenomena of life.

Readers with a specific interest in the early research into respiration and metabolism should consult FRANK, which shows how 17th-century British scientists sought to integrate Harvey's discovery of the circulation of the blood into a wider understanding of the nature of vital phenomena. Frank reveals, in particular, how these researchers drew on new experimental techniques, particularly from the chemical sciences, to develop a coherent and empirically grounded account of animal heat and breathing. He is also attentive to the social circumstances within which such work was conducted, and his analysis of the networks of collaboration and correspondence between scientists working in this area does much to reinstate physiology as one of the key fields of endeavour in what we now regard as the scientific revolution.

A considerable body of work has focused on the biochemical aspects of respiration, including both the transport of respiratory gases in the blood, and the intracellular processes of metabolism in which those gases are implicated. FRUTON covers the development of the whole field from the late 18th to the mid-20th century in two lengthy chapters, the first dealing chiefly with intracellular respiration, the second with emerging knowledge of the processes of intermediary metabolism. Like Goodfield, Fruton stresses the creative tension between reductionist and more organismic conceptions of vital phenomena. Particular aspects of this story are developed by KEILIN, who concentrates on the processes of tissue and cell respiration, particularly in more recent work. The first 140 pages survey the emergence of the notion of cell respiration up to 1925, while the remaining 200 pages offer a detailed account of research into cytochrome and its role in intracellular respiration – work in which Keilin himself played a leading role. A complementary perspective may be found in ASTRUP & SEVERINGHAUS, who provide a useful overview of the development of knowledge of blood gas transport, including work on the chemistry of haemoglobin and on the effects of blood pH. Their volume is of particular interest for the attention it pays to the clinical dimension of work on blood gases and pH, including the recent development of clinical technologies for measuring such factors.

By far the most detailed work in this field, however, has been conducted by Frederic L. Holmes. Two massive biographical studies deal with the work of Antoine Lavoisier on respiration (HOLMES, 1985) and Hans Krebs on cellular metabolism (HOLMES, 1991–93). HOLMES (1974), tangentially related to these, analyses Claude Bernard's work on the chemistry of nutrition, including the metabolism of foodstuffs. Each study carefully locates the experimental and theoretical work of the protagonists within the context of ongoing research and debate over the nature of metabolic processes, and does as much to illuminate this wider context as to analyse the investigative practices of the main subjects. Holmes has also produced a very valuable, sophisticated, and accessible overview of the history of intermediary metabolism, which synthesises and summarises many of the insights he has developed in the course of these more local and fine-grained studies. HOLMES (1992) looks in particular at the very different disciplinary programmes within which metabolic research was conducted during the period between about 1840 and 1940, and analyses some of the social and intellectual factors that led to their gradual convergence into a coherent field of concerted research. Just over 100 pages in length, this little volume stands out from other books in the field for the way in which it combines a synoptic understanding of the development of technical knowledge of metabolic research with a sensitive awareness of new forms of sociologically-oriented historiography of science.

STEVE STURDY

See also Biochemistry; Experimental Physiology; Nutrition; Physiology: France

Rhetoric

Bazerman, Charles, *Shaping Written Knowledge: The Genre and Activity of the Experimental Article in Science*, Madison: University of Wisconsin Press, 1988

Dear, Peter (ed.), *The Literary Structure of Scientific Argument: Historical Studies*, Philadelphia: University of Pennsylvania Press, 1991

Gilbert, G. Nigel and Michael Mulkay, *Opening Pandora's Box: A Sociological Analysis of Scientists' Discourse*, Cambridge and New York: Cambridge University Press, 1984

Gross, Alan G., *The Rhetoric of Science*, Cambridge, Massachusetts: Harvard University Press, 1990

Krips, Henry, J.E. McGuire and Trevor Melia (eds), *Science, Reason, and Rhetoric*, Pittsburgh: University of Pittsburgh Press, and Konstanz, Germany: Universitätsverlag Konstanz, 1995

Latour, Bruno and Steve Woolgar, *Laboratory Life: The Social Construction of Scientific Facts*, Beverley Hills, California: Sage, 1979; as *Laboratory Life: The Construction of Scientific Facts*, with a new postscript, Princeton, New Jersey: Princeton University Press, 1986

McCloskey, Donald N., *The Rhetoric of Economics*, Madison: University of Wisconsin Press, 1985

Myers, Greg, *Writing Biology: Texts in the Social Construction of Scientific Knowledge*, Madison: University of Wisconsin Press, 1990

Shapin, Steven, "Pump and Circumstance: Robert Boyle's Literary Technology", *Social Studies of Science*, 14 (1984): 481–520

The field of the rhetoric of science has only developed since the 1980s; of course, rhetoric *per se* has been a legitimate area of inquiry since the ancient Greeks, but the distinction in Aristotle between rhetoric and science has meant that a "rhetoric of science" seemed an impossibility, because the very distinctiveness of science as a body of valid reasoning came from its difference from rhetoric. With the development of the sociology of scientific knowledge (SSK), scholars started to investigate how the contents of well-accepted scientific knowledge could be examined using the tools of rhetorical and literary analysis. If science was to be regarded as a social construct, then it was surely constructed in part by literary and rhetorical means. Indeed, the importance of the literary constitution of scientific knowledge was emphasized as early as 1979 in LATOUR & WOOLGAR, which described scientists as literary reasoners who construct scientific facts by arguing over and interpreting inscriptions.

One of the first attempts to apply a full-blooded rhetorical analysis to an area of science was McCLOSKEY's pioneering book on economics, which showed how economic arguments are cast within a set of standard rhetorical tropes. McCloskey is himself an economic historian, and part of the weight of his argument was to contrast this rhetoric of economics with actual economic practice. His approach therefore carries with it a whiff of the sociology of error; i.e. the equating of rhetoric with error.

Another early attempt at a rhetoric of science can be found in BAZERMAN, which examines the changing form of the scientific article since the establishment of the Royal Society. There are examples from articles on physics and from American political science, with Bazerman offering a Vygotskian model of language in order to show how the semiotic community of science is constructed. This differs from the radical social constructivism of Latour & Woolgar, because, although Bazerman acknowledges the predominant role played by language in science, he does not treat scientific findings as being solely rhetorically constituted.

A more fully-fledged treatment of science as rhetoric is to be found in GROSS, whose intention it is to restore the power of rhetoric as a discipline. Rather than rhetoric being an inferior and subservient form of knowledge, Gross argues provocatively that science itself is a limited form of rhetoric. Gross makes connections between rhetoric in science and other forms of rhetoric, and analyzes the power of analogy in the context of the political oratory of F.D. Roosevelt, the scholarly arguments of the Popper-Kuhn debate, and the attempts by Watson and Crick to unravel the genetic code. A variety of textual examples are used throughout, including papers on taxonomy, Darwin's notebook, the Copernican revolution, Newton's optics, the priority dispute over the calculus, and recent debates concerning recombinant DNA research.

MYERS is an investigation of how textual and representational practices have shaped knowledge in several areas of modern biology. The work is notable because it focuses on fine-grain material, such as the textual revisions scientists make to articles as they seek to get them published. Popular science and the controversy over Wilson's sociobiology are also examined.

That a variety of materials traditionally collected by sociologists and historians, such as letters and interviews, can be subject to rhetorical analysis is the central tenet of GILBERT & MULKAY – a study of a controversy in modern biology known as oxidative phosphorylation. Developing a form of "discourse analysis", the authors argue that rhetorical strategies, and a variety of accounting practices, can be found within and between different sources of data – for example, interviews and scientific articles. This radical skepticism toward traditional sociological and historical enquiry – such as the imputation of motives, interests, and desires to actors – means that all the analyst can do is examine textual fragments, and examine how such texts are ordered in different discursive contexts. Among the topics treated are scientific humor and scientific diagrams.

In contrast to Gilbert & Mulkay, SHAPIN argues that rhetoric cannot be separated from material and social practice. Shapin shows that matters of experimental fact concerning the air pump were established by Boyle with the aid of a material technology (the air pump itself), a literary technology (the form the experimental reports took, whereby it would seem that the reader had witnessed a demonstration), and a social technology (whereby matters of fact would alone seem decisive).

The importance of literary and rhetorical analysis for the history of science is shown by DEAR. This collection of essays by historians of science spans three centuries and includes a variety of disciplines, including mathematics and medicine, as well as physiology and physics. One particular noteworthy theme is how disciplinary boundaries are textually constituted and reconstituted.

A variety of current approaches towards scientific rhetoric is exhibited in KRIPS, McGUIRE & MELIA. These essays are penned by philosophers of science who desire to defend scientific realism, and by sociologists of science who argue that science is totally rhetorically constituted. Other pieces by literary scholars illustrate how fresh light can be thrown on scientific texts by teasing out the nuanced readings more familiar to work on fictional genres. The aim of the collection as a whole is to try and strike a middle path between reason and rhetoric.

TREVOR J. PINCH

Rittenhouse, David   1732–1796

American astronomer

Barton, William, *Memoirs of the Life of David Rittenhouse, LLD F.R.S. – late President of the American Philosophical Society, &c. Interspersed with various notices of many distinguished men: with an Appendix, containing sundry philosophical and other papers, most of which have not hitherto been published*, Philadelphia: Edward Parker, 1813

Ford, Edward, *David Rittenhouse: Astronomer–Patriot, 1732–1796*, Philadelphia, University of Pennsylvania Press, 1946

Hindle, Brooke, *David Rittenhouse*, Princeton, New Jersey: Princeton University Press, 1964; reprinted New York: Arno Press, 1980

Hindle, Brooke (ed.), *The Scientific Writings of David Rittenhouse*, Princeton, New Jersey: Princeton University Press, 1964

Hindle, Brooke, entry on Rittenhouse in *Dictionary of Scientific Biography*, edited by Charles Coulston Gillispie, vol. 11, New York: Scribner, 1975

Rice Jr, Howard C., *The Rittenhouse Orrery: Princeton's Eighteenth-Century Planetarium, 1767–1954 – A Commentary on an Exhibition Held in the Princeton University Library*, Princeton, New Jersey: Princeton University Press, 1954

Rush, Benjamin, *An Eulogium, Intended to Perpetuate the Memory of David Rittenhouse, Late President of the American Philosophical Society, Delivered before the Society in the First Presbyterian Church, in High-Street, in Philadelphia, on the 17th Dec. 1796*, Philadelphia: Ormrod and Conrad, 1796

David Rittenhouse was a farmer's son who became first a clockmaker and instrument-maker and then rose steadily, through participation in the 1769 transit of Venus and membership of the American Philosophical Society, to a position at the heart of political power in the newly independent United States. He was an austere and disciplined man whose main activities all related to numbers: either he produced quantifying instruments, or else he manipulated numbers on paper. He is often compared to Isaac Newton, who also crowned a career in the exact sciences with an appointment to the management of money at the heart of state power.

HINDLE's entry in the *Dictionary of Scientific Biography* is the most convenient introduction to Rittenhouse. It gives a short description of his achievements and a brief bibliography of the main sources. HINDLE's 1964 book is the best biography for academic purposes. In close to 400 pages, it covers Rittenhouse's life chronologically and is based on a great variety of historical sources, ranging from manuscripts in the American Philosophical Society through correspondence with illuminaries of the American Revolution to government records. There is a very good bibliographical note at the end. Hindle is attentive to the historical context, be it religious, political or scientific. For example, Benjamin RUSH's eulogy to Rittenhouse shortly after his death is revealed to have been controversial, as not all constituencies agreed with Rush's presentation of Rittenhouse as a self-taught man, unfettered by academic artificialities. The famous physician and signatory of the Declaration of Independence's eulogy was highly conspicuous, as it was attended by the President, the Senate and House of Representatives of the United States, foreign ministers, consuls, judges of US and Pennsylvania courts, and many Philadelphia dignitaries. Hindle is good at uncovering the different reactions to such events in (and shortly after) Rittenhouse's life. The biography was reprinted in 1980 to coincide with the publication of Rittenhouse's scientific papers: HINDLE's 1980 work, which reproduces Rittenhouse's writings published in bona fide scientific journals, primarily in the *Transactions of the American Philosophical Society*. The papers are grouped by topic and not chronologically. There is a brief introduction by the editor, but no footnotes or scholarly apparatus.

FORD is a celebration of Rittenhouse. It has covered most of the historical sources listed by Hindle, but it stays very close to those dealing directly with Rittenhouse. It only barely refers to general developments in science or politics, and seems unaware of the ways in which Rittenhouse or his image could be used for particular partisan purposes, and assumes that everyone took Rittenhouse to be self-evidently heroic. None the less, it is highly readable and only half as long as Hindle's biography.

BARTON is a Victorian-style "Life and Letters", and its more than 600 pages makes it quite formidable. It quotes liberally but selectively from Rittenhouse's correspondence and from other letters about him. Some of the material used by

Barton is no longer extant and for serious historical study it is thus indispensable. Hindle has compared Barton's quotes with still extant sources and finds him reliable.

RICE's 1954 work was published to accompany an exhibition on an orrery that Rittenhouse made for the College of New Jersey (now Princeton University). It contains information on orreries in England and America, and on how orreries presented the Newtonian system as exemplified in planetary motion. It also contains a history of this particular orrery from 1767 to 1948.

ARNE HESSENBRUCH

See also Astronomy: general works; Franklin; Instrument Makers

Rockefeller Foundation

Brown, E. Richard, *Rockefeller Medicine Men: Medicine and Capitalism in America*, Berkeley: University of California Press, 1979

Bullock, Mary Brown, *An American Transplant: The Rockefeller Foundation and Peking Union Medical College*, Berkeley: University of California Press, 1980

Cueto, Marcos (editor), *Missionaries of Science: The Rockefeller Foundation and Latin America*, Bloomington: Indiana University Press, 1994

Fisher, Donald, *Fundamental Development of the Social Sciences: Rockefeller Philanthropy and the United States Social Science Research Council*, Ann Arbor: University of Michigan Press, 1993

Fosdick, Raymond Blaine, *The Story of the Rockefeller Foundation*, New York: Harper, 1952

Jonas, Gerald, *The Circuit Riders: Rockefeller Money and the Rise of Modern Science*, New York: Norton, 1989

Kay, Lily E., *The Molecular Vision of Life: Caltech, the Rockefeller Foundation, and the Rise of the New Biology*, New York and Oxford: Oxford University Press, 1993

Kohler, Robert E., *Partners in Science: Foundations and Natural Scientists, 1900–1945*, Chicago: University of Chicago Press, 1991

Shaplen, Robert, *Toward the Well-Being of Mankind: Fifty Years of the Rockefeller Foundation*, New York: Doubleday, 1964

The Rockefeller Foundation is a philanthropic foundation that has had a major influence on the history of science in the 20th century. It has funded various activities in a great many countries: public health, education, the social sciences, agriculture, and population. In the 1960s and 1970s in-house histories were produced that celebrated the Foundation's achievements. Since then, there has been a flowering of work on its history. Most of this work has also been supported by the Foundation itself, either through direct support of scholarship or indirectly through permitting and facilitating access to Foundation records at a well-equipped archive near New York City. The more recent histories, however, are generally critical of the impact which the Foundation has had upon science and society, both at home in the US and also in the Third World.

FOSDICK was President of the Rockefeller Foundation for 12 years and he had complete access to the Foundation's files. The book is addressed to "laymen" and the author is at pains to emphasize that it is not merely a shield against public censure and to recognise that the Foundation has made mistakes. None the less, given the great political difficulties in the 20th century, Fosdick summarizes the work of the Foundation as having contributed to the well-being of mankind throughout the world, as the stated aim of the Foundation has it. Fosdick pays much attention to the finances of the Foundation while humbly revealing the philanthropical work done to spread sanitation and scientific medicine. This emphasis was chosen by the Foundation because it avoided entanglements in religious, political, and social issues. The book also describes the Foundation's involvement in agriculture, social science, astrophysics, and the humanities.

SHAPLEN is an in-house history of the years since 1952, the publication date of Fosdick's volume. It is in large format and with many illustrations of happy Third-Worlders. The book is structured under the following headings: health, to feed the world, the world of ideas (academe and arts), and outlook.

By contrast, BROWN is a critique of the US medical system. Brown argues that the political-economic organization of American society generates certain types of technical innovation to the exclusion of others, which then feed back and generate new social forces. Within this feedback system, both Foundation and government policy have served the interests of some medical groups, but only because these coincided with those of the larger corporate class.

FISHER also finds the Foundation's policies to have been less than beneficial. Focusing on institutional history, he argues that the causes for the development of the social sciences in the US are to be found in external factors, such as changes in the economy, class structure, ideology, and hegemony. The 1920s and 1930s were particularly important, because it was in this period that a bargain was struck between social scientists, the Foundation, and the State. In this bargain, the role of academics was defined largely by the philanthropic foundations, and not by the academics themselves.

Working from the archival papers of leading American scientists and Foundation officers, KOHLER is able to construct an intimate portrait of the patronage relationships between academic scientists and philanthropists in the early 20th-century US. Kohler addresses the role of philanthropy in the growth of academic research, and the changes this wrought in universities, as well as the shaping of the ways in which scientists sought funding for "pure" research, first from the foundations and during and after World War II from the federal government. Academic research funded directly by commercial concerns created a different set of expectations and had a different form. The demonstration of the importance of Foundation priorities in choosing which lines of research, which methods, and which instruments to bankroll presents a significant mechanism through which to understand how social or individual priorities can shape the kind of knowledge that is created.

KAY discusses some of the same scientists as Kohler, but takes her analysis in a very different direction. Arguing that molecular biology was a key to scientific "social control," sought both by Foundation officers and scientists, Kay invokes a hegemonic world-view shared by her actors by virtue of common race, class, gender, and socialization. Kay's analysis concentrates on the California Institute of Technology in order to keep the study focused and manageable.

CUETO is a collection of papers paying special attention to the local reception of and responses to US philanthropy. Armando Solorzano, for example, relates how the Foundation had to adapt to different circumstances even in two Mexican provinces (Yucatan and Veracruz) when combating yellow fever. There is also much emphasis on the interests of the scientists in the North. For instance, while the Foundation instituted several programs in yellow fever in Latin America, the etiology of the disease was also of special interest to scientists at the Rockefeller Institute for Medical Research in New York City. The book contains papers on the Foundation's surveys of Latin America in the 1920s, on yellow fever and public health in Brazil (1920s) and Mexico (1900–22), on agriculture in Mexico in the mid-20th century, on physiology, and on genetics in Brazil (1943–60).

BULLOCK describes the history of the Peking Union Medical College (PUMC) which was funded by the Foundation and which became the most important institution through which the Chinese encountered and adopted Western medicine organized around hospital and laboratory. Instigated in the years after the Flexner report, the PUMC was to become a "Johns Hopkins for China". Bullock endeavours to get beyond an account of passive reception by the Chinese, and there is much emphasis on the student population and its diffusion throughout China. The printed historical sources are almost exclusively in English; Bullock has also conducted a number of interviews.

JONAS is a defense of the Foundation that addresses some of the charges of modern critics. It is thorough and well-written, emphasizing the difficulty of gauging the impact that scientific philanthropy will have. The author's stance may be judged from the conclusion that a philanthropic entity, as a friendly outsider, may play a useful role not just in supplying the cash but also in helping creative people decide what their needs are in the first place.

CARLA KEIRNS AND ARNE HESSENBRUCH

Romanticism

Broman, Thomas, "University Reform in Medical Thought at the End of the Eighteenth Century", *Osiris*, n.s., 5 (1989): 36–53

Clark, William, "On the Dialectical Origins of the Research Seminar", *History of Science*, 27 (1989): 111–54

Cunningham, Andrew and Nicholas Jardine (eds), *Romanticism and the Sciences*, Cambridge and New York: Cambridge University Press, 1990

Eichner, Hans, "The Rise of Modern Science and the Genesis of Romanticism", *Publications of the Modern Language Association of America*, 97 (1982): 8–30

Engelhardt, Dietrich von, *Hegel und die Chemie: Studie zur Philosophie und Wissenschaft der Natur um 1800*, Wiesbaden: Pressler, 1976

Engelhardt, Dietrich von, *Historisches Bewusstsein in der Naturwissenschaft: Von der Aufklärung bis zum Positivismus*, Freiburg: Alber, 1979

Gode von Aesch, Alexander, *Natural Science in German Romanticism*, New York: Columbia University Press, 1941

Haym, Rudolf, *Die romantische Schule: Ein Beitrag zur Geschichte des deutschen Geistes*, Berlin: Görtner, 1870

Heine, Heinrich, *The Romantic School*, in *Selected Works*, edited and translated from the German by Helen M. Mustard and Max Knight, New York: Random House, 1973

Kuhn, Thomas S., "Energy Conservation as an Example of Simultaneous Discovery", in his *The Essential Tension: Selected Studies in Scientific Tradition and Change*, Chicago: University of Chicago Press, 1977

Lenoir, Timothy, *The Strategy of Life: Teleology and Mechanics in Nineteenth-Century German Biology*, Dordrecht and Boston: Reidel, 1982

Levere, Trevor H., *Poetry Realized in Nature: Samuel Taylor Coleridge and Early Nineteenth-Century Science*, Cambridge and New York: Cambridge University Press, 1981

Taylor, Charles, *Hegel*, Cambridge and New York: Cambridge University Press, 1975

Wetzels, Walter D., *Johann Wilhelm Ritter: Physik im Wirkungsfeld der deutschen Romantik*, Berlin: De Gruyter, 1973

Ziolkowski, Theodore, *German Romanticism and Its Institutions*, Princeton, New Jersey: Princeton University Press, 1990

In the period between 1780 and 1830, Romanticism dominated poetry, art, music, philosophy, and politics, mirroring the intellectual, cultural, political, and social ferment of that era. Romanticism is well known for its attacks on Enlightenment science, but recent work has shown that it was also important in the creation of new sciences.

The diverse legacies of Romanticism are apparent in the radically different treatments of the "Romantic School" by Heinrich Heine and Rudolf Haym. HEINE's brilliant commentary on the school to which he once belonged is an iconoclastic, tendentious, witty, satirical, and deeply ironic essay that displays a carefree attitude to scholarly standards. HAYM's work, on the other hand, is magisterial and judicious, as encyclopedic in its treatment of the sources as it is narrow in its focus – a monument to the erudite and disciplined historical scholarship that developed out of the Romantic fascination with history. Both authors saw Romanticism as a German literary movement, but where Heine's concerns are literary–political, Haym's are literary–philosophical. Neither author suggested that Romanticism was important in the history of science.

Heine wrote his work to introduce a French audience to Romanticism, and to correct Madame de Staël's *De l'Allemagne*. His proximity to his subjects, especially German reactionary politics, brings his account to life and helps explain its polemical character. Heine addressed Romanticism in general, which he depicted as the revival of medieval poetry, and the Romantic School in particular, a very specific group that arose in Jena in the 1790s under the shrewd direction of the brothers

August Wilhelm and Friedrich Schlegel. He dismissed the notion that the school based itself on idealism, *Naturphilosophie*, or any philosophy whatever, arguing instead that it could only be understood within the political context of the German lands, especially during and after the Napoleonic occupation. Conditions were then favourable for the resurgence of a mystical, superstitious, Catholic, "medieval–Christian movement" that rejected democracy, Enlightenment, all things French, and the cosmopolitanism of Herder, Goethe and Schiller.

Haym addressed only the Romantic School in its narrow sense, a group that included Ludwig Tieck, Novalis, Hölderlin, the Schlegels, J.F.W. Schelling, F.E.D. Schleiermacher, and the natural scientists J.W. Ritter and H. Steffens. These individuals, all of whom were born between 1767 and 1775 and most of whom gathered in Jena around 1800, were taken as representative of broader trends. Haym saw Schelling's *Naturphilosophie* as a pinnacle of Romanticism: the union of Goethe's vision of nature with Fichtean idealism. *Die romantische Schule* lends itself to consultation and reference, but it must not be confused with a compendium. It is a book with an argument representative of 19th-century *Geistesgeschichte*. Whereas Heine argued that the fascination with "spirit" so typical of the Romantic School was a sign of mysticism and political reaction, Haym believed that the German "literary revolution" of Romanticism was directly analogous to the French Revolution, and attributes the dissolution of the Romantic School to its literal and metaphorical drift toward the mysticism of the Catholic south of Germany – giving rise to a general crisis that found its resolution not in political life, but in Hegel.

An updated version of *Geistesgeschichte* is available through the philosopher Charles Taylor's treatment of how the aims of the Romantic era informed Hegel's thought. Adopting the terminology employed by I. Berlin and M.H. Abrams, TAYLOR argues that Romanticism was characterized by an "expressive" theory of art and language. Expressivism, which Taylor associates with Rousseau and Herder, was strongly anti-dualist, held that the individual developed within organic communities, and rejected the mechanistic, atomistic, and utilitarian understanding of life it associated with the *philosophes*. Taylor's account only touches on science, but it suggests that the philosophical anthropology of Herder and the Romantics needs to be studied within the context of natural history and philosophy.

Well aware of the difficulties of defining Romanticism, GODE VON AESCH organized his book around the "age of Goethe", not because Goethe's life encompassed the Romantic epoch, but because Goethe embodied the strivings of the age – especially its captivation with the idea of unity. The Romantic, Goethean project was to do for its era what Lucretius did for his: the creation of a poem of the world that would unite humanity, nature, science, and literature in a modern myth. Gode von Aesch's erudite account finds these tendencies in many literary figures, and also in scientists such as Alexander von Humboldt and L. Oken.

In an important paper, KUHN argued that Schelling's belief in the interrelation of magnetic, electrical, chemical, and organic phenomena, and his constant search for conversion and transformation processes, gave scientists certain philosophical predispositions that led to the simultaneous discovery of the conservation of energy. Kuhn was not the first historian of science to consider *Naturphilosophie* seriously, but his paper came at an important time, when the history of science was becoming a fully independent discipline, setting its own questions and no longer guided by the agendas of scientists.

The fruits of such confidence in the methods of the history of science can be seen in the work of Dietrich von Engelhardt, Timothy Lenoir, Trevor Levere, and Walter Wetzels. ENGELHARDT (1976) is a useful book, both because it makes sense of Hegel's chemistry and, even more importantly, because it does so through a general discussion of Romantic science, especially chemistry. Hegel sought neither to undermine current chemistry nor to create an alternative to it, but rather to develop a philosophy that explained nature according to logical categories that underlie human consciousness and the historical world. Engelhardt brings clarity to general discussions of Romantic science by distinguishing between the transcendental *Naturphilosophie* of Kant, J.G. Fichte and scientists such as J.F. Blumenbach and J.J. Fries; metaphysical *Naturphilosophie*, which had a speculative version in Schelling and Hegel, and a Romantic version in the science of Ritter, Steffens and Oken; and, "scientific *Naturphilosophie*", or the empirical research methods and progress of modern science. By 1830, the scientific version prevailed, the transcendental version had a few adherents, and metaphysical *Naturphilosophie*, though barely remembered, was thought to have hindered scientific progress.

LENOIR argues that Kant's *Critique of Judgement*, and the biology of Blumenbach, J.C. Reil and K.F. Kielmeyer, laid out a "teleo-mechanist research program" that shaped German biology through the first half of the 19th century. Unlike the notions of teleology common in Britain, teleo-mechanism did not depend on religious arguments. Thus Blumenbach's *Bildungstrieb* (formative drive) was the emergent property of an organism, not an external agent acting upon it. Lenoir's provocative and original thesis makes sense of a large body of refractory evidence, and demonstrates the importance of non-Darwinian biology, but his broad application of I. Lakatos's notion of a "research program" has been criticized for succeeding at the expense of historical accuracy.

The life of the physicist J.W. Ritter is emblematic of Romantic science. His discovery of ultra-violet light and his chemical interpretation of galvanism earned him a place in historical reference works, while his growing fascination with mysticism and magical galvanism (especially after his move to Munich in 1805), his self-experimentation, and his untimely death led Haym to see his work as "Romanticism grown wild". WETZELS shows that Ritter's science was not half-baked philosophy papered over with some chemistry and physics. His study of the oscillations and periodicity of the voltaic pile, pendulum, and balance, especially in their relation to the human body, gave concrete expression to the Romantic belief in the unity of humans and nature. Moreover, Wetzels argues that the Munich period was not a break from, but rather a natural continuation of his study of galvanism.

The relationship between science and Romanticism might have been most evident in Germany, but it also made itself felt in Britain. LEVERE's meticulous study treats Coleridge's first-hand experience with *Naturphilosophie*, as well as his knowledge of British empiricism, and shows the shape that both took in his work. Coleridge saw value in empiricism, but he feared that its associations with materialism would lead Britain down the path to social strife. Unlike some sympathizers with *Naturphilosophie*, Coleridge gave a central place to Christianity and Trinitarianism in his natural philosophy. Levere explains the relationship between Coleridge's poetic and scientific pursuits, the part he played in the dissemination of German thought, and his involvement with the British scientific community.

Over the course of his career, the literary historian Hans EICHNER has studied the multiple meanings of Romanticism, a problem that also preoccupied A.O. Lovejoy and René Wellek. In an essay of broad scope, Eichner describes Romanticism as a reaction against the mechanistic science of the 17th and 18th centuries. The Romantic fascination with organicism, the uniqueness of the individual and historical explanations, as well as the emphasis on intuition, insight, and imagination were all aimed at overcoming the consequences of mechanistic materialism. Eichner puts the work of Schelling, Ritter, and Steffens at the centre of the Romantic project, but he concludes that their scientific forays were colossal failures: the Romantic historical turn gave us *Geisteswissenschaft*, but after recovering from its Romantic delirium *Naturwissenschaft* returned to its Enlightenment sources. Eichner thus implies that historians of science are well-suited to understand Romanticism, but his conclusion is oddly ahistorical, for it implies that either the biology, geology and physics of 1830 were directly continuous with the natural history and natural philosophy of 1780, or that Romanticism had no part in shaping the new structure of science.

Eichner's paper could serve as an example of the historiographic strategies ENGELHARDT (1979) describes in his study of historical consciousness in the sciences. Just as the historiography of the Enlightenment insisted that scholasticism and Aristotelianism needed to be overcome before science could progress, so also "positivist" science after 1830 regarded Romantic science as an obstacle to its progress. Engelhardt shows that such a historiography, which the Romantics themselves directed against their enlightened predecessors, is more useful for legitimating current scientific practices than for understanding the past.

The papers in CUNNINGHAM & JARDINE provide an overview of recent work and point to some new directions for scholarship. Thus Simon Schaffer's essay explores the ways in which genius, a concept rampant in Romantic thought, played an important part in the cultural politics that undid 18th-century natural philosophy and helped to establish the new role of the scientist. Madness and abnormal psychology, topics not unrelated to genius, are the subject of Nigel Reeves's paper on the playwright Heinrich von Kleist, which suggests the importance of medicine and medical institutions for studies of Romanticism and science.

Thomas Broman and William Clark address the transition from the 18th-century *Gelehrter* (scholar) to the 19th-century research professor. BROMAN links Reil's plans to create a professoriate of medical theory (distinct from medical practitioners) with *Naturphilosophie*'s ideal of a unified *Wissenschaft*. Instead of portraying *Naturphilosophie* as a set of doctrines concerning polarity and harmony, Broman sees it as a program to create a unified *Wissenschaft*, with science at its

head. The plans of Schelling and Reil failed, but they were among the first to envision the new research professor, free to pursue *Wissenschaft* without the practical concerns of a profession. CLARK finds the origins of the research professor in the philological seminar. In a panoramic presentation of the history of scholarship, Clark traces the origin of the seminar to the early modern era, when the "juridical–theological" conceptual space of the medieval college gave way to the "economic–political" space of the early modern cathedra, collegium, seminar, and society. These institutions were themselves sublimated into the modern research institute, where the modern researcher, member of a bureaucratic class, pursued the Romantic ideal of "originality". The work of Broman and Clark shows that the research professorship was not simply an outgrowth of the expansion of scientific knowledge, but part of a historically made professional identity.

The Romantics are typically associated with a life that was unusual, unconventional, and unstructured, but while the years at Jena c.1800 were unsettled for many, Romanticism was not an especially impractical era. Novalis was a mining engineer, a number of prominent Romantics studied at the mining academy in Freiberg, Goethe was trained in the law before he worked in mines and was a minister in several departments in Weimar, and many of the rest became successful professors. ZIOLKOWSKI looks at these more practical aspects of Romanticism in his exploration of five Romantic institutions: mines, the law, madhouses, universities, and museums. His primary aim is to show their relation to literature, but his discussion – particularly of mines, madhouses, and universities – is important for historians of science, as the *Geist* of Romanticism also manifested itself in institutions, or was created by them. Ziolkowski reminds us that if we are to understand the Romantic era, we would do well to remember the political analysis of Romanticism by Heine, himself trained as a lawyer. The Romantics were never so insular or other-worldly as their ideology suggests.

ERNST P. HAMM

See also Genius; Germanophone Areas

Röntgen, Wilhelm Conrad   1845–1923

German physicist

Beier, Walter, *Wilhelm Conrad Röntgen*, Stuttgart and Leipzig: Teubner, 1985, 2nd edition, 1995

Brachner, Alto *et al. Röntgenstrahlen-Entdeckung, Wirkung, Anwendung*, Munich: Deutsches Museum, 1995

Dessauer, Friedrich, *Die Offenbarung einer Nacht: Leben und Werk von Wilhelm Conrad Röntgen*, Frankfurt: Josef Knecht, 1958; 4th edition, 1988

Fölsing, Albrecht, *Wilhlem Conrad Röntgen: Aufbruch ins Innere der Materie*, Munich: Hanser, 1995

Glasser, Otto, *Wilhelm Conrad Röntgen and the Early History of the Roentgen Rays*, translated from the German by Margaret Boveri, Springfield, Illinois: Thomas, 1934 (original edition, 1931)

Lemmerich, Jost, *100 Jahre Röntgenstrahlen* (exhibition catalogue), Universität Würzburg, 1995

Nitske, W. Robert, *The Life of Wilhelm Conrad Röntgen, Discoverer of the X-Ray*, Tucson: University of Arizona Press, 1971

Turner, Gerard L'E., entry on Röntgen in *Dictionary of Scientific Biography*, edited by Charles Coulston Gillispie, vol. 11, New York: Scribner, 1975

Many books were published to celebrate the 100th anniversary of the discovery of X-rays, including at least five monographs onWilhelm Conrad Röntgen, and there are also a number of important earlier publications.

How did Röntgen arrive at this crucial discovery, the multiple and lasting effects of which extend beyond medicine to modern X-ray astronomy? Unfortunately, the discovery of X-rays is shrouded in mystery, as in his lifetime Röntgen refused to give the full story and in his will decreed that all his notes and records be destroyed. Despite the difficulties, BRACHNER *et al.* give a brief and fluent biography of Röntgen as a man and as a scientist, and also provide selected information on the history of X-ray physics and technology. There is also a more comprehensive chapter of more than 100 pages on Röntgen's life in the standard biography by GLASSER, whose tone, however, may seem too euphorically baroque. Those interested in an (at times critical) account of the interplay between the scientist and the man should consult FÖLSING, while BEIER is for readers who are happy with a less detailed (and less critical) account. LEMMERICH is especially suitable for all those who love instruments, details, and original source material. However, for an intensive scholarly account of the history of X-rays, one must return to Glasser. Originally published in 1931, this work went through a slightly revised edition in 1959, and was reprinted with a new and extensive introduction in 1995 (the characterization as a "revised edition" is misleading). These are, in sum, the most interesting books on Röntgen that appeared in the centenary year, 1995.

However, regarding the current decline of the medical importance of X-rays (at least in terms of their traditional use), and the beginning of a new stage in their scientific application – such as structural identifications in physics, chemistry, and biology with the aid of synchrotron radiation from accelerators, or the analysis of X-rays from cosmic objects in X-ray astronomy – these books offer little information. The only exceptions are Lemmerich, which provides a few, fairly incidental references to the literature, and Brachner *et al.*, which gives more detailed information. In 1896, X-rays had caused a gigantic revolution in medical diagnosis (and a little later in therapy), but in more recent years the public has come to associate them with "dangerous" physics, and frequently to equate them with radioactivity. However, in the field of computerized tomography – for example, in medical diagnosis – X-rays are still indispensable, and the intensity and frequency of their application on the human body has been greatly reduced to minimize harm.

In the early years of the 20th century, however, X-rays were seen as the means by which human anatomy could be completely revealed and understood. The development of this myth – the Röntgen craze – is described in Fölsing and Glasser, the latter including a separate chapter on how contemporary caricatures mirror the mythical aura around X-rays. In neither of these books is there much critical reflection regarding the myth, but Fölsing speaks briefly about early experiences with radiation damage. Glasser's compilation of sources on the history of the discovery remains useful; dates and facts, quotations (especially private ones) by Röntgen and his contemporaries, reprints of the first three publications by Röntgen, and extensive summaries of the relevant (including technological) history until just after 1900 (and occasionally up to the 1920s), give a detailed impression of the sensation the discovery created at that time. Röntgen's work before and after the discovery is barely touched upon, however. Brief consideration of Röntgen's early scientific research can be found in Beier and Brachner *et al.* – for example, the "Röntgen current", a current that James Clerk Maxwell had predicted would occur when a dielectric is moved to and fro within an electric field. He predicted that the shifting of the electric charge within the dielectric would generate an electric current, producing a surrounding magnetic field, which was detected by Röntgen with a sensitive magnetic needle. The catalogue of the exhibition at the Deutsches Museum also provides material on Röntgen's work before 1896, but since it merely describes and comments on the historical context of the objects on display one after another, this account is somewhat fragmented. Brachner *et al.* also offer a survey of original apparatus housed by the Deutsches Museum.

None of the books listed here provide any useful information concerning Röntgen's work in Munich, following his famous discovery. Although Röntgen did not publish for a few years after 1897, his work with the Russian physicist A. Joffe on the interactions of X-rays with crystals (from 1905 onwards) did have an impact on the development of solid state physics. Their chief joint publication did not appear in the *Annalen der Physik* until 1921, mainly because Röntgen delayed it with his customary care and pedantry. The article received very little attention on publication, and even today remains completely in the shadow of both X-rays and nuclear physics, which upstaged solid state physics from 1900 to c.1960.

In English, there is a translation of Glasser (the original edition), and also the popular biography by NITSKE, which contains reprints of the first three famous publications by Röntgen. Unfortunately, Nitske relates much in a suggestive manner, without admitting either that his tale is scantily supported by sources, or that there are alternative interpretations. On the other hand, he skilfully incorporates original sources into his narrative, and, overall, the book is more accessible than Glasser and more informative than Beier. Nevertheless, Nitske almost completely ignores Röntgen's research before and after the discovery of X-rays. An earlier, but similarly popular biography of Röntgen in German is DESSAUER, which again focuses on the great discovery, but uses source material somewhat more carefully.

One last article deserves to be mentioned: TURNER's contribution to the *Dictionary of Scientific Biography*. Though brief, it provides balanced information on Röntgen's personal biography, his entire research career, and his famous discovery, and remains the best introduction to the subject. Of course, Röntgen can also be explored in two museums: the Deutsches Röntgen Museum in Remscheid-Lennep, his place of birth, and the Deutsches Museum in Munich, which gives Röntgen's original apparatus a central role in its physics exhibition. However, the definitive biography of Röntgen – the account linking his unique discovery with the person, the experimental physics with the theoretical background, and the status of professors around 1900 with the impact of science on society – has yet to be written.

JÜRGEN TEICHMANN
translated by Anna-Katherina Mayer

See also Radiology

Rowland, Henry Augustus   1848–1901

American physicist

Henry, Richard C., David H. DeVorkin and Peter Beer (eds), "Henry Rowland and Astronomical Spectroscopy: Celebration of the 100th Anniversary of Henry Rowland's Introduction of the Concave Diffraction Grating", special edition of *Vistas in Astronomy*, 29 (1986): 119–236

Hentschel, Klaus, "The Discovery of the Redshift of Solar Frauenhofer Lines by Rowland and Jewell in Baltimore around 1890", *Historical Studies in the Physical and Biological Sciences*, 23/2 (1993): 219–77

Kevles, Daniel J., *The Physicists: The History of a Scientific Community in Modern America*, New York: Knopf, 1978; revised edition, Cambridge, Massachusetts: Harvard University Press, 1995

Miller, John David, *Henry Augustus Rowland and His Electromagnetic Researches*, PhD dissertation, Oregon State University, 1970

Miller, John David, "Rowland and the Nature of Electric Currents", *Isis*, 63 (1972): 5–27

Reingold, Nathan, *Science in Nineteenth Century America: A Documentary History*, New York: Hill and Wang, 1964

Rezneck, Samuel, "The Education of an American Scientist: H.A. Rowland, 1848–1901", *American Journal of Physics*, 28 (1960): 155–62

Rezneck, Samuel, "An American Physicist's Year in Europe: Henry A. Rowland, 1875–1876", *American Journal of Physics*, 30 (1962): 877–86

Serafini, Anthony, *Legends in Their Own Time: A Century of American Physical Scientists*, New York: Plenum Press, 1993

Wise, M. Norton (ed.), *The Values of Precision*, Princeton, New Jersey: Princeton University Press, 1995

It is somewhat surprising that Henry Augustus Rowland, a "borderland physicist–engineer hybrid" so characteristic of late 19th-century American science, has not yet been the subject of a fully-fledged scientific biography. However, some of his experimental research program, especially the electrodynamic and spectroscopic aspects, have been analyzed in some depth, although a thorough study of Rowland's efforts to redetermine the mechanical equivalent of heat, which was the first real step forward in this regard since Joule's measurements three decades earlier, is still missing.

SERAFINI's somewhat hagiographic chapter on Rowland is typical of popular biographical accounts. His inclusion of Rowland, the "first modern physicist", among the select crowd of "legends in their own time" is justified firstly on social grounds, by his prominent role as a spokesman for pure science and as founding president of the American Physical Society, and secondly on scientific grounds, by the great importance of his work on diffraction gratings.

After Serafini's briefing, the text to turn to is KEVLES, originally published in 1978 but reprinted several times as a result of its extraordinary quality of giving a well-balanced history of the evolution of the discipline of physics in America. Kevles provides statistics on physicists and student enrolment and a discussion of qualitative trends (such as the dominant Baconian tradition of data-gathering), as well as background information on the founding of new research institutions such as the Johns Hopkins University, where Rowland became the first professor of physics. Robert Kargon's contribution in HENRY, DEVORKIN & BEER supplements this social historian's perspective by a closer look at Rowland's impact as a physics professor who supervised a total of 165 graduate students, 45 of whom later starred in the American Men of Science, a clear mark of distinction. One generation later, many of these men held central positions in the rapidly expanding discipline of physics.

In two biographical essays on Rowland's education, Samuel Rezneck covers Rowland's civil engineering studies at the Rensselaer Polytechnic Institute in Troy, New York to 1870 (REZNECK, 1960), as well as describing his stay abroad in 1875–76 (REZNECK, 1962). With the financial support of the first president of Johns Hopkins University, Rowland travelled from Ireland to France, Germany, and Switzerland, in order to work at European physical laboratories and inspect their facilities. Upon his return to Baltimore, not only was Rowland able to set up one of the best-equipped physics laboratories in the world, but he had also acquired first-hand experience of state-of-the-art physical research. REINGOLD's anthology of original documents, with brief introductory remarks relating to science in 19th-century America, serves as a good companion to Kevles's history and Rezneck's two papers. The section "The Rise of physics" contains two letters by Rowland concerning his first scientific paper, which had been rejected by the *American Journal of Science* and was later published in the *Philosophical Magazine* thanks to Maxwell's support, as well as several other letters relating to Rowland's travels in Europe.

MILLER (1970) provides an in-depth account of Rowland's electromagnetic researches, describing the scientific background and the intentions behind his electromagnetic experiments while working at Helmholtz's Berlin laboratory in the winter of 1875. According to Miller, Rowland had already been pondering convective currents since reading Faraday in 1868, and he simply took advantage of the good instrumentation in Helmholtz's laboratory to test whether both convective and conductive electricity induced magnetic fields (as implied in Maxwell's theory). Helmholtz's motives for promoting Rowland's efforts are also analyzed. Finally, Miller connects these early electric convection experiments of 1876 with Hall's detection of another magnetic effect of electricity (discovered in Baltimore in 1879 under Rowland's supervision), and points out the dependency of their work on a fluid model of electricity later abandoned in favor of electric interaction with the aether. Rowland's work on electric currents is also described in MILLER (1972).

The best introduction to Rowland's spectroscopic work, for which he became most famous, is provided by HENRY, DEVORKIN & BEER's collection of papers, delivered at the 100th anniversary of Rowland's introduction of concave gratings at Baltimore. Deborah J. Warner gives an excellent overview of the contemporary technology of ruling gratings, one of the few specialties of American instrument-makers (such as J. Saxton, W.A. Rogers, and L.M. Rutherfurd) even before Rowland. John Strong's contribution is noteworthy for its insights into the practice of the ruling of gratings – he himself was one of the last living inheritors of Rowland's legacy in the grating art. Strong also speculates on possible paths for the development of concave gratings, Rowland's second major innovation, apart from improvements to the ruling screw and to the guiding mechanism of the ruling engine.

Additional information on Rowland's spectroscopic work can be obtained from HENTSCHEL's account of the discovery in Baltimore c.1890 of red shift in the solar spectrum. The impact of Rowland's new grating technology is documented by a close comparison of research practice in spectroscopy before and after 1880. The whole set of practices and skills needed to achieve optimal performance of the precision ruling machine is described in full, and Rowland's dependence on the skills of his mechanician and his assistant who were in charge of the actual production and quality testing of the gratings is emphasized. It is Hentschel's thesis that when unexpected shifts of Fraunhofer lines relative to terrestrial comparison lines were detected, Rowland tended to dismiss them as unexplained artefacts, while it was his assistant, Lewis E. Jewell, who established the existence of the solar red shift, thereby questioning the accuracy of Rowland's extensive tables of solar wavelengths.

Further reflections on the broader implications of precision in Rowland's cultural setting are found in George Sweetnam's contribution to WISE's anthology. Sweetnam emphasizes the economic aspects of the production of diffraction gratings, and the interdependency of the instrument-producer John Brashear and the experimentalist Rowland, who also depended on Brashear for the distribution of the gratings to researchers all over the world at production cost. Sweetnam ends with a wider discussion of Rowland's emphasis on action over contemplation, on "active" over "passive instruments", and on empirical accuracy over theoretical understanding. Taking up an idea of Lorraine Daston, he comes to the conclusion that for Rowland "precision in the study of nature possessed moral as well as technical value". Thus, a "moral economy" is attached to precision measurements, which "cultivated certain personal idiosyncrasies . . . and, especially, the character traits of diligence, fastidiousness, thoroughness, and caution".

KLAUS HENTSCHEL

See also Astrophysics; Electromagnetism; Spectroscopy

Royal Institution

Archives of the Royal Institution, Minutes of the Managers' Meetings, 1799–1903, 15 vols, bound in 7, London, 1971–76

Berman, Morris, "The Early Years of the Royal Institution, 1799–1810: A Re-evaluation", *Science Studies*, 2 (1972): 205–40

Berman, Morris, *Social Change and Scientific Organization: The Royal Institution, 1799–1844*, London: Heinemann, and Ithaca, New York: Cornell University Press, 1978

Caroe, A.D.R., *The House of the Royal Institution*, London: Royal Institution, 1963

Caroe, Gwendy, *The Royal Institution: An Informal History*, London: Murray, 1985

Chilton, Donovan and Noel G. Coley, "The Laboratories of the Royal Institution in the Nineteenth Century", *Ambix*, 27 (1980): 173–203

Forgan, Sophie, *The Royal Institution of Great Britain, 1840–1873*, PhD dissertation, University of London (Westfield College), 1977

Jones, Bence, *The Royal Institution: Its Founder and Its First Professors*, London: Longman's Green, 1871; reprinted, New York: Arno Press, 1975

McCabe, Irena M. and Frank A.J.L. James, "Collections X: History of Science and Technology Resources at the Royal Institution of Great Britain", *British Journal for the History of Science*, 17 (1984): 205–59

Martin, Thomas, *The Royal Institution,* London: Longman's Green, 1942; revised edition, 1949

Throughout the 19th century, the Royal Institution possessed one of the finest scientific laboratories in Europe. For much of that time it was the only laboratory in Britain where experimental science could be pursued effectively. It was in this laboratory that Humphry Davy and Michael Faraday conducted their fundamental chemical and physical researches, particularly in the area of electricity. Later, John Tyndall, James Dewar, William Henry Bragg, his son William Lawrence Bragg, George Porter, and others held professorial appointments at the Royal Institution. Much concerning the history of the Royal Institution can therefore be learned from reading accounts of their lives. With such a distinguished record of research, it was thus natural that, when the history of the Royal Institution came to be written, there was a tendency to concentrate on this at the expense of the many other activities that also take place there.

This approach skewed accounts of the founding of the Royal Institution and its early history, since scientific research was never envisaged by the founders as one of the aims of the Royal Institution; rather, the dissemination of scientific knowledge was its initial primary aim. JONES, the first history of the Royal Institution to be written, gave Benjamin Thompson, Count Rumford, the leading role in its foundation. This perspective allowed Jones to stress the importance of research, and hence Davy's significance as a scientific discoverer; indeed, this account ends with Davy's departure from the Royal Institution. Moreover, as the first account to be published, Jones formed the agenda for much subsequent writing on the Royal Institution; for example, both MARTIN and G. CAROE follow his lead in their accounts of the early years of the Institution, by concentrating on research.

The archives of the Royal Institution contain a remarkably large and comprehensive collection of institutional records, which more recent historians have used to provide a different account of the early Royal Institution. Some of the Royal Institution's records were published in ARCHIVES OF THE ROYAL INSTITUTION, which photographically reproduced and indexed the minute books of the Managers of the Royal Institution. It provides a good picture of the management of the Royal Institution during its first century, though the informative quality of the minutes is variable depending on who the Assistant Secretary was at a given time. McCABE & JAMES provide a brief overview of the archival holdings of the Royal Institution, both as administrative records and as personal papers of the professors.

Using such archival sources, BERMAN draws attention to the importance of agricultural and imperial interests, as well as those of social reform, in the formation and early years of the Royal Institution. Berman rightly pointed out the importance of Joseph Banks, Lord Spencer, and Thomas Bernard, among others, to the Royal Institution and thus reduced the significance of the crucial role assigned previously to Rumford. Berman, however, swung too far in the opposite direction from other historians of the subject, by neglecting almost completely the role of research. He somewhat overstated the case, by portraying Faraday as a instrument of government policy (for example, in the enquiry of 1844 into the Haswell Colliery disaster) which, he argued, did violence to Faraday's supposed commitment to "pure science".

FORGAN takes a more balanced view of the development of the Royal Institution in the middle third of the 19th century. She examines the role of the managers who ran the Institution and its two secretaries during this period, John Barlow and Bence Jones, showing that they had more influence than the professors, including Faraday and Tyndall. One of the major concerns of the secretaries, Forgan shows, was the success or failure of the lecture courses from which the Royal Institution earned much of its income. It was only towards the end of this period, under the influence of Bence Jones, that research was seen to be an integral part of the activities of the Royal Institution, rather than just of its professors.

For the remainder of the 19th century, and indeed for the 20th century, knowledge of the history of the Royal Institution is sketchier than for the years before 1873. CHILTON & COLEY contains useful information for the whole of the 19th century, including floor plans showing the development of the laboratory, while A. CAROE looks at the development of the building as a whole up to c.1940. Chilton & Coley also provide some detail of laboratory finance and, very rare in any kind of historical literature, a list of technicians working in the Royal Institution up to 1925.

Bence Jones's aspirations to make research central to the activities of the Royal Institution were further reinforced in 1896, when the new Davy-Faraday Research Laboratory was opened following an endowment by Ludwig Mond. It was in this laboratory that Dewar, the Braggs, Porter, and more recent directors have conducted their scientific research. These developments are covered in Martin and G. Caroe (a daughter of William Henry Bragg). Apart from brief mentions in the latter, however, many of the recent major developments in the Royal Institution, such as the Schools Lectures, the televising of the Christmas Lectures, and the Institution's expanding role in the promotion of the public understanding of science, have received little or no attention.

FRANK A.J.L. JAMES

See also Davy; Faraday; Performance; Popularization

Royal Society of London

Atkinson, Dwight, *Scientific Discourse in Sociohistorical Context: The Philosophical Transactions of the Royal Society of London, 1675–1975*, Mahwah, New Jersey: Erlbaum, 1999

Barton, Ruth, "'An Influential Set of Chaps': The X-Club and Royal Society Politics, 1864–85," *British Journal for the History of Science*, 23 (1990): 53–81

Feingold, Mordechai, "Of Records and Grandeur: The Archive of the Royal Society," in *Archives of the Scientific Revolution: The Formation and Exchange of Ideas in Seventeenth-Century Europe*, edited by Michael Hunter, Woodbridge, Suffolk: Boydell Press, 1998, 171–84

Gascoigne, John, *Science in the Service of Empire: Joseph Banks, the British State and the Uses of Science in the Age of Revolution*, Cambridge and New York: Cambridge University Press, 1998

Hall, Marie Boas, *All Scientists Now: The Royal Society in the Nineteenth Century*, Cambridge and New York: Cambridge University Press, 1984

Hall, Marie Boas, *Promoting Experimental Learning: Experiment and the Royal Society, 1660–1727*, Cambridge: Cambridge University Press, 1991

Hunter, Michael, *Establishing the New Science: The Experience of the Early Royal Society*, Woodbridge, Suffolk: Boydell Press, 1989

Lyons, Henry, *The Royal Society, 1660–1940: A History of Its Administration under Its Charters*, Cambridge: Cambridge University Press, 1944; New York: Greenwood Press, 1968

McClellan, James E. III, *Science Reorganized: Scientific Societies in the Eighteenth Century*, New York: Columbia University Press, 1985

Shapin, Steven, *A Social History of Truth: Civility and Science in Seventeenth-Century England*, Chicago: University of Chicago Press, 1994

Sorrenson, Richard, "Towards a History of the Royal Society in the 18th century," *Notes and Records of the Royal Society of London*, 50 (1996): 29–46

Sprat, Thomas, *History of the Royal-Society of London for the Improving of Natural Knowledge*, London: Martyn and Allestry, 1667; edited by Jackson I. Cope and Harold Whitmore Jones, St Louis: Washington University, and London: Routledge and Kegan Paul, 1959

Weld, Charles Richard, *A History of the Royal Society, with Memoirs of the Presidents*, 2 vols, London: J. W. Parker, 1848

As the oldest still active scientific institution, the Royal Society of London has naturally attracted much scholarship. Nearly all important English and most Scottish, Welsh, and Irish scientific figures, as well as those from beyond the British Isles, have been members. It has been a significant venue that has organized the pursuit of science for more than three centuries, both within its walls and over the entire globe. It was widely copied throughout the British empire and the United States, and its history can be usefully split into three eras: from its founding to the 1830s, from the 1840s to World War I, and from World War I to the present. The beginnings of the first era have attracted a huge amount of modern scholarship, the rest of this era comparatively little; the beginnings of the second era quite large amounts, the rest of it less so; the third era none. I have selected the most significant and representative literature on the Society; there is very much more available that can be traced by following the footnotes in the works cited here.

The history of the Society has not been easy to interpret. It was supposedly founded to support the new experimental philosophy, but, as HALL (1991) points out, experimentation was not the dominant mode of investigation, even in the Society's early years. The Royal Society was meant to be useful, but, as HUNTER argues, its members had virtually no interest in practical matters. It was not even particularly Royal at its founding. Charles II gave it a charter and a mace in 1662, and little else. This was quite in contrast to the Royal Greenwich Observatory, the only other significant Stuart scientific institution, which the king in Parliament funded fairly consistently. Subsequent Stuarts and Hanoverians continued this policy of zero funding for the Royal Society with very few specific exceptions. Therefore, according to Hunter, Fellows had to look to their own resources; it was they who paid the Society, not the Society them. They were members of a London club that turned out to be rather important; they were not pensioned Academicians. These simple facts had profound consequences. To survive the Society had to recruit many members – often numbering into the hundreds, but never female – to pay the bills for the rooms, the secretary, the demonstrator of experiments, the instruments themselves, and the publication of the Society's journal, *Philosophical Transactions*. It also had to provide enough intriguing or important scientific material to keep the general membership interested. Thus a Fellow might be an obscure country parson with only a passing interest in botany or he could be Isaac Newton. This huge range in the abilities and interests of the membership made the Society, as McCLELLAN demonstrates, very different from the more exclusive European academies.

While the Society may not have been particularly empiricist, utilitarian, Royal, or academic, it has, however, as FEINGOLD's account shows, taken a deep interest in its past, and its Fellows have produced several histories. But when a Fellow wrote one, did he speak for himself, or the Society? This question has bedeviled Sprat, Weld, and Lyons whose interests as Fellows and their position in the Society must be carefully considered when reading their accounts. SPRAT has been particularly problematic in this regards. Written only seven years after the Society's founding, it was a programmatic announcement of the Society's ideals as held by a certain number of the Fellows, not a dispassionate account of the actual activities of the entire membership. WELD, though an apologetic text, is still surprisingly good in its treatment of the Society's transition from a place where experimental effects were shown to a place where they were instead talked about. It is also important for its material on the presidents of the Society in the 18th and early 19th centuries. LYONS contains some useful details on the administrative structure of the Society, but is unusually Whiggish in its attempts to decide which Fellows were "scientific" and which were not.

The modern scholarship surrounding the founding of the Society, which is substantial and interesting, can only be touched upon. HUNTER provides an excellent introduction to that literature, which concerns, among other things: the founding rhetoric of the Society; the relations between science and religion; and the social status of the Fellows and the science they advocated. The Society's early attempts to establish an appropriate scientific discourse – both spoken and written – and to maintain a regularly published journal have attracted rhetorical analysis, most recently and extensively in ATKINSON, which gives a detailed analysis of the *Philosophical Transactions*. The Fellows' early attempts to make experiments and instruments work, and to create norms for assigning credit for discoveries, have been the subject of much sociological work, including the always interesting SHAPIN, which, however, tends rather too easily to take one Fellow, Robert Boyle, as representative of all the Fellows.

While the Society underwent no dramatic changes in the 18th century, it was not therefore unimportant. SORRENSON notes that it continued to follow its founding principles in respecting the plain fact, and those who could produce it, and to be suspicious of generalizations and generalizers. While it revered its greatest Fellow, Sir Isaac Newton, its Fellows mostly ignored his mathematizing methodology and concentrated on the production of novel experimental effects, accurate measurement, and meticulous natural history. The Society remained a club, but one that used shared correspondence networks, economic interests, observations, instruments, and readings of papers to maintain sociability. GASCOIGNE studies Sir Joseph Banks' very long presidency (1778–1820), which coincided with the almost continuous conflict of the American and French Revolutions and the Napoleonic Wars. The Society made vigorous attempts to be useful to its nation, while the social makeup of the Fellowship and the self-funded nature of the Society remained relatively unchanged.

BARTON describes the substantial, but none the less rather slow, changes which the Society underwent after Banks' presidency, and these constitute the beginning of the second era. The Royal Society had to adjust to the fact that it was no longer the only substantial scientific society in London once a host of single-discipline societies, such as the Geological, sprung up. It also chose to stop electing members who were more patrons than practitioners of science and sought and received more state support. The political struggles that accompanied these changes have attracted much scholarly attention. HALL (1984) gives a broad but scholarly overview of the entire 19th century with especial emphasis on just when the Society became "scientific". Thereafter, quite remarkably, the scholarship dries up. The Society changed greatly in its third era from World War I onwards – as the British state took a much greater interest in all aspects of science and university dons came almost completely to dominate the Fellowship – but there are no works devoted to the Society's 20th-century history.

RICHARD SORRENSON

Russia

Bailes, Kendall E., *Technology and Society under Lenin and Stalin: Origins of the Soviet Technical Intelligentsia, 1917–1941*, Princeton, New Jersey: Princeton University Press, 1978

Fortescue, Stephen, *The Communist Party and Soviet Science*, London: Macmillan, 1986; Baltimore: Johns Hopkins University Press, 1986

Graham, Loren R., *The Soviet Academy of Sciences and the Communist Party, 1927–1932*, Princeton, New Jersey: Princeton University Press, 1967

Graham, Loren R., *Science and Philosophy in the Soviet Union*, New York: Knopf, 1972; London: Allen Lane, 1973

Graham, Loren R., *Science, Philosophy and Human Behaviour in the Soviet Union*, New York: Columbia University Press, 1987

Graham, Loren R., *Science in Russia and the Soviet Union: A Short History*, Cambridge and New York: Cambridge University Press, 1993

Joravsky, David, *Soviet Marxism and Natural Science, 1917–1932*, New York: Columbia University Press, and London: Routledge and Kegan Paul, 1961

Medvedev, Zhores A., *Soviet Science*, New York: Norton, 1978; Oxford: Oxford University Press, 1979

Popovsky, Mark, *Manipulated Science*, New York: Doubleday, 1979

Vucinich, Alexander, *Science in Russian Culture*, 2 vols, Stanford, California: Stanford University Press, 1963–70; London: Peter Owen, 1965

Vucinich, Alexander, *Empire of Knowledge: The Academy of Sciences of the USSR (1917–1970)*, Berkeley: University of California Press, 1984

As with all analyses of the Russian empire, its scientific history must be separated into two parts, before and after the Bolshevik *coup d'état* of October 1917, as, from the 1920s onwards, ideology and Marxist philosophy increasingly impinged upon scientific theory and practice.

A good general introduction is provided by GRAHAM (1993). With a keen eye for the context within which science develops, Graham examines how social, economic, and political factors shaped scientific theories and institutions. There are sections on the tsarist period, the impact of the Russian Revolution, and the relationship between science and Soviet society. Graham also discusses the changes brought about in Russia and the other republics by the collapse of communism.

The ambitious VUCINICH (1963–70) provides the best overview in the English language of science in Russia before 1917. Used in the broad sense of "learning", Vucinich's science includes the social sciences and some of the humanities. His main concern is the influence of social environment – including ideology, education, and religion – on scientific thought, but he also considers the effects of literary currents, economic and technological developments, political upheavals, and urbanization. The book is thus a wide-ranging study of cultural change as reflected in the development of science and scientific attitudes.

Medvedev, a Russian biologist, and Popovsky, a Russian journalist, write about science in the USSR from a more personal perspective. MEDVEDEV offers a brief history of science in the USSR since 1917. He analyzes the effects of totalitarianism on scientific progress, and paints a picture of bureaucratic controls, which includes engrossing descriptions of the actual workings of the Soviet system, and accounts of how scientists were promoted or censored. In a similar vein, POPOVSKY focuses on how secrecy, professional manipulation, and Russian chauvinism had destructive effects upon the lives of many individuals. His work is a candid view of a regime that boasted of more than a million scientists, but suppressed so much original thought that the Soviet scientist was even more brow-beaten and grasping than his predecessors, cowed into submission by the tsars. Popovsky describes the faking of theses, the rigid scientific hierarchy, the paranoid suspicion of any contact with foreign scientists, and the failures of state-run research. Medvedev's style tends to be heavier than Popovsky's, but both authors convey a sense of the bizarre and the tragic.

BAILES examines the central role played by technologists and engineers in the political and social development of the USSR between 1917 and the German invasion of 1941. He offers a succinct account of Russian engineering before the Bolshevik coup, and an analysis of its problems during the first decade of Soviet rule. Bailes concentrates on the expansion of technology's role during the rapid industrialization beginning in 1928, and then examines the destruction of the old technostructure from 1928 to 1933, and its replacement with a new group of young "red specialists". He also analyzes the social origins, training, and working conditions of the new technical class. There are case studies built around major policy controversies designed to show how the technical intelligentsia interacted with other elements of the Soviet society. In the end, applied scientists emerged as the single largest element in the ruling class; in 1966, 65% of members of the Central Committee had a higher technical education. The work is a study of the nature of the Stalinist system, and includes observations on the origins of the Great Purge, the consequences of the rapid pace imposed by Stalin on industry, and the reasons for the slow rate of innovation in Soviet industry.

Joravsky, Graham (1972), and Fortescue examine the role of Marxism in shaping scientific practice. JORAVSKY deals with the development of the Soviet Marxist philosophy of natural science in the 1920s and early 1930s. He argues that tensions inherent in the Marxist tradition were resolved arbitrarily and narrowly in this period, while an inherited conflict within dialectical materialism, between positivism and metaphysics, remained unsettled, setting the stage for further conflicts. In the end, both were condemned and "narrow partyness" triumphed. Dialectical materialism became dogma, narrowly interpreted and used as a weapon in the war against ideologically alien scientists.

GRAHAM (1972) deals largely with the later periods. The author lucidly sketches out the nexus of scientific–philosophical–

political issues in the 20th century, and their evolution in the USSR. He contrasts materialism and idealism, and writes that the core of dialectical materialism consists of two parts: an assumption of the independent and sole existence of matter-energy, and an assumption of a continuing process in nature in accordance with dialectical laws. He devotes chapters to the genetics controversy, relativity physics, quantum mechanics, resonance chemistry, cybernetics, cosmology, the origin of life, and psychophysiology. Graham contends that, of all the sciences, quantum mechanics most closely touches dialectical materialism as a philosophy of science. After 1947, a great debate on the subject was mounted in the USSR, during which several interpretations of quantum mechanics evolved. In contrast, the famous genetics controversy erupted, not as a result of philosophy, but because Lysenko's viewpoint was endorsed by Communist Party organs. GRAHAM (1987) expands and updates the earlier book to cover events up to the mid-1980s.

FORTESCUE analyzes the political role of Soviet science, and its management by the Communist Party from the end of the Stalin era to the 1980s, illustrating important, sometimes arcane, aspects of science policy and administration often with the aid of political anecdotes. Fortescue attempts to place his analysis within the framework of three different models of Soviet policy: the totalitarian, the "vanguard party", and pluralist models. There are chapters on the Central Committee and Politburo, and on local and regional party organs. The book is dense and hard going in places, and likely to appeal only to a narrow group of specialists in Soviet politics, because it contains many untranslated Russian terms, copious but unhelpful footnotes, and an insufficient index.

Graham (1967) and Vucinich (1984) specifically analyze the central role of the Academy of Sciences in the intellectual and scientific life of the USSR. GRAHAM (1967) is short, lucidly argued, and meticulously documented. It describes the takeover and restructuring of the Academy by the Soviet regime during the period of the first Five-Year Plan, when there was intense controversy over the goals, organization, and functions of scientific research. One of the Soviet goals was to establish "socialist science" as superior to "capitalist science". The book is an excellent summary of Russia's pre-revolutionary scientific achievements and academic traditions, the Communist Party's views on science and its place in a socialist society, and Lenin and Stalin's efforts to "bolshevize" traditional Russian scholarship. There is a useful bibliography and several organizational charts.

VUCINICH (1984) is a more general work. After a review of the ancestry of the Academy, Vucinich traces developments between 1917 and 1970, showing how the USSR set out to make the Academy of Sciences an agency of the government and a bastion of scientific ideology. Its basic social function was to formulate and execute national science policy; it had to co-ordinate the national effort in basic research, and to guide the growth and activities of the academies of individual republics. According to Vucinich, the most dramatic pages in the Academy's history concern the conflict between scientists as guardians of the scientific legacy and philosophers as defenders of ideology. He shows that only after Stalin's death could the Academy regain some of its intellectual integrity. Wide ranging, admirably researched, and clearly written, this work is an excellent point of departure for those who want to know more about the organization and administration of Soviet science.

ELIZABETH V. HAIGH

See also Russian Academy of Sciences

Russian Academy of Sciences

Alekseeva, M.A. *et al.*, *Graviroval'naia Palata Akademii nauk XVIII veka: Sbornik documentov*, Leningrad: Nauka, 1985

Black, J.L. , *G.F. Müller and the Imperial Russian Academy*, Kingston: McGill-Queen's University Press, 1986

Filippov, M.S. (ed.), *Istoriia Biblioteki Akademii nauk SSSR (1714–1964)*, Moscow and Leningrad: Nauka, 1964

Gnucheva, V.F. (ed.), *Geograficheskii Department Akademii Nauk XVIII veka*, Moscow and Leningrad: Publishing House of the USSR Academy of Science, 1946

Graham, Loren R., *Science in Russia and the Soviet Union: A Short History*, Cambridge and New York: Cambridge University Press, 1993

Komkov, G.D., B.V. Levshin and L.K. Semenov, *Akademiia nauk SSSR: Kratkii istoricheskii ocherk*, 2 vols, Moscow: Nauka, 1977

Kopelevich, I.K., *Osnovanie Peterburgskoi Akademii nauk*, Leningrad: Nauka, 1977

Ostrovitianov, K.V. (ed.), *Istoriia Akademii nauk SSSR*, 2 vols, Moscow: Publishing House of the USSR Academy of Science, 1958–64

Pekarskii, P.P. (ed.), *Istoriia imperatorskoi Akademii nauk*, 2 vols, St Petersburg: Imperial Academy of Science Press, 1870–73

Staniukovich, T.V., *Kunstkamera Peterburgskoi Akademii nauk*, Moscow and Leningrad: Publishing House of the USSR Academy of Science, 1953

Sukhomlinov, M.I. (ed.), *Istoriia Rossiiskoi Akademii*, 8 vols, St Petersburg, 1875–88

Sukhomlinov, M.I. (ed.), *Materialy dlia istorii imperatorskoi Akademii nauk*, 10 vols, St Petersburg: Imperial Academy of Science Press, 1885–1900

Vucinich, Alexander, *Science in Russian Culture: A History to 1860*, 2 vols, Stanford, California: Stanford University Press, 1963–70

Zubov, V.P., *Istoriografiia estestvennykh nauk v Rossii*, Moscow: Publishing House of the USSR Academy of Science, 1956

This essay discusses literature concerning the Russian Academy of Sciences from its foundation in 1725 to 1800. GRAHAM provides an extensive bibliographic essay on the Academy during the 19th century and Soviet era. KOPELEVICH includes a long bibliographical essay of Soviet works on 18th-century Russian science, while ZUBOV gives an excellent critical account of histories of Russian science in the 18th and 19th centuries.

Even today, the most detailed and objective study of the Russian Academy of Sciences in the 18th century remains that of the archeologist and historian, Petr Petrovich PEKARSKII. Volume 1 consists of a historical introduction followed by long biographical essays on academicians enlisted before 1742, while volume 2 is devoted to biographies of M.V. Lomonosov and Vasilii Tatishchev. Both volumes are indexed and list primary biographical sources for each academician. Although discussion of important non-academicians (such as A.K. Nartov) is minimal, Pekarskii does describe interpersonal disputes and patronage connections not appearing in more sanitized Soviet works. Pekarskii's history, which ends around 1770, may be supplemented with similarly thorough biographical essays by SUKHOMLINOV (1874–88), dealing with academicians such as Lepekhin, Rumovskii, Kotelnikov, Severgin, and Ozeretskovskii.

Understandably, later Soviet histories have been marred by an overstatement of academic achievement and a lack of critical judgement, interpretation, and contextualization of events. Volume 1 of OSTROVITIANOV, the best and most extensive of these works, covers the period 1724–1803, and includes an index and appendices of major decrees concerning the Academy. However, its contrived editorial argument that the Academy quickly arose from a rich pre-Petrine culture to become a major scientific center, together with its disconnected essays listing facts about academic publications, departments, and activities, make the work valuable for reference but little else. Lomonosov, the "father of Russian science", receives excessive attention – the book is divided into periods before, during, and after Lomonosov – while the significance of foreign contributions is downplayed. The same faults appear in volume 1 (1724–1917) of the 250th-anniversary history of the Academy edited by KOMKOV, LEVSHIN & SEMENOV, except that much of the factual information obtainable in Ostrovitianov is missing.

American histories of Russian science avoid the excesses of Soviet works, but often maintain their underlying assumptions. VUCINICH provides the only comprehensive English-language history of the Academy, focusing on events up to 1860, with particular emphasis on the second half of the 18th century. Vucinich's argument is reminiscent of the now-debunked conflict theses of Draper and White, as he allies the rise of Russian science with social-progressive movements, the fall of a tyrannical church, and a state founded on mysticism and superstition. "Progressive" heroes such as Lomonosov receive most attention, while foreign academicians, apart from the ubiquitous Euler, are often ignored.

Soviet studies of Academic departments often avoid the generalizations of broader histories. The detailed historical introduction to ALEKSEEVA et al. by M.A. Alekseeva assesses the place of the engraving department in 18th-century Russian culture, occasionally calling attention to the Academy's role in defining the image of both the autocracy and natural philosophy through art. Fully annotated documents relating to the department from 1724 to 1805 are included, with short biographies of personnel, both major and minor. GNUCHEVA's discussion of the geographical department in the years 1726–99 is similarly well informed, but offers little interpretation of important episodes, such as the creation of the first Russian atlas. Annotated correspondence, reports, and decrees relating to cartography are appended, as well as a list of all maps produced by the department in the 18th century.

The Kunstkammer is dealt with by STANIUKOVICH, but his discussion, which attempts to equate the increasing popularity of the museum with a rising populist intelligentsia, is superficial and filled with unnecessary details. Similarly, the lengthy history of the Academy's Library from 1714 to 1964, edited by FILIPPOV, lists endless facts and figures on budgets, personnel, and acquisitions, and avoids any coherent arguments. In contrast, BLACK provides a worthy appraisal of the Academy's historical work, focusing on the career of G.F. Müller, and particularly his disputes with Lomonosov over the Normanist theory of Russian origins. However, discussion is confined within a narrow academic context, with little attention given to cultural or political circumstances contributing to the events described.

Finally, for those cautious of Soviet interpretations, published archive material concerning the Academy is in abundant supply, at least for the first half of the 18th century. Some 8,000 documents appear in SUKHOMLINOV (1885–1900), a large, albeit somewhat random, selection of letters, decrees, protocols, and contracts drawn from the Academy's chancellory and conference archives, covering the period 1726–50. Although contents are not listed, documents are presented in strict chronological order over the 10 volumes, each covering approximately two years. Sadly, the absence of notes can occasionally lead to confusion, but a comprehensive name index is provided for each volume.

SIMON WERRETT

See also Russia

Rutherford, Ernest   1871–1937

New Zealand-born nuclear physicist

Andrade, Edward N. da C., *Rutherford and the Nature of the Atom*, New York: Doubleday, and London: Heinemann, 1964

Badash, Lawrence, "Ernest Rutherford and Theoretical Physics", in *Kelvin's Baltimore Lectures and Modern Theoretical Physics: Historical and Philosophical Perspectives*, edited by Robert Kargon and Peter Achinstein, Cambridge, Massachusetts: MIT Press, 1987

Birks, John B. (ed.), *Rutherford at Manchester*, London: Heywood, 1962; New York: Benjamin, 1963

Bunge, Mario and William R. Shea (eds), *Rutherford and Physics at the Turn of the Century*, Folkestone, Kent: Dawson, and New York: Science History Publications, 1979. [contents include Lawrence Badash, "The Origins of Big Science: Rutherford at McGill"; J.L. Heilbron, "Physics at McGill in Rutherford's Time"; Norman Feather, "Some Episodes of the Alpha-Particle Story, 1903–1977"; Thaddeus J. Trenn, "Rutherford in the McGill Physics Laboratory"; Stanley L. Jaki, "The Reality Beneath: The World View of Rutherford"]

Eve, Arthur S., *Rutherford: Being the Life and Letters of the Rt Hon. Lord Rutherford, OM*, New York: Macmillan, and Cambridge: Cambridge University Press, 1939

Feather, Norman, *Lord Rutherford*, Glasgow: Blackie, 1940; revised edition, London: Priory Press, 1973

Heilbron, J.L., "The Scattering of α and ß Particles and Rutherford's Atom", *Archive for History of Exact Sciences*, 4 (1968): 247–307

Malley, Marjorie, "The Discovery of Atomic Transmutation: Scientific Styles and Philosophies in France and Britain", in *History of Physics: Selected Reprints*, edited by Stephen G. Brush, College Park, Maryland: American Association of Physics Teachers, 1988, 184–95

Stuewer, Roger, "Rutherford's Satellite Model of the Nucleus", *Historical Studies in the Physical and Biological Sciences*, 16 (1986): 321–52

Trenn, Thaddeus J., *The Self-Splitting Atom: The History of the Rutherford-Soddy Collaboration*, London: Taylor and Francis, 1977

Wilson, David, *Rutherford: Simple Genius*, Cambridge, Massachusetts: MIT Press, and London: Hodder and Stoughton, 1983

Several full-length biographies of the nuclear physicist, Ernest Rutherford, as well as numerous biographical articles, have been written by his former students. These acclaim Rutherford's personality, character, and scientific ability, recount the great discoveries attributed to him, and add a liberal dose of personal and scientific anecdotes.

The book written by Rutherford's former student, Arthur S. EVE, was for many years considered the standard biography. It consists mainly of portions of Rutherford's voluminous personal and scientific correspondence, complemented with personal reminiscences of Eve and others, as well as excerpts from official documents, published papers, and newspaper articles. The overall organization is chronological, and comprises both personal and scientific aspects of Rutherford's life. An index is provided, but, as was common at the time, complete notes and a bibliography are not included.

Eve's goal in writing this biography was "to hold up a mirror in which Rutherford may reveal himself, just as he was" (Preface). Hence, he uses text mainly in order to connect the various documents, without providing much analysis. No attempt is made to supply broad themes, historical interpretations, or context, beyond the immediate environs of Rutherford's life. Within these limitations, Eve supplies interesting and colorful views of persons, places, and events germane to his subject. His biography of Rutherford is useful primarily for these anecdotes and eyewitness accounts, and for its copious examples of correspondence.

By concentrating on Rutherford's best known scientific achievements – transmutation theory, the atomic nucleus, and artificial disintegration – FEATHER provides a more unified narrative. He traces Rutherford's early interest in research, discerns aspects of character and personality that contributed to his successes, and rounds out his laudatory scientific biography with material on Rutherford's humanitarian activities. However, he does not supply much information on the scientific context within which Rutherford worked.

ANDRADE's biography, originally part of the Science Study series for high school students, attempts to place Rutherford's work within its scientific context. Andrade supplies pertinent background information on the 1890s and on scientific laboratories during Rutherford's time, and intersperses the scientific discussions with personal recollections and impressions of Rutherford.

The commemorative volume edited by BIRKS contains speeches from the Rutherford Jubilee International Conference of 1961, copies of the Rutherford Memorial Lectures, reprints of nine scientific papers by Rutherford and his colleagues at Manchester, bibliographies, and a few other items. Contributors include Rutherford's former students Ernest Marsden, Charles Darwin, E.N. da C. Andrade, Niels Bohr, H.R. Robinson, A.S. Russell, and P.M.S. Blackett. Some correspondence of Arthur Schuster is included. The book contains a wealth of anecdotes and personal impressions of Rutherford, although much less has been included to enlighten the reader about the internal development of Rutherford's scientific work. As is customary for a memorial volume, the tone throughout is of high praise for its subject.

WILSON has written a comprehensive, detailed, well-researched, and sympathetic biography that integrates Rutherford's life and work. He has gone far beyond his predecessors in the use of unpublished materials, his thoughtful analysis of Rutherford's personal and professional relationships, and his presentation of Rutherford's life as a coherent whole. Wilson seems to have left no stone unturned in his search for documentary materials, whether this meant undertaking interviews with Rutherford's acquaintances or tracking down previously unknown, confidential, or untapped resources. His well-written biography is a mine of information and a pleasure to read. Especially noteworthy are the chapters that establish the extent and importance of Rutherford's wartime work, his post-war services to the British government, his relationship with the Russian physicist, Peter Kapitza, and the development of his political contacts and negotiation skills. The presentation of Rutherford's New Zealand background and his early work on radio waves is illuminating. Wilson believes that the crucial role played by Rutherford and the experimental physics tradition in the development of atomic physics has been eclipsed by theoretical physics and the Americans, and he strives to correct this misperception. The book is weakest in its treatment of the scientific milieu within which Rutherford worked; the author was apparently unaware of significant features of late 19th- and early 20th-century science, and has drawn a number of anachronistic analogies and conclusions and made occasional errors of fact, while omitting information that would enable the reader to place Rutherford and his contemporaries in proper perspective.

A number of authors discuss characteristics of Rutherford's research style in the useful collection of essays edited by BUNGE & SHEA. John L. Heilbron shows how Rutherford utilized the research strengths of McGill University in Montreal, and compares Rutherford's work to that of his colleague Howard T. Barnes, the theoretical breadth and scope of whose research was limited by the time needed for his high-precision experimental research. Meanwhile, Rutherford, who was content to leave the next significant digit to others, was able to achieve far-reaching theoretical and experimental breakthroughs. Thaddeus J. Trenn's article reveals that Rutherford, unwittingly aided by calculation errors, adjusted assumptions and juggled data to arrive at the result he expected for the velocity of alpha rays in crossed magnetic and electric fields. Surprisingly, Trenn's analysis leads him only to praise Rutherford's "high degree of ingenuity and creativity" (p. 106), rather than to draw further implications for either Rutherford's methodology in particular or the philosophy of science in general.

In a related vein, Norman Feather (within an article discussing alpha-particle research over several decades) shows how Rutherford remained silent in his publications (until many years later, when he was able to explain the matter) about a contradiction between his expectation and his experimental finding for the charge of the alpha-particle. Finally, although Rutherford's knack for improvizing with limited resources was legendary, Lawrence Badash's article paradoxically locates elements of the beginnings of the transition to "Big Science" in Rutherford's tenure at McGill University. Badash supports his conclusion by identifying certain characteristics of Rutherford's scientific practices and leadership with key features of today's Big Science, whereas Wilson disagrees with this interpretation, pointing to contrary evidence.

MALLEY compares the investigations that led Rutherford and Soddy to propose the transmutation theory to the parallel researches of Pierre Curie and André Debierne in France. She finds the different outcomes of the British and French teams to have resulted largely from differences in their styles and philosophies of science. While Rutherford and Soddy proceeded as unselfconscious realists, favoring concrete, material hypotheses, the French were inhibited by their positivism. Likewise, the article by Stanley L. Jaki (in Bunge & Shea) underlines Rutherford's "epistemological realism", regarding it as key to Rutherford's scientific success in general.

Rutherford's fame as an experimental physicist, coupled with his habit of directing barbs towards theoretical physicists, may have led many to misjudge his real attitudes and underestimate his role as a theoretician. In a well-documented article, BADASH shows that Rutherford had great respect for theory if it was accessible to, and guided by, experiment, particularly when it elucidated his own research areas. Rutherford sup-ported theoretical work in his own laboratory, and advanced numerous theories himself.

Several writers have analyzed key researches of Rutherford. TRENN presents a detailed, step-by-step account of the conceptual processes leading to the discovery of atomic transmutation, in which Rutherford collaborated with the chemist, Frederick Soddy. Basing his study largely on textual analyses, he focuses on the development of scientific ideas and conceptual change, and shows that the strengths of each partner were essential for this work.

Rutherford's experiments with α particle scattering in matter are usually presented as attempts to unravel the mysteries of atomic structure, which culminated in the discovery of the nuclear atom. In contrast to this popularized view, HEILBRON concludes from a detailed analysis that Rutherford's aim was to develop a theory of α and β particle scattering superior to that of J.J. Thomson and Thomson's collaborator, James Crowther. The nuclear atom emerged from these studies almost as an afterthought, and although Rutherford considered it important, his suggestion was hardly noticed at the time. Not only was the idea not original, it could not be reconciled with classical mechanics. Only after Bohr had developed his atomic theory did Rutherford's nuclear atom find its niche, and hence its significance, in the new atomic physics.

STUEWER traces the development of Rutherford's nuclear models from 1919, when Rutherford postulated satellite hydrogen nuclei to explain artificial disintegration, to 1929–30, when he adopted Gamow's quantum mechanical explanation of radioactive disintegration. Stuewer shows how Rutherford successfully altered and adapted his satellite model to fit new experimental evidence. His strong preference for visual models, together with the unifying power of this particular model, made Rutherford reluctant to discard it completely.

MARJORIE MALLEY

See also Atomic Theory; Nuclear Physics

S

Scheele, Carl Wilhelm 1742–1786

Swedish chemist

Anonymous, "Carl Wilhelm Scheele – Pharmacist and Chemist: A Brief Account of his Life and Work, *Pharmaceutical Journal* (January 1893)

Boklund, Uno (ed.), *Carl Wilhelm Scheele: His Work and Life*, vols 1–2: *The Brown Book*, translated from the Swedish, Stockholm: Roos, 1968 (original edition, 1961)

Boklund, Uno, entry on Scheele in *Dictionary of Scientific Biography*, edited by Charles Coulston Gillispie vol. 11, New York: Scribner, 1981

Cassenbaum, Heinz and George B. Kauffman, "The Analytical Concept of the Chemical Element in the Work of Bergman and Scheele", *Annals of Science*, 33 (1976): 447–56

The Chemical Essays of Charles-William Scheele: Translated from the Transactions of the Academy of Sciences at Stockholm, with Additions, London: John Murray, 1786

Dobbin, Leonard (ed. and trans.), *The Collected Papers of Carl Wilhelm Scheele*, London: Bell, 1931

Hermbstädt, Sigismund Friedrich (ed.), *Sämmtliche physische und chemische Werke*, by Scheele, 2 vols, Berlin: Rottmann, 1793; reprinted Niederwalluf bei Wiesbaden: Sandig, 1971

Nechaev, I., *Chemical Elements: The Fascinating Story of Their Discovery and of the Famous Scientists, Who Discovered Them*, translated from the Russian by Beatrice Kinkead, New York: Coward McCann, 1942; London: Lindsay Drummond, 1944

Oseen, C.W. (ed.), *Carl Wilhelm Scheele: Handschriften 1756-1777*, Stockholm: Schwedische Akademie der Wissenschaften, 1942

Partington, J.R., *A History of Chemistry*, vol. 3, London: Macmillan, and New York: St Martin's Press, 1962

Thorpe, T.E., *Essays in Historical Chemistry*, London and New York: Macmillan, 1894

Carl Wilhelm Scheele was born in Stralsund in Swedish Pomerania. Many of his papers were written in German, but he settled in Sweden proper, and throughout his career he worked with both languages: German and Swedish. There are some factual differences about details of his life, including the type of school he attended, but most, starting with ANONYMOUS, agree that he had only an elementary education. In his youth, Scheele was said to be shy but hardworking. He was apprenticed to Martin Bauch in Gothenburg, a pharmacist, where he stayed for eight years. He worked as an assistant in pharmacies in Malmö in 1865, in Stockholm in 1868, and in Uppsala in 1870. In 1875, he set up on his own in Köping, purchasing a pharmacy from the widow of a recently deceased pharmacist.

BOKLUND (1981) is the most useful starting point for research on Scheele. It gives a short description of his life and science and a brief overview of the primary and secondary sources. PARTINGTON is a general history of chemistry, which in its examination of the chemical revolution discusses the claims for three scientists to have discovered oxygen: Priestley, Lavoisier, and Scheele. Partington clearly establishes Scheele's priority.

Even though there is no definitive biography, Scheele's personality and research have been fairly thoroughly explored in a variety of ways, and many of his papers and manuscripts have been published. THORPE's biographical essay is a virtual hagiography of Scheele. This is a problem similar to the one encountered with studies of Faraday: there are very few unkind words said about either. Thorpe argues that Scheele was hampered by poverty and harassed by debt. He was, however, the son of a merchant, who worked as a pharmacist all his life, so although he was not wealthy and worried a lot about money, he probably did not have to live in grinding poverty. Thorpe also states that Scheele had an excellent relationship with the other great contemporary Swedish chemist, Torbern Bergman, though he was deeply upset that the latter rejected his first two scientific papers.

It is vital to examine the primary and secondary education of famous scientists in for a variety of reasons, such as providing role models or as a way of understanding the history of certain academic issues. Scheele tends not to feature in recent collections of scientific biographies for schools, although NECHAEV's work may have been useful for an earlier generation. Nechaev provides a number of anecdotes about Scheele's experimental work, but he is presented as being so hardworking and virtuous that it is doubtful that these stories would entertain the present generation.

Scheele also discovered chlorine, which he called "dephlogisticated acid of salt", and a host of other substances. CASSENBAUM & KAUFFMAN examine the views of Bergman and Scheele on the concept of elements, showing that Scheele had theoretical views, as well as being a brilliant experimentalist. The difficulty in understanding Scheele's work is the problem of explaining how he could make so many discoveries, while still espousing the "phlogiston" theory which was becoming an untenable position even as he was researching.

Uno Boklund started to publish Scheele's manuscripts in preparation for a full-scale biography that never materialized. BOKLUND (1968) consists of the first two volumes of the seven planned. The missing volumes would have provided a biography and a printed version of his laboratory notes and correspondence. The volumes actually published contain Scheele's so-called "Brown Book" in facsimile and in deciphered form: it is full of Scheele's notes on chemistry in the now odd-seeming chemical notation of the day. There are helpful comments and an introduction, without which the "Brown Book" would remain inaccessible.

OSEEN has deciphered the manuscripts that Scheele's widow sent to J.C. Wilcke, when the latter was preparing an obituary. The manuscripts themselves are now kept in the Swedish Academy of Sciences.

Scheele was translated into English and French already during his lifetime. The *CHEMICAL ESSAYS* contains many of his papers and includes a preface by Thomas Beddoes, who explains to a British audience why Scheele's work is of interest. The "additions", to which the title refers, are papers on similar topics by Wiegleb, Meyer, Crell, and Beddoes himself. Guiton de Morveau translated some of Scheele's papers into French. HERMBSTÄDT, a German edition of his papers, was published soon after his death in two volumes, the second of which also includes excerpts from his correspondence. There is an interesting 14-page obituary by Crell, who praises Scheele's analytical skills ("der grosse Scheidekünstler") and claims him as a fellow German. DOBBIN provides a translation into 20th-century English of all Scheele's main publications, such as the *Chemical Treatise on Air and Fire*, and also a few scientific letters. A handy appendix translates the names of substances into the modern terminology.

WILLIAM PALMER

Schelling, Friedrich Wilhelm Joseph von 1775–1854

German philosopher

Durner, Manfred, Francesco Moiso and Jörg Jantzen, *Friedrich Wilhelm Joseph Schelling: Ergänzungsband zu Werke Band 5 bis 9: Wissenschaftshistorischer Bericht zu Schellings naturphilosophischen Schriften, 1797–1800*, Stuttgart-Bad Cannstatt: Frommann-Holzboog, 1994

Esposito, Joseph L., *Schelling's Idealism and Philosophy of Nature*, Lewisburg, Pennsylvania: Bucknell University Press, and London: Associated University Presses, 1977

Fischer, Kuno, *Schellings Leben, Werke und Lehre*, 3rd edition, Heidelberg: Winter, 1902

Gerabek, Werner E., *Friedrich Wilhelm Joseph Schelling und die Medizin der Romantik: Studien zu Schellings Würzburger Periode*, Frankfurt: Peter Lang, 1995

Hasler, Ludwig (ed.), *Schelling: Seine Bedeutung für eine Philosophie der Natur und der Geschichte: Referate und Kolloquien der Internationalen Schelling-Tagung Zürich 1979*, Stuttgart-Bad Cannstatt: Frommann-Holzboog, 1981

Heckmann, Reinhard, Hermann Krings and Rudolf W. Meyer (eds), *Natur und Subjektivität: Zur Auseinandersetzung mit der Naturphilosophie des jungen Schelling: Referate, Voten und Protokolle der II. Internationalen Schelling-Tagung Zürich 1983*, Stuttgart-Bad Cannstatt: Frommann-Holzboog, 1985

Heuser-Kessler, Marie-Luise, *Die Produktivität der Natur: Schellings Naturphilosophie und das neue Paradigma der Selbstorganisation in den Naturwissenschaften*, Berlin: Duncker & Humblot, 1986

Tilliette, Xavier (ed.), *Schelling im Spiegel seiner Zeitgenossen*, vols 1–2, Turin: Bottega D'Erasmo, 1974–81; vol. 3, Milan: Mursia, 1988

The literature on Friedrich Wilhelm Joseph von Schelling's impact on contemporary, and even modern, natural science is the main subject of this entry. It is now considered self-evident that Schelling's philosophy of nature (especially in the period 1797–1801) was influenced by contemporary natural science, and that his work had an impact upon the development of theories and research in the empirical sciences, especially the organic sciences and medicine. A renaissance in Schelling studies has taken place in the last 40 years in Germany, but this has not been matched in Anglophone countries.

Only two standard biographical works should be stressed here, of which FISCHER is still the most comprehensive and detailed. Volume 1 presents Schelling's life and writings, chronologically by his places of employment: Leipzig, Jena (especially his relationship with Karoline Schlegel), Würzburg, Munich (first time around, his controversy with Friedrich Heinrich Jacobi and Carl August Eschenmayer; second time around, his work at the University and Bavarian Academy of Sciences), Erlangen, and Berlin. In volume 2, Fischer considers Schelling's doctrines: the philosophy of nature, the philosophy of identity (including philosophy of arts), and the philosophy of religion (including philosophy of mythology and revelation). Fischer always attempts to understand Schelling's thinking within its historical and ideological context.

TILLIETTE provides a very comprehensive collection of printed biographical documents – quotations, reports, and statements on Schelling – based on contemporary correspondence (for example, by Voigt-Goethe, Creuzer-Günderode, Humboldt-Varnhagen, Humboldt-Bunsen, and Herbart), diaries (for example, by Melchior Meyr, Heinrich Puchta, Johann Andreas Schmeller, and Sulpiz Boisserée), memoirs, and memorabilia (ordered according to Schelling's place of residence), which reflect Schelling's personality. This study also contributes to an understanding of the chronology and contents of Schelling's lectures, and provides material for a new comprehensive biography.

HASLER and HECKMANN, KRINGS & MEYER all express the recent appreciation of the Romantic *Naturphilosophie*, in particular that of Schelling. Hasler contains essays on Schelling's relations to natural science (by D. von Engelhardt, H. Querner, and D. von Uslar) and with medicine (by K.E. Rothschuh, R. Toellner, and N. Tsouyopoulos). Heckmann, Krings & Meyer contain essays on Schelling's reaction to contemporary sciences (chemistry, biology, and electricity), and the systematical extension of his "speculative physics" (Krings explaining its central concept as "nature as a subject"). There are also essays on the importance of Schelling's speculative physics for the history of German Idealism, and on his *Naturphilosophie* from a modern viewpoint (cosmology, medicine, and the theory of evolution).

ESPOSITO investigates Schelling's idea of nature, his World System, and the connections between science and *Naturphilosophie* that evolved out of the ideas of Fichte and his *Theoretical Groundwork of the Philosophy of Nature* (1796). He stresses Schelling's critics – the anti-Idealists Franz Berg, Friedrich Köppen, and Wilhelm Traugott Krug, Karl Leonhard Reinhold (who is wrongly included), and the attack by Hegel – and examines Schelling's influence on 19th-century American philosophers (for example, Frederic Hedge, Caleb Sprage Henry, James March, Laurens P. Hickok, Charles S. Peirce, Josiah Royce), and on Idealism of more recent times (e.g., that of J.H. Muirhead and Nicholas Rescher, and on such critics of Idealism as Bertrand Russell). Esposito argues that Schelling's achievements in *Naturphilosophie* (for example, in the theory of organisation) warrant him a firm place in the history of science.

HEUSER-KESSLER inaugurates a new discussion on Schelling's *Naturphilosophie* within the context of the modern paradigm of self-organisation in biochemistry and biophysics. After describing the state of physics and biology c.1800 and discussing the influence of *Naturphilosophie* on the natural sciences, she points out the connection between Schelling's mature philosophical thoughts on nature – especially his view of magnetism and electrical phenomena, and his understanding of self-organisation as an infinite endeavour ("unendliches Bestreben") of the human mind – and the theories of Ilya Prigogine (thermodynamics) and Hermann Haken (synergetics) based on the idea of self-organisation, and demonstrates that Schelling is a third factor in modern bio-physical discussion.

GERABEK considers Schelling's intense interest in medical science during his Würzburg sojourn, and points out the meaning of experience and experiment for Schelling's theories using primary sources for *Naturphilosophie*: monographs, articles, and Schelling's correspondence of 1803–06. Against the background of Romantic *Naturphilosophie* and medicine, Gerabek shows Schelling's defining influence on discussions concerning such issues as the organism, physiology, Brownianism in the Würzburg Schelling Circle (which included, for example, I. Döllinger, A. Röschlaub, and L. Oken), and academic appointments.

DURNER, MOISO & JANTZEN is a "scientific-historical report" presenting Schelling's resources in 17th- and 18th-century natural science, and providing a very detailed and comprehensive bibliography. Originally conceived as a supplementary volume to the historical–critical edition of Schelling's works, it also serves as a separate history of natural science in the 17th and 18th centuries. Durner introduces contemporary theories of chemistry, including the beginnings of chemistry as a science, theories of chemical processes (Lavoisier and Kirwan), theories of combustion (phlogistic/antiphlogistic theories of Stahl, Buffon and Lavoisier), different kinds of gases (Hales, Black, Cavendish, and Priestley), and water (e.g., Le Roy, Saussure, and Deluc). Moiso deals with theories of magnetism (e.g., Newton, Franklin, Coulomb, Lesage, and

Prevost), electricity (e.g., Franklin, Volta, and Priestley), and galvanism (e.g., Galvani, Soemmering, Fowler, and Hunter). Finally, Jantzen covers theories of physiology (including irritability and sensibility (Haller)), vitality (e.g., Blumenbach and Kielmeyer), and reproduction and regeneration (Harvey and Blumenbach).

BEATRICE RAUSCHENBACH

See also Germanophone Areas; Romanticism

Schrödinger, Erwin 1887–1961
Austrian physicist

Götschl, Johann (ed.), *Erwin Schrödinger's World View: The Dynamics of Knowledge and Reality*, Dordrecht and Boston: Kluwer, 1992

Hermann, A. (ed.), *Die Wellenmechanik*, Stuttgart: Battenberg, 1963

Hoffmann, Dieter, *Erwin Schrödinger*, Leipzig: Teubner, 1985

Kerber, G., A. Dick and W. Kerber, *Dokumente, Materialien und Bilder zur 100: Wiederkehr des Geburtstages von Erwin Schrödinger*, Vienna: Fassbänder, 1987

Mehra, Jagdish and Helmut Rechenberg, *Erwin Schrödinger and the Rise of Wave Mechanics*, 2 vols, New York: Springer, 1987

Moore, Walter, *Schrödinger: Life and Thought*, Cambridge and New York: Cambridge University Press, 1989

Oberkofler, G. and P. Goller, *Erwin Schrödinger: Briefe und Dokumente aus Zürich, Wien und Innsbruck*, Innsbruck: Universitätsverlag, 1992

Schrödinger, Erwin, *Gesammelte Abhandlungen/Collected Papers*, edited by Österreichischen Akademie der Wissenschaften, 4 vols, Vienna and Braunschweig: Vieweg, 1984

Schrödinger, Erwin, *Mein Leben, Meine Weltansicht*, Vienna: Zsolnay, 1985

Scott, William T., *Erwin Schrödinger: An Introduction to His Writings*, Amherst: University of Massachusetts Press, 1967

Erwin Schrödinger's life and work are treated in numerous biographies, in representations of the historical development of wave mechanics, and in editions of his scientific and popular writings. Much of the German material has been translated into English.

SCHRÖDINGER (1985) – the autobiographic notes – constitute the most useful entry. They provide a synopsis of the person and the physicist by Schrödinger himself, and make clear how much of Schrödinger's work in physics was based on philosophy and on his *Weltanschauung* (world view). Physics was for him never a purely technical problem, but always primarily a question of knowledge. This applies to his revolutionary work on wave mechanics, to his work on field theory, and particularly to his research on the thermodynamics of open systems leading to his *What is Life?*

The omnibus volume by GÖTSCHL gives a deeper insight into these problems; here, 15 separate studies, by such authors as Y. Elkana, H. Poser, E. Scheibe, and F.M. Wuketis, all focus on Schrödinger's *Weltanschauung*. The range of subjects under discussion is very wide, from the holistic aspects of Schrödinger's wave equation and his interpretation of quantum physics, to his influence on modern (molecular) biology, and the extent to which Schrödinger's visions of a unity of nature and culture have influenced our view of life. This volume contains what is probably the most comprehensive study of Schrödinger's papers.

Although the Götschl volume yields a general view of Schrödinger's life and work, the following biographies are essential for detailed information concerning Schrödinger's life and his role in the history of science. The German-language biography by HOFFMANN, intended for a large audience, is a good introduction, as it covers the major stages of Schrödinger's life and his most important scientific achievements. SCOTT's biography is much more detailed and comprehensive. Concentrating on the representation of Schrödinger as a revolutionary in physics, Scott examines the development of modern quantum physics and Schrödinger's contribution to it. In addition, the biography analyses the impact of Schrödinger's Viennese origins upon his physics, in particular pointing to the connection with Boltzmann and the Viennese tradition of statistical physics. Whereas Hoffmann and Scott foreground Schrödinger's work in their biographies, MOORE focuses his analysis on the scholar's life and fascinating personality. He does occasionally overshoot the mark in a sensationalist manner, however, dwelling excessively on private matters and presenting as fact that which is only presumed and supposed.

The above systematic biographies are completed by OBERKOFLER & GOLLER's collection of letters and documents which presents Schrödinger's life in Zürich, Vienna, and Innsbruck in greater detail. KERBER, DICK & KERBER, a volume accompanying an exhibition dedicated to Schrödinger's centenary, contains many illustrations and thus provides not only an excellent impression of the existing "Schrödingeriana", but also illustrates how deeply the polyglot and cosmopolitan Schrödinger was influenced by his Austrian origins.

The fifth volume of MEHRA & RECHENBERG's series in the *Historical Development of Quantum Theory* is dedicated to Schrödinger's work on wave mechanics and its physical implications. The first part is a historical biography, and the second a representation of Schrödinger's wave mechanics, very much within the genre of the history of ideas. Both parts of the volume are impressive in that they are truly encyclopedic, amassing an enormous amount of material, but this is also their disadvantage, as the material is frequently not treated consistently or in a historically adequate manner. Furthermore, not enough credit is given to historians who had already published on Schrödinger's wave mechanics, such as Hanle, Kragh and Wessels.

Meanwhile, HERMANN is a pioneering work, which condenses all of Schrödinger's classic research on wave mechanics, supplemented by a few (unfortunately too few) remarks and a biographical essay that integrates Schrödinger's life and work. Finally, SCHRÖDINGER (1984), the collected papers, conveniently brings together all the scattered publications by Schrödinger in four volumes.

DIETER HOFFMANN
translated by Klaus Staubermann

See also Quantum Mechanics

Science Fiction

Aldiss, Brian and David Wingrove, *Trillion Year Spree: The History of Science Fiction*, London: Gollancz, and New York: Atheneum, 1986

Brantlinger, Patrick, "The Gothic Origins of Science Fiction", in *Problems in Materialism and Culture*, edited by Raymond Williams, London: Verso, 1980

Christie, John, "A Tragedy for Cyborgs", *Configurations*, 1 (1993): 171–96

Clute, John and Peter Nicholls, *The Encyclopedia of Science Fiction*, London, Orbit, and New York: St Martin's Press, 1993

Haraway, Donna J., "A Cyborg Manifesto", in her *Simians, Cyborgs, and Women: The Re-Invention of Nature*, London: Free Association Books, 1990; New York: Routledge, 1991

James, Edward, *Science Fiction in the Twentieth Century*, Oxford: Oxford University Press, 1994

Science Fiction Studies, 1973–

Sontag, Susan, "The Imagination of Disaster", in her *Against Interpretation, and Other Essays*, New York: Farrar Straus, 1966; London: Eyre and Spottiswoode, 1967

Suvin, Darko, *Metamorphoses of Science Fiction: On the Poetics and History of a Literary Genre*, New Haven, Connecticut: Yale University Press, 1979

Suvin, Darko, *Victorian Science Fiction in the UK: Discourses of Knowledge and Power*, Boston: G.K. Hall, 1983

Williams, Raymond, *Problems of Materialism and Culture: Selected Essays*, London: Verso, 1980

Wolfe, Gary K., *The Known and the Unknown: The Iconography of Science Fiction*, Kent, Ohio: Kent State University Press, 1979

Most authorities agree that science fiction emerged out of the gothic novel of the later 18th and early 19th centuries. Mary Shelley's fascinating and deeply flawed *Frankenstein* is, sometimes rather obsessively, presented as the *ur*-text of the genre. "Scientific romances" then proliferated around 1860. Authors such as Edward Bulwer Lytton, Samuel Butler, Edwin Abbot, Jules Verne, and H.G. Wells (an extremely selective sample, it should be noted) responded to scientific and technological advances in narratives that were politically charged and alternately celebratory and satirical. In the early 20th century the historical focus shifted to the United States. The emergence in the 1920s of mass circulation magazines such as John Campbell's *Astounding* and Hugo Gernsback's *Amazing Stories* was a crucial development; Gernsback popularized the term "science fiction" to describe stories that he and others were beginning to serve up. The writing was often, but not always, formulaic and uninspired, the illustrations crude, the whole package designed to appeal to an audience of lonely male midwestern teenagers: Rampaging monster, beneficent robots, thrusting spacecraft, and terrorized females became, and have to an extent remained, the icons of the genre. From this time science fiction was established as a powerful, perhaps ubiquitous, brand of pulp fiction, despised by connoisseurs of "mainstream" literature. The success of George Lucas's film *Star Wars* in 1977 expanded the market for science fiction books still further, and it is now a mass industry with a mass readership.

Science fiction critics have taken seriously its engagement with science and technology. For some its defining characteristics, shared with science itself, are extrapolation, reason, and experiment. Other examinations of science fiction reveal coded warnings of the violence and irrationality underlying scientific method. Pessimistic interpretations of the history of the genre read it as an indication of man's progressive alienation from his technological environment, while optimists extol writings that, inspired by cutting-edge technoscience, might prefigure political liberation.

The essential reference work is CLUTE & NICHOLLS. It is authoritative, well-documented, and provocative. The thematic entries that account for more than a quarter of the book have real interpretative bite. It should be supplemented by ALDISS & WINGROVE, who provide an entertaining and idiosyncratic jaunt through 200 years of the history of science fiction, which they represent as a field of oscillation between "thinking" and "dreaming" poles. "Thinking" science fiction is a rational engagement with science and technology: writers at the "dreaming" pole are conscious of humanity's alienation from its scientific productions. SUVIN (1983) exhaustively catalogues and analyses the vast corpus of 19th-century science fiction, its ideological underpinnings, and the social status (generally professional and bourgeois) of its authors and readers. Edward JAMES applies a nuanced historical understanding of the phenomenon of science fiction in the 20th century. Particularly impressive is his account of that strange and despised beast, the science fiction community: an arena in which authors of international repute mix with an assortment of scientologists and other millenarians, occultists, hobbits, and heavy metal munchkins.

Darko Suvin has been perhaps the most influential of all science fiction theorists, despite a tendency to repetition and a grinding prose style. His most influential claim (propounded in SUVIN, 1979) is that science fiction is characterized by what he terms cognitive estrangement; the narrative probing of the world as it is through the imagination of the world as it is not. The alternative worlds of science fiction, whether past, near, or far-future are unfamiliar but possible. This plausibility distinguishes the genre from myth, fairytale, and mere fantasy; deep space, unlike fairyland and the enchanted garden, is a laboratory of counterfactuals. Gary WOLFE also regards science fiction as an essentially experimental genre. Drawing on Mircea Eliade, he writes that the "transformation of Chaos into Cosmos, of the unknown into the known, is the central action of a great many works of science fiction". His elegant book charts the iconography of science fiction, the "embodiments" of this process of making the unknown knowable, realized in sealed spaces – e.g. spaceships – and through liminal figures – e.g. cyborgs, mutants, etc. While Suvin stresses the significance of technological and scientific novelties (or *novums* as he prefers) in science fiction narratives, for Wolfe the genre is straightforwardly extrapolative. As he suggests, for historians of science schooled on Kuhn, science fiction is often peculiarly unimaginative: "it accepts the dominant paradigms of contemporary science and projects them linearly in time and space".

Aligned to the dreaming pole, Susan SONTAG's influential essay on science fiction films of the 1950s and 1960s denies that they have anything to do with pure science at all, but are rather fantasies of technology. They invite an "aesthetic view of destruction and violence" that privileges technological

artefacts – spaceships, ray guns, thermonuclear devices – as the locus of value over "helpless" humanity. The pleasure and problem of such films, which enjoyed a renascence in the mid-to late 1970s and again in the mid-1990s, is that they inure us to the idea of destruction – and perhaps lead to a state of passive, and therefore unhealthy anticipation of destruction. In a fine essay indebted to Sontag's analysis Patrick BRANTLINGER has examined the emergence of science fiction in the 19th century as an offshoot of the gothic novel. Both genres, he claims, are organized around the idea that reason taken to extremes "produces monsters". In the gothic romance these monsters are the images of lunacy and nightmare; in science fiction they are projections of mankind's technological capability. Aliens and robots are science fiction's signs of alienation. They acquire personalities, usually demonic, and act against the interests of human protagonists.

Raymond WILLIAMS is perhaps the only major scholar in the Leavisite tradition – in which character development and psychological realism are preferred over extrapolative skill as literary marks of value – who takes science fiction seriously. He allows for science fiction's dystopian potential, but prefers to stress the progressive understandings of such writers as William Morris in the 19th century and Ursula Le Guin in the 20th. The crucial distinction he makes is between technological instrumentality and human agency, and argues that good (i.e. progressive, moral) science fiction does not commit the error of conflating these. The future state, for better or worse, will be the product of human desire directing technological transformations. Somewhat paradoxically he claims that literary representation can allude only to the form these transformations will take. The best science fiction is thus both quixotic and genuinely transgressive in a Kuhnian sense: "it is part of the power of science fiction that it is always potentially a mode of authentic shift; a crisis of exposure which produces a crisis of possibility; a reworking; in imagination, of *all* forms and conditions".

The notion that science fiction is liberating has appealed to the current generation of theorists. Donna HARAWAY's manifesto has already achieved canonical status. It opens with the famous assertion that "the boundary between science fiction and social reality is an optical illusion". The cyborg, the bastard offspring of cybernetics, genetics and information theory, is neither earth nor metal, human nor inhuman, male nor female, oppressor nor oppressed. It challenges traditional social narratives, and determinisms of every kind, including those of divinity, biology, gender, and technology. Haraway recognizes that science and technology are the tools of familiar political oppressions, but vests an almost transcendent faith in the liberating power of cyborgs. "Our best machines are made of sunshine", she writes. "People are nowhere near so fluid." Some critics have found this rather difficult to take. Drawing on recent cyberpunk science fiction, John CHRISTIE argues that the cyborg threatens confinement, the limitation of human potential, as much as it promises liberation.

SCIENCE-FICTION STUDIES is the main journal in the field. The most frequently examined authors are Le Guin, doyenne of woolly Marxists and gender warriors, Philip K. Dick, hero of the terminally estranged, and, of course, Mary Shelley.

HENRY ATMORE

See also Literature and Science

Scientific Illustration

Blum, Ann Shelby, *Picturing Nature: American Nineteenth-Century Zoological Illustration*, Princeton, New Jersey: Princeton University Press, 1993

Crary, Jonathan, *Techniques of the Observer: On Vision and Modernity in the Nineteenth Century*, Cambridge, Massachusetts: MIT Press, 1990

Daston, Lorraine and Peter Galison, "The Image of Objectivity", *Representations*, 40 (1992): 81–128

Dennis, Michael Aaron, "A Graphic Understanding: Instruments and Interpretation in Robert Hooke's *Micrographia*", *Science in Context*, 3 (1989): 309–64

Edgerton, Samuel Y. Jr, *The Heritage of Giotto's Geometry: Art and Science on the Eve of the Scientific Revolution*, Ithaca, New York: Cornell University Press, 1991

Kemp, Martin, *The Science of Art: Optical Themes in Western Art from Brunelleschi to Seurat*, New Haven, Connecticut: Yale University Press, 1990

Lynch, Michael and Steve Woolgar (eds), *Representation in Scientific Practice*, Cambridge, Massachusetts: MIT Press, 1990

Pang, Alex Soojung-Kim, "Victorian Observing Practices, Printing Technology, and Representations of the Solar Corona", *Journal for the History of Astronomy*, 25 (1994): 249–74; 26 (1995): 63–75

Rudwick, Martin J.S., "The Emergence of a Visual Language for Geological Science, 1760–1840", *History of Science*, 14 (1976): 149–95

Rudwick, Martin J.S., *Scenes from Deep Time: Early Pictorial Representations of the Prehistoric World*, Chicago: University of Chicago Press, 1992

Shapin, Steven, "The Politics of Observation: Cerebral Anatomy and Social Interests in the Edinburgh Phrenology Disputes", *Sociological Review Monographs*, 27 (1979): 139–78

Smith, Bernard, *Imagining the Pacific: In the Wake of the Cook Voyages*, New Haven, Connecticut: Yale University Press, 1992

Stafford, Barbara Maria, *Body Criticism: Imaging the Unseen in Enlightenment Art and Medicine*, Cambridge, Massachusetts: MIT Press, 1991

Wilson, Catherine, *The Invisible World: Early Modern Philosophy and the Invention of the Microscope*, Princeton, New Jersey: Princeton University Press, 1995

The relationship between science and art was of major interest to the pioneering historians of science in the 1940s and 1950s, but the discovery by historians and sociologists in the 1960s and 1970s that "science" was not a stable, timeless object seemed to make the examination of its relationship with "art" – another suspiciously broad term – a dead end. However, recent studies of instruments and scientific practices have given a new impetus to the study of "visual representation" in science, by providing a more interesting and methodologically rewarding foundation for the analysis of scientific pictures and picturing techniques. Visual records are among the basic products of a wide variety of instruments, and the analysis of visual reasoning, argument, and recording as forms of practice offer a means of showing how pictures reflect professional pressures, research agendas, and social interests.

The revival of interest in scientific illustration began with RUDWICK's (1976) examination of the role that the "visual language" of stratigraphy played in the development of geology in the early 19th century, and with SHAPIN's study of the influence of social interests on drawings of the brain made by Edinburgh phrenologists and their critics. These works connected the study of visual representation with the sociology of knowledge, and scholars soon added rhetoric, laboratory ethnography, discourse analysis, and literary theory to their tools for analyzing pictures, as the essays in LYNCH & WOOLGAR (originally produced in the mid-1980s) demonstrate. This work in turn inspired historians and sociologists of science to attend to scientific illustration and imagery in broader studies of natural history, modern physics, anthropology, astronomy, and other fields. DASTON & GALISON's study of the changing definitions of objectivity, for example, was based on an analysis of scientific atlases produced from the 1600s to the 1900s. Art historians, most notably STAFFORD and CRARY, have also used scientific illustration as a medium for detecting changes in aesthetics and visual culture.

None the less, most studies of scientific illustration can be clustered into several large areas. The first is the period from the Renaissance to the 17th century. Foremost among the works on this period is EDGERTON's book on the impact of Renaissance innovations in painting – in particular chiaroscuro and linear perspective – on Renaissance technical illustrations, Galileo's drawings of the moon, and technical European books sent to China. Most provocative are his claims that Galileo's Florentine artistic training, with its deep concern for representing chiaroscuro, linear perspective, and reflection of light between objects, "contributed crucially" to his discovery of "the true physical appearance of the surface of the moon". KEMP surveys the uses of geometry, optics, and color theory in art from the Renaissance to the 19th century. Early modern microscopy has been the subject of several works: DENNIS's study of Robert Hooke's *Micrographia* shows how natural philosophers of the Restoration period confronted the practical problems of using instruments and visual records as cornerstones for a new philosophy, while WILSON argues that microscopy had a profound effect on early modern philosophy.

Visual records produced by Enlightenment explorers have been a second focus of scholarly attention. Most notable is SMITH's survey of the impact of Cook's voyages on European science and art. The book ranges widely, but Smith's studies of Pacific landscape painting and representations of native peoples are particularly noteworthy. In the course of attempting to reconcile the multiple and conflicting demands of polite audiences, scientists and naval officers, and the Pacific landscape itself, landscape artists developed styles that pushed landscape painting closer to an empirical vision, which prefigured Romantic and Pre-Raphaelite art. These artists also called attention to the relationship between climate, atmosphere, and ecology in a way that influenced Alexander von Humboldt and Charles Darwin. Smith's analysis of portraiture embeds ethnographic drawing within a network of exchange, revealing its products to be the outcome of careful negotiation. The experience of observing Pacific islanders at close range encouraged

Cook's artists to produce works notable for their sensitivity and attention to detail: coarse, lurid paintings of savages were produced by 19th-century artists who never left Europe. Further, Smith notes that Tahitian and Maori subjects had something to gain from the exchange: a portrait was as valuable a rarity as could be acquired from Europeans in trade.

The history of botanical and zoological illustration has been a third area of focus. RUDWICK's 1992 study of pictures of prehistoric Earth shows how illustrators and naturalists dealt with the problem of illustrating "deep time", events that occurred before the appearance of humans and for which pictorial records were absent. BLUM's history of American zoological illustration from the colonial period to 1900 argues that changes in illustrators' styles reflected artistic influences, technical opportunities and limits, and disciplinary pressures. Thus, the dramatic but precise plein-air style of early naturalist-illustrators such as William Bartram and Rembrandt Peale reflected assumptions about the wild character of American nature and the importance of fieldwork and empiricism to American natural history, while the mid-19th-century illustrators' arrangement of their subjects in symmetrical rows, like specimens in a glass case, and their attention to fine anatomical detail, reflected a de-emphasis on fieldwork in favor of laboratory work and comparative anatomy.

Recent studies of scientific representation have several features in common. All dispense with the search either for overarching similarities or essential differences between science and art, and instead focus on the interaction of particular disciplines with certain artistic practices at specific times. While attention was previously confined to science's relationship to painting and other fine arts, scholars now study engravings, photographs, sketches, and computer models. They also pay more attention to the role that technologies and materials play in shaping visual records: for example, Blum demonstrates that photography first encouraged illustrators to greater verisimilitude, but later encouraged simplification of illustrations and a revival of line drawings, while PANG shows that astronomers treated photography as a complement to visual observation until the 1880s, and that photographs were judged in part on aesthetic standards developed for drawings. Dennis, Smith, Blum and Pang have all shown that copying processes require careful oversight and management, and that reproduction technologies (whether mezzotint, lithograph, or photomechanical technologies such as halftone engraving) introduce decisive changes in the content of original illustrations.

ALEX SOOJUNG-KIM PANG

See also Printing; Reading Culture and Science; Representation

Scientific Instruments: general works

Clifton, Gloria C., *Directory of British Scientific Instrument Makers, 1550–1851*, London: Zwemmer National Maritime Museum, 1995

Daumas, Maurice, *Scientific Instruments of the Seventeenth and Eighteenth Centuries*, translated from the French and edited by Mary Holbrook, London: Batsford, and New York: Praeger, 1972 (original edition, 1953)

Dictionary of British Scientific Instruments, issued by the British Optical Instruments Manufacturers' Association, London: Constable, 1921

Field, Judith V., "What is Scientific about a Scientific Instrument?", *Nuncius*, 3 (1988): 3–26

Hackmann, W.D., "Instrumentation in the Theory and Practice of Science: Scientific Instruments as Evidence and as an Aid to Discovery", *Annali dell'Istituto e Museo di Storia della Scienza di Firenze*, 10 (1985): 87–115

Hackmann, W.D., "Scientific Instruments: Models of Brass and Aids to Discovery", in *The Uses of Experiment: Studies in the Natural Sciences*, edited by David Gooding, Trevor Pinch and Simon Schaffer, Cambridge: Cambridge University Press, 1989

Turner, A.J., *Early Scientific Instruments: Europe, 1400–1800*, London: Sotheby's, and New York: Philip Wilson, 1987

Turner, A.J., *Mathematical Instruments in Antiquity and the Middle Ages: An Introduction*, London: Vade-Mecum Press, 1994

Turner, Gerard L'E., *Antique Scientific Instruments*, Poole, Dorset: Blandford Press, 1980

Turner, Gerard L'E., "Scientific Instruments", in *Information Sources in the History of Science and Medicine*, edited by Pietro Corsi and Paul Weindling, London and Boston: Butterworth, 1983

Turner, Gerard L'E., *Nineteenth-Century Scientific Instruments*, London: Sotheby's, and Berkeley: University of California Press, 1983

Van Helden, Albert, "The Birth of the Modern Scientific Instrument, 1550–1700", in *The Uses of Science in the Age of Newton*, edited by John G. Burke, Berkeley: California University Press, 1983

Van Helden, Albert and Thomas L. Hankins (eds), "Instruments", *Osiris*, n.s., 9 (1994)

Warner, Deborah Jean, "What is a Scientific Instrument, When Did It Become One, and Why?", *British Journal for the History of Science*, 23/76 (1990): 83–93

Wise, M. Norton (ed.), *The Values of Precision*, Princeton, New Jersey: Princeton University Press, 1995

In recent years both historians and philosophers of science have shown an increased interest in the role of instruments for the study of nature. More recently still, even some art historians have become fascinated by the images produced by such devices. Nevertheless, the study of the artefacts of science was for a long time the Cinderella of the history of science. Science historians, in line with historians generally, have always been more familiar with the written records, while instrument historians, on the other hand, are interested in the material objects of scientific culture. Thus, their inspiration and working practices have come from other disciplines which study cultural artefacts: for example, art historians, anthropologists, and especially archaeologists. Perhaps the discipline closest to the study of scientific instruments is industrial archaeology, for, unlike traditional archaeology which is wholly reliant on the study of the artefact, industrial archaeologists have access both to the artefact and written records.

The study of scientific instruments takes a number of forms that can be broadly categorized as "antiquarian", "intellectual", and "museological". These categories do, of course, overlap, but it is useful to have them in mind when reviewing the literature on the history of scientific instruments. HACKMANN (1985) provides a brief overview of these different approaches. Examples are given of morphological and taxonomic (including chemical and metallographical) studies for the dating of instruments, the identification of instruments with particular workshops, the authentication of doubtful specimens, the determination of the output of different workshops, and the elucidation of the routes along which instrument technology was disseminated. Also discussed are some of the problems associated with such studies. A typical example is the study of decorative gold-tooling motifs on some 70 vellum-covered microscopes and telescopes from the 17th and 18th centuries initiated by G. L'E. Turner in 1966. He demonstrated that the same tools were used to decorate instruments by different makers, and that these tooling motifs fell into distinct stylistic groups which could be used as a rough guide to dating. Thus, this study threw new light on the structure of the instrument maker's trade, even though the approach would not have surprised archaeologists or art historians. In other studies, the workshop output of certain instruments has been determined by plotting production graphs of serial numbers. A useful literature review is provided by G. L'E TURNER (1983, "Scientific Instruments"), although this is now rather out of date. The subject still lacks a general bibliography. CLIFTON is a recent seminal work on the organization of the scientific instrument-making trade, presenting a comprehensive directory of British makers from 1550 to the Great Exhibition of 1851, based on trade directories, guild records, rent books, etc. It will be up to future instrument historians to use this information in their studies.

Any general overview of this subject is problematized by the difficulty of defining what is meant by "scientific instruments". Not only are there many different ways (and reasons) for studying these instruments, but there are also many definitions of them. For instance, should clocks, astrolabes, orreries, telescopes, electrical machines, air pumps, voltaic piles, and an arsenal of other devices used in the laboratory, all be defined as "scientific" instruments? The extraordinary diversity of devices is highlighted by the list issued by the British Optical Instrument Manufacturers' Association in their *DICTIONARY OF BRITISH SCIENTIFIC INSTRUMENTS*: one suspects that few clock historians would see themselves as members of the fraternity of historians of scientific instruments.

The problem of definition is very apparent in the literature. Scholars find that it is almost impossible not to be anachronistic when attempting a comprehensive overview of this subject in terms of chronology and interment types. VAN HELDEN's assumption that a scientific instrument is a tool developed to investigate nature qualitatively or quantitatively may be true for laboratory devices of the late 17th century onwards, but is distorting for the period 1550–1700 which, according to van Helden, is the period of the birth of the modern scientific instrument. Neither the astrolabe nor the pendulum clock are easily categorized. A. TURNER (1994) appreciates the problem of inflexible definitions and consciously uses the term "mathematical instrument" as being more appropriate in this study of instruments from antiquity to the Middle Ages, while in A. TURNER (1987), which covers

the period 1400–1800, he uses what he considers to be the anachronistic term "scientific instrument". His three categories of instruments – 1) as used in the study of a particular aspect of the natural world; 2) as used by practitioners of mathematically and astronomically based professional activities (categorized by other historians as "practical mathematics"); and 3) as everyday devices dependent on scientific or mathematical principles – are historiographically sensitive, but what is lacking from his book of 1987 is a discussion of instruments in terms of laboratory devices. On the other hand, both G. L'E. TURNER (1980) and especially G. L'E. TURNER (1983, *Nineteenth-Century Scientific Instruments*) contain lucid descriptions of the whole spectrum of scientific instruments. The former is a very popular account, while the latter focuses mostly on 19th-century devices used in the laboratory for experimental and didactic purposes. Both books are mainly intended for the collector.

FIELD is concerned with the relationship between scientific instruments and their corresponding fields of science, but with particular reference to astronomy and related mathematical sciences from about 1400 to 1650. Her inclusion of the dome of a Florence Cathedral, which provided the framing for a gnomon, again highlights the difficulty of categorization. She argues that instrument studies should be taken seriously by historians who are interested in exploring the social context of science. DAUMAS is a truly pioneering study that emphasizes the mutual dependence of scientific practice and contemporary craft technology, although its indiscriminate use of the word "scientific" makes it less sophisticated than later works.

VAN HELDEN & HANKINS, undoubtedly influenced by the growing literature on scientific instruments of the last decade, attempt a much more pragmatic definition than that of Van Helden (1983). The two authors appreciate that the term "scientific instrument" has multiple meanings – encompassing models (orreries, ether models), sense-extending devices (telescopes, microscopes), and measuring devices (chemical balances, electrometers) – and conclude that scientific instrumentation constitutes a technology of science that has greatly expanded since the 17th century. In an attempt to facilitate discussion about the role of instruments in the study of natural phenomena, HACKMANN (1989) distinguishes between "passive" observers (observational instruments such as telescopes and microscopes) and "active" explorers of nature (laboratory devices, such as electrical machines and air pumps). However, these two categories blur at the edges, as certain instruments can be used either passively or actively.

It can be demonstrated from the contemporary literature that categories such as "scientific instrument" have always been rather fluid in their meaning. The contributors to WISE analyse different aspects of precision, accuracy, measurement, and instrumentation. The central theme is that quantitative ideas of accuracy and precision emerged from the social and institutional nexus of science and politics during the 18th century, but the concept of "scientific instrument" is not problematized.

WARNER argues that the category of "scientific instruments" cannot be applied to 17th-century science, as it was not until the mid-19th century that the terms "natural philosophical" and "philosophical" were replaced by "scientific" with regard to instruments. James Clerk Maxwell may well have been the first to spell out the scientist's meaning of the term "scientific instrument" in his capacity as a member of the British Committee of Council on Education that organized the Special Loan Collection of Scientific Apparatus in 1867. Perhaps the most useful conclusion is that there is no such simple category as a "scientific instrument", and that historians of science are now well attuned to such difficulties of categorization.

WILLEM HACKMANN

See also Astronomical Instruments; Instrument Makers; Medical Instruments; Microscopes; Scientific Instruments: France; Telescopes

Scientific Instruments: France

Bennett, J.A., *Le Citoyen Lenoir: Scientific Instrument Making in Revolutionary France*, Cambridge: Whipple Museum, 1989

Blondel, Christine *et al.* (eds), *Studies in the History of Scientific Instruments*, London: Rogers Turner, 1989

Blondel, Christine and Matthias Dörries (eds), *Restaging Coulomb: Usages, controverses et réplications autour de la balance de torsion*, Florence: Olschki, 1994

Brenni, Paolo, "L'industria degli strumenti scientifici in Francia nel XVIII e XIX secolo", in *Gli strumenti*, edited by Gerard L'E. Turner, Milan: Banca Popolare di Milano, 1990, 450–63

Brenni, Paolo, "Nineteenth-Century French Industry Makers", *Bulletin of the Scientific Instrument Society*: 38 (1993): 11–13; 39 (1993): 11–14; 40 (1994): 3–6; 41 (1994): 4–8; 43 (1994): 12–15; 44 (1995): 13–17; 45 (1995): 19–24; 46 (1995): 12–17; 48 (1996): 10–14; 49 (1996): 3–8

Daumas, Maurice, *Scientific Instruments of the Seventeenth and Eighteenth Centuries and Their Makers*, translated from the French and edited by Mary Holbrook, London: Batsford, and New York: Praeger, 1972; reprinted, London: Portman Books, 1989 (original edition, 1953)

Payen, Jacques, "Les Constructeurs d'instruments scientifiques en France au XIXe siècle", *Archives internationales d'histoire des sciences*, 36/116 (1986): 84–161

Shinn, Terry, "The Bellevue grand électroaimant, 1900–1940: Birth of a Research-Technology Community", *Historical Studies in the Physical and Biological Sciences*, 24/1 (1993): 157–87

Syndicat des constructeurs en instruments d'optique et precision, *L'Industrie française des instruments de precision*, Paris: Corbeil, 1902; reprinted, Paris: Brieux, 1980

Turner, A.J., *From Pleasure and Profit to Science and Security: Etienne Lenoir and the Transformation of Precision Instrument-Making in France, 1760–1830*, Cambridge: Whipple Museum, 1989

Turner, A.J., *Of Time and Measurement: Studies in the History of Horology and Fine Technology*, Aldershot, Hampshire: Variorum, 1993

Williams, Mari E.W., *The Precision Makers: A History of the Instruments Industry in Britain and France, 1870–1939*, London and New York: Routledge, 1994

The literature on scientific instruments in France can be divided up into general overviews, works on particular instrument makers or instruments, and collected volumes with diverse contents.

There are two general overviews: Brenni (1990) and Daumas. BRENNI (1990) is an introductory overview addressed to the public at large and not specifically to professional historians of science. The topic is described in very general terms with no footnotes, but there is a large bibliography. Brenni's paper provides the easiest access to the history of scientific instruments in France for the beginner. The founding text of the history of scientific instrument making in France is DAUMAS. Although the emphasis is on the 17th and 18th centuries, Daumas provides a grand view and, unlike much of the instrument literature produced for collectors, attempts an ambitious contextualisation, in particular by linking the history of manufacture and science with the history of instrumentation and workshop practice. Written in the 1950s, it remains a useful monograph, although it does not use all the sources available to the modern historian. It is also somewhat old-fashioned, in the sense that it follows a classically linear and teleological model of historical progress.

In a series of papers, BRENNI (1993–96) presents a study of several instrument makers in France. The makers chosen are generally the most successful in terms of sales and exports and innovation, and each paper provides a short biography and an overview of the historical sources. The focus is on the instruments, many of which are illustrated. Brenni plans to expand these essays into a monograph in the near future.

Whereas the series of papers by Brenni deals with the most prominent instrument makers, PAYEN provides a great deal of data on a wide variety of makers. Unfortunately, he does not always refer to the primary sources. Payen primarily lists his amassed information, but there is an introduction, in which he attributes the decline of the international standing of French makers to their proclivity for the artistic.

TURNER (1989) is the most detailed study of the French industry in the late 18th and early 19th centuries, dealing not only with Lenoir but also with his contemporaries in the trade. Much of the information is based on previously unused primary sources.

The focus of BENNETT is again the work of Etienne Lenoir, who is shown to have played a pivotal role in the revival of the French industry after the Revolution. This is a catalogue of an exhibition held at the Whipple Museum of the History of Science in Cambridge, comprising French instruments and related books and prints from the early 18th to the mid-19th centuries.

BLONDEL & DÖRRIES takes up a number of issues arising from the replication of Coulomb's torsion balance carried out by Peter Heering as a part of the programme to rebuild historical scientific instruments at the University of Oldenburg. They show that replication revealed a number of problems in experimental practice, such as the fact that even wood conducts electricity, and that Coulomb's law could not be replicated except when the instrument was placed within a Faraday cage. Such issues point to the vital importance of tacit knowledge in scientific experimentation, and highlight the necessity of training, and the importance of material culture and of the control of the surroundings in which the experiment takes place. Within this context, the question of the relevance of the fact that Coulomb was an engineer is raised. In addition, it was found that much of the tacit knowledge was available in the 18th-century historical sources (such as wood conducting electricity) and that, generally, the historical sources and the replication threw light on each other in a number of ways. Finally, the specificity of local scientific culture is addressed; Coulomb's simple law turns out not to have been embraced in equal measure by all Western scientists – as, for example, one had to be a Newtonian to make sense of Coulomb, and Germans were generally not Newtonians.

SYNDICAT DES CONSTRUCTEURS EN INSTRUMENTS D'OPTIQUE ET PRECISION is a publication by the French profession of scientific instrument makers, who, unlike their German counterparts, had no catalogue at the 1900 Paris Exhibition. In response, the French published this catalogue after the event. As might be expected of a publication intended to advertise the strengths of French instrument makers, it is lavishly illustrated, with details of 50 makers, their addresses, and a description of their area of expertise and specialisation.

SHINN describes French scientific instruments in the 20th century, in particular giving an account of the development of the large Bellevue electromagnet during the first half of the century. In terms of scientific theory, the project has been considered a failure, as no significant discoveries were made. However, Shinn argues that it would be too narrow to judge the project by such standards alone; it provided an opportunity for the physics community to devote themselves to the study of instrumentation and materials in its own right, and much was learned about the manufacture of magnets and cryogenics in the process. In addition, it brought experience with Big Science projects, funding to the physics community, and links with industry. In other words, the grand electromagnet project was productive at the frontier between science and technology, both in institutional and techno-scientific terms. Terry Shinn is currently working on a monograph on this topic.

WILLIAMS is an interesting analysis of the history of scientific instruments, seen from the perspective of economic history. Her argument is that innovation constitutes the driving force within economic history, and thus historians would be well-advised to pay more attention to scientific instrument makers. Despite its title, the book is in fact more concerned with England than with France, and within France it covers mainly optics, a field in which the author has previously worked. However, it does provide broad links with industrial history and to some extent military history, especially in relation to World War I. In accordance with her economic emphasis, Williams's history differs from many of the works discussed here in that she does not delve into technical details, nor does she provide any illustrations of the instrumentation.

TURNER (1993) is a collection of previously-published articles, covering early gnomonics, navigation at the time of Berthoud, the work of Danfrie, and the slide-rule in the 17th century.

BLONDEL *et al.* consists of several dozen papers that were originally given at a conference. As a result, the papers are very diverse, although most consider French scientific instruments to some extent. The topics covered range from 17th- and 18th-century instrument makers, innovations in clock

making, psychological instruments, and the use of the induction coil in medicine and physics, to range finders employed during World War I.

CHRISTINE BLONDEL AND JIM BENNETT

See also Instruments Makers; Scientific Instruments: general works

Scientific Revolution

Bacon, Francis, *The New Organon and Related Writings*, edited by Fulton H. Anderson, Indianapolis: Bobbs-Merrill, 1960

Butterfield, Herbert, *The Origins of Modern Science, 1300–1800*, London: Bell, 1949

Cohen, H. Floris, *The Scientific Revolution: A Historiographical Inquiry*, Chicago: University of Chicago Press, 1994

Duhem, Pierre, *The Origins of Statics, the Sources of Physical Theory*, translated from the French by Grant F. Leneaux *et al.*, Dordrecht and Boston: Kluwer Academic, 1991 (original edition, 2 vols 1905–06)

Hall, A. Rupert, *The Scientific Revolution, 1500–1800*, London: Longmans Green, 1954; as *The Revolution in Science, 1500–1750*, London: Longman, 1983

Jacob, Margaret C., *The Cultural Meaning of the Scientific Revolution*, New York: Knopf, 1988

Koyré, Alexandre, *From the Closed World to the Infinite Universe*, Baltimore: Johns Hopkins Press, 1957

Koyré, Alexandre, *Études Galileenes*, Paris: Hermann, 1939; as *Galileo Studies*, translated from the French by John Mepham, Atlantic Highlands, New Jersey: Humanities Press, and Hassocks, Sussex: Harvester Press, 1978 (original edition, 1939)

Kuhn, Thomas S., *The Copernican Revolution: Planetary Astronomy in the Development of Western Thought*, Cambridge, Massachusetts: Harvard University Press, 1957

Kuhn, Thomas S., *The Structure of Scientific Revolutions*, Chicago: University of Chicago Press, 1962; revised edition, 1970

Lindberg, David C. and Robert S. Westman (eds), *Reappraisals of the Scientific Revolution*, Cambridge and New York: Cambridge University Press, 1990

Porter, Roy and Mikuláš Teich (eds), *The Scientific Revolution in National Context*, Cambridge and New York: Cambridge University Press, 1992

Shapin, Steven and Simon Schaffer, *Leviathan and the Air-Pump: Hobbes, Boyle, and the Experimental Life*, Princeton, New Jersey: Princeton University Press, 1985

Yates, Frances A., *Giordano Bruno and the Hermetic Tradition*, Chicago: University of Chicago Press, and London: Routledge and Kegan Paul, 1964

The era of the "scientific revolution" has been the focus of debates concerning the origins of modern science throughout the 20th century. For its adherents, it is nothing less than the founding moment of science in early modern Europe, signifying a radical intellectual break with the past. This revolution was allegedly accomplished by Copernicus, Galileo, Descartes, and their contemporaries, and opened the way for all future scientific progress. Despite being subjected to severe criticisms over the years, the notion of a scientific revolution has proved extremely resilient. Even today, when the scientific revolution is no longer widely accepted as an accurate historical account, it still provides the framework of debate for much scholarly work on early modern science. The literature on the scientific revolution is, of course, enormous. The following is no more than a small selection, designed to outline the main lines and currents of interpretation prevalent in this field during the 20th century.

The notion of a radical break with the past was not the invention of historians of science, but was bequeathed to them by the early modern promoters of science themselves. Francis BACON, for example, in aphorism 96 of his *Novum organum*, complained that "we have as yet no natural philosophy that is pure; all is tainted and corrupted", and he therefore took it upon himself to correct this situation by promoting a new method of investigation, based on systematic observations and careful generalizations. Descartes and Galileo expressed similarly disparaging views on the knowledge they inherited from their medieval predecessors, while each promoted his own reform program. While the proper scientific methodology remained in dispute, the historical chronology went largely unchallenged until the late 19th century. It was generally acknowledged that a radically new scientific methodology emerged in Europe in the 16th and 17th centuries, and that this was responsible for the great advances in knowledge that have been achieved since that time.

The first modern challenge to this view was advanced by DUHEM. While researching his history of statics, Duhem came across the works of the medieval schoolmen Jordanus de Nemore and Albert of Saxony. Their scientific methodology, according to Duhem, was no different from Galileo's approach three centuries later. Furthermore, he argued, Galileo's work can only be understood against the background of the achievement of his medieval predecessors. Science, according to Duhem, advances gradually by minute increments throughout human history. "The so called 'Renaissances'", he claimed in his introduction, "were frequently nothing but unjust and sterile reactions".

The defense of the scientific revolution was taken up in the 1930s by Koyré. The work of Galileo and Descartes, he argued in KOYRÉ (1939/1978), constituted a radical break with their predecessors on two counts: the dissolution of the cosmos as a presupposition in accounts of the universe, and the geometrization of space. Elsewhere, Koyré described the scientific revolution in somewhat different terms, emphasizing the move from "the world of the more or less to the world of precision", or describing it as a philosophical revolution in which Plato's mathematical approach to nature replaced Aristotle's qualitative approach. But while the precise emphasis of Koyré's interpretation varied somewhat, the basic outlook remained the same: the scientific revolution, for Koyré, was fundamentally a revolution in world-view. A closed, non-geometrical, qualitative world was replaced by an infinite universe, existing in Euclidean space and governed by mathematical laws.

Koyré's scholarship inspired a full generation of works, of which I will mention only two. BUTTERFIELD was not a professional historian of science, and his importance to the field lies not in any original contributions, but in the immense popularity of his book. The very term "scientific revolution", while in use previously, gained universal currency through Butterfield's eminently readable work. For Butterfield, the scientific revolution was a momentous event in human history, "reducing the Renaissance and Reformation to the rank of mere episodes". He generally accepts Koyré's account of a transformation of world-views, but enlarges the historical boundaries of the transformation. His first chapter deals with the medieval theory of impetus, while his last gives an account of the "postponed" 18th-century revolution in chemistry. The core of the revolution remained, as before, in the 16th and 17th centuries.

In contrast to Butterfield, who was an outsider to the field, Hall devoted his entire career to the study of the scientific revolution, and thus HALL (1983, revised from 1954) is far richer in detail, though rather less readable, than Butterfield. As the title of his book makes clear, Hall generally follows Koyré's thesis of a scientific revolution in early modern Europe, and even accepts Koyré's view that the most important part of this shift was the application of mathematics to the study of nature. Hall insists, however, that there can be no single cause for the scientific revolution: the legacy of medieval universities, and social and economic shifts in the period, take their place alongside the revival of mathematical Platonism as plausible explanations. While Koyré sought to pinpoint the precise nature of the scientific revolution, Hall is satisfied to present it as a wide array of interrelated developments.

KUHN (1957) was clearly written in the tradition established by Koyré. According to Kuhn, with the emergence of Renaissance humanism and Neoplatonism, the ancient Ptolemaic universe suddenly appeared untenable. Copernicus provided an alternative universe, which was more in accord with the contemporary emphasis on mathematical symmetries and internal coherence. For Kuhn, as for Koyré, the revolution consisted of one world-view completely displacing another, and for both Platonism was a major factor in this shift.

In KUHN (1962), Koyré's thesis is pushed beyond anything intended by its author. For Koyré, science originated in a wholesale philosophical shift, substituting mathematical Platonism for an outmoded Aristotelian perspective. This was a significant departure from the older tradition, in which the origins of science were described as a methodological shift, substituting an erroneous method for a correct one. Koyré and his followers tacitly assumed that the philosophical revolution was a one-time occurrence, after which science settled down to explore its newly-constructed universe. This, however, was no more than an assumption: world-views may change, and if science is dependent upon them, then it too may be subject to occasional revolutionary transformations. This was precisely the point elaborated by Kuhn (1962); science, according to Kuhn, periodically goes through revolutionary "paradigm shifts", and each of these establishes a new world-view that sets the agenda for a period of "normal science", before it too is displaced by a new revolutionary change. The singular "Copernican revolution" of his previous work was here replaced by consecutive "scientific revolutions", occurring periodically in the course of scientific work.

While Kuhn questioned the uniqueness of the scientific revolution, YATES challenged its rationality. Like Koyré, Yates viewed the emergence of science as a transformation in world-view. The medieval notion of man, according to Yates, was of a fallen creature, a passive spectator to a world dominated by superior powers. In contrast, the Renaissance saw the emergence of man as magus – a great operator and manipulator of the secret powers of nature. This magus, Yates argues, was the precursor of the scientific virtuosi of the 17th century. Significantly, this shift in the view of man, according to Yates, was the result of the translation of the ancient Hermetic corpus by Marsilio Ficino in the 15th century. Paradoxically then, modern rational science has its roots in a magical mystical treatise of dubious origin.

The theses of both Kuhn and Yates were widely criticized on historical, as well as philosophical, grounds. The blow they dealt to the unity of the scientific revolution, however, proved irreparable. In the past three decades, works relating to the topic are characterized mostly by their fragmentation. For the most part, they either deal with particular specialized aspects of early modern science, or relate the scientific revolution to a myriad of early modern social and cultural trends.

At first glance, JACOB would appear to be an exception to this rule, as she is one of the few authors in recent years attempting to treat the scientific revolution as a whole. Her project, however, is very different from that of Koyré, Butterfield, or Hall. While she accepts the rational nature of the scientific revolution, this in itself, she argues, does little to explain the immense success of the new sciences. The acceptance of science, for Jacob, is always dependent on the local cultural meaning attributed to it in each historical setting. She therefore proceeds to discuss issues such as the usefulness of Galilean science for the educated laity in Italy, the alliance of science and Puritanism in 17th-century England, and the role of the Royal Society in promoting the new social order of the Restoration. On each and every one of these issues, Jacob provides interesting insights. One may, none the less, question the usefulness of the concept the scientific revolution, which has to be explained in so many different ways in so many different contexts.

Unlike Jacob, SHAPIN & SCHAFFER focus on a particular episode of early modern science, namely the debate between Robert Boyle and Thomas Hobbes over Boyle's air-pump experiments. Whereas Jacob was concerned only with the social acceptance of science, Shapin & Schaffer address its social construction, describing how the establishment of scientific facts became the battleground for rival conceptions of the proper social and political order in Restoration England. Science, for Shapin & Schaffer, is not merely affected by external cultural factors, but is itself a social and political activity.

It is no coincidence, given the fragmentation of the field, that some of the latest books on the scientific revolution are not overarching interpretations, but collections of articles. For PORTER & TEICH there can be no single interpretation; the scientific revolution in England was different from that in France, Italy, Spain, or Portugal. Each of these requires a separate interpretation that is provided by a specialist in that particular area. LINDBERG & WESTMAN attempt to focus on the scientific revolution as a whole; the articles in their collection, however, end up highlighting an array of separate issues relating to the topic, such as patronage, occultism, and religion.

The studies themselves are fascinating and highly instructive; their diversity, however, merely emphasizes how problematic the unifying concept of a "scientific revolution" has become.

COHEN is not a historical work, but a historiographical study. It is very informative, and provides excellent source material on the literature of the scientific revolution. It is perhaps symptomatic of what the scientific revolution has become in recent years, that this recent work in the field is a book about books. For the scientific revolution is no longer a historical event, nor an academic field; it is, above all, a tradition of historical writing that dominated the study of early modern science in the 20th century.

AMIR ALEXANDER

See also Hermeticism; Merton Thesis

Scientification of Education

Cravens, Hamilton, *Before Head Start: The Iowa Station and America's Children*, Chapel Hill: University of North Carolina Press, 1993

Joncich, Geraldine M., *The Sane Positivist: A Biography of Edward L. Thorndike*, Middletown, Connecticut: Wesleyan University Press, 1968

Noble, Douglas D., *The Classroom Arsenal: Military Research, Information Technology, and Public Education*, London and New York: Falmer, 1991

Petrina, Stephen, "Psychology, Technology, and Clinical Procedures in Education: The Cases of Luella W. Cole and Sidney L. Pressey, 1917–1934" (dissertation), University of Maryland, 1994

Rose, Nikolas S., *The Psychological Complex: Psychology, Politics, and Society in England, 1869–1939*, London and Boston: Routledge and Kegan Paul, 1985

Rose, Nikolas S., *Governing the Soul: The Shaping of the Private Self*, London and New York: Routledge, 1990

Ross, Dorothy, *G. Stanley Hall: The Psychologist as Prophet*, Chicago: University of Chicago Press, 1972

Woodridge, Adrian, *Measuring the Mind: Education and Psychology in England, 1860–1990*, Cambridge and New York: Cambridge University Press, 1994

Education in Europe and North America became more scientific with the rationalization of natural history and other social practices during the mid-1800s. PETRINA describes how chairs in education and pedagogy were established in universities, and teaching became a subject of professional study. Scientific practice and thought penetrated the entire process of education, from administration to school services to teaching. Meanwhile, materials and procedures – such as school surveys, medical inspections, and standardized tests – were commercialized during the early 1900s, and the science of education became big business. As in the scientification of business and social work, it was economists, psychologists, and sociologists who saw education as a social domain for their techniques; economics and sociology, along with scientific management, were to define the terms for administrative science, and psychology was to underwrite the "new" pedagogy. The "medicalization" of education, occurring earlier in Belgium, France, Norway, and

Sweden than in other countries, aligned medical sciences with school and mental hygiene. Meanwhile, natural and social Darwinism selectively guided an anthropology of education on the African and Asian continents. Indeed, viewing the "science of education" as an idiom in the domain of education can be helpful; looking for a "science" as opposed to an anthropology, psychology, or sociology of education in history is futile.

Within education, the term "research" became synonymous with "science" during the first decades of the 20th century, and it was not until the mid-1980s that non-positivistic forms of educational research were widely accepted. While a huge investment of scientific technique was made in schooling in most countries of the world during the late 19th and 20th centuries, educational practice has proven to be less a science than a political improvisation. This is a new insight, however, and many regarded education as Thomas Kuhn had the human sciences in 1962: a pre-paradigmatic social endeavor en route toward becoming normal science.

Throughout the last 150 years, there have been those who have claimed an intrinsic content of educational science, and those who have pointed to scientific sources for education. The monitorial schools of England and Scotland demonstrated the uses of disciplinary psychologies during the early 1800s, while Alexander Bain argued, in his *Education as a Science* (1879), that education was intrinsically a science. In the same period, Herbert Spencer (in England) and Johann Herbart (in Germany) rationalized pedagogy through sociological or psychological techniques. By the turn of the century, there was a cadre of psychologists and sociologists specializing in education, and making scientific technique and content common sources for administrative and pedagogical practice.

In the United States, G. Stanley Hall and Edward L. Thorndike were two of the better-known psychologists who worked to found a science of teaching and learning. Hall's biographer, ROSS, provides a detailed narrative portrait, combining intellectual history with biography. She documents Hall's work in domesticating science through his "child study", but suspends analysis of the networks of "naturalists" – parents, physicians, psychologists, social workers, and teachers. As a result, the historical processes underlying this convergence of education, medicine, and psychology remain unclear; while Ross documents the intellectual paper trail of Hall's studies of the contents of children's minds, she does not link up to the broader cultural implications of these processes. For example, as child study helped bring science and child-welfare together, it made a particular type of scientific practice accessible to a large number of female parents, social workers, and teachers. While many of Hall's peers dismissed child study, or educational and clinical psychology, for their lack of rigor, these same scientists rejoiced (or protested) in the late 1910s when psychology boasted more women scientists than any other discipline except domestic science. Similarly, Hall's naturalism and genetic psychology had much to do with bridging charity, social welfare, and teaching with the new "scientific" social casework and pedagogy. Similar (and linked) to social medicine at the time, Hall's work helped to posture school children as legitimate subjects for scientific investigation, intervention, and policy in the US.

While Hall hinged the field study of school children on science, Thorndike linked the experimental laboratory directly to school practice. Like Ross's portrait, JONCICH's biography of Thorndike is heavy on factual narrative and intellectual history and light on interpretation. Where Hall was presented as elder statesman for psychology and child study, Thorndike is painted as the educator *qua* scientist of Teachers College, Columbia University. Thorndike, along with John B. Watson, brought animal psychology to education and child-rearing via behaviorism. During the 1910s, Thorndike was noted for postulating two "provisional" laws to account for the acquired behavior in chickens, fish, cats, and monkeys he had repeatedly noted over roughly a 12-year period of experimentation: the "Law of Effect" suggests that rewards strengthen connections in the brain and punishment weakens them, while the "Law of Exercise" suggests that repetition strengthens connections over time. Thus, by reinforcing the common classroom practices of drill and recitation, these laws were postured as evidence of the new science of learning without threatening the status quo. Behaviorism, as exemplified by Thorndike, underwrote the intellectual legitimacy, and in turn the textbooks, of a nascent educational psychology during the 1910s. As a result, educational psychology, predominantly behaviorist learning theory, hygiene, and testing were valued above all other courses in the teacher training institutes in the US, and in most of England, Scotland, and Germany, during the 1920s.

While the intellectual fashion in historical practice during the late 1960s can be found in the works of Ross and Joncich, the politics of psychological apparatus, discourses, practices, and knowledge in education are to be found in more recent texts. Nikolas Rose has, for at least the last two decades, been reworking interpretations, in the mode of Foucault's archeology and genealogy, of the interrelations between psychology, social life, and the self in liberal democratic societies. In ROSE (1985), the school is just one site from 1875 to 1925, albeit a particularly effective one, for moralizing and regulating behavior into manageability or governability. Rather than a scientific technique to be applied, psychology was in fact shaped in the schools. Through deployment of such techniques as intelligence testing and clinical treatment in English schools during the 1910s, psychology for practitioners such as Cyril Burt became a science of individuals and differences. In the name of hygienics, and tied to medical practice and eugenics, intelligence testing was popularized in schools on both administrative and instructional grounds. By the mid-1920s, tests of all sorts had become the primary apparatus for psychological practice in England and the US, and education its primary domain. Burt, and a large contingency of psychopathologists, psychologists, psychiatrists, and social workers, helped to reassemble the school, and army, court, family, and prison – social life in general – along with their science. Indeed, ROSE (1990) extends the analysis from the school to social life writ large.

Thus, Rose has begun to address theoretical issues of education, science, and power. By contrast, WOODRIDGE offers a detailed and sometimes overly intellectual history of education and psychology in England and Wales. Relying on the work of 11 English psychologists, including Burt and Susan Isaacs, Woodridge's account addresses "internal" questions concerning the professionalization of educational psychology, and the rise of meritocratic schooling via the competitive intelligence examination system. For Woodridge, Isaacs instituted and established child development in England, and, like Burt or Hall, was a tireless popularizer of psychology. Isaacs co-founded the Malting House School in Cambridge during 1924, a psychologized "discovery" school for children aged two to eight. Reminiscent of the probationary regime of Scottish playgrounds of the early 1880s, Malting House was an institutional apparatus for moralizing young children. Through Isaacs's vision, psychoanalytic theory was embedded in the school architecture and practice, and the children at play were monitored through observation and detailed record-keeping. Malting House would lose its patron and close within a decade, however, as Isaacs, like many of her clinical or educational psychologist peers, turned to the state-sponsored child study centers and clinics for access to the emotions, morals, and minds of young children.

While the history of psychological clinics and their role in education has been under-analyzed, CRAVENS's case study of the Iowa Child Welfare Research Station has extended our understanding of these complex institutions. Cravens presents a detailed history of the rise of one of the most important and productive research bureaux in the US during the 1920s and 1930s. Politically-charged accession of philanthropic and state support kept the Iowa Station in business, and annexed to the University of Iowa, from 1917. Cravens's attempt to uncover a psychological position and program that was alternative to the "mainstream" of the science of individuals is notable, presenting us with a picture of what came to be known as the "Iowa point of view" on the psychology of intelligence and the nature–nurture controversy. Iowa Station psychologists, Bird Baldwin, George Stoddard, Kurt Lewin, and Beth Wellman were not merely paying lip-service to refuting the hereditarian and racist ideas of the Intelligence Quotient (IQ), but were informing their arguments with clinical investigations. From the Iowa Station, during the mid- to late 1930s, came a series of studies debunking scientific notions of fixed IQs, suggesting that education and child-rearing did matter. The research was as controversial at the time as that of the hereditarians, but Cravens none the less champions the Iowa research as a "science of democracy". The Iowa Station would continue to function as a research clinic through the mid-1970s, but the post-World War II terms and conditions for education and science in the US had shifted.

NOBLE is an attempt to bring to light the military context of the interrelations between psychology and education during the 1950s and 1960s. Contending that computer-based education (CBE) was shaped, and its use controlled, by psychologists financially wedded and intellectually indebted to the military, Noble uses five case studies to support his "militarization" thesis – that within the technologies themselves are the values of cognitive science, cybernetics, and the military ethos of command and control. For example, the Programmed Logic for Automatic Teaching Operations (PLATO) project at the University of Illinois, supported by the US Army, Navy, and Air Force at different times from the 1960s to the 1980s, reflected the military and psychological ambition to automate instruction and examinations. The first PLATO system, produced in 1961, was a single-station, computer-based teaching machine, with pre-programmed feedback or diagnostic capabilities. The system's design embedded Thorndike's Laws of Learning, and a behaviorist psychology reinforced through B.F. Skinner's experimentation. Subsequent PLATO models would eventually be mass-marketed to schools through the big business tactics of the Control Data Corporation during the mid-1980s.

Currently, in democratic societies, it is evident that education, defined either narrowly as schooling or broadly as growth, is irrevocably bound up with defense, medicine, science, technology, disciplinary power, and liberal rationality. Perhaps it is here, at this intersection of history and genealogy, that the most productive accounts of a "scientification of education" will be written. Certainly, Rose's work provides impetus for this direction. None the less, absent from the histories reviewed here are accounts from the children's perspective. Perhaps the child in Peter Hoeg's story of education and psychology *Borderliners* should be given the final verdict: "It is a plan", says Katarina. "When you look at it with awareness, or start to touch it, then it starts to disintegrate. That is the conclusion of the first phase of the experiment."

STEPHEN PETRINA

See also Human Sciences; Social Sciences

Seki Kowa 1642?–1708

Japanese mathematician

Endo, Tosisada and Y. Mikami (eds), *Zoshu Nihon Sugakusi*, 1896; revised edition by A. Hitayama, Tokyo: Koseisha-koseikaku, 1981

Hirayama, A., K. Shimodaira and H. Hirose, *Takakazu Seki Zenshu*, Osaka: Kyoiku Tosho, 1974

Horiuchi, Annick, *Les Mathématiques japonaises a l'époque d'Edo, (1600–1867): Une étude de travaux de Seki Takakazu (?–1708) et de Takebe Katahiro (1664–1739)*, Paris: Vrin, 1994

Kato, H., *Nihon Sugakusi*, vol. 1, Tokyo: Maki-shoten, 1967

Ogura, K., *Chugoku – Nihon no Sugaku*, Tokyo: Keiso-shobo, 1978

Smith, David Eugene and Yoshio Mikami, *A History of Japanese Mathematics*, Chicago: Open Court, 1914

SMITH & MIKAMI's pioneering work on the history of Japanese mathematics is unfortunately now a rare book, but it is indispensable for the serious student of Seki's contributions to mathematics, as it contains an influential 50-page account of his work. It is also the only substantial piece of literature on Seki in the English language.

More recently, Seki's collected works have been published by HIRAYAMA, SHIMODAIRA & HIROSE, enabling access to Seki's work as a founder of the *Wasan* school (the school of Japanese mathematics) in the early Edo period (Edo is now Tokyo, the period 1603–1868). At present, this collection of Seki's work includes 28 items (books or manuscripts) treating 18 problems, such as algebraic expressions, the completion of Horner's method, Newton's approximation method and interpolation formulae, the finding of determinants, and solutions to problems of the calculus of finite differences. One of the most remarkable facts uncovered by the authors is that Seki left seven astronomical works, which seem to have prompted his subsequent endeavours in mathematics.

HORIUCHI discusses the mathematical achievements of Seki and his immediate follower, Takebe Katahiro (1664–1739). The Chinese astronomical system, *Shoushi li*, was introduced into Japan from the 13th century, and in 1684 the Edo government successfully supported Shibukawa Harumi's use of this system as the basis for calendrical reform of the *Jokyo Reki*, which prompted work on astronomical problems. Seki sought to determine the orbits of the sun and the moon, in order to be able to predict eclipses with precision; his work on astronomical tables for the semidiurnal arc of the sun's orbit, as seen from Edo, shows that he must have improved on the formula imported from China. Horiuchi reviews Seki's works, arguing that he learned the algebraic method called *tianyuan shu* from the Chinese mathematical works *Yang hui suanfa* (1275) and Chu Shijie's *Suanxue qi meng* (1299). From these he also acquired the method of solving algebraic equations with numerical coefficients (Horner's methods), and then developed this method in the name of the *Tenzan jutsu*. One of his achievements, discussed in volume 4 of his *Katsuyo sampo* (1680), is the development of a theory of the circle (*Enri*). Although Seki was not able to express pi with an infinite series, he did employ an interpolation formula for the numerical calculation of the value that is very similar to Newton's method.

It is unfortunate that so few works on Seki exist in Western languages; if one were to judge him on the basis of this literature alone, one would perforce get the wrong impression. For a proper understanding, one has to turn to Japanese works, such as the three books singled out below: Kato, Ogura, and Endo, Mikami & Hirayama.

In his *A History of Mathematics in Japan*, KATO argues that Seki's by-name *sansei* (saint of mathematics) is thoroughly justified, since he completely changed the character of Japanese mathematics. Kato's discussion of Seki's achievements includes his discovery of the determinant for the solution of an equation. In his wake a school was established in his name: the Seki-*ryu*.

By contrast, OGURA criticises the claims by many Japanese mathematicians that Seki's theory of the circle made Newton redundant. He rightly asserts that, although Seki and Newton were contemporaries, the immense distance between Japan and England means that it makes no sense to compare the two without taking into consideration the concrete historical situation. Ogura's work is entitled *Mathematics in China and Japan*, and discussion of Seki is not the main concern of the book.

Endo's writings from the late 19th century (in ENDO, MIKAMI & HIRAYAMA) constitute a monumental, and indeed the most prestigious, work on the history of mathematics in Japan. Endo argues that Seki's work marks the beginning of the fourth stage (1673–1771) of Japanese mathematical history; on the basis of the previous period, Seki was able to make significant developments in the Japanese type of mathematics, which eventually declined and was officially abolished during the Meiji restoration (1868). The enlarged version of Endo's writings of 1981 contains detailed notes by Hirayama. It is this publication (*Enlarged Version of the History of Japanese Mathematics*) that initiated the modern studies of Japanese mathematics.

KEIZO HASHIMOTO

See also China: general works; astronomy; Japan

Set Theory

Garciadiego, Alejandro R., *Bertrand Russell and the Origins of the Set-Theoretic "Paradoxes"*, Basel: Birkhäuser, 1992

Grattan-Guinness, Ivor (ed.), *From the Calculus to Set Theory, 1630–1910: An Introductory History*, London: Duckworth, 1980

Hallett, Michael, *Cantorian Set Theory and Limitation of Size*, Oxford: Clarendon Press, and New York: Oxford University Press, 1984

Hawkins, Thomas, *Lebesgue's Theory of Integration: Its Origins and Development*, Madison: University of Wisconsin Press, 1970; 2nd edition, New York: Chelsea, 1975

Johnson, Phillip E., *A History of Set Theory*, Boston: Prindle Weber and Schmidt, 1972

Lavine, Shaughan, *Understanding the Infinite*, Cambridge, Massachusetts: Harvard University Press, 1994

Manheim, Jerome H., *The Genesis of Point Set Topology*, New York: Macmillan, and Oxford: Pergamon Press, 1964

Moore, Gregory H., *Zermelo's Axiom of Choice: Its Origins, Development, and Influence*, New York: Springer, 1982

Tiles, Mary, *The Philosophy of Set Theory: An Historical Introduction to Cantor's Paradise*, Oxford and Cambridge, Massachusetts: Blackwell, 1989

The modern theory of sets, whether in the abstract form used by most mathematicians today, or in the axiomatic form preferred by logicians, has its origins in the 19th century and the concrete problems of point sets, topology, and the theory of functions. All of these came together in the pioneering work of Georg Cantor in the 1870s, when he resolved a fundamental theorem in the theory of trigonometric series – namely, the question of the uniqueness of representations of arbitrary functions by trigonometric series. Although Cantor at first managed to prove his theorem over continuous domains, and then over domains in which there were only a finite number of exceptional points, he eventually managed to show that the theorem remained valid even if there was an infinite number of exceptional points. This was the case so long as the infinite sets of points in question were distributed in a very specific way, i.e., what Cantor called infinite sets of the first species.

In the process of defining sets of the first species, Cantor discovered that he had not only to define clearly the concept of real numbers, but to investigate their properties in detail, and he eventually showed that there were distinct orders of magnitude between different infinite sets. That is, the infinite was not a single concept; there was not a single "infinity" that sufficed to account for all infinite sets, but rather a distinct and unending hierarchy of infinities. In 1874, Cantor showed that the set of all real numbers was infinitely larger, in a carefully specified way, than the set of common integers or fractions. Further study revealed special properties of sets of points, which Cantor later generalized to his theory of abstract sets and transfinite numbers, for which he also devised a corresponding transfinite arithmetic. The theory soon provided a powerful, unifying foundation for much of mathematics, until concerns were raised about the consistency of the theory in the light of certain paradoxes, discovered first by Cantor himself and later by a number of mathematicians, most notably

Cesare Burali-Forti and Bertrand Russell. To resolve the paradoxes of set theory – or at least to eliminate them by restricting the scope of set theory itself – these mathematicians sought a more careful definition of the basic concept of "set" than Cantor's, which some believed was the root of the problem. Others sought to provide axiomatic foundations for set theory that were designed to restrict the notion of "set" in such a way that the paradoxes were eliminated from mathematics. It was also hoped that both the consistency and completeness of the axiomatic systems themselves could be proven.

MANHEIM represents an early effort to survey the motivation that initially led Cantor to develop his theory of point sets, beginning with the earliest historical problems with calculus and concepts of functions, derivatives, and infinite series. Manheim explains how Cantor's interest in trigonometric series eventually led him to introduce the concept of derived sets, and to distinguish between different classes of infinite sets. However, little attention is devoted to Cantor's own subsequent development of a more powerful, abstract set theory, nor is there much about the equally important development of topology in general, as opposed to the study of linear point sets. Brief mention is made of work by Maurice Fréchet and Felix Hausdorff, along with discussion of the foundations of abstract spaces in Hausdorff's *Grundzüge der Mengenlehre* (1914).

JOHNSON focuses primarily on Georg Cantor and his pioneering contributions, although it does briefly discuss developments leading to axiomatic set theory, and includes a lengthy bibliography.

HAWKINS provides a detailed discussion of set theory in the years 1870–1900, as a background to Lebesgue's development of a new theory of integration. Here the primary emphasis is on theories of integration, beginning with Augustin Louis Cauchy and Riemann and leading finally to Lebesgue. Hawkins pays particular attention to the importance of Fourier and trigonometric series, Cantorian set theory, and, above all, foundational concerns relating to rigor and various reformulations of the fundamental theorem of the calculus. Chapters 4–6 and the Epilogue concern the development of measure and integration in the years 1900–15. Beginning with Borel's theory of measure, these chapters culminate in Hawkins's discussion of the Lebesgue integral, its applications (especially the Riesz-Fischer Theorem), and Radon's extension of measure to more general spaces.

GRATTAN-GUINNESS offers a collection of six articles covering different periods. One essay is specifically devoted to the history of set theory, whereas three others raise significant issues relating to the development of set theory in the 19th and early 20th centuries: J. Dauben, chapter 5: "The Development of Cantorian Set Theory"; I. Grattan-Guinness, chapter 3: "The Emergence of Mathematical Analysis and its Foundational Progress, 1780–1880"; T. Hawkins, chapter 4: "The Origins of Modern Theories of Integration"; and R. Bunn, chapter 6: "Developments in the Foundations of Mathematics, 1870–1910".

MOORE provides a full-length historical study of one of the early critical problems set theory had to face – the Axiom of Choice, and its role in 20th-century mathematics. Moore's first chapter treats the prehistory of the Axiom, particularly the use of arbitrary choices in analysis and the pivotal role played by

Georg Cantor's development of transfinite set theory. The second chapter analyzes the controversy provoked by Zermelo's proof of Cantor's conjecture that every set can be well-ordered, a central problem of set theory that led to Zermelo's explicit formulation of the Axiom of Choice. In response to the controversy raised by the Axiom and his proof of the well-ordering theorem, Zermelo axiomatized set theory in the hope of establishing the rigor of his arguments beyond any doubt. The third chapter deals with Zermelo's axiomatization, along with applications of the Axiom of Choice in other areas of mathematics, notably algebra and analysis. The fourth and final chapter deals with applications of equivalents of the Axiom of Choice (such as Zorn's Lemma) in diverse fields of mathematics, as well as Kurt Gödel's results on the consistency of the Axiom. A brief epilogue discusses developments since 1940.

HALLETT provides a philosophical discussion of the various reactions to the flaws discovered in set theory, focusing on "limitation of size" theories as one alternative. The first half of Hallett's book is devoted to a description of the basic elements of Cantor's set theory, which is followed by a consideration of early attempts to limit the concept of set as a means of avoiding the paradoxes, including early limitation of size theories devised by P.E.B. Jourdain and D. Mirimanoff. The basic claim of Hallett's book is that set theory bears the stamp of many of its creator's idiosyncrasies, whose faith in its correctness, despite the paradoxes, rested on theological and philosophical assumptions. Whereas Cantor was not apparently troubled by the paradoxes of set theory, it was left to others to rescue it from the paradoxes that Cantor himself discovered, but from which he was unable to free transfinite set theory. The second part of Hallett concentrates on a number of axiomatic theories, including those devised by Ernst Zermelo, Adolf Fraenkel, and John von Neumann. The book draws to a large extent on historical examples, but the focus throughout is the philosophical analysis of set theory and its limitations – namely, the fact that there is an inherent conflict between Cantor's original formulation of set theory and its later development in terms of the power set axiom.

The aim of TILES is "to persuade philosophers that the philosophy of mathematics is not an isolated specialty but is inseparably intertwined with what are standardly regarded as mainstream philosophical issues". In the course of her discussion, Tiles asks whether set theory was invented or discovered, whether Cantor's Continuum Hypothesis can be said to be either true or false, and how such questions may be related to larger issues of meaning. Tiles maintains that, despite opposition to the infinite, and the debate since the time of Zeno and Aristotle over whether or not an infinite number of points can constitute a continuous line or a continuum can be reduced to an infinite set of discrete points, neither the infinite in general, nor Cantor's famous transfinite numbers in particular, can be dismissed as nonsense. Much of the discussion in Tiles is carried out in terms of activity (what mathematicians actually do), rather than approaching the infinite from either a strictly realist or anti-realist mathematical position. In the process, Tiles considers Cantor's transfinite "paradise", Frege's views on logic and arithmetic, Russell's Logicism, axiomatizations of set theory, and Gödel's independence results, with a final chapter on "Mathematical Structure – Construct and Reality". The basic problem of set theory, Tiles concludes, is that it attempts to be both "mathematical object" and "framework" at the same time. This, however, is the essence of paradox, since "the set theoretic converse cannot simultaneously be both object of study and framework within which to study".

GARCIADIEGO explores in detail the role played by Bertrand Russell in the appreciation of the significance of the set-theoretic "paradoxes". In addition to sketching briefly the antecedents and basic foundations of Cantor's theory of transfinite numbers, he goes on to examine in detail the consequences of the Burali-Forti paradox and the Cantorian paradoxes of set theory. This leads to a discussion of the philosophical and mathematical background to Russell's *Principles of Mathematics* (1903). Garciadiego ends with a discussion of "semantic paradoxes" due to Berry, König, Richard, Dixon, and others.

LAVINE is concerned with the basic question of set theory: how can we know anything abut the infinite? And if we can know anything about it, what exactly is it that we know, and what warrants any conclusions we may be able to draw about it? In turning first to history, Levine emphasizes that Cantor's original set theory was not an abstract theory of sets or collections, nor was it naive or paradoxical, but instead it "grew seamlessly" in so far as sets were collections that could be counted, albeit with transfinite rather than finite ordinal or cardinal numbers. Lavine's major point is that Cantor actually had a "smooth theory that broke down in the 1890s" with the introduction of his famous "diagonalization" method to prove the nondenumerability of the real numbers. This ultimately rested on what came to be known as the Power Set Axiom, and it is this that Lavine blames for causing "big trouble", because Cantor did not know how to count the collections to which power sets gave rise.

Nevertheless, Lavine insists that Cantorian set theory was not riddled with paradoxes, and was never in such dire straits as many have supposed. We understand the infinite, he points out, through two straightforward developments – one is counting, the other is the construction of power sets. Lavine maintains that the source of our understanding of the infinite is "experience of the indefinitely large"; what we know about the infinite is drawn from processes that seem indefinitely long, and in support of this point of view, he offers an analysis of the indefinitely large based upon the mathematical theory of Jan Mycielski. Ultimately, what Lavine finds most remarkable about set theory is the fact that it enables us, with no direct experience of infinite sets, not only to conceive of them, but to construct powerful, even beautiful theories to deal with the infinite.

JOSEPH W. DAUBEN

See also Cantor

Sexuality

Abramson, Paul R. and Steven D. Pinkerton, *Sexual Nature/Sexual Culture*, Chicago: University of Chicago Press, 1995

Allgeier, Albert R. and Elizabeth R. Allgeier, *Sexual Interactions*, Lexington, Massachusetts: D.C. Heath, 1985; 5th edition, 1995

Bullough, Vern L., *Science in the Bedroom: A History of Sex Research*, New York: Basic Books, 1994

Ellis, Havelock, *Studies in the Psychology of Sex*, 7 vols, Philadelphia: F.A. Davis, 1905–28; reprinted New York: Random House, 1936–42

Hirschfeld, Magnus, *Die Homosexualität des Mannes und des Weibes*, Berlin: Marcus, 1914

Hirschfeld, Magnus, *The Transvestites: The Erotic Drive to Cross-Dress*, translated from German by Michael A. Lombardi-Nash, Buffalo, New York: Prometheus, 1991 (original edition, 1910)

Hyde, Janet Shibley, *Understanding Human Sexuality*, New York: McGraw Hill, 1979; 5th edition, 1994

Kinsey, Alfred C. , Wardell B. Pomeroy and Clyde E. Martin, *Sexual Behavior in the Human Male*, Philadelphia: Saunders, 1948

Krafft-Ebing, Richard von, *Psychopathia Sexualis*, translated from the 12th edition by F.J. Rebman (1906): reprinted New York: Physicians and Surgeons, 1925; revised edition, London: Heinemann, 1928; New York: Physicians and Surgeons, 1933

Masters, William H. and Virginia C. Johnson, *Human Sexual Response*, Boston: Little Brown, and London: Churchill, 1966

Masters, William H. and Virginia C. Johnson, *Human Sexual Inadequacy*, Boston: Little Brown, and London: Churchill, 1970

Money, John and Anke A. Ehrhardt, *Man & Woman, Boy & Girl: The Differential of Dimorphism of Gender Identity from Conception to Maturity*, Baltimore: Johns Hopkins University Press, 1972

The study of sex poses unique difficulties as a scientific discipline, since it encompasses so many different areas of knowledge, some of which are less scientific than others. Probably the best overall introduction to modern research on the topic is BULLOUGH.

Although biology is a key area, and despite the obvious external differences between the sexes, scientific explanations of sex began to appear only in the early 20th century. Modern sex research began in German-speaking areas, primarily motivated by the need for a better legal understanding of what was then labelled as sexual pathology – i.e. effectively all non-procreative sexual activity. KRAFFT-EBING was a pioneer but, despite being a physician, perhaps the only thing scientific about his book was his attempt to classify different sexual behaviours. Others soon followed, the major attempt to put the study of sex on a scientific basis being by HIRSCHFELD, who established an institute for research into sexuality in Berlin and a scholarly journal, and made large-scale studies of both homosexuality and what he called transvestism.

In the English-speaking world, the major researcher was Havelock ELLIS, whose seven volumes on various aspects of sexual behavior included case histories, historical studies, and a good summary of what was known in the 1920s. Although both Hirschfeld and Ellis were physicians, their approach to sex was more that of the social scientist or historian. Many of the physicians who studied sexuality did so from the point of view of treatment, and from the 1920s to the 1950s most writings on sex were by psychiatrists, based on a small number of clients.

The most significant research studies, however, took place in the laboratory, and here the emerging field of endocrinology led to major breakthroughs in understanding human sexuality. A good description of this is in Bullough. The scientist who was perhaps most important in applying endocrinological studies to human sexual behavior was John MONEY who, beginning in the 1950s, published a series of volumes on what he called "gender", in which he emphasized that sexuality involved more than anatomical sex, and that humans are influenced by factors other than genitalia – in particular, social conceptions of what might be called "masculinity" and "femininity".

The 1930s also saw the beginning of major sex surveys, the most notable of which were by Alfred KINSEY, although these were not published until the late 1940s and early 1950s. Although Kinsey was a biologist, his studies were essentially sociological, breaking new ground by their attention to the variety of sexual behavior in which humans engaged.

Another area of investigation that grew out of endocrinology research led to the development of oral contraceptives, and brought a renewed emphasis on the study of female sexuality. The major breakthrough in this area was by MASTERS & JOHNSON in the 1960s, when new technology allowed exploration of the female orgasm, impotence in men, and anorgasmia in women. It was out of this new field that sex therapists emerged, frequently challenging many of Masters & Johnson's ideas concerning therapy.

One of the current areas of contention is the influence of biology versus culture, or nature versus nurture. This has been explored in a number of books, including ABRAMSON & PINKERTON. Research continues today on a variety of topics, from sexually transmitted diseases to gender dysphoria, although much of the cutting edge material is in journals, the quality of which has risen considerably in the past decade. Two major publications specializing in sexuality are the *Journal of Sex Research* and *Archives of Sexual Behavior*, and there are a number of specialty journals. One of the problems unique to sexuality in terms of scientific investigation is the popularity of the topic, which inevitably means that there is much pseudo-science in the field. Perhaps the best way to find a summary of the current state of knowledge in this rapidly changing, and increasingly scientific, field is a good, college-level textbook, such as ALLGEIER & ALLGEIER, and HYDE.

VERN L. BULLOUGH

See also Gender and sex

Siemens, Werner von 1816–1892

German electrical engineer and entrepreneur

Burhenne, Karl, *Werner Siemens als Sozialpolitiker*, Munich: Beck, 1932

Feldenkirchen, Wilfried, *Werner von Siemens: Inventor and International Entrepreneur*, translated from the German, Columbus: Ohio State University Press, 1994 (original edition, 1992)

Heintzenberg, Friedrich (ed.), *Werner von Siemens in Briefen an seine Familie und an Freunde*, Stuttgart: Anstalt, 1953

Hoffmann, Dieter and W. Schreier (eds), *Werner von Siemens (1816–1892). Studien zu Leben und Werk: PTB-Texte*, 2 vols, Braunschweig: Physikalisch-Technische Bundesanstalt, 1995

Matschoss, Conrad, *Werner von Siemens: Ein kurzgefasstes Lebensbild nebst einer Auswahl seiner Briefe*, 2 vols, Berlin: Springer, 1916

Siemens, Georg, *Der Weg der Elektrotechnik: Geschichte des Hauses Siemens*, 3 vols, Freiburg and Munich: Karl Alber, 1949–53; 2nd edition 1961

Siemens, Werner von, *Wissenschaftliche Anhandlungen und Vorträge*, 2 vols, Berlin: Springer, 1889–91

Siemens, Werner von, *Lebenserinnerungen*, Berlin: Springer, 1892

Weiher, Sigfried von, *Werner von Siemens: Ein Leben für Wissenschaft, Technik und Wirtschaft*, Göttingen: Musterschmidt, 1966

The life and work of Werner von Siemens caught the attention of biographers and historians of technology and economics very early. The best introductory text is SIEMENS (1892), which contains Siemens's autobiographical recollections, and it is worth taking a glance at the collected scientific publications in two volumes, SIEMENS (1889–91). The recollections were completed immediately before his death, and give a first-hand impression of Siemens's personality and his rise, from the son of a country estate leaseholder, to his position as one of the most important entrepreneurs of 19th-century Germany and one of the founders of electrical engineering. The memoirs document Siemens's almost boundless optimism and belief in progress, which was not just limited to science and technology but extended also to society: in Siemens's view, modern technological and economic development was dependent on a high level of scientific achievement, just as social progress was driven by success in science and technology. This interrelation was expressed most popularly and programmatically in his metaphor of a "scientific age", at his remarkable lecture during the "Berliner Naturforscherversammlung" of 1886. Siemens's recollections have reached 18 editions, because the Siemens company supports its distribution.

The biography published by MATSCHOSS, the grand old man of German technological history, on the occasion of Siemens's centenary, can be considered now more of a historical document than a comprehensive and historically-balanced biography. It is at its most engaging when describing the technological context of Siemens's work, and when rendering some of his letters. These published letters remain an important source, since a comprehensive edition of Siemens's correspondence is still lacking. HEINTZENBERG fills some of the more significant gaps left by Matschoss, but important parts of Siemens's correspondence remain accessible only through the not very user-friendly archives of the Siemens company in Munich.

WEIHER attempts a synthesis of the biographies of Siemens that appeared between 1916 and 1966 within the history of science and technology. His overview of Siemens's life and work is comprehensive and instructive, but it is also somewhat one-sided and hagiographic. Weiher focuses on Siemens as an engineer and electrical engineer, while his social position and his importance as an entrepreneur are only hinted at – despite the fact that the development of electrical engineering, and of the electrical industry, were to a large extent shaped by his technical genius. Indeed, it could be argued that Siemens's role as an entrepreneur should be rated higher than that of his contemporary and competitor, Emil Rathenau, the head of AEG.

Siemens the industrialist and his company are placed in the foreground in G. SIEMENS and BURHENNE, although both are again somewhat one-sided in their treatments. G. SIE-MANS, Werner's grandson, presents an economic and managerial history of the company within a narrow technological context. By contrast, BURHENNE is concerned primarily with the social context of Siemens's managerial initiatives, which included housing, health, and leisure facilities for employees. Burhenne praises Siemens as a "capitalist with social awareness", who pioneered social legislation in Germany. This judgement is not completely amiss, but has become more differentiated in recent research.

The biography by FELDENKIRCHEN, the Siemens company's in-house historian, gives a good insight into modern approaches in research on Siemens. This offers not only a good overview of Siemens's life and work, but also emphasizes Siemens's impact on management and business, thus linking the history of science and technology with social and economic history. The edition published on the occasion of the centenary of Siemens's death (HOFFMANN & SCHREIER) also focuses on newer approaches to research on Siemens. This includes the role of Siemens as entrepreneur, his (non-)participation in the institutionalization of electrical engineering, and the close relationship between physics and electrical engineering, both in terms of science proper and in terms of institutional development in the last third of the 19th century.

DIETER HOFFMANN
translated by Klaus Staubermann

See also Electrical Engineering; Physikalisch-Technische Reichsanstalt; Telegraphy

Skill

Aronowitz, Stanley and William Di Fazio, *The Jobless Future: Sci-Tech and the Dogma of Work*, Minneapolis: University of Minnesota Press, 1994

Bell, Daniel, *The Coming of Post-Industrial Society: A Venture in Social Forecasting*, New York: Basic Books, 1973

Blauner, Robert, *Alienation and Freedom: The Factory Worker and His Industry*, Chicago: University of Chicago Press, 1964

Braverman, Harry, *Labor and Monopoly Capital*, New York: Monthly Review Press, 1974

Collins, H.M., *Changing Order: Replication and Induction in Scientific Practice*, Beverly Hills, California: Sage, 1985

Collins, Randall, *The Credential Society: An Historical Sociology of Education and Stratification*, New York: Academic Press, 1979

Cooley, Mike, *Architect or Bee? The Human/Technology Relationship*, edited by Shirley Cooley, Slough, Berkshire: Langley Technical Services, 1980; Boston: South End Press, 1982; as *Architect or Bee? The Human Price of Technology*, London: Hogarth, 1987

England, Paula, *Comparable Worth: Theories and Evidence*, New York: De Gruyter, 1992

Polanyi, Michael, *Personal Knowledge: Towards a Post-Critical Philosophy*, Chicago, University of Chicago Press, and London: Routledge, 1958; revised edition, 1962

Star, Susan Leigh (ed.), *Ecologies of Knowledge: Work and Politics in Science and Technology*, Albany: State University of New York Press, 1995

Stinchcombe, Arthur L., *Information and Organizations*, Berkeley: University of California Press, 1990

Wajcman, Judy, *Feminism Confronts Technology*, University Park: Pennsylvania State University Press, and Cambridge: Polity Press, 1991

Wood, Stephen (ed.), *The Transformation of Work? Skill, Flexibility, and the Labour Process*, London and Boston: Unwin Hyman, 1989

Work and Occupations (special issue on skill), 17/4 (1990)

Zuboff, Shoshana, *In the Age of the Smart Machine*, New York: Basic Books, 1988

As a result of the changes in work patterns and the use of technology, the meaning of skill is in flux in the second half of the 20th century. The message from the policy world is that new automation technologies are creating jobs only for the "high-skilled" – meaning those who are trained in computers, are at least minimally proficient in mathematics and science, and are able to work on multiple tasks. Historians and sociologists agree that traditional craft work no longer captures the notion of skill. However, they are much more divided on how exactly science and technology have transformed skill requirements in industrial work. While this issue has generated a huge literature, a smaller tradition in the sociology of science shows that scientific practice itself has the character of craft work – suggesting that old notions of skill might still be relevant.

BLAUNER made one of the earliest surveys of skill in post-war factory jobs. He found that craft work in the textile and automobile industries was being degraded by continued reliance on assembly-line technology, but this was more than offset by upgrading in chemical manufacturing and oil refining industries under continuous flow processes. Blauner believed that the most important historical trend in the evolution of blue-collar work was in place, with traditional skill giving way to "responsibility". He claimed that continuous process technology required the capacity to exercise mental judgement (nous) rather than manual dexterity (skill).

A decade later, Bell and Braverman made diametrically opposed claims regarding the future of skill, across both white-collar and blue-collar work. BELL argued that science and technology were the new productive forces in the shift to "post-industrial" society. Work was becoming largely knowledge-based with the elimination of unskilled manual work, the creation of new forms of professional and service work, and the upgrading of the shrinking proportion of manufacturing jobs. Like Blauner, therefore, he associated skill with manual work, and proclaimed a shift to cognitive work across the workforce.

Bell's claims concerning skill depended mostly on his analysis of occupational shifts. Focusing more on the labour process within occupations, BRAVERMAN found that work was largely becoming deskilled. That is, work processes were being broken down into routine, repetitive tasks executed by workers and controlled by engineers and managers. This was even happening to many sections of the white-collar workforce, contradicting Bell's arguments. While deskilling emerged from the application of science to work (in line with Frederick Taylor's methods), and the introduction of new technologies, Braverman argued that the managerial ideology of worker control was the real cause.

The large number of studies that followed these conflicting claims of upskilling and deskilling are surveyed in Wood, and in *Work and Occupations*. ZUBOFF is one of the most original attempts to synthesize the conflicting perspectives. In her much-cited study, she argues that there is a tension between the skills actually demanded by new information technologies and the prevailing structure of managerial authority. To be most effective, these technologies required workers to develop what she called "intellective" (conceptual) skills. This meant that they would have more autonomy and more access to the production knowledge that had been appropriated by managers under Taylorism. Zuboff believed that the managerial logic of expertise would ultimately have to bow to the logic of the "smart machine", leading to a "post-hierarchical" workplace.

A prominent claim in the upskilling tradition, examined by WOOD, is that new forms of skill are being created that require flexibility; i.e. the ability to integrate a wide range of tasks, conceptual and manual. The empirical studies in the book tend to emphasize the contingency of outcomes of skill change; there is no clearly discernible overall shift toward either the upgrading or the downgrading of skills. Eschewing technological determinism, the writers argue that skill change varies from industry to industry, and even from firm to firm.

The special issue of the journal *WORK AND OCCUPATIONS* takes a more critical look at skill studies, focusing on the largely taken-for-granted concept of skill itself. The authors find that skill is a social construction. Skill is relational: what counts as skill depends on who has it as well as how many do not, and who is allowed to define it. Kenneth Spenner argues that many claims for upskilling or deskilling do not distinguish between content shifts (skill change in a job) and compositional shifts (skill change across the labour force, via creation of new occupations and destruction or shrinking of old ones). Paul Attewell criticizes positivist measures of skill that assume that skill is inherent to a job, and human capital theories that take skill to be a quality possessed by individuals. He discusses Jean Lave's situated learning theory, which argues that skills are grounded in the group context of their use, rather than being an individual property. Ethnomethodological approaches question the assumption in Marxist theories, as well as in positivist measures of skill, that routine activities are low-skilled. Research in this vein uncovers the complexity in repetitive activity, which is ironically more difficult to automate than, say, expert decision-making.

POLANYI is well-known for arguing that "tacit knowledge" is central to the understanding of scientific practice. While others use the concept to argue against the devaluation of so-called unskilled work, he sought to protect scientific work from external control. Describing science as a practice that cannot be reduced to laws and procedures, he claimed that there are things scientists know but cannot tell – just as the cyclist or swimmer knows how to cycle or swim, without being able to explain the laws of physics that they obey. Tacit knowledge blurs the distinction between mental and manual facilities, making them both impermeable to rule-bound explanations.

H.M. COLLINS (1985) develops this idea further in his sociological account of replication in science. He argues that the ability to build a particular form of laser was not transferred simply by a formal algorithm. Rather than being a simple transfer of written information, it involved the mastery of a great many skills – which, once absorbed from personal contacts between scientists and trial-and-error, became difficult to pinpoint. Science, Collins argues, is a skilled practice involving the acquisition of tacit knowledge, much as in other everyday social activities.

The anthology edited by STAR brings together recent work in the social studies of science that extends this theme of science as akin to a craft-activity. Where the early works in the field focused on the micro level of the laboratory, this volume also considers economic and political factors, such as funding patterns. The repertoire of skills of the scientist is extended to include their behaviour in response to such macro factors.

Drawing on Weber's theory of occupations as competing status groups, R. COLLINS (1979) argues that modern professional work (including science) is able to sustain an image of skilled work because of the uncertainty and open-endedness of its work conditions. Like medieval craft guilds, professions restrict entry, require new entrants to go through long periods of training (ostensibly to acquire skills), retain authority to define the standards of the occupation, and develop specialized discourses. Occupations that are unable to restrict entry – such as clerical work in the 19th century – typically lose their skilled status. Attributions of skill therefore depend also on supply and demand: what is scarce is more likely to be called skilled. STINCHCOMBE, on the other hand, associates skill with the very same uncertainty of work situations that Collins believes makes them unaccountable and impossible to scrutinize. He defines skill as the capacity to routinize most of the activity that is part of a job carried out in an uncertain environment.

Both England and Wajcman survey feminist challenges to definitions of skill. Their main thesis is that the existing measures of skill, particularly in regards to overwhelmingly female jobs, rarely reflect their actual complexity. ENGLAND reviews theories of comparable worth, a pay equity policy that developed in response to the sex-based segregation in labour markets. Comparable worth argues for equal pay for jobs of equal worth. Central to it is the idea that society has defined skills in such a way that "women's work" – nursing, school teaching, child care – is consistently undervalued. Jobs given formal authority (e.g. doctors) are overwhelmingly male and treated as high-skilled, but a close look at other work practices reveals the range of important decisions taken by ostensibly low-skilled workers (e.g. nurses).

WAJCMAN extends this argument to consider how gender relations shape technological change and, therefore, skill change in the workplace. Feminist research criticizes both the upskilling and deskilling schools. Some studies show that even as technology has altered the skill and task range of jobs, the distinction between "men's work" and "women's work" persists, with men holding on to the ostensibly skilled jobs. Others show how managers use women and new technologies to displace powerful, highly paid male workers. In some cases, women and men may do the same machining work, but are stratified into separate occupations with different skill measures.

Writing in a Marxist vein, COOLEY argues that intellectual work, such as science and engineering, has become Taylorized under the logic of capitalism. This is the irony of engineers developing scientific techniques to control and deskill production workers, as they threaten to be engulfed by their own practices. For instance, computer-aided design can be used to routinize the skilled activity of engineering design and break it down into minor tasks for drafters to perform. Based on their case studies of engineering, architecture, academic research, and teaching, ARONOWITZ & DiFAZIO agree with this prediction. They proclaim the "end of skill" under the existing techno-scientific regime of capitalism. As abstract knowledge becomes central to production across the economy, large sections of the knowledge class are open to harsh, insecure working conditions.

SUJANTHA RAMAN

See also Management Sciences; Marxism; Practice; Work

Smith, Adam 1723–1790

British philosopher and economist

Brown, Vivienne, *Adam Smith's Discourse: Canonicity, Commerce and Conscience*, London and New York: Routlege, 1994

Haakonssen, Knud, *The Science of a Legislator: The Natural Jurisprudence of David Hume and Adam Smith*, Cambridge and New York: Cambridge University Press, 1981

Hollander, Samuel, *The Economics of Adam Smith*, Toronto: University of Toronto Press, and London: Heinemann, 1973

Hont, Istvan and Michael Ignatieff (eds), *Wealth and Virtue: The Shaping of Political Economy in the Scottish Enlightenment*, Cambridge and New York: Cambridge University Press, 1983

Hutchison, T.W., *Before Adam Smith: The Emergence of Political Economy, 1662–1776*, Oxford and New York: Blackwell, 1988

Minowitz, Peter, *Profits, Priests, and Princes: Adam Smith's Emancipation of Economics from Politics and Religion*, Stanford, California: Stanford University Press, 1993

Ross, Ian Simpson, *The Life of Adam Smith*, Oxford: Clarendon Press, and New York: Oxford University Press, 1995

Teichgraeber, Richard F., III, *"Free Trade" and Moral Philosophy: Rethinking the Sources of Adam Smith's Wealth of Nations*, Durham, North Carolina: Duke University Press, 1986

Werhane, Patricia H., *Adam Smith and His Legacy for Modern Capitalism*, Oxford and New York: Oxford University Press, 1991

Adam Smith is most celebrated for *An Inquiry into the Nature and Causes of the Wealth of Nations* (1776), although many scholars of the period also pay tribute to his *Theory of Moral Sentiments* (1759) and to his related essays and lectures on philosophy, rhetoric, and jurisprudence. Historians of science might find interesting Smith's essays on the history of astronomy, ancient physics, and ancient logic and metaphysics, if only as a partial record of what was known on the subject during the Enlightenment.

If one included all the textbooks on the history of economics – many of which devote a chapter to Smith – in addition to the hundreds of articles and books, then there are well over 1000 scholarly interpretations of Adam Smith to be considered. A newcomer to the densely-populated world of "Smithiana" might find this wealth of material daunting, but fortunately the recent publication by ROSS of the first full-length biography of Adam Smith since the 19th century is an extremely useful guide to the literature. Built upon some 30 years of concentrated research, Ross's study is both comprehensive and judicious, and evinces the same virtue of self-command that Smith preached on many occasions.

For decades, scholars have grappled with the apparent inconsistency of Smith's model of human nature in the *Theory of Moral Sentiments* with that of the *Wealth of Nations*, whereby individuals are portrayed first as motivated by sympathy for others, and in the latter work by self-interest. However, there is now general agreement that "Das Adam Smith Problem", as it came to be known, has been resolved. WERHANE, among others, argues that Smith appreciated the complexity of human nature, and saw different motivating forces operating in different spheres of activity; both sympathy and self-interest are derivative of the more fundamental desire for the approval of others, which is engendered by the cultivation of friendship and civil society, as well as by the accumulation of wealth.

HUTCHISON's detailed study of economic inquiry from William Petty to Adam Smith (1662–1776) provides the most detailed account of Smith's immediate predecessors. While Hutchison appreciates the sophistication of pre-Smithian thought, he none the less exonerates Smith of Joseph Schumpeter's ridiculous charge that there was nothing new in the *Wealth of Nations*. Hutchison in fact emphasizes Smith's critical role in instigating classical political economy, to the point of identifying a "Smithian revolution".

The most detailed study of Smith's economic theory is by HOLLANDER, who elucidates Smith's powers of scientific analysis. Smith, it is argued, had a firm grasp of the equilibrating mechanisms of the economy, whereby price adjustments serve to clear markets. Moreover, Smith's recognition of the role of capital accumulation was not restricted to an agrarian economy. Hollander argues, contrary to many other scholars (for example, Charles Kindleberger), that Smith was fully aware of the Industrial Revolution unleashed by the 1770s. Hollander highlights Smith's strong orientation toward economic development, both in the agrarian and manufacturing sectors, as well as his interest in the overall accumulation of capital and the growth of commerce. Hollander also places

Smith's work within the broader context of the history of economic ideas and economic development.

Various essays in the HONT & IGNATIEFF collection provide a rich contextual analysis of Scottish political economy, considering Smith as conjoined with, for example, David Hume and James Steuart, in a more overarching programme to grapple with the so-called "rich country–poor country debate". Although Smith cast many shadows over commercial advancement, there was little doubt that he looked to capital investment in the agrarian sector as the key to growth. Donald Winch's essay, "Adam Smith's 'Enduring Particular Result': A Political and Cosmopolitan Perspective", argues persuasively that scholars have yet to come close to fathoming Smith's grand vision. The situation is not made simpler by the fact that, close to his death, Smith had so much of his work burned.

HAAKONSSEN highlights the sense in which Smith viewed political economy as the science of the legislator, and it is in this context that Smith's work on jurisprudence becomes of much greater significance, as a means of reconciling the opposing elements of his two more substantial works on moral philosophy and economics. Smith's concept of justice was grounded in a doctrine of rights, and was less aligned with utilitarianism than has commonly been supposed.

TEICHGRAEBER builds upon Haakonssen's efforts to link Hume and Smith, a difficult task given how little Smith acknowledged the work of others, and given the dearth of correspondence between these two close friends. One important point of difference was their respective commitments to theism. MINOWITZ, however, has argued quite forcefully that Smith was much closer to Hume's secular beliefs than has often been appreciated. BROWN has underscored Smith's indebtedness to the Stoics, which may well have provided him with an alternative to Christian arguments for an ordered and harmonious world, while preserving a modicum of deism. Brown's book is strikingly original insofar as she treats Smith's corpus as replete with unresolved dialogues on the question of virtue. Arguing that Smith privatized morality by locating it within the inner-self's capacity for deliberation and striving for self-command, the multitude of voices Brown reconstructs draws on some of the analytical apparatus of contemporary literary theory, and is part of a broader movement among historians and philosophers of economics to elucidate the rhetorical component of economic discourse.

MARGARET SCHABAS

See also Political Economy

Smithsonian Institution

Carmichael, Leonard and J.C. Long, *James Smithson and the Smithsonian Story*, New York: Putnam, 1965

Danilov, Victor J., *America's Science Museums*, New York: Greenwood Press, 1990

Goode, George Brown (ed.), *The Smithsonian Institution, 1846–1896: The History of Its First Half Century*, New York: Arno Press, 1980

Hafertepe, Kenneth, *America's Castle: The Evolution of the Smithsonian Building and Its Institution, 1840–1878*, Washington, DC: Smithsonian Institution Press, 1984

Hellman, Geoffrey T., *The Smithsonian Octopus on the Mall*, Philadelphia: Lippincott, 1967

MacCloskey, Monro, *Our National Attic: The Library of Congress, the Smithsonian Institution, the National Archives*, New York: Rosen Press, 1968

Oehser, Paul Henry, *The Smithsonian Institution*, New York: Praeger, 1970; 2nd edition, Boulder, Colorado: Westview Press, 1983

Smithsonian Institution, *The Smithsonian Institution*, Washington, DC: Smithsonian Institution Press, 1951

Smithsonian Insitution, *Snakes, Snails and History Tails: Building Discovery Rooms and Learning Labs at the Smithsonian Institution*, Washington, DC: The Institution, 1991

True, Webster P., *The Smithsonian Institution*, Washington, DC: Smithsonian Institution, 1929

True, Webster P., *The First Hundred Years of the Smithsonian Institution, 1846–1946*, Washington, DC, 1946

True, Webster P., *The Smithsonian: America's Treasure House*, New York: Sheridan House, 1950

Much of the writing on the Smithsonian Institution, apart from anniversary commemorative pamphlets or texts, focuses on specific areas of research taking place at any one of the Smithsonian-sponsored centres. This is particularly true of journal articles of the 1980s and 1990s. These are not included in this list, but are a valuable source of criticism on specific changes in funding, research, and division of scholarship within the institution.

Generally, the Smithsonian Institution is viewed reverently and affectionately, almost as a living entity, by those most intimately associated with it, and part of this reverence manifests itself in the texts that are written by ex-Smithsonian staff. One such example is the history by OEHSER, a member of the editorial staff at the Smithsonian from 1931 to 1966. In less than 200 pages Oehser takes the reader through James Smithson's life, the twists and turns of the story of his bequest and its fruition 17 years later, all the way to the Institution of the 20th century. Among the most valuable features of this work are the appendices, which include selected Smithsonian publications and the text of the Act establishing the "Smithsonian Institution", as well as a bibliography of further reading, which offers more on the institution and its major players, such as Joseph Henry and George Brown Goode.

GOODE, a noted American naturalist, was appointed assistant secretary of the Smithsonian in charge of the National Museum in 1887. His 856-page tome was completed after his death to celebrate the 50th anniversary of the Smithsonian, 1896; fortunately, much of the work in progress had been delegated or finished by Goode himself before he died. The wide scope of Goode's book includes articles on the building and the grounds, the establishment of the Board of Regents, benefactors and secretaries, as well as 11 chapters on research in chemistry, geology and mineralogy, botany, physics, mathematics, astronomy, palaeontology, meteorology, zoology, anthropology, and geography. Although the book covers only 50 years, it is the most comprehensive on the period.

Like Oehser, True was a member of the editorial staff at the Smithsonian, and TRUE (1929), published as volume 1 of the Smithsonian Scientific Series, and supplementing the Annual

Reports and volumes of technical papers abounding at this time, is essentially a public relations initiative. As such it takes the reader on a tour, in part 1, of the major halls of the Smithsonian, such as the United States National Museum, the National Zoo, the Freer Gallery of Art, and the National Gallery of Art, and then in part 2 the history of the Institution is outlined, including the origins of the Weather Bureau and Bureau of Fisheries. True also has other works to his credit on the Smithsonian including TRUE (1950), which is almost a catalogue or souvenir book for tourists, offering only highlights (and 64 black and white plates) of the exhibits and work of the scientists associated with the Smithsonian. For example, one can see and read about George Washington's uniform and mess kit, anthropologist T. Dale Stewart at work "tracing the coronal suture of a Sioux Indian skull", Renoir's *A Girl with the Watering Can*, Charles Lindbergh's *Spirit of St Louis*, or a shrunken head.

HELLMAN (1967) is a similar "labour of love", and one of a number of books published on the Smithsonian in the 1960s. He confesses to having a bias to the Smithsonian, and this, coupled with his friendship with Smithsonian Secretary S. Dillon Ripley, seems to be the motivation for his engaging, first-person reflections. This is a general history and personal account of the "octopus on the Mall", and more of a guide through his best and worst experiences of the Institution than any reworking of previous histories.

Where Hellman and Oehser are unyielding in their praise of the concept and reality of the Smithsonian Institution, MacCLOSKEY is far more utilitarian in his brief essay. Better known as a retired Brigadier General in the United States Air Force, and for his numerous books about the service, MacCloskey's history of the Institution (18 pages) shares editorial space with lengthier profiles of the Library of Congress and The National Archives (138 pages and 20 pages, respectively). His purpose is to outline the holdings and services available to the public at each of the three institutions, and he states, unequivocally, that Smithson would be pleased with how the Smithsonian of 1968 so unfailingly represented the objectives of his bequest.

HAFERTEPE's book is also specific in its theme, dealing with the architecture of the Smithsonian in the period 1840 to 1878. He describes the controversial first decades when the direction and physical shape of the Institution were being fought over, as well as the fire of 24 January 1865, that caused the collapse of the roof, the loss of almost 50,000 of Henry's letters, the loss of library collections, and the near total loss of the art gallery. The only thing that prevented the entire building from going up in flames was the architecture, for the iron beams were fireproof.

Another chronicle from the 1960s is CARMICHAEL & LONG. Written as a collaborative effort, Carmichael (then Seventh Secretary of the Smithsonian) wrote the first of three parts, covering the history, structure, and future developments (as of 1965) of the institution. Long contributed the second part, a biography of Smithson, and a third section on the history of the constituent parts, and of the philosophies of the "increase" and "diffusion" of knowledge that served as the cornerstone in conceptualizing this new endeavour. For anyone researching the Smithsonian of the mid-1960s, there is also a useful appendix that lists all officers, committees, and staff, including the heads of departments, divisions, and affiliated scientists, and countless black and white photos of exhibits.

The Smithsonian also published its own pamphlets, which range from generally descriptive to subject specific studies of museology. SMITHSONIAN INSTITUTION (1951) is a pamphlet which, in its 49 pages, places the Institution within a mid-20th-century appreciation of pure as well as applied science, and also brings the evolution of the Smithsonian up to date for the period, noting the ongoing and future projects – such as the "new" Museum of History and Technology approved by Congress in 1955, and under construction at the time of writing for a scheduled opening in 1963.

An example of the work published by the Smithsonian specific to museum studies is SMITHSONIAN INSTITUTION (1991). This report documents the concept and implementation of "discovery rooms", from the first experiment by the psychologist Caryl Marsh at the National Museum of Natural History in the late 1960s, to the five that have evolved since then, at the National Museum of Natural History, the National Zoo, and the National Museum of American History.

Finally, the Smithsonian features prominently in any guide to American museums. One of the most recent is DANILOV (1990), a guide to American science museums. In his preface, Danilov points out that a study by the National Endowment for the Arts showed that 38 per cent of all museum visits were to science museums, making them the most popular type of museum in the United States. This is a reference text, and its 587 listings cover 480 museums or related institutions, including 10 associated with the Smithsonian Institution. Listings are relatively brief, and entries include exhibit or museum highlights and information, such as addresses, opening hours, and admission details.

MARIANNE P. FEDUNKIW

See also Museums

Social Sciences

Barnes, Harry Elmer, *Social Thought from Lore to Science*, 2 vols, Boston: Heath, 1938; 3rd edition, with Howard Becker, 3 vols, New York: Dover, 1961

Brown, Robert, *The Nature of Social Laws: Machiavelli to Mill*, Cambridge and New York: Cambridge University Press, 1984

Collini, Stefan, Donald Winch and John Burrow, *That Noble Science of Politics: A Study in Nineteenth Century Intellectual History*, Cambridge and New York: Cambridge University Press, 1983

Deutsch, Karl W., Andrei S. Markovits and John Platt (eds), *Advances in the Social Sciences, 1900–1980: What, Who, Where, How?*, Lanham, Maryland: University Press of America, 1986

Fuller, Steve, *Philosophy, Rhetoric and the End of Knowledge: The Coming of Science and Technology Studies*, Madison: University of Wisconsin Press, 1993

Kelley, Donald R., *The Human Measure: Social Thought in the Western Legal Tradition*, Cambridge, Massachusetts: Harvard University Press, 1990

Lepenies, Wolf, *Between Literature and Science: The Rise of Sociology*, translated from the German by R.J. Hollingdale, Cambridge and New York: Cambridge University Press, 1988 (original edition, 1985)

Manicas, Peter T., *A History and Philosophy of the Social Sciences*, Oxford and New York: Blackwell, 1987

Proctor, Robert N., *Value-Free Science? Purity and Power in Modern Knowledge*, Cambridge, Massachusetts: Harvard University Press, 1991

Ross, Dorothy, *The Origins of American Social Science*, Cambridge and New York: Cambridge University Press, 1991

Sorokin, Pitirim A., *Contemporary Sociological Theories*, New York: Harper, 1928

Wagner, Peter, Bjorn Wittrock and Richard Whitley (eds), *Discourses on Society: The Shaping of the Social Science Disciplines*, Dordrecht and Boston: Kluwer Academic, 1991

As introductions to the history of the social sciences, SOROKIN and BARNES merit special consideration, because, as both were written before sociology had established a distinct disciplinary history, they examine virtually every major social scientific theory put forth from classical antiquity to the first quarter of the 20th century. Bibliographically, both books are extremely useful in their coverage of theorists whose works are difficult to locate in English. Moreover, the aim of both books is to distil from each theory the kernel that contributes to the advancement of general social science, which is understood to be the search for socio–historical generalizations.

Barnes is organized in broadly chronological terms, except for the recent period that is divided into national schools. Sorokin is organized according to the source of the theory's inspiration, which makes the author especially alert to whether a theory is legitimized mainly by data or by its metaphorical resonances within natural scientific theories.

Once we move beyond such textbooks, there is considerable historiographical difference over how to proceed. LEPENIES defends the bold thesis that the differences between the humanities and the natural and social sciences are ultimately differences of genre. He draws mainly on the 19th-century German attempts to develop a distinct discourse for the social sciences (the "third culture") by adapting elements of scientific and literary discourses. DEUTSCH, MARKOVITS & PLATT, themselves practising social scientists, pursue the equally bold thesis that, whereas progress in the natural sciences is plausibly portrayed as paradigm-driven, in the social sciences progress is more likely to come from techniques that arise from the solutions to real-world problems, which are then incorporated into one or more disciplinary agendas. Their thesis is backed by an analysis of the historical conditions under which social science innovations had been developed and diffused.

The idea that the history of the social sciences is best seen as a history of discipline formation has been increasingly challenged at a variety of levels. WAGNER, WITTROCK & WHITLEY reveal important differences in the institutionalization of the social sciences across the national university systems of Europe. ROSS makes an interesting case for linking the reform-minded positivism of early American social scientists to the popular image of the United States as a unique social experiment. The implied thesis here is that the national culture prevailed over any distinct disciplinary traditions that had emerged in Europe, which in turn provided much of the basis on which European social science was subsequently (i.e. post-World War II) professionalized.

FULLER argues that the development of canonical disciplinary histories for the social sciences has been an effective vehicle for justifying the ignorance of relevant work in neighbouring fields, and for concealing the blind spots of one's own. According to COLLINI, WINCH & BURROW, historians may be led astray if they assume at the start that a field such as "politics" would have eventually become an academic discipline of some sort, when there were doubts on this score in 19th-century Britain, both from professional academics and practising politicians.

BROWN and MANICAS are two wide-ranging and erudite histories that use past ideas and events to undercut the legitimacy of the recent positivist philosophy in the social sciences. Brown shows that despite their periodic genuflection to Newton, social theorists before the mid-19th century rarely modelled their idea of social law on physical law. Indeed, they typically spoke in the language of rational agency. The emergence of the natural sciences as the standard of academic knowledge may be responsible for the subsequent change in emphasis. Manicas finds more fault with the original theorists, whom he accuses of misunderstanding the nature of Newton's accomplishment, which involved explanation, not prediction and control. The conflation of explanation and prediction as goals of science is the reason Manicas gives for the fragmented character of contemporary social science. His solution is the deep-structural realism associated with Rom Harré and Roy Bhaskar.

KELLEY and PROCTOR are probably the works that come closest to the professional historian's ideal, being full of hard-to-find and useful information, while remaining studiously ambivalent concerning the ultimate lessons that should be drawn regarding the contemporary scene. However, despite their professional scruples, it is clear that both authors disapprove of the tendency of the social sciences to wrap themselves in the mantle of the natural sciences so as to escape political scrutiny. Kelley pursues an original path in tracing how social theorists since the pre-Socratics have tried to confer "natural" status on conventional aspects of the social order. This leads him to focus on the history of law as a key to understanding the history of the social sciences. Proctor follows the rhetoric of value-free enquiry, starting with the Charter of the Royal Society, and proceeding through the debates surrounding the founding of the major social science disciplines, especially those that sought to disentangle social science from socialism.

STEVE FULLER

See also Political Economy; Sociology

Societies

Berman, Morris, *Social Change and Scientific Organization: The Royal Institution, 1799–1844*, London: Heinemann, and Ithaca, New York: Cornell University Press, 1978

Biagioli, Mario, "Etiquette, Interdependence, and Sociability in Seventeenth-Century Science", *Critical Inquiry*, 22 (1996): 193–238

Crosland, Maurice P., *Science under Control: The French Academy of Sciences, 1795–1914*, Cambridge and New York: Cambridge University Press, 1992

Hahn, Roger, *The Anatomy of a Scientific Institution: The Paris Academy of Sciences, 1666–1803*, Berkeley: University of California Press, 1971

Hall, Marie Boas, *All Scientists Now: The Royal Society in the Nineteenth Century*, Cambridge and New York: Cambridge University Press, 1984

Hunter, Michael, *Science and Society in Restoration England*, Cambridge and New York: Cambridge University Press, 1981

Hunter, Michael, *The Royal Society and Its Fellows, 1660–1700: The Morphology of an Early Scientific Institution*, Chalfont St Giles, Buckinghamshire: British Society for the History of Science, 1982; 2nd edition, 1994

Inkster, Ian and Jack Morrell (eds), *Metropolis and Province: Science in British Culture, 1780–1850*, London: Hutchinson, and Philadelphia: University of Pennsylvania Press, 1983

McClellan III, James E., *Science Reorganized: Scientific Societies in the Eighteenth Century*, New York: Columbia University Press, 1985

McClellan III, James E., *Colonialism and Science: Saint Domingue in the Old Regime*, Baltimore: Johns Hopkins University Press, 1992

Merton, Robert K., *Science, Technology and Society in Seventeenth-Century England*, in *Osiris*, edited by George Sarton, Bruges, Belgium: St Catherine Press, 1932; published separately, New York: Harper, 1970

Morrell, Jack and Arnold Thackray (eds), *Gentlemen of Science: Early Years of the British Association for the Advancement of Science*, Oxford: Clarendon Press, and New York: Oxford University Press, 1981

Roberts, Gerrylynn K., "Scientific Academies Across Europe", in *The Rise of Scientific Europe*, 1500–1800, edited by David Goodman and Colin A. Russell, Sevenoaks, Kent: Hodder and Stoughton/Open University, 1991

Roche, Daniel, *Le Siècle des lumières en province: Académies et académiciens provinciaux, 1680–1789*, 2 vols, Paris and The Hague: Mouton, 1978

Shapin, Steven, *A Social History of Truth: Civility and Science in Seventeenth-Century England*, Chicago: University of Chicago Press, 1994

Although they had important precursors, major scientific societies originated in the 17th century with the foundation of the Accademia dei Lincei in Rome(1603), the Accademia del Cimento in Florence(1657), the Royal Society of London (1660), and the Paris Académie des Sciences (1666). Such societies proliferated in the 18th century, including the Berlin Academy (1700), the St Petersburg Academy (1724), and the American Philosophical Society (1769). In the 19th and 20th centuries, scientific societies became more widespread, being founded in provincial towns of developed nations and also in the developing world. These societies also became more specialised, reflecting the escalating specialisation of science itself. However, even as they multiplied, scientific societies became less important to the scientific enterprise; from the late 19th century onwards, they were no longer the major sites of scientific exchange, having been eclipsed by universities, and corporate and government laboratories.

The literature on scientific societies reflects this change in their status, and also changes in the historiography of science. Much has been written on the early societies as embodiments of the first scientific communities, while they have also been used as a window on the role of science in societies undergoing political revolution, industrialization, and rapid social change. The study of these early societies was an important part of the growth of the externalist history of science, as a site at which the interaction of science and wider social forces could be explored. However, more recent developments in the sociology of scientific knowledge, involving microsociological concern with particular experiments or scientific discourses, for example, have tended to relegate macrosociological (or contextual) studies of the institutions of science to the background.

ROBERTS gives a good overview of the nature and extent of scientific societies up to 1800, and their importance as indications and embodiments of the new enthusiasm for scientific inquiry. McCLELLAN (1985) gives a wide-ranging account of societies in the 18th century, with an emphasis on the development of international networks of institutions. There is widespread agreement that scientific societies came to serve crucial communication and control functions in science, although it should be noted that certain functionalist approaches can prove anachronistic.

Scientific societies have been important foci for the contextual study of relations between science and the wider society. MERTON's pioneering and controversial study examined the extent to which the Royal Society of London (and the new science) was spurred on by economic and religious imperatives. HUNTER's detailed and valuable researches (1981 and 1982) have contested the Merton thesis and the work of those who have broadly supported Merton's approach. Thus, Hunter questions both the degree to which concerns with utility guided the scientific activities of the Society's Fellows, and also the value of Merton's rather vague characterisation of the Puritanism that, he argued, provided a crucial stimulus to scientific inquiry.

HAHN provides a classic study of the French Academy of Sciences as a relatively exclusive, centralised organ of the state, while CROSLAND carries the study through to 1914. The Royal Society of London was, by contrast, a voluntary association without a strong formal state role, though, as HALL shows, it did perform important public functions in a more informal way. While metropolitan institutions have received most attention, provincial ones reveal much about the wider cultural significance and resonance of the pursuit of science.

ROCHE is a *tour de force* of pre-revolutionary French provincial institutions. INKSTER & MORRELL provides a good way into a large literature on science in the British provinces during the industrial revolution, including some important insights into the role of science and scientific societies in industrialisation.

BERMAN's account of the Royal Institution reveals the varied social and political groups contesting the uses of science in British society around 1800. MORRELL & THACKRAY's prosopographically based study of the peripatetic British Association for the Advancement of Science depicts the formation of a dominant group in science in early Victorian culture. McCLELLAN (1992), a study of the *Cercle des Philadelphes* in Saint Domingue, indicates how much can be learned – in this case about the relations between French science and French colonialism – from the study of "peripheral" and otherwise obscure institutions.

To the functional and contextual approaches to the study of scientific societies has recently been added an approach that regards scientific societies as spaces within which cultural forms of science, such as experimentalism, and the bases of credibility and authority in creating knowledge are partially developed and instantiated. SHAPIN emphasises the notion that scientific truth – establishing matters of fact in the new science – depended crucially on answers to the question of "who was to be believed?" Issues of trust, of gentlemanly status, and credibility are seen as at the heart of modern science. Although Shapin does not study institutional settings in detail, the scientific societies were one crucial venue where these issues were worked through. BIAGIOLI pursues similar themes, although concentrating on European examples. This sort of approach has been pursued almost exclusively in relation to 17th-century institutions, and its depiction of dominant moral codes in science is likely to fracture as efforts are made to integrate it with contextual studies of scientific societies in later times.

Despite their unpopularity in recent years, much remains to be done by way of contextual studies of scientific societies, especially of those societies outside the major metropolitan centres. Colonial settings would prove particularly rewarding. The limited, but still important, role of scientific societies and academies in generating the public face of science in the 20th century is a neglected area of research.

DAVID PHILIP MILLER

See also Académie des Sciences; Journals; Royal Society of London; Universities

Sociology

Abrams, Philip, *The Origins of British Sociology, 1834–1914*, Chicago: University of Chicago Press, 1968

Aron, Raymond, *Main Currents in Sociological Thought*, 2 vols, translated from the French by Richard Howard and Helen Weaver, New York: Basic Books, and London: Weidenfeld and Nicolson, 1965–67 (original edition, 1960)

Barnes, Harry Elmer, *Social Thought from Lore to Science*, 2 vols, Boston: Heath, 1938; 3rd edition, with Howard Becker, 3 vols, New York: Dover, 1961

Barnes, Harry Elmer, *An Introduction to the History of Sociology*, Chicago: University of Chicago Press, 1948

Bauman, Zygmunt, *Intimations of Postmodernity*, London and New York: Routledge, 1991

Besnard, Philippe (ed.), *The Sociological Domain: The Durkheimians and the Founding of French Sociology*, Cambridge and New York: Cambridge University Press, 1983

Bottomore, Tom and Robert Nisbet (eds), *A History of Sociological Analysis*, New York: Basic Books, 1978

Bulmer, Martin (ed.), *Essays on the History of British Sociological Research*, Cambridge and New York: Cambridge University Press, 1985

Gurvitch, Georges and Wilbert E. Moore (eds), *Twentieth Century Sociology*, New York: Philosophical Library, 1945

Hawthorn, Geoffrey, *Enlightenment and Despair: A History of Sociology*, Cambridge and New York: Cambridge University Press, 1976; 2nd edition, 1987

Lazarsfeld, Paul, "Notes on the History of Quantification in Sociology: Trends, Sources and Problems," *Isis*, 52/2 (1961): 277–333

Levine, Donald N., *Visions of the Sociological Tradition*, Chicago: University of Chicago Press, 1995

Nisbet, Robert A., *The Sociological Tradition*, New York: Basic Books, 1966

Platt, Jennifer, *A History of Sociological Research Methods in America, 1920–1960*, Cambridge and New York: Cambridge University Press, 1996

Turner, Stephen Park and Jonathan H. Turner, *The Impossible Science: An Institutional Analysis of American Sociology*, Newbury Park, California: Sage, 1990

The term sociology was coined by Auguste Comte in the 1830s. The discipline, however, dates from the last decades of the 19th century.

Some historians include sociology within the broader history of social thought, treating sociology proper as simply one chapter of a much longer story. BARNES (1948) presents "a comprehensive summary and critical appraisal of the growth of sociological thought [sic] from the ancient Near East to our own day". BARNES (1938) begins his history with a similarly broad rubric, the attempt to understand "man's ideas about life with his fellows". In such treatments, modern sociology shares a common past with all the other social sciences, and indeed with history, philosophy, and literature as well.

Most historians of sociology, however, date the beginnings of the subject in the latter part of the 19th century, and their concerns are typically to delineate and to understand what precipitated this new, specifically sociological discourse. A good deal still hinges on how a given historian defines the enterprise of sociology. ARON poses the problem thus: "How is one to reconstruct the past of a discipline whose objectives, methods, and boundaries are not exactly determined?" His own, somewhat arbitrary, solution is to think of sociology as "the would-be *science* of the *social*", a formula he applies to a succession of philosopher–sociologists from Montesquieu to Weber. He thereby constructs a lineage of sociological thought, although along the way the meanings of both "science" and "the social" are subtly altered in order to establish some kind of continuity.

NISBET sees sociology as a deliberate reaction to the industrial and democratic revolutions at the close of the 18th century and after. A "golden age" of social thinking, c.1830–1900, constituted a sociological tradition organized around core ideas (community, authority, status, the sacred, alienation) which continue to give identity and direction to modern sociology. BOTTOMORE & NISBET organize their collaborative work around the "break in social thought which produced sociology". According to their view, the otherwise widely different founders of sociology (Marx, Weber, Durkheim) shared "a new and more precise conception of 'society' as an object of study to be clearly distinguished from the state and the political realm, from a vague universal history of humanity, and from the particular histories of 'peoples', 'states' or 'civilizations'". Similarly BAUMAN, a contemporary theorist, regards sociology as singularly associated with modernity. Its focal conception, "society", he argues, is a distinctly modern creation, in sharp contrast to the *polis* or the household (the original core concepts of political science and economics). HAWTHORN traces the burden of sociology back to questions posed during the Enlightenment, notably by Rousseau and Kant, about "the connection between individuals and societies". He treats the discipline's implicit retreat from facing such philosophically-laden questions as a signal failure, which has condemned the field to a series of theoretically rootless "limited empiricisms".

Among authors who have treated the considerable national differences within sociological traditions, GURVITCH & MOORE offer authoritative overviews of the origins and development of the field in the first half of the 20th century. LEVINE argues that the approaches to sociology followed in the different countries "were embedded in contrasting traditions of moral philosophy", and that subsequently "the originative figures of modern sociology mainly cite fellow nationals"; hence his discrete sketches of British, French, German, Italian, and American traditions. ABRAMS reconstructs the early development of sociology in Britain, attributing its relative weakness there in part to the corresponding strength of social statistics and social administration. BESNARD provides a series of essays on the institutionalization of sociology in France, largely as the work of the Durkheim school. TURNER & TURNER sketch an overview of sociology in the United States, interpreting its course as "intimately connected to the nature and level of resources that have been available to sociologists". They try, in particular, to account for the shift from a practical and activist orientation among early sociologist–reformers to a precocious interest in developing research methodology as a special field, and conclude rather provocatively that "the organization of sociology as a whole hinders its development as science".

The history of empirical social research has often been treated as a separate topic, or a sub-field in itself. LAZARSFELD provides an interesting excursus into the history of quantification of social data, which both illuminates the importance of the topic in the heritage of sociology, and demonstrates its virtual independence from the history of social thought. BULMER presents a series of historical reflections on the uses of sociological research in Britain, and several case studies of landmarks in empirical research. PLATT analyses the development of research methods and of empirical research in the United States from 1920 to 1960, the period "during which

American sociology became dominant quantitatively and qualitatively". She considers her book to be a corrective to the usual theory-centered approach in histories of sociology, and hence an effort "to shift the balance of historical concern further in the direction of empirical research".

MICHAEL DONNELLY

See also Quantification; Social Sciences

Sociology of Science

Bloor, David, *Knowledge and Social Imagery*, London and Boston: Routledge and Kegan Paul, 1976; 2nd edition, Chicago: University of Chicago Press, 1991

Collins, H.M., *Changing Order: Replication and Induction in Scientific Practice*, Beverly Hills, California: Sage, 1985

Latour, Bruno and Steve Woolgar, *Laboratory Life: The Social Construction of Scientific Facts*, Beverley Hills, California: Sage, 1979; as *Laboratory Life: The Construction of Scientific Facts*, with a new postscript, Princeton, New Jersey: Princeton University Press, 1986

Latour, Bruno, *Science in Action: How to Follow Scientists and Engineers through Society*, Cambridge, Massachusetts: Harvard University Press, and Milton Keynes, Buckinghamshire: Open University Press, 1987

Lynch, Michael, *Scientific Practice and Ordinary Action: Ethnomethodology and Social Studies of Science*, Cambridge and New York: Cambridge University Press, 1993

Pickering, Andrew (ed.), *Science as Practice and Culture*, Chicago: University of Chicago Press, 1992

Shapin, Steven and Simon Schaffer, *Leviathan and the Air Pump: Hobbes, Boyle, and the Experimental Life*, Princeton, New Jersey: Princeton University Press, 1985

Shapin, Steven, *A Social History of Truth: Civility and Science in Seventeenth-Century England*, Chicago: University of Chicago Press, 1994

Woolgar, Steve (ed.), *Knowledge and Reflexivity: New Frontiers in the Sociology of Knowledge*, London: Sage, 1988

The sociology of science has seen rapid development since the 1970s, the sociology of scientific knowledge (SSK) having taken over from the previously predominant approach of Mertonian sociology of science. The older approach was more a sociology of scientists, including scientific institutions and careers, because Merton was concerned with the types of social arrangements that were conducive to the production of certified knowledge. However, SSK attempts to understand how the very technical content of the sciences can be understood sociologically. This approach has had an enormous influence on science studies in general, including the history and philosophy of science.

The wider intellectual roots of SSK are to be found in phenomenology (especially the strand from Alfred Schutz through Peter L. Berger and Thomas Luckmann), in the later writings of Ludwig Wittgenstein, in ethnomethodology, and in Karl Mannheim. All the major works in SSK are indebted in one way or another to these traditions.

A "Strong Programme" in the sociology of scientific knowledge is set out by BLOOR, which is a manifesto for the extension of Mannheim's sociology of knowledge into the hard sciences and mathematics. Bloor argues that such a programme should seek causal explanations, be impartial to the truth or falsity of the knowledge claims under investigation, be symmetrical in the type of sociological explanation sought (e.g. the same sorts of explanation should be posited for true and false claims), and be reflexive. Examples are drawn from the Popper-Kuhn debate and from the history of mathematics.

COLLINS provides a number of detailed case studies in SSK. He examines parapsychology, laser building, and the detection of gravity waves in order to show how scientists build up a network of inductive generalizations in the course of skilled activities such as building, replicating, and calibrating experiments. By focusing much of his work on areas of contestation such a scientific controversies, Collins is able to investigate the possibilities for radical change in science. He concludes that scientific order is made primarily through the tools for making human order.

Another important empirical research site for SSK has been that of detailed studies of laboratory life. LATOUR & WOOLGAR is the pioneering example of this genre. The mundane activities of bio-chemists at the Salk Institute are examined in the same way as an anthropologist might treat an exotic tribe. They show how scientists are literary reasoners, and how scientific facts, such as the existence of the hormonal factor TRF, are socially constructed in the course of a series of linguistic transformations.

The semiotic and French philosophical roots of Latour & Woolgar become more obvious in the fully worked out actor-network theory offered in LATOUR. This extremely influential book contains a wealth of examples drawn from both science and technology – technoscience – which shows how a variety of human and non-human actors get enrolled and translated into networks. Technoscience is treated as "politics by other means", and Latour follows many different scientific and technological actors as they attempt to build and stabilize actor-networks.

Another important ethnographic strand in the study of science has stemmed from the influence of Harold Garfinkel and ethnomethodology. LYNCH provides a detailed account of the origins of this approach, which focuses upon the local accounting practices and work traditions where scientific activities are carried out. Lynch also provides one of the most authoritative reviews of SSK.

The influence of SSK on the history of science is exemplified in SHAPIN & SCHAFFER. This historical study of the debate between Hobbes and Boyle over the establishment of matters of fact to do with the working of air pumps has been widely heralded as a key text in the recent history of science. The detailed negotiations over the working of air pumps are set in the wider context of Restoration politics, and in this case we can see how the making of natural knowledge can be shaped by political events. Shapin & Schaffer show how Boyle developed not only a new experimental practice, but the literary, social, and material technologies that enabled the Royal Society as a whole to provide an authoritative means for the establishment of new facts about the natural world.

The reflexivity postulate of the Strong Programme, and the problems and pitfalls of a fully-reflexive sociology of science, are explored in WOOLGAR. Does SSK apply to itself and what are the implications of this? This edited collection of essays by many leading sociologists of science shows a variety of approaches towards dealing with reflexivity. Woolgar and Ashmore in their introduction argue for, and demonstrate, how post-structuralist, playful approaches towards language might offer a way of solving notorious reflexive conundrums. The general influence of cultural studies, anthropology, poststructuralism, and feminist epistemology on SSK can be seen in PICKERING. This edited collection provides the most up-to-date reading of the rich variety of approaches now available within the sociology of science. Debates between different approaches, such as the merits of actor-network theory and the different interpretations of Wittgenstein within SSK, are a prominent feature. This book reveals a field fragmented and polarized around a number of debates. The earlier unity of the Strong Programme seems to have been lost, and, paradoxically, at the very moment when SSK has been achieving greater impact within the academy at large.

SHAPIN is an example of one of the most thorough-going attempts to extend sociological thinking into science. By tracing relationships of trust within science, and in gentlemanly courtly society, Shapin turns full-circle, back to the Mertonian project of establishing the institutional prerequisites that make scientific knowledge possible.

TREVOR J. PINCH

See also Fact; Measurement; Performance; Rhetoric

Solid State Physics

Braun, Ernest and Stuart Macdonald, *Revolution in Miniature: The History and Impact of Semiconductor Electronics*, Cambridge and New York: Cambridge University Press, 1978; revised edition, 1982

Eckert, Michael and Helmut Schubert, *Kristalle, Elektronen, Transistoren: Von der Gelehrtenstube zur Industrieforschung*, Reinbek bei Hamburg: Rowohlt, 1986; as *Crystals, Electrons, Transistors: From Scholar's Study to Industrial Research*, translated by Thomas Hughes, New York: American Institute of Physics, 1989

Forman, Paul, "Behind Quantum Electronics: National Security as a Basis for Physical Research in the United States, 1940–1960", *Historical Studies in the Physical and Biological Sciences*, 18/1 (1987): 149–229

Hoddeson, Lillian, "The Discovery of the Point-Contact Transistor", *Historical Studies in the Physical Sciences*, 12 (1981): 41–76

Hoddeson, Lillian, *et al.* (eds), *Out of the Crystal Maze: Chapters from the History of Solid-State Physics*, New York and Oxford: Oxford University Press, 1992

Keith, Stephen T. and Paul Hoch, "Formation of a Research School: Theoretical Solid State Physics at Bristol, 1930–54", *British Journal for the History of Science*, 19 (1986): 19–44

Mott, Sir Nevill (ed.), *The Beginnings of Solid State Physics: A Symposium*, London: Royal Society, 1980

Slater, John C., *Solid-State and Molecular Theory: A Scientific Biography*, New York: Wiley, 1975

Szymborski, Krzysztof, "The Physics of Imperfect Crystals – A Social History", *Historical Studies in the Physical Sciences*, 14/2 (1984): 317–55

Teichmann, Jürgen, *Zur Geschichte der Festkörperphysik: Farbzentrenforschung bis 1940*, Stuttgart: Steiner, 1988

Warnow-Blewett, Joan and Jürgen Teichmann, *Guide to Sources for the History of Solid State Physics*, New York: American Institute of Physics, 1989

Since solid state physics was the scientific impetus behind the revolution in information and communication technologies, it might be called the most important scientific activity of the 20th century. However, it is only within the last 15 that historians of science have recognized its historical significance. The initial impetus came from a meeting in London organized by the theoretical physicist Sir Nevill Mott in 1979, where leading solid state physicists presented their recollections. The conference proceedings, edited by MOTT, are a collection of short and personal accounts of the participants' ideas on the history of their field.

The only monograph that predates the London meeting is SLATER's autobiography, which contains a detailed history of the events at the Massachusetts Institute of Technology (MIT) in Cambridge. As head of the physics department from 1930 to 1951, Slater oversaw a period of massive change and expansion. Thus, the central chapters of his book emphasize the institutional development of the MIT physics department, whereas the first and last chapters discuss the internal developments of research in solid state physics in general.

In the aftermath of the London conference, an international project for the history of solid state physics was established. The final report on this project, edited by HODDESON *et al.*, is a massive work divided into nine independent chapters (700 pages with c.2500 footnotes). With the exception of the first and last chapters, the chapters are divided by internal physical criteria, such as Band Theory, Magnetism, and Semiconductors. In the first chapter, Michael Eckert *et al.* examine the period before solid state physics existed as a distinct field (pre-1930). The study incorporates an analysis of the institutional settings, the financial support of research, the new experimental techniques (i.e. X-ray diffraction), and the theoretical investigations. The emergence of solid state physics as a distinct discipline, and the scientific community associated with it, is the subject of the final chapter written by Spencer R. Weart. Through social analysis, Weart provides an account of the increasing specialization of the field of solid state physics, as physicists (beginning in the 1930s) were able to devote their entire careers to the field. By 1960, as the proliferation of autonomous research groups, institutes, conferences, and journals devoted to solid state physics clearly demonstrates, this sub-discipline was firmly established as a distinct field of physics. The other chapters of Hoddeson *et al.* are primarily devoted to the intellectual development of the field, from about 1920 to 1960, and demonstrate several fascinating aspects of the emergence of ideas in solid state physics. Topics include the Electron Theory of Metals (chapter 2), Band Theory (chapter 3), Point Defects and Color Centers (chapter 4), Mechanical Properties (chapter 5), Magnetism (chapter 6), Semiconductors (chapter 7), and Collective Phenomena (chapter 8).

Despite this internalist division of solid state physics, the authors of the individual chapters generally demonstrate the interrelations of politics, industry, and science, and provide the most comprehensive accounts of their respective topics to date. To stimulate further studies on the history of the field, they draw attention to relevant source material, for which a separate "Guide to Sources" has been published by WARNOW-BLEWETT & TEICHMANN.

The concept of the formation of research schools has been an important tool in the historiography of solid state physics. Teichmann, Szymborski and Keith & Hoch all provide detailed studies of the local aspects of the history of solid state physics.

TEICHMANN explores the history of point defects and color centers in ionic crystals, by concentrating on the famous school of Robert Wichard Pohl in Göttingen. During the 1920s and 1930s, Pohl's distrust of theory led him to reject every interpretation of his group's measurements that employed the modern quantum theory. Nevertheless, in the 1940s, these experiments were considered to be crucial for the further development of the field and therefore to demonstrate Pohl's deep intuitive sense concerning physical quantities. In the last chapters of his book, Teichmann compares Pohl's school to other contemporary schools, and investigates its importance for the development of solid state physics in general. Due to Teichmann's emphasis on the research actually done in Pohl's laboratory, the reader will need a sound knowledge of physics to reap the full benefit of his detailed analysis.

SZYMBORSKI provides a comparative analysis of the four major schools working on imperfect crystals up to the 1940s: Göttingen (Pohl), Halle (Smekal), Leningrad (Joffe), Vienna (Przibram). He focuses on the social modes of operation within the groups, as well as their research methodologies. However, the reason why Pohl's school was so singularly successful remains unclear in both Szymborski's and Teichmann's analyses.

KEITH & HOCH discuss the formation of the school of theoretical solid state physics at Bristol. Starting, first, with a research grant for theoretical investigation of the properties of the solid state in 1930, the Bristol school achieved international reputation within only a few years. One of the salient features of the research done in Bristol was the continued emphasis on the practical use of theoretical physics, which grew out of the close connection with metallurgists and crystallographers. The policy of welcoming visiting foreign scholars before 1933 helped to integrate many refugee physicists from Nazi-Germany in later years. Keith & Hoch show in their analysis how social and institutional factors influenced the direction, success, and failures of physical research.

ECKERT & SCHUBERT use the history of solid state physics to exemplify the general transformation of physics from an academic discipline in the 19th century to a modern techno-science in the middle of the 20th century. They begin with the institutionalization of science in the 19th century, and follow the development of the electron theory of metals through to the emergence of schools of solid state physics in the 1930s. The radar project during World War II is regarded as the foundation for the invention of the transistor and the emergence of the semiconductor industry. Eckert & Schubert's account demonstrates how this growing industry shaped the methods of physics and how, conversely, scientific inventions changed society. Thus, the book is a good introduction to the study of science within the social context, and, additionally, is accessible to non-specialists.

The transistor has been the focus of several historical studies. For example, HODDESON gives a detailed micro-analysis of the underlying concepts used, and the experimental steps taken toward the invention of the point-contact transistor. BRAUN & MACDONALD, on the other hand, explore the history of the semiconductor industry. They trace this history from the invention of the transistor to the integrated circuit, as well as the general patterns of the new industry. Their analysis provides a good example of the interaction between technological and economic history.

Finally, FORMAN points to the importance of the military–scientific complex for the emergence of this new industry in the United States. In a detailed study, he shows the tremendous increase of funding for physical research by the military, and its impact on the cognitive development of physics.

KAI HANDEL

See also Physics: 20th century; Quantum Theory

Space Science

Corliss, William R., *Scientific Satellites*, Washington, DC: Government Printing Office/NASA, 1967

DeVorkin, David H., *Science with a Vengeance: How the Military Created the US Space Sciences after World War II*, New York: Springer, 1992

Ezell, Edward Clinton and Linda Neuman Ezell, *On Mars: Exploration of the Red Planet, 1958–1978*, Washington, DC: Government Printing Office/NASA, 1984

Hall, R. Cargill, "Early US Satellite Proposals", *Technology and Culture*, 4 (1963): 410–34

Hall, R. Cargill, *Lunar Impact: A History of Project Ranger*, Washington, DC: Government Printing Office/NASA, 1977

Hirsh, Richard F., *Glimpsing an Invisible Universe: The Emergence of X-Ray Astronomy*, Cambridge and New York: Cambridge University Press, 1983

Hufbauer, Karl, *Exploring the Sun: Solar Science since Galileo*, Baltimore: Johns Hopkins University Press, 1991

McDougall, Walter A., *The Heavens and the Earth: A Political History of the Space Age*, New York: Basic Books, 1985

Massey, Harrie and M.O. Robins, *History of British Space Science*, Cambridge and New York: Cambridge University Press, 1986

Newell, Homer E., *Beyond the Atmosphere: Early Years of Space Science*, Washington, DC: Government Printing Office/NASA, 1980

Roland, Alex, "Science and War", *Osiris*, new series, 1 (1985): 247–72

Smith, Robert W., *The Space Telescope: A Study of NASA, Science, Technology, and Politics*, Cambridge and New York: Cambridge University Press, 1989

Tatarewicz, Joseph N., *Space Technology and Planetary Astronomy*, Bloomington: Indiana University Press, 1990

Although there are academic departments, institutes, and high level advisory committees incorporating the name in their title, space science does not exist as a distinct discipline, but rather as a locus of activity for a wide range of specialties – from orbit theory and rocketry engineering, to environmental science, physics, comparative planetology, geophysics, meteorology, and astronomy. Here the term is confined to the definition suggested by Homer E. Newell, a long-term chief scientist at NASA and formerly a charter member of a scientific rocketry group at the Naval Research Laboratory. In 1980 he characterized space science as, "those scientific investigations made possible or significantly aided by rockets, satellites, and space probes". Newell's argument was that, in its origins, space science was defined by the use of a particular type of vehicle that carried instrumentation and equipment into realms otherwise inaccessible by ordinary means of transport. Thus, although the disciplinary elements may well have already existed – such as in areas like astronomy, meteorology, ionospheric physics, and cosmic ray physics – what was created in the 1940s was a new professional space, which DeVORKIN argues was defined in terms of a vehicle for research by patrons interested primarily in the vehicle itself. This definition was as much an artefact of institutional and promotional efforts as it was a conscious act on the part of practitioners. Given Newell's definition as a working hypothesis, the history of the subject becomes intimately connected with the social forces that created rocketry and space flight, as McDOUGALL and many others have shown, and, if treated within this context, offers rich territory for illuminating how scientific practice reflects national security policy and international relations – as explored by MASSEY & ROBINS in the case of British space science.

Many popular writers claim that all matters relating to space research originate with Sputnik in 1957 but, by Newell's definition, it all began with the German V-2 missile, as DeVorkin argues. Indeed, Sputnik produced a huge rush of activity in many countries, but the organizations that were created in its wake, in the United States at least, and the policies that helped to frame the national response, were built out of parts of pre-existing institutions which had already created significant infrastructures for rocket research.

One must also appreciate that space science was made possible not only by the presence of a vehicle, but by the interests of new patrons who could afford that vehicle. Thus, space science is an artefact of government and military patronage, which, in the post-World War II era, has profoundly altered the direction and character of scientific research. ROLAND explores the literature generated by historians, policy analysts, and practitioners on shifts in direction and methodology caused by this new patronage, which helps to contextualize space science.

US scientists who reminisce about their participation in space science typically describe how they either created or adapted new tools for on-going research. In fact, as DeVorkin has shown, the first generation of scientists to use rockets for scientific study were mainly instrument-makers who found themselves tackling totally new and untried areas of research: the requirements of space science, whether with balloons, rockets, satellites, or space probes, went way beyond the capabilities of traditional academic institutions. Enormous investments in manpower, time, new types of equipment, to say nothing of the development and operational costs of the vehicles themselves, created huge technical and managerial challenges that placed the science itself in a secondary role. This was a new type of scientific practice, created in the process of what commentators then called the "permanent mobilization of science".

NEWELL provides a very broad and insightful technical introduction to the growth of space science, from the 1940s to 1970. His earlier works, plus his many reviews for the US Navy and for NASA, contribute to the technical history, which can be augmented by the detailed inventories created by CORLISS. Reminiscences and memoirs by practitioners often provide valuable information; beyond memoirs by James Van Allen, Herbert Friedman, Richard Tousey, and Bernard Lovell, the history series of the American Astronautical Society has devoted considerable attention to European and Soviet pioneers.

In the post-Sputnik era, space science acquired its full arsenal of vehicles. Scientific research was universally considered to be a viable element in Cold War policies and pressures, since it held out the potential to enhance both national prestige and national security. Thus, there was an enormous amount of programmatic activity to study the sun from space and to explore the high-energy universe, which is examined by both HIRSH and HUFBAUER – the former as the growth of instrument specialty groups and the latter as an academic specialty. Equally, such social forces led to efforts to send probes and landers to the moon and the planets for scientific exploration, as HALL has chronicled and TATAREWICZ has explored in terms of NASA's need to acquire scientific expertise to meet mission goals. Finally, efforts to build hugely expensive multipurpose earth-orbiting space telescopes created an entirely new type of scientist in modern society, as SMITH has argued in his study of the Hubble Space Telescope.

Some writers have contributed useful perspectives on the political and military aspects of the US's post-Sputnik space program, placing it, along with the space sciences, within the national security state. Massey & Robins, and the sweeping political history by McDougall, are useful in this regard; the latter has become a standard of interpretive reference, against which the social forces promoting space activities are now being examined.

The NASA History Series has been especially prolific in areas relating to the space sciences (see Hall, Hufbauer, and EZELL & EZELL on the exploration of Mars). Several disciplinary histories – on X-ray astronomy by Hirsh, planetary astronomy by Tatarewicz, the Space Telescope by Smith, and solar physics by Hufbauer – have identified the communities that eventually formed to conduct space research from satellites and space probes, and demonstrate how, through changing scientific priorities, manpower pools, infrastructural needs, and funding patterns, many of the physical sciences in America were transformed socially and professionally through access to space.

DAVID H. DEVORKIN

See also Astronomy: general works; Astrophysics; Big Science; Physics: 20th century

Spain

Capel, Horacio, Joan Eugeni Sanchez and Omar Moncada, *De Palas a Minerva: La formación científica y la estructura institucional de los ingenieros militares en el siglo XVIII*, Barcelona: Serbal, and Madrid: Consejo Nacional de Investigaciones Científicas, 1988

Glick, Thomas F., *Einstein in Spain: Relativity and the Recovery of Science*, Princeton, New Jersey: Princeton University Press, 1988

Kottek, Samuel S. and Luis García Ballester (eds), *Medicine and Medieval Ethics in Medieval and Early Modern Spain*, Jerusalem: Magnes Press, 1996

López Piñero, Jose María, *Ciencia y técnica en la sociedad española de los siglos XVI y XVII*, Barcelona: Labor Universitaria, 1979

López Piñero, Jose María *et al.*, *Diccionario histórico de la ciencia moderna en España*, 2 vols, Barcelona: Editorial Península, 1983

López Piñero, Jose María (ed.), *La ciencia en la España en el siglo XIX*, Madrid: Marcial Pons, 1992

Millás Vallicrosa, José María, *Estudios sobre historia de la ciencia española*, Barcelona: Instituto Luis Vives de Filosofia, 1949

Sánchez Ron, José M. (ed.), *1907–1987: La junta para ampliación de estudios e investigaciones científicas, 80 años después*, 2 vols, Madrid: Consejo Nacional de Investigaciones Científicas, 1989

Sellés, Manuel, José Luis Peset and Antonio Lafuente (eds), *Carlos III y la ciencia de la ilustración*, Madrid: Alianza, 1988

Vernet, Juan, *De Abd al-Rahman I a Isabel II: Recopilación de estudios dispersos sobre Historia de la ciencia y de la cultura española ofrecida al autor por sus discípulos con ocasión de su LXV aniversario*, Barcelona: PPU, 1989

The history of Spanish science emerged, as was the case in many other countries, as an offshoot of the history of medicine at the end of the 1970s. This explains the closer connection between both disciplines than between the history of science and subjects such as sociology or the philosophy of science, both thriving fields in other countries but still only nascent in Spain. This also explains the fact that the pioneer of current studies of the Spanish scientific tradition was López Piñero, originally a medical historian and disciple of Laín Entralgo, the chief historian of medicine and the doyen of the Spanish history of science. LÓPEZ PIÑERO (1983) is an indispensable dictionary of the subject; though less thorough than the *Dictionary of Scientific Biography*, it covers four and a half centuries (from the period of Catholic Kings to the Civil War), and includes more than 800 entries, with information on Spanish scholars who have contributed to the history of world science, and on some foreign ones who exerted a powerful influence in the Iberian peninsula.

The three leading authors on medieval Spain are Millás Vallicrosa, Juan Vernet and García Ballester. To study science in Muslim Spain (al-Andalus), it is necessary to refer to Juan Vernet's works, one of the world's leading Arabists and a prominent disciple of Millás Vallicrosa, the pioneer and founder of

Spain's more firmly established school of Arabic science, the Catalonian school. The vastness of their work does not allow for comprehensive coverage here, and so only two compilations will be mentioned, MILLÁS VALLICROSA and VERNET. In MILLÁS VALLICROSA, readers will find Vernet's insightful assessment of the achievements of this school. Vernet demonstrates that Europe had access to the classical legacy, through Arabic versions coming from Catalonia from the 10th century, before the classical works reached Europe directly via William de Moerbecke's and other translations a few centuries later, and proves that Arabic science was more than a mere imitation of Greek science, and that its influence was crucial for the development of astronomy during the Renaissance. KOTTEK & GARCÍA BALLESTER's work provides English readers with a valuable collection of contributions to a Spanish–Israeli conference on medicine in medieval and early modern Spain. It includes articles by García Ballester and some of his disciples (Arrizabalaga, Salmón), and others who study medical procedures in the cultural "melting pot" (Christian, Jewish and Muslim) of the Iberian peninsula.

LÓPEZ PIÑERO (1979), on science in modern Spain, deserves special mention as it represents a turning-point in Spanish historiography on the subject. Its introduction is highly recommended as it sums up, in just a few pages, the studies carried out on Spanish science to date. The author reveals the staleness of the so-called "polemic about Spanish science": the ideological forces that, ever since Masson de Morvilliers's virulent article in the *Encyclopédie méthodique* (1782), led to the emergence of two irreconcilable groups, one of detractors and the other of apologists for the Spanish contribution to world science. Influenced by Pierre Vilar, and by the aspiration to construct a "total history", the book constitutes, furthermore, a vigorous analysis of the articulation of scientific activities in Spanish society at its zenith during the 16th century, and its subsequent period of decay during the 17th century, a time of crisis and isolation from Europe.

On science during the Enlightenment, a field assiduously studied since the 1980s, the manual edited by SELLÉS, PESET & LAFUENTE is still the most thorough. Essays in the volume include a detailed summary of the most relevant aspects of the endeavour by the Bourbon dynasty (and its successive ministries), the so-called Enlightened Despotism, to renew and modernize science in Spain. The institutionalization of knowledge at universities and academies is also described, with emphasis on the colonial dimension of this process, a vital subject for any historical analysis of Spanish science. The end product is a coherent text that provides insights into the Spanish Enlightenment, less rationalist, homogeneous and influenced by French thought than usual. This volume reflects, on the other hand, the concerns prevalent in the period in which it was written – the reassertion of Enlightenment ideals and scientific activity by the fledgling Spanish democracy.

Horacio Capel, historian of geography and doyen of leading specialists (such as Luis Urteaga, Francesco Nadal), is another indispensable author. In CAPEL, he examines the academies of military engineers in the 18th century, a sector that, together with the Navy, played a leading role in the institutionalization of science. The presence of the military in this process was more pronounced than in other Western countries, in which civil institutions were predominant.

The 19th century has attracted less attention than other periods. A comprehensive assessment of the period can be found, however, in a book edited by the pervasive LÓPEZ PIÑERO (1992), which comprises articles by Peset, Sánchez Ron, Josa and Puerto, among others. Despite some omissions (geology, navigation, engineering), it provides basic information on the progress of physics and the mathematical sciences, universities, natural history, chemistry, pharmacy and medicine throughout the turbulent 19th century in Spain. The 20th century is suitably covered by GLICK and SÁNCHEZ RON. Glick, also the author of well-known studies on the spread of the ideas of Darwin and Freud in Spain, reconstructs the history of the incorporation of Einstein's theories into Spanish society, and their impact in the inter-war period. The book is not confined to scientific circles: it studies figures such as Blas Cabrera, Gregorio Marañón and Esteve Terradas, but also others such as Antonio Machado, Ortega y Gasset, Unamuno, and other intellectuals whose activity is crucial in order to obtain a balanced vision of the "Silver Age" of Spanish culture. Finally, the work edited by Sánchez Ron (undoubtedly the greatest specialist in contemporary Spanish science) describes, following a comparative approach, the trajectory of the Junta para Ampliación de Estudios e Investigaciones Científicas (the precursor of the modern Consejo Superior de Investigaciones Científicas, CSIC), and, at the same time, a sizeable span of Spanish scientific activity in the 20th century.

JUAN PIMENTEL

See also Latin America; Religion and Science: Islam

Spectroscopy

Arabatzis, Theodore, "The Discovery of the Zeeman Effect: A Case Study of the Interplay between Theory and Experiment", *Studies in History and Philosophy of Science*, 23 (1992): 365–88

Forman, Paul, "The Doublet Riddle and Atomic Physics circa 1924", *Isis*, 59 (1968): 156–74

Forman, Paul, "Alfred Landé and the Anomalous Zeeman effect", *Historical Studies in the Physical Sciences*, 2 (1970): 153–261

Hearnshaw, J.B., *The Analysis of Starlight: One Hundred and Fifty Years of Astronomical Spectroscopy*, Cambridge and New York, Cambridge University Press, 1986

James, Frank A.J.L., *The Early Development of Spectroscopy and Astrophysics*, PhD dissertation, University of London (Imperial College), 1981

James, Frank A.J.L., "The Establishment of Spectro-Chemical Analysis as a Practical Method of Qualitative Analysis, 1854–1861", *Ambix*, 30 (1982): 30–53

James, Frank A.J.L., "The Creation of a Victorian Myth: The Historiography of Spectroscopy", *History of Science*, 23 (1985): 1–24

James, Frank A.J.L., "The Discovery of Line Spectra", *Ambix*, 32 (1985): 53–70

Kragh, Helge, "The Fine Structure of Hydrogen and the Gross Structure of the Physics Community", *Historical Studies in the Physical Sciences*, 15 (1984–85): 67–125

Maier, Clifford Lawrence, *The Role of Spectroscopy in the Acceptance of the Internally Structured Atom, 1860–1920*, New York: Arno Press, 1981

McGucken, William, *Nineteenth-Century Spectroscopy: Development of the Understanding of Spectra, 1802–1897*, Baltimore: Johns Hopkins University Press, 1969

Sutton, Michael A., "Spectroscopy and the Structure of Matter: A Study in the Development of Physical Chemistry", (dissertation), University of Oxford, 1972

Sutton, Michael A., "Sir John Herschel and the Development of Spectroscopy in Britain", *British Journal for the History of Science* (1974): 42–60

Sutton, Michael A., "Spectroscopy and the Chemists: A Neglected Opportunity?", *Ambix*, 23 (1976): 16–26

Although a vital research field of the second half of the 19th century, spectroscopy has received surprisingly little attention from historians of science. The two most notable exceptions to this rule are the two monographs by Maier and McGucken, which both focus on the development of theoretical interpretations of spectra. The criticisms in the papers by Frank James, however, at least hint at the important aspects of instrumental practice that need to be considered for a full history of spectroscopy, taking into account spectroscopical practice and the development of the pertinent apparatus.

McGUCKEN's book on the development of the understanding of spectra between 1802 and 1897 serves as a good introductory textbook; it only briefly describes the origins of spectrum analysis before 1859, and focuses on the interrelations between the "quest for spectral series formulae" and on models of the atom that tried to make sense of the regularities found in spectral series. It is McGucken's claim that Zeeman's search for a magnetic effect on spectral lines stems in part from his interest in William Thomson's vortex atom theory, and that only after he found the effect named after him did he then shift to Lorentz's electron theory interpretation. A different, and more convincing, interpretation of this episode is offered in ARABATZIS's paper on the Zeeman effect; Arabatzis shows how closely Zeeman's findings and Lorentz's interpretation went hand-in-hand in this case, and this paper is a good example of a well-researched study on the interplay between theory and experiment. MAIER, like McGucken, emphasises the search for spectral series, and their interpretation in analogy with harmonic overtones: for example, both texts discuss extensively Lockyer's dissociation theory and the controversies regarding the differences between band spectra and line spectra. However, Maier does not end his discussion with the advent of J.J. Thomson's discovery of the electron, but continues with a discussion of the interplay of atomic concepts in relation to spectroscopy from c.1900 to the rise of Bohr's quantum theory of 1913. Thus, Maier discusses how Bohr's quantized Kepler-orbits of the electrons around the positive nucleus gave a satisfactory account, not only of the hydrogen line spectrum, but also of ionized helium and X-ray spectra.

SUTTON (1972) complements Maier and McGucken by focusing on the contributions of British scientists, such as John F.W. Herschel, David Brewster, and Fox Talbot, in the early 19th century. SUTTON (1974) focuses on Herschel, and

SUTTON (1976) elaborates the notion that, due to "something of a breakdown in communication among specialists in different disciplines at this time", the majority of chemists between 1826 and 1860 missed a good opportunity by not realizing what potential lay in these discoveries. Sutton's forerunner-perspective has been severely challenged by JAMES (1985, "The Discovery of Line Spectra"), and in JAMES (1985, "The Creation of a Victorian Myth: The Historiography of Spectroscopy"), he criticizes Sutton, McGucken, Dingle, and others for constructing a Victorian-style myth of a tradition of "spectro-chemical analysis" long before Kirchhoff's and Bunsen's breakthrough of 1859. According to JAMES (1982), the establishment of spectral analysis as a practical method of qualitative analysis only occurred in the period 1854–61, as a result of a shift in perspective towards chemical questions, while the earlier studies were essentially scattered bits of observations originating from quite different, more physical, research contexts, such as the measuring of the absorption of light, and the probing of the nature of the spark. James claims that initially the Fraunhofer rays were merely a means to a different end, based on Fraunhofer's and Brewster's desire to obtain monochromatic light sources in order to achieve the improved gauging of the refractive powers of the various types of glass that was needed for the development of achromatic lenses.

For anyone interested in the astronomical applications of spectroscopy, HEARNSHAW is a good place to start, although it is structured along a Whiggish line of continuous progress, with no exploration of the many dead-ends. Richly illustrated, concisely written, and with several bibliographies of specialized topics interspersed in the text, this work focuses on stellar spectroscopy, and includes the application of the Doppler principle to determine radial velocities, stellar spectral classification, and the quantitative analysis of stellar spectra.

Among the huge literature on quantum theory and quantum mechanics, the papers by FORMAN (1968 and 1970) and KRAGH stand out as particularly precise accounts of interesting episodes in the interplay of theory and experiment involving spectroscopic data. While Forman's papers deal with the anomalous Zeeman effect, the doublet riddle, and other anomalies of the old quantum theory, Kragh's paper scrutinizes the story of Paschen's allegedly clear confirmation of Sommerfeld's relativistic quantum theory on the fine structure of hydrogen spectrum lines. According to Kragh's analysis, based on the contemporary physics literature, the issue was considered extremely complicated and controversial at the time, both on empirical and theoretical grounds.

KLAUS HENTSCHEL

See also Astrophysics; Chemistry; Fraunhofer; Scientific Instruments: general works

Spencer, Herbert 1820–1903

British philosopher and social reformer

Duncan, David, *The Life and Letters of Herbert Spencer*, London: Methuen, 1908

Francis, Mark, "Herbert Spencer and the Mid-Victorian Scientists", in *Metascience*, 1986

Hofstadter, Richard, *Social Darwinism in American Thought, 1860–1915*, Philadelphia: University of Pennsylvania Press, 1944, London: Oxford University Press, 1945; revised edition, Boston: Beacon Press, 1955

Lightman, Bernard, *The Origins of Agnosticism*, Baltimore: Johns Hopkins University Press, 1987

Moore, James, "Herbert Spencer's Henchmen", in *Darwinism and Divinity: Essays on Evolution and Religious Belief*, edited by John Durant, Oxford: Blackwell, 1985

Peel, J.D.Y., *Herbert Spencer: The Evolution of a Sociologist*, London: Heinemann, and New York: Basic Books, 1971

Richards, R.J., *Darwin and the Emergence of Evolutionary Theories of Mind and Behavior*, Chicago: University of Chicago Press, 1987

Spencer, Herbert, *Autobiography*, 2 vols, London: Williams and Norgate, 1904

Taylor, M.W., *Men versus the State: Herbert Spencer and Late Victorian Individualism*, Oxford: Clarendon Press, 1992

Wiltshire, David, *The Social and Political Thought of Herbert Spencer*, Oxford: Oxford University Press, 1978

Young, Robert M., *Mind, Brain, and Adaptation in the Nineteenth Century*, Oxford: Clarendon Press, 1970

A great deal of Spencer scholarship has focused on his political ideas and his evolutionary sociology. Recently, however, more work has been done on his psychological and religious theories.

The crucial starting point is the *Autobiography*, supplemented by DUNCAN's *Life and Letters*. SPENCER styled the former "a natural history of myself", reflexively indicating the congruence of his dissenting background and the later shape of his ideas. Nonconformity manifested itself in the Spencer family as an instinctive and vituperative rejection of established authority, he argued, and it was from this that both his extreme individualism and normative stress on the process of natural (as opposed to forced) development derived. Twentieth-century historians of Spencer's thought and influence have frequently picked up on his self-presentation. HOFSTADTER, who, within the context of New Deal economics deplored Spencer's enthusiastic reception by "Gilded Age" laisser-faire industrialists such as Andrew Carnegie, described him as a "secular Calvinist". For American Spencerians nature, personified as a harsh, unbending mistress, was the secular equivalent of a jealous, ruthless Calvinist God. Drawing upon the Weberian relation of Protestantism to industrial progress, Hofstadter presented Spencer's ideas as befitting an age of unprecedented industrial development and class exploitation. MOORE has recently offered a multi-layered account of Spencer's influence upon the "liberal Protestant" justification of laisser-faire capitalism in late 19th-century America.

PEEL and WILTSHIRE each incorporate material relating to Spencer's background and youth into their respective treatments of his sociological and political thought. Peel argues that Spencer's Lamarckianism, picked up in the 1840s, enabled him to describe a relationship between the individual and society based on the (environment-led) acquisition of mental and cultural characteristics, which avoided recourse to "social facts", separable from individual agency. He proceeds to describe the more polemical aspects of Spencer's sociological enterprise: the distinction between militant and industrial social organisation, and repudiation of the institutions characteristic of the former, among which Spencer counted status. Far from legitimating social inequality and exploitation, he viewed such institutions as indications of barbarism. Peel accounts for the discrepancy between this, and the image of Spencer as the philosopher of laisser-faire, by the somewhat dubious device of distinguishing Spencerian ideals – the utopian visions of an essentially detached mind – from Spencerian ideology – the practical use of his ideas.

WILTSHIRE, whose tone is consistently drier, offers an alternative, more critical, description of the apparent contradictions in Spencer's life and thought. He suggests that in the space between absolute and relative ethics, (the former referring to the rights and duties of perfect men, the latter to the utilitarian principle guiding present-day action), Spencer found a "loophole" through which he could slip if his theory ever seemed to necessitate state intervention. Despite his reference to Spencer's "drift to conservatism"; Wiltshire seems impervious to the notion that Spencer's thought might have altered substantially over time, and hence fails to place it within any particular context, intellectual or otherwise. Wiltshire is also less than sympathetic to Spencer's use of the organic analogy; he contends that the main flaw in Spencer's thought was his failure to reconcile his individualist politics to his evolutionary sociology. Thus, for Wiltshire, there is no "loophole" through which Spencer's theories, in their totality, can be saved.

Spencer's "drift to conservatism" is TAYLOR's main concern. While recognising that Spencer fully formulated his critique of government in his *Social Statics* (1850), Taylor contends that is was in the 1880s that his political ideas received widespread attention, and traces Spencer's influence on the somewhat disparate group of individuals associated with the Liberty and Defence of Property League (fl. 1882). Social evolutionism was to members of the League a profoundly conservative doctrine, with which they argued that the organic development of social institutions denied the efficacy of positive government. Spencerian psychology, which stressed the relationship of environment to racial rather than individual psychology, bolstered this position. Taylor fails, however, to convince that these beliefs were anything other than the province of a handful of cranky extremists.

Spencer's psychological theories are described in YOUNG and in Richards. Young's is the more technical approach, tracing Spencer's belief in the specialisation of mental functions to his interest in phrenology in the 1840s, while recognising the evolutionary perspective of the *Principles of Psychology* (1855) as the crucial aspect of the mature theory. This perspective enabled Spencer to refute one of the most powerful idealist objections to associationist psychology – namely, how the limited and various experiences of individuals can possibly be constitutive of the complexity and homogeneity of the ideas people have. By describing mental operations as evolved, Spencer could account for the seemingly universal "fit" of certain ideas to the environment in terms of a natural evolutionary process: the increasing correspondence, acquired and inherited, of inner subjective relations to outer objective relations. The introduction of the temporal element, Young argues, produced an extremely powerful psychology.

RICHARDS portrays Spencer as being rather more amenable to idealism than Young allows. He characterises Spencer's psychology as "evolutionary Kantianism", in which a concept, the opposite of which is inconceivable, such as space, is the product of a mechanism of the acquisition and inheritance of "fitting" associations. Richards also provides more detail on the wider intellectual context of Spencer's "breakthrough" in the mid-1850s, and on the anti-interventionist implications of his mature psychology.

The thorny issue of Spencer's religious beliefs has been explored by FRANCIS and LIGHTMAN. Francis describes Spencer as contributing to the construction of a "new religion" in the 1850s and 1860s, one based on naturalistic, but not necessarily mechanistic, principles. This religion had its basis in science, which indicated the holistic relationship of man and nature. The cornerstone of this edifice was the notion of the "Unknown", a metaphysics immune to reason, but none the less capable of being demonstrated rationally to exist, and one highly amenable to scientists eager to deny the authority of the Church, yet not immune to the legitimating charms of theology. Lightman has described in greater detail the context within which Spencer formulated his ideas about the "Unknown". For Spencer, science, like religion, revealed the essential mystery underlying the operation of natural law. It was, Lightman suggests, this religious aspect to Spencer's evolutionary thought that guaranteed its normative status.

HENRY ATMORE

See also Darwinism; Evolution

Spiritualism

Barrow, Logie, *Independent Spirits: Spiritualism and English Plebeians, 1850–1910*, London and New York: Routledge and Kegan Paul, 1986

Collins, H.M. and T.J. Pinch, *Frames of Meaning: The Social Construction of Extraordinary Science*, London and Boston: Routledge and Kegan Paul, 1982

Gauld, Alan, *The Founders of Psychical Research*, London: Routledge and Kegan Paul, and New York: Schocken Books, 1968

Hess, David J., *Science in the New Age: The Paranormal, Its Defenders and Debunkers, and American Culture*, Madison: University of Wisconsin Press, 1993

Inglis, Brian, *Natural and Supernatural: A History of the Paranormal from Earliest Times to 1914*, London: Hodder and Stoughton, 1977

Inglis, Brian, *Science and Parascience: A History of the Paranormal, 1914–1939*, London: Hodder and Stoughton, 1984

Moore, R. Laurence, *In Search of White Crows: Spiritualism, Parapsychology and American Culture*, New York: Oxford University Press, 1977

Oppenheim, Janet, *The Other World: Spiritualism and Psychical Research in England, 1850–1914*, Cambridge and New York: Cambridge University Press, 1985

Owen, Alex, *The Darkened Room: Women, Power and Spiritualism in Late Nineteenth-Century England*, London: Virago, 1989; as *The Darkened Room: Women, Power and Spiritualism in Late Victorian England*, Philadelphia: University of Pennsylvania Press, 1989

Podmore, Frank, *Modern Spiritualism: A History and a Criticism*, 2 vols, London: Methuen, 1902

Turner, Frank M., *Between Science and Religion: The Reaction to Scientific Naturalism in Late Victorian England*, New Haven, Connecticut: Yale University Press, 1974

The history of spiritualism has typically served the divergent concerns of psychical researchers, converted spiritualists, and sceptical debunkers, who have all combed the historical record to assess the veracity of the people who have produced and investigated spiritual manifestations. Recently, however, historians have shown much more agnosticism, and have examined spiritual phenomena as functions of particular social, cultural and intellectual settings.

Podmore and Inglis were both members of the Society for Psychical Research in London (SPR) and produced classic general surveys of spiritualism. Although both are short on argument, they remain useful reference guides. PODMORE's history reflects the SPR's programme of subjecting historical records of spiritual phenomena to harsh tests of plausibility. It traces the roots of spiritualism to medieval witchcraft, alchemy, and animal magnetism, dwells at length on the Victorian heyday, and boasts a comprehensive coverage of European and American spiritualism. He questions "not what agencies may be inferred from the facts, but whether the facts justify the inference of any new agency at all", and concludes that Victorian investigators' frequent suppositions of spiritual agencies were unjustified, given their poor experimental protocol, the possibility of hallucination, and the strong likelihood of trickery by the mediums.

Inglis's preference for "supernatural" rather than "spiritual" beliefs generates an engaging and plausible narrative that connects prehistoric tribal communities with psychical research in the 1930s. In INGLIS (1977), he is relatively sympathetic to his subjects, but in INGLIS (1984) his appraisal is harsher: for instance, he castigates British psychical researchers for not undertaking potentially interesting research programmes, such as the examination of "physical" phenomena. The latter volume has a constant and rather misleading emphasis on English speaking (and mainly SPR) psychical researches, but includes a valuable chapter on continental mediums (such as Rudi Schneider), details the SPR's conflicts with Harry Price and Conan Doyle, and charts the rise of Joseph Banks Rhine's ESP research. Early 20th-century psychical research appears as a doomed enterprise, ruined by political fights, changing research agendas, and declining credibility among physicists and psychologists. The books's readability and scholarship are marred by awkwardly placed and often erroneous references.

OPPENHEIM adopts a drier style and produces a veritable catalogue of the geographies, literature, and personalities of Victorian and Edwardian spiritualism and psychical research. This is the best place to start and an enduring reference guide. Oppenheim explores the internal tensions within the heterogeneous and socially élite worlds of spiritualism, and its difficult relationships with psychical research, theosophy, orthodox science, and Christianity. The underlying motivation of Spiritualists and psychical researchers to reconcile science and religion, she suggests, was undermined by the metaphysical implications of their work and by unscientific protocol. However, this static and anachronistic portrayal of Victorian science undermines any attempt to understand why mesmerism and spiritual phenomena were appealing lines of enquiry for scientists.

COLLINS & PINCH regard scientific authority as a social accomplishment and offer powerful analytical techniques for historians of science and psychical research. Their sociological study of paranormal metal-bending stresses that expertise, rationality, authority, and evidence are only meaningful in the scientifico–social group that produced them (for instance, modern physicists); therefore, they cannot be used unproblematically to judge the claims of a radically different group (notably parapsychologists). The authors suggest that final "scientific" judgements of the paranormal have to appeal instead to wider social and cultural factors.

Turner and Gauld agree that the interest of Victorian intellectuals in the spirit world derived from their quest to discover a universe that was both friendly and devoid of suffering. As TURNER's case studies (including Henry Sidgwick, F.W.H. Myers, A.R. Wallace, and Samuel Butler) show, neither orthodox Christianity (on which they had been reared), nor the dogmatic pronouncements of scientific naturalists such as T.H. Huxley, John Tyndall, and William Clifford Kingdon could resolve these or other fundamental questions in ethics, immortality, and human consciousness. However, spiritualism and psychical research – which, for many of these men were only short-lived interests – promised to fulfil these desires by "the possible discovery of natural entities that could render the natural order commensurable to the ideals of human beings dwelling therein". GAULD makes much less of the broader cultural opposition between science and religion in his intimate studies of the SPR élite of Sidgwick, Myers, and Edmund Gurney. He suggests that, although their evidence for telepathy and the survival of the human personality is inconclusive, it is still admissible and was partly responsible for the successful erosion of the "materialist synthesis" of the 1870s.

MOORE's book covers aspects of American spiritualism and psychical research from the early 19th to the late 20th centuries. Through a series of short biographies of key American spiritualists, he illustrates how spiritual phenomena gave apostates substantial proof of the afterlife and informed post-Civil War social reforms, and how mediumship presented a viable though controversial profession for women. Proceeding to the 20th century, Moore's focus shifts from spiritualism to the controversial establishment of parapsychology; most notably, Rhine's laboratory. Ultimately, the search for the white crows of psychical research – those enduring phenomena that confound scientific generalisation – were undermined not merely because of their rarity and poor replicability, but because of "their meaningless to existing research in terms of either clarifying a problem or pointing toward a line of profitable theoretical and experimental work".

The marked enthusiasm for spiritualism among predominantly 19th-century northern English plebeians has been explored by BARROW, thus complementing the élite's spiritualism examined in Turner, Inglis, and Oppenheim. Plebeian spiritualists, with working-class, anti-Christian and politically radical backgrounds, both reacted to and built on the mid 19th-century secularism and millenarianist ideas of socialists such as Robert Owen. Spiritualism shared with militant atheism and heterodox medical practices a "democratic epistemology" – a knowledge available to everybody, acquired through a self-reliant, anti-dogmatic, and empirical examination of phenomena. Spiritualism's emphasis on self-education resonated well with the autodidact plebeians' desire to reassert control over their lives and gain mental and physical independence from orthodox priestly and medical authorities.

Compared with Moore, OWEN attributes more fluidity to the gendered power relations operating in the séance. Her scholarly study sees the rise of female spiritual mediumship within the context of late Victorian society's shifting perceptions of women, realised in reformed divorce laws and women's rising professional status. Owen interprets the séance as a battle ground in which women could negotiate and subvert patriarchal ideals of femininity. Passivity and spirituality were normative attributes of femininity, but also the very qualities required for control by and communication with invisible spirits. Materialisation séances, spiritual healing, and public inspirational lecturing extended female powers far beyond their legitimate localities, and therefore threatened culturally imposed limits.

Hess's study of three groups in the modern American paranormal scene – New Agers, parapsychologists, and sceptics – has some important methodological lessons for understanding the cultural locus of spiritualism. Drawing on recent work in French structuralist anthropology and the sociologist Thomas Gieryn's useful concept of scientists's "boundary-work", Hess argues that each group uses similar discursive forms to construct disciplinary boundaries: they all legitimize their own practices in relation to symbolically-similar desired and undesired "others", and they all claim superior scientific and social worth, accusing each other of atavism, greed, and fraud. According to Hess, the content of these battles over mind/body and nature/culture can be traced to divergent conceptions of gender. Like Collins & Pinch, this book denies that experimental evidence can authoritatively settle problems of the paranormal, but is optimistic that warring factions can reach some consensus by discussing the cultural, social, and political implications of their work.

RICHARD NOAKES

See also Aether; Gender: general works; Mesmerism

Standardization

Brain, Robert, "Standards and Semiotics", in *Inscribing Science: Scientific Texts and the Materiality of Communication*, edited by Timothy Lenoir, Stanford, California: Stanford University Press, 1998

Foucault, Michel, *Discipline and Punish: The Birth of the Prison*, translated from the French by Alan Sheridan, New York: Pantheon, and London: Allen Lane, 1977 (original edition, 1975)

Grindley, Peter, *Standards, Strategy, and Policy: Cases and Stories*, Oxford and New York: Oxford University Press, 1995

Hawkins, Richard, Robin Mansell and Jim Skea (eds), *Standards, Innovation and Competitiveness: The Politics and Economics of Standards in Natural and Technical Environments*, Aldershot, Hampshire: Elgar, 1995

Kohler, Robert E., *Lords of the Fly: Drosophila Genetics and the Experimental Life*, Chicago: University of Chicago Press, 1994

Krislov, Samuel, *How Nations Choose Product Standards and Standards Change Nations*, Pittsburgh: University of Pittsburgh Press, 1997

Rothery, Brian, *Standards and Certification in Europe*, Aldershot, Hampshire, Gower, 1996

Schmidt, Susanne K. and Raymund Werle, *Coordinating Technology: Studies in the International Standardization of Telecommunications*, Cambridge, Massachusetts: MIT Press, 1998

Within the history of science, metrology has been the main area of concern within the larger topic of standardization. This entry covers the literature on standards that does not fit neatly under metrology. There are general histories of standardization and analyses of the phenomenon of standardization from the perspective of economics, business strategy, and science policy. Finally, there is literature on standardization within science narrowly construed, but which is not about the precision measurement of numbers: language standards and standard organisms.

KRISLOV, a political scientist, aims to give a taxonomy of all kinds of standards worldwide. The core of the book describes the infrastructures for standardization in the US, Europe, Japan, and the Soviet Union. In the US a substantial part of standardization is done outside the main federal institution, the National Standards Bureau, in voluntary associations. This is in contrast to the process in Europe where voluntary associations play a much smaller role and where the nation-state, and now the European Union, is the driving force. Krislov sees a general development toward more flexible standards.

GRINDLEY addresses an audience concerned primarily with business strategy. He examines the development of particular products and processes in which standardization played a crucial role: the video cassette recorder, digital audio, the personal computer, open systems, high-definition television, and telepoint. With the help of these examples, he shows that proprietary standards can drive users to a competitor with a non-proprietary standard, who may then come to define the standard. Business strategists thus have to choose between high margins and isolation on the one hand and low margins and the possibility of a larger network of consumers on the other. Grindley argues that traditional economic theory does not equip the business strategist to deal with such dilemmas. He also discusses the advantages of market-determined standards over regulated standards.

SCHMIDT & WERLE cut a sociologically inspired trail through the thicket of modern telecommunications standard-setting. They describe the maze of institutions involved in the process and describe three case studies of standards negotiated within one of the main institutions, the Comité Consultatif International Télégraphique et Téléphonique. These cases are interactive videotex, telefax, and electronic mail handling (X.400). They argue that, at least within telecommunications, the main form of standardization today occurs in committees of such institutions, and they arrive at a general model for

describing the standardization process by integrating game theory and institutional analysis. The authors deviate from game theory mainly in emphasizing that individual participants cannot always discern the payoff of their decisions, and that much of the work is technical. While acknowledging that participants are also negotiating from established interests, Schmidt & Werle demonstrate that most of the work is carried out in an ethos of compromise, and that finding the technically best solution is more of an impetus toward consensus than is raw politics.

HAWKINS *et al.* deal with standards mainly from a science policy perspective. There are eight papers on the public and private interest in standardization, including one by Paul David, a main contributor to path dependency models according to which the market fails in network technologies because suppliers have an interest in locking in their customers. Here, David reiterates his stance, arguing that governments can constructively intervene by keeping the market from developing monopolistic standards, not by creating standards itself but by subsidizing diversity. He also describes the recent development toward "meta-standards", flexible architectures for system technologies, rather than narrow technical specifications. There are four papers on standard-setting institutions. Much emphasis is given to the newer European Union policies and their integration into national legislation.

ROTHERY is a useful short introduction to the main present-day standards bodies in Europe, excluding the national institutes; their structures are described, with brief histories. The focus is on the institutions of the European Union, such as the European Committee for Standardization (CEN), the European Committee for Electrotechnical Standardization (CENELEC), and the European Telecommunications Standards Institute (ETSI), but the book also covers the International Organization for Standards (ISO) and the International Electrotechnical Commission (IEC). It describes the basic legal structure of each body within the European Union and also the EU's system of environmental and health and safety regulations.

BRAIN places the origins of modern linguistics within the context of the French Third Republic, which vigorously pursued a policy of language standardization along with the dissemination of a whole host of scientific and technical standards. Brain shows how French linguists focused on the spoken language as opposed to the written language with which philologists in the enemy country across the Rhine concerned themselves. The French linguists allied themselves with physiologists who employed scientific apparatus for measuring speech and making sound visible as traces, as in the graphical method. Finally, Brain argues that the patriarch of linguistics, Ferdinand de Saussure, wrote his seminal *Cours de linguistique générale* very much with laboratory phonetics in mind. Furthermore, Saussure thought of semiotics in terms of the metrological conundrum of money: coinage, monetary or verbal, must remain in all cases arbitrary. Value can be determined only by a given unit's relational placement within the system, and not by reference to an external measure.

In the late 20th century research in the life sciences has become standardized to a large extent. There are several institutional bodies that supply not only mass-produced instrumentation, but also mass-produced and certified organic materials, such as the American Type Culture Collection.

KOHLER is the most influential history of standardized organic material. Interestingly, it does not explicitly situate itself within other discussions of standards, and is entirely free of jargon. The book is a history of *Drosophila melanogaster*, the common fruit fly, which was the single most important organism in the development of genetics (and still remains so for the teaching of the discipline). Kohler describes the research in T.H. Morgan's laboratory, especially that by Alfred Sturtevant, Calvin Bridges, and Theodosius Dobzhansky. He describes the tremendous productivity of their work on the fruit fly and how they became the hub of genetics research, supplying flies within a growing network. Kohler also discusses the relationship between the realities of this economy and the research done.

In the French and German languages, the word for standard is norme (or Norm). For this reason, the history of standardization is sometimes seen in a broader context. FOUCAULT's influential text on the history of the prison contrasts the violence of punishment in the old regime with the corrective micro-punishments of 19th-century penitentiaries. He traces the historical creation of norms against which deviance could be defined. He finds this general form of corrective punishment spreading throughout 19th-century society, from prisons to other institutions, such as schools and asylums.

ARNE HESSENBRUCH

See also Measurement; Metrology

Statistics

Ben-David, Joseph, *The Scientist's Role in Society: A Comparative Study*, Englewood Cliffs, New Jersey: Prentice-Hall, 1971

Coleman, William, *Death is a Social Disease: Public Health and Political Economy in Early Industrial France*, Madison: University of Wisconsin Press, 1982

Cullen, M.J., *The Statistical Movement in Early Victorian Britain: The Foundations of Empirical Social Research*, New York: Barnes and Noble, and Hassocks, Sussex: Harvester Press, 1975

Daston, Lorraine, *Classical Probability in the Enlightenment*, Princeton, New Jersey: Princeton University Press, 1988

Eyler, John M., *Victorian Social Medicine: The Ideas and Methods of William Farr*, Baltimore: Johns Hopkins University Press, 1979

Gigerenzer, Gerd *et al.*, *The Empire of Chance: How Probability Changed Science and Everyday Life*, Cambridge and New York: Cambridge University Press, 1989

Krüger, Lorenz, Lorraine J. Daston and Michael Heidelberger (eds), *The Probabilistic Revolution*, vol. 1: *Ideas in History*, Cambridge, Massachusetts: MIT Press, 1987

MacKenzie, Donald A., *Statistics in Britain, 1865–1930: The Social Construction of Scientific Knowledge*, Edinburgh: Edinburgh University Press, 1981

Matthews, J. Rosser, *Quantification and the Quest for Medical Certainty*, Princeton, New Jersey: Princeton University Press, 1995

Morgan, Mary, Lorenz Krüger and Gerd Gigerenzer (eds), *The Probabilistic Revolution*, vol. 2: *Ideas in the Sciences*, Cambridge, Massachusetts: MIT Press, 1987

Porter, Theodore M., *The Rise of Statistical Thinking, 1820–1900*, Princeton, New Jersey: Princeton University Press, 1986

Porter, Theodore M., "The Quantification of Uncertainty after 1700: Statistics Socially Constructed?", in *Acting under Uncertainty: Multidisciplinary Conceptions*, edited by George M. von Furstenberg, Dordrecht and Boston: Kluwer, 1990

Stigler, Stephen M., *The History of Statistics: The Measurement of Uncertainty before 1900*, Cambridge, Massachusetts: Belknap Press of Harvard University Press, 1986

Within the last 15 to 20 years, the history of statistics has emerged as a major field of scholarly inquiry within the history of science. Although the reasons for this upsurge of interest are multifaceted, one explanation may be the highly ambiguous position of statistical reasoning within the history of modern scientific thinking, as both culturally pervasive (numbers can be used to explain almost anything) and philosophically problematical (as it offers only probabilities, rather than the ideal of scientific certainty). In addition, the term itself has undergone numerous mutations during the past three centuries and its meaning is often highly context-dependent; it can refer to a purely descriptive enterprise concerned only with the cataloguing of social facts, or to a highly sophisticated set of mathematical techniques used to make inferences about aggregative data. Since this intellectual diversity is reflected in the literature on the history of statistics, this survey will highlight the following thematic approaches: "heroic" accounts of pioneering statistical theoreticians; statistics as a tool for social description; the professionalization of statistics; and the role of statistics in remaking modern scientific disciplines and society itself.

There is a well-established tradition within the history of science that focuses on "heroic" scientific theorists. Within the literature on the history of statistics, the books by STIGLER and PORTER (1986) fall into this broad category, despite notable methodological differences between the two authors. Stigler writes as a statistician, focusing on the technical and mathematical aspects, whereas Porter is a historian of science, and focuses more on placing the important statistical theorists within their broader social and intellectual contexts. Although addressing different audiences, the works are complementary in that together they provide both the "internal" and "external" factors that motivated such statistical pioneers as P.S. Laplace, L.A.J. Quételet, H.T. Buckle, W.H. Lexis, G.T. Fechner, Francis Galton, Richard Lovell Edgeworth, Karl Pearson, and G. Udny Yule.

Even though these statistical theorists are often remembered today for their mathematical aptitude, the term "statistics" had little connection with mathematics prior to the late 19th century. As can be inferred etymologically, "state-istics" was associated from the mid-18th century onwards with descriptive numbers that were of interest to political states. This interest intensified during the first half of the 19th century, following in the wake of the political, economic, and public health changes wrought by the French and industrial revolutions. Accounts of early statistical enthusiasts can be found in Daston, Cullen, Coleman, and Eyler. Even though DASTON'S focus is on probabilistic rather than statistical theorists, she does discuss the role of statistical methods within the emerging life insurance industry in the 18th and 19th centuries. CULLEN writes a social history of politically-motivated early statistical advocates, while COLEMAN and EYLER provide biographies of two important players in these movements – the physicians Louis René Villermé and William Farr respectively. The section on "Society" in KRÜGER, DASTON & HEIDELBERGER offers multiple perspectives on statistics as social-fact-gathering during the 19th century within a myriad of national contexts.

With Francis Galton's discovery of the method of correlation in 1888, a process began whereby statistics acquired the additional meaning of a tool of mathematical inference, paving the way for the professionalization of statistics as an applied mathematical discipline. Within the history of science, the professionalization of new scientific disciplines has become an increasingly active area of scholarly inquiry, particularly as the focus has shifted from the study of "science as ideas" toward the study of "science as social practice". Nevertheless, there are methodological differences even among those who write from a more sociological orientation, as the works by Ben-David and MacKenzie demonstrate. BEN-DAVID adopts the view that society provides the institutional settings within which science takes place; however, society does not determine which scientific theories eventually triumph. Applied specifically to the professionalization of statistics, Ben-David argues that it emerged as a new scholarly discipline in the United States rather than Britain (the home of the major statistical pioneers) because the American university system was less rigid, thereby permitting the creation of new scholarly specialities. MACKENZIE, by contrast, adopts the view that society actually determines the content of scientific theory, and that scientific knowledge is "socially constructed". Applying this idea to the professionalization of statistics, MacKenzie argues that the structure of modern statistical theory reflects the interest in eugenics held by the early statistical theoreticians. A historiographical overview of these various sociologically-informed accounts is provided by PORTER (1990). The story of statistical professionalization is told as a continuous historical narrative in GIGERENZER.

With the emergence of statistics as a standard technique of scientific inference, new standards of rigor and objectivity have been introduced in such varied fields as psychology, sociology, economics, biology, and physics. In addition, entirely new domains have been subjected to the rule of number, ranging from baseball to mental testing, public opinion, and the determination of therapeutic efficacy in medicine. These developments are broadly surveyed in Gigerenzer, and the application of statistics to 20th-century scientific disciplines is given fuller treatment in MORGAN, KRÜGER & GIGERENZER. The history of statistical attempts to establish therapeutic efficacy in the 19th and 20th centuries is surveyed in MATTHEWS.

J. ROSSER MATTHEWS

See also Biometrics; Error Theory; Probability; Public Health

Steno, Nicolaus *see* Stensen, Niels

Stensen, Niels   1638–1686
Danish anatomist, geologist, and bishop

Bierbaum, Max and Adolf Faller, *Niels Stensen*, Münster: Aschendorff, 1979

Heida, Ulrike, *Niels Stensen in seinen Beziehungen zu medizinischen Fachkollegen seiner Zeit*, Berlin: Grosse, 1986

Hsu, Kuang-Tai, *Nicolaus Steno and His Sources: The Legacy of the Medical and Chemical Traditions in His Early Geological Writings*, dissertation, University of Oklahoma, 1992

Kardel, Troels, *Steno: Life, Science, Philosophy*, Copenhagen: Munksgaard, 1994

Larsen, Knud and Gustav Scherz (eds), *Nicolai Stenonis opera theologica*, 2 vols, Copenhagen: Nyt Nordisk, 1944–47

Maar, Vilhelm (ed.), *Nicolai Stenonis opera philosophica*, 2 vols, Copenhagen: Vilhelm Tryde, 1910

Poulsen, Jacob E. and Egill Snorrason (eds), *Nicolaus Steno, 1638–1686: A Reconsideration by Danish Scientists*, Gentofte, Denmark: Nordisk Insulinlaboratorium, 1986

Rudwick, Martin J.S., *The Meaning of Fossils: Episodes in the History of Paleontology*, London: Macdonald, and New York: Elsevier, 1972; revised edition, New York: Science History Publications, 1976

Scherz, Gustav, assisted by Hans Ræder (eds), *Nicolai Stenonis Epistolae*, 2 vols, Copenhagen: Nyt Nordisk, 1952

Scherz, Gustav (ed.), "Steno Geological Papers", translated by Alex J. Pollock, in *Acta Historica Scientiarum Naturalium et Medicinalium*, vol. 20, Odense: Odense University Press, 1969

Scherz, Gustav, *Niels Stensen: Eine Biographie*, 2 vols, edited by Harriet M. Hansen and Franz Peter Sonntag, Leipzig: St Benno, 1987–88

The literature on Niels Stensen, also known as Nicolaus Steno, is immense, and includes several thousand articles. This is partly because he contributed to fields that are now considered distinct: anatomy, geology, and theology. Moreover, Stensen is credited with several discoveries in science, and is also a prominent figure in Catholicism; indeed, he was beatified and canonized in 1986. The literature is very much framed by the disciplinary boundaries of the 20th century, and there is barely any literature that attempts to contextualize Stensen in the way that has been done for other figures of early modern Europe, such as Galileo.

This division of Stensen's activities into distinct spheres is apparent in the collections of his voluminous writings. MAAR started off this trend with his collection of the writings deemed to be philosophical or scientific. LARSEN & SCHERZ then collected the "theological" writings, and SCHERZ (1952) the correspondence. All volumes contain Stensen's writings in the original language, which is mainly Latin. It is possible to find translations of many of these, but they are scattered and so cannot been mentioned here – with the exception of SCHERZ

(1969), in which the "geological" papers are collated and translated into English.

The standard biography of Niels Stensen is SCHERZ (1987–88), who is also responsible for the entry in the *Dictionary of Scientific Biography*. Scherz is an Austrian-born Danish Redemptorist, and sharply separates Stensen's scientific and ecclesiastical life: volume 1 deals with the former, and volume 2 with the latter. He distinguishes four periods in Stensen's scientific life. The first period was devoted to research on glands and the lymph system, and covers his discovery of the duct of the parotid gland, described in his *De musculis et glandulis* (1664). During the next period of two to three years, Stensen studied the heart, and concluded in his *Elementorum myologiæ specimen* (1666–67) that the heart was no hearth, as Descartes had believed, but a muscle. The third period covers his anatomical research of the brain and the embryo, *Discours . . . sur l'anatomie du cerveau* (1669), in which Stensen repudiated Cartesian speculations on the function of the epiphysis, and for the first time offered a correct explanation of the female reproductive system. Finally, during the fourth period, Stensen established geology and crystallography as scientific disciplines, publishing *De solido intra solidum naturaliter contento dissertationis prodromus* (1669) and *Indice de cose naturali* (1671–72). Stensen undertook his investigations in palaontology and mineralogy, mostly in Tuscany and in the Alps, in the service of Grand Duke Ferdinand II of Medici and the Accademia del Cimento. Scherz documents how he developed an increasingly critical attitude towards the teachings of Descartes, and, although initially attracted to Spinoza's system, eventually also turned away from that. Scherz argues that Stensen felt himself much closer to Galileo. In 1667, Stensen converted to Catholicism, after which his scientific work gradually decreased until it ceased altogether with his ordination in 1675, and he subsequently served as bishop in Hannover, Münster, Hamburg, and finally Schwerin.

BIERBAUM & FALLER stress the inner unity of Stensen's adventurous career, not in the sense that his scientific and religious ideas were one, but that he concentrated wholeheartedly on his activities, whether engaged in research or charity.

MAAR, a Danish physiologist and medical historian, in his brief and clear introduction to Stensen's philosophical works, concludes that Stensen distinguished himself through his method: "He asked his questions and gave his answers as a scientist of the 20th century; and, deeply religious though he was, he never for a moment introduced any supernatural element into his solutions of problems of natural science". HEIDA, a German historian of science, also highlights Stensen's inductive empiricism, as opposed to the deductions of Cartesian rationalism.

The contributors to POULSEN & SNORRASON discuss the relationship between Stensen's scientific research and religious beliefs. Billeskov Jansen contributes a biographical piece, and there are essays on Stensen's work on glands, muscles, the brain, paleontology and crystallography, geology, and on Steno's relationship with Ray. Finally, Snorrason discusses Stensen as "illustrative expositor"; Stensen did a great number of anatomical drawings himself, and some of them are reproduced here.

RUDWICK, a historian of science, finds that Stensen abandoned the earlier encyclopedic tradition of compiling all previous opinions on the subject, and made a sharp distinction between his observed facts and his "conjectures", listing the observations first, and then citing them at appropriate points in his arguments, almost in the manner of a mathematical theorem. In contrast, HSU, a historian of geology, has interpreted the timidity of Stensen's conjectures as a matter of style and presentation.

KARDEL, a general medical practitioner, sees no such timidity in Stensen's writings, but rather straightforward arguments against his professors in both Amsterdam and Copenhagen, and against Descartes's followers in Paris. Furthermore, Kardel emphasizes Stensen's persistent effort to collect arguments against his own propositions; only when having failed to find contradictory evidence, did Stensen make known his conclusion.

DAN CH. CHRISTENSEN

See also Anatomy; Denmark; Geology; Paleontology

Surgery

Allbutt, T. Clifford, *The Historical Relations of Medicine and Surgery to the End of the Sixteenth Century*, London and New York: Macmillan, 1905; reprinted, New York: AMS Press, 1978

Atkinson, Richard S. and Thomas B. Boulton (eds), *The History of Anaesthesia*, London: Royal Society of Medicine Services, 1988

Billings, John Shaw, "The History and Literature of Surgery", in *System of Surgery*, vol. 1, edited by Frederic S. Dennis, Philadelphia: Lea Brothers, 1895, 17–144

Breasted, James Henry, *The Edwin Smith Surgical Papyrus: Published in Facsimile and Hieroglyphic Transliteration with Translation and Commentary*, 2 vols, Chicago: University of Chicago Press, 1930

Cooter, Roger, *Surgery and Society in Peace and War: Orthopaedics and the Organization of Modern Medicine, 1880–1948*, London: Macmillan, 1993

Dally, Ann, *Women under the Knife: A History of Surgery*, London: Hutchinson Radius, 1991; New York: Routledge, 1992

De Moulin, Daniel, *A History of Surgery: with Emphasis on the Netherlands*, Dordrecht and Boston: Nijhoff, 1988

Faulconer, Albert, Jr. and Thomas E. Keys, *Foundations of Anesthesiology*, Springfield, Illinois: Thomas, 1965

Gelfand, Toby, *Professionalizing Modern Medicine: Paris Surgeons and Medical Science and Institutions in the Eighteenth Century*, Westport, Connecticut: Greenwood Press, 1980

Haller, Albrecht von, *Bibliotheca Chirurgica: Qua Scripta ad artem Chirurgicam Facientia a rerum intiis recensentur*, 2 vols, Bern: Haller, and Basel: Schweighauser, 1774–75

Lawrence, Christopher (ed.), *Medical Theory, Surgical Practice: Studies in the History of Surgery*, London and New York: Routledge, 1992

Majno, Guido, *The Healing Hand: Man and Wound in the Ancient World*, Cambridge, Massachusetts: Harvard University Press, 1975

Malgaigne, J.F., *Surgery and Ambroise Paré*, translated by Wallace B. Hamby, Norman: University of Oklahoma Press, 1965

Pouchelle, Marie Christine, *The Body and Surgery in the Middle Ages*, New Brunswick, New Jersey: Rutgers University Press, and Cambridge: Polity Press/Blackwell, 1990

Reilly, Philip, *The Surgical Solution: A History of Involuntary Sterilization in the United States*, Baltimore: Johns Hopkins University Press, 1991

George Tiemann and Co., *The American Armamentarium Chirurgicum and the American Surgical Instrument Trade*, New York: Ludwig, 1889; with an introduction by James E. Edmonson and F. Terry Hambrecht, San Francisco: Norman Publishing, and Boston: Printer's Devil, 1989

Wangensteen, Owen H. and Sara D. Wangensteen, *The Rise of Surgery: From Empiric Craft to Scientific Discipline*, Minneapolis: University of Minnesota Press, 1978

Zimmerman, Leo and Ilza Veith, *Great Ideas in the History of Surgery*, Baltimore: Williams and Wilkins, 1961; 2nd revised edition, New York: Dover, 1967

More than their medical counterparts, surgeons have been trained to acquire specific manual skills. Handbooks and manuals of surgery have typically retained the ancient four-fold classification of surgery as an art, or craft, whose practitioners (i) joined unnaturally separated parts, (ii) separated preternaturally joined parts, (iii) removed superfluous parts, and (iv) supplied those parts that were wanting. Surgical writings, such as Richard Boulton's *A System of Rational and Practical Chirurgery* (1713), also specified that surgery was a "manual" operation, through which its practitioners "by the use of Instruments, or the Assistance of Hands" would aim to "relieve those accidental diseases" that their patients were "externally subject to".

Surgical histories have appeared in print as far back as the Enlightenment. HALLER's two-volume *Bibliotheca Chirurgica* provided contemporaries with the most comprehensive, topically-organized, bibliographical reference source of key works on surgical history. Its historical usefulness as a source book of early texts and treatises remains unparalleled.

The earliest medical papyrus, known today as the Smith papyrus, describes 48 cases of surgical operations, including those on injuries to the head, chest, and spine. BREASTED's facsimile and hieroglyphic transliteration and translation claims to disclose, "for the first time the human mind peering into the mysteries of the human body, and recognizing conditions and processes there as due to intelligible causes".

MAJNO gathered evidence from Mesopotamia to Rome from the time of Galen (AD 130–200), and persuasively argues that of all surgical conditions, examining the historical care of wounds provides the most insight towards understanding the surgical treatments of the past. Unlike any other surgical source book, this work reports the findings of reconstructed ancient experiments in 20th-century laboratory settings, whereby the efficacy of ancient remedies in treating modern experimentally-produced wounds are evaluated.

Allbutt, Billings, and Wangensteen & Wangensteen all provide chronologically descriptive accounts of what they deem to be the key advances or progresses of surgery. ALLBUTT's is a thorough history, while BILLINGS provides what remains the most complete, yet concise, bibliographical guide to surgeons and their practices. WANGENSTEEN & WANGENSTEEN's 785-page "assessment of surgery's progress" takes the form of an "appraisal of achievements, in the operations of emergency and dire necessity, followed by an inquiry into factors that led surgery from empiricism to an acceptance of scientific observation and discoveries in other disciplines". Their exhaustively descriptive reviews of surgery are topographically divided into sections on specific surgical conditions, including wound management in amputation, lithotomy, gastric surgery, ectopic pregnancy, and vascular surgery. The historical importance of anesthesia, antiseptic technique, hospital design, and the germ theory of disease also receive considerable coverage. The extensive bibliography, which includes full citations of most of the key primary surgical sources, provides a thorough repository of information.

In order to further understanding of the most influential surgical writings, ZIMMERMAN & VEITH have reprinted key passages from primary sources discussing surgical concepts and techniques. The GEORGE TIEMANN & CO. catalogue provides an excellent visual accompaniment to studies of 19th- and 20th-century tools and technologies of surgery.

The Renaissance surgeon, Ambroise Paré, popularized Andreas Vesalius's revolutionary work *De Humani Corporis Fabrica Libri Septum*, in a condensed version for surgeons. Following the monumental ideas of Vesalius, Paré broke from a long tradition of orthodox practice and urged his readers to observe and gather their own information about the body. MALGAIGNE thoroughly establishes the social and medical contexts within which Paré worked, in order to allow for a fuller appreciation of his specific contributions. Most notably, Paré's exposure to the horrors of war provided him with ample opportunity to treat the wounds inflicted from the new military tool, gunpowder. This work also reviews his reintroduction of the use of ligatures to stop bleeding vessels, a procedure that improved the success of amputations, and his self-designed experiments to test the reputed efficacy of antidotes on specific poisons.

Renaissance thinking also features prominently in DE MOULIN's chronological description of Dutch surgery. Although this work spans the course of western history, it is most useful in its survey of Dutch innovations and influences on surgery from the 14th to the 20th centuries. Like Malgaigne's work on the French Paré, De Moulin describes surgical progress within the cultural and political background of the Netherlands.

Nowhere does the socio–political influence on surgery appear more pronounced that in post-revolutionary France. GELFAND deftly constructs an account of how changing social, institutional, and conceptual factors were all interlinked with the professionalization of surgery in France. The pre-revolutionary structure of surgery – already exalted from its age-old apprentice craft image – was well-suited for the post-1794 citizenry, who deemed anatomy as a more practical basis for a profession than the speculative physiology of medical practice. Although French surgeons and their techniques had long been emulated by their continental and British counterparts, the new official view of surgical education after the French

Revolution created a successful model for the subsequent professionalization of medicine.

Apart from Gelfand's work, those works previously discussed focus on the progressive rise of surgery, brought about, so their authors would have us believe, by the introduction of new techniques. However, Pouchelle and Lawrence contribute more pithy accounts of surgical thinking. POUCHELLE focuses on the life of the 14th-century surgeon, Henri de Mondeville, in an elaborate attempt to infer from a surgeon's writing a more general description of contemporary society. Beyond describing the surgeons "profession", she uses his *Chirurgerie* to develop a broad account of medieval attitudes toward the body.

LAWRENCE has offered a promising "theoretical model" for redirecting the literature of surgical history. He explicitly draws upon a suggestion by Owsei Temkin for thinking about surgical "theory" in order to construct a historical account from the "surgical point of view": for example, surgical "theory" of the late Enlightenment may be discussed as the integration of a surgeon's interest in local pathology with his understanding and treatment of "surgical" disease. In addition to his own introduction on the history and historiography of surgery, Lawrence has collected writings from other authors, including the following studies: a profile of the types of patients and diseases treated by a 17th-century London surgeon; scrofula from a culturally-constructed viewpoint; the usefulness of "surgical modes of thought" in developing methods of physical examination; the physiological underpinning of John Hunter's surgical writings; the Listerian "revolution" of surgery; the shift from conservative to radical surgical operations; distinctive clinical and anatomical approaches to rectal surgery and to the use of chloroform; and the use of surgical instruments as documents of surgical history.

COOTER analyzes the conceptual, political, and technical reorganization of British medicine from the late 19th- to the mid-20th centuries. He argues that a new "category" of patients developed from the crippled children, wounded soldiers, and injured workers of wartime, which were ultimately placed at the center of welfare policy-making. Using surgical conditions, Cooter shows that modern medicine was shaped by philanthropy, war, labor, capital, and the state. Although the focus of this work is British medicine, Cooter makes extensive comparisons with the United States.

Although few topics in medical history have attracted as much attention as anesthesia, there are few reliable comprehensive historical overviews. FAULCONER & KEYS reproduce various original works, from Andreas Vesalius's *Artificial Respiration on a Sow* (1543) to Linus Pauling's *A Molecular Theory of General Anesthesia* (1961). The editors have focused on the topics of respiratory physiology, inhalation anesthesia, conduction anesthesia, intravenous anesthesia, as well as accessory techniques including hypodermic injection, blood pressure measurement, and premedication. Investigations into measuring the depth of anesthesia, and theories of narcosis are also covered. ATKINSON & BOULTON is the collection with the most varied topics on the history of anesthesia; its articles focus on the origins of anesthesia, the introduction and spread of various techniques, the organization of this specialty of medical practice, and the history of resuscitative care, in addition to the important agents, apparatuses, and individuals of the field.

Reilly and Dally each provide an in-depth view of two popular, but unrelated, surgical topics. REILLY focuses on the era of the American eugenics movement of the early to mid-19th century, which aimed at improving the genetic condition of human society by preventing those individuals deemed "socially inadequate" or physically "defective" from reproducing through enforced surgical sterilization. DALLY has produced perhaps the most historically acceptable account of women's surgery, by balancing the over-rhetorical, ahistorical accounts of many feminist authors with the factual evidence of many historical cases.

PHILIP K. WILSON

See also Anatomy; Medical Instruments; Plastic Surgery

Sweden

Beretta, Marco and Tore Frängsmyr (eds), *Sidereus Nuncius and Stella Polaris: The Scientific Relations between Italy and Sweden in Early Modern History*, Canton, Massachusetts: Science History Publications, 1997

Broberg, Gunnar and Nils Roll Hansen (eds), *Eugenics and the Welfare State: Sterilization Policy in Denmark, Sweden, Norway, and Finland*, East Lansing: Michigan State University Press, 1996

Crawford, Elisabeth, *The Beginnings of the Nobel Institution: The Science Prizes, 1901–1915*, Cambridge and New York: Cambridge University Press, 1984

Crawford, Elisabeth, *Arrhenius: From Ionic Theory to the Greenhouse Effect*, Canton, Massachusetts: Science House Publishing, 1996

Fehrman, Carl and Håkan Westling, *Lund and Learning: An Informal History of Lund University*, translated by Alan Crozier, Lund: Lund University Press, 1987

Frängsmyr, Tore (ed.), *Science in Sweden: The Royal Swedish Academy of Sciences, 1739–1989*, Canton, Massachusetts: Science History Publications, 1989

Friedman, Robert Marc, *Appropriating the Weather: Vilhelm Bjerknes and the Construction of a Modern Meterology*, Ithaca, New York: Cornell University Press, 1989

Fries, Robert E., *A Short History of Botany in Sweden*, Uppsala: Almqvist & Wiksell, 1950

Klinge, Matti, *Professorer*, Helsingfors: Söderström, 1989

Lindqvist, Svante (ed.), *Center on the Periphery: Historical Aspects of 20th Century Swedish Physics*, Canton, Massachusetts: Science History Publications, 1993

Lindroth, Sten (ed.), *Swedish Men of Science 1650–1950*, translated by Burnett Anderson, Stockholm: Swedish Institute, 1952

Lindroth, Sten, *Kungl. Svenska vetenskapsakademiens historia*, 3 vols, Stockholm: Almqvist & Wiksell, 1967

Lindroth, Sten, *Svensk lärdomshistoria* [A History of Swedish Learning], 4 vols, Stockholm: Norstedts, 1975–81

Lindroth, Sten, *A History of Uppsala University, 1477–1977*, Uppsala: Almqvist & Wiksell, 1977

Naturvetenskapernas historia i Sverige intill år 1800/Natural science in Sweden up to 1800, Uppsala: Lychnosbibliotek. (including volumes by N.V.E. Nordenmark on astronomy,

1959; Hugo Olsson on chemistry, 1971; Herman Richter
on geography, 1959; Gunnar Eriksson on botany, 1969)

Schück, Henrik *et al.*, *Nobel: The Man and His Prizes*,
Stockholm: Sohlman, and Norman: University of
Oklahoma Press, 1950; 2nd edition, Amsterdam: Elsevier,
1962

There is a great deal of literature on the history of science in
Sweden, although most of it is only obtainable in Swedish, and
there is no general handbook. However, in English there is a
growing number of monographs published in the series
Uppsala Studies in the History of Science. The Uppsala department of History of Science and Learning also publishes a
newsletter on Scandinavian activities within the field.

LINDROTH (1952) covers 29 prominent Swedish scientists.
With the exception of Lindroth himself, all the contributors
to this volume were scientists who gave a short portrait of
the "father figure" of their respective scientific disciplines. The
selection is reasonably balanced, with an emphasis on the
period before 1800, which might be called the golden age
of Swedish science, and including individuals such as Olaus
Rudbeck, Emanuel Swedenborg, Anders Celsius, Carl
Linnaeus, Pehr Wilhelm Wargentin, and Torbern Bergman. At
the other end of the time-scale, there are short essays on the
Nobel prize winners Svante Arrhenius, Allvar Gullstrand, The
Svedberg, and Manne Siegbahn. This mainly biographical
handbook is, of course, to some extent outdated, but it remains
a useful introduction to the subject despite its avoidance of
more problematic subjects, such as the geneticist Herman
Nilsson Ehles's attraction to Nazi ideology.

LINDROTH (1975–81), in four volumes, is a very comprehensive history of Swedish science and learning. The first three
volumes give a full and authoritative narrative of Swedish academic scholarship, and are especially strong on the Latin culture
of the 17th century. (Lindroth began as a historian of
Renaissance medicine.) Objections could be raised against his
overly academic and, perhaps, non-theoretical standpoint, but
this work remains an impressive feat and a classic. Unfortunately, it was never completed. The fourth volume, of which
approximately half was written, covered the romantic period
and was posthumously published by Lindroth's successor to
the chair in Uppsala, Gunnar Eriksson.

LINDROTH (1967), a three-volume history of the Swedish
Academy of Sciences, covers the classical period of Swedish
science from 1739, the founding year of the Academy, to 1818,
the end of the period in which Berzelius was General Secretary,
after which the Academy experienced a period of decline. As
could be expected from a poly-historian such as Lindroth, the
account is rich in detail and colour, and makes massive use of
the archival material. Throughout, much attention is paid to
the external aspects of 18th-century science; certainly, it was
not only natural science that was on the agenda, but also
philology, husbandry, and philanthropy. Thanks to Lindroth's
work, the history of the Academy is unusually well-covered,
although neither of these two works are available in any other
language. As a supplement, however, FRÄNGSMYR is useful.
In 10 essays, various aspects of the activities of the Academy
are considered up to the post-war period, including such
general themes as the utilitarian aspects of Swedish science,
scientific travel in Sweden, the polar expeditions, and environ-

mental protection. There is also a chapter on the "Benefits of
the Nobel Prizes" by Elisabeth Crawford.

The Nobel archives (at the Royal Academy of Sciences) have
been used by CRAWFORD (1996) and FRIEDMAN in their
monographs on Svante Arrhenius and Vilhelm Bjerknes.
Crawford and Friedman both shed light on the committees,
the conditions, and the coteries of the physical sciences at the
Stockholm Högskola and Uppsala University, where the prizes
were decided. Crawford in particular describes in detail the
small Swedish scientific community, located not so much on
the periphery as might be expected, and with good contacts
with the important German universities. Her story mainly
covers physics and chemistry, and leaves out the other sciences.
The only general history in English on the Nobel prize was
edited by the literary historian Henrik SCHÜCK, but this is
mainly a reference rather than an analytical work.

LINDROTH (1977) brings the history up to modern times
in a short but useful survey, published on the occasion of the
university's fifth centennial in 1977. The University of Lund
has one text in English on its history, by FEHRMAN & WEST-
LING, although this is fairly brief. Åbo (Turku) University in
Finland, a part of the Swedish empire up to 1809, has been
the object of a massive study by KLINGE, which is a gold
mine of information on the inner life of north Germanic
science and learning during the period of the Swedish Baltic
power (available in Finnish, Swedish and (abridged) German
versions). BERETTA, in an instructive catalogue of an exhibition at the Stockholm Museum of Natural History, covers the
relationship between Italian and Swedish science in the period
1500–1800 in pictures, with a long introduction by the editor.

There are not many special histories of Swedish science. In
Swedish, there is the series on different disciplines up to 1800
(*NATURVETENSKAPERNAS*). In English, there is only FRIES
on botany, which covers the whole history up to its year of
publication, and is a useful reference work containing a large
number of names. The 500-page volume edited by LINDQVIST
contains a multifaceted history of 20th-century Swedish
physics, including a shrewd essay by the editor on the role of
physics in cultural discourse. About 20 scholars contribute,
which sometimes makes the narrative fragmentary, but the
systematic bibliography, of some 60 pages, adds to the usefulness of this volume, which also focuses on the general problem
of the interplay between a small nation and the general development of science elsewhere. BROBERG & ROLL HANSEN,
a recent comparative volume on the Scandinavian eugenics
movement, should also be mentioned, because it attempts to
understand science (or pseudo-science) within a Lutheran,
social democratic context. In Nordic countries, and particularly Sweden, sterilization became especially prevalent as part
of a progressive, scientistic programme during the inter-war
period, which continued into the 1950s.

GUNNAR BROBERG

See also Nobel Institution

Sydenham, Thomas 1624–1689

English physician

Cook, Harold J., *The Decline of the Old Medical Regime in Stuart London*, Ithaca, New York: Cornell University Press, 1986

Debus, Allen G. (ed.), *Medicine in Seventeenth-Century England: A Symposium*, Berkeley: University of California Press, 1974

Dewhurst, Kenneth (ed.), *Dr Thomas Sydenham, 1624–1689: His Life and Original Writings*, London: Wellcome Historical Medical Library, and Berkeley: University of California Press, 1966

Payne, Joseph Frank, *Thomas Sydenham*, London: Fisher Unwin, and New York: Longmans Green, 1900

Pechey, John (ed.), *The Whole Works of That Excellent Practical Physician, Dr Thomas Sydenham*, translated from the Latin by Pechy, London: Printed for Wellington and Castle, 1696

Sloan, A.W., *English Medicine in the Seventeenth Century*, Durham: Dirham Academic Press, 1996

Williamson, Richard Thomas, *English Physicians of the Past: Short Sketches*, Newcastle upon Tyne: Reid, 1923

Thomas Sydenham, generally regarded as the leading physician of his day, was a soldier before he became a physician, which probably accounts for his empirical and practical attitude towards medicine. After a few months as a student at Oxford in 1642, he joined the Parliamentary army in which he served with distinction. He returned to Oxford in 1646 and, in 1648, became a Bachelor of Medicine by "actual creation", without undergoing all the classical studies normally required for the degree. He studied medicine privately at Montpellier under Charles Barbeyrac, and then spent his professional life as a private physician, first in Westminster and then in London, licensed by the College of Physicians, but seeking no Fellowship, although he became eligible on becoming a Doctor of Medicine at Cambridge in 1676.

Sydenham believed and taught that more could be learned about disease from studying the patient than from books, and he ignored the considerable advances in medical science made in his lifetime by William Harvey, Marcello Malpighi, Thomas Willis, and others. His medical treatment was traditional, usually ineffective, and often dangerous, although he rid the pharmacopoeia of many dangerous and obnoxious remedies. His contribution to medicine was his insistence on the careful examination and follow-up of the patient, recommended by Hippocrates but not usual in the 17th century. His contribution to science was an attempt to classify diseases as contemporary botanists and zoologists were attempting to classify plants and animals, an early stage in what was to become the important science of vital statistics.

PECHEY, a close associate and friend of Sydenham, published in 1696 *The Whole Works of that Excellent Practical Physician, Dr Thomas Sydenham*. In his preface he refers briefly to Sydenham's life and to his character: "He was religious, loyal, learned, and of a solid judgement and sterling honesty. But I shall say no more of him; his book will be the best and most lasting monument of his face." Pechey's book contains all Sydenham's medical writings, including the "Epistolary Discourses" to other physicians who had sought his advice. He was particularly interested in epidemic diseases and, like Hippocrates, recognised that these tended to occur in particular localities and in particular seasons. Later translations of Sydenham's works are by Swan (1743), Latham (1848), and Comrie (1992).

PAYNE wrote an excellent biography of Thomas Sydenham, in which he points out that "he had the good fortune to obtain a degree at the beginning instead of the end of his student's course". At Oxford, Sydenham would meet many students destined to achieve distinction in science, including Willis, Wren, Boyle, Hooke, and Lower, but he seems to have been little influenced by them, and later tended to ignore the advances in science for which they were responsible. According to Payne, Sydenham usually wrote in English but, to make his works more "respectable", they were translated into Latin by his friends, especially Gilbert Havers (a classical scholar) and John Mapletoft (a medical colleague). They were then translated back into English by various people.

WILLIAMSON calls Sydenham the "father" of English clinical medicine, and quotes him as saying "that the art of medicine was to be learnt only from its practice and its exercise". He had little faith in book-learning and believed that the greatest advances in medicine come from careful study of individual patients. Williamson records the formation of the Sydenham Society in 1843, and its revival in 1858. The object of the society was to reprint rare and expensive books, and translations of foreign works, for the benefit of English medical practitioners.

DEWHURST's biography is rather adulatory. He writes, "The sound judgement and acute observations of Thomas Sydenham, the English Hippocrates, freed clinical medicine from the last vestiges of medievalism and set the pattern for further progress." However, although Sydenham certainly sustained the Hippocratic doctor–patient relationship, his treatment remained essentially medieval. Dewhurst includes several of Sydenham's "Epistolary Discourses".

DEBUS is the editor of a *Festschrift* in honour of C.D. O'Malley, a distinguished medical historian. The key references to Sydenham are the chapters by L.J. Rather entitled "Pathology of Mid-Century: A Reassessment of Thomas Willis and Thomas Sydenham", and A.W. Franklin on "Clinical Medicine". Rather stresses the difference in approach by Willis and by Sydenham to the study of disease. Willis, himself a distinguished anatomist and experimental scientist, was greatly influenced by the discoveries being made at the time by other scientists. However, these were largely ignored by Sydenham, who believed that no useful medical knowledge could be gained from pathological anatomy or laboratory experiments. In the chapter on clinical medicine, Franklin again emphasises the differences between Sydenham and Willis, and also describes the practice of some other contemporary physicians. Willis and Sydenham both examined their patients carefully, but Willis continued his study post-mortem when practicable. He rejected the traditional theory that disease is due to an imbalance of the four "humours", whereas Sydenham still accepted this classical doctrine, merely adding the observation that individual diseases might attack particular organs.

COOK makes only brief reference to Sydenham, but stresses his belief that medicine should be learnt by apprenticeship and not from books, and that neither anatomy nor physiology would advance the practice of medicine. Cook states that Sydenham did not attribute disease to an imbalance of the humours, which contradicts some of Sydenham's own writings and that of most other writers on the subject, but all are agreed that Sydenham believed that some individual diseases could be identified, and that he attempted to classify fevers.

SLOAN praises Sydenham's return to the Hippocratic tradition by examining the actual patient, instead of merely his horoscope and possibly his urine, as was common practice. His description of some diseases, including gout and "Sydenham's chorea", are unrivalled. Unfortunately, Sydenham's antipathy to the discoveries in experimental science and in anatomy that were being made by his contemporaries, coupled with his own great prestige, did more to impede than to advance the progress of medicine. Sydenham and other physicians of the time were working within the limits of a traditional, though false, concept of disease, and there were few effective cures at the time; in fact the therapy of the period, which usually included bleeding and polypharmacy, often did more harm than good. Sydenham famously acknowledged this when he confessed that on occasion, "I have consulted my patient's safety and my own reputation most effectively *by doing nothing at all.*"

A.W. SLOAN

T

Taxonomy

Allen, David Elliston, *The Naturalist in Britain: A Social History*, London: Allen Lane, 1976; 2nd edition, Princeton, New Jersey: Princeton University Press, 1994

Douglas, M., *Purity and Danger: An Analysis of Concepts of Pollution and Taboo*, London: Routledge and Kegan Paul, 1960; New York: Praeger, 1969

Foucault, Michel, *The Order of Things: An Archaeology of the Human Sciences*, translated from the French by Alan Sheridan, New York: Pantheon Books, and London: Tavistock, 1970 (original edition, 1966)

Lovejoy, A.O., *The Great Chain of Being: A Study of the History of an Idea*, Cambridge, Massachusetts: Harvard University Press, 1936

Mayr, Ernst, *The Growth of Biological Thought: Diversity, Evolution, and Inheritance*, Cambridge, Massachusetts: Harvard University Press, 1982

Sloan, P.R., "John Locke, John Ray, and the Problem of the Natural System", *Journal of the History of Biology*, 5 (1972): 153

Vernon, K., "Desperately Seeking Status: Evolutionary Systematics and the Taxonomists' Search for Respectability", *British Journal for the History of Science*, 26 (1993): 207-27

Winsor, Mary P., *Starfish, Jellyfish and the Order of Life: Issues in Nineteenth-Century Science*, New Haven, Connecticut: Yale University Press, 1976

Taxonomy concerns the theory and practice of classification. It is not confined solely to scientific areas, but is a more general issue concerning the ordering of knowledge and the way we interpret the world. DOUGLAS's classic anthropological text is an excellent general consideration of some of the wider issues surrounding classification, and a useful corrective to the narrower concerns of scientific taxonomy as understood in the modernised world. Biological taxonomy is also an inherently historical activity, in that it traces its modern origins back to the 18th century. Taxonomists are thus inevitably bound up in both historical and philosophical issues, and many practising scientists have written worthy studies on the subject.

MAYR is one such scientist–historian, and part of his vast compendium of observations on biological thought covers taxonomy, providing a useful overview of the development of taxonomic thought from Aristotle to the present day. He sees three phases of development: the construction of overarching systems of classification, usually at higher taxonomic levels, based on generally Aristotelian methods of the division of organisms into groups, according to their essence; a second phase, ushered in by Darwin, who provided a properly scientific basis for taxonomy on common ancestry; and a third, more recent emphasis on the study of species and sub-specific categories. Throughout, Mayr reveals his own interests as one of the foremost evolutionary taxonomists of the 20th century, but, providing one can ignore the biases, it is a useful place to begin.

Immeasurably more complex is LOVEJOY's analysis of the origin and development of the concept of the Great Chain of Being, which, he argues, provided a central intellectual framework for Western thought from ancient to early modern times. Lovejoy is a historian of ideas, and he identifies three core concepts – Plato's principle of plenitude, Aristotle's notions of a scale, and gradation of complexity in animals – which combine to produce a vast, continuous chain of being, from the lowest to the highest. He analyses the operation of the notion in a range of philosophical and scientific areas, up to its most influential period in the 18th century, when, he suggests, the discoveries of ever more variation in organisms supported the idea of continuity inherent in the Great Chain of Being.

FOUCAULT's wide-ranging excavation in the archaeology of knowledge attempts to chart a fundamental shift in the pattern of understanding, from the classical period of the 17th and 18th centuries, to a recognisably modern state of affairs in the early 19th century, within three areas of knowledge – language, systems of exchange, and biological classification. He seeks to unearth the underlying patterns and structures of knowledge although, typically, he offers no real explanation of how changes in the patterns came about. In his classical period, organisms came to be arranged according to visible attributes of specifically identifiable characteristics; for example, Linnaeus's sexual system ignored the traditional utilitarian or mythical criteria, and allowed a more scientific classification, although one effectively based on the arrangement of disembodied characteristics on a flat, grid-like space of perception. Cuvier, in the early 19th century, however, constructed a hierarchy of characteristics built around central plans of organismal structure. In a fundamental discontinuity with classical knowledge, the Great Chain of Being was broken into Cuvier's four great, and equivalent, *embranchements* of animals.

WINSOR's is a much more detailed, empirical study of the work of taxonomists during the first half of the 19th century, and in particular on animals contained in Cuvier's *embranche-ments* – Radiata – which resulted in the disintegration of the group. In an implicitly teleological argument, Winsor suggests that taxonomists made these changes with very ambiguous perceptions of the grounds on which they were working. The theoretical explanation for the arrangement of organisms was finally provided by Darwin, but his theory did not result in any major revolution in taxonomy; rather, Darwin's task was to explain what taxonomists already recognised.

SLOAN's paper, although focusing on a fairly restricted debate in the history of taxonomy, raises wider issues. Biological taxonomists seek to create natural classifications that will reflect real relationships occurring in nature. The history of taxonomy, however, has been bedevilled by debate between taxonomists with different perceptions of what counts as natural. In the early 18th century, the dominant view was Aristotelian essentialism, which emphasised those characteristics that were assumed to reflect the real essences of organisms. John Ray, drawing on Locke's ideas, adopted a more empirical approach, in not weighting any particular characteristics on supposed essential importance, and trying to assess the overall resemblance between organisms based on numerous characteristics. In an important concluding note, Sloan suggests that subsequent debates in the history of taxonomy may have rehearsed essentially the same dispute, between those who classify according to certain specially weighted characteristics, and those who classify on more general, overall resemblance.

There is much less literature on the practise, and institutions, as opposed to the theory, of taxonomy. ALLEN's empirically detailed, and entertaining, study of natural history as a social activity captures something of its enormous popularity, especially in the 19th century, when field clubs took to the hills, coast and countryside in search of new species, additions to collections, or the romance of nature. Although separated to an extent from the more systematic or scientific activity of taxonomy, the amateur tradition was a crucial element. Taxonomy may have dominated biological sciences throughout the 19th century, but it was popularly perceived as old fashioned in the century following. VERNON considers the fortunes of taxonomy in the 20th century, and tries to show that the frequent attempts at modernisation, which have also given rise to considerable controversy, were in fact attempts to improve and update the image of a fundamental, but poorly regarded, activity.

KEITH VERNON

See also Botany: general works

Technology

Aitken, Hugh G.J., *The Continuous Wave: Technology and American Radio, 1900–1932*, Princeton, New Jersey: Princeton University Press, 1985

Bijker, Wiebe E., Thomas P. Hughes and Trevor J. Pinch (eds.), *The Social Construction of Technological Systems: New Directions in the Sociology and History of Technology*, Cambridge, Massachusetts: MIT Press, 1987

Daumas, Maurice (ed.), *A History of Technology and Invention: Progress Through the Ages*, 3 vols, translated from the French by Eileen B. Hennessy, New York: Crown, 1969–79 (original edition, 4 vols, 1962–79)

Hounshell, David A., *From the American System to Mass Production 1800–1932: The Development of Manufacturing Technology in the United States*, Baltimore: Johns Hopkins University Press, 1984

Hughes, Thomas P., *Networks of Power: Electrification of Western Society, 1880–1930*, Baltimore: Johns Hopkins University Press, 1984

Kranzberg, Melvin and Carroll W. Pursell, Jr, *Technology in Western Civilization*, vol 1: *The Emergence of Modern Industrial Society: Earliest Times to 1900*; vol. 2: *Technology in the Twentieth Century*, New York: Oxford University Press, 1967

Lerman, Nina E., Arwen Palmer Mohun and Ruth Oldenziel (eds), "Gender Analysis and the History of Technology" (special issue) *Technology and Culture*, 38 (1997): 1–213

Lindqvist, Svante, *Technology on Trial: The Introduction of Steam Power Technology into Sweden, 1715–1736*, Stockholm: Almqvist & Wiksell, 1984

Mackenzie, Donald, *Inventing Accuracy: A Historical Sociology of Nuclear Missile Guidance*, Cambridge, Massachusetts: MIT Press 1990

Mumford, Lewis, *Technics and Civilization*, London: Routledge and Kegan Paul, and New York: Harcourt Brace, 1934

Needham, Joseph, *Science and Civilization in China*, Cambridge and New York: Cambridge University Press, 1954–

Nye, David E., *Electrifying America: Social Meanings of a New Technology 1880–1940*, Cambridge, Massachusetts: MIT Press, 1990

Singer, Charles, *et al.*, *A History of Technology*, 8 vols, Oxford and New York: Oxford University Press, 1954–84

Smith, Merritt Roe, *Harpers Ferry Armory and the New Technology: The Challenge of Change*, Ithaca, New York: Cornell University Press, 1977

In the 1960s and 1970s, a number of grand surveys of the history of technology were published, covering western developments "from Plato to NATO", while literature in the 1980s has tended to be much more focused on particular topics or particular locales. The argument in favour of the specialized story is that the complexity of technology in its economic, social, institutional, or scientific setting is lost in the grand sweep, which can lead to misrepresentations. None the less, the general overview remains useful. This entry will first present these "grand sweeps", and then proceed to discuss the most influential "case studies" of the last 20 years.

The first and largest grand survey is SINGER. The monumentality of the eight volumes makes it unlikely that anyone would want to read it from cover to cover, but it is a valuable reference work, with essays on most technologies throughout the ages. The underlying plot is one of technological progress through the improvement of machines and other technical artefacts. The first five volumes, published under the patronage of the Imperial Chemical Industries, cover the period up to 1900, with each volume dedicated to a particular time-span and then divided into essays on individual technologies – such as steam engines, bridges, spinning, and weaving. Many line drawings render the technological artefacts very clearly. Volumes 6 and 7 were published decades after the first five, and here Singer attempted to move away from an emphasis on what and how things were made towards a consideration of the impact of economic, social, and political factors. These two volumes cover the period 1900–50, with chapters on such themes as the economics of technological development, management, atomic energy, paint, railways, and cinematography. The subject matter is thus still largely organized by technology, but the line drawings are replaced by photographs. Volume 8 contains consolidated indexes.

KRANZBERG & PURSELL, designed for a one-year course, was intended to remedy the fact that no single available text sufficiently stressed the cultural, economic, and social implications of technology in history. The first of two volumes has a world-wide scope but focuses on Britain; the second volume focuses on the US. Each volume is divided into essays largely defined by novel technologies; for example, part 3 of volume 1, on the Industrial Revolution (1750–1830), contains essays on the prerequisites for industrialization, the textile industry, the steam engine, metallurgical and machine tool development, steam transportation, and the social impact of the Industrial Revolution. Although much recent history of technology does not accept this form of compartmentalization, this is by no means simply a catalogue of machines, and the essays are well-written.

DAUMAS is also a monumental survey, although not quite in the league of Singer. The historical scope is from the "origins of technological civilization" to 1860, and emphasis is placed on the history of mechanization. Daumas excludes the contexts of accountancy, banking, and war, but includes the technologies of the written text within the context of mechanization. The title indicates the author's concern with the role of innovation, which he argues is a collective experience – as opposed to the sudden insight of a genius – that takes the form of a progressive evolution. He also argues for a historical change in the role of innovation: during the first half of the 19th century, science began to influence technology, but, since the early 20th century, science has become the principal factor of innovation.

The grand surveys of the history of technology focus almost exclusively on western technology, and NEEDHAM's work was intended to balance the often parochial attitudes in the history of science, medicine, and technology. Famously, he cited Francis Bacon to the effect that the history of the western world had been changed irrevocably by the inventions of printing, gunpowder, and the magnetic compass, and went on to show how all three had been discovered in China significantly in advance of the scientific revolution. Despite the title, much of what is described in this series is technological, such as agricultural technology, ship-building technology, or those technologies mentioned by Bacon. The trail-blazing scholarship and meticulous footnotes makes this a tremendous resource, although it can make difficult reading.

MUMFORD is also extensive in its coverage of time and space, but, in contrast to the three works above, it aims to reveal the constant interplay between the social milieu – monasticism, capitalism, science, play, luxury, war – and the more specific achievements of the inventor, the industrialist, and the engineer. Mumford had an idiosyncratic and provocative view of history that led to sweeping generalizations. For example, he divided history into three periods: the eotechnic, the paleotechnic, and the neotechnic (what others have called the Industrial Revolution). He also believed that in the 1930s the world was on the verge of a transition from a mechanical to an electrical phase, and that with the coming of electricity, especially hydroelectric power, the vagaries of a society organized by capitalist greed would give way to a more rational world, run by scientific engineers and scientists. Mumford was to become far more sceptical of technology by the 1970s.

There are many excellent studies of the history of technology and, although not all can be covered here, the following have been very influential. SMITH has analyzed the early 19th-century emergence of the "American system" – machine production with exchangeable parts – which has traditionally been seen as one of the greatest achievements of American technology. By focusing upon one of the US Army's weapon factories, he shows that the development was by no means as linear or straightforward as had been previously assumed. By contrast, for differing reasons, both management and employees fought the new technology tooth and nail. Smith describes the political, social, and economic factors that made people in one army factory resist new technology that had been assimilated without problem elsewhere.

HOUNSHELL covers the development of the American system from its inception in the army factories to the breakthrough of the car industry in the 20th century. Hounshell describes the spread of the American system into civil production in companies such as Singer (sewing machines), McCormick (harvesting machines), Pope (bicycles), and Ford (cars), and shows the greatly increased production in Singer and McCormick, although the principle of exchangeable parts was not carried through completely until the 1880s. He also documents how true mass production was only achieved with Ford's assembly lines in Detroit c.1915, and the resulting radical change in workers' conditions.

LINDQVIST describes the failed technology transfer of the steam engine from Britain to Sweden in the early 18th century. In an impressively clear and entertaining style, he describes the reasons for this failure, which were not primarily "technological". The steam engine needed many elements found in Britain's mining culture (but not in Sweden's) to function: for instance, the price of alternative sources of energy, and the infrastructure for repairs, differed, and even the appropriate Swedish vocabulary had to be invented: a cylinder had to be paraphrased as resembling a butter churn. The steam engine was thus not simply a black box that could be transported with ease. There are many resonances with current problems in technology transfer to the Third World.

HUGHES is perhaps the single most influential text on the history of technology. Describing the introduction of electrical lighting and power within a number of local contexts – Berlin, London, Chicago, north-east England, and California – he examines the different technical and organizational solutions found in order to introduce electricity into quite different political and social cultures. Hughes's conceptual apparatus has become dominant in the history of technology: the main concept is that of "systems", which may consist not only of hardware, devices, machines, and processes, but also of the networks connecting them, such as transmission lines and, crucially, utility companies, manufacturing enterprises, and even regulatory bodies. Hughes describes the development of systems using a military metaphor: the system advances in a front, and at times encounters difficulties when some parts of the front lag behind the others; these constitute "reverse salients", and efforts are then concentrated on eliminating such reverse salients in order to enable the system as a whole to proceed. The development in Berlin, London, Chicago, etc. is shown to have presented different reverse salients that were eliminated with appropriate local solutions.

NYE also describes the process of electrification, but whereas Hughes's story focuses on supply, Nye concentrates on demand. By choosing "the typical American town: Middletown", he describes the waves of electrification from the point of view of the citizens and consumers – from lighting, to trams, an amusement park, factory conveyor belts, and domestic electricity. The story alternates between large and small events, and is always well documented.

In very elegant prose, AITKEN describes the shift from wireless telegraphy, based on Marconi's spark transmitter, to radio, based on continuous radio waves. In the first half of the book, Aitken describes the early 20th-century development of three continuous wave technologies: high frequency generators, arc transmitters, and vacuum tubes. Aitken emphasizes that not only was scientific and technical knowledge important, but that a new conception of the potentialities of radio communication was essential too. In the second half of the book, attention is shifted away from the contact between individual scientists and inventors towards the interplay between the new technology and large enterprises and military institutions. Radio technology was considered to be of national interest, and much effort was put into keeping the US at the forefront, resulting in the foundation of the Radio Corporation of America in 1919.

Many of the essays in BIJKER, HUGHES & PINCH introduced sociological concepts into the analysis of technological systems. Hughes elaborates on his concepts of "system builder", "technological momentum", and "reverse salients". Michel Callon describes Renault's project of the electrical car in the early 1970s, pointing to the alliances that are necessary for the production of successful technology; his catch-phrase is "heterogeneous actor-network theory". Bijker and Pinch show that there was nothing inevitable about the development of the bicycle, and that the end result was in many ways contingent. "Relevant social groups", "variation", "selection", and "closure" are some of their (almost Darwinist) conceptual tools.

MacKENZIE's story of the increased accuracy of nuclear missiles during the Cold War emphasizes the contingency and multiple processes of negotiation, and the central notion of accuracy. On the basis of this well-documented account of ambitious scientists and technologists, prestigious laboratories, large companies, and political and military institutions and their leaders, Mackenzie convincingly repudiates the notion of technological determinism – a natural technological trajectory leading inevitably to higher accuracy.

The special issue of *Technology and Culture* edited by LERMAN, MOHUN & OLDENZIEL on gender analysis and the history of technology gives, as an introduction, a historical survey of the literature in the relevant genres. Gender analysis is convincingly presented as a versatile tool in the history of technology, in part to counter the still widespread misconception that it involves merely the counting of female engineers. Techniques of social history are marshalled for a multi-layered conception of gender in technology: 1) gender is part of human identity – the ways in which people see themselves and their lives as men and women; 2) gender plays structural roles in societies, defining barriers and boundaries, and is embedded in all manner of institutions, such as education and labour markets; 3) gender ideologies show up in symbolic forms: images and ideals of manhood and womanhood, gendered metaphors, and masculine and feminine connotations of objects and activities. The issue also contains half a dozen articles illustrating these layers; for example, one article analyses the Fisher Body Company, which throughout most of the 20th century supplied American boys with model cars. An emblematic advert renders a boy showing a model to an admiring girl, thus illustrating the intimate connection between masculinity and technology in education and play.

HENRY NIELSEN AND ARNE HESSENBRUCH

See also Capitalism and Science; Computing; Electricity; Engines: steam; Mechanization; Technology Transfer; Telegraphy

Technology Transfer

Etzkowitz, Henry and Loet Leydesdorff (eds), *The University in the Global Knowledge Economy: A Triple Helix of University-Industry-Government Relations*, London: Cassell, 1997

Gibbons, Michael *et al.*, *The New Production of Knowledge: The Dynamics of Science and Research in Contemporary Societies*, Beverly Hills, California, and London: Sage, 1994

Headrick, Daniel R., *The Tentacles of Progress: Technology Transfer in the Age of Imperialism, 1850–1940*, New York: Oxford University Press, 1988

Inkster, Ian, *Science and Technology in History: An Approach to Industrial Development*, New Brunswick, New Jersey: Rutgers University Press, and London: Macmillan, 1991

Jeremy, David J., *Transatlantic Industrial Revolution: The Diffusion of Textile Technologies Between Britain and America, 1790–1830s*, Cambridge, Massachusetts: MIT Press, 1981

Kenwood, A.G. and A.L. Lougheed, *Technological Diffusion and Industrialization Before 1914*, New York: St Martin's Press, and London: Croom Helm, 1982

Landes, David S., *The Unbound Prometheus: Technological Change and Industrial Development in Western Europe from 1750 to the Present*, Cambridge and New York: Cambridge University Press, 1969

Misa, Thomas J., *A Nation of Steel: The Making of Modern America, 1865–1925*, Baltimore: Johns Hopkins University Press, 1995

Tarr, Joel A. and Gabriel Dupuy (eds), *Technology and the Rise of the Networked City in Europe and America*, Philadelphia: Temple University Press, 1988

Tod, Jan, *Colonial Technology: Science and the Transfer of Innovation to Australia*, Cambridge and New York: Cambridge University Press, 1995

Technology transfer is the movement of particular inventions, entire technological systems or knowledge of how to construct them across national or organizational boundaries. The processes of technology transfer have been noted to occur across time and space, during the medieval period in the diffusion of such basic technologies as the water wheel, windmill and heavy plough and in the relations among civilizations such as China and the West, in which both organizational technologies such as bureaucracy and physical technologies such as gunpowder moved westward. Technology transfer is a key element of economic growth, perhaps even more important than the invention and development of technology.

Technology transfer is a complex process that requires appropriate organizational and cultural "software" as well as technical "hardware" to be accomplished in its most productive form. More than the relocation of a physical artefact, technology transfer also involves entrepreneurship, specific skills, even government finance or patronage as well as commercial demand. MISA argues, on the basis of the American steel industry, that technology transfer in its most developed form is the ability to obtain knowledge and skills from an originating source, adapt them to use in a different economic and social structure and then diffuse them into new technical applications in other industrial sectors.

Equal partners freely entering into agreements, the contemporary positive image of technology transfer, has a reverse, mirror image. HEADRICK shows how colonial powers have used technology transfer as a means to increase their economic and political influence, without necessarily having to use military force. In this inherently unequal patron/client relationship the "sender" typically restricted the transfer process to a narrow domain and limited access to the knowledge transferred by having its nationals operate the relocated technology. For example, British engineers operated locomotives for as long as three quarters of a century after the construction of the first railroad in India, keeping this skill out of the hands of the "receivers" for as long as possible.

The purpose of colonial technology transfer was to draw the less developed country more fully into the colonizer's economonic and political orbit. Thus, colonizers in India and Africa put transportation technologies, such as rail and road, in place to assist in the extraction of resources and the movement of troops. Communication technologies such as telegraph and telephone systems were installed to help a few colonial administrators maintain political control over vast regions and large populations. Nevertheless, once installed these technologies became a double-edged sword, used by indigenous peoples for their own purposes, including creation of networks and organizations to displace their colonial rulers. When Tata built steel mills, with technology imported from the US, they were at one and the same time viewed as a bulwark of empire by British officials and the groundwork for an independent economy by nationalist Indian entrepreneurs.

After independence, technology transfer as an economic development strategy becomes clear to both sides, as the former colonizer and newly-independent nation, struggle to assert their opposing interests. JEREMY delineates the workings of this process overall as favorable to the emerging nation, at least in the growth of the US textile in the early 19th century. American manufacturers sought to obtain knowledge and devices from Britain through socially mobile individuals willing to leave their home country and recreate devices upon their arrival in the US. Although it could not prevent the movement of technology the British government was able to exact an additional cost on its transfer through export and immigration controls.

Jeremy argues that on the US side, technology transfer was facilitated and magnified by the availability of technologically knowledgeable individuals who adapted the technology to local circumstances. Thus, far more important than machine models, however were skilled managers and mechanics. This illustrates the crucial human dimension of technology transfer. In this analysis particular bits of technology were moved by specific individuals across national boundaries within the same industrial sector.

Jeremy's case study of textile technology exemplifies INKSTER's category of narrow technology transfer. In this mode a particular technology is tranferred from its place of origin as a technological process in a particular industry to another geographical site within the same industrial context. On the other hand, in broad technology transfer a technology is moved from its place of origin to a variety of applications across several industries. For the latter to be more likely to take place a local R&D capacity is required.

What are the preconditions for successful technology transfer? LANDES emphasizes conditions at the receptor site as a prerequisite for successful technology transfer: the importance of a stable political and legal environment, with reliable contracts replacing force as the guarantor of relationships. TARR & DUPUY also emphasize the importance of the unique physical, economic and social context into which techology is transferred. If technology is not appropriately modified to fit local circumstances it may well fail to take hold. Thus, British "destructor" technology for incinerating urban wastes that was economical in a dense urban setting where even outlying land was too costly to be devoted to a dump, worked less well in the US in the late 19th and early 20th centuries, where burying wastes was a viable alternative.

There are fascinating anomalies in technology transfer. The movement of technology across national borders has been found to be more rapid than diffusion within them. For example, KENWOOD & LOUGHEED show that Watt's steam engine patented in Britain in 1776, came into use in France in 1779 and Germany in 1788, yet its use was not widespread in Britain until the 1830s and 1840s. Their finding suggests the salience of regional disparities to the potential for technology transfer and the greater likelihood for transfer among "high-tech" areas, wherever they are located. TOD focuses on the question: Can technology transfer generate a capacity for innovation? in the Australian context. The answer is at least in part dependent upon the ability to move newly acquired technical capabilities more broadly acrss the economy.

GIBBONS *et al.* argue that technology transfer has taken on a new meaning with the decline of colonialism and protectionism. Now the issue is the movement of technology across institutional spheres such as between academia and industry. Beginning with the contractual sale of specific pieces of intellectual property between firms, technology transfer becomes a way of integrating inventors and manufacturers, producers and users of technology. ETZKOWITZ & LEYDES-DORFF analyse how technology transfer can grow into a two way flow of ideas and techniques among a variety of partners who come to see themselves as participants in a virtual joint enterprise.

HENRY ETZKOWITZ

See also Research and Development; Technology

Telegraphy

Appleyard, Rollo, *The History of the Institution of Electrical Engineers, 1871–1931*, London: Institution of Electrical Engineers, 1939

Bright, Charles, *Submarine Telegraphs*, London: Lockwood, 1898; New York: Arno Press, 1974

Fleming, J.A., *Fifty Years of Electricity*, London: Wireless Press, 1921

Headrick, Daniel R., *The Invisible Weapon: Telecommunications and International Politics, 1851–1945*, Oxford and New York: Oxford University Press, 1991

Hollister-Short, Graham and Frank A.J.L. James, *History of Technology*, vol. 13, London: Mansell, 1991

Kieve, Jeffrey L., *The Electric Telegraph*, Newton Abbott, Devon: David and Charles, 1973

Smith, Willoughby, *The Rise and Extension of Submarine Telegraphy*, London: Virtue, 1891; New York: Arno Press, 1974

This essay concerns itself with electric telegraphy, and takes no account of visual systems. Most of the books considered concentrate on submarine telegraphy, as this technology was more complex and problematic than its land-based relative. Submarine telegraphy demanded considerable scientific input, and had remarkable economic and political effects which, in a sense, heralded modern communication systems.

There have been very few general, technical histories of telegraphy, but FLEMING, reminiscing in 1921, reviewed 50 years of the history of electrical engineering. The first and last chapters of his book provide a comprehensive account of cable and wireless telegraphy from a purely technical point of view. For a quick and relatively easy introduction to the technology of telegraphy, Fleming's book is invaluable. His explanations of some of the more complicated sending and receiving instruments have yet to be improved upon, and particularly clear are his descriptions of duplexing and multiplexing, both of which were important in rendering telegraphy increasingly economic. There are many illustrations, and the niceties of the technology are well explained, although the work must be viewed more as a primary source for the later developments. The book is also of interest for its description of electrical engineering artefacts in general. On a more specialist level, BRIGHT, first published in 1898, remains the most comprehensive history of submarine telegraphy to date. Based on an earlier, French treatise, Bright covered every subject touching upon telegraphy. Of course, his interpretation of the signifi-

cance and effects of long distance, deep sea cables are restricted, and cannot be accepted without much qualification, but his descriptions of the technicalities of cable construction, laying and working have yet to be surpassed.

Recently, historians of technology have begun to reassess the history of telegraphy, particularly that of submarine telegraphy, with a view to applying modern methods of analysis to the subject. Some of the papers in HOLLISTER-SHORT & JAMES go some way to providing a new synthesis of telegraphy. In particular, taken together, the articles by Bruce Hunt ("Michael Faraday and the Rise of Field Theory"), Iwan Morus ("Telegraphy and the Technology of Display"), Graeme Gooday ("Teaching Telegraphy and Electrotechnics in the Physics Laboratory: William Ayrton and the Creation of an Academic Space for Electrical Engineering in Britain, 1873–1884"), and Colin Hempstead ("An Appraisal of Fleeming Jenkin, 1833–1855), Electrical Engineer"), allow telegraphy to be placed within a wide context, demonstrating how it related to theoretical issues, how it was introduced to the public, how its technology, techniques, and science were incorporated into academic institutions and courses, and how individuals were part of its history.

In the first two chapters of APPLEYARD, the introduction and developments of electric telegraphy are outlined, showing how the political, technical, and economic importance of the first wide-scale application of electricity necessitated the formation of an association of engineers. Although this is a triumphalistic and hagiographic work, Appleyard's account of the techniques of telegraphy, and the global importance of submarine cables for imperial Britain, serve as a good, although dated, introduction to the appearance and use of rapid, long distance electrical communication systems. A more modern approach is provided by HEADRICK, a broad study of the importance of international cable systems for imperialism, economic dominance, political, military and industrial intelligence, and national rivalries. Headrick mentions only briefly purely technological considerations, giving his attention mainly to the consequences of electrical communications – for example, he uses the story of the deep sea cables as a means of charting the rise and decline of the British Empire. Cable telegraphy is contrasted with radio, but both systems are embedded within political and economic history.

The books by Kieve and Smith are, in their own ways, useful contributions to the human and social histories of telegraphy. KIEVE's work is a comprehensive study of the non-technical aspects of telegraphy in the United Kingdom. He deals with commercial issues, and provides information on investments, profits, charges, and salaries. Structural changes in the industry are also described, with public and private enterprise contrasted, and the effects of legislation on the development of telegraphy, and later, telephony analysed. The story is extended beyond World War II in order to end the narrative with an account of the final demise of telegraphy, with telephony ousting the older technology in the 1960s. The appendices contain a short selection of economic information, and there are extensive footnotes and a bibliography, although now dated. SMITH was, from the early 1850s, one of the pioneers of submarine telegraphy. Towards the end of his life he recorded his own view of its history, and in so doing produced not only a highly personal account, but also recorded his experiences of designing, laying, testing, and using submarine cables. The work is arranged chronologically, and outlines the story of submarine telegraphy from 1850 to c.1875, including descriptions of the technologies, problems associated with the laying of deep sea cables, developments in the structure of cables, clashes of personality, and his ideas on the "future". It is not, in itself, a balanced history, but taken with the other works above it brings a human element to the predominantly scientific and technological picture of the progress and demise of this important engineering innovation.

COLIN A. HEMPSTEAD

See also Electrical Engineering; Electricity; Measurement

Telescopes

Bennett, J.A., "'On the Power of Penetrating into Space': The Telescopes of William Herschel", *Journal for the History of Astronomy*, 7 (1976): 75–108

DeVorkin, David H., *The History of Modern Astronomy and Astrophysics: A Selected, Annotated Bibliography*, New York: Garland, 1982

Gingerich, Owen (ed.), *Astrophysics and Twentieth-Century Astronomy to 1950* (vol. 4 of *General History of Astronomy*), Cambridge and New York: Cambridge University Press, 1984

King, Henry C., *The History of the Telescope*, Cambridge, Massachusetts: Sky, and London: Griffin, 1955

Kuiper, Gerard P. and Barbara M. Middlehurst (eds), *Telescopes*, Chicago: University of Chicago Press, 1960

Osterbrock, Donald E., *Pauper & Prince: Ritchey, Hale & Big American Telescopes*, Tucson: University of Arizona Press, and Cambridge: Cambridge University Press, 1993

Preston, Richard, *First Light: The Search for the Edge of the Universe*, New York: Atlantic Monthly Press, 1987

Smith, Robert W. *et al.*, *The Space Telescope: A Study of NASA, Science, Technology, and Politics*, Cambridge and New York: Cambridge University Press, 1989

Smith, Robert W., "Engines of Discovery: Scientific Instruments and the History of Astronomy and Planetary Science in the United States in the Twentieth Century", *Journal for the History of Astronomy* (February 1997)

Van Helden, Albert, *The Invention of the Telescope*, Philadelphia: American Philosophical Society, 1977

Van Helden, Albert, "Telescope Building, 1850–1900", in *Astrophysics and Twentieth-Century Astronomy to 1950*, edited by Owen Gingerich, Cambridge and New York: Cambridge University Press, 1984

Warner, D.J. and R.B. Ariail, *Alvan Clark & Sons, Artists in Optics*, 2nd edition, Richmond, Virginia: Willmann-Bell, 1995

Wright, Helen, Joan N. Warnow and Charles Weiner, *The Legacy of George Ellery Hale*, Cambridge, Massachusetts: MIT Press, 1972

VAN HELDEN has argued that one of the most interesting aspects of the history of the telescope is that it has served as the "prototype of modern scientific instruments", and its history thereby provides critical insight into the history of scientific practice. Here we limit our attention to observational astronomy with optical telescopes, keeping in mind the fact that, notwithstanding van Helden's prescient observation, little as yet has appeared in monograph form that explores that connection.

There are few comprehensive historical reviews of telescope design and use. The most accessible are the classic chronicle by KING, and a shorter study by van Helden in GINGERICH, which draws from rich early primary sources such as Repsold, Danjon, and Couder. Classic works such as Repsold and Ambronn's magisterial *Handbuch der astronomischen Instrumentenkunde* (1899) are excellent sources for high-quality woodcut images of telescopes, but they do not venture beyond description. However, over the past decades, several articles have explored both technical and conceptual aspects of this history. For example, BENNETT described the invention of the achromatic lens and the growth of huge speculum-metal reflectors, while two articles in Gingerich have explored the problem of producing large glass lenses of high optical quality, making modern long-focus refractors possible in the late 19th century (van Helden), and the transformation of telescopic astronomy by photography (Lankford). Annotated citations to the secondary literature (to 1980) can be found in DeVORKIN.

Many forces caused telescopes to become larger and larger, and eventually propelled them into space. Although, in general, the historical literature on this subject is not vast, there are a number of distinctly valuable studies available. There were certainly large technical obstacles to overcome, such as those described by Bennett in the casting of large speculum mirrors for reflectors by Herschel and Rosse, or those reviewed by van Helden in Gingerich, in producing optically pure glass for refractors. There were also many intellectual reasons for improving telescopes, but this area is less well-studied and much work remains to be done. Beyond purely technical or intellectual forces, other factors drove astronomers, craftsmen, and their patrons to build large telescopes; the themes of public and private patronage, politics, and local pride have been examined in more detail by essayists in Gingerich, and more recently by SMITH (1989), in his study of the Space Telescope. However, there are many gaps in the literature.

One of the most important issues is still the relationship of optical craftsman to patron. Although there are some helpful studies that illuminate this area in the journals cited here, most deal with other forms of instrumentation, and few monographs explore this theme for optical telescopes specifically. OSTERBROCK has therefore provided valuable new insight into one particular case, that of George Ritchey and George Ellery Hale, but here the relationship is particularized by clashing egos and differing agendas, and there are few useful generalities to be drawn that might illuminate a broader landscape. Some fertile ground has been broken by WARNER & ARIAIL's new study of one important name in the American telescope trade, and, although the authors only hint here at the various social and cultural drives that made telescopes desirable objects to procure for personal and professional reasons, Warner is presently developing the subject.

Technical reviews of modern telescope design and development appear frequently in the scientific review literature, the most accessible being KUIPER & MIDDLEHURST. Chapters by Bowen and Baustian describe the 200-inch and 120-inch telescopes, whereas other astronomers such as Mayall, McMath and Orren Mohler, Bolton, and Frank Drake address more general design issues, such as the various classes of modern reflecting telescope, the Schmidt Camera, radio telescopes, mountings and drive mechanisms, site selection, and the limitations of the atmosphere. The chapters by Bowen and Shane in WRIGHT, WARNOW & WEINER provide broader insight into the technical issues facing those involved in the design of large classical 20th-century telescopes.

It is quite interesting to contrast these contemporary essays by scientists with the perspective provided by historians such as van Helden and Lankford in Gingerich, who have examined the design choices made by earlier generations. Similar comparisons can be made with contemporary descriptions in the *Annual Reviews of Astronomy and Astrophysics*, numerous monographs issued by specialists, or even popular magazines like *Sky & Telescope* – which has always chronicled the establishment of new observatories, providing descriptive detail on design, construction, and operation, as well as noting new trends, such as the shift away from heavy equatorial-mounted instruments toward lighter, optically faster systems built around computerized alt-azimuth mountings.

Contemporary scientific reviews can typically provide useful focused studies of astronomical instrumentation, but they do not address the equally important question of the influence of new technologies on the changing nature of the discipline – a factor considered more by historians, who address this and related issues in the volume edited by Gingerich, as well as in a special volume of the *Journal for the History of Astronomy* (February 1991), and in a particularly insightful, popular study by PRESTON.

SMITH (1997), exploring issues raised by Van Helden and others, has provided a thoughtful historiographical review of contemporary questions such as those already mentioned, but primarily of what the study of instruments can reveal about how disciplines and specialties form and change. He points out that interest in instruments has increased among historians, who share a growing concern for getting to the root of the experimental process, and that instruments should be studied because they have stimulated the coalescence of communities around efforts to standardize practice.

DAVID H. DEVORKIN

See also Astronomical Instruments; Astronomy: general works; Space Science

Themata

Holton, Gerald, *Thematic Origins of Scientific Thought: Kepler to Einstein*, Cambridge, Massachusetts: Harvard University Press, 1973, 2nd edition 1988

Holton, Gerald, *The Scientific Imagination: Case Studies*, Cambridge and New York: Cambridge University Press, 1978

Holton, Gerald, *The Advancement of Science, and Its Burdens*, Cambridge and New York: Cambridge University Press, 1986

Kragh, Helge, *An Introduction to the Historiography of Science*, Cambridge and New York: Cambridge University Press, 1987

Losee, John, *Philosophy of Science and Historical Enquiry*, Oxford: Clarendon Press, and New York: Oxford University Press, 1987

Merton, Robert K., "Thematic Analysis in Science: Notes on Holton's Concept", *Science*, 188 (1975): 335–38

Truppi, Carlo, *Continuità e mutamento: Il tempo nell'innovazione delle tecniche e nell'evoluzione dell'architettura*, Milan: Franco Angeli, 1994

The approach to historical research known as thematic analysis originated in the recognition by Gerald Holton in the early 1960s that the older, well established approaches, although useful, were not contributing to an understanding of the choice of conceptual models, the motivation of scientists for pursuing research problems, or the treatment of data. Laboratory notes, letters, and other documents reveal that during the nascent, "private" period of work, some scientists, whether consciously or not, use a relatively small number of highly motivating and very general presuppositions or hypotheses that are not directly derivable from the phenomena, that are not provable or disprovable, and that have generally been in use for a long time. These presuppositions may lead to error or to success; but in either case, when such work is then recast for presentation in the "public" phase of science, these motivating aids (which Holton has termed thematic presuppositions, or thematic hypotheses) tend to be suppressed and disappear from view – although they are also frequently the basis for the acceptance or rejection of the work by other scientists, who are guided by their own thematic preferences.

HOLTON (1973) uses case studies to show this mechanism at work, how certain themata (singular "thema", from the Greek: that which is laid down; proposition; primary word) can rule the scientific imagination. The cases include Kepler's ability to move among three basic presuppositions (the universe as a physical machine, as a mathematical harmony, and as a central theological order); Niels Bohr's invention of a new thema, complementarity; and Albert Einstein's obstinate attachment to the themata of unification, formal explanation, logical parsimony, symmetry, continuum, and classical causality – all of which help to explain the fact that Einstein distanced himself from the basic tenets of Bohr and the experiments of A.A. Michelson.

HOLTON (1978) adds the case study of R.A. Millikan, which describes his habit of discarding data that would undermine his prior, thematic decision to regard the electron's charge as uniquely quantized. It also studies the path by which Enrico Fermi arrived at the insight that slow (i.e. "moderated") neutrons can cause artificial radioactivity – a large first step to designing nuclear reactors. HOLTON (1986) then elaborates on Einstein's research program and world picture, and describes the contrary presuppositions of J. Robert Oppenheimer and Werner Heisenberg.

It turns out that thematic analysis proved useful in a variety of fields of study beyond those presented above. The postscript to the 1988 edition of Holton (1973) cites some of the numerous articles and books that have made explicit use of these concepts within various contexts – the history and philosophy of science, the sociology of science, physics, biology, psychology, sociology, literary criticism, and linguistics. It appears that each special statement of a thema is an aspect of its more general conception; thus, a general thema Q would take on a specific form in physics that may be symbolized by Qf, in psychological investigation by Qj, in studies on mythology and folklore by Qm, and so on. For example, TRUPPI demonstrates in detail the dominant role of themata in the progressive evolution of architectural forms, and in the cultural mechanisms that underlie the variety of real constructions throughout history.

LOSEE is concerned with the relationship between the philosophy of science and the history of science. He locates the significance of the thematic analysis of cases to the history of science in its contribution to a descriptive, rather than a normative, philosophy of science. Meanwhile, Helge KRAGH sees thematic analysis as a particular application of the "thesis of invariance of historical themes", which manifest themselves at different times "in all important branches of culture". He finds it most useful when applied "vertically", over a relatively short span of time and to individual scientists.

An insightful discussion of the general applications of thematic analysis is the article by Robert K. MERTON, in which he traces predecessors of thematic analysis in Michael Polanyi's "tacit knowledge", in Harold Lasswell's "content analysis", in the studies of "post-mature discoveries" by Joshua Lederberg and Harriet Zuckerman, and in the literature on the meaning of "progress" in science.

GERALD HOLTON

See also Paradigm

Third Reich and Science

Beyerchen, Alan D., *Scientists under Hitler: Politics and the Physics Community in the Third Reich*, New Haven, Connecticut: Yale University Press, 1977

Deichmann, Ute, *Biologen unter Hitler: Vertreibung, Karrieren, Forschung*, Frankfurt and New York: Campus, 1992

Geuter, Ulfried, *The Professionalization of Psychology in Nazi Germany*, translated from the German by Richard J. Holmes, Cambridge and New York: Cambridge University Press, 1992 (original edition, 1988)

Ludwig, Karl-Heinz, *Technik und Ingenieure im Dritten Reich*, Dusseldorf: Athenäum-Droste, 1974

Mehrtens, Herbert and Steffen Richter (eds), *Naturwissenschaft, Technik und NS-Ideologie. Beiträge zur Wissenschaftsgeschichte des Dritten Reichs*, Frankfurt: Suhrkamp, 1980

Meinel, Christoph and Peter Voswinckel (eds), *Medizin, Naturwissenschaft, Technik und Nationalsozialismus: Kontinuitäten und Diskontinuitäten*, Stuttgart: Verlag für Geschichte der Naturwissenschaften und der Technik, 1994

Olff-Nathan, Josiane (ed.), *La Science sous le Troisième Reich*, Paris: Editions du Seuil, 1993

Renneberg, Monika and Mark Walker (eds), *Science, Technology and National Socialism*, Cambridge and New York: Cambridge University Press, 1994

Rössler, Mechtild, *"Wissenschaft und Lebensraum": Geographische Ostforschung im Nationalsozialismus: Ein Beitrag zur Disziplingeschichte der Geographie*, Berlin and Hamburg: Reimer, 1990

Walker, Mark, *German National Socialism and the Quest for Nuclear Power, 1939–1949*, Cambridge and New York: Cambridge University Press, 1989

Weindling, Paul, *Health, Race, and German Politics between National Unification and Nazism, 1870–1945*, Cambridge and New York: Cambridge University Press, 1989

In recent years, the subject of "the sciences under National Socialism" has evolved into a recognised research topic within the historiography of science, and one that is almost unique in its establishment of an indisputable connection between scientific activity and political conditions. In this instance, the political context consists of a criminal regime that employed the argument of German racial superiority to justify suppression, enslavement, and genocide. Historians of science and others have taken up the question of the personal guilt or responsibility of individuals who were directly involved in this process. Closely linked with this line of inquiry is the study of scientific (sub-)disciplines that can be termed Nazi, both in that they count as characteristic of the political system that gave rise to them, and in that they can be distinguished from other, non-Nazi sub-disciplines. In general, the topic offers a paradigmatic case for the general discussion of the relations between sciences, scientists, and the political systems in which they are situated, and also of the technological potential with which scientists supply political systems.

There is as yet no comprehensive monograph on the sciences under National Socialism, but the topic is accessible through a wealth of publications on the lives of individual scientists, collective biographies, studies of particular disciplines, scientific institutions, specific scientific projects, and even ideological concepts that derive from, or were introduced to, natural science. A guide to the state of research is offered by four collections. As the oldest volume, MEHRTENS & RICHTER represents the initial stage in the development of the topic; its seven essays deal with individual disciplines and their representatives, among others mathematics, physics, chemistry, and their ideology-governed "Aryan" variants. Very instructive is the extensive introduction by Mehrtens, which not only offers a detailed survey of the older literature, but also develops the questions that have shaped subsequent research. The volume by OLFF-NATHAN comprises a section on so-called "hard" science, which deals with various aspects of mathematics and physics, as well as the biological and human sciences. MEINEL & VOSWINCKEL presents the results of a congress in 29 brief case studies that are classified under the headings "institutions", "disciplines", "careers", "amnesias", and "historicisations". Again, the introductory essay by Herbert Mehrtens, which takes another look at historiographical developments, deserves special mention. The essays in RENNEBERG & WALKER cover a large variety of scientific and technical disciplines as well as projects, and, since they all pursue their subject across the political ruptures of 1933 and 1945, the volume supplies a wide spectrum of answers to the questions regarding what features of contemporary science were specifically Nazi, and what continuities can be observed across these political thresholds.

The focus of research on science under National Socialism has changed over time. In the 1960s, the student movement engendered a wave of publications fuelled by the "will to come to terms with the past". While this wave ended the silence concerning the victims of National Socialism (a large portion of this literature deals with the persecution, expulsion, and extinction of the Jews), it also signalled the advent of an apologetic and justificatory historiography, which was undertaken especially in a number of university lecture series on their respective institutions during the Nazi era. Scientists who commented on the issue chose to distance themselves from the problem as such, by stipulating that there was a gap between the abuse of science and science itself. Literature regarding this phenomenon is discussed in Mehrtens & Richter.

The first detailed historical analyses of science and technology were undertaken in the 1970s. Their number increased enormously during the 1980s, above all in relation to the commemorative occasions in 1983 and 1985. The first historical studies focused particularly on the most striking features of National Socialism, namely the expulsion of Jewish scientists, the attacks on academic autonomy, and the pretensions of the *völkisch*, racist ideology. Because, in general, National Socialism was widely assumed to be pervaded by anti-scientism, research on the developments of individual disciplines focused mainly on the various *völkisch* variations (from the so-called German physics to racial biology) as pathological cases within the evolution of science. The literature on this problem is discussed in the introduction to Renneberg & Walker, and BEYERCHEN provides a classical study of the *Gleichschaltung* of a discipline, i.e. the conformation of physicists to the norms set by the Nazi regime. This study stresses the ideological pressures to which the discipline of physics was subjected during the early years of National Socialism, and the author criticizes earlier studies of the subject for representing the discipline merely through prominent members who were mainly engaged in fundamental research.

The inclusion of the "normal" sciences in the historiography of science under National Socialism resulted in a broadening of the historical outlook. In Mehrtens & Richter, Mehrtens broke through the older historiographical pattern (which had equated the *völkisch* variants with what counted as specifically Nazi in the sciences), by stipulating that the ideology of "service for the people" also assisted the economic machinery sustaining the Nazi system. Mehrtens's own studies, and a number of analyses of various disciplines, have revealed that those who actively sought to integrate the Nazi ideology into their research programme found ample opportunity for doing so in research legitimation strategies that argued for the significance of the work for the economic and military goals of the Third Reich. Conversely, the material and political support for science increased enormously with the intensification of rearmament after 1936, and again during World War II. LUDWIG provides a survey of the numerous organizations for the promotion of scientific research, set within the context of competing Nazi institutions. The collections listed here also include individual case studies of the "normal sciences", which make visible how, through the expertise they embodied, individual disciplines and their representatives served and actively supported the technocratic side of National Socialism. A good example is provided by WALKER, who chose a prominent case

(once again from physics) in the project for the harnessing of nuclear energy. Walker shows that modern physics was not merely subjected to ideological offensives, but that the subject effectively profited from the support by technocrats in public administration, industry, and the military. DEICHMANN's broad study of biology likewise dispels the notion that National Socialism universally obstructed scientific activity, while RÖSSLER has established that there is no simple way to distinguish between the technocratic and the ideological sides of National Socialism, since they had common goals. Her study of the discipline "Geography of Eastern Europe" reveals close links between the ideology of *Lebensraum*, racist population politics, and scientific planning.

With the integration of developments prior to 1933, the historical outlook of the topic has once again been broadened. It is widely known that the racist foundations of Nazi ideology are rooted in the tradition of biologistic and social Darwinist thinking of the Wilhelmian period. The most prominent studies of the precursors of Nazi science concern themselves with research in the field of racial hygiene and eugenics, and WEINDLING may be seen as representative of the sizeable body of literature on this topic. Other studies of disciplines or projects extending beyond the threshold of 1933 emphasize not only internalist elements within the historical continuity, but also an urge for professional security and a desire to realize projects already conceived. Such desires were fulfilled during the Third Reich, when disciplines, concepts, or projects were either geared towards (or turned out to already be serviceable to) Nazi goals. Individual examples for this can be found in Renneberg & Walker, and GEUTER is especially instructive in its study of the extremely successful professionalization of psychology in alliance with the state, business, and, above all, the military. The newer university histories which include the years before 1933 (again, Renneberg & Walker give extensive references to this literature) have emphasized how smoothly and uncritically the universities entered the Third Reich. The quest for motives behind this process has identified the political disposition of academics, the rejection of the Weimar Republic, Nazi sympathies, and anti-semitism. Indeed, the academic ethos totally failed to serve as an ethical bulwark against National Socialism.

MONIKA RENNEBERG
translated by Anna-Katherina Mayer

See also Eugenics; Planck; Race

Thomson, J.J. 1856–1940
British physicist

Anderson, David L., *The Discovery of the Electron: The Development of the Atomic Concept of Electricity*, Princeton, New Jersey: Van Nostrand, 1964

Buchwald, Jed Z., *From Maxwell to Microphysics: Aspects of Electromagnetic Theory in the Last Quarter of the Nineteenth Century*, Chicago: University of Chicago Press, 1985

Cavendish Laboratory, *A History of the Cavendish Laboratory 1871–1910*, London and New York: Longmans Green, 1910

Crowther, J.G., *British Scientists of the Twentieth Century*, London: Routledge and Kegan Paul, 1952

Crowther, J.G., *The Cavendish Laboratory, 1874–1974*, London: Macmillan, 1974

Davis, E.A. and I.J. Falconer, *J.J. Thomson and the Discovery of the Electron*, London: Taylor and Francis, 1997

Falconer, Isobel J., "Corpuscles, Electrons and Cathode Rays: J.J. Thomson and the Discovery of the Electron", *British Journal for the History of Science*, 20 (1987): 241–76

Falconer, Isobel J., "J.J. Thomson and 'Cavendish' Physics", in *The Development of the Laboratory: Essays on the Place of Experiment in Industrial Civilization*, edited by Frank A.J.L. James, London: Macmillan, and New York: American Institute of Physics, 1989

Hunt, Bruce, *The Maxwellians*, Cornell: Cornell University Press, 1991

Rayleigh, Robert John Strutt, Lord, *The Life of Sir J.J. Thomson, OM, Sometime Master of Trinity College*, Cambridge: Cambridge University Press, 1942; reprinted, London: Dawsons, 1969

Thomson, George P., *J.J. Thomson and the Cavendish Laboratory*, London: Thomas Nelson, 1964; New York: Doubleday, 1965

Thomson, J.J., *Recollections and Reflections*, London: Bell, 1936; New York: Macmillan, 1937; reprinted, New York: Arno Press, 1975

Sir Joseph John Thomson, Cavendish Professor of experimental physics at Cambridge University, was one of the most influential British scientists of the early 20th century. He commanded great respect through his own work on gaseous conduction, electrons, atomic theory, and the structure of light, and, through his influence on his research students, he set the agenda for British physics up to World War II. Many early works, largely based on the reminiscences of his students, explained his success as the product of uncomplicated "experimental genius" coupled with a vivid personality. Such works often portray his "discovery" of the corpuscle (now known as the electron) as the outcome of a long-lasting controversy over the nature of cathode rays, his electric and magnetic deflection measurement of the charge-to-mass ratio of the rays as the crucial experiment which revealed the presence of electrons, and the discovery of the isotopes of Neon as the intended outcome of his positive ray work. All these positions have been shown to be untenable by recent scholarship, such as FALCONER (1987), although they can still be found in many of the articles appearing in 1997, the centenary year of the electron. Among the older works of this type, most notable are those by Anderson and Crowther; ANDERSON focuses on the electron, which he treats as almost synonymous with cathode rays, drawing together relevant discharge experiments by Thomson and others, while CROWTHER (1952) attempts to give a social and psychological outline of Thomson, and also describes his experimental work.

A more rounded view is given in RAYLEIGH, the earliest, and still the best, biography. Rayleigh was one of Thomson's students, and he chronicles Thomson's life in great detail, describing his family background and home life as well as his scientific achievements. The great experimentalist theme is implicit, but Rayleigh was close enough to Thomson in time and philosophy not to discount theoretical ideas entirely. This is the only work to devote much space to Thomson's later years as Master of Trinity College and as a senior spokesman for science to the government.

Along the same lines, but briefer, is the biography by GEORGE P. THOMSON, Thomson's son. The scientific principles of his experiments are well described, and illustrated with diagrams, and there is a useful appendix on vacuum pumps which the author regards as essential to the experiments. However, although the theory is described, its relation to the experiments is unclear.

DAVIS & FALCONER, the only recent biography, attempts a more complete integration of Thomson and his environment, bringing out the various influences, both scientific and social, which informed his work. In their examination of the way in which Thomson arrived at the idea of a corpuscle, the authors bring out his underlying metaphysics and theoretical conceptions. The book reproduces a number of Thomson's original papers, selected for their readability and significance in the development of his ideas. A lengthy foreword by his grandson, David Thomson, gives new personal information.

Recent works on the development of Maxwellian electrodynamics provide essential background for some of the scientific influences on Thomson. It is evident in both Buchwald and Hunt that Thomson played only a minor role in this development, yet it formed a significant part of his underlying preconceptions. BUCHWALD is devoted exclusively to the theoretical ideas by which discrete charges (electrons) were introduced to the Maxwellian continuum. On this restricted topic the book is enlightening, covering an important, though often neglected, area of Thomson's work, but it is heavy going for the non-mathematician. HUNT concentrates more on the "Maxwellians" as a social group, to which Thomson was peripheral although, like them, he used the ether as a foundation of his scientific work. Hunt examines the mechanical tradition underlying Maxwellian ideas, and the ontological significance they assigned to the ether.

The best source for Thomson's position at the Cavendish is CAVENDISH LABORATORY. Produced in 1910 to commemorate 25 years of Thomson's professorship, it is divided up chronologically, with each chapter written by a research student present in the laboratory at the time. Inevitably, the quality of the historical information varies with the author of the chapter. The volume reviews all the research done at the Cavendish Laboratory, and also discusses the development of practical teaching, while a survey by Thomson also considers the role of technicians. Appendices list most of the publications emanating from the Cavendish, and nearly all the scientists who have worked there, including their previous education and positions held in 1910.

The works by Crowther and Falconer on the Cavendish rely heavily on the book prepared by the Cavendish Laboratory for their information. CROWTHER (1974) is a detailed social history of the laboratory, covering its first 100 years, and examining research, teaching, technicians, finance, and biographical details of many of the scientists. Five chapters are devoted to its development under Thomson, pulling together material from Rayleigh and J.J. Thomson, as well as from the Cavendish Laboratory. The book is a useful source, but has two irritating flaws: first, its uncritical reliance on secondary sources, which renders much of the discussion of Thomson's work suspect; and second, the lack of integration of references with text. The aim of FALCONER (1989) is more limited in scope. Looking at the change in the nature of the Cavendish Laboratory during Thomson's professorship, both in the type of research done and the characteristics of the students produced, she analyses this in terms of the different scientific traditions that Thomson represented, and in the way he exerted his influence within the laboratory.

Finally, the autobiography, J.J. THOMSON, is essential reading for anyone wishing for an insight into his personality. Relegating his own scientific work to one chapter near the end of the book, Thomson dwells at length on people he has encountered, and phenomena that have excited his interest, while remaining tantalisingly unclear concerning the role he played in many of the developments – scientific, social, and political – that he describes. Inevitably, also, there is very little information about his marriage or home life. His pride in his students is revealed in the appendix, which lists all those who have been elected Fellows of the Royal Society, and the professorships his students have taken up all over the world.

ISOBEL FALCONER

See also Atomic Theory; Electricity; Electromagnetism

Time

Barnett, Jo Ellen, *Time's Pendulum: The Quest to Capture Time – From Sundials to Atomic Clocks*, New York and London: Plenum, 1998

Borst, Arno, *The Ordering of Time: From the Ancient Computus to the Modern Computer*, translated from the German by Andrew Winnard, Chicago: University of Chicago Press, and Cambridge: Polity Press, 1993

Burchfield, Joe D., *Lord Kelvin and the Age of the Earth*, New York: Science History Publications, 1975

Glennie, Paul and Nigel Thrift, "Reworking E. P. Thompson's 'Time, Work-Discipline and Industrial Capitalism'", *Time and Society*, 5 (1996): 275–99

Gould, Stephen Jay, *Time's Arrow, Time's Cycle : Myth and Metaphor in the Discovery of Geological Time*, Cambridge, Massachusetts: Harvard University Press, 1987

Howse, Derek, *Greenwich Time and the Discovery of the Longitude*, Oxford and New York: Oxford University Press, 1980

Kern, Stephen, *The Culture of Time and Space, 1880–1918*, Cambridge, Massachusetts: Harvard University Press, 1983

Le Goff, Jacques, *Time, Work, and Culture in the Middle Ages*, translated from the French by Arthur Goldhammer, Chicago: University of Chicago Press, 1980 (original edition, 1977)

Macey, Samuel L. (ed.), *Encyclopedia of Time*, New York: Garland, 1994

Macey, Samuel L., *Time: A Bibliographic Guide*, New York: Garland, 1991

O'Malley, Michael, *Keeping Watch: A History of American Time*, New York: Viking, 1990

Schaffer, Simon, "Astronomers Mark Time: Discipline and the Personal Equation", *Science in Context*, 2/1 (1988): 115–45

Schivelbusch, Wolfgang, *The Railway Journey: Trains and Travel in the 19th Century*, translated from the German by Anselm Hollo, New York: Urizen, 1979, Oxford: Blackwell, 1980; as *The Railway Journey: The Industrialization of Time and Space in the 19th Century*, Berkeley, University of California Press, and Leamington Spa, Warwickshire, Berg, 1986 (original edition, 1978)

Selin, Helaine (ed.), *Encyclopaedia of the History of Science, Technology, and Medicine in Non-Western Cultures*, Dordrecht: Kluwer, 1997

Thompson, E.P., "Time, Work-Discipline, and Industrial Capitalism", *Past and Present*, 38 (1967): 56–97

Toulmin, Stephen and June Goodfield, *The Discovery of Time*, London: Hutchinson, and New York: Harper and Row, 1965

TOULMIN & GOODFIELD is a *tour-de-force* journey through time in Western thought, upon which most subsequent general histories of time are based. It examines historical and ahistorical conceptions within several spheres of learning: ancient history, the authority of the Scriptures, the revival of civil history, geological time, evolution, history as an academic discipline, and modern physical cosmology. Toulmin & Goodfield suggest that human history and natural history were separated at the time of Thucydides, and that this separation was important within a debate on the permanence of the world. They point to Giambattista Vico as the first to bring history back into natural philosophy, very much against the grain of Newtonian emphases on the timelessness of natural laws. They describe 1800 as a turning point. Before that date the world was generally viewed as static; afterwards, notions of dynamic change gained ground.

BARNETT is in a sense a popular rendering of Toulmin & Goodfield. It is divided into two parts, one on the history of clocks and one on the history of time as treated in Toulmin & Goodfield. It is a highly readable account offering good general coverage. It is thoroughly whiggish – past thought is evaluated in the terms of the latest science – making the narrative straightforward and simple.

Perhaps the single most influential text on the history of time is THOMPSON. It correlates industrial working habits and people's inward notion of time during the Industrial Revolution, in particular the replacement of task orientation (organization of time according to the necessity of performing particular tasks) with time orientation (work organized by time as given by the clock). Indeed, Thompson argues that a general diffusion of clocks took place in the late 18th century, just at the moment when the Industrial Revolution required a greater synchronization of labour. Thompson's article has had tremendous influence, especially for its suggestion that a time-sense could be internalized and was specific to particular historical periods.

Most of the literature on time takes one of the themes initiated in Toulmin & Goodfield and examines a Thompsonian time-sense.

LE GOFF has examined this theme for the Middle Ages. He traces the diffusion of time measurement in the Middle Ages, especially in the form of church clocks. He emphasizes two different sensibilities of time in ecclesiastical and commercial contexts, which he terms merchant's time and church time. A main part of Le Goff's story is the increasing use of merchant's time for the purposes of lengthening the working day, in other words, as a tool of exploitation.

BORST describes how medieval Europeans reckoned their time. He centres his account on the *computus*, a procedure for fixing dates and times taught to clerics in their *quadrivium* studies throughout the Middle Ages. Borst follows the development of this procedure and examines the neologisms it spawned, such as account and compute. One of his points is, *contra* Thomas Nipperdey, that the orientation toward the future, as opposed to living in the present, is not a feature of modernity but characterized medieval life to a large degree.

GOULD describes the discovery of deep time in geology, the notion that earth has existed for such a long time as to be almost incomprehensible. The book is structured to demolish the whiggish account of geology in most textbooks: geology progressing from superstition to science by increasingly facing the incontrovertible facts. In particular, Gould inverts the status of the villain (Thomas Burnet) and the two heroes (James Hutton and Charles Lyell) in order to debunk cardboard myths about science as pure observation and applied logic. Burnet is described instead as a rationalist whose reconstruction of the earth's history incorporated the need for both time's arrow (unidirectional time) and time's cycle (immutable laws). Hutton and Lyell, by contrast, focused exclusively upon the unidirectionality of time and are presented by Gould as narrowly denying the richness of history.

BURCHFIELD describes the encounter between geology and physics between 1850 and 1930, a debate that was almost exclusively British. Lyell's principle of geological forces working uniformly over vast periods of time was tempered by the calculations of the age of the earth by William Thompson (later Lord Kelvin), bringing the tools of thermodynamics to bear on the time required for our planet to cool to its present temperature. Burchfield describes the impact that this had upon geology. Thomson found the earth to be much younger than Lyell had suggested, and this presented a challenge to the very slow forces suggested within uniformitarianism. Burchfield also emphasizes the impact of physics-style quantification upon geology, and he takes the story up past Kelvin's death to include radioactive dating. Burchfield pays little attention to the popular and public aspects of the debate.

SCHIVELBUSCH is a highly entertaining account of railway culture in the 19th century. It covers briefly many aspects, such as the structure of the railway compartment, the disappearance of conversation between passengers, the fatigue of materials and human bodies, and the need to soften the hard industrial appearance of railroads with the use of upholstery and classical architecture for the public face of railway stations. He argues that the railway journey fundamentally altered the experience of time and space. One now travelled quickly from point to point without being able to notice the sights, smells, and sounds of the places in between. This caused "panoramic vision", a sense of large-scale structures with an attendant loss of fine-grained detail. Schivelbusch intriguingly juxtaposes this with commodification: merchandise could be much more widely distributed because of the railroads and was increasingly divorced from the local context of production, becoming characterized primarily by a price tag.

O'MALLEY is an account of the development from local to standard time in the US in the period 1825 to 1925. Rich with entertaining anecdotes, the book examines the impact of such things as train schedules and factory punch clocks upon everyday life, including the rise of an ethic of punctuality. The end point of the book, the Scopes trial, characterizes its general theme. This trial resulted in the replacement of a biblical measure of time with "scientific" time, fed by a large infrastructure of precision measurement and telecommunication.

HOWSE is an account that developed out of the exhibition galleries at the Old Royal Observatory in Greenwich, London. It covers all manners of time-keeping from antiquity to the atomic clock. Special emphasis is placed on the history of Greenwich Mean Time, that is the establishment of an infrastructure encompassing high-precision astronomical observation and a telegraphic network for the distribution of time signals. It describes some of the politics at national and international conferences on the coordination and standardization of time, but the main strength of the book is in its clear exposition of technicalities, such as escapements and quartz crystal clocks. The book also contains a wealth of amusing anecdotes.

SCHAFFER describes the actual work and its organization at the Greenwich Observatory under the stern leadership of George Biddell Airy (1801–92). Significantly, this was the first place where employees had to clock in. The routine observation of stars crossing the meridian by shift workers could result in a precise measurement of time only with strict management of the personal differences of the observers. Schaffer reveals the technical and managerial tools employed to control each observer's individuality. He also describes how experimental psychology was born in this setting where individual differences were reduced to nothing more than reaction times.

KERN argues that the introduction of world standard time at the turn of the century had an enormous impact upon communication, industry, war, art, science, literature, and the everyday life of the masses. He adopts Thompson's notion of age-specific time-sense (and space-sense). He notices its reductionism, but argues that it results in interesting historical narratives. Kern's technique is to juxtapose thematically related developments from all cultural domains. The result is a highly learned and suggestive text covering, among other things, science, philosophy, painting, poetry, literature, psychoanalysis, diplomacy, and music ("sometimes a link can be found"). Kern finds the most interesting aspect of time-sense to be that while standard time was being increasingly enforced, a plurality of private times was explored.

GLENNIE & THRIFT is a spirited attack on Thompson. It argues convincingly that all historial eras had many contemporary time-senses. They historicize Thompson's article itself by pointing to the 1960s as a high point of societal synchronization: national radio and television, standardized working days (from 9 to 5), etc., making it plausible that Thompson should have seen societies as sharing one general time-sense. Glennie & Thrift conveniently array a substantial amount of historical research on time-sense in order to refute Thompson.

There are also useful reference works for the history of time.

MACEY (1991) is a bibliography that contains lists of literature without further comment. The material is structured simply by the chapter headings: multidisciplinary studies, aging, archaeology, art and architecture, biology, chemistry, economics, geography, geology and geophysics, history and historiography, horology, law, literature and language, mathematics, medicine, music, navigation, philosophy, physics, political science, psychology, religion, sociology and anthropology, time management, time's measurements and division. The book contains an author index and a subject index.

MACEY (1994) is an encyclopedia of more than 700 pages with some 360 entries. The entries under headings that are not explicitly about time (e.g. Derrida or Music: Western) deal only with the time-related aspects of that topic. Each entry contains a short list of suggested further reading.

SELIN's edited volume covers all manner of science-related topics in the non-Western world providing a useful corrective to the exclusively Western literature discussed above. It includes entries on time for many cultures on most continents: Africa, China, India, the Islamic world, Maya culture, and the Pueblo world. In addition, there is a general entry giving an overview of anthropological literature on time. Calendars are treated in separate entries, again for a broad range of cultures. All entries have helpful lists for further reading.

ARNE HESSENBRUCH

See also Clocks

Toxicology

Amberger-Lahrmann, Mechthild and Dietrich Schmähl (eds), *Gifte: Geschichte der Toxikologie*, Berlin, Heidelberg, and New York: Springer, 1988

Bartrip, Peter, "A 'Pennurth of Arsenic for Rat Poison': The Arsenic Act, 1851 and the Prevention of Secret Poisoning", *Medical History*, 36 (1992): 53–69

Coley, Noel G., "Alfred Swaine Taylor, MD, FRS (1806–1880): Forensic Toxicologist", *Medical History*, 35 (1991): 409–27

Earles, Melvin P., "Early Theories of the Mode of Action of Drugs and Poisons", *Annals of Science*, 17 (1961): 97–110

Grmek, Mirko Drazen, *Raisonnement expérimental et recherches toxicologiques chez Claude Bernard*, Geneva and Paris: Droz, 1973

Hoppe, Brigitte, "Louis Lewin (1850–1929): Sein Beitrag zur Entwicklung der Ethnopharmakologie, Toxikologie und Arbeitsmedizin", (dissertation), Berlin: Freie Universität, 1985

Knoefel, Peter K., *Felice Fontana: Life and Work*, vol. 2, Trento, Italy: Società di Studi Trentini di Scienze Storiche, 1984

Lewin, Louis, *Die Gifte in der Weltgeschichte: Toxikologische, allgemeinverständliche Untersuchungen der historischen Quellen*, Berlin: Springer, 1920

Maehle, Andreas-Holger, *Johann Jakob Wepfer (1620–1695) als Toxikologe: Die Fallstudien und Tierexperimente aus seiner Abhandlung über den Wasserschierling (1679)*, Aarau, Switzerland: Sauerländer, 1987

Porter, Roy and Mikuláš Teich (eds), *Drugs and Narcotics in History*, Cambridge and New York: Cambridge University Press, 1995

The most comprehensive history of toxicology has been edited by AMBERGER-LAHRMANN & SCHMÄHL. Written by experts in the present toxicological sub-disciplines, it covers narcotics, social drugs, toxic side-effects of medicines, forensic toxicology, radiation toxicology, carcinogenic substances, occupational toxicology, and legal requirements in industrial toxicology. It is mainly useful as a reference work on the progress of medical knowledge since the 19th century, although some general problems are also highlighted – such as the relativity of toxicity in the tradition of the Paracelsian *dosis sola facit venenum* (the dose alone makes a poison), adequate risk assessment in new medicines and industrial chemicals, and the ethical conflict between the demands of consumer protection and animal welfare in obligatory animal testing.

The social aspects of drugs and poisons, alongside the scientific, are a central theme in the collection of essays edited by PORTER & TEICH, which covers the period from antiquity to the present day and gives an interdisciplinary perspective. The medico–historical approach is adopted by John Scarborough and Andreas-Holger Maehle. Scarborough demonstrates detailed knowledge of opium in Hellenistic and Roman medicine, which pertain to both the drug's medicinal benefits and its dangers. He argues that the latter were seen rather in its potential toxicity than in its habit-forming properties. This was still true in the 18th century, and Maehle emphasizes the wide therapeutic use of opium in Western medicine at this time, and shows the drug's important role in the development of methods and theories of experimental pharmacology, toxicology, and neurophysiology. A piece of comparative cultural history is provided by Rudi Matthee, who observes a pattern in the global spread of tobacco, coffee, cacao, tea, and distilled liquors from the late 16th to the early 18th centuries. All these now so-called "social drugs" were introduced as medicinal agents, and their social acceptance was linked to moral and religious controversies, which gave way to economic interests (taxation), before popularization set in. Epidemiological and anthropological perspectives are employed by Stephen E. Kunitz and Jerrold E. Levy in a study on alcohol-related health problems in North American Indians.

The most common approach in this volume is that of social history, directed broadly to the question of access to and use of drugs and poisons that have been demarcated and controlled. S.W.F. Holloway sees the Arsenic Act of 1851, the first restriction on the sale of poisons in Britain, as an example of bureaucratic control that needs to be distinguished from the model of professional control, via improved qualifications of druggists and chemists, that had been advocated by the Pharmaceutical Society. His view is at variance with that of BARTRIP, who has argued for a close connection between the Arsenic Act and subsequent pharmaceutical reform. The Harrison Narcotic Act of 1914, which made opiates and cocaine legally available in the US on prescription only- and soon prevented doctors from prescribing maintenance doses for addicts, is at the centre of the contribution by Caroline J. Acker. She suggests that the American medical profession's support for this legal restriction was motivated by the wish to be exonerated of responsibility for the problem of iatrogenic addiction. This coincided with changes in the perception of addiction by the American public, which are elucidated by John Parascandola in a semantic study of the word "drug". The growing importance of the chemical and pharmaceutical industry for the development and testing of new substances since the late 19th century is illustrated by essays from Erika Hickel (on Germany) and Judy Slinn (on Britain). Finally, contemporary issues are considered by Virginia Berridge, who analyses British drug policies in the face of AIDS, and by the psychiatrist Ann Dally, who makes critical and controversial observations on the current "war on drugs".

To complete the social dimension of toxicology, readers with an interest in the historical role of poisons as a means of murder and suicide will find rich and carefully documented information in the classic compilation by the Berlin toxicologist, LEWIN. Written shortly after World War I, it also includes a historical account of poisons as warfare agents.

While – with the exception of Lewin – the social history of drugs and poisons is a relatively new field, there are a number of studies on the scientific development of toxicology. MAEHLE has examined the animal experiments of the Swiss physician Johann Jakob Wepfer in the 1670s, which are generally regarded as the first example of a systematic, scientific testing of poisons. Changes in toxicological theories from the 17th to the early 19th centuries have been investigated by EARLES, and the numerous poison experiments of the Abbé Felice Fontana in the late 18th century – including viper venom, curare, cherry-laurel, and opium – have been analysed by KNOEFEL.

Three studies give insights into 19th-century toxicology after the introduction of chemical analysis and the systematization of the subject by Mathieu J.B. Orfila. GRMEK has examined Claude Bernard's laboratory work on carbon oxide intoxication and arrow poisons (curare, strychnine) as a key to the French physiologist's scientific thought. In this way, Grmek's study illustrates the importance of toxicology for the development of experimental physiology and vice versa, epitomized in Bernard's concept of the localized action of poisons on specific anatomo-physiological elements. COLEY has studied the forensic toxicology of Alfred Swaine Taylor against the background of 19th-century improvements in both inorganic and organic analysis. Finally, the scientific biography of Louis Lewin by HOPPE gives a well-documented overview of this outstanding toxicologist's research, which encompassed various psychotropic drugs and addiction, the side-effects of medicines, occupational toxicology, arrow poisons, abortifacients, and the historical aspects of poisons.

Despite its broad coverage, there are still considerable gaps in the historiography of toxicology. A comprehensive study of the development of toxicology as an academic discipline and of its institutionalization is much needed. Interdisciplinary work remains to be done on the emergence of forensic toxicology, and a history of modern environmental toxicology would certainly be desirable.

ANDREAS-HOLGER MAEHLE

See also Anti-Vivisection; Drugs; Experimental Physiology; Forensic Medicine

Traditional Medicine

Brown, Diana DeG., *Umbanda: Religion and Politics in Urban Brazil*, Ann Arbor, Michigan: UMI Research Press, 1986

Coreil, J., "Innovation Among Haitian Healers: The Adoption of Oral Rehydration Therapy", *Human Organization*, 47 (1988): 48–57

Fabrega, Horacio and Daniel B. Silver, *Illness and Shamanistic Curing in Zinancantan: An Ethnomedical Analysis*, Stanford, California: Stanford University Press, 1973

Foster, George M. and Barbara Gallatin Anderson, *Medical Anthropology*, New York: John Wiley, 1978

Fulder, Stephen, *The Handbook of Complementary Medicine*, Sevenoaks, Kent: Coronet, 1984; 2nd edition, Oxford and New York: Oxford University Press, 1988

Helman, Cecil, *Culture, Health, and Illness: An Introduction for Health Professionals*, Bristol: Wright-PSG, 1984; 2nd edition, London and Boston: Wright, 1990; 3rd edition, Oxford and Boston: Butterworth-Heinemann, 1994

Kleinman, Arthur, *Patients and Healers in the Context of Culture: An Exploration of the Borderland Between Anthropology, Medicine, and Psychiatry*, Berkeley: University of California Press, 1980

Last, M., "Professionalization of Indigenous Healers", in *Medical Anthropology: A Handbook of Theory and Method*, edited by Thomas M. Johnson and Carolyn F. Sargent, New York: Greenwood Press, 1990, 349–66

Martin, M., "Native American Healers: Thoughts for Post-Traditional Healers", *Journal of the American Medical Association*, 245 (1981): 141–43

McGuire, Meredith B., *Ritual Healing in Suburban America*, New Brunswick, New Jersey: Rutgers University Press, 1988

Ngubane, H., "Aspects of Clinical Practice and Traditional Organization of Indigenous Healers in South Africa", *Social Science and Medicine*, 15B (1981): 361–65

Snow, Loudell F., *Walkin' over Medicine*, Boulder, Colorado: Westview Press, 1993

Velimirovic, B., "Is Integration of Traditional and Western Medicine Really Possible?", in *Anthropology and Primary Care*, edited by J. Coreil and J.D. Mull, Boulder, Colorado: Westview Press, 1990

World Health Organization, *The Promotion and Development of Traditional Medicine*, Geneva: World Health Organization, 1978

World Health Organization, *Traditional Birth Attendants: An Annotated Bibliography on Their Training*, Geneva: World Health Organization, 1979

World Health Organization, *Traditional Birth Attendants: A Joint WHO/UNFPA/UNICEF Statement*, Geneva: World Health Organization, 1990

Traditional or folk medicine usually refers to those forms of indigenous healing that were once common in the pre-industrial era, but which still survive in many parts of the world. There is no universal form of traditional medicine: its beliefs and behaviours differ widely from one culture to the next, often with marked variations even at the local or village level. A great number of these diverse forms have been described from different parts of the world; in each case, the type of traditional medicine practised is always the product of a particular time and place, and a specific local social and cultural context. In many countries, syncretic forms of healing are becoming increasingly common, combining traditional, modern, and imported elements. Apart from South and East Asia, traditional medicine normally features in non-literate societies. For that reason, most of the literature stems from the industrialized world or from global institutions such as the World Health Organization (WHO). For the same reason, most literature covers traditional medicine of the present and recent past.

Despite this diversity, KLEINMAN describes some of the broad generalizations that can be made about traditional practitioners – particularly, the division between "sacred" and "secular" healers. The former (including shamans, diviners, and astrologers) generally deal with supernatural explanations for illness, while the latter (including bone-setters, herbalists, and midwives) have mainly technical skills. In practice, though, these roles often overlap. Kleinman's book is a detailed ethnographic study of the range of traditional healers, sacred and secular, found in modern Taiwan – especially the shaman of *tang-ki*.

HELMAN describes some of the many paths into folk healing, used by traditional practitioners world-wide. These include the acquisition of skills and healing powers through inheritance (being born into a "healing family"), through one's position within a family (such as the "seventh son of a seventh son" in parts of rural Ireland), through revelation (becoming aware of one's "gift" after an intense emotional experience, such as illness, trance, or dream), through apprenticeship to an established healer, or through the acquisition of a particular skill on one's own (such as the "injectionist").

The literature on traditional healers usually emphasizes their mastery of certain practical and psychological techniques, sometimes based on esoteric knowledge – either inherited within a family, or acquired from others. These may include forms of divination, and the use of herbal and other remedies. Helman describes how the therapeutic approach of traditional healers is usually holistic, incorporating physical, psychological, religious, and social forms of intervention, and that they often aim to treat not only the individual, but also their family and community at the same time.

FABREGA & SILVER give a detailed ethnography of one particular type of traditional healer, the *h'ilol* or shaman in the community of Zinancantan, Mexico. Unlike Western doctors, the shaman's relationship with his community is characterized by a shared world-view, and by personal closeness, warmth, informality, and the use of everyday language in consultations. He is a figure of high prestige in the community, whose tasks include articulating and reinforcing their cultural values. He is believed to act not only for the patient's benefit, but also for the benefit of their family, community, and even the gods.

MARTIN describes how, in Native American traditional healing, the focus of attention is often the family, as well as the patient. As in other cultural groups, the family is often intimately involved, in both diagnosis and treatment, and takes part in all the appropriate healing rituals on behalf of its sick relative.

Perhaps the most common form of traditional healer, especially in developing countries, is the folk midwife or traditional birth attendant. These include the *parteras* of Mexico, the *comadronas* of Puerto Rico, the *nanas* of Jamaica, the *dais* of India, and the *dayas* of Egypt. As well as assisting at labour and birth, traditional birth attendants often supervise antenatal and post-natal care, perform important rituals during pregnancy and birth, and in some countries perform female circumcision. They usually work within the local cultural premises, and have an important social and ritual role within those communities, their practice thus having both "sacred" and "secular" components. The World Health Organization, despite reservations about the lack of formal training of most traditional birth attendants, and the limitations of their techniques, now regards them as a major resource in health care. It is promoting their further training and integration into national health care programmes, while at the same time emphasizing the need for the "continuation of traditional art", and for respect for their roots in traditional cultures. The three WHO reports describe how traditional birth attendants, who are almost always female, are found in virtually every village, and in many urban neighbourhoods, throughout Africa, Asia, Latin America, and the Caribbean. The report of 1978 estimates that in Africa and rural India, 80 % of women are assisted during birth by a traditional birth attendant, and that world-wide they deliver an estimated 60–80 % of all babies.

WHO (1990) suggests further that, after training, traditional birth attendants could also act as community health educators, giving advice on nutrition, family planning, immunisations, AIDS prevention, the importance of personal and environmental hygiene, and the need to bring babies and children to local health clinics.

As well as traditional birth attendants, WHO (1978) also recommends that other forms of traditional medicine be promoted, developed, and integrated wherever possible with modern, scientific medicine in developing countries (where medical manpower is in short supply). However, they stress the need "to ensure respect, recognition and collaboration among the practitioners of the various systems concerned". Traditional healers have been used successfully in several national and local health programmes. COREIL describes how some Haitian traditional healers have proved successful in promoting the use of oral rehydration therapy for diarrhoeal diseases.

As the title indicates, WHO (1979) gives an extensive bibliography. VELIMIROVIC, however, sees the WHO initiative on traditional medicine as well-meaning, but misguided. He argues that its integration with the formal sector of health care since 1978, "has contributed virtually nothing to solving the monumental health problems of the developing world", or to the attainment of the WHO aim of "health for all by the year 2000". This is due in part to an unclear definition of what constitutes "traditional medicine", and to the uncritical assumption of its efficacy and safety. In many cases, he writes, the beliefs and behaviours of traditional healers can be detrimental to health, and so they themselves are part of the problem. Furthermore, in many developing countries, it "is often not as popular with the people themselves as health planners believe".

In most societies, traditional healers are often linked, formally and informally, with other such healers. NGUBANE describes how, among Zulu traditional healers in South Africa, these links tend to be by informal networks. Each Zulu diviner of *isangoma* may make informal contact, over a 3–5-year period, with over 400 fellow diviners all over the country. This provides them with an opportunity to exchange information and techniques, and to monitor each other's behaviour.

In other cases, the links between healers have recently become more formalized. LAST describes how, as a result of the 1978 Alma–Ata Declaration of "Health for All by the Year 2000", the "professionalization" of traditional healers has markedly increased, especially in Africa. By forming professional organizations, they hope to advance their interests and those of their clients, to raise their prestige, to improve standards or practice, to gain official support, and to define an area of health care that only they can provide. Some – like the Zimbabwe National Traditional Healers Association – have become recognized by their governments as professional bodies in their own right. Last points out, however, that in many cases folk healers are too diffuse a group, and too rooted within local contexts, to be standardized or organized. Often their legitimacy can derive only from local tradition, or their own charisma, and not from some distant government bureaucracy.

Traditional healers are not just a rural phenomenon. With the growth of urbanization in developing countries, they are now found in many urban communities and shanty-towns, where they often practice within healing cults or churches, which may be organized around a single charismatic leader. BROWN, for example, describes the diverse forms and socio–cultural context of Umbanda, a popular Afro-Brazilian religion and healing-system that has millions of adherents, especially in urban areas. Its forms of healing incorporate traditional West African, Catholic, and spiritist elements. Similar syncretic religions, particularly with African roots, are found in many other Latin American and Caribbean countries.

FULDER describes how traditional medicine is not only a phenomenon of non-industrialized societies, as examples can be found in most Western societies. His survey reveals the overlap that exists between many forms of traditional and "alternative" (or "complementary") healing currently practised in Britain. Some (such as herbalism and spiritual healing) have indigenous roots, while others (such as acupuncture, traditional Chinese medicine, and Shiatsu) have been imported from the Far East. Similarly, McGUIRE describes the many forms of non-medical healing practised in suburban America, including the various new forms of psychotherapy, the manifestations of the Human Potential Movement, Christian and "New Age" healing, and other types of healing derived from Buddhism, Hinduism, Jainism, and other oriental religions. SNOW describes the wide variety of folk healers found in the many low-income African–American neighbourhoods in the US. These commonly include "herb doctors", "root doctors", spiritualists, "conjure" men and women, healing ministers and faith healers, Voodoo "houngans" or "mambos", neighbourhood "prophets", "granny women", and the vendors of magical herbs, roots, and patent medicines.

Fulder also describes two regions – India, and the People's Republic of China – where there has been a successful integration of Western and traditional forms of health care. In both cases, indigenous healing traditions enjoy almost the same legitimacy and official support as Western medicine. In China, traditional Chinese medicine provides a complementary system

of health care for much of the population, especially in rural areas. In India, there are 91 recognized Ayurvedic (Hindu) medical schools, and 10 Unani (Muslim) medical schools, and Ayurvedic medicine, in particular, serves a large proportion of the Indian population. Similarly, an official Central Council for Homeopathy has recognized 200,000 homeopathic practitioners and supervizes their training. The government supports 130–50 homeopathic hospitals, and 1,500 homeopathic dispensaries.

At present, despite the growth of professionalization and the support of WHO, the situation of traditional medicine is in flux. FOSTER & ANDERSON, in a wide-ranging review of the subject, note that in recent years the actual number of traditional healers in many countries has declined. This may be due to urbanization, often associated with increasing levels of education and availability of medical services, as well as to low pay and a reluctance to undergo a lengthy apprenticeship to an older healer.

CECIL G. HELMAN

See also Africa: health and healing; China: medicine; Complementary Medicine; Holistic Medicine; India: medicine; Quackery

Tuberculosis

Barnes, David S., *The Making of a Social Disease: Tuberculosis in Nineteenth-Century France*, Berkeley: University of California Press, 1995

Bates, Barbara, *Bargaining for Life: A Social History of Tuberculosis, 1876–1938*, Philadelphia: University of Pennsylvania Press, 1992

Bryder, Linda, *Below the Magic Mountain: A Social History of Tuberculosis in Twentieth-Century Britain*, Oxford: Clarendon Press, and New York: Oxford University Press, 1988

Cummins, Lyle S., *Tuberculosis in History: From the 17th Century to Our Own Times*, London: Ballière, Tindall and Cox, and Baltimore: Williams and Wilkins, 1949

Dubos, Rene and Jean Dubos, *The White Plague: Tuberculosis, Man, and Society*, Boston: Little Brown, 1952; 2nd edition, New Brunswick, New Jersey: Rutgers University Press, 1987

Ryan, Frank, *Tuberculosis: The Greatest Story Never Told: The Search for the Cure and the New Global Threat*, Bromsgrove, Worcestershire: Swift, 1992; as *The Forgotten Plague: How the Battle Against Tuberculosis Was Won – and Lost*, Boston: Little Brown, 1993

Smith, Francis B., *The Retreat of Tuberculosis, 1850–1950*, London and New York: Croom Helm, 1988

Szreter, Simon, "The Importance of Social Intervention in Britain's Mortality Decline, 1850–1914: A Re-Interpretation of the Role of Public Health", *Social History of Medicine*, 1 (1988): 1–37

A major killer in the West before the 20th century, tuberculosis has attracted considerable historical attention. Particular points of interest in respect of the disease's history have been its role as a metaphor for social ideologies, its behaviour in the 19th and 20th centuries, the so-called "conquest" of the disease, and the fashionable sanatorium treatment of the period c.1880–1940.

The historical literature on tuberculosis deals almost exclusively with the disease in its respiratory form, and falls into three broad categories. The first of these belongs essentially to the older, heroic tradition of medical history that emphasises the progress of medicine from a largely ineffective art to a highly successful science in the late 20th century. Superior examples of this genre are DUBOS & DUBOS and Ryan. The former has classic status, partly as an account of the social and scientific history of tuberculosis since the late 18th century, and partly as an explanation of the disease in terms of the relationships between disease agent, host, and environment – an approach that Dubos & Dubos elaborated in later work, and which has been highly influential. RYAN's work, by contrast, focuses on the story of Selman Waksman, the man who claimed credit for the discovery of streptomycin, the first effective drug to be deployed against the disease. Despite a number of inaccuracies, Ryan offers the most detailed study of the process of this scientific discovery, making use of diaries, letters, and oral history sources to illuminate the personal histories of his protagonists. Also in this category is CUMMINS's brief account of the changing medical views of tuberculosis from the late 17th to the late 19th centuries. Cummins presents a series of studies on contributions to the study and knowledge of tuberculosis, beginning with early English medical writers such as Sydenham and Thomas Willis, progressing through the early 19th-century French school, and concluding with that century's two most influential figures, Edward Livingstone Trudeau and Robert Koch. The section on the latter has been superseded, but the book remains a useful guide to the earlier tuberculosis literature.

The second category of works on tuberculosis is of the modern type, which seeks to place the history of the disease within a social, political, and ideological framework, and to balance the old triumphalist literature by detailing the wider context of scientific backcasts, dissension, compromise, and competition in which the celebrated achievements were enmeshed. These studies generally focus on the experience of one country, but SMITH discusses a range of issues relating to tuberculosis by drawing on evidence from a number of Western countries. His sometimes dogmatic overview is principally concerned with etiologies of the disease, and medical and popular responses to them. To this end he also examines the phenomenon of the sanatorium, and the specific remedies purported to cure tuberculosis. The account is framed within a wider discussion of the incidence, morbidity, and mortality of the disease.

Most Western countries identified tuberculosis as a critical national problem during the 19th century. In Britain and France, this discovery was associated with concerns about national efficiency; in the United States Koch's discovery of the bacillus of tuberculosis stimulated the campaign against the disease. Three interpretative studies offer more intimate perspectives on the tuberculosis experience of these countries. France was early to identify tuberculosis as a national problem, and BARNES offers the only English-language account of tuberculosis in France (there is a useful French-language literature). His work explores the social, medical, literary, and

political responses provoked by a disease that came to symbolise both an ideal of redemptive suffering and a model of vice and degeneration to respectable French society. The account includes a local study of public health measures against the disease in Le Havre, and uncovers the part that tuberculosis played in the narratives of working-class French politics at the turn of the century. BATES documents the experiences of American tuberculosis patients, using a wide range of sources, notably the correspondence of Lawrence Flick, one of the pioneers in tuberculosis treatment. Within the context of the campaigns to control and cure the disease, Bates shows how its victims coped with their illness and the social problems it created. Adopting a rather different perspective, BRYDER examines the rise of the anti-tuberculosis movement in Britain from c.1890, focusing particularly on the institutional responses as exemplified in private sanatoria and in the dispensaries and treatment centres established as a result of the National Insurance Act of 1911. The methods used in these institutions, and the patients' points of view, form an integral part of this account, which amplifies our understanding of the extent to which tuberculosis conveyed a social stigma upon its sufferers.

The third important category of tuberculosis literature is concerned with the role of the disease in the decline of mortality in the West since 1850, and with the reasons for the decline of tuberculosis mortality that dates from well before medicine was able to offer a hope of cure. Although the issue is inevitably touched on in the different modern studies of the disease, the great bulk of the specialist literature on this topic is to be found in periodicals published since 1988. The *agent provocateur* of this literature was the article published by SZRETER, in which he challenged Thomas McKeown's hypotheses of 1876 that the decline of tuberculosis was due to improving levels of nutrition after 1840, and that the decline of mortality was in turn initiated by the reduction in tuberculosis.

ANNE HARDY

See also Bacteriology; Epidemics; Public Health

Turing, Alan   1912–1954

British mathematician

Bernstein, Jeremy, "A Portrait of Alan Turing", in his *Cranks, Quarks, and the Cosmos: Writings on Science*, New York: Basic Books, 1993

Gandy, R.O., "Dr. A.M. Turing, O.B.E., F.R.S.", *Nature* (18 September 1954): 535–56

Good, I.J., "Early Work on Computers at Bletchley", *Annals of the History of Computing*, 1 (1979): 38–48

Hilton, Peter, "Working with Alan Turing", *Mathematical Intelligencer*, 13/4 (1991): 22–25

Hodges, Andrew, *Alan Turing: The Enigma*, New York: Simon and Schuster, and London: Burnett Books, 1983

Murray, Joan, "Hut 8 and Naval Enigma, Part I", in *Codebreakers: The Inside Story of Bletchley Park*, edited by F.H. Hinsley and Alan Stripp, Oxford and New York: Oxford University Press, 1993

Newman, M.H.A., "Alan Mathison Turing", in *Biographical Memoirs of Fellows of the Royal Society of London*, 1 (1955): 253–63

Turing, Sara, *Alan M. Turing*, Cambridge: Heffer, 1959

Despite the fact that Alan Turing's work in cryptanalysis is regarded as crucial to the Allied Forces's victory during World War II, and his work on computable numbers is seminal in computer science and artificial intelligence, accounts of his life are scant. He remained, in fact, an obscure figure until the 1970s, largely because of the British government's enforced secrecy around his cryptanalysis work during World War II and because of British society's censure of his overt homosexuality.

A typical example of this obsessive secrecy is the formal obituary by GANDY for *Nature*. Turing was Gandy's PhD supervisor at Cambridge and, after the war, became a close friend. Gandy lists Turing's mathematical and technical accomplishments, but Turing's role in breaking the German Enigma code for the Government Code and Cypher School from 1939 to 1945 is reduced to "the work he did during the war".

NEWMAN's more extensive obituary was published a year after Gandy's. Newman was the first to read Turing's paper on computable numbers before the war and, much later, was a character witness at Turing's criminal trial for gross indecency. His account follows the life of a pure mathematician and provides technical details of Turing's major research projects: the notion of computable numbers and the Turing machine; the pioneering work in the design of subroutines for the ACE, the automatic computer at the National Physical Laboratory; the Turing test for machine intelligence; and his theory of morphogenesis. As Gandy had done, Newman refers to the six years during the war as "his work for the Foreign Office", and characterized this period as an interruption to his scientific work. Newman also minimizes the times in Turing's life during which he showed great eagerness and competence in the hands-on work necessary for the application of his theoretical achievements.

In her attempt to fashion a worthier public account of Turing's life, Sara TURING wrote a tribute to her son that labors under several constraints: limited literary competence, no scientific expertise, no knowledge of Alan's wartime work, and no admission of his homosexuality. Her eulogy reads like a school report and is filled with flattering quotations from letters and memoirs. Nevertheless, it has become one of the main sources for subsequent encyclopedia entries on Turing.

With the relaxation in the early 1970s of the Official Secrets Act, Turing's World War II work was finally mentioned by several of his colleagues at the British code-breaking facility at Bletchley Park. GOOD and HILTON, who were both part of Turing's area called Hut 8, and MURRAY, who was Turing's erstwhile fiancée, provide accounts of a more three-dimensional character with their details about Turing's style of working, but they say little of his crytanalytic techniques.

By far the most detailed and comprehensive biography of Turing's life is that by HODGES. Although he never met Turing personally, Hodges draws from a treasury of Turing's personal papers and on a plethora of interviews with his friends and associates. The result is a biography that integrates the many facets of Turing's personality with his views on philosophical and scientific questions. This biography delves deeply into both the personal details of Turing's life and into the technical details of his research.

Hodges's biography corrects earlier accounts, in that he brings to light Turing's interest and work in the political and practical aspects of his efforts to build a computer, and deals with the social, cultural, and historical context within which Turing lived. The highlight of this biography is the last chapter, which shows how Turing's life was an allegory for the ideals that he espoused: first, his so-called desert-island mentality for crafting his own resources; second, his comparable strategies for developing theories, which led him to work always from first principles and to remain unaffected by received opinion; third, his personal struggle to reconcile his beliefs about the deterministic nature of the human mind with his experience of his own obsession over free will, and finally his uncompromising regard for the truth.

Because it towers above all previous accounts, Hodges's biography is the source for all subsequent accounts. Hugh Whitmore's stage play, *Breaking the Code*, for example, is based solely on Hodges's book, as is the derivative PBS video of the same name. In fact this biography is so thorough that it seems to have discouraged any new original inquiries into Turing's life.

At least one of these subsequent accounts, however, complains that Hodges's level of detail may have gone too far and in fact might be regarded as lurid and obsessive at times, especially when it focuses on Turing's homosexuality. BERNSTEIN feels that Hodges's biography is too polemical and seems ideologically motivated, written as it is by someone who claims membership of the London Gay Liberation Front. However, in as much as he denies the relevance of some of the flesh-and-blood details of Turing's private life to his public biography, Bernstein's own account devotes considerable attention to Turing's last homosexual affair and his subsequent trial, conviction, and punishment for gross indecency.

LAWRENCE SOUDER

See also Artificial Intelligence; Computing

U

United States: general works

Bruce, Robert V., *The Launching of Modern American Science, 1846–1876*, New York: Knopf, 1987

Daniels, George H., *American Science in the Age of Jackson*, New York: Columbia University Press, 1968

Dupree, A. Hunter, *Science in the Federal Government: A History of Policies and Activities to 1940*, Cambridge, Massachusetts: Belknap Press of Harvard University Press, 1957

Dupree, A. Hunter, "The History of American Science – A Field Finds Itself", *American Historical Review* (1966): 863–74

Greene, John C., *American Science in the Age of Jefferson*, Ames: Iowa State University Press, 1984

Hindle, Brooke, *The Pursuit of Science in Revolutionary America, 1735–1789*, Chapel Hill: University of North Carolina Press, 1956

Kevles, Daniel J., *The Physicists: The History of a Scientific Community in Modern America*, New York: Knopf, 1978; revised edition, Cambridge, Massachusetts: Harvard University Press, 1995

Kohlstedt, Sally Gregory and Margaret W. Rossiter (eds), *Historical Writing on American Science: Perspectives and Prospects*, Baltimore: Johns Hopkins University Press, 1986

Reingold, Nathan, *Science, American Style*, New Brunswick, New Jersey: Rutgers University Press, 1991

Rosenberg, Charles E., *No Other Gods: On Science and American Social Thought*, Baltimore: Johns Hopkins University Press, 1976

Rossiter, Margaret W., *Women Scientists in America: Struggles and Strategies to 1940*, Baltimore: Johns Hopkins University Press, 1982

Stearns, Raymond P., *Science in the British Colonies of America*, Urbana: University of Illinois Press, 1970

Historical writing on science in the United States is essentially, although not entirely, a post-World War II phenomenon. Characteristic of that writing is the recognition that science is a human activity carried out within a particular cultural and political context. For most Americanists, the proper subjects of historical research are humans and their institutions, not the evolution of abstract scientific ideas, and to understand the history of science, the historian must also understand the history of the nation within which the science was practised.

This position has been most clearly articulated by DUPREE (1966), who sees the history of US science as part of US history, and rejects George Sarton's insistence that historians of science must have scientific expertise.

One approach to the history of science in the United States which has been very fruitful has been chronological. There are monographs that describe and analyse US science from the 16th to the late 19th centuries. For the most part, these monographs emphasize the importance of patronage and an institutional infrastructure for the successful prosecution of scientific research.

STEARNS underscores the role of the Royal Society of London and of individual British scientists in promoting scientific activity in the colonies. His focus is the transatlantic exchange of information and specimens from the time of the earliest English exploration. By including those colonies that did not later become part of the United States, he provides some useful comparisons. In contrast, while not ignoring European connections, HINDLE emphasizes the development of a North American scientific community and its early efforts at institution-building, and is also interested only in the proto-United States. Both books look at the significant role of communication among scientists.

GREENE organizes his appraisal of US science in the years 1780–1820 by geographical site and scientific discipline. Like Hindle, he views science primarily as an urban phenomenon, and regards this period as one in which Americans assimilated European developments and established institutional bases. President Thomas Jefferson is seen as important both as an active promoter of science and as a symbol of the high status accorded to science in the United States.

The focus of DANIELS is the elite members of the American scientific community between 1815 and 1845. His is one of a number of quantitative studies that demonstrate that American scientists active prior to 1876 were likely to be specialists, professionals, and almost as concerned with the physical as the biological sciences. Compared to Hindle, Greene, or Bruce, Daniels is much more concerned with ideas, especially philosophical ideas, than with institutions. In an effort to explain the relative lack of achievement in abstract science compared to the Europeans, Daniels argues that American scientists were overwhelmingly naive Baconians, collecting facts, rejecting theorizing, and identifying all science with taxonomy.

Integrating narrative and quantitative analysis, BRUCE describes the rise of institutions and the development of scientific careers in the mid-19th century. He asserts that the configuration of the American scientific community and its institutions established during this period endured for over a century.

There is an enormous literature on special themes within the history of US science. The essays in KOHLSTEDT & ROSSITER, which originally appeared in *Osiris* (1985), provide some guidance to the literature in eight areas of research.

One of the classic themes in the history of US science is the role of government as patron. The starting point for all discussions of science and government is DUPREE (1957). Relying substantially on printed sources, he demonstrates, 1966, that federal support of US science was a key factor in its progress from the birth of the Republic. However, the volume ends at a time when government patronage was primarily through the employment of scientists. There is no equivalent study for the post-World War II era, when federal funds were almost universally made available to scientists through grants and contracts.

A theme tat has attracted attention more recently has been the role of gender in US science. The fundamental study on this theme is ROSSITER, who provides an inventory of the community of US scientists, and identifies two forms of discrimination facing women: hierarchical, which limited their advancement, and territorial, which limited their activities to certain fields.

A third approach is disciplinary history. Again, Kohlstedt & Rossiter offer guidance. Much US disciplinary history is written by the participants, with enormous differences in quality and utility, ranging from the insightful analysis of the work of one's predecessors to self-serving accounts of one's own work. However, there has been a growing body of work by historians whose model is KEVLES, that examines the contradiction between the elitism practised by the physics community in the distribution of funds and the ideals of American democracy. Not only does Kevles provide a synthetic overview of the development of physics in the US, but he also furnishes insights that may be applicable to other disciplines.

Some of the most important insights into the development of science in the United States have appeared in essays, not monographs. Fortunately, collections are available by two of the leading essayists. The 13 essays in ROSENBERG elucidate the relationship between science and American society, revealing science as a motivator of behavior and as a supplier of social images. They also consider the role of the scientist in society and the impact of society upon the scientist. Rosenberg draws his examples from the biomedical disciplines, including genetics, eugenics, public health, and agriculture. REINGOLD uses examples from the history of the physical sciences, and his 17 essays are concerned with many of the larger historiographic issues that have dominated the field: the alleged American indifference to basic research; the role of science in the history of science; the significance of Thomas S. Kuhn's theories; the relationship between theory and practice; and the relationship between science and technology. Both essayists also consider the portrayal of the scientist in popular culture.

MARC ROTHENBERG

See also Big Science

United States: women in science

Abir-am, Pnina G. and Dorinda Outram (eds), *Uneasy Careers and Intimate Lives: Women in Science, 1789–1979*, New Brunswick, New Jersey: Rutgers University Press, 1987

Bailey, Martha J., *American Women in Science: A Biographical Dictionary*, Santa Barbara, California: ABC-CLIO, 1994

Bonta, Marcia Myers, *Women in the Field: America's Pioneering Women Naturalists*, College Station: Texas A&M University Press, 1991

Grinstein, Louise S., Rose K. Rose and Miriam H. Rafailovich (eds), *Women in Chemistry and Physics: A Bio-Bibliographic Sourcebook*, Westport, Connecticut: Greenwood Press, 1993

Kass-Simon, G. and Patricia Farnes (eds), *Women of Science: Righting the Record*, Bloomington: Indiana University Press, 1990

Kohlstedt, Sally Gregory, "In from the Periphery: American Women in Science, 1830–1880", *Signs*, 4 (1978): 81–96

Rossiter, Margaret W., *Women Scientists in America: Struggles and Strategies to 1940*, Baltimore: Johns Hopkins University Press, 1982

Rossiter, Margaret W., *Women Scientists in America: Before Affirmative Action, 1940–1972*, Baltimore: Johns Hopkins University Press, 1995

Siegel, Patricia Joan and Kay Thomas Finley, *Women in the Scientific Search: An American Bio-Bibliography, 1724–1979*, Metuchen, New Jersey: Scarecrow Press, 1985

Works on women scientists in any part of the world have been small in number until recently, and only a few biographical entries appear in most of the older reference sources. However, this is beginning to change. SIEGEL & FINLEY attempt the first comprehensive look at women scientists in the US, covering 251 women almost all of whom were born in the 19th century. The aim is to provide a starting point for future work, and the authors concentrate on published studies of biography, many of which are from periodicals. The scientists are grouped by field, and entries briefly describe the life and work, with secondary bibliographies arranged chronologically. BAILEY followed with a second comprehensive biographical resource on American women scientists. She focuses on 285 women, primarily in the physical and natural sciences during the 19th and 20th centuries, but only including women who began their careers before 1950. She identifies women located in the first three editions of *American Men of Science*, those whose names were starred in the 4th–7th editions, as well as in other sources. Bailey notes the difficulty in finding information on many of her subjects because they did not have the same opportunities as men for education, research, or publication. Science for women during much of the past was often a collaborative effort with male relatives, and women scientists have been concentrated in biology, medicine, psychology and mathematics.

GRINSTEIN, ROSE & RAFAILOVICH selected 75 women, most from the 19th and 20th centuries, of whom 58 were born or worked in the United States. They were chosen because they satisfied several of the following criteria: they had gained advanced degrees in spite of social or family pressures, had accomplished innovative research, were influential teachers, were leaders in professional societies or had extensive scholarly publications. Particular attention is paid to the circumstances that influenced the scientist's career, and her work is evaluated for significance. Primary and secondary bibliographies are provided.

BONTA states that early in the 19th century botany became the acceptable science for women to study. They became involved in natural history through gardening, drawing or writing, all considered acceptable pastimes for women. Few became professionals, but many performed research, collected plants and helped to found and run botanical organizations. Bonta studies 25 naturalists, arguing that these women did important work, mostly overlooked in the standard chronicles of American natural history. Dividing their biographies by field of study, she includes naturalists, botanists, entomologists, ornithologists, and ecologists, such as Rachel Carson, who became a household name after publishing *Silent Spring*. Other, less important, contributors are briefly mentioned in the introduction to each section.

KOHLSTEDT maintains that women engaged in scientific work were only marginal members of the scientific community during most of the 19th century. The too "learned" woman was an object of disapproval; therefore, specialized associations and established journals excluded them. Her essay divides women scientists of this period into three generations. The first group, including those such as Jane Colden who learned botany from her father, pursued relatively isolated study and generally came from the upper, educated classes. The second group were illustrators and teachers, such as Almira Hart Lincoln Phelps, who was a pioneer in the education of women in the sciences. Her first textbook on botany, published in 1829, aimed to encourage its study by women, and was very successful, selling 275,000 copies by 1872. The third generation gained advanced training, public recognition, and access to scientific associations, as in the case of Maria Mitchell, the astronomer. After the Civil War the women's colleges such as Mount Holyoke and Vassar offered the most effective support for women in science.

ROSSITER (1982) was immediately recognized as a landmark study. Extensively researched and well documented, her work provides invaluable data on the lives of many American women scientists within the context of the struggle for equality. She asserts that, following Emma Willard's pioneering work for women's education in the 1820s, women began their involvement in science employed as assistants or within specific "sex-typed" fields such as home economics. Starting in the 1840s, they created their own scientific organizations because they were excluded from the male-dominated societies. Women scientists were "atypical" as science was perceived to be a masculine field, and women's education was merely to make them better wives and mothers. During the years 1880–1910 economic, social and demographic change in the US led to the negotiation of acceptable conditions for women in science but a new rigidity set in after 1910, when the male establishment erected barriers in higher education and elsewhere. Some women protested, but most accepted separate organizations, prizes and under-employment.

ROSSITER (1995) looks at the "golden age" of science. Women, however, came out of World War II only slightly stronger than before in spite of manpower shortages, and although record numbers had been encouraged to study science and engineering. Men returned from the war to re-establish themselves in the scientific hierarchy; public opinion about women's role in society had not really changed. During the Cold War American women were again exhorted to study science, especially by the federal government, but attitudes of employers remained basically unchanged. Women faculty members at the prestigious schools were few in number, and had marginal status and power. The highest ranking and most numerous were still concentrated in home economics. Some women, such as Barbara McClintock, forged successful careers at non-profit institutions, although, here too, they were underpaid and rarely promoted. It was not until 1972 that the legal revolution in women's education and employment rights seemed to guarantee that more American women would become prominent scientists.

KASS-SIMON & FARNES collect 11 essays describing the contributions of a number of "forgotten" women scientists. They find a correlation between women's socially-defined role and the extent of their scientific achievement. Before 1920, women moved into low paid jobs that required attention to detail but resulted in important contributions. Pamela Mack's essay on American women astronomers notes the importance of the independent status of observatories for these women. Kass-Simon & Farnes provide valuable data on American women in archaeology, biology, mathematics, physics and crystallography. Women in the last field gained high visibility not because of their numbers but because of the achievements of a few.

ABIR-AM & OUTRAM examine how the interplay between career and personal life has affected the participation of women in science. The first essays are social–historical studies: a new definition of the family in the 18th century tied women more emotionally to their children, while encouraging men to identify with the external "objective" world. These studies show that women's position in science is as much a product of their own perception of it as of the fact of domination by the male scientific establishment or cultural stereotypes. Nancy Slack's essay dealing with American women botanists explores their work in relation to their status as single women or married partners. Marianne Ainley's essay on North American women ornithologists in the years 1900–50 demonstrates how women could progress in a discipline that accepted many amateurs.

JOAN GARRETT PACKER

See also United States; Women in Science: general works

Universities

Armytage, W.H.G., *Civic Universities: Aspects of a British Tradition*, London: Ernest Benn, 1955; New York: Arno Press, 1977

Ashby, Eric, *Technology and the Academics: An Essay on Universities and the Scientific Revolution*, London: Macmillan, 1963; New York: St Martin's Press, 1966

Ben-David, J. and A. Zloczower, "Universities and Academic Systems in Modern Societies", *European Journal of Sociology*, 3 (1962): 45–84

Geiger, Roger L., *To Advance Knowledge: The Growth of American Research Universities, 1900–1940*, Oxford and New York: Oxford University Press, 1986

Grant, Edward, "Science and the Medieval University", in *Rebirth, Reform and Resilience: Universities in Transition, 1300–1700*, edited by James M. Kittelson and Pamela J. Transue, Columbus: Ohio State University Press, 1984, 68–102

McClelland, Charles E., *State, Society and University in Germany, 1700–1914*, Cambridge and New York: Cambridge University Press, 1980

Sanderson, Michael J., *The Universities and British Industry, 1850–1970*, London: Routledge and Kegan Paul, 1972

A very great deal has been written concerning the history of universities, but only a small proportion attempts any sort of critical appraisal. Similarly, while science has been a crucial element, particularly of modern universities, it remains only a relatively minor issue in the literature, and there are few major studies of science and the university.

GRANT's chapter surveys the place of science during the transition from the medieval to the early modern period, and argues that, far from being inimical to the study of the natural world, medieval curricula placed considerable emphasis on science. The "trivium" of liberal arts brought natural philosophy on a par with moral philosophy and metaphysics, while the alternative "quadrivium", the study of arithmetic, geometry, astronomy and music, was essentially scientific. However, it is perhaps stretching the point to argue that the formally disputatious methodology of scholasticism represented the same sense of enquiry that underlay the scientific revolution, when, as Grant acknowledges, the major events of the scientific and, later industrial, revolutions occurred largely independently of the universities.

ASHBY's influential essay, written during a period of considerable ferment in British universities, takes up the issue of modernization, which began during the 19th century. Initially in France, and then most importantly in the German states, universities finally began to break with medieval tradition and to take up the new science, and much of their subsequent development has involved the gradual adoption of the German model. An important part of the literature on universities uses historical work to make contemporary points; Ashby's complaint is that, if scientific study was accepted at European universities, technology and applied science were much less readily assimilated, frequently being consigned to other, usually lesser, institutions. In a somewhat similar vein, ARMYTAGE examines British universities from the medieval period, and argues that they have always had a strong civic and scientific tradition, most fully realised in the creation at the turn of the 20th century of the civic universities, those integrated with local communities. These universities effectively became "community service stations", and Armytage's plea is for the preservation of the university ideal concerned with providing local and national services.

The crucial transformation in the nature of the university, substantially based around the development and incorporation of science, occurred in Germany in the early 19th century, a period McCLELLAND considers as part of his wider study. In the wake of defeat during the Napoleonic Wars, the German states sought to establish a form of international credibility through cultural eminence, centred around their revitalised universities. The central notion of *Wissenschaft*, originally a Hegelian ideal of personal self-development through the quest for pure knowledge, fostered a critical approach to education and research that produced spectacular results in the new scientific research laboratories. The phenomenal production of new knowledge impressed not only the German states, who gave ever greater sums for research, but educators across the developed world, who saw it as the means of progress. Much of the applied science and technology, however, was developed in non-university institutions of similar intellectual, but not social, status, and McClelland points out that the majority of students continued to use the universities principally in order to enhance their job prospects in the professions or administrative bureaucracy.

The article by BEN-DAVID & ZLOCZOWER is an extremely interesting, if brief, schematic analysis of the relationships between university systems and wider social structures in several countries. They argue that the rapid modernisation in Germany was impelled by the competition between universities in the different states and the structure of the professoriate. Britain, by contrast, had an extremely centralised university system dominated by Oxford and Cambridge, and did not experience the same dynamic development spurred by competition. The highly de-centralised American university arrangement put a premium on innovation of any kind, resulting in an extremely wide range of studies, institutionalized in different ways. The arguments are necessarily highly superficial, but nevertheless offer an important, comparative interpretation.

The question of the relationships between universities and applied or industrial demands is the subject of SANDERSON's hugely informative study, primarily of the civic universities. He shows that industrial and commercial concerns were closely associated with these, and other new universities as they developed during the 20th century, and that the civic universities may be regarded as the counterpart of similar institutions found throughout the industrial world, such as the German technical high schools and American land-grant universities. It is a problem, not restricted to Sanderson's book, that only universities are considered, when a considerable amount of scientific and technical work, at the highest level, was conducted in other institutions.

GEIGER's account considers the development of around a dozen elite universities in the US, which perhaps represent the furthest extension of the idea of the university as a place of *Wissenschaft*, or the search for pure knowledge. During the late 19th century, this handful of institutions began to re-orientate themselves towards advanced, specialist study and research, particularly in the sciences. With expansion, scientific professionalization, and the growth of research, these universities fostered a massive growth and concomitant fragmentation of science. The momentum in research was maintained with enormous benefactions from philanthropic organisations, which also oversaw the concentration on pure scientific research through the early 20th century. With further expansion of the higher education system, the research universities turned themselves into an increasingly selective elite, with an even greater emphasis on graduate and postgraduate level work and research.

KEITH VERNON

See also Education; France: scientific and technical education

V

Vacuum

Dear, Peter, *Discipline & Experience: The Mathematical Way in the Scientific Revolution*, Chicago: University of Chicago Press, 1995

Drachmann, A.G., *Ktesibios, Philon and Heron: A Study in Ancient Pneumatics*, Copenhagen: Munksgaard, 1948

Duhem, Pierre, *Le Système du monde: Histoire des doctrines cosmologiques de Platon à Copernic*, 10 vols, Paris: Hermann, 1913–59

Grant, Edward, *Much Ado about Nothing: Theories of Space and Vacuum from the Middle Ages to the Scientific Revolution*, Cambridge and New York: Cambridge University Press, 1981

Hesse, Mary B., *Forces and Fields: The Concept of Action at a Distance in the History of Physics*, London: Thomas Nelson, and New York: Philosophical Library, 1961

Jammer, Max, *Concepts of Space: The History of the Theories of Space in Physics*, Cambridge, Massachusetts: Harvard University Press, 1954; 2nd edition, New York: Harper, 1960

Koyré, Alexandre, *From the Closed World to the Infinite Universe*, Baltimore: Johns Hopkins Press, 1957

Middleton, W.E. Knowles, *The History of the Barometer*, Baltimore: Johns Hopkins Press, 1964

Segre, Michael, *In the Wake of Galileo*, New Brunswick, New Jersey: Rutgers University Press, 1991

Shapin, Steven and Simon Schaffer, *Leviathan and the Air-Pump: Hobbes, Boyle, and the Experimental Life*, Princeton, New Jersey: Princeton University Press, 1985

Waard, Cornelis de, *L'Expérience barométrique: ses antécédents et ses explications. Étude historique*, Thouars: Imprimerie Nouvelle, 1936

Historical interest in the concept of void space has focused primarily on the problems of how, and why, the vacuum came to be seen as a real possibility, and eventually superseded the dominant ancient view, represented most influentially in Western culture by Aristotle, that empty space was a meaningless or contradictory concept. Accordingly, studies of the concept of vacuum concentrate on the period before the establishment of the Newtonian concept of absolute space, which, by providing the theoretical basis for experimental work that seemed to point to the possibility of void space, rendered the concept of vacuum largely unproblematic. A major feature of the literature on void space is its links to theological considerations about the power and presence of God. In more recent historiography, however, arguments about the possibility of vacuum have involved issues concerning the establishment of intellectual authority and correct scientific method.

DRACHMANN provides a clear account and analysis of the work of three ancient mechanicians, Ctesibios, Philo of Byzantium and Hero (or Heron) of Alexandria, who developed a number of devices that now would be described as depending for their action on the pressure of the atmosphere or other hydrostatic phenomena, but which for these Hellenistic thinkers seemed to depend on the principle of *horror vacui*. In the works of these thinkers, however, this principle did not signify the absolute impossibility of vacuum, but rather suggested that an artificially created vacuum could be put to practical use. This book can be seen, therefore, as a study of an alternative tradition to the dominant Platonic and Aristotelian rejection of the notion of void space.

There were, of course, other alternative traditions within ancient Greek thought that allowed for the possibility of void space, notably atomism and Stoicism, but these ideas are best pursued in more general surveys of atomist or stoic thought. JAMMER does consider ancient theories of void space in his opening chapter in a brief general survey of concepts of space from antiquity to the mid-20th century, but the analysis lacks depth. Moreover, Jammer is concerned with theories of space in general, although theories of vacuum are included, at least up to the emergence of Newton's absolute space. Jammer seems to have been inspired to write his survey as a result of the profound impact of relative theory on contemporary conceptions of space and he declares that his intention is to deal with the history of space "from the standpoint of physics". However, the result is often extremely anachronistic; for example, in discussing Aristotle's rejection of empty space beyond the sphere of the fixed stars, he writes,

"It is perhaps not wholly unjustified to suggest a comparison between the notion of physical space in Aristotle's cosmology and the notion of Einstein's 'spherical space' as expounded in early relativistic cosmology. In both theories a question of what is 'outside' finite space is nonsensical."

More often than not this kind of exposition serves to obscure, rather than illuminate, the intellectual concerns of the natural philosophers under discussion. It is perhaps significant, also, that although Jammer recognises the need for a chapter on "Judaeo–Christian Ideas About Space", he sees this as an "interruption" to his account of the development of physical concepts of space.

The monumental survey of cosmological doctrines from Plato to Copernicus in DUHEM provides a more detailed consideration of theories of void space. Nevertheless, this forms only a very small part of Duhem's much more ambitious project to establish the medieval origins of modern science, and, incidentally, to show the importance for scientific progress of traditional French Catholicism.

While Duhem was effectively the founder of the history of medieval science, his work has long since been superseded. By far the richest and most historically-informed study of medieval and early modern theories of space and vacuum is provided by GRANT. Based on extensive reading of primary and secondary sources and comprehensively annotated, this book covers the three major kinds of void space considered in the pre-modern era: interstitial vacua (small-scale vacua conceived to exist in between particles of matter); large scale intracosmic vacua or *vacua separata* (artificially produced, or merely hypothetical void spaces within the world system); and extracosmic void space (a supposed empty space beyond the fixed stars). Taking Aristotle as his starting point, Grant provides a detailed survey of medieval and Renaissance thought, and takes the story as far as early modern thinkers, such as Pierre Gassendi, Otto von Guericke, Isaac Newton, G.W. Leibniz, and John Locke. An important aspect of Grant's thesis is that, while medieval scholastics accepted Aristotle's rejection of intracosmic vacua, they rejected his denial of extracosmic space and earnestly debated the nature of the extracosmic void. The infinite space beyond the fixed stars, within which the world was located, came to be identified with the supposed infinite immensity of God, even though the conception of the extension of God in three dimensions had to be avoided. This tradition of theological debate can be seen to culminate in Newton, who finally advocated the three-dimensional extension of God and saw absolute space as one of God's attributes. Grant shows that whereas the three-dimensional infinite space of the atomists and the Stoics failed to have any significant influence on Christian-dominated Western culture, the theological tradition of void space that developed within scholasticism enabled the emergence of Newtonian absolute space.

KOYRÉ also deals with the development of the idea of infinite space, not as existing beyond the fixed stars, but as the space within which the fixed stars become scattered. Taking theology, rather than Aristotelian natural philosophy, as his starting point, Koyré is primarily concerned with ideas about infinity and the immensity of God, and only incidentally, therefore, with arguments about the existence of void space. However, he provides, among other things, a useful discussion of Descartes's rejection of void space (not considered by Grant), and a fuller discussion of the dispute between Newton and Leibniz on the nature of space and void.

None of the above discusses the phenomenon of the Torricellian vacuum and its impact on theories of void space. This is provided by WAARD, who is chiefly concerned with tracing the origins of the concept of atmospheric pressure, and its displacement of the older theory of *horror vacui*. After a preliminary survey of ancient and medieval attitudes to the concept of void, Waard sees the earliest appreciation of atmospheric pressure in the writings of the Dutch physico–mathematician Isaac Beeckman, but goes on to discuss Giovanni Baliani, Gasparo Berti, Galileo, and Evangelista Torricelli.

MIDDLETON is concerned with the history of the barometer as a scientific instrument, and largely takes the existence of vacuum for granted. The first part of the book does provide, however, what the author calls a prehistory of the barometer, looking at early 17th-century theories about the action of pumps and the development of the experimental production of void space, and the subsequent work of Robert Boyle, Robert Hooke, and Edme Mariotte. SEGRE traces Galileo's influence on his Italian disciples, and provides a brief, but useful, account of the local context of Torricelli's barometric experiments – the outcome, he suggests, of Galileo's own speculations on the nature of vacuum.

While providing a detailed account of Boyle and Hooke's experiments with the newly invented air-pump, SHAPIN & SCHAFFER's overall aim is to show how Boyle and like-minded, self-styled "experimental philosophers" believed that their experimentalism was the only secure way of commanding a general assent from all investigators, so dispelling dispute. They seek to demonstrate this principally through analysis of the dispute between Boyle and the rationalist Thomas Hobbes on the status of the air-pump experiments, but there is also important material on related disputes with other philosophers, including Christiaan Huygens. Shapin & Schaffer is a vital resource for a full understanding of the development of early modern science, and can be used, also, to show the broader, historical significance of post-Torricellian arguments on the possibility of void space.

This idea is reinforced by DEAR, who, while describing changing conceptions of how scientific truth can best be established, shows how the French philosopher, Blaise Pascal, presented his barometric experiments in accordance with the conventions of the so-called mixed mathematical sciences, in order to invest particular experiences with universal philosophical significance (chapter 7). Once again, experimental claims about the existence of void space are shown to have played an important role in contests concerning intellectual authority.

The possibility, or otherwise, of void space plays little part in historical discussions of space after the (temporary) triumph of Newtonian absolute space during the 18th century. Nor does it re-enter historical discussions when, towards the end of the 19th century, Newtonian space began to be replaced by a more relativistic conception. Certainly, there is no discussion of vacuum in Jammer's last chapter on post-Newtonian developments, although Albert Einstein, in his "Foreword", suggests that there can be no such thing as empty space in the field theories that derive from the work of Michael Faraday and Robert Maxwell. HESSE makes a similar point in her historical study of theories of action at a distance; however, her study is principally concerned with establishing a philosophical position about the role of analogies and models in physics, and theories of vacuum make only an incidental appearance.

JOHN HENRY

See also Meterological Instruments; Newton; Relativity

Valence

Benfey, Otto Theodor (ed.), *Classics in the Theory of Chemical Combination*, New York: Dover, 1963

Kohler, Robert E., "The Origins of G.N. Lewis's Theory of the Shared Pair Bond", *Historical Studies in the Physical Sciences*, 3 (1971): 343–76

Kohler, Robert E., "Irving Langmuir and the 'Octet' Theory of Valence", *Historical Studies in the Physical Sciences*, 4 (1972): 39–87

Kohler, Robert E., "The Lewis-Langmuir Theory of Valence and the Chemical Community, 1920–1928", *Historical Studies in the Physical Sciences*, 6 (1975): 431–68

Novitski, Mary Eunice, *August Laurent and the Prehistory of Valence*, Chur, Switzerland, and Philadelphia: Harwood Academic, 1992

Russell, Colin A., *The History of Valency*, Leicester: Leicester University Press, and New York: Humanities Press, 1971

Sadoun Goupil, Michelle, *Du Flou au clair? Histoire de l'affinité chimique*, Paris: Éditions du Comité des Travaux Historiques et Scientifique, 1991

Vidal, B., *La Liaison chimique: Le concept et son histoire*, Paris: VRIN, 1989

This entry covers general histories of chemical combination and notions of affinity and valence, but also more specialised works on chemists who were prominent in the development of the concept of valence.

SADOUN GOUPIL presents the history of the concept of affinity from the end of the 16th century to the 20th century, although the changes to the concept effected by quantum mechanics are not examined. The author aims to show how a vague concept, which could be expressed by many words that carry anthropomorphic connotations, can become a quantifiable and measurable scientific concept, and one of the most useful classificatory concepts in chemistry. The development of the notions of affinity and attraction within the context of the Newtonian programme are traced among British, Dutch, and French physicists, and there is also a discussion of the anti-Newtonianism of the French chemists. The work ends with the work by August Horstmann, François Massieu, Hermann von Helmholtz, J.W. Gibbs, Pierre Duhem, and Théophile de Donder on the use of the notion of potential in the development of chemical thermodynamics.

VIDAL's book is a comprehensive narrative of the history of chemical bonding. More than half of the book deals with developments after the birth of quantum mechanics, which had provided theoretical grounds for understanding the stability of the chemical bond. Vidal gives an analytic presentation of Burrau's calculation of the hydrogen molecule ion, of Heisenberg's paper on the helium atom and his introduction of quantum mechanical resonance, of Walter Heitler's and F.W. London's solution of the problem of the covalent bond, of Linus Pauling's resonance structures, of Pauling's and Slater's concept of hybridization, and of Friedrich Hund and Robert S. Mulliken's molecular orbitals. The method of self-consistent field calculation is dealt with in detail. There are also numerous comments on the condemnation of Pauling's theory of resonance by the Academy of Sciences of the USSR, Pauling's subsequent indecision, and the position of the French Marxists on this incident.

NOVITSKI argues that Auguste Laurent and C.F. Gerhard, in their unitary system of chemistry, had employed a method of formulation that signalled the presence of phenomena due to valence. However, Novitski warns that his study is from the anachronistic perspective of a modern observer, and that neither Laurent nor Gerhard ever conceived of the modern bond theory. Nevertheless, Laurent's hypothesis that chemical atoms can be divided, and that variations in the number and arrangement of their internal parts could explain why even a single element could behave in different ways, was analogous in reasoning to the later rationale that would explain chemical combination in terms of the distribution of electrons in atoms.

RUSSELL traces the developments in the conceptions concerning valence, which originated in the work of F.A. Kekulé and Edward Frankland. These developments are described in detail as they impinge on aromatic chemistry, the classification of the elements, the theory of organic structure, and stereochemistry. The influences of electrochemistry on the further refinement of the notion of valency is systematically presented, as is the impact of the study of atomic spectra on the understanding of the bonding between atoms, the introduction of the concept of electron-sharing in order to account for the covalent bond, and the theoretical novelties brought about by quantum mechanics in the understanding of the covalent bond. These discussions are placed within the broader context of the social and intellectual history of the time, and the author stresses the dependence upon factors such as education, as well as the internal structure of chemistry research and the personalities of the participants.

In a series of papers, KOHLER (1971, 1972, and 1975) discusses the origins and development of one of the most useful notions for the understanding of the formation of molecules – namely the concept of shared electrons. As Kohler shows, although G.N. Lewis was not the first to suggest such a mechanism, he was the person who applied it successfully to many chemical problems, and fiercely propagandized the significance of the notion. However, the reception of electron-pairing was less than enthusiastically received by the physics community, and it was only through the writings of Irving Langmuir that physicists were gradually converted to its heuristic value. Langmuir's negative appraisal of Bōhr's atomic theory contrasted with his favorable view of Lewis's static model of the atom, which, along with Parson's proposal of an electron endowed with magnetic properties, was an important resource for the development of Langmuir's own theory of atomic structure. Langmuir's model of the atom, in contrast to Lewis's, was not based on the assumption of a completely stationary electron, and he modified Lewis's theory in order to reconcile it with Bohr's model of the atom.

BENFEY is a collection of papers that refer to aspects of chemical combination by prominent scientists in the field: Friedrich Wöhler and Justus Liebig, Laurent, A.W. Williamson, Frankland, Kekulé, A.S. Couper, J.H. van't Hoff and J.A. Le Bel. Useful editorial notes accompany the papers.

KOSTAS GAVROGLU

See also Affinity; Chemistry; Quantum Mechanics

Venereal Disease

Brandt, Allan M., *No Magic Bullet: A Social History of Venereal Disease in the United States since 1880*, New York and Oxford: Oxford University Press, 1985

Cassel, Jay, *The Secret Plague: Venereal Disease in Canada, 1838–1939*, Toronto: University of Toronto Press, 1987

Davenport-Hines, Richard, *Sex, Death, and Punishment: Attitudes to Sex and Sexuality in Britain since the Renaissance*, London: Collins, 1990

McHugh, Paul, *Prostitution and Victorian Social Reform*, London: Croom Helm, and New York: St Martin's Press, 1980

Mort, Frank, *Dangerous Sexualities: Medico-Moral Politics in England since 1830*, London and New York: Routledge and Kegan Paul, 1987

Oriel, J.D., *The Scars of Venus: A History of Venereology*, London and New York: Springer, 1994

Quétel, Claude, *History of Syphilis*, translated from the French by Judith Braddock and Brian Pike, Cambridge: Polity Press/Blackwell, and Baltimore: Johns Hopkins University Press, 1990

Rosebury, Theodor, *Microbes and Morals: The Strange Story of Venereal Disease*, New York: Viking Press, 1971; London: Secker and Warburg, 1972

Walkowitz, Judith R., *Prostitution and Victorian Society: Women, Class and the State*, Cambridge and New York: Cambridge University Press, 1980

In 1972, ROSEBURY commented that, although the history of the venereal diseases combined the "fascination of murder and bubonic plague" with sex, "the most engrossing of all subjects", it has been unpopular with writers. His book emerged in the context of traditional, rather triumphalist, writing about sex in history, which assumed progression from ignorance to the enlightenment generated by the "sexual revolution" of the 1960s. It is an easy read, taking a broad overview "for ordinary people rather than for specialists or scholars", and raising most of the important issues in the history of the subject.

ORIEL, writing from the perspective of a clinician rather than a professional historian, provides another useful overview, synthesizing much material, including research since Rosebury: his bibliography is an excellent guide to scattered articles. He is sensibly cautious about claims for the existence of syphilis in pre-modern societies (although he probably just missed reports of skeletal remains suggesting the presence of syphilis in Europe before 1493). His account of changing medical understanding of these diseases is lucid, and there are comparative accounts of the development of venereology and public health measures for VD control in Britain, continental Europe, and the US.

There is, however, a great lack of detailed monographs on medical developments, attitudes to, and policies intended to control, venereal diseases in different countries at different historical periods. The state of the historiography of sexually transmitted diseases is improving, but still rather sporadic.

One topic around which there is already something of a developed historiographical debate is the British Contagious Diseases Acts of 1864, 1866, and 1868. This legislation, its administration, its effects, and the campaigns to both extend and repeal the Acts, are the subject of two excellent studies, by WALKOWITZ and McHUGH, which both appeared in 1980. McHugh deals more with the intricacies of the political campaign for repeal, while Walkowitz includes a valuable study of the operation of the Acts, and the local repeal campaigns, in two port towns. Both studies discuss the existing state of understanding of the diseases and the efficacy of the Acts. The Contagious Diseases Acts also form a significant element in MORT – although this study of "medico–moral politics" extends considerably beyond sexually transmitted diseases – and are discussed by Davenport-Hines. The debates still continue in the journals, and within the broader context of studies of women, and of sex, in Victorian Britain.

DAVENPORT-HINES, though one of the few works to venture far outside this particular episode, needs to be read with some caution, as the author's approach is somewhat coloured by the AIDS hysteria of the late 1980s. Instead of critically and cautiously evaluating his sources, Davenport-Hines amasses evidence to support a particular thesis about enduring British attitudes to sexuality, and in particular behaviour defined as deviant. This might result in certain misconceptions in the reader; for example, one would not necessarily realize from the book that the incidence of VD in Britain declined radically between 1918 and 1939. There are a number of careless inaccuracies, and some chronological inexactitude where evidence from widely-separated periods is adduced in support of his arguments. However, the work deploys considerable detailed primary research in often obscure sources, and is a valuable guide to the literature.

The rise of AIDS in the last decades of the 20th century has provided a considerable stimulus to historical investigation of venereal diseases. BRANDT is particularly concerned with the cultural construction of these diseases in the United States, and emphasizes the problems, persisting well into the 20th century, for the formulation and implementation of policy. The root of these problems lies in the dichotomy between those who regarded the actual diseases as the greater public menace, and those who feared that controlling these diseases would simply encourage immorality, regarded by some as far more deleterious for the nation than the diseases themselves – a conflict that has dogged control of sexually transmitted diseases, at least in Anglo–Saxon Protestant cultures. Brandt also explores the tensions arising between the competing claims by public health officials and private practitioners for authority, and for responsibility for "scientific" prevention and treatment.

CASSEL explicitly criticizes Brandt for drawing a rather simplistic picture, and provides useful points of comparison between two contiguous cultures, in particular the rather different relationships between public health and private practice. In Canada as in the UK and the US World War I was a pivotal period of anxiety about, and discussion of, VD, but it had been preceded by developing public concern and developments in diagnosis and treatment during the first decade of the 20th century. A particular strength of Cassel's account is his discussion of the means by which new curative methods were put into practice. He indicates that the Canadian view of these diseases as a problem for state intervention was consistent, with the level of public provision between the wars contrasting favourably with the US. However, the work concludes just before antibiotics radically changed the picture.

One of the few authors to deal in any detail with a non-Anglo–Saxon Protestant culture, QUÉTEL writes from a French perspective and concentrates on syphilis, which he claims, supported by numerous examples from French literature, has provoked more cultural responses than any other disease. Although he demonstrates some acquaintance with the situation in the UK, and alludes to Brandt's work on the US, Quétel does not really engage with preceding historiographical debates, though he does indicate that the French system of regulating prostitution, often held up as a model for emulation in the UK and the US, was by no means a reliable prophylactic measure.

While these monographs all have their value for the history of venereal disease, much of the most interesting historiographical debate has taken place, and continues to take place, in scattered articles, to which the bibliographies of these monographs provide some guide.

LESLEY A. HALL

See also Public Health; Sexuality

Vesalius, Andreas 1514–1564

Belgian anatomist

Carlino, Andrea, *La Fabbrica del Corpo: Libri e Dissezione nel Rinascimento*, Turin: Einaudi, 1994

Cunningham, Andrew, *The Anatomical Renaissance: The Resurrection of the Anatomical Projects of the Ancients*, Aldershot, Hampshire, and Brookfield, Vermont: Scolar, 1997

Eriksson, Ruben (ed.), *Andreas Vesalius' First Public Anatomy at Bologna, 1540: An Eyewitness Report by Baldasar Heseler, Together with His Notes on Matthaeus Curtius' Lectures on Anatomia Mundini*, Uppsala and Stockholm: Almqvist & Wiksell, 1959

Ferrari, Giovanna, "Public Anatomy Lessons and the Carnival: The Anatomy Theatre of Bologna", *Past and Present*, 117 (1987): 50–106

Ivins, William M. Jr., "What about the 'Fabrica' of Vesalius?", in *Three Vesalian Essays to Accompany the Icones Anatomicae of 1934*, by Samuel W. Lambert, Willy Wiegand and Ivins, New York: Macmillan, 1952, 43–130

Lind, L.R., *Studies in Pre-Vesalian Anatomy: Biography, Translations, Documents*, Philadelphia: American Philosophical Society, 1975

O'Malley, Charles D., *Andreas Vesalius of Brussels, 1514–1564*, Berkeley: University of California Press, 1964

Richardson, W.F. and J.B. Carman, *Book One of the Fabrica of Vesalius*, San Francisco: Norman, 1997

Roth, M., *Andreas Vesalius Bruxellensis*, Berlin: Reimer, 1892

Saunders, J.B. de C.M. and C.D. O'Malley (eds), *The Illustrations from the Works of Andreas Vesalius of Brussels*, New York: 1950

Schultz, Bernard, *Art and Anatomy in Renaissance Italy*, Ann Arbor: UMI Research Press, 1985

Schupbach, William, *The Paradox of Rembrandt's "Anatomy of Dr Tulp"*, London: Wellcome Institute, 1982

Singer, Charles (ed.), *The Fasciculo di Medicina, Venice, 1493*, by Johannes de Ketham, Florence: Lier, 1925 (contains a translation of the *Anatomia* of Mundinus, 1316)

Singer, Charles (ed. and trans.), *Vesalius on the Human Brain*, London and New York: Oxford University Press, 1952

Vesalius is normally credited with the introduction of "modern" anatomising. His major work *De Humani Corporis Libri Septem* (Seven Books on the Fabric of the Human Body) was published in 1543 and caused a wide stir, both because of the striking woodcuts of the human body and its parts, and because Vesalius was thought to be criticising the work of Galen, hitherto the chief authority on anatomy.

Given his importance, it is remarkable how little literature there is on Vesalius. There are two basic biographies. ROTH's 19th-century German hagiographic study brings together a lot of information concerning Vesalius's life, and is still the primary resource for basic documentation. O'MALLEY's more recent biography enlivens the characterisation of Vesalius, but the approach is still hagiographic. O'Malley's view that Vesalius rejected the Galenic tradition has now been challenged by CUNNINGHAM, who argues that Vesalius was in fact seeking to emulate Galen's anatomical project, but on man rather than the ape. Cunningham places Vesalius's anatomical project within a wider tradition of the revival of ancient anatomical research programmes during the Renaissance, and argues that Vesalius's teachers, Jacobus Sylvius (1478–1555) and Johannes Guenther (1487–1574), Vesalius himself, and subsequent anatomists in Padua, such as Realdus Colombus (1515?–59) and Hieronymus Fabricius ab Aquapendente (1533–1619), were all engaged in reviving a sequence of anatomical traditions from antiquity. Vesalius's role was to revive the Galenic tradition, and to dissect the human body, which Galen had been unable to do. If one wishes to imagine Vesalius at work, dissecting human bodies in front of his students, there is nothing to touch ERIKSSON's translation into English of an eye-witness account of a long dissection by Vesalius, held at Bologna in 1540, which also gives the reactions of his professors and students.

The tradition of anatomising that Vesalius displaced was modelled on the text of Mundinus's *Anatomia* (1316), which had been the main guide to dissecting in the universities. A translation of Mundinus has been published in SINGER (1925). For the attitudes and opinions of anatomists in the late 15th and early 16th centuries (i.e. the period just before Vesalius), LIND provides translations into English of works by Alessandro Achillini (1463–1512), Alessandro Benedetti (1450?–1512), Garbiele Zerbi (1445–1505), Berengario da Carpi (1470–1530), Niccolo Massa (1485–1569), Andres de Laguna (1499–1560), Johannes Dryander (1500–60), and Giovanni Battista Canano (1515–79).

There are two recent studies that have placed Vesalius and his work within the 16th-century context. SCHUPBACH has made an excellent study of the significance to 16th-century anatomising of the ancient injunction, "Know thyself". This is the most sophisticated study yet made of the aims and preoccupations of 16th-century anatomists, and it brings insights from art history to the reading of representations of dissection.

One of Vesalius's achievements was to increase the importance of the anatomy theatre, with respect to the teaching of anatomy for medicine. FERRARI deals with the wider social role of the anatomy theatre, and its importance within the world of the carnival.

Vesalius's main text, the famous *Fabrica* , has not been completely translated into any modern language. SINGER (1952) has translated Book 7, on the human brain, into English, and O'Malley's biography includes a translation of the introductory material as an appendix. RICHARDSON & CARMAN have translated Book 1, on the bones. The *Fabrica* remains a difficult text, as it is written in Ciceronian Latin, and demands extensive anatomical knowledge and acquaintance with 16th-century anatomising practices for its proper understanding.

The many woodcut figures of the *Fabrica*, reproduced in SAUNDERS & O'MALLEY, are of outstanding quality, both artistically and in their technical execution as wood-blocks. Titian was long thought to be responsible for the figures, but there is no consensus currently on the identity of the artist. As the woodcuts in the *Fabrica* are so important, it is useful to know how they were made. IVINS, an expert on art history and printing, is essential reading on the process of production of these figures, from drawing through to cutting of the blocks, and printing from them. Sixteenth-century anatomists often worked with artists, who needed to learn how to portray the human figure and its muscles, and SCHULTZ presents a good guide to the relation of anatomising to Renaissance art and artists. CARLINO discusses the role of representation and iconography, anatomical practices, traditions of dissection, and the relation of the body to textual authorities in 16th-century anatomising.

There is, unfortunately, no study of the long-term influence of Vesalius on later anatomising.

ANDREW CUNNINGHAM

See also Anatomy; Performance; Scientific Illustration

Veterinary Science

Karasszon, Denes, *A Concise History of Veterinary Medicine*, translated from the Hungarian by E. Farkas, translation revised by Iringo K. Kecskes, Budapest: Akadémiai Kiadó, 1988

Leclainche, E., *Histoire de la médecine vétérinaire*, Toulouse: Office du Livre, 1936

Michell, A.R. (ed.), *History of the Healing Professions: Parallels between Veterinary and Medical History*, vol. 3: *The Advancement of Veterinary Science: The Bicentenary Symposium Series*, Wallingford: C.A.B. International, 1993

Pugh, L.P., *From Farriery to Veterinary Medicine, 1785–1795*, Cambridge: Royal College of Veterinary Surgeons, 1962

Schwabe, Calvin W., *Veterinary Medicine and Human Health*, Baltimore: Williams and Wilkins, 1964; London: Baillière, Tindall and Cassell, 1969

Smith, Sir Frederick, *The Early History of Veterinary Literature and Its British Development*, 4 vols, London: Baillière, Tindall and Cox, 1913–33

Smithcors, James Frederick, *Evolution of the Veterinary Art: A Narrative Account to 1850*, Kansas City: Veterinary Medicine Publishing Company, 1957; London: Baillière, Tindall and Cox, 1958

Wilkinson, Lise, *Animals and Disease: An Introduction to the History of Comparative Medicine*, Cambridge and New York: Cambridge University Press, 1992

As the cave paintings of Paleolithic artists testify, humans have always studied animals. From the earliest times, man has striven to maintain the health of animals of agricultural and commercial importance, such as cows and horses, and, although Plato famously disapproved, animal physiology and animal pathology have long been studied in order to learn more about the human body.

To date, the history of veterinary science has been dwarfed by the history of medical science. In the history of medicine, animals and their care-givers remain invisible, despite the obvious importance of both to medical science. There is a large literature on vivisection and physiology, in which veterinarians and veterinary science are largely ignored. Similarly, in the history of bacteriology, the important role of animal diseases in the development of the germ theory of disease is often obscured. This relative lack of interest in the history of the study of animals has its roots in the tendency of humans to see themselves as both separate from animals and superior to them.

Most works in the history of veterinary science are chronological overviews, which attempt to encompass large time-periods and vast geographies. A typical example is SMITHCORS, which relies heavily on Smith, and presents a narrative that begins in prehistory and ends in the 19th century. In a similar fashion, LECLAINCHE, emphasizing the development of veterinary instruction, is divided into two parts: the first covers the period from antiquity to the Renaissance, and the second systematically (and alphabetically) outlines the history of the veterinary profession in over 50 countries up to 1936. SMITH's four-volume account remains the classic in the field, although its usefulness is limited by, as Roy Porter notes (in his article in Michell's volume), Smith's "relentless contempt for pre-19th century writings". This inability to place the ideas and events of earlier eras within context remains a failing of much veterinary history, an exception being the articles in MICHELL. In his own encyclopedic account, KARASSZON reveals his prejudices with his section headings; his narrative begins with the "era of intuitive, naïve–empiric, and superstitious–magic animal healing", and he devotes a large amount of his book to "the rise of scientific reasoning". WILKINSON, in one of the more thoughtful surveys, gives an overview of the subject from antiquity to the appearance of bovine spongiform encephalopathy (BSE) or "mad cow disease".

Of those monographs that are not broad surveys, PUGH's book, which begins with the establishment of the London Veterinary College in 1791 and ends with the establishment in 1844 of a Royal Charter for the Royal College of Veterinary Surgeons, is typical. Pugh outlines how farriery, an occupation that could be lucrative but was generally despised, was transformed into a profession that remained of lower status than its medical rival, but achieved the stamp of its own Royal College. This narrative is representative of the two dominant themes of veterinary history: professionalization, and how veterinarians have lagged behind medics in establishing both professional bodies and schools.

Doctors were always keen to maintain their more elevated social and professional position, and, unsurprisingly, veterinarians and doctors were often actively hostile to each other. Some veterinary schools banned students who had previously trained as medics, and, as Wilkinson highlights, even among veterinarians there were rivalries. Veterinarians with academic aspirations tended to study horses, rather than lowly livestock, such as cattle. It was the cattle plagues of the 18th and 19th centuries that finally drew the attention of veterinary researchers to livestock, and even when governments did support research into cattle plague in the late 19th century, they preferred to hire the expertise of men like John Burdon Sanderson in England and Robert Koch in Germany, who were not trained as veterinarians. The cattle plague played an important role in the emergence of the field of bacteriology, from its inception through to the era of the colonial research institutes, while the germ theory itself, which underpinned bacteriology, depended, as Wilkinson succinctly states, on "animal experiments based on specific infectious diseases attacking both man and one or other mammalian species".

Events in France are a particular focus of interest, since it was at the forefront of veterinary professionalization. The first veterinary schools were established in Lyons in 1762 and at Alfort in 1766. Other schools followed at Turin in 1769, and in the 1780s veterinary schools were established in Copenhagen, Vienna, Dresden, Hannover, and Budapest. A secondary theme is how Britain was slow, relative to France and the Continent, in establishing its veterinary profession. Pugh attributes this to the dominant laissez-faire attitude in Britain, which meant that would-be veterinary professors had to raise funds privately, in contrast with the more interventionist ideology of the continental powers, whose governments funded the new veterinary institutions because of their hoped-for military or agricultural significance. However, as Wilkinson points out, it was in Britain in the mid-19th century that the first institute of comparative medicine was established with private funding – the Brown Institution in London, headed by Burdon Sanderson. The interest in Britain's progress relative to other countries is partly an artefact of the literature itself, which is centred mainly on Britain and France, although Karasszon, Smithcors, and Leclainche successfully broaden their scope.

SCHWABE, uniquely, organizes his book thematically around the many roles of veterinarians. There were (and are) many facets of veterinary practice. Veterinarians were responsible for health and disease among non-humans. They were investigators in pathological zoology, or in comparative medicine. In many ways their activities were a branch of agriculture, with broad economic implications. They could be, through their care of wild or domestic animals, responsible for the environment as a whole, and, Schwabe argues, should remain an exemplar of the humane treatment of animals.

Despite this holistic approach, Schwabe – like the other authors mentioned in this essay – privileges the history of veterinary science. Thus, although these monographs aim to be histories of veterinary medicine, which has many intersections with social, economic, environmental, and agricultural history, their main focus is the history of veterinary science, narrowly defined.

TERRIE M. ROMANO

See also Anti-Vivisection; Bacteriology; Botanical and Zoological Gardens

Virchow, Rudolf 1821–1902

German physician, anthropologist, and statesman

Ackerknecht, Erwin Heinz, "Beiträge zur Geschichte der Medizinalreform von 1848", *Sudhoffs Archiv für Geschichte der Medizin und der Naturwissenschaften* 25 (1932): 61–183

Ackerknecht, Erwin Heinz, *Rudolf Virchow: Doctor, Statesman, Anthropologist*, Madison: University of Wisconsin Press, 1953

Bauer, Arnold, *Rudolf Virchow, der politische Arzt*, Berlin: Stapp, 1982

Boyd, Byron A., *Rudolf Virchow: The Scientist as Citizen*, New York: Garland, 1991

Gregory, Frederick, *Scientific Materialism in Nineteenth Century Germany*, Dordrecht and Boston: Reidel, 1977

Hacking, Ian, *The Taming of Chance*, Cambridge and New York: Cambridge University Press, 1990

Hall, Thomas S., *Ideas of Life and Matter: Studies in the History of General Physiology 600 BC–1900 AD*, Chicago: University of Chicago Press, 1969

Heinz, David, *Rudolf Virchow und die Medizen des 20. Jahrhunderts*, Munich: Quintessenz, 1993

Latour, Bruno, *The Pasteurization of France*, translated from the French by Alan Sheridan, Cambridge, Massachusetts: Harvard University Press, 1988 (original edition, 1984)

Lenoir, Timothy, *The Strategy of Life: Teleology and Mechanics in Nineteenth Century German Biology*, Dordrecht and Boston: Reidel, 1982

Maulitz, Russell, "Rudolf Virchow, Julius Cohnheim and the Program of Pathology", *Bulletin of the History of Medicine*, 52 (1978): 162–82

Mazzolini, Renato J., "Stato e organismo, individui e celluli nell'opera di Rudolf Virchow negli anni 1845–1860", *Annali, Istituto storico italo-germanico*, 5 (1983): 1–140

Pagel, Walter, *Virchow und die Grundlagen der Medizin des XIX Jarhunderts*, Jena: Gustav Fisher, 1931

Rather, Lelland J. (ed. and trans) *Disease, Life and Man: Selected Essays* by Virchow, with an introduction by Rather, Stanford, California: Stanford University Press, 1958

Schlumberger, H.G., "Rudolf Virchow and the Franco–Prussian War", *Annals of Medical History*, 4 (1942): 23–7

Temkin, Owsei, *The Double Face of Janus and Other Essays in the History of Medicine*, Baltimore: Johns Hopkins University Press, 1977

Vasold, Manfred, *Rudolf Virchow: Der grosse Arzt und Politiker*, Stuttgart: Deutsche Verlag-Anstalt, 1988

Weindling, Paul, "Theories of the Cell State in Imperial Germany", in *Biology, Medicine and Society, 1840–1940*, edited by Charles Webster, Cambridge and New York: Cambridge University Press, 1981

Major works in English on Rudolf Virchow are few and far between. This is perhaps because of the awesome definitiveness of the standard biography of Virchow by ACKERKNECHT (1953). Ackerknecht presents Virchow's life as a trilogy of interrelated careers of "doctor, statesman and anthropologist", each revolutionary in its own right, in the construction of "cellular pathology", political liberalism, and quantitative anthropology respectively. Nevertheless, the work should be recommended with a gentle warning. After World War II, Virchow was resurrected as a role-model for left-wing, liberal Germans untainted by the romanticism and racism of the Nazi era. Ackerknecht, once very politically active in the far left (Trotskyist) movement in Europe in the 1930s, had, by the 1950s, altered his beliefs and turned to a defence of standard individualistic liberalism. In his thesis of 1931, written in Leipzig under Henry Sigerist, ACKERKNECHT (1932) brings a Marxist analysis to bear on the medical reform movement of 1848, and locates Virchow as part of a class struggle for medical and political reform – thus, the two movements of politics and biology are intertwined. By the biography of 1953, however, Virchow seems a changed man, a reasoned defender of classic liberalism, the "last of the individualists and universalists in Germany". The sense of the whole is now lost, and Virchow's careers become separated and disconnected.

German biographies are equally loaded with defences of liberalism and disciplinary isolation, ranging from tinges of hagiography in VASOLD to the traditional triumphalism of HEINZ. A succinct account by a German literary historian is to be found in BAUER, who chronicles the main events of Virchow's life and again portrays him as a fighter for individual freedom and a "democratic Germany".

A fairly complete political biography is to be found in BOYD, which contains a fine bibliography of mainly German printed and archival sources. Boyd is fairly complete, discussing Virchow's rise from radical medical student pioneering epidemiology and social medicine to the sorry affair of Virchow's enthusiastic participation in Bismarck's *Kulturkampf* against the Catholics. Yet, Boyd can also verge on hagiography and over-caution in making cross-disciplinary causal and methodological claims. This caution is evident in Boyd's treatment of the famous convergence of Virchow's revolutionary ideas on cellular pathology – wherein all activities of the body, both pathological and normal, are reduced to actions of individual self-interested cells (atoms) – and his political views of radical individualist liberalism. Virchow himself was the first to make the "analogy" explicit; in his "Atome und Individuen" (Atoms and Individuals) of 1859 (translated and introduced in RATHER), he claimed that the relation between cells and individuals was not one of metaphor but "identity" – that the cell in the body is identical to the individual in the state - a point reiterated in his classic scientific text, *Cellular Pathology* of 1858. This comparison has been both a puzzle and a delight to historians of science, offering a fine example of the social shaping of science and the role of metaphor in the construction of scientific beliefs.

However, most commentators linger at the level of metaphor and forget that Virchow himself was inverting the long-held organic view of the state, wherein the political and biological were identified as one in the same, in favour of a reductionist view of the individual in the state. Virchow retained the received structure of the state/organism comparison, yet denied its substantive organicist grounds. Theories of the cell state and their relationship to earlier organic views are discussed in WEINDLING, while MAZZOLINI carefully analyses the relationship between scientific and political ideas during the formative years of Virchow's career. Boyd does not go so far, however, resigning himself to suggesting the "similarities between the two realms" of the scientific and the political, while making no causal judgements.

For a classification of this sort of "vitalistic" materialism, and its place between "idealist vitalism" and mechanical materialism, one may turn to the works by Pagel, Lenoir, Temkin, Gregory, and Hall. The essays on this topic included in TEMKIN are by far the most philosophical, and reveal Temkin's orientation towards locating medical ideas within the wider context of philosophical debate. PAGEL found strong hints of Romanticism in Virchow's attitude towards "cells" as vital and irreducible individuals. LENOIR represents the whole movement towards "vitalism" and organicism as part of a Lakatosian "research program", arising out of the Kantian and Romantic approach to teleology and the organism. Lenoir sees Virchow as a middle figure, sitting between vitalism and materialism. GREGORY gives a powerful account of the rise and fall of the militancy of the mechanical materialists and their critique of vitalism in the second half of the 19th century. He has little to say about Virchow, but he does set the scene of the struggle of ideas, both political and scientific. Virchow, for Gregory, reflects the beginning of the compromise by bourgeois materialists in the face of the more militant "dialectical" materialism of the Social Democratic Party – a compromise that resulted in the famous debate between Ernst Haeckel and Virchow on the scientific and political grounds of evolution. HALL ignores the social and political, and confines himself to a straight history and classification of ideas, presenting Virchow as the leading figure among the mitigated mechanists. A full-length study of the place of this formative model in the history of German politics has yet to be written.

So far, we have seen Virchow's multiple personalities as detached and unallied, and most work on Virchow still lies within separate histories of ideas. Yet, if anything, Virchow was instrumental in fashioning those very disciplines and institutions within which the "ideas" were formed and demarcated. Thus, it is here, among the institutions, that possibilities for an interesting integration start to appear. MAULITZ makes the pregnant suggestion that Virchow's flexibility and dogmatism with respect to cellular pathology is best seen as a classic case of institution-building. Whereas older histories, including those of Hall and Lenoir, told how Virchow seized the cell theory of M.J. Schleiden and Theodore Schwann and refashioned it as a tool to "extirpate" scientific medicine from humoral, neural, and otherwise ontologically-tainted notions of pathology, Maulitz sees the attack on humoral pathology as part of Virchow's Prussian institution-building. This suggests that the lure of the microscope is inexorably linked with Virchow's marginalisation of the institutions and practices of humoral medicine, and his successful attempt to institutionalize "scientific medicine" in his Berlin Pathological Institute. The microscope and the new laboratory science were inexorably linked within the new Institute, and thus were tied to the political programme of social epidemiology. (The similarities to LATOUR's Pasteur are remarkable.) This, claims Maulitz, explains why later Virchow could be much more flexible in his toleration of a reformed cellular pathology which, in the work of his student, Cohnhem, went well beyond the localised and static to a more dynamic conception of pathology. This was possible only because the development took place within, and reinforced the structures of, the Berlin Institute. Maulitz runs the danger of reducing Virchow's cellular pathology to pragmatic considerations of institutional power within science. (It is ironic, that early interpretations of the cell/state analogy leaned entirely towards this sort of pragmatic interpretation.) Yet, Maulitz's programme promises one way in which to unify the separate elements in Virchow studies. However, the study needs to go further and analyse Virchow's attempt at institution-building in anthropology and politics.

There are few works, beyond Ackerknecht, that discuss the role of Virchow in the history of anthropology, yet his role in the formation of that discipline is crucial, both as an institution-builder and teacher of Franz Boas. Virchow's role in the deconstruction of the idea of a German race during the Franco–Prussian war is detailed by Ackerknecht. Again, Ackerknecht's account should be read in its post-World War II context: for Ackerknecht, Virchow sets a fine example of how to be a good, peaceful, anti-racist German. (See SCHLUMBERGER for an explicitly political use of Virchow's position during the war.) However, Virchow's motives were mildly nationalistic and liberal. The French were at pains to show that racial characteristics lay at the core of Prussian aggression during the conflict, but Virchow's massive statistical studies indicated that this was not the case, and that there was no Prussian "race". (It is interesting to compare Boyd and Ackerknecht on this matter, because they radically differ in the details of the conflict.)

In his chapter on "Prussian Statistics", HACKING discusses the Foucaultian "epistemic grounds" or "deep knowledge" underlying the necessity of turning a debate about war and the state to the demarcation of race. Virchow is seen as part of a general tendency towards the use of statistics in the settling of social programmes and the construction of the "normal" state – a tendency that would easily absorb both holistic and reductionist accounts of the individual. On a deep level, says Hacking, Virchow was responsible for the manufacture of the modern bio–political state, and thus doctor, statesman, and anthropologist become one.

GORDON McOUAT

See also Anthropology; Neumann; Pathology

Virology

Chastel, Claude, *Histoire des virus: De la variole au sida*, Paris: Société nouvelle des éditions Boubée, 1992
Fenner, F. and A. Gibbs (eds), *Portraits of Viruses: A History of Virology*, Basel and New York: Karger, 1988
Grafe, Alfred, *A History of Experimental Virology*, translated from the German by Elvira Rechendorf, Berlin and New York: Springer, 1991
Hughes, Sally Smith, *The Virus: A History of the Concept*, London: Heinemann, and New York: Science History Publications, 1977
Théodoridès, J., "Les Maladies virales", in *Des miasmes aux virus*, Paris: Pariente, 1991
Waterson, A.P. and Lise Wilkinson, *An Introduction to the History of Virology*, Cambridge and New York: Cambridge University Press, 1978
Williams, Greer, *Virus Hunters*, New York: Knopf, 1959; London: Hutchinson, 1960

Virology is one of a number of related academic disciplines – including immunology, molecular biology, and genetics – that have emerged and grown to prominence as specialist subjects in the 20th century. It existed for half a century as a not very well-defined subsidiary of bacteriology and microbiology, but in the early 1950s its emergence as an academic subject in its own right was marked by the publication of S.E. Luria's classic textbook, *General Virology*, and the appearance of the first issue of the journal *Virology*. Eventually, separate departments of virology were established in universities and medical schools.

On the basis of evidence obtained at a steadily accelerating pace during the 1940s and 1950s, including the identification of the "double helix" and the DNA and RNA nucleic acids as carriers of genetic information, understanding of the nature and *modus operandi* of viruses entered its final definitive phase. As a corollary of such new knowledge and understanding, it became possible for historians to begin to trace the evolution of 20th-century ideas and evolutionary processes in the subject.

WILLIAMS was the first to be published. This is a readable, popular account, by a sometime public health teacher and medical journalist, of some of the important people and events of the long prehistory of virology, from 1900 to 1960. The focus of the text is on a few key incidents in the development of vaccines, from the pure empiricism of William Jenner's cow pox vaccine, via Louis Pasteur's rabies experiments, to Max Theiler's achievements with yellow fever, and the polio vaccines of Jonas Salk and Albert Sabin. Also included are sketches of early basic research on tobacco mosaic disease, and of the difficulties in determining the cause of influenza. The style and chapter headings are journalistic in style, and there are a number of illustrations portraying key players, and also electron micrographs of selected viruses and bacteriophages.

In complete contrast, HUGHES, published nearly 20 years later, is the first (if brief) scholarly history of the concept. The author pays particular attention to the early work on virology in the latter decades of the 19th century which, having culminated in M.W. Beijerinck's perceptive research on the agent of tobacco mosaic disease, led to the identification of "filterable" and "invisible" viruses as a separate class of infectious agents, and provided the foundations for a general understanding of the nature of viruses. The account is strongest on this early history before and around the turn of the 20th century. Illustrations are few and far between, but tables of "Landmarks in Bacteriology (1877-1900)" and "Landmarks in Viral Research" help to identify major advances and their authors.

At nearly twice the number of pages, and published only a year later, WATERSON & WILKINSON is a useful supplement to Hughes as a history of virological research and ideas. The authors also attempt to relate the development of these ideas to the working methods of individual scientists, and to reconstruct the creative processes that both preceded, and resulted from, their observations. There are a number of illustrations and biographical notes on contributors to developments in this field, and a full cross-referenced author index.

By far the most complete history of virology to date is CHASTEL, written by a professor of microbiology at Brest University. It contains detailed accounts of past and present research and methodology, and also includes accounts of the sinister viruses that have emerged, in a blaze of publicity, from exotic regions in the final decades of the 20th century: Lassa fever, Marburg disease, Ébola, AIDS, and the as yet to be identified "prions" of scrapie in sheep, BSE in cattle, and Creutzfeldt-Jakob disease in man. The book is well illustrated, and there is an extensive and helpful bibliography of nearly 900 original books and articles.

Among more specialised accounts, THÉODORIDÈS constitutes one chapter in a beautifully illustrated account of infectious diseases through the ages. It is lucidly written and has numerous illustrations, many reproduced from original documents.

GRAFE is a thorough, factual, and highly technical account, perhaps more suitable as an introductory text for students considering specialisation in virological research than for the average reader of the history of science. For the specialist it is a handy collection of information and references, clearly organised in short sections, with a helpful index.

Finally, FENNER & GIBBS is an aptly-named collection of essays by some of the best known workers in the field – active research scientists, rather than historians – who each presents his individual assessment of the importance of past work on one of 15 different viruses. Written by virologists and molecular biologists working in increasingly specialised fields, each essay might have been better subtitled, "One Man's View of Virology". Nevertheless, the 15 papers included are highly readable and largely enjoyable.

LISE WILKINSON

See also Bacteriology; Immunology; Molecular Biology

Vision

Arnheim, Rudolf, *Visual Thinking*, Berkeley: University of California Press, 1969

Crary, Jonathan, *Techniques of the Observer: On Vision and Modernity in the Nineteenth Century*, Cambridge, Massachusetts: MIT Press, 1990

Edgerton, Samuel Y., *The Heritage of Giotto's Geometry: Art and Science on the Eve of the Scientific Revolution*, Ithaca, New York: Cornell University Press, 1991

Foucault, Michel, *Madness and Civilization: A History of Insanity in the Age of Reason*, translated from the French by Richard Howard (abridged edition), New York: Pantheon Books, 1965; London: Tavistock, 1967 (original edition, 1961)

Foucault, Michel, *The Order of Things: An Archaeology of the Human Sciences*, translated from the French by Alan Sheridan, New York: Pantheon Books, and London: Tavistock, 1970 (original edition, 1966)

Foucault, Michel, *The Birth of the Clinic: An Archaeology of Medical Perception*, translated from the French by A.M. Sheridan Smith, New York: Pantheon Books, and London: Tavistock, 1973 (original edition, 1963)

Gombrich, Ernst H., *Art and Illusion: A Study in the Psychology of Pictorial Representation*, New York: Pantheon Books, 1960; 5th edition, London: Phaidon, 1977

Hanson, Norwood Russell, *Patterns of Discovery: An Inquiry into the Conceptual Foundations of Science*, Cambridge: Cambridge University Press, 1958

Ivins Jr, William M., *Art and Geometry: A Study in Space Intuitions*, Cambridge, Massachusetts: Harvard University Press, 1946

Jay, Martin, *Downcast Eyes: The Denigration of Vision in Twentieth-Century French Thought*, Berkeley: University of California Press, 1994

Kemp, Martin, *The Science of Art: Optical Themes in Western Art from Brunelleschi to Seurat*, New Haven, Connecticut: Yale University Press, 1990

Kuhn, Thomas S., *The Structure of Scientific Revolutions*, Chicago: University of Chicago Press, 1962; revised edition, 1970

Levin, David Michael (ed.), *Modernity and the Hegemony of Vision*, Berkeley: University of California Press, 1993

Miller, Arthur I., *Imagery in Scientific Thought: Creating Twentieth Century Physics*, Boston: Birkhäuser, 1984

Pastore, Nicholas, *Selective History of Theories of Visual Perception, 1650–1950*, Oxford and New York: Oxford University Press, 1971

Stafford, Barbara Maria, *Body Criticism: Imaging the Unseen in Enlightenment Art and Medicine*, Cambridge, Massachusetts: MIT Press, 1991

Stafford, Barbara Maria, *Artful Science: Enlightenment, Entertainment, and the Eclipse of Visual Education*, Cambridge, Massachusetts: MIT Press, 1994

Turner, R. Steven, *In the Eye's Mind: Vision and the Helmholtz-Hering Controversy*, Princeton, New Jersey: Princeton University Press, 1994

Vitz, Paul C. and Arnold B. Glimcher, *Modern Art and Modern Science: The Parallel Analysis of Vision*, New York: Praeger, 1984

Vision is a doubly important concept for historians of science; it has been the subject of scientific study through optics, psychology, and medicine, and it also has been one of the most important means by which scientists have gained information about the world. Of course, these two conceptions are related, since new scientific theories about vision change the way we perceive the world, and (conversely) scientists' observations have led to new theories of vision.

Most of the historical treatments of visual perception have discussed the history of optics more generally, but there are several studies solely on theories of vision. The most chronologically comprehensive is PASTORE, who reviews three centuries of empirical studies of vision, focusing on the conflict between nativists – who claim that seeing is an innate, psychological attribute – and empiricists – who claim that vision develops as a result of the organism's environment. Rather than proclaim the triumph of empiricism (as Pastore does), TURNER prefers to leave unsettled the uneasy compromise between nativism and empiricism, by looking at a crucial episode in the history of visual perception theories – namely, the late 19th-century debate between Hermann von Helmholtz (an empiricist) and Ewald Hering (a nativist). Turner's approach is detailed and often technical, as he attempts to show that scientific controversies sometimes never reach a final conclusion.

Through such studies of optics and visual perception, and histories of technology, some historians reasoned that science must have guided the development of artistic vision. For instance, the development of photography and color theories have been shown to be crucial to changes in art. VITZ & GLIMCHER present a strong version of this thesis, claiming that modern art is derivative of modern science. In fact, they argue that modern science is a fundamentally theoretical and verbal pursuit that has produced a similar theoretical approach in art. While IVINS is not nearly so dogmatic about the beholdenness of art to science, he does argue that since ancient Greek geometry had a metrical rather than perspectival notion of space, space in Greek art was "tactile-muscular" rather than visual. In other words, the ancient Greeks were not visual thinkers, and their culture consequently was overly compartmentalized and disorganized.

Conversely, many art historians and philosophers of science have claimed that art, and aesthetics more generally, have guided the way scientists have perceived the world. Through historical and philosophical argument, ARNHEIM seeks to establish vision as the key to cognition, and outlines a theory of thought based on imagery. He thereby challenges the *modus operandi* of many historians of science, who rely on texts as the only source material. HANSON, a philosopher of science, took up this charge by examining how scientific vision is shaped by prior knowledge, and how changes in scientific opinion occur through gestalt switches rather than gradual conversion. KUHN borrows liberally from Hanson in order to argue that at any one time different scientists can have incommensurable visions of the world; disputes between old and new world views are settled by a conversion of the majority of the scientific community, who are convinced more by social pressures than by the gradual accumulation of empirical evidence (which can often be explained under each of the incompatible world views). Focusing on the creative origins of scientific ideas rather than the controversy, MILLER shows that visual thinking was crucial for 20th-century physicists, even when their images did not accord with commonsensical "reality".

Postmodernists and relativists have posed a further challenge to the study of scientific vision, by arguing that penetrating, objective vision is a myth. Instead, our knowledge is an outcome of our place in time, space, and culture (and previous knowledge) rather than a pure view of the world "out there". As an explanatory survey of this position, JAY's lengthy book is not for those who are made faint-of-heart by continental philosophy, but provides a masterful history of the predominant place of vision in natural philosophy from Plato onward. Jay uses this history to explain why some French postmodernists (such as Foucault, Barthes, Irigaray, and Derrida) have discarded vision as the proper means for understanding the world. This book's informative references to other works provides an excellent reading list. Likewise, LEVIN's contributors (one of whom is Jay) question whether vision really has the dominant place in modern culture that conventional wisdom dictates. Chapters on the visual theories of Descartes, Hegel, Nietzsche, Sartre, Heidegger, Derrida, and Foucault provide indispensable postmodern interpretations of the history of vision. Among the postmodern works cited by Jay and Levin, FOUCAULT's studies (1965, 1970 and 1973) are especially important to the history of science. While Foucault does not consider himself a historian, his thesis, that for those in power objective vision – transformed here into the "gaze" – acts as a surveillance mechanism rather than as disinterested perception, has been enormously influential for many historians of science. GOMBRICH, probably the most frequently cited among scholars on vision and science, argues that art never presents an unmediated view of the world, and spectators perceive art through their cultural expectations. Different cultures in different time periods have different "languages" for depicting reality, so that photography seems to us the most objective mode of representation only because we have been trained to understand its visual code.

Many of the most recent scholars who write on the seamless history of vision, art, and science may challenge the reader who has little background in philosophy – but their works are often the most rewarding. CRARY, an art historian, has written a brief but dense book on visual technologies in the late 18th and 19th centuries, especially the camera obscura and the photographic camera. As opposed to many historians before him, Crary argues that photography marked the end, rather than the beginning, of a visual revolution – the science of vision would no longer concentrate on the abstract and mechanical transmission of light, but rather on the human subject. STAFFORD (1991 and 1994), another art historian, has written several intriguing books on the visual culture of the Enlightenment. In a sense, she challenges Crary's thesis, for if the observer was becoming more embodied in the 19th century, the human subject of scientific inquiry became less embodied between the Enlightenment and today. Where once the scientist's eye was directed at seeing the interior of a material human body, X-rays and magnetic resonance imaging are ghostly, mechanized versions of the "real" thing.

While he shows few of the postmodernist signs of Crary and Stafford, EDGERTON agrees that the visual apparatuses of science and art have co-evolved. While Renaissance artists such as Giotto and Leonardo were beholden to Euclid's geometry, scientists such as Galileo were influenced in turn by artistic developments, such as chiaroscuro and perspective. Edgerton also compares Western vision to the very different approach of the Chinese during the same period. Similarly, for the period from the Renaissance to the 19th century, KEMP notes that both science and art relied on vision as their primary means for understanding nature, although, as his extended comparison of color science and pigment theory during the Newtonian period illustrates, scientific and artistic theories and techniques did not always match seamlessly. Kemp is also more skeptical than Edgerton about art's role in scientific revolutions, and prefers intellectual to social explanations for changes in science and art.

ELIZABETH GREEN MUSSELMAN

See also Optics; Photography; Physiology: Germany; Representation

Vitalism

Burwick, Frederick and Paul Douglass (eds), *The Crisis in Modernism: Bergson and the Vitalist Controversy*, Cambridge and New York: Cambridge University Press, 1992

Duchesneau, François, *La Physiologie des lumières: Empirisme, modèles, et théories*, The Hague and Boston: Nijhoff, 1982

Freyhofer, Horst H., *The Vitalism of Hans Driesch: The Success and Decline of a Scientific Theory*, Frankfurt: Peter Lang, 1982

Grogin, Robert C., *The Bergsonian Controversy in France, 1900–1914*, Calgary, Alberta: University of Calgary Press, 1988

Haigh, Elizabeth J., *Xavier Bichat and the Medical Theory of the Eighteenth Century*, London: Wellcome Institute, 1984

King, Lester S., *The Road to Medical Enlightenment, 1650–1695*, London: Macdonald, and New York: Elsevier, 1970

King, Lester S., *The Philosophy of Medicine: The Early Eighteenth Century*, Cambridge, Massachusetts: Harvard University Press, 1978

Roger, Jacques, *Les Sciences de la vie dans la pensée française du XVIIIe siècle: La génération des animaux de Descartes à l'Encyclopédie*, Paris: Colin, 1963; revised edition, Paris: Michel, 1993

Schubert-Soldern, Rainer, *Mechanism and Vitalism: Philosophical Aspects of Biology*, translated from the German by C.E. Robin, edited by Philip G. Fothergill, Notre Dame, Indiana: University of Notre Dame Press, and London: Burns and Oates, 1962

The mechanist–vitalist debate concerning the nature of organic functions and the appropriate means for studying them flourished during the Enlightenment. After a hiatus, in which the matter seemed to be resolved on behalf of the mechanists, the debate surfaced again in the first half of the 20th century. This time, the controversy focused largely on the question of whether or not there is a purposefulness to organic processes, and whether or not there is an evolutionary direction towards progressively increasing consciousness.

Roger, Duchesneau, and Haigh each deal in a general way with the first of these periods, describing and analysing the evolution of vitalist theory and evaluating its role in the development of physiology. A good place to start is ROGER's large but eminently readable book. His wide-ranging study is divided into three sections: "La Fin de la renaissance (1600–1670)",

"La Philosophie des savantes (1670–1745)", and "La Science des philosophes (1745–1770)". Rogers examines the major debates that preoccupied scholars in each period, including embryology, heredity, and pre-existence. In the second section, there is a chapter on "Les Mésaventures du mécanisme" and another on "La Renaissance des forces vitales". Moreover, the entire volume addresses issues involved in the mechanist–vitalist debate, and the book synthesizes a massive amount of material clearly and lucidly.

DUCHESNEAU's detailed, but rather more turgid, analysis examines the debate about the nature of life as it unfolded in the 18th century. It is organized around the work of 14 individual thinkers, each of whom is presented as facing a set of determinate problems raised by his field of study, and by the contributions of his predecessors and contemporaries. He begins with the "*antimécanisme*" and animist theory of G.E. Stahl, discusses the mechanist theories of Friedrich Hoffmann and Herman Boerhaave, and then the notions of "irritability" and "sensibility" in Robert Whytt and Victor Haller. In fact, Haller is Duchesneau's central figure, chronologically and conceptually. He distinguishes between the tradition of K.F. Wolff and J.F. Blumenbach, who attached vitalism to epigenesis, and the Montpellier tradition, which developed the notion of the organism as a network of quasi-organisms in which living forces reside. Using the perspective of a philosopher, he thus examines the method of formulation of scientific theories and their function, and explores such problems as the role of experimental method, the genesis of hypotheses, the role and nature of models, and the evolution of concepts.

Using the figure of Xavier Bichat as the apogee of vitalist theory, HAIGH argues that physiology was born of 18th-century vitalist philosophy. She distinguishes between animism and vitalism, both of which were opposed to iatromechanism, and argues that Bichat's theory was a synthesis of the vital theory developed in Montpellier and the notions of sensibility and irritability analyzed at length by Whytt, Haller, Denis Diderot, and others. In the process, she distinguishes a variety of viewpoints that in the 18th century were subsumed under the terms "vitalism" and "mechanism".

King's works deal with the epistemology of medicine and with the relationship between philosophy and medical theory. KING (1970) examines the history of medical and philosophical ideas in the years 1660–1740, including those concerning the relationship between the mind, the soul, and the body, and embraces metaphysical, natural–theological, and methodological reflections. The author discusses theories about the nature of matter and of humoural theory, and looks at the nature of iatrochemical and iatromechanical theories, focusing on such central figures as a J.B. von Helmont, Boerhaave, Hoffmann, and Stahl.

KING (1978) is concerned with the theories that underlay 18th-century medical practice. The book reviews particular topical areas in order to reveal the views of philosophers, physicians, and others on subjects central to an understanding of early 18th-century medicine. In a chapter on "iatromechanism", King presents G.A. Borelli, Archibald Pitcairn, Hoffmann, and Boerhaave as the major spokesmen for the concept. In another chapter devoted to "Soul, Mind, and Body", he considers Van Helmont, Thomas Willis, and Stahl, all of whom opted for an animist solution to the mind–body problem.

SCHUBERT-SOLDERN's work addresses questions that emerged early in the 20th century. His purpose is to conduct a scientific inquiry into the nature of life, and he presents a wealth of biological data that must be accounted for by any philosophical consideration of life science. In the process, he gives a clear comparison, partly historical, of how mechanists and vitalists attempt to correlate observed data with their philosophical system. He finds that neither system is completely satisfactory, and he develops a "holistic" position that leans, however, more towards vitalism. Schubert-Soldern contends that "modern vitalism" originated in research into the origin of the living form. He emphasizes the importance of the vitalism of Hans Driesch and the mechanism of August Weismann, devoting space to their "Entelechial Wholeness Factor", and mechanist "Germplasm Theory" respectively, and argues that the controversy in biology since the 1920s is largely a continuation of that which they began.

Grogin and Burwick & Douglass discuss Henri Bergson's vitalistically-grounded theory of evolution, with a view to evaluating his influence on the 20th century. GROGIN skilfully expounds Bergson's philosophy, showing how his doctrines evolved and the principal influences on his thought, and succeeds admirably in elucidating Bergson's concept of *élan vital*, which was at the heart of his controversial *Évolution créatrice* of 1907. In this carefully argued work, Grogin shows that, between 1907 and 1914, Bergson was an international celebrity and perhaps the world's most controversial philosopher.

BURWICK & DOUGLASS's book is very wide ranging. It deals largely with the political and intellectual conflict concerning vitalist issues from 1917 to the 1930s. In an introductory article, Burwick distinguishes between "naive vitalism", which had posited a vital force, and "critical vitalism", as in the work of Bergson and Driesch, which emerged in the 19th-century transition from matter-based to energy-based physics. The latter, he argues, was joined to German *Naturphilosophie*, and to the aesthetic and social vitalism of Friedrich Nietzsche, such that "as the century closed, the vitalist tradition was being powerfully reinterpreted by some of the most celebrated intellectuals in the West". Ten essays in the book examine how mechanist and vitalist thinking infiltrated literature, the arts, and philosophy. One author finds French existentialism deeply indebted to Bergson, and another demonstrates his impact on poststructuralism. One even sees Bergson's ideas persisting into the "chaos" and "systems" philosophers of the late 20th century.

FREYHOFER sets out to evaluate why vitalism, as propounded by the zoologist Hans Driesch, enjoyed a considerable following in the first three decades of the 20th century, and why it then declined in influence. A book almost exclusively for philosophers, it offers only a glance at the man himself, and instead concentrates on the development of Driesch's vitalist theory. Freyhofer claims that this theory led Driesch to a general theory of knowledge and reality, but shows how, in the 1920s and 1930s, his vitalism tended to attract parapsychologists, fundamentalists, and fascists. Although it lacks an index, the book has an extensive bibliography of relevant German and English literature.

ELIZABETH V. HAIGH

See also Evolution; Mechanization

Volta, Alessandro   1745–1827

Italian physicist

Barona, Josep Lluís, *Fisiología: origen histórico de una disciplina experimental*, Madrid: Akal, 1991

Brazier, Mary Agnes Burniston, *A History of the Electrical Activity of the Brain: The First Half-Century*, London: Pitman, 1961

Dibner, Bern, *Alessandro Volta and the Electric Battery*, New York: Watts, 1964

Dibner, Bern, *Galvani-Volta: A Controversy That Led to the Discovery of Useful Electricity*, Norwalk, Connecticut: Burndy Library, 1952

Hackmann, W.D., *Electricity from Glass: The History of the Frictional Electrical Machine, 1600–1850*, Alphen aan den Rijn, Netherlands: Sijthoff & Noordhoff, 1978

Heilbron, J.L., entry on Volta in *Dictionary of Scientific Biography*, edited by Charles Coulston Gillispie, vol. 14, New York: Scribner, 1976

Heilbron, J.L., *Electricity in the 17th and 18th Centuries: A Study of Early Modern Physics*, Berkeley: University of California Press, 1979

Papp, Desiderio, *Historia de la Física*, Madrid: Espasa Calpe, 1961

Polvani, Giovanni, *Alessandro Volta*, Pisa: Domus Galileana, 1942

Premuda, Loris, *Storia della fisiologia: Problemi e figure*, Udine: Del Bianco, 1966

Volpati, Carlo, *Alessandro Volta nella gloria e nell'intimità*, Milan: Fratelli Treves, 1927

Alessandro Volta's interests within the field of physics were quite broad, and included electrostatics, meteorology, pneumatics, galvanism, and animal electricity. All these aspects, and some information on his biography and his social and family environment, are covered in HEILBRON (1976), which also includes a sound description of works published by Volta. In his monograph on electricity in the 17th and 18th centuries, HEILBRON (1979) provides much information on Volta's academic career, his contributions to instrumentation, his collaboration with Lavoisier and Laplace, and his important work in the fields of electricity and pneumatics, and in other areas of physics. POLVANI also offers an insightful and laudable general study of Volta's scientific contributions, and constitutes an excellent summary of the various facets of his work.

Other books analyze specific aspects of Volta's life or writings. VOLPATI represents one of the best general assessments of the main highlights of Volta's life and his scientific biography. The most assiduously studied aspects of Volta's scientific activity are those concerning electrostatics, and his dispute with Galvani about physiological stimulation and animal electricity. HACKMANN's book analyzes the first of these aspects, placing Volta's contribution within the context of the rise and development of electricity, whereas DIBNER (1952 and 1964) describes the work that led to the fabrication of the electric battery, undoubtedly the most renowned of Volta's achievements and the one that had the greatest influence on the development of electricity. In his history of physics, PAPP devotes two long chapters to the emergence and development of electricity, and places the discovery of the electric current by Volta in historical perspective.

Volta's role in the controversy with Galvani, and the rise of electrophysiology in the second half of the 18th century as a new field of research, are treated in some of the best-known books on the history of physiology. BARONA devotes a chapter to these issues, in which he explores the significance of electrophysiology as an experimental innovation, and the electric interpretation of nervous and muscular impulses. Adopting the same approach, PREMUDA describes Volta's work in electrophysiology and his disagreements with Galvani.

JOSEP LLUÍS BARONA

See also Electricity; Galvani; Galvanic Battery

Von Neumann, John   1903–1957

Hungarian-born American mathematician

Aspray, William, *John von Neumann and the Origins of Modern Computing*, Cambridge, Massachusetts: MIT Press, 1990

Bródy, F. and Tibor Vámos, *The Neumann Compendium*, Singapore and River Edge, New Jersey: World Scientific, 1995

Dore, Mohammed, Sukhamoy Chakravarty and Richard Goodwin (eds), *John von Neumann and Modern Economics*, Oxford: Clarendon Press, and New York: Oxford University Press, 1989

Glimm, James, John Impagliazzo and Isadore Singer (eds), *The Legacy of John von Neumann*, Providence, Rhode Island: American Mathematical Society, 1990

Goldstine, Herman H., The Computer: From Pascal to von Neumann, *Princeton, New Jersey: Princeton University Press, 1972*

Heims, Steve J., *John Von Neumann and Norbert Wiener: From Mathematics to the Technologies of Life and Death*, Cambridge, Massachusetts: MIT Press, 1980

Legendi, Tamás and Tibor Szentivanyi, *Leben und Werk von John von Neumann: Ein zusammenfassender Überblick*, translated from the Hungarian, Mannheim: Bibliographisches Institut, 1983 (original edition, 1979)

Macrae, Norman, *John von Neumann*, New York: Pantheon Books, 1992

Nagy, Ferenc (ed.), *Neumann János és a "Magyar Titok"*, Budapest: Országos Műszaki, 1987

Taub, Abraham H. (ed.), *Collected Works*, 6 vols, Oxford and New York: Pergamon Press, 1961–63

Ulam, Stanislaw (ed.), "John von Neumann, 1903–57", *Bulletin of the American Mathematical Society* (special issue), 64 (1958): 1–129

John Von Neumann's mathematical work is unique both in its versatility and in its applicability to various physical, economic and social domains, although his undiminished fame is largely a result of his contribution to the foundation of computer science and his collaboration with US military research (atomic weapons, hydrodynamics). Nevertheless his work on economic theory, mathematical physics, and pure mathematical research are also highly esteemed and a source of inspiration for specialists.

The pre-eminence of Von Neumann's contribution to the theory and practice of the electronic, digital, stored program computer is revealed in editions and books by several of his collaborators such as Goldstine and Taub, as well as by younger scholars, among them several Hungarian compatriots, such as Aspray, Glimm, Legendi, Nagy, Szentivanyi, and Vamos.

GOLDSTINE gives, in the second part of his book, a lively account of his close collaboration with John von Neumann on the ENIAC and EDVAC projects since 1944, and on the subsequent "von Neumann machine" at the Institute for Advanced Study in Princeton. Based on a large amount of unpublished material and personal recollections, Goldstine traces the historical origins of notions such as "flow diagram", "programming", "coding", and "cellular automata" in von Neumann's work.

ASPRAY's book was written almost two decades later, when the role of the computer as a scientific instrument as well as a social factor had become much clearer. Among other things, the impact of computers on meteorology and numerical analysis are studied in much more detail here. Both Goldstine and Aspray focus on US-related events, while developments in computers and numerical analysis elsewhere in the world are not fully covered.

The historical roots of von Neumann's understanding of automata are partly to be found in the correspondence between von Neumann and his childhood acquaintance, Rudolf Ortvay (1885–1945), the director of the Theoretical Physics Institute of the University of Budapest. Their correspondence between 1928 and 1941 is collected in NAGY, along with facsimiles of documents and photographs relating to von Neumann's life.

Another Hungarian collection, by LEGENDI & SZENTIVANYI, also focuses on von Neumann's work on computers, especially his work on cellular automata. Besides neurophysiology, another source of von Neumann's interest in computers and automata was his early work in the 1920s on the foundations of mathematics and logics. While this work is reproduced in volume 1 of TAUB and is still influential with logicians, a full investigation of its connection with von Neumann's work on the logical theory of computers is still missing. A useful feature of TAUB's edition is the inclusion of reviews by competent mathematicians of many of von Neumann's unpublished papers.

BRODY & VAMOS exclude from their selective edition of von Neumann's papers all work before 1930, which was written mostly in German, among them his contributions to Hilbert space theory. As to von Neumann's work on quantum mechanics, Bródy & Vámos concentrate on von Neumann's theory of measurement and quantum logics, both still a source of inspiration to mathematical physicists. The main focus of this most recent edition, however, is von Neumann's work on operator algebras ("von Neumann algebras") and its relation to mathematical physics.

In the collection edited by GLIMM, IMPAGLIAZZO & SINGER, leading experts analyse von Neumann's contributions to ergodic theory (G.W. Mackey, D.S. Ornstein, H. Furstenberg), operator algebras (F.J. Murray, R.V. Kadison), scientific computing (J. Glimm, N. Pippenger, J.D. Cowan, W. Aspray), and the ramifications of von Neumann's work for mathematical physics (H. Araki, A.M. Jaffe, I.E. Segal). This collection partly supersedes and updates an earlier honorary issue, dedicated to von Neumann, of the *Bulletin of the American Mathematical Society*, edited by von Neumann's friend and collaborator Stanisław ULAM. Ulam's introductory essay, which has recently been reproduced in Brody & Vámos, is still the most comprehensive and balanced biography of John von Neumann. Moreover, the honorary issue of the *Bulletin* remains valuable for its commentaries by leading American mathematicians on von Neumann's work in lattice theory (G. Birkhoff), measurement theory (P. Halmos), automata theory (C.E. Shannon), and the theory of games and mathematical economics (H.W. Kuhn, A.W. Tucker).

Von Neumann's work on economics is investigated in more detail in the collection edited by DORE, CHAKRAVARTY & GOODWIN. This work centres on von Neumann's article of 1937 on the model of an expanding economy, and stresses "von Neumann's shift of emphasis within economics in a combinatorial direction". The volume acknowledges, however, that von Neumann's joint book with O. Morgenstern (1944) lacked substantive significance for economics, since it focused mainly on zero-sum two person game theory.

An edition of von Neumann's extensive correspondence with influential scientists and politicians remains a desideratum for future scholarship. This correspondence is still scattered throughout archives and private collections in a number of countries and it is written in at least three languages. Such an edition should be an important contribution to the historiography of Jewish emigration from Europe and may, at the same time, enable final judgments on von Neumann's controversial political position, especially on his relation to the US Atomic Energy Commission after 1950.

HEIMS's critical monograph of von Neumann and Norbert Wiener stresses von Neumann's anti-communist attitudes and his support of the "old military masculine ideal of toughness and ruthlessness". Meanwhile, the economist and journalist MACRAE, with less sophistication in his argument but with the benefit of historical hindsight after the collapse of communism, defends von Neumann's promotion of the arms race. This popular account of von Neumann's life draws partly on biographical material, collected by Stanisław Ulam, which may yet serve as the basis for a full intellectual biography of von Neumann.

REINHARD SIEGMUND-SCHULTZE

See also Computing; Hungary

W

Watt, James   1736–1819

British engineer and inventor

Arago, M., *Historical Eloge of James Watt*, translated from the French by James Patrick Muirhead, London: John Murray, 1839

Dickinson, H.W., *James Watt, Craftsman and Engineer*, Cambridge: Cambridge University Press, 1936; New York: Kelley, 1967

Dickinson, H.W. and Rhys Jenkins, *James Watt and the Steam Engine*, Oxford: Clarendon Press, 1927

Dickinson, H.W. and H.P. Vowles, *James Watt and the Industrial Revolution*, London and New York: Longmans Green, 1943

Muirhead, James Patrick, *The Origin and Progress of the Mechanical Inventions of James Watt Illustrated by His Correspondence with His Friends and the Specifications of His Patents*, 3 vols, London: John Murray, 1854

Musson, A.E. and Eric Robinson, *Science and Technology in the Industrial Revolution*, Manchester: Manchester University Press, and Toronto: Toronto University Press, 1969

Robinson, Eric and A.E. Musson, *James Watt and the Steam Revolution: A Documentary History*, London: Adams and Dart, and New York: Kelley, 1969

Robinson, Eric and Douglas McKie (eds), *Partners in Science: Letters of James Watt and Joseph Black*, London: Constable, and Cambridge, Massachusetts: Harvard University Press, 1970

Smiles, Samuel, *Lives of the Engineers: The Steam-Engine: Boulton and Watt*, revised edition, London: John Murray, 1878

Williamson, George, *Memorials of the Lineage, Early Life, Education and Development of the Genius of James Watt*, London: Constable, 1856

James Watt's crucial improvements to the steam engine have rightly dominated biographical works about him, but this has generally been to the exclusion of most of his other inventions and discoveries. The invention for which he is best remembered is the addition of the separate condenser to the Newcomen engine. Not only did this make a much more powerful and economical engine, but it led to his development of the steam engine from a machine that could only pump water into one that could turn rotating machinery directly. Watt solved the problems he faced by the application of scientific principles, and so he may be said to be the originator of scientific engineering.

Another problem with the published sources is that most authors have written with an adulatory slant, and have not examined Watt's work critically. This is certainly true of ARAGO, who was writing at a time when the effects of Watt's steam engine in increasing mill and mine productivity were becoming more apparent, and when moves were afoot to create various Watt memorials. Ever since Arago, biographies of Watt have been produced regularly every 20 or 30 years; a number of these have essentially relied on information from earlier publications, and few will therefore be discussed here.

One such derivative biography is WILLIAMSON, who concentrates on Watt's ancestors and his early life at Greenock. It is now virtually impossible to check the veracity of Williamson's stories because few papers have survived from this period of Watt's life. Similarly, MUIRHEAD gives a short introductory life followed by extracts of Watt's correspondence with such people as John Roebuck, Small, and Matthew Boulton concerning principally the development of his steam engine in Scotland and then in Birmingham. Together with the text of Watt's patents, these volumes are a source of much important material.

For the best general account of Watt's life, we must turn to SMILES, who begins with Watt's early career in Scotland, and then covers the rest of his life in Birmingham together with that of Matthew Boulton. Smiles had access to some of the mass of Watt's papers, then still with the family but now available at Birmingham Central Library. One difficulty for biographers was that access to the papers held in Watt's house at Doldowlod was restricted for many years. DICKINSON & JENKINS, 70 years after Smiles, had access to these papers and hence gave a much fuller, more accurate account than earlier works. Starting with a sketch of Watt's life in Scotland, the book does not really tackle Watt's development of his engine with the vital separate condenser, but gives instead a comprehensive treatment of the later developments, after Watt had moved to Birmingham in 1774, showing the many improvements to the pumping engines, especially those in Cornwall, and how Watt pioneered his rotative engines. DICKINSON's later book does describe other inventions, such as Watt's perspective and copying machines, but inevitably concentrates on both the pumping and rotative engines. Dickinson examined the correspondence between Watt, Boulton, and Roebuck over the separate condenser in the Muirhead collection, but it seems unlikely that he was able to refer to other papers in the Doldowlod archives and he fails to explain the problems Watt had with his invention. On the steam engine, it is not as detailed as Dickinson's earlier collaborative work with Jenkins.

Access to these crucial Doldowlod papers was given to ROBINSON & MUSSON, who published a small fraction of them in celebration of the 200th anniversary of Watt's crucial patent for the separate condenser of 1769. Much of this material had already appeared in Muirhead, but this later book does contain some new additions.

DICKINSON & VOWLES sets the story against the background of other developments and inventions that were helping to launch the industrial revolution at that time. For accounts of some of Watt's scientific contributions and discoveries, we have to turn to other works by Robinson. ROBINSON & McKIE published the correspondence between Watt and his mentor, Professor Joseph Black, who moved to Edinburgh from Glasgow in 1766, and died in 1799. There are also letters to and from Professor John Robison, who was often involved in their scientific experiments, and subjects covered include the steam engine, alkali from sea salt, the copying press, chlorine bleaching, and many other chemical and scientific problems. A more detailed examination of some of these scientific inquiries can be found in MUSSON & ROBINSON, which covers in detail Watt's attempts in both alkali and chlorine manufacture, as well as his interests in dyeing. Their article, "Training Captains of Industry", describes the education of James Watt Jr.

In spite of all these publications, the challenge of writing an adequate biography remains. The acquisition of the Doldowlod papers for the public domain means that a more thorough appraisal of Watt's career, as first a scientific instrument-maker and then a civil engineer at Glasgow, can now be made, for it was in these professions that he laid the foundations for his later work on the steam engine.

RICHARD L. HILLS

See also Energy; Engines: steam

Whewell, William 1794–1866

British philosopher of science

Ashworth, William J. (ed.), *A Calendar of the Correspondence of William Whewell*, Cambridge: Trinity College, 1996

Becher, Harvey, "William Whewell and Cambridge Mathematics", *Historical Studies in the Physical Sciences*, 11 (1980): 1–48

Fisch, Menachem, *William Whewell: Philosopher of Science*, Oxford: Clarendon Press, and New York: Oxford University Press, 1991

Fisch, Menachem and Simon Schaffer (eds), *William Whewell: A Composite Portrait*, Oxford: Clarendon Press, and New York: Oxford University Press, 1991

Stair-Douglas, Janet, *The Life and Selections from the Correspondence of William Whewell*, London: Kegan Paul, Trench, 1881

Todhunter, I., *William Whewell, DD: Master of Trinity College Cambridge: An Account of His Writings with*

Selections from His Literary and Scientific Correspondence, 2 vols, London: Macmillan, 1876; reprinted, New York: Johnson, and Farnborough, Hampshire: Gregg International, 1970

Yeo, Richard, *Defining Science: William Whewell, Natural Knowledge and Public Debate in Early Victorian Britain*, Cambridge and New York: Cambridge University Press, 1993

In October 1811, William Whewell began the tedious trek from Lancaster to Cambridge, the start of a journey that would take him from being the son of a carpenter and joiner to Master of Trinity College. When he first arrived in Cambridge, the war with France was still raging, and the English physical and mental landscape was gradually changing to meet the needs of a developing industrial economy – for many, these changes heralded a new morality expunged of religion, and a very real threat to the English constitution. It was within this context that Whewell assimilated himself into the traditional Anglican culture of the 18th century, and, within the walls of Trinity College, he laboured to protect English culture from what he regarded as the illusory and destructive effects of French abstract reason, as well as the growing interests stemming from the new industrial cities. Indeed, Whewell devoted his life to preserving and ensuring that political and intellectual (especially scientific) changes did not adversely affect the constitutional marriage between church and state, and the intrinsic role that Oxbridge played in this holy alliance.

Whewell's work in trying to safeguard this institutional set-up can best be seen in his correspondence, found in the under-used volumes by STAIR-DOUGLAS and TODHUNTER. Both, especially the former, contain a wealth of information on Whewell's private views, and reveal the total centrality of Trinity College to his work. This has recently been bolstered by ASHWORTH's selected calendar of Whewell's correspondence, which provides a chronological slice (some 2,000 letters) of his ideas and opinions exchanged with his core network of close friends and colleagues. Perhaps the most important part of Whewell's correspondence is the 480 letters he exchanged with the Anglican political economist, Richard Jones. This long correspondence reveals that intrinsic to Whewell's historical approach was a variation of the German historical method and an emphasis on etymology.

It is through Whewell's ideas on political economy, history, and language that his political and intellectual views are united. This is supported by a number of the papers presented in FISCH & SCHAFFER, especially the entries by Harvey Becher, Geoffrey Cantor, Simon Schaffer, Perry Williams, and Richard Yeo. The book as a whole is an attempt to present a synthesis of Whewell's vast array of interests. All these authors have shown how Whewell's use of history, and his onslaught on Ricardian political economy and pure French algebraic analysis, were particularly targeted to counter abstract reasoning and to seek an appropriate scientific morality – reflecting Whewell's rejection of a utilitarian legitimation of science, and his desire to establish a moral and intellectual one.

For Whewell, as the entries by Cantor and Yeo show, great men of science were not bound by strict rules but used their imagination. His history and the study of language, as Schaffer's paper reveals, were intrinsic to his discursive weaponry, and he utilised these resources to slay the foul language of the radical press, and the stench of abstract arguments spewing from the mouths of atheists and utilitarian philosophers. Language was intrinsic to permanent knowledge, and history was the tool in which to find it. In his metascientific project, Whewell did not seek the ground rules of science, but rather he sought to generalise the pattern in which subjects were translated into scientific disciplines. Only established science, in Whewell's sense, could be assimilated into the traditional structure of a liberal education. This form of education was defined by an equilibrium between new and old knowledge, in which active discovery had no place. Whewell's moral philosophy, in particular, was designed to restore this balance through the correct training of the Cambridge mind. Whewell used his philosophy both to legitimate a particular stance (as opposed to the use of pure reason), and to show that science did not progress through sudden changes, but rather accommodated old claims within a new perspective.

Both BECHER and FISCH examine Whewell's textbooks, but come to different conclusions. Fisch believes that these books reveal Whewell's attempt to reconcile Lagrangian formalism with Baconian empiricism, and he tries to reconstruct Whewell's philosophy by tracing the intellectual difficulties he encountered and his attempts to overcome them. Fisch concludes that the roots of Whewell's later inductive philosophy lie in his mechanics textbooks. Conversely, Becher argues that Whewell was essentially anti-Lagrangian, and locates his textbooks within the traditional requirements of a liberal education.

YEO sets out to explore Whewell's role in trying to define science within the rich milieu of early Victorian culture; for example, debates occurred in theology, science, philology, history, literature, and political economy, and Whewell was active in varying degrees in all these areas. A discussion of this "metascientific discourse" occupies much of the first part of Yeo's book, giving a sense of Whewell's seemingly diverse interests and of a culture still far removed from the specialist disciplinary boundaries of the 20th century. Yeo has not written a biography of Whewell, but rather uses him as a scholar who drew upon a whole range of media to define science and its cultural meaning. It was this task, argues Yeo, that Whewell began to see as his vocation. He describes how Whewell developed a philosophy of science in order to counter the materialist and utilitarian epistemology with one which proposed fundamental ideas as the basis of the scientific–human mind, and shows how Whewell's philosophy was then made the foundation of his later work in the moral sciences. His mission was to sever the growing link perceived between the material and moral sphere, and to replace it with a philosophy that stressed the role of both empiricism and idealism.

For Whewell, scientific progress operated through a philosophy of induction, in which advances still retained old truths revealed in a new light. Intellectually, Whewell saw purely deductive habits of thinking as destructive to this view. One of the more neglected areas of Whewellian scholarship is his work on moral philosophy; Yeo rightly stresses its central role in Whewell's activities, and reminds us that before 1840 "the key philosophical contest was mainly fought over ethics, not science. This was the conflict between utilitarianism and some version of intuitionism." Whewell's targets were the Cambridge textbooks of John Locke and William Paley. (Moral concerns were apparent from Whewell's earliest reflections and cannot be seen simply as a later development of his work.) Yeo traces the debates and resources Whewell drew upon in moving from within a Baconian framework to the anti-Lockean stance that defined his philosophy of science within a moral constituency. There is thus a sense in which Whewell's work is incredibly straightforward: it can be seen as essentially a quest to preserve the institution of Cambridge University, and especially Trinity College, from increasingly vociferous onslaughts and political interference during the first half of the 19th century.

WILLIAM J. ASHWORTH

See also Faraday; Philosophy of Science; Political Economy

Wind Turbines

Baker, T. Lindsay, *A Field Guide to American Windmills*, Norman: University of Oklahoma Press, 1985

Gipe, Paul, *Wind Energy Comes of Age*, New York: Wiley, 1995

Golding, Edward William, *The Generation of Electricity by Wind Power*, London: Spon, 1955; New York: John Wiley, 1976

Hansen, Hans Christian, *Poul la Cour, Grundtvigianer, Opfinder og Folkeoplyser*, Vejen: Askov Højskoles, 1985

Heymann, Matthias, *Die Geschichte der Windenergienutzung, 1890–1990*, Frankfurt: Campus, 1995

Karnøe, Peter, *Dansk Vindmølleindustri – en overraskende international succes: Om innovationer, industriudvikling og teknologipolitik*, Frederiksberg: Samfundslitteratur, 1991

Le Gourières, Désiré, *Wind Plants: Theory and Design*, translated from the French, Oxford: Pergamon Press, 1982 (original edition, 1980)

Neumann, Friedrich, *Die Windmotoren, Beschreibung, Konstruktion und Berechnung der Windflügel, Windturbinen und Windräder*, Weimar: Voigt, 1881; reprinted Hanover: Libri Rari, 1984

Putnam, Coslett Palmer, *Power from the Wind*, New York: Van Nostrand, 1948

Righter, Robert W., *Wind Energy in America: A History*, Norman: University of Oklahoma Press, 1996

Schieber, Walther, *Energiequelle Windkraft*, Berlin: Fackelträger, 1941

Van Heys, Johann Wilhelm, *Was jeder Deutsche über Windkraft wissen muß*, Berlin: Mittelbach, 1933

Wind turbines have for a long time been a field of marginal interest in the history of science and technology, although some literature, comprising historical overviews or historical descriptions of particular developments, has been published by those actively involved in wind technology development. Only recently, after wind power use experienced an enormous boom in countries such as California, Denmark, and Germany, has historical interest in wind turbines markedly increased, and a number of comprehensive scientific historical analyses have appeared. Though wind power remains a comparably small energy source, its great symbolic value as an abundant and clean source of energy has motivated considerable historical research and prompted much discussion.

NEUMANN described and collected data on windmills and a great number of newly developed wind turbines in the second half of the 19th century. The turbines he described mostly remained immature and technically inferior to the conventional windmill, but his book gives a good impression of the numerous efforts at that time to improve wind technology.

As a government official, VAN HEYS had to describe wind turbine types and review proposals of mostly utopian "big wind power plants", which caused enthusiastic discussions in Nazi Germany. In spite of his engineering experience, he neglected construction problems of large-scale turbines and proved to be as confident about German technological power as many other German experts of that time. SCHIEBER, by contrast, collected a great deal of information on, and photographs of, small wind turbines still in use in order to illustrate the opportunities provided by wind power. His work did not aim at propagating the "big wind power plants" like Van Heys, but at reviving the use of small wind turbines, which were declining rapidly in number.

From the 1930s, Putnam had planned to construct a big wind power plant and he managed to erect the largest wind turbine of the early 1940s in Vermont, US. In PUTNAM, he described these efforts, providing much information on wind technology and wind power use. In a similar manner, GOLDING recounted the efforts in Britain after the war; the British Electrical and Allied Industries Research Association (ERA) undertook comprehensive investigations on optimum design features and the costs of wind power use, and developed several prototype wind turbines. Like Putnam's, many of Golding's observations still apply in the 1990s.

In the 1960s, cheap oil and the advent of nuclear power ended interest in wind power abruptly, but only 10 years later energy and environmental crises prompted a new flurry of publications on wind turbines. LE GOURIÈRES is one example of many (although one of very few French contributions), and at the time was one of the first modern technical books on wind turbine design. For the historian, it is useful for its most thorough documentation of early French wind turbines, and for its numerous sketches of small wind turbines manufactured during the late 1970s. GIPE is the most comprehensive and up-to-date book intended for the expert; the author provides a large amount of technical and economic information on wind turbines, and gives much historical detail on wind technology development and wind power use since the 1970s. Especially useful are his accounts of different turbine designs, and the success of the Danish wind technology style, which Gipe considered superior.

In the past years a growing number of historical works on wind turbines have appeared. BAKER collected enormous amounts of material on American water-pumping wind turbines, the predecessor of modern wind turbines, which first appeared in the US in the mid-19th century, and within a few decades they turned large areas of the "Great American Desert" into the fertile "Great Plains". Baker lists as many as 1000 producers and 1100 turbine types, and provides detailed information on some of the most important. Twentieth-century wind technology development, however, was strongest in Europe. HANSEN reconstructs the pioneering work of the "Danish Edison" Poul la Cour, and carefully describes la Cour's experiments and innovations in his attempt to develop an "ideal windmill", and his first successful, reliable, and cheap electricity-generating wind turbines. Drawing on many primary sources, Hansen shows that la Cour strongly supported rural electrification based on wind power and that he contributed to a continuing tradition of wind power use in Denmark.

A comprehensive reconstruction of the history of wind technology and wind power use in the 20th century has been provided by HEYMANN. Focusing on developments in Germany, Denmark, and the US, and drawing on a large variety of primary and secondary sources, Heymann shows that the impediments to wind power use in the 20th century were not primarily the cost of wind turbines, but rather its "structural incompatibility" with central and monopolized electricity supply, as well as the underestimation of technical problems. Since the 1980s, Danish wind technology has proved most successful and has supported wind power booms in Denmark, California, and Germany; this is because it originated from a Danish craftsmen tradition, which since the 1970s has proved an ideal social, political, and technical environment, and has avoided the over-ambition of engineers in other countries.

KARNØE analyzed the success of Danish wind technology since the 1980s from the perspective of innovation management research. He described Danish wind technology development as having a "bottom-up" style of development, while ambitious research and development projects in the US and other countries adopted a "top-down" approach. Karnøe's interpretation caused numerous discussions among social scientists. A comprehensive narrative history of the American effort to utilize the wind for electricity production has been written by RIGHTER. Righter dedicates half of his book to recent developments (since the 1970s), and emphasizes political and legal discussions and changes, which helped to create the strong wind power boom in California in the 1980s.

MATTHIAS HEYMANN

See also Electricity; Technology

Women in Science: general works

Abir-Am, Pnina and Dorinda Outram (eds), *Uneasy Careers and Intimate Lives: Women in Science, 1789–1979*, New Brunswick: Rutgers University Press, 1987

Donnison, Jean, *Midwives and Medical Men: A History of Inter-Professional Rivals and Women's Rights*, London: Heinemann, and New York, Schocken Books, 1977; 2nd edition, New Barnet: Hertfordshire: Historical Publications, 1988

Faruqui, Aktar, Mohamed Hassan and Gabriella Sandri (eds), *The Role of Women in the Development of Science and Technology in the Third World*, Singapore and Teaneck, New Jersey: World Scientific, 1991

Mozans, H.J., *Woman in Science: With an Introductory Chapter on Woman's Long Struggle for Things of the Mind*, 1913; Cambridge, Massachusetts: MIT Press, 1974

Pycior, Helena, Nancy G. Slack and Pnina G. Abir-Am (eds), *Creative Couples in the Sciences*, New Brunswick: Rutgers University Press, 1996

Rossiter, Margaret W., *Women Scientists in America: Struggles and Strategies to 1940*, Baltimore: Johns Hopkins Press University, 1982

Rossiter, Margaret W., *Women Scientists in America: Before Affirmative Action, 1940–1972*, Baltimore: Johns Hopkins Press University, 1995

Schiebinger, Londa, *The Mind Has No Sex? Women in the Origins of Modern Science*, Cambridge, Massachusetts: Harvard University Press, 1989

Shiva, Vandana, *Staying Alive: Women, Ecology, and Development*, London: Zed Books, 1988

Weisbard, Phyllis and Rima Apple, *The History of Women and Science, Health, and Technology*, University of Wisconsin System Women's Studies Librarian, 1993

For centuries women were barred from universities (from the 12th century until late into the 19th century) and scientific societies for no reason other than their sex. This exclusion was justified often by empirical investigations that found women incapable of producing great science, claiming that something either in their physical, psychological, or intellectual constitution impeded progress in this field. (See also "Gender and Sex, Scientific Treatments of".)

Historically, the first challenge was to prove that women have contributed to the development of science. The 18th and 19th centuries produced a number of lexicons of scientific women, including the French astronomer Jérôme de Lalande's *Astronomie des dames* (1786), Christian Harless's *Verdienste der Frauen um Naturwissenschaft, Gesundheits-, und Heilkunde* (The Contributions of Women to Natural Science, Health, and Healing); (1830), and Elise Oelsner's *Leistungen der deutschen Frau* (The Achievements of the German Woman); (1894). This tradition culminated in MOZANS (pseudonym for the Catholic priest, J.A. Zahm), which detailed women's contributions to each recognized field of science. Zahm argued that whatever women have achieved in science has been through defiance of conventional codes, which compelled them to confine their activities to the ordinary duties of the household. These early lexicons were augmented by biographies and autobiographies of great women scientists, which generally explored their achievements within the context of the barriers they encountered. WEISBARD & APPLE have produced the most comprehensive bibliography treating women in the various sciences.

More recently historians have begun to move away from the "great woman of science" model, in which women's achievements are measured against those of men, to examine more general patterns in the scientific work of women. ROSSITER (1982) and ROSSITER (1995) chart the fortunes of women scientists against shifting government and university policies, changing economic circumstances, and changing attitudes toward women. Her first volume introduced the important concept of "women's work" in science: the tendency of women to be concentrated in certain scientific fields or jobs, such as, for example, tedious and poorly paid sorting and classifying of astronomic photographs, or computing (before computers). World War II and the GI bill form the focus of her second volume, which documents how the lavish benefits awarded to returning veterans increased doctorates among men five-fold, while the number of women was held steady, effectively blocking the scientific pipeline for women during a period of massive growth in US science. SCHIEBINGER's history of women scientists in early modern Europe pays close attention to class issues – to the differing experience of women artisans and women aristocrats – and also to national differences. Arguing that women were trained and ready to take their place in modern science at its origins, Schiebinger analyses how the culture of science was refashioned both ideologically and institutionally to make the exclusion of women seem natural. The essays in ABIR-AM & OUTRAM explore the tensions between career and personal life that have traditionally affected women more than men. Looking at the professionalization of science and the privatization of the home, the authors reveal that while men followed the path of ever bigger science in the 20th century, women remained fixed in domestic arrangements, relying on support for their professional work from their family members – parents, husbands, or children. The volume edited by PYCIOR, SLACK & ABIR-AM examines scientific couples; since the time of the guilds (Schiebinger), wives have assisted in their husbands' profession, with varying degrees of acknowledgement. The book contains analyses of the changing configurations of collaboration between scientific couples, such as Marie and Pierre Curie, Albert Einstein and Mileva Marić, Irène and Frédéric Joliot-Curie, and more contemporary figures.

Studies of women scientists have focused mainly on women in the United States and Europe. Studies of minority women in science (a "Black Artemis" to complement Ken Manning's *Black Apollo* of science), and cross-cultural studies (a Joseph Needham of Chinese women in science, for example) are much needed. FARUQUI, HASSAN & SANDRI, one of the few books on women in Third World science, reveals that women occupy sometimes surprisingly high positions in sciences in these countries. Women, for example, constitute over half of all the chemists in Argentina, and are better represented in Turkish science overall than in most highly industrialized, first world countries. Some scholars suggest that this is because the sciences do not carry the privilege and prestige they do elsewhere, or because advantages of class outweigh the disadvantages of sex in a particular scientific setting.

Voltaire's proclamation of 1764 that "all the arts have been invented by man, not by woman" was echoed recently in the assertion by two prominent sociologists of science that women have achieved less than men in science, no matter how achievement is measured. Women are generally considered recipients, not generators of knowledge. Historians of women in science have traditionally considered the role of women in what are now defined as mainstream sciences: astronomy, physics, chemistry, biology, botany, entomology, and so forth. More recently historians are asking whether there also exist sciences that have been developed and practised primarily by women. Schiebinger argues that midwifery provides such an example. DONNISON documents how the rise of professional man-midwives (later known as obstetricians and gynecologists) sounded the death knell for the traditional midwife. In another example, SHIVA discusses how women have developed certain aspects of agriculture, including water management and preservation, land fertility, and forest management. Home economics and nursing provide further examples. These fields have tended to be ignored by historians of science because they have not been considered as sciences. Such a view may depend more on the fact that these sciences have been practised by women, than on the knowledge of nature involved, or the value of services rendered. Further studies are needed, using ethnographic tools, in order to explore the ways in which the limits of science are demarcated, and how, within this area, women's contributions are evaluated. A United Nations commission has recently opened the question of globally evaluating women's indigenous knowledge. Nevertheless, there is nothing sacred or mystical about the fact that particular knowledge has been developed by women; women's work in birthing or seed preservation is a response to sexual divisions of labor in particular cultures – the same kinds of knowledge could have been developed by men under different conditions.

LONDA SCHIEBINGER

See also Gender and Sex; Home Economics; Obstetrics and Midwifery; United States: Women in Science

Women in Science: astronomy

Abir-am, Pnina G. and Dorinda Outram (eds), *Uneasy Careers and Intimate Lives: Women in Science, 1789–1979*, New Brunswick, New Jersey: Rutgers University Press, 1987

Bailey, Solon, *The History and Work of Harvard Observatory, 1839–1927*, New York: McGraw-Hill, 1931

Haramundanis, Katherine (ed.), *Cecilia Payne-Gaposchkin: An Autobiography and Other Recollections*, Cambridge and New York: Cambridge University Press, 1984

Hill, Edward, *My Daughter Beatrice: A Personal Memoir of Dr Beatrice Tinsley, Astronomer*, New York: American Physical Society, 1986

Hoffleit, Dorrit, *Women in the History of Variable Star Astronomy*, Cambridge, Massachusetts: American Association of Variable Star Astronomers, 1993

Hoffleit, Dorrit, *The Education of American Women Astronomers Before 1960*, Cambridge, Massachusetts: American Association of Variable Star Astronomers, 1994

Jones, Bessie Zaban and Lyle Gifford Boyd, *The Harvard College Observatory: The First Four Directorships, 1839–1919*, Cambridge, Massachusetts: Belknap Press of Harvard University Press, 1971

Kass-Simon, G. and Patricia Farnes (eds), *Women of Science: Righting the Record*, Bloomington: Indiana University Press, 1990

Lubbock, Constance A., *The Herschel Chronicle: The Life Story of William Herschel and His Sister Caroline Herschel*, New York: Macmillan, and Cambridge: Cambridge University Press, 1933

Rossiter, Margaret W., *Women Scientists in America: Struggles and Strategies to 1940*, Baltimore: Johns Hopkins University Press, 1982

Rossiter, Margaret W., *Women Scientists in America: Before Affirmative Action, 1940–1972*, Baltimore: Johns Hopkins University Press, 1995

Wright, Helen, *Sweeper in the Sky: The Life of Maria Mitchell, First Woman Astronomer in America*, New York: Macmillan, 1947

Interest in the considerable contribution made by women to astronomy has grown steadily in the past 20 years. Publications in this area are twofold: biographical works of specific individuals, and studies of the role of women at specific institutions or in specific countries. In addition to the rich literature in science and history journals, the books detailed below give a good overview of work in this area.

Caroline Herschel was one of the earliest successful woman astronomers. LUBBOCK, Herschel's great-niece, based the work on family correspondence and Herschel's personal papers. This often-quoted work describes how Herschel was both housekeeper to her famous brother and an astronomical observer, both as assistant to William Herschel and in her own right. This is a valuable illustration of the way in which, prior to the 20th century, female astronomers commonly worked as assistants to male relatives.

Maria Mitchell, the first American woman astronomer and first astronomy professor at Vassar, has been the subject of a number of works. Indeed, Mitchell and Caroline Herschel seem to be favorite topics for juvenile literature. The definitive (adult) biography of Mitchell was written by WRIGHT, herself an astronomer. This well-researched work is the result of careful study of the Mitchell archives at Nantucket, Vassar and elsewhere. The style is engaging and uplifting. Wright captures the spirit of Mitchell and her deep affection for her home island as well as her love for astronomy.

HILL documents the brief life of his daughter, Beatrice Tinsley, a brilliant theoretical astronomer whose prolific pen was silenced at the age of 40 by cancer. The book, based on letters and personal recollections, documents Tinsley's childhood and education, as well as her struggle to balance her personal and professional lives in the face of physical adversity. It also contains an introduction by the well-known astronomer Sandra Faber, and an obituary written by Yale colleagues.

Cecilia Payne-Gaposchkin, the first woman astronomy professor at Harvard, was also one of the most distinguished astrophysicists of the 20th century. Her daughter, Katherine HARAMUNDANIS, published her autobiography in a collection that includes Haramundanis's recollections, an introduction by the astronomer Jesse Greenstein – which places Payne-Gaposchkin's work within the context of the astrophysics community in the early 1920s – and an introduction by the historian Peggy Kidwell – which focuses on the development of Payne-Gaposchkin's groundbreaking doctoral thesis (the first that Harvard awarded).

Several collections of essays focusing on women scientists in general have been published. ABIR-AM & OUTRAM include three relevant papers among the 12 in their volume: Marilyn Bailey Ogilvie's "Marital Collaboration: An Approach to Science", which discusses Margaret Huggins; Sally Gregory Kohlstedt's "Maria Mitchell and the Advancement of Women in Science", which, unlike many other Mitchell biographies, concentrates on her political work for the Association for the Advancement of Women; and Peggy A. Kidwell's "Cecilia Payne-Gaposchkin: Astronomy in the Family", which focuses on Payne-Gaposchkin's partnership with her husband and colleague, Sergei, as well as her unrelenting dedication to the combined role of wife, mother, and astronomer.

KASS-SIMON & FARNES include, among their 10 chapters, the impressively researched work of Pamela E. Mack,

"Straying from Their Orbits: Women in Astronomy in America". Based on her pioneering Harvard undergraduate thesis (which is a must-have for serious researchers in the field), it describes the opportunities for, and contributions of, women astronomers at women's colleges and observatories in the late 19th and early 20th centuries, with a special emphasis on Harvard College Observatory.

Two histories of Harvard College Observatory are valuable resources in this field. BAILEY, a long-time staff member and Acting Director (1919–21), gives a detailed and well footnoted (although somewhat technical) synopsis of the work of the Observatory in the late 19th and early 20th centuries. The tremendous role played by women is evident because their contributions are recounted alongside those of male staff members. While little biographical data is presented, the list of observatory staff members and their dates of service is a valuable resource.

The best account of women astronomers at Harvard, apart from Mack's thesis, is usually considered to be JONES & BOYD, who take a more personal approach to the history of the Observatory. While much of the same scientific work is recounted, the strength of this work lies in the biographical information and personal correspondence it includes. Women feature in every chapter, although a special chapter is devoted to women astronomers at Harvard and elsewhere. Informative endnotes add to the usefulness of this well-documented volume.

ROSSITER (1982) quickly became a standard reference for the study of women in science, and, with the completion of ROSSITER (1995), valuable statistics for women in the sciences in the 20th century have now been properly documented. Thoroughly researched and laden with facts, this ambitious study of women's changing role in science is the standard against which other works must be measured. Biographical information on a number of women astronomers is included in both volumes, and the bibliography is a valuable starting point for independent research on this topic.

Hoffleit has written two important, albeit not widely-known, reference works on women in astronomy. Herself an astronomer at Harvard and then Yale for much of the 20th century, she blends personal anecdotes with well-researched facts on American women astronomers. In HOFFLEIT (1993), she recounts the valuable contributions of women in the US and abroad to variable star research, as well as the pivotal role they have played in the American Association of Variable Star Observers. Statistics of discoveries and publication rates are the main focus of this work. HOFFLEIT (1994) describes the education of women at the Seven Sister Colleges, and the important role of Maria Mitchell and her students. Statistics on women's employment and college degrees are included, as well as brief biographies of a number of women astronomers. A list of more than 120 American women astronomers before 1960 (with their degrees) is a useful resource. Both works include rich and useful bibliographies.

KRISTINE LARSEN

See also Astronomy; Women in Science: general works

Women in Science: chemical sciences

Ainley, Marianne Gosztonyi (ed.), *Despite the Odds: Essays on Canadian Women in Science*, Montreal: Véhicule Press, 1990

Grinstein, Louise S., Rose K. Rose and Miriam H. Rafailovich (eds), *Women in Chemistry and Physics: A Biobibliographic Sourcebook*, Westport, Connecticut: Greenwood Press, 1993

Kass-Simon, G. and Patricia Farnes (eds), *Women of Science: Righting the Record*, Bloomington: Indiana University Press, 1990

Laidler, Keith J., *The World of Physical Chemistry*, Oxford and New York: Oxford University Press, 1993

Ogilvie, Marilyn Bailey, *Women in Science: Antiquity through the Nineteenth Century: A Biographical Dictionary with Annotated Bibliography*, Cambridge, Massachusetts: MIT Press, 1986

Rayner-Canham, Marlene F. and Geoffrey W. Rayner-Canham, *Harriet Brooks: Pioneer Nuclear Scientist*, Montreal: McGill-Queen's University Press, 1992

Siegel, Patricia Joan and Kay Thomas Finley, *Women in the Scientific Search: An American Bio-Bibliography, 1724–1979*, Metuchen, New Jersey: Scarecrow Press, 1985

Women in the chemical sciences are frequently obscure, because the entry point into science was, for many, a husband, brother, other male family member or friend, and consequently their contribution was often blended with that of the male. While Marie Curie and Irène Joliot-Curie, both of whose husbands were involved in science, may come to mind, few others are so well-known.

AINLEY's book is a helpful entry point into this subject, because it takes a balanced approach by examining some of the historical aspects, the biographies of a few women, and some contemporary concerns. Typical of many books on women in science, several disciplines are covered, including a chapter on Canadian women and careers in the chemical sciences. The book includes a selected bibliography which is useful for finding journal articles; the contributors are grouped together and bibliographic details are supplied, along with detailed notes and acknowledgements.

KASS-SIMON & FARNES also address the broader topic of women in science, and include a chapter dedicated to chemistry, and a second on crystallography, a branch of chemistry in which women have made significant contributions. One of their objectives was to identify the true role played by women in the development of science: were their achievements few, or were they hidden and unacknowledged? Although it has now become obvious that the latter is the case, few had previously undertaken such a comprehensive investigation.

Harriet Brooks was one of Canada's first researchers in the field of radioactivity, and RAYNER-CANHAM & RAYNER-CANHAM undertook the extensive primary research necessary to compile her biographical details. Their text discusses her life, her contributions to science, and why these have remained untold until recently. Brooks is probably the only person to work with the three "big names" in the field of radioactivity: Ernest Rutherford, J. J. Thomson and Marie Curie, and yet for many years she was simply a name on some research papers. Since she often published alone, literature searches focusing on the better-known scientists have not drawn attention to her work until now.

The *Journal of Chemical Education* remains one of the best sources of information on women in the chemical sciences. While authors may not have found sufficient researched material for book-length works, there is ample material for journal articles, and since the target audience of this journal is those in teaching, it is an ideal venue for promoting the role of women.

Another productive path when looking for information on women in the chemical sciences is through the use of general references such as bio-bibliographies. GRINSTEIN, ROSE & RAFAILOVICH's bio-bibliography is much more than a list or dictionary; each entry includes a biography, a section on the scientist's work, and a bibliography, which includes both the scientist's publications and those about her. OGILVIE is a biographical dictionary with annotated bibliography, and there is an additional list of women about whom little is known. SIEGEL & FINLEY includes less on individual women, but the names are divided up into sections rather than alphabetically, which makes the identification of the chemists and biochemists much easier, since they are grouped together. Of these three publications, Grinstein, Rose & Rafailovich's is the best for basic information, as the list of the scientist's own publications is not included in either of the other two.

While bio-bibliographic sources are useful for identifying women and learning about their specific contributions to science, a more contextual image may be gleaned from publications on a specific subject area. LAIDLER's recent book is a good example, as it incorporates information on women involved in physical chemistry into the history of that particular field of chemistry, which is where it really should be found. The contributors are discussed on equal footing, regardless of gender. Mary Somerville and Agnes Pockels are the subject of two of the more than 30 detailed biographies, which also include Sir Isaac Newton and Michael Faraday. Laidler made an effort to feature people, "whose lives are of particular interest and a few whose contributions to science seem to have been underrated". More than 140 contributors to the field are included in the biographical notes, along with references. It is refreshing to find both biographical and scientific information on all contributors, of both genders, together in one place.

The 1990s have signalled an increased interest in women's contributions to science. Children's literature is certainly the area with the greatest number of publications on women in chemical sciences, as there is now a strong movement to encourage girls and young women to consider careers in mathematics and science, but the information is increasingly available in an adult format. Women have always made contributions to the chemical sciences and, with sustained interest, over the next decade the number of adult publications will undoubtedly grow.

HELEN P. GRAVES SMITH

See also Chemistry; Women in Science: general works

Women in Science: life sciences

Bonta, Marcia Myers, *Women in the Field: America's Pioneering Women Naturalists*, College Station: Texas A&M University Press, 1991

Keller, Evelyn Fox, *A Feeling for the Organism: The Life and Work of Barbara McClintock*, San Francisco: W.H. Freeman, 1983

Ogilvie, Marilyn Bailey, *Women in Science: Antiquity through the Nineteenth Century: A Biographical Dictionary with Annotated Bibliography*, Cambridge, Massachusetts: MIT Press, 1986

Schipperges, Heinrich, *Hildegard von Bingen: Ein Zeichen für unsere Zeit*, Frankfurt: Knecht, 1981

Siegel, Patricia Joan and Kay Thomas Finley, *Women in the Scientific Search: An American Bio-Bibliography, 1724–1979*, Metuchen, New Jersey: Scarecrow Press, 1985

Veglahn, Nancy J., *Women Scientists*, New York: Facts on File, 1991

Wilson, Carol Green, *Alice Eastwood's Wonderland: The Adventures of a Botanist*, San Francisco: California Academy of Sciences, 1955

BONTA's very detailed study gives biographies of 25 women naturalists, botanists, entomologists, ornithologists, ecologists, and what she terms "pioneers". Some of them are well known – such as Agnes Chase, Alice Eastwood, Elizabeth Gertrude Knight Britton, and Rachel Carson – others less so – such as Jane Colden, Martha Maxwell, and Kate Brandegee. The women are depicted as individuals, as members of disciplines, as professionals, and as friends. A selected bibliography provides the reader with further readings on each woman.

KELLER's portrait of Barbara McClintock, who in her mid-forties conducted research on the cytogenetics of maize and revolutionized orthodox genetics, is based on interviews with McClintock and her colleagues. The work functions on three levels: to readers who are not biologists, it serves as an introduction to an unfamiliar world; to people who have studied classical genetics, it serves to reveal the person behind the name; and to professional biologists, it serves as a book on scientific language and discourse. Keller stresses McClintock's discovery of transposition as the key to the complexity of genetic organization. The notes include a bibliography, mostly of journal articles.

OGILVIE combines biographical accounts with bibliographical information (divided into chronological sections) on women in the Western world born before 1885. It includes women in the life sciences, including the ornithologist Florence Merriam Bailey, the botanist Jane Colden (later Farquhar), Alice Eastwood, Margaret Clay Ferguson, Hildegard of Bingen, Jane Webb Loudon, Ethel Sarjant, and others.

SCHIPPERGES, one of the editors of the German language Hildegard edition, paints a complex picture of Hildegard's life and work, which is not influenced by feminism or the "New Age". He "translates" her writings from Latin and the medieval symbolism into modern (scientific) language. His main subjects are the knowledge of nature and medical science (in particular the understanding of "disease" and "remedy"), the conception of man against the background of a philosophy of corporality (man as *opus Dei, opus alterum per alterum,* and *opus cum creatura*), and questions concerning creation, the world, the cosmic order, and the life and sufferings of Jesus Christ, including the Trinitarian structure of God and of being.

SIEGEL & FINLEY's bio-bibliography, which concentrates on published studies of biography, provides items on women in the life sciences, especially bacteriologists, biologists, botanists, embryologists, entomologists, medical scientists, ornithologists, psychologists, and finally zoologists, mostly 19th- and 20th-century women, several of whom are not mentioned in *Notable American Women*.

VEGLAHN describes the lives and achievements of 11 American women, including women in the life sciences, such as the botanist Alice Eastwood, the zoologist Nettie Maria Stevens, Alice Hamilton, the founder of industrial medicine in the US, the biochemist Gerty Cori, the anthropologist Margaret Mead, the geneticist Barbara McClintock, and the physicist and medic Rosalyn Yalow. Each biography includes an introduction, a chronology, and a list of further reading. Other women are just mentioned briefly; for example, the botanist Elizabeth Britton, the ichthyologist Eugenie Clark, the biochemist Gladys Anderson Emerson, the physiologist Helen Hyde, and the physician Helen Brook Taussig.

WILSON's biography is based on the author's personal contact with Alice Eastwood, who is known, for example, to have created new varieties of geraniums. It also draws on Eastwood's memoirs, letters, published writings, and on official records of the California Academy of Sciences. However, this is not primarily a scientific biography, and does not refer to any literature or contain any footnotes.

BEATRICE RAUSCHENBACH

See also Botany; Gender; Molecular Biology; Women in Science: general works

Women in Science: medicine

Blake, Catriona, *The Charge of the Parasols: Women's Entry to the Medical Profession in Britain*, London: Women's Press, 1990

Bonner, Thomas Neville, *To the Ends of the Earth: Women's Search for Education in Medicine*, Cambridge, Massachusetts: Harvard University Press, 1992

Geyer-Kordesch, Johanna, "Women and Medicine", in *Companion Encyclopedia of the History of Medicine*, edited by W.F. Bynum and Roy Porter, vol. 2, London and New Yorks: Routledge, 1993

Hall, Lesley A., "Chloe, Olivia, Isabel, Letitia, Harriette, Honor, and Many More: Women in Medicine and Biomedical Science, 1914–1945", in *This Working-Day World: Women's Lives and Culture(s) in Britain, 1914–1945*, edited by Sybil Oldfield, London: Taylor and Francis, 1994

Hurd-Mead, Kate Campbell, *A History of Women in Medicine: From the Earliest Times to the Beginning of the Nineteenth Century*, Haddam, Connecticut: Haddam Press, 1938

Leneman, Leah, *In the Service of Life: The Story of Elsie Inglis and the Scottish Women's Hospitals*, Edinburgh: Mercat Press, 1994

Morantz-Sanchez, Regina Markell, *Sympathy and Science: Women Physicians in American Medicine*, New York and Oxford: Oxford University Press, 1985

The historiography of women in medicine is surprisingly patchy and unsatisfactory. Most of the works listed above are relatively recent, because earlier studies of the struggle for women's medical education and their entry into the profession tend to be old-fashioned - in the "exemplary lives of great women" mould – though not without merit. (See the bibliographies of, for example, Blake, Geyer-Kordesch, and Morantz-Sanchez.) The struggle was closely related to other feminist campaigns, and it is no coincidence that the "second feminist wave" has generated fresh studies. Now that women's history has largely emerged from a simplistic model of male doctor–villains tyrannizing female patient–victims (or heroines battling against male opposition to enter the profession), we can anticipate nuanced studies that take account of those complex interplays of class, gender, ethnicity, and power that have characterized the increasing presence of women in medicine since the end of the 19th century.

It is, however, distressing that the history of women as doctors still remains very largely bogged down in the heroic struggles of the later 19th century. While it is welcome that these struggles are being reinterpreted in a more subtle and nuanced way, the achievement of access to medical education and entry to the profession was very far from being the end of the story (as Morantz-Sanchez in particular makes clear). Important primary source materials are now becoming more accessible to the researcher, and probably, over the next decade, a brief bibliography such as this will alter quite dramatically.

HURD-MEAD was influenced by the first feminist wave. In what was intended as the first volume of a two-part study, she provided an extensive historical overview of women's participation in medical practice, before the professionalization of medicine in the 19th century first excluded them and then obliged them to find ways of successfully negotiating its increasingly stringent gate-keeping procedures. Conscious of the way that "with women . . . tradition has been prone to garble and distort the original data", Hurd-Mead goes a long way towards redressing the balance, by showing the presence of, and contribution by, women in medicine from ancient Egypt to the end of the 18th century. It has been extensively drawn upon in subsequent syntheses, and, for those in search of visual depictions of women in the past engaging in medical care, contains a number of useful illustrations.

GEYER-KORDESCH's encyclopedia article, though brief, is a useful supplement. Within a wider consideration of the complex relations between women and medicine, which have generated so much recent historiography, this article looks at the role of women healers and the economic, social, and cultural factors that did or did not favour their participation in medical practice. Its European (as opposed to British / US) perspective is commendable, and there are useful hints for further reading.

BLAKE's volume on the entry of women to the British medical profession is a lucid account intended for the general reader as much as the scholar. It locates the subject firmly within the context of wider Victorian debates on the role and needs of women, with all their contradictions and ambiguities.

There is a useful chronology, and brief biographies of some significant early medical women. The notes and references provide a good introduction to primary sources and secondary studies.

The issue of women needing to demonstrate themselves fully the equals of men in the medical profession, as contrasted with the belief in a particular womanly contribution they might make to the practice of medicine, is a central theme in MORANTZ-SANCHEZ's study of women doctors in America, whom she perceives as continually plagued by the problem of striking the balance between separatism and assimilation. Such differences were also an issue in the attempts to define orthodox medicine and the appropriate paths of entry in the US, during the 19th-century shift from earlier entrepreneurial models of medical practice to a closely regulated profession. The bulk of this book deals with the 19th century, but the final chapters do provide a look at the continuing problems that faced women doctors in the US during the 20th century. There is an extremely useful bibliographical essay on selected secondary source materials.

Access to medical education was central to the struggle to enter the medical profession. Many of the women discussed by Blake and Morantz-Sanchez obtained this, in part at least, at institutions in France or Switzerland. BONNER looks at the reasons for this, and thus sets the British and American struggles within a wider context. He makes a strong case for the importance of the medical school at Zurich in its pioneering role in opening its doors to women, covers the wider campaign for medical education, and also gives attention to the rather neglected topic of Russian woman doctors. The whole subject is illuminated by being shown against the wider contemporary European political and cultural background.

A work that brings the story a little further forward in historical time is LENEMAN's study. Again, as one can see from its bibliography, the work of women doctors during World War I, like the heroic events of the 19th century, produced a considerable number of contemporary or near contemporary accounts, as well as later historical or biographical studies. Women's desire to serve in war, though in an appropriately female role of tending the sick and wounded, was another episode that, like the entry of women into the profession, by its nature tended to generate a narrative of heroic struggle.

Although most of these works do go some way towards deconstructing earlier simplistic narratives of such heroic struggles, it is to be hoped that the increasingly productive encounter between the history of medicine and women's history will bear fruit in revealing less dramatic but no less significant stories. HALL's brief article is a preliminary approach towards identifying some of the issues and individuals that might repay further study, and suggests some sources worth pursuing.

LESLEY A. HALL

See also Nursing; Obstetrics and Midwifery; Women in Science: general works

Women in Science: physical sciences

Ajzenberg-Selove, Fay, *A Matter of Choices: Memoirs of a Female Physicist*, New Brunswick, New Jersey: Rutgers University Press, 1994

Ceranski, Beate, *"Und sie fürchtet sich vor niemandem": Die Physikerin Laura Bassi*, Frankfurt: Campus, 1996

Curie, Eve, *Madame Curie*, translated from the French by Vincent Sheean, New York: Doubleday, 1937; London: Heinemann, 1938

Dash, Joan, "Maria Goeppert-Mayer", in her *A Life of One's Own: Three Gifted Women and the Men They Married*, New York: Harper and Row, 1973, 229–346

Ernst, Sabine (ed.), *Lise Meitner an Otto Hahn: Briefe aus den Jahren 1912 bis 1924*, Stuttgart: Wissenschaftliche Verlagsgesellschaft, 1992

Freeman, Joan, *A Passion for Physics: The Story of a Woman Physicist*, Bristol and Philadelphia: Hilger, 1991

Grinstein, Louise S., Rose K. Rose and Miriam H. Rafailovich (eds), *Women in Chemistry and Physics: A Biobibliographic Sourcebook*, Westport, Connecticut: Greenwood Press, 1993

Kerner, Charlotte, *Lise, Atomphysikerin: Die Lebensgeschichte der Lise Meitner*, Weinheim and Basel: Beltz, 1986

Klens, Ulrike, *Mathematikerinnen im 18. Jahrhundert: Maria Gaetana Agnesi, Gabrielle-Emilie DuChâtelet, Sophie Germain: Fallstudien zur Wechselwirkung von Wissenschaft und Philosophie im Zeitalter der Aufklärung*, Pfaffenweiler: Centaurus, 1994

Ogilvie, Marilyn Bailey, *Women in Science: Antiquity Through the Nineteenth Century: A Biographical Dictionary with Annotated Bibliography*, Cambridge, Massachusetts: MIT Press, 1986

Quinn, Susan, *Marie Curie: A Life*, New York: Simon and Schuster, and London: Heinemann, 1995

Rife, Patricia, *Lise Meitner: Ein Leben für die Wissenschaft*, Dusseldorf: Claassen, 1990

Schiebinger, Londa, *The Mind Has No Sex? Women in the Origins of Modern Science*, Cambridge, Massachusetts: Harvard University Press, 1989

Sime, Ruth Lewin, *Lise Meitner: A Life in Physics*, Berkeley: University of California Press, 1996

As the above list shows, biography has been the most important genre for "women in the physical sciences". Ever since Eve Curie's famous biography of her mother, the lives of eminent women physicists have attracted attention. Recently, this biographical genre has been deeply influenced by the development of gender and women's studies, as has the history of science in general. Biographies of women physicists will certainly continue to be an essential part of the field, although comparative studies and collective biographies, analyzed under a common perspective such as marital collaboration or discipline formation, should become increasingly important. However, because the non-biographical studies which are currently available deal with women from all scientific disciplines they have been omitted from this entry, with the exception of Schiebinger.

In her groundbreaking study, SCHIEBINGER gives a lucid introduction to the gendering of science in the 17th and 18th centuries and the consequences for women's participation in science. She deals with social structures (e.g. patronage and artisanal culture) as well as with philosophical aspects (e.g. female allegories of science, and the emerging concept of polarity of the sexes). The women discussed include Du Châtelet, Caroline Herschel, and Margaret Cavendish.

Although KLENS's title refers to women mathematicians, she in fact thoroughly analyzes the contributions to natural philosophy and mathematical physics of three important Enlightenment women scientists. Klens is mainly interested in the interactions between these women's philosophical attitudes and their scientific contributions, and in the process she pays much attention to gender issues and, probably for the first time, properly evaluates the scientific contributions of her subjects. Her study of Agnesi, for example, counterbalances both the mythologizing and the discriminating attitudes that dominate a large part of Agnesi studies.

While a number of interesting articles on Laura Bassi, the first female professor, have appeared recently, CERANSKI is the first full-scale biography. This microstudy of scientific culture in Enlightenment Italy shows how the specific science culture at Bologna, combined with Bassi's ability to take advantage of it, contributed to her unique career. Ceranski links the multiple aspects of Bassi's life to the underlying contexts of gender and science, and thus presents an analytical approach that is transferable to the study of other women in Enlightenment science.

There is considerably less literature on women involved in scientific research, teaching, and popularization during the 19th century, probably because fewer women were involved. To obtain information on particular individuals, such as Mary Somerville or Margaret Maltby, one has to resort to reference works, two of which provide access to basic biographical as well as bibliographical material. While OGILVIE covers the whole range of scientific disciplines and includes a significant number of women from antiquity to the end of the 19th century, GRINSTEIN, ROSE & RAFAILOVICH focuses on physics and chemistry (there is an equivalent volume for women mathematicians), and deals almost exclusively with women of the 19th and 20th centuries (born before 1933). The volumes are organized alphabetically and provide biographical surveys, a list of each woman's publications (selected, if there are too many), and a guide to secondary literature. Both works are a valuable starting point for further studies on women physicists, but unfortunately both display a heavy American bias which slightly diminishes their merit.

Of all female scientists, the physicist and chemist Marie Curie has received the most attention. The two titles selected from the vast literature on her highlight the development of the biographical genre. The still enchanting, but hardly historically critical (indeed, the rather hagiographical), biography by her daughter Eve CURIE shaped the image of the shy tragic heroine devoted to science which has influenced the whole biographical corpus on "Madame Curie". QUINN, on the other hand, is not only the latest and most comprehensive work on Curie, but draws on important source material hitherto inaccessible, at least as regards the Langevin affair.

Both books provide a lively account that does not require any special scientific knowledge.

Lise Meitner probably comes second in popularity after Marie Curie, especially in the light of her tragic life, aspects of which prevented her from reaping the rewards of a long collaboration with Otto Hahn. With SIME, there is now a comprehensive and well-written biography available which will certainly be the standard work for years to come. In particular, Sime takes pains to show that Meitner's contribution has been swept under the carpet, both before and after World War II. The most penetrating German language work on Meitner is probably ERNST, although she covers only a part of Meitner's life. The book is primarily a collection of Meitner's letters to Hahn between 1912 and 1924, but it also contains a thorough book-length introduction to Meitner's life and work during that period. Both Kerner and Rife tend to be popular rather than scholarly: KERNER won a prestigious German youth book award, and is a readable yet substantial introduction, whereas RIFE remains rather superficial, and draws heavily (and often clumsily) on well-known secondary literature.

Maria Goeppert-Mayer, the second woman physicist to win the Nobel prize, is one of three famous women examined in DASH. Again, this biography is aimed at a wide readership and, although sometimes heavily stereotyped (e.g. in its depiction of German academic life, or on the issue of gender), it is based on interviews with Goeppert-Mayer and her husband and serves as a valuable introduction to her work. A comprehensive scientific biography by Karen Johnson will soon be available, as will Maushart's study of Hertha Sponer, a woman physicist with origins in Göttingen who had a distinguished career in the US.

Finally, book-length autobiographies by contemporary women constitute an exciting addition to the field in recent years. Both AJZENBERG-SELOVE and FREEMAN give thoughtful accounts of their own careers as highly successful nuclear physicists, thus participating in a subfield that has been exceptionally sympathetic to women physicists. Both autobiographies reveal the subtle but effective sexual discrimination encountered by these women, so typical of the experiences of later generations of women physicists. However, in both cases the prevailing picture is of fun, support, and success rather than defeat and bitterness.

BEATE CERANSKI

See also Gender: general works; Nuclear Physics; Radioactivity; Women in Science: general works

Women in Science: technology

Berg, Maxine, *The Age of Manufacturers: Industry, Innovation and Work in Britain, 1700–1820*, Oxford: Blackwell/Fontana, 1985; New York: Oxford University Press, 1986; 2nd edition, London and New York: Routledge, 1994

Bindocci, Cynthia Gay, *Women and Technology: An Annotated Bibliography*, New York: Garland, 1993

Cockburn, Cynthia, *Brothers: Male Dominance and Technological Change*, London: Pluto Press, 1983

Cockburn, Cynthia and Susan Ormrod, *Gender and Technology in the Making*, London and Thousand Oaks, California: Sage, 1993

Cooper, Patricia A., *Once a Cigar Maker: Men, Women and Work Culture in American Cigar Factories, 1900–1919*, Urbana: University of Illinois Press, 1987

Cowan, Ruth Schwartz, *More Work for Mother: The Ironies of Household Technology from Open Hearth to Microwave*, New York: Basic Books, 1983

Donnison, Jean, *Midwives and Medical Men: A History of Inter-Professional Rivalries and Women's Rights*, London: Heinemann and New York: Schocken Books, 1977; 2nd edition, as *Midwives and Medical Men: A History of the Struggle for the Control of Childbirth*, New Barnet, Hertfordshire: Historical Publications, 1988

Easlea, Brian, *Fathering the Unthinkable: Masculinity, Scientists and the Nuclear Arms Race*, London: Pluto Press, 1983

Hacker, Sally, *Pleasure, Power and Technology: Some Tales of Gender, Engineering, and the Cooperative Workplace*, Boston: Unwin Hyman, 1989

Hardyment, Christina, *From Mangle to Microwave: The Mechanization of Household Work*, Cambridge: Polity Press, and New York: Blackwell, 1988

Herlihy, David, *Opera Muliebria: Women and Work in Medieval Europe*, Philadelphia: Temple University Press, 1990

Jellison, Katherine, *Entitled to Power: Farm Women and Technology, 1913–1963*, Chapel Hill: University of North Carolina Press, 1993

Lipartito, Kenneth, "When Women Were Switches: Technology, Work and Gender in the Telephone Industry, 1890–1920", *American Historical Review*, 99 (1994): 1074–111

Martin, Michèle, *"Hello Central?" Gender, Technology and Culture in the Formation of Telephone Systems*, Montreal: McGill-Queen's University Press, 1991

McGaw, Judith A., *Most Wonderful Machine: Mechanization and Social Change in Berkshire Paper Making, 1801–1885*, Princeton, New Jersey: Princeton University Press, 1987

Rossiter, Margaret W., *Women Scientists in America: Struggles and Strategies to 1940*, Baltimore: Johns Hopkins University Press, 1982

Rothschild, Joan (ed.), *Machina ex Dea: Feminist Perspectives on Technology*, New York: Pergamon Press, 1983

Stanley, Autumn, *Mothers and Daughters of Invention: Notes for a Revised History of Technology*, Metuchen, New Jersey: Scarecrow Press, 1993

Strom, Sharon Hartman, *Beyond the Typewriter: Gender, Class and the Origins of Modern American Office Work, 1900–1930*, Urbana: University of Illinois Press, 1992

Summerfield, Penny, *Women Workers in the Second World War: Production and Patriarchy in Conflict*, London: Croom Helm, 1984; 2nd edition, London and New York: Routledge, 1989

Tilly, Louise A. and Joan W. Scott, *Women, Work and Family*, New York: Holt, Rinehart and Winston, 1978

Trescott, Martha Moore (ed.), *Dynamos and Virgins Revisited: Women and Technological Change in History: An Anthology*, Metuchen, New Jersey: Scarecrow Press, 1979

Wajcman, Judy, *Feminism Confronts Technology, London: Polity Press, and University Park, Philadelphia: Pennsylvania State University Press, 1991*

Webster, Juliet, *Office Automation: The Labour Process and Women's Work in Britain*, Hemel Hempstead, Hertfordshire: Harvester Wheatsheaf, 1989

Wilson, Adrian, *The Making of Man-Midwifery: Childbirth in England, 1660–1770*, Cambridge, Massachusetts: Harvard University Press, and London: University College London Press, 1995

Scholars interested in women and technology have only recently turned their attention to the relationships between the two, with few studies appearing before the mid-1970s. The collections edited by TRESCOTT and ROTHSCHILD bring together a range of perspectives and styles, marking out the terrain for subsequent research. Historians have made a much more limited contribution to the field than sociologists. Indeed, WAJCMAN's comprehensive and accessible overview reflects this balance, but is none the less essential preliminary reading for historians. In addition, this volume demonstrates clearly that the majority of studies have concerned themselves with women and technology rather than women in technology, in the sense that women are discussed more often as users of technologies than they are as its creators.

The literature is concentrated around four themes: domestic technologies, reproductive and medical technologies, technology in the workplace, and women as technologists. Along with other branches of women's history, the study of women and technology has moved away from an initial focus on recovering the achievements of forgotten women, and towards analysing the gendered nature of technology. This has been accompanied by a shift away from seeing women as passive victims of technologies shaped by men, towards exploring technology as a social process in which gender and technology shape and reshape each other. COCKBURN & ORMROD provides a good example of this approach.

The masculine nature of technology has been explored in depth by EASLEA. Other writers including Wajcman, HACKER, and Cockburn & Ormrod focus more on the masculine nature of technological knowledge, and the extent to which technological skills have been defined as masculine attributes. Underlying the work of these scholars lies an explicit feminist political agenda seeking to challenge men's monopoly over technology, which is seen as an important source of patriarchal authority. MARTIN, however, suggests that while women did not have control over the initial development of new technologies, such as the telephone, they were not simply passive users trapped by the visions of the men who designed the system. Instead, they were able to shape the way the telephone was used, thus imposing their own meanings on it.

COWAN has done much to bring the study of women into the mainstream of the history of technology, and her work on domestic technologies has been a starting point for many who have followed. She argues that, far from having the liberating effect on women that is often supposed, the introduction of new technologies into the home did not lead to a reduced burden of domestic labour for women. Instead, these technologies eliminated many of the jobs once done by other members of the household, leaving women as increasingly isolated workers within their own homes. New domestic technologies, developed by commercial corporations in a patriarchal society, simply reflected the dominant power structures of that society, reinforcing the sexual division of labour and female subordination. HARDYMENT concentrates on the development of the machines themselves, and includes examples of discarded designs.

Reproductive and medical technologies have given rise to an extensive literature, which continues to be dominated by the conclusion that male control of these technologies has served to reinforce patriarchal domination. Wajcman provides a good overview and useful bibliography. DONNISON documents in detail the contest between female midwives and the male-dominated medical profession for control over the birthing process, arguing that the male monopoly of the use of forceps was decisive in ensuring their triumph, even though it did not necessarily benefit mothers or children. WILSON has challenged this interpretation; instead of portraying women as passive victims of the medical profession, he suggests that they themselves chose to place their trust in man-midwives, because they saw them as offering a better option.

The majority of work on the relationship between workplace technologies and women's experiences of work, both inside and outside the home, covers the period since the onset of industrialisation in 18th-century Europe. HERLIHY, however, provides a useful and wide-ranging textbook-style survey of the literature on women's work in medieval Europe, arguing that women's participation in productive enterprise changed dramatically during the medieval period as they lost their central role. TILLY & SCOTT analyse the role of women's work in the family economy, from the early modern period to the 1960s, setting the scene for much subsequent scholarship by arguing that this work needs to be examined within the context of family responsibilities. They also argue that there was a considerable degree of continuity between the type of work done by women before and after industrialisation, a theme taken up by BERG, who gives much more explicit attention to the role of technology in the gender division of labour.

Studies of the 19th century bring technology to the fore as an important element in shaping the nature of women's work. McGAW demonstrates that increasing levels of mechanisation did not fundamentally affect the gender division of labour: men often gained positions that used new technology, leaving women to perform much of the hand-work that remained. Men's work continued to be defined as skilled, while what women did was generally regarded as unskilled. When employers did seek to replace male labour with female labour, they generally met fierce resistance, as both COOPER and COCKBURN document, presenting evidence of a working class deeply divided along gender lines. Only the extraordinary demands of war-time production threatened these boundaries, but as SUMMERFIELD demonstrates, these shifts were often only temporary, and serve to highlight the strength of existing divisions.

STROM and LIPARTITO draw attention to the way in which new workplace technologies contributed to the emergence of feminised occupations, offering women new opportunities while at the same time confirming their subordinate position in the labour market. Strom focuses on this process in office work, while Lipartito examines the work of women in the telecommunications industry. WEBSTER demonstrates how the introduction of new office technologies during the 1980s served to entrench the gender division of labour, which had been established with the introduction of the typewriter many decades earlier.

The relationship between technological change and women's work in agriculture is analysed by JELLISON, who reveals how farm women resisted efforts to create separate spheres of labour in the house and in the field, preferring their role as producers to the domestic ideal that was actively promoted to them.

Given the absence of women technologists from standard biographical collections, the listing provided by BINDOCCI and STANLEY's comprehensive study of women inventors are the best starting points for researching individual women, although they are both heavily biased towards European and, especially, North American material. Stanley draws on a wide range of material, from archaeology and anthropology as well as history, to argue that women as well as men have always invented. She sets out to revise the accepted definition of technology, so that inventions that are important for women in their everyday lives are granted equal status with those deemed important to men. To support these arguments, she presents a wealth of detailed information on women and their inventions, and although this is heavily biased towards women resident in the US during the 19th and 20th centuries, she does include evidence from non-Western cultures also. Unfortunately, little effort is made to draw more general conclusions on the nature of female inventive activity. An indication of how women's work as technologists can be integrated into a broader economic and social context is provided by ROSSITER, who includes in her account women scientists working in industry.

SALLY HORROCKS

See also Gender: general works; Technology; Women in Science: general works; Work

Work

Applebaum, Herbert, *The Concept of Work: Ancient, Medieval, and Modern*, Albany: State University of New York Press, 1992

Aronowitz, Stanley and William DiFazio, *The Jobless Future: Sci-Tech and the Dogma of Work*, Minneapolis: University of Minnesota Press, 1994

Bell, Daniel, *Work and Its Discontents*, Boston: Beacon Press, 1956

Braverman, Harry, *Labor and Monopoly Capital: The Degradation of Work in the Twentieth Century*, New York: Monthly Review Press, 1974

Cowan, Ruth Schwartz, *More Work for Mother: The Ironies of Household Technology from the Open Hearth to the Microwave*, New York: Basic Books, 1983

Kuhn, Thomas, "Energy Conservation as an Example of Simultaneous Discovery", in *Critical Problems in the*

History of Science, edited by Marshall Clagett, Madison: University of Wisconsin Press, 1959

Merton, Robert K., *Science, Technology and Society in Seventeenth Century England*, Bruges, Belgium: St Catherine's Press, 1932; New York: Fertig, 1970

Oakley, Ann, "Domestic Work", in *Work, Employment and Unemployment: Perspectives on Work and Society*, edited by Kenneth Thompson, Milton Keynes, Buckinghamshire: Open University Press, 1984

Pahl, R.E. (ed.), *On Work: Historical, Comparative and Theoretical Approaches*, Oxford and New York: Blackwell, 1988

Rabinbach, Anson, *The Human Motor: Energy, Fatigue, and the Origins of Modernity*, New York: Basic Books, 1990

Robertson, James, *The Future of Work: Jobs, Self-Employment and Leisure after the Industrial Age*, London: Gower, 1985

Sohn-Rethel, Alfred, *Intellectual and Manual Labour: A Critique of Epistemology*, Atlantic Highlands, New Jersey: Humanities Press, and London: Macmillan, 1978

Tilgher, Adriano, *Work: What It Has Meant to Men Through the Ages*, translated from the Italian by Dorothy Canfield Fisher, New York: Harcourt Brace, 1930

Wise, M. Norton with Crosbie Smith, "Work and Waste: Political Economy and Natural Philosophy in Nineteenth Century Britain", *History of Science*, 27–28 (1989–90) [in 4 sections]

For the physicist and the engineer, work is a measure of mechanical output – the product of force and distance moved (f.s). In the human sciences, work refers to the social institution around which life is organized, so that specific activities must be considered in context. For the historian of science, this broader study of "work" is relevant for the following three reasons. First, science and technology have been closely associated with the organization and (continuing) transformation of work since the late 19th century. Second, socially dominant ideas about work are important for understanding the development of science and technology throughout history. Finally, the rise of Big Science and current debates over the future of work place in sharp relief the notion of science itself as a labour process.

APPLEBAUM provides an encyclopedic review of how work has been regarded throughout the history of Western civilization. He traces changing attitudes to work from early Greece, the Christian era, the Reformation and the rise of capitalism, to 20th-century efforts to re-evaluate the work ethic. Work in early non-market societies did not exist separately from the household. In modern societies, the universal market mechanism separates producers and users, but transforms various concrete activities into the abstract activity of "work". The contempt for manual trades in classical Greece meant also that there could be no fertile interaction between science and technology – science itself could only be theoretical. Following on from Weber's thesis that the rise of capitalism was influenced by the Reformation's transformation of the conception of work and the rise of the work ethic, MERTON makes a similar argument for the rise of experimental science.

KUHN argues that the concept of work as a dynamical quantity (i.e. as in f.s) played a crucial role in the quantification of the law of energy conservation. The quantity force times distance – known variously as mechanical effect, mechanical power, and finally as work – had been in use since the industrial revolution to measure what different engines could achieve. To compute the conversion coefficients comparing one engine's capacity with another, the pioneers of the first law relied on this concept.

Rabinbach and Wise & Smith demonstrate how 19th-century discourses of work, based on natural philosophy and political economy respectively, shaped each other under the imperatives of industrialization. WISE & SMITH focuses on the influence of political economy on the origins of thermodynamics and field theory, specifically in Lord Kelvin's contribution. For Kelvin, work was not just an engineering measure but a motivation for action, a source of value and progress. Work in this sense had to be juxtaposed against "waste", an indicator of decadence and decline, in order to sort out conservation of total energy from the inevitable dissipation of some useful energy in conversion processes (the second law). Engineers and political economists needed to be aware of this waste in order to improve productivity.

RABINBACH considers the impact of thermodynamic views on the new social "science" of work, found in both Taylorism and European socialism. To these social reformers, the new energy doctrine translated into the idea that the human body and the industrial machine were both motors that converted energy into productive work. Rabinbach argues that the image of labour was thus radically transformed, from one associated with human will to "labour power", a neutral expenditure of energy. The Christian proscription of idleness was transformed into a scientific concern for "fatigue", understood as an inevitable dissipation of energy by the "human motor". Once understood in these terms, the body could be controlled to maximize efficiency.

Daniel Bell is best known for his 1973 prophecy of the post-industrial society, a vision that has been interpreted as a conservative celebration of technocracy. But in the late 1950s, BELL produced a critique of the harsh conditions of industrial work under both the older efficiency cult of scientific management and its successor, the human relations school. However, he thought that the continuous flow processes of automation would make it impossible to persist with the Tayloristic fetish of measuring individual work.

The possibility that automation would eliminate the drudgery of manual work, transform muscle-based activity into a higher cognitive form, and create more time for leisure was a prominent theme in the 1960s – particularly among French socialists calling for a re-evaluation of the work-centred society. The debates around this issue are reviewed by Rabinbach, Applebaum, and Robertson. Many of these themes were foreshadowed by TILGHER in 1930, in his synoptic treatise on conceptions of work. Tilgher noted that, unlike the Calvinist who worked in order to attain salvation, modern "man" was driven toward an incessant transformation of the external world as an end in itself. At the same time, the plethora of goods and wealth produced by this religion of work was leading to the opposite creed of consumption and recreation.

By the 1980s, when it became clear that the economy was not opening up routes to liberation, the "future of work" debates began also to focus on the rise of unemployment in the Western world. ROBERTSON argued that the job ethic is at odds with reality; jobless growth is made possible by increased productivity, which itself is due to new technology. On the other hand, there is much socially useful work that could be done by people coming together in local settings to exchange services, or even, to do science. Just as Luther taught people to see the Catholic Church as a mere buffer between themselves and God's will, he claimed that we should likewise recognize that the organizations of the formal economy keep us from fulfilling our needs.

In the 1970s, Braverman and Sohn-Rethel offered Marxist critiques of the division between intellectual and manual labour. BRAVERMAN is a classic study challenging the post-war belief that electronic technologies are making work more high-skilled. He starts with an analysis of how Taylor's methods of scientific management created a separation between conception and execution of industrial work in the early 20th century. He then goes on to examine how science and technology continue to be applied in order to break down the work processes – in many white-collar occupations also – into routine tasks, leaving managers with a monopoly over the conceptual elements. SOHN-RETHEL argues that intellectual labour originally arose as something separate from manual labour, as a means by which the ruling classes could appropriate the products of the latter – for example, the arithmetic operations used to collect taxes and tributes. Mathematics is the ultimate expression of the dividing-line between "head" and "hand". Forms of knowledge are also specific to the context of their economic system; thus, while Greek philosophy was rooted in a society of slave-labour, modern science grew out of a system of wage-labour.

Oakley and Cowan demystify the notion that advances in science and technology have decreased the burdens of housework. OAKLEY examines the domestic hygiene movement that developed in the late 19th century in the US and Europe. Pasteur's germ theory suggested that disease could be controlled by man – or rather, by women's efforts in maintaining clean surroundings. With women (domestic servants and housewives) as guardians of public health, housework had to be carried out in consultation with experts producing new knowledge. Efforts to improve housework via biochemistry, economics, and scientific management ended up creating more work for women.

COWAN reminds us that industrialization was not just a process occurring outside the home. The industrial revolution created the distinction between home and workplace, and transformed the newly demarcated "housework". Cowan uses the concept of work process to show that microwave ovens, vacuum cleaners, washing machines, and other gadgets of the modern home increased the amount of work done by women, for, with the new implements, housewives took over several tasks previously performed by other members of the household. Further, the technology changed socially acceptable standards of the good home.

The papers in PAHL exemplify the range of post-1960s social science approaches to studying work. Male, industrial work was traditionally the bread-and-butter of the sociology of work. The field has progressed via significant feminist challenges: one, to the demarcation of household labour ("non-work") from paid work; two, by the recognition that through most of history and continuing today, women have always been doing so-called men's work; and three, by revealing the crucial role of various tasks done by women in the Third World.

After a century of the science of work, the work conditions of scholars and scientists has itself become an area of inquiry. ARONOWITZ & DiFAZIO scrutinize all kinds of knowledge work, academic and industrial, against the backdrop of budget crises and the un- and under-employment of professionals. They argue that because abstract, codified knowledge is now central to industrial work processes, knowledge workers – scientists, engineers, managers – have themselves become replaceable. Therein lies the contradiction of, for example, CAD (computer-aided design) engineers who are working ultimately to displace themselves from their jobs.

SUJANTHA RAMAN

See also Capitalism and Science; Home Economics; Management Sciences; Political Economy; Skill

BOOKLIST INDEX

Books and articles discussed in the entries are listed here under the name of the author/editor.
The page numbers refer to the lists themselves, where full publication information is given.

GENERAL INDEX

Page numbers in **bold** refer to subjects with their own entries.

deposition 19
origins 19
Oresme, Nicole 47
organ transplantation
antibiotics 261
ethics 90
organic chemistry 59, 69, 360, **535–36**
Berzelius 76, 77
dyes 186, 187
theoretical 565
organic compounds 75
dyes 186, 187
Fischer 258
organic material, standardized 705–06
organic phenomena 657
organicism 658
organicists 219
organisms 566
phenotype 291
Schelling 671
structure 715
theory 396
organization of science, Bacon 66
organization theory 671
organizational skills 435
Organon of the Rational Art of Healing
(Hahnemann) 347
orgasm, female 686
Orient, ancient 295
Oriental philology, Denmark 172
orientalism **536–37**
origin of life
dialectical materialism 175
theology issues 640
Origin of Species (Darwin; 1859) 165, 166,
167, 238, 239, 271
ornithology **537–38**
professionalization 600
women 737, 764, 765
orphanages 54
orreries 48, 654, 676
Ørsted, Hans Christian 203, 206, 212, 430,
538–39
electromagnetism 205
Ortega y Gasset 700
orthodox medicine 145
orthodoxy
Islamic scholars 642
Protestant 640
orthopaedics 458
Osborn, Henry Fairfield 545
oscillograph 203
osteopathy 145
Ostwald, Wilhelm 143, 428, **539–41**,
565
other, construction 429
otoplasty 577, 578
Oughtred, William 42
Oughtred Society 112
*Our Wandering Continents: An Hypothesis
of Continental Drifting* (Du Toit)
149
outliers, rules for rejection 227
ovarian compression 125
ovariectomy 314
ovariotomists 459

Owen, Richard 97, 107
fossils 545
homology concept 272
rivalry with Huxley 297
Owen, Robert 704
Oxford Botanic Gardens, England 97, 100
Oxford Group 259, 260, 261
Oxford (UK)
botany 101
physiologists 103
scientific community in Commonwealth /
Restoration periods 323
Oxford University (UK) 738
oxidation, biological 81
oxidative phosphorylation 653
oxides 408
oxygen 128
biological systems 82
discovery 669
Lavoisier's theory 75, 408, 409
Priestley 594
Ozeretskovskii 666
ozone hole 403

Pacific
eastward diffusion of science 295
European representation of experiences
71
expeditions 243
Pacific islanders 674–75
pacifism 540
women's science 343
paediatrics 458, 459
paganism in classical antiquity 218
pain **543–44**
anti-vivisectionists 35
lesionless 544
theories 183
pain relief
childbirth 528
homeopathy 347
Paine, Thomas 5
pain-killers 183
paintings 647, 674, 717
time-sense 727
Palaeolithic man 231
palaeomagnetism 149
palaeontology **544–45**
Buckland 108
Cuvier 160–62
embryology 67
environmental sciences 221
evolutionary synthesis 240
fossil record interpretation 238
Huxley (Thomas) 363
natural selection 504
plant 98, 99
progressive development 611
Smithsonian Institution 690
Stensen 708
palaeotechnic revolution 717
Palaeozoic geology 297
palaetiological sciences 296
Paley, William 759
Pallas, Simon 583
Pallas perturbations 281

Palomar Observatory 320
Panama-Pacific International Exposition
(San Francisco) 483
pancreatic juice function 73
pandemics 223
AIDS 23
bubonic plague 575
pangenesis 239
Darwin's hypothesis 278
pansophistic thought 156
pantheism, Goethe 309
papal infallibility 640
papal patronage, Accademia dei Lincei 3
paper making 390
paper mills 485
Papert, Seymour 43
Pappus 299, 356
papyrus, medical 709
Paracelsian experimentation at Accademia
dei Lincei 3
Paracelsian influence, Tycho Brahe 104
Paracelsian tradition 728
Paracelsus, Philippus 24, 152, 347, 496,
545–46
fire concept 328
hysteria 366
therapeutic theory 557
parachute 411
paradigm **546–48**
conflict 127
model 312
parallel postulate 233
paranoia, Cantor 116
paranoid–schizoid positions 604
paranormal 704
experiences 391, 704
parapsychology 696, 704, 753
Paré, Ambrose 709
parental authority 125
Parent-Duchâtelet, Alexandre 326
parenthood, biological 649
Paris Academy, Maupertuis 447
Paris Observatory, Newton 516
Paris school
pathological signs of disease 256
theoretical organic chemistry 565
Paris University (France) 490
Jesuit influences 388
Middle Ages 644
Parkinson, John 333
Parliament of Science 599
Parmenides 40, 579
Parsons, C.E. Auguste 216
partial differential equations 488
particle acceleration 409
particle physics 520, **548–49**
astrophysics 52
CERN 122, 123
cosmology interface 79
Denmark 172
elementary 567
neutrinos 549
Newton's alchemical studies 25
postwar funding 567
particle scattering 668
particle theory 534

NOTES ON ADVISERS
AND CONTRIBUTORS

Albree, Joe. Assistant Professor of Mathematics and Pre-Engineering, Auburn University at Montgomery, Alabama. Author of *A Station Favorable to the Pursuits of Science* (with David C. Arney and V. Frederick Rickey, 2000). Contributor to the journals *Mathematics Magazine*, *Alabama Journal of Mathematics*, *Bulletin of the London Mathematical Society*, *Historica Mathematica*, and *Mathematical Intelligencer*. Managing editor of the *Alabama Journal of Mathematics* since 1996; reviewer for the history section of *Library Recommendations for Undergraduate Mathematics* edited by Lynn Arthur Steen (1992). **Essay:** Arithmetic.

Alexander, Amir. Faculty Member, Center for 17th and 18th Century Studies, University of California at Los Angeles. Author of "The Imperialist Space of Elizabethan Mathematics", *Studies in History and Philosophy of Science* (1995) and "Lunar Maps and Coastal Outlines", *Studies in the History and Philosophy of Science* (1998). **Essay:** Scientific Revolution.

Anderson, Katharine. Visiting Professor, Department of the History of Science, Harvard University. Author of several articles including "The Weather Prophets: Science, Reputation and Forecasting in Victorian Britain", *History of Science* (forthcoming). **Essays:** CERN, Meteorology.

Andrews, B.J. Assistant Professor and Head Tutor, Department of the History of Science, Harvard University. Co-author of *The Making of Modern Chinese Medicine* (in preparation). Editor of *Western Medicine as Contested Knowledge* (with Andrew Cunningham, 1997). Author of several articles on the history of medicine and science in East Asia. **Essay:** China: medicine.

Apple, Rima D. Professor, School of Human Ecology and the Women's Studies Program, University of Wisconsin. Author of *Vitamania* (1996) and *Mothers and Medicine* (1987). Editor of *Women, Health, and Medicine in America* (1990), *Mothers and Motherhood* (with Janet Golden, 1997). Contributor of an article on nutrition to the *Journal of Food and Society*. Co-editor of *Advancing the Consumer Interest*, 1994–98, and associate editor of *Isis*, 1989–92. **Essay:** Home Economics.

Arrizabalaga, Jon. Researcher in the History of Science at CSIC, Barcelona. Author of *The Great Pox: The French Disease in Renaissance Europe* (with John Henderson and Roger French, 1997) and *La salut en la historia d'Europa* (with Alvar Martínez Vidal and José Pardo Tomas, 1998). Editor of *Practical Medicine from Salerno to the Black Death* (with Luís García-Ballester, Roger French and Andrew Cunningham, 1994). Member of the editorial board of the journals *History of Medicine*, *Science*, *Asclepio*, and *Dynamis*. **Essay:** AIDS.

Ashcroft, Richard. Sir Siegmund Warburg Lecturer in Medical Ethics, Imperial College School of Medicine, London. Specialist in the ethics of medical and scientific research. Contributor of an article on the ethics of clinical trials to *Health Technology Assessment*, and contributor to the journals *Bioethics*, *Journal of Medical Ethics*, *Health Care Analysis*, *Medicine Healthcare and Philosophy*, and *British Medical Journal*. **Essay:** Medical Ethics.

Ashworth, William J. Lecturer, School of History, University of Liverpool, and former member of the William Whewell Calendar Project. Author of "Labour Harder than Thrashing" in *Flamsteed's Stars: New Perspectives on the Life and Work of the First Astronomer Royal, 1646–1719* edited by Frances Willmoth (1997). Contributor to *Canadian Journal of History*, *History of Science*, *Social History*, *Isis*, and *British Journal for the History of Science*. **Essays:** Accountability, Whewell.

Atmore, Henry. Independent Scholar. **Essays:** Science Fiction, Spencer.

Ball, Mike. Senior Lecturer in Anthropology and Sociology, Staffordshire University. Author of *The Passage of Time in Occupations* (1980), *Analysing Visual Data* (with G.W.H. Smith, 1992), and *Annual Company Reports as Visual Numerical and Written Modes of Representation* (with N. Barrow, 1993). Contributor to *Collins Dictionary of Sociology* edited by David and Julia Jary (1991; 2nd edition, 1995), and to the journals *Local Organisation*, and *Communication and Cognition*. **Essays:** Boas, Evans-Pritchard, Lévi-Strauss, Rationality.

Barona, Josep Lluís. Professor of the History of Science and Director of the Department of History of Science and Documentation, University of Valencia. Author of *Fisiología, origen histórico de una ciencia experimental* (1991), *La doctrina y el laboratorio: fisiología y experimentación en la sociedad española de siglo XIX* (1992), *Sobre medicina y filosofía natural en el renacimiento* (1993), *Ciencia e historia* (1994), *Malaltia í cultura* (1995), and *Història del pensament biològic* (1998). Contributor to the journals *Asclepia*, *Gesnerus*, *History and Philosophy of the Life Sciences*, *Mencina nei Secoli*, *Physis*, and *Dynamis*. Essays: Medieval Science and Medicine, Phrenology, Ramón y Cajal, Volta.

Belhoste, Bruno. Researcher at the Institut National de Récherche Pédagogique, Paris, and Assistant Professor at the École Nationale des Ponts et Chaussées, Marne-la Vallée, France. Author of *Augustin-Louis Cauchy: A Biography* (1991) and *Les Sciences dans l'enseignement secondaire français, textes officiels*, vol. 1: 1794–1914 (1995). Editor of *La Formation Polytechnicienne, 1794–1994* (with Amy Dahan Dalmedico and Antoine Picon, 1994), *La France des X: deux siècles d'histoire* (with Amy Dahan Dalmedico, Dominique Pèstre, and Antoine Picon, 1995), and *Les Sciences au lycée* (with H. Gispert and N. Hulin, 1996). Essays: École Polytechnique, Monge.

Bellon, Richard. Doctoral candidate, University of Washington, Seattle. Contributor of articles on Joseph Hooker and the professionalization of science to the *Journal of the History of Biology*. Essay: Hooker.

Bennett, Jim. Adviser. Director of the Museum of the History of Science, University of Oxford. Author of several books including *Catalogue of the Archives and Manuscripts of the Royal Astronomical Society* (1978) and *The Divided Circle: A History of Instruments for Astronomy, Navigation and Surveying* (1987). Essays: Navigational Instruments, Scientific Instruments: France (with Christine Blondel).

Bivins, Roberta E. Adviser. Research Associate, Centre for the History of Science, Technology and Medicine, University of Manchester. Author of *Acupuncture, Expertise, and Cross-Cultural Medicine* (2000). Contributor to *Medicine: A History of Healing* edited by Roy Porter (1997), and to the journals *Journal for the History of Biology* and *History of Science*. Essays: Acupuncture, India: medicine.

Blondel, Christine. Senior Programme Manager, Family Firms, INSEAD, France. Author of "Large Family Capitalism: Cases of Multi-Generation Families Controlling Large, Publicly Quoted Firms", *FBN Newsletter* (with Ludo Van der Heden, August 1999), "Fair Process: Seeking Justice in Family Firms", *Proceedings of FBN Conference* (with Randel Carlock and Ludo Van der Heyden, October 2000), *Niraj: Successor's Dilemma in an Indian Family Firm* (in preparation). Essay: Scientific Instruments: France (with Jim Bennett).

Bohlin, Ingemar. Research Fellow, Section of Science and Technology Studies, University of Gothenburg. Author of *Through Malthusian Specs? A Study in the Philosophy of Science Studies* (1995). Contributor to the journals *Social Studies of Science*, *Studies in History and Philosophy of Science*, and *Science as Culture*. Essay: Darwin.

Bonah, Christian. Assistant Professor, Département d'Histoire et de Philosophie des Sciences de la Vie et de la Santé, Louis Pasteur University, Strasbourg. Author of *Les Sciences physiologiques en Europe: analyses comparées du XIXème siècle* (1995), "Physiology, Periodicals, and National Differences at the End of the 1860s" in *Essays in the History of the Physiological Sciences* edited by Claude Debru (1995), "Pathological Anatomy versus Pathological Physiology: A Franco-German Dispute over a 'Province for Pathology'" in *Pathology in the 19th and 20th Centuries* edited by C.R. Prüll (1998), and *Instruire, guérir, servir: formation et pratique médicales en France et en Allemagne* (2000). Contributor to the journal *Archives Internationales d'Histoire des Sciences*. Essays: Physiology: France, Physiology: Germany.

Borossa, Julia. Freelance writer. Author of articles on Freud and psychoanalysis in *Case Material and Clinical Discourse* edited by Ivan Ward (1997), and contributor to *Oxford Literary Review* (1997), *Angelaki* (1998), and *Paragraph* (1998). Editor of *Sandor Ferenczi: Selected Writings* (1999). Essays: Freud, Klein, Psychoanalysis: gender, Psychoanalysis: institutional.

Bowler, Peter J. Professor of History and Philosophy of Science, Queen's University Belfast. Author of *The Eclipse of Darwinism* (1983), *Evolution: The History of an Idea* (1984), *The Non-Darwinian Revolution* (1988), *Charles Darwin: The Man and His Influence* (1991), and *Biology and Social Thought, 1850–1914* (1993). Essays: Evolution, Natural Selection, Paleontology.

Bracegirdle, Brian. Research Consultant in Microscopy. Former Chief Curator, Science Museum, London. Author of *The Archaeology of the Industrial Revolution* (with Brian Bowers and others, 1973), *A History of Microtechnique* (1978), *Scientific Photomacrography* (1995), and *Microscopial Mounts and Mounters* (1998). Editor of *Quekett Journal of Microscopy*. Essay: Microscopes.

Bracegirdle, Patricia H. Doctoral candidate, Wellcome Institute for the History of Medicine, London. Former Director of Educational Services and Chief Inspector, Royal Borough of Kensington and Chelsea. Essay: Histology.

Brain, Robert. Assistant Professor of the History of Science, Harvard University. Research interests include the cultural history of 19th-century science, technology and medicine, the history of the life sciences and scientific instruments. Essays: Exhibitions, Graphical Method, Marey.

Bravo, Michael T. Head of Science and Development Group, Scott Polar Research Institute, Cambridge University. Author of *The Accuracy of Ethnoscience* (1996). Contributor to *Enlightenment and Geography* edited by D. Livingstone and C. Withers (1999) and the journal *Ecumene*. Essays: Expeditions (with Juan Pimentel), Polar Science.

Bray, Francesca. Adviser. Professor of Anthropology, University of California at Los Angeles. Author of *Science and Civilization in China* (1984), *The Rice Economies: Technology and Development in Asian Societies* (1986), and *Technology and Gender: Fabrics of Power in Late Imperial China* (1997). Member of the editorial committee, University of California Press, 1991–94, and since 1993, member of the advisory board for *Chinese Science*. **Essay:** China: agriculture.

Broberg, Gunnar. Professor, History of Science and Ideas, Lund University, Sweden. Author of *Homo Sapiens L* (1975), *Linnaeus and His Garden* (with Allan Ellenius and Bengt Jonsell, 1983), *Golden Apples* (textbook/anthology on Swedish history of science and ideas) (1993), and *Eugenics and the Welfare State* (with Nils Roll-Hansen, 1996). Editor of the *Yearbook of the Linnean Society*. **Essays:** Linnaeus, Sweden.

Brock, William. Adviser. Visiting Professor, Centre for History and Cultural Studies of Science, University of Kent at Canterbury. Author of several books including *The Fontana History of Chemistry* (1992; as *The Norton History of Chemistry*, 1993), *Science for All: Studies in the History of Victorian Science and Education* (1996), and *Justig von Liebig: Chemical Gatekeeper* (1997).

Brooks, Nathan. Assistant Professor of History, New Mexico State University. Contributor to the journals *Annals of Science* and *Ambix*. Advisory editor of the journal *Isis*, 1995–98. **Essay:** Mendeleev.

Brooks, Randall C. Curator, Physical Sciences and Space, National Museum of Science and Technology, Ottawa. Editor, *Rittenhouse*. Contributor to the journals *Bulletin of Scientific Instrument Society*, *Canadian Journal of Civil Engineering*, *Transactions of the Newcomen Society*, and *Journal of the Royal Astronomical Society of Canada*. **Essays:** Astronomical Instruments, Canada.

Brüning, Reinhart. Science journalist and freelance writer. Author of *Entstehung des Neuen: Peirce' konzept der Abduktion, das allgemeine Korrespondenzprinzip und Metaphern in der Wissenschaft: Historische Fallstudie: Die Förderband metapher in der Ozeanographie* (1999). **Essay:** Discovery.

Bud, Robert. Head of Information and Research, Science Museum, London. Author of several books including *Science versus Practice: Chemistry in Victorian Britain* (with Gerrylyn K. Roberts, 1984), and *The Uses of Life: A History of Biotechnology* (1993). Editor of *Instruments of Science* (with Deborah Jean Warner, 1996), *Manifesting Medicine: Bodies and Machines* (with Bernard Finn and Helmuth Trischer, 1999), and *Cold War, Hot Science* (with Philip Gummett, 1999). **Essay:** Biotechnology.

Bugos, Glenn E. Historian, The Prologue Group, California. Author of *Engineering the F-4 Phantom II: Parts Into Systems* (1996). **Essay:** Management Sciences.

Buiter, Hans. Department of Technology Management, Eindhoven University of Technology. Author of *Nederlands-Indie, 1830–1949* (1993). **Essay:** Netherlands: technology.

Bullough, Vern L. Visiting Professor, University of Southern California, Los Angeles, and Distinguished Professor Emeritus, State University of New York at Buffalo. Author of numerous books on sexuality, and the history of science and medicine, including *Cross-Dressing, Sex and Gender* (with Bonnie Bullough, 1993), *Human Sexuality: An Encyclopedia* (1994), *Science in the Bedroom* (with Bonnie Bullough, 1994), *Sexual Attitudes: Myths & Realities* (with Bonnie Bullough, 1995), and *Gender Blending* (with Bonnie Bullough and James Elias, 1997). Senior editor of *Free Inquiry*, and consulting editor for Prometheus Books. **Essay:** Sexuality.

Bynum, W.F. Professor, Wellcome Trust Centre for the History of Medicine at University College London. Author of several books including *Science and the Practice of Medicine in the Nineteenth Century* (1994). Editor of *Companion Encyclopedia of the History of Medicine* (with Roy Porter, 1993), *The Anatomy of Madness: Essays in the History of Psychiatry* (with Roy Porter and Michael Shepherd, 1985–88), and *The Beast in the Mosquito: The Correspondence of Ronald Ross and Patrick Manson* (with Caroline Overy, 1998). **Essays:** Clinical Science, Epidemiology, Experimental Physiology, Fevers, Medical Specialization, Pathology.

Campbell-Kelly, Martin. Reader, Department of Computer Science, University of Warwick. Author of *ICL: A Business and Technical History* (1989) and *Computer: A History of the Information Machine* (with William Aspray, 1996). Editor of *The Moore School Lectures* (with M.R. Williams, 1985), *The Works of Charles Babbage* (1989), *The Early British Computer Conferences* (with M.R. Williams, 1989), and *Passages from the Life of a Philosopher* (1994). Editor of the Charles Babbage Institution Reprint Services for the History of Computing, 1982–91, and member of the editorial boards of *Annuals of the History of Computing* and *Computer Journal*. **Essay:** Computing.

Ceranski, Beate. Wissenschaftliche Assistentin [Assistant Professor], Historisches Institut, University of Stuttgart. Author of *Und sie fürchtet sich vor niemandem: Die Physikerin Laura Bassi, 1711–1778* (1996). Contributor to *Instrument – Experiment: Historische Studien* edited by Christoph Meinel (2000) and *Formatting Gender: Transitions, Breaks, and Discontinuites in German-Speaking Europe* edited by Ulrike Gleixner and M. Gray (in preparation), and to the journal *Nuncius*. **Essays:** Particle Physics, Women in Science: physical sciences.

Chamak, Brigitte. Researcher in the History of Science in IRESCO, Paris. Author of "The Emergence of Cognitive Science in France: A Comparison with the USA", *Social Studies of Science* (1999) and "Les Sciences cognitives", in *Dictionnaire d'histoire et de philosophie des sciences* (1999). **Essay:** Artificial Intelligence.

Chavot, Philippe. Maître de Conférence, IUT-Louis Pasteur/ GERSULP, Louis Pasteur University, Strasbourg. Editor of *L'Animal dans les sciences: médicine, ecologie et sociobiologie* (1995) and *L'Animal, objet ou miroir de l'homme?* (in preparation). Contributor to *Les Sciences, les techniques et leurs publics: Actes des XVIIIe JIES* edited by A. Giordan, J.L. Martinand, and D. Raichvarg (1996), *Jardins d'essais, jardins laboratoires: Actes du 120 congrès des sociétés historiques et scientifiques* (1999), *L'éducation aux risques: Actes des XXIIe JIES* edited by C. Giordan, J.L. Martinand, and D. Raichvarg (in preparation), *Ethique et transplantation d'organes* edited by Jean-François Collange (with Felt Ulrike and Anne Masseran, in preparation), *Encyclopedia of the World's Zoos* edited by Catharine Bell (in preparation), and to the journals *Revue Passerelles, Bulletin d'Histoire et d'Epistémologie des Sciences de la Vie, Revue d'Histoire des Sciences, Bulletin SFECA, Bulletin de Liaison SQEBC,* and *Musées et Recherchés.* **Essays:** Lorenz, Muséum National d'Histoire Naturelle (with Claude Schnitter and Anne Masseran).

Chen, Xiang. Assistant Professor of Philosophy at California Lutheran University, Thousand Oaks. Author of *Instrumental Traditions and Theories of Light* (2000). Contributor to *Scientific Methods* edited by Peter Achinstein (1994) and to the journals *Archive for History of Exact Science, Annals of Science, Studies in the History and Philosophy of Science, Studies in the History and Philosophy of Modern Physics, Perspectives on Science, Journal for General Philosophy of Science, Philosophy of Science, Synthèse, Philosophical Psychology, Journal of Natural Dialects, Exploration,* and *Physical Bulletin.* **Essay:** Optics.

Childs, Peter E. Lecturer in Chemistry, Department of Chemical and Environmental Sciences, University of Limerick. Author of "From Hydrogen to Meitnerium" in *Chemical Nomenclature* edited by K.J. Thurlow (1998) and *Aughinish Alumina* (3rd edition, 1998). Contributor to *Irish Chemical News, Chemistry in Action!* and *Education in Chemistry.* Director of the Schools Information Centre on the Irish Chemical Industry since 1989. Editor of *Chemistry in Action!* **Essay:** Industrial Chemistry.

Christensen, Dan Ch. Lecturer in the History of Science, Roskilde University, Denmark. Contributor to *Land Productivity and Agro Systems in the North Sea Area: Elements for a Comparative History* edited by Bas J.P. van Bavel and Eric Thoen (1999) and *English Instrument Makers Observed by Predacious Danes* edited by Jesper Lützen (in preparation). Author of articles in *Intellectuals Reading Technology: Proceedings from the Nordic Symposium on Technology* (1991) and the journals *Centaurus, Kultur & Technik,* and *Annals of Science.* Editor of *European Historiography of Technology: Proceedings from the TISC Conference* (1993). **Essays:** Ørsted, Stensen.

Clark, John F.M. School of History, Rutherford College, University of Kent at Canterbury. Contributor to the journals *History Today* and *British Journal for the History of Science.* **Essays:** Ethology and Animal Behaviour, Ideology.

Cox-Maksimov, D.C.T. Former doctoral candidate, Wellcome Unit for the History of Medicine, Wolfson College, Cambridge. Author of "The Making of the Clinical Trial in Britain: Expertise, the State and the Public" (PhD dissertation, 1998). **Essay:** Clinical Trials.

Crawford, Catherine. Lecturer, Department of History, University of Essex. Author of *Legal Medicine in History* (with Michael Clark, 1994) and contributor to *Companion Encyclopedia of the History of Medicine* edited by Roy Porter and W.F. Bynum (1993) and *Legal Medicine and the Law* edited by Y. Otsuka and S. Saki (1998). **Essay:** Forensic Sciences.

Crawford, Elisabeth. Senior Research Fellow, Centre National de la Récherche Scientifique, Strasbourg. Author of numerous books and articles including *The Beginnings of the Nobel Institution: The Science Prizes, 1901–1915* (1984), *The Nobel Population 1901–1937: A Census of the Nominators and Nominees for the Prizes in Physics and Chemistry* (with J.L. Heilbron and R. Ullrich, 1987), *Nationalism and Internationalism in Science, 1880–19939: Four Studies of the Nobel Population* (1990) and *Arrhenius: From Ionic Theory to the Greenhouse Effect* (1996). **Essay:** Nobel Institution.

Crosland, Maurice. Professor Emeritus, Centre for the History of Science, University of Kent at Canterbury. Author of *Historical Studies in the Language of Chemistry* (1962; revised edition, 1978), *The Society of Arcueil: A View of French Science at the Time of Napoleon 1* (1967), *Gay-Lussac: Scientist and Bourgeois* (1978), *The Science of Matter* (1992), *Science Under Control: The French Academy of Sciences, 1795–1914* (1992), *In the Shadow of Lavoisier: The "Annales de Chimie" and the Emergence of a New Science* (1994), and *Studies in the Culture of Science in France and Britain since the Enlightenment* (1995). Editor of *Science in France in the Revolutionary Era Described by Thomas Bugge* (1969) and *The Emergence of Science in Western Europe* (1975). Former editor of *British Journal for the History of Science.* **Essays:** Berthollet, Gay-Lussac, Lavoisier.

Cunningham, Andrew. Adviser. Formerly Acting Director, Wellcome Unit, University of Cambridge and Affiliated Lecturer, Department of History and Philosophy of Science, University of Cambridge. Author of "Paracelsus Fat and Thin: Thoughts on Reputations and Realities" in *Paracelsus: The Man and His Reputation. His Ideas and their Transformation,* edited by Orel Peter Grell (1998) and "Une Vérité á Contrecoeur [on William Harvey]" *Les Cahiers de Science et Vie: 1000 Ans de Sciences* (1998). Editor of *The Medical Enlightenment of the Eighteenth Century* (with Roger French, 1990), *Before Science: The Invention of the Friars' Natural Philosophy* (with Roger French, 1996), and *Health Care and Poor Relief in Counter Reformation Europe* (with Ole Peter Grell and Jon Arrizabalga, 1997). **Essay:** Vesalius.

Cuomo, Serafina. Lecturer in the History of Science and Technology, Imperial College, London. Author of *Pappus of Alexandria and the Mathematics of Late Antiquity* (2000). Contributor to the journals *History of Science* and *Studies in History and Philosophy of Science.* **Essays:** Archimedes, Euclid, Leonardo da Vinci, Pythagoras.

Dally, Ann. Research Associate, Wellcome Institute for the History of Medicine, London. Author of *Inventing Motherhood: The Consequences of an Ideal* (1982), *A Doctor's Story* (1990), *Women Under the Knife* (1991), and *Fantasy Surgery, 1880–1930* (1996). Editor of *Maternal and Child Care*, 1965–70. **Essays:** Gynaecology, Obstetrics and Midwifery.

D'Ambrosio, Ubiratan. Professor Emeritus of Mathematics, Universidade Estadual de Campinas, Saõ Paolo, Brazil. President of the Brazilian Society of the History of Mathematics (SBHMat). Author of *Etnomatemática* (1990) and *Ethnomathematics: The Art or Technique of Explaining and Knowing* (1999). Contributor to several books including *O Cálculo das variações no século XIX e a transição para a Análise Moderna* edited by Fernando Raul Neto (1998) and *Ethnomathematics: Where Does it Come From and Where Does It Go?* edited by Claudi Alsina *et al.* (1998). Contributor to the journals *Current Anthropology*, *Episteme*, Saber y Tiempo, and *PRISTEM*. **Essay:** Ethnoscience.

Dauben, Joseph W. Professor of the History of Science, Herbert H. Lehman College, City University of New York. Author of several books including *Georg Cantor: His Mathematics of the Infinite* (1979; 2nd edition, 1990) and *Abraham Robinson: The Creation of Nonstandard Analysis* (1995). Editor of *The Intersection of Science and Mathematics* (with Sasaki Chikara and Sugiura Mitsuo, 1994) and *History of Mathematics* (with others, 1996). **Essays:** Botanical and Zoological Gardens, Cantor, Gödel, Merton Thesis, Set Theory.

Dawbarn, Frances. Postdoctoral Teaching and Research Assistant, University of Lancaster. Author of articles on physicians and patronage in Early Modern England in the *British Journal for the History of Science* and *Endeavour*, and contributor of reviews to *Medical History*. **Essay:** Paracelsus.

Dean, Dennis R. Former Professor of English and Humanities, University of Wisconsin, Madison, and University Research Professor, Istanbul Technical University. Author of *Tennyson and Geology* (1985), *James Hutton and the History of Geology* (1992), and *Gideon Mantel and the Discovery of Dinosaurs* (1999); editor of *James Hutton in the Field and in the Study* (1997), and contributor to numerous journals. **Essay:** Hutton.

De Chadarevian, Soraya. Senior Research Associate, and Affiliated Lecturer, Department of the History and Philosophy of Science, University of Cambridge. Author of *Zwischen den Diskursen: Maurice Merleau-Ponty und die Wissenschaften* (1990). Editor of *Molecularising Biology and Medicine* (with Harmke Kamminga, 1998). Contributor to the *Journal for the History of Biology*. **Essays:** DNA, Molecular Biology.

De Renzi, Silvia. Research Fellow, Wellcome Unit for the History of Medicine, University of Cambridge. Contributor to *Bibliothecae Selectae* edited by E. Gahone (1993), *Health Care Provision and Poor Relief in Southern Counter Reformation Europe* edited by Andrew Cunningham, Ole Peter Grel and Jon Arrizabalaga (1997), and *Medicine, Mortality and the Book Trade* edited by Robin Myers and Michael Harris (1998), and to the journal *Intersezioni*. **Essays:** Accademia dei Lincei, Accademia del Cimento.

DeVorkin, David H. Curator, History of Science, National Air and Space Museum, Smithsonian Institution, Washington, DC. Author of numerous articles and books including *Practical Astronomy* (1986), *Race to the Stratosphere* (1989), *Science with a Vengeance* (1992), and *Henry Norris Russell: Dean of American Astronomers* (2000). **Essays:** Astrophysics, Space Science, Telescopes.

Diamond, Jr, Arthur M. Professor of Economics, University of Nebraska at Omaha. Contributor to the journals *Science*, *History of Political Economy*, *Research in the History of Economic Thought and Methodology*, *Journal of Economic History*, *Science, Technology and Human Values*, *Economic Inquiry: The Journal of Human Resources*, *Journal of Economic Education*, *Theory and Discussion*, *Scientometrics*, *Journal of Gerontology*, *Perspectives in Biology and Medicine*, and *Journal of Economic Studies*. **Essays:** Keynes, Marshall.

Dijksterhuis, Fokko Jan. Lecturer, Department of History, University of Twente. Contributor to *Zeventiende Eenw* (1996), and to the journal *Metascience*. **Essay:** Huygens.

Divall, Colin. Professor of Railway Studies, University of York. Contributor to *Railway Management and Its Organisational Structure* edited by J. Armstrong, C. Bouneau, and J. Vidal Olivares (1998), *History and Heritage* edited by John Arnold, Kate Davies and Simon Ditchfield (1998), *Determinants in the Evolution of the European Chemical Industry, 1900–1939* edited by Anthony S. Travis, Harm G. Schröter and Ernst Homburg (with Sean Johnston, 1998), *Professional Identities in Transition* edited by Inga Hellberg, Mike Saks and Cecilia Benoit (with Sean Johnston, 1999), *The History and Practice of Britain's Railways* edited by R.W. Ambler (1999), *Scaling Up: The Institution of Chemical Engineers and the Making of a New Profession* (with Sean Johnston, in preparation), *Moving On: Making Histories in Transport Museums* (with Andrew Scott, in preparation), and of articles on the engineering professions to the journals *Technology and Culture*, *Minerva*, *Contemporary British History*, *Journal of Contemporary History*, and *Social Studies of Science*. Member of the editorial board, since 1997, and exhibitions reviews editor, since 2000, of the *Journal of Transport History*. Reviews editor of *Science and Public Policy*, 1993–95. **Essay:** Engineering Schools.

Dmitriev, Igor S. Director of D.I. Mendeleev Museum and Archives of St Petersburg State University and Professor of the History of Science, St Petersburg State University of Pedagogical Art. Author of numerous publications including *Formation of Spin-Valency Theory* (1980) and *Molecules without Chemical Bonds* (1981). Contributor to the volumes *Quantum Chemistry* (1980) and *The History of Classical Organic Chemistry* (1992). **Essays:** Avogadro, Berzelius.

Dobson, Mary J. Director, Wellcome Unit for the History of Medicine, Reader in the History of Medicine, University of Oxford, and Fellow of Green College, Oxford. Author of *From Old England to New England: Changing Patterns of Mortality* (1987) and *Contours of Death and Disease in Early Modern England* (1997). **Essay:** Malaria.

Dolan, Brian. Wellcome Research Lecturer at the University of East Anglia. Author of *Exploring European Frontiers: British Travellers in the Age of Enlightenment* (2000). Editor of *Science Unbound* (1998) and *Malthus, Medicine, and Morality* (2000). **Essays:** Affinity, Blowpipe, Galvanic Battery, Professionalization.

Donnelly, Michael. Professor of Sociology, Bard College, New York. Author of *Managing the Mind: A Study of Medical Psychology in Early-Nineteenth-Century Britain* (1983), *The Politics of Mental Health in Italy* (1992), and "From Political Arithmetic to Social Statistics" in *The Rise of the Social Sciences and the Formation of Modernity* edited by Johan Heilbron, Lars Magnusson and Bjorn Wittrock (1998). **Essays:** Asylums, National Styles of Reasoning, Sociology.

Dorn, Harold. Professor of the History of Science and Director of the Department of Humanities and Social Sciences, Stevens Institute of Technology, Hoboken, New Jersey. Author of *The Geography of Science* (1991) and *Science and Technology in World History* (with James E. McClellan III, 1999). Contributor to numerous journals including *Scientific American* and *Technology and Culture*. **Essays:** Geography of the Sciences, Marxism and Science.

Dreger, Alice D. Assistant Professor of Science and Technology Studies, Lyman Briggs School and Center for Ethics and Humanities in the Life Sciences, Michigan State University. Author of "Hermaphrodites in Love" in *Science and Homosexualities* edited by Vernon A. Rosario (1997), *Hermaphrodites and the Medical Invention of Sex* (1998), *Intersex in the Age of Ethics* (1999), and "'Ambiguous Sex' – or Ambivalent Medicine?" in *Meaning and Medicine* edited by James Lindemann Nelson and Hilde Lindemann Nelson (1999). Editor of the special issue on intersex, *Journal of Clinical Ethics* (1998). **Essay:** Gender and Sex (with Londa Schiebinger).

Drolias, Basileios. Research Assistant in Astrophysics, Imperial College, London. **Essay:** Acoustics.

Dunn, Richard. Loans Officer, Victoria and Albert Museum, London. Author of *The True Place of Astrology among the Mathematical Arts* (1994) and *Astrology in Harriot's Time* (1994). **Essays:** Almanacs, Astrology, Dee.

Egerton, Frank N. Professor of History, University of Wisconsin, Parkside. Author of *Overfishing or Pollution?* (1985). Editor of *History of American Ecology* (1977) and *Edward Lee Greene* (1983). Contributor to *Encyclopedia of American Forest and Conservation History* (1983), *Breaking New Waters* edited by Annamarie L. Beckel (1987), *Humans as Components of Ecosystems* edited by Mark J. McDonnell and S.T.A. Pickett (1993), *Dictionnaire du Darwinisme et de l'évolution* edited by Patrick Tort (1996), *American National Biography* (1999), *Encyclopedia of Environmental Issues* (1999), and *New Dictionary of National Biography* (in preparation), and to the journals *Isis*, *Journal of the History of Biology*, *Environmental Review*, *Newsletter for History and Sociology of Marginality in Science*, *Essays in Arts and Sciences*, and *Environmental History Review*. **Essay:** Ecology.

Eglash, Ron. Assistant Professor, Science and Technology Studies, Rensselaer Polytechnic Institute. Author of *African Fractals: Modern Computing and Indigenous Design* (1999). Contributor to *The Cyborg Handbook* edited by Chris Gray (1995), *Exploring Fractals on the Macintosh* edited by Bernt Wahl (1995), and to the journals *American Anthropologist*, *Science Technology and Human Values*, *Social Studies of Science*, *Complexity*, *Ekistics*, *Mathematics Teacher*, *Journal of Social and Evolutionary Structures*, *Technoscience*, *Dynamics Newsletter*, and *Investigations on Cetacea*. **Essays:** Chaos Theory, Indigenous Knowledge Systems.

Elston, M.A. Senior Lecturer in Sociology, Department of Social and Political Science, Royal Holloway, University of London. Author of "The Antivivisectionist Movement and the Science of Medicine" in *Challenging Medicine* edited by J. Gabe *et al.* (1994) and "Women and Anti-vivisection in Victorian Britain" in *Vivisection in Historical Perspective* edited by Nicolaas A. Rupke (1987). Editor of *The Sociology of Medical Science and Technology* (1997). **Essay:** Anti-Vivisection.

Epple, Moritz. Heisenberg Research Fellow, Mathematical Insitute, University of Bonn. Co-author of *Die Entstehung der Knotentheorie* (1999) and author of "Grundlagen der Analysis, 1860–1910" in *Geschichte der Analysis* edited by H.N. Jahnke (1999). Contributor of articles on the history of topology and the history of the philosophy of mathematics to the journals *Historica Mathematica*, *Archive for History of Exact Sciences*, and *Mathematische Semesterberichte*. Associate editor of *Historica Mathematica*. **Essay:** Mathematical Modernity.

Erneling, Christina. Assistant Professor, College of Communication, Lund University, Sweden. Author of *Understanding Language Acquisition* (1993) and "Language Development" in *Discursive Psychology in Practice* edited by R. Harre and P. Stearns (1995). Editor of *The Future of the Cognitive Revolution* (with David M. Johnson, 1997) and *The Mind as a Scientific Object* (with David M. Johnson, in preparation). Contributor to the journals *Interchange* and *Canadian Women Studies*. **Essay:** Piaget.

Etzkowitz, Henry. Director, Science Policy Institute, State University of New York, Purchase. Author of *Athena Unbound: Overcoming Barriers to Women in Science* (in preparation). Editor of *Universities in the Global Knowledge Economy: A Triple Helix of University-Industry-Government Relations* (with Loet Leyesdorff, 1997) and *Capitalizing Knowledge* (with Andrew Webster and Peter Healey, 1998). **Essay:** Technology Transfer.

Falconer, Isobel. Independent scholar. Author of *J.J. Thomson and the Discovery of the Electron* (with E.A. Davis, 1997). Contributor to *The Development of the Laboratory* edited by Frank A.J.L. James (1989), *The Electron and the Birth of Microphysics* edited by Jed Buchwald (in preparation) and to the journals *Physics Education*, *British Journal for the History of Science*, *Historical Studies in the Physical Sciences*, and *Measurement Science and Technology*. Editor of the newsletter *Education Forum*, and former curator of the Cavendish Laboratory Museum. **Essay:** Thomson.

Fan, Fa-Ti. Faculty Member, Max Planck Institute for the History of Science, Berlin. Author of articles on China including "Hybrid Discourse and Textual Practice: Sinology and Natural History in the Nineteenth Century", *History of Science* (2000). **Essays:** China: general works, China: natural history, Orientalism.

Fara, Patricia. Fellow, Clare College, and Affiliated Lecturer, Department of History and Philosophy of Science, University of Cambridge. Author of *Computers* (1982) and *Sympathetic Attractions: Magnetic Practices, Beliefs, and Symbolism in Eighteenth-Century England* (1996). Editor of *The Changing World* (with Peter Gathercole and Ronald Laskey, 1996) and *Memory* (with Karalyn Patterson, 1998). Contributor to *The Global Warming Debate* edited by John Emsley (1996), *History of the Geosciences* edited by Gregory Good (1998), *Heroic Reputations and Exemplary Lives* edited by Geoffrey Cubitt and Allen Warren (2000), *The Cambridge History of Science: Science in the Eighteenth Century* edited by Roy Porter (in preparation), and to the *British Journal for the History of Science, Endeavour, History Today, Studies in the History and Philosophy of Science, British Journal for 18th-Century Studies, Notes and Records of the Royal Society, History Workshop Journal, Journal for the History of Astronomy, Enlightenment and Dissent, History of Science,* and *Museums Journal.* **Essays:** Banks, Halley, Magnetism.

Farber, Paul Lawrence. Distinguished Professor of History of Science, Oregon State University, Corvallis. Author of *The Emergence of Ornithology as a Scientific Discipline* (1982), *Biology: The Network of Life* (with Michael Mix and Keith King, 1992), *The Temptations of Evolutionary Ethics* (1994), and *Finding Order in Nature* (2000). **Essay:** Ornithology.

Fedunkiw, Marianne P. Associated Scholar, Institute for the History and Philosophy of Science and Technology (IHPST), University of Toronto. Contributor to *Notable Twentieth Century Scientists* (1994), *Gale Encyclopedia of Multicultural America* (1995), and *American National Biography* (1997). Writer for the *Globe and Mail*, Toronto, and Chase Producer for the *Discovery Channel*. **Essays:** Harvey, Radiology, Smithsonian Institution.

Figueirõa, Silvia F. de M. Assistant Professor, Institute of Geosciences, Campinas State University, Brazil. Editor of *O conhecimento geológico na América Latina* (with M.M. Lopes, 1990), *Geschichte der Wissenschaften in Lateinamerika* (with M. Guntau, 1992), *Geological Sciences in Latin America* (with M.M. Lopes, 1994), *As ciências geológicas no Brasil* (1997), and *Um olhar sobre o passado* (2000). Contributor to numerous books on geoscientific topics and to many journals including *Interciencia, Quipu, Asclepio, Antilia, Earth Sciences History,* and *Osiris.* **Essay:** Brazil.

Finlay, Mark R. Associate Professor, Armstrong Atlantic State University, Savannah, Georgia. Contributor to *World Views and Scientific Discipline Formation* edited by William R. Woodward and Robert S. Cohen (1991) and *The Science and Culture of Nutrition, 1840–1940* edited by Andrew Cunningham and Harmke Kamminga (1995). Contributor to the journals *Ambix, Bulletin of the History of Medicine, Agricultural History,* and *Georgia Historical Quarterly.* **Essays:** Liebig, Nutrition.

Finn, Bernard S. Curator, Smithsonian Institution, Washington, DC, and Adjunct Professor at the University of Maryland for Seminar on Museums since 1996. Author of *A Retrospective Technology Assessment: Submarine Telegraphy* (with Vary Coates, 1979), "The Museum of Science and Technology" in *The Museum: A Reference Guide* edited by Michael Shapiro (1989), and *The History of Electrical Technology: An Annotated Bibliography* (1991). Editor of *Manifesting Medicine: Bodies and Machines* (with Robert Bud and Helmuth Trischler, 1999). Contributor to the journal *Technology and Culture.* Managing editor of the journal *Isis,* 1963–79, and co-editor of the journal *Artefacts* since 1999. **Essay:** Museums.

Forrester, John. Adviser. Reader in the History and Philosophy of Science, University of Cambridge. Author of *Language and the Origins of Psychoanlysis* (1980; 2nd edition, 2000), *The Seductions of Psychoanalysis* (1990), *Freud's Women* (with Lisa Appignanesi, 1992; 2nd edition, 2000), *Dispatches from the Freud Wars* (1997), and *Truth Games: Lies, Money and Psychoanalyis* (1997). Contributor to *Dismantling Truth* edited by Hilary Lawson and Lisa Appignanesi (1989), *100 Years of Psychoanalysis* edited by André Haynal and Ernst Falzeder (1994), *Fathers, Families and the Outside World* edited by Val Richards and Gillian Wilce (1997), "*Meine . . . alten und dreckigen Götter*" edited by Lydia Marinelli (1998), *Whose Freud?* edited by Peter Brooks and Alex Woloch (2000), and to the journals *Psychoanalysis and History, History Workshop Journal, History of the Human Sciences, Economy and Society,* and *Studies in the History and Philosophy of Science.*

Fox, Robert. Adviser. Professor of History, Faculty of Modern History, Oxford University. Author and editor of numerous publications including *The Caloric Theory of Gases from Lavoisier to Regnault* (1971), *The Culture of Science in France, 1700–1900* (1992), *Science, Industry, and the Social Order in Post-Revolutionary France* (1995), and *Laboratories, Workshops and Sites: Concepts and Practices of Research in Industrial Europe, 1800–1914* (with Anna Guagnini, 1999).

Fuller, Steve. Professor of Sociology, University of Warwick. Author of *Social Epistemology* (1988), *Philosophy of Science and Its Discontents* (1989; 1993), *Philosophy, Rhetoric and the End of Knowledge* (1993), *Science* (1997), *The Governance of Science* (2000), and *Thomas Kuhn* (2000). Founding executive editor of *Social Epistemology: A Journal of Knowledge, Culture, and Policy* since 1987. **Essays:** Discipline, Internalism versus Externalism, Linguistics, Progress, Race, Social Sciences.

Galgano, Michael J. Professor of History and Head of Department, James Madison University, Virginia. **Essay:** Medicine, Disease, and Health.

Galison, Peter L. Adviser. Mallinckrodt Professor of the History of Science, Harvard University. Author of *How Experiments End* (1987) and *Image and Logic* (1997). Editor of *Big Science* (with Brian Hevly, 1992), *The Disunity of Science* (with David

J. Stump, 1996), *Picturing Science, Producing Art* (with Caroline A. Jones, 1998), *The Architecture of Science* (with Emily Thompson, 1999), and *Atmospheric Flight in the Twentieth Century* (with Alex Roland, 2000).

Galle, Karl. Former Postgraduate student, Imperial College, London. **Essay:** Galvani.

Gambaro, Ivana. Researcher and teacher trainer at SSIS, University of Genoa. Author of *Astronomia e tecniche di ricerca nelle lettere di G.B. Riccioli ad A. Kircher* (1989) and *The Development of Electronic Detectors at CERN* (1992). Contributor of articles on the history of accelerators and of elementary partical physics to the journals *Rivista di Storia delle Scienze*, *Quaderni di Storia della Fisica*, and *Giornale di Fisica*. **Essay:** Fermi.

Gavroglu, Kostas. Professor of the History of Science, University of Athens. Author of *Methodological Aspects of the Development of Low Temperature Physics 1881–1957* (with Yorgos Goudaroulis, 1989) and *Fritz London (1900–1954)* (1995). Editor of *Imre Lakatos and Theories of Scientific Change* (with Yorgos Goudaroulis and Pantelis Nikolakopoulos, 1989), *Through Measurement to Knowledge: The Selected Papers of Heike Kamerlingh Onnes, 1853–1926* (with Yorgos Goudaroulis, 1991), *Festschrift for Robert S. Cohen* (with J. Stachel and M. Wartofsky, 1996–97), *Archimedes* (vol. 2, 1998), and "Studies in History and Philosophy of Theoretical Chemistry", special issue of *Studies in the History and Philosophy of Modern Physics* (in preparation). Contributor to several books including *Computers and Mathematical Applications* edited by H. Hargittai (1988), *The Nobel Prizes Winners: Physics* edited by Frank N. Magill (1990), *Problems of Realism* edited by R.S. Cohen (1994), *Philosophers in the Laboratory* edited by V. Mossini (1995), *Scientific Controversies* edited by P. MacHamer, M. Pera and A. Baltas (2000), and to numerous journals including *Historical Studies in the Physical Sciences*, *Annals of Science History*, *Archives for the History of the Exact Sciences*, *Methodology and Science*, *Historia Scientiarum*, *Studies in the History and Philosophy of Science*, *Synthèse*, and *Perspectives in Physics*. **Essays:** Cryogenics, Physical Chemistry, Valence.

Gerdes, Paulus. Professor of Mathematics, Ethnomathematics Research Centre, Maputo, Mozambique. Author of *Une Tradition géométrique en Afrique* (1995), *Lusona: Geometrical Recreations from Africa* (1997), *Ethnomathematik dargestellt am Beispiel der Sona Geometrie* (1997), *Women, Art and Geometry in Southern Africa* (1998), *Geometry from Africa* (1999), and *Le Cercle et le carrée* (2000). Editor of *Mathematics, Education, and Society* (with C. Keitel, A. Bishop and P. Damerow, 1989) and *Explorations in Ethnomathematics and Ethnoscience in Mozambique* (1994). **Essays:** Africa: south of the Sahara, Ethnomathematics.

Gingerich, Owen. Research Professor of Astronomy and History of Science, Harvard-Smithsonian Center for Astrophysics. Author of *The Great Copernicus Chase and Other Adventures in Astronomical History* (1992), *The Eye of Heaven: Ptolemy, Copernicus, Kepler* (1993), *An Annotated Census of Copernicus' De revolutionibus (Nuremberg, 1543) and (Basel, 1566)* (in preparation), and more than 500 technical and educational articles and reviews. Associate editor, *Journal for the History of Astronomy*. **Essay:** Kepler.

Gladstein, Jay E. Independent scholar. Assistant editor of *History of Science Society Newsletter*, 1995–96. **Essay:** Hunter.

Goldbloom, Alexander. Research Associate, the Wellcome Institute for the History of Medicine, London. Author of "A Dance to the Music of Bethlem" *The Welcome Trust* (1997). **Essay:** Quackery.

Goldstein, Catherine. Researcher, Centre National de la Recherche Scientifique, University of Paris-South. Author of *Un théorème de Fermat et ses lecteurs* (1995). Editor of *Mathematical Europe* (with Jeremy Gray and Jim Ritter, 1996). Contributor to *Eléments d'histoire des sciences* edited by M. Serres (1989), *Geschichte der Algebra* edited by E. Scholz (1990), and *Dictionnaire d'histoire et philosophie des sciences* edited by D. Lecourt (1999). Book review co-editor of *Historia Mathematica*. **Essays:** Egypt and Mesopotamia, Fermat, Number Theory.

Gooday, Graeme J.N. Lecturer in History and Philosophy of Science, University of Leeds. Contributor to *The Values of Precision* edited by M. Norton Wise (1995) and to the journals *History of Technology*, *British Journal for the History of Science*, and *History of Universities*. **Essays:** Electrical Instruments, Instrument as Embodied Theory, Measurement, Practice.

Goodfellow, Sarah. Graduate student, Department of History, Pennsylvania State University. Special interests include the history of science, sexuality and modern Europe. **Essay:** The Body.

Goodrum, Matthew R. Staff member, Indiana University Press. Author of "The British Sea Side Studies, 1820–1860" (PhD dissertation, University of Indiana, 1997). **Essay:** Prehistory: archaeology and anthropology.

Gordin, Michael D. Doctoral candidate, Department of the History of Science, Harvard University. Contributor of articles on Soviet biological warfare, standardization, Russian chemistry, and the Russian Academy of Sciences to the journals *Ambix*, *Journal of the History of Biology*, and *Isis*. **Essays:** Atomic Weapons, Dialectical Materialism.

Gorman, Michael John. Fellow, Dibner Institute for the History of Science and Technology, Massachussets Institute of Technology. Contributor to the journals *Mélanges de l'Ecole Française de Rome, Italie et Méditerranée*, and *Perspectives on Science*. Member of the editorial board of the journal *Nuncius*, and organizer of the publication of Athunasius Kircher Correspondence Project on the internet. **Essay:** Jesuits.

Gradmann, Christoph. Research Assistant, Institut für Geschichte Medizin, University of Heidelberg. Author of *Ärztelexikon: Von der Antike bis zum 20. Jahrhundert* (with

Wolfgang U. Eckart, 1995), and editor of *Die Medizin und der Erste Weltkrieg* (with Wolfgang U. Eckart, 1996). Contributor to the journals *Populäre historische Biographien in der Weimarer Republik*, *Medizin Gesellschaft und Geschichte*, and *Tractrix: Yearbook for the History of Science, Medicine, Technology and Mathematics* (1993). **Essay:** Koch.

Graham, Sally S. Assistant Librarian, Wood Library-Museum of Anesthesiology, Park Ridge, Illinois, and Behavioural Medicine Therapist, Good Shepard Hospital, Barrington, Illinois. Contributor to *ASA Newsletter*. **Essay:** Adler.

Graves Smith, Helen P. Assistant to the Curators, Collection and Research Branch, National Museum of Science and Technology, Ottawa. Research interests include science education and popularization of the sciences. **Essay:** Women in Science: chemical sciences.

Gray, Jeremy. Adviser. Senior Lecturer in Mathematics, Open University, and Affiliated Research Scholar, Department of History and Philosophy of Science, University of Cambridge. Special interest includes the history of mathematics in the 19th and 20th centuries, with a particular interest in complex function theory and geometry, and also on issues in the philosophy and social significance of mathematics. Author of several books including *The Hilbert Challenge* (2000) and *Linear Differential Equations and Group Theory from Riemann to Poincaré* (2nd edition, 2000). Editor of *The Symbolic Universe* (1999). **Essays:** Algebra, Axiomatics, Function, Geometry, Group Theory.

Green Musselman, Elizabeth. Assistant Professor of History, Southwestern University. Author of "Science as a Landed Activity" in *Surveying the Record: North American Exploration to 1900* edited by Edward L. Carter (1999) and contributor of articles on John Dalton and John Herschel to *History of Science* and *British Journal for the History of Science*. **Essay:** Vision.

Gross, Joe. Independent Scholar, Oxford. **Essay:** Leibniz.

Hackmann, Willem. Senior Assistant Keeper, Museum of the History of Science, Oxford. Author of *Apples to Atoms: Portraits of Scientists from Newton to Rutherford* (exhibition catalogue, 1983). Editor of *Learning, Language, and Invention* (with Anthony John Turner, 1994), *Catalogue of Pneumatical, Magnetical, and Electrical Instruments* (1995). **Essay:** Scientific Instruments: general works.

Haigh, Elizabeth V. Professor of History, Saint Mary's University, Halifax, Nova Scotia. Author of *Xavier Bichat and the Medical Theory of the Eighteenth Century* (1984). Contributor to *L'Homme et la Nature* (1985) and *British Medicine in an Age of Reform* edited by William French and Andrew Weir (1990). **Essays:** Bichat, Lysenko, Russia, Vitalism.

Hall, Lesley A. Senior Assistant Archivist (Outreach), Wellcome Library for the History and Understanding of Medicine, London. Author of *Hidden Anxieties: Male Sexuality 1900–1950* (1991), *The Facts of Life: The Creation of Sexual Knowledge in Britain, 1650–1950* (with Roy Porter, 1995), and *Sex, Gender and Social Change in Britain since 1880* (2000). Editor of *Sexual Cultures in Europe: National Histories* (with Franz X. Eder and Gert Hekma, 1999), *Sexual Cultures in Europe: Themes in Sexuality* (with Franz X. Eder and Gert Hekma, 1999), and *Sex, Sin and Suffering* (with Roger Davidson, in preparation). Contributor to the journals *Social History of Medicine*, *Journal of Contemporary History*, *Journal of History of Sexuality*, *Women's History Notebooks*, *Genitourinary Medicine*, *Social History*, and *Women's History Review*. Fellow of the Royal Historical Society. **Essays:** Malthusianism, Venereal Disease, Women in Science: medicine.

Hamm, Ernst P. Assistant Professor, Science and Technology Studies, Atkinson Faculty of Liberal and Professional Studies, York University, Toronto. Contributor of articles on 18th- and early 19th-century science in Germany to the journals *History of Science*, *Earth Sciences History*, and *Studies in History and Philosophy of Science*. Currently researching Goethe, geology, and the culture of science in classical Weimar. **Essays:** Enlightenment, Romanticism.

Handel, Kai. Postdoctoral Research Fellow, Institut für Wissenschafts- und Technikgeschichte, TU Bergakademie Freiberg. Author of "Research Styles in Particle and Solid State Theory" in *The Emergence of Modern Physics* edited by F. Bevilacqua, D. Hoffmann, and R. Stuewer (1995) and *Anfänge der Halbleiterforschung* (in preparation). Contributor to the journals *Berichte zur Wissenschaftgeschichte* and *Wechelwirkung*. General Secretary of the Georg-Agricola-Society for the History of Science and Technology from 2001. **Essay:** Solid State Physics.

Haraway, Donna J. Adviser. Professor, History of Consciousness Department, University of California at Santa Cruz. Author of *Crystals, Fabrics, and Fields* (1976), *Primate Visions* (1989), *Simians, Cyborgs, and Women* (1990), *Manifesto Cyborg* (1995), and *Modest Witness* (1997). Contributor to *Cultural Studies* edited by Larry Grossberg, Cary Nelson and Paula Treichler (1992), *Feminists Theorize the Political* edited by Joan Scott and Judith Butler (1992), *The Sociology of Gender* edited by Sarah Franklin (1997), *Cyborgs and Citadels* edited by Gary Downey and Joseph Dumit (1998), *Primate Encounters* edited by Shirley Strum and Linda Fedigan (2000), and to numerous journals.

Hardcastle, Gary L. Associate Professor, Department of Philosophy, University of Wisconsin, Stevens Point. Contributor to the journals *Philosophy of Science*, *History of Psychology*, *Southern Journal of Philosophy*, *Studies in the History and Philosophy of Science*. **Essay:** Paradigm.

Hardy, Anne. Lecturer in the History of Modern Medicine, Wellcome Trust Centre for the History of Medicine, University College, London. Author of *The Epidemic Streets: Infectious Disease and the Rise of Preventative Medicine, 1856–1900* (1993), *Prevention and Cure* (with Lise Wilkinson, 2000), and *Health and Medicine in Britain since 1860* (in preparation). Contributor to numerous journals. **Essays:** Epidemics, Tuberculosis.

Harris, Benjamin. Professor of Psychology, University of Wisconsin, Parkside. Contributor to *In Shadows of the Past* (1984), *The Rise of Experimentation in American Psychology* (1988), and to the journals *American Psychologist, Isis, History of Psychology, Journal of the History of the Behavioral Sciences, History of Psychiatry, Bulletin of the History of Medicine, Rethinking Marxism, Psychology of Women Quarterly,* and *Journal of Social Issues.* Co-founder of *Forum for History of Human Science* and Fellow of American Psychological Society. **Essay:** Psychology.

Hashimoto, Keizo. Professor of History and Technology of Science, Kansai University, Japan. Author of *Hsu Kuang-ch'i and Astronomical Reform* (1988) and co-editor of *East Asian Science* (with Catherine Jami and Lowell Skar, 1995). **Essays:** China: astronomy and mathematics, Seki.

Hayward, Rhodri Lloyd. Research Fellow, Wellcome Unit for the History of Medicine, University of East Anglia. Author of articles on the psychologization of religious inspiration in *Prophecy* edited by Bertrand Taithe and Tim Thornton (1997), on the biopolitics of Arthur Keith and Morley Roberts in *Regenerating England* edited by Lawrence and Mayer (2000), on the history of British cybernetics in *Psychology in Britain* edited by G. Bunn, Lovie and Richards (in preparation), and on Victorian dream interpretation in *History Workshop Journal.* Contributor of book reviews to *British Journal of the History of Science, Journal of the History of the Neurosciences, History of Psychiatry, Journal of the History of Behavioural Sciences,* and *Social History of Medicine.* **Essays:** Charcot, Foucault, Human Sciences, Knowledge and Power, Neurosciences.

Heidelberger, Michael. Institüt für Philosophie, Humbolt-Universität, Berlin. Editor of *Probability and Conceptual Change in Scientific Thought* (with Lorenz Kruger, 1981). **Essays:** Experiments, Psychophysics.

Helman, Cecil G. Associate Professor, Department of Human Sciences, Brunel University, and Senior Lecturer, Department of Primary Care and Population Sciences, Royal Free and University College Medical School, London. Honorary Research Fellow, Department of Anthropology, University College London. Author of *Body Myths* (1991) and *Culture, Health and Illness* (1994, 4th edition, 2000). Contributor to the journals *Anthropology and Medicine, British Medical Journal, Social Science and Medicine, British Anthropology and Medicine,* and *Lancet.* International corresponding editor, *Medical Anthropology Quarterly* since 1986; international consulting editor, *Culture, Medicine and Psychiatry,* 1984–93; member of the editorial boards of *Anthropology and Medicine,* 1997–2000, and *Medical Humanities* since 1999. **Essay:** Traditional Medicine.

Hempstead, Colin A. Visiting Research Fellow, formerly Reader in the History of Technology, School of Law, Arts and Humanities, University of Teeside, Middlesbrough. Author of *A Victorian Scientist and Engineer: Fleeming Jenkin and the Birth of Electrical Engineering* (with Gillian Cookson, 2000). Contributor to several journals including *History of Technology, Engineering Science and Education Journal,* and *History of Technology.* **Essays:** Electrical Engineering, Telegraphy.

Heng, John. Assistant Professor, Department of Philosophy and Religious Studies, King's College, University of Western Ontario. Author of "Ethical Issues Relating to Consent in Providing Treatment and Care" in *Developmental Disabilities in Ontario* edited by Ivan Brown and Maire Percy (1999). Contributor to the journals *Canadian Philosophical Reviews* and *Quaderni di Niccolò Stenone.* **Essay:** Humanism.

Henry, John. Senior Lecturer in the Science Studies Unit, University of Edinburgh. Author of *The Scientific Revolution and the Origins of Modern Science* (1997), contributor to *The Books of Nature and Scripture* edited by James E. Force and Richard H. Popkin (1994), *Hugh Miller and the Controversies of Victorian Science* edited by Michael Shortland (1996), and *Journal of the History of Ideas.* **Essays:** Atomism, Hermeticism, Occult Sciences, Religion and Science: general works, Religion and Science: Renaissance, Vacuum.

Hentschel, Klaus. Assistant Professor, Institute for the History of Science, University of Göttingen. Author of *Interpretations and Misinterpretations of Einstein's Theory of Relativity* (1990), *The Einstein Tower* (1997), and *On the Interplay of Experimentation, Instrument-Making, and Theory Construction* (1998). Editor of *Physics and National Socialism* (1996), *Heinrich Kayser's Autobiography Lebenserinnerungen* (with M. Doerries, 1996), *Letter Diary of Max Planck, Carl Runge, Bernhard Karsten and Adolf Leopold* (with R. Tobies, 1999), and *The Role of Visual Representations in Astronomy* (with A. Wittmann, 2000). Contributor to the journals *Studies in the History of Science/Modern Physics, Historical Studies in the Physical Sciences, Annals of Science, Physics in Perspective,* and *Journal for the History of Astronomy.* **Essays:** Bohr, Heisenberg, Mach, Michelson, Planck, Rowland, Spectroscopy.

Hessenbruch, Arne. Research Fellow, Dibner Institute for the History of Science and Technology, Massachusetts Institute of Technology. Co-author of *Sir William Siemens* (1993) and co-editor of *The Correspondence of Charles Darwin* (vols 10 and 11, 1997–98). Contributor to *Geschlechterverhältnisse in Medizin, Naturwissenschaft und Technik* edited by Christoph Meinel and Monika Renneberg (1996), *The Sciences in the European Periphery during the Enlightenment* edited by Kostas Gavroglu (1999), *Wissenschaft und Öffentlichkeit in Berlin um 1900* edited by Constantin Goschler (2000), *Radioactivity: History and Culture, 1896–1930s* edited by John Krige and Christine Blondel (2000), and to the journals *Social Studies of Science, Archive for the History of Exact Sciences, VEST: Tidskrift för Vetenskapsstudier, British Journal for the History of Science, Annals of Science, Isis, Bulletin of the Social History Society, Social History of Medicine, European Journal of Physics,* and *Physikalische Blätter.* **Essays:** Astronomy: general works, Brahe, Cartography, Clocks, Denmark, Franklin, Gauss, History of Science: general works, Metrology, Oppenheimer, Ostwald, Physical and Human Geography; Priestley, Rational Mechanics (with Simon Schaffer), Rittenhouse, Rockefeller Foundation (with Carla Keirns), Standarization, Technology (with Henry Nielsen), Time.

Heymann, Matthias. Researcher, Munich Centre for the History of Science and Technology. Author of *Development Prospects for Emission Inventories and Atmospherical Transport and Chemistry Models (DEMO)* (with Rainer Friedrich and Alfred Trukenmüller, 1993), *Die Geschichte der Windenergienutzung 1890–1990* (1995), and contributor to *Umwelt, Technik und Politik* edited by Helmut Maier (1999), and *Proceedings of the EUROTRAC-2 Symposium 1998* edited by Patricia M. Borrell and Peter Borrell (1999). Contributor to *NTM, Centaurus, Technology and Culture,* and *Technikgeschichte.* **Essay:** Wind Turbines.

Hill, Katherine. Visiting Research Lecturer in Science and Technology, University College of Cape Breton, Sydney, Nova Scotia, and doctoral candidate, University of Toronto. Author of articles on the history of mathematics in *Notes and Records of the Royal Society* and *Proceedings of the Canadian Society for the History & Philosophy of Mathematics.* **Essay:** Napier.

Hillam, Christine. Deceased. Former Honorary Research Fellow, Department of Clinical Dental Sciences, University of Liverpool. Author of *Brass Plate and Brazen Impudence: Dental Practice in the Provinces, 1755–1855* (1991). Editor of *The Roots of Dentistry* (1990) and *Dental Practice in Europe in the Late Eighteenth Century* (in preparation). Contributor to the journals *British Dental Journal, Medical Historian, Community Dental Health, Dental Historian, Pharmaceutical History, Orvosi Hetilap,* and *Bulletin of History of Medicine.* **Essay:** Dentistry.

Hills, Richard L. Honorary Reader, History of Science and Technology Group, Institute of Science and Technology, University of Manchester. Author of several books including *Power in the Industrial Revolution* (1970), *Richard Arkwright and Cotton Spinning* (1973), *Beyer, Peacock: Locomotive Builders to the World* (1982), *Papermaking in Britain, 1488–1988* (1988), *Power from Steam* (1989), and *Power from Wind* (1994). Author of numerous articles on related subjects, has contributed to several journals including *History of Technology, Transactions of the Newcomen Society,* and *Technology and Culture.* Director of the North Western Museum of Science and Industry, Manchester, 1968–85. **Essays:** Engines: steam, Mills and Waterwheels, Watt.

Hodgkiss, Andrew. Consultant Liaison Psychiatrist, St Thomas' Hospital, and Honorary Senior Lecturer in Liaison Psychiatry, GKT Medical School, King's College, University of London. Author of *From Lesion to Metaphor: Chronic Pain in British, French and German Medical Writings, 1800–1914* (in preparation). Contributor to *A History of Clinical Psychiatry* edited by German E. Berrios and Roy Porter (1995). Former assistant editor and clinical book reviews editor of the journal *History of Psychiatry.* **Essay:** Pain.

Hoecker-Drysdale, Susan. Former Professor of Sociology (retired), Concordia University, Montreal. Author of *Harriet Martineau: First Woman Sociologist* (1992), *Harriet Martineau: Theoretical and Methodological Perspectives* (with Michael R. Hill, in preparation). Contributor to *Despite the Odds: Essays on Canadian Women and Science* edited by Marianne

Gosztonyi Ainley (1990), *Creative Couples in the Sciences* edited by Helena Pycior, Nancy Slack and Pnina Abir-Am (1996), *Frauen in der Soziologie: Neun Portrats* edited by Claudia Honegger and Theresa Wobbe (1998), *Blackwell Companion to Major Social Theorists* edited by George Ritzer (2000) and to the journals *Women's Writing: The Victorian Period* and *Le Revue.* **Essays:** Alienation, Martineau.

Hoffmann, Dieter. Research Scholar at the Max Planck Institute for History of Science, Berlin. Author and editor of many books and articles including *Erwin Schrödinger* (1985), *Robert Havemann* (1990), *Ernst Mach* (1991), *Robert Havemann* (1991), *Operation Epsilon* (1993), *Gustav Magnus und sein Haus* (1995), *The Emergence of Modern Physics* (1997), *Science under Sozialism* (1999), and *Who Was Who in the GDR* (2000). Curator of "Physikalische Blätter" (Physics in Perspective) and chairman of the History of Physics Group of the German Physical Society. **Essays:** Helmholtz, Laue, Meitner, Nernst, Physikalisch-Technische Reichsanstalt, Schrödinger, Siemens.

Hollister-Short, Graham. Honorary Lecturer in History of Technology, Centre for the History of Science, Technology and Medicine, Imperial College, London. Author of *Discovering Wrought Iron* (1970). Contributor to the *Oxford Companion to the Decorative Arts* (1975) and to the journals *The Connoisseur, History of Technology, Industrial Archaeology, British Journal for the History of Science, Polhem, Quaderni Storici, Der Anschnitt, Arbor, Antique Collector, Icon,* and *Vierteljahrschrift für Sozial – und Wirtschaftesgeschichte.* Editor of *History of Technology* since 1990, and editor of *Icon,* 1995–98. **Essays:** Agricola, Mechanization.

Holloway, S.W.F. Formerly, Senior Lecturer, University of Leicester. Author of *Royal Pharmaceutical Society of Great Britain, 1841–1991* (1991). Contributor to *Drugs and Narcotics in History* edited by Roy Porter and M. Teich (1995). **Essay:** Pharmacy.

Holton, Gerald. Mallinckrodt Professor of Physics and Professor of History of Science Emeritus, Harvard University. Author of *Thematic Origins of Scientific Thought* (1973; revised edition, 1988), *Albert Einstein: Historical and Cultural Perspectives* (1982), *Foundations of Modern Physical Science* (1985), *The Advancement of Science, and Its Burdens* (1986), *Einstein, History and Other Passions* (with Gerhard Sonnert, 1995), *Who Succeeds in Science? The Gender Dimension* (with Gerhard Sonnert, 1995), and *Gender Differences in Science Careers: The Project Access Study* (1995). Founding editor of *Daedalus, The Journal of the American Academy of Arts and Sciences,* and Founder of *Science, Technology and Human Values.* Member of the editorial committee, *The Collected Papers of Albert Einstein.* **Essay:** Themata.

Home, R.W. Professor of History and Philosophy of Science, University of Melbourne. Author of *Aepinus's Essay on the Theory of Electricity and Magnetism* (with P.J. Connor, 1979), *The History of Classical Physics: A Selected, Annotated Bibliography* (1984), and *Electricity and Experimental Physics in Eighteenth-Century Europe* (1992). Editor of *Australian*

Science in the Making (1988), *Physics in Australia to 1945: Bibliography and Biographical Register* (1990), and *International Science and National Scientific Identity: Australia between Britain and America* (with Sally Gregory Kohlstedt, 1991); co-editor of *Regardfully Yours: Selected Correspondence of Ferdinand von Mueller* (1998–). Editor of *Historical Records of Australian Science*, general editor of *Australasian Studies in History and Philosophy of Science*, and founder, Australian Science Archives Project (now Australian Science and Technology Heritage Centre). **Essay:** Australia and New Zealand.

Honner, John. Formerly, Professor of Philosophy at the United Faculty of Theology, Queen's College, University of Melbourne. Author of *The Description of Nature: Niels Bohr and the Philosophy of Quantum Physics* (1988). Contributor to numerous collections and journals including *Compass*, *Studies in the Philosophy of Science*, *Studies in the History and Philosophy of Science*, *Zygon*, *Australian Journal of Chemistry*, *Heythrop Journal*, *Eureka Street*, and *Pacifica: Australian Theological Studies*. **Essay:** Atomic Theory.

Hoppe, Brigitte. Professor of the History of Science, Institut für Geschichte der Naturwissenschaften, Ludwig-Maximilians-Universität, Munich. Author of *Das Kräuterbuch des Hieronymus Bock: Wissenschaftshistorische Untersuchung* (1969), *Biologie, Wissenschaft von der belebten Materie von der Antike zur Neuzeit* (1976), and *Aus der Frühzeit der Chemischen Konstitutionsforschung: die Tropanalkaloide Atropin und Cocain in Wissenschaft und Wirtschaft* (1979). Editor of *Biology Integrating Scientific Fundamentals* (1979) and *Fundamental Changes in Cellular Biology in the 20th Century* (with C. Galperin and S.F. Gilbert, 1999). Contributor to many journals including *Sudhoffs Archiv*, *Medizinhistorisches Journal* and *Pharmazeutische Zeitung*. Corresponding member of the International Academy of History of Sciences, Paris, and member of the management board of several journals. **Essays:** Baer, Botany: general works, Drugs, Herbalism, Mendel.

Hopwood, Nick. University Assistant Lecturer, Department of History and Philosophy of Science, University of Cambridge. Contributor of articles on socialist science to *History Workshop Journal* and *History of Science*, and on late 19th-century embryology to *Isis* and the *Bulletin of the History of Medicine*. **Essay:** Haeckel.

Horden, Peregrine. Wellcome Trust Research Lecturer in the History of Medicine, Department of History, Royal Holloway College, University of London. Author of *Man and Environment in the Mediterranean World* (1996) and *The Corrupting Sea: A Study of Mediterranean History* (with Nicholas Purcell, 2000). Editor of *Freud and the Humanities* (1985), *The Locus of Care* (with Richard Smith, 1998), *Music as Medicine* (2000), and *The Year 1000: Medical Practice at the End of the First Millennium* (with Emilie Savage-Smith, 2000). **Essay:** Plague.

Horrocks, Sally. Lecturer, Department of Economic and Social History, Leicester University. Secretary of the British Society for the History of Science and review editor of the *Economic History Review*. Research interests include modern British business history with particular emphasis on research and development. **Essays:** Research and Development, Women in Science: technology.

Horwitz, Steven. Associate Professor of Economics, St Lawrence University in Canton, New York. Author of *Monetary Evolution: Free Banking, and Economic Order* (1992) and *Microfoundations and Macroeconomics: An Austrian Perspective* (2000). Editor of *Advances in Austrian Economics* (with Peter J. Boettke, 1997). Contributor to *The Elgar Companion to Austrian Economics* edited by Peter J. Boettke (1994), *Methodological Issues in the Subjectivist Paradigm: Essays in Memory of Ludwig Lachmann* edited by Roger Koppl and Gary Mongiovi (1998), *Socialism: Not Half Right but All Wrong* (in preparation), and to the journals *Review of Austrian Economics*, *History of Political Economy*, *Journal of the History of Economic Thought*, and *Southern Economic Journal*. **Essay:** Hayek.

Howell, Joel D. Professor, Department of Internal Medicine and Department of History, University of Michigan. Author of *Technology and American Medical Practice, 1880–1930* (1988), *Medical Lives and Scientific Medicine at Michigan, 1891–1969* (1993), *Technology in the Hospital: Transforming Patient Care in the Early Twentieth Century* (1995), and of articles on the history of medical technology. **Essay:** Cardiology.

Hudson, Robert G. Center for Interdisciplinary Studies, Virginia Polytechnic Institute. Contributor of articles on the epistemology of observation, Carnap, experimental reasoning, and early quantum theory to the journals *Studies in History and Philosophy of Science*, *Philosophy of Science*, *Erkenntnis*, *History of Philosophy Quarterly*, and *Synthese*. **Essay:** Observation.

Huff, Toby E. Chancellor Professor of Sociology, University of Massachusetts, Dartmouth. Author of *Max Weber and the Methodology of the Social Sciences* (1984) and *The Rise of Early Modern Science: Islam, China and the West* (1993). Editor of *On the Roads to Modernity: Conscience, Science and Civilizations (Selected Writings by Benjamin Nelson)* (1981) and *Max Weber and Islam* (with Wolfgang Schluchter, 1999). **Essays:** Arabic Science, Religion and Science: Islam.

Hughes, Jeff. Lecturer, Centre for the History of Science, Technology and Medicine, University of Manchester. Contributor to *The Historiography of Contemporary Science and Technology*, edited by Thomas Soderqvist (1997), *The Invisible Industrialists: Manufactures and the Construction of Scientific Knowledge* edited by Jean-Paul Gaudillere and Ilana Löwy (1998), *Cold War, Hot Science: Applied Research in Britain's Defence Laboratories 1945–1990* edited by Robert Bud and Philip Gummett (1999), and to the journal *History and Technology*. **Essay:** Nuclear Physics.

Hume, Brad D. Lecturer, Department of History, University of Dayton. Author of "The Romantic and the Technical in Early Nineteenth-Century American Exploration" in *Surveying the Record: North American Exploration to 1900* edited by Edward Carter (1999). Contributor to the *Journal of the*

History of Sexuality. Managing and editorial assistant for *Discourse: A Journal for Studies in Media and Culture,* 1985–87. **Essay:** Anthropometry.

Hunter, Michael. Professor of History, Birkbeck College, University of London. Author of *Science and Society in Restoration England* (1981, 1992), *The Royal Society and Its Fellows 1660–1700* (1982; 2nd edition, 1994), *Establishing the New Science* (1989), *Science and the Shape of Orthodoxy* (1995), and *Robert Boyle, 1627–91* (2000). Editor of *Robert Boyle Reconsidered* (1994), *Robert Boyle by Himself and His Friends* (1994), *Archives of the Scientific Revolution* (1998), *The Works of Robert Boyle* (with Edward B. Davis, 1999–2000), and *The Correspondence of Robert Boyle* (with Antonio Clericuzio, in preparation). **Essay:** Boyle.

Israel, Paul. Managing Editor, Book Edition, Thomas A. Edison Papers, Rutgers University. Author of *From Machine Shop to Industrial Laboratory: Telegraphy and the Changing Context of American Invention, 1830–1920* (1992), *Edison's Electric Light* (with Robert Friedel, 1986), and *Edison: A Life of Invention* (1998). Co-editor of *The Papers of Thomas A. Edison* (vols 1–4, 1989–99). **Essay:** Edison (with Robert Rosenberg)

Jackson, Myles W. Assistant Professor, Department of History, Willamette University, Salem, Oregon. Contributor to the journals *Social Studies of Science, Studies in History and Philosophy of Science, Science and Context,* and *Journal of the History of Biology.* **Essays:** Fraunhofer, Germanophone Areas, Goethe.

James, Frank A.J.L. Reader in History of Science, The Royal Institution, London. Editor of *Faraday Rediscovered* (with David Goodling, 1985), *The Development of the Laboratory: Essays on the Place of Experiment in Industrial Civilization* (1989), *The Correspondence of Michael Faraday* (1991–), *Renaissance and Revolution* (with J.V. Field, 1993), and *Semaphores to Shortwaves* (1998). Editor of the *Newsletter* of the British Society for the History of Science since 1989, and editor of *History of Technology,* 1989–96. **Essays:** British Association for the Advancement of Science, Davy, Electricity, Faraday, Royal Institution.

Johns, Adrian. Associate Professor, Division of Humanities and Social Sciences, California Institute of Technology, Pasadena. Author of *The Nature of the Book: Print and Knowledge* (1998). **Essay:** Reading Culture and Science.

Johnson, Stephen B. Assistant Professor, Department of Space Studies, University of North Dakota. Author of *The Secret of Apollo* (in preparation) and *The United States Air Force and the Culture of Innovation, 1945–1965* (in preparation). Contributor to *American National Biography* (1999), *Symposium on Developing US Launch Capability* edited by Roger Launius (in preparation), *Systems, Experts, and Computers* edited by Thomas P. Hughes and Agatha C. Hughes (in preparation), and to the journals *History of Technology, Technology and Culture,* and *Space Times.* Editor of *Quest: The History of Spaceflight Quarterly.* **Essay:** Heat.

Johnston, Stephen. Assistant Keeper, Museum of the History of Science, University of Oxford. Author of *The Geometry of War, 1500–1750* (with Jim Bennett, 1996) and *Solomon's House in Oxford: New Finds from the First Museum* (with Jim Bennett and A.V. Simcock, 2000). Associate editor, *Instruments of Science* edited by Robert Bud and Deborah Jean Warner (1998). **Essays:** Calculating Devices, Mathematical Instruments.

Jonsson, Fredrik. Faculty Member, Department of Physics, Royal Institute of Technology, Sweden. **Essays:** Cartesianism, Descartes.

Junker, Thomas. Fakultät für Biologie, Lehrstuhl für Ethik in den Biowissenschaften, University of Tübingen. Author of *Darwinismus und Botanik* (1989). Editor of *Charles Darwin's Correspondence with German Naturalists* (with Marsha Richmond, 1996), *Ethik der Biowissenschaften* (with Eve-Marie Engels and Michael Weingarten, 1998), *Die Entstehung der Synthetischen Theorie: Beiträge zur Geschichte der Evolutionsbiologie in Deutschland 1930–1950* (vol.2, with Eve-Marie Engels, 1999), and *Repräsentationsformen in den biologischen Wissensahften* (vol.3, with others, 1999). Contributor to *Die Rezeption von Evolutionstheorien im 19. Jahrhundert* edited by Eve-Marie Engels (1995), *Geschichte der Biologie* edited by Ilse Jahn (1998), and *In Evolutionsbiologie von Darwin bis heute* edited by Rainer Brömer, Uwe Hossfeld, and Nicolaas A. Rupke (2000). Contributor to the journals *Sudhoffs Archiv, History and Philosophy of the Life Sciences, Journal of the History of Biology, Isis,* and *Theory in Biosciences.* **Essays:** Darwinism, Darwinism in Germany.

Kaiser, David. Assistant Professor, Program in Science, Technology, and Society, and Lecturer, Department of Physics, Massachusetts Institute of Technology. Author of *Drawing Theories Apart: The Dispersion of Feynman Diagrams in Postwar Physics* (in preparation). Editor of *Reading Einstein's Relativities* (with Peter Galison and Michael Gordin, in preparation) and *American Science and the Long War, 1940–1990* (with Peter Galison and Michael Gordin, in preparation). Contributor to *Niels Bohr in Contemporary Philosophy* edited by Jan Faye and Henry Folse (1994), *Conceptual Foundations of Quantum Field Theory* edited by Tian Yu Cao (1998), and *Le Vide: l'autre côte de la matière* edited by Simon Diner and Edgard Gunzig (with Sam Schweber, in preparation). Contributor of articles to numerous journals including *Representations, Science in Context, Studies in History and Philosophy of Modern Physics, British Journal for the History of Science,* and *Studies in History and Philosophy of Science.* **Essays:** Feynman, Physics: 20th century.

Kant, Horst. Research Scholar, Max Planck Institute for the History of Science, Berlin. Author of *Alfred Nobel* (1983), *J. Robert Oppenheimer* (1985), and *Abram Fedorovic Ioffe* (1989). Editor of *Fixpunkte: Wissenschaft in der Stadt und der Region* (1996). Contributor to *Wissenschaft in Berlin* edited by Hubert Laitko (1987), *Geschichte der Physik: Ein Abriss* edited by W. Schreier (1988), *Naturwissenschaft und Technik in der Geschichte* edited by H. Albrecht (1993), *Die Kaiser-Wilhelm /Max-Planck-Gesellschaft und ihre Institute* edited by

Bernhard vom Brocke and Hubert Laitko (1996), and *Harenberg Lexikon der Nobelpreistrager* (1998). **Essay:** Kaiser-Wilhelm-Gesellschaft.

Keirns, Carla. Doctoral candidate, University of Pennsylvania. Visiting Curator, US National Library of Medicine exhibition *Breath of Life: Historical Perspectives on Asthma*. Author of "Is There a Chemist in the House?" *Chemical Heritage* (1998) and "Seeing Patterns" *Journal of the History of Biology* (1999). **Essays:** Africa: health and healing, Evolutionary Synthesis, Health, Mortality, and Social Class, Rockefeller Foundation (with Arne Hessenbruch).

Kellman, Jordan. Instructor, History Department and Honors College, Louisiana State University. **Essay:** Buffon.

Kinsella, William J. Assistant Professor, Department of Communication, Lewis and Clark College, Portland, Oregon. Author of *Communication and the Construction of Knowledge in a Scientific Community: An Interpretive Study of the Princeton University Plasma Physics Laboratory* (dissertation, 1996), "From Big Science to Postmodern Science" in *Technical Expertise and Public Decisions: Proceedings of the 1996 International Symposium on Technology and Society* edited by C. Andrews (1996), and "Theorizing Nuclear Communication" in *Proceedings: Fifth Biennial Conference on Communication and Environment* edited by B. Short (in preparation). Contributor to the journals *Management Communication Quarterly* and *New Jersey Journal of Communication*. Member of the editorial board of *New Jersey Journal of Communication*. **Essay:** Big Science.

Knight, David. Professor, Department of Philosophy, University of Durham, England. Author of numerous works including *The Age of Science* (1988), *Humphry Davy: Science and Power* (1992), *Ideas in Chemistry* (1995), *Science in the Romantic Era* (1996). Editor of the *British Journal for the History of Science*, 1982–88, *The Development of Chemistry* (1998), and editor of Blackwell Science Biographies series. **Essay:** Chemistry.

Kragh, Helge. Professor of the History of Science, University of Aarhus, Denmark. Author of *Dirac: A Scientific Biography* (1990), *Cosmology and Controversy: The Development of Two Theories of the Universe* (1996), and *Quantum Generations: A History of Physics in the Twentieth Century* (1999). **Essays:** Big Bang Theory, Cosmology.

Kreuzman, Henry B. Assistant Professor of Philosophy, College of Wooster, Ohio. Currently working on a book on the concept of rationality in epistemology and philosophy of science. Contributor to *Proceedings of the Ohio Philosophical Association*. **Essays:** Fact, Philosophy of Science.

Kühne, Andreas. Research Fellow, Ludwig Maximilians University, Munich. Co-editor of the Nicolaus-Copernicus-Gesamtausgabe. Contributor to the journals *Nuncius* and *Berichte zur Wissenschaftsgeschichte*. **Essays:** Copernicanism, Copernicus.

Kuklick, Henrika. Adviser. Professor and Chair, Department of History and Sociology of Science, University of Pennsylvania. Author of *The Savage Within: The Social History of British Anthropology, 1885–1945* (1991). Editor of *Science in the Field* (with Robert E. Kohler, 1996) and *A New History of Anthropology* (in preparation). Contributor to *Colonial Situations* edited by George W. Stocking Jr (1991) and *Cambridge and the Torres Strait* edited by Anita Herle and Sandra Rouse (1998), and of articles on the history of anthropology and other human sciences to the journals *American Ethnologist*, *Annual Review of Sociology*, *Journal of the History of the Behavioral Sciences*, *Sociological Quarterly*, and *Theory and Society*.

Larsen, Kristine. Assistant Professor of Astronomy and Physics, Central Connecticut State University, New Britain. Contributor to *Jewish Women in America: An Historical Encyclopedia*, edited by Paula E. Hyman and Deborah Dash Moore (1997), *Historical Dictionary of Women's Education in the United States*, edited by Linda Eisenmann (1998), and to the journals *Mercury*, *American Journal of Physics*, and *Physical Review*. **Essay:** Women in Science: astronomy.

Lenoir, Timothy. Adviser. Professor of History and Chair of the Program in History and Philosophy of Science, Stanford University. Author of numerous books and articles including *The Strategy of Life: Teleology and Mechanics in Nineteenth Century German Biology* (1982), *Politik im Tempel der Wissenschaft: Forschung und Machtausübung im deutschen Kaiserreich* (1992), *Instituting Science: The Cultural Production of Scientific Disciplines* (1997), and editor of *Inscribing Science: Scientific Texts and the Materiality of Communication* (1998).

Lesney, Mark S. Adjunct Professor, Science and Technology in International Affairs Program, Georgetown University, Washington, DC; Adjunct Professor, Science and Technology Studies Program, Virginia Polytechnic Institute, Falls Church. Senior Editor, American Chemical Society special publications: *Today's Chemist at Work* and *Modern Drug Discovery*. **Essays:** Bateson, Genetics: general works.

Lewenstein, Bruce V. Associate Professor, Departments of Communication and Science and Technology Studies, Cornell University. Author of *The Establishment of American Science* (with Sally Gregory Kohlstedt and Michael M. Sokal, 1999). Editor of *When Science Meets the Public* (1992) and *Cornell Cold Fusion Archive Funding Aid* (1994). Contributor to the journals *Osiris*, *Social Studies of Science*, and *Science Technology and Human Values*. Editor of *Public Understanding of Science*, former managing editor of *Osiris*, and former member of AAAS Committee on Public Understanding of Science and Technology. **Essay:** Popularization.

Lindberg, David C. Adviser. Hilldale Professor of the History of Science, University of Wisconsin, Madison. Author of *Theories and Vision from Al-Kindi to Kepler* (1976), *Roger Bacon's Philosophy of Nature* (1983), *Studies in the History of Medieval Optics* (1983), and *The Beginnings of Western Science* (1992). Editor of *Science in the Middle Ages* (1978),

God and Nature (with Ronald L. Numbers, 1986), and *Reappraisals of the Scientific Revolution* (with Robert S. Westman, 1990). General editor (with Ronald L. Numbers) of the forthcoming *Cambridge History of Science*, editorial board member of *Isis*, *Osiris*, and the *British Journal for the History of Science*, and president of the History of Science Society, 1994–95. **Essay:** Religion and Science: Medieval.

Lindee, M. Susan. Associate Professor, University of Pennsylvania. Author of *Suffering Made Real: American Science and the Survivors at Hiroshima* (1994), and *The DNA Mystique: The Gene as a Cultural Icon* (with Dorothy Nelkin, 1995). Contributor to the journals *Osiris*, *Bulletin of the History of Medicine*, and *Journal of the History of Biology*. **Essay:** Genetics: post-DNA.

Lloyd, Sir Geoffrey. Adviser. Emeritus Professor of Ancient Philosophy and Science, Department of Classics, University of Cambridge. Author of several books including most recently *Adversaries and Authorities* (1996) and *Aristotelian Explorations* (1996). Editor of *Le Savoir grec* (with Jacques Brunschwig, 1996).

López-Beltrán, Carlos. Researcher, Instituto de Investigaciones Filosóficas, Universidad Nacional Autónoma de México, Mexico City. Contributor to the journals *Studies in History and Philosophy of Science*, and *Revue d'Histoire des Sciences*. Contributor to the *Oxford Spanish Dictionary*. **Essay:** Heredity.

Low, Morris F. Senior Lecturer, Department of Asian Languages and Studies, University of Queensland, Brisbane. Author of *Science, Technology and Society in Contemporary Japan* (with Shigeru Nakayama and Hitoshi Yoshioka, 1999). Editor of *Japanese Science, Technology and Economic Growth Down Under* (with Helen Marriott, 1996), *Beyond Joseph Needham: Science, Technology and Medicine in East and Southeast Asia* (1998), and *The Politics of Knowledge: Science and Evolution in Asia and the Pacific* (with Christine Dureau, 1999). Contributor to *Scientists and the State* edited by Etel Solingen (1994), *Nationality and Nationalism in East Asia* edited by Alan J.K. Sanders (1996), *Technological Change* edited by Robert Fox (1996), *Universities and the Global Knowledge Economy* edited by Henry Eztkowitz and Loet Leydesdorff (1997), and to the journals *Annals of Science*, *Asian Studies Review*, *Higher Education*, *Historia Scientiarum*, *Historical Studies in the Physical and Biological Sciences*, *Humanities Research*, *Studies in History and Philosophy of Science*, *Isis*, *Japanese Studies*, *Progress in Theoretical Physics Supplement*, and *Social Studies of Science*. President of the Japanese Studies Association of Australia, 1995–97. **Essays:** Japan: general works, Japan: medicine, Japan: technology.

Löwy, Ilana. Adviser. Senior Research Fellow, INSERM (Institut National de la Santé et de la Recherche Medicale), France. Author of *The Polish School of Philosophy of Medicine* (1990), *Between Bench and Bedside: Science, Healing and Interleukin-2 in a Cancer Ward* (1996), *Medical Acts and Medical Facts: The Polish Tradition of Practice* (2000), and *Moustiques et modernité: la lutte contre la fièvre jaune au*

Brésil, 1900–1950 (in preparation). Editor of *The Invisible Industrialist* (with Jean-Paul Gaudillière, 1998), *L'Invention du naturel: les sciences et la fabrication du masculin et du feminin* (with D. Gardey, 2000), *The Rockefeller Foundation and Biomedical Sciences*, special issue of *Studies in History and Philosophy of Biological and Biomedical Sciences* (with P. Zylberman, 2000), and *Transmission: Diseases between Heredity and Infection* (with Jean-Paul Gaudillière, in preparation). Contributor to *Science in the Twentieth Century* edited by John Krige and Dominique Pèstre (1997), *Molecularization of Biology and Medicine* edited by Soraya de Chadarevian and Harmke Kamminga (1998), *Greater Than the Parts: Holism in Medicine, 1920–1950* edited by Christopher Lawrence and George Weisz (1998), and *Living and Working with New Medical Technologies* edited by Margaret Lock, Alan Young and Alberto Cambrosio (in preparation). Contributor to the journals *Studies in the History and Philosophy of Science*, *Annales HSS*, *Science in Context*, *Journal of the History of Biology*, and *Gender and History*.

McClellan III, James E. Professor, History of Science, Stevens Institute of Technology, Hoboken, New Jersey. Author of *Science Reorganized: Scientific Societies in the Eighteenth Century* (1985), *Colonialism and Science: Saint Domingue in the Old Regime* (1992), *Science and Technology in World History* (with Harold Dorn, 1999), and contributor to the journals *Isis*, *Dix-Huitième Siecle*, *Annals of Science*, and *Revue d'Histoire des Sciences*. **Essays:** Académie des Sciences, Colonialism and Science.

McOuat, Gordon. Director, History of Science and Technology Programme, and Associate Professor, Contemporary Studies Programme, University of King's College/ Dalhousie University, Halifax, Nova Scotia. Contributor to *Science and Society* edited by David McGee *et al.* (1989) and *Terra Borealis* edited by Micheline Manseau (1999), and to the journals *Annals of Science*, *British Journal for the History of Science*, and *Studies in History and Philosophy of Science*. **Essays:** Anthropology, Virchow.

Maehle, Andreas-Holger. Professor of History of Medicine and Medical Ethics, Department of Philosophy, University of Durham. Author of *Johann Jakob Wepfer (1620–1695) als Toxikologe* (1987), *Kritik und Verteidigung des Tierversuchs* (1992), and *Drugs on Trial* (1999). Contributor to the journals *Gesnerus*, *Medical History*, *Medizinhistorisches Journal*, *Clio Medica*, *Medizin, Gesellschaft und Geschichte*, and *Würzburger Medizinhistorische Mitteilungen*. Member of the editorial staff of *Medizinhistorisches Journal* and of the editorial board of *Medical History*. **Essay:** Toxicology.

Magnello, M. Eileen. Staff Member, Wellcome Unit for the History of Science, London. Contributor of articles on Karl Pearson to the journals *Annals of Science*, *History of Science*, and *British Journal for the History of Science*. **Essays:** Biometrics, Galton, Pearson.

Maier, Helmut. Faculty Member, Ruhr-Univeristät Bochum. Editor of *Technische Intelligenz und "Kulturfaktor" Technik* (with Burkard Dietz and Michael Fressner, 1996), *Umwelt, Technik und Politik* (1999). **Essay:** Materials Science.

Main, Roderick. Visiting Research Fellow, Centre for Psychoanalytic Studies, University of Essex. Editor of *Jung on Synchronicity and the Paranormal* (1997). Contributor to the journal *Harvest: Journal for Jungian Studies*. **Essay:** Jung.

Malley, Marjorie. Instructor, Rogers State College, Oklahoma. Contributor to several journals including *Isis*, *Archive for History of Exact Sciences*, and *Annals of Science*. **Essays:** Curie, Hahn, Radioactivity, Rutherford.

Marks, Lara. Senior Lecturer in the History of Science, Technology and Medicine, Imperial College, London. Author of *Metropolitan Maternity: Maternal and Infant Welfare Services in Early Twentieth Century London* (1996) and *Sexual Chemistry: An International History of the Contraceptive Pill* (in preparation). Editor of *Women and Children First: International Maternal and Infant Welfare 1870–1950* (with Valerie Fildes and Hilary Marland, 1992) and *Migrants, Minorities and Health* (with Michael Worboys, 1997). Contributor to *Narrative Based Medicine: Dialogue and Discourse in Clinical Practice* edited by T. Greenhalgh and B. Hurwitz (with S. Hogarth, 1998), *Molecularising Biology and Medicine* edited by Harmke Kamminga and Soraya De Chadarevian (1998), *Women and Modern Medicine* edited by A. Hardy and L. Conrad (in preparation), *Localizing and Globalizing Technologies* edited by A.R. Saetnan, N. Oudshoorn, and M. Kirejczyk (in preparation), *Remedies and Healing Cultures in Britain and the Netherlands in the Twentieth Century* edited by M. Gijswijt-Hofstra and T. Tansey (in preparation), and to the journals *Social Science and Medicine*, *British Journal of Sexual Medicine*, *History and Technology*, *Social History of Medicine*, *Immigrants and Minorities*, *Twentieth Century British History*, *Economic History Review*, and *Oral History Journal*. **Essay:** Birth Control.

Marsden, Ben. Lecturer in Cultural History, University of Aberdeen. Author of *Engineering and Empire: Science and Technology in Nineteenth-Century Britain* (with Crosbie Smith, in preparation), contributor to *Making Space for Science* edited by Crosbie Smith and Jon Agar (1998), and to the journals *History of Science* and *British Journal for the History of Science*. **Essays:** Energy, Music and Science: antiquity to 1700, Music and Science: since 1700.

Martin, R.N.D. Independent scholar. Author of *Pierre Duhem: Philosophy and History in the Work of a Believing Physicist* (1991). Editor and translator of *Discourse on Metaphysics and Related Writings* by Leibniz (with Stuart Brown, 1988). Contributor to *Christianisme et Science* (1989) and to the journals *Annals of Science*, *History of Science*, and *Synthèse*. **Essay:** Duhem.

Masseran, Anne. Independent scholar, Paris. **Essay:** Muséum National D'Histoire Naturelle (with Claude Schnitter and Philippe Chavot).

Matthews, J. Rosser. Lecturer, Department of the History of Medicine, University of Wisconsin-Madison. Author of "Probabilistic and Statistical Methods in Medicine" in *Com-panion Encyclopedia of the History and Philosophy of the Mathematical Sciences* edited by I. Grattan-Guinness (1994) and *Quantification and the Quest for Medical Certainty* (1995). Contributor of articles on quantification in medicine and health care policy to the journals *Bulletin of the History of Medicine* and *Journal of Health Politics, Policy and Law*. **Essay:** Statistics.

Mauskopf, Seymour H. Professor of History, Duke University, Durham, North Carolina. Author of several books including *Crystals and Compounds: Molecular Structure and Composition in Nineteenth-Century French Science* (1976) and *The Elusive Science: Origins of Experimental Psychical Research 1915–1940* (with Michael R. McVaugh, 1980); editor of *The Reception of Unconventional Science by the Scientific Community* (1979); and *Chemical Sciences in the Modern World* (1993). **Essay:** Chemical Revolution.

Mehrtens, Herbert. Adviser. Professor of Modern History, Technische Universität Braunschweig. Author of *Die Entstehung der Verbandstheorie* (1979) and *Moderne Sprache Mathematik* (1990). Editor of *Social History of Nineteenth Century Mathematics* (with Ivo Schneider, 1981) and *Normalität und Abweichung* (with Werner Sohn, 1990).

Mendelsohn, Everett. Adviser. Professor of the History of Science, Harvard University. Founder and former editor of *Journal of the History of Biology* and past president of the International Council for Science Policy Studies. Editor of *Science, Technology and the Military* (with Merritt Roe Smith and Peter Weingart, 1988), *Technology, Pessimism and Postmodernism* (1993), *Biology as Society, Society as Biology: Metaphors* (with Sabine Maaens and Peter Weingart, 1995), and *The Practices of Human Genetics* (with Michael Fortun, 1999).

Miller, David Philip. Head, School of Science and Technology Studies, University of New South Wales. Editor of *Visions of Empire* (with Peter Hanns Reill, 1996). Contributor to *The Politics and Rhetoric of Scientific Method* edited by John A. Schuster and Richard R. Yeo (1986), *Lord Bute* edited by Karl W. Schweizer (1988), *Visions of Empire* edited by David Philip Miller and Peter H. Reill (1996), and of articles on Joseph Banks, the 18th-century Royal Society, and the physical sciences in early 19th-century Britain to the journals *British Journal for the History of Science*, *History of Science*, *Osiris*, and *Notes and Records of the Royal Society of London*. **Essays:** Herschel, Journals, Societies.

Mills, Eric L. Professor of History of Science and of Oceanography, Dalhousie University, Halifax, Canada. Author of *Biological Oceanography: An Early History 1870–1960* (1989), *The Scripps Institution* (1993), and of articles on biological oceanography and the history of science. **Essay:** Oceanography.

Morus, Iwan Rhys. Lecturer, School of Anthropological Studies, Queen's University of Belfast. Author of *Frankenstein's Children: Electricity, Exhibition and Experiment in Early Nineteenth-Century London* (1998). **Essay:** Performance.

Moulin, A.M. Director of Research, Centre National de la Recherche Scientifique, Paris. Author of *Le Dernier Langage de la médecine: histoire de l'immunologie de Pasteur au Sida* (1991), editor of *Science and Empires* (with Patrick Petitjean and Catherine Jami, 1992), and contributor to the journals *Research and Immunology*, *History and Philosophy of Life Sciences*, *La Recherche*, and *Transplantation Reviews*. **Essays:** Immunology, Medical Instruments (with Kim Pelis), Pasteur (with Kim Pelis).

Neushul, Peter. Visiting Researcher, University of California at Santa Barbara. Contributor to *Magill's Survey of Science: Space Exploration Series* edited by Frank N. Magill (1989), *Seaweed Cultivation for Renewable Resources* edited by K.T. Bird and P.H. Benson (1987), *Great Events from History: Science and Technology Series* edited by Frank N. Magill (1991), and *Magill's Survey of Science: Applied Science series* edited by Frank N. Magill (1993–98). Contributor to the journals *Technology and Culture*, and *Discovery*. **Essays:** Fleming, Florey.

Nicholls, Phillip A. Senior Lecturer in Sociology, Staffordshire University. Author of *Homeopathy and the Medical Profession* (1988). Contributor to *Alternative Medicine in Britain* edited by Mike Saks (1992), *The Homoeopathy Discussion Group* edited by Helle Johannessen, Soren Gosvig Oleson and Jorgen Ostergard Anderson (1995), *A Hearing for Homoeopathy* edited by Soren Gosvig Oleson and Erling Hog (1996), *Laienpraktiker und haretische Mediziner: Grosbritannien, Weltgeschichte der Homoopathie* edited by Martin Dinges (with Peter Morrell, 1996), and *Central Aspects of Methodology in Research on Alternative Therapies* edited by Soren Gosvig Oleson et al. (1997). Associate editor of the *Collins Dictionary of Sociology* (2nd edition, 1995). **Essay:** Homoeopathy.

Nielsen, Henry. Faculty Member, Aarhus University, Denmark. Editor of *Made in Denmark: Nye Studier i dansk teknologi-historie* (with Hans Buhl, 1994), and *Neighbouring Nobel: Denmark and the Nobel Prize* (with Keld Nielsen, in preparation). **Essay:** Technology (with Arne Hessenbruch).

Nightingale, Simon A. Independent scholar. **Essays:** Agriculture, Chemical Analysis.

Noakes, Richard. Leverhulme Postdoctoral Research Fellow, Division of History and Philosophy of Science, School of Philosophy, University of Leeds, and Centre for Nineteeth-Century Studies, Department of English Literature, University of Sheffield. Editor of *From Newton to Hawking: A History of Cambridge University's Lucasian Professors of Mathematics* (with Kevin C. Knox, in preparation). Contributor of articles on Victorian telegraphy and spiritualism to the *British Journal for the History of Science* and on early 19th-century electricity to *Victorian Studies*. **Essays:** Aether, Spiritualism.

Nuttall, Derek. Former college lecturer, and Honorary Correspondent to the National Printing Heritage Trust. Author of *A History of Printing in Chester from 1658 to 1965* (1969), *A Brief History of Platen Presses* (1973). Editor of *The Book Trade in Cheshire to 1850: A Directory* (1992) and *Cheshire History*. **Essay:** Printing.

O'Donovan, Perry. Editor, Darwin Correspondence project, Cambridge University Library. **Essay:** Botany: Britain.

Oldroyd, David. Honorary Visiting Professor, School of Science and Technology Studies, University of New South Wales. Author of *Darwinian Impacts* (1980), *The Arch of Knowledge* (1986), *The Highlands Controversy* (1990), *Thinking about the Earth* (1996), and *Sciences of the Earth* (1998). Co-editor of *The Wider Domain of Evolutionary Thought* (with Ian Langham, 1983). Member of the editorial boards of *Annals of Science*, *Social Epistemology*, *Australian Studies in History and Philosophy of Science*, and *Studies in the History and Philosophy of the Earth Sciences*. Secretary-General of the International Commission on the History of Geological Sciences. **Essays:** Geology, Lyell.

Packer, Joan Garrett. Head, Reference Department, Elihu Burritt Library, Central Connecticut State University, New Britain. Author of *Margaret Drabble: An Annotated Bibliography* (1988), *Rebecca West: An Annotated Bibliography* (1991). Contributor to *Notable Women in the Life Sciences* edited by Benjamin F. Shearer and Barbara S. Shearer (1996) and *Notable Women in the Physical Sciences* edited by Benjamin F. Shearer and Barbara S. Shearer (1997). **Essays:** Cuvier, United States: women in science.

Palló, Gábor. Senior Researcher, Institute of Philosophy, Hungarian Academy of Science. Has written many articles on the early radioctivity research in Hungary and on the migration of Hungarian scientists. **Essay:** Hungary.

Palmer, William. Independent scholar. **Essay:** Scheele.

Pang, Alex Soojung-Kim. Lecturer, University of California, Davis. Contributor to *Louis I. Kahn: In the Realm of Architecture* edited by David B. Brownlee and David G. DeLong (1991). Book review editor for *HSPS*. **Essay:** Scientific Illustration.

Pelis, Kim. Assistant Professor, Johns Hopkins University. Author of articles on blood, Edward Jenner, and Charles Nicolle in *Bulletin for the History of Medicine*, *Annals of Science*, *Vox Sanguinis*, and *Journal of the Royal College of Physicians of London*. **Essays:** Medical Instruments (with A.M. Moulin), Pasteur (with A.M. Moulin).

Pèstre, Dominique. Adviser. Director of Research, Centre Alexandre Koyré, École des Hautes Études en Sciences Sociales, Paris. Author of *Physique et physiciens en France, 1818–1940* (1984) and editor of *Science in the Twentieth Century* (with John Krige, 1997).

Petrina, Stephen. Assistant Professor, Department of Curriculum Studies, University of British Columbia. Contributor to *International Journal of Technology and Design Education* (1998) and *Journal of Technology Education* (1998). **Essay:** Scientification of Education.

Pfeffer, Naomi. Senior Lecturer, School of Community Health, Psychology and Social Work, University of North London. Author of *The Experience of Infertility* (with Anne Woollett, 1983), *The Stork and the Syringe: A Political History of Reproductive Medicine* (1993). Member of the editorial advisory board for *Journal of Medical Ethics*. **Essay:** Reproductive Medicine.

Pickstone, John. Adviser. Director of the Centre for the History of Science, University of Manchester. Author of several books and articles including *Medicine and Industrial Society: A History of Hospital Development in Manchester and Its Region, 1752–1946* (1985). Editor of *Medical Innovations in Historical Perspective* (1992). Contributor to numerous journals including *History of Science, Social Analysis,* and *British Journal for the History of Science.*

Pimentel, Juan. Faculty Member, Department of the History of Science, CSIC, Madrid. **Essays:** Expeditions (with Michael T. Bravo), Latin America, Spain.

Pinch, Trevor J. Professor, Department of Science and Technology Studies, Cornell University. Author of *The Golem: What Everyone Should Know about Science* (with Harry Collins, 1993; 2nd edition, 1998), and *Confronting Nature: The Sociology of Solar Neutrino Detection* (1986). Editor of *The Social Construction of Technological Systems* (with Wiebe E. Bijker and Thomas P. Hughes, 1987) and *The Uses of Experiment* (with Simon Schaffer and David Gooding, 1989). Contributor to the journals *Social Studies of Science, Science Technology and Human Values,* and *Technology and Culture.* Series editor of *Inside Technology* for MIT Press. **Essays:** Rhetoric, Sociology of Science.

Porter, Dorothy. Professor of the History of Science and Medicine, Birkbeck College, University of London. Author of *In Sickness and in Health: The British Experience, 1650–1850* (with Roy Porter, 1988), *Patient's Progress: Doctors and Doctoring in Eighteenth-Century England* (with Roy Porter, 1989), and *Health, Civilisation and the State: A History of Public Health from Ancient to Modern Times* (1999). **Essay:** Public Health.

Porter, Roy. Adviser. Professor of the Social History of Medicine, Wellcome Institute for the History of Medicine, London. Author of numerous books including *Mind Forg'd Manacles: Madness in England from the Restoration to the Regency* (1987), *A Social History of Madness* (1987), *In Sickness and in Health: The British Experience, 1650–1850* (with Dorothy Porter, 1988), *London: A Social History* (1994), *The Facts of Life: The Creation of Sexual Knowledge in Britain, 1650–1950* (with Lesley A. Hall, 1995), *The Greatest Benefit to Mankind: A Medical History of Humanity* (1997), *Gout: The Patrician Malady* (with G.S. Rousseau, 1998), and *Quacks: Fakers and Charlatans in English Medicine* (2000). Editor of many books including most recently *Companion Encyclopedia of the History of Medicine* (with W.F. Bynum, 1993), *The Hutchinson Dictionary of Scientific Biography* (1994; revised edition, 2000), *The Cambridge Illustrated History of Medicine* (1996), *Cultures of Psychiatry and Mental Health Care in Postwar Britain and the Netherlands* (with Marijke Gijswijt-Hofstra, 1998). **Essays:** Hysteria, Madness, Psychiatry.

Porter, Theodore M. Adviser. Professor of History, University of California at Los Angeles. Author of *The Rise of Statistical Thinking, 1820–1900* (1986), *The Empire of Chance: How Probability Changed Science and Everyday Life* (with Gerd Gigerenzer et al., 1989), and *Trust in Numbers: The Pursuit of Objectivity in Science and Public Life* (1995). Editor of *Modern Social Sciences* (with Dorothy Ross, in preparation). **Essays:** Quantification, Quételet.

Power, Michael. P.D. Leake Professor of Accounting and Director, Centre for the Analysis of Risk and Regulation, London School of Economics. Author of *The Audit Society: Rituals of Verification* (1997). Editor of *Accounting and Science* (1996). Member of the editorial boards of the journals *Accounting* and *Organisations and Society.* **Essay:** Accountancy.

Proctor, Robert N. Distinguished Professor of the History of Science, Pennsylvania State University. Author of *Racial Hygiene: Medicine under the Nazis* (1988), *Value-Free Science? Purity and Power in Modern Knowledge* (1991), *Cancer Wars: How Politics Shapes What We Know and Don't Know about Cancer* (1995), and *The Nazi War on Cancer* (1999). Contributor of an article on the role of historians of science as expert witnesses in US courts to the journal *Nature.* **Essay:** Cancer.

Pumfrey, Stephen. Lecturer, Department of History, University of Lancaster. Author of *Science Culture and Popular Belief in Renaissance Europe* (1991), contributor to several books including *Planetary Astronomy from the Renaissance to the Rise of Astrophysics* edited by René Taton and Chris Wilson (1989), *L'Étude sociale des sciences* edited by Dominique Pestre (1992), and *Paracelsus* edited by Ole Peter Grell (1996) and to numerous journals including *History of Science, Physis, Annals of Science,* and *British Journal for the History of Science.* **Essay:** Gilbert.

Raj, Kapil. Independent scholar, Paris. Contributor to *Science and Empire* edited by Deepak Kumar (1991) and to the journals *Annales, Revue de Synthèse,* and *History and Technology.* **Essay:** India: general works.

Raman, Sujantha. Graduate School of Public and International Affairs. University of Pittsburgh. Contributor to *Nuclear Technology Debates* edited by Regis Cabral (1992). **Essays:** Information, Skill, Work.

Rauschenbach, Beatrice. Scientific Assistant, Bavarian Academy of Sciences, Munich. Board member of, and author of several articles in, the *Neues Bibel-Lexicon,* 1989–95, and the historical critical edition of the Bavarian Academy of sciences, *Schelling.* **Essays:** Comte, Gesellschaft Deutscher Naturforscher und Ärzte, Kant, Plato, Positivism, Schelling, Women in Science: life sciences.

Ray, Hillary. Lawyer. Committee Member of the New South Wales Young Lawyers and member of the International Committee of Jurists. **Essay:** Natural Law.

Regneri, Günter. Independent scholar, Berlin. **Essay:** Neumann.

Remane, Horst. Fachbereich Physik, Fachgruppe Geschichte der Naturwissenschaften und der Technik, Martin-Luther-Universität, Halle. Author of *Emil Fischer* (1984), *Wissenschaftsgeschichte en miniature: Neun Kapitel aus der Geschichte der Mathematik und der Naturwissenschaften* (with H. Wussing, 1989) and *Chemie an der Universitaet Halle* (with C. Schmoll, 1997). Editor of *Richard Willstaetter im Briefwechsel mit Emil Fischer 1895–1919* (with W. Schweitzer) and *Briefwechsel von Emil Fischer mit Svante Arrhenius aus den Jahren 1902 bis 1919* (with L. Tansjö, 2000). **Essays:** Baeyer, Fischer.

Renneberg, Monika. Institut für Wissenschafts-und Technikgeschichte, Frieberg. Author of *Grundung und Ausbau des GUSS: Forschungszentrums Geesthacht* (1995), and editor of *Science, Technology and National Socialism* (with Mark Walker, 1994). **Essay:** Third Reich and Science.

Reynolds, Brian R. Postgraduate student, Institute for the History and Philosophy of Science, University of Toronto. Assistant Curator, Canadian Automotive Museum, Ottawa, and former archivist, National Museum of Science and Technology, Ottawa. **Essays:** Automobiles, Engines: turbo.

Rodine, Craig. Knowledge Media Institute, Open University, Milton Keynes, Buckinghamshire. **Essay:** Mersenne.

Romano, Terrie M. Faculty Member, History of Medicine Program, Queen's University, Ontario. Contributor to *Bulletin of the History of Medicine* (1997). **Essay:** Veterinary Science.

Rosenberg, Robert. Director, Thomas A. Edison Papers, Rutgers University. Editor of *The Papers of Thomas A. Edison*, vols 1–4 (1989–94), *Thomas A. Edison Papers* microfilm (1985–); *Thomas A. Edison Papers* electronic (1997–). **Essay:** Edison (with Paul Israel).

Rothenberg, Marc. Smithsonian Institution, Washington, DC. Editor of *Joseph Henry* vols 3–7 (1979–95), *A Scientist in American Life: Essays and Lectures of Joseph Henry* (1980), *The History of Science and Technology in the United States: A Critical and Selective Bibliography* vol. 1 (1982) and vol. 2 (1993), and *Scientific Colonialism: A Cross-Cultural Comparision* (with Nathan Reingold, 1987). **Essay:** United States: general works.

Rothman, Harry. Research Professor of Science and Technology Policy, University of the West of England, Bristol. Editor of *Workshop on Social, Political and Ethical Issues in Human Genome Research* (double issue of *Genetic Engineer and Biotechnologist*) (with Peter Glasner, 1995) and *Genetic Imaginations: Ethical, Legal and Social Issues in Human Genome Research* (with Peter Glasner, 1998). Contributor to *Instruments of Science* (1996) and to the journals *Genetic Engineer and Biotechnologist, Biomedical Technology, Industrial Biotechnology International, Nature,* and *Science and Public Policy.* Editor of the journal *Technology Analysis and Strategic Management.* **Essays:** Genetic Engineering, Human Genome Project.

Rupke, Nicolaas A. Professor of the History of Science and Director, Institut für Wissenschaftsgeschichte, Georg-August-Universität Göttingen, Germany. Author of *The Great Chain of History* (1983) and *Richard Owen* (1994). Editor of *Vivisection in Historical Perspective* (1987), *Science, Politics and the Public Good* (1988), *Ideas and Ideologies* (1994), and *Medical Geography in Historical Perspective* (2000). **Essays:** Continental Drift, Functionalism and Structuralism: biological sciences, Humboldt.

Rüting, Torsten. Research Fellow, Institut für Geschichte der Naturwissenschaften, Mathematik und Technik, Universität Hamburg. Contributor to *Darwin und Darwinismus: Ergebnisse eines Symposiums* (1995), and *Learning and Memory* edited by Norbert Elsner and Randolf Menzel (1995). Contributor to the journals *Naturwissenschaft und Technik,* and *Biologisches Zentralblatt.* **Essay:** Pavlov.

Saks, Mike. Dean of Faculty of Health and Community Studies, De Montfort University, Leicester. Author of *Professions and the Public Interest: Medical Power, Altruism and Alternative Medicine* (1995). Editor of *Alternative Medicine in Britain* (1992) and *Health Professions and the State in Europe* (with T. Johnson and G. Larkin, 1995). Contributor to *Challenging Medicine* edited by Jonathan Gabe, David Kelleher and Gareth Williams (1994), *Medicine: A History of Healing* edited by Roy Porter (1997), *Modernity, Medicine and Health* edited by Graham Scambler and Paul Higgs (1998), *Religion, Health and Suffering* edited by John R. Hinnells and Roy Porter (1999), and to the journals *Complementary Therapies in Nursing and Midwifery, European Journal of Oriental Medicine,* and *Journal of Interprofessional Care.* **Essays:** Complementary Medicine, Holistic Medicine.

Salazar, Christine F. Affiliated Research Scholar, Department of History and Philosophy of Science, University of Cambridge. Translator of "Historical Consciousness in the German Romantic Naturforschung" (from the German) in *Romanticism and the Sciences* edited by Andrew Cunningham and Nicholas Jardine (1990), *Philip Melanchthon: Orations on Philosophy and Education* edited by Sachiko Kusakawa (1999), and "Tradition and Truth: Forms of Philosophical-Scientific Historiography in Galen's *De Placitis*" in *Ancient Histories of Medicine* edited by Philip J. Van der Eijk (1999). Contributor to *Classical Quarterly* and *Sudhoffs Archiv.* **Essays:** Galen, Greece: medicine, Hippocrates.

Samuel, Andrew M.M. Postgraduate student, Lancaster University. Contributor to the journal *Technoscience.* **Essay:** Representation.

Sánchez-Ron, José M. Professor of History of Science, Department of Theoretical Physics, Universidad Autonoma de Madrid. Author of *El poder de la ciencia* (1992), editor of

National Military Establishments and the Advancement of Science and Technology (with Paul Forman, 1996), and contributor to the journal *Osiris*. **Essay:** Maxwell.

Schabas, Margaret. Adviser. Professor, Department of Philosophy, York University, Toronto. Author of *A World Ruled by Number* (1990), and contributor to the journals *Isis*, *Dialogue*, *Studies in the History and Philosophy of Science*, *History of Political Economy*, and *Victorian Studies*. Member of the editorial board for the journals *History of Political Economy* and *Economics and Philosophy*. **Essays:** Mill, Political Economy, Smith.

Schaffer, Simon. Adviser. Reader in History and Philosophy of Science, University of Cambridge. Author of *Leviathan and the Air-Pump* (with Steven Shapin , 1985), and editor of *Robert Hooke* (with Michael Hunter, 1989), *The Uses of Experiment* (with David Gooding and Trevor J. Pinch, 1989), and *The Sciences in Enlightened Europe* (with William Clark and Jan Golinski, 1999). **Essays:** Electromagnetism, Rational Mechanics (with Arne Hessenbruch).

Schiebinger, Londa. Edwin E. Sparks Professor of the History of Science, Pennsylvania State University. Author of several books including *Nature's Body: Gender in the Making of Modern Science* (1993), *Has Feminism Changed Science?* (1999), and the article "Why Mammals Are Called Mammals: Gender Politics in Eighteenth-Century Natural History" *American Historical Review* (1993). Editor of *Feminism and the Body* (2000). **Essays:** Gender: general works, Gender and Sex (with Alice D. Dreger), Women in Science: general works.

Schirrmacher, Arne. Research Fellow, Munich Centre for the History of Science and Technology. Author of "The Establishment of Quantum Physics in Göttingen 1900–24" in *History of Modern Physics* edited by H. Kragh, P. Marage, and G. Vanpaemel (2000). **Essay:** Hilbert.

Schmaus, Warren. Professor of Philosophy, Illinois Institute of Technology, Chicago. Author of *Durkheim's Philosophy of Science and the Sociology of Knowledge: Creating an Intellectual Niche* (1994), and contributor to the journals *Sociological Perspectives*, *Social Epistemology*, *Philosophy of the Social Sciences*, *Studies in History and Philosophy of Science*, *Philosophy of Science*, *History and Theory*, *Economics and Philosophy*, and *Science, Technology and Human Values*. Associate editor of *Perspectives on the Professions*, 1981–87. **Essay:** Durkheim.

Schnitter, Claude. Independent scholar, Paris. Contributor to *Revue d'Histoire des Sciences* and *Histoire des Sciences Médicales*. **Essay:** Muséum National d'Histoire Naturelle (with Anne Massaran and Philippe Chavot).

Schroeder-Gudehus, Brigitte. Professor, Department of Political Science, University of Montreal. Author of *Les Scientifiques et la paix: la communauté scientifique pendant l'entre-deux-guerres* (1978), and *Les Fastes du progrès: le guide des expositions universelles, 1851–1992* (1992). Contributor to *Fair Representations: World's Fairs in the Modern World* edited by Robert W. Rydell and Nancy E. Gwinn (1994), and to the journals *Relations Internationales*, and *Les Congrès Scientifiques Internationaux*. **Essays:** Global Organizations, International Science.

Secord, Jim. Adviser. Reader in History and Philosophy of Science, University of Cambridge. Author of *Controversy in Victorian Geology* (1986) and *Victorian Sensation: The Extraordinary Publication, Reception, and Secret Authorship of Vestiges of the Natural History of Creation* (2000). Editor of *Cultures of Natural History* (with Nicholas Jardine and E.C. Spary, 1996).

Segre, Michael. Teacher of the history of science, University of Munich. Author of *In the Wake of Galileo* (1991). **Essays:** Galilean School, Galilei.

Selin, Helaine. Science Librarian, Hampshire College, Amherst, Massachusetts. Editor of *Science across Cultures: An Annotated Bibliography of Books on Non-Western Science, Technology and Medicine* (1992), *Encyclopedia of the History of Science, Technology, and Medicine in Non-Western Cultures* (1997), *Astronomy across Cultures* (2000), and *Mathematics across Cultures* (2000). Contributor of articles on non-Western science to *Science Teacher and College Teaching*. **Essay:** Astronomy: non-European.

Shinn, Terry. Director of Research, Centre National de la Récherche Scientifique, Paris. Author of *Savior scientifique et pouvoir social: École Polytechnique* (1980); editor of *Expository Science: Forms and Functions of Popularisation* (with Richard Whitley, 1985), *Denationalizing Science* (with Elisabeth Crawford and Sverker Sörlin, 1993), and *Science and Technology in a Developing World* (with Jack Spaapen and Venni Krishna, 1997). Contributor to the journals *Sociology of the Sciences Yearbook*, *Social Studies of Science*, *Science Studies*, *Social Science Information*, *Revue Française de Sociologie*, and *Minerva*. **Essay:** France: scientific and technical education.

Siegmund-Schultze, Reinhard. Professor for History of Mathematics, Agder University College, Kristiansand, Norway. Author of *Mathematische Berichterstattung in Hitlerdeutschland* (1993), *Mathematiker auf der Flucht vor Hitler* (1998), and *Terror and Exile* (with J. Bruening and D. Ferus, 1998). Editor of *K. Weierstrass: Ausgewaehlte Kapitel aus der Funktionenlehre* (1998). Contributor to *World Views and Scientific Discipline Formation* edited by William R. Woodward and Robert S. Cohen (1991), *Companion Encyclopedia of the History and Philosophy of the Mathematical Sciences* edited by I. Grattan-Guinness (1994), *Geschichte der Analysis* edited by H.N. Jahnke (1999), *Science under Socialism* edited by Kristie Macrakis and Dieter Hoffmann (1999), and to the journals *Archive for History of Exact Sciences*, *Historia Mathematica*, *Geschichte und Gesellschaft*, and *Naturwissenschaft, Geschichte, Medizin*. **Essay:** Von Neumann.

Sismondo, Sergio. Assistant Professor, Department of Philosophy, Queen's University, Kingston, Ontario. Author of *Science Without Myth: On Constructions, Reality, and Social Know-*

ledge (1996), and contributor to *Perspectives on Science*, *Metaphilosophy*, and *Social Studies of Science*. **Essays**: Bacon, Metaphor, Objectivity.

Slater, Leo B. Director, Historical Services, Chemical Heritage Foundation. Contributor to the journals *Historical Studies in the Physical and Biological Sciences*, *Bulletin for the History of Chemistry*, *International Journal for Peptide and Protein Research*, *Isis*, and *Chemical Heritage Magazine*. **Essays**: Organic Chemistry (with Tracy L. Sullivan), Plastics and Polymers (with Tracy L. Sullivan).

Sloan, A.W. Deceased. Former Professor of Physiology, University of Cape Town, South Africa. Author of *Physiology for Students and Teachers of Physical Education* (1970), *The Physiological Basis of Physiotheraphy* (1979), *Man in Extreme Environments* (1979), *English Medicine in the Seventeenth Century* (1996), and of articles on plague epidemics, and William Harvey, Thomas Sydenham, Claude Bernard, and François Magendie. **Essays**: Bernard, Sydenham.

Smith, David N. Associate Professor, Department of Sociology, University of Kansas. Author of *Marx's Kapital for Beginners* (1982) and *Orwell for Beginners* (1984). Editor of *Patriarchy and Property: The Ethnological Notebooks of Karl Marx* (in preparation), *The Classical Theory Reader* (in preparation), and *Ernest Manheim* (vol. 2, in preparation). Contributor to *Ethnohistorische Wege und Lehrjahre eines Philosophen* edited by Dittmar Schorkowitz (1995), *The Seductiveness of Jewish Myth* edited by S. Daniel Breslauer (1997), *The Coming Age of Scarcity: Preventing Mass Death and Genocide in the 21st Century* edited by Isidor Wallimann and Michael Dobkowski (1998), *After the Science Wars* edited by Keith Ashman and Philip Baringer (in preparation), *On the Edge of Scarcity* edited by Isidor Wallimann and Michael Dobkowski (in preparation), and to the journals *American Psychologist*, *Sociological Theory*, *Sociological Quarterly*, *Social Thought and Research*, *Sociological Inquiry*, *Humanity and Society*, *Etudes Durkheimiennes/Durkheimian Studies*, and *Current Perspectives in Social Theory*. **Essays**: Capitalism and Science, Marx.

Somsen, Geert. Assistant Professor, History Department, Faculty of Arts and Culture, Universiteit Maastricht, The Netherlands. Author of *"Wetenschappelijk Onderzoek en Algemeen Belang": de chemie van H.R. Kruyt 1882–1959* (1998). Editor of *Pursuing the Unity of Science: Ideology and Scientific Practice in the Interwar Period* (with Harmke Kamminga, in preparation). Contributor of articles on Dutch science to *Determinants in the Evolution of the European Chemical Industry, 1900–1939* edited by Anthony S. Travis *et al.* (1998) and to the journals *Annals of Science* and *Gewina*. **Essay**: Colloid Chemistry.

Sörlin, Sverker. Head, Department of History of Science and Ideas, Umeå University, Sweden. Author of numerous books and articles including *Denationalizing Science* (with Elisabeth Crawford and Terry Shinn, 1993), *De lärdas republik: Om vetenskapens internationella tendenser* (1994), *Universiteten som drivkrafter: Globalisering, kunskapspolitik och den nya intellektuella geografin* (1996), *Jorden en ö: En global miljöhis-*

toria (with Anders Öckerman, 1998), *Den globala nationalismen: Nationalstatens historia och framtid* (with Björn Hettne and Uffe Östergård, 1998). Editor of several books including *Sustainability: The Challenge: People, Power, and the Environment* (with L. Anders Sandberg, 1998). **Essays**: Environmental Sciences, Nature.

Sorrenson, Richard. Assistant Professor, Department of History and Philosophy of Science, Indiana University, Bloomington. Author of *The Ship as a Scientific Instrument* (1996), *Towards a History of the Royal Society* (1996), *George Graham, Visible Technician* (1999), and "From Captain Cook to Captain Kirk: Expeditionary Science in the Last Two Centuries" in *Modern Science in National and International Context* edited by Ronald L. Numbers (in preparation). Editor of *Did the Royal Society Matter in the Eighteenth Century?* (1999). Contributor of articles on scientific instrument makers, the Royal Society of London, and scientific voyages to the journals *Osiris*, *British Journal for the History of Science*, and *Notes and Records of the Royal Society of London*. **Essay**: Royal Society of London.

Souder, Lawrence. Instructor, Drexel University, Philadelphia. Contributor to *Notable Twentieth Century Scientists* (1995) and *Encyclopaedia of the History of Science, Technology and Medicine in Non-Western Cultures* (1997). **Essays**: Aristotle, Hodgkin, The Mind, Raman, Turing.

Staley, Richard. Visiting Assistant Professor, Department of the History of Science, University of Wisconsin, Madison. Author of *Empires of Physics: A Guide to the Exhibition* (with Jim Bennett *et al.*, 1993), *1900: The New Age: A Guide to the Exhibition* (with Jim Bennett, 1994) and "Michelson's Interferometer" in *Instrument–Experiment: Historische Studien* edited by Christoph Meinel (2000). Editor of *The Physics of Empire: Public Lectures* (1994), Contributor of articles on the histories of relativity to *Isis*. **Essays**: Einstein, Quantum Mechanics, Quantum Theory, Relativity.

Stewart, Larry. Professor, Department of History, University of Saskatchewan. Author of *The Rise of Public Science: Rhetoric, Technology, and Natural Philosophy in Newtonian Britain, 1640–1750* (1995), and contributor to the journals *Isis*, *British Journal for the History of Science*, and *Medieval History*. **Essay**: Public and the Private.

Sturdy, Steve. Lecturer in History of Medicine, Science Studies Unit, University of Edinburgh. Editor of *War, Medicine and Modernity* (with Roger Cooter and Mark Harrison, 1998) and *Medicine and the Management of Modern Warfare* (with Roger Cooter and Mark Harrison, 1999). Contributor to *Medical Innovations in Historical Perspective* edited by John Pickstone (1992), *Molecularizing Biology and Medicine* edited by Soraya De Chadarevian and Harmke Kamminga (1998), and *Greater than the Parts: Holism in Biomedicine 1920–1950* edited by Christopher Lawrence and George Weisz (1998). Contributor to the journals *History of Science*, *Medical History*, *Philosophy of Science*, *Isis*, and *British Journal for the History of Science*. **Essays**: Endocrinology, Hospitals, Pharmacology, Respiration.

Sullivan, Tracy L. Writer and Editor, Elliott School of International Affairs, George Washington University. **Essays**:

Organic Chemistry (with Leo B. Slater), Plastics and Polymers (with Leo B. Slater).

Summers, Anne. Curator in the Department of Manuscripts, British Library, and Honorary Professor of History, Middlesex University, London. Author of *Angels and Citizens: British Women as Military Nurses 1854–1914* (1988), *How To Find Source Materials: British Library Collections on the History and Culture of Science, Technology and Medicine* (1996), and *Female Lives, Moral States: Women, Religion and Public Life 1800–1930* (2000). Contributor to *Patriotism* edited by R. Samuel (1989), *Victorian Values* edited by G. Marsden (1990), *Nichts als Unterdrückung?* edited by L. Barrow, D. Schmidt and J. Schwarzkopf (1991), *Lieux de femmes dans l'espace public 1800–1930: Histoire et Société Contemporaines* (vol.13, 1992), *Borderlines* edited by B. Melman (1998), and to the journals *History Today, History Workshop Journal, English Historical Review, Victorian Studies, British Medical Journal, Medicine and Charity, RCN History of Nursing Society Journal,* and *Historical Research.* Member of the editorial board of *History Workshop Journal* since 1975. **Essay:** Nursing.

Susskind, Charles. Professor, Department of Engineering, University of California, Berkeley. Author of several books including *Fundamentals of Microwave Electronics* (with Marvin Chodorow, 1964), *Understanding Technology* (1975), *Twenty-Five Engineers and Inventors* (1976), *Ferdinand Braun* (with Friedrich Kurylo, 1981), *Electricity and Medicine: History of Their Interaction* (with Margaret Rowbottom, 1984), *Janáček and Brod* (1985), *Heinrich Hertz: A Short Life* (1995), and 24 entries in the *Dictionary of Scientific Bibliography* edited by Charles Coulston Gillispie (1970–80). Editor of *Encyclopedia of Electronics* (1962). **Essays:** Hertz, Lawrence, Millikan.

Swijtink, Zeno G. Professor of Philosophy, Sonoma State University, California. Author of *The Empire of Chance* (with others, 1989). **Essays:** Error Theory, Probability.

Teichmann, Jürgen. Professor of History of Science and Museum's Director, Institut für Geschichte der Naturwissenschaften, Ludwig-Maximilians-Universität, Munich and Deutsches Museum, Munich. Author of *Zur Entwicklung von Grundbegriffen der Elektrizitätslehre, insbesondere des elektrischen Stromes bis 1820* (1974), *Wandel des Weltbildes* (1980, 1985, 1999), *Out of the Crystal Maze* (1992), and *Experimente, die Geschichte machten* (1995). **Essay:** Röntgen.

Terrall, Mary. Assistant Professor, Department of History, University of California, Los Angeles. Contributor to *The Sciences in Enlightened Europe* edited by William Clark, Jan Golinski and Simon Schaffer (1999) and *Books and the Sciences in History* edited by Nicholas Jardine and Marina Frasca-Spada (2000). Contributor of articles on Maupertuis to the journals *Isis, Configurations,* and *History of Science.* **Essay:** Maupertuis.

Tighe, Janet. Member of the Teaching Faculty, University of Pennsylvania, contributing courses to the History and

Sociology Department, the American Civilization Program, the History Department and to the Language and Cultural Perspectives Program, Lauder Institute of Management, of the Wharton School. Contributor to *Framing Disease* edited by Charles E. Rosenberg and Janet Golden (1992) and to the journals *Transactions and Studies of the College of Physicians of Philadelphia, Temple Review, The International Journal of Law and Psychiatry, Bulletin of the History of Medicine,* and *American Journal of Legal History.* **Essay:** Medicine and Law.

Travis, Anthony S. Deputy Director, Sidney M. Edelstein Center for the History and Philosophy of Science, Technology and Medicine, Hebrew University of Jerusalem. Author of *The Rainbow Makers: The Origins of Synthetic Dyestuffs Industry in Western Europe* (1993) and *Heinrich Caro and the Creation of Modern Chemical Industry* (with Carsten Reinhardt, 2000). Editor of *Determinants in the Evolution of the European Chemical Industry, 1900–1939* (with Ernst Homburg and Harm G. Schröter, 1998) and *The Chemical Industry in Europe, 1850–1914* (with Ernst Homburg, Peter J.T. Morris, and Harm G. Schröter, 1998). Former advisory editor, *Technology and Culture.* **Essay:** Dyestuffs.

Tucker, Jennifer. Assistant Professor of History, Wesleyan University. Contributor of an article on photography to *Victorian Science in Context* edited by Bernard Lightman (1997) and articles to *Osiris.* **Essay:** Photography.

Tuttle, Julianne. Doctoral candidate, Indiana University, Bloomington. **Essay:** Genius.

Van Helvoort, Ton. Freelance technical translator and scientific writer, based in the Netherlands. Contributor to the journals *History of Science, Journal of the History of Biology, History and Philosophy of the Life Sciences, Medical History, Annals of Science,* and *Studies in History and Philosophy of Science.* **Essays:** Bacteriology, Biochemistry.

Van Riper, A. Bowdoin. Adjunct Professor, Department of Social and International Studies, Southern Polytechnic State University, Marietta, Georgia. Author of *Men Among the Mammoths* (1993), *Science in Popular Culture* (in preparation), *Looking Up: Aviation and the Popular Imagination* (in preparation), and of chapters in *History in Dispute* edited by Robert J. Allison (vols 2 and 3; 2000) and *Science and Its Times* edited by Neil Schlager (vols 4, 6, and 7; in preparation). Contributor to the journal *Film and History.* **Essays:** Age of the Earth, Archaeology, Buckland.

Vernon, Keith. Senior Lecturer in Social History, Department of Historical and Critical Studies, University of Central Lancashire, Preston. Author of "Science and Technology" in *The First World War in British History* edited by Stephen Constantine *et al.* (1995) and "The Numerical Taxonomy Debates" in *Studies in History and Philosophy of the Life Sciences* (in preparation). Contributor to the journals *Annals of Science, History of Science,* and *British Journal for History of Science.* **Essays:** Degeneration, Education, Taxonomy, Universities.

Videira, Antonio Augusto Passos. Associate Professor, Department of Philosophy, State University of Rio de Janeiro, and Invited Researcher at Centro Brasileiro de Pesquisas Físicas, Brazil. Author of several books including *Algumas Observações Históricas e Epistemologicas Sobre o Conceito de Átomo Clássico* (1993) and *Atomismo, Energetismo e Pluralismo Teórico no Pensamento Epistemológico de Ludwig Boltzmann* (1994), and *Oque é vida* (2000). **Essays:** Boltzmann, Poincaré.

Vogel, Brant. Doctoral candidate, Emory University, Atlanta. Consultant, New York. Author of *Weather Prediction and Weather Theory in Early Modern Europe* (in preparation). **Essay:** Meteorological Instruments.

Wagner, Donald B. External Lecturer, Department of Asian Studies, University of Copenhagen. Author of *Dabiesha* (1985), *Pattern and Loom* (with John Becker, 1987), *Iron and Steel in Ancient China* (1993), *The Traditional Chinese Iron Industry and Its Modern Fate* (1997), "The Earliest Use of Iron in China" in *Metals in Antiquity* edited by Suzanne M.M. Young et al. (1999), and *The State and the Iron Industry in Han China* (2000). Contributor to the journals *Historia Mathematica*, *Acta Orientalia*, *Archeomaterials*, *Journal of the Historical Metallurgy Society*, *Chinese Science*, and *Journal of East Asian Archaeology*. **Essay:** Metallurgy.

Ward, Helen M. Assistant Librarian, Royal Horticultural Society. **Essay:** Horticulture.

Weathers, Kimberly. Independent scholar, Houston, Texas. **Essay:** Lister.

Weindling, Paul. Wellcome Trust Research Professor in the History of Medicine, School of Humanities, Oxford Brookes University. Author of *Darwinism and Social Darwinism in Imperial Germany* (1988), *Health, Race and German Politics* (1989), *L'Hygiene de la race* (1998), and *Epidemics and Genocide in Eastern Europe 1890–1945* (2000). Editor of *Information Sources in the History of Science and Medicine* (with Pietro Corsi, 1983), *The Social History of Occupational Health* (1985), and *International Health Organisations and Movements 1918–1939* (1995). Contributor to articles on the Nuremberg Code in *Bulletin for the History of Medicine* and the Nuremberg medical trial in *Holocaust and Genocide Studies*. **Essays:** Behring, Ehrlich.

Weiss, Sheila Faith. Associate Professor of History, School of Liberal Arts, Clarkson University, New York. Author of *Race Hygiene and National Efficiency: The Eugenics of Wilhelm Schallmayer* (1987). Contributor to the journals *Isis*, *Osiris*, and *Medizin-historisches Journal*. **Essay:** Eugenics.

Werrett, Simon. Postdoctoral Research Fellow, University of Cambridge. Research interests include a social history of rocketry. **Essay:** Russian Academy of Sciences.

Westfall, Richard S. Deceased. Formerly, Henry H.H. Remak Distinguished Scholar, Distinguished Professor Emeritus of History and Philosophy of Science, Indiana University, Bloomington. Author of numerous books and articles including a biography of Isaac Newton, *Never at Rest* (1980). **Essays:** Newton, Newtonianism.

White, Paul. Associate Editor, Darwin Correspondence Project, and Affiliated Research Scholar, Department of History and Philosophy of Science, University of Cambridge. Author of "Genius in Public and Private" in *Thomas Henry Huxley's Place in Science and Letters* edited by Alan P. Barr (1997), *Thomas Huxley* (in preparation), and "Cross-Cultural Encounters" in *Encounters: Transactions in Science and Culture in Victorian Britain* edited by R. Lockhurst and J. McDonagh (in preparation). Co-editor of *The Correspondence of Charles Darwin* (vols 12 and 13, in preparation). Contributor of an article on T.H. Huxley and scientific identity to the journal *History of Science*. **Essays:** Gender and Identity, Huxley, Literature and Science.

Widmalm, Sven. Adviser. Department of History and Philosophy of Science, University of Cambridge. Author of numerous articles and papers on the history of Swedish science, and contributor to several books including *The Quantifying Spirit in the 18th Century* edited by Tore Fränsmyr, J.L. Heilbron and Robin E. Rider (1990), *The Scientific Revolution in National Context* edited by Roy Porter and Mikulás Teich (1992), and *Center on the Periphery: Historical Aspects of 20th-Century Swedish Physics* edited by Svante Lindqvist (1993). **Essay:** Hale.

Wiesenfeldt, Gerhard. Doctoral candidate, Institut für Geschichte der Naturwissenschaften, Mathematik und Technik, Hamburg. **Essays:** Boerhaave, Instrument Makers.

Wilkinson, Lise. Research Associate, Wellcome Institute for the History of Medicine, London. Author of *An Introduction to the History of Virology* (with A.P. Waterson, 1988), *Animals and Disease* (1992), and *Prevention and Cure* (with Anne Hardy, 2000). Contributor to the *Cambridge World History of Human Disease* (1993), *History of Healing Professions* (1993), and *Companion Encyclopedia of the History of Medicine* (1993), and contributor to numerous journals such as *History of Medicine*. **Essay:** Virology.

Williams, Carolyn D. Lecturer, Department of English, Reading University. Author of *Pope, Homer and Manliness* (1993), and contributor to the journals Studies in *English Literature*, *British Journal for Eighteenth Century Studies*, *International Journal of Hermetic Studies*, *Essays in Criticism*, *Yearbook of English Studies*, *Journal of Beckett Studies*, and *The Scriblerian*. **Essays:** Alchemy, Malthus.

Wilson, Philip K. Historian of Medicine, Penn State College of Medicine, Milton S. Hershey Medical Center, Hershey, Pennsylvania, and Biomedical and Health Editor, *Encyclopaedia Britannica*, Chicago. Author of *Surgery, Skin, and Syphilis: Daniel Turner's London (1667–1741)* (1999). Editor of *Childbirth: Changing Ideas and Practices in Britain and America, 1600 to the Present* (1996). Contributor to *The History of Medical Popularization, 1650–1850* (1992), *Medicine in the Enlightenment* (1994), and to the journals *Annals of Science*, *Journal of the Royal Society of Medicine*,

St Thomas's Hospital Gazette, The London Journal, and to numerous dictionaries and encyclopedias. **Essays:** Anatomy, Embryology, Plastic Surgery, Surgery.

Winter, Alison. Associate Professor of History, California Institute of Technology, Pasedena. Author of *Mesmerized: Mind and Authority in Victorian England* (1998) and contributor to *Historical Journal* and *Knowledge Incarnate: The Physical Presentation of Intellectual Selves* edited by Christopher Lawrence and Stephen Shapin (1998). **Essays:** Doctor–Patient Relationship, Mesmerism.

Wintroub, Michael. Assistant Professor, Department of History, University of Michigan, Ann Arbor. Contributor of articles on science and collecting in the 16th century to the journals *Studies in History and Philosophy of Science*, *Sixteenth Century Journal*, and *History of Science*. **Essays:** Astrolabes, Court Society.

Yeo, I. Richard. Associate Professor (Reader) in History of Science, School of Humanities, Griffith University, Brisbane, Australia. Author of *Defining Science: William Whewell, Natural Knowledge and Public Debate in Early Victorian Britain* (1993), "Classifying the Sciences" in *The Cambridge History of Science*, vol. 4: *The Eighteenth Century* edited by Roy Porter (in preparation), and *Encyclopaedic Visions: Scientific Dictionaries and Enlightenment Culture* (in preparation). Editor of *The Politics and Rhetoric of Scientific Method* (with John Schuster, 1986) and *Telling Lives in Science* (with Michael Shortland, 1996). Contributor to the *Journal for the History of Ideas*. Member of the editorial board of *Australian Studies in History and Philosophy of Science*, and former member of the editorial board of *British Journal for the History of Science*. **Essay:** Encyclopedias.

Yglesias, Elmer. Doctoral candidate, Department of the History of Science, Harvard University. **Essay:** Greece: general works.

Young, Robert M. Independent scholar, London. Author of *Mind, Brain and Adaptation in the Nineteeth Century* (1970). **Essay:** Psychoanalysis: conceptual.